Foreword

Chris R. Brewin, Research Professor, Department of Psychology, Royal Holloway, University of London

In the period from 1950 to the mid-1970s behaviour therapists developed clearly defined procedures such as desensitization and response prevention that could readily be described and taught. These techniques required little investigation of the individual, only a careful description of the behaviour, its antecedents, and its consequents. However, their usefulness tended to be restricted to the treatment of fairly circumscribed disorders such as specific phobias and compulsions. When behaviour therapists came to address depression and more generalized anxiety disorders, the significance of personal meanings assumed great importance. The investigation of individual thought processes, as recommend by Albert Ellis and Aaron Beck, became the cornerstone of the new cognitive–behavioural approaches.

These new techniques were not embraced, however, without a prolonged period of soul-searching by behaviour therapists. There was great anxiety that investigating individual cognitions was not as 'scientific' or methodologically rigorous as purely behavioural approaches. The new approaches were eventually adopted because they worked, but many expressed unease. The fear was frequently expressed that, in taking this step, behaviour therapy could no longer be so clearly differentiated from psychoanalysis. It was perceived that the project of creating a truly 'scientific' type of therapy was being abandoned for ever in favour of an explicit search for personal meaning.

These fears and uncertainties about the scientific status of psychotherapy, particularly when contrasted with the status of biological psychiatry, are still very much with us. It is hard for the identification of pathogenic personal meanings, no matter how plausible and no matter how successful the outcome, to appear as valuable scientifically as identifying the existence of too large or too small quantities of a neurotransmitter. These issues contribute not only to individual unease, but also to external perceptions of the mental health sciences to internal demarcations, and to decisions about how best to spend limited research funds. This book therefore addresses a topic that is of central importance to all those working in mental health.

Bolton and Hill's important and far-reaching analysis goes right to the heart of these controversial issues. By approaching the problem from the standpoint of the philosophy of science and the philosophy of mind, they avoid the taking of sides and any sterile argument about what is 'better'. Rather, they oblige the reader to see the problem in a wholly new way, one which distinguishes the causality inherent in physics and chemistry from the causality inherent in biological systems that have inbuilt goals and are constantly working towards more or less well specified objectives.

As they point out, explanations that are couched in terms of meaning or intention are extremely powerful in biology and psychology. They also show convincingly that these explanations work just as well for many examples of abnormal behaviour as they do for normal behaviour that follows predictable rules. The divide between the biological and the psychosocial approach to mental illness is shown to be profoundly misleading — instead, Bolton and Hill argue, the divide is between intentional explanations and non-intentional explanations. According to intentional explanations, symptoms arise because normally functioning biological and psychological systems are attempting to deal with information that is either internally inconsistent or is inconsistent with the person's goals. According to non-intentional explanations, the biological or psychological systems are themselves malfunctioning, probably as a result of some disease process. Both types of explanation may apply at different times, and both are equally 'scientific'.

This analysis, while not minimizing the inherent difficulties, clearly defines the unique contribution of psychotherapy and explains why the psychiatric problems of the majority of sufferers will never be explicable in terms of biological or psychological malfunctioning arising from non-intentional causes. From this perspective, all psychotherapies aim to specify what information is in the system, how accurate this is, and whether there is conflict with the person's goals. Where they differ is in their methods of assessment and in their techniques for resolving conflict.

As well as placing psychotherapy within a broader context of the explanation of psychiatric disorder, Bolton and Hill's analysis also defines a scientific project of categorizing and describing regularities in the personal meanings attached to psychiatric symptoms. Although ambitious, its completion is probably considerably more achievable than that of mapping the entire human genome. This book suggests that, as far as the majority of psychiatric patients are concerned, it will also be of considerably more value.

MIND, MEANING, AND MENTAL DISORDER

The Nature of Causal Explanation In Psychology And Psychiatry

DEREK BOLTON
Institute of Psychiatry and
Maudsley Hospital, London

and

JONATHAN HILL
University of Liverpool and
Royal Liverpool
Children's Hospital

Oxford New York Tokyo
Oxford University Press

Oxford University Press, Great Clarendon Street, Oxford OX2 6DP

Oxford New York
Athens Auckland Bangkok Bogota Bombay Buenos Aires
Calcutta Cape Town Dar es Salaam Delhi Florence Hong Kong Istanbul
Karachi Kuala Lumpur Madras Madrid Melbourne Mexico City
Nairobi Paris Singapore Taipei Tokyo Toronto Warsaw
and associated companies in
Berlin Ibadan

Oxford is a trade mark of Oxford University Press

Published in the United States
by Oxford University Press Inc., New York

© Derek Bolton and Jonathan Hill, 1996

First published 1996
First published in paperback 1998

A catalogue record for this book is available from the British Library

Library of Congress Cataloging in Publication Data
(Data available)

ISBN 0 19 261504 1 (Hbk)
ISBN 0 19 262936 0 (Pbk)

Printed in Great Britain by
Bookcraft Ltd, Avon

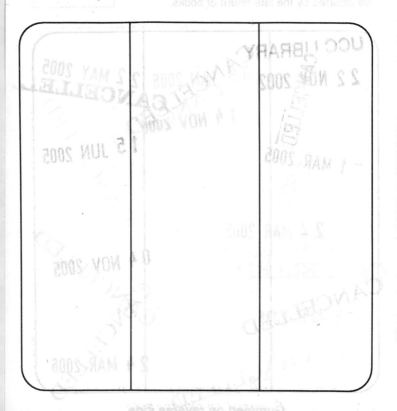

LIBRARY
TEL: 01244 375444 EXT: 3301

Chester
A College of the
University of Liverpool

This book is to be returned on or before the last date stamped below. Overdue charges will be incurred by the late return of books.

LIBRARY

UNIVERSITY
COLLEGE
CHESTER

A College of the
University of Liverpool

Preface

Philosophical ideas about the mind, brain, and behaviour can seem theoretical and unimportant when placed alongside the urgent questions of mental distress and disorder. However, there is a need to give attempts to answer these questions some direction. On the one hand, a substantial research effort is going into the investigation of brain processes and the development of drug treatments for psychiatric disorders, and, on the other, a wide range of psychotherapies and forms of counselling are becoming available to adults and children with mental health problems. These two strands reflect a long Western tradition of dividing body and mind, and attempting to resolve questions of the explanation of disturbance either in favour of the malfunctioning brain, or the disordered psyche. It is crucial in determining the direction of research and clinical practice to clarify whether these are competing incompatible perspectives, or whether they are complementary and in need of integration.

However, it is unlikely that philosophical ideas will illuminate central questions in psychology and psychiatry without themselves being informed by the concepts and findings from areas such as learning theory, developmental psychology, artificial intelligence, and psychoanalysis. The book therefore starts with a review of key issues in the philosophy of mind and philosophy of science as they relate to questions of cognition, emotion, and behaviour. Intentionality emerges as a central concept in human functioning, but we go on to make the case that it is a distinguishing feature of biological systems in general. Human psychological faculties then emerge as particularly sophisticated elaborations of intentional processes, which create the conditions both for intelligence and culture, and also for instability and disorder.

Throughout the discussion philosophical theories are brought to bear on the particular questions of the explanation of behaviour, the nature of mental causation, and eventually the origins of major disorders, including depression, anxiety disorders, schizophrenia, and personality disorder.

The book has been written for philosophers and academic and clinical psychologists and psychiatrists, but we would be delighted if anyone whose business or interest is to understand human behaviour were to make use of it. In that it presents a particular thesis it is aimed at a postgraduate readership, but the advanced undergraduate will find that many contemporary themes in philosophy, psychology, and psychiatry are covered, and provided the ideas proposed are treated with some caution under exam conditions, the more innovative content may not prove too hazardous.

The authors came to have an interest in philosophical problems in psychology and psychiatry by different routes. Before training as a clinical psychologist D. B. read philosophy and researched on Wittgenstein. J. H. read natural sciences before training in medicine, psychiatry, and family therapy. Both of us were undergraduates at Cambridge University where our belief in the value of ideas and cross-disciplinary thinking was reinforced and informed. We published papers independently about 12 years ago which overlapped in subject-matter—meanings, reasons, and causes—and conclusions, whence came our idea of co-writing a book. During the 1980s we were very fortunate to be part of a group of people working at the Institute of Psychiatry and the Maudsley Hospital in London that met regularly to present papers and discuss philosophical issues in relation to psychology and psychiatry. This provided a containing and critical setting in which to try out new ideas, many of which appear in this book, and we are very pleased to acknowledge and thank the other members of that group, Jim Birley who particularly encouraged its formation, Adrian Grounds, Peter Hobson, Alan Lee and Digby Tantam.

The book as a whole is co-written, although some chapters were written mainly by one or other of us. Chapters 1–4 were written mainly by D. B., 5 and 7 mainly by J. H., while 6, 8, and 9 have been co-written.

D. B.'s contribution was written partly during tenure of a Jacobsen Research Fellowship in Philosophy at University College London during 1989–91, and he gratefully acknowledges this support. A different kind of support came from Stacia, Henry, and Matthew, who for many years gave his attempts to make time to write the book their whole-hearted backing.

J. H. would like to thank his father for teaching him the value of asking questions and his mother for her insight that they cannot all be answered. He is very grateful to his wife Judy, and his children Susannah, Jessie, and Rosalind for their support, and belief that this book would be completed. Alison Richards helped in the ordering of the ideas, and David Lyon provided valuable assistance in the use of clear language. Dudley Ankerson and Bernard Wood provided inspiration on broader but equally important fronts.

Both authors would like to thank friends and colleagues for their comments and advice on all or parts of the work at various stages of completion, including Simon Baron-Cohen, Chris Brewin, Andy Clark, Bill Fulford, Sebastian Gardner, Peter Hobson, David Papineau, and Mick Power.

D. B., *London*
J. H., *Liverpool*
1995

Contents

Introduction

The starting point of this book is an assumption that theories of the mind need to provide an account of order and disorder, which have been traditionally the domain of psychology and psychiatry; and that psychology and psychiatry need to understand the nature of their explanations, which is the province of the philosophy of mind and philosophy of science. In the ensuing chapters we start with the philosophical issues, reviewing the problems and arguing for a thesis which is in some respects novel. We then show how this thinking can be applied to biological systems in general and to the mind and its functioning, both in order and disorder, and in the ground between the two. We start by way of introduction at the other end of that pathway with the most common adult mental health problem, depression, in order to illustrate briefly how the philosophical, research, and clinical issues are closely linked.

Depressive episodes involve changes of behaviour, mood, and thinking about the self, the outside world, the past, and the future. They may be understood in two contrasting ways. In the first, it is assumed that being depressed is like any other human emotional state and that there is a reason for it, in a loss or threat or other similar adverse external circumstance. In the second, it is inferred that this is not part of the person's usual set of emotional responses to events, and is a form of illness. We will be concerned in this book to make clear how either interpretation gives rise to questions, to offer some solutions to those questions, and above all to show how important it is to keep alive several lines of thought in the investigation and treatment of psychiatric or psychological disorder.

The difference between the two types of explanation, broadly speaking, lies in whether or not they refer to the meaning of the mood, beliefs, and behaviours. In the first they are thought to be meaningful in relation to the rest of the person's life, his or her past and present experiences. Why is this problematic? Where the precipitants are clear, such an account may be straightforward, but often they are not. The person appears to have nothing to be depressed about, or can think of no reason to be depressed. The depressed person does not feel or seem to be his/her normal self. The depression is experienced as happening to the person, rather than being part of them. In other words, the experience and the observed phenomena have the qualities of an illness that intrudes inexplicably and uncontrollably into the life of the individual. Many psychiatric conditions have the quality, to a greater or lesser extent, that the person's mood, beliefs, experiences, or behaviours do not fit their circumstances and are experienced as intrusive, or inexplicable, and in some ways as alien.

A further question arises from the meaningful account, where we are able to identify reasons for the depression. In what sense could a loss such as the death of a loved one be the cause of the depression? We can describe in human terms how that might be: because the two people had shared happy experiences, had supported each other, confided intimate concerns; in short, because they meant a lot to each other. Does this mean that the loss caused the depression in the same sense that loss of support causes an apple to fall? Apples fall off trees all over the world in the same way, following the same laws of nature, yet the death of one person has a quite different emotional effect from the death of another. The difference appears to be related to the significance of one and not the other. We must conclude either that our concepts of meaning and significance must be capable of translation into other terms more like those of physics, or that different ideas of cause and effect are operating. If it is the latter, are cause and effect in the mind different from cause and effect in the rest of the world? In the course of the book we shall argue that states of mind are genuinely causal, that the causal processes are different from those of physics, but not different from those in biology generally. We will also find that even mental states that are experienced as intrusive, inappropriate, and uncontrollable may arise from the experiences and personality of the individual. Then the clinical and research implication is that therapeutic approaches should address those areas.

We will see also that the second kind of explanation of depression, as a form of illness, may be appropriate. However, we will not be able to entertain that possibility until we have addressed a further set of questions. If one constellation of emotions, beliefs, or behaviours, such as those of depression, are not linked to the rest of a person's life or experiences, is there a difference between this and their other mental states which we readily think of as meaningful? For instance, if I was happy last year because I got a good new job, and now I am depressed for no apparent reason, was the job really the cause of my happiness, or was my happiness as inexplicable as my depression? If I suppose that my depression arose from an abnormality of my brain function, could I then put last year's happiness down to brain function? This has a certain appeal because it must have involved alterations in brain function, but does that mean that the new job was not really part of the causal chain? As we shall see, attempts have been made to argue that those meaningful events that we think of as causing our feelings, thoughts, and behaviours do not really do that, and only brain processes are genuinely causal, but these attempts do not succeed. The alternative is to suppose that different causal processes might have operated in last year's happiness and this year's depression. If this is the case, we will need again two forms of causal process. From the research and clinical perspectives, the questions do not stop there. Even if we can elucidate two different kinds of origin of mental events and behaviours, how do we determine when each is operating separately or in combination? Our aim is to provide an approach to this question, first through an analysis of causal processes in the operation of the mind, then through a consideration of these within the context of biology and development, and finally in an enquiry into the origins of some of the major psychiatric disorders.

The problem area with which we are concerned has historical roots, and an understanding of these helps to make the issues clearer. We continue in this introduction with a brief review of some of the historical background.

The distinction between meaning and causality, and the related distinction between understanding and explaining, arose at the turn of the century within the new cultural sciences, the *Geisteswissenschaften*. The distinctions signified a major problem, the apparent misfit between the phenomena studied by these new sciences—human beings and culture, and specifically the *meaning* which pervades them—and the assumptions and methods of the natural sciences, developed since the seventeenth century. Meaningful phenomena show a particularity ('uniqueness') uncaptured by general laws. They apparently cannot be subsumed under causal laws of the natural sciences. Further, meaning bears a loose relation to 'hard facts', so that understanding of it tends to appear subjective. It seemed, therefore, that knowledge of meaningful phenomena could not be accomodated by the methodology of the natural sciences, based in assumptions of generality, causality, and objectivity. Hence there arose a dichotomy between the natural sciences and the sciences of meaning, implying the autonomy of the latter. This whole problem, subsequently endorsed and elaborated in hermeneutic readings of the cultural sciences, and evident currently in various post-modernist critiques, was expressed by the turn-of-the-century distinctions between meaning and causality, and understanding and explaining (for an historical, critical review of these distinctions see von Wright 1971).

The problem of meaning in relation to scientific method and explanation as it arose at the turn of the century was recognized immediately as relevant to the new psychiatry by Jaspers. His *Allgemeine Psychopathologie* (1923) attempted to construct a psychiatry that can embrace both causal explanation in terms of material events and empathic understanding of non-causal meanings, but the tension between the two methodologies was covered over rather than resolved. Jaspers' problem was psychiatry's problem. He anticipated what was to become a split within psychiatry between explanation of disorder in terms of brain pathology and 'explanation' in terms of (extraordinary) meanings. The former had no room for meaning; the latter became subject to much philosophical stick, because of its pretensions to be science.

Psychoanalytic theory, as the main and uncompromising proponent of meaningful explanation of disorder, has carried the burden of the problematic status of meaning in relation to scientific method. Problems identified for it included apparent lack of objectivity of data, the non-empirical character of its hypotheses (alleged unfalsifiability), and the questionable assumption that meanings are causes. The pressure, mounting in the 1960s, contributed to the development of the hermeneutic readings of psychoanalytic theory popular in the 1970s, which accepted, with more or less regret, the demarcation between understanding and causal, or more generally, scientific, explanation (Ricoeur 1970; Habermas 1971; Klein 1976; Schafer 1976; and for critical commentary Grünbaum 1984, 1986). The hermeneutic reading of psychoanalytic theory, important and presumably inevitable as it was at the time, was relatively short-lived. In part this was because of its implausibility: psychoanalytic theory, like all psychological theories, did seem interested in the aetiology of behaviour, and not just in, as it were, spinning meanings out of the air. But also, at about this time, the terms of the problem were being transformed. In psychology, behaviourism was in the process of being dismantled by a new kind of psychological science, in which mental states played centre stage. This was of course the 'cognitive revolution' in psychology, which began roughly in the 1960s and which continues apace.

The recent appearance of this cognitive paradigm has powerful implications for the problems embodied in the traditional distinctions between meaning and causality, and between understanding and explaining. The new paradigm establishes mental states and processes as subjects for scientific enquiry, and as having a role in the scientific explanation of behaviour. At the same time, the working assumption is apparently that mental states are causal, or, to put the point more fully, that mental states are invoked in causal explanations of behaviour. Furthermore, although here we encounter many problems and controversies, the prima-facie implication is that the meaning that characterizes mind comes within the domain of scientific enquiry, implicated in mental causation.

Inevitably psychiatry has inherited all the philosophical or conceptual problems of psychology, including the problem of meaning and causality, but it faces further specific ones of its own. There are certainly problems with construing meaningful mental states as causes of behaviour already in the normal case, but there is a further reason for doubting the relevance of meaningful explanation in the case of disorder. The reason is simple, on the surface, namely, that the notion of disorder is applied precisely at the point where meaning comes to an end. Roughly, the question of disorder is raised when there is (serious) failure of meaningful connection between mental states and reality, or among mental states, or between mental states and action. In the apparent absence of meaningful connections, we may posit different kinds of mechanism, involving physical causation, mechanisms that have nothing to do with meaning, with beliefs, desires, plans, etc. Given breakdown in meaning, in mental order, it is plausible to suppose that we require explanation in terms of non-meaningful processes, specifically disruption by some form of biological abnormality. This a priori consideration lends weight to the so-called 'medical model' in psychiatry, in so far as it seeks to explain psychological disorder by reference to biological pathology.

The simplicity of this line of thought is overshadowed, however, because the issue of where the limits of the meaningful lie presses hard. Psychological theory may find meaning beyond the point at which common sense runs out. Many controversies within and around psychiatry turn on this point. The various alternatives to, and critiques of, mainstream, medical psychiatry share in common the charge that it has abandoned the search for meaning prematurely, has over-hastily opted for the lower-level form of explanation in terms of biological causation, because of a poverty-stricken theory of meaning. Freudian theory extended the limits of the meaningful beyond what was envisaged by the common sense, and the psychiatry, of the time. The diverse critiques of the 'medical model' which appeared in the 1960s and which came to be known collectively as the 'anti-psychiatry' movement, likewise charged psychiatry with having a blinkered perception of meaning. Szasz (1961) questioned the legitimacy of the very idea of 'mental illness' as used in psychiatry, and attacked the associated medicalization of what he described rather as (comprehensible) 'personal problems of living'. Laing (1960) reframed madness, schizophrenia, as being an understandable, indeed the only sane, response to a confused and contradictory family life. In examining the historical presuppositions of the relatively recent idea of 'mental illness', Foucault (1965) sought to show that it arose as an inevitable consequence of the excessive rationality of the Enlightenment, as the mere negation of reason, meaning, and validity, that this essentially negatively defined madness was expelled, as it were, from consciousness, so also geographically, out of the community, into the asylums. The general criticism is that there is more meaning in so-called mental illness than meets the eye of psychiatry, and behind that, of the culture in which modern psychiatry has arisen.

Having surveyed from an historical perspective the problem space within which we are working, let us sketch our position once more. Concerning the central problem of meaning and causality, we argue that explanations that invoke meaning (meaningful mental states) are causal, but they are in critical respects different from causal explanations of the sort found in the physical sciences. In this way we draw a distinction between two varieties of causal explanation, which we call the *intentional* and the *non-intentional*. This distinction obviously differs from the distinction between meaning and causality because it is not drawn in terms of what is or is not causal. But also, the distinction we propose appears at a different place in the spectrum of the sciences, not between the 'hard' natural sciences and the 'soft' cultural sciences, but rather between the natural sciences of physics and chemistry, and the (equally natural) biological sciences. In the biological sciences we find concepts of function, design, rules, information, and information-processing, which are the essential ingredients of intentional-causal explanation as understood here. Marking the distinction at this point, between the pre-biological and the biological sciences, has the effect of assimilating biology to psychology, and indeed to the cultural sciences. Our point can be put briefly by saying that meaning is akin to, or is on a continuum with, the information that pervades biological systems and functioning. This proposal stands in contrast to those that, in one way or another, endorse a radical distinction between the meaning of mind, language and culture, and anything to be found in the natural sciences, biological or otherwise. These alternative positions, which otherwise of course vary greatly among themselves, include materialism and hermeneutics, and the views of such contemporary philosophers as Quine and Davidson.

For psychiatry, which seeks models of aetiology and intervention, the exploration of meaningful processes is of interest only in so far as meanings are causes. Once this claim, in the form outlined above, is defined and established in the first part of the essay, through chapters 1–6, we turn in the second part of the essay, chapters 7–9, to explore breakdown of intentionality, and the nature and limits of intentional explanations of psychological disorder. The notion of breakdown of intentionality is also relevant to the first part of the essay, however. Intentional-causal explanations, our whole way of conceiving the phenomena that they explain, are permeated by concepts involving normative distinctions, such as function, and hence dysfunction, design more-or-less suited to the environment and task, normal as opposed to abnormal environmental conditions, true/false belief, adaptive as opposed to maladaptive behaviour, and so on. In this sense themes concerning disorder and its explanation run through all of the chapters.

While the philosophy of psychology has a long and familiar history, and is currently flourishing, the philosophy of psychiatry has been relatively neglected. The most thorough and influential analysis of the philosophical foundations of psychiatry was Jaspers', and there the distinction between meaningful and causal connections was fundamental. Since Jaspers, it would be fair to say that philosophical study of general psychiatry has been in limbo. Philosophers have perhaps been wary of tackling the problems of psychiatry because of unfamiliarity. In part this would be modesty appropriate in the philosophy of any science, art, or scholarly discipline, but a further factor here is probably the one identified by Foucault, that in the modern age 'madness' became alienated from culture, delegated then solely to the psychiatric profession. This has been a result detrimental to all concerned. While the philosophical foundations of psychiatry suffered from inevitable neglect, attention focused rather on the two broad areas referred to earlier: the scientific status or otherwise of psychoanalytic theory, and the diverse 'anti-psychiatry' critiques. The former debate did not concern primarily the concept of disorder, nor, a related point, psychiatry in general. The latter debates certainly were about psychiatry and the notion of 'mental illness', but their problems were social, political, and historical, not primarily philosophical. Controversy about the scientific status of psychoanalytic theory continues (Grünbaum 1984, 1986), and mainstream, medical psychiatry had, and continues, to defend itself against the radical critiques (Clare 1976; Wing 1978; Roth and Kroll 1986; Reznek 1991).

We do not attempt in this essay to weigh into these well-known debates. Our aim is rather as stated above, to examine some philosophical aspects of the problem of meaning and causality, in the light of contemporary theory in philosophy of mind and cognitive psychology, and its bearing on the concepts of mental order and disorder. This examination is relevant to the controversies surrounding psychoanalytic theory, and the notion of mental illness, but these are not the main focus. If the essay can claim allegiance to any 'tradition' in the philosophy of psychiatry, it would be to that represented by Jaspers. That said, we have no pretensions to follow Jaspers in the non-philosophical direction of his work, concerned with the details of psychiatric phenomenology and its classification. This emphasis belonged with the idea that meaningful phenomena have no causal role: all that was to be done, in this case, was to describe and classify them. By contrast, in so far as meaningful phenomena are implicated in causal processes, the task is to try to explicate some basic principles of their operation.

There are various reasons why the time is right for increased communication between philosophy and psychiatry; in particular, the divide between philosophy and psychology has become more flexible, with shared interest in the nature of mind and of psychological explanation. One upshot of this increased flexibility is that problems of mental disorder and its explanation are more available to philosophy. Several books on the philosophy of psychiatry have appeared in recent years, compared with few or none in previous decades. Fulford (1988) emphasized the value-laden, normative nature of concepts in psychiatry, and Hundert (1989) identified disorder in the forms of interaction between subject and object, organism and environment. Themes of these kinds are also prominent in the present essay.

REFERENCES

Clare, A. (1976). *Psychiatry in dissent*. Tavistock Publications, London.

Foucault, M. (1965). *Madness and civilization*. Random House, New York.

Fulford, K. W. M. (1988). *Moral theory and medical practice*. Cambridge University Press, Cambridge.

Grünbaum, A. (1984). *The foundations of psychoanalysis: a philosophical critique*. University of California Press, Berkeley.

Grünbaum, A. (1986). Precis of *The foundations of psychoanalysis: a philosophical critique*, with peer commentary. *The Behavioral and Brain Sciences*, 9, 217–84.

Habermas, J. (1971). *Knowledge and human interests* (trans. J. J. Shapiro). Beacon Press, Boston.

Hundert, E. M. (1989). *Philosophy, psychiatry, and neuroscience*. Oxford University Press, Oxford.

Jaspers, K. (1923). *Allgemeine Pychopathologie*. Springer Verlag, Berlin. (English translation: Hoenig, J. and Hamilton, M. W. (1963) *General Psychopathology*. Manchester University Press, Manchester.)

Klein, G. S. (1976). *Psychoanalytic theory*. International Universities Press, New York.

Laing, R. D. (1960). *The divided self*. Penguin, Harmondsworth, Middlesex.

Reznek, L. (1991). *The philosophical defence of psychiatry*. Routledge, London.

Ricoeur, P. (1970). *Freud and philosophy*. Yale University Press, New Haven, Connecticut.

Roth, M. and Kroll, J. (1986). *The reality of mental illness*. Cambridge University Press, Cambridge.

Schafer, R. (1976). *A new language for psychoanalysis*. Yale University Press, New Haven, Connecticut.

Szasz, T. (1961). *The myth of mental illness: foundations of a theory of personal conduct*. Harper and Row, New York.

von Wright, G. H. (1971). *Explanation and understanding*. Routledge and Kegan Paul, London.

Wing, J. (1978). *Reasoning about madness*. Oxford University Press, Oxford.

1
Mind, meaning,
and the explanation of action

1.1 MAIN IDEA OF THE CHAPTER

The main idea of this chapter is that explanations of behaviour in terms of meaningful, mental states have theory-driven predictive power. Three sections work out various aspects of this idea. Section 1.2 looks at its expression in psychological science, specifically in the cognitive paradigm which superceded behaviourism. Section 1.3 works around the meaning of meaning and related concepts including intentionality and information. Section 1.4 examines aspects of the theory of mind. These sections, the substantial part of the chapter, deal with issues central to current philosophy of mind and psychological theory, and are intended to be of interest in their own right. But they also serve to substantiate the claim that meaningful, mental explanations of action are good at prediction. From this main claim of the chapter is then derived, in Section 1.5, its main conclusion, that such explanations are *causal*.

This conclusion has practical significance for psychological theory: in seeking causal explanations of action, we should construct models that refer to meaningful, mental states. On the other hand, the significance of all this, both the conclusion and its implication, owes much to historical considerations. The *problem* here, and hence the solution, is hard to understand in isolation from the history of ideas. The relevant history includes the emergence of the *Geisteswissenschaften* and the problem of meaning in the late nineteenth century, this against the background of dualism and the problematic status of mind which was axiomatic to the modern science of the seventeenth century, and the effects of both problematics on the development of a scientific psychology.

In the absence of this context, it is hard to see the problem or the interest in the solution. The problem of whether mental, meaningful explanations are causal or not is a typically philosophical one, apparent only at a highly theoretical level. Typically, observation and experiment do not touch it at all. The question is not about the phenomena, not even about this or that theory of the phenomena, but concerns rather the status of a particular kind of psychological theory, whether it is causal or not, and hence, for example, whether it belongs within the domain of the empirical sciences. It is also hard to grasp what the problem is, or that there is a problem at all, within the terms of common sense. Common sense and ordinary language have no difficulty with the idea that meaningful, mental states are causes, in the sense that explanations which invoke beliefs, desires, and so on, typically use terms such as 'because', 'cause', etc. The problem is not apparent here. It becomes apparent only in relation to preconceptions about the nature of mind, its relation to the body, and about the nature of meaning and causality. The problem has relatively little to do with common sense, and not much to do with this or that theory, but is much more to do with background philosophical assumptions. These assumptions have been constructed during the few hundred years or so since the beginnings of modern Western thought. Both mind, and then later meaning, have been correctly regarded as highly problematic from the point of view of the methodological assumptions of the natural sciences.

Dualism is discussed at the beginning of subsection 1.2.1 and some historical aspects of the problem of meaning in subsection 1.3.8. These historical discussions are relatively brief: for the most part the chapter concentrates on contemporary issues in philosophy of mind and psychological theory.

The argument is, as indicated, from the (theory-driven) predictive power of explanation of action in terms of mind and meaning to the causal status of such explanation. There are various other positions and pathways in this area well-known in the contemporary philosophical literature. One very influential position quite distinct from what is proposed here is due to Davidson. While Davidson assumes that reason-giving explanations are causal, he does not derive this from the premise that they belong to a theory with predictive power, and he sees them as discontinuous with the endeavour of empirical science (for example, Davidson 1963, 1970; Evnine 1991; Malpas 1992). In this respect Davidson's work is in the tradition of the dichotomy between '*verstehen*' and '*erklären*', and between meaning and causality, which this essay aims to deconstruct. Dennett and Fodor, both of whom will be discussed frequently in this essay, have each emphasized the predictive power of the kind of explanation in question. Fodor (for example 1987) infers causality, but links it to a strong version of mind/meaning–brain identity theory which will be discussed and rejected in the second chapter. Dennett (for example 1988) steers away from the question of causality, perhaps linked to his wanting to avoid a problematic realism, such as Fodor's, about mind and meaning. The problem of realism here, the question of what mental states are, particularly if they are to be credited with causal power, will be discussed in the second and third chapters. Many problems arise once we embrace the conclusion that mental, meaningful states are causal, and these will occupy us through many subsequent chapters. In this chapter we lay the foundations for the conclusion, by spelling out how such states figure in theories that predict.

1.2 THE 'COGNITIVE PARADIGM' IN PSYCHOLOGICAL SCIENCE

1.2.1 Previous paradigms defined by dualism

Since the beginnings of the modern scientific view of the world, mind and its place in nature have been problematic. The problems were expressed by Cartesian dualism, the theory of two quite distinct substances, *res extensa* and *res cogitans*, which accompanied the development of the scientific world-picture. As Burtt argued in his classic study, Cartesian dualism accompanied the growth of the modern scientific world-picture not only in time, but was an inevitable complement to it (Burtt 1932; see also Bolton 1979, pp. 51–3, for a summary of philosophical themes in Burtt's argument). The world described by the new physics was spatial (geometrical), material, independent, and objective. Mind, by contrast, was immaterial, non-spatial, and essentially subjective. This modern dualism effectively split the human being in two. The human body was conceived as matter like the rest of nature, and then mind comprised everything human that could not be construed as material. In this way not only was the spiritual, or rational, soul distinguished from the body and from nature, but so also sensation, perception, appetite, and will, which would seem so clearly to be bodily qualities and functions, except in so far as the body, like the rest of nature, had been stripped of all sensitivity and life. Modern dualism split the *natural* human being in two; in this respect it was a new conception, distinct from the various kinds of dualism found in ancient and scholastic thought (Burtt 1932, pp. 113ff.; Copleston 1960, pp. 120ff.).

The modern distinction between matter and mind raised very many problems, including the problem of causal interaction. It always was unclear how mental processes, being immaterial, could causally influence matter, specifically the body and the brain, or vice versa. Furthermore, in so far as the material universe constituted a closed system in which energy remained constant, it seemed impossible that events within it should be affected by, or should affect, events in a different reality altogether. In brief, it was apparently impossible for Cartesian mental events to cause material events; in particular, they apparently could not be causes of behaviour. From here it may be seen that if explanations of behaviour in terms of mental events are causal, the mental events in question are unlikely to be of the sort defined by Cartesian dualism; and, in turn, the implication would then be that the behaviour to be explained would not be of the sort defined by Cartesian dualism, either. The Cartesian concepts of mind and matter (including the body and behaviour) stand or fall together.

In positing two such distinct substances as mind and matter, modern dualism made the prospect of relation between them irredeemably problematic. So far as concerned mind and body in particular, a relatively straightforward sign of the problem was the apparent impossibility of causal interaction between the two. But the same underlying difficulty gave rise to a variety of problems concerning the expression of mind in behaviour, among which was the 'problem of knowledge of other minds'.

Cartesian mind was private: mental states, according to dualism, are known directly in one's own case, but otherwise they can be known only indirectly, by problematic inference from behaviour and speech. This epistemological problem did not arise at the start. The great seventeenth-century epistemological problem was not knowledge of other minds, but knowledge of the reality posited by the new physics. It should be emphasized that this reality was not the familar one apparent in perception. Rather, the epistemological problem followed on the distinction between the world of sensory appearance and the *absolute* reality 'behind' it, a distinction fundamental to seventeenth-century science and made explicit in Cartesian dualism (Burtt 1932). The problem of knowledge of the external world (nature itself) remained the 'scandal of philosophy' until Kant. Within the Cartesian (seventeenth century) metaphysics, matter and mind were both problematic, each in their own, though interdependent, ways. Within this context, however, there was no problem of knowledge of other minds. This question, as to how one subject can know another, was beside the point, indeed could not arise, while there remained the problem of the (one) subject's knowledge of object. Rather, the problem of intersubjectivity began to make its appearance, through the nineteenth century, within post-Kantian idealism, as the subject came to be seen as embodied, within nature, and among others (Bolton 1982; Mensch 1988).

The problem of knowledge of mind, that is to say, of 'other minds', arose in a particularly stark form within the foundations of psychological science in the latter decades of the nineteenth century. The possibilities and the problems of the new science were defined by dualism. Given acceptance of the Cartesian concept of mind, scientific psychology confronted two main tasks: study of mental phenomena (consciousness, sensation, perception, memory, and so on), and study of their relation to physical events. The first programme constituted the core of psychology, the second was the subsidiary psychophysiology. Both required a method of observing mental events, and the methodology implied by dualism was clear: mental phenomena are observed directly by their subject in introspection, while they are known only indirectly by others, on the basis, primarily, of the subject's introspective reports. However, this introspectionist methodology was problematic on various counts, such as reliability and its restrictive reliance on language-use. Behind such practical disadvantages lay the fundamental problem that Cartesian mental states were epistemically private, inaccessible to public observation and verification. This privacy, and the ontological status of mind as distinct from matter, were thoroughly problematic from the point of view of science method.

New options were needed. An alternative was indeed available within dualism, for inherent in it was the possibility of an alternative methodology concerned exclusively with the material world, and to what is accessible to public observation, namely, *behaviour*. While behaviourism represented a radically new approach to psychological science, still it operated within the thought-space defined by Cartesian dualism. Behaviourism was defined by dualism, negatively and positively. Dualism defined what it was that behaviourism was excluding as irrelevant to science, namely, the Cartesian mind. Further, and positively, Cartesian dualism bequethed to behaviourism its general model of the topic of the new science, according to which the body, as Cartesian matter, is fundamentally non-intelligent, or *mechanical*, in particular, governed by the operation of reflex arcs. Behaviourism as a methodology eschewed reference to mental states for the purpose of explaining behaviour. Without a role in explanation, mental states were, from the point of view of psychological science, non-existent: there was no reason to posit them. Explanation of behaviour confined itself to causes in the environment, to stimuli affecting the agent. There was, however, available to methodological behaviourism a limited notion of something going on within the organism, namely, direct causal connections between stimuli and responses. These direct stimulus–response connections could be innately wired in, as anticipated in the Cartesian notion of the reflex arc, or made in learning procedures, according to the principles of association, in classical or operant conditioning. (On the early development of modern psychological science see, for example, Zangwill 1950; Robinson 1976; Gardner 1985; Baars 1986; Brennan 1986; Leahey 1994.)

1.2.2 Explanation of behaviour in terms of cognitive states

Methodological behaviourism combined with stimulus–response psychology dominated animal learning theory in the first decades of the twentieth century. There were signs of dissent even within animal learning theory, however, as psychologists in the 1930s and 1940s sought to model 'higher' forms of behaviour, and apparently found the need to invoke cognitive states and processes. Two related features of behaviour were particularly important here. First, animal behaviour is characteristically *purposive*, or *goal-directed*, and secondly, that this purposive behaviour is frequently *plastic*, that is to say, is flexible according to circumstances. One kind of example of plasticity is that of rats which, having learnt to run through a maze to the goal-box will, if the maze is flooded, swim to it (Macfarlane 1930). Flexible, purposive behaviour exhibits certain *higher-order invariants* which are not evident at the level of simple, physical (geometrical) descriptions of behaviour. Distinct sequences of behaviour can have in common that they lead to the same goal, and also, as in the example above, two behavioural sequences can follow the same path. It is then plausible to suppose that behaviour exhibits these invariants because the relevant features of the environment are *represented in (encoded in)* the animal. This is to say, what the animal acquires in the learning process is a 'map' of the maze, and an 'expectancy' of the goal. In this way plastic, purposive behaviour lends itself to cognitive modes of description and explanation, while non-purposive, or uniform, stereotyped behaviour, does not. Many experiments were devised to demonstrate the purposive nature of behaviour, and, in particular, various types of plasticity of means to end.[1]

Cognitive learning theory stands in contrast to the more straightforward stimulus–response model. According to the former, associations between stimuli are acquired, not only associations between stimuli and responses. The contrast here can be expressed in various ways. One is to say that the cognitive model posits *representations* of the environment, something like a 'mental map', the most simple form of which would be patterns of stimulus–stimulus associations. On the other hand, it is worthwhile noting that the stimulus–response model can be construed as positing a kind of representation: stimuli are represented at least in the sense that they cause specific responses. The connection between representation of the environment and the behaviour it gives rise to is very clear in stimulus–response theory. In fact, however, the connection is made too close, so that the difference between representation and the behaviour caused collapses, and we are left only with the latter. What happens in cognitive theory is that representations of stimuli are allowed *to interact with one another* before the production of behaviour. This feature of the theory accomodates the fact that there is (in 'higher' behaviour) no one–one link between particular stimuli and particular responses. Hence also the frequently cited characterization of cognitive as opposed to stimulus–response theory, namely, that it explains behaviour as a response to *interpretations* of stimuli, not to stimuli immediately; or again, that the connection between stimuli and responses is mediated by representations.

Another way of making out the difference between the cognitive paradigm and the earlier stimulus–response psychology uses the term *information*. According to the cognitive model, information is picked up from the environment, processed, which processing includes assimilation into pre-existing cognitive maps, and states carrying processed information mediate between between stimulus and response. Stimulus–response explanation, on the other hand, needs a notion of information defined only in terms of the S–R linkage, a notion so minimal that it does not require separate consideration.

Stimulus–response psychology belonged with behaviourist methodology, as noted above, and so naturally the theoretical move towards the cognitive paradigm implied also a methodological shift. The methodological question is: what is required for an adequate explanation of behaviour? Given Cartesian preconceptions according to which mental states are immaterial and causally irrelevant, it follows readily enough that they will have no role in the explanation of behaviour, that our methodological presuppositions should be confined to environmental stimuli, and their direct causal effect on behaviour. The question, then, was whether this alone could do all the required explanatory work. And the answer seemed to be 'no' in the case of explanation of the goal-directed and plastic characteristics of higher animal behaviour. And in so far as these characteristics require for their explanation the postulate of representations, or information-carrying states, then this postulate becomes a methodological presupposition.

In the background of this move away from behaviourism is an epistemological change on a large scale. A fundamental reason why early psychological science eschewed mental states was that they were epistemically private, accessible only to the subject, by introspection. The issues in animal learning theory, however, were already well removed from this Cartesian concept of mind. The issues, of course, had nothing to do with rats introspecting mental states, but rather concerned what was needed in theory for the explanation of behaviour and, together with that, for predictive power. In psychological science, mental states are introduced into the picture, if they are introduced at all, if theory requires them for the purposes of explanation and prediction of behaviour. As already indicated, their role in theory is essentially a matter of carrying information, used in the control of action. This use of the notion of mental states is quite different from the Cartesian. In the Cartesian framework the definition of mental states is fundamentally epistemological: mental states are known immediately, infallibly, by their subject. It is precisely this property that makes mental states so far irrelevant to psychological science. Mental states become relevant to psychological science in so far as postulating them facilitates the purposes of scientific theory, these being, briefly, explanation and prediction. This handle on the notion of mental states presupposes, indeed is, an epistemology. The theory of knowledge of mental states is, in very broad terms, as follows: mental states are known (beliefs about them are evaluated) with reference to the predictive power and success of theory which postulates them.

Two features of this new epistemology may be noted here. First, it suits primarily a third-person perspective, and owes an account of any special characteristics of first-person (subjective) knowledge of mental states. The position here is exactly the opposite to the Cartesian. Secondly, the new epistemology of mental states, with its appeal to theory as opposed to direct observation, belongs with a more general 'post-empiricist' epistemology. These two points, concerning post-empiricist epistemology, and knowledge of one's own mental states, will be taken up later in the chapter, in section 1.4.

There was much to be said on either side of the debate within animal learning theory between the stimulus–response and cognitive approaches, but as is well-known, and as just implied, the issue was not at all just a local one. A paradigm shift in and around psychological science was beginning. The debate within animal learning theory came to be settled decisively in favour of the cognitive model, largely under the influence of external developments, which showed up inadequacies in the concepts of stimulus–response theory, and which replaced rigidly construed behavioural methodology by methodologies explicitly employing cognitive concepts. These developments were particularly in linguistics, artificial intelligence and mathematical information theory, and they promoted what has come to be called the 'cognitive revolution' in psychology in the 1950s and 1960s. Let us review briefly these external influences.[2]

We consider first Chomsky's well-known critique (1959) of Skinner's project of explaining language learning and use in terms of the concepts and principles of stimulus–response theory. Chomsky's criticisms illustrate the points discussed above concerning the weaknesses of stimulus–response theory and its accompanying strict behavioural methodology. Early in the paper Chomsky remarks on the reason why Skinner's programme appears so 'bold and remarkable' (Chomsky 1959, pp. 48–49, original italics):

> It is not primarily the fact that he has set functional analysis as his problem, or that he limits himself to study of *observables*, i.e., input–output relations. What is so surprising is the particular limitations he has imposed on the way in which the observables of behaviour are to be studied, and, above all, the particularly simple nature of the *function* which, he claims, describes the causation of behaviour. One would naturally expect that prediction of the behavior of a complex organism (or machine) would require, in addition to information about external stimulation, knowledge of the internal structure of the organism, the ways in which it processes input information and organizes its own behavior.

Such reference to 'internal' structure and processes was precisely what Skinner wished to avoid, emphasizing rather external factors, such as stimulus, reinforcement, etc. Chomsky proceeded to argue, however, that these (and related) fundamental concepts of conditioning theory, while they may be given relatively specific operational definitions in the experimental paradigms of animal learning theory, come to lose clear meaning outside of these contexts, and the principles (laws) which employ them become vacuous or trivial. On the notion of *stimulus-control* of an utterance, for example, Chomsky writes (Chomsky 1959, p. 52, original italics):

> A typical example . . . would be the response to a piece of music with the utterance *Mozart* or to a painting with response *Dutch*. These responses are asserted to be 'under the control of extremely subtle properties' of the physical object or event [Skinner 1957, p. 108]. Suppose instead of saying *Dutch* we had said *Clashes with the wall-paper, I thought you liked abstract work, Never saw it before, Tilted, Hanging too low, Beautiful, Hideous, Remember our camping trip last summer?*, or whatever else might come into our minds when looking at the picture . . . Skinner could only say that each of these responses is under the control of some other stimulus property of the physical object. If we look at a red chair and say *red*, the response is under the stimulus control of the stimulus *redness*; if we say *chair*, it is under the control of the collection of properties *chairness* . . ., and similarly for any other response. This device is as simple as it is empty.

The point at issue here is that in complex behaviour, such as speaking a language, there is plasticity in response: we can respond in many ways to the same stimulus. Or better, in many ways to the same stimulus *as described in physical terms*. To say in *these* terms that behaviour is under stimulus-control is false. On the other hand, we can adopt an alternative way of characterizing the stimulus, namely, the stimulus *as represented by*, or, *as described by*, the subject; but then, we lose complete objectivity in the description, and rely on the familiar concepts of common-sense, mentalistic psychology. And to say in *these* terms that behaviour is under stimulus-control may well be true, but if so, trivially. Thus, Chomsky continues (ibid.):

> Since properties are free for the asking . . . we can account for a wide class of responses in terms of Skinnerian functional analysis by identifying the *controlling stimuli*. But the word *stimulus* has lost all objectivity in this usage. Stimuli are no longer part of the outside physical world; they are driven back into the organism. We identify the stimulus when we hear the response. It is clear from such examples, which abound, that the talk of stimulus control simply disguises a complete retreat to mentalistic psychology.

The problem for the claim that utterances are under stimulus control can be put briefly as follows. Either the stimulus is identified independently of the meaning of the utterance (e.g. in physical terms) or its identification depends on the meaning of the utterance. But on the first reading the claim is false, and on the second it is vacuous. What is vacuous here is any purported explanation of uttering sentences with this or that meaning.

The same general obstacle faces the attempt to define the meaningful content of information-carrying states in terms of their causes. Such a proposal goes under the name of causal semantics; it will be discussed in Chapter 4 and faced with a line of argument similar to Chomsky's against Skinner. We anticipated these sorts of issues earlier in the discussion of the cognitive paradigm in contrast with stimulus–response psychology, concluding that, at least in the psychological explanation of higher behaviour, the content of representation cannot be defined primarily in terms of the stimuli represented, but rather with reference to the activity which, in interaction with other representations, it regulates.

Related problems are encountered in the definition of *response*. One problem pointed out by Chomsky is that Skinner does not attempt to specify what kind of similarity in form is required for two physical events to be considered instances of the same operant. Chomsky, as Skinner, is concerned here of course with identifying units of verbal behaviour, but the problem of *criteria of identification of responses* is a general one for operant theory. Consider an example that is not to do with language: the movement, physically defined, of lifting one's arm. This could count as a variety of actions (or behaviours), such as stretching, greeting, holding up the traffic, surrendering, depending on the context, internal and external. The same physical event (bodily movement) can be many behaviours. But also vice versa: the same behaviour (or action) can be instanced by a variety of bodily movements. In this critical sense the notions of *same behaviour*, and of *behaviour* itself, await definition. As Chomsky observes in connection with linguistic utterances, 'extrapolation' of the definition of response from the limited experimental paradigms is of no use: operational definitions cannot (by definition) be applied to a different class of phenomena (Chomsky p. 1959, 53).

The issue here is nothing less than the nature of the *explanandum* for psychological theory, and it can be usefully expressed in terms of 'intentionality', a concept that will be discussed in Section 1.3. Stimulus–response theory is most happy with the response being understood as being a physically defined movement of the body. Behaviour in this sense has no intentionality—in brief, it is not about anything—and is likely not to require any posit of regulation by intentional states for its explanation. But on the other hand, and of course, it is also taken for granted that the behaviour of interest to (any) psychological theory does have intentionality, whether the behaviour be, for example, bar-pressing, or speech production. Typically, as Chomsky observes, S–R theory trades on ambiguity between construing behaviour as being non-intentional on the one hand and intentional on the other, with the heavy reliance on operational definition in terms of experimental paradigms allowing and obscuring this ambiguity. The significance of this is that what is required in theory critically depends on the nature of the behavioural *explanandum*. While non-intentional behaviour can be regarded as the effects of non-intentional causes, explanation of intentional behaviour, with its characteristic goal-directedness and adapativeness, requires the notion of regulation by intentional states. Aspects of this point have been considered earlier in this section, and it is discussed further below (subsection 1.3.6).

The correspondence between behavioural movements and the actions thereby performed is a loose and variable one. Here we see an expression of the plasticity which causes profound trouble for behaviourism and S–R theory. There is no simple one–one mapping between physically defined stimuli and stimuli that control behaviour, and none either between physically defined bodily movements and behaviour. The (considerable) slack between physically defined events and the behavioural phenomena is precisely what is taken up with reference to internal, cognitive processes. And so, in attempting to make plausible his operant theory, Skinner repeatedly lapses into (for him) illicit reliance on mentalistic concepts. This happens again, Chomsky notes (1959, pp. 53–4), in the case of response-strength, defined as 'probability of emission': Skinner's detailed treatment of examples relies on appeal to concepts such as *interest, intention, belief.*

The trouble with Skinner's notion of reinforcement, and the law of effect which invokes it, is even more acute. Since reinforcement is defined as a stimulus capable of increasing response-strength, the claim of the Law of Effect, that reinforcement increases response-strength, is patently a tautology. Skinner is forced into this trivialization because of the impossibility of finding a non-vacuous characterization of reinforcement, that is, colloquially, of what living beings are motivated to work for. Of course, examples abound, but can they be captured without reference to what living creatures in fact do work for? Presumably not. And consequently, the so-called law of effect is doomed to vacuousness, or, at the very least, it has no advantages over our common-sense, mentalistic explanations. Having reviewed many of Skinner's examples of reinforcement, Chomsky concludes (Chomsky pp. 1959, 56–7, original italics):

> The phrase 'X is reinforced by Y . . .' is being used for a cover term for 'X wants Y', 'X likes Y', 'X wishes that Y were the case', etc. Invoking the term *reinforcement* has no explanatory force, and any idea that this paraphrase introduces any new clarity or objectivity into the description of wishing, liking, etc., is a serious delusion. . . . A mere terminological revision, in which a term borrowed from the laboratory is used with the full vagueness of the ordinary vocabulary, is of no conceivable interest.

Following his critique of Skinner's programme, Chomsky outlined a positive way forward, namely, consideration of the syntactic structure of language, and of the way in which knowledge of grammer, internalized in the speaker, contributes to verbal behaviour. In this way the notion of *internalized structures and rules* became central to a cognitive, non-behavioural, theory of language learning and use. The details, however, of Chomsky's new linguistics are not our concern in the present argument. The relevant points may be summarized as follows: that stimulus–response psychology, and the concepts of conditioning on which it is based, are inadequate for the explanation of complex, plastic behaviour; that its systematic attempt to down-play the subject's contribution in such behaviour becomes combined with implicit and illicit reliance on the mentalistic concepts of common sense; and that an explicit theory of the subjective contribution to complex behaviour typically postulates internalized structures and rules. This latter idea became pivotal in the new 'cognitive revolution' in psychology.

A second major influence contributing to this revolution in the 1950s and 1960s was the application in psychology of methods and models from the new discipline of artificial intelligence (AI), that is, the construction of machines, computers, real or ideal, which can simulate aspects of (natural) intelligence. The relevance of AI methodology to cognitive psychology is profound. It provides ways of conceiving and modelling mental processes, such as (obviously) computation, and (less obviously) attention and perception, which, on the one hand, permit experimental investigation and test, and which, on the other, carry no implication that these mental processes operate within some non-physical medium. In these ways the new methodology removed two major obstacles to the scientific study of the mind, obstacles that had given rise, inevitably but temporarily, to behaviourism. AI terminology and methodology greatly influenced the theory of and research into particular cognitive capacities: attention, perception, memory, language comprehension, etc. (Neisser 1967; Anderson 1983; Johnson-Laird 1988; Boden 1988). But in addition to this influence in faculty-specific research, and of course related to it, the new AI gave new and powerful form to cognitive theories of behaviour. It endorsed and elaborated the idea that cognitive processes are involved in the organization and regulation of complex, plastic, rule-guided behaviour (Miller *et al.* 1960). It is this contribution of AI which is of particular relevance to the present theme.

It may be remarked immediately, however, that the AI model of cognitive processes at work in the mediation of behaviour raises as well as solves conceptual problems. As noted in the above discussion of cognitive theories of animal learning, what seems to be required for the explanation of complex behaviour is the concept of a *representation of the environment*. Now while AI offers a model of internal processes which underlie intelligent behaviour, the model is essentially one of *computations*, that is, roughly, rule-following manipulations of (transformations of) symbols; but there is apparently no mention yet of anything like *representation of the environment*. This is to say, the concepts in AI pertain, at least in the first instance, to the *syntax* of symbols, but they do not yet explicate their *semantics*, that is, their meaning, or their representational properties. This indeed has been regarded as one of the major inadequacies of AI models of mental processes. Or, the argument can be turned the other way round: success of computational models of mind can be used to cast doubt on the legitimacy of concepts of mind which invoke meaning. These issues are taken up in the next chapter.

Let us finally mention briefly a third major influence contributing to the cognitive revolution in psychology, mathematical communication theory (MCT) (Shannon and Weaver 1949). MCT is concerned with certain statistical quantities associated with 'sources', 'channels', and 'receivers'. When a particular condition is realized at a source, and there are other conditions which could have been realized, the source can be regarded as a *generator of information*. For example, in throwing a dice the result reduces six possibilities to one actuality, and therefore generates information, quantified as log (2) 6, = 2.6 bits. The amount of information generated is relative to a receiver, in particular, to the amount of information already in the receiver about the source; in the example above it is assumed that prior to the throw we know only that six results are equally possible. Various applications of MCT to psychology were made, for example in psychophysical models (Miller 1953; Attneave 1959; Garner 1962).

However, in addition to specific applications of details of MCT, it reinforced use of the information-processing terminology which has come to pervade cognitive psychology and the cognitive sciences generally. The terminology can be used to formulate the basic tenets of cognitive psychology such as the following: information is picked up from the environment, by the sense-receptors, processed (transformed, encoded) in certain ways, including into representations of the environment, which then serve in the organization and regulation of complex (purposive, plastic, rule-guided) behaviour.

On the other hand, it must be noted that the concept of information used in this way is quite distinct from, though related to, the concept as used in MCT. The concept required in cognitive psychology is, as we have already seen, a semantic one: we are interested in the fact that particular signals carry information from (and about) the environment, that this informational content is employed in the production of representations and the regulation of organism/environment interactions. The idea of informational content does not, however, figure in MCT. The mathematical theory is concerned with *how much* information is carried, not with *what* information is carried. Indeed, it does not deal with particular signals at all, hence not with their content, but with classes of signals, and the statistical averages of the amounts of information carried. In this sense the mathematical theory is of no immediate relevance in explicating the concept of semantic information which underpins theorizing in cognitive psychology, and cognitive explanations of behaviour in particular.[3]

Following this partial and brief survey of some of the major influences on the cognitive revolution in psychology, let us return to the issue with which we began, the conflict within psychology between cognitive and stimulus–response learning theories. The characteristics of animal behaviour cited in order to introduce the concepts of cognition were its goal-directedness and its plasticity. Traditionally, behaviours with these characteristics have been contrasted with behaviours, such as salivation, for which stimulus–response theory seems adequate. From a biological point of view, however, there is every reason to say that the systems serving responses such as salivation are goal-directed. Furthermore, the information-processing paradigm of course applies here. So the distinction between behaviour explicable in terms of stimulus–response connections, and 'higher' behaviour of the sort emphasized by the cognitive learning theories cannot be brought out in terms of goal-directness and information-processing. The notion of 'higher' here requires explication in some other way, and the implication of the above considerations is that it has to do with *plasticity*.

Plasticity is of two basic types: first, in cases where the same response is made to a variety of stimuli, secondly in cases where a variety of responses are made to the same stimulus. In brief, the S–R relation is not one–one, but is one–many or many–one. Both these types of plasticity occur in the context of goal-directed behaviour, and they have the function precisely to serve in the attainment of the relevant goal. The goal is constant, but if it is to be achieved under varying patterns of environmental conditions, the behaviour of the living being has to be adaptive, plastic in one or other or both of the ways described. Adaptive behaviour thus exhibits *invariants* across physically distinct stimuli, responses, and sequences of interaction. It is in this respect that we distinguish 'higher' animal behaviour (such as flexible route-finding, problem-solving) from conditioned behaviour, and even more so from the operation of biological subsystems, which, though goal-directed and mediated by information, exhibit no, or relatively less, plasticity.

The above remarks suggest a connection between behavioural plasticity and the nature of informational content. In the absence of plasticity, it is plausible to say that patterns of information are already in the environment, requiring only to be picked up and used (acted upon) by an appropriately designed system. But to the extent that there is plasticity, patterns of information already in the environment are not of the kind apparently at work in the regulation of behaviour. Rather, what regulates behaviour has to be considered the result of work done within the living being. The information has to be more 'processed'. For example, two physically distinct stimuli, or two physically distinct sequences of behaviour, have to come to be treated as the same. The conclusion is, then, that information-processing systems are more complex, 'higher', indeed increasingly 'cognitive', to the degree that the result of processing which regulates behaviour of the system is different from the information being received. Or again: to the degree that behaviour is determined by 'subjective' as well as 'objective' factors.

All these considerations, concerning plasticity, informational content, the importance of contribution of the agent, the distinction between lower and higher forms of cognition, will recur repeatedly in one context or another throughout this essay.

We consider next what the cognitive psychology paradigm has to say about two large topics: consciousness and affect. These brief discussions are included to make more adequate the characterization of the cognitive paradigm used here, with particular attention to points directly relevant to the main themes of the essay, concerning the explanation of behaviour in terms of meaningful, mental states.

1.2.3 In living beings cognition is already affective

It is obvious enough, given the formative influence of such disciplines as transformational linguistics, AI modelling, and mathematical communication theory, that cognitive psychology erred on the side of saying little about affect. Producers of syntactic strings of symbols, computers, and mathematically defined signal exchangers are, so far, unemotional. On the other hand, and as made prominent in the presentation in the preceding section, fundamental to cognitive psychology was the project of explaining animal behaviour in terms of cognitive states. The cognitive theory of action has to posit at least goals, methods of achieving them, and means of determining success or failure, and these elements are enough to provide a basis for the concept of affect (Miller *et al.* 1960; Pfeifer 1988; Oatley 1988). The absence of the notion from the models that helped to form cognitive psychology was connected to the fact that these critical elements were more or less obviously absent. The production of well-formed syntax so far has no point, except itself. Neither does information exchange between mathematically defined systems. Computers can be made to perform tasks, but they don't mind whether they achieve them or not, and in this sense the tasks, and the notions of success and failure, are ours rather than theirs. The notions of goals, and success and failure in achieving them, belong primarily to biological systems, for which success as opposed to failure *matters*.

Living beings depend for their survival on achieving certain outcomes and avoiding others. They show a definite preference for success in these tasks, and hence interest in the environment and the results of their actions. We refer here to the activity of the living being as a whole, but the notions of goals, success, and failure can be applied secondarily to biological subsystems, in so far as their normal functioning is essential for the integrity of the whole. The adaptiveness and plasticity of action is designed precisely for the achievement of goals in the face of variation and adversity. The position for living as opposed to inanimate systems is that they strive to achieve whatever is required for their integrity. Adaptiveness, plasticity, urgency, rest, and motion are examples of the kind of behavioural characteristics that the notion of 'striving to achieve' seeks to capture and interpret.

This is the context in which the notion of affect starts to work. States of affairs have a 'valency' for the living being, positive or negative, according to whether they promote or disrupt its integrity and capacity for action. Perception of states of affairs as being in this sense positive or negative is linked closely to plans for appropriate action, such as approach or avoidance. In this way affective responses to situations are associated with motives for action. Commonly cited as basic emotions are happiness, anger, fear, sadness, and disgust. With the possible exception of the latter, these emotions involve perceptions of situations as affecting integrity and action, and are closely linked to behavioural responses. Happiness is linked to achievement of goals and perhaps temporary absence of others; anger is a response to being hurt, and includes the impulse to retaliate, fear includes perception of threat and leads to fleeing or fighting, sadness follows loss of what is valued, and involves yearning, and so on. The notion of 'basic emotions' here belongs to biology and evolutionary theory in particular, but also to the a priori (philosophical) theory of action. There is a close link between these two kinds of theory, exploited throughout the essay, in so far as each seeks to define what is fundamental to action.[4]

Cognition and affect are both defined in terms of action: cognition serves action by processing information; affect signifies the point of it all. But these are interwoven, aspects of one activity. The goals of action have to be represented, and its methods have to have an aim. From the point of view of the philosophy and psychology of action, emotion has cognitive structure and content, and cognition is in the service of achieving aims, and hence involves affect.

These principles will recur in a variety of contexts as we proceed. They affirm close links between cognition and emotion, but this is not to say that the two are indistinguishable. Clearly they are, to some extent, depending on the type of case in hand. Cognitive processing can be relatively affect-less, in the absence of any real goal or, again, if divorced from action. How far processing here is typical of cognition in everyday life is open to doubt, and this is reflected in the increasing shift of focus in cognitive psychology from articifical experimental paradigms to those with more ecological (and biological) validity. Also, emotion may be in various ways independent of cognition, and this is exploited in research on the effects of mood on cognition. It is, for example, possible to make someone unhappy by giving her information (e.g. about a loss) and then to study what effects this negative mood state has on memory, for example that she remembers negative events, such as previous losses. Clearly, this kind of interaction does not count against the general principle that emotions are cognitive and cognitions emotional.[5]

On the other hand, emotion may be experienced in the apparent absence of appropriate cognition. However, assuming that the emotion is salient (intense, persistent, with effects on behaviour), the apparent absence of appropriate cognition raises the question of abnormal function. A possible explantion is that the emotion has been caused not by the processing of information but by lower-level interference to the physiological structures and processes which serve the emotions, for example by naturally occurring biochemical imbalance. Another kind of explanation is that emotion and cognition have become dissociated for psychological reasons: the object of the emotion may be intolerable to the person, for example. In the same way there are, broadly speaking, two ways of explaining cognition in the apparent absence of the appropriate emotion. One posits lower-level disruption of information-processing, the other invokes rules at the level of the information-carrying states themselves. The distinction between these two kinds of causal pathway, and their roles in the generation of disorder, will be developed as major themes in the essay, and need not detain us here. For now the main point is simply that the apparent absence of connection between (strong) emotion and appropriate cognition so far suggests a breakdown in normal functioning, and in this sense such cases are exceptions that prove the rule.

The interwoven nature of cognition and emotion in living beings may be expressed by saying that cognitive states, to the extent that they are emotionally charged, are already sources of energy, specifically motivators of action. The formulation is relevant to the conclusion drawn in this chapter, that explanations which invoke mental, meaningful states are causal, and to the claim worked out through chapters 4 and 5 that information-processing, or intentionality, is the basis of a distinctive form of causal explanation.

1.2.4. Consciousness: empirical questions and philosophical problems

We turn now to consider the role of consciousness in the cognitive psychology paradigm. Cognitive states are posited as representations (information-carrying states) involved in the regulation of action. This conception, or definition, of cognition stands in marked contrast to the Cartesian. In Cartesian dualism, cognition is a feature of mind, as opposed to matter, and the defining characteristic of mind is that it is known indubitably to the subject. In this conception, it is not at all part of the definition of cognition that it serves action, nor indeed that it represents anything external: Cartesian mind could, in principle, be just as it is even in the absence of the body and of the rest of the external, material world. The absence in the Cartesian famework of any role for mind in the running of behaviour shows up clearly in its conception of behaviour as mechanical, as 'non-intelligent'. But just as the Cartesian conception has little to say about those features of mind, cognition and behaviour, which are treated as axiomatic in cognitive psychology, so conversely, cognitive psychology has some difficulty encompassing what is fundamental in Cartesian dualism: subjective awareness, or consciousness. This is to say, these concepts are not built into the foundations of the theory, historically or logically.

Within the cognitive psychology paradigm, the essential function of cognitive states is to serve in the regulation of action, and it does not belong to their definition that they are known to the subject. Indeed, and this is the point already implicit in the paragraph above, the paradigm so far has nothing to say about cognitive states 'being known to the subject'. Cognitive psychology can accomodate the notions of consciousness and subjective awareness in its own terms, that is, in so far as they have a role in explanation of certain features of information-processing and (ultimately) the regulation of action. These features would include selective attention, high levels of analysis (processing), executive control, and the subjective report in language of information-processing and information-carrying states. It is typically for the purpose of explaining phenomena of these kinds that cognitive psychological models invoke the notion of consciousness. A corollary, unsuprising in the context sketched above, is that in terms of these sorts of criteria of consciousness, most information-processing is pre-conscious or unconscious. Conscious states and processes are a subset of those that regulate behaviour, for example, as already indicated, those with an executive role, and/or closely linked (in language-users) to verbal report.

In this general context many kinds of question arise, more or less connected to one another. One immediate issue is whether the external criteria of consciousness can diverge. Can there be cognitive states which regulate behaviour but which are, in principle, inaccessible to conscious reporting? Do unconscious cognitive states use something other than language-like symbolism? Are they linked particularly with drives, or emotions? Can conscious and unconscious regulations of action come into conflict, with the implication of disorder in case they do? Aspects of some of these issues will be considered later, for example conflict and disorder in subsection 1.4.3 and Chapter 8, and distinction between kinds of encoding in AI models in the next chapter (Section 2.2). Otherwise, we leave aside details of the distinction between conscious and unconscious in terms of the cognitive psychology paradigm, making only the general observation that in the paradigm what is essential to cognitive states is regulation of behaviour, as opposed to 'subjective awareness'. This general conception permits subsequent distinctions between conscious and unconscious modes of cognition and the formulation of empirical questions about them as indicated above.[6]

We shall return to the role of consciousness later, in a developmental context (Section 6.4), but before leaving the topic at this stage we may note that philosophical as well as empirical questions surround the concept. These 'philosophical problems' derive from the Cartesian concept of mind and the deep theory change involved in its replacement by the cognitive-behavioural paradigm. The dualism between mind and matter in seventeenth-century philosophy, as formulated by Descartes, was overdetermined, being many distinctions at once. Mind was equivalent to consciousness, to appearance, and to representation (thought), in contrast to matter, which was the reality represented by thought. The seventeenth-century picture as a whole was highly and irredeemably problematic, mainly because the postulated reality lay beyond the appearances and could be not be known directly, or at all, by the subject of thought, the *cogito*. But notwithstanding this major anomaly, the theory stood, supported by fundamental assumptions. As already indicated (subsection 1.2.1), a major assumption of the modern world-view was that the material world described by the new philosophy of nature (physics) was absolute, and therefore had to be distinguished from the objects given in sense-appearances, which are relative objects, tainted by subjectivity.

Moving beyond this original seventeenth-century metaphysics, a more superficial dualism takes for granted the material world, including (human) bodies, and then wonders whether these bodies (other than one's own) have immaterial minds. This 'problem of other minds' has already been mentioned (in subsection 1.2.1) as implicated in methodological behaviourism. It is essentially a hotchpotch problem, a transitionary thought-stage between the original Cartesian dualism and the non-dualist idea that mind is revealed in the activity of the human body (being), an idea which in turn permits knowledge of one subject by another. The view that mental processes regulate higher activity, and hence can be inferred on the basis of that activity, has become commonplace, and, accordingly, scepticism about other minds has become out of date, a 'philosophical' problem only, or one belonging to the early history of psychological science.

However, the hotchpotch problem still lives on, just about, in a still more emaciated form, as the (or one of the) 'philosophical' problems of *consciousness*. Do living beings, or some of them, have conscious states (sometimes called 'qualia'), or some special quality of awareness, over and above particular forms of information-processing, undetectable by any means known to man or woman? What can be detected, from the outside, are (only), we are inclined to say, *signs* of consciousness, of particular forms of information-processing, such as selective attention and self-report. But consciousness itself, so this line of thought continues, seems unknowable, except in one's own case. But then—and here we have the feeling of a typically philosophical conundrum—in one's own case one seems to be aware of *nothing but* objects of consciousness. After all—and here we remind ourselves of the original Cartesian problem (subsection 1.2.1)—what one knows in one's own case are conscious sense-experiences (sights, sounds, touch, etc.), not any material substance over and above (or underneath) these.

The correct inference here is that consciousness cannot be thought of as something separable from the objects of empirical knowledge. There is, however, a distinction to be drawn between the subject's knowledge of objects and the subject's knowledge of other subjects. In the former, consciousness is indistinguishable from the experience of reality. In the latter, consciousness in another subject is indistinguishable from its appearances in the person's activity, and this is the methodological assumption suited to cognitive science.[7]

1.2.5 'Folk psychology' within the paradigm

The cognitive paradigm in psychological science posits cognitive, information-carrying states for the purpose of explaining and predicting complex behaviour. Now it is apparent—when looked at in this way—that folk psychology does the same sort of thing.

Explanation of behaviour in terms of the mental states of the agent are familiar in everyday discourse. In order to explain why a person is acting in such-and-such a way we suppose that she has, at least, certain beliefs and a desire: beliefs about current circumstances and about the effects of her actions, and desire for a particular result. This form of psychological explanation is apparently used in all cultures including our own, and prior to any psychological science, and it has come to be called in the recent literature 'folk psychology' (Stich 1983; Fodor 1987; Astington *et al.* 1988; Mele 1992). A critical point here is that folk psychology does not serve only the hermeneutic purpose of making sense of the phenomena retrospectively, but also facilitates the prediction of action. This may be made by a detached observer, but prediction here also, and most importantly, means the mutual anticipation which is a condition of social life.

Folk psychology includes explanations of action in terms of beliefs and desires, but also accounts of the origin of beliefs in terms of experience, of experience in terms of reality, and of desire in terms of need. These sorts of explanation are characteristic of folk psychology, but they are also used in the social sciences and in some branches of psychology, such as social, developmental, and clinical psychology, especially in the psychoanalytic tradition.

Crucial to folk psychological mental states is their so-called meaningful content, typically specified by propositional clauses of natural languages, referring to actual or possible states of affairs. A person has the belief that such-and-such is the case, or the desire that it should be the case; and so on. The meaning of mental states is critical to the interconnections among them, and to their relation to action.

The at least superficial similarity between cognitive-behavioural psychology and folk psychology may give rise to surprise and consternation. The surprise is that while scientifically respectable paradigms, such as conditioning theory and physiological psychology, say little or nothing about mind and meaning, these being matters for the unscientific folk, including the pseudo-scientific psychoanalytic theorists, we now have a scientifically respectable paradigm, the successor to conditioning theory, and compatible with an up-dated physiological psychology, which essentially posits something like mental, meaningful, intervening states for the purpose of explaining behaviour. Then the consternation: so does not the cognitive paradigm here come up against all that looked problematic about this sort of alleged explanation? How can there be a 'science' of mind, or of meaning? One response then is to back-peddle: cognitive psychology does not really posit anything like meaningful, mental states, after all. This skirmish will be discussed later (in subsection 1.3.8, and again in Section 4.4), but first we turn in the next section to work around the problem of meaning, specifically bringing out its intimate link with action (interaction) and hence its fundamental role in psychological theory.

1.3 INTENTIONALITY AND MEANING: THE MARK OF MIND AND ACTION

1.3.1 Some (rough) definitions

Intentionality is a concept much used in current philosophy of mind and psychological theory. It has two main aspects. First, it refers to *aboutness* (or *directedness*). To say that a belief (or fear, or hope, or any other information-carrying state) has intentionality means partly that it is *about something*, typically an object, or state of affairs. Furthermore, and this is the second aspect of intentionality, it is not necessary that this 'something', that which, for example, the belief is about, exists in reality. One can believe that such-and-such is the case, when it is not; one can fear something that does not exist; and so on. The proposal that intentionality is the defining characteristic of mind, credited to Brentano (1874), has become the focus of many issues in contemporary philosophical and theoretical psychology.[8]

Readers unfamiliar with this term of philosophical art should note that intentionality as meant here has nothing specifically to do with intentions in the everyday sense, except in so far as intentions, like any other mental states, have intentionality, and the concept has still less to do with conscious, verbally expressed intentions.

A philosophical term of art distinct though connected to *intentionality* is *intensionality* (spelt with an 's' rather than a 't'). It may be thought of as applying directly to sentences, and secondarily to the states they describe. Two characterizations of intensionality may be given, though they can be made into one. One of the characterizations is plainly close to the definition of intentionality: a compound sentence is intensional if its truth-value does not depend on the truth-value of its component. Thus, it may be true that John believes that angels exist irrespective of whether they do.

The second way of characterizing the intensionality of sentences is as follows: a sentence is intensional if its truth-value is not preserved by substitution of co-extensive terms. John may want the biggest teddy bear in the room, though he still may not want Jill's teddy, even if . . ., etc. We can also take an example relevant to attempts to define informational content in terms of evolutionary theory, discussed at length in Chapter 4 (Section 4.5). Frogs snap at flies but also at small, ambient black dots which are not flies. What is the content of the informational states driving the behaviour: 'fly' or '(any) ambient black dot'? In effect we are asking here about the nature of the intentional object of the information-carrying state and of the behaviour that it regulates, and this can usefully be understood as a question about the appropriate intensional description.

Most mental states are described by sentences that are intensional in one or both of the above senses. Implications include that we can believe and want things that do not exist, and that we may believe or want certain things under some descriptions but not under others. These are, of course, enormously important facts about us, about our mentality in particular, to which we shall return in various ways throughout the essay. The main point may be stated briefly by saying that the mental states are about reality conceived in specific ways, in certain ways rather than others, and may be about what in reality does not exist.

Concepts closely linked to intentionality (and intensionality), include thought, representation, meaning, and information. All of these are essentially to do with 'aboutness' and 'inexistence' in the senses outlined above. The link between intentionality and thought (or thinking) suggests that Brentano's thesis is to some extent anticipated in the Cartesian idea that the *cogito* defines the mind. The close link between intentionality and meaning is expressed in the fact that intentional objects may also be called the meaning, or the meaningful content, of the intentional states. Information, too, seems to have intentionality: signals carry information about, for example, relative spatial position, or the information *that* such-and-such, etc., and it is also possible for informational content to be in *error*.

A main theme in the essay will be that intentionality, in the technical sense defined above, in terms of *aboutness* and 'inexistence', characterizes the 'information' invoked in cognitive psychological models, and indeed also that invoked in the information-processing models that permeate biology (subsection 1.3.7; Chapter 5). It is obviously critical to these lines of thought that intentionality is understood in the technical sense and is not restricted by definition to conscious, verbally expressed states of mind.

One way of expressing the line of argument to be developed later, referred to in the preceding paragraph, is to say that it extends Brentano's thesis downwards, the proposal being that intentionality characterizes not only states of mind, but more generally, the information-carrying states in functional, biological systems.

The connection between intentionality, activity, and function will be discussed briefly below (subsections 1.3.3, 1.3.4), and in more detail in chapters 4 and 5. We begin by discussing in the next subsection what the proposed view stands opposed to, this being, briefly, that intentionality (representation, thought, meaning) is a matter of being something like a picture of reality.

1.3.2 An old theory: resemblance (pictures)

In cognitive-behavioural psychology mental states are attributed to an agent, and on this basis action is explained and predicted. An essential feature of at least some of these mental states is that they carry information about the environment, about the scene of action. Such information-carrying, meaningful states are variously known as perceptions, beliefs, representations, mental models, and so on.

At this stage many questions arise. What is a representation? How does anything represent anything else, and some particular thing? How can a meaningful sign serve in the generation of action? These questions are all very closely linked together: the answer to any one of them already fixes the terms of answers to the others. Before considering them, it should be remarked that the issues are general ones, independent of the vehicle by which meaning is carried. Many kinds of item can carry information: mental states, but also pictures, words, written and spoken, and presumably states of the brain. In what follows we approach the problems of representation and meaning in relation to pictures and language. Questions as to how and in what sense the brain is a semantic system will occupy us throughout Chapter 2.

First consider the question: 'What is a representation?' It may be noticed straightaway that the word 'represent' apparently has the connotation that something (some object or state of affairs) is being in some sense *replicated*, presented again, in the sign. This in turn belongs with the idea, of which more later, that a representation must be in some sense like a picture, or image. Not all of the terms that require explication have this connotation; not, for example, 'belief' or 'information-carrying state'. But, in any case, the line of thought that links representations to pictures and images is a very powerful one. It belongs, however, to a past paradigm (to seventeenth-century philosophy, including Cartesianism and empiricism), not to the present.

The idea that representation is a matter of one item (the sign, or model) copying another (reality) has a very long history. It was conscripted into use in seventeenth-century philosophy, in the context of Cartesian dualism, but it has other origins and applications. In its most clear and strong form the idea is simply this: A represents (means) B by being a *resemblance of* B. This account looks most plausible in the case of pictures and images, and has therefore been applied primarily to mental representation, in which pictures and images seem to play a role. The account seems less well-suited to that other paradigm of meaning and representation, language.

At the start, Plato saw (in the *Cratylus*), that words apparently do not *sound like* what they represent. Characteristically, Plato was concerned with spoken language rather than with written. But it is equally true that written language does not *look like* what it represents. If the resemblance theory of meaning and representation is to be made to work for language, it has to be argued that in *some sense* 'beneath the surface', despite appearances, there is indeed a resemblance between language and the world. Plato considered, without enthusiasm, the possibility that resemblance could be found in the history (etymology) of words. In the twentieth century, a very different form of resemblance theory for language was constructed by Wittgenstein in his *Tractatus* (1921). The proposal was that propositions are pictures of states of affairs, though the pictorial form of language is beneath the surface, to be revealed by logical analysis.

Neither Plato nor Wittgenstein were led to a resemblance theory for language because of superficial plausibility, which indeed it conspicuously lacks. They were led to it rather under pressure from a profound argument, concerning the fact that language can, like other forms of representation, be *true or false* of the world. The problem is to explain how signs can be meaningful (can represent something in reality) without thereby being true; or again, it is to explain how a meaningful sign can be false. The problem can be posed as a paradox: if a sign is meaningful (is a *sign* at all), then it must stand for something in reality—but false signs correspond to nothing. The theory of meaning as resemblance serves to resolve this paradox of the false proposition. As we shall see later, in section 4.3, causal accounts of meaning have great difficulty accounting for the fact that a meaningful, information-carrying state can be false as well as true. The solution offered by the resemblance theory, expressed as in the *Tractatus*, runs briefly as follows: a picture is meaningful because its parts stand for objects in reality, but can nevertheless be false, if the objects signified do not stand in the relationship shown in the picture. Conversely, the proposition as picture is true if it is *like* the state of affairs depicted.

This theory of representation as resemblance gives clear expression to the idea of *truth as correspondence with reality*. The implication is that once the resemblance theory of representation is abandoned, we shall require an account of truth and falsity which is not based in the notions of correspondence and failure of correspondence between signs and reality. Aspects of this implication will be pursued in later chapters.

The picture theory of language encounters many problems, not the least of which is the one already mentioned, that sentences simply do not look like pictures of what they mean. However, this problem, like others, can be handled by appropriate saving devices, including particularly the notion of a logical form hidden beneath surface grammar. The overthrow of the picture theory required not only pressure from anomalies, but primarily the construction of a radically different theory of language and meaning.

Wittgenstein went on to propose a new theory in his later period. The proposal was, in brief, that *the meaning of a sign is given by its use in human activity*. Wittgenstein's account is simple on the surface but is philosophically exceedingly complex. It pervades all the works of his later period, being introduced for example in the first pages of the *Philosophical Investigations* (Wittgenstein 1953, §§1–37; with commentaries in, for example, Folgelin 1976; Bolton 1979; Pears 1988). Wittgenstein's theory of meaning as use in activity is thoroughly conducive to the proposals worked through in this essay, and will be referred to frequently. In the next subsection we note that Wittgenstein's account clearly endorses the proposal that runs though this chapter, that there are strong connections between concepts such as meaning and intentionality, and action. Wittgenstein's later-period theory of meaning is also invoked explicitly in Chapter 2, in defining the sense in which the brain encodes meaning (Section 2.6). The theory is explored further in Chapter 3, when we consider Wittgenstein's account of what it means to follow a rule (Section 3.3).

1.3.3 Intentionality based in action

The present essay adopts the view that intentionality (meaning, thought, representation) is grounded in activity. So far, following the general method of cognitive behavioural science, we have introduced meaningful mental states essentially in relation to the explanation and prediction of action. It is to be expected that the theory of meaning which belongs with this approach will likewise affirm a fundamental connection between meaning and action—and this is what Wittgenstein's later-period account does.

Broadly speaking it would be fair to say that the link between intentionality and action is relatively clear in psychological theory, in the context of its aim of explaining behaviour. The link was already apparent in the primitive stimulus–response theoretical definition of meaning (Skinner 1957; see also subsection 1.2.2, on Chomsky's critique). It is fundamental to the whole enterprise of explaining behaviour by appeal to cognitive states, as already noted, and it remains explicit in contemporary psychological theorizing (for example Looren de Jong 1991; Vedeler 1991).

On the other hand, in philosophy there is no general acceptance of the idea that there is a conceptual link between intentionality or meaning and action. It would be fair to say that since the *Tractatus* philosophers have abandoned the idea that language represents by virtue of resemblance, or, what comes more or less to the same, the idea that the truth of a proposition consists of a quasi-spatial matching between (complex) sign and state of affairs. So-called causal theories of meaning, in which the connection between meaning and activity generally does not appear as fundamental, have largely taken its place. The definition of meaning in terms of causal relations makes meaning dynamic as opposed to static, and in this sense moves away from the resemblance/picture theory and towards the connection with action. However, it fails to capture the normative distinctions essential to meaning, in this sense achieving less than the older theory, and it fails to grasp the various kinds of *creativity* involved in meaning. Making good these shortfalls leads us in effect to the link between meaning and action, in so far as action is activity which admits of normative distinctions and which is creative in various connected senses. Action as the creation of order is discussed in the context of rule-following in Chapter 3 (Section 3.3), and the weaknesses of causal semantics and the need for a functional, action-based semantics are discussed in the fourth chapter (Sections 4.3 and 4.5).

The account of meaning as being use in practice applies to signs generally, not just to those of language. Consider those signs which are paradigms for the resemblance theory of representation: pictures and images. It is plausible to suppose that we represent kinds, for example triangles or horses, in the form of mental pictures or images which resemble the items in question. But even in these most favourable cases the details are problematic. We would want to suppose that the representing mental image was like all the instances of the kind. The difficulty is, however, that instances of a kind are generally not all like one another, so that a particular mental image would have to be like some instances but not others. As Berkeley observed in connection with Locke's doctrine of general ideas, it is hard to conceive how we could form in our minds the idea of a triangle which is neither oblique nor right-angled, etc. (Berkeley 1710, p. 13). The underlying problem is that instances of a kind generally do not exhibit a common feature; rather, they are united by what Wittgenstein called 'family resemblances' (1953, §66). The absence of a common feature, in analogue or verbal form, has given rise in contemporary cognitive psychology to more sophisticated models of the representation of classes (Rosch and Mervis 1975; Fodor *et al.* 1980; Smith and Medin 1981; with recent review in Eysenck and Keane 1990, for example).

The fact that, in a plain sense, instances of a given kind generally do not all look alike disrupts the idea, fundamental to the resemblance theory of representation, that the meaning of a sign is fixed by the nature of the sign. This idea serves to make the use of a sign in practice a result of, rather than the origin of, its meaning. But it does not work. A picture of a chair, say, does not mean 'chair' by virtue of looking like all chairs; nothing can look like all (and only) chairs. Moreover, a picture of a particular chair can (be used to) mean various things, not only 'chair', but also, for example, 'antique chair', 'something to sit on', etc. Pictures determine no unique meaning. Rather, what is critical is not the nature of the picture itself, but the *use* to which it is put, for example its use in sorting out *these* items from *these*. In general, pictures can be used in a variety of ways, and their meaning varies with their use (Wittgenstein 1953, for example §139). In so far as meaning is determined by use, there is as yet no need to distinguish signs that resemble things from those, such as words, that do not. Resemblance then no longer appears as a fundamental concept in the theory of meaning and representation. What is fundamental to representation is not the nature of the sign, but is rather the way the sign is used in activity.

Typical of Wittgenstein's critique would be something like the following line of argument (cf. Wittgenstein 1953, for example sections *c*. §191–239; commentary in, for example, Folgelin 1976, Bolton 1979, Pears 1988). How can a person sort out items into categories, for example according to shape? Well, she uses cards with shapes drawn on, and consults these as she goes. So how does she know how to use the cards, when this or that item is close enough to the sample, or that size doesn't matter, and so on? Now the answer here can't come in the form of appeals to more samples. This is clear enough in the case of cards held in the hands, but then we are tempted by the idea of samples in the mind, which of course have special *mental properties*, so that in particular they don't need interpreting (they can be used in only one way). The explanation short-circuits. It admits that ordinary samples do very little work. Witness this also by 'giving' cards to a cat, for example. The cat simply has no idea what to do with them, or what we are requiring of it. So we presuppose a great deal when we think that the sorting procedure makes use of samples, in particular we presuppose that the person can participate in the procedure, in this 'form of life'. Make sense of this ability to participate, and then by all means add that samples on cards might sometimes be helpful—but these are the last and a relatively small part of the story.

Activity is obscured by appeal to resemblance between sample and items in the class. The various theories of universals, and the empiricist doctrine of abstract ideas, all have the effect of denying the role of creative activity in classification. It is as if the sample (the universal or abstract idea) does all the work of classifying, so that the activity of sorting this with that is irrelevant, or at most the acting out of an order (a classification) that already exists.

1.3.4 Rules and regulations

The notion of resemblance has been used to explicate the ordering of particulars into classes. We saw earlier (subsection 1.3.2) that it has also been used to provide a solution to the problem of true-or-false representation. The implication of abandoning the resemblance theory is that this solution also is abandoned. We can say that the use of signs, whether in classifying, or representation of states of affairs, is true or false, correct or incorrect. As Wittgenstein saw, this normative feature of our use of signs can be expressed using the concepts of *rules* and *rule-following*. In saying that someone is using a sign we are supposing that its use in practice is governed by a rule, that particular applications of it are correct as opposed to incorrect, or vice versa. What is required then is an account of what it means for a sign (or any representation) to be used correctly or incorrectly, according to a rule. These issues will be taken up in later parts of the essay, mainly in Chapters 3 and 4.

Another aspect of what is essentially the same point is that representations serve in the regulation of behaviour, in its direction according to a rule. The notion of regulation is central to the theory of action, and generally to cybernetics and the theory of (functional) systems (Wiener 1948; von Bertalanffy 1968; Sayre 1976; Varela 1979).

The notions of rules and regulation are introduced into explanations of systemic activity at a very abstract (philosophical) level. They capture the fundamental idea that activity (interaction with the environment) is 'right' or 'wrong'. But there is no commitment here yet to the idea that representations as rules are *objects*. It may be that ordered activity involves the use of object-like items, various 'expressions of rules', in the form of language or pictures, but this is so far speculation, philosophical or empirical. What has to be guarded against particularly is philosophical pressure to suppose that there *must be* object-like representations, hidden in the mind or brain, if not evident in the hands. As we have seen, this supposition belongs primarily with the idea that representation is something done by objects, whereas the conception of representation as a rule belongs with the idea that representation is achieved by activity. These issues surface again in the second chapter (Section 2.2), when we consider various models of how reality is represented (how information is encoded) in the brain.

It may be noted that the account of meaning in terms of rule-following practice makes transparent what remains obscure according to the resemblance theory, namely, the intimate connection between meaning and the prediction of action. Theories which invoke meaningful (information-carrying) states are effective in the prediction of action because they attribute to the agent the propensity to follow certain rules, and therefore they can be used to predict, rightly or wrongly, what the agent will do.

1.3.5 The intentional stance

In this section we consider a framework proposed by Dennett (1979, 1987, 1988), which clarifies the logic of mentalistic explanations of behaviour, their predictive power, and their relation to other forms of explanation. The framework is fruitful not only in the philosophy of psychology generally, but also in the philosophy of psychiatry.

Dennett proposed that three stances can be used in the prediction of behaviour: the physical stance, the design stance, and the intentional stance. He illustrated these in application to what is apparently the simplest case, artificial intelligence, taking the chess-playing computer as an example (Dennett 1979). The moves of the computer could be, in principle, predicted from knowledge of the physical constitution of the machine and of the physical laws governing its operation. This would be prediction from the physical stance. Prediction of the computer's moves could also be based on knowledge of the design of the machine, including its program. This would be prediction from the design stance. It requires no knowledge of the physical constitution of the machine. Dennett argues that while the physical and design stances can, in principle, be used for prediction, they are in practice inapplicable in the case of the more sophisticated chess-playing computers. There is, however, a third possibility, one that requires neither knowledge of the physical constitution of the machine and covering physical laws, nor knowledge of the program. It consists, simply, in predicting that the computer will make the most 'rational' move! This is prediction from the intentional stance. In the intentional stance we attribute to the computer, in scare quotes, certain 'beliefs' and 'desires'. This is to say, we attribute regulation by intentional states, carrying information about the state of play, and about goals.[9]

Dennett's framework is relevant to many themes of the present essay, concerning the mind–body relation, the power of explanations that invoke information-carrying states, and the concept of psychological disorder. The relevance of the framework to these issues may be summarized as follows.

Dennett brings out the fact that a form of explanation at least akin to that familiar in folk psychology as applied to human beings is applicable also to artificial intelligent systems. The implication is that some aspects of folk psychological explanation, in particular those concerned with prediction of behaviour, do not invoke dualist concepts of mind. There is no (not much) temptation to suppose that computers have immaterial mental states. This move away from dualism is, of course, one of the main philosophical implications of the new discipline of artificial intelligence, and it opens up possibilities of relationship between mind and body which were excluded by the dualist dichotomy.

Dennett's elucidation of the intentional stance reinforces one of the main points of the present chapter, that explanation in terms of meaningful states is efficient in prediction of behaviour. Further, it suggests that such explanation is the best we have for the purpose, at present, and indeed for the foreseeable future. Prediction of human behaviour from the physical stance would require at least knowledge of brain processes far exceeding what is currently available in neuroscience. Similarly, prediction from the design stance would await at least major developments in cognitive psychology. In the meantime, we use folk psychology. But furthermore, even supposing that neuroscience and cognitive psychology progressed to the point of being able, in principle, to predict behaviour as efficiently as explanation in terms of meaningful mental states, it would still be doubtful whether, for practical purposes of prediction, either could replace folk psychology. If Dennett is right, even in the case of chess-playing computers, for which we already have adequate theories of hardware and software, the complexity of explanations involving them prohibit their use for the prediction of moves. And the complexity of human behaviour, of its physical basis and underlying information-processing, exceeds that of the chess-playing computer by orders of magnitude.

There remains, on the other hand, the theoretical question of whether the intentional stance could, in principle, be eliminated in favour eventually of the physical stance. An argument against this supposition is proposed later in this chapter (subsection 1.4.3), and is developed in various contexts in later chapters (sections 2.4.2, 2.5.6, 5.5).

Dennett's framework is also relevant to analysis of the concept of psychological disorder. Dennett makes the plausible suggestion, in passing, that in order to explain breakdown of function, for example in the chess-playing computer, we have to drop to the physcial stance, there to appeal to short-circuits, overheating or blown fuses, for example (Dennett 1979, pp. 4–5). The point behind this suggestion is that when function fails we have to abandon the intentional stance, with its reference to rules, strategies, etc. and look instead for physically defined causes.

A priori inference of this kind lends support, in the case of psychological disorder, to the 'medical model' in psychiatry, in so far as it favours theories of organic aetiology. Psychological disorder is the breakdown of psycho-logic, that is, of meaning, rationality, and so on, and beyond this limit we apparently have to abandon our normal intentional forms of explanation (the theory of mind) and posit instead causal processes at the biological level which disrupt normal processes. However, the supposition that breakdown of function can be explained only from the physical stance is invalid, even in the relatively simple case of the chess-playing computer. There are options from within the design stance, and also some from within the intentional stance, although these are more complicated. Dennett, by the way, does not develop these other options, since they lie outside his primary concerns, but they are not incompatible with his account.

Consider first the option of explaining disorder from the design stance. The chess-playing computer makes irrational moves, inappropriate to winning the game, because it follows the wrong rules (for this purpose). Here we envisage a causal pathway to breakdown of function in which there is no physical disruption to information-processing, but rather use of inappropriate rules. Contemporary models of major psychological disorders such as autism or schizophrenia, discussed in Chapter 9, may be seen in Dennett's terms as making use of the design stance as well as, or instead of, the cruder physical stance. On the other hand, as will be discussed later (subsection 7.2.2), the notion of 'design' is considerably more complex, and problematic, in the case of living beings as compared with computers.

As to the possibility of explaining disorder from within the intentional stance, this seems to be ruled out a priori—at least at first sight. Apparently disorder is precisely the breakdown of intentionality, and hence it does not admit of explanation in terms of intentional processes. In the psychological case, the concept of disorder signifies the point at which there is (serious) breakdown of meaning: disorder means, roughly, (serious) breakdown in meaningful connections. Hence it cannot be explained in terms of such connections. This simple and powerful line of thought is fundamental to the problems with which we are concerned, the role of meaning in the causal explanation of order and disorder. Its simplicity and power derive primarily, however, from limiting consideration to systems which have only one function. We are in fact concerned with complex systems with many goals and subgoals, routines and subroutines, and in this case there are several possibilities that avoid the apparent contradiction in explaining breakdown of intentionality in terms of intentional processes. One possibility is that two or more sets of rules come into conflict, leading to disorder in action. Another is that one goal can be abandoned in order to achieve a higher goal; that in this sense one function will be sacrificed, but as part of an intentional strategy. In these kinds of ways intentional processes can be implicated in breakdown, and they are elaborated on in later chapters (7, 8, and 9).

Having described Dennett's framework and its relevance to the present essay, we should remark on a major divergence of emphasis between Dennett's theorizing and ours, on the fundamental issue of how the intentional stance and the intentional systems to which it applies are to be defined. Dennett tends to define the intentional stance in terms of the assumption of rationality, and intentional systems (trivially) as those to which the intentional stance can be usefully applied (Dennett 1987, Chapter 2, 1988). The way taken here is different. We begin by defining intentional systems in terms of the behavioural characteristics already discussed in subsection 1.2.2 as supporting cognitive as opposed to S–R models of animal behaviour. These characteristics are, briefly, goal-directedness and flexibility according to circumstances. The intentional stance is then seen to explain and predict the behaviour of systems with these characteristics precisely because it posits regulation by states which carry information about goals and the current environment (or organism–environment interactions).

These differences in definition have several consequences. Dennett's approach suggests that the intentional stance is restricted in application to 'rational' systems. Rationality is a high-level cognitive capacity of human beings, some other relatively advanced animals, and artificial simulators. The behavioural definition of intentional systems proposed here, by contrast, has to do only with ends and means, and applies far down the phylogenetic scale, and to biological subsystems as well. Secondly, and connected, Dennett's approach apparently does not envisage the intentional stance being used for predicting irrational behaviour. But it can be. We may learn for example that the chess-playing computer prefers its black bishop to its queen (systematically moves in such a way as to retain the former rather than the latter given these alternative outcomes), and this rule is as useful for prediction as the more rational opposite. What matters to the use of the intentional stance is that some or other identifiable strategy is being used to achieve some identifiable end-state; it is not also necessary that the strategy or the end-state is reasonable. This point is of course critical to the problem tackled later in the essay, concerning the role of intentional processes in disorder. A third consequence of Dennett's approach is that by understating in the foundations of the theory the role of behavioural criteria in warranting attributions of intentionality, their objectivity looks less secure than it might otherwise. The problem of objectivity, with reference to Dennetts' remarks on it, is discussed in Section 3.4.

1.3.6 The intentional stance predicts intentional behaviour

The behavioural characteristics that warrant use of the intentional stance, goal-directness and plasticity, are invariants which are not apparent at the level of physical or geometrical description of the behaviour. This point may be expressed briefly, though with caution, by saying that the characteristics are not apparent at the 'behavioural' level, where 'behavioural' here refers to spatially–defined movements of the body. In general there is no one–one correspondence between behavioural descriptions (in this restricted sense) and intentional descriptions. For example, two distinct behavioural sequences may have in common that they lead to the same goal.

Connected with this point is that intentional predictions can, and frequently do, show an indeterminacy relative to behaviour as physically defined. For example, if I know that Jack plans to meet Jill in Clapham at 2.15, I can predict that at 2 o'clock he will be making his way there, but I may not be able to predict whether is proceeding by foot, bus, or car. My prediction, though indeterminate, is nevertheless informative: many possibilities are excluded. In order to make a more precise behavioural prediction, I require more information. Similarly, in the case of the chess-playing computer: I may predict that the computer will develop an attack on the queen's side, without knowing exactly how it will do so. Nevertheless, the prediction is that some moves, or patterns of moves, are more likely than others.

The intentional stance is effective in the prediction of behaviour. The predicted behaviour is, in general, not defined in physical or geometrical terms, but is rather brought under intentional descriptions. The distinction here between behavioural movements and (intentional) action has been much discussed in the philosophical literature (Anscombe 1957; Davidson 1971; Hornsby 1986). The kind of behaviour predicted by intentional psychology is behaviour that itself has significance, meaning, and intentionality. It may be noted that actions have intentionality in the same sense as applies to the cognitive states that regulate them (subsection 1.3.1). That is to say, actions are typically object-directed, and this 'object' may not exist in reality. For example, an animal trying to find food searches in the same way whether or not there is any food to find.

The point at issue here is not simply that 'we can describe behaviour in two ways', that is as physical movement and as intentional. Behind this contrast are the important issues concerning the point of modes of description, and what practices they belong to. Specifically, intentional, in contrast with non-intentional, characterizations of behaviour belong with the aim of trying to capture, to understand, explain, and predict, complex interaction between living beings and their environment. Further, because this interaction is what we are trying to explain, the mental states we invoke have intentionality, or meaning. Intentionality and meaning, which can seem utterly mysterious or suspect, or both, in fact appear as clear and inevitable in the context of this simple connection. Let us consider this point further.

What is it that explanations of behaviour seek to explain? It is true, just about, that we can describe behaviour narrowly, without mentioning the environment, as bodily movements. Supposing the *explanandum* to be of this kind, it would presumably follow that the *explanans* also would not require reference to the environment. Explanation in terms of inner processes would then not invoke information, or meaning. But of course behaviour in this restricted sense is precisely not what interests us. We don't want to know, for example, why Jones moved his arm in such-and-such a geometrically defined way; we want to know why he picked up the cup; why and how the rat found found its way round the maze to the goal-box, etc. The behavioural *explanandum*, that is to say, is typically an (invariant in the) interaction between the living being and its environment. This being so, it is not surprising that, indeed it has to be the case that, the *explanans* cites facts about the agent, facts about the environment, and (primarily) facts about the interactions between the two. We say, for example, Jones saw the cup, wanted a drink, so picked it up; the rat learnt that the sequence L–R–L leads to food, etc.

Such explanations cite features, actual or possible, of the environment, but these as being represented, stored, or encoded within the subject. They are applicable in both psychology and biology: in the former semantic or representational properties are attributed to mental states, in the latter to material processes in the brain. The mind/matter distinction is less critical here than the fact that in both types of explanation of behaviour the concepts of information-processing are fundamental. The contents of information-bearing states, mental or material, have to be characterized by reference to environmental features precisely in so far as they are invoked to explain behaviour as interaction between the organism and its environment.

Information-processing concepts are justified by their role in providing adequate causal explanation of interactions between the living being and its environment. A fundamental concept here is that information about the environment is stored (in some code) within the agent. One simple aspect of the logic of such attribution can be brought out by comparison with the notion of stored or potential energy in physics. Explanations of clockwork, for example, invoke the concept of potential energy stored within the spring-mechanism, in order to explain why energy expended in interaction between the mechanism and something else, during winding of the clock, affects the behaviour of the mechanism at a later time. The concept of energy storage serves here at least to preserve the principle that causation is spatio-temporally local. The same general logic underlies the notion of information-storage in biology and psychology. It is invoked at least in order to explain how information picked up in interaction between the living being (or biological subsystem) and its environment at one time can affect its behaviour at a later time.

The fact that the bio-psychological concept of information, and even more so of highly processed information, is more complex that the concept of energy in physics is connected, of course, with the complexity of the behaviour of living beings as compared with, for example, clockwork. There are diverse relations between input and output, stimulus and response; there is evidence of interpretation, construal of a stimulus as a this or a that, of success or failure in relation to apparent goals, of behaviour based on error, or on imagination; and so on. To cut a long but familiar story very short: it is the 'intelligent' behaviour of livings beings in their environment, its evidence of learning, variety, plasticity, creativity, goal-directedness, etc. which underlies attribution to the living being of information-carrying states with particular, more or less processed, contents.

It may be noted that there is a qualified argument here for the impossibility of eliminating the concept of intentionality or meaning from behavioural science. It is perfectly possible to manage without intentional concepts, but what can then be predicted is only non-intentional behaviour. *If* the goal is explanation and prediction of intentional behaviour (complex organism–environment interactions), *then* the methodological assumption has to be that the agent is regulated by information about the environment, that is, by intentional states, either mental, or encoded in the brain, or both.

This line of thought is invoked repeatedly through Chapter 2, as we consider various objections to the claim that information (or meaning) is encoded in the brain. For example, it runs counter to the widely held assumption that brain states cannot encode so-called 'broad' content (subsection 2.5.6).

1.3.7 Cognitive psychological information and folk psychological meaning

As discussed in subsection 1.2.5, there are evidently strong connections between the relatively recent paradigm of cognitive psychology, and our familiar folk psychology.

Both are committed to the fundamental idea that cognitive or mental states are involved in the organization and regulation of behaviour. Folk psychology formulates explanations of behaviour in terms of beliefs, desires, etc., while cognitive psychology uses specialist terms concerning information-processing, and end-(goal-) states, as well as borrowing fairly freely from folk psychology colloquial notions such as plans, decisions, etc. Further, the meaningful content that characterizes folk psychological mental states apparently has a counterpart in the information-content carried by cognitive psychological states. Both sorts of state have the critical property of *intentionality*: they are about something, and they may be in error. It is reasonable to say that intentionality is a, or the, fundamental feature of meaningful states, but this feature also belongs to the information-carrying states which are fundamental to the cognitive psychology paradigm. That there is a close connection between cognitive psychology and our familiar folk psychology might seem obvious enough, but there are difficult issues concealed here, particularly to do with the possible commitment of cognitive psychology to the notion of meaning, which has long been regarded as problematic and probably irrelevant from a scientific point of view. We shall consider these issues in the next subsection, but first let us define in more detail the relation between the notion of information as it is used in cognitive psychology, and the folk psychological notion of meaning.[10]

The first point to make is that the folk psychological notion of meaningful content does not cover all the kinds of informational content invoked in cognitive psychology. Rather, and this is the main proposal of this subsection, the folk psychological notion refers particularly to that highly processed information which is involved in the regulation of action. The cognitive psychology paradigm applied to human action requires the concept of highly processed information which serves in the regulation of that action. The proposal is that the concept required here is captured by the familiar common-sense notion of belief with meaningful content. In brief: the information regulating action is typically specified by statements of the form 'S believes that p'. Such statements play a role in explanations of action roughly as follows: 'A person S is doing such and such because S believes that p is the case, wants it to be that q, and believes that by performing the action in question in context p, the result will be that q'. This form of complex proposition can, of course, also be adapted to make a prediction that S will perform the action in question in the said circumstances given the requisite beliefs and desire, other things being equal.

We take it that cognitive psychology as part of behavioural science aspires to be of use in the prediction of behaviour. For this purpose, according to the information-processing paradigm, it is necessary to include among the posited conditions of action, specification of the information involved in its regulation. Our proposal is that it is at this point that the theory requires the notion of meaningful content familiar in everyday usage.

However and of course, cognitive psychology has aims other than the prediction of action. In particular, it seeks to determine methods of information pick-up and processing which precede the use of information in action. On these issues folk psychology has conspicuously little to say. Its grasp of perception, for example, is pretty well exhausted by the simple description 'S sees that p', a description that refers to the result of much processing. In general what matters to folk psychology is not the input side of information-processing, but rather the end-result: highly processed, meaningful states involved in the organization and regulation of action. This is what matters to folk psychology, because the prediction of such action is what matters to the folk.

A further point to make by way of clarification of the main proposal is that the information invoked in cognitive psychology is not restricted to what is or to what can be encoded in linguistic form. In the early stages of sensory information-processing, as in visual perception for example, coding structures are non-linguistic, and it is plausibly only the later stages of perception, approaching production of the conscious perceptual image, which can be described as aquisition of a belief specifiable in words. There is evidence that analogical structures, such as spatial images, as well as propositional descriptions in linguistic form, are implicated in some thinking and problem-solving, and there may also be a more generic, non-propositional form of encoding meaning. The representations regulating action may themselves be sensorimotor in form.[11]

In proposing that the informational content regulating action is specified by the meaningful content of belief, the intention is not to deny any of the above points. It is true that beliefs are typically identified by propositional clauses of natural languages. However, attribution of a belief identified in this way does not presuppose that the belief is encoded in language. This is evident in the fact that we attribute beliefs to living beings that have no language, such as very young children or animals. The grounds of such attribution is intelligent behaviour which, we suppose, is mediated by perceptual and other non-linguistic images. Neither is our concept of belief restricted in the case of language users to the precise words they use to express beliefs. We can attribute to someone the belief 'that p' without supposing that the person has uttered or indeed ever could utter the expression 'p'; the person may speak another language for example. In general, our concepts of belief and meaningful content exhibit an appropriate neutrality with respect to the particular form in which information regulating action is encoded, notwithstanding the fact that specifying informational content *in words* inevitably requires words, particular words of a particular language.

The main argument of this section is, then, that the concept of belief with meaningful content is (or is very closely connected to) the concept of informational content regulating action, such as is required by the cognitive psychology paradigm. The connection is between folk psychology and that aspect of cognitive psychology concerned with the prediction of behaviour. Folk psychology has little or nothing to say about the stages of information-processing prior to regulation of action, but in description of the informational content involved in regulation folk psychology comes into its own. It is in this respect that folk psychology, with its concepts of mental states with meaningful contents, has got matters just about right. Unless this claim is correct, it is hard to see, indeed, how folk psychology could be as effective as it is in the prediction of action. Its success would be a mystery.

The proposed account of the relation between cognitive psychology and folk psychology stands opposed to the idea, to be considered further in the following subsection, that folk psychology is only a relatively weak, pre-scientific theory, the key concepts of which, and the notion of meaning in particular, await replacement by a mature cognitive psychology. This view implies that the domain of interest of the two theories coincide, with the scientific, naturally enough, doing better than the pre-scientific. The account proposed here is rather that folk psychological theory is a proper subset of cognitive psychological theory, namely, that part dealing with the regulation of action by meaningful mental states. This account implies that cognitive psychology not only will win, but always has won hands down, over the business of defining information pick-up and processing prior to the regulation of action by meaningful mental states: folk psychology never was a contender here. The proposed account implies, on the other hand, that the more cognitive psychology attempts to define the information-carrying states involved in the regulation of action (particularly action with ecological validity), the more it is bound to draw on the familar concepts and contents of folk psychology.

1.3.8 Cognitive science and meaning: the historical problem

The above conclusion involves accepting, notwithstanding conceptual problems familiar in the recent history of ideas, that meaning after all has a role in scientific theory. The problems, already referred to in the Introduction, may be sketched as follows.

The last decades of the nineteenth century saw the emergence of new sciences, particularly history and social science, which had as their subject-matter the expression of mind in society. To the extent that these new *Geisteswissenschaften* had their roots in German idealism, rather than in the seventeenth-century dichotomy between mind and matter, knowledge of mind was not a problem for them: the activity of mind in culture and society was a given. But there arose then a fundamentally new problem, which remains ours, namely, that knowledge of mind and its expression in activity does not conform readily to the methodological assumptions and rules of the natural sciences. The tension found expression in the celebrated distinctions between *meaning* and *causality*, and between *understanding* and *explaining* (see von Wright 1971 for an historical, critical review). Human activity is permeated by meaning, understanding of which is a fundamental aim of the cultural sciences. Meaningful phenomena, however, and the way they are known, seem to be different in fundamental ways from the subject-matter and methods of the natural sciences. One contrast is that meaningful phenomena (such as an historical event, or a cultural practice) are singular or even unique, whereas natural science deals (mostly) with repeated and/or repeatable phenomena. Another, connected contrast is that physics seeks and uses general causal laws in its explanations, while the cultural sciences produce diverse meaningful accounts of diverse events. A third contrast is more explicitly epistemological: understanding plausibly draws on empathy, is subjective, and varies between subjects, while the methods of observation in the natural sciences are objective, and the results should be the same for all.

The problems of mind and meaning have to do with a tension between meaningful phenomena and scientific method, the method used by the hugely successful paradigm of knowledge, modern natural science. They are distinct from the problems of mind and body, concerning the apparent impossibility of causal interaction, and the epistemological privacy of mind. As already remarked, the roots of the two sets of difficulties are distinguishable: the new cultural sciences grew within the context of nineteenth-century idealism, which had already left seventeenth-century dualism behind. On the other hand, of course, it was inevitable that the two problematics became muddled up. This is perhaps specially true for psychology, where both the mind/body issues and the problems of meaning and scientific method are of fundamental relevance. The Cartesian framework remained enormously influential, in philosophy and in the sciences, including the new psychology. The older Cartesian problems of mind and body then overlapped and combined with the new problems of mind, meaning, and scientific method, both contributing to the idea that meaningful mental (immaterial) states, and the meaningful activity which they allegedly produce, were thoroughly problematic within the scientific world-picture.

Conflict-resolution was achieved by splitting: causality as opposed to meaning, explanation as opposed to understanding, behavioural science as opposed to hermeneutic non-science. This solution becomes undermined, however, in so far as cognitive psychology, the legitimate heir to experimental behavioural psychology, is committed to anything like meaningful states.

This has been a major problematic for cognitive science from the beginning. The paradigm was, and continues to be, surrounded by controversy about the status, definition, and role of meaning. We referred above (subsection 1.2.2) to three external influences which helped to bring about the cognitive revolution in psychology: transformational linguistics, AI, and the mathematical theory of communication (information theory). It is remarkable and significant that all three in fact explicitly eschewed reference to meaning. The exclusion of meaning was already noted above in connection with AI and information theory, but the same point applies in the case of transformational linguistics: Chomsky's theory was about syntax, not semantics (Chomsky 1957; Katz and Fodor 1963). The fact that these three paradigms of the new cognitive science all, for one reason or another, excluded semantics reinforced the pre-existing scepticism about meaning from the point of view of science, expressed in the turn-of-the-century distinction between meaningful and causal connections.

While linguistics, AI models, and the mathematical theory of communication could, all for different reasons and in different ways, exclude semantics, the same is apparently not true of the cognitive theory of behaviour, which now lies at the centre of behavioural science. The cognitive theory which replaced stimulus–response theory invokes regulation by information-carrying states for the purpose of explaining and predicting behaviour. The states involved in the regulation of behaviour, that is, in the regulation of interactions between the living being and the environment, carry information about those interactions. The notion of information at work here is, and has to be, a semantic one, involving the characteristic intentional properties of directness, and the possibility of error. That the cognitive states invoked by cognitive theory have semantic, intentional properties is essential to the theory, not just incidental, at least in so far as it is being used to explain and predict organism/environment interactions. And it seems then that we are marginally close to saying that the cognitive theory of behaviour has to invoke meaning.

The idea that cognitive psychology can manage without meaning was given a good run for its money by Stich in his well-known *From folk psychology to cognitive science* (1983). Stich proposed that cognitive psychology can and should eschew the notion of meaningful content fundamental to folk psychology (Stich 1983, Chapter 1, *et passim*). The advantage to be gained from this manoeuvre is that cognitive psychology would not be saddled with those features of meaning which are problematic from the point of view of scientific method, such as vagueness, context-dependence and observer-relativity (Stich 1983, Chapter 5). But is the exclusion of meaning from cognitive psychology possible? Stich argues that it is not only possible but mandatory. His argument concerns the problem of supervenience of meaningful states on states of the brain (Stich 1983, pp. 164ff.). This kind of argument will be discussed and rejected in the next chapter (Section 2.5). For now the point to be made is simply that Stich apparently fails to consider whether the baby—the cognitive psychological notion of information—would not be thrown out along with the bathwater—the folk psychological notion of meaning. It would seem that Stich's position is tenable only under either or both of the following assumptions: that the notions of meaningful content and informational content are fundamentally distinct, and/or that cognitive psychology requires no notion of informational content. As to this latter claim, it is not at all obvious how the information-processing models of cognitive psychology could manage without the notion of information (or informational content) being processed. The basis of the former claim is also unclear. Rather, as noted above, the information-carrying states posited by cognitive psychology share fundamental characteristics with the meaningful states posited by folk psychology. In particular, both are invoked in the explanation and prediction of complex behaviour, and both have the features characteristic of intentionality: they are about reality, and its interaction with the living being, and they can be in error.

In so far as the cognitive states posited by cognitive psychology have meaningful content, then apparently scientific explanation and meaning have to be compatible after all. This conclusion implies that we have to find answers to a number of difficult questions: What do explanations of behaviour in terms of meaning have to do with those with face scientific validity, namely, explanations in terms of brain processes? Secondly, how do we accomodate within the theory of scientific explanation the subjectivity which characterizes attributions of meaning? These two questions are tackled in the following two chapters. And further, to be considered in chapters 4 and 5, there is the problem defined explicitly in the distinction between meaningful and causal connections: Are meaningful explanations after all causal? And if so, in what sense?

1.4 THEORY AND THEORY OF MIND

1.4.1 The idea of theory in post-empiricist epistemology

The assumption that psychological explanation of behaviour, scientific or folk, is embedded in a theory has been made throughout the chapter so far. Further aspects of the 'theory of mind' are considered later in this section, but first we consider in general terms the notion of 'theory' and its role in post-empiricist epistemology. As we shall see, this topic interacts with many of the themes in this chapter and in the essay as a whole.

Empiricism was a major theory of knowledge from the seventeenth-century onwards. It began life, in Locke and Hume, as much psychology as philosophy, and it assumed a central role in the development of psychological science towards the end of the nineteenth century. Also, during the nineteenth century, empiricism increasingly dominated conceptions of the physical sciences. In philosophy empiricism assumed a new form in the first decades of the twentieth century, as logical empiricism, or logical positivism, which applied some empiricist assumptions to the theory of meaning (of language). Throughout the twentieth century, however, in very many and diverse ways, empiricism has been deconstructed, and we are now the owners and users of a different kind of theory of knowledge, at its most clear, perhaps, when defined in contrast to what it replaces. Post-empiricist epistemology interacts with so many themes of this essay, and will be used or referred to so frequently, that a statement of some principles in this one place will prove useful.[12]

Empiricist epistemology supposed that all knowledge (except of the logical truths) is based in experience. This implies a one–one or one–many mapping between beliefs and experiences, and it presupposes that experience is given as independent of beliefs, as so-called 'hard' (uninterpreted, infallible) data. These empiricist assumptions have been dismantled in the twentieth century. It has been recognized that empirical beliefs form a theory in which there is no mapping of the required kind between individual beliefs and experience, and that there is no sharp distinction between theory and empirical data. This latter point is usually expressed by saying that all observation is theory-laden. The fundamental idea of empiricism is that knowledge is derived from sense-experience, conceived as an absolute (unconditional) given. Sense-experience is, on this view, essentially passive, involving no activity on the part of the subject, but only simple 'awareness'. By contrast, once the subject is an agent, perception has to be active, in various senses. Sense-data have to be processed into information relevant to action, to its aims and methods, in the context of information already held. Sense-experience involves cognitive activity. Another aspect of the same point is that perception is fundamentally in the service of action, in the sense of activity of the living being as a whole. Hence also, when perception is conscripted into use for planning action, it essentially involves hypotheses (expectations) about the scene and outcomes of action. Beyond a certain level of complexity, these hypotheses assume the form of a systematic theory.

The above characterization of post-empiricism runs together two themes: first, a set of interrelated claims about theory and experience (that theory is systemic in relation to experience, that the distinction between the two is not sharp, etc.), and secondly, that sense-experience (and cognition generally) is in the service of action. The first is the most familiar theme in post-empiricism. We suggest, however, that the second also belongs to the epistemology which replaces empiricism. Fundamental to empiricism was the view of sense-experience as being a passive reflection of reality, whereas, by contrast, experience in post-empiricism is active, in various senses but including that experience (and cognition generally) is essentially in the service of action. This same view of cognition is, of course, also axiomatic in biology, evolutionary theory, and cognitive-behavioural psychology. Philosophical and bio-psychological theory coincide here.

In order to make as clear as possible the context for, and relevance of, what is inevitably a much oversimplified and very partial discussion of empiricism and post-empiricism, let us list their points of contact with issues discussed elsewhere in the essay. The list is of some of the more obvious points only, and they are all connected with one another.

First, as already noted, empiricism belonged with the idea that the subject is a passive observer of ready-made images, whereas post-empiricism, by contrast, posits activity in many connected senses. The assumption that cognition is essentially involved in the regulation of action, axiomatic to cognitive-behavioural psychology, is typical of post-empiricist epistemology. The present essay is based on this assumption, and invokes it throughout. The sixth point to be made below also directly concerns the active nature of cognition.

Secondly, Locke's empiricism was closely linked to the Cartesian concept of mind (discussed above, subsection 1.2.1), in particular to the theory of introspection, that is the Cartesian theory of first-person knowledge of mental states, the inference being that post-empiricism implies a new kind of account of self-knowledge (subsection 1.4.3).

Thirdly, Hume's empiricism comprised a theory of learnt connections between mental states, one which relied heavily on the notion of *association*. This notion re-appeared within psychological science, in particular in the theory of conditioning. Association (in space and time) has nothing much to do with *content*. The implication is that post-empiricist psychology will invoke connections between mental states other than (mere) association, and in particular connections which depend on semantic content. This is linked to the shift from conditioning to cognitive psychological theories discussed in subsection 1.2.2, and also directly to the problem of causality and meaning, which is the next point.

Fourthly, Hume's analysis of causality turns precisely on association only and not internal connections between events (subsection 4.2.1). The implication is that post-empiricism can envisage a different kind of causality, involving internal, content-based connections. Such a form of causal explanation will be explicated through chapters 4 and 5.

Fifthly, empiricism promotes a particular view of psychological science, namely, that is seeks generalizations over hard empirical data (e.g. movements of the body). Post-empiricism envisages a more theoretical view of hypotheses, and indeed of the data. This is reflected in psychology in liberation from behaviourism by the cognitive paradigm (subsection 1.2.2). But along with this shift in the methodological assumptions of psychological science there is a corresponding shift in the conception of its subject-matter.

As a sixth point, empiricism implies that the subjects under study in psychological science are in the business of learning generalizations over (associations between) hard empirical data (R–S or S–S links, etc.). In contrast, post-empiricist psychology envisages that subjects, at any rate beyond a certain level of cognitive development, are engaged in a task more like theory-building. The capacity of cognitive psychology to handle cognitive processing more complex than conditioning (subsection 1.2.2) is a sign of its close relation to post-empiricism. A connected point is that within the cognitive paradigm, the role of cognitive states in mediating between sensory data and action is a function not only of the sensory data but also of interaction among the cognitive states themselves. The mediating role of cognitive states is thus systemic, in a sense consistent with post-empiricist epistemology. There is no simple one–one mapping between what presents to the senses and the cognition, or behaviour, to which it gives rise.

Finally, among the higher-level theories envisaged by post-empiricism would be one for the explanation and prediction of behaviour in terms of mental states, the theme of this chapter. Such a theory can be called a 'theory of mind' (subsection 1.4.2). We move away here from the Cartesian idea that mental events are inaccessible, ghostly processes, towards regarding them as something more like theoretical constructs, which is the kind of status they have in cognitive psychology.

In brief, the shift from empiricist epistemology to post-empiricism interacts at various levels with many issues relevant to psychology and addressed in this essay. Furthermore, the issues concern not only mind, causality, and the nature of explanation, as indicated above, but also mental disorder. This implication will be brought out in subsection 1.4.4. Essential background to that discussion are those parts of post-empiricist epistemology which deal with the preservation of theoretical order. The issues here have been well worked through in the philosophy of science. They are of central importance in many contexts and we turn next to consider them briefly.

As already discussed, empiricism implies that particular beliefs correspond to particular conditions of experience. The claim can be expressed by saying: in the case of any proposition (which purports to represent reality) we should, in principle, be able to say what conditions of experience would make it true or would make it false, or, would lead to its acceptance or rejection. The kind of claim was presupposed in Popper's attempt to distinguish science from non-science using the principle of falsifiability. The principle seemed to presuppose that all propositions in scientific theory could be unambiguously falsified by certain experimental data. This supposition is apparently empiricist in the sense outlined above, and in so far as this is so, it would be correct to say that Popper's principles of falsifiability and demarcation were among the last expression of empiricist dogma. The principles were applied in various ways, including in highly influential criticism of psychoanalytic theory, for being non-falsifiable non-science.[13]

Subsequent work in the philosophy and history of science, in particular Lakatos's classic paper (1970), dismantled these remaining empiricist assumptions. It became clear that there was no definite mapping between observations and theoretical propositions. If a theory as a whole made empirical predictions that turned out to be false, diagnosis of error in the theory was so far ambigous: it could be inferred that there was error somewhere in the system, but not yet where. Further, some propositions within the theory were likely to be protected from refutation, to be in this sense treated as unfalsifiable. These would be propositions fundamental to the theory as a whole, typically referring to 'unobservables' and the principles governing their causal interactions. Such propositions constitute the 'core' of the scientific theory. Further, however, the theory as a whole has to contain a more or less explicit theory of observation, which in effect links the theoretical, unobservable processes to the instruments and procedures of measurement. Observation and experiment, at least in so far as it is taken to be relevant to (confirming or disconfirming) theory, has to be interpreted by the theory of observation. The notion of hard, theory-free, incorrigible data is undermined in this way.

The history of science is replete with cases in which the theory ostensibly under test has been saved from anomalies by adjustment within the theory of observation. An example cited by Lakatos (1970, p. 130n) is the Newtonian theory of gravitation applied to lunar motion, which was at first incompatible with the observations made by the first Astronomer Royal at Greenwich: Newton corrected Flamsteed's data for the effects of atmospheric refraction, and the amended observations were, after all, as predicted by the gravitational theory. This is, of course, a remarkable and famous example of success. It illustrates that adjustments that save a theory from anomalies can be desirable, in fact can constitute advance in knowledge. The ammended theory turns anomalies into confirmations, but it achieves this by increasing the scope and predictive power of the theory. This type of move is called by Lakatos a progressive theory-change, and it stands in contrast to degenerating changes, which preserve theory by restricting its predictive power (Lakatos 1970, pp. 118f.). There are diverse ways in which the predictive power of theories can degenerate: for example, by multiplication of *ad hoc* hypotheses, or by stretching the definition and application of key explanatory terms.

Lakatos makes clear the ways in which scientific theory can degenerate. These problems and issues are familiar in psychological theorizing. Consider the charge referred to above, that psychoanalytic theory is unfalsifiable. Even if the charge of intrinsic unfalsifiability is misconceived, the criticism can stand in the form: in some respects psychoanalytic theory may have *come to be used* unfalsifiably, hedged about by so many possibilities and qualifications that it becomes a match for any phenomena we can imagine, so that it predicts everything and excludes nothing. Over-elaboration is certainly a particular hazard for an elaborate theory, particularly one that deals in unconscious mental states and mechanisms. The opposite kind of risk exists for theory that errs on the side of parsimony. For example, as discussed in subsection 1.2.2, Chomsky showed that operant theory applied to language learning stretches the meaning of its few key terms to the point of vacuity.

It should be emphasized that the tendency to protect core theory from refutation, even at high cost, is not adequately explained by appeal to such as whim, pride, or perversity. There is a methodological principle at work here, which has logical and psychological justification. The core theory, defining the underlying phenomena and causal principles, is essential for making predictions. For this reason it cannot (psychologically) and should not (logically) be given up easily. Without it we would not be able to make any predictions, and therefore neither would we know how to act: action would so far cease. In scientific investigation this means: we would have no reason to set up an experiment, since there would be nothing to put to the test. The implication is that fundamental theories generally are not given up even if experience apparently contradicts them. Indeed, as Lakatos observed, theories in science are typically launched amidst an array of anomalies, and they stay afloat notwithstanding the apparent contradictions: the anomalies are either ignored, or it is assumed that they can be handled by the theory, somehow or other.

In general, theories are not abandoned under the weight of counter-evidence, in so far as the counter-evidence can be deflected away from what is essential to the theory. This raises the issue of what more is required for radical theory change. The general answer is that a new theory has to be on offer, one that can replace the old one and that can, in particular, make sense of, explain and predict, what were anomalies for the old theory (Lakatos 1970). Large-scale changes of this kind may be described as 'paradigm-shifts' (Kuhn 1962). They can be seen throughout the history of the sciences, for example, the change from the Ptolemeic to the Copernican view of the Earth's place in the solar system; the change from Newtonian to relativistic mechanics; and in psychology recently, the change from behaviourist to cognitive psychology.

The above considerations concern scientific theory and practice (experimentation), but they apply equally to the epistemology of daily life. The implication is that the knowledge or belief used in daily life has the form of theories. In the remainder of this section we consider how this applies to activities generally, to the knowledge-base of interaction with other social beings (subsection 1.4.2), and indeed to knowledge of one's own actions (subsection 1.4.3). The section ends with discussion of 'core' beliefs fundamental to the possibility of action as such, a matter which brings us to the interplay between psychological order and disorder, a principal theme of the essay as a whole (subsection 1.4.4).

Before proceeding to apply the insight of post-empiricism, that knowledge and belief in daily life have the form of theories, two caveats or complications should be noted. To the extent that the term 'theory' connotes only propositional knowledge (knowledge expressed in sentence-like structures), the claim that all knowledge is theoretical neglects various forms of analogical representation. Qualifications along these lines are discussed for example by Feyerabend (1988). In the particular case of the theory of mind, to be discussed in subsection 1.4.2, analogical knowledge would involve something like mental simulation, or empathy, and this epistemology will be discussed in the third chapter (Section 3.2).

A further complication is the fact that a person's behaviour, or indeed an animal's behaviour, may be best predicted by attribution of a theory, an interconnected set of beliefs and desires, not withstanding the fact that the person (still less the animal) does not, or could not, come up with any such theory. This consideration has led to distinctions between 'explicit' and 'tacit' theory, and between explicit and tacit knowledge generally.[14] Broadly speaking, the assumption we make in this chapter and throughout the essay is that attribution of a theory to a person or animal is warranted in so far as it facilitates prediction of their behaviour. It is certainly a further issue whether the agent can or does articulate such a theory. The capacity to give an account of oneself plausibly depends on language, and hence is uniquely human, and it matures relatively late even in human cognitive development, during adolescence (subsection 6.5.3). Furthermore, even when a person formulates a theory about the beliefs and desires regulating his or her own actions, it may not be the one that best predicts those actions. In this sense the person's explicit theory may be partial or false, and as we shall see, these kinds of failure of self-knowledge can generate psychological difficulties (subsection 1.4.3).

So far in this section we have considered mainly scientific theories and experimentation, but post-empiricist epistemology has a quite general application. Practice is guided by systems of belief, pictures or models of the world in which action takes place. They define the preconditions of action, its nature and its consequences. This context determines the significance (meaning) of what we do, and the beliefs that define it are brought to bear in the planning and execution of courses of action. Human practices are endless in number, and boundless in diversity and complexity: farming, marrying, teaching, travelling, painting, calculating, experimenting, praying, and so forth. The order in an activity finds expression in the beliefs belonging to it; order concerning the various presuppositions of the activity, the variety in the course of action, and its purpose. Agriculture, for example, is a way of life dependent on many things in nature and in human beings, and comprises many stages, and this complexity is mirrored in interconnected beliefs, concerning such things as seeds, soil, sun, rain, and the importance of right timing. There may be theories also about crop rotation, about the breeding of new strains, and in magical cultures, theories about the collaboration of spirits, and so on. So it is that within and around practices we have systems of belief, in agriculture, as in making machinery, conducting a scientific experiment, making friends, etc. The systematic nature of belief corresponds to the systematic nature of activity. One belief in isolation prompts no single action, but from a combination of beliefs action does follow, indeed many interwoven and interrelated actions. As a point about predicting practices of another agent, the implication is that the mental states and meanings which are attributed have the form of a theory, corresponding to the systematic nature of what is being predicted.

The strong links between theory and practice are reflected in the intimate connection between theory and experience emphasized in post-empiricism. These are two aspects of the same point, since experience is action, from the point of view of the agent.

Thus, experience is completely interwoven with beliefs about the reality that we are experiencing, with the former conditioning the latter, but also the latter the former. Among our beliefs are those that state fundamental convictions about the world in which we act; these beliefs define the world, and therefore the content of experience itself. Preconceptions determine what can be experienced, so far as we are concerned. What we *really see*, as opposed to imagine, or simply 'feel in ourselves', depends on what we believe is there to be seen. For example, if the world-picture excludes spirits, then, it will be said, there is no experience of spirits, but at most only hallucinations of them, or mistaken inferences from what is really seen. Our ideas concerning reality influence experience, or at least our interpretation of experience.

The notion of interpretation here, though valid, does not imply that there is an absolute, uninterpreted experience. All experience, at least by the time it is used for action, is interpreted, and it is generally possible to construct various interpretations. Further, to speak of interpretation here, though legitimate, is to speak from the outside: it acknowledges the role of thought in the formation of intelligible experience; it is perhaps to compare one system of thought with an alternative. Seen from within, however, one's beliefs do not 'interpret' experience, they define what one's experience *is*; perceptions and thought, including thought in language, form a unified experience of reality.

Empiricism was right to join together the concepts of experience and idea. But it wrongly gave priority to the one (experience) over the other (idea). Further, it conceived both too narrowly, in terms only of qualities given immediately in the five modes of sensation. Most importantly, empiricism conceived both in absolute terms, independently of activity and interpretation.

1.4.2 Theory of action in terms of mind

We may bring together the idea that intentional concepts are useful in explanation and prediction of action, and post-empiricist epistemology, fundamental to which is the notion of theory. Combining these two themes we are led to the idea that we explain and predict action using a theory of intentional states and processes. In brief, we are led to the idea of a 'theory of mind', and to a particular way of looking at our familiar folk psychology.

Folk psychology, our familiar language of mental states and processes, admits of several interpretations. Within the framework of Cartesian metaphysics, the language refers to a private, immaterial realm, independent of the body. Part of this picture is that first-person knowledge of mind is direct and certain, while third-person knowledge is indirect and (probably irredeemably) uncertain. This whole problematic, inherited from seventeenth-century philosophy, was played out in the first decades of psychological science, with introspectionism followed by behaviourism. The philosophical work of dismantling the Cartesian interpretation of mind was accomplished, for example, by Wittgenstein (1953) and by Ryle (1949). These philosophers were able to show that mental concepts do not refer to some private process running parallel to behaviour, but are intimately (logically) linked to behaviour itself. It would be fair to say that in these writers the negative part of the argument, the deconstruction, was clearer than the positive part. It became clear what mentalistic language was *not* doing. But then, what *was* it doing? What is it for?

The answer to this post-Cartesian question emerged clearly first in experimental psychology, naturally so given its nature, briefly as follows: mental states are invoked in psychological theory as regulators of action, for the purpose of explaining and predicting complex forms of behaviour. In other words, the post-Cartesian response in psychological science has been the cognitive paradigm.

There are striking similarities, as well as differences, between cognitive psychological science and our familiar folk psychology (subsection 1.3.7). Given the similarities, it is natural enough to suppose that folk psychology is also in the business of, among other things, explaining and predicting behaviour, and is in this sense a (quasi-scientific) theory. Hence we arrive at the idea of the 'theory of mind'.

Another theme in the same movement of thought is this. As behavioural scientists became accustomed to the explicit and deliberate use of mentalistic concpets in explanation and prediction of the behaviour of their experimental subjects, it becames possible to think that those participants might be using a similar theory to make sense of and anticipate social behaviour, including, indeed, interactions with the experimenters. It was in fact in this kind of context, interplay between the subject, a chimpanzee, and the scientist, that the expression 'theory of mind' was created (Premack and Woodruff 1978). The implication for our familiar folk psychological language is then that it is an explicit formulation of a 'theory of mind' (Stich 1983; Fodor 1987; Whiten 1991).

The idea that folk psychology is a scientific-like theory for the explanation and prediction of behaviour is thus new. Its appearance required not only the dismantling of Cartesian assumptions, but also firm familiarity with the cognitive paradigm in behavioural science. Previous to this the idea is conspicuous by its absence. For example, Piaget studied development of the child's theories of many things, from the physical world to morality, but not yet development of the child's theory of mind. This is now, however, a flourishing topic in developmental psychology (Astington *et al.* 1988; Harris 1989; Wellman 1990; Butterworth *et al.* 1991; Bennett 1993).

The idea that propositions about mental states serve in the explanation and prediction of action is fundamental to the post-Cartesian cognitive paradigm. It is taken as the starting-place for the present essay, and runs through most of its themes and arguments. That propositions about mind have a form of a theory, in the sense of post-empiricist epistemology, is an (inevitable) corollary of the basic idea, and is explicitly explored and used in various places as we proceed.

In the next section, knowledge of one's own mind, as well as knowledge of the other's mind, is construed as having the form of a theory. In Chapter 4 (Section 4.6) we discuss the status of theoretical generalizations over meaningful mental states. In Chapter 8 we explore further a topic to be introduced below (Subsection 1.4.4), that there are aspects of the theory of the self in relation to the world which are essential to action, such that action and thought itself are threatened if they are threatened.

The notion of a theory of mind draws attention to certain features of explanation of behaviour in terms of mental states: the explanations 'go beyond' immediately known phenomena; they can be used to make sense of, and predict, what is observable; they function within a hierarchically organized system of propositions; etc. In brief, knowledge of mind is being understood in a typically post-empiricist way. The contrast is basically with *direct* acquaintance with the objects of knowledge. In the case of mental objects this direct acquaintance would be introspection, though it always appeared problematic in the third person case. The point of the shift to post-empiricism is not, however, that we can imagine giving up the theory that other people have minds, as if it were a disposable option. Such a claim is dubious psychology (Hobson 1991), and dubious philosophy. It has already been argued (in subsection 1.3.6), that the intentional stance is mandatory, while the purpose is prediction of intentional activity.

1.4.3 Self-knowledge, error, and disorder

The considerations so far in this chapter have concerned primarily the attribution of intentional states on the basis of 'intelligent' (goal-directed, plastic) behaviour, seen in human beings, but also in animals and even artificial intelligent systems. In this subsection we move on to consider a capacity which is uniquely human, namely, the ability to give an account of one's own intentional states. We have the capacity to give an account of the beliefs, desires, plans, and so on, according to which we act. This is a very high-level cognitive capacity, perhaps the highest of all, one inimately involved in concepts such as self-consciousness, autonomy, freedom, and responsibility.[15]

The capacity to give an account of one's own cognitive states may be called the capacity for second-order intentionality. Intentionality consists in the possession of cognitive states such as beliefs and desires. Second-order intentionality consists in the possession of beliefs about those beliefs and desires, or desires about desires, etc. It is expressed in propositions of the form: 'I believe that I believe (or desire) that p'.

The capacity to give an account of oneself is of great importance, and so, therefore, is the matter of its failure. It is no surprise to find that the capacity is characteristically—although not universally—disrupted in cases of what we call psychological or psychiatric disorder. A person experiences a strong emotion, or finds herself engaged in some course of action, but has no idea of the reason why. Typically the person feels ignorant, perplexed, and overwhelmed. Another kind of case is that in which the person has an account, but it is 'irrational', in the opinion of others, and perhaps even in his or her own. Of course, ignorance, or an irrational account of the beliefs and desires regulating one's action, is not sufficient for 'disorder'. There are many aspects of daily action of which we have no account: we simply act, respond in the way we do, without preoccupation as to the reasons. Or again, we may have a whimsical account, bordering on the eccentric. However, in so far as an activity or mood is salient for us, especially if it is disruptive or distressing in frequency and/or intensity, then generally we do seek a valid understanding of why it is occurring, at least so that it becomes predictable, and perhaps manageable. Apart from problems of clinical severity, we are all more or less familiar with difficulties in making sense of problematic patterns of behaviour and feeling, such as in personal relations, or in attitudes to work. Disruption in self-knowledge is thus involved in psychological difficulties of clinical severity, and in 'problems of living', to adopt Szasz's (1961) phraze. So the issues here are relevant to the main themes of this essay.

The account of self-knowledge that has dominated philosophy and psychology since about the seventeenth century through to relatively recently, may be called the traditional theory of introspection. The main idea is that mental states are immediately manifest to the self. This metaphor has three specific implications: completeness, infallibility, and 'priviledged access'. The self knows *all* of its own mental states, it *cannot make a mistake* about them, and its knowledge of them is direct, qualitatively superior to the indirect, inferential knowledge (or belief) possible for another subject.

This seventeenth-century conception of self-knowledge has collapsed with the appearance of the cognitive psychological paradigm, from Freud onwards, in which the defining characteristic of mental states is their regulation of behaviour, not their appearance in consciousness (or self-report) (see Subsection 1.2.4). It is evident within this paradigm that people sometimes make mistakes about, or have no idea about, the intentional processes regulating their behaviour.

What replaces the theory of introspection, broadly speaking, is the idea that self-knowledge *has the form of a theory*. A version of this new epistemology was proposed by Nisbett and Wilson in their well-known paper (1977), and will be discussed further below. The proposal that self-knowledge has the form of a theory has the immediate advantages of accomodating the phenomena which are anomalous for the traditional theory of introspection, namely, ignorance and error. Theories in general are partial, as opposed to complete, and they are subject to error, as opposed to infallible. These features of self-knowledge become comprehensible, if self-knowledge is construed as a theory.

The construal of self-knowledge as a theory extends the notion of 'theory of mind', discussed in the previous subsection, to one's own case: knowledge of one's own mind is seen as having the same form as knowledge of other minds, namely, the form of a theory. In the context of post-empiricist epistemology generally, the point is that knowledge of the self has the same or similar form to knowledge of reality in general. This suggestion was indeed already in classical empiricism. Locke grouped together introspection ('reflection') with the 'external' senses, assimilating knowledge of the internal world to knowledge of the external (1690, Book II, Chapter 1, §4).

The construal of self-knowledge as a theory is plausible in the contexts of current theories of the mind and knowledge, but it is also somewhat counter-intuitive. Is it true that knowledge of one's own mind is just like one's knowledge of someone else's? Is it true that in reporting one's mental states one is invoking a theory ranging over unobservables? Certainly we would be very far from the notion of introspection; in fact too far.

There are empirical and philosophical reasons for making certain qualifications to the idea that self-knowledge is theoretical. These qualifications concern two features of self-knowledge which are highlighted by, though overstated by, the traditional theory of introspection: infallibility and priviledged access. (Nothing remains, by the way, of the third claim of the theory, completeness, once we adopt the model of cognitive psychology.) Let us consider the issues of priviledged access and infallibility in connection with Nisbett and Wilson's (1977) proposal that self-knowledge has the form of a theory.

Nisbett and Wilson emphasize that a feature of their account is first person/third person symmetry in knowledge of (beliefs about) mental states: an observer has the same source of belief about my mental states as I do, namely theory. On the other hand, Nisbett and Wilson allow that the subject has 'indeed direct access to a great storehouse of private knowledge', or at least knowledge 'quantitatively superior' to that of any observer, such as concerning personal historical facts, the focus of current attention, current sensations, also emotions, evaluations, and plans (Nisbett and Wilson 1977, p. 255). This qualification by Nisbett and Wilson to their generally anti-introspectionist stance is exploited and elaborated by Ericsson and Simon, who add to Nisbett and Wilson's catalogue: awareness of on-going processes (Ericsson and Simon 1980, p.245). They propose that priviledged subjective information of the above sorts is in, or can be retrieved into, short-term memory, whence it is available for verbal reports (loc. cit. *et passim*). Ericsson and Simon cite (interpretations of) much experimental evidence in support of the conclusion that subjective reports of mental states and processes, in so far as they draw on information of the above kinds held in short-term memory, do indeed show high degrees of accuracy as judged by behavioural criteria. In brief, introspection can indeed be a direct, reliable source of knowledge about the mental states and processes regulating our behaviour.

The implication is that we have to qualify the proposal of first-person/third-person epistemological symmetry. While it may be true that both subject and observer alike draw on theory, the observer has as information only behaviour (including speech), while the subject has maybe that, but in any case also priviledged information of the sort described above, roughly, what is conscious in perception and short-term memory.

The issue of priviledged access is connected to the issue of infallibility in the reporting of subjective states. There are circumstances in which the statement 'I believe that p', even when sincerely made, can be wrong. For example, a social psychologist may demonstrate to me, following controlled observation of my behaviour in a selection procedure, that I discriminate on the basis of sex or ethnic group, even though I was not only unaware of this, but sincerely believed the opposite. The general point, illustrated in various contexts in Nisbett and Wilson's review (1977), is that first-person reporting of mental states is fallible in so far as it may conflict with the person's actions.[16]

On the other hand, there is a way in which sincerely made statements of belief can be infallible. In so far as I resolve to act in accord with a belief—in so far as, as we colloquially say, I 'make a point of it'—then in general my behaviour will indeed accord with that belief. In the circumstances envisaged above, the psychologist's demonstration would have the effect, we may suppose, of ensuring that I do not continue making the same mistake. Nisbett and Wilson make the point that if subjects in experimental situations were to be (made) aware of being influenced by (what they would regard as) factors irrelevant to the task, then they would probably correct for them (Nisbett and Wilson 1977, pp. 239, 247). This is connected to another point made by Nisbett and Wilson, that when we consciously, deliberately apply rules for decision-making, then the verbal report of these rules will indeed accurately predict behaviour (1977, p. 244). The position in such a case could be described by saying that we have a correct *theory about* what is regulating behaviour, but it would be better to say instead, or as well, that the theory *serves in* the regulating procedure. In these circumstances the verbal expression is not so much a (true or false) report of a mental process, but is rather an affirmation of the intent to follow such-and-such a procedure. Hence there is (in normal circumstances) no possibility of error.

Analogous points apply in the case of desire. The assertion 'I desire that p' may be false, as judged by concurrent behaviour incompatible with that desire, or as judged by the speaker's disillusionment on achieving its object. Nevertheless, the assertion (assuming it is sincere) is likely to be true in the sense that (at least some of) the speaker's behaviour is, or would be in appropriate circumstances, appropriate to the expressed desire. The expression of desire, as of belief, can be the expression of intent.

Nisbett and Wilson emphasize the fallible use of self-report, in which, for example, 'I believe that p' is offered, perhaps mistakenly, as the best explanatory account of the speaker's behaviour. But Nisbett and Wilson tend to neglect the infallible usage of first-person statements of belief and desires, in which they are more akin to expressions of intent. Related arguments were proposed in early commentaries on Nisbett and Wilson's paper, particularly by Morris (1981) and by Shotter (1981). The critical point in the present context is that infallibility of self-reports is being explained by supposing that they function not only as (true-or-false) descriptions but also as expressions of states of mind and inclinations to action.

Neglect of the expression of intention has the effect of neglecting also an important consequence of being in error. According to the simplest version of the proposal that self-knowledge has the form of a theory, the issue of correctness or incorrectness in reports of one's own mental states is just the same as in other theoretical explanations, a matter of criteria familiar in the philosophy of science: predictive efficacy, coherence, parsimony, etc. If we make a mistake then so be it; we adjust the theory. While this may be an adequate model of correctness/incorrectness so far as concerns precisely the theoretical aspects of statements of beliefs and desires, we need another kind of model in relation to their use as expressions of commitment to a course of action. In so far as sincere statements of belief express the intention to act in accord with that belief, even when there is behavioural evidence of a contrary belief at work, so that the expressed belief is in that sense mistaken, then the consequence of being mistaken is not simply that the subject happens to be wrong; it is rather that there are *two conflicting systems* of belief, in fact two conflicting systems of belief–desire–behaviour complexes.

Verbally expressed beliefs and desires regulate certain actions. This set of beliefs, desires, and actions is either congruent with (consistent with) other relevant actions, and the beliefs and desires which (we suppose) regulate them; or they are not. If the two sets are consistent, then second-order intentional statements, of the form 'I believe that I believe that, or desire that, p' are indistinguishable from the first-order statements

'I believe that, desire that, p'. But if the two sets are inconsistent, then first-order and second-order intentionality have fallen apart. In the first case, the person 'knows herself': what she is doing and why. In the second case the person is in a (more or less serious) muddle, engaged in two incompatible courses of action. There is failure of self-knowledge, long recognized as the source of much of our trouble.

Knowledge of one's own mind, like knowledge of other minds, has the form of a theory. This post-empiricist formulation has a surprising, radically non-Cartesian result, namely, that self-knowledge is closely interwoven with the social. This follows from the fact that the theory of mind, like theories generally, has essentially social origins. Let us explore this point further.

Post-empiricist epistemology is defined by at least the negative claim, that knowledge is not derived from experience (alone), but also by the positive claim that knowledge, in the form of theory, is acquired in education, broadly conceived. Knowledge is acquired as it were by 'revelation', by all means no longer divine, but given in the teachings of social groups. Underlying this change in epistemological emphasis from individual experience to social teaching is a shift in the idea of thought itself. In empiricism thoughts are something like mental images, and hence they are plausibly derived from experience. Post-empiricism, by contrast, characteristically for the twentieth century, emphasizes language as a fundamental medium of thought; and language is manifestly social, acquired in education.

Post-empiricist epistemology thus emphasizes that knowledge of mind is theoretical, and further, that the source of the theory is social. This applies to knowledge of one's own mind, just as much as to knowledge of someone else's.

The theory of mind as acquired in education, including one's theory about one's own mind, is essentially partial, and more or less right or more or less wrong. There is truth or error here, in our view of ourselves, depending on the way we have been taught.

It is, on the other hand, possible to steer away from the idea that socially constructed theory can be in error. This tendency is inherent in post-empiricism. To the extent that experience is conditioned by socially constructed theory, it cannot be an independent measure of the theory's truth or falsity. Then perhaps the distinction between true or false theory collapses altogether, or, less drastically, it seems to turn on distinction between agreement and disagreement, so that truth comes to be seen as a matter of *consensus*. Emphasis on the theoretical and hence social origins of theory as opposed to its empirical basis, inevitably leads to the drawing of a strong link between being right and being in accord with the relevant social group. This line of thought, in connection with the theory of mind, is apparently followed by Nisbett and Wilson in the following quotation (1977, p. 255):

> In general we may say that people will be accurate in reports about the causes of their behaviour and evaluations whenever the culture, or a subculture, specifies clearly what stimuli should produce which responses, and especially where there is continuing feedback from the culture or subculture concerning the extent to which the individual is following the prescribed rules for input and output.

Nisbett and Wilson make this generalization from experiments in which trained experts (stockbrokers and clinical psychologists) can say what decision procedures they are following. Now we have seen that, in general, when people follow an explicit rule then some, at least, of their behaviour will accord with the explicit rule. But we have also remarked that even so they may be following other, contrary rules, without being aware of it. In the experiments cited by Nisbett and Wilson this was presumably not the case. But if it is the case, then the explicit rule is *not* an accurate representation of the underlying psychological processes: it fails to explain and predict that behaviour which accords with the contrary rules. Further, and of course, this misrepresentation can occur *whether or not* the explicit rule is socially prescribed. For the point here is simply that not only individuals, but also cultures and subcultures can be in error about the cognitive and affective states which mediate between stimuli and behaviour.

Rejection of the idea that there is any essential connection between accuracy of self-reports and consensus follows simply on the assumption, used throughout this essay, that attribution of mental states generally serves to predict behaviour, and is accurate or inaccurate according as to whether it does so correctly or otherwise. The distinction here is not a matter of agreement as opposed to disagreement. If a person reports that she is following such-and-such a rule, then (in the normal case) she will indeed be following it and the report will be, in this respect, right. This applies whether the rule in question is socially prescribed or idiosyncratic. Further, and in either case, the self-report may be wrong in the sense that it fails to account for other, conflicting patterns of behaviour.

Our intention here is not to understate the role of social learning, and indeed of consensus, in acquisition of the theory of mind. The point being made is rather, and just, that truth of the theory and of particular judgements within it cannot be defined in those terms. It is important to press this point because otherwise it would seem that self-knowledge is achieved whenever we follow socially prescribed rules, whereas the reality is that this method is just as likely to be lead us into error.

The theory of mind includes hypotheses of the following kinds: as to what kind of experiences should give rise to what beliefs and feelings, and conversely, as to what such-and-such beliefs and feelings are the result of; as to what behaviour appropriately belongs with what beliefs and emotions; as to what people do desire, or do rationally desire, etc. The fact is that we are not omniscient about such matters, not at all. A given psychological theory (individual or social) has a partial range, like any theory, so that it is silent on, for example, the emotions caused by such-and-such a type of experience. Further, it will have false components, for example that such-and-such a belief is an unreasonable response to such-and-such an experience, when in fact the link between them is entirely inevitable. The individual acquires such a theory, with all its blind spots and errors, and applies it in his own case, with, let us suppose, due social reinforcement, and he will then be—like his fellows—quite out of touch with what is actually going on in him, that is, with his relation to experience and his own actions.

Examples of inadequate or incorrect psychological theory, more or less contentious, abound. The following are intended only to illustrate what seems obvious, that groups just as much as individuals can get psychological theory thoroughly wrong. At the cultural level there is much to be said for Foucault's general indictment of the modern European age for its excessive use of Reason and its systematic ignorance, denial, or disqualification of other psychological forces (Foucault 1965). A connected point is that if Freud was right, the common-sense psychology of his time was woefully inadequate.

The above are plausible examples of inadequate or false theory at the cultural level. The smallest subcultural unit, the family, is of particular interest because it is here that the child learns most immediately such psychological theory as is on offer. Children's ability to recognize emotions, say, depends on family discourse about emotional states, their causes and their effects (Brown and Dunn 1991; Dunn *et al.* 1991*a,b*).

Partiality and error are occupational hazards. In the clinic can be seen examples, often of course extreme, of what happens in general: children being taught inadequate or plainly wrong accounts of (mental) life. No connection is made for the child between, say, withdrawal and feeling angry, or depressed, or between the experience of loss and sadness. Or false theories are proposed, such as: father never gets angry (so his withdrawal cannot be a sign of anger); we are a happy family (so whatever misgivings you may have are illegitimate); crying is wrong (so is not an appropriate response to loss); whatever mother does, she is beyond criticism (or beyond praise); mother loves you totally (so whatever else you are suffering from, it isn't lack of love). Such theories, or lack of theory, are passed on to the child and adherence to them is ensured by positive and negative feedback to the child's contributions. Often, as is the case with other types of theory, they are the product of more than one generation (cf. the family therapy literature on 'family myths', for example Byng-Hall 1973). In these ways, the child acquires no good theory as to the relation between experience, cognitive and affective states, and behaviour.

The above considerations point to many themes central to the essay. This is because, as remarked at the beginning of the subsection, self-knowledge in the sense explicated here belongs with the highest mental functions, and is thereby crucially implicated in human psychological order and disorder. The capacity to affirm in language the intentionality of one's own activity brings with it, as the other side of the coin, the possibility of conflict between deliberate, rule-guided activity and the cognitive states which otherwise regulate affect and behaviour.

Regardless of whether a psychological theory acquired in education, and in the family specifically, is adequate, once acquired ('internalized'), it generates behaviour appropriate to it. In the case of error, as emphasized earlier, the problem is not just that the child has the wrong theory; it is rather that she tries to live according to rules that run counter to her natural inclinations. For example, the child may ignore—or believe she should be able to ignore—a significant loss, so she might not cry, or otherwise grieve. Or again, a child will generally tend to feel miserable, even despairing, if left alone (for too long), but it may be a rule in the family, implicit and explicit, that everyone should be, providing they are normal, happy. Following this rule, as well as her natural inclinations, the child will be both miserable and happy at the same time, or in succession. Either way the emotions, and the actions to which they would give rise, are inhibited.

In this simple example can be seen the characteristic point that one of the conflicting mental states is not given the right name. Happiness is correctly named, but misery is given no name, or is misnamed. The 'right' name here means: use of the name leads to expectations that are fulfilled. As generally, the use of intentional language is justified by its success in prediction. The child learns that happiness is associated with feelings such as of satisfaction and gratitude, and with the natural expressions of these feelings. But if the word is applied in cases in which the child is neglected, then so far she is unprepared for her feelings and inclinations; they make no sense. So far the child does not know what she is believing, feeling, or inclined to do.

Psychological disorder can result from acquisition of a false or inadequate theory of mind. The shortcomings in theory which we have been considering have to do with the *content* of mental states and the relations between contents, as opposed to their *form*. Let us explore the contrast further. Folk psychology has a form, defined by attribution of intentional states and connections between them, of increasing theoretical complexity. It is plausible to say that this form is relatively constant across cultures, perhaps that it is innately conditioned rather than learnt, and that disorder in the capacity to use this form of theory is likely to be drastic. On this last point, it has been hypothesized that failure in development of the theory of mind, of certain of its formal features beyond a certain level of complexity, is implicated in one of the major developmental psychological disorders, autism (Baron-Cohen *et al.* 1993). The failures of theory considered in this subsection concern content rather than form in this sense. Content, in contrast to form, is relatively culture-sensitive, and, a connected point, is presumably learnt rather than innately determined. Given that a child is prepared to develop a complex theory of cognitive-affective states in application to others and to the self, she relies on adults to teach her the content of such states in particular cases, and here there is room for error. The more serious the error, the more it has to do with conditions fundamental to action, the more serious would be the confusion and conflict to which it gives rise.

A sense of 'form' used by logicians, and distinct from that indicated above, concerns adherence to logical principles, such as non-contradiction. The 'laws of logic' of course do not turn on content. Arguably, however, their acquisition and use are sensitive to the vagaries of education. Communications to children can include more or less subtle contradictions, which can be expected to inhibit development of the capacity to think (straight). This line of thought found expression in the hypothesis that contradictory communication, in the special (inescapable) form of so-called 'double-binds', is implicated in the genesis of the major cognitive disorder, schizophrenia (Bateson *et al.* 1956; and, for discussion, Hirsch and Leff 1975. Cf. subsection 8.2.2, p. 308 and section 9.2). The form/content distinction is complicated and many-sided, and hence also is its relevance to psychological disorder.

The intimate link between failure of self-knowledge and psychological disorder is evident in the fact that some of the major pioneering work of dismantling the Cartesian theory of introspection, hence in effect the Cartesian concept of mind, has been in the area of psychological disorder, specifically by Freud. The view of self-knowledge sketched in this subsection reaffirms the close connection between ignorance about ourselves and disorder, but in other general respects it apparently differs markedly from Freudian theory. First, Freud viewed the processes involved in self-knowledge and ignorance as intrapsychic, whereas the view outlined here emphasizes their interpersonal nature. Secondly, one of Freud's crucial observations was that failure of self-knowledge typically serves a defensive function, protecting the self from intolerable intentional states, such as beliefs, memories, feelings, or impulses. By contrast, in the account given so far here nothing has been said about failure of self-knowledge having a defensive function; ignorance appears so far as no more than a failure of education. These differences are more superficial than deep, however. As will be suggested in various places as we proceed, the intrapsychic and the interpersonal, although distinguishable, are interwoven (subsection 3.3.3, sections 6.3 and 6.4); as are ignorance, or distortion of reality, and defence (subsections 1.4.4 and 8.2.3).

In the following subsection, continuing explication of post-empiricist epistemology, we consider the question of rules (beliefs) that are fundamental to action and cognition. This is linked to the issues raised above concerning the definition and role of logic in psychological order, and in the defence against disorder.

1.4.4 Fundamental rules: logic and psychologic

The post-empiricist perspective allows us to see that theories have a 'core' of fundamental beliefs, or rules, which cannot be given up without the threat that thought and action itself fall into disarray (subsection 1.4.1). Thus, if the chemical theory embodied in the periodic table of elements, or particular hypotheses essential to it, were to be given up, in the absence of a viable alternative, the cost would be confusion in, and cessation of, chemical experimentation and thinking. We would not know what to think, or what to do. This kind of point is well recognized and (relatively) well understood in application to scientific theory. Its applications to psychology and clinical psychology are of interest here. The critical point is that some theory is essential to us, either because it belongs with activities we cannot do without, or because it belongs with action as such. We apparently do not have to continue with chemistry, for example, so we could carry on despite the demise of current theory, and do something else instead. Though of course even this point is relative and needs qualification: it might not apply to someone whose identity as a chemist was fundamental to the person's view of him or herself. There are cultural and individual differences in what are taken to be essential practices and beliefs. It can be said, on the other hand, that some very general beliefs are essential to action as such, though again, what this amounts to may vary from individual to individual, and between cultures and subcultures. But insofar as there are such convictions, they maintain psychological order: what lies beyond them is breakdown.

Issues of this kind were explored philosophically by Wittgenstein in *On certainty* (1969). Wittgenstein saw that knowledge, or certainty, was intimately linked to what we need in order to act. For example, at §414 Wittgenstein writes:

> How do I *know* that it is my hand? Do I even here know what it means to say it is my hand?—When I say 'how do I know' I do not mean that I have the least *doubt* of it. What we have here is a foundation for all my action.

Again, at §411:

> If I say '*we assume* that the earth has existed for many years past' (or something similar), then of course it sounds strange that we should *assume* such a thing. But in the entire system of our language-games it belongs to the foundations. The assumption, one might say, forms the basis of action, and therefore, naturally, of thought.

An implication of these and many other passages in *On certainty* is that the foundations of knowledge coincide with the foundations of thought and meaning. We have to know, or at least be certain of, judgement itself. In this general respect Wittgenstein's proposal follows the original Cartesian epistemology: the method *de omnibus dubitandum* came to an end precisely at the *Cogito*. But while in Descartes thought consisted of (subjective) mental events, such as images of perception, thought in Wittgenstein's philosophy pertains essentially to action. Hence the conclusion that the foundations of certainty are what is required for action.

The connection between these points and the empiricist theory of knowledge may be brought out in the following way. Empiricism acknowledged that the truths of logic were (alone) not based in experience. 'Logic' here refers to what is essential to thought. In the philosophical tradition logic variously comprised the law of identity and the laws of the syllogism, later elaborated into the propositional and predicate calculi. In post-empiricism, however, logic acquires a significance broader than these formalities. It comes to include core assumptions within systems of belief which serve as rules for the interpretation of experience, as opposed to beliefs which might be overthrown by experience. Further, the boundary line here between logic and empirical belief is no longer clear-cut. Wittgenstein brings out such points in the following passages, for example, at §§94–8:

> I did not get my picture of the world by satisfying myself of its correctness; nor do I have it because I am satisfied of its correctness. No: it is the inherited background against which I distinguish between true and false.
>
> The propositions describing this world-picture might be part of a kind of mythology. And their role is like that of rules of a game; and the game can be learned purely practically, without learning any explicit rules.
>
> It might be imagined that some propositions, of the form of empirical propositions, were hardened and functioned as channels for such empirical propositions as were not hardened but fluid; and that this relation altered with time, in that fluid propositions hardened, and hard ones became fluid.
>
> . . . But if someone were to say 'So logic too is an empirical science, he would be wrong. Yet this is right: the same proposition may get treated at one time as something to test by experience, at another as a rule of testing.

A similar point is made at §319:

> But wouldn't one have to say then, that there is no sharp boundary between propositions of logic and empirical propositions? The lack of sharpness *is* that of the boundary between *rule* and empirical proposition.

If core propositions, or rules, within the system of belief were to be questioned, then the entire system would be under threat. Reference to the law of identity in this connection is made at §494:

> 'I cannot doubt this proposition without giving up all judgement'.
> But what sort of proposition is that? (It is reminiscent of what Frege said about the law of identity.) It is certainly no empirical proposition. It does not belong to psychology. It has rather the character of a rule.

A strange consequence of this broadening of the scope of logic is brought out, and softened, at §628:

> When we say 'Certain propositions must be excluded from doubt', it sounds as if I ought to put these propositions—for example that I am called L. W.—into a logic-book. For if it belongs to the description of a language-game, it belongs to logic. But that I am called L. W. does not belong to any such description. The language-game that operates with people's names can certainly exist even if I am mistaken about my name,—but it does presuppose that it is nonsensical to say that the majority of people are mistaken about their names.

But it may be added here that even though the language-game certainly continues given radical error or doubt by one person, that person's participation may well come to an end. At §§613–14, for example:

> But what could make me doubt whether this person here is N. N., whom I have known for years? Here a doubt would seem to drag everything with it and plunge it into chaos.
>   That is to say: If I were contradicted on all sides and told that this person's name was not what I had always known it was (and I use 'know' here intentionally), then in that case the foundation of all judging would be taken away from me.

Given these high stakes, the point is precisely that we are hardly inclined to give up core beliefs. Under pressure, their rule-like function takes over: counter-evidence is deflected away. Thus, at §516, for example:

> If something happened (such as someone telling me something) calculated to make me doubtful of my own name, there would certainly also be something that made the grounds of these doubts themselves seem doubtful, and I could therefore decide to retain my old belief.

A similar point is made at §§360–2 (with allusion perhaps to the Cartesian appeal to divine good faith):

> I KNOW that this is my foot. I could not accept any experience as proof to the contrary.—That may be an exclamation; but what *follows* from it? At least that I shall act with a certainty that knows no doubt, in accordance with my belief.
>   But I might also say: it has been revealed to me by God that it is so. God has taught me that this is my foot. And therefore if anything happened that seemed to conflict with this knowledge I should have to regard *that* as deception.
>   But doesn't it come out here that knowledge is related to a decision?

The notion of revealed truth, antithetical to empiricism, ironically re-appears, in mundane not divine form, in the post-empiricist epistemology. Theories are passed on to the individual in education, as remarked already in the preceding subsection in the case of 'theory of mind'. Particularly for the child, belief in adults is essential to learning. On this, Wittgenstein (1969) writes, for example:

> §160. The child learns by believing the adult. Doubt comes *after* belief.

Belief in the teacher has to be one of the child's fundamental rules. Allow us to give an anecdote that illustrates this point specifically in relation to the current theme concerning logic. A child (aged 5) of one of the authors came home from school saying that he had been learning about shapes, and had learned among other things that a rectangle was not a rectangle. Gentle scepticism and suggestions of alternatives were met with the firm and repeated declaration that Miss had said so. For this 5-year-old, when it came to a choice between what Miss said and the law of identity, the law of identity came a clear second.

The question arises as to what those propositions are that we claim to know for certain, and which ones form the basis of our judgement. The general answer is just that they are those propositions that we need in order to act and to think. We can give extreme generalities, but beyond those we are limited to giving examples.

In *On certainty* Wittgenstein makes much reference to the work of G. E. Moore. In papers aimed at defending common sense against scepticism Moore cited examples of certainties that define extremely general conditions of our action (life): the body, the hand in particular, space and time, experience, and other human beings (Moore 1925, 1939). The level of generality here is appropriately philosophical. Other examples of certainties cited by Wittgenstein include somewhat less general facts, of for example history, geography, and biology, as well as judgements made by a person about his or her personal history and circumstances. It is evident here that the examples that could be given are endless. There is great diversity between cultures, sub-cultures, and individuals, and variation through time. So we can cite more or less general, and more or less particular cases of propositions which have the property of logical certainty, but it is not possible to define the conditions of thought and action once and for all.

It has been implicit in the discussion so far that there is an intimate connection between propositions that define our picture of the world, and mental order. Doubt or error concerning fundamental rules raises the issue of breakdown of psychological function. The connection here is of central concern to the themes of the present essay.

While our certainty has foundations in logic, these foundations are not absolute. There is no suggestion that our knowledge is infallible. It is possible for a person to be in doubt about, or in error about, even fundamental things. But in such cases, doubt arises as to the person's soundness of mind. Wittgenstein makes this point throughout *On certainty*. For example, at §71:

> If my friend were to imagine one day that he had been living for a long time past in such and such a place, etc. etc., I should not call this a *mistake*, but rather a mental disturbance (Geistesstorung), perhaps a transient one.

And at §155, concerning Moore's 'common-sense' propositions:

> In certain circumstances a man cannot make a *mistake*. ('Can' is here used logically, and the proposition does not mean that a man cannot say anything false in those circumstances.) If Moore were to pronounce the opposite of those propositions which he declares certain, we should not just not share his opinion: we should regard him as demented (geistesgestort).

Certain false judgements cast doubt on the speaker's state of mind. The inference would be that there is something wrong with the person's capacity to make judgements. The nature of the impairment would be so far unclear; it may involve perception, memory, language-comprehension, or reason itself. That there are judgements which define the capacity for judgement is presupposed in neurological and psychiatric examination. When a clinician asks a patient questions such as: 'How many fingers am I holding up?' or, 'Where are we now?', the aim is not to elicit information, but is rather to test the measure.

These considerations bring out the nature of certainty. A person can say: 'I *must* be right about this (for example that this is my hand), providing I am able to make judgements at all'. Of course, from the person's point of view this qualification can hardly be doubted: what lies on the other side is chaos (madness).

The philosophical theory of judgement and knowledge has to include an account of radical error, which will be 'mental disorder'. This link between philosophical theory and the notion of mental disorder is clear in Wittgenstein's work in post-empiricist epistemology, but in the previous tradition it was submerged beneath the weight of the problem of knowledge (of the external world). At the beginning of modern thought Descartes made the connection between error in fundamental matters and madness. In pursuing the method of doubt beyond the bounds of common sense, beyond what is apparently beyond rational doubt—for example that he has a body—Descartes in his *First meditation* observes that he has to cite circumstances in which contrary, bizarre beliefs can occur, in particular in insanity and in dreaming (1641, p. 145). But it then becomes an insoluble problem to distinguish wakefulness from sleep (ibid. p. 146); or again, we could add, to distinguish sanity from delusion. Descartes continues (loc. cit.):

> Now let us assume that we are asleep and that all these particulars, e.g. that we open our eyes, shake our head, extend our hands, and so on, are but false delusions; and let us reflect that possibly neither our hands nor our whole body are such as they appear to us to be.

The Cartesian problem can be formulated in terms of mental disorder, or dreaming, but the real problem had nothing much to do with either. Rather, as has been suggested (subsection 1.2.1), the real problem in the modern world-picture was how absolute objects could be known on the basis of relative, subjective experience. The Cartesian problem belonged to an age in which subjective experience (delusional or otherwise) was more certain than (absolute) objectivity. For us, on the other hand, the common, though not absolute, world of objects is obvious enough, so that it hardly needs affirmation. The issue remains relevant in psychiatry, however, since in mental disorder even what appears obvious to us all is brought into question.

In *On certainty* Wittgenstein examined the certainty that we attach to some beliefs of a factual nature, general or personal. In focusing on factual beliefs, Wittgenstein followed traditional theory of knowledge, the originality being the characteristically post-empiricist insight that certainty in such beliefs was a matter of their being essential to action, and hence to judgement itself. But the acknowledgement of the fundamental connection between certainty and action opens up a different area, concerning beliefs that are actually about the self's activity, and in particular about what is essential to it. Such beliefs constitute what can be called the core of the theory of action.

Action presupposes at least the following core beliefs, or expectations: that the self is competent (enough) to act, that the world is predictable (enough), and that the world provides (enough) satisfaction of needs. Such expectations have to be preserved if activity is to continue. If they were to be abandoned, action would appear to be either impossible or pointless: there would be, so far, no reason to act.

Beliefs of this kind have a special epistemological and logical role. They will be expressed, if they are expressed at all, with certainty. Or again, the agent will be extremely reluctant to abandon them, on pain, so far, of abandoning action itself. This means, for example, that any experience that seems to contradict them will, if at all possible, be re-interpreted in such a way as to preserve the beliefs, and hence action itself.

Another way of bringing out the special epistemological and logical role of such propositions is to describe them as a priori. This has various connotations. The involvement of such beliefs in the regulation of action follows from the definition of (belongs to the concept of) action itself. Further, such beliefs are not based in experience, but rather serve in the interpretation of experience: counter-evidence will tend to be re-construed so as to remove threat to the core beliefs. It is possible also that such beliefs or expectations are a priori in the sense of being innate, designed in at birth. It is at least plausible to suppose that living beings are designed by evolutionary selection so as to expect such as predictability and satisfaction of needs, these expectations being preconditions of attempts to act. Another sign of the special status of these beliefs and expectations, one which directly links the philosophical and psychological senses of being a priori (or innate) is the fact that their attribution is valid providing the subject is acting at all, regardless of the particular nature of the action.

It is true that we rarely have occasion to articulate or attribute core assumptions of action explicitly. Typically, fundamental principles may remain implicit, until the theory is faced with repeated recalcitrant experiences. The presuppositions of action show up when they apparently fail to apply. Thus, for example, in the learned helplessness experimental paradigm animals apparently give up the expectation that what they do makes a difference, and consequently they do nothing (Seligman 1975). It is evident in this example that fundamental rules underlying action can be (are) attributed to animals, such as rats, which have no language. The only presuppositions are those that underlie the attribution of mental (cognitive) states generally. Core beliefs or expectations can be attributed to a living being in so far as they best explain and predict intentional activity. And so also, as in the case of learned helplessness just cited, the negation of such beliefs or expectations can be attributed in so far as they best explain and predict the giving up of intentional activity.

It belongs to post-empiricism that action is regulated by cognitive states in the form of a theory, which has a core, essential to the enterprise, which will be protected more or less at any cost, by whatever resources the living, cognitive being has at its disposal. Beliefs at the core of the theory are essential for action, but also essential for thought (cognition) itself. Their opposites are not possible thoughts, or at least, not ones that can be used in the planning of action. In this sense the belief that the world is enough for life is a 'logical truth': its negation cannot be thought. The implication here, which belongs both to philosophy (logic) and to psychology, is that major assaults on the core of the theory of action not only require drastic defensive manoeuvres, but they also, at the same time, have profoundly adverse effects on the capacity for thought.

These issues will be taken up later, in Chapter 8, under the headings of psychological trauma and psychic defences.

1.5 THEORY-DRIVEN PREDICTIVE POWER IMPLIES CAUSALITY

1.5.1 Introduction

Throughout this chapter we have explored various aspects of the fact that explanations of behaviour in terms of intentional states have predictive power. In this section we draw the conclusion that such explanations are causal. This conclusion is relatively less surprising in the case of explanations in cognitive-behavioural psychology, with their scientific credentials and terminology, but is more contentious when applied to folk psychological explanations. This is because folk psychology is often thought of as pre-, merging into non-scientific, and because its central notion of meaning has been regarded as nothing to do with science generally or with causal explanation in particular. We consider some of these issues concerning folk psychology first, before moving on to the connection between predictive power and causal explanation.

1.5.2 Folk psychology as a theory for prediction

Cognitive psychology had more explanatory and predictive power than the paradigm that it replaced, S–R theory (Subsection 1.2.1), as one would expect of a scientific paradigm-shift. Folk psychology too, however, can be, and is, used for prediction. Using our familiar method of understanding in terms of mental states, we anticipate actions and reactions, by all means fallibly, but generally with remarkable accuracy. Any kind of course of action and its separable components, whether it be, to chose at random from countless possible types of example, playing a game, making friends, building a house, conducting an experiment, is understood by us according to the beliefs, motives, and strategies of the participants. And generally, notwithstanding ample scope for misunderstanding, we anticipate what goes on with enough success, enough of the time. To the extent that we make mistakes, then our grasp of the activity, and our own participation, is confounded.

That folk psychology has predictive power is from one point of view not surprising at all. Predictive power is closely linked to practical utility, and given that the folk have practical concerns, it makes sense that they should have developed a theory which has predictive power. On the other hand, response to this line of thought probably depends on which examples of folk theories we have in mind. We can think of, say, folk physics in support of it, but as against it, examples such as astrology and magic, as cited by Churchland (1988). It may be that the appraisal of folk theories generally depends on their compatibility with current scientific paradigms.

Here we come across a consideration specific to folk psychology, that its characteristic posits, mental states and their meaning, have been thoroughly problematic from the point of view of modern science, and resisted within psychological science particularly (subsections 1.2.1, 1.3.8). Against this background, our familiar ordinary explanations of people's actions in terms of such as beliefs, desires, motives, and plans, with examples obvious to the point of being trite, may be dismissed as *merely* 'folk psychology', with little or no relevance to hard psychological science, whether behavioural or neurophysiological.

Nevertheless it has become clear recently, as folk psychology has come to be regarded as a theory akin to cognitive psychology, that there is a decisive objection to simply dismissing it as scientifically invalid or irrelevant. The objection, as we have anticipated, is just that folk psychology generates powerful predictions. Fodor has made this point with particular force.[17]

Predictive efficacy, of course, is one of the fundamental aims of scientific theory. The point is exactly not that folk psychology is being praised for such as literary or poetic qualities, which might indeed be regarded as irrelevant to its scientific value.

This is connected with the fact that the same considerations also count against 'hermeneutic' vindications of the discourse of mind and meaning, which would endorse and make a virtue of its non-scientific status. According to the line of argument adopted here, the language of mind and meaning has at least one fundamental feature in common with scientific theory, namely predictive function. This function is critical to the scientific endeavour, and to the extent that it belongs also to our understanding of mind and meaning, the dichotomy between these two forms of discourse deconstructs.

1.5.3 The inference to causal explanation

Explanations of action in terms of meaningful mental states are effective in prediction. The point to be made at this stage is just that there is a close relation between predictive efficacy and causal explanation. It is relatively uncontroversial to say that predictive power is a necessary condition for an explanation to be causal. It is not by itself, however, a sufficient condition. Accidental connections (for example between being a swan and being white) can be used for prediction, without being causal. It is characteristic of accidental generalizations that their truth is accidentally restricted in space and/or time (in the example just cited restricted to Europe, before zoos), and also that they do not belong to or follow from a systematic theory. Neither of these points applies in the case of explanation of behaviour in terms of mind and meaning. There are various plausible responses to the apparent fact that attribution of mental states predicts behaviour, but supposition that the connection is mere coincidence is not among them. The next possibility is more interesting.

Generalization may be reliable, and may indeed signify causal connection, but the associated phenomena may be linked by a common cause, rather than one kind being a cause of the other. An example would be the association between migrating behaviour of birds in different parts of the world. Typically we construe an association as signifying a common cause in case we have, or can at least envisage, a theory that would specify the causal mechanisms and hence the connection between the several sets of phenomena. It is possible to look at the connection between mental states and behaviour in this way. The idea would be: there are reliable connections between mental states of certain kinds and behaviour of certain kinds, such that the former predict the latter, but mental states are not causes of behaviour, rather they are both products of a common cause, the most likely candidate for which role is activity of the brain. This is a reasonable answer but it is out of date: it is reasonable only in the context of assumptions that have been replaced in current theory. The assumptions are Cartesian, or neo-Cartesian, namely, that mental events are immaterial processes, running in parallel to material events, neural or bodily, and that there is no essential connection between the mental and the material. The Cartesian dual-process theory has no role in cognitive psychology or cognitive science generally, including AI in particular. To put the point another way, we are beyond the stage at which the predictive power of the theory of mind can be understood in these terms.

The situation is rather that the pressure mounts to adopt some form of mind/brain identity theory, the main idea being that mental events are *in some sense* brain events and (therefore can be) *in some sense* causes of behaviour. Subsequent chapters are dedicated to making sense of the italicized phrases in this solution! These chapters, particularly 2, 4, and 5, are in this sense elaborations of the conclusion reached at this point.

Although it awaits explication, the conclusion stands that explanation of action in terms of mental states and their meaningful contents is causal, and it collapses the traditional dichotomy between meaningful and causal explanations.

1.6 SUMMARY

The main idea of this chapter is that explanations of behaviour in terms of meaningful, mental states have theory-driven predictive power. Three sections, 1.2–1.4, work out various aspects of this idea, and the conclusion is then drawn in 1.5 that such explanations are *causal*.

Section 1.2 concerned psychological science. The section began (1.2.1) with a sketch of dualism and the problematic role of mind in seventeenth-century science. The ill-fit between mind and science became starkly apparent at the turn of the nineteenth century with attempts to construct a science of the mind, leading first to a methodologically weak introspectionism and then to the other alternative within the framework of Cartesian dualism, behaviourism. The logic of cognitive explanations of behaviour and influences on the cognitive revolution in psychology were discussed in subsection 1.2.2. Cognitive animal learning theory drew attention to the fact that the behaviour of man and of higher animals is 'intelligent' (goal-directed and plastic), apparently not only a matter of mechanical conditioning, and proposed that cognitive processes are implicated in the organization and regulation of such behaviour. The following two subsections considered briefly the role within the cognitive paradigm of two major psychological faculties: affect and consciousness. The cognitive paradigm can look, especially from the point of view of some its formative influences, affectless. But this appearance is misleading: affect, or emotion, is essential to cognition, in so far as it regulates the activity of living beings (1.2.3). On the other hand, it is true that the concept of consciousness is not essential to the general paradigm. It assumes importance for the explanation of certain high-level features of action, most, though not all, of which are characteristically human (1.2.4). The section closed (1.2.5) by remarking on similarities between cognitive and folk psychology, a theme that recurs throughout the chapter.

In Section 1.3 we began a task that will occupy us throughout the essay, clarification of that family of concepts that includes notions such as intentionality, representation, meaning, and information. After some preliminary definitions (subsection 1.3.1), we considered the attractive idea, which has a very long history, that such concepts are grounded in *resemblance* between sign and signified (subsection 1.3.2). We saw reasons to reject the resemblance theory, however, in favour of the view that signs have meaning (represent, have intentionality, carry information) in so far as they are used in activity (subsection 1.3.3). Such use is subject to normative descriptions (right/wrong, etc.), and can in this sense be described as rule-following (subsection 1.3.4). The intimate connection between concepts of meaning and rule-following begins to clarify a central theme in this chapter, that explanations that invoke meaningful states are effective in prediction: they attribute propensity to follow rules, and hence serve to predict what the agent will do. The predictive power of intentional explanations is emphasized by Dennett. In Subsection 1.3.5 we considered his notion of the intentional stance for the explanation of systemic, functional behaviour, in comparison and contrast with the design and physical stances. The intentional stance predicts intentional behaviour, a feat that cannot be accomplished from the lower-level physical stance (subsection 1.3.6). This is an argument for the ineliminability of intentional explanations of action. It is argued in subsection 1.3.7 that there is a strong connection between the folk psychological notion of meaning and the cognitive psychological notion of (semantic) information. Folk psychological attributions of belief seek specifically to identify the highly processed information involved in the regulation of action. By contrast, folk psychology has little or nothing to say about earlier stages of information-processing. The implication of this argument is that folk psychology has a share of the scientific legitimacy of cognitive psychology, but also that the cognitive psychology paradigm inherits the traditional problems of meaning from the point of view of scientific assumptions and methods (subsection 1.3.8). It was not only Cartesian mind that was problematic in the modern scientific world-picture. As attention came to focus on the meaningful character of mind, this too was recognized as problematic from the point of view of science. Meaningful phenomena were seen to involve subjectivity, and were apparently not among the causes envisaged by the natural sciences. Hence the pressure to keep meaningful phenomena, including meaningful mental states, out of psychological science.

In Section 1.4 we noted that various themes so far and to follow throughout the essay interact strongly with the shift from empiricist to post-empiricist epistemology. Critical to post-empiricism is the idea that knowledge is not derived directly from unconditionally given experience, but is mediated by theory, hierarchically organized systems of belief (subsection 1.4.1). We went on to consider the currently influential idea that we use a 'theory of mind' to predict behaviour (subsection 1.4.2). In subsection 1.4.3 we considered our capacity to represent our own mental states, to hold beliefs about the states of mind regulating our own action. It was argued that this second-order intentionality has two aspects. On the one hand, it is similar to the third-person case: a person can have a theory about her own mental states, just as she has a theory about those of another. A person's theory about herself, like theories generally, can be wrong. On the other hand, (sincere) statements of belief and desire, can function more like expressions of intention. Even if they incorrectly identify the mental states at work in a particular course of behaviour, nevertheless they tend to generate actions and affect appropriate to what is avowed. In such circumstances, there is conflict within the system. Rule-conflict generally is critical in psychological disorder, and we return to the notion in that context in later chapters. Of the many and various connections between post-empiricism and themes of the essay, one concerns the boundary between order and disorder (subsection 1.4.4): the theory underlying action has a core which is essential to action, such that its breakdown would threaten action itself.

The effectiveness of explanations in terms of meaningful, mental states in delivering predictions of behaviour points to the conclusion that such explanations are causal. This inference was drawn in Section 1.5. The argument is indeed relatively straightforward. The problem is not so much the argument but making sense of its conclusion. At its starkest, the conclusion is that meaningful mental states are causes of action (or behaviour). The conclusion, however, raises many problems, immediately two: 'What is the ontological status of mental states?' and, 'What is the nature of mental causation?'. A third problem, pressing from the direction of the theory of knowledge is this: causal processes are surely within, or have, objective reality, but meanings are notoriously tainted by subjectivity. The ontological problem will be addressed in Chapter 2, the epistemological issues in Chapter 3, and the special nature of meaningful, mental causation in chapters 4 and 5.

NOTES

1.   For accounts of animal learning theory see, for example, Hilgard and Bower (1966) and Mackintosh (1983). The brief discussion in the text of early cognitive theory refers mainly to the work of Tolman (1932, 1948). Brewer (1974) and Dulany (1974) provide helpful, brief critiques of the transition from conditioning to cognitive learning models.

2.   The following review is very partial as well as brief. It omits theories within psychology which, as well as cognitive learning theory, anticipated the cognitive paradigm, Piaget's developmental psychology, and Heider's attribution theory. For comprehensive treatments of the cognitive revolution in psychology see Gardner (1985) and Baars (1986).

3.   For discussion of the relation between the concept of information in MCT and in cognitive psychology see Dretske (1981, 1983). Dretske's main aim in these works was to work out a causal theory of semantics, a topic to be discussed in Chapter 4.

4.   Classic philosophical studies of the emotions include Aristotle's *De Anima*, and Spinoza's *Ethics* Part III. The biological/evolutionary theoretic approach to the emotions was elaborated by Darwin (1872). The close connection between affect, cognition, and action is apparent conceptually and in psychological theory (Gordon 1987; Oatley 1988; Barnard and Teasdale 1991). The central role of affect can also be defined using cybernetic theory, e.g. Ciompi 1991. On the notion of valency and basic emotions in current cognitive psychology see, for example, Davidson (1992) and other papers in Stein and Oatley (1992). Oatley and Johnson-Laird (1987)

have proposed that emotions are linked specifically to the managing of multiple goals, an issue that occupies us in Chapter 6 (Section 6.4).

5. The early statement of the problem of ecological validity for cognitive psychology was Neisser's (1976), with recent discussion in relation to memory including Conway (1991) and Ceci and Bronfenbrenner (1991). The question of independence of emotion from cognition was hotly debated in the 1980s (Zajonc 1980, 1984; Zajonc *et al.* 1982; Lazarus 1982, 1984; Mandler 1982), with eventually a degree of consensus that emotion *can be* independent of *conscious* cognitive processing, though normally involves unconscious processing (Mandler 1982; Brewin 1988; Williams *et al.* 1988). This conclusion is compatible with what is proposed in the text. The literature on influence of mood on cognitive processing is reviewed in Williams *et al.* (1988) and Brewin (1988). Recent theorizing about the links between cognition and emotion include, in philosophy, Greenspan (1988) and Nash (1989) and, in psychology, the very detailed model proposed by Barnard and Teasdale (Barnard and Teasdale 1991; Teasdale and Barnard 1993).

6. This is the briefest allusion to a complicated, contentious, and expanding area of cognitive psychological research (see, for example, Lycan 1987; Gillett 1988; Marcel and Bisiach 1988; Clark 1990; Pickering and Skinner 1990; Velmans 1991; Baddeley 1992; Davies and Humphreys 1992; Smith 1992; Baddeley and Weiskrantz 1993). An excellent review of the issues from the point of view of clinical psychology, which emphasizes connections between current cognitive science and early work by theorists such as Freud and Janet, is given by Power and Brewin (1991).

7. The distinction here is often drawn in terms of first-and third-person perspectives on the objects of knowledge and on mental states in particular (see, for example, Nagel 1986; Dennett 1987). Various recent approaches to consciousness work to break the down the Cartesian distinction between reality and consciousness, from the point of view of cognitive psychology (Velmans 1990), in relation to quantum mechanics (Lockwood 1989; see also Goertzel 1992), and by, for example, Davidson (1989) and Dennett (1991) in the philosophy of mind. Philosophical problems of consciousness are discussed also by, for example, Hannay (1990), Searle (1990, 1992), Flanagan (1992), and in Davies and Humphreys (1992).

8. The definition of *intentionality* given here, and the definition of *intensionality* to be given below in the text, while sufficient for our purposes, are rough and ready, and readers seeking detailed accuracy are advised to consult the account of Brentano's thesis and some of its more recent formulations and versions in Dennett (1969); see also Searle (1983). Full discussions of intentionality in relation to modern philosophical psychology are given by Lyons in his series of articles (1990, 1991, 1992). These articles consider various approaches to intentionality, exemplified by Carnap and Dennett (in the first article), by Chomsky and Fodor (in the second), and by the teleological semantics (in the third article). Lyons's range is reflected in the present essay. Dennett's approach is discussed in subsection 1.3.5, Fodor's language of thought hypothesis is discussed in Chapter 2, Section 2.2, and causal and teleological (or functional) semantics throughout Chapter 4.

9. Dennett's analysis raises the question whether it is possible or necessary to distin-

guish between systems such as computers which have merely 'derived' intentionality from those like ourselves who have 'intrinsic' or 'original' intentionality (Dennett 1987; Newton 1992) The issues under this heading are diverse and complicated. They include the problem of defining when such systems are 'in error', which is considered at length throughout Chapter 4. Another issue discussed under this heading concerns the ways in which intentional systems are 'designed': computers by human beings, human beings by evolution. We touch on aspects of this issue in Chapter 5, arguing that the intentionality of biological systems specifically is characterized by a range of connected structural and functional features. Generally speaking, however, nothing in the present essay relies heavily on any distinction between 'derived' and 'intrinsic' (or 'original') intentionality.

10. This is a complex topic, only some aspects of which will be addressed in the text; see also, for example, Dretske (1981, 1983, 1988), Jackendoff (1987), Bogdan (1988), Israel (1988), Greenwood (1991), Cummins (1991), and Hanson (1990). Information and meaning together are the topics for causal and functional semantics, to be discussed in Chapter 4.

11. A discussion of the relation between language and the various levels of visual information-processing described by Marr (1982) can be found in Jackendoff (1987). The issue of analogical as opposed to propositional and linguistic representation has been the subject of much research and debate, for example Shepard and Metzler (1971), Kosslyn and Pomerantz (1977), Kosslyn (1981), Pylyshyn (1981), Johnson-Laird (1983), Weiskrantz (1988), Finke (1989), and Tye (1991). Barnard's interacting cognitive subsystems framework posits nine types of information and two levels of meaning, specific propositional coding and a more generic level (Barnard 1985; Barnard and Teasdale 1991; Teasdale and Barnard 1993). The question of symbolic encoding of information as it arises in AI models is discussed in section 2.2, and the grounding of meaning in sensorimotor representations is discussed in Section 2.3. Recent philosophical commentary on the relation between thought and language includes Gillett (1992). The problem of linguistic as opposed to non-linguistic specification of mental contents is excellently discussed by Clark (1990).

12. Source material for empiricism includes Locke (1690) and Hume (1777). On logical empiricism see, for example, Ayer (1936, 1959). Major statements of post-empiricism include Quine (1953), Feyerabend (1965), Wittgenstein (1969), and Lakatos (1970). Aspects of these last two works are discussed in subsection 1.4.4 and in this subsection, respectively.

13. On the demarcation criterion, see Popper (1959), Kuhn (1962), Lakatos and Musgrave (1970), including particularly Lakatos (1970) and Feyerabend (1975), with commentary in O'Hear (1989). On its application to psychoanalytic theory, see Popper (1962, 1974), and for commentary Grünbaum (1984, 1986, 1993).

14. These distinctions are many-sided, complex, and controversial. They arose early in cognitive science (Chomsky 1965; Fodor 1968; Turvey 1974), and remain influential in contemporary theorizing (Chomsky 1980; Evans 1985; Stich and Nichols 1992). The simple position adopted in this essay is stated below in the text.

15. 'Self-knowledge' has various meanings, of which the capacity to give an account

of one's own intentional states is one. For critical discussion of the varieties of self-knowledge see, for example, Neisser (1988) and Cassam (1994).

16. This way of qualifying first-person infallibility and authority, in terms of possible conflict with the person's actions, is quite distinct from another method currently popular in the philosophical literature, in which the qualification appeals to the so-called 'broad' content of mental states (Davidson 1984, 1987; Burge 1988; Boghossian 1989; McKinsey 1991). The notion of broad content invoked here derives from Putnam's (1975) argument that 'meaning ain't in the head', and will be discussed at length in the next chapter (Section 2.5).

   Both ways of qualifying first-person authority have in common the critical point that self-reports of mental states are committed to the existence of something 'non-subjective', and hence can be wrong. In the account proposed here this something non-subjective is the person's (objective) behaviour, while in the other account it is typically some independently defined feature of the external world. Criticisms of the generally accepted notion of broad content are made in subsection 2.5.4 from the standpoint of a behavioural criterion of content, and those criticisms are of a piece with the behavioural criterion of failure of self-knowledge proposed here.

   An advantage of this behavioural criterion is that it can deliver an account not only of possible error in first-person reports, but also of 'infallible' uses of such reports. The approach to infallibility, based on the fact that self-reports normally regulate action, is considered below in the text.

17. See, for example, Fodor (1987, Chapter 1). Much recent discussion has concerned the role in folk psychological explanation and prediction of *ceteris paribus* clauses (that is, of qualifying clauses to the effect: 'other things being equal'), and particularly the question whether reliance on such clauses invalidates the alleged explanations and predictive power (for example, Fodor 1987, 1991; Schiffer 1991). We assume here that this is not the case. Indeed, it will be argued later, in Chapters 4 and 5, that one particular type of folk psychological (and cognitive psychological) *ceteris paribus* clause, referring in some way to 'normal' psychological function, is critical to the logic of explanations which invoke intentional states, and to their special causal status.

REFERENCES

Anderson, J. R. (1983). *The architecture of cognition*. Harvard University Press, Cambridge, Mass.

Anscombe, G. E. M. (1957). *Intention*. Blackwell, Oxford.

Astington, J. W., Harris, P. L. and Olson, D. R. (ed.) (1988). *Developing theories of mind*. Cambridge University Press, Cambridge.

Attneave, F. (1959). *Applications of information theory to psychology: a summary of basic concepts, methods and results*. Henry Holt, New York.

Ayer, A. J. (1936). *Language, truth and logic*. Gollanz, London. (2nd edn, revised, 1946.)

Ayer, A. J. (ed.) (1959). *Logical positivism.* The Free Press, Glencoe, Illinois.

Baars, B. (1986). *The cognitive revolution in psychology.* Guildford, New York.

Baddeley, A. (1992). Editorial: Consciousness and working memory. *Consciousness and Cognition*, 1, 3–6.

Baddeley, A. and Weiskrantz, L. (ed.) (1993). *Attention: selection, awareness, and control.* Oxford University Press, Oxford.

Barnard, P. (1985). Interacting cognitive subsystems: a psycholinguistic approach to short-term memory. In *Progress in the psychology of language*, (ed. A. Ellis), Vol. 2, pp. 197–258. Lawrence Erlbaum Associates, London.

Barnard, P. and Teasdale, J. (1991). Interacting cognitive subsystems: a systemic approach to cognitive-affective interaction and change. *Cognition and Emotion*, 5, 1–39.

Baron-Cohen, S., Tager-Flusberg, H., and Cohen, D. (ed.) (1993). *Understanding other minds: perspectives from autism.* Oxford University Press, Oxford.

Bateson, G., Jackson, D., Haley, J., and Weakland, J. (1956). Toward a theory of schizophrenia. *Behavioral Science*, 1, 251–64.

Bennett, M. (ed.) (1993). *The child as psychologist.* Harvester, Sussex.

Berkeley, G. (1710). The principles of human knowledge. In *The works of George Berkeley*, (ed. A. A. Luce and T. E. Jessop), Vol. ii. Thomas Nelson and Sons, London, 1949.

Boden, M. (1988). *Computer models of mind.* Cambridge University Press, Cambridge.

Bogdan, R. J. (1988). Information and cognition: an ontological account. *Mind and Language*, 3, 81–122.

Boghossian, P. (1989). Content and self-knowledge. *Philosophical Topics*, 17, 5–26.

Bolton, D. (1979). *An approach to Wittgenstein's philosophy.* Macmillan, London.

Bolton, D. (1982). Life-form and idealism. In *Idealism, past and present*, (ed. G. Vesey), pp. 269–84. Cambridge University Press, Cambridge.

Brennan, J. F. (1986). *History and systems of psychology*, (3rd edn). Prentice Hall, Englewood Cliffs, NJ.

Brentano, F. (1874). *Psychologie vom empirischen standpunkt*, Vol. I. Leipzig.

Brewer, W. (1974). There is no convincing evidence for operant or classical conditioning in adult humans. In *Cognition and the symbolic processes*, (ed. W. B. Weimer and D. S. Palermo), pp. 1–42. Lawrence Erlbaum Associates, Hillsdale, NJ.

Brewin, C. R. (1988). *Cognitive foundations of clinical psychology.* Lawrence Erlbaum, Hove.

Brown, J. and Dunn, J. (1991). 'You can cry, mum': the social and developmental implications of talk about internal states. *British Journal of Developmental Psychology*, 9, 237–56.

Burge, T. (1988). Individualism and self-knowledge. *Journal of Philosophy*, 85, 649–63.

Burtt, E. A. (1932). *The metaphysical foundations of modern physical science*, (2nd edn). Routledge and Kegan Paul, London.

Butterworth, G., Harris, P., Leslie, A., and Wellman, H. (ed.) (1991). *Perspectives on the child's theory of mind.* Oxford University Press, Oxford.

Byng-Hall, J. (1973). Family myths used as defence in conjoint family therapy. *British Journal of Medical Psychology*, 46, 239–49.

Cassam, Q. (ed.) (1994). *Self-knowledge*. Oxford University Press, Oxford.

Ceci, S. J. and Bronfenbrenner, U. (1991). On the demise of everyday memory. *American Psychologist*, **46**, 27–31.

Chomsky, N. (1957) *Syntactic structures*. Mouton, The Hague.

Chomsky, N. (1959). Review of B. F. Skinner's *Verbal behavior. Language*, **35**, 26–58. (Reprinted in Block, N. (ed.) (1980). *Readings in philosophy of psychology*, Vol. I, pp. 48–63. Methuen, London. Page references to this volume.

Chomsky, N. (1965). *Aspects of the theory of syntax*. MIT Press, Cambridge, Mass.

Chomsky, N. (1980). Rules and representations. With peer commentary. In *The Behavioral and Brain Sciences*, **3**, 1–61.

Churchland, P. M. (1988). *Matter and consciousness*. MIT Press, Cambridge, Mass. (1984, revised 1988.)

Ciompi, L. (1991). Affects as central organizing and integrating factors. *British Journal of Psychiatry*, **159**, 97–105.

Clark, A. (1990). Belief, opinion and consciousness. *Philosophical Psychology*, **3**, 139–54.

Conway, M. A. (1991). In defense of everyday memory. *American Psychologist*, **46**, 19–26.

Copleston, F. (1960). *A history of philosophy*, Vol. iv. Burns and Oates, London.

Cummins, R. (1991). The role of mental meaning in psychological explanation. In *Dretske and his critics*, (ed. B. McLaughlin), pp. 102–17. Blackwell, Oxford.

Darwin, C. (1872). *The expression of the emotions in man and animals*. Reprinted by University of Chicago Press, 1965.

Davidson, D. (1963). Actions, reasons, and causes. Reprinted in Davidson, D. (1980). *Essays on actions and events*, pp. 3–19. Clarendon Press, Oxford.

Davidson, D. (1970). Mental events. In *Experience and theory*, (ed. L. Foster and J. Swanson). MIT Press, Cambridge, Mass. (Reprinted in Davidson, D. (1980). *Essays on actions and events*, pp. 207–27. Clarendon Press, Oxford.)

Davidson, D. (1971). *Agency*. In *Agent, action, and reason*, (ed. R. Binkley, R. Bronaugh, and A. Marras). University of Toronto Press, Toronto. (Reprinted in Davidson, D. (1980). *Essays on actions and events*, pp. 43–61. Clarendon Press, Oxford.)

Davidson, D. (1984). 1st Person Authority. *Dialectica*, **38**, 101–11.

Davidson, D. (1987). Knowing one's own mind. *Proceedings and Addresses of the American Philosophical Association*, **60**, 441–58.

Davidson, D. (1989). The myth of the subjective. In *Relativism: interpretation and confrontation*, (ed. M. Krausz, pp. 159–72. Notre Dame University Press, Notre Dame, Ind.

Davidson, R. J. (1992). Prolegomenon to the structure of emotion: Gleanings from neuropsychology. In *Basic emotions*, (ed. N. L. stein and K. Oatley), pp. 245–68. Lawrence Erlbaum Associates, Hove.

Davies, M. and Humphreys, G. W. (ed.) (1992). *Consciousness*. Blackwell, Oxford.

Dennett, D. (1969). *Content and consciousness*. Routledge and Kegan Paul, London.

Dennett, D. (1979). *Brainstorms: philosophical essays on mind and psychology*. Harvester, Sussex.

Dennett, D. (1987). *The intentional stance*. MIT Press, Cambridge, Mass.

Dennett, D. (1988). Precis of *The intentional stance* with peer commentary. *The Behavioral and Brain Sciences*, **11**, 495–546.

Dennett, D. (1991). *Consciousness explained*. Penguin, Harmondsworth.

Descartes, R. (1641). *Meditations on first philosophy*. (Quotations from and page references to *The philosophical works of Descartes*, trans. E. S. Haldane and G. R. T. Ross, Cambridge University Press, Cambridge, 1911, reprinted 1967.)

Dretske, F. (1981). *Knowledge and the flow of information*. MIT Press, Cambridge, Mass.

Dretske, F. (1983). Precis of *Knowledge and the flow of information*, with peer commentary. *Behavioral and Brain Sciences*, **6**, 55–63.

Dretske, F. (1988). Commentary: Bogdan on information. *Mind and Language*, **3**, 141–44.

Dulany, D. (1974). On the support of cognitive theory in opposition to behaviour theory: a methodological problem. In *Cognition and the symbolic processes*, (ed. W. B. Weimer and D. S. Palermo), pp. 43–56. Lawrence Erlbaum Associates, Hillsdale, NJ.

Dunn, J., Brown J., and Beardsall, L. (1991a). Family talk about feeling states and children's later understanding of others' emotions. *Developmental Psychology*, **27**, 448–55.

Dunn, J., Brown J., Slomkowski, C., Tesla, C., and Youngblade, L. (1991b). Young children's understanding of other people's feelings and beliefs: individual differences and their antecedents. *Child Development*, **62**, 1352–66.

Ericsson, K. A. and Simon, H. A. (1980). Verbal reports as data. *Psychological Review*, **87**, 215–51.

Evans, G. (1985). Semantic theory and tacit knowledge. In *Collected papers*, (ed. G. Evans), pp. 322–42. Oxford University Press, Oxford.

Evnine, S. (1991). *Donald Davidson*. Polity Press, Cambridge.

Eysenck, M. W. and Keane, M. T. (1990). *Cognitive psychology. A student's handbook*. Lawrence Erlbaum Associates, Hove.

Feyerabend, P. (1965). Problems of empiricism. In *Beyond the edge of certainty*, (ed. R. Colodny), Prentice Hall, Englewood Cliffs.

Feyerabend, P. (1975). *Against method*. New Left Books, London.

Feyerabend, P. (1988). Knowledge and the role of theories. *Philosophy and Social Sciences*, **18**, 157–78.

Finke, R. A. (1989). *Principles of mental imagery*. MIT Press, Cambridge, Mass.

Flanagan, O. (1992). *Consciousness reconsidered*. MIT Press, Cambridge, Mass.

Fodor, J. (1968). The appeal to tacit knowledge in psychological explanation. *Journal of Philosophy*, **65**, 627–40.

Fodor, J. (1987). *Psychosemantics*. MIT Press, Cambridge, Mass.

Fodor, J. (1991). You can fool some of the people all of the time, everything else being equal; hedged laws and psychological explanation. *Mind*, **100**, 19–34.

Fodor, J., Garrett, M. F., Walker, E. C. T., and Parkes, C. H. (1980). Against definitions. *Cognition*, **8**, 263–367.

Folgelin, R. (1976). *Wittgenstein*. Routledge and Kegan Paul, London.

Foucault, M. (1965). *Madness and civilization*. Random House, New York.

Gardner, H. (1985). *The mind's new science: A history of the cognitive revolution*.

Basic Books. (Reprinted 1987 with new epilogue.)

Garner, W. R. (1962). *Uncertainty and structure as psychological concepts*. Wiley, London.

Gillett, G. (1988). Consciousness and brain function. *Philosophical Psychology*, 1, 327–41.

Gillett, G. (1992) *Representation, meaning, and thought*. Clarendon Press, Oxford.

Goertzel, B. (1992). Quantum theory and consciousness. *Journal of Mind and Behavior*, 13, 29–36.

Gordon, R. M. (1987). *The structure of emotions: investigations in cognitive philosophy*. Cambridge University Press, Cambridge.

Greenspan, P. S. (1988). *Emotions and reasons: an inquiry into emotional justification*. Routledge, New York.

Greenwood, J. (ed.) (1991). *The future of folk psychology: Intentionality and cognitive science*. Cambridge University Press, Cambridge.

Grünbaum, A. (1984). *The foundations of psychoanalysis: A philosophical critique*. University of California Press, California.

Grünbaum, A. (1986). Precis of *The foundations of psychoanalysis: A philosophical critique*, with peer commentary. *The Behavioral and Brain Sciences*, 9, 217–84.

Grünbaum, A. (1993). *Validation in the clinical theory of psychoanalysis*. International Universities Press, Madison, CT.

Hannay, A. (1990). *Human consciousness*. Routledge, New York.

Hanson, P. (ed.) (1990). *Information, language, and cognition*. University of British Columbia Press, Vancouver.

Harris, P. L. (1989). *Children and emotion: the development of psychological understanding*. Blackwell, Oxford.

Hilgard, E. R. and Bower, G. H. (1966). *Theories of learning*, (3rd edn). Appleton-Century-Crofts, New York.

Hirsch, S. and Leff, J. (1975). *Abnormalities in parents of schizophrenics*, Maudsley Monographs 22. Oxford University Press, Oxford.

Hobson, P. (1991). Against the theory of 'Theory of Mind'. *British Journal of Developmental Psychology*, 9, 33–51.

Hornsby, J. (1986). Physicalist thinking and conceptions of behaviour. In *Subject, thought and context*, (ed. P. Pettit and J. McDowell), pp. 95–115. Clarendon, Oxford.

Hume, D. (1777). *An enquiry concerning human understanding*, (ed. L. A. Sclby-Bigge, 1902, (2nd edn)). Oxford University Press, Oxford.

Israel, D. (1988). Commentary: Bogdan on information. *Mind and Language*, 3, 123–40.

Jackendoff, R. (1987). *Consciousness and the computational mind*. MIT Press, Cambridge, Mass.

Johnson-Laird, P. (1983). *Mental models: towards a cognitive science of language, inference and consciousness*. Cambridge University Press, Cambridge.

Johnson-Laird, P. (1988). *The computer and the mind*. Cambridge University Press, Cambridge.

Katz, J. and Fodor, J. (1963). The structure of a semantic theory. *Language*, 39, 170–210.

Kosslyn, S. M. (1981). The medium and the message in mental imagery: a theory. *Psychological Review*, **88**, 44–66.

Kosslyn, S. M. and Pomerantz, J. R. (1977). Imagery, propositions, and the form of internal representations. *Cognitive Psychology*, **9**, 52–76.

Kuhn, T. S. (1962). *The structure of scientific revolutions*. University of Chicago Press, Chicago.

Lakatos, I. (1970). Falsification and the methodology of scientific research programmes. In *Criticism and the growth of knowledge*, (ed. I. Lakatos and A. Musgrave), pp. 91–196. Cambridge University Press, Cambridge.

Lakatos, I. and Musgrave, A. (ed.) (1970). *Criticism and the growth of knowledge*. Cambridge University Press, Cambridge.

Lazarus, R. G. (1982). Thoughts on the relation between emotion and cognition. *American Psychologist*, **37**, 1019–24.

Lazarus, R. G. (1984). On the primacy of cognition. *American Psychologist*, **39**, 124–9.

Leahey, T. H. (1994). *A history of modern psychology*, (2nd edn). Prentice Hall, Englewood Cliffs, NJ.

Locke, J. (1690). *An essay concerning human understanding*, (ed. P. H. Nidditch, 1975). Oxford University Press, Oxford.

Lockwood, M. (1989). *Mind, brain and quantum*. Blackwell, Oxford.

Looren de Jong, H. (1991). Intentionality and the ecological approach. *Journal for the Theory of Social Behavior*, **21**, 91–109.

Lycan, W. G. (1987). *Consciousness*. MIT Press, Cambridge, Mass.

Lyons, W. (1990). Intentionality and modern philosophical psychology, I: The modern reduction of intentionality. *Philosophical Psychology*, **3**, 247–69.

Lyons, W. (1991). Intentionality and modern philosophical psychology, II: The return to representation. *Philosophical Psychology*, **4**, 83–102.

Lyons, W. (1992). Intentionality and modern philosophical psychology, III: The appeal to teleology. *Philosophical Psychology*, **5**, 309–26.

Macfarlane, D. A. (1930). The role of kinesthesis in maze learning. *University of California Publications in Psychology*, **4**, 277–305.

McKinsey, M. (1991). Anti-individualism and privileged access. *Analysis*, **51**, 9–16.

Mackintosh, N. J. (1983). *Conditioning and associative learning*. Oxford University Press, New York.

Malpas, J. E. (1992). *Donald Davidson and the mirror of meaning: holism, truth, interpretation*. Cambridge University Press, Cambridge.

Mandler, J. (1982). The structure of value: accounting for taste. In *Affect and cognition*, (ed. M. S. Clarke and S. T. Fiske), pp. 3–36. Lawrence Erlbaum, Hillsdale NJ.

Marcel, A. J. and Bisiach, E. (ed.) (1988). *Consciousness in contemporary science*. Clarendon, Oxford.

Marr, D. C. (1982). *Vision: a computational investigation into the human representation and processing of visual information*. Freeman, San Francisco.

Mele, A. R. (1992). *Springs of action: understanding intentional behavior*. Oxford University Press, New York.

Mensch, J. R. (1988). *Intersubjectivity and transcendental idealism*. SUNY Press, Albany.

Miller, G. A. (1953). What is information measurement? *American Psychologist*, 8, 3–11.

Miller, G. A., Gallanter, E., and Pribram, K. (1960). *Plans and the structure of behavior*. Holt, Rinehart and Winston, New York.

Moore, G. E. (1925). A defence of common sense. (Reprinted in Moore, G. E. (1959). *Philosophical papers*, pp. 32–59. George Allen and Unwin, London.)

Moore, G. E. (1939). Proof of an external world. (Reprinted in Moore, G. E. (1959). *Philosophical papers*, pp. 127–50. George Allen and Unwin, London.)

Morris, P. (1981). The cognitive psychology of self-reports. In *The psychology of ordinary explanations of social behaviour*, (ed. C. Antaki) pp. 183–203. Academic Press, London.

Nagel, T. (1986). *The view from nowhere*. Oxford University Press, Oxford.

Nash, R. (1989). Cognitive theories of emotion. *Nous*, 23, 481–504.

Neisser, U. (1967) *Cognitive psychology*. Appleton-Century-Crofts, New York.

Neisser, U. (1976). *Cognition and reality*. Freeman, San Francisco.

Neisser, U. (1988). Five kinds of self-knowledge. *Philosophical Psychology*, 1, 35–59.

Newton, N. (1992). Dennett on Intrinsic Intentionality. *Analysis*, 52, 18–23.

Nisbett, R. and Wilson, T. (1977). Telling more than we can know: verbal reports on mental processes. *Psychological Review*, 84, 31–59.

Oatley, K. (1988). Plans and the communicative function of emotions: a cognitive theory. In *Cognitive perspectives on emotion and motivation*, (ed. V. Hamilton, G. Bower, and N. Frijda), pp. 345–64. Kluwer, Dordrecht.

Oatley, K. and Johnson-Laird, P. (1987). Towards a cognitive theory of emotions. *Cognition and Emotion*, 1, 29–50.

O'Hear, A. (1989). *An introduction to the philosophy of science*. Oxford University Press, Oxford.

Pears, D. (1988). *The false prison: A study of the development of Wittgenstein's philosophy*, Vol. 2. Clarendon Press, Oxford.

Pfeifer, R. (1988). Artificial intelligence models of emotion. In *Cognitive perspectives on emotion and motivation*, (ed. V. Hamilton, G. Bower, and N. Frijda), pp. 287–320. Kluwer, Dordrecht.

Pickering, J. and Skinner, M. (1990). *From sentience to symbols: readings on consciousness*. Harvester, Sussex.

Popper, K. (1959). *The logic of scientific discovery*. Hutchinson, London.

Popper, K. (1962). *Conjectures and refutations*. Routledge and Kegan Paul, London.

Popper, K. (1974). Replies to my critics. In *The philosophy of Karl Popper*, (ed. P. A. Schilpp), Book II, pp. 961–1197. Open Court, Lasalle, Illinois.

Power, M. and Brewin, C. (1991). From Freud to cognitive science: a contemporary account of the unconscious. *British Journal of Clinical Psychology*, 30, 289–310.

Premack, D. and Woodruff, G. (1978). Does the chimpanzee have a theory of mind?. *The Behavioral and Brain Sciences*, 4, 515–26.

Putnam, H. (1975). The meaning of 'meaning'. In *Mind, language and reality*, pp. 215–71. Cambridge University Press, Cambridge.

Pylyshyn, Z. (1981). The imagery debate: analogue media versus tacit knowledge. *Psychological Review*, 88, 16–45.

Quine, W. V. O. (1953). Two Dogmas of empiricism. In *From a logical point of view*, (ed. W. V. O. Quine), pp. 20–46. Harvard University Press, Cambridge, Mass.

Robinson, D. N. (1976). *An intellectual history of psychology*. Macmillan, New York.

Rosch, E. and Mervis, C. B. (1975). Family resemblances: studies in the internal structure of categories. *Cognitive psychology*, 7, 573–605.

Ryle, G. (1949). *The concept of mind*. Hutchinson, London.

Sayre, K. M. (1976). *Cybernetics and the philosophy of mind*. Routledge and Kegan Paul, London.

Schiffer, S. (1991). *Ceteris paribus clauses*. Mind, 100, 1–17.

Searle, J. R. (1983). *Intentionality: an essay in the philosophy of mind*. Cambridge University Press, Cambridge.

Searle, J. R. (1990). Consciousness, explanatory inversion and cognitive Science. *Behavioral and Brain Sciences*, 13, 585–642.

Searle, J. R. (1992). *The rediscovery of the mind*. MIT Press, Cambridge, Mass.

Seligman, M. (1975). *Helplessness: on depression, development, and death*. W. H. Freeman, San Francisco.

Shannon, C. and Weaver, W. (1949). *The mathematical theory of communication*. University of Illinois Press, Urbana.

Shepard, R. N. and Metzler, J. (1971). Mental rotation of three-dimensional objects. *Science*, 171, 1–17.

Shotter, J. (1981). Telling and reporting: prospective and retrospective uses of self-ascriptions. In *The psychology of ordinary explanations of social behaviour*, (ed. C. Antaki), pp. 157–81. Academic Press, London.

Skinner, B. (1957). *Verbal behaviour*. Appleton-Century-Crofts, New York.

Smith, D. W. (1992). Consciousness in action. *Synthese*, 90, 119–43.

Smith, E. E. and Medin, D. L. (1981). *Categories and concepts*. Harvard University Press, Cambridge, Mass.

Stein, N. L. and Oatley, K. (ed.). (1992). *Basic emotions*. Lawrence Erlbaum Associates, Hove.

Stich, S. (1983). *From folk psychology to cognitive science*. MIT Press, Cambridge, Mass.

Stich, S. and Nichols, S. (1992). Folk psychology: simulation or tacit theory? *Mind and Language*, 7, 35–71.

Szasz, T. S. (1961). *The myth of mental illness: Foundations of a theory of personal conduct*. Harper and Row, New York.

Teasdale, J. and Barnard, P. (1993). *Affect, cognition and change*. Lawrence Erlbaum Associates, Hove.

Tolman, E. C. (1932). *Purposive behavior in animals and men*. Appleton-Century-Crofts, New York.

Tolman, E. C. (1948). Cognitive maps in rats and men. *Psychological Review*, 55, 189–208.

Turvey, M. T. (1974). Constructive theory, perceptual systems, and tacit knowledge. In *Cognition and the symbolic processes*, (ed. W. B. Weimer and D. S. Palermo), pp. 165–80. *Lawrence Erlbaum Associates, Hillsdale, NJ*.

Tye, M. (1991). *The imagery debate*. MIT Press, Cambridge, Mass.

Varela, F. (1979). *Principles of biological autonomy*. North Holland, New York.

Vedeler, D. (1991). Infant intentionality as object directness: an alternative to representationalism. *Journal for the Theory of Social Behavior*, 21, 431–48.

Velmans, M. (1990). Consciousness, brain and the physical world. *Philosophical Psychology*, 3, 77–99.

Velmans, M, (1991). Is human information processing conscious? *Behavioral and Brain Sciences*, 14, 651–726.

von Bertalanffy, L. (1968). *General systems theory: foundations, developments, applications*. George Braziller, New York.

von Wright, G. H. (1971). *Explanation and understanding*. Routledge and Kegan Paul, London.

Weiskrantz, L. (ed.) (1988). *Thought without language*. Clarendon Press, Oxford.

Wellman, H. (1990). *The child's theory of mind*. MIT Press, Cambridge, Mass.

Whiten, A. (ed.) (1991). *Natural theories of mind: evolution, development and simulation of everyday mindreading*. Blackwell, Oxford.

Wiener, N. (1948). *Cybernetics of control and communication in the animal and the machine*. MIT Press, Cambridge, Mass.

Williams, J. M. G., Watts, F. N., Macleod, C., and Matthews, A. (1988). *Cognitive psychology and emotional disorders*. Wiley, Chichester.

Wittgenstein, L. (1921). *Tractatus logico-philosophicus*. (Trans. D. F. Pears and B. F. McGuiness (1961). Routledge and Kegan Paul, London.

Wittgenstein, L. (1953). *Philosophical investigations*, (ed. G. E. M. Anscombe and R. Rhees, trans. G. E. M. Anscombe). Blackwell, Oxford.

Wittgenstein, L. (1969). *On certainty*, (ed. G. E. M. Anscombe and G. H. von Wright, trans. D. Paul and G. E. M. Anscombe). Blackwell, Oxford.

Zajonc, R. B. (1980). Feeling and thinking: preferences need no inferences. *American Psychologist*, 35, 151–75.

Zajonc, R. B. (1984). On the primacy of affect. *American Psychologist*, 39, 117–23.

Zajonc, R., Pietromonaco, P., and Bargh, J. (1982). Independence and interaction of affect and cognition. In *Affect and cognition*, (ed. M. S. Clarke and S. T. Fiske), pp. 211–27. Lawrence Erlbaum Associates, Hillsdale, NJ.

Zangwill, O. L. (1950). *An introduction to modern psychology*. Methuen, London.

2
Mind, Meaning, and Neural Causation

2.1 THE PROBLEM, AND A FAMILIAR SOLUTION: THE BRAIN ENCODES MEANING

2.1.1 Mind–brain identity as a quick solution

It was concluded in the first chapter that explanations of action in terms of meaningful, mental states are causal; or again, that such states are causes of (intentional) behaviour.

This conclusion raises many questions, including the following: 'How do meaningful mental states cause behaviour?'; 'What are such states, that they *can* cause behaviour?'; and 'How do they relate to brain states, which we suppose (also) cause behaviour?'[1]

Mental states now appear in the best scientific theory we have of complex, higher behaviour. The problem of the causal status of mind is therefore not only of philosophical relevance (or irrelevance); it presses hard in science itself. On the other hand, the issues here are inevitably entangled with long-standing philosophical controversies. These include the traditional problems of dualism: the apparent causal powerlessness of mind, and its incompatibility generally with materialist assumptions in the natural sciences (subsection 1.2.1). Given the forced choice between dualism and materialism, any new science of behaviour apparently has no choice but to opt for the latter. It should be recalled that in the considerations in the preceding chapter there was no commitment to dualism. The argument emphasized the functional role of mental states as mediating causes between stimuli and behaviour, without reference to their ontological status. A tempting response at this stage is to suppose that mental events are just material events in the brain, and that this is how and why they have causal influences on behaviour.

In brief, the materialist theory of mind can be derived from two premises: first, that mental processes mediate causally between stimuli and behaviour; and secondly, that the causal processes which mediate between stimuli and behaviour are material processes in the brain. The first premise can plausibly be construed either as a basic postulate of cognitive psychology or as a conceptual presumption of folk psychology, or as both. The second premise is plausibly construed as derived from two claims, one a priori the other a posteriori. The former is to the effect that all causes of material events are material, while the empirical claim is that the material causes of behaviour are, in fact, in the brain. Hence we infer that mental events, as causes of behaviour, are contingently (as a matter of empirical fact) identical with brain events.

This move, identifying the mind with the brain, would apparently solve the problem of mental causation at one stroke, in terms highly satisfactory to materialism and natural science.

2.1.2 The legacy of Cartesianism: inevitable problems

Predictably enough, however, the philosophical problem cannot be disposed of so fast. Philosophical problems typically have the form of forced choice dichotomies, which have their origins in genuine tensions and contradictions in deep theory. Dogmatic statements of one side or another of the split express rather than solve the underlying conflicts. In the present case, identifying the mind with the material brain encounters difficulties which are all variations of the fact that the material brain lacks properties of the mind.

The problematic here derives largely from seventeenth-century philosophy, which, as outlined in the previous chapter (subsection 1.2.1), stripped 'matter' of all but the primary (mathematical, absolute) qualities, consigning the rest to 'the mind', which hence became the container for all sensibility. To say that the mind is identical with the brain will not work if the brain is understood in the spirit of seventeenth-century dualism, as being matter with only physically defined properties. Cartesian mind was defined in various ways: as a thinking substance, conscious, subjective, known with certainty, and as immaterial. These characteristics all are bound to present as problems to be deconstructed or resolved before mind–brain identity theory or any post-Cartesian concept of mind can be made to work. But, certainly, no theory is going to be adequate which just affirms one or other half of Cartesian dualism. If there is going to be an adequate materialism, it will have to envisage the brain as being something like the Cartesian mind, not as non-mental Cartesian matter. This is the very general idea, expressed in historical terms, which we will be working around in this chapter.

The materialist theory of mind has been subject to various kinds of objection. One kind of objection rests on the fact that mental states have properties which material states do not (such as manifestation in consciousness, epistemic privacy), and vice versa (such as spatial location). Since, according to Liebniz' 'law of identity' two identical things have all properties in common, it would follow that mental states cannot be material states. However, it has been argued, controversially, that the thesis of contingent identity, as opposed to conceptual or analytic identity, can avoid or otherwise cope with problems of this sort. These issues have been much debated in the philosophical literature (for example Boyd 1980, and other papers in Block 1980 *a*, Part Two).

We already considered briefly in the first chapter (subsection 1.2.2) the distinction between first-person (subjective) and third-person (objective) perspectives on the mind. In large part the obvious objections to the materialist theory have to do with the 'subjective' aspects of mind: mind as viewed by the subject. From this point of view mental states are manifest in consciousness, and have phenomenal qualities, but neither of these characteristics obviously belongs to brain states. However, we shall focus here on problems for the materialist theory that arise from the objective, or scientific perspective. This is, after all, the context in which mind–brain identity is inferred: the claim never was grounded in introspection. From the objective perspective, mental states make their appearance as posits in the theory of behaviour, as mediators between stimulus and response. The question is whether from this external, scientific point of view mental states can be identified with material states of the brain. In effect we are questioning here the fast derivation of the materialist theory of mind with which we concluded the preceding subsection.

In considering inadequacies of mind–brain identity from the objective, scientific perspective, we are in one sense already far removed from Cartesianism, which viewed mind from a subjective point of view only. On the other hand, a (or the) defining attribute of Cartesian mind was *thinking*, which is closely linked to representation, meaning, and intentionality, and these are none other than the characteristics of mental states which are essential for the purposes of cognitive explanations of behaviour. The explanation of action in terms of mental states depends on the fact that mental states are about the scene of action, and about agent–environment interactions (subsection 1.3.6). So it turns out that what was essential to the Cartesian mind is essential also to mind as posited by cognitive-behavioural explanations. This means that the latter will not be satisfied with any definition of mental states that makes them 'material' *as opposed to* 'thoughtful'. Put the other way round, from the point of view of the explanation of behaviour in terms of mental states, if mind is going to be identified with the material brain, then the material brain will have to be—like Cartesian mind—a 'thinking substance'.

2.1.3 On the irreducibility of mind and meaning

The language of mind and meaning used in the description and explanation of action is, no doubt, vastly different from the language used to describe the material processes in the brain. As discussed in the first chapter, the mental states that have to do with action have meaningful content, or intentionality; they are subject to normative descriptions, pertaining to rules, to distinctions such as right/wrong, reasonable/unreasonable, etc.; they are attributed to the agent 'holistically', in the form of a theory about many (meaningfully) connected states. These are the characteristics of mental states as invoked in the explanation and prediction of behaviour, and they apparently have no counterpart in brain states, at least when physically defined. The implication is that the mind cannot be identified with the material brain, or, at least, that mental state descriptions cannot be reduced to descriptions of the brain. The various, related meaningful aspects of mental states prohibit any (simple) reduction of the mental to the physical, since, to put it briefly, meaning would be lost in the reduction.[2]

An aid to understanding the attractiveness of the mind–brain identity theory and the problems that it conceals is provided by Hornsby (1986). She presents two pictures of the mediation between 'inputs' and 'outputs': one is the intentional psychological, the other is the neurophysiological. As follows (Hornsby 1986, p. 95):

Hornsby observes (loc. cit.) that one has only to look at these two pictures to be tempted to make a superimposition. She proceeds to argue that such superimposition is invalid, in particular at the 'output' end. One theme in Hornsby's argument is that intentional actions do not map on to, and cannot be identified with, bodily movements. This lack of correspondence has been referred to already in the first chapter (subsection 1.3.6). The general problem with the superimposition at the 'input' end is that the objects of perception and of belief typically cannot be captured by physical descriptions because, in brief, they carry more and different kinds of meaning (information). This critical point has been considered already in the preceding chapter (subsection 1.2.2), will be discussed later in this chapter (subsection 2.5.4) and at length in Chapter 4 (sections 4.3 and 4.4).

The main question for this chapter concerns the superimposition of the 'central' mediating states. Can mental states be identified with neurophysiological states? In so far as there is no identity between the *relata* of these two kinds of central states, it can be expected that the answer to this question is negative, and further, that the reasons are closely related to those in the cases of inputs and outputs; they concern the *meaning* carried by mental states. The conclusion is, in brief, that the meaning of mental states prohibits their being identified with neural states.

2.1.4 The brain encodes meaning

However, while there is something correct about the preceding line of thought, it is not difficult to see a way of softening the implied contrast between mind and brain. At its starkest, the problem may be expressed by saying that mental states have meaning—carry information—while neural states do not. But, of course, the reply is then simply that this is not true: neural states do carry information. It is axiomatic in the area of overlap between cognitive science and neuroscience that information-processing is implemented by the brain. In brief: neural states encode, and process, information. In what follows, this will sometimes be called the 'encoding thesis' for short.

The question under consideration is whether from the external point of view, in the context of explaining behaviour in terms of mental states, these states can be identified with material states of the brain. The answer is that it is possible, provided that the latter are described in terms of informational content and processing. If, on the other hand, neural states and processes are described in a lower-level, non-intentional language, without reference to information, then it is a mistake to make the identification, for an essential feature of mental states is not captured in these lower-level descriptions.

In the historical terms sketched in subsection 2.1.2 the point can be expressed in the following way: from the point of view of the cognitive-behavioural sciences, the theory of mind–brain identification can be made to work, but on condition that the brain is doing the kind of thing that was done by the Cartesian mind, in particular *thinking* (or representing). In contemporary terms this proposal is the familiar one, that the brain is an information-processing system.

It should be exphasized that the concept of information required in the present context has to be a *semantic* one, linked to meaning, intentionality, representation, etc. The context in question is the modelling of, and hence the explanation and prediction of, organism–environment interactions. In this context, for this purpose, the information processed by the brain has to be *about* something (it has to *represent* something), namely, actual or possible states of the environment, results of action, etc. When brain function is described in these terms, in terms of intentionality, it is in effect being regarded as functioning like the mind.

This proposal is not most happily expressed by saying that mental (or meaningful) states and processes *are identical with* brain states and processes. It is better expressed using terms such as 'are realized by'. This shift in terminology signifies a relationship which is not static, but which is more like that between process and function. It is recommended already by the functionalist theory of mental states, which defines them in terms of their causes and effects. The functionalist theory can be used to derive the theory of mind–brain identity, along the lines of the argument given at the beginning of the section, but it can also be turned against a strong version of the identity theory.

The objection emphasizes precisely function rather than composition: functional states in general can be 'realized' in a variety of ways, so they cannot be identified with a particular material structure or process. The functional states of computing systems, for example, can be realized in diverse kinds of hardware. In biology it is familiar that the same function can be served by a variety of structures and processes in different species. Similarly, the argument proceeds, mental states as functional states cannot be identified with the material states that realize them. According to this argument, the valid sense of 'identity' here would have to be that in which functional states are 'realized by', 'served by', or 'implemented by' material processes. It may be that, as a matter of fact, the same kind of mental state is realized in different cases by different neural structures and processes. The same belief as a functionally defined state may be realized in one way in human beings, in another in cats, or in different ways in different members of the same species, or even differently in the same person at different times. Considerations of this sort have led to a distinction between *type* and *token* mind–brain identity theories. (These terms are taken from philosophical logic: 'type' means kind, 'token' means instance. Thus, the following quotation marks, 'A A', contain one letter type and two letter tokens.) Type identity theory proposes that each type of mental event is identical with a type of brain event. This strong version of the identity theory has come to be regarded as mistaken, for the kind of reasons adduced above, and has been replaced by token identity theory. According to this weaker version, each token mental event is identical with (in the sense of realized by) some token brain event. Token identity theory acknowledges that it cannot be assumed that kinds of mental event correspond to kinds of brain events. Thus, functional characterization of mental states, whether in terms of causal role, or in terms of carrying information, or both, requires that the mind–brain identity theory be ammended to read as follows: each mental event (token) is realized by (and in this sense only 'is identical with') some (token) brain event.[3]

Let us summarize some steps of the argument so far. Causation by mental states can be reconciled with material, neural causation, by adopting a materialist theory of mind, according to which mental states are identical with states of the brain. However, the theory immediately runs up against objections that mental states have properties brain states do not. Some of the peculiarly mental properties have to do with the mind as subjectively experienced, but others are postulated from the perspective of the scientific observer, pertaining to the role of mental states in the production of behaviour, and it is this which is primarily the concern of the present essay. We saw in the first chapter that for the purposes of explaining and predicting complex, higher action (organism–environment interactions) the cognitive psychology paradigm supposes that such activity is regulated by mental states of the living being which have intentionality (which carry information, or meaning). The question is then this: can these mental states be identified with the neural states that cause behaviour?; and the answer is a relatively simple 'yes': the intentional states which regulate behaviour are states of the brain. Certainly, and essentially, this proposed relatively simple solution presupposes that brain states have semantic properties, or again, that intentional states are 'realized in' brain states. The proposed solution can be expressed in the terms characteristic of the interface between cognitive psychology and neuroscience by saying that neural states 'encode' information (or meaning). The implication here is that the causal role of information-carrying neural states in the regulation of organism–environment interactions depends on the information they encode. This critical point will be expanded below in subsections 2.5.5–6, and developed through chapters 4 and 5.

It should be emphasized that the proposed solution makes no commitment to causation by meaningful states *in addition to* causation by neural states. The first kind of causal explanation essentially makes use of intentional concepts (it runs in terms of information-processing). But the point is that causal explanation of action which invokes neural states and processing *also* uses intentional concepts, is run in these same terms. In other words, the distinction between causation by intentional states and causation by non-intentional states does not signify a distinction between causation by non-material states (whatever that might be) and causation by material states. Rather, there are two forms of causal explanation, one of which does and one of which does not invoke intentional states, but both invoke material as opposed to immaterial states (whatever they might be). Hence this proposal undermines the Cartesian mind/matter distinction rather than endorsing one side of it (matter) at the expense of the other (mind). Both kinds of causal explanation invoke material states, but in one of them material states are credited with properties of the Cartesian mind, namely, representation ('thought'). The distinction between, and definition of, the two forms of causality being proposed here will be taken up later, in chapters 4 and 5.

There is no commitment here to dualism, to the idea that there is a mental (meaningful) substance in addition to matter. The point would be rather than there are two forms of description of the material brain. One form of description employs intentional concepts, in particular the concept of information, while the other uses only non-intentional concepts, drawn from basic sciences such as physics and chemistry. The proposal is in effect that the irreducibility of meaning does not signify a dichotomy between mind and matter, but rather a distinction between meaningful (intentional) descriptions and non-meaningful (non-intentional) descriptions. Material processes in the brain can be described in either way, and are described in both ways at the interface between cognitive psychology and neuroscience. In particular, when the purpose is to explain interactions between the organism and the environment, neural processes are described as being concerned precisely with the pick-up, processing, and utilization of information (or meaning).

It follows that intentional language in the brain sciences is essential, and cannot be eliminated in favour of non-intentional descriptions, *for certain purposes, specifically the explanation and prediction of organism–environment interactions.* This is to say, what is known in psychology as cognitive-behavioural science, and in philosophy as the theory of action, will not be able to manage without intentional concepts, and, to make a point of more philosophical interest, it is a philosphical error to think that they could or should be run in non-intentional terms. As anticipated in the first chapter (Subsection 1.3.6), these points are fundamental to the issues addressed in this chapter, and will recur through it.

The solution proposed here to the problem of reconciling mental, meaningful, and material causation includes what Kim (1991) has usefully called the 'dual explanandum strategy'. Kim formulates the problem as follows: 'Given that every physical event has a physical cause, how is a mental cause also possible?' (Kim 1991, p. 57). He points out that a promising general strategy is just to say that there are two behavioural *explananda*, and that there is therefore no problem about there being two kinds of *explanans*. This is the approach adopted here, the critical distinctions being drawn in terms of the presence or absence of intentionality. Kim's main concern is with Dretske's version of the dual explanadum strategy, different from the one proposed here, but he argues that a general point about the strategy is that it requires commitment to dualism, specifically to non-physical causes (Kim 1991, pp. 59–60). But as argued above, the dual explanadum strategy, at least in the version proposed here, and particularly in combination with the encoding thesis, does not imply dualism. Let us take for granted that there are only physical causes, and specifically that the behaviour of a system has physical causes within the system. Even so, when we wish to explain and predict intentional (functional, goal-directed) system–environment interactions, we have to attribute to those physical causes encoded intentionality.

2.1.5 Review of objections, 1–5

The proposed solution to the problem of reconciling meaningful/ mental causation with material causation by the brain is simply that the neural states that cause behaviour encode meaning, with the implication that the causal role of these states is a function of the meaning (or information) they encode.

This familiar idea, however, runs up against a number of powerful and influential theoretical objections, at least five. They are all more or less directly to the effect that mental states with meaningful content, at least as characterized in ordinary language and folk psychology, cannot be construed as being encoded in the brain, and hence not as causes of behaviour. If this conclusion were valid, we would have to preserve something like the turn-of-the-century distinction between meaning and causality. The five objections to the proposed solution, which will be considered in the next five sections of this chapter, may be characterized briefly as follows:

1. The hypothesized encoding is incompatible with connectionist models of psychological function.
2. You can't get semantics out of syntax (not even neural syntax).
3. In any case, it would be the neural syntax doing the causing, and the alleged causal role of semantics drops out as irrelevant.
4. Meanings ain't in the head. (They don't supervene on brain states.)
5. It ascribes to brains what properly belongs to people (and relationships, and culture).

The first objection is based mainly on powerful computer models of mental function, the second is a practically an axiom of philosophical logic, the third is combination of much the same point with plausible assumptions about causality, the fourth is a highly influential line of thought deriving from Putnam linked to a materialist definition of content, and the fifth objection has strong Wittgensteinian credentials. In any circumstances this would be a curious alliance of disparate views, and it is remarkable that they converge in objecting in one way or another to the proposal that meaning is encoded in the brain and thereby has a causal role.

The proposal, on the other hand, has much to be said for it. As already indicated, it manages to reconcile in a relatively straightforward way the role of meaning in the explanation of action, explored in the previous chapter, with the idea that the brain controls behaviour. Cognitive psychology and neuroscience readily use the idea that the brain encodes information (meaning), which in effect defuses conflict between the regulating role of information (or meaning) and the regulating role of the brain. It seems possible, then to combine the claims that ascriptions of meaningful, intentional states provide powerful explanations of behaviour; that such states are causes of behaviour; and that the causes of behaviour are in the brain, specifically, neural states that encode information (meaning). In this combination of claims, fundamental tenets of folk psychology, cognitive psychology, and of neuroscience appear as compatible, indeed as complementary. What is critical in the reconciliation is the apparently simple idea that the brain can encode meaning. This is what in effect collapses dichotomies in deep theory: matter/mind, matter/intentionality, and causality/ meaning.

2.2 OBJECTIONS TO THE PROPOSED SOLUTION, 1: 'ARE THERE "SENTENCES IN THE HEAD"?'

2.2.1 The language of thought hypothesis

It is an axiom of folk psychology, and arguably of cognitive psychology, that behaviour is caused by (regulated by) meaningful states, which are typically identified by propositional clauses of natural languages. Take this as a first (composite) premise. Take as second premise: behaviour is caused by neural states. Plausible conclusion: brain states are (encode) meaningful states, with the implication that brain states must be something like propositional clauses of natural languages. In brief: there must be 'sentences in the head'.

Following this line of thought we come to the area of Fodor's so-called language of thought hypothesis. This hypothesis is sophisticated and complicated, comprising many interrelated components, among which are the following: mental states with meaningful content have an articulated syntactic structure (analogous to the syntactic structure of sentences of natural languages); the causal role of a mental state in relation to other mental states and to behaviour is determined by its syntactic structure; mental states are realized in neural states, which also have 'syntactic' structure; the causal role of such neural states is determined by their 'syntactic' structure (Fodor 1975, and for critical commentary see, for example, Clark 1989; Warmbrod 1989; Maloney 1990; Loewer and Rey 1991; as well as below).

In a more recent work Fodor introduces the language of thought (LOT) hypothesis as follows (Fodor 1987, p. 135):

> LOT wants to construe propositional-attitude tokens as relations to symbol tokens. According to standard formulations, to believe that P is to bear a certain relation to a token of a symbol which means that P. (It is generally assumed that tokens of the symbol in question are neural objects, . . .). Now, symbols have intentional contents and their tokens are physical in all the known cases. And—qua physical—symbol tokens are the rights sorts of things to exhibit causal roles.

The language of thought hypothesis (in its full form not recorded here) is the most rigorous working out of the view that mental, meaningful causality is equivalent to, or reducible to, the material causality of the brain, and is much admired for this reason.

The hypothesis can also be understood as giving a particularly literal interpretation to the claim, endorsed in general terms in this chapter, that meaningful mental states are encoded in brain states. The implied interpretation is that if, for example, a person believes that p, then this meaningful mental state is encoded in the person's brain in the sense that there is in the brain a neural state, with a syntactic structure, which has the same meaning as the sentence 'p'. There are, literally, meaningful sentence-like structures in the brain.

The language of thought hypothesis claims that the neural states that realize cognitive functions have the syntactic structure of sentences of natural language. This apparently amounts to an empirical claim about the 'cognitive architecture' of the states which realize cognitive functions, and as such interacts with the theory of artificial intelligence (AI).

AI, with its theoretical and working models of machines, computers, which can perform intelligent functions, has been among the most powerful influences in the development of cognitive psychology (subsection 1.2.2). It constructs models of how intelligent performance can be achieved, and hence perhaps of how it is in fact achieved by the brain. By providing such models, AI theory has helped to make cognitive function accessible to psychological theory and experiment, to free psychology from the confines of behaviourism, which notoriously had little or nothing to say about internal processes mediating stimulus and response, about processes inside the so-called 'black box'. Our interest in AI modelling in the present context has to do with its implications for the problem of mental causation generally and the neural encoding of meaning in particular.[4]

AI constructs models of the structures that serve mental functions, so what do these models have to say about the claim that there are sentence-like structures in the head? In brief, although the position becomes much more complicated, the claim is endorsed by 'good old-fashioned', symbolic, AI models, but is apparently incompatible with the more recent connectionist models of neural structure and function.

The language of thought hypothesis is closely connected, via the so-called computational theory of mind (on which more below, subsection 2.3.1) to the classical (von Neumann–Turing) theory of computation. In this classical theory, computation is performed on symbol systems, symbols, and strings of symbols, and these, and the rules that govern their manipulation, are defined in terms of syntactic form only. Syntactic form is some physical characteristic of a symbol, such as the shape. In the case of computation in the brain, syntax would be a matter of some physical property of the brain, such as electromagnetic characteristics of neuronal activity. When applied in AI models of cognition, the classical theory of computation gives rise to two sorts of issues. First, there is the problem whether and how syntactically defined states and operations have anything to do with *meaning*. This problem is relevant to our themes of mind, meaning, and material states as they are formulated within AI theory, and we shall consider it in Section 2.3. Secondly, it may be that the brain is not a classically defined computer, and this is the point of the connectionist alternatives, to which we now turn.

2.2.2 Objections based on connectionist models

Fodor's language of thought hypothesis belongs with traditional, symbolic AI models of the sort based in the classical theory of computation. In these models explicitly stored formal-synatic rules are applied to explicit and localizable symbolic structures, including structures with the syntactic form of sentences. If a computing device can be ascribed the information that p, the ascribed state can be identified with a localized state of the device.

However, and on the other hand, connectionist models of 'computation' (now in scare quotes) typically do not involve operations on discrete structures that can be identified as symbols. The representational or symbolic features of connectionist systems are embodied as parallel patterns of activity among subsymbolic units, distributed over the system as a whole. There is no physical (hardware) counterpart to a symbol, or sentence.[5]

There is thus apparent conflict between traditional, symbolic AI models and connectionist models, and hence also conflict between theories of cognitive function that appeal to the one or to the other. Assuming this incompatibility, it is possible to construct the following argument: if connectionist models of neural structure and function are correct, then there are no sentence-like structures in the brain of the sort presupposed by folk psychology, and explicitly posited by the language of thought hypothesis, and the brain does not encode the meaningful states envisaged in folk psychology. Whence:

(1) folk psychology and the language of thought hypothesis can be eliminated; and

(2) neural causation has nothing to do with 'meaningful causation', which notion goes the same way as its folk psychological origin.

An argument along these lines has been proposed by Ramsey *et al.* (1990). They write:

> The crucial folk psychological tenets in forging the link between connectionism and eliminativism are the claims that propositional attitudes are *functionally discrete, semantically interpretable,* states that play a *causal role* in the production of behaviour. (Ramsey *et al.* 1990, p. 121.)

The proposal that folk psychology is committed to functional discreteness is implausible given the systemic, holistic nature of attribution of the propositional attitudes (referred to above, subsection 2.1.3; cf. also 1.4.1–2). This is linked to the reasons why the argument proposed by these authors turns out to be unsatisfactory, but for the present let us continue with the development of their argument. Ramsey *et al.* proceed to describe connectionist models which are apparently incompatible with the assumptions in question (1990, pp. 128–9):

> In many connectionist networks it is not possible to localize propositional representation beyond the input layer. That is, there are no particular features or states of the system which lend themselves to a straightforward semantic evaluation. ... It is connectionist networks of this sort ... that we have in

mind when we talk about the encoding of information in the biases, weights and hidden nodes being *widely distributed* rather than *localist*.

... It is often plausible to view such networks as collectively or holistically encoding a set of propositions, although none of the hidden units, weights or biases are comfortably viewed as *symbols*. When this is the case we will call the strategy of representation invoked in the model *subsymbolic*.

Ramsey *et al.* then draw their conclusion that a particular kind of connectionist model is incompatible with what they take to be fundamental to folk psychology (1990, p. 141):

The connectionist models in question are those which are offered as models at the *cognitive* level, and in which the encoding of information is widely distributed and subsymbolic. In such models . . . there are no *discrete, semantically interpretable* states that play a *causal role* in some cognitive episodes but not others. Thus there is, in these models, nothing with which the propositional attitudes of common sense psychology can plausibly be identified. If these models turn out to offer the best accounts of human belief and memory, we will be confronting an *ontologically radical* theory change—the sort of theory change that will sustain the conclusion that propositional attitudes, like caloric and phlogiston, do not exist.

In brief, the argument is that if connectionism is right about neural structure, folk psychology is wrong, and is up for 'elimination'. No loss, it will be added, by those who believe that the idea of mental, meaningful causation belongs peculiarly to a pre-scientific, out-of-date, folk psychology. (For related arguments for eliminativism see also, for example, Churchland, P.M. 1989 and Churchland, P.S. 1986.)

In reply to this kind of argument there are several points to be made. First, the conclusion—that folk psychology may turn out to be simply wrong—looks false in the light of its predictive efficacy, discussed in the first chapter. Secondly, the incompatibility between connectionist and traditional AI models is probably less sharp than the argument supposes. Thirdly, in any case there is nothing in connectionist models incompatible with the general idea, endorsed and defended in this chapter, that information (meaning) is encoded in the brain; on the contrary, the models aim to show *how* this could be achieved. And finally, such strength as the argument has derives from the fact that it credits (saddles) folk psychology with an unnecessarily strong claim about the neural encoding of meaning. These four points are discussed in turn below.

Arguments of the kind described in the first chapter counsel against the dismissal (supposed eliminability) of folk psychology. Folk psychology has predictive power, but this fact would apparently be a mystery if it were simply a false theory. Moreover, it is not just folk psychology that is at issue here. As argued (in subsection 1.3.7), the cognitive psychology paradigm, based as it is on the notion of information-processing, is committed to something very like the folk psychological meaningful mental states. The suggestion that this commitment is simply wrong mystifies the predictive power of models within this cognitive psychology paradigm, as well as that of folk psychology. This is the basic reason for suspecting the soundness of any argument that concludes that explanation of behaviour in terms of meaningful mental states is invalid.

What can be said in reply, then, to the claim that such states fail to show up in powerful connectionist models of mental function? The distinction between symbolic AI models, based on the classical theory of computation, and connectionist models is valid, but in various ways blurred. Connectionist models can be (and are) implemented by traditional computers using symbol-based programmes. This fact, however, is of doubtful relevance to understanding the implementation of cognitive function in the brain, since it is likely that if the brain is a computing system at all, it is a massive parallel distributed, connectionist system, not a digital, serial computer. Connectionist theories have aimed explicitly at compatibility with what is known of the micro-structure and -function of the brain. Of more relevance to cognitive psychology and neuroscience is the possibility that symbolic programs could be implemented in connectionist hardware. If this is possible, the conflict between symbolic AI models of cognitive function and connectionist models of brain function would be lessened. The position would be that while the latter are valid models of implementation in the brain, the former are valid models of 'emergent' properties of the system, namely, of manipulation of (meaningful) symbols according to rules. This idea receives support from the fact that there are statistical cluster analyses of connectionist networks the results of which do admit of semantic labelling. On the other hand, certain cognitive tasks, particularly those involving reasoning and inference with symbols, are most readily modelled in the traditional symbolic programs, while others, including sensori- and motor-functions, are most readily modelled in connectionist programs. This fact points to a different way of reconciling the two kinds of model. It may be that the brain is engaged in both types of processing, serial-symbolic, and parallel-connectionist, with interactions between them.[6]

Be that (the relation between traditional and connectionist AI models), as it may, the claim that meaning (information) is encoded in the brain is unaffected. This, to recall, is the main idea endorsed and defended in the present chapter, proposed as a solution to the problem of reconciling meaningful/mental causation with the causation of behaviour by the brain. But of course, connectionism has no objections to the idea, fundamental to the cognitive neuroscience enterprise, that the brain processes, and hence has to encode, information about the environment. There is no question about *whether* the brain encodes and processes information, but only about *how* it does so. In connectionist systems information is stored as parallel patterns of activity among subsymbolic units, not in symbols. It can be seen in the second quotation above from Ramsey *et al.* (1990, pp. 128–9), that they apparently have no problem with the idea that connectionist networks encode information, even 'sets of propositions'.

To repeat, the issue between connectionist and traditional AI models of brain function is not *whether* the brain encodes information (meaning), but *how*. It is usual and valid to say that the traditional models invoke symbols, while the connectionist models do not. The notion of symbol at work here is basically a syntactic one, to be understood superficially by way of examples such as letters and numerals, and defined formally within the so-called classical theory of computation, (referred to in subsection 2.2.1, and in more detail in subsection 2.3.1). An equally valid conception of symbolism, however, is the semantic one. According to this, a symbol may be defined as *whatever carries meaning* (information). In *this* sense, which to repeat is valid though distinct from that in classical computation theory, connectionist models do indeed envisage 'symbols', namely, as patterns of activity within the system. It can be seen that this conception of neural symbolism is broadly consistent with there being a fundamental link between the meaning of a sign and its use in activity, an idea adopted in the first chapter (subsections 1.3.2–4) and applied throughout the essay. Issues in the definition of symbolism and syntax, and their relation to semantics are of course critical to the concept of 'encoded meaning' and will be addressed further in subsequent sections.

We have been considering the argument proposed by Ramsey *et al.* (1990) which would eliminate folk psychology on connectionist grounds, and we suggested above that such strength as the argument has derives from the fact that it credits (saddles) folk psychology with an unnecessarily strong presupposition about the neural encoding of meaning. The argument assumes that attribution of mental states with (linguistically identified) meaning presupposes that there are in-the-head items similar to such states. Fodor's language of thought hypothesis, we should note and emphasize, makes just this same assumption. As is quite characteristic of philosophical claims and counter-claims, the two opposed positions here, Fodor's on the one hand, and Ramsey *et al.*'s on the other, the one vindicating folk psychological explanation, the other which would eliminate it, in fact share critical preconceptions. In this case the critical shared assumption is roughly as follows, that meaningful mental states are real, and causal, only if they correspond to discrete, localizable micro-states of the brain. Under this assumption it will indeed appear as though Fodor's language of thought hypothesis is the only way of saving the validity of folk psychology, and equally, that folk psychology, like Fodor's hypothesis, may well fall foul of connectionist models of brain function. However, it is by no means obvious that common sense does or should make the kind of assumption in question. We consider in the next subsection reasons for saying that both the hypothesized language of thought vindication of folk psychological explanation and the arguments that would eliminate folk psychological explanation mistake its logic and hence its ontological commitments.

2.2.3 Reply: there don't have to be such sentences

Let us leave questions as to what is in the brain and how it does what it does, whatever that is, and return to a relatively clear position, where we started the essay, with what is open to view, namely, that theory-driven attribution of psychological states with meaningful content, whether in folk or scientific theory, is based in and predicts behaviour.

For example, we describe a rat as having acquired (by normal learning procedures) information about a maze including a goal-box containing food, and as being hungry (on the grounds that it hasn't eaten for a while), then we can predict, other things being equal (including 'normal'), that the rat, given free run of the maze, will run along to the goal-box and eat. Attribution of the psychological states is based on observation of behavioural patterns, and it predicts further behavioural patterns. But the question under consideration is whether these attributions are valid only if there are discrete and localizable micro-states of the brain which correspond to such terms as 'information about the maze', or 'expectation of food in the goal-box'. The general problem here concerns the relation between descriptions that are based on patterns of behavioural interaction, and descriptions that refer to states and events inside what is behaving. Clark (1988) clarifies the issues here by use of analogy with descriptions of cars.

Clark notes that cars admit of (at least) two general kinds of description. One kind may be called 'performance' descriptions: they refer to how the car performs (behaves) when driven in particular ways in particular conditions. They include descriptions concerning such as road-holding while cornering, acceleration, and fuel consumption. A second type of description concerns what may be called 'engineering' characteristics, such as weight-distribution, wheel-size, gear-ratios. Three connected points are apparent about the relation between performance and engineering descriptions. First, the same performance description, such as 'corners well at high speeds', can apply to cars with very different engineering characteristics. Secondly, in any particular car, a performance feature does not correspond to an isolated engineering characteristic, but rather to the interaction of many such characteristics, and moreover, to these in interaction with the conditions in which the car is driven. In this sense performance features are 'emergent' properties; a particular performance feature appears precisely when a car (with any one of a variety of engineering profiles) is performing, that is, when it is being driven in such-and-such conditions. Thirdly, and again related, terms used in describing performance may have no analogues in terms used in describing engineering features; for example neither the expression 'holds the road badly in the wet' nor any expression with similar meaning will appear in description of the car's engineering profile. In summary of these three points, it may be concluded that performance descriptions do not 'map on to' engineering characteristics.

Clark (1988) goes on to apply this simple analysis to the case of psychological propositions. Such propositions attribute properties to the agent, semantic properties essentially defined as being about the environment, and on the basis of such attribution we make predictions about interactions between the agent and the environment. In these ways psychological propositions are akin to performance descriptions. (In terms of the car analogy, performance features are attributed to a car, these features are defined explicitly or implicitly with reference to (environmental) driving conditions, and such attribution enables prediction of how the car will behave in such-and-such conditions.) But performance descriptions refer to 'emergent' characteristics, to characteristics that appear in the course, precisely, of performance. And we have seen that, at least in the case of cars, it is a mistake to suppose that such emergent characteristics map on to internal mechanisms. So it is at least questionable to assume that psychological propositions, as performance descriptions, map on to internal, neural states and processes, still more so to assume that the validity of such propositions presupposes such a mapping.

The above considerations suggest that there are two distinct though related types of explanation of behaviour. The first is concerned with behaviour considered essentially as interaction with the environment. It proceeds on the basis of observation of regularities in interactions, and it constructs explanations and predictions of such regularities by attributing to the agent states which are 'about the environment' (that is, semantic, meaningful, information-carrying states). Folk psychology is the paradigm of this type of explanation, and it generally works well (enough) for the purposes of daily life. The same basic method is used, with extensions and refinements for particular purposes, by various forms of 'cognitive-behavioural' science. The second type of explanation of behaviour concerns the neural mechanisms and processes that underlie the behavioural capacities. The link between these two types of explanation is provided (currently) by AI models of neural function, which seek to explicate how 'intelligent' behaviour is produced by the brain.

The language of thought hypothesis clarifies and explicitly endorses, with its use of the symbolic AI model, the claim that the two types of explanation described above will coincide: the hypothesis is that states with the same structure as meaningful states, as described in ordinary language, will be found in the brain. The problem is that, if the brain is indeed correctly modelled as a connectionist system, the hypothesis is false, at least at a micro-level of analysis.

However, there is no need to suppose, and there is good reason not to suppose, that the two types of explanation must coincide. In particular, the validity of the first type, explanation of behaviour in terms of cognitive, meaningful states, does not require that such states are manifest in the micro-structure and -function of the brain, and in particular, therefore, it is not undermined by connectionist models of neural function. What is required is rather that the explanations correspond to at least emergent characteristics of neural processing. We have indicated above several ways in which this requirement is met. First, to the extent that connectionist systems admit of higher-level descriptions in terms of symbolic processing. Secondly, that statistical analysis of micro-function in connectionist systems reveals clusters that admit of semantic labelling. Thirdly, that attributions of mental states with content are 'performance' descriptions, based in observation of regularities, and in this sense they correspond to emergent characteristics of the agent, to characteristics that appear in the course of action. The first two senses in which psychological propositions are valid concerns particularly AI modelling of neural function. But the third runs free of an scientific discovery concerning the the way in which behaviour is generated by the brain. It locates the subject-matter of psychological propositions in action (in interaction), not inside the brain.

While folk psychological descriptions are not committed to the existence of corresponding in-the-head items, it would be fair to say that they presuppose that there is *some 'mechanism' or other* in the person which can produce intelligent, intentional behaviour. What this presupposition is taken to amount to will depend on background metaphysics. In the Cartesian framework, the assumption is more or less only that of immaterial mind. In our post-dualist age, neural mechanisms of the appropriate kinds are required, as modelled currently in AI.

On the basis of the above understanding of psychological descriptions, it remains possible to say that they provide causal explanations, and possible to say also that the states they invoke are encoded in the brain.

By all means, the notions of causality and of encoding require particular interpretations. The nature of encoding will continue to occupy us through this chapter, and causality will be discussed at length in chapters 4 and 5, but some points are apparent here. Characteristics of a system which appear in interaction with the environment can be cited in causal explanations. In the case of cars, for example, a performance characteristics such as poor road-holding can be cited in causal explanation of (and in prediction of) a crash. It may be noted that engineering characteristics will serve such a purpose only in so far as they contribute to, in such-and-such circumstances, performance characteristics. This is, in a very simple way, analogous to the fact that neural states explain intentional behaviour only in so far as they encode intentional states. In the psychological case, for example, a rat's behaviour in a maze, expectation that there is food in the goal-box, neurally encoded, can be cited in causal explanation of (and in prediction of) running to the box. The performance characteristics cannot be identified with, and do not necessarily correspond to, internal, physically defined states. In this case we have to envisage a form of causal explanation that does not consist in saying that one material state gives rise to another, and, in particular, that is not based in observation of constant conjunction between the cause and the effect. In other words, while psychological propositions are causal, they are not captured by physicalist descriptions, nor by the Humean analysis. Chapters 4 and 5 will be occupied with the task of identifying a non-physicalist, non-Humean concept of causality appropriate to the explanation of action.

2.3 OBJECTIONS TO THE PROPOSED SOLUTION, 2: '(NEURAL) SYNTAX ISN'T ENOUGH FOR SEMANTICS'

2.3.1 Searle and the computational theory of mind

As noted in the previous section, the language of thought hypothesis is closely connected to the so-called computational theory of mind, which in turn is based in the classical (von Neumann–Turing) theory of computation. According to classical theory, computation is performed on symbol systems, physical tokens (of some kind), and strings of tokens; the rules that govern their manipulation are defined in terms of shape, in terms of syntatic form only. In particular, computation is defined without reference to meaning; symbols may be 'interpreted' as having meaning, as representing objects and states of affairs, but this is not essential to the definition or to the practice of computation. If this classical, 'symbolic' theory of computation is applied to cognitive psychology, the result is the so-called computational theory of mind, according to which, in brief, cognitive states and processes are defined in terms of syntax, not (essentially) in terms of meaning (Fodor 1975; Newell 1980; Pylyshyn 1980, 1984).

The claim that cognition can be adequately characterized as computational in the sense of classical theory, which seemed to be the assumption behind AI, and which was spelt out in the computational theory of mind, has been the subject of much debate in the cognitive science literature. The debate was sparked by Searle in the early 1980s by his 'Chinese room argument' in support of the conclusion that symbol manipulation cannot be sufficient for understanding (or meaning, or intentionality). The argument is very well known and for our purposes a very brief formulation will suffice.

Imagine you are handed Chinese symbols and asked to manipulate (transform) them according to a rule book, then no matter how efficiently you receive symbols at inputs, follow the rules, and dispose of the symbols produced as outputs, still this process of symbol-manipulation is compatible with you having no understanding whatsoever of the meaning of the symbols. Human beings with brains, however, do understand the meaning of symbols. So if AI theory says that cognitive activity of the brain is symbol-manipulation only, then it's wrong.

In a recent formulation of the argument, Searle draws out his main point about the Chinese room as follows (1987, p. 214):

> The point of the story is to remind us of a conceptual truth that we knew all along; namely, that there is a distinction between manipulating the syntactical elements of languages and actually understanding the language at a semantic level. What is lost in the AI *simulation of* cognitive behaviour is the distinction between syntax and semantics. . . . In the case of actually understanding a language, we have something more than a formal or syntactical level. We have a semantics. We do not just shuffle uninterpreted formal symbols, we actually know what they mean.

Searle's Chinese room argument, together with its strengths and weaknessness, and proposed solutions to the problems it raises, have been much discussed in the literature (Searle 1980, 1982, 1984, 1987; and, among others Russow 1984; Rey 1986; Gray 1987; Newton 1988; Harnad 1989, 1990). In what follows we draw out some points directly related to biology and psychology.

A recurring theme in criticisms of the attempt to analyse cognitive processes in terms of syntax alone, and of the computational theory of mind in particular, is that it is insufficiently biological. In his discussions of the Chinese room argument Searle (1987) makes such a point by saying that emphasis on computation alone without regard to its implementation, neglects the special properties of the brain as biological material, which in some way uniquely could achieve intentionality. The problem can be formulated in this way: what do you have to add to, or have instead of, symbol manipulation in order to achieve intentionality? The answer probably has something to do with biology. But to respond: 'the brain (as opposed to an inanimate system)', is to give a disappointingly empirical answer, even if true, to what seems more like a conceptual question.

To bring out the inadequacy of the computational theory of mind from the point of view of biology or psychology we have to consider what is fundamental to those sciences, specifically in what they have to say about intentionality. There are reasons to expect a deep and large-scale paradigm clash between the computational theory of mind and the bio-pyschological sciences, one which can hardly be resolved just by appeal to the special material composition of the brain. The concept and theory of computation on which the computational theory of mind was based was developed in formal logic, a context quite distinct from the concerns of biology and (most) psychology. Specifically, biology is concerned with animal functions necessary for successful action (survival) and the structures which realize them, including sensory, mediating, and motor systems, systems for digestion, energy production, internal temperature regulation, etc. , all these being designed to work in (being selected in) particular environmental conditions. All this, with the implications concerning functions, designs, and implementation of biological information-processing has nothing to do with formal logic. Or put the other way round, formal logic, the classical theory of computation, and the computational theory of mind, have nothing to say about the functions of and design contraints on information-processing in biological systems. We pass by the details here, which are excellently clarified by Clark (1989), in order to highlight the very general feature of information-processing (intentionality) as conceived in biology and psychology, namely, that it essentially serves action.

2.3.2 Reply: symbols are linked to activity and hence carry meaning

If we bring the aforementioned conception of intentionality, basic to biology and psychology and adopted throughout this essay, to bear on the problem identified by Searle, we arrive at something like the following: what you have add to, or have instead of, symbol manipulation, in order to achieve intentionality is the regulation of action, that is, meaningful (goal-directed, plastic) interactions with the environment. In his discussions of the Chinese room, Searle (1987) rejects this frequently made response, on the grounds, roughly, that robots don't understand anything either. Probably not, but still there are abundant reasons for keeping in mind the connection, fundamental to biology and psychology, between meaning and action.

Explanation in terms of intentional states get a grip on artificial systems in so far as they 'behave intelligently' (e.g. solve problems), even though for *many* reasons we would not be inclined to say that they 'really' understand or mean anything. These many reasons mostly, or perhaps all, have to do with the fact that we human beings are paradigms of intentionality, and AI systems are not like us: they are simpler, more circumscribed; they are inanimate (they do not show the behavioural signs of being alive), including that they don't mind what happens to them, that they are not made of biological material, that they don't look like us; and so on. All these sorts of background considerations support the intuition that AI systems do not have 'real' intentionality as we do, but they concern what is open to view, including appearance and particularly behaviour, and they are therefore consistent with the main idea that attributions of meaning are based in behavioural considerations. No other criterion of meaning is involved here. It is in particular misleading to suppose that the critical question is whether machines do, or can, have the 'subjective feeling of understanding (or meaning)', in so far as this is an updated AI version of the outdated problem of other minds. As already discussed in the first chapter (subsection 1.2.4) this problem turns on the remnants of Cartesian dualism, and has no proper place in the cognitive-behavioural paradigm, which posits intentional states essentially as regulators of activity, not as subjective experiences.

In biology and cognitive-behavioural science, cognition (or information-processing) is regarded as being primarily in the service of action, and hence also the content of cognitive states (the information picked up, processed, and utilized) is likewise to be understood in terms relevant to action. This assumption is found in one form or another in the various domains of psychology. Cognitive learning theory defines cognitive states as mediating between stimulus and response. Developmental psychology has long taken cognition to be grounded in sensorimotor capacities (Piaget 1950). This same connection is apparently supported by general considerations about neural structure. Sensory and motor pathways permeate into and pervade the cortex (Brodal 1991), and were these to be stripped away, there would be practically no cognitive processing system left which could be engaged in the manipulation of uninterpreted symbols. Within the framework of cognitive-behavioural science, with its primary aim of explaining sensorimotor capacities such as discrimination, recognition, manipulation, and catagorization, cognitive states and processes will be, in general, defined as precisely serving such capacities, and hence cannot be adequately characterized as manipulation of meaningless symbols. At the very least, the symbols must have (for the agent) semantic interpretation, namely, as being about action. But the point is better made in this way: the 'symbols' already have meaning, because they are linked intrinsically to sensori-cognitive-motor capacities. A detailed response to Searle's problem along these lines, using traditional symbolic and connectionist modelling, has been made out by Harnad (1989, 1990).

It should be emphasized that the point here is not that connectionist models of mental function automatically avoid or solve the general problem identified by Searle, the problem of how to model intentionality and not just syntax (symbolism). According to connectionist models of neural function, the brain encodes information, though not in symbolic form, but as patterns of activity. However as noted above (subsection 2.2.2), these patterns are indeed 'symbols', precisely in so far as they encode information. But the point is that we can ask of any proposed model of encoding information: 'In what sense is there anything *semantic* here?' It is always possible to raise the question identified by Searle: 'Why is there intentionality here, over and above "symbol manipulation" (in a broad sense)?' The point is then, as Harnad argues (1989, 1990), that connectionist modelling can provide an answer to this question in so far as the 'symbols' (the patterns of activity within the system) already have meaning. The 'symbols' are essentially involved in the regulation of intentional (rule-guided) system/environment interaction, intrinsically linked to sensori-cognitive-motor capacities.

It is significant that the AI models of sensori-cognitive-motor capacities are typically connectionist, not those of symbolic AI, of the kind presupposed by the computational theory of mind. On the other hand, just as connectionist models do not automatically solve Searle's problem, but only when they accomodate a theory of meaning, so too symbolic AI models do not necessarily fail to solve the problem.

However, they do indeed get off to a poor start, particularly in their usual context of the computational theory of mind. For this theory fails to make axiomatic the link between symbolism and meaning, particularly meaning as grounded in (rule-guided) system/environment interactions. It defines mental states in terms of syntactic properties, not semantic ones. It can add (on) a semantics, but typically this involves no essential link between the semantics of mental states and action. The computational theory of mind can approach the idea of mental states having semantic properties in two main ways. First, following the classical theory of computation, it can construe semantic properties as dependent on (mirrored in) syntactic properties, and secondly, it defines the semantic properties in terms of the causal role of mental states. Both approaches, in the context of mind–brain identity theory, help to make up Fodor's language of thought hypothesis as already discussed (section 2.2). However, and as Fodor is well aware, this otherwise ingenious combination of several plausible doctrines leaves open the possibility that, so far as concerns the causal explanation of behaviour, semantic properties of mental/neural states are irrelevant, that what does the explanatory work are their syntactic properties. We turn now to consider this problem, in McGinn's formulation.

2.4 OBJECTION TO THE PROPOSED SOLUTION, 3: 'IF THERE IS NEURAL SYNTAX, THEN THIS IS WHAT CAUSES BEHAVIOUR AND ENCODED MEANING DROPS OUT AS IRRELEVANT'

2.4.1 McGinn's statement of the argument

There is a plausible line of thought in this area to the effect that semantic properties cannot play a causal role, or at least, not unless they correspond to synactic ones. Let us consider this, beginning with a lengthy quote from McGinn (1989, pp. 132–4):

> I come now to what I take to be the most serious and challenging argument against content based psychology. . . . The argument proceeds from certain principles about causation (so let us call it 'the causal argument')—specifically, about how mental causation must be seen to work. . . . (It) presupposes externalism, . . . according to which contentful states are identified by reference to entities that lie outside the subject's body (including, of course, his head): . . . Now this implies that contentful states are (as we might say) extrinsically relational: they essentially consist in relation to extrinsic non-mental items (objects, properties, etc.). . . . For example, for John to have the concept *square* (and so to be capable of believing that the box is square) is for John to stand in a certain relation to the *property* of being a square. So when we ascribe that concept to John we report him as standing in this extrinsic correspondence relation to that objective property. And now the causal objection to citing such contents in psychological explanations is just this: *if such explanations purport to be causal, then these correspondence relations cannot themselves be implicated in the causal transaction being reported* [italics added]. This is because what happens at the causal nexus is local, proximate, and intrinsic: the features of the cause that lead to the effect must be right there where the causal interaction takes place. Causation is the same with brains and minds as it is with billiard balls.

In brief, and to use an illustration closer to the cognitive explanation of action, if we cite in explanation of the rat's running to the goal-box its belief that there is food there, this explanation can only be causal, the belief can only be a causal item, if it is local to the rat's movements. It cannot be part of the causal power of the belief state that it relates to something external. This is, roughly, what McGinn refers to as the 'causal argument'.[7]

  The argument under consideration here points back to where we started at the beginning of this chapter. Whatever might be going on under the name of meaningful, mental causation, we know in any case, practically for certain, that the causes of behaviour are in the brain. Brain processes are at least the local causes, the disruption of which, for example, puts paid to action. So somehow, whatever mental meaningful causation is, it has to be compatible with this fact. But this is of course where the encoding thesis comes in. It enables us to formulate a resolution along the following lines: local brain events cause behaviour, but they encode meaning; or even, the causes are 'encoded meanings'.

  McGinn outlines this sort of response as follows (1989, pp. 136–7):

Since only the 'shape' (syntax, orthography) of internal symbols can be relevant to their causal powers, not their semantic relations to items in the world, we need, if we are to save content for psychology, to find a way of *linking* shape with semantics. We need, that is, to suppose that content is somehow reflected in intrinsic features of the symbol: that distinctions of content are mirrored by distinctions of shape. Let us call the claim that there are such shape/content links the *encoding thesis*. The encoding thesis says that semantic properties are perfectly matched by syntactic properties—semantics is coded into syntax. . . . And it is in virtue of this one–one correspondence that content gets a causal foothold. For whenever a content enters into a causal explanation we know that there exists some intrinsic syntactic property of the underlying symbol that is turning the wheels of the causal mechanism. In other words, content attributions can occur legitimately in causal explanations because they are guaranteed to have syntactic *proxies*.

McGinn defines the encoding thesis in a strong form, as proposing something like a structural similarity between syntax and meaning. This strong form of the thesis is in the area of Fodor's language of thought hypothesis discussed in Section 2.2. We saw connectionist reasons to be less literal about how meaning may be neurally encoded. McGinn cites a different reason for doubting such a strong structural similarity between syntax and semantics, namely, that it is plainly absent in the case of natural languages (McGinn 1989, p. 138; see also subsection 1.3.2). In any case, McGinn goes on to allow a weaker version of the encoding thesis (loc. cit.):

A less literal construal would be more charitable. By 'syntax' is meant whatever intrinsic states underlie the causal dispositions associated with an internal symbol—presumably brain states at some level of description.

This more liberal reading of the notion of encoding is of the kind being endorsed here. It would be compatible, for example but in particular, with connectionist models of neural encoding.

To recapitulate, the so-called causal argument proposes that while (neural) syntax can cause behaviour, semantic features, being non-locally defined, cannot. Faced with this consideration the encoding thesis tries to retain semantics as causally relevant by saying that meaning is encoded in syntax. McGinn argues, however, that this attempt to secure the causal relevance of meaning fails (1989, p. 137):

If (content) does its causal work by proxy, then it seems redundant to invoke it—we could simply stick with syntax. (This would be) an application of Occam's razor: keep your theoretical entities down to a minimum, compatibly with preservation of explanatory power. The encoding thesis, by guaranteeing a translation from content to syntax, invites the elimination of talk of content in favour of syntactic talk.

Thus, the alleged causal role of meaning depends entirely on the causal role of syntax, and in this case we can, and should, invoke the latter only, and the former drops out of consideration as redundant.

McGinn presents this objection to the encoding thesis in its strong form, but essentially it applies to the weaker form as well. However loose the notion of 'neural syntax', even if it means 'whatever neural organization encodes meaning', the point apparently still stands, that these local states and processes will be doing the causal work, and there is no need to invoke encoded meaning in the causal story.

2.4.2 Reply: semantic concepts are essential when what is to be causally explained is action

In the preceding subsection we presented the so-called causal argument against the causal role of meaning, and the alleged failure of the encoding thesis to meet it. Such a failure would contradict the main idea of this chapter, so we have to respond.

We have already in the first chapter (subsection 1.3.6) considered reasons for rejecting the hypothetical conclusion of the argument, that explanation of action can be run in terms of non-semantic concepts. The point is in brief that *if* the goal is explanation and prediction of intentional behaviour (complex organism–environment interactions), *then* the methodological assumption has to be that the agent is regulated by information about the environment, that is, by intentional states, either mental, or encoded in the brain, or both. It is, on the other hand, perfectly possible to do away with intentional concepts, but then only non-intentional behaviour can be predicted, for example physical movements of the body, not intentional interactions with the environment.

This main point holds regardless of the interpretations given to the notion of encoding, whether strong or weak, regardless whether semantic properties are or are not mirrored in the syntactic structure of symbols.

The claim against which the causal argument is directed is that explanations of behaviour which invoke meaningful content, correspondence to what is external, are causal. The argument can be summarized as follows, to quote again McGinn (1989, p. 134):

> *If such explanations purport to be causal, then these correspondence relations cannot themselves be implicated in the causal transation being reported* [italics added]. This is because what happens at the causal nexus is local, proximate, and intrinsic: the features of the cause that lead to the effect must be right there where the causal interaction takes place. Causation is the same with brains and minds as it is with billiard balls.

And our reply may be summarized as follows. It depends what is to be explained. What can be explained in terms of causes defined intrinsically, proximately, and locally is behaviour defined intrinsically, proximately, and locally, for example a leg moving. But if what we want to explain is extrinsically defined goal-directed, plastic behaviour, for example an animal finding its way to a goal-box, then the causes we need to invoke have to be defined extrinsically, as intentional states. But are these extrinsically defined states invoked for this purpose proximate and local? Yes of course, that is the point of the notion of encoding. The intentional, semantic property of representation is encoded in the local, proximate neural state.

As to whether causation is (all) the same with brains and minds as it is with billiard balls, probably it isn't. Causal explanations run in non-intentional terms apply to billiard balls and to brain–behaviour interactions, but in the latter case, unlike the former, there is also the possibility of constructing causal explanations in intentional terms; indeed this is mandatory when what is to be explained is intentional behaviour. This distinction between two forms of causality is developed through Chapter 4 and elaborated in Chapter 5.

The conclusion that explanation of intentional behaviour in terms of intentional states is causal was drawn in Chapter 1. The argument in the present chapter is that this conclusion is compatible with neural causation because neural states, in so far as they regulate intentional behaviour, themselves have (encode) intentional features. This ensures that causation is material, and proximate to the effects.

The implication is that the causal role of these material, proximate states depends on the semantic features that they encode. This implication can hardly be understood while we have in mind as a model of causation, in seventeenth-century style, interactions between billiard balls. The causal role of semantic features can be seen clearly at one level, in AI models of mental function, in so far as those structural and functional characteristics that encode information vary with the information they encode, and these same variable features also determine how such characteristics interact with one another and eventually cause certain outputs of the system. This is obvious enough, but it invites the response, which we have been considering under the name of the 'causal argument', that all we are really seeing here is the causal role of syntax, not the causal role of semantics. To get at semantics we need to stand back and take a broader view, taking in not just what is going on inside the system, but also the intentional activity of the system within the environment.

Intentional activity is best explained and predicted by attributing to the agent systems of intentional states. The inference about causality, drawn in the first chapter, can be expressed by saying either that the intentional states posited are casual, or that the explanations that invoke them are causal explanations. These two formulations are more or less equivalent, at least in the sense that it would be unattractive to have to argue for one and against the other. However, probably they can be understood with different emphases or connotations, and perhaps particularly when it comes to handling the critical implication that causality here turns on intentionality. In one of the two formulations, this implication will read: it is the intentional properties of intentional states which determine their causal role. Obvious though this implication may look, and indeed it is obvious, it becomes obscured by the so-called causal argument which we have been considering. All we see when we look at intentional states, for example in AI models, is syntax not semantics, and it is unclear how semantic features can play, or need to play, any causal role; still less, then, is it clear how or why such a causal role should depend on particular semantic features rather than others.

For the particular purpose of getting unstuck here, we need to remind ourselves of the other route, the other formulation of the claim that intentionality involves causality. That is: explanations that attribute intentional states to an agent and thereby predict intentional activity, are causal explanations. From here, it is not at all difficult to see that causal explanations of this kind run differently, generate different predictions, as a function of the particular semantic contents attributed to the agent. This is really obvious.

Of course it is possible to reach the same conclusion by the other route, by considering the causal role of intentional states. But this is more complicated and therefore hazardous. The complication is that it has to go via the idea that material states encode information, and the proposal that reference to the fact that such states do encode information cannot be omitted *while the purpose is to explain and predict intentional activity*. In brief, *for this purpose*, semantic talk cannot be eliminated in favour of syntactic talk. The critical turnings here are easy to miss, or are controversial. They lead away from the intentional states in themselves, and the causal role they have in virtue of intrinsic, syntactical, physical features. We take into account rather what else such states have to be credited with if we are adequately to explain and predict intentional activity, namely: semantic contents, and causal roles which are a function of the particular contents that are encoded.

2.4.3 Overview of the problem of syntax and semantics

The previous three sections have all been involved with the problem of syntax and semantics, in the attempt to defend and clarify the encoding thesis. Let us at this stage take a broad view of the problem.

Syntax may be defined as being a physical property of a symbol, such as the shape of a letter or numeral. In the context of mind–brain identity theory, the physical property would be such as the electromagnetic characteristics of neuronal networks. But this kind of definition alone, though suited to formal logic (particularly of course with the usual example of shape), does little work in logic understood as the a priori theory of representation. For logic in this sense, the notion of syntax is generally invoked in the service of semantics, of the theory of meaning. The problem of meaning can be put simply like this: how can one thing—a sign—signify another, its object? And the notion of syntax can play a role in answering this question.

One kind of solution to the problem of meaning, discussed already in the first chapter (subsection 1.3.2) appeals to something like *resemblance* between sign and signified. In some applications of this very general theory, particularly in the philosophy of language, the notion of the syntax of a sign readily plays a crucial role. The syntax of a sign, its intrinsic structure or shape, represents possible structures in reality. This kind of theory, of which Wittgenstein's *Tractatus* (1921) is probably the best worked-out example, illustrates the general point that what matters about the sign is fundamentally only what contributes to its having meaning (i.e. is only what makes it a *sign*). In this sense syntactic definitions of signs presuppose or imply a semantic theory. In particular, then, if we define syntax in terms of shape, we are presupposing that what matters to meaning (what achieves meaning) is shape, and this is a *massive* assumption in the theory of meaning, linked indeed to the resemblance theory just mentioned. But, important for our purposes, the assumption stands opposed to the definition of representation endorsed here, in terms of the regulation of action (subsection 1.3.3).

Before going on to consider what notion of 'syntax' belongs with this semantic theory, let us note a further very general point which is plain enough in the resemblance theory. Sign and signified have something *in common*, a form, the possibility of having such-and-such a structure, in virtue of which the sign can be a correct or incorrect (true or false) representation of reality. This idea is, again, worked out clearly in the *Tractatus*, in its doctrines of the identity between pictorial form, the form of thought, and the form of reality.[8] Form here means something like 'order', the fact that things are this way rather than that, or are truly or falsely represented as being this way or that. Sign and signified have something—a form—in common. In the case of picture-representations it is the (possibility of) structural configuration, and this is apparent in the syntactic description of signs. But what is 'form' in the case of representations as regulators of activity?

We have, as discussed in the first chapter (subsections 1.3.3–4), abandoned the theory of resemblance, and supposed rather that signs represent reality in so far as they are used in rule-following activities, activities which are 'right' or 'wrong'. Because the order is now seen as a property of the activity, that is, of the interaction between agent and environment, we do not *also* have to assume that there has to be some structured sign (sign with a shape) which achieves the representation of reality. The essential feature of a sign is now its use in rule-following activity, not its shape. The analogue of the theory of syntax in the new theory of representation naturally presupposes or implies a semantics. How does a sign refer to something in reality? Basically, because the users of the sign interact with things in reality. To take Wittgenstein's example at the start of the *Philosophical investigations* (1953): men are building, one man calls out the word 'slab', and another picks up and brings a certain kind of building stone.

The question arises as to how, in what sense, the use of a sign is 'right' or 'wrong'? One possibility is that the distinction between correct and incorrect uses of signs is based partly in the fact that the activity in which they are used goes right or wrong. For example, some kinds of building stone can be fitted together to make a wall, others cannot. This line of thought will be pursued in this essay, although it is not to be found in Wittgenstein. Its plausibility can be seen as follows. Action essentially admits of normative distinctions: 'right'/'wrong', 'successful/unsuccessful', 'achieves goal'/ 'fails to do so', etc. This is a reasonable enough claim in philosophy, but it is in any case axiomatic in the bio-psychological sciences. It would be extraordinary, then, if normative distinctions in the use of signs were not linked to those in practice, especially given the background theory that it is use in practice that gives a sign meaning.

The shift from the *Tractatus* theory of meaning to the one in the *Philosophical investigations*, from pictures to rule-guided activity, may be expressed as the replacement of the notion of spatial form by form of activity, or again, by 'form of life' (Bolton 1982). Continuing in the terminology of the *Tractatus*, normative distinctions can be made out in the new theory in the following way. The 'form of the sign' is the activity of the agent, and the form of reality is the interwoven movement of objects in reality, and these two are in more or less agreement: action either works in reality or not. This 'pragmatic' approach to the true/false distinction is elaborated in the next chapter (Section 3.2).

If the notion of syntax were to be retained in this context, it would refer primarily to the order in intentional activity, not the physically defined order in a sign, such as a sentence, on paper, or in the brain. Indeed, and this is the main point, sentences (on paper or in a neural code) are not yet, according to this theory, *signs* at all. They become signs only when, and only in so far as they are, involved in rule-guided activity. This point is pivotal in the shift from the resemblance theory of meaning to the understanding of meaning as use in activity (subsection 1.3.2). It can indeed be used to launch a critique of the idea that the brain encodes meaning, and we shall discuss it further in this connection later, in Section 2.6. But here the point is that the notion of *order* which is central to the theory of representation is already captured in the notion of activity according to a rule: actions are 'right' or 'wrong', subject for example to positive or negative feedback, either from reality itself, or in the form of judgements from other people. In this context we do not *also* need the idea that the order in action emanates from a more fundamental order inside the brain. On this issue, anticipating some themes in the shift from symbolic to connectionist AI modelling, Wittgenstein remarked (1967, §608):

> No supposition seems to me more natural than that there is no process in the brain correlated with or associating with thinking; so that it would be impossible to read off thought-processes from brain processes. I mean this: if I talk or write there is, I assume, a system of impulses going out from my brain and correlated with my spoken or written thoughts. But why should the *system* continue further in the direction of the centre? Why should this order not proceed, so to speak, out of chaos?

The issue in this area most directly relevant to the problems tackled in this chapter is the following. The syntax of a sign may be defined as that by virtue of which it has meaning (and the particular meaning it has). The resemblance theory in its various forms, consistent with classical computation theory, implies that the syntax of a sign is a matter of physically defined properties, specifically shape. This is obviously compatible with physicalism, which envisages only such properties as being fundamental. In the case of encoding of information in the brain, it is obviously necessary to extend the range of physical properties constituting syntax to neural properties. This line of thought can be made to mesh with the idea that information-carrying neural states cause behaviour, and with the assumption that all causation is a matter of physical events following physical laws. In brief, information-carrying neural states will have causal power by virtue of their physically defined syntactic properties of neural states. Thus, (Fodor 1987, p. 5, with an Endnote):

> Here . . . is how the new story is supposed to go: You connect the causal properties of a symbol with its semantic properties *via its syntax*. The syntax of a symbol is one of its higher-order physical properties. To a metaphorical first approximation, we can think of the syntactic structure of a symbol as an abstract feature of its shape.
>
> *Endnote: Any* nomic property of symbol tokens, however—any property in virtue of the possession of which they satisfy causal laws—would, in principle, do just as well. (So, for example, syntactic structure could be realized by relations among electromagnetic states rather than relations among shapes; as, indeed, it is in real computers.)
>
> [*Text continued*] Because, to all intents and purposes, syntax reduces to shape and because the shape of a symbol is a potential determinant of its causal role, it is fairly easy to see how there could be environments in which the causal role of a symbol correlates with its syntax. It's easy, that is to say, to imagine symbol tokens interacting causally *in virtue of* their syntactic structures. The syntax of a symbol might determine the causes and effects of its tokenings in much the way that the geometry of a key determines which locks it will open.

This story backs up Fodor's position as outlined in subsection 2.2.1, but the powerful assumptions it makes about semantics, syntax, and causality are questionable.

It is possible to tell a different story. It begins with the kind of semantic theory being endorsed here, to the effect that neurally encoded semantic states essentially regulate intentional action. We then have to construct a syntactic theory compatible with this. As already noted, 'syntax' always, in any theory, has to be defined in a way that makes sense of semantics. Definition in terms of shape will do if representation is essentially a matter of spatial resemblance. Definition in terms of relations between electromagnetic states will do if semantics can be defined in terms of such relations. But according to the story we are now running, semantic properties cannot defined in those or any other physical terms. Semantic properties *and therefore also syntactic properties* have to be understood in terms of the regulation of intentional action. Hence the view of neural syntax arrived at in subsection 2.3.2: neural 'symbols' are essentially involved in the regulation of intentional system–environment interaction, and are linked intrinsically to sensori-cognitive-motor capacities.

The proposal that synactic properties are not physically definable hangs together with the point made earlier (subsections 1.3.6, 2.1.4) and which will be made again (subsection 2.5.6), that causal explanation of intentional as opposed to non-intentional behaviour has to posit intentional states in the acting system. Invoking physically defined properties will not do the required work.

The implication of diverging in this way from Fodor's account of semantic causation is that we have to envisage causal laws that are not couched in terms of physical properties, but rather in terms of semantic ones. This idea, already anticipated for example at the end of subsection 2.4.2, is worked out in chapters 4 and 5. Another aspect of this implication is that information-carrying neural states have causal generating power by virtue of being semantic states, or again, that there is something like 'semantically defined energy'. This sort of conclusion was anticipated in earlier discussion of the intimate link between cognition and affect (subsection 1.2.3). The connection between information and the generation of order in functional, intentional systems appears also as a consequence of the shift from causal to functional semantics in Chapter 4 (subsection 4.6.3).

2.5 OBJECTIONS TO THE PROPOSED SOLUTION, 4: 'ARE MEANINGS IN THE HEAD?'

2.5.1 Introduction

In this section we discuss Putnam's highly influential claim that 'meanings ain't in the head' (Putnam 1975). Putnam's proposal, based on so-called 'twin-Earth' thought-experiments, along with variations, interpretations, and elaborations of its implications, are the subjects of a very large literature in philosophy and some theoretical cognitive science. Our interest here is partial and selective, concerning specifically implications for meaningful, mental causation. Putnam's proposal can be used to construct an argument against the idea that meaningful, mental states are causal, and so we need to consider it here.[9]

Among the various ways of approaching Putnam's claim and its implications, let us start with the issues discussed in the preceding section, to do with whether semantic characteristics can be causal. In subsection 2.4.1 we considered a line of thought which may be summarized briefly as follows: the meaning of any 'sign' in the brain (of any information-carrying neural state) must involve a relation between the brain and something external, the reality represented. But causality has to be local. Therefore meaning can't be causal.

To which the reply, given in subsection 2.4.2, was, in brief: if you want to explain non-local behaviour, that is behaviour which is environment directed, then you need to cite non-locally defined causes, which can be done while preserving local causation by positing that brain states encode meaning. This solution was meant to follow the lead of the information-processing paradigm within the behavioural sciences. The aim is to explain action in terms of information-carrying (cognitive) states, and these are regarded as encoded in the brain.

Essential to this explanatory paradigm, however, is a particular way of defining the informational content of cognitive states, namely, in terms of the interactivity between agent and the environment. The conceptual linkage between meaning and action is already implied by the fact that cognitive states are posited for the purpose of explaining action. This has been implicit or explicit throughout the first chapter and the present one. However, quite different assumptions about meaning can be made, so that there is in particular no conceptual linkage between meaning and action, in which case the proposal that meaning is encoded in the brain is lost, and with it the compatibility between material (neural) causation, and mental, meaningful causation, the latter of which then has to be jettisoned. This move belongs with the idea that meaningful characterizations of behaviour are in some business other than causal explanation, and runs counter to what is being argued for throughout this essay.

In brief, what we will be considering in this section of the chapter is the way that a definition of meaning that precludes interaction between the agent and what is represented undermines the idea that meaning is encoded in the brain and thereby has a causal role. We will in effect be arguing that in the context of cognitive explanation of behaviour such a definition of meaning, omitting agent–environment interactions, is a mischief-maker.

The position is, however, somewhat complicated by the fact that the view of meaning that we will be arguing against is frequently combined with a plausible proposal that we endorse, namely, that meaningful mental states are 'broad' or 'world-involving'. This is to say that their definition makes reference to the world other than the subject. This proposal is correct, and adopted, and indeed emphasized, here, but the 'world-involving' nature of meaningful states is compatible with the causal role of meaning, assuming these states are encoded in the brain. But, to repeat, this reconciliation only works if meaningful content is defined in terms of agent–environment interactions. Without this definition, the world-involving nature of meaningful states precludes their being encoded in the brain, and precludes their having any causal role.

One more issue, a matter of terminology prominent in the literature, has to be mentioned in this introductory subsection. The dictum 'meanings ain't in the head' may be taken to sum up the claim that the meaningful content of mental states is not dependent solely on the state of the brain. The notion of dependence at work here is defined using the technical term *supervenience*. The claim is that the meaningful content of mental states does not supervene on states of the brain. The notion of supervenience may be defined, roughly, as follows: states of type X supervene on states of type Y if and only if there is no difference among X states without a corresponding difference among Y states.[10]

In what follows we shall assume that there is a link between the technical notion of supervenience and the notion of encoding familiar in cognitive science. At least in this sense: that the supervenience of states of type X on states of type Y is a *necessary* condition of states of type Y encoding states of type X. While nothing in the arguments to follow depends on this linkage between supervenience and encoding, it helps to make explicit connections between Putnam's thesis and the philosophical literature to which it has given rise, and the cognitive science paradigm which is our main concern here.

The claim to be considered is that meaningful states do not supervene on brain states, with its implication that they cannot be causes of behaviour. In terms of encoding, the claim would be that such states are not encoded in brain states: meanings are not '(encoded) in the head'. The implication, again, being that meaningful states cannot be causes of behaviour. This in effect is the contraposition of the argument being proposed here, namely: since meaningful mental states are causes of behaviour they are encoded in brain states.

We have to consider, then, the basis of the claim that meaningful states do not supervene on brain states. Putnam came to this conclusion by means of what have come to be called twin-Earth thought-experiments, to which we turn next.

2.5.2 A twin-Earth thought-experiment and its standard interpretation: meaning does not supervene on the brain

In order to answer the question whether mental states with meaning supervene on brain states we have to consider the variation. We have to conduct an 'experiment' which holds brain states constant, and then see whether meaningful mental content can nevertheless vary: if it does, then there is no supervenience. It is of course important that the 'experiment' here is not, and cannot be, an empirical one. There is the practical impossibility of finding two identical brains and knowing that they are identical. But further, it is unclear what scientific test would show whether or not meaningful contents were identical under these conditions; apparently we should have to use 'intuitions' about meaning. So for more than one reason we are squarely in the philosophical arena here: the experiment has to be a thought-experiment, and it is heavily dependent on intuition.

Consider, then, the following thought-experiment, due to Putnam (1975), which seems to show that meaning fails to depend on states of the brain.

We are to imagine there to be in another world a person P* who is an exact replica of person P on Earth; in particular their brain states are identical. Further, the world P* inhabits is exactly similar to Earth in all respects except one: it has a substance with physico-chemical composition XYZ where we have the substance with composition H_2O. XYZ is the same as H_2O according to any casual test, though they can be distinguished in a chemical laboratory. Given this imaginary situation, we are invited to share the intuition that P and P* differ in semantic characteristics, that the meaning of their words differ, and the meaningful contents of their thoughts. Specifically, the suggestion is that the words 'water is wet' means something different when uttered by P than when uttered by P*, and that the content of P's thought that water is wet is different from the the corresponding thought entertained by P*. Indeed the intuition is meant to be that P* can neither say nor think that water is wet. The source of the alleged difference in meaningful content is due to the difference in the environments, defined in physico-chemical terms. Since the meaningful content of the *doppelgänger's* thoughts differs even though their brain states are identical, the conclusion is that meaningful content does not supervene on the brain. In brief, meaning ain't in the head.[11]

The intuitions that support this conclusion are of a piece with the physicalist or materialist criterion of meaning which refers to the physical (or physico-chemical) nature of what is represented. On this basis we reach the conclusion that mental states, individuated by meaningful content, do not supervene on brain states.

The same conclusion is reached by means of a different type of thought-experiment, formulated by Burge in a series of papers (1979, 1982*a*, *b*, 1986 *a*, *b*). In this type of case, the difference in mental contents between the *doppelgänger* is not due to a difference in their (physical) environments, but is due rather to a difference in their linguistic communities. Burge's arguments (or intuitions) have a broad range, unresricted to contents which can plausibly be construed as referring to physico-chemical kinds. They point to the conclusion that *no* mental contents (expressible in language) supervene on brain events. We shall assume in what follows that if the *doppelgänger* thought-experiments exclude content–brain supervenience at all, they do so for all content. However, we shall not discuss Burge's type of thought-experiment, since our comments on the Putnam type apply to what both types have in common, namely, the claim that meaningful content can differ notwithstanding identity of brain states. We shall call this claim the 'standard interpretation' of the *doppelgänger* thought-experiments.

We shall argue in the next section that the standard interpretation of the thought-experiments is mistaken; or, to put the point more cautiously, that it is incompatible with the criterion of mental content required for a cognitive-behavioural science. First let us consider the drastic consequences of accepting the standard reading of the *doppelgänger* thought-experiments, and proposals which have been made for handling them. These consequences, as anticipated at the beginning of the section, concern primarily meaning and causality.

2.5.3 Lack of supervenience implies that mental states are not causal; or they have no (ordinary) meaning

According to the standard interpretation of the twin-Earth thought-experiments, mental states identified in terms of meaningful content do not supervene on states of the brain. Now we introduce a premise to the effect that all causes of behaviour supervene on local material events, namely, in the brain. This plausible premise serves only to exclude both non-material causation (whatever that might be), and distal causation (unmediated by local). Thus from a combination of the standard interpretation of the thought-experiment plus a plausible premise about causality, it follows that mental states identified in terms of meaningful content are not causes of behaviour.

The meaningful content at issue is that as specified in folk psychological ordinary language. The problem with meaningful content as envisaged by folk psychology and ordinary language is that it is 'broad', or 'world-involving': it supervenes on (varies with) the states of the world, not only on states of the brain (see, for example, Stich 1983; McGinn 1982, 1989).

The argument is, then, that the broad, world-involving mental states posited by folk psychology cannot play a role in the causal explanation of behaviour, and therefore in particular have no role to play in the causal explanations of cognitive-behavioural science.

The conclusion that broad content does not supervene on brain states and therefore cannot be causal threatens the cognitive-behavioural explanatory paradigm. If the paradigm is to be preserved, desperate remedies are required and have been proposed. Roughly, the saving principle has to be that cognitive states can have a causal role, but broad content has to be irrelevant to it. In which case, either cognitive states have causal role but content drops out altogether, or some notion of content is retained as relevant to causal role, namely 'narrow' content as opposed to 'broad'. Narrow content is not world-involving, does supervene on the brain, and therefore can be causal. Hence we find proposed both theories of content-less (meaning-less) cognitive causation (Stich 1983), and narrow content theories (Fodor 1980; McGinn 1982).

The idea of narrow content appears, however, highly problematic. Content, one supposes by definition, has intentionality, aboutness, hence is world-involving, and so broad. The idea of narrow content seems at best extraordinary and at worst self-contradictory. On the other hand, narrow content can be defined in terms of causal role. In this case narrow content theories become similar to the proposal to define cognitive states in terms of causal role, omitting reference to content altogether. This shifts the problem, however, rather than solving it. The cognitive-behavioural explanatory paradigm, like the folk psychological, describes not only the content of mental states in broad, world-involving terms, but also in those terms the behaviour that such states cause. We say, for example, 'having learnt that the goal-box contained food, and being hungry, the rat ran towards it'. The causal role of cognitive states is to be defined in terms of interactions among them and the behaviour they generate, but in the kind of explanation in question, the behaviours generated are typically world-involving, or broad. Hence the causal roles of the cognitive states are defined in broad terms, so also then is any notion of content tied to causal role. There seems to be no way of managing without our familiar broad, world-involving characterizations of intentional activity and the cognitive states that regulate it. Attempts to do so have to envisage an extraordinary, not yet invented, behavioural language. In Stich's terms, what is required are 'autonomous' behavioural descriptions. Stich admits to difficulties clarifying their nature, and remarks negatively: 'there is no reason to expect that the autonomous behavioural-description terminology ultimately to be found most useful will be a purely physical description of movements of the sort that behaviourists sought but never found' (1983, p. 169). Elsewhere he notes that 'perhaps an appropriate autonomous behavioural descriptive language does not yet exist' (1983, p. 136fn).

But this is, we suggest, a problematic solution to an ill-conceived problem.[12] There is no need to jettison our familiar broad, world-involving definition of the mental content involved in the regulation of action. On the contrary, this is just what is required for the causal explanation of intentional action. Basically this just repeats the point made earlier, for example in reply to the so-called casual argument in subsection 2.4.2.

We have to reassess the problem. As remarked at the beginning of this subsection, the conclusion that mental states identified in terms of meaningful content are not causes of behaviour follows from two premises. First, the standard interpretation of the twin-Earth thought-experiments, according to which mental states identified in terms of meaningful content do not supervene on (depend on) states of the brain. Secondly, that all causes of behaviour supervene on local material events, namely, in the brain.

Since we are rejecting the conclusion, we have to reject one of the premises. Attempts have been made to manage without the second premise, by distinguishing between types of causal explanation and in particular by defining a type that depends on content in the absence of supervenience. Jackson and Pettit (1988) distinguish between causal explanations which cite a *causally efficacious feature* and those which cite a *feature which 'causally programmes' without causing*. Explanations of behaviour in terms of broad mental content are then held to be indeed legitimate causal explanations, but of the causal programming variety. This proposal ensures the relevance of broad mental states to causal explanation and seems to avoid the problems inherent in the idea of narrow content. On this last point, however, the difficulty is that causal programming explanations generally seem to presuppose causal efficacious explanations, so that in particular, causal programming explanations of behaviour in terms of broad mental states apparently presuppose causal efficacious explanations in terms of narrow mental states (Rowlands 1989). A related suggestion is Dretske's distinction between 'triggering' and 'structuring' causes of behaviour, again designed to show how content can be causal even though it fails to supervene on brain states (Dretske 1988, with critical commentary in McLaughlin 1991).

Our suggestion is, however, to retain the principle in question, namely that causes of behaviour supervene on local material events in the brain. It is an apparently plausible principle, and is embraced by the idea characteristic of the information-processing based behavioural sciences and adopted here, that semantic characteristics are encoded in brain states. This means that what has to be rejected is the standard interpretation of the twin-Earth thought-experiments, according to which mental states identified in terms of meaningful content do not supervene on (depend on) states of the brain. From the point of view of the general account being proposed here, this is the real culprit.

The encoding thesis makes it possible to hold both that meaningful states are world-involving and that they act as local causes, the implication being that they satisfy the supervenience condition. This in turn implies that semantic content involves interaction between the subject of the mental states and what is represented. Such a definition of meaning is suited to the cognitive-behavioural sciences, but it is not captured by the standard interpretation of the twin-Earth experiments. Let us consider these issues in more detail.

2.5.4 Reply: meaning stands in need of behavioural criteria

The standard interpretation of the thought-experiments is that the *doppelgänger*, while identical in brain states, nevertheless have mental states with different meaningful content. As against this we can say that in the circumstances envisaged, mental contents are indeed identical, at least according to behavioural criteria of content, since the behaviours of the *doppelgänger* are the same. Use of behavioural criteria is appropriate to cognitive-behavioural science, which posits mental states with semantic contents in order to explain behaviour.

The obvious reply to this suggestion is that the *doppelgänger* do indeed differ in behaviour: one drinks, tries to find, etc. H_2O, while the other drinks, tries to find, etc. XYZ. Just as mental content varies with the environment, so does the appropriate description of behaviour. This reply serves as a quick defence of the standard reading of the thought-experiments, but it fails to recognize the point behind the suggestion that we have in these cases identity of behaviour. The suggestion is not simply the superficial one that the relevant behaviours can be described in the same way; this can indeed be met with a flat denial, consistent with the standard reading of the thought-experiment. The important point is rather that there is identity of behaviour *because a critical behavioural difference is missing, namely, behaviour which discriminates between H_2O and XYZ.*

Fundamental to the standard interpretation of the thought-experiments is that it discriminates between mental contents in the absence of corresponding discriminative behaviour. Since the *doppelgänger ex hypothesi* do not (and could not) discriminate between H_2O and XYZ in their behaviour, there is no justification for ascribing to them mental states with content H_2O as opposed to XYZ, or vice versa. At least, there is no justification from the point of view of a cognitive science of behaviour, which on the grounds of parsimony posits only those mental states and contents required for an adequate explanation of behaviour, including of discriminative behaviour. In this sense, the standard reading of the thought-experiments invokes a criterion of mental content different from, and incompatible with, the criterion appropriate to psychology.

This line of thought has some similarities with Fodor's more recent argument for the notion of narrow content in cognitive science, the so-called modal argument (Fodor 1987, 1991). Fodor criticizes the standard reading of the *doppelgänger* cases on the grounds that it invokes a difference in mental content which does no causal-explanatory work. Fodor goes on to suggest that specification of mental content should be relativized to context, in such a way that the *doppelgänger* share mental states. Fodor and his twin-Earth replica share the same mental state, the content of which is H_2O in case of being on Earth, or XYZ in case of being on twin-Earth. Content so defined would be 'narrow' in the sense of being supervenient, and causal. But it would at the same time be 'broad' in the sense of referring to a disjunctively specified environment. Fodor's argument and the notion of narrow content which it defends has been much discussed (Burge 1989; Block 1991; Crane 1991; McGinn 1991; Wilson 1992; Adams 1993*a*,*b*; Manfredi 1993; Russow 1993).

The position being proposed in this section is similar to Fodor's in key ways. We endorse the behavioural criterion of content suited to the cognitive-behavioural explanatory paradigm, and hence in particular the methodological principle: no difference in content to be invoked which does not explain a behavioural difference. On the other hand, our emphasis in the notion of 'behavioural difference' is not essentially concerned with differences in the environmental scene of behaviour, but is specifically to do with *discriminative* behaviour. Our proposal is to define content *only* in terms of what makes a difference to behaviour, to organism–environment interactions, in which case neither the term H_2O nor the term XYZ, nor therefore thier disjunction, has a role to play in the characterization of mental states in the twin-Earth experiments as described. This proposal delivers broad meaning and causal power, jettisons only the idea of broad content defined by reference to what makes no difference to behaviour, and in this context the idea of narrow as opposed to broad content drops out as redundant. These implications are discussed below.

The proposal, then, is to use a behavioural criterion of content with the emphasis, as indicated, on discriminative behaviour. Such a criterion stands in clear contrast to the one at work in the setting up of, and the standard interpretation of, the type of thought-experiment we are considering, which has to do with the physico-chemical nature of the environment.

On the other hand, it can be argued that the physicalist (or materialist) criterion of mental content is supported by considerations of causal history, the supposition being that the causal history of the pyschological states in question involves causation by H_2O in the one case and XYZ in the other (Davidson 1989). However, since the thought-experiments are set up in such a way that the brain states of *doppelgängers* are identical, H_2O has effects on the brain indistinguishable from those of XYZ. So whatever it is about these substances that has to be invoked in order to explain their causal effects on the brain, it is not their chemical composition. Presumably, then, within the terms of the causal theory of mental content, there are no grounds for distinguishing between the causal histories of the *doppelgänger's* mental states. In this way the causal criterion of mental content seems to point to the same conclusion as the behavioural criterion, and for similar reasons.

If mental content in the *doppelgänger* cases is not to be identified in physico-chemical terms, how else should it be specified? The line of thought in the preceding paragraph provides one approach to this question. We take it as obvious that living beings are sensitive to only some of the properties of water; obvious because we are speaking of beings with particular needs and aims, with limited sensory and cognitive capacities, not of God. Expressed in the information-processing language of biology and psychology, the point is that livings beings are sensitive to and encode only part of the hypothetical totality of information pertaining to water. In the case of human beings, and the *doppelgängers* in the thought-experiments in particular, let us call this subset of information IE: information encoded. IE includes, say: fluid, colourless, drinkable, fire-extinguishing. But in particular it excludes, *ex hypothesi* in the *doppelgänger* cases, being composed of H_2O rather than XYZ, or vice versa. Then we may say that the *doppelgänger* have the same information-bearing states, the content of which is characterized in terms of IE. The general proposal is that the mental content which regulates behaviour is to be defined in terms of encoded information, which is essentially a product of organism–environment interactions.

As indicated, such a definition of mental content in terms of encoded information is distinct from what is presupposed in the standard reading of the thought-experiments. It is the kind of definition appropriate to biology and psychology, and it hangs together with behavioural criteria of mental content. Living beings are sensitive to some features of the environment but not others: they encode particular information, salient to their activity. The criterion of whether a certain type of information is or is not encoded and used in the regulation of activity is precisely behavioural, including specifically evidence of discriminative behaviour. Thus, for example, a creature's behaviour may show that it possesses information that a pool of water is drinkable, or is polluted, but may show that it does not possess the information that water is composed of the chemical elements hydrogen and oxygen as opposed to others; and so on.[13]

2.5.5 Behaviourally defined content supervenes on the brain, is 'world-involving', and is causal

The definition and criteria of mental content being proposed are unlike those at work in the standard reading of the thought-experiments. It may be expected, then, that they give no support to the (apparently paradoxical) implications of the standard reading. According to the account proposed here, mental content does supervene on brain states, even though it is 'world-involving', and thereby it is relevant to the causal role of mental states. Let us consider these points in turn.

The content of cognitive states as identified by this method supervenes on brain states. According to behavioural criteria of content, which attend specifically to discriminative behaviour, there is no reason to distinguish between the mental contents of the *doppelgänger*. In the thought-experiment we have been considering, distinction between mental contents is based on differences in the physico-chemical nature of the environments. But the reply is that the physico-chemical nature of their environments is irrelevant to the *doppelgänger*: they simply do not detect it. This is how the thought-experiment is set up. By contrast, consider the environmental features which, as shown in their behaviour, the *doppelgänger* do detect, that water is fluid, drinkable, etc. In respect of these features, the environments of the *doppelgänger* are indeed identical, and this identity hangs together with the identity of their behaviour, brain states, and mental contents.[14]

Let us consider the dictum that meaning ain't in the head, in relation to the argument in the above paragraph. The meaning in question is tied to the physico-chemical composition of the environment. However, the thought-experiments are set up precisely in such a way that the *doppelgänger* fail to detect this feature of the environment. No wonder, then, that meaning ain't in the head! When the basis of this dictum is spelt out as above, it is (more or less) tautological. As is the following proposition: meaning is encoded in, and hence is supervenient on, states of the brain (is 'in the head') in so far as it pertains to features of the environment to which the living being is sensitive. Thus, according to the way the thought-experiment is set up, meaning pertaining to such as fluidity is in the *doppelgänger's* heads, but there is nothing in their heads about chemical composition.

Nothing in the above argument, of course, precludes there being mental states with meaningful content individuated in terms of concepts of physics and chemistry. Anyone who has learnt these sciences has them; the *doppelgänger* apparently haven't. Further, mental states with such content, according to the present argument, supervene on brain states; they are 'in the head'. The point is not that concepts of physics and chemistry cannot be used to individuate mental states, but is rather that the use of any concepts for this purpose stands in need of justification by behavioural criteria.

Mental content, defined by behavioural criteria, not only supervenes on the brain, but is essentially 'world-involving'. Contrary to the standard reading of the thought-experiments, this latter characteristic of mental content does not preclude supervenience.

According to the proposed analysis, mental content is 'broad', or 'world-involving', in the sense that it is defined and individuated by reference to features of the world. These may include, in the thought-experiment we have taken as example, features such as fluidity or transparency. It is essential to our notion of mental content that environmental properties enter into its definition. This correct insight, however, has been misconstrued in the standard interpretation of the *doppelgänger* thought-experiments as being incompatible with content–brain supervenience. It has been wrongly supposed that if content is world-involving then it cannot supervene on states of the brain, and vice versa.

The conclusion that mental content is both world-involving and supervenient on the brain belongs straightforwardly with the assumption characteristic of biology and psychology that information about the environment is encoded in the brain. This assumption is fundamental to the causal explanation of behaviour in terms of information-processing. The main point is that the contents of information-bearing states, mental or material, have to be characterized by reference to environmental features precisely in so far as they are invoked to explain behaviour as interaction between the organism and its environment. In other words, content is world-involving because of its role in the explanation of behaviour. This understanding of the world-involving character of mental content is, however, quite distinct from, and opposed to, the conception at work in the thought-experiments. In that context, the world-involving character of content is entirely irrelevant to behaviour, and this is the reason why the thought-experiments give rise to conundrums.

Meaningful content defined as information encoded within the living being supervenes on states of the brain and its effects are evident in behaviour. Given these propositions, there is apparently no reason to deny, while there is reason to affirm, that the content of cognitive states is relevant to their causal role. The causal effects of cognitive states on other such states and on behaviour depend on what information they encode. We consider these points further in the next subsection.

2.5.6 'Individualism' and causal role

We are proposing that content is attributed to the subject's mind or brain, even though it is individuated broadly, with reference to features of the environment. This conclusion may be compared and contrasted with the doctrine of 'individualism' against which Burge has argued in a number of papers (1979, 1982a,b, 1986a,b,c, 1989).

This doctrine may be stated briefly in the following form: that intentional states are fixed by, supervene on, bodily states the nature of which are specifiable without reference to external, environmental conditions. Burge has taken individualism to be refuted by the *doppelgänger* thought-experiments, his own (which have not been discussed here) and Putnam's. The standard interpretation of the thought-experiments apparently refutes individualism by the two claims, first that intentional states are individuated with reference to external conditions, and secondly that such states do not supervene on the brain.

The view proposed in this section affirms the first of these claims but not the second. According to what we are proposing, individualism is correct: the states of the brain on which intentional states supervene may be described in intrinsic terms, even though the intentional states that they encode are specified with reference to extrinsic conditions.

That said, and here we return to a line of thought already discussed in several places so far (for example, subsections 1.3.6, 2.4.2): for the purpose of causal explanation of behaviour in the environment (as opposed to behaviour as motor movement), descriptions of brain processes will be couched in the language of information-processing, including specification of information about the environment which is coded. When this language is used, brain processes themselves are characterized broadly, with reference to external conditions.

This possibility of choice between (to put it briefly) intrinsic and extrinsic description exists in the case of brain states, but probably not in the case of mental or cognitive states: here extrinsic (information-processing) description only is possible. This is connected with Brentano's thesis, that the mental is essentially characterized by its intentionality, its 'aboutness'. In the context of cognitive-behavioural science, the point is that cognitive states are posited essentially in order to explain behaviour in the environment, and so they have to specified by reference to (actual or possible) environmental states. Cognitive-behavioural science does not have as *explanandum* behaviour as motor acts, considered in isolation from the environment. Or again, there is no need to posit *cognition* in the explanation of behaviour so defined: explanation in (non-information -processing) neurophysiological terms will suffice, and is appropriate.

The suggestion is, then, that non-intentional characterization of mental states is an impossibility, or at least is useless for the purpose of cognitive-behavioural explanation. Functionalism, in so far as it is committed to a non-intentional, 'narrow', definition of the causal role of mental states, then appears as mistaken. Burge takes functionalism to be a contemporary version of individualism, and hence false. The present argument endorses this criticism. The only viable version of functionalism would define the causal role of mental states essentially in terms of information-carrying and -processing. This link between the notion of causality applicable in psychology and biology and the concept of information-processing will be argued for in detail in Chapter 5.

We have argued that mental content has the following three characteristics: it supervenes on states of the brain and is relevant to the causal role of mental states, but also it is 'world-involving', individuated in terms of environmental features. The standard interpretation of the *doppelgänger* thought-experiments, by contrast, splits these characteristics of mental content apart, making the third appear incompatible with the first two: but all three are essential for adequate causal explanation in biology and psychology.

In the way the thought-experiments are set up and standardly interpreted, the world-involving nature of mental content is indeed incompatible with supervenience and causal role, precisely because it is defined in such a way as to make no difference to the brain or to behaviour. But the incompatibility inferred from this kind of case shows up as problematic when we consider world-involving characteristics of mental states which are reflected in behaviour and which therefore presumably do supervene on the brain. This kind of case is encountered as soon as we turn from the imaginary world of the thought-experiments to consider a working psychological theory.

In support of his claim that content is world-involving, Burge cites the fact that 'the best empirical theory that we have [Marr's] individuates the intentional content of visual representations by specific reference to specific physical characteristics of visible properties and relations' (1986c, p. 38). So such content is broad and world-involving. But then let us raise the critical questions: 'Is content so defined relevant or not relevant to the causal role of representations, and do representations with content so defined supervene on brain states or not?' We take it that the answer to both these questions is going to have to be 'Yes'. However, Burge cannot give this answer, because it contradicts the standard conclusion drawn from the thought-experiments, to which Burge remains heavily committed, that mental states individuated broadly are neither causal nor supervenient on the brain. This conclusion, when applied to the theory of visual perception, leads to what appears to be the puzzling position that while the content of visual representations is individuated by reference to visible environmental conditions, this fact is irrelevant to the causal role of the representations, is unreflected, for example, in discriminative behaviour, and fails to supervene on physical states of the visual system. This is the kind of problematic position which Burge seems obliged to formulate and defend (Burge 1986c, 1989; Francescotti 1991).

It makes sense in the thought-experiments to suppose that broad, world-involving content is non-supervenient and lacks causal role because their aim is not to explicate causal explanation, and indeed they define content in such a way that it makes no difference to (discriminative) behaviour. But in working cognitive psychology, the aim is to explain intentional activity, including discrimination, and in this context it is to be expected that content will play a causal role, and will be neurally encoded (will supervene on the brain), while being at the same time 'world-involving', that is, specified as being about such-and-such an object or feature in the environment as opposed to some other.

In this context of cognitive-behavioural explanation the claim that broad content is neither causal nor supervenient creates paradoxes because the kind of content such explanation invokes is typically a matter of perceptible properties, that is, properties which can be perceived, and which when perceived make a difference to the brain and to behaviour. Of course 'perceptible' here does not mean 'consciously perceptible': what is required is that the agent be sensitive to the properties in question, consciously or otherwise. Some of these properties may coincide with the categories of physics and chemistry, such as shape and mass (within certain ranges), or oxygen in solution. Others are plainly relative to the living being, such as being non-poisonous or dangerous. In biology and psychology, the environment that is represented in information-carrying states cannot be defined without reference to the sensitivity, aims, and interests of the living being.

2.5.7 Meaning and action: post-empiricist qualifications

Mental content supervenes on brain states, has causal role, and is world-involving, individuated by reference to environmental features, these being of a particular sort, namely, features which matter to, and may be frankly relative to, the subject. The standard reading of the thought-experiments fails to insert this qualification concerning features that individuate content, indeed flatly contradicts it, and therefore leads to the conclusion that meaningful content, broadly individuated, fails to supervene on brain states and has no causal role. Meaningful content is then irrelevant to cognitive-behavioural science. At this point it may be recalled that the meaningful content that is and has been in question is meaningful content as specified in folk psychological ordinary language. The standard reading of the thought-experiments thus threatens to consign ordinary language, and folk psychology with it, into scientific oblivion.

The arguments in the preceding three subsections, against the standard interpretation of the thought-experiments, serve, if correct, to counter this attack. Moreover, they bring out that the folk psychological method of specifying mental content is, in form, correct. For the purpose of explaining intelligent behaviour in the environment, as opposed to motor movements in a vacuum, the meaningful content of cognitive states is appropriately specified by reference to (perceptible) environmental conditions. This is precisely the method used in folk psychology. The fact that mental content as specified in ordinary language is broad, or world-involving, is not at all a drawback in the context of cognitive-behavioural explanation, rather it is a virtue. Further, broadly individuated, world-involving mental contents of the sort familiar in folk psychology presumably supervene on brain states, in so far as they make a difference to behaviour, that is, in so far as the explanations which invoke them are effective in the prediction of behaviour.

An implication of the view being proposed is that the meaning of ordinary language, used among other purposes for specifying the meaningful content of mental states, is grounded in behaviour. The meaning of a sign derives from its use in action, not from, for example and in particular, the fact that it is used within an environment with such-and-such physico-chemical constitution (save in so far as such constitution makes a difference to the activity of the users of the sign, hence to the use of the sign within that activity). The contrast in the philosophy of language and meaning here is between the view proposed by the later Wittgenstein, and subsequent theories that seek to anchor linguistic meaning in a materialist reality. There is much to be said on either side of this debate, but the philosophy of language is not our primary concern here. What does follow, however, from the above arguments in the philosophy of mind is that it is Wittgenstein's view of meaning as use in activity which belongs with cognitive-behavioural science; in this context the other definition of meaning leads to paradoxes.

As it stands, the proposed definition ties meaning to the sphere of interaction between the living being and the environment, hence to experience (though not necessarily conscious experience). In this sense the claim that meaning is grounded in action is close to empiricism. On the other hand, as outlined in the first chapter (subsection 1.4.1), empiricism neglects theoretical representation of realities that cannot be reduced to experience. Human beings at least, beyond a certain level of cognitive maturation, can represent a greater reality which includes but exceeds what is given in experience; we represent, for example, events in distant regions of space and time, perhaps also spirit worlds, and so on. Plausibly such representation is dependent on our use of language; in any case, we are less inclined to attribute such world-pictures to creatures without language, to animals or infants. So what remains of the idea that meaning must be grounded in action? At the very least, it has to be qualified and elaborated to allow for the kind of case just described: meaning is grounded in interaction between the living being and its environment, though on that basis, representation may be made of reality which exceeds what is immediately encountered in action.

An elaboration of this general kind can be seen in Wittgenstein's work, by comparing the *Philosophical investigations* with *On certainty*. The former introduces the new theory of meaning in connection with simplified examples of simple activities, such as shopping and building (Wittgenstein 1953, §§1–37). The latter deals with daily activities, simple but no longer simplified, and these are now shown as surrounded by systems of belief, or world-views (Wittgenstein 1969; see also subsection 1.4.4).

The gradual freeing of concepts from action is also a prominent theme in psychological development, to be considered later (Chapter 6). Whether looked philosophically or psychologically, however, the roots of meaning in action and experience remain evident. Our conception of realities that lie beyond experience typically uses images, categories, and analogies from experience, and they presuppose that those realities interact with what is nearer to hand, so that experience contains signs of what lies beyond it. It follows from this last point that some kinds of activity require for their cognitive explanation the ascription of mental content concerned with 'distant realities'. In order to understand and predict the behaviour of a physicist, chemist, palaeontologist, priest, or tribal magician, it is necessary to suppose that their beliefs and actions concern (what they take to be) signs of realities beyond what is directly experienced in practice.

2.6 OBJECTIONS TO THE PROPOSED SOLUTION, 5: 'PEOPLE NOT BRAINS HAVE MEANING'

2.6.1 The objection

We have proposed that meaning is encoded in the brain, and thereby plays a role in the regulation of action. This proposal is intended to reconcile meaningful with neural causation, and to follow the lead of the information-processing paradigm in the brain-behavioural sciences. We have considered so far four interconnected objections to this proposal, and we turn now to the fifth and final one.

It has some superficial similarities to the one just discussed, in so far as it invokes the general idea that meaning involves the world and is therefore not the kind of thing that can be in the brain. But instead of being based in materialist preconceptions about reality and meaning, or in ultimately problematic thought-experiments, the objection in the form to be considered next is based in what may be called a Wittgensteinian view of language and meaning, as being essentially involved in forms of life.

As discussed earlier (subsection 2.4.3), Wittgenstein in his early work, the *Tractatus* (1921), proposed that the pictorial structure of the sign alone (its syntax) has meaning, is a true-or-false representation of reality. This view is given up in the later period: signs have meaning not because they are distributed in a spatial or quasi-spatial structure, but because they are 'distributed in' a rule-guided activity. Our activities are typically social, and are surrounded by cultural theories, in the way described by post-empiricist epistemology (subsection 1.4.1). In short, meaning is embedded within human social practices and culture.

Whereas the view articulated in the *Tractatus* fits well with the idea that there are signs in the brain, 'picturing' the world, Wittgenstein's later view makes this idea look odd. How can the sign with meaning be in the brain? Is it not rather in practices and culture? It seems that the idea of encoding, and all the information-processing language that goes along with it, might be something like a muddled category mistake.

Considerations along these Wittgensteinian lines have been made by various philosophers, such as Hacker (1987).[15] After quoting distinguished biologists and psychologists working within the information-processing paradigm, Hacker writes (1987, p. 488):

> The general conception at work involves the supposition that the brain has a *language* of its own, which consists of *symbols* that *represent* things. It uses the *vocabulary* of this language to *encode information* and it produces *descriptions* of what is seen . . . .

This general conception is then dismissed as a 'mythology of neural processes' (Hacker 1987, p. 490).

So on what grounds? Hacker goes on to remind us of familiar facts about language, to do with natural languages, the speakers being human, showing rule-following skills, using words in the course of diverse activities, explaining meanings, correcting errors, etc. He continues (1987, p. 492):

> I mention these platitidues because they are easily forgotten. For if one remembers them it should be obvious that it *makes no sense* to speak of the brain as having or using a language. Only of a creature that can perform acts of speech does it make sense to say that it has, understands, uses, a language. But it is literally unintelligible to suggest that a brain, let alone a part of a brain, might ask a question, have or express an intention, make a decision, describe a sunset, . . . To have, and to have mastered a language is to have a repertoire of behaviour. . . . But the repertoire of 'behaviour' of a brain or part of a brain does not lie on the same parameters as the behavioural repertoire of language users.

Hacker concludes that neurophysiologists and biological scientists are muddled, conceptually confused, etc. (1987, p. 500, *et passim*).

This sort of objection would of course silence just about the whole of behavioural/ brain science.

2.6.2 Agreed, but still . . .

The objection presented above is based on something correct, and endorsed in the essay, namely the broadly Wittgensteinian view that meaning is grounded in social practices, embedded in culture. But, as against Hacker's line of argument, we propose that this view of meaning can be combined with the information-processing paradigm, and in particular with the claim that meaning is encoded in the brain. Indeed we have to stress here that the encoding thesis *has been explicated and defended* by appeal to the broadly Wittgensteinian view of meaning just referred to.

Throughout this chapter we have steered away from the idea that there are signs (signs with syntactic structure) in the brain doing the representing, as it were, all on their own. This strong formulation of the encoding thesis is in fact what provokes the various objections to the thesis, which has therefore to be rescued from it. The strong formulation of the encoding thesis runs into trouble because it is incompatible with connectionist models (section 2.2), because it tries to reduce (neural) semantics to (neural) syntax (section 2.3), and because it fails to explain why (neural) semantic properties rather than syntactic properties do any work in the causal explanation of behaviour (Section 2.4). At each stage of the defence of the encoding thesis we have had to restrain the presumption that meaning, specifically meaning encoded in the brain, is essentially a matter of syntactic, language-like, structures, and to substitute the view that meaning essentially pertains to rule-guided activity, or again, of intentional agent/environment interactions.

The route we have taken to the notion of neural encoding has several steps. The first step, argued for throughout Chapter 1, is that explanation of action in terms of meaningful states has predictive power; the second is the conclusion of that chapter, that such explanation is causal; the third is the assumption taken for granted in this chapter that the brain causally regulates action, all of which can be made compatible on the methodological assumption that the meaning (information) that regulates action is encoded in the brain. This route to the encoding thesis does not end at 'sentences in the head', but with the proposal that the brain encodes meaning *somehow or other*. This proposal is of course much weaker empirically, but this is appropriate enough given its philosophical, conceptual origins. But in return for (appropriate) empirical vagueness, it makes the strong a priori claim that an adequacy condition of any theory of encoding is that the critical connection between meaning and the regulation of action is not lost. The strong interpretation of encoding, which posits signs with syntactic structure in the brain doing the representing, inevitably neglects this connection between meaning and action, and indeed runs the risk of neglecting meaning (in favour of syntax) altogether.

Thus we have, through sections 2.2–2.4 of this chapter, proposed a notion of meaning *and of encoded meaning* as being essentially involved with activity. This same idea was, of course, used again to protect the encoding thesis in Section 2.5, in considering whether meaning supervenes on brain states.

In brief, then, the claim that the brain encodes meaning, as defended and explicated here, far from being incompatible with the kind of view of meaning proposed by Wittgenstein, actually presupposes it.

Rule-following activity, activity which can be performed 'rightly' or 'wrongly', is what warrants the attribution of meaning to the agent, or to the brain, which as a matter of fact is the material system most of all involved in the regulation of action. To take a relatively simple case, we attribute to a rat, and in particular to the rat's brain, information about the maze, on the grounds that the animal relates to the maze in an ordered, methodical, goal-directed way. In the indefinitely more complicated case of human beings, actions have many and various meanings, and these include (perceived) relationships to realities defined by theories embedded deep in the culture. As remarked at the end of the previous section, in order to understand the actions of such as a physicist, or tribal magician, we have to understand their theories about reality and their relation to it, for these theories guide what the people do. In brief, action is regulated here by meaning as much as in the much simpler cases, and there is as much reason to invoke meanings encoded in the brain.

But of course in this context it is clear, as stressed throughout the chapter, that it is not the brain in isolation which carries meaning, but the brain in its role as regulating action. If the brain is described in intrinsic, non-relational, non-intentional terms, in terms of physical or physico-chemical processes, without reference to information-processing, then all that can explained and predicted is intrinsic, non-relational, non-intentional behaviour: the motion of the body, not the meaning of the act, which depends on nature and culture. If one is to explain and predict behaviour in relation to these realities, then the regulating neural processes have to be credited with information relating to them.

Before leaving the current objection to the idea of encoding, presented in the preceding subsection, one further point should be remarked, concerning the attribution of intentionality to parts as opposed to the whole.

While folk psychology in general attributes meaningful states to the person, cognitive psychology need not be so restricted. The concept of encoded meaning does not have to be based in the activity of the whole person, but can be based in the interaction between functional subsystems and their local environments. If an information-processing system is described as encoding information, this description is based on interaction between the system and whatever it is that the encoded information is about. This 'environment' may be the scene of action of the person as a whole, in which case the proper subject of the ascription of information is the person as a whole, and is to subpersonal systems only secondarily. The belief that this is the bus to Clapham, for example, belongs to the person, and only thereby to a subpersonal system, in particular to the brain. But the 'environment' may be less than the scene of action of the person as a whole, in which case the proper subject of the ascription is some subpersonal system, and is to the person only secondarily. To cite examples that will be discussed later, in Chapter 5, it is in this sense the retina that encodes information about light intensities (and only thereby the person); or again, it is the baroreceptors of the cardiovascular system (and probably not the person at all) that pick up information about blood pressure. And so on.

The idea that meaning belongs to the person as a whole, participating in cultural practices, and not to the brain, is linked to the 'hermeneutic' separation of meaning from anything familiar in the sciences, as if there were nothing like it lower down, in the phylogenetic scale for example, or in biological subsytems. This hermeneutic idea is the alternative to the approach being adopted and explored in this essay, which emphasizes continuities rather than dichotomies. In the present context the claim is that some meaning, and certainly some information, can be attributed to something less than the whole.

2.7 SUMMARY

The main claim of the first chapter was that explanations of action in terms of meaningful mental states are effective in prediction, and the inference was drawn that such explanations are causal. The main burden of the present chapter has been to reconcile this conclusion with the material causation of behaviour by the brain.

In Section 2.1 we saw that mind–brain identity theory promises a quick reconciliation, but it runs against several obstacles, chief of which in the present context is that mental states have intentionality while brain states arguably do not. It was suggested, on the other hand, that brain processes can be legitimately regarded as carrying (encoding) information, and indeed are so regarded at the interface between cognitive psychology and neuroscience, particularly for the purpose of explaining the role of the brain in regulating action. Subsequent sections were devoted to explication of this idea that brain states encode information, or meaning, and in particular to defending it from various lines of thought much discussed in the current literature.

In Section 2.2 we considered Fodor's language of thought hypothesis, according to which there are sentence-like structures in the brain, which serve both to encode meaning and to regulate (cause) behaviour. However, as noted in subsection 2.2.2, this particularly literal reading of the encoding thesis is apparently incompatible with connectionist models of cognitive function and its implementation in the brain. In these models, there are, at least at a micro-level of analysis, no physical (hardware) counterparts to meaningful symbols, or sentences. The relation between connectionist models of cognitive function and those of traditional, symbolic AI, the ones conducive to the language of thought hypothesis, is complex. The philosophical assumption relevant here is that, if attribution of meaningful mental states is valid, in particular if it affords causal explanations of action, then such attributions must pick out corresponding states in the brain. This assumption can be combined with affirmation of its antecedent in order to derive its consequent, in the (sophisticated) form of the language of thought hypothesis. Alternatively, the assumption can be combined with denial of its consequent (on connectionist grounds), leading to denial of its antecedent, to the 'elimination' of folk psychology. Either way the assumption is problematic, and reasons for rejecting it were presented in Section 2.2.3. Psychological descriptions attribute meaningful states to the brain, or better, to the person as agent. However, they are based on (high-level) regularities in organism–environment interactions, and it is on this basis that they predict such interactions well (enough). There is no reason to suppose that in accomplishing this task, psychological descriptions also have to pick out neural structures that correspond to them. The assumption that folk psychology seeks to define the neural structures that serve information-processing and action, still more that this is its primary aspiration, is based on a misconception of the logic of psychological description, and hence of its ontological commitments.

The upshot of these considerations is that the brain can be said to encode meaning, or information, though not because there is a one–one correspondence between meaningful states and neural states. The language of meaning and of encoded meaning is based in organism–environment interactions, and can be applied to the brain only in so far as the brain serves in the regulation of those interactions. The main claim of the chapter—that meaningful mental causation can be reconciled with neural causation by appeal to the idea that the brain encodes meaning—can thus be preserved, though with these qualifications.

We turned next to related issues in AI theory, concerning the relation between syntax and semantics. In Section 2.3 we considered Searle's well-known 'Chinese room argument' against the conflation of semantics with syntax: symbol-manipulation is not enough for intentionality. As to what is, we invoke again the claim, as throughout the essay, that intentionality is grounded in activity. Made in terms of semantics and syntax, the point would be that the 'symbols' that carry meaning must be essentially involved in the mediation of sensorimotor pathways.

The considerations in the next two sections, 2.4. and 2.5, have to do particularly with the idea that meaning encoded in the brain plays a causal role. This claim about causality is, as indicated in the first section, the main rationale of the encoding thesis. In Section 2.4 we consider a line of argument pervasive in the literature, the main thrust of which is that it would have to be neural syntax that causes behaviour, not the alleged neural semantics, because only the former is local to the effects. Semantic properties, so the argument runs, are about distal features and therefore cannot be causes. Our reply is that locally defined neural causes will have locally defined effects, namely motor behaviour which is not about the environment. By contrast, causal explanation of intentional behaviour has to cite intentional causes, causes that are about what the behaviour is about. Such causes are identified in non-local terms, though they are local to the behaviour that they regulate. This combination of intentional features with local realization is, of course, precisely the point of the thesis that meaning (information) is encoded in the brain.

We turned in Section 2.5 to a distinct though related argument which would refute the main proposal, an extremely influential argument based on Putnam's so-called twin-Earth thought-experiments. It leads to the conclusion that 'meanings ain't in the head', and hence (among other things) are not causes of behaviour. The argument, presented in some detail in subsections 2.5.2 and 2.5.3, seeks to establish the claim that mental states as individuated by meaningful content can (be imagined to) vary while brain states remain the same, this variation being due to variation in the represented states of affairs. This claim has been accepted by most commentators, leading either to the more or less reluctant dismissal of folk psychological meaning as being irrelevant to causal explanation, or else to the problematic attempt to define a 'narrow' as opposed to a 'broad' content. Putnam's argument was criticized in the remainder of the section. The standard reading of the twin-Earth thought-experiments, the one that supports the conclusion that meanings 'ain't in the head', posits differences in mental contents which are not reflected in behavioural differences, in particular, not in discriminative behaviours. This dissociation between mental content and behavioural criteria, whatever can be said for it on other grounds, is at odds with what is required in the context of a cognitive-behavioural science. In this context, the postulate of meaningful states serves the purpose of explaining and predicting action, in particular discriminative behaviour, and is otherwise unjustified. The implication is that meaningful content is to be defined essentially in terms of organism–environment interactions. Given this kind of definition of content, several features of folk psychological meaning which are problematic or incompatible according to the standard reading of the *doppelgänger* thought-experiments appear as valid. Folk psychological meaning, intentionality in general, is and should be all of the following: 'world-involving', supervenient on neural states which regulate action, and invoked in the causal explanation of action.

We considered in Section 2.6 a Wittgensteinian kind of objection to the encoding thesis. The objection emphasizes the basis of meaning in human practices and culture, and resists the idea that meaning is 'in the brain'. The underlying point is accepted, and indeed has been emphasized throughout the chapter to rescue the encoding thesis from the various objections to it. However, the language of encoding, appropriately understood, remains valid in this context. Meaningful psychological 'states' are manifested in action. It is possible to describe these states as being encoded in the brain, but this description presupposes that the brain is functioning within the person, and that the person is acting in the environment. In this sense, the subject of psychological states is primarily the person (as agent). Nevertheless it is possible and legitimate to say that the brain encodes these meaningful states: this is the way in which brain function has to be described when the task is to explain how it regulates action.

The main claim of the present chapter, that meaningful mental causation is compatible with neural causation, is thus defended against various lines of alleged refutation. Attempts to invalidate the notion of causation by meaningful mental states in effect assume that such states are either too tied to the subject or too tied to the object, with interaction between the two being ignored in both cases. The assumption has been that meaningful states have to be found in the brain (in neural syntax), independently of action, or else defined by what is outside the brain, or person, again independent of action. The replies to the objections, in Sections 2.2–2.5, were all variations on the theme that meaning (intentionality) has to do essentially with action, that is, with higher-order invariants in organism–environment interactions. For in this case there is no need to find symbolic syntax in the brain divorced from the regulation of action, and nor can meaning be defined in terms of reality independent of the sensitivity of the representing being.

The claim that attribution of mental states with meaningful content is based on, and is concerned with, regularities in organism–environment interactions hangs together with the point, made in the first chapter, that such attribution serves to predict action. This theory-driven predictive power apparently makes unavoidable the conclusion that explanations that invoke meaningful mental states are in some sense causal, and it lies at the basis of replies to all arguments to the contrary. The conclusion stands, but we have so far said little about 'in what sense'! Consideration of this major issue will occupy us in chapters 4 and 5. In the next chapter we turn to an issue that has been pressing more or less strongly in the discussions so far, namely relativity and the problem of objectivity.

NOTES

1. These issues to be addressed in this chapter, along with many ramifications neglected here, are the subjects of a large and expanding literature. Selective references will be made as we proceed. Useful collections of papers covering many of the issues to be raised include Silvers (1989), Tomberlin (1989, 1990),

Cole *et al.* (1990), Lycan (1990), Loewer and Rey (1991), and Heil and Mele (1993).

2. Davidson has emphasized the holistic and normative characteristics of mental state ascriptions, in support of his doctrine of 'anomalous monism' (Davidson 1980, Essays 11–13). Commentary includes Vermazen and Hintikka (1985), Antony (1989), Evnine (1991), Bickle (1992), and Malpas (1992). The irreducibility of the mental to the physical, and the problems of reducibility to the physical in general, are the subjects of a large literature: recent papers and collections include Crane (1990), Lennon (1990), Montogomery (1990), Charles and Lennon (1992), and Robinson (1993).

3. On points in this paragraph see, for example, Block (1980*b*) and other papers in Block (1980*a*), Part Three. A recent discussion of multiple realization is given by Kim (1992).

4. AI is a mathematical and experimental discipline of great complexity, and is beyond the concerns as well as the competence of the present essay, except to the limited extent indicated in the text. The literature in and surrounding AI is extensive and rapidly expanding. A useful sourcebook is Partridge and Wilks (1990). On AI applications to cognitive psychology see, for example, Boden (1988, 1989), Johnson-Laird (1993), and Broadbent (1993). Collections of papers on philosophical issues in AI theory include Graubard (1988), Boden (1990), and Cummins and Pollock (1991). Further references will be made to selected topics below.

5. Detailed consideration of connectionism is beyond the scope of this essay. Source material and material on applications in neurobiology and psychology include McClelland *et al.* (1986), Rumelhart *et al.* (1986), Boden (1988, 1989), Morris (1989), Arbib and Robinson (1990), Hanson and Olsen (1990), Bechtel and Abrahamsen (1991), Hinton (1991), Quinlan (1991), Davis (1992), Nadel *et al.* (1992), Broadbent (1993), and Johnson-Laird (1993). Discussion of connectionism and its philosophical implications may be found in Churchland (1986), Graubard (1988), Clark (1989), Bechtel (1990), Boden (1990), Cummins and Pollock (1991), Ramsey *et al.* (1991), and Churchland and Sejnowski (1992).

   The main point at issue in the present context is the very general one that in connectionist models there are no, or no clear, counterparts to (meaningful) symbols. This fact can be developed into an argument against Fodor's Language of Thought hypothesis particularly, and generally against the idea that folk psychological meaning has anything corresponding to it in the brain, and hence, anything corresponding to it at all. This line of thought and replies to it are the subject of the remainder of this section.

6. On the possible relations between the two kinds of model see, for example, Fodor and Pylyshyn (1988), Russell (1988), Smolensky (1988), Clark (1989, 1989–90, 1990), Hawthorne (1989), and Bechtel (1990). Power and Brewin (1991) discuss the issues particularly from the perspective of clinical psychology.

7. For another formulation see, for example, Jacob (1992). Generally this line of thought pervades the literature around Putnam's claim that 'meaning ain't in the head', to be considered in the next section.

8. See Wittgenstein (1921), for example 2.01–2.04, 2.1–2.2. Secondary sources include, for example, Folgelin (1976), Bolton (1979), and Pears (1987).

9. Recent critical commentaries on the issues around Putnam's claim include McGinn (1989) and Bilgrami (1992). Selected further references relevant to points discussed in the text will be cited as we proceed. It is fair to say that the twin-Earth thought-experiments, sketched after this introductory subsection, represent a peculiarly philosophical methodology, not user over-friendly to non-philosophers. This introductory subsection links the issues to the rest of the chapter, and some main points are summarized at the end of the chapter. Perhaps the best known application to theoretical psychology is Fodor's 'methodological solipsism' (1980), which will be discussed in the fourth chapter (subsection 4.4.2). The crucial point for the present essay is that the twin-Earth thought-experiments have been widely accepted in the philosophical community as showing that meaningful mental states do not supervene on brain states and hence cannot be causes of behaviour. Any proposal that there is causality here has to find a way around or through this standard reading of the thought-experiments, and this is the main aim of the current section.

10. This brief formulation of supervenience is Fodor's (1987, p. 30), and suffices in the present context. There are alternative, related definitions; see, for example, Stich (1983), Kim (1984), and Lennon (1990). The notion of supervenience of the mental on the physical has been invoked to accomodate anti-reductionist considerations of the kind cited in subsection 2.1.3, and to save some plausibility for physicalism (see, for example, Von Kutschera 1992; Poland 1994). Our interest in this section is the supervenience of mental content and specifically the causal role of content.

11. Putnam's original argument had a form which may be summarized as follows. Consider two plausible assumptions: first, that knowing the meaning of a term is just a matter of being in a certain psychological (dispositional) state, and secondly, that the meaning (intension) of a term determines its extension. From these it follows that the psychological state that consitutes knowing the meaning of a term determines the extension of the term. But this is the claim that the thought-experiments show to be false, demonstrating the possibility, in the case of using words, of the same psychological (subjective, mind/brain) state, but different extension. In brief, in the sense of meaning which determines extension, meaning ain't in the head (Putnam 1975, especially pp. 215–27). This line of thought was turned into a problem for the cognitive science explanatory paradigm, which invokes cognitive states as having a causal role dependent on their meaning, by Fodor (1982). This problem is our main concern and will be considered in the next subsection.

12. Dale (1990) also criticizes Stich's attempt to run the causal story with only syntax and no semantics. The general problem for the narrow content theorist of describing either content or behaviour in a useful, or indeed in any, way is well-stated by Owens (1987). A later version of narrow content theory which avoids this sort of criticism has been proposed by Fodor (1987, 1991) and will be discussed in the next subsection.

13. The contrast drawn in this subsection between behavioural criteria of mental

content and the one presupposed in the standard reading of the *doppelgänger* thought-experiments was anticipated in Chapter 1 in connection with self-knowledge and error (subsection 1.4.3, Note 16).

The connected proposal that the mental content regulating behaviour is defined in terms of interactions is approached by another route, by way of causal to functional semantics, in Chapter 4. This proposal has some connections with Dennett's notion of the 'notional world' of the organism/agent in his complex discussion in 'Beyond belief' (Dennett 1982).

14. This statement and defence of the supervenience thesis ignores the issue of demonstrative terms, such as 'this' and 'that'. It is likely that demonstratives play a critical role is specifying mental content for the purpose of explaining action (Peacocke 1981). But this specification by reference to something external is not incompatible with supervenience, as least so far as the *doppelgänger* thought-experiments are concerned. It is true that my replica cannot see, think of, or touch *this* (very same) keyboard. But by the same token, he does not have this (very same) brain. In these cases, in the sense in which *doppelgänger* have different mental contents they have different brains as well, and there is nothing of interest here about supervenience (encoding, causality, etc.).

15. See also Hamlyn (1990) for distinct though related criticisms of the information-processing cognitive science paradigm from a broadly Wittgensteinian perspective, and compare also Mendonca (1988).

REFERENCES

Adams, F. (1993a). Fodor's modal argument. *Philosophical Psychology*, 6, 41–56.
Adams, F. (1993b). Reply to Russow. *Philosophical Psychology*, 6, 63–5.
Antony, L. (1989). Anomalous monism and the problem of explanatory force. *Philosophical Review*, 98, 153–87.
Arbib, M. A. and Robinson, J. A. (ed.) (1990). *Natural and artificial parallel computation*. MIT Press, Cambridge, Mass.
Bechtel, W. (1990). Connectionism and the philosophy of mind: an overview. In *Mind and cognition: A reader*, (ed. W. G. Lycan), pp. 252–73. Blackwell, Oxford.
Bechtel, W. and Abrahamsen, A. (1991). *Connectionism and the mind: an introduction to parallel processing in networks*. Blackwell, Oxford.
Bickle, J. (1992). Mental anomaly and the new mind–brain reductionism. *Philosophy of Science*, 59, 217–30.
Bilgrami, A. (1992). *Belief and meaning: the unity and locality of mental content*. Blackwell, Oxford.
Block, N. (ed.) (1980a). *Readings in philosophy of psychology*, Vol. I. Methuen, London.
Block, N. (1980b). Introduction: what is functionalism? In *Readings in philosophy of psychology*, (ed. N. Block), Vol. I, pp. 171–84. Methuen, London.
Block, N. (1991). What narrow content is not. In *Meaning in mind: Fodor and his critics*, (ed. B. Loewer and G. Rey), pp. 33–64. Blackwell, Oxford.

Boden, M. (1988). *Computer models of mind*. Cambridge University Press, Cambridge.

Boden, M. A. (ed.) (1989). *Artificial intelligence in psychology: interdisciplinary essays*. MIT Press, Cambridge, Mass.

Boden, M. (ed.) (1990). *The philosophy of artificial intelligence*. Oxford University Press, Oxford.

Bolton, D. (1979). *An approach to Wittgenstein's philosophy*. Macmillan, London.

Bolton, D. (1982). Life-form and idealism. In *Idealism, past and present*, (ed. G. Vesey), pp. 269–84. Cambridge University Press, Cambridge.

Boyd, R. (1980). Materialism without reductionism: what physicalism does not entail. In *Readings in philosophy of psychology*, (ed. N. Block), Vol. I, pp. 67–106. Methuen, London.

Broadbent, D. (ed.) (1993). *The simulation of human intelligence*. Blackwell, Oxford.

Brodal, P. (1991). *The central nervous system: structure and function*. Oxford University Press, Oxford.

Burge, T. (1979). Individualism and the mental. *Midwest Studies in Philosophy*, **IV**, 73–121.

Burge, T. (1982*a*). Two thought experiments reviewed. *Notre Dame Journal of Formal Logic*, **23**, 284–93.

Burge, T. (1982*b*). Other bodies. In *Thought and object*, (ed. A. Woodfield), pp. 97–120. Clarendon Press, Oxford.

Burge, T. (1986*a*). Cartesian error and the objectivity of perception. In *Subject, thought and context*, (ed. C. Pettit, and J. McDowell), pp. 117–36. Oxford University Press, Oxford.

Burge, T. (1986*b*). Intellectual norms and foundations of mind. *Journal of Philosophy*, **83**, 697–720.

Burge, T. (1986*c*). Individualism and psychology. *Philosophical Review*, **95**, 3–45.

Burge, T. (1989). Individuation and causation in psychology. *Pacific Philosophical Quarterly*, **70**, 303–22.

Charles, D. and Lennon, K. (ed.) (1992). *Reduction, explanation, and realism*. Clarendon Press, Oxford.

Churchland, P. M. (1989). *A neurocomputational perspective. The nature of mind and the structure of science*. MIT Press, Cambridge, Mass.

Churchland, P. S. (1986). *Neurophilosophy: towards a unified science of the mind–brain*. MIT Press, Cambridge, Mass.

Churchland, P. S. and Sejnowski, T. J. (1992). *The computational brain*. MIT Press, Cambridge, Mass.

Clark, A. (1988). Critical Notice of Fodor's *Psychosemantics*. *Mind*, **97**, 605–17.

Clark, A. (1989). *Microcognition: philosophy, cognitive science and parallel distributed processing*. MIT Press, Cambridge, Mass.

Clark, A. (1989–90). Connectionist minds. *Proceedings of the Aristolelian Society*, **90**, 83–102.

Clark, A. (1990). Connectionism, competence, and explanation. In *The philosophy of artificial intelligence*, (ed. M. Boden), pp. 281–308. Oxford University Press, Oxford.

Cole D., Fetzer, J. and Rankin, T. (ed.) (1990). *Philosophy, mind, and cognitive enquiry*. Kluwer, Dordrecht.

Crane, T. (1990). There is no question of physicalism. *Mind*, 99, 185–206.

Crane, T. (1991). All the difference in the world. *Philosophical Quarterly*, 41, 1–25.

Cummins, R. and Pollock, J. (1991). *Philosophy and AI: essays at the interface*. MIT Press, Cambridge, Mass.

Dale, J. (1990). Intentionality and Stich's theory of brain sentence syntax. *Philosophical Quarterly*, 40, 169–82.

Davidson, D. (1980). *Essays on actions and events*. Clarendon Press, Oxford.

Davidson, D. (1989). What is present to the mind. In *The mind of Donald Davidson*, (ed. J. Brandl and W. L. Gombocz), pp. 3–18. Rodopi, Amsterdam.

Davis, S. (ed.) (1992). *Connectionism: theory and practice*. Oxford University Press, Oxford.

Dennett, D. (1982). Beyond Belief. In *Thought and object*, (ed. A. Woodfield), pp. 1–95. Clarendon Press, Oxford. (Reprinted with an addition in Dennett, D. (1987). *The intentional stance*, pp. 117–211. MIT Press, Cambridge, Mass.)

Dretske, F. (1988). *Explaining behaviour: reasons in a world of causes*. MIT Press, Cambridge, Mass.

Evnine, S. (1991). *Donald Davidson*. Polity Press, Cambridge.

Fodor, J. (1975). *The language of thought*. Crowell, New York.

Fodor, J. (1980). Methodological solipsism considered as a research strategy in cognitive psychology. With peer commentary. *The Behavioural and Brain Sciences*, 3, 63–109.

Fodor, J. (1982). Cognitive science and the twin-Earth problem. *Notre Dame Journal of Formal Logic*, 23, 116–17.

Fodor, J. (1987). *Psychosemantics*. MIT Press, Cambridge, Mass.

Fodor, J. (1991). A modal argument for narrow content. *Journal of Philosophy*, 87, 5–26.

Fodor, J. and Pylyshyn, Z. (1988). Connectionism and cognitive architecture. *Cognition*, 28, 3–71.

Folgelin, R. (1976). *Wittgenstein*. Routledge and Kegan Paul, London.

Francescotti, R. (1991). Externalism and Marr's theory of vision. *British Journal for the Philosophy of Science*, 42, 227–38.

Graubard, S. R. (ed.) (1988). *The artificial intelligence debate: false starts, real foundations*. MIT Press, Cambridge, Mass.

Gray, J. A. (1987). Mind–brain identity as a scientific hypothesis: a second look. In *Mindwaves. Thoughts on intelligence, identity and consciousness*, (ed. C. Blakemore and S. Greenfield), pp. 461–83. Blackwell, Oxford.

Hacker, P. (1987). Languages, minds and brain. In *Mindwaves. Thoughts on intelligence, identity and consciousness*, (ed. C. Blakemore and S. Greenfield, pp. 485–505. Blackwell, Oxford.

Hamlyn, D. W. (1990). *In and out of the black box*. Blackwell, Oxford.

Hanson, S. J. and Olsen, C. L. (1990). *Connectionist modeling and brain function: the developing interface*. MIT Press, Cambridge, Mass.

Harnad, S. (1989). Minds, machines and Searle. *Journal of Experimental and Theoretical Artificial Intelligence*, 1, 5–25.

Harnad, S. (1990). The symbol grounding problem. *Physica*, D 42, 335–46.

Hawthorne, J. (1989). On the compatibility of connectionist and classical models. *Philosophical Psychology*, 2, 5–16.

Heil, J. and Mele, A. (ed.) (1993). *Mental causation*. Clarendon Press, Oxford.

Hinton, G. E. (ed.) (1991). *Connectionist symbol processing*. MIT Press, Cambridge, Mass.

Hornsby, J. (1986). Physicalist thinking and conceptions of behaviour. In *Subject, thought and context*, (ed. P. Pettit and J. McDowell), pp. 95–115. Clarendon, Oxford.

Jackson, F. and Pettit, P. (1988). Functionalism and broad content. *Mind*, 97, 381–400.

Jacob, P. (1992). Externalism and mental causation. *Proceedings of the Aristotelian Society*, 92, 203–19.

Johnson-Laird, P. (1993). *The computer and the mind: an introduction to cognitive science*, (2nd edn revised). Fontana, London.

Kim, J. (1984). Concepts of supervenience. *Philosophy and Phenomenological Research*, 65, 153–76.

Kim, J. (1991). Dretske on how reasons explain behavior. In *Dretske and his critics*, (ed. B. McLaughlin), pp. 52–72. Blackwell, Oxford.

Kim, J. (1992). Multiple realization and the metaphysics of reduction. *Philosophy and Phenomenological Research*, 52, 1–26.

Lennon, K. (1990). *Explaining human action*. Duckworth, London.

Loewer, B. and Rey, G. (ed.) (1991). *Meaning in mind: Fodor and his critics*. Blackwell, Oxford.

Lycan, W. G. (ed.) (1990). *Mind and cognition. A reader*. Blackwell, Oxford.

McClelland, J. L., Rumelhart, D. E. and the PDP Research Group (1986). *Parallel distributed processing: explorations in the microstructure of cognition* Vol. 2. *Psychological and biological models*. MIT Press, Cambridge Mass.

McGinn, C. (1982). The structure of content, In *Thought and object*, (ed. A. Woodfield), pp. 207–58. Clarendon Press, Oxford.

McGinn, C. (1989). *Mental content*. Blackwell, Oxford.

McGinn, C. (1991). Conceptual causation: some elementary reflections. *Mind*, 100, 573–86.

McLaughlin, B. (ed.) (1991). *Dretske and his critics*. Blackwell, Oxford.

Maloney, J. C. (1990). *The mundane matter of the mental language*. Cambridge University Press, Cambridge.

Malpas, J. E. (1992). *Donald Davidson and the mirror of meaning: holism, truth, interpretation*. Cambridge University Press, Cambridge.

Manfredi, P. (1993). Two routes to narrow content: both dead ends. *Philosophical Psychology*, 6, 3–21.

Mendonca, W. P. (1988). Brain and mind: on the sequences of conceptual confusion in cognitive psychology. *Epistemologia*, 11, 29–54.

Montgomery, R. (1990). The reductionist ideal in cognitive psychology. *Synthese*, 85, 279–314.

Morris, R. G. M. (ed.) (1989). *Parallel distributed processing: implications for psychology and neurobiology*. Clarendon Press, Oxford.

Nadel, L. N., Cooper, L. A., Culicover, P. and Harnish, R. M. (ed.) (1992). *Neural connections, mental computations*. MIT Press, Cambridge, Mass.

Newell, A. (1980). Physical symbol systems. *Cognitive Science*, 4, 135–83.

Newton, N. (1988). Machine understanding and the Chinese room. *Philosophical Psychology*, **1**, 207–16.

Owens, (1987). In defense of a different doppelganger *Philosophical Review*, **96**, 521–54.

Partridge, D. and Wilks, Y. (ed.) (1990). *The foundations of artificial intelligence: a sourcebook*. Cambridge University Press, Cambridge.

Peacocke, C. (1981). Demonstrative thought and psychological explanation. *Synthese*, **XLIX**, 187–217.

Pears, D. (1987). *The false prison: A study of the development of Wittgenstein's philosophy*, vol. 1. Clarendon Press, Oxford.

Piaget, J. (1950). *The child's construction of reality*. Routledge and Kegan Paul, London.

Poland, J. (1994). *Physicalism. The philosophical foundations*. Clarendon Press, Oxford.

Power, M. and Brewin, C. (1991). From Freud to cognitive science: a contemporary account of the unconscious. *British Journal of Clinical Psychology*, **30**, 289–310.

Putnam, H. (1975). The meaning of 'meaning'. In *Mind, language and reality*, pp. 215–71. Cambridge University Press, Cambridge.

Pylyshyn, Z. W. (1980). Computation and cognition: issues in the foundations of cognitive science, with peer commentary, *Behavioral and Brain Sciences*, **3**, 111–69.

Pylyshyn, Z. W. (1984). *Computation and cognition*. MIT Press, Cambridge Mass.

Quinlan, P. (1991). *Connectionism and psychology*. Harvester, New York.

Ramsey, W., Stich, S., and Garan, J. (1990). Connectionism, eliminativism and the future of folk psychology. In *Philosophy, mind, and cognitive enquiry*, (ed. D. Cole, J. Fetzer, and T. Rankin) pp. 117–44. Kluwer, Dordrecht.

Ramsey, W., Stich, S. and Rumelhart, D. (ed.) (1991). *Philosophy and connectionist theory*. Lawrence Erlbaum Associates, Hillsdale, N. J.

Rey, G. (1986). What's really going on in Searle's 'Chinese Room'? *Philosophical Studies*, **50**, 169–85.

Robinson, H. (ed.) (1993). *Objections to physicalism*. Clarendon Press, Oxford.

Rowlands, M. (1989). Discussion of Jackson & Pettit. *Mind*, **98**, 269–76.

Rumelhart, D. E., McClelland, J. L. and the PDP Research Group (1986). *Parallel distributed processing: explorations in the microstructure of cognition*, Vol. 1. *Foundations*. MIT Press, Cambridge, Mass.

Russell, J. (1988). Cognisance and cognitive science. Part one: the generality constraint. *Philosophical Psychology*, **1**, 235–58.

Russow, L. (1984). Unlocking the Chinese room. *Nature and System*, **6**, 221–7.

Russow, L. (1993). Fodor, Adams, and causal properties. *Philosophical Psychology*, **6**, 57–62

Searle, J. (1980). Minds, brains and programs. With peer commentary. *Behavioral and Brain Sciences*, **3**, 417–57.

Searle, J. (1982). The Chinese room revisited. *Behavioral and Brain Sciences*, **5**, 345–8.

Searle, J. (1984). *Minds, brains and science*. BBC Publications, London.

Searle, J. (1987). Minds and brains without programs. In *Mindwaves. Thoughts on intelligence, identity and consciousness*, (ed. C. Blakemore and S. Greenfield), pp. 209–33. Blackwell, Oxford.

Silvers, S. (ed.) (1989). *Rerepresentation. Readings in the philosophy of mental representation*. Kluwer, Dordrecht.

Smolensky, P. (1988). On the proper treatment of connectionism, *Behavioral and Brain Sciences*, **11**, 1–74.

Stich, S. (1983). *From folk psychology to cognitive science*. MIT Press, Cambridge, Mass.

Tomberlin, J. E. (ed.) (1989). *Philosophical Perspectives, 3. Philosophy of Mind and Action Theory*. Ridgeview, Atascadero, CA.

Tomberlin, J. E. (ed.) (1990). *Philosophical Perspectives, 4. Action Theory and Philosophy of Mind*. Ridgeview, Atascadero, CA.

Vermazen, B. and Hintikka, M. (ed.) (1985). *Essays on Davidson: Actions and Events*. Clarendon, Oxford.

Von Kutschera, F. (1992). Supervenience and reductionism. *Erkenntnis*, **36**, 333–43.

Warmbrod, K. (1989). Beliefs and sentences in the head. *Synthese*, **79**, 201–30.

Wilson, R. (1992). Individualism, causal powers, and explanation. *Philosophical Studies*, **68**, 103–9.

Wittgenstein, L. (1921). *Tractatus logico-philosophicus*, (trans. D. F. Pears and B. F. McGuiness, 1961). Routledge and Kegan Paul, London.

Wittgenstein, L. (1953). *Philosophical investigations*, (ed. G. E. M. Anscombe and R. Rhees, trans. G. E. M. Anscombe). Blackwell, Oxford.

Wittgenstein, L. (1967). *Zettel*, (ed. G. E. M. Anscombe and G. H. von Wright, trans. G. E. M. Anscombe). Blackwell, Oxford.

Wittgenstein, L. (1969). *On certainty, (ed. G. E. M. Anscombe and G. H. von Wright, trans. D. Paul and G. E. M. Anscombe). Blackwell, Oxford.*

3
Relativity in knowledge of mind and meaning; and in knowledge generally

3.1 Introduction: intentionality is observer-relative
3.2 Theory of mind and empathy ('mental simulation')
    3.2.1 The empirical basis includes intentional behaviour
    3.2.2 Recognition of intentional behaviour involves empathy
    3.2.3 Empathy as thought-experiment, interwoven with theory
    3.2.4 Sources of error, and infallibility
    3.2.5 Empathic knowledge is originally subject-less
    3.2.6 Perspectives on psychological development
3.3 Rule-following
    3.3.1 The role of rules: order through time
    3.3.2 Rule-following as creation of order
    3.3.3 The role of agreement
    3.3.4 Relativity and the independent constraints on action
3.4 Relativity and reality in the natural and bio-psychological sciences
    3.4.1 Is what is relative really real?
    3.4.2 Relativity in physics, and on upwards, with increasing differentiation
    3.4.3 Reliability, validity, and the subject/object distinction
    3.4.4 Bio-psychological measures and realities
3.5 Summary

3.1 INTRODUCTION: INTENTIONALITY IS OBSERVER-RELATIVE

To a large extent philosophical preconceptions determine whether or not the theory of knowledge of mind is of scientific interest. In Cartesian theory knowledge of mind other than one's own is problematic, at best an inference from mindless, mechanical behaviour, with no possibility of checking its validity. Such an inference is also scientifically idle: it has no incremental explanatory/predictive value. This position shifts once non-Cartesian assumptions are brought to bear, specifically the assumption that mental states serve in the regulation of intentional activity. The behaviour that signifies mind is already mind-like, characterized by intentionality, and the regulation of action is more epistemically accessible than private, immaterial, parallel processes. In so far as knowledge of mind facilitates prediction of the behaviour of living beings, then it becomes of scientific interest, appearing not only in the methodology of the behavioural sciences, but also among the objects of study. There are developmental issues in the epistemology of mind, along the phylogenetic scale, studied in biology and ethology (Byrne and Whiten 1988; Whiten 1991), and along the ontogenetic scale, studied in developmental psychology (Astington *et al.* 1988; Whiten 1991). Clinical psychology also has an interest in knowledge of mind, specifically radical gaps and errors of various kinds (Fonagy 1991; Baron-Cohen *et al.* 1993; Hobson 1993; see also subsections 1.4.2, 1.4.3, and 8.2.2, pp. 311–12).

However, problematic aspects of knowledge of mind, particularly from the point of view of the sciences, do not disappear easily. It was remarked at the beginning of the previous chapter, in relation to dualism and mind–brain identity theory, that philosophical dichotomies generally are not resolved by dogmatic assertion of one side or the other. Rather, something like a compromise is required, the deeper aspect of which is deconstruction of the terms of the dichotomy. In the present case, the point is that resolution of the problem of knowledge of mind requires deep shifts in seventeenth-century assumptions concerning both knowledge and mind. The latter have already been indicated: mind has to be seen not as a Cartesian parallel process, but as involved in the regulation of intentional activity. Likewise, shifts have to made in traditional epistemological dichotomies, specifically between subjective knowledge (of mind), and objective knowledge (of matter). We shall be working towards a position in which this dichotomy (as a dichotomy) cannot be recognized at all.

Once dualism is abandoned, with the acknowledgement that mind is involved in meaningful behaviour, there is no longer space for a radical scepticism about mind. On the other hand, as noted already in the Preface and chapter 1 (subsection 1.3.8), there arises a different though related problem, concerning the objectivity of perceptions of intentionality. This lack of objectivity, compared with the objectivity in the natural sciences, was one ground of the turn-of-the-century distinction between meaningful and causal connections. Attribution of intentionality tends to be subjective and unreliable, and hence so far inadequate for the purpose of scientific explanation, as noted, for example, by Jaspers in relation to clinical intuition (1923, p. 2). The problem is at least that inter-observer reliability in perceptions of meaningful phenomena can be poor. The corollary is that their (objective) validity is no better. In other words, the appearance of subjectivity in the purported knowledge of the phenomena casts doubt on their objective reality.

In clinical psychology and psychiatry, debate of the problem of objectivity has focused largely on psychoanalytic theory, as has frequently been the case with other problems of meaning. Psychoanalytic theory has been accused of being able to find not only different but mutually incompatible meanings in the same set of phenomena, the implication being that attribution of meaning in the theory has no objective validity (see subsection 1.4.1). The problem of objectivity of meaning is, however, a general one, not confined to psychoanalysis.

A related point is that the problem is not especially about unconscious as opposed to conscious mental states. It is tempting to suppose that attribution of conscious mental states based on subjective self-report is relatively unproblematic, but this assumption is misconceived. It presupposes that subjective self-reports are infallible, and we have already noted in the first chapter (subsection 1.4.3) that this assumption is not generally valid. The problem of determining objective criteria for ascription of mental states cannot be solved just by appeal to what the subject is inclined to say.

Knowledge of mind, and of the intentional behaviour regulated by mental states, is not 'purely objective', like knowledge of the physical movements of bodies. Rather there is an element of subjectivity in our knowledge of mind, as recognized, though exaggerated, by the Cartesian theory. This subjectivity shows up as a variation in attributions of intentionality between observers: different people viewing the same activity may see different patterns of intentionality at work, including the vacuous case of seeing no such patterns. In brief, knowledge of intentionality involves *observer-relativity*. Inevitably this has been cited as among the main reasons why the notion of meaning should have no role in a mature cognitive science (for example, Stich 1983, p. 136; discussed in subsection 1.3.8). The nature and implications of this relativity need explication, and this is the main theme running through this chapter. We approach the problem in two main ways, both already marked out as critical in the first chapter, one concerning theory of mind, and the other rule-following.

Mental states can be 'known' in the sense that they are posits in a theory of behaviour. In other words the idea explored in various ways in the first chapter, that mental states are invoked in order to explain and predict behaviour, constitutes the core of an epistemology. We might expect clear objectivity here, as usually in scientific theories, specially when we think of cognitive learning theory (discussed in subsection 1.2.2). In contrast, perhaps, it is the folk psychological theory of mind, our day-to-day way of knowing the mental states of others (subsection 1.4.2), which shows relativity and subjectivity. There may be, however, something left out by the proposal that knowledge of mind is an exercise in theory, and we consider in the next section an alternative, or complementary, epistemology based in empathy. This theory of knowledge of mind has a long history, but has recently been revived in terms of so-called 'mental simulation'.

Our second approach to the epistemology of mind is via the question of what it means to follow a rule. We shall consider Wittgenstein's arguments to the effect that rule-following involves agreement, specifically participation in a form of life.

Both routes lead to similar conclusions, including that attributions of intentionality depend on the intentional states of the one making the attributions. This observer-relativity of these judgements calls into question their objective validity, as already remarked. The question whether intentional states have objective reality, and if so, of what kind, interacts strongly with issues of brain—mind identity, discussed in the previous chapter. But the discussion in this chapter will focus more on the epistemological problem of the observer-relativity of intentional state ascriptions. This problem will be considered with reference to the relativity involved in the move from the lower-level to the higher-level sciences, from physics through to psychology.

3.2 THEORY OF MIND AND EMPATHY ('MENTAL SIMULATION')

3.2.1 The empirical basis includes intentional behaviour

In the first chapter (subsection 1.2.2) we noted that cognitive psychology posits cognitive states in order to explain and predict goal-directed, flexible behaviour. We went on to remark, in subsection 1.2.5, that folk psychology can be plausibly regarded in a similar light, as being a quasi- or proto-scientific theory used to explain and anticipate behaviour. The behavioural phenomena constitute the empirical basis of cognitive psychological and folk psychological theory: they are evidence for ascription of mental states, and they are what is predicted from such ascriptions.

The empirical basis of any scientific theory should be defined as objectively as possible. This means at least that there should be high levels of agreement between observers as to the empirical facts. Further, it is plausible to require that the empirical basis be defined independently of the theoretical constructs used in its explanation. This may be seen as a special case of the first requirement: observers with competing theories of the phenomena should at least be able to agree on the nature of the evidence which could distinguish between them. In application to the case of cognitive-behavioural science, the fundamental requirement is that there should be high levels of agreement between observers as to what behaviour is being observed. Further, it is plausible to require that behavioural evidence should be definable without explicit or implicit reference to mental states. That is to say, behavioural description should be couched in non-intentional language. These two connected requirements are apparently met by behavioural descriptions of motor and speech acts. The proposal that mental state ascriptions are, or at least should be, for the purposes of cognitive-behavioural science, based on behavioural evidence of this kind constitutes a 'purely objective' epistemology of mind.

The proposal, however, has its problems. Behaviour to which mental state ascriptions are relevant already has intentionality: it cannot be described in non-intentional language (alone). The intentional stance generally explains and predicts behaviour under intentional description, as noted in subsection 1.3.6. This characteristic was discussed further in the second chapter (subsection 2.4.2, 2.5.6) in terms of the 'world-involving' nature of mental states and their role in the causal explanation of behaviour. It was argued that mental states are 'world-involving', defined by reference to (encoded) environmental features, precisely because behaviour itself is world-involving. The *explanandum* of cognitive-behavioural explanation is not isolated motor acts, but is rather interaction between the living being and its environment. Such interactions are patterns extended through time, the actual or attempted achievement of goals, plasticity of mean to ends, depending on circumstances, etc. The terms used to describe these patterns re-appear in specification of the mental (informational) content invoked to explain and predict them. The language is in both cases intentional: mental states are about the environment, but so is behaviour. The implication here is that non-intentional behaviour is inadequate as a basis for ascription of mental states. Or, put differently, the point is that it is only when behaviour is perceived as, or conceived as, intentional, that there is need to postulate regulation by mental states.

The behavioural evidence relevant to any theory of mind already has intentionality, or meaning. It may be anticipated that this bears directly on the issue of reliability of ascriptions of meaningful, mental states. Generally observers agree as to the occurrence or non-occurrence of motor acts, such as the lifting of an arm, or movement from one place to another. On the other hand, in the case of behavioural patterns extended through time and across varying circumstances, manifesting more or less apparent goals, and more or less apparent plasticity of means to ends, etc., it is less obvious that all observers will see the same. In so far as the behavioural evidence includes intentionality, agreement between observers becomes less certain; there is more scope for interpretation.

It can be said that attributions of intentionality involve subjectivity, and are thus not entirely objective. But note how this subjectivity arises. Primarily it arises out of *individual differences* between observers, of a sort that leads to variation in the results of observation. Individual differences are typically on a continuum rather than in dichotomous categories. The implication is that the contrast between 'subjective' and 'objective' ways of knowing is wrongly conceived as a dichotomy, but is rather a matter of degree.

Relativity in ascriptions of intentionality are apparent even in the case of predicting the behaviour of artificially intelligent systems. As generally in the discussion of mind and meaning, many critical points do not turn on the mind/matter distinction, nor on the animate/inanimate distinction, but rather on the distinction between behaviour that is and behaviour that is not functional, rule-guided, mediated by information, etc. Consider the example of the chess-playing computer, used already in the first chapter (subsection 1.3.5). In order to describe its moves in intentional terms we use observation by the senses no less than if we wish to describe just the movements of pieces from squares to squares. However, it is clear that something more is required for the use of intentional descriptions, namely, *knowledge of the game*. In the absence of such knowledge, descriptions and explanations from the intentional stance are unavailable. Someone who is ignorant of the game will be able to record the moves made, but not the logic behind them. In this case, attempts at prediction would remain at the purely 'behavioural' level, proceeding by induction from past observations, and typically this method would have little success, particularly as the game develops. Recognition of intentionality in sequences of moves, the attribution of strategy and the formulation of prediction on that basis, requires familiarity with the game, over and above the ability to see what (physical) movements are being made.

3.2.2 Recognition of intentional behaviour involves empathy

The question arises as to what is involved in knowledge of a game, or generally, any rule-guided, goal-directed activity. There are, broadly speaking, two kinds of answer, with a complicated and contentious relationship between them. One draws on the notion of *theory*. This epistemology has been the one assumed and endorsed through the essay so far. It is highly suited to cognitive science (subsection 1.2.2), belongs clearly with post-empiricist epistemology (subsections 1.4.1–2) and has generated much research in various areas of psychology (section 3.1). The core of this epistemology is that attribution of intentionality is driven by a theory that posits intentional states of various kinds and contents, and interactions among such states and between them and stimuli and activity. There is, however, a different kind of epistemology of intentionality, which has less to do with using theory.

In the case of chess-playing, especially when the game develops beyond a certain stage, into positions so far unencountered, the ability to perceive strategies apparently depends increasingly on the ability to play the game oneself. The recognition of intentionality in the other's moves draws on one's own inclinations to adopt this or that strategy at a given stage in the game. It can be seen here, in this simple case, that something like 'empathy' is involved in the attribution of intentional states. Consider now the more complicated, psychological case. A particular kind of cognitive-affective state has characteristic causes and characteristic expressions in behaviour. An observer who knows the emotion in his or her own case may recognize it in another, and thereby form expectations concerning the other's behaviour. In contrast, the observer who is unfamiliar with the emotion in herself will at best be able to record the other's behaviour, and not the emotion as cause (or reason): the various expressions of the emotion will pass unnoticed, or will appear as unconnected phenomena, without underlying psychological unity. Expressions of grief, for example, would be ignored, or attributed, say, to influenza, or to other stresses. In general, perception of intentional states and connections in the other person is facilitated by the perceiver's familiarity with such states and connections in his or her own case.

Theories of knowledge of mind in which a notion something like empathy plays a critical role have recently been proposed in the philosophical literature (Gordon 1986; Heal 1986; Ripstein 1987; Goldman 1989). This kind of epistemology was soon taken into developmental psychological theory (Harris 1989; and below, subsection 3.2.6) although it is yet to appear in scientific clinical psychology. The idea that the therapist uses himself or herself to understand (and anticipate) the patient is, of course, fundamental to psychoanalysis and its derivatives, but it can hardly be envisaged in the scientific paradigm of knowledge.

The recent formulations of the theory of empathy vary among themselves, and some explicitly use the term 'empathy' while others, particularly Gordon's (1986) relies more on the technical term 'mental simulation'. Interestingly, this epistemology has been generally understood as being an *alternative* to the proposal that knowledge of mind is an exercise in theory. For example, in introducing his version of the theory in a more recent paper Gordon characterizes it as follows (1992, p. 5):

> Human competence in predicting and explaining behavior depends chiefly on a capacity for mental simulation, particularly for decision-making within a pretend context. . . . The Simulation Theory competes with the so-called 'Theory' Theory, the view that a common-sense psychological theory, a 'folk psychology', underlies human competence in explaining and predicting behavior and implicitly defines our concepts of the various mental states.

In exploring the notion of empathy or mental simulation in what follows, however, we shall not be suggesting that there is here an alternative to the epistemology that invokes theory. We shall propose that the exercise of theory, emphasized in the first chapter, and the role of empathy, endorsed here, are not at all incompatible, but are, on the contrary, interwoven. This falls out as a clear consequence of interpreting empathy, or mental simulation, as belonging to the empirical basis of the theory of mind, specifically as a form of thought-experiment, an idea to which we turn next.[1]

3.2.3 Empathy as thought-experiment, interwoven with theory

The recognition of patterns of intentionality in behaviour is part of the empirical basis for the theory of mind. But information from observed cases alone has a number of limitations. It so far fails to apply to novel, unfamiliar circumstances, and it may not permit discrimination between causal and accidental associations.

Now it is well known in the case of knowledge of (inanimate) objects that experiment, that is, intervention into what is observed, is typically more powerful than simply observation of what happens to happen. Experimentation permits observations of phenomena which might, or would otherwise, not occur, and may, in particular, facilitate definition of necessary and sufficient causal conditions, using Mill's methods of agreement and difference. A by all means *very special* sort of experiment is the so-called 'thought-experiment', that is, manipulation of reality and observation of results, all in the imagination. While thought-experiments have limited, though interesting, application in relation to knowledge of (inanimate) objects, it can be said a priori that they are particularly suited to knowledge of subjects, to knowledge of, as it were, intentional objects. The reason is just that in this case, the subject of knowledge is also among the objects of knowledge, and information dependent on the nature of the subject alone also provides information about the objects of knowledge. Since thought-experiments can, in this special case, enhance information from cases observed in reality, and since thought-experiments are easier and faster to run than experiments in reality, there is a priori reason to suppose that they figure in the empirical basis of the theory of mind.

Suppose, then, that the task is to judge how someone is feeling or would be feeling in such-and-such circumstances, hence to anticipate what she is, or would be, inclined to do; or, that it is to make a judgement as to what emotional state is giving rise to such-and-such behaviour, hence again to anticipate what the person is likely to go on to do. A possible method is to run thought-experiments along the following lines: imagine, consciously or otherwise, the initial conditions in question, and the feelings, inclinations to behaviour, etc. to which they (in the imagination) give rise.

It is clear that thought-experiments, in so far as they are experiments, go hand in hand with theory. Empirical knowledge generally requires both theory and experience. Theory requires an empirical basis, which in the special case of the theory of mind, the suggestion is, includes the results of thought- or imagination-experiments. Of course such results, like those of any experiment, are of varying reliability and validity, depending on the accuracy of the surrounding theory. There is a complementary relationship here. On the one hand, experimental manipulation in the imagination of experiences, mental states, and behavioural tendencies provides information relevant to knowledge of mind. And on the other, (use of) this information is theory-dependent: thought- or imagination-experiments, as experiments, involve assumptions and interpretations.[2]

3.2.4 Sources of error, and infallibility

The fact that information from one's own case is like the result of an experiment, and involves theory, is connected with the fact that the method as a whole is fallible. Let us consider in more detail this issue of error, which here as always is fundamental to epistemology. At the same time we shall have to address the issue of *infallibility*, the necessary absence of error, which has a special role in the case of self-knowledge.

One source of error in attribution of intentionality to others, as with all empirical hypotheses, is insufficient evidence. But there are further interconnected possibilities of error created by use of information from one's own case: this information is partial (incomplete), fallible, and subjective. Let us consider each of these points in turn.

Consider the case of failure to recognize grief. The problem may be that the observer has no information available from his or her own case concerning the psycho-logic of the emotion, or has but fails to use it. The observer's information, or theory of mind, is incomplete. Then an incorrect intentionality will be attributed, such as malingering; or a non-intentional causal attribution will be made, such as post-viral syndrome.

Suppose, on the other hand, that the observer does draw on self-knowledge in the attempt to understand the other. It cannot be assumed that this self-knowledge is infallible: we make mistakes about our own mental states, as noted already in the first chapter (subsection 1.4.3). It is likely that the use of language in articulating psychological theory, in representing relations between experience, belief, feeling, and action, is a particularly potent source of error. Theory expressed in language very often misrepresents, for example, the 'natural expression' of the emotions. A child in grief, for example, may not be helped to articulate the emotion, its causes and effects: the emotion is left unremarked, or called by the wrong name, for example weakness, illness, or boredom. The resulting incompletness or error in self-knowledge will then reappear as incompleteness or error in the child's, or later the adult's understanding of others.

It should be remarked in passing that it would be hazardous to assume that the information from the observer's own case has to be explicitly or implicitly formulated in (coded in) language. Pre-linguistic infants, and perhaps non-linguistic animals, demonstrate in their social behaviour the ability to recognize intentionality in others, and in so far as this depends on information about their own reactions, it is non-linguistic information. The way of knowing here would be primarily analogic: patterns of intentionality in the other would be compared with those in the observer. In our own case, as mature human beings, pre- or non-linguistic, analogical coding of information relevant to the perception of intentionality may be assumed to exist alongside, more or less compatibly, theory expressed in language.

Even if self-knowledge, however derived, is valid, still its use in understanding others remains a further source of error. Attribution of intentionality to another, straightforwardly on the basis of one's own, will be valid only to the extent that the other is like oneself. Otherwise it will lead to the wrong result. For example, I may correctly interpret the other's crying as the expression of perceived loss because that is how I respond in those circumstances. But equally, I may fail to recognize the experience of loss in another if I assume that the experience is always expressed in this way. There are individual differences in the expression of emotion, and in the case of difference between myself and the other, identification will be invalid. In case of difference the use of empathy has to be modified. I have to represent what it is like to be someone unlike myself. The implied paradox here is a genuine one: *I* do indeed have to imagine being *someone else*. This modified form of empathic identification involves subtle interplay between acknowledgement of difference and presumption of similarity.

There has to be acknowledgement of difference. On the other hand, in order to make sense of what it is like to have different experiences, beliefs, and feelings, I still have to draw on information from my own case. I remember having been in similar, though still distinct, circumstances, and my responses in them, or I imagine what my responses would be were I hypothetically to be in the other's position; or, to obtain the best result possible for me, I use both methods in combination. I remember, for example, what it is like to be bereaved, and I imagine what it would be like to be bereaved while at the same time believing that one should not show signs of distress to others; I then notice what I am inclined to feel, say, and do in this position.

Experience and imagination are used together in 'knowing'—more or less well—the mind of another. The method is certainly subjective, but this is appropriate and necessary: knowledge of another's subjectivity is going to have to involve one's own. The method is by all means prone to error, and leads us into much trouble. On the other hand, whatever is prone to error is also capable of being right. If there are (objective) criteria for the one, there are (objective) criteria for the other. We make mistakes, more or less serious, in our understanding of others, and these mistakes show up as failure to anticipate each other's actions, and in particular as failure in co-operative endeavour. But equally, and here we return to the theme of the first chapter concerning attribution of intentionality and prediction: we are right often enough to make social life possible.

Knowledge of mental states, one's own or someone else's, is highly prone to error. On the other hand, there is some infallibility in self-knowledge. As noted in subsection 1.4.3, reports of the mental states regulating, or about to regulate, one's own current (salient) activity tend to be correct. These self-reports, when infallible, were construed not as beliefs about one's behaviour, but rather as expressions of intent to put such beliefs into practice.

This construal of self-report is linked to a point due to Wittgenstein: if a statement is (functioning as) a description of a process, mental or otherwise, then it can go wrong; so conversely, if a statement cannot go wrong, then it is not functioning as a description of a process.[3] Arguably this appeal to non-descriptive uses of language is the only way of making sense of incorrigible statements, but in any case it cannot be done in Cartesian terms, by appeal to mental states being manifest to the self. Even if (all or some) mental states are manifest to the self, still they are not manifest with verbal labels attached, still less with (necessarily) the right verbal labels attached. There is no way through here to the notion of an infallible description. To explain infallibility we need to invoke, rather than description, something like affirmation, or commitment.

This point is in turn linked to others previously discussed with reference to Wittgenstein. They may be collected together here as all relevant to the knowledge of mind, specifically in one's own case. We saw in subsection 1.4.4 in the context of post-empiricism that some propositions hold fast as methodological rules necessary for action and thought itself. Some of these refer to the world in which we live, but some refer to oneself, and specifically to one's capacity to act. We cannot afford to be wrong about (sincerely made) statements such as 'I see the door in front of me', 'I will go out of the door', 'This is my hand', and so on. I cannot be wrong about this sort of thing, not *in normal circumstances*. This means roughly: not if my basic faculties are working as they seem to be. What lies on the other side of this qualification is so far unthinkable to me. There is a commitment here to belief, to putting aside doubt, which is necessary in order to continue to act (cf. also below, subsection 6.4.5).

In summary then, there is something like infallible self-knowledge, but only in so far as we express a resolution to act, or to respond, in such-and-such a way. Once we *describe*, we make a true-or-false representation of a process (a pattern of intentionality), and then inevitably there is the possibility of error.

Another way of making this point is to say that infallible self-report is not based on information. Hence the information from one's own case used in empathy is not infallible self-knowledge. This conclusion leads on to an issue that has been pressing for some time, concerning the relation between self-knowledge and knowledge of the other.

3.2.5 Empathic knowledge is originally subject-less

So far we have talked of empathy as using information about oneself as a way of trying to know another person. We ask, for example, 'What would I feel if I had just experienced such-and-such?', intending the answer to help in knowing what the other might be feeling given the experience in question. This a natural description, but superficial. Behind it lies the epistemological point that empathic knowledge is originally subject-less, that is to say, is not about a (particular) subject at all. This point has the corollary that knowledge of the other is not based on knowledge of the self: rather both arise in the same way and on the same basis.

In terms of the proposal being developed here, simulations as thought-experiments are not primarily a source of self-knowledge, though they can be used for this purpose. The theory of mind required to run thought-experiments has to include methodological assumptions covering the move from current results to predictions about other cases. The simplest such assumption uses the straight rule: it will be in other cases just as it is in the present one. More sophisticated rules take into account differences between cases, such as differences in spatio-visual perspective, in ways of expressing emotion, or in beliefs, etc. It is, by all means, tempting to describe the methodological assumption of the straight rule as being that the other is like the self, while the more complex rules allow for differences between oneself and others. This way of describing the assumption behind the straight rule, however, presupposes that the distinction between self and other is being made, and the point is that this distinction comes into operation only with the more complex rules, which allow for differences in perspective. The thought-experiments are not about mental states of the self as opposed to mental states of the other. They provide information which is, so far, subject-less. The information is primarily about intentional states and their (apparent) connectedness, but these are not yet states of the self as opposed to states of the other. Attribution of patterns of intentionality to the self as opposed to the other requires recognition of, and allowances for, features that distinguish the self from others, and vice versa. This is to say, self-knowledge is not the basis for knowledge of the other, but rather they share the same origins, and develop in parallel.

Rules are required to make predications about other cases from the present observation or experiment. The rules become more sophisticated as they take into account relevant differences between the current case and others, but these differences are not correctly characterized in terms of differences between self and other. The first distinction to be drawn is between *this present* case and *other* cases. The 'other cases' by all means include other people, but they also, and equally, include myself in conditions other than those in the present case, for example, myself at different times, places, or with different relevant beliefs and goals, etc. The aim is to use the current observation or experiment to predict as accurately as possible what will or would happen in other cases. Accuracy will be achieved to the extent that the rules of inference become increasingly sensitive to differences in perspective, in the broadest sense. This increasing sensitivity plausibly involves increasing capacity or skill in imaginative manipulation of perspectives (visual, cognitive, emotional, etc.), in other words, increasing aptitude for thought-experiments of the sort already discussed. But it seems equally plausible to suppose that sensitivity to perspective depends on a theory, concerning at least the idea that perception and belief do indeed depend on perspective, as opposed to being determined just by reality as it appears (at present) to be. It would be reasonable to suppose, further, that these two capacities, for thought-experiments with perspectives, and for theory about perspectives, are inextricably linked.

3.2.6 Perspectives on psychological development

The epistemological points made in the previous subsection can be applied to the question of what is involved in the child's acquisition of knowledge of mind. As remarked earlier, there has been a tendency in the philosophical literature to assume that the theory of empathy, or mental simulation, stands opposed as an alternative to the epistemology which construes knowledge of mind as an exercise in theory. This opposition has carried over into psychological theories of the child's acquisition of knowledge of mind. We find, on the one hand, developmentalists emphasizing the child's increasing theoretical sophistication (Gopnik and Wellman 1992; Perner and Howes 1992), while proponents of the Simulation Theory emphasize the child's increasing understanding of the role of perspective (Harris 1992). An advantage of combining the two epistemologies is that one does not have to choose between these two themes in psychological development, both of which are apparently major. Indeed, the implication of the line of argument proposed in the preceding subsection is not just that these two kinds of maturation are compatible, but is more that they are inextricably interwoven. Development in scientific theory characteristically goes hand in hand with innovations in techniques of observation and experimentation; by all means at times one jumps ahead of the other, which then catches up, but in general and in principle they are interdependent.

A particularly crucial development in the theory of mind, highlighted by proponents of the 'theory-theory', is towards the idea of mental states as true-or-false representations (for example, Gopnik and Wellman 1992). This important theoretical development is, however, intimately linked, as a matter of logic, to recognition of and facility with variation in perspective. The main point, which will be presented in more detail below (subsections 3.3.3–4 and 3.4.3), is that the distinction between true and false cannot be made out on the basis of the present point of view alone, still less is it made out by comparing the present point of view with an absolute reality; rather it arises in comparison and contrast between perspectives. The distinction between true and false, as also between appearance and reality, depends on the power of discriminating between me-now/me-then and me (-now)/him (-now). In effect, what is required is discrimination between the current perspective and others, and this in turn requires that the current perspective is construed precisely *as a perspective*. Thus, what appear to be advances in theory, concerning true-or-false representation, or the difference between appearance and reality, intimately involve the idea of perspective, and hence plausibly both facilitate and are facilitated by experience and imaginative play with perspectives. The argument leads, once again, round and round: from theory to experience or experiment, back to theory, and so on.

A further consequence of the mutual dependence here between theory and experiment is that prior to the development of the idea that the current perspective (whether visual, or more elaborately cognitive-affective) is a perspective, there cannot be any imaginative play with perspective. This type of experiment cannot be run; or again, the question it is designed to answer cannot be asked. Without distinction between true and false, appearance and reality, or indeed between self and other, rudimentary attribution of intentionality would be determined by what was being experienced at the time. In this developmental stage, or state of mind, attribution would use a very straight rule: primitive, and powerful.[4]

The suggestion is that development in the theory of mind is interwoven with development of imaginative play with perspectives. It should be noted at this point that in children this imaginative play is most apparent indeed in *play*. The implication here is that children use play to improve their knowledge of mind, whether in theory or simulation (Leslie 1987; Harris 1989; Hobson 1990).

The proposal in subsection 3.2.3 that the empirical basis for the theory of mind included thought-experiments was supported by the remark that experiments, that is, concerning the relation between experiences, mental states, and behaviour, were difficult and time-consuming to conduct in reality. But some of the difficulties do not arise in play, and, all being well, the child has plenty of time. Play can be used to experiment with diverse circumstances, emotions, beliefs, capacities, tasks; to try out perspectives and activities different from the child's own. This play is in a space between reality and the imagination. The experiments are neither in reality nor in thought alone; the simulations are neither on-nor off-line. Experimentation in play seems to occupy the child as much as, or more than, experimentation in the mind alone; or perhaps skill in the latter is acquired by practice in the former. These observations on the significance of play qualify earlier remarks that have focused exclusively on thought-experiments.

Experimentation with perspectives, whether manifestly in play or covertly in thought alone, is a source of self-knowledge and of knowledge of others equally. As has already been argued, the information provided is so far subject-less. It is a matter of what it is (or seems) like to have such-and-such experiences, including being in certain kinds of social role or interpersonal relationship, what it is like to have such-and-such feelings, beliefs, tasks, inclinations to action, etc. The initial conditions of the experiment can be at any point along this continuum, and the experiment is to investigate what these give rise to, or what gave rise to them. Hence the child plays at being for instance a carer, a baby, a teacher, a goody or a baddy, kind or nasty; and so on, and on. What the child finds out in this play is so far not about herself rather than anyone else, or vice versa. It is primarily, and precisely, about the mental (intentional) states themselves: particular experiences, feelings, tasks, intentions, inclinations to actions. Application of information of this sort to understanding another person, or oneself, in a real situation involves further judgement, that is, attribution of the mental states, and estimation of their interaction with others operating at the same time.

3.3 RULE-FOLLOWING

3.3.1 The role of rules: order through time

There is a close connection, already remarked in the the first chapter (subsection 1.3.4), between mental states, regulation, and rule-following. We describe behaviour as caused by mental states in so far as it is goal-directed and adaptive, and this 'causation' involves regulation, the modification of behaviour according to circumstances towards a goal. These intentional behaviour sequences are hence also typically subject to normative decriptions: appropriate/inappropriate, successful/unsuccessful, right/wrong. This normative quality can be captured by saying that the behaviour in question is subject to a rule, or is rule-following. So the central questions for this chapter concerning the epistemology of mind can be framed using the notion of rule-following. How do I know that someone is following a rule? How do I know which rule? What is this knowledge knowledge of? In this section we consider aspects of Wittgenstein's influential discussion of rule-following in the *Philosophical investigations* (1953).[5]

At the beginning of his *Investigations*, Wittgenstein criticizes the general idea that signs have meaning because they stand for objects; rather their meaning derives from use in activity (1953, §§ 1 to *c*. 37). He proceeds to criticize various doctrines familiar in the philosophical tradition which express the idea that meaning is correlation with an object, in such a way as to exclude the use of signs in activity as redundant, or even as incomprehensible. These include doctrines which invoke universals (ibid. *c*. §§ 57–78), and various logical theories, including Wittgenstein's own in the *Tractatus* (ibid. *c*. §§ 39–64 and 89–116).

Before considering briefly Wittgenstein's treatment of such doctrines below, we should note that the issues here are not only of interest to the history of philosophy, but are relevant to contemporary theories of meaning and mental content. Highly influential theories still draw on, or make a virtue of, the view that meaning and reference do not essentially involve human activity. These include the materialist theory of mental content, discussed in the context of the problem of supervenience in the previous chapter (Section 2.5), and the causal theory of semantics, to be discussed in the next chapter (Section 4.3).

Meaningful signs, whether written or spoken language, or mental representations, or information-carrying neural states, pick out, *in some sense*, the order (or *form*) in reality. It is possible to conceive this order as already given, both in the sense of already given in time, and in the sense of given without contribution from the activity of an agent. At least until the Kantian revolution, such an absolute conception of order has been dominant in the tradition. It has had various expressions, which fall broadly into two categories, concerning classes and spatial relations. In both cases the notion of resemblance between sign and signified, discussed in subsection 1.3.2, is fundamental.

The various theories of universals in ancient thought, and the theories of general and abstract ideas in modern thought, all seek to explain the unity of classes in terms of an object which is, or which resembles, what all and only members of the class have in common. Such a special and problematic 'universal (or general) object' is the meaning of any sign which represents a class.

Relation between objects in space is a different kind of order, which assumed paramount importance in the modern period. In seventeenth-century philosophy of nature it too was conceived as given absolutely: independently of time, of experience, of frames of reference, to be measured by rigid rods. The order of objects in space, the natural order, could perhaps be represented in perception, though the details were irredeemably problematic. In particular, perceptual experience is relative, dependent on the nature and position of the subject, and further, it was meant to be mental, and hence not spatial. In brief, perceptions are not rigid rods, indeed they are not rods at all. Such paradoxes point to the murky incoherence of this modern world-picture. In the *Tractatus* (Wittgenstein 1921) the problems of relativity and mind were bypassed by logic: spatial states of affairs are represented by (more) spatial states of affairs, configurations of signs, involving no relativity, nothing at all which could be called contribution by the subject. As discussed in Chapter 1 (subsection 1.3.2), the picture theory of thought and language is derived in the *Tractatus* as a solution to the problem of how a sign can be meaningful (can stand for something in reality) while yet being false (while failing to correspond to reality). The pictures are the 'real signs', hidden beneath the surface of language, which does indeed conspicuously not look like what is represented.

The theory that the meaning of a general term is a feature common to all members of a class, and the theory that a true-or-false proposition is something like a picture of a state of affairs, though otherwise distinct, both affirm the idea that meanings are essentially static, object-like structures which resemble or reflect the pre-given order in reality. These structures—universals, ideas, pictures—do all the work of representation. Or rather, there is no need for work: the 'real signs' simply *are* what reality is like. In this general picture there is no use for such concepts as time, the creation of order, activity, relativity, and subjectivity (and still less, of intersubjectivity). These excluded concepts are all intimately related to one another.

During this century, theories of meaning that turn on the notion of resemblance have become unattractive, particularly, but not only, because they fare badly when applied to language. The theories posit signs that 'resemble reality', but the signs of (everyday, natural) languages typically do not. If we persist with the question: 'How does a sign signify reality?', and if we do *not* allow ourselves to invoke resemblance, then we are led towards the idea that some *form of activity*, specifically human activity, is required to link the two. This reading inevitably introduces relativity into the theory of meaning and reference, a relativity to human activity and the community of language-users. These are familiar themes in Wittgenstein's later philosophy.

This line of thought will be resisted by those who want to preserve a non-relativistic, (purely) 'objective' philosophy. One such resistance is provided by causal semantics, probably in combination with the materialist theory of content: the dynamic relation between sign and reality is defined in causal terms, and the reality in terms of the basic natural sciences. No subjectivity or relativity here. These alternative approaches are considered and rejected elsewhere (sections 2.5 and 4.4–4.6). In this section we shall pursue the Wittgensteinian approach, which as indicated soon leads us towards relativity. In the next section, however, we go on to argue that this relativity does not dispose of, but rather re-defines, the notion of objectivity, in a way, moreover, suited to the sciences.

Wittgenstein begins his *Philosophical investigations* very simply, by citing the fact that people engage in co-operative activity, such as building, using language for communication. This is to be the starting-place for the theory of meaning and language. Starting-place means: it is not derived from deeper assumptions. In particular, it is not to be *explained away* by other theories (such as the ones described above). Philosophy always begins with what is obvious, beyond all reasonable doubt. The starting-place that Wittgenstein adopts may be contrasted with others in the philosophical tradition. Of particular relevance in the present context is the contrast with the dominant (though noriously problematic) axiom of modern epistemology, namely, the certainty of subjective experience, used, for example, by Locke as the basis for the empiricist theory of representation (ideas). The proposal underlying Wittgenstein's choice of starting-place is that the reality of action, community, and language is now more obvious, more clear, than the reality of subjective experience. Plausibly this same assumption characterizes most contemporary psychology, and it has been adopted in the present essay: our conception of mind and meaning is based in their relevance to action and mutual understanding, not in contemplation of one's own mental states.

Wittgenstein's proposal is, then, that the meaning of a sign derives from its use in activities such as making requests, sorting out one kind of thing from another, fetching and carrying, etc. This claim may indeed appear as relatively innocuous, but in fact it contradicts presuppositions about meaning and the order in reality which pervade the tradition, and which still influence our current thinking.

Given that meaning is grounded in action, the notion of *order* makes its appearance in the following way: the activity which is the origin of meaning is not random, but is ordered, essentially 'right' or 'wrong'. We may express the fact that practice is ordered by saying that it proceeds in accordance with a rule. This concept of ordered practice, practice that follows a rule, is what replaces the traditional concepts of static representation, expressed in the theories of universals, ideas of perception, picture-propositions, of truth-conditions as states of affairs; and so forth.

In their most pure expressions, these traditional theories of meaning are alien to the idea that signs are used through time, in practice, according to a rule. Nothing needs to be done to create meaning. But, if something has to be said about the use of (ordinary) signs in practice, it will be this: the order —the distinction between right and wrong—in practice and in our use of signs will be secondary to, based in, an order which is already given; either in the nature of 'real signs', or in some mental *act*. Deconstruction of various expressions of this general idea is the main negative theme in Wittgenstein's treatment of judgement and rule-following in the *Investigations*, beginning at about § 134. The contrary and new conclusion for which Wittgenstein argues may be summarized briefly thus: *meaning—the rule—is not determined in advance.*

3.3.2 Rule-following as creation of order

The simplest account of the rule for using a sign would be that the sign itself determines its application. This account does not refer to the ordinary signs of language, but rather to pictures or exemplars of things. Even so, the attempt to explain meaning in terms of the instrinsic nature of a sign only works if it is supposed that the sign is not *used* at all. For the idea was that the picture simply represents how things stand; nothing is *done* with the picture, so there is no question of doing different things with it. But once we grant that signs are used, for example in our activities of collecting things together, it becomes apparent that signs themselves can dictate no method of application, and hence no meaning. Any sign, whether verbal or pictorial, can be used in a variety of ways. This use is the source of meaning, not the object itself (Wittgenstein 1953, §§139–141; cf. above, subsection 1.3.2).

Another possibility is that the rule for the use of a sign is simply what its use *is intended to be*. According to this kind of account, a child who is learning the use of the word 'chair' by being shown examples, must try to see what meaning the teacher has in mind. And if the child goes on to make a mistake, applying the word to a sofa, say, the suggestion is that this counts as a mistake because it conflicts with the meaning that was intended, and which has been already given to the word.

Wittgenstein considers this suggestion using an analogy with continuing an arithmetical series (1953, §§ 143f., 185f.). Suppose we teach a child to expand the series '+2', giving examples at the beginning. The child then proceeds alone, correctly up to 1000, but then continues: 1004, 1008, 1012. We could point out the mistake, and the child may make corrections. What requires definition, however, is the sense in which a 'mistake' has been made. Or: 'Why is 1002 the *right* number to write after 1000?' According to the suggestion under consideration, the answer is that this is what we meant the pupil to do when we gave the instruction to continue the series '+2' from the examples given. Meaning is conceived here as a kind of intention which defines in advance the expansion of the formula, or, in general, the correct use of a sign. But the objection is that we cannot lay down all the steps in advance, because there are infinitely many of them. It may be true to say that when we gave the instruction to expand the series we *meant at the time* that 1002 should be written after 1000. But even though we meant the step then, still we did not take it then; and if we did, there are indefinitely many others that we did not take. We meant the step at the time in so far as, if the child had asked at the time how to continue after 1000, we should have replied '1002'. And we can affirm this counter-factual proposition because as soon as the issue is raised, we reply without hesitation: write 1002 after 1000. But to say that the issue can be settled at any time without hesitation does not mean, and cannot mean, that it has been settled already, in advance.

We are evaluating the idea that the correct use of sign is determined by the meaning that we give the sign. And the conclusion is that the opposite is so: it is the correct use of a sign which determines its meaning. The correct use of a sign cannot be defined in advance, but is created as we proceed. What can seem as it if were an 'act of meaning', is rather a *process*.

On the other hand, perhaps the analogy between using a sign and being able to expand an arithmetic formula is misleading in an important respect. The series of numerals associated with a formula such as '+2' is a conventional one. It is perhaps for this reason that knowing the formula alone is no help in knowing the series, that the series has to be made up—albeit with no hesitation—as we go along. But by contrast, *judgement made about the world* is not just a matter of convention. It is plausible to suppose that a series of such judgements, say the classification of many things into one class, is held together by an independent, objective regularity. So that, for example, repeated uses of the sentence 'This is red' mark a regularity in the world, and understanding how to use the sentence is a matter of perceiving and representing this regularity. It would follow then that there would be a truly informative expression of the rule for using the sentence, namely, a table with the word written opposite a sample of red. Understanding the word would then be acquaintance with such a table in the mind, a mental state that underlies and explains the practice of making judgements.

The suggestion is, then, that to follow a rule is to read off judgements from some expression of the rule, perhaps in the form of a table relating signs to samples. Wittgenstein shows, however, that this kind of suggestion does not work (1953, §§ 156 to *c.* 171). The problem is that expressions of rules, such as tables, can be 'read' in various ways, that they can determine no unique usage. Or again, expressions of rules, of whatever kind, admit of many 'interpretations'. These interpretations can be expressed by more expressions of rules, for example by more tables, perhaps with more or less complicated systems of arrows linking signs and samples, but such further expressions of rules are again open to various interpretations, to diverse applications. So one difficulty is that a particular expression of a rule, together with any number of expressions for its interpretation, can be used in various ways. But the further and related difficulty is that they can also be used in entirely random ways, *in ways which are not rule-following at all.*

The conclusion is, then, that we cannot capture the notion of following a rule in terms of intended use, nor in terms of expressions of rules. This is the negative conclusion of Wittgenstein's discussion of rule-following.[6]

This negative conclusion may be expressed also by saying that nothing short of order *in practice* will count as rule-following; that is, nothing short of making judgements (in words or in action) which are right as opposed to wrong. And this points towards a more positive doctrine, to the effect that following a rule is a practice.

In § 201, Wittgenstein refers to the difficulties that arise when we try to define action according to a rule in terms of interpretations of expressions of rules, which in turn require further interpretations, and so on. But he continues (1953, §§ 201–2):

> What this shows is that there is a way of grasping a rule which is *not* an *interpretation*, but which is exhibited in what we call 'obeying the rule' and 'going against it' in actual cases.
>
> Hence there is an inclination to say: every action according to the rule is an interpretation. But we ought to restrict the term 'interpretation' to the substitution of one expression of the rule for another.
>
> And hence also 'obeying a rule' is a practice . . . .

Nothing short of ordered practice will count as obeying a rule. In particular, no amount of mental manipulation of expressions of rules is sufficient. There are, of course, mental processes, conscious and unconscious, involved in rule-guided practice: processes such as feelings of recognition of items in the environment, feelings of being guided by samples, inspection of samples, tables, formulae, etc. But the activity that results from such processes may or may not be ordered (rational, intelligent). Whether someone is or is not following a rule depends on what they do in practice; for example, on what items they call or treat as the same. Only if a person's judgements and actions are of a certain kind do we say that she is 'going by regularities in the world'. Our concept of regularities in the world is of a piece with our concept of regularities in action. This is an aspect of the correspondence between reality and thought.

The concept of following a rule cannot be explained in terms of perception of regularities in the world, since following a rule and perceiving regularities come to the same thing. In a similar way, the practice of following a rule cannot be explained in terms of *reason*. Here the point is not that we have no reasons for proceeding as we do, but rather that our reasons run out. Wittgenstein writes (1953, § 211):

> How can he *know* how he is to continue a pattern by himself—whatever instruction you give him?—Well, how do *I* know?—If that means 'have I reasons?' the answer is: my reasons will soon give out. And then I shall act, without reasons.

Reasons come to an end once we have described, in the various ways in which we can describe, the fact that we are following the rule. We can, for example, refer to our training, saying that we are carrying on as we were taught, or we may point to a sample, saying that it guides us, etc. But if someone were to press the question: 'But why call *this* the same way as before?' or 'Why is *this* near enough to the sample?' then sooner or later we run out of answers, and carry on regardless, in the way we are inclined. The concept of following a rule—of ordered judgement and practice—is (of course) a very fundamental one, and does not rest on any more fundamental notion of reason. To say that someone is following a rule so far means, among other things, that they are acting rationally.

The rules followed in practice and in our use of signs are not laid down in advance, by pictures, or by acts of mind; rather they are formed in practice, as we take action which is right or wrong. Nor can following a rule be explained in terms of an independently defined 'following of regularities', nor in terms of independently defined 'reasons'. Right or wrong practice is not derived from a more fundamental principle of order: the practice itself is what is fundamental. The conclusion is that the origin of the rule—of meaning, of the measure of reality—is neither more nor less than *our natural inclination to proceed in one way rather than another*.

But now the paradox is: in what sense is there a *rule* here at all? We have considered attempts to define an order already made, but apparently there is none. But then, what kind of order is it that can be made up as we go along? Why is one way of proceeding any more 'correct' than any other?

3.3.3 The role of agreement

Towards the end of his discussion of rule-following, Wittgenstein begins to speak of shared practice and judgement. Thus, obeying a rule is a custom (Wittgenstein 1953,

§ 198); a rule cannot be obeyed privately (ibid. § 202), the word 'agreement' and the word 'rule' are related to one another, they are cousins (ibid. § 224).

The implication of Wittgenstein's remarks here may be that a person's practice accords with a rule in so far as it is shared with other people. However, the justification for such a move at this stage of Wittgenstein's discussion of rule-following is far from clear. So far it has been established what following a rule *is not*; it is not to follow what is laid down in advance in some act of meaning, or in some expression of a rule. But what is the justification of a move from this negative conclusion to the positive conclusion that following a rule is a matter of being in accord with other people? Why is agreement in practice either a necessary or a sufficient condition of following a rule?

It is difficult to see why *mere numbers* should make a difference to the issue. On the one hand, we can imagine a group of people all acting and speaking in similar ways, but apparently without rhyme or reason. On the other, we can presumably imagine a person on his own—perhaps on a desert island—acting and using signs in an orderly way, regardless of any relation to a present, past, or hypothetical community.[7] It is by all means the case that people (usually) do live in communities, and that their rule-following practices are shared. It may also be true to say, on biological and psychological grounds, that children have to be taught how to act and how to use signs, so that in fact no human being could ever come to follow a rule in isolation from others. But such empirical considerations and speculations so far fail to bring out the conceptual connection between rule-following and agreement. Nor is it clear that the empirical facts unformly support such a connection. Frequently we do have to follow rules on our own; others are not so preoccupied with us that they attend to, offer guidance on, or pass opinion on our every move.

We suggest that the point is *not* that we ascribe rule-following to groups as opposed to individuals; rather, we make the ascription in both cases and on the same grounds, namely, to the extent that we find practices, whether group or individual, comprehensible.

This point about grounds for ascription of rule-following indicates a radically different way of introducing the notion of agreement into the arena. The notion of agreement is relevant to the judgement whether a person's practice is rule-governed, not because a person cannot follow a rule without others there to share it, but because, if the judgement is made at all, it is made by other people, and then on the basis of whether they can follow and share in the person's activity. This can be expressed by saying that agreement is relevant to judgement about rule-following because *one person is the measure of another*. When a person is inclined to make a judgement, he or she supposes that the judgement is correct. What seems right, is right, so far as the person is concerned. Under what conditions, then, do we say that the other is following the rule? The answer is clear: when the other does what we are ourselves inclined to do. In this way, so far as a person is concerned, the notion of agreement with his or her own judgement is intertwined with the notion of following a rule. Agreement is critical in the same way to related notions such as intentionality and rationality.

The clearest cases of agreement are those in which two people are inclined to proceed in the same way, but there are of course other, critical possibilities related to these straightforward cases. In order to judge that the other is following some rule or other, it is not necessary that their practice be the same as one's own; it is enough to see some sense in what the person is doing. This involves acknowledgement that the other's action is right (reasonable, understandable), given his or her purposes and experience. Understanding of the other is like, and is based on, understanding of oneself: both are a matter of acknowledging inclinations to action. We experience tendencies and responses in directions other than those in which we act. These inclinations to action—these meanings—can be seen at work in the actions of others, which therefore make sense, even though these actions are unlike our own. Mutual understanding has to be achieved in the midst of individual differences.

Thus we come by this route to conclusions similar to those already reached in the previous section, namely, that understanding of intentionality in others is based in empathy (straightforward or otherwise). This coincidence is to be expected, in view of the intimate connection between intentionality and rule-following. Examination of the concept of rule-following leads to the conclusion that subjective inclinations form the basis of expectations about the behaviour of others.

However, unlike the considerations in the previous section concerning empathy in knowledge of intentionality, the considerations so far in this section concerning rule-following do not apply only to expectations about social behaviour, but rather to *judgement in general*, including about the natural (apart from the social) world. This great generality is of course typical of philosophical enquiry, and is to be expected of Wittgenstein's analysis of what it means to following a rule.

The argument that rules are formed in practice, outlined in subsection 3.3.2 included the point that the concept of following a rule cannot be explained in terms of perception of regularities in the world: following a rule and perceiving regularities come to the same thing. This means that subjective responses to reality, the inclination to act in one way rather than another (e.g. to treat *this* as the same as or different to *that*) form the basis of judgements about sameness and difference, classes and properties, in the natural world.

This conclusion stands opposed to those various doctrines described at the start of this section, according to which meanings are static measures which reflect pre-given order in reality. If we were to speak in the present context of measures, it would be ourselves, our responses to reality.

The implication is that our concept of reality is thoroughly interwoven with interpersonal relations, with the comparison of views. The position is not, however, that the notion of reality collapses into the notion of agreement. This is too simple, and it neglects the role of reality as independent of judgement. In the course of action through time, a person proceeds in the way she judges to be right. If another person agrees, then what seems right to the one seems right also to the other; but this does not yet mean that they *are* right. Agreement does not turn 'seems' into 'is'. But then, what is the relation between appearance and reality? All we have concluded so far, in the absence of rigid, fixed measures, is that human responsiveness is the vehicle of representation. And so far as this measure is concerned (and in fact the same would apply to any measure), what seems right, is right. These points are pursued below.

3.3.4 Relativity and the independent contraints on action

By considering Wittgenstein's treatment of rule-following we have arrived at the conclusion that the human being is the measure of things, with its puzzling and disturbing implication that the distinction between 'seems' and 'is', between appearance and reality, seems to collapse. Although it represents a diversion from the mainly contemporary focus of the present essay, it can hardly be allowed to escape our attention that this problem had a lively, though brief, airing at the beginnings of Western philosophical thought. Since, for reasons to be indicated below, the problem in this form has only recently been revived, it is worthwhile to consider briefly its fate in Plato.

The claim that man is the measure was one of the three interconnected doctrines criticized and rejected by Socrates in the *Theaetetus*:

> And it has turned out that these three doctrines coincide: the doctrine of Homer and Heracleitus and all their tribe that all things move like flowing streams; the doctrine of Protagoras, wisest of men, that Man is the measure of all things; and Theaeteus' conclusion that, on these grounds, it results that perception is knowledge. (*Theaetetus*, 160D–E; translation from Cornford 1935.)

Socrates criticizes all of these doctrines, but the most sustained argument is directed at the doctrine of Protagoras, that the human being is the measure of things. This doctrine means, according to Socrates, that individual things are to me such as they appear to me, and to you such as they appear to you (152–152C). Socrates argues that this doctrine has no place for the concept of falsity, and is therefore wrong. The claim is that the doctrine can give no account of false judgement, since it implies that all judgements are true. Or again: if the human being is the measure of things, there would be no distinction between subjective appearance and reality, indeed there would be no concept of objective reality. Socrates' claim, in brief, was that if the human being is the measure of things, then there is *loss of objectivity*.

This Socratic interpretation has been of enormous significance, setting the scene for struggles between scepticism, the claim that knowledge is impossible, and various forms of dogmatism, which claimed for knowledge an absolute, non-relative, and therefore non-human, basis. Common to both scepticism and dogmatism was the assumption that knowledge, if it exists at all, must have absolute foundations. Behind this was the assumption that beliefs acquired by relative measures involved subjectivity, that is to say, absence of objectivity. The relative measures delivered results dependent on the point of view: on sensory capacity, on relative position; on culture and ideology; and so on. But these shifting, apparently incompatible representations could hardly be representations of the one, independent reality. If this was to be known at all, there had to be absolute measures. Reason, as conceived in rationalist epistemology, and experience as conceived by empiricism, were the two absolute measures in modern thought. As these lost credibility through the nineteenth century, relativity has made its appearance in this. This long-lost, newly re-discovered relativity has been both resisted and welcomed, both on the grounds that it involves loss of (absolute) objectivity.

But what is lost is neither more nor less than the idea of an absolute, non-relative object. The idea of a 'relativistic object' remains, involved in the relativistic epistemology, though by all means such a notion of object is not the traditional one. But in any case it is wrong to suppose that relativity implies subjectivity without objectivity; on the contrary, it is obvious enough in general terms that relativity involves both subject and object in interaction.

The notion of objectivity which belongs properly with relativity is in fact familiar to common sense and language, but it is obscured by deep theoretical preconceptions. Socrates in the *Theaetetus* criticizes Protagoras' doctrine because it offers no account of false judgement, but the everyday examples of being right rather than wrong, or vice versa, which are cited, do not turn on absolute standards. Rather, the distinctions turn on mundane features of judgement that turn out to be quite compatible with the claim that human beings are the measure. Socrates cites cases in which a person is skilled at a practice, is good at achieving an intended result, as for example a physician at healing the body, or a gardner at cultivating plants (167B–C). He also cites cases of disagreement, addressing Theodorus as follows (170D–E, translation from Cornford 1935):

> When you have formed a judgement on some matter in your own mind and express an opinion about it to me, let us grant that, as Protagoras' theory says, it is true for you; but are we so to understand that it is impossible for us, the rest of the company, to pronounce any judgement on your judgement; or, if we can, that we always pronounce your opinion to be true? Do you not rather find thousands of opponents who set their opinion against yours on every occasion and hold that your judgement and belief are false?

To which Theodorus replies:

> I should just think so, Socrates; thousands and tens of thousands, as Homer says; and they give me all the trouble in the world.

Finally, Socrates cites cases where we know that not every person's opinion can be correct; as for example when a patient disagrees with his physician about the future course of his illness, or when legislators dispute whether some law will be advantageous to the state (177C–179C).

Thus Socrates illustrates the ways in which a person's judgement can be, or can be judged by others to be, false, even though it seems right to the person at the time. The examples are, of course, taken from everyday life, in which activities achieve or fail to achieve their goals, and in which expectations are realized or not, and in which people agree with one another or not. But then, it is not at all obvious that Protagoras' doctrine cannot account for the notion of false judgement defined in these ways. On the contrary, the doctrine arguably comprises such a notion, in the following way. If the human being, specifically in activity, is the measure of things, then this measure will be 'right' or 'wrong' according to whether it fulfils its goals or not. Further, since the measuring activity is extended through time, results obtained at one time may accord or conflict with results obtained later: judgements as predictions turn out 'right' or 'wrong'. Further, the human measures are multiple, and in so far as human beings differ from one another, they will disagree in the results of their measurement.

Judgement, whether in words or action, is made from a particular perspective, on the basis of particular sensory mechanisms and information, and on the basis of certain background expectations. Judgement, which consists in the inclination to say or do something, is to the effect that *this* is how things are. At the time, there is no distinction between 'seems' and 'is', between appearance and reality. It can be thought at the time, however, for example with the words: 'It seems so me now, but I may be wrong'. But what enables this thought, and what enables the distinction to be made, is the fact that judgement made from one perspective may conflict with judgement made from another, for example by another person, or by oneself at a later time. In brief, the appearance/reality distinction is based in comparison between appearances. This central point was anticipated above (subsection 3.2.6) in discussing the relation between theory and empathy in the developing mind, and it recurs again in subsection 3.4.4, in the definition of the objectivity in intentional attributions.

The relativistic way of making out the distinction between appearance and reality, in terms of comparison between appearances, stands in contrast to the idea common to dogmatism and scepticism alike, that reality lies behind the appearances, independent of them. This idea by all means holds on to a fixed reality behind the flux, but the cost is typically that knowledge of this reality tends to be insolubly problematic, at least for human beings. The relative measures are apparently all we have, and it is not clear how they signify a non-relative reality. This problematic was manifest in Classical thought and is also one way of expressing the modern (Seventeenth century) problem of knowledge (Subsection 1.2.1).

The relativistic account of appearance and reality gives a central place to agreement between appearances, between observers. On the other hand, agreement is not all that is at issue here. In general terms, the aim of judgement is not just to agree with others, but is also, or is primarily, to find agreement *with reality*. So far, particularly in consideration of Wittgenstein's discussion of rule-following, the focus has been on agreement between people rather than on correspondence with reality. This emphasis may arise particularly when we have in mind the use of language. In so far as language is a conventional means of representation, and particularly in so far as we do share language, it may seem as if agreement on the rule is primarily what matters. But according to Wittgenstein's own account, language has meaning (*is* language) because it is used *in activity*, for example, in the course of building. When we turn attention to the practical consequences of using signs in one way rather than another, then we see what is obvious, that our use of language is not at all subject only to conventional constraints, a matter of agreement with others. On the contrary, language is used in our activity, and it is subject to the same constraints in reality, as is our practice.

For example, imagine a person building a shelter. She makes separate collections of different kinds of stone, each kind with its own name. On one occasion she makes a mistake, putting a round stone in the pile of square ones. When she comes to put this stone in place in the building, it does not fit; she has to start again; or perhaps, in a more complicated case, she is bewildered, and gives up. So the person made an error, in her action and her use of words. But this is not simply in the sense that other people would call it an error, nor indeed only because the person concerned would call it an error. Rather, the error shows up because her course of action goes astray; it is disrupted.

The importance of practical constraints have sometimes been neglected in commentary on Wittgenstein's discussion of rule-following. Kripke, for example, imagines the strange case of a person who insists that the sum of 68 and 57 is 5, and he goes on to discuss in what sense this is an error, if not because of facts about past usage, then in terms of our inclination to disagree with him (Kripke 1980). But the *application* of arithmetic is not brought into the discussion. If someone used such a calculation in planning how much water he needs to cross a desert, then he would soon come to see that he had got it wrong—and if he remained adamant until the end, then he would be slow to learn as well as dead. In any case the error speaks for itself.

The consequences of incorrect judgement are evident, and they run their course regardless whether we agree among ourselves or not. A person's judgement by all means is measured by others: they agree or disagree. But also, judgement is measured by reality itself. Reality passes judgement on our judgement. By all means it does not speak English! But rather, the order of reality is involved in the ordered activity that underlies our use of language. Between these two, there is correspondence or lack of correspondence. Human activity is the measure of reality. This reality is not a state, but is rather modes of movement and interaction, and hence it is encountered directly in practice. Judgements guide activity; they lead us to anticipate certain events, certain patterns of action and consequence, and we plan our activity accordingly. If a judgement misleads us, so that our action is confounded, then that judgement has turned out to be wrong. Reality lets us know when we are in error; we take notice, and adapt, if we are to carry on.

Another way of making this point is to say that action is interaction between the living being, the means of representation, and independent reality. Not everything in this interaction depends on the living being; and what is independent in the interaction is 'reality'. Thus reality already appears in the appearances, which are therefore not 'merely subjective'. I cannot, for example, make a closed door appear immaterial by walking through it.

Acknowledgement of relativity does not entail subjectivity or scepticism, an abandonment of the idea of objectivity. Objectivity can be defined in relativistic terms. In so far as thought and language are used in practice, in the organization and planning of action, there are 'objective' constraints on them, and hence distinctions between getting it right and getting it wrong, or more or less right or wrong.

It is dialectically necessary to emphasize that there are real, practical constraints on judgement as well as, and as opposed to, accord or discord with other people. The relativistic point stands, however, that other perspectives, in the form of other people, help make up the individual's view as to what is real and what is not. Our knowledge of reality is inextricably bound to interpersonal relations. In development, the point is the general one that social processes interact with individual cognitive development (Vygotsky 1934; Butterworth and Light 1982; Hinde *et al.* 1985; Gellatly *et al.* 1989). At any age the point remains that much of our activity is social, dependent on mutual understanding and help: we cannot construct a tower, for example, if we cannot communicate about the building.

3.4 RELATIVITY AND REALITY IN THE NATURAL AND BIO-PSYCHOLOGICAL SCIENCES

3.4.1 Is what is relative really real?

Relativity in the knowledge of intentionality raises problems concerning its objectivity. In so far as relativity is taken to mean subjectivity as opposed to objectivity, then this purported knowledge will seem illusory, more apparent than real, particularly in comparison with what we expect from and find in the natural sciences.

The observer-relativity in folk psychological attributions of meaning is cited by Stich, for example, as one reason why cognitive science had better do without them (Stich 1983, p. 136). It was argued in the first chapter (Subsection 1.3.8) that this avoidance strategy has to make the dubious assumption that the information-carrying states posited by cognitive psychology can be characterized without references to meaningful content, and would deny cognitive science access to the predictive utility of explanations which invoke meaningful content. We have argued that cognitive science can, and has to, use such explanations, at least when modelling intentional behaviour. But here, as it were, we pick up the tab. If the argument is going to be that cognitive science can, and has to, use the notion of meaning (for the purpose of explaining and predicting intentional behaviour), then we owe an account of how science can include a relativistic epistemology.

It may, on the other hand, be possible to grant the predictive utility of intentional explanations without supposing that they posit anything objectively real. This would be a so-called *instrumentalist* (or perhaps 'interpretationist') as opposed to a *realist* construal of intentional language. It has advantages particularly if it is supposed that the only real states that intentional states could be are brain states, but it turns out, for example on connectionist grounds, that there are no brain states of the requisite kind (cf. above, subsection 2.2.2).

Dennett's views on these matters are appropriately complicated, and this is one way in which he sets off to explain his position (1988, p. 496):

> Sometimes attributions of belief appear entirely objective and unproblematic, and sometimes they appear beset with subjectivity and infected with cultural relativism. Catering to these two families of cases are two apparently antithetical theoretical options: *realism*, the view that beliefs are objective things in the head which could be discovered ... by physiological psychology; and *interpretationism*, the view that attributing a belief is a highly relativistic undertaking . . .—'it all depends what you're interested in'.
>
> It is a common mistake to see these alternatives as mutually exclusive and exhaustive. . . . My thesis is that while belief is a perfectly objective phenomenon (which apparently makes me a realist), it can be discerned only from the point of view of someone who adopts a certain predictive strategy, the *intentional stance* (which apparently makes me an interpretationist).

Dennett's version of realism emphasizes the grounding of intentional attributions in patterns of activity more than correspondence with in-the-head items (Dennett 1988; cf. also above, subsection 2.2.3). These patterns are typically not captured by physicalist descriptions: they are higher-order invariants which cut across physically (geometrically) defined movements, concerning such as variable routes to the same goal (Dennett 1988; also below and subsection 1.3.6). Referring to hypothetical super-physicists who predict everything on the basis of a completed physical theory, using therefore only the physical stance and not the intentional stance, Dennett writes (1987, p. 37):

My view is, I insist, a *sort* of realism, since I maintain that the patterns the Martians miss are really, objectively there to be noticed or overlooked. How could the Martians, who 'know everything' about the physical events in our world, miss these patterns? What could it mean to say that some patterns, while objectively there, are visible only from one point of view?

Now of course invariance relations as such are not problematic in science or philosophy, but in the present case the particular problem is their *relativity* to the observer. On this point Dennett writes (1987, p. 39):

> I claim that the intentional stance provides a vantage point for discerning . . . useful patterns. These patterns are objective—they are *there* to be detected—but from our point of view they are not *out there* entirely independent of us, since they are patterns composed partly of our own 'subjective' reactions to what is out there; they are the patterns made to order for our narcissistic concerns . . .

The question is whether our patterns of intentionality are objectively real (like the invariance relations recognized in physics and chemistry), or whether they are more like beauty. Dennett steers a course here between objectivity and subjectivity, though one indeed that he has had repeatedly to explain and defend. Thus Dennett, (1987, p. 37):

> Perhaps the major source of disquiet about my position over the years has been its delicate balancing act on the matter of the observer-relativity of attributions of belief and other mental states. On my view, is belief attribution (or meaning) in the eye of the beholder? Do I think there are *objective truths* about what people believe, or do I claim that all attributions are just *useful fictions*?

In what follows we propose a position like Dennett's in that it tries to define a notion of objectivity as well as of subjectivity in attributions of intentionality. It rests on relativistic definitions of the kind invoked so far in this section. By all means we are unlikely to have as much success as Dennett, let alone more, in vindicating such a view!

The assumption that relativity involves subjectivity as opposed to objectivity was criticized in the preceding subsection. It was argued there that with relativity we lose the notion of *absolute* objectivity, but we gain instead a relativistic notion. Fundamental to the relativistic definition are the following points: the 'object' is that which in an interaction is independent of the subject's control, and further, is that which appears from different points of view (in different interactions). The absolute object, by contrast, is defined independently of any interactions with the subject of knowledge. In the context of a relativistic epistemology, finding relativity in any particular domain of knowledge is so far nothing to get excited about. Relativity looks problematic, of course, only against the background of absolutist preconceptions, only if we think that knowledge ought to be, or in the paradigm case is, relativity-free. And this is where a certain view of the sciences makes its appearance. The idea would be that the best or most fundamental science, physics (and perhaps chemistry), just describe reality *as it is*, untainted by anything like relativity (subjectivity). Such a view assigns physics (and perhaps chemistry) a privileged position as compared with the rest of the sciences, and suggests that any theory that wants to envisage intentionality, with its manifest observer-relativity, is in danger of falling off the edge of the scientific world.

The question that presents itself here is therefore this: 'What notion of objectivity belongs to the natural sciences, the absolute or the relativistic?' The latter answer is at least superficially suggested by the fact that we live in the age of relativity theory, as opposed to Newtonian mechanics. Is the notion of relativity in the new physics anything to do with the relativity evident in psychology, or is all that there is here just verbal coincidence?

In order to tackle this question we consider briefly at the start of the next subsection some aspects of relativity expressed at the start of twentieth-century physics, arguing that the new physics is indeed relativistic in the sense defined so far. The inference then is that, just so far as concerns the involvement of relativity, knowledge of mind is in the same position as knowledge in the natural sciences.

In effect the argument is that relativity is implicated in *all* knowledge, whether in physics or elsewhere. The generality of this conclusion is consistent with conclusions reached in the preceding section by considering what is meant by saying that someone is following a rule (as opposed to behaving randomly). The enquiry ended with relativistic conclusions, but the route went by way of considering what is involved in making judgement, including about natural regularities. In brief, and as was anticipated at the beginning of the section (subsection 3.3.1), the remit of the notion of rule-following is very wide, concerning judgement as such. It is, then, not likely that some judgement is a matter of rule-following activity, while other judgement is a matter of static structures resembling possible states of affairs. This would be peculiar hotchpotch philosophy—just a mistake. But it would be equally a mistake, indeed it would be the corresponding mistake in the theory of knowledge, to suppose that much, or even most, forms of knowledge were relative, involving (activity of) the subject, while some special type, inevitably alone considered 'genuine', managed to avoid this altogether. There would just be two epistemologies here, unconnected except in their anachronistic juxtaposition.

On the other hand, there are *differences* as well as similarities to account for. In some sense which awaits explication, the methods of physics and the phenomena with which it is concerned are more objective, less subjective, than empathic methods and the intentional phenomena which are thereby known. After briefly considering relativity in physics we shall go on to argue that there is a matter of degree here, a continuity in the sciences which can be accomodated by a relativistic epistemology. By contrast, epistemologies that posit absolutes typically dictate choices: (absolutely) objective, or else (absolutely) subjective.

3.4.2 Relativity in physics, and on upwards, with increasing differentiation

Within the special theory of relativity, observers in different positions in space-time measure spatio-temporal relations with different results.[8] The results of measurement depend partly on the nature of the observer with respect to the quantities being measured. In this sense, measurement is an 'interaction' between observer and observed. Differences in results are apparent in so far as the observers differ (with respect to the quantities being measured). However, these differences do not imply that the various results obtained are incompatible with one another: the apparent incompatibility is resolved by taking into account the differences between observers.

There are rules linking results obtained from one spatio-temporal framework to results obtained from another, these being the so-called Lorentz transformations. Contrary to what is presupposed in Newtonian mechanics, there is no priviledged framework for measurement, and no corresponding 'absolute' length of an object, nor 'absolute' time of an event: spatio-temporal relations are always relative to one or another framework from which they are measured.

In the beginnings of modern science, the great division between absolute and relative qualities was imposed by prising apart the primary qualities of objects, including mass, shape, and velocity, from the so-called secondary qualities, the sensory qualities of colour, smell, etc. The primary qualities were absolute properties of objects, independent of human perception of them. The secondary qualities, on the other hand, were relative (involved interaction). Hence they belonged not to the (absolute) object, but rather to the subjective 'mind', created for this purpose, to be the bearer of the non-absolute qualities. One sign of the problem in all this was the fact that properties of mass, space, and time were, as much as the secondary qualities, evident in sensory perception and hence, of course, appeared just as relative. This point was made early on by Berkeley as part of his attempt to dismantle mind–matter dualism (Berkeley 1710).

There are, no doubt, interesting differences as well as similarities between primary and secondary qualities of objects (for recent discussion see, for example, McGinn 1983; Hacker 1987), but whatever these differences may be, it is not possible, in the context of relativity physics, to define them in the seventeenth-century way, in terms of what is or is not absolute. In contemporary physics the primary qualities are measured by interactions, and the results of measurement are relative to the measure. The critical difference between primary and secondary qualities therefore cannot turn on the absence of interaction and relativity in the former case.

Distinctions here will have to be made out in *another* way, specifically, in terms of the nature of the measures involved. Space and time are measured by rods and clocks, whereas colour, for example, is apparent only to more complicated, specialist measuring instruments. Within a relativistic framework it is possible to make discriminations between *more or less general* measures and realities. This line of thought is pursued below.

Let us take what is, by all means, a long jump, from physics to psychology, to the 'measurement' of mental states. Knowledge of such states depends partly on the nature of the observer with respect to the qualities being measured, that is, on the mental states of the observer. In this sense knowledge of mental states is an interaction between observer and observed. Different results will be obtained to the extent that observers differ. But this apparent incompatibility can be resolved by taking into account differences between observers. There is no absolute truth concerning mental states on particular occasions: their measurment is always relative to the mental state of one or another observer.

So far, then, the epistemology of mental states is formally similar to the epistemology of space-time. In this case there is no reason to say, indeed there is reason to deny, that psychology is committed to a form of knowledge second-rate compared with that in physics; neither is there reason to doubt the reality of its objects, any more than there is to doubt the reality of spatio-temporal relations.

On the other hand, the argument has, by all means, made a long jump: knowledge of mental states seems and is very different from knowledge of physical magnitudes, in particular because subjectivity and relativity are much more apparent. Let us put down some stepping-stones.

Subjectivity and relativity become apparent to the extent that observers differ in respect of what is being measured. Since generally we share the same spatio-temporal framework, we agree in measurement of spatial and temporal relations. Likewise, we have in common basic perceptual systems, so there is broad consensus concerning familiar perceptual properties of objects, including the so-called secondary qualities. The focus of the present discussion is, by contrast, the lack of agreement between observers in the attribution of intentionality, the manifest appearance of subjectivity and relativity. However, lack of agreement here is just what is expected from the point of view of a relativistic epistemology. To the extent that the measures differ (with respect to what is being measured), the results of measurement also vary, and in the particular case of mentality and intentionality there are high degrees of individual differences. Along the phylogenetic scale there is increasing systemic organization and increasing differentiation of species. Along the ontogenetic scale in humans, there is also increasing systemic organization and increasing differences among individuals. There is in both cases a logical connection between increasing complexity of systemic function and increasing differentiation (individuality). The 'higher' behaviour of humans, and the mentality that regulates it, represent the extreme of biological, or bio-psychological, differentiation. This differentiation characterizes both the 'object' of measurement and the measuring instrument. Here, then, we find most disagreement. But this does not mean that subjectivity and relativity arise in knowledge *for the first time*, still less that there can really be no *knowledge* here. On the contrary, subjectivity and relativity characterize all (empirical) knowledge. It is just that what was before hidden among what we have in common becomes apparent in our differences. Disagreement in judgement concerning the intentionality at work in higher behaviour is a logical consequence of individual differences in cognitive organization.

3.4.3 Reliability, validity, and the subject/object distinction

Agreement in judgement is greatest in those respects in which people are alike in constitution and competence, for example in judgement whether a needle is at a certain position on a dial, or whether such-and-such is red. But as perception, cognition, and emotion become more complex, individuality is increasingly apparent. And since the perception of psycho-logic depends on psychological characteristics of the perceiver, this perception may vary from person to person. Indeed a person may fail entirely to register a desire, say, in another, if the person knows no such motivation in his or her own case. The measurement of higher cognitive-affective phenomena will certainly be less reliable in a group picked at random than measurement of, say, the number of ticks on a questionnaire. This reflects the individuality of human beings in the relevant respects. But agreement will be apparent in so far as observers are alike in respect of the qualities being observed. The implication is that even the most complex psychological interpretation of behaviour can be reliable among observers, provided they are similar with respect to cognitive-affective characteristics.

The above remarks concern reliability. Let us consider now validity, which refers to accuracy of measurement, or truth, and is not secured by reliability alone. In epistemology that takes interaction as fundamental, there is no place for a conception of truth as static correspondence between measure and what is measured (cf. Subsections 1.3.2–3). The appropriate conception of truth is dynamic, to do with interactions and relations between them, and indeed turns out to be closely connected to reliability.

All attempts at measurement, as interactions, are valid in the restricted sense of providing information. The procedure of observation produces a certain result, which is real, and which in principle at least is repeatable. The result depends on qualities in the measure and qualities in the object measured. The question then arises as to what is due to one or the other. This question, however, cannot be answered on the basis of a single case. The distinction between objective and subjective arises not in one appearance but in many. Roughly, features that are common in many interactions are defined as due to qualities in the object, and those that are particular to any one are defined as due to qualities in the subject. The concept of interaction is fundamental, and the concepts of 'subject' and 'object' are derivative. This idea is fundamental to theory in various areas of psychology (Hundert 1989), including development (Piaget 1955; Russell 1995) and personality (Bowers 1973; Mischel 1979).

A valid observation may be defined as one that correctly represents the object. Bearing in mind the above conception of object, we may say that a reliable observation, that is, one constant between several observers (or conditions of observation), is already valid. On the other hand, we have the idea that reliable observation can still be wrong. However, according to relativistic epistemology, this possibility of error is not to be understood in terms of failure to correspond to an absolute object. It concerns rather failure to predict correctly the results of further measurement. The 'object' is revealed in, and is defined in terms of, its interactions with measuring instruments. Thus the valid measurement—the one true to the object—is that which correctly predicts the results of other measurements. In brief, validity is a matter of generalizability, and the distinction between validity and reliability becomes blurred. The intimate connection between agreement and truth falls out as a natural consequence of relativistic philosophy, whereas according to a simple correspondence theory of truth it has to remain fundamentally obscure. This relativistic idea is clearly expressed in contemporary statistical theory of reliability and validity. Generalizability theory blurs the distinction between the two, in contrast to the so-called classical definition of validity in terms of the 'true score' (Cronbach *et al.* 1963).

The above remarks concern judgement generally but, of course, apply to attributions of intentionality, the topic of this chapter. The implication is that any attribution of intentionality (or meaning) provides information concerning the observer and what is observed. To the extent that the judgement provides the former only, it tells us nothing about the object of judgement; it is subjective and invalid. Still, we may infer something, concerning the one making the judgement, for example that he or she always sees the same meanings, and is inclined always to say roughly the same thing. Conversely, to the extent that a judgement provides information about the person being observed, we may infer correct predictions concerning what he or she will do in various circumstances. To the extent that a judgement supports such predictions, it is objective and valid. Thus we arrive at the unsurprising conclusion (implicit thoughout the first chapter) that attribution of meaning is objectively valid in so far as it takes account of, and successfully predicts, the relevant observable phenomena.

In practice our opinions will differ more or less as we attempt to see the meaningful connections at work in behaviour. But the appearance of disagreement is no reason for scepticism about our endeavours. The issue of truth runs deeper than agreement or disagreement in opinions. Science aims not at agreement, but at correct representation of the phenomena.

In relativistic theories, the phenomena are conceived as being fundamentally interactions between the subject and object of measurement. Within this framework, it is predicted that there will be differences in the results of measurement made from different points of view, but these differences are subsumed under rules that take into account the different points of view from which measurements are made. In the special theory of relativity, these are the Lorentz transformations. An adequate psychological theory of intentionality, one which accurately represents the phenomena, should seek coherence in conflicting interpretations of intentionality among different individuals, by taking into account their diverse psychological characteristics. There is no reason why the theory of intentionality should become paralysed when faced with disagreement in judgement: on the contrary, conditions of agreement and of disagreement become part of its subject-matter. In other words, one aim of cognitive psychology is to find 'invariance laws' in the midst of individual differences (cf. Shaw and McIntyre 1974).

3.4.4 Bio-psychological measures and realities

The proposal is, then, that relativity in knowledge of intentional states does not in itself imply that the objects of such knowledge are less real than the objects known to physical theory. Perception of patterns of intentionality depends partly on our subjective reactions and concerns, that is to say, on intentional characteristics of the perceiver. But results of measurement of spatio-temporal magnitudes also depend partly on the observer's relevant characteristics, namely, position in space and time. In both cases subjectivity is combined with objectivity: measurement made from one point of view can be right or wrong, this distinction being drawn by reference to measurements made from other points of view.

It is true that patterns of intentionality do not appear as such in physics, nor would they appear (let us suppose) in a completed physics. A physical description of a chess game would not distinguish between intentional strategies and random sequences of moves, or indeed between either of those and the table being overturned by the wind. So if (a completed) physics describes all that is in reality, then patterns of intentionality are excluded as unreal, as perhaps fictions useful for prediction but no more.

But what is the basis for the claim that physics describes all that is real? Presumably this claim rests partly on the idea that physics describes reality free of any reference to subjectivity and relativity of measurement. But it does not: this idea is a leftover from seventeenth-century science. A completed physics, if current trends are any indication, will include reference to observers in space-time using rods and clocks, etc. To say that physics is free of observer-relativity, while higher-level sciences such as psychology are not, marks the distinction in entirely the wrong way, in any case in a way long past its sell-by date, and to say on these grounds that the one deals with reality (or real reality) while the other deals with convenient (or inconvenient) fictions compounds the error.

Another way of marking the differences is needed now, and it has nothing to do with the reality of physical objects as opposed to the unreality of everything else. Rather, it falls out of what is fundmental to the new epistemology, namely, the nature of the measure and its sensitivity. The distinction between physics and the behavioural sciences lies not in the absence as opposed to the presence of observer-relativity, but rather in the nature of the measuring instruments and consequently in the nature of what is measured; and this distinction is not absolute, but is a gradation. Measurement of spatio-temporal relations presupposes observers within space-time using spatio-temporal measures. But there are more and different kinds of measures in reality which are not the concern of physics. Biology and psychology study sensory and cognitive systems of increasing complexity which are sensitive to patterns of similarity and difference in the environment relevant to life, action, and social intercourse (cf. Chapter 6). Along the phylogenetic and ontogenetic scales, these measures of reality become increasingly differentiated, diverse, and individual, with consequent manifestation of subjectivity and relativity of measurement. However, what is perceived by the bio-psychic measures are no less real from the point of view of those measures than space and time are to the observer limited to the use of rods and clocks. The point is rather that the bio-psychic measures are sensitive to aspects of reality which are inaccessible to the measuring instruments of physics.

The central problem for this chapter has been knowledge of mind and meaning, in particular its apparent subjectivity which compares unfavourably with the objectivity of the natural sciences. We have argued, however, that this subjectivity is properly described as relativity, and that relativity characterizes all knowledge, including the physical sciences. Relativity pervades one subject's knowledge of another, but also the subject's knowledge of the object. By the same considerations, objectivity is also relativistic, defined in terms of invariance in interactions. It is inevitable that if the measure is relative, so is what is measured; just as absolute measures belong with absolute objects.

While it would be fair to say that concepts of absolutes are being replaced by concepts of relativity, still the influence of the former remains strong. Conceptions of representation and reality as absolute characteristically define them in advance, a priori; they circumscribe the limits of thought and reality. Relativistic definitions, by contrast, are more fluid and flexible.

Empiricism and materialism, both aspects of positivism, are examples of dogmatic philosophies that define the nature of reality and thought in advance. Empiricism proposed an account of thought and the reality represented in terms of sense-experience. It is now acknowledged, however, that in general the content of thought and language cannot be so defined (Chapter 1, subsection 1.4.1).

The materialist world-picture, however, remains pervasive in contemporary thought, and it exerts powerful pressure to adopt the materialist definition of content. Materialism claims that ultimately or fundamentally all that exists is the reality postulated by (a completed) physics. An apparent consequence of this view is that ultimately or fundamentally this reality is alone what is available for representation in thought. However, since many or most familiar concepts apparently do not coincide with physical categories, the materialist definition of content tends to be restricted to so-called 'natural kinds'. For example, the meaning of 'water' is taken to be anchored by its reference to H_2O, as in the thought-experiments discussed in Chapter 2 (subsection 2.5.2). The use of the expression 'natural' rather than 'physical' kind here signifies the materialist preconception that nature is to be identified with physical nature (with nature as defined by physics).

The materialist definition was, however, rejected (in subsection 2.5.4), as being inappropriate for biology and psychology. These are the sciences that (unlike physics and chemistry) use the concepts of functional behaviour regulated by information processing and informational content. They invoke such concepts in order to achieve adequate explanation of interactions between living systems and their environment, and the criterion of content appropriate to such explanation is fundamentally behavioural. Physical or physico-chemical kinds define informational content only to the extent that sensitivity to such kinds shows up in behaviour (in some behavioural response of the system), including specifically in discriminative behaviour. In general, the content of informational states, what they are about, is defined in terms of interaction, with explicit or implicit reference to the capacities and aims of the living being (subsection 2.5.4, also Section 4.5). In the context of the present discussion, the point is that this definition of meaning broadens out the notions of representation and what is represented beyond what can be described in terms of the natural sciences, to include also the bio-psychological measures and the realities they represent. The bio-psychological measures—living beings—are sensitive to aspects of reality which are salient to action; these aspects may include, though in any case they certainly exceed, those aspects accessible to the measures of physics.

A working assumption of cognitive-behavioural science is that ('higher') behaviour is to be explained in terms of regulation by mental states which carry processed information. Definition of the processed information carried by mental states involved in the regulation of action will include reference to its regulatory, or causal, role. Now it is also a conceptual truth that mental states represent reality. Integrating these two characterizations of mental states leads towards the idea that reality is—to put it briefly—*that which is encountered in action*. Another way of putting this point is to say that the reality represented in perception and thought is relative to cognitive processes within the living being, processes that serve in the regulation of activity.

This kind of approach to the definition of reality belongs with cognitive-behavioural science. However, it runs counter to several preconceptions of the traditional scientific world-picture. It is incompatible with materialism, since the reality encountered as relevant to action cannot generally be defined in the terms of physics. Beneath materialism lies a still deeper metaphysical prejudice, that reality should be defined independently of any reference to the subject. But the reality of action obviously cannot be defined in this way: it is an interaction between subject and object, between the living being and its environment.

If there are a priori categories of thought, they will be determined by what it means to be a living being; they will be biological and psychological categories, not primarily categories of physics and chemistry. Here would be included, for example, information concerning orientation in space and time, consumption of food (energy), threat, reproduction, and so on, and also, where appropriate, information necessary to social interaction, for example concerning the meaning of conventional signs.

Underlying such definitions of content are assumptions concerning the aims of action. It is a moot point, however, whether the aims of action, and therefore the categories of thought, can be circumscribed a priori. As noted above (subsection 3.4.2), the phylogenetic and ontogenetic scales are characterized by increasing complexity and differentiation of function: ends become served by increasingly diverse means, and new ends and means appear. For human beings in particular, the purposes of action and the contents of thought are diverse and unlimited.

The impossibility of circumscribing the content of human thought is connected partly to our use of language: in language diverse and unlimited 'meanings' become available as guides for action. This claim follows on from rejection of attempts to define the meaning of language and thought a priori, in particular from rejection of empiricist and materialist (positivist) definitions of meaning. Further, the content of thought as expressed in language apparently exceeds what is relevant to the necessities of life as envisaged by (evolutionary) biology.

To illustrate this point, consider the case of a person perceiving a shadow in the darkness. This perception may cause the belief that something rectangular-shaped is present, or further, the belief that there is danger, but also, given the requisite pre-existing system of thought, for which presumably language is required, the perception may give rise to the belief that there is concealed in the shadows an angel carrying a message. The first content can be defined in terms of physics, and can be envisaged by empiricist and materialist accounts of meaning; the first and the second content can be envisaged by (evolutionary) biology; but the third is the thought of a reality far removed from what can be defined in the terms of those philosophical and scientific theories.

All three types of content, however, have to be envisaged by psychology as a cognitive-behavioural science. The third is no less relevant than the first two to the cognitive explanation and prediction of behaviour. Psychology has to acknowledge whatever mental content makes a difference. The logic of psychological explanation and prediction is, of course, all the same whether the cognitive states invoked are true or false, scientifically valid or otherwise. For the purposes of explanation, psychology is not committed to the reality of the object of thought, only to the reality of the thought and its effects in action.

The answer to the general question as to how we determine mental content is that we observe what people do and listen to what they say, and compare the one with the other. The content of thought revealed by these methods exceeds what is countenanced by traditional attempts to circumscribe the objects of thought a priori. In general the behavioural criterion of mental content is an empirical one, dependent on observation. It stands opposed to preconceptions about what thought and the reality represented in thought *must* be like.

The proposal is, then, that it is impossible to prescribe the meanings at work in the regulation of action. The point is not that no categories of thought are fixed for us, only that not all are. Our position in the nature described by physics, and our position as living beings within nature as described by biology, provides the basis for, and places constraints on, all action and therefore all meaning.

As already noted in the previous and in the present section, intersubjectivity is fundamental to the relativistic definition of thought and reality. This aspect of relativity is still further removed from, and alien to, empiricist and materialist theories. They conceive thought solipsistically: the subject represents sense-experience or physical reality, in which realms other people appear as a special, though according to fundamental theory not so special, case.

The appearance of conflict here between relativistic and dogmatic philosophies over the role of intersubjectivity is genuine, not superficial. It is specifically *not* a matter of a philosophical theory of cognitive content (e.g. a materialist one) running parallel to, above or below, empirical theory which recognizes the role of the interpersonal in cognition. The empirical theory (such as was mentioned at the end of the preceding section) does not belong with empiricism and materialism, but with a priori principles which make fundamental the role of the interpersonal in cognition. The concept of 'reality' can be defined generally as that which determines the correctness or otherwise of thought. If reality is defined as an absolute object, the only constraint on thought is the independent nature of the absolute object represented. This idea if found in all dogmatic philosophies, including materialism in its current form. There is no essential connection between the true-or-false representation of reality and intersubjectivity. In relativistic conceptions of measurement, however, what determines the correctness or otherwise of measurement is not correspondence or lack of correspondence with an absolute object, but is rather comparison, agreement or otherwise, between points of view. This communication is fundamental to reality, taking the place of the dogmatically postulated object.

3.5 SUMMARY

The observer-relativity in knowledge of mind and meaning, and the various problems to which it gives rise, have long been recognized (Section 3.1). The issues were approached in Section 3.2 by considering the role of empathy (mental simulation), as well as theory, in our knowledge of mind. The behaviour which signifies mental states itself has intentionality (subsection 3.2.1), and perception of this plausibly involves the observer's own intentional states (subsection 3.2.2). Mental simulations construed as thought-experiments provide a fast, easy to perform means of experimenting with the causal relations among mental states and between mental states and tendencies to behaviour, and hence, along with observation of actual cases, can be part of the empirical basis of the theory of mind (subsection 3.2.3). Knowledge of mind, like other forms of empirical–theoretical knowledge, is surrounded by the possibility of error (subsection 3.2.4). The theory of empathy seems to give priority to first-person knowledge, with knowledge of oneself being the basis for understanding the other, but this appearance is deceptive: the simulations (or thought-experiments) in question are about intentional states and their connectedness, and attribution of the states and connections to this or that subject is a further step (subsection 3.2.5). This attribution involves both facility with perspectives and theory, the implication being that in developmental theory we do not have to choose between the child's increasing theoretical sophistication and the child's increasing facility with perspectives: both are fundamental and they are linked logically (subsection 3.2.6).

In Section 3.3 we approach knowledge of intentionality, and its observer-relativity, by way of Wittgenstein's discussion of rule-following. The notion of rule-following serves to capture the concept of *order* in reality and thought, as being through time, in activity, as opposed to being static, in the form of objects (subsection 3.2.1). The negative conclusion of Wittgenstein's analysis of rule-following is that the rule is not laid down in advance; the positive implication is that it is created in practice (subsection 3.3.2). The concept of agreement enters here as critical. This is not, however, because agreement is a necessary or a sufficient condition of someone's following a rule. The point is rather that one person's judgement about another that they are following a rule, is based on the observer's inclination to agree with what the other is doing (subsection 3.3.3). Relativity has traditionally been thought (since Plato's critique in the *Theaetetus*) to imply subjectivity and the collapse of objectivity. What is lost, however, is (only) the notion of an *absolute* object. The object makes many appearances, and in particular in those cases not under the control of the observer (subsection 3.3.4).

The relativity of attributions of intentionality, particularly in contrast to the objectivity in the physical sciences, seems to suggest that they describe no objective reality (subsection 3.4.1). However, consistent with the conclusions reached in the preceding section, it is argued that relativity pervades all the sciences, including physics. However, with increasing differentiation in phylogenesis and ontogenesis, subjectivity in the form of individual differences increasingly appears, both in the measures and in what is measured (subsection 3.4.2). In the context of relativity, validity and objectivity are defined in terms of multiple measurements made from different points of view, with comparisons and contrasts between them being dependent on invariance relations (subsection 3.4.3). Bio-psychological measures are sensitive to more and different aspects of reality as compared to those in the physical sciences. Contrary to what is envisaged by dogmatic philosophies such as empiricism and materialism, the implication of relativistic epistemology is that the reality we represent cannot be determined in advance, and is in its foundations interpersonal (subsection 3.4.4).

NOTES

1. We assume that this interpretation of empathy, or mental simulation, as being a form of thought-experiment, is plausible and interesting, but it is only more or less compatible with the various detailed proposals to be found in the literature. Recent collections of papers on comparisons and contrasts between empathy and theory-based epistemologies of mind are those of Davies and Stone (1995a,b). These include reprints of original papers and commentaries that appeared in a special issue of *Mind and Language* in 1992, as well as new papers. One of these is by one of the present authors (Bolton 1995) and it brings together themes running through this chapter and chapters 1 and 8.

2. In brief, thought-experimentation interweaves with theory, and hence the conclusion anticipated at the end of the previous subsection, that in so far as empathy or mental simulations involve anything like thought-experiments, they cannot be run without theory. If this interpretation of empathy is valid, the assumption of incompatibility

between empathy-based and theory-based epistemologies is mistaken. As already noted, this assumption is common, among proponents and opponents of simulation theory alike (for example, Gopnik and Wellman 1992; Gordon 1992; Stich and Nichols 1992). On the other hand, other commentators have seen it as obvious that simulations are going to require theory (Blackburn 1992). We endorse this line, and also the converse, that the theory of mind would work better if it made use of simulations in its empirical basis.

3. See Wittgenstein (for example 1953, sections 244 and 288ff.), and for commentary, for example, Bolton (1979, pp. 194–208) and Pears (1988, pp. 346–50).

4. The reference here is to Klein's notion of projective identification (Klein 1946; Sandler 1988). Klein described projective identification as being a basis for fundamental distinctions, as between self and non-self, as well as being among the mechanisms of defence, to be discussed in Chapter 8 (subsection 8.2.3).

5. Commentaries are numerous, and include, for example, Folgelin (1976), Kripke (1980), and Pears (1988). The treatment in the text of rule-following is most similar to the one in Bolton (1979), and discussion of the closely related problem of *form* (or *order*) summarizes some points in Bolton (1982).

6. In his influential commentary, Kripke (1980, Chapter 2) argues that Wittgenstein's analysis of rule-following leads to a major sceptical paradox about meaning, to the effect that there really is no such thing as meaning anything by a word. Kripke focuses on Wittgenstein's negative arguments, concerning what following a rule is not, and in particular, on the conclusion that the rule is not laid down in advance. Kripke then infers that, according to Wittgenstein's arguments, there is no rule, and hence no meaning. But he neglects Wittgenstein's positive proposal, that the rule is made in practice, to which we now turn in the text. Similar rejoinders to Kripke have been made by other commentators, for example McGinn (1984), Pears (1988).

   We may remark briefly on interesting positive proposals that Kripke goes on to make, which interact with the topics of the present chapter, and of the essay as a whole. He suggests (1980, Chapter 3) that Wittgenstein does not rest content with the alleged sceptical paradox about rule-following and meaning, but rather offers a 'sceptical solution' to it, involving reference to the community. Kripke uses the expression 'sceptical solution' to recall Hume's famous treatment of causality. Kripke notes (1980, pp. 66f.) that Hume's sceptical solution involved two features of causal inferences: first, that they are based in custom (habit, or natural inclination), and secondly, that they pertain essentially to a number of cases, not to one in isolation. Plausibly, considerations of these kinds play a role in Wittgenstein's account of rule-following, as we shall see. However, it is not *these* features that make Hume's solution a *sceptical* one. Hume's positive account remains 'sceptical' because, according to it, causal inference is is based in custom *as opposed to reason* (Hume 1777, V, I, 35–8). By contrast, Wittgenstein draws on a notion of custom (and natural inclination) in his account of rule-following, but such a notion is *not* opposed to reason. On the contrary, the account of rule-following is at the same time an account (or part of an account) of rationality, as discussed below in the text. A preconceived absolute definition of reason, against which the human measure is adversely compared, is a (or the) sure route to scepticism. And conversely, one way of avoiding scepticism is to countenance non-absolute, relativistic methods of representation and knowledge, as through this chapter.

7. The question whether an isolated individual, a Robinson Crusoe, could or could not follow a rule has been much debated in commentaries, usually in connection with Wittgenstein's 'private language argument', for example Ayer (1954), Rhees (1954), Kripke (1980), Peacocke (1981), McGinn (1984), Davies (1988), Pears (1988), and Budd (1989).

8. The following sketch is, of course, highly simplified and selective, emphasizing points to be taken up subsequently. For the interested reader unfamiliar with relativity theory, Einstein's own popular exposition (1920) is the best introduction. Berstein's commentary (1973) is excellent on the philosophical background of Einstein's revolution. A purely philosophical treatment, emphasizing relations between relativity theory in physics and the 'relativistic' conception of measurement and knowledge generally, can be found in Bolton (1979); this gives a more detailed version of the argument in the text. The main proposal to be made is that observer-relativity characterizes the theory of measurement in contemporary physics. This point is made in connection with the special theory of relativity because it appears there simply and clearly. The same point in much the same form appears also in the extended general theory. The issue of observer-relativity in the other great foundation of contemporary physics, quantum mechanics, requires a different kind of treatment, even superficial consideration of which is beyond the scope of the present essay. That said, it may be noted at least that the issue arises there in a radical form.

REFERENCES

Astington, J. W., Harris, P. L. and Olsen, D. R. (ed.) (1988). *Developing theories of mind*. Cambridge University Press, Cambridge.

Ayer, A. J. (1954). Can there be a private language? *Proceedings of the Aristotelian Society Suppl.*, 28, 63–76.

Baron-Cohen, S., Tager-Flusberg, H., and Cohen, D. (ed.) (1993). *Understanding other minds: perspectives from autism*. Oxford University Press, Oxford.

Berkeley, G. (1710). *The principles of human knowledge*. Reprinted in *The works of George Berkeley*, (ed. A. A. Luce and T. E. Jessop), vol. ii. Thomas Nelson and Sons, London, 1949.

Berstein, J. (1973). *Einstein*. Fontana, London.

Blackburn, S. (1992). Theory, observation, and drama. *Mind and Language*, 7, 187–203. (Reprinted in Davies, M. and Stone, A. (ed.) (1995). *Folk psychology: the theory of mind debate*, pp. 274–90. Blackwell, Oxford.

Bolton, D. (1979). *An approach to Wittgenstein's philosophy*. Macmillan, London.

Bolton, D. (1982). Life-form and idealism. In *Idealism, past and present*, (ed. G. Vesey), pp. 269–84. Cambridge University Press, Cambridge.

Bolton, D. (1995). Self-knowledge, error and disorder. In *Mental simulation: evaluations and applications*, (ed. M. Davies and A. Stone), pp. 209–34. Blackwell, Oxford.

Bowers, K. S. (1973). Situationalism in psychology. *Psychological Review*, **80**, 307–30.

Budd, M. (1989). *Wittgenstein's Philosophy of Psychology*. Routledge, London.

Butterworth, G. and Light, P. (ed.) (1982). *Social cognition: Essays on the development of understanding*. Harvester, Sussex.

Byrne, R. W. and Whiten, A. (ed.) (1988). *Machiavellian intelligence*. Clarendon Press, Oxford.

Cornford, F. M. (1935). *Plato's theory of knowledge*. Routledge and Kegan Paul, London.

Cronbach, L. J., Rajaratnam, N., and Gleser, G. C. (1963). Theory of generalizability: a liberalization of reliability theory. *British Journal of Statistical Psychology*, **16**, 137–63.

Davis, M. and Stone, A. (ed.) (1995*a*). *Folk psychology: the theory of mind debate*. Blackwell, Oxford.

Davies, M. and Stone, A. (ed.) (1995*b*). *Mental simulation: evaluations and applications*. Blackwell, Oxford.

Davies, S. (1988). Kripke, Crusoe and Wittgenstein. *Australian Journal of Philosophy*, **66**, 52–66.

Dennett, D. (1987). *The intentional stance*. MIT Press, Cambridge, Mass.

Dennett, D. (1988). Precis of *The intentional stance*, with peer commentary. *The Behavioral and Brain Sciences*, **11**, 495–546.

Einstein, A. (1920). *Relativity*, trans. R. W. Lawson. Methuen, London. (University Paperback, 1960.)

Folgelin, R. (1976). *Wittgenstein*. Routledge and Kegan Paul, London.

Fonagy, P. (1991). Thinking about thinking: some clinical and theoretical considerations in the treatment of a borderline patient. *International Journal of Psychoanalysis*, **72**, 639–56.

Gellatly, A., Rogers, D., and Sloboda, J. (ed.) (1989). *Cognition and social worlds*. Clarendon Press, Oxford.

Goldman, A. (1989). Interpretation psychologized. *Mind and Language*, **4**, 161–85. (Reprinted in Davies, M. and Stone, A. (ed.) (1995). *Folk psychology: the theory of mind debate*, pp. 74–99. Blackwell, Oxford.)

Gopnik, A. and Wellman, H. (1992). Why the child's theory of mind really is a theory. *Mind and Language*, **7**, 145–71. (Reprinted in Davies, M. and Stone, A. (ed.) (1995). *Folk psychology: the theory of mind debate*, pp. 232–58. Blackwell, Oxford.)

Gordon, R. M. (1986). Folk psychology as simulation. *Mind and Language* **1**, 158–71. (Reprinted in Davies, M. and Stone, A. (ed.) (1995). *Folk psychology: the theory of mind debate*, pp. 60–73. Blackwell, Oxford.)

Gordon, R. M. (1992). The Simulation Theory: objections and misconceptions. *Mind and Language*, **7**, 11–34. (Reprinted in Davies, M. and Stone, A. (ed.) (1995). *Folk psychology: the theory of mind debate*, pp. 100–22. Blackwell, Oxford.)

Hacker, P. (1987). *Appearance and reality*. Blackwell, Oxford.

Harris, P. L. (1989). *Children and emotion: the development of psychological understanding*. Blackwell, Oxford.

Harris, P. L. (1992). From simulation to folk psychology: the case for development. *Mind and Language*, **7**, 120–44. (Reprinted in Davies, M. and Stone, A. (ed.) (1995). *Folk psychology: the theory of mind debate*, pp. 207–31. Blackwell, Oxford.)

Heal, J. (1986). Replication and functionalism. In *Language, mind and logic*, (ed. J. Butterfield), pp. 135–50. Cambridge University Press, Cambridge. (Reprinted in Davies, M. and Stone, A. (ed.) (1995). *Folk psychology: the theory of mind debate*, pp. 45–59. Blackwell, Oxford.)

Hinde, R., Perret-Clermont, A. N., and Stevenson-Hinde, J. (ed.) (1985). *Social relationships and cognitive development*. Oxford University Press, Oxford.

Hobson, R. (1990). On acquiring knowledge about people and the capacity to pretend: response to Leslie (1987). *Psychological Review*, 97, 114–21.

Hobson, R. (1993). *Autism and the development of mind*. Lawrence Erlbaum Associates, Hillsdale, NJ.

Hume, D. (1777). *An enquiry concerning human understanding*, (ed. L. A. Selby-Bigge, 1902, (2nd edn). Oxford University Press, Oxford.

Hundert, E. (1989). *Philosophy, psychiatry and neuroscience. Three approaches to the mind*. Oxford University Press, Oxford.

Jaspers, K. (1923). *Allgemeine Psychopathologie*. Springer Verlag, Berlin. (English translation by Hoenig, J. and Hamilton, M. W. (1963). *General Psychopathology*. Manchester University Press.)

Klein, M. (1946). Notes on some schizoid mechanisms. *International Journal of Psychoanalysis*, 27, 99–110.

Kripke, S. (1980). *Wittgenstein on rules and private language*. Blackwell, Oxford.

Leslie, A. (1987). Pretense and representation: the origins of 'Theory of Mind'. *Psychological Review*, 27, 412–26.

McGinn, C. (1983). *The subjective view: secondary qualities and indexical thoughts*. Oxford University Press, Oxford.

McGinn, C. (1984). *Wittgenstein*. Blackwell, Oxford.

Mischel, W. (1979). On the interface of cognition and personality. *American Psychologist*, 34, 750–4.

Peacocke, C. (1981). Rule-following: the nature of Wittgenstein's arguments. In *Wittgenstein: to follow a rule*, (ed. S. H. Holtzman and C. M. Leich). Routledge and Kegan Paul, London.

Pears, D. (1988). *The false prison: a study of the development of Wittgenstein's philosophy*, Vol. 2. Clarendon Press, Oxford.

Perner, J. and Howes, D. (1992). 'He thinks he knows': and more developmental evidence against the simulation (role taking) theory. *Mind and Language*, 7, 72–86. (Reprinted in Davies, M. and Stone, A. (ed.) (1995). *Folk psychology: the theory of mind debate*, pp. 159–73. Blackwell, Oxford.)

Piaget, J. (1955) *The child's construction of reality*, (trans. M. Cook). Routledge and Kegan Paul, London.

Rhees, R. (1954). Can there be a private language? *Proceedings of the Aristotelian Society, Suppl.*, 28, 77–94.

Ripstein, A. (1987). Explanation and empathy. *Review of Metaphysics*, 40, 465–82.

Russell, J. (1995). At two with nature: agency and the development of self-world dualism. In *The body and the self*, (ed. J. Bermúdez, A. J. Marcel, and N. Eilan), pp. 127–51. MIT Press. Cambridge, Mass.

Sandler, J. (ed.) (1988). *Projection, identification, projective identification*. Karnac Books, London.

Shaw, R. and McIntyre, M. (1974). Algoristic foundations for cognitive psychology. In *Cognition and the symbolic processes*, (ed. W. Weimer and B. Palermo), pp. 305–62. Erlbaum Associates, Hillsdale, NJ.

Stich, S. (1983). *From folk psychology to cognitive science*. MIT Press, Cambridge, Mass.

Stich, S. and Nichols, S. (1992). Folk psychology: simulation or tacit theory? *Mind and Language*, 7, 35–71. (Reprinted in Davies, M. and Stone, A. (ed.) (1995). *Folk psychology: the theory of mind debate*, pp. 123–58. Blackwell, Oxford.)

Vygotsky, L. (1934). *Thought and language*, (Trans. Hanfmann, E. and Vakar, G. (1962). MIT Press, Cambridge, Mass).

Whiten, A. (ed.) (1991). *Natural theories of mind: the evolution, development and simulation of everyday mindreading*. Blackwell, Oxford.

Wittgenstein, L. (1921). *Tractatus logico-philosophicus*. (Trans. Pears, D. F. and McGuiness, B. F. (1961). Routledge and Kegan Paul, London.)

Wittgenstein, L. (1953). *Philosophical Investigations*, (ed. G. E. M. Anscombe and R. Rhees, trans. G. E. M. Anscombe). Blackwell, Oxford.

4

The definition of meaning: causal and functional semantics

4.1 INTRODUCTION

In the first chapter it was remarked that explanations of action in terms of mental states with meaning are effective in prediction, and the conclusion was drawn that such explanations must be, in some sense, causal. In the second chapter it was argued that the causal status of such explanations is compatible with the fact that the material causes of behaviour are in the brain, provided we assume that mental states are realized in brain states, and in particular that the brain encodes meaning. In the third chapter we turned to issues concerning mind, meaning, and objectivity. To some extent this was a diversion from the problem of meaning and causality, although emphasis in that discussion on the close connection between meaning and relativity belongs with the emphasis throughout the essay on action, on organism–environment interactions. In this chapter we return to meaning and causality.

Our task, pursuing the conclusion of the first chapter, is to explicate the sense in which explanations in terms of meaningful mental states are causal. In accordance with the conclusion of the second chapter, the task here is not to explicate a notion of immaterial as opposed to material causality, but is rather to explore the relation between causal explanation which does, and causal explanation which does not, appeal to the notion of encoded meaning (or information).

Meaningful states appear to be causes of behaviour, but also, they appear as effects of environmental causes. In the language of cognitive-behavioural psychology, cognitive (information-carrying) states mediate between stimuli and responses, being effects of the one and causes of the other.

At this stage of the argument, with the conclusion that meaningful or information-carrying states enter into causal relations, there is a powerful pressure to construe this 'semantic causation' as being simply 'causation' of the kind known in the physical sciences. Otherwise there is apparently a threat to the 'unity of science' and perhaps also to the physicalist assumption that all causing ultimately goes on at the physical level.

The pressure here is linked to the fast and plausible route to mind–brain identity considered at the beginning of Chapter 2, running as follows: 'so if, after all, mental states are causes of behaviour (if they figure in good scientific explanations), then, since we already know from physical theory that the material brain causes behaviour, mental states must be material brain states'. The parallel line of thought concerning causality runs roughly as follows: 'if, after all, semantic states are causes of behaviour (if they figure in good scientific physical causes, best identified in the physical sciences, then causal explanation that invokes semantic states must ultimately be, or be like, causal explanation in those sciences'.

On the other hand, there is an old problem here, the difference (dichotomy) between meaningful and causal connections. It was noted in the Introduction and first chapter (subsection 1.3.8) that the dichotomy between meaning and causality drawn in the cultural sciences at the turn of the century was based on what appear to be genuine differences between explanations in terms of beliefs, desires, reasons, etc., and causal explanations of the sort familiar in the natural sciences and physics in particular. The differences include that meaningful connections are evident already in particulars, while causal connections as determined in the natural sciences essentially involve generality: repeated or repeatable events, covered by general laws. It is difficult, in other words, to construe meaningful explanations as being causal in the sense familiar in the natural sciences, and entrenched in the scientific world-picture. This was the underlying problematic which prompted the turn-of-the-century dichotomy between meaning and causality.

The contemporary position, however, looks like this: respectable empirical sciences, including cognitive psychology, now envisage semantic states and their involvement in causal interactions, and hence there is pressure to break down the dichotomy between meaning and causality. There are broadly two ways of going about this: either causal explanations in terms of semantic states have to be shown to be (ultimately) the same, after all, as causal explanations in the natural sciences; or, it has to be shown that they are a distinctive, new form of causal explanation.

The first option is taken up by the doctrine known as causal semantics. It attempts to explicate the notion of meaning, or information, in terms an analysis of causality suited to the physical sciences. In Section 4.3 we see that the attempt fails. Before moving to a more positive thesis, we pause to consider in Section 4.4 a somewhat desperate suggestion, the only appeal of which is that it retains the requisite analysis of causality even though it cannot capture meaningful relations. The suggestion is that cognitive psychology should manage without semantics, and in particular should omit study of organism–environment interactions. This line of thought can reasonably be turned into a *reductio ad absurdum* argument against the assumption that the old view of causality is appropriate to meaningful connections.

In rejecting causal semantics, the argument is in effect that the original distinction between meaning and causality *as familiar in the natural sciences* is valid. It follows then that meaningful causal connections represent a distinctive form of causality. In other words, we pursue the second of the two options defined above.

Causal semantics explicates meaning using a notion of causality suited to the physical sciences. Its other distinguishing feature is that it defines meanings primarily in terms of their environmental causes rather than in terms of the interactions among them and their regulation of behaviour. This is connected with the fact that causal semantics envisages no fundamental role for systemic activity in the creation of meaning. This in turn goes along with the notion of causality at work here, in which nothing like systemic activity has any work to do. The implication is that the rejection of causal semantics involves a shift in the definition of meaning away from emphasis on 'input' towards emphasis on interactions between information-carrying states and their regulation of motor 'output'. The chief significance of this shift is that the definition of content can then take account of the contribution of the semantic processing system. Of course this kind of definition of meaning belongs with the idea invoked in all the preceding chapters, that meaningful states are invoked in order to explain (intentional) activity, and hence are to be understood essentially in terms of the difference they make to behaviour.

We consider in Section 4.5 so-called 'functional semantics', according to which information is defined with reference to the function of information-processing systems. Implicit in the discussion is the implication that the type of causal explanations that apply to functional, information-processing systems have distinctive features not apparent in the lower-level sciences. This conclusion is made explicit and explored in Section 4.6, with reference particularly to causal necessity and generality. Thus we develop through this chapter an argument for the claim that the form of causal explanation that applies to non-intentional phenomena (to phenomena under non-intensional descriptions), fails to capture the logic of causal explanation of intentional phenomena (of phenomena under intensional descriptions). In this way we will be working towards a distinction between two types of causal explanation, which may be called for convenience the non-intentional, and the intentional. This distinction will be elaborated in Chapter 5.

It should be remarked here that the distinction we are working towards is not that between non-functional and functional explanations. Functional (or teleological) explanations, which appeal to principles such as 'The function of cholorophyll in plants is to enable plants to perform photosynthesis', are characteristic of biology, and in their appeal to function, or purpose, they appear different from the non-functional explanations found in the sub-biological sciences. On the other hand, standard philosophy of science is that explanations of this type can be analysed into a set of non-functional, non-teleological statements (Nagel 1961). But this distinction and its apparent superficiality is not what is at issue here. We are concerned rather with the distinction between explanations which do, and explanations which do not, invoke semantic concepts (information-processing). A functional–teleological explanation of an information-processing system may be given in the form: 'A system of such-and-such kind encodes/processes information in order to facilitate such-and-such kind of activity'. It may be possible, along the lines of the standard analysis (Nagel 1961), to render this as a set of non-functional, non-teleological propositions, but the expression 'encodes/processes information' survives the analysis untouched. It is this expression, we suggest, that signifies a form of causal explanation distinct from what is found in the sub-biological natural sciences.

We begin in Section 4.2 by covering in more detail issues that we have sped past in this introduction, particularly concerning the analysis of causality. It should be said straightaway that the relevant issues in the philosophy of science and metaphysics are complicated, and even the 'more detail' will be exceedingly sketchy. The story has to start with Hume's analysis of causality in terms of constant conjunction (subsection 4.2.1), which prompts the problem of necessary connection (subsection 4.2.2). Consideration of Hume's problem leads to a widely accepted view that causality essentially involves *generality covered by a law of nature* (subsection 4.2.3). Further, there is a natural enough, common presupposition that the laws of nature are (ultimately) physical laws, or again, that all real causing goes on at the physical level. This presupposition leads to what will be called the 'physicalist' construal of causality (subsection 4.2.4). Causal connections, so understood, are apparently quite distinct from meaningful connections, as recognized in the turn-of-the-century dichotomy between the two (subsection 4.2.5). But this dichotomy, and the assumptions about causality that underlie it, have to be deconstructed in so far as meaningful explanations do seem to be causal. This task occupies the remainder of the chapter.

4.2 HUME'S ANALYSIS OF CAUSALITY, SOME STANDARD ELABORATIONS, AND THE PROBLEM OF MEANING

4.2.1 Correlation and generality

In his *Enquiry concerning human understanding*, Hume argued that our knowledge of cause and effect arises from experience of constant conjunction (1777, Sections IV and VII). This is to say: the judgement that event A causes event B is based in the observation that events of type A are always followed by events of type B. This aspect of Hume's analysis of causality is fundamental, and has to be kept in sight amidst the various complications that surround it, some of which we consider next.

In practice, on any one occasion we observe an event of type B preceded by complex of circumstances, C, in addition to an event of type A. To establish a causal link between A and B the relevance of those circumstances has to be determined. To establish whether A is a *necessary* condition of B we observe C without A, as naturally occurring or by contrivance, and observe whether or not B follows. To establish whether or not A is a *sufficient* condition of B we observe A without C, as naturally occurring or by contrivance, and observe whether or not B follows. These principles, elucidated by Mill (1843) in his 'methods of agreement and difference', underlie our modern idea of controlled experimentation.

In practice, particularly in the life-sciences, psychology, and the social sciences we rarely find universal generalizations, but rather partial ones, of the form: A is followed by B in a certain proportion of observed cases. Presumably whether or not B occurs following A depends on other, so far unknown factors, and the assumption is that there are universal, causal generalizations, even if we cannot determine them. One function of a universal generalization is to license the simple inductive inference: the next observed A will be followed by B. In the absence of a universal generalization, the problem is to determine the *probability* of the next A being followed by B, given that a certain proportion of As so far observed have been followed by B. This is the problem for the theory of statistical inference. Its complexity compounds in interaction with the problem cited above, that of controlling for potentially relevant variables. (The problem comes to concern the validity of the assumption that the circumstances associated with the next A are typical of those in the sample so far observed.) The life-sciences, psychological, and social sciences rely heavily, then, on statistical methodology rather than on simple induction from universal generalizations; the universal, causal generalizations are assumed rather than known.

Thus practical application of Hume's analysis of causal propositions in terms of constant conjunction between events is complicated by the need for controlled observation and statistical inference. Nevertheless, the analysis remains firm as the underlying basis of these scientific methods.

4.2.2 The problem of necessary connection

We consider now a very different kind of problem concerning Hume's analysis, philosophical rather than methodological. This is the problem, identified by Hume (1777, Section VII), as to whether constant conjunction is *all there is* to our notion of causality, whether, in particular, there is a connotation of *necessary connection* in our notion of causality which is not captured by the notion of constant conjunction.

It should be emphasized that this is not the problem frequently encountered in scientific practice, as to whether an observed association between two types of event signifies that the one causes the other, or is mere coincidence, or perhaps signifies a common cause of both. The alternatives here can be resolved in principle by application of Mill's methods, that is, by controlled observation or experiment. The distinction here between causal connection and constant conjunction is the distinction between observation of constant conjunction which does and which does not control for other relevant factors.

The *further* problem identified by Hume remains after application of the requisite scientific methodology, which is why it is philosophical rather than methodological.

Even in case it has been established that one kind of event is a sufficient (or necessary and sufficient) condition for the occurrence of another, is this all that is required to establish a causal connection between the two? Does the concept of causal connection also connote an element of necessary connection, which we could express by saying that if the one kind of event occurs, then the other *must* occur.

Hume gave a sceptical answer to the problem that he had identified: he could find no resources in his empiricist philosophy capable of explicating any such notion of (empirical) necessity. According to empiricism the phenomena are known by experience. Thus also, any correlation among the phenomena is to be known only on the basis of observation, and is simply a matter of contingent fact, not of any 'necessity'. What comes more or less to the same is that Hume supposed cause and effect to be discrete—entirely separate—events; so that we can, for example, always imagine the cause without the effect (Hume 1777, Section IV). Imaginative capacities aside, the point is that there is no logical, a priori, or conceptual linkage between the description of the cause and description of the event. There is in this sense at least no necessary connection between cause and effect, only observed association between kinds of event. This association, and no more, is all that is allowed by a strict empiricism.

The failure of empiricism to capture a priori conditions of experience, in particular necessity in causation, became a major rationale for Kant's subsequent 'Copernican revolution' in philosophy. For the present purpose, however, we omit discussion of the Kantian post-empiricist response, and consider rather a more contemporary solution.

4.2.3 The standard assumption: causality involves generality covered by natural law

It is widely acknowledged that there has to be a distinction between 'merely accidental' generalizations and generalizations with nomic, law-like necessity. For the statement 'A-events cause B-events' to be true there has to be a correlation between the two kinds of event, but also this correlation has to be, or to be a consequence of, a law of nature: it is not enough for the correlation to be merely accidental.

Braithwaite, for example, distinguishes laws of nature from 'more generalizations', and defines causal laws as a subclass of the former (1953, chapter IX).

Davidson's complex views on a range of issues concerning causation include endorsement of the following (Davidson 1967, p. 160):

A singular causal statement '*a caused b*' entails that there is a law to the effect that 'all the objects similar to *a* are followed by objects similar to *b*, . . .'

Thus also Fodor, in setting up a major argument which we shall consider in detail later (subsection 4.4.2), puts the point as follows (1980, p. 70):

If one assumes that what makes my thought about Robin Roberts a thought *about Robin Roberts* is some causal connection between the two of us, then we'll need a description of RR such that the causal connection obtains in virtue of him satisfying that description. And *that* means, presumably, that we'll need a description under which the relation between him and me instantiates a law.

The idea may be expressed briefly as being that causality implies generality covered by (natural) law. Such a view is very widely accepted and for convenience it will be called in what follows the 'standard assumption' about causality.

The next main point, to be taken up in the next subsection, is that the natural law invoked in this standard assumption is usually and plausibly taken to be *physical law*. But before going on to consider this, let us briefly make some links with empiricism and post-empiricism which will become important as we proceed.

As remarked above, empiricism was intimately involved, in Hume, with the analysis of causation in terms of correlation and the problem of necessary connection. However, the empiricist claim that all empirical knowledge is derived from experience has come to be recognized as mistaken. As discussed in the first chapter (subsection 1.4.1) post-empiricist epistemology sees that empirical knowledge typically has the form of a theory that posits unobservables, and which cannot be analysed in terms of statements about sense-experience. It may be expected that the new epistemology has implications for Hume's empiricist treatment of causality. An obvious implication is that some statements of empirical associations will have an element of necessity in so far as they are deducible from theory: they *must hold, if* the theory is correct (Braithwaite 1953; Popper 1959). In effect, the 'empirical' necessity here derives from a deduction from other propositions. While this account clearly exceeds what is envisaged by empiricism, it remains true to one fundamental aspect of Hume's empiricist analysis. The account defines a sense in which empirical generalizations 'must' hold, but this element of necessity is added, as it were, from the outside, by the covering theory. It is not a matter of internal linkage between cause and effect, which remain, as in Hume, discrete, entirely separate from one another.

The relation between the above approach to causal necessity and what has been called above the standard assumption about causality is controversial. The standard assumption links causal necessity to natural law, or 'necessity in nature', and it is not obvious that this law-like necessity can be equated with something like inferential role in theory (Armstrong 1983). The theory in question would have to be a true, yet to be discovered, representation of reality. Even so, it may be objected, the necessity of natural law derives from necessity in nature, not from necessity within the representation. This controversy is not, however, relevant to the line of argument here. From the epistemological point of view, if not the metaphysical, the status of natural law is bound up with belonging to theory. We shall assume in what follows that natural law underlies causal necessity, and that our best estimate of what is or is not a natural law is current theory.

4.2.4 Natural laws understood to be physical (the physicalist construal)

The standard assumption about causality, as involving generality covered by natural law, has the pretty well inevitable consequence that causality comes to be seen as the province of the natural sciences, of physics and chemistry in particular. After all, it is (trivially) the natural sciences which aim to identify laws of nature, and among the natural sciences physics and chemistry apparently capture unlimited generality. A connected point is that these are the sciences in which generalizations can be seen to follow from covering theory in something like a hypothetico-deductive form. The idea that the natural laws involved in causal relations are (or are ultimately) physical laws will be called for convenience in what follows the 'physicalist construal' of natural laws (or of causality).

This construal of natural law and causality belongs with the physicalist view that ultimately *all causing goes on at the physical level*. One source of this view is the metaphysical assumption that there are only physical things. The strength and the weakness of this assumption, however, is that it may stand opposed only to (often outdated) metaphysics, claims to the effect that there are, for example, minds as well as bodies, or Platonic forms outside of nature. It is plausible enough to say that there are no entities of these kinds, and that even if there were they could have no causal role in nature. This ontological approach combines with the construal of natural law and causality now under consideration, providing support for the view that ultimately all causing goes on at the physical level.

This physicalist view—that ultimately all causing goes on at the physical level—is widespread in contemporary phiolosophy, including major positions in the philosophy of mind. It is one pressure behind adopting mind–brain identity theory as soon as mental causation has been acknowledged. As discussed in the previous chapter (subsection 2.2.1), Fodor's language of thought hypothesis allows mental, meaningful causation only because it coincides with material (neural), syntactic causation. Davidson's doctrine of anomalous monism (1970) has the consequence that the laws implicated in causal interaction between the mental and the physical must be physical. Dennett appears ambiguous over the question whether intentional states are real or (merely) constructs useful for prediction, as noted in the previous chapter (subsection 3.4.1), but in any case proposes that explanations which invoke them are causal only in so far as they supervene on physical conditions (Dennett 1987, p. 57). These diverse and influential views in the philosophy of mind apparently share the assumption that ultimately causation must be physical, involving physical laws.

Although the physicalist construal of natural causality is commonly accepted, the line of thought followed in this essay runs counter to it. The view argued for in Chapter 2, intended to endorse the current paradigm in neuroscience/cognitive psychology, is that mental, meaningful causation is compatible with material causation because mental states are encoded in brain states. This proposal stays with the idea that all causation is at the physical level, at least in the sense that it posits no immaterial (e.g. Cartesian mental) causal objects, but it draws away from the presumption that the causal laws (the theoretical explanations) in question here belong to physics (or physics/chemistry). Rather, the implication is that the logic of explanation here is distinct from what we find in physics and chemistry, invoking what we find in the natural sciences only in biology and upwards, namely, systemic function involving information-processing.

According to the account to be worked towards in this chapter and the next, we find in the biological sciences upwards a form of causal explanation which in critical respects is unlike what we find in the sub-biological natural sciences. In distancing ourselves from the idea that the 'natural laws' underlying causality have to be physical laws, we move away also from corresponding conceptions of generality and necessity. Causal explanations in biology upwards are of course theory-driven, but they do not have the generality found in the sub-biological sciences: the 'laws', and the necessity, invoked concern not nature generally, but the (normal) functioning of particular kinds of information-processing system.

4.2.5 Meaningful connections apparently not causal in these commonly accepted senses

Neither the standard assumption about causality, defined in subsection 4.2.3, nor its physicalist construal, defined in 4.2.4, are a very good fit with our familiar explanations of actions in terms of meaningful mental states such as beliefs and desires. Such explanations hardly look as if they are, or are derived from, natural laws, still less physical laws. In brief, meanings apparently are not causes.

On the other hand, we do find in meaningful explanations something like generality and necessity. A person does such-and-such because of having various beliefs and wishes, and anyone else who had exactly the same beliefs and wishes, and no other contrary ones, would do the same. There is a generalizing principle here, even if the particular statement applies to just one person on one occasion! Further, if a person has reasons for doing such-and-such, in the form of the requisite beliefs and wishes, then she must, other things being equal, do it. 'Other things being equal' here includes 'has no conflicting beliefs/desires'. But the qualification also includes 'if the person is behaving rationally', which in turn can be glossed as 'if she is behaving normally as a rational agent'. This logic of necessity will be explored later, but for the moment the point is that it has apparently little or nothing to do with causal necessity due to natural laws. Further, and worse still from the point of view of familiar assumptions about causality, the necessary connections here are due to meaning, or reason, as opposed to being contingent. In all the familiar approaches to causality considered so far, whether causal necessity is seen as based only in our experience of constant conjunctions, or in natural law, or in our hypotheses about nature, there is the clear assumption that causal necessity is fundamentally contingent, based in matters of fact about nature, which in principle could be different, not in laws of reason, or the connections between meanings, which in principle could not.

In the case of reasons, or meaningful connections, putative cause and effect are apparently not entirely separate, indicated by the fact that the mental state is typically specified in the same way, with the same meaningful content, as the action that it is said to generate. Connected with this, we do not need to make field observations, still less experiments, to establish generalizations over meaningful connections: they are apparently a priori, or conceptual, in fact linked by meaning. This kind of necessary connection is quite unlike what is proposed in Hume, and in the other accounts we have considered, where the necessary connection is a posteriori. The necessity in meaningful connections apparently does not (have to) follow from a covering natural law. Similar problems arise over the issue of whether environmental events are the causes of meaningful states. It is notoriously difficult in cognitive psychology, and in folk psychology it is frankly impossible, to define the stimulus as cause of a mental state without reference to (the meaningful content of) the mental state itself.

Meaningful connections are apparently not causal according to the standard assumption about causality, that it involves generality covered by natural law. *A forteriori*, they are poor candidates for being causal connections according to the physicalist construal of natural law, where also new problems arise, namely, that it is hard or impossible to conceive the causes of meaningful states, the states themselves, and their effects in action, in the terms of physics, in order to being them under covering physical laws.

In brief, for all these reasons (at least), meanings are not causes, and hence the turn-of-the-century dichtomies between meaning and causality, understanding and (causal) explanation.

Before proceeding, a note on terminology is necessary. The problem of the relation between meaning and causality arises under a particular interpretation, or set of interpretations, of causality, namely, those sketched in this section so far. In brief, the interpretations are to the effect that causality involves generality and natural laws, particularly laws of physics. The arguments to follow in this chapter require specification of causality as understood in these ways. So widespread are these interpretations that the term 'cause' in the literature, though used in these senses, is usually used unqualified. Where there is no ambiguity we shall follow this briefer, customary usage, in arguing for example that meaning is not causal, that it cannot be viewed as causal relation. But the sense of causality here is as outlined above: generality covered by natural, particularly physical law. Another sense of causality will be defined as we proceed, one in which meaningful connections are causal.

4.3 NEVERTHELESS, CAUSAL SEMANTICS: MEANING DEFINED AS A CAUSAL RELATION

4.3.1 The theory and overview of what is wrong with it

The conclusion that meaningful explanations are not causal may not matter much if the only 'body of knowledge' that employed them was folk psychology. But in so far as they are invoked by sciences, particularly applied sciences, which aim to make a difference, the conclusion is problematic and controversial. Much of the controversy here, as remarked earlier (subsection 1.3.8), has revolved around psychoanalysis. From the hard-headed scientific point of view, psychoanalysis can be grouped together with the folk psychology that it extends, and disposed of as non-science. But the position looks different, and becomes again thoroughly problematic, with the turn of events in which authentic, experimentally based psychological science has become involved with something very like mental states with meaning (semantic information). It is (almost) quite impossible to dismiss cognitive psychology as pseudo-science, and it is a very uninviting prospect to suppose that this behavioural science is dealing not with causes but with meanings, as if it, too, were a hermeneutic exercise, along with psychoanalysis and textual criticism. This line of thought suggests that the meaning/causality distinction really has to go. It is a polemical argument, by all means, but this is suited to the fact that the distinction between meaning and causality has often enough been used and abused in polemical arguments.

In this chapter we consider various responses to the dilemma in its contemporary form, as outlined in the introductory section, starting here with *causal semantics*. Causal semantics tries to capture meaning within the familiar net of causal relations, preferably in terms consistent with physicalism. This involves dismantling the dichotomy between meaning and causality by defining the former in terms of the latter. In general terms the problem with this proposal is that it tries to dismantle a philosophical dichotomy by acknowledging only one of its terms. We have come across this philosophical strategy earlier, mainly in connection with (simple) mind–brain identity theory (subsection 2.1.2), where it was identified as one most likely to fail. The general problem is that distinctive characteristics emphasized by, though exaggerated by, the category to be absorbed, are not captured by the category doing the absorbing, which always was defined in opposition to the other. In the present case this means: the definition of meaning as being a causal relation omits the specificity of meaning, its relation to the subject, and the origin of its necessity within these factors. Causal semantics makes meaning too general, too objective, and too necessary, with no possibility of it 'breaking down'.

Causal semantics seeks to construe the relation between meaningful mental states (or information-carrying states generally) and what they mean, as being a matter of association covered by natural, probably physical, law. If causal semantics can be made to work, then the critical intentional concepts will be analysed in the familiar terms of causality, and then presumably explanations which invoke concepts of information and meaning could be eliminated in favour of explanations which invoke no such concepts. In brief, semantics would be 'naturalized' (Fodor 1990). However, we shall argue that causal semantics cannot be made to work. As implied in the preceding paragraph, the reason why the theory does not work is connected with the fact that the dichotomy between meaning and causality marked a genuine tension which cannot just be glossed over, a tension between meaningful phenomena and explanation, and the methodological assumptions suited to the (sub-biological) natural sciences.

Causal semantics has been much discussed in the literature (Dretske 1981, 1983; Fodor 1990; also, for example, Baker 1989; Villanueva 1990). Various forms of causal semantics have been proposed, the most rigorous and sophisticated being those of Dretske (1981, 1983), and of Fodor (1990). Some aspects of these versions will be considered as we proceed. For purposes of bringing out some critical features and problems of causal semantics, a brief statement of its main idea from Fodor will suffice, as follows (Fodor 1990, p. 57):

S-events carry information about P-events if 'Ps cause Ss' is a law.

A similar analysis can be given of the expression 'S-events *mean* P-events'. It can be applied to cognitive states or to linguistic utterances, though the distinction here is blurred. (An account of the meaningful content of the cognitive state 'believes that p' or 'possesses the information that p' will be closely linked to a theory as to the meaning of the sentence p, and vice versa.) A precursor in psychology of more recent theories of causal semantics, as Fodor remarks (1990, pp. 53ff.), was Skinner's attempt to extend operant theory to verbal behaviour (Skinner 1956), the proposal being that (meaningful) utterances are under 'stimulus control'. This proposal could be expressed in the form: utterances are caused by environmental stimuli, and thereby have meaning.

Causal semantics is subject to two main criticisms. First, its explanation of the content of meaningful states tends to be either vacuous or inadequate. The underlying problem is the one anticipated in the preceding section: it is unclear that the 'causes' of meaningful states can be identified independently of the meaningful states themselves, their alleged effects. The second main criticism of causal semantics is that it cannot adequately explain the fact that informational or meaningful states can come to represent what has no existence in reality. Two kinds of case come under this heading. One concerns our capacity to use meaningful though 'empty' terms or concepts, whether in myth or in play (e.g. 'unicorn'), or in scientific theory (e.g. 'phlogiston'). The other concerns the fact that information-carrying states can be *false*.

We suggest that the diagnoses of both failings are the same. In both cases the problem is that causal semantics (explicitly) seeks to define information entirely 'objectively', without reference to the 'subjective' contribution to information processing and content. Or again: the basic fault of causal semantics is its attempt to define information without acknowledging its relativity to a 'receiver' (and user).[1]

4.3.2　First problem: the definition of meaning is vacuous or inadequate

According to causal semantics, cognitive states (or utterances with meaningful content) are caused by events in the environment, and thereby carry information about, or mean, those events. The critical question concerns the definition of environmental events. Broadly speaking, there are two options. Either the events are defined *independently of* the contents they are alleged to cause, or they are defined by appeal to their alleged affects. In neither way, however, do we have an adequate explanation of mental content. The former option cannot account for the diversity of content; the latter can, but vacuously.

Environmental stimuli can be defined independently of the informational states which, according to causal semantics, they cause. Physical descriptions can be given, of the stimulus or of the sensory stimulation to which it gives rise. Or again, low-level phenomenal descriptions can be given, concerning shape, colour, etc. But either way there is so far no account of the richness and variety of informational states. Informational content is, in general, not determined by physical or low-level phenomenal characteristics. For example, a person sees a dog and comes to believe (with or without conscious thought) that is it dangerous, and so runs away, or that it is friendly, and so pats it. If the contents of such beliefs are determined by the stimuli that cause the beliefs, then these stimuli cannot be defined in physical terms, or in terms of perceived shapes and colours.

Since this option is unpromising, causal semantics tends to rely on the alternative: environmental stimuli come to be defined by reference to the informational states that they are held to cause. It is in making this move that the theory lapses into vacuity. The environment is populated with whatever properties are required to explain the corresponding mental states. If I see a dog and believe it to be dangerous, my belief has this content because it is caused by (an instance of) the property *dangerousness*, etc. In this way causal semantics comes to embrace a prolific realism concerning properties, the assumption being that at least all meaningful predicates of all natural languages are associated with independently existing properties. But whatever the philosophical attractions or otherwise of this realism, it is of little or no use in the explanation of meaningful states or events, mental or verbal. In general, the grounds for positing the existence of causal properties is the existence of their alleged effects, that is, meaningful mental states or linguistic utterances, not the other way round. The postulate of environmental causes becomes merely an *ad hoc* device for explaining the content of representational states. The classic statement of this kind of objection to causal semantics is Chomsky's critique of Skinner's proposal that verbal behaviour is under 'stimulus control', already discussed in the first chapter (subsection 1.2.2). Fodor's recent rigorous formulation of causal semantics (Fodor 1990), to be discussed below, continues to rely on the same kind of prolific realism as was exploited by Skinner.

Causal semantics seeks to capture meaning within the notion of causal association by identifying the meaning of information-carrying states with their environmental causes. But the problem is how to determine these environmental causes without reference to their alleged effects. Let us contrast the causal approach to semantics with another, which draws essentially on the notion of information-processing. What does a cognitive psychological, information-processing, story about the production of informational states look like? A rough answer will serve the present purpose:

At the input end, in stimulation, information is picked up by sensory systems. The information picked up depends partly on the physically defined nature of the stimulus, and partly on characteristics of the sensory system. As a rule, sensory systems are designed to pick up information of kinds relevant to the animal's behaviour and needs, at least to its survival. This information is then processed, which includes assimilation into innate or acquired patterns of association or expectation, of greater or lesser complexity, these being again of kinds relevant to the animal's behaviour and needs. Processing eventually produces informational states which serve in the regulation of behaviour. The more information becomes processed, the more it differs from the low-level information picked up at the periphery. The information that this is thirst-quenching water, for example, is not what is encoded on the retina. The processed information not only does not allow definition in terms of physics (e.g. the content 'water' cannot be defined as H_2O), but it essentially implicates the animal's needs (drives), which have even less to do with physics. The environment has to be defined in physical terms to tell the first part of the information-processing story, in specifying what can be and is picked up at the sensory level, but after that physical definition of informational content becomes decreasingly relevant. What becomes relevant in its place is the way in which low-level information is interpreted, the criterion of which, at any given stage, is a matter of behavioural responses of information-processing subsystems, eventually of the animal (as a whole) as it acts in the environment.

We assume, crude though the above sketch is, that it captures some essential features of the cognitive psychological account of the causal history and content of information-carrying states, and it is apparent that in such an account physical descriptions of the environment represented in cognitive states (as opposed to bio-psychological descriptions) play a limited, though by all means a fundamental, role.[2]

Cognitive psychology acknowledges that there are properties of environmental stimulation which can be specified without reference to information-carrying states, physical properties such as shape, orientation, energy patterns, etc. But it proceeds to explain how these are processed in ways dependent on the living being (the receiver, perceiver, and agent), producing cognitive states with content which cannot be defined in physical terms, which is richer and more diverse.

It is in this critical respect that the information-processing story in cognitive psychology diverges from causal semantics, which seeks to explain content by reference to environmental causes. If causal semantics acknowledges that the environmental causes sufficient to explain content cannot be captured by physical definitions, then it has to define them, in a circular way, by reference to the content of the information-carrying states themselves. In this way the environment is credited with properties corresponding to mental states which involve much interpretation or processing of physical characteristics, mental states concerning, for example, dangerousness. In effect, the results of interpretation and processing are explained in terms of ready-made features of the world. In this sense the subjective contribution to concept-formation (meaning) is denied.

There is nothing wrong with attributing to the environment characteristics such as dangerousness. Certainly this is what the frightened animal does, notwithstanding the fact that physics countenances no such property. The issue is rather how we proceed in scientific explanation. The *explanation* of how the animal becomes frightened is not simply that it 'sees an instance of the property *dangerousness*'. The explanation has rather to cite information-processing capacities of the animal, and the interests that they serve. The postulate of the property of dangerousness can be added as an after-thought to the account in terms of interpretation and processing, but it does no explanatory work. The significance of such a postulate is in fact metaphysical rather than scientific. The claim that meaningful content is caused by ready-made, independently existing properties ensures that the results of interpretation are 'objective' rather than 'subjective'. The effect is that the subjective contribution to meaning is denied. In this way the theory of causal semantics stands in the venerable (and diverse) realist tradition, which posits reality as ready-formed, then simply impressed on the mind (or brain), with nothing for the mind (or brain) to do except register the way things are. Empiricism was a theory of representation and knowledge of this kind, and causal semantics is one of its not so distant descendents. Causal semantics is true to the realist tradition in two related ways. First, in that the mode of representation is objectively defined (i.e. as a causal association); second, in that the representational content is objectively defined, in terms of already-made, independent properties.

Causal semantics, in the version that makes profligate appeal to environmental properties, has difficulty in remaining causal, in so far as the criterion for the existence of such properties is the existence of their alleged effects, mental states with the corresponding content. Further, the theory seems to have little to do with the information-processing account characteristic of cognitive psychology. In brief, causal semantics in this version seems to be neither causal nor scientific.

4.3.3 Second problem: no explanation of empty terms or false propositions

The above problem for causal semantics is intensified when the theory has to deal with 'empty' content, signified by terms such as 'unicorn' or 'phlogiston'. Up to this point, causal semantics can appeal to the causal role of *instances* of properties in generating mental states which mean, or carry information about them. But in the case of empty concepts, there are no such instances. To cope with this kind of case, causal semantics has to run the causal story in terms of properties, not instances of properties (Fodor 1990, p. 100). The idea would be that, for example, beliefs about phlogiston were caused by the *property* 'phlogiston'.

The theory has to run in the same way even in case of mental content that is not empty. This is partly to achieve simplicity and consistency in the theory, but also, and more importantly, because we have to allow for the possibility in principle that a concept such as 'electron' may turn out to be empty after all, in some future physical theory. Even well-entrenched notions are replaceable. Generally, theories of meaning have to secure meaning in the absence of truth. Beliefs about phlogiston, though false, never were meaningless; no more would beliefs about electorns turn out to be senseless, and to have always been senseless, in case the theory in which those beliefs are embedded came to be superceded. This general point applies in the theory of linguistic meaning and in the theory of mental content, and specifically, in the theory of the role of mental content in regulating action. Explanation of Lavoisier's and Priestley's 'experimental behaviour' (their behaviour as they conducted their critical experiments on burning) in terms of their beliefs and conjectures has to include reference to the content *phlogiston*. It is, of course, entirely irrelevant to the cognitive-behavioural explanation that this content is, and always was, empty.

To handle the problem of empty content, casual semantics tells the causal story in terms of properties, not instances. But in making this move, causal semantics is not only forced to rely heavily on the problematic notion of properties, it is also faced with the additional problem of explaining their causal role. What are properties (as opposed to their actual instances), and how do they exert causal influence? How should we proceed to investigate the processes by which a property, such as *phlogiston*, or *electron*, gives rise to beliefs?

Neither in common-sense psychology nor in cognitive psychology do these baffling questions arise. Both theories proceed in a different way. Beliefs are acquired by *interpretation of* relatively simpler experiences or stimuli, and are empty or otherwise, true or false, according to whether the interpretation is correct or incorrect. Thus, for example, the story of the acquisition of the concept *phlogiston* involves reference to a plausible though mistaken interpretation of the fact that usually, that is in open systems, the products of combustion are less substantial than what is burnt. False belief is understood here in terms of mistaken interpretation. This is the approach taken in common sense, or at least, in the philosophy of science. Cognitive psychology can appeal to such interpretative processes which are open to view, and also to others which are not, concerning, for example, the pick-up of low-level physical stimulation and its subsequent (largely unconscious) processing. But in neither case is there anything about properties causing mental states with corresponding contents.

As a version of realism, causal semantics allows no fundamental role for creation of meaning by the subject, whether in construction of scientific theory or in imaginative play. But this drive for what may be called an excessive objectivity is exactly what makes the theory inadequate. What requires explanation, including from the point of view of a cognitive-behavioural science, is that mental states with informational or meaningful content determine behaviour (and affect) regardless of whether or not they correspond to anything in reality. It is just at this stage that we require subjective contribution to meaning as well as objective determination. This is the natural route taken by common sense and cognitive psychology. But this subjectivity cannot be envisaged by realism, which therefore postulates that (possibly) instance-less properties are the objectively real determinants of meaningful content. This postulate, however, affords nothing recognizable as a scientific explanation of the origin of meaning.

Let us consider briefly another way in which causal semantics might approach the problem of empty concepts, other than by appeal to instance-less properties. The proposal would be that ideas that are, or that might be, empty, are essentially *complex*, that is to say, composed of simpler ideas, such as colour and shape, which do derive from real instances. This proposal is characteristic of empiricism (Locke 1690, II, Chapter XII; see also Fodor 1990, p. 101). It has advantages compared with prolific realism about properties, including that it posits activity within the mind, this activity being the generation of complex ideas from simple, according to the principles of association elaborated by empiricism and later by conditioning theory. So we work here towards the idea of subjective contribution to meaning, which can be described in a general way as interaction among representations, or as information-processing, which results in the production of something new. Note, however, that while the complex idea is produced by mental activity, its ultimately simple constituents are not, but are simply impressed on the mind by reality. In *this* sense nothing new is ever produced, only rearrangements of what is already given. What has to added to this picture, or what has to transform it, is the post-empiricist critique, which brings out the theory-dependent nature of experience and the hierarchical functioning of theory, in the light of which it cannot be maintained that all concepts are analysable into simple, given, ideas (see above, subsection 1.4.1). Perhaps the concept *unicorn* is composed of simple ideas such as colour and shape, but this is only to the extent that we have no (not much) theory about them. If we believed in unicorns, and they mattered to us, we presumably would want a theory about them, about their signs, appearances, and effects, and about their activities behind the scenes, and the concept then would exceed what is envisaged by empiricism. A main thrust of the post-empiricist critique is that propositions about theoretical entities, for example about phlogiston in the theory of combustion, typically cannot be reduced to propositions about observational data.

The post-empiricist account of concept-formation provides another perspective on the main point of this section, namely, that information depends on the information-processing system, and that this relativity is denied by causal semantics. In its clearest form, causal semantics posits properties in reality, no matter how complex or abstract, which just 'cause' representations with that content. There is no need here for any activity within, or contribution by, an information-processing system. Indeed in the fundamentals of the theory the notion of such a system does not appear. Causal semantics is in this sense akin to S–R psychology, which proposes a direct, one–one, relation between environmental causes and effects in the organism, without mediation by the mind (or brain), which concept has little, if any, theoretical use (see above, subsections 1.2.1–2).

We have been discussing the fact that meaningful content can be about what does not exist. Content expressible by empty terms is one kind of case, another is content expressible by false propositions. The two kinds of case are connected, but we turn now to consider briefly the second in its own right. The falsity of meaningful content, like the presence of empty concepts, presents causal semantics with a probably insurmountable problem.

The problem can be expressed as follows: according to causal semantics, an event A means or carries information about an event B in case A is caused by B, but, if A is not caused by B, then A carries not false information about B, but rather carries no information about B at all. Correlations between types of event can be more or less reliable, but there seems to be no apparent sense to the notion of a *miscorrelation*, and hence none so far to the notion of false or incorrect information. In brief, the problem is *how to obtain a distinction between right and wrong in terms of the notion of causal association*. Attempts by proponents of causal semantics to solve this fundamental problem have not met with much success.[3]

The problem of empty content (of concepts) and the problem of false content (of judgements) are closely linked together, both arising from the fact that what is represented need not exist. This feature is, of course, none other than the *intentionality* of representation (subsection 1.3.1). Any aspiring theory of content has to account for this; it constitutes a very clear adequacy condition for the theory of meaning. The problem for causal semantics is that it seems to fail just this critical test.

We first considered the problem of error, which is as just remarked another name for the problem of intentionality, in the first chapter (subsection 1.3.2). We began to tackle the question: how can one item represent, or mean (or carry information about) another? We saw that the simplest answer would be just that sign and signified are 'correlated' in some way or other, so that the one stands for the other. But even at this superficial level the problem of error makes itself felt. An empty or false sign stands for nothing, but then what is the difference between this and not being a sign at all? How can a sign be meaningful even though there is nothing it is correlated with? The notion of *resemblance* provides an excellent solution to this problem, though its plausibility depends on the extent to which signs do in fact resemble what they signify. Signs of language, in particular, apparently do not. In the absence of resemblance we can define meaning in terms of the *use* of signs in activity, acknowledging the distinction between right and wrong actions, and uses of signs, in terms of the notion of rule-following.

The question as to what following a rule amounts to was taken up in the third chapter, Section 3.3. The problem of making out a difference between 'right' and 'wrong' presses hard in the account of meaning in terms of rule-following, as it does in any theory of meaning. We arrived at the apparent paradox that when a person follows a rule what seems right is right, so far as the person is concerned for the time being, and so far as we have defined no sense to 'but is wrong' (subsection 3.3.2). The proposed solution was a relativistic one, which made out the normative distinctions in two connected ways, in terms of agreement or disagreement between judgements made from various points of view, and in terms of success or otherwise of action (subsections 3.3.3–4). An implication of these relativistic distinctions between right and wrong, or between appearance and reality, is that the vehicle of meaning (of true or false representation) has to be a system which can compare representations from various points of view, which can predict one from another, and which can modify them as appropriate. We arrive, in brief, at a conception of the vehicle of meaning (the measure of reality) as being an active system with the capacity to process information. The contrast here is with theories of meaning which posit static, object-like measures which mirror, or resemble, absolute states of affairs (cf. subsections 1.3.2, 3.3.1).

We are working our way towards this idea from another direction, by considering what is wrong with causal semantics. The point argued so far in this section is that this theory apparently comes to grief on what is a decisive testing ground for theories of meaning, the problem of empty content. We have considered two aspects of the same problem, namely, the creativity and error in ideas and judgement. No account of these features of meaning, both aspects of the fact that meaning can run free of reality, can be gleaned simply from the idea of 'objective' causal correlation between events. So what is the alternative? A more promising account has been indicated in the discussion so far. In the course of criticizing causal semantics we have invoked an account that looks more promising, namely, one which acknowledges what causal semantics is concerned to deny, namely, that there is a subjective contribution to meaning, one that derives from the measuring system itself. This idea will be taken up in later sections. In the next section we continue to consider the consequences of trying to apply standard concepts of causality to explanations in cognitive psychology.

4.4 TRYING TO MANAGE WITH NO SEMANTICS AT ALL

4.4.1 Stich's meaning-less cognitive science

We have already mentioned in various contexts Stich's attempt to avoid the problem of meaning in cognitive science by trying to characterize cognitive states only in terms of causal role, not content. One objection was spelled out in the first chapter (subsection 1.3.8), briefly as follows: information-processing is axiomatic to cognitive psychology, but there cannot be information-processing without information to process, and once information is allowed in, so is meaning. The concepts of meaning and information are closely related: the problem of meaning and causality can be run in exactly the same way using the expression 'information' instead of 'meaning'; what matters here is what they have in common, namely intentionality (subsection 1.3.7). Another problem emerged in the discussion of so-called narrow content in the second chapter (subsection 2.5.3): without intentional language there is apparently no way of characterizing the behavioural effects of cognitive causes.

We turn in this section to consider a related, though different, recommendation to the effect that cognitive science should run without semantics, due to Fodor. Unlike in Stich, there is no wedge inserted between meaning and causal relations, on the contrary the two are held together, but since, so the argument runs, cognitive science cannot encompass causal relations, nor can it encompass semantics. As anticipated, the sense of causality presupposed here is as previously defined: generality covered by natural, specifically physical, law.

4.4.2 Fodor's 'methodological solipsism' as a research strategy for cognitive science

Causal semantics seeks to define the content of information-carrying states in terms of their environmental causes. As noted in the preceding section, this attempt runs straight on to a well-known cleft stick: either the environmental stimuli are defined independently of the mental states they are said to cause, in physical terms, or they are defined in terms of their alleged effects. The former option looks untenable because the content of mental states, the reality they mean, exceeds physically definable aspects of the environment. The latter option looks untenable because it can provide no non-vacuous, causal explanations. Moreover, it leads to a profligate realism concerning properties, and to the scientifically odd idea that properties (as opposed to their instances) have causal power.

No one is better aware of this cleft stick, and the problem of escaping it, than Fodor. This is so notwithstanding the fact that in his (1990) paper Fodor proposes a causal semantics, adopting the second of the above options, apparently choosing to ignore for the sake of argument the risk of vacuousness.

Earlier, in his well-known paper 'Methodological solipsism considered as a research strategy in cognitive science', Fodor endorses the other option open to causal semantics, definition of meaningful content in terms of its *physically defined* environmental causes.

This physicalist version of causal semantics is consistent with the physicalist construal of causality (subsection 4.2.4), as involving coverage by physical laws. It is also closely related to the idea, discussed and rejected in the second chapter (Section 2.5), that 'meaning is not in the head'. The main point in the background here is that if the key concepts of meaning and causality are interpreted in a physicalist way, they turn out to have nothing to do with cognitive behavioural psychology.

Thus we find that Fodor in his (1980) paper endorses the physicalist version of causal semantics, but he does not recommend its use in cognitive psychology. On the contrary, he argues that it offers to cognitive psychology an impossible methodology! The implication, then, is that cognitive psychology has to manage without any semantics at all. Indeed, Fodor proposes, it has to manage without any account of the (causal) interactions between organism and the environment. Rather, cognitive psychology is confined to a 'solipsist' methodology. In this way Fodor provides a salutary lesson on the consequences of applying the physicalist construal of causality to psychology.

Fodor's paper is complex, and we shall draw out for discussion only those themes relating directly to the notion of causality and causal law at work in psychological explanation.

The working assumptions in Fodor's argument are that mental states are legitimately invoked in the explanation of behaviour, and that interactions between mental states, behaviour, and the environment are essentially causal. Specifically, mental states have a causal role in the production of behaviour, and the environment has a causal role in the production of mental states. Further, it is the causal interactions between organism and the environment which fix the meaning of mental states. Granted these working assumptions (which are all of the kind endorsed in this essay) what should psychology be aiming for?

According to Fodor, one research strategy, recommended by what he calls 'naturalistic psychology', is to determine organism–environment interactions and the causal laws that govern them (1980 p. 64 et passim). Naturalistic psychology thus aims to comprise a semantics (1980, pp. 70–1).

But, Fodor's line of thought continues, causality implies nomological necessity, that is, deducibility from scientific law, in particular, from physics (loc. cit.). Granted this, determination of causal laws in general requires that the *relata* of causal connections are specified in terms of physics. Therefore, in particular, the determination of causal laws in organism–environment interactions requires specification in such terms. The requirement is at least that the environmental causes of behaviour and mental states would have to be specified in terms of physics, including such as H_2O and NaCl. Causes so defined would determine the content of mental states (loc. cit.). Thus causal semantics naturally belongs with the materialist (physicalist) definition of content, as remarked above and anticipated in Chapter 2 (subsection 2.5.3). In this way Fodor concludes that naturalistic psychology, with its associated semantics, has to rely on physical theory as to the nature of environmental causes. We have to wait for physical theory to tell us what it is that cognitive states are about. But this conclusion Fodor takes to be untenable; the argument apparently has the form of a *reductio ad absurdum*.

Before considering the closing step of the argument, however, let us consider what alternative Fodor offers in place of a discredited naturalistic methodology. It would have to be one that eschews the study of organism–environment causal interactions, being concerned with the organism and its representations without reference to the environment. Such a strategy is in this sense 'solipsistic'. Fodor takes methodological solipsism to be characteristic of what he calls the tradition of 'Rational' psychology, and in particular of the recent expression of that tradition, the computational theory of mind (discussed in Chapter 2, subsection 2.3.1). According to this theory, mental processes satisfy the so-called *formality condition*, that is to say: they have access only to the formal properties of representations, hence no access to their semantic properties, including truth and reference, and 'indeed, no access to the property of being representations *of the environment*' (Fodor 1980, p. 65, original italics).

In summary, Fodor assumes the standard, physicalist analysis of causality as involving coverage by natural, physical law, and argues on this basis that psychology cannot aim to determine causal interactions between organism and environment; further, since these causal interactions are what determine the meaning of mental states, cognitive psychology cannot comprise semantics. The argument sketched above, extracted from Fodor's complex discussion, apparently has the form of a *reductio ad absurdum*, though we have yet to consider the nature of the alleged absurdity.

What is wrong with naturalistic psychology's dependence on physical science? At one critical point Fodor suggests that, on the basis as set out, naturalistic psychology would have to wait for *completion* of the natural sciences, in which case the research strategy on offer would indeed be hopeless. No doubt, Fodor remarks, it's alright to have a research strategy which says 'wait awhile', but who wants to wait for ever? (1980, p. 70).

But this move is dubious. Why should psychology, in the circumstances envisaged, have to wait for a completed physics? Why could it not proceed in the meantime with the physics we have? After all, chemistry, for example, manages on this basis, as docs physics itself!

Elsewhere in the paper Fodor apparently envisages another argument, to do with the division of labour between psychology and physics. The objection to a naturalistic psychology as the study of causal interactions between organism and environment is that it would have to specify relevant causal properties of the environment, but this is the task of physics, not psychology (1980, p. 70). This alternative argument also seems questionable, however. Why should the science of organism–environment interaction not make use of, and partly rest on, physical theory about the environment? It is unclear why such a science would thereby not be psychology, if this is what Fodor is suggesting, unless we assume what Fodor is seeking to show, that psychology must use a solipsistic methodology.

So far, then, Fodor's arguments against the possibility of a naturalistic psychology seem weak. That said, there is another type of argument against the possibility of a naturalistic psychology, at least in the sense defined by Fodor. The point is simply that physical descriptions of the environment as represented in thought are generally not the appropriate kind for the purpose of cognitive explanations of behaviour. Following the arguments against naturalistic psychology, Fodor writes (1980, p. 71):

> It is important to emphasize that these sorts of arguments do *not* apply against the research program embodied in 'Rational psychology'; viz., to the program which envisions a psychology that honours the formality condition. The problem we've been facing is: under what description does the object of thought enter into scientific generalizations about the relations between thoughts and their objects. It looks as though the naturalist is going to have to say: under a description that's law-instantiating; e.g. under physical description. Whereas the rational psychologist has a quite different answer. What *he* wants is *whatever description the organism has in mind* when it thinks about the object of thought, . . . It's our relation to these sorts of descriptions that determines what psychological state type we're in in so far as the goal of taxonomizing psychological states is explaining how they affect behaviour [original italics].

Fodor thus proposes that what might be called an 'organism-based' definition of mental content is what is required for cognitive-behavioural explanation. This, we may note, is the kind of definition of content endorsed in the present essay (particularly subsections 2.5.4 and 3.4.2, also Section 4.5 below). Fodor, however, takes the proposal to be characteristic of so-called rational psychology, of the computational theory of mind in particular, and of solipsistic methodology. This is certainly not the position adopted here.

But Fodor's line of thought as sketched above is dubious. It is unclear why a psychology which invokes 'organism-based' descriptions of the environment represented in thought, for the purpose of explaining behaviour, belongs with a methodology unconcerned with semantics and organism–environment interactions. On the contrary, such a psychology seems straightforwardly to be concerned with both.

Suppose we attribute to an animal thirst, and the belief that the liquid before it is thirst-quenching. These cognitive–affective states are specified in terms that the animal has in mind, and these terms may not coincide with physical descriptions of the environment. From attribution of these states, we predict that the animal will lower its head and initiate drinking-behaviour. The belief state invoked essentially has semantic properties, in particular the property of being about the environment. And the prediction concerns organism–environment interactions: it is not 'solipsistic'.

By all means truth and successful reference are irrelevant to explanation and prediction. The animal may be deceived in believing that the liquid before it is thirst-quenching, and, in conditions of illusion or hallucination, there may be no liquid there at all. Nevertheless, the explanation runs the same way: it predicts at least *attempted* behavioural interaction. For example, the animal spits out polluted water, or starts with surprise when it bends its head and encounters sand. In action, or at least in attempted action, the animal has no access to the truth or successful reference of its cognitive states; it proceeds, as it were, by appearances only. But the animal must have access to at least one semantic property of its information-carrying states, namely, that they are about the environment. Without access to this minimal but fundamental property of cognitive states, it would have no reason, or cause, (to try) to act in the way it does. Action regulated by cognitive states, whether successful or otherwise, is intentional, it has 'aboutness', and is not 'solipsistic'. This same semantic property essentially characterizes the regulating cognitive states, whether these are invoked from the outside, for the purpose of explanation and prediction of action, or whether they are accessed from the inside, for the purpose of planning and carrying out action.

The above argument amounts to a rejection of the 'formality condition' imposed in particular by the computational theory of mind, that is, the condition that mental processes have access only to formal, not to (any) semantic properties of representations (see above, and Fodor, 1980, p. 65).

The main topic of this chapter concerns causality, and the main question for this section concerns the effects of applying to cognitive psychology a familiar philosophical analysis of causal necessity, viz. that it involves coverage by scientific law, in particular by physics. Fodor shows that application of this analysis to psychology reaps havoc. In the extreme, the consequence is that cognitive psychology is prohibited from studying the causal interactions between the organism and its environment, and hence also has to exclude semantics. Since Fodor endorses the standard, physicalist view of causality, he is obliged, and is willing on other grounds (particularly the computational theory of mind), to embrace this consequence.

The consequence is, however, highly implausible! Cognitive psychology, and artificial intelligence, are pervaded by studies of organism–environment interactions, as many of the commentators on Fodor's paper were quick to point out (Fodor 1980, open peer commentary). Assuming that the interactions under study are indeed causal interactions, the inference apparently has to be that the familiar, physicalist construal of causality does not apply to cognitive psychology.

The problem is not that a physicalist theory of organism–environment interactions could never get off the ground, because of waiting for ever for physical theory to be completed. The problem is rather that for the purpose of explaining and predicting an organism's behavioural responses in terms of cognitive states, what matters is the way in which the environment is encoded and represented within the organism, and such informational content generally cannot be specified in the categories of physics.

It has already been argued, contrary to what Fodor claims, that the requisite organism-based definitions of the environment represented in cognitive states belong to a psychology of organism–environment interactions. So is a naturalistic psychology possible after all? It is, but not in the sense defined by Fodor. Naturalistic psychology as defined by Fodor is a combination of two doctrines. The first is the methodological proposal that psychology can and should study causal interactions between organism and environment. The second is the philosophical assumption that, given this aim, psychology has to describe these interactions in such a way that they can be covered by causal laws of the natural sciences (physics and chemistry). Adoption of an organism-based definition of mental content requires rejection of this philosophical assumption, but the methodological proposal remains intact.

4.4.3 Summary of difficulties and likely solution

The conclusion reached in the preceding subsection was that while it was possible for there to be a cognitive psychology of causal interactions between organism and environment, the notion of causality at work here cannot be the physicalist one. This physicalist construal of causality requires the materialist theory of mental content, and the arguments against the latter in the second chapter (subsection 2.5.3) are, as already remarked, closely connected to the arguments against the latter in this section. The fundamental problem is that the categories and explanations of physics are of very restricted value when we want to construct a cognitive-behavioural psychology, that is, a theory of the regulation of higher behaviour by cognitive states. In brief, the *meaning* in higher behaviour, in the mental states which regulate it, and in the environment as perceived and acted on, resists capture in the concepts of physics.

This 'failure' of the physical sciences appears as problematic from the point of view of the materialism and physicalism that dominates much current philosophical thinking, and there is much pressure to deny it. It is denied precisely by the materialist theory of content and the physicalist construal of causality, according to which meaningful content and connections can be captured within the physicalist net. But then the tension between meaning and the physical sciences certainly does not go away, but is manifest in various conundrums in the philosophy of psychology. Given the materialist theory of content, it appears that meanings ain't in the head and therefore aren't causes of behaviour (subsection 2.5.2). Given the physicalist construal of causality, it seems that psychological theory cannot cope with causal organism–environment transactions at all (subsection 4.4.2).

We have suggested, however, that this last, pretty implausible conclusion can be resisted, provided we abandon the physicalist construal of causality, along with the materialist definition of content. In this way we preserve as a possible and legitimate area of study for psychology the causal interactions between living beings and their environments, and in particular their mediation by semantic processing.

The question then arises as to what notion of causality psychology presupposes. The general implication of the argument so far is that causal explanations of interactions between organism and the environment have to take into account information-processing characteristics of the organism, and the functions that they serve. In brief, the causal connections in question, and the meaning they determine, are 'organism-based'. Several distinguishable though closely related points come under this heading, and will be discussed in remaining sections of this chapter:

First, informational content is relative to functional systems.

Secondly, explanations that invoke informational content and its processing are essentially relative to functional systems, and the 'laws' covering such systems must be of a kind distinct from those in physics and chemistry, concerned with the design, means, and ends of particular functional systems. The necessity in these laws will turn on the assumption of 'normal' functioning. Causal concepts and normative concepts coincide here.

Hence, thirdly, since these 'laws' are specific to particular information-processing systems, we lose the *generality* characteristic of the physical sciences.

These points are taken up in the next two sections.

4.5 FUNCTIONAL SEMANTICS: MEANING DEFINED IN TERMS OF SYSTEMIC FUNCTION

4.5.1 General principles

Causal semantics defines meaning in terms of causality as understood in the physical sciences. Further, it defines meaning primarily in terms of environmental causes rather than behavioural effects. These two features of causal semantics hang together with the fact the theory does not envisage, indeed goes out of its way to deny, that there is any systemic contribution to the production of meaning. Properties are posited as already in the environment, able to cause mental states with corresponding content, which causal process hence involves no subjective contribution (subsections 4.3.2–3). This negative conclusion is plainly demanded by the physicalist construal of causality. The implication is that the rejection of causal semantics involves not only a shift away from the physicalist construal of causality, but also a shift in the definition of meaning away from emphasis on 'input' towards emphasis on interactions among information-carrying states and their role in regulating 'output'. The chief significance of this change is that the definition of content can begin to take account of the contribution of the semantic processing system. This kind of definition of meaning belongs with the idea invoked in all the preceding chapters, that meaningful states are invoked in order to explain (intentional) activity, and hence are to be understood essentially in terms of the difference they make to behaviour.

Another way of looking at what is essentially the same point about the move from causal to functional semantics is in terms of the theory of error. We saw in subsection 4.3.3 that causal semantics flounders on the problem that information-carrying states can be false as well as true. This fundamental feature of such states apparently defines capture by the notion of causality alone: either events of one kind are causally associated with another or they are not, but there is no obvious sense in the notion of a 'mis-association'. In this section we explore the possibility indicated at the time, that solution of the problem of error requires reference to the system that picks up, processes, and utilizes information. Error will be down to something like 'misinterpretation', or 'misapplication'.

By whichever route we approach functional semantics, meaning comes to be defined with reference to information-processing systems. The first version of functional semantics to be considered retains the essential claim of causal semantics, namely, that the content of an information-carrying state is defined by its environmental causes. We shall call this version 'causal-functional semantics', and it will be contrasted later with a 'behavioural-functional' version, which defines content primarily in terms of the difference it makes to the behaviour of the system.

4.5.2 Millikan's version: content defined by normal biological/evolutionary causes

The problem for functional semantics in its causal version is to define the normative characteristic of informational content—that it can be true or false, correct or incorrect—in terms of a normative distinction among its environmental causes.

The task is to define a sense in which some causes of information-carrying states are 'right' and others are 'wrong'. Such a normative distinction between types of cause is not afforded by a straightforward causal semantics, but it can be drawn once we make explicit reference to functional systems. The basic idea of functional semantics is that error arises in informational states of a system in case they are caused by conditions unlike those in which the system has been designed to function. The required assumptions concerning design, function, and conditions can be based in considerations of evolutionary biology. Functional (or teleological) theories of content along these lines have been proposed, for example, by Millikan (1984, 1986) and Papineau (1987).[4] What follows is a brief version of some of their key features.

Biological systems and subsystems have been selected in the evolutionary process in so far as they fulfil certain advantageous functions in particular environmental conditions. These latter may be called for short the 'normal' conditions for particular systems. Consider now specifically the case of systems whose function it is to represent (carry information about) the environment. Such representational systems, like others, have evolved in normal conditions. Normal conditions define the content of a representational state, as follows: a representational state carries the information that it is caused by normal conditions. In these terms it is possible to apply a normative description to particular representational states of a system. We may distinguish between representational states which are caused by normal conditions, and those which are caused by abnormal conditions: the former are 'correct' representations, the latter 'incorrect'.

In this way we can apparently capture a distinction between correct and incorrect representations, and one, moreover, with scientific credibility. The basic idea that in incorrect representation something has gone wrong is explicated in terms of informational states of a system being triggered by conditions unlike those that the system has been designed to respond to.

4.5.3 Fodor's objection: these causes are ambiguous

An objection to the analysis outlined above has been forcibly put by Fodor (1990). Fodor makes the objection using the example of fly-detection and -snapping behaviour in the frog, the subject of the seminal paper of Lettvin *et al.* (1959), 'What the frog's eye tells the frog's brain'.

An account of the frog's behaviour according to the proposal being considered would include the following claims. There is in the frog an information-processing mechanism selected in the evolutionary process for detecting and snapping at flies. On occasion the frog detects and snaps at ambient black dots which are not flies. However, in this case the mechanism is responding to environmental conditions unlike those in which it has evolved. Thus we may say that in this case and in this sense the informational content carried in some state of the mechanism is 'incorrect'. Hence we achieve a distinction between correct/ incorrect, true/false informational content.

Fodor's objection is, however, that we can apparently run the account in another way, blocking the conclusion. We can say that there is in the frog a mechanism selected in the evolutionary process for detecting and snapping at ambient black dots. If the function of the mechanism is described in this way, detection and snapping at a non-fly ambient black dot is *not* an error. By all means, in the frog's normal ecology, all or most ambient black dots are in fact flies, so the result of the selection process is indeed a mechanism that, all or most of the time, succeeds in detecting and snapping at flies. The choice is therefore in the description of the 'intentional object' of the frog's information-carrying state, as being flies or ambient black dots. But, Fodor objects, the evolutionary story can be told either way, and in the latter case the proposed distinction between correct and incorrect informational content collapses (1990, pp. 71ff.). Dretske (1986) makes a similar point.

4.5.4 Rejoinder: evolutionary theory delivers intensional specifications of functions and stimuli

But is the objection outlined above valid? Can the evolutionary story be told either way? According to evolutionary theory a given mechanism is selected for a particular function. Plausibly this means something like: it would not have been selected unless it performed that function. So then, what function has the frog's 'fly(?)-detecting-snapping' mechanism been selected for? Surely the answer has to be: for catching flies *as food*, not for catching inedible ambient black dots. That is, the mechanism would not have been selected but that it performs the function of securing flies (as food); not, . . . but that it performs the function of catching ambient (inedible) black dots.

The point may be expressed in terms of *intensional descriptions* (as defined in subsection 1.3.1). Evolutionary theory demands an intensional description of the function of the mechanism for detecting and catching flies, as being for securing *food*, and hence also it vindicates the corresponding intensional description of the normal conditions in which the mechanism has been selected.

Nevertheless, there is something right about Fodor's objection. Its valid aspect can be brought out by asking the question: 'How could a biological information-processing system ever come to represent environmental conditions which it has not been selected to represent?' In so far as there is no answer to this question, the proposed distinction between true and false representation seems to collapse. Let us unpack this line of thought. It appeals to features of biological information-processing systems such as specialized detectors, and capacity for being deceived, which will be emphasized and elaborated on in the next chapter.

Not any state of an information-processing system counts as an information-carrying state. For example, a state of the brain caused by massive haemorrhage so far carries no information at all, and in particular none about the cause of the state. A state of an information-processing system is information-carrying only in so far as it results from the processing (coding, translation, etc.) of information picked up from the environment, characteristically by specialized detectors. The problem for the theory of error under consideration is that the only environmental states that can cause information-processing systems to go into information-carrying states *are those that the system is designed to respond to*. In the case of biological information-processing systems this means: only normal environmental conditions. So the proposed distinction between true and false information-carrying states cannot be made out.

In the particular case of the frog's behaviour there is, then, a reason for describing the regulating information as being about ambient black dots. It is simply that frogs are just as good at detecting and snapping at non-fly ambient black dots as at dealing with flies. It is hard to avoid the conclusion, endorsed by the considerations in the preceding paragraph, that the relevant mechanism is designed to process and respond to information about ambient black dots, regardless whether they happen to be flies or not.

So we have here two apparently conflicting intuitions, backed by biological and behavioural considerations. But is the conflict genuine? There is no escaping the conclusion that the frog's mechanism is designed in such a way that it detects and responds to ambient black dots, flies or otherwise. The behavioural evidence is clear. But equally, there is no escaping the demand of evolutionary theory that this mechanism has been selected because it fulfils the function of detecting and catching flies (as food). It is on the basis of theory of function that biology speaks pervasively and unhesitatingly of 'deception' in biological systems. But 'deception' is itself possible only because the system is designed in such a way as to receive and respond to information which is in fact irrelevant to, which does not serve, its function (the function for which it has been selected). The notion of deception, and in general a distinction between correct and incorrect information, can be vindicated on the basis of an (intensional) specification of systemic function. Such specification can in turn be based on evolutionary theoretic considerations, as indicated above.

4.5.5 Systemic behaviour is also a basis for intensional specifications of function

The question arises as to whether specification of systemic function has to be based in evolutionary theory, or whether it can be based in behavioural evidence alone. Plausibly behavioural evidence alone will do, bearing in mind that we are concerned here with behaviour which exhibits intentionality. To bring out the nature of the behavioural evidence sufficient to determine function, and hence to afford various normative distinctions, let us start with evolutionary theoretic considerations. It will be seen then that such evidence can stand on its own, detached from evolutionary theory.

Part of the evolutionary story about the frog's information-processing system is that it would not have evolved but for the fact that it enabled ingestion of flies as food. If the environment had been different (too few ambient black dots were flies) the system would have been de-selected and, let us suppose, replaced by another, more discriminatory one. This notion of *adaptation* is of course fundamental to evolutionary theory. As things are, the system fails to discriminate between flies and other ambient black dots. Frogs snap at and ingest the one as much as the other. They have, in particular, no 'corrective' mechanisms that arrest the routine of snapping at and ingesting non-flies at any stage. The evidence for such mechanisms would, of course, be behavioural: we would observe 'corrective behaviour', which is essentially a matter of arrest, possibly with replacement of, an initiated behavioural routine. Frogs—we are assuming—show no such corrective behaviour in the case of a non-fly; they do not desist from snapping on the basis on a closer look, nor do they spit it out. All this gives reason for saying that so far as the frog is concerned, non-flies are all the same as flies.[5]

Thus there is no evidence that an individual frog regards non-fly routines as an error; it does not behave as if it has made a mistake. We, on the other hand, because we know the function that the behavioural routine is meant to serve, that for which it has been selected, can call its application to non-flies an error. Connected with this, it might also be said, briefly and therefore in scare quotes, that the ecosystem consisting of the species frog and its environment also 'treats the non-fly routine as an error': too much in the species and it would be discarded.

The above remarks define the kind of behavioural evidence required to support the hypothesis that the frog regards catching non-flies as a mistake. Imagine an adapted frog species, members of which show either or both of the following sorts of behaviour. First, on sighting any ambient black dot, the frog prepares for snapping, but makes closer inspection (in some way): the frog then usually snaps if the dot is in fact a fly, but otherwise usually does not. Secondly, in case the frog snaps at and takes into its mouth a non-fly, it promptly spits it out. Here we would have behavioural evidence that the frog treats snapping at and/or ingesting non-flies as a mistake, the evidence being arrest of either or both the snapping and the ingestion behaviours. Such behaviour is evidence of discriminatory mechanisms, and of regulation of behavioural routines on the basis of information received at particular stages.

The discriminatory and corrective behaviour of this (hypothetical) frog constitutes evidence that it is after flies but not any other ambient black dots. The behaviour itself shows what the function of the behaviour is. In particular, the function may be determined on the basis of behavioural evidence alone, without the need for an evolutionary theoretic definition of function.

Indeed, it is arguable that even with frogs being the way they are, there is behavioural evidence that it is flies they are after, not any other ambient black dots. It is true that the frog, as it were, happily snaps and ingests non-flies. But the behavioural evidence is broader than just this. The behavioural consequences of at least persistent non-fly snaps are presumably different from those of persistent fly snaps. In the former case the frog stays hungry, an affective state which would show up in various ways; in the latter the frog is satiated, with different behavioural effects. Observation of these behavioural differences would be grounds for saying that the function of snapping behaviour is to secure flies (as food). In this case, contrary to what has been assumed so far, evolutionary theory is not required in order to define the function of snapping behaviour as being to catch flies (as food); this definition of the function can be based on behavioural evidence alone.

We may note in passing that these considerations to the effect that there are behavioural criteria of content of information-carrying states characterized intensionally runs counter to the claim that attempts to naturalize intentional explanation have failed because they have rendered intentional states non-intensional (Rosenberg 1986), but without restriction to language-users (Emmett 1989). Of course the line of argument we propose is based on the assumption, made back in the first chapter (subsection 1.3.6), that the behavioural evidence for meaningful states already has (to be seen) to have intentionality. In this sense there is here no sympathy with the aim characteristic of causal semantics, to 'naturalize' meaning (Fodor 1990, with critical commentary in, for example, Baker 1991; see also subsection 4.3.1 above).

Function may be specified using behavioural evidence, not only by appeal to evolutionary theory. Moreover, it may be argued that there is a sense in which behavioural determination of function *has to precede* evolutionary considerations. The point is the simple one that until we have determined, on the basis of observation of behaviour, the function of a behavioural routine, and hence of the information-processing mechanisms that serve it, we cannot even begin to construct an evolutionary explanation of its development.

But of course, as we may suspect given post-empiricism (subsection 1.4.1), the implied contrast here between observation and theory is artificial and unnecessary. 'Observation' of basic patterns of animal behaviour is laden with biological/evolutionary theory. The point for the present purpose is simply this: the function of functional behaviour is generally manifest in the behaviour, particularly in such characteristics as discrimination, modification of strategy, and satiation or otherwise.

The fact that we can get a handle on function, and on what counts as error, without recourse to evolutionary theory has particular importance, however, in relation to 'higher' forms of activity about which evolutionary theory has nothing definite to say. The scale of 'higher' and 'lower' forms of activity concerns at least degree of discrimination, of complexity and length of behavioural routines, and hence degree of regulation. 'Higher' behaviour is thus precisely of the kind in which function, or at least distinction between getting it right and getting it wrong, shows up in the behaviour itself. In this way behavioural criteria of function and error are increasingly available as we move up the scale from lower to higher activities, and the need for evolutionary theoretic definitions decreases. Indeed, such definitions become less and less helpful, particularly as we consider cultural practices, which constitute much of human activity, and which interact with our 'natural' behaviour. It is arguably degrading, but in any case notoriously difficult, to define the function of cultural activities, and the complex processes by which they are regulated, in terms of basic biological needs and natural selection.[6]

Let us summarize some of the main points made so far in this section. Causal semantics fails to allow the possibility of informational content being wrong. The suggested diagnosis of this failure is neglect of the contribution to informational content by the system which receives, processes, and uses information. This neglect is made good by functional semantics. Given an intentional specification of the function of a system, of what it (its response) is 'meant to achieve', we can define what counts as success or failure, and hence define other normative distinctions. If, on a particular occasion, a system fails to achieve its function, it has made an error somewhere along the line. Intentional specification of systemic function can be derived from evolutionary theoretic considerations, or on the basis of (intentional) behavioural evidence alone.

Let us grant that functional semantics in the form so far considered affords a solution to the problem of error, and in this respect improves on causal semantics. Still, in so far as functional semantics seeks to retain an essential claim of causal semantics, the claim that content is defined by its environmental causes, it inherits other problems of causal semantics, reviewed in Section 4.3. Thus, what is to be said about environmental causes that define the content of 'empty' informational states, for example those carrying information about (and regulating behaviour about) unicorns or phlogiston? There are no corresponding conditions in the environment. Or again, do we have to adopt a profligate (and vacuous) realism, ascribing to the environment whatever properties are needed in order to explain the existence of informational states with the corresponding content? Of course such problems are minimized, though certainly not removed, while we stay within the context of basic biological mechanisms and functions, the context in which the theory of functional semantics has usually been worked out. But they arise explicitly and in full force when we come to consider highly processed informational content which frankly exceeds characteristics of its environmental causes as defined in physics, or in psychological theories of perception. Here we think of content such as *dangerous*, or *edible*, but also, for example, *beautiful, democratic*, etc. In brief, in so far as functional semantics seeks to remain a genuine causal theory, to define informational content in terms of environmental causes, it continues to run up against problems of the kind faced by causal semantics.

4.5.6 A behavioural version of functional semantics: meaning defined in terms of action (again)

It was suggested in subsection 4.3.1 that the failures of causal semantics all arise from the same source, namely, its neglect of the systemic contribution to informational content. Functional semantics in the causal version so far considered, does not sufficiently free itself of this error. In order to explain this criticism, let us sketch a different form of the theory, to be called for convenience 'behavioural functional semantics', which avoids the problematic definition of content in terms of environmental causes. The basic claim of functional semantics in this form is that informational content is defined by its effects on the outputs of the system rather than by inputs (McGinn 1989; Papineau 1993). The point may be expressed by saying that behavioural functional semantics defines informational content in terms of what the information-processing system *makes of* input. Thus functional semantics captures the idea that there is indeed a systemic contribution to information, or meaning.

As we have seen, all semantic theories have to explain how information or meaningful content can be true or false. We have seen that causal semantics apparently fails in this task, while functional semantics in its causal form succeeds. But consider how it succeeds. The normative distinction applied to content is based in a normative distinction among environmental causes. This distinction in turn is based in a definition of systemic function, in considerations of what the system has been designed to achieve, of that function for which it has been selected in evolution. Systemic function has to be specified here intensionally, and we saw that such specification is indeed legitimate in the context of evolutionary biology. It was argued, however, that definition of systemic function essentially refers to the behaviour of the system, in particular to its intended effects, that is, the effects that the system has been designed or selected for. The implication, then, is that normative distinction among environmental causes of information-carrying states rests ultimately on normative distinction among the behavioural effects of these states. The implication is that the latter distinction is fundamental, and this point is what functional semantics in its behavioural version seeks to make explicit.

Let us consider in some detail how behavioural functional semantics works, and in particular how it approaches the problem of error.

How might error in informational content be defined in functional terms? Functional systems pick up information from the environment, process it, and use the result in regulating responses. It is in this systemic process that we find the possibility of error.

In brief, a functional, information-processing system *makes a mistake* if it interprets a signal P as being a sign of (as being caused by) environmental condition C1, when in fact P emanates from (is caused by) environmental condition C2.

For this proposal to work, we obviously require a definition of 'interprets signal S as a sign of C', and it is at this critical point that we need to refer to behaviour. The definition required is something like the following: a system 'interprets a signal P as a sign of C' if reception of P causes the system to respond in way appropriate to it being the case that C.

This definition in turn requires definition of when system responses are appropriate or otherwise to particular environmental conditions. This runs along the following lines. In order to know whether a systemic response is appropriate to the environment being in such-and-such a condition, we have to know what the behaviour is 'meant to achieve'. In other words, definition of what counts as a response being appropriate or inappropriate requires a theory about the function of the behaviour in question, or generally, of the system. This theory has to specify function intensionally, and we have already considered in the previous subsection the kind of principles used in such specification.

In summary, the proposed account of correctness or error in informational content runs as follows: a system emits a certain response R, regulated by an information-carrying state Si with a particular content. The response (we assume) is meant to achieve a particular result, typically some change in the environment to a condition CR. The response is appropriate to achieving CR if the initial condition of the environment is CI. In this sense the response is appropriate to it being the case that CI. The informational state Si is then true if CI is in fact the case, and is otherwise false. Whether the state is true or false will then (tend to) show up in the success or otherwise of the behaviour to which it gives rise.

As would be expected, the above account of truth and error in informational states defines also informational content. In brief, an information-carrying state Si has a particular content, C (that is, carries the information that the environment is in condition C), in case it tends to cause, other things being equal, behaviour appropriate to it being the case that C.

This kind of definition of content may seem to raise problems. Causal semantics was charged with the problem of being unable to specify the environmental causes of information-carrying states independently of the contents which they are supposed to cause (subsection 4.3.2). But now it looks as if behavioural functional semantics might be faced with a behavioural version of the same problem, namely, that of identifying the content of information-carrying states independently of the behaviour they are supposed to cause. In so far as mental content is defined in terms of its alleged behavioural effects, it seems that it cannot be taken to have a causal role. This echoes one of the considerations underlying the traditional distinction between meaningful and causal connections (subsection 4.2.5). However, this line of thought presupposes a narrow reading of what is involved in understanding cognitive states in terms of their role in regulating behaviour. The definition of content suggested above was as follows: an information-carrying state Si has a particular content, C, in case it tends to cause, other things being equal, behaviour appropriate to it being the case that C. This definition of content so far cites no specific behaviour, and therefore avoids the alleged circularity. The specific behaviours which are 'appropriate to it being the case that C' will depend on many factors, including, as already indicated, on what the system is trying to achieve, and on interaction with other relevant information-carrying states. For example, the behaviour appropriate to it being the case that there is a bull before me is a function of my desire to escape it, and my belief that this can best be done by climbing a tree, if there is one, or otherwise by running. Thus the content of my belief that there is a bull before me can be defined simply in terms of its tendency to generate behaviour appropriate to that being the case, but what this amounts to is specifiable in non-trivial ways. There is therefore so far no obstacle to saying that the belief has a causal role in relation to the behaviour generated in particular circumstances.

In the definitions given above of correctness and incorrectness, and of informational content, information-carrying is a property of states of the information-processing system, not, as in causal semantics, a property of the signal itself. Further, and related, the proposed definition of content appeals primarily not to the environmental causes of information-carrying states, but rather to their role in the regulation of behaviour. In brief, content is defined not in terms of input, but rather in terms of what the system *makes of* input. The contribution of the system to content is what gives scope for error. Also it creates the possibility of 'empty' content, content which corresponds to no reality. Both these features of informational content are problematic for causal semantics, precisely because it neglects the systemic contribution to content.

We have considered two versions of functional semantics. One defines content and the true/false distinction by reference to the role of information-carrying states in the regulation of intentional activity; the other by reference to a certain type of environmental cause of such states, namely, their normal causes as defined by evolutionary theory. In any given case, however, given the same intensional specification of function, both versions of functional semantics will deliver the same results, the same specification of content, and the same evaluation, true or false.

The behaviour-based version has several advantages, however. It avoids those problems that the causal version inherits from causal semantics *simpliciter*, namely, the problem of identifying environmental causes independently of their alleged representational effects, and the problem of empty content. Further, it is not restricted to behaviour and informational content of the limited kind addressed by evolutionary biology. But aside from these advantages, the behavioural version of functional semantics makes explicit what is misleadingly only implicit in the causal version; namely, that specification of informational content and normative description of it rest fundamentally on considerations of (intentional) behaviour.

We are led by this route, via discussion of causal and functional accounts of meaning, to themes and conclusions already familiar from the first three chapters. Attribution of meaningful content rests on behavioural criteria. The behaviour in question is essentially interactive: it already has intentionality. Hence explanations that invoke meaningful states are effective in the prediction of action. Such explanations attribute propensities to follow rules: the behaviour they predict is essentially subject to normative descriptions: correct/incorrect, appropriate/inappropriate, successful/unsuccessful, etc.

4.6 SYSTEMIC FUNCTION, MEANING, AND WHAT WE EXPECT OF CAUSAL EXPLANATION

4.6.1 Necessity, linked to norms of function and dysfuction

The main conclusion of the first chapter was that explanations of action in terms of meaningful, information-carrying states are causal, though it was left open in what sense. In Section 4.2 we outlined various familiar views about causality, noting their well-known apparent incompatibility with meaningful explanations. We sketched first Hume's analysis in terms of correlation and generality (subsection 4.2.1). This idea of causality is taken into causal semantics, but it provides no adequate basis for a definition of meaning, specifically because it is too simple to provide a theory of error, and generally because it sets out to ignore systemic contribution to meaning (Section 4.3).

Other familiar views about causality were sketched in the second section. Within the confines of empiricism, Hume could find nothing necessary in causal connections, nothing over and above mere conjunction between events (subsection 4.2.2). This apparent gap in the analysis of causality can be made good by appeal to natural laws, and in practice by deducibility from scientific theory (subsection 4.2.3), specifically by appeal to physical laws (4.2.4). But this analysis fails to apply to cognitive psychology. As noted in subsection 4.4.2, application of such a notion of causality leads to the apparently false conclusion that cognitive psychology cannot aspire to study causal interactions between organism and environment, and in particular can say nothing about those interactions that are relevant to meaning (or information-carrying). If cognitive psychology does study causal interactions, then we have to abandon the idea that causality and causal necessity must be a matter of physical laws. The implication was that such laws as are invoked in bio-psychological explanation have to do with the functioning of particular systems (4.4.3).

This implication hangs together with the conclusions reached in Section 4.5, that the shortcomings in causal semantics are addressed by functional semantics, which defines meaning essentially by reference to the functional activity of information-processing systems.

We return in this section to the problem of causal necessity, to discuss in the light of considerations so far its relation to explanations that invoke meaning.

It was noted in subsection 4.2.3 that the problem of necessary connection in causality can be solved by appeal to covering natural laws. It is tempting to construe these as physical laws (subsection 4.2.4), but as this does not suit psychology (subsection 4.4.2), why not just drop this physicalist construal, and draw back to the weaker position that causal explanation is committed to there being some covering natural law or other? This line of thought leads to the idea that the causal status of cognitive explanations derives from their place within a well-entrenched systematic empirical theory about relations between stimuli, cognitive states, and behaviour. There is something correct about this suggestion, but it is not yet complete. It omits special features of descriptions of functional systems, namely, that they essentially invoke *norms* of function, and that this accounts for their necessity.

If a person believes such-and-such, then she *must*, in appropriate circumstances, act in a way that accords with that belief. This 'must', however, has nothing to do with scientific theory or natural law. If the consequent of the hypothetical fails, no scientific theory has been refuted, still less has there been a miracle! Rather, the inference would be that, for one reason or another, the person has apparently acted irrationally. The nomological character of the prediction pertains to the 'laws' of reason, not to laws of an empirical science.

It is true that cognitive explanations are embedded in theory, but it is also true that the theory is permeated by reference to norms. Let us expand on this point in relation to Dennett's notion of the intentional stance, already described in Chapter 1, subsection 1.3.5.

Dennett is clear that use of the intentional stance as a predictive strategy involves adoption of several working assumptions: we treat the living being as a rational agent, assuming that it acts on beliefs and desires according to rational rules; we attribute the beliefs it ought to have, given its place in the world and its purposes (including here all truths relevant to its interests which are available from its experience); in a similar way we attribute desires the creature ought to have, and make predictions on this basis (Dennett 1987, for example p. 17). The critical first assumption is one of 'perfect' rationality, and this ideal is revised downwards, presumably in the light of the creature's behaviour. Attribution of what beliefs and desires the creature actually has, as opposed to those it ought to have, is presumably subject to revision downwards in the same way.

It may be seen that application of the intentional stance in the way Dennett proposes requires assumptions about the creature's sensory and cognitive capacities (which determine what is 'available from experience'), and about its purposes and interests. Some of these assumptions are presumably made in advance; for example, all living beings must have an interest in food, and information-processing capacities appropriate to its securement. Apart from such cases, however, determination of what desires and beliefs a creature has requires observation of what it actually strives for, and how.

Given that application of the intentional stance is partly based on, and is answerable to, observation of behaviour, it is tempting to suppose that the methodology could proceed straightforwardly a posteriori: we observe the behaviour of the system, find that its prediction is best served by positing drives and information-carrying states, attribute these in accord with behavioural criteria, adjusting such attributions as predictions fail. No a priori assumption of perfection in rationality would be made in this method, nor any assumption of appropriateness of beliefs and desires. In other words, it is tempting to suppose that application of the intentional stance as a predictive strategy can proceed 'bottom-up' just as well as 'top-down'. However, the supposition that attribution of intentionality can proceed entirely a posteriori, on the basis of observation alone, though plausible, is unsound. Dennett is right in claiming that non-empirical assumptions are being made, assumptions which are specifically *normative*.

Application of the intentional stance involves the assumption that the system in question has a design (natural or artificial) relevant to the achievement of certain ends. This assumption is essentially normative, presupposing distinctions between good and poor design, between function and malfunction. The non-empirical character of the assumption of design in the intentional stance shows up in the options open when its predictions fail. It is true that specification of ends and means can, and should, be based on observation of the behaviour of the system, that predictions of the theory then succeed or fail, and that, if they fail, the theory can be modified. So far, then, the theory acts simply as an empirical hypothesis. However, there are always other possibilities open when predictions fail, namely, that the system is poorly designed, or is malfunctioning. When these possibilities are considered, the assumption of design is held fast, and is used for the purpose of diagnosing failure in the system. In these contexts the assumption of design assumes an a priori role, held fast in the face of anomalies, and used in the detection of error elsewhere. The error is located, as it were, within the phenomena, not within the theory. Only in biology and psychology is such a diagnosis of error possible; there is nothing corresponding to it in physics and chemistry. This is because these basic sciences are not concerned with functional systems (as functional systems), and therefore have no use for normative descriptions of their subject-matter.

Psychological generalizations and their predictions in particular cases allow for the possibility of system failure. They are typically qualified by provisos to the effect 'if all other things are equal', by so-called *ceteris paribus* clauses, which include particularly explicit or implicit reference to 'normal' functioning. It can be said, for example, that perception of danger in the immediate environment will lead to avoidance behaviour, other things being equal. If in a particular case the creature in question fails to take evasive action, it may be inferred that other things are not equal, and one particular kind of possibility here is that the creature is not functioning normally.

It is clear, however, that while generalizations can be rescued in the face of anomaly by this method, the risk is that they become unfalsifiable, empty of empirical content, compatible with everything and excluding nothing. If this were the case, then the proposal that explanations that invoke intentional states are useful in predicting behaviour, the premise of the present essay, would be invalid: the appearance of predictive efficacy here would be an illusion.

This argument can be turned the other way round, however: since explanations that invoke intentional states are useful in prediction, they cannot be trivial or vacuous, notwithstanding their reliance on *ceteris paribus* clauses. The argument is turned this way round by Fodor (1987, chapter.1). Fodor goes on to observe that reliance on *ceteris paribus* clauses is characteristic of generalizations in other sciences, with physics being the possible exception, without lapse into triviality (Fodor 1987; see also Fodor 1991; Schiffer 1991).

It may be noted, however, that while scientific theory and prediction typically rely on *ceteris paribus* clauses, the theory and prediction of functional systems invoke them for a special reason. The point is not just that the phenomena are complicated, and generalizations in practice always partial. It is also that in the case of functional systems, theory and its predictions refer essentially to the *normal* case, and provisos are then added to allow for the abnormal.

Many examples from folk psychology and from the various fields of psychological science could be used to illustrate this point. Consider, for example, the following familiar case of a principle based in meaningful connections: intense sadness is precipitated, other things being equal, by experience of major loss. Anomalies include cases of intense sadness appearing in the absence of self-report of recent major loss, in the absence of such a loss in the recent history, or following recent experience of minor loss only, such as the death of a pet cat. In the face of such anomalies the principle can be preserved in one of two ways. It can be hypothesized that memory of past major losses, perhaps cued by one or several minor losses, is regulating current mood, consciously or otherwise. Alternatively, disruption to normal psychological function by lower-level (non-meaningful) causes, such as hormonal imbalance, can be hypothesized. In general, the explanation of breakdown of meaningful connections can proceed by positing either other meaningful connections or lower-level (non-semantic) disruption.

These points about the explanation of breakdown will occupy us through subsequent chapters. For now the point is that in the case of functional systems, including human beings, theory and its predictions refer essentially to the *normal* case, and provisos are then added to allow for the abnormal. We cited above the psychological principle: intense sadness is precipitated, other things being equal, by experience of major loss. We noted that 'other things being equal' in this case includes: unless experience of recent minor loss is intensified by memory of past major loss, and, unless there is biochemical disruption to normal psychic function.

Both of the above qualifications are reasonable. Others would (probably) not be, such as: unless the person's birth sign is Scorpio. This means, both cited applications of the *ceteris paribus* clause are plausible on the basis of current theory and empirical data. But the clause does not license salvage of the theory in any which way we choose. It has more or less specific, but in any case circumscribed, content. It leads, in case of anomaly, to more or less specific, but in any case circumscribed, predictions, concerning early learning history, or the underlying biochemistry. The psychological principle, together with its specified *ceteris paribus* clauses, serves as a methodological rule for distinguishing between normal and abnormal function, and for the investigation of apparently abnormal cases.

It can be seen here that the relation between a meaningful generalization and its *ceteris paribus* clause is an intimate, 'internal' one. In brief, the former is about what happens *normally*, while the latter is (partly) about what happens *abnormally*.

Another aspect of this point is that psychological generalizations do not even purport to hold good in *all* cases, only, and by definition, in normal ones. In this sense anomalies are not properly described as 'counter-examples' to the generalization; they are rather, and only, the abnormal cases which the generalization already envisages. The internally related *ceteris paribus* clause then serves to explain why and how conditions are abnormal. The position is different in sciences unconcerned with systemic function, and therefore with the distinction between normal and abnormal function. In these sciences anomalies for a generalization are indeed counter-examples which so far contradict it, unless a *ceteris paribus* clause can be invoked to explain away the counter-example and hence save the generalization.

In summary, then, the relative immunity of meaningful explanations from revision, their use of *ceteris paribus* clauses, and in particular the fact that they express norms of function, does not preclude their usefulness in prediction.

It is important to stress that we have here only *relative* immunity from revision. It is true that theories of meaningful content and connections, with more or less specific *ceteris paribus* clauses, are well entrenched. But in principle they can be given up, and some have been. In effect this involves radical revision in the theory of functions of particular biological or psychological (sub-)systems, and of their norms of operation.

Consider, for example, assumptions concerning the accessibility of mental states to consciousness and self-report, a topic already discussed in the first chapter (subsection 1.4.3). A principle in the Cartesian mould would run something like the following: if a person believes that p, then, other things being equal, she is aware that she believes that p, and will assent to the statement that p. 'Other things being equal' includes: all the relevant psychological functions are working normally, but also, for example, the person is being sincere. Anomalies for the generalization, disavowal, or denial of a belief apparently present according to other (behavioural) criteria, would be dealt with by invoking one or other component of the *ceteris paribus* clause. In this way the principle can be maintained, and was for a long time. However, it has been overturned, regarded now as valid only within a limited domain, by the combined operation of two factors. First, accumulation of (or attention to) anomalies that can be dealt with only by *ad hoc* explanations with no independent support, and secondly, and essentially, by the emergence of a new paradigm, according to which the definitive function of mental states is regulation of action, not appearance in consciousness. The processes by which even well-entrenched theories can be overthrown, or at least radically demoted, are described by Lakatos in his classic paper, (1970), as discussed in the first chapter (subsection 1.4.1). Lakatos was concerned with the physical sciences, but the basic rules are the same for psychological theory, whether philosophical, folk, or scientific.

It has been argued that explanations of action in terms of meaningful states are not causal in the sense of Hume's analysis and its standard elaborations, at least because they typically involve rational norms. These claims are familiar in the literature (Collingwood 1946, with commentary by, for example, Martin 1991; also Strawson 1985; Roque 1987–88; Haldane 1988; Henderson 1991). To the extent that it is assumed, then, that the neo-Humean accounts have a monoploy on causality, it follows that the explanation of action in terms of reasons, the bringing of behaviour under rational norms, must be a different kind of enterprise from causal explanation. This inference in effect preserves something like the dichotomies between meaning and causality, and between understanding and (causal) explanation. The position being argued for here is quite different. The proposal is that reason-giving explanation is causal: it is what causal explanation comes to look like in the case of the action of rational agents.

This interpretation of the general idea that reasons are causes is distinct from Davidson's very influential thesis. Davidson has argued that explanations in terms of reasons are causal, but the causal laws envisaged here are not content-based but rather refer to physical properties (Davidson 1963, with commentary in, for example, Lepore and McLaughlin 1985; Dretske 1989; Evnine 1991). Our quite different proposal is that the causal nature of explanations in terms of reasons involves precisely those reasons, and hence meaning and norms. As above, our argument is that reason-giving explanation is what causal explanation comes to look like in the case of the action of rational agents. In physics, causal laws have nothing to do with either intentionality or functional norms. These concepts make their appearance in the bio-psychological sciences, and they come eventually, as we move along the phylogenetic and ontogenetic scales, to involve beliefs, desires, and reasons for human action. But the logic of explanation which cites reasons as causes can be seen already in the foundation of biological science, the fundamental point being that the causal explanation of functional behaviour typically invokes information-processing and norms.

Dretske (1988*a*) has proposed an influential account according to which reasons function in causal explanations, and do so, moreover, by virtue of their content. This represents an improvement on Davidson's position, but it is again distinct from what is being argued for here. As discussed in subsection 2.5.3, Dretske's account is constructed to allow for the alleged lack of supervenience of content on neural states, whereas we are assuming that content supervenes on and specifically is encoded in such states. The assumption that information is encoded in material states of systems is evident in biology as well as psychology, and is central to our version of the claim that explanations in terms of information-carrying states, of which reasons are a particularly advanced form, are causal.

The suggestion that we should speak of *causality* in the case of meaning and reason may seem unattractive from the point of view of a philosophy which assumes that the lower-level natural sciences have a monopoly on the notion of causal law. Normative concepts pervade conceptions of psychological order, and hence also definitions of disorder (Fulford 1989). But are they implicated in causal explanation? If normative concepts such as rationality have to do with the causal explanation of behaviour, what is to prevent the involvement of the even more frankly unscientific concepts of ethics? Probably nothing, at least in the case of explanation of human behaviour, of its order and disorder, normality and abnormality. But uninviting though this prospect might be to the scientific mind, the vantage point from which it appears is unavoidable. The normative character of our conception of living beings, which reaches up to the level of rationality and morality, appears already well below that level. As Dennett's exposition makes clear, normative concepts concerning good and bad design, function and malfunction, with respect to certain ends, are presupposed in all applications of the intentional stance, and, it might be added, of the design stance. They are found in biological explanations of systemic function, and indeed in AI. It cannot be reasonably denied, we take it, that these sciences are in the business of finding causes, necessary and sufficient conditions of systemic responses. The analysis of the concept of causal explanation has to be broad enough to encompass the explanations of these sciences, which explicitly involve normative assumptions.

4.6.2 Generality, though decreasing with differentiation

Hume saw that generality is fundamental to the notion of causality. The proposition that one event has caused another implies the generalization that events of the one kind are followed by events of the other kind. How might this insight be applied in biology and psychology, to the relation between stimuli and responses? Hume's analysis would be applicable most straightforwardly in case the same stimulus always gave rise to the same response. In other words, the paradigm causal connection would be the reflex arc (as in the knee-jerk), axiomatic to seventeenth-century physiology and to bio-psychological schools which continued that tradition. The relation between stimulus and response in living systems is, however, not always one-one. Particularly as systemic complexity increases, the relation is more often one-many and/or many-one. Explanation of such variability requires postulation of mediating processes within the system, operating in a way dependent on the system's design. Therefore such generalizations, or partial (statistical) generalizations, as exist are essentially relative to the design of particular systems. Systems with different designs give rise to different correlations between stimuli and responses. Of course there is so far nothing to prevent us calling the correlations causal in Hume's sense, nor is there need to deny the implication of generality.

Generalization of this kind will be possible, however, only across systems with similar designs, and this condition severely restricts the scope of generalization in the biological sciences and upwards. By way of compensation, there can be generalizations over systems with different designs but the same function, though these generalizations are so far unconcerned with details of the mediating mechanisms. Either way, the result is that there is no 'general theory' of biological function. What we have rather is many specific (sub-) theories, concerning the function and design of such as the heart, kidney, liver, limbic system, etc., with often different theories for different species.

In psychology the same point applies, even more so as we deal with more highly differentiated cognitive-affective functions. We have (sub-) theories of vision and of memory, for example, more or less varying across different species, and often different depending on the kind of information being processed. In psychology, as in biology, there is no 'general theory' of function.

In psychology there was an attempt to construct a general theory of at least one fundamental function, learning, which would be applicable across the phylogenetic and ontogenetic scales, that is, the theory of conditioning. The theory explicitly aspired to the status of the general laws of the natural (sub-biological) sciences. But such aspiration is misconceived. Once we deal (explicitly) with systemic function, generality of the kind achieved in physics and chemistry is unattainable, and more importantly, inappropriate. Bio-psychological systems have diverse functions and fulfil them by diverse means. The scientific method appropriate in the case of such systems is investigation of specifics.

The above considerations raise the question to what extent we can expect to find generalizations concerning cognitive-affective states, their environmental causes, and their behavioural effects. Such connections are essentially relative to the perceiving, acting living being concerned. Given species' differences, individual differences within species, particularly in human beings, and given the diversity of contexts in which action occurs, it would seem so far that the prospects for generalization are slim.

That said, there is in fact no shortage of generalizations concerning cognitive-affective states, their causes and effects. However, generalization here is of a special kind, and is achieved at some cost.

Examples of generalizations over cognitive-affective states include the following. Fear is caused by (perception of) stimuli which are (interpreted as) threatening, for example because they are associated with pain, or just because they are novel; and it results, depending on many factors, including (perceived) context, in such behaviours as search, defence, avoidance, or preparation for attack (Gray 1982). Or again, the cognitive-affective state of helplessness results from persistent or traumatic (perceived) lack of control over major aversive events, such as pain, or deprivation, and ensues in behavioural inertia (Seligman 1975).

Such generalizations invoke informational content, or meaning. Stimuli are perceived as having a certain significance, resulting in a cognitive-affective state with a particular content, which in turn, generates in a way depending on perceived meaning of context and on aims, appropriate intentional, meaningful behaviour (or, in the case of helplessness in particular, appropriate cessation of intentional behaviour). In this sense, the generalizations are over 'meaningful connections'. Jaspers cites other examples: attacked people become angry and spring to the defence, cheated people grow suspicious (1923, p. 302).

So there are generalizations over cognitive-affective states, their causes and effects, and they typically invoke meaningful connections. It may be seen, however, that such generalizations are somewhat vague, or *non-specific*. This is, of course, connected to the well-known multifactorial nature of the processes involved. There is variation among species, among individuals, this in turn compounded by variation in (perceived) characteristics of particular situations. The generalizations cover many different kinds of case, and many different particular cases. What counts as threat, novelty, pain, defence, lack of control, deprivation, attack, cheating, suspicion, etc. differs, more or less, between species, individuals, and contexts.

Although the generalizations are vague, their instances can in principle be described in highly specific ways. *This* person, in *this* mental state, finds that such-and-such is intolerably offensive, and so retaliates in these ways ... Description of the details in particular cases contains much information, in principle as much as is being used (consciously or otherwise) by the agent. Hence the familiar idea that meaningful connections are by their nature highly specific, even to the extent of being 'unique', instanced in but one particular case. On this particularity Jaspers writes (1923, p. 314):

> We all know a great many psychic connections which we have learnt from experience (not only through repetition but through having understood one real case which opened our eyes) ... Such meaningful connections as we all know and as constantly conveyed by our language lose all their force if we try to give them a general formulation. Anything really meaningful tends to have a concrete form and generalization destroys it.

Compared with the particular instance, the corresponding generalization is less informative. The implication is that specificity in particular cases makes generalization problematic: it can be achieved, but at the expense of information. Generalizations concerning meaningful connections thus do not capture the data inherent in particular cases, but are rather abstractions achieved by reduction of content. In this respect such generalizations stand in marked contrast to those in the (sub-biological) natural sciences.

As summaries of observations of particular cases, generalizations concerning meaning leave much to be desired. However, summary of observations is not the only function of such generalizations. As noted in the preceding subsection, they also have a 'non-empirical' role in theory, as expressions of norms. Consider again Jaspers' examples: attacked people become angry and spring to the defence, cheated people grow suspicious. These propositions possess an element of non-empirical necessity. If they seemed not to hold in a particular case, we would be inclined to investigate further to see whether first appearances were deceptive, and in so far as investigations were negative, the generalization can still be retained, by considering the possibility that the person is not acting appropriately (meaningfully, rationally). It can be seen in these and similar examples that generalizations concerning meaning are not simply the result of observation, but rather serve as *rules* for the interpretation and investigation of the phenomena, and in particular, for the diagnosis of disorder.

Jaspers was right to emphasize the particularity of meaningful phenomena. It is a mistake, however, to suppose that generalization here is impossible. Generalization over meaningful connections is possible, though, as Jaspers again recognized, it is unlike empirical generalization. It is not grounded in induction from observed cases, nor, a related point, is it overthrown by anomalies. This non-empirical character of generalizations about meaning is not, however, derived from a covering general theory. Rather, meaningful generalizations function as expressions of norms of appropriateness (rationality) for particular kinds of cognitive-affective states, their causes and effects. They concern norms for specific cognitive-affective subsystems: trust, fear, grief, anger, curiosity, rationality, and so on. In these contexts the laws are 'logical'—'psycho-logical'—rather than empirical.

The distinction at issue here may also be drawn in this way. Empirical generalization is grounded in enumeration of instances. In meaningful, psychological generalization, by contrast, single instances already contain the general. If connections are perceived as meaningful in just one instance, the perceived meaning immediately assumes the status of a rule for the interpretation and investigation of other, similar cases. In this sense generality is inherent in meaning. Hence the inevitable although hazardousness ease with which we move here from the particular to the general.

Meaningful generalizations can be used in such a way as to be immune from revision by experience. If they seem to fail in a particular case, appeal can be made to one or another mitigating circumstance, and in particular, to failure of 'normal' function. However, as noted in the preceding subsection, what we have here is only *relative* immunity from revision. Theories of normal function can change, from pressure of empirical anomalies, consolidated by paradigm shifts, and what was at one time a rule for the interpretation of phenomena can become treated as an empirical generalization which turns out to be false.

The dual aspect of propositions that invoke meaningful connections, which function on the one hand as summaries of empirical correlations and on the other as rules of normal function, is relevant to an aspect of the issue of discreteness of cause and effect, discussed in subsection 4.2.5 and subsequently in relation to functional semantics (subsection 4.5.6). Hume's analysis emphasized that if two events are causally related they (their descriptions) must be logically independent. However, some propositions that invoke meaningful connections apparently flout this condition. We can say, for example, that if someone believes that p, then she tends to act in a way that accords with that belief. In this formulation the belief and the action fall under the same intensional description. It is tempting then to suppose that the generalization is simply true 'by definition', without substantial content; in particular that it does not specify an empirical association between two independent events, and is for that reason not a causal proposition.

However, this line of thought, which would support the dichotomy between meaning and causality, can be seen in the light of considerations in this and the preceding subsection to be oversimple and invalid. Meaningful generalizations are not true 'by definition', at least, not by definition of words. One might say that they are true by definition of the meaningfulness of psychological processes. They are true in so far as agents are behaving meaningfully: normally, appropriately, with 'everything intact'. The generalizations can fail in so far as the condition of normality is not met. We can imagine cases, indeed there are of course actual cases, in which a person shows clear signs of having such-and-such a belief, but nevertheless behaves in ways incompatible with that belief. The implication of this possibility of failure is that a belief and its normal effects can become dissociated, so that there are indeed two independent states (processes) at work here. This being so, one more support for the dichotomy between meaningful and causal connections appears invalid.

4.6.3 Agency: actions as self-caused, with 'inner necessity'

The considerations so far in this section lead to a perspective on the problem of free will and causality. This problem is in fact a set of interrelated problems, each of which and the connections between them are complicated. But consider something like the following line of thought, which brings into question not so much freedom as action itself.

In so far as we suppose that all of nature proceeds according to laws, then it seems as though what we are inclined to call human action is rather part of a larger process, following these laws of nature, in which nothing new, nothing not covered by law, could appear. Each branch of knowledge, each 'science' in the broadest sense, could give its own account of this process and the laws that it followed, as in theology, in mechanics, and to some extent also in evolutionary biology, psychology, and sociology. So we have the idea of natural law, of what happens under natural law, but no fundamentally distinct notion of *action; a forteriori*, then, no notion of *free action*.

The only concept on offer in this thought space seems to be just that *the law can sometimes be broken*. In the case of divine law, theology struggled with the problem of free will. In the case of natural law, in the modern scientific world-view picture, the idea that the law can fail, can be broken, is out of place. In any case, lawlessness, what looks at though it may be caprice or chance, may offer no attractive analysis of (free) action. Thus there seems to be a choice between action being subsumed under general laws, and its being law-less. It is possible, however, to deconstruct this dichotomy.[7]

The argument in this section has been that our notion of causality, and the notion of law-like necessity to which it is linked, is inevitably modified in application from the lower-level natural sciences, to the biological, then up into psychology. The 'laws' involved in causality become increasingly specific. At the same time, by the same considerations, the *origin of law* appears increasingly specific, from the whole of nature, to parts. This point may be illustrated as follows.

Explanation of why a living being, a dog say, when unsupported falls to the ground, appeals to the nature of the physical body as one among all others. Explanation of food-seeking appeals to the nature of the dog as a living being. More particular types of styles of action are explained in terms of the dog being a dog. To the extent that one dog behaves much like another, at least so far as we are concerned, we attribute the cause of the dog's behaviour to the nature of its species, rather than to the individual. As to human beings, there are perhaps also actions, or reactions, which are common to all, or to all human beings of a particular culture, and for these we may want to find causes within human nature, or within society, rather than in individuals. The question is where the authorship lies. The concept of individual action takes hold in cases where human beings act differently from one another. It is by experiencing the diversity of the actions of others that a human being can realize her own possibilities, between which she must chose. When a person acts in the way she has chosen, the reason for the action can be attributed to no nature other than her own. What a person does then is self-caused, with inner necessity due to the person's nature. In this sense such an action is the agent's responsibility, and 'free'.

Human action does conform to laws, but these laws become increasingly specific, reaching the point at which the law is the 'inner law' of the agent. Another way of expressing the point would be to say that human action does not simply conform with, but nor does it 'break', natural laws. Within these terms, the point would be rather that our action creates natural law, that we are in this sense small, human-size, miracles. By all means we are at this point a long way away from general natural law of the kind known in the physical sciences, but the transition here is developmental: individual agency is what general natural law has become.

This conclusion is consistent with the line of thought from Wittgenstein (1953), considered above (Section 3.3), concerning what it means to follow a rule. The argument is to the effect that the rule is made in practice, as opposed to being given in advance, in acts of mind, or in pictures, formulae, tables, and other expressions of rules. The argument is a priori, a matter of logic, and is not concerned with *causes* of action. However, at the philosophical level of generality, these various kinds of point tend to merge. If logic comes to the conclusion that action involves the creation of order, it is likely that the analysis of causal law will come to something like the same conclusion, that action is self-caused, etc. Also, in the sciences themselves there is expression of the very general idea that action involves the creation of order, for example in Schroedinger's (1967) suggestion that living systems are *local* areas in which the second law of thermodynamics does not hold. This suggestion in turn belongs with the shift from causal to functional semantics recommended in the previous section, the implication of which is that systemic functional activity creates information (cf. Sayre 1976, 1986; Oyama 1985; Wicken 1987).

There are deep and complicated connections between concepts such as order, entropy, information, action, and intentionality, anticipated early in our considerations, in the intimate link between cognition and affect (subsection 1.2.3). But let us pass these by and focus back on the particular line of argument proposed in this subsection, to note some problem areas which it implies.

The argument was that as behaviour becomes more particular and less general, then its causes are seen correspondingly as more particular and less general. This process reaches its height in the case of human action, which is seen as self-caused; that is, as opposed to being attributable to our nature as physical bodies, living beings, human beings, of a particular culture, etc. But this perception is by all means highly theory-dependent! Roughly, the methodological rule is to attribute the origins of action to the entity which is acting, . . . until we find out more about the general laws under which it falls. So then it would follow that the more we know about, say, the psychological principles governing human behaviour, the less we are inclined to say that the particular person is the cause of the act. This, we have to note in passing, apparently threatens the moral idea of individual responsibility for action. So it may be that after all we have to envisage a form of determinism which seems to rule out (individual) action, not linked to mechanics, but to the twentieth-century paradigm for explaining human behaviour.

On the other side, we have the fact that there is, objectively, according to current deeply entrenched biological and psychological theory, increasing differentiation along the phylogenetic scale, and then along the ontogentic scale. Generality decreases, specificity (individuality) increases. This spectrum is not just a matter of observer/theory-relativity, a matter of what we happen to know, but is in the phenomena (in nature). Another aspect of the same point is the special characteristic of generalization which emerges as we deal with increasingly specific systems. As noted in the previous subsection, there are generalizations in biology and in psychology, but they are achieved at the expense of loss of information about specifics. They assume the role more of methodological propositions for the investigation of specifics, as opposed to being empirical generalizations which summarize individual instances. In this way, even as we learn more about the psychological principles of human behaviour, this theoretical knowledge will always be in the service of, and cannot replace, the understanding of why the individual person behaves as she or he does.

4.7 SUMMARY

The conclusion that meaningful explanations of action are causal was reached in the first chapter, based primarily on the fact that they deliver theory-driven predictive power. The explanations in question are those of folk psychology, but they include those in cognitive psychology, and indeed in biology, which share the fundamental idea that functional systemic activity is regulated by information-carrying states. The main argument of the present chapter has been that while explanations of this general kind are causal, their logic is not captured by certain familiar interpretations of causality.

The traditional analyses of causality were sketched in the second section. Hume proposed that causal propositions are based in observation of association between kinds of event (subsection 4.2.1). However, this analysis failed to capture the necessity in causal propositions (4.2.2), a gap which has to be made good by distinguishing mere generalizations from those which are, or which are covered by, natural law (4.2.3), in particular of physics (4.2.4). Essential features of causal propositions according to this kind of analysis are thus empirical correlation covered by a general physical law. Meaningful explanations do exhibit the features that are expected of causal explanation—necessity and generality—but not in the way envisaged by the views of causality already outlined (subsection 4.2.5).

Nevertheless, once it is granted that meaningful explanations are causal, there is great pressure to bring them into the domain of the physical sciences and the notion of causality appropriate to them. Causal semantics, discussed in the third section, is one way of doing this. The proposal is (briefly and roughly) that A carries information about B in case B causes A, that is, in case there is a correlation between events of kind A and events of kind B covered by a natural law (subsection 4.3.1). This proposal tends to be either vacuous or inadequate (4.3.2), and fails to capture two linked features of the representation relation, that intentional states can be empty, and false (4.3.3).

In the fourth section we considered further the point that the objects of intentional states cannot, in general, be defined in terms of physical theory. A consequence is that semantic relations cannot be captured in the net of physical theory. Fodor embraces the unattractive conclusion that cognitive psychology cannot study the causal interactions between organism and environment, and in particular not those which ground semantics (subsection 4.4.2). The correct inference is not that causal relations here are ungraspable, but rather that an inappropriate model of causality is being applied (4.4.3).

The causal processes that serve information-processing essentially involve the activity, hence the design and function, of the processing system. Neglect of the systemic contribution to information processing and content is the main failing of causal semantics, and is made good by so-called functional semantics, to which we turned in the fifth section. The main idea of functional semantics is that information (or meaning) has to be defined with reference to the (normal) function of the information-processing system (subsection 4.5.1). Two versions of functional semantics were considered. In its 'causal' version, the notion of normal function is used to make a normative distinction among the causes of information-carrying states, and hence a normative dictinction among the contents of such states, with the critical task of defining the normative distinction among causes to be performed by biological/evolutionary theory (subsection 4.5.2). Contrary to an argument of Fodor's, evolutionary theory can deliver intensional descriptions of functions and objects, and hence also a theory of error (subsections 4.5.3–4). It was subsequently argued that a behavioural version of functional semantics can deliver the same (4.5.5). Causal-functional semantics disguises the fact that the notion of normal function affords primarily a normative distinction among behavioural responses, and that it is this which grounds the distinction between true and false informational content. Functional semantics in its behavioural version makes this explicit (subsection 4.5.6).

The intimate connection between intentional states and functional systems is what gives rise to the special causal status of intentional explanations. The familiar account of causality in terms of generality covered by natural law is appropriate for the lower-level sciences, physics and chemistry, up to, but not including, biology. With the appearance of (the study of) functional systems, in biology and psychology, different principles of causality come into play. In particular, the critical principles of necessity and generality have to be re-thought. The issues are considered in the sixth section.

In subsection 4.6.1 we returned to the problem of causal necessity. If prediction from physical theory fails, and statements of initial conditions are sound, then there is an error somewhere in the theory. Either that or there has been a miracle! By contrast, if prediction from a meaningful generalization fails in a particular case, then certainly the generalization can be abandoned, but there is another possibility, namely, that the system in question is failing to function normally. This possibility is analogous to the breakdown of law, which the physical sciences never envisage. But in the case of systems, breakdown can and does occur. The 'laws' being broken are not general laws of nature, but are rather rules or norms which apply specifically to one or another kind of functional system. In this way the causal necessity in explanations of systemic function is based in norms of function, not in general laws of nature. Hence one aspect of the difference between intentional causality and the type envisaged in the standard analyses.

There are further implications concerning generalization, drawn out in subsection 4.6.2. While it is possible to make generalizations concerning systemic function, and meaning in particular, they are restricted to, precisely, one or another kind of functional system. The sciences from biology upwards are concerned with specifics. A connected point is that generalization tends to be at the expense of information about particular cases. This point increases in relevance as specificity of function increases, in particular as we make generalizations about meaningful connections among higher-level cognitive-affective states and action. On the other hand, as implied by the considerations above, summary of empirical data is not the only function of generalizations concerning meaning. The propositions function also as expressions of norms or rules. This function gives rise to the well-known difficulties in attempting to construe meaningful connections between phenomena as being empirical associations. This is a further aspect of the distinction between meaningful causation and what may be called neo-Humean causation.

Implications for the concept of agency fall out of the analysis (subsection 4.6.3). Causal power is attributed to what is specific to the agent to the extent that explanation cannot be given in terms of a more general nature. In the extreme case, the individual person is identified as the causal origin of the act.

In this chapter we have worked towards the conclusion that there are two types of causal explanation, which may be called for convenience the non-intentional and the intentional. The first of these is defined in neo-Humean terms as based in observation of empirical correlations, covered by general natural law. This notion of causality belongs to the lower-level natural sciences, physics and chemistry. Intentional-causal explanation, by contrast, is distinctively embedded within concepts of functional, information-processing systems. This type of causal explanation makes its appearance in biology, pervades psychology, and also provides the appropropriate model for folk psychological explanations of action in terms of meaningful mental states. The distinction between the two kinds of causal explanation, the logic of each kind, and the relation between them, are explored in more detail in the next chapter.

NOTES

1. It may be noted that the mathematical theory of information, or communication, (Shannon and Weaver 1949) is concerned with quantities of information and explicitly not with informational content, and it is therefore irrelevant to the definition of the latter (Dretske 1981, 1983; see also above, subsection 1.2.2). That said, the mathematical theory defines quantity of information as essentially relative to the receiving system, in particular to the information already possessed. Our main objection to causal semantics to be made in this section is that it neglects this essential relativity in the case of informational content.

2. This account is intended to be relatively uncontentious cognitive psychology.

Cognitive psychological theories of vision are concerned with physical features and particularly their invariance relations, but acknowledge more advanced stages of processing which involve the 'semantics' of objects, including use and purpose (e.g. Marr 1982). The points made in the text against causal semantics, that it neglects the agent-relativity of informational content, and that content exceeds what can be specified in physicalist terms, echo the arguments in the second chapter against Putnam's claim that 'meaning ain't in the head' (Section 2.5).

3. Dretske (1981, 1983), attempted to allow for error by distinguishing between causal links between sign and signified established during learning and causal links established subsequently, and perhaps wrongly. Fodor has argued convincingly that this does not work (1987, p. 102f.). Fodor proceeds to develop a highly sophisticated causal semantic theory which does indeed afford distinction between correct and incorrect content, resting on what Fodor calls the principle of asymmetric dependence (1987, 1990). However, there are, in our view, two weaknesses in Fodor's theory. One is that it depends essentially on the idea that properties (as opposed to their instances) are the causes of mental content. This idea has already been criticized in the text for its apparent obscurity, not least from the point of view of scientific investigation and explanation. The other weakness concerns specifically the principle of asymmetric dependence. The principle solves the problem of error, and the closely related problem of ambiguity of mental content, but at the critical point of solution Fodor appeals to the behavioural characteristics, specifically to 'recovery from error' (Fodor 1990, p. 107). In this way the distinction between truth and error turns fundamentally on systemic behaviour, and the principle of asymmetric dependence, with its apparatus of properties and causal associations, appears only as an embellishment. This criticism of Fodor's solution is elaborated below, subsection 4.5.5, Note 5.

4. See also Bogdan (1988), McGinn (1989), and Papineau (1993). For critical commentary on functional semantics, in one or another version, see, for example, Dretske (1988b), Israel (1988), Forbes (1989), and Lyons (1992).

5. Fodor's (1990) sophisticated causal semantics seeks to secure what a simple causal semantics cannot secure, solution of the problem of ambiguity of content and of the related problem of error. Fodor's solution rests on appeal to what he calls the principle of asymmetric dependence. It was remarked above in 4.3.3 (Note 3), that while Fodor's principle succeeds, it does so only because it helps itself to criteria that go beyond what is available to causal semantics. This remark can now be justified. Fodor argues, by application of the principle of asymmetric dependence, that the intentional object of the frog's fly snaps is ambient black dots rather than flies, and hence that non-fly snaps are not errors. Crucial to the argument, however, is appeal to behavioural characteristics. Thus: frogs 'are prepared to go on going for bee-bees *forever*', they are not 'in a position to recover', they '*have no way at all* of telling flies from bee-bees', in particular no discrimination by use of another modality (Fodor 1990, p. 107 and note 19, original italics). By contrast, Fodor observes, *he* can tell the difference between a fly and a bee-bee, and if he swats at the latter he has made a mistake, from which he can 'recover' (loc. cit.), that is, presumably, he makes a mistake which he can correct. In this way Fodor appeals to discriminative and

corrective behaviour, or their absence, in his definition of content and error. The position is, then, that Fodor's sophisticated causal semantics, by use of the principle of asymmetric dependence, can indeed resolve ambiguity of content and provide a solution to the problem of error. But it rests on appeal to concepts that exceed what is permitted to causal semantics, concepts concerning (presence or absence of) discriminative and/or functional behaviour. That content and error are defined in terms of these phenomena is a claim belonging rather to functional semantics.

6. Recent critical discussion of sociobiology includes Sterelny (1992).
7. The problems here are discussed in the literature in connection with two positions, usually called compatibilism and incompatibilism (Searle 1984; Honderich 1988; Bishop 1989; Ginet 1989; Dretske 1992). According to the former, free will is compatible with the fact that our action conforms to natural laws, while according to the latter it is incompatible. The proposal to be made in the text identifies with neither of these views.

REFERENCES

Armstrong, D. (1983). *What is a law of nature?* Cambridge University Press, Cambridge.

Baker, L. R. (1989). On a causal theory of content. In *Philosophical perspectives, 3: philosophy of mind and action theory*, (ed. J. E. Tomberlin), pp. 165–86. Ridgeview, Atascadero.

Baker, L. R. (1991). Has content been naturalized? In *Meaning in mind: Fodor and his critics*, (ed. B. Loewer and G. Rey), pp. 17–32. Blackwell, Oxford.

Bishop, J. (1989). *Natural agency. An essay on the causal theory of action*. Cambridge University Press, Cambridge.

Bogdan, R. J. (1988). Information and cognition: an ontological account. *Mind and Language*, 3, 81–122.

Braithwaite, R. (1953). *Scientific explanation*. Cambridge University Press, Cambridge.

Collingwood, R. G. (1946). *The idea of history*. Clarendon, Oxford.

Davidson, D. (1963). Actions, reasons, and causes. Reprinted in Davidson, D. (1980). *Essays on actions and events*, pp. 3–19. Oxford University Press, Oxford.

Davidson, D. (1967). Causal relations. Reprinted in Davidson, D. (1980). *Essays on actions and events*, pp. 149–62. Oxford University Press, Oxford.

Davidson, D. (1970). Mental events. Reprinted in Davidson, D. (1980). *Essays on actions and events*, pp. 207–25. Oxford University Press, Oxford.

Dennett, D. (1987). *The intentional stance*. MIT Press, Cambridge, Mass.

Dretske, F. (1981). *Knowledge and the flow of information*. MIT Press, Cambridge, Mass.

Dretske, F. (1983). Precis of *Knowledge and the flow of information*, with peer commentary. *Behavioral and Brain Sciences*, 6, 55–90.

Dretske, F. (1986). Misrepresentation. In *Belief*, (ed. R. Bogdan), pp. 17–36. Oxford University Press, Oxford.

Dretske, F. (1988a). *Explaining behavior: reasons in a world of causes*. MIT Press, Cambridge, Mass.

Dretske, F. (1988*b*). Commentary: Bogdan on information. *Mind and Language*, **3**, 141–4.

Dretske, F. (1989). Reasons and causes. In *Philosophical perspectives, 3: philosophy of mind and action theory*, (ed. J. Tomberlin), pp. 1–15. Ridgeview, Atascadero.

Dretske, F. (1992). The metaphysics of freedom. *Canadian Journal of Philosophy*, **22**, 1–13.

Emmett, K. (1989). Must intentional states be intenSional? *Behaviorism*, **17**, 129–36.

Evnine, S. (1991). *Donald Davidson*. Polity Press, Cambridge.

Fodor, J. (1980). Methodological Solipsism considered as a research strategy in cognitive psychology. With peer commentary. *The Behavioral and Brain Sciences*, **3**, 63–109.

Fodor, J. (1987). *Psychosemantics*. MIT Press, Cambridge, Mass.

Fodor, J. (1990). A theory of content, I & II. In *A theory of content and other essays*, pp. 51–136. MIT Press, Cambridge, Mass.

Fodor, J. (1991). You can fool some of the people all of the time, everything else being equal; hedged laws and psychological explanation. *Mind*, **100**, 19–34.

Forbes, G. (1989). Biosemantics and the normative properties of thought. In *Philosophical perspectives, 3: philosophy of mind and action theory*, (ed. J. E. Tomberlin), pp. 533–47. Ridgeview, Atascadero.

Fulford, K. (1989). *Moral theory and medical practice*. Cambridge University Press, Cambridge.

Ginet, C. (1989). Reasons explanation of action: an incompatibilist account. In *Philosophical perspectives, 3: philosophy of mind and action theory*, (ed. J. E. Tomberlin), pp. 17–46. Ridgeview, Atascadero.

Gray, J. (1982). *The neuropsychology of anxiety*. Clarendon Press, Oxford.

Haldane, J. (1988). Folk psychology and the explanation of human behaviour. *Proceedings of the Aristotelian Society, Suppl.* LXII, 223–54.

Henderson, D. (1991). Rationalizing explanation, normative principles, and descriptive generalizations. *Behaviour and Philosophy*, **19**, 1–20.

Honderich, T. (1988). *A theory of determinism. The mind, neuroscience and life hopes.* Oxford University Press, Oxford.

Hume, D. (1777). *An enquiry concerning human understanding*. (Ed. Selby-Bigge, L. A. (1902) (2nd edn). Oxford University Press, Oxford.)

Israel, D. (1988). Commentary: Bogdan on information. *Mind and Language*, **3**, 123–40.

Jaspers, K. (1923). *Allgemeine Psychopathologie*. Springer Verlag, Berlin. (English translation by Hoenig, J. and Hamilton, M. W. (1963). *General Psychopathology*. Manchester University Press.)

Lakatos, I. (1970). Falsification and the methodology of scientific research programmes. In *Criticism and the growth of knowledge*, (ed. I. Lakatos and A. Musgrave), pp. 91–196. Cambridge University Press, Cambridge.

Lepore, E. and McLaughlin, B. (ed.) (1985). *Actions and events. Perspectives on the philosophy of Donald Davidson*. Blackwell, Oxford.

Lettvin, J. Y., Maturana, H. R. McCulloch, W. S., and Pitts, W. H. (1959). What the frog's eye tells the frog's brain. *Proceedings of the Institute of Radio Engineers*, 1940–51.

Locke, J. (1690). *An essay concerning human understanding.* (Ed. Nidditch P. H. (1975). Oxford University Press, Oxford.)

Lyons, W. (1992). Intentionality and modern philosophical psychology, III the appeal to teleology. *Philosophical Psychology,* 5, 309–26.

McGinn, C. (1989). *Mental content.* Blackwell, Oxford.

Marr, D. C. (1982). *Vision: a computational investigation into the human representation and processing of visual information.* Freeman, San Francisco.

Martin, R. (1991). Collingwood on reasons, causes, and the explanation of action. *International Studies in Philosophy,* 23, 47–62.

Mill, J. S. (1843). *A system of logic.* John W. Parker, London.

Millikan, R. (1984). *Language, thought, and other biological categories.* MIT Press, Cambridge, Mass.

Millikan, R. (1986). Thoughts without laws: cognitive science with content. *Philosophical Review,* 95, 47–80.

Nagel, E. (1961). *The structure of science: problems in the logic of scientific explanation.* Routledge and Kegan Paul, London.

Oyama, S. (1985). *The ontogeny of information: developmental systems and evolution.* Cambridge University Press, Cambridge.

Papineau, D. (1987). *Reality and representation.* Blackwell, Oxford.

Papineau, D. (1993). *Philosophical naturalism.* Blackwell, Oxford.

Popper, K. (1959). *The logic of scientific discovery.* Hutchinson, London.

Roque, A. J. (1987–88). Does action theory rest on a mistake? *Philosophy Research Archives,* 13, 587–612.

Rosenberg, A. (1986). Intentional psychology and evolutionary biology, Parts I and II. *Behaviorism,* 14, 15–27 and 125–38.

Sayre, K. M. (1976). *Cybernetics and the philosophy of mind.* Routledge and Kegan Paul, London.

Sayre, K. M. (1986). Intentionality and information processing: an alternative model for cognitive science, with peer commentary. *The Behavioral and Brain Sciences,* 9, 121–66.

Schiffer, S. (1991). Ceteris Paribus laws. *Mind,* 100, 1–17.

Schroedinger, E. (1967). *What is life?* and *Mind and matter.* Cambridge University Press, Cambridge.

Searle, J. (1984). *Minds, brains and science.* BBC Publications, London.

Seligman, M. (1975). *Helplessness: on depression, development, and death.* Freeman, San Fransisco.

Shannon, C. and Weaver, W. (1949). *The mathematical theory of communication.* University of Illinois Press, Urbana.

Skinner, B. F. (1956). *Verbal behavior.* Appleton-Century-Crofts, New York.

Sterelny, K. (1992). Evolutionary explanations of human behaviour. *Australian Journal of Philosophy,* 70, 156–73.

Strawson, P. (1985). Causation and explanation. In *Essays on Davidson. Actions and events,* (ed. B. Vermazen and M. B. Hintikka), pp. 115–35. Oxford University Press, Oxford.

Villanueva, E. (ed.) (1990). *Information, semantics and epistemology.* Blackwell, Oxford.

Wicken, J. S. (1987). Entropy and information: suggestions for a common language. *Philosophy of Science*, 54, 176–93.

Wittgenstein, L. (1953). *Philosophical investigations*, (ed. G. E. M. Anscombe and R. Rhees, trans. G. E. M. Anscombe). Blackwell, Oxford.

5
Two forms of causality in biological and psychological processes

5.1 INTRODUCTION

We have seen in the first chapter that explanations of behaviour which invoke mental, intentional states have predictive power, and that both folk psychology and cognitive psychology exploit this fact. It was argued further that, in respect of predictive power, explanations in terms of mental states are apparently akin to causal explanations. Several major questions to which this conclusion gives rise were outlined at the end of the first chapter.

One set of issues concerns the logic of causal explanation in terms of mental states, in itself, and in relation to the type of causal explanation familiar in the natural, physical sciences. The most straightforward, the most parsimonious manoeuvre here is to suppose that explanations in terms of mental, intentional states are causal in the same sense as explanations in the physical sciences, that there is no distinct notion of causality at work in psychological explanation. A particularly clear expression of this line of thought is the theory known as causal semantics, which seeks to explicate the critical notions of meaning and information in terms of the notion of causality as it applies in the physical sciences (Dretske 1983). This attempt was considered and rejected in Chapter 4. It was argued that while explanations which invoke intentional states have several features characteristic of casual explanation, including predictive power and (a qualified) generality, they possess other features which are not captured by the standard Humean and neo-Humean analyses of causality which apply to explanations in the physical sciences. The conclusion was drawn that it is necessary to distinguish between two kinds of causal explanation, given the names 'intentional' and 'non-intentional' causality.

The task of this chapter is to elaborate the distinctive character of intentional causality and its relation to non-intentional causality. We shall see that causal explanations that invoke mental states have many features that distinguish them from non-intentional-causal explanations. However, the proposal is far from raising any possibility of a mind–body dualism. Rather, we argue that both forms of causal explanation apply throughout biological systems, whether psychological, physiological, or biochemical. In particular, intentional-causal processes can be seen to operate throughout the phylogenetic scale, throughout biological processes of any given organism, and throughout human psychological development. This form of causality was referred to in a previous paper (Hill 1982) in terms of 'reasons', but we have preferred to use 'intentional causes' here in order to underline their causal role, and to emphasize that the concept does not refer only to psychological causality.

The proposal is biological but not 'downward', or reductionist. It runs counter to a prevalent assertion that the aim of biology is the explanation of living processes in physico-chemical terms, and instead highlights the levels of abstraction and intentionality already present in non-psychological living systems. It will be seen that this is of crucial importance in the area of psychology and psychiatry where a very specific reductionist interpretation of the meaning of 'biological' has been widely espoused (Guze 1989; Scadding 1990). It is equally relevant in other areas. For instance Ingold (1990) has outlined the consequences for social anthropology, of a psychobiology that leaves phenomena such as culture stranded as in some way 'non-biological'.

The method employed will consist first of a presentation of the characteristics of intentional causes, contrasted with non-intentional causes. We will illustrate the application of the analysis to a number of biological processes. We will then show that explanations that invoke intentional causality cannot be translated into accounts that invoke non-intentional causality, and that for the same reasons a reduction of biological and psychological processes to physico-chemical terms cannot on a priori grounds be effected. The general point to be made is that processes characterized by intentional causes cannot be redescribed in a reduction that is unable to specify the same informational content. However, it will be seen that this holds only where the system is functioning normally, and that under conditions of malfunction the explanation may be in terms of a non-intentional cause, such as that where pathology is identified in disease. This in some ways resembles a reduction in the level of explanation from the physiological or psychological to the physico-chemical.

Having established the case for biological systems in general, we will examine in Chapter 6 examples from different points in the phylogenetic scale, and at different stages in human psychological development, and this will constitute a further test, and an illustration of the utility, of the proposition. We will argue further that this and other approaches should be tested not only in relation to discrete acts of perception, or computational tasks, but should provide an analysis of real life activities, including those where there is distress or disturbance. There will be a discussion of the interplay between intentional and non-intentional causes, and a specification of conditions under which each is sought in giving an account of psychological function and dysfunction, which will lead in chapters 7, 8, and 9 to a more detailed consideration of psychiatric disorder.

5.2 INTENTIONAL CAUSALITY

5.2.1 The principles of intentional causality

The features of the operation of intentional causes can be specified generally, with reference to any biochemical or physiological processes, and the regulation of blood pressure in the cardiovascular system will be used to illustrate the points. The description of such regulation will be of the form: 'pressure receptors in the walls of the major arteries (baroreceptors) respond to changes in arterial blood pressure leading to an alteration in the frequency of impulses in the nerves which travel to the specialized (vasomotor) centre in the medulla oblongata region of the brain, resulting in an alteration in the frequency of impulses in the (sympathetic and parasympathetic) nerves running to the blood vessels and the heart. Alterations in blood pressure lead via this mechanism to changes in the diameter of the blood vessels and heart rate, with consequent compensatory changes in blood pressure.'

Normal and abnormal processes

First, we note that the description is of the normal functioning of the system. The response of the regulatory systems is referred to as 'normal', 'correct', or 'appropriate', and it follows that incorrect, abnormal, or inappropriate responses can be identified. In the absence of these or equivalent terms, there would not be an adequate explanation of the regulation of blood pressure nor of the failure to regulate blood pressure.

Goals

Secondly, the definition of normal functioning of the system requires a specification of its goals. In the absence of mention of this, when talking of the maintenance of blood pressure, we will not have criteria for normal or abnormal functioning. Ethological explanations of animal behaviours, similarly, entail a specification of their goals (Tinbergen 1948; Hinde 1982).

Purpose

Thirdly, wider reference is made to the purpose of this system. This specifies the task that is achieved in relation to survival, and places the organism within an evolutionary framework. In these second and third points it will be clear that we are talking of a teleological account, and two rather contrasting points need to be made about this. There is no doubt that this account joins those of Polanyi (1958), Tinbergen (1948), and Hinde (1982) in asserting that *descriptively* a teleological explanation is required. For many purposes this will put the ultimate purpose in terms of survival, although as we shall see, as our thesis develops, the concept of purpose in human psychological functioning changes. It does not, however, disappear. We will see that descriptions that lack teleology will also lack intentionality, and so both are crucial to the prediction of the behaviour of biological systems. Nevertheless, at no point will it be argued that the teleological account includes an explanation of the way any particular function has come about. Certainly, once the role of intentional causality is described, some questions may be posed regarding its origins in biological systems, but these are not the concern of this analysis.

Information and intentionality

Fourth, what is contained within the receptors, nerves, and brain is information about blood pressure. The physical state of each of these elements is of no causal relevance apart from its capacity to encode the level of blood pressure. Thus the events in this system have intentionality in the sense that Searle has used the term to refer to their 'directedness'. Searle (1983) has discussed intentionality primarily in terms of mental states such as beliefs, wishes, and desires. He emphasizes that they consist both of a representation and a states of affairs that is represented. Thus the mental state is systematically linked with a state of affairs, but that state of affairs may not obtain, in which case a mistake has been made. Searle argues that human perception, and some non-human psychological states, for instance those of dogs, have intentionality. In arguing for the intentionality of visual experience Searle writes, 'the visual experience is as much directed at or of objects and states of affairs in the world as any of the paradigm intentional states (such as beliefs, wishes, desires) . . .'. Searle does not allow intentionality a role in non-psychological functioning, but a central plank of our case is that it is pervasive in biological systems. Here, in the example of the regulation of the cardiovascular system, the patterning of the impulses in the regulatory system is directed at or of the blood pressure, and the system has intentionality with respect to blood pressure. This patterning is linked systematically with blood pressure, but may be found also in the absence of that blood pressure, in which case a mistake has been made.

Range of function and preoccupation

Fifth, the frequency of the nerve impulses to the brain is not defined by the blood pressure but by the preoccupation of the system, which is to monitor the blood pressure in relation to its normal level. Below an arterial blood pressure of 50 mmHg there are no impulses, the frequency increases slowly over the next 30 mmHg, and then the rate of increase accelerates between 80 and 160 mmHg, and plateaus at about 200 mmHg. Thus it shows a maximum response in relation to the point round which it is required to regulate blood pressure. Other blood pressures are of no 'interest'. Here, and throughout biological systems, we need a concept of what matters to the system. This does not amount to semantics in the usual sense of the term, nor would it be useful to stretch it this far, nevertheless it is a precursor of what we recognize as meaning when referring to the activities of the mind.

Action

Next, the response of the cardiovascular system is an action. Action here refers to behaviour that is informed by the implication of the stimulus for the system, and is an appropriate response to it. In general, intentional-causal processes, whether within the internal environment of the organism (*milieu interieur*) or in the organism in its external environment (*milieu exterieur*), have implications for action. Thus events in the environment, the preoccupations of the system or organism, and actions are closely linked elements of intentional-causal processes. As we shall see in examples of animal behaviour, and normal human behaviour, perceptual and cognitive responses generally lead to effective action. Similarly, in interpersonal functioning the capacity for appropriate action in social settings is crucial. In considering the possibility of disorder, we will be concerned with the difference between behaviour and action, and with conditions under which effective action is not possible.

Selectivity and accuracy

This leads to the seventh point, which is that the responses are selective (depending on the preoccupation of the system) and they have to be correct. There is not a response to what is 'out there' in terms of a complete objective account, but to those aspects of what is out there that are relevant to what the system is up to. When we come to a consideration of the relationship of organisms to events in the environment we shall see that the same point applies. The analysis has to place the organism as central to the process in that it determines which aspects of the environment are relevant, but having done that it must read the position accurately, otherwise for most species the consequence is death.

Differences

Eighth, the system deals predominantly in differences. It is most exquisitely tuned to departures from the normal. As we shall see in further examples, biological systems in general respond to departures from the expected in terms of key features rather than by detection or perception of the object as a whole.

Rules, convention, and agreement

The ninth feature is that the changes in blood pressure and the alterations in the frequencies of impulses in the nerves require rules that specify what the frequencies will stand for. In their absence there could be no systematic link between the pressure of the blood in the arteries and the frequencies of transmitted impulses. The tenth feature follows directly from the ninth and it is that the rules are conventionalized. That is to say, they take the form of 'let frequency X stand for blood pressure Y where X is open to a range of possibilities limited by the properties of the nerves'. Thus, the physical properties of the nerve provide some constraints, but the convention linking the frequencies to the blood pressure changes provides the specification of those frequencies. This point is easily missed because we are familiar with conventions that are created among people, but not with those that are wired in within organisms and not, in practice, subject to change. Nevertheless, the principle is the same, for we could envisage a system that conveyed the same information about blood pressure but had a starting frequency of X_1 impulses per second that corresponded to a blood pressure of up to 50 mmHg and increased to X_2 impulses per second at 200 mmHg. Provided these frequencies changed in a manner that bore the same systematic relation to blood pressure, their absolute values would not matter. It follows (principle eleven) from the specification of conventionalized rule-bound responses that this convention has to apply throughout the system. Thus the convention covering the relationship between blood pressure and frequency of impulses that are generated at the receptor has to be 'read' in the same way at the brain, otherwise the information will be lost. As we shall see, in more sophisticated sensory systems, such as that of the visual system, the convention must be shared among several elements. We can speak, therefore, of an agreement among the elements of the system about the information that is carried by a given physical state, such as the frequency of impulses in the nerves.

Physical—intentional asymmetry

The twelfth principle is that the information (about blood pressure) can be encoded in a wide range of physical entities, and the intentionality is not specifiable by the physical state of the system only. A non-neuronal system might encode the information in terms of exactly the same range of frequencies as those seen in the nervous impulses, but the physical entities along which such frequencies were transmitted might be quite different. In one sense the physical entity is seen to be the servant of the functioning of the system. This point is made intentionally in a way which underlines the abstract nature of the processes. However, it is made with a further qualification, namely that the materials do matter. The physico-chemical laws are not violated and the processes have to take advantage of these physico-chemical properties in order to perform functions. Put another way, biological systems consist of both form and substance, and a separation of the two is not sought in this analysis.

Processes not specifiable by energy equations

A further, thirteenth feature of intentional causes, which brings them into sharp contrast with non-intentional causes, is that they cannot be specified using energy equations. The energy of neuronal transmission is generated within the nerve and is not caused by the force of the blood pressure. The energy or force entailed in a change of blood pressure does not enter into the equation specifying its representation, as this is defined by the convention that we have already described. It follows that the blood pressure could, in theory, be represented by a range of frequencies each involving different levels of energy expenditure. Thus, the link between the stimulus and the response does not violate the laws of physics, nor, however, do these laws enable us to define the response.

Specialist receptors

The fourteenth distinctive element of intentional causality is that it can act only via specialized receptors. The link between the blood pressure and the impulses in the nerves, which we could now reasonably call signals, requires an apparatus that translates blood pressure into the specified frequencies of nervous impulses. This is the interface between the physical changes of blood pressure and the encoded frequencies of the afferent nerves. The change of blood pressure stretches the baroreceptors, that is to say the force of the blood causes the stretching without the mediation of intentional processes, but the output of the receptor is variable depending on the blood pressure to which it is most sensitive. Thus, the physical changes induced in the receptor by the blood pressure are exploited to provide a measure of that blood pressure over a range that is closely linked to the task of maintaining a normal blood pressure. Although changes in blood pressure can initiate frequency changes via the baroreceptors, they will not have this effect at other points in the regulatory system where these receptors are absent. For instance, pressure applied directly to the nerve will have a local effect proportional to its force that may well damage it, but will not lead to a volley of impulses that represents such a pressure.

Deception

Finally, the regulatory system is capable of making mistakes or being deceived. Stimulation of the nerves from the baroreceptors at the same frequency as that produced by the rise and fall of blood pressure would lead to a response of the vasomotor centre and the sympathetic and parasympathetic nerves the same as that which would be observed if there were a change of blood pressure. Simulation leads to the same response as the actual stimulus.

5.2.2 The interrelationship of the principles of intentional causality

The purpose of enumerating these 15 principles is to make them explicit and available for inspection as we proceed. They are, however, closely interlocking and exist in relation to each other. Two examples will illustrate the point. The notion of correct and incorrect responses can be seen to be linked directly to that of rules. The rules provide the basis from which the judgement of failure or breakdown can be made. Responses either follow the rules or break them. We should note that in the absence of rules, that is to say when only non-intentional causality applies, reference is made to the general laws of nature. These cannot by definition be broken except in a miracle, or in another universe. There may be observations that depart from the laws, but these are either disregarded, or provide a basis for the revision of those laws. However, when intentional responses depart from the prevailing rules, the rules may still hold although the responses are faulty. It is important to emphasize that we are considering here only the case where one set of rules applies, so that departures from them can be taken to be incorrect. As we shall see later, the position is different where more than one set of rules may be operating.

Similarly, the concept of purpose cannot be disconnected from intentionality and convention. The intentionality of the state of the system, for instance of nervous impulses, is related to the function that is performed by the system as a whole, and the set of rules provides the conditions under which the desired outcomes can be achieved.

5.3 NON-INTENTIONAL CAUSALITY

The implication thus far has been that the enumerated features of intentional causality are not to be found in the physical sciences. It is beyond the scope of this book to explore at any length the nature of physical causality. It has, after all, merited a substantial literature of its own. In the previous chapter (Section 4.2) we considered several closely connected interpretations of causality appropriate to the physical sciences, none of which of course involved intentional concepts, noting some of the unresolved issues.

Here we will re-emphasize that the nature of causality in physics and chemistry is not straightforward. The mechanistic classical mechanics of Newton have been supplanted by uncertainty, probability, and relativity, the last of which has been discussed in Chapter 3 (subsection 3.4.2). This has led to questions about the possibility of determinist explanations in which outcomes can be predicted precisely from a given set of physical conditions, and a considerable controversy that started with Einstein and Bohr over whether physics can deal only in probabilities, or whether uncertainty about outcomes is an expression of current ignorance. Thus the question of the extent to which available explanations are a function of what is 'out there' or of the observer, or an interaction between the two are unresolved. These ideas of the new physics, with their emphasis on the fit between the physical phenomenon and the process of the mind of the scientist, are entirely consistent with the argument presented so far and the one which will be further unravelled over the next chapters. At the same time, the nature of the explanations employed in that human activity, which must significantly reflect aspects of the reality, differ in key respects from those employed in our explanations of biology and psychology. This is our current focus. Therefore, we will not attempt, even briefly, a further review of current models or ideas in physics, but highlight further the *difference* between explanations that refer to non-intentional causality and those that involve intentional causality.

Non-intentional causality makes no reference to normal or correct functioning (first principle). There may be unexpected or unusual results, but these are by definition not contained within the general law to which the explanation appeals, and lead to its modification or occasionally to its abandonment. Similarly, the concepts of goals and purposes are not required in the elaboration of physical laws or the prediction of events (second and third principles). The concept of information has no place in physical or chemical descriptions (fourth principle). All terms such as signal, representation, or language, which denote information-processing are absent. Physical states do not have intentionality, although the human preoccupation with intentionality has led to the interpretation of physical events as 'warnings' or 'indicators'. Explanations of this kind, for instance linking a fall in atmospheric pressure to cloud and rain, involve the exploitation of the regular association of events rather than the representation of one event by another in the physical world. The fifth, sixth, and seventh properties of intentional causes, referring to the preoccupation of the system, the selectivity of responses, and response to differences, have no place in physico-chemical explanations. Nor does the concept of action as directed and informed (eighth principle). The ninth, tenth, and eleventh principles refer to rules, conventions, and agreements, none of which are to be found in physio-chemical explanations. As we have seen already, the physical laws stand in a similar relationship to physical events as do rules to biological events, but they are universal, not alterable, and cannot be broken.

In relation to the thirteenth principle, explanations in physics and chemistry are contrasted with those of intentional causality in that they involve the writing of energy equations, and both Newtonian and relativistic physics make predictions on the basis of these. The fourteenth feature of intentional causality was the requirement for specialized receptors as mediators between physical events and intentional-causal links. In contrast, physico-chemical interactions can take place at any point, and depend only on the physical features, such as the spacial configuration or electrical charges of the atoms and molecules. Finally, the concept of deception or mistaken responses is absent from physico-chemical systems.

5.4 THE RELATIONSHIP BETWEEN INTENTIONAL AND NON-INTENTIONAL CAUSALITY

Having outlined the case for two distinctive types of causal process, we move to examine the relationship between the two. As we have made clear previously, there is no disguised dualism in this theory, and the operation of the two forms of causality are closely linked. This will become apparent as we survey a range of non-psychological and psychological examples. However, at this stage we can summarize the relationship by saying that intentional processes, whether psychological or not, take advantage of the physical properties of matter in order to achieve their ends. In the case of neuronal conduction, the impulses are generated by the movement of sodium and potassium ions, which alter the electrical potential across the cell membrane, which in turn leads to an alteration of the permeability of the membrane, thus leading to further movement of ions. This is done in such a way that the information is transmitted accurately. Thus although we can give a non-intentional account of the way in which the end-result is achieved, the parameters of the end-result, and the judgement about whether it is the right one, can be made only with reference to the functioning of the system, the information carried, and the ensuing action. This is the domain of intentional causality. We shall see later in this chapter that DNA makes use of the structure of nucleotides to encode genetic information, and that the structure of haemoglobin creates a spatial organization of atoms so that oxygen is transported and released to the tissues of the body. There is, therefore, a very close link between the physico-chemical properties of the ions, atoms, and molecules, and the organization of these which employs the principles of intentional causality.

This can be summarized with reference to physical-intentional asymmetry. Taking again the example of the conduction of nerve impulses in the control of the cardiovascular system, then the relationship of intentional and non-intentional causality can be expressed in the form of three statements. The same frequency of impulses may have no intentionality, the same frequency may have a different intentionality, and a different frequency may have the same intentionality. The first condition would apply where the nerves were stimulated by an electrode. The second would occur if the nerves could be transplanted and connected to receptors that monitored something different, such as the acidity of the blood, in which case the same frequencies would have a quite different intentionality. In the third condition the same information about blood pressure would be embodied in a different set of frequencies. This would be possible provided the frequencies of impulses bore the same systematic relationship to blood pressure as the existing ones.

This principle will be seen in further examples in later chapters and we do not want anticipate their working out yet. However Fodor (1981) has provided a graphic argument for the same point applied to economics, and we include it here because of its clarity, and because it provides an indication of the extent of the applicability of the principle. He assumes that some general laws of economic transactions can be stated, and considers the range of possible physical manifestations of those laws (p. 134), 'Some monetary exchanges involve strings of wampum. Some involve dollar bills. And some involve signing one's name to a check', and then, '. . . what is interesting about monetary exchange is surely not their commonalities under *physical* description. A kind like a monetary exchange *could* turn out to be coextensive with a physical kind; but if it did, that would be an accident on a cosmic scale.'

Returning to the principles of intentional causality, the intentionality of the frequency of the nerve impulses and that of money are guaranteed where there are rules that follow a convention, and these are observed by the participant elements; whether in a neuronal circuit or monetary system.

5.5 INTENTIONAL CAUSALITY CANNOT BE REPLACED BY NON-INTENTIONAL

5.5.1 Introduction

What then of the possibility that intentional descriptions could, in principle, be recast in non-intentional terms. It will be clear by now to the reader that we believe that it is not possible. After all, the starting point of this chapter, taking up themes from earlier chapters, was that attempts to describe psychological processes using the same causal principles as those of physics and chemistry have led to major problems. The proposal presented here is intended to solve these. Furthermore, we have indicated already that intentional causality entails processes that are not found in physico-chemical processes. Nevertheless, it might be objected, surely the only real causality is physico-chemical and non-intentional, and in any case it is widely assumed in areas of psychiatry and psychology that the causes of disorder are likely to be established at a molecular level.

We will come at the issue of the possible elimination of the intentional from three directions in this section. First, there are the arguments that intentional explanations could be replaced by physics and chemistry by a reduction of one to the other. Secondly, there is the case, put particularly strongly by Searle, that non-mental intentional explanations are fine as a manner of speaking, but are not really explanatory. Thirdly, the question is posed what might be the consequences of trying to describe an intentional system with reference only to its physical components?

5.5.2 Intentional explanations are not reducible

'Reductionism' has had a long history, and has been interpreted in many different ways. We are interested in the strongest form of reduction, whereby the claim is made that explanations, given in terms of intentional causality, could be replaced by the 'lower-level' explanations of physics and chemistry. Following the argument from earlier in the book, we will require a reduction to provide at least as good, and preferably a better, explanatory framework. This should enumerate the general principles by which the causal processes work, and should be effective at prediction.

As we saw in Chapter 2, there are powerful arguments against the reducibility of intentional states of mind and actions, and examples such as that provided by Fodor of the impossibility of a physical specification of the laws of economics, provide further support to the case. The question then arises as to whether non-psychological biological processes can be reduced. If they can, we will have to entertain the possibility of a dualism, whereby explanations of the mind are in some fundamental way different from those of biology more generally.

Nagel's (1961) argument for the possibility of the reduction of a 'secondary science' such as biology to the 'primary sciences' of physics and chemistry provides a useful starting point. He wrote (p. 352), 'A reduction is effected when the experimental laws of the secondary science (and if there is an adequate theory, its theory as well) are shown to be the logical consequences of the theoretical assumptions of the primary science.' However, he continues, 'If the laws of the secondary science contain terms that do not occur in the theoretical assumptions of the primary discipline ... the logical derivation of the former from the latter is prima facie impossible.' It is clear from the example of the regulation of the cardiovascular system, and it will be apparent in further examples, that this is the case with biological processes. Numerous terms, such as 'normal', 'function', 'mistake', 'information', and 'rules', do not occur in the primary sciences. Nagel proposes that under such conditions the reduction might still be made if the secondary and primary sciences can be linked in accordance with the 'condition of connectability' and the 'condition of derivability', where the first must be satisfied before the second is applicable. Fodor (1981) has similarly argued that the reduction of one science to another requires 'bridge' laws or conditions.

According to Nagel's first condition, the terms may be connected either if they are analysable in physico-chemical terms, or if they are associated by a co-ordinating definition, or if there are empirical connections. The intentional terms cannot be re-analysed in physico-chemical terms for the same reasons that this cannot be done in economics. Specific physico-chemical examples of normal blood pressure can be given, but the meaning of the term within a description of the cardiovascular system, and in the prediction of its behaviour, cannot be provided in physico-chemiocal terms, and similarly for 'information', 'signal', 'rules', and so on. A second way in which the condition of connectability might be fulfilled is through a co-ordinating definition. It would seem, however, that in the absence of concepts corresponding to those found in intentional causality, a definition or convention that might link these to physico-chemical processes will not be possible. The third of Nagel's conditions of connectability is the presence of an empirical link. It might be tempting to suppose that where the molecular structure has been established, as is the case with many protein molecules, then an empirical link between the physico-chemical and intentional has been established. However, the protein molecule is part of a system that includes its synthesis and its actions, for instance as an enzyme. Information is required for its construction, criteria for correct and incorrect assembly are needed, and these are to be found in relation to its effective function. Empirical evidence that protein molecules assemble themselves in the absence of encoded information is lacking. Indeed, the evidence is that amino acids polymerize under certain conditions in sequences that are determined partly by the different reactivity of amino acids with different substituent groups and partly by chance (see, for example, Fox and Dose 1972). In other words, they do not assemble preferentially into functional protein molecules. It seems, therefore, that the condition of connectability cannot be met, and the reduction cannot be effected.

A somewhat less technical objection to the reducibility of biological processes can be put briefly by drawing on our earlier consideration of intentionality. Intentional states carry information about, and refer to, other states, events or conditions, and cannot be reduced beyond the point where that information has been lost.

As we saw in the previous section, our argument does not propose that there is not a relationship between the intentional and the non-intentional, but that many of those functions we expect a causal explanation to perform cannot be reduced. The point can be illustrated with reference to two opposing views on the reducibility of biochemical explanations. Kincaid (1990) has argued along similar lines to those described here, that an attempted reduction of biochemistry will not work for a range of reasons, including that the same function may be served by different physical entities, and that any one particular physical entity may serve different functions, depending upon context. Robinson (1992) countered with the assertion that 'Biological entities and processes are being equated to chemical entities and processes increasingly day by day'. This, however, does not bear directly on the issue of the reduction of causal mechanisms. The discovery of the physico-chemical structure illuminates the detail and the realization of intentional processes. Furthermore, in the process of discovery there will be an interaction between the studies of functions and structure. Robinson provides details of the relationship between a range of neurotransmitter substances and receptor sites, and describes the way in which different chemicals may have similar effects at those sites, 'For it is through examination of the structure of the *receptors* [his italics] that biochemical unity is revealed. The triumph for biochemical simplification and generalization is in recognizing that these chemically diverse mediators work through two different classes of receptors.' In spite of his emphasis on the chemistry, Robinson inadvertently demonstrates that he is interested in the physical realization of intentional processes, through reference to transmitters, mediators, and receptors. This is further illustrated in his comments on structure and function, 'Knowledge of function has been a guide and reference for biochemistry research, but, . . . the biochemical studies not only reveal common themes for achieving that function, they also can add to the catalog of functions.' The point is that biochemistry is the study of structure in relation to function, and these belong to the area of intentional causality. The study of structure may indicate further functions, and the study of function lead to the elucidation of structures.

The claim that intentional-causal explanations are reducible to physics and chemistry has been subjected to a softening by some authors, so that the case is no longer one that biological explanations can be replaced by physico-chemical ones. For instance, with reference to scientific domains, such as those of psychology and neuroscience, Hardcastle (1992) has proposed that, 'reduction merely sets out a relationship between the two domains', and Sarkar (1992) has argued for constitutive reductionsim which refers to, 'Those models of reduction that assert, at least, that upper-level (intuitively larger) systems are composed of lower-level (intuitively smaller) systems and conform to the laws governing the latter.' These 'reductionist' theories do not run counter to our thesis. They require an elucidation of the organizing principles and rules that will determine the onset, the direction, the content, the duration, the outcome, and the cessation of biological responses. This is, after all, what we demand of laws in physics, and require also of causal explanations in biology.

In concluding this section it is important to emphasize that the identity of the domains of function and explanation should not be taken to be clearly demarcated. It will be evident in later chapters that the intentional response to an external event will often be psychological, physiological, biochemical, and neuroendocrinological. Our prediction is only that in order for the causal process to take place there must be a capacity to encode information about the stimulus. Thus it will not be useful to determine whether, *in general*, psychology can be reduced to neuroscience, but rather how is the intentional state of the organism represented and placed in the service of action. As Hardcastle observes, 'no easy or obvious division of labour exists between psychology and neuroscience'.

5.5.3 Intentionality is not 'as if'

A second assault on our proposed demarcation between intentional and non-intentional causality could take a rather different form. This would argue that the proposed intentionality is spurious and that it constitutes what Searle (1984, 1990) has termed 'as if intentionality'. He has claimed that once intentionality is ascribed to biological processes other than mental processes, then there will be no limit to the phenomena that will be included, 'everything in the universe follows laws of nature, and for that reason everything behaves with a degree of regularity, and for that reason behaves as if it is following a rule, trying to carry out a certain project, acting in accordance with certain desires and so on. For instance suppose I drop a stone. The stone *tries* to reach the centre of the earth, and in doing so follows the rule $s = 1/2gt^2$.' Searle rightly objects to the ascription of mental processes to biological processes in general, but wrongly denies their intentionality. His fears that this would lead to a universal intentionality can be countered by the application of the principles that have been enumerated already in this chapter. In brief, the falling stone cannot fall incorrectly, its fall can be described without reference to information, it does not give priority to some speeds rather than others, it follows universal laws of nature that cannot in this universe be conceived of differently and do not entail a convention, the fall is described using an energy equation, there are no special receptors involved, nor could there be deception. There is, therefore, a very clear demarcation between intentionality, including non-mental intentionality, and the non-intentional world of physics and chemistry.

5.5.4 The Martian needs intentionality

In a third approach to the problem let us suppose that we wish to instruct a Martian, who knows nothing of intentionality, to assemble the regulatory apparatus of the cardiovascular system. We will assume that the mechanics of this process are fully understood. Would it be possible to assemble a working replica of the regulatory system without reference to intentional concepts? Let us suppose that we have already a conducting apparatus that can transmit electrical impulses in the same way as that of the relevant neurons, with the same frequency range as that found in the regulation of the cardiovascular system. We now need the receptors that will convert blood pressure to nervous impulses. It would be possible to tell the Martian how to construct the receptor, and he (or she) would have to carry this out on the basis of 'that goes there'. If the Martian were to ask 'why?' then the answer would be either that this must be obeyed without question, or that 'this is how it is done in order to convert a range of blood pressures into a given frequency range'. Thus the construction could be carried out either by submission to an authority, or with reference to the intentionality of the system. Further, if the Martian knew only the physical laws governing the components he would not know when he had made a mistake. This could be identified only by the instructor, or by a Martian who knew about the intentionality of the system. Similarly, he would not know when to stop, unless either he was instructed, or he was aware of when the receptor had been completed according to the function it was designed to perform. The general point is that knowledge of intentional causality would be required for the Martian to understand what he was doing and to act appropriately, and in its absence he would have to depend on the instruction of another, who did know about the intentionality of the baroreceptor.

5.6 THE PLACE OF NON-INTENTIONAL CAUSALITY IN THE EXPLANATION OF BREAKDOWN

Thus far we have focused on processes that cannot be described adequately in physico-chemical terms, and for which a reduction to such terms is not possible. Surely, it would be objected, the history of medicine especially over the past 100 years has rested on the replacement of explanations which involved intentional causes by physico-chemical and reductionist explanations. Thus syphilis is the cause of general paralysis of the insane, a brain lesion is the cause of temporal lobe epilepsy, and Alzheimer's disease is a cause of dementia. Here we come to a further element in the application of the distinction between intentional and non-intentional causes to biological systems in general. The general case was put by Polanyi (1958) who argued that we look for reasons for the way biological systems work, and causes of their failure. Restated within the terms of this book we invoke intentional causes to describe the way biological systems function, and non-intentional causes for the account of their breakdown. (It should be emphasized that although this holds for the great generality of non-psychological examples, it cannot be assumed for human psychological functioning. Indeed, possible intentional origins of psychological disorder will provide a major focus of Chapter 8.) The example of the regulation of blood pressure will serve again to illustrate the issues. When the regulation breaks down, and there is, for example, low blood pressure, we look for a non-intentional cause. The judgement that this has taken place is based on a knowledge of normal functioning and this is an issue to which we will return in the next section. At this stage it will be assumed that it has been established that the blood pressure is low. The origins of this can be found in any medical textbook under the heading of 'The causes of hypotension'. The headings from *Harrison's principles of internal medicine* include hypovolaemia (low blood volume), cardiogenic causes, obstruction to blood flow, and neuropathic (due to abnormalities in the nervous control of blood vessels). The list illustrates a number of points that provide a sharp contrast with those made regarding the way the system works. Here the causes of disruption do not act with reference to information about blood pressure. Examples include a laceration to a blood vessel, an injury to heart muscle, an obstruction to blood flow along an artery, or nerve damage. A description of the cause and effect is a physico-chemical one without the mediation of information. The amount of damage is related to the volume of the toxin, or the force of the injury. The cardiovascular system does not have a detection apparatus nor a state of readiness for such disruptive agents, and they can, in principle, have their effect at any part of the system. Finally there is no question of failure resulting from mistaken identity or deception.

It seems then that in clear cases of dysfunction or disease at least some of the causal story does not entail intentional-causal processes. However, the position is somewhat different from that of eliminating an intentional account, for instance through a reduction to physics and chemistry, because here we are seeking to explain those cases where intentionality has run out. Taking the example of low blood pressure, this is no longer performing its function adequately, and it is the departure from the correct intentional response that needs to be explained. Just as in Chapter 1 we saw that as long as behaviour was described only in terms of movement, and not as action or similar functional response, then only a physical causal story was required, so this is also the case in breakdown. If the explanandum (low blood pressure) lacks intentionality so will the explanans, at least in part. This is not therefore a reduction in the sense considered by Nagel, Fodor, and others, whereby intentional phenomena are explained in the physical sciences, but it resembles a reduction in as much as one type of event in the biological system (that representing disruption of function) may have a non-intentional explanation.

5.7 DISRUPTION OF FUNCTION AND THE CONDITIONS FOR NON-INTENTIONAL CAUSALITY

If questions of function and dysfunction, normal or abnormal, are central to the identification of intentional or non-intentional causal processes, then we need to clarify the conditions under which each is sought. Often it is quite clear that breakdown has occurred, as function has been quite dramatically disrupted. However, this is not always the case, and it may well be very unclear, especially in examples of psychological functioning. In the regulation of the cardiovascular system, if the frequencies of impulses in the nerves were not to rise in the normal rule-bound manner in relation to a rise in blood pressure, then we would look for a (non-intentional) cause of the disruption of function. However, the behaviour of a part of an intentional system does not necessarily indicate whether a disruption of the rules has taken place. Take the example of pulse rate. A low pulse rate, or bradycardia, might lead the physician to suspect dysfunction on the grounds that this was a departure from normal. One possibility would be that there had been an interruption of the functioning of the conducting tissues of the heart leading to the bradycardia. This would have involved non-intentional causality; for instance a toxin or reduced level of oxygen supplied to the tissues might have damaged the nerve. However, the same bradycardia could arise in a very fit person. In this case it would be a response to the increased capacity of the heart, and would therefore be an appropriate response mediated by information about cardiac output. Furthermore, we would find in this case that when the person exercised the pulse rate would increase in a way that was systematically linked to the increased need of the body for oxygen. The damaged heart, by contrast, would not respond appropriately. The general principle is that we pay attention to apparent disruption of normal functioning and of the operation of rules, and such an apparent disruption may originate from intentional processes or may represent breakdown arising from a physical, non-intentional cause. Either way our starting point is a study of the integrity of the intentional system. The conditions for establishing breakdown of function, and the question of whether intentional or non-intentional explanations are relevant will provide a recurring focus in later chapters.

5.8 BIOLOGICAL PROCESSES: A FURTHER EXAMINATION

Thus far we have considered only one example in order to explore the distinction between intentional and non-intentional causality and the relationship between the two. In concluding this chapter we will take further examples in order to illustrate the general applicability of the argument, and to provide, at least in part, an examination of the proposals.

5.8.1 DNA and protein synthesis

At first sight the elucidation of the role of deoxyribonucleic acid (DNA) in determining the structure and function of complex biological structures, with the accompanying possibilities of the modification of such structures through the alteration of the molecule, appear to support the physico-chemical re-analysis of living processes. However, it provides one of the most dramatic demonstrations of the opposite thesis—the one argued here. For the DNA molecule has significance only by virtue of the vast quantity of information that is stored within the molecule, and because it is linked in a systematic way with protein synthesis, a process that is characterized by intentional causality. Briefly, the sequence involves the reading (transcription) of the nucleotide triplet codes in the DNA, by the messenger ribonucleic acid (mRNA) molecule, which acts as a template for the assembly of amino acids in the synthesis of proteins. Amino acids are brought to the mRNA by smaller transfer RNA (tRNA) molecules, which have the task of delivering specific amino acids to the correct sites on the mRNA. This process is referred to as the 'translation' of the genetic code into proteins.

Taking the 15 principles of intentional causality;

1. The process can take place normally or correctly, and there can be mistakes, often with devastating results.
2. The goal of the DNA–RNA protein synthesis system is the accurate construction of protein molecules from amino acids.
3. The purpose is to provide a means whereby adaptive structure and function are passed down the generations.
4. The DNA molecule carries information about, or has intentionality with respect to, protein structure, and this in turn has intentionality in relation to a range of functions.

5. and 6.   Only certain features of the DNA molecules are of interest to the

mRNA, namely the nucleotide sequence.

7. The DNA provides the information that directs the assembly of the RNA and protein molecules; it informs actions.

8. The DNA code is read as this sequence in contrast to another sequence; the system deals in differences.

9. The nucleotide code follows the rule that links particular triplets to particular amino acids.

10. This code is conventionalized. From the point of view of the physics it could take many different forms. The criterion for a fault is given by the convention. Thus some amino acids are coded by more than one triplet code, which means that in some cases a difference of nucleotide is not a mistake, but in other cases it is.

11. The crucial feature that enables the convention to work is that there is agreement throughout the sequence. For instance, amino acids are brought to the mRNA by the tRNA, molecules which have sites that fit selectively to certain mRNA triplets. Thus the structure that systematically links a particular amino acid (say AA1) to the tRNA site for AA1 must correspond to the triplet code for AA1 in the mRNA, and the triplet code for AA1 in the DNA.

12. The information about protein structure or mRNA could be encoded in a different physical structure. However the DNA, mRNA, and protein molecules make use of the physical properties of the nucleotides in order to carry out the task of protein synthesis with great efficiency.

13. The sequence cannot be specified by an energy equation.

14. Specialized receptors are involved. Notably the tRNA has a specific site at which it binds to the mRNA.

15. The system can be deceived. This can be demonstrated, for instance, in relation to the synthesis of the enzyme (a protein) lactase in bacteria. This enzyme takes part in the metabolism of lactose, and the rate of its synthesis increases in the presence of lactose. However, if a molecule is introduced that resembles lactose in some key respects, but is not metabolized by lactase, the cell is deceived into producing more lactase than is appropriate to the level of lactose.

An attempted elimination of the intentional account of DNA and protein synthesis would have to define in physico-chemical terms items such as triplet coding, the role of mRNA as a messenger, and the nature of correct functioning and mutations. Similarly, although the terms 'transcription' and 'translation' may seem to refer inappropriately to human language, in many respects the process more closely resembles that of human communication than it does physico-chemical processes.

5.8.2 The haemoglobin molecule

We can explore the relationship between intentional and non-intentional causality further using the example of a particular protein, the haemoglobin molecule. This large and complex molecule is the main component of the red blood cells which carry oxygen from the lungs to the tissues and help to carry carbon dioxide back to the lungs. The presence of the haemoglobin molecule increases the oxygen-carrying capacity of the blood by 70 times, and without haemoglobin large animals could not get enough oxygen to exist. In order to perform this function it has to operate over a very precise range of oxygen pressures, such that it absorbs oxygen in the lungs and releases it in the tissues. If this does not occur, either it will carry insufficient oxygen from the lungs, or it will release insufficient at the tissues.

Consider an attempted reduction or redefinition of the synthesis of haemoglobin in physico-chemical terms. As we have seen, according to Nagel's condition of connectability a reduction is effected if there can be a re-analysis in physico-chemical terms, a co-ordinating definition, or an empirical connection. The possibility of a re-analysis can be explored with reference to normal or correct versus abnormal or incorrect sequences of amino acids. The re-analysis of the normal sequence of amino acids in the haemoglobin molecule would simply be a recitation of the amino acid sequence. However, it is known that the substitution of one amino acid (valine for glutamic acid) has serious consequences for the functioning of the haemoglobin molecule and leads to sickle-cell disease. In this condition, the red cells become mishapen, leading to blocking of blood vessels, and reduction of blood supply and hence lack of oxygen at the tissues. The substitution of valine for glutamic acid gives rise to an abnormal or incorrect sequence. As long as the re-analysis of the sickle-cell haemoglobin molecule was simply the enumeration of a sequence of amino acids, it would be neutral as to whether it was normal or abnormal. It would not be able to specify the crucial difference which leads to malfunction and illness.

The second possibility, namely that a co-ordinating definition might enable the condition of connectability to be met, fails for similar reasons. Given that physico-chemical processes lack the features described in biological processes, a co-ordinating definition cannot be envisaged. There remains the possibility of an empirical link. However, as we have seen, the experimental evidence shows that amino acids polymerize in sequences that are determined partly by the different reactivity of amino acids with different substituent groups and partly by chance. The probability of a given sequence is very low, and the chance of the sequence appearing repeatedly is remote. Thus Nagel's criteria of connectability are not met.

The sickle-cell example illustrates very clearly the way in which abnormality is identified in relation to function, and is not given by any particular physical facts. Thus, if the shape of the red cells were not affected by the substitution of valine for glutamic acid, it would be a normal variant. Or, if the shape of the red cell in relation to the size of the blood vessels did not matter to their flow, and if the transport of oxygen to the tissues were not a central function of haemoglobin, then the substitution might not be a fault. This is to certain extent the case for individuals who live in parts of Africa where there is a risk of malaria. The sickle-cell trait, whereby only some of the haemoglobin molecules are affected, confers some protection from malaria and so if resistance to malaria is specified as a property of haemoglobin, then under certain conditions those with this trait have advantages over those that lack it. The question of which form of haemoglobin has a fault then is less clear. The general point is that the condition is determined by the function that the molecule serves in relation to particular features of the environment, and by the effect that the physical variation has on that function.

Once an abnormality has been identified, a non-intentional causal factor may be sought. For instance a protein abnormality might be traced back to faulty DNA. This would require that the mistake in the DNA had been transcribed and translated correctly in the synthesis of the protein. Once the mistake in the DNA has been identified it might be possible to give a non-intentional account, for instance where a chemical agent had, by virtue of its physical properties, affected the nucleotide sequence. It seems then that an elimination of intentionality, and reduction to physics could be achieved. However, the intentionality has already been eliminated in that what has to be explained is the abnormal behaviour of the haemoglobin and red blood cells. There is therefore not a reduction from the intentional to the non-intentional, but from abnormal behaviour to abnormal molecule. At the same time, the fault is defined by contrast with the correct behaviour and amino acid sequence, and the integrity of the rest of the intentional system is required for the chemical to be the cause of the abnormal protein.

5.9 SUMMARY

In this chapter we have sought to lay the foundations for the argument that intentional and non-intentional causal processes occur throughout biological systems, including those involved in human psychological functioning. Our purpose has been to state, and in some degree demonstrate, the differences between the two, and to anticipate ways in which this analysis will provide an account that is biological and psychological, of order and disorder in the mind.

REFERENCES

Dretske, F. I. (1983). Precis of knowledge and the flow of information. *Behavioural and Brain Sciences*, **6**, 55–90.

Fodor, J. A. (1981). *Representations: philosophical essays on the foundations of cognitive science*. Harvester Press, Sussex.

Fox, S. W and Dose, K. (1972). *Molecular evolution and the origin of life*. Freeman, San Francisco.

Guze, S. B. (1989). Biological psychiatry: is there any other kind?. *Psychological Medicine*, **19**, 315–23.

Hardcastle, V. G. (1992). Reduction, explanatory extension, and the mind/brain sciences. *Philosophy of Science*, **59**, 408–28.

Hill, J. (1982). Reasons and causes: the nature of explanations in psychology and psychiatry. *Psychological Medicine*, **12**, 501–14.

Hinde, R. A. (1982). *Ethology*. Fontana.

Ingold, T. (1990). An anthropologist looks at biology. *Man*, **25**, (2), 208–9.

Kincaid, H. (1990). Molecular biology and the unity of science. *Philosophy of Science*, **57**, 575–93.

Nagel, E. (1961). *The structure of science*. Routledge and Kegan Paul, London.

Polanyi, M. (1958). *Personal knowledge: towards a post-critical philosophy*. Routledge and Keegan Paul, London.

Robinson, J. D. (1992). Aims and achievements of the reductionist approach in biochemistry/molecular biology/cell biology: a response to Kincaid. *Philosophy of Science*, 59, 465–70.

Sarkar, S. (1992). Models of reduction and categories of reductionism. *Synthese*, 91, 167–94.

Scadding, J. G. (1990). The semantic problems of psychiatry. *Psychological Medicine*, 20, 243–8.

Searle, J. R. (1983). *Intentionality: an essay in the philosophy of mind*. Cambridge University Press, Cambridge.

Searle, J. R. (1984). *Minds, brains and science*. BBC Publications, London.

Searle, J. R. (1990). Consciousness, explanatory inversion and cognitive science. *Behavioural and Brain Sciences*, 13, 585–642.

Tinbergen, N. (1948). Social releasers and the experimental methods required for their study. *Wilson Bulletin*, 60, 6–51.

6
Intentional causality, neurobiology, and development

6.1 INTRODUCTION

We turn in this chapter from physiology and biochemistry to animal and human neurobiology and psychology. There is a shift from systems that respond to stimuli from the '*milieu interieur*', such as changes in blood pressure or blood sugar, to those that respond to features of the external environment. The external environment is comprised both of inanimate objects and other living creatures. Intentional-causal processes with the features described in the previous chapter, will be seen to operate throughout.

The method in the first place will be to determine whether there is a break at any point in the phylogenetic (evolutionary) or ontogenetic (human developmental) scales, whereby the analysis applied to physiological processes ceases to be appropriate. However, this alone will not be sufficient. An analysis that showed a common form of causality would provide a valuable unity of explanation, but would run the risk either of an inappropriate elevation of basic biological processes to a level analogous to that of complex human psychological functioning, or an implied reduction of such functioning to a more basic form. Our argument does neither. Rather it proposes that there is a potential inherent in the simplest biological processes which has been elaborated during evolution, and is seen at its most sophisticated in human psychological functioning. Where the operation of intentional causal processes is 'wired in', through particular neuronal connections, then the rules, conventions, and agreements and their relationship to action are fixed. However, where the organism has the capacity to learn, there is scope for different rules and representations to apply under different circumstances and at different times. Where this is the case there will be a need for the capacity to represent representations, to monitor them, and to link them to action. These requirements follow inevitably from our specification of the features of intentional causality, once they are open to acquisition, testing, and variability. The analysis will then be seen to specify functions that are fulfilled by sophisticated human capabilities, including consciousness and language. As the extent of the sophistication of this evolutionary 'play' on intentional causality becomes evident, so will the scope for its malfunction. Our discussion in this chapter will lay some of the foundations for a consideration of the basis of disordered psychological functioning in chapters 7 and 8.

6.2 NEUROBIOLOGY

6.2.1 The basic units

The basic units of the nervous system are the neurons, which are the signalling units of behavioural responses (Kandel *et al.* 1991). Neurons possess the capacity to generate all-or-none action potentials which can convey information encoded in the frequency of the impulses. Where sensory data are involved, there exist sense receptors that transduce physical events, such as pressure or light, into patterns of impulses that bear a systematic relationship to the relevant features of the stimulus. Information is passed from one neuron to another at synapses via a range of chemical neurotransmitters. The release of these transmitters is brought about by the arrival of the electrical impulses, and they act at receptor sites on the next neuron (the post-synaptic membrane) to bring about further transmission of impulses. Synapses are points of integration where several neurons from different locations, or with different actions, can converge. The transmitted chemicals are released and taken up again in a precise manner, so that the information in the signal is retained. The *raison d'être* of the neuron is information processing.

6.2.2 The visual system

This point may be illustrated with reference to the function of the visual system. Much of what is known about the visual system has been derived from work on animals, and so our analysis of intentional causality does not yet need to refer to human psychological functioning. Nevertheless, in all animals the visual system enables discriminations to be made that influence behaviour, and therefore it participates in processes that are at least precursors of human psychological functioning.

Briefly, the visual system of a wide range of organisms may be described as follows (Bruce and Green 1990). The eye contains a lens that focuses images on the retina where there are cells that are responsive to particular frequencies of light. These cells convert (transduce) light into electrical events, and these lead to the release of transmitters into synapses with bipolar cells. These bipolar cells synapse with ganglion cells which send axons via the optic nerve to the lateral geniculate nucleus and thence to the visual cortex. Horizontal cells and amacrine cells in the retina modulate the flow of information. Particular structures in the visual cortex respond to specified features of the stimulus, and a representation of the stimulus is utilized in the elaboration of action.

How do the features of intentional causality that we enumerated in the previous chapter apply to the operation of the visual system? The role of the specialized receptor is very clear. Intensity, shape, pattern, and colour are features of the stimulus that play a causal role in perception and action, but only if they are detected by receptors capable of translating the key features of the stimulus into patterns of neuronal firing. Light is absorbed by the cells and leads to a change of molecular conformation of retinal, a form of vitamin A. This molecular change leads to the separation of retinal from opsin, which is a protein, and a consequent hyperpolarization of the receptor cell membrane, and this is mediated by a messenger (cyclic guanosine monophosphate (GMP)). The hyperpolarization of the membrane leads to the release of transmitters to the bipolar cells. There is an exact correspondence between the action of one photon and the amount of cyclic GMP synthesized, and therefore, a relationship between the amount of light and the amounts of transmitter released. Much of the information about the image on the retina is contained in the spatial arrangement of the retinal receptors and their systematic connections with the visual cortical cells. Thus, the retinal receptors make use of a photochemical process to generate information about light.

It might be supposed that in the initial, peripheral processing of visual stimuli, processes that most resemble non-intentional causality might be seen. For instance it might be predicted that there would be a direct correspondence between light intensity and intensity of response of retinal cells. Then it might be possible to apply, at least initially, an analysis along the lines of causal semantics (discussed in subsection 4.3.1). However, the reverse is the case. The function and organization of retinal cells in invertebrates and vertebrates appear to be suited to the transformation of sensory stimuli into information, according to a set of rules that is tightly linked to the functioning of the organism in its environment. The extensive research into the visual apparatus of the horseshoe crab (*Limulus*) will illustrate many of the points. One of the first discoveries made by Hartline and Graham (1932) was that the frequency of impulses that pass along the optic nerve is roughly proportional to the logarithm of light intensity. This means that although the frequency is systematically related to the intensity, the changes of frequency are not uniform over the whole range of light intensities. *Limulus* is exposed to light intensities that may vary by a factor of 10^6–10^7, and if there were a linear correspondence the frequencies would have to cover the same range. Given that the maximum rate at which impulses can pass down an axon is 1000 per second, the dimmest light would be coded by a frequency of one impulse every several thousand seconds. Thus, even in this 'primitive' organism, the most peripheral visual processes entail a rule linking intensity of light to the frequency of impulses. This rule leads to function over a wide range of light intensities, corresponding to the range of conditions experienced by the organism and in which action must be possible. It also preserves the quality of information over the range. In the absence of this mechanism it would be difficult to discriminate differences in frequency at the lowest end of the frequency range, and the time required to make that discrimination would put the crab at risk from predators.

The extent of peripheral processing is seen further in the phenomena of light and dark adaptation, and lateral inhibition. The response of the *Limulus* cell axon when light is shone on it, is first to show a rapid increase in the frequency of impulses, which rises to a peak and then falls to a steady state. Both the peak rate and the steady level are related to the intensity of the light. This therefore provides information both about the change, and the intensity of the light. Thus discrimination of some features of the environment is enhanced. Lateral inhibition (Hartline *et al.* 1956) improves spatial discrimination. When photoreceptors are stimulated they inhibit the firing of those cells that surround them. This means that if the whole eye is evenly and diffusely illuminated, excitation of receptor cells by light will be largely cancelled by inhibition from neighbouring cells. However, if there is a sharp boundary between bright and dimly lit areas, lateral inhibition will enhance the difference in rates of firing of the neurons. Thus it is clear that the *Limulus* eye does not represent the objective characteristics of what is 'out there'; rather it selects and highlights some features at the expense of others. Slow temporal changes and gradual spatial differences are not perceived, while rapidly changing, sharply contrasted stimuli elicit maximal firings of neurons. This enhances the quality of the information about events in the environment that matter to the organism. The process is both selective and places a premium on accuracy.

The vertebrate eye is, in general, more complex, but performs similar functions. The role of the peripheral visual system in selecting and discriminating is similarly striking. Each ganglion cell has a receptive field: a region of the retina in which stimulation affects the ganglion cell's firing rate. In the cat, these receptive fields are concentric (Kuffler 1953). Some ganglion cells respond with a burst of impulses when a spot of light is shone on the centre of the field, and when light ceases to shine on the surround. This is referred to as a centre-on response. Other ganglion cells respond in the opposite fashion, and are termed centre-off cells. Ganglion cells are further differentiated into X and Y cells. X cells show a graded response depending on the extent of illumination in different areas of the field. Y cells, by contrast, show a non-linear response, and respond preferentially to movement. These selective mechanisms increase discrimination and hence quality of information. Clearly, the priority of the system is once again effective discrimination of stimuli.

This example highlights also the points made earlier about rules, convention, and agreement. A stimulus with the same physical property leads to opposite responses in different neurons, and these are therefore not specified by the physical properties of the stimulus. Similarly, in the distinction between X and Y cells the same physical stimulus may lead to a response in one, but not in the other. The systematic relationship between the stimulus and the response therefore requires a rule and a convention that extends throughout the visual system, so that, for instance, bursts in some neurons are read as onset and others as offset. There will need to be in effect an agreement within the system that this is the case. This is reflected in the very precise mapping of the retinal fields in the areas of the brain to which fibres from the eye travel via the lateral geniculate nucleus and the occipital cortex. Some occipital cortex cells have concentric fields like the retinal cells, but others have excitatory and inhibitory areas which are straight lines. In some cells there are two boundaries with a central excitatory area and an inhibitory area on either side, and vice versa. Clearly these will have to be linked systematically to neurons in the visual pathway in such a way that a burst of firing is 'taken' to signify onset or offset of light.

Overall, the structure of the striate cortex shows a very precise regular arrangement of cell types. This 'functional architecture' (Hubel and Wiesel 1962, 1968) ensures that a wide range of features of stimuli are mapped on to the cortical structure. For instance, some cortical cells are arranged in columns according to their preference for the orientation of the stimulus. Each column covers approximately a 10° arc. Here, then, the responses of the cells are selective, precise, and make discriminations. They provide information about particular features of the stimulus.

Now let us turn to two broader questions in vision: possible mechanisms in the assembly of perceptions, and the relationship between vision and action. A detailed consideration of the psychophysiology of perception is beyond the scope of our discussion, but some of the recent work is highly relevant. Marr (1982) argued that an explanation of the components of the system can be provided only once its overall function has been described. This requires a computational theory that specifies what the visual system must do, a specification of the way in which problems are solved (algorithm), and an understanding of ways in which these are implemented. A specific example of Marr's approach is found in his theory of the role of the primal sketch in vision. He hypothesized that this is comprised of a number of representations of light intensity differences present in the image. Typically an image will contain numerous gradations of light intensity, not all of which are of similar significance. The task of the raw primal sketch is to identify those changes of intensity that are crucial to the identity of the image, rather like the key lines in an artist's sketch, say, of the human face. Marr and Hildreth (1980) derived an algorithm in which the gradients of intensity are measured using the second derivative of the intensity values. This mathematical operation provides a value which reflects the rate of change of intensity of light over distance, and therefore will provide specific information about the extent to which the intensity gradient in an image is changing. They implemented the algorithm using a computer, and showed how it could produce patterns of light that might constitute raw primal sketches. This, of course, does not demonstrate that such an algorithm applies in living visual pathways, and the evidence concerning this is rather conflicting (Bruce and Green 1990). The method used by Marr and his colleagues does, however, underline the distinctive nature of the intentional causal processes that are to be elucidated. The task is taken to be the identification of crucial edges or boundaries in the image, and then the algorithm refers to the method. Clearly, if there is one method, there could also be others. The method will take account of the nature of the stimulus, but equally the priorities of the organism. The method as formulated is not embodied in any paricular physical entity. Any arrangement of physical entities that could carry out the transformation of the light intensities will do. It is not that the physical entity is irrelevant, but that its definition will follow the specification of the operation. This we referred to earlier as the intentional-physical asymmetry. Interestingly, in Marr and Hildreth's algorithm the rule is defined by a mathematical procedure, but this might not have been the case. For instance, they also postulate another set of operations which are effectively filters of different widths. These determine the intensity of light to which responses are made, and their setting is not specified by a mathematical operation.

Vision is linked clearly to action. Even in a simple organism such as a fly the mechanism is quite complex (Gotz *et al.* 1979). The fruitfly, *Drosophila melanogaster*, turns to follow stripes within a rotating drum by a combination of altered wing action and a sideways deflection of the abdomen and hind legs. The visual system detects a difference in the environment and action is taken to lessen it. In more complex examples corrective action is taken to ensure that a goal is achieved. For the insect, accurate landing is crucial. Then there will be a relationship between perceptions of key aspects of the surroundings, and of the fly's speed and position in relation to them, with action taken to ensure an effective landing. The vision must be selective and accurate, and the external state of affairs must be represented and compared with current actions in order to determine what is required for the landing. The principle is the same as that for the cardiovascular system, but the goal, of landing, is one that is performed under many varied circumstances. It therefore requires the detection of differences, and corrective action, under a much wider range of circumstances. Equally, the complexity of the processes is much lower than that entailed in human action. Nevertheless, as we shall see, the human capacities for learned skills, multiple goals, and complex actions are all sophisticated elaborations of the potential in these more simple examples of intentional causal systems.

Now that we have reviewed some of the key principles of the visual system in a range of organisms, let us recapitulate on their implications for causal explanations in biological systems in general, and, more specifically, for perception and behaviour. We have argued that external stimuli, linked systematically to representations by the organism, with behavioural consequences, constitute genuine causal pathways. When we describe the visual system we cannot omit reference to any of the features that we enumerated in Chapter 5. We are referring to the normal functioning of the system and there are numerous points at which it could fail. This is not merely normative, as an infinity of other forms of functioning would not serve this purpose, with serious implications for the organism. Abnormality is not given by the physical make-up, but by the implications for functioning in relation to environment. It is defined ecologically. The visual system highlights some aspects of the environment in its representation in order to detect crucial differences between different features of the environment, and particularly those that have implications for different actions. In other words, the totality of what is 'out there' is not represented, but what it is about 'out there' that matters to action. There are no 'raw' perceptual experiences, as physical stimuli are transformed and coded via sets of rules at peripheral receptors and made available for complex processing. The transmission of information entails the coding of a wide range of features of visual stimuli in frequencies of neuronal impulses, their spatial arrangement, and their interconnections at a range of points in the visual pathway. The rules require a convention that must be preserved throughout. Marr has referred to the intentional-physical asymmetry in terms of the algorithm and the implementation.

The physical apparatus is given the task of carrying out the procedure. As we described earlier, the implications are:

(1) that the same physical events need not have intentionality—if, for instance, the same physical state of affairs were triggered by electrical or chemical stimuli;

(2) the same elements of the system could have different intentionality—this is seen in the contrast between those neurons that show bursts of activity to onset of light and those to offset of light; and

(3) that a different physical state, for instance a different frequency of impulses, could represent the same intentionality.

Where the frequency range is optimal, it is because the organism has evolved an effective algorithm in relation to need, not because of a physico-chemical definition of a specific frequency for a given stimulus. It will be evident from these considerations that the energy of the physical stimulus does not enter into the energy equation of the perceptual response or the actions. The energy of the light may be represented but that will entail a rule-bound set of processes and not a series of events that are definable by a physical equation which includes the energy of the stimulus.

6.2.3 Representation and behaviour in animals—some further examples

Our consideration of further animal examples will cover the bat, the bee, and the stickleback. Take first the bat. This mammal has poor eyesight and flies at night. It emits pulses of sound waves and is able to perceive when these are returned from objects. The auditory cortex is very large compared with that of other mammals, and it is subdivided into distinct areas, each of which provides information about some feature of the bat's insect prey (Suga *et al.* 1981). Separate regions are concerned with the distance, size, relative velocity, and wing-beat frequency of the prey. Bats compute prey distance with great precision from the delay between emission of the orientation sound and time of arrival of the returning echo reflected from the insect. The frequency of emitted impulses is greater when the bat is near the ground, which gives it better resolution for small objects. In one area of the auditory cortex, single neurons hardly respond to either the outgoing sound or the echo alone, but fire strongly to pairs of such sounds with a particular delay between them. Neurons sensitive to the same delay are grouped together, and the delay producing maximal response alters progressively along the cortex from a fraction of a millisecond (ms) to about 18 ms, equivalent to target distances ranging from just under 10 cm to 3 m.

This system has to be described in terms of what is carried out, and the fact that this can occur correctly or incorrectly, requires special senses, is capable of representing information about the physical world, and could be deceived. The reflected sound waves are the cause of the bat's behaviour, and in their absence the bat would collide with some objects, and fail to catch others. This example provides a good illustration of the way in which the properties of the physical world, here the effect of objects on sound wave, are exploited by the organism. The sequence of events from the emission of the sound waves to their return is governed by the laws covering the transmission of sound through gasses, which are not variable, but the processes whereby the emitted and returning signals are compared require rules and a convention within the bat as to how the frequencies are represented. This transforms the sounds into signals. A different species of bat could have evolved in which the same patterns of firing could have denoted a different range of target distances, say between 3 and 10 m.

The representation of key features of the external world may be transmitted among organisms, and the behaviour of bees provides a good example. Bees returning to the hive perform a dance which indicates the direction and distance of nectar-bearing flowers, in relation to the position of the sun (von Frisch 1967). The subsequent flight of other bees in the swarm is influenced by the features of the dance. The dance goes in a figure of eight, and the information is in the straight run through the middle of the figure eight. The angle from the vertical on the honeycomb gives the angle between a line from the nest to the sun, and a line from the nest to the flowers. The duration of the straight run gives the distance, at a ratio of 75 ms/100 m.

In this example of social interaction among organisms, all of the principles of intentional causality are to be found. In brief, it serves a function, it can occur normally or there can be mistakes, it has intentionality with respect to the location of nectar, only some features of the dance count as sources of information, and only certain aspects of the terrain are conveyed, namely the ones that are crucial to the finding of nectar. The dance has the relationship to the location of nectar as has a map to a geographical location, and requires a set of rules and a convention that is held in common by all the participating bees. The rules must specify not only how direction is coded in the dance, but also that it is direction to which reference is being made. Not only what distance, but also that distance is what is referred to. Not only where and how far, but also that what is referred to is nectar. However, there is no reason why a species of bees should not have evolved a convention that used, for instance, the angle with the horizontal to give direction, or a different ratio of time of run to distance of flowers, or that used the same dance to indicate a different set of information. Thus, here again, before the evolution of human minds, there evolved the operation of rules, requiring conventions, and these have been utilized within social organizations so that both what is referred to and the content of that reference is shared.

Tinbergen (1948) demonstrated the significance of the red belly of the three-spined stickleback which develops during the breeding season when the fish establishes its territory. If there is an incursion by one male into the territory of another, the threatened male will attack if the intruder has a red belly. It has been shown that very crude models of the stickleback elicit attack from other males provided the red belly is present, and conversely, life-like models that lack the red belly are relatively ineffective. There is no doubt that the red belly is the explanation for the behaviour, in that it meets all the conditions for a cause, viz. the behaviour is elicited in its presence, is not elicited in its absence, and there is a regular conjunction of antecedent and consequent under specifiable conditions. However, the process involves all the features described earlier in relation to the regulation of the cardiovascular system. There are normal and abnormal responses, the responses depend upon the capacity of the recipient to represent 'red', the response is selective and it depends crucially on the distinction 'red' versus 'non-red'. The stickleback shows no 'interest' in other qualities, such as whether the object is life-like. Referring back to the visual system, it is highly selective but has to be accurate with respect to this stimulus. There has to be a rule covering the relationship between the colour and behaviour, and this must be shared within the species. This is conventionalized in the sense that it is quite feasible to envisage that another colour, or another perceptual quality such as size, could have the same causal function if there had a evolved a convention within the species that such perceptual stimuli signified threat.

6.3 EARLY HUMAN PSYCHOLOGICAL DEVELOPMENT

6.3.1 Introduction

How will our analysis stand up in relation to human psychological functioning? To repeat, we have proposed that it should:

(1) apply without a break across biological examples both psychological and non-psychological;
(2) stand up to detailed scrutiny in relation to complex human behaviours; and
(3) make predictions about human psychological functioning, and in particular address both normal and abnormal processes.

6.3.2 The newborn infant

The newborn infant provides us with a useful starting point. He or she is in many respects helpless and incompetent. His/her survival capability is lower than that of most other animals, and this vulnerability will persist longer than that of any others. Yet, given that, for infants, adult caregivers are a normal part of the environment, they are equipped to detect and respond to those features of the outside world that are necessary for survival. Two examples will illustrate this.

Suckling is an activity that is seen in most infants from birth. By contrast with the other motor capabilities of the newborn which are very poor, suckling is fully developed. It occurs in response to a stimulus such as a nipple, and consists of a well-coordinated activity involving sucking, swallowing, and breathing. Whether or not it is readily characterized as psychological, it entails perception, the encoding in the afferent nerves of information about a nipple-like stimulus, and a highly integrated delivery of efferent messages to a range of muscles. This highlights how a relationship between the stimulus, the assessment of the stimulus, and the behaviour may occur in a way that is closely analogous to, and involves the same principles as, those of the cardiovascular system and the stickleback, yet is higher up the continuum towards psychological processes.

The second example is of the visual capabilities of the newborn infant. Newborn infants appear to make relatively few perceptual discriminations; however, they do look preferentially at face-like patterns, compared to patterns that do not resemble faces (Fantz 1963). Here is a perception that is selective with respect to the stimuli, a receiving agent that is ready for such an input, and a response that requires a set of rules in the infant about patterns which are of interest or matter. In the light of the subsequent emergence of relationships with adults as a primary source of protection, stimulation, and affective development, this preference can be seen to perform an important function. Here is a process that most would describe as psychological and yet at a relatively low level of sophistication. It undoubtedly involves intentional causality.

6.3.3 The first months

Now let us take our account on a few weeks in the life of the infant. At around 4–6 weeks infants start to smile socially, and interactions with adults take off (Stern 1977). Infants show clearly that they enjoy contact with other people, through smiling, open facial expressions, gurgling, and excited body movements. Parents and other caregivers experience them as having elements of what appears later as mature psychological functioning. Much of the developmental research into the early months has focused on the pleasurable, excited face-to-face exchanges between caregivers and infants (Stern *et al.* 1974; Trevarthen 1980). These are constructed jointly by adult and infant and require the accurate and sensitive participation of each. The infant plays an important part in the initiation, maintenance, and termination of the exchanges. Here then in early infant development, and within the context of an environment of other people, perception and action are tied together closely. Perception leads to action which leads to further perception, and further action. And what is that draws the attention of the infant? The behaviour of adults with infants is characterized by exaggerated, repeated, and rhythmic movements and vocalizations. It is as if adults know that it is helpful in the development of perception to create well-marked regularities, and indeed infants respond to this. Equally, infants are interested in repetition only if there is variability woven into it (Kagan 1967; Kagan *et al.* 1978). As Stern has put it, 'Infants are [also] constantly "evaluating", in the sense of asking, is this different from or the same as that? How discrepant is what I have just encountered from what I have previously encountered?' (Stern 1985, p. 42). It seems that the infant is interested in the fact of regularity and departures from it, which suggests that once a set of rules about the stimulus is established the variations become of interest. The infant deals in (constructed) norms and differences from them. However, if the difference is too great then the infant is likely to pause or withdraw. The variations are welcome provided they do not undermine the background set of expectancies developed by the infant, and if there is a major difference in caregiver behaviour, a new appraisal is required. Here then perceptions are selective and related to what matters to the infant. By contrast with most of our previous examples, the sets of rules against which stimuli are judged are constructed by the infant. Even at this age we are beginning to see the exploitation of the potential inherent in all intentional-causal processes. If events can be judged within one set of rules, they can also be construed and acted upon under others.

It is evident also from the study of early infant processes that aspects of the external world are represented. We have argued (in subsection 1.3.2) against a pictorial concept of representations, and throughout earlier chapters have argued in favour of representation as construction with respect to key aspects of the environment in relation to the preoccupations and needs of the organism. Further, representation will exist at a level of abstraction whereby the information is given by the rules and patterns, rather than any given physical state of the organism. Two further examples from early infant development will illustrate this. The first relates to the capabilities of 3-week-old infants. In an experiment carried out by Meltzoff and Borton (1979) the infants were blindfolded and given one of two different dummies (pacifiers) to suck, one which had a spherical-shaped nipple, and the other a nipple with nubs protruding from various points on its surface. After an infant had sucked one nipple, both were placed in front of him/her and the blindfold was removed. Following a quick visual comparison the infants looked more at the nipple they had just sucked. Thus the infant's representation of what was sucked was sufficiently abstract that it could be related to a visual stimulus. It did not consist only of what it felt like, or what it looked like.

With age the level of abstraction becomes greater. Infants of 10 months of age were shown a series of schematic face drawings in which each face was different in length of nose or placement of the ears or eyes. Then the infants were 'asked', using a task that involved the distinguishing of familiar and novel faces, which single drawing best 'represented' the entire series. They chose a drawing that averaged the features of all the faces that had been seen, but was not one of the individual drawings of the series (Strauss 1979). The representation was related systematically to the stimuli but also took a form that was linked to the needs of the developing child. The representation had sufficient generality that it could provide a basis for future perceptions and actions, including faces that had not previously been seen. Equally it had certain defining characteristics such that some stimuli could have fallen outside its range.

6.3.4 Attachment

Between 6 and 9 months there occurs the emergence of selective attachments, a phenomenon which is particularly informative. Attachment theory and the relevant research now constitutes a major body of knowledge, and only the basic principles will be outlined here in order to illustrate a number of points. Although there is no doubt that infants distinguish between familiar and unfamiliar adults before the age of 6–9 months, at about this time the preference for their principal caregivers becomes very striking. This is manifest in a very specific way. The infant will look for comfort from attachment figures, especially when under perceived threat, or tired or ill, but will move away from that person and explore when not under threat. The attachment figure is said to act as a secure base for exploration and play, as well as a comforter at times of anticipated or actual distress (Bowby 1969). Different patterns of behaviour in relation to the attachment figure can be identified reliably using the Ainsworth Strange Situation Test, and these different patterns are related both to the preceding quality of parent–infant interactions, and a number of aspects of subsequent development (Bretherton 1985). These have been assessed several years later, and blind to the original attachment classification, and there is an association between the classification and subsequent characteristics such as quality of peer relationships, self-esteem, and effectiveness at coping with difficulties or in tackling novelty (Sroufe *et al.* 1990). It should be emphasized that an association does not ensure a mechanism, but it is reasonable to conclude that the quality of early relationships is relevant to later personal functioning.

What does this tell us about the developmental progression in intentional-causal processes? First, it underlines the importance to the infant of other people, and by this age, specific people. In the context of the points made earlier, other people matter to the infant. Secondly, it reinforces the proposition that any theory of causality in relation to the mind must encompass perceptual, cognitive, emotional, and behavioural aspects of interpersonal functioning. Thirdly, the behaviour of the infant can be predicted only on the basis of an internalized set of rules or schema. Earlier attempts to predict behaviour on the basis of frequencies of specific behaviours did not work (Sroufe and Waters 1977). Thus, for instance, smiling and laughing with mother do not predict smiling and laughter with a stranger. Indeed, typically the securely attached infant demonstrates quite different behaviours with mother and with a stranger; differences which appear to represent inconsistencies of behaviour, but which can be reliably predicted under the terms of an internalized set of rules. Fourthly, the attachment pattern is related to the preceding interactions of mother and infant (Crittenden 1992). These have entailed contributions from both mother and infant, and it is difficult to separate the relative contributions of each; however, undoubtedly the characteristics of the mother's handling of the infant play an important part. Thus the set of rules is assembled significantly from the infant's experience of his or her mother (Stern 1985). Each sequence between the mother and infant can be seen both as a manifestation of the sets of rules regarding attachment, and a test of them. It has been shown that when mothers are exposed to significant distress, the attachment category of their infants is more likely to change over a period of 6 months, than otherwise (Vaughn *et al.* 1979). It is likely that the rules and expectancies have changed in the light of experience. Fifthly, the evidence from the follow-up into later childhood indicates that the internalized attachment schema may have considerable stability, and influence subsequent sets of rules (Sroufe *et al.* 1990). Such sets of rules about the worth of the self, and about competence are likely to be crucial to an understanding of the causation of psychological states and behaviours.

6.3.5 Play

At around 18 months we see the emergence of perhaps the most dramatic demonstration of the potential of intentional-causal processes; in play. This is characterized by the creation, using convention and agreement, of identities and stories related to objects or other people. As this activity becomes more sophisticated with age, the actual physical properties of objects act increasingly only as cues for their imagined identities. The story, a series of events tied together by an intentional explanation, makes use of these imagined identities, which are conventionalized and rule bound (Garvey 1977). In general, by the age of 3 years, children are at home with repeated changes of sets of rules. Sometimes this is clarified by the words 'let's pretend . . .' or a statement that implies pretending, such as 'I'm the mummy and you're the daddy'. There is no requirement, however, that the participants are male and female, nor that the performance is an exact replica of the children's experiences. Equally, it is likely to reflect some key elements of their experiences or preoccupations. In joint play it is crucial that the participants share the same set of rules. The actions of each has a causal role in the actions of the other, which can be predicted only by reference to the agreed, conventionalized, jointly constructed frame of reference.

In order for this to work the children must have a firm grasp of what is and what is not play in their shared interactions. If this is in doubt, there needs to be the capacity to check, from outside the play.

Consider examples from Garvey (1977). The first is the following sequence. X sits on a three-legged stool that has a magnifying glass in the centre:

X. I've got to go to the potty.
Y. (turns to him) Really?
X. (grins) No, pretend.
Y. (smiles and watches X).

For this sequence to work it must be assumed that there can be a conversation in which an assertion is untrue but playful, and that there are communications which can be relied upon to comment truthfully on whether this is the case.

The capacity to play requires a high level of abstraction of joint rules, and of actions within those rules. Take this example: X and Y conduct a game that consists of X discovering a stuffed snake, Y sharing the discovery, X playing the straight man, and Y expressing fear.

X. (holds up the snake)
Y. (draws back in alarm) What's that?
X. It's a snake! (laughs at Y's exaggerated fear)
Y. Do it again.
X. (holds up snake)

Here there are clear rules, unspoken but communicated, and an understanding that 'it' refers to the sequence, and again that 'Do it again' is spoken from outside the sequence and is about it.

The extent to which children familiarize themselves with rules and conventions of communication is seen in their play with the conventions of language, in which it is used as non-play and then experimented with, and then returned to non-play again. X and Y are discussing their feelings about the playroom.

X. Don't you wish we could get out of this place?
Y. Yeah, 'cause it has yucky things.
X. Yeah.
Y. 'cause it's fishy too, 'cause it has fishes.
X. And it's snakey too 'cause it has snakes. And it's beary too 'cause it has bears.
Y. And it's hatty too 'cause it has hats.
X. Where's the hats? (X ends the game).

The conventions of social exchange may be played with and create humour. For instance, if I ask you a question the convention is either that I do not know and need the information, or that I do know and I want to test your knowledge. In the following sequence two children relaxing together enjoy a series of pointless questions and answers:

X. (picks up dress-up items) What's this?
Y. It's a party hat.
X. What's this?
Y. Hat.
X. Funny. And what's this?

Y. Dress.

X. Yuck.

Y. Tie.

X. It's all yucky stuff.

X did not need the information nor was he testing Y's knowledge. They jointly violated the convention.

There is an extensive research literature on the purposes of play which undoubtedly extend beyond our current considerations; however, they clearly include the experimentation with movement among different sets of rules of interpretation, different solutions, and their associated feelings, wishes, fears, beliefs, and actions (cf. subsection 3.2.6). This is personal and interpersonal, it requires that play and non-play are distinguished, that fantasy and reality are differentiated, and that true and false may be identified accurately.

6.4 RULE MULTIPLICITY:
SELECTION AND COMMUNICATION

6.4.1 The problems and forms of solution

Consideration of rules about rules brings us to a crucial developmental issue, and one that is of great importance to our thesis. We return to our argument about intentional-casual processes. In order for these processes to be effective, their elements must operate in harmony. This is to say, the representation, the rules, the convention, the range of function, the needs of the organism, and the action must be compatible. As long as the intentional systems are comprised of fixed biological structures, these rules and the underlying conventions are also fixed. Their harmonious operation has evolved over long periods and they have an established survival value. However, now we are considering examples in which the rules are in some degree acquired, and may vary rapidly depending upon internal states and needs, and external circumstances. In other words, the appearance of novel intentional sequences, which in evolution have occurred over thousands of years, may appear as new perceptions, cognitions, or action sequences, in humans from moment to moment. It is not surprising then that the developing child practises from the first weeks of life, in play and relationships, the skills required to move among internal sets of rules, representations, and states of mind.

In the context of this variability a certain general condition has to be met if action is to be possible: there has to be means for determining which set of rules applies at any one time. The necessary functions here are closely linked, in the theory and in practice, and they may be classified and described in various ways, such as the following:

1. An executive function, to exercise some control over multiple rules, and specifically to select those used for immediate action. Presupposed here is a capacity for monitoring, so that the executive can access states of mind and relate them to external context prior to selection.
2. In the case of social, co-operative action, a method of sharing information as

to which among the multiplicity of rules are being used, or are about to the used is required. In brief, social beings need communication.

Broadly speaking, the former grouping has to do with what is within the organism, with the intrapsychic, and with consciousness specifically, while the latter has to do with intersubjectivity, including the use of language. These divisions are somewhat arbitrary in that the phenomena in question, though distinguishable, are closely interwoven.

Concepts which span all the phenomena with which we are concerned here are those of self, and person. These concepts highlight particularly continuity through time, which is at the heart of action. Action presupposes continuity through time specifically in the form of access between memory and plans. From the point of view of the agent this continuity, and the access on which it is based, may appear subjectively as the sense of self, at least for those agents who can say and think 'I'. Monitoring, selection, and communication of mental states, presuppose an I which thinks (which remembers, plans, wills). From the outside, from the point of another, co-operative agent, the continuity of self appears as the perception of an understandable, predictable-enough person.

In summary, along the phylogenetic scale we see the release of the potential within intentional processes, specifically the freeing-up of rules and conventions from what is innately fixed, the generation of multiple possibilities, which requires, if action is to continue, methods of monitoring, selection, and, for co-operative beings, communication. These hypothesized functions are closely linked to concepts of consciousness, self, communication, and language. In this way the theme of the present chapter comes across these very large ideas. They are considered in the remainder of this section, which ends with some epistemological implications. The discussions are inevitably partial, with the emphasis on connections with the current theme and with other parts of the essay.

6.4.2 Consciousness

Consciousness is a thriving research area within the cognitive psychology paradigm and has already been referred to in this context in the first chapter (subsection 1.2.4.). Some points may be summarized as follows. Most information-processing occurs without the subject's conscious awareness. Processing of incoming sensory information, for example, is monitored and selected for conscious attention under certain conditions, including relevance to the regulation of ongoing activity. Consciousness presupposes monitoring of subliminal processing and plays an executive role in the control of action. The main point to be made in the present context is that consciousness is implicated in selection from among multiple rules and representations for the purposes of action.

6.4.3. Self and personality

Continuity and consistency in conscious awareness, and control of mental states and action, are closely linked to the concepts of self, subjectively experienced, and person or personality, as experienced by others. The extent to which individuals vary from situation to situation, and the extent to which they show consistency has been a source of extended and unresolved debate (Mischel 1968, 1973, 1979; Bem 1983). However, in summary, the evidence may be taken to indicate that there is both variability and consistency, and that, in general, the consistency is less in individual behaviours than in underlying organizational principles. Personality may be seen as that which gives order and congruence to different kinds of behaviour in which the individual engages (Hall and Lindzey 1978) and personality traits are 'enduring patterns of perceiving, relating to, and thinking about the environment and oneself and are exhibited in a wide range of important social and personal contexts' (American Psychiatric Association 1994, p. 630). This is consistent with the idea that there is an overarching mechanism that provides substantial continuity over time and place. Clearly, the statement in schematic form of the need for this agency will lead to many questions that are beyond the scope of this chapter. For instance is this 'self' seen best in everyday events and encounters, or is it that which is seen under particular circumstances such as extreme passions or duress? Is self as subjectively experienced co-extensive with the monitoring and executive mechanism, the function of which we outlined earlier?

Notwithstanding these questions, the developmental findings provide considerable illumination. Stern (1985) has provided an account of the development of the self system, that draws on developmental findings and theories, and is highly pertinent to this issue. He argues that in the first weeks of life there is evident a capability for representation that reflects the first steps in the development of the self. As we saw earlier in the chapter, the infant possesses, from the first days of life, the capacity to represent aspects of the external world. Thus the perception of a difference in the shape of nipple that has been experienced only through touch is manifest when two nipples are seen. This requires a representation of difference in shape that is not tied to one perceptual route. Even at this age we see capacities of sufficient abstraction and generality that they may form the basis of what will become more recognizable as self functions, and Stern has referred to the presence in the first 2 months of life of the 'emergent self'. However, in the succeeding 4 months capabilities appear that more clearly fulfil our requirements. Here, as Stern has argued, the infant develops the senses of self-agency, self-coherence, self-affectivity, and self-history. Self-agency refers to a sense of authorship of one's own actions derived from a range of action-related processes: the formation of motor-plans for actions, feedback via nerves from joints and muscles that actions have occurred (proprioception), and the regularity of consequences for actions. Stern and colleagues carried out experiments with 4-month-old Siamese twins, which showed that although each sucked the other's fingers, they distinguished between their own and those of their twin. This reflected differences in proprioception and action plans. Schedules of reinforcement for actions carried out by the self, and those carried out by others, will be different, and infants as young as 3 months are able to make these distinctions. This experience of self-agency will provide the infant with an experience of continuity. Also in this age period, from 2 to 6 months, the sophisticated interpersonal exchanges with caregivers include many different games, and interactions which are not games, which means that they take place under different rules. Putting the two together, self-agency is a domain in which actions may be performed under different sets of rules, and are also experienced as having the same agent. It seems then, again, that action is crucial to the account. Not only is the elaboration of effective action a crucial outcome of intentional-causal processes, it also provides a basis for the organization of intentional-causal processes, representations, and plans of actions. Subjectively, it contributes to the continuity of the sense of self, with implications that where the conditions for action are significantly curtailed the sense of self-agency and continuity may be threatened.

The argument concerning self-affectivity is similar. The young infant experiences the same affects, notably pleasure, and distress, in a range of circumstances. Stern comments that 'affects are excellent high-order self-invariants because of their relative fixity: the organisation and manifestation of each emotion is well fixed by innate design and changes little over development' (Stern 1985, p. 89). Stern continues, 'mother's making faces, grandmother's tickling, father's throwing the infant in the air, the baby-sitter's making sounds, and uncle's making the puppet talk may all be the experience of joy' (Stern 1985, p. 90). The rules of engagement with each of these people are likely to be different, and with development that differentiation will become sharper, yet it is the same joy with each encounter, and this provides support for the sense of self. In this analysis innate responses are taken to provide the underpinning of the self and its metarepresentational function. Different representations are linked to a common, wired-in affective response, and this in turn leads to an overarching affectively laden representation.

Further on in development, we find an increasing capacity to formulate in language one's own mental states, in particular to give reasons for one's actions and to announce one's intentions. This capacity to give an account of oneself, in language, is fundamental to our concepts of self and person, as already noted in the first chapter (subsection 1.4.3). Some developmental aspects of the capacity are referred to in subsections 6.4.4 and 6.5.3.

6.4.4 Communication, metacommunication, and language

We have seen already that even at a few weeks of age infants are able to participate in joint activities with caregivers in which there are shared rules of engagement. At around 9 months of age it is evident that the establishment of which set of rules will apply is simultaneously personal and interpersonal. Two examples will illustrate this. Sroufe and Waters (1976) asked mothers to put masks over their faces in the presence of their 9-month-old infants, under a range of conditions. The authors described the typical responses of the infants. There was initially a cessation of previous activity and a period during which the infant looked closely at his/her mother, often with an expression of puzzlement. This was followed either by crying and other manifestations of distress, or by laughter. The type of reaction was influenced significantly by factors such as whether the infant was in familiar surroundings. Thus it seemed that the central question that the experiment presented to the child was, 'Has my mother gone and am I under threat, or is she still there and am I OK?' The cues were both internal and external, and the search was for an individual and shared frame of reference. Once the solution was established, action ensued, but prior to this it was not possible; the infant was immobile.

The second example illustrates the use of another person in order to determine which rules apply to a state of affairs in the physical world. One-year-old infants may be lured with a toy to crawl across a visual cliff (an apparent drop off on the floor which is mildly frightening to a child of this age). When infants encounter this situation they often give evidence of uncertainty; action is unclear. Emde and Sorce (1983) found that they then look towards a parent to read her face for its affective (emotional) content. If the mother has been instructed to show facial pleasure by smiling, the infant crosses the visual cliff, but if she has been instructed to show facial fear, the infant turns back and sometimes becomes upset. Thus the infant appears to find out from the other what her state of mind should be. Here the elements of intentional causality are interpersonal and the rules, convention, and agreement are shared between the participants. These also need a metaframe which has the form of shared action and commitment. Here is scope for variability and creativity, provided the communications from the other person can be relied upon. If they cannot, further disruptions of intentionality, with threats to effective action, may arise.

Increasingly, non-verbal communication, and communication about communication, is joined, to some extent covered over, and is elaborated by, the use of language. It has been emphasized throughout this chapter that early human development is characterized by finely tuned sensitivity to social interaction; that the aspects of reality that matter to the infant are largely interpersonal. Social interaction requires agreement on tasks and methods. Social animals generally require ways of communicating which, among various sets of rules, are to be applied on given occasions, rules relating to such as hunting, avoiding predators, feeding, playing, etc. It is plausible to suppose that among the functions served by the development of language phylogenetically and ontogenetically is that of facilitating communication of which sets of rules are to be used in co-operative endeavours.

It was noted at the beginning of this section that selection among multiple sets of rules is linked to consciousness within the agent, and to language (as well as non-verbal conventions) in relation to shared activities. It was anticipated that these divisions are somewhat blurred, however, and this point can be expanded upon here. There is an intimate relationship between cognition and social relationships, as was discussed throughout Chapter 3, and with particular reference to Vygotsky's developmental psychology at the end of subsection 3.3.4. Cognition here, of course, includes features of consciousness. The carer–infant relationship guides development of the infant's cognitive capacities, including aspects of consciousness itself. For example, Vygotsky proposed that the capacity for attention to aspects of the environment and to current activity, one function of consciousness, is an internalization of shared attention-behaviour within the infant–carer relationship (Vygotsky 1934). At a later stage, and more obviously, the acquisition of language depends on teaching, but this socially acquired language is internalized, as linguistically encoded rules, and these come to play an increasing role in regulating action in the developing child (Vygotsky 1934; Luria 1961; see also subsection 6.5.2). In this way, while both attention and language have social origins, both become crucial to the regulation of the individual's actions.

The connections here between individual and social, thought and language, are many and complicated. For example, joint attention-behaviour is arguably (one of) the earliest signs in the infant of the capacity for representing the other's mental states, this being in turn at the basis of acquiring the 'theory of mind', problems with which may be implicated in autism (Baron-Cohen 1991). It has already been remarked that selective attention is one aspect of consciousness (subsections 6.4.2, 1.2.4). The capacity to say what rules one is following is another aspect of consciousness, linked to what we call self-consciouness, as noted in the fuller discussion in the first chapter (subsection 1.4.4).

A further strong link between consciousness and social activity has been suggested from an evolutionary point of view by Humphreys (1983). He proposes that consciousness delivers information about the mind–brain states of the agent, and has evolved particularly with the function of facilitating analogic knowledge of the intentionality of others. This proposal is linked to the so-called simulation epistemology of mind discussed in Chapter 3 (Section 3.2).

6.4.5 Cognition and commitment

In the context of multiple rules and representations, what is required is a cognitive function which selects one plan of action, with its associated representations, from among various possibilities, a function which 'decides what to do'. So far in this section the need for a mental executive function has been considered from the point of view of biology and psychology. As generally in this essay, however, similar conclusions can be reached by an a priori, epistemological route. In the present case this has to do with the close connection in post-empiricism between cognition and commitment.

In the first chapter we outlined general characteristics of post-empiricism (subsection 1.4.1) and went on to discuss links between epistemology and logic, that is, between the theory of knowledge and the theory of representation (subsection 1.4.4). It was an insight of modern, seventeenth-century epistemology, in the Cartesian system, and in empiricism, that the a priori basis of certainty is to be found in logic, in the nature of thought itself. According to the logic of Wittgenstein's *On certainty* (1969), this insight assumes the form: the a priori basis of certainty lies in our methods of thinking, and beneath those, our ways of acting. Commitment to the methods being used, rejection of what is incompatible with them, is a precondition of action, and of thought itself. Doubts about the methods, indecision between alternatives, is incompatible with practice, leading to perpetual hesitation, to no action. Conversely, in so far as we do act and think, we expel doubt and proceed with certainty. This commitment, or certainty, is necessary in practice. But it also belongs to logic, to the very idea of judgement. On this, Wittgenstein remarks (1969, § 150):

> ... somewhere I must begin with not-doubting; and that is not, so to speak, hasty but excusable: it is part of judging.

We have, and must have, certainty in action, and in methods of judgement. This means that in particular procedures some beliefs have to stand fast; these beliefs are not so much assumptions, as instruments essential to the activities in question. This applies to everyday actions. For example (Wittgenstein 1969, §§ 148, 150):

> Why do I not satisfy myself that I have two feet when I want to get up from a chair? There is no why. I simply don't. This is how I act.

> How does someone judge which is his right and which his left hand? How do I know that my judgement will agree with someone's else's? How do I know that this colour is blue? If I don't trust *myself* here, why should I trust anyone else's judgement? That is to say: somewhere I must begin with not-doubting; and that is not, so to speak, hasty but excusable: it is part of judging.

The point applies also to the most cognitively complex activities, such as scientific enquiry (Wittgenstein 1969, §§ 341–3):

> ... The *questions* that we raise and our *doubts* depend on the fact that some propositions are exempt from doubt, are as it were hinges on which those turn.

> That is to say, it belongs to the logic of our scientific investigations that certain things are *indeed* not doubted.

> But it isn't that the situation is like this: we just *can't* investigate everything, and for that reason we are forced to rest content with assumption. If I want the door to turn, the hinges must stay put.

The beliefs which stand firm are those which define particular methods of interpretation and action. They have the form, typically, of affirmations of what is presupposed by application of a particular method, and at the same time they rule out alternative methods of interpretation and enquiry. Whatever activity we are engaged in, some things have to be taken for granted. The point here is of course a very general one. Thus (Wittgenstein 1969, § 344): 'My *life* consists in my being content to accept many things.'

Another expression of the same point is that methodological rules guide the interpretation of experience and the planning of action (subsections 1.4.1 and 1.4.4). These tend not to be given up in the face of anomalous experiences. Rather, these core rules are preserved by denying or reconstruing what seems to go against them. This is necessary if judgement, in general, or of particular kinds, is to continue. Related here also is the account given earlier of the incorrigibility of self-reports (subsections 1.4.3 and 3.2.4). Reports of the mental states regulating one's own current activity or the actions about to be performed function in part as statements of intent, and hence cannot, in normal circumstances, be wrong. In various ways the knowledge—or certainty—required for action and thought appears in the form of a *decision* (Wittgenstein 1969, for example §§ 516, 360–62; quoted from and discussed in subsection 1.4.4). What is needed is *commitment* by the agent, or an *executive function* within the information-processing system.

These issues are central to post-empiricism, because it frees thought and knowledge from something pre-given and fixed, from 'experience' construed as an absolute category, and thereby emphasizes creative activity. There are then many possibilities, and in the midst of these decisions are necessary.

In biology this requirement appears as sketched through this chapter. Along the phylogenetic scale, rules and representations are progessively less pre-given and fixed, becoming more acquired, created, and diverse. Hence the need for decision-making procedures and communication, appearing as aspects of consciousness and language.

In the history of epistemology the same underlying problematic can be seen at work in the problem of knowledge, particularly in its Classical form and in its present-day form. As remarked in Chapter 1 (subsection 1.2.1), the seventeenth-century problem was generated by and preoccupied with the split between sense–experience and the absolute nature posited by modern science. There is, however, a more accessible problem of knowledge, related to, though obscured by, this modern extreme.

The problem arises from the *relativity* of what passes for human knowledge, relativity to the senses, to personal opinions, to culture, and may be expressed in the form: how in all this flux can we identify anything really fixed, anything that we can really know? This was the Classical problem, identified by Plato, for example in the *Theaetetus* (discussed above, subsection 3.3.4) and expounded at length by the Pyrrhonists. Thus Sextus Empiricus propounds the various modes of sceptical argument, citing many and diverse examples of variation and opposition among experiences, theories, beliefs, and customs (Sextus Empiricus *c.* AD 200 chapters 14–16). To any one may be opposed another of apparently equal validity, so that there is no way of deciding which is right, and the sceptic therefore judges neither way, saying only 'perhaps', 'possibly', or 'it seems so' (op.cit. chapters 21–2). This state of affairs invites the sophists to propose that being right or true can be a matter only of power, alleged values assigned to the opinions and interests of the dominant group. Such cynicism, which has much to be said for it, is well expounded by contemporary post-modernist writers such as Foucault (1977; and for critical commentary see for example Norris 1993).

The sceptical problem arises where there is consciousness of variety, of the many possibilities, the relativity, and the apparent absence of absolutes. One response is to believe that one's own beliefs have absolute validity, untainted, unlike everybody else's, by relativity, but this position is essentially undermined by the sceptical critique. The conclusion that there are no absolute truths may appear inevitable. There is, however, the exception that we can affirm the world which generates this conclusion, a world in which relativity and difference are recognized rather than disqualified. A further qualification to scepticism, connected because it belongs with the same relativistic episteme, is that we have to have to affirm some beliefs rather than others in order to be able to think and act at all. This is a non-sceptical thought characteristic of twentieth-century epistemology, the positive side of the relativity, found when it is in an affirming rather than a sceptical mood, as for example in Wittgenstein's *On certainty*: we know, are certain of, what we need to know in order to be able to act.

To put the point another way, the sceptical suspense of judgement is nothing for a living being. It essentially presupposes an 'I' which sits and thinks rather than does anything. This kind of criticism was made by Hume in his *Treatise* (1739, p. 160):

> He [the Pyrrohonian] must acknowledge, if he will acknowledge anything, that all human life must perish, were his principles universally and steadily to prevail. All discourse, all action would immediately cease; and men remain in a total lethargy, till the necessities of nature, unsatisfied, put an end to their miserable existence. It is true; so fatal an event is very little to be dreaded. Nature is always too strong for principle.

Central to the sceptical problem is that *more of the same*—more experience, thought, opinions, reasons—will not solve it. *More cognition* makes no difference. Rather, what is required is a decision, or commitment, to do (or believe) this rather than that. The implication here is that, at basis, activity and thought are unsupported by reason. This certainly does not imply 'irrationality'. On the contrary, it belongs to the definition of action that it is justified by reasons, with reference to beliefs and desires. Rather, reasons in the end run out, and what remains then are our inclinations, the will, to act and think in this way rather than that, according to our nature, as living beings, as human beings, and as the particular person that we are. These points have been discussed in other contexts. In Chapter 3 (subsection 3.3.2) in discussion of Wittgenstein's critique of rule-following we concluded that reasons run out, leaving inclinations. In Chapter 4 (subsection 4.6.3) we argued that explanations of action cite the nature of the agent, in terms of theories which have more or less generality, from those which cite general biological nature to those which appeal to personality.

6.5 THOUGHT AND REASON

6.5.1 Introduction

The main task of this chapter is explication of the proposal that intentionality and intentional causality run right though from relatively elementary biological processes to the most complex psychological processes, up to mature human cognition, including reason. Essential to this developmental story is the seamless transition from biology to developmental psychology as considered in sections 6.2 and 6.3. We saw in section 6.3 that principles of intentionality can be seen at work in early development, and that their creative potential begins to be realized in children's play. This creative potential, the freeing of rules and representations from fixed patterns, is of enormous significance in nature and culture, and was viewed from various perspectives in section 6.4. In this closing section we return to the developmental story of the chapter, extending it from the early stages of human cognitive development to its maturity.

6.5.2 Origins in action

Notwithstanding the evident, great differences between intentionality in the beginnings of life and in the mature human mind, the transitions are seamless. The links between early biological and psychological function in human development are made clear in the claim, fundamental to Piagetian theory, that cognition has its origin in action (Piaget 1937, with commentary in Flavell 1963). Thus Piaget (1970, pp. 103–4):

> In the common view, the external world is entirely separate from the subject ... Any objective knowledge, then, appears to be simply the result of a set of perceptive recordings, motor associations, verbal descriptions, which all participate in producing a sort of figurative copy or 'functional copy' (in Hull's terminology) of objects and the connections between them. The only function of intelligence is systematically to file, correct, etc., these various sets of information; in this process, the more faithful the critical copies, the more consistent the final copies will be. In such an empiricist prospect, the content of intelligence comes from outside, and the coordinations that organize it are only the consequences of language and symbolic instruments.
>
> But this passive interpretation of the act of knowledge is in fact contradicted at all levels of development and, particularly, at the sensorimotor and pre-linguistic levels of cognitive adaptation and intelligence. Actually, in order to know objects, the subject must act upon them, and therefore transform them: he must displace, connect, combine, take apart, and reassemble them.
>
> From the most elementary sensorimotor actions (such as pushing and pulling)

to the most sophisticated intellectual operations, which are interiorized actions, carried out mentally (e.g., joining together, putting in order, putting into one-to-one correspondence), knowledge is constantly linked with actions or operations, that is, with *transformations*.

Piaget here correctly suggests that the main idea, that cognition is grounded in action, stands opposed to a variety of traditional and contemporary doctrines, as has been argued thoughout this essay, such as the resemblance theory of representation (subsections 1.3.1–2), the computational theory of mind (section 2.2, also 2.4), and empiricism (section 1.4).

Vygotsky, too, endorses the link between higher mental functions and action. We have noted already that he typically emphasizes social action (subsection 3.3.4), and the role of language in regulating (or controlling) action (subsection 6.4.4). Thus Vygotsky (1981, pp. 69–70):

> Children master the social forms of behavior and transfer these forms to themselves. With regard to our area of interest, we could say that the validity of this law is nowhere more obvious than in the use of the sign. A sign is always originally a means used for social purposes, a means of influencing others, and only later becomes a means of influencing oneself.
>
> According to Janet, the word initially was a command to others and then underwent a complex history of imitations, changes of functions, etc. Only gradually was it separated from action. According to Janet, it is always a command, and that is why it is the basic means of mastering behavior. Therefore, if we want to clarify genetically the origins of the voluntary function of the word and why the word overrides motor responses, we must inevitably arrive at the real function of commanding in both ontogenesis and phylogenesis.

Separation of thought and language from their beginnings in action is a major developmental task, involving creation of many distinctions, between self and object, appearance and reality, sign and signified. Such distinctions remain blurred in what may be called pre-rational, or magical thought. In this stage (or state of mind), imagination, wish, sign and reality merge, while through childhood the rational mentality draws more precise boundaries (Piaget 1937; Vygotsky 1981; Subotskii 1985; Harris 1994).

6.5.3 Cognitive maturation in adolescence

Further cognitive development occurs at or around puberty. As would be expected, this is linked to further maturation in brain structure and function, specifically in the frontal regions (Jernigan *et al.* 1991), which characteristically serve the organization and regulation of action (Luria 1966).

In his formulation of cognitive development during adolescence, Piaget emphasized the appearance of so-called formal operations, basic to which is application of propositional logic. Indeed the study was called *The growth of logical thinking* (Inhelder and Piaget 1958). The propositional calculus specifies rules for making complex propositions from simple ones, using connectives such as *not*, *and*, *or*, and *implies*.

Inhelder and Piaget's emphasis on formal logic as the high point of reason is connected to themes in early twentieth-century philosophy referred to in the first chapter. The propositional calculus had a fundamental role in both Wittgenstein's *Tractatus* (1921) (subsection 1.3.2) and logical empiricism (1.4.1). In both cases it was the structure which contained the combinations of all simple propositions which represented reality. It defined the permissible relations between propositions, and the validity of inferences between one (complex) proposition and another. In brief, and in these senses, the propositional calculus defined 'reason'. Against this logico-philosophical background, it was plausible to regard human cognitive development as culminating in competence with the propositional calculus, and other formal logical systems (such as set theory).

This whole background metaphysics was being overturned at the same time, however, giving way to post-empiricism, with its emphasis on activity and theory. Representation is seen primarily as being in the service of action, as opposed to being pictures or images of states of affairs, and it employs hierarchically organized theory, and is not simply a passive reflection of experience (Chapter 1, subsection 1.4.1). Of course, Piaget himself was a main contributor to both aspects of the paradigm shift as it has occurred in psychology. His emphasis on the intimate connection between thought and action in early cognitive development is well known, and referred to above (subsection 6.5.2), as is his emphasis on the role of cognitive structures.

The paradigm shift in the definition of cognition has immediate implications for logic in the broader sense of the theory of judgement. The inference is that what matters to logic is the role of cognition in regulating action, and the role of theory in the interpretation of experience. In the new paradigm, what matters to logic, to the a priori definition of the conditions of thought and reason, is whatever is essential to theory in the regulation of action (Chapter 1, subsection 1.4.4).

Emphasis on the development of the power to theorize can, in fact, be found in Inhelder and Piaget's theory of cognitive maturation in adolescence, but at the end, in the final chapter, after all the material on the development of formal logic. The authors write (1958, pp. 339–40):

> The adolescent is the individual who commits himself to possibilities although we certainly do not mean to deny that his commitment begins in real-life situations. In other words, the adolescent is the individual who begins to build begins to build 'systems' or 'theories', in the largest sense of the term. The child does not build systems. His spontaneous thinking may be more or less systematic . . . but it is the observer who sees the system from outside, while the child is never aware of it since he never thinks about his own thought . . . The child has no powers of reflection, i.e. no second-order thoughts which deal critically with his own thinking. No theory can be built without such reflection. In contrast, the adolescent is able to analyse his own thinking and construct theories. The fact that these theories are oversimplified, awkward, and usually contain very little originality is beside the point.

Inhelder and Piaget go on to emphasise the developmental function of the adolescent's theories (1958, p. 340):

> From the functional standpoint . . . they furnish the cognitive and evaluative bases for the assumption of adult roles . . . They are vital in the assimilation

of the values which delineate societies or social classes as entities in contrast to simple interindividual relations.

Consistent with the point made throughout this chapter, that developmental processes create also new possibilities of misrepresentation, Inhelder and Piaget remark on the fantasies of omnipotence which can accompany the adolescent's newly acquired powers of thought, a theme to which we will return in chapter 8 under the heading of psychological defences (Inhelder and Piaget 1958, pp. 345–6):

> The adolescent goes through a phase in which he attributes an unlimited power to his own thoughts so that the dream of a glorious future or of transforming the world through Ideas (even if this idealism takes a materialistic form) seems to be not only fantasy but also an effective action which in itself modifies the empirical world. This is obviously a form of cognitive egocentrism.

6.6 SUMMARY

In this chapter we have reviewed the operation of intentional causal processes in an ascent from the perceptual apparatus of primitive organisms to the complex interpersonal life of the developing child. Such processes are, we have argued, pervasive and unifying in biology. Equally, there are marked differences between the operation of non-human organisms and that of the human mind. These can be seen to be based on an extraordinary, explosive, and rich elaboration of intentionality, characterized by the capacity for the acquisition of multiple sets of rules of perception, thought, emotions, and actions. This implies immense scope for creativity and change, but also the need for the capacity to represent representations, to monitor them, and to link them to action, including social interaction. These functions are among those served by consciousness and language. As the extent of the sophistication of this evolutionary 'play' on intentional causality becomes evident, so will the scope for its malfunction.

REFERENCES

American Psychiatric Association (1994). *Diagnostic and statistical manual of mental disorders*, (4th edn). American Psychiatric Association, Washington, DC.

Baron-Cohen, S. (1991). Precursors to a theory of mind: understanding attention in others. In *Natural theories of mind: evolution, development and simulation of everyday mindreading*, (ed. A. Whiten, pp. 233–51). Blackwell, Oxford.

Bem, D. (1983). Constructing a theory of triple typology: some (second) thoughts on nomothetic and ideographic approaches to personality. *Journal of Personality*, 51, 566–77.

Bowlby, J. (1969). *Attachment and loss: I. Attachment*. Hogarth Press, London.

Bretherton, I. (1985). *Attachment theory: retrospect and prospect*. In *Growing points of attachment theory and Research*, (ed. I. & V. E. Horton and E. Waters). Monographs of the Society for Research in Child Development, 50, Serial No. 209, 3–38. University of Chicago Press.

Bruce, V. and Green P. R. (1990). *Visual perception*. Lawrence Erlbaum Associates, London.

Crittenden, P. M. (1992). Treatment of anxious attachment in infancy and early childhood. *Development and Psychopathology*, 4, 575–602.

Emde, R. N. and Sorce, J. E. (1983). The rewards of infancy: emotional availability and maternal referencing. In *Frontiers of Infant Psychiatry*, (ed. J. D. Call, E. Galenson, and R. Tyson), Vol. 2. Basic Books, New York.

Fantz, R. L. (1963). Pattern vision in new-born infants. *Science*, 140, 296–7.

Flavell, J. H. (1963). *The developmental psychology of Jean Piaget*. D. van Nostrand, New York.

Foucault, M. (1977). *Language, counter-memory, practice*, (ed. D. F. Bouchard and S. Simon). Blackwell, Oxford.

Garvey, C. (1977). *Play*. Fontana, London.

Gotz, K. G., Hengstenberg, B., and Biesinger, R. (1979). Optomotor control of wingbeat and body posture in *Drosophila. Biological Cybernetics*, 35, 101–12.

Hall, C. S. and Lindzey, G. (1978). *Theories of personality*, (3rd ed). Wiley, New York.

Harris, P. L. (1994). Unexpected, impossible and magical events: children's reactions to causal violations. *British Journal of Developmental Psychology*, 12, 1–7.

Hartline, H. K. and Graham, C. H. (1932). Nerve impules from single receptors in the eye. *Journal of Cellular and Comparative Physiology*, 1, 227–95.

Hartline, H. K., Wagner, H. G., and Ratliff, F. (1956). Inhibition in the eye of the *Limulus. Journal of General Physiology*, 39, 651–73.

Hubel, D. H. and Wiesel, T. N. (1962). Receptive fields, binocular interaction, and the functional architecture in the cat's visual cortex. *Journal of Physiology*, 160, 106–54.

Hubel, D. H. and Wiesel, T. N. (1968). Receptive fields and functional architecture of monkey striate cortex. *Journal of Physiology*, 195, 215–43.

Hume, D. (1739). *A treatise of human nature*. (Ed. Selby-Bigge, L. A. (1888). Oxford University Press, Oxford.)

Humphreys, N. (1983). *Consciousness regained*. Oxford University Press, Oxford.

Inhelder, B. and Piaget, J. (1958). *The growth of logical thinking from childhood to adolesence*. Basic Books, New York.

Jernigan, T., Trauna, D., Hesselink, J., and Tallal, P. (1991). Maturation of human cerebrum observed *in vivo* during adolescence. *Brain*, 114, 2037–49.

Kagan, J. (1967). Stimulus–schema discrepancy and attention in the infant. *Journal of Experimental Child Psychology*, 5, 381–90.

Kagan, J., Kearsley, R. B., and Zelazo, P. R. (1978). *Infancy: its place in human development*. Harvard University Press, Cambridge Mass.

Kandel, E. R., Schwartz, J. H., and Jessel, T. M. (1991). *Principles of neural science*. Elsevier, New York.

Kuffler, S. W. (1953). Discharge patterns and functional organization of mammalian retina. *Journal of Neurophysiology*, 16, 37–68.

Luria, A. R. (1961). *The role of speech in the regulation of normal and abnormal behavior*. Liveright, New York.

Luria, A. R. (1966). *The higher cortical functions in man*. Basic Books, New York.

Marr, D. (1982). *Vision: a computational investigation into the human representation and processing of visual information.* W. H. Freeman, San Francisco.

Marr, D. and Hildreth, E. (1980). Theory of edge detection. *Proceedings of the Royal Society of London, Series B,* **207**, 187–216.

Meltzoff, A. N. and Borton, W. (1979). Intermodal matching by human neonates. *Science,* **282**, 403–4.

Mischel, W. (1968). *Personality and assessment.* Wiley, New York.

Mischel, W. (1973). Toward a cognitive social learning reconceptualization of personality. *Psychological Review,* **80**, 252–83.

Mischel, W. (1979). On the interface of cognition and personality: beyond the person–situation debate. *American Psychologist,* **34**, 740–54.

Norris, C. (1993). *The truth about postmodernism.* Blackwell, Oxford.

Piaget, J. (1937). *The construction of reality in the child.* (Trans. Cook, M. (1954). Basic Books, New York.)

Piaget, J. (1970). Piaget's theory. In *Carmichael's manual of child psychology,* (ed. P. H. Mussen), pp. 703–32. Wiley, London. (Reprinted in P. H. Mussen (ed.) (1983) *Handbook of child psychology,* Vol. I, pp. 103–28. Wiley, London. Page reference to this volume.)

Sextus Empiricus (*c.* AD 200) *Outlines of Pyrrhonism.* (Selections with commentary in Hallie, P. (ed. (1985). *Sextus Empiricus: selections from the major writings on scepticism, man, and God.* Hackett, Indianapolis, Ind.)

Sroufe, L. A. and Waters, E. (1976). The ontogenesis of smiling and laughter: a perspective on the organization of development in infancy. *Psychological Review,* **83**, 173–89.

Sroufe, L. A. and Waters, E. (1977). Attachment as an organizational construct. *Child Development,* **48**, 1184–99.

Sroufe, L. A., Egeland, B., and Kreutzer, T. (1990). The fate of early experience following developmental change: longitudinal approaches to individual adaptation in childhood. *Child Development,* **61**, 1363–73.

Stern, D. (1977). *The first relationship, mother and infant.* Fontana, London.

Stern, D. (1985). *The interpersonal world of the infant.* Basic Books, New York.

Stern, D. N., Jaffe, J., Beebe, B., and Bennett, S. L. (1974). Vocalizing in unison and in alternation: Two modes of communication within the mother–infant dyad. *Annals of the New York Academy of Science,* **263**, 89–100.

Strauss, M. S. (1979). Abstraction of proto typical information by adults and ten-month-old infants. *Journal of Experimental Psychology: Human Learning and Memory,* **5**, 618–32.

Subotskii, E. V. (1985). Preschool children's perception of unusual phenomena. *Soviet Psychology,* **23**, 91–114.

Suga, N., Kuzirai, K., and O'Neill, W. E. (1981). How biosonar information is represented in the bat cerebral cortex. In *Neuronal mechanisms of hearing,* (ed. J. Syka and L. Aitkin). Plenum, New York.

Tinbergen, N. (1948). Social releasers and the experimental methods required for their study. *Wilson Bulletin,* **60**, 6–51.

Trevarthen, C. (1980). The foundations of intersubjectivity: development of interpersonal and cooperative understanding in infants. In *The social foundation of language and thought: essays in honor of Jerome Bruner* (ed. D. R. Olson) Norton, New York.

Vaughn, B., Egeland, B., Sroufe, L. A., and Waters, E. (1979). Individual differences in infant–mother attachment at twelve and eighteen months: stability and change in families under stress. *Child Development*, 50, 971–5.

Von Frisch, K. (1967). *The dance, language and orientation of bees*. Harvard University Press, Cambridge, Mass.

Vygotsky, L. (1934). *Thought and language*. (Trans. Hanfmann, E. and Vakar, G. (1962). MIT Press, Cambridge, Mass.)

Vygotsky, L. (1981). The genesis of higher mental functions. In *The concept of activity in Soviet psychology*, (ed. J. V. Wertsch, pp. 144–88. M. E. Sharpe, New York. (Reprinted in K. Richardson and S. Sheldon (ed.) (1990). *Cognitive development to adolescence*, pp. 61–80. Lawrence Erlbaum Associates, Hove. Page reference to this volume.)

Wittgenstein, L. (1921). *Tractatus logico-philosophicus*. (Trans. Pears, D. F. and McGuiness, B. F. (1961). Routledge and Kegan Paul, London.

Wittgenstein, L. (1969). *On certainty, (ed. G. E. M. Anscombe and G. H. von Wright, trans. D. Paul and G. E. M. Anscombe). Blackwell, Oxford.*

7
Psychiatric disorder and its explanation

7.1 INTRODUCTION

We turn now to order and disorder in human psychological functioning. In doing this we build on the conclusions of the previous chapters. We assume that intentional states such as beliefs and fears are genuinely causal, and that they underpin action. We expect that the analysis of intentional-causal processes which applied to non-psychological biological and psychological processes in development will apply also to descriptions of adult psychological functioning. Inasmuch as intentional processes have throughout been seen to require the specification of function and dysfunction, this will apply also to psychological order and disorder. In other words, the analysis of order in psychological functioning inevitably leads to one of disorder. We will illustrate the application of the analysis through a detailed consideration of a relatively unremarkable example of danger and fear. Even in such a simple example there is scope for a complex interplay between intentional- and non-intentional-causal processes. This will lead to a more general consideration of the ways in which we might specify physical and psychiatric disorder, and the extent to which psychiatry has borrowed a model from general medicine. It will be evident that it is the examination of intentionality, rather than the issue of biological causation, that is central. We will suggest that the failure to identify the role of intentional-causal processes in established medical diagnoses has led to a rather narrow concept of biological psychiatry.

7.2 THE OPERATION OF INTENTIONALITY IN PSYCHOLOGICAL PROCESSES

7.2.1 Introduction

Our 'ascent' through physiology, phylogeny, and development brings us to adult human psychological functioning. This forms the final part of the thesis that intentional-causal processes are seen throughout biological systems. Our initial, and most detailed example will be of human behaviour in response to an external threat. We have chosen this because it provides a very clear basis on which to illustrate quite substantial complexity. The case could be made that we need to go further, to sequences of behaviours, to relationships, families, social groupings, and societies, and some of these will be considered in relation to a range of possible mechanisms in order and disorder, in this and the following two chapters. Nevertheless, we will not in this book attempt to carry the analysis into a detailed consideration of the functioning of complex human organizations.

7.2.2 An analysis of the response to danger

Take the example of a state of fear induced in a person (who will be referred to henceforward either as 'the man' or 'the subject') standing in a field, at the sight of a bull in the same field. The state of fear is a normal or appropriate response. It is mediated by information about the bull. There is a series of physical events set in train, starting at the retina and proceeding via the visual pathways to the visual cortex, and thereafter a number of complex processes involving other cortical and subcortical structures. These events have to be described in terms of being about a state of affairs in the outside world; they have intentionality.

The response is not determined by the inherent properties of the bull but by the preoccupation of the individual. Thus the size of the bull might be a determining factor; however, it is likely that, in a manner rather analogous to that of the response of the cardiovascular regulatory system, there will be a threshold below which fear is not induced, then a range over which fear is related to the size of the bull, and a point above which fear is reduced on the grounds that at a certain weight the bull would be unlikely to be sufficiently mobile to pose a threat. The point is that the response is determined by a quality such as 'dangerousness' which is a function of the perceiving organism; the subject in relation to the stimulus.

The perception is rule-bound and conventionalized. It could be represented in many different ways provided the information were retained. Thus is would be possible to induce fear if the observer were looking in the opposite direction to the bull, at a person who had a prearranged signal which meant 'bull'. This could be any action provided it had been agreed previously what it meant. The rules governing the response of the man in the field are likely to be a combination of wired in and learnt. Those linking light impinging on the retina, bursts of impulses in the visual pathway, and visual cortical responses were considered in the previous chapter. These rules, or the capacity to acquire them, are likely to be determined genetically, although as we shall see, the experiments of Hubel and Wiesel and others have indicated that exposure to light early in development may also have an important role. Further brain processes are likely to interpret shape or movement in terms of previous experiences. Influential experiences may include seeing bulls or even having been charged by a bull, but equally may consist only of having read about, or having been told about bulls and their behaviour. Thus the internalized sets of rules may have been generated in a number of different ways. Further, there is a wide range of ways in which the link between the bull and the emotional and behavioural response could be mediated. It could be in the form of a belief of the form 'bulls are dangerous' or 'Aberdeen Angus bulls are dangerous'. Equally there could be, depending on history and culture, other internalized sets of rules that would lead to the same response, of the form 'all animals over 5 feet high are dangerous' or 'all four-legged animals are dangerous', or 'all animals with rings in their noses are dangerous', and so on. Such beliefs would be embedded in further beliefs such as that 'animals are stronger than humans', or that 'these animals move faster than humans', and beliefs such as those concerning the efficacy and the value of the self. Thus the internalized rules may vary substantially and they may be generated through very different routes.

The term 'belief' is here a shorthand for a wide range of states of mind. Thus the man in the field might be a farmer whose knowledge of bulls is based on 40 years of experience but no reading, or he may have had no experience of bulls directly but might have read extensively about cattle. The beliefs of the former might be manifested in behaviour that is systematically related to the behaviour of the bull but in few words, and the latter predominantly in conversation. Alternatively, the man in the field might be a French student with exactly the same amount of book knowledge regarding bulls as a student whose first language is English. Each of these will have used entirely different words, and hold beliefs that are expressed differently, but are linked to the phenomenon in the same systematic way. Within the context of the analysis of intentional causality, a belief is an example of the way in which we describe to ourselves the set of rules governing the construction that is to be placed on our experiences. This is true of all intentional states, including those that are predominantly cognitive, and those that are predominantly affective.

The indirect association between the energy of the stimulus and that of the response is well illustrated in this example. Clearly, a charging bull has momentum and energy. However, the response of the person to the presence of the bull is not mediated by that energy. If we suppose that the presence of the bull is indicated to the man by a third gesticulating party, then a large energetic gesture could mean 'bull standing still' whereas a small gesture might convey 'bull charging'. This will depend entirely upon the convention that has been adopted. The process is fundamentally the same whether we refer to signalling among the neurons of the visual system, or signalling among people. Just as the responses of neurons to light may be an increase or decrease of the rate of firing—via on-centre and off-centre receptors—so human signalling systems utilize increases or decreases of magnitude or energy of responses to denote the presence of the object.

The perception of the bull entails the detection of difference. We saw on p. 242 how this occurs in the peripheral visual system. Higher perceptual processes need to discriminate between numerous possibilities such as bull versus cow, and dead versus alive. The extent of the discrimination will depend upon the experience of the observer. For instance, for many people the perception of the bull would be sufficient to provide the basis for action, however a farmer might discriminate 'Aberdeen Angus' and 'Hereford', and in the latter case (because Hereford bulls are not generally aggressive) he will not be anxious. The response is based on the presence of sufficient cues to make the distinction.

Just as in the case of the baroreceptor, so here the response depends upon the presence of a specialized receptor, the visual apparatus. In the absence of this, and if no alternative sensory apparatus were used, the bull, no matter how fierce, could not be the cause of the fear.

Finally, the person in the field was capable of being deceived. Clearly this could be achieved easily by the gesticulating mediator. However, provided that the cues which were taken as crucial to make the distinction were available, so could a bull-like object. The conditions under which this requirement were met would vary. For instance at dusk, a bull-like shape may suffice, while in daylight and close up, the resemblance would have to be closer. Nevertheless the bull-like object would be the intentional cause of the fear in exactly the same way as a volley of impulses from the baroreceptors to the vasomotor centre.

7.3 THE DISRUPTION OF INTENTIONALITY

How then do we construct criteria for judging normal and abnormal responses? Thus far, we have stated that fear is a normal response to a bull which is perceived as a potentially dangerous animal. This can be further clarified with reference to the person's beliefs about bulls, about this bull in relation to bulls in general, beliefs about the self, and information about the person's current circumstances. All of these are relevant to a description of the state of anticipation or readiness of the person in the field. Let us assume that we are observing the man in the field. If he is clearly in a state of fear, as evidenced by sweating, rapid heart rate, or alteration of speech or behaviour, we would be likely to ask no further questions. This is because we have used the information about the situation and our knowledge of the concerns, perceptions, and beliefs of other people in general, and concluded that the response is consistent with the set of rules under which we expect it to take place.

7.3.1 The identification of an apparent break in intentionality

Suppose, however, the man does not show fear under these circumstances. The observer cannot provide an account according to the set of rules, or expectations that he assumes are operating. *There is a discontinuity in the account that can be given*. However, if the observer then notices that the man in the field is carrying a rifle, he is less likely to be puzzled, because he has further information that tells him about the assumptions or expectancies of the person in the field. The rifle can be said to be the intentional cause of the lack of fear, provided the observer can interrogate the man further to establish that the gun is loaded, and he knows how to use it, or, following the point about deception, that he believes the gun is loaded, and he believes he knows how to use it. The observer can only account for the behaviour if he has the same information as that which is influencing the man in the field.

Suppose now that there are no such observable items which might enable the observer to give a satisfactory account. There are four possibilities:

(1) that the observer does not have sufficient knowledge of the sets of rules or expectations that inform the behaviour;
(2) the man in the field has not seen the bull and so does not have relevant information;
(3) the man in the field does not have the relevant set of concerns, expectancies, or beliefs; and
(4) that there has been disruption of the functioning of his perceptual, cognitive, or motor capabilities.

The first explanation would apply if the man turned out to be a Spanish bullfighter who relished an encounter with a bull. In terms of Dennett's analysis, which we reviewed in Chapter 1 (Dennett 1987), this would be a design stance explanation, in that this was the framework in which the response could be predicted. The man had been trained to perceive bulls as a challenge and source of excitement, and the intentionality of his response could be described within that framework. This would have nothing to do with design in the sense of an immutable wired-in feature, but as an acquired set of rules and expectancies, an issue to which we will return later in this chapter.

In the second case the man in the field has not received the information about the bull and so there cannot be a response which has intentionality with respect to the bull.

The third type of account would apply if the animal were unfamiliar to the man, either from direct experience or through other sources of information, in which case he would not have the 'equipment' with which to respond. The experience of the bull would then fall outside the range of the information-processing capability of the man, and this would be another modified 'design stance' explanation.

There remains the possibility that function has been disrupted. This may have been the result of disease or trauma to one or more elements of the pathway linking perception and action. For instance, there may have been damage to the optic nerve, to the visual cortex, or he may have a condition that affects thinking or emotional responses. The damaging agents operate in the same ways as those that might disrupt the cardiovascular system. For instance, a blow to the head or a tumour may disrupt the functioning of the optic nerve by virtue of its physical force or pressure. The energy of the trauma does enter into the equation, no special receptors are required, and the system does not have a set of rules that underpin the representation of the trauma. If a blow to the head is the cause of injury to the optic nerve, there will be no requirement that the man 'saw it coming' or that he in any sense perceived the blow. Indeed it could have had the same effect if it were administered while he was asleep or under an anaesthetic. Here then, the cause of the disruption would be non-intentional and would depend crucially on the physical make-up of the nerve and the extent of the injury. Thus far we need make no reference to intentional processes; and only to physico-chemical laws. The significance of the physical injury would, however, depend upon the role of the molecules, atoms, or ions in the intentional system. If the change of physical state had no implications for functioning, then it would not be a significant injury, and equally a small change of physical state might have serious consequences. Here then, the envisaged link between the disruptive agent and the visual system does not entail intentional causality, but its significance does.

7.3.2 The experience of the individual

We turn next to the experience of the man in the field. In the straightforward case, he is likely to provide an explanation of his fear in similar terms to those that have been used by the observer. Common-sense, or folk psychology, accounts are close to those of intentional-causal explanations. He would be likely to explain similarly his lack of fear if he possessed an object such as a gun which made him feel safe. His explanation of those instances where he did not show fear, and there were no aspects of the circumstances that were hidden from the observer, are of great interest. Here, to a greater or lesser extent, the man is likely at the time to have been unaware of the cause of his lack of response. The Spanish bullfighter might, if asked subsequent to the event, say that when he was younger he was afraid of bulls, or that he knew of people who were afraid of bulls. Then he would be able to refer to a different set of rules in which bulls were seen as fearsome, but it would be crucial to his competence as a bullfighter that the contradictory sets of rules, 'I must fight' and 'I must run away' did not operate together if effective action were to ensue. We will return at length to the consequences of the operation of contradictory sets of rules in the next chapter.

If he did not see the bull, then only afterwards when we say something like 'You seemed very calm in the field with the bull', and he replies 'Oh my God was there a bull? I probably didn't see it as the sun was in my eyes', does the cause of the lack of fear become apparent. Where bulls fall outside the range of experience or knowledge of the man, at the time he will have nothing to report. Questioned afterwards he will report the perception but not its significance. Once the significance of bulls is explored, it is likely that he will be able to provide the explanation of his lack of fear.

The physical cause of disruption of vision is similar. The man is not aware that the disruption has occurred. It is, however, different in that neither can he perceive its origins. Although he has an intentional apparatus which perceives the sun as the origin of the blinding light, this is not the case for the physical agent. Thus he cannot give an account of the way in which his perceptual apparatus was disrupted. This is an example of the general principle, which is that non-intentional-causal agents have their effect without the awareness or the activity of the person, who has the experience of something happening to him. This follows from our observation that non-intentional-causal agents do not require sensory or information-processing facilities, which in relation to psychological functioning means forms of perception.

Before taking our example further, we will summarize the general points covered so far. Human psychological responses are explained in terms of states of mind which entail intentional-causal processes. These require internalized sets of rules and frames, and where responses are seen to be consistent with these, there will be many questions to be addressed about the origins and mechanisms, but there will not be doubt about the functioning of the system. Where the observer notes a discontinuity between the stimulus and the expected response then further questions will be asked. Answers may entail further information about circumstances, further information about the subject's perceptions, expectations or beliefs; or they may specify stimuli outside the range of the subject's perceptual or cognitive range; or there may be disruption of functioning. Where the apparent discontinuity has arisen from lack of information its provision will remove the discontinuity and provide an explanation of the apparent dysfunction. Where the stimulus is outside the range of functioning or there has been a disruption, then the discontinuity will remain. The subject, on interrogation, may be able to provide an account of the intentional origins of the discontinuity where, for instance, he was using a set of beliefs that were unknown to the observer. Where there has been disruption of the intentional processes, the origins of discontinuity will be outside the awareness of the subject, at the time, and on subsequent reflection.

7.3.3 Accounting for a change in behaviour

Now let us return to our example and consider a change of behaviour, for this eventually is one of the key issues to be addressed in the area of psychological disturbance. The man looks at the bull, he starts to sweat and look around for an escape route; suddenly he stops. Now the discontinuity is clearly a feature of the man in the field. Provided the observer is correct in assuming that up to the change of behaviour the man was responding appropriately, then we cannot postulate the modified design stance explanation whereby the stimulus is outside the range of the subject's experience or expectations. The explanation could still be that this is only an apparent discontinuity in that he believes, for instance, that the best strategy for dealing with the bull is first to show fear and then indifference. However, other possibilities are more likely. The first is that he has remembered, following the initial response, that the best strategy is not to show fear, and has put this into practice. In other words he has employed a new set of rules to govern the response. The second possibility is that he has acquired or discovered that he has an agent that makes the position safer. For instance, he has reached into his pocket and there has found a pistol. Thirdly, in a revision of the perceptual processes of the sort described earlier, he may have discovered that it is not a real bull, or only a Hereford bull. Fourthly, there may have been a disruption of his appreciation of the situation. Thus an agent which induced clouding of consciousness, such as epilepsy, or a drug administered unknown to him, could have been the cause. The general point is that disruptions or apparent disruptions in the account that can be given can arise from the intrusion or introduction of another set of rules, additional information, or a disruption of the intentional apparatus by a physical agent. In the latter case the search for further rules or information will not remove the disruption. Of crucial interest here is the fact that from the observer's point of view an apparent disruption in the rule-following may arise either from the interaction of sets of rules, or from the acquisition of new information by the subject, or a disruptive cause, and the extent to which the observer considers alternative sources of such rules or information, will influence his or her explanation.

7.4 LEVELS OF EXPLANATION AND THE REDUCTION OF MENTAL PROCESSES

We have seen that intentional causality makes reference to principles that are not found in chemistry and physics, but the operation of the principle takes advantage of physical processes to achieve their ends. Intentional causality is not reducible to the non-intentional where the system is functioning, but dysfunction can arise from disruption that can be explained at least in part by non-intentional-causal processes. There is implied in this analysis a concept of levels of functioning that needs to be spelt out in relation to psychological functioning.

Intuitively, it would seem, and many authors have proposed (Nagel 1961; Darnell *et al.* 1990), that a hierarchy of levels may be constructed which places physics at the bottom and proceeds via chemistry, biochemistry, physiology, and neuropsychology to psychology and psychiatry. This has led to a continuing discussion regarding the reducibility of mental processes (Fodor 1983; Putnam 1983; Dennett 1987; Hardcastle 1992). We have argued that if biological causality is not reducible to physico-chemical processes, then by the same argument neither will that branch of the biological, referred to as the psychological. The argument against reduction of the psychological therefore in part borrows from that in Chapter 5.

Many recent authors have also argued against the reduction of mental processes (e.g. Davidson 1980; Fodor 1983), but, as we have seen, the accompanying danger is that mental processes are stranded without a causal story, or one that separates them from other biological processes. However, once the case for the pervasiveness of intentional processes in biology is presented, then explanations of psychological processes are no more stranded than those of molecular biology. Nevertheless, we do need to be quite specific about what can and cannot be reduced, and how far. We need also to be clear about levels of causal processes, for we are not referring to distinctions such as those of mental versus non-mental, or neuroscience versus biochemistry. That would be to create a dualism (or multilevelism) that is totally at odds with our analysis. For instance a rapid heart beat is part of the intentional response of fear, and an erection is part of male sexual excitement. These physiological responses have intentionality with respect to the stimulus in just the same way as mental processes.

In one sense then, the concept of 'level' becomes redundant. This is, however, different from the concept 'level' that emerges from our proposition; one that is defined by the nature of the analysis of information. Just as intentional explanations cannot be reduced to chemistry and physics where the words and concepts have no parallel, so they cannot be reduced to a point where the rules of interpretation of information no longer exist. The location of this point will depend upon the way in which information is encoded, and the relevant rules are stored. Take the distinction between the neurosciences and psychology. These may be taken to denote different levels of explanation whereby one might be invoked to explain the other. In our analysis the relevant issue is, how is the representation and its link with action elaborated?

Often, this means that reduction will not be the appropriate way to characterize the link between the neurosciences and psychology (Hardcastle 1992). Thus the rules for transforming light from the bull into patterns of neuronal firing are present throughout the visual system and underpin the intentionality of the system with respect to features such as dark and light, orientation and movement. The specification of these rules belongs to the neurosciences. However, the determinant of the response is the perception of 'bull' or 'particular breed of bull' and this will require the representation of the person's knowledge of the bull also under a range of relevant beliefs and expectations about them. As we have argued earlier, such mental events are genuinely causal in the mediation of stimulus and response, and here it is clear that the response requires the internalized rules which underpin the perception and discrimination. The question of level of analysis relates only to the level at which such rules are present and capable of being utilized in perception and judgement.

The identification of level requires a specification of the intentional 'work' that is entailed. For instance, what would be entailed in envisaging a lower-level account of perceptions or beliefs? It would be necessary to specify how the same information could be represented without these psychological entities. This would, in effect, require a parallel system with the same ability as a psychological system but non-psychological. It would need to have access to the information derived from sources such as reading, talking, and direct experience, and it would have to partake of the generation of internalized rules, and of the movement among them, while not being psychological. Further, if we take consciousness to be a key feature of psychological functioning, and the monitoring of the wide range of internalized rules to be an important function of consciousness, this lower level activity would have to do without that facility to monitor movement among sets of rules. Thus in postulating a lower-level capability we would have to envisage it functioning without some of the capacity that appeared in our developmental account to be crucial to the handling of multiple sets of rules. It is likely that such a system would be inefficient and mistake-prone. Further, from our perspective, it would not do any explanatory work. To return to the fundamental point, 'level' here refers to level of intentional analysis and response, and this may correspond to a range of academic disciplines.

The interplay between different levels of intentionality may be illustrated using two further variations of the story of a man in the field with the bull. In the first he is not anxious, and there is no explanation, and when asked about it subsequently the man says he was surprised at his response because previously he had been very frightened by bulls. The explanation is that unknown to him he has been given a drug which reduces anxiety. This drug interrupts the intentional link between the stimulus, the perception, emotional and physiological responses, and the behaviour. It acts like other physical agents without the subject's perception.

Drugs are interesting agents in relation to the intentionality of physiological and biological systems. For instance, many antibiotics mimic the features of molecules that are important for the synthesis or division of bacteria, and hence fool the organisms into absorbing them. However, they do not perform the usual function of such molecules and the biochemistry of the bacteria is disrupted. In other words, they make use of intentional features to cause interruption.

Anxiety-reducing agents, such as beta-blockers, use the same principle. The molecules of these drugs are similar to those of the receptors for the naturally occurring transmitters. Interestingly, there is more than one receptor, and the effect of the transmitter differs depending on the nature of the receptor. The beta-blocker sits on beta-receptors so that the apparatus is effectively 'blinded'. The effects of the sympathetic nervous system transmitters to stimulate nervous impulses and hence sympathetic activity, which is a part of the anxiety response, are therefore decreased. Here then, the blockade has an intentional component in that the beta-blocker mimics to some degree the transmitter, but lacks the features required to stimulate a response. It therefore acts to deceive the system. If the receptor only accepted the correct molecule, that is, made finer discriminations, the blockade could not work. Function is disrupted because of the interruption of the intentional causal link. This is then observed and experienced as an interruption of the link between the bull and fear. That part of the link we call psychological has been interrupted and the effect of the drug does not entail psychological processes such as awareness and perception. Therefore in relation to psychological processes and the relevant information for them, there is a non-intentional-causal effect. However, inasmuch as sympathetic activity is also part of the intentional response to the bull, and the blockade requires mimicry at the receptor site, it performs the same function as that which a cardboard bull might if it were to deceive the man into being afraid.

The second case makes a different point. The man is in the field and there is no bull, or at least he hasn't seen it. Nevertheless he feels anxious and has a tachycardia. The explanation is that he has not eaten for some time, and is hypoglycaemic (has low blood sugar). In this case his state has intentionality with respect to glucose metabolism, but not anxiety-provoking agents. There is then an intentional cause of his state, but not in relation to anxiety-provoking agents. Inasmuch as he is not anxious about anything, the anxiety does not have an intentional cause. In this example we see the intrusion of the effect of intentional processes at one level (physiology) into another level, the psychological.

The purpose of these examples is to underline two rather contrasting points. The first is that the concept of levels of functioning is misleading if it obscures the extent to which responses with the same intentionality may occur at multiple levels. Equally, there are differences in levels of representation such that intentionality with respect to 'dangerous bull' has a different logic and degree of complexity than intentionality with respect to 'lack of glucose'.

7.5 DISORDER

We have, earlier in this chapter, considered the possibility that a medical condition might account for a disruption in the function of perceptions, emotional states, cognitions, or behaviours in response to the presence of a potentially dangerous animal. We turn now to the general description of illness or medical condition, before going on to psychiatric disorder. The definition of physical illness is not straightforward because, depending on the condition, different features such as pain, disability, or threat to life will be more or less prominent. However, frequently, abnormality of biochemistry or physiology will be crucial, and the concept of abnormality will refer to the elements of intentional-causal processes outlined in Chapter 5. Conditions such as diabetes, renal (kidney) failure, high blood pressure, and various endocrine conditions such as Addison's disease or Cushing's disease, entail their failure to regulate the relevant systems appropriately.

It is crucial to emphasize that frequently specification of the physical state of a system does not give the diagnosis. Take the example of a tachycardia (rapid pulse). This may have intentionality, for instance with respect to a decrease in atmospheric oxygen, or vigorous exercise. Thus if a physician were working in Cuzco (Peru) at a height of 12 000 ft, and a patient came to her with a pulse rate of 100, she would ask them how long they had been at this altitude. If the answer were 'one day' she might well look no further. This would be because she had made the judgement based on the normal functioning of a system that is able to detect a change of oxygen and respond with appropriate action. However if this were a long-term resident of the town she might look for another explanation. One possibility might be that a disturbance in the conducting mechanism of the heart could have led to the tachycardia, and this would have taken place via non-intentional-causal links. The tachycardia would not have intentionality with respect to the effective functioning of the cardiovascular system, and evidence of this disruption might be found in the form of an identifiable lesion.

The account of physical disorder is, however, not so straightforward, because in medical conditions non-intentional causality is seldom found in isolation from intentional causality. Indeed, it is one of the most striking features of living organisms that they detect and respond to agents such as infections or injuries, which may present threats to their integrity. They have available compensatory (intentional) responses. Take the example of blood-clot formation and the healing of tissues in response to injury. Here the injury that occurs by a non-intentional mechanism is detected and a response is elaborated that restores normal functioning. All of the criteria of intentional causality apply, but the stimulus is breakdown of functioning. In general, although we can point to pathology or noxious agents as the cause of breakdown, it is rare that this is seen in the absence of compensatory mechanisms. In the examples of healing, it is usually clear which components arise from the disruptive agent, and which are part of the compensatory mechanism (although scar tissue can cause considerable damage), but in other examples they may be closely related. For instance, a further explanation for a tachycardia might be that substantial blood loss has taken place, in which case the increased pulse rate forms part of an adaptive response to a fall in blood volume, which is designed to maintain blood pressure in the face of this reduced volume of circulating blood. In some susceptible individuals this tachycardia might lead to chest pain due to relative insufficiency of the oxygen supply to the heart, so that the clinical picture arises from a complex interplay of intentional and non-intentional causality. Where there is injury there also is compensation, and where there is threat there also is adaptation.

Another source of complexity arises from the fit between the organism and the environment. We noted in Chapter 5 that where intentional causality operates, there is a normal range of function that is defined in terms of fit between the system and the environment. Where this is the *milieu interieur* there is little scope for change, but where it is the external environment there is considerable scope. In general the environment relevant to the range of functioning will be that in which the animal evolved, 'the environment of evolutionary adaptiveness' (Bowlby 1969). It is evident that in Westernized societies the physical and social environment is substantially different from that in which humans evolved. It seems also that the nutritional environment is different and that this has consequences for physical health. It is not within our scope to examine the evidence for and against such explanations; however, the emerging role of diet in disease is illuminating. Research over the past 20 years has focused on the role of diet in the genesis of diseases of Western society such as large bowel cancer and coronary heart disease. Western diets differ from those of more traditional societies, in having less fibre and a higher proportion of animal fat. In some cases, such as those related to high transit times for low fibre food through the gut, there may be a toxic effect; in other words a non-intentional cause. However, in other cases, such as that of raised blood cholesterol, with its associated increased risk of coronary heart disease, there may be a greater demand placed on the regulatory system than that for which it was designed (and in which it has evolved), or an alteration of the setting of that mechanism. The mechanism would be that the intake of dietary animal fat is greater than that which can be metabolized without an increase of blood cholesterol, and the system is overloaded, or that there is, in effect, an adjustment of the normal level, that is to say of the one the system seeks to restore. In either case, intentional processes are important. Once the cholesterol has persisted at an abnormal level it may in turn lead to other processes that proceed beyond their normal range of functioning, and hence lead to atheroma (fat deposits in the blood vessels) and coronary heart disease. Similarly, the normal regulatory process for cholesterol may include exercise and in its absence the regulation may be impeded.

Mechanisms that entail functioning at the limits of the range of the intentional apparatus and alteration of setting can be illustrated through two further examples. Many individuals who live at high altitudes have a condition called polycythaemia, in which there is an increased number of red cells in the blood. This is a response of the red cell manufacturing system to lack of oxygen at altitude and therefore mediated through intentional-causal processes. However, these individuals also have an increased risk of stroke, a condition that arises from blockage of an artery to the brain consequent upon the thickness of the blood, and secondary to the polycythaemia. The explanation of the stroke therefore includes intentional and non-intentional causality. A mechanism which is adaptive over some ranges of oxygen levels, may be maladaptive when humans live under conditions which are near the limits of their physiological design.

An alteration in the 'setting' of the system is seen in sufferers with chronic lung disease who often have a permanently raised level of carbon dioxide in their blood, to which their brains have become accustomed. When there is a worsening of the condition, usually because of chest infection, the carbon dioxide level rises and they become more breathless. Thus the intentional system continues to work, but over a different range. The aim of treatment is to return the patient to his or her previous state, including the previous carbon dioxide level in the blood and not to a more general normal level.

In summary, we may say that medical illnesses are characterized by disruption of functioning which often entails an interplay between intentional and non-intentional-causal processes. These processes are equally physiological but radically different. The intentional processes entail causal links in which there may be correct or incorrect responses, there is rule-following, there is a detection apparatus with rules for the interpretation of events, there is a range of functioning, there is effective action, and there could be deception. Explanations such as those involving a blow to the head or laceration of a blood vessel are also physiological but do not entail any of these elements, and refer to the disruption of the integrity of the intentional system.

7.6 PSYCHIATRIC DISORDER

7.6.1 The definition of psychiatric disorder

Over the past 20 years there has been a substantial international effort to create a effective classification of psychiatric and psychological disorder. The two principal systems, those of the World Health Organization (1992) and the American Psychiatric Association (1994) have provided detailed criteria for disorder, and research questionnaires and interviews based on them have been developed. These have introduced substantial comparability among studies of psychiatric conditions. However, a number of problems remain unresolved, and it is important to review these briefly before going on to the explanation of psychiatric disorder.

First, the definitions of psychiatric syndromes are, in many respects, arbitrary. For instance, definitions of depression differ over the symptoms that are required, their duration, and whether they have to be associated with impaired functioning before a diagnosis is made.

Secondly, 'comorbidity' between psychiatric conditions is very common. People with one psychiatric condition often have two or more (Cloninger *et al.* 1990). For instance, depression and panic disorder are classified separately but they occur together commonly (Andrade *et al.* 1994). Clearly this could deflect two or more conditions with a common cause, or that one condition confers vulnerability for another, or that there is a lack of distinctiveness between the hypothesized diagnostic categories.

Thirdly, it is not clear that psychiatric disorders are best captured by a categorical model. This assumes that the subject either has a condition or he/she has not. Clearly this is appropriate where there is a definable pathology with a clear clause, which is the case for many medical conditions. However, most psychiatric conditions may also be satisfactorily characterized by scores on a dimension such as depression, anxiety, or aggression.

Fourthly, even when the syndrome definition may appear to be reasonably satisfactory, the condition may be heterogeneous. For instance, it has been argued that schizophrenia may be heterogeneous, with genetic and environmental factors playing a role to different extents in different subgroups (Murray *et al.* 1985, 1991).

It may be that these difficulties will prove so substantial that a quite different approach to psychological disorder will be required. It is more likely that the classification system will be modified gradually. We are interested here to understand what it has borrowed from medicine and what are the *implied* causal processes.

Psychiatric diagnoses are generally characterized by a mixture of 'abnormal' beliefs, experiences, emotions, or behaviours, and often include impaired social functioning as part of the definition. These features are referred to as symptoms, with the implication that they signify illness or disease. Thus psychiatry has borrowed from general medicine the concept of symptom constellations with clearly identifiable pathologies. This has been supported by medical findings of the early twentieth century:

> ... the clinical correlations between postmortem pathological findings and the behavioural sequelae of strokes, and the identification of the basis of general paresis (syphilis) filled the imagination of a generation of psychiatrists who believed that the application of such approaches would yield similar results for other psychiatric conditions. (Tsuang 1993.)

The conditions referred to here are clearly the result of a disruption of functioning by a physical agent. The explanation of a discrete condition could be provided by reference to a non-intentional cause, together with the functioning of the system in which there is a specification of the role of blood supply to, or neuronal circuits in, the brain.

Thus psychiatric classification has borrowed the assumption that intentionality has run out, that there has been a disruption of functioning, and that a non-intentional-causal process is responsible. Let us review the requirements that this is the case. There will be a disruption of the intentionality of states of mind or behaviours in relation to external stimuli, or in relation to previous behaviour, or both. There must be an identifiable disruptive agent that is absent in subjects who do not show this condition and in those that do prior to its onset, and this agent should have identifiable physical properties, such that a mechanism for the prediction of mental states or behaviours via bridge conditions can be envisaged. It will be evident as we consider a range of examples that these conditions are not met for any psychiatric diagnosis, but that some elements of the requirement may be present in some conditions.

7.6.2 The disruption of intentionality

Our analysis starts with a further consideration of the intentionality of mental states and behaviour. In one sense the judgement about intentionality looks as though it might be rather uncertain. After all, an extensive analysis of the man in the field with the bull was based upon the judgement of the observer as to what might be expected. If that judgement is highly individual, then my analysis and yours may differ substantially, and our capacity to describe what is going on will be limited. However, for most purposes our judgements of the expected behaviour of others is good, because we are good at guessing at their thoughts, attitudes, and emotions. Indeed, if it were not so, our capacity to cope socially would be very limited as we would not be able to predict the behaviour of others, nor moderate our behaviours in relation to the expectations of others. We are generally good monitors of the intentionality of other people. (Some indication of the consequences of a deficit in this ability may be seen in conditions such as autism or Asperger's syndrome, where the capacity to understand the rules of social interaction and the likely state of mind of others is limited. Sufferers make serious errors in social situations and require special educational and social supports. Many are of average or above-average intelligence and so it seems that the capacity to understand the intentionality of others is distinctively different from that of a general problem-solving capacity (Hobson 1993).)

The judgement of the intentionality of possible psychiatric disorder, such as anxiety or depression, may not be as straightforward as that of the man in the field. Where symptoms follow a major loss, such as the death of a close relative or friend, the link will be clear. Suppose, however, that the depressed mood and associated difficulties, such as poor concentration, poor sleep, and lack of appetite, come on apparently unexpectedly. From the perspective of the sufferer the episode has the characteristics of an illness, in which he/she is the passive recipient of a state which has intruded inexplicably into his/her life. One possibility is that the depression has intentionality that was not immediately apparent to the person. George Brown and Tirril Harris and colleagues have made an explicit approach to this possibility through the investigation of life events and depression in women (Brown and Harris 1978; Brown 1989). In measuring life events they assumed that their meaning would be important, and they operationalized this in terms of the extent of contextual threat. Threat was taken to be comprised of a combination of the nature of the event and the circumstances of the person, so that the same event could have a different rating of threat depending on circumstances. In order to avoid the possible 'colouring' effect of depressed mood, their ratings were made by trained researchers who were given details of the event and the circumstances, but not whether the person had become depressed. These assessors made a rating based on what might be expected under those circumstances. Thus the method explicitly assumed that there exist general sets of rules of perception and interpretation of events, provided circumstances can be specified adequately. The prediction of depression was strongest where there was a combination of vulnerability factors such as lack of confiding partner, and life events. Brown and Harris have not reported on the extent to which the women in their studies themselves believed these factors were important; however, they showed that for a substantial group of women with depression there may be intentionality with respect to current adversities and circumstances. (We say 'may be' because some evidence indicates that the association between provoking agents and depression may be due to a 'third variable', namely an influence that leads both to increased life events and depression (McGuffin *et al.* 1988). This does not, however, undermine the strategies used by Brown and Harris in the investigation of the intentionality of depression.)

If these findings endure, will it mean that depression should not be considered a psychiatric condition? Clearly other factors, such as the extent of distress or inability to function adequately, will be relevant to that judgement. However, they do indicate that in some cases the assumption of disrupted intentionality, which has been borrowed from the concept of illness, may not be appropriate.

A second approach to the ascertainment of intentionality was that of Jaspers (1963) who sought to drive a wedge between meaningful and causal connections, and argued that meaningful connections are accessed for the self through introspection and in others through empathy. Our concept of intentional causality is much wider than that of Jaspers' concept of meaningful connections; however, our approach has much in common with his. He proposed that some beliefs, both normal and abnormal, were understandable in the context of the person's history and beliefs and current circumstances. These were to be contrasted with primary delusions which are direct, intrusive, unmediated by thought, and not understandable. Jaspers defined personality as, 'the term we give to the individually differing and characteristic totality of understandable connections in any one psychic life' (Jaspers 1963, p. 428), and against this background a primary delusion is one that intrudes into and distorts existing understandable connections (Walker 1991). Jaspers is here making two claims together; that the question of understandability is central, and that it can be resolved by reference to the form of the mental phenomenon. The latter claim remains uncertain. Schneider proposed that 'first rank symptoms', ones which are least likely to be understandable, will demarcate schizophrenia from other psychotic disorders (Schneider 1959). These first rank symptoms are, however, found in association with other symptom constellations which are not typical of schizophrenia, and their utility is not proven. Nevertheless, within Jaspers' framework the use of understandability is clearly central to the determination of the intentionality of mental states and behaviours.

7.6.3 Non-intentional-causal explanations

An alternative approach to the question of intentionality and disorder may be made from the other end of the hypothesized causal chain. If possible candidates for non-intentional causation of psychiatric disorder could be identified, then perhaps a non-intentional explanation would be supported. Depression provides us with an example of a condition in which a wide range of candidates for such an explanation has been identified. These have included neuroendocrine abnormalities in the regulation of thyroid and adrenal functioning. The results have, however, been rather inconsistent, and have not discriminated consistently between depressed and non-depressed adults. Let us suppose that further research provides firmer evidence for an association between endocrine abnormalities and depression. What would we require if they were playing a causal role? At least that the administration of the relevant hormone increased the risk of depression, that a reduction in the circulating hormone was associated with remission, and that where people became depressed the changes in hormone level preceded the mood changes.

Some supporting evidence comes from Cushing's syndrome. Here the pituitary gland at the base of the brain produces excess adrenocorticotrophic hormone (ACTH) which stimulates the adrenal gland to produce excess corticosteroids. There is a non-intentional cause of the increased steroids. Depression is seen in roughly half the cases of Cushing's syndrome and usually remits after treatment for the Cushing's disease (Kelly *et al.* 1980). Thus increased corticosteroids *may* have a causal role in depression, but given that Cushing's syndrome is a very rare cause of depression, unless there exists a more covert form of the disease, it is not the usual explanation.

Numerous studies have demonstrated an association between depression and abnormalities in the regulation of corticosteroids (Checkley 1992). Mere association between hormonal changes and depression will not, however, provide us with the causal story. Altered corticosteroid levels may be a consequence either of other causally relevant factors or they may form part of the physiological component of the depressive syndrome. It has been demonstrated in animals that corticosteroid levels in the blood rise in response to stress, and this introduces (the as yet untested) possibility that an increase in corticosteroids might provide part of the intentional-causal link between stressful life events and depression (Checkley 1992). Such a possibility serves to underline, yet again, that in an examination of intentional- and non-intentional-causal links the division between psychological and physiological, or mental and neuroendocrine, ceases to be appropriate.

Two further examples make the point. Patients with panic attacks have been shown, using positron emission tomography, to have significant increases in cerebral blood flow in a number of regions of the brain during lactate (chemically) induced attacks. It would be tempting, therefore, to deduce that the altered cerebral blood flow represents a non-intentional cause of the panic attacks. However, normal individuals during states of anticipatory anxiety (when awaiting an unpleasant stimulus) have also been shown to have significant increases in cerebral blood flow in identical regions of the brain (Reiman *et al*. 1989). Here the altered cerebral blood flow was a consequence of the state of anxiety, or at least an integral part of it, and the mechanism entailed intentional causality. In the case of the patients, the altered cerebral blood flow may have been a cause, consequence, or integral part of the anxiety state, which was induced by a non-intentional-causal route. One possible explanation could bring the findings together along the lines of: repeated episodes of anxiety for which there are intentional-causal explanations, could lead to an altered sensitivity of cerebral blood vessels (in other words an altered setting of the cerebral blood vessels) to the blood chemistry, and that this instability might lead to the triggering of alterations of cerebral blood flow, possibly when the acidity of blood changed, giving rise to further episodes of panic. This explanation would invoke an intentional explanation with respect to anxiety, leading to alterations of the physiology of cerebral blood vessels, with consequent panic episodes of non-intentional origin with respect to anxiety.

A similar mechanism may well operate in the association between levels of aggression and raised levels of male hormones in young men. In non-human primates, individuals who are dominant within a troop show a rise in androgen levels in response to a challenge, and socially dominant non-aggressive delinquent boys have higher levels of androgens in their blood than less-dominant peers (Ehrenkranz *et al*. 1974). It seems then that androgen levels may *reflect* social position and behaviour, and there is an intentional-causal explanation. However, delinquent aggressive boys have higher levels of androgens than either of the other two non-aggressive delinquent groups. These levels may simply reflect the aggression, or it may be that androgen levels were, in the first place, increased as a consequence of their social behaviour, and this in turn led to, or contributed to, aggressive behaviour. This would mean that there was an intentional-causal link for the raised androgens, which in turn contributed to the level of aggression via a non-intentional-causal route.

7.6.4 Interactions between intentional- and non-intentional-causal processes

We have seen so far that our investigation of intentional- and non-intentional-causal links will need to focus on mental states and behaviours and their relationship with preceding or concurrent events, and on the physiological accompaniments of these states and behaviours. Throughout, the analysis will be of the extent of, and possible disruption of, intentionality. We can illustrate this further by reference to the same mechanisms as those that we considered earlier in relation to physical conditions. First there was the role of compensation in response to non-intentional disruption. Such a mechanism might operate in schizophrenia. Neuropsychological theories of schizophrenia have postulated that sufferers have difficulty in sorting out which features of a situation should be attended to, and which can be taken for granted or are irrelevant (Gray *et al.* 1991). They therefore have to deal with more uncertainty than most people. One possible explanation for the fixed ideas of delusions is that they create certainty, and that because testing or questionning these beliefs would open the person to substantial uncertainty, a better strategy is to insist on their truth. Support for the proposal that delusions have a value to individuals, comes from a study by Roberts (1991). He compared patients who were deluded with a group that had recovered from delusions, and comparison groups of psychiatric nurses and trainee priests. The deluded patients and those who had recovered showed marked contrasts. The deluded scored much higher than the recovered patients on a measure of meaning and purpose in life, and were less depressed with fewer suicidal ideas. In all the measures, the deluded patients resembled closely the nurses and the trainee priests. This study suggests that symptoms may have intentionality with respect to difficulties, of which cognitive deficits would be one example. We will consider this in more detail in Chapter 9.

Next we reviewed mechanisms that entailed functioning beyond the normal range. 'Normal' here referred to the environment of evolutionary adaptiveness and the design features of the organism. A similar mechanism may be envisaged in the case of schizophrenia. Numerous studies have shown that individuals with schizophrenia are more likely to relapse if they are living in a family where there is a high level of expressed emotion, which is characterized by high levels of criticism, hostility, or overinvolvement. Cross-cultural studies have demonstrated that the level of expressed emotion is lower in non-Westernized societies, such as that of rural India, and that schizophrenia runs a more benign course in these societies (Kuipers and Bebbington 1988). Putting the neuropsychological theory and these findings together, it may be that information-processing which has been adaptive in environments experienced during evolution, is not adequate in the altered interpersonal climate of contemporary Western societies.

Finally, we considered mechanisms which entail alterations in the 'setting' of the system. These may be considered alterations of the design features such that responses have intentionality, but over a different range. For instance, there is good evidence that psychotic episodes are linked to life events as well as to high expressed emotion (Norman and Malla 1993). Equally, only a minority of individuals who are exposed to these experiences develop psychotic episodes. It may be that the critical issue is the level of stress that can be handled, and that for some individuals the threshold is low and for others high for responding with psychotic symptoms. Those with a low threshold may have a design fault with non-intentional origins, but episodes are provoked via an intentional-causal mechanism.

7.7 GENETICS, 'DESIGN', AND DISORDER

7.7.1 Introduction

We have referred in earlier chapters to 'design fault' as one type of origin of disorder. In doing this we have made use of the framework described in Chapter 1 and outlined by Dennett (1987). Thus far Dennett's proposal *re* design and the chess-playing computer has served us well. We return to it at this point because, in the light of our discussion of intentional causality and development, it requires some additions and some modifications. The concept of 'design' provided a useful framework against which intentionality could be understood to have run out. Further, design stance explanations might seem to resemble genetic explanations. By analogy with the chess-playing computer it might be that in human psychological development the design would refer to genetically determined, 'hard-wired' constitutional factors. The match between these and the demands of the environment would then provide us with part of the description of function, and design faults with part of the explanation of disorder. However, neither the application of the concept of design, nor the operation of genetic influences are so straightforward.

7.7.2 Dennett, development, and design

The concept of design

In order to examine this we need to start by explicating the meaning of the term 'design'. We will follow Dennett in considering a non-biological example, but one that is adapted to a rather more extensive range of conditions than the chess-playing computer, the aeroplane. The term 'design' refers to a number of features of construction and operation. First, it refers to the objective of the construction of the object, namely that it should be able to fly. Just as in the biological examples, this leads immediately to criteria for normal or correct design and construction and to criteria for mistakes. Secondly, it refers to the means by which this will be achieved, and therefore to the functioning served by components and their intentionality. Thirdly, it provides a specification in relation to the environment. Here this might include temperature, wind speeds, height of flying, and length of runways. The physical construction can be judged only in relation to these environmental demands. Fourthly, the design refers to what goes in at the outset, in the construction, and remains constant. It therefore provides a reference point against which any particular event can be judged. Fifthly, it has a high degree of generality in that it covers most or all of what the aeroplane is up to. We can see that in many respects this analysis conforms with that implied by Dennett's chess-playing computer. Nevertheless, the complexity of the computer may obscure the extent to which its functioning is defined very narrowly. Its relationship to the environment is defined by a keyboard input and by an agent that understands the rules of chess. This is in marked contrast to the range of environments that might be encountered by the aeroplane, or indeed by a biological organism. Dennett's example does not contradict this, but it may obscure it, and it is crucial at this stage to bring out the relationship of 'design' to complex environments.

Biology and design

How might the concept of 'design' stand up in relation to human psychological functioning? We can examine this using the 'method' used so far in the book. We first require that it works in non-psychological biological examples on the grounds that it must work here if it is to succeed with psychological functioning, and then examine it in relation to the observation that psychological functioning is subject to development during which there is a complex interplay between person and environment. This will lead to a consideration of design in relation to multiple sets of rules, and the generation of these within human functioning.

Taking examples from previous chapters, the term 'design' could be applied to the cardiovascular system, the genetics of protein synthesis, or the visual system. In each of these it would refer to the purpose of the system, and to the means by which it is achieved. The means would include the specification of the rules, and the convention and agreement within the signalling and control systems. As we have seen earlier, the environments of the cardiovascular system and the DNA are the *milieu interieur* which have further links with the external world, and that of the visual system is the external world. The example of haemoglobin and sickle-cell disease provided an illustration of the intimate relationship between structure, function, and environment in the definition of 'correct' or 'incorrect', and these could all be taken to be aspects of 'design'. As in the example of the aeroplane the 'design' of these biological examples will often refer to what is there from the start, and what remains constant, although in more complex perceptual systems this may not be the case. Finally, the design can be taken to refer to the functioning of the system in general. It would seem then that the concept of 'design' will apply to many biological systems, and it is entirely compatible with our analysis of intentional causality.

Design and 'wiring'

The position is rather different when we come to development and multiple sets of rules. How are we to interpret the notion of what is 'wired in', stable, and general? Take first the issue of wiring. In human development, in contrast to that of other organisms, the neuronal connections of the brain develop substantially after birth (Changeux 1985). Evidence from animal experiments, where postnatal neuronal development is more limited, indicates that neuronal connections are influenced by experience. Hubel and Wiesel (1962) showed that cats or monkeys that have been reared with one eye sutured closed have no vision in that eye and there is shrinkage of the area of the lateral geniculate body devoted to that eye, with a corresponding diminution in the number of branches sent by the deprived cells to the cortex. At the cortex there is a shift in the number of connections from the deprived to the non-deprived eye. This effect is seen only following monocular deprivation in the first 3 months of life, and after that age even extended periods of deprivation seem to have little effect. Furthermore, the effect of environment on neurodevelopment can be quite specific. Blakemore and Cooper (1970) showed that kittens raised in environments in which there were only horizontal stripes are blind to other orientations, and this is reflected in the preferential responses of neurons in the visual cortex. Human infants show a loss of visual capacity in an eye that has been subject to 'monocular deprivation', for instance where there is a squint. It is probable that this is accompanied by similar brain changes to those demonstrated in cats and monkeys. It seems therefore likely that, given the greater level of postnatal development of neuronal connections in humans during the first years of life, there may be a similar process whereby connections that are required for a wide range of psychological functioning are influenced by environmental experiences. Wiesel (1982) wrote:

> ... deprivation experiments demonstrate that neuronal connections can be modulated by environmental influences during a critical period of postnatal development. We have studied this process in detail in one set of functioning properties of the nervous system, but it may well be that other aspects of brain function, such as language, complex perceptual tasks, learning, memory and personality, have different programmes of development. Such sensitivity of the nervous system to the effects of experience may represent the fundamental mechanism by which the organism adapts to its environment during the period of growth and development.

It seems then that the wiring might be influenced by organism–environment interaction through a process that is similar to learning. If we are to retain the concept of design, we will at least need to talk of a succession of designs each related to, but different from, the previous one, and we will need to understand the relationship between them, and the environment.

Design, stability, and generality

The question of stability brings us back to the generation of sets of rules and expectancies, and their role in providing the basis for action, and further testing of the rules in development. Theories of the development of intimate (attachment) relationships and of cognitive development have emphasized the interplay between internal mental models or schemata, and experience, whereby sometimes new evidence may be incorporated into existing schemata, and at others may contribute to the development of new ones. The implication is that the internalized general models will be more or less stable, depending on:

(1) the extent to which they are tested;
(2) the extent to which experience supports or undermines them;
(3) the extent of the person's need to hold on to them, for instance in order to maintain the basis for actions; and
(4) their general utility.

We will refer to points (1), (2), and (3) extensively in the next chapter as they provide an important basis for further considerations of disorder. However, we should note here, and will return to the point, that (4) has a resemblance to that made by Polanyi (1958) and Popper (1969) in relation to beliefs in the sciences. Theories or 'laws' will be held strongly and persist, even in the light of contradictory evidence, if their wider utility is great and there is nothing to replace them; indeed one might argue, provided they are effective in directing further action. So that we can say at this point that the candidates for the persistence of sets of rules or schema, especially those with great generality, may relate to considerations other than those of whether they are wired in.

The developmental story leads to further inroads into the straightforward concept of 'design'. Development clearly entails the generation of succeeding sets of rules, schemata, cognitive-affective models, and ways of interpreting and feeling. Developmentalists of diverse origins, including Freud, Klein, Erikson, Piaget, Kagan, Bowlby, and Stern, have all postulated such successions. Each has striven to articulate the *differences* in *general* frameworks within which children operate at different phases of development, and to provide an account of what links these. While not opposing this proposal, Rutter and Rutter (1992) have argued that in development the identification of what constitutes a continuity or discontinuity is not straightforward. Thus the emergence of a butterfly from a chrysalis preceded by a caterpillar is clearly in many respects a discontinuity, but in that the information for the butterfly is already present in the caterpillar this is a continuity. Indeed, it must be assumed that the design information for the butterfly is present in the caterpillar. Similarly the child may take one set of expectancies from an environment in which they were appropriate to one in which they are not. What might be generated then is a different set of expectancies and behaviours, that can be understood best as the outcome of the interactions between the previous ways of seeing things and the current environment. Where then does this leave the concept of design? Either that it will have to be reserved for those aspects of psychological functioning that are not subject to such changes, or it will be necessary to talk of successive designs. Our analysis must, however, go further in relation to multiple sets of rules. The chess-playing computer is just that until a further design feature is built it. But what of the chess-playing human being? Strikingly, he or she can perform that function for a relatively brief period, and simultaneously perform other functions, such as that of being a parent. Indeed, a feature of the behaviour of young children in play is the way they experiment with different 'designs'. Clearly it would be possible to subsume this under the overall description of a 'playful child', which might then be referred to in terms of the design. However, clinical experience suggests that if such a child were to experience a major trauma his/her play might decrease quite dramatically. Would we then refer to a 'new design' or revise the design to be 'playful child, sensitive to trauma'? The point is that in development and in maturity human psychological functioning operates under a range of sets of rules, schemas, or assumptions, all of which have some of the features attributed to design in machines or non-psychological biological systems. However, they vary in the extent of their generality and stability.

In summary, it seems that the concept of 'design' can provide a useful shorthand, and we will use it, together with the caveats reviewed here, in relation to examples of disturbance. However, the analysis presented earlier provides a different emphasis. It suggests that although rule-bound responses probably evolved in ways that have clear survival value, there is inherent in the use of rules a creative potential whereby goals and activities can have their own intrinsic value. In other words, if it is possible to see the same thing in many different ways, then those different ways of seeing may become the focus of interest, for instance in play. This is not to propose a mechanism but to point out that the freeing of sets of rules, assumptions, or ways of seeing, and of the accompanying emotional states and behaviours, from being wired in, has potential for the elaboration of goals which might not be essential to survival. Once psychological states are conceptualized in terms if rule-bound processes there is no prediction as to whether or not they are wired in, or to the extent to which they are the outcome of an interaction with the environment. Similarly, there is no prediction as to their stability or generality. They may be wired in and stable in the case of physiological and some psychological processes, or patterned in ways that are open to change. They may have great generality, or they may be quite specific. Thus it may be more valuable to talk of sets of rules governing internal models of relationships, beliefs, or patterns of emotional response, which have greater or lesser degrees of generality, are related to a greater or lesser extent to previous experiences, and are more or less stable.

7.7.3 Genetic influences

Genes and environment

Genetic influences enter into our account in a fascinating and somewhat paradoxical way. This arises from the frequent contrast that is made between genetic and environmental influences, as if each were a separate commodity that taken together could explain outcome. As we shall see, this may fit some particular cases but does not work well in the general analysis.

Our argument will again start with non-psychological examples. The genetic code contains information about structure and function, both of which have a close fit with the environment of the organism. Indeed, the analysis of the principles of intentional causality when applied to the perceptual apparatus, specified that the system must anticipate and detect key aspects of the environment. The performance then is that of the 'organism in the environment'. This means that what has to be understood is the process whereby structure and function relate to the environment, and in that sense the questions are not primarily or necessarily genetic.

We will return to the example of sickle-cell trait and sickle-cell disease. Under some atmospheric conditions it will be apparent that the inheritance follows a straightforward recessive pattern, and it might be understood purely as a genetic condition. However, in a country in which people lived at different altitudes it might emerge that the prevalence of the symptoms was substantially different in one area compared to another, thus indicating an important environmental effect. In one environment the contribution of the environment would be practically zero, but when comparing the two environments it would be substantial. Furthermore, the environments could differ substantially in all respects other than that of the pressure of oxygen in the air and make no difference, and similarly the two altitudes might be indistinguishable in all respects except for atmospheric oxygen and still make a major difference. Thus the feature of the environment that *matters* is that which is specified in the structure and function of the system, which in this example is directly and simply related to genetic structure. The contribution of the genetic influence could be elucidated *only* in relation to that structure and function.

Just as we saw in Chapter 5 that the physical composition of the haemoglobin molecule does not provide a definition of 'fault', so the definition of genetic fault is not given by the physical fact. This is seen particularly clearly in this example because in some areas of the world the sickle-cell trait confers resistance to malaria and so is advantageous. Thus the same physical fact may be either a deficit or advantageous depending on the relationship between the structure, function, and environment. Differences can be destructive or creative! That physical differences may have such contrasting consequences depending on the relationship between the structure, function, and environment may introduce some unwished for complexity; however, if they did not, we would be without a theory of the way in which mutations can have survival value.

The extent to which genetic influences have consequences that are environmentally sensitive varies. Some, it seems, are destructive of structure and function irrespective of environments; for instance those that give rise to cystic fibrosis or Huntington's chorea. Others, such as sickle-cell disease, cause symptoms and damage only under certain environmental conditions. When we come to human psychological functioning there are extensive possibilities for organism–environment interactions.

Genes and 'design'

As we have seen, the term 'design' describes well what is encoded genetically for the haemoglobin molecule, and 'design fault' refers to a difference that is stable and that interacts in a relatively straightforward manner with the environment. Where studies show greater concordance for a condition among those who are genetically more related than those who are genetically less similar, this may be interpreted as reflecting a design fault.

The interpretation of such studies in relation to human psychological functioning is not, however, so straightforward. To some extent this follows from our previous examination of the concept of 'design' in the developing person. In particular, we saw that the brain develops substantially after birth and that the interaction with the environment is probably very important. Most of the evidence comes from experiments with the visual system of cats and monkeys, in which it is evident that the development of the brain is related in very specific ways to environmental stimuli. It is possible that similar considerations apply to social development in some animals. Perhaps the strongest evidence for an effect of experience on 'wiring' comes from studies of imprinting and critical periods in birds and animals. Birds, such as geese, will become imprinted on to a moving object if they are exposed to it at a particular time early in development (Lorenz 1965). These objects are, in the environment of evolutionary adaptiveness, adult birds, but have included Konrad Lorenz and other humans, and other animals. The young birds then follow the animal or object on which they have been imprinted. Imprinting takes place only over a defined (critical) period, and if exposure does not occur at this time, imprinting does not take place. It seems likely that the critical period is determined by a neurodevelopmental process, and that the identity of the object of the imprinting is then similarly wired in. In lower animals the stimulus acts only as a releaser of the imprinting and its qualities are relatively unimportant; however, in higher animals, such as monkeys, the quality of the experience matters. Newborn monkeys exposed to punitive artificial 'maternal' figures show increased clinging behaviour (Harlow 1961). Monkeys reared in social isolation for the first 6 years of their life have been shown to display substantial and persistent abnormalities of social and sexual behaviour in adult life (Harlow and Harlow 1969). An effect of early social experience on brain development would be difficult to demonstrate in monkeys, and probably impossible in humans. However, it is possible that early social experiences may affect brain development. As we have seen, at about 9 months the infant forms selective attachments and this is a phenomenon seen throughout a wide range of cultures. Assessments of the quality of attachments during this period have substantial predictive capability up to 10 years later (Sroufe *et al.* 1990), which suggests that a relatively enduring 'design' feature is established early in life. In a study of children who were in institutions for the first 4 years of their lives, and then adopted, Hodges and Tizard (1989) showed that in adolescence these early institutionalized individuals still had interpersonal difficulties. This was in spite of the very advantageous circumstances of their adoptive homes. This does not demonstrate an effect of early experiences on the 'wiring' of the brain but is consistent with it.

Whatever the role of external environmental experiences in brain development, it is clear that the genetic code cannot specify the wiring of the brain. It is striking that only 1 per cent of the human genome differs from that of the ape, which suggests that the enormous differences in intellectual, aesthetic, and interpersonal capabilities are encoded in a general strategy for brain development which unfolds in relation to experience. There is substantial evidence that this proceeds via the creation of an internal environment in which a complex signalling process guides the formation of neuronal connections (Jones and Murray 1991). It is possible that, as Wiesel proposed, this internal environment takes its cues from the external; after all, the function of the brain is to mediate through beliefs, emotions, and actions, between internal and external worlds (Hundert 1988).

Genetics, development, and disorder

Now we turn to the interpretation of studies of genetic influences on development and disorder. Until recently, strategies for the assessment of genetic influences have used predominantly twin and adoption studies. Although there has been some criticism of these, much of the evidence for genetic influences has been derived from such studies. Both strategies depend upon the comparison of groups that can be predicted to differ in a consistent way in their genetic make-up. Twin studies entail an estimation of the co-occurrence of a condition in both twins (concordance) and a comparison of identical (monozygotic) and non-identical (dizygotic) twins. If there is a difference in the concordance between the identical and non-identical twins, this is taken to reflect the extent of genetic influence. This is based on the assumption that twins in general have a shared environment, and that higher concordance among monozygotic twins will reflect the fact that genetically, they are identical. There is now considerable evidence that twins do not experience identical environments in the same family, and so the interpretation will become more complex (Plomin and Daniels 1987; Goodman 1991). Adoption studies compare the rate of a disorder in children of parents with that disorder who have been adopted, with other adopted children whose parents do not have this disorder. A significant difference between the two groups is taken to result from genetic factors. This method also has its limitations. For instance, adopted children may not be representative of the wider population of the children of parents with the disorder. It could be that the parents of children who are adopted have a variant of the condition that is more severe or has some different features, compared with parents whose children are not adopted. This may not therefore provide an examination of wider genetic mechanisms in the condition.

We will focus on issues that arise from our earlier discussion. In the account of the intentionality of behaviour there cannot be a specification of the environment independent of the selective perceptions, needs, and functioning of the organism. This means that genetic influences will be definable only in relation to specific aspects of the environment. Let us consider this point in relation to twin studies. This method requires first the identification of an affected twin, and then the assertainment of whether the other has the condition. If environmental factors play a part in the genesis of the condition, then it is possible that by identifying an affected twin one is at the same time identifying a particular environmental feature. This would then mean that the comparison of monozygotic and dizygotic twins was a study of genetic influences under certain environmental conditions. By environment, we mean not the general characteristics of families and other important social influences, but those which matter to the condition. For instance, adoption studies of schizophrenia suggest that there is a genetic effect but only where the adoptive parents show particular characteristics (Tienari 1990). Given the care with which adoptive families are generally chosen, it is unlikely that this represents global dysfunction, but rather specific features of relevance to the condition. Where such a specific feature is influential, it may contribute to the genesis of vulnerability early in development; that is to say, through a relatively persistent design difference; or in the presence of such a vulnerability it may affect whether the condition is manifest. The extent of specificity in the fit between organism and environmental features means that genetic studies have to specify environments quite precisely.

As we saw earlier in our discussion of the concept of design, a physical difference may have design implications, depending on function, and a design difference may, under some conditions, lead to a functional deficit, and in others confer advantage. The difference between genetic fault and useful mutation is not given by the physical fact but by the organism and environment fit. Thus the investigation of genetic vulnerability will not be straightforward. Let us suppose that the quality of 'sensitivity to others' is a genetically determined trait. This trait would include an awareness of the state of mind of others, and a concern about it, combined with a difficulty in ignoring other people. This is likely to be an asset in a family where there is mutual concern and respect, but a disadvantage where there is discord and violence. The trait might emerge as a valuable quality in a study of the normal range of family functioning, and an inherited 'vulnerability' in a study that included adverse family environments.

The concept of range of function is of relevance to our discussion. As we have seen, in some cases quite specific aspects of the environment may influence outcome. However, the environmental demands may be so great that avoidance of disorder requires an exceptional capacity to cope. This is likely to be the case where there is parental violence or physical or sexual abuse. Then genetic studies may find no apparent effect because genetic differences are overwhelmed by a level of adversity that is outside of the range normal psychological experience. The effects of such traumas will provide an important focus for the next chapter. Conversely, there may be detectable genetic effects whose operation is quite different from those seen in studies of less severe experiences. The genetics of resilience may be different from the genetics of vulnerability.

Finally, intentionality entails representation and action. This opens up important interactional possibilities in the relationship between genetic influences and environmental factors. This is illustrated by the role of attachment in development. It is probable that the security of attachment of the young infant (see p. 250) is related to the contribution of the mother or other principal caregiver, but maternal behaviour is also influenced by the temperamental characteristics of the infant. Given the genetic influences in temperament, it is likely that the security of attachment is related to genetic processes via temperament and maternal behaviour. In turn, securely attached infants are treated differently by teachers later in life (Sroufe *et al.* 1990). So they continue to have an effect on their environment. Thus a twin study might find a significant genetic effect, but in the absence of an examination of developmental processes, might omit crucial elements in the story.

7.8 'BIOLOGICAL' PSYCHIATRY AND PSYCHOLOGY

In psychiatric research the field of biological psychiatry has expanded rapidly, and although the causal assumptions are rarely spelt out, 'biological' here is generally taken to refer to the disruptive effect of biochemical or neuroendocrine abnormalities on psychological functioning. Thus Scadding (1990) writes 'I will take it that "biology" is being used here to mean the study of living organisms directed towards explanation in physicochemical terms'. He goes on, 'some disorders of behaviour can already be explained in this way, and it is to be expected that with advances in knowledge, more and more of psychology and behavioural science will become biological'. These quotations come from an editorial in a leading psychiatric journal. The same journal contains an editorial by Guze (1989) entitled 'Biological psychiatry: is there any other kind?' in which he emphasizes that human evolution has been substantially the evolution of the brain and its capacity for thought, language, and culture. He acknowledges the complex interaction between individuals and the environment. He argues that in relation to psychiatry:

> [if] it could be asserted that few if any of the states or conditions that constitute the forms of psychiatry are the result of differences in the development or physiology of the brain, biology would be of only marginal interest. If it could be argued that all or most of our patients develop their disorders primarily, if not exclusively through normal learning processes, that are independent of human variability, the emphasis on biology might justifiably be seen as excessive and unjustifiable.

He goes on to suggest that, 'if environmental factors play a part in psychiatric conditions, these putative causes of psychiatric disorder seem to reflect only the normal range of human trouble that most people experience without becoming ill'. Later in the paper he writes, 'the conclusion appears inescapable to me that what is called psychopathology is the manifestation of disordered processes in various brain systems that mediate psychological functioning. Psychopathology thus involves biology'.

Reference to these papers has been included in some detail in order to indicate the particular ways in which the term 'biological' is being used. How does it stand up in relation to the analysis presented here? Let us first take Scadding's assertion, implied also by Guze, that 'biology' can be taken to refer to the study of living organisms 'directed towards explanation in physicochemical terms'. We have seen throughout that biology consists of the elucidation of the processes whereby environments are represented, functioning is regulated, and responses are elaborated. These processes have intentional properties and a level of abstraction, none of which is available in physico-chemical descriptions. The examples of DNA and protein synthesis were emphasized in order to highlight how the description in terms of molecules may distract us from paying proper attention to the information processing and representational processes.

Guze makes a central point of the explanation of disorder arising from differences in brain function. It should be pointed out that his assertion about the effects of environmental influences is incorrect and a considerable body of research has demonstrated the effects of childhood experiences on adult psychiatric functioning (Rutter *et al.* 1990; Bifulco *et al.* 1992). However, no developmentalist would argue that individual differences do not matter. The central issue is, what is the brain up to? As we have seen, it is crucially concerned with the elaboration of sets of rules, in the form of beliefs, wishes, fears, and of internal models of relationships. These may be more or less wired in. The extent to which this is the case has nothing to do with 'more or less biological'. Inasmuch as the brain elaborates these intentional processes, and the intentional processes are the explanations of behaviour, brain function has to be considered in relation to these processes. Just as the molecular mechanism that is employed to translate blood pressure into efferent impulses has to be described in terms of its successful transmission of the information, so the brain processes invoked in perception have to refer to the information transmitted to the visual cortex. According to the analysis presented earlier in Chapter 5, the biological view should not anticipate the relative importance of innate versus processes, nor can it predict the source of variation among individuals.

A third point concerns the distinction between function and dysfunction. Scadding appears to have assumed that because 'some disorders of behaviour' can already be explained in terms of physical agents, that 'with advances in knowledge more and more psychological and behavioural science will become biological'. We see here a failure to distinguish function from dysfunction which leads to an unjustified generalization from cases that involve breakdown to those that do not.

There is to be found in such analyses of 'biological psychiatry and psychology' an implicit reductionism or implicit dualism. Thus Scadding takes biology to refer to a study which will eventually yield physico-chemical descriptions, and Guze looks forward to a time when psychology and psychiatry will be replaced by neuroscience. However Guze, hinting perhaps that the enterprise might not work, argues that if learning turned out to be central to the origins of dysfunction, then psychiatry would have less need for neuroscience and more need for cultural anthropology, sociology, and social psychology. Presumably these are seen as 'non-biological' and therefore refer to aspects of brain function which are 'non-biological'. Ingold (1990), a social anthropologist, has argued that the effect of sociobiology has been to account for some phenomena as biological by reference 'down' to neurological structures, while explaining others with reference to culture, by implication a phenomenon that is non-biological. Once it is clear that intentional processes pervade biological systems, then biological psychiatry will expect to refer to disciplines such as anthropology and social psychology without abandoning the biological stance.

7.9 SUMMARY

We have now taken our account of intentional-causal processes into the explanation of adult human behaviour. As was the case with non-psychological and non-human examples, the description of the normal or functional response is inseparable from that of the abnormal or dysfunctional, and the key is the integrity of the intentional-causal process. In human psychological functioning this is more complex but the principles are the same.

The definition of psychiatric disorder is essentially descriptive and probably refers to a heterogeneous set of phenomena, but the apparent disruption of intentionality is central to its identity. The explanation may entail further, previously unidentified, intentional contributions, or disruption arising from a non-intentional-causal agent. In many respects psychiatric practice has borrowed from general medicine the assumption that in disorder intentionality has been interrupted, or run out, and in some instances this will be the case. In general, even where there is a non-intentional cause of breakdown, both in psychological and non-psychological systems there are compensatory, intentional-causal responses.

The interplay between intentional- and non-intentional-causal processes, and between developing individuals and specific environmental factors, are important in a consideration of genetic influences. The concept of genetically influenced 'design fault' is useful once it has been modified to take account of the developmental issues that we reviewed in Chapter 6. In the light of our analysis of causal processes, 'biological psychiatry' is seen to have made use of a restricted sense of the term 'biological'. Further, where it has assumed that biological processes are reducible to physics and chemistry, it has departed from an intentional-causal analysis which is needed both in biology and psychology.

REFERENCES

American Psychiatric Association (1994). *Diagnostic and statistical manual of mental disorders*, (4th edn). American Psychiatric Association, Washington, DC.

Andrade, L., Eaton, W. W. and Chilcoat, J. (1994). Lifetime comorbidity of panic attacks and major depression in a population-based study. Symptom profiles. *British Journal of Psychiatry*, 165, 363–9.

Bifulco, A., Harris, T. O., and Brown, G. (1992). Mourning or early inadequate care? Reexamining the relationship of maternal loss in childhood with adult depression and anxiety. *Development and Psychopathology*, 4, 433–49.

Blakemore, C. and Cooper, G. F. (1970). Development of the brain depends on the visual environment. *Nature*, 228, 477–8.

Bowlby, J. (1969). *Attachment and loss: I. Attachment*. Hogarth Press, London.

Brown, G. W. (1989). Introduction: life events and measurement. In *Life events and illness* (ed. G. W. Brown and T. O. Harris). Guilford Press, New York.

Brown, G. W. and Harris, T. (1978). *Social origins of depression: a study of psychiatric disorders in women*. Tavistock Publications, London.

Changeux, J. P. (1985). *Neuronal man: the biology of mind*. Pantheon, New York.

Checkley, S. A. (1992). Neuroendocrine mechanisms, life events and depression. *British Journal of Psychiatry*, **160**, (Suppl. 15), 7–15.

Cloninger, C. R. *et al.* (1990). The empirical structure of psychiatric comorbidity and its theoretical significance. In *Comorbidity of mood and anxiety disorders*, (ed. J. D. Maser and C. R. Cloninger), pp. 439–62. American Psychiatric Press, Washington, DC.

Darnell, J., Lodish, H., and Baltimore, D. (1990). *Molecular cell biology*, (2nd edn). Freeman, New York.

Davidson, D. (1980). *Essays on actions and events*. Clarendon Press, Oxford.

Dennett, D. (1987). *The intentional stance*, pp. 43–68. MIT Press, Cambridge, Mass.

Ehrenkranz, J., Bliss, F., and Sheard, M. H. (1974). Plasma testosterone correlation with aggressive behaviour and social dominance in men. *Psychosomatic Medicine*, **36**, 469–75.

Fodor, J. (1983). *Representations: philosophical essays on the foundations of cognitive science*, pp. 127–45. MIT Press, Cambridge, Mass.

Goodman, R. (1991). Growing together and growing apart: the non-genetic forces on children in the same family. In *The new genetics of mental illness*, (ed. P. McGuffin and R. Murray), pp. 212–24. Heinemann Medical Books, Oxford.

Gray, J. A., Feldon, J, Rawlins, J. N. P., Hemsley, D. R. and Smith, A. D. (1991). The neuropsychology of schizophrenia. *Behavioural and Brain Sciences*, **14**, 1–84.

Guze, S. B. (1989). Biological psychiatry: is there any other kind? *Psychological Medicine*, **19**, 315–23.

Hardcastle, V. G. (1992). Reduction, explanatory extension, and the mind/brain sciences. *Philosophy of Science*, **59**, 408–28.

Harlow, H. F. (1961). The development of affectional patterns in infant monkeys. In *Determinants of infant behaviour*, (ed. B. M. Foss), Vol. 1. Methuen, London.

Harlow, H. F. and Harlow, M. K. (1969). Effects of various mother–infant relationships on rhesus monkey behaviours. In *Determinants of infant behaviour*, (ed. B. M. Foss), Vol. 4. Methuen, London.

Hobson, R. P. (1993). The emotional origins of social understanding. *Philosophical Psychology*, **6**, (3); 227–49.

Hodges, J. and Tizard, B. (1989). IQ and behavioural adjustment of ex-institutional adolescents. *Journal of Child Psychology and Psychiatry*, **30**, 53–75.

Hubel, D. H. and Wiesel, T. N. (1962). Receptive fields, binocular interaction, and the functional architecture in the cat's visual cortex. *Journal of Physiology*, **160**, 106–54.

Hundert, E. M. (1988). *Philosophy, psychiatry and neuroscience*. Clarendon, Oxford.

Ingold, T. (1990). An anthropologist looks at biology. *Man*, **25**, (2), 208–9.

Jaspers, K. (1963). *General psychopathology* (transl. J. Hoenig and M. W. Hamilton). Manchester University Press, Manchester.

Jones, P. and Murray, R. M. (1991). The genetics of schizophrenia is the genetics of neurodevelopment. *British Journal of Psychiatry*, **158**, 615–23.

Kelly, W. F., Checkley, S. A. and Bender, D. A. (1980). Cushing's syndrome, tryptophan and depression. *British Journal of Psychiatry*, **136**, 125–32.

Kuipers, L. and Bebbington, P. (1988). Expressed emotion research in schizophrenia: theoretical and clinical implications. *Psychological Medicine*, **18**, 893–909.

Lorenz, K. Z. (1965). *Evolution and modifications of behaviour*. University of Chicago Press, Chicago.

McGuffin, P., Katz, R., and Bebbington, P. E. (1988). The Camberwell Collaborative Depression Study: III. Depression and adversity in the relatives of depressed probands. *British Journal of Psychiatry*, 152, 775–82.

Murray, R. M., Lewis, S., and Reveley, A. M. (1985). Towards an aetiological classification of schizophrenia. *Lancet*, i, 1023–6.

Murray, R. M., Jones, P., and O'Callaghan, E. (1991). Fetal brain development and later schizophrenia. In *The childhood environment and adult disease*, CIBA Foundation Symposium 156, pp. 155–70. Wiley, Chichester.

Nagel, E. (1961). *The structure of science*. Routledge and Kegan Paul, London.

Norman, R. M. G. and Malla, A. K. (1993). Stressful life events and schizophrenia. I: A review of the literature. *British Journal of Psychiatry*, 162, 161–6.

Plomin, R. and Daniels, D. (1987). Why are children in the same family so different from one another? *Behavioural and Brain Sciences*, 10, 1–60.

Polanyi, M. (1958). *Personal knowledge: towards a post-critical philosophy*. Routledge and Keegan Paul, London.

Popper, K. R. (1969). *Conjectures and refutations*, (3rd edn). Routledge and Kegan Paul, London.

Putnam, H. (1983). Reductionism and the nature of psychology. In *Mind design: philosophy, psychology, artificial intelligence*, (ed. J. Haugland), pp. 205–19. MIT Press, Cambridge, Mass.

Reiman, E. M. *et al.* (1989). Involvement of temporal poles in pathological and normal forms of anxiety. *Journal of Blood Flow and Metabolism*, 9, (Suppl. 1), S589.

Roberts, G. (1991). Delusional belief systems and meaning in life. *British Journal of Psychiatry*, 159, (Suppl. 14), 19–28.

Rutter, M. and Rutter, M. (1992). *Developing minds: challenge and continuity across the life span*. Penguin, London.

Rutter, M., Quinton, D., and Hill, J. (1990). Adult outcome of institution reared children: males and females compared. In *Straight and devious pathways from Childhood to adulthood*, (ed. L. Robins and M. Rutter), pp. 135–57. Cambridge University Press, Cambridge.

Scadding, J. G. (1990). The semantic problems of psychiatry. *Psychological Medicine*, 20, 243–8.

Schneider (1959). *Clinical Psychopathology* (transl, by M. W. Hamilton), Grune and Stratton, New York.

Sroufe, L. A., Egeland, B., and Kreutzer, T. (1990). The fate of early experience following developmental change: longitudinal approaches to individual adaptation in childhood. *Child Development*, 61, 1363–73.

Tienari, P. (1990). Genes, family environment or interaction? Findings from an adoption study. In *Etiology of mental disorder*, (ed. E. Kringlen, N. Lavik, and S. Torgersen), pp. 33–48. University of Oslo, Vindern.

Tsuang, M. T. (1993). Genotypes, phenotypes, and the brain. A search for connections in schizophrenia. *British Journal of Psychiatry*, 163, 299–307.

Walker, C. (1991). Delusion: What did Jaspers really says? *British Journal of Psychiatry*, 159 (suppl. 14), 94–103.

Weiner, I., Feldon, J., and Ziv-Harris, D. (1987). Early handling and latent inhibition in the conditioned suppression paradigm. *Developmental Psychobiology*, 20, 233–40.

Wiesel, T. N. (1982). The postnatal development of the visual cortex and the influence of environment. Nobel Lecture report. *Bioscience Reports*, 2, 351–77.

World Health Organization (1992). The ICD-10 classification of mental and behavioural disorders—clinical descriptions and diagnostic guidelines. WHO, Geneva.

8
Intentionality in disorder

8.1 TWO APPROACHES: LOGIC AND BIOLOGY

In psychological disorder we find apparent disruption at one or more stages in the intentional-causal pathways linking stimulus, perception, thought, emotion, and behaviour. Another aspect of this point is that psychological disorder essentially involves disorder of (intentional) action (cf. Fulford 1989). Physical disruption will be a major candidate for the explanation along the lines discussed in Chapter 7. In this chapter we examine the possibility that interruption of intentionality could have intentional-causal origins. In doing this we find ourselves considering questions and solutions formulated at the beginnings of the psychological theory of disorder. Freud can be regarded as starting from the same central question: could psychological phenomena that display the same qualities as those seen in unequivocal cases of physically caused conditions, of persistent, intrusive disruption of normal function, have their origins in psychological processes? This is to say, in the terms used here: could they have their origins in intentional-causal processes? In his analysis of hysterical conversion syndromes, Freud postulated disruption of normal function by states of mind deriving from early intolerable, traumatic experiences and impulses. Similar principles were being invoked at around the same time in an otherwise very different psychological theory of disorder, namely Watson's account of phobias. In this account, the disorder was due to the inappropriate generalization of learnt fear, this learning having occurred in a one-trial traumatic experience. Thus at the beginnings of clinical psychological theory at the turn of the century, in the two early models which, it would be fair to say, gave rise to all the rest, what we find is the fundamental idea that memories of traumas intrude into, and hence disrupt, normal function. The notion of trauma is fundamental to the explanation of breakdown of intentionality in terms of intentional processes, though broader concepts are also required.

We shall take two approaches to the problem. One draws on general logical and epistemological considerations of the sort discussed in the first chapter. In that chapter we, in effect, gave an outline definition of a family of concepts including representation, thought, and intentionality. The linkage to action, and the organization into theory, were critical to the definition. In this chapter we show how from these very general considerations it is possible to derive conditions of psychological disorder with particular characteristics. This is done in Section 8.2.

The second approach takes further the account given in the previous chapter of disruption of function, which placed emphasis on the disruption of intentionality. Just as intentional causality was seen to operate throughout biological systems, both psychological and non-psychological, so disruption of intentionality was seen to be the hallmark of disorder throughout biological systems. The consideration of possible intentional origins of such disruption will draw on our consideration of intentional causality in biological systems given in Chapter 5 and of our proposition in Chapter 6 that the psychological development of the child may be seen to represent the exploitation of a potential inherent in the simplest biological processes. In particular, the development of multiple internalized rules and representations with their immense potential for flexibility and creativity, will be seen also to entail substantial risks.

8.2 THE LOGIC AND EPISTEMOLOGY OF DISORDER

8.2.1 Radical error

Persistent misrepresentation and rule-conflict

We have defined representations as being involved essentially in the regulation of action, and we have remarked that they are typically hierarchically organized, in the way highlighted by post-empiricist theory of knowledge. From these assumptions it is possible to derive general features of psychological disorder and general principles for its explanation.

We will be working towards defining a form of explanation of disorder in intentionality which is couched at the level of the intentional processes themselves. Such a form of explanation therefore has to derive from the definition of intentionality, in this sense from logic. It turns out that it has basically the following form: radical failures of intentionality arise in case intentional processes subvert their own nature, that is to say, their role in the planning of action. Post-empiricist epistemology provides the framework for elaborating this basic idea. The investigation will take us close to familiar psychological models of disorder, from conditioning models to those in the more cognitively elaborate psychoanalytic tradition.

We begin with a priori remarks on psychological disorder. In so far as intentionality is the defining characteristic of mind, all mental disorder involves breakdown of intentionality. Intentionality is, of course, a broad concept here, concerning the representational (cognitive) capacities of mind. We may provisionally distinguish two kinds of way in which representation may fail: it may fail to represent reality correctly, or it may fail to regulate action appropriately. This distinction is blurred, however, in so far as misrepresentation leads to inappropriate action.

We make mistakes all of the time, however, and so far this has nothing to do with what we mean by 'mental disorder'. To begin to capture this notion, we need some idea of *radical* misrepresentation. We may expect that the understanding of 'radical' here should follow from the nature of representation itself. In so far as representation regulates action, and action is extended though time, it belongs to the nature of representation that error is subject to discovery and correction through time, in the course of action. This general idea underlies the definition of at least one kind of radical misrepresentation, namely, as being misrepresentation that fails to be corrected through time. In the phenomena of persistent error we begin to recognize something of what is meant by 'mental disorder'.

However, regulation of action may fail even if representation of the environment is correct. The circumstances are simply those in which two or more representations are correct, but give rise to incompatible plans for action. In brief, the circumstances involve one or another kind of *rule-conflict*. As outlined in Chapter 6, human psychological functioning is characterized by a multiplicity of sets of rules, with the implication that there is ample scope for rule-conflict. While misrepresentation can in principle be due to lower-level disrupting causes, rule-conflict is generally unamenable to this type of explanation. This is to say, it arises generally in the context of normal psychological functioning. The representations and their regulation of action are individually in order, but in combination they are in disorder. Once again, as in the case of misrepresentation, it should be noted that rule-conflict is common, and has nothing to do yet with what is meant by 'mental disorder'. Again as in the case of misrepresentation, we begin to capture this notion when we envisage *persistence* despite continuing failure of action. In other words, in persistent, unresolved rule-conflict, leading to persistent disarray in action, we begin to recognize signs of 'mental disorder'.

Avoidance and re-enactment (re-experiencing)

What stands in need of explanation, then, is persistent misrepresentation, and persistent, unresolved rule-conflict. Various forms of explanation are possible a priori, of which our main interest here are those that run in terms of the intentional processes themselves, those that may be called 'psychological'.

As already remarked, in rule-conflict representations are in order, but only opposed, and there is typically no lower-level, reductive explanation. Persistent misrepresentation, on the other hand, may have an explanation in terms of physical disruption of information-processing systems, as when, for example, visual images are produced by electrical stimulation of the visual cortex. On the other hand, persistent misrepresentation may essentially involve intentional processes, specifically the fulfilment of a wish, or the enactment of fear, as in the case of Don Quixote, who in search of adventure perceived windmills as monstrous giants, or Macbeth, who falsely perceived the image and ghost of his murderous action. Something like hallucination may occur from either kind of cause. In the framework of Dennett's three explanatory stances (subsection 1.3.5), hallucination admits of explanation from the physical and the intentional stances.

Persistent error in representing the environment may be explained also from Dennett's design stance, in the sense that it is innately determined. Consider, for example, the case of the frog's fly-snapping behaviour discussed in Chapter 4, (Section 4.5). The frog may mistake an ambient non-fly black dot for a fly, this being a mistake at least from our point of view, and the mistaken representation is due to innate features of cognitive design, in particular to the absence of a mechanism for discriminating between flies and other fly-like objects.

Error in representing the environment is also an intrinsic risk during learning. The principle is relatively simple: representations acquired in and appropriate to one environment are wrongly applied to another, different environment, and the error naturally shows up in failure of action. For example, a rat learns its way though a complicated maze to the goal-box, and is then put in a more or less subtly different maze, where cues lead to unexpected results, for example dead-ends. Consequently action is thwarted, desires remain unsatisfied. Breakdown of function shows up in, for example, frustration-behaviour, randomness, repetitiveness, or inertia.

However, the fact is that we are continuously exposed to new situations, more or less different from what we have experienced before, and we are not constantly falling into confusion. Normally we change the old rules, or learn new ones. What has to be explained in clinical psychology, as we have already noted, is precisely the *persistence* of maladaptive rules and representations, their failure to respond to new information.

Broadly speaking, the explanations of this failure invoke the fact that new information is *avoided*. Avoidance includes the straightforwardly behavioural variety, but may also include complex forms of mental denial and disqualification. But further, whatever type of avoidance is used, there is typically a kind of experience, after all, of what is being avoided, and this experience confirms the old rules and representations, even if they are, otherwise, quite invalid. This may be called *re-enactment* (or re-experiencing).

These points, in one form or another, are familiar in clinical psychological theory, and the main aim of this section is to explicate them from the more general, philosophical perspectives presented in the first part of this essay. Before embarking on this task, a sketch of some examples of what is to be explained, and the kinds of explanation in question, may be helpful.

Consider for example phobias, irrational fears and avoidance, regulated by the (persistent) representation of an object as extremely dangerous, when in fact it is not. A psychological explanation of the phobia, for example of enclosed spaces, would run as follows: in the past the person has been exposed to real danger in a situation from which escape was or was thought to be impossible, and this representation of enclosed space as dangerous has generalized to all other (similar) enclosed spaces. The question arises as to why the representation is not modified by subsequent exposure to safe enclosed spaces.

That example is of the kind emphasized by conditioning or behavioural theories. Consider another example of the kind emphasized in psychoanalytic theory, with its characteristic concern with interpersonal relations. A person experiences persistent breakdown in intimate friendships. Examination reveals a pattern, one theme in which is that the person begins to act as if she were about to be rejected, in circumstances in which there is apparently no objective evidence for this expectation. An obvious psychological explanation of this theme, one which draws again on simple principles of learning, is that the person has experienced rejection in past intimate relationships, and the representation of them as involving rejection has generalized to all other (similar) intimate relationships. But again, the problem for theory is this: why has the representation not been modified by subsequent exposure to friendships that work?

Answers to the problem of persistence run in terms of avoidance. Phobias are characterized by behavioural avoidance, so one reason why a learnt fear of enclosed spaces would not be modified by subsequent contrary experience is simply that the person avoids enclosed spaces and therefore never experiences them as safe. By the same principle, someone who has experienced devastating rejection in past important relationships may subsequently avoid similar relationships, and hence the representation of them as involving rejection is never put to the test.

On the other hand, in the second case as described we are supposing that the person continues to try, and still the earlier acquired representation persists. So explanation of persistence in terms of avoidance does not apply here. Implicit in the sketch of the case is that the person responds in accord with the earlier acquired representation. She selectively attends to (the slightest) signs of rejection, or interprets behaviour of her partner as signifying rejection, even though (we are supposing) no rejection is intended. The perception of rejection leads by psychologic to emotions of hurt and anger, hence to such as irritation and withdrawal, which in turn, we may surmise, prompts similar responses in her partner. In short, the relationship progresses into difficulties, and the outcome is one that readily lends itself to the interpretation by the person that she is being rejected. In this way the representation that is brought to the relationship from the beginning generates a pattern and sequence of responses the outcome of which is confirmation of the representation. This kind of pathway to persistent misrepresentation is distinct from avoidance. The same principle can operate in phobia, in case the person does not avoid the feared situation completely. Here the representation of the situation as dangerous gives rise to anticipatory anxiety, which may intensify when in the situation to the extreme of panic. In this way the situation comes to be experienced after all as threatening and dangerous, even when objectively it is not. The expectation is fulfilled: the representation is confirmed.

The examples of persistent misrepresentation outlined above involve expectations that, in some way or other, action will not achieve desired goals. In the first case there is fear of physical danger, in the second fear of rejection by significant others. The proposed explanation of persistent misrepresentation turns on this feature. If the results of action are represented as threatening or useless, then there will tend to be either avoidance, or generation of confirming experiences in situations which might otherwise be disconfirming.

We can, on the other hand, envisage something like inappropriate and uncorrected representations which involve expectations of success. For example, the child is likely to persist for a considerable time in the expectation that her parents or other adults in charge will take care of her, notwithstanding ample evidence to the contrary. But here we have a plausible case of an expectation, a hope, which is innately determined, and which therefore stands relatively firm no matter what experience is like. As remarked earlier, persistent error in representation arises in case of inadequate match between the design of the living being, between the reality for which it is designed, and the world into which it is born.

All the examples cited above involve conflict among representations. In phobic anxiety, the person (usually) also believes that the feared situations are safe, that the fear is irrational. Otherwise, indeed, there would be no disorder, at least not so far as the person was concerned. Similarly, we tend to persist in the expectation that action, for example in relation to others, can and should satisfy needs, notwithstanding evidence to the contrary. The conflict generally is between the need to act, the expectation that action can and must succeed, and the perception that in one way or another it does not work. The conflict is among the cognitive-affective representations, in so far as they are to be used in the regulation of action. Conflict may arise in various ways: if the same object is perceived as both desirable and undesirable; if two objects, which cannot both be achieved, are both desired; or if two objects, which cannot both be avoided, are both undesired. Normally such conflict can be resolved, but it stays unresolved, persistent, if there is unpreparedness to tolerate negative consequences of action, these being either some kind of punishment, or at least failure to achieve one of two desired ends. It may be inferred that from the point of view of the agent action is impossible: it would would lead to intolerable danger, or to intolerable loss.

It is here that we return to the proposal made at the beginning of this subsection. Radical failure of intentionality arises in case intentional processes subvert their own nature, that is to say, their role in the planning of action. The point is that representation incompatible with action is in some sense also impossible. This is the origin of the paradox already implied in the juxtaposition of avoidance and re-enactment.

8.2.2 Threats to action and thought: trauma and paradox

Introduction: a priori approaches

The distinction between conditions that are conducive to the agent and those that are not, between 'pleasure' and 'pain', and the interaction between them, has a long history in attempts to understand and explain behaviour. Severe pain, or threat, appears typically under the name of 'trauma' in psychological theories of disorder. We shall make use of something like this notion, emphasizing, in accord with our approaches up to now, intentional and developmental perspectives.

The distinction between conditions favourable to action, and conditions that make action difficult to impossible, is relevant not only to psychology and clinical psychology, but also, given a certain assumption, to philosophy, specifically to the a priori theory of representation. The assumption in question is that representation essentially serves action. In terms of the cognitive-behavioural paradigm defined by this assumption there arises the prospect of profound paradox in case representation is of conditions in which action cannot proceed. The underlying logical problem is that there are conditions of reality which cannot be represented.

It is possible to see from within logic the logical form or forms that psychological disorder can assume. The critical point is that thought is for the planning of action, and therefore it must represent the possibility of action: if it cannot do this it undermines itself. Thought goes on, but is impossible. This defines the central, paradoxical idea of psychological disorder.

We will approach this idea in two ways. First, via post-empiricist epistemology, and secondly via the idea of the limits of thought.

Core theory and negative critical experiments

According to post-empiricist epistemology, as outlined in the first chapter (Section 1.4), beliefs are hierarchically organized, in the form of a theory. The theory interprets experience and is used in the planning of action. It typically has a core of working assumptions, which define essential characteristcs of reality and knowledge. These core assumptions are essential to the theory: without them the theory, the interpretation of experience, and the planning of action would fall into disarray. If the theory makes a prediction that turns out to be false, it can be inferred that there is a mistake somewhere in the system, but not yet where. There is room for manoeuvre in the diagnosis of error. A sound methodological rule is to make as little adjustment as is necessary, though in the case of repeated, or serious failures of prediction, major revision in the theory may be indicated. In any case, there has to be resistance to giving up core beliefs, which are fundamental to the whole enterprise. Thus apparent anomalies are deflected away from the core, to be handled in some way or other elsewhere. Occasionally in the sciences there are attempts to construct a so-called critical experiment, which has the aim of putting the core of a theory to the test. Generally, however, this can happen only when there is an alternative theory standing by to pick up the pieces: in the absence of a viable alternative theory which can handle the recalcitrant data, no experiment is likely to be regarded as critical (Lakatos 1970).

In the first chapter (subsection 1.4.4) we applied post-empiricist epistemology to the theory of action. Action presupposes at least the following beliefs, or expectations: that the self is competent (enough) to act, that the world is predictable (enough), and that the world provides (enough) satisfaction of needs. Such expectations have to be preserved if activity is to continue. If they were to be abandoned, action would appear to be either impossible or pointless: there would be, so far, no reason to act.

We may ask, then, what would happen if fundamental convictions of these kinds were to be apparently challenged by experience? Suppose they were put to the test by apparently critical experiences, in the absence, moreover, of an alternative theory which could handle them. There would be major cognitive problems, in both representation and knowledge. From the point of view of the theory, particularly the core theory, apparent anomalies have a highly peculiar status. On the one hand, they represent an enormous threat, signifying the downfall of the theory and the end of action itself, and have maximum salience. But on the other hand, they cannot be true, or really true, according to the theory, and so should be only discounted. So the theory of action in relation to these apparently critical anomalies gets into profound confusion.

The limits of thought

The same idea can be approached by considering the idea that there are limits of thought. It is natural enough to presuppose that whatever exists, or at least whatever is known to the subject, can be represented. We find this assumption in the philosophical tradition, but alongside it we find also the recognition that there are limits to representation, deriving from the nature of representation itself. The most rigorous working out of this idea is by Wittgenstein in his *Tractatus logico-philosophicus* (1921). We considered the *Tractatus* account of representation in the first chapter (subsection 1.3.2) as a particularly clear expression of a theory which has a long history, namely, that representation is a matter of *resemblance* between sign and the reality signified. In the *Tractatus* theory, thoughts and linguistic propositions alike are pictures, or combinations of pictures, of possible states of affairs. The general form of proposition is: This (the picture) is how things stand. This account implies limits to representation, namely: only what can be pictured can be represented in thought or in language.

However, the *Tractatus* account also implies that there are things that cannot be pictured. Pictures cannot represent, for example, that the relation between representation and reality is pictorial, nor that the world is the totality of facts, nor any of the philosophical theory of the *Tractatus*. The paradoxical implication, which the young Wittgenstein was quite prepared to embrace, was that his book expressed what was inexpressible in thought and language, and was therefore itself nonsense. The appearance of paradox here is inevitable, however, because definition of the limits of thought requires that we think both sides of the limit. (The primary material referred to here includes mainly Wittgenstein 1921, 4.11s, 4.12s, 4.5s, 5.1–6.1 and 6.1–7, the last proposition in the book. Unfamiliar readers would, however, be advised to consult commentaries, practically all of which address the major and integral theme of the 'inexpressible'.)

As noted in the first chapter (subsection 1.3.3), the *Tractatus* picture-theory has little to do directly with the theory of representation at work in the present essay. We explicate representation not in terms of pictures (or images) but rather primarily with reference to the regulation of action. We adopt, in other words, the axiom of cognitive psychology, and indeed of biology, that information-processing generally is in the service of action. But just as the *Tractatus* theory recognizes that there are limits to what can be represented, limits that derive from the nature of representation itself, so too the present theory of representation implies corresponding limitations, and indeed also the paradoxes to which such limitations inevitably give rise.

The key here is the definition of representation as serving action. Suppose that there are circumstances in which action is, or is perceived to be, impossible. Suppose that these circumstances are represented as such. But then the representation cannot be used to facilitate (to regulate, to plan) action, which is, according to the representation, not possible. But in so far as the representation cannot be used in the service of action, in so far as it is incompatible with action, it is not a possible representation. The paradox here can be expressed by saying that the reality in question has to be both represented and not represented.

The considerations in this and the preceding subsections are closely connected, and in the end come to the same. Definition of the limits of thought, in terms of thought itself, and its paradoxical consequences, are of the general form clarified in the *Tractatus* account. But in order to apply these insights to the theory of representation adopted here, we leave behind the *Tractatus* idea of passive pictures, and consider representation in the form of action. This takes us to post-empiricism.

Post-empiricism, like the empiricism that it replaced, is as much a theory of representation as a theory of knowledge. As a theory of representation it emphasizes the active nature of cognition, in a variety of senses. These include that beliefs are flexible in relation to experience, organized in a theory, and also that beliefs are used to plan action. We considered in the preceding subsection what happens in case such a theory, such a vehicle of representation, comes up against what it defines as its limits, which involves acknowledging the other side, the possibility of critical experiences which would refute the core of the theory.

Trauma

We have invoked the notion of experiences that constitute a major threat to the conditions of action, and which lead to radical disorder in cognition. The concept in clinical psychology and psychiatry that comes closest to this idea, sketched so far in a purely a priori way, is the concept of (psychological) *trauma*. The concept of trauma is a broad one, and is invoked in whole or partial explanation of many kinds of psychological disorder. It is of relevance, however, not only to clinical psychology and psychiatry but also to logic, the a priori theory of representation, provided that logic defines representation essentially as serving in the regulation of action. The underlying problem, logical and psychological, is that representation of reality in which action is impossible or pointless subverts itself: it makes itself impossible, or pointless.

The most apparent traumas are experiences that threaten life itself, as in war, fires and other disasters, and serious physical attacks on the person. The most immediate effect is terror; fear of death or damage. It is clear that the traumatic events are experienced and represented; otherwise there would be no (psychological) problem. Indeed, typically they are persistently *re-experienced*, in one way or another. On the other hand, in some sense (or senses) the trauma is not and cannot be represented. For example, there may be amnesia for critical periods in the sequence of events, or the events are remembered, but not the terror; or the events are recalled with a third-person perspective, as though observed from the outside rather than experienced from within them; or the memory images have an unreal, dream-like quality. These points will be discussed further in the next chapter, under the heading of Post-traumatic Stress Disorder (subsection 9.3.3).

The points made so far in this section apply to manifest traumas such as involvement in disasters. It has to be emphasized, however, that 'trauma' in the sense at work in this section, namely, experience that radically subverts the conditions of intentionality, is not confined to such cases of obvious 'psychological shock'. In a developmental context particularly, a broader notion is required. The development of action and cognition requires certain forms of experience, and is inhibited in their absence. Children have to learn how to how to relate, how to act, how to think, and how to speak. Children are no doubt biologically designed for these tasks, but they require the right kind of help from adults. They need, for example, a secure space for action (for play), encouragement and help in planning and in achieving goals, and in finding the right descriptions of, predictive patterns for, reality. Parent–child interactions that include patterns such as neglect, excessive prohibition on, or rejection of, the child's spontaneous attempts to act and speak, excessive (for example age-inappropriate) demands, confused or contradictory communications, may be expected, on a priori grounds alone, to inhibit or distort development of the child's capacity to act and to think. As in the case of manifest disaster, the result will tend to be experience of a world in which action is perceived as impossible, or pointless, or both. This broader notion of what subverts conditions of intentionality, based in developmental considerations, will be explored in more detail in the next section (8.3).

Theory of mind: further possibilities of disorder

We have been discussing so far in this section threats to core beliefs in the theory of action which have to do with apparently disconfirming experience. There are other kinds of threat, however, involving apparently opposed socially acquired beliefs. Here belongs the fact, already discussed in the first chapter (subsection 1.4.2), that we use an explicit theory of mind and action which is, like theories generally, socially acquired. In this case the possibility arises that children are taught to have beliefs which seem to contradict the assumptions required for action to be viable. A child may be taught in words as well as in practice that he or she is too demanding, or is incompetent, or that the world is too dangerous, or unsatisfying; and so on. Thus we can envisage threats to the core assumptions underlying action arising not only from acute or chronic traumatic experiences, but from conflicting propositions which come with the force of parental authority. In these circumstances there is a similar adverse and paradoxical effect on the capacity for thought: the assertions assault what has to be believed if action is to continue, and hence they have to be both taken seriously and ignored. This kind of threat to intentionality will be discussed also in the next section (8.3), where the focus is explicitly on developmental processes.

Wherever there is threat to what is fundamental to action, whether in the form of obvious or hidden disasters, or breakdown in the conditions of child development, including perverse instruction, the assault has to be dealt with in some way if action is to carry on. Protection is needed.

8.2.3 Psychic defences

Behavioural strategies, mental analogues, and elaborations

In the previous section we considered threats to the core of the theory presupposed by action, to assumptions or expectations of safety, competence, and satisfaction of needs, for example. Such attacks require defensive manoeuvres. At their simplest, these are behavioural. Living beings respond to threats to their integrity by escape or fighting. And if the environment fails to provide for needs, alternative sources of satisfaction are sought. In so far as living beings have the capacity for representation, however, there are alternatives to these real actions: they can create analogues within the realm of representation itself. Threats can be denied representation, or they can be attacked and destroyed in thought. Satisfaction of needs can likewise be thought, even if not really achieved. Such strategies operate within the mind as opposed to reality: they are acts of the imagination, and they involve departure from, or distortion of, reality.

Pursuing this line of thought rapidly leads to points of a kind familiar in psychoanalytic theory. However, our aim in this section is not to explicate or endorse specific psychoanalytic models of particular psychic defences, but is rather to sketch some principles for understanding the concept which belongs with proposals made so far in this essay. The reason that we come across here points familiar in psychoanalytic theory is just that Freud was the first to see clearly the problem-space in question. Its definition required various conceptual assumptions which contradicted and superceded what was envisaged by mainstream scientific psychology until fairly recently. These assumptions included the following, all of which were discussed in the first chapter: preparedness to use the intentional stance, the language of intentional states, in psychological explanation and prediction, as in common-sense folk psychology; but departure from common sense (Cartesian common sense) by not restricting intentionality to what is available to consciousness and expressed in self-report; the post-empiricist recognition that some intentional states constitute the core of belief, to be protected from counter-evidence, and the inevitable conclusion then that while such protection averts perceived catastrophe, it involves at least distortion of reality, and perhaps manifest disorder.

As indicated above, there is a model for intrapsychic defences in the post-empiricist conception of scientific theories discussed in the first chapter (Section 1.4). In this context, unlike the unconscious mind, cognitive maneouvres to protect the core of theory are open to view. The defensive strategies have been well documented by Lakatos in his seminal paper (1970) and discussed in subsections 1.4.1 and 1.4.4. They include simple denial of the anomalies, which works well until replication, and degenerating theory changes, such as *ad hoc* elaborations which involve restriction of scope. We should note also an extreme reaction to pressure within theory, namely, the splitting of the scientific community, where one side takes the old theory and all its evidence, ignoring, disqualifying the new, and the new school envisages only its domain of evidence. In these circumstances there can be little (genuine) communication between the two schools of thought. An example would be the splitting of psychoanaltyic and scientific paradigms in psychology under the weight of the dichotomy between meaningful and causal connections. All these sorts of manoeuvre under radical pressure, which are familiar in science—denial, theory-restriction, and splitting—have intrapsychic analogues.

Simple denial in the face of unwanted or inexplicable phenomena is common enough. It is likely to be unsustainable, however, in any form in the face of trauma, whether a single catastrophe, or chronic adverse experience. One way of responding to undeniable conflict involves what may be called splitting: the traumatic experiences, and in particular their apparent meaning, are kept isolated from the convictions presupposed by action. Cognitive responses to gross and subtle trauma may include that the trauma is represented, indeed persistently re-experienced and re-enacted, but it is split off from the representation of reality as one in which it is possible to live. This splitting off is a form of denial, of not allowing the trauma to access basic, necessary beliefs. Splitting, and the dissociation which it implies, thus present as relatively simple ways of protecting fundamental assumptions. The precise nature and modelling of these and related psychic mechanisms has been, and remains, a subject of debate (Breuer and Freud 1895; Klein 1946; Hilgard 1977/1986; Power and Brewin 1991; Gardner 1993).

Denial and splitting can be readily identified within a post-empiricist philosophy of mind as possible defensive manoeuvres. The possibility of dissociation belongs with the idea explored in detail in Chapter 6, that human cognition is characterized by multiple sets of rules, concerning subsystems of cognitive-affective-behavioural states. Coherence and integrity among these subsystems are not a given, but have to be achieved, and this process can be threatened, as will be discussed in more detail in the next section. Also, however, dissociation can be conscripted into use as a defence. As generally with cognitive phenomena, even otherwise maladaptive mechanisms can be made use of, including as defences, a point that will recur through the remainder of this section.

Other types of defence familiar in psychoanalytic theory have a more complicated, though still strong, relation to the kind of assumptions we have been using in this essay. Consider, for example, projection (or projective identification), one of the main primitive defences posited in Kleinian theory (Klein 1946; Sandler 1988). To understand projection from the standpoint of the considerations adduced so far in this chapter, we need to elaborate on the view of the self which is essential for action. It includes competence, or power. However, if the self is seen as *too powerful* further problems arise, in particular in case the self is perceived as capable of destroying the source of needs, and is inclined to because that source is not sufficiently satisfying. The idea of an 'impossible reality' is then complicated by the idea of an 'impossible self', that is to say, a self that is inclined to attack and destroy the source of satisfaction of its needs. Destructive attack is a familiar, effective response to threat. It is, however, a particularly problematic response in the specific case of frustration of needs. In early development, it would appear as destructive impulses, anger or rage, against the carer, prompted by perceived deprivation. In general, and at any developmental stage, intolerable destructive impulses would include those directed at any outside object, or any aspect of the self, which is valued. Such impulses are bound to create conflict. One solution to the conflict is to project the destructive impulses into the source of needs. Projection then appears as a primitive defence against such impulses, by ascribing them not to the self, but to the outside world, either to a natural object, or to another subject. In this way projection presents as a radical misuse of the 'theory of mind'. As in the case of all defences there is a cost. In this case the cost is that the self is stripped of power, and confronts a frightening reality.

So far we have considered the defences of denial, splitting, and projection. More positive strategies include self-gratification. If the real world fails as a source of satisfaction of needs, such as for comfort and affirmation, it is possible to create an imaginative world in which the self can please itself. Pleasure in this state of mind may include sexual self-satisfaction as an expression of power to elicit comfort and love. At another level, there may be dreams of praise and acclaim. Reality is given up as a source or object of love, and the self is substituted. Such are the procedures involved in the so-called narcissistic defence (Freud 1914). On the surface is the thought that the world is inferior and unworthy of love; beneath is the fear that the self has these awful qualities. As with other defences, there is dissociation, with more or less rapid switching between contrary states of mind.

Failure of self-knowledge as defence

So far we have considered psychic defences which are in effect developmentally primitive, without any essential dependence on language. The issues, here as elsewhere, become complicated by the use of a theory about one's own mental states. More sophisticated, 'rational' forms of denial of unacceptable states of mind become available, including such as re-construal, intellectualizing, and explaining away. These defences are typically added to the repertoire with the theorizing that makes them possible during adolescence (Freud 1936, see also Chapter 6, subsection 6.5.3). These intellectual responses to intolerable mental states are akin to the defensive, degenerating strategies used in scientific theory when it is faced with anomalies. As in scientific theory, the cost is typically restriction of scope and predictive power, but what is secured is at least certainty within the restricted domain. Once there is an explicit, working theory of mind, moreover, primitive defensive strategies such as straightforward denial, splitting, projection, and narcissism, can all be elevated into theoretical form. The theory of the self and others can be conscripted into the service of defence, by selective attention to, and distortions of, the phenomena.

We described self-knowledge in the first chapter (subsection 1.4.3) as having the form of a theory. The account belongs with post-empiricist epistemology, and stands opposed basically to the Cartesian idea of introspection. We noted that failure of self-knowledge leads to confusion and rule-conflict, endorsing the long-recognized close connection between failure of self-knowledge and psychological problems. On the other hand, we did not in the earlier discussion refer to the defensive function of failure of self-knowledge, a further point emphasized by Freud and subsequent psychoanalytic theorists. We noted that the theory of mind, applied to the self as well as to others, is, like all theories, acquired in education, which thus appears as a major source of error. Hence this new model of self-knowledge apparently differs from the psychoanalytic view in implicating education rather than defensive function in the production of error. And to this we may add another apparent difference, that Freud viewed the processes involved in self-knowledge and ignorance as intrapsychic, whereas the account endorsed here emphasizes their interpersonal nature. On the other hand, while it is true that psychoanalytic theory has emphasized the intrapsychic nature of processes involved in self-knowledge and its failure, the contrast with interpersonal accounts is not that sharp. Psychoanalytic theory has always been concerned with interpersonal relations, whether internalized in the mind of the individual or played out in reality. This is connected with the fact that there is no tension between Freud's insight that failure of self-knowledge typically serves a defensive function, and the view of self-knowledge and its failures as originating in social and family life. It has been emphasized by family therapists working within a psychoanalytic framework that the blind spots and error intrinsic to the family's psychological theory typically have a defensive function (for example, Byng-Hall 1973). The theory includes rules, explicit or implicit, which systematically promote ignoring, disqualification, or distortion of certain beliefs and desires. Moreover, among the methods for achieving this result are the developmentally primitive defence mechanisms described in psychoanalytic theory. These mechanisms may be called 'intrapsychic', and they may indeed be subjective in origin, but in any case they are also modelled, selectively reinforced, and maintained by family function. Children have ample opportunity to learn from parents the use of various forms of denial, such as splitting and projection.

Defence benefit/cost analysis: avoidance and re-enactment (re-experiencing)

We have been considering the proposal that certain core assumptions have to be preserved if action is to be possible. They concern a view of the self as competent, of the world as safe and predictable, and sufficiently gratifying. If this view is threatened in some way, the first response is to act so as to remove the threat. But of course special problems arise in case intervention is impossible or unsuccessful, when the circumstances for some reason cannot be altered. The living being is then obliged to remain in a situation in which action is either impossible or pointless or both. In this condition the tendency will be for action to become random, or irrelevant, or it may cease altogether. Such are the signs in behaviour. As to cognition, it may be inferred a priori that there are similarly radical disorders: thought may cease altogether, or may become random, or it frees itself from reality.

The risks involved in abandoning core beliefs testify to their necessity, to the importance of defending them at practically any cost. The consequences of giving them up, in more or less circumscribed areas of life, include the two most common themes in psychological disorder: profound anxiety, and depression. The anxious person lives in fear of danger, and has to restrict his or her sphere of activity more or less drastically. In depression the view of action is hopeless: the self is powerless, the world provides no pleasure, and there is no prospect of change. To the extent that the depressed person sees no point in it, she does not act. The extreme is suicide, the act that brings action to an end.

Anxious or depressed beliefs signify the failure of attempts at defence, the failure to preserve convictions that action can carry on. As discussed in the previous section, they may arise from traumatic experience of some kind, or they may have been acquired from parental instruction, or both.

Depressed and anxious beliefs are maladaptive in the sense that they inhibit action. But there is another possiblity here, that maladaptive beliefs may themselves function as defences, as protection of something considered necessary to carry on. This complicated and paradoxical possibility is consistent with the general assumption used in this essay, that the fundamental direction of mental phenomena is to ensure the continuation of action. The methodological assumption is that this continues to be true even in, and indeed plausibly *especially* in, the most difficult bio-psychological circumstances. This implies that 'symptoms' may well be serving functions, an idea that has always been central to psychoanalytic theory and its derivatives.

Consider, for example, one of the well-known psychoanalytic models of depression, as being aggression towards the carer, as a response to perceived neglect or abuse, turned against the self. The view of the self as weak and useless may serve as a defence against the view that the self is too powerful, and in particular inclined to assault the one who should be helping. Further, helplessness may be expected to elicit care. The point here is that maladaptiveness, like threat, admits of degrees, and is hierarchically organized. Certain assumptions will be given up, even valued ones, in order to preserve what is still more important.

Or again, consider the issue of excessively contradictory parental instruction, which is closely connected to themes of this chapter (p. 308 and subsection 8.3.5). The child is persistently given contradictory instruction, information, and commands, so that, for example, statements of affirmation are combined with verbal or non-verbal rejection, or the child is informed that what he or she experiences is not really happening; and so on. In such circumstances the distinction between right and wrong judgement is not made out clearly enough, and so far there are no rules by which to act or to think. Doing nothing, the giving up of action and thought, may be the most viable response in the circumstances. This solution works but only until independent action is required, which becomes increasingly unavoidable through adolescence. Moreover, the adolescent is faced with the task of constructing a theory of this apparently nonsensical world. What kind of theory would this be? One option would be construction of solipsistic independence from reality, especially from other people, and a theme in the theory would inevitably be profound fear of chaos.

The psychic defences serve to protect core assumptions perceived as necessary for action. If these assumptions are abandoned, in the light of experience or parental instruction, the result is that action is perceived as in some way impossible, or pointless. Further, some basic assumptions may be given up in order to preserve others perceived as even more essential. Whatever the origin of the maladaptive cognitions, they likewise assume the status of rules for the interpretation of experience, to be held with certainty, and protected from apparent counter-evidence.

The psychic defences are self-perpetuating; their aim is to preserve the status quo. This means: core beliefs are to be maintained, contrary experience is to be kept at a distance by forms of denial and distortion. It is reality itself which is being denied and distorted. But reality being what it is, that in experience and action which is independent of the will, it continues to have its effects, to make itself known. What is feared is continually re-experienced and re-enacted. In anxiety states, reality is avoided, but is still represented and feared; in depression, inaction fails to elicit enough care and maintains absence of reward; the narcissistic personality acts so as to extinguish love from others; in delusion, the person may seem to make sense to himself, but communication with others fails drastically.

The psychic defences have the benefit of protection of the view of the world and the self as tolerable. The costs involve distortion of the phenomena, restriction of theory and consequently life style, and re-experiencing (re-enactment) of the original threat, typically without comprehension.

It was remarked at the beginning of this section that radical failure of intentionality has two connected forms: persistent misrepresentation and persistent rule-conflict. These are what require explanation. We went on to note, in subsection 8.2.2, that the explanation invokes the notion of trauma, broadly conceived. Persistent misrepresentation and persistent rule-conflict appear as the re-experiencing, or re-enactment, of the orginal threats to the integrity of action. We then went on, in the present subsection, to consider psychic defences, and we have arrived at the conclusion that these defences characteristically involve persistent misrepresentation and persistent rule-conflict, these being, again, the re-experiencing, or re-enactment, of the original traumatic experience. The solution to the problem plays out the problem. The disorder is an attempt to preserve order by the repetition of disorder. The position here is thus a matter of complex identities and paradoxes, inevitably, since we are considering the undermining of cognition by cognition, and its reconstruction.

Integration

Traumatic experience, broadly conceived, undermines conditions of action. The conflict may be resolvable, depending on many factors and circumstances. Resolution requires a single frame of reference in which, first, danger and safety are acknowledged, and secondly, the world is construed as, on balance, safe enough. As already discussed, in the absence of such a meta-frame, there remains a split between two conflicting systems of representation, affect and behaviour. The two systems run in parallel, without communication between them. In particular, the fear that the world is as experienced in the trauma remains split off from the expectation and evidence to the contrary. In this way the fear persists, notwithstanding subsequent experience that may contradict it.

Change in these circumstances is, needless to say, not easy to achieve. It is necessary to distinguish between kinds of change. As implied throughout this discussion, we characteristically find in psychological disorder conflicting systems of cognition, affect, and behaviour. The conflict is generally between what is tolerable and what is intolerable. Shifts between these states of mind, more or less rapid, constitute what may be called first-order change. Second-order change, by contrast, requires integration, and is more difficult to achieve. It requires dismantling of defences, whether these be simple avoidance, or more subtle mental strategies. With this dismantling, the feared outcome is realized, namely, threat to core assumptions about the self and its relation to reality. These core assumptions have to be adjusted to take account of, to make sense of and predict, what before was denied or distorted. A new and better theory is required. The kind of change required here is akin to what occurs in scientific theory, when under the weight of anomalies, and on condition that a more powerful theory can be constructed, it shifts from one paradigm to another.

8.3 INTENTIONAL CAUSALITY AND DISORDER

8.3.1 Introduction: threats to the integrity of intentional causality

In the previous section possible intentional origins of psychological disorder were considered in relation to representation, cognition, motivation, and action. Our method was essentially philosophical and psychological. We pursue now the same issues taking our discussion of chapters 5, 6, and 7 as a starting point. We will, in effect, press our account of intentional causality and show that it leads to similar proposals as those of the previous section, and further supports the convergence of accounts from epistemology and philosophy of mind on the one hand, and biology and development on the other.

It was evident in our earlier discussion that where intentional causal processes are wired in then elements are likely to be harmoniously linked. Provided the environment remains roughly that in which the organism evolved, representation and action will be possible. Humans are physiologically adapted to a narrow range of environmental conditions, but they possess the capacity to devise a wide range of strategies for action, and hence are able to live in very varied environments. The possession of multiple and acquired internalized rules for action, which may be matched to contrasting environmental demands, has therefore been of considerable survival value. However, with the capacity to acquire rules of perception, thought, and action, there has arisen the possibility that the operation of intentional-causal processes will not be smooth. In contrast to non-intentional causality, the elements of intentional-causal processes that we specified in Chapter 5 do not necessarily work in harmony. This point may be obscured where the process is biochemical or physiological, because the elements are not acquired or multiple. There is also a dramatic difference in the time periods over which the intentional processes of biochemistry and physiology, and those of the child, develop. If we assume that the efficient function of an intentional-causal sequence in a physiological system has evolved over several million years, then the learning of new rules for perceptions and actions over hours, days, months, or even a few years, may seem to be a precarious truncation of the process!

In the next sections we examine some of the ways in which the elements of intentional causality might not be in harmony, and hence give rise to psychological disorder. Our discussion is derived directly from that of Chapter 5. We need only take the features of intentional causality as seen in biological processes generally and ask what will happen if these are inappropriate, contradictory, or in competition.

First, there are those conditions in which accurate representation and action are incompatible. We ask what will be the consequences when accurate representation does not create the grounds for action, and what are the consequences if accuracy of perception must be sacrificed for action to take place? Just as when we took a philosophical starting point, we are interested in coping and psychological survival in the face of severe adversity and trauma. Secondly, there are risks arising from the requirement that internalized sets of rules should be both sufficiently general that they may inform action in different circumstances, and sufficiently differentiated that they can distinguish among different environmental demands. Thirdly, acquired internalized rules require stability if they are to inform action, and need to be available to revision in the light of experience. Threats to the integrity of representation and action will arise where either there is insufficient stability or there are conditions under which testing is not possible. Finally, intentional processes may be threatened where the monitoring and metarepresentational capacity is undermined. Each of the first three types of threat may be so persistent and pervasive that this more radical breakdown occurs, or there may be a direct assault on the basic sense of self and the experience of the external world.

8.3.2 Incompatibility between representation and action

Take first the requirement that representation is in the service of action. This is unlikely to contain a contradiction provided that accurate perceptions and effective actions have evolved together in harmony with the needs of the organism. As we have seen, problems arise where events in the outside world do not fall within the range of representations that an organism is able to link to action; for instance, where a threat is so great that neither fight or flight are possible. Then the alternatives are either that the animal reprocesses the threat as falling within the usual scope of representation and action, or that action is not possible. A further possibility arises where the individual is capable of generating multiple representations. This is seen in animals, especially non-human primates, but to a much greater extent in humans, and we have reviewed in Chapter 7 the flexible and creative potential of such a capability in activities such as play. There exists then in human development the possibility that this capacity for multiple representations will provide a means of coping with trauma and other circumstances under which action is not possible. The child may cope by generating two representations, one which omits reference to the threat but is compatible with action, and the other which includes the threat and the accompanying thoughts and emotions and is split off in the mind so that it does not underpin action. There is then the scope for an inaccurate representation which is compatible with action, and an accurate representation that is incompatible with action. Having considered this possibility in detail earlier in relation to post-empiricist theory of knowledge, we encounter it now as a risk pursuant on the freeing-up of elements of intentional causality in human development. The evolutionary perspective enables us to see clearly how dangerous this could be. For children, psychological and physical survival depends upon the capacity to act in relation to caregivers. Actions will need to preserve close contact with those who might provide for the child, and this will be straightforward if the representations of the behaviours of the caregivers are compatable with these actions. But suppose they are not. Suppose the perceptions of the child are of neglect, hostility, or physical or sexual abuse. How is the child to act and still retain the link with caregivers? The child has a need to be looked after, and to find a reasonably tolerable emotional state, but accurate perception reveals something different.

Then there is the possibility of an undermining of the flow of intentional causal sequences with a consequent inability to act, or incoherence of action. We have referred already to the possibility that this may contribute to some clinical pictures, but it is also evident in development. The study of infants with their caregivers in the Strange Situation Test (Ainsworth *et al.* 1978) has indicated that most have a strategy in their relating; that is to say they act in ways that are related systematically to the behaviours of their parents. A minority, comprised predominantly of those who come from families at risk for mental health or parenting problems, show a different pattern. Their behaviours with their parents are characterized by sudden cessation of actions, freezing, and actions that are contradictory either together or in sequence. The behaviours of the parents of these infants have been described as unpredictable or frightening (Main and Hesse 1990). The context is that the infant is with the person who, above all others, should be a source of protection and care, but who is also frightening. The consequence of the preservation of accuracy of perception is an undermining of the conditions of action.

It seems from the evidence so far that this 'disorganized' attachment pattern does not generally persist beyond infancy, and is replaced by others in which actions are possible. The evidence from non-human primates is that in a competition between accuracy of perception and the need for care, the latter will prevail. Baby monkeys will cling to surrogate 'mothers' that punish them (Harlow 1961) and children have often been observed to continue to seek comfort and care from parents who reject them (Bowlby 1969). If we assume that representations of some kind are required for these actions to take place, then they must omit whatever information is incompatable with the actions. It might be argued that this information could simply be forgotten, but the act of forgetting some specific items of information is likely also to entail their representation. Not only that, but there will be required the mental effort of making sure that this information is not used in the regulation of action. Put simply, the forgetting of painful and frightening information is probably not an option. Thus in effect there are established two different sets of internalized rules, one that preserves accuracy but does not meet the needs of the individual, and one that sacrifices accuracy but allows those needs to be met, both in terms of personal comfort and the survival of the relationship with key caregivers. It is likely that the one that meets some needs will prevail, whereas the other is predominantly non-operative. The non-operative perceptions, affects, and cognitions will then be unconscious, untested, and in contradiction to those that underpin actions. It will be evident that where this mechanism applies, the task of the overarching agency, of the self, or representer of representations, will be made particularly complex because of the contradictions between the schemata. Contradictions between representations, especially partial representations, will provide important examples of possible sources of disruption of functioning.

We return, then, to an analysis which is similar to that of the previous section, albeit via a somewhat different route. We find ourselves again, in some respects, in agreement with Melanie Klein's view that the child may separate representations which, broadly speaking, may be 'good' or 'bad'; while not espousing her particular developmental account. Here the inactivation of a representation of some aspects of the environment, in order to permit action, arises as a prediction from the operation of intentional-causal processes.

How might such inactivated representations operate? Suppose the accurate perception is 'I am being abused' there will be many associated perceptions such as 'I am in pain', 'I am angry', 'I am helpless'. If the relationships of the child demand that these are not acknowledged, then they cannot provide the basis for action, and it is likely that they will be maintained out of consciousness, and will not be available for testing that might establish their truth and their range of applicability. It is then possible that such a constellation of beliefs and emotions may be activated later, perhaps by events or people that in some way resemble the original, and then they may intrude into the life of the individual. The extent of generalization, the lack of relationship with the severity of the precipitating event, and the subjective experience of intrusion will arise from the extent to which this state of mind has been kept separate and untested. Pain, hopelessness, and helplessness erupting in this way might lead to an episodic disorder such as depression. This proposal assumes that the observing capacity of the self remains relatively intact. That is to say, the individual reports the intrusion into the continuity of his/her life. Often this is the case in depression where the state of mind is experienced as different from the person's usual self, unwanted, something that is suffered. Those elements of self, of the identification with, and commitment to, the depressed state of mind are lacking. The observing capacity retains its contact with that prior to the episode, and encounters a state of mind which is experienced as unfamiliar.

Repetition of traumatic experiences, especially in childhood, might lead to a rather different state of affairs which may have implications for the integrity of the self. We saw in Chapter 6 that the self probably develops out of a combination of innate capabilities and the repetition and generalization of emotional states, perceptions, and actions across situations and over time. This in turn allows for a benign diversity of states of mind and behaviours that may vary considerably but do not contradict or undermine each other. If, however, the young child's experiences require a repeated splitting of perceptions, thoughts, and emotional states, then what is split off may become a representational framework with so great a generality and commitment that it resembles that of the self. Nevertheless it will remain split off from the 'day to day' self. Here then, is a possible mechanism for intrusions into the activity of the self which are not apparent from the individual's perspective because there is a different observing agent. Those close to the individual often refer to 'Jekyll and Hyde' or to 'two people', and for the individual one state of mind and accompanying behaviours is strikingly inaccessible from the other. Here the commitment to, and conviction of the rightness of, each is very strong. Examples might include outbursts of relatively unprovoked violence, the rapid changes of state of mind of 'borderline' functioning (Chapter 9), and some types of psychotic episodes.

8.3.3 The generalization and differentiation of representations

Our second possible mechanism is derived from a consideration of the extent of generalization and differentiation of rules of perception, thought, and action. As we have seen, this changes with development. The young infant is responsive to human faces in general, but at around 9 months he/she makes a very sharp distinction between familiar adults (attachment figures) and strangers. However, this is not rigid, and the infant acquires new attachment figures through interaction and familiarity. The recognition of the difference between relating to special people and others underpins relationships throughout life. Similarly, the ability to judge the different interpersonal requirements of settings such as parties, job interviews, or funerals is crucial to effective social functioning. This requires sets of rules of sufficient generality that they may provide a guide for action under these different conditions, and sufficient differentiation that they are able to support appropriate behaviour. Difficulties may arise where there is either too restricted a range, or overgeneralization of the representations.

Clearly overgeneralization may simply arise from faulty learning. Fear or salivation may be elicited by association with conditioned stimuli that are, in themselves, not threatening nor nutritious. Such conditions should be open to relatively straightforward corrective action. Equally, overgeneralization may appear as a strategy in order to cope with difficult circumstances. Take the dilemma of the child for whom accuracy and need are in conflict, in relation to parents. If the representation that has to do with emotional needs is widened to include other adults, then potentially some further needs may be met. This is seen in some children who are insecurely attached, and in particular in children who have been in institutions where there have been many caretakers (Hodges and Tizard 1989). Here the overgeneralization may be linked clearly to survival, and may not be open to such ready revision. Such an overgeneralization may have consequences for the accurate perception of the differences between different relationships, and varied social circumstances.

Sets of rules, or schemata, that are too narrow may have implications for the development of the self and the metarepresentational systems. As we have seen, generalizations of a sense of agency and of affects are likely to be crucial mechanisms in the development of the self. In the case of affects this will require a reciprocal process. Joy is experienced with different people in relation to different joint frameworks but is the same experience, thus supporting the continuity of the sense of self (Stern 1985). Experiences of sorrow may be linked in similar fashion. However, crucially, there will also be required the sense of self that is capable either of joy or of sorrow. This may be provided by other indicators of continuity, such as continuity of a sense of agency and memory. However, where the child's experiences are predominantly of a narrow range of affective states, and where only these affective states are reinforced or permitted in the family, then these may generalize to the point where the self and its narrow range of emotional states are closely identified. If we assume that a priority for the self is ensuring the conditions for action, problems may arise if these have been clearly identified with a particular restricted constellation of affective states. Circumstances that have implications for emotional states outside this range, such as bereavement, may lead to representations that undermine these conditions, and hence helplessness and possibly depression.

8.3.4 The stability and testing of representations

A further, third, source of disruption of intentional causality may arise if the conditions that sets of rules should both be testable but also relatively enduring are threatened. If they are not testable, they are likely to become inappropriate to the demands of the environment. If they are open continuously to revision, then they will cease to provide a map or model in relation to which testing can take place. As we have seen, the interplay between relatively enduring and general hypotheses and testability is prominent in many theories, including those of Piaget, in relation to cognitive development, and Lakatos, in relation to the development of scientific paradigms. In each of these cases the hypotheses not only provide the bridge with reality, but also the conditions for thought, and for action. During development, children continually test internalized sets of rules concerning beliefs, fears, wishes, and motives. The test may concern the truth of a belief, for instance about the cause of an event. It is common for children to blame themselves for events that have, in fact, been accidents, or have been brought about by adults. Expression of that belief through talking about it, or through play, will be important if it is to be examined. Where a child faces harsh or critical parents, the truth of her beliefs may be particularly difficult to establish. For instance, a child may blame herself for the abuse that a sibling has received. If she is to locate the harm as coming from a parent, this may need to be identified by a trusted adult; however, she will take a risk in seeking to check that perception with the perpetrator, or the other parent. So she may continue to blame herself. Similarly, for the abused child there is often a requirement that the acts be kept secret, so it may be impossible for the child to test the belief 'I am being abused' and so an important truth may not be available to the child. We will return to this issue in the next chapter.

A need for constant revision of expectations is likely to be necessary where the behaviours of parents or other caregivers are inconsistent and unpredictable. Inconsistencies of parenting are common in the families of children with behaviour problems (Patterson 1982). Plans for effective action are then likely to be difficult to establish, and this may be reflected in the high frequency of impulsive and aggressive responses of the children.

8.3.5 The integrity of the metarepresentational system

So far, we have traced possible mechanisms for the disruption of function from contradictions among the elements of intentional causality in human psychological functioning. It seems that the more repeated and generalized these are, the greater the scope for a more radical malfunction of the metarepresentational and organizational agency. However, it is possible that there are routes to disruption that primarily affect this organizing process.

Take first the processes described by Stern (1985) in relation to the development of the self after around 6 months of age. At this stage the infant refers to the parent for guidance as to which set of rules applies, for instance regarding the visual cliff. But what do the infant and mother have to achieve? They have to establish their joint frame of reference, along the lines of 'I (the infant) am asking you a question and need guidance'. And then the content of that communication has to be applied to the task. Of course, the infant cannot check with the parent whether they do have that joint frame of reference because the checking would require that framework. In other words, interactions require an organizing principle that frames them, and establishes their rules, just as do individual states of mind. These are established by metacommunications, which convey what are the rules of social exchange. It is interesting to note that the a priori nature of the statement of the rules often is provided by the explicit or implicit rules of institution, dress, titles, or architecture. These are especially useful where the individuals do not know each other well. Where they do, the metacommunications are likely to be more particular to the relationships.

There will normally be a reciprocal support between the metacommunications and the content of the communications. Thus to take an everyday example, the child stands on the table and checks with the parent whether this is permissible. The parent answers 'no' using the metacommunication (through posture, facial expression, and tone of voice), 'this is serious and I mean it'. The child continues, falls off, and discovers both that the content was correct, and that he had read correctly the rules underpinning his relationship with the parent. Now suppose the parent does not indicate unequivocally that she is serious, perhaps by smiling, or walking out of the room while saying 'no'. Then the child ignores the content but follows the metamessage 'I am not serious' and falls of the table. If he is blamed, then either he has to point out that there was another component to the message (i.e. you did not appear to mean it), or accept what the parent says and deny that component. If the metacommunication has been experienced along the lines of 'I don't care whether you fall off the table' it will remain an unacknowledged hostile element in the relationship. The general point is the same as that considered earlier in relation to split off aspects of individual representations. The child has to find a basis for action in the relationship. If the content and the metacommunication are in conflict, he must choose which to follow, otherwise he has to tolerate contradictory elements in the intentional-causal processes, and this will preclude action. It is likely, with the parent, that he will choose the route that least threatens the relationship, and in this case it is hypothesized to be the one that does not mention a possible lack of care or hostility. Where the majority of exchanges do not contain such contradictions, and where it is clear that angry or hostile emotions can be acknowledged, such interactions are not likely to have a major impact. Where they are repeated then the child may develop split off states of mind of the form 'I hate my mother' which are not accessible or testable.

A second source of disruption to the observing and overarching representational agent may arise from a direct assault. It is likely that this high-invariant agent, or self, contains some general and some core assumptions. These, as our discussion of Stern's work has indicated, are related to the sense of self as having continuity, and to a differentiation of the continuity of the self from that of the external world. In other words, the predictability of the physical world, the world of other people, and of the individual, with their different rhythms, promotes the differentiation into the distinctive sense of self. Crucially, a central assumption is that action is possible. Where elements of intentional-causal processes are contradictory, and hence do not provide the basis for action, elements of that contradiction may be ignored in the service of action. Suppose, however, that action is not possible. Severe trauma may pose a threat to the self because of the break in the continuity of experience, and by creating conditions in which action is not possible. Disasters, such as those seen in football stadia or on ships, entail a breakdown of the predictability of the physical world, of the individual's relationship to it, and of the conditions for action. There has then occurred a break in the basic condition for intentionality. For some individuals a solution may be found in denial that would create or recreate conditions for action, but for many the representation is so powerful that it persists and includes the representation that action was not possible. As we have seen, such a paradoxical representation may provide the basis for the repetitive intrusive thoughts in reaction to trauma. These phenomena are seen also after sustained childhood sexual abuse where usually the child has been helpless, and following bereavement when, at least in relation to one person, action cannot change the circumstances.

8.4 PSYCHOLOGICAL MODELS OF DISORDER AND TREATMENT

8.4.1 Introduction

We are now in a position to explore similarities and differences between the analysis proposed so far in this chapter and current theories of psychological disorder. Our account has not emphasized a particular theoretical framework in psychology and psychiatry. It is not our purpose to do so, nor to attempt to elaborate a new theory. Rather, we have been examining the kind of account of order and disorder that follows from bringing together considerations in the philosophy of mind and knowledge, and in the theory of causal processes in biological systems. Nevertheless, this has led us to a point where it is possible to be quite specific about mechanisms, and the question arises as to the relation of this account to the available theoretical frameworks, of which we consider six briefly below. There is no attempt to do justice to the models, but only to indicate links with the proposals made so far in this chapter.

8.4.2 Conditioning theory

The principles of classical and operant conditioning supported models of various kinds of psychological disorder. Among the most elaborated and important was the formulation of phobic anxiety as a conditioned fear response. Conditioning theories of phobic anxiety invoked intentional processes of the kind described so far in this section, including hypothesized origin in traumatic experience (or in at least repeated, adverse, subtraumatic experiences), inappropriate generalization of fear, avoidance which precludes unlearning, and/or re-experiencing of the original fear in similar situations (Eysenck 1979).

Conditioning models, and particularly the behavioural therapies to which they gave rise, remain important, but generally they have been superseded by more sophisticated theories within the cognitive psychological paradigm outlined in the first chapter (subsection 1.2.2).

8.4.3 Social learning theory

Social learning theory extends conditioning theory by acknowledging social influences on learning, including the acquisition of behaviours by observation of others, and by recognizing cognitive processes in behaviour, including the regulating role of verbally expressed rules (Bandura 1977; Hodgson 1984).

One of the main applications of social learning theory has been to severe and persistent aggressive and disruptive behaviours in children. There is ample evidence that behaviour problems in children often occur against a background of inconsistent parental discipline, a high level of instructions, a high level of criticism or hostility, inadvertent reinforcement of aggressive behaviours, and a lack of explanation of the reason for instructions or reprimands (Patterson 1982). This may lead to a set of internalized rules in which the actions of others are readily construed as aggressive and aggressive responses are seen as appropriate. In studies that made use of videotapes of cartoon characters, young children who had been physically abused and showed high levels of aggressive behaviour, when compared with non-abused, non-aggressive children, construed the actions of the participants as more aggressive, and were more likely to indicate that aggressive solutions to interpersonal encounters were preferable (Dodge *et al.* 1990). This would indicate that the children had stable coherent representations and action plans that were inappropriate. Equally it is possible that inconsistency of experiences will not provide the setting for consistent internalized sets of rules, in which case contradictory schemata might be established along lines described earlier. This process may be more likely where, as Patterson has shown for some parents, discipline is determined by the mood of the parent, rather than the objective characteristics of the behaviour. This will make it difficult for the child to identify under which sets of rules the parental injunction falls. Is it to be understood as a function of the parent's mood, and therefore requiring a response that falls within a general strategy for dealing with mood changes, or is it to be construed as linked to the child's behaviour? In opting for one, the child may leave the other unexpressed, untested, and unexplored.

Interventions based on the teaching of new skills to parents, and thereby creating a setting in which children may acquire new internalized rules for behaviour, have had significant success (Kazdin 1993). These techniques focus also on effective action. It is characteristic of children with aggressive and disruptive behaviours that though they 'act' frequently, they provoke aversive responses from, or frustration by, others. Thus their experience of effective action is low. Parent training techniques place considerable emphasis on the creation by the parents of situations where the child has more control, and hence is able to act effectively; for instance in periods of play in which the parent is encouraged to follow the child's requests. A further way in which the child's experience of being able to act effectively is undermined arises where interactions have become so negative that her helpful or competent behaviours are no longer noticed by the parents. They are not acknowledged to be making an effective contribution to the relationships. The therapeutic approaches help the parents to notice, and then to praise prosocial behaviours. Through the reinforcement of such behaviours they become effective agents of social (inter)action. For some children the restoration in this way of a sense of agency may have important consequences for the recovery of the experience of a coherent self.

8.4.4 Cognitive therapy

Cognitive therapy is based on the assumption that cognition, in the form of beliefs and expectations, has a causal role in the generation of affect and behaviour. This proposal has been applied particularly in models of depression and anxiety (Beck 1976; Beck *et al.* 1986). Cognitions said to be implicated in the generation of depression include such as: 'I will be ineffective at this task, I am generally ineffective', 'Other people are better at doing things than I am', or 'I did not do that well, I don't do things well'. While cognitive therapy is clearly related in some ways to cognitive psychology (Brewin 1988), its scientific basis is not yet clearly elaborated (Teasdale 1993).

Cognitive therapy was developed partly to add value to behaviour therapy. Behaviour therapy confronts cognition with experience: irrational (inappropriate) fear is treated by safe, contained exposure to feared stimuli; depression by promoting activity which may bring satisfaction. Such experiences serve to disconfirm anxious or depressed views of the world, and also as evidence, despite expectations to the contrary, that the person can cope. On the other hand, behavioural methods can fail if a person uses theory to re-construe the relevant experiences. If a person is convinced that he and the world are hopeless, then any experience which seems to contradict this assumption is at risk for being avoided, denied, reconstrued, or rationalized away. Such cognitive manoeuvres fall outside the scope of behavioural intervention, but they are precisely what can be addressed and questioned in cognitive therapy. On the other hand, a possible weakness of cognitive therapeutic intervention at the level of verbally expressed beliefs alone is that it may fail to engage with, make a difference to, the underlying cognitive-affective states. For these sorts of reason, a combination of the two kinds of approach, under the name of cognitive-behavioural therapy, is commonly indicated.

Recently an extension of this idea has been recommended, on the basis of a complex model, in the direction of using active, 'experiential' therapeutic methods, such as those usually associated with Gestalt therapy (Teasdale 1993).

Cognitive therapy focuses on the person's theory of his or her own mental states, through attempting to make explicit underlying assumptions and rules, at first unavailable for self-report. Beck (1976) writes:

> These [cognitive schemata] will operate without the person's being aware of his rulebook. He screens selectively, integrates, and sorts the flow of stimuli and forms his own responses without articulating to himself the rules and concepts that dictate his interpretations and action.

How do these internalized sets of rules explain the disruption of functioning which occurs with the onset of a depressive episode? The theory is that the cognitions have developed prior to the episode and often are unconscious. At some point these sets of rules or schemata are then triggered into action, where they become the predominant set of rules that determine mood and behaviour, resulting in depression. A central assumption in the treatment is that these sets of rules of interpretation of events and other people may not have been tested, and the therapist examines the basis for them jointly with the patient. Therefore in cognitive therapy an explicit link is made between the monitoring and observing capacity of the individual and the therapist. On the basis of the thesis discussed earlier (subsection 8.3.2) it might be expected to be effective only where that observing agency appears to be intact. This is a prediction that remains to be tested.

Cognitive therapy is not much concerned with the origins of maladaptive cognitions, though it is presumably likely that in some cases they have an understandable connection to previous experience. There is, similarly, relatively little attention to the other aspect of the intentionality of maladaptive cognitions, namely, that they may in some cases serve a function. As remarked above (p. 313), maladaptive cognitions, for example in depression, may serve as protection from some greater threat, such as an assault on a valued other.

8.4.5 Psychoanalytic theories

Freud's early career was as a physician, working with neurological disorders which had clear, non-intentional, organic origins (Glymour 1991). He found himself attempting to explain apparently identical conditions for which no organic pathology could be identified. In his therapy of women with hysterical conversion syndromes Freud sought to establish whether an intentional account might be found for a disruption of functioning, which to the person and to an observer appeared intrusive and lacking in intentionality. He concluded that the activity of unconscious wishes which for much of the individual's life had been maintained inactive could provide an explanation (Izenberg 1991). Furthermore, the conflict between the conscious representation, and the separate unconscious representations created the conditions in which action was not possible, and hence paralysis.

The general principles underlying this proposal include ones that we have considered earlier in this chapter, such as the preparedness to invoke intentional states in explanation of disorder, departure from (Cartesian) common sense by not restricting intentionality to what is available to consciousness and expressed in self-report, and recognition that some intentional states constitute the core of belief to be protected from counter-evidence at any cost, including sacrifice of perceptions of reality or aspects of the self.

Psychoanalytic theories, and especially that of Freud, have been criticized for using a nineteenth-century hydraulic model of the effect of unconscious processes. This is seen to attribute qualities of force and energy inappropriately to brain states which might be better understood in terms of information-processing. While it is quite evident that information-processing is going on, intentionality entails also the registering of what matters to the organism, especially in its emotional charge, and action in avoiding or countering threat, or achieving a goal. The concepts of force and energy capture graphically what it is that energizes the response of the organism, whether animal or person. Furthermore, they provide pointers to the implications of conditions under which these states of mind and actions are disallowed. When we consider that the disallowing or splitting off of representations together with their very powerful emotions may have arisen in the context of painful, frightening, and immobilizing experiences, then their psychological impact when they are reactivated may be best described in the language of force and energy. Such an activation of a set of unconscious, untested, unintegrated, beliefs, wishes, and fears is likely to be experienced as intrusive, uncontrollable, and not understandable, in the same way as a physical (non-intentional) disruption of functioning. It seems then that Freud saw how intentional processes could, while remaining intentional, lead to causal pathways that produce phenomena with the same form as those arising from non-intentional origins, and hence apparently share their force, energy, and lack of intentionality.

The importance of early interpersonal experiences in psychological development was argued for by Melanie Klein (1946), and subsequent object-relations theorists. Klein's proposition that representations may be split into good and bad, and that if these are not in contact with each other there is a price to be paid, is a form of explanation that is highly compatible with a consideration of the consequences of threats to intentionality. However, and with hindsight perhaps surprisingly, Klein assumes that this is the basic universal human condition in early infancy which is 'cured' by good parenting. The evidence, which we reviewed briefly in Chapter 6, would suggest that infants possess substantial integrative capabilities from birth, and that disorder is more likely to arise from threats to the integrity of intentionality. Notwithstanding this difference, both analyses lead to the conclusion that parents, or other committed caregivers, are important to the developmental processes whereby a child comes to represent reasonably accurately key aspects of the external world, and his/her own internal world, and to elaborate appropriate and effective actions. In the absence of such development there arise the risks of inaccurate or partial representations, for instance where aspects of reality are split off, and an unintegrated and therefore more unpredictable and frightening mental life. This explicit linking of accuracy of representation of the external world and integration of mental life is clearly consistent with our previous considerations of epistemology and intentional-causal processes.

Winnicott (1971) also belonged to the object-relations school of psychoanalysis and his writings continue to exert a powerful influence on psychoanalytic theory. We find in them glimpses of ideas rather than an explicit and overarching framework. Two particular aspects of his work illuminate a consideration of function and dysfunction. He proposed, using extremely confusing terminology, that the infant needs to make the move in development from 'relating to' an object to 'using' an object. Roughly speaking, this means that the child ceases to need to control the other person, normally the parent, and becomes able to have a more mature multifaceted connection that is intimate but not controlling. The route is via an attack on the person, that he/she survives. Although Winnicott does not use the same language, he is referring to the testing of internalized schemata of the form 'I fear that my aggression is too dangerous for you', 'I will be rejected if I show aggression', 'I fear you will retaliate if I show aggression'. The survival of the parents, the lack of retaliation, and the absence of rejection provide containment for the child through the creation of a sense of safety. In addition, they may be seen to serve the function of contributing to the frame in which multiple, and often anxiety-provoking representations may be explored. They have the quality of commitment, and stating 'here are the boundaries', that are needed in order to promote the development of the metarepresentational system, the self. Put another way, the parent is a source of certainty and of what has to be to some extent just asserted, in order to provide a framework in which uncertainty and multiple rules of interpretation and action can be explored. The containment offered by parents has both an emotional and an epistemological function.

Winnicott's emphasis on the role of play has similar implications. He refers to play as taking place in a 'transitional space', that is to say in a domain of experience that is neither subjective and therefore unconnected to reality, nor objective and therefore representational of reality. In play crucial issues are explored with intensity and in detail, but without the consequences that would occur in the real world. These issues concern sex, loss, death, aggression, fears, wishes, and adult roles. Here the representations and their implications for action can be given life within the containing boundary of the 'this is play' metacognitions and communications. One side of a conflict, such as that concerning love and hate for a parent, may be worked out to the point of action, in the knowledge that the consequences may be enacted but will not actually ensue. This might entail a benign form of splitting in order to explore the consequence of the actions, but within a containing frame. Thus in Winnicott's theory play provides another epistemological and emotional container for the development, explanation, and testing of sets of rules and representations.

8.4.6 Family systems theories

The theories that we have considered thus far take as their starting point that disruption of function has taken place, and that this is the individual's problem. Family therapy has in some respects proposed that this is a case of mistaken identity. We say 'in some respects' because currently there is a wide diversity of emphases in family therapy (Hoffman 1982; Boscolo *et al.* 1987), and some will not be captured in this brief overview.

A major influence on the analysis of psychological problems has come from systems theory and the work of Gregory Bateson (1971). It is agreed that disruption of function is a key issue, but that the disruption is only apparent. By analogy with the physician who may ascribe a tachycardia to the effects of altitude, systems theory and family therapy have led therapists to examine further sources of intentionality within a person's context. For instance, a person may suffer from depression and there may be no apparent precipitants in the form of life events that involve loss or threat. We may then look for an agent that might have disrupted function, or for the intrusion of affective/cognitive representations along the lines described earlier. A family systems approach might lead to an interview with the family, in which the pattern of relationships prior to the depression and after its onset provide the focus for investigation. Take the example of a woman in her thirties who is married with children. It might be that her own mother had been widowed and that the depression provided a focus for the maternal grandmother's care for the patient, and hence brought them closer, without overtly challenging the marriage between the patient and her spouse. This would not provide an explanation of the intentionality of the origin of the depression, but would suggest that its maintenance was linked to the family relationships. The depression that had been seen previously as malfunction would then be 'reframed' as forming an important component of the family functioning. The behaviour is therefore seen to come under a different set of rules from that which the patient and the family first envisaged. Previously these rules, approximating to 'she is ill' placed the action in the hands of the physician, whereas under the new sets of rules, which include the question of how to care for the mother and preserve the marriage, the possible actions are in the hands of the family members. The family systems model can be widened in order to emphasize, that, before it is assumed that intentionality has run out, many contexts will need to be examined. However, the application of systems theory to therapy has a major difference from the analysis presented in this chapter in that it does not have a theory of breakdown. It is claimed that all apparent disorder may be analysed in terms of context. Whether this is the case is an empirical issue; however, at this stage it seems unlikely that such a position will be tenable. Serious individual psychological dysfunction can be substantial and seen across many contexts, each of which no doubt creates the setting for the disturbed behaviour, but also to which that individual contributes significantly.

Although family therapy has generally stopped short of an attempt to understand the implications of family functioning for the individual's development, different schools of family therapy have focused on some of the features of intentional causality that we have described. Much early interest centred on the origins of schizophrenia and the role of double-bind communications (Bateson *et al.* 1956). Bateson argued that communication has a content and a frame (metacommunication) and if the recipient is not to be confused, these must be congruent. Where they are contradictory and there is an implied prohibition on accurately reading one of the elements of the contradiction, then the participants will be confused. Bateson suggested that some symptoms of schizophrenia might represent attempts to bring order to the confusion, for instance through the generation of a clear fixed delusional belief, and others might reflect the confusion, for instance in the disturbed logic of formal thought disorder. This is close to our discussion of the possible impact on the developing child of confusing and contradictory communications, with implications for the integration of states of mind and the self (subsection 8.3.5; cf. also the discussion at the end of subsection 1.4.3). However Bateson's theory was expressed in terms of an attempted solution to current relationship difficulties, rather than a developmental process. His theory of schizophrenia is almost certainly incorrect. However, subsequent family systems approaches, especially those of the 'Milan School' have analysed family functioning in terms of communication deviance (Palazzoli *et al.* 1978), and have derived interventions that have been designed to lead to clarity.

Another 'school' has placed emphasis on the organization of the family (Minuchin 1974; Minuchin and Fishman 1981). Presenting problems are analysed in terms of current relationships, and are postulated to arise where the patient occupies a position that is inappropriate to his/her developmental stage and that of the family. For instance, in the example of the depressed woman, her role as mother of young children might have been taken over by the grandmother, leaving the mother functioning more like one of the children than a parent. The maintenance of the depression might then be seen to be related to this position in the family, and the solution might be for the mother to regain some of her role. This approach emphasizes the importance of family structure for children, and therefore addresses containment in development in a way that has points of contact with approaches based on psychoanalytic and social learning theory.

Recent developments in family therapy have included the system of the family and therapist in the analysis (Boscolo *et al.* 1987; McNamee and Gergen 1992). This has therefore moved away from a description of the intentionality of the presenting problem, to one that addresses behaviours seen in therapy. This is clearly related to an issue that arises in all psychotherapeutic approaches, namely one of the identity of the metaframe. As an observer I may be able to identify the frame and set of rules within which a person is functioning; however, when I engage in the therapeutic relationship a joint frame must be established. This, after all, will provide the container in which different representations of actions may be explored. In doing this, however, the therapist enters the frame that he/she is attempting to understand. Family therapists have for a long time made use of one-way screens and teams of observers in an attempt to commentate from the outside, but of course at the point where such groupings also participate in the therapeutic process the same considerations will apply. While it is the case that in order to understand the intentionality of behaviour within therapy it will be important to include the metarules of that engagement, including the role of therapist variables such as age, gender, and professional identity, our analysis would predict that behaviours seen in therapy can also be understood in relation to individual and family biography. The therapeutic task then is one of determining which sets of rules, representations, and actions are most relevant.

8.4.7 Attachment theory

Attachment theory (Bowlby 1969) differs from those discussed so far in that it has not developed in relation to psychological treatments. However, some of the research findings, to which we referred also in subsection 8.3.2, are of direct relevance to the issue of the intentional explanation of disorder. Infants who have been been assessed as 'secure', and those who have displayed behaviour that may be classified 'insecure avoidant' and 'insecure ambivalent' appear to have a coherent strategy with respect to attachment. It is not clear whether these insecure patterns have implications for subsequent disorder. On the one hand, they do not appear to be adaptive ways of dealing with distress and it is possible that, with repetition, lack of containment and splitting along the lines that we have outlined might occur. Equally there may be sufficient flexibility for change. A third 'disorganized' insecure category may signify already at 12 months of age an organization of internalized representations which has the intrusive and unpredictable qualities that we have associated with disorder. Infants in this group are described as showing sequential displays of contradictory behaviour patterns, especially on reunion with the parent. Examples include 'immediately following strong proximity seeking and a bright full greeting with raised arms, the infant moves to the wall or into the centre of the room and stills or freezes with a "dazed" expression' (Main and Solomon 1990). Disorganized infants are described as also showing simultaneous displays of contradictory behaviour patterns. An infant approaches her mother 'by moving backward towards on her stomach, face averted'. It seems that either in sequence, or simultaneously these infants show behaviours that reflect incompatible, intrusive representations. Each may separately preserve the conditions for action; however, 'freezing' or 'dazed expressions' lasting for 20 seconds or more, even while being held by a parent, are common. Thus it seems that the conditions for action here are not maintained. The category 'disorganized' is common in high-risk groups, especially where there has been maltreatment (Main and Hesse 1990). The developmental path of disorganized infants is of great interest to the account proposed here, in that often it is replaced at 4 or 5 years of age by a 'controlling' pattern. This is characterized by taking control of interactions with the parent through bossing her about, insulting her, or controlling through caregiving (Cassidy and Marvin 1991; Wartner *et al.* 1994). It seems that in these children the imperative to act has taken over, but at the expense of reciprocity and of receipt of care in the relationship. It is likely that representations of the unpredictable or frightening parental behaviours are now inactivated or split off.

Parental attachment representations can be assessed using the Adult Attachment Interview Schedule (Main and Hesse 1990). This yields a classification of 'secure autonomous', 'insecure dismissing', 'insecure preoccupied', 'insecure unresolved with respect to loss or trauma'. The ratings are made on the basis of the way in which the adult describes relationships with his or her own parents in childhood. The secure autonomous account is characterized by significant realistic detail, emotional content that does not become overwhelming, and a capacity to reflect on experiences. The insecure dismissing category is characterized by brief and emotionally neutral descriptions, and the insecure preoccupied by long, emotionally entangled accounts. The unresolved category is rated where there is a lack of coherence of the account, lapses in the metacognitive monitoring of reasoning processes or of the process of the discourse, or where the account is derailed by the intensity of emotion, associated with loss or trauma. Here then, the research instrument has taken the intrusion into the account, and disruption of the observing capacity, to which we have attached great importance, as the key to the rating. Studies of mothers and infants have shown a strong association between this unresolved category and the disorganized infant status, which suggests that adults who are prone to such intrusions and failures of metarepresentations may, as parents, behave in ways that contribute to similar development in their children (Ward 1990; Ward and Carlson 1995). Recent attachment research has therefore provided an indication of the role of intrusive disruptive internalized sets of rules in relation to adverse childhood experiences, and this provides a promising avenue for the understanding of the intentional basis of psychiatric disorder.

8.5 SUMMARY

In this chapter we have considered explanation of psychological disorder in terms of intentional processes. We approached the problem in two ways, first, in Section 8.2, as it were top-down, via consideration of the logic of representation, and secondly, in Section 8.3, as it were bottom-up, by considering conditions of intentionality in biological systems. We noted in subsection 8.2.1 that radical error in intentionality is a matter of persistent misrepresentation or persistent rule-conflict, and that these admit of psychological explanation in terms of avoidance and re-enactment of unacceptable outcomes. This idea was taken up and explored at some length in subsection 8.2.2. The broad notion of trauma and the cognitive paradoxes to which it gives rise was approached from the direction of post-empiricist epistemology (pp. 305–6), and via Wittgenstein's early work on the limits of thought (pp. 306–7). Reference was then made to post-traumatic stress reactions, to be taken up in the next chapter. Along with the notion of threat to psychic integrity comes the notion of psychic defences, and this was explored in subsection 8.2.3, using two quite different sources. First, analogy with threats to scientific theory, relatively open to view and well understood. And secondly, with reference to psychoanalytic theory, where the psychic defences have been first identified and explained. Several defences were discussed (pp. 308–11), including simple denial, splitting, projection, and narcissism. More intellectualized defences, and intellectualization of the primitive defences, become possible in the context of an explicit theory of mind (pp. 311–12). Defences typically entail costs as well as benefits, and in the special case of psychic defences these costs involve perpetual movement between avoidance and re-enactment. In this paradoxical sense the problem coincides with the solution (pp. 312–14).

From a biological perspective it was evident that where rules of interpretation are wired in, or there is limited scope for the acquisition of new representations, events that fall outside the range of the rules that are able to underpin action are not recognized as such, or lead to disorganized action or inaction. The position is different where multiple sets of rules of intentional processes can be generated. The elaboration of these intentional processes in psychological and social development, seen most dramatically in childhood, provides the basis for flexible, intelligent, and creative development. The integrity of intentional processes is, however, no longer guaranteed. The child may cope with trauma and other threats in development through the creation of contradictory representations, some that are accurate but cannot underpin action, and others that are inaccurate but lead to action, and especially action that retains crucial relationships with adults (subsection 8.3.2). This creates the possibility of internal disruptions of the integrity of intentional processes and hence intentional origins of psychological disorder. Further mechanisms include the generation of mental representations that are either insufficiently differentiated or too narrow (subsection 8.3.3), representations that are either lacking in sufficient stability or unavailable for testing and revision (8.3.4), and a metarepresentational system that is unable to monitor and integrate individual and interpersonal processes (8.3.5).

In Section 8.4 the nature of explanations of disorder in a range of theoretical, research, and therapeutic frameworks was discussed in the light of the operation and disruption of intentional processes.

REFERENCES

Ainsworth, M. D., Blehar, M. C., Waters, E., and Wall, S. (1978). *Patterns of attachment*. Erlbaum, Hillsdale, NJ.

Bandura, A. (1977). *Social learning theory*. Prentice Hall, Englewood Cliffs, NJ.

Bateson, G. (1971). *Steps to an ecology of mind*. Ballentine, New York.

Bateson, G., Jackson, D., Haley, J., and Weakland, J. (1956). Toward a theory of schizophrenia. *Behavioural Science*, 1, 251–64.

Beck, A. T. (1976). *Cognitive therapy and the emotional disorders*. International Universities Press, New York.

Beck, A. T., Emery, G., and Greenber, R. C. (1986). *Anxiety disorders and phobias: a cognitive perspective*. Basic Books, New York.

Boscolo, L., Cecchin, G., Hoffman, L., and Penn, P. (1987). *Milan systemic family therapy: conversations in theory and practice*. Basic Books, New York.

Bowlby, J. (1969). *Attachment and loss:I. Attachment*. Hogarth Press, London.

Breuer, J. and Freud, S. (1985). *Studies in hysteria*. Standard Edition 2, (1964). Hogarth Press, London.

Brewin, C. (1988). *Cognitive foundations of clinical psychology*. Lawrence Erlbaum Associates, London.

Byng-Hall, J. (1973). Family myths used as defence in conjoint family therapy. *British Journal of Medical Psychology*, 46, 239–49.

Cassidy, J. and Marvin, R. S., with the Working Group of the John D. and Catherine T. MacArthur Foundation on the Transition from Inancy to Early Childhood (1991). Attachment organization in three- and four-year olds: coding guidelines. Unpublished manuscript, University of Virginia, Charlottesville.

Dodge, K. A., Bates, J. E., and Pettit, G. S. (1990). Mechanisms in the cycle of violence. *Science*, 250, 1678–83.

Eysenck, H. (1979). The conditioning model of neurosis. *The Behavioral and Brain Sciences*, 2, 155–99.

Freud, A. (1936). *The ego and the mechanisms of defence*. International Universities Press, New York.

Freud, S. (1914). *On narcissism: an introduction*. Standard Edition 14, (1957), pp. 73–102. Hogarth Press, London.

Fulford, K. W. M. (1989). *Moral theory and moral practice*. Cambridge University Press, Cambridge.

Gardner, S. (1993). *Irrationality and the philosophy of psychoanalysis*. Cambridge University Press, Cambridge.

Glymour, C. (1991). Freud's Androids. In *The Cambridge companion to Freud*, (ed. J. Neu), pp. 44–85. Cambridge University Press, Cambridge.

Harlow, H. F. (1961). The development of affectional patterns in infant monkeys. In *Determinants of infant behaviour*, (ed. B. M. Foss), Vol. 1. Methuen, London.

Hilgard, E. (1977/1986). Divided consciousness: multiple controls in human thought and action. Wiley, New York. (Expanded edition 1986.)

Hodges, J. and Tizard, B. (1989). IQ and behavioural adjustment of ex-institutional adolescents. *Journal of Child Psychology and Psychiatry*, 30, 53–75.

Hodgson, R. (1984). Social learning theory. In *The scientific principles of psycho-pathology*, (ed. P. McGuffin, M. Shanks, and R. Hodgson), pp. 361–82. Academic Press, London.

Hoffman, L. (1982) *Foundations of family therapy*. Basic Books, New York.

Izenberg, G. N. (1991). Seduced and abandoned. The rise and fall of Freud's seduction theory. In *The Cambridge companion to Freud*, (ed. J. Neu), pp. 25–43. Cambridge University Press, Cambridge.

Kazdin, A. E. (1993). The treatment of conduct disorder: progress and directions in psychotherapy research. *Development and Psychopathology*, 5, 277–310.

Klein, M. (1946). Notes on some schizoid mechanisms. *International Journal of Psychoanalysis*, 27, 99–110.

Lakatos, I. (1970). Falsification and the methodology of scientific research programmes. In *Criticism and the growth of knowledge*, (ed. I. Lakatos and A. Musgrave), pp. 91–196. Cambridge University Press, Cambridge.

McNamee, S. and Gergen, K. (1992). *Therapy as a social construction*. Sage, London.

Main, M. and Hesse, P. (1990). Lack of resolution of mourning in adulthood and its relationship to infant disorganization: some speculations regarding causal mechanisms. In *Attachment in the preschool years*, (ed. M. Greenberg, D. Cicchetti, and E. M. Cummings), pp. 161–82. University of Chicago Press, Chicago.

Main, M. and Solomon, J. (1990). Procedures for identifying infants as disorganized/disorientated during the Ainsworth Strange Situation. In *Attachment in the preschool years*, (ed. M. Greenberg, D. Cicchetti, and E. M. Cummings), pp. 161–82. University of Chicago Press, Chicago.

Minuchin, S. (1974). *Families and family therapy*. Harvard University Press, Cambridge, Mass.

Minuchin, S. and Fishman, H. C. (1981). *Family therapy techniques*. Harvard University Press, Cambridge, Mass.

Palazzoli, S., Boscolo, L., Cecchin, G., and Prata, G. (1978). *Paradox and counter-paradox*. Jason Aronson, New York.

Patterson, G. R. (1982). *Coercive family process*. Castalia, Eugene, OR.

Power, M. and Brewin, C. (1991). From Freud to cognitive science: a contemporary account of the unconscious. *British Journal of Clinical Psychology*, 30, 289–310.

Sandler, J. (ed.) (1988). *Projection, identification, projective identification*. Karnac Books, London.

Stern, D. N. (1985). *The interpersonal world of the infant*. Basic Books, New York.

Teasdale, J. (1993). Emotion and two kinds of meaning: cognitive therapy and applied cognitive science. *Behaviour Research and Therapy*, 31, 339–54.

Ward, M. J. (1990). Predicting infant–mother attachment from adolescent mother's prenatal working models of relationships. Paper presented at the International conference on Infant Studies, Montreal, Canada.

Ward, M. J. and Carlson, E. A. (1995). Associations among adult attachment representations, maternal sensitivity, and infant–mother attachment in a sample of adolescent mothers. *Child Development*, **66**, 69–79.

Wartner, U. G., Grossman, K., Fremmer–Bombik, E., and Suess, G. (1994). Attachment patterns at age six in South Germany: predictibility from infancy and implications for preschool behaviour. *Child Development*, **65**, 1014–27.

Winnicott, C. (1971). *Playing and reality*. Basic Books, New York.

Wittgenstein, L. (1921). *Tractatus logico-philosophicus*. (Trans. Pears, D. F. and McGuiness, B. F. (1961) Routledge and Kegan Paul, London).

9
Psychiatric conditions

9.1 INTRODUCTION

We are now in a position to take further our consideration of causal processes in biology and psychology in relation to disorder. The purpose of this is to outline the way in which these causal processes might operate. Emphasis will be on causal routes for which there is good evidence. Where the evidence does not point strongly in any particular direction, we shall rely on theory and some speculation. After all, if this enterprise is to be useful or valid, it should be able to go beyond the evidence. We shall consider three kinds of syndrome: schizophrenia; anxiety disorders, mainly obsessive-compulsion and post-traumatic stress disorder; and personality disorder. We have selected these, obviously not with any aim of covering all of psychopathology, but because they illustrate various kinds of issue in the explanation of disorder. Schizophrenia has been addressed by all, or most, orientations in psychiatry and clinical psychology, with theories about it from practically every point of view, invoking non-intentional- and intentional-causal pathways of various kinds. The task is set, therefore, of assessing which are valid and how they hang together. Obsessive-compulsive disorder is less researched, but it has the special interest of suggesting alternative aetiological models, one of which emphasizes intentionality while the other posits non-intentional-causal pathways. Post-traumatic stress disorder is included because of the clarity of its intentionality, its relation to environmental stressors, which is indeed (unusually) built into the definition of the disorder. The relatively transparent nature of post-traumatic stress reactions may serve as a partial model for more obscure problems, as will be discussed. Personality disorder represents both a problem and an opportunity for research and clinical practice. The problem arises from the attempt to encompass the complexity of personality functioning in diagnostic categories, and the opportunity from the recognition of the role of the person in our understanding of psychiatric disturbance. This demands an analysis that is developmental, and that attends to the interplay between intentional and non-intentional processes.

In what follows we use diagnostic terms because they will orient the reader and provide general pointers to boundaries between conditions. However, this does not imply a commitment either to the assumption that each is unitary, or that explanations might not cross their boundaries.

9.2 SCHIZOPHRENIA

9.2.1 Introduction: syndromes

Schizophrenia has a central place in the practice, theory, and research endeavours of psychiatry and clinical psychology. The term probably covers a range of conditions with different aetiologies, although their separation has not been achieved with any certainty. A distinction that has had substantial utility is that between Type 1 and Type 2 syndromes (Crow 1985; Tsuang 1993). The Type 1 syndrome refers typically to the symptoms of acute episodes characterized by delusions (firmly held, culturally inappropriate erroneous beliefs), hallucinations (perceptual experiences without basis in the external world), and disorders of thinking. The Type 2 syndrome is comprised of the so-called negative symptoms of restriction of emotional range, poverty of thought and speech, decreased motor activity, apathy, lack of spontaneity, and diminished interpersonal interactions. These syndromes are not distinct and the same individuals often show signs of both. However, there is some evidence that the inheritance of each may be distinctive and that there may therefore be differences in aetiology. In this consideration of schizophrenia (and this caveat will become familiar throughout this chapter) we cannot assume that our review of possible causal explanations will apply equally across all cases. Nevertheless, studies to which reference is made have used a standardized definition of schizophrenia, either that of the World Health Organization or the American Psychiatric Association, so that, in general, the clinical pictures presented by subjects in the investigations will be broadly comparable.

9.2.2 Biochemical contributions

Some of the earliest 'biological' explanations of schizophrenia provided examples of non-intentional-causal accounts. The 'dopamine hypothesis' contained the following propositions. Amphetamines can lead in normal individuals to a disturbed state that closely resembles that seen in sufferers with schizophrenia. Amphetamines increase the level of dopamine in the relevant parts of the brain (see later) and drugs that are effective in episodes of schizophrenia also block the effects of dopamine at receptor sites. It is therefore possible that an episode of schizophrenia is the result of excess dopamine. The explanation is that the level of dopamine in the system will be outside the normal range, or that there is deception of the system, with levels of dopamine that might be expected in the presence of certain sensory stimuli, but occurring in their absence. With respect to this biochemical system there would be an intentional explanation (e.g. deception), but with respect to stimuli that are relevant to the intentionality of beliefs or experiences there is an intrusion and a non-intentional explanation. Episodes might be precipitated by psychological factors if, for instance, these led to increased arousal that was associated with a consequent alteration of dopamine levels. Then there would be an intentional explanation for the altered dopamine level, and a non-intentional explanation of the altered state of mind and behaviour. The origin of this susceptibility to altered dopamine might be genetic. Evidence from twin and adoption studies indicates a substantial heritability for schizophrenia, although the nature of the genetic contribution is unclear (Roberts 1991).

9.2.3 Neuropathology and neuropsychology

Evidence for a neuropathological deficit in schizophrenia is increasing. The area of the brain that is most consistently identified is the parahippocampal gyrus on the median side of the temporal lobe (Jakob and Beckman 1986; Falkai *et al.* 1988). How might this contribute to the development of schizophrenia? Medial temporal lobe structures are believed to have a crucial role in the integration and processing of the inputs from a wide range of areas of the brain. They act as a kind of 'gate' for information, selecting only certain items for further processing (Frith and Done 1988; Gray *et al.* 1991). It is possible, then, that at least some patients with schizophrenia have deficits in information processing. Gray *et al.* (1991) have proposed that a central deficit in the functioning of the schizophrenic patient is found in a problem in the linking of stored memories to current stimuli. As we saw in Chapter 6, the ability to do this is present in very young infants. Repeated stimuli are of great interest provided they are accompanied by variations. Clearly, variations may be detected only by comparison with previous, remembered stimuli. This theory suggests that for the schizophrenic patient each stimulus appears as if new. The authors cite, in support of this, findings that schizophrenic patients show deficits in experimental conditions that test the influence of stored memories of regularities of previous input on current perception. It is hypothesized that in the acute schizophrenic state the individual is unable to determine which aspects of sensory stimuli are familiar and which are novel, and so attends to incidental stimuli. Those aspects of monitoring the surroundings and the self that are usually carried out unconsciously have to be done consciously and the individual is overloaded by the task. This leads to disorientation of thought and speech.

This theory is linked to the dopamine hypothesis via results of experiments on learning in rats. Rats, like other animals, including humans, can be trained to respond to a conditioned stimulus when it is paired to an unconditioned stimulus. Famously, Pavlov's dogs learned to salivate to the sound of a bell, after the bell had been paired with the sight of food. However, if rats have been exposed to the conditioned stimulus in the absence of the unconditioned stimulus prior to the pairing of the two, they take longer to link the conditioned to the unconditioned stimulus. In other words, their previous experience of the conditioned stimulus has taught them that it is not linked to a reward (such as food) and so they take longer to adopt a different 'interpretation'. In the language of our previous discussion, they have one internalized set of rules for the interpretation of the stimulus, and take time to replace it with another. This phenomenon of latent inhibition can be abolished with amphetamine and restored by the administration of a drug that blocks the effect of dopamine; a drug of the same type as that used in the treatment of schizophrenia.

Gray and colleagues (Gray *et al.* 1991) have argued that these deficits arise from an interruption of the brain's capacity to integrate sensory inputs with a person's current motor state and stored memories, which is required in order to make judgements about current circumstances and the possible need for action. They propose that this deficit is caused by excess dopamine activity and so they postulate a non-intentional origin for the limited information-processing capacity of the brain. This reduces the ability of the individual to generate internalized sets of rules, and to use them in perception and the regulation of action. Under certain conditions, say those where the perceptual demands are high, the task may be too great and thoughts and behaviour become disorganized. Thus against this background, any particular episode may have intentional origins in the extent of sensory overload. As we saw in Chapter 7 the concept of 'design' is derived from a consideration of organism and environment. This model postulates a combination of the two in the generation of the psychotic (schizophrenic) breakdown. Whether environmental factors appear to be important will depend upon the critical range over which they make a difference. It is possible that, at least for some individuals, the limitation of information processing is so profound that all or most levels of environmental demand will be sufficient to lead to psychosis, and for others that it is of an order that some commonly encountered environmental requirements can be accommodated whereas others cannot. Then differences in environment will be seen to be critical to the incidence of psychosis. Clearly, the earlier non-intentional account and this one may be combined. For instance, a deficit in the regulation of dopamine might lead to an increase in its level, thus impeding the information-processing capability of the individual and hence precipitating psychosis.

What then of the origins of the hypothesized deficit? We return to the neuropathology of schizophrenia. One possibility is that neuronal damage occurs shortly prior to the onset of the first psychotic episode, so that the episode is an immediate consequence of the development of the lesion. This would suggest a degenerative brain condition; however, the evidence does not support this (Murray *et al.* 1988). It is more likely that there is a disturbance in brain development, either before birth, or in the first few months of life. Here we enter an area of some controversy. The case has been made that environmental factors, such as viral infection or perinatal injury, may contribute to the neurodevelopmental deficit (Jones and Murray 1991), and conversely that the deficit generally arises from genetic influences (Roberts 1991).

9.2.4 Neurodevelopment and psychological development

The proposition that schizophrenia may arise from a neurodevelopmental deficit takes us back to our consideration of development, design, and intentional-causal processes. If the deficit is present at an early stage, what might be the consequences in childhood? Further neuropsychological hypotheses are of great interest in this respect. Frith (1992) has argued that an important deficit in schizophrenia is in the link between willed intentions and the monitoring of actions. Under experimental conditions schizophrenic patients have been shown to be poorer than other individuals at correcting their actions when they are unable to see their effects, which suggests that their central monitoring is poorer (Mlakar *et al.* 1994). A consequence of such a deficit is likely to be that the schizophrenic sufferer does not recognize that he is the cause of his own actions, and this may form the basis of the experience of having one's actions controlled by another agent, and by analogy with action, the experience of thoughts being controlled. There is a failure of (meta)representation of the individual's own mental activities. Frith has also emphasized that a problem for many schizophrenics is to understand context. In human communication it is necessary to understand the meaning of the words, and also the way in which they are being used in a particular context, and schizophrenics tend to be bad at this. In other words, they have difficulties in identifying metacommunications accurately. If these hypotheses are correct, and at this stage they must be viewed as informed speculations, the person with schizophrenia suffers from deficits in processes which in infancy appear to be crucial to the development of the self, and its metarepresentational capabilities. The linking of memory to event provides a sense of continuity over time, the sense of agency repeated over time and place creates continuity, and the accurate identification of context links self to different circumstances.

If it is hypothesized that the neurodevelopmental deficit is present in infancy, is it possible that analogous psychological deficits might be present also early in development? If so, what would be the implications for the infant's experience of the caregiver, and the caregiver's experience of the infant? We do not know the answer to these questions, but our speculations will focus on information-processing and the development of the self. We may guess that the infant whose capacity to generate internalized regularities and to detect and enjoy novelty is impaired might appear rather puzzled and unresponsive, which might impede the development of pleasurable, rhythmic, face-to-face interactions which are so characteristic of the first months of life, and appear to form the basis of subsequent forms of communication and relating. Difficulties in understanding interpersonal context might have similar consequences. We do not know whether the hypothesized deficit might be overcome, at least in part, by the use of appropriate strategies. Clearly, the generation of expectations and departures from them arises both from the capacity of the infant, and the nature of the stimuli, provided predominantly in infancy by a caregiver. Might some parents be more able than others to provide sufficient scaffolding on which to create such internalized rules, perhaps through substantial repetition, or more marked variations against such a background? Conversely, might some parents give up the task of close sustained interactions in the face of an apparently uncomprehending infant? Consideration of such possibilities highlights the way in which the development of representations and metarepresentations might be impeded or facilitated. They entail variants of the design stance explanation, in the sense outlined in Chapter 7. The common strand is the acquisition of the rules for the interpretation of events. The extent to which these are wired in, how pervasive they are, and extent to which they are open to modification is not prejudged.

We should make clear that there are other possibilities. For instance, it could be argued that the neurodevelopmental deficit, although present from early childhood, is not expressed until the time when schizophrenia is commonly first seen, in adolescence, perhaps as a result of neuronal maturation at that age. Then our analysis might not apply. It seems, however, that at least a significant number of children who are at risk for schizophrenia do show differences from other children. Studies of the children of parents with schizophrenia have shown that they have more attentional deficits, and that these are associated with subsequent social insensitivity, social indifference, and social isolation (Cornblatt *et al.* 1992). Clearly studies such as this are complicated by the presence of parents with schizophrenia who might have the same or similar hypothesized deficits as their children; however, they provide some preliminary evidence that deficits may be present in childhood which could disrupt early parent–child interactions, with implications for subsequent development.

In our discussion of the design stance, it was emphasized that even where intentional causal processes are wired in, in humans the 'wiring' may be influenced by experience. If the development of the visual system is influenced by visual experience then why not information-processing? In rats the phenomenon of latent inhibition is not seen if they have not been handled during the first days of life (Weiner *et al.* 1987), which suggests that early experiences may have long-term structural implications. This does not lead us away from the role of genetic influences, but rather to an interactive theory in which the information-processing capacity is central and the origins are in genetically determined variability and variability in early intentional-causal processes.

Further indirect support comes from studies where both inheritance and environment have been assessed. In the Finnish Adoption Study the rate of schizophrenia or schizophrenia spectrum disorders in the adopted children of schizophrenic parents was 30 per cent, with 15 per cent in a control group. However, these differences were apparent only in a comparison of adopting families which were rated (without knowledge of the adopted children's mental health) as showing confusing patterns of communication. These might be expected to make difficult the identification of metacommunications concerning the rules of social interaction and hence, in vulnerable individuals, lead to an impaired understanding of the actions of others (Tienari *et al.* 1994).

In the context of a developmental interactional account, the capacity for multiple representational systems may be important to outcome. Thus the infant with the hypothesized deficit may, as a result of a parent's ability to compensate, develop a secure attachment relationship, which will increase the chances of instrumental and interpersonal competence. This may act as a protective factor in relation to a persistent deficit and the risk of psychosis. Conversely, the development of insecure attachment may increase the risk. Children who as infants have been classified as 'insecure', later in life elicit less supportive responses from their teachers than those rated 'secure'. If a similar effect applies between parents and children, and if the vulnerability of infants makes it more difficult for parents to establish a secure attachment relationship, then these parents might later be less supportive and more critical of their children. There is ample evidence that the emotional atmosphere in the home, and especially the level of criticism, hostility, and over-involvement (which together are termed 'expressed emotion'), influences the course of schizophrenia (Bebbington and Kuipers 1994), and the relapse rate can be reduced substantially if the expressed emotion of the parents is lowered through a family-based intervention (Jesus Mari and Streiner 1994). It is not clear whether expressed emotion is a factor in the onset of schizophrenia, however if developmental processes of the kind described here are important, it is likely to be the transaction between vulnerability and parenting style that matters.

9.2.5 Psychosis, certainty, and action

Is it possible to take further the account of the formation of psychotic symptoms, especially those of the acute phase, delusions and hallucinations? The simplest dopamine hypothesis would predict that the symptoms are the consequence of overstimulation of neurons; a non-intentional explanation. However, it may be that the origin and nature of these abnormal beliefs and experiences is not qualitatively different from those of individuals who are not psychotic. The diagnostic classifications and research instruments create a sharp distinction but in practice it is not clear-cut (Strauss 1992). If we put this together with the neuropsychological theories of schizophrenia, we may emerge with a different formulation. The theory provides an explanation of disordered, chaotic, overwhelmed, and unpredictable thoughts and behaviours. Delusions and hallucinations are, by contrast, clear, unambiguous, and relatively or absolutely uninfluenced by evidence. Consider further contrasts. The experience of self predicted by the neuropsychological theory is fragmented and discontinuous in time; the experience of self in relation to delusions and hallucinations is likely to be coherent, and to have continuity. The experience of external reality where stimuli require constant reassessment, and where context is indecipherable, is likely to be one of uncertainty in which high vigilance is required. The experience of external reality through delusions and hallucinations is likely to contain substantial predictability. The neuropsychological theory predicts a deficit in information-processing which renders action impossible or at best fragmented and inconsistent; delusions and hallucinations will often have clear implications for action. For these reasons the symptoms, at least of some sufferers, may be seen as the outcome of coping strategies which restore coherence to representations, and provide a basis for action. They are possible attempts to restore the integrity of intentional-causal processes. Evidence in support of this proposition comes from several sources.

Studies of the attributional style of deluded and hallucinated patients have shown that, compared to non-psychotic individuals, they make use of less evidence in coming to conclusions, and when making causal inferences they ascribe more global, stable, and external origins to events (Bentall *et al.* 1991). This is evident in relation to tasks that have nothing to do with their abnormal beliefs. It seems possible therefore that they are using a particular strategy for making inferences; that they have a characteristic set of internalized rules for the interpretation of events. This is a style which restricts attention to incoming stimuli and creates certainty. The attributions have much in common with depressive (global, stable) cognitions, but favour externality over internality. It could be argued that such external (paranoid) attributions provide a better basis for action than the depressive.

Roberts (1991) compared currently deluded patients, with patients who had recovered from delusions, and with psychiatric nurses and Anglican ordinands, on measures of purpose in life and depression. The groups with the highest purpose in life scores were the deluded and the ordinands, with the nurses slightly lower, and those who had recovered from delusions substantially (and statistically significantly) lower than all other groups. The recovered patients were also the most depressed. The explanation could be in part that the content of more of those with persistent delusions was grandiose or erotic, although persecutory delusions were equally common in both groups. It seems then that the delusions, although in some respects maladaptive, also provided coherence and meaning. Strauss (1992) has similarly described contrasting examples from a major follow-up study of schizophrenic patients:

> At the two year follow-up, a woman who was still very delusional was functioning socially in a way better than many 'normal' people. She was working, looking after her child, and taking care of her house on a relatively limited income, all while frequently being psychotic. Another patient I saw, a woman whose symptoms had essentially disappeared, was sitting in darkened room in her house, and had not worked or had contact with friends for most of the time since I had seen her at the initial evaluation, two years before.

This does not demonstrate that the delusions were important to effective functioning and action, but it is consistent with that proposition. However, a patient from the study of Roberts, who had recovered from delusions, expressed himself directly on the issue, 'I always felt everything I said was worthless, but as Jesus everything I said was important—it came from God . . . I just want to hide away, I don't feel able to cope with people . . . I always feel lonely, I don't know what to say.'

In these examples we see the operation of compensatory mechanisms, comparable to those of the increase in heart rate in response to blood loss. However, there is the added element that we described in the previous chapter. Intentionality in psychological processes entails the experience of continuity, coherence, and efficacy. Where the environment is reasonably benign and decipherable, and where action is possible and effective, these experiences are supported. Threats arising either internally or externally or in combination, may be countered via mechanisms that entail sacrifice in order to restore meaning and action. The sacrifice of accuracy of perception in the pursuit of clarity and action may be a particular (but not exclusive) schizophrenic strategy.

9.3 ANXIETY DISORDERS

9.3.1 Intentionality, development, and content

Central to the anxiety disorders is excessive or unrealistic anxiety. Various kinds of anxiety disorder may be distinguished according to the object of the fear and the behavioural and physiological responses. The main kinds of anxiety disorder defined by DSM-IV (American Psychiatric Association 1994) include phobias, characterized by avoidance; obsessive-compulsion, in which anxiety is relieved by compulsive neutralizing rituals; generalized anxiety disorder, involving persistent worrying; panic disorder, comprising unexpected anxiety attacks; and post-traumatic stress disorder, involving persistent re-experiencing of the trauma, avoidance, and emotional numbing.

In this section we consider anxiety disorders using the approach to psychological function and dysfunction proposed in previous chapters. The approach to psychological function takes intentionality, embedded in developmental processes, to be fundamental. Underpinning this core assumption is the very general idea that it is principles of intentionality which are going to deliver causal explanations of bio-psychological phenomena. Without this background philosophical assumption, intentionality, involving meaningful connections between the contents of intentional states and processes, will tend to be neglected or regarded as secondary, and in particular will not be put to work in the explanation of psychological disorder, where meaning seems, in any case, to have run out.

In the case of anxiety disorders, unlike some other kinds of psychopathology, we can begin with a good grasp of the relevant 'normal' function and its intentionality. As discussed under the heading of functional semantics in Chapter 4. (subsection 4.5.2), 'normal' is most readily understood in this sort of context in terms of evolutionary biology: the normal function of a biological or biopsychological system is that which it was selected in evolution to serve (Millikan 1984, 1986). The normal function of anxiety is relatively easy to define in broad terms, as involving detection of danger to the living being. Thus for example, Eysenck (1992, p. 4):

> In considering the potential value of a cognitive approach to anxiety, it is important to consider anxiety from the evolutionary perspective. Anxiety is an unpleasant and aversive state, and it is perhaps not immediately obvious what (if any) biological significance it might have. However, it is clear that rapid detection of the early warning signs of danger possesses considerable survival value . . . The key purpose or function of anxiety is probably to facilitate the detection of danger or threat in potentially threatening environments.

Given the function of detection of danger, anxiety typically involves intensification of, and selection in, various pre-attentional and attentional processes, including hypervigilance towards and mental preoccupation with danger, and danger and safety signals (Gray 1982; Oatley and Johnson-Laird 1987; Eysenck 1992).

It has been assumed throughout this essay that psychological functions generally are dedicated to action. In the case of anxiety this means generating solutions to the problem of the perceived danger. Once detected, threat has to be appropriately responded to. Relatively primitive (from the evolutionary point of view) ways of doing this include behavioural avoidance and physical destruction of the source of danger. Avoidance and destruction have in common that they get rid of the danger: they get the living being out of harm's way, or vice versa. A different kind of coping strategy can be called 'problem-solving', as opposed to problem avoidance or problem destruction. It involves interacting with the source of danger in such an adaptive way that, after all, it does no harm to the agent.

It is also relatively easy to see ways in which the function of anxiety is elaborated in phylogenesis and ontogenesis. Danger comes to include not only assaults on physical integrity and deprivation of biological necessities, but also, for example in social beings, threat to status in the group, and in human beings, threat to various aspects of 'self-esteem'. Development also elaborates the response side of anxiety. Increased cognitive resources create more possibilities of problem-solving. Specifically, the behavioural coping skills of avoidance and attack find mental analogues (analogues in mental representations) in living beings with the requisite cognitive capacity. This means, roughly, that some possible dangers need not be thought about at all, or if at all, that they can be disqualified in the imagination. There are also problem-solving analogues within the realm of mental representations, which involve making plans as to how to cope with the difficult situation if and when it arises.

The detection of danger and the solving of the perceived problem are intimately linked. This implies that along with detection of danger, appraisal of coping skills is fundamental to anxiety (Lazarus and Averill 1972; Eysenck 1992). Hence perceived absence of being able to cope, in the form of perceived unpredictability or uncontrollability of significant events, is critical in the generation of anxiety, in animals (Mineka and Kihlstrom 1978) and in human beings (Olah *et al.* 1984; Edwards 1988; Endler and Parker 1990). If, in the face of threat, no coping skills can be found which work, the result tends to be runaway anxiety (panic).

According to the approach taken here, principles of intentionality and development of the kind sketched above make up the foundations of the theory of anxiety. They constitute the core of theory in the sense of post-empiricist epistemology (subsection 1.4.1). Core assumptions, it may be recalled, are less concerned with particular facts established by particular methods, and more concerned with defining the nature and aetiology of the phenomena, and formulating critical questions about them. They are at work in the selection and interpretation of data, and they typically drive research programmes.

The assumptions about anxiety sketched so far are intended to be relatively uncontroversial in the sense that they are supported by a great deal of empirical data and are compatible with many other relevant, well-supported approaches. The question concerns rather what is at the core of the theory. We have begun with intentionality in the context of development, but there are certainly other places for the theory of anxiety to start. For example, Gray (1982) takes as his main problem the question as to what brain systems serve anxiety, and approaches this by studying the operation and effects of anxiolytic pharmacological agents. Eysenck (1992) applies another paradigm to anxiety, namely the explanation of individual differences in terms of personality traits. Another approach is study of what are inevitable side-effects of the normal function of anxiety, such as lowered interest in (lowered concentration on, and motivation for) other situations and tasks (Williams *et al.* 1992). Important though all these models and accompanying methodologies are, they are designed to focus on issues other than the intentionality of anxiety and its developmental complexities. While such differences in emphasis and direction are already in the models of normal anxiety, they are perhaps most apparent in application to the problem of disorder.

When applied to disorder, the model proposed here defines the primary problems as being in the area of intentional and non-intentional processes and possible interactions between them. Critical questions include: to what extent are biologically normal, intentional processes operating in cases of anxiety disorder? At what point if any are they disrupted by non-intentional-causal processes?

The assumption that the anxiety system functions to facilitate detection of, and response to, threat is a methodological principle rather than an empirical generalization (a distinction discussed in subsection 4.6.2). It defines the 'normal' case, and by implication the 'abnormal', this distinction being most readily understood in this sort of context in terms of evolutionary biology, as already indicated. The methodological principle envisages that normal function can break down. This is to say, the anxiety system may run free of the detection of danger. In this case the system is functioning abnormally, that is, it is not serving the function for which it was selected. Abnormal function can be caused in various ways, but all are variations on abnormalities in the physiological structures and functions which realize the anxiety system, such that this system operates in the absence of appropriate (in the sense of evolutionary theory) information-processing.

At this point, of course, we encounter squarely the problems posed by anxiety disorder. Commonly the person will say what his or her anxiety is about, will describe the intentional object of the fear, but the anxiety is inappropriate to this object, being either excessive or unrealistic in relation to it. It may be inferred that in such cases the anxiety system is operating in a biologically abnormal way, in the absence of appropriate (in the sense of evolutionary theory) information-processing, in which case it would be appropriate to look for neurological or cognitive 'design flaws' (cf. Gray 1982; Eysenck 1992; Williams *et al.* 1991).

On the other hand, it would be agreed that the person's self-report is no infallible guide here. Absence of an account of perceived real threat by the person so far hardly counts against there being one. The cognitive processing which permeates anxiety is not necessarily conscious, in the sense of conscious awareness or verbal report (Tyrer *et al.* 1978; Dixon 1981; Kemp-Wheeler and Hill 1987). The assumption that anxiety has intentionality, specifically perception of threat, is thus independent of whether or not the person is aware of, or can say, what the perceived danger is. In general, the information-processing which mediates between perception and action (affective responses and behaviour) may be unconscious, in the sense of being unavailable for, and perhaps misrepresented by, self-report (subsections 1.2.4, 1.4.3).

The question arises, therefore, as to how we get a hold on the intentional objects of psychological states without reliance on self-report. Earlier discussions of the epistemology of mind and meaning (subsection 1.4.2, Section 3.2, subsections 4.5.4–5) focused on three closely interwoven methods: observation of intentional behaviour, application of a theory of mind, and perhaps mental simulation (thought-experiments) in one's own case. A fourth source of information is, of course, other relevant self-reports which may be assumed to be reliable.

Consider, for example, the case of a child presenting with excessive and unrealistic fear about his own health. Assessment of such a case, described in more detail in, for example, Bolton (1994), would involve gaining information about events in the family, the child's patterns of intentional behaviour, application of theory about the kind of thing that would make a child really afraid, perhaps supplemented by use of empathy, and information about the child's relevant beliefs and views, and all of these in combination could lead to an hypothesis about the real object of the child's fear, for example, in the context of medical anxieties in the family, that the father is in danger of having a heart attack.

In general, not only is there no reason to assume that the self-report of the intentional object of fear (what it is about) is accurate, but there is reason positively to doubt it. This is just because real causes of anxiety have to be dealt with, and one great way is avoidance, including in its mental form, denial. As indicated earlier, gaps and error in the theory of mind are frequently in the service of defence, in the individual and in the family (pp. 311–12).

The approach proposed here is based simply on the methodological assumption that normal biopsychological function is *persistent*. And normal function has, of course, to do with detection of *real* danger, not imagined. The evolutionary hypothesis is that the anxiety system would not have been selected had it not served the function of detecting danger, but it makes no sense to interpret 'danger' in this context as things that really represent no threat at all. The search is for something that *really matters to* a human being of such-and-such a kind. If a toddler, for example, seems to get into something like a panic state when a toy is taken from him, it is plausible to suppose that the appropriate intensional description of the event is one that brings out its highly threatening nature for the child, so that it means to him, for example, the collapse of plans and the disintegration of action, or his powerlessness. A second-choice hypothesis in this case is that the child's anxiety is excessive or unrealistic, that the anxiety system, the detection of significant threat, is functioning abnormally due to some design fault.

This is not to say, of course, that the anxiety system, or any other bio-psychological system, cannot go wrong. As already discussed, the methodological assumption of normal function may have to be given up in particular cases or kinds of case. There may be direct evidence of non-intentional causation of activity of the autonomic nervous system, and in this case hypotheses about intentional causation would be discounted, or there may be interactions between the two kinds of causal pathway. Otherwise the reason for abandoning the assumption of normal function is likely to be the negative one, that is, failing to find any plausible hypotheses about real threats to the person which the expressed intentional object means. What guides the search for meaning here is primarily bio-psychological theory, in which developmental issues are fundamental.

Threat is, of course, readily understandable in the form of, for example, a predatory animal, as is the response of fleeing or attacking. For social beings, particularly slowly maturing ones like ourselves, the role of carers is equally a matter of life and death. For the infant, avoidance or attack by carers constitute major, life-threatening, dangers. Given the vulnerability of infants, it is plausible to envisage no lower limit to the age at which patterns of anxiety and its management are generated. Psychoanalytic theory has emphasized that these patterns belong from the beginning to the mother–infant interaction, and the first critical type of coping task is attributed naturally enough to mother. Mother has to contain the infant's anxiety, which means, briefly, that her task is to not, out of her own anxiety, avoid or panic in the face of the child's, but is rather to stay with the baby, physically and mentally, holding him calm (cf. Winnicott 1971; see also subsection 8.4.5). This kind of task and its vagaries become apparent enough as the child grows older. The theme of dependence on adults runs through all the variety in the child's developmental and life-tasks, and the evolving child–carer relationship therefore remains closely implicated in fear and coping.

A related approach to the objects and causes of anxiety concerns the development of self. The general principle is that perceived threats to self-preservation generate high anxiety (Oatley and Johnson-Laird 1987). What that amounts to depends on what is essential to, or perceived as essential to, the self, and this is a complicated matter for human beings. As discussed in Chapter 6 (subsections 6.4.3, 6.5.2), the foundations of various aspects of the sense of self are established early in life (Stern 1985), and these are developed and elaborated at least through childhood and adolescence (Erikson 1963). ·Formation of the sense (or senses) of the self depends on the accomplishment of a wide and complex variety of tasks, including physical actions, affective responding, interpersonal relating, speech, education, and so on. Tasks generate anxiety, and solutions require effective coping skills.

Psychological theory here moves into social theory. It is impossible to know what is essential to the sense of self in human beings, and therefore what signifies a major threat to them, without understanding culture. Superficially the same event may have very different meanings between societies. A certain kind of practice may be innocent according to one set of values, but sin in another, and so on. If an event generates high anxiety, it can and should be construed in a way that brings out its highly dangerous significance. Failure of a child at school, to take another kind of example, may signify to an immigrant family loss of hope of improvement for generations.

The issues in meaningful explanation encountered here have been discussed in previous chapters. The meanings available in culture, and which guide human activity, are diverse and cannot be circumscribed, exceeding what is visible from the point of view of evolutionary biology (subsections 2.5.7, 3.4.4, 4.5.5). It is possible to make generalizations about meaningful connections, but they are achieved by abstraction from specific cases, with loss of information and explanatory/predictive power concerning specific cases (subsection 4.6.2). The generalizations are less like summaries of the data and more like methodological principles for the investigation of cases. Thus we can say in very general terms that anxiety involves detection of threat, but what this comes to in particular cases stands in need of further investigation. The specifics are differentiated in phylogenesis and ontogenesis. Some things, such as physical assault and deprivation of nutrition, are dangerous to us, as to all living beings. More specific dangers arise for us as social beings. Also, different dangers can arise for women as opposed to men, and vice versa, for one kind of social group rather than another, and so on. Meaningful explanations can be made progressively more particular, referring eventually to a particular person (subsection 4.6.3).

Another aspect of the investigation and definition of meaning lies on the borderline between psychological theory and epistemology. Empiricism envisaged several ways in which one event may signify another, according to principles of resemblance and learned association. As discussed in subsection 1.4.1, post-empiricism makes this picture much more complicated. The perception of events is theory-laden, as is the perceived connection between events. Appreciation of the meaning that events have for a person requires study of his or her system of beliefs.

These points may be applied to the methodological assumption that unrealistic content in anxiety disorder may stand for something realistic. Empiricist conditioning principles may do some work here. Simple phobias may be caused by one or more really threatening, traumatic experiences of the feared object. In post-traumatic stress disorder the overgeneralization of realistic fear, the overinclusiveness of resemblance, is manifest. In other cases the link may be less evident in content, due to contiguity in time and place only, as when a person fears a particular smell, for example, because of its previous coincidence with real danger. The *meaning* in such a case is just an association, in the context of a particular conditioning history. Alongside such cases, emphasized in the conditioning theory/behavioural paradigm, are those involving more complex symbolism and theory, as for example fear of contamination meaning guilt. These are familiar more in psychoanalytic theory, which has always worked with characteristic post-empiricist principles, including specifically the idea that there are core features of self which the person seeks to preserve (pp. 308–11). However, all these various types of case encountered in the anxiety disorders involve meaning and intentionality. All can be brought under the heading: the person is anxious about something which means to him or her something really threatening. Intentional-causal pathways are involved, and clinicians of diverse psychological persuasions are alike engaged in trying to track them.

We have been discussing the search for meaning in the case of anxiety and the anxiety disorders. Biological, psychological, and social theory guide the search for real threats which the person is perceiving. They include involvement in gross disasters such as serious accidents or war. Real threats include also the more subtle developmentally defined traumas discussed in the previous chapter (pp. 307–8 and Section 8.3). In general terms these developmental traumas involve deprivation of what the growing child needs in order to be able to learn how to act. Of specific relevance in the present context, the child may fail to learn adequate, effective coping skills. These considerations suggest that life in the family is likely to be critical in the generation and maintenance of anxiety in various ways.

The child begins with practically no coping skills, so starts off, according to our working definitions of anxiety, highly prone to anxiety, being dependent more or less entirely on adults to get things to work. To the extent that the adults have poor coping skills, the child has no experience, no modelling, of adaptive problem-solving. At a more complex level, including theory explicit in language, carers' appraisal of the child's attempts at problem-solving is likely to influence the child's self-appraisal of his coping skills. Pessimism, worry, disqualification, criticism of the child's attempts to work out solutions (for example in making friends, or learning to read) are all bound, other things being equal, to make or keep the child anxious.

Another aspect is learning from parental modelling. Two main kinds of cases come under this general heading: learning excessive anxiety reactions, and failing to learn appropriate coping strategies to carry into adult life. As emphasized above, failure to cope with anxiety-provoking situations is an important aspect of anxiety, but it has particularly strong relevance under the plausible assumption that many childhood fears are innate, or at least an inevitable theme in bio-psychological maturation. For, in this case, what stands in need of explanation in the case of disorder is not so much the appearance of anxiety but failure to handle it and the situations that give rise to it. This learning process, like most others, is highly sensitive to parental example and instruction.

A further, major way in which family function may be causally linked to childhood anxiety disorder concerns the content of the anxiety. Family life may be a source of major stressors, including death or serious illness within the family, parental mental illness, chronic marital conflict, and of course sexual abuse.

The hypothesis that family function plays a major role in the aetiology of anxiety disorders, both in childhood and in continuations into adulthood, is well supported. Evidence from a wide range of studies, using a variety of designs, supports the general conclusion that anxiety disorders, and related difficulties such as depression, tend to run in families. A high proportion of the mothers of children with anxiety disorders themselves have a lifetime history of anxiety disorder (Last *et al.* 1987), and children of anxious parents are at increased risk for anxiety disorder (Sylvester *et al.* 1987; Turner *et al.* 1987). There is raised incidence of anxiety disorders and other types of psychopathology in the relatives of individuals with anxiety disorders (Carey and Gottesman 1981; Harris *et al.* 1983), and there are relationships between anxiety and depression and familial patterns of psychopathology (Leckman *et al.* 1983; Weissman *et al.* 1984; Livingston *et al.* 1985; Bernstein and Garfinkel 1988; Bernstein *et al.* 1990).

Evidence of a genetic contribution to anxiety disorders is relatively weak, although the story may be different for different anxiety disorders. Where physiological signs dominate, there may be a constitutional, genetically based, low threshold for functioning of the anxiety system. There is evidence of more genetic contribution to panic disorder than to generalized anxiety disorder (Torgersen 1990), where the evidence so far is for purely environmental familial transmission (Eysenck 1992). Adult patients with generalized anxiety disorder reported more trauma in the family as children than patients with panic disorder (Torgersen 1986).

The methodological assumption that even in excessive or unrealistic cases anxiety may still be fulfilling its normal biological function, applies not only to the detection of significant threat but also to the generation of solutions. This implies that the symptoms of anxiety disorder are unsuccessful attempts to solve real problems. The anxiety presents as a persistent perception of danger, and the cognitive and behavioural symptoms are the accompanying persistent attempts to find a solution.

Coping strategies include avoidance, destruction of the problem, and problem-solving. Such strategies may work in given circumstances, but if the perceived threat cannot be managed satisfactorily, they tend in one way or another to get out of hand, leading to the exaggerated and persistent combinations of avoidance, perhaps destructive acts, at least in the imagination, vain attempts at problem-solving, and panic, which are the anxiety disorders. Overreliance on coping with anxiety by avoidance, physical and mental, tends to alternate with surprise panic, as in panic disorder. Physical avoidance is an efficient strategy for keeping safe and therefore calm, but is maladaptive in case the feared situation is also desired for some reason, as usually in agoraphobia, or social phobia. The worry characteristic of generalized anxiety disorder, verging on panic, endless and fruitless, appears as a form of cognitive avoidance in adults (Borkovec *et al.* 1991), and in children, once they develop the prerequisite cognitive capacities (Vasey 1993). Avoidance is mandatory when situations are seen as really dangerous, as life-threatening, but for the very same reason they demand attention and vigilance: paradoxical attempts to do both at the same time, in reality and in the imagination, are seen most clearly in post-traumatic stress disorder. Obsessive-compulsive disorder may represent a pre-rational coping style getting out of hand, exhibiting the characteristic, paradoxical combinations of coping and not coping, being in and out of control, and panic. The fundamental fear is of being out of control where coping is essential, and this leads to excessive, out-of-control coping. In general, the problem and the solution become timelessly muddled, this being characteristic of intentional processes in disorder (pp. 312–14).

In this opening subsection we have considered in general terms intentional-causal models of anxiety disorder, based in assumptions about the biologically normal function of anxiety. In what follows we consider the points raised in more detail in relation to two particular anxiety disorders, obsessive-compulsion and post-traumatic stress. In the first of these, intentional and non-intentional theories are both plausible in the current state of research, and the form of solution to this inter-theoretic tension is unclear. By contrast, an intentional-causal model is clearly appropriate for post-traumatic stress disorder, and may have application to other kinds of mental state involving recurring, intrusive, distressing cognition.

9.3.2 Obsessive-compulsive disorder

It is very plausible to view obsessive-compulsive disorder (OCD) as an anxiety disorder, and it is so classified in all the standard nosologies. Anxiety is typically involved in the phenomenology: the person has preoccupying, anxiety-provoking thoughts, usually about some unrealistic danger, and compulsively attempts to neutralize these thoughts and to relieve the anxiety they engender by activities such as counting, cleaning, or checking, carried out in stereotyped or ritualized ways. Anxiety is apparently implicated also in normal, non-clinical phenomena which may be akin to obsessive-compulsion phenomena, in children's magical thinking and actions, and in adult life, particularly in people with so-called obsessional traits.

Broadly speaking, the classification of OCD as a kind of anxiety disorder goes along with emphasizing its intentionality. Obsessional fears are typically quite irrational, but it may be hypothesized that they have meaning, along the lines discussed in the previous subsection. Profound fear of losing control, perhaps specifically with destructive results, is a plausible candidate for a general theme in many cases of obsessional anxiety. The obsessive-compulsive rituals have obvious intentionality so far as the person is concerned: they are about preventing feared catastrophe. At a more symbolic level, it may be that rituals serve to produce the feeling of control in otherwise senseless activities, in response to the perception of being out of control in a realistic area of life. This function of ritualistic behaviour was noted by Freud (1913) and by later theorists (Rachman and Hodgson 1980; Leonard 1989). Psychoanalytic theory also emphasizes the developmentally early fear that the self may become uncontrollably aggressive, making mess, or chaos (Freud 1966). More recent theorizing in the cognitive-behavioural tradition has retained the assumption of intentionality while emphasizing the person's appraisal of the thoughts concerned. It has been hypothesized that fantastic thoughts, for example of causing great harm, are found also in the non-clinical population, but an abnormally exaggerated sense of responsibility for these otherwise ordinary thoughts, negative evaluation of the self for having them, can give rise to recurring distressing thoughts and attempts to neutralize them (Salkovskis 1985; Rachman 1993).

All these psychological theories characteristically point to continuities between the clinical and the non-clinical phenomena, between the abnormal and the normal case. This hangs together with accepting the intentionality of obsessive-compulsive phenomena, in which case the search is for meaning in the otherwise apparently meaningless. The 'meaning' of the obsessional thoughts for the person may be to do with being out of control in some suitably profound sense, or, or as well, it may be that they signify a negative evaluation of the self.

So far, so understandable. On the other hand, there has recently been an accumulation of evidence to suggest that intentional-causal connections of such kinds can hardly be the whole story about OCD. In the past 5 years evidence has accumulated of neurological soft signs and neuropsychological deficits in OCD (Cox *et al.* 1989; Denkla 1989; Head *et al.* 1989; Hollander *et al.* 1990, 1993; Hymas *et al.* 1991; Christensen *et al.* 1992). More direct evidence of neurological structural abnormalities has been detected using computed tomography (CT) and magnetic resonance imaging (MRI) (Luxenberg *et al.* 1988; Scarone *et al.* 1992). There are also associations between OC phenomena and known kinds of neurological disorder, including postencephalitic Parkinson's disease (von Economo 1931), Sydenham's chorea (Swedo *et al.* 1989), and brain injury (McKeon *et al.* 1984), and some response to psychosurgery (Chiocca and Martuza 1990). The range of evidence indicated above has been plausibly cited in support of the hypothesis that OCD has an abnormal neurological basis, probably specifically in the basal ganglia (Wise and Rapoport 1989; Rapoport 1990). This model is complex in various ways, comprising both neurological and psychological hypotheses. It proposes that the basal ganglia serve sensory and cognitive, as well as motor functions, and that specified neurological dysfunctions cause psychological dysfunctions characteristic of OCD. Specifically, the model regards OC symptoms as *displacement activities* (in the ethological sense) 'run wild', triggered in the absence of, or in any case unregulated by, normal processing of external stimuli.

Wise and Rapoport introduce the notion of displacement activities as follows (1989, pp. 336–7):

> [Our hypothesis] is based on a simple model of an innate releasing mechanism in the basal ganglia: a detection mechanism for recognizing specific aspects of stimuli (key or sign stimuli) and a releasing mechanism for the species-typical behavioral response (sometimes known as a fixed-action pattern). Usually detection of the key stimulus causes release (i.e. execution) of the appropriate behavior. But two sorts of behavior can occur in the absence of a key stimulus. Vacuum behaviors . . ., for example, are often actions which would be appropriately directed toward a specific object but when the object is not present. A bird may snap at insects absent and go through the motions of preparing the non-existent bugs for its meal . . . Similarly, displacement behaviors are released when there are 'conflicts between two strongly activated antagonistic drives', or 'when the normal outlet for a certain motivation is blocked'.

The authors go on to remark that displacement activity is of particular relevance in the case of OCD, and quote the following passage from Lorentz (1981, p. 251):

> A vast majority of motor patterns appearing as displacement activities are common 'everyday' activities ... the so-called comfort activities of birds and mammals, such as scratching, preening, shaking, furnish the most common examples of displacement activities; when embarrassed, even humans tend to scratch behind the ear—and in other places.

Wise and Rapoport proceed on the basis of neuroanatomical considerations to conjecture that in OCD hyperactivity in the cingulate cortex causes execution of displacement activities in the absence of the appropriate sensory input and in the absence of motivation to perform them (1989, p. 338).

It may be seen that the ethological strand in this model of OCD is compatible with a psychological story invoking intentional causality. Strong drive conflict or blocking may trigger 'easy', innate behaviour patterns with a low performance threshold, but such behaviours would then acquire the function of reducing the high anxiety generated by the drive frustration (Stein *et al.* 1992). The processes involved here would be biologically normal, and indeed suggestive of the psychological models of obsessive-compulsion already discussed. The assumption would be that displacement activities acquired anxiety-reducing functions as just outlined, and this relatively simple biological beginning was elaborated in development into something like a coping strategy in salient situations perceived as uncontrollable: otherwise senseless routines would serve at least to create the 'illusion of control'. An obsessive-compulsive disorder in intentionality would thus come about within the intentional processes themselves, in the way described in general terms in the previous chapter.

So far, then, there is nothing in the ethological approach to OCD incompatible with the psychological, and there may indeed be developmental connections between the two. In the ethological model, as in the psychological, there is so far nothing to do with neurological deficit. The further step proposed in Wise and Rapoport's model, is the claim that displacement activities are not being triggered by intentional-causal processes, but by lower-level, non-intentional, interference with normal information processing. This shift in the model from intentional- to non-intentional-causal explanation has the consequence that it says nothing about compulsive behaviour having functional, specifically anxiety-reducing, properties.

There are anomalies for the basal ganglia hypothesis, acknowledged by its proponents, including less than perfect fit between known basal ganglia damage and OCD, and also anomalies for the general hypothesis of neurological deficit: the course of OCD (sometimes late onset, sometimes episodic), cognitive-behavioural specificity in the disorder (certain thoughts and actions only), and the efficacy of behaviour therapy, including anxiety-reduction techniques (Wise and Rapoport 1989).

The position in the current state of OCD research is thus that we have two apparently conflicting types of aetiological model of OCD: one type invokes only intentional-causal mechanisms, the other only, or mainly, non-intentional-causal mechanisms. Apparently they are each consistent with different sorts of evidence. The psychological models with their emphasis on anxiety and anxiety reduction are plainly consistent with the typical phenomenology of OCD, and with the efficacy of behaviour therapy. The neurological deficit model is more consistent with a variety of evidence of neurological impairment as listed above. What is evidence for the one, is anomalous for the other. Thus efficacy of behaviour therapy is at least superficially analomous for hypothesis of neurological deficit, while there is apparently no way that the psychological models (in their current form at least) predict neurological impairment. The fact that there are differential predictions here shows that the conflict between the two kinds of model is a genuine one. It is not that the two sorts of model 'say the same thing in two ways', in neurological and psychological language. This reflects the general point, made back in the first chapter (subsection 1.3.5), that intentional stance explanation of breakdown of function is distinct from physical stance explanation of breakdown: they invoke quite different sorts of causal pathway, and point to different sorts of remedy.

The most elegant solution to the conflict is that OCD is heterogeneous in the appropriate respects. According to this line of thought, OCD would exist on a spectrum. At one end we would have an anxiety disorder, blending into non-clinical phenomena of similar kinds, akin to other neurotic disorders in various ways, while, at the other end of the spectrum would be found disorder associated with neurological dysfunction. The prediction is that markers of functional neurosis cluster together and markers of neurobiological deficit cluster together, and the two clusters are dissociated. The hypothesis of such a neat solution is worth testing, though by all means it is not necessarily the most likely. It puts to sea among known anomalies, including conspicuous lack of correlation between neurological soft signs and neuropsychological test abnormalities in the many studies referred to above. Preliminary analysis from a study designed for the purpose of testing this heterogeneity hypothesis also indicates more or less entirely negative results (Shafran, Bolton, and Gray, in preparation).

Alternatives to this kind of solution to the conflict between 'psychological' models of OCD, which invoke intentionality, and 'neurological deficit' models, which do not, will have to be more complicated, even messy, though none the less likely for that. In one way or another, the different kinds of evidence will have to be reassessed and/or reinterpreted. It is possible that, for example, soft neurological signs in OCD signify comorbidity rather than abnormal neural aetiology. As to neuropsychological test abnormalities, a recent study by Cohen *et al.* (in press), not yet replicated, has shown that some are associated with anxiety not OCD specifically, and hence may not, after all, signify any neurological deficit. On the other side, it may be necessary to re-frame in some kinds of case the response of OCD to behaviour therapy: perhaps it is misleading to speak of cure here, or of remission, it being rather that the person learns how better to manage a chronic neurological disability.

9.3.3 Post-traumatic stress disorder and other cases of recurring, instrusive, distressing thoughts

Trauma is a most fertile ground for psychological theory, and it is no accident that right at the start of clinical psychology it figured prominently in the two paradigms that were to set the scene for the century to come: Freud's and Watson's. Irrational fear lends itself to the simple explanation of inappropriate generalization. This model is at its simplest in Watson, and at its most complex in Freud, complicated by cognitive and developmental processes. Of course, backwards trauma hunting has been problematic in both traditions: Freud didn't know whether he had found real or fantasized trauma, and the behaviourists often failed to find the hypothesized one-trial learning in the history of patients with irrational fears. In trying to model post-traumatic stress disorder (PTSD) we do not have this sort of problem, because generally matters are much more open to view. In the paradigm case envisaged by the standard diagnostic systems (such as DSM to be discussed below) the traumatic shock is clear in time and in broad outlines in nature. It is, generally speaking, clear enough whether a person has experienced trauma, when, and of what kind.

Post-traumatic overgeneralization of fear, with physiological arousal and behavioural avoidance, can be explained relatively straightforwardly in conditioning theory. Trauma also affects more complex cognition. We have already considered (in subsection 9.3.1) the effects of anxiety on information-processing. The main function of the anxiety system is detection of and response to danger, and hence involves intensification of and selection in various pre-attentional and attentional processes, including hypervigilance towards and mental preoccupation with danger, and danger and safety signals. Inevitable side-effects of anxiety then include lowered interest in (lowered concentration on, and motivation for) other situations and tasks. All of this is plausibly a natural response to a major, life-threatening experience. The development of core post-traumatic stress symptoms following major trauma appears as biologically normal. The problem is not so much understanding why they develop, but is rather explaining why they are so persistent, sometimes over many, many years.

We consider these sorts of issues in what follows, bringing to bear proposals from previous chapters. To begin with, it may be helpful to readers unfamiliar with post-traumatic stress disorder to see a summary of standard diagnostic criteria.

DSM-IV introduces the diagnostic criteria for post-traumatic stress disorder in the following way (American Psychiatric Association 1994, pp. 427–8):

> The person experienced, witnessed, or was confronted with an event or events that involved actual or threatened death or serious injury, or a threat to the physical integrity of self or others . . . [and] the person's response involved intense fear, helplessness, or horror. **Note:** In children this may be expressed instead by disorganized or agitated behaviour.

The core of PTSD is then persistent re-experiencing of the traumatic event, in one or more of the following ways (loc. cit.):

- recurrent and intrusive distressing recollections of the event including images, thoughts, or perceptions. **Note:** In young children, repetitive play may occur in which themes or aspects of the trauma are expressed.
- recurrent distressing dreams of the event. **Note:** in children there may be frightening dreams without recognizable content.
- acting or feeling as if the traumatic event were recurring (includes a sense of reliving the experience, illusions, hallucinations, and dissociative flashback episodes, including those that occur on wakening or when intoxicated). **Note:** In young children trauma-specific reenactment may occur.
- intense psychological distress at exposure to internal or external cues that symbolize or resemble an aspect of the traumatic event.

- physiological reactivity upon exposure to internal or external cues that symbolize or resemble an aspect of the traumatic event.

A second group of symptoms has to do with persistent avoidance of stimuli associated with the trauma or numbing of general responsiveness, at least three of which are required for diagnosis, as follows:

- efforts to avoid thoughts, feelings or conversations associated with the trauma
- efforts to avoid activities, places, or people that arouse recollections of the trauma
- inability to recall an important aspect of the the trauma
- markedly diminished interest or participation in significant activities
- feeling of detachment or estrangement from others
- restricted range of affect (e.g., unable to have loving feelings)
- sense of a foreshortened future, e.g., does not expect to have a career, marriage, or children, or a normal life span

A further diagnosic criterion is persistent symptoms of increased arousal, as indicated by at least two of the following:

- difficulty falling or staying asleep
- irritability or outbursts of temper
- difficulty concentrating
- hypervigilance
- exaggerated startle response

What is described here as the diagnostic criteria for PTSD are responses to trauma which are, for the most part, readily understandable from a bio-psychological point of view. It would be difficult to imagine contrary responses to trauma as being normal. Any living being that narrowly escaped death and, as it were, shrugged it off, would so far be taking chances, would be at risk for being less lucky the next time. If a person experiences severe threat, then she should be anxious about what may have happened, what she could have done, if anything, to avoid or escape the danger, and whether it may happen again. In other words, cognitive resources would be focused on the trauma and its possible recurrence. In effect this comprises the cognitive symptoms in the first group, persistent re-experiencing, and the consequent symptoms of physiological arousal in the third group. Symptoms in the second group, significantly, pull the other way: traumatic experience, as well as demanding constant attention, also, and for the same reason, makes us want to avoid it like anything. The avoidance of trauma-like memories, feelings, and situations can generalize, so as to cover practically any stresses, including otherwise normal demands, such as interpersonal relationships and future planning.

Before considering approach-avoidance conflict further, we may note in passing the signs of tension here between bio-psychological normality and the notion of disorder. Emphasis on the bio-psychological normality of post-traumatic stress reactions suggests that any disorder here has more to do with these reactions failing to decay over time. The position would be akin to the distinction between bereavement and depressive episode. Grief can give rise to thoughts, emotions, and behaviour barely, if at all, distinguishable from a depressive syndrome, but diagnosis of major depressive episode is excluded in case the disturbance is a normal reaction to the death of a loved one (American Psychiatric Association 1994, p. 323). Signs of bereavement becoming complicated by depression include morbid preoccupation with worthlessness, suicidal ideation, marked functional impairment or psychomotor retardation, or prolonged duration. It would be possible in a similar vein to envisage a 'normal' post-traumatic stress reaction which could become complicated by 'disorder', signs of which would include, for example, high degrees of generalization of fear reactions, or of withdrawal, or prolonged duration. These remarks, by the way, are not at all a criticism of the standard definition of post-traumatic stress disorder, but are intended only to clarify what otherwise might seem odd, that bio-psychological normality and the appearance of disorder can be closely linked, particularly following major stressors.

The theme in the background here has to do with the paradoxes inherent in the experience of and response to trauma, discussed in Chapter 8 (Section 8.2), in subsection 9.3.1, and further below. A sign of paradox is that bio-psychologically normal coping strategies when applied to apparently insoluble problems can themselves become maladaptive, disrupting normal activity. The symptom follows from and re-enacts the perception of the impossibility of carrying on. Lines between normal response and disorder are, in these circumstances, difficult to draw sharply. Death of a loved one is distinguished as a normal cause of what otherwise could be called depressive disorder, but other major losses which also lead to grief reactions, such as loss of physical capacity following serious accident or illness, are not so distinguished. The issues here are complicated, and the lines to be drawn are bound to be vague.

These considerations, however, point to the fact that what needs explanation in the case of post-traumatic stress disorder is not so much the appearance of the signs of post-traumatic stress, but their failure to decay over time. Why is the trauma persistently re-experienced, often over many years?

PTSD can be regarded as a phobic reaction, and modelled accordingly in conditioning theory. Recurring re-experiencing is accounted for by this model, for example as a result of a high degree of generalization which makes avoidance impossible (Keane *et al.* 1985). The CS–CR link is preserved because the CS is endured with great anxiety, that is, is never perceived as (responded to as) safe, and anxiety incubates rather than decays (Eysenck 1979). A broadly similar, though more explanatory story can be told in terms of more complex information-processing models. The task for the person traumatized in, for example, a shipping disaster, is to acquire the information that, nevertheless, ships are really safe (enough), but assimilation and accommodation of this information from experience is ruled out in so far as there are expectations of danger, leading to search for danger signals, leading to lowered threshold for such interpretations, leading to the perception that ships are dangerous after all. A model along these lines, applied to the post-traumatic stress of war veterans, is worked out by Chemtob *et al.* (1988). A related formulation is proposed by Foa and Steketee (1989), to be discussed further below; and see also Creamer *et al.* (1992).

The idea, then, is that traumatic experience produces a massive effect on information-processing, on the anxiety system specifically, so that it becomes, as it were, permanently on, sensitive to danger signals and unprepared to recognize security. This is very likely to be a major part of the story. But so far it does not easily address the persistent re-experiencing of the trauma itself, in waking thought, in dreams, or other re-enactments. Why does the victim go through it over and over again? Here we come across the idea that the traumatic experience is in some way 'unresolved'. But what does this mean, and why does it happen?

Directly relevant to this central question is Rachman's (1980) notion of *failure of emotional processing*. He invoked it to explain a variety of phenomena: obsessions, the return of fear, incubation of fear, abnormal grief reactions, failures to respond to fear-reducing procedures, and nightmares. Although Rachman was not concerned in the paper explicitly with post-traumatic stress disorder, the notions could be applied to it, and have been by Foa and Steketee (1989), using a model proposed by Foa and Kozak (1986). Much discussion in all these papers concerns the criteria or signs that emotional processing has or has not occurred. There is a risk, of which the proponents of the model are aware, that signs of its failure coincide with the phenomena to be explained. This issue is basically one of operational definition of a highly theoretical construct. In fact two sorts of definition are required: theoretical and operational. In his original paper Rachman concentrated on the latter somewhat at the expense of the former. He suggested that, 'as a start, emotional processing is regarded as a process whereby emotional disturbances are absorbed, and decline to the extent that other experiences and behaviour can proceed without disruption' (Rachman 1980, p. 51). The notion of emotional processing in this way rests heavily on the theoretical construct of 'absorption'. But what is this?

Further progress was made by Foa and Kozak, who defined emotional processing as the modification of memory structures that underlie emotions, particularly acquisition of new, incompatible information (Foa and Kozak 1986, p. 22). Concerning post-traumatic stress disorder in particular, Foa and her colleagues proposed that what distinguishes it from other anxiety disorders is that the traumatic event was of monumental significance and violated formerly held 'basic concepts of safety' (Foa and Steketee 1989, p. 166). They propose that this violation establishes massive fear structures (information-processing biased towards danger) which then inhibit new learning, specifically of safety (Foa and Steketee 1989, pp. 167–70).

This was the proposal discussed above. It is likely to be correct, but, as already suggested, it apparently does not directly address the issue of repeated re-experiencing the trauma itself. The hope was that the concept of 'failure of emotional processing' would cast light here, but it is not yet clear how.

We suggest that some very general consideration about the nature of cognition can be brought to bear on these issues, mainly the post-empiricist assumption that we use hierarchically organized systems of belief for the purpose of action. This was discussed in the first chapter (subsections 1.4.1, 1.4.4) and linked to trauma in the previous chapter (pp. 305–6). In these terms it is possible to elaborate on key theoretical notions such as 'basic concepts of safety', 'size' of fear structures, and resistance to change. It is specifically possible to gain a distinctive theoretical grip on the key problem of persistent re-experiencing of the trauma through time, of failure to decay.

The basic idea, as outlined in the previous chapter (Section 8.2, 8.3), is that trauma comes into conflict with core assumptions in the theory of action, such as that the world is a safe enough place for action, and that the self is competent enough. The conditions of action include 'safety' in the broadest sense, a notion invoked by Foa and her colleagues (Foa and Steketee 1989). If reality is being represented as incompatible with the conditions of action, then representation itself is confounded, having to both exist and not exist. The paradox of representation and non-representation, extended through time, finds dramatic expression in the most characteristic of post-traumatic signs, namely, in persistent and intrusive re-experiencing of the traumatic events. These points will be expanded on later, but first we may consider another theoretical approach close to what we are proposing, one that relies heavily on the notion of 'basic assumptions'.

Janoff-Bulman (1985) argues that the stress syndrome of PTSD is largely attributable to the shattering of victims' 'basic assumptions' about themselves and their world. She cites various theorists in explanation of the notion of basic assumptions at work in daily life, and notes that traumatic experience clashes with these on a scale comparable to threats to 'paradigms' in Kuhn's sense. This passing reference to post-empiricist philosophy of science directly points in the direction we are taking. As basic assumptions threatened by traumatic experience Janoff-Bulman cites three, as follows (1985, pp. 16f.):

- the belief in personal invulnerability
- the perception of the world as meaningful and comprehensible
- the view of ourselves in a positive light.

And she goes on to discuss their implication in post-traumatic stress disorder.

We do not disagree with the proposal that these three assumptions can be fundamental and involved in the response to trauma. However, in accord with the general approach of the essay, we would start by viewing the 'basic assumptions' of action from a more biological perspective, and indeed from a more general epistemological one. This approach points to assumptions of action being more like the following:

(1) the world is safe enough;
(2) predictable enough;
(3) satisfies enough needs; and
(4) the agent is competent enough.

If these assumptions were to be given up, action would appear as either impossible or pointless, or both. The assumptions, the consequences of giving them up, and the need to hang on to them have been discussed earlier (subsections 1.4.4, 8.2.2).

This second set of assumptions we are proposing stands in contrast to the first set, listed above as proposed by Janoff-Bulman, in three main ways. First, the second set applies down the phylogenetic scale, without restriction to specifically human characteristics such as positive self-image or perceived invulnerability. The theory of anxiety certainly has to be applicable early in phylogenesis, but arguably animals can also show something specifically like post-traumatic stress syndrome, including learned helplessness aspects (Foa *et al.* 1992; Peterson and Seligman 1983). Secondly, the concept of 'good enough', due famously to Winnicott (1971), permeates all these matters: it is not necessary to have perfect control, competence, and so on. Thirdly, as already mentioned, the second set of assumptions *have to* be preserved if action is to continue. Giving them up means that it is either impossible to perform (intentional) behaviour, or pointless to, which implies, for example, random behaviour, freezing/paralysis, or withdrawal. In brief, the second set of expectations are minimal, attributable to animals, and essential to action as such, and all these features hang together.

On this basis we can develop our proposals further. It was remarked above that traumatic experience on the one hand demands attention from the victim, but on the other hand avoidance is also an adaptive response. This certainly includes behavioural avoidance of similar situations, but also mental avoidance of the terror. Mental approach-avoidance conflict in effect means that the same phenomena *have to be both thought about and not thought about*. The paradoxical effects of traumatic experience on cognition were considered in some detail in Chapter 8, in relation to post-empiricist epistemology (pp. 305–6) and the philosophical notion of limits of thought (pp. 306–7).

The key here is the *definition of representation (thought) as serving action*. Consider circumstances in which action is, or is perceived to be, impossible, and which are represented as such. The representation cannot be used to facilitate (to regulate, to plan) action, which, according to the representation, is not possible. But in so far as the representation cannot be used in the service of action, in so far as it is incompatible with action, it is not a possible representation. Thus the reality in question has to be in some way thought about and not thought about. It is clear that the traumatic events are experienced and represented; otherwise indeed there would be no (psychological) problem. But they also have to be in some way not represented.

The paradox here shows up in various ways. For example, there may be amnesia for critical periods in the sequence of events, or the events are remembered but not the terror; or the events are recalled with a third-person perspective, as though observed from the outside rather than experienced from within; or the memory images have an unreal, dream-like quality. All of these are ways of remembering the trauma and not remembering the trauma at the same time. Another form of the paradox is to alternate remembering with not remembering through time. This involves mental avoidance some of the time, feeling fine, as if nothing had happened, or as if the self had not really been affected, with this fragile sense of well-being repeatedly being interrupted by intrusive, distressing preoccupation with the traumatic experience, or by unexpected panic attacks.

Persistent and intrusive re-experiencing of the traumatic events is the dramatic core of post-traumatic stress. It can appear in several forms, as in DSM-IV's first group of diagnostic signs listed above: in waking thought, in dreams, in re-enactment (for example in children's play), and in situations which resemble or symbolize the trauma. The representation is thus clearly in evidence, though it may be partial in one or more of the ways described above (e.g. remembered as if unreal), and it has the special quality of intrusive repetition. The intrusiveness here can be seen as a measure of the salience of the experience for the bio-psychological being—it demands attention—and the repetition can be seen as the expression through time of the paradox of representation and non-representation. It is forgotten during the day, say, when life continues more or less as usual, and provides distraction, but it is remembered as soon as cognitive resources are available, at night, or when the mind wanders off some other task. The energy involved in both preoccupation with the trauma (trying to understand it, trying to withstand the fear) and in mental avoidance of the trauma (trying to forget, to keep oneself engaged in distracting tasks) is substantial. These mental tasks typically leave the person exhausted, much less able to cope with the stresses of daily living, which he or she may then avoid.

In terms of post-empiricist epistemology, as discussed in the previous chapter (pp. 305–6), the point is that traumatic experience contradicts deep convictions in the theory of action, to the effect, for example, that the world is predictably a possible place in which to act, or that the self is able to cope. This creates two cognitive responses. On the one hand, the traumatic experience is impossible, according to these convictions, and thus cannot have happened (to me), and warrants only being put out of mind. On the other hand, still more powerfully, the traumatic experience is, according to the same convictions of massive importance, apparently signifying the impossibility of action (life) itself, so not only cannot be forgotten, but has to be attended to above all else.

The trauma and the core of the theory of action are incompatible, so they cannot both be believed, and this leads to circular cognitive sequences which may be schematically represented as follows:

Step 1: trauma occurred,
Step 2: therefore the core theory is false,
Step 3: but the theory must be preserved: or else 'life is unbearable',
Step 4: so the trauma cannot really have happened,
but, Step 5: it certainly did, that is, back to Step 1 again, and so on.

Traumatic experience signifies that core theory presupposed in action is wrong. But if it is wrong, action comes to an end. But this is impossible (we are inclined to carry on). But if the theory that action is possible is retained, then the traumatic experience cannot have happened. On the other hand, it is remembered. There is a massive conflict here between theory—theory that we have to hang on to—and experience. And paradoxes press: if the experience happened, the theory is wrong, but it can't be wrong . . . Or the other way round, if the theory is right, the experience cannot have happened, but it did . . . and is of huge significance (i.e. overthrows the conditions of survival), therefore needs much attention, cognitive resources. But it implies that action is impossible, which is impossible . . .. And so round and round. This is by all means confusing. The fundamental problem is that traumatic experience apparently contradicts the conditions of action, and will therefore be both rejected, and attended to, both for dear life.

Another way of putting the problem is that core convictions and the trauma cannot both be believed, but must be each believed. Solution of this problem requires drastic mental measures. Both cannot be believed at the same time, with the same mind. One kind of solution is dissociation, as discussed above, in third-person memories or dreams of the event, in remembering without affect, in memories experienced as unreal, in forgetting the worst times. These are ways of believing that the trauma was experienced, and believing that it was not, at the same time. The alternative is persistent re-experiencing, alternating with persistent forgetting/denial, thus achieving beliefs in each side of the contradiction at different times.

There is in post-traumatic stress reaction a *failure to integrate the trauma into the system of belief about the self and reality*. There is frequently, in fact, resistance to such integration, taking the form of explicit thoughts to the effect that the trauma cannot, or should not, have happened. This protest of despair and outrage marks the contrast between reality as it is and reality as it must be, or ought to be. Life requires that reality is benign enough, and the thought that it is not is not a possible thought, at least, not one that can be used as a basis for action. This thought has no use; its meaning cannot be understood. Hence there is a pattern of repetition in which the trauma is persistently re-experienced and its apparent meaning, that core beliefs are false, is rejected.

The proposed explanation of re-experiencing and re-enactment is partly, then, that it cannot be accommodated within the core of theory. This amounts to a theoretical definition of the idea of failure of emotional processing discussed earlier. However, this negative feature exists alongside a more positive mechanism. As indicated above, it is very plausible to suppose that following narrow escape from serious danger cognitive resources should be dedicated to understanding what happened and how, with a view to making sure that it never happens again, or if it does, that the person knows what to do. This problem-solving may be a function of persistent re-experiencing and re-enactment of the trauma. This possibility was envisaged in Freud's notion of attempts at 'completion' following trauma, interestingly discussed in the context of more recent theories by Horowitz (1986, Chapter 6). The person may, for example, think or dream about the disaster, with alternating endings, some worse than what actually happened, but some better. A successful resolution, in representations unmarked by time, may even serve to undo the traumatic experience, or it may restore a positive view. However, unsuccessful attempts to work out a better ending, in dreams, in waking thought, or in patterns of behaviour, in effect only re-enact the trauma, over and over again. In this case, the attempts to find a solution have become the problem, a typical sign of intentional processes in disorder as discussed earlier (pp. 312–14, 348–9).

Attempts to work out a more successful, tolerable outcome of a traumatic experience may also, however, be a kind of denial, a refusal to accept that the experience was as awful as it was. This denial would then characteristically alternate with the repeated realization through re-enactment that it was, after all, that bad. This pattern persists in so far as the representations of past and present lack distinctive time or context markers, and are hardly distinguished.

A quite different strand in the attempt to adapt to traumatic experience is construction of a representation which acknowledges how awful it was, but which forsees the possibility of a different, better outcome next time. Or, what comes close to the same thing, construction of a representation in which the the trauma is recognized as both awful but despite that somehow possible to survive. Either way, what is envisaged is a world, or a self and a world, which is both dreadful and yet possible.

Here we come across the key idea of integrating the traumatic experience into the person's system of belief, noted in the previous chapter (p. 314). The psychological conflicts and tasks of adjustment here can be compared with the problems of anomalies and theory adaptation which are manifest in the progress of the sciences. As noted above, Janoff-Bulman (1985), in introducing the idea of basic assumptions with a view to conceptualizing the effects of trauma, refers to Kuhn's (1962) notion of paradigm in science. We also suggest that the epistemological principles linking theory and experiment, visible in science, are similar to those operating in the case of psychological adjustment to trauma. The principles are specifically those of post-empiricism (subsections 1.4.1, 1.4.4., pp. 305–6).

Trauma may be defined as experience which scores pretty well a direct hit on the core of the theory which regulates action, contradicting the conviction that the world is, in various senses, safe enough. To achieve this the event has to be one which cannot simply be ignored. It may be experienced fast and dramatically, in one trial, as in disasters. Or it may be experienced repeatedly, as for example child sexual abuse in the family. Either way the trauma is forcibly experienced. As already discussed, a natural response to this blatent conflict between the undeniable force of the trauma and the unmoveable core of belief is something like dissociation, or splitting (pp. 309–10, and above). Both are held on to, but in different states of mind, through time, or even at the same time. What is required in these circumstances if the trauma is not to be repeatedly re-experienced, is construction of a representation which can accommodate both the traumatic experience and the view of the self and the world as, on balance, secure enough. This kind of resolution following a disaster may be apparent in thoughts to the effect: 'It did happen, I nearly died, I was terrified; but I survived (without too much loss), it is over, and all being well, taking into account reasonable estimation of probabilities, it is unlikely to happen to me again'. Or following sexual abuse: 'It did happen, but it was not my fault; my mother did not stop it, or did not believe me, but she is not all bad'. And so forth.

By all means whether such a resolution can be achieved in practice depends on many circumstances and factors. Some of these will have to do with the severity of the trauma and the losses sustained. Thinking particularly of trauma experienced in adult life, it may be expected that pre-existing personality characteristics are also relevant, specifically concerning core assumptions about the self and world. We can envisage several broad kinds of case here. One is the kind emphasized by Janoff-Bulman (1985), in which the person's core assumptions are somewhat extreme, such as the assumption of personal invulnerability, or super-competence. Highly successful men and women may 'fall apart' following trauma and fail to recover, often developing depression. In such cases the person simply cannot stand the vulnerability and failure to cope, or the loss of function in the initial post-traumatic reaction. Adjustment to trauma against the background of excessively self-confident assumptions can be extremely difficult, and Janoff-Bulman is right to draw attention specifically to them. Something critical to the person's view of themselves is lost, and post-traumatic stress can be then complicated by depression in response to this loss. The task in such cases is to achieve a view of the self as 'good enough'. Similar sorts of considerations apply to cases in which the pre-existing core assumptions about the world are overoptimistic. Experience contradicting this is quite unprepared for, and is particularly devastating. This is one aspect of the reason why young children are so vulnerable to traumatic abuse in the family: they have, and they have to have, more or less unquestioning trust in those meant to be looking after them.

Another kind of case is that in which pre-traumatic core assumptions are already of a balanced, not black-and-white kind. Here one would find already in the one scheme of things acknowledgement that there was safety and danger, coping and not coping, succeeding and failing, and so on. The prediction would be that such a view, or way of thinking, would serve to facilitate adjustment to trauma, other things being equal.

A third kind of case might be in people whose view of the self and world was already pretty negative, as the result of experiences and achievements that were perceived as not good enough. Here it might be predicted that the adjustment to trauma, or certain kinds of trauma, might be facilitated, in so far as it did not in fact contradict basic assumptions. But, on the other hand, the trauma would serve to give massive confirmation to the person's depressive outlook.

It can be assumed that variations in the theory of self and world are highly conditioned by learning. In other words, we suppose that from the beginnings the child's view of the world and self is shaped by experience and education to become more or less like the three kinds described above. The child may come to have a highly negative view of carers, or other people, or the self. He may be competent, and brought up so as to believe that he is wonderful, and that everything goes and should go his way. In certain circumstances these two views can even coexist, unintegrated, reflecting unresolved ambivalance in the family and in the mind. A different possibility is development of a view of the self and world as positive and negative, and on balance good enough. This would require a combination of not too much adverse experience, enough good experience, together with help from carers to do the integrative work of containing positive and negative, security and anxiety, possession and loss, success and disappointment, in the one mental space.

The concept in developmental cognitive psychology which comes closest to what is at issue here is that of attachment representation, discussed previously (subsections 6.3.4, 8.4.7). We have suggested that post-traumatic stress reactions will more readily decay to the extent that the person's pre-existing core beliefs about the self and world already contain positive and negative features with negotiation among them. Assuming that core beliefs are associated specifically with secure attachment representation, the prediction would be that secure attachment representation facilitates recovery from post-traumatic shock. As with all hypotheses about personality variables as protective or risk factors in post-traumatic stress, there is the problem that they are measured after the event and hence are confounded by the post-traumatic effects themselves. However, the methodological problem is soluble using large samples and control groups.

We have proposed that trauma is persistently re-experienced or re-enacted in so far as it contradicts the representation of a tolerable, secure reality. The traumatic experience is remembered alongside the experience of safety, with persistent, recurring alternation between the two states of mind. This cycle resolves to the extent that the traumatic experience can be integrated into a representation of the self and world as being, on balance, safe enough.

Finally in this subsection we consider briefly other possible applications of the model sketched so far. As remarked above, Rachman (1980) invoked failure of emotional processing in order to explain a variety of cases of repetitive, intrusive distressing thoughts, including obsessions and abnormal grief reactions. The model proposed here applies most transparently to post-traumatic stress disorder. It applies readily also to persistent grief reactions, unsurprisingly since bereavement typically involves trauma. In grief the loss of the loved one is both represented and not represented. Representation may take the form of persistent memories of aspects of the death or discovery or news of the death. Alternating with this is non-representation of the loss, by seeing the dead person, in hallucination, or mistaken first appearances, and by other diverse forms of denial, including the wish to carry on as before as though nothing had changed. So far, as remarked in connection with trauma in general, this is normal. The problem is more when this splitting persists, when there is no integration, when the person does not adjust to the loss, but carries on alternating between a fragile sense of well-being, and depressive episodes.

A problem much more challenging to the model is explanation of the obsessions in obsessive-compulsive disorder. The model as outlined works best in cases of real traumatic experiences contradicting reasonable basic assumptions about the self and the world. It is so far unclear that this could have anything to do with the fantastic world of obsessional beliefs and rituals. On the other hand, even if destined for failure, it is worthwhile considering possibilities here.

The core ideas would be as before. The proposal would be that obsessional thoughts signify something quite contrary to basic assumptions about the self and the world, that they repeatedly, intrusively recur in the absence of any integration of the thoughts, or what they mean, into a tolerable self- and world-view. Aspects of these hypotheses fit fairly readily with the clinical presentation. According to psychological formulations, the best candidates for the meaning of obsessional thoughts have to do with fear of uncontrolled loss, or destruction, for which the self is in some way responsible (subsection 9.3.2). This interpretation is an example of construing the intentional object of apparently irrational fear in such a way as to bring out its bio-psychological significance (subsection 9.3.1). Apparently irrational compulsions would be construed in a corresponding way, as symbolizing the person's capacity to keep things in order. It is also plausible to hypothesize something like splitting or dissociation in at least some people with obsessive-compulsive disorder. Fear of being out of control shows up alongside, alternating with, keeping in precise control, these two contradictory themes being timelessly entangled together in the compulsions themselves.

A critical feature of obsessive-compulsive disorder is as yet untouched by this approach, however. This is the characteristic blurring of the distinction between mind and reality. Obsessions are expressions of fear of serious harm, typically some catastrophe to the self, or destruction of (the person's) world by the self. The person is unclear (in this state of mind) between imagined destruction (or destruction in the imagination) and real destruction. At the same time the individual believes that his or her special stereotyped, ritualized actions can avert the feared catastrophe.

At this point it is possible, in line with themes in previous chapters, to introduce a developmental aspect into the model of recurring, intrusive thoughts when applied to obsessive-compulsive disorder. 'Irrationality' can be construed as *pre-rationality*. All the above-listed irrational characteristics of the obsessive-compulsive have early developmental analogues, concerning blurring of the distinctions known to reason and the reliance on 'magical' thinking (Piaget 1937; Vygotsky 1981; Harris 1994; see also Chapter 6, subsection 6.5.2). There are in pre-rational thought in children inflated views of the power of the self, linked to egocentricism, including feelings of omnipotence, linked then to perceived responsibility, the other side of which is fear of helplessness and destruction. There is also blurred appearance/reality distinction, and belief in the power of ritual (in thought or action) to influence otherwise uncontrollable reality. In the face of possible catastrophe, pre-reason uses magic. Mind is experienced as powerful, which has the following implication: if the mind can destroy reality, it can also save it. Apparent similarities between pre-rational thought and activity and obsessive-compulsive phenomena have long been recognized (Freud 1913; A. Freud 1965). There are also, of course, differences, specifically in persistence and in distress caused, which are emphasized by those who see obsessive-compulsion as a neurological disorder (Leonard 1989; see also subsection 9.3.2).

It may be possible, then, to apply the model of intrusive, distressing thoughts worked out in the case of post-traumatic stress to obsessive-compulsive disorder. The adult experiences trauma in reality. The young child, by contrast, is in a world in which fantasy and reality are not yet reliably distinguished, in which imagined catastrophe might be real catastrophe, or in which real catastrophe, such as loss or prolonged separation from a carer, might be due to his imagination. The adult responds to real catastrophe by cognitive preoccupation alternating with avoidance. The young child (the mind in that developmentally early stage) responds also by preoccupation, and the problem-solving strategy is the exercise of magical powers of control.

9.4 PERSONALITY DISORDER

9.4.1 Introduction

The concept of personality disorder has a long and rather chequered history. At worst its use has been pejorative, non-developmental, and anti-therapeutic. Notwithstanding the difficulties, it provides a pointer to important aspects of disturbance that are not characterized by episodic occurrences of relatively clearly defined syndromes, such as depression. The two main classificatory systems include a number of different categories of personality disorder, but they assume that there is a unified underlining concept which is characterized by the presence of abnormal traits. The *Diagnostic and statistical manual of mental disorders*, (4th edn) (commonly known as DSM-IV) states that:

> Personality traits are enduring patterns of perceiving, relating to, and thinking about the environment and one's self that are exhibited in a wide range of social and personal contexts. Only when personality traits are inflexible and maladaptive and cause significant functional impairment or subjective distress do they constitute personality disorders. (American Psychiatric Association 1994, p. 630.)

In practice, the different personality disorder categories include very widely differing kinds of items, including those that refer to states of mind (e.g. uncertainties of self-image), mood states, (e.g. marked shifts from normal mood to depression, irritability or anxiety), interpersonal difficulties (e.g. a pattern of unstable and intense interpersonal relationships), and specific behaviours, such as failure to accept social norms. Given this heterogeneity, attempts to provide one explanatory framework are likely to prove frustrating. It is clear also that each personality disorder category is not distinct, and co-occurrence of several diagnoses is common (Oldham *et al.* 1992), so that in considering one particular category we cannot be confident of its separate identity. These limitations, combined with the tendency for the concept to be misused, might make it seem a poor subject for our concluding chapter. However, from a mental health perspective, its value lies in drawing our attention to the presence of recurring maladaptive patterns of attributions, emotional states, cognitions and actions. These persistent patterns of personal dysfunction are found in over 50 per cent of patients referred to mental health facilities with problems such as depression and other non-psychotic conditons, such as anxiety and eating disorders (Pfohl *et al.* 1984; Gartner *et al.* 1989; Shea *et al.* 1990). When we turn to the possible intentionality of personality disorder, the most striking findings are those that indicate that frequently it is preceded by behavioural disturbance, or severe adversity in childhood, or a combination of the two (Robins 1966, 1986; Ogata *et al.* 1990).

9.4.2 Borderline personality disorder

Notwithstanding the problems of definition, we will examine one particular personality disorder, 'borderline personality disorder', in relation to intentionality and development. Borderline personality disorder is characterized by intense and unstable intimate relationships, rapid changes of mood, and impulsive aggressive behaviour often towards the self, in the form of overdoses or cutting the wrists or other parts of the body. It is commonly preceded by a history of physical or sexual abuse (Ogata *et al.* 1990). How might these childhood experiences be related to the adult disorder?

We start with an examination of borderline processes in relation to our earlier considerations, particularly those in Chapter 8. Clinical experience and a range of psychotherapeutic formulations (e.g. Kernberg 1984) have provided a valuable picture of borderline processes. The mind of the individual is characterized by sharp and unpredictable shifts of mood and perceptions. The contrast is often between a view of the self and those around that is optimistic and confident, and one dominated by anger and unhappiness. In the happy state of mind, often it seems that facts that do not fit that state are not recognized, or if they are, they lead to catastrophic change to pessimism and anger. These facts may be derived from current circumstances, or from reference to the person's previous states of mind or behaviours. When in one state of mind the individual appears not to have access to others. This applies also in the other direction, so that when he/she is pessimistic and angry, good experiences are forgotten and angrily denied, and there appears to be little scope to consider some modification of that way of seeing things. Here then, representations and the rules of perception and experience are contradictory and are subject to rapid, intense, and unpredictable change. Furthermore each will tolerate only certain kinds of information, so that its range of function is narrow and open to catastrophic failure.

Relationships are subject to a similar roller-coaster effect as the individual. Typically they are seen as filled with love and perfection, or as useless or destructive, and they may become violent. Then relationships seem to reflect in part the individual's need to keep states of mind pure and lacking in doubt or difficulty, and in part a particular pattern of communication. As long as a relationship is in one state or another and the individual can keep hold of it that way, communication of departures from this are ignored or are not tolerated. Communication, as a means of adding new information to interactions between people, is eliminated. Put another way, there is a lack of negotiation of a joint frame of reference between the individuals, and instead a demand by at least one of the participants of what has to be the case, for instance that it is a perfect relationship. Thus both the individual and his/her relationships are characterized by rapid shifts between contradictory states, and a lack of individual or interpersonal metarepresentational systems.

Repeated injury to the body is common in borderline functioning. Sometimes this represents a suicide attempt, but usually it does not. Often the individual will cut him/herself when frustrated or angry. This is a complicated phenomenon and many different explanations have been offered for it. Here we will focus on one aspect, the attack on a part of oneself. In evolution, anger and attack appear to be part of an intentional response which has survival value for the individual and species through reducing danger. They form part of effective action with respect to the environment. In self-injury it seems that part of the intentional sequence, entailing the emotion and the action, is subverted so that action is not effective in bringing about change. It is an example of a contradiction in the intentional process, (referred to earlier, subsection 9.3.3), of action both occurring but not occurring, simultaneously. The way this is achieved may be through a split in the representation of the self (or at least of the body) so that a part of oneself can become the object of action. In one sense that creates the appearance of effective action, but in reality it is ineffective because it is part of the same person. In summary, in borderline processes we have contradictory unpredictable states of mind and relationships, lack of effective communication and negotiations, and action that is not action.

9.4.3 Sexual abuse and borderline processes

How might these be related to childhood experiences of adversity? We reviewed some of the relevant mechanisms in the previous chapter, and return to them here in more detail. We will focus on sexual abuse, although many of the processes are likely to be found in other forms of abusive, punitive or neglectful parenting. Sexual abuse of young children is usually painful, intrusive, confusing, and frightening. Typically it occurs under conditions of secrecy with threats from the perpetrator of injury or loss, for instance through break-up of the family, if the child discloses. Whether it is carried out by a parent or an adult from outside the family, it involves a transgression of the assumed protective role of adults. It may well be carried out in a perverse manner within the day to day events of family life. Furniss (1992) described a father who signalled to his daughter that the abuse was about to take place with the words, 'Go and wash your hands', and once it was over would say, 'Now it is time to do your homework'. Abused children may show signs characteristic of trauma in general, of hyperarousal, irritability, and flashbacks, but may manage to hide the distress and maintain an appearance of normality. Then, in spite of severe trauma, they continue to act in ways that preserve their relationships, including those in the family. How does the child cope? He/she is faced with representations of the facts of what are going on, and with the accompanying emotions of fear and anger, without a means of acting on them. These representations would, under other circumstances, lead to report of the act, but as physical danger and loss of family are threatened if that happens, the secrecy is preserved. Furthermore the actions that are required, to behave as if nothing is happening, require quite different representations in the mind. So here are the conditions under which the child may split off cognitive-emotional states of the form 'I am being hurt, I am frightened' which cannot be linked to action, and 'I am fine', which is inaccurate but may provide the basis for survival and action. He/she learns to segregate the components of the mind so that what is known is not known. Here then, may be the conditions for the development of contradictory states of mind, that are maintained separate in order to preserve the conditions for action in childhood.

Not only is sexual abuse likely to lead to segregated thoughts and feelings, but also ones that are not linked systematically to external events. The scope for establishing their applicability, and for their testing and modification, is likely therefore to be limited. Thus if the child learns to split off the emotions labelled 'I am frightened' when being abused, the question arises as to how to deal with the same emotions arising at other times. How is he/she to distinguish those times when the state of mind can be registered and talked about, and when this is not possible? It is unlikely that there will be help available from adults in sorting this out, and so there is the possibility that events which might not usually be frightening will come to be feared. Similarly, if such a state cannot be registered and talked about, there will be little scope for exploring those conditions under which being frightened might be modified. This is the reverse of the benign exploration of perceptions, fears, and wishes that goes on in the play and relationships of most children, and may lead to mental representations that are inflexible, inappropriate to external circumstances, and not readily open to modifications.

The example of the father's use of everyday language to signal the beginning and end of episodes of abuse, illustrates the way in which trust in what is said can be undermined, in abuse. If some sentences are uttered under one set of metarules and others under different rules, but the difference cannot be acknowledged, then the child is likely to feel uncertain about the meaning of apparently straightforward communications. This will have implications for the monitoring of the individual's state of mind, and for his/her understanding of what is happening between people. In contrast to the infant who looks to the parent for help in deciding whether to cross the visual cliff (subsection 6.4.4), the child who is being abused may not have adults with whom communications are sufficiently unambiguous that such checking could be possible. One possible solution then is to attempt to constrict the range of individual and interpersonal emotions, thoughts, and actions in order to reduce uncertainty, and enable actions to be preserved. This, in turn, is likely to reduce the scope for negotiations in relationships, as these require confidence that what is said is what is meant, and that areas of uncertainty can be entered with relative safety. This constricting of communication may provide another basis for the splitting of representations. If communications allow only 'normal' family life to be acknowledged, then the unacknowledged aspects have to be kept separate in the minds of the participants, and hence for the child this may become an habitual way of coping.

The child not only has to cope with the knowledge that the abuse is taking place, but also with the fact of it. This frequently involves physical pain and revulsion and many survivors have described dividing their mind from their body so that, in effect, what happens to the body is not experienced as happening to them. This is yet a further division in the representation of what is going on, but with somewhat different consequences. If the child comes to see the body as in some ways not part of the self, then the body can be treated as if it is that of someone else, and in particular may be neglected or attacked. Not only that, by creating a split between mind and body, the child runs the risk of separating representation and the agent of action, the body.

9.4.4 Development, intentional, and borderline processes

Let us summarize now the developmental processes that may be impaired when a child is abused sexually or in other ways, and underline the links with the function and dysfunction of intentional processes. First children need to register the presence of perceptions, thoughts, and emotions, and their differences, and to move among them without fear, just as happens in their play. When certain states of mind are not allowed they may become disconnected, unintegrated, and disruptive. Secondly, the content of these representations needs to be tested for their applicability, truth, and possible modification. In the language of our earlier discussion, the underlying rules have specificity and generality so that they can mediate between events and actions. Where such mental representations cannot be tested, for instance through play with other children, or through being brought into relationships with adults, they are likely to become rigid, and inappropriate. The child, and the adult, is likely to find none reflects reality satisfactorily so that one is held until it can no longer bear the strain of the evidence, only to be replaced by another with similar limitations. Thirdly, children need to be confident of the truth of communications within their social networks, and in particular that they can be clear about the convention that is being followed in the use of language. The metarepresentational framework in which communications take place must have clarity. Then language can be used to express needs, state views, and enter areas of uncertainty, in short to negotiate effectively within relationships. This basic assumption that what is said is meant often cannot be made by the child who is being abused. Fourthly, the child needs an integrated experience of mind and body. Our accounts of development and of post-empiricist thought have underlined the close connection between thoughts and action, and of the experience of effective agency as crucial to the sense of self. Under conditions of repeated helplessness and of dissociation from the body, this link in intentional processes is likely to be undermined, leading to inaction, or action that is ineffective and turned on the person's own body. In many ways the child is faced with representing the unrepresentable, acting the impossible action, and dividing the basis of intentionality. The features of borderline functioning that we considered earlier, the intense unstable relationships in which negotiation and communication are limited, and the rapid changes of moods, beliefs and actions, can be seen to follow from these processes.

Of all the borderline phenomena, self-injury is perhaps one of the most striking and puzzling. We see now several ways in which the person who has been abused may come to injure herself repeatedly in adult life. The child searches for an explanation and blames herself, but the conditions for testing her explanations are undermined by secrecy and fear. Her experience of her body is separated from her experience of herself because she has coped with the trauma by dissociating herself from her body. Then via a similar mechanism she may blame parts of her body for the abuse. Her sense of self does not include an experience of her body as an agent of effective action, through the impossibility of action being linked to representation. With subsequent development the 'choice' when faced with stress, loss, or maltreatment is either to deny the difficulties, hence using the childhood coping strategy; or to allow them to be represented with implications for action. Where she sees herself or her body as the cause of the difficulties, where she does not have the previous experience of action as effective, where her body has not been integrated into her sense of self, action may be turned on to her own body.

9.4.5 Protection and resilience

Our account has so far indicated ways in which threats to intentional processes may arise through coping with experience, with possible borderline functioning later in life. It is important to keep in mind that at this stage we do not know why some people show this kind of disturbance in adult life following child sexual abuse, while many do not, nor whether sexual abuse has specific effects when compared to other forms of abusive and neglectful parenting. The implications for the intentionality of adverse experiences may vary considerably. For instance, some children may be able to keep some areas of relatively integrated mental life alive, while still coping in ways that we have discussed here. If that is the case, that might be a function of constitutional factors, early pre-abuse experiences, or other valued previous or current relationships. Here the fit between the child and the experience may be crucial. For instance, some children who are abused are preoccupied with the welfare of other members of the family and do not disclose in order to protect them from the knowledge. Then a sensitivity to others may be a greater risk factor for coping later in ways that are maladaptive, than lack of sensitivity. Such a difference of sensitivity might have its roots in earlier experiences, or in inherited differences.

The capacity of a parent to envisage the infant or child as a mental entity may be a further source of resilience (Fonagy *et al.* 1994). Then the child will experience her wide range of intentions, feelings, and desires as contained within her parent's mind, within the relationship, and therefore containable within her own mind. Containment, as we saw in Chapter 8, is both epistemological and psychological. This may enable the child to reflect emotionally and cognitively on her own states of mind, even in the face of trauma, so that she may then be less vulnerable to the radical undermining that we have considered earlier. Fonagy and his colleagues have provided evidence that this self-reflective capacity may confer resilience in the face of adversity, and its role in protection from severe consequences of abuse will be an important focus of future research.

9.5 CONCLUSION

In reviewing psychiatric syndromes, some themes recur. This does not lead to a general theory of disorder, but to an analysis that has some general features. When seen against a developmental background, disorder is viewed in relation to the tasks that must be achieved where multiple sets of mental rules are possible. These include the monitoring of internal and interpersonal rules, the maintenance of the individual's experience of continuity in the presence of multiple states of mind, and the capacity to understand the mental states and actions of others. Many of the overarching, metarepresentational functions could also be characterized as functions of the self, and these appear to be disrupted in conditions that are as widely different as schizophrenia and borderline personality disorder. In schizophrenia the monitoring of the individual's own thoughts or actions may be impaired, whereas in borderline functioning the continuity of states of mind is undermined. If the sense of self is derived from the awareness of being the author of one's own actions or thoughts over time, then in these conditions it is undermined in different ways. In as much as the coherence of the self is in turn central to action, disturbances of action are the result of these different forms of disruption of the self.

In both conditions further contrasting factors may undermine action. In schizophrenia inefficient information-processing may lead either to action based on incidental aspects of a situation, or to inaction based on information overload. In borderline personality disorder experiences in which action has been impossible may lead to action turned on itself, in self-injury. However, in both, there may be elements that represent the attempt to preserve action in the face of such threats. In schizophrenia delusions and hallucinations may, in part, be compensatory mechanisms that reduce uncertainty, hence providing the basis for action. In borderline personality disorder the splitting of mental representations may similarly, by excluding elements that are incompatible with action, provide (partial) representations that provide the basis for action. Thus in both conditions elements of accurate representation are sacrificed, in order for action to continue.

Conditions in which action is preserved may be contrasted with those, such as depression, where it is not. In either case a range of intentional and non-intentional origins may be envisaged. In situations of helplessness, depression may be seen to be an appropriate and accurate representation that action is not possible. Depression seen in the absence of such a threat may result from the intrusion of cognitive and emotional states that undermine action, arising from a physical, non-intentional interruption of perceptions, thoughts, feelings, or actions. Equally, depression may arise where mental representations that have been maintained inactive or out of consciousness are activated, and are incompatible with action.

In post-traumatic stress disorder there appears to be a lack of resolution in favour of either representation or action. While some of the elements, such as denial of aspects of the trauma, seem to be attempts to limit the scope of the representation, this is not as comprehensive or complete as that seen for instance in borderline processes. Instead there is a circular repeated movement back and forth between the representation of the trauma and hence threat to action, and an assertion that action and therefore life is possible and so the representation must be denied or limited: and so on. Perhaps in this 'disorder' we find the clearest statement of the need to represent and to act, and the price paid when these requirements are in conflict.

We conclude by revisiting our starting point. Mental entities, perceptions, feelings, thoughts, and wishes are genuinely causal and must provide sufficient certainty that the individual can act effectively. Throughout biology, intentional states of organisms, from the simplest cellular creatures to non-human primates, have provided the basis for action, and in general the certainty has been derived from the evolution of those intentional states over long periods of time. In this and the preceding chapters we have seen how, in the activities of the human mind, is seen an infinite elaboration of the potential inherent in all intentional processes in biology. This has introduced novelty, creativity, and flexibility, which are seen in the achievements of language, custom, technology, and culture. It has also increased the risks of uncertainty, confusion, and the undermining of action. These are reduced through an interplay between the sophisticated integrative capacities of the human brain and the continuities of human relationships, skills, beliefs, and social organizations. Disorder is found in the failure of intentional states to underpin action, either where these are undermined by the external world, or where they are distorted, contradictory, or unintegrated, and action is undermined or ineffective.

REFERENCES

American Psychiatric Association (1994). *Diagnostic and Statistical Manual of Mental Disorders*, (4th edn). American Psychiatric Association, Washington, DC.

Bebbington, P. and Kuipers, L. (1994). The predictive utility of expressed emotion in schizophrenia: an aggregate analysis. *Psychological Medicine*, 24, 707–18.

Bentall, R. P., Kaney, S., and Dewey, M. E. (1991). Paranoia and social reasoning: an attribution theory analysis. *British Journal of Clinical Psychology*, 30, 13–23.

Bernstein, G. A. and Garfinkel, B. D. (1988). Pedigrees, functioning, and psychopathology in families of school phobic children. *American Journal of Psychiatry*, 142, 1497–9.

Bernstein, G. A., Svingen, P. H., and Garfinkel, B. D. (1990). School phobia: patterns of family functioning. *Journal of the American Academy of Child and Adolescent Psychiatry*, 29, 24–30.

Bolton, D. (1994). Family systems interventions. In *Handbook of phobic and anxiety disorders of children*, (ed. T. Ollendick, W. Yule and N. King), pp. 397–414. Plenum, New York.

Borkovec, T. D., Shadick, R., and Hopkins, M. (1991). The nature of normal and pathological worry. In *Chronic anxiety: generalized anxiety disorder and mixed anxiety-depression*, (ed. R. Rapee and D. H. Barlow), pp. 29–51. Guildford Press, New York.

Carey, G. and Gottesman, I. (1981). Twin studies of anxiety, phobic, and obsessive disorders. In *Anxiety: new research and changing concepts*, (ed. D. F. Klein and J. Rabkins), pp. 117–33. Raven Press, New York.

Chemtob, C., Roitblat, H. L., Hamada, R. S., Carlson, J. G., and Twentyman, C. T. (1988). A cognitive action theory of post traumatic stress disorder. *Journal of Anxiety Disorders*, 2, 253–75.

Chiocca, E. A. and Martuza, R. L. (1990). Neurosurgical therapy of obsessive-compulsive disorder. In *Obsessive-compulsive disorders: theory and management*, (ed. M. A. Jenicke, L. Baer and W. E. Minichiello), pp. 283–94. Year Book Medical, Chicago.

Christensen, K. J., Kim, S. W., Dysken, M. W., and Hoover, K. M. (1992). Neuropsychological performance in obsessive-compulsive disorder. *Biological Psychiatry*, 31, 4–18.

Cohen, L., Hollander, E., DeCaria, C. M., Stein, D. J., Simeon, D., Liebowitz, M. R., and Aronowitz, B (in press). Specificity of neuropsychological impairment in obsessive compulsive disorder: a comparison with social phobic and normal controls. *Journal of Neuropsychology and Clinical Neuroscience.*

Cornblatt, B. A., Lenzenweger, M. F., Dworkin, R. H., and Erlenmeyer–Kimling (1992). Childhood attentional dysfunctions predict social deficits in unaffected adults at risk of schizophrenia. *British Journal of Psychiatry*, **161**, (suppl. 18), 59–64.

Cox, C., Fedio, P., and Rapoport, J. (1989). Neuropsychological testing of obsessive-compulsive adolescents. In *Obsessive-compulsive disorder in children and adolescents*, (ed. J. L. Rapoport), pp. 73–85. American Psychiatric Press Inc., Washington.

Creamer, M., Burgess, P., and Pattison, P. (1992). Reaction to trauma: a cognitive processing model. *Journal of Abnormal Psychology*, **101**, 452–9.

Crow, T. J. (1985). The two syndrome concept: origins and current status. *Schizophrenia Bulletin*, **11**, 471–86.

Denckla, M. (1989). Neurological examination. In *Obsessive-compulsive disorder in children and adolescents*, (ed. J. L. Rapoport), pp. 107–15. American Psychiatric Press Inc., Washington.

Dixon, N. F. (1981). *Preconscious processing*. Wiley, Chichester.

Edwards, J. R. (1988). The determinants and consequences of coping with stress. In *Causes, coping, and consequences of stress at work*, (ed. C. L. Cooper and R. Payne) pp. 233–63. Wiley, Chichester.

Endler, N. S. and Parker, J. D. A. (1990). Multidimensional assessment of coping: a critical evaluation of coping. *Journal of Personality and Social Psychology*, **58**, 844–54.

Erikson, E. (1963). *Childhood and society*. Norton, New York.

Eysenck, H. (1979). The conditioning model of neurosis. *The Behavioral and Brain Sciences*, **2**, 155–99.

Eysenck, M. W. (1992). *Anxiety: the cognitive perspective*. Lawrence Erlbaum Associates, Hove.

Falkai, P., Bogerts, B., and Rozumek, M. (1988). Limbic pathology in schizophrenia: the entorhinal region — a morphometric study. *Biological Psychiatry*, **24**, 515–21.

Foa, E. B. and Kozak, M. J. (1986). Emotional processing and fear: exposure to corrective information. *Psychological Bulletin*, **99**, 20–35.

Foa, E. B. and Steketee, G. (1989). Behavioral/cognitive conceptualizations of post-traumatic stress disorder. *Behavior Therapy*, **20**, 155–76.

Foa, E. B., Zinbarg, R., and Rothbaum, B. (1992). Uncontrollability and unpredictability in post traumatic stress disorder: an animal model. *Psychological Bulletin*, **112**, 218–38.

Fonagy, P., Steele, M., Steele, H., Higgitt, A., and Target, M. (1994). The Emanuel Miller Memorial Lecture 1992. The theory and practice of resilience. *Journal of Child Psychology and Psychiatry*, **35**, (2), 231–57.

Freud, A. (1965). *Normality and pathology in childhood: assessments of developments*. New York: Interbational Universities Press.

Freud, A. (1966). Obsessional neurosis: a summary of psychoanalytic views as presented at the Congress. *International Journal of Psychoanalysis*, **47**, 116–22.

Freud, S. (1913). *Totem and taboo*. Standard Edition **13**, (1953), pp. 1–161. Hogarth Press, London.

Frith, C. D. (1992). *The cognitive neuropsychology of schizophrenia*. Lawrence Erlbaum Associates, Hove.

Frith, C. D. and Done, D. J. (1988). Towards a neuropsychology of schizophrenia. *British Journal of Psychiatry*, **153**, 437–43.

Furniss, T. (1992). Lecture, First European Conference of the Association of Child Psychology and Psychiatry and Allied Disciplines, York, England.

Gartner, A. F., Marcus, R. N., Halmi, K., and Loranger, A. W. (1989). DSM-III-R personality disorders in patients with eating disorders. *American Journal of Psychiatry*, **146**, 1585–91.

Gray, J. A. (1982). *The neuropsychology of anxiety*. Clarendon, Oxford.

Gray, J. A., Feldon, J., Rawlins, J. N. P., Hemsley, D. R., and Smith, A. D. (1991). The Neuropsychology of Schizophrenia. *Behavioral and Brain Sciences*, **14**, 1–84.

Harris, E. L., Noyes, R., Crowe, R. R., and Chaudery, M. D. (1983). A family study of agoraphobia. *Archives of General Psychiatry*, **40**, 1061–4.

Harris, P. L. (1994). Unexpected, impossible and magical events: children's reactions to causal violations. *British Journal of Developmental Psychology*, **12**, 1–7.

Head, D., Bolton, D., and Hymas, N. (1989). Deficit in cognitive shifting ability in patients with obsessive-compulsive disorder. *Biological Psychiatry*, **23**, 323–7.

Hollander, E. *et al.* (1990). Signs of central nervous system dysfunction in obsessive-compulsive disorder. *Archives of General Psychiatry*, **47**, 27–32.

Hollander, E., Cohen, L., Richards, M., Mullen, L., Decaria, C., and Stern, Y. (1993). A pilot study of the neuropsychology of obsessive-compulsive disorder and Parkinson's Disease: basal ganglia disorders. *Journal of Neuropsychiatry and Clinical Neurosciences*, **5**, 104–7.

Horowitz, M. (1986). *Stress response syndromes*, (2nd edn). Jason Aronson, New York.

Hymas, N., Lees, A., Bolton, D., Epps, K., and Head, D. (1991). The neurology of obsessional slowness. *Brain*, **114**, 2203–33.

Jakob, H. and Beckman, H. (1986). Prenatal developmental disturbances in the limbic allocortex in schizophrenics. *Journal of Neural Transmission*, **65**, 303–26.

Janoff-Bulman, R. (1985). The aftermath of victimization: rebuilding shattered assumptions. In *Trauma and its wake*, (ed. C. Figley), Vol. 1, pp. 15–35. Brunner/Mazel, New York.

Jesus Mari, J. De and Streiner, D. L. (1994). An overview of family interventions and relapse on schizophrenia: meta-analysis of research findings. *Psychological Medicine*, **24**, 565–78.

Jones, P. and Murray, R. M. (1991). The genetics of schizophrenia is the genetics of neurodevelopment. *British Journal of Psychiatry*, **158**, 615–23.

Keane, T. M., Zimmerling, R. T., and Caddell, J. M. (1985). A behavioral formulation of post-traumatic stress disorder in Vietnam veterans. *The Behavior Therapist*, **8**, 9–12.

Kemp-Wheeler, S. M. and Hill, A. B. (1987). Anxiety responses to subliminal experience of mild stress. *British Journal of Psychology*, **78**, 365–74.

Kernberg, O. (1984). *Severe personality disorders*. Yale University Press, New Haven.

Kuhn, T. S. (1962). *The structure of scientific revolutions*. University of Chicago Press, Chicago.

Last, C. G., Hersen, M., Kazdin, A. E., Francis, G., and Grubb, H. J. (1987). Psychiatric illness in the mothers of anxious children. *American Journal of Psychiatry*, **144**, 1580–3.

Lazarus, R. S. and Averill, J. R. (1972). Emotion and cognition: with special reference to anxiety. In *Anxiety: current trends in theory and research*, (ed. C. D. Spielberger), Vol. 2, pp. 241–83. Academic Press, New York.

Leckman, J. F., Weissman, M. M., Merikangas, K. R., Pauls, D. L., and Prusoff, B. (1983). Panic disorder and major depression. *Archives of General Psychiatry*, **40**, 1055–60.

Leonard, H. (1989). Childhood rituals and superstitions: developmental and cultural perspective. In *Obsessive-compulsive disorder in children and adolescents*, (ed. J. L. Rapoport), pp. 289–309. American Psychiatric Press Inc., Washington.

Livingston, R., Nugent, H., Rader, L., and Smith, R. G. (1985). Family histories of depressed and anxious children. *American Journal of Psychiatry*, **142**, 1497–9.

Lorentz, K. Z. (1981). *The foundations of ethology*. Springer-Verlag, New York.

Luxenberg, J., Swedo, S., Flament, M., Friedland, R., Rapoport, J., and Rapoport, S. (1988). Neuroanatomical abnormalities in obsessive-compulsive disorder detected with quantitative X-ray computed tomography. *American Journal of Psychiatry*, **145**, 1089–93.

McKeon, J., McGuffin, P., and Robinson, P. (1984). Obsessive-compulsive neurosis following head injury: a report of four cases. *British Journal of Psychiatry*, **144**, 190–2.

Millikan, R. (1984). *Language, thought, and other biological categories*. MIT Press, Cambridge, Mass.

Millikan, R. (1986). Thoughts without laws: cognitive science with content. *Philosophical Review*, **95**, 47–80.

Mineka, S. and Kihlstrom, J. (1978). Unpredictable and uncontrollable aversive events. *Journal of Abnormal Psychology*, **87**, 256–71.

Mlakar, J., Jensterle, J., and Frith, C. D. (1994). Central monitoring deficiency and schizophrenic symptoms. *Psychological Medicine*, **24**, 557–64.

Murray, R. M., Lewis, S. W., Owen, M. J., and Foerster, A. (1988). The neurodevelopmental origins of dementia praecox. In *Schiziphrenia: the major issues*, (ed. P. Bebbington and P. McGuffin), pp. 90–106. Heinemann/Mental Health Foundation, Oxford.

Oatley, K. and Johnson-Laird, P. N. (1987). Towards a cognitive theory of the emotions. *Cognition and Emotion*, **1**, 29–50.

Ogata, S. N., Silk, K. R., Goodrich, S., Lohr, N. E., Western, D., and Hill, E. M. (1990). Chidhood sexual and physical abuse in adult patients with borderline personality disorder. *American Journal of Psychiatry*, **147**, 1008–13.

Olah, A., Torestad, B., and Magnusson, D. (1984). *Coping behaviours in relation to frequency and intensity of anxiety provoking situations*. Reports of the Department of Psychology, 629. University of Stockholm.

Oldham, J. M., Skodol, A. A., Kellman, D., Hyler, S. E., Rosnick, L., and Davies, M. (1992). Diagnosis of DSM-III-R personality disorders by two structured interviews: patterns of comorbidity. *American Journal of Psychiatry*, **149**, (2), 213–20.

Peterson, C. and Seligman, M. (1983). Learned helplessness and victimization. *Journal of Social Issues*, **2**, 103–16.

Pfohl, B., 'Stangl, D., and Zimmerman, M. (1984). The implications of DSM-III Personality disorders for patiients with major depression. *Journal of Affective Disorders*, **7**, 309–18.

Piaget, J. (1937). *The construction of reality in the child*. (Trans. Cook, M. (1954). Basic Books, New York.

Rachman, S. (1980). Emotional processing. *Behaviour Research and Therapy*, **18**, 51–60.

Rachman, S. (1993). Obsessions, responsibility and guilt. *Behaviour Research and Therapy*, **31**, 149–54.

Rachman, S. J. and Hodgson, R. (1980). *Obsessions and compulsions*. Prentice Hall, Englewood Cliffs, N. J.

Rapoport, J. L. (1990). Obsessive compulsive disorder and basal ganglia dysfunction. *Psychological Medicine*, **20**, 465–9.

Roberts, G. (1991). Delusional belief systems and meaning in life. *British Journal of Psychiatry*, **159**, (Suppl. 14), 19–28.

Robins, L. N. (1966). *Deviant children grown up*. Williams and Wilkins, Baltimore.

Robins, L. N. (1986). The consequences of conduct disorder in girls. In *Development of antisocial and prosocial behaviour*, (ed. D. Olweus, J. Block, and M. Radke-Yarrow), pp. 385–414. Academic Press, Orlando.

Salkovskis, P. (1985). Obsessional-compulsive problems: a cognitive-behavioural analysis. *Behaviour Research and Therapy*, **23**, 571–83.

Scarone, S. *et al.* (1992). Increased right caudate nucleus size in obsessive-compulsive disorder: detection with magnetic resonance imaging. *Psychiatry Research, Neuro-imaging*, **45**, 1115–21.

Shea, M. T. *et al.* (1990). Personality disorders and treatment outcome in the NIMH treatment of depression collaborative research program. *American Journal of Psychiatry*, **147**, 711–18.

Stein, D., Shoulberg, N., Helton, K., and Hollander, E. (1992). The neuroethological approach to obsessive-compulsive disorder. *Comprehensive psychiatry*, **33**, 274–81.

Stern, D. (1985). *The interpersonal world of the infant*. Basic Books, New York.

Strauss, J. S. (1992). The person — key to understanding mental illness: towards a new dynamic psychiatry, III. *The British Journal of Psychiatry*, **161**, (suppl. 18), 19–26.

Swedo, S. E. *et al.* (1989). High prevalence of obsessive-compulsive symptoms in patients with Sydenham's chorea. *American Journal of Psychiatry*, **146**, 246–9.

Sylvester, C., Hyde, T. S., and Reichler, R. J. (1987). The diagnostic interview for children and personality interview for children in studies of children at risk for anxiety disorders and depression. *Journal of the American Academy of Child and Adolescent Psychiatry*, **26**, 668–75.

Tienari, P., Wynne, L. C., Moring, J., Lahti, I., Naarala, M., Sorri, A., Wahlberg, K.–E., Saarento, O., Seitamaa, M., Kaleva, M., and Laksy, K. (1994). The Finnish adoptive family study of schizophrenia. Implications for family research. *British Journal of Psychiatry*, **164** (suppl 23), 20–6.

Torgersen, S. (1986). Childhood and family characteristics in panic and generalized anxiety disorder. *American Journal of Psychiatry*, **143**, 630–9.

Torgersen, S. (1990). Genetics of anxiety and its clinical implications. In *Handbook of anxiety*, Vol. 3: *The neurobiology of anxiety*, (ed. G. D. Burrows, M. Roth and R. Noyes), pp. 381–406. Elsevier, Amsterdam.

Tsuang, M. T. (1993). Genotypes, phenotypes, and the brain. A search for connections in schizophrenia. *British Journal of Psychiatry*, 163, 299–307.

Turner, S. M., Beidel, D. C., and Costello, A. (1987). Psychopathology in the offspring of anxiety disorders patients. *Journal of Consulting and Clinical Psychology*, 55, 229–35.

Tyrer, P., Lewis, P., and Lee, I. (1978). Effects of subliminal and supraliminal stress on symptoms of anxiety. *Journal of Nervous and Mental Disease*, 166, 88–95.

Vasey, M. W. (1993). Development and cognition in childhood anxiety: the example of worry. In *Advances in clinical child psychology*, (ed. T. H. Ollendick and R. J. Prinz), Vol 15, pp. 1–39. Plenum, New York.

von Economo, C. (1931). *Encephalitis lethargica: its sequelae and treatment*. Oxford University Press, Oxford.

Vygotsky, L. (1981). The genesis of higher mental functions. In *The concept of activity in Soviet Psychology*, (ed. J. V. Wertsch), pp. 144–88. M. E. Sharpe, New York. (Reprinted in Richardson, K. and Sheldon, S. (ed.) (1990). *Cognitive development to adolescence*, pp. 61–80. Lawrence Erlbaum Associates, Hove.

Weiner, I., Feldon, J., and Ziv–Harris, D. (1987). Early handling and latent inhibition in the conditioned suppression paradigm. *Developmental Psychobiology*, 20, 233–40.

Weissman, M. M., Leckman, J. F., Merikangas, K. R., Gammon, G. D., and Prusoff, B. (1984). Depression and anxiety disorders in parents and children. *Archives of General Psychiatry*, 41, 845–52.

Williams, J. M. G., Watts, F. N., Macleod, C., and Matthews, A. (1992). *Cognitive psychology and emotional disorders*. Wiley, Chichester.

Winnicott, D. W. (1971). *Playing and reality*. Tavistock, London.

Wise, S. and Rapoport, J. (1989). Obsessive-compulsive disorder: is it basal ganglia dysfunction? In *Obsessive-compulsive disorder in children and adolescents*, (ed. J. L. Rapoport), pp. 327–44. American Psychiatric Press Inc., Washington.

Index

ECONOMICS

Pearson

ECONOMICS

Tenth edition

John Sloman

The Economics Network, University of Bristol

Visiting Professor, University of the West of England

Dean Garratt

Nottingham Business School

Jon Guest

Aston Business School

Aston University

 Pearson

Harlow, England • London • New York • Boston • San Francisco • Toronto • Sydney
Dubai • Singapore • Hong Kong • Tokyo • Seoul • Taipei • New Delhi
Cape Town • São Paulo • Mexico City • Madrid • Amsterdam • Munich • Paris • Milan

PEARSON EDUCATION LIMITED
KAO Two
KAO Park
Harlow
CM17 9NA
United Kingdom
Tel: +44 (0)1279 623623
Web: www.pearson.com/uk

———————

First edition published 1991 (print)
Second edition published 1994 (print)
Updated second edition published 1995 (print)
Third edition published 1997 (print)
Updated third edition published 1998 (print)
Fourth edition published 2000 (print)
Fifth edition published 2003 (print)
Sixth edition published 2006 (print)
Seventh edition published 2009 (print)
Eighth edition published 2012 (print and electronic)
Ninth edition 2015 (print and electronic)
Tenth edition 2018 (print and electronic)

978-1-292-18785-3 (print)
978-1-292-18790-7 (PDF)
978-1-292-18786-0 (ePub)

British Library Cataloguing-in-Publication Data
A catalogue record for the print edition is available from the British Library

Library of Congress Cataloguing-in-Publication Data
Names: Sloman, John, 1947- author. | Garratt, Dean, 1970- author. | Guest,
  Jon, author.
Title: Economics / John Sloman, The Economics Network, University of Bristol,
  Visiting Professor, University of the West of England, Dean Garratt,
  Nottingham Business School, Jon Guest, Aston University.
Description: Tenth Edition. | New York : Pearson, [2017] | Revised edition of
  Economics, [2015]
Identifiers: LCCN 2017048463| ISBN 9781292187853 (Print) | ISBN 9781292187907
  (PDF) | ISBN 9781292187860 (ePub)
Subjects: LCSH: Economics.
Classification: LCC HB171.5 .S635 2017 | DDC 330--dc23
LC record available at https://lccn.loc.gov/2017048463

10 9 8 7 6 5 4 3 2 1
22 21 20 19 18

Front cover images and all Part and Chapter opener images: John Sloman

Typeset in 8/12 pt Stone Serif ITC Pro by SPi Global
Printed in Slovakia by Neografia

NOTE THAT ANY PAGE CROSS REFERENCES REFER TO THE PRINT EDITION

About the Authors

John Sloman is Visiting Fellow at the University of Bristol and Associate of the Economics Network (www.economicsnetwork.ac.uk), a UK-wide organisation, where, until his retirement in 2012, he was Director. The Economics Network is based at the University of Bristol and provides a range of services designed to promote and share good practice in learning and teaching economics. The Network is supported by grants from the Royal Economic Society, the Scottish Economic Society and university economic departments and units from across the UK.

John is also Visiting Professor at the University of the West of England, Bristol, where, from 1992 to 1999, he was Head of School of Economics. He taught at UWE until 2007.

John has taught a range of courses, including economic principles on Economics, Social Science and Business Studies degrees, development economics, comparative economic systems, intermediate macroeconomics and managerial economics. He has also taught economics on various professional courses.

John is the co-author with Dean Garratt of *Essentials of Economics* (Pearson Education, 7th edition 2016), with Dean Garratt; Elizabeth Jones of the University of Warwick and Jon Guest of *Economics for Business* (Pearson Education, 7th edition 2016); and with Elizabeth Jones of *Essential Economics for Business* (Pearson Education, 5th edition 2017). Translations or editions of the various books are available for a number of different countries with the help of co-authors around the world.

John is very interested in promoting new methods of teaching economics, including group exercises, experiments, role playing, computer-aided learning and the use of audience response systems and podcasting in teaching. He has organised and spoken at conferences for both lecturers and students of economics throughout the UK and in many other countries.

As part of his work with the Economics Network he has contributed to its two sites for students and prospective students of economics: Studying Economics (www.studyingeconomics.ac.uk/) and Why Study Economics? (http://whystudyeconomics.ac.uk).

From March to June 1997, John was a visiting lecturer at the University of Western Australia. In July and August 2000, he was again a visiting lecturer at the University of Western Australia and also at Murdoch University in Perth.

In 2007, John received a Lifetime Achievement Award as 'outstanding teacher and ambassador of economics', presented jointly by the Higher Education Academy, the Government Economic Service and the Scottish Economic Society.

Dr Dean Garratt is a Principal Lecturer in Economics at Nottingham Business School (NBS) and the Course Leader for MSc Economics, MSc Economics and Investment Banking and MSc International Finance.

Dean teaches economics at a variety of levels, including modules in macroeconomics, applied economics and career development for economists. He is passionate about encouraging students to communicate economics more intuitively, to deepen their interest in economics and to apply economics to a range of issues.

Earlier in his career Dean worked as an economic assistant at both HM Treasury and at the Council of Mortgage Lenders. While at these institutions he was researching and briefing on a variety of issues relating to the household sector and to the housing and mortgage markets.

Dean is a Senior Fellow of the Higher Education Academy and an Associate of the Economics Network which aims to promote high-quality teaching practice. He has been involved in several projects promoting a problem-based learning (PBL) approach in the teaching of economics.

In 2006, Dean was awarded the Outstanding Teaching Prize by the Economics Network. The award recognises exemplary teaching practice that deepens and inspires interest in economics. In 2013, he won the student-nominated Nottingham Business School teacher of the year award.

Dean is an academic assessor for the Government Economic Service (GES) helping to assess candidates at Economic Assessment Centres (EACs). In this role he assesses candidates looking to join the GES, the UK's largest employer of professional economists.

Dean runs sessions on HM Treasury's Graduate Development Programme (GDP). These sessions cover principles in policy making, applying economics principles and ideas to analyse policy issues and contemporary developments in macroeconomics.

Outside of work, Dean is an avid watcher of many sports. Having been born in Leicester, he is a season ticket holder at both Leicester City Football Club and Leicestershire County Cricket Club.

Jon Guest is a Senior Teaching Fellow at Aston Business School and a Teaching Associate at Warwick Business School. He joined Aston University in September 2017 having previously been a Senior Lecturer at Nottingham Business School, a Principal Teaching Fellow at Warwick Business School and a Senior Lecturer at Coventry University.

Jon has taught on a range of courses including Principles of Microeconomics, Intermediate Microeconomics, Economic Issues and Behavioural Economics. He has also taught economics on various professional courses for the Government Economic Service and HM Treasury.

Jon has worked on developing teaching methods that promote a more active learning environment in the classroom. In particular, he has published journal articles and carried out a number of funded research projects on the impact of games and experiments on student learning. These include an online version of the TV show *Deal or No Deal* and games that involve students acting as buyers and sellers in the classroom. He has recently included a series of short videos on economics topics and implemented elements of the flipped classroom into his teaching. Jon is also interested in innovative ways of providing students with feedback on their work.

Through his work as an Associate of the Economics Network, Jon has run sessions on innovative pedagogic practices at a number of universities and major national events. He is also an academic assessor for the Economics Assessment Centres run by the Government Economic Service. This involves interviewing candidates and evaluating their ability to apply economic reasoning to a range of policy issues. He has also acted as an External Examiner for a number of UK universities.

The quality of his teaching was formally recognised when he became the first Government Economic Service Approved Tutor in 2005 and won the student-nominated award from the Economics Network in the same year. Jon was awarded the prestigious National Teaching Fellowship by the Higher Education Academy in 2011.

Jon is a regular contributor and editor of the *Economic Review* and is a co-author of the 7th edition of the textbook, *Economics for Business*. He has published chapters in books on the economics of sport and regularly writes cases for the 'Sloman in the News' website. He has also published research on the self-evaluation skills of undergraduate students.

Outside of work Jon is a keen runner and has completed the London Marathon. However, he now has to accept that he is slower than both of his teenage sons – Dan and Tom. He is also a long-suffering supporter of Portsmouth Football Club.

Brief Contents

Contents

Part D   MICROECONOMIC POLICY

11   Inequality, Poverty and Policies to
     Redistribute Income   316

Part G THE WORLD ECONOMY

Supporting Resources

Visit www.pearsoned.co.uk/sloman to find valuable online resources:

MyLab Economics

For students

- Study guide with exercises, quizzes and tests, arranged chapter by chapter
- Multiple-choice questions to test your learning
- Glossary with Flashcards to check your understanding
- Link to Sloman Economics News site
- Online textbook chapters
- Link to additional resources on the companion website (listed below)

For lecturers

- MyLab's gradebook, which automatically tracks student performance and progress
- Extensive test bank, allowing you to generate your own tests, assessments and homework assignment
- Access to a wealth of lecturer resources on the companion website (listed below)

Companion website

For students

- Answers to all in-chapter questions in the book
- Over 200 case studies with questions and activities, organised by chapter
- Over 130 audio animations explaining all the key models used in the book
- Regularly updated and searchable blog, featuring current news items with discussion of the issue, questions and links to articles and data
- Hotlinks to 285 sites relevant to the study of economics
- Maths case studies illustrating the key mathematical concepts used in the book

For lecturers

- Comprehensive range of PowerPoint slides, including figures and tables from the book, as well as animated slide shows for use in lectures, organised chapter by chapter. There are various versions of these slide shows, some including questions that can be used with 'clickers'
- Animated key models in PowerPoint
- Teaching and learning case studies, discussing ways of increasing student engagement and improving student learning
- 20 workshops in Word for use in large or small classes, plus a guide on ways of using the workshops. These can easily be customised to suit lecturers' needs. Answers are given to all the workshop questions.
- Over 200 case studies with questions and student activities (as on student website). Answers to all questions in case studies
- Answers to all questions in the book (end-of-chapter questions, box questions and in-text questions) and to questions in maths case studies

Also: The companion website provides the following features:
- Search tool to help locate specific items of content
- Online help and support to assist with website usage and troubleshooting

For more information please contact your local Pearson Education sales representative or visit www.pearsoned.co.uk/sloman.

Preface

Economics affects all our lives. As consumers we try to make the best of our limited incomes. As workers – or future workers – we take our place in the job market. As citizens of a country our lives are affected by the decisions of our government and other policy makers: decisions over taxes, decisions over spending on health and education, decisions on interest rates, decisions that affect unemployment, inflation and growth. As dwellers on the planet Earth we are affected by the economic decisions of each other: the air we breathe, the water we drink and the environment we leave to our children are all affected by the economic decisions taken by the human race.

Economics thus deals with some of the most challenging issues we face. It is this that still excites us about economics after many years of teaching the subject. We hope that some of this excitement rubs off on you.

The first nine editions of *Economics* have been widely used in Britain and throughout the world. Like them, this new edition is suitable for all students of economics at first-year degree level, A level or on various professional courses where a broad grounding in both principles and applications is required. It is structured to be easily understood by those of you who are new to the subject, with various sections and boxes that can be left out on first reading or on shorter courses; yet it also has sufficient depth to challenge those of you who have studied the subject before, with starred sections (appearing on a grey background) and starred case studies that will provide much that is new. There are also optional short mathematical sections for those of you studying a more quantitatively focused course.

The book gives a self-contained introduction to the world of economics and is thus ideal for those who will not study the subject beyond introductory level. But by carefully laying a comprehensive foundation and by the inclusion of certain materials in starred sections that bridge the gap between introductory and second-level economics, it provides the necessary coverage for those of you going on to specialise in economics.

The book looks at the world of the early twenty-first century. Despite huge advances in technology and despite the comfortable lives led by many people in the industrialised world, we still suffer from unemployment, poverty and inequality, and in many countries (the UK included) the gap between rich and poor has grown much wider; our environment is polluted; our economy still goes through periodic recessions; conflict and disagreement often dominate over peace and harmony.

In today's world there are many challenges that face us, including:

- A growing interdependence of the economies of the world, with a seemingly inexorable process of 'globalisation', which links us all through a web of telecommunications and international trade into a world of Amazon, Facebook, Coca-Cola, Nike trainers, Google, Netflix and the English Premier League.
- New challenges for the UK arising from the Brexit vote.
- A rise in populism as the lower paid and unemployed see their incomes stagnating while the wealthy get richer. This has led to many people calling for policies to protect their jobs and communities from cheap imports.
- Large-scale migration of people across and within continents placing pressures on resources, but also creating new economic opportunities.
- Evidence that economic problems spread like a contagion around the world, tying domestic economic growth to global events.
- The effects of financialisation, by which we mean the increasing economic importance of the financial sector, and its impact on the financial health of people, businesses and governments as well as its potential to destabilise economies.
- The continuing hangover from the turmoil on international financial markets that culminated in the banking crisis of 2007–8, with many countries today still trying to tackle high levels of public and private debt and with austerity policies acting as a brake on growth.
- Rapid economic growth of some developing countries, such as India and China, which are increasingly influential in the global economy.
- A move away from the ideological simplicity of a 'free-market' solution to all economic problems.

- An EU struggling to reform its institutions and processes and to stimulate economic growth.
- An ever-deepening crisis for many of the poorest developing countries, often ravaged by disease, conflict and famines, and seemingly stuck in a cycle of poverty.

Economists are called on to offer solutions to these and many other problems. We shall be seeing what solutions economists can offer as the book progresses.

But despite our changing environment, there are certain economic fundamentals that do not change. Although there are disagreements among economists – and there are plenty – there is a wide measure of agreement on how to analyse these fundamentals.

Critical thinking and employability

When you are approaching graduation and start applying for jobs, you will need to demonstrate to potential employers that you have the range of skills necessary for analysing and solving problems and for communicating ideas and solutions to colleagues and clients. This requires the ability to think critically and to apply core concepts and ideas to new situations. Universities recognise this and 'employability' is a key objective of courses nowadays.

Employability is a core focus of this book. Critical thinking is developed through questions positioned throughout the text to encourage you to reflect on what you have just read and thereby improve and deepen your learning. Answers to these questions are freely available on the website to enable you to check your progress. Critical thinking is also developed through the use of Boxes of case studies and applications occurring several times in each chapter. These apply the economics you're learning to a variety of real-world issues and data. There are many additional case studies with questions on the student website.

If your lecturer recommends the use of MyEconLab to accompany the text, you will find there large banks of additional questions and the ability to monitor your progress. These questions enable you to reflect on your learning and on where additional work is required.

Critical thinking is also encouraged through the use of fifteen 'threshold concepts'. These are core ideas and concepts that recur throughout economics. Understanding and being able to apply these core economic concepts helps you to 'think like an economist' and to relate the different parts of the subject to each other. An icon appears in the margin wherever the concept recurs so that you can easily recognise its use in a new context.

In addition there are 40 'Key ideas' that encourage you to relate new material to a toolkit of ideas. Again, there are icons in the margin to help you identify the relevant idea.

The whole way through the book, you are encouraged to reflect on your learning, to apply it to the real world and to use real-world data to make sense of economic issues and problems.

In addition to the book, there is a news blog with new news items added several times per month. Each blog post discusses economic issues in the news and relates these news items to key economic concepts and theories. Links are given to a range of articles, videos, podcasts, data and reports and each blog post finishes with a set of discussion questions. You can access the blog from the book's website at www.pearsoned.co.uk/sloman. Archived articles go back many months. You can also search the news articles by key word, chapter of this book or by month. Again, the use of real-world news topics, questions and data help you apply the theories and ideas you will learn in this book and develop these all-important critical thinking skills that are so central to employability.

In terms of employability, employees who can think flexibly and apply concepts and theories in new and perhaps strange situations to analyse and solve problems will be much more valuable to their employer. This book helps you to develop these skills. What is more, the use of data in the book and in the blogs and other web resources, and the hyperlinks in the e-text to data sources and relevant articles, will allow you to gain experience in using evidence to support and assess arguments.

Employers value these problem-solving skills. Indeed, they like to employ graduates with an economics degree, or some element of economics in their degree, because of the skills you will develop. And it's not just for jobs as economists, but for a large number of professions where studying economics is seen to equip you with a valuable set of skills that are transferable to a range of non-economics situations.

We hope that this book will give you an enjoyable introduction to the economist's world and that it will equip you with the tools to understand and criticise the economic policies that others pursue.

Good luck and have fun.

John, Dean and Jon

TO LECTURERS AND TUTORS

In the light of the financial crisis and the struggle of many countries to tackle its aftermath, there has been much soul-searching amongst economists about the appropriateness of the models we use and what should be taught to our students. These concerns were debated at an international conference at the Bank of England in 2012. One outcome of this was the publication of a book, *What's the Use of Economics?*[1] This considers how undergraduate courses could be reformed to meet the needs of employers and how economic models and syllabuses could be revised to reflect the real world and to provide a foundation for devising effective economic policy. A second, follow-up conference, *Revisiting the State of Economics Education,* took place at the Bank of England in 2015 and the debate continues.[2]

We have attempted to address these concerns in the past two editions of this book and have gone further still in this new edition. In particular, we have incorporated recent developments in macroeconomics, including stressing the importance of balance sheets, credit cycles, financial instability and systemic risk, the increased use of the *DAD/DAS* framework and the integration of the expectations-augmented Phillips curve and the *IS/MP* model. But these have been treated at a level wholly suitable for first-year students.

We have also given further weight to behavioural economics in analysing the behaviour of both consumers, firms and workers. In particular, there is more detailed discussion of loss aversion and the endowment effect, present bias and self-control issues, reference points and biases when making decisions under conditions of uncertainty. More weight is given to the importance of institutional structures and culture and we have also strengthened microeconomic analysis in several places, such as game theory and price discrimination.

We have also thoroughly revised the applied chapters and sections to reflect changes in policies. For example, we have included the implications of the Brexit vote and also of the Trump administration's policies in several parts of the book.

In addition, we show how many of the theories developed to explain the problems that existed at the time and how they have evolved to reflect today's issues. We have thus continued to emphasise the link between the history of economic thought and economic history.

This new edition also retains many of the popular features of the previous edition:

■ A style that is direct and to the point, with the aim all the time to provide maximum clarity. There are numerous examples to aid comprehension.

1 Diane Coyle (ed.), *What's the Use of Economics?* (London Publishing Partnership, 2012).

2 Peter Day, 'Are economics degrees fit for purpose', *BBC News,* 5 February 2016).

■ All economic terms highlighted in the text where they first appear and defined at the foot of that page. Each term is also highlighted in the index, so that the student can simply look up a given definition as required. By defining them on the page where they appear, the student can also see the terms used in context in the text.

■ Key ideas highlighted and explained when they first appear. There are 40 of these ideas, which are fundamental to the study of economics. Students can see them recurring throughout the book, and an icon appears in the margin to refer back to the page where the idea first appears.

■ Fifteen 'threshold concepts'. Understanding and being able to relate and apply these core economic concepts helps students to 'think like an economist' and to relate the different parts of the subject to each other. Again, an icon appears in the margin wherever the concept recurs.

■ A wealth of applied material in boxes (177 in all), making learning more interesting for students and, by relating economics to the real world, bringing the subject alive. The boxes allow the book to be comprehensive without the text becoming daunting and allow more advanced material to be introduced where appropriate. Many of the boxes can be used as class exercises and virtually all have questions at the end.

■ Extensive use of data, with links in the online version to general data sources and individual datasets, with many opportunities for students to explore data to help them reflect on policy choices.

■ Full-page chapter introductions. These set the scene for the chapter by introducing the students to the topics covered and relating them to the everyday world. The introductions also include a 'chapter map'. This provides a detailed contents listing, helping students to see how the chapter is structured and how the various topics relate to each other.

■ A consistent use of colour in graphs and diagrams, with explanations in panels where appropriate. These features make them easier to comprehend and more appealing.

■ Starred sections and boxes for more advanced material (appearing with a grey background). These can be omitted without interrupting the flow of the argument. This allows the book to be used by students with different abilities and experience, and on courses of different levels of difficulty.

■ 'Looking at the maths' sections. These short sections express a topic mathematically. Some use calculus; some do not. They are designed to be used on more quantitatively focused courses and go further than other textbooks at introductory level in meeting the needs of students on such courses. Most refer students to worked examples in Maths Cases on the student website. Some of these use simultaneous equations; some use simple unconstrained optimisation techniques; others use constrained optimisation, using both substitution and Lagrange multipliers. The 'Looking at the maths' sections are short and can be omitted by students on non-mathematical courses without any loss of continuity.

- An open learning approach, with questions incorporated into the text so as to test and reinforce students' understanding as they progress. This makes learning a much more active process.

- End-of-chapter questions. These can be set as work for students to do in class or at home. Alternatively, students can simply use them to check their comprehension at the end of a topic.

- Summaries given at the end of each section, thus providing a point for reflection and checking on comprehension at reasonably frequent intervals.

- An even micro/macro split.

- The book is divided into seven parts. This makes the structure transparent and makes it easier for the student to navigate.

Despite retaining these popular features, there have been many changes to this tenth edition.

Extensive revision

Economics (10th edition) uses a lot of applied material, both to illustrate theory and policy, and to bring the subject alive for students by relating it to contemporary issues. This has meant that, as with the previous edition, much of the book has had to be rewritten to reflect contemporary issues. Specifically this means that:

- Many new boxes have been included on topical and controversial issues, including the secondary ticket market, the dominance of Google, the Financial Accelerator and primary surpluses/sustainable debt. Existing boxes have been extensively revised.

- There are many new examples given in the text.

- Theoretical coverage has been strengthened at various points in the book to reflect developments in the subject. This includes:
  - an increased emphasis on the role of borrowing, debt, financial markets, balance sheets and risk at the government, corporate and household levels;
  - the development of macroeconomic models, including the interaction between the *IS/MP* model, the *DAD/DAS* model and the expectations-augmented Phillips curve models;
  - increased emphasis on behavioural economics at the level of both the consumer and the firm, including the impact of present bias, loss aversion, preferences for fairness and biases when making decisions in an uncertain environment;
  - a deepening of the exposition of game theory and more detailed analysis of price discrimination, externalities and public goods.

- The text provides extensive coverage of the recent developments in money and banking and their impact on the economy.

- All policy sections reflect the changes that have taken place since the last edition, including changes to the regulation of businesses and the protection of the environment, and the continuing international responses to the financial crisis and policies adopted in various countries to reduce levels of public-sector deficits and debt. The text enables students to see how they can apply fundamental economic concepts to gain a better understanding of these important issues. Hence, students will be in a better position to analyse the actual responses of policy makers as well as the alternatives that could perhaps have been pursued.

- All tables and charts have been updated, as have factual references in the text.

- Most importantly, every single section and every single sentence of the book has been carefully considered, and if necessary redrafted, to ensure both maximum clarity and contemporary relevance. The result, we hope, is a text that your students will find exciting and relevant to today's world.

SUGGESTIONS FOR SHORTER OR LESS ADVANCED COURSES

The book is designed to be used on a number of different types of course. Because of its comprehensive nature, the inclusion of a lot of optional material and the self-contained nature of many of the chapters and sections, it can be used very flexibly.

It is suitable for one-year principles courses at first-year degree level, two-year economics courses on non-economics degrees, A level, HND and professional courses. It is also highly suitable for single-semester courses, either with a micro or a macro focus, or giving a broad outline of the subject.

The following suggests chapters which are appropriate to different types of course and gives some guidance on chapters that can be omitted while retaining continuity:

Alternative 1: Less advanced but comprehensive courses

Omit all starred sections, starred sub-sections and starred boxes.

Example of a comprehensive course, omitting some of these chapters: Chapters 1–8, 10, 12–14, 15, 17–22, 24–25.

Alternative 2: Economics for Business courses

Chapters 1–3, 5–9, 12–15, 18, 21, 23–6.

Example of an Economics for Business course, omitting some of these chapters: Chapters 1–3, 6–10, 14, 15, 18, 22, 24–25.

Alternative 3: Introduction to microeconomics

Chapters 1–14, 24. The level of difficulty can be varied by including or omitting starred sections and boxes from these chapters.

Example of an Introduction to Microeconomics course, omitting some of these chapters: Chapters 1–4, 6–8, 10, 12, 24.

Alternative 4: Introduction to macroeconomics

Chapters 1, 2, 15–26. The level of difficulty can be varied by including or omitting starred sections and boxes from these chapters.

Example of an Introduction to Macroeconomics course, omitting some of these chapters: Chapters 1, 2, (if microeconomics has not previously been covered) 15, 17–23, 25.

Alternative 5: Outline courses

Chapters 1, 2, 6, 7, 15, 17, 18, 22, 24, 25 (section 25.1). Omit boxes at will.

Alternative 6: Courses with a theory bias

Chapters 1, 2, 4–10, 12, 15–21, 23, 24, 25. The level of difficulty can be varied by including or omitting starred sections and boxes from these chapters.

Alternative 7: Courses with a policy bias (and only basic theory)

Chapters 1–3, 6, 7, 11–15, (17), 22–6.

COMPANION RESOURCES

MyEconLab (for students)

MyEconLab is a comprehensive set of online resources developed for the tenth edition of *Economics*. The book is available with an access card, but if your book did not come with one, you can purchase access to the resources online at www.MyEconLab.com.

MyEconLab provides a variety of tools to enable students to assess their own learning, including exercises, quizzes and tests, arranged chapter by chapter. There are many new questions in this edition and each question has been carefully considered to reflect the learning objectives of the chapter. A personalised Study Plan identifies areas to concentrate on to improve grades, and specific tools are provided to each student to direct their studies in the most efficient way.

Student website

In addition to the materials on MyEconLab, there is an open-access companion website for students with a large range of other resources, including:

- Animations of key models with audio explanations. These can be watched online or downloaded to a computer, MP4 player, smart phone, etc.;

- Links to the Sloman Economics news blog with news items added several times each month by a small team of authors;
- 201 case studies with questions for self study and a range of activities for individual students or groups. These case studies are ordered chapter by chapter and referred to in the text;
- Maths cases with exercises, related to the 'Looking at the Maths' sections in the book;
- Updated list of 285 hotlinks to sites of use for economics;
- Answers to all in-chapter questions;

Note that the companion website, news blog and hotlinks can also be accessed directly from **www.pearsoned. co.uk/sloman**.

See the Student resources chart on page xxi.

MyEconLab (for lecturers)

You can register online at www.myeconlab.com to use MyEconLab, which is a complete virtual learning environment for your course or embedded into Blackboard, WebCT or Moodle. You can customise its look and feel and its availability to students. You can use it to provide support to your students in the following ways:

- MyEconLab's gradebook automatically records each student's time spent and performance on the tests and Study Plan. It also generates reports you can use to monitor your students' progress.
- You can use MyEconLab to build your own tests, quizzes and homework assignments from the question base provided to set for your students' assessment.
- Questions are generated algorithmically so that they use different values each time they are used.
- You can create your own exercises by using the econ exercise builder.

Additional resources for lecturers

There are also many additional resources for lecturers and tutors that can be downloaded from the lecturer section of MyEconLab or from the separate lecturer website. These have been thoroughly revised from the tenth edition. These include:

- PowerPoint® slideshows in full colour for use with a data projector in lectures and classes. These can also be made available to students by loading them on to a local network. There are several types of these slideshows:
  - All figures from the book and most of the tables. Each figure is built up in a logical sequence, thereby allowing them to be shown in lectures in an animated form. They are also available in a simple version suitable for printing for handouts or display on an OHP or visualiser.
  - A range of models. There are 41 files, each containing one of the key models from the book, developed in an animated sequence of between 20 and 80 screens.
  - Customisable lecture slideshows. There is one for each chapter of the book. Each one can be easily edited, with points added, deleted or moved, so as to suit particular lectures. A consistent use of colour is made to show how the points tie together. It is not intended that all the material is covered in a single lecture; you can break at any point. It's just convenient to organise them by chapter. They come in various versions:
    - o Lecture slideshows with integrated diagrams. These include animated diagrams, charts and tables at the appropriate points.
    - o Lecture slideshows with integrated diagrams and questions. These include multiple-choice questions to allow lectures to become more interactive and can be used with or without an audience response system (ARS). ARS versions are available for InterWrite PRS® and for two versions of Turning-Point® and are ready to use with the appropriate 'clickers'.
    - o Lecture plans without the diagrams. These allow you to construct your own diagrams on the blackboard, whiteboard or visualiser.

- Answers to all questions in *Economics* (10th edition): i.e. questions embedded in the text, box questions and end-of-chapter questions. These can be edited as desired and distributed to students.
- Answers to the case studies and maths cases found in MyEconLab.
- Case studies. These 201 cases, also available to students on the student website, can be reproduced and used for classroom exercises or for student assignments. Most cases have questions, to which answers are also provided (not available to students). Each case also has an activity for individual students or for groups, and most would be suitable for seminars.
- Extended case studies. These have a range of student activities, questions, data and multimedia, and can be used for project work, group work, work for and during seminars and as part of assessment.
- Maths cases. These 27 maths cases with exercises, also available to students in MyEconLab, relate to the 'Looking at the Maths' sections in the book. Answers to the exercises are also provided (not available to students).
- Workshops. There are 20 of these (10 micro and 10 macro/international). They are in Word® and can be reproduced for use with large groups of students (up to 200). They can also be amended to suit your course. Suggestions for use are given in an accompanying file. Answers to all workshop questions are given in separate Word® files.
- Teaching/learning case studies. These 20 case studies examine various ways to improve student learning of introductory economics. They have been completely revised with new hyperlinks where appropriate.

The following two pages show in diagrammatic form all the student and lecturer resources.

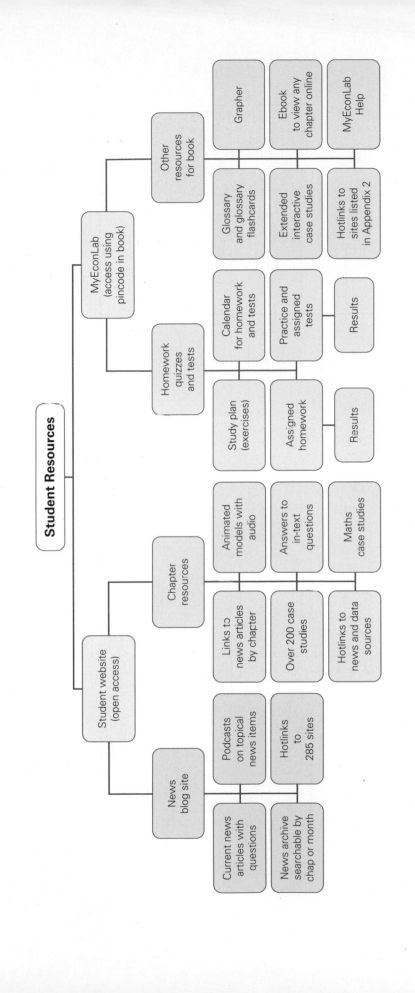

Student Resources

Student website (open access)

MyEconLab (access using pincode in book)

News blog site
- Current news articles with questions
- Podcasts on topical news items
- News archive searchable by chap or month
- Hotlinks to 285 sites

Chapter resources
- Animated models with audio
- Links to news articles by chapter
- Answers to in-text questions
- Over 200 case studies
- Maths case studies
- Hotlinks to news and data sources

Homework quizzes and tests
- Study plan (exercises)
- Calendar for homework and tests
- Assigned homework
- Practice and assigned tests
- Results
- Results

Other resources for book
- Glossary and glossary flashcards
- Grapher
- Extended interactive case studies
- Ebook to view any chapter online
- Hotlinks to sites listed in Appendix 2
- MyEconLab Help

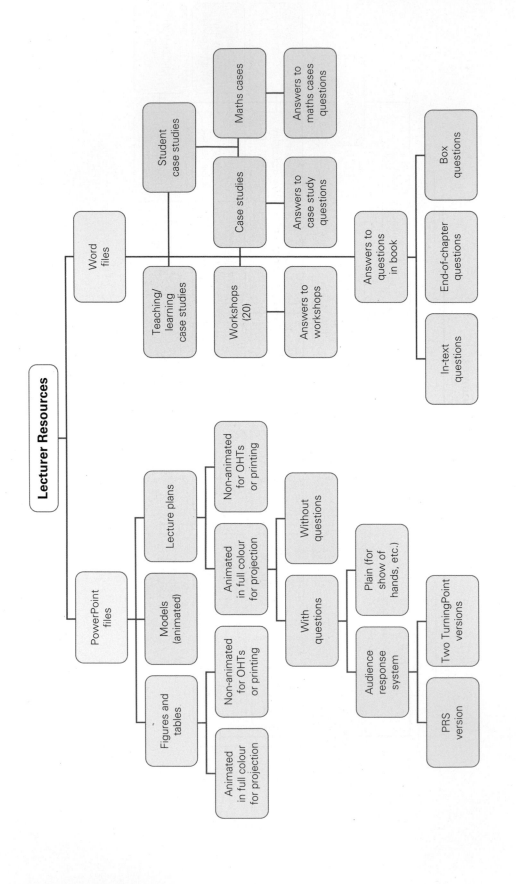

Acknowledgements

As with previous editions, we owe a debt to various people. The whole team from Pearson has, as always, been very helpful and supportive. Thanks in particular to Natalia Jaszczuk and Catherine Yates, the editors, who have offered great support throughout the long process of bringing the book to print. Thanks also to Joan Dale Lace, who, as previously, meticulously copyedited the manuscript and to Sue Gard who carefully proofread everything.

A huge thanks goes to Alison Wride from EML Learning who co-authored the previous three editions. She has decided to concentrate her efforts on her work with the Government Economic Service, but many of her ideas are still retained in this edition. And a special thanks, as previously, to Mark Sutcliffe from the Cardiff School of Management. He provided considerable help and support for the first few editions and it's still much appreciated.

Thanks too to colleagues and students from many universities who have been helpful and encouraging and, as in previous editions, have made useful suggestions for improvement. We have attempted to incorporate their ideas wherever possible. Please do write or email if you have any suggestions. Especially we should like to thank the following reviewers of the previous editions. Their analysis and comments have helped to shape this new edition.

Review of the 9th Edition:

Professor Francesco Feri, Royal Holloway, University of London, UK.

Helen Arce Salazar, The Hague University of Applied Sciences, Netherlands.

Dr Marie Wong, Middlesex University, UK.

Professor Peter Schmidt, Hochschule Bremen, City University of Applied Sciences, Germany.

Dr Sambit Bhattacharyya, University of Sussex, UK.

Review of 10th Edition:

Dr Giorgio Motta, Lancaster University, UK.

Dr Eric Golson, University of Surrey, UK.

Dr Giancarlo Ianulardo, University of Exeter, UK.

A special thanks to Peter Smith from the University of Southampton who has again thoroughly revised and updated the MyEconLab online course. It's been great over the editions to have his input and ideas for improvements to the books and supplements.

Finally, our families have been remarkably tolerant and supportive throughout the writing of this new edition. A massive thanks to Alison, Pat and Helen, without whose encouragement the project would not have been completed.

Publisher's acknowledgements

We are grateful to the following for permission to reproduce copyright material:

Figures

Figure 11.1 adapted from Household disposable income and inequality 2015/16, Table 1 (ONS, January 2017), Contains public sector information licensed under the Open Government Licence (OGL) v3.0.http://www.nationalarchives.gov.uk/doc/open-government-licence.; Figure 11.3 adapted from Household disposable income and inequality (ONS, 2017) https://www.ons.gov.uk/peoplepopulationandcommunity/personalandhouseholdfinances/incomeandwealth/datasets/householddisposableincomeand inequality, Contains public sector information licensed under the Open Government Licence (OGL) v3.0.http://www.nationalarchives.gov.uk/doc/open-government-licence.; Figure 11.6 adapted from *Dataset*: *Income and source of income for all UK Households*, National Statistics (2017) Table 18, Contains public sector information licensed under the Open Government Licence (OGL) v3.0.http://www.nationalarchives.gov.uk/doc/open-government-licence.; Figure 11.7 adapted from *Dataset*: *Occupation (4 digit SOC) - Annual Survey of Hours and Earnings*: *Table 14*, National Statistics (2016) Table 14.2a, Contains public sector information licensed under the Open Government Licence (OGL) v3.0.http://www.nationalarchives.gov.uk/doc/open-government-licence.; Figure 11.8 adapted from *The effects of taxes and benefits on household income*, National Statistics (2016) Table 19, Contains public sector information licensed under the Open Government Licence (OGL) v3.0.http://www.nationalarchives.gov.uk/doc/open-government-licence.; Figure 11.9 adapted from *The effects of taxes and benefits on household income*, National Statistics (2016) Table 28, Contains public sector information licensed under the Open Government Licence (OGL) v3.0.http://www.nationalarchives.gov.uk/doc/open-government-licence.; Figure 11.10 adapted from *Distribution of personal wealth statistics*, National Statistics (HMRC 2016) Table 13.1, Contains public sector information licensed under the Open Government Licence (OGL) v3.0.http://www.nationalarchives.gov.uk/doc/open-government-licence.; Figure 13.4 adapted from *Family Spending Reference Tables*, National Statistics (2017) Table 3.2, Contains public sector information licensed under the Open Government Licence (OGL) v3.0.http://www.nationalarchives.gov.uk/doc/open-government-licence.;

Figure 15.4 adapted from Time Series Data, series YBHA and ABMI (Office for National Statistics), Contains public sector information licensed under the Open Government Licence (OGL) v3.0.http://www.nationalarchives.gov.uk/doc/open-government-licence.; Figure 15.7 adapted from Quarterly National Accounts, series KGZ7, KG7T and IHYR (National Statistics), Contains public sector information licensed under the Open Government Licence (OGL) v3.0.http://www.nationalarchives.gov.uk/doc/open-government-licence.; Figure 15.9 adapted from Dataset UNEM01 SA: Unemployment by age and duration (seasonally adjusted) (ONS), Contains public sector information licensed under the Open Government Licence (OGL) v3.0.http://www.nationalarchives.gov.uk/doc/open-government-licence.

Tables

Tables 1.1, 1.2 adapted from Time Series data, series MGSC (ONS, 2017), Contains public sector information licensed under the Open Government Licence (OGL) v3.0.http://www.nationalarchives.gov.uk/doc/open-government-licence.; Table 1.3 adapted from The Effects of Taxes and Benefits on Household Income, financial year ending 2016, Table 29 (ONS, 2017) https://www.ons.gov.uk/peoplepopulationandcommunity/personalandhouseholdfinances/incomeandwealth/datasets/theeffectsoftaxesandbenefitsonhouseholdincomefinancialyearending2014, Contains public sector information licensed under the Open Government Licence (OGL) v3.0.http://www.nationalarchives.gov.uk/doc/open-government-licence.; Table 1.5 adapted from Time Series data, series K22A (ONS, 2017)., Contains public sector information licensed under the Open Government Licence (OGL) v3.0.http://www.nationalarchives.gov.uk/doc/open-government-licence.; Table on page 192 adapted from *United Kingdom Input–Output Analyses, 2006 Edition* National Statistics (2006) Table 8.31, Contains public sector information licensed under the Open Government Licence (OGL) v3.0.http://www.nationalarchives.gov.uk/doc/open-government-licence.; Table on page 222 adapted from *United Kingdom Input–Output Analyses, 2006 Edition*, National Statistics (2006) Table 8.31, Contains public sector information licensed under the Open Government Licence (OGL) v3.0.http://www.nationalarchives.gov.uk/doc/open-government-licence.; Table on page 272 from How do UK companies set prices?, *Bank of England Quarterly Bulletin*, Q2, Table D, p.188 (Hall, S., Walsh, M. and Yates, T. 1996); Table on page 272 from How do UK companies set prices?, *Bank of England Quarterly Bulletin*, Q2, Table E, p.189 (Hall, S., Walsh, M. and Yates, T. 1996), http://www.bankofengland.co.uk/archive/Documents/historicpubs/qb/1996/qb9602.pdf; Table on page 273 from Price-setting behaviour in the United Kingdom, *Bank of England Quarterly Bulletin*, Q4, Table E, p.408 (Greenslade, J. & Parker, M. 2008), http://www.bankofengland.co.uk/publications/Documents/quarterlybulletin/qb080403.pdf; Table on page 294 adapted from *Dataset: All Employees - Annual Survey of Hours and Earnings: Table 1*, National Statistics (2016) Table 1.6a, Contains public sector information licensed under the Open Government Licence (OGL) v3.0.http://www.nationalarchives.gov.uk/doc/open-government-licence.; Table on page 294 adapted from *Dataset: Occupation (4 digit SOC) - Annual Survey of Hours and Earnings: Table 14*, National Statistics (2016) Table 14.6a, Contains public sector information licensed under the Open Government Licence (OGL) v3.0.http://www.nationalarchives.gov.uk/doc/open-government-licence.; Table 11.2 adapted from *Dataset: Household disposable income and inequality*, National Statistics (2017) Table 2, Contains public sector information licensed under the Open Government Licence (OGL) v3.0.http://www.nationalarchives.gov.uk/doc/open-government-licence.; Table on page 382 after *Economic Case for HS2 (Department for Transport, October 2013)* High Speed Two (HS2) Limited (2013) Table 15, p.85, http://assets.hs2.org.uk/sites/default/files/inserts/S%26A1_Economiccase_0.pdf, Contains public sector information licensed under the Open Government Licence (OGL) v3.0.http://www.nationalarchives.gov.uk/doc/open-government-licence.; Table on page 401 after Government revenue from environmental taxes in the UK, 1997 to 2016, *Dataset: Environmental Taxes*, Table 1, Contains public sector information licensed under the Open Government Licence (OGL) v3.0.http://www.nationalarchives.gov.uk/doc/open-government-licence.; Table 13.2 adapted from *Transport Statistics of Great Britain Database 2016*, Department for Transport (2017) Table TSGB0101, Contains public sector information licensed under the Open Government Licence (OGL) v3.0.http://www.nationalarchives.gov.uk/doc/open-government-licence.; Table 15.5 adapted from Balance of Payments (ONS) https://www.ons.gov.uk/economy/nationalaccounts/balanceofpayments, Contains public sector information licensed under the Open Government Licence (OGL) v3.0.http://www.nationalarchives.gov.uk/doc/open-government-licence.; Tables 15.6, 15.7 adapted from *UK National Accounts, The Blue Book: 2016*, ONS, Contains public sector information licensed under the Open Government Licence (OGL) v3.0.http://www.nationalarchives.gov.uk/doc/open-government-licence.; Table on page 528 adapted from National Balance Sheet and Quarterly National Accounts (National Statistics), Contains public sector information licensed under the Open Government Licence (OGL) v3.0.http://www.nationalarchives.gov.uk/doc/open-government-licence.; Table on page 720 adapted from Capital Stocks, Consumption of Fixed Capital, 2016 and Quarterly National Accounts (series YBHA) (National Statistics), Contains public sector information licensed under the Open Government Licence (OGL) v3.0.http://www.nationalarchives.gov.uk/doc/open-government-licence.; Table on page 804 adapted from Economist

Text

Poetry on pages 862-863 from *The Apeman Cometh*, Jonathan Cope (Adrian Mitchell 1975) © Adrian Mitchell, Reprinted by kind permission of United Agents LLP; General Displayed Text on page 382 from *Economic Case for HS2 – the Y network and London–West Midlands*, Department for Transport (2011), Contains public sector information licensed under the Open Government Licence (OGL) v3.0.http://www.nationalarchives.gov.uk/doc/open-government-licence.; Box 12.2 after Commons Sense, *The Economist*; General Displayed Text 12.6 from *Economic Case for HS2 – the Y network and London–West Midlands*, Department for Transport (High Speed Two 2013) Table 15, p.85, Contains public sector information licensed under the Open Government Licence (OGL) v3.0.http://www.nationalarchives.gov.uk/doc/open-government-licence.; General Displayed Text on page 394 from *The Economics of Climate Change: The Stern Review*, HM Treasury (Stern, N. 2007) p. i, Contains public sector information licensed under the Open Government Licence (OGL) v3.0.http://www.nationalarchives.gov.uk/doc/open-government-licence.; Box 23.6 after Intricate workings: Tackling unemployment requires a careful mixture of policies, *The Economist*.

A Part

Introduction

This opening part of the book introduces you to economics – what it is, some of the fundamental concepts and, most of all, why it is a great subject to study. Economics is not a set of facts or theories to be memorised; it is both more interesting and more useful than that. Studying economics enables you to think about the world in a different way; it helps you to make sense of the decisions people make: decisions about what to buy or what job to do; decisions governments make about how much to tax or what to spend those taxes on; decisions businesses make about what to produce, what prices to charge and what wages to pay. This makes economics relevant for everyone, not only those who are going on to further study.

After studying economics you will be able to apply this 'way of thinking' to your life both now and in the future. You will be able to think more analytically and to problem-solve more effectively; this helps explain why economics graduates are so highly valued by employers. Studying economics therefore opens up a variety of career opportunities.

Economics contains some simple core ideas which can be applied to a wide range of economic problems. We will start examining these ideas in Chapter 1, but we begin on the next four pages, in 'Why Economics is Good for You', with a look at some interesting questions and puzzles that make the subject such a rich one. By the time you have studied the book, you'll be able to answer these and more.

Why Economics is Good for You

You may never have studied economics before, and yet when you open a newspaper what do you read? – a report from 'our economics correspondent'. Turn on the television news and what do you see? – an item on the state of the economy. Talk to friends and often the topic will turn to the price of this or that product, or whether you have got enough money to afford to do this or that.

The fact is that economics affects our daily lives. We are continually being made aware of local, national and international economic issues, such as price increases, interest rate changes, fluctuations in exchange rates, unemployment, economic recessions or the effects of globalisation.

We are also continually faced with economic problems and decisions of our own. What should I buy for lunch? Should I save up for a summer holiday, or spend more on day-to-day living? Should I go to university, or should I try to find a job now? If I go to university, should I work part-time?

This 'mini chapter' is an easy read to get you started on the road to thinking like an economist.

WHAT IS ECONOMICS?

If we told you that economics is a problem of maximisation subject to constraints, you'd probably drop this book and find something else to do. So let's put it a different way. Economics is a way of answering some of the most important questions societies face. It's also a way of answering much 'smaller' questions: ones that affect all of us. We are going to set out some of these questions, and start you off on your economics journey. But be warned – once you start thinking like an economist, you probably won't be able to stop.

An island economy

In Chapter 1 we will introduce various core economic concepts and some formal definitions of the economic problems faced by individuals and society. But let's start with a flight of fancy.

Let's suppose that we wake up tomorrow and find ourselves in charge of an island economy. Who is 'we' in this case? Well perhaps it is the authors, plus the reader. Or perhaps it is your economics tutorial group, or a group of random strangers. It really doesn't matter, since it *is* just an imaginary problem.

Once we got over the excitement of being in charge of a whole economy, we might begin to appreciate that it's not going to be all palm trees and days at the beach. An economy has people who need to eat, be housed and will need access to health care. It may have other islands, nearby, that are friendly and want to trade – or are not friendly and may want to invade.

Being in charge suddenly seems to involve quite a few decisions. What is this island going to produce so that people can live? Is it going to be self-sufficient, or to 'swap' goods with other countries? How are people going to know what to produce? How will the products be shared out? Will they be allocated to everyone, even those who do not work? What will we do if some people are too old to work and haven't got savings or families? What should we do if the island bank runs out of money? How can we be sure that we will have enough resources to support the people next year, as well as this?

At the end of the book (page 862) you will see a poem about people cast away on a desert island. Hopefully, after reading this book, you will understand their plight better. But you might find it interesting to read it now before embarking on your studies.

Of course, we are never actually going to be parachuted in to be in charge of an island, except, perhaps, in a reality TV show – although some of you reading this book may aspire to go into politics. But the questions we have posed above are a reflection of the real challenges countries face. We will look at the role of government throughout this book: choices that need to be made, decisions that need to be taken, different approaches policy makers can take, and what happens when governments need to work together.

Books and media

Economics has undergone something of a makeover in the past few years. There are two main reasons.

In 2007–8 there was a major financial crisis, which led to the collapse of banks across the world and a downturn in the global economy. It also led to a close scrutiny of why economists had not predicted the crisis. The outcome was a great deal more coverage of economics and economists than had been seen previously – an interesting example of the Oscar Wilde saying, 'There is only one thing worse than being talked about, and that is not being talked about.' Indeed, it stimulated a lot of interest in studying economics at university!

The second reason has less to do with actual economics and more to do with the way it has been written about. The first decade of the century saw the publication of a number of books which presented economics as a series of thought-provoking puzzles, rather than as a purely academic subject. These included *The Undercover Economist*[1] by Tim Harford and the *Freakonomics*[2] titles, which resulted from collaboration between University of Chicago economist Steven Levitt and New York Times journalist Stephen J. Dubner.

Today, coverage of economics is widespread: in papers, on the Internet, in blogs and radio and television programmes. If you are reading this book because you are studying for a degree or other qualification, you may feel that you are just too busy to read more than the recommended reading list. But try to think more broadly than that. You will find that you can develop your 'economics' brain by spotting the issues. Whether you read papers, or look at news sites online, if you get into the habit of identifying economic issues and puzzles, you will be going a long way towards being an economist.

You could start by Googling the Sloman Economics News site.[3] This not only gives you links to up-to-date articles, with some analysis and questions, it also links through to chapters in this book.

---

1 Tim Harford, *The Undercover Economist* (Little, Brown, 2005).
2 Steven D. Levitt and Stephen J. Dubner, *Freakonomics: A Rogue Economist Explores the Hidden Side of Everything* (William Morrow and Company, 2005).
3 **www.pearsoned.co.uk/sloman**

PUZZLES AND STORIES

Let's look at some examples of economic puzzles and ideas. The ones we discuss below are just a few that you might find interesting.

A pay rise, how exciting

Do you work? By which we mean, do you work for money? If so, make a note of your hourly pay and how many hours you work per week.

Let's assume you are earning £7.50 per hour. Would you like a pay rise to £15 per hour? You would? And what will you do with the extra money you earn? You might go on holiday, or save more, or perhaps you'll simply go out for an extra evening per week, or buy nicer food when you go shopping.

But before we start talking about that, we need to go back to that note of yours. If your rate of pay doubled, how many hours would you work now? You might work the same number of hours; you might think it's worth working more hours; or, you might decide that you can work fewer hours and have more time for other things. It's an interesting puzzle for you to think about. You could ask your friends how they might react in this situation. Perhaps you, or some of your friends, aren't working at the moment, but might do so if higher rates of pay were on offer.

We've thought about this from your point of view. Who else might be interested in the puzzle? Employers are obviously involved. If they want people to do more work, they might consider whether offering higher hourly rates will achieve that. Imagine how annoying it would be if instead people want to work fewer hours, not more. We will see in Chapters 10 and 11 that governments might be interested, too.

Do we have too much debt?

If you are thinking about your student loan or credit card debt, then you will probably immediately say yes. Debt arises from borrowing – the more you borrow and the less you pay back the bigger your debt will be. But borrowing is not always a bad thing. You might not like having to borrow to go to university, but you probably thought it was your best option. You hope that, by getting a degree, you will get a higher salary and that this will more than compensate for the extra debt. It is the same when people buy a house or apartment. People are willing to take out a mortgage so that they can have a place of their own now and 'get on the housing ladder'.

But what about governments? After the financial crisis of 2007–8, governments around the world borrowed large amounts of money to support their economies. They used the money to fund ailing banks and to spend on infrastructure, such as roads, hospitals and broadband. But then, as government debt rocketed, many governments decided they were borrowing too much. They did an about-turn. They started an austerity drive of cutting government expenditure and raising taxes. But was this the right thing to do? Was the debt too high, or should they have continued borrowing to invest in infrastructure and boost the economy? This is something that economists and politicians are still debating to this day.

Of course I want to know

One thing that economists spend a lot of time talking and thinking about is information. We will see in the rest of this book how important it is when making decisions. And, as you've already seen, most of economics is about making decisions. For example, how can you decide which university to apply for? You need to have all sorts of information: what the entry requirements are, what the structure of the course is, how good the lecturers are at teaching and making the subject interesting, how many people get good jobs at the end of the course, how good the social life is, what the accommodation is like. You can probably think of at least three or four other questions you would want answering.

Let's take another example. Suppose you are trying to decide whether to see a film that's just been released. You can get information about the plot, the actors, the special effects, the rating, etc. You can talk to friends who've seen it. You can also read opinions of critics and reviewers on the quality of the film. Hopefully all this information will help you choose whether to spend money and time going to see it.

Similarly, you can get information about many of the other goods and services you might want to buy, by talking to friends or family, researching on the Internet or browsing in shops.

What about a bigger piece of information? Suppose someone could tell you exactly how long you will live if you continue with your current lifestyle? Would that be a useful piece of information? How would it change your day-to-day choices? Would you behave differently right away? Does your answer depend on who gives the information? You might be more inclined to believe a scientist than an astrologer!

In practice, no one is going to be able to tell you your exact life expectancy (to the day). Accidents can happen and medicine moves on. So the best you could currently expect is an informed prediction based, usually, on statistical probability. But such informed predictions about life expectancy are crucial for insurance companies deciding on premiums.

Information is all around us – in fact, we are said to live in the information age. So the problem is often not one of a lack of information, but one of selecting what information is reliable. We hope, by reading this book, you will be better able to assess information and its usefulness for making economic decisions.

We need to save more; we need to spend more

Puzzles like the two above involve decisions of individual people and these are probably the easiest type to identify. But there are some which apply to a whole economy or country. The second half of this book, Chapters 15 onwards, looks at 'whole economy' economics, so let's identify an issue in that area.

How much do you save? The answer is likely to depend on your income, your spending habits and probably on things that are hard to pin down, such as your current level of confidence or how 'good' you are at saving.

Now let's think about saving on a national basis. You may have heard people say that we need to save more. There are all sorts of reasons why saving is a 'good thing'. We are living longer and, unless we save more, we may not have enough to be comfortable in our old age. When we save, we have a buffer against emergencies. When we save, we are not (generally) borrowing, so we don't have to pay interest; instead, we receive interest and so our income is higher.

All of these reasons can be scaled up to the whole economy. You have probably heard politicians say that the country needs to save for the future, especially if we are all going to live longer. The nation, they argue, needs to reduce its debts so that we can reduce the interest we have to pay, leaving more over for the things people want, such as a better health service and better education. And if emergencies arise (the financial crisis of 2007–8 is a really good example) the country will be in a better position if banks have plenty of money. It's also true that saving by individuals provides a source of funds for businesses that want and need to borrow for investment.

You might be wondering why this is a puzzle, since it seems pretty straightforward.

Let's think about the opposite of saving. If you don't save, what do you do with your money? You spend it and, hopefully, enjoy it. Imagine the opposite – that you saved a lot of your income, much more than you do now. Imagine that you only bought the barest of necessities, grew your own food, wore the same clothes for years and didn't buy any new technology, or even have an occasional night out. You might have a pretty miserable life.

Now scale this up to the whole economy again. If people start spending less, what will happen? Businesses will very quickly be in trouble. The banks will be full of our savings, but no one will be borrowing. With spending falling, many firms won't be able to make profits and will have to close. The economy will move into recession and very soon could be in severe crisis.

Of course this is an exaggerated example. But you can see the puzzle, can't you? Saving is good, but so is spending. What should we do? What should the government encourage us to do?

APPLYING THE PRINCIPLES

Thinking like an economist – a word of warning

As you go through the rest of this book, whether you study all of it or just some sections, try to spot the puzzles we have talked about above. And look out for other puzzles and issues. You can do this outside formal study. Economics is about people and society. It isn't a dry subject; it is something that is all around us. Try to get into the habit of thinking like an economist on a daily basis. If there's a decision to be made, there's an economic way of thinking about it.

To help you think like an economist, we've identified 15 'threshold concepts'. Understanding these concepts and being able to apply them in various contexts helps you gain a deeper understanding of economic problems and choices. We describe each concept when we first come across it and then, each time we use it, there is an icon in the margin to remind you and to refer you back to the page where it's described.

Where will this approach of 'thinking like an economist' take you? It will make you more analytical; it will help you make better decisions. There's evidence that it can get you a better job and it will certainly make you better at your job.

We'd like to offer one word of warning though. Once you're thinking like an economist, there's no turning back. It's a skill that will be with you for life. Just bear in mind that the non-economists around you may need convincing about the beauty of the subject.

Enjoy the book, but, more importantly, enjoy your journey through economics and the new light it will shed on the world around you.

BOX A.1   WHAT'S THE LATEST ECONOMICS NEWS?   CASE STUDIES AND APPLICATIONS

- Government says that the UK cannot remain in the EU single market or customs union when it leaves the EU.
- The Bank of Japan engages in another round of quantitative easing to boost the ailing Japanese economy.
- Severe droughts cause crops to fail across sub-Saharan Africa: higher grain prices expected soon.
- There is widespread criticism of Donald Trump's policies on trade, with fears that US exports might suffer if America cuts back on imports.
- Unemployment falls and economic growth accelerates, leading to expectations of higher interest rates.

- The age at which UK workers can draw their state pension is raised further. Many predict that those currently under 30 will be working until at least the age of 70.
- Lack of training helps to explain low levels of productivity.
- Oil prices set to remain low for many years as more and more countries engage in fracking.
- Interest rates likely to rise; house prices likely to fall.

1. *What is it that makes each one of the above news items an economics item?*
2. *In each case identify two different individuals or groups who might be affected by the news item.*

Economics and Economies

In the introductory chapter we discussed some of the questions and puzzles that make economics such an interesting subject to study. Now we turn to explaining those ideas in a bit more detail. We also introduce some of the tools you will need to help you analyse the puzzles posed and answer the questions.

Economics contains some core ideas. These ideas are simple, but can be applied to a wide range of economic problems. We start examining these ideas in this chapter. We begin on the journey to help you to 'think like an economist' – a journey that we hope you will find fascinating and will give you a sound foundation for many possible future careers.

In the introductory chapter, we asked what economics is about. In this chapter, we will attempt to answer that question and give you greater insight into the subject you are studying. We will see how the subject is divided up and we will distinguish between the two major branches of economics: microeconomics and macroeconomics.

We will also look at the ways in which different types of economy operate, from the centrally planned economies of the former communist countries to the more free-market economies of most of the world today. We will ask just how 'markets' work.

1.1 WHAT DO ECONOMISTS STUDY?

Many people think that economics is about *money*. Well, to some extent this is true. Economics has a lot to do with money: with how much money people earn; how much they spend; what various items cost; how much money firms make; the total amount of money there is in the economy. But, as we shall see later in the book, money is only important because of what it allows us to do; money is a tool and economics is more than just the study of money.

It is concerned with the following:

■ The *production* of goods and services: how much an economy produces, both in total and of individual items; how much each firm or person produces; what techniques of production are used; how many people are employed.
■ The *consumption* of goods and services: how much people spend (and how much they save) ; how much people buy of particular items; what individuals choose to buy; how consumption is affected by prices, advertising, fashion, people's incomes and other factors.

 Could production and consumption take place without money? If you think they could, give some examples.

But we still have not got to the bottom of what economics is about. Is there one crucial ingredient that makes a problem an economic one? The answer is that there is a central problem faced by all individuals and all countries, no matter how rich. It is the problem of *scarcity* – an issue underlying all other economic problems. For an economist, scarcity has a very specific definition.

 Before reading on, how would you define 'scarcity'? Must goods be at least temporarily unattainable to be scarce?

The problem of scarcity

Ask people if they would like more money, and the vast majority would answer 'Yes'. But they don't want more money for its own sake. Rather they want to be able to buy more goods and services, either today or in the future.

These 'wants' will vary according to income levels and tastes. In a poor country 'wants' might include clean water, education and suitable housing. In richer nations 'wants' might involve a second car, longer holidays and more time with friends and family. As countries get richer, human wants may change but they don't disappear. Wants are virtually unlimited.

Yet the means of fulfilling wants are limited. At any point, the world can only produce a finite amount of goods and services because the world has a limited amount of *resources*. These resources, or *factors of production* as they are often called in economics, are of three broad types:

■ Human resources: *labour*. The labour force is limited in number, but also in skills. This limits the productivity of labour: i.e. the amount labour can produce.
■ Natural resources: *land and raw materials*. The world's land area is limited, as are its raw materials.
■ Manufactured resources: *capital*. Capital consists of all those inputs that have themselves had to be produced. The world has a limited stock of factories, machines, transportation and other equipment. The productivity of this capital is limited by the current state of technology.

 Could each of these types of resources be increased in quantity or quality? Is there a time dimension to your answer?

So this is the fundamental economic problem: human wants are virtually unlimited, whereas the resources available to meet those wants are limited. We can thus define scarcity as follows:

 KEY IDEA 1 *Scarcity* is the excess of human wants over what can actually be produced. Because of scarcity, various choices have to be made between alternatives.

 If we would all like more money, why does the government not print a lot more? Could it not thereby solve the problem of scarcity 'at a stroke'?

Definitions

Production The transformation of inputs into outputs by firms in order to earn profit (or to meet some other objective).

Consumption The act of using goods and services to satisfy wants. This will normally involve purchasing the goods and services.

Factors of production (or resources) The inputs into the production of goods and services: labour, land and raw materials, and capital.

Labour All forms of human input, both physical and mental, into current production.

Land and raw materials Inputs into production that are provided by nature: e.g. unimproved land and mineral deposits in the ground.

Capital All inputs into production that have themselves been produced: e.g. factories, machines and tools.

Scarcity The excess of human wants over what can actually be produced to fulfil these wants.

Of course, we do not all face the problem of scarcity to the same degree. A poor family who may not be able to afford enough to eat, or a decent place to live, will hardly see it as a 'problem' that a rich family cannot afford a second skiing holiday. But economists do not claim that we all face an equal problem of scarcity. In fact this is one of the major issues economists study: how resources are distributed, whether between different individuals, different regions of a country or different countries of the world.

This economic problem – limited resources but limitless wants – makes people, both rich and poor, behave in certain ways. Economics studies that behaviour. It studies people at work, producing goods that people want. It studies people as consumers, buying the goods that they want. It studies governments influencing the level and pattern of production and consumption. It even studies why people get married and what determines the number of children they have! In short, it studies anything to do with the process of satisfying human wants.

Demand and supply

We have said that economics is concerned with consumption and production. Another way of looking at this is in terms of *demand* and *supply*. Demand and supply and the relationship between them lie at the very centre of economics. How does this relate to the problem of scarcity?

Demand is related to wants. If every good and service were free, people would simply demand whatever they wanted. In total, such wants are likely to be virtually boundless, perhaps only limited by people's imaginations. *Supply,* on the other hand, is limited. It is related to resources. The amount that firms can supply depends on the resources and technology available.

Given the problem of scarcity – that human wants exceed what can actually be produced – *potential* demands will exceed *potential* supplies. Society has to find some way of dealing with this problem, to try to match demand with supply. This applies at the level of the economy overall: total or 'aggregate' demand needs to be balanced against total or *aggregate* supply. In other words, total spending in the economy should balance total production. It also applies at the level of individual goods and services. The demand and supply of cabbages should balance, and so should the demand and supply of cars, houses, tablets and holidays.

But if potential demand exceeds potential supply, how are *actual* demand and supply made equal? Either demand has to be reduced, or supply has to be increased, or a combination of the two. Economics studies this process. It studies how demand adjusts to available supplies, and how supply adjusts to consumer demands.

Dividing up the subject

Economics is traditionally divided into two main branches – *macroeconomics* and *microeconomics,* where 'macro' means big and 'micro' means small.

Macroeconomics is concerned with the economy as a whole. It is concerned with *aggregate demand* and *aggregate supply*. By 'aggregate demand' we mean the total amount of spending in the economy, whether by consumers, by customers outside the country for our exports, by the government, or by firms when they buy capital equipment or stock up on raw materials. By 'aggregate supply' we mean the total national output of goods and services.

Microeconomics is concerned with the individual parts of the economy. It is concerned with the demand and supply of particular goods, services and resources such as cars, butter, clothes, haircuts, plumbers, accountants, blast furnaces, computers and oil.

 Which of the following are macroeconomic issues, which are microeconomic ones and which could be either depending on the context?
  (a) Inflation.
  (b) Low wages in certain sectors.
  (c) The rate of exchange between the pound and the euro.
  (d) Why the prices of fresh fruit and vegetables fluctuate more than that of cars.
  (e) The rate of economic growth this year compared with last year.
  (f) The decline of traditional manufacturing industries.
  (g) Immigration of workers.

Macroeconomics

Because scarcity exists, societies are concerned that their resources should be used *as fully as possible* and that over time their national output should grow.

Why should resources be used as fully as possible? If resources are 'saved' in one time period surely they can be used in the next time period? The answer is that not all resources can be saved. For example, if a worker doesn't go to work one week then that resource is lost: labour can't be saved up for the future.

Why do societies want growth? To understand this, think back to the discussion of endless wants: if our output grows, then more of our wants can be satisfied. Individuals and society can be made better off.

> ### Definitions
>
> **Macroeconomics** The branch of economics that studies economic aggregates (grand totals): e.g. the overall level of prices, output and employment in the economy.
>
> **Aggregate demand** The total level of spending in the economy.
>
> **Aggregate supply** The total amount of output in the economy.
>
> **Microeconomics** The branch of economics that studies individual units: e.g. households, firms and industries. It studies the interrelationships between these units in determining the pattern of production and distribution of goods and services.

The achievement of growth and the full use of resources are not easy. This is demonstrated by periods of high unemployment and stagnation that have occurred from time to time throughout the world (for example, in the recessions of the 1930s, the early 1980s and the period following the financial crisis of 2007–8). Furthermore, attempts by governments to stimulate growth and employment can result in inflation and rising imports. Economies have often experienced cycles where periods of growth alternate with periods of recession, such periods varying from a few months to a few years. This is known as the 'business cycle'.

Macroeconomic problems are closely related to the balance between aggregate demand and aggregate supply.

If aggregate demand is too *high* relative to aggregate supply, inflation and trade deficits are likely to result.

- *Inflation* refers to a general rise in the level of prices throughout the economy. If aggregate demand rises substantially, firms are likely to respond by raising their prices. If demand is high, they can probably still sell as much as before (if not more) even at the higher prices, and make higher profits. If firms in general put up their prices, inflation results. By comparing price levels between different periods we can measure the **rate of inflation**. Typically, the rate of inflation reported is the *annual* rate of inflation: the percentage increase in prices over a 12-month period.
- *Balance of trade* deficits are the excess of imports over exports. If aggregate demand rises, people are likely to buy more imports. So part of the extra spending will go on goods from overseas, such as Japanese TVs, Chinese computers, German cars, etc. Also, if the rate of inflation is high, home-produced goods will become uncompetitive with foreign goods. We are likely to buy more foreign imports and people abroad are likely to buy fewer of our exports.

If aggregate demand is too low relative to aggregate supply, unemployment and recession may well result.

- *Recession* is where output in the economy declines for two successive quarters or longer. In other words, during this period growth becomes negative. Hence, not all periods during which the economy contracts are termed 'recessions'. It is the duration and persistence of the contraction that distinguishes a recession. Recessions are associated with low levels of consumer spending. If people spend less, shops are likely to find themselves with unsold stock. Then they will buy less from the manufacturers; they will cut down on production; and buy fewer capital goods such as machinery.
- *Unemployment* is likely to result from cutbacks in production. If firms are producing less, they will need to employ fewer people.

Macroeconomic policy, therefore, tends to focus on the balance of aggregate demand and aggregate supply. It can be

Definitions

Inflation A general rise in the level of prices throughout the economy

(Annual) Rate of inflation The percentage increase in the level of prices over a 12-month period.

Balance of trade Exports of goods and services minus imports of goods and services. If exports exceed imports, there is a 'balance of trade surplus' (a positive figure). If imports exceed exports, there is a 'balance of trade deficit' (a negative figure).

Recession A period where national output falls for two or more successive quarters.

Unemployment The number of people of working age who are actively looking for work but are currently without a job. (Note that there is much debate as to who should officially be counted as unemployed.)

Demand-side policy Government policy designed to alter the level of aggregate demand, and thereby the level of output, employment and prices.

Supply-side policy Government policy that attempts to alter the level of aggregate supply directly.

demand-side policy, which seeks to influence the level of spending in the economy. This in turn will affect the level of production, prices and employment. Or it can be *supply-side policy*. This is designed to influence the level of production directly: for example, by trying to create more incentives for firms to innovate.

Microeconomics

Microeconomics and choice

Because resources are scarce, choices have to be made. There are three main categories of choice that must be made in any society:

- *What* goods and services are going to be produced and in what quantities, since there are not enough resources to produce everything people want? How many cars, how much wheat, how much insurance, how many iPhones, etc. will be produced?
- *How* are things going to be produced? What resources are going to be used and in what quantities? What techniques of production are going to be adopted? Will cars be produced by robots or by assembly-line workers? Will electricity be produced from coal, oil, gas, nuclear fission, renewable resources such as wind farms or a mixture of these?
- *For whom* are things going to be produced? In other words, how will the country's income be distributed? After all, the higher your income, the more you can consume of the total output. What will be the wages of shop workers, MPs, footballers and accountants? How much will pensioners receive? How much of the country's income will go to shareholders or landowners?

BOX 1.1   **LOOKING AT MACROECONOMIC DATA**   **CASE STUDIES AND APPLICATIONS**

Assessing different countries' macroeconomic performance

Rapid economic growth, low unemployment, low inflation and the avoidance of current account deficits[1] are major macroeconomic policy objectives of most governments around the world. To help them achieve these objectives they employ economic advisers. But when we look at the performance of various economies, the success of governments' macroeconomic policies seems decidedly 'mixed'.

The table shows data for the USA, Japan, Germany[2] and the UK from 1961 to 2018.

Macroeconomic performance of four industrialised economies (average annual figures)

	Unemployment (% of workforce)				Inflation (annual %)				Economic growth (annual %)				Balance on current account (% of national income)			
	USA	Japan	Germany	UK	USA	Japan	Germany	UK	USA	Japan	Germany	UK	USA	Japan	Germany	UK
1961–70	4.8	1.3	0.6	1.7	2.4	5.6	2.7	3.9	4.2	10.1	4.4	3.0	0.5	0.6	0.7	0.2
1971–80	6.4	1.8	2.2	3.8	7.0	8.8	5.1	13.2	3.2	4.4	2.8	2.0	0.9	0.5	1.1	−0.7
1981–90	2.5	2.5	6.0	9.6	4.5	2.2	2.5	6.2	3.2	3.9	2.3	2.6	−1.7	2.3	2.6	−1.4
1991–2000	3.3	3.3	7.9	7.9	2.2	0.4	2.3	3.3	3.3	1.5	1.9	2.4	−1.6	2.5	−0.7	−1.5
2001–07	5.3	4.6	9.2	5.2	2.8	−0.1	1.9	1.9	2.1	1.0	2.3	2.5	−4.8	3.3	3.8	−2.1
2008–18	6.9	3.9	5.3	6.6	1.6	0.3	1.3	2.3	1.7	0.7	1.3	1.2	−2.7	2.7	7.1	−3.5

Note: Years 2017 and 2018 are forecasts.
Source: *Statistical Annex of the European Economy* (Commission of the European Communities, various tables and years) and *World Economic Outlook* (IMF, April 2017).

1. Has the UK generally fared better or worse than the other three countries?
2. Was there a common pattern in the macroeconomic performance of each of the four countries over these 58 years?

If the government does not have much success in managing the economy, it could be for the following reasons:

- Economists have incorrectly analysed the problems and hence have given the wrong advice.
- Economists disagree and hence have given conflicting advice.

- Economists have based their advice on inaccurate statistics or incorrect forecasts.
- Governments have not listened to the advice of economists. This could be for political reasons, such as the electoral cycle.
- There is little else that governments could have done: the problems were insoluble or could not have been predicted.

1 The current account balance is the trade balance plus any incomes earned from abroad minus any incomes paid abroad. These incomes could be wages, investment incomes or government revenues (see section 15.7 for details).
2 West Germany from 1961 to 1991.

All societies have to make these choices, whether they are made by individuals, groups or the government. They can be seen as microeconomic choices, since they are concerned not with the total amount of national output, but with the individual goods and services that make it up: what they are, how they are made, and who gets to consume them.

Choice and opportunity cost

Choice involves sacrifice. The more food you choose to buy, the less money you will have to spend on other goods. The more food a nation produces, the fewer resources there will be for producing other goods. In other words, the production or consumption of one thing involves the sacrifice of alternatives. This sacrifice of alternatives in the production (or consumption) of a good is known as its *opportunity cost*.

If the workers on a farm can produce either 1000 tonnes of wheat or 2000 tonnes of barley, then the opportunity cost of producing 1 tonne of wheat is the 2 tonnes of barley forgone. The opportunity cost of buying a textbook is the new pair of jeans that you have had to go without. The opportunity cost of saving for your old age is the consumption you sacrifice while younger.

KEY IDEA 2   The *opportunity cost* of any activity is the sacrifice made to do it. It is the best thing that could have been done as an alternative.

Definition

Opportunity cost The cost of any activity measured in terms of the best alternative forgone.

| THRESHOLD CONCEPT 1 | CHOICE AND OPPORTUNITY COST | THINKING LIKE AN ECONOMIST |

KI 1
p7

Scarcity, as we have seen, is at the heart of economics.

We all face scarcity. With a limited income we cannot buy everything we want. And even if we had the money, with only 24 hours in a day, we would not have time to enjoy all the things we would like to consume. The same applies at a national level. A country has limited resources and so cannot produce everything people would like. Of course, this is also true on a global scale: our planet has finite resources, and the technology and our abilities to exploit these resources are also limited.

With limited resources and endless wants, we have to make choices. In fact, virtually every time we do something, we are making a choice between alternatives. If you choose to watch television, you are choosing not to go out. If you buy a pair of trainers for £70, you are choosing not to spend that £70 on something else. Likewise, if a country devotes more of its resources to producing manufactured goods, there will be less to devote to the provision of services. If we devote more resources to producing a cleaner environment, we may have to produce less of the material goods that people want to consume.

What we give up in order to do something is known as its **opportunity cost.** Opportunity cost is the cost of doing something measured in terms of the best alternative forgone. It's what you would have chosen to do with your time or money if you had not made the choice you did. This is one of the most fundamental concepts in economics. It is a threshold concept: once you have seen its importance, it affects the way you look at economic problems. When you use the concept of opportunity cost, you are thinking like an economist. And this may be different from thinking like an accountant or from the way you thought before.

It may sound deceptively simple, but in some cases working out the opportunity cost of an activity can be a tricky process. We will come across this concept many times throughout this book.

By looking at opportunity cost we are recognising that we face trade-offs. To do more of one thing involves doing less of something else. For example, we trade off work and leisure. The more we work, the less leisure time we will have. In other words, the opportunity cost of working is the leisure we have sacrificed. Nations trade off producing one good against others. The more a country spends on defence, the less it will have to spend on consumer goods and services. This has become known as the 'guns versus butter' trade-off. In other words, if a country decides to use more of its resources for defence, the opportunity cost is the consumer goods sacrificed. We examine such trade-offs at a national level on pages 15–17, when we look at the 'production possibility curve'.

We therefore have to make decisions between alternatives. To make sensible decisions we must weigh up the benefits of doing something against its opportunity cost. This is known in economics as 'rational decision making'. It is another of our threshold concepts (no. 8): see page 109.

1. *Think of three things you did last week. What was the opportunity cost of each one?*
2. *Assume that a supermarket has some fish that has reached its sell-by date. It was originally priced at £10, but yesterday was marked down to £5 'for quick sale'. It is now the end of the day and it still has not been sold. The supermarket is about to close and there is no one in the store who wants fish. What is the opportunity cost for the store of throwing the fish away?*

TC 1
p11

Opportunity cost as the basis for choice is the first of our 'Threshold concepts' (see above). There are 15 of these threshold concepts, which we shall be exploring throughout the book. Once you have grasped these concepts and seen their significance, they will affect the way that you understand and analyse economic problems. They will help you to 'think like an economist'.

Rational choices

Economists often refer to **rational choices**. This simply means that people are weighing up the *costs* and *benefits* of different activities and picking the option that allows them to maximise their objective. For consumers and workers this means making choices that maximise their happiness. For a firm it may mean choosing what and how much to produce to maximise profits.

Definition

Rational choices Choices that involve weighing up the benefit of any activity against its opportunity cost so that the decision maker successfully maximises their objective: i.e. happiness or profits.

Imagine you are doing your shopping in a supermarket and you want to buy a chicken. Do you spend a lot of money and buy a free-range organic chicken, or do you buy a cheap bird instead? To make a rational (i.e. sensible) decision, you will need to weigh up the costs and benefits of each alternative. The free-range chicken may taste better and it may meet your concerns about animal welfare, but it has a high opportunity cost: because it is expensive, you will need to sacrifice quite a lot of consumption of other goods if you decide to buy it. If you buy the intensively farmed chicken, however, although you will not enjoy it so much, you will have more money left over to buy other things: it has a lower opportunity cost.

Thus rational decision making, as far as consumers are concerned, involves choosing those items that give you the best value for money – i.e. the *greatest benefit relative to cost.*

The same principles apply to firms when deciding what to produce. For example, should a car firm open up another production line? A rational decision will again involve weighing up the benefits and costs. The benefits are the revenues the firm will earn from selling the extra cars. The costs will include the extra labour costs, raw material costs, costs of component parts, etc. It will be profitable to open up the new production line only if the revenues earned exceed the costs entailed: in other words, if it increases profits.

In the more complex situation of deciding which model of car to produce, or how many of each model, the firm must weigh up the relative benefits and costs of each – i.e. it will want to produce the most profitable product mix.

 Assume that you are looking for a job and are offered two. One is more enjoyable, but pays less. How would you make a rational choice between the two jobs?

Marginal costs and benefits

In economics we argue that rational choices involve weighing up **marginal costs** and **marginal benefits**. These are the costs and benefits of doing a little bit more or a little bit less of a specific activity. They can be contrasted with the total costs and benefits of the activity.

Take a familiar example. What time will you set your alarm to go off tomorrow morning? Let us say that you have to leave home at 8:30. Perhaps you will set the alarm for 7:00. That will give you plenty of time to get ready, but it will mean less sleep. Perhaps you will decide to set it for 8:00. That will give you a longer lie-in, but more of a rush in the morning to get ready.

So how do you make a rational decision about when the alarm should go off? What you have to do is to weigh up the costs and benefits of *additional* sleep. Each extra minute in bed gives you more sleep (the marginal benefit), but means you'll be more rushed when you get up (the marginal cost). The decision is therefore based on the costs and benefits of *extra* sleep, not on the total costs and benefits of a whole night's sleep.

This same principle applies to rational decisions made by consumers, workers and firms. For example, the car firm we were considering just now will weigh up the marginal costs and benefits of producing cars: in other words, it will compare the costs and revenue of producing *additional* cars. If additional cars add more to the firm's revenue than to its costs, it will be profitable to produce them.

Rational decision making, then, involves weighing up the marginal benefit and marginal cost of any activity. If the marginal benefit exceeds the marginal cost, it is rational to do the activity (or to do more of it). If the marginal cost exceeds the marginal benefit, it is rational not to do it (or to do less of it).

Rational decision making is Threshold Concept 8 and this is examined in Chapter 4, page 109.

 How would the principle of weighing up marginal costs and benefits apply to a worker deciding how much overtime to work in a given week?

Microeconomic objectives

Microeconomics is concerned with the allocation of scarce resources: with the answering of the *what, how* and *for whom* questions. But how satisfactorily will these questions be answered? Clearly this depends on society's objectives. There are two major objectives that we can identify: *efficiency* and *equity*.

Efficiency. If altering what was produced or how it was produced could make us all better off (or at least make some of us better off without anyone losing), then it would be efficient to do so. For a society to achieve full **economic efficiency**, three conditions must be met:

- Efficiency in production (**productive efficiency**). This is where production of each item is at minimum cost. Producing any other way would cost more.
- Efficiency in consumption. This is where consumers allocate their expenditures so as to get maximum satisfaction from their income. Any other pattern of consumption would make people feel worse off.
- Efficiency in specialisation and exchange. This is where firms specialise in producing goods for sale to consumers, and where individuals specialise in doing jobs in order to buy goods, so that everyone maximises the benefits they achieve relative to the costs of achieving them.

These last two are collectively known as **allocative efficiency**. In any economic activity, allocative efficiency will be increased as long as doing more of that activity (and hence less of an alternative) involves a greater marginal benefit than marginal cost. Full efficiency will be achieved when all such improvements have been made.

Definitions

Marginal costs The additional cost of doing a little bit more (or 1 unit more if a unit can be measured) of an activity.

Marginal benefits The additional benefits of doing a little bit more (or 1 unit more if a unit can be measured) of an activity.

Rational decision making Doing more of an activity if its marginal benefit exceeds its marginal cost and doing less if its marginal cost exceeds its marginal benefit.

Economic efficiency A situation where each good is produced at the minimum cost and where individual people and firms get the maximum benefit from their resources.

Productive efficiency A situation where firms are producing the maximum output for a given amount of inputs, or producing a given output at the least cost.

Allocative efficiency A situation where the current combination of goods produced and sold gives the maximum satisfaction for each consumer at their current levels of income. Note that a redistribution of income would lead to a different combination of goods that was allocatively efficient.

| BOX 1.2 | THE OPPORTUNITY COSTS OF STUDYING | | CASE STUDIES AND APPLICATIONS |

What are you sacrificing?

You may not have realised it, but you probably consider opportunity costs many times a day. We are constantly making choices: what to buy, what to eat, what to wear, whether to go out, how much to study, and so on. Each time we make a choice to do something, we are in effect rejecting doing some alternative. This alternative forgone is the opportunity cost of the action we choose.

Sometimes the opportunity costs of our actions are the direct monetary costs we incur. Sometimes it is more complicated.

Take the opportunity costs of your choices as a student.

Buying a textbook costing £59.99

This choice does involve a direct money payment. What you have to consider are the alternatives you could have bought with the £59.99. You then have to weigh up the benefit from the best alternative against the benefit of the textbook.

1. *What might prevent you from making the best decision?*

Coming to lectures

Even though students now pay fees for their degrees in many countries, there is no extra (marginal) monetary cost in coming to classes once the fees have been paid. You will not get a refund by missing a lecture. The fees, once you've paid them, are what we call a 'sunk cost'.

So are the opportunity costs zero? No: by coming to a lecture you are not working in the library; you are not sleeping; you are not undertaking paid work during that time. If you are making a rational decision to come to classes, then you will consider such possible alternatives.

2. *If there are several other things you could have done, is the opportunity cost the sum of all of them?*
3. *What factors would make the opportunity cost of attending a class relatively high?*

Revising for an economics exam

Again, the opportunity cost is the best alternative to which you could have put your time. This might be revising for some other exam. You will probably want to divide your time sensibly between your subjects. A *sensible* decision is not to revise economics on any given occasion if you will gain a greater benefit from revising another subject. In such a case the (marginal) opportunity cost of revising economics exceeds the (marginal) benefit.

Choosing to study at university or college

What are the opportunity costs of being a student in higher education?

At first it might seem that the costs of higher education would include the following:

- Tuition fees.
- Books, stationery, etc.
- Accommodation, food, entertainment, travel and other living expenses.

But adding these up does not give the opportunity cost. The opportunity cost is the *sacrifice* entailed by going to university or college *rather than* doing something else. Let us assume that the alternative is to take a job that has been offered. The correct list of opportunity costs of higher education would include:

- Books, stationery, etc.
- Additional accommodation and travel expenses over what would have been incurred by taking the job.
- Wages that would have been earned in the job, less any income received as a student.
- The tuition fees paid by the student.

4. *Why is the cost of food not included? Should the cost of clothing be included?*
5. *What impact would it have on the calculation of opportunity costs if you really disliked the nature of the work in the best alternative job?*
6. *Is the opportunity cost to the individual of attending higher education different from the opportunity costs to society as a whole? Do the benefits of higher education for society differ from those for the individual?*

KEY IDEA 3

Economic efficiency is achieved when each good is produced at the minimum cost and where individual people and firms get the maximum benefit from their resources.

Equity. Even though the current levels of production and consumption might be efficient, they could be regarded as unfair, if some people are rich while others are poor. Another microeconomic goal, therefore, is that of *equity*.

Income distribution is regarded as equitable if it is considered to be fair or just. The problem with this objective, however, is that people have different notions of fairness. A rich person may well favour a much higher degree of inequality than will a poor person. Likewise, socialist governments will generally be in favour of a greater redistribution of income from the rich to the poor than will Conservative governments. Equity is therefore described as a value judgement: notions of equity will depend on the values of individuals or society.

KEY IDEA 4 *Equity* is where income is distributed in a way that is considered to be fair or just. Note that an equitable distribution is not the same as an equal distribution and that different people have different views on what is equitable.

Would it be desirable to have total equality in an economy, so that everyone receives the same share of resources?

The social implications of choice

In practice, the choices that people make may be neither efficient nor equitable. Firms may use inefficient techniques or be poorly managed; people often make wrong decisions about what to buy or what job to take; governments may be wasteful or inefficient in their use of tax revenues; there may be considerable inequality and injustice.

What is more, the effects of people's choices often spill over to other people. Take the case of pollution. It might be profitable for a firm to tip toxic waste into a river. But what is profitable for the firm will not necessarily be 'profitable' for society. Such an action may have serious environmental consequences.

Throughout the book we will be considering how well the economy meets various economic and social objectives, whether micro or macro. We will examine why problems occur and what can be done about them.

Illustrating economic issues: the production possibility curve

Economics books and articles frequently contain diagrams. The reason is that diagrams are very useful for illustrating economic relationships. Ideas and arguments that might take a long time to explain in words can often be expressed clearly and simply in a diagram.

Two of the most common types of diagram used in economics are graphs and flow diagrams. In this and the next section we will look at one example of each. These examples are chosen to illustrate the distinction between microeconomic and macroeconomic issues.

We start by having a look at a *production possibility curve*. This diagram is a graph. Like many diagrams in economics it shows a simplified picture of reality – a picture stripped of all details that are unnecessary to illustrate the points being made. Of course, there are dangers in this.

Definitions

Equity A distribution of income that is considered to be fair or just. Note that an equitable distribution is not the same as an equal distribution and that different people have different views on what is equitable.

Production possibility curve A curve showing all the possible combinations of two goods that a country can produce within a specified time period with all its resources fully and efficiently employed.

KI 1
p7

| BOX 1.3 | SCARCITY AND ABUNDANCE | CASE STUDIES AND APPLICATIONS |

Is lunch ever free?

The central economic problem is scarcity. But are *all* goods and services scarce? Is anything we desire truly abundant?

First, what do we mean by *abundance*? In the economic sense we mean something where supply exceeds demand at a *zero* price. In other words, even if it is free, there is no shortage. What is more, there must be no opportunity cost in supplying it. For example, if the government supplies health care free to the sick, it is still scarce in the economic sense because there is a cost to the government (and hence the taxpayer).

Two things that might seem to be abundant are air and water.

Air

In one sense air *is* abundant. There is no shortage of air to breathe for most people for most of the time. But if we define air as clean, unpolluted air, then in some parts of the world it is scarce. It costs money to clean polluted air. We may not pay directly – the cleaned-up air may be free to the

'consumer' – but the taxpayer or industry (and hence its customers) will have to pay.

Even if you live in a non-polluted part of the country, you may well have spent money moving there to escape the pollution. Again there is an opportunity cost to obtain the clean air.

Water

Whether water is abundant depends again on where you live. It also depends on what the water is used for.

Water for growing crops in a country with plentiful rain *is* abundant. In drier countries, resources have to be spent on irrigation. Water for drinking is not abundant. Reservoirs have to be built. The water has to be piped, purified and pumped.

1. There is a saying in economics, 'There is no such thing as a free lunch' (hence the subtitle for this box). What does this mean?
2. Are any other (desirable) goods or services truly abundant?

Figure 1.1   A production possibility curve

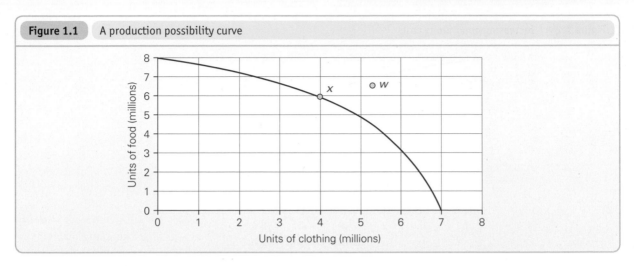

Table 1.1   Maximum possible combinations of food and clothing that can be produced in a given time period

Units of food (millions)	Units of clothing (millions)
8.0	0.0
7.0	2.2
6.0	4.0
5.0	5.0
4.0	5.6
3.0	6.0
2.0	6.4
1.0	6.7
0.0	7.0

In the attempt to make a diagram simple enough to understand, we run the risk of oversimplifying. If this is the case, the diagram may be misleading.

A production possibility curve is shown in Figure 1.1. The graph is based on the data shown in Table 1.1.

Assume that some imaginary nation devotes all its resources – land, labour and capital – to producing just two goods: food and clothing. Various possible combinations that could be produced over a given period of time (e.g. a year) are shown in the table. Thus the country, by devoting all its resources to producing food, could produce 8 million units of food but no clothing. Alternatively, by producing, say, 7 million units of food it could release enough resources – land, labour and capital – to produce 2.2 million units of clothing. At the other extreme, it could produce 7 million units of clothing with no resources at all being used to produce food.

The information in the table can be transferred to a graph (Figure 1.1). We measure units of food on one axis (in this case the vertical axis) and units of clothing on the other. The curve shows all the combinations of the two goods that can

be produced with all the nation's resources fully and efficiently employed. For example, production could take place at point x, with 6 million units of food and 4 million units of clothing being produced. Production cannot take place beyond the curve. For example, production is not possible at point w: the nation does not have enough resources to do this.

Note that there are two simplifying assumptions in this diagram. First, it is assumed that there are just two types of good that can be produced. We have to assume this because we only have two axes on our graph. The other assumption is that there is only one type of food and one type of clothing. This is implied by measuring their output in particular units (e.g. tonnes). If food differed in type, it would be possible to produce a greater tonnage of food for a given amount of clothing simply by switching production from one foodstuff to another.

These two assumptions are obviously enormous simplifications when we consider the modern complex economies of the real world. But despite this, the diagram still allows important principles to be illustrated simply. In fact, this is one of the key advantages of using diagrams.

Microeconomics and the production possibility curve

A production possibility curve illustrates the microeconomic issues of choice and opportunity cost.

If the country chose to produce more clothing, it would have to sacrifice the production of some food. This sacrifice of food is the opportunity cost of the extra clothing.

The fact that to produce more of one good involves producing less of the other is illustrated by the downward-sloping nature of the curve. For example, the country could move from point x to point y in Figure 1.2. In doing so it would be producing an extra 1 million units of clothing, but 1 million units less of food. Thus the opportunity cost of the 1 million extra units of clothing would be the 1 million units of food forgone.

It also illustrates the phenomenon of ***increasing opportunity costs***. By this we mean that as a country produces more

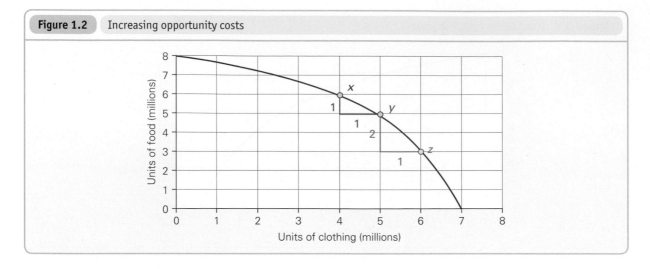

Figure 1.2 Increasing opportunity costs

Definition

Increasing opportunity costs of production When additional production of one good involves ever-increasing sacrifices of another.

of one good it has to sacrifice ever-increasing amounts of the other. The reason for this is that different factors of production have different properties. People have different skills; land varies across different parts of the country; raw materials differ one from another; and so on. Thus, as a country concentrates more on the production of one good, it has to start using resources that are less suitable – resources that would have been better suited to producing other goods. In our example, then, the production of more and more clothing will involve a growing *marginal cost*: ever-increasing amounts of food have to be sacrificed for each additional unit of clothing produced.

It is because opportunity costs increase that the production possibility curve is bowed outward rather than being a straight line. Thus in Figure 1.2, as production moves from point x to y to z, so the amount of food sacrificed rises for each additional unit of clothing produced. The opportunity cost of the fifth million units of clothing is 1 million units of food. The opportunity cost of the sixth million units of clothing is 2 million units of food.

1. *What is the opportunity cost of the seventh million units of clothing?*
2. *If the country moves upward along the curve and produces more food, does this also involve increasing opportunity costs?*
3. *Under what circumstances would the production possibility curve be (a) a straight line; (b) bowed in towards the origin? Are these circumstances ever likely?*

Macroeconomics and the production possibility curve

There is no guarantee that resources will be fully employed, or that they will be used in the most efficient way possible. The nation may thus be producing at a point inside the curve: for example, point v in Figure 1.3.

What we are saying here is that the economy is producing less of both goods than it is possible for it to produce, either because some resources are not being used (for example, workers may be unemployed), or because it is not using the most efficient methods of production possible, or a combination of the two. By using its resources to the full, the nation could move out onto the curve: to point x or y, for example. It could produce more clothing *and* more food.

Here we are concerned not with the combination of goods produced (a microeconomic issue), but with whether the total amount produced is as much as it could be (a macroeconomic issue).

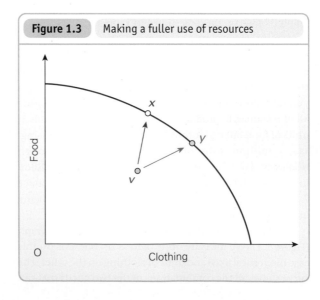

Figure 1.3 Making a fuller use of resources

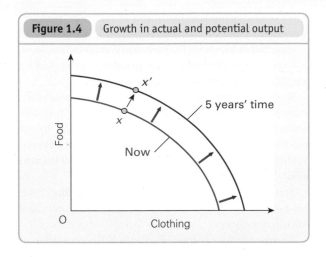

Figure 1.4 Growth in actual and potential output

Over time, the production possibilities of a nation are likely to increase. *Investment* in new plant and machinery will increase the stock of capital; new raw materials may be discovered; technological advances are likely to take place; through education and training, labour is likely to become more productive. This growth in potential output is illustrated by an outward shift in the production possibility curve. This will then allow actual output to increase: for example, from point *x* to point *x′* in Figure 1.4.

 Will economic growth always involve a parallel outward shift of the production possibility curve?

Illustrating economic issues: the circular flow of goods and incomes

The process of satisfying human wants involves producers and consumers. The relationship between them is two-sided and can be represented in a flow diagram (see Figure 1.5).

The consumers of goods and services are labelled 'households'. Some members of households, of course, are also workers, and in some cases are the owners of other factors of production too, such as land. The producers of goods and services are labelled 'firms'.[1]

Firms and households are in a twin 'demand and supply' relationship with each other.

First, in the top part of the diagram, households demand goods and services, and firms supply goods and services. In the process, exchange takes place. In a money economy (as opposed to a *barter economy*), firms exchange goods and services for money. In other words, money flows from households to firms in the form of consumer expenditure, while

Definition

Investment The production of items that are not for immediate consumption.

1 In practice, much of society's production takes place within the household for its members' own consumption. Examples include cooking, cleaning, growing vegetables, decorating and childcare. Also, firms buy from and sell to each other – whether it be raw materials, capital goods or semi-finished goods. Nevertheless, it is still useful to depict the flows of goods and services and money between households and firms when explaining the operation of markets.

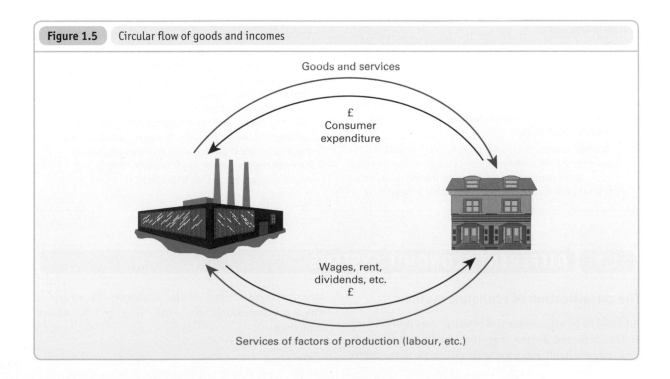

Figure 1.5 Circular flow of goods and incomes

goods and services flow the other way – from firms to households.

This coming together of buyers and sellers is known as a *market* – it could be a street market, a shop or a website offering online shopping. Thus we talk about the market for apples, for oil, for houses, for televisions, and so on.

Second, firms and households come together in the market for factors of production. This is illustrated in the bottom half of Figure 1.5. This time the demand and supply roles are reversed. Firms demand the use of factors of production owned by households – labour, land and capital. Households supply them. Thus the services of labour and other factors flow from households to firms, and in exchange firms pay households money – namely, wages, rent, dividends and interest. Just as we referred to particular goods markets, so we can also refer to particular factor markets – the market for bricklayers, for footballers, for land, and so on.

So there is a circular flow of incomes. Households earn incomes from firms and firms earn incomes from households. The money circulates. There is also a circular flow of goods and services, but in the opposite direction. Households supply factor services to firms, which then use them to supply goods and services to households.

This flow diagram, like the production possibility curve, can help us to distinguish between microeconomics and macroeconomics.

Microeconomics is concerned with the composition of the circular flow: what combinations of goods make up the goods flow; how the various factors of production are combined to produce these goods; for whom the wages, dividends, rent and interest are paid out.

Macroeconomics is concerned with the total size of the flow and what causes it to expand and contract.

Definitions

Barter economy An economy where people exchange goods and services directly with one another without any payment of money. Workers would be paid with bundles of goods.

Market The interaction between buyers and sellers.

Section summary

1. The central economic problem is that of scarcity. Given that there is a limited supply of factors of production (labour, land and capital), it is impossible to provide everybody with everything they want. Potential demands exceed potential supplies.

2. The subject of economics is usually divided into two main branches: macroeconomics and microeconomics.

3. Macroeconomics deals with aggregates such as the overall levels of unemployment, output, growth and prices in the economy.

4. Microeconomics deals with the activities of individual units within the economy: firms, industries, consumers, workers, etc. Because resources are scarce, people have to make choices. Society has to choose by some means or other *what* goods and services to produce, *how* to produce them and *for whom* to produce them. Microeconomics studies these choices.

5. Rational choices involve weighing up the marginal benefits of each activity against its marginal opportunity costs. If the marginal benefits exceed the marginal costs, it is rational to choose to do more of that activity.

6. The production possibility curve shows the possible combinations of two goods that a country can produce in a given period of time. Assuming that the country is already producing on the curve, the production of more of one good will involve producing less of the other. This opportunity cost is illustrated by the slope of the curve. If the economy is producing within the curve as a result of idle resources or inefficiency, it can produce more of both goods by taking up this slack. In the longer term, it can only produce more of both by shifting the curve outwards through investment, technological progress, etc.

7. The circular flow of goods and incomes shows the interrelationships between firms and households in a money economy. Firms and households come together in markets. In goods markets, firms supply goods and households demand goods. In the process, money flows from households to firms in return for the goods and services that the firms supply. In factor markets, firms demand factors of production and households supply them. In the process, money flows from firms to households as incomes for factor services.

1.2 DIFFERENT ECONOMIC SYSTEMS

The classification of economic systems

All societies face the problem of scarcity. They differ considerably, however, in the way they tackle the problem. One important difference between societies is in the degree of government control of the economy: the extent to which government decides 'what', 'how' and 'for whom' to produce.

KI 1
p7

At the one extreme lies the completely *planned or command economy*, where all the economic decisions are taken by the government.

At the other extreme lies the completely *free-market economy*. In this type of economy there is no government intervention at all. All decisions are taken by individuals and firms. Households decide how much labour and other factors to supply, and what goods to consume. Firms decide what goods to produce and what factors to employ. The pattern of production and consumption that results depends on the interactions of all these individual demand and supply decisions in free markets.

In practice, all economies are a mixture of the two; it is the *degree* of government intervention that distinguishes different economic systems. In China, the government plays a large role, whereas in the USA, the government plays a much smaller role.

It is still useful to analyse the extremes, in order to put the different *mixed economies* of the real world into perspective. The mixture of government and the market can be shown by the use of a spectrum diagram such as Figure 1.6. It shows where particular economies of the real world lie along the spectrum between the two extremes.

The diagram is useful in that it provides a simple picture of the mixture of government and the market that exists in various economies. It can also be used to show changes in the mixture over time.

The problem with this type of classification is that it is one-dimensional and oversimplified. Countries differ in the *type* of government intervention as well as the level. For example, governments can intervene through planning, public ownership, regulation, taxes and subsidies, partnership schemes with private industry, and so on. Two countries could be in a similar position along the spectrum but have very different types of government intervention.

Notice that there has been a general movement to the right along the spectrum since the 1980s. In former communist countries this has been a result of the abandonment of central planning and the adoption of private enterprise. In Western economies it has been a result of deregulation of private industry and privatisation (the selling of nationalised industries to the private sector).

 How do you think the positions of these eight countries will change over the next decade?

The informal sector: a third dimension

In all societies, many economic decisions are made, whether individually or in groups, which involve neither the government nor the market. For example, many of the activities taking place in the home, such as cooking, cleaning, gardening and care for children or the elderly, can be seen

> ### Definitions
>
> **Centrally planned or command economy** An economy where all economic decisions are taken by the central authorities.
>
> **Free-market economy** An economy where all economic decisions are taken by individual households and firms and with no government intervention.
>
> **Mixed economy** An economy where economic decisions are made partly by the government and partly through the market. In practice all economies are mixed.

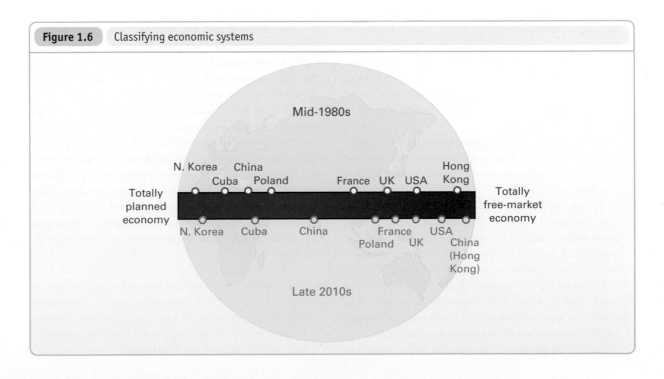

Figure 1.6   Classifying economic systems

as 'economic' activities. There is an output (such as a meal or a service provided) and there is an opportunity cost to the provider (in terms of alternative activities forgone). And yet no money changes hands. Similarly, many of the activities done in groups, such as clubs and charities, involve the provision of goods and/or services, but again, no money changes hands.

These activities are taking place in the *informal sector*. The relative size of the informal sector varies from one country to another and over time. In rich countries, as more women continue to work after having children, and as working hours have increased, many people employ others to do the jobs, such as cleaning and childcare, that they once did themselves. What was once part of the informal sector is now part of the market sector.

In many developing countries, much of the economic activity in poorer areas involves *subsistence production*. This is where people grow their own food, build their own shelter, etc. While some of the inputs (e.g. building materials) may have to be purchased through the market, much of this production is in the informal sector and involves no exchange of money. The importance of the informal sector, particularly to developing countries, should not be underestimated. This is an area of increasing interest to many economists, particularly those interested in the downsides of economic growth.

The command economy

The command economy is usually associated with a socialist or communist economic system, where land and capital are collectively owned. The state plans the allocation of resources at three levels:

- It plans the allocation of resources between current consumption and investment for the future. By sacrificing some present consumption and diverting resources into investment, it could increase the economy's growth rate.

    The amount of resources it chooses to devote to investment will depend on its broad macroeconomic strategy: the importance it attaches to growth as opposed to current consumption.

- At a microeconomic level, it plans the output of each industry and firm, the techniques that will be used, and the labour and other resources required by each industry and firm.

    In order to ensure that the required inputs are available, the state would probably conduct some form of *input–output analysis*. All industries are seen as users of inputs from other industries and as producers of output for consumers or other industries. For example, the steel industry uses inputs from the coal and iron-ore industries and produces output for the vehicle and construction industries. Input–output analysis shows, for each industry, the sources of all its inputs and the destination of all its output. By using such analysis the state attempts to

match up the inputs and outputs of each industry so that the planned demand for each industry's product is equal to its planned supply.

- It plans the distribution of output between consumers. This will depend on the government's aims. It may distribute goods according to its judgement of people's needs; or it may give more to those who produce more, thereby providing an incentive for people to work harder. It may distribute goods and services directly (for example, by a system of rationing); or it may decide the distribution of money incomes and allow individuals to decide how to spend them. If it does the latter, it may still seek to influence the pattern of expenditure by setting appropriate prices: low prices to encourage consumption, and high prices to discourage consumption.

Assessment of the command economy

With central planning, the government could take an overall view of the economy. It could direct the nation's resources in accordance with specific national goals.

High growth rates could be achieved if the government directed large amounts of resources into investment. Unemployment could be largely avoided if the government carefully planned the allocation of labour in accordance with production requirements and labour skills. National income could be distributed more equally or in accordance with needs. The social repercussions of production and consumption (e.g. the effects on the environment) could be taken into account, provided the government was able to predict these effects and chose to take them into account.

In practice, a command economy could achieve these goals only at considerable social and economic cost. The reasons are as follows:

- The larger and more complex the economy, the greater the task of collecting and analysing the information essential to planning, and the more complex the plan. Complicated plans are likely to be costly to administer and involve cumbersome bureaucracy.

KI 3
p13

- If there is no system of prices, or if prices are set arbitrarily by the state, planning is likely to involve the inefficient use of resources. It is difficult to assess the relative efficiency of two alternative techniques that use different inputs if there is no way in which the value of those inputs can be ascertained. For example, how can a rational decision be made between an oil-fired and a coal-fired furnace if the prices of oil and coal do not reflect their relative scarcity?

- It is difficult to devise appropriate incentives to encourage workers and managers to be more productive without a reduction in quality. For example, if bonuses are given according to the quantity of output produced, a factory might produce shoddy goods, since it can probably produce a larger quantity of goods by cutting quality. To avoid this problem, a large number of officials may have to be employed to check quality.

- Complete state control over resource allocation would involve a considerable loss of individual liberty. Workers would have no choice where to work; consumers would have no choice what to buy.

- If production is planned, but consumers are free to spend money incomes as they wish, there will be a problem if the wishes of consumers change. Shortages will occur if consumers decide to buy more; surpluses will occur if they decide to buy less.

Most of these problems were experienced in the former Soviet Union and the other Eastern bloc countries, and were part of the reason for the overthrow of their communist regimes (see Box 1.4).

The free-market economy

Free decision making by individuals

In a free market, individuals are free to make their own economic decisions. Consumers are free to decide what to buy with their incomes: free to make demand decisions. Firms are free to choose what to sell and what production methods to use: free to make supply decisions. The demand and supply decisions of consumers and firms are transmitted to each other through their effect on prices: through the **price mechanism**. The prices that result are the prices that firms and consumers have to accept.

The price mechanism

The price mechanism works as follows. Prices respond to shortages and surpluses. Shortages result in prices rising. Surpluses result in prices falling. Let us take each in turn.

If consumers want more of a good (or if producers decide to cut back supply), demand will exceed supply. The resulting shortage will cause the price of the good to rise. This will act as an incentive to producers to supply more, since production will now be more profitable. At the same time it will discourage consumers from buying so much. *The price will continue rising until the shortage has been eliminated.*

If, on the other hand, consumers decide they want less of a good (or if producers decide to produce more), then supply will exceed demand. The resulting surplus will cause the price of the good to fall. This will act as a disincentive to producers, who will supply less, since production will now be less profitable. It will encourage consumers to buy more. *The price will continue falling until the surplus has been eliminated.*

This price, where demand equals supply, is called the **equilibrium price**. By **equilibrium** we mean a point of balance or a point of rest: in other words, a point towards which there is a tendency to move.

1. *Try using the same type of analysis in the labour market to show what will happen if there is an increase in demand for labour. What is the 'price' of labour?*
2. *Can you think of any examples where prices and wages do not adjust very rapidly to a shortage or surplus? For what reasons might they not do so?*

The response of demand and supply to changes in price illustrates a very important feature of how economies work: *people respond to incentives*. It is important, therefore, that incentives are appropriate and have the desired effect. This is the fifth of our 15 threshold concepts (see Chapter 2, page 50).

TC 5
p50

The effect of changes in demand and supply

How will the price mechanism respond to changes in consumer demand or producer supply? Patterns of consumer demand will change over time: for example, people may decide they want more fixed gear bikes and fewer mountain bikes. Likewise the pattern of supply changes: for example, changes in technology may allow the mass production of microchips at lower cost, while the production of hand-built furniture becomes relatively expensive.

In all cases of changes in demand and supply, the resulting changes in price act as both signals and incentives.

A change in demand.   A rise in demand is signalled by a rise in price, which then acts as an incentive for supply to rise. The high price of these goods relative to their costs of production signals that consumers are willing to see resources diverted from other uses. This is just what firms do. They divert resources from goods with lower prices relative to

---

Definitions

Price mechanism The system in a market economy whereby changes in price in response to changes in demand and supply have the effect of making demand equal to supply.

Equilibrium price The price where the quantity demanded equals the quantity supplied: the price where there is no shortage or surplus.

Equilibrium A position of balance. A position from which there is no inherent tendency to move away.

BOX 1.4   COMMAND ECONOMIES

The rise and fall of planning

Russia

The Bolsheviks under the leadership of Lenin came to power in Russia with the October revolution of 1917. Communism was introduced and the market economy abolished. Industries were nationalised; workers were told what jobs to do; food was taken from peasants to feed the towns; workers were allocated goods from distribution depots.

With the ending of the civil war in 1921, the economy was in bad shape and Lenin embarked on the New Economic Policy. This involved a return to the use of markets. Smaller businesses were returned to private hands and peasants were able to sell their crops. The economy began to recover; however Lenin died in 1924 and Stalin came to power.

The Russian economy underwent a radical transformation from 1928 onwards. The key features of the Stalinist approach were collectivisation, industrialisation and central planning. Peasant farms were abolished and replaced by large-scale collective farms where land was collectively owned and worked, and by state farms, owned by the state and run by managers. This caused disruption and famine, with peasants slaughtering their animals rather than giving them up. However, in the longer term more food was produced. Both collective and state farms were given quotas of output that they were supposed to deliver, for which the state would pay a fixed price.

Alongside the agricultural reforms a drive to industrialisation took place and a vast planning apparatus was developed. At the top was *Gosplan*, the central planning agency. This prepared five-year plans, which specified the general direction in which the economy was to move, and annual plans, which gave details of what was to be produced and with what resources for some 200 or so key products. The system operated without either the price mechanism or the profit motive, although incentives existed with bonuses paid to managers and workers if targets were achieved.

Stalin died in 1953, but the planning system remained largely unchanged throughout the Soviet Union until the late 1980s. Initially, high growth rates had been achieved, though at a cost of low efficiency. Poor flows of information led to inconsistencies in the plans. Targets were often unrealistic,

and as a result there were frequent shortages and sometimes surpluses. There was little product innovation and goods were frequently of poor quality. A large 'underground economy' flourished in which goods were sold on the illegal market and in which people did second 'unofficial' jobs.

Moves to the market

By the time Gorbachev came to power in 1985 many people were pressing for economic reform. Gorbachev responded with his policy of perestroika (economic reconstruction), which involved managers preparing their own plans and managers and workers being rewarded for becoming more efficient. Under the new system, one-person businesses and larger co-operatives were allowed, while the price mechanism was reintroduced with the state raising prices if there were substantial shortages.

These reforms, however, did not halt the economic decline. Managers resented the extra responsibilities and people were unclear as to what to expect from the state. Queues lengthened in the shops and people became disillusioned with *perestroika*.

Communism fell apart in 1989 and both the Soviet Union and the system of central planning came to an end. Russia embarked upon a radical programme of market reforms in which competition and enterprise were intended to replace state central planning (see Case Studies 1.5, Free-market medicine in Russia; 14.9, Privatisation in transition economies; and 14.10, Forms of transition in transition countries, on the student website).

Initially, the disruption of the move to the market led to a sharp decline in the Russian economy. GDP fell by an average of 5.5 per cent per annum between 1993 and 1998. This was followed by a period of rapid economic growth, which averaged 7 per cent from 2000 to 2008. But the economy declined by nearly 8 per cent in the 2009 recession. Although this was followed by growth rates of 4.5 and 4.3 per cent in 2010 and 2011, since then growth has been around 2 per cent. Many commentators point to decades of underinvestment in industry and in road and rail infrastructure, corruption, disillusionment and continuing political uncertainty as root causes of this sluggish growth rate. From 2014, the economy was further dampened by Western

---

costs (and hence lower profits) to those goods that are more profitable.

A fall in demand is signalled by a fall in price. This then acts as an incentive for supply to fall. The goods are now less profitable to produce.

A change in supply.   A rise in supply is signalled by a fall in price. This then acts as an incentive for demand to rise. A fall in supply is signalled by a rise in price. This then acts as an incentive for demand to fall.

The fact that markets adjust so as to equate demand and supply is our fourth 'Threshold Concept', which is discussed in Chapter 2, page 47.

Changes in demand or supply cause markets to adjust. Whenever such changes occur, the resulting 'disequilibrium' will bring an automatic change in prices, thereby restoring equilibrium (i.e. a balance of demand and supply).

TC 4
p47

1. *Why do the prices of fresh vegetables fall when they are in season? Could an individual farmer prevent the price falling?*
2. *If you were the manager of a supermarket, how would you set about deciding what prices to charge for food approaching its sell-by date?*
3. *Demand for downloaded music has grown rapidly, yet the prices of downloads have fallen. Why?*

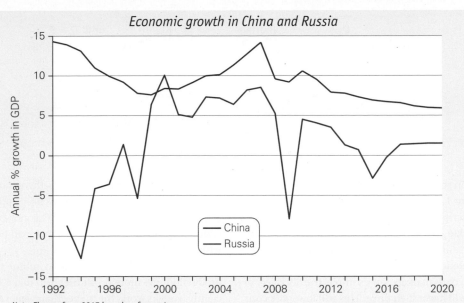

Economic growth in China and Russia

Note: Figures from 2017 based on forecasts.
Source: Data drawn from *World Economic Outlook Database* (IMF, April 2017).

economic sanctions in response to Russia's annexation of Crimea and the continuing conflict in Eastern Ukraine. Russia went into recession in 2015, but rebounded in 2017.

China

In contrast to the Soviet Union, China's move towards a more market-based economy has been carefully managed by the ruling Communist Party. From the 1940s to the 1970s central planning, combined with the removal of all property rights, resulted in low productivity, a creaking infrastructure and famine.

But after the death of Party Chairman Mao Zedong in 1976, a new breed of Chinese leaders came to power, and they were increasingly pragmatic. There was a focus on making use of aspects of capitalism alongside government control of the economy. Productivity was valued equally with political stability, while consumer welfare was considered as important as the elimination of unemployment. Economic zones were set up, where foreign investment was encouraged, and laws on patents and other intellectual property encouraged innovation. This approach was developed further over the following decades and from 1992 to 2010 China averaged growth of 10.5 per cent per annum – the highest in the world.

Today, China is the world's second largest economy and, although growth has slowed somewhat to around 6.5 per cent, is poised to overtake the USA by 2020 albeit with much lower output *per head*. Yet its human rights record remains a concern to many around the world; economic liberalisation and growth have not been accompanied by political freedom. Furthermore, it is experiencing some of the problems of capitalism: pollution, income inequality and potential instability of the financial system. It remains unclear how long the combination of capitalist economics alongside tight political control can continue to deliver.

The interdependence of markets

The interdependence of goods and factor markets.   A rise in demand for a good will raise its price and profitability. Firms will respond by supplying more. But to do this they will need more inputs. Thus the demand for the inputs (factors of production) will rise, which in turn will raise the price of the inputs. The suppliers of inputs will respond to this incentive by supplying more. This can be summarised as follows:

KI 5
p22

1. Goods market
   - Demand for the good rises.
   - This creates a shortage.
   - This causes the price of the good to rise.
   - This eliminates the shortage by reducing demand and encouraging firms to produce more.

2. Factor market
   - The increased supply of the good causes an increase in the demand for factors of production (i.e. inputs) used in making it.
   - This causes a shortage of those inputs.
   - This causes their prices to rise.
   - This eliminates their shortage by reducing demand and encouraging the suppliers of inputs to supply more.

| Figure 1.7 | The price mechanism: the effect of a rise in demand |

Goods market

$$D_g \uparrow \longrightarrow \begin{array}{c} \text{shortage} \\ (D_g > S_g) \end{array} \longrightarrow \boxed{P_g \uparrow} \begin{array}{c} \nearrow S_g \uparrow \\ \searrow D_g \downarrow \end{array} \text{until } D_g = S_g$$

Factor market

$$S_g \uparrow \longrightarrow D_f \uparrow \longrightarrow \begin{array}{c} \text{shortage} \\ (D_f > S_f) \end{array} \longrightarrow \boxed{P_f \uparrow} \begin{array}{c} \nearrow S_f \uparrow \\ \searrow D_f \downarrow \end{array} \text{until } D_f = S_f$$

So changes in goods markets will lead to changes in factor markets. Figure 1.7 summarises this sequence of events, where the subscripts 'g' and 'f' refer to the good and the factors used in making it respectively. (It is common in economics to summarise an argument like this by using symbols.)

Interdependence exists in the other direction too: factor markets affect goods markets. For example, the discovery of raw materials will lower their price. This will lower the costs of production of firms using these raw materials and will increase the supply of the finished goods. The resulting surplus will lower the price of the good, which will encourage consumers to buy more.

 Summarise this last paragraph using symbols like those in Figure 1.7.

The interdependence of different goods markets. A rise in the price of one good will encourage consumers to buy alternatives. This will drive up the price of alternatives. This in turn will encourage producers to supply more of the alternatives.

 Are different factor markets similarly interdependent? What would happen if the price of capital equipment rose?

Conclusion

Even though all individuals are merely looking to their own self-interest in the free-market economy, they are in fact being encouraged to respond to the wishes of others through the incentive of the price mechanism. (See Case Study 1.4, The interdependence of markets, on the student website; see also Box 1.5.)

Assessment of the free-market economy

The fact that a free-market economy functions automatically is one of its major advantages. There is no need for costly and complex bureaucracies to co-ordinate economic decisions. The economy can respond quickly to changing demand and supply conditions.

When markets are highly competitive, no one has great power. Competition between firms keeps prices down and acts as an incentive for efficiency. The more firms there are competing, the more responsive they will be to consumer wishes.

The more efficiently firms can combine their factors of production, the more profit they will make. The more efficiently workers work, the higher their wages are likely to be. The more carefully consumers decide what to buy, the greater the value for money they will receive.

Thus people pursuing their own self-interest through buying and selling in competitive markets helps to minimise the central economic problem of scarcity, by encouraging the efficient use of society's resources in line with consumer wishes. From this type of argument, the following conclusion is often drawn by defenders of the free market: 'The pursuit of private gain results in the social good.' This claim is the subject of much debate and has profound moral implications (see Threshold Concept 2).

Problems of the free market

In practice, however, markets do not achieve maximum efficiency in the allocation of scarce resources, and governments therefore feel it necessary to intervene to rectify this and other problems of the free market. The problems of a free market include:

- Power and property may be unequally distributed. Those who have power and/or property (e.g. big business, unions and landlords) will gain at the expense of those without power and property.
- Competition between firms is often limited. A few firms may dominate an industry, charging high prices and making large profits.
- Consumers and firms may not have full information about the costs and benefits associated with different goods and factor inputs and may thus make the wrong decisions.
- Rather than responding to consumer wishes, firms may attempt to persuade consumers by advertising.

BOX 1.5 ADAM SMITH (1723–90)

The 'invisible hand' of the market

Many economists would argue that modern economics dates from 1776, the year in which Adam Smith's *An Inquiry into the Nature and Causes of the Wealth of Nations* was published – one of the most important books on economics ever written.

The work, in five books, is very wide-ranging, but the central argument is that market economies generally serve the public interest well. Markets guide production and consumption like an *invisible hand*. Even though everyone is looking after their own private self-interest, their interaction in the market will lead to the social good.

In book I, chapter 2, Smith writes:

Man has almost constant occasion for the help of his brethren and it is in vain for him to expect it from their benevolence only . . . It is not from the benevolence of the butcher, the brewer, or the baker that we expect our dinner, but from their regard to their own interest. We address ourselves, not to their humanity but to their self-love, and never talk to them of our own necessities, but of their advantages.

Later, in book IV, chapter 2, he continues:

Every individual is continually exerting himself to find out the most advantageous employment of whatever capital he can command. It is his own advantage, indeed, and not that of the society, which he has in view. But the study of his own advantage naturally, or rather necessarily, leads him to prefer that employment which is most advantageous to the society . . . he intends only his own gain, and he is in this, as in many other cases, led by an invisible hand to promote an end which was no part of his intention. Nor is it always the worse for the society that it

was no part of it. By pursuing his own interest he frequently promotes that of society more effectually than when he really intends to promote it.

He argued, therefore, with one or two exceptions, that the state should not interfere with the functioning of the economy. It should adopt a laissez-faire or 'hands-off' policy. It should allow free enterprise for firms and free trade between countries.

This praise of the free market has led many on the political right to regard him as the father of the 'libertarian movement' – the movement that advocates the absolute minimum amount of state intervention in the economy (see Box 12.7 on page 388). In fact, one of the most famous of the libertarian societies is called the Adam Smith Institute.

But Smith was not blind to the drawbacks of unregulated markets. In book I, chapter 7, he looks at the problem of monopoly:

A monopoly granted either to an individual or to a trading company has the same effect as a secret in trade or manufactures. The monopolists, by keeping the market constantly under-stocked, by never fully supplying the effectual demand, sell their commodities much above the natural price, and raise their emoluments, whether they consist in wages or profit, greatly above their natural rate.

Later on he looks at the dangers of firms getting together to pursue their mutual interest:

People of the same trade seldom meet together, even for merriment or diversion, but the conversation ends in a conspiracy against the public or in some contrivance to raise prices.

- Lack of competition and high profits may remove the incentive for firms to be efficient.
- The practices of some firms may be socially undesirable. For example, a chemical works may pollute the environment.
- Some socially desirable goods would simply not be produced by private enterprise. Who would carry out counter-terrorism activities if this were not funded by governments?
- A free-market economy may lead to macroeconomic instability. There may be periods of recession with high unemployment and falling output, and other periods of rising prices.
- Finally, there is the ethical objection, that a free-market economy, by rewarding self-interested behaviour, may encourage selfishness, greed, materialism and the acquisition of power.

The fact that free markets may fail to meet various social objectives is Threshold Concept 3.

The mixed economy

Because of the problems of both free-market and command economies, all real-world economies are a mixture of the two systems.

In *mixed market economies*, the government may control the following:

- *Relative prices* of goods and inputs, by taxing or subsidising them or by direct price controls.
- Relative incomes, by the use of income taxes, welfare payments or direct controls over wages, profits, rents, etc.

Definitions

Mixed market economy A market economy where there is some government intervention.

Relative price The price of one good compared with another (e.g. good X is twice the price of good Y).

THRESHOLD CONCEPT 2 | PEOPLE GAIN FROM VOLUNTARY ECONOMIC INTERACTION

Economic interaction between people can take a number of different forms. Sometimes it takes place in markets. For example, when goods are exchanged, there is interaction between the consumer and the shop. When someone is employed, there is interaction between the employer and the employee. When a firm buys raw materials, there is interaction between the purchasing firm and the selling firm.

In each case there is expected to be a mutual gain. If there wasn't, the interaction would not take place. If you go on a holiday costing £400, then assuming the holiday turns out as you expected, you will have gained. You would rather have the holiday than spend the £400 on something else. The marginal benefit to you exceeds the marginal cost. The travel agent and tour operator also gain. They make a profit on selling you the holiday. It is a 'win–win situation'. This is sometimes called a *positive sum game*: an interaction where there is a positive net gain.

Another example is international trade (the subject of Chapter 24). If two countries trade with each other, there will be a net gain to both of them. If there wasn't, they would not trade. Both countries will end up consuming a greater value of products than they could without trade. The reason is that each country can specialise in the products it is relatively good at producing (compared to the other country) and export them, and import from the other country the goods it is relatively poor at producing.

That there is a net gain from voluntary interaction is a *threshold concept* because realising this tends to change the way we look at economic activity. Often it is important to identify what these overall gains are so that we can compare them with alternative forms of interaction. For example, even though both workers and their employer respectively gain from the wages currently paid and the output currently produced, it might still be possible to reorganise the workforce in a way that increases production. This could allow the employer to pay higher wages and still gain an increase in profits. Both sides could thus gain from constructive negotiation about wages and new work practices.

Sometimes it may appear that voluntary interaction results in one side gaining and the other losing. For example, a firm may raise its price. It gains and the consumer loses. But is this strictly true? Consumers are certainly worse off than before, but as long as they are still prepared to buy the product, they must consider that they are still gaining more by buying it than by not. There is still a gain to both sides: it's just that the firm is gaining more and the consumer is gaining less.

1. *Would you ever swap things with friends if both of you did not gain? Explain your answer.*
2. *Give one or two examples of involuntary (i.e. compulsory) economic interaction, where one side gains but the other loses.*

THRESHOLD CONCEPT 3 | MARKETS MAY FAIL TO MEET SOCIAL OBJECTIVES

We have seen that market forces can automatically equate demand and supply. The outcomes of the process may be desirable, but they are by no means always so. Unrestrained market forces can result in severe problems for individuals, society and the environment.

Markets tend to reflect the combined actions of individual consumers and firms. But when consumers and firms make their decisions, they may act selfishly and fail to take account of the broader effects of their actions. If people want to buy guns, market forces will make their supply profitable. If people want to drive fuel-hungry cars, then this will create the market for firms to supply them. Market forces are not kind and caring. They mechanically reflect human behaviour.

And it's not just selfish behaviour that markets reflect, but ignorance too. You may be unaware that a toy you buy for a child is dangerous, but by buying it, you encourage unscrupulous firms to supply them. A firm may not realise that a piece of machinery it uses is dangerous until an accident happens. In the meantime, it continues using it because it is profitable to do so.

If wages are determined purely by demand and supply, then some people, such as footballers and bankers, may be very well

paid. Others, such as cleaners and shop workers, may be very poorly paid. If the resulting inequality is seen as unfair, then market forces alone will not be enough to achieve a fair society.

Recognising the limitations and failings of markets is a *threshold concept*. It helps us to understand how laws or taxes or subsidies could be framed to counteract such failings. It helps us to relate the mechanical operation of demand and supply to a whole range of social objectives and ask whether the market system is the best way of meeting such objectives.

But to recognise market failures is only part of the way to finding a solution. Can the government put things right, and if so, how? Or do the limitations of government mean that the solution is sometimes worse than the problem? We examine these issues in many parts of the book. We set the scene in Threshold Concept 7 on page 81.

1. *If global warming affects all of us adversely, why in a purely market economy would individuals and firms continue with activities that contribute towards global warming?*
2. *In what ways do your own consumption patterns adversely affect other people?*

- The pattern of production and consumption, by the use of legislation (e.g. making it illegal to produce unsafe goods), by direct provision of goods and services (e.g. education and defence) or by taxes and subsidies.
- The macroeconomic problems of unemployment, inflation, lack of growth, balance of trade deficits and exchange rate fluctuations, by the use of taxes and government expenditure, the control of bank lending and interest rates, the direct control of prices and the control of foreign exchange rates.

The fact that government intervention can be used to rectify various failings of the market is Threshold Concept 7 (see Chapter 3, page 81). It is important to realise, however, that government actions may bring adverse as well as beneficial consequences. For more on government intervention in the mixed economy see Chapters 11 to 14.

Section summary

1. The economic systems of different countries vary according to the extent to which they rely on the market or the government to allocate resources.

2. At the one extreme, in a command economy, the state makes all the economic decisions. It plans amounts of resources to allocate for present consumption and amounts for investment for future output. It plans the output of each industry, the methods of production it will use and the amount of resources it will be allocated. It plans the distribution of output between consumers.

3. A command economy has the advantage of being able to address directly various national economic goals, such as rapid growth and the avoidance of unemployment and inequality. A command economy, however, is likely to be inefficient and bureaucratic; prices and the choice of production methods are likely to be arbitrary; incentives may be inappropriate; shortages and surpluses may result.

4. At the other extreme is the free-market economy. In this economy, decisions are made by the interaction of demand and supply. Price changes act as the mechanism whereby demand and supply are balanced. If there is a shortage, price will rise until the shortage is eliminated. If there is a surplus, price will fall until that is eliminated.

5. A free-market economy functions automatically and if there is plenty of competition between producers this can help to protect consumers' interests. In practice, however, competition may be limited; there may be great inequality; there may be adverse social and environmental consequences; there may be macroeconomic instability.

6. In practice, all economies are some mixture of the market and government intervention. It is the degree and form of government intervention that distinguishes one type of economy from another.

1.3 THE NATURE OF ECONOMIC REASONING

Economics is one of the social sciences. So in what sense is it a *science*? Is it like the natural sciences such as physics and astronomy? What is the significance of the word 'social' in social science? What can economists do, and what is their role in helping governments devise economic policy?

Economics as a science

The methodology employed by economists has a lot in common with that employed by natural scientists. Both attempt to construct theories or *models* which are then used to *explain* and *predict*. An astronomer, for example, constructs models of planetary movements to *explain* why planets are in the position they are and to *predict* their position in the future.

Models in economics

In order to explain and predict, the economist constructs models which show simplified relationships between various economic phenomena. The simplification is deliberate – economists know their models look nothing like the real world they hope to explain. It is referred to as abstraction. An example of a model is one showing the relationships between demand, supply and price of a product. Although most models can be described verbally, they can normally be represented more precisely in graphical or mathematical form.

Building models

Models are constructed by making general hypotheses about the causes of economic phenomena: for example, that consumer demand will rise when consumer incomes rise. These hypotheses will often be based on observations. This process of making general statements from particular observations is known as *induction*.

Definitions

Economic model A formal presentation of an economic theory.

Induction Constructing general theories on the basis of specific observations.

Using models

Explanation. Models explain by showing how things are caused: what the causes of inflation are, why workers in some industries earn more than others, and so on. A model is constructed to help explain a particular relationship or set of phenomena. An economic model might be really useful for one purpose but not very useful for another.

Prediction. Models are sometimes used to make simple forecasts: for example, inflation will be below 5 per cent next year. Usually, however, predictions are of the 'If . . . then . . .' variety: for example, if demand for good *x* rises, its price will rise. This process of drawing conclusions from models is known as **deduction**.

When making such deductions it has to be assumed that nothing else that can influence the outcome has changed in the meantime. For example, if demand for good *x* rises, its price will rise *assuming* the cost of producing good *x* has not fallen. This is known as the **ceteris paribus** assumption. *Ceteris paribus* is Latin for 'other things being equal'.

Assessing models

Models can be judged according to how successful they are in explaining and predicting. They are not judged by how closely they resemble the real world.

If the predictions are wrong, the first thing to do is to check whether the deductions were correctly made. If they were, the model must be either adapted or abandoned in favour of an alternative model with better predictive ability. But in economics, as with many other disciplines, academics are often unwilling to abandon their models. Instead they prefer the minimum adaptation necessary. This can lead to lively debates between different 'schools of thought', each claiming that their models paint a more accurate picture of the economy.

There has been a great deal of debate recently about why economic models failed to forecast the financial crisis of 2007–8. In September 2010, Ben Bernanke, the then Federal Reserve Board Chairman, said the failure of the economic models did not mean that they were irrelevant or significantly flawed. Rather than throwing out the models, more

work was needed to capture how the financial system impacts on growth and stability. Some people argued that the models were simply misused: i.e. used for a purpose they were not designed for. John Kay argued it was like using a London Underground map to work out the best walking route![2]

Others disagreed. They claimed that many of the main models that had failed to predict the crisis were fundamentally flawed and needed replacing with other models – perhaps amended versions of older ones; perhaps new ones.

We look at these debates in Parts E and F of the book.

Economists as detectives

Because of a lack of conclusive evidence about just how many parts of the economy function, economists also need the skills of detectives. This involves a third type of reasoning (in addition to induction and deduction), known as **abduction**. This involves making informed guesses or estimates from limited evidence. It is using the scraps of evidence as clues to what might be really going on. It is how many initial hypotheses are formed. Then the researcher (or detective) will use the clues to search for more evidence that can be used for induction that will yield a more robust theory. The clues may lead to a false trail, but sometimes they may allow the researcher to develop a new theory or amend an existing one. A good researcher will be alert to clues; to seeing patterns in details that might previously have been dismissed or gone unnoticed.

Before the banking crisis of 2007–8 and the subsequent credit crunch and recession in the developed world, many

---

Definitions

Deduction Using a theory to draw conclusions about specific circumstances.

Ceteris paribus Latin for 'other things being equal'. This assumption has to be made when making deductions from theories.

Abduction Using pieces of evidence to develop a plausible explanation. This can then be tested by gathering more evidence.

---

2 John Kay, *Obliquity* (Profile Books, 2010).

| BOX 1.6 | *CETERIS PARIBUS* | CASE STUDIES AND APPLICATIONS |

Because of the complexities of the real world, economic models have to make various simplifying assumptions. Sometimes, however, economists are criticised for making unrealistic assumptions, assumptions that make their models irrelevant. The following joke illustrates the point.

There were three people cast away on a desert island: a chemist, an engineer and an economist. There was no food on the island and their plight seemed desperate.

Then they discovered a crate of canned food that had been washed up on the island. When they realised that they had no

means of opening the cans, they decided that each of them should use their expertise to find a solution.

The chemist searched around for various minerals that could be heated up to produce a compound that would burn through the lids of the cans.

The engineer hunted around for rocks and then worked out what height of tree they would have to be dropped from in order to smash open the cans.

Meanwhile the economist sat down and thought 'Assuming we had a can opener . . .'.

economists were picking up clues and trying to use them to develop a theory of systemic risk in financial markets. They were using the skills of an economic detective to try to discover not only what was currently going on but also what might be the consequences for the future. Some used abductive reasoning successfully to predict the impending crisis; most did not.

Economics as a social science

Economics concerns human behaviour. One problem here is that individuals often behave in very different ways. People have different tastes and different attitudes. This problem, however, is not as serious as it may seem at first sight. The reason is that people *on average* are likely to behave more predictably. For example, if the price of a product goes up by 5 per cent, we might be able to predict, *ceteris paribus,* that the quantity demanded will fall by approximately 10 per cent. This does not mean that every single individual's demand will fall by 10 per cent, only that *total* demand will. Some people may demand a lot less; others may demand the same as before.

Even so, there are still things about human behaviour that are very difficult to predict, even when we are talking about whole groups of people. How, for example, will firms react to a rise in interest rates when making their investment decisions? This will depend on things such as the state of business confidence, something that is notoriously difficult to predict. How will a business respond to price changes by its rivals? This will often depend on how it thinks its rivals themselves will react to its own response. How will people respond to a crisis, such as the global banking and credit crisis of 2007–8? This depends very much on the mood of financial and other companies and individuals. A mood of pessimism (or optimism for that matter) can quickly spread, but not to a degree that is easily predictable.

For these reasons there is plenty of scope for competing models in economics, each making different assumptions and leading to different policy conclusions. As a result, economics can often be highly controversial. As we shall see later on in the book, different political parties may adhere to different schools of economic thought. Thus the political left may adhere to a model which implies that governments must intervene if unemployment is to be cured, whereas the political right may adhere to a model which implies that unemployment will be reduced if the government intervenes less and relies more on the free market.

One branch of economics that has seen considerable growth in recent years is behavioural economics, which adds elements of psychology to traditional models in an attempt to gain a better understanding of decision making by investors, consumers and other economic participants. Much of the early evidence in support of behavioural economics came from laboratory experiments where people made decisions in simulated environments – normally a computer room. More recent evidence has come from field experiments, where people make decisions in a more natural environment and do not know their behaviour is being observed. For more on behavioural economics see Chapters 4, 5, 9, 10, 13 and 14.

The fact that there are different economic theories does not mean that economists always disagree. Despite the popular belief that 'if you laid all the economists of the world end to end they would still not reach a conclusion', there is in fact a large measure of agreement between economists about how to analyse the world and what conclusions to draw.

Economics and policy

Economists play a major role in helping governments to devise economic policy. In order to understand this role, it is necessary to distinguish between 'positive' and 'normative' statements.

A ***positive statement*** is a statement of fact. It may be right or wrong, but its accuracy can be tested by appealing to the facts. 'Unemployment is rising', 'Inflation will be over 6 per cent by next year' and 'If the government cuts taxes, imports will rise' are all examples of positive statements.

A ***normative statement*** is a statement of value: a statement about what ought or ought not to be, about whether something is good or bad, desirable or undesirable. 'It is right to tax the rich more than the poor', 'The government ought to reduce inflation' and 'State pensions ought to be increased' are all examples of normative statements. They cannot be proved or disproved by a simple appeal to the facts.

Economists can only contribute to questions of policy in a positive way. That is, they can analyse the consequences of following certain policies. They can say which of two policies is more likely to achieve a given aim, but they should not, as economists, say whether the aims of the policy are desirable. For example, economists may argue that a policy of increasing government expenditure will reduce unemployment and raise inflation, but they cannot, as economists, decide whether such a policy is desirable.

TC 1
p11

KEY IDEA 6

The importance of the positive/normative distinction. Economics can only contribute to policy issues in a positive way. Economists, as scientists, should not make normative judgements. They can make them only as individual people, with no more moral right than any other individual.

Definitions

Positive statement A value-free statement which can be tested by an appeal to the facts.

Normative statement A value judgement.

Which of the following are positive statements and which are normative?

(a) Cutting the higher rates of income tax will redistribute incomes from the poor to the rich.

(b) It is wrong that inflation should be targeted if the consequence is higher unemployment.

(c) It is incorrect to state that putting up interest rates will reduce inflation.

(d) The government should introduce road pricing to address the issue of congestion.

(e) Current government policies should be aimed at reducing the deficit rather than stimulating growth.

Section summary

1. The methodology used by economists is similar to that used by natural scientists. Economists construct models, which they use to explain and predict economic phenomena. These models can be tested by appealing to facts and seeing how successfully they have been predicted or explained by the model. Unsuccessful models can be either abandoned or amended.

2. Being a social science, economics is concerned with human actions. Making accurate predictions in economics is very difficult given that economics has to deal with a constantly changing environment.

3. Economists can help governments to devise policy by examining the consequences of alternative courses of action. In doing this, it is important to separate positive questions about what the effects of the policies are from normative ones as to what the goals of policy should be. Economists in their role as economists have no superior right to make normative judgements. They do, however, play a major role in assessing whether a policy meets the political objectives of government (or opposition).

END OF CHAPTER QUESTIONS

1. Imagine that a country can produce just two things: goods and services. Assume that over a given period it could produce any of the following combinations:

   Units of goods

0	10	20	30	40	50	60	70	80	90	100

   Units of services

80	79	77	74	70	65	58	48	35	19	0

   (a) Draw the country's production possibility curve.

   (b) Assuming that the country is currently producing 40 units of goods and 70 units of services, what is the opportunity cost of producing another 10 units of goods?

   (c) Explain how the figures illustrate the principle of increasing opportunity cost.

   (d) Now assume that technical progress leads to a 10 per cent increase in the output of goods for any given amount of resources. Draw the new production possibility curve. How has the opportunity cost of producing extra units of services altered?

2. Imagine that you won millions of pounds on the National Lottery. Would your 'economic problem' be solved?

3. Assume that in a household one parent currently works full-time and the other stays at home to look after the family. How would you set about identifying and calculating the opportunity costs of the second parent now taking a full-time job? How would such calculations be relevant in deciding whether it is worth taking that job?

4. When you made the decision to study economics, was it a 'rational' decision (albeit based on the limited information you had available at the time)? What additional information would you like to have had in order to ensure that your decision was the right one?

5. In what way does specialisation reduce the problem of scarcity?

6. Would redistributing incomes from the rich to the poor reduce the overall problem of scarcity?

7. Assume that fracking becomes common across the UK. The result is that supplies of shale gas and oil increase sharply. Trace through the effects of this on the market for oil, gas and the market for other fuels.

8. Give two examples of positive statements about the economy, and two examples of normative ones. Now give two examples that are seemingly positive, but which have normative implications or undertones.

Online resources

Additional case studies on the student website

1.1 **Buddhist economics.** A different perspective on economic problems and economic activity.

1.2 **Green economics.** This examines some of the environmental costs that society faces today. It also looks at the role of economics in analysing these costs and how the problems can be tackled.

1.3 **Global economics.** This examines how macroeconomics and microeconomics apply at the global level and identifies some key issues.

1.4 **The interdependence of markets.** A case study in the operation of markets, examining the effects on a local economy of the discovery of a large coal deposit.

1.5 **Free-market medicine in Russia.** This examines the operating of the fledgling market economy in Russia and the successes and difficulties in moving from a planned to a market economy.

1.6 **Alternative measures of well-being.** This case study takes a preliminary look at how we measure the well-being of society. Should we use output (GDP) per head or some other measure?

Websites relevant to this chapter

Numbers and sections refer to websites listed in the Web Appendix and hotlinked from this book's website at **www.pearsoned.co.uk/sloman**.

- For news articles relevant to this chapter, see the *Sloman Economics News* site link from MyEconLab or the *Economics News* section on the student website.

- For a tutorial on finding the best economics websites, see site C8 (*Internet for Economics*).

- For general economics news sources, see websites in section A of the Web Appendix at the end of the book, and particularly A1–9, 24, 25, 35, 36. See also A39–44 for links to newspapers worldwide.

- For sources of economic data, see sites in section B and particularly B1–5, 21, 33, 34, 38, 47.

- For general sites for students of economics, see sites in section C and particularly C1–7, 10 and 28.

- For sites giving links to relevant economics websites, organised by topic, see sites I2, 3, 7, 12, 13, 14, 16.

- For news on the Russian economy (Box 1.4 and Case Study 1.5 on the student website), see sites A14, 15.

- For an excellent site giving details of the lives, works and theories of famous economists from the history of economic thought (including Adam Smith from Box 1.5), see C18.

Foundations of Microeconomics

In the first half of the book, we focus on microeconomics. Despite being 'small economics' – in other words, the economics of the individual parts of the economy, rather than the economy as a whole – it is still concerned with many of the big issues of today. To understand how the economy works at this micro level, we must understand how markets work. This involves an understanding of demand and supply.

In Chapter 2, we look at how demand and supply interact to determine prices (and so allocate resources) in a free-market economy. We will also see just how responsive they are to changing circumstances.

Markets, however, are not always free: governments frequently intervene in markets. In Chapter 3, we look at some of the reasons why governments may choose to reject the free market and examine the methods they use to influence prices, output and allocation.

We look at markets, their efficiency and government intervention in more detail in Parts C and D.

2 Chapter

Supply and Demand

As we saw in Chapter 1, in a free-market economy prices play a key role in transmitting information from buyers to sellers and from sellers to buyers. This chapter examines this 'price mechanism' in more detail.

We examine what determines demand, what determines supply and what the relationship is between demand, supply and price. We see how the price mechanism transmits information both from consumers to producers, and from producers to consumers; and how prices act as incentives – for example, if consumers want more European city breaks, how this increased demand leads to an increase in their price and hence to an incentive for firms to increase their production.

What we will see is the mechanism whereby the free market responds to changes in demand or supply – and responds in a way that balances demand and supply at a position of 'equilibrium'.

But we will also need to see just how much prices and output respond to changes in demand and supply. How much will the demand for music downloads go up if their price comes down? How much will the supply of new houses go up if the price of houses rises? In section 2.4 we develop the concept of elasticity of demand and supply to examine this responsiveness.

Finally, we look at how quickly markets adjust and also examine how people's expectations of price changes affect what actually happens to prices. In particular, we look at speculation – people attempting to gain from anticipated price changes.

The markets we will be examining are highly competitive ones, with many firms competing against each other. In economics we call this *perfect competition*. This is where consumers and producers are too numerous to have any control over prices: they are *price takers*.

In the case of consumers, this means that they have to accept the prices as given for the things that they buy. On most occasions this is true; when you get to the supermarket checkout you cannot start haggling with the checkout operator over the price of a can of beans or a tub of ice cream.

In the case of firms, perfect competition means that producers are small and face too much competition from other firms to be able to raise prices. Take the case of foreign exchange traders selling euros. They have to sell the currency at the current market price. If individually they try to sell at a higher price, no one will buy, since purchasers of currency can get all the euros they want at the market price.

Of course, many firms *do* have the power to choose their prices. This does not mean that they can simply charge whatever they like. They will still have to take account of overall consumer demand and their competitors' prices. Hewlett-Packard (HP), when setting the price of its laptop computers, will have to ensure that they remain competitive with those produced by Dell, Toshiba, Lenovo, etc. Nevertheless, most firms have some flexibility in setting their prices: they have a degree of 'market power'.

If this is the case, then why do we study *perfect* markets, where firms are price takers? One reason is that they provide a useful approximation to the real world and give us many insights into how a market economy works. Many markets, such as those in agriculture and finance, do function very similarly to those we shall be describing.

Another is that perfect markets provide an ideal against which to compare the real world, since in perfect markets we see resources being used and allocated efficiently. Economists can therefore use them as a benchmark when comparing the prices, output, profit, etc. in different types of market. For example, will the consumer end up paying higher prices in a market dominated by just a few firms than in one operating under perfect competition? Will Sky respond to an increase in demand for television services in the same way as a farmer does to an increase in the demand for cauliflowers?

Markets with powerful firms are examined in Chapters 7 and 8. For now we concentrate on price takers.

2.1 DEMAND

The relationship between demand and price

The headlines announce 'Major crop failures in Brazil and East Africa: coffee prices soar'. Shortly afterwards you find that coffee prices have increased sharply in the shops. What do you do? You will probably cut back on the amount of coffee you drink. Perhaps you will reduce it from, say, six cups per day to four. Perhaps you will give up drinking coffee altogether.

This is simply an illustration of the general relationship between price and consumption: *when the price of a good rises, the quantity demanded will fall*. This relationship is known as the *law of demand*. There are two reasons for this law:

- People will feel poorer. They will not be able to afford to buy as much of the good with their money.

The purchasing power of their income (their *real income*) has fallen. This is called the *income effect* of a price rise.

- The good will now cost more than alternative or 'substitute' goods, and people will switch to these. This is called the *substitution effect* of a price rise.

Similarly, when the price of a good falls, the quantity demanded will rise. People can afford to buy more (the income effect), and they will switch away from consuming alternative goods (the substitution effect).

Therefore, returning to our example of the increase in the price of coffee, we will not be able to afford to buy as much as before, and we will probably drink more tea, cola, fruit juices or even water instead.

Definitions

Perfect competition (preliminary definition) A situation where the consumers and producers of a product are price takers. (There are other features of a perfectly competitive market; these are examined in Chapter 7.)

Price taker A person or firm with no power to be able to influence the market price.

Law of demand The quantity of a good demanded per period of time will fall as price rises and will rise as price falls, other things being equal (*ceteris paribus*).

Income effect The effect of a change in price on quantity demanded arising from the consumer becoming better or worse off as a result of the price change.

Substitution effect The effect of a change in price on quantity demanded arising from the consumer switching to or from alternative (substitute) products.

KEY IDEA 7

The income and substitution effects are useful concepts as they help to explain why people react to a price rise by buying less. The size of these effects depends on a range of factors. These factors determine the shape of the demand curve.

A word of warning: be careful about the meaning of the words *quantity demanded*. They refer to the amount that consumers are willing and able to purchase at a given price over a given period (e.g. a week, or a month, or a year). They do not refer to what people would simply *like* to consume. You might like to own a luxury yacht, but your demand for luxury yachts will almost certainly be zero at the current price. Quantity demanded may also be different from the quantity actually purchased. A consumer may be willing and able to purchase the good but cannot find a supplier willing to sell at that price.

The demand curve

Consider the hypothetical data in Table 2.1, which shows how many kilograms of potatoes per month would be purchased at various prices.

Columns (2) and (3) show the *demand schedules* for two individuals, Kate and Simon. Column (4) shows the total *market demand schedule*. This is the total demand by all consumers. To obtain the market demand schedule for potatoes, we simply add up the quantities demanded at each price by *all* consumers: i.e. Kate, Simon and everyone else who demands potatoes. Notice that we are talking about demand *over a period of time* (not at *a point* in time). Thus we could talk about daily demand or weekly demand or annual demand.

Assume that there are 200 consumers in the market. Of these, 100 have schedules like Kate's and 100 have schedules like Simon's. What would be the total market demand schedule for potatoes now?

The demand schedule can be represented graphically as a *demand curve*. Figure 2.1 shows the market demand curve for potatoes corresponding to the schedule in Table 2.1. The price of potatoes is plotted on the vertical axis. The quantity demanded is plotted on the horizontal axis.

Point *E* shows that at a price of 100p per kilo, 100 000 tonnes of potatoes are demanded each month. When the price falls to 80p we move down the curve to point *D*. This shows that the quantity demanded has now risen to 200 000 tonnes per month. Similarly, if the price falls to 60p we move down the curve again to point *C*: 350 000 tonnes are now demanded. The five points on the graph (*A*−*E*) correspond to the figures in columns (1) and (4) of Table 2.1. The graph also enables us to read off the likely quantities demanded at prices other than those in the table.

1. *How much would be demanded at a price of 30p per kilogram?*
2. *Assuming that demand does not change from month to month, plot the annual market demand for potatoes.*

Table 2.1	The demand for potatoes (monthly)			
	Price (pence per kg) (1)	Kate's demand (kg) (2)	Simon's demand (kg) (3)	Total market demand (tonnes: 000s) (4)
A	20	28	16	700
B	40	15	11	500
C	60	5	9	350
D	80	1	7	200
E	100	0	6	100

Definitions

Quantity demanded The amount of a good that a consumer is willing and able to buy at a given price over a given period of time.

Demand schedule for an individual A table showing the different quantities of a good that a person is willing and able to buy at various prices over a given period of time.

Market demand schedule A table showing the different total quantities of a good that consumers are willing and able to buy at various prices over a given period of time.

Demand curve A graph showing the relationship between the price of a good and the quantity of the good demanded over a given time period. Price is measured on the vertical axis; quantity demanded is measured on the horizontal axis. A demand curve can be for an individual consumer or group of consumers, or more usually for the whole market.

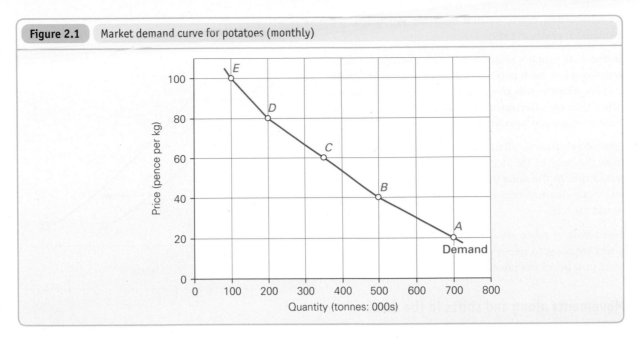

Figure 2.1   Market demand curve for potatoes (monthly)

A demand curve could also be drawn for an individual consumer. Like market demand curves, individuals' demand curves generally slope downwards from left to right: they have negative slope. The lower the price of the product, the more a person is likely to buy.

1. *Draw Kate's and Simon's demand curves for potatoes on one diagram. Note that you will use the same vertical scale as in Figure 2.1, but you will need a quite different horizontal scale.*
2. *At what price is their demand the same?*
3. *What explanations could there be for the quite different shapes of their two demand curves? (This question is explored in section 3.1 below.)*
4. *Assume that Kate and Simon are the only two consumers in the market. Show how the market demand curve can be derived from their individual demand curves.*

Two points should be noted at this stage:

- In textbooks, demand curves (and other curves too) are only occasionally used to plot specific data. More frequently they are used to illustrate general theoretical arguments. In such cases the axes will simply be price and quantity, with the units unspecified.
- The term 'curve' is used even when the graph is a straight line. In fact when using demand curves to illustrate arguments we frequently draw them as straight lines – it's easier.

Other determinants of demand

Price is not the only factor that determines how much of a good people will buy. Demand is also affected by the following.

Tastes.   The more desirable people find the good, the more they will demand. Tastes are affected by advertising, by trends and fashion, by observing other consumers, by considerations of health and by the experience of consuming the good on previous occasions. For example, the recent fashion for men to grow beards has had a negative impact on the demand for razors.

The number and price of substitute goods (i.e. competitive goods). The higher the price of **substitute goods**, the higher will be the demand for this good as people switch from the substitutes. For example, the demand for e-cigarettes will be influenced by the price of cigarettes. If the price of cigarettes increases, the demand for e-cigarettes will rise.

The number and price of complementary goods.   **Complementary goods** are those that are consumed together; cars and petrol, paper and ink cartridges, fish and chips. The higher the price of complementary goods, the fewer of them will be bought and hence the less will be the demand for the good under consideration. For example, the demand for games will depend on the price of games consoles, such as the Sony PlayStation® and Microsoft Xbox®. If the price of games

---

Definitions

Substitute goods A pair of goods which are considered by consumers to be alternatives to each other. As the price of one goes up, the demand for the other rises.

Complementary goods A pair of goods consumed together. As the price of one goes up, the demand for both goods will fall.

consoles comes down, so that more are purchased, the demand for games will rise.

Income. As people's incomes rise, their demand for most goods will rise. Such goods are called **normal goods**. There are exceptions to this general rule, however. As people get richer, they spend less on **inferior goods**, such as supermarket 'value' ranges, and switch to better quality goods.

Distribution of income. If national income were redistributed from the poor to the rich, the demand for luxury goods would rise. At the same time, as the poor got poorer they might have to buy more inferior goods; demand for these would rise too.

Expectations of future price changes. If people think that prices are going to rise in the future, they are likely to buy more now before the price does go up.

Movements along and shifts in the demand curve

A demand curve is constructed on the assumption that 'other things remain equal' (*ceteris paribus*). In other words, it is assumed that none of the determinants of demand, other than price, changes. The effect of a change in price is then simply illustrated by a movement along the demand curve: for example, from point *B* to point *D* in Figure 2.1 when the price of potatoes rises from 40p to 80p per kilo.

What happens, then, when one of these other determinants does change? The answer is that we have to construct a whole new demand curve: the curve shifts. If a change in one of the other determinants causes demand to rise – say, income rises – the whole curve will shift to the right. This shows that at each price more will be demanded than before. Thus, in Figure 2.2, at a price of *P*, a quantity of Q_0 was originally demanded. But now, after the increase in demand, Q_1 is demanded. (Note that D_1 is not necessarily parallel to D_0.)

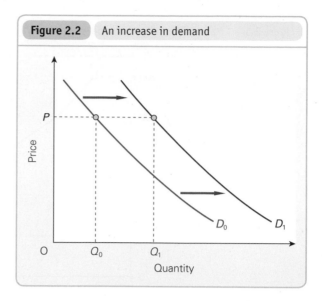

Figure 2.2   An increase in demand

If a change in a determinant other than price causes demand to fall, the whole curve will shift to the left.

To distinguish between shifts in and movements along demand curves, it is usual to distinguish between a change in *demand* and a change in the *quantity demanded*. A shift in the demand curve is referred to as a **change in demand**, whereas a movement along the demand curve as a result of a change in price is referred to as a **change in the quantity demanded**.

1. Assume that in Table 2.1 the total market demand for potatoes increases by 20 per cent at each price – due, say, to substantial increases in the prices of bread and rice. Plot the old and the new demand curves for potatoes. Is the new curve parallel to the old one?
2. The price of blueberries rises and yet it is observed that the sales of blueberries increase. Does this mean that the demand curve for blueberries is upward sloping? Explain.

Definitions

Normal good A good whose demand rises as people's incomes rise.

Inferior good A good whose demand falls as people's incomes rise.

Change in demand The term used for a shift in the demand curve. It occurs when a determinant of demand other than price changes.

Change in the quantity demanded The term used for a movement along the demand curve to a new point. It occurs when there is a change in price.

*LOOKING AT THE MATHS

We can represent the relationship between the market demand for a good and the determinants of demand in the form of an equation. This is called a ***demand function***. It can be expressed either in general terms or with specific values attached to the determinants.

Simple demand functions

Demand equations are often used to relate quantity demanded to just one determinant. Thus an equation relating quantity demanded to price could be in the form

$$Q_d = a - bP \qquad (1)$$

For example, the actual equation might be:

$$Q_d = 10\,000 - 200P \qquad (2)$$

From this can be calculated a complete demand schedule or demand curve, as shown in the table and diagram. As price (P) changes, the equation tells us how much the quantity demanded (Q_d) changes.

Demand schedule for equation (2)

P	Q_d
5	9000
10	8000
15	7000
20	6000
25	5000

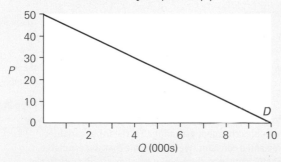

Demand curve for equation (2)

1. *Complete the demand schedule in the table up to a price of 50.*
2. *What is it about equation (2) that makes the demand curve (a) downward sloping; (b) a straight line?*

Definitions

Demand function An equation which shows the mathematical relationship between the quantity demanded of a good and the values of the various determinants of demand.

Regression analysis A statistical technique which allows a functional relationship between two or more variables to be estimated.

Econometrics The science of applying statistical techniques to economic data in order to identify and test economic relationships.

This equation is based on a *ceteris paribus* assumption: it is assumed that all the other determinants of demand remain constant. If one of these other determinants changed, the equation itself would change. There would be a shift in the curve: a change in demand. If the *a* term alone changed, there would be a parallel shift in the curve. If the *b* term changed, the slope of the curve would change.

Simple equations can be used to relate demand to other determinants too. For example, an equation relating quantity demanded to income would be in the form

$$Q_d = a + bY \qquad (3)$$

1. *Referring to equation (3), if the term 'a' has a value of −50 000 and the term 'b' a value of 0.001, construct a demand schedule with respect to total income (Y). Do this for incomes between £100 million and £300 million at £50 million intervals.*
2. *Now use this schedule to plot a demand curve with respect to income. Comment on its shape.*

More complex demand functions

In a similar way, we can relate the quantity demanded to two or more determinants. For example, a demand function could be of the form:

$$Q_d = a - bP + cY + dP_s - eP_c \qquad (4)$$

This equation says that the quantity demanded (Q_d) will fall as the price of the good (P) rises, will rise as the level of consumer incomes (Y) rises, will rise as the price of a particular substitute (P_s) rises and will fall as the price of a particular complement (P_c) rises, by amounts *b, c, d* and *e* respectively.

Estimated demand equations

Surveys can be conducted to show how demand depends on each one of a number of determinants, while the rest are held constant. Using statistical techniques called ***regression analysis***, a demand equation can be estimated.

For example, assume that it was observed that the demand for butter (measured in 250g units) depended on its price (P_b), the price of margarine (P_m) and total annual consumer incomes (Y). The estimated weekly demand equation may then be something like

$$Q_d = 2\,000\,000 - 50\,000P_b + 20\,000P_m + 0.01Y \qquad (5)$$

Thus if the price of butter were 50p, the price of margarine were 35p and consumer incomes were £200 million, and if P_b and P_m were measured in pence and *Y* was measured in pounds, then the demand for butter would be 2 200 000 units. This is calculated as follows:

$$\begin{aligned} Q_d &= 2\,000\,000 - (50\,000 \times 50) + (20\,000 \times 35) \\ &\quad + (0.01 \times 200\,000\,000) \\ &= 2\,000\,000 - 2\,500\,000 + 700\,000 + 2\,000\,000 \\ &= 2\,200\,000 \end{aligned}$$

The branch of economics that applies statistical techniques to economic data is known as ***econometrics***. Econometrics is beyond the scope of this book. It is worth noting, however, that econometrics, like other branches of statistics, cannot produce equations and graphs that allow totally reliable predictions to be made. The data on which the equations are based are often incomplete or unreliable, and the underlying relationships on which they are based (often ones of human behaviour) may well change over time.

*BOX 2.1   THE DEMAND FOR LAMB

A real-world demand function[1]

UK consumption of lamb: 1974–2015

Source: Based on data in *Family food Datasets* Table 2.1 (Defra).

The diagram shows what happened to the consumption of lamb in the UK over the period 1974–2015. How can we explain this dramatic fall in consumption? One way of exploring this issue is to make use of a regression model, which should help us to see which variables are relevant and how they are likely to affect demand.

The following is an initial model fitted[2] (using *Gretl,* a free, open source, statistical software package) to annual data for the years 1974–2010.

$$Q_L = 144.0 - 0.137P_L - 0.034P_B + 0.214P_P - 0.00513Y + \varepsilon \qquad (1)$$

where:

Q_L is the quantity of lamb sold in grams per person per week;

P_L is the 'real' price of lamb (in pence per kg, 2000 prices);[3]

P_B is the 'real' price of beef (in pence per kg, 2000 prices);

P_P is the 'real' price of pork (in pence per kg, 2000 prices);

Y is households' real disposable income per head (£ per year, 2000 prices);

ε is the error term that attempts to capture the impact of any other variables that have an impact on the demand for lamb.

This model makes it possible to predict what would happen to the demand for lamb if any one of the four explanatory variables changed, assuming that the other variables remained constant. We will assume that the estimated coefficients used throughout this box are all statistically significant.

Using equation (1), calculate what would happen – ceteris paribus – to the demand for lamb if:
(a) the real price of lamb went up by 10p per kg;
(b) the real price of beef went up by 10p per kg;
(c) the real price of pork fell by 10p per kg;
(d) real disposable income per head rose by £100 per annum.
Are the results as you would expect?

There is a serious problem with estimated demand functions like these if there are unobserved factors that change over time and have an impact on the demand for lamb. By omitting explanatory variables, we can say that the model is mis-specified and this introduces a bias into the estimated coefficients. For example, the estimated coefficient on Y is negative and quite close to zero. This suggests that household income has little effect on demand. Is this what we would expect? Also, the coefficient on P_B is negative which suggests that lamb and beef are complements in consumption. Once again this appears to be a counterintuitive result.

One factor that did change over time was tastes. During the 37-year period covered by the data there was a shift in demand away from lamb and other meats, partly for health reasons, and partly because of an expansion in the availability of and demand for vegetarian and low-meat alternatives.

On the assumption that this shift in taste took place steadily over time, a new demand equation was estimated for the same years:

$$Q_L = 121.4 - 0.151P_L - 0.0213P_B$$
$$+ 0.180P_P - 0.000391Y - 1.728 \, TIME \tag{2}$$

where $TIME = 1$ in 1974, 2 in 1975, 3 in 1976, etc.

1. *How does the introduction of the variable TIME affect the relationship between the demand for lamb and (a) its real price; (b) real disposable income per head?*
2. *Does lamb appear to be a normal good or an inferior good?*
3. *What does the negative coefficient of P_B indicate?*

It can be argued that model (2) is a better model than model (1) because it appears to have a better 'goodness of fit'. This is indicated by something called the 'R-squared' statistic. If $R^2 = 1$ this suggests the model can explain all the variation in the data on the demand for lamb, whereas if $R^2 = 0$ this indicates that the model cannot explain any of the variation in the data.

In model (2), $R^2 = 0.913$ compared with 0.908 for model (1). This means that model (2) can explain 91.3 per cent of the variation in the consumption of lamb during the period 1974 to 2010, whereas model (1) can explain 90.8 per cent.

Whilst model (2) appears to be a small improvement on model (1),[4] it still has problems. The estimated coefficient of Y remains negative and is very close to zero while the

coefficient on P_B remains negative. The model might still be mis-specified because of other omitted variables. For example, consumers' purchases of lamb in any given year might be influenced by what they were consuming the previous year. The model also includes the real price of two substitutes for lamb, but does not include the real prices of any complements.

To take the above points into account, the following third model was estimated, using data for 1975 to 2010.

$$Q_L = -37.520 - 0.128P_L + 0.0757P_B + 0.122P_P + 0.00415Y$$
$$- 1.529TIME + 0.679LQ_L - 0.0519P_C \tag{3}$$

where LQ_L is the lagged consumption of lamb (i.e. consumption in the previous year) and P_C is the real price of a complement (potatoes). $R^2 = 0.958$ and all the coefficients are significant.

1. *To what extent is model (3) an improvement on model (2)? (Hint: is lamb now a normal or inferior good?)*
2. *Use the three equations and also the data given in the table below to estimate the demand for lamb in 2000 and 2010. Which model works the best in each case? Why? Explain why the models are all subject to error in their predictions.*
3. *Use model (3) and the data given in the table to explain why the demand for lamb fell so dramatically between 1980 and 2010.*

	Q_L	LQ_L	P_L	P_B	P_P	Y	$TIME$	P_C
1980	128	121	421.7	546.0	414.6	10 498	7	26.7
2000	54	56	467.0	480.5	381.1	17 797	27	44.9
2010	44	46	506.2	470.1	381.1	19 776	37	53.5

1 Thanks to Tony Flegg, John's 'office mate' at UWE, for contributing to this box and to Andrew Hunt from Plymouth University for updating the figures.
2 Nominal food prices were calculated by dividing expenditure by consumption. These nominal prices in pence per kg were then adjusted to 'real' prices by dividing by the RPI (retail price index) for total food (2000 = 100) and multiplying by 100. See www.gov.uk/government/statistical-data-sets/family-food-datasets (expenditure and consumption).
3 The R^2 must be adjusted for the number of variables because simply adding more variables will always cause the unadjusted R^2 figure to increase.
4 Care must be taken not to judge a model by simply looking at the R^2 figure, which is sometimes called 'the most over-used and abused of all statistics'.

Section summary

1. When the price of a good rises, the quantity demanded per period of time will fall. This is known as the 'law of demand'. It applies both to individuals' demand and to the whole market demand.

2. The law of demand is explained by the income and substitution effects of a price change.

3. The relationship between price and quantity demanded per period of time can be shown in a table (or 'schedule') or as a graph. On the graph, price is plotted on the vertical axis and quantity demanded per period of time on the horizontal axis. The resulting demand curve is downward sloping (negatively sloped).

4. Other determinants of demand include tastes, the number and price of substitute goods, the number and price of complementary goods, income, distribution of income and expectations of future price changes.

5. If price changes, the effect is shown by a movement along the demand curve. We call this effect 'a change in the quantity demanded'.

6. If any other determinant of demand changes, the whole curve will shift. We call this effect 'a change in demand'. A rightward shift represents an increase in demand; a leftward shift represents a decrease in demand.

*7. The relationship between the quantity demanded and the various determinants of demand (including price) can be expressed as an equation.

2.2 SUPPLY

Supply and price

Imagine you are a farmer deciding what to do with your land. Part of your land is in a fertile valley, while part is on a hillside where the soil is poor. Perhaps, then, you will consider growing vegetables in the valley and keeping sheep on the hillside.

Your decision will depend to a large extent on the price that various vegetables will fetch in the market and the price you can expect to get for meat and wool. As far as the valley is concerned, you will plant the vegetables that give the best return. If, for example, the price of potatoes is high, you might use a lot of the valley for growing potatoes. If the price gets higher, you may well use the whole of the valley. If the price is very high indeed, you may even consider growing potatoes on the hillside, even though the yield per acre is much lower there.

In other words, the higher the price of a particular farm output, the more land will be devoted to it. This illustrates the general relationship between supply and price: *when the price of a good rises, the quantity supplied will also rise*. There are three reasons for this:

- As firms supply more, they are likely to find that beyond a certain level of output, costs rise more and more rapidly. In the case of the farm just considered, if more and more potatoes are grown, then the land which is less suitable for potato cultivation has to be used. This raises the cost of producing extra potatoes. It is the same for manufacturers. Beyond a certain level of output, costs are likely to rise rapidly as workers have to be paid overtime and as machines approach capacity working. If higher output involves higher costs of producing each unit, producers will need to get a higher price if they are to be persuaded to produce extra output.

- The higher the price of the good, the more profitable it becomes to produce. Firms will thus be encouraged to produce more of it by switching from producing less profitable goods.

- Given time, if the price of a good remains high, new producers will be encouraged to enter the industry. Total market supply thus rises.

The first two determinants affect supply in the short run. The third affects supply in the long run. We distinguish between short-run and long-run supply in section 2.5 on page 70.

The supply curve

The amount that producers would like to supply at various prices can be shown in a *supply schedule*. Table 2.2 shows a monthly supply schedule for potatoes, both for an individual farmer (farmer X) and for all farmers together (the whole market). (Note, however, that the amount they supply at a given price may not be the same as the amount they actually sell. Some supply may remain unsold.)

Definition

Supply schedule A table showing the different quantities of a good that producers are willing and able to supply at various prices over a given time period. A supply schedule can be for an individual producer or group of producers, or for all producers (the market supply schedule).

Table 2.2	The supply of potatoes (monthly)		
	Price of potatoes (pence per kg)	Farmer X's supply (tonnes)	Total market supply (tonnes: 000s)
a	20	50	100
b	40	70	200
c	60	100	350
d	80	120	530
e	100	130	700

The supply schedule can be represented graphically as a *supply curve*. A supply curve may be an individual firm's supply curve or a market curve (i.e. that of the whole industry).

Figure 2.3 shows the *market* supply curve of potatoes. As with demand curves, price is plotted on the vertical axis and quantity on the horizontal axis. Each of the points *a–e* corresponds to a figure in Table 2.2. Thus, for example, a price rise from 60p per kilogram to 80p per kilogram will cause a movement along the supply curve from point *c* to point *d*: total market supply will rise from 350 000 tonnes per month to 530 000 tonnes per month.

1. *How much would be supplied at a price of 70p per kilo?*
2. *Draw a supply curve for farmer X. Are the axes drawn to the same scale as in Figure 2.3?*

Not all supply curves will be upward sloping (positively sloped). Sometimes they will be vertical, or horizontal or even downward sloping. This will depend largely on the time period over which firms' response to price changes is considered. This question is examined in the section on the elasticity of supply (see section 2.4 below) and in more detail in Chapters 6 and 7.

Other determinants of supply

Like demand, supply is not simply determined by price. The other determinants of supply are as follows.

The costs of production. The higher the costs of production, the less profit will be made at any price. As costs rise, firms will cut back on production, probably switching to alternative products whose costs have not risen so much.

The main reasons for a change in costs are as follows:

- Change in input prices: costs of production will rise if wages, raw material prices, rents, interest rates or any other input prices rise.
- Change in technology: technological advances can fundamentally alter the costs of production. Consider, for example, how the microchip revolution has changed production methods and information handling in virtually every industry in the world.
- Organisational changes: various cost savings can be made in many firms by reorganising production.
- Government policy: costs will be lowered by government subsidies and raised by various taxes. Government regulation may also increase costs; examples include minimum wages and obligations for employers to provide and contribute to employee pensions.

Definition

Supply curve A graph showing the relationship between the price of a good and the quantity of the good supplied over a given period of time.

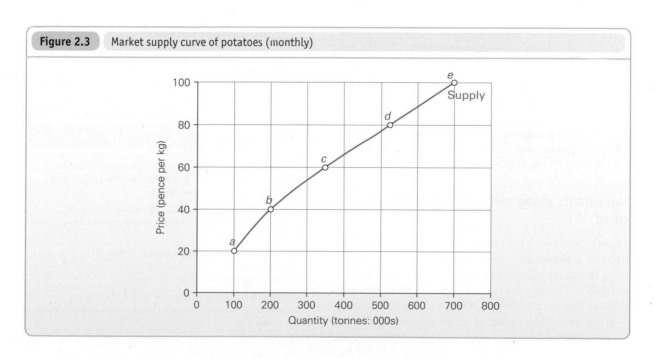

Figure 2.3 Market supply curve of potatoes (monthly)

The profitability of alternative products (substitutes in supply). If a product which is a **substitute in supply** becomes more profitable to supply than before, producers are likely to switch from the first good to this alternative. Supply of the first good falls. Other goods are likely to become more profitable if their prices rise and/or their costs of production fall. For example, if the price of carrots goes up, or the cost of producing carrots comes down, farmers may decide to cut down potato production in order to produce more carrots.

The profitability of goods in joint supply. Sometimes when one good is produced, another good is also produced at the same time. These are said to be **goods in joint supply**. An example is the refining of crude oil to produce petrol. Other grade fuels will be produced as well, such as diesel and paraffin. If more petrol is produced due to a rise in demand and hence its price, then the supply of these other fuels will rise too.

Nature, 'random shocks' and other unpredictable events. In this category we would include the weather and diseases affecting farm output, wars affecting the supply of imported raw materials, the breakdown of machinery, industrial disputes, earthquakes, floods and fire, etc. For example, in April 2017 the grape harvest in both France and the UK was significantly affected by heavy frosts leading to a reduction in the supply of wine.

The aims of producers. A profit-maximising firm will supply a different quantity from a firm that has a different aim, such as maximising sales. For most of the time we shall assume that firms are profit maximisers. In Chapter 9, however, we consider alternative aims.

Expectations of future price changes. If price is expected to rise, producers may temporarily reduce the amount they sell. They may build up their stocks and only release them on to the market when the price does rise. At the same time they may install new machines or take on more labour, so that they can be ready to supply more when the price has risen.

The number of suppliers. If new firms enter the market, supply is likely to increase.

 By referring to each of the above determinants of supply, identify what would cause (a) the supply of potatoes to fall and (b) the supply of leather to rise.

Movements along and shifts in the supply curve

The principle here is the same as with demand curves. The effect of a change in price is illustrated by a movement along the supply curve: for example, from point *d* to point *e* in Figure 2.3 when price rises from 80p to 100p. Quantity supplied rises from 530 000 to 700 000 tonnes per month.

If any other determinant of supply changes, the whole supply curve will shift. A rightward shift illustrates an

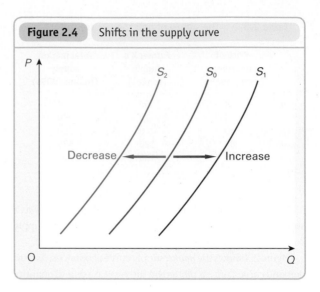

Figure 2.4   Shifts in the supply curve

increase in supply. A leftward shift illustrates a decrease in supply. Thus in Figure 2.4, if the original curve is S_0, the curve S_1 represents an increase in supply (more is supplied at each price), whereas the curve S_2 represents a decrease in supply (less is supplied at each price).

A movement along a supply curve is often referred to as a **change in the quantity supplied**, whereas a shift in the supply curve is simply referred to as a **change in supply**.

 This question is concerned with the supply of oil for central heating. In each case consider whether there is a movement along the supply curve (and in which direction) or a shift in it (and whether left or right).
(a) New oil fields start up in production.
(b) The demand for central heating rises.
(c) The price of gas falls.
(d) Oil companies anticipate an upsurge in demand for central-heating oil.
(e) The demand for petrol rises.
(f) New technology decreases the costs of oil refining.
(g) All oil products become more expensive.

Definitions

Substitutes in supply These are two goods where an increased production of one means diverting resources away from producing the other.

Joint supply goods These are two goods where the production of more of one leads to the production of more of the other.

Change in the quantity supplied The term used for a movement along the supply curve to a new point. It occurs when there is a change in price.

Change in supply The term used for a shift in the supply curve. It occurs when a determinant other than price changes.

*LOOKING AT THE MATHS

Using survey data and regression analysis, equations can be estimated relating supply to some of its determinants. Note that not all determinants can be easily quantified (e.g. nature and the aims of firms), and they may thus be left out of the equation.

The simplest form of supply equation relates supply to just one determinant. Thus a function relating supply to price would be of the form

$$Q_s = c + dP \qquad (1)$$

Using regression analysis, values can be estimated for c and d. Thus an actual supply equation might be something like

$$Q_s = 500 + 1000P \qquad (2)$$

1. *If P was originally measured in pounds, what would happen to the value of the d term in equation (2) if P were now measured in pence?*
2. *Draw the schedule (table) and graph for equation (2) for prices from £1 to £10. What is it in the equation that determines the slope of the supply 'curve'?*

If any determinant other than price changed, a new equation would result. For example, if costs of production fell, the equation might then be

$$Q_s = 1000 + 1500P \qquad (3)$$

More complex supply equations would relate supply to more than one determinant. For example:

$$Q_s = 200 + 80P - 20a_1 - 15a_2 + 30j \qquad (4)$$

where P is the price of the good, a_1 and a_2 are the profitabilities of two alternative goods that could be supplied instead, and j is the profitability of a good in joint supply.

Explain why the P and j terms have a positive sign, whereas the a_1 and a_2 terms have a negative sign.

Section summary

1. When the price of a good rises, the quantity supplied per period of time will usually also rise. This applies both to individual producers' supply and to the whole market supply.

2. There are two reasons in the short run why a higher price encourages producers to supply more: (a) they are now willing to incur the higher costs per unit associated with producing more; (b) they will switch to producing this product and away from products that are now less profitable. In the long run, there is a third reason: new producers will be attracted into the market.

3. The relationship between price and quantity supplied per period of time can be shown in a table (or schedule) or as a graph. As with a demand curve, price is plotted on the vertical axis and quantity per period of time on the horizontal axis. The resulting supply curve is upward sloping (positively sloped).

4. Other determinants of supply include the costs of production, the profitability of alternative products, the profitability of goods in joint supply, random shocks and expectations of future price changes.

5. If price changes, the effect is shown by a movement along the supply curve. We call this effect 'a change in the quantity supplied'.

6. If any determinant *other* than price changes, the effect is shown by a shift in the whole supply curve. We call this effect 'a change in supply'. A rightward shift represents an increase in supply; a leftward shift represents a decrease in supply.

*7. The relationship between the quantity supplied and the various determinants of supply can be expressed in the form of an equation.

2.3 PRICE AND OUTPUT DETERMINATION

Equilibrium price and output

We can now combine our analysis of demand and supply. This will show how the actual price of a product and the actual quantity bought and sold are determined in a free and competitive market.

Let us return to the example of the market demand and market supply of potatoes, and use the data from Tables 2.1 and 2.2. These figures are given again in Table 2.3.

What will be the actual price and output? If the price started at 20p per kilogram, demand would exceed supply by 600 000 tonnes $(A - a)$. Consumers would be unable to obtain all they wanted and would thus be willing to pay a higher price. Producers, unable or unwilling to supply enough to meet the demand, will be only too happy to accept a higher price. The effect of the shortage, then, will be to drive up the price. The same would happen at a price of 40p per kilogram. There would still be a shortage; price would still rise. But as the price rises, the quantity demanded falls and the quantity supplied rises. The shortage is progressively eliminated.

Table 2.3 The market demand and supply of potatoes (monthly)

Price of potatoes (pence per kg)	Total market demand (tonnes: 000s)	Total market supply (tonnes: 000s)
20	700 (A)	100 (a)
40	500 (B)	200 (b)
60	350 (C)	350 (c)
80	200 (D)	530 (d)
100	100 (E)	700 (e)

 Explain the process by which the price of houses would rise if there were a shortage.

What would happen if the price of potatoes started at a much higher level: say, at 100p per kilogram? In this case supply would exceed demand by 600 000 tonnes ($e - E$). The effect of this surplus would be to drive the price down as farmers competed against each other to sell their excess supplies. The same would happen at a price of 80p per kilogram. There would still be a surplus; price would still fall.

In fact, only one price is sustainable – the price where demand equals supply: namely, 60p per kilogram, where both demand and supply are 350 000 tonnes. When supply matches demand the market is said to **clear**. There is no shortage and no surplus.

TC 4
p47

As we have already seen in section 1.2, the price where demand equals supply is called the *equilibrium price* and we return to this in more detail in Threshold Concept 4 on page 47. In Table 2.3, if the price starts at anything other than 60p per kilogram, it will tend to move towards 60p. The equilibrium price is the only price at which producers' and consumers'

wishes are mutually reconciled: where the producers' plans to supply exactly match the consumers' plans to buy.

KEY IDEA 8
Equilibrium is the point where conflicting interests are balanced. Only at this point is the amount that demanders are willing to purchase the same as the amount that suppliers are willing to supply. It is a point that will be automatically reached in a free market through the operation of the price mechanism.

Demand and supply curves

The determination of equilibrium price and output can be shown using demand and supply curves. Equilibrium is where the two curves intersect.

Figure 2.5 shows the demand and supply curves of potatoes corresponding to the data in Table 2.3. Equilibrium price is P_e (60p) and equilibrium quantity is Q_e (350 000 tonnes).

At any price above 60p, there would be a surplus. Thus at 80p there is a surplus of 330 000 tonnes ($d - D$). More is supplied than consumers are willing and able to purchase at that price. Thus a price of 80p fails to clear the market. Price will fall to the equilibrium price of 60p. As it does so, there will be a movement along the demand curve from point D to point C, and a movement along the supply curve from point d to point c.

At any price below 60p, there would be a shortage. Thus at 40p there is a shortage of 300 000 tonnes ($B - b$). Price will

Definition

Market clearing A market clears when supply matches demand, leaving no shortage or surplus.

Figure 2.5 The determination of market equilibrium (potatoes: monthly)

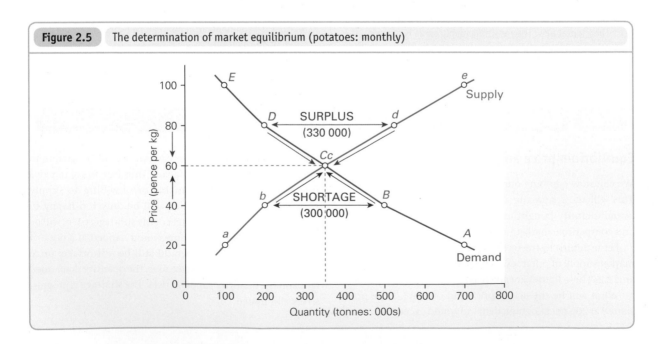

rise to 60p. This will cause a movement along the supply curve from point *b* to point *c* and along the demand curve from point *B* to point *C*.

Point *Cc* is the equilibrium: where demand equals supply.

Movement to a new equilibrium

The equilibrium price will remain unchanged only so long as the demand and supply curves remain unchanged. If either of the curves shifts, a new equilibrium will be formed.

KI 5
p22

A change in demand

If one of the determinants of demand changes (other than price), the whole demand curve will shift. This will lead to a movement *along* the *supply* curve to the new intersection point.

For example, in Figure 2.6, if a rise in consumer incomes led to the demand curve shifting to D_2, there would be a

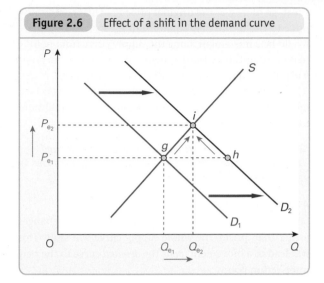

Figure 2.6 Effect of a shift in the demand curve

THRESHOLD CONCEPT 4 **MARKETS EQUATE DEMAND AND SUPPLY**

'Let the market decide.' 'Market forces will dictate.' 'You can't buck the market.'

These sayings about the market emphasise the power of market forces and how they affect our lives. Markets affect the prices of the things we buy and the incomes we earn. Even governments find it difficult to control many key markets. Governments might not like it when stock market prices plummet or when oil prices soar, but there is little they can do about it.

In many ways a market is like a democracy. People, by choosing to buy goods, are voting for them to be produced. Firms finding 'a market' for their products are happy to oblige and produce them. The way it works is simple. If people want more of a product, they buy more and thereby 'cast their votes' (i.e. their money) in favour of more being produced. The resulting shortage drives up the price, which gives firms the incentive to produce more of the product. In other words, firms are doing what consumers want – not because of any 'love' for consumers, or because they are being told to produce more by the government, but because it is in their own self-interest. They supply more because the higher price has made it profitable to do so.

This is a *threshold concept* because to understand market forces – the forces of demand and supply – is to go straight to the heart of a market economy. And in this process, prices are the key. It is changes in price that balance demand and supply. If demand exceeds supply, price will rise. This will choke off some of the demand and encourage more supply until demand equals supply – until an equilibrium has been reached. If supply exceeds demand, price will fall. This will discourage firms from supplying so much and encourage consumers to buy more, until, once more, an equilibrium has been reached.

In this process, markets act like an 'invisible hand' – a term coined by the famous economist Adam Smith (see Box 1.5 on page 25). Market prices guide both producers to respond to

consumer demand and consumers to respond to changes in producer supply.

In many circumstances, markets bring outcomes that people want. As we have seen, if consumers want more, then market forces will lead to more being produced. Sometimes, however, market forces can bring adverse effects. We explore these in various parts of the book. It is important, at this stage, however, to recognise that markets are rarely perfect. Market failures, from pollution to the domination of our lives by big business, are very real. Understanding this brings us to Threshold Concept 7 (see page 81).

Partial equilibrium

The type of equilibrium we will be examining for the next few chapters is known as 'partial equilibrium'. It is partial because what we are doing is examining just one tiny bit of the economy at a time: just one market (e.g. that for eggs). It is even partial within the market for eggs because we are assuming that price is the *only* thing that changes to balance demand and supply: that nothing else changes. In other words, when we refer to equilibrium price and quantity, we are assuming that all the other determinants of both demand and supply are held constant.

If another determinant of demand or supply *does* change, there would then be a new partial equilibrium as price adjusts and both demanders and suppliers respond. For example, if a health scare connected with egg consumption causes the demand for eggs to fall, the resulting surplus will lead to a fall in the equilibrium price and quantity.

1. *If there is a shortage of certain skilled workers in the economy, how will market forces lead to an elimination of the skills shortage?*
2. *If consumers want more of a product, is it always desirable that market forces result in more being produced?*

shortage of $h-g$ at the original price P_{e_1}. This would cause price to rise to the new equilibrium P_{e_1}. As it did so, there would be a movement along the supply curve from point g to point i, and along the new demand curve (D_2) from point h to point i. Equilibrium quantity would rise from Q_{e_1} to Q_{e_2}.

The effect of the shift in demand, therefore, has been a movement *along* the supply curve from the old equilibrium to the new: from point g to point i.

 What would happen to price and quantity if the demand curve shifted to the left? Draw a diagram to illustrate your answer.

A change in supply

Likewise, if one of the determinants of supply changes (other than price), the whole supply curve will shift. This will lead to a movement *along* the *demand* curve to the new intersection point.

For example, in Figure 2.7, if costs of production rose, the supply curve would shift to the left: to S_2. There would be a shortage of $g - j$ at the old price of P_{e_1}. Price would rise from P_{e_1} to P_{e_3}. Quantity would fall from Q_{e_1} to Q_{e_3}. In other words, there would be a movement along the demand curve from point g to point k, and along the new supply curve (S_2) from point j to point k.

To summarise: a shift in one curve leads to a movement along the other curve to the new intersection point.

Sometimes a number of determinants might change. This might lead to a shift in *both* curves. When this happens, equilibrium simply moves from the point where the old curves intersected to the point where the new ones intersect.

 What will happen to the equilibrium price and quantity of butter in each of the following cases? You should state whether demand or supply (or both) have shifted and in which direction. (In each case assume ceteris paribus.*)*
(a) A rise in the price of non-dairy spread.
(b) A rise in the demand for cream.
(c) A rise in the price of bread.

(d) A rise in the demand for bread.
(e) An expected rise in the price of butter in the near future.
(f) A tax on butter production.
(g) The invention of a new, but expensive, process for removing all saturated fat from butter, alongside the passing of a law which states that all butter producers must use this process.

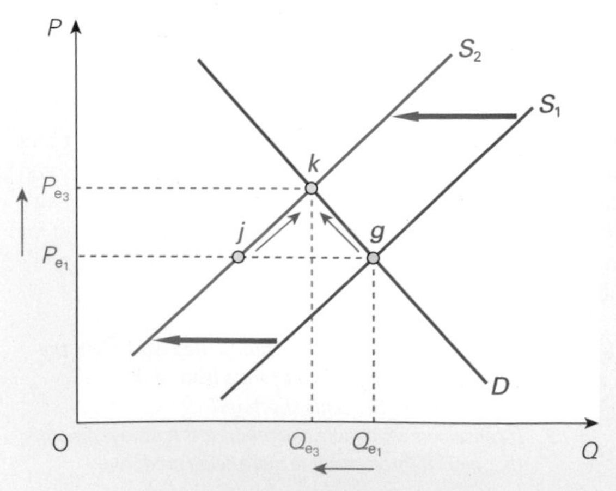

Incentives in markets

Throughout this chapter we have seen that people and firms respond to incentives. In all cases of changes in demand and supply, the resulting changes in price act as both signals and incentives. This is Threshold Concept 5.

*LOOKING AT THE MATHS

We saw on pages 39 and 45 how demand and supply curves can be represented by equations. Assume that the equations for the supply and demand curves in a particular market are as follows:

$$Q_D = a - bP \qquad (1)$$

$$Q_S = c + dP \qquad (2)$$

We can find the market equilibrium price by setting the two equations equal to each other, since, in equilibrium, the quantity supplied (Q_S) equals the quantity demanded (Q_D). Thus:

$$c + dP = a - bP$$

Subtracting c from and adding bP to both sides gives:

$$dP + bP = a - c$$
$$\therefore (d + b)P = a - c$$
$$\therefore P = \frac{a - c}{d + b} \qquad (3)$$

We can then solve for equilibrium quantity (Q_e) by substituting equation (3) in either equation (1) or (2) (since $Q_D = Q_S$). Thus, from equation (1):

$$Q_e = a - b\left(\frac{a - c}{d + b}\right)$$
$$= \frac{a(d + b) - b(a - c)}{d + b}$$
$$= \frac{ad + ab - ba + bc}{d + b} = \frac{ad + bc}{d + b} \qquad (4)$$

or, from equation (2):

$$Q_e = c + d\left(\frac{a - c}{d + b}\right)$$
$$= \frac{cd + cb + da - dc}{d + b} = \frac{cb + da}{d + b} \qquad (5)$$

Thus:

$$Q_e = \frac{ad + bc}{d + b} \text{ (equation (4))} = \frac{cb + da}{d + b} \text{ (equation(5))}$$

A worked example is given in Maths Case 2.1 on the student website.

Figure 2.7 Effect of a shift in the supply curve

*Identifying the position of demand and supply curves

Both demand and supply depend on price, and yet their interaction determines price. For this reason it is difficult to identify just what is going on when price and quantity change, and to identify just what the demand and supply curves look like.

Let us say that we want to identify the demand curve for good X. We observe that when the price was 20p, 1000 units were purchased. At a later date the price has risen to 30p and 800 units are now purchased. What can we conclude from this about the demand curve? The answer is that without further information we can conclude very little. Consider Figures 2.8 and 2.9. Both are consistent with the facts.

In Figure 2.8 the demand curve has not shifted. The rise in price and the fall in sales are due entirely to a shift in the supply curve. The movement from point *a* to point *b* is thus a movement along the demand curve. If we can be certain that the demand curve has not shifted, then the evidence allows us to identify its position (or, at least, two points on it).

In Figure 2.9, however, not only has the supply curve shifted, but so also has the demand curve. Let us assume that people's tastes for the product have increased. In this case a movement from *a* to *b* does *not* trace out the demand curve.

We cannot derive the demand curve(s) from the evidence of price and quantity alone.

The problem is that when the supply curve shifts, we often cannot know whether or not the demand curve has shifted, and if so by how much. How would we know, for example, just how much people's tastes have changed?

The problem works the other way round too. It is difficult to identify a supply curve when the demand curve shifts. Is the change in price and quantity entirely due to the shift in the demand curve, or has the supply curve shifted too?

This is known as the *identification problem*. It is difficult to identify just what is causing the change in price and quantity.

Definition

Identification problem The problem of identifying the relationship between two variables (e.g. price and quantity demanded) from the evidence when it is not known whether or how the variables have been affected by other determinants. For example, it is difficult to identify the shape of a demand curve simply by observing price and quantity when it is not known whether changes in other determinants have shifted the demand curve.

| Figure 2.8 | Problems in identifying the position and shape of the demand curve: shift in supply curve alone |

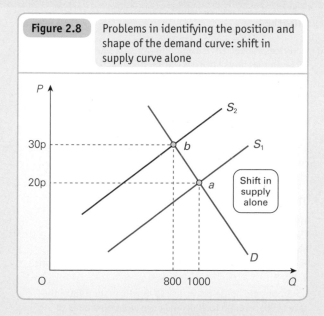

| Figure 2.9 | Problems in identifying the position and shape of the demand curve: shift in supply *and* demand curves |

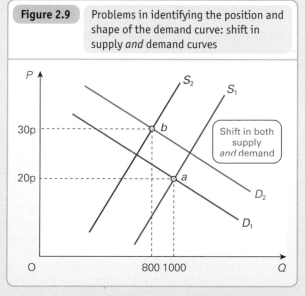

THRESHOLD CONCEPT 5   PEOPLE RESPOND TO INCENTIVES

So it's important to get them right

What gets you out of bed and into an economics lecture on time? What helps decide whether you wear a cycle helmet when out for a bike ride? What motivates a firm to invest in extra training for its workforce? Incentives drive the way individuals and businesses behave – even when we don't see that the incentive exists.

Financial and non-financial incentives

When there is a shortage of a good, its market price will rise, the opportunity cost goes up and there is an incentive for us to consume less. Similarly there is an incentive for firms to produce more. After all, the good is now more profitable to produce. This is an example of a financial incentive, for both buyers and producers. Other financial incentives include wages (i.e. being paid to work), bursaries for students and tax relief on investment for businesses.

But when we look at what motivates people making decisions, we see that non-financial incentives also play an important role. When we give to charity, support a football team, buy presents for our family or decide to run across a busy road rather than use a crossing, we are reacting to non-financial incentives.

Do incentives lead to desirable outcomes?

Let us return to the example of a shortage of a good, leading to a price rise. The resulting incentives could be seen as desirable, the shortage is eliminated and consumers are able to buy more of a good where demand initially exceeds supply.

However, there are plenty of instances where incentives may be 'perverse'. In other words, they could have undesirable effects. For example, if a particular course or module on your degree is assessed by two pieces of coursework, this may act as an incentive for you to concentrate solely on these two pieces and do little work on the rest of the syllabus.

There are plenty of other examples where incentives can be perverse. Making cars safer may encourage people to drive faster. Increasing top rates of income tax may encourage high earners to work less or to evade paying taxes by not declaring income – tax revenues may end up falling.

If an economic system is to work well, it is important, therefore, that the incentives are appropriate and do not bring about undesirable

BOX 2.2   UK HOUSE PRICES

The ups and downs (and ups again) of the housing market

The housing market is very important to consumers, firms and government in the UK. Households spend more on housing as a proportion of their income than any other good or service. Higher house prices tend to increase consumer confidence, leading to higher levels of spending and economic growth. Banks may also feel more confident about lending money to both consumers and firms. If house prices fall, the opposite is true. It is therefore not surprising that so many people take such a keen interest in both house prices and the outlook for the market.

The chart shows what happened to house prices in the period 1984 to 2017. It clearly illustrates the volatility of the market. For example, in the late 1980s, there was a boom with prices doubling between 1984 and 1989. By the end of 1988, prices were rising at an astonishing annual rate of 34 per cent.

However, this boom came to an end in late 1989. Between 1990 and 1995, house prices fell by 12.2 per cent, causing many households to move into 'negative equity'. This is where the size of a household's mortgage is greater than the value of their house, meaning that if they sold their house, they would still owe money. Many people during this period, therefore, found that they were unable to move house.

In the latter part of the 1990s the housing market started to recover, with prices rising at around 5 per cent per annum. This steady increase turned into another boom, with house prices rising at an annual rate of 26 per cent at the peak (in the 12 months to January 2003). With the financial crisis of 2007–8, house prices started to decline rapidly once again and in 2009 they fell by 19 per cent. They remained flat for several years, mirroring the lack of growth in the economy.

Prices started to rise again in late 2013 and by July 2014 annual house price inflation had reached 11.7 per cent. However, there was significant regional variation across the UK. Similar trends continued into 2015 and early 2016. For example, in June 2016 house prices grew at an annual rate of 13.2 per cent in the East of England compared with 4.7 per cent in Yorkshire and the Humber. This growth began to slow after the EU referendum. Then in April 2017, house prices recorded their first quarterly fall since 2012.

The determinants of house prices

House prices are determined by demand and supply. If demand rises (i.e. shifts to the right) or if supply falls (i.e. shifts to the left), the equilibrium price of houses will rise. Similarly, if demand falls or supply rises, the equilibrium price will fall.

So why did house prices rise so rapidly in the 1980s, the late 1990s through to 2007 and once more from 2013 to 2016? Why did they also fall in the early 1990s and again from 2008 to 2013? The answer lies primarily in changes in the *demand* for housing. Let us examine the various factors that affected the demand for houses.

Incomes (actual and anticipated).   The second half of the 1980s, 1996 to 2007 and 2013 to 2016 were periods of rising incomes. The economy was experiencing an economic 'boom', or recovery in the later period. Many people wanted to spend much of their extra income on housing: either buying a house for the first time, or moving to a better one. What is more,

side effects. This is a *threshold concept* because virtually every action taken by households or firms is influenced by incentives. We need to understand just what the incentives are, what their effects are likely to be, and how the incentives could be improved.

We can see the outcome of inappropriate incentives, when we look at what happened in the former Soviet Union in the days of central planning. The targets given to factory managers (see Box 1.4 on pages 22–3) were often inappropriate. For example, if targets were specified in tonnes, the incentive was to produce heavy products. Soviet furniture and cooking utensils tended to be very heavy! If targets were set in area (e.g. sheet glass), then the incentive was to produce thin products. If targets were set simply in terms of number of units, then the incentive was to produce shoddy products.

Despite the lessons that should have been learnt from the failures of Soviet planning, we still see a lack of real understanding of incentives and the role they can play. If banks are told to increase the amount of financial capital they hold, they may cut down on lending to small businesses. If a university's quality is measured by how many first and upper second-class degrees it awards, then

there is an incentive to make it easier for students to get high marks.

We will examine the role of incentives in more detail later in the book, particularly when we look at behavioural economics. One crucial incentive is that of profit. In a competitive environment, firms striving for increased profit may result in better products and a lower price for consumers as firms seek to undercut each other. In other cases, however, firms may be able to make bigger profits by controlling the market and keeping competitors out or by colluding with them. Here the profit incentive has a perverse effect: it leads to higher prices for consumers and less choice.

1. *Give two other examples of perverse incentives. How could the incentives be improved?*
2. *Suppose that the kitchen is very untidy – what are the incentives for you to address this? What incentives could you use to get someone else to do it for you?*
3. *Many students undertake voluntary work while at university. What do think the incentives are for this? Identify any perverse incentives associated with volunteering and how they could be addressed.*

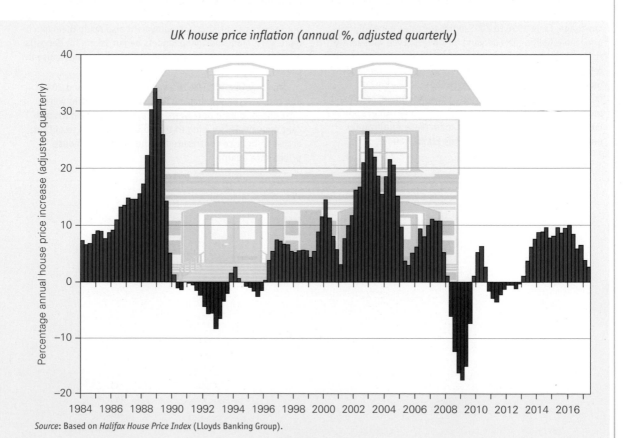

UK house price inflation (annual %, adjusted quarterly)

Source: Based on *Halifax House Price Index* (Lloyds Banking Group).

many people were confident that their incomes would continue to grow and were prepared to stretch themselves financially in the short term by buying an expensive house, assuming that their mortgage payments would become more affordable over time.

The early 1990s and late 2000s, by contrast, were periods of recession or low growth, with rising unemployment and flat or falling incomes. For example, average real earnings (i.e. earnings after taking inflation into account) fell by 9 per cent between 2008 and 2013. People were less confident about their ability to afford large mortgages. In 2017, rising inflation caused real wages to fall once again. This, combined with uncertainty about the future of the economy following the UK's decision to leave the European Union, had a negative impact on demand.

The number of households.   Social and demographic changes have resulted in a sharp increase in the number of households over the past 30 years. In 1981, there were 20.18 million households in Great Britain; by 2016 this had increased to 27.1 million. Reasons include more lone parents, increased life expectancy and flows of workers from abroad. Although average household size was lower, the overall impact was an increase in demand for housing.

The cost of mortgages.   During the second half of the 1980s, mortgage interest rates were generally falling. Although they were still high compared with rates today, in real terms they were negative.

In 1989, however, this trend went into reverse. Mortgage interest rates started rising. Many people found it difficult to maintain their existing payments, let alone take on a larger mortgage. From 1996 to 2003 mortgage rates generally fell, once more fuelling the demand for houses. Even with gently rising interest rates from 2003 to 2007, mortgages were still relatively affordable. Between 2009 and 2017, interest rates remained at an all-time low, which reduced the cost of mortgage repayments. However, a combination of continued uncertainty following the financial crisis and cautious lenders meant that demand did not start to increase significantly until around 2013. The result of the EU referendum

introduced more uncertainty back into the market from the second half of 2016.

The availability of mortgages.   In the late 1980s, mortgages were readily available. Banks and building societies were prepared to accept smaller deposits on houses and to grant mortgages of 3.5 times a person's annual income (compared with 2.5 times in the early 1980s). In the early 1990s, however, banks and building societies became much more cautious. They were aware that, with falling house prices, rising unemployment and the increasing problem of negative equity, there was a growing danger that borrowers would default on payments.

With the recovery of the economy in the mid-1990s and with increased competition between lenders, mortgages became more readily available and for greater amounts relative to people's incomes. This helped to push up prices. The belief that prices would continue to rise led lenders to relax their requirements even further. After all, if borrowers were to default, lenders would still have a good chance of getting their money back if house prices continued to rise. By the mid-2000s, many lenders were allowing borrowers to self-certificate their income and were increasingly willing to lend to those with a poor credit history. This was the 'sub-prime' market. In 2001, the average house price was 3.4 times greater than average earnings. By 2007, this figure had risen to 5.74. Problems in the mortgage market were a key contributing factor to the financial crises of 2007–8.

From late 2007 to 2012 the willingness of lenders to issue mortgages changed dramatically. The credit crunch in 2008–9 meant that the banks had less money to lend. Falling house prices and rising unemployment also made them much more wary. Many mortgage lenders began asking for deposits of at least 25 per cent – over £40 000 for an average house in the UK.

This requirement was relaxed through 2013 and 2014 and the government-backed 'Help to buy' schemes were introduced to help borrowers get a mortgage with a 5 per cent deposit. This easing in the ability of people to obtain access to finance contributed to the increase in house prices once again.

Speculation.   A belief that house prices will continue to move in a particular direction can exacerbate house price movements. In other words, speculation tends to increase house price movements. In the 1980s, 1997–2007 and 2013–16, people generally believed that house prices would continue rising. This encouraged them to buy, and to take out the biggest mortgage possible, before prices went up any further. There was also an effect on supply. Those with houses to sell held back until the last possible moment in the hope of getting a higher price. The net effect was a rightward shift in the demand curve for houses and a leftward shift in the supply curve. The effect of this speculation, therefore, was to help bring about the very effect that people were predicting (for more on the impact of speculation see section 2.5).

In the early 1990s and late 2000s, the opposite occurred. People thinking of buying houses held back, hoping to get a better deal when prices had fallen. People with houses to sell tried to sell as quickly as possible before prices fell any further. Again the effect of this speculation was to aggravate the change in prices – this time a fall in prices.

The impact of speculation has also been compounded by the growth in the 'buy-to-let' industry, with mortgage lenders entering this market in large numbers and a huge amount of media attention focused on the possibilities for individuals to make very high returns.

Supply.   While speculation about changing house prices is perhaps the biggest determinant of housing supply in the short run, over the long term supply depends on house building. Governments' housing policy is often focused on how to encourage the building industry by providing tax and other incentives and streamlining planning regulations. But house building may bring adverse environmental and social problems and people often oppose new developments in their area. Building on the 'Green Belt' has become a controversial issue.

What of the future?

The Institute of Fiscal Studies[1] forecast that average real wages will be lower in 2021 than they were in 2008. If this forecast is accurate, the decade from 2012 to 2021 will represent the worst period of pay for workers in 70 years and will have a negative impact on the future demand for housing. Data from the Office of National Statistics[2] suggest that house prices are the least affordable they have ever been. Between 1997 and 2016 the cost of an average home increased by 259 per cent while average real earnings increased by 68 per cent. The average house cost 7.6 times more than average earnings in 2016. As we saw above, the corresponding figure in 2001 was 3.4.

Will these negative factors on the demand side of the market lead to falling house prices? Many observers believe that they will continue to rise because of a lack of supply. The number of new households has exceeded the number of new houses built in every year since 2008, with the gap growing in recent years. Estimates suggest that 250 000 to 300 000 new homes would have to be built every year to keep up with demand. The figure for the year to June 2016 was 139 030. It looks increasingly likely that the government will fail to meet its target of building a million new homes by May 2020.

1. *Draw supply and demand diagrams to illustrate what was happening to house prices (a) in the second half of the 1980s and the period from 1997 to 2007; (b) in the early 1990s and 2008–12; (c) 2014–16 in London, and in a region outside SE England.*
2. *What determines the supply of housing? How will factors on the supply side influence house prices?*
3. *What is the role of the prices of 'other goods' in determining the demand for housing?*
4. *Find out what forecasters are predicting for house prices over the next year and attempt to explain their views.*

1 'Earnings and the labour market', *IFS Budget Analysis* (2017).
2 'Housing affordability in England and Wales: 1997 to 2016', *Statistical Bulletin* (ONS, March 2017).

BOX 2.3	STOCK MARKET PRICES

Demand and supply in action

Firms that are quoted on the stock market can raise money by issuing shares. These are sold on the 'primary stock market'. People who own the shares receive a 'dividend' on them, normally paid six-monthly. The amount varies with the profitability of the company.

People or institutions that buy these shares, however, may not wish to hold on to them for ever. This is where the 'secondary stock market' comes in. It is where existing shares are bought and sold. There are stock markets, primary and secondary, in all the major countries of the world.

There are 2226 companies (as of April 2017) whose shares and other securities are listed on the London Stock Exchange and trading in them takes place each weekday. The prices of shares depend on demand and supply. For example, if the demand for Tesco shares at any one time exceeds the supply on offer, the price will rise until demand and supply are equal. Share prices fluctuate throughout the trading day and sometimes price changes can be substantial.

To give an overall impression of share price movements, stock exchanges publish share price indices. The most famous one in the UK is the FTSE ('footsie') 100, which stands for the 'Financial Times Stock Exchange' index of the 100 largest companies' shares. The index represents an average price of these 100 shares. The chart shows movements in the FTSE 100 from 1995 to 2017. The index was first calculated on 3 January 1984 with a base level of 1000 points. It reached a peak of 6930 points on 30 December 1999 and fell to 3287 on 12 March 2003, before rising again to a high of 6730 on 12 October 2007. However, with the financial crisis, the index fell to a low of 3512 on 3 March 2009. During the latter part of

2009 and 2010, the index began to recover, briefly passing the 6000 mark at the end of 2010, but fluctuating around 5500 during 2011/12. The index then started on an upward trend in 2013, peaking at 7104 on 27 April 2015, before falling back to around 6000 in early 2016.

After the initial shock of the Brexit vote in June 2016, it rose again to over 7000 in June 2016. Part of the reason for this was the fall in the sterling exchange rate that occurred because of the uncertainty over the nature of the Brexit deal. With many of the FTSE 100 companies having assets denominated in dollars, a falling sterling exchange rate meant that these dollar assets were now worth more pounds.

What causes share prices to change? Why were they so high in 1999, but only just over half that value only three years later? Why did this trend occur again in the late 2000s and what is likely to happen as the time for the UK leaving the EU approaches? The answer lies in the determinants of the demand and supply of shares.

Demand

There are five main factors that affect the demand for shares.

The dividend yield.   This is the dividend on a share as a percentage of its price. The higher the dividend yields on shares the more attractive they are as a form of saving. One of the main explanations of rising stock market prices from 2003 to 2007 was high profits and resulting high dividends. The financial crisis and slowdown in the world economy explains the falling profits and dividends of companies from

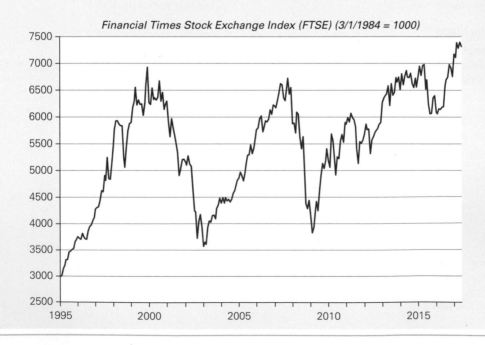

Financial Times Stock Exchange Index (FTSE) (3/1/1984 = 1000)

2007 and the subsequent recovery in the global economy caused them to increase once again.

The price of and/or return on substitutes. The main substitutes for shares in specific companies are other shares. Thus if, in comparison with other shares, Tesco shares are expected to pay high dividends relative to the share price, people will buy Tesco shares. As far as shares in general are concerned, the main substitutes are other forms of saving. Thus if the interest rate on savings accounts in banks and building societies fell, people with such accounts would be tempted to take their money out and buy shares instead.

Another major substitute is property. If house prices rise rapidly, as they did in 2002 and 2003, this will reduce the demand for shares as many people switch to buying property in anticipation of even higher prices. If house prices level off, as they did in 2005/6, this makes shares relatively more attractive as an investment and can boost the demand for them. With the global slowdown in 2008 pushing both house and share prices downwards, investors looked for other substitutes. Gold and government debt became more popular, as they were considered to be a safer investment.

Incomes. If the economy is growing rapidly and people's incomes are rising rapidly, they are likely to save some of their extra income and therefore buy more shares. Thus in the mid-to-late 1990s, when UK incomes were rising at an average annual rate of over 3 per cent, share prices rose rapidly (see chart). As growth rates fell in the early 2000s, so did share prices. The trend then repeated itself with growth rates picking up from 2003 to 2007 and then declining again with the onset of recession from 2007. With signs of a global economic recovery, share price rose again between 2012 and mid-2015.

Wealth. 'Wealth' is people's accumulated savings and property. Wealth rose in the 1990s and many people used their increased wealth to buy shares. It was a similar picture in the mid-2000s.

Expectations. From 2003 to 2007, people expected share prices to go on rising. They were optimistic about continued growth in the economy and that certain sectors, such as leisure and high-tech industries, would grow particularly strongly. As people bought shares, this put more upward pressure on prices, thereby fuelling further speculation that they would go on rising and encouraging further share buying.

With the financial crisis and fears of recession, there was a dramatic fall in share prices as confidence was shaken. As people anticipated further price falls, they held back from buying, thereby reducing demand and pushing prices lower. Prices remained volatile after the financial crisis, as uncertainty remained about the prospects for the global economy. Only when people

became increasingly confident about the chances of an economic recovery did share prices begin to rise consistently once more.

However, uncertainty has increased again with concerns about the slow recovery in Europe, falling growth in China and many other developing countries, and the consequences of the UK's exit from the EU. The impact of speculation is examined in more detail in section 2.5.

Supply

The factors affecting supply are largely the same as those affecting demand, but in the opposite direction.

If the return on alternative forms of saving falls, people with shares are likely to hold on to them, as they represent a better form of saving. The supply of shares to the market will fall. If incomes or wealth rise, people again are likely to want to hold on to their shares.

As far as expectations are concerned, if people believe that share prices will rise, they will hold on to the shares they have. Supply to the market will fall, thereby pushing up prices. If, however, they believe that prices will fall, as they did in 2008, they will sell their shares now before prices do fall. Supply will increase, driving down the price.

Share prices and business

Companies are crucially affected by their share price. If a company's share price falls, this is taken as a sign that 'the market' is losing confidence, as was the case with Tesco during the latter part of 2014. This will make it more difficult to raise finance, not only by issuing additional shares in the primary market, but also from banks. It will also make the company more vulnerable to a takeover bid. This is where one company seeks to buy out another by offering to buy all its shares. A takeover will succeed if the owners of more than half of the company's shares vote to accept the offered price. Shareholders are more likely to agree to the takeover if they have been disappointed by the recent performance of the company's shares.

1. *If the rate of economic growth in the economy is 3 per cent in a particular year, why are share prices likely to rise by more than 3 per cent that year?*
2. *Find out what has happened to the FTSE 100 index over the past 12 months and explain why (see site B27 on the hotlinks part of the website).*
3. *Why would you expect the return on shares to be greater than that offered by a bank savings account?*

2.4   ELASTICITY

Price elasticity of demand

When the price of a good rises, the quantity demanded will fall. But in most cases we will want to know more than this. We will want to know by just *how much* the quantity demanded will fall. In other words, we will want to know how *responsive* demand is to a rise in price.

Take the case of two products: oil and cabbages. In the case of oil, a rise in price is likely to result in a relatively small fall in the quantity demanded. If people want to continue driving, they have to pay the higher prices for fuel. A few may turn to riding bicycles, and some people may make fewer journeys, but for most people, a rise in the price of petrol and diesel will make little difference in the short term to how much they use their cars.

In the case of cabbages, however, a rise in price may lead to a substantial fall in the quantity demanded. The reason is that there are alternative vegetables that people can buy. Many people, when buying vegetables, will buy whatever is reasonably priced.

We call the responsiveness of demand to a change in price the ***price elasticity of demand***, and it is one of the most important concepts in economics. For example, if we know the price elasticity of demand for a product, we can predict the effect on price and quantity of a shift in the *supply* curve for that product.

Figure 2.10 shows the effect of a shift in supply with two quite different demand curves (D and D'). Curve D' is more elastic than curve D over any given price range. In other words, for any given change in price, there will be a larger change in quantity demanded along curve D' than along curve D.

Assume that initially the supply curve is S_1, and that it intersects with both demand curves at point a, at a price of P_1 and a quantity of Q_1. Now supply shifts to S_2. What will happen to price and quantity? In the case of the less elastic demand curve D, there is a relatively large rise in price (to P_2) and a relatively small fall in quantity (to Q_2): equilibrium is at point b. In the case of the more elastic demand curve D', however, there is only a relatively small rise in price (to P_3), but a relatively large fall in quantity (to Q_3): equilibrium is at point c.

Measuring the price elasticity of demand

What we want to compare is the size of the change in quantity demanded with the size of the change in price. But since price and quantity are measured in different units, the only sensible way we can do this is to use percentage or

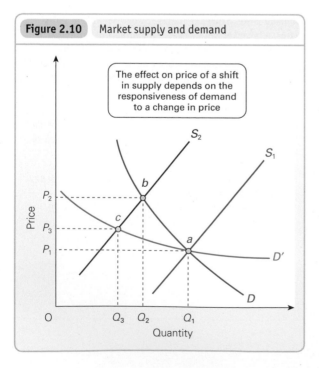

Figure 2.10   Market supply and demand

The effect on price of a shift in supply depends on the responsiveness of demand to a change in price

Definition

Price elasticity of demand The responsiveness of quantity demanded to a change in price.

proportionate changes. This gives us the following *formula for the price elasticity of demand* ($P\epsilon_D$) for a product: percentage (or proportionate) change in quantity demanded divided by the percentage (or proportionate) change in price. Putting this in symbols gives:

$$P\epsilon_D = \frac{\%\Delta Q_D}{\%\Delta P}$$

where ϵ (the Greek epsilon) is the symbol we use for elasticity, and Δ (the capital Greek delta) is the symbol we use for a 'change in'.

Thus if a 40 per cent rise in the price of oil caused the quantity demanded to fall by a mere 10 per cent, the price elasticity of oil over this range will be

$-10\%/40\% = -0.25$

whereas if a 5 per cent fall in the price of cabbages caused a 15 per cent rise in the quantity demanded, the price elasticity of demand for cabbages over this range would be

$15\%/-5\% = -3$

Cabbages have a more elastic demand than oil, and this is shown by the figures. But just what do these two figures show? What is the significance of minus 0.25 and minus 3?

Interpreting the figure for elasticity

The use of proportionate or percentage measures
Elasticity is measured in proportionate or percentage terms for the following reasons:

- It allows comparison of changes in two qualitatively different things, which are thus measured in two different types of unit: i.e. it allows comparison of *quantity* changes with *monetary* changes.
- It is the only sensible way of deciding *how big* a change in price or quantity is. Take a simple example. An item goes up in price by £1. Is this a big increase or a small increase? We can answer this only if we know what the original price was. If a can of beans goes up in price by £1 that is a huge price increase. If, however, the price of a house goes up by £1 that is a tiny price increase. In other words, it is the percentage or proportionate increase in price that determines how big a price rise is.

The sign (positive or negative)
Demand curves are generally downward sloping. This means that price and quantity change in opposite directions. A *rise* in price (a positive figure) will cause a *fall* in the quantity demanded (a negative figure). Similarly a *fall* in price will cause a *rise* in the quantity demanded. Thus when working out price elasticity of demand, we either divide a negative figure by a positive figure, or a positive figure by a negative. Either way, we end up with a negative figure.

The value (greater or less than 1)
If we now ignore the negative sign and just concentrate on the value of the figure, this tells us whether demand is *elastic* or *inelastic*.

Elastic ($\epsilon > 1$).   This is where a change in price causes a proportionately larger change in the quantity demanded. In this case, the value of elasticity will be greater than 1, since we are dividing a larger figure by a smaller figure. Hence, if the elasticity figure is -2.5 it tells us that if prices were increased by 1 per cent, demand would fall by 2.5 per cent. Customers are very sensitive to a change in the price.

Inelastic ($\epsilon < 1$).   This is where a change in price causes a proportionately smaller change in the quantity demanded. In this case, elasticity will be less than 1, since we are dividing a smaller figure by a larger figure. Hence, if the elasticity figure is -0.3 it tells us that if prices were increased by 1 per cent, demand would fall by 0.3 per cent. Customers are relatively insensitive to a change in the price.

Unit elastic ($\epsilon = 1$).   **Unit elasticity of demand** occurs where price and quantity demanded change by the same proportion. This will give an elasticity equal to 1, since we are dividing a figure by itself. An increase in price by 1 per cent leads to a fall in demand by 1 per cent.

Determinants of price elasticity of demand

The price elasticity of demand varies enormously from one product to another. For example, the demand for a holiday in any given resort typically has a price elasticity greater than 5, whereas the demand for electricity has a price elasticity less than 0.5 (ignoring the negative signs). But why do some products have a highly elastic demand, whereas others have a highly *in*elastic demand? What determines price elasticity of demand?

The number and closeness of substitute goods.   This is the most important determinant. The more substitutes there are and the closer they are to the good, the more people will switch

KI 9
p66

> ### Definitions
>
> **Formula for price elasticity of demand ($P\epsilon_D$)** The percentage (or proportionate) change in quantity demanded divided by the percentage (or proportionate) change in price: $\%\Delta Q_D \div \%\Delta P$.
>
> **Elastic demand** Where quantity demanded changes by a larger percentage than price. Ignoring the negative sign, it will have a value greater than 1.
>
> **Inelastic demand** Where quantity demanded changes by a smaller percentage than price. Ignoring the negative sign, it will have a value less than 1.
>
> **Unit elasticity of demand** Where quantity demanded changes by the same percentage as price. Ignoring the negative sign, it will have a value equal to 1.

to these alternatives when the price of the good rises: the greater, therefore, will be the price elasticity of demand. The number of substitutes is strongly influenced by how broadly a market is defined.

A broadly defined market, such as alcohol, has very few substitutes. Customers tend to be relatively insensitive to the price. Using data from the *General Household Survey* and the *Expenditure and Food Survey* (now the *Living Costs and Food Survey*), researchers from the University of Sheffield estimated an elasticity figure for alcohol of −0.40 in the UK.[1] A more narrowly defined market such as beer is likely to have more substitutes (i.e. wine, spirits and cider) so consumers will tend to be less price inelastic. A figure of between −0.98 and −1.27 has been estimated for off-trade beer: i.e. sold in supermarkets and licensed shops.[2] The elasticity of demand for a good produced by a single firm (i.e. a particular brand of whisky or beer) is likely to be even more price sensitive. Consumers can switch to another supplier of the same product.

 Why will the price elasticity of demand for holidays in Crete be greater than that for holidays in general? Is this difference the result of a difference in the size of the income effect or the substitution effect? Is there anything the suppliers of holidays in Crete can do to reduce this higher price elasticity?

The proportion of income spent on the good. The higher the proportion of our income we spend on a good, the more we will be forced to cut consumption when its price rises: the bigger will be the income effect and the more elastic will be the demand.

Thus salt has a very low price elasticity of demand. Part of the reason is that there is no close substitute. But part is that we spend such a tiny fraction of our income on salt that we would find little difficulty in paying a relatively large percentage increase in its price: the income effect of a price rise would be very small. By contrast, there will be a much bigger income effect when a major item of expenditure rises in price. For example, if mortgage interest rates rise (the 'price' of loans for house purchase), people may have to cut down substantially on their demand for housing – being forced to buy somewhere much smaller and cheaper, or to live in rented accommodation.

 Will a general item of expenditure such as food or clothing have a price-elastic or inelastic demand? (Consider both the determinants we have considered so far.)

1 Petra Meier et al., 'Modelling the potential impact of pricing and promotion policies for alcohol in England: results from the Sheffield Alcohol Policy Model Version 2008 (1-1)', *Independent Review of the Effects of Alcohol Pricing and Promotion* (University of Sheffield, 2008).

2 Y. Meng, A. Brennan, R. Purshouse et al., 'Estimation of own and cross price elasticities of alcohol demand in the UK: A pseudo-panel approach using the Living Costs and Food Survey 2001–2009', *Journal of Health Economics*, vol. 34 (White Rose Research Online, 2014).

The time period.   When price rises, people may take time to adjust their consumption patterns and find alternatives. The longer the time period after a price change the more elastic the demand is likely to be.

To illustrate this, let us return to our example of oil. The Office for Budget Responsibility estimates that the price elasticity of demand for fuel is −0.07 in the short run and −0.13 in the medium term. Other studies have estimated a long-run figure of approximately −0.85.[3] Why is the figure for fuel so much more inelastic in the short run than the long run? If fuel prices rise, people will find it difficult to reduce their consumption by a significant amount in the short run. If public transport options are limited, they still have to drive their cars to work and for leisure purposes. Although the number of journeys they make may remain unchanged, some people may be able to reduce their fuel consumption slightly by driving more economically. Firms still have to use fuel to transport their goods and oil may be a major source of energy in a production process that cannot easily be changed.

Over time, people can find other ways to respond, such as purchasing new fuel-efficient vehicles, car sharing or moving closer to their work. Firms can also change their production methods and the way they transport their goods.

 Demand for oil might be relatively elastic over the longer term, and yet it could still be observed that over time people consume more oil (or only very slightly less) despite rising oil prices. How can this apparent contradiction be explained?

Price elasticity of demand and consumer expenditure

One of the most important applications of price elasticity of demand concerns its relationship with the total amount of money consumers spend on a product. ***Total consumer expenditure** (**TE**)* is simply price multiplied by quantity purchased.

$$TE = P \times Q$$

For example, if consumers buy 3 million units (Q) at a price of £2 per unit (P), they will spend a total of £6 million (TE).

Total consumer expenditure will be the same as the ***total revenue** (**TR**)* received by firms from the sale of the product (before any taxes or other deductions).

> ## Definitions
>
> **Total consumer expenditure on a product (*TE*) (per period of time)** The price of the product multiplied by the quantity purchased: $TE = P \times Q$.
>
> **Total revenue (*TR*) (per period of time)** The total amount received by firms from the sale of a product, before the deduction of taxes or any other costs. The price multiplied by the quantity sold: $TR = P \times Q$.

3 *Analysis of the Dynamic Effects of Fuel Duty Reductions* (HM Treasury, April 2014).

What will happen to consumer expenditure (and hence firms' revenue) if there is a change in price? The answer depends on the price elasticity of demand.

Elastic demand

As price rises, so quantity demanded falls and vice versa. When demand is elastic, quantity demanded changes proportionately more than price. Thus the change in quantity has a bigger effect on total consumer expenditure than does the change in price. For example, when the price rises, there will be such a large fall in consumer demand that *less* will be spent than before. This can be summarised as follows:

- *P* rises; *Q* falls proportionately more; thus *TE* falls.
- *P* falls; *Q* rises proportionately more; thus *TE* rises.

In other words, total expenditure changes in the same direction as *quantity*.

This is illustrated in Figure 2.11. The areas of the rectangles in the diagram represent total expenditure. Why? The area of a rectangle is its height multiplied by its length. In this case, this is price multiplied by quantity bought, which is total expenditure. Demand is elastic between points *a* and *b*. A rise in price from £4 to £5 causes a proportionately larger fall in quantity demanded: from 20 million to 10 million. Total expenditure *falls* from £80 million (the striped area) to £50 million (the pink area).

When demand is elastic, then, a rise in price will cause a fall in total consumer expenditure and thus a fall in the total revenue that firms selling the product receive. A reduction in price, however, will result in consumers spending more, and hence firms earning more.

Inelastic demand

When demand is **inelastic,** it is the other way around. Price changes proportionately more than quantity. Thus the change in price has a bigger effect on total consumer

expenditure than does the change in quantity. To summarise the effects:

- *P* rises; *Q* falls proportionately less; *TE* rises.
- *P* falls; *Q* rises proportionately less; *TE* falls.

In other words, total consumer expenditure changes in the same direction as *price*.

This is illustrated in Figure 2.12. Demand is inelastic between points *a* and *c*. A rise in price from £4 to £8 causes a proportionately smaller fall in quantity demanded: from 20 million to 15 million. Total expenditure *rises* from £80 million (the striped area) to £120 million (the pink area).

In this case, firms' revenue will increase if there is a rise in price and fall if there is a fall in price.

 Assume that demand for a product is inelastic. Will consumer expenditure go on increasing as price rises? Would there be any limit?

Special cases

Figure 2.13 shows three special cases: (a) a totally inelastic demand ($P\epsilon_D = 0$), (b) an infinitely elastic demand ($P\epsilon_D = \infty$) and (c) a unit elastic demand ($P\epsilon_D = -1$).

Totally inelastic demand.   This is shown by a vertical straight line. No matter what happens to price, quantity demanded remains the same. It is obvious that the more the price rises, the bigger will be the level of consumer expenditure. Thus in Figure 2.13(a), consumer expenditure will be higher at P_2 than at P_1.

 Can you think of any examples of goods which have a totally inelastic demand (a) at all prices; (b) over a particular price range?

Infinitely elastic demand.   This is shown by a horizontal straight line. At any price above P_1 in Figure 2.13(b), demand is zero. But at P_1 (or any price below) demand is 'infinitely' large.

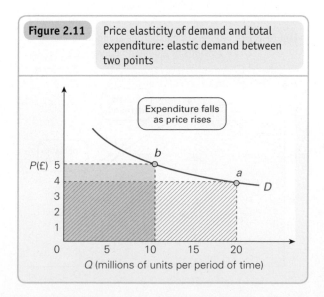

Figure 2.11   Price elasticity of demand and total expenditure: elastic demand between two points

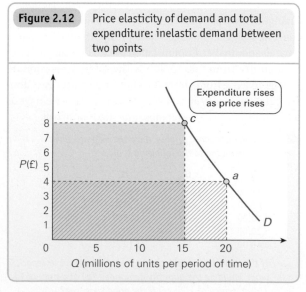

Figure 2.12   Price elasticity of demand and total expenditure: inelastic demand between two points

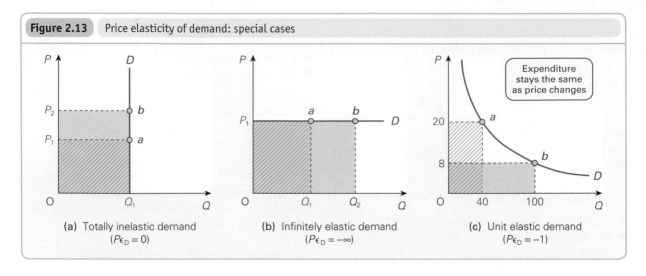

Figure 2.13 Price elasticity of demand: special cases

(a) Totally inelastic demand ($P\epsilon_D = 0$)

(b) Infinitely elastic demand ($P\epsilon_D = -\infty$)

(c) Unit elastic demand ($P\epsilon_D = -1$)

This seemingly unlikely demand curve is in fact relatively common for an *individual producer.* In a perfect market, as we have seen, firms are small relative to the whole market (like the small-scale grain farmer). They have to accept the price as given by supply and demand in the *whole market,* but at that price they can sell as much as they produce. (Demand is not *literally* infinite, but as far as the firm is concerned it is.) In this case, the more the individual firm produces, the more revenue will be earned. In Figure 2.13(b), more revenue is earned at Q_2 than at Q_1.

Unit elastic demand. This is where price and quantity change in exactly the same proportion. Any rise in price will be exactly offset by a fall in quantity, leaving total consumer expenditure unchanged. In Figure 2.13(c), the striped area is exactly equal to the pink area: in both cases, total expenditure is £800.

You might have thought that a demand curve with unit elasticity would be a straight line at 45° to the axes. Instead it is a curve called a *rectangular hyperbola.* The reason for its shape is that the proportionate *rise* in quantity must equal the proportionate *fall* in price (and vice versa). As we move down the demand curve, in order for the *proportionate* change in both price and quantity to remain constant there must be a bigger and bigger *absolute* rise in quantity and a smaller and smaller absolute fall in price. For example, a rise in quantity from 200 to 400 is the same proportionate change as a rise from 100 to 200, but its absolute size is double. A fall in price from £5 to £2.50 is the same percentage as a fall from £10 to £5, but its absolute size is only half.

 To illustrate these figures, draw the demand curve corresponding to the following table.

P	Q	TE
£2.50	400	£1000
£5.00	200	£1000
£10.00	100	£1000
£20.00	50	£1000
£40.00	25	£1000

If the curve had an elasticity of −1 throughout its length, what would be the quantity demanded (a) at a price of £1; (b) at a price of 10p; (c) if the good were free?

The measurement of elasticity: arc elasticity

We have defined price elasticity as the percentage or proportionate change in quantity demanded divided by the percentage or proportionate change in price. But how, in practice, do we measure these changes for a specific demand curve? We shall examine two methods. The first is called the *arc method.* The second (in an optional section) is called the *point method.*

A common mistake that students make is to think that you can talk about the elasticity of a *whole curve.* In fact in most cases the elasticity will vary along the length of the curve.

Take the case of the demand curve illustrated in Figure 2.14. Between points *a* and *b,* total expenditure rises ($P_2Q_2 > P_1Q_1$): demand is thus elastic between these two points. Between points *b* and *c,* however, total expenditure falls ($P_3Q_3 < P_2Q_2$). Demand here is inelastic.

Normally, then, we can only refer to the elasticity of a *portion* of the demand curve, not of the *whole* curve. There are, however, two exceptions to this rule.

Figure 2.14 Different elasticities along different portions of a demand curve

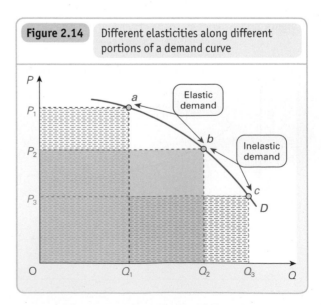

How to increase sales and price

When we are told that a product will make us more attractive, enrich our lives, make our clothes smell great or allow us to save the planet, just what are the advertisers up to? 'Trying to sell the product', you may reply.

In fact there is a bit more to it than this. Advertisers are trying to do two things:

- Shift the product's demand curve to the right.
- Make it less price elastic.

This is illustrated in the diagram.

Effect of advertising on the demand curve

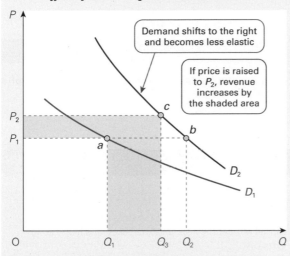

Demand shifts to the right and becomes less elastic

If price is raised to P_2, revenue increases by the shaded area

D_1 shows the original demand curve with price at P_1 and sales at Q_1. D_2 shows the curve after an advertising campaign. The rightward shift allows an increased quantity (Q_2) to be sold at the original price. If the demand is also made highly inelastic, the firm can raise its price and still have a substantial increase in sales. Thus, in the diagram,

price can be raised to P_2 and sales will be Q_3 – still substantially above Q_1. The total gain in revenue is shown by the shaded area.

How can advertising bring about this new demand curve?

Shifting the demand curve to the right

This can occur in two ways. First, if advertising brings the product to more people's attention, then the market for the good grows and the demand curve shifts to the right. Second, if the advertising increases people's desire for the product, they will be prepared to pay a higher price for each unit purchased.

Making the demand curve less elastic

This will occur if the advertising creates greater brand loyalty. People must be led to believe (rightly or wrongly) that competitors' brands are inferior. This can be done directly by comparing the brand being advertised with a competitor's product. Alternatively, the adverts may concentrate on making the product seem so special that it implies that no other product can compete. These approaches will allow the firm to raise its price above that of its rivals with no significant fall in sales. The substitution effect will have been lessened because consumers have been led to believe that there are no close substitutes.

1. *Think of some advertisements which deliberately seek to make demand less elastic.*
2. *Imagine that 'Sunshine' sunflower spread, a well-known brand, is advertised with the slogan 'It helps you live longer'. What do you think would happen to the demand curve for a supermarket's own brand of sunflower spread? Consider both the direction of shift and the effect on elasticity. Will the elasticity differ markedly at different prices? How will this affect the pricing policy and sales of the supermarket's own brand? What do you think might be the response of government to the slogan?*

The first is when the elasticity just so happens to be the same all the way along a curve, as in the three special cases illustrated in Figure 2.13. The second is where two curves are drawn on the same diagram, as in Figure 2.10. Here we can say that demand curve D is less elastic than demand curve D' at any given price. Note, however, that each of these two curves will still have different elasticities along its length.

Although we cannot normally talk about the elasticity of a whole curve, we can nevertheless talk about the elasticity between any two points on it. This is known as **arc elasticity**. In fact, the formula for price elasticity of demand that we have used so far is the formula for arc elasticity. Let us examine it more closely. Remember the formula we used was:

$$\frac{\text{Proportionate } \Delta Q}{\text{Proportionate } \Delta P} \text{(where } \Delta \text{ means 'change in')}$$

The way we measure a proportionate change in quantity is to divide that change by the level of Q: $\Delta Q/Q$. Similarly, we measure a proportionate change in price by dividing that change by the level of P: $\Delta P/P$. Price elasticity of demand can thus now be rewritten as

$$\frac{\Delta Q}{Q} \div \frac{\Delta P}{P}$$

But just what value do we give to P and Q? Consider the demand curve in Figure 2.15. What is the elasticity of

Definition

Arc elasticity The measurement of elasticity between two points on a curve.

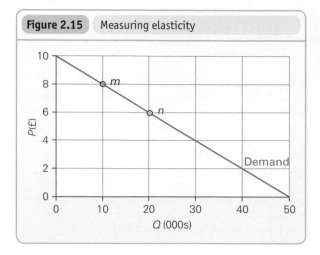

Figure 2.15 Measuring elasticity

Similarly, the proportionate change in quantity between points m and n is $^{10}/_{15}$, since 15 is midway between 10 and 20.

Thus using the **average (or 'midpoint') formula**, arc elasticity between m and n is given by:

$$\frac{\Delta Q}{\text{average } Q} \div \frac{\Delta P}{\text{average } P} = \frac{10}{15} \div \frac{-2}{7} = -2.33$$

Since, ignoring the negative sign, 2.33 is greater than 1, demand is elastic between m and n.

 Referring to Figure 2.15, use the midpoint formula to calculate the price elasticity of demand between (a) $P = 6$ and $P = 4$; (b) $P = 4$ and $P = 2$. What do you conclude about the elasticity of a straight-line demand curve as you move down it?

demand between points m and n? Price has fallen by £2 (from £8 to £6), but what is the proportionate change? Is it $-^{2}/_{8}$ or $-^{2}/_{6}$? The convention is to express the change as a proportion of the average of the two prices, £8 and £6: in other words, to take the midpoint price, £7. Thus the proportionate change is $-^{2}/_{7}$.

Definition

Average (or 'midpoint') formula for price elasticity of demand $\Delta Q_D/\text{average } Q_D \div \Delta P/\text{average } P$.

BOX 2.5 **ANY MORE FARES?**

CASE STUDIES AND APPLICATIONS

Pricing on the buses

Imagine that a local bus company is faced with increased costs and fears that it will make a loss. What should it do?

The most likely response of the company will be to raise its fares. But this may be the wrong policy, especially if existing services are underutilised. To help it decide what to do, it commissions a survey to estimate passenger demand at three different fares: the current fare of 50p per mile, a higher fare of 60p and a lower fare of 40p. The results of the survey are shown in the first two columns of the table.

Demand turns out to be elastic. This is because of the existence of alternative means of transport. As a result of the elastic demand, total revenue can be increased by reducing the fare from the current 50p to 40p. Revenue would rise from £2m to £2.4m per annum.

But what will happen to the company's profits? Its profit is the difference between the total revenue from passengers and its total costs of operating the service. If buses are currently

underutilised, it is likely that the extra passengers can be carried without the need for extra buses, and hence at no extra cost.

At a fare of 50p, the old profit was £0.2m (£2.0m − £1.8m). After the increase in costs, a 50p fare now gives a loss of £0.2m (£2.0m − £2.2m).

By raising the fare to 60p, the loss is increased to £0.4m. But by lowering the fare to 40p, a profit of £0.2m can again be made.

 1. *Estimate the price elasticity of demand between 40p and 50p and between 50p and 60p.*
2. *Was the 50p fare the best fare originally?*
3. *The company considers lowering the fare to 30p, and estimates that demand will be 8.5 million passenger miles. It will have to put on extra buses, however. How should it decide?*

Fare (£ per mile)	Estimated demand (passenger miles per year: millions)	Total revenue (£ millions per year)	Old total cost (£ millions per year)	New total cost (£ millions per year)
(1)	(2)	(3)	(4)	(5)
0.40	6	2.4	1.8	2.2
0.50	4	2.0	1.8	2.2
0.60	3	1.8	1.8	2.2

*The measurement of elasticity: point elasticity

Rather than measuring elasticity between two points on a demand curve, we may want to measure it at a single point: for example, point *r* in Figure 2.16. In order to measure *point elasticity* we must first rearrange the terms in the formula $\Delta Q/Q \div \Delta P/P$. By doing so we can rewrite the formula for price elasticity of demand as:

$$\frac{\Delta Q}{\Delta P} \times \frac{P}{Q}$$

Since we want to measure price elasticity at a *point* on the demand curve, rather than between two points, it is necessary to know how quantity demanded would react to an *infinitesimally small* change in price. In the case of point *r* in Figure 2.16, we want to know how the quantity demanded would react to an infinitesimally small change from a price of 30.

An infinitesimally small change is signified by the letter *d*. The formula for price elasticity of demand thus becomes

$$\frac{dQ}{dP} \times \frac{P}{Q}$$

where dQ/dP is the differential calculus term for the rate of change of quantity with respect to a change in price (see Appendix 1). And conversely, dP/dQ is the rate of change of price with respect to a change in quantity demanded. At any given point on the demand curve, dP/dQ is given by the *slope* of the curve (its rate of change). The slope is found by drawing a tangent to the curve at that point and finding the slope of the tangent.

The tangent to the demand curve at point *r* is shown in Figure 2.16. Its slope is −50/100. Thus, dP/dQ is −50/100 and dQ/dP is the inverse of this, −100/50 = −2.

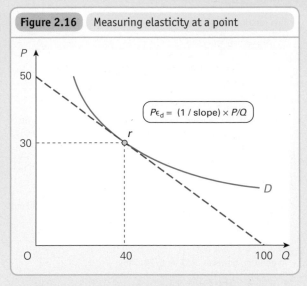

Figure 2.16 Measuring elasticity at a point

$$P\epsilon_d = (1 / \text{slope}) \times P/Q$$

Returning to the formula $dQ/dP \times P/Q$, elasticity at point *r* equals

$$-2 \times 30/40 = -1.5$$

Rather than having to draw the graph and measure the slope of the tangent, the technique of differentiation can be used to work out point elasticity as long as the equation for the demand curve is known. An example of the use of this technique is given in Box 2.6 (on page 64).

Definition

Point elasticity The measurement of elasticity at a point on a curve. The formula for price elasticity of demand using the point elasticity method is $dQ/dP \times P/Q$, where dQ/dP is the inverse of the slope of the tangent to the demand curve at the point in question.

*LOOKING AT THE MATHS

Elasticity of a straight-line demand curve

A straight-line demand curve has a different elasticity at each point on it. The only exceptions are a vertical demand curve ($P\epsilon_D = 0$) and a horizontal demand curve ($P\epsilon_D = \infty$). The reason for this differing elasticity can be demonstrated using the equation for a straight-line demand curve:

$$Q = a - bP$$

The term '−*b*' would give the slope of the demand curve if we were to plot *Q* on the vertical axis and *P* on the horizontal. Since we plot them the other way around,[1] the term '*b*' gives the inverse of the slope as plotted. The slope of the curve as plotted is given by dP/dQ; the inverse of the slope is given by $dQ/dP = -b$).

The formula for price elasticity of demand (using the point elasticity method) is

$$P\epsilon_D = \frac{dQ}{dP} \cdot \frac{P}{Q}$$

Different elasticities along a straight-line demand curve

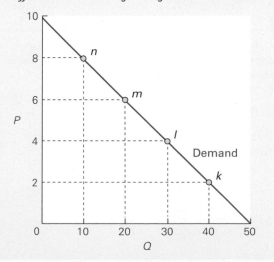

This can thus be rewritten as

$$P\epsilon_D = -b\frac{P}{Q}$$

This is illustrated in the diagram, which plots the following demand curve:

$$Q = 50 - 5P$$

The slope of the demand curve (dP/dQ) is constant (i.e. $-10/50$ or -0.2). The inverse of the slope (dQ/dP) is thus -5, where 5 is the 'b' term in the equation. In this example, therefore, price elasticity of demand is given by

$$P\epsilon_D = -5\frac{P}{Q}$$

The value of P/Q, however, differs along the length of the demand curve. At point n, $P/Q = 8/10$. Thus

$$P\epsilon_D = -5(8/10) = -4$$

At point m, however, $P/Q = 6/20$. Thus

$$P\epsilon_D = -5(6/20) = -1.5$$

These questions refer to the diagram.
1. *What is the price elasticity of demand at points l and k?*
2. *What is the price elasticity of demand at the point (a) where the demand curve crosses the vertical axis; (b) where it crosses the horizontal axis?*
3. *As you move down a straight-line demand curve, what happens to elasticity? Why?*
4. *Calculate price elasticity of demand between points n and l using the arc method. Does this give the same answer as the point method? Would it if the demand curve were actually curved?*

1 It is contrary to normal convention to plot the independent variable (P) on the vertical axis and the dependent variable (Q) on the horizontal axis. The reason why we do this is because there are many other diagrams in economics where Q is the *independent* variable. Such diagrams include cost curves and revenue curves, which we will consider in Chapter 6. As you will see, it is much easier if we *always* plot Q on the horizontal axis even when, as in the case of demand curves, Q is the dependent variable.

| *BOX 2.6 | USING CALCULUS TO CALCULATE THE PRICE ELASTICITY OF DEMAND | EXPLORING ECONOMICS |

(A knowledge of the rules of differentiation is necessary to understand this box. See Appendix 1.)

The following is an example of an equation for a demand curve:

$$Q_d = 60 - 15P + P^2$$

(where Q_d is measured in thousands of units). From this the following table and the graph can be constructed.

P	60	$-15P$	$+P^2$	$=$	Q_d (000s)
0	60	-0	$+0$	$=$	60
1	60	-15	$+1$	$=$	46
2	60	-30	$+4$	$=$	34
3	60	-45	$+9$	$=$	24
4	60	-60	$+16$	$=$	16
5	60	-75	$+25$	$=$	10
6	60	-90	$+36$	$=$	6

Point elasticity can be easily calculated from such a demand equation using calculus. To do this you will need to know the rules of differentiation (see pages A: 9–12). Remember the formula for point elasticity:

$$P\epsilon_D = dQ/dP \times P/Q$$

The term dQ/dP can be calculated by differentiating the demand equation:

Given $Q_d = 60 - 15P + P^2$
then $dQ/dP = -15 + 2P$

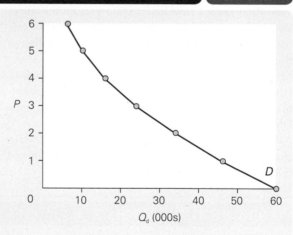

Thus at a price of 3, for example,

$$dQ/dP = -15 + (2 \times 3)$$
$$= -9$$

Thus price elasticity of demand at a price of 3

$$= -9 \times P/Q$$
$$= -9 \times 3/24$$
$$= -9/8 \text{ (which is elastic)}$$

Calculate the price elasticity of demand on this demand curve at a price of (a) 5; (b) 2; (c) 0.

Price elasticity of supply ($P\epsilon_s$)

When price changes, there will be not only a change in the quantity demanded, but also a change in the quantity supplied. Frequently we will want to know just how responsive quantity supplied is to a change in price. The measure we use is the *price elasticity of supply*.

Figure 2.17 shows two supply curves. Curve S_2 is more elastic between any two prices than curve S_1. Thus, when price rises from P_1 to P_2 there is a larger increase in quantity supplied with S_2 (namely, Q_1 to Q_3) than there is with S_1 (namely, Q_1 to Q_2). For any shift in the demand curve there will be a larger change in quantity supplied and a smaller change in price with curve S_2 than with curve S_1. Thus the effect on price and quantity of a shift in the demand curve will depend on the price elasticity of supply.

The *formula for the price elasticity of supply* ($P\epsilon_s$) is: the percentage (or proportionate) change in quantity supplied divided by the percentage (or proportionate) change in price. Putting this in symbols gives

$$P\epsilon_s = \frac{\%\Delta Q_s}{\%\Delta P}$$

In other words, the formula is identical to that for the price elasticity of demand, except that quantity in this case is quantity *supplied*. Thus if a 10 per cent rise in price caused a 25 per cent rise in the quantity supplied, the price elasticity of supply would be

$25\%/10\% = 2.5$

and if a 10 per cent rise in price caused only a 5 per cent rise in the quantity, the price elasticity of supply would be

$5\%/10\% = 0.5$

In the first case, supply is elastic ($P\epsilon_s > 1$); in the second it is inelastic ($P\epsilon_s < 1$). Notice that, unlike the price elasticity of demand, the figure is positive. This is because price and quantity supplied change in the *same* direction.

Determinants of price elasticity of supply

The amount that costs rise as output rises. The less the additional costs of producing additional output, the more firms will be encouraged to produce for a given price rise: the more elastic will supply be.

Supply is thus likely to be elastic if firms have plenty of spare capacity, if they can readily get extra supplies of raw materials, if they can easily switch away from producing alternative products and if they can avoid having to introduce overtime working, at higher rates of pay. The less these conditions apply, the less elastic will supply be.

Time period

- Immediate time period. Firms are unlikely to be able to increase supply by much immediately. Supply is virtually fixed, or can only vary according to available stocks. Supply is highly inelastic.

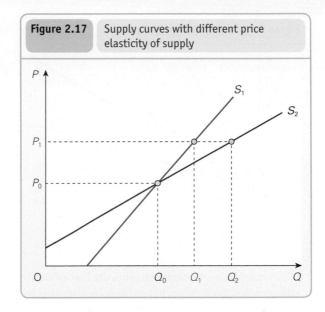

Figure 2.17 Supply curves with different price elasticity of supply

- Short run. If a slightly longer period of time is allowed to elapse, some inputs can be increased (e.g. raw materials) while others will remain fixed (e.g. heavy machinery). Supply can increase somewhat.
- Long run. In the long run, there will be sufficient time for all inputs to be increased and for new firms to enter the industry. Supply, therefore, is likely to be highly elastic in many cases. In some circumstances the long-run supply curve may even slope downwards. (See the section on economies of scale in Chapter 6, pages 162–3.)

The measurement of price elasticity of supply

A vertical supply has zero elasticity. It is totally unresponsive to a change in price. A horizontal supply curve has infinite elasticity. There is no limit to the amount supplied at the price where the curve crosses the vertical axis.

When two supply curves cross, the steeper one will have the lower price elasticity of supply (e.g. curve S_1 in Figure 2.17). Any straight-line supply curve starting at the origin, however, will have an elasticity equal to 1 throughout its length, *irrespective of its slope*. This perhaps rather surprising result is illustrated in Figure 2.18. This shows three supply curves, each with a different slope, but each starting from the origin. On each curve two points are marked. In each case there is the *same* proportionate rise in Q as in P. For example, with curve S_1 a doubling in price from £3 to £6 leads to a doubling of output from 1 unit to 2 units.

Definitions

Price elasticity of supply The responsiveness of quantity supplied to a change in price.

Formula for price elasticity of supply (P_{ϵ_s}) The percentage (or proportionate) change in quantity supplied divided by the percentage (or proportionate) change in price: $\%\Delta Q_s \div \%\Delta P$. Using the arc formula, this is calculated as $\Delta Q_s/\text{average } Q_s \div \Delta P/\text{average } P$

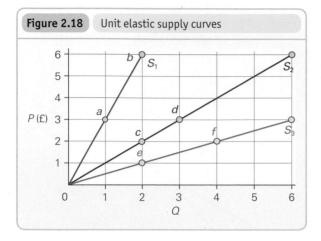

Figure 2.18 Unit elastic supply curves

This demonstrates nicely that it is not the *slope* of a curve that determines its elasticity, but its proportionate change.

Other supply curves' elasticities will vary along their length. In such cases we have to refer to the elasticity either between two points on the curve, or at a specific point. Calculating elasticity between two points will involve the **arc method**. Calculating elasticity at a point will involve the point method. These two methods are just the same for supply curves as for demand curves: the formulae are the same, only the term Q now refers to quantity supplied rather than quantity demanded.

Income elasticity of demand

So far we have looked at the responsiveness of demand and supply to a change in price. But price is just one of the determinants of demand and supply. In theory, we could look at the responsiveness of demand or supply to a change in *any* one of their determinants. We could have a whole range of different types of elasticity of demand and supply.

KEY IDEA 9

Elasticity. The responsiveness of one variable (e.g. demand) to a change in another (e.g. price). This concept is fundamental to understanding how markets work. The more elastic variables are, the more responsive is the market to changing circumstances.

In practice, there are just two other elasticities that are particularly useful to us, and both are demand elasticities.

The first is the *income elasticity of demand* (Y_{ϵ_D}). This measures the responsiveness of demand to a change in consumer incomes (Y). It enables us to predict how much the demand curve will shift for a given change in income. The *formula for the income elasticity of demand* is: the percentage (or proportionate) change in demand divided by the percentage (or proportionate) change in income. Putting this in symbols gives

$$Y_{\epsilon_D} = \frac{\%\Delta Q_D}{\%\Delta Y}$$

Definitions

Formula for price elasticity of supply (arc method)
ΔQ_s/average $Q_s \div \Delta P$/average P.

Income elasticity of demand The responsiveness of demand to a change in consumer incomes.

Formula for income elasticity of demand (Y_{ϵ_D}) The percentage (or proportionate) change in demand divided by the percentage (or proportionate) change in income: $\%\Delta Q_D \div \%\Delta Y$.

In other words, the formula is identical to that for the price elasticity of demand, except that we are dividing the change in demand by the change in income that caused it rather than by a change in price. Thus if a 2 per cent rise in income caused an 8 per cent rise in a product's demand, then its income elasticity of demand would be:

8%/2% = 4

The major determinant of income elasticity of demand is the degree of 'necessity' of the good. In a developed country, the demand for luxury goods expands rapidly as people's incomes rise, whereas the demand for basic goods rises only a little. Thus items such as designer handbags and foreign holidays have a high income elasticity of demand, whereas items such as vegetables and socks have a low income elasticity of demand.

If income elasticity of demand is positive and greater than 1 then this tells us that the share of consumers' income spent on the good increases as their income rises. If the figure is positive but less than 1 then this tells us that the share of consumers' income spend on the good falls as income rises. In both of these cases people demand more of the good as incomes rise. However, the demand for some goods actually *decreases* as people's incomes rise beyond a certain level. These are inferior goods such as supermarkets' 'value lines' and bus journeys. As people earn more, so they switch to better quality products. Unlike **normal goods**, which have a positive income elasticity of demand, **inferior goods** have a negative income elasticity of demand.

 Look ahead to Table 3.1 (page 96). It shows the income elasticity of demand for various foodstuffs. Explain the difference in the figures for milk, bread and fresh fish.

Income elasticity of demand is an important concept to firms considering the future size of the market for their product. If the product has a high income elasticity of demand, sales are likely to expand rapidly as national income rises, but may also fall significantly if the economy moves into recession. (See Case Study 2.5, *Income elasticity of demand and the balance of payments*, on the student website. This shows how the concept of income elasticity of demand can help us understand why so many developing countries have chronic balance of payments problems.)

Cross-price elasticity of demand ($C\epsilon_{D_{AB}}$)

This is often known by its less cumbersome title of *cross elasticity of demand*. It is a measure of the responsiveness of demand for one product to a change in the price of another (either a substitute or a complement). It enables us to predict how much the demand curve for the first product will shift when the price of the second product changes.

The *formula for the cross-price elasticity of demand* ($C\epsilon_{D_{AB}}$) is: the percentage (or proportionate) change in demand for good A divided by the percentage (or proportionate) change in price of good B. Putting this in symbols gives

$$C\epsilon_{D_{AB}} = \frac{\%\Delta Q_{D_A}}{\%\Delta P_B}$$

If good B is a *substitute* for good A, A's demand will *rise* as B's price rises. In this case, cross elasticity will be a positive figure. For example, if the demand for butter rose by 2 per cent when the price of margarine (a substitute) rose by 8 per cent, then the cross elasticity of demand for butter with respect to margarine would be

2%/8% = 0.25

If good B is *complementary* to good A, however, A's demand will *fall* as B's price rises and thus as the quantity of B demanded falls. In this case, cross elasticity of demand will be a negative figure. For example, if a 4 per cent rise in the price of bread led to a 3 per cent fall in demand for butter, the cross elasticity of demand for butter with respect to bread would be

−3%/4% = −0.75

The major determinant of cross elasticity of demand is the closeness of the substitute or complement. The closer it is, the bigger will be the effect on the first good of a change in the price of the substitute or complement, and hence the greater the cross elasticity – either positive or negative. For example, a figure of 1.169 has been estimated for the cross-price elasticity of demand for on-trade spirits (i.e. whisky, vodka, etc.) with respect to the price of on-trade beer. This suggests they are moderately close substitutes in consumption.

Firms need to know the cross elasticity of demand for their product when considering the effect on the demand for their product of a change in the price of a rival's product or of a complementary product. These are vital pieces of information for firms when making their production plans.

Definitions

Normal goods Goods whose demand increases as consumer incomes increase. They have a positive income elasticity of demand. Luxury goods will have a higher income elasticity of demand than more basic goods.

Inferior goods Goods whose demand decreases as consumer incomes increase. Such goods have a negative income elasticity of demand.

Cross-price elasticity of demand The responsiveness of demand for one good to a change in the price of another.

Formula for cross-price elasticity of demand ($C_{\epsilon_{D_{AB}}}$) The percentage (or proportionate) change in demand for good A divided by the percentage (or proportionate) change in price of good B: $\%\Delta Q_{DA} \div \%\Delta P_B$.

| THRESHOLD CONCEPT 6 | ELASTICITY: OF A VARIABLE TO A CHANGE IN A DETERMINANT | THINKING LIKE AN ECONOMIST |

As we have seen in the case of price elasticity of demand, elasticity measures the responsiveness of one variable (e.g. quantity demanded) to change in another (e.g. price). This concept is fundamental to understanding how markets work. The more elastic variables are, the more responsive is the market to changing circumstances.

Elasticity is more than just a technical term. It's not difficult to learn the formula

$$P\epsilon_D = \frac{\%\Delta Q_D}{\%\Delta P}$$

in the case of price elasticity of demand, and then to interpret this as

$$P\epsilon_D = \frac{\Delta Q_D}{\text{average } Q_D} \div \frac{\Delta P}{\text{average } P}$$

using the arc elasticity method, or as

$$P\epsilon_D = \frac{dQ_D}{dP} \times \frac{P}{Q}$$

using the point elasticity method.

We can also very simply state the general formula for any elasticity as

$$\epsilon_{XY} = \frac{\%\Delta X}{\%\Delta Y}$$

where the formula refers to the responsiveness of variable X to a change in variable Y (where X could be quantity supplied or demanded, and Y could be price, income, the price of substitutes, or any other determinant of demand or supply). Again, we could use the arc or point elasticity methods. Although students often find it hard at first to use the formulae, it's largely a question of practice in mastering them.

What makes elasticity a *threshold concept* is that it lies at the heart of how economic systems operate. In a market economy, prices act as signals that demand or supply has changed. They also act as an incentive for people to respond to the new circumstances. The greater the elasticity of demand, the bigger will be the response to a change in supply; the greater the elasticity of supply, the bigger will be the response to a change in demand.

Understanding elasticity and what determines its magnitude helps us understand how an economy is likely to respond to the ever-changing circumstances of the real world.

In a perfect market economy, firms face an infinitely elastic (horizontal) demand curve: they are price takers (see pages 59–60 and Figure 2.13(b)). What this means is that they have no power to affect prices: they are highly dependent on market forces.

By contrast, big businesses (and some small ones too) are in a very different position. If there are only one or two firms in a market, each is likely to face a relatively inelastic demand. This gives them the power to raise prices and make more profit. As we have seen, if demand is price inelastic, then raising price will increase the firm's revenue (see Figure 2.13(b)). Even if demand is elastic (but still downward sloping) the firm could still increase profit by raising prices, provided that the fall in revenue was less than the reduction in costs from producing less. The general point here is that the less elastic is the firm's demand curve, the greater will be its power to raise prices and make a bigger profit.

It's not just price elasticity of demand that helps us understand how market economies operate. In a perfect market, market supply is likely to be highly elastic, especially in the long run after firms have had time to enter the industry. Thus, if a new lower-cost technique is discovered, which increases profits in an industry, new firms will enter the market, attracted by the higher profits. This increased supply will then have the effect of driving prices down and hence profit rates will fall back. What this means is that in highly competitive industries firms are very responsive to changing economic circumstances. If they are not, they are likely to be forced out of business; it's a question of survival of the fittest. We explore this process in more detail in section 7.2.

If there is less competition, firms have an easier life. But what is good for them may be bad for us as consumers. We may end up paying higher prices and having poorer quality goods – although not necessarily. We explore this in sections 7.3 and 7.4 and in Chapter 8.

So, getting to grips with elasticity is not just about doing calculations. It's about understanding the very essence of how economies operate.

1. *What would you understand by the 'wage elasticity of demand for labour'? How would the magnitude of this elasticity affect the working of the market for (a) plumbers and (b) footballers?*
2. *How can income elasticity of demand help explain how the structure of economies changes over the years?*

Another application of the concept of cross elasticity of demand is in the field of international trade and the balance of payments. How does a change in the price of domestic goods affect the demand for imports? If there is a high cross elasticity of demand for imports (because they are close substitutes for home-produced goods), and if prices at home rise due to inflation, the demand for imports will rise substantially, thus worsening the balance of trade.

Which are likely to have the highest cross elasticity of demand: two brands of coffee, or coffee and tea?

*LOOKING AT THE MATHS

Calculating income and cross-price elasticities from a demand equation

The following demand equation relates quantity demanded (Q_A) for good A to its own price (P_A), consumer income (Y) and the price of a substitute good B (P_B).

$$Q_A = a - bP_A + cY + eP_B$$

Note that this is a 'linear' equation because it has no power terms, such as P^2 or Y^2. The formula[1] for income elasticity of demand for good A will be

$$Y\epsilon_D = \frac{\partial Q_A}{\partial Y} \cdot \frac{Y}{Q_A}$$

But since the term $\partial Q_A / \partial Y$ represents the amount that Q_A will change for a given change in Y (i.e. the value of c), then

$$Y\epsilon_D = c\frac{Y}{Q_A}$$

Similarly, the formula for cross-price elasticity of demand for good A with respect to good B will be

$$C\epsilon_{D_{AB}} = \frac{\partial Q_A}{\partial P_B} \cdot \frac{P_B}{Q_A} = e\frac{P_B}{Q_A}$$

A worked example of these two formulae is given in Maths Case 2.2 on the student website. We can also use calculus to work out the two elasticities for both linear and non-linear demand equations. A worked example of this is given in Maths Case 2.3 on the student website.

1 Note that in this case we use the symbol '∂' rather than 'd' to represent an infinitesimally small change. This is the convention when the equation contains more than one independent variable (in this case P_A, Y and P_B). The term $\partial Q_A / \partial Y$ is the 'partial derivative' (see page A:13) and refers to the rate of change of Q_A to just one of the three variables (in this case Y).

Section summary

1. Elasticity is a measure of the responsiveness of demand (or supply) to a change in one of the determinants.

2. It is defined as the proportionate change in quantity demanded (or supplied) divided by the proportionate change in the determinant.

3. If quantity changes proportionately more than the determinant, the figure for elasticity will be greater than 1 (ignoring the sign): it is elastic. If the quantity changes proportionately less than the determinant, the figure for elasticity will be less than 1: it is inelastic. If they change by the same proportion, the elasticity has a value of 1: it is unit elastic.

4. Price elasticity of demand measures the responsiveness of demand to a change in price. Given that demand curves are downward sloping, price elasticity of demand will have a negative value. Demand will be more elastic the greater the number and closeness of substitute goods, the higher the proportion of income spent on the good and the longer the time period that elapses after the change in price.

5. When demand is price elastic, a rise in price will lead to a reduction in total expenditure on the good and hence a reduction in the total revenue of producers.

6. Demand curves normally have different elasticities along their length. We can thus normally refer only to the specific value for elasticity between two points on the curve or at a single point.

7. Elasticity measured between two points is known as arc elasticity. When applied to price elasticity of demand the formula is

$$\frac{\Delta Q_d}{\text{average } Q_d} \div \frac{\Delta P}{\text{average } P}$$

*8. Elasticity measured at a point is known as *point elasticity*. When applied to price elasticity of demand the formula is

$$\frac{dQ}{dP} \times \frac{P}{Q}$$

where dQ/dP is the inverse of the slope of the tangent to the demand curve at the point in question.

9. Price elasticity of supply measures the responsiveness of supply to a change in price. It has a positive value. Supply will be more elastic the less costs per unit rise as output rises and the longer the time period.

10. Income elasticity of demand measures the responsiveness of demand to a change in income. For normal goods it has a positive value. Demand will be more income elastic the more luxurious the good and the less rapidly demand is satisfied as consumption increases. For inferior goods, income elasticity has a negative value.

11. Cross-price elasticity of demand measures the responsiveness of demand for one good to a change in the price of another. For substitute goods the value will be positive; for complements it will be negative. The cross-price elasticity will be higher the closer the two goods are as substitutes or complements.

2.5 THE TIME DIMENSION

The full adjustment of price, demand and supply to a situation of disequilibrium will not be instantaneous. It is necessary, therefore, to analyse the time path which supply takes in responding to changes in demand, and which demand takes in responding to changes in supply.

Short-run and long-run adjustment

As we saw in the previous section, elasticity varies with the time period under consideration. The reason is that producers and consumers take time to respond to a change in price. The longer the time period, the bigger the response, and thus the greater the elasticity of supply and demand.

This is illustrated in Figures 2.19 and 2.20. In both cases, as equilibrium moves from points *a* to *b* to *c*, there is a large short-run price change (P_1 to P_2) and a small short-run quantity change (Q_1 to Q_2), but a small long-run price change (P_1 to P_3) and a large long-run quantity change (Q_1 to Q_3).

Price expectations and speculation

In a world of shifting demand and supply curves, prices do not stay the same. Sometimes they go up; sometimes they come down.

If people think prices are likely to change in the foreseeable future, this will affect the behaviour of buyers and sellers *now*. If, for example, it is now December and you are thinking of buying a new television, you might decide to wait until the January sales, and in the meantime make do with your

set. If, on the other hand, in December you see a summer holiday advertised that you like, you might well book it then and not wait until nearer the summer for fear that the price will have gone up by then. Thus a belief that prices will go up will cause people to buy now; a belief that prices will come down will cause them to wait.

The reverse applies to sellers. If you are thinking of selling your house and prices are falling, you will want to sell it as quickly as possible. If, on the other hand, prices are rising sharply, you will wait as long as possible so as to get the highest price. Thus a belief that prices will come down will cause people to sell now; a belief that prices will go up will cause them to wait.

> **KEY IDEA 10**
>
> ***People's actions are influenced by their expectations.*** People respond not just to what is happening now (such as a change in price), but to what they anticipate will happen in the future.

This behaviour of looking into the future and making buying and selling decisions based on your predictions is called *speculation*. Speculation is often based on current

Definition

Speculation Where people make buying or selling decisions based on their anticipations of future prices.

Figure 2.19 Response of supply to an increase in demand

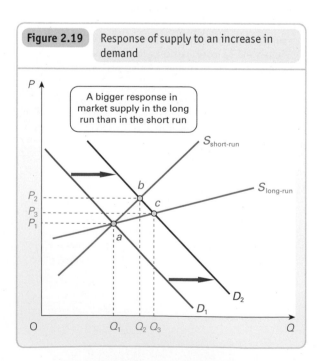

Figure 2.20 Response of demand to an increase in supply

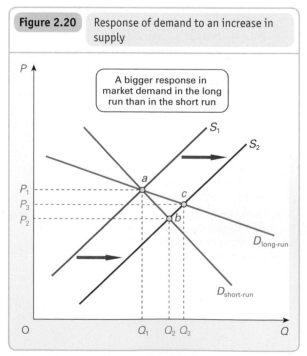

trends in prices. If prices are currently rising, people may try to decide whether they are about to peak and go back down again, or whether they are likely to go on rising. Having made their prediction, they will then act on it. Their actions will then affect demand and supply, which in turn will affect price. Speculation is commonplace in many markets: the stock exchange, the foreign exchange market and the housing market are three examples.

Sometimes people will take advantage of expected price rises purely to make money and have no intention of keeping the item they have bought. For example, if shares in a particular company are expected to rise in price, people may buy them now while they are cheap and sell them later when the price has risen, thereby making a profit from the difference in price.

Similarly, people will sometimes take advantage of expected price reductions by selling something now only to buy it back later. For example, if you own shares and expect their price to fall, you may sell them now and buy them back later when their price has fallen. Again, you make a profit from the difference in price.

Sometimes the term *speculation* is used in this narrower sense of buying (or selling) commodities or financial assets simply to make money from later selling them (or buying them back) again at a higher (or lower) price. The term **speculators** usually refers to people engaged in such activities.

In the extreme case, speculators need not part with any money. If they buy an item and sell it back fairly soon at a higher price, they may be able to use the money from the sale to pay the original seller: just pocketing the difference. Alternatively, speculators may sell an item they do not even possess, as long as they can buy it back in time (at a lower price) to hand it over to the original purchaser. Again, they simply pocket the difference in price.

It may sound as if speculators are on to a good thing, and often they are, but speculation does carry risks: the predictions of individual speculators may turn out to be wrong, and then they could make losses rather than profits.

Nevertheless, speculators on average tend to gain rather than lose. The reason is that speculation tends to be *self-fulfilling*. In other words, the actions of speculators tend to bring about the very effect on prices that they had anticipated. For example, if speculators believe that the price of Barclays shares is about to rise, they will buy some. But by doing this they will contribute to an increase in demand and ensure that the price *will* rise; the prophecy has become self-fulfilling.

Speculation can either help to reduce price fluctuations or aggravate them: it can be stabilising or destabilising.

Stabilising speculation

Speculation will tend to have a **stabilising** effect on price fluctuations when suppliers and/or demanders believe that a change in price is only *temporary*.

An initial fall in price.   In Figure 2.21 demand has shifted from D_1 to D_2; equilibrium has moved from point *a* to point *b*, and price has fallen to P_2. How do people react to this fall in price?

Given that they believe this fall in price to be only temporary, suppliers *hold back,* expecting prices to rise again: supply shifts from S_1 to S_2. After all, why supply now when, by waiting, they could get a higher price?

Definitions

Speculators People who buy (or sell) commodities or financial assets with the intention of profiting by selling them (or buying them back) at a later date at a higher (lower) price.

Self-fulfilling speculation The actions of speculators tend to cause the very effect that they had anticipated.

Stabilising speculation Where the actions of speculators tend to reduce price fluctuations.

Figure 2.21   Stabilising speculation: initial price fall

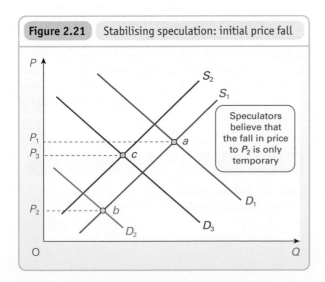

Figure 2.22   Stabilising speculation: initial price rise

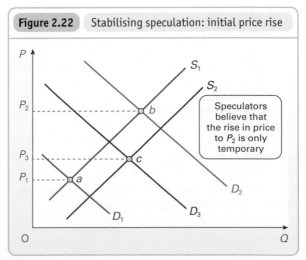

Buyers *increase* their purchases, to take advantage of the temporary fall in price. Demand shifts from D_2 to D_3.

The equilibrium moves to point *c*, with price rising back towards P_1.

An initial rise in price.   In Figure 2.22 demand has shifted from D_1 to D_2. Price has risen from P_1 to P_2.

Suppliers bring their goods to market now, before price falls again. Supply shifts from S_1 to S_2. Demanders, however, hold back until price falls. Demand shifts from D_2 to D_3. The equilibrium moves to point *c*, with price falling back towards P_1.

An example.   A good example of stabilising speculation is that which occurs in agricultural commodity markets. Take the case of wheat. When it is harvested in the autumn, there will be a plentiful supply. If all this wheat were to be put on the market, the price would fall to a very low level. Later in the year, when most of the wheat would have been sold, the price would then rise to a very high level. This is all easily predictable.

So what do farmers do? The answer is that they speculate. When the wheat is harvested, they know price will tend to fall, and so instead of bringing it all to market they put some into store. The more the price falls, the more they will put into store *anticipating that the price will later rise*. But this holding back of supplies prevents prices from falling. In other words, it stabilises prices.

Later in the year, when the price begins to rise, they will gradually release grain onto the market from the stores. The more the price rises, the more they will release on to the market *anticipating that the price will fall again by the time of the next harvest*. But this releasing of supplies will again stabilise prices by preventing them from rising so much.

Rather than the farmers doing the speculation, it could be done by grain merchants. When there is a glut of wheat in the autumn, and prices are relatively low, they buy wheat on the grain market and put it into store. When there is a shortage in the spring and summer they sell wheat from their stores. In this way they stabilise prices just as the farmers did when they were the ones who operated the stores.

 In Figures 2.21 and 2.22, the initial change in price was caused by a shift in the demand curve. Redraw these two diagrams to illustrate the situation where the initial change in price was caused by a shift in the supply curve (as would be the case in the wheat market that we have just considered).

Destabilising speculation

Speculation will tend to have a ***destabilising*** effect on price fluctuations when suppliers and/or buyers believe that a change in price heralds similar changes to come.

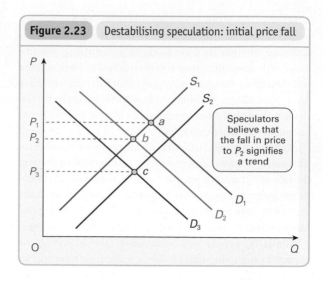

Figure 2.23   Destabilising speculation: initial price fall

Speculators believe that the fall in price to P_2 signifies a trend

An initial fall in price.   In Figure 2.23 demand has shifted from D_1 to D_2 and price has fallen from P_1 to P_2. This time, believing that the fall in price heralds further falls in price to come, suppliers sell now before the price does fall. Supply shifts from S_1 to S_2. And demanders wait: they wait until price does fall further. Demand shifts from D_2 to D_3.

Their actions ensure that price does fall further: to P_3.

An initial rise in price.   In Figure 2.24 a price rise from P_1 to P_2 is caused by a rise in demand from D_1 to D_2. Suppliers wait until price rises further. Supply shifts from S_1 to S_2. Demanders buy now before any further rise in price. Demand shifts from D_2 to D_3. As a result, price continues to rise: to P_3.

In section 2.3 we examined the housing market (see Box 2.2). In this market, speculation is frequently destabilising. Assume that people see house prices beginning to move upwards. This might be the result of increased demand brought about by a cut in mortgage interest rates or by growth in the economy. People may well believe that the rise in house prices signals a boom in the housing market: that prices will go on rising. Potential buyers will thus try to buy as soon as possible before prices rise any further. This will increase demand (as in Figure 2.24) and will thus lead to even bigger price rises. This is precisely what happened in the UK housing market in 1999–2007 and from mid-2013 (see chart in Box 2.2 on page 50). Conversely, in early 2008 prices started to fall; potential buyers believed that they would fall

Definition

Destabilising speculation Where the actions of speculators tend to make price movements larger.

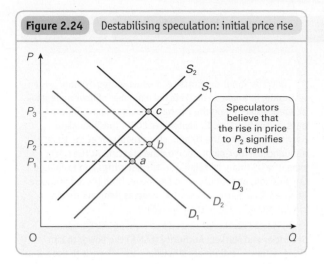

Figure 2.24 Destabilising speculation: initial price rise

Speculators believe that the rise in price to P_2 signifies a trend

further and thus held off entering the market, leading to even bigger price falls.

Estate agents consistently 'talk up' the housing market, often predicting price rises when other commentators are more cautious. Explain why they might have a vested interest in doing so.

Conclusion

In some circumstances, then, the action of speculators can help to keep price fluctuations to a minimum (stabilising speculation). This is most likely when markets are relatively stable in the first place, with only moderate underlying shifts in demand and supply.

In other circumstances, however, speculation can make price fluctuations much worse. This is most likely in times of uncertainty, when there are significant changes in the determinants of demand and supply. Given this uncertainty, people may see price changes as signifying some trend. They then 'jump on the bandwagon' and do what the rest are doing, further fuelling the rise or fall in price.

Redraw Figures 2.23 and 2.24 assuming, as in the previous question, that the initial change in price was caused by a shift in the supply curve.

Dealing with uncertainty and risk

When price changes are likely to occur, buyers and sellers will try to anticipate them. Unfortunately, on many occasions no one can be certain just what these price changes will be. Take the case of stocks and shares. If you anticipate that the price of, say, Marks & Spencer shares is likely to go up substantially in the near future, you may well decide to buy some now and then sell them later after the price has risen. But you cannot be certain that they will go up in price: they may fall instead. If you buy the shares, therefore, you will be taking a gamble.

Now, gambles can be of two types. The first is where you know the odds. Let us take the simplest case of a gamble on the toss of a coin. Heads you win; tails you lose. You know that the odds of winning are precisely 50 per cent. If you bet on the toss of a coin, you are said to be operating under conditions of **risk**. *Risk is when the probability of an outcome is known.* Risk itself is a measure of the *variability* of an outcome. For example, if you bet £1 on the toss of a coin, such that heads you win £1 and tails you lose £1, then the variability is −£1 to +£1.

The second form of gamble is the more usual. This is where the odds are not known or are known only roughly. Gambling on the stock exchange is like this. You may have a good idea that a share will go up in price, but is it a 90 per cent chance, an 80 per cent chance or what? You are not certain. Gambling under this sort of condition is known as operating under **uncertainty**. *This is when the probability of an outcome is not known.*

You may well disapprove of gambling and want to dismiss people who engage in it as foolish or morally wrong. But 'gambling' is not just confined to horses, cards, roulette and the like. Risk and uncertainty pervade the whole of economic life, and decisions are constantly having to be made whose outcome cannot be known for certain. Even the most morally upright person will still have to decide which career to go into, whether and when to buy a house, or even something as trivial as whether or not to take an umbrella when going out. Each of these decisions and thousands of others are made under conditions of uncertainty (or occasionally risk).

Definitions

Risk When a (desirable) outcome of an action may or may not occur, but the probability of its occurring is known. The lower the probability, the greater the risk involved in taking the action.

Uncertainty When an outcome may or may not occur and its probability of occurring is not known.

BOX 2.7   SHORT SELLING

Gambling on a fall in share prices

A form of speculation that can be very damaging to stock markets is the practice of *short selling*. This is where people take advantage of anticipated falls in share prices by selling shares they do not possess. How does this work?

Assume that a share price is currently £10 per share and traders on the stock market believe that the price is about to fall. They want to take advantage of this but don't possess any. What they do is borrow shares from dealers who do own some and agree to return them on a specified date. They pay a fee for doing this. In the meantime they sell the shares on the market at the current price of £10 and wait for it to fall. They are now 'short' of the shares (i.e. they don't possess them but still owe them).

Assume that just before the agreed time comes for returning the shares the price has fallen to £8. The trader then buys the shares, returns them to the dealer who had lent them and pockets the difference of £2 (minus the fee).

Although anyone can short sell shares, it is largely traders from various financial institutions who engage in this practice. Huge bonuses can be earned from their employers if the short selling is profitable. This encourages an atmosphere of risk-taking and looking to short-term gains rather than providing long-term capital to firms.

Short selling in the banking crisis of 2008

The practice of short selling had become rife and added to the instability of markets, driving share prices down that were anticipated to fall. This was a particular problem in 2008, when worries about bad debts and losses in the banking sector led many traders to short sell the shares of banks and other financial institutions felt to be most at risk.

The short selling of Halifax Bank of Scotland (HBOS) shares in September 2008 was a major contributing factor to the collapse in its share price. HBOS, the UK's largest mortgage lender, had been suffering losses as a result of falling house prices and difficulties of many house owners in keeping up with their monthly mortgage payments. The share price plummeted by over 70 per cent in the space of a few days. The fall was driven on by speculation, much of it short selling. On 17 September it was announced that HBOS would be taken over by Lloyds TSB.

Concerns about the practice of short selling driving instability in financial markets led a number of governments – or agencies acting on their behalf – to introduce temporary bans on the practice. In September 2008, the Financial Services Authority, the UK industry's regulator at the time, announced a four-month ban on the practice. At the same time, the US financial regulator, the Securities and Exchange Commission, announced a similar move. Both these bans were imposed for a matter of months, whereas Denmark held a similar policy for more than two years.

In May 2012, the EU passed a law giving the European Securities and Markets Authority (ESMA) the power to ban short selling in emergency situations: i.e. where it threatens the stability of the EU financial system. The UK government opposed the legislation but the EU Court of Justice rejected the challenge in 2014.

Is short selling always profitable?

Short selling, as with other forms of speculation, is a type of gambling. If you gamble on a price fall and the price does fall, your gamble pays off and you make a profit. If you get it wrong, however, and the price rises, you will make a loss. In the case of short selling, you would have to buy the shares (to give back to the lender) at a higher price than you sold them for.

This is just what happened in September 2008. With central banks around the world supporting markets, with the US government announcing that it would take over the bad debts of banks and with future short selling temporarily banned, share prices rapidly increased. The FTSE rose by a record 8.8 per cent on 19 September. Those with 'short positions' – i.e. those who had sold shares they had borrowed – then had to buy them back at a much higher price. Losses of hundreds of millions of pounds were made by short sellers. But they gained little sympathy from the general public, who blamed their 'greed' for much of the falls in share prices of the previous weeks.

1. *Why would owners of shares, such as pension funds, lend them to short sellers rather than selling the shares themselves and then buying them back later?*
2. *What are the potential benefits of short selling for the economy?*
3. *'Naked' short selling has been banned in many countries. What exactly is naked short selling?*

Definition

Short selling (or shorting) Where investors borrow an asset, such as shares, oil contracts or foreign currency; sell the asset, hoping the price will soon fall; then buy it back later and return it to the lender. Assuming the price has fallen, the short seller will make a profit of the difference (minus any fees). There is always the danger, however, that the price may have risen, in which case the short seller will make a loss.

BOX 2.8   **DEALING IN FUTURES MARKETS**

A way of reducing uncertainty

One way of reducing or even eliminating uncertainty is by dealing in **futures** or **forward markets**. Let us examine first the activities of sellers and then those of buyers.

Sellers

Suppose you are a farmer and want to store grain to sell at some time in the future, expecting to get a better price then than now. The trouble is that there is a chance that the price will go down. Given this uncertainty, you may be unwilling to take a gamble.

An answer to your problem is provided by the *commodity futures market*. This is a market where prices are agreed between sellers and buyers today for delivery at some specified date in the future.

For example, if it is 20 October today, you could be quoted a price today for delivery in six months' time (i.e. on 20 April). This is known as the six-month **future price**. Assume that the six-month future price is £160 per tonne. If you agree to this price and make a six-month forward contract, you are agreeing to sell a specified amount of wheat at £160 on 20 April. No matter what happens to the **spot price** (i.e. the current market price) in the meantime, your selling price has been agreed. The spot price could have fallen to £140 (or risen to £180) by April, but your selling price when 20 April arrives is fixed at £160. There is thus *no risk to you whatsoever of the price going down*. You will, of course, have lost out if the spot price is *more* than £160 in April.

Buyers

Now suppose that you are a flour miller. In order to plan your expenditures, you would like to know the price you will have to pay for wheat, not just today, but also at various future dates. In other words, if you want to take delivery of wheat at some time in the future, you would like a price quoted *now*. You would like the risks removed of prices going *up*.

Let us assume that today (20 October) you want to *buy* the same amount of wheat on 20 April that a farmer wishes to sell on that same date. If you agree to the £160 future price, a future contract can be made with the farmer. You are then guaranteed that purchase price, no matter what happens to the spot price in the meantime. There is thus *no risk to you whatsoever of the price going up*. You will, of course, have lost out if the spot price is *less* than £160 in April.

The determination of the future price

Prices in the futures market are determined in the same way as in other markets: by demand and supply. For example, the six-month wheat price or the three-month coffee price will be that which equates the demand for

those futures with the supply. If the five-month sugar price is currently £220 per tonne and people expect by then, because of an anticipated good beet harvest, that the spot price for sugar will be £170 per tonne, there will be few who want to buy the futures at £220 (and many who want to sell). This excess of supply of futures over demand will push the price down.

Speculators

Many people operate in the futures market who never actually handle the commodities themselves. They are neither producers nor users of the commodities. They merely speculate. Such speculators may be individuals, but they are more likely to be financial institutions.

Let us take a simple example. Suppose that the six-month (April) coffee price is £1300 per tonne and that you, as a speculator, believe that the spot price of coffee is likely to rise above that level between now (October) and six months' time. You thus decide to buy 20 tonnes of April coffee futures now.

But you have no intention of taking delivery. After four months, let us say, true to your prediction, the spot price (February) has risen and as a result the April price (and other future prices) have risen too. You thus decide to *sell* 20 tonnes of April (two-month) coffee futures, whose price, let us say, is £1500. You are now 'covered'.

When April comes, what happens? You have agreed to buy 20 tonnes of coffee at £1300 per tonne and to sell 20 tonnes of coffee at £1500 per tonne. All you do is to hand the futures contract to buy to the person to whom you agreed to sell. They sort out delivery between them and you make £200 per tonne profit.

If, however, your prediction had been wrong and the price had *fallen,* you would have made a loss. You would have been forced to sell coffee contracts at a lower price than you bought them.

Speculators in the futures market thus incur risks, unlike the sellers and buyers of the commodities, for whom the futures market eliminates risk. Financial institutions offering futures contracts will charge for the service: for taking on the risks.

 If speculators believed that the price of cocoa in six months was going to be below the six-month future price quoted today, how would they act?

Definitions

Futures or forward market A market in which contracts are made to buy or sell at some future date at a price agreed today.

Future price A price agreed today at which an item (e.g. commodities) will be exchanged at some set date in the future.

Spot price The current market price.

KEY IDEA 11

People's actions are influenced by their attitudes towards risk. Many decisions are taken under conditions of risk or uncertainty. Generally, the lower the probability of (or the more uncertain) the desired outcome of an action, the less likely people will be to undertake the action.

Give some examples of decisions you have taken recently that were made under conditions of uncertainty. With hindsight do you think you made the right decisions?

We shall be examining how risk and uncertainty affect economic decisions on several occasions throughout the book. For example, in Chapter 5 we will see how it affects people's attitudes and actions as consumers and how taking out insurance can help to reduce their uncertainty. At this point, however, let us focus on firms' attitudes when supplying goods.

Stock holding as a way of reducing the problem of uncertainty

A simple way that suppliers can reduce the problem of uncertainty is by holding stocks. Take the case of the wheat farmers we saw in the previous section. At the time when they are planting the wheat in the spring, they are uncertain as to what the price of wheat will be when they bring it to market. If they keep no stores of wheat, they will just have to accept whatever the market price happens to be at harvest time. If, however, they have storage facilities, they can put the wheat into store if the price is low and then wait until the price goes up. Alternatively, if the price of wheat is high at harvest time, they can sell the wheat straight away. In other words, they can choose the time to sell.

Section summary

1. A complete understanding of markets must take into account the time dimension.

2. Given that producers and consumers take a time to respond fully to price changes, we can identify different equilibria after the lapse of different lengths of time. Generally, short-run supply and demand tend to be less price elastic than long-run supply and demand. As a result, any shifts in *D* or *S* curves tend to have a relatively bigger effect on price in the short run and a relatively bigger effect on quantity in the long run.

3. People often anticipate price changes and this will affect the amount they demand or supply. This speculation will tend to stabilise price fluctuations if people believe that the price changes are only temporary. However, speculation will tend to destabilise these fluctuations (i.e. make them more severe) if people believe that prices are likely to continue to move in the same direction as at present (at least for some time).

4. Many economic decisions are taken under conditions of risk or uncertainty. Uncertainty over future prices can be tackled by holding stocks. When prices are low, the stocks can be built up. When they are high, stocks can be sold.

END OF CHAPTER QUESTIONS

1. The weekly demand and supply schedules for T-shirts (in millions) in a free market are as follows:

Price (£)	8	7	6	5	4	3	2	1
Quantity demanded	6	8	10	12	14	16	18	20
Quantity supplied	18	16	14	12	10	8	6	4

(a) What are the equilibrium price and quantity?

(b) Assume that changes in fashion cause the demand for T-shirts to rise by 4 million at each price. What will be the new equilibrium price and quantity? Has equilibrium quantity risen as much as the rise in demand? Explain why or why not.

(c) Now plot the data in the table and mark the equilibrium. Also plot the new data corresponding to (b).

2. On separate demand and supply diagrams for bread, sketch the effects of the following: (a) a rise in the price of wheat; (b) a rise in the price of butter and margarine; (c) a rise in the price of rice, pasta and potatoes. In each case, state your assumptions.

3. For what reasons might the price of overseas holidays rise? In each case, identify whether these are reasons affecting demand, supply, or both.

4. If both demand and supply change, and if we know which direction they have shifted but not how much, why is it that we will be able to predict the direction in which *either* price *or* quantity will change, but not both? (Clue: consider the four possible combinations and sketch them if necessary: (a) *D* left, *S* left; (b) *D* right, *S* right; (c) *D* left, *S* right; (d) *D* right, *S* left.)

5. If you were the owner of a clothes shop, how would you set about deciding what prices to charge for each garment at the end-of-season sale?

6. Is there any truth in the saying that the price of a good is a reflection of its quality?

7. Assume that oil begins to run out and that extraction becomes more expensive. Trace through the effects of this on the market for oil and the market for other fuels.

8. Why are both the price elasticity of demand and the price elasticity of supply likely to be greater in the long run?

9. Which of the following will have positive signs and which will have negative ones: (a) price elasticity of demand; (b) income elasticity of demand (normal good); (c) income elasticity of demand (inferior good); (d) cross elasticity of demand (with respect to changes in price of a substitute good); (e) cross elasticity of demand (with respect to changes in price of a complementary good); (f) price elasticity of supply?

10. What are the advantages and disadvantages of speculation from the point of view of (a) the consumer; (b) firms?

Online resources

Additional case studies on the student website

2.1 **Adjusting to oil price shocks.** A case study showing how demand and supply analysis can be used to examine the price changes in the oil market since 1973.

2.2 **Coffee prices.** An examination of the coffee market and the implications of fluctuations in the coffee harvest for growers and coffee drinkers.

2.3 **Shall we put up our price?** This uses the concept of price elasticity of demand to explain why prices are higher where firms face little or no competition.

2.4 **Response to changes in petrol and ethanol prices in Brazil.** This case examines how drivers with 'flex-fuel' cars responded to changes in the relative price of two fuels: petrol and ethanol (made from sugar cane).

2.5 **Income elasticity of demand and the balance of payments.** This examines how a low income elasticity of demand for the exports of many developing countries can help to explain their chronic balance of payments problems.

2.6 **The role of the speculator.** This assesses whether the activities of speculators are beneficial or harmful to the rest of society.

Maths Case 2.1 Finding equilibrium price and quantity using algebra. This gives an example of solving equilibrium price and quantity from a demand and a supply equation using the method of simultaneous equations.

Maths Case 2.2 Calculating income and cross-price elasticities from a demand equation: a worked example (Part 1: not using calculus). This gives an example of working out cross and income elasticities from a particular demand function.

Maths Case 2.3 Calculating income and cross-price elasticities from a demand equation: a worked example (Part 2: using calculus). This shows how simple differentiation can be used to work out elasticity values. It gives an example of working out cross and income elasticities from a particular demand function.

Websites relevant to this chapter

Numbers and sections refer to websites listed in the Web Appendix and hotlinked from this book's website at www.pearsoned.co.uk/sloman.

- For news articles relevant to this chapter, see the *Economics News* section on the student website.
- For general news on markets, see websites in section A, and particularly A1, 2, 3, 4, 5, 8, 9, 18, 23, 24, 25, 26, 36. See also links to newspapers worldwide in A38, 39, 43 and 44, and the news search feature in Google at A41.
- For links to sites on markets, see the relevant sections of I7, 14 and 23.
- For data on the housing market (Box 2.2), see sites B7–11.
- For sites favouring the free market, see C17 and E34.
- For student resources relevant to this chapter, see sites C1–7, 9, 10, 19, 28.
- For a range of classroom games and simulations of markets, see sites C23, 24 and 27 (computer-based) and C20 (non-computer-based).

Government and the Market

In the previous chapter we looked at free markets: markets where there is no government intervention. However, as we saw in Chapter 1 the real world is one of mixed economies. Indeed, the government intervenes in many markets, even highly competitive ones. This intervention can take a number of forms:

- Fixing prices, either above or below the free-market equilibrium.
- Taxing the production or sale of various goods, such as petrol.

- Subsidising the production or sale of various goods, such as public transport.
- Producing goods or services directly (e.g. defence and health care).
- Regulation. Various laws could be passed to regulate the behaviour of firms. For example, some activities, such as the dumping of toxic waste, could be made illegal; or licences or official permission might have to be obtained to produce certain goods; or a regulatory body could supervise the activities of various firms and prevent any that it felt to be against the public interest (e.g. the production of unsafe toys).

Supply and demand analysis is a useful tool for examining the effects of government intervention. First, in section 3.1, we examine what could happen if a government fixes prices, either above or below the equilibrium. Then, in the following section, we look at the effects of government taxes on products. We see the impact on prices and output and how this depends on the price elasticity of demand and supply.

In section 3.3 we examine what happens if the government seeks to do away with a market system of allocation altogether, either by providing things free to consumers, or by banning certain harmful activities.

Finally, we look at the impact of government intervention in agriculture – a sector that has received massive government support in many countries of the world. We look at the economic arguments for such intervention and then examine some specific measures that governments have taken.

The role of government in the economy is examined further in Chapters 11 to 14.

3.1 THE CONTROL OF PRICES

TC 3
p26

TC 7
p81

At the equilibrium price, there will be no shortage or surplus. The equilibrium price, however, may not be the most desirable price. The government, therefore, may prefer to keep prices above or below the market clearing level.

If the government sets a *minimum price* above the equilibrium (a price floor), there will be a surplus. This is illustrated in Figure 3.1. With curves S and D, the surplus is $Q_s - Q_d$ ($b - a$). Legislation prevents the price from falling to eliminate this surplus.

The size of the surplus at any given minimum price will depend on the price elasticity of demand and supply. For example, if supply and demand are less elastic (S_1 and D_1 instead of S and D) the same minimum price will create a smaller surplus: $Q_{s_1} - Q_{d_1}$ ($d - c$). Given the impact of

time on elasticity, the surplus will tend to be larger in the long run.

If the government sets a *maximum price* below the equilibrium (a price ceiling), there will be a shortage. This is illustrated in Figure 3.2. With curves S and D the shortage is

Definitions

Minimum price A price floor set by the government or some other agency. The price is not allowed to fall below this level (although it is allowed to rise above it).

Maximum price A price ceiling set by the government or some other agency. The price is not allowed to rise above this level (although it is allowed to fall below it).

Figure 3.1 Minimum price: price floor

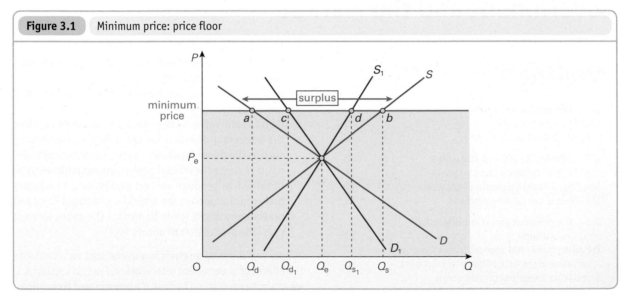

Figure 3.2 Maximum price: price ceiling

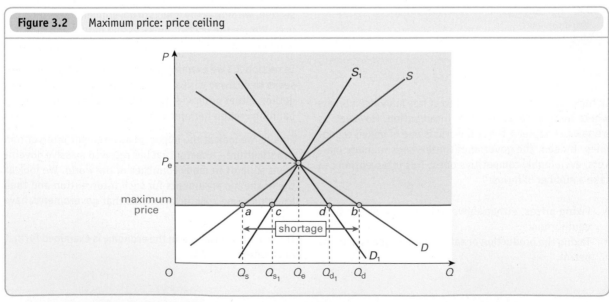

THRESHOLD CONCEPT 7   **GOVERNMENTS CAN SOMETIMES IMPROVE MARKET OUTCOMES**   THINKING LIKE AN ECONOMIST

Threshold Concept 3 was that markets may fail to meet social objectives; this implies that there may be a need for government intervention. Governments have a number of policy instruments that they can use, either to influence markets or to replace them altogether. These policy instruments include taxation, benefits and subsidies, laws and regulations, licences and permits, and direct provision by government departments or agencies (such as the National Health Service in the UK).

The threshold concept here is not merely that governments intervene, but that they can correct, or at least lessen, market failures. Once we have understood the nature of a market failure, we can then set about designing a policy to correct it. For example, if we could identify that the cost to society of producing a product in a way which created pollution was £20 per unit more than the benefit that society gained from the product, then the government could tax the producer £20 per unit.

In Chapters 11 to 14 we consider a number of these policy instruments and seek to identify the *optimum* level of government intervention to meet social objectives. In this chapter we have a preliminary look at some of these instruments.

Governments themselves, however, are imperfect organisations with a number of different motivations. For an economic adviser to recommend a particular policy as the best means of correcting a market failure does not mean that the government will carry it out efficiently or, indeed, carry it out at all. In fact sometimes intervention can make things worse rather than better.

1. *What market failures could be corrected by the use of welfare benefits? Does the payment of such benefits create any problems for society?*
2. *Assume that the government sees litter as a market failure that requires government action. Give some examples of policies it could adopt to reduce litter.*

$Q_d - Q_s$ $(b - a)$. Legislation prevents the price from rising to eliminate this shortage.

The size of the shortage at any given maximum price will again depend on the price elasticity of demand and supply. For example, if demand is less elastic (D_1 instead of D) the same maximum price will create a smaller shortage: $Q_{d_1} - Q_{s_1}$ $(d - c)$.

Setting a minimum (high) price

The government sets minimum prices to prevent them from falling below a certain level. It may do this for various reasons:

- To protect producers' incomes. If the industry is subject to supply fluctuations (e.g. fluctuations in weather affecting crops), prices are likely to fluctuate severely. Minimum prices will prevent the fall in producers' incomes that would accompany periods of low prices. (This is examined further in section 3.4 in the context of agricultural intervention.)
- To create a surplus (e.g. of grains) – particularly in times of plenty – which can be stored in preparation for possible future shortages.
- To deter the consumption of particular goods. Some people may consume more of a good than is in their own self-interest because they do not fully appreciate the future costs to their health. They may also act irrationally because of self-control and addiction issues. See chapter 5 for more detail.
- In the case of wages (the price of labour), minimum wage legislation can be used to prevent workers' wage rates from falling below a certain level. This may form part of a government policy on poverty and inequality (see Box 11.2).

Draw a supply and demand diagram with the price of labour (the wage rate) on the vertical axis and the quantity of labour (the number of workers) on the horizontal axis. What will happen to employment if the government raises wages from the equilibrium to some minimum wage above the equilibrium?

The government can use various methods to deal with the surpluses associated with minimum prices.

- The government could buy the surplus and store it, destroy it or sell it abroad in other markets. This is illustrated in Figure 3.3, where the government purchases the unsold surplus of $b - a$ (i.e. $Q_s - Q_d$). The cost to the government of buying this surplus is the shaded area (abQ_sQ_d). This is what happened in the EU's Common Agricultural Policy where 'Intervention Boards' bought up surpluses and in most cases (e.g. grains, milk, powder and beef) put them in storage. The expense of storage would have to be added to the shaded area in Figure 3.3 to obtain the full cost to the government of the policy. These costs would be lower if the government could sell surpluses on the world market.
- Supply could be artificially lowered by restricting producers to particular quotas. For example, in Figure 3.1, supply could be reduced to Q_d (or Q_{d_1} in the case of D_1). This would reduce the costs to the government of having to purchase the surplus, but it might be a difficult policy to enforce.
- Demand could be raised by advertising, by finding alternative uses for the good, or by reducing consumption of substitute goods (e.g. by imposing taxes or quotas on substitutes, such as imports).

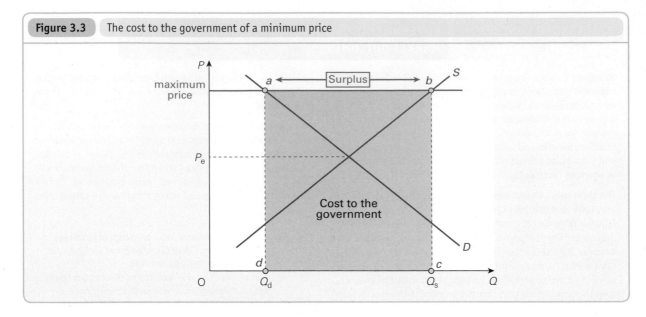

Figure 3.3   The cost to the government of a minimum price

One of the problems with minimum prices is that firms with surpluses on their hands may try to evade the price control and cut their prices.

Another problem is that high prices may cushion inefficiency. Firms may feel less need to find more efficient methods of production and to cut their costs if their profits are being protected by the high price. Also, the high price may discourage firms from producing alternative goods which they could produce more efficiently or which are in higher demand, but which nevertheless have a lower (free-market) price.

Setting a maximum (low) price

The government may set maximum prices to prevent them from rising above a certain level. The rationale for this type of policy is usually one of fairness, with the government setting maximum prices for basic goods so that people on lower incomes can afford to buy them. This may be a particular issue in times of famine or war.

The resulting shortages, however, create further problems. If the government merely sets prices and does not intervene further, the shortages will lead to sellers having to allocate the good amongst its potential customers in one or more of the following ways:

■ *'First-come, first-served' basis.* This is likely to lead to queues developing outside shops, or websites crashing if people try to purchase the good on line. To try to deal with these issues firms may have to adopt waiting lists. Queues have been a common feature of life in Venezuela and Argentina where the governments have kept the prices of many basic goods below the level necessary to equate demand and supply.
■ *Random ballot.* The seller puts the name of every customer willing to pay the maximum price into a random draw.

Only those who are lucky enough to have their name drawn receive the good.
■ *Favoured customers.* This could be the seller's friends, family and/or regular customers.
■ *A measure of merit.* For example, the number of students who want a place on a particular course at a university and are willing to pay the tuition fee may exceed the number of places available. In this instance, the university may allocate places to those who achieve the highest grades.
■ *A rule or regulation.* State schools facing excess demand often allocate places based on the distance children live from the school (in the case the maximum price is zero). Preference is also given to applicants who have an older sibling already at the school.

None of the above may be considered fair since some people in need may be forced to go without. Therefore, the government may adopt a system of **rationing**. People could be issued with a set number of coupons for each item rationed.

A major problem with maximum prices is likely to be the emergence of **illegal markets** (sometimes called **underground** or **shadow markets**), where customers, unable to buy enough in legal markets, may well be prepared to pay very high prices: prices above P_e in Figure 3.2 (see Box 3.2).

> ### Definitions
>
> **Rationing** Where the government restricts the amount of a good that people are allowed to buy.
>
> **Illegal or underground or shadow markets** Where people ignore the government's price and/or quantity controls and sell illegally at whatever price equates illegal demand and supply.

| BOX 3.1 | A MINIMUM UNIT PRICE FOR ALCOHOL | CASE STUDIES AND APPLICATIONS |

A way of reducing alcohol consumption?

A market where the use of minimum pricing has been extensively discussed is that of alcohol. In early 2010, the UK House of Commons Health Select Committee[1] proposed the introduction of a form of minimum pricing. Known as a 'minimum unit price' (MUP), the price floor is set according to the alcoholic content of the drink rather than the volume of liquid. The Select Committee report suggested that a MUP of 50p would save more than 3000 lives per year.

In March 2012, the UK government announced its intention to introduce MUP following a period of consultation with industry stakeholders. The Scottish government passed legislation for the introduction of a 50p MUP in June 2012.

What impact would a 50p MUP have on the price of alcoholic drinks in the UK? The table provides some examples across a range of products.

Effect of a 50p MUP on the price of various alcoholic drinks

Product	Volume	Strength (% abv)	Units of alcohol	Minimum price
Vodka	70cl	37.5	26.25	£13.13
Whisky	70cl	40.0	28.00	£14.00
Alcopop	70ml	4.0	2.80	£1.40
Lager (4 pack)	440 ml × 4	5.0	2.20	£4.40
Wine (white)	750ml	12.0	9.00	£4.50

Minimum unit pricing versus higher taxes

What are the advantages of introducing a MUP rather than simply increasing tax and duties on alcohol?

Evidence from researchers at Sheffield University[2] indicates that it is a more effective way of targeting heavy drinkers. Economic simulations undertaken to forecast the impact of a 50p MUP found that the policy would have a very small impact on people who consume moderate amounts of alcohol: i.e. men who drink fewer than 22 units per week and women who drink fewer than 15 units. On average, this group responds by drinking only 3 fewer units per year, equivalent to one pint of strong beer.

The simulations suggest that the impact of the policy on heavy drinkers would be much stronger. Men who drink over 50 units per week and women who drink over 35 units respond on average by consuming 134 fewer units per year. The impact on heavy drinkers in the poorest 20 per cent of households is even greater still. They respond by consuming 372 fewer units per year.

One disadvantage of an MUP is that any extra revenue goes to the retailers rather than to the government. Research by the Institute of Fiscal Studies,[3] suggests it would reduce competition and lead to windfall profits for the alcohol and retail industry. They argue that reforming taxes on alcohol is a more effective way of targeting heavy drinkers.

In July 2013, the UK government announced that it was not going ahead with its proposed MUP policy. The then Home Secretary, Theresa May, stated:

> Consultation has been extremely useful. But it has not provided evidence that conclusively demonstrates that Minimum Unit Pricing will actually do what it is meant to do: reduce problem drinking without penalising all those who drink responsibly.[4]

The government instead introduced a minimum price at a much lower level. In May 2014, it became illegal for firms to sell alcoholic drinks at prices below the amount of duty and VAT levied on them. In 2016, this was £1.56 for four cans of average strength lager and £8.72 for a standard bottle of vodka.

At the time of writing, the MUP of 50p is yet to be introduced in Scotland because of a series of legal cases. After the legislation was passed, alcohol trade associations argued that the policy contravened European Union law by impeding trade between member states. They took their case to the Scottish Court of Session (SCS). The SCS initially concluded that the MUP did not infringe EU law but referred the case to the European Court of Justice (ECJ) for more guidance.

In December 2015, the ECJ ruled that the MUP was a restraint on trade but could be justified on the grounds that it protects human life. It referred the case back to the SCS. In October 2016, the SCS ruled that an MUP was consistent with EU law. However, the Scottish Whisky Association has submitted another appeal to the UK Supreme Court. The case is expected to be heard at some point in 2017.

1. Draw a diagram to illustrate the likely impact of setting a minimum price based on duty and VAT levels.
2. Explain how price elasticity of demand determines the impact of a 50p MUP on the consumption of alcohol.
3. In the 2017 Budget, the Chancellor introduced plans to introduce a minimum excise tax on cigarettes. Explain how this effectively imposes a price floor.

1 *Alcohol: First Report of Session 2009–10* (House of Commons Health Committee, April 2010).
2 'Minimum pricing for alcohol effectively targets high risk drinkers, with negligible effects on moderate drinkers with low incomes', *The University of Sheffield News*, February 2014.
3 'Reforms to alcohol taxes would be more effective than minimum unit pricing', Institute for Fiscal Studies, March 2013.
4 Home Office, 'Next steps following the consultation on delivering the government's alcohol strategy', July 2013, p. 3.

BOX 3.2 THE RISE IN ILLEGAL LENDING

The consequence of a maximum price in the payday loan market

Governments in countries such as Venezuela and Argentina have imposed maximum prices on a large number of different goods. However, there are far fewer instances of this type of policy in the UK.

One historical case is the use of rent controls in the housing market. First introduced in 1915 as a response to wartime housing shortages, they were finally abolished as part of the 1988 Housing Act. Since January 1989, no new private sector lettings in the UK have been subject to rent controls. Jeremy Corbyn, the leader of the Labour Party, has, however, argued in favour of their re-introduction.

The introduction of maximum pricing in the payday loan market

A recent example of maximum pricing in the UK is in the market for high-cost short-term credit (HCSTC). Otherwise known as the 'payday loan market', this is where customers typically borrow a few hundred pounds for a short time period, usually two to four weeks. One common reason given for this type of borrowing is the need to pay an unexpected bill. The expectation is that the loan will be repaid when the borrower receives the next pay cheque.

What is the price of borrowing (i.e. buying money) in the credit market? It is the interest rate plus any other fees charged by the lender. If the market is competitive and unregulated then this price is determined by the interaction of the demand and supply. This is illustrated at point a in the diagram at the equilibrium price P_e.

The payday loan market grew dramatically after the financial crisis of 2007–8 and reached its peak in 2013 when the Financial Conduct Authority (FCA) estimated that approximately 400 firms made 10 million loans with a market value of £2.5 billion. However, as the market grew, politicians and even the Archbishop of Canterbury began to express concerns about the level of interest rates. For example, a borrower would typically have to pay around £38 for a 30-day loan of £100. This was an interest rate of 1.26 per cent per day or 4670 per cent per annum! Similar concerns were also expressed about the size of penalty charges imposed on borrowers when they failed to meet repayment deadlines.

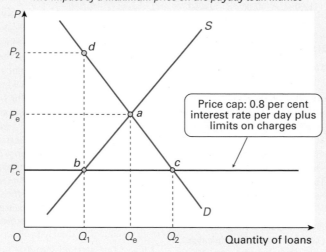

The impact of a maximum price on the payday loan market

Price cap: 0.8 per cent interest rate per day plus limits on charges

In an attempt to deal with these issues, the FCA announced a series of regulations in July 2014.[1] They came into effect in January 2015 and were as follows:

- The interest rate was capped at 0.8 per cent per day: i.e. a maximum price was introduced. This means that the maximum amount a lender can charge for a 30-day loan of £100 is £24 (assuming it is repaid on time).
- Charges for late repayments of loans were limited to a maximum amount of £15. The interest rate on outstanding debts was also capped at 0.8 per cent per day.
- The total amount borrowers could be charged, even if they defaulted, was limited to double the amount they borrowed.

The impact of maximum prices in the payday loan market

What is the impact of the maximum price on a competitive market if it is set below its equilibrium level? This is also illustrated in the diagram. With a price cap of P_c, the simple demand and supply model predicts that the quantity of the loans supplied falls from Q_e to Q_1 while the quantity demanded increases from Q_e to Q_2. The supply side of the market dominates and so the amount of loans issued falls to Q_1. There is a shortage of loans of $Q_2 - Q_1$ ($c - b$).

The FCA anticipated that the number of loans would fall, causing many lenders to go out of business. It forecast that, out of the 400 businesses registered as official payday lenders prior to the regulation, only four (one high street and three online) would survive. In reality, the reduction has been far smaller. In December 2016, the FCA announced that the number had fallen from 400 to 144.

The demand and supply model also predicts that the imposition of a maximum price gives an opportunity for the development of an illegal market. If supply is restricted to Q_1, the market clearing price would now be P_2 (point d), where demand also equals Q_1. If the legal price, therefore, is only P_c, there will be many people who would be willing to pay far more.

Let us say that an individual borrower is prepared to pay P_2. Individual payday lenders may be willing to break the law and charge a price above P_c, but below P_2, depending on their position on the supply curve. Thus both the borrower and the lender would be better off if they made a loan agreement at any price between the price the borrower is willing to pay and the price the lender is willing to accept.

However, the maximum price legislation prevents this mutually beneficial transaction from taking place legally. If potential borrowers are willing to go to the unofficial market they may find illegal lenders (loan sharks) willing to lend them money at an interest rate above the capped level of 0.8 per cent per day but below the maximum rate they are willing to pay.

When discussing the impact of an interest-rate cap, Steve Davies of the Institute of Economic Affairs argued that:

> the demand for these types of loans would remain but would now be met by truly unsavoury characters. If you want to help loan sharks and low life money lenders then restricting legitimate firms is the way to go.[2]

In November 2016, the FCA announced that it was launching a review of its payday market regulations and, in particular, it was:

> keen to see if there is any evidence of consumers turning to illegal money lenders directly as a result of being excluded from high-cost credit because of the price cap.[3]

It will be interesting to see, once more evidence is available, if the benefits of the regulations on the payday loan industry outweigh the costs. The FCA is also considering whether to introduce a similar cap on interest rates and charges for bank overdrafts.

1. Using the concept of elasticity, explain why the impact of a maximum price, such as the one introduced by the FCA, may be different in the economic long run as opposed to the short run.
2. Discuss the economic rationale for introducing a maximum price into the market for payday lending.

1 'FCA proposes price cap for payday lenders', Financial Conduct Authority press release, 15 July 2014.
2 'Cracking down on payday lenders will hurt the poor', Institute for Economic Affairs, July 2013.
3 'FCA launches call for input on high-cost credit and overdrafts', press release, 29 November 2016.

BOX 3.3   HOW CAN TICKET TOUTS MAKE SO MUCH MONEY?

Some pricing issues in the market for tickets

Some organisations set prices below market clearing levels. Take the example of the ticketing industry.

Tickets for live music, theatre, comedy and sporting events are sold by event organisers or authorised ticketing websites such as Ticketmaster®. This is the 'primary market' where the organiser or promoter sets the prices. There is evidence that ticket prices in the primary market are consistently below market clearing levels. For example, research by Media Insight Consulting found that, on average, fans were willing to pay £181 to see Adele in concert in the spring 2016 tour, whereas the tickets cost £65.

Organisers often set ticket prices below the market clearing level because of uncertainty over demand and the desire to avoid half-empty venues. They may also want to make the tickets available at reasonable prices to fans. However, by setting prices below market clearing levels in the primary market, it creates the opportunity for people to make large amounts of money in the secondary market.

The 'secondary market' is where someone resells a ticket they previously purchased in the primary market. The event organiser has no control over prices in this sector. One type of seller in the secondary market is someone who, because of changes in their circumstances, is no longer able to attend the event. Such people are simply trying to get their money back. However, another type of seller purchases tickets deliberately to resell them at a mark-up in the secondary market. This type of seller is sometimes called a 'ticket tout' or 'scalper' and the potential returns are considerable. The worldwide value of the secondary ticketing market has been estimated at around $8 billion.

The scope for profit by ticket touts

Why can ticket touts sell for such large profits? The diagram helps to explain how it is possible. The supply curve is perfectly inelastic in the short run as the capacity of the venue holding the event (stadium, concert hall, theatre, etc.) is fixed at Q_c. The market-clearing price is P_e where the quantity of tickets demanded is equal to the quantity supplied. The price in the primary market is P_p. So there is a shortage of tickets: i.e. $Q_d > Q_c$.

Suppose that ticket touts are able to purchase half of the tickets on sale in the primary market (Q_t) using computer programs called bots. These automated pieces of software enable the user to make multiple transactions at the same time.

Assuming that none of the people with the highest willingness to pay (represented by points a to b on the demand curve) purchase the tickets in the primary market, the ticket touts will be able to resell all of their tickets for a price of P_s. The shaded area represents the potential profit.

The secondary ticketing market

Media reports have highlighted cases where tickets for sale in the primary market have sold out in less than an hour, with ticket touts suspected of purchasing large numbers using bots. These same tickets quickly start reappearing for prices far in excess of their face value on one of the four websites that dominate the secondary ticket market: Viagogo (based in Switzerland), Stubhub (owned by eBay), Seatwave and GetMeIn (both owned by Ticketmaster). In one extreme case

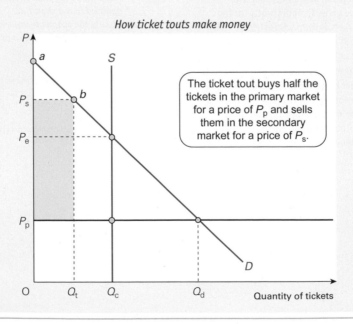

How ticket touts make money

The ticket tout buys half the tickets in the primary market for a price of P_p and sells them in the secondary market for a price of P_s.

an £85 ticket for an Adele concert at the O2 arena in 2016 was advertised by a seller on GetMeIn for a price of £24 840!

The resale of tickets for football matches in England and Wales without the clubs' permission was made illegal in 1994. Ticket touting was also prohibited for events at the London Olympic Games in 2012. Some pressure groups have argued that the existing legislation should be extended so that either the secondary ticket market for all music, cultural and sporting events is banned or limits placed on resale prices.

Attempts to control the secondary ticketing market in the UK

Consumer Rights Act

In response to these concerns the government introduced the Consumer Rights Act (CRA) in 2015. This came into force in May 2015 and placed the following requirements on people offering tickets for resale in the secondary market:

- The face value of the ticket, the seat location (i.e. its block, row and seat number) and any usage restrictions must be prominently displayed.
- Any relationship between the seller and the event organiser or official website must be clearly shown.
- Tickets puchased in the secondary market cannot be cancelled by the event organiser unless this condition has been made very clear in the original terms of sale.

The Waterson Review

The Act also stipulated that a review of the secondary ticketing market should take place within 12 months of the new legislation coming into force. In October 2015, the government commissioned the review and announced that its chair would be an economist, Professor Michael Waterson. Final recommendations were published in May 2016[1] and included the following:

- Increased responsibility should be placed on secondary ticketing websites to make sure that sellers using their sites adhere to the conditions stipulated in the CRA 2015.
- The sale of tickets in the primary market should be made much more transparent. For example, event organisers should clearly indicate the proportion of tickets already sold before they go on general sale.
- More actions should be taken to make sure that consumers understand the difference between the primary and secondary market.

Professor Waterson opposed an outright ban of the secondary market as he thought it would (a) drive sellers into the illegal sector so increasing the chances of fraud; (b) reduce consumer welfare, as evidence for the review indicated that prices were often below their face value. He also opposed a cap on resale prices as he argued that sellers respond to this type of regulation by finding innovative ways of circumventing the rules. He also questioned whether the cost of the resources required to enforce a price cap would exceed the benefits the regulation would provide.

The government stated in March 2017 that it fully accepted all of the report's recommendations. It also announced that a new clause would be added to the Digital Economy Bill 2016 which would make the use of bots to purchase large numbers of tickets illegal and subject to unlimited fines.

CMA review.   In June 2016, the Competition and Markets Authority (CMA) began a completely separate review of secondary ticketing websites. In December 2016, it announced an enforcement investigation of the sector as potential violations of consumer protection law had been identified in its initial findings.

Culture Media and Sport Select Committee hearings. The House of Commons Culture Media and Sports Select Committee also held sessions on 15 November 2016 and 21 March 2017 where its members listened to evidence from a number of interested parties. After the hearings it concluded that there were 'far-ranging and disturbing factors in the market'.

Changes in the primary market.   The management of a number of bands and solo artists have taken measures in an attempt to reduce ticket touting. In particular, they have switched to paperless tickets where the person attending the event has to present the debit/credit card used to purchase the ticket in the primary market and some form of photo ID in order to gain entry. Some websites such as Twickets, Swap My Ticket only allow resale at the face value of the ticket.

The secondary ticketing market is a controversial area and its workings continue to be scrutinised by both the media and the government.

1. *Are there any potential conflicts of interest when a primary market seller such as Ticketmaster owns secondary market websites such as Seatwave and GetMeIn?*
2. *To what extent is it in the interests of society to allow people to resell tickets at a price far in excess of their face value? What is the impact on allocative efficiency?*

1 'Independent review of consumer protection measures concerning online secondary ticketing facilities', *Waterson Review*, May 2016.
2 'Secondary ticket platforms compliance review', CMA, July 2016.

Another problem is that the maximum prices reduce the quantity produced of an already scarce commodity. For example, artificially low prices in a famine are likely to reduce food supplies: if not immediately, then at the next harvest, because of less being sown. In many developing countries, governments control the price of basic foodstuffs in order to help the urban poor. The effect, however, is to reduce incomes for farmers, who are then encouraged to leave the land and flock into the ever-growing towns and cities.

To minimise these types of problem the government may attempt to reduce the shortage by encouraging supply: by drawing on stores, by direct government production, or by giving subsidies or tax relief to firms. Alternatively, it may attempt to reduce demand: by the production of more alternative goods (e.g. home-grown vegetables in times of war) or by controlling people's incomes.

Another example of maximum prices is where the government imposes rent controls in an attempt to make rented accommodation more affordable. Here the 'price' is the rent people are charged. The danger of this policy is that it will create a shortage of rental property. The policy is examined in Case Study 3.3 on the student website.

Every year the number of people who want to run the London Marathon far exceeds the number of places available. For example, 253 000 applicants were willing to pay £35 to enter the 2017 event. Unfortunately, there were only 17 500 places for these applicants and so the majority ended up very disappointed. Find out the different methods used by the organisers to allocate all 40 000 places and consider their advantages and disadvantages.

Section summary

1. There are several ways in which the government intervenes in the operation of markets. It can fix prices, tax or subsidise products, regulate production, or produce goods directly itself.

2. The government may fix minimum or maximum prices. If a minimum price is set above the equilibrium, a surplus will result. If a maximum price is set below the equilibrium price, a shortage will result. The size of the surplus or shortage will depend on the price elasticity of demand and supply.

3. Minimum prices are set as a means of protecting the incomes of suppliers or creating a surplus for storage in case of future reductions in supply. If the government is

not deliberately trying to create a surplus, it must decide what to do with it.

4. Maximum prices are set as a means of keeping prices down for the consumer. The resulting shortages will lead to sellers of the good having to allocate the good among its potential customers in a number of ways including: first-come, first-served; random ballot; favoured customers; measures of merit; rules/regulations. Alternatively, the government could introduce a system of rationing. With maximum prices, underground markets are likely to arise. This is where goods are sold illegally above the maximum price.

3.2   INDIRECT TAXES AND SUBSIDIES

The effect of imposing taxes on goods

We now turn to another example of government intervention – the imposition of taxes on goods. These *indirect taxes*, as they are called, include taxes such as value added tax (VAT) and excise duties on cigarettes, petrol and alcoholic drinks.

These taxes can be a fixed amount per unit sold – a *specific tax*. An example is the tax per litre of petrol. Alternatively,

they can be a percentage of the price or value added at each stage of production – an *ad valorem tax*. An example is VAT.

When a tax is levied on a good, this has the effect of shifting the supply curve upwards by the amount of the tax (see Figure 3.4). In the case of a specific tax, it will be a parallel shift, since the amount of the tax is the same at all prices. In the case of an *ad valorem* tax, the curve will *swing* upwards. At a zero price there would be no tax and hence no shift in the supply curve. As price rises, so the gap between the original

Definitions

Indirect tax A tax on the expenditure on goods. Indirect taxes include value added tax (VAT) and duties on tobacco, alcoholic drinks and petrol. These taxes are not paid directly by the consumer, but indirectly via the sellers of the good. Indirect taxes contrast with direct taxes (such as

income tax) which are paid directly out of people's incomes.

Specific tax An indirect tax of a fixed sum per unit sold.

Ad valorem tax An indirect tax of a certain percentage of the price of the good.

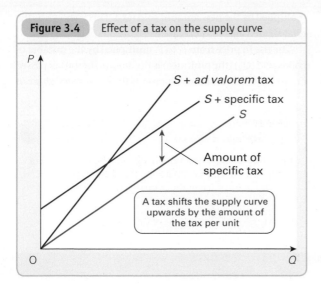

Figure 3.4 Effect of a tax on the supply curve

S + *ad valorem* tax

S + specific tax

S

Amount of
specific tax

A tax shifts the supply curve
upwards by the amount of
the tax per unit

incidence of such taxes is distributed between consumers and producers. Consumers pay to the extent that price rises. Producers pay to the extent that this rise in price is not sufficient to cover the tax.

> ### Definition
>
> **Incidence of tax** The distribution of the burden of tax between sellers and buyers.

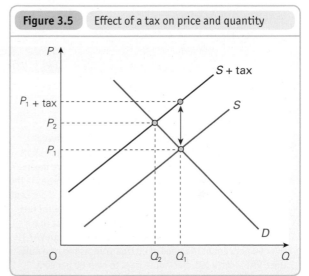

Figure 3.5 Effect of a tax on price and quantity

P_1 + tax

P_2

P_1

S + tax

S

D

Q_2 Q_1

and new supply curves will widen, since a given *percentage* tax will be a larger *absolute* amount the higher the price.

But why does the supply curve shift upwards by the amount of the tax? This is illustrated in Figure 3.5. To be persuaded to produce the same quantity as before the imposition of the tax (i.e. Q_1), firms must now receive a price which allows them fully to recoup the tax they have to pay (i.e. P_1 + tax).

The effect of the tax is to raise price and reduce quantity. Price will not rise by the full amount of the tax, however, because the demand curve is downward sloping. In Figure 3.5, price rises only to P_2. Thus the burden or

*LOOKING AT THE MATHS

Assume that a specific tax per unit of t is imposed on producers of a good. This is then added to the pre-tax price of P_1. The price paid by consumers is thus $P_1 + t$.

Assuming linear demand and supply equations (see page 48), these can be written as:

$$Q_D = a - b(P_1 + t) \qquad (1)$$

$$Q_S = c + dP_1 \qquad (2)$$

In equilibrium, $Q_D = Q_S$. Thus:

$$a - b(P_1 + t) + c + dP_1$$

We can rearrange this equation to give:

$$bP_1 + dP_1 = a - c - bt$$

Thus:

$$P_1 = \frac{a - c - bt}{b + d}$$

Take the following example. If the demand and supply equations were

$$Q_D = 120 - 10(P_1 + t) \qquad (4)$$

and

$$Q_S = 10 + 5P_1 \qquad (5)$$

and $t = 2$, then from equation (3):

$$P_1 - \frac{120 - 10 - (10 \times 2)}{10 + 5} = 6$$

and from equations (4) and (5):

$$Q_D = 120 - 80 = Q_S = 10 + 30 = 40$$

The market price will be

$$P_1 + t = 6 + 2 = 8$$

Assuming that the pre-tax equations were

$$Q_D = 120 + 10P$$

and

$$Q_S = 10 - 5P$$

what is (a) the consumer share of the tax and (b) the producer share?

Elasticity and the incidence of taxation

TC 6
p68

The incidence of indirect taxes depends on the elasticity of demand and supply of the commodity in question.

Consider cases (1)–(4) in Figure 3.6. In each of the diagrams (which are all drawn to the same scale), the size of the tax is the same: the supply curve shifts upwards by the same amount. Price rises to P_2 in each case and quantity falls to Q_2; but, as you can see, the size of this increase in price and decrease in quantity differs in each case, depending on the price elasticity of demand and supply.

The total tax revenue is given by the amount of tax per unit (the vertical difference between the two supply curves)

multiplied by the new amount sold (Q_2). This is shown as the total shaded area in each case in Figure 3.6.

The rise in price from P_1 to P_2 multiplied by the number of goods sold (Q_2) (the pink area) is the amount of the tax passed on to consumers and thus represents the *consumers' share* of

Definitions

Consumers' share of a tax on a good The proportion of the revenue from a tax on a good that arises from an increase in the price of the good.

BOX 3.4 **ASHES TO ASHES?**

A moral dilemma of tobacco taxes

Revenue from tobacco taxes

The price elasticity of demand for cigarettes is relatively inelastic at current prices (approximately −0.6 in the short run: see below), and so taxing tobacco is an effective means for the government to generate revenue. Tobacco duties in the UK are forecast to raise £9.2 billion in 2016/17 or 1.3 per cent of total tax revenue. This compares with 3.9 per cent for fuel duties and 1.5 per cent for alcohol duties. (Note that these figures exclude the additional revenue raised through VAT.) Over 60 per cent of the price of 20 cigarettes is tobacco duty. Once VAT is included, this figure rises to over 80 per cent.

Clearly, then, tobacco duties are a major source of revenue for the government. The fewer people who respond to higher taxes by either quitting or smoking less, the greater the increase in revenue. In fact, if the government encouraged people to smoke, it would raise more money. However, this creates an interesting dilemma as a strong pressure exists on governments around the world to discourage people from smoking: the more they succeed, the lower will be their tax revenue.

This is not a new problem. Cabinet papers released in May 2008 revealed that in 1956 the then Chancellor, Harold Macmillan, argued against issuing a government health warning about cigarettes, despite being presented with statistical evidence that it was harmful. He was concerned that an official warning would lead to reduced tax revenue from tobacco.

The costs of smoking

What is the impact of fewer people smoking on government finances? Tax revenues would clearly fall, but there would also be less spending on smoking-related health care. Estimates of the amount spent on smoking-related illness by the National Health Service vary between £3 billion and £6 billion per annum. One study by the Department of Public Health at Oxford University,[1] put the figure at £5.2 billion in 2005/6. This, however, is less than the £9.2 billion revenue raised from tobacco taxes. Clearly smokers more than pay for their own treatment. Indeed, the state and the NHS may acquire further financial benefit from smokers. The benefits

stem from the fact that smokers die younger. The NHS gains from avoiding many of the high-cost treatments required by elderly patients and the state gains from having to pay out less in pensions and other benefits.

There are other potential costs of people smoking. The think tank Policy Exchange estimated some figures for the following different categories.

- Loss in output from premature death of smokers — £4.1 billion
- Increased absenteeism from work — £2.5 billion
- Loss in productivity from smoking breaks — £2.9 billion
- Cost of smoking-related house fires — £507 million
- Cost of cleaning up cigarette butts — £342 million

Although some people have questioned the accuracy of these data, they do help to illustrate the wide range of potential costs.

There is also the human cost from suffering and deaths. Data from the Office of National Statistics indicated that 78 000 deaths in 2014 were attributable to smoking – 17 per cent of all deaths. In 2014/15, there was an average of 4700 admissions to hospital every day for conditions that could have been caused by smoking.

The effects of raising tobacco taxes

So perhaps raising tobacco taxes would be doubly beneficial. Not only would it raise revenue, but also it would help to support other anti-smoking measures. The UK government is currently using a tobacco duty escalator – a policy of raising tobacco duty by 2 per cent above the rate of inflation each year. There are, however, three problems with this policy.

The first concerns smuggling and tobacco-related crime. Smuggled cigarettes accounted for around 13 per cent of the UK market in 2015/16. Not only is the high price differential between tobacco prices in the UK and abroad encouraging criminality, but estimates for 2015/16 suggest that smuggled tobacco products meant the government lost around £2.4 billion in tax revenue.

the tax. The remainder (the green area) is the **producers' share**. This is the amount by which the producers' net price ($P_2 - t$) is below the original price (P_1) multiplied by Q_2.

The following conclusions can be drawn:

- Quantity will fall less, and hence tax revenue for the government will be greater, the less elastic are demand and supply (cases (1) and (3)).

Definitions

Producers' share of a tax on a good The proportion of the revenue from a tax on a good that arises from a reduction in the price to the producer (after the payment of the tax).

- Price will rise more, and hence the consumers' share of the tax will be larger, the less elastic is demand and the more elastic is supply (cases (1) and (4)).
- Price will rise less, and hence the producers' share will be larger, the more elastic is demand and the less elastic is supply (cases (2) and (3)).

Cigarettes, petrol and alcohol have been major targets for indirect taxes. Demand for each of them is high and fairly inelastic. Thus the tax will not curb demand greatly. They are good sources, therefore, of tax revenue to the government (see Box 3.4).

Another issue concerns the disproportionate impact on those with low incomes. The proportion of people smoking in the poorest 40 per cent of households is approximately double the proportion smoking in the richest 40 per cent of households. In 2015/16, 1.2 per cent of total household expenditure by the poorest 20 per cent of the population was on cigarettes. The figure for the richest 10 per cent was just 0.2 per cent. Therefore, the higher the tax on tobacco, the more it redistributes incomes from the poor to the rich.

The third problem is that raising tobacco taxes does *not* have a very marked effect on the consumption of cigarettes; taxes are an ineffective way of discouraging smoking. Why is this? Think back to the discussion on elasticity in section 2.4; demand for cigarettes is inelastic because there are few substitutes and cigarette smokers are often addicted to their habit. A study by HM Revenue and Customs in December 2010[2] estimated the short-run elasticity of demand at approximately −0.57, with long-run elasticity of −1.05. In 2015, the long-run figure was updated to −1.19. The work suggests that a 1 per cent increase in specific duty will raise an extra £25 million each year.

The use of alternative policies

This dilemma helps explain the move away from using taxes as a method of reducing smoking and towards policies that more directly affect smokers' behaviour. In 2006 and 2007, legislation came into force in the UK banning smoking in workplaces and public places such as shops, bars and restaurants. This followed similar moves in other countries and was supported by an earlier report by the Chief Medical Officer,[3] which suggested that the policy would save up to £2.7 billion from a healthier workforce. In October 2015, it also became illegal in England and Wales to smoke in a vehicle carrying children.

Other measures are targeted at the promotion and advertising of tobacco. For example, large shops selling cigarettes have to keep them hidden from public view. A law on the plain packaging of cigarettes came into full effect in May 2017. This includes the following restrictions:

- Picture and text health warnings must cover at least 65 per cent of the front and back of the packet.

- The only advertising allowed on the packet are the product name and brand variant in a standard font size and colour.
- Packets must be cuboid in shape and contain a minimum of 20 cigarettes.

These measures appear to have had some impact, although a substantial minority continues to smoke. In 2014, 19 per cent of all adults in Great Britain were smokers, down from a peak of 46 per cent in 1974.

If smokers continue to give up in substantial numbers then the government will find itself having to look elsewhere for a source of replacement tax revenue. A number of countries are investigating the possibility of introducing new duties on e-cigarettes to make up for some of the shortfall. In 2015, 4 per cent of adults in the UK were e-cigarette users – more than triple the number in 2012.

1. *You are a government minister. What arguments might you put forward in favour of maximising the revenue from cigarette taxation?*
2. *What has been the likely impact on businesses and individuals of the ban on smoking in public places?*
3. *As we saw in the box, an HMRC study on smoking estimates the long-term price elasticity of demand as −1.19, with a short-term elasticity of −0.57. Explain these figures.*
4. *Many people think that if tobacco were to be discovered today it would be an illegal substance, as is the case with cannabis. What problems would a government face if it tried to ban smoking completely (see section 3.3)?*

1 S. Allender, R. Balakrishnan, P. Scarborough, P. Webster and M. Rayne, 'The burden of smoking-related ill health in the United Kingdom', *Tobacco Control*, vol. 18, no. 4 (BMJ, 2009).

2 Magdalena Cuzbek and Surjinder Johal, *Econometric Analysis of Cigarette Consumption in the UK* (HMRC Working Paper 2010 and update 2015).

3 L. Donaldson, *Annual Report of the Chief Medical Officer 2003* (Department of Health, 2004).

4 'Detailed household expenditure as a percentage of total expenditure by disposable income decile group, UK', Table 3.2 (ONS, 2017).

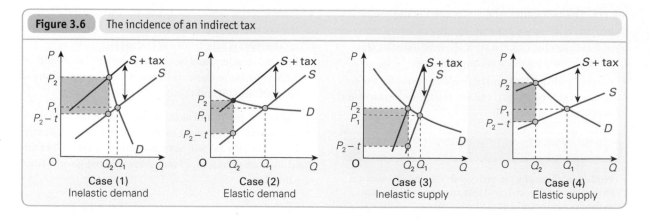

Figure 3.6 The incidence of an indirect tax

Case (1) Inelastic demand

Case (2) Elastic demand

Case (3) Inelastic supply

Case (4) Elastic supply

Supply tends to be more elastic in the long run than in the short run. Assume that a tax is imposed on a good that was previously untaxed. How will the incidence of this tax change as time passes? How will the incidence be affected if demand too becomes more elastic over time?

The effect of subsidising products

A subsidy is a payment by the government to a producer or consumer and so is the opposite of a tax. For example, in 2015/16 the train operating company Northern received 10.7p from the government per passenger kilometre travelled. This provided a total subsidy of £249 million. Investment in renewable energy such as wind farms has also received considerable government support.

When a government pays a subsidy per unit of a product to the producer it has the effect of shifting the market supply curve downwards by the amount of the subsidy. Why is this? Take the example of a fixed subsidy per unit sold (a specific subsidy) illustrated in Figure 3.7.

The market is initially in equilibrium at point a where the quantity demanded equals the quantity supplied. Price and quantity are P_0 and Q_0 respectively. Now assume the government introduces a subsidy per unit of an amount $a - b$. Firms are now willing to supply the same quantity (Q_0) for a lower market price (P_2) because the government is paying the difference ($P_0 - P_2$) via the subsidy. This willingness to supply at lower market prices is true for all quantities of output and so the whole market supply curve shifts downwards by the amount of the subsidy to S + subsidy. As the amount of the subsidy paid by the government is the same at all prices the shift is a parallel one.

The subsidy reduces the equilibrium price from P_0 to P_1 and increases the equilibrium quantity from Q_0 to Q_1. However, as you can see, the price does not fall by the full amount

Figure 3.7 Effect of a subsidy on price and quantity

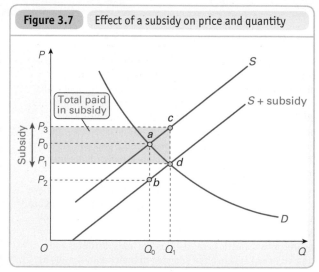

of the subsidy. As with the analysis of tax, the extent to which the subsidy is passed on to the consumer depends on the price elasticity of demand and supply. The consumer's share of the subsidy will be greater (i.e. the price fall will be greater), the less elastic the demand and the more elastic the supply.

Demonstrate with a supply and demand diagram the incidence of a subsidy when demand is price elastic and supply is price inelastic.

How much does the subsidy cost the taxpayer? This will depend on two things – the size of the per-unit subsidy and the quantity sold after it has been introduced. This is illustrated by the shaded area in Figure 3.7: i.e. the per-unit subsidy ($P_3 - P_1$) multiplied by the quantity produced (Q_1).

Section summary

1. If the government imposes a tax on a good, this will cause its price to rise to the consumers, but it will also cause the revenue to producers (after the tax has been paid) to fall.

2. The 'incidence of tax' will depend on the price elasticity of demand and supply of the good.

3. The consumers' burden will be higher and the producers' burden correspondingly lower, the less elastic the demand and the more elastic the supply of the good. The total tax revenue for the government will be higher the less elastic are both demand and supply.

4. A subsidy is a payment by the government to a producer or consumer. It will cause the equilibrium price to fall and quantity to increase.

5. The cost of a specific subsidy for the government will depend on the size of the per unit payment and the equilibrium quantity after it has been introduced.

3.3   GOVERNMENT REJECTION OF MARKET ALLOCATION

Sometimes the government may consider that certain products or services are best not allocated through the market at all.

This section examines two extreme cases. The first is goods or services that are provided free at the point of delivery, such as treatment in National Health Service hospitals and education in state schools. The second is goods and services whose sale is banned, such as certain drugs, weapons and pornography.

Providing goods and services free at the point of delivery: the case of hospital treatment

When the government provides goods and services free to consumers, this often reflects the public's view that they have a *right* to such things. Most people believe that it would be wrong to charge parents for their children's schooling or for having treatment in a hospital, certainly emergency treatment. However, there are also economic reasons that lie behind the provision: for example, educating children brings a benefit to *all* society.

But what are the consequences of not charging for a service such as health? The analysis is similar to that of a maximum price, only here the maximum price is zero. Figure 3.8 illustrates the situation. It shows a demand and a supply curve for a specific type of treatment in a given hospital.

The demand curve is assumed to be downward sloping. If people had to pay, the amount of treatment demanded would fall as the price went up – partly because some people would feel that they could not afford it (the income effect), and partly because people would turn to alternative treatments, such as prescription drugs. The fewer the alternatives, and the less close they are to hospital treatment, the less elastic would be the demand curve.

The supply curve is assumed to be totally inelastic, at least in the short run, given current space and equipment. In the longer run, the supply curve may be upward sloping, but only if any charges made could be used to employ extra staff and buy more equipment, and even build extra wards and theatres, rather than the money simply going to the government.

At a price of zero, there is a shortage of $Q_d - Q_s$. Only at the equilibrium price of P_e will demand equal supply.

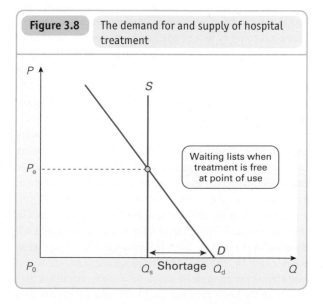

Figure 3.8   The demand for and supply of hospital treatment

The shortage will have to be dealt with and some form of rationing will be required. One way to ration health care is to have a waiting list system. Most hospitals in the UK have waiting lists for non-emergency treatments. The trouble with this 'solution', however, is that waiting lists will continue to lengthen unless the shortage is reduced. There is also the problem that some people on the waiting list may require urgent treatment; these cases will get faster treatment than non-urgent cases. A consequence is that people waiting for non-urgent treatments, such as hip replacements or the treatment of varicose veins, may have to wait a very long time. Public health care systems that do not make any charges for treatment are sometimes criticised for being unresponsive to the needs of patients.

Changes in demand and supply

One of the problems for the provision of health care is that the demand has grown more rapidly than people's incomes. Unless an increasing proportion of a nation's income is devoted to health care, shortages are likely to get worse. The demand curve in Figure 3.8 will shift to the right faster than the supply curve.

But why has demand grown so rapidly? There are two main reasons. The first has to do with demography. People in developed countries are living longer and the average age of the population is rising. But elderly people require a larger amount of medical treatment than younger people. The second has to do with advances in medical science and technology. More and more medical conditions are now treatable, so there is now a demand for such treatment where none existed before.

What is the solution? The answer for most people would be to increase supply, while keeping treatment free. Partly this can be done by increases in efficiency, and, indeed, various initiatives have been taken by government and health managers to try to reduce costs and increase the amount of treatment offered. Often, however, such measures are highly controversial; examples include reducing the length of time people are allowed to stay in hospital after an operation, or moving patients to hospitals, often at a distance, where operations can be done more cheaply.

The only other way of increasing supply is to allocate more funds to health care, and this means either increasing taxes or diverting resources from other forms of public expenditure, such as education or social security. But then, as we know, scarcity involves choices! Between 2000 and 2012, spending on the National Health Service in the UK increased from 5.5 per cent of GDP to 8.2 per cent, but fell back to 7.8 per cent by 2015. It is projected to fall further to 6.6 per cent by 2020/21, despite an ageing population and rapidly rising treatment costs. However, attention has increasingly been focused on improving outcomes and reducing administrative costs.

? *Schooling is free in state schools in most countries. If parents are given a choice of schools for their children, there will be a shortage of places at popular schools (the*

analysis will be the same as in Figure 3.8, with the number of places in a given school measured on the horizontal axis). What methods could be used for dealing with this shortage? What are their relative merits?

Prohibiting the sale of certain goods and services: the case of illegal drugs

It is illegal to sell certain goods and services, and yet many of these goods have flourishing markets. Billions of pounds change hands worldwide in the illegal drugs, arms and pornography trades. What, then, is the impact of making certain products illegal? How would the effect compare with other policies, such as taxing these products?

Note that as economists we can examine the effects of such policies and hence help to inform public debate: we cannot, however, *as economists* make judgements as to whether such policies are *morally* right or wrong (see pages 29–30 on the distinction between positive and normative statements).

TC 1
p11

The market for illegal products

Figure 3.9 illustrates the market for a product such as a drug. If it were not illegal, the demand and supply curves would look something like D_{legal} and S_{legal}. The equilibrium price and quantity would be P_{legal} and Q_{legal}.

Now assume that the drug is made illegal. The effect will be to reduce supply and demand (i.e. shift both curves to the left), as both suppliers and users of the drug fear being caught and paying the penalty (fines or imprisonment). Also, some people will stop supplying or using the drug simply because it is illegal and irrespective of any penalty. The harsher the penalties for supplier or user, and the more likely they are to get caught, and also the more law-abiding people are, the bigger will be the leftward shift in the respective supply or demand curve.

In Figure 3.9, the supply curve shifts to $S_{illegal}$ and the demand curve shifts to $D_{illegal}$. The quantity sold will fall to

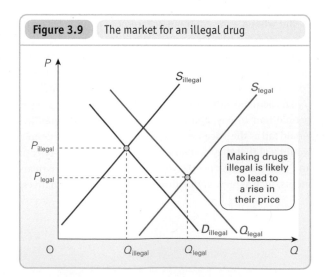

Figure 3.9   The market for an illegal drug

Making drugs illegal is likely to lead to a rise in their price

$Q_{illegal}$ and the price will rise to $P_{illegal}$. It is assumed that there will be a bigger shift in the supply curve (and hence a rise in price) as the penalties for supplying drugs are usually higher than those for merely possessing them.

 Under what circumstances would making a product illegal (a) cause a fall in its price; (b) cause the quantity sold to fall to zero?

A comparison of prohibition with taxing the product

Cocaine is illegal. Other drugs, such as tobacco and alcohol, are taxed. But the effect in both cases is to reduce consumption. So are there any differences in the results of using taxation and prohibition?

A *tax* on a product, like making a product illegal, will have the effect of shifting the supply curve upwards to the left (as we saw in Figure 3.5 on page 89). Unlike making the product illegal, however, a tax will not shift the demand curve. A bigger shift in the supply curve would therefore be needed than in Figure 3.9 for a tax to have the same effect as prohibition on the level of consumption. It would also result in a higher price for any given level of consumption.

So why not simply use taxes rather than making goods illegal? Those in favour of legalising various drugs argue that this would avoid the associated criminal activity that goes with illegal products (such as drugs gangs, violence and money laundering) and the resulting costs of law enforcement. It would also bring in tax revenue for the government.

The reason given by governments for keeping drugs illegal is that it sends out important messages to society and reflects what the majority wants. Taxing something, by contrast, implies that the product is acceptable. Also, if taxes were to be set high enough to reduce legal consumption to a politically acceptable level, there would then develop a large illegal market in the drugs as people sought to evade the tax.

 What are the arguments for and against making the sale of alcoholic drinks illegal? To what extent can an economist help to resolve the issue?

Section summary

1. Sometimes the government will want to avoid allocation by the market for a particular good or service. Examples include things provided free at the point of use and products that are prohibited by the government.

2. If products are provided free to consumers, demand is likely to exceed supply. This is a particular problem in the case of health care, where demand is growing rapidly.

3. If products such as drugs are prohibited, an illegal market is likely to develop. Demand and supply would be less than in a free market. The price could be either higher or lower, depending on who faces the harshest penalties and the greatest likelihood of being caught – suppliers or users.

4. A similar reduction in consumption could be achieved by using taxation. Other effects, however, such as on the price, on allied crime and on public perceptions of the acceptability of the product, will be different.

3.4 AGRICULTURE AND AGRICULTURAL POLICY

If markets for agricultural products were free from government intervention, they would be about as close as one could get to perfect competition in the real world. There are thousands of farmers, each insignificantly small relative to the total market. As a result, farmers are price takers.

Yet despite this high degree of competition, there is more government intervention in agriculture throughout the world than in virtually any other industry. For example, nearly half of the EU budget is spent on agricultural support. Agricultural markets therefore pose something of a paradox. If they are so perfect, why is there so much government intervention?

Why intervene?

The following are the most commonly cited problems of a free market in agricultural products.

Agricultural prices are subject to considerable fluctuations. This has a number of effects:

- Fluctuating prices cause fluctuating farm incomes. In some years, farm incomes may be very low.
- In other years, the consumer will suffer by having to pay very high prices.
- Fluctuating prices make the prediction of future prices very difficult. This in turn makes rational economic decision making very difficult. How is a farmer to choose which of two or more crops to plant if their prices cannot be predicted?
- This uncertainty may discourage farmers from making long-term investment plans. A farmer may be reluctant to invest in, say, a new milking parlour if in a couple of years it might be more profitable to switch to arable farming. A lack of investment by farmers will reduce the growth of efficiency in agriculture.

Low incomes for those in farming.   Over the years, farm incomes have tended to decline relative to those in other sectors of the economy. What is more, farmers have very little market power. A particular complaint of farmers is that they have to buy their inputs (tractors, fertilisers, etc.) from non-competitive suppliers who charge high prices. Then they often have to sell their produce at very low prices to food processors, packers, distributors and supermarkets. Farmers thus feel squeezed from both directions.

KI 4
p14

Traditional rural ways of life may be destroyed.   The pressure on farm incomes may cause unemployment and bankruptcies; smaller farms may be taken over by larger ones; village life may be threatened – with the break-up of communities and the closure of schools, shops and other amenities.

Competition from abroad.   Farming may well be threatened by cheap food imports from abroad. This may drive farmers out of business.

Against all these arguments must be set the argument that intervention involves economic costs. These may be costs to the taxpayer in providing financial support to farmers, or costs to the consumer in higher prices of foodstuffs, or costs to the economy as a whole by keeping resources locked into agriculture that could have been more efficiently used elsewhere.

Then there is the question of recent trends in food prices. With the rise in demand for food from rapidly growing countries, such as China and India, and with the increased use of land for growing biofuels rather than food crops, world food prices have risen. Farming in many parts of the world is becoming more profitable.

Causes of short-term price fluctuations

Supply problems.   A field is not like a machine. It cannot produce a precisely predictable amount of output according to the inputs fed in. The harvest is affected by a number of unpredictable factors such as the weather, pests and diseases. Fluctuating harvests mean that farmers' incomes will fluctuate.

Demand problems.   Food, being a basic necessity of life, has no substitute. If the price of food in general goes up, people cannot switch to an alternative: they have either to pay the higher price or to consume less food. They might consume a bit less, but not much. The price elasticity for food in general, therefore, is very low, as Table 3.1 shows.

KI 9
p66

It is not quite so low for individual foodstuffs because if the price of one goes up, people can always switch to an alternative. If beef goes up in price, people can buy pork or lamb instead. Nevertheless, certain foodstuffs still have a low price elasticity, especially if they are considered to be basic foods rather than luxuries, there are no close substitutes, or they account for a relatively small portion of consumers' income.

With an inelastic demand curve, any fluctuations in supply will cause large fluctuations in price. This is illustrated in Figure 3.10.

TC 6
p68

Table 3.1	Price and income elasticities of demand in the UK for various foodstuffs	
Foodstuff	Price elasticity of demand (average 2001–9)	Income elasticity of demand (1998–2000)
Milk	−0.70	−0.17
Cheese	−0.60	0.23
Poultry	−0.94	0.16
Lamb	−0.59	0.15
Pork	−0.77	0.13
Fish	−0.36	0.27
Eggs	−0.57	−0.01
Fresh vegetables	−1.00	0.22
Potatoes	−0.51	0.09
Fresh fruit	−0.99	0.30
Bananas	−0.62	0.12
Canned and dried fruit	−0.78	0.37
Fruit juice	−0.79	0.45
All foods	−0.07	0.20

Sources: Price elasticity data: based on and averaged from multiple tables by JS in Richard Tiffin, Kelvin Balcombe, Matthew Salois and Ariane Kehlbacher *Estimating Food and Drink Elasticities* (University of Reading, 2011); Income elasticity data: *National Food Survey 2000* (National Statistics, 2001), extracted by JS from Tables 6.3 and 6.5.

Figure 3.10	Inelastic demand for food

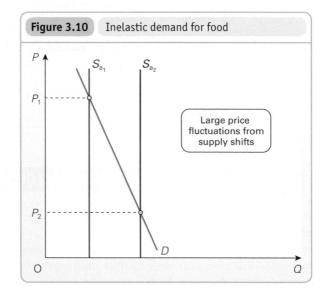

 Why is the supply curve drawn as a vertical straight line in Figure 3.10?

Causes of declining farm incomes

Demand problems.   There is a limit to the amount people wish to eat. As people get richer, they might buy better cuts of meat, or more convenience foods, but they will spend very little extra on basic foodstuffs. Their income elasticity of demand for basic foods is very low (see Table 3.1).

BOX 3.5   THE FALLACY OF COMPOSITION

Or when good is bad

Ask farmers whether they would like a good crop of potatoes this year, or whether they would rather their fields be ravaged by pests and disease, and the answer is obvious. After all, who would wish disaster upon themselves!

And yet what applies to an individual farmer does not apply to farmers as a whole. Disaster for all may turn out not to be disaster at all.

Why should this be? The answer has to do with price elasticity. The demand for food is highly price inelastic. A fall in supply, due to a poor harvest, will therefore cause a proportionately larger rise in price. Farmers' incomes will thus rise, not fall.

Look at diagram (a). Farmer Giles is a price taker. If he alone has a bad harvest, price will not change. He simply sells less (Q_2) and thus earns less. His revenue falls by the amount of the shaded area. But if all farmers have a bad harvest the picture is quite different, as shown in diagram (b). Supply falls from Q_1 to Q_2, and consequently price rises from P_1 to P_2. Revenue thus rises from areas (1 + 2) to areas (1 + 3).

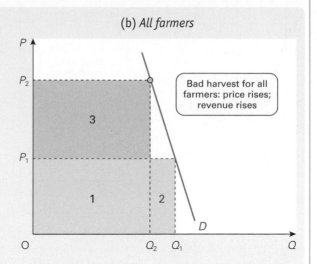

(b) *All farmers*

Bad harvest for all farmers: price rises; revenue rises

And so what applies to a single farmer in isolation (a fall in revenue) does not apply to farmers in general. This is known as the 'fallacy of composition'.

KEY IDEA 12 — *The fallacy of composition.* What applies in one case will not necessarily apply when repeated in all cases.

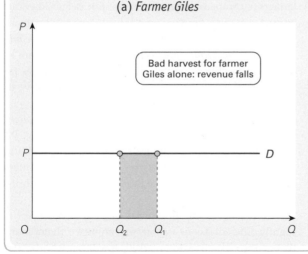

(a) *Farmer Giles*

Bad harvest for farmer Giles alone: revenue falls

1. *Can you think of any other (non-farming) examples of the fallacy of composition?*
2. *Would the above arguments apply in the case of foodstuffs that can be imported as well as being produced at home?*

Why don't farmers benefit from a high income elasticity of demand for convenience foods?

This very low income elasticity of demand has a crucial effect on farm incomes. It means that a rise in national income of 1 per cent leads to a rise in food consumption of considerably less than 1 per cent. As a result, total farm incomes will grow much more slowly than the incomes of other sectors, farmers' incomes will grow less rapidly than those of the owners of other businesses, and farm workers' wages will grow less rapidly than those of other workers.

Supply problems. Farming productivity has grown dramatically over the years as farmers have invested in new technology and improved farming methods. But, given the price-inelastic demand for food, increased supply will have the effect of driving down agricultural prices, thus largely offsetting any reduction in costs. And given the income-inelastic demand for food, the long-term rise in demand will be less than the long-term rise in supply.

Figure 3.11 shows a basic foodstuff like potatoes or other vegetables. Rising productivity leads to an increase in supply from S_1 to S_2. But given that demand is price inelastic and shifts only slightly to the right over time, from D_1 to D_2, price falls from P_1 to P_2.

As we saw above, this national effect of low price and income elasticities of demand and rising supply has been offset in recent years by growing *world* demand for food and

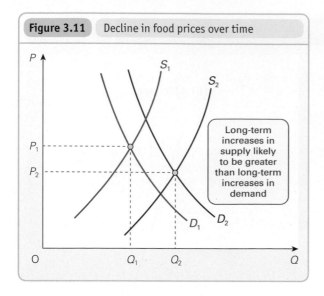

Figure 3.11 Decline in food prices over time

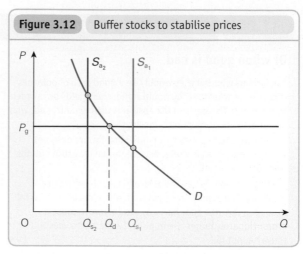

Figure 3.12 Buffer stocks to stabilise prices

problems with world supply, such as poor harvests, rising input costs (such as diesel and fertilisers) and the diversion of land to growing biofuels – in 2013, some 35 per cent of the US maize (corn) crop was being used for ethanol production. The effect of all this is a substantial increase in the prices of many foodstuffs, and in particular wheat, rice, maize and soya.

Government intervention

There are five main types of government intervention that can be used to ease the problems for farmers.

Buffer stocks
Buffer stocks involve the government buying food and placing it in store when harvests are good, and then releasing the food back on to the market when harvests are bad. They can thus only be used with food that can be stored: i.e. non-perishable foods, such as grain; or food that can be put into frozen storage, such as butter. The idea of buffer stocks is a very ancient one, as Case Study 3.4 on the student website demonstrates.

What the government does is to fix a price. Assume that this is P_g in Figure 3.12. At this price demand is Q_{d_1}. If there is a good harvest (S_{a_1}), the government buys up the surplus, $Q_{s_1} - Q_d$, and puts it into store. If there is a bad harvest (S_{a_2}), it releases $Q_d - Q_{s_2}$ from the store on to the market.

This system clearly stabilises price, at P_g. At this price, though, farm incomes will still fluctuate with the size of the harvest. It is possible, however, to have a buffer stock system that stabilises *incomes*. Such a system is examined in Case Study 3.5 on the student website.

To prevent stores mounting over time, the government price will have to be the one that balances demand and supply over the years. Surpluses in good years will have to match shortages in bad years. Buffer stocks, therefore, can only

stabilise prices or incomes; they do not *increase* farm incomes over the long term.

Subsidies
The government can pay subsidies or grant tax relief to farmers to compensate for low market prices. Subsidies can be used to increase farm incomes as well as to stabilise them. The simplest form of subsidy is one known as **direct income support** or **direct aid**. Here farmers are paid a fixed sum of money irrespective of output. Given that such subsidies are unrelated to output, they do not provide an incentive to produce more.

An alternative system is to pay a subsidy *per unit of output*, which we examined in section 3.2. Figure 3.7 on page 92 illustrates the impact of a specific subsidy on an agricultural product in which the country is self-sufficient – farmers have an incentive to produce more, and the market price falls.

When some of the product is imported, the effect is slightly different. Let us assume, for simplicity, that a country is a price taker in world markets. It will face a horizontal world supply curve of the product at the world price. In other words, consumers can buy all they want at the world price. In Figure 3.13 the world price is P_w. Without a subsidy, domestic supply is Q_{s_1}. Domestic demand is Q_d. Imports are therefore the difference: $Q_d - Q_{s_1}$.

Assume now that the government wants farmers to receive a price of P_g. At that price, domestic supply increases

> ## Definitions
>
> **Buffer stocks** Stocks of a product used to stabilise its price. In years of abundance, the stocks are built up. In years of low supply, stocks are released on to the market.
>
> **Direct income support or direct aid** A fixed grant to farmers that does not vary with current output. It may be based on acreage, number of livestock or past output.

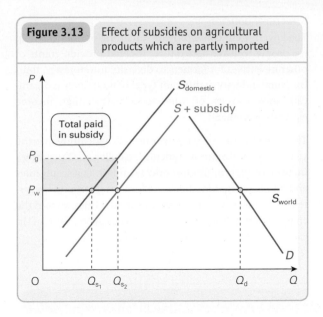

Figure 3.13 Effect of subsidies on agricultural products which are partly imported

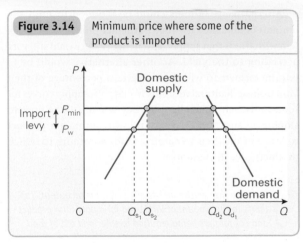

Figure 3.14 Minimum price where some of the product is imported

to Q_{s_2}, but the price paid by the consumer does not fall. It remains at P_w. The subsidy paid per unit is $P_g - P_w$. The cost to the taxpayer is again shown by the shaded area.

A problem with subsidies of a fixed amount per unit is that the price the farmer receives will fluctuate along with the market price. An alternative, therefore, would be to let the size of the subsidy vary with the market price. The lower the price, the bigger the subsidy.

An advantage of subsidies is that they result in lower prices for the consumer. On the other hand, they have to be paid from tax revenues and therefore result in higher taxes.

High minimum prices

If the government considers agricultural prices to be too low, it can set a minimum price for each product above the free-market level as we discussed in section 3.1. This was the traditional approach adopted in the EU. In recent years, however, forms of intervention in the EU have become more diverse.

Once again, the effect of high minimum prices will vary between products, depending on whether the country is a net importer or self-sufficient. If the country is self-sufficient, Figure 3.3 on page 82 would illustrate its impact.

How would Figure 3.3 change if the government were able to sell the surplus food on the world market.

Agricultural products where the country is a net importer.   Assuming that the minimum price is above the world price, the government will need to impose customs duties (known alternatively as **tariffs** or **import levies**) on imported products to bring them up to the required price. Given that the world price will fluctuate, these import levies would need to be variable.

The effects of this system are illustrated in Figure 3.14. If trade took place freely at the world price P_w, Q_{d_1} would be demanded and Q_{s_1} supplied domestically. The difference $(Q_{d_1} - Q_{s_1})$ would be imported.

If a minimum price P_{min} is now set and a levy imposed on imports to raise their price to P_{min}, domestic prices will also rise to this level. Demand will fall to Q_{d_2}. Domestic supply will rise to Q_{s_2}. Imports will fall to $Q_{d_2} - Q_{s_2}$. The amount paid in import levies is shown by the shaded area.

What would be the amount paid in Figure 3.14 if instead of the government buying the surpluses, export subsidies were given to farmers so as to guarantee them a price (plus subsidy) of P_{min}?

Reductions in supply

An alternative approach would be to find some way of reducing supply. This would lead to a higher market price and could avoid the cost to the taxpayer of buying surpluses or paying subsidies.

In open markets, however, a reduction in domestic supply could simply lead to an increase in imports, with the result that the price would not rise to the desired level. In such a case, a combination of a reduction in domestic supply and import levies (or other import restrictions) would be required.

But how could supply be reduced? The simplest way would be to give farmers a quota specifying how much each was allowed to produce. Milk quotas, which have been in force in the EU since 1984, are an example of this system.

Definition

Tariffs or import levies Taxes on imported products: i.e. customs duties.

Alternatively, farmers could be required to limit the amount of *land* they use for a particular product. The problem with this is that supply, and hence price, would still vary according to the yield. Another alternative would be to require farmers to withdraw a certain percentage of their land from agricultural use. This would shift supply curves for food to the left generally, but they would still be upward sloping because farmers could still switch from one product to another on their remaining land, according to which products gave the best price.

Compare the relative merits of (a) quotas on output, (b) limits to the amount of land used for a particular product and (c) farmers being required to take land out of food production.

Structural policies

The government could provide retraining or financial help for people to leave agriculture. It could provide grants or other incentives for farmers to diversify into forestry, tourism, rural industry or different types of food, such as organically grown crops, or other foods with a high income elasticity of demand.

The EU has made major interventions in agriculture over the years under its Common Agricultural Policy or 'CAP' using a mixture of high minimum prices, import levies, subsidies and supply restrictions. It has made major reforms to the system over the years in response to various criticisms and the changing agricultural environment. The CAP is examined in Case Study 3.8 on the student website.

Section summary

1. Despite the fact that a free market in agricultural produce would be highly competitive, there is large-scale government intervention in agriculture throughout the world. The aims of intervention include preventing or reducing price fluctuations, encouraging greater national self-sufficiency, increasing farm incomes, encouraging farm investment, and protecting traditional rural ways of life and the rural environment generally.

2. Price fluctuations are the result of fluctuating supply combined with a price-inelastic demand. The supply fluctuations are due to fluctuations in the harvest.

3. The demand for food is generally income inelastic and thus grows only slowly over time. Supply, on the other hand, has generally grown rapidly as a result of new technology and new farm methods. This puts downward pressure on prices – a problem made worse for farmers by the price inelasticity of demand for food.

4. Government intervention can be in the form of buffer stocks, subsidies, price support, quotas and other ways of reducing supply, and structural policies.

5. Buffer stocks can be used to stabilise prices. They cannot be used to increase farm incomes over time.

6. Subsidies will increase farm incomes but will lower consumer prices to the world price level (or to the point where the market clears).

7. Minimum (high) prices will create surpluses, which must be bought by the government and possibly resold on international markets. In the case of partly imported foodstuffs, the high price is achieved by imposing variable import levies.

8. Supply can be reduced by the imposition of quotas on output or restricting the amount of land that can be used.

END OF CHAPTER QUESTIONS

1. Assume that the (weekly) market demand and supply of tomatoes are given by the following figures:

Price (£ per kilo)	4.00	3.50	3.00	2.50	2.00	1.50	1.00
Q_d (000 kilos)	30	35	40	45	50	55	60
Q_s (000 kilos)	80	68	62	55	50	45	38

(a) What are the equilibrium price and quantity?

(b) What will be the effect of the government fixing a *minimum* price of (i) £3 per kilo; (ii) £1.50 per kilo?

(c) Suppose that the government paid tomato producers a subsidy of £1 per kilo.

   (i) Give the new supply schedule.

(ii) What will be the new equilibrium price?

(iii) How much will this cost the government?

(d) Alternatively, suppose that the government guaranteed tomato producers a price of £2.50 per kilo.

   (i) How many tomatoes would it have to buy in order to ensure that all the tomatoes produced were sold?

   (ii) How much would this cost the government?

(e) Alternatively, suppose it bought *all* the tomatoes produced at £2.50.

   (i) At what single price would it have to sell them in order to dispose of the lot?

   (ii) What would be the net cost of this action?

2. Think of two things that are provided free of charge. In each case, identify whether and in what form a shortage might occur. In what ways are/could these shortages be dealt with? Are they the best solution to the shortages?

3. Discuss the relative merits of the different methods used by the All England Tennis Club to allocate tickets for Wimbledon each year.

4. If the government increases the tax on a litre of petrol by 5p, what will determine the amount by which the price of petrol will go up as a result of this tax increase?

5. Illustrate on four separate diagrams (as in Figure 3.6) the effect of different elasticities of demand and supply on the incidence of a subsidy.

6. The Soft Drinks Industry Levy will take effect in the UK from April 2018. Explain how this tax will work and discuss its potential impact on consumer behaviour.

7. Why are agricultural prices subject to greater fluctuations than those of manufactured products?

8. Compare the relative benefits of subsidies and high minimum prices to (a) the consumer; (b) the producer.

Online resources

Additional case studies on the student website

3.1 Rationing. A case study in the use of rationing as an alternative to the price mechanism. In particular, it looks at the use of rationing in the UK during the Second World War.

3.2 Underground (or shadow) markets How underground markets can develop when prices are fixed below the equilibrium.

3.3 Rent control. The effect of government control of rents on the market for rental property

3.4 Seven years of plenty and seven years of famine. This looks at how buffer stocks were used by Joseph in biblical Egypt.

3.5 Buffer stocks to stabilise farm incomes. This theoretical case shows how the careful use of buffer stocks combined with changes in set prices can be used to stabilise farm incomes.

3.6 Agricultural subsidies. This considers who gains and who loses from the use of subsidies on the production of agricultural products.

3.7 The CAP and the environment. This case shows how the system of high intervention prices had damaging environmental effects. It also examines the more recent measures the EU has adopted to reverse the effects.

3.8 The Common Agricultural Policy of the EU. This case study looks at the various forms of intervention in agriculture that have been used in the EU. It looks at successes and problems and at various reforms that have been introduced.

Websites relevant to this chapter

Numbers and sections refer to websites listed in the Web Appendix and hotlinked from this book's website at **www.pearsoned.co.uk/sloman.**

■ For news articles relevant to this chapter, see the *Economics News* section on the student website.

■ For general news on markets and market intervention, see websites in section A, and particularly A1-5, 7-9, 18, 21, 25, 26, 35, 36. See also A38, 39, 42, 43 and 44 for links to newspapers worldwide; and A40 and 41 for links to economics news articles from newspapers worldwide.

■ For information on taxes in the UK, see sites E25, 30 and 36.

■ For information on agriculture and the Common Agricultural Policy, see sites E14 and G9.

■ For sites favouring the free market, see C17 and E34.

■ For student resources relevant to this chapter, see sites C1-7, 10, 19, 28.

■ For a range of classroom games and simulations of markets and market intervention, see sites C23, 24 and 27 (computer-based) and C20 (non-computer-based).

Microeconomic Theory

We now examine in more detail how economies function at a micro level. In doing so, we look at some of the big questions of our time. How do consumers choose between different goods? Why do some firms make such large profits? Why is there such a gap between the rich and the poor?

Chapters 4 to 6 examine demand and supply in more detail. Then in Chapters 7 to 9 we look at how the degree of competition a firm faces affects its prices and profits. Finally, in Chapter 10 we look at the distribution of income: why some people are rich while others are poor.

4

Chapter

Background to Demand: the Rational Consumer

In this chapter we take a more detailed look at consumer demand. If we had unlimited income and time we would not have to be careful with our money. In the real world, however, given limited incomes and the problem of scarcity, we have to make choices about what to buy. You may have to choose between buying textbooks and going to a festival, between a new pair of jeans and a meal out, between saving for a car and having more money to spend on everyday items.

We start by assuming in this chapter that consumers behave 'rationally'. Remember in Chapter 1 we defined rational choices, those that involve weighing up the costs and benefits of our actions. As far as consumption is concerned, rational action involves considering the relative costs and benefits to us of the alternatives we could spend our money on. We do this in order to gain the maximum satisfaction possible from our limited incomes.

Of course, this does not mean that you look at every item on the supermarket shelf and weigh up the satisfaction you think you would get from it against the price on the label. Nevertheless, you have probably learned over time the sort of things you like and what they cost and can make out a 'rational' shopping list quite quickly.

There are two main approaches to analysing consumer behaviour: the marginal utility approach and the indifference approach. We examine both of them in this chapter.

We also look at the problem of making rational choices when benefits occur over a period of time, as is the case with durable goods, or later, as is the case with goods where there is a waiting list or where orders take some time to deliver.

As we start by examining the **rational consumer**, it is important to understand what we mean by the term. Economists use it to refer a person who attempts to get the best value for money from their purchases, given a limited income. Thus the rational consumer tries to ensure that the benefits of a purchase are worth the expense.

Sometimes we may act 'irrationally'. We may buy goods impetuously or out of habit. In general, however, economists believe it is reasonable to assume that people behave rationally.

Do you ever purchase things irrationally? If so, what are they and why is your behaviour irrational?

Two words of warning before we go on. First, don't confuse irrationality and ignorance. In this chapter we assume that consumers behave rationally, (something we query in the next chapter) but that does not mean they have perfect information. Have you ever been disappointed after buying something? Perhaps it was not as good as you had expected from an advert? Or perhaps you found later that you could have bought an alternative more cheaply? Perhaps a holiday may not turn out to be as good as the website led you to believe. This is a problem of ignorance rather than irrationality.

Second, the term 'rational' does not imply any approval of the decision involved. It is simply referring to behaviour that is consistent with your own particular goals: behaviour directed to getting the most out of your limited income. People may disapprove of the things that others buy – their clothes, junk food, lottery tickets – but as economists we should not make judgements about people's goals. We can, however, look at the implications of people behaving rationally in pursuit of those goals. This is what we are doing when we examine rational consumer behaviour: we are looking at its implications for consumer demand.

4.1 MARGINAL UTILITY THEORY

Total and marginal utility

People buy goods and services because they get satisfaction from them. Economists call this satisfaction 'utility'.

An important distinction must be made between *total utility* and *marginal utility*.

Total utility (*TU*) is the total satisfaction a person gains from all those units of a commodity consumed within a given time period. If Lucy drinks 10 cups of tea a day, her daily total utility from tea is the satisfaction derived from those 10 cups.

Marginal utility (*MU*) is the additional satisfaction gained from consuming one *extra* unit within a given period of time. Thus we might refer to the marginal utility that Lucy gains from her third cup of tea of the day or her eleventh cup.

A difficulty arises with the utility approach to explaining demand: how do you measure utility? Utility is subjective. There is no way of knowing what another person's experiences are really like. How satisfying does Nick find his first cup of tea in the morning? How does his utility compare with Lucy's?

For the moment, we will assume that a person's utility *can be measured*. We use an imaginary measure called utils, where a **util** is one unit of satisfaction.

Diminishing marginal utility

Up to a point, the more of a commodity you consume, the greater will be your total utility. However, as you become more satisfied, each extra unit that you consume will probably give you less additional utility than previous units. In other words, your marginal utility falls, the more you consume. This is known as the **principle of diminishing marginal utility**.

KEY IDEA 13

The principle of diminishing marginal utility. The more of a product a person consumes, the less will be the additional utility gained from one more unit.

For example, the second cup of tea in the morning gives you less additional satisfaction than the first cup. The third cup gives less satisfaction still.

At some level of consumption, your total utility will be at a maximum. No extra satisfaction can be gained by the consumption of further units within that period of time. Thus marginal utility will be zero. Your desire for tea may be fully satisfied at seven cups per day. An eighth cup will yield no extra utility. It may even give you displeasure (i.e. negative marginal utility).

Definitions

Rational consumer A person who weighs up the costs and benefits to them of each additional unit of a good purchased.

Total utility The total satisfaction a consumer gets from the consumption of all the units of a good consumed within a given time period.

Marginal utility The extra satisfaction gained from consuming one extra unit of a good within a given time period.

Util An imaginary unit of satisfaction from the consumption of a good.

Principle of diminishing marginal utility As more units of a good are consumed, additional units will provide less additional satisfaction than previous units.

Are there any goods or services where consumers do not experience diminishing marginal utility?

Total and marginal utility curves

If we could measure utility, we could construct a table showing how much total and marginal utility a person would gain at different levels of consumption of a particular commodity. This information could then be transferred to a graph. Table 4.1 and Figure 4.1 do just this. They show the imaginary utility that Ollie gets from consuming packets of crisps.

Referring first to the table, if Ollie consumes no crisps, he obviously gets no satisfaction from crisps: his total utility is zero. If he now consumes one packet a day, he gets 7 utils of satisfaction. (Sorry if this sounds silly, but we will tackle this question of measurement later.) His total utility is 7, and his marginal utility is also 7. They must be equal if only one unit is consumed.

If he now consumes a second packet, he gains an extra 4 utils (*MU*), giving him a total utility of 11 utils (i.e. 7 + 4). His marginal utility has fallen because, having already eaten one packet, he has less craving for a second. A third packet gives him less extra utility still: marginal utility has fallen to 2 utils, giving a total utility of 13 utils (i.e. 11 + 2).

By the time he has eaten five packets, he would rather not eat any more. A sixth actually reduces his utility (from 14 utils to 13): its marginal utility is negative.

The information in Table 4.1 is plotted in Figure 4.1. Notice the following points about the two curves:

■ The *MU* curve slopes downwards. This is simply illustrating the principle of diminishing marginal utility.
■ The *TU* curve starts at the origin. Zero consumption yields zero utility.
■ The *TU* curve reaches a peak when marginal utility is zero. When marginal utility is zero (at five packets of crisps), there is no addition to total utility. Total utility must be at the maximum – the peak of the curve.
■ Marginal utility can be derived from the *TU* curve. It is the slope of the line joining two adjacent quantities on the curve. For example, the marginal utility of the third packet of crisps is the slope of the line joining points *a* and *b*. The slope of such a line is given by the formula

$$\frac{\Delta TU}{\Delta Q} (= MU)$$

In our example $\Delta TU = 2$ (total utility has risen from 11 to 13 utils), and $\Delta Q = 1$ (one more packet of crisps has been consumed). Thus $MU = 2$.

Table 4.1	Ollie's utility from consuming crisps (daily)	
Packets of crisps consumed	**TU in utils**	**MU in utils**
0	0	–
1	7	7
2	11	4
3	13	2
4	14	1
5	14	0
6	13	−1

Figure 4.1	Ollie's utility from consuming crisps (daily)

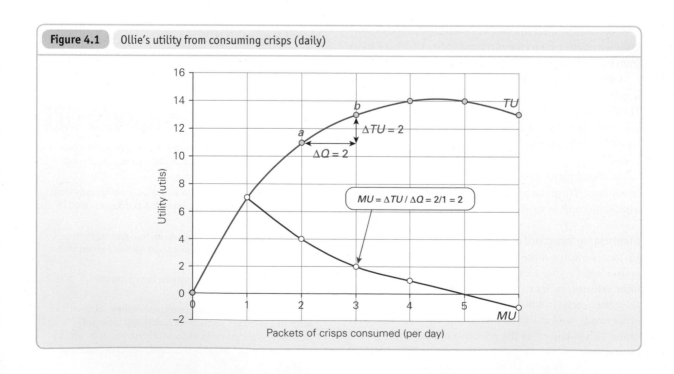

*BOX 4.1   USING CALCULUS TO DERIVE A MARGINAL UTILITY FUNCTION

The relationship between total utility and marginal utility can be shown using calculus. If you are not familiar with the rules of calculus, ignore this box (or see Appendix 1, pages A:9–13).

A consumer's typical utility function for a good might be of the form

$$TU = 600Q - 4Q^2$$

where Q is the quantity of the good consumed. This would give the figures shown in the following table.

Q	60Q	$-4Q^2$	=	TU
1	60	−4	=	56
2	120	−16	=	104
3	180	−36	=	144
4	240	−64	=	176
.	.	.		.

1. **Complete this table to the level of consumption at which TU is at a maximum.**

Marginal utility is the first derivative of total utility. In other words, it is the rate of change of total utility. Differentiating the *TU* function gives

$$MU = \frac{dTU}{dQ} = 600 - 8Q$$

This gives the figures shown in the following table.

Q	60Q	−8Q	=	MU
1	60	−8	=	52
2	60	−16	=	44
3	60	−24	=	36
4	60	−32	=	28
.	.	.		.

Note that the marginal utility diminishes.

The *MU* function we have derived is a straight-line function. If, however, the *TU* function contained a cubed term (Q^3), the *MU* function would be a curve.

2. **Derive the MU function from the following TU function:**

$$TU = 200Q - 25Q^2 + Q^3$$

From this MU function, draw a table (like the one above) up to the level of Q where MU becomes negative. Graph these figures.

If Ollie were to consume more and more crisps, would his total utility ever (a) fall to zero; (b) become negative? Explain.

The ceteris paribus *assumption*

The table and graph we have drawn are based on the assumption that other things do not change.

In practice, other things *do* change – and frequently. The utility that Ollie gets from crisps depends on what else he eats. If on Saturday he has a lot to eat he will get little satisfaction from crisps. If on Monday, however, he is too busy to eat proper meals, he would probably welcome one or more packets of crisps.

Each time the consumption of *other* goods changed – whether substitutes or complements – a new utility schedule would have to be drawn up. The curves would shift. Remember, utility is not a property of the goods themselves. Utility is in the mind of the consumer, and consumers change their minds. Their tastes change; their circumstances change; their consumption patterns change.

The optimum level of consumption: the simplest case – one commodity

Just how much of a good should people consume if they are to make the best use of their limited income? To answer this question we must tackle the problem of how to measure utility, given that in practice we cannot measure 'utils'.

One solution to the problem is to measure utility with money. In this case, utility becomes the value that people place on their consumption. Marginal utility thus becomes the amount of money a person would be prepared to pay to obtain one more unit: in other words, what that extra unit is worth to that person. If Ollie is prepared to pay 60p to obtain an extra packet of crisps, then we can say that packet yields him 60p worth of utility: $MU = 60p$.

So how many packets should he consume if he is to act rationally? To answer this we need to introduce the concept of *consumer surplus*.

Marginal consumer surplus

Marginal consumer surplus (*MCS*) is the difference between what you are willing to pay for one more unit of a good and what you are actually charged. If Ollie were willing to pay 45p for another packet of crisps which in fact only cost him 40p, he would be getting a marginal consumer surplus of 5p.

$$MCS = MU - P$$

Definitions

Consumer surplus The excess of what a person would have been prepared to pay for a good (i.e. the utility) over what that person actually pays.

Marginal consumer surplus The excess of utility from the consumption of one more unit of a good (*MU*) over the price paid: $MCS = MU - P$.

Total consumer surplus

Total consumer surplus (*TCS*) is the sum of all the marginal consumer surpluses that you have obtained from all the units of a good you have consumed. It is the difference between the total utility from all the units and your expenditure on them. If Ollie consumes four packets of crisps, and if he would have been prepared to spend £2.60 on them and only had to spend £2.20, then his total consumer surplus is 40p.

$$TCS = TU - TE$$

where *TE* is the total expenditure on a good: i.e. $P \times Q$.

Let us define **rational consumer behaviour** as the attempt to maximise consumer surplus. How do people set about doing this?

People will go on purchasing additional units as long as they gain additional consumer surplus: in other words, as long as the price they are prepared to pay exceeds the price they are charged ($MU > P$). But as more is purchased, so they will experience diminishing marginal utility. They will be prepared to pay less for each additional unit.

Their marginal utility will go on falling until $MU = P$: i.e. until no further consumer surplus can be gained. At that point, they will stop purchasing additional units. Their optimum level of consumption has been reached: consumer surplus has been maximised. If they continue to purchase beyond this point, *MU* would be less than *P,* and thus they would be paying more for the last units than they were worth to them.

The process of maximising consumer surplus can be shown graphically. Let us take the case of Tanya's annual purchases of petrol. Tanya has her own car, but as an alternative she can use public transport or walk. To keep the analysis simple, let us assume that Tanya's parents bought her the car and pay the licence duty, and that Tanya does not have the option of selling the car. She does, however, have to buy the petrol. The current price is £1.30 per litre. Figure 4.2 shows her consumer surplus.

If she were to use just a few litres per year, she would use them for very important journeys for which no convenient alternative exists. For such trips she may be prepared to pay up to £1.60 per litre. For the first few litres, then, she is getting a marginal utility of around £1.60 per litre, and hence a marginal consumer surplus of around 30p (i.e. £1.60 − £1.30).

By the time her annual purchase is around 200 litres, she would be prepared to pay only around £1.50 for additional litres. The additional journeys, although still important, would be less vital. Perhaps these are journeys where she could have taken public transport, albeit at some inconvenience. Her marginal consumer surplus at 200 litres is 20p (i.e. £1.50 − £1.30).

Gradually, additional litres give less and less additional utility as less important journeys are undertaken. The 500th litre yields £1.40 worth of extra utility. Marginal consumer surplus is now 10p (i.e. £1.40 − £1.30).

By the time she gets to the 900th litre, Tanya's marginal utility has fallen to £1.30. There is no additional consumer

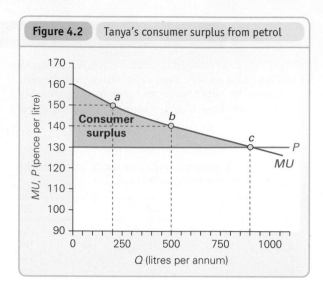

Figure 4.2 Tanya's consumer surplus from petrol

surplus to be gained. Her total consumer surplus is at a maximum. She thus buys 900 litres, where $P = MU$.

Her total consumer surplus is the sum of all the marginal consumer surpluses: the sum of all the 900 vertical lines between the price and the *MU* curve. This is shown by the total *area* between *P* and *MU* up to 900 litres (i.e. the pink shaded area in Figure 4.2).

This analysis can be expressed in general terms. In Figure 4.3, if the price of a commodity is P_1, the consumer will consume Q_1. The person's total expenditure (*TE*) is

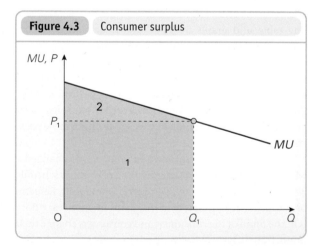

Figure 4.3 Consumer surplus

Definitions

Total consumer surplus The excess of a person's total utility from the consumption of a good (*TU*) over the total amount that person spends on it (*TE*): $TCS = TU - TE$.

Rational consumer behaviour The attempt to maximise total consumer surplus.

THRESHOLD CONCEPT 8   **RATIONAL DECISION MAKING INVOLVES CHOICES AT THE MARGIN**   THINKING LIKE AN ECONOMIST

Rational decision making involves weighing up the marginal benefit and marginal cost of any activity. If the marginal benefit exceeds the marginal cost, it is rational to do the activity (or to do more of it). If the marginal cost exceeds the marginal benefit, it is rational not to do it (or to do less of it).

Let's take the case of when you go to the supermarket to do shopping for the week. Assume that you have £50 to spend. Clearly, you will want to spend it wisely. With each item you consider buying, you should ask yourself what its marginal benefit is to you: in other words, how much you would be prepared to spend on it. This will depend on the prices and benefits of alternatives. Thus if you were considering spending £3 from the £50 on wholemeal bread, you should ask yourself whether the £3 would be better spent on some alternative, such as white bread, rolls or crackers. The *best* alternative (which might be a combination of products) is the marginal opportunity cost. If the answer is that you feel you are getting better value for money by spending it on the wholemeal bread, then you are saying that the marginal benefit exceeds the marginal opportunity cost. It is an efficient use of your money to buy the wholemeal bread and forgo the alternatives.

Most decisions are more complex than this, as they involve buying a whole range of products. In fact, that is what you are doing in the supermarket. But the principle is still the same. In each case, a rational decision involves weighing up marginal benefits and marginal costs.

This is another example of a *threshold concept* because it is a way of thinking about economic problems. It is a general principle that can be applied in a whole host of contexts: whether it is individuals deciding what to buy, how much to work, what job to apply for, or whether to study for a degree or take a job; or firms deciding how much to produce, whether to invest in new capacity or new products, or what type of people to employ and how many; or governments deciding how much to spend on various projects, such as roads, hospitals and schools, or what rates of tax to impose on companies that pollute the environment.

In each case, better decisions will be made by weighing up marginal costs and marginal benefits.

1. *Assume that a firm is selling 1000 units of a product at £20 each and that each unit on average costs £15 to produce. Assume also that to produce additional units will cost the firm £19 each and that the price will remain at £20. To produce additional products will therefore reduce the average profit per unit. Should the firm expand production? Explain.*
2. *Assume that a ferry has capacity for 500 passengers. Its operator predicts that it will typically have only 200 passengers on each of its midweek sailings over the winter. Assume also that each sailing costs the company £10 000. This means that midweek winter sailings cost the company an average of £10 000/200 = £50 per passenger. Currently tickets cost £60.*
   Should the company consider selling stand-by tickets during the winter for (a) less than £60; (b) less than £50? (Clue: think about the marginal cost of taking additional passengers.)

P_1Q_1, shown by area 1. Total utility (*TU*) is the area under the marginal utility curve: i.e. areas 1 + 2. Total consumer surplus (($TU - TE$)) is shown by area 2.

 If a good were free, why would total consumer surplus equal total utility? What would be the level of marginal utility at the equilibrium level of consumption?

Marginal utility and the demand curve for a good

An individual's demand curve

Individual people's demand curve for any good will be the same as their marginal utility curve for that good, where utility is measured in money.

This is demonstrated in Figure 4.4, which shows the marginal utility curve for a particular person and a particular good. If the price of the good were P_1, the person would consume Q_1, where $MU = P_1$. Thus point *a* would be one point on that person's demand curve. If the price fell to P_2, consumption would rise to Q_2, since this is where $MU = P_2$. Thus point *b* is a second point on the demand curve. Likewise if

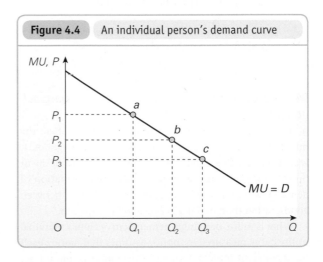

Figure 4.4   An individual person's demand curve

price fell to P_3, Q_3 would be consumed. Point *c* is a third point on the demand curve.

Thus as long as individuals seek to maximise consumer surplus and hence consume where $P = MU$, their demand curve will be along the same line as their marginal utility curve.

The market demand curve

The market demand curve will simply be the (horizontal) sum of all individuals' demand curves and hence *MU* curves.

The shape of the demand curve. The price elasticity of demand will reflect the rate at which *MU* diminishes. If there are close substitutes for a good, it is likely to have an elastic demand, and its *MU* will diminish slowly as consumption increases. The reason is that increased consumption of this product will be accompanied by decreased consumption of the alternative product(s). Since total consumption of this product plus the alternatives has increased only slightly (if at all), the marginal utility will fall only slowly.

For example, the demand for a certain brand of petrol is likely to have a fairly high price elasticity, since other brands are substitutes. If there is a cut in the price of Texaco petrol (assuming the prices of other brands stay constant), then consumption of Texaco petrol will increase a lot. The *MU* of Texaco petrol will fall slowly, since people consume less of other brands. Petrol consumption *in total* may be only slightly greater, and hence the *MU* of petrol only slightly lower.

> *Why do we get less total consumer surplus from goods where our demand is relatively elastic?*

Shifts in the demand curve. How do shifts in demand relate to marginal utility? For example, how would the marginal utility of (and hence demand for) tea be affected by a rise in the price of coffee? The higher price of coffee would cause less coffee to be consumed. This would increase the marginal utility of tea since if people are drinking less coffee, their desire for tea is higher. The *MU* curve (and hence the demand curve) for tea thus shifts to the right.

> *How would marginal utility and market demand be affected by a rise in the price of a complementary good?*

Weaknesses of the one-commodity version of marginal utility theory

A change in the consumption of one good will affect the marginal utility of substitute and complementary goods. It will also affect the amount of income left over to be spent on other goods. Thus, a more satisfactory explanation of demand would involve an analysis of choices between goods, rather than looking at one good in isolation.

What is more, deriving a demand curve from a marginal utility curve measured in money assumes that money itself has a constant marginal utility. The trouble is that it does not. If people have a rise in income, they will consume more. Other things being equal, the marginal utility of the goods that they consume will diminish. Thus an extra £1 of consumption will bring less satisfaction than previously. In other words, it is likely that the *marginal utility of money diminishes as income rises.*

Unless a good occupies only a tiny fraction of people's expenditure, a fall in its price will mean that their real income has increased: i.e. they can afford to purchase more goods in general. As they do so, the marginal utility of their money will fall. We cannot, therefore, legitimately use money to measure utility in an absolute sense. We can, however, still talk about the relative utility that we get from various goods for a given increase in expenditure.

The following sections thus look at the choice between goods, and how it relates to marginal utility.

The optimum combination of goods consumed

We can use marginal utility analysis to show how a rational person decides what combination of goods to buy. Given that we have limited incomes, we have to make choices. It is not just a question of choosing between two obvious substitutes, like a holiday in Greece and one in Spain, but about allocating our incomes between all the goods and services we might like to consume. If you have, say, an income of £20 000 per year, what is the optimum 'bundle' of goods and services for you to spend it on?

The rule for rational consumer behaviour is known as the **equi-marginal principle**. This states that a consumer will get the highest utility from a given level of income when the ratio of the marginal utilities is equal to the ratio of the prices. Algebraically, this is when, for any pair of goods, A and B, that are consumed:

$$\frac{MU_A}{MU_B} = \frac{P_A}{P_B} \tag{1}$$

To understand this, suppose that the last unit of good A you consumed gave three times as much utility as the last unit of B. Yet good A only cost twice as much as good B. You would obviously gain by increasing your consumption of A and cutting your purchases of B. But as you switched from B to A, the marginal utility of A would fall due to diminishing marginal utility, and conversely the marginal utility of B would rise.

To maximise utility you would continue this substitution of A for B until the ratios of the marginal utilities (MU_A/MU_B) equalled the ratio of the prices of the two goods (P_A/P_A). At this point, no further gain can be made by switching from one good to another. This is the optimum combination of goods to consume.

Equation (1) is a specific example of the general equi-marginal principle in economics, which applies to all rational

---

> **Definition**
>
> **Equi-marginal principle (in consumption)** Consumers will maximise total utility from their incomes by consuming that combination of goods where
> $$\frac{MU_A}{MU_B} = \frac{P_A}{P_B}$$

> **BOX 4.2**   **THE MARGINAL UTILITY REVOLUTION: JEVONS, MENGER, WALRAS**   **EXPLORING ECONOMICS**
>
> ### Solving the diamonds–water paradox
>
> What determines the market value of a good? We already know the answer: demand and supply. So if we find out what determines the position of the demand and supply curves, we will at the same time be finding out what determines a good's market value.
>
> This might seem obvious. Yet for years economists puzzled over just what determines a good's value.
>
> Some economists like Karl Marx and David Ricardo concentrated on the supply side. For them, value depended on the amount of resources used in producing a good. This could be further reduced to the amount of labour time embodied in the good. Thus, according to the labour theory of value, the more labour that was directly involved in producing the good, or indirectly in producing the capital equipment used to make the good, the more valuable would the good be.
>
> Other economists looked at the demand side. But here they came across a paradox.
>
> Adam Smith in the 1760s gave the example of water and diamonds. 'How is it', he asked, 'that water which is so essential to human life, and thus has such a high "value-in-use", has such a low market value (or "value-in-exchange")? And how is it that diamonds which are relatively so trivial have such a high market value?' The answer to this paradox had to wait over a hundred years until the marginal utility revolution of the 1870s. William Stanley Jevons (1835–82) in England, Carl Menger (1840–1921) in Austria and Léon Walras (1834–1910) in Switzerland all independently claimed that the source of the market value of a good was its marginal utility, not its total utility.
>
> This was the solution to the diamonds–water paradox. Water, being so essential, has a high total utility: a high 'value in use'. But for most of us, given that we consume so much already, it has a very low marginal utility. Do you leave the cold tap running when you clean your teeth? If you do, it shows just how trivial water is to you at the margin. Diamonds, on the
>
> other hand, although they have a much lower total utility, have a much higher marginal utility. There are so few diamonds in the world, and thus people have so few of them, that they are very valuable at the margin. If, however, a new technique were to be discovered of producing diamonds cheaply from coal, their market value would fall rapidly. As people had more of them, so their marginal utility would rapidly diminish.
>
> Marginal utility still only gives the demand side of the story. The reason why the marginal utility of water is so low is that supply is so plentiful. Water is very expensive in Saudi Arabia! In other words, the full explanation of value must take into account both demand and supply.
>
>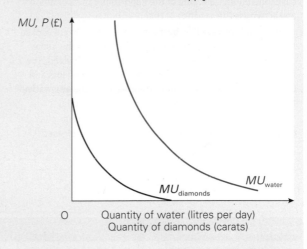
>
> *The diagram illustrates a person's MU curves of water and diamonds. Assume that diamonds are more expensive than water. Show how the MU of diamonds will be greater than the MU of water. Show also how the TU of diamonds will be less than the TU of water. (Remember: TU is the area under the MU curve.)*

---

choices between two alternatives, whether in production, consumption, employment or whatever.

The multi-commodity version of marginal utility and the demand curve

How can we derive a demand curve from the above analysis?

Let us simply reinterpret equation (1) so that it relates the *MU* and *P* of good A to the *MU* and *P* of *any* other good. In

other words, the equation would be the same for goods B, C, D, E and any other good. For any given income, and given prices for good A and all other goods, the quantity a person will demand of good A will be that which satisfies equation (1). One point on the individual's demand curve for good A has been determined.

If the price of good A now falls, such that

$$\frac{MU_A}{MU_B} > \frac{P_A}{P_B} \text{ (and similarly for goods C, D, E, etc.)}$$

the person would buy more of good A and less of all other goods (B, C, D, E, etc.), until equation (1) is once more satisfied. A second point on the individual's demand curve for good A has been determined.

Further changes in the price of good A would bring further changes in the quantity demanded, in order to satisfy equation (1). Further points on the individual's demand curve would thereby be derived.

 KEY IDEA 14 — *The equi-marginal principle.* The optimum amount of two alternatives consumed (or produced) will be where the marginal benefit ratios of the two alternatives are equal to their marginal cost ratios:

$$\frac{MU_A}{MU_B} = \frac{P_A}{P_B}$$

If the price of *another* good changed, or if the marginal utility of any good changed (including good A), then again the quantity demanded of good A (and other goods) would change, until again equation (1) were satisfied. These changes in demand will be represented by a *shift* in the demand curve for good A.

TAKING ACCOUNT OF TIME

Do you take a taxi or go by bus? How long do you spend soaking in the bath? Do you cook a meal from scratch, or will you get a take-away?

We have argued that if decisions are to be rational, they should involve weighing up the relative marginal utilities of these activities against their relative marginal costs. As economists, of course we are interested in considering all costs, including time. One of the opportunity costs of doing any activity is the sacrifice of time.

A take-away meal may be more expensive than one cooked at home, but it saves you time. Part of the cost of the home-cooked meal, therefore, is the sacrifice of time involved. The full cost is therefore not just the cost of the ingredients and the fuel used, but also the opportunity cost of the alternative activities you have sacrificed while you were cooking.

Given the busy lives many people lead in affluent countries, they often put a high value on time. Increased sales of ready meals and the employment of home cleaners are consequences of this valuation.

Of course, leisure activities also involve a time cost. The longer you spend doing pleasurable activity 'a', the less time you will have for doing pleasurable activity 'b'. The longer you laze in the bath, the less TV you will be able to watch (unless you have a TV in the bathroom).

1. *We have identified that consumers face limits on their income and time. Can you think of any other constraints that we face when making consumption decisions?*
2. *Give some examples of business opportunities that could arise as a consequence of people being 'cash-rich, but time-poor'.*
3. *If someone hires a cleaner, does this imply that they are 'cash-rich, but time-poor'? How about hiring a personal trainer?*

Section summary

1. The satisfaction people get from consuming a good is called 'utility'. Total utility is the satisfaction gained from the total consumption of a particular good over a given period of time. Marginal utility is the extra satisfaction gained from consuming one more unit of the good.

2. The marginal utility tends to fall the more that people consume. This is known as the 'principle of diminishing marginal utility'.

3. The utility that people get from consuming a good will depend on the amount of other goods they consume. A change in the amount of other goods consumed, whether substitutes or complements, will shift the total and marginal utility curves.

4. 'Rational' consumers will attempt to maximise their consumer surplus. Consumer surplus is the excess of people's utility (measured in money terms) over their expenditure on the good. This will be maximised by purchasing at the point where the *MU* of a good is equal to its price.

5. In the simple case where the price and consumption of other goods is held constant, a person's *MU* curve will lie along the same line as that person's demand curve.

6. The market demand curve is merely the horizontal sum of the demand curves of all the individual consumers. The elasticity of the market demand curve will depend on the rate at which marginal utility diminishes as more is consumed. This in turn depends on the number and closeness of substitute goods. If there are close substitutes, people will readily switch to this good if its price falls, and thus marginal utility will fall only slowly. The demand will be elastic.

7. Measuring the marginal utility of a good in money avoids the problem of using some imaginary unit such as utils, but it assumes that money has a constant utility. In reality, the marginal utility of money is likely to decrease as income rises.

8. A more satisfactory way of analysing the demand for goods is to look at people's choices between goods. A consumer will maximise utility from a given income by consuming according to the 'equi-marginal principle'. This states that goods should be consumed in that combination which equates the *MU/P* ratio for each good.

4.2 THE TIMING OF COSTS AND BENEFITS

The exact timing of the costs incurred and the benefits received varies between different types of consumption. This has implications for the way the rational choice model is applied. In some cases, all the costs and benefits of a decision are virtually instantaneous with only a very small delay in time between them. For example, if you purchase a coffee the cost is immediate (unless you use a credit card) and the total pleasure from consuming the drink occurs shortly afterwards.

However, for a whole range of other consumption decisions all the costs and benefits are not instantaneous and occur over a more prolonged period of time. There may also be significant delays between the point in time the costs are incurred and the benefits received. This is called intertemporal choice.

Take the example of buying a consumer durable, such as a mobile phone, dishwasher or car. The major cost of purchasing many of these products is often immediate, or virtually so (unless paying by instalments), while the stream of benefits they provide occurs for months or years after the initial costs are paid. In other cases, all the benefits from consumption are instantaneous, while some of the costs occur in the future. For example, when considering whether or not to purchase cigarettes, the consumption benefits and monetary cost are fairly immediate, while the health costs occur in the future. The same would be true about decisions to purchase alcohol and unhealthy food. For a rational person, intertemporal decision making would be required in all of these examples.

Optimum consumption with intertemporal choice

How can the rational choice model be extended to analyse and explain these types of intertemporal choices?

In standard economic theory it is assumed that most people are impatient most of the time. They would prefer to consume the things they like immediately rather than having to wait until a later date. They would also prefer to delay any costs until later: i.e. paying for goods using a credit card.

This impatience can be illustrated by the following simple example. Imagine that it is 10:00am on Monday morning and you are given the choice between receiving a payment of £500 immediately or having to wait until 10:00am on Tuesday morning. When asked this type of question most people prefer to have the £500 immediately.

The key to understanding this impatience is to think about the point in time from which the decision is being judged. If a person prefers to receive £500 on Monday rather than having to wait until Tuesday, then the following must be true.

$$U^{\text{Monday}}: u(£500_{\text{Monday}}) > u(£500_{\text{Tuesday}})$$

This is simply stating that from the person's point of view on Monday (U^{Monday}), the utility from receiving the money on Monday ($u(£500_{\text{Monday}})$) is greater than the utility of having to wait until Tuesday ($u(£500_{\text{Tuesday}})$).

This does not mean that from their point of view on Tuesday that £500 received on Tuesday would give them any less pleasure than it would on Monday. In other words:

$$U^{\text{Monday}}: u(£500_{\text{Monday}}) = U^{\text{Tuesday}}: u(£500_{\text{Tuesday}})$$

From the person's point of view on Tuesday (U^{Tuesday}), £500 received on Tuesday provides the same utility as receiving the £500 on Monday, from their point of view on Monday. Impatience in this example means that judging the decision from Monday's perspective, receiving £500 immediately would give the person more pleasure than having to wait 24 hours.

 What is the minimum amount by which the pay-off of £500 would have to increase in order for you personally to agree to wait for another 24 hours before receiving it?

Discounting: measuring impatience

From Monday's perspective, how much more utility does receiving £500 immediately provide rather than having to wait until Tuesday? To capture this impatience, standard economic theory uses a method of weighting future costs and benefits. It is called *exponential discounting* and multiplies any costs and benefits that occur in the future by a fraction of less than one to adjust them to what they are worth to the person immediately: i.e. their *present value*. This fraction is called the *discount factor*.

To illustrate this idea, assume a person is considering a consumption decision when all the costs occur immediately, while all the benefits occur in the future. To keep the example as simple as possible, assume the benefits all occur at one point in time in the future rather than being spread out over a number of days, weeks or months. The good costs £10,

Definitions

Exponential discounting A method of reducing future benefits and costs to a present value. The discount rate depends on just how much less, from the consumer's perspective, *future* utility and costs (from a decision made today) are than gaining the utility/incurring the costs *today*.

Present value (in consumption) The value a person places today on a good that will not be consumed until some point in the future.

Discount factor The value today of deciding to consume a good one period in the future as a proportion of the value when it is actually consumed.

which is payable immediately, and provides £20 of utility in exactly one month's time (perhaps there is a month's delay before it can be delivered). As all the costs are immediate, they are weighted at 100 per cent of their value. However, impatience means that the future benefits have to be weighted by a fraction of less than one to adjust them to what they are worth to the person immediately.

If the person's impatience could be captured by a monthly discount factor of, say, 0.9 then £20 of pleasure in a month would be worth £18 (0.9 × £20) to that person today. The present value of the benefits from consuming the good (£18) would still be greater than the immediate cost (£10); so a rational person would purchase the product and be prepared to wait for delivery.

Levels of impatience will vary from one individual to another. The more impatient people are, the lower their discount factor and the less they will value benefits and costs that occur at some point in the future. For example, imagine that in the previous example a person's greater level of impatience could be captured by a discount factor of 0.4. This makes £20 of benefits received in a month's time worth only £8 to that person now. As the immediate cost of £10 is now greater than the discounted value of the future benefits, this more impatient individual would not purchase the good.

The further into the future any costs and benefits occur, the greater their values have to be reduced to adjust them to what they are worth to an individual today. If the benefits from consuming the product all occur in two months' time the discount factor will be less than 0.9.

How is the discount factor for a two-month delay calculated? The per-period discount factor is the amount by which each discount factor in one period has to be multiplied in order to work out the discount factor for the following period. Assuming the size of the delay between each period remains the same (i.e. in this case it is always a month) the per-period discount factor remains constant. Therefore, the discount factor of 0.9 for a one-month delay would have to be multiplied by 0.9 to calculate the discount factor for a two-month delay. It would equal 0.81. A benefit of £20 in two months has a present value of 0.81 × £20 or £16.20.

1. (a) What discount factor is used to weight benefits that occur in three months' time for a person with a per-monthly discount factor of 0.9?
    (b) What does this make the present value of £20 of benefits received in three months' time?

2. Assume that the good costs £10, which has to be paid today. How long would the maximum delay in months before receiving the £20 of benefits have to be before a person with a monthly discount of 0.9 would no longer purchase the good?

*LOOKING AT THE MATHS

How do we calculate the present value of the purchase of a product whose utility occurs over a period of time? Let us assume that a person's discount factor is 0.8. In other words, a good yielding £100 of benefits one period in the future would be valued at only 0.8 × £100 = £80 today.

But what about a product that yields utility in several future periods? The formula we use for calculating its present value (i.e. its utility over its lifetime expressed in a value today) is:

$$U = \sum_{t=0}^{t=n} \delta^t U_t \qquad \textbf{(1)}$$

where U is the total present utility value of a good consumed over various time periods, $t = 0$ to $t = n$; δ is the discount factor applied for each time period t and U_t is the utility gained in each specific time period t.

Let us assume that a good has a life of three years and yields £100 of utility at the end of year 1, £300 at the end of year 2 and £200 at the end of year 3. Its total present utility is not the simple sum of the three utilities that will be experienced; it is not £100 + £300 + £200 = £600. Instead it is found by applying the above formula. Again, let us assume that the discount factor is 0.8. Substituting the figures for the three years in equation (1) gives:

$$U = (0.8 \times £100) + (0.8^2 \times £300) + (0.8^3 \times £200)$$
$$= (0.8 \times £100) + (0.64 \times £300) + (0.512 \times £200)$$
$$= £80 + £192 + £102.40$$
$$= £374.40$$

What is the present value (utility) of a good which yields £50 of utility at the end of year 1, £60 at the end of year 2, £100 at the end of year 3 and £50 at the end of year 4, assuming a discount factor of 0.9? Would it be worth the consumer paying £200 for it today?

Section summary

1. The benefits, and sometimes the costs, of some consumer goods occur over a period of time rather than instantaneously. Consumers are thus faced with making intertemporal choices.

2. Because consumers would generally rather have goods now than later, benefits (and costs) that occur in the future have to be discounted to give them a present value.

3. The higher the discount factor, the lower will be the present value for any given future benefit or cost.

*4.3   INDIFFERENCE ANALYSIS

The limitations of the marginal utility approach to demand

Even though the multi-commodity version of marginal utility theory is useful in demonstrating the underlying logic of consumer choice, it still has a major weakness. Utility cannot be measured in any absolute sense. We cannot really say, therefore, by how much the marginal utility of one good exceeds another.

An alternative approach is to use *indifference analysis*. This does not involve measuring the *amount* of utility a person gains, but merely *ranking* various combinations of goods in order of preference. In other words, it assumes that consumers can decide whether they prefer one combination of goods to another. For example, if you were asked to choose between two baskets of fruit, one containing four oranges and three pears and the other containing two oranges and five pears, you could say which you prefer or whether you are indifferent between them. It does not assume that you can decide just *how much* you prefer one basket to another or just how much you like either.

The aim of indifference analysis, then, is to analyse, *without having to measure utility,* how a rational consumer chooses between two goods. As we shall see, it can be used to show the effect on this choice of (a) a change in the consumer's income and (b) a change in the price of one or both goods. It can also be used to analyse the income and substitution effects of a change in price.

Indifference analysis involves the use of *indifference curves* and *budget lines*.

Indifference curves

An *indifference curve* shows all the various combinations of two goods that give an equal amount of satisfaction or utility to a consumer.

To show how one can be constructed, consider the following example. Imagine that a supermarket is conducting a survey about the preferences of its customers for different types of fruit. One of the respondents is Ali, a student who likes a healthy diet and regularly buys fresh fruit. He is asked his views about various combinations of oranges and pears. Starting with the combination of 10 pears and 13 oranges, he is asked what other combinations he would like the same amount as this one. From his answers a table is constructed (Table 4.2). What we are saying here is that Ali would be equally happy to have any one of the combinations shown in the table.

This table is known as an *indifference set*. It shows alternative combinations of two goods that yield the same level of satisfaction. From this we can plot an indifference curve. We measure units of one good on one axis and units of the other good on the other axis. Thus in Figure 4.5, which is

| Table 4.2 | Combinations of pears and oranges that Ali likes the same amount as 10 pears and 13 oranges |

Pears	Oranges	Point in Figure 4.5
30	6	a
24	7	b
20	8	c
14	10	d
10	13	e
8	15	f
6	20	g

based on Table 4.2, pears and oranges are measured on the two axes. The curve shows that Ali is indifferent as to whether he consumes 30 pears and 6 oranges (point *a*) or 24 pears and 7 oranges (point *b*) or any other combination of pears and oranges along the curve.

Notice that we are not saying *how much* Ali likes pears and oranges; merely that he likes all the combinations along the indifference curve the same amount. All the combinations thus yield the same (unspecified) utility.

The shape of the indifference curve

As you can see, the indifference curve we have drawn is not a straight line. It is bowed in towards the origin. In other words, its slope gets shallower as we move down the curve. Indifference curves are normally drawn this shape. But why?

Let us see what the slope of the curve shows us. It shows the rate at which the consumer is willing to exchange one good for the other, holding their level of satisfaction the same. For example, consider the move from point *a* to point *b* in Figure 4.5. Ali gives up 6 units of pears and requires 1 orange to compensate for the loss. The slope of the indifference curve is thus $-6/1 = -6$. Ignoring the negative sign, the slope of the indifference curve (that is, the rate at which the consumer is willing to substitute one good for the other) is known as the *marginal rate of substitution* (*MRS*). In this case, therefore, the *MRS* = 6.

Definitions

Indifference curve A line showing all those combinations of two goods between which a consumer is indifferent: i.e. those combinations that give the same level of utility.

Indifference set A table showing the same information as an indifference curve.

Marginal rate of substitution (between two goods in consumption) The amount of one good (Y) that a consumer is prepared to give up in order to obtain one extra unit of another good (X): i.e. $\Delta Y / \Delta X$.

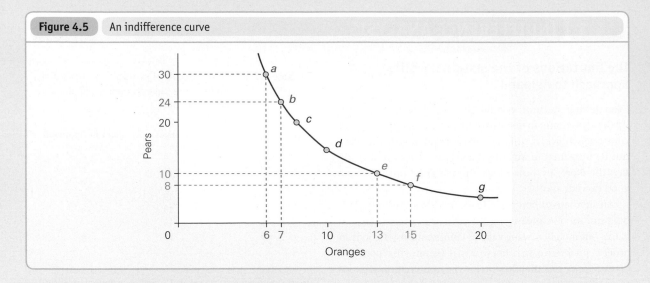

Figure 4.5   An indifference curve

Note that as we move down the curve, the marginal rate of substitution diminishes as the slope of the curve gets less. For example, look at the move from point *e* to point *f*. Here the consumer gives up 2 pears and requires 2 oranges to compensate. Thus, along this section of the curve, the slope is $-2/2 = -1$ (and hence the *MRS* = 1).

The reason for a *diminishing marginal rate of substitution* is related to the *principle of diminishing marginal utility* that we looked at in section 4.1. This stated that individuals will gain less and less additional satisfaction the more of a good that they consume. This principle, however, is based on the assumption that the consumption of other goods is held *constant*. In the case of an indifference curve, this is not true. As we move down the curve, more of one good is consumed but *less* of the other. Nevertheless the effect on consumer satisfaction is similar. As Ali consumes more pears and fewer oranges, his marginal utility from pears will diminish, while that from oranges will increase. He will thus be prepared to give up fewer and fewer pears for each additional orange. *MRS* diminishes.

The relationship between the marginal rate of substitution and marginal utility

In Figure 4.5, consumption at point *a* yields equal satisfaction with consumption at point *b*. Thus the utility sacrificed by giving up six pears must be equal to the utility gained by consuming one more orange. In other words, the marginal utility of an orange must be six times as great as that of a pear. Therefore, $MU_{\text{oranges}}/MU_{\text{pears}} = 6$. But this is the same as the marginal rate of substitution. With *X* measured on the horizontal axis and *Y* on the vertical axis, then

$$MRS = \frac{MU_X}{MU_Y} = \text{slope of indifference curve} \atop \text{(ignoring negative sign)}$$

 Although indifference curves will normally be bowed in towards the origin, on odd occasions they might not be. Which of the following diagrams correspond to which of the following? Explain the shape of each curve.

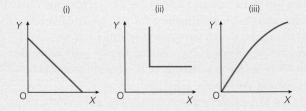

(a) *X and Y are left shoes and right shoes.*
(b) *X and Y are two brands of the same product, and the consumer cannot tell them apart.*
(c) *X is a good but Y is a 'bad' – like household refuse.*

An indifference map

More than one indifference curve can be drawn. For example, referring back to Table 4.2, Ali could give another set of combinations of pears and oranges that all give him a higher (but equal) level of utility than the set shown in the table. This could then be plotted in Figure 4.5 as another indifference curve.

Although the actual amount of utility corresponding to each curve is not specified, indifference curves further out to the right would show combinations of the two goods that yield a higher utility, and curves further in to the left would show combinations yielding a lower utility.

In fact, a whole *indifference map* can be drawn, with each successive indifference curve showing a higher level of utility. Combinations of goods along I_2 in Figure 4.6 give a higher

Definitions

Diminishing marginal rate of substitution The more a person consumes of good X and the less of good Y, the less additional Y will that person be prepared to give up in order to obtain an extra unit of X: i.e. $\Delta Y/\Delta X$. diminishes.

Indifference map A graph showing a whole set of indifference curves. The further away a particular curve is from the origin, the higher the level of satisfaction it represents.

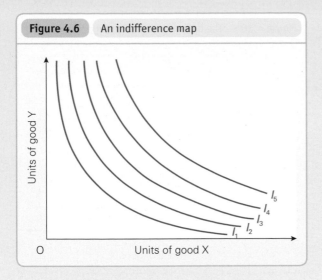

Figure 4.6 An indifference map

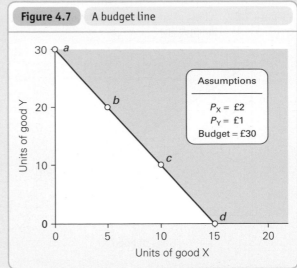

Figure 4.7 A budget line

Assumptions

P_X = £2
P_Y = £1
Budget = £30

utility to the consumer than those along I_1. Those along I_3 give a higher utility than those along I_2, and so on. The term 'map' is appropriate here, because the indifference curves are rather like contours on a real map. Just as a contour joins all those points of a particular height, so an indifference curve shows all those combinations yielding a particular level of utility.

 Draw another two indifference curves on Figure 4.5, one outward from and one inward from the original curve. Read off various combinations of pears and oranges along these two new curves and enter them on a table like Table 4.2.

The budget line

We turn now to the **budget line**. This is the other important element in the analysis of consumer behaviour. Whereas indifference maps illustrate people's preferences, the actual choices they make will depend on their incomes. The budget line shows what combinations of two goods you are able to buy, given (a) your income available to spend on them and (b) their prices.

Just as we did with an indifference curve, we can construct a budget line from a table. The first two columns of Table 4.3 show various combinations of two goods X and Y

Table 4.3 Consumption possibilities for budgets of £30 and £40

	Budget of £30		Budget of £40	
Units of good X	Units of good Y	Point on budget line in Figure 4.7	Units of good X	Units of good Y
0	30	A	0	40
5	20	B	5	30
10	10	C	10	20
15	0	D	15	10
			20	0

Note: It is assumed that P_X = #2, P_Y = #1.

that can be purchased assuming that (a) the price of X is £2 and the price of Y is £1 and (b) the consumer has a budget of £30 to be divided between the two goods.

In Figure 4.7, then, if you are limited to a budget of £30, you can consume any combination of X and Y along the line (or inside it). You cannot, however, afford to buy combinations that lie outside it: i.e. in the darker shaded area. This area is known as the *infeasible region* for the given budget.

We have said that the amount people can afford to buy will depend on (a) their budget and (b) the prices of the two goods. We can show how a change in either of these two determinants will affect the budget line.

A change in income

If the consumer's income (and hence budget) increases, the budget line will shift outwards, parallel to the old one. This is illustrated in the last two columns of Table 4.3 and in Figure 4.8, which show the effect of a rise in the consumer's budget from £30 to £40. (Note that there is no change in the prices of X and Y, which remain at £2 and £1 respectively.)

More can now be purchased. For example, if the consumer was originally purchasing 7 units of X and 16 units of Y (point *m*), this could be increased with the new budget of £40, to 10 units of X and 20 units of Y (point *n*) or any other combination of X and Y along the new higher budget line.

A change in price

The relative prices of the two goods are given by the slope of the budget line. The slope of the budget line in Figure 4.7 is 30/15 = 2. (We are ignoring the negative sign: strictly speaking, the slope should be −2.) Similarly, the slope of the

Definition

Budget line A graph showing all the possible combinations of two goods that can be purchased at given prices and for a given budget.

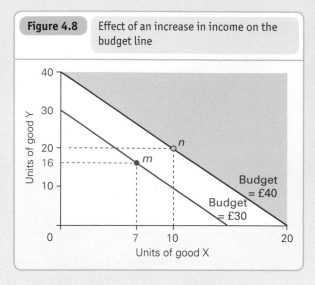

Figure 4.8 Effect of an increase in income on the budget line

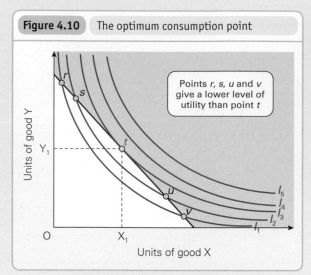

Figure 4.10 The optimum consumption point

Points *r*, *s*, *u* and *v* give a lower level of utility than point *t*

new higher budget line in Figure 4.8 is 40/20 = 2. But in each case this is simply the ratio of the price of X (£2) to the price of Y (£1).

Thus the slope of the budget line equals

$$\frac{P_X}{P_Y}$$

If the price of either good changes, the slope of the budget line will change. This is illustrated in Figure 4.9 which, like Figure 4.7, assumes a budget of £30 and an initial price of X of £2 and a price of Y of £1. The initial budget line is B_1.

Now let us assume that the price of X falls to £1 but that the price of Y remains the same (£1). The new budget line will join 30 on the Y axis with 30 on the X axis. In other words, the line pivots outwards on point *a*. If, instead, the price of Y changed, the line would pivot on point *b*.

1. Assume that the budget remains at £30 and the price of X stays at £2, but that Y rises in price to £3. Draw the new budget line.
2. What will happen to the budget line if the consumer's income doubles and the prices of both X and Y double?

The optimum consumption point

We are now in a position to put the two elements of the analysis together: the indifference map and a budget line. This will enable us to show how much of each of the two goods the 'rational' consumer will buy from a given budget. Let us examine Figure 4.10.

The consumer would like to consume along the highest possible indifference curve. This is curve I_3 at point *t*. Higher indifference curves, such as I_4 and I_5, although representing higher utility than curve I_3, are in the infeasible region: they represent combinations of X and Y that cannot be afforded with the current budget. The consumer *could* consume along curves I_1 and I_2, between points *r* and *v*, and *s* and *u* respectively, but they give a lower level of utility than consuming at point *t*.

The optimum consumption point for the consumer, then, is where the budget line touches (is 'tangential to') the highest possible indifference curve.

If the budget line is tangential to an indifference curve, they will have the same slope. (The slope of a curve is the slope of the tangent to it at the point in question.) But as we have seen, the slope of the budget line is

$$\frac{P_X}{P_Y}$$

and the slope of the indifference curve is

$$MRS = \frac{MU_X}{MU_Y}$$

Therefore, at the optimum consumption point

$$\frac{P_X}{P_Y} = \frac{MU_X}{MU_Y}$$

But this is the *equi-marginal principle* that we established in the first part of this chapter: only this time, using the indifference curve approach, there has been no need to measure utility. All we have needed to do is to observe, for any two combinations of goods, whether the consumer preferred one to the other or was indifferent between them.

Figure 4.9 Effect on the budget line of a fall in the price of good X

We can express the optimum consumption point algebraically. With a limited budget of B, the objective is to maximise utility subject to this budget constraint. This can be expressed as

$$\text{Max}\,TU(X,Y) \qquad \qquad (1)$$

subject to the budget constraint that

$$P_X X + P_Y Y = B \qquad \qquad (2)$$

Equation (1) is known as the 'objective function' and says that the objective is to maximise utility, which depends on the consumption of two goods, X and Y. For example, assume that the utility function is

$$TU = X^{3/4} Y^{1/4}$$

This is known as a 'Cobb–Douglas utility function' and will give smooth convex indifference curves. Assume also that the price of X is 4, the price of Y is 2 and the budget is 64. Thus:

$$4X + 2Y = 64$$

Rearranging this constraint to express X in terms of Y gives

$$X = 16 - \frac{Y}{2}$$

By first substituting this value of X into the utility function (so that it is expressed purely in terms of Y) and then differentiating the resulting equation and setting it equal to zero, we can solve for the value of Y and then X that yields the maximum utility for the given budget. The answer is:

$$X = 12 \text{ and } Y = 8$$

The workings of this are given in Maths Case 4.1 on the student website.

An alternative method, which is slightly longer but is likely to involve simpler calculations, involves the use of 'Lagrangian multipliers'. This method is explained, along with a worked example, in Maths Case 4.2.

The effect of changes in income

As we have seen, an increase in income is represented by a parallel shift outwards of the budget line (assuming no change in the price of X and Y). This will then lead to a new optimum consumption point on a higher indifference curve. A different consumption point will be found for each different level of income.

In Figure 4.11, a series of budget lines are drawn representing different levels of consumer income. The corresponding optimum consumption points (r, s, t, u) are shown. Each point is where the new higher budget line just touches the highest possible indifference curve.[1] The line

[1] We can always draw in an indifference curve that will be tangential to a given budget line. Just because we only draw a few indifference curves on a diagram, it does not mean that there are only a few possible ones. We could draw as many as we liked. Again it is rather like the contours on a real map. They may be drawn at, say, 10 metre intervals. We could, however, if we liked, draw them at 1 metre or even 1cm intervals, or at whatever height was suitable to our purpose. For example, if the maximum height of a lake were 32.45 metres above sea level, it might be useful to draw a contour at that height to show what land might be liable to flooding.

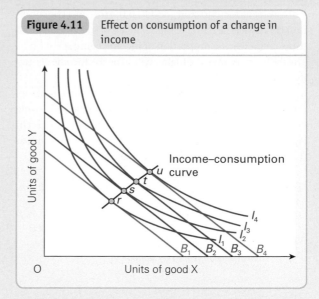

Figure 4.11 Effect on consumption of a change in income

joining these points is known as the *income–consumption curve*.

If your money income goes up and the price of goods does not change, we say that your *real income* has risen. In other words, you can buy more than you did before. But your real income can also rise even if you do not earn any more money. This will happen if prices fall. For the same amount of money, you can buy more goods than previously. We analyse the effect of a rise in real income caused by a fall in prices in just the same way as we did when money income rose and prices stayed the same. Provided the *relative* prices of the two goods stay the same (i.e. provided they fall by the same percentage), the budget line will shift outwards parallel to the old one.

Income elasticity of demand and the income–consumption curve

The income–consumption curve in Figure 4.11 shows that the demand for both goods rises as income rises. Thus both goods have a positive income elasticity of demand: they are both normal goods.

Definitions

Income–consumption curve A line showing how a person's optimum level of consumption of two goods changes as income changes (assuming the prices of the goods remain constant).

Real income Income measured in terms of how much it can buy. If your *money* income rises by 10 per cent, but prices rise by 8 per cent, you can buy only 2 per cent more goods than before. Your *real* income has risen by 2 per cent.

Now let us focus just on good X. If the income–consumption curve became flatter at higher levels of income, it would show an increasing proportion of income being spent on X. The flatter it became, the higher would be the income elasticity of demand for X.

If, by contrast, X were an inferior good, such as cheap margarine, its demand would fall as income rose; its income elasticity of demand would be negative. This is illustrated in Figure 4.12. Point b is to the left of point a, showing that at the higher income B_2, less X is purchased.

1. The income–consumption curve in Figure 4.12 is drawn as positively sloped at low levels of income. Why?
2. Show the effect of a rise in income on the demand for X and Y where, this time, Y is the inferior good and X is the normal good. Is the income–consumption curve positively or negatively sloped?

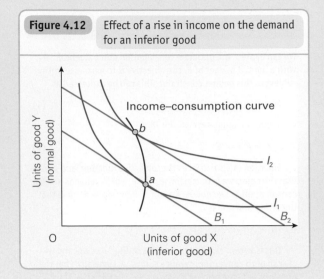

Figure 4.12   Effect of a rise in income on the demand for an inferior good

---

*BOX 4.4   LOVE AND CARING

An economic approach to family behaviour

We have been using indifference analysis to analyse a single individual's choices between two goods. The principles of rational choice, however, can be extended to many other fields of human behaviour. These include situations where people are members of groups and where one person's behaviour affects another. Examples include how friends treat each other, how sexual partners interrelate, how parents treat children, how chores are shared out in a family, how teams are organised, how people behave to each other at work, and so on.

In all these cases, decisions constantly have to be made. Generally, people try to make the 'best' decisions – ones which will maximise the interests of the individual or the members of the group: decisions that are 'rational'. This will involve weighing up (consciously or subconsciously) the costs and benefits of alternative courses of action to find out which is in the individual's or group's best interests.

One of the pioneers of this approach was Gary Becker (1930–2014). Becker was a professor at Chicago University from 1970 and was a member of the 'Chicago school', a group of economists from the university who advocate the market as the best means of solving economic problems.

Gary Becker attempted to apply simple economic principles of rational choice to a whole range of human activities, including racial and sexual discrimination, competition in politics and criminal behaviour. Much of his work, however, focused on the family, a field previously thought to be the domain of sociologists, anthropologists and psychologists. Even when family members are behaving lovingly and unselfishly, they nevertheless, according to Becker, tend to behave 'rationally' in the economists' sense of trying to maximise their interests, only in this case their

'interests' include the welfare of the other members of their family.

A simple illustration of this approach is given in the diagram below. It assumes, for simplicity, that there are just two members of the family, Judy and Warren. Warren's consumption is measured on the horizontal axis; Judy's on the vertical. Their total joint income is given by Y_T. The line $Y_T Y_T$ represents their consumption possibilities. If Warren were to spend their entire joint income on himself, he would consume at point g. If Judy were to spend their entire joint income on herself, she would consume at point f.

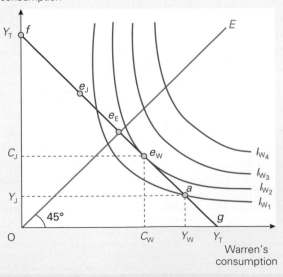

The effect of changes in price

If either X or Y changes in price, the budget line will 'pivot'. Take the case of a reduction in the price of X (but no change in the price of Y). If this happens, the budget line will swing outwards. We saw this effect in Figure 4.9 (on page 118). These same budget lines are reproduced in Figure 4.13, but this time we have added indifference curves.

The old optimum consumption point was at *j*. After the reduction in the price of good X, a new optimum consumption point is found at *k*.

Illustrate on an indifference diagram the effects of the following:
(a) A rise in the price of good X (assuming no change in the price of Y).
(b) A fall in the price of good Y (assuming no change in the price of X).

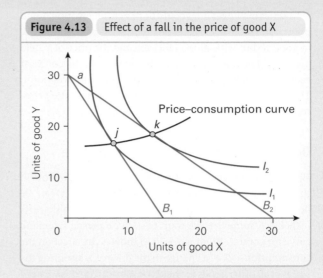

| Figure 4.13 | Effect of a fall in the price of good X |

CASE STUDIES AND APPLICATIONS

Let us assume that Warren works full-time and Judy works part-time. As a result, Warren earns more than Judy. He earns Y_W; she earns Y_J. If each spent their own incomes on themselves alone, they would consume at point *a*.

But now let us assume that Warren loves Judy, and that he would prefer to consume less than Y_W to allow her to consume more than Y_J. His preferences are shown by the indifference curves. Each curve shows all the various combinations of consumption between Warren and Judy that give Warren equal satisfaction. (Note that because he loves Judy, he gets satisfaction from her consumption: her happiness gives him pleasure.)

Warren's optimum distribution of consumption between himself and Judy is at point e_W. This is the highest of his indifference curves that can be reached with a joint income of Y_T. At this point he consumes C_W; she consumes C_J.

If he loved Judy 'as himself' and wanted to share their income out equally, then the indifference curves would be shallower. The tangency point to the highest indifference curve would be on the 45° line OE. Consumption would be at point e_E.

Similar indifference curves could be drawn for Judy. Her optimum consumption point might be at point e_J. But if she loved Warren 'as herself', her optimum point would then be at point e_E.

Some interesting conclusions can be drawn from this analysis:

- Income redistribution (i.e. consumption redistribution) within the family can be to the benefit of all the members. In the case we have been considering, both Warren and Judy gain from a redistribution of income from point *a* to point e_W.

The only area of contention is between points e_W and e_J. Here negotiation would have to take place. This might be in return for some favour. 'If you'll let me have the money I need for that new coat, I'll do the washing up for a whole month.'

- In the case of each one loving the other as themself, there is no area of contention. They are both happiest with consumption at point e_E.
- In the case of 'extreme love', where each partner would prefer the other to have more than themselves, point e_W would be above point e_E, and point e_J would be below point e_E. In this case, each would be trying to persuade the other to have more than they wanted. Here a different type of negotiation would be needed. 'I'll only let you buy me that coat if you let me do the washing up for a whole month.'
- Some forms of consumption benefit both partners. Household furniture or a new car would be cases in point. Any such purchases would have the effect of shifting the consumption point out beyond line Y_TY_T, and could lead to both partners consuming on a higher indifference curve. This shows the 'economic' advantages of the collective consumption that can be experienced in households or other groups (such as clubs).

1. *If Judy earned more than Warren, show how much income she would redistribute to him if (a) she cared somewhat for him; (b) she loved him 'as herself'. Draw her indifference curves in each of these two cases.*
2. *In the case where they both love each other 'as themselves', will their two sets of indifference curves be identical?*

A series of budget lines could be drawn, all pivoting round point *a* in Figure 4.13. Each one represents a different price of good X, but with money income and the price of Y held constant. The flatter the curve, the lower the price of X. At each price, there will be an optimum consumption point. The line that connects these points is known as the *price–consumption curve*.

Deriving the individual's demand curve

We can use the analysis of price changes to show how in theory a person's demand curve for a product can be derived. To do this we need to modify the diagram slightly.

Let us assume that we want to derive a person's demand curve for good X. What we need to show is the effect on the consumption of X of a change in the price of X assuming the prices of all other goods are held constant. To do this we need to redefine good Y. Instead of being a *single* good, Y becomes the total of *all other* goods. But what units are we to put on the vertical axis? Each of these other goods will be in different units: litres of petrol, loaves of bread, kilograms of cheese, numbers of haircuts, etc. We cannot add them all up unless we first convert them to a common unit. The answer is to measure them as the total amount of money spent on them: i.e. what is *not* spent on good X.

With expenditure on all other goods plotted on the vertical axis and with income, tastes and the price of all other goods held constant, we can now derive the demand curve for X. This is demonstrated in Figure 4.14.

We illustrate the changes in the price of X by pivoting the budget line on the point where it intersects the vertical axis. It is then possible, by drawing a price–consumption line, to show the amount of X demanded at each price. It is then a simple matter of transferring these price–quantity relationships on to a demand curve. In Figure 4.14, each of the points *a, b, c* and *d* on the demand curve in the lower part of the diagram corresponds to one of the four points on the price–consumption curve. (Note that P_2 is half of P_1, P_3 is one-third of P_1 and P_4 is one-quarter of P_1.)

 As quantity demanded increases from Q_1 to Q_2 in Figure 4.14, the expenditure on all other goods decreases. (Point b is lower than point a.) This means, therefore, that the person's total expenditure on X has correspondingly increased. What, then, can we say about the person's price elasticity of demand for X between points a and b? What can we say about the price elasticity of demand between points b and c, and between points c and d?

The income and substitution effects of a price change

In Chapter 2 we argued that when the price of a good rises, consumers will purchase less of it for two reasons:

■ They cannot afford to buy so much. This is the *income effect*.

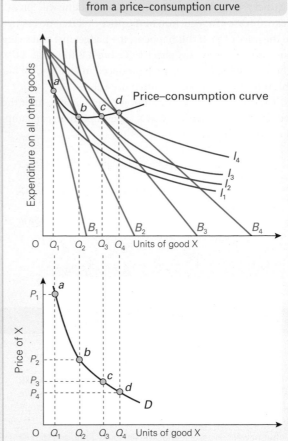

■ The good is now more expensive relative to other goods. Therefore consumers substitute alternatives for it. This is the *substitution effect*.

We can extend our arguments from Chapter 2 by demonstrating the income and substitution effects with the use of indifference analysis. Let us start with the case of a normal good and show what happens when its price changes.

Definitions

Price–consumption curve A line showing how a person's optimum level of consumption of two goods changes as the price of one of the two goods changes (assuming that income and the price of the other good remain constant).

Income effect of a price change That portion of the change in quantity demanded that results from the change in real income.

Substitution effect of a price change That portion of the change in quantity demanded that results from the change in the relative price of the good.

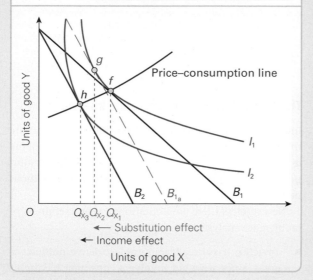

Figure 4.15 The income and substitution effects of a rise in the price of good X if X is a normal good

A normal good

In Figure 4.15 the price of **normal good** X has risen and the budget line has pivoted inwards from B_1 to B_2. The consumption point has moved from point f to point h. Part of this shift in consumption is due to the substitution effect and part is due to the income effect.

The substitution effect. To separate these two effects a new budget line is drawn, parallel to B_2 but tangential to the original indifference curve I_1. This is the line B_{1a}. Being parallel to B_2, it represents the new price ratio (i.e. the higher price of X). Being tangential to I_1, however, it enables the consumer to obtain the same utility as before: in other words, there is no loss in real income to the consumer. By focusing, then, on B_{1a}, which represents no change in real income, we have excluded the income effect. The movement from point f to point g is due purely to a change in the relative prices of X and Y. The movement from Q_{x_1} to Q_{x_2} is the substitution effect.

The income effect. In reality, the budget line has shifted to B_2 and the consumer is forced to consume on a lower indifference curve I_2: real income has fallen. Thus the movement from Q_{x_2} to Q_{x_3} is the income effect.

In the case of a normal good, therefore, the income and substitution effects of a price change reinforce each other. They are both negative: they *both* involve a *reduction* in the quantity demanded as price *rises* (and vice versa).[2]

[2] It is important not to confuse the income effect of a price change with the simple effect on demand of an increase in income. In the latter case, a rise in income will cause a rise in demand for a normal good – a positive effect (and hence there will be a positive income elasticity of demand). In the case of a price reduction, although for a normal good the resulting rise in real income will still cause a rise in demand, it is in the opposite direction from the change in price – a negative effect with respect to price (and hence there will be a negative price elasticity of demand).

The bigger the income and substitution effects, the higher will be the price elasticity of demand for good X.

 Illustrate on two separate indifference diagrams the income and substitution effects of the following:
(a) A decrease in the price of good X (and no change in the price of good Y).
(b) An increase in the price of good Y (and no change in the price of good X).

An inferior good

As we saw above, when people's incomes rise, they will buy less of **inferior goods** such as poor-quality margarine and cheap powdered instant coffee, since they will now be able to afford better-quality goods instead. Conversely, when their income falls, they will have to reduce their living standards: their consumption of inferior goods will thus rise.

The substitution effect. If the price of an inferior good (good X) rises, the substitution effect will be in the same direction as for a normal good: i.e. it will be negative. People will consume less X relative to Y, since X is now more expensive relative to Y. For example, if the price of inferior-quality margarine (good X) went up, people would tend to use better-quality margarine or butter (good Y) instead. This is illustrated in Figure 4.16 by a movement along the original indifference curve (I_1) from point f to point g. The quantity of X demanded falls from Q_{x_1} to Q_{x_2}.

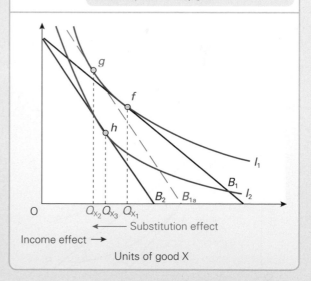

Figure 4.16 The income and substitution effects of a rise in the price of good X if X is an inferior (non-Giffen) good

Definitions

Normal good A good whose demand increases as income increases.

Inferior good A good whose demand decreases as income increases.

The income effect. The income effect of the price rise, however, will be the opposite of that for a normal good: it will be positive. The reduction in real income from the rise in price of X will tend to increase the consumption of X, since with a fall in real income more inferior goods will now be purchased – including more X. Thus point *h* is to the right of point *g*: the income effect increases quantity back from Q_{x_2} to Q_{x_3}.

A Giffen good: a particular type of inferior good

If the inferior good were to account for a very large proportion of a consumer's expenditure, a change in its price would have a significant effect on the consumer's real income, resulting in a large income effect. It is conceivable, therefore, that this large abnormal income effect could outweigh the normal substitution effect. In such a case, a rise in the price of X would lead to more X being consumed!

This is illustrated in Figure 4.17, where point *h* is to the *right* of point *f*. In other words, the fall in consumption (Q_{x_1} to Q_{x_2} as a result of the substitution effect is more than offset by the rise in consumption (Q_{x_2} to Q_{x_3}) as a result of the large positive income effect.

Such a good is known as a **_Giffen good_**, after Sir Robert Giffen (1837–1910), who is alleged to have claimed that the consumption of bread by the poor rose when its price rose. Bread formed such a large proportion of poor people's consumption that, if its price went up, the poor could not afford to buy so much meat, vegetables, etc., and had to buy more bread instead. It is possible that in countries in Africa today with very low incomes, staple foods such as manioc (cassava) and maize are Giffen goods. Naturally, such cases must be very rare indeed and some economists remain unconvinced of their existence, except as a theoretical possibility.

 Could you conceive of any circumstances in which one or more items of your expenditure would become Giffen goods? Apply the same analysis to an elderly couple on a state pension.

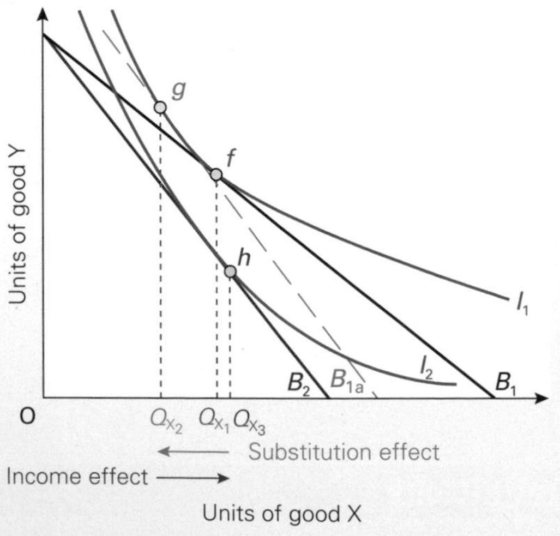

The usefulness of indifference analysis

Indifference analysis has made it possible to demonstrate the logic of 'rational' consumer choice, the derivation of the individual's demand curve, and the income and substitution effects of a price change. All this has been done without having to measure utility.

Nevertheless there are limitations to the usefulness of indifference analysis:

■ In practice, it is virtually impossible to derive indifference curves, since it would involve a consumer having to imagine a whole series of different combinations of goods and deciding in each case whether a given combination gave more, equal or less satisfaction than other combinations.

■ Consumers may not behave 'rationally', and hence may not give careful consideration to the satisfaction they believe they will gain from consuming goods. They may behave impetuously.

■ Indifference curves are based on the satisfaction that consumers believe they will gain from a good. This belief may well be influenced by advertising. Consumers may be disappointed or pleasantly surprised, however, when they actually consume the good. In other words, consumers are not perfectly knowledgeable. Thus the 'optimum consumption' point may not in practice give consumers maximum satisfaction for their money.

■ Certain goods are purchased only now and again, and then only one at a time. Examples would include consumer durables such as cars, televisions and washing machines. Indifference curves are based on the assumption that marginal increases in one good can be traded off against marginal decreases in another. This will not be the case with consumer durables.

Figure 4.17 | The income and substitution effects of a rise in the price of good X if X is a Giffen good

---

Definition

Giffen good An inferior good whose demand increases as its price increases as a result of a positive income effect larger than the normal negative substitution effect.

Characteristics theory

Characteristics theory was developed in the mid-1960s by Kelvin Lancaster. He argued that people demand goods not for their own sake, but for the characteristics they possess.

Take cars, for example. When choosing between the different makes, consumers do not just consider their relative prices, they also consider their attributes: comfort, style, performance, durability, reliability, fuel consumption, etc. It is these characteristics that give rise to utility.

Characteristics theory, then, is based on four crucial assumptions:

■ All goods possess various characteristics.
■ Different brands possess them in different proportions.
■ The characteristics are measurable: they are 'objective'.
■ The characteristics (along with price and income) determine consumer choice.

Let us assume that you are choosing between three different goods or brands of a good (e.g. a foodstuff). Each one has a different combination of two characteristics (e.g. protein and calories). Your choices can be shown graphically.

The choice between brands of a product: each brand has different characteristics

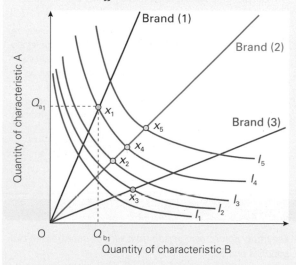

The levels of two characteristics are shown on the two axes. An indifference map can be constructed, showing the different combinations of the two characteristics that yield given levels of utility. Thus any combination of the two characteristics along indifference curve I_4 in the diagram gives a higher level of utility than those along I_3, and so on. The shape of the indifference curves (bowed in) illustrates a diminishing marginal rate of substitution between the two characteristics.

The amounts of the two characteristics given by the three brands are shown by the three rays. The more that is consumed of each brand, the further up the respective ray will the consumer be. Thus at x_1, the consumer is gaining Q_{a_1} of characteristic A and Q_{b_1} of characteristic B.

Assume that, for the same money, the consumer could consume at x_1 with brand (1), x_2 with brand (2) and x_3 with brand (3). The consumer will consume brand (1): x_1 is on a higher indifference curve than x_2 or x_3.

Now assume that the price of brand (2) falls. For a given expenditure, the consumer can now move up the brand (2) ray. But not until the price has fallen enough to allow consumption at point x_4 will the consumer consider switching from brand (1). If price falls enough for consumption to be at point x_5, clearly the consumer will switch.

The characteristics approach has a number of advantages over conventional indifference curve analysis in explaining consumer behaviour.

■ It helps to explain brand loyalty. When price changes, people will not necessarily gradually move from one brand to another. Rather they will stick with a brand until a critical price is reached. Then they will switch brands all at once.
■ It allows the choice between several goods to be shown on the same diagram. Each good or brand has its own ray.
■ It helps to explain the nature of substitute goods. The closer substitutes are, the more similar will be their characteristics and hence the closer will be their rays. The closer the rays, the more likely it is that there will be a shift in consumption to one good when the price of the other good changes.
■ A change in the quality of a good can be shown by rotating its ray.

There are weaknesses with the approach, however:

■ Some characteristics cannot be measured. Such characteristics as beauty, taste and entertainment value are subjective: they are in the mind of the consumer.
■ Only two characteristics can be plotted. Most goods have several characteristics.

1. *Make a list of the characteristics of shoes. Which are 'objective' and which are 'subjective'?*
2. *If two houses had identical characteristics, except that one was near a noisy airport and the other was in a quiet location, and if the market price of the first house were £280 000 and that of the second £300 000, how would that help us to put a value on the characteristic of peace and quiet?*

Characteristics theory is examined in more detail in Case Study 4.6 on the student website.

Section summary

1. The indifference approach to analysing consumer demand avoids having to measure utility.

2. An indifference curve shows all those combinations of two goods that give an equal amount of satisfaction to a consumer. An indifference map can be drawn with indifference curves further to the north-east representing higher (but still unspecified) levels of satisfaction.

3. Indifference curves are usually drawn convex to the origin. This is because of a diminishing marginal rate of substitution between the two goods. As more of one good is purchased, the consumer is willing to give up less and less of the other for each additional unit of the first. The marginal rate of substitution is given by the slope of the indifference curve, which equals MU_X/MU_Y.

4. A budget line can be drawn on an indifference diagram. A budget line shows all those combinations of the two goods that can be purchased for a given amount of money, assuming a constant price of the two goods. The slope of the budget line depends on the relative price of the two goods. The slope is equal to P_X/P_Y.

5. The consumer will achieve the maximum level of satisfaction for a given income (budget) by consuming at the point where the budget line just touches the highest possible indifference curve. At this point of tangency, the budget line and the indifference curve have the same slope. Thus $MU_X/MU_Y = P_X/P_Y$, which is the 'equi-marginal principle' for maximising utility from a given income that was established in section 4.1.

6. If the consumer's real income (and hence budget) rises, there will be a parallel outward shift of the budget line. The 'rational' consumer will move to the point of tangency of this new budget line with the highest indifference curve. The line that traces out these optimum positions for different levels of income is known as the 'income–consumption curve'.

7. If the price of one of the two goods changes, the budget line will pivot on the axis of the other good. An outward pivot represents a fall in price; an inward pivot represents an increase in price. The line that traces the tangency points of these budget lines with the appropriate indifference curves is called a 'price–consumption curve'.

8. By measuring the expenditure on all other goods on the vertical axis and by holding their price constant and money income constant, a demand curve can be derived for the good measured on the horizontal axis. Changes in its price can be represented by pivoting the budget line. The effect on the quantity demanded can be found from the resulting price–consumption curve.

9. The effect of a change in price on quantity demanded can be divided into an income and a substitution effect. The substitution effect is the result of a change in relative prices alone. The income effect is the result of the change in real income alone.

10. For a normal good, the income and substitution effects of a price rise will both be negative and will reinforce each other. With an inferior good, the substitution effect will still be negative but the income effect will be positive and thus will to some extent offset the substitution effect. If the good is 'very' inferior and the (positive) income effect is bigger than the (negative) substitution effect, it is called a Giffen good. A rise in the price of a Giffen good will thus cause a rise in the quantity demanded.

11. Indifference analysis, although avoiding having to measure utility, nevertheless has limitations. Indifference curves are difficult to derive in practice; consumers may not behave rationally; the 'optimum' consumption point may not be optimum if the consumer lacks knowledge of the good; indifference curves will not be smooth for items where single units each account for a large proportion of income.

END OF CHAPTER QUESTIONS

1. Imagine that you had £10 per month to allocate between two goods, A and B. Imagine that good A cost £2 per unit and good B cost £1 per unit. Imagine also that the utilities of the two goods are those set out in the table below. (Note that the two goods are not substitutes for each other, so that the consumption of one does not affect the utility gained from the other.)

   (a) What would be the marginal utility ratio (MU_A/MU_B) for the following combinations of the two goods: (i) 1A, 8B; (ii) 2A, 6B; (iii) 3A, 4B; (iv) 4A, 2B? (Each combination would cost £10.)

   (b) Show that where the marginal utility ratio (MU_A/MU_B) equals the price ratio (P_A/P_B), total utility is maximised.

   (c) If the two goods were substitutes for each other, why would it not be possible to construct a table like the one given here?

The utility gained by a person from various quantities of two goods: A and B

Good A			Good B		
Units per month	MU (utils)	TU (utils)	Units per month	MU (utils)	TU (utils)
0	–	0.0	0	–	0.0
1	11.0	11.0	1	8.0	8.0
2	8.0	19.0	2	7.0	15.0
3	6.0	25.0	3	6.5	21.5
4	4.5	29.5	4	5.0	26.5
5	3.0	32.5	5	4.5	31.0
			6	4.0	35.0
			7	3.5	38.5
			8	3.0	41.5
			9	2.6	44.1
			10	2.3	46.4

2. Is it reasonable to assume that people seek to equate the marginal utility/price ratios of the goods that they purchase, if (a) they have never heard of 'utility', let alone 'marginal utility'; (b) marginal utility cannot be measured in any absolute way?

3. Consider situations where you might think about swapping items with someone. Why are such situations relatively rare? Can you think of circumstances in which this might be more common?

4. Explain why the price of a good is no reflection of the total value that consumers put on it.

*5. Sketch a person's indifference map for two goods X and Y. Mark the optimum consumption point. Now illustrate the following (you might need to draw a separate diagram for each):

   (a) A rise in the price of good X, but no change in the price of good Y.

   (b) A shift in the person's tastes from good Y to good X.

   (c) A fall in the person's income and a fall in the price of good Y, with the result that the consumption of Y remains constant (but that of X falls).

*6. Distinguish between a normal good, an inferior good and a Giffen good. Use indifference curves to illustrate your answer.

*7. Assume that commuters regard bus journeys as an inferior good and car journeys as a normal good. Using indifference curves, show how (a) a rise in incomes and (b) a fall in bus fares will affect the use of these two modes of transport. How could people's tastes be altered so that bus journeys were no longer regarded as an inferior good? If tastes were altered in this way, what effect would it have on the indifference curves?

Online resources

Additional case studies on the student website

4.1 Bentham and the philosophy of utilitarianism. This looks at the historical and philosophical underpinning of the ideas of utility maximisation.

4.2 Utility under attack. This looks at the birth of indifference analysis, which was seen as a means of overcoming the shortcomings of marginal utility analysis.

4.3 Applying indifference curve analysis to taxes on goods. Assume that the government wants to raise extra revenue from an expenditure tax. Should it put a relatively small extra tax on all goods, or a relatively large one on just certain selected goods?

4.4 Income and substitution effects: the Slutsky approach. This looks at an alternative way of using indifference analysis to analyse income and substitution effects.

4.5 Deriving an Engel curve. Income elasticity of demand and the income–consumption curve.

4.6 The characteristics approach to analysing consumer demand. This is an extension of the analysis of Box 4.5.

Maths Case 4.1 Finding the optimum consumption point: Part 1. This case looks at how the utility maximisation point can be discovered with a Cobb–Douglas utility function with given prices and a given budget constraint.

Maths Case 4.2 Finding the optimum consumption point: Part 2. This case uses the Lagrange method to solve the same problem as in Maths Case 4.1

Websites relevant to this chapter

See sites listed at the end of Chapter 5 on page 147.

Consumer Behaviour in an Uncertain World

In this chapter we examine consumer choices when people
have only limited information and when they do not necessarily behave as the 'rational' consumers we examined in
Chapter 4.

When we buy goods or services there is often the risk that
the benefits will not turn out as we had expected. The quality may be poorer or the good may not last as long as we
had anticipated. In section 5.1 we look at consumption
decisions when consumers are faced with uncertainty. We
also look at how consumers may take out insurance to
safeguard against uncertainty and at how the firms providing insurance may behave.

In section 5.2 we look at how people actually behave when
buying goods and services. They might not have the time
to weigh up the costs and benefits or all possible purchases. Instead they may behave impulsively or according
to simple rules of thumb. Economists conduct experiments
and surveys to see just how consumers do behave in various situations and we shall examine some of their
findings.

5.1   DEMAND UNDER CONDITIONS OF RISK AND UNCERTAINTY

The problem of imperfect information

In the previous chapter, we assumed that when we buy a good or service, we know the price and how much value we put on it. In many cases this is a reasonable assumption. When you buy a bar of chocolate, you know how much you are paying for it and have a good idea how much you will like it. But what about a mobile phone, or a car, or a laptop, or any other *consumer durable*? In each of these cases you are buying something that will last you a long time, and the further into the future you look, the less certain you can be of its costs and benefits to you.

Take the example of purchasing a laptop computer that costs you £300. If you pay cash, your immediate outlay involves no uncertainty: it is £300. But the computer can break down. In 12 months' time you could face a repair bill of £100. In other words, when you buy the laptop, you are uncertain as to the full 'price' you will have to pay over its lifetime.

KEY IDEA 15

Good decision making requires good information. Where information is poor, decisions and their outcomes are also likely to be poor.

If the costs of the laptop are uncertain, so too are the benefits. You might have been attracted in the first place by the description in an online advert or at a shop. Once you have used the laptop for a while, however, you might discover things you had not anticipated. Perhaps it takes longer than you had anticipated to boot up, or to connect to the Internet or to run various types of software/games.

Buying consumer durables thus involves uncertainty. So too does the purchase of assets, whether a physical asset such as a house or financial assets such as shares. In the case of assets, the uncertainty is over their future *price*. If you buy shares in a company, what will happen to the price? Will it shoot up, thus enabling you to sell them at a large profit, or will it fall? You cannot know for certain.

The problems surrounding making decisions today based on expectations of the future are explored in Threshold Concept 9.

Definition

Consumer durable A consumer good that lasts a period of time, during which the consumer can continue gaining utility from it.

THRESHOLD CONCEPT 9   **PEOPLE'S ACTIONS DEPEND ON THEIR EXPECTATIONS**   THINKING LIKE AN ECONOMIST

Many, if not most, economic actions are taken before the benefits are enjoyed. You work first and get paid at the end of the month; you buy something in a shop today, and consume it later. In the case of a bar of chocolate, you may consume it fairly soon and pretty well all at once, in the case of many 'consumer durables', such as electrical goods, you will enjoy them over a much longer period.

It is the same with firms. What they produce today will be sold at some point in the future. In other words, firms typically incur costs first and receive revenues later. In the case of investing in new buildings or equipment, it may be a very long time before the firm starts seeing profits from the investment.

In each of these cases, then, the decision is made to do something now in anticipation of what will happen in the future. The threshold concept here is that decision making is only as good as the information on which it is based. If your expectations turn out to be wrong, a seemingly good decision may turn out disastrously. Part of what we do as economists is to examine how people get information and on what basis they form their expectations; part of what we do is to forecast the future.

When information about the future is imperfect, as it nearly always will be, there are risks involved in basing decisions on such information. Businesses constantly have to live with risk: risk that market prices will decline, that costs will rise, that machinery will break down, that competitors will launch new products, and so on. But in our everyday lives, we too face risks because of poor information about the future. Do you spend money on a holiday in this country and risk having a wet week? Do you go to the cinema to see a film, only to find out that you don't enjoy it?

Sometimes you lack information simply because you have not taken the time or paid the money to acquire it. This could apply to the specifications of a product. A little research could give you the information you require. Sometimes, however, the information is simply not available – at least not in the form that will give you certainty. A firm may do market research to find out what consumers want, but until a product is launched, it will not be certain how much will be sold. A market analyst may give you a forecast of what will happen to stock market prices or to the dollar/euro exchange rate, but analysts frequently get it wrong.

1. *What risks are involved in buying the latest version of the iPhone? Compare these with the risks of buying a house?*
2. *Give some examples of ways in which it is possible to buy better information. Your answer should suggest that there is profitable business to be made in supplying information.*
3. *Is there a role for government intervention in the provision of information? (We return to this in Chapter 12).*

Attitudes towards risk and uncertainty

So how will uncertainty affect people's behaviour? The answer is that it depends on their attitudes towards taking a gamble. To examine these attitudes let us assume that people do at least know the chances involved when taking a gamble (i.e. they know the exact *probabilities* of different outcomes occurring). In other words, they operate under conditions of risk rather than uncertainty.

Explain the difference between 'risk' and 'uncertainty' (see Chapter 2, pages 66–76).

Consider the following example. Imagine that as a student you only have £105 left to spend out of your student loan and have no other income or savings. You are thinking of buying an instant lottery ticket/scratch card. The lottery ticket costs £5 and there is a 1 in 10 or 10 per cent chance that it will be a winning ticket. A winning ticket pays a prize of £50. Would you buy the lottery ticket? This will depend on your attitude towards risk.

In order to explain people's attitude towards risk it is important to understand the concept of expected value. The **expected value** of a gamble is the amount the person would earn on average if the gamble was repeated on many occasions. To calculate the expected value of a gamble you simply multiply each possible outcome by the probability that outcome will occur. These values are then added together.

In our example the gamble has only two possible outcomes – you purchase a winning ticket or a losing ticket. There is a 10 per cent chance it is a winning ticket, which will give you a total of £150 to spend (£100 left out of your loan after you have purchased the ticket plus a £50 prize). There is a 90 per cent chance it is a losing ticket, in which case you will only have £100 left to spend out of your student loan. Therefore, the expected value of this gamble is:

$$EV_{gamble} = 0.1(£150) + 0.9(£100) = 105$$

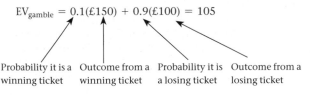

| Probability it is a winning ticket | Outcome from a winning ticket | Probability it is a losing ticket | Outcome from a losing ticket |

If you do not purchase the ticket you will have £105 to spend for sure.

$$EV_{no\ gamble} = 1(105) = 105$$

There are three possible categories of attitude towards risk.

Risk neutral. If people are risk neutral, they will always choose the option with the highest expected value. Therefore, in this example, a student who is risk neutral would be indifferent between buying or not buying the instant lottery ticket, as each outcome has the same expected value of £105.

Risk averse. If people are risk averse they will never choose a gamble if it has the same expected value as a certain pay-off. Therefore, a student who is risk averse would definitely not buy the instant lottery ticket.

It is too simplistic, however, to say that a risk-averse person will never take risks. Such a person may choose a gamble if it has a greater expected value than a certain pay-off. If the probability of purchasing a winning instant lottery ticket in the previous example was 20 per cent instead of 10 per cent, then a risk-averse student might buy the ticket, as the expected value of the gamble (£110) is greater than the certain pay-off (£105).

Whether or not risk-averse people do take gambles depends on the strength of their aversion to risk, which will vary from one individual to another. The greater a person's level of risk aversion, the greater the expected value of a gamble they are willing to give up in order to obtain a certain pay-off.

The certain amount of money that gives a person the same utility as the gamble is known as the gamble's **certainty equivalent**. The more risk averse a person is, the lower the gamble's certainty equivalent for them. The expected value of a gamble minus a person's certainty equivalent of that gamble is called the **risk premium**. The more risk averse someone is, the greater their positive risk premium.

Risk loving. If people are risk loving they would always choose a gamble if it had the same expected value as the pay-off from not taking the gamble. Therefore, a risk-loving student would definitely purchase the lottery ticket.

Once again, it is too simplistic to say that risk-loving people will always choose a gamble. They may choose a certain-pay-off if it has a higher expected value than the gamble. For a risk-loving person the certainty equivalent of a gamble is greater than its expected value. For example, if the probability of purchasing a winning instant lottery ticket in the previous example was 1 per cent instead of 10 per cent, then even a risk-loving student might choose not to buy the ticket. It would depend on the extent to which that person enjoyed taking risks. The more risk loving people are, the greater the return from a certain pay-off they are willing to sacrifice in order to take a gamble. Because the certainty equivalent of a gamble is greater than its expected value the risk premium is negative.

1. *What is the expected value of the above lottery ticket gamble if the chances of purchasing a winning ticket with a prize of £50 are 30 per cent? How much of the expected value of the gamble is a risk-averse person willing to sacrifice if they decide against purchasing the ticket? If they were indifferent between purchasing and not purchasing the ticket, what is their certainty equivalent and risk premium of the gamble?*

Definitions

Expected value The average value of an outcome of an activity when the same activity takes place many times.

Certainty equivalent The guaranteed amount of money that an individual would view as equally desirable as the expected value of a gamble. Where a person is risk averse, the certainty equivalent is less than the expected value.

Risk premium The expected value of a gamble minus a person's certainty equivalent.

2. *What is the expected value of the lottery ticket gamble if the chances of purchasing a winning ticket are 1 per cent? How much of the certain pay-off is a risk-loving person willing to sacrifice if they decide to purchase the lottery ticket? If they were indifferent between purchasing and not purchasing the ticket what is their certainty equivalent and risk premium of the gamble?*

Diminishing marginal utility of income and attitudes towards risk taking

Avid gamblers may be risk lovers. People who spend lots of money on various online betting websites or at the race track may enjoy the thrill of taking a risk, knowing that there is always the chance that they might win. On average, however, such people will lose. After all, the bookmakers have to take their cut and thus the odds they offer are generally unfavourable.

Most people, however, are risk averse most of the time. We prefer to avoid insecurity. But is there a simple reason for this? Economists use marginal utility analysis to explain why.

They argue that the gain in utility to people from an extra £100 is less than the loss of utility from forgoing £100. Imagine your own position. You have probably adjusted your standard of living to your income, or are trying to do so. If you unexpectedly gained £100 that would be very nice: you could buy some new clothes or have a meal out. But if you lost £100, you might have serious difficulties in making ends meet. Thus if you were offered the gamble of a 50:50 chance of winning or losing £100, you might well decline the gamble.

 Which gamble would you be more likely to accept, a 60:40 chance of gaining or losing £10 000, or a 50:50 chance of gaining or losing £1? Explain why.

This risk-averse behaviour accords with the principle of *diminishing marginal utility*. In the previous chapter we focused on the utility from the consumption of individual goods: Lucy and her cups of tea; Ollie and his packets of crisps. In the case of each individual good, the more we consume, the less satisfaction we gain from each additional unit: the marginal utility falls. But the same principle applies if we look at our *total* consumption. The higher our level of total consumption, the less additional satisfaction will be gained from each additional £1 spent.

What we are saying here is that there is a ***diminishing marginal utility of income***. The more you earn, the lower will be the utility gained from each *extra* £1. If a person on £15 000 per year earned an extra £1000, they will feel a lot better off: their marginal utility from that income will be relatively very high. If a person already earning £500 000 per year earned an extra £1000, however, their gain in utility will be far less.

? *Do you think that this provides a moral argument for redistributing income from the rich to the poor? Does it prove that income should be so redistributed?*

Why income make us risk averse? The answer is illustrated in Figure 5.1, which shows the *total* utility you get from your income.

The slope of this curve gives the *marginal* utility of your income. As the marginal utility of income diminishes, so the

Definition

Diminishing marginal utility of income Where each additional pound earned yields less additional utility than the previous pound.

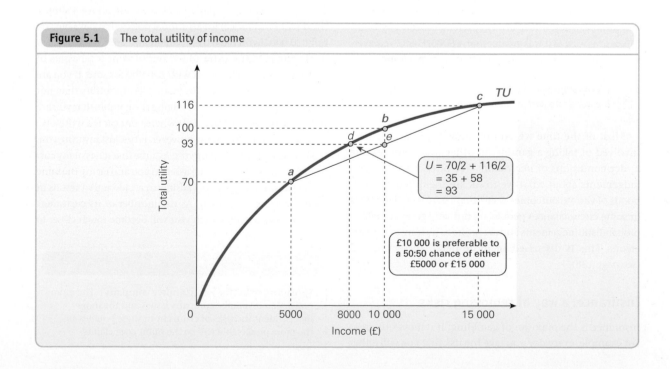

Figure 5.1   The total utility of income

U = 70/2 + 116/2
  = 35 + 58
  = 93

£10 000 is preferable to a 50:50 chance of either £5000 or £15 000

curve gets flatter. Assume a person experiences 70 units or utils of pleasure from spending £5000 on the goods they like. This is shown at point *a* on Figure 5.1.

If the person's income now rises from £5000 to £10 000 their total utility increases by 30 utils, from 70 to 100 utils. This is shown as the movement along the total utility curve from point *a* to point *b*. A similar rise in income from £10 000 to £15 000 leads to a move from point *b* to point *c*. This time, however, total utility has increased by only 16 utils, from 100 to 116 utils. Marginal utility has diminished.

Now assume that your income is £10 000 and you are offered the following gamble: a 50:50 chance of gaining an extra £5000 or losing £5000. Effectively, then, you have an equal chance of your income rising to £15 000 or falling to £5000. The expected value of the gamble is £10 000 – the same as the pay-off from not taking the gamble.

At an income of £10 000, your total utility is 100. If your gamble pays off and increases your income to £15 000, your total utility will rise to 116: i.e. an increase of 16. If it does not pay off, you will be left with only £5000 and a utility of 70 utils: i.e. a decrease of 30. Therefore you have a 50:50 chance of experiencing either 116 or 70 utils of pleasure. Your *average* or expected utility will be (116 + 70)/2 = 93 utils.

This point can be illustrated on Figure 5.1 by drawing a straight line or chord between points *a* and *c*. Points along this chord represent all the possible weighted averages of the utility at point *a* and point *c*. In this example, because the probability is 50:50, expected utility is represented half way along the chord at point *e*. As you can see from the *TU* curve, the expected utility from the gamble is the same as the utility experienced from receiving £8000 for certain (point *d*). This is the certainty equivalent of the gamble.

The risk premium is £2000: i.e. the expected value of £10 000 minus the certainty equivalent of £8000. For this individual, £10 000 for certain provides greater utility than the gamble. They would always prefer a certain pay-off in this case as long as it was greater than £8000. Hence risk aversion is part of rational utility-maximising behaviour.

 If people are generally risk averse, why do so many around the world take part in national lotteries?

Most of the time we do not know the exact chances involved of taking a gamble. In other words, we operate under conditions of *uncertainty*. We often have to make judgements about what we think are the different likelihoods of various outcomes occurring. There is evidence that in some circumstances people are not very good at making probabilistic judgements and are prone to making systematic errors. This is discussed in more detail in section 5.2 (see page 138).

Insurance: a way of removing risks

Insurance is the opposite of gambling. It removes the risk. For example, every day you take the risk that you will either lose your mobile phone or drop and break it. In either case you will have to incur the cost of purchasing a new handset to replace it. Alternatively, you can remove the risk by taking out an appropriate insurance policy that pays out the cost of a new handset if the original one gets lost or broken.

Given that many people are risk averse, they may be prepared to pay a premium for an insurance policy even though it will leave them with less than the expected value of not buying the insurance and taking the gamble. The total premiums paid to the insurance companies, and hence the revenue generated, will be *more* than the amount the insurance companies pay out: that is, after all, how such companies make a profit.

But does this mean that the insurance companies are less risk averse than their customers? Why is it that the insurance companies are prepared to shoulder the risks that their customers were not? The answer is that the insurance company is able to **spread its risks**.

The spreading of risks

Take the following simple example. Assume you have £100 000 worth of assets (i.e. savings, car, property, etc.). You drive your car to school/university every day and there is a 1 in 20 (or 5 per cent) chance that at some point during the year you will be responsible for an accident that results in your car being a write-off. Assume the market value of the car is currently £20 000 and remains unchanged for the following 12 months. The expected value of taking the gamble for the year (i.e. not purchasing comprehensive car insurance) is 0.95(100 000) + 0.05(80 000) = £99 000.

If you are risk averse you would be willing to pay more than an additional £1000 to purchase a fully comprehensive car insurance policy that covers you for a year. For example, you may be willing to pay £1100 (over and above a simple third-party insurance) for an annual policy that pays out the full £20 000 if you have the accident and are responsible for it. Having paid the extra £1100 out of your total assets of £100 000, you would be left with £98 900 for sure. If you are risk averse, this may give you a higher level of utility than not purchasing the insurance and taking the gamble that you are not responsible for an accident where your car is a write-off.

The insurance company, however, is not just insuring you. It is insuring many others drivers. Assume that it has many customers with exactly the same assets as you and facing the same 5 per cent risk every year of causing an accident that results in their car being a write-off. As the number of its customers increases, the outcome each year will become much closer to

KI 11
p76

Definition

Spreading risks (for an insurance company) The more policies an insurance company issues and the more independent the risks of claims from these policies are, the more predictable will be the number of claims.

its expected or average value. Therefore, the insurance company can predict with increasing confidence that, on average, 5 out of every 100 of its customers will cause an accident every year and make a claim on their own insurance for £20 000, while the other 95 out of every 100 will not cause an accident and so not make a claim on their insurance for their own car.

This means that the insurance company will pay out £100 000 in such claims for every 100 of its customers. This works out as an average pay-out of £1000 per customer. If each customer is willing to pay £1100 extra for such a policy, the insurance company will generate more in revenue from its customers than it is paying out in claims. Assuming that the administrative costs of providing each policy per customer is less than £100, the insurance company can make a profit.

This is an application of the *law of large numbers*. What is unpredictable for an individual becomes highly predictable in the mass. The more people the insurance company insures, the more predictable the final outcome becomes. In other words, an insurance company will be able to convert your *uncertainty* into their *risk*.

In reality, people taking out insurance will not all have the same level of wealth and the same chances of having an accident. However, using statistical data the insurance company will be able to work out the average chances of an event occurring for people in similar situations. Basing premiums on average chances can, however, create some problems for the insurance company, which will be discussed later in the chapter.

The independence of risks

The spreading of risks does not just require that there should be a large number of policies. It also requires the risks to be **independent**. This means that if one person makes a claim it does not increase the chances of another person making a claim too. If the risks are independent in the previous example, then if one person has a car accident the chances of another person having a car accident remain unchanged at 5 per cent.

Now imagine a different example. If an insurance company insured 1000 houses *all in the same neighbourhood,* and then there were a major fire in the area, the claims would be enormous. The risks of fire would *not* be independent, as if one house catches fire it increases the chances of the surrounding houses catching fire. If, however, a company provided fire insurance for houses scattered all over the country, the risks *are* independent.

1. Why are insurance companies unwilling to provide insurance against losses arising from war or 'civil insurrection'?
2. Name some other events where it would be impossible to obtain insurance.
3. Explain why an insurance company could not pool the risk of flooding in a particular part of a country? Does your answer imply that insurance against flooding is unobtainable?

Another way in which insurance companies can spread their risks is by *diversification*. The more types of insurance a company offers (car, house, life, health, etc.), the greater the likelihood the risks would be independent.

Problems for unwary insurance companies

A major issue for insurance companies is that they operate in a market where there is significant **asymmetric information**. Asymmetric information exists in a market if one party has some information that is relevant to the value of that transaction that the other party does not have. In the insurance market the buyer often has private information about themselves that the insurance company does not have access to.

Asymmetric information is often split into two different types – unobservable characteristics and unobservable actions. Each separate type of asymmetric information can potentially generate a different problem. Unobservable characteristics could generate the problem of *adverse selection*; unobservable actions could generate the problem of *moral hazard*. We consider each in turn.

Potential problems caused by unobservable characteristics – adverse selection

Different potential consumers of insurance will have different characteristics. Take the case of car insurance: some drivers may be very skilful and careful, while others may be less able and enjoy the thrill of speeding. Or take the case of life assurance: some people may lead a very healthy lifestyle by eating a well-balanced diet and exercising regularly; others may eat large quantities of fast food and do little or no exercise.

In each of these cases the customer is likely to know more about their own characteristics than the insurance company. These characteristics will also influence the cost to the firm of providing insurance. For example, less able drivers are more

---

Definitions

Law of large numbers The larger the number of events of a particular type, the more predictable will be their average outcome.

Independent risks Where two risky events are unconnected. The occurrence of one will not affect the likelihood of the occurrence of the other.

Diversification Where a firm expands into new types of business.

Asymmetric information Where one party in an economic relationship has better information than another.

likely to be involved in an accident and make a claim on their insurance than more able drivers. The problems this might cause can best be explained with a simple numerical example.

In the previous car insurance example, considered earlier (page 132), we assumed that all the customers had the same characteristics: i.e. they all had a 5 per cent chance per year of being responsible for a car accident where damage to their own car costs, on average, £20 000. In reality, because of their different characteristics, the chances of having a car accident will vary from one customer to another. To keep the example simple, we will assume that an insurance company has only two types of potential customer. One half of them are very skilful drivers and have a 1 per cent chance per year of causing a car accident, while the other half are less able drivers who each have a 9 per cent chance per year of causing an accident. The problem for the insurance company is that when a customer purchases the insurance they do not know if they are a skilful or a less able driver.

When faced with this situation the insurance company could set a profit-making risk premium on the assumption that half of its customers will be highly competent drivers, while the other half will have relatively poor driving skills. Using the law of large numbers, the firm can predict that 5 per cent of its customers will make a claim and so the average pay-out would be £1000 per customer (i.e. £20 000/20). Once again, assuming administration costs of less than £100 per customer, the insurance company could potentially make a profit on each policy.

The problem is that the skilful drivers might find this premium very unattractive. For them the expected value of the gamble (i.e. not taking out the insurance) is $0.99(100\,000) + 0.01(80\,000) = \#99\,800$. Taking out the extra insurance would leave them with £98 900: i.e. their initial wealth of £100 000 minus the premium of £1100. Unless they were very risk averse, the maximum amount they would be willing to pay is likely to be far lower than £1100.

On the other hand, the less skilful drivers might find the offer from the insurance company very attractive. Their expected value from taking the gamble is $0.91(100\,000) + 0.09(80\,000) = \#98\,200$. Their maximum willingness to pay is likely to be greater than £1100. In fact, if they were all risk averse they would all purchase the policy if it was £1800, as this would leave them with £98 200 – the same as the expected value of the gamble.

The insurance company could end up with only the less able drivers purchasing the insurance. If this happens, then 9 out of every 100 customers would make a claim of 20 000 each. The average pay-out per customer would be £1800. Therefore the firm would be paying out far more in claims than it would be generating from the premiums.

If, however, the insurer *knew* a potential customer was a skilful driver, then it could offer the insurance policy at a much lower price: one that the risk-averse skilful driver would be willing to pay. If all the customers purchasing the policy were skilful drivers, then 1 in 100 would make a claim for £20 000. The average claim per customer would only be £200. All the skilful and risk-averse customers would be willing to pay more than £200 for the insurance policy.

But if the insurance company does not know who is careful and who is not, this asymmetric information will block mutually beneficial trade from taking place.

This example has illustrated the problem of ***adverse selection*** in insurance markets. This is where customers with the least desirable characteristics from the sellers' point of view (i.e. those with the greatest chance of making a claim) are more likely to take out the insurance policy at a price based on the average risk of *all* the potential customers. This can result in the insurance market for low-risk individuals collapsing even though mutually beneficial trade would be possible if symmetric information were present.

The potential problem of adverse selection is not unique to the insurance market. Unobservable characteristics are present in many other markets and may relate to the buyer, the seller or the product that is being traded. A well-known example is that of a second-hand car dealer who sells a 'lemon' (a car with faults) to an unsuspecting buyer who does not have the technical knowledge to check on the car. Another is a shop buying second-hand items paying a low price for a valuable antique from a seller who does not know its value. Table 5.1 provides some other examples.

We can define adverse selection more generally as follows. It is Key Idea 16.

Table 5.1   Adverse selection in various markets

Market	Hidden characteristic	Informed party	Uniformed party
The labour market	Innate ability of the worker/ preference for working hard	The potential employee: i.e. the seller of labour services	The employer: i.e. the buyer of labour services
The credit market	Ability of people to manage their money effectively	The customer applying for credit	The firm lending the money
A street market with haggling	How much the person is willing to pay	The customer	The seller of the product
The electronic market: e.g. eBay	The quality/condition of the product	The seller of the product	The buyer of the product

Adverse selection A market process whereby buyers, sellers or products with certain unobservable characteristics (e.g. high risk or low quality) are more likely to enter the market at the current market price. This process can have a negative impact on economic efficiency and cause some potentially profitable markets to collapse.

Tackling the problem of adverse selection. Are there any ways that the potential problems caused by adverse selection can be overcome? One way would be for the party who is uninformed about the relevant characteristics of the other parties to ask them for information. For example, an insurance company may require people to fill out a questionnaire giving details about their lifestyle and family history, or undergo a medical, so that the company can assess the particular risk and set an appropriate premium. There may need to be legal penalties for people caught lying! This process of the uninformed trying to get the information from the informed is called 'screening'.

An alternative would be for the person or party who is informed about the relevant characteristics taking action to reveal it to the uninformed person or party. This is called 'signalling'. For example, a potentially hardworking and intelligent employee could signal this fact to potential employers by obtaining a good grade in an economics degree or working for a period of time as an unpaid intern.

What actions can either the buyers or sellers take in each of the examples in Table 5.1 to help overcome some of the potential problems caused by the unobservable characteristics?

Potential problems caused by unobservable actions – moral hazard

Imagine in the previous example if the different characteristics of the drivers were perfectly observable to the insurance company: i.e. the insurance company could identify which drivers were more able or careful and could charge them a lower premium than those who were less able or careful. The company might still face problems caused by *unobservable actions* – again, a problem of asymmetric information.

Once drivers have purchased comprehensive insurance their driving behaviour may change. All types of driver now have an incentive to take less care when they are driving. If they are involved in an accident, all the costs will be covered by the insurance policy and so the marginal benefit from taking greater care will have fallen. This will result in the chances of a skilful driver having an accident rising above 1 per cent and of the less skilful driver rising above 9 per cent.

The problem for the insurer is that these changes in driving behaviour are difficult to observe. The companies may end up in a position where the amount of money claimed by both the skilful and less skilful drivers increases above the revenue that they are collecting in premiums based on the risk before the insurance was taken out.

This is called *moral hazard* and can more generally be defined as where the actions/behaviour of one party to a transaction change in a way that reduces the pay-off to the other party. It is caused by a change in incentives once a deal has been reached. It can only exist if there are unobservable actions.

Moral hazard Following a deal, the actions/behaviour of one party to a transaction may change in a way that reduces the pay-off to the other party. In the context of insurance, it refers to customers taking more risks when they have insurance than when they do not have insurance.

The problem of moral hazard may occur in many different markets and different situations.

- Once a person has a permanent contract of employment they might not work as hard as the employer would have expected.
- If someone else is willing to pay your debts (e.g. your parents) it is likely to make you less careful in your spending! A similar type of argument has been used for not cancelling the debts of poor countries.
- If a bank knows that it will be bailed out by the government and not allowed to fail, it may undertake more risky lending strategies.
- If you hire a car, you may be rough with the clutch or gears, knowing that you will not bear the cost of the extra wear and tear on the car.
- When working in teams, some people may slack, knowing that more diligent members of the team will cover for them (giving them a 'free ride').

Tackling moral hazard. What are the most effective ways of reducing moral hazard? One approach would be for the uninformed party to devote more resources to *monitoring* the actions and behaviour of the informed party – in other words, to reduce the asymmetry of information. Examples

---

Definitions

Adverse selection in the insurance market Where customers with the least desirable characteristics from the sellers' point of view are more likely to purchase an insurance policy at a price based on the average risk of all the potential customers.

Moral hazard Where one party to a transaction has an incentive to behave in a way which reduces the pay-off to the other party.

include: insurance companies employing loss adjusters to assess the legitimacy of claims; lecturers using plagiarism detection software to discourage students from attempting to pass off other people's work as their own. However, monitoring may often be difficult and expensive.

An alternative is to change the terms of the deal so that the party with the unobservable actions has an incentive to behave in ways which are in the interests of the uninformed party. Examples include: employees who take sick leave being required to produce a medical certificate to prevent people taking 'sickies'; students doing group project work being assessed on their own contribution to the project rather than being given the same mark as everyone else in the group, thereby discouraging free riding.

 How will the following reduce the moral hazard problem?
(a) A no-claims bonus in an insurance policy.
(b) Having to pay the first so many pounds of any insurance claim (an 'excess').
(c) The use of performance-related pay

Section summary

1. When people buy consumer durables, they may be uncertain of their benefits and any future costs. When they buy financial assets, they may be uncertain of what will happen to their price in the future. Buying under these conditions of imperfect knowledge is therefore a form of gambling.

2. The expected value of a gamble is the amount the person would earn on average if the gamble were repeated on many occasions. If we know the expected value of such gambles we are said to be operating under conditions of risk. If we do not know the expected value, we are said to be operating under conditions of uncertainty.

3. People can be divided into risk lovers, those who are risk averse and those who are risk neutral. Because of the diminishing marginal utility of income, it is rational for people to be risk averse (unless gambling is itself pleasurable).

4. Insurance is a way of eliminating risks for policy holders. If people are risk averse they will be prepared to pay premiums in order to obtain insurance. Insurance companies, on the other hand, are prepared to take on these risks because they can pool risk by selling a large number of policies. According to the law of large numbers, what is unpredictable for a single policy holder becomes highly predictable for a large number of them provided that their risks are independent of each other.

5. Insurance markets arise as an institutional response to risk aversion. Their existence potentially makes society 'better off' as they can increase individual utility. Insurance market failure may arise as a result of asymmetric information, through either adverse selection or moral hazard. Adverse selection is where customers with the least desirable characteristics from the sellers' point of view are more likely to purchase an insurance policy at a price based on the average risk of all the potential customers. Moral hazard occurs when insured people have an incentive to take more risks.

6. Both adverse selection and moral hazard are likely to occur in a range of economic relationships whenever there is a problem of asymmetric information. They can both be reduced by tackling asymmetry of information. Better information can be provided by screening, signalling or monitoring, or there can be incentives for providing more accurate information.

5.2 BEHAVIOURAL ECONOMICS

The field of behavioural economics has developed rapidly over the past 20 years. It integrates some simple insights from psychology into standard economic theory in an attempt to improve its ability to explain and predict behaviour. Here we focus on consumer behaviour. In Chapter 9 we look at the contribution of behavioural economics to explaining the behaviour of firms.

What is behavioural economics?

It is important to understand that the development of modern behavioural economics is not an attempt to replace mainstream economic theory. It aims, instead, to complement and enhance existing theory.

Standard economic theory

In order to understand fully what behavioural economics is, it is useful to think back to standard economic theories. These are built on the key assumption that people attempt to maximise their own self-interest – that they make 'rational choices'. They do this by accurately assessing all the costs and benefits involved when making even the most complicated of decisions. They then successfully make choices that maximise their own happiness. In most theories it is assumed that people's happiness depends only on the pay-offs to themselves.

However, this does not mean that economists actually believe that everyone in the real world makes rational choices. They accept that real human beings make mistakes and often care about the pay-offs to others. What economists are assuming is that the people in their theoretical models behave in a rational and selfish manner.

But why assume that people in theories, such as consumer choice, behave differently from people in the real world? This is an example of *abstraction*. If theories built upon this simplified view of human behaviour can effectively explain and predict real-world behaviour, then it is a useful assumption to make.

The alternative would be to assume that people in the theories are as complicated as their real-word counterparts. This would introduce much greater complexity into the analysis and make it much more difficult to understand and apply. If the simpler model is doing a good job at explaining and predicting real-world behaviour, why make it any more complicated than it needs to be?

How appropriate are the assumptions of standard models?   Economists have also argued that rational choice does generally approximate to human behaviour because:

■ People will tend to make mistakes in a haphazard and random manner that cancel each other out.
■ Those individuals who do not behave in a manner that is consistent with perfect rationality and self-interest will be driven out of the market by competitive forces.
■ People will learn how to make rational decisions from experience.

To what extent does conventional economic theory successfully explain and predict real-world behaviour? In many instances it does a pretty good job, which explains why this textbook and many others are full of economic theories built on these assumptions. But sometimes people's behaviour seems to run counter to traditional theory. We examine such occasions in this section and in Chapter 9.

Evidence on human behaviour and the challenge to standard theory

Part of the basis for behavioural economics is evidence from research using laboratory experiments. These have produced some results that are inconsistent with the predictions of mainstream theory. For example, studies found that people appear to have a far greater dislike of losses than would be predicted by mainstream theories. They also appear to be willing to pay to avoid outcomes that they believe are unfair.

Some evidence from some naturally occurring data also appears to be inconsistent with mainstream theory. The financial crisis demonstrated a real-world situation where people seemed to make repeated mistakes. Also, large amounts of money contributed by individuals to charities every year suggest that people are influenced by the impact of their decisions on the utility of others. Other studies have found evidence of behaviour that is inconsistent with the rational choice model in a number of areas, including (a) gym membership; (b) the housing market; (c) trading in financial markets; (d) the labour supply decisions of taxi drivers.

A number of theories have been developed, therefore, that are more consistent with some of the results in the research literature. Some of the more influential of these theories will be briefly explained in the remainder of this section.

BOX 5.1   EXPERIMENTAL ECONOMICS   EXPLORING ECONOMICS

A way of understanding human behaviour

In Chapter 1 (see page 27) we explained that economics is a social science, with methodologies in common with the natural sciences; both construct models which can be used to explain and predict.

In the natural sciences it is common to use experiments to test models or to determine their design features. This, however, was generally not the case with economics. But with the rise of behavioural economics, the use of experiments has become increasingly popular, both for research and teaching purposes.

An experiment will normally involve simulating some economic scenario, with various actors, such as buyers and sellers, or firms and employees. Volunteers (perhaps students!) will play the role of these actors and be offered various incentives, such as cash or forfeits, to see how these affect behaviour. The idea of these incentives is to mimic real-world situations. Often the simulation is set up in the form of a game with the incentive being simply to win.

In these experimental 'laboratories' economists can study how people behave under a range of conditions, changing one variable at a time.

Experiments are now a well-established method of looking at consumer behaviour, but are also increasingly being used by policy makers to understand outcomes that traditional theory might not predict (see Box 5.4).

It is important to realise that experiments do not always suggest that rationality is a mistaken assumption. In many circumstances individuals do behave in exactly the way traditional theory suggests – but in many other circumstances they do not. Experiments can help to understand why individuals behave the way they do and how changing incentives will affect this behaviour.

 What are the limitations of using laboratory experiments and games to understand consumer behaviour?

Bounded rationality

A person might in principle want to maximise utility, but faces complex choices and imperfect information. Sometimes it *would* be possible to obtain better information. But on other occasions people may decide that it is not worth the time and effort, and perhaps expense, of getting more information. Their ability to be 'rational' is thus limited or '*bounded*' by the situation in which they find themselves.

Too much choice and limited information

Although choice is generally thought to be a good thing, sometimes consumers can be baffled by having too much choice and this can hamper their decision making. They do not have the time and information to look through all the alternatives.

A well-known experiment conducted by Sheena Iyengar and Mark Lepper[1] suggested that, in some circumstances, choice may be bad for consumers. The experiment involved setting up stalls offering shoppers the chance to sample a number of jams. It showed that while shoppers were most attracted to the stall that offered 24 samples, they were in fact 10 times more likely actually to buy when offered only 6 varieties. Too much choice appeared to hinder decision making and so to reduce consumers' utility.

Limited information is a particular problem with consumer durables. For example, when purchasing a laptop computer, a customer may be unsure about (a) how well it will perform, (b) how useful it will be and (c) the chances it will break down.

Although people may not know the exact costs and benefits of many decisions for certain, will they still attempt to be rational? In many cases the answer is yes. They simply do the best they can.

 How good are you at making probabilistic judgements? Here is an interesting example. Suppose that one out of every hundred people in the population has a genetic medical condition. There is a test for this medical condition that is 99 per cent accurate. This means that if a person has the condition, the test returns a positive result with a 99 per cent probability; and if a person does not have the condition, it returns a negative result with 99 per cent probability. If a person's test comes back positive (and you know nothing else about that person), what is the probability that s/he has the medical condition?

Heuristics

To simplify the choice problem, people often revert to using mental short-cuts, referred to as *heuristics*, which require only modest amounts of time and effort. A heuristic technique is any approach to problem-solving, such as deciding what to buy, which is practical and sufficient for the purpose, but not necessarily optimal.

For example, people may resort to making the best guess, or to drawing on past experiences of similar choices that turned out to be good or bad. Sometimes, when people are likely to face similar choices again, they resort to *trial and error*. They try a product. If they like it, they buy it again; if not, they don't.

On other occasions, they may use various *rules of thumb*: buying what their friends do, or buying products on offer or buying trusted brands. For example, people may have found that a particular brand of products is to their liking. When they want a new type of product, they may thus decide to use the same brand, even though they have never bought that particular product before. For example, you may have had a Sony TV before and liked it and so, when buying a laptop, choose a Sony. This 'brand loyalty' is something that companies recognise and strive to develop in their customers.

These rules of thumb can lead to estimates that are reasonably close to the utility people will actually get and can save on time and effort. However, they sometimes lead to systematic and predictable misjudgements about the likelihood of certain events occurring.

Behavioural economists seek to understand the different assumptions people make and their different responses in situations of bounded rationality. Such an understanding is also important to those working in the advertising and marketing industry: they want to know the most effective ways of influencing people's spending decisions.

Framing and the reference point for decisions

As we have seen, the use of heuristics can be consistent with the assumption of people attempting to maximise their self-interest under conditions of bounded rationality. Sometimes, however, people will make decisions that seem to run counter to rational choice theory – even allowing for limited time and information and the use of heuristics. This is because of the way they perceive or 'frame' their decisions.

Framing options affects choice

In traditional models of consumer choice, individuals aim to maximise their utility when choosing between goods, or bundles of goods. The context in which the choices are offered or made is not considered. Yet in real life we see that

1 Sheena S. Iyengar and Mark R. Lepper, 'When choice is demotivating: can one desire too much of a good thing?', *Journal of Personality and Social Psychology*, vol. 79, no. 6 (American Psychological Association, 2000).

Definitions
Bounded rationality When the ability to make rational decisions is limited by lack of information or the time necessary to obtain such information or by a lack of understanding of complex situations.
Heuristic A mental short-cut or rule of thumb that people use when trying to solve complex problems or when faced with limited information. They reduce the computational or research effort required but sometimes lead to systematic errors.

context is important; people will often make different choices when they are perceived, or *framed*, in different ways. For example, people will buy more of a good when it is flagged up as a special offer than they would if there is no mention of an offer, *even though the price is the same*.

This principle has led to the development of **nudge theory**, which underpins many marketing techniques. Here people can be persuaded to make a particular choice by framing it in an optimistic way or presenting it in a way that makes it easy to decide. We look at governments' use of nudge theory in Box 5.4 (see page 144).

Biases when assessing the likelihood of uncertain events

People's choices also reflect various biases or preconceptions they may have. This can make choices less than optimal.

Biased use of information.   People tend to give a disproportionate weight to single events that are easy to imagine or retrieve from memory. Here are some potential examples of this heuristic:

- A tendency to overweight the single experience of a friend or relative and underweight the experience of a large number of consumers you have never met. For example, assume that you are thinking of buying a particular laptop and are trying to determine its reliability. A friend has recently purchased the same model and has had to send it back to the manufacturer for costly repairs. This may lead you to underestimate the reliability of this particular model and overestimate the chances of it breaking down. When making the probability assessment you underweight the information from a survey based on the experience of 10 000 users of the same laptop.
- A tendency to assign too much weight to the most recent information that can be retrieved from memory and not enough weight to older information. For example, you may have bought a particular type of cheese in the past, but have not done so for a while. You see it again in a supermarket, but because you cannot remember how much you liked it, you stick to a different type which you have consumed recently and know you like.
- Hindsight bias – events that actually take place are easier to imagine and visualise than those that do not.

Definitions

Framing The way in which a choice is presented or understood. A person may make different decisions depending on whether a choice is presented optimistically or pessimistically.

Nudge theory The theory that positive reinforcement or making the decision easy can persuade people to make a particular choice. They are 'nudged' into so doing.

Therefore, people have a tendency to (a) overestimate the chances that an event would happen after it has actually occurred; (b) underestimate the chances that an event would happen that did not occur. For example, after watching their team lose, football fans believe that the tactics chosen by the manager were always more likely to fail than they actually were before the game began.

Gambler's fallacy.   This is the false belief that past outcomes have an impact on the likelihood of the next outcome occurring when, in reality, they are independent of one another. For example, assume a coin is tossed four times and comes up heads each time. You may mistakenly believe that a tail is more likely on the next toss. Another example is the choice of holiday destination. Assume that the actual chances of it being a sunny week in a particular resort is 50:50. Last year you went there and it rained. So you think, let's go there this year and because it rained last year it is more likely to be sunny this year.

The reference point for decision making

We saw in section 5.1 that people tend to be loss averse. The diminishing marginal utility of income makes this rational behaviour. But depending on how a choice is framed, the choice may seem to be at odds with rational behaviour. For example, take the following two ways that the same choice could be framed:

- 'If you switch to using this environmentally friendly product it will save you £200 per year in lower energy costs.'
- 'If you don't switch to using this environmentally friendly product you are wasting £200 per year in higher energy costs.'

The first presentation may lead to people perceiving the £200 as a potential gain; the reference point is the current situation before the choice is made. The second presentation is designed to switch the consumer's reference point to having switched, so that the £200 is perceived as a loss of not switching. If people are more sensitive to a potential loss than a forgone gain, then presenting the choice in the second way is more likely to persuade people to purchase the environmentally friendly product. Again, the advertising and marketing industry is well aware of this.

The reference point used by people to judge an outcome as a gain or a loss could be influenced by a range of factors. For example, it might be influenced by the following:

- *Their expectations.* Imagine that Dean and Jon are both students on an economics course. They have both exerted the same level of effort writing an assessed essay and each receives a mark of 60 per cent. Will they both be equally happy? If Dean expected to get 70 per cent, then this might be his reference point. He might 'code' the result as a 10 percentage point loss and feel very unhappy. If Jon, on the other hand, expected to get a mark of 50 per cent, he

An example of loss aversion

Consider the following two slightly different situations for the same person, Clare: (a) she is thinking of buying a good such as a coffee mug; (b) she has already purchased it and now owns it. In each case we can think of a way of measuring her valuation of that good.

In the first case it could be measured as the maximum amount she is willing to pay for the mug. This is known as her willingness to pay (WTP). In the second case it could be measured as the minimum amount she needs to be offered in order for her to be willing to sell it to someone else. This is known as her willingness to accept (WTA).

Apart from a few exceptions, traditional economic theory predicts that ownership of a product should have no impact on peoples' valuation of that product. Therefore, their WTP for the product should be equal to their WTA for the same product.

This means that utility functions and indifference curves should be unaffected by people purchasing and owning a product. For example, the diagram illustrates Clare's total utility from coffee mugs. If she purchases one mug, her utility increases from 0 to U_1: i.e. she moves from point a to point b along her utility function. If she were then to sell this mug, her total utility would decrease from U_1 to 0: i.e. she would move back along the same utility function from point b to point a, merely giving up the utility from owning the mug. In other words, her utility function is reversible. As the gain in utility from buying the mug is the same as the loss in utility from selling the same mug, WTP should equal WTA.

The endowment effect: when WTA is greater than WTP

In a famous study, Kahneman, Knetch and Thaler[1] carried out a series of experiments with students on a Law and Economics degree at Cornell University. They were randomly divided into two equal-sized groups. Students in one group were each given a coffee mug and told that they could sell it if they wished. They were asked for their WTA. Students in the other group could each examine the mugs and make an offer to buy one. They were asked their WTP. The authors found that the median WTA

of the students who were given the mugs was $5.25 whereas the median WTP in the other group was only $2.25.

As the students had been randomly allocated into the two groups, standard theory predicts that WTP should be equal to WTA. However, the evidence suggests that those who were given ownership of the mugs at the start of the experiment valued them far more than those who were not.

A similar exercise was carried out with pens. In this experiment the median WTP remained constant at $1.25, while the median WTA varied between $1.75 and $2.50. Once again, ownership seemed to have an impact on valuation.

After purchase, ownership becomes the new reference point

One explanation for these results is that ownership of a good influences a person's reference point. Those who do not already own the good perceive (or 'code') its purchase as a *gain* in utility and would move from point a to b in the diagram. However, once they have purchased a good its ownership is included in their reference point. Selling the good would be coded as a *loss*.

If people are loss averse then the sale of the good has a much bigger negative impact on their utility than the gain in utility from purchasing the product. This creates a discrete kink in the utility function at point b; the utility function is no longer reversible. Sale of the good would cause a movement from b to a^L. The negative impact on utility of selling the good (U_1 to U^L) is greater than the gain in utility from purchasing the good (0 to U_1). This discrete kink in the utility function helps to illustrate people's WTA being greater than their WTP.

1.   *What explanations other than the endowment effect could help to explain any differences between a buyer's WTP and a seller's WTA?*
2. * *Illustrate the impact of the endowment effect on indifference curves.*

1   D. Kahneman, J. L. Knetch and R. H. Thaler, 'Experimental tests of the endowment effect and the Coase theorem', *Journal of Political Economy*, vol. 98, no. 6 (1990), pp. 1352–75.

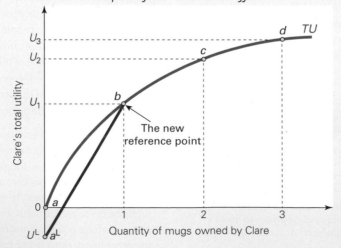

Impact of the endowment effect

might code the result as a gain of 10 percentage points and feel much happier. A similar argument could be made if a worker was expecting to receive a real wage increase of 3 per cent but only received one of 2 per cent.

■ *By making comparisons with others.* If customers obtain a 10 per cent discount on a product they purchase, they may initially feel happy and code the outcome as a gain. However, if they subsequently find out that other customers obtained a 20 per cent discount on the same product, this might change their reference point and they might begin to code the outcome as a loss.

■ *Adjusting slowly to a changed income/asset position.* Contestants on the game show *Who Wants to be a Millionaire?* who have already won £16 000 may still take a 50:50 gamble of winning another £16 000 (i.e. having a total prize of £32 000) or losing £15 000 (i.e. having a total prize of £1000). When asked why they took the gamble, participants are likely to explain that even if they lose they will still have £1000 more than before they played the game. Comments such as these suggest that the contestants' reference point while playing the game remains at their income level *before* playing the game: i.e. every pay-off is coded as a gain. However, as they play the game, their income/asset position is changing. When they take the gamble they have already won £16 000. If their perception of their income position had fully adjusted, the reference income level would include the £16 000 and the chances of losing would be coded as a £15 000 loss.

Reference dependent loss aversion.   People are generally loss averse – we saw this in section 5.1 (pages 139–41) when looking at the diminishing marginal utility of income. However, this loss aversion can be amplified by the reference point for a decision. The theory of **reference dependent loss aversion** is illustrated by the **endowment effect**, sometimes known as **divestiture aversion**. This is where people ascribe more value to things when they already own them, and are faced with selling them or otherwise giving them up, than when they are merely considering purchasing or acquiring them in the first place. In other words, when the reference point is one of ownership of an item, people put a higher value on it than when the reference point is one of non-ownership.

This suggests that the dislike of losses may be even stronger than is predicted by diminishing marginal utility of income in conventional economic theory (see page 131). Box 5.2 examines the endowment effect and shows how it produces a discrete kink or change in the slope of the utility function at the reference point.

 According to rational choice theory, the money you've already spent – known as 'sunk costs' (see page 156) – should be excluded from decision making. However, there is considerable evidence that it does affect consumer behaviour. Using loss aversion, can you explain why this might be the case.

Present bias and self-control issues

Traditional theory assumes that if people plan to do something at some specific point in time in the future, such as going to a lecture at 10am next Monday, they do indeed do so when the time arrives. This is referred to as **time consistency**.

The only reason time-consistent people would change their mind is if new information came to light about the relative size of the costs and benefits of their decisions. For example, at 3:00pm on Monday you might plan to go to the gym at 5:00pm on Monday. However, at 4:00pm you might change your mind because you find out your best friend is coming to see you at 5:00pm. This is still time-consistent behaviour, as the only reason you have changed your mind is because information has changed: the opportunity cost of going to the gym turns out to be greater than you had thought at 3:00pm.

In practice, people often exhibit *time-inconsistent* behaviour. This is likely when some of the costs or benefits occur before other ones. People may then change their minds. For example, you may plan to start revising at 10:00am on Monday, but when that time arrives you may instead watch TV or play a computer game and plan to start revising on Tuesday!

Many people make New Year's resolutions; most do not stick to them! People are weak willed; people put things off.

 Can you think of any other examples of decisions where people often change their mind with the passage of time once the costs or benefits become immediate.

Behavioural economists refer to this form of time inconsistency as **present bias**. This is where people put a greater

---

Definitions

Reference dependent loss aversion Where people value (or 'code') outcomes as either losses or gains in relation to a reference point. This can mean that losses are disliked more than would be predicted by standard diminishing marginal utility.

Endowment effect (or divestiture aversion) The hypothesis that people ascribe more value to things when they own them than when they are merely considering purchasing or acquiring them – in other words, when the reference point is one of ownership rather than non-ownership.

Definitions

Time consistency Where a person's preferences remain the same over time. For example, it is time consistent if you plan to buy a book when your student loan arrives and then actually do so when it does.

Present bias Time-inconsistent behaviour whereby people give greater weight to present pay-offs relative to future ones than would be predicted by standard discounting techniques.

weight on present benefits and/or costs than would be implied by a standard discounting approach. This means that they put excess weight on the costs of doing things they don't like doing, but believe are good for them (such as exercise or dieting); and excess weight on the benefits of doing things they want to do, but believe are bad for them (such as eating lots of chocolates or going out rather than revising). According to the well-known saying, 'hard work often pays off after time, but laziness pays off now'.

This suggests that when comparing pay-offs (benefits minus costs) in, say, a month with those today, people use a higher discount factor than when comparing pay-offs between two points in time a month apart, but both in the future. See Box 5.3 for a more detailed example.

Present bias helps explain why many people have difficulty in sticking to commitments. Indeed, some behavioural economists have actually created a website called *stickK*, which enables people to make their own commitment contracts to help them stick to their plans.

Taking other people into account

Our behaviour as consumers, as in many other aspects of our lives, is often influenced by other people – both the effect we have on them and the effect they have on us.

Reciprocity
We start by looking at the effect of our consumption on other people. Behavioural economists have tried to develop utility functions that capture the idea that consumers care about the pay-offs to other people as well as themselves.

For example, having *altruistic* preferences in economics means that you might be willing in some circumstances to increase the pay-offs to another person or group of people at

---

*BOX 5.3 | **MODELLING PRESENT BIAS**

A case study of gym attendance

A student, Jake, is considering whether or not to go to the gym at 5:00pm for an hour after his classes have finished for the day. Assume he has paid a monthly membership fee and there are no additional charges per visit. Therefore, the only cost of going to the gym is the opportunity cost of his time: e.g. giving up the chance to watch TV or meet his friends. To make the example as simple as possible, assume that all the benefits, such as health and general feelings of well-being, occur in the hour after he has finished at 6:00 pm.

If the benefits and opportunity cost of going to the gym can be valued at £20 and £10 respectively, will he decide to go? Are the discounted benefits greater than the discounted costs? Does the decision change with the passage of time? If Jake makes the decision at 3:00pm, will he still plan to go when considering the decision at 5:00pm?

Time-consistent behaviour

To begin with, consider the decision from his point of view at 3:00pm. At this moment in time, all the costs and benefits are in the future. Assuming he is impatient, the value of these costs and benefits at 5:00pm and 6:00pm respectively need to be adjusted to their value to Jake at 3:00pm.

Let δ (Jake's per hourly discount factor) $= 0.9$. Using standard exponential discounting, the costs (C) that occur in two hours' time (i.e. at 5:00pm) need to be multiplied by $\delta \times \delta$ (or δ^2) to adjust their value to the student at 3:00pm. The benefits (B), which all occur in three hours' time (i.e. at 6:00pm), need to be multiplied by $\delta \times \delta \times \delta$ (or δ^3) to adjust their value to the student at 3:00pm. The net benefit in

pounds (NB) (i.e. benefit minus cost) from his point of view at 3:00pm, is given by the following:

$$NB^{3pm} = \delta^3 B_{6pm} - \delta^2 C_{5pm} = 0.729(20)$$
$$- 0.81(10) = 14.58 - 8.1 = 6.48$$

Although the benefits occur one hour after the costs, their greater discounted value means that at 3:00pm Jake will plan to go to the gym at 5:00pm.

Now consider the decision from his point of view at 5:00pm. The costs are immediate while the benefits are an hour away. Therefore, they have to be weighted by 1 and δ respectively, giving:

$$NB^{5pm} = \delta B_{6pm} - C_{5pm} = 0.9(20) - 1(10)$$
$$= 18 - 10 = 8$$

When 5:00pm arrives, therefore, Jake will follow through on his intention of going to the gym.

This simple example illustrates how the standard model of exponential discounting with a constant discount factor per period of time imposes time consistency (try using different values for δ, B and C and you will see that this remains so). The weighting factor used to adjust the benefits at 6:00pm is always 90 per cent of the size of the weighting factor used to adjust the costs at 5:00pm. This percentage difference remains the same no matter from what point in time the decision is being judged.

Therefore, if Jake discovers no new information about the size of the costs and benefits with the passage of time, his preferences remain the same. If at 3:00pm he plans to go to the gym at 5:00pm, he will indeed go to the gym when 5:00pm arrives.

a personal cost to yourself: e.g. making donations to a charity or buying presents for people (see also Box 4.4 on page 120, which looks at love and caring for another person). Having *spiteful* preferences, on the other hand, means that you might be willing to *reduce* the pay-offs of another person or group of people at a cost to yourself.

Evidence from experiments suggest that the same people are often willing to increase the pay-offs to others at a personal cost to themselves in some situations while reducing the pay-offs to others at a personal cost to themselves in other situations. In other words, people can have both altruistic and spiteful preferences.

To capture these ideas, behavioural economists have developed a number of models of **reciprocity**. Some of these suggest that people may experience an increase in their own utility by being kind to people they believe have been kind to them. Their utility may also increase if they are unkind to people they believe have been unkind to them.

> **Definition**
>
> **Reciprocity (in economics)** Where people's behaviour is influenced by the effects it will have on others.

 Are such models consistent with standard theories of rational behaviour?

Relativity matters

Not only are we likely to consider the effect we have on others and be motivated by either altruism or spite, but we are also likely to be influenced by other people's behaviour. For example, if you are making a choice about buying a car, you might be influenced by the car your brother drives; if he chooses an Audi, perhaps you would like a more expensive car, a Mercedes possibly (assuming that you have graduated

Time-inconsistent behaviour: present bias

In the real world we often observe people behaving in a time-*inconsistent* way. They plan to do things at points in time when all the costs and benefits occur in the future. However, they have a tendency to change their mind with the passage of time once some of the costs or benefits are experienced immediately.

A more formal study carried out by DellaVigna and Malmendier (2006)[1] analysed data from three health clubs in the USA where consumers had a choice between paying $80 per month with no payment per visit or $10 per visit with no monthly fee. The authors found that 80 per cent of those who chose the monthly membership option ended up paying more per visit on average than they would have paid if they had simply opted to pay per visit. These customers overestimated how many times they would go and did not learn from their mistakes as they did not change their membership.

One simple way the previous model can be extended to capture this type of behaviour idea is called *quasi-hyperbolic discounting*. All the costs and benefits, apart from those that occur immediately, are now multiplied by an additional weighting factor (β). What happens in the previous example if $\beta = 0.5$?

Jake will still plan to go to the gym from his perspective at 3:00pm as shown below:

$$NB^{3pm} = \beta\delta^3 B_{6pm} - \beta\delta^2 C_{5pm} = 0.3645(20) - 0.405(10)$$
$$= 7.29 - 4.05 = +3.24$$

By multiplying both costs and benefits by a constant fraction of 0.5 their relative weighting has not changed: i.e. the weighting factor used to adjust the benefits is still 90 per cent of the one used to adjust the costs. This would be true from any vantage point (i.e. 1:00pm, 2:00pm, etc.) as long as the costs and benefits were both in the future and remained an hour apart.

However, things change once the costs become immediate. Having planned to go to the gym at 3:00pm, Jake now changes his mind when 5:00pm finally arrives. The costs are now immediate and hence are not multiplied by β.

$$NB^{5pm} = \beta\delta B_{6pm} - C_{5pm} = 0.45(20) - 10$$
$$= 9 - 10 = -1$$

Once the costs become immediate, while the benefits are still an hour away, the difference between the weighting changes from 90 per cent to 45 per cent. This has the effect of magnifying the size of the immediate cost relative to the future benefit. This is an example of *present bias* and can create time-inconsistent preferences.

The quasi-hyperbolic discounting model illustrates a situation where a person's weighting of the present/immediate over a later point in time is even greater than would be suggested by standard models of exponential discounting.

1. *The bias for the present will vary from one individual to another. What happens in the previous example if the student has a smaller bias for the present that can be captured by $\beta = 0.7$.*
2. *Imagine a decision where all the benefits occur exactly an hour before the costs. Assume the benefits = £10 and the costs = £20 Using the quasi-hyperbolic discounting model, show how a person's preferences will change with the passage of time.*
3. *Assume you have a present bias but are fully aware of the inconsistent nature of your preferences. What actions could you take to make sure you actually carry out your planned decisions?*

1 Stefano DellaVigna and Ulrike Malmendier, 'Paying not to go to the gym', *American Economic Review*, vol. 96, no. 3 (June 2006).

and now have a well-paid job!). If he switches to a Jaguar, then perhaps you will opt for a Porsche. You want a better (or faster or more expensive) car than your brother; you are concerned not only with your choice of car but with your *relative* choice.

This does not disprove that choice depends on perceived utility. But it does demonstrate that utility often depends on your consumption *relative* to that of other people. Again, this is something that the advertising industry is only too well aware of. Adverts often try to encourage you to buy a product by showing that *other* people are buying it.

Herding and 'groupthink'

Being influenced by what other people buy, and thus making relative choices, can lead to herd behaviour. A fashion might catch on; people might grab an item in a sale because other people seem to be grabbing it as well; people might buy a particular share on the stock market because other people are buying it.

Now, part of this may simply be the use of a heuristic under bounded rationality; sometimes it may be a good rule of thumb to buy something that other people want, as they might know more about it than you do. But there is a danger in such behaviour: other people may also be buying it because other people are buying it, and this builds a momentum. Sales may soar and the price may be driven well above a level that reflects the utility people will end up gaining. People have been persuaded to buy various risky financial assets because other people have been buying them and hence their price has been rising. This type of behaviour helps us to understand some of the aspects of destabilising speculation that we examined in section 2.5 (page 72–73).

BOX 5.4 | **NUDGING PEOPLE** EXPLORING ECONOMICS

How to change behaviour without taking away choice

One observation of behavioural economists is that people make many decisions out of habit. They use simple rules, such as: 'I'll buy the more expensive item because it's bound to be better'; or 'I'll buy this item because it's on offer'; or 'I always take the car to work, so I don't need to consider alternatives'; or 'Other people are buying this, so it must be worth having'.

Given that people behave like this, how might they be persuaded to change their behaviour? Governments might want to know this. Are there 'nudges' which will encourage people to act in their own self-interest: e.g. stop smoking, take more exercise or eat more healthy food? Will these 'nudges' impose a cost on those people who are acting in a rational manner? Firms too will want to know how to sell more of their products or to motivate their workforce. Even parents might want to make use of behavioural economics.

Opting in versus opting out

An interesting example concerns 'opting in' versus 'opting out'. In some countries, with organ donor cards, or many company pension schemes or charitable giving, people have to opt in. In other words, they have to make the decision to take part. Many as a result do not, partly because they never seem to find the time to do so, even though they might quite like to. With the busy lives people lead, it's too easy to think, 'Yes, I'll do that some time', but never actually get round to doing it: i.e. they have present bias.

With an 'opt out' system, people are automatically signed up to the scheme, but can freely choose to opt out. Thus it would be assumed that organs from people killed in an accident who had not opted out could be used for transplants. If you did not want your organs to be used, you would have to join a register. It could be the same with charitable giving. Some firms add a small charitable contribution to the price of their products (e.g. airline tickets or utility bills), unless people opt out. Similarly, under UK pension arrangements introduced from 2012, firms automatically deduct pension contributions from employees' wages unless they opt out of the scheme.

Opt-in schemes have participation rates of around 60 per cent, while otherwise identical opt-out funds retain between 90 and 95 per cent of employees. It is no wonder that Adair Turner, in his report on pensions, urged legislation to push pension schemes to an opt-in default position and that policy is moving in this direction.[1]

This type of policy can improve the welfare of those who make systematic mistakes (i.e. suffer from present bias) while imposing very limited harm on those who act in a time-consistent manner. If it is in the interests of someone to opt out of the scheme, they can easily do so. Policies such as these are an example of what behavioural economists call 'soft paternalism'.

The Behavioural Insights Team

The UK Coalition government (2010–15) established the Behavioural Insights Team (BIT) (also unofficially known as the Nudge Unit) in the Cabinet Office in 2010. A major objective of this team is to use ideas from behavioural economics to design policies that enable people to make better choices for themselves.

BIT was partially privatised in 2014 and is now equally owned by the UK government, the innovation charity Nesta and the Team's employees.

1. *How would you nudge members of a student household to be more economical in the use of electricity?*
2. *How could the government nudge people to stop dropping litter?*
3. *In the 2011 Budget, the then Chancellor of the Exchequer, George Osborne, announced that charitable giving in wills would be exempt from inheritance tax. Do you think this will be an effective way of encouraging more charitable donations?*

1 Richard Reeves, 'Why a nudge from the state beats a slap', *Observer*, 20 July 2008.

Is what's best for the individual best for others?

Many of the choices we make are not made as individuals purely for ourselves. If you are a member of a family or living with friends, many of your 'consumption' decisions will affect the other members of the household and many of their decisions will affect you.

Some things will be decided jointly: what to have for dinner, what colour to paint the hall, whether to have a party. Put it another way: when you gain utility, the other members of the household will often gain too (e.g. from things 'jointly' consumed, such as central heating).

Sometimes, however, it is the other way round. When things are jointly purchased, such as food, then one person's consumption will often be at the expense of other members of the household. 'Who's finished all the milk?' 'I want to watch a different television programme.'

What we are saying is that when individuals are in a group, such as a family, a club or an outing with a group of friends, their behaviour will affect and be affected by the other members of the group. For this reason, we have to amend our simple analysis of 'rational' choice. Let us consider two situations. The first is where people are trying to maximise their own self-interest within the group. The second is where people are genuinely motivated by the interests of the other members – whether from feelings of love, friendship, moral duty or whatever. We will consider these two situations within a family.

Self-interested behaviour

If you do not consider the other members of the family, this could rebound on you. For example, if you do not clean out the bath after yourself, or do not do your share of the washing up, then you may have to 'pay the price'. Other family members may get cross with you or behave equally selfishly themselves.

When considering doing things for their own benefit, therefore, the 'rational' person would at the very least consider the reactions of the other members of the family. We could still use the concept of marginal utility, however, to examine such behaviour. If marginal utility were greater than the price ($MU > P$), it would be 'rational' to do more of any given activity. Here, though, marginal utility would include utility not only from directly consuming goods or services within the household, but also from the favourable reactions to you from other family members. Likewise, marginal utility would be reduced if there were any unfavourable reaction from other family members. The 'price' (i.e. the marginal cost to you) would include not only the monetary costs to you of consuming something, but also any other sacrifice you make in order to consume it. In other words, the price would be the full opportunity cost.

Take first the case of goods or services jointly consumed, such as a family meal. Do you offer to cook dinner? If you were motivated purely by self-interest, you would do so if the marginal benefit (i.e. marginal utility) to you exceeded the marginal cost to you. The marginal benefit would include the benefit to you of consuming the meal, plus any pleasure you got from the approval of other family members, plus any entitlement to being let off other chores. The marginal cost to you would include any monetary costs to you (e.g. of purchasing the ingredients) and the sacrifice of any alternative pleasurable activities that you had to forgo (such as watching television). Whether the actual preparation of the meal was

regarded as a marginal benefit or a marginal cost would depend on whether the individual saw it as a pleasure or a chore.

Clearly, these benefits and costs are highly subjective: they are as you perceive them. But the principle is simple: if you were behaving purely out of self-interest, you would cook the meal if you felt that you would gain more from doing so than it cost you.

Now take the case of consuming something individually where it deprives another household member of consuming it (such as taking the last yoghurt from the fridge). Again, if you were behaving purely out of self-interest, you would have to weigh up the pleasure from that yoghurt against the cost to you of incurring the irritation of other family members.

Behaviour in the interests of the family as a whole

However, most people are not totally selfish, especially when it comes to relating to other members of their family. In fact, family members are often willing to make personal sacrifices or put in considerable effort (e.g. with household chores or child rearing) for the sake of other family members, without being motivated by what they individually can get out of it.

In such cases, consumption decisions can be examined at two levels: that of the individual and that of the whole family.

As far as individuals are concerned, analysis in terms of their own marginal benefit and marginal cost would be too simplistic. Often it is a more accurate picture to see household members, rather than behaving selfishly, instead behaving in the self-interest of the whole household. So a decision about what food to buy for the family at the supermarket, if taken by an individual member, is likely to take into account the likes and dislikes of other family members, and the costs to the whole household budget. In other words, it is the whole family's marginal benefits and marginal costs that the individual family member is considering.

Other forms of altruism

It can be argued that unselfish behaviour within a family, or social circle, is not truly altruistic. After all, it is not unreasonable to suppose that others will treat you better as a consequence. But outside the circle of family and friends we do see behaviour that does appear to be altruistic. Individuals choose to give money to charity, to return other people's property when they find it and to give blood that will help save strangers.

This is a further area of economic theory that behavioural economists find interesting and it is providing a focus for economic research. The apparent contradiction between net utility maximisation and the actions of individuals provides an opportunity to gain further understanding about motivation and utility.

1. *Imagine that you are going out for the evening with a group of friends. How would you decide where to go? Would this decision-making process be described as 'rational' behaviour?*
2. *Think of some examples of altruistic behaviour towards strangers. In each case list some of the reasons why individuals might behave 'unselfishly'.*

Implications for economic policy

Governments, in designing policy, will normally attempt to change people's behaviour. They might want to encourage people to work harder, to save more, to recycle rubbish, to use their cars less, to eat more healthily, and so on. If the policy is to be successful, it is vital for the policy measures to contain appropriate incentives: whether it be a tax rise, a grant or subsidy, a new law or regulation, an advertising campaign or direct help.

But whether the incentives are appropriate depends on how people will respond to them, and to know that, the policy makers will need to understand people's behaviour. This is where behavioural economics comes in. People might respond as rational maximisers; but they might not. It is thus important to understand how context affects behaviour and adjust policy incentives appropriately.

 Remember the question we asked at the beginning of Chapter 4 (page 105): 'Do you ever purchase things irrationally? If so, what are they and why is your behaviour irrational?' Can you better explain this behaviour in the light of behavioural economics?

Section summary

1. Traditional economics is based on the premise that consumers act rationally, weighing up the costs and benefits of the choices open to them. Behavioural economics acknowledges that real-world decisions do not always appear rational; it seeks to understand and explain what economic agents actually do.

2. Experiments and observations provide useful insights into the ways individuals act when faced with choices and decisions. They allow economists to test existing models and theories, but also provide motivation for the construction of new theories of human behaviour.

3. People's ability to make rational decisions is bounded by limited information and time. Thus people resort to using heuristics – rules of thumb.

4. The choices they make may also depend on how these choices are framed – the way in which they are presented or are perceived. People can be nudged to frame choices differently.

5. Sometimes people appear to behave irrationally. This may be because of a biased use of information: putting undue weight on the experience of friends or on their own experiences, especially recent ones. It may be because of the belief that independent things are really connected (the gambler's fallacy).

6. Seemingly irrational behaviour may arise from the choice of reference point for decision taking. The reference point used by people to judge an outcome as a gain or a loss can be influenced by a range of factors, including their expectations, comparisons with others and adjusting slowly to new information.

7. People who are loss averse may value things more highly when they own them than when they are considering buying them (the endowment effect) or when the costs or benefits are immediate. This reference-dependent loss aversion may result in people giving additional weight to loss than would occur simply from the diminishing marginal utility of income.

8. Giving additional weight to immediate benefits or costs is called 'present bias' and can lead to time-inconsistent behaviour, with people changing their minds and not acting in accordance with previous plans.

9. Apparently irrational behaviour may also be the result of taking other people into account. Altruism and spite are two emotions affecting choice here. People may also be influenced by other people's tastes.

10. Governments, in devising policy, are increasingly looking at ways to influence people's behaviour by devising appropriate incentives. Behavioural economics provides useful insights here.

END OF CHAPTER QUESTIONS

1. A country's central bank (e.g. the Bank of England or the US Federal Reserve Bank) has a key role in ensuring the stability of the banking system. In many countries the central bank is prepared to bail banks out which find themselves in financial difficulties. Although this has the benefit of reducing the chance of banks going bankrupt and depositors losing their money, it can create a moral hazard. Explain why.

2. Discuss the EU ruling that gender may not be used to differentiate insurance premiums. Which insurance markets would be affected by outlawing age 'discrimination' in a similar manner? What would be the impact?

3. The European New Car Assessment Programme (Euro NCAP) carries out crash tests on new cars in order to assess the extent to which they are safer than the minimum required standard. The cars are given a percentage score in four different categories, including adult occupant protection and child occupant protection. An overall safety rating is then awarded. Based on the test results in November 2014, the Volvo V40 hatchback was judged to be the safest car on the market. If you observed that these cars were *more* likely to be involved in traffic accidents, could this be an example of adverse selection or moral hazard? Explain.

4. How does economics predict rational consumers will treat spending on credit cards compared with spending cash? Do you think that there are likely to be differences in the way people spend by each? If so, can you explain why?

5. How does behavioural economics differ from standard economics?

6. Give some example of heuristics that you use. Why do you use them?

7. For what reasons may branded products be more expensive than supermarkets' own-brand equivalents? How can behavioural economics help to explain this?

8. If you buy something in the shop on the corner when you know that the same item could have been bought more cheaply two miles up the road in the supermarket, is your behaviour irrational? Explain.

9. Why do gyms encourage people to take out monthly or even annual membership rather than paying per visit?

10. Many European countries operate organ donor schemes, some with schemes requiring that potential donors opt in, others with a system of opting out, or presumed consent. Explain why a system of presumed consent is likely to result in much higher numbers of donors. Does your answer suggest that all countries should move to presumed consent for organ donors?

Online Resources

Websites relevant to Chapters 4 and 5

Numbers and sections refer to websites listed in the Web Appendix and hotlinked from this book's website at **www.pearsoned.co.uk/sloman**.

- For news articles relevant to this chapter, see the *Economics News* section on the student website.
- For general news on demand and consumers, see websites in section A, and particularly A2, 3, 4, 8, 9, 11, 12, 23, 25, 36. See also site A41 for links to economics news articles on particular search topics (e.g. consumer demand and advertising).
- For data, information and sites on products and marketing, see sites B1, 3, 17, 11, 13, 17, 39, 48.
- For student resources relevant to Part C, see sites C1–7, 19.
- For more on behavioural economics, see sites C1, 6, 7, 23.
- For material on consumer behaviour see the consumer behaviour section in site D3.
- For experiments and games examining consumer behaviour see D13, 14, 17–20.

Background to Supply

So far we have assumed that supply curves are upward sloping: that a higher price will encourage firms to supply more. But just how much will firms choose to supply at each price? It depends largely on the amount of profit they will make. If a firm can increase its profits by producing more, it will normally do so.

Profit is made by firms earning more from the sale of goods than they cost to produce. A firm's total profit ($T\Pi$) is thus the difference between its total sales revenue (TR) and its total costs of production (TC):

$$T\Pi = TR - TC$$

In order then to discover how a firm can maximise its profit or even get a sufficient level of profit, we must first consider what determines costs and revenue.

The first four sections build up a theory of short-run and long-run costs. They show how output depends on the inputs used, and how costs depend on the amount of output produced. Section 6.5 then looks at revenue. Finally, in section 6.6, we bring cost and revenue together to see how profit is determined. In particular, we shall see how profit varies with output and how the point of maximum profit is found.

Chapter 4 went behind the demand curve. It saw how the 'rational' consumer weighs up the *benefits* (utility) of consuming various amounts of goods or combinations of goods against their *costs* (their price).

We now need to go behind the supply curve and find out just how the **rational producer** (or 'firm' as we call all producers) will behave.

In this case, we shall be looking at the benefits and costs to the firm of producing various quantities of goods and using various alternative methods of production. We shall be asking:

- How much will be produced?
- What combination of inputs will be used?
- How much profit will be made?

Profit and the aims of a firm

The traditional theory of supply, or **theory of the firm**, assumes that firms aim to *maximise profit*; this is a realistic assumption in many cases. The traditional profit-maximising theory of the firm is examined in this and the following two chapters. First, we examine the general principles that govern how much a firm supplies. Then, in Chapters 7 and 8, we look at how supply is affected by the amount of competition a firm faces.

In some circumstances, however, firms may not seek to maximise profits. Instead they may seek to maximise sales, or the rate of growth of sales. Alternatively, they may have no *single* aim, but rather a series of potentially conflicting aims held by different managers in different departments of the firm. Sometimes there may be a conflict between the owners of the firm and those running it. Not surprisingly, a firm's behaviour will be influenced by what its objectives are: i.e. what it is trying to achieve. Chapter 9 looks at the implications of firms having different aims and objectives. It also considers some ideas from behavioural economics.

6.1   THE SHORT-RUN THEORY OF PRODUCTION

The cost of producing any level of output will depend on the amount of inputs (or 'factors of production') used and the price the firm must pay for them. Let us first focus on the quantity of factors used.

 KEY IDEA 18

Output depends on the amount of resources and how they are used. Different amounts and combinations of inputs will lead to different amounts of output. If output is to be produced efficiently, then inputs should be combined in the optimum proportions.

Short- and long-run changes in production

If a firm wants to increase production, it will take time to acquire a greater quantity of certain inputs. For example, a manufacturer can use more electricity by turning on switches, but it might take a while to obtain and install more machines, and longer still to build a bigger, or a second, factory.

If the firm wants to increase output relatively quickly, it will only be able to increase the quantity of certain inputs. It can use more raw materials and more fuel. It may be able to use more labour by offering overtime to its existing workforce, or by recruiting extra workers if they are available. But it will have to make do with its existing buildings and most of its machinery.

The distinction we are making here is between *fixed factors* and *variable factors*. A *fixed* factor is an input that cannot be increased within a given time period (e.g. buildings). A *variable* factor is one that can.

The distinction between fixed and variable factors allows us to distinguish between the **short run** and the **long run**.

The short run is a time period during which at least one factor of production is fixed. Output can be increased only by using more variable factors. For example, if a coffee bar became more successful it could serve more customers per day in its existing shops, if there was space. It could increase the quantity of milk and coffee beans it purchases. It may be able to hire more staff, depending on conditions in the local labour market, and purchase additional coffee machines if

Definitions

Rational producer behaviour When a firm weighs up the costs and benefits of alternative courses of action and then seeks to maximise its net benefit.

Theory of the firm The analysis of pricing and output decisions of the firm under various market conditions, assuming that the firm wishes to maximise profit.

Fixed factor An input that cannot be increased in supply within a given time period.

Variable factor An input that can be increased in supply within a given time period.

Short run The period of time over which at least one factor is fixed.

Long run The period of time long enough for *all* factors to be varied.

BOX 6.1   MALTHUS AND THE DISMAL SCIENCE OF ECONOMICS   EXPLORING ECONOMICS

Population growth + diminishing returns = starvation

The law of diminishing returns has potentially cataclysmic implications for the future populations of the world.

If the population of the world grows rapidly, then food output may not keep pace with it. There could be diminishing returns to labour as more and more people crowd on to the limited amount of land available.

This is already a problem in some of the poorest countries of the world, especially in sub-Saharan Africa. The land is barely able to support current population levels. Only one or two bad harvests are needed to cause mass starvation – witness the appalling famines in recent years in Ethiopia and Sudan.

The relationship between population and food output was analysed as long ago as 1798 by the Reverend Thomas Robert Malthus (1766–1834) in his *Essay on the Principle of Population*. This book was a bestseller and made Robert Malthus perhaps the best known of all social scientists of his day.

Malthus argued as follows:

I say that the power of population is indefinitely greater than the power in the earth to produce subsistence for man.

Population when unchecked, increases in a geometrical ratio. Subsistence increases only in an arithmetical ratio. A slight acquaintance with numbers will show the immensity of the first power in comparison with the second.[1]

What Malthus was saying is that world population tends to double about every 25 years or so if unchecked. It grows geometrically, like the series 1, 2, 4, 8, 16, 32, 64, etc. But food output, because of diminishing returns, cannot keep pace with this. It is likely to grow at only an arithmetical rate, like the series 1, 2, 3, 4, 5, 6, 7, etc. It is clear that population, if unchecked, will soon outstrip food supply.

So what is the check on population growth? According to Malthus, it is starvation. As population grows, so food output per head will fall until, with more and more people starving, the death rate will rise. Only then will population growth stabilise at the rate of growth of food output.

Have Malthus' predictions been borne out by events? Two factors have mitigated the forces that Malthus described:

■ The rate of population growth tends to slow down as countries become more developed. Although improved health prolongs life, this tends to be more than offset by a decline in the birth rate as people choose to have smaller families. This is illustrated in the table below. Population growth peaked in the 1960s, has fallen substantially since then and is projected to fall further in future decades.
■ Technological improvements in farming have greatly increased food output per hectare. These include better fertilisers and the development of genetically modified crops. (See Case Study 6.1 on the student website for an example.)

The growth in food output has thus exceeded the rate of population growth in developed countries and in some developing countries too. Nevertheless, the Malthusian spectre is very real for some of the poorest developing countries, which are simply unable to feed their populations satisfactorily. It is these poorest countries of the world which have some of the highest rates of population growth – around 3 per cent per annum in many African countries.

A further cause for concern arises from the move in Asia towards a westernised diet, with meat and dairy products playing a larger part. This further increases pressure on the land, since cattle require considerably more grain to produce meat than would be needed to feed humans a vegetarian diet.

A third factor is cited by some commentators, who remain unconvinced of the strength of Malthus' gloomy prognostication for the world. They believe that he seriously underestimated humankind's capacity to innovate; perhaps human ingenuity is one resource that doesn't suffer from diminishing returns.

1. *Why might it be possible for there to be a zero marginal productivity of labour on many family farms in poor countries and yet just enough food for all the members of the family to survive? (Illustrate using MPP and APP curves.)*
2. *The figures in the following table are based on the assumption that birth rates will fall faster than death rates. Under what circumstances might these forecasts underestimate the rate of growth of world population?*

World population levels and growth: actual and projected

Year	World population (billions)	Average annual rate of increase (%)		
		World	More developed regions	Less developed regions
1950	2.5			
1960	3.0	1.8	1.2	2.1
1970	3.7	2.0	1.0	2.4
1980	4.4	1.9	0.7	2.3
1990	5.3	1.6	0.6	2.2
2000	6.1	1.4	0.4	1.7
2010	6.9	1.2	0.4	1.4
2020	7.8	1.1	0.3	1.3
2030	8.5	0.9	0.1	1.1
2040	9.2	0.8	0.0	0.9
2050	9.7	0.6	0.0	0.7

Source: *World Population Prospects: The 2015 Revision* (United Nations, Department of Economic and Social Affairs) (Medium variant for predictions).

1 T. R. Malthus, *First Essay on Population* (Macmillan, 1926), pp. 13–14.

there was space to install them. However, in the short run it could not extend its existing shops or have new ones built. This would take more time.

The long run is a time period long enough for all inputs to be varied. Given enough time, a firm can build additional factories and install new plant and equipment; a coffee shop can have new shops built.

The actual length of the short run will differ from firm to firm and industry to industry. It is not a fixed period of time. It might take a farmer a year to obtain new land, buildings and equipment; if so, the short run is any time period up to a year and the long run is any time period longer than a year. If it takes a mobile phone handset manufacturer two years to get a new factory built, the short run is any period up to two years and the long run is any period longer than two years.

1. *How will the length of the short run for the airline depend on the state of the aircraft industry?*
2. *Up to roughly how long is the short run in the following cases?*
    (a) A firm supplying DJs for clubs and parties.
    (b) Nuclear power generation.
    (c) A street food wagon.
    (d) 'Superstore Hypermarkets Ltd'.
    In each case specify your assumptions.

For the remainder of this section we will concentrate on short-run production.

The law of diminishing returns

Production in the short run is subject to *diminishing returns*. You may well have heard of 'the law of diminishing returns': it is one of the most famous of all 'laws' of economics. To illustrate how this law underlies short-run production let us take the simplest possible case where there are just two factors: one fixed and one variable.

Take the case of a farm. Assume the fixed factor is land and the variable factor is labour. Since the land is fixed in supply, output per period of time can be increased only by increasing the amount of workers employed. But imagine what would happen as more and more workers crowd on to a fixed area of land. The land cannot go on yielding more and more output indefinitely. After a point the additions to output from each extra worker will begin to diminish.

We can now state the law of diminishing (marginal) returns.

The law of diminishing marginal returns states that when increasing amounts of a variable factor are used with a given amount of a fixed factor, there will come a point when each extra unit of the variable factor will produce less extra output than the previous unit.

A good example of the law of diminishing returns is given in Case Study 6.1 on the student website. It looks at diminishing returns to the application of nitrogen fertiliser on farmland.

The short-run production function: total physical product

Let us now see how the law of diminishing returns affects the total output of a firm in the short run. When a variable factor is added to a fixed factor the total output that results is often called **total physical product** (*TPP*).

The relationship between inputs and output is shown in a **production function**. In the simple case of the farm with only two factors – namely, a fixed supply of land ($\bar{L}n$) and a variable supply of farm workers (Lb) – the short-run production function would be

$$TPP = f(\bar{L}n, Lb)$$

This states that total physical product (i.e. the output of the farm) over a given period of time is a function of (i.e. depends on) the quantity of land and labour employed. The total physical output illustrated by the short-run production function shows the maximum output that can be produced by adding more of a variable input to a fixed input: i.e. it shows points that are all *technically efficient*.

In reality, total output from any given combination of inputs may be lower than the production function indicates because of inefficient management and methods of production. This issue is discussed in more detail in Box 7.5 in the next chapter. The level of technology is also assumed to be constant. (If there is technological progress, the whole production function would change.)

We could express the production function using an equation (an example is given in Box 6.4).

Alternatively, the production function could be expressed in the form of a table or a graph. Table 6.1 and Figure 6.1 show a hypothetical short-run production

Definitions

Law of diminishing (marginal) returns When one or more factors are held fixed, there will come a point beyond which the extra output from additional units of the variable factor will diminish.

Total physical product The total output of a product per period of time that is obtained from a given amount of inputs.

Production function The mathematical relationship between the output of a good and the inputs used to produce it. It shows how output will be affected by changes in the quantity of one or more of the inputs used in production holding the level of technology constant.

Technical efficiency The firm is producing as much output as is technologically possible given the quantity of factor inputs it is using.

Table 6.1	Wheat production per year from a particular farm		
	Number of workers (*Lb*)	TPP	APP (= TPP/Lb)	MPP (= ΔTPP/ΔLb)

	Number of workers (*Lb*)	TPP	APP (= TPP/Lb)	MPP (= ΔTPP/ΔLb)
a	0	0	–	
	1	3	3	3
b	2	10	5	7
	3	24	8	14
c	4	36	9	12
	5	40	8	4
d	6	42	7	2
	7	42	6	0
	8	40	5	−2

function for a farm producing wheat. The first two columns of Table 6.1 and the top diagram in Figure 6.1 show how total wheat output per year varies as extra workers are employed on a fixed amount of land.

With nobody working on the land, output will be zero (point *a*). As the first farm workers are taken on, wheat output initially rises more and more rapidly. The assumption behind this is that with only one or two workers

productivity is low, since the workers are spread too thinly. With more workers, however, they can work together – each, perhaps, doing some specialist job – and thus they can use the land more productively. In Table 6.1, output rises more and more rapidly up to the employment of the third worker (point *b*). In Figure 6.1 the *TPP* curve gets steeper up to point *b*.

After point *b*, however, diminishing marginal returns set in: output rises less and less rapidly, and the *TPP* curve correspondingly becomes less steeply sloped.

When point *d* is reached, wheat output is at a maximum: the land is yielding as much as it can. Any more workers employed after that are likely to get in each other's way. Thus beyond point *d* output is likely to fall again: eight workers actually produce less than seven workers.

All the points along the total physical product are technically efficient. Any point below it is technically inefficient. For example, if production were at point *e* with five workers producing 30 tonnes, it would be technically possible for those five workers to produce 40 tonnes at point *f*.

 What would happen to the TPP curve if the quantity of the fixed factor used in production were to increase to a new higher fixed level?

Figure 6.1	Wheat production per year (tonnes)

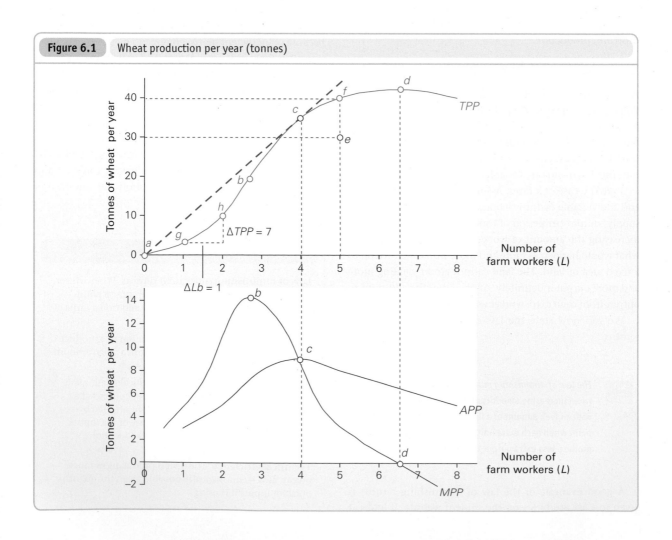

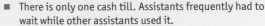

BOX 6.2   **DIMINISHING RETURNS IN THE BREAD SHOP**   CASE STUDIES AND APPLICATIONS

Is the baker using his loaf?

Just up the road from where John lives is a bread shop. Like many others, he buys his bread there on a Saturday morning. Not surprisingly, Saturday morning is the busiest time of the week for the shop and as a result it takes on extra assistants.

During the week only one assistant serves the customers, but on a Saturday morning there used to be five serving. But could they serve five times as many customers? No, they could not. There were diminishing returns to labour.

The trouble is that certain factors of production in the shop are fixed:

- The shop is a fixed size. It gets very crowded on Saturday morning. Assistants sometimes had to wait while customers squeezed past each other to get to the counter, and with five serving, the assistants themselves used to get in each other's way.

- There is only one cash till. Assistants frequently had to wait while other assistants used it.
- There is only one pile of tissue paper for wrapping the bread. Again the assistants often had to wait.

The fifth and maybe even the fourth assistant ended up serving very few extra customers.

John is still going to the same bread shop and they still have only one till and one pile of tissue paper. But now only three assistants are employed on a Saturday! The shop, however, is just as busy.

How would you advise the baker as to whether he should (a) employ four assistants on a Saturday; (b) extend his shop, thereby allowing more customers to be served on a Saturday morning; (c) extend his opening hours on a Saturday?

The short-run production function: average and marginal product

In addition to total physical product, two other important concepts are illustrated by a production function: namely, **average physical product** (*APP*) and **marginal physical product** (*MPP*).

Average physical product

This is output (*TPP*) per unit of the variable factor (Q_v). In the case of the farm, it is the output of wheat per worker.

$APP = TPP/Q_v$

Thus in Table 6.1 the average physical product of labour when four workers are employed is $36/4 = 9$ tonnes per year.

Marginal physical product

This is the *extra* output (ΔTPP) produced by employing *one more* unit of the variable factor.

Thus in Table 6.1 the marginal physical product of the fourth worker is 12 tonnes. The reason is that by employing the fourth worker, wheat output has risen from 24 tonnes to 36 tonnes: a rise of 12 tonnes.

In symbols, marginal physical product is given by

$MPP = \Delta TPP/\Delta Q_v$

Thus in our example:

$MPP = 12/1 = 12$

The reason why we divide the increase in output (ΔTPP) by the increase in the quantity of the variable factor (ΔQ_v) is that some variable factors can be increased only in multiple units. For example, if we wanted to know the *MPP* of

fertiliser and we found out how much extra wheat was produced by using an extra 20kg bag, we would have to divide this output by 20 (ΔQ_v) to find the *MPP* of *one* more kilogram.

Note that in Table 6.1 the figures for *MPP* are entered in the spaces between the other figures. The reason is that *MPP* can be seen as the *difference* in output *between* one level of input and another. Thus in the table the difference in output between five and six workers is 2 tonnes.

The figures for *APP* and *MPP* are plotted in the lower diagram of Figure 6.1. We can draw a number of conclusions from these diagrams:

- The *MPP* between two points is equal to the slope of the *TPP* curve between those two points. For example, when the number of workers increases from 1 to 2 ($\Delta Lb = 1$), *TPP* rises from 3 to 10 tonnes ($\Delta TPP = 7$). *MPP* is thus 7: the slope of the line between points *g* and *h*.
- *MPP* rises at first: the slope of the *TPP* curve gets steeper.
- *MPP* reaches a maximum at point *b*. At that point the slope of the *TPP* curve is at its steepest.
- After point *b*, diminishing returns set in. *MPP* falls. *TPP* becomes less steep.

KI 19
p151

Definitions

Average physical product Total output (*TPP*) per unit of the variable factor in question: $APP = TPP/Q_v$.

Marginal physical product The extra output gained by the employment of one more unit of the variable factor: $MPP = \Delta TPP/\Delta Q_v$.

- *APP* rises at first. It continues rising as long as the addition to output from the last worker (*MPP*) is greater than the average output (*APP*): the *MPP* pulls the *APP* up (see Box 6.3). This continues beyond point *b*. Even though *MPP* is now falling, the *APP goes on* rising as long as the *MPP* is still above the *APP*. Thus *APP* goes on rising to point *c*.

- Beyond point *c*, *MPP* is below *APP*. New workers add less to output than the average. This pulls the average down: *APP* falls.

BOX 6.3   THE RELATIONSHIP BETWEEN AVERAGES AND MARGINALS   EXPLORING ECONOMICS

In this chapter we have just examined the concepts of *average* and *marginal* physical product. We shall be coming across several other average and marginal concepts later on. It is useful at this stage to examine the general relationship between averages and marginals. In all cases there are three simple rules that relate them.

To illustrate these rules, consider the following example.

Imagine a room with 10 people in it. Assume that the *average* age of those present is 20.

Now if a 20-year-old enters the room (the *marginal* age), this will not affect the average age. It will remain at 20. If a 56-year-old now comes in, the average age will rise: not to 56, of course, but to 23. This is found by dividing the sum of everyone's ages (276) by the number of people (12). If then a child of 10 were to enter the room, this would pull the average age down.

From this example we can derive the three universal rules about averages and marginals:

- If the marginal equals the average, the average will not change.
- If the marginal is above the average, the average will rise.
- If the marginal is below the average, the average will fall.

 Suppose a course you are studying has five equally weighted pieces of coursework. Assume each one is marked out of 100 and your results are shown in the table below.

Coursework	1	2	3	4	5
Mark	60	60	70	70	20

Each number in the second row of the table is the marginal mark from each piece of coursework. Calculate your total and average number of marks after each piece of coursework. Show how your average and marginal marks illustrate the three rules above.

---

*BOX 6.4   THE RELATIONSHIP BETWEEN *TPP*, *MPP* AND *APP*   EXPLORING ECONOMICS

Using calculus again

The total physical product of a variable factor (e.g. fertiliser) can be expressed as an equation. For example:

$$TPP = 100 + 32Q_f + 10Q_f^2 - Q_f^3 \qquad (1)$$

where *TPP* is the output of grain in tonnes per hectare, and Q_f is the quantity of fertiliser applied in kilograms per hectare.

From this we can derive the *APP* function. *APP* is simply TPP/Q_f: i.e. output per kilogram of fertiliser. Thus:

$$APP = \frac{100}{Q_f} + 32 + 10Q_f - Q_f^2 \qquad (2)$$

We can also derive the *MPP* function. *MPP* is the rate of increase in *TPP* as additional fertiliser is applied. It is thus the first derivative of *TPP*: $dTPP/dQ_f$. Thus:

$$MPP = 32 + 20Q_f - 3Q_f^2 \qquad (3)$$

From these three equations we can derive the table shown.

 Check out some figures by substituting values of Q_f into each of the three equations.

Maximum output (484 tonnes) is achieved with 8kg of fertiliser per hectare. At that level, *MPP* is zero: no additional output can be gained.

Q_f	TPP	APP	MPP
1	141	141	49
2	196	98	60
3	259	86	65
4	324	81	64
5	385	77	57
6	436	72	44
7	471	67	25
8	484	60	0
9	469	52	−31

This maximum level of *TPP* can be discovered from the equations by using a simple technique. If *MPP* is zero at this level, then simply find the value of Q_f where

$$MPP = 32 + 20Q_f - 3Q_f^2 = 0 \qquad (4)$$

Solving this equation[1] gives $Q_f = 8$.

1 By applying the second derivative test (see Appendix 1) you can verify that $Q_f = 8$ gives the *maximum TPP* rather than the *minimum*. (Both the maximum *and* the minimum point of a curve have a slope equal to zero.)

- As long as *MPP* is greater than zero, *TPP* will go on rising. new workers add to total output.
- At point *d*, *TPP* is at a maximum (its slope is zero). An additional worker will add nothing to output: *MPP* is zero.
- Beyond point *d*, *TPP* falls; *MPP* is negative.

1. What is the significance of the slope of the line a–c in the top part of Figure 6.1?
2. Given that there is a fixed supply of land in the world, what implications can you draw from Figure 6.1 about the effects of an increase in world population for food output per head? (See Box 6.1.)

Section summary

1. A production function shows the relationship between the amount of inputs used and the amount of output produced from them (per period of time). It assumes technical efficiency in production.

2. In the short run it is assumed that one or more factors (inputs) are fixed in supply. The actual length of the short run will vary from industry to industry.

3. Production in the short run is subject to diminishing returns. As greater quantities of the variable factor(s) are used, so each additional unit of the variable factor will add less to output than previous units: marginal physical product will diminish and total physical product will rise less and less rapidly.

4. As long as marginal physical product is above average physical product, average physical product will rise. Once *MPP* has fallen below *APP*, however, *APP* will fall.

6.2 COSTS IN THE SHORT RUN

We have seen how output changes as inputs are varied in the short run. We now use this information to show how costs vary with the amount a firm produces. Obviously, before deciding how much to produce, it has to know the precise level of costs for each level of output.

But first we must be clear on just what we mean by the word 'costs'. The term is used differently by economists and accountants.

Measuring costs of production

When measuring costs, economists always use the concept of **opportunity cost**. Remember from Chapter 1 how we defined opportunity cost. It is the cost of any activity measured in terms of the *sacrifice* made in doing it: in other words, the cost measured in terms of the value of the best alternative forgone.

How do we apply this principle of opportunity cost to a firm? First we must discover what factors of production it is using. Then we must measure the sacrifice involved. To do this it is useful to put factors into two categories.

Factors not owned by the firm: explicit costs

The opportunity cost of using factors not already owned by the firm is simply the price that the firm has to pay for them. Thus if the firm uses £100 worth of electricity, the opportunity cost is £100. The firm has sacrificed £100, which could have been spent on something else. The same would be true for machinery or buildings (factories/shops/units) that have been rented from other organisations. These costs are called *explicit costs* because they involve direct payment of money by firms.

Factors already owned by the firm: implicit costs

When the firm already owns factors (e.g. machinery), it does not as a rule have to pay out money to use them. Their opportunity costs are thus **implicit costs**. They are equal to what the factors could earn for the firm in some alternative use, either within the firm or hired out to some other firm. Implicit costs do not involve actual cash outlays. They are less visible than explicit costs but just as important in decision making.

Here are some examples of implicit costs:

- A firm owns some buildings. The opportunity cost of using them in production for a year is the highest rent that could have been earned by letting them out to another firm over the same period.

- A firm draws £100 000 from the bank out of its savings in order to invest in new plant and equipment. The opportunity cost of this investment is not just the £100 000 (an explicit cost), but also the interest it thereby forgoes (an implicit cost).

- The owner of the firm could have earned £40 000 per annum by working for someone else. This £40 000 is then the opportunity cost of the owner's time running the business over the same period.

The opportunity costs of any decision in production are the implicit and explicit costs that are relevant to that

---

Definitions

Opportunity cost Cost measured in terms of the value of the best alternative forgone.

Explicit costs The payments to outside suppliers of inputs.

Implicit costs Costs that do not involve a direct payment of money to a third party, but which nevertheless involve a sacrifice of some alternative.

particular decision. By relevant we mean the costs that are incurred if the firm chose one particular course of action: e.g. expand output or stay in business. If a different decision is taken these costs would be avoided.

 What implicit and explicit costs would a firm avoid if it decided not to expand production?

Some costs may remain unaffected by whatever decision a firm makes. These are not opportunity costs and so are irrelevant. They are called *sunk costs* and should be completely disregarded.

A sunk cost often exists when a firm has paid for a factor of production in the past and that factor of production no longer has value in any alternative uses. For example, a firm may have previously purchased a piece of machinery that is highly specialised and tailored to its own production process. If this machinery is of no value to any other firms and has no scrap value, the opportunity cost of using it is *zero*. No matter what decisions the firm makes in the future, the money used to purchase the machinery – its *historic cost* – is irrelevant. Not using the machine will not bring that money back – it cannot be recovered. In such a case, if the output from the machinery is worth more than the cost of all the *other* inputs involved, the firm might as well use the machine rather than let it stand idle.

It is important to remember that the cost of the machine was not always a sunk cost. Before its purchase, the opportunity cost of buying the machine was the money paid for it. It was only after its purchase that it became a sunk cost and had an opportunity cost of zero. The timing of a decision is crucial when deciding whether a cost is relevant or sunk.

 The 'bygones' principle states that sunk costs should be ignored when deciding whether to produce or sell more or less of a product. Only those costs that can be avoided should be taken into account.

KEY IDEA 20

Costs and inputs

A firm's costs of production will depend on the factors of production it uses. The more factors it uses, the greater will its costs be. More precisely, this relationship depends on two elements:

- The productivity of the factors. The greater their physical productivity, the smaller will be the quantity of them required to produce a given level of output, and hence the lower will be the cost of that output. In other words, there is a direct link between *TPP, APP* and *MPP* and the costs of production.
- The price of the factors. The higher their price, the higher will be the costs of production.

In the short run, some factors are fixed in supply. Their total costs, therefore, are fixed, in the sense that they do not

Definitions

Sunk costs Costs that cannot be recouped (e.g. by transferring assets to other uses). Examples include specialised machinery or the costs of an advertising campaign.

Historic costs The original amount the firm paid for factors it now owns.

BOX 6.5   THE FALLACY OF USING HISTORIC COSTS

EXPLORING ECONOMICS

Or there's no point crying over spilt milk

If you fall over and break your leg, there is little point in saying 'If only I hadn't done that, I could have gone on that skiing holiday; I could have done so many other things [sigh].' Wishing things were different won't change history. You have to manage as well as you can with your broken leg.

It is the same for a firm. Once it has purchased some inputs, it is no good then wishing it hadn't. It has to accept that it has now got them, and make the best decisions about what to do with them.

Take a simple example. The local greengrocer decides in early December to buy 100 Christmas trees for £10 each. At the time of purchase, this represents an opportunity cost of £10 each, since the £10 could have been spent on something else. The greengrocer estimates that there is enough local demand to sell all 100 trees at £20 each, thereby making a reasonable profit.

But the estimate turns out to be wrong. On 23 December there are still 50 trees unsold. What should be done? At this stage the £10 that was paid for the trees is irrelevant. It is an historic cost. It cannot be recouped: the trees cannot be sold back to the wholesaler, nor can they be kept for next year.

In fact, the opportunity cost is now zero. It might even be negative if the greengrocer has to pay to dispose of any unsold trees. It might, therefore, be worth selling the trees at £10, £5 or even £1. Last thing on Christmas Eve it might even be worth giving away any unsold trees.

1. *Why is the correct price to charge (for the unsold trees) the one at which the price elasticity of demand equals −1? (Assume no disposal costs.)*
2. *Supermarkets have to pay for the rubbish they produce to be disposed of. Given this, what should they do with food that is approaching the sell-by date?*

KI 20
p156

BOX 6.6 **ARE FIXED COSTS ALWAYS THE SAME AS SUNK COSTS?** EXPLORING ECONOMICS

All sunk costs are fixed costs, but not all fixed costs are sunk costs

Within a given time period (i.e. the economic short run) some costs of production are completely insensitive to the quantity of output a firm produces. They remain the same whether the firm produces zero or a million units of output. These are called fixed costs. Other costs are responsive to the amount the firm produces. If it expands production, these costs will increase and if it reduces output they will fall. These are known as variable costs.

A variable cost can never be an example of a sunk cost as its size depends on the decision taken by a firm. A variable cost is always an opportunity cost. What about fixed costs? Is a fixed cost always a sunk cost? Could they be different in some circumstances?

Consider the following examples of costs that are likely to remain fixed for a number of different firms across a range of different sectors.

- Developing a new product – this could involve R&D.
- Advertising campaign to launch a new product.
- Physical capital:
  – machinery;
  – business premises.
- Human capital:
  – recruitment/training.
- Heating and lighting the business premises.
- Complying with government regulation.

If a firm temporarily shuts down then some of these costs cannot be avoided. For example, the costs of (a) developing a new product, (b) an advertising campaign and (c) complying

with government regulation can never be recovered. These categories of fixed cost are also examples of sunk costs. They remain the same no matter what the firm decides to do.

What about the cost of heating and lighting the business premises? Although these are fixed costs of production it is highly likely that they could be avoided if the firm temporarily shut down: i.e. with no staff in the building, the heating and lighting could simply be turned off. This is an example of a fixed cost that is *not* a sunk cost.

It may be possible for the firm to avoid some of the fixed costs associated with physical capital. If the firm temporarily shuts down, it might be able to rent the business premises and machinery to other firms. The higher the rental value of these assets, the greater the proportion of the fixed cost that is not a sunk cost.

The chances of a firm being able to rent out its physical capital to other businesses will depend on how much it has been tailored to its own particular use. Is the physical capital very specialised or is it more generic (such as a lorry) and so of value to a large number of other firms?

You need to think very carefully before deciding whether a fixed cost is also a sunk cost.

 A firm currently rents a piece of machinery for £500 per month. The rental contract stipulates that this fee must be paid for the next 12 months. If the firm temporarily shut down it could rent the machinery to another business for £300 per month. To what extent is this fixed cost also a sunk cost?

KI 20 p156

---

vary with output. Rent on land is a **fixed cost**. It is the same whether the firm produces a lot or a little.

The total cost of using variable factors, however, does vary with output. The cost of raw materials is a **variable cost**. The more that is produced, the more raw materials are used and therefore the higher is their total cost.

 The following are some costs incurred by a sports footwear manufacturer. Assume the manufacturer wants to increase output over a relatively short time period: i.e. in the economic short run. Decide whether each one of the following is a fixed or a variable cost of expanding production in the short run or has some element of both. Clearly explain any assumptions you have made.
(a) The cost of synthetic leather and mesh materials.
(b) The fee paid to an advertising agency.
(c) Wear and tear on machinery.
(d) Business rates on the factory.
(e) Electricity for heating and lighting.
(f) Electricity for running the machines.
(g) Basic minimum wages agreed with the union.
(h) Overtime pay.
(i) Depreciation of machines as a result purely of their age (irrespective of their condition).

Total cost

The **total cost** (*TC*) of production is the sum of the *total variable costs* (*TVC*) and the *total fixed costs* (*TFC*) of production:

$$TC = TVC + TFC$$

Consider Table 6.2 and Figure 6.2. They show the total costs for firm X of producing different levels of output (*Q*). Let us examine each of the three cost curves in turn.

Total fixed cost (TFC)

In our example, total fixed cost is assumed to be £12. Since this does not vary with output, it is shown by a horizontal straight line.

Definitions

Fixed costs Total costs that do not vary with the amount of output produced.

Variable costs Total costs that do vary with the amount of output produced.

Total cost The sum of total fixed costs and total variable costs: $TC = TFC + TVC$.

Table 6.2	Total costs for firm X		
Output (Q)	**TFC (£)**	**TVC (£)**	**TC (£)**
0	12	0	12
1	12	10	22
2	12	16	28
3	12	21	33
4	12	28	40
5	12	40	52
6	12	60	72
7	12	91	103
.	.	.	.

Total variable cost (TVC)

With a zero output, no variable factors will be used. Thus $TVC = 0$. The TVC curve, therefore, starts from the origin.

The shape of the TVC curve follows from the law of diminishing returns. Initially, *before* diminishing returns set in, TVC rises less and less rapidly as more variable factors are added. Take the case of a factory with a fixed supply of machinery: initially as more workers are taken on the workers can do increasingly specialist tasks and make a fuller use of the capital equipment. This corresponds to the portion of the TPP curve that rises more rapidly (up to point *b* in Figure 6.1 on p. 152).

As output is increased beyond point *m* in Figure 6.2, diminishing returns set in. Since extra workers (the extra variable factors) are producing less and less extra output, the extra units of output they do produce will cost more and more in terms of wage costs. Thus TVC rises more and more rapidly. The TVC curve gets steeper. This corresponds to the

portion of the TPP curve that rises less rapidly (between points *b* and *d* in Figure 6.1).

Total cost (TC)

Since $TC = TVC + TFC$, the TC curve is simply the TVC curve shifted vertically upwards by £12.

Average and marginal costs

Average cost (AC) is cost per unit of production:

$$AC = TC/Q$$

Thus if it cost a firm £2000 to produce 100 units of a product, the average cost would be £20 for each unit (£2000/100).

Like total cost, average cost can be divided into the two components, fixed and variable. In other words, average cost equals *average fixed cost* (AFC = TFC/Q) plus *average variable cost* (AVC = TVC/Q):

$$AC = AFC + AVC$$

Definitions

Average (total) cost Total cost (fixed plus variable) per unit of output: $AC = TC/Q = AFC + AVC$.

Average fixed cost Total fixed cost per unit of output: $AFC = TFC/Q$.

Average variable cost Total variable cost per unit of output: $AVC = TVC/Q$.

Figure 6.2 Total costs for firm X

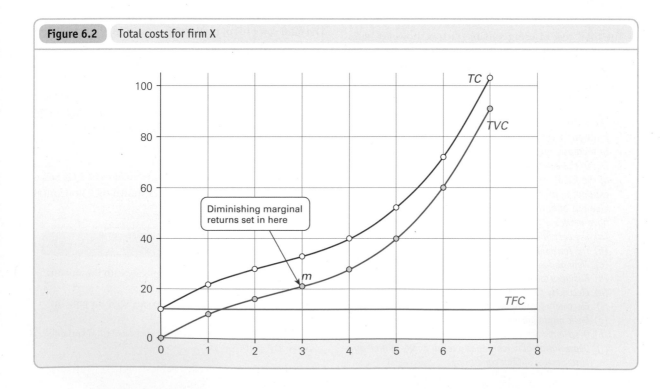

Marginal cost (MC) is the extra cost of producing one more unit: that is, the rise in total cost per one unit rise in output:

$$MC = \frac{\Delta TC}{\Delta Q}$$

For example, assume that a firm is currently producing 1 000 000 boxes of matches a month. It now increases output by 1000 boxes (another batch): $\Delta Q = 1000$. As a result, its total costs rise by £30: $\Delta TC = £30$. What is the cost of producing one more box of matches? It is

$$\frac{\Delta TC}{\Delta Q} = \frac{\#30}{1000} = 3p$$

(Note that all marginal costs are variable, since, by definition, there can be no extra fixed costs as output rises.)

Given the *TFC, TVC* and *TC* for each output, it is possible to derive the *AFC, AVC, AC* and *MC* for each output using the above definitions.

For example, using the data of Table 6.2, Table 6.3 can be constructed.

 Fill in the missing figures in Table 6.3. (Note that the figures for MC come in the spaces between each level of output.)

What will be the shapes of the *MC, AFC, AVC* and *AC* curves? These follow from the nature of the *MPP* and *APP* curves that we looked at in section 6.1 above. You may recall that the typical shapes of the *APP* and *MPP* curves are like those illustrated in Figure 6.3.

Marginal cost (MC)

The shape of the *MC* curve follows directly from the law of diminishing returns. Initially, in Figure 6.4, as more of the variable factor is used, extra units of output cost less than previous units. *MC* falls. This corresponds to the rising portion of the *MPP* curve in Figure 6.3 and the portion of the *TVC* curve in Figure 6.2 to the left of point *m*.

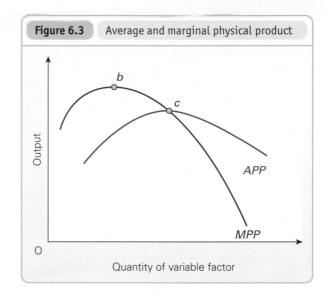

Figure 6.3   Average and marginal physical product

Beyond a certain level of output, diminishing returns set in. This is shown as point *x* in Figure 6.4 and corresponds to point *b* in Figure 6.3 (and point *m* in Figure 6.2). Thereafter *MC* rises as *MPP* falls. Additional units of output cost more and more to produce, since they require ever-increasing amounts of the variable factor.

Average fixed cost (AFC)

This falls continuously as output rises, since *total* fixed costs are being spread over a greater and greater output.

Definitions

Marginal cost The extra cost of producing one more unit of output: $MC = \Delta TC/\Delta Q$.

Table 6.3   Total, average and marginal costs for firm X

Output (Q) (units)	TFC (£)	AFC (TFC/Q) (£)	TVC (£)	AVC (TVC/Q) (£)	TC (TFC + TVC) (£)	AC (TC/Q) (£)	MC (ΔTC/ΔQ) (£)
0	12	–	0	–	12	–	
							10
1	12	12	10	10	22	22	
							...
2	12	6	16	...	28	14	
							5
3	...	...	21	7	...	...	
							7
4	...	3	28	...	40	...	
							12
5	...	2.4	...	8	52	10.4	
							...
6	...	...	...	10	...	12	
							31
7	...	1.7	91	13	103	14.7	

Figure 6.4   Average and marginal costs

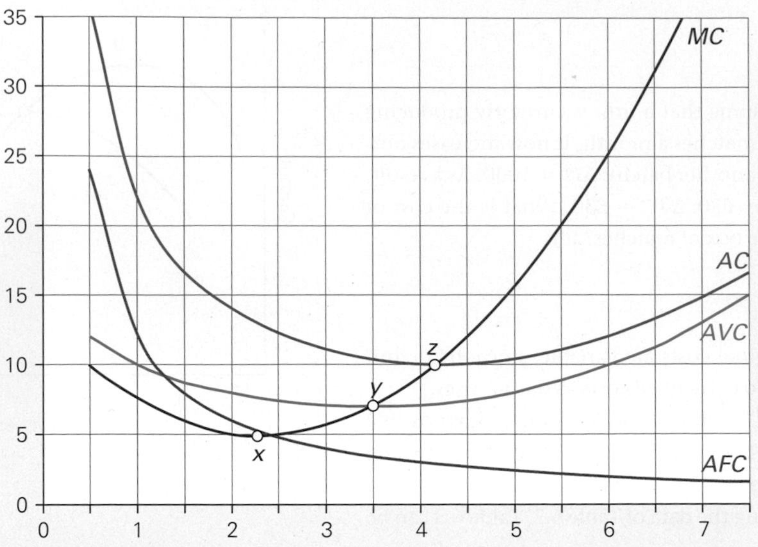

Average variable cost (AVC)

The shape of the *AVC* curve depends on the shape of the *APP* curve. As the average product of workers rises (up to point *c* in Figure 6.3), the average labour cost per unit of output (the *AVC*) falls: as far as point *y* in Figure 6.4. Thereafter, as *APP* falls, *AVC* must rise.

Average (total) cost (AC)

This is simply the vertical sum of the *AFC* and *AVC* curves. Note that as *AFC* gets less, the gap between *AVC* and *AC* narrows.

The relationship between average cost and marginal cost

This is simply another illustration of the relationship that applies between *all* averages and marginals (see Box 6.3).

As long as new units of output cost less than the average, their production must pull the average cost down. That is, if *MC* is less than *AC*, *AC* must be falling. Likewise, if new units cost more than the average, their production must drive the average up. That is, if *MC* is greater than *AC*, *AC* must be rising. Therefore, the *MC* crosses the *AC* at its minimum point (point *z* in Figure 6.4).

Since all marginal costs are variable, the same relationship holds between *MC* and *AVC*.

> **?** *Why is the minimum point of the AVC curve at a lower level of output than the minimum point of the AC curve?*

---

*LOOKING AT THE MATHS

The total, average and marginal cost functions can be expressed algebraically as follows:

$$TFC = a \tag{1}$$

$$TVC = bQ - cQ^2 + dQ^3 \tag{2}$$

$$TC = a + bQ - cQ^2 + dQ^3 \tag{3}$$

where *a* is the constant term representing fixed costs, and the signs of the terms in the *TVC* equation have been chosen to give *TVC* and *TC* curves shaped like those in Figure 6.2. Dividing each of the above by *Q* gives:

$$AFC = \frac{a}{Q} \tag{4}$$

$$AVC = b - cQ + dQ^2 \tag{5}$$

$$AC = \frac{a}{Q} + b - cQ + dQ^2 \tag{6}$$

Differentiating equation (3) or (2) gives:

$$MC = b - 2cQ + 3dQ^2 \tag{7}$$

A worked example of each of these is given in Maths Case 6.1 on the student website.

| BOX 6.7 | COST CURVES IN PRACTICE | | EXPLORING ECONOMICS |

When fixed factors are divisible

Are cost curves always the shape depicted in this chapter? The answer is no. Sometimes, rather than being U-shaped, the *AVC* and *MC* curves are flat-bottomed, like the curves in the diagram below. Indeed, they may be constant (and equal to each other) over a substantial range of output.

The reason for this is that fixed factors may sometimes not have to be in full use all the time. Take the case of a firm with 100 identical machines, each one requiring one person to operate it. Although the firm cannot use more than the 100 machines, it could use fewer: in other words, some of the

machines could be left idle. Assume, for example, that instead of using 100 machines, the firm uses only 90. It would need only 90 operatives and 90 per cent of the raw materials.

Similarly, if it used only 20 machines, its total variable costs (labour and raw materials) would be only 20 per cent. What we are saying here is that average variable cost remains constant – and over a very large range of output, using anything from 1 machine to 100 machines.

The reason for the constant *AVC* (and *MC*) is that by varying the amount of fixed capital used, the proportions used of capital, labour and raw materials can be kept the same and hence the average and marginal productivity of labour and raw materials will remain constant.

Only when all machines are in use (at Q_1) will *AVC* start to rise if output is further expanded. Machines may then have to work beyond their optimal speed, using more raw materials per unit of output (diminishing returns to raw materials), or workers may have to work longer shifts with higher (overtime) pay.

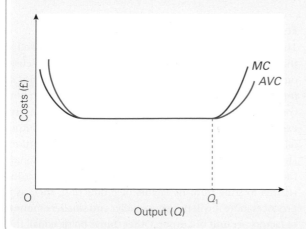

1. Assume that a firm has five identical machines, each operating independently. Assume that with all five machines operating normally, 100 units of output are produced each day. Below what level of output will AVC and MC rise?
2. Manufacturing firms like the one we have been describing will have other fixed costs (such as rent and managerial overheads). Does the existence of these affect the argument that the AVC curve will be flat bottomed?

Section summary

1. When measuring costs of production, we should be careful to use the concept of opportunity cost. In the case of factors not owned by the firm, the opportunity cost is simply the explicit cost of purchasing or hiring them. It is the price paid for them. In the case of factors already owned by the firm, it is the implicit cost of what the factor could have earned for the firm in its next best alternative use.

2. In the short run, some factors are fixed in supply. Their total costs are thus fixed with respect to output. In the case of variable factors, their total cost will increase as more output is produced and hence as more of the variable factor is used.

3. Total cost can be divided into total fixed and total variable costs. Total variable cost will tend to increase less rapidly

at first as more is produced, but then, when diminishing returns set in, it will increase more and more rapidly.

4. Marginal cost is the cost of producing one more unit of output. It will probably fall at first (corresponding to the part of the TVC curve where the slope is getting shallower), but will start to rise as soon as diminishing returns set in.

5. Average cost, like total cost, can be divided into fixed and variable costs. Average fixed cost will decline as more output is produced since total fixed cost is being spread over a greater and greater number of units of output. Average variable cost will tend to decline at first, but once the marginal cost has risen above it, it must then rise.

6.3 THE LONG-RUN THEORY OF PRODUCTION

In the long run, *all* factors of production are variable. There is time for the firm to build a new factory, to install new machines, to use different production techniques and to combine its inputs in whatever proportion and in whatever quantities it chooses.

In the long run, then, there are several decisions that a firm has to make: decisions about the scale and location of its operations and what techniques of production it should use. These decisions affect the costs of production. It is important, therefore, to get them right.

KI 18
p149

| Table 6.4 | Illustrating figures derived from a production function |

		Number of machines				
		1	2	3	4	5
Number of workers	1	4	7	13	13	12
	2	11	16	19	20	21
	3	16	21	24	25	26
	4	19	24	27	29	30
	5	21	25	28	30	32

The distinction between long-run and short-run production is illustrated in Table 6.4. The numbers in the table show the maximum output (the technically efficient output) that can be produced by employing different combinations of capital and labour. The impact of increasing the quantity of labour can be seen by working down each column. For example, if one worker is employed with one machine the maximum output that can be produced is 4. If a second worker is employed with one machine the total output is 11 and so on. The impact of increasing the amount of capital – i.e. the number of machines – can be seen by working across each row.

The scale of production

If a firm were to double all of its inputs – something it could do in the long run – would it double its output? Or will output more than double or less than double? We can distinguish three possible situations:

Increasing returns to scale. This is where a given percentage increase in inputs leads to a *larger* percentage increase in output. For example, look what happens in Table 6.4 if the both the number of workers and machines used in production are both doubled from 1 to 2. Total output increases from 4 to 16 (look diagonally downwards). In this case a 100 per cent increase in the inputs used in production leads to a 400 per cent increase in output. Production exhibits increasing returns to scale.

Constant returns to scale. This is where a given percentage increase in inputs leads to the *same* percentage increase in output. This is illustrated in Table 6.4 when the number of workers and machines are both increased from 2 to 3. This 50 per cent increase in inputs leads to a 50 per cent increase in output: i.e. total output increases from 16 to 24.

Decreasing returns to scale. This is where a given percentage increase in inputs leads to a *smaller* percentage increase in output. If, in the table, both the number of workers and machines are increased from 3 to 4 (a 33.3 per cent increase) then output increases from 24 to only 29 (a 20.8 per cent increase).

Notice the terminology here. The words 'to scale' mean that *all* inputs increase by the same proportion. Increasing and decreasing returns *to scale* are therefore quite different from increasing and diminishing returns to a variable factor (where only the *variable* factor increases). Returns to a variable factor is a characteristic of *short-run* production and can be illustrated in Table 6.4 by working down each of the columns – assuming labour is the variable factor and capital is the fixed factor.

 Table 6.4 illustrates five different short-run productions functions: i.e. where the number of machines remains constant at one, two, three, four or five. In each case explain if there are diminishing or increasing marginal returns?

Economies of scale

The concept of increasing returns to scale is closely linked to that of **economies of scale**. Whereas returns to scale focuses on how output changes in proportion to the quantity of inputs used in production, economies of scale looks at how costs change in proportion to the output produced. A firm experiences economies of scale if costs per unit of output fall as the scale of production increases: i.e. the proportionate increase in total costs is lower than the proportionate increase in output. Clearly, if a firm is getting increasing returns to scale from its factors of production, then as it produces more it will be using smaller and smaller amounts of factors per unit of output. Other things being equal, this means that it will be producing at a lower unit cost.

There are several reasons why firms are likely to experience economies of scale. Some are due to increasing returns to scale; some are not.

Specialisation and division of labour. In large-scale plants workers can often do simple, repetitive jobs. With this **specialisation and division of labour** less training is needed; workers can become highly efficient in their particular job, especially with long production runs; there is less time lost in workers switching from one operation to another; and supervision is easier. Workers and managers can be employed who have specific skills in specific areas.

Indivisibilities. Some inputs are of a minimum size: they are indivisible. The most obvious example is machinery. Take the case of a combine harvester. A small-scale farmer could

---

Definitions

Economies of scale When increasing the scale of production leads to a lower cost per unit of output.

Specialisation and division of labour Where production is broken down into a number of simpler, more specialised tasks, thus allowing workers to acquire a high degree of efficiency.

not make full use of one. They only become economical to use, therefore, on farms above a certain size. The problem of **indivisibilities** is made worse when different machines, each of which is part of the production process, are of a different size. For example, if there are two types of machine, one producing 6 units a day, and the other packaging 4 units a day, a minimum of 12 units would have to be produced, involving two production machines and three packaging machines, if all machines are to be fully utilised.

The 'container principle'. Any capital equipment that contains things (blast furnaces, oil tankers, pipes, vats, etc.) tends to cost less per unit of output the larger its size. The reason has to do with the relationship between a container's volume and its *surface area.* A container's cost depends largely on the materials used to build it and hence roughly on its surface area. Its output depends largely on its *volume.* Large containers have a bigger volume relative to surface area than do small containers.

For example, a container with a bottom, top and four sides, with each side measuring 1 metre, has a volume of 1 cubic metre and a surface area of 6 square metres (six surfaces of 1 square metre each). If each side were now to be doubled in length to 2 metres, the volume would be 8 cubic metres and the surface area 24 square metres (six surfaces of 4 square metres each). Thus an eightfold increase in capacity has been gained at only a fourfold increase in the container's surface area, and hence an approximate fourfold increase in cost.

Greater efficiency of large machines. Large machines may be more efficient in the sense that more output can be gained for a given amount of inputs. For example, only one worker may be required to operate a machine whether it be large or small. Also, a large machine may make more efficient use of raw materials.

By-products. With production on a large scale, there may be sufficient waste products to enable some by-product or by-products to be made.

Multi-stage production. A large factory may be able to take a product through several stages in its manufacture. This saves time and cost in moving the semi-finished product from one firm or factory to another. For example, a large cardboard-manufacturing firm may be able to convert trees or waste paper into cardboard and then into cardboard boxes in a continuous sequence.

All the above are examples of *plant economies of scale.* They are due to an individual factory or workplace or machine being large. There are other economies of scale, however, that are associated with the *firm* being large – perhaps with many factories.

Organisational economies. With a large firm, individual plants can specialise in particular functions. There can also be centralised administration of the firm; for example, one human resources department could administer all the wages. Often, after a merger between two firms, savings can be made by *rationalising* their activities in this way.

Spreading overheads. Some expenditures are economic only when the *firm* is large: for example, research and development – only a large firm can afford to set up a research laboratory. This is another example of indivisibilities, only this time at the level of the firm rather than the plant. The greater the firm's output, the more these *overhead* costs are spread.

Financial economies. Large firms are often able to obtain finance at lower interest rates than small firms, since they are seen by banks to be lower risk. They may be able to obtain certain inputs cheaper by buying in bulk.

Economies of scope. Often a firm is large because it produces a range of products. This can result in each individual product being produced more cheaply than if it was produced in a single-product firm. The reason for these *economies of scope* is that various overhead costs and financial and organisational economies can be shared among the products. For example, a firm that produces a whole range of DVD players, televisions and hard disk recorders can benefit from shared marketing and distribution costs and the bulk purchase of electronic components.

1. *Which of the economies of scale we have considered are due to increasing returns to scale and which are due to other factors?*
2. *What economies of scale is a large department store likely to experience?*

Diseconomies of scale

When firms get beyond a certain size, costs per unit of output may start to increase. There are several reasons for such **diseconomies of scale**:

- Management problems of co-ordination may increase as the firm becomes larger and more complex, and as lines of communication get longer. There may be a lack of personal involvement by management.

Definitions

Indivisibility The impossibility of dividing a factor into smaller units.

Plant economies of scale Economies of scale that arise because of the large size of a factory.

Rationalisation The reorganising of production (often after a merger) so as to cut out waste and duplication and generally to reduce costs.

Overheads Costs arising from the general running of an organisation, and only indirectly related to the level of output.

Economies of scope When increasing the range of products produced by a firm reduces the cost of producing each one.

Diseconomies of scale Where costs per unit of output increase as the scale of production increases.

- Workers may feel 'alienated' if their jobs are boring and repetitive, and if they feel that they are an insignificantly small part of a large organisation. Small to medium-sized companies often report that workers feel they 'make a difference'; this may be lost in a large firm and as a consequence lower motivation may lead to shoddy work.
- Industrial relations may deteriorate as a result of these factors and also as a result of the more complex interrelationships between different categories of worker. More levels of 'people management' may therefore be required.
- Production-line processes and the complex interdependencies of mass production can lead to great disruption if there are hold-ups in any one part of the firm.

Whether firms experience economies or diseconomies of scale will depend on the conditions applying in each individual firm.

 Why are firms likely to experience economies of scale up to a certain size and then diseconomies of scale after some point beyond that?

Location

In the long run, a firm can move to a different location. The location will affect the cost of production since locations differ in terms of the availability and cost of raw materials, suitable land and power supply, the qualifications, skills and experience of the labour force, wage rates, transport and communications networks, the cost of local services, and banking and financial facilities. In short, locations differ in terms of the availability, suitability and cost of the factors of production.

Transport costs will be an important influence on a firm's location. Ideally, a firm will wish to be as near as possible to both its raw materials and the market for its finished product. When market and raw materials are in different locations, the firm will minimise its transport costs by locating somewhere between the two.

In general, if the raw materials are more expensive to transport than the finished product, the firm should be located as near as possible to the raw materials. Thus heavy industry, which uses large quantities of coal and various ores, tends to be concentrated near the coal fields or near the ports. If, on the other hand, the finished product is more expensive to transport (e.g. bread and beer), the firm will probably be located as near as possible to its market.

When raw materials or markets are in many different locations, transport costs will be minimised at the 'centre of gravity'. This location will be nearer to those raw materials and markets whose transport costs are greater per mile.

 How has the opening up of trade and investment between eastern and western Europe likely to have affected the location of industries within Europe that have (a) substantial economies of scale; (b) little or no economies of scale?

The size of the whole industry

As an *industry* grows in size, this can lead to **external economies of scale** for its member firms. This is where a firm, whatever its own individual size, benefits from the *whole industry* being large. For example, the firm may benefit from having access to specialist raw material or component suppliers, labour with specific skills, firms that specialise in marketing the finished product, and banks and other financial institutions with experience of the industry's requirements. What we are referring to here is the **industry's infrastructure**: the facilities, support services, skills and experience that can be shared by its members.

1. *Name some industries where external economies of scale are gained. What are the specific external economies in each case?*
2. *Would you expect external economies to be associated with the concentration of an industry in a particular region?*

The member firms of a particular industry might experience **external diseconomies of scale**. For example, as an industry grows larger, this may create a growing shortage of specific raw materials or skilled labour. This will push up their prices, and hence the firms' costs.

The optimum combination of factors: the marginal product approach

In the long run, all factors can be varied. The firm can thus choose what techniques of production to use: what design of factory to build, what types of machine to buy, how to organise the factory, whether to use highly automated processes or more labour-intensive techniques. It must be very careful in making these decisions. After all, once it has built a factory and installed machinery, these then become fixed factors of production, and the subsequent 'short-run' time period may in practice last a very long time. **KI 18 p149**

For any given scale, how should the firm decide what technique to use? How should it decide the optimum 'mix' of factors of production?

> ### Definitions
>
> **External economies of scale** Where a firm's costs per unit of output decrease as the size of the whole industry grows.
>
> **Industry's infrastructure** The network of supply agents, communications, skills, training facilities, distribution channels, specialised financial services, etc. that supports a particular industry.
>
> **External diseconomies of scale** Where a firm's costs per unit of output increase as the size of the whole industry increases.

The profit-maximising firm will obviously want to use the least costly combination of factors to produce any given output. It will therefore substitute factors, if by so doing it can reduce the cost of a given output. What then is the optimum combination of factors?

The simple two-factor case

Take first the simplest case where a firm uses just two factors: labour (L) and capital (K). The least-cost combination of the two will be where

$$\frac{MPP_L}{P_L} = \frac{MPP_K}{P_K}$$

in other words, where the extra product (MPP) from the last pound spent on each factor is equal. But why should this be so? The easiest way to answer this is to consider what would happen if they were not equal.

If they were not equal, it would be possible to reduce cost per unit of output by using a different combination of labour and capital. For example, if

$$\frac{MPP_L}{P_L} > \frac{MPP_K}{P_K}$$

more labour should be used relative to capital, since the firm is getting a greater physical return for its money from extra workers than from extra capital. As more labour is used per unit of capital, however, diminishing returns to labour set in. Thus MPP_L will fall. Likewise, as less capital is used per unit of labour, MPP_K will rise. This will continue until

$$\frac{MPP_L}{P_L} = \frac{MPP_K}{P_K}$$

At this point, the firm will stop substituting labour for capital.

Since no further gain can be made by substituting one factor for another, this combination of factors or 'choice of technique' can be said to be the most efficient. It is the least-cost way of combining factors for any given output. Efficiency in this sense of using the optimum factor proportions is known as **productive efficiency.**

The multi-factor case

Where a firm uses many different factors, the least-cost combination of factors will be where

$$\frac{MPP_a}{P_a} = \frac{MPP_b}{P_b} = \frac{MPP_c}{P_c} \cdots = \frac{MPP_n}{P_n}$$

where a . . . n are different factors. This is a variant of the equi-marginal principle that we examined on page 111.

The reasons are the same as in the two-factor case. If any inequality exists between the MPP/P ratios, a firm will be able to reduce its costs by using more of those factors with a high MPP/P ratio and less of those with a low MPP/P ratio until they all become equal.

A major problem for a firm in choosing the least-cost technique is in predicting future factor price changes.

If the price of a factor were to change, the MPP/P ratios would cease to be equal. The firm, to minimise costs, would then like to alter its factor combinations until the MPP/P ratios once more became equal. The trouble is that, once it has committed itself to a particular technique, it may be several years before it can switch to an alternative one. Thus if a firm invests in labour-intensive methods of production and is then faced with an unexpected wage rise, it may regret not having chosen a more capital-intensive technique. While there is no simple solution to this issue, there are a number of companies that have made a business of predicting trends across different sectors to assist firms in their decision making.

If factor X costs twice as much as factor Y ($P_X/P_Y = 2$), what can be said about the relationship between the MPPs of the two factors if the optimum combination of factors is used?

*LOOKING AT THE MATHS

We can express the long-run production function algebraically. In the simple two-factor model, where capital (K) and labour (L) are the two factors, the production function is

$$TPP = f(K, L)$$

A simple and widely used production function is the **Cobb–Douglas production function.** This takes the form

$$TPP = AK^\alpha L^\beta$$

Box 6.8 demonstrates that where $\alpha + \beta = 1$ there are constant returns to scale; where $\alpha + \beta > 1$, there are increasing returns to scale; and where $\alpha + \beta < 1$, there are decreasing returns to scale.

A multiple-factor Cobb–Douglas production function would take the form

$$TPP = AF_1{}^\alpha F_2{}^\beta F_3{}^\gamma \cdots F_n{}^\omega$$

where $F_1, F_2, F_3 \ldots F_n$ are all the factors. For example, if there were six factors, n would be factor 6. Again, it can be shown that where $\alpha + \beta + \gamma + \ldots + \omega = 1$ there are constant returns to scale; where $\alpha + \beta + \gamma + \ldots + \omega > 1$, there are increasing returns to scale; and where $\alpha + \beta + \gamma + \ldots + \omega < 1$, there are decreasing returns to scale.

Definitions

Productive efficiency The least-cost combination of factors for a given output.

Cobb–Douglas production function Like other production functions, this shows how output (TPP) varies with inputs of various factors (F_1, F_2, F_3, etc.). In the simple two-factor case it takes the following form:

$$TPP = f(F_1, F_2) = AF_1{}^\alpha F_2{}^\beta$$

If $\alpha + \beta = 1$, there are constant returns to scale; if $\alpha + \beta > 1$, there are increasing returns to scale; if $\alpha + \beta < 1$, there are decreasing returns to scale.

---

*BOX 6.8   THE COBB–DOUGLAS PRODUCTION FUNCTION   EXPLORING ECONOMICS

Exploring its properties

Let us take the simple Cobb–Douglas production function (see Looking at the Maths box on page 165):

$$TPP = AK^\alpha L^\beta \tag{1}$$

Returns to scale and the Cobb–Douglas production function

What would happen if you were to double the amount of both K and L used (in other words, the scale of production doubles)? If output doubles, there are constant returns to scale. If output more than doubles, there are increasing returns to scale; if it less than doubles, there are decreasing returns to scale. Let us see what happens when we double the amount of K and L in equation (1).

$$\begin{aligned} TPP &= A(2K^\alpha)(2L^\beta) \\ &= A2^\alpha K^\alpha 2^\beta L^\beta \\ &= A2^{\alpha+\beta} K^\alpha L^\beta \end{aligned}$$

If $\alpha + \beta = 1$, then $2^{\alpha+\beta} = 2$. Thus

$$TPP = 2AK^\alpha L^\beta$$

In other words, doubling the amount of K and L used has doubled output: there are constant returns to scale.

If $\alpha + \beta > 1$, then $2^{\alpha+\beta} > 2$. In this case, doubling inputs will more than double output: there are increasing returns to scale. Similarly, if $\alpha + \beta < 1$, then $2^{\alpha+\beta} < 2$ and there are decreasing returns to scale.

Finding the marginal physical products of labour and capital

The marginal physical product (MPP) of a factor is the additional output obtained by employing one more unit of that factor, while holding other factors constant. The MPP of either factor in the above Cobb–Douglas production function can be found by differentiating the function with respect to that factor (see pages A:12–13 for the rules of partial differentiation). Thus

$$MPP_K = \frac{\partial(TPP)}{\partial K} = \alpha AK^{\alpha-1} L^\beta \tag{2}$$

and

$$MPP_L = \frac{\partial(TPP)}{\partial L} = \beta AK^\alpha L^{\beta-1} \tag{3}$$

For example, if the production function were

$$TPP = 4K^{3/4} L^{1/2} \tag{4}$$

and if $K = 81$ and $L = 36$, then, from equations (2) and (4),

$$\begin{aligned} MPP_K &= \alpha AK^{\alpha-1} L^\beta \\ &= \frac{3}{4} \times 4(81^{-1/4})(36^{1/2}) \\ &= 3 \times \frac{1}{3} \times 6 = 6 \end{aligned}$$

and $MPP_L = \beta AK^\alpha L^{\beta-1}$

$$\begin{aligned} &= \frac{1}{2} \times 4(81^{3/4})(36^{-1/2}) \\ &= 2 \times 27 \times \frac{1}{6} = 9 \end{aligned}$$

In other words, an additional unit of capital will produce an extra 6 units of output and an additional unit of labour will produce an extra 9 units of output.

Assume that the production function is given by

$$TPP = 36K^{1/3} L^{1/2} R^{1/4}$$

where R is the quantity of a particular raw material used.

(a) Are there constant, increasing or decreasing returns to scale?
(b) What is the marginal productivity of the raw material if $K = 8$, $L = 16$ and $R = 81$?

---

*The optimum combination of factors: the isoquant/isocost approach

This section is optional. You can skip straight to page 170 without loss of continuity.

A firm's choice of optimum technique can be shown graphically. This graphical analysis takes the simplest case of just two variable factors – for example, labour and capital. The amount of labour used is measured on one axis and the amount of capital used is measured on the other.

The graph involves the construction of *isoquants* and *isocosts*.

Isoquants

Imagine that a firm wants to produce a certain level of output: say, 5000 units per year. Let us assume that it estimates all the possible combinations of labour and capital that could produce that level of output. Once again this is assuming technical efficiency in production. Some of these estimates are shown in Table 6.5.

Technique *a* is a capital-intensive technique, using 40 units of capital and only 5 workers. As we move towards technique *e*, labour is substituted for capital. The techniques become more labour intensive.

These alternative techniques for producing a given level of output can be plotted on a graph. The points are joined to form an *isoquant*. Figure 6.5 shows the 5000 unit isoquant corresponding to Table 6.5.

Definitions

Isoquant A line showing all the alternative combinations of two factors that can produce a given level of output.

Table 6.5	Various capital and labour combinations to produce 5000 units of output per year				
	a	b	c	d	e
Units of capital (K)	40	20	10	6	4
Number of workers (L)	5	12	20	30	50

The isoquant shows the whole *range* of alternative ways of producing a given output. Thus Figure 6.5 shows not only points *a* to *e* from the table, but all the intermediate points too.

Like an indifference curve, an isoquant is rather like a contour on a map. As with contours and indifference curves, a whole series of isoquants can be drawn, each one representing a different level of output (*TPP*). The higher the output, the further out to the right will the isoquant be. Thus in Figure 6.6, isoquant I_5 represents a higher level of output than I_4, and I_4 a higher output than I_3, and so on.

1. *Could isoquants ever cross?*
2. *Could they ever slope upwards to the right? Explain your answers.*

The shape of the isoquant. Why is the isoquant 'bowed in' towards the origin? This illustrates a diminishing **marginal rate of factor substitution** (*MRS*). This, as we shall see very soon, is due to the law of diminishing returns.

The MRS[1] is the amount of one factor (e.g. K) that can be replaced by a 1 unit increase in the other factor (e.g. L), if output is to be held constant. So if 2 units of capital

---

1 Note that we use the same letters *MRS* to refer to the marginal rate of factor substitution as we did in the previous chapter to refer to the marginal rate of substitution in consumption. Sometimes we use the same words too – just 'marginal rate of substitution' rather than the longer title. In this case we must rely on the context in order to tell which is being referred to.

($\Delta K = 2$) could be replaced by 1 unit of labour ($\Delta L = 1$) the *MRS* would be 2. Thus:

$$MRS = \frac{\Delta K}{\Delta L} = \frac{2}{1} = 2$$

The *MRS* between two points on the isoquant will equal the slope of the line joining those two points. Thus in Figure 6.7, the *MRS* between points *g* and *h* is 2 ($\Delta K/\Delta L = 2/1$). But this is merely the slope of the line joining points *g* and *h* (ignoring the negative sign).

When the isoquant is bowed in towards the origin, the slope of the isoquant will diminish as one moves down the curve, and so too, therefore, will the *MRS* diminish. Referring again to Figure 6.7, between points *g* and *h* the *MRS* = 2. Lower down the curve between points *j* and *k*, it has fallen to 1.

Calculate the MRS moving up the curve in Figure 6.5 between each pair of points: e–d, d–c, c–b and b–a. Does the MRS diminish moving in this direction?

The relationship between MRS and MPP. As one moves down the isoquant, total output, by definition, will remain the same. Thus the loss in output due to less capital being used (i.e. $MPP_K \times \Delta K$) must be exactly offset by the gain in output due to more labour being used (i.e. $MPP_L \times \Delta L$). Thus:

$$MPP_L \times \Delta L = MPP_K \times \Delta K$$

Definitions

Marginal rate of factor substitution The rate at which one factor can be substituted by another while holding the level of output constant:

$$MRS = \Delta F_1/\Delta F_2 = MPP_{F_2}/MPP_{F_1}$$

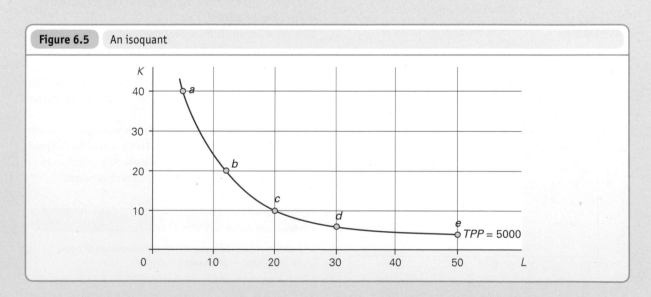

Figure 6.5 An isoquant

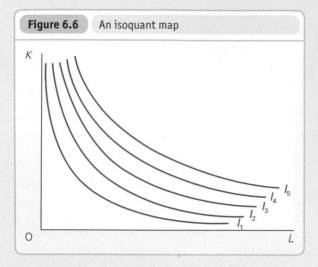

Figure 6.6   An isoquant map

Table 6.6   Combinations of capital and labour costing the firm £300 000 per year

Units of capital (at £20 000 per unit)	0	5	10	15
No. of workers (at a wage of £10 000)	30	20	10	0

Assume that factor prices are fixed. A table can be constructed showing the various combinations of factors that a firm can use for a particular sum of money.

For example, assuming that P_K is £20 000 per unit per year and P_L is £10 000 per worker per year, Table 6.6 shows various combinations of capital and labour that would cost the firm £300 000 per year.

These figures are plotted in Figure 6.8. The line joining the points is called an **isocost**. It shows all the combinations of labour and capital that cost £300 000.

As with isoquants, a series of isocosts can be drawn. Each one represents a particular cost to the firm. The higher the cost, the further out to the right will be the isocost.

This equation can be rearranged as follows:

$$\frac{MPP_L}{MPP_K} = \frac{\Delta K}{\Delta L}(=MRS)$$

Thus the *MRS* is equal to the inverse of the marginal productivity ratios of the two factors.

Diminishing MRS and the law of diminishing returns.   The principle of diminishing *MRS* is related to the law of diminishing returns. As one moves down the isoquant, increasing amounts of labour are being used relative to capital. This, given diminishing returns, would lead the *MPP* of labour to fall relative to the *MPP* of capital. But since *MRS* = MPP_L/MPP_K, if MPP_L/MPP_K diminishes, then, by definition, so must *MRS*.

The less substitutable factors are for each other, the faster *MRS* will diminish, and therefore the more bowed in will be the isoquant.

Isocosts

We have seen how factors combine to produce different levels of output, but how do we choose the level of output? This will involve taking costs into account.

1. *What will happen to an isocost if the prices of both factors rise by the same percentage?*
2. *What will happen to the isocost in Figure 6.8 if the wage rate rises to £15 000?*

The slope of the isocost equals

$$\frac{P_L}{P_K}$$

This can be shown in the above example. The slope of the isocost in Figure 6.8 is 15/30 = ½. But this is P_L/P_K (i.e. £10 000/£20 000).

Isoquants and isocosts can now be put on the same diagram. The diagram can be used to answer either of two questions: (a) What is the least-cost way of producing a particular level of output? (b) What is the highest output that can be achieved for a given cost of production?

These two questions are examined in turn.

The least-cost combination of factors to produce a given level of output

First the isoquant is drawn for the level of output in question: for example, the 5000 unit isoquant in Figure 6.5. This is reproduced in Figure 6.9.

Then a series of isocosts are drawn representing different levels of total cost. The higher the level of total cost, the further out will be the isocosts.

The least-cost combination of labour and capital is shown at point *r*, where *TC* = £400 000. This is where the isoquant just touches the lowest possible isocost. Any other point on the isoquant (e.g. *s* or *t*) would be on a higher isocost.

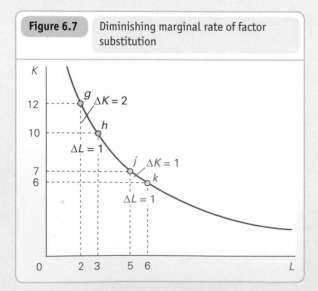

Figure 6.7   Diminishing marginal rate of factor substitution

Definitions

Isocost A line showing all the combinations of two factors that cost the same to employ.

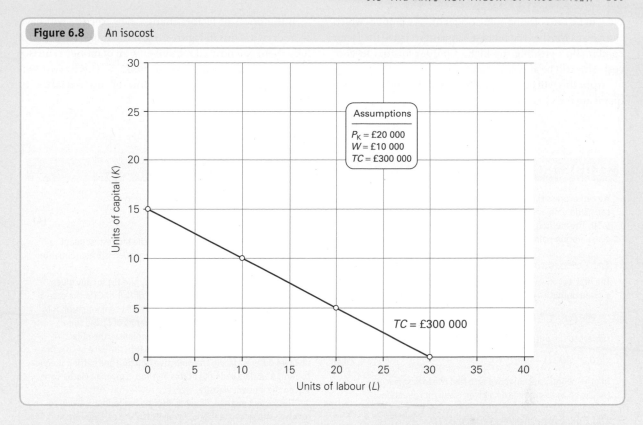

Figure 6.8   An isocost

Assumptions

$P_K = £20\ 000$
$W = £10\ 000$
$TC = £300\ 000$

$TC = £300\ 000$

Comparison with the marginal productivity approach. We showed earlier that the least-cost combination of labour and capital was where

$$\frac{MPP_L}{P_L} = \frac{MPP_K}{P_K}$$

In this section it has just been shown that the least-cost combination is where the isoquant is tangential to an isocost (i.e. point *r* in Figure 6.9). Thus their slope is the same. The slope of the isoquant equals *MRS*, which equals MPP_L/MPP_K; and the slope of the isocost equals P_L/P_K.

$$\therefore \frac{MPP_L}{MPP_K} = \frac{P_L}{P_K}$$

$$\therefore \frac{MPP_L}{P_K} = \frac{MPP_K}{P_K}$$

Thus, as one would expect, the two approaches yield the same result.

Highest output for a given cost of production

An isocost can be drawn for the particular level of total cost outlay in question. Then a series of isoquants can be drawn, representing different levels of output (*TPP*). This is shown in Figure 6.10. The higher the level of output, the further

Figure 6.9   The least-cost method of production

$TC = £200\ 000$
$TC = £300\ 000$
$TC = £400\ 000$
$TC = £500\ 000$
$TPP = 5000$ units

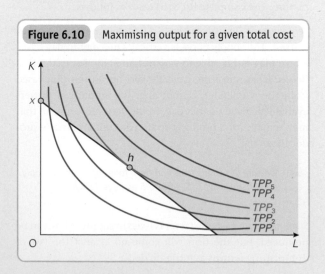

Figure 6.10   Maximising output for a given total cost

TPP_5
TPP_4
TPP_3
TPP_2
TPP_1

out will lie the corresponding isoquant. The point at which the isocost touches the highest isoquant will give the factor combination yielding the highest output for that level of cost. This will be at point *h* in Figure 6.10.

Again this will be where the slopes of the isocost and isoquant are the same: where $P_L/P_K = MRS$.

If the prices of factors change, new isocosts will have to be drawn. Thus in Figure 6.10, if the wage rate goes up, less labour can be used for a given sum of money. The isocost will swing inwards round point *x*. The isocost will get steeper. Less labour will now be used relative to capital.

---

*LOOKING AT THE MATHS

We can express the optimum production point algebraically. This can be done in either of two ways, corresponding to Figures 6.9 or 6.10. The method is similar to that used for finding the optimum consumption point that we examined on page 118.

(a) Corresponding to Figure 6.9

The first way involves finding the least-cost method of producing a given output (*Q*). This can be expressed as

$$\text{Min } P_K K + P_L L \tag{1}$$

subject to the output constraint that

$$Q = Q(K, L) \tag{2}$$

In other words, the objective is to find the lowest isocost (equation 1) to produce on a given isoquant (equation 2).

(b) Corresponding to Figure 6.10

The second involves finding the highest output that can be produced for a given cost. This can be expressed as

$$\text{Max } Q(K, L) \tag{3}$$

subject to the cost constraint that

$$P_K K + P_L L = C \tag{4}$$

In other words, the objective is to find the highest isoquant (equation 3) that can be reached along a given isocost (equation 4).

There are two methods of solving (a) and (b) for any given value of P_K, P_L and either *Q* (in the case of (a)) or *C* (in the case of (b)). The first involves substituting the constraint equation into the objective function (to express *K* in terms of *L*) and then finding the value of *L* and then *K* that minimises the objective function in the case of (a) or maximises it in the case of (b). This involves differentiating the objective function and setting it equal to zero. A worked example of this method is given in Maths Case 6.2 on the student website.

The second method, which is slightly longer but is likely to involve simpler calculations, involves the use of 'Lagrangian multipliers'. This method is explained, along with a worked example, in Maths Case 6.3. It is the same method as we used in Maths Case 4.2 when finding the optimal level of consumption of two products.

Postscript: decision making in different time periods

We have distinguished between the short run and the long run. Let us introduce two more time periods to complete the picture. The complete list then reads as follows.

Very short run (immediate run).   All factors are fixed. Output is fixed. The supply curve is vertical. On a day-to-day basis, a firm may not be able to vary output at all. For example, a flower seller, once the day's flowers have been purchased from the wholesaler, cannot alter the amount of flowers available for sale on that day. In the very short run, all that may remain for a producer to do is to sell an already produced good.

 Why are Christmas trees and fresh foods often sold cheaply on Christmas Eve? (See Box 6.5 on page 156.)

Short run.   At least one factor is fixed in supply. More can be produced, but the firm will come up against the law of diminishing returns as it tries to do so.

Long run.   All factors are variable. The firm may experience constant, increasing or decreasing returns to scale. But although all factors can be increased or decreased, they are of a fixed *quality*.

Very long run.   All factors are variable, *and* their quality and hence productivity can change. Labour productivity can increase as a result of education, training, experience and social factors. The productivity of capital can increase as a result of new inventions (new discoveries) and innovation (putting inventions into practice).

Improvements in factor quality will increase the output they produce: *TPP, APP* and *MPP* will rise. These curves will shift vertically upwards.

Just how long the 'very long run' is will vary from firm to firm. It will depend on how long it takes to develop new techniques, new skills or new work practices.

It is important to realise that decisions *for* all four time periods can be made *at* the same time. Firms do not make short-run decisions *in* the short run and long-run decisions *in* the long run. They can make both short-run and long-run decisions today. For example, assume that a firm experiences an increase in consumer demand and anticipates that it will continue into the foreseeable future. It thus wants to increase output. Consequently, it makes the following four decisions *today*:

- (*Very short run*) It accepts that for a few days it will not be able to increase output. It informs its customers that they will have to wait. In some markets the firm may temporarily raise prices to choke off some of the demand.
- (*Short run*) It negotiates with labour to introduce overtime working as soon as possible, to tide it over the next few weeks. It orders extra raw materials from its suppliers. It launches a recruitment drive for new labour so as to avoid paying overtime longer than is necessary.
- (*Long run*) It starts proceedings to build a new factory. What would this involve? In some cases the firm may talk to the bank directly about finance and start investigating sites. A different approach might be to discuss requirements with a firm of consultants.
- (*Very long run*) It institutes a programme of research and development and/or training in an attempt to increase productivity.

1. Could the long run and the very long run ever be the same length of time?
2. What will the long-run and very-long-run market supply curves for a product look like? How will the shape of the long-run curve depend on returns to scale?
*3. In the very long run, new isoquants will have to be drawn as factor productivity changes. An increase in productivity will shift the isoquants inwards towards the origin: less capital and labour will be required to produce any given level of output. Will this be a parallel inward shift of the isoquants? Explain.

Although we distinguish these four time periods, it is the middle two we are primarily concerned with. The reason for this is that there is very little the firm can do in the *very* short run. And concerning the *very* long run, although the firm will obviously want to increase the productivity of its inputs, it will not be in a position to make precise calculations of how to do it. It will not know precisely what inventions will be made, or just what will be the results of its own research and development.

Section summary

1. In the long run, a firm is able to vary the quantity it uses of all factors of production. There are no fixed factors.

2. If it increases all factors by the same proportion, it may experience constant, increasing or decreasing returns to scale.

3. Economies of scale occur when costs per unit of output fall as the scale of production increases. This can be due to a number of factors, some of which result directly from increasing (physical) returns to scale. These include the benefits of specialisation and division of labour, the use of larger and more efficient machines, and the ability to have a more integrated system of production. Other economies of scale arise from the financial and administrative benefits of large-scale organisations.

4. Long-run costs are also influenced by a firm's location. The firm will have to balance the needs to be as near as possible both to the supply of its raw materials and to its market. The optimum balance will depend on the relative costs of transporting the inputs and the finished product.

5. To minimise costs per unit of output, a firm should choose that combination of factors which gives an equal marginal product for each factor relative to its price: i.e. $MPP_a/P_a = MPP_b/P_b = MPP_c/P_c$, etc. (where a, b and c are different factors). If the MPP/P ratio for one factor is greater than for another, more of the first should be used relative to the second.

6. An isoquant shows the various combinations of two factors to produce a given output. A whole map of such isoquants can be drawn with each isoquant representing a different level of output. The slope of the isoquant ($\Delta K/\Delta L$) gives the marginal rate of factor substitution (MPP_L/MPP_K). The bowed-in shape of isoquants illustrates a diminishing marginal rate of factor substitution, which in turn arises because of diminishing marginal returns.

7. An isocost shows the various combinations of two factors that cost a given amount to employ. It will be a straight line. Its slope is equal to the price ratio of the two factors (P_L/P_K).

8. The tangency point of an isocost with an isoquant represents the optimum factor combination. It is the point where MPP_L/MPP_K (the slope of the isoquant) $= P_L/P_K$ (the slope of the isocost). By drawing a single isoquant touching the lowest possible isocost, we can show the least-cost combination of factors for producing a given output. By drawing a single isocost touching the highest possible isoquant, we can show the highest output obtainable for a given cost of production.

9. Four distinct time periods can be distinguished. In addition to the short- and long-run periods, we can also distinguish the very-short- and very-long-run periods. The very short run is when all factors are fixed. The very long run is where not only the quantity of factors but also their quality is variable (as a result of changing technology, etc.).

6.4 COSTS IN THE LONG RUN

We turn now to *long-run* cost curves. Since there are no fixed factors in the long run, there are no long-run fixed costs. For example, the firm may rent more land in order to expand its operations. Its rent bill therefore goes up as it expands its output. In the long run, then, all costs are variable costs.

 Fixed costs and the time period. Fixed costs occur only in the short run, since in the long run all inputs can be varied.

Long-run average costs

Long-run average cost (LRAC) curves can take various shapes, but a typical one is shown in Figure 6.11.

It is often assumed that as a firm expands, it will initially experience economies of scale and thus face a downward-sloping *LRAC* curve. After a point, however, all such economies will have been achieved and thus the curve will flatten out. Then (possibly after a period of constant *LRAC*) the firm will get so large that it will start experiencing diseconomies of scale and thus a rising *LRAC*. At this stage, production and financial economies will begin to be offset by the managerial problems of running a giant organisation.

 Given the LRAC curve in Figure 6.11, what would the firm's long-run total cost curve look like?

Assumptions behind the long-run average cost curve

We make three key assumptions when constructing long-run average cost curves.

Factor prices are given. At each level of output, it is assumed that a firm will be faced with a given set of factor prices. If factor prices *change*, therefore, both short- and long-run cost curves will shift. Thus an increase in nationally negotiated wage rates would shift the curves upwards.

However, factor prices might be different at *different* levels of output. For example, one of the economies of scale that many firms enjoy is the ability to obtain bulk discount on raw materials and other supplies. In such cases, the curve does *not* shift. The different factor prices are merely experienced at different points along the curve, and are reflected in the shape of the curve. Factor prices are still given for any particular level of output.

The state of technology and factor quality are given. These are assumed to change only in the *very* long run. If a firm gains economies of scale, it is because it is able to exploit *existing* technologies and make better use of the existing availability of factors of production.

Firms choose the least-cost combination of factors for each output. The assumption here is that firms operate efficiently: that they choose the cheapest possible way of producing any level of output. In other words, at every point along the *LRAC* curve, the firm will adhere to the cost-minimising formula (see page 164):

$$\frac{MPP_a}{P_a} = \frac{MPP_b}{P_b} = \frac{MPP_c}{P_c} = \ldots = \frac{MPP_n}{P_n}$$

where $a \ldots n$ are the various factors the firm uses.

If the firm did not choose the optimum factor combination, it would be producing at a point above the *LRAC* curve.

Definitions

Long-run average cost curve A curve that shows how average cost varies with output on the assumption that *all* factors are variable. (It is assumed that the least-cost method of production will be chosen for each output.)

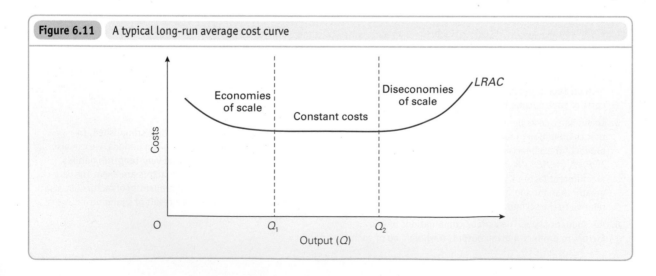

Figure 6.11 A typical long-run average cost curve

Long-run marginal costs

The relationship between long-run average and *long-run marginal cost* curves is just like that between any other averages and marginals (see Box 6.3). This is illustrated in Figure 6.12.

If there are economies of scale (diagram (a)), additional units of output will add less to costs than the average. The *LRMC* curve must be below the *LRAC* curve and thus pulling the average down as output increases. If there are diseconomies of scale (diagram (b)), additional units of output will cost more than the average. The *LRMC* curve must be above the *LRAC* curve, pulling it up. If there are no economies or diseconomies of scale, so that the *LRAC* curve is horizontal,

---

Definitions

Long-run marginal cost The extra cost of producing one more unit of output assuming that all factors are variable. (It is assumed that the least-cost method of production will be chosen for this extra output.)

---

any additional units of output will cost the same as the average and thus leave the average unaffected (diagram (c)).

1. *Explain the shape of the LRMC curve in diagram (d) in Figure 6.12.*
2. *What would the LRMC curve look like if the LRAC curve were 'flat bottomed', as in Figure 6.11?*

The relationship between long-run and short-run average cost curves

Take the case of a firm which has just one factory and faces a short-run average cost curve illustrated by $SRAC_1$ in Figure 6.13.

In the long run, it can build more factories. If it thereby experiences economies of scale (due, say, to savings on administration), each successive factory will allow it to produce with a new lower $SRAC$ curve. Thus with two factories it will face $SRAC_2$, with three factories $SRAC_3$, and so on. Each $SRAC$ curve corresponds to a particular amount of the factor that is fixed in the short run: in this case, the factory.

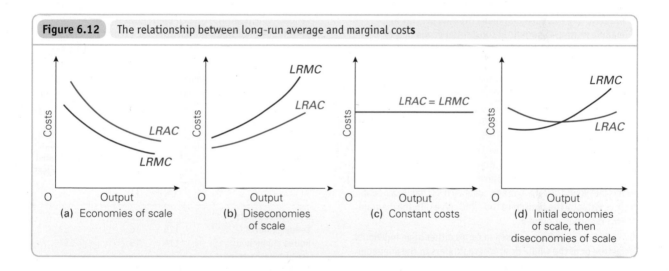

Figure 6.12   The relationship between long-run average and marginal costs

(a) Economies of scale

(b) Diseconomies of scale

(c) Constant costs

(d) Initial economies of scale, then diseconomies of scale

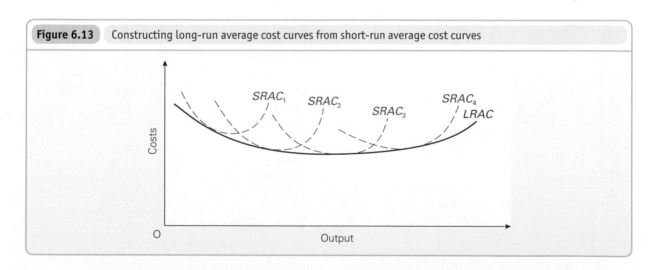

Figure 6.13   Constructing long-run average cost curves from short-run average cost curves

(There are many more *SRAC* curves that could be drawn between the ones shown, since factories of different sizes could be built or existing ones could be expanded.)

From this succession of short-run average cost curves we can construct a long-run average cost curve, as shown in Figure 6.13. This is known as the *envelope curve*, since it envelopes the short-run curves.

Definitions

Envelope curve A long-run average cost curve drawn as the tangency points of a series of short-run average cost curves.

 Will the envelope curve be tangential to the bottom of each of the short-run average cost curves? Explain why it should or should not be.

Long-run cost curves in practice

Firms do experience economies of scale. Some experience continuously falling *LRAC* curves, as in Figure 6.12(a). Others experience economies of scale up to a certain output and thereafter constant returns to scale.

Evidence is inconclusive on the question of diseconomies of scale. There is little evidence to suggest the existence of *technical* diseconomies, but the possibility of diseconomies due to managerial and industrial relations problems cannot be ruled out.

BOX 6.9	MINIMUM EFFICIENT SCALE

The extent of economies of scale in practice

Two of the most important studies of economies of scale are those by C. F. Pratten[1] in the late 1980s and by a group advising the European Commission[2] in 1997. Both studies found strong evidence that many firms, especially in manufacturing, experienced substantial economies of scale.

In a few cases, long-run average costs fell continuously as output increased. For most firms, however, they fell up to a certain level of output and then remained constant.

The extent of economies of scale can be measured by looking at a firm's *minimum efficient scale* (*MES*). The *MES* is the size beyond which no significant additional economies of scale can be achieved: in other words, the point where the *LRAC* curve flattens off. In Pratten's studies, he defined this level as the minimum scale above which any possible doubling in scale would reduce average costs by less than 5 per cent (i.e. virtually the bottom of the *LRAC* curve). In the diagram, *MES* is shown at point *a*.

The *MES* can be expressed in terms either of an individual factory or of the whole firm. Where it refers to the minimum efficient scale of an individual factory, the *MES* is known as the *minimum efficient plant size* (*MEPS*).

The *MES* can then be expressed as a percentage of the total size of the market or of total domestic production. Table (a), based on the Pratten study, shows *MES* for plants and firms in various industries. The first column shows *MES* as a percentage of total UK production. The second column shows *MES* as a percentage of total EU production. Table (b), based on the 1997 study, shows *MES* for various plants.

Expressing *MES* as a percentage of total output gives an indication of how competitive the industry could be. In some

Table (a)

Product	MES as % of production		% additional cost at ½ MES
	UK	EU	
Individual plants			
Cellulose fibres	125	16	3
Rolled aluminium semi-manufactures	114	15	15
Refrigerators	85	11	4
Steel	72	10	6
Electric motors	60	6	15
TV sets	40	9	9
Cigarettes	24	6	1.4
Ball-bearings	20	2	6
Beer	12	3	7
Nylon	4	1	12
Bricks	1	0.2	25
Carpets	0.3	0.04	10
Footwear	0.3	0.03	1
Firms			
Cars	200	20	9
Lorries	104	21	7.5
Mainframe computers	>100	n.a.	5
Aircraft	100	n.a.	5
Tractors	98	19	6

Source: See footnote 1 below.

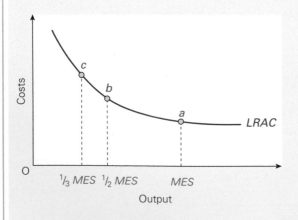

Some evidence on economies of scale in the UK is considered in Box 6.9.

*Derivation of long-run costs from an isoquant map[2]

Cost curves are drawn on the assumption that, for any output, the least-cost combination of factors is used: that is, that production will take place at the tangency point of the isoquant and an isocost, where $MPP_L/MPP_K = P_L/P_K$: i.e. where $MPP_L/P_L = MPP_K/P_K$. By drawing a series of isoquants and isocosts, long-run costs can be derived for each output.

2 This optional section is based on the material in the optional section on pages 166–70.

In Figure 6.14, isoquants are drawn for a hypothetical firm at 100 unit intervals. Up to 400 units of output, the isoquants are getting closer together. Thereafter, the gap between the isoquants widens again.

The line from *a* to *g* is known as the **expansion path**. It traces the tangency points of the isoquants and isocosts,

Definitions

Expansion path The line on an isoquant map that traces the minimum-cost combinations of two factors as output increases. It is drawn on the assumption that both factors can be varied. It is thus a long-run path.

industries (such as footwear and carpets), economies of scale were exhausted (i.e. *MES* was reached) with plants or firms that were still small relative to total UK production and even smaller relative to total EU production. In such industries, there would be room for many firms and thus scope for considerable competition.

Table (b)

Plants	MES as % of total EU production
Aerospace	12.19
Agricultural machinery	6.57
Electric lighting	3.76
Steel tubes	2.42
Shipbuilding	1.63
Rubber	1.06
Radio and TV	0.69
Footwear	0.08
Carpets	0.03

Source: See footnote 2 below.

In other industries, however, even if a single plant or firm were large enough to produce the whole output of the industry in the UK, it would still not be large enough to experience the full potential economies of scale: the *MES* is greater than 100 per cent. Examples from Table (a) include factories producing cellulose fibres, and car manufacturers. In these industries, there is no possibility of competition from within the country. In fact, as long as the *MES* exceeds 50 per cent, there will not be room for more than one firm large enough to gain full economies of scale (unless they export). In this case, the industry is said to be a natural monopoly.

As we shall see in the next few chapters, when competition is lacking, consumers may suffer by firms charging prices considerably above costs.

A second way of measuring the extent of economies of scale is to see how much costs would increase if production

were reduced to a certain fraction of *MES*. The normal fractions used are ½ or ⅓ *MES*. This is illustrated in the diagram. Point *b* corresponds to ½ *MES*; point *c* to ⅓ *MES*. The greater the percentage by which *LRAC* at point *b* or *c* is higher than at point *a*, the greater will be the economies of scale to be gained by producing at *MES* rather than at ½ *MES* or ⅓ *MES*. For example, in Table (a) there are greater economies of scale to be gained from moving from ½ *MES* to *MES* in the production of electric motors than in cigarettes.

The main purpose of the studies was to determine whether the single EU market is big enough to allow both economies of scale and competition. The tables suggest that in all cases, other things being equal, the EU market is indeed large enough for this to occur. The second study also found that 47 of the 53 manufacturing sectors analysed had scope for further exploitation of economies of scale.

In the 2007–13 research framework the European Commission agreed to fund a number of research projects, to conduct further investigations of *MES* across different industries and to consider the impact of the expansion of the EU.

1. Why might a firm operating with one plant achieve MEPS and yet not be large enough to achieve MES? (Clue: are all economies of scale achieved at plant level?)
2. Why might a firm producing bricks have an MES which is only 0.2 per cent of total EU production and yet face little effective competition from other EU countries?

1 C. F. Pratten, 'A survey of the economies of scale', in *Research into the 'Costs of Non-Europe'*, Volume 2 (Commission of the European Communities, Luxembourg, 1988).

2 European Commission/Economists Advisory Group Ltd, 'Economies of scale', *The Single Market Review*, Sub-series V, Volume 4 (Commission of the European Communities, Luxembourg, 1997).

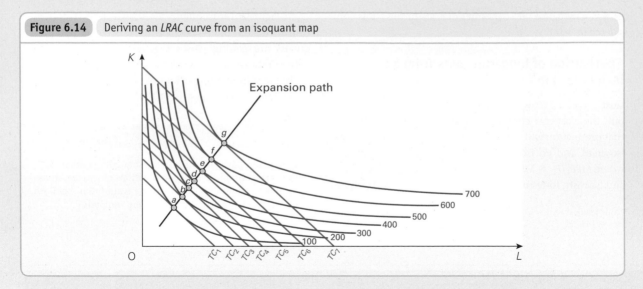

Figure 6.14 Deriving an *LRAC* curve from an isoquant map

and thus shows the minimum-cost combinations of labour and capital to produce each output: the (long-run) total cost being given by the isocost.

Up to point *d*, less and less *extra* capital (*K*) and labour (*L*) are required to produce each extra 100 units of output. Thus long-run marginal cost is falling. Above point *d*, more and more extra *K* and *L* are required and thus *LRMC* rises.

Thus the isoquant map of Figure 6.14 gives an *LRMC* curve that is ⌣-shaped. The *LRAC* curve will therefore also be ⌣-shaped (only shallower) with the *LRMC* coming up through the bottom of the *LRAC*.

 What would the isoquant map look like if there were
(a) continuously increasing returns to scale;
(b) continuously decreasing returns to scale?

Section summary

1. In the long run, all factors are variable. There are thus no long-run fixed costs.

2. When constructing long-run cost curves, it is assumed that factor prices are given, that the state of technology is given and that firms will choose the least-cost combination of factors for each given output.

3. The *LRAC* curve can be downward sloping, upward sloping or horizontal, depending in turn on whether there are economies of scale, diseconomies of scale or neither. Typically, *LRAC* curves are drawn saucer-shaped or ⌣-shaped. As output expands, initially there are economies of scale. When these are exhausted, the curve will become flat. When the firm becomes very large, it may begin to experience diseconomies of scale.

   If this happens, the *LRAC* curve will begin to slope upwards again.

4. The long-run marginal cost curve will be below the *LRAC* curve when *LRAC* is falling, above it when *LRAC* is rising and equal to it when *LRAC* is neither rising nor falling.

5. An envelope curve can be drawn which shows the relationship between short-run and long-run average cost curves. The *LRAC* curve envelops the short-run *LRAC* curves: it is tangential to them.

6. Costs can be derived from an isoquant map. Long-run total costs are found from the expansion path, which shows the least-cost combination of factors to produce any given output. It traces out the tangency points of the isocosts and isoquants.

6.5 REVENUE

Remember that we defined a firm's total profit as its total revenue minus its total costs of production. So far in this chapter we have examined costs. We now turn to revenue.

As with costs, we distinguish between three revenue concepts: total revenue (*TR*), average revenue (*AR*) and marginal revenue (*MR*).

Total, average and marginal revenue

Total revenue (TR)

Total revenue is the firm's total earnings per period of time from the sale of a particular amount of output (*Q*). For example, if a firm sells 1000 units (*Q*) per month at a price of £5 each (*P*), then its monthly total revenue will be £5000: in other words, £5 × 1000 (*P* × *Q*). Thus

$$TR = P \times Q$$

Average revenue (AR)

Average revenue is the amount the firm earns per unit sold. Thus

$$AR = TR/Q$$

So if the firm earns £5000 (*TR*) from selling 1000 units (*Q*), it will earn £5 per unit. But this is simply the price! Thus

$$AR = P$$

(The only exception to this is when the firm is selling its products at different prices to different consumers. In this case, *AR* is simply the (weighted) average price.)

Marginal revenue (MR)

Marginal revenue is the extra total revenue gained by selling one more unit (per time period). So if a firm sells an extra 20 units this month compared with what it expected to sell, and in the process earns an extra £100, then it is getting an extra £5 for each extra unit sold: *MR* = £5. Thus

$$MR = \Delta TR/\Delta Q$$

We now need to see how each of these three revenue concepts (*TR*, *AR* and *MR*) varies with output. We can show this graphically in the same way as we did with costs.

The relationships will depend on the market conditions under which a firm operates. A firm that is too small to be able to affect market price will have different-shaped revenue curves from a firm that is able to choose the price it charges. Let us examine each of these two situations in turn.

Revenue curves when price is not affected by the firm's output

Average revenue

If a firm is very small relative to the whole market, it is likely to be a **price taker**. That is, it has to accept the price given by the intersection of demand and supply in the whole market. But, being so small, it can sell as much as it is capable of producing at that price. This is illustrated in Figure 6.15.

The left-hand part of the diagram shows market demand and supply. Equilibrium price is £5. The right-hand part of the diagram looks at the demand for an individual firm that is tiny relative to the whole market. (Look at the differences in the scale of the horizontal axes in the two parts of the diagram.)

Being so small, any change in its output will be too insignificant to affect the market price. It thus faces a horizontal demand 'curve' at the price. It can sell 200 units, 600 units, 1200 units or whatever without affecting this £5 price.

Average revenue is thus constant at £5. The firm's average revenue curve must therefore lie along exactly the same line as its demand curve.

Definitions

Total revenue A firm's total earnings from a specified level of sales within a specified period: *TR* = *P* × *Q*.

Average revenue Total revenue per unit of output. When all output is sold at the same price, average revenue will be the same as price: *AR* = *TR*/*Q* = *P*.

Marginal revenue The extra revenue gained by selling one more unit per period of time: *MR* = *ΔTR*/*ΔQ*.

Price taker A firm that is too small to be able to influence the market price.

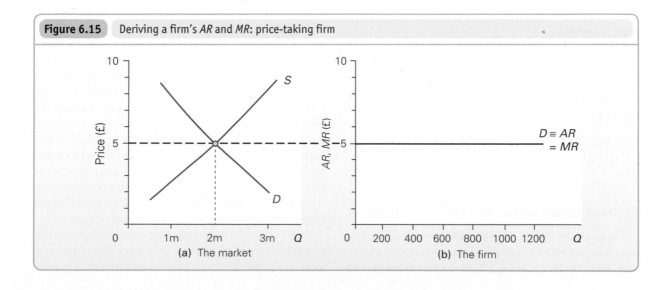

Figure 6.15 Deriving a firm's *AR* and *MR*: price-taking firm

Table 6.7	Deriving total revenue for a price-taking firm

Quantity (units)	Price ≡ AR = MR (£)	TR (£)
0	5	0
200	5	1000
400	5	2000
600	5	3000
800	5	4000
1000	5	5000
1200	5	6000
.	.	.

Table 6.8	Revenues for a firm facing a downward-sloping demand curve

Q (units)	P = AR (£)	TR (£)	MR (£)
1	8	8	
2	7	14	6
3	6	18	4
4	5	20	2
5	4	20	0
6	3	18	−2
7	2	14	−4
.	.	.	.

Figure 6.16 Total revenue for a price-taking firm

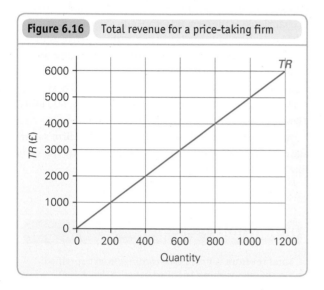

Marginal revenue

In the case of a horizontal demand curve, the marginal revenue curve will be the same as the average revenue curve, since selling one more unit at a constant price (*AR*) merely adds that amount to total revenue. If an extra unit is sold at a constant price of £5, an extra £5 is earned.

Total revenue

Table 6.7 shows the effect on total revenue of different levels of sales with a constant price of £5 per unit. As price is constant, total revenue will rise at a constant rate as more is sold. The *TR* 'curve' will therefore be a straight line through the origin, as in Figure 6.16.

 What would happen to the TR curve if the market price rose to £10? Try drawing it.

Revenue curves when price varies with output

The three curves (*TR*, *AR* and *MR*) look quite different when price does vary with the firm's output. If a firm has a relatively large share of the market, it will face a downward-sloping demand curve. This means that if it is to sell more, it must lower the price. It could also choose to raise its price. If it does so, however, it will have to accept a fall in sales.

Average revenue

Remember that average revenue equals price. If, therefore, price has to be lowered to sell more output, average revenue will fall as output increases.

Table 6.8 gives an example of a firm facing a downward-sloping demand curve. The demand curve (which shows how much is sold at each price) is given by the first two columns.

Note that, as in the case of a price-taking firm, the demand curve and the *AR* curve lie along exactly the same line. The reason for this is simple: *AR* = *P*, and thus the curve relating price to quantity (the demand curve) must be the same as that relating average revenue to quantity (the *AR* curve).

Marginal revenue

When a firm faces a downward-sloping demand curve, marginal revenue will be less than average revenue, and may even be negative. But why?

If a firm is to sell more per time period, it must lower its price (assuming it does not advertise). This will mean lowering the price not just for the extra units it hopes to sell, but also for those units it would have sold had it not lowered the price.

Thus the marginal revenue is the price at which it sells the last unit, *minus* the loss in revenue it has incurred by reducing the price on those units it could otherwise have sold at the higher price. This can be illustrated with Table 6.8.

Assume that the price is currently £7. Two units are thus sold. The firm now wishes to sell an extra unit. It lowers the price to £6. It thus gains £6 from the sale of the third unit, but loses £2 by having to reduce the price by £1 on the two units it could otherwise have sold at £7. Its net gain is therefore £6 − £2 = £4. This is the marginal revenue: it is the extra revenue gained by the firm from selling one more unit. (Notice that in Table 6.8 the figures for *MR* are entered in the spaces between the figures for the other three columns.)

There is a simple relationship between marginal revenue and *price elasticity of demand*. Remember from Chapter 2 (page 59) that if demand is price elastic, a *decrease* in price will lead to a proportionately larger increase in the quantity demanded and hence an *increase* in revenue. Marginal revenue will thus be positive. If, however, demand is inelastic, a decrease in price will lead to a proportionately smaller increase in sales. In this case, the price reduction will more than offset the increase in sales and as a result revenue will fall. Marginal revenue will be negative.

KI 9
p66

If, then, at a particular quantity sold marginal revenue is a positive figure (i.e. if sales per time period are 4 units or less in Figure 6.17), the demand curve will be elastic at that quantity, since a rise in quantity sold (as a result of a reduction in price) would lead to a rise in total revenue. If, on the other hand, marginal revenue is negative (i.e. at a level of sales of 5 or more units in Figure 6.17), the demand curve will be inelastic at that quantity, since a rise in quantity sold would lead to a *fall* in total revenue.

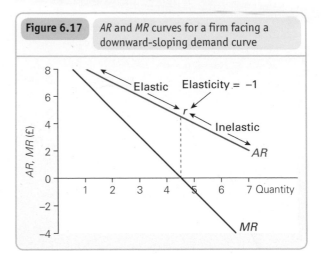

Figure 6.17 *AR* and *MR* curves for a firm facing a downward-sloping demand curve

*LOOKING AT THE MATHS

As with cost curves (see page 160), we can express revenue curves algebraically.

Price-taking firms

Let us take *TR, AR* and *MR* in turn. They will take the following forms:

$$TR = bQ \qquad (1)$$

This equation will give an upward-sloping straight-line *TR* 'curve', with a slope of *b*. Note that the absence of a constant (*a*) term means that the line passes through the origin. This is obviously the case, given that if sales (*Q*) are zero, total revenue will be zero.

$$AR = \frac{TR}{Q} = b \qquad (2)$$

This will give a horizontal *AR* curve at an *AR* (i.e. price) of *b*.

$$MR = \frac{d(TR)}{dQ} = b \qquad (3)$$

Differentiating the *TR* function gives a value of *b*. As we have seen, *AR = MR* when the firm is a price taker and faces a horizontal demand curve (at the market price).

Price-making firms: a straight-line demand 'curve'

'Price makers' face a downward-sloping demand curve. If this is a straight-line demand curve, the revenue equations will be as follows:

$$TR = bQ - cQ^2 \qquad (4)$$

The negative cQ^2 term will give a revenue curve whose slope gets less until a peak is reached (see Figure 6.18). Thereafter, as the cQ^2 term becomes bigger than the bQ term, *TR* will fall.

$$AR = \frac{TR}{Q} = b - cQ \qquad (5)$$

This gives a straight-line downward-sloping *AR* curve (demand curve) with a slope of −*c*, which crosses the horizontal axis when *cQ* becomes bigger than *b*.

$$MR = \frac{d(TR)}{dQ} = b - 2cQ \qquad (6)$$

This again gives a straight downward-sloping line, this time with a slope of −2*c*. Note that this means that the slope of the *MR* curve is twice that of the *AR* curve.

But what if the demand curve is actually curved? What will the three revenue equations be then? We explore this in Maths Case 6.4 on the student website and relate the equations to the relevant diagrams.

The relationship between marginal revenue and price elasticity of demand

You can see from Figure 6.17 how price elasticity of demand and marginal revenue are related. We can express this relationship algebraically as follows:

$$MR = P(1 + (1/P\epsilon_D)) \qquad (7)$$

or

$$P = \frac{MR}{1 + (1/P\epsilon_D)}$$

Proof of this relationship is given in Maths Case 6.2 on the student website, but for now we can see how equation (7) relates to Figure 6.17. The *P* term must be positive. If demand is elastic, then $P\epsilon_D$ must have a value less than −1 (i.e. the figure for elasticity, ignoring the negative sign, must be greater than 1). Thus the term $1/P\epsilon_D$ must have a negative value between 0 and −1. This means, therefore, that the term $(1 + (1/P\epsilon_D))$ must be positive, and hence *MR* must be positive.

If, however, demand is inelastic, then $P\epsilon_D$ must have a value between −1 and zero. Thus the term $1/P\epsilon_D$ must have a negative value less than −1 (i.e. an absolute value, ignoring the negative sign, that is greater than 1). This means, therefore, that the term $(1 + (1/P\epsilon_D))$ must be negative, and hence *MR* must be negative.

Finally, if demand is unit elastic, then the term $1/P\epsilon_D$ must have a value of −1 and hence the term $(1 + (1/P\epsilon_D))$ must have a value of zero. *MR* must be zero.

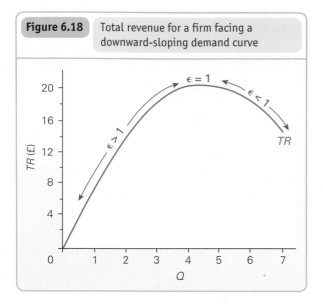

Figure 6.18 Total revenue for a firm facing a downward-sloping demand curve

But why? As long as marginal revenue is positive (and hence demand is price elastic), a rise in output will raise total revenue. However, once marginal revenue becomes negative (and hence demand is inelastic), total revenue will fall. The peak of the *TR* curve will be where $MR = 0$. At this point, the price elasticity of demand will be equal to 1.

Shifts in revenue curves

We saw in Chapter 2 that a change in *price* will cause a movement along a demand curve. It is similar with revenue curves, except that here the causal connection is in the other direction. Here we ask what happens to revenue when there is a change in the firm's *output*. Again the effect is shown by a movement along the curves.

A change in any *other* determinant of demand, such as tastes, income or the price of other goods, will shift the demand curve. By affecting the price at which each level of output can be sold, there will be a shift in all three revenue curves. An increase in revenue is shown by a shift upwards; a decrease by a shift downwards.

Thus the demand (*AR*) curve in Figure 6.17 is elastic to the left of point *r* and inelastic to the right.

Total revenue

Total revenue equals price times quantity. This is illustrated in Table 6.8. The *TR* column from Table 6.8 is plotted in Figure 6.18.

Unlike the case of a price-taking firm, the *TR* curve is not a straight line. It is a curve that rises at first and then falls.

Copy Figures 6.17 and 6.18 (which are based on Table 6.8). Now assume that incomes have risen and that, as a result, two more units per time period can be sold at each price. Draw a new table and plot the resulting new AR, MR and TR curves on your diagrams. Are the new curves parallel to the old ones? Explain.

Section summary

1. Total revenue (*TR*) is the total amount a firm earns from its sales in a given time period. It is simply price times quantity: $TR = P \times Q$.

2. Average revenue (*AR*) is total revenue per unit: $AR = TR/Q$. In other words, $AR = P$.

3. Marginal revenue is the extra revenue earned from the sale of one more unit per time period.

4. The *AR* curve will be the same as the demand curve for the firm's product. In the case of a price taker, the demand curve and hence the *AR* curve will be a horizontal straight line and will also be the same as the *MR* curve. The *TR* curve will be an upward-sloping straight line from the origin.

5. A firm that faces a downward-sloping demand curve must obviously also face the same downward-sloping *AR* curve. The *MR* curve will also slope downwards, but will be below the *AR* curve and steeper than it. The *TR* curve will be an arch shape starting from the origin.

6. When demand is price elastic, marginal revenue will be positive and the *TR* curve will be upward sloping. When demand is price inelastic, marginal revenue will be negative and the *TR* curve will be downward sloping.

7. A change in output is represented by a movement along the revenue curves. A change in any other determinant of revenue will shift the curves up or down.

6.6 PROFIT MAXIMISATION

We are now in a position to put costs and revenue together to find the output at which profit is maximised, and also to find out how much that profit will be.

There are two ways of doing this. The first and simpler method is to use total cost and total revenue curves. The second method is to use marginal and average cost and marginal and average revenue curves. Although this method is a

little more complicated (but only a little!), it is more useful when we come to compare profit maximising under different market conditions.

We will look at each method in turn. In both cases, we will concentrate on the short run: namely, that period in which one or more factors are fixed in supply. In both cases, we take the instance of a firm facing a downward-sloping demand curve.

Table 6.9 Total revenue, total cost and total profit

Q (units)	TR (£)	TC (£)	TΠ (£)
0	0	6	−6
1	8	10	−2
2	14	12	2
3	18	14	4
4	20	18	2
5	20	25	−5
6	18	36	−18
7	14	56	−42
.	.	.	.

Figure 6.19 Finding maximum profit using totals curves

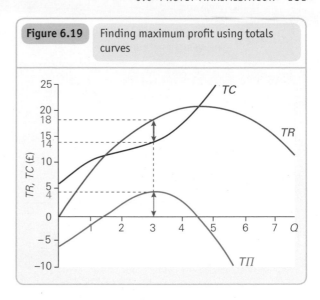

Short-run profit maximisation: using total curves

Table 6.9 shows the total revenue figures from Table 6.8. It also shows figures for total cost. These figures have been chosen so as to produce a *TC* curve of a typical shape.

Total profit (*TΠ*) is found by subtracting *TC* from *TR*. Check this out by examining the table. Where (*TΠ*) is negative, the firm is making a loss. Total profit is maximised at an output of 3 units, where there is the greatest gap between total revenue and total costs. At this output, total profit is £4 (£18 − £14).

The *TR*, *TC* and (*TΠ*) curves are plotted in Figure 6.19. The size of the maximum profit is shown by the arrows.

 What can we say about the slope of the TR and TC curves at the maximum profit point? What does this tell us about marginal revenue and marginal cost?

Short-run profit maximisation: using average and marginal curves

Table 6.10 is based on the figures in Table 6.9.

 1. *Fill in the missing figures (without referring to Table 6.8 or 6.9).*
2. *Why are the figures for MR and MC entered in the spaces between the lines in Table 6.10?*

Finding the maximum profit that a firm can make is a two-stage process. The first stage is to find the profit-maximising output. To do this we use the *MC* and *MR* curves. The second stage is to find out just how much profit is at this output. To do this we use the *AR* and *AC* curves.

Stage 1: Using marginal curves to arrive at the profit-maximising output

There is a very simple *profit-maximising rule*: if profits are to be maximised, *MR must equal MC*. From Table 6.10 it can be seen that it *MR* = *MC* at an output of 3. This is shown as point *e* in Figure 6.20.

But why are profits maximised when *MR* = *MC*? The simplest way of answering this is to see what the position would be if *MR* did not equal *MC*.

Definitions

Profit-maximising rule Profit is maximised where marginal revenue equals marginal cost.

Table 6.10 Revenue, cost and profit

Q (units)	P = AR (£)	TR (£)	MR (£)	TC (£)	AC (£)	MC (£)	TΠ (£)	AΠ (£)
0	9	0		6	–		−6	–
			8			4		
1	8	8		10	10		...	−2
			...			2		
2	7	14		12	...		2	1
			4			2		
3	6	18		14	4²/₃		4	1¹/₃
			2			4		
4	5	20		18	4¹/₂		2	¹/₂
			0			7		
5	4	20		25	5		−5	−1
			−2			...		
6	3	18		36	...		...	...
			...			20		
7	2	14		56	8		−42	−6
.	.	.	.	.	.	.	.	.

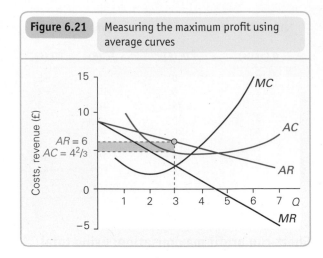

Figure 6.20 Finding the profit-maximising output using marginal curves

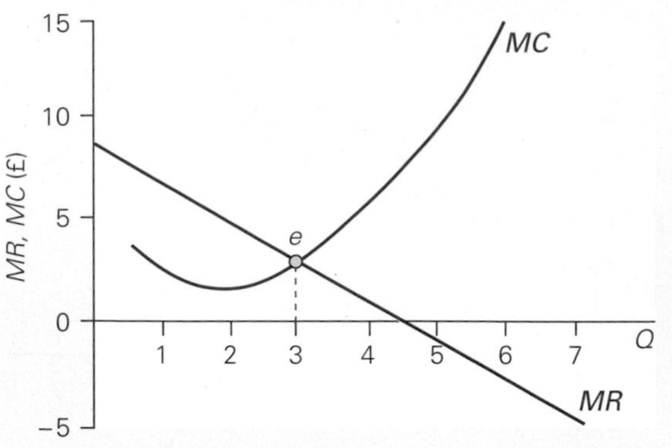

Figure 6.21 Measuring the maximum profit using average curves

Referring to Figure 6.20, at a level of output below 3, *MR* exceeds *MC*. This means that by producing more units there will be a bigger addition to revenue (*MR*) than to cost (*MC*). Total profit will *increase. As long as MR exceeds MC, profit can be increased by increasing production.*

At a level of output above 3, *MC* exceeds *MR*. All levels of output above 3 thus add more to cost than to revenue and hence *reduce* profit. *As long as MC exceeds MR, profit can be increased by cutting back on production.*

Profits are thus maximised where $MC = MR$: at an output of 3. This can be confirmed by reference to the $T\Pi$ column in Table 6.10.

Students worry sometimes about the argument that profits are maximised when $MR = MC$. Surely, they say, if the last unit is making no profit, how can profit be at a *maximum*? The answer is very simple. If you cannot *add* anything more to a total, the total must be at the maximum. Take the simple analogy of going up a hill. When you cannot go any higher, you must be at the top.

Stage 2: Using average curves to measure the size of the profit

Once the profit-maximising output has been discovered, we use the average curves to measure the *amount* of profit at the maximum. Both marginal and average curves corresponding to the data in Table 6.10 are plotted in Figure 6.21.

First, average profit (*A*) is found. This is simply $AR - AC$. At the profit-maximising output of 3, this gives a figure for $A\Pi$ of $£6 - £4^2/_3 = £1^1/_3$. Then total profit is obtained by multiplying average profit by output:

$$T\Pi = A\Pi \times Q$$

This is shown as the shaded area. It equals $£1^1/_3 \times 3 = £4$. This can again be confirmed by reference to the $T\Pi$ column in Table 6.10.

*LOOKING AT THE MATHS

As we have seen, the rule for profit maximisation is that firms should produce where $MC = MR$. This can be derived algebraically as follows. Profit is defined as

$$T\Pi = TR - TC \quad (1)$$

Profit is maximised at the point where an additional unit of output will add no more to profit – that is, where

$$\frac{\Delta T\Pi}{\Delta Q} = M\Pi = 0 \quad (2)$$

or, from (1), where

$$\frac{\Delta TR}{\Delta Q} - \frac{\Delta TC}{\Delta Q} = 0 \quad (3)$$

or

$$\frac{\Delta TR}{\Delta Q} = \frac{\Delta TC}{\Delta Q} \quad (4)$$

that is, where $MR = MC$.

Equation (2) can be related to Figure 6.19. Profits are maximised at the highest point of the $T\Pi$ curve. At the top of any curve (or bottom for that matter), its slope is zero. Thus $\Delta T\Pi/Q = M\Pi = 0$. Put another way, the tangent to the top of the $T\Pi$ curve is horizontal.

? *From the information for a firm given in the table below, construct a table like 6.10.*

Q	0	1	2	3	4	5	6	7
P	12	11	10	9	8	7	6	5
TC	2	6	9	12	16	21	28	38

Use your table to draw diagrams like Figures 6.19 and 6.21. Use these two diagrams to show the profit-maximising output and the level of maximum profit. Confirm your findings by reference to the table you have constructed.

| *BOX 6.10 | USING CALCULUS TO FIND THE MAXIMUM PROFIT OUTPUT | EXPLORING ECONOMICS |

Imagine that a firm's total revenue and total cost functions were

$$TR = 48Q - Q^2$$
$$TC = 12 + 16Q + 3Q^2$$

From these two equations the following table can be derived.

Q	TR	TC	TΠ (= TR − TC)
0	0	12	−12
1	47	31	16
2	92	56	36
3	135	87	48
4	176	124	52
5	215	167	48
6	252	216	36
7	287	271	16
.	.	.	.

1. How much is total fixed cost?
2. Continue the table for $Q = 8$ and $Q = 9$.
3. Plot TR, TC and TΠ on a diagram like Figure 6.19.

It can clearly be seen from the table that profit is maximised at an output of 4, where $TΠ = 52$.

This profit-maximising output and the level of profit can be calculated without drawing up a table. The calculation involves calculus. There are two methods that can be used.

Finding where $MR = MC$

Marginal revenue can be found by differentiating the total revenue function.

$$MR = dTR/dQ$$

The reason is that marginal revenue is the rate of change of total revenue. Differentiating a function gives its rate of change.

Similarly, marginal cost can be found by differentiating the total cost function:

$$MC = dTC/dQ$$

Differentiating TR and TC gives

$$dTR/dQ = 48 - 2Q = MR$$

and

$$dTC/dQ = 16 + 6Q = MC$$

Profit is maximised where $MR = MC$, in other words, where

$$48 - 2Q = 16 + 6Q$$

Solving this for Q gives

$$32 = 80$$
$$\therefore Q = 4$$

The equation for total profit $(TΠ)$ is

$$TΠ = TR - TC$$
$$= 48Q - Q^2 - (12 + 16Q + 3Q^2)$$
$$= -12 + 32Q - 4Q^2$$

Substituting $Q = 4$ into this equation gives

$$TΠ = -12 + (32 \times 4) - (4 \times 4^2)$$
$$\therefore TΠ = 52$$

These figures can be confirmed from the table.

Maximising the total profit equation

To maximise an equation we want to find the point where the slope of the curve derived from it is zero. In other words, we want to find the top of the $TΠ$ curve.

The slope of a curve gives its rate of change and is found by differentiating the curve's equation. Thus to find maximum $TΠ$ we differentiate it (to find the slope) and set it equal to zero (to find the top).

$$TΠ = -12 + 32Q - 4Q^2 \text{ (see above)}$$
$$\therefore dTΠ/dQ = 32 - 8Q$$

Setting this equal to zero gives

$$32 - 8Q = 0$$
$$\therefore 8Q = 32$$
$$\therefore Q = 4$$

This is the same result as was found by the first method. Again $Q = 4$ can be substituted into the $TΠ$ equation to give

$$TΠ = 52$$

Given the following equations:

$$TR = 72Q - 2Q^2; TC = 10 + 12Q + 4Q^2$$

calculate the maximum profit output and the amount of profit at that output using both methods.

Some qualifications

Long-run profit maximisation

Assuming that the *AR* and *MR* curves are the same in the long run as in the short run, long-run profits will be maximised at the output where *MR* equals the *long-run MC*. The reasoning is the same as with the short-run case.

The meaning of 'profit'

One element of cost is the opportunity cost to the owners of the firm of being in business. This is the minimum return the owners must make on their capital in order to prevent them from eventually deciding to close down and perhaps move into some alternative business. It is a *cost* because, just as with wages, rent, etc., it has to be covered if the firm is to continue producing. This opportunity cost to the owners is sometimes known as ***normal profit***, and is *included in the cost curves*.

What determines this normal rate of profit? It has two components. First, someone setting up in business invests capital in it. There is thus an opportunity cost. This is the interest that could have been earned by lending it in some riskless form (e.g. by putting it in a savings account in a bank). Nobody would set up a business unless they expected to earn at least this rate of profit. Running a business is far from riskless, however, and hence a second element is a return to compensate for risk. Thus:

normal profit (%) = rate of interest on a riskless loan
+ a risk premium

The risk premium varies according to the line of business. In those with fairly predictable patterns, such as food retailing, it is relatively low. Where outcomes are very uncertain, such as mineral exploration or the manufacture of fashion garments, it is relatively high.

Thus if owners of a business earn normal profit, they will (just) be content to remain in that industry. If they earn more than normal profit, they will also (obviously) prefer to stay in this business. If they earn less than normal profit, then after a time they will consider leaving and using their capital for some other purpose. We will see in Chapter 7 that the level of profits that a firm can make plays a pivotal role in the way markets are structured.

? *How will the size of 'normal profit' vary with the general state of the economy?*

Given that normal profits are included in costs, any profit that is shown diagrammatically (e.g. the shaded area in Figure 6.21) must therefore be over and above normal profit. It is known by several alternative names: ***supernormal profit***, ***pure profit***, ***economic profit*** or sometimes simply ***profit***. They all mean the same thing: the excess of total profit over normal profit.

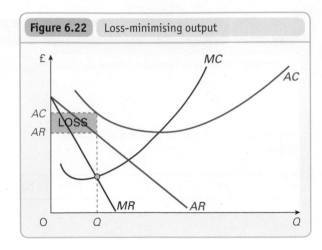

Figure 6.22 Loss-minimising output

Loss minimising

It may be that there is no output at which the firm can make a profit. Such a situation is illustrated in Figure 6.22: the *AC* curve is above the *AR* curve at all levels of output.

In this case, the output where *MR* = *MC* will be the loss-minimising output. The amount of loss at the point where *MR* = *MC* is shown by the shaded area in Figure 6.22. Even though the firm is making losses, there is no 'better' level of output at this point.

Whether or not to produce at all

The short run.   Fixed costs have to be paid even if the firm is producing nothing at all. Rent and business rates have to be paid, etc. It was explained in Box 6.6 how some of these could sometimes be avoided if the firm temporarily shut down. However, to keep the following discussion as simple as possible it is assumed that all fixed costs are also sunk costs. This means that providing the firm is able to cover its *variable* costs, it is no worse off than it would be if it temporarily shut down. Therefore it should continue to produce because, if shut down, its losses would be greater. Of course, if the firm's revenues are more than its variable costs, then it is able to go some way to covering the fixed costs and again it will continue to produce.

Definitions

Normal profit The opportunity cost of being in business: the profit that could have been earned in the next best alternative business. It is counted as a cost of production.

Supernormal profit (also known as pure profit, economic profit or simply profit) The excess of total profit above normal profit.

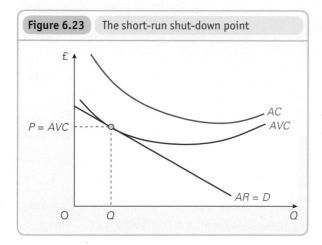

Figure 6.23   The short-run shut-down point

costs and it will shut down production. This situation is known as the ***short-run shut-down point***.

The long run.   All costs are variable in the long run. If, therefore, the firm cannot cover its long-run average costs (which include normal profit), it will close down. The ***long-run shut-down point*** will be where the *AR* curve is tangential to the *LRAC* curve.

> ## Definitions
>
> **Short-run shut-down point** Where the *AR* curve is tangential to the *AVC* curve. The firm can only just cover its variable costs. Any fall in revenue below this level will cause a profit-maximising firm to shut down immediately.
>
> **Long-run shut-down point** Where the *AR* curve is tangential to the *LRAC* curve. The firm can just make normal profits. Any fall in revenue below this level will cause a profit-maximising firm to shut down once all costs have become variable.

What happens if the firm's revenue is not enough to cover its variable costs: that is, if the *AVC* curve is above, or the *AR* curve below, the position illustrated in Figure 6.23? In that case the firm is worse off than if it only has fixed

---

BOX 6.11   THE LOGIC OF LOGISTICS   *CASE STUDIES AND APPLICATIONS*

Driving up profits

One key to a company's success is the logistics of its operations. 'Logistics' refers to the management of the inflow of resources to a company and the outflow of finished goods from it; in other words, it refers to 'supply-chain management'. This includes the purchasing of raw materials, transporting them, production sequencing, stock control, delivery to wholesalers or retailers, and so on.

Logistics depends on the provision of high-quality and timely information. As IT systems have become increasingly sophisticated, they have enabled modern developments in logistics to transform the operation of many industries.

Driving down costs

With the widespread use of containerisation and development of giant distribution companies, such as UPS and DHL, transporting materials and goods around the world has become much faster and much cheaper. Instead of having to make parts in-house, companies can now use the logistics industry to obtain them at lower cost elsewhere, often from the other side of the world.

With improved systems for ordering materials, and deliveries becoming more and more reliable, firms no longer need to keep large stocks of parts; they simply buy them as they need them. The same opportunity to save costs lies with the finished product: a company can keep lower levels of stocks when its own delivery mechanisms are more efficient.

The globalisation of logistics, with increasing use of the Internet, has resulted in a hugely complex logistics industry. Firms that were once solely concerned with delivery are now employed to manage companies' supply chains and achieve substantial cost savings for them.

Driving up revenues

Efficient logistics has not just resulted in lower costs. The flexibility it has given firms has allowed many to increase their sales.

Carrying lower levels of stocks and switching from supplier to supplier, with the process often being managed by a logistics company, can allow companies to change the products they offer more rapidly. They can be more responsive to consumer demand and thereby increase their sales.

A well-known example of a company benefiting from this approach is Primark. This low-cost fashion retailer focuses much more on buying, logistics and supply-chain management than on branding or advertising.

1. *What dangers are there in keeping stocks to a minimum and relying on complex supply chains?*
2. *Which industries do you think would benefit most from reduced transport times for their finished products? Think of an industry, other than low-cost fashion, which would benefit from the ability to switch rapidly the products offered.*

*LOOKING AT THE MATHS

We can state the short- and long-run shut-down points algebraically. Remember that total profit ($T\Pi$) is defined as

$$T\Pi = TR - TC = TR - (TFC + TVC) \qquad (1)$$

A negative value for $T\Pi$ means that the firm makes a loss. This will occur when

$$TR - (TFC + TVC) < 0$$

or

$$TR < (TFC + TVC)$$

But when should the firm shut down?

Short-run shut-down point

If the firm shuts down, TR and TVC will be zero, but in the short run it will still incur total fixed costs (TFC) and thus

$$T\Pi = -TFC \qquad (2)$$

In other words, it will make a loss equal to total fixed costs. From this it can be seen that the firm should close in the short run only if

$$T\Pi < -TFC$$

i.e.

$$(TR - TFC - TVC) < -TFC \qquad (3)$$

In other words, the loss should not exceed fixed costs. Put another way (i.e. by rearranging (3)), it should continue in production as long as

$$TR \geq TVC \qquad (4)$$

or, dividing both sides of (4) by quantity, where

$$AR \geq AVC \qquad (5)$$

The firm, therefore, should shut down if

$$AR < AVC$$

This is shown in Figure 6.23.

Long-run shut-down point

In the long run, there are no fixed costs. Thus

$$T\Pi = TR - TVC = TR - TC \qquad (6)$$

If the firm shuts down, it will earn no revenue, but incur no costs. Thus

$$T\Pi = TR - TC = 0 - 0 = 0$$

The firm should therefore continue in production as long as

$$(TR - TC) \geq 0$$

i.e.

$$TR \geq TC$$

or, dividing both sides by quantity, as long as

$$AR \geq AC$$

where AC in this case is long-run average cost. The firm, therefore, should shut down if

$$AR < AC$$

Section summary

1. Total profit equals total revenue minus total cost. By definition, then, a firm's profits will be maximised at the point where there is the greatest gap between total revenue and total cost.

2. Another way of finding the maximum profit point is to find the output where marginal revenue equals marginal cost. Having found this output, the level of maximum profit can be found by finding the average profit ($AR - AC$) and then multiplying it by the level of output.

3. Normal profit is the minimum profit that must be made to persuade a firm to stay in business in the long run. It is counted as part of the firm's costs. Supernormal profit is any profit over and above normal profit.

4. For a firm that cannot make a profit at any level of output, the point where $MR = MC$ represents the loss-minimising output.

5. In the short run, a firm will close down if it cannot cover its variable costs. In the long run, it will close down if it cannot make normal profits.

END OF CHAPTER QUESTIONS

1. The following table shows the average cost and average revenue (price) for a firm at each level of output.

Output	1	2	3	4	5	6	7	8	9	10
AC (£)	7.00	5.00	4.00	3.30	3.00	3.10	3.50	4.20	5.00	6.00
AR (£)	10.00	9.50	9.00	8.50	8.00	7.50	7.00	6.50	6.00	5.50

(a) Construct a table to show TC, MC, TR and MR at each level of output (put the figures for MC and MR midway between the output figures).

(b) Using MC and MR figures, find the profit-maximising output.

(c) Using TC and TR figures, check your answer to (b).

(d) Plot the AC, MC, AR and MR figures on a graph.

(e) Mark the profit-maximising output and the AR and AC at this output.

(f) Shade in an area to represent the level of profits at this output.

*2. Draw the isoquant corresponding to the following table, which shows the alternative combinations of labour and capital required to produce 100 units of output per day of good X.

K	16	20	26⅔	40	60	80	100
L	200	160	120	80	53⅓	40	32

(a) Assuming that capital costs are £20 per day and the wage rate is £10 per day, what is the least-cost method of producing 100 units? What will the daily total cost be? (Draw in a series of isocosts.)

(b) Now assume that the wage rate rises to £20 per day. Draw a new set of isocosts. What will be the least-cost method of producing 100 units now? How much labour and capital will be used?

3. Choose two industries that you believe are very different. Identify factors used in those industries that in the short run are (a) fixed; (b) variable.

4. Taking the same industries, identify as many economies of scale as you can.

5. 'Both short-run and long-run average cost curves may be ⌣-shaped, but the explanations for their respective shapes are quite different.' Explain this statement.

6. Why do marginal cost curves intersect both the average variable cost curve and the average cost curve at their lowest point?

7. Draw a diagram like that in Figure 6.21. Now illustrate the effect of a rise in demand for the product. Mark the new profit-maximising price and output. Will the profit-maximising output, price, average cost and profit necessarily be higher than before?

8. Why might it make sense for a firm which cannot sell its output at a profit to continue in production for the time being? For how long should the firm continue to produce at a loss?

Online resources

Additional case studies on the student website

6.1 Diminishing returns to nitrogen fertiliser. This case study provides a good illustration of diminishing returns in practice by showing the effects on grass yields of the application of increasing amounts of nitrogen fertiliser.

6.2 Deriving cost curves from total physical product information. This shows how total, average and marginal costs can be derived from total product information and the price of inputs.

6.3 Division of labour in a pin factory. This is the famous example of division of labour given by Adam Smith in his *Wealth of Nations* (1776).

6.4 Followers of fashion. This case study examines the effects of costs on prices of fashion-sensitive goods.

6.5 Putting on a duplicate. This examines the effects on marginal costs of additional passengers on a coach journey.

6.6 Comparing the behaviour of long-run and short-run costs. This is an application of isoquant analysis.

Maths Case 6.1 Total, average and marginal cost. Looking at the mathematical functions for these curves and deriving specific types of cost from a total cost equation.

Maths Case 6.2 Finding the optimum production point: Part 1. Examples using the method of substituting the constraint equation into the objective function.

Maths Case 6.3 Finding the optimum production point: Part 2. The same examples as in Maths Case 6.2, but this time using the Lagrangian methods.

Maths Case 6.4 Total, average and marginal revenue. Looking at the mathematical functions for these curves for both price-taking and price-making firms and relating them to revenue curves.

Websites relevant to this chapter

Numbers and sections refer to websites listed in the Web Appendix and hotlinked from this book's website at **www.pearsoned.co.uk/sloman.**

- For news articles relevant to this chapter, see the *Economics News* section on the student website.
- For student resources relevant to this chapter, see sites C1–7, 9, 10, 14, 19, 20 and 28.
- For a case study examining costs, see site D2.
- For sites that look at companies, their scale of operation and market share, see B2 (third link); E9, 10; G7, 8.
- For links to sites on various aspects of production and costs, see sites I7 and 11.

Profit Maximising under Perfect Competition and Monopoly

As we saw in Chapter 6, a firm's profits are maximised where its marginal cost equals its marginal revenue: $MC = MR$. But we will want to know more than this.

- What determines the amount of profit that a firm will make? Will profits be large, or just enough for the firm to survive, or so low that it will be forced out of business?
- Will the firm produce a high level of output or a low level?
- Will it be producing efficiently, making best use of resources?
- Will the price charged to the consumer be high or low?
- More generally, will the consumer and society as a whole benefit from the decisions a firm makes? This is, of course, a normative question (see section 1.3). Nevertheless, economists can still identify and analyse the wider effects of these decisions.

The answers to these questions largely depend on the amount of competition that a firm faces. A firm in a highly competitive environment will behave quite differently from a firm facing little or no competition. In particular, a firm facing competition from many other firms will be forced to keep its prices down and be as efficient as possible, simply to survive. If, however, the firm faces little or no competition (like a local water company or a major pharmaceutical company), it may have considerable power over prices, and we may end up paying considerably more as a result.

In this chapter and the next, we consider different types of market structure. Here we focus on the extremes: perfect competition (very many firms competing) and monopoly (only one firm in the industry).

7.1 ALTERNATIVE MARKET STRUCTURES

It is traditional to divide industries into categories according to the degree of competition that exists between the firms within the industry. There are four such categories.

At one extreme is **perfect competition**, where there are very many firms competing. Each firm is so small relative to the whole industry that it has no power to influence price. It is a price taker. At the other extreme is **monopoly**, where there is just one firm in the industry, and hence no competition from within the industry. In the middle come **monopolistic competition**, which involves quite a lot of firms competing and where there is freedom for new firms to enter the industry, and **oligopoly**, which involves only a few firms and where entry of new firms is restricted.

To distinguish more precisely between these four categories, the following must be considered:

- How freely firms can enter the industry. Is entry free or restricted? If it is restricted, just how great are the barriers to the entry of new firms?
- The nature of the product. Do all firms produce an identical product, or do firms produce their own particular brand or model or variety?
- The firm's degree of control over price. Is the firm a price taker or can it choose its price, and if so, how will changing its price affect its profits? What we are talking about here is the nature of the demand curve it faces. How elastic is it? If the firm puts up its price, will it lose (a) all its sales (a horizontal demand curve), or (b) a large proportion of its sales (a relatively elastic demand curve), or (c) just a small proportion of its sales (a relatively inelastic demand curve)?

KI 9
p66

KEY
IDEA
22

Market power. When firms have market power over prices, they can use this to raise prices and profits above the perfectly competitive level. Other things being equal, the firm will gain at the expense of the consumer. Similarly, if consumers or workers have market power, they can use this to their own benefit.

Table 7.1 shows the differences between the four categories.

1. *Give two more examples in each category.*
2. *Would you expect builders and restaurateurs to have the same degree of control over price?*

The market structure under which a firm operates will determine its behaviour. Firms under perfect competition will behave quite differently from firms which are monopolists, which will behave differently again from firms under oligopoly or monopolistic competition.

TC 5
p50

This behaviour (or 'conduct') will in turn affect the firm's performance: its prices, profits, efficiency, etc. In many cases,

it will also affect other firms' performance: *their* prices, profits, efficiency, etc. The collective conduct of all the firms in the industry will affect the whole industry's performance.

Economists thus see a causal chain running from market structure to the performance of that industry.

Structure → *Conduct* → *Performance*

First we shall look at the two extreme market structures: perfect competition and monopoly. Then in Chapter 8 we shall look at the two intermediate cases of monopolistic competition and oligopoly.

The two intermediate cases are sometimes referred to collectively as **imperfect competition**. The vast majority of firms in the real world operate under imperfect competition. It is still worth studying the two extreme cases, however, because they provide a framework within which to understand the real world. Some industries tend more to the competitive extreme, and thus the behaviour and performance of firms with these industries corresponds more closely to the predictions of perfect competition. Other industries tend more to the other extreme: for example, when there is one dominant firm and a few much smaller firms. In such cases, the behaviour and performance of firms corresponds more closely to the predictions of monopoly.

Chapters 7 and 8 assume that firms, under whatever market structure, are attempting to maximise profits. Chapter 9 questions this assumption. It looks at alternative theories of the firm: theories based on assumptions *other* than profit maximising.

Definitions

Perfect competition A market structure where there are many firms, none of which is large; where there is freedom of entry into the industry; where all firms produce an identical product; and where all firms are price takers.

Monopoly A market structure where there is only one firm in the industry. (Note that this is the economic definition of a pure monopoly. In UK competition law, the part that applies to the abuse of monopoly power covers firms that are in a position of 'market dominance'. Such firms will have a large share, but not necessarily a 100 per cent share of the market. See Chapter 14 for more on this.)

Monopolistic competition A market structure where, as with perfect competition, there are many firms and freedom of entry into the industry, but where each firm produces a differentiated product and thus has some control over its price.

Oligopoly A market structure where there are few enough firms to enable barriers to be erected against the entry of new firms.

Imperfect competition The collective name for monopolistic competition and oligopoly.

Table 7.1	Features of the four market structures				
Type of market	Number of firms	Freedom of entry	Nature of product	Examples	Implication for demand curve for firm
Perfect competition	Very many	Unrestricted	Homogeneous (undifferentiated)	Cabbages, carrots, foreign exchange (these approximate to perfect competition)	Horizontal. The firm is a price taker
Monopolistic competition	Many/several	Unrestricted	Differentiated	Builders, restaurants, hairdressers, garage mechanics	Downward sloping, but relatively elastic. The firm has some control over price
Oligopoly	Few	Restricted	1. Undifferentiated 2. Differentiated	1. Petrol, cement 2. Cars, electrical appliances, supermarkets, retail banking	Downward sloping, relatively inelastic but depends on reactions of rivals to a price change
Monopoly	One	Restricted or completely blocked	Unique	Prescription drugs produced under a patent, local water companies	Downward sloping, more inelastic than oligopoly. The firm has considerable control over price

7.2 PERFECT COMPETITION

Assumptions of perfect competition

The model of perfect competition is built on four assumptions:

- Firms are *price takers*. There are so many firms in the industry that each one produces an insignificantly small portion of total industry supply, and therefore has no power whatsoever to affect the price of the product. It faces a horizontal demand 'curve' at the market price: the price determined by the interaction of demand and supply in the whole market.
- There is complete *freedom of entry* into the industry for new firms. Existing firms are unable to stop new firms setting up in business. Setting up a business takes time, however. Freedom of entry, therefore, applies in the long run.
- All firms produce an *identical product*. (The product is 'homogeneous'.) There is therefore no branding and no advertising, since there would be no point in the firm incurring this cost.
- Producers and consumers have *perfect knowledge* of the market. Producers are fully aware of prices, costs and market opportunities. Consumers are fully aware of the price, quality and availability of the product.

These assumptions are very strict. Few, if any, industries in the real world meet these conditions. Certain agricultural markets are perhaps closest to perfect competition. The market for fresh vegetables is an example.

Nevertheless, despite the lack of real-world cases, the model of perfect competition plays a very important role in economic analysis and policy. Its major relevance is as an 'ideal type' for society. Many argue that achieving perfect competition would bring a number of important advantages, such as keeping prices down to marginal cost and preventing firms from making supernormal profit over the long run. The model can thus be used as a standard against which to judge the shortcomings of real-world industries. However, we will also see that it has disadvantages, when compared with other market structures.

1. *It is sometimes claimed that the market for various stocks and shares is perfectly competitive, or nearly so. Take the case of the market for shares in a large company like Apple. Go through each of the four assumptions above and see if they apply in this case. (Don't be misled by the first assumption. The 'firm' in this case is not Apple itself.)*
2. *Is the market for gold perfectly competitive?*

TC 9
p129

BOX 7.1   CONCENTRATION RATIOS

EXPLORING ECONOMICS

Measuring the degree of competition

We can get some indication of how competitive a market is by observing the number of firms: the more the firms, the more competitive the market would seem to be. However, this does not tell us anything about how *concentrated* the market might be. There may be *many* firms (suggesting a situation of perfect competition or monopolistic competition), but the largest two firms might produce 95 per cent of total output. This would make these two firms more like oligopolists.

Thus, even though a large number of producers may make the market *seem* highly competitive, this could be deceiving. Another approach, therefore, to measuring the degree of competition is to focus on the level of concentration of firms.

Firm concentration ratios for various industries (by output)

Industry	5-firm ratio	15-firm ratio
Sugar	99	99
Tobacco products	99	99
Oils and fats	88	95
Confectionery	81	91
Gas distribution	82	87
Soft drinks, mineral water	75	93
Postal/courier services	65	75
Telecommunications	61	75
Inorganic chemicals	57	80
Pharmaceuticals	57	74
Alcoholic beverages	50	78
Soap and toiletries	40	64
Accountancy services	36	47
Motor vehicles	34	54
Glass and glass products	26	49
Fishing	16	19
Advertising	10	20
Wholesale distribution	6	11
Furniture	5	13
Construction	5	9

Source: Based on data in *United Kingdom Input–Output Analyses*, 2006 edition (National Statistics, 2006), Table 8.31.

The simplest measure of industrial concentration involves adding together the market share of the largest so many firms: e.g. the largest 3, 5 or 15. This would give what is known as the '3-firm', '5-firm' or '15-firm' 'concentration ratio'. There are different ways of estimating market share: by revenue, by output, by profit, etc.

The table shows the 5-firm and 15-firm concentration ratios of selected industries in the UK by output. As you can see, there is an enormous variation in the degree of concentration from one industry to another.

One of the main reasons for this is differences in the percentage of total industry output at which economies of scale are exhausted. If this occurs at a low level of output, there will be room for several firms in the industry which are all benefiting from the maximum economies of scale.

The degree of concentration will also depend on the barriers to entry of other firms into the industry (see pages 201–4) and on various factors such as transport costs and historical accident. It will also depend on how varied the products are within any one industrial category. For example, in categories as large as furniture and construction there is room for many firms, each producing a specialised range of products.

So is the degree of concentration a good guide to the degree of competitiveness of the industry? The answer is that it is *some* guide, but on its own it can be misleading. In particular, it ignores the degree of competition from abroad.

1. What are the advantages and disadvantages of using a 5-firm concentration ratio rather than a 15-firm, a 3-firm or even a 1-firm ratio?
2. Why are some industries, such as bread baking and brewing, relatively concentrated, in that a few firms produce a large proportion of total output (see Box 7.2 and Case Study 7.4 on the student website), and yet there are also many small producers?

The short run and the long run

Before we can examine what price, output and profits will be, we must first distinguish between the short run and the long run as they apply to perfect competition.

In the **short run**, the number of firms is fixed. Depending on its costs and revenue, a firm might be making large profits, small profits, no profits or a loss; and in the short run, it may continue to do so.

In the **long run**, however, the level of profits affects entry and exit from the industry. If supernormal profits are made (see page 184), new firms will be attracted into the industry, whereas if losses are being made, firms will leave.

Note that although we shall be talking about the *level* of profit (since that makes our analysis of pricing and output decisions simpler to understand), in practice it is usually the

rate of profit that determines whether a firm stays in the industry or leaves. The **rate of profit** (*r*) is the level of profit ($T\Pi$) as *a proportion of the level of capital (K) employed*: $r = T\Pi/K$. If $T\Pi$ is measured as profit before tax and interest payments, *r* is

Definitions

Short run under perfect competition The period during which there is insufficient time for new firms to enter the industry.

Long run under perfect competition The period of time that is long enough for new firms to enter the industry.

Rate of profit Total profit ($T\Pi$) as a proportion of the capital employed (*K*): $r = T\Pi/K$. Often measured by using ROCE in the real world.

BOX 7.2   IS PERFECT BEST?

Be careful of the word 'perfect'.

'Perfect competition' refers to competition that is complete. Perhaps 'complete competition' would be a better term. There is a complete absence of power, a complete absence of entry barriers, a complete absence of product differentiation between producers, and complete information for producers and consumers on the market. It is thus useful for understanding the effects of power, barriers, product differentiation and lack of information.

Perfect does not mean 'best', however.

Just because it is at the extreme end of the competition spectrum, it does not follow that perfect competition is desirable. After all, you could have a perfect killer virus – i.e. one that is totally immune to drugs, and against which humans have no natural protection at all. Such a thing, though perfect, is hardly desirable.

To say that perfect competition is desirable and that it is a goal towards which government policy should be directed are normative statements. Economists, in their role as economists, cannot make such statements.

This does not mean, of course, that economists cannot identify the effects of perfect competition, but whether these effects are *desirable* or not is an ethical question.

The danger is that by using perfect competition as a yardstick, and by using the word 'perfect' rather than 'complete', economists may be surreptitiously persuading their audience that perfect competition is a goal we *ought* to be striving to achieve.

---

referred to as the return on capital employed (ROCE). As you would expect, larger firms will need to make a larger *total* profit to persuade them to stay in an industry. Total normal profit is thus larger for them than for a small firm. The *rate* of normal profit, however, will probably be similar.

1. Why do economists treat normal profit as a cost of production?
2. What determines (a) the level and (b) the rate of normal profit for a particular firm?

Thus whether the industry expands or contracts in the long run will depend on the rate of profit. Naturally, since the time a firm takes to set up in business varies from industry to industry, the length of time before the long run is reached also varies from industry to industry.

The short-run equilibrium of the firm

The determination of price, output and profit in the short run under perfect competition can best be shown in a diagram.

Figure 7.1 shows a short-run equilibrium for both an industry and a firm under perfect competition. Both parts of the diagram have the same scale for the vertical axis. The horizontal axes have totally different scales, however. For example, if the horizontal axis for the firm were measured in, say, thousands of units, the horizontal axis for the whole industry might be measured in millions or tens of millions of units, depending on the number of firms in the industry.

Let us examine the determination of price, output and profit in turn.

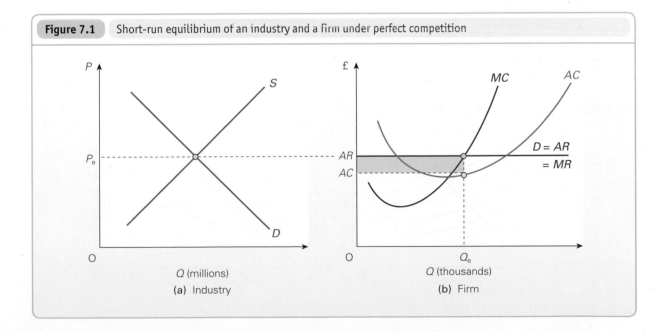

Figure 7.1   Short-run equilibrium of an industry and a firm under perfect competition

(a) Industry

(b) Firm

Price. The price is determined in the industry by the intersection of demand and supply. The firm faces a horizontal demand (or average revenue) 'curve' at this price. It can sell all it can produce at the market price (P_e), but nothing at a price above P_e.

Output. The firm will maximise profit where marginal cost equals marginal revenue ($MR = MC$), at an output of Q_e. Note that, since the price is not affected by the firm's output, marginal revenue will equal price (see pages 177–8 and Figure 6.15).

Profit. If the average cost (AC) curve (which includes normal profit) dips below the average revenue (AR) 'curve', the firm will earn supernormal profit. Supernormal profit per unit at Q_e is the vertical difference between AR and AC at Q_e. Total supernormal profit is the shaded rectangle in Figure 7.1.

What happens if the firm cannot make a profit at *any* level of output? This situation would occur if the AC curve were above the AR curve at all points. This is illustrated in Figure 7.2, where the market price is P_1. In this case, the point where $MC = MR$ represents the *loss-minimising* point (where loss is defined as anything less than normal profit). The amount of the loss is represented by the shaded rectangle.

As we saw in section 6.6, whether the firm is prepared to continue making a loss in the short run or whether it will close down immediately depends on whether it can cover its *variable* costs – assuming all fixed costs are also sunk costs.

Provided price is above average variable cost (AVC), the firm will still continue producing in the short run: it can pay its variable costs and go some way to paying its fixed costs. It will shut down in the short run only if the market price falls below P_2 in Figure 7.2.

The firm's short-run supply curve
The *firm's* short-run supply curve will be a section of its (short-run) marginal cost curve.

A supply curve shows how much will be supplied at each price: it relates quantity to price. The marginal cost curve relates quantity to marginal cost. But under perfect competition, given that $P = MR$, and $MR = MC$, P must equal MC. Thus the supply curve and the MC curve will follow the same line.

For example, in Figure 7.3(b), if price were P_1, profits would be maximised at Q_1 where $P_1 = MC$. Thus point *a* is one point on the supply curve. At a price of P_2, Q_2 would be produced. Thus point *b* is another point on the supply curve, and so on.

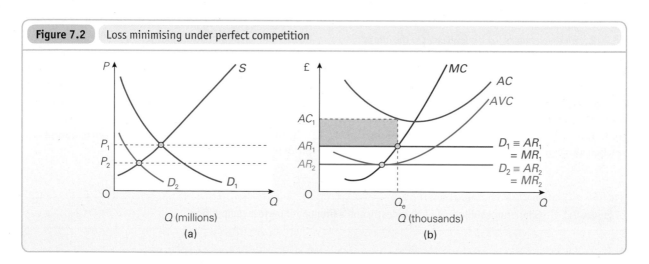

Figure 7.2   Loss minimising under perfect competition

(a) Q (millions)

(b) Q (thousands)

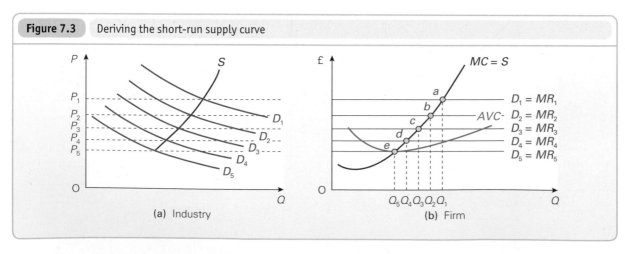

Figure 7.3   Deriving the short-run supply curve

(a) Industry

(b) Firm

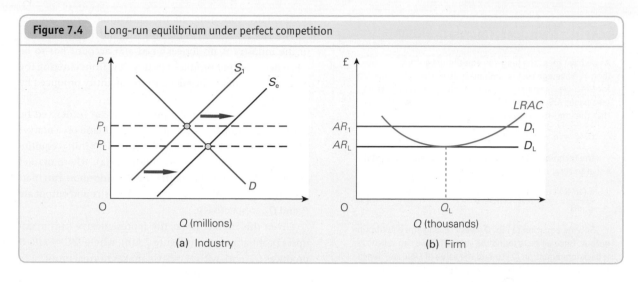

Figure 7.4 Long-run equilibrium under perfect competition

(a) Industry

(b) Firm

So, under perfect competition, the firm's supply curve is entirely dependent on costs of production. This demonstrates why the firm's supply curve is upward sloping. Given that marginal costs rise as output rises (due to diminishing marginal returns), a higher price will be necessary to induce the firm to increase its output.

Note that, assuming all fixed costs are also sunk costs, the firm will not produce at a price below AVC. Thus the supply curve is only that portion of the MC curve above point e.

The short-run industry supply curve

What is the short-run supply curve of the whole *industry*? This shows the total quantity supplied by all the firms already in the industry at each possible price. It does not include the output produced by any new entrants as this would only apply in the long run. To calculate short-run industry supply at any price we simply add up how much each individual firm wants to supply at that price. For example, if there were 100 firms in the market which all wanted to supply 10 units at a price of £5, then the market supply at £5 would be 1000. To derive the industry supply curve, therefore, we simply sum the short-run supply curves (and hence MC curves) of all the firms already in the industry. Graphically this will be a *horizontal* sum, since it is only the *quantities* that are added at each price.

 Will the industry supply be zero below a price of P_5 in Figure 7.3?

The long-run equilibrium of the firm

TC 5
p50 In the long run, if typical firms are making supernormal profits, new firms will be attracted into the industry. Likewise, if established firms can make supernormal profits by increasing the scale of their operations, they will do so, since all factors of production are variable in the long run.

The effect of the entry of new firms and/or the expansion of existing firms is to increase industry supply. This is

illustrated in Figure 7.4. At a price of P_1 supernormal profits are earned. This causes industry supply to expand (the short-run industry supply curve shifts to the right). This in turn leads to a fall in price. Supply will go on increasing and price falling until firms are making only normal profits. This will be when price has fallen to the point where the demand 'curve' for the firm just touches the bottom of its long-run average cost curve. Q_L is thus the long-run equilibrium output of the firm, with P_L the long-run equilibrium price.

 Illustrate on a diagram similar to Figure 7.4 what would happen in the long run if price were initially below P_L.

Since the $LRAC$ curve is tangential to all possible short-run AC curves (see section 5.4), the full long-run equilibrium will be as shown in Figure 7.5 where

$$LRAC = AC = MC = MR = AR$$

Figure 7.5 Long-run equilibrium of the firm under perfect competition

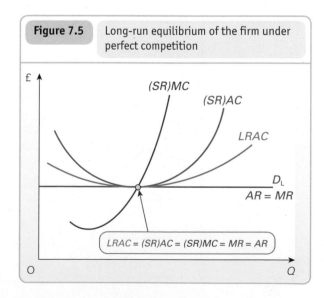

$$LRAC = (SR)AC = (SR)MC = MR = AR$$

As we have seen, the long-run equilibrium output is where long-run average cost is minimised. If we know the equation for *LRAC*, we can simply use the techniques of minimisation (see pages A:9–13) to find the equilibrium output. Assume that the long-run average cost function is

$$LRAC = a - bQ + cQ^2$$

The technique is to differentiate this function and set it equal to zero, i.e.

$$\frac{d\,(LRAC)}{dQ} = -b + 2cQ = 0 \qquad \textbf{(1)}$$

Solving equation (1) for Q gives the long-run equilibrium output. Once we have found the value of Q, we can substitute it back into equation (1) to find the value of *LRAC* and hence the equilibrium price (since $P = LRAC$).

We can then use the second derivative test (see page A:12) to check that this indeed does represent a minimum, not a maximum, *LRAC*. An example of this is given in Maths Case 7.1 on the student website.

The firm's long-run supply curve

The firm's long-run supply curve is derived in a very similar way to the firm's short-run supply curve. The major difference is that, in the long run, the firm can adjust all of its inputs. This means that all of its costs are now variable and hence the long-run average cost curve is the same as long-run average variable cost curve. Therefore, the firm's long-run supply curve is the portion of its long-run marginal cost curve above the point where it is cut by the average cost curve. At prices below this level it would be loss minimising for the firm to produce zero.

The long-run industry supply curve

The long-run industry supply curve cannot be derived in the same way as the short-run industry supply curve: i.e. by

horizontally summing all the individual firms' supply curves. This is because, in the long run, the number of firms in the industry is no longer fixed and account has to be taken of the output produced by any new firms entering the industry. This has to be added to the quantity produced by existing firms.

The long-run industry supply curve can be derived by analysing the impact of an increase in demand on a market that is initially in long-run equilibrium. This initial equilibrium is shown at point a in Figure 7.6(a), where market demand (D_{M_1}) is equal to both long-run and short-run market supply (LRS_M and SRS_{M_1}). The market price and output are P_1 and Q_{M_1} respectively.

Given this market price, the representative firm maximises profit at point x in Figure 7.6(b), where $MC = MR$. It produces Q_{F_1} and, with $P_1 = AC_1$, makes normal profit.

Assume now that the market demand curve increases from D_{M_1} to D_{M_2}. Firms in the market respond to the higher prices by increasing production. The market equilibrium in the short run moves from point a to point b – a movement up along the short-run market supply curve (SRS_{M_1}). The market price and quantity increase to P_2 and Q_{M_2}.

Given this new higher market price of P_2, the profit-maximising response of the representative firm is to move upwards along its supply or MC curve from point x to point y. Its output increases from Q_{F_1} to Q_{F_2} and, as the price is now greater than the firm's average cost, it makes supernormal profit.

In the long run, this supernormal profit will act as a signal to entrepreneurs and new firms will enter the market. The arrival of new entrants will cause the short-run market supply curve to shift to the right (to SRS_{M_2}), putting downward pressure on the market price.

Not only will the new entrants affect the market for the final product, they will also have an impact on the various markets for different factors of production. For example, the demand for raw materials required to produce the good will increase as new entrants and existing firms try to purchase

---

Figure 7.6   Long-run industry supply curve (increasing cost industry)

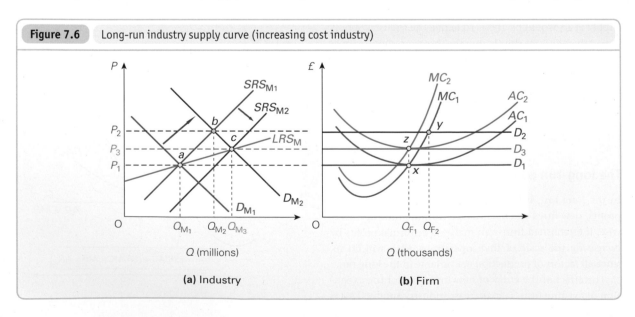

(a) Industry

(b) Firm

them. This might put upward pressure on the prices of various input prices, such as raw materials, energy, labour and physical capital. If the price of factor inputs does rise, this will cause the firm's AC and MC curves in Figure 7.6(b) to shift upwards: e.g. from AC_1 to AC_2 and MC_1 to MC_2.

Given this rise in the costs of production, new firms will stop entering the industry once the short-run industry supply curve has shifted to SRS_{M_2}. The new long-run market equilibrium is at point c with the price falling back to P_3 and industry output increasing to Q_{M_3}. At the new lower market price of P_3 the firm will maximise profits at point z. The market price is now equal to the firm's new higher AC curve (AC_2) – profits have returned to the normal level. There is thus no longer any incentive for other firms to enter the industry.

The long-run market supply curve (LRS_M) goes through points a and c: i.e. the two positions of long-run equilibrium.

Increasing cost industry – upward-sloping long-run supply curve. In the example in Figure 7.6, the long-run industry supply curve is upward sloping because the extra demand for factor inputs generated by new entrants puts upward pressure on their prices. This is referred to as an ***increasing-cost industry*** (i.e. where there are external diseconomies of scale – see page 164). It is likely to occur when the demand for factor inputs from firms within one industry make up a relatively large proportion of the total demand for those inputs. This is more likely when most of the factor inputs are industry specific: i.e. specialist capital equipment tailored to the production of a particular good. In these circumstances, any increase in demand from new entrants will have a significant impact on the total demand for the inputs, making an increase in their price more probable.

Constant-cost industry – horizontal long-run supply curve. In some industries the majority of factor inputs will be far less specialised. Take the example of an input such as electricity. The demand for electricity from firms in a particular industry will be small relative to the total demand for electricity across the whole economy. If the demand from new entrants in one industry increased, it is unlikely to affect the market price of electricity. If this was true for all factor inputs used by firms then it would be a ***constant-cost industry***. As new firms entered, the average total cost curve of the individual firms would remain unchanged. A constant-cost industry would have a horizontal long-run industry supply curve.

Decreasing-cost industry – downward-sloping long-run supply curve. Another possibility is that increasing demand from new entrants within the industry causes the price of factor inputs to decrease. This is called a ***decreasing-cost industry***. It can occur when the increased demand for inputs enables the suppliers of these inputs to exploit internal economies of scale. It can also occur when firms in the industry share

common transport, training or other infrastructure. These external economies of scale (see page 164) cause the cost curves in Figure 7.6(b) to shift downwards. A decreasing-cost industry will therefore have a downward-sloping long-run industry supply curve.

 Use a diagram similar to Figure 7.6 to derive a long-run market supply curve for (a) a constant-cost industry; (b) a decreasing-cost industry.

The incompatibility of perfect competition and substantial economies of scale

Why is perfect competition so rare in the real world – if it even exists at all? One important reason for this has to do with economies of scale.

In many industries, firms may have to be quite large if they are to experience the full potential economies of scale. But perfect competition requires there to be *many* firms and that each one is a price taker. Firms must therefore be small under perfect competition: too small in most cases for economies of scale.

Once a firm expands sufficiently to achieve economies of scale, it will usually gain market power. It will be able to undercut the prices of smaller firms, which will thus be driven out of business. Perfect competition is destroyed.

Perfect competition could only exist in any industry, therefore, if there were no (or virtually no) economies of scale.

 1. What other reasons can you think of why perfect competition is so rare?
2. Why does the market for fresh vegetables approximate to perfect competition, whereas that for aircraft does not?

Perfect competition and the public interest

Benefits of perfect competition
There are a number of features of perfect competition which, it could be argued, benefit society:

■ Price equals marginal cost. As we shall see in Chapter 12, this has important implications for the allocation of resources between alternative products. Given that price equals marginal utility (see Chapter 4), marginal utility will equal marginal cost. This is argued to be an *optimal* position.

TC 8
p109

| BOX 7.3 | E-COMMERCE AND MARKET STRUCTURE |

Has technology shifted market power?

The relentless drive towards big business over the decades has seen many markets become more concentrated and dominated by large producers. And yet there are forces that undermine this dominance, bringing more competition to markets. One of these forces is *e-commerce*.

In this case study, we will consider the impact of e-commerce on the competitive environment and market power.

What do we mean by e-commerce?

E-commerce or e-shopping is a shorthand term for buying and selling products through electronic means, in most cases through the Internet. It has grown rapidly in the last 10 years and shows no sign of slowing down. The chart shows the rise in online retail sales as a proportion of all retail sales in the UK between 2007 and 2016. Note that the proportion of Internet sales rises each year in the run-up to Christmas as many people buy gifts online.

According to the EU's 2016 survey on *ICT usage and e-commerce in enterprises*,[1] approximately two-thirds of Internet users in the EU had purchased a good online in the previous 12 months. The figure was highest in the UK at 83 per cent. The most popular products purchased online were clothes/sports goods, tickets for events and books. Unsurprisingly, the fastest growth in the use of e-shopping has occurred amongst 16–24-year-olds.

Moving markets back towards perfect competition?

In an article published in the *Economist*[2] in 2000 it was stated that 'the internet cuts costs, increases competition and improves the functioning of the price mechanism. It thus moves the economy closer to the textbook model of perfect competition, which assumes abundant information, zero transaction costs and no barriers to entry'.

To see if this is true, let's look at the assumptions of this market structure.

Large numbers of buyers and sellers. The growth of e-commerce has led to many new firms starting up in business. The majority of these are small companies that often sell directly to consumers via their own websites or use online marketplaces such as eBay or Amazon. In 2016, eBay had approximately 160 million active buyers and 25 million active sellers, while Amazon had approximately 310 million active customers and 2 million third-party sellers. Approximately 50 per cent of the units shipped by Amazon are goods sold by a third-party seller.

The global reach of the Internet increases the potential number of buyers and sellers that can trade with one another. For example, in 2016, 32 per cent of consumers in the EU who purchased online did so from sellers in other member states, while 20 per cent purchased from sellers outside of the EU.

Perfect knowledge. The Internet has significantly reduced some of the transaction costs of using a market. Consumers can easily compare the prices and other features of the goods they are interested in purchasing by using search engines, such as Google Shopping, NexTag and PriceGrabber. Indeed, it is common to see people in shops (physical shops in this case) browsing competitors' prices on their mobile phones. This places the high street retailer under intense competitive pressure. Interestingly, four of the top five online retailers in the UK in 2016 – Tesco, Argos, John Lewis, Next – also have physical shops. Success for some firms now means having both physical and online stores.

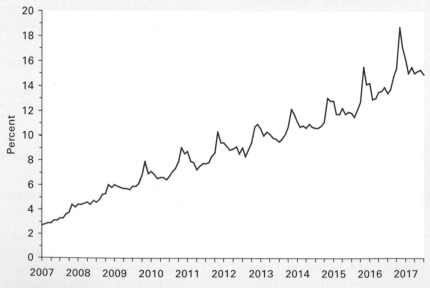

Value of Internet retail sales as a percentage of total retail sales

Source: Based on series J4MC from *Time Series Data* (National Statistics).

Although the competitive pressures seem to have increased in 'B2C' (business-to consumers) e-commerce the impact may be even greater in 'B2B' (business-to-business) e-commerce. Many firms are constantly searching for cheaper sources of supply, and the Internet provides a cheap and easy means of conducting such searches.

Freedom of entry   Internet companies often have lower start-up costs than their conventional rivals. Their premises are generally much smaller, with no 'shop-front' costs and lower levels of stockholding; in fact many of these businesses are initially operated from their owners' homes and garages with little more required than a computer and good Wi-Fi connection. An e-commerce website for the business can be set up in a matter of hours. Marketing costs will also be lower if the new entrant's website can easily be located by a consumer using a search engine.

Internet companies are often smaller and more specialist, relying on Internet 'outsourcing' (buying parts, equipment and other supplies through the Internet), rather than making everything themselves. They are also more likely to use delivery firms rather than having their own transport fleet. All this can make it relatively cheap for new firms to set up and begin trading over the Internet.

One consequence of the rise in e-commerce is that the distinction between firms and consumers has become increasingly blurred. With the rise of online marketplaces such as eBay and Amazon, more and more people have found going into business incredibly easy. Some people sell products they produce at home, while others specialise in selling-on products using the marketing power of these online marketplaces.

Not only do these factors make markets more price competitive, they can also bring other benefits. Costs might be driven down as firms economise on stockholding, rely more on outsourcing and develop more efficient relationships with suppliers.

What are the limits to e-commerce?

In 20 years, will the majority of us be doing all our shopping on the Internet? Will the only shopping malls be virtual ones? Although e-commerce is revolutionising markets, it is unlikely that things will go that far.

One of the key benefits of shopping in physical shops is that you get to see the good, touch it and possibly try it out before buying. You can buy the good there and then and take instant possession: you don't have to wait. Although you can order things online and often get next-day delivery, it is not quite the same as instant possession.

Furthermore, shopping can be an enjoyable experience. Many people like wandering round the shops, meeting friends, trying on clothes, playing with the latest electronic gadgets, and so on. 'Retail therapy' can be a pleasurable leisure activity and one that some people are willing to pay for in the form of higher prices.

Rather than traditional and online shopping being seen as alternatives for one another, there is an increasing tendency for people to see them as complementary. Many people go onto the High Street, try on clothes and try out electronic appliances before going home to order them on the Internet. This enables consumers to get the best possible prices, while also having more certainty about the characteristics of the product they are purchasing.

The extent to which people can use online shopping may be limited by current technology and infrastructure. Although the quality of Internet access has significantly improved as broadband has become widely available, online purchases might still be hampered by busy sites that cannot effectively handle the number of users.

Some consumers may also be deterred by fears that delivery of the product will be late or fail completely. Research by Citizens Advice[3] found that, in 2015/16, people experienced problems with 4.8 million deliveries and spent 11.8 million hours trying to sort out any issues. Consumers had difficulty making contact with the relevant company to find out exactly where their missing parcel had gone and in many situations did not know who was responsible for sorting out any problems.

A final constraint on the spread of online shopping is that access to a credit or debit card is often required to make a purchase. This option might not be available to everyone, particularly younger consumers and those on lower incomes.

Increasing market power

There are some concerns that the rise of e-commerce could actually reduce competition and result in the growth of more firms with substantial market power. Greater price transparency could actually result in *less* competition. For example, sellers may have previously reduced their prices in the belief that they could make extra sales before their competitors responded. However, the greater price transparency provided by the Internet means that rivals are able to spot price changes and respond more quickly. This reduces the incentive for some firms to reduce their prices in the first place.

If firms can more easily monitor their rivals' pricing behaviour, it might also increase the likelihood of price-fixing agreements. The topic of collusion will be discussed in more detail in Chapter 8.

It was previously explained how the marketing costs for start-ups in e-commerce might be lower than those in more traditional retailing. However, simply creating a website is not enough to make online businesses successful – potential customers also have to visit them. New firms might have to spend considerable amounts of money on marketing to increase consumers' awareness of their brands and websites. The majority of this expenditure could be a sunk cost and so would act as a significant barrier to entry. Promotional costs might be reduced if the new entrant's website was listed on a search engine's results page. However, customers are most likely to visit the links that appear towards the top of the results page. These will be

(continued)

those with the greatest number of hits, which are likely to be the more established firms.

Although comparison websites increase price transparency they could also result in consumers paying higher prices. Many of these websites make considerable profits. They earn revenue by charging a fee every time a customer is referred to a listed firm's website via the price comparison website. These fees add to costs and could result in firms charging higher prices. One important issue is the size of the fee. If consumers only use one price comparison website it would have considerable market power and the ability to charge listed firms high fees.

If users build up a familiarity and knowledge of using a particular website it might create switching costs. Consumers are then less likely to visit other rival websites and so this reduces competition.

There may also be significant economies of scale in logistics: i.e. the storage, packaging and shipping of the products to the consumer. Amazon has invested heavily in automating its distribution centres using Kiva robots. This type of capital investment will only reduce a firm's average costs if it sells a large volume of products. Interestingly, the

Head of Amazon UK stated in 2004 that 'one of the greatest myths in the 1990s was there are no barriers to entry in e-commerce'.

There is no doubt that e-commerce is here to stay in all sectors. Many large companies recognise that their retail outlets have effectively become display space for their online activities. It will be interesting to see if the continued growth of e-commerce results in either increasing competition or more market power.

1. *Why may the Internet work better for replacement buys than for new purchases?*
2. *Give three examples of products that are particularly suitable for selling over the Internet and three that are not. Explain your answer.*
3. *As Amazon has grown in size it has acquired substantial monopoly power. What are the barriers to entry for other companies wishing to act as a marketplace for B2C and B2B business?*

1 *Community Survey on ICT Usage in Enterprises* (Europa, 2016).
2 'A thinkers' guide', *The Economist*, 30 March 2000.
3 'Shoppers will spend two and a half hours sorting out a delivery problem this Christmas', *Citizens Advice Press Release*, 7 December 2016.

To demonstrate why, consider what would happen if they were not equal. If price were greater than marginal cost, this would mean that consumers were putting a higher value ($P = MU$) on the production of extra units than they cost to produce (MC). Therefore more ought to be produced. If price were less than marginal cost, consumers would be putting a lower value on extra units than they cost to produce. Therefore less ought to be produced. When they are equal, therefore, production levels are just right. But, as we shall see later, it is only under perfect competition that $MC = P$.

- Long-run equilibrium is at the bottom of the firm's long-run *AC* curve. That is, for any *given* technology, the firm, in the long run, will produce at the least-cost output.
- Perfect competition is a case of 'survival of the fittest'. Inefficient firms will be driven out of business, since they will not be able to make even normal profits. This encourages firms to be as efficient as possible.
- The combination of (long-run) production being at minimum average cost and the firm making only normal profit keeps prices at a minimum.
- If consumer tastes change, the resulting price change will lead firms to respond (purely out of self-interest). An increased consumer demand will result in extra supply with only a short-run increase in profit.

Because of these last two points, perfect competition is said to lead to **consumer sovereignty**. Consumers, through the market, determine what and how much is to be produced. Firms have no power to manipulate the market. They cannot control price. The only thing they can do to increase profit is to become more efficient, and that benefits the consumer too.

Definition

Consumer sovereignty A situation where firms respond to changes in consumer demand without being in a position in the long run to charge a price above average cost.

Possible disadvantages of perfect competition

Even under perfect competition, however, the free market has various limitations. For example, there is no guarantee that the goods produced will be distributed to the members of society in the *fairest* proportions. There may be considerable inequality of income. (We examine this issue in Chapter 10.) What is more, a redistribution of income would lead to a different pattern of consumption and hence production. Thus there is no guarantee that perfect competition will lead to the optimum combination of goods being produced when society's views on equity are taken into account.

Another limitation is that the production of certain goods may lead to various undesirable side effects, such as pollution. Perfect competition cannot safeguard against this either.

What is more, perfect competition may be less desirable than other market structures such as monopoly.

- Even though firms under perfect competition may seem to have an incentive to develop new technology (in order to gain supernormal profits, albeit temporarily), the long-run normal profits they make may not be sufficient to fund the necessary research and development. Also, with complete information available, if they did develop new, more efficient methods of production, their rivals would merely copy them, in which case the investment would have been a waste of money.

■ Perfectly competitive industries produce undifferentiated products. This lack of variety might be seen as a disadvantage to the consumer. Under monopolistic competition and oligopoly there is often intense competition over the quality and design of the product. This can lead to innovation and improvements that would not exist under perfect competition. The issue of the efficiency or otherwise of perfect markets and the various failings of real-world markets is examined in more detail in Chapters 12–14.

Section summary

1. The assumptions of perfect competition are: a very large number of firms, complete freedom of entry, a homogeneous product and perfect knowledge of the good and its market on the part of both producers and consumers.

2. In the short run, there is not time for new firms to enter the market, and thus supernormal profits can persist. In the long run, however, any supernormal profits will be competed away by the entry of new firms.

3. The short-run equilibrium for the firm will be where the price, as determined by demand and supply in the market, is equal to marginal cost. At this output, the firm will be maximising profit. The firm's short-run supply curve is the same as its marginal cost curve (that portion of it above the *AVC* curve).

4. The long-run equilibrium will be where the market price is just equal to firms' long-run average cost. The long-run industry supply curve will thus depend on what happens to firms' *LRAC* curves as industry output expands. If their *LRAC* curves shift upwards due to increasing industry costs (external diseconomies of scale), the long-run industry supply curve will slope upwards. If their *LRAC* curves shift downwards due to decreasing industry costs (external economies of scale), the long-run industry supply curve will slope downwards.

5. There are no substantial (internal) economies of scale to be gained by perfectly competitive firms. If there were, the industry would cease to be perfectly competitive as the large, low-cost firms drove the small, high-cost ones out of business.

6. Under perfect competition, production will be at the point where $P = MC$. This can be argued to be optimal. Perfect competition can act as a spur to efficiency and bring benefits to the consumer in terms of low costs and low prices.

7. On the other hand, perfectly competitive firms may be unwilling to invest in research and development or may have insufficient funds to do so. They may also produce a lack of variety of goods. Finally, perfect competition does not necessarily lead to a fair distribution of income or guarantee an absence of harmful side effects of production.

7.3 MONOPOLY

What is a monopoly?

This may seem a strange question because the answer seems obvious. A monopoly exists when there is only one firm in the industry.

But whether an industry can be classed as a monopoly is not always clear. It depends how narrowly the industry is defined. For example, a confectionary company may have a monopoly on certain chocolate bars, but it does not have a monopoly on chocolate in general. A pharmaceutical company may have a monopoly of a certain drug, but there may be alternative drugs for treating a particular illness.

To some extent, the boundaries of an industry are arbitrary. What is more important for a firm is the amount of monopoly *power* it has, and that depends on the closeness of substitutes produced by rival industries. A train company may have a monopoly over railway journeys between two towns, but it faces competition in transport from cars, coaches and sometimes planes.

 As an illustration of the difficulty in identifying monopolies, try to decide which of the following are monopolies: BT; a local evening newspaper; food sold in a university outlet; a village post office; Interflora®; the London Underground; ice creams in the cinema; Guinness; the board game 'Monopoly'. (As you will quickly realise in each case, it depends how you define the industry.)

Barriers to entry

For a firm to maintain its monopoly position, there must be *barriers to entry* that make it difficult for new firms to enter

---

Definition

Barrier to entry Anything that prevents or impedes the entry of firms into an industry and thereby limits the amount of competition faced by existing firms.

the market. Barriers also exist under oligopoly, but in the case of monopoly they must be high enough to block the entry of all new firms.

Economists sometimes distinguish between *structural* and *strategic* barriers.

- Structural or natural barriers exist because of the characteristics of the industry. The firm is not deliberately seeking to construct such barriers. Rather, they are a side effect of attempts by the monopoly to run its business more efficiently.
- Strategic barriers, on the other hand, are the result of actions by the firm for the sole purpose of deterring potential entrants.

In reality, this distinction between structural and strategic barriers is often blurred. Firms might take advantage of the underlying characteristics of the industry to increase the size of any barriers that occur naturally.

Barriers can exist for a number of different reasons.

Economies of scale. If an industry experiences substantial economies of scale, it may have lower long-run average costs of production when one firm supplies the entire output of the industry. This is illustrated in Figure 7.7. D_1 represents the industry demand curve, and hence the demand curve for the monopoly. P_{BE} and Q_{BE} represent the break-even price and output of the industry. The profit-maximising level of output will be below this level (not illustrated on this diagram).

The long-run average costs of producing any level of output up to Q_{BE} are lower if one firm supplies the whole market. This can be illustrated by imagining a situation where two firms (A and B) compete against one another and share the market with each producing half of the total industry output. The demand curve for each firm would, in effect, be

D_2. Assuming that both firms have equal access to the same technology and factor inputs at the same prices, they would have identical long-run average cost curves, as shown by *LRAC*.

If each firm produced an output of Q_A and Q_B respectively, total industry output would be $Q_A + Q_B$ and the market price would be P_1, given by point e on the market demand curve. Both firms have a long-run average cost of $LRAC_1$ of producing Q_A and Q_B respectively and make long-run average supernormal profits of $b - c$. However, if the firms merged and the new unified business produced the same total output of $Q_A + Q_B$, its long-run average costs would be lower: i.e. $LRAC_2$ (point e).

This is an example of a **natural monopoly** where long-run average costs are lower if one firm supplies the entire market.

In some extreme cases of natural monopoly it might be impossible for two or more firms to charge any price that would enable them to cover their long-run average costs. This would be true in Figure 7.7 if the *LRAC* curve was above the demand curve for the individual firms (D_2) for its entire length.

A natural monopoly is most likely to occur if the market is relatively small and/or the industry has relatively high capital/infrastructure costs (i.e. fixed costs) and relatively low marginal costs. One real-world example is the network of pipelines that supply gas to homes and businesses. If two

Definition

Natural monopoly A situation where long-run average costs would be lower if an industry were under monopoly than if it were shared between two or more competitors.

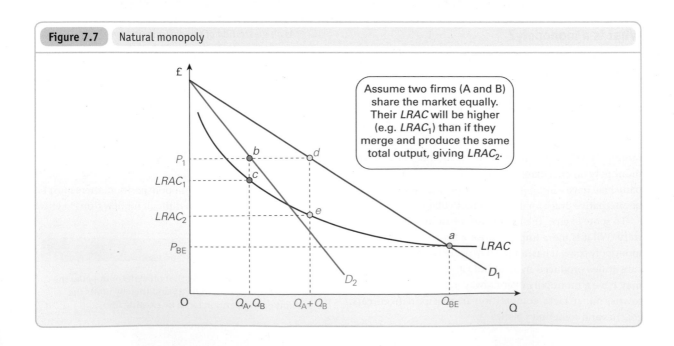

Figure 7.7 Natural monopoly

Assume two firms (A and B) share the market equally. Their *LRAC* will be higher (e.g. *LRAC₁*) than if they merge and produce the same total output, giving *LRAC₂*.

competing firms each built a national network of pipes it might be difficult for them both to make a profit as they would share the customers but each have the same infrastructure costs. A monopoly that supplies all customers could make a profit as it would have much lower average total costs from supplying the whole market. Electricity transmission via a national grid is another example of a natural monopoly.

 BT Openreach is responsible for providing and maintaining the fixed-line network connections to customers in the UK. This includes the huge system of telegraph poles and cable ducts (small underground tunnels) that carry telecom lines between BT exchanges and houses/business premises. To what extent do you think this it is a natural monopoly?

An industry may not be a natural monopoly, but significant economies of scale might still act as a barrier to entry. For example, potential new businesses might be deterred from trying to enter a market in the knowledge that they would have to sell large volumes of output before they could compete. The monopolist already experiencing economies of scale could charge a price below the cost of the new entrant and drive it out of business. There are, however, some circumstances where a new entrant may be able to survive this competition – if, for example, it is a firm already established in another industry. For example, Virgin Money entered the UK retail banking market in 2010 when it purchased Church House Trust, and Amazon entered the UK online grocery market in 2016.

Absolute cost advantages. If a monopolist has an absolute cost advantage, its average cost curve will be below that of any potential entrants at all levels of output. What might give a monopolist such a cost advantage?

- *More favourable access or control over key inputs.* In some markets the monopolist might be able to obtain access to important factor inputs on more favourable terms for a certain period of time. For example, if there was a supplier that provided a much higher quality of a factor input than its rivals, the monopoly could either sign a long-term exclusive contract with this firm or take ownership via a merger. For example, in 2012 Amazon purchased Kiva Systems. This company was the leading supplier of robotics for a number of warehouse operators and retailers. After the takeover, Kiva only supplied Amazon and was renamed Amazon Robotics in 2015. In more extreme cases the monopolist may be able to gain complete control if there is only one supplier of that input. For many years the De Beers company owned both the majority of the world's diamond mines and the major distribution system.
- *Superior technology.* The monopolist may have access to superior technology that is difficult for rival firms either to copy or to imitate. For many years, Google's search ranking algorithm helped it to provide a results page that many people found more useful than those of its rivals.
- *More efficient production methods.* Through years of experience of running the business an established monopoly

might have learnt the most efficient way of organising the production of its good or service. Much of this knowledge is tacit. It is developed and refined through a process of trial and error and cannot be written down in a way which could be easily understood by others. The new entrant would have to go through the same learning experience over a number of years before it could operate on the same cost curve as the monopolist.

- *Economies of scope.* A firm that produces a range of products is also likely to experience a lower average cost of production. For example, a large pharmaceutical company producing a range of drugs and toiletries can use shared research, marketing, storage and transport facilities across its range of products. These lower costs make it difficult for a new single-product entrant to the market, since the large firm could undercut its price to drive it out of the market.

 Under what circumstances might a new entrant succeed in the market for a product, despite existing firms benefiting from economies of scale?

Switching costs for consumers. Sometimes, if customers are considering whether or not to buy a product from a different firm, they may decide against it because of the additional costs involved. These are called **switching costs** and some examples include:

TC 1 p11

- *Searching costs.* How easy is it for the consumer to find and compare the price and quality of goods/services offered by alternative suppliers? The more time and effort it takes, the greater the switching costs. Some firms have been accused of deliberately making it more difficult for consumers to make these comparisons. For example, a report into the retail banking market by the Competition and Markets Authority in 2016[1] found low switching rates amongst current account holders, because they found it almost impossible to compare 'prices'. The price in this case is a combination of the account fees, overdraft charges and forgone interest.
- *Contractual costs.* In some markets customers have to sign a contract which stipulates that they purchase the good or service from the same supplier for a certain period of time: e.g. energy, mobile phones, broadband. A termination fee has to be paid if the customer wants to switch to a different supplier before the end of the contract period. Some firms also provide incentives for repeat purchases: e.g. loyalty cards, frequent flyer programmes.
- *Learning costs.* These may occur if the consumer invests time and effort in learning how to use a product or

Definitions

Switching costs The costs to a consumer of switching to an alternative supplier.

1 *Retail Banking Market Investigation: Final Report,* Competition and Markets Authority (9/8/16), see section 14.

service. The switching costs increase as this knowledge becomes more specific to the brand/product supplied by a particular firm. For example, a consumer might have spent a considerable amount of time learning how to use applications with the iOS operating system on an iPhone®. This may deter them from switching to a smartphone that uses Google's Android operating system.

- *Product uncertainty costs.* Consumers might not fully discover either the quality or how much they like a good until after they have purchased and used it for some time. This might make them reluctant to change supplier once they have found and experienced a particular brand or product they like.

- *Compatibility costs.* Some products have two elements to them. One part is more durable, while the other needs replacing more regularly. Once customers have purchased the more durable element from a supplier, they are 'locked in' to purchasing the non-durable part from the same supplier for compatibility reasons. Examples include razor handles and razor blades, coffee machines and coffee pods, printers and ink cartridges.

Some goods or services have very large switching costs because of the existence of network externalities. A **network externality** exists when consumers' valuation of a good is influenced by the number of other people who also use the same product. For example, the benefits of having a mobile phone increase with the number of other people who also have one. In some cases, a consumer's valuation will depend on the extent to which other people use one particular brand. For a specific social media website, such as Facebook, its success depends on lots of people using the same website. Buyers and sellers are willing to pay higher fees to use Amazon and eBay as an online marketplace because so many other buyers and sellers use the same websites.

When a good or service has significant network externalities it makes it difficult for a new entrant. Even if it produces a far superior and/or cheaper version of a product, it is difficult to get people to switch because they are unwilling to give up the network benefits associated with their current supplier. Other examples of products with network externalities include Microsoft's Windows (see Case Study 7.4 on the student website), Adobe's Acrobat (for PDF files) and airlines operating interconnecting routes (see Box 7.7).

Product differentiation and brand loyalty. If a firm produces a clearly differentiated product, where the consumer associates the product with the brand, it will be very difficult for a new firm to break into that market.

> ### Definitions
>
> **Network externalities or network economies** The benefits a consumer obtains from consuming a good/ service increase with the number of other people who use the same good/service.

In 1908, James Spengler invented, and patented, the electric vacuum cleaner. Later that year he sold the patent to his cousin's husband, William Hoover, who set about putting mass production in place. Decades after their legal monopoly (see below) ran out, people still associate vacuum-cleaning with Hoover and many of us would say that we are going to 'Hoover the carpet', despite using a Dyson, or other machine. When looking for some information by using an Internet search engine people often say 'they googled it'.

Other examples of strong brand image include Guinness®, Kellogg's® Cornflakes, Coca-Cola®, Nescafé® and Sellotape®. In many cases, strong brand presence would not be enough to *block* entry, but it might well reinforce other barriers.

More favourable or complete control over access to customers. If a firm can gain more favourable access or control over the best outlets through which the product is sold, this can hinder the ability of new entrants to gain access to potential customers. For example, approximately 50 per cent of public houses (pubs) in the UK operate on tenancy contracts known as the 'tied lease model'. This is effectively an exclusive supply contract which means that landlords of such pubs have to purchase almost all of their beverages from the pub company (e.g. Enterprise Inns, Punch Taverns and J. D. Wetherspoon) that owns the pub.

Legal protection. The firm's monopoly position may be protected by patents on essential processes, by copyright, by various forms of licensing (allowing, say, only one firm to operate in a particular area) and by tariffs (i.e. customs duties) and other trade restrictions to keep out foreign competitors. Examples of monopolies protected by patents include most new medicines developed by pharmaceutical companies, Microsoft's Windows operating systems and agro-chemical companies, such as Monsanto, with various genetically modified plant varieties and pesticides.

Mergers and takeovers. The monopolist can put in a takeover bid for any new entrant. The mere threat of takeovers may discourage new entrants.

Aggressive tactics. An established monopolist can probably sustain losses for longer than a new entrant. Thus it can start a price war, mount massive advertising campaigns, offer an attractive after-sales service, introduce new brands to compete with new entrants, and so on.

Intimidation. The monopolist may resort to various forms of harassment, legal or illegal, to drive a new entrant out of business.

Equilibrium price and output

Since there is, by definition, only one firm in the industry, the firm's demand curve is also the industry demand curve.

Compared with other market structures, demand under monopoly will be relatively inelastic at each price. The

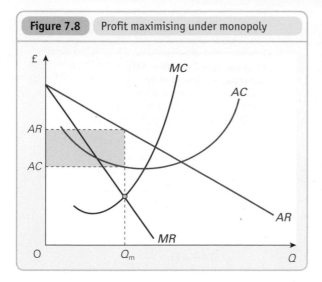

Figure 7.8 Profit maximising under monopoly

monopolist can raise its price and consumers have no alternative firm in the industry to turn to. They either pay the higher price or go without the good altogether.

Unlike the firm under perfect competition, the monopoly firm is a 'price maker'. It can choose what price to charge. Nevertheless, it is still constrained by its demand curve. A rise in price will lower the quantity demanded. Be careful not to fall into the trap of thinking that a monopoly can control both price *and* output simultaneously.

As with firms in other market structures, a monopolist will maximise profit where $MR = MC$. In Figure 7.8, profit is maximised at Q_m. The supernormal profit obtained is shown by the shaded area.

These profits will tend to be larger the less elastic is the demand curve (and hence the steeper is the MR curve), and thus the bigger is the gap between MR and price (AR). The actual elasticity will depend on whether reasonably close substitutes are available in *other* industries. The demand for a rail service will be much less elastic (and the potential for profit greater) if there is no bus service to the same destination.

Since there are barriers to the entry of new firms, these supernormal profits will not be competed away in the long run. The only difference, therefore, between short-run and long-run equilibrium is that in the long run the firm will produce where $MR = long\text{-}run\ MC$.

 Try this brain teaser. A monopoly would be expected to face an inelastic demand. After all, there are no direct substitutes. And yet, if it produces where $MR = MC$, MR must be positive and demand must therefore be elastic. Therefore the monopolist must face an elastic demand! Can you solve this conundrum?

Limit pricing

If the barriers to the entry of new firms are not total, and if the monopolist is making very large supernormal profits, there may be a danger in the long run of potential rivals

breaking into the industry. In such cases, the monopolist may keep its price down and thereby deliberately restrict the size of its profits in the short run so as not to attract new entrants. This practice is known as **limit pricing**.

In Figure 7.9, three AC curves are drawn: one for the monopolist (firm M), one for a potential entrant (firm A) and one for another potential entrant (firm B). It is assumed that the monopolist has an absolute cost advantage over both potential entrants (e.g. more favourable access to factor inputs) so it has a lower AC curve over all levels of output. Any potential new entrant, if it is to compete successfully with the monopolist, must charge the same price or a lower one (assuming no product differentiation).

The short-run profit-maximising position for the monopolist is to produce where $MC = MR$. This is illustrated at point a in Figure 7.9. The firm will produce an output of Q_1 and charge a price of P_1. If it faces potential competition from a new entrant such as firm A, it can charge this price without any fear of entry. Firm A's average costs are above this profit-maximising price and so it would not be profitable to enter the market at this price or any level below it. The barriers to entry for firm A are total.

Definition

Limit pricing Where a monopolist (or oligopolist) charges a price below the short-run profit-maximising level in order to deter new entrants.

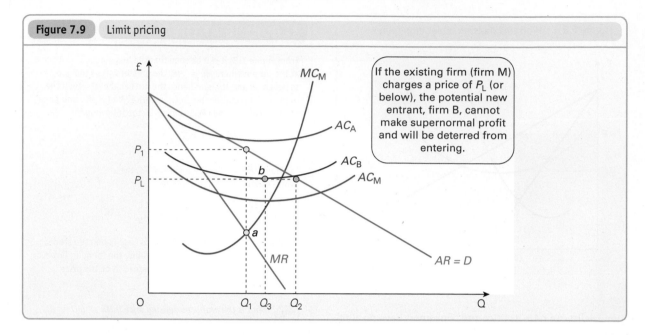

Figure 7.9　Limit pricing

> If the existing firm (firm M) charges a price of P_L (or below), the potential new entrant, firm B, cannot make supernormal profit and will be deterred from entering.

However, if a potential new entrant, such as firm B, had average costs below P_1, it could make supernormal profits by entering at that price. In such a case, it is in the monopolist's interests to charge the lower price of P_L, and produce Q_2, to deter firm B from entering the market. At a price of P_L, the best firm B could do would be to make just normal profit by producing Q_3 (point b). However, if it did enter the market and the monopolist continued to produce Q_2, the market price would fall below P_L and the new entrant would make a loss at any output. Thus, P_L can be seen as a *limit price* – a price ceiling, at or below which potential new entrants will be deterred from entering the industry.

P_L may be below the monopolist's short-run profit-maximising price, but it may prefer to limit its price to P_L to protect its long-run profits from the damage caused by competition.

Fear of government intervention to curb the monopolist's practices may have a similar restraining effect on the price that the monopolist charges. In the UK, the Competition and Markets Authority may undertake an investigation, see section 14.1 for more on this.

1. What does this analysis assume about the price elasticity of demand for the new entrant (a) above P_L; (b) below P_L?
2. Can you think of any limitations with the limit price model?

Monopoly and the public interest

Disadvantages of monopoly

There are several reasons why monopolies may be against the public interest. As we shall see in Chapter 14, these have given rise to legislation to regulate monopoly power and/or behaviour.

Higher price and lower output than under perfect competition (short run). Figure 7.10 compares the profit-maximising position for an industry under monopoly with that under perfect competition. The monopolist will produce Q_1 at a price of P_1. This is where $MC = MR$.

If the same industry operated under perfect competition, however, it would produce at Q_2 and P_2 – a higher output and a lower price. This is where industry supply under perfect competition equals industry demand. (Remember, we showed in section 7.2 that the firm's supply curve under perfect competition is its MC curve and thus the industry's supply curve is simply the *industry MC* curve: the MC curve shown in Figure 7.10.)

This analysis is based on the assumption that the industry has the *same AC* and *MC* curves whether under perfect competition or run as a monopoly. For example, suppose some potato farmers initially operate under perfect competition.

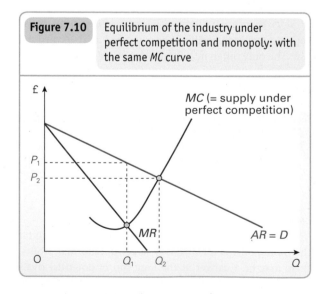

Figure 7.10　Equilibrium of the industry under perfect competition and monopoly: with the same *MC* curve

The market price is P_2 in Figure 7.10. Then they set up a marketing agency through which they all sell their potatoes. The agency therefore acts as a monopoly supplier to the market and charges a price of P_1. Since it is the same farmers before and after, production costs are unlikely to have changed much. But as we shall see below, even if an industry has *lower* *AC* and *MC* curves under monopoly than under perfect competition, it is still likely to charge a higher price and produce a lower output.

When we were looking at the advantages of perfect competition, we said that the level where $P = MC$ could be argued to be the *optimum* level of production. Clearly, if a monopolist is producing below this level (e.g. at Q_1 in Figure 7.10 – where $P > MC$), the monopolist can be argued to be producing at *less* than optimal output. Consumers would be prepared to pay more for additional units than they cost to produce.

Higher price and lower output than under perfect competition (long run). Under perfect competition, freedom of entry eliminates supernormal profit and forces firms to produce at the bottom of their *LRAC* curve. The effect, therefore, is to keep long-run prices down. Under monopoly, however, barriers to entry allow profits to remain supernormal in the long run. The monopolist is not forced to operate at the bottom of the *AC* curve. Thus, other things being equal, long-run prices will tend to be higher, and hence output lower, under monopoly.

Possibility of higher cost curves due to lack of competition. The sheer survival of a firm in the long run under perfect competition requires that it uses the most efficient known technique, and develops new techniques wherever possible. The monopolist, however, sheltered by barriers to entry, can still make large profits even if it is not using the most efficient technique. It has less incentive, therefore, to be efficient (see Box 7.4).

On the other hand, if it can lower its costs by using and developing more efficient techniques, it can gain extra supernormal profits which will not be competed away.

Unequal distribution of income. The high profits of monopolists may be considered as unfair, especially by competitive firms, or anyone on low incomes for that matter. The scale of this problem obviously depends on the size of the monopoly and the degree of its power. The monopoly profits of the village store may seem of little consequence when compared to the profits of a giant national or international company.

> **?** *If the shares in a monopoly (such as a water company) were very widely distributed among the population, would the shareholders necessarily want the firm to use its monopoly power to make larger profits?*

In addition to these problems, monopolies may lack the incentive to introduce new product varieties, and large monopolies may be able to exert political pressure and thereby get favourable treatment from governments.

Advantages of monopoly

Despite these arguments, monopolies can have some advantages.

Economies of scale. The monopoly may be able to achieve substantial economies of scale due to larger plant, centralised administration and the avoidance of unnecessary duplication (e.g. a monopoly water company would eliminate the need for several sets of rival water mains under each street). If this results in an *MC* curve substantially below that of the same industry under perfect competition, the monopoly will produce a *higher* output at a *lower* price. In Figure 7.11, the monopoly produces Q_1 at a price of P_1, whereas the perfectly competitive industry produces Q_2 at the higher price P_2.

Note that this result follows only if the monopoly *MC* curve is below point *x* in Figure 7.11. Note also that since an industry cannot exist under perfect competition if substantial economies of scale can be gained, it is somewhat hypothetical to make the comparison between a monopoly and an alternative situation that could not exist. What is more, were the monopolist to follow the $P = MC$ rule observed by perfectly competitive firms, it would charge an even lower price (P_3) and produce an even higher output (Q_3).

Possibility of lower cost curves due to more research and development and more investment. Although the monopolist's sheer survival does not depend on its finding ever more efficient methods of production, it can use part of its supernormal profits for research and development and investment. It thus has a greater ability to become efficient than has the small firm with limited funds.

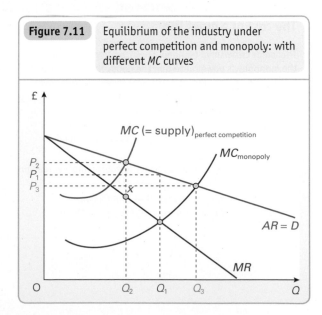

Figure 7.11 Equilibrium of the industry under perfect competition and monopoly: with different *MC* curves

BOX 7.4   GOOGLE – A MONOPOLY ABUSING ITS MARKET POWER?

Searching for market dominance?

The early days of search engines and the rise of Google

Google is in a dominant position in the general Internet search engine market. In January 2017, it had a 80.47 per cent share of the global desktop search engine market and a 94.87 per cent share of the global mobile/tablet search engine market.

However, this has not always been the case. It is hard to imagine now but when the company began in 1997 it was a new entrant, doing battle with other established firms that dominated this new dynamic and growing market.

In 1994, Lycos® and Webcrawler® were the first businesses to introduce modern search engine services, where a user could input a general query and obtain a results page. AltaVista® entered the market in 1995 and soon became the dominant player as it provided a results page that users found the most useful. By the end of 1997, this search engine was receiving 80 million hits per day and was the sole provider of Internet search software for Yahoo.

Other companies such as Inktomi and HotBot entered the market successfully but Google began to rise to prominence at the turn of the century. Its global market share grew dramatically from less than 5 per cent at the beginning of 2000 to over 50 per cent by 2003. By 2007, it had reached the dominant position it has today.

Google appears to have obtained a dominant position in the market by using superior technology to search the web. Its initial success is largely credited to it providing a results page that its users found far more useful than those of its rivals. It has now remained in a dominant position for over 10 years.

Google's barriers to entry

Is there any evidence that Google has engaged in business activities whose sole purpose is to prevent or limit competition? Has it created any strategic barriers to entry?

Some switching costs may exist because of the existence of *network externalities.* As more people use the same search engine it enables the provider to collect more data about users' search behaviour. This information helps the firm to improve its search-engine results page making it more difficult for a new entrant to compete with a much smaller user base. This is an example of a structural barrier to entry because it is a result of the underlying characteristics of the industry. The size of these network externalities are smaller, however, in the Internet search market than for companies in other digital industries such as Facebook in the social media market.

Other switching costs appear to be trivial. Any search engine can be used irrespective of the device (desktop or mobile), the operating system or the web browser being used. The service is free so there are no contractual switching costs. The search costs are minimal – a search engine can be used to find its rivals. The learning costs are also small. Although there may be some variation in the presentation of the results, once users have become accustomed to one search engine they can easily use another.

It is hard to see how Google does anything to 'lock-in' its users: i.e. strategically increasing switching costs to such a level that consumers are prevented from switching to other search engines they would find more useful. If Google introduced a small fee for its search services, the majority of users would probably quickly switch to one of its rivals.

BOX 7.5   X INEFFICIENCY

The cost of a quiet life

KI 3
p13

The major criticism of monopoly has traditionally been that of the monopoly's power in selling the good. The firm charges a price above *MC* (see Figure 7.10). This is seen as *allocatively inefficient* because at the margin consumers are willing to pay more than it is costing to produce *(P > MC);* and yet the monopolist is deliberately holding back, so as to keep its profits up. Allocative inefficiency is examined in detail in section 12.1.

But monopolies may also be inefficient for another reason: they may have higher costs. Why is this?

Higher costs may be the result of *X inefficiency*[1] (sometimes known as *technical inefficiency*). Without

competitive pressure on profit margins, cost control may become lax. The firm may employ too many staff and spend on prestigious buildings and equipment. There may be less effort to keep technologically up to date, to research new products, or to develop new domestic and export markets.

The more comfortable the situation, the less may be the effort which is expended to improve it. The effect of this X inefficiency is to make the *AC* and *MC* curves higher than they would otherwise be. The outcome is that consumers pay higher prices and the firm moves even further away from the efficient, competitive, outcome.

EU investigation

However, after an investigation that began in 2010, the European Commission (EC) sent Google a 'Supplementary Statement of Objections' in July 2016. One of these objections relates to the way the general search page displays the results from a product search enquiry. The EC has accused Google of taking advantage of its dominant position in the general search engine market to suppress competition in another market where it faces much greater competition – the comparison shopping services market.

Comparison shopping websites collect product information together from participating retailers and display them on a single results page in response to a shopper's search enquiry. The EC argued that Google had systematically favoured its own comparison shopping service – Google Shopping. The shopping service appears as a very prominent box of images and links at the top of the general search results page. By doing this, Google is accused of potentially preventing consumers from seeing the comparison shopping websites they would find the most useful.

The EC noted that Google's first comparison shopping service 'Froogle' was not very successful. The subsequent services 'Google Product Search' and 'Google Shopping' have grown far more rapidly after changes to the presentation of results were introduced. Concerns have been expressed that Google's actions have significantly weakened its rivals in the comparison shopping market and deterred potential new entrants.

Google responded to the objections in November 2016 by complaining about the way the online shopping market was defined. In its report, the EC concluded that comparison shopping services and merchant platforms such as eBay and Amazon were separate markets. Google argued that general search engines, comparison shopping sites, supplier websites and merchant platforms are all effectively in competition with each other. It referred to studies in the USA which found that 55 per cent of customers start their online shopping using Amazon, 28 per cent start on a search engine, while 16 per cent start by going straight to the individual suppliers' website. Although Google is becoming increasingly dominant in comparison shopping services, it argues that this is just one small part of a much bigger market.

The EC argues they are separate markets as companies such as Amazon pay comparison shopping service websites for referrals. Google's response is that it is quite possible for companies simultaneously to compete and co-operate with one another.

In June 2017, the EC imposed a record fine of €2.4 billion on Google for abusing its dominant market position. Google appealed against this fine to the General Court in September 2017. It will be interesting to see how this legal battle develops over the next few years.

1. *Explain why network externalities are much smaller in the general Internet search market than they are for social media.*
2. *Provide a critique of Google's responses to the European Commission.*

[1] 'Antitrust: Commission takes further steps in investigations alleging Google's comparison shopping and advertising-related practices breach EU rules', European Commission, Press release, 14 July 2016.

Following the financial crisis in 2007/8 and subsequent recession, there were significant reductions in X inefficiency in many countries. To cope with falling sales, and a fall in both sales and profits, many firms embarked on cost-cutting programmes. Much out-of-date plant was closed down, and employment was reduced. Those firms that survived the recession (and many did not) tended to emerge both more competitive and more efficient.

A further factor in the reduction in X inefficiency has been the growth in international competition. Even if a firm has monopoly power at home, the growth in global markets and e-commerce (see Box 7.3), and reductions in customs duties and other barriers to trade (see section 24.2), provide fiercer competition from abroad.

1. *How might you measure X inefficiency?*
2. *Another type of inefficiency is productive inefficiency. What do you think this is? (Clue: it has to do with the proportions in which factors are used.)*
3. *Explain why X inefficiency might be more common in state monopolies than those owned by shareholders.*

1 This term was coined by Harvey Leibenstein, 'Allocative efficiency or X efficiency', *American Economic Review,* June 1966.

BOX 7.6 CUT-THROAT COMPETITION

The UK razor market

The market for wet razors and their blades is worth approximately £400 million in the UK. It was traditionally dominated by two producers, Gillette® and Procter & Gamble (P&G), with more than two thirds of sales between them. When they merged in 2007, the result was a new unified firm with substantial monopoly power. The Wilkinson Sword brand, owned by Edgewell Personal Care, was the next largest manufacturer in the UK, with around 18 per cent of sales. These two businesses also dominate the $3 billion US market.

The industry displays many of the characteristics we would expect of a market dominated by one large firm – very high levels of advertising and strong branding that make it difficult for new entrants. There is also evidence of ongoing innovation: where once the twin-blade razor was a novelty, now five blades are the norm.

New entrants: the US market

Yet, despite all the potential barriers to entry, some new firms have successfully entered the market in recent years and changed the way that many customers purchase their razors. The most successful of all these businesses is the Dollar Shave Club. Founded in California in 2011, this company has had a significant impact on the US market. It introduced an innovative subscription service: customers sign up via the company's website for a year's supply of 60 standard twin-blade razor cartridges, which are delivered to their homes for $1 per month.

Perhaps the most novel aspect of this business was its marketing strategy. As a new start-up, it did not have the multimillion-dollar advertising budget to compete with Gillette and Wilkinson Sword in traditional methods of marketing. It decided, instead, to launch its products using humorous YouTube videos featuring the company's CEO Michael Dublin. Its first video cost $4500 and included advertising messages such as 'Do you think your razor needs a vibrating handle, a flashlight, a back scratcher and 10 blades? . . . So stop paying for shave tech you don't need.'

The focus of the business is clearly on price rather than product differentiation.

Within two hours of posting its first video the company's website crashed and within six hours it had completely sold out of stock. The video has been viewed over 20 million times and has proved to be a very successful marketing tool. Sales increased from $4 million in 2012 to $200 million in 2016 and the company has a 15 per cent share of the US market for razor cartridges. Its impact on the way many customers purchase razors has been dramatic. Online sales in the USA have increased rapidly and now account for 8 per cent of the razor market.

Other new start-ups, such as Harry's, Razor Co and Shave Mob, have also entered the growing online market. In the USA, P&G has responded to this competition by launching its own subscription service for its Gillette brand in 2014.

New entrants: the UK market

Similar changes have also occurred in the UK market. The King of Shaves razor was launched in 2008, with a view to building on the success of the brand's shaving gel and foams. The company worked on developing a lower-cost, lightweight alternative to the products offered by Gillette and Wilkinson Sword. It also tried to make greater use of online advertising, e-mail and social media to market its product.

However, the company has found it tough to compete successfully. It made losses of £959 000 in 2014 before making a profit in 2016 for the first time since 2009. Its recent improvement in performance appears to have come from switching more of its sales to its online subscription service.

Cornerstone also operates a subscription service in the UK where customers can have razor blades and skincare products delivered every 2, 6 or 18 weeks.

Perhaps the biggest threat to P&G's dominant position in this global industry will come from the decision of Unilever to enter the razor market. In July 2016, it purchased the Dollar Shave Club for $1 billion. With the financial backing of the third largest consumer goods company in the world, this new entrant could now pose serious competition. It will be interesting to see if the Gillette brand name can maintain its dominant market position.

1. What are the characteristics of the razor market that present barriers to entry for new firms? How have companies, such as Dollar Shave Club, sought to overcome these barriers?
2. High levels of innovation have been a key characteristic of the market for wet razors for many years. Do these always benefit the consumer?
3. It has been estimated that Gillette makes a profit of 3000 per cent on each razor blade sold. Explain how this figure might have arisen.

Competition for corporate control. Although a monopoly faces no competition in the goods market, it may face an alternative form of competition in financial markets. A monopoly, with potentially low costs, which is currently run inefficiently, is likely to be subject to a takeover bid from another company. This *competition for corporate control* may thus force the monopoly to be efficient in order to avoid being taken over.

KI 3 p13

Innovation and new products. The promise of supernormal profits, protected perhaps by patents, may encourage the

TC 5 p50

Definition

Competition for corporate control The competition for the control of companies through takeovers.

development of new (monopoly) industries producing new products.

Monopoly and price discrimination

One further characteristic of monopoly is that it allows firms to price discriminate: to charge different prices either to all customers or to different groups of customers. Firms undertake this as a way of further increasing profits. The ability to price discriminate rests on the firm having some monopoly power, although this need not be a complete monopoly. Price discrimination is discussed in more detail in section 8.4, pages 238–40.

Section summary

1. A monopoly is where there is only one firm in an industry. In practice, it is difficult to determine that a monopoly exists because it depends on how narrowly an industry is defined.

2. Barriers to the entry of new firms are usually necessary to protect a monopoly from competition. They may be either structural or strategic barriers.

3. Such barriers include cost advantages: these include economies of scale – perhaps with the firm being a natural monopoly – and absolute cost advantages, such as more favourable access or control over key inputs, the use of superior technology, more efficient production methods or economies of scope.

4. Barriers also include switching costs for customers, more favourable or complete control over access to customers, product differentiation, patents or copyright and tactics to eliminate competition (such as takeovers or aggressive advertising).

5. Profits for the monopolist (as for other firms) will be maximised where $MC = MR$. In the case of monopoly, this will probably be at a higher price relative to marginal cost than for other firms, due to the less elastic nature of its demand at any given price.

6. Monopolies may be against the public interest to the extent that they charge a higher price relative to cost than do competitive firms; if they cause a less desirable distribution of income; if a lack of competition removes the incentive to be efficient and innovative; and if they exert undesirable political pressures on governments.

7. On the other hand, any economies of scale will in part be passed on to consumers in lower prices, and the monopolist's high profits may be used for research and development and investment, which in turn may lead to better products at possibly lower prices.

7.4 THE THEORY OF CONTESTABLE MARKETS

Potential competition or monopoly?

In recent years, economists have developed the theory of contestable markets. This theory argues that what is crucial in determining price and output is not whether an industry is *actually* a monopoly or competitive, but whether there is the real *threat* of competition.

If a monopoly is protected by high barriers to entry – for example, it controls the supply of the key raw materials – then it will be able to make supernormal profits with no fear of competition.

If, however, another firm *could* potentially take away all of its customers with little difficulty, it will behave much more like a competitive firm. The threat of competition has a similar effect to actual competition.

As an example, consider a catering company engaged by a university to run its cafés and coffee bars. The catering company has a monopoly over the supply of food to the students at the university assuming there are no other eating places nearby. If, however, it starts charging high prices or providing a poor service, the university could offer the running of the cafés to an alternative catering company. This threat may force the original catering company to charge 'reasonable' prices and offer a good service.

Perfectly contestable markets

A market is **perfectly contestable** when potential rivals (a) face no costs of entry and exit (b) can rapidly enter the market before the monopolist has time to respond. In such cases, the instant it becomes possible to earn supernormal profits, new firms will quickly enter the market and charge a price below the monopolist's price.

If the monopolist is unable to respond immediately, the new entrant sells to all of the customers in the market and makes supernormal profit. When the monopolist finally

---

Definition

Perfectly contestable market A market where there is free and costless entry and exit and the monopolist cannot immediately respond to entry.

does respond by cutting its own prices, profits are driven back down towards their normal level. At that stage the new entrant is able to exit the market costlessly. This is known as '*hit and run*'.

The sheer threat of this happening, so the theory goes, will ensure that the firm already in the market will (a) keep its prices down, so that it just makes normal profits, and (b) produce as efficiently as possible, taking advantage of any economies of scale and any new technology. If it did not do this, rivals would enter, and potential competition would become actual competition.

This is illustrated in Figure 7.12. Assume that there is only one firm in the industry, which faces a long-run average cost curve given by *LRAC*. Assume that profits are maximised at a price of P_1, with supernormal profits being shown by the shaded area. If entry and exit costs are high, the price will remain at this level. If entry and exit costs are low, however, rival firms may be tempted to enter, charge a slightly lower price than the monopoly and take all of its customers.

To avert this, the existing firm will have to lower its price. In the case of zero entry and exit costs, the monopolist will have to lower its price to P_2, where price equals *LRAC*, and where, therefore, profits are normal and would not attract rival firms to enter. At the same time, the monopolist will have to ensure that its *LRAC* curve is as low as possible (i.e. that it avoids any X inefficiency (see Box 7.5)).

Contestable markets and natural monopolies

So why in such cases are the markets not *actually* perfectly competitive? Why do they remain monopolies?

The most likely reason has to do with economies of scale and the size of the market. To operate close to its minimum efficient scale, the firm may have to be so large relative to the market that there is only room for one such firm in the industry. If a new firm does come into the market, then one or other of the two firms will not survive the competition. The market is simply not big enough for both of them. This is the case in Figure 7.12. The industry is a natural monopoly, given that the *LRAC* curve is downward sloping even at output *c*.

If, however, there are no entry or exit costs, new firms will be perfectly willing to enter even though there is only room for one firm – either because they believe that they are more

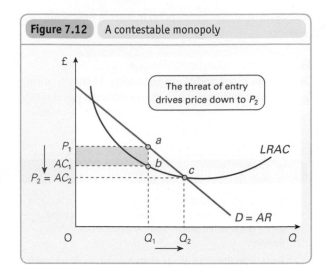

Figure 7.12 A contestable monopoly

efficient than the established firm or because they are willing to engage in hit-and-run competition. The established firm, knowing this, will be forced to produce as efficiently as possible and with only normal profit.

The importance of costless exit

There is always an element of risk whenever a firm is thinking of entering an industry. It is often difficult to forecast its costs and future demand accurately and there is no guarantee these forecasts will prove to be correct. For example, there could be an unanticipated fall in demand for the product caused by a negative shock such as a recession; the technology used by the entrant might quickly become obsolete, especially if it is entering an industry with high levels of innovation; the established firm may respond far more quickly to the new firm's entry than anticipated, leaving it unable to make any supernormal profit.

But does this risk matter? Cannot a new entrant engage in hit-and-run competition and quickly leave a market? This depends on the costs of exit – on the extent of *sunk costs* (see page 156). Setting up in a new business often involves large expenditures on physical capital (plant and machinery), advertising and complying with government regulations. Once this money is spent, it may not be possible to recover. For example, the losing firm may be left with capital equipment that it cannot use or sell. The firm may therefore be put off entering in the first place. The market is not perfectly contestable; the established firm can make supernormal profit.

If, however, the capital equipment does generate the same return in *alternative* uses, the exit costs will be zero (or at least very low), and new firms will be more willing to make the necessary investment and take the risks of entry. For example, a rival coach company may open up a service on a route previously operated by only one company, and where there is still only room for one operator. If the new firm loses the resulting battle, it can still use the coaches it has purchased. It simply uses them for a different route. The cost of the coaches is not a sunk cost.

Costless exit, therefore, encourages firms to enter an industry, knowing that, if unsuccessful, they can always transfer their capital elsewhere.

The lower the exit costs, the more contestable the market. This implies that firms already established in other similar markets may provide more effective competition against monopolists, since they can simply transfer capital from one market to another. For example, studies of airlines in the USA show that entry to a particular route may be much easier for an established airline, which can simply transfer planes from one route to another (see Box 7.7).

 In which of the following industries are exit costs likely to be low: (a) steel production; (b) market gardening; (c) nuclear power generation; (d) specialist financial advisory services; (e) production of a new drug; (f) street food; (g) car ferry operators? Do these exit costs depend on how narrowly the industry is defined?

Assessment of the theory

The theory of contestable markets is an improvement on simple monopoly theory, which merely focuses on the existing structure of the industry and makes no allowance for potential competition.

Perfectly contestable markets may exist only rarely. But, like perfect competition, they provide an *ideal type* against which to judge the real world. It can be argued that they provide a more useful ideal type than perfect competition, since they provide a better means of predicting firms' price and output behaviour than does the simple portion of the market currently supplied by the existing firm.

One criticism of the theory, however, is that it does not take sufficient account of the possible reactions of the established firm. There could be a contestable market, with no barriers to entry or exit, but the established firm may signal very clearly that it will respond immediately if any firm dares to enter its market. The threat of facing an immediate price war might deter any potential entrant, allowing the established firm to continue charging high prices and making supernormal profits.

Perhaps the most important contribution of the theory is to help us focus on the importance of sunk costs when determining the threat of entry and performance of a market. Many of the factors that create barriers to entry, such as economics of scale and product differentiation/advertising, may only actually create a barrier to a new entrant if they involve expenditures that cannot be recovered if it later exits the market.

Contestable markets and the public interest

If a monopoly operates in a perfectly contestable market, it might bring the 'best of both worlds'. Not only will it be able to achieve low costs through economies of scale, but also the potential competition will keep profits and hence prices down.

For this reason, the theory has been seized on by politicians on the political right to justify a policy of laissez-faire (non-intervention) and deregulation (e.g. coach and air routes). They argue that the theory vindicates the free market. There are two points in reply to this:

- Few markets are *perfectly* contestable. If entry and exit are not costless, a monopoly can still make supernormal profits in the long run.
- There are other possible failings of the market beside monopoly power (e.g. inequality, pollution). These failings are examined in Chapters 11 and 12.

Nevertheless, the theory of contestable markets has highlighted the importance of sunk costs in determining monopoly behaviour. Monopolists may deliberately spend large amounts of money on advertising as they realise it increases the sunk costs of entry and hence deters new firms from entering its market. Many policy makers now focus on sunk costs when considering anti-monopoly policy.

BOX 7.7 **AIRLINE DEREGULATION IN THE USA AND EUROPE**

A case study of contestable markets

If a market is highly contestable, the mere threat of competition may successfully keep prices and profits down to near-competitive levels. Of course, established firms would be keen to erect barriers to entry and to make exit more costly for any firm that did enter.

Governments around the world are generally in favour of increased competition and frown on the erection of entry barriers (see section 14.1). This means that they generally prefer not to intervene if markets are competitive or highly contestable, but may attempt to regulate the prices, profits or behaviour of firms where competition or contestability is limited. Conversely, if markets have been regulated and yet are potentially competitive, many governments have then deregulated them (i.e. removed regulations).

A good case study of deregulation and contestability (or lack of it) is the airline industry. Here the reduction of regulations over decades has allowed low-cost airlines to build market share and challenge the large network carriers.

The USA

The airline industry in the United States was deregulated in 1978. Prior to that, air routes were allocated by the government, with the result that many airlines operated as monopolies or shared the route with just one other airline. Now there exists a policy of 'open skies'.

Initially the consequences were dramatic, with lower fares and, over many routes, a greater choice of airlines. The Brookings Institute calculated that, in the first 10 years of deregulation, the lower fares saved consumers some $100 billion. One consequence of the increased competition was that many long-established US airlines went out of business.

Even where routes continued to be operated by just one or two airlines, fares still fell if the route was *contestable*: if the entry and exit costs remained low. In 1992, despite the bankruptcies, 23 new carriers were established in North America, and many routes were taken over by existing carriers.

But deregulation did not make all routes more contestable. In some cases the reverse happened. In a situation of rising costs and falling revenues, there were mergers and takeovers of the vulnerable airlines. By 2000, just 7 airlines accounted for over 90 per cent of American domestic air travel, compared with 15 in 1984. With this move towards greater monopolisation, some airlines managed to make their routes *less* contestable. The result was that air fares over the 1990s rose faster than prices in general.

A key ingredient in making routes less contestable was the development of a system of air routes radiating out from about 30 key or 'hub' airports. With waves of flights scheduled to arrive and depart within a short space of time, passengers can make easy connections at these hub airports.

The problem is that several of these hub airports became dominated by single airlines which, through economies of scale and the ownership or control of various airport facilities, such as boarding gates or check-in areas, could effectively keep out potential entrants. By 2002, at 15 of the hub airports, including some of the busiest, the dominant airline had a market share in excess of 70 per cent.

The airlines also used measures to increase contractual switching costs and thereby make entry barriers higher. These measures include frequent flier rewards, deals with travel agents and code sharing with 'partner' airlines.

The rise of the low-cost airlines. In the 2000s, however, the domestic US airlines market became more competitive again, thanks to the growth of low-cost carriers (LCCs), the largest being Southwest Airlines. These accounted for just 7 per cent of US domestic passengers in 1990; by 2009 this had risen to 34 per cent and in 2013, for the first time, LCCs had a greater market share than the network carriers. The response of the major airlines was to create their own low-cost carriers, such as Delta's 'Song' in 2004 and United's 'Ted' in 2004.

A danger here is that big airlines may use their LCCs to undercut the prices of small new entrants to drive them out of the market. Such 'predatory pricing' (see pages 246 and 422) is illegal, and the Department of Justice investigated several cases. However, predatory pricing is very difficult to distinguish from price competition between firms. Thus cases have been consistently dismissed by juries, who have concluded that there was insufficient proof that the big airlines were breaking the law. This issue re-emerged in 2011, when Delta Airlines was criticised for adopting predatory practices in order to maintain a monopoly position at Minneapolis St Paul Airport.

With the rise in fuel prices in 2006–8 and lower passenger numbers from 2007, resulting from the global recession, some of these new LCCs went out of business. Delta shut its Song division in 2006 and United shut Ted in 2008.

The whole industry has gone through a period of major consolidation with five big mergers reducing the number of large airlines from nine to four. For example, in 2011 Southwest acquired AirTran, another major low-cost carrier. This deal enabled it to remove one of its leading rivals. American, United, Delta and Southwest now control 80 per cent of the US market and some observers have expressed concerns about the lack of competition on prices. At 40 of the largest US airports, one airline now has the majority of the market. This was the case at 34 airports 10 years ago.

The US airline market is more competitive than it was before the industry deregulated in 1978. However, the level of competition has fallen dramatically in the past 10 years. It will be interesting to see if the threat of potential competition constrains the pricing behaviour of the four big airlines in the future.

Europe

Until the early 1990s, the European air transport industry was highly regulated, with governments controlling routes. National routes were often licensed to the national airline and international routes to the two respective national airlines. Since 1993, the industry has been progressively deregulated and competition has increased, with a growing availability of discount fares. Now, within the EU, airlines are free to charge whatever they like, and any EU airline can fly on any route it wants, providing it can get the slots at the airports at either end.

As in the USA, however, whilst increased competition has benefited passengers, many of the airlines have tried to make their routes less contestable by erecting entry barriers. Predatory pricing occurred, as the established airlines tried to drive out new competitors. The proliferation of fare categories made it hard for consumers to compare prices, and established carriers' highly publicised fares often had many restrictions, with most people having to pay considerably higher fares. As in the USA, code sharing and airline alliances have reduced competition. Finally, at busy airports, such as Heathrow, the shortage of check-in and boarding gates, runways and airspace provided a major barrier to new entrants.

Nevertheless, new low-cost airlines, such as easyJet, Ryanair and Flybe, provided effective competition for the established national and short-haul international carriers, which were forced to cut fares on routes where they directly competed. British Airways went as far as re-badging their loss-making subsidiary regional airline as BA Connect in 2006, adopting a low-cost model and pledging to 'cut one third from standard domestic fares'. However, the company accrued further losses that year and was sold to Flybe in early 2007.

Low-cost airlines have been able to enter the market by using other airports, such as Stansted and Luton in the case of London, and various regional airports throughout Europe. Many passengers showed themselves willing to travel further at the beginning and end of their journey if the overall cost remained much lower. Ryanair, in particular, has made use of smaller airports located some way from major cities.

Lower costs

How do the LCCs compete? The airline industry does not on the face of it seem to be a highly contestable one. Apart from anything else, aircraft would appear to be a high-cost input.

The answer lies in a variety of cost-saving opportunities. The LCCs are able to lease planes rather than buy them; even when they own their own planes, the aircraft are generally older and more basic, offering a standard accommodation rather than different classes. The result is reduced exit costs, increasing contestability. In addition, by charging extra for each item of luggage, they reduce the amount they carry, thus saving fuel.

There is also evidence of lower staff costs. Initially, LCCs paid less than the traditional airlines; however, this is no longer the case. Peter Belobaba, of MIT, has reported that since 2006 salaries and benefits for LCC employees have equalled those available to employees of the larger carriers. Yet productivity is measurably higher, with 15 per cent more available seat miles per employee.

The large hub-and-spoke carriers have also found that the very nature of their operations constricts their ability to compete with the LCCs on city-to-city routes. Not only are the hubs themselves expensive, but the movement of passengers in and out of the terminals takes longer than with smaller airports. Thus the LCCs, with operating costs some 25 to 50 per cent lower than the traditional carriers, have become a highly effective competitive force on these routes between various city pairs and have forced down prices.

Despite these successes, a period of increasing fuel prices and falling consumer demand from 2008 led some commentators to suggest that the LCCs were unlikely to survive. However, although they experienced some tough years, the LCCs have proved to be very resilient. They now account for about 40 per cent of the European aviation market and this share is forecast to grow in the future.

Ryanair and easyJet have also tried to make improvements to customer service. For example, Ryanair made changes to its website to make it easier and quicker to book tickets. Both companies have also tried to target more business customers. Ryanair introduced 'business plus' tickets, which give extra baggage allowance and premium seats at the front of the plane while remaining very price competitive.

Four of the biggest airlines in Europe are LCCs and it seems that the market will remain highly contestable for the foreseeable future.

1. *Make a list of those factors that determine the contestability of a particular air route.*
2. *In the UK, train operators compete for franchises to run services on a particular route. The franchises are normally for 7, 10, 12 or 15 years. The franchise specifies prices and minimum levels of services (frequency, timing and quality). Would this be a good system to adopt in the airline market over particular routes? How is the airline market similar to/different from the rail market in this regard?*
3. *In a period of rising fuel prices, and thus higher airfares, do you think that the low-cost carriers are more or less vulnerable than the traditional carriers in the short term? Would your answer differ when we look at the longer-term decisions of passengers?*
4. *In a recession, do you think that the low-cost carriers are more or less vulnerable than the traditional carriers? And in a boom?*

Section summary

1. Potential competition may be as important as actual competition in determining a firm's price and output strategy.

2. The threat of this competition increases as entry and exit costs to and from the industry diminish. If the entry and exit costs are zero, the market is said to be perfectly contestable. Under such circumstances, an existing monopolist will be forced to keep its profits down to the normal level if it is to resist entry by new firms. Exit costs will be lower, the lower are the sunk costs of the firm.

3. The theory of contestable markets provides a more realistic analysis of firms' behaviour than theories based simply on the existing number of firms in the industry.

END OF CHAPTER QUESTIONS

1. A perfectly competitive firm faces a price of £14 per unit. It has the following short-run cost schedule:

Output	0	1	2	3	4	5	6	7	8
TC (£)	10	18	24	30	38	50	66	91	120

   (a) Copy the table and put in additional rows for average cost and marginal cost at each level of output. (Enter the figures for marginal cost in the space between each column.)

   (b) Plot *AC, MC* and *MR* on a diagram.

   (c) Mark the profit-maximising output.

   (d) How much (supernormal) profit is made at this output? t

   (e) What would happen to the price in the long run if this firm were typical of others in the industry? Why would we need to know information about long-run average cost in order to give a precise answer to this question?

2. If the industry under perfect competition faces a downward-sloping demand curve, why does an individual firm face a horizontal demand curve?

3. If supernormal profits are competed away under perfect competition, why will firms have an incentive to become more efficient?

4. Is it a valid criticism of perfect competition to argue that it is incompatible with economies of scale?

5. On a diagram similar to Figure 7.4, show the long-run equilibrium for both firm and industry under perfect competition. Now assume that the demand for the product falls. Show the short-run and long-run effects.

6. Why is the profit-maximising price under monopoly greater than marginal cost? In what way can this be seen as inefficient?

7. On three diagrams like Figure 7.8, illustrate the effect on price, quantity and profit of each of the following: (a) a rise in demand; (b) a rise in fixed costs; (c) a rise in variable costs. In each case, show only the *AR, MR, AC* and *MC* curves.

8. Think of three examples of monopolies (local or national) and consider how contestable their markets are.

Online resources

Additional case studies on the student website

7.1 **B2B electronic marketplaces.** This case study examines the growth of firms trading with each other (business-to-business or 'B2B') over the Internet and considers the effects on competition.

7.2 **Measuring monopoly power.** This case study examines how the degree of monopoly power possessed by a firm can be measured.

7.3 **Competition in the pipeline?** This examines monopoly in the supply of gas.

7.4 **Windows cleaning.** This discusses the examination of Microsoft's market dominance by the US Justice Department and the European Commission.

Maths Case 7.1 Long-run equilibrium under perfect competition. Using calculus to find equilibrium output and price.

Maths Case 7.2 Price elasticity of demand and the profit-maximising price. A proof of the profit-maximising rule relating price elasticity of demand, price and marginal revenue.

Websites relevant to this chapter

See sites listed at the end of Chapter 8 on page 249.

8 Chapter

Profit Maximising under Imperfect Competition

Very few markets in practice can be classified as perfectly competitive or as a pure monopoly. The vast majority of firms do compete with other firms, often quite aggressively, and yet they are not price takers: they do have some degree of market power. Most markets, therefore, lie between the two extremes of monopoly and perfect competition, in the realm of 'imperfect competition'.

There are two types of imperfect competition: monopolistic competition and oligopoly.

Under monopolistic competition, there will normally be quite a large number of relatively small firms. Think of the number of car repair garages, builders, hairdressers, restaurants and other small traders that you get in any large town or city. They are in fierce competition with each other, and yet competition is not perfect. They are all trying to produce a product that is different from their rivals.

Under oligopoly, there will be only a few firms competing. Most of the best-known companies, such as Ford, Coca-Cola, Nike, BP and Apple, are oligopolists. Sometimes oligopolists will attempt to collude with each other to keep prices up. On other occasions, competition will be intense, with rival firms trying to undercut each other's prices, or developing new or better products in order to gain a larger share of the market. We will examine both collusion and competition between oligopolists and show when each is more likely to occur.

8.1   MONOPOLISTIC COMPETITION

We will start by looking at monopolistic competition. This was a theory developed in the 1930s by the American economist Edward Chamberlin. Monopolistic competition is nearer to the competitive end of the spectrum. It can best be understood as a situation where there are a lot of firms competing, but where each firm does nevertheless have some degree of market power (hence the term 'monopolistic' competition): each firm has some choice over what price to charge for its products.

Assumptions of monopolistic competition

- There are *quite a large number of firms*. As a result, each firm has an insignificantly small share of the market, and therefore its actions are unlikely to affect its rivals to any great extent. This means that when each firm makes its decisions it does not have to worry how its rivals will react. It assumes that what its rivals choose to do will *not* be influenced by what it does.

  This is known as the assumption of **independence**. (As we shall see later, this is not the case under oligopoly. There we assume that firms believe that their decisions *do* affect their rivals, and that their rivals' decisions will affect them. Under oligopoly, we assume that firms are *inter*dependent.)

- There is *freedom of entry* of new firms into the industry. If any firm wants to set up in business in this market, it is free to do so.

  In these two respects, therefore, monopolistic competition is like perfect competition.

- The situation differs from perfect competition, however, in that each firm produces a product or provides a service in some way different from those of its rivals. As a result, it can raise its price without losing all its customers. Thus its demand curve is downward sloping, although it will be relatively elastic given the large number of competitors to which customers can turn. This is known as the assumption of **product differentiation**.

  Restaurants, hairdressers and builders are all examples of monopolistic competition.

Give some other examples of monopolistic competition. (Try looking at www.yell.com if you are stuck.)

Definitions

Independence (of firms in a market) Where the decisions of one firm in a market will not have any significant effect on the demand curves of its rivals.

Product differentiation Where one firm's product is sufficiently different from its rivals' to allow it to raise the price of the product without customers all switching to the rivals' products. A situation where a firm faces a downward-sloping demand curve.

Equilibrium of the firm

Short run

As with other market structures, profits are maximised at the output where $MC = MR$. The diagram will be the same as for the monopolist, except that the AR and MR curves will be more elastic. This is illustrated in Figure 8.1(a). As with perfect competition, it is possible for the monopolistically competitive firm to make supernormal profit in the short run. This is shown as the shaded area.

Just how much profit the firm will make in the short run depends on the strength of demand: the position and elasticity of the demand curve. The further to the right the demand curve is relative to the average cost curve, and the less elastic the demand curve is, the greater will be the firm's short-run profit. Thus a firm facing little competition and whose product is considerably differentiated from that of its rivals may be able to earn considerable short-run profits.

1. *Why may a food shop charge higher prices than supermarkets for 'essential items' and yet very similar prices for delicatessen items?*
2. *Which of these two items is a petrol station more likely to sell at a discount: (a) oil; (b) sweets? Why?*

Long run

If typical firms are earning supernormal profit, new firms will enter the industry in the long run. As they do, they will take some of the customers away from established firms. The demand for the established firms will therefore fall. Their demand (AR) curve will shift to the left, and will continue doing so as long as supernormal profits remain and thus new firms continue entering.

Long-run equilibrium is reached when only normal profits remain: when there is no further incentive for new firms to enter. This is illustrated in Figure 8.1(b). The firm's demand curve settles at D_L, where it is tangential to the firm's $LRAC$ curve. Output will be Q_L: where $AR_L = LRAC$. (At any other output, $LRAC$ is greater than AR and thus less than normal profit would be made.)

1. *Why does the $LRMC$ curve cross the MR_L curve directly below the tangency point of the $LRAC$ and AR_L curves?*
2. *Assuming that supernormal profits can be made in the short run, will there be any difference in the long-run and short-run elasticity of demand? Explain.*

Limitations of the model

There are various problems in applying the model of monopolistic competition to the real world:

- Information may be imperfect. Firms will not enter an industry if they are unaware of what supernormal profits are being made, or if they underestimate the demand for the particular product they are considering selling.

Figure 8.1   Equilibrium of the firm under monopolistic competition

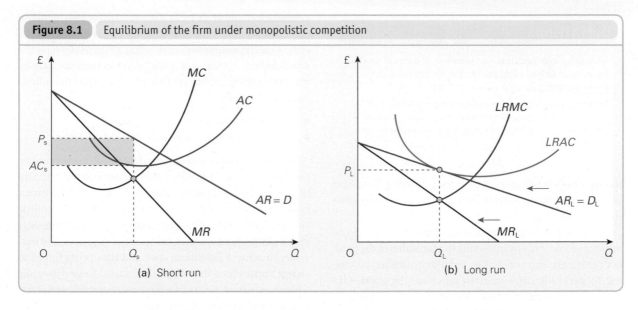

(a) Short run

(b) Long run

- Given that the firms in the industry produce different products, it is difficult if not impossible to derive a demand curve for the industry as a whole. Thus the analysis has to be confined to the level of the firm.

- Firms are likely to differ from each other not only in the product they produce or the service they offer, but also in their size and cost structure. What is more, entry may not be *completely* unrestricted. Two petrol stations could not set up in exactly the same place – on a busy crossroads, say. Thus although the typical or 'representative' firm may earn only normal profit in the long run, other firms may be able to earn long-run supernormal profit. They may have some cost advantage or produce something that is impossible to duplicate perfectly.

- One of the biggest problems with the simple model shown in Figure 8.1 is that it concentrates on price and output decisions. In practice, the profit-maximising firm under monopolistic competition also has to decide the exact variety of product to produce and how much to spend on advertising it. This will lead the firm to take part in non-price competition.

Non-price competition

Non-price competition involves two major elements: product development and advertising.

The major aims of *product development* are to produce a product that will sell well (i.e. one in high or potentially high demand) and that is different from rivals' products (i.e. has a relatively inelastic demand due to lack of close substitutes). For shops or other firms providing a service, 'product development' takes the form of attempting to provide a

---

SELLING ICE CREAM AS A STUDENT   CASE STUDIES AND APPLICATIONS

John's experience of monopolistic competition

When I was a student, my parents lived in Exeter in Devon, and at that time the city's bypass became completely jammed on a summer Saturday as holidaymakers made their way to the coast. Traffic queues were several miles long.

For a summer job, I drove a small ice-cream van. Early on, I had the idea of selling ice cream from a tray to the people queuing in their cars. I made more money on a Saturday than the rest of the week put together. I thought I was on to a good thing.

But news of this lucrative market soon spread, and each week new ice-cream sellers appeared – each one reducing my earnings! By the middle of August there were over thirty ice-cream sellers from five different ice-cream companies. Most tried to get to the beginning of the queue, to get ahead of their rivals.

Imagine the scene. A family driving to the coast rounds a bend and is suddenly met by a traffic jam and several ice-cream sellers all jostling to sell them an ice cream. It was quite surreal. Not surprisingly, many of the potential customers refused to buy, feeling somewhat intimidated by the spectacle. It was not long before most of us realised that it was best to disperse and find a section of the road where there were no other sellers.

But with so many ice-cream sellers, no one made much money. My supernormal earnings had been reduced to a normal level. I made about the same on Saturday to people stuck in queues as I would have done if I had driven my van around the streets.

1. *Was there totally free entry to this market?*
2. *What forms of product differentiation were there?*

> ### Definitions
>
> **Non-price competition** Competition in terms of product promotion (advertising, packaging, etc.) or product development.
>
> **Excess capacity (under monopolistic competition)** In the long run, firms under monopolistic competition will produce at an output below their minimum-cost point.

service which is better than, or at least different from, that of rivals: personal service, late opening, certain lines stocked, and so on.

The major aim of *advertising* is to sell the product. This can be achieved not only by informing the consumer of the product's existence and availability, but also by deliberately trying to persuade consumers to purchase the good. Like product development, successful advertising will not only increase demand, but also make the firm's demand curve less TC 6 p50 elastic since it stresses the specific qualities of this firm's product over its rivals' (see Box 2.4 on page 61).

Product development and advertising not only increase a firm's demand and hence revenue, they also involve increased costs. So how much should a firm advertise to maximise profits?

For any given price and product, the optimal amount of advertising is where the revenue from *additional* advertising (MR_A) is equal to its cost (MC_A). As long as $MR_A > MC_A$, additional advertising will add to profit. But extra amounts spent TC 8 p109 on advertising are likely to lead to smaller and smaller increases in sales. Thus MR_A falls, until $MR_A = MC_A$. At that point, no further profit can be made. It is at a maximum.

Why will additional advertising lead to smaller and smaller increases in sales?

Two problems arise with this analysis:

- The effect of product development and advertising on demand will be difficult for a firm to forecast.
- Product development and advertising are likely to have different effects at different prices. Profit maximisation, therefore, will involve the more complex choice of the optimum combination of price, type of product, and level and variety of advertising.

Monopolistic competition and the public interest

Comparison with perfect competition

It is often argued that monopolistic competition leads to a less efficient allocation of resources than perfect competition.

Figure 8.2 compares the long-run equilibrium positions for two firms. One firm is under perfect competition and thus faces a horizontal demand curve. It will produce an output of Q_1 at a price of P_1. The other is under monopolistic

competition and thus faces a downward-sloping demand curve. It will produce the lower output of Q_2 at the higher price of P_2. A crucial assumption here is that a firm would have the *same* long-run average cost (*LRAC*) curve in both cases. Given this assumption, monopolistic competition has the following disadvantages:

- Less will be sold and at a higher price.
- Firms will not be producing at the least-cost point.

By producing more, firms would move to a lower point on their *LRAC* curve. Thus firms under monopolistic competition are said to have **excess capacity**. In Figure 8.2 this excess capacity is shown as $Q_1 - Q_2$. In other words, monopolistic competition is typified by quite a large number of firms (e.g. petrol stations), all operating at an output less than that necessary to achieve minimum cost, and thus being forced to charge a price above that which they could charge if they had TC 3 p26 a bigger turnover. How often have you been to a petrol station and had to queue for the pumps.

Does this imply that if, say, half of the petrol stations were closed down, the consumer would benefit? (Clue: what would happen to the demand curves of the remaining stations?)

On the other hand, it is often argued that these wastes of monopolistic competition may be insignificant. In the first place, although the firm's demand curve is downward sloping, it is still likely to be highly elastic due to the large number of substitutes. In the second place, although the firm under monopolistic competition will not be operating quite at the bottom of its *LRAC* curve, the nature of the industry may allow some economies of scale to be gained. The *LRAC* curve would thus be lower than in the case of the larger

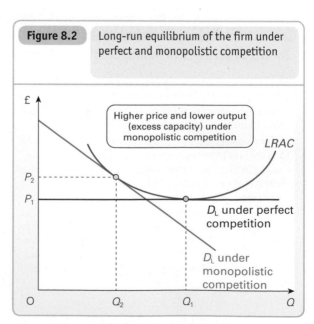

| Figure 8.2 | Long-run equilibrium of the firm under perfect and monopolistic competition |

Higher price and lower output (excess capacity) under monopolistic competition

LRAC

D_L under perfect competition

D_L under monopolistic competition

number of smaller firms that would be necessary to keep the industry perfectly competitive. The size of the economies of scale, if any, will obviously vary from industry to industry.

Perhaps more importantly, consumers are likely to benefit from monopolistic competition by having a greater variety of products to choose from. Given that we all have individual tastes and preferences, our utility will be higher with choice.

 Which would you rather have: five restaurants to choose from, each with very different menus and each having spare tables so that you could always guarantee getting one; or just two restaurants to choose from, charging less but with less choice and making it necessary to book well in advance?

Comparison with monopoly

The arguments here are very similar to those comparing perfect competition and monopoly.

On the one hand, freedom of entry for new firms and hence the lack of long-run supernormal profits under monopolistic competition are likely to help keep prices down for the consumer and encourage cost saving. On the other hand, monopolies are likely to achieve greater economies of scale and have more funds for investment and research and development.

Section summary

1. Monopolistic competition occurs where there is free entry to the industry and quite a large number of firms operating independently of each other, but where each firm has some market power as a result of producing differentiated products or services.

2. In the short run, firms can make supernormal profits. In the long run, however, freedom of entry will drive profits down to the normal level. The long-run equilibrium of the firm is where the (downward-sloping) demand curve is tangential to the long-run average cost curve.

3. The long-run equilibrium is one of excess capacity. Given that the demand curve is downward sloping, its tangency point with the *LRAC* curve will not be at the bottom of the *LRAC* curve. Increased production would thus be possible at *lower* average cost.

4. In practice, supernormal profits may persist into the long run: firms have imperfect information; entry may not be completely unrestricted; firms may use non-price competition to maintain an advantage over their rivals.

5. Non-price competition may take the form of product development or product promotion (advertising, etc.).

6. Monopolistically competitive firms, because of excess capacity, may have higher costs than perfectly competitive firms, but consumers may gain from a greater diversity of products.

7. Monopolistically competitive firms may have fewer economies of scale than monopolies and conduct less research and development, but the competition may keep prices lower than under monopoly.

8.2 OLIGOPOLY

Oligopoly occurs when just a few firms between them share a large proportion of the industry.

There are, however, significant differences in the structure of industries under oligopoly and similarly significant differences in the behaviour of firms. The firms may produce a virtually identical product (e.g. metals, chemicals, sugar, petrol). Most oligopolists, however, produce differentiated products (e.g. cars, soap powder, soft drinks, electrical appliances). Much of the competition between such oligopolists is in terms of the marketing of their particular brand. Marketing practices may differ considerably from one industry to another.

The two key features of oligopoly

Despite the differences between oligopolies, two crucial features distinguish oligopoly from other market structures.

Barriers to entry

In contrast to the situation under monopolistic competition, there are various barriers to the entry of new firms. These are similar to those under monopoly (see pages 201–4). The size of the barriers, however, varies from industry to industry. In some cases entry is relatively easy, whereas in others it is virtually impossible.

Interdependence of the firms

Because there are only a few firms under oligopoly, each has to take account of the others. This means that they are mutually dependent: they are **interdependent**. Each firm is affected by its rivals' actions. If a firm changes the price or specification of its product, for example, or the amount of its advertising, the sales of its rivals will be affected. The rivals may then respond by changing their price, specification or advertising. No firm can afford to ignore the actions and reactions of other firms in the industry.

 KEY IDEA 23

People often think and behave strategically. How you think others will respond to your actions is likely to influence your own behaviour. Firms, for example, when considering a price or product change will often take into account the likely reactions of their rivals.

Definition

Interdependence (under oligopoly) One of the two key features of oligopoly. Each firm will be affected by its rivals' decisions. Likewise its decisions will affect its rivals. Firms recognise this interdependence. This recognition will affect their decisions.

BOX 8.2   INCREASING CONCENTRATION

CASE STUDIES AND APPLICATIONS

Losing innocence

We have identified barriers to entry under oligopoly as a factor in keeping the number of firms low. But why does market power grow in some oligopolies, with the number of firms decreasing? The answer can be found in mergers and acquisitions, tough economic conditions and increasing brand loyalty, all of which can reduce competition.

As we saw in Box 7.1, one of the simplest ways of assessing the extent of market power is to look at concentration ratios – the market share of the leading firms. The table below gives some extracts of the table in that box.

Five-firm concentration ratios for various industries (by output)

Industry	Five-firm ratio	Industry	Five-firm ratio
Sugar	99	Fishing	16
Tobacco products	99	Advertising	10
Confectionary	81	Wholesale distribution	6
Soft drinks, mineral water	75	Furniture	5
Motor vehicles	34	Construction	5

Source: Based on data in *United Kingdom Input–Output Analyses,* Table 8.31 (Office of National Statistics, 2006).

1. *Can you identify which firms make up the majority of the soft drinks industry?*
2. *What are the characteristics that make fishing so 'unconcentrated'?*
3. *Does the relatively low concentration in the car industry surprise you? Explain your answer.*

Unsurprisingly, the industries with the highest concentration ratios display a number of varying characteristics. They often involve high capital costs, allowing firms to benefit from economies of scale. Alternatively, a small number of firms have control of the required resources; sugar is a good example here.

In industries with differentiated products, such as confectionary, there are high levels of branding and advertising. On the other hand, the industries with the lowest

ratios tend to have lower costs of entry. In many cases their advertising spend is likely to be local, if it exists at all.

Innocent

But why do concentration ratios change over time? One factor is mergers and takeovers. Take the case of Innocent. In 1999 three friends set up the Innocent® Drinks Company. Specialising in smoothies, it was a new entrant to the soft drinks industry, one which is dominated by Coca-Cola®, Pepsi™ and Cadbury Schweppes (now the Dr Pepper Snapple® Group).

Over the next decade the company grew, from three employees to more than 250, achieving a market share of over 77 per cent by 2007. (By 'market' here we are referring to smoothies and yoghurt drinks rather than all soft drinks.) Making good profits and with a reputation for outstanding corporate social responsibility, life seemed good for the three entrepreneurs.

However, even the most successful of firms is vulnerable to takeover and in 2009 it was announced that Coca-Cola had acquired an 18 per cent stake in Innocent. By 2013, this had increased to 90 per cent, with Coca-Cola taking full control. The outcome was uproar from those who had 'bought-in' to the Innocent mission, and of course an increase in the concentration ratio of the soft drinks industry. However, one of the three entrepreneurs who established Innocent Drinks, Richard Reed, has argued that without the backing of Coca-Cola the firm would have been unable to achieve its global success.

Innocent drinks has approximately 60 per cent of the UK market. However, this once new entrant is itself now under increasing competition from a number of new start-ups including Savse®, Plenish®, Radiance, Moju, Love Smoothies, Blend & Press and Juice Warrior.

1. *Are there any advantages to consumers in a highly concentrated industry?*
2. *Explain why the measurement of the concentration ratio will be dependent on the definition of the market, referring to the Innocent story.*
3. *Do small independent burger companies have any market advantages over the global firms such as McDonald's® and Burger King®?*

It is impossible, therefore, to predict the effect on a firm's sales of, say, a change in its price without first making some assumption about the reactions of other firms. Different assumptions yield different predictions. For this reason there is no one single theory of oligopoly. Firms may react differently and unpredictably.

KI 10
p70

Competition and collusion

The interdependence of firms in an oligopolistic market pulls them in two very different directions:

- Each firm, by carefully studying the market and its rivals' strategy may believe that, by competing, it can gain a greater share of industry profits.
- On the other hand, firms may conclude that competition will be destructive and lead to lower profits: i.e. through retaliatory price-cutting. So instead, they may prefer to collude with each other by making agreements about price, output, product design, etc. By acting together as if they were a monopoly, the firms could take actions that jointly maximise industry profits and share these profits between them.

These two policies are incompatible. The more fiercely firms compete to gain a bigger share of industry profits, the smaller these industry profits will become. For example, price competition will drive down the average industry price, while competition through advertising will raise industry costs. Either way, industry profits will fall.

Sometimes firms collude, sometimes not. The following sections examine first *collusive oligopoly* (both open and tacit), and then *non-collusive oligopoly*.

Industry equilibrium under collusive oligopoly

When firms under oligopoly engage in collusion, they may agree on output, prices, market share, advertising expenditure, etc. Such collusion reduces the uncertainty they face. It reduces the fear of engaging in competitive price cutting or retaliatory advertising, both of which could reduce total industry profits.

A formal collusive agreement is called a *cartel*. The cartel will maximise profits if it acts like a monopoly: if the members behave as if they were a single firm. This is illustrated in Figure 8.3.

The total market demand curve is shown with the corresponding market *MR* curve. The cartel's *MC* curve is the *horizontal* sum of the *MC* curves of its members (since we are adding the *output* of each of the cartel members at each level of marginal cost). Profits are maximised at Q_1 where $MC = MR$. The cartel must therefore set a price of P_1 (at which Q_1 will be demanded).

TC 8
p109

KI 22
p190

Having agreed on the cartel price, the members may then compete against each other using *non-price competition*, to gain as big a share of resulting sales (Q_1) as they can.

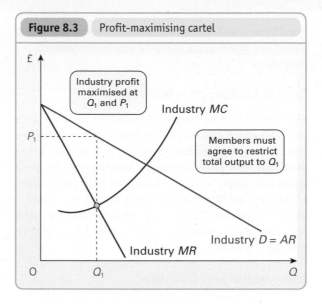

Figure 8.3 Profit-maximising cartel

 How will advertising affect the cartel's MC and AR curves? How will this affect the profit-maximising output? Is there any problem here for the cartel in fixing the price?

Alternatively, the cartel members may somehow agree to divide the market between them. Each member would be given a *quota*. The sum of all the quotas must add up to Q_1. If the quotas exceeded Q_1, either there would be output unsold if price remained fixed at P_1, or the price would fall.

But if quotas are to be set by the cartel, how will it decide the level of each individual member's quota? The most likely method is for the cartel to divide the market between the members according to their current market share. This is the solution most likely to be accepted as 'fair'.

 If this 'fair' solution were adopted, what effect would it have on the industry MC curve in Figure 8.3?

In many countries, cartels are illegal – being seen by the government as a means of driving up prices and profits, and thereby as being against the public interest (see section 14.1). Where open collusion is illegal, however, firms may simply break the law, or get round it. Alternatively, firms may stay

Definitions

Collusive oligopoly Where oligopolists agree (formally or informally) to limit competition between themselves. They may set output quotas, fix prices, limit product promotion or development, or agree not to 'poach' each other's markets.

Non-collusive oligopoly Where oligopolists have no agreement between themselves, formal, informal or tacit.

Cartel A formal collusive agreement.

Quota (set by a cartel) The output that a given member of a cartel is allowed to produce (production quota) or sell (sales quota).

within the law, but still *tacitly* collude by watching each other's prices and keeping them similar. Firms may tacitly 'agree' to avoid price wars or aggressive advertising campaigns.

Tacit collusion: price leadership

One form of **tacit collusion** is where firms keep to the price set by an established leader. The leader may be the largest firm: the one dominating the industry. This is known as **dominant firm price leadership**. Alternatively, the price leader may simply be the one that has proved to be the most reliable one to follow: the one that is the best barometer of market conditions. This is known as **barometric firm price leadership**. Let us examine each of these two types of price leadership in turn.

Dominant firm price leadership

How in theory does the leader set the price? The leader will maximise profits where its marginal revenue is equal to its marginal cost. Figure 8.4(a) shows the total market demand curve and the supply curve of all followers. These firms, like

perfectly competitive firms, accept the price as given, only in this case it is the price set by the leader, and thus their joint supply curve is simply the sum of their MC curves – the same as under perfect competition.

The leader's demand curve can be seen as that portion of market demand unfilled by the other firms. In other words, it is market demand minus other firms' supply. At P_1 the whole of market demand is satisfied by the other firms, and so the demand for the leader is zero (point a). At P_2 the other firms' supply is zero, and so the leader faces the full market demand (point b). The leader's demand curve thus connects points a and b.

The leader's profit will be maximised where its marginal cost equals its marginal revenue. This is shown in Figure 8.4(b). The diagram is the same as Figure 8.4(a) but with the addition of MC and MR curves for the leader. The leader's marginal cost equals its marginal revenue at an output of Q_L (giving a point l on its demand curve). The leader thus sets a price of P_L, which the other firms then duly follow. They supply Q_F (i.e. at point f on their supply curve). Total market demand at P_L is Q_T (i.e. point t on the market demand curve), which must add up to the output of both leader and followers (i.e. $Q_L + Q_F$).

 Draw a pair of diagrams like those in Figure 8.4. Illustrate what would happen if market demand rose but the costs of neither leader nor followers rose. Would there be an equal percentage increase in the output of both leader and followers?

In practice, however, it is very difficult for the leader to apply this theory. The leader's demand and MR curves depend on the followers' supply curve – something the leader will find virtually impossible to estimate with any degree of accuracy. The leader will thus have to make a rough estimate of what its profit-maximising price and output will be, and simply choose that. That is the best it can do.

> ### Definitions
>
> **Tacit collusion** Where oligopolists take care not to engage in price cutting, excessive advertising or other forms of competition. There may be unwritten 'rules' of collusive behaviour such as price leadership.
>
> **Dominant firm price leadership** Where firms (the followers) choose the same price as that set by a dominant firm in the industry (the leader).
>
> **Barometric firm price leadership** Where the price leader is the one whose prices are believed to reflect market conditions in the most satisfactory way.

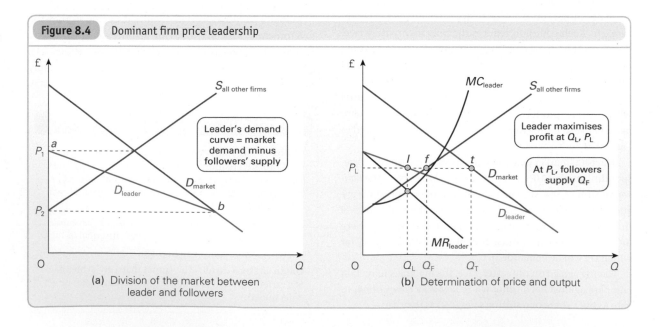

Figure 8.4   Dominant firm price leadership

(a) Division of the market between leader and followers

(b) Determination of price and output

In Figure 8.4, the various curves can be represented by equations and this would allow us to solve for P_L, Q_L, Q_F and Q_T. An example of this is given in Maths Case 8.1 on the student website.

Note that we derived all the curves in Figure 8.4 from just three: the market demand curve, the followers' supply curve and the leader's *MC* curve. It follows that, if we know the functions for these three curves, we can derive the functions for the remainder.

A simpler model is where the leader assumes that it will maintain a constant *market share* (say, 50 per cent). It makes this assumption because it also assumes that all other firms will follow its price up and down. This is illustrated in Figure 8.5. It knows its current position on its demand curve (say, point *a*). It then estimates how responsive its demand will be to industry-wide price changes and thus constructs its demand and *MR* curves accordingly. It then chooses to produce Q_L at a price of P_L: at point *l* on its demand curve (where $MC = MR$). Other firms then follow that price. Total market demand will be Q_T, with followers supplying that portion of the market not supplied by the leader, namely $Q_T - Q_L$.

There is one problem with this model: the assumption that the followers will want to maintain a constant market share. If the leader raises its price, the followers may want to supply more, given that the new price (=MR for a price-taking follower) may well be above their marginal cost. On the other hand, the followers may decide merely to maintain their market share for fear of retaliation from the leader, in the form of price cuts or an aggressive advertising campaign.

Barometric firm price leadership

A similar exercise can be conducted by a barometric firm. Although such a firm does not dominate the industry, its price will be followed by the others. It merely tries to estimate its demand and *MR* curves – assuming, again, a constant market share – and then produces where $MR = MC$ and sets price accordingly.

In practice, which firm is taken as the barometer may frequently change. Whether we are talking about oil companies, car producers or banks, any firm may take the initiative in raising prices. Then, if the other firms are merely waiting for someone to take the lead – say, because costs have risen – they will all quickly follow suit. For example, if one of the banks raises its mortgage rates by 1 per cent, then this is likely to stimulate the others to follow suit.

Tacit collusion: rules of thumb

An alternative to following an established leader is to follow an established set of simple 'rules of thumb'. These rules do not involve setting *MC* equal to *MR*, and thus may involve an immediate loss of profit. They do, however, help to prevent an outbreak of competition, and thus help to maintain profits into the longer term.

One example of a rule of thumb is **average cost pricing**. Here, producers simply add a certain percentage for profit on top of average costs. Thus, if average costs rise by 10 per cent, prices will automatically be raised by 10 per cent. This is a particularly useful rule of thumb in times of inflation, when all firms will be experiencing similar cost increases.

 If a firm has a typically shaped average cost curve and sets prices 10 per cent above average cost, what will its supply curve look like?

Another rule of thumb is to have certain **price benchmarks**. Thus clothes may sell for £19.95, £24.95 or £49.95 (but not £18.31 or £36.42). If costs rise, then firms simply raise their price to the next benchmark, knowing that other firms will do the same.

Rules of thumb can also be applied to advertising (e.g. you do not criticise other firms' products, only praise your own); or to the design of the product (e.g. lighting manufacturers tacitly agreeing not to bring out an everlasting light bulb).

Definitions

Average cost pricing Where a firm sets its price by adding a certain percentage for (average) profit on top of average cost.

Price benchmark A price that is typically used. Firms, when raising a price, will usually raise it from one benchmark to another.

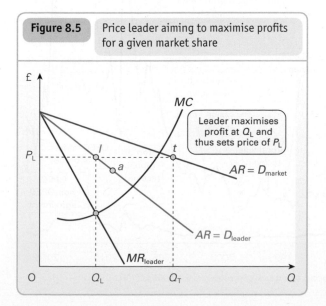

Figure 8.5 Price leader aiming to maximise profits for a given market share

Leader maximises profit at Q_L and thus sets price of P_L

MC

$AR = D_{market}$

$AR = D_{leader}$

MR_{leader}

BOX 8.3 | **OPEC**

The history of the world's most famous cartel

OPEC, the Organization of the Petroleum Exporting Countries, is probably the best known of all cartels. It was set up in 1960 by the five major oil-exporting countries: Saudi Arabia, Iran, Iraq, Kuwait and Venezuela. Today it has 13 members, including Nigeria, Angola, Libya and Ecuador. Its stated objectives were as follows:

- The co-ordination and unification of the petroleum policies of member countries.
- The organisation of means to ensure the stabilisation of prices, eliminating harmful and unnecessary fluctuations.

The years leading up to 1960 had seen the oil-producing countries increasingly in conflict with the international oil companies, which extracted oil under 'concessionary agreement'. The oil-producing countries had little say over output and price levels.

The early years

Despite the formation of OPEC in 1960, it was not until 1973 that control of oil production was effectively transferred from the oil companies to the oil countries, with OPEC making the decisions on how much oil to produce and thereby determining its oil revenue. By this time OPEC consisted of 13 members.

OPEC's pricing policy over the 1970s consisted of setting a market price for Saudi Arabian crude (the market leader), and leaving other OPEC members to set their prices in line with this. This was a form of dominant 'firm' price leadership.

As long as demand remained buoyant, and was price inelastic, this policy allowed large price increases with consequent large revenue increases. In 1973/4, after the Arab–Israeli war, OPEC raised the price of oil from around $3 per barrel to over $12. The price was kept at roughly this level until 1979. And yet the sales of oil did not fall significantly.

 Illustrate what was happening here on a demand and supply diagram. Remember that demand was highly inelastic and was increasing over time.

After 1979, however, following a further increase in the price of oil from around $15 to $40 per barrel, demand did fall. This was largely due to the recession of the early 1980s which, in turn, was largely caused by governments' responses to the oil price increases.

The use of quotas

Faced by declining demand, OPEC after 1982 agreed to limit output and allocate production quotas in an attempt to keep

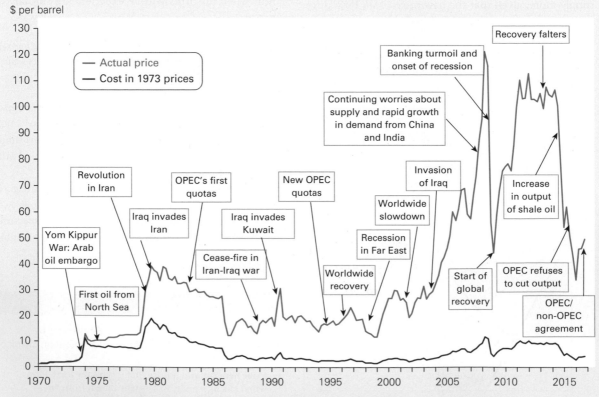

Oil prices

Source: Nominal oil price data from *Global Economic Monitor (GEM), Commodities* (World Bank); Price Index from *Data Extracts* (OECD).

the price up. However, the cartel was beginning to break down. Reasons included:

- The world recession and the resulting fall in the demand for oil.
- Growing output from non-OPEC members.
- 'Cheating' by some OPEC members who exceeded their quota limits.

With a glut of oil, OPEC could no longer maintain the price. As the chart shows, the oil price fell.

The trend of lower oil prices was reversed in the late 1980s. With the world economy booming, the demand for oil rose and along with it the price. Then in 1990, Iraq invaded Kuwait and the first Gulf War ensued. With the cutting off of supplies from Kuwait and Iraq, the supply of oil fell and there was a sharp rise in its price.

But with the ending of the war and the recession of the early 1990s, the price rapidly fell again and only recovered slowly as the world economy started expanding once more.

On the demand side, the development of energy-saving technology plus increases in fuel taxes led to a relatively slow growth in consumption. On the supply side, the growing proportion of output supplied by non-OPEC members, plus the adoption in 1994 of a relatively high OPEC production ceiling of 24.5 million barrels per day, meant that supply more than kept pace with demand.

The situation for OPEC deteriorated further in the late 1990s, following the recession in the Far East. Oil demand fell by some 2 million barrels per day. By early 1999, the price had fallen to around $10 per barrel – a mere $2.70 in 1973 prices! In response, OPEC members agreed to cut production by 4.3 million barrels per day. The objective was to push the price back up to around $18–20 per barrel.

But, with the Asian economy recovering and the world generally experiencing more rapid economic growth, the price rose rapidly and soon overshot the $20 mark. By early 2000 it had reached $30: a tripling in price in just 12 months. With the world economy then slowing down, however, the price rapidly fell back, reaching $18 in November 2001.

However, in late 2001 the relationship between OPEC and non-OPEC oil producers changed. The 10 members of the OPEC cartel decided to cut production by 1.5 million barrels a day. This followed an agreement with five of the major oil producers outside of the cartel to reduce their output too, the aim being to push oil prices upwards and then stabilise them at around $25 per barrel. The alliance between OPEC and non-OPEC oil producers is the first such instance of its kind in the oil industry. As a result, it seemed that OPEC might now once again be able to control the market for oil.

The price surge of 2003–8

But how successfully could this alliance cope with crisis? With worries over an impending war with Iraq and a strike in Venezuela, the oil price rose again in late 2002, passing the $30 mark in early 2003. In 2004, the situation worsened with supply concerns related to the situation in Iraq, Saudi Arabia, Russia and Nigeria, and the oil price rose to over $50 in October 2004. OPEC tried to relax the quotas, but found it difficult to adjust supply sufficiently quickly to make any real difference to the price.

From 2006, oil prices increased more sharply than they ever had before and, for the first time in years, the real price of oil exceeded that seen in the 1970s. The major cause of the increases was very substantial increases in demand, particularly from India and China, coupled with continuing concerns about supply. The implications of the sharp price increases were substantial: inflationary pressures built up across the world, while the income of OPEC nations doubled in the first half of 2008.

By July 2008 the price reached $147. Some analysts were predicting a price of over $200 per barrel by the end of the year.

... and then a fall but rise again

But then, with the growing banking turmoil and fears of a recession, the price began to fall, and rapidly so, reaching $34 by the end of the year – less than a quarter of the price just five months previously. While this was good news for the consumer, it was potentially damaging for investment in oil exploration and development and also for investment in alternative energy supplies.

OPEC responded to the falling price by announcing cuts in production, totalling some 14 per cent between August 2008 and January 2009. But with OPEC producing less than a third of global oil output, this represented less than 5 per cent of global production. Nevertheless, as global demand recovered, so oil prices rose again from 2009, peaking in March 2012 at $118.

A new threat to OPEC

Prices remained relatively stable from 2012 to mid-2014. However, OPEC was facing increased competition from a big new entrant into the market – US shale oil production. US shale oil production doubled between 2011 and 2014, contributing to a fall in the oil price from $112 a barrel in June 2014 to just $30 a barrel in February 2016.

OPEC responded to this fall in prices, not by cutting output, but by announcing that it would retain output. This strategy was relying on the fact that although production from shale oil wells has low marginal costs, it often only lasts two or three years. Investment in new shale oil wells, by contrast, tends to be relatively expensive. By OPEC maintaining production, it was hoping to use its remaining market power to reduce supply of competitors over the medium to long term.

However, with revenues from oil falling so dramatically, OPEC and non-OPEC producers (such as Russia) reached an agreement in December 2016 to cut production. This is the first time such an agreement had occurred since 2001 and it was estimated that the countries involved were responsible

(Continued)

BOX 8.3 | **OPEC (continued)**

for producing about 55 per cent of global output. The oil price immediately started to increase again.

Early reports suggest record adherence to the agreement. The problem for OPEC is that the increase in oil price has made US shale production profitable once again. A number of rigs that temporarily shut down have become operational again and production has increased by 9 million barrels a day. It will be interesting to see what influence OPEC can have on the price of oil in the future given the increase in non-conventional extraction, such as in shale formations.

1. *What conditions facilitate the formation of a cartel? Which of these conditions were to be found in the oil market in (a) the early 1970s; (b) the mid-1980s; (c) the mid-2000s; (d) 2016?*
2. *Could OPEC have done anything to prevent the long-term decline in real oil prices seen from 1981 to 2002?*
3. *Does the increased demand seen from China and India imply that the era of cheap energy is over? What impact could technology have in the long run on (a) demand; (b) supply?*

Factors favouring collusion

Collusion between firms, whether formal or tacit, is more likely when firms can clearly identify with each other or some leader and when they trust each other not to break agreements. It will be easier for firms to collude if the following conditions apply:

- There are only very few firms all well known to each other.
- They are not secretive with each other about costs and production methods.
- They have similar production methods and average costs, and are thus likely to want to change prices at the same time and by the same percentage.
- They produce similar products and can thus more easily reach agreements on price.
- There is a dominant firm.
- There are significant barriers to entry and therefore little fear of disruption by new firms.
- The market is stable. If industry demand or production costs fluctuate wildly, it will be difficult to make agreements, partly due to difficulties in predicting and partly

because agreements may frequently have to be amended. There is a particular problem in a declining market where firms may be tempted to undercut each other's prices in order to maintain their sales.

- There are no government measures to curb collusion.

In which of the following industries is collusion likely to occur: bricks, beer, margarine, cement, crisps, washing powder, blank DVDs, carpets?

Non-collusive oligopoly: the breakdown of collusion

In some oligopolies, there may only be a few (if any) factors favouring collusion. In such cases, the likelihood of price competition is greater.

Even if there is collusion, there will always be the temptation for individual oligopolists to 'cheat', by cutting prices or by selling more than their allotted quota.

Let us take the case of a cartel consisting of five equal-sized firms. The whole cartel is illustrated in Figure 8.6(a). Assume that the cartel sets the industry profit-maximising

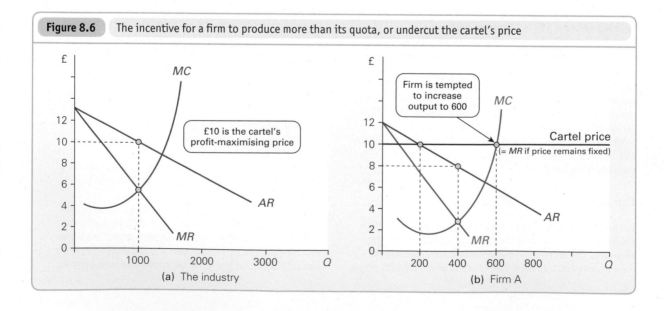

Figure 8.6 The incentive for a firm to produce more than its quota, or undercut the cartel's price

price of £10. This will give an industry output of 1000 units, which the cartel divides equally between its five members: i.e. each member is assigned a quota of 200 units.

Now consider Figure 8.6(b). This shows the position for one of the members of the cartel, firm A. Provided the cartel's price remains fixed at £10, then £10 would also be the marginal revenue for the individual firm. This will create an incentive for cartel members to cheat: to sell more than their allotted quota. Firm A would maximise its own profits by selling 600 units, where $MC = P (= MR)$, provided it could do this by taking market share off the other members, and thus leaving total industry output (and hence price) unaffected.

Alternatively, individual members might be tempted to undercut the cartel's price. Again, provided the rest of the cartel maintained its price at £10, firm A would face a relatively elastic demand curve (shown by AR in Figure 8.6(b)). A modest cut in its price would attract considerable custom away from the other members of the cartel. Firm A would maximise its profit by cutting its price to £8 and thereby increasing its sales to 400 units.

The danger, of course, with either selling above quota or cutting price is that this would invite retaliation from the other members of the cartel, with a resulting price war. Price would then fall and the cartel could well break up in disarray.

Non-collusive oligopoly: assumptions about rivals' behaviour

Even though oligopolists might not collude, they will still need to take account of rivals' likely behaviour when deciding their own strategy. In doing so, they will probably look at rivals' past behaviour and make assumptions based on it. There are three well-known models, each based on a different set of assumptions.

The Cournot model: firms choose quantity and the market determines the price

One of the earliest models of oligopoly was developed by the French economist Augustin Cournot in 1838. The simplest version of the **Cournot model** has the following assumptions.

- Each firm has to choose an output level for a given period without knowing its rivals' production plans (although, except in the case of new firms, they will know how much their rivals have produced in the past). In other words, firms have to make decisions about production simultaneously.
- Production has long lead times and is relatively inflexible. For example, imagine a business investing in a factory or unit that has a specific production capacity. Once the building work begins and the specialised machinery has been ordered and installed, it is difficult for the firm to alter its planned output.

- Whereas output has long lead times, the market price adjusts instantly so that each firm is able to sell all the output it produces.
- The good is homogenous and each firm has the same costs. This means that all the firms in the market sell their output for the same price.

This combination of flexible prices and inflexible output creates an interesting strategic environment. The price the firm receives for its output, in any given period, depends on the production decisions of other firms as well as its own. To calculate its profit-maximising output it has to estimate the most likely output its rivals will produce. The Cournot model assumes that each firm expects its rival(s) to produce the same amount in the current period as it did in the previous period.

To make the analysis as simple as possible we will assume that the industry is a **duopoly** and that the two firms, A and B, each have the same costs.

Figure 8.7(a) illustrates the profit-maximising price and output for firm A. The total market demand curve is shown as D_M. Assume that firm B produced Q_{B_1} units last year. Firm A, according to the model's assumption, therefore believes that firm B will continue to produce Q_{B_1} units this year.

To calculate firm A's profit-maximising output we need to identify its **residual demand curve**: i.e. the curve showing how much of the total demand is left for firm A, after B has supplied the market with its output. With firm B's output assumed to be Q_{B_1}, firm A perceives its own residual demand curve to be D_{A1}. This is the market demand curve, D_M, minus Q_{B_1} units: i.e. the horizontal gap between D_M and D_{A_1} in Figure 8.7(a).

The marginal revenue curve corresponding to D_{A_1} is MR_{A_1} and the profit-maximising output is Q_{A_1}, where $MR_{A_1} = MC_A$. The market will adjust instantly so that firm A can sell Q_{A_1} units and firm B can sell Q_{B_1} units of this homogenous product for a price of P_1.

If firm A believed that firm B would produce *more* than Q_{B_1}, its residual demand and MR curves would be further to the left and the profit-maximising quantity and price would both be lower. This illustrates that the outputs are strategic substitutes – as firm A believes that firm B will produce more, its best response is to produce less.

TC 8
p109

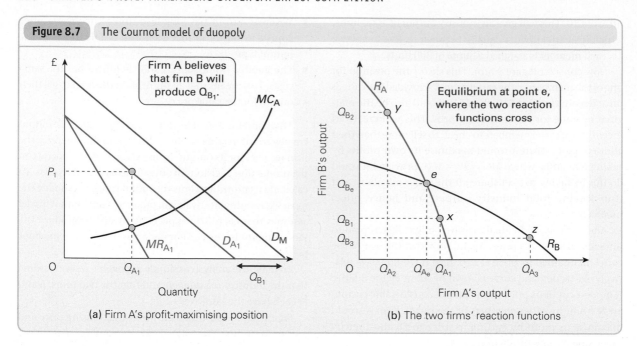

Figure 8.7 The Cournot model of duopoly

(a) Firm A's profit-maximising position

(b) The two firms' reaction functions

One limitation of the analysis so far is that it only illustrates firm A's profit-maximising best response to one predicted level of output: i.e. that firm B produce Q_{B_1} units. Firm A's *reaction function*, illustrated by curve R_A in Figure 8.7(b), shows its profit-maximising best responses to *all* the different outputs its rival could produce. It has a negative slope because outputs are strategic substitutes: the more firm B produces, the less will firm A produce. Thus if it perceived that firm B would produce Q_{B_2} units, it would produce Q_{A_2} units (point *y*).

Figure 8.7(b) also illustrates firm B's reaction function, assuming that firm B behaves similarly to firm A and assumes that its rival will produce a particular level of output. Firm B's reaction function is given by the curve R_B. Thus if firm B perceived that A would produce Q_{A_3} units, firm B would produce Q_{B_3} units (point *z*)

What is the *Cournot equilibrium*? This will occur at point *e* in Figure 8.7(b). Only at this point will neither firm choose to adjust its output once it has discovered the production level of its rival. How is this point reached if neither firm currently produces that level of output?

Assume that production is at point *x*. Firm A predicts that firm B will produce Q_{B_1}. Although firm A is on its reaction

curve, firm B is not. If firm B predicts that firm A will produce Q_{A_1} its best move is *not* to produce Q_{B_1}. It will instead produce at a point on its reaction curve vertically above this (i.e. an output *greater* than Q_{B_1}). Firm A will discover that firm B has produced a greater output than it predicted. It will respond by reducing its own production level – it will move up along its reaction curve. This process will continue until point *e* is reached. Only at this point will the levels of production chosen by each firm (in the light of what the other one chooses) add up to the total amount demanded.

Profits in the Cournot model. Industry profits will be *less* than under a monopoly or a cartel. The reason is that price will be lower than the monopoly price. This can be seen from Figure 8.7(a). If this were a monopoly, then to find the profit-maximising output, we would need to construct an *MR* curve corresponding to the market demand curve (D_M). This would intersect with the *MC* curve at a higher output than Q_{A_1} and a *higher* price (given by D_M).

Nevertheless, profits in the Cournot model will be higher than under perfect competition, since price is still above marginal cost. However, as the number of firms in the industry increases the price would move closer to the level in a competitive market and industry profits would fall.

Maths Case 8.2 on the student website shows how the Cournot equilibrium can be derived algebraically from the market demand function and the cost functions of the two firms.

The Bertrand model: firms set prices and the market determines the quantity sold

Another famous model of oligopoly was developed by the French economist, Joseph Bertrand, in 1883. He criticised the Cournot model as he argued that firms are more likely

---

Definitions

Reaction function (or curve) This shows how a firm's optimal output varies according to the output chosen by its rival (or rivals).

Cournot equilibrium Where each of two firm's actual output is the same as what the other firm predicted it would produce: where the two firms' reaction curves cross.

to set prices and let the market determine the quantity sold. Bertrand again took the simple case of a duopoly where both firms have the same costs of production. However, the conclusions of the model apply equally to oligopolies with three or more firms. It is based on the following assumptions:

- Each firm has to choose its price without knowing the price set by the other firm. It assumes its rival will charge the same price in the current period as it did in the previous period.
- Firms have to set prices in advance and decisions cannot be easily changed: i.e. prices are inflexible.
- The good is homogenous – the only thing that customers care about when they purchase the product is its price.
- Each firm can adjust its output instantly and has no capacity constraints. Therefore, if a firm charges a lower price than its rival it can immediately supply the entire market.

The model predicts that each firm will keep reducing its price until all supernormal profits are competed away. The reason for this result is simple. If firm A assumes that its rival, firm B, will hold price constant, then firm A predicts that by undercutting this price by a small amount it will gain the whole market, which it can instantly supply. By following the same line of reasoning firm B will be forced to respond by cutting its price. The model, therefore, predicts a price war with prices being reduced until they equal average total cost, with only normal profits remaining.

This outcome is very different from the one predicted by the Cournot model. It is referred to as the *Bertrand Paradox* because the result seems counterintuitive: i.e. a duopoly results in an outcome very similar to that of perfect competition. The prediction changes significantly if product differentiation and/or limits in the ability of the firm to supply the entire market (i.e. capacity constraints) are introduced into the model. Firms may also seek to collude long before profits have been reduced to a normal level. Alternatively, firms may put in a *takeover bid* for their rival(s).

Nash equilibrium.   The equilibrium outcome in either the Cournot or Bertrand models is not in the *joint* interests of the firms. In each case, total profits are less than under a monopoly or cartel. But, in the absence of collusion, the outcome is the result of each firm doing the best it can, given the assumptions it makes about what its rivals are doing. The resulting equilibrium is known as a *Nash equilibrium*, after John Nash, a US mathematician (and subject of the film *A Beautiful Mind*) who introduced the concept in 1951. This concept will be discussed in more detail in section 8.3.

 Can you think of any reasons why the predictions of the Cournot and Bertrand models of oligopoly are so different?

The kinked demand curve assumption

In 1939, a theory of non-collusive oligopoly was developed simultaneously on both sides of the Atlantic: in the USA by Paul Sweezy and in Britain by R. L. Hall and C. J. Hitch. This *kinked demand theory* has since become perhaps the most famous of all theories of oligopoly. The model seeks to explain how it is that, even when there is no collusion at all between oligopolists, prices can nevertheless remain stable.

The theory is based on two asymmetrical assumptions:

- If an oligopolist cuts its price, its rivals will feel forced to follow suit and cut theirs, to prevent losing customers to the first firm.
- If an oligopolist raises its price, however, its rivals will *not* follow suit since, by keeping their prices the same, they will gain customers from the first firm.

The logic that follows from these assumptions, is that each oligopolist will face a demand curve that is *kinked* at the current price and output (see Figure 8.8). A rise in price will lead to a large fall in sales as customers switch to the now

Definitions

Takeover bid Where one firm attempts to purchase another by offering to buy the shares of that company from its shareholders.

Nash equilibrium The position resulting from everyone making their optimal decision based on their assumptions about their rivals' decisions. Without collusion, there is no incentive for any firm to move from this position.

Kinked demand theory The theory that oligopolists face a demand curve that is kinked at the current price, demand being significantly more elastic above the current price than below. The effect of this is to create a situation of price stability.

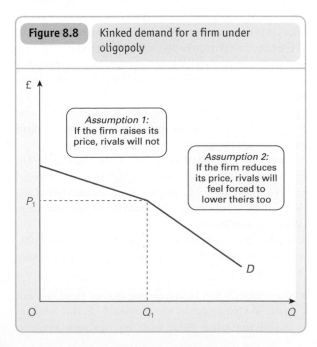

| **Figure 8.8** | Kinked demand for a firm under oligopoly |

Figure 8.9 Stable price under conditions of a kinked demand curve

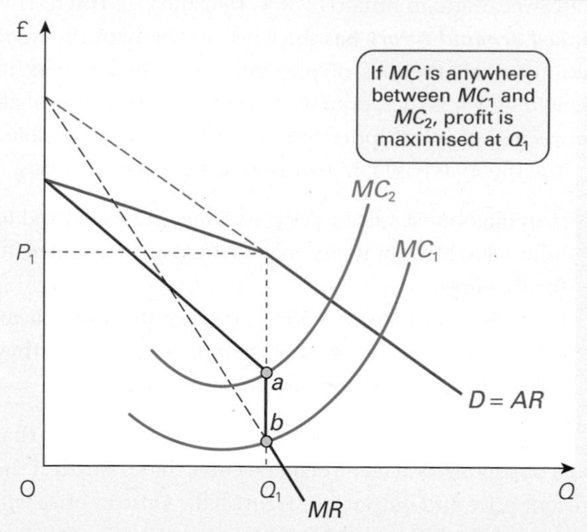

If *MC* is anywhere between MC_1 and MC_2, profit is maximised at Q_1

---

predictions and revaluing stocks of finished goods, and it may upset customers. Price stability, therefore, is not proof of the accuracy of the model.

- Although the model can help to explain price stability, it does not explain how prices are set in the first place. To do this, some other model would be required. This is a serious limitation in times of inflation, when oligopolists, like other firms, raise prices in response to higher costs and higher demand. What the model does predict, however, is that the price will be raised only after marginal cost has risen above MC_2 in Figure 8.9, and that once it has been raised, a new kink will form at that price. Price will then remain fixed at that level until higher costs once more force a further price rise.

Oligopoly and the public interest

If oligopolists act collusively and jointly maximise industry profits, they will in effect be acting together as a monopoly. In such cases, the disadvantages to society experienced under monopoly will also be experienced under oligopoly (see section 7.3).

Furthermore, in two respects, oligopoly may be more disadvantageous than monopoly:

- Depending on the size of the individual oligopolists, there may be less scope for economies of scale to mitigate the effects of market power.
- Oligopolists are likely to engage in much more extensive advertising than a monopolist (see Case Study 8.10 on the student website).

These problems will be less, however, if oligopolists do not collude, if there is some degree of price competition and if barriers to entry are weak.

Also, the power of oligopolists in certain markets may to some extent be offset if they sell their product to other powerful firms. Thus oligopolistic producers of baked beans sell a large proportion of their output to giant supermarket chains, which can use their market power to keep down the price at which they purchase the beans. This phenomenon is known as ***countervailing power***.

relatively lower-priced rivals. The firm will thus be reluctant to raise its price. Demand is relatively elastic above the kink. On the other hand, a fall in price will bring only a modest increase in sales, since rivals lower their prices too and therefore customers do not switch. The firm will thus also be reluctant to lower its price. Demand is relatively inelastic below the kink. Therefore oligopolists will be reluctant to change prices at all.

This price stability can be shown formally by drawing in the firm's marginal revenue curve, as in Figure 8.9.

To see how this is done, imagine dividing the diagram into two parts, one on either side of Q_1. At quantities less than Q_1 (the left-hand part of the diagram), the *MR* curve will correspond to the shallow part of the *AR* curve. At quantities greater than Q_1 (the right-hand part), the *MR* curve will correspond to the steep part of the *AR* curve. To see how this part of the *MR* curve is constructed, imagine extending the steep part of the *AR* curve back to the vertical axis. This and the corresponding *MR* curve are shown by the dotted lines in Figure 8.9.

As you can see, there will be a gap between points *a* and *b*. In other words, there is a vertical section of the *MR* curve between these two points.

Profits are maximised where $MC = MR$. Thus, if the *MC* curve lies anywhere between MC_1 and MC_2 (i.e. between points *a* and *b*), the profit-maximising price and output will be P_1 and Q_1. Thus prices will remain stable *even with a considerable change in costs*.

Despite its simple demonstration of the real-world phenomenon of price stability, the model does have two major limitations:

- Price stability may be due to *other* factors. Firms may not want to change prices too frequently as this involves modifying price lists, working out new revenue

?

Which of the following are examples of effective countervailing power?
(a) Tour operators purchasing seats on charter flights.
(b) A large office hiring a photocopier from Xerox®.
(c) Marks & Spencer buying clothes from a garment manufacturer.
(d) A small village store (but the only one for miles around) buying food from a wholesaler.

Definition

Countervailing power Where the power of a monopolistic/oligopolistic seller is offset by powerful buyers who can prevent the price from being pushed up.

BOX 8.4 BUYING POWER

The UK grocery sector

Over the past few years there has been increasing concern about the power of large supermarket chains in the UK. This has resulted in a number of Competition Commission investigations. Many of these have focused on anti-competitive practices such as rival chains agreeing not to set up in the same town and price collusion on some staple products. (For more on government competition policy, see Chapter 14, pages 429–30).

However, more recently, focus has turned to the supermarkets' power not as sellers, but as buyers. If a wholesale manufacturer of ready-meals, or a supplier of sausages, wants to reach a wide customer base, it will need to deal with the four largest supermarket chains, which control over 75 per cent of the market. A market like this, where there are a few large purchasers of goods and services, is known as an *oligopsony*. (A single large buyer of goods, services or factors of production is known as a *monopsony* and we look at this in Chapter 10, pages 287–90).

Market power

Over the years a number of unfair practices by the supermarkets towards their suppliers have been identified. These include retrospectively changing contracts and forcing suppliers to fund special offers such as 'buy one, get one free'. Furthermore, there is evidence that firms were regularly asked for very substantial payments, in order to be included on 'preferred supplier' lists.

After a lengthy investigation, the Competition Commission (one of the predecessors to the Competition and Markets Authority) concluded that the supermarkets were passing on excessive risks and unexpected costs to their suppliers. As a consequence, a stronger Grocery Supplies Code of Practice

(GSCP) was introduced in 2009. This recognised the power that large grocery retailers wield over their smaller suppliers and outlawed the practices detailed above.

In January 2013, the government appointed a 'Groceries Code Adjudicator' (GCA) to make sure the supermarkets were complying with the GSCP. In January 2016, the GCA concluded that Tesco had not been complying with the code. In particular, she concluded that the company had 'knowingly delayed paying money to suppliers in order to improve its own financial position'. In June 2016, Morrisons was also judged to have broken the code by requiring suppliers to make lump-sum payments even though they were not required according to the supply contracts.

Who benefits?

It would be easy to conclude that the power of supermarkets, both as purchasers and as retailers, is so great that they are a 'bad thing'. However, that would be overly simplistic. There is evidence that they compete on price and as a consequence have held down the cost of food bills in the UK. They have also introduced a variety of products and offer very convenient shopping for many people, particularly those who work full-time. The grocery market is a good example of a sector where growth and market power can be identified as both beneficial and harmful to other economic agents.

1. *Explain why manufacturers of food products continue to supply supermarkets, despite concerns that they are not always treated fairly.*
2. *Is the supermarket sector an oligopoly or monopolistically competitive, in your opinion? Justify your answer.*

The power of oligopolists will also be reduced if the market in which they operate is contestable (see section 7.4). The lower the entry and exit costs for new firms, the more difficult it will be for oligopolists to collude and make supernormal profits.

Which of the following markets do you think are contestable: (a) credit cards; (b) brewing; (c) petrol retailing; (d) insurance services; (e) compact discs?

In some respects, oligopoly may have *advantages* to society over other market structures:

- Oligopolists, like monopolists, can use part of their supernormal profit for research and development. Unlike monopolists, however, oligopolists will have a considerable *incentive* to do so. If the product design is improved, this may allow the firm to capture a larger share of the market, and it may be some time before rivals can respond with a similarly improved product. If, in addition, costs

Definition

Oligopsony A goods market with just a few buyers (or employers in the case of labour markets).

are lowered by technological improvement, the resulting higher profits will improve the firm's capacity to withstand any price war.

- Non-price competition through product differentiation may result in greater choice for the consumer. Take the case of stereo equipment. Non-price competition has led to a huge range of different products of many different specifications, each meeting the specific requirements of different consumers.

It is difficult, however, to draw any general conclusions, since oligopolies differ so much in their performance.

Section summary

1. An oligopoly is where there are just a few firms in the industry with barriers to the entry of new firms. Firms recognise their mutual dependence.

2. Oligopolists will want to maximise their joint profits. This will tend to make them collude to keep prices high. On the other hand, they will want the biggest share of industry profits for themselves. This will tend to make them compete.

3. They are more likely to collude if there are few of them; if they are open with each other; if they have similar products and cost structures; if there is a dominant firm; if there are significant entry barriers; if the market is stable; and if there is no government legislation to prevent collusion.

4. Collusion can be open or tacit.

5. A formal collusive agreement is called a 'cartel'. A cartel aims to act as a monopoly. It can set price and leave the members to compete for market share, or it can assign quotas. There is always a temptation for cartel members to 'cheat' by undercutting the cartel price if they think they can get away with it and not trigger a price war.

6. Tacit collusion can take the form of price leadership. This is where firms follow the price set by either a dominant firm in the industry or a firm seen as a reliable 'barometer' of market conditions. Alternatively, tacit collusion can

simply involve following various rules of thumb, such as average cost pricing and benchmark pricing.

7. Even when firms do not collude, they will still have to take into account their rivals' behaviour. In the Cournot model, firms assume that their rivals' output is given and then choose the profit-maximising price and output in the light of this assumption. The resulting price and profit are lower than under monopoly, but still higher than under perfect competition.

8. In the Bertrand model, firms assume that their rivals' price is given. This will result in prices being competed down until only normal profits remain.

9. In the kinked demand curve model, firms are likely to keep their prices stable unless there is a large shift in costs or demand.

10. Whether oligopoly behaviour is in the public interest depends on the particular oligopoly and how competitive it is; whether there is any countervailing power; whether the firms engage in extensive advertising and of what type; whether product differentiation results in a wide range of choice for the consumer; how much of the profits are ploughed back into research and development; and how contestable the market is. Since these conditions vary substantially from oligopoly to oligopoly, it is impossible to state just how well or how badly oligopoly in general serves the public interest.

8.3 GAME THEORY

When firms operate in a competitive environment and recognise their interdependence, what is the most probable outcome? If each firm aims to maximise its profits it needs to think strategically: it needs to work out its optimal response to the actual or most likely actions of its rivals.

At first sight, this might seem like an almost impossible task given the complexity of the reasoning involved. However, economists have developed *game theory* as a useful framework and set of tools for thinking about these situations. By helping to identify the best strategy that each firm can adopt for each assumption about its rivals' behaviour, game theory can help economists to predict the most likely outcome in markets with strategic interdependence.

This section will show how game theory can provide useful insights into firms' behaviour in oligopolistic markets. It is important to remember that it can also be applied to a broad range of issues, including the negotiations over the UK's exit from the European Union. For some types of games, however, game theory offers few insights. For example, where the outcomes are determined purely by chance: e.g. lotteries, bingo, etc. or where there is only one player: e.g. solitaire. Nevertheless, there are many economic situations where game theory can provide considerable insights.

Simultaneous single-move games

As we have seen, the firm's profit-maximising strategy in a competitive oligopoly market depends, in part, on how it thinks its rivals will react to its decisions on prices, output, product development, advertising, etc. If this competition is a one-off event (such as firms competing for a specific contract) then it can be modelled as a *simultaneous single-move game*. This type of game is also called a single-period or one-shot game.

Definitions

Game theory A mathematical method of decision making in which alternative strategies are analysed to determine the optimal course of action for the interested party, depending on assumptions about rivals' behaviour. Widely used in economics, game theory is also used as a tool in biology, psychology and politics.

Simultaneous single-move game A game where each player has just one move, where each player plays at the same time and acts without knowledge of the actions chosen by other players.

A 'complete-information' simultaneous single-move game has the following characteristics. Each firm:

- is aware of all the choices available to its rival: i.e. all the decisions it could possibly make about pricing, output, advertising, product development, etc.
- is able to calculate the impact of each of these potential decisions on its own profits;
- makes its own decision without knowing the choice of its rival.

These assumptions are very similar to those found in the Bertrand and Cournot models of oligopoly discussed in section 8.2. Economists have actually reinterpreted both of these models as examples of simultaneous single-move games. Another example is the Rock–Paper–Scissors game. Each player knows the three choices available to both participants and has to decide without knowing the choice made by the other player. A sealed bid auction is another example, where each bidder submits a price without knowing any of the bids submitted by their competitors.

This type of environment poses a significant challenge for a firm. As a first step it can work out the impact of each of its rivals' actions on its own profit. However, to determine its best response it would usually need to know which of these actions its rival has actually taken. In a simultaneous single-move game it does not have this information. How can a firm work out its best response to a rival's decision that it cannot observe.

TC 9
p129

Simultaneous single-move games with dominant strategies

In some strategic environments the firm does not have to worry about trying to work out the most likely actions of its rivals. Its best response remains the same, no matter what assumptions it makes about its rivals' behaviour. In the terminology of game theory, the firm has a ***dominant strategy***.

One of the best ways of illustrating this idea is to represent the strategic environment facing the firms as a ***normal-form game***. A normal (or strategic) representation of a game is presented as a matrix. This matrix illustrates the pay-offs (e.g. profits) from each of the different available decisions. A simple example of a pay-off is shown in Table 8.1.

This example illustrates the various profits two firms (X, and Y) could earn from charging two different prices – £2 and £1.80. To keep the example simple, we assume the firms have identical costs, products and demand and can only choose one or other of the two prices.

Let us initially consider firm Y's position. Should it set its price at £2 or £1.80? Which decision would make it the most profit? To answer this question we need to look at the impact of firm X's different pricing decisions on the profits of firm Y and work out its best response. If firm Y assumes that firm X chooses a price of £2, it needs to focus on the left-hand column of the pay-off matrix. Firm Y's best response is clearly to charge £1.80, earning it £12 million in profits, as illustrated in cell C. If firm Y sets its price at £2, it makes a lower profit of £10 million, as illustrated in cell A.

What happens if firm Y now assumes that firm X chooses a price of £1.80? All the relevant information is now in the right-hand column of the pay-off matrix. Firm Y's best response once again is to charge £1.80, earning it profits of £10 million, as illustrated in cell D. If firm Y sets its price at £2, it makes a lower profit of £5 million, as illustrated in cell B.

Therefore, no matter which of the two prices firm Y assumes that firm X will charge, firm Y's best response is always to charge £1.80 as this will yield the highest possible profits. Charging £1.80 is a dominant strategy for firm Y.

If we now look at the game from firm X's viewpoint we get exactly the same result. No matter what price firm X assumes that firm Y will charge, its best response is always to charge £1.80. Therefore charging £1.80 is also a dominant strategy for firm X.

Because both firms have a dominant strategy, the outcome of the game is easy to predict. Both firms charge £1.80 and earn £8 million in profit, as illustrated in cell D. This is the dominant strategy equilibrium of the game.

This game is an example of the ***prisoners' dilemma***. The original scenario with two prisoners is discussed in more detail in Box 8.5. What exactly is the dilemma in the game above? By pursuing a strategy to maximise its own individual profit, each firm makes less money than it could have if it had acted collectively. If they both co-operated with one another (i.e. colluded) and agreed to charge the higher price

Table 8.1	Profits for firms X and Y at different prices

		X's price	
		£2.00	**£1.80**
Y's price	**£2.00**	A £10m, £10m	B £5m, £12m
	£1.80	C £12m, £5m	D £8m, £8m

Definitions

Dominant-strategy game Where the firm's optimal strategy remains the same, irrespective of what it assumes its rivals are going to do.

Normal-form game Where the possible pay-offs from different strategies or decisions are presented as a matrix.

Prisoners' dilemma Where two or more firms (or people), by attempting independently to choose the best strategy, think about what their rivals are likely to do, end up in a worse position than if they had co-operated in the first place.

of £2 they would each have made a profit of £10 million (cell A) instead of £8 million (cell D). The game clearly illustrates the incentive each firm has to cheat on a collusive arrangement in the absence of any binding agreements.

 Is the incentive structure in the single-move prisoners' dilemma game in the interests of society?

More complex simultaneous single-move games

In many instances, one or both firms will not have a dominant strategy. In these cases, a firm's best response will vary depending on what it thinks its rival will do. Take the example shown in Table 8.2. This is very similar to the example in Table 8.1, but has a different profit structure.

Let us once again consider firm Y's position. If firm Y assumes that firm X chooses a price of £2, its best response is to charge £1.80, earning £20 million in profits as shown in cell C. However, if it assumes that firm X chooses a price of £1.80, its best response is to charge £2, earning £15 million in profits as shown in cell B. Hence, its best response changes depending on what price it thinks firm X will charge.

Accurately predicting firm X's decision is important for firm Y if it wants to maximise its profits. If its belief turns out to be wrong, it will make less profit. What is the most effective way of anticipating what your rival will do? The answer is for firm Y to try to examine the decision from the perspective of firm X. Can it successfully put itself in its rival's shoes and analyse the competition from their viewpoint?

If firm Y looks at the pricing decision from firm X's point of view it will see that firm X actually has a dominant strategy. If firm Y charges £2 it can see that firm X's best response is to charge £1.80 (making a profit of £6m rather than £5m). If firm Y charges £1.80, firm X's best response is also to charge £1.80 (making a profit of £4m rather than £3m). Therefore, firm Y can predict with a high level of certainty that firm X will charge £1.80 – its dominant strategy. Firm Y's best response, therefore, is to charge £2.00 and make a profit of £15m rather than £12m. This combination of prices in cell B is the equilibrium in the game.

Some games can be much more complicated than the one shown in Table 8.2. For example, neither firm could have a dominant strategy; there could be more than two firms and more than two choices. How can we predict the most likely

outcome in these circumstances? At what point will every firm have no incentive to change its strategy?

Nash equilibrium and expected behaviour

In section 8.2 (page 231), we looked at the concept of the Nash equilibrium. This is the position that results from everyone making their optimal decision based on their assumptions about their rivals' decisions. The dominant strategy equilibrium in the prisoners' dilemma and the equilibrium in Table 8.2 are both examples of a Nash equilibrium. In each case, neither firm has an incentive to change its decision as it is choosing its best price in response to the price chosen by its rival.

In fact, all dominant strategy equilibria (i.e. where both firms have a dominant strategy) are examples of Nash equilibria. Identifying any dominant strategies, if they exist, makes it easier to find the Nash equilibrium.

In many games, there is more than one Nash equilibrium. In these cases, it is more difficult to predict the most likely outcome.

If a firm's actual behaviour was *different* from its expected behaviour, then the decisions of it rivals do not represent a Nash equilibrium. In these circumstances, what the firm perceives to be its best response, based on the expected behaviour of its rival, proves not to be the case when the actual behaviour of the other firm is observed. The firm will have an incentive to change its behaviour.

Repeated simultaneous-move games

The previous analysis of simultaneous single-move games gives some useful insights but instances of one-off interactions are relatively unusual. In most real-world settings, firms in oligopolistic markets compete against one another on a repeated basis. Decisions about pricing, advertising, product development, etc., are made continually over the months and years that firms are in business. For example, Apple and Samsung launch new versions of their smartphone handsets on an annual basis. Do the predicted outcomes of single-move games remain the same when the game is repeated?

We previously examined a single-move prisoners' dilemma game in which the most likely outcome was for both firms to charge the lower price of £1.80 (see Table 8.1 on page 235). There was a strong incentive for both firms to cheat on any collusive agreement to fix prices at £2.00. Does repeated interaction between the same firms change the predicted outcome of the game? For example, if firms X and Y make the same simultaneous pricing decisions repeatedly, could their optimal strategy change so that they both start charging £2.00?

The big difference between a single-move game and a repeated game is that each firm can now see what its rivals did in previous periods. This creates the possibility that whatever firms choose to do in one period might have an impact on the behaviour of their rivals, and hence their own profits, in later periods. In particular, decisions that generate

Table 8.2	A more complicated game		
		X's price	
		£2.00	£1.80
Y's price	£2.00	A £18m, £5m	B £15m, £6m
	£1.80	C £20m, £3m	D £12m, £4m

BOX 8.5   THE PRISONERS' DILEMMA

Game theory is not just relevant to economics. A famous non-economic example is the prisoners' dilemma.

Nigel and Amanda have been arrested for a joint crime of serious fraud. Each is interviewed separately and given the following alternatives:

- First, if they say nothing, the court has enough evidence to sentence both to a year's imprisonment.
- Second, if either Nigel or Amanda *alone* confesses, he or she is likely to get only a three-month sentence but the partner could get up to ten years.
- Third, if both confess, they are likely to get three years each.

What should Nigel and Amanda do?

		Amanda's alternatives	
		Not confess	Confess
Nigel's alternatives	Not confess	**A** Each gets 1 year	**C** Nigel gets 10 years Amanda gets 3 months
	Confess	**B** Nigel gets 3 months Amanda gets 10 years	**D** Each gets 3 years

Let us consider Nigel's dilemma. Should he confess in order to get the short sentence? This is better than the year he would get for not confessing. There is, however, an even better reason for confessing. Suppose Nigel doesn't confess but, unknown to him, Amanda does confess. Then Nigel ends up with the long sentence. Better than this is to confess and to get no more than three years. Nigel's best response is always to confess.

Amanda is in exactly the same dilemma, so the result is simple. When both prisoners act in their own self-interest by confessing, they both end up with relatively long prison terms. Only when they collude will they end up with relatively short prison terms, the best combined solution.

Of course, the police know this and will do their best to prevent any collusion. They will keep Nigel and Amanda in separate prison cells and try to persuade each of them that the other is bound to confess.

Thus the choice of strategy depends on:

- Nigel's and Amanda's risk attitudes: i.e. are they 'risk lovers' or 'risk averse'?
- Nigel's and Amanda's estimates of how likely the other is to own up.

1. *Why is this a dominant-strategy 'game'?*
2. *How would Nigel's choice of strategy be affected if he had instead been involved in a joint crime with Rikki, Kate, Amrita and Dave, and they had all been caught?*

KI 12
p97

The prisoners' dilemma is a good illustration of *the fallacy of composition* that we examined in Box 3.5 (see page 97). What applies at the level of the individual does not apply to the group as a whole. It might be in the individual's interests to confess. It is clearly not in the interests of both, however, for both to confess.

Let us now look at two real-world examples of the prisoners' dilemma.

Standing at football

When people go to some public event, such as a football match, they often stand in order to get a better view. But once people start standing, everyone is likely to do so: after all, if they stayed sitting, they would not see at all. If everyone stands, no one has an incentive to sit down, since they would then see nothing. In this Nash equilibrium, most people are worse off, since, except for tall people, their view is likely to be worse and they lose the comfort of sitting down.

Too much advertising

Why do firms spend so much on advertising? If they are aggressive, they do so to get ahead of their rivals. If they are cautious, they do so in case their rivals increase their advertising. Although in both cases it may be in the individual firm's best interests to increase advertising, the resulting Nash equilibrium is likely to be one of excessive advertising: the total spent on advertising (by all firms) is not recouped in additional sales.

1. *Give some other non-economic examples of the prisoners' dilemma.*
2. *Can collusion by firms overcome the prisoners' dilemma?*

higher profits today could lead to lower profits in the future. The potential impact of this trade-off can be illustrated by using the prisoners' dilemma example in Table 8.1.

Assume that firm X and Y have an agreement to charge £2.00 (or simply follow each other's lead in doing so). Each firm will thus continue charging £2 as long as the other firm does too. If, however, firm Y ever cut its price to £1.80 in one period, then firm X would do the same in all future periods. Once this has happened, no matter what firm Y then does, firm X is unlikely to charge a price of £2 ever again. In game theory, this new strategy employed by firm Y is known as the *trigger strategy*.

Figure 8.10   Profits for firm Y in a repeated game

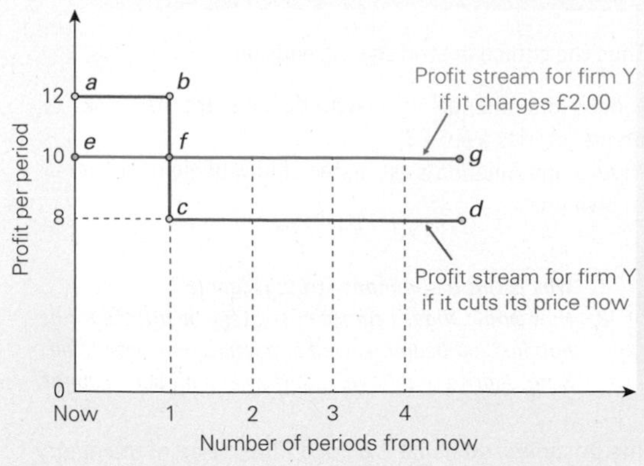

The profit profile for firm Y of following two different pricing strategies is illustrated in Figure 8.10. By following the same dominant strategy as in the single-move game and charging a price of £1.80 (i.e. breaking the agreement), firm Y can increase its profit in the first period from £10 million to £12 million. The downside of this strategy is that its profits in all future periods will fall to £8 million as firm X responds by also charging £1.80. This is illustrated by the profit profile of $a \to b \to c \to d$ in Figure 8.10.

Alternatively, firm Y could stick to the agreement and charge £2.00 in the first period. Its profit of £10 million is £2 million lower than it would have earned by charging £1.80. However, as long as it maintains its price at this level, firm X will also charge £2.00. Firm Y's profits in all future period will thus be £10 million as opposed to £8 million. This is shown by the profit profile $e \to f \to g$.

After a while, both Y and X will realise that the Nash equilibrium (£1.80) is not to the advantage of either. This may persuade them to set up a stronger collusive agreement to restore prices to £2. This outcome is most likely to occur when:

- firms value future profits quite highly;
- firms compete against each other very frequently – there are more future time periods to benefit from the higher profits of charging £2 and area *fgdc* is larger;
- the higher profits from charging £1.80 in the first period are relatively small. This reduces the size of area *abfe*;
- a firm can quickly observe that its rival is charging the lower price. This reduces the length of time over which a firm will benefit from the higher profits of charging £1.80, again reducing the size of area *abfe*;
- both firms adopt the trigger strategy, putting them in a similar position.

Backwards induction and movement to the Nash equilibrium.   Another issue is whether both firms know just how long the current product designs and costs will last – in other words, when the current round of repeated price

Definitions

Trigger strategy Once a firm observes that its rival has broken some agreed behaviour it will never co-operate with them ever again.

Backwards induction A process by which firms think through the most likely outcome in the last period of competition and then work backwards step by step thinking through the most likely outcomes in earlier periods of competition.

settings will end. If they do, then the chances of the firm co-operating and charging higher prices is much lower. The most likely outcome is the same as for a single-move game, with the dominant strategy being to cut price.

To understand why this is the case both firms need to think about the most likely outcome in the last period of competition (i.e. the last time prices are set before any changes in product design, costs, etc.) and then work backwards to think about the most likely outcome in earlier periods. This is called **backwards induction**.

The incentive for each firm to charge £2 in any period is to influence the behaviour of its rivals in future periods. However, in the last period of competition there is no future to affect, as the firms will never compete against one another again with the same product. Therefore, the last period is effectively the same as a simultaneous single-move game and both firms are highly likely to follow their dominant strategies of charging £1.80.

If both firms realise in the last-but-one period of competition that they cannot influence what their rival will do in the last period of competition then their best strategy is also to charge £1.80. If they keep following the same line of reasoning they will both charge £1.80 in every period of competition.

Therefore, the chances of the firms charging a higher price is much greater when they both believe that competition between them will carry on indefinitely: i.e. neither of them knows the precise date when the current type of interaction between them will come to an end.

Another type of strategy firms can follow in a repeated game is the 'tit-for-tat' strategy. What is the 'tit-for-tat' strategy? What impact will it have on the most likely outcome in a repeated game?

Sequential-move games

So far we have looked at simultaneous games: where firms take decisions at the same time without seeing the decision of the other firm(s). However, in many real-world competitive environments, one firm (the first mover) makes and implements a decision (i.e. it produces a certain output, sets a particular price or introduces a new product) *before* its rivals (the second movers). The second movers are then able to observe the actions of the first mover before deciding on their best response. These strategic environments can be studied by using *sequential-move games*.

Take the case of a new generation of large passenger aircraft that can fly further without refuelling. Assume that there is a market for a 500-seater version of this type of aircraft and a 400-seater version, but that the market for each size of aircraft is not big enough for the two manufacturers, Boeing and Airbus, to share it profitably. Let us also assume that the 400-seater market would give an annual profit of £50 million to a single manufacturer and the 500-seater would give an annual profit of £30 million, but that if both manufacturers produced the same version, they would each make an annual loss of £10 million.

Assume that Boeing is the first mover and announces which plane it will build: the 400-seater or the 500-seater. Airbus then has to respond to the decision and decide which plane it will build.

This scenario can be illustrated as a sequential-move game and is shown in Figure 8.11. Sequential-move games are typically illustrated in 'extensive form' by use of a *decision tree*, which identifies the possible sequence of events. The small square on the left of the decision tree shown in Figure 8.11 is Boeing's decision point (point A). If it decides to build the 500-seater plane, we move up the top branch. Airbus would now have to make a decision (point B_1). If it too decides to build the 500-seater plane, we would move to outcome 1: a loss of £10 million for both manufacturers.

Clearly, with Boeing building a 500-seater plane, the best response for Airbus would be to choose the 400-seater plane: we would move to outcome 2, with Boeing making a profit of £30 million and Airbus a profit of £50 million. Airbus would be very pleased!

Boeing's best strategy at point A, however, would be to build the 400-seater plane. We would then move to Airbus's decision point B_2. In this case, Airbus's best response is to build the 500-seater plane. Its profit would be only £30 million (outcome 3), but this is better than a £10 million loss if it too built

the 400-seater plane (outcome 4). With Boeing deciding first, the Nash equilibrium will thus be outcome 3.

There is clearly a *first-mover advantage* here. Once Boeing has decided to build the more profitable version of the plane, the best response for Airbus is to build the less profitable one. Naturally, Airbus would like to build the more profitable one and be the first mover. Which company succeeds in going first depends on how advanced they are in their research and development and in their production capacity.

The importance of threats and promises

In a sequential-move game, a second mover could threaten or promise to behave in a certain way in an attempt to influence the behaviour of the first mover. For example, in the above game Airbus could announce that it was going to build a 400-seater plane irrespective of what Boeing decides to do. Why would Airbus do this? If Boeing believed Airbus' announcement then its best move is to build a 500-seater plane, making a profit of £30 million as opposed to a loss of £10 million. Hence, the announcement influences Boeing's behaviour in a manner that is favourable to Airbus – it earns greater profits.

However, there is a problem with Airbus' announcement – Boeing will probably not believe it! If Boeing

---

Definitions

Sequential-move game One firm (the first mover) makes and implements a decision. Rival firms (second movers) can observe the actions taken by the first mover before making their own decisions.

Decision tree (or game tree) A diagram showing the sequence of possible decisions by competitor firms and the outcome of each combination of decisions.

First-mover advantage When a firm gains from being the first one to take action.

Figure 8.11	A decision tree

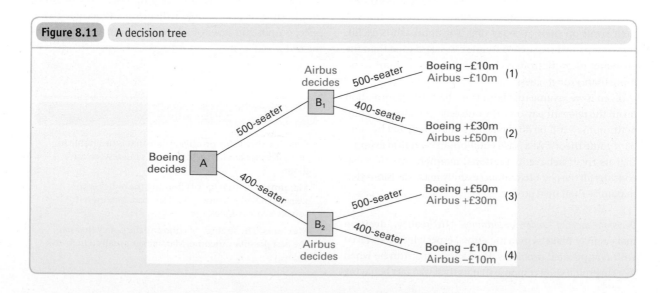

actually built a 400-seater plane, Airbus' best move would be to build a 500-seater plane. Boeing can clearly see that it is not in Airbus' own self-interest to do what it said it was going to do. Therefore the strategy is not *credible* and Boeing will build the 400-seater plane.

Could Airbus take some irreversible actions so it is committed in advance to building the 400-seater plane? The key to the success of this policy is that Boeing must believe it: it must be credible. If this was possible, then by limiting its own options, Airbus could actually make greater profits. In some circumstances, inflexibility can actually improve the competitive position of the firm by altering its rivals' expectations about how it will behave.

More complex sequential-move games

The aircraft example is the simplest version of a sequential-move game, with just two companies and each one making only one key decision. In many business situations, much more complex trees could be constructed. The 'game' would be more like one of chess, with many moves and several options on each move. If there were more than two companies, the decision tree would be more complex still.

Assessing the simple theory of games

Game theory provides a very useful framework for helping us to think about competitive environments where there is strategic interdependence. It highlights the importance of each firm trying to think through situations from their rival's viewpoint in order to work out their own profit-maximising decision.

In this section, we have considered a number of quite simple games, with just two firms having to choose between just two different options. In reality, many oligopolistic markets will consist of a number of firms that each have to choose from multiple options on pricing, product design, advertising, etc. Therefore it would be very difficult if not impossible for them to obtain precise information on (a) the pay-offs to all their rivals from all the possible actions they could take and (b) the impact of all the possible actions of their rivals on their own pay-offs. The approach is useful, therefore, only in relatively simple cases, and even then the estimates of profit from each outcome may amount to no more than a rough guess.

Even if we assume that both firms have full information on all the relevant pay-offs, the outcome of real-world competition may still be different from that predicted by standard game theory. At a Nash equilibrium each firm assumes that its rivals behave in a rational manner: that they can consider all the pay-offs and successfully make decisions that maximise their own profits.

Decision making under uncertainty. In reality, decision makers may make systematic errors, especially when faced with complicated problems. How sure can a firm be when working out its best response that its rival is in fact behaving in a rational manner? Could it mistakenly choose a suboptimal strategy?

If firms believe there is a strong chance that their rivals will behave in an irrational manner, then the outcome of competition is much harder to predict. In response to this uncertainty they might play it safe by choosing the strategy that minimises their losses from the worst-case scenario from the unpredictable behaviour of their rival. Such a strategy is known as *maximin*. Alternatively, if they were more risk loving, they could gamble and choose the outcome that maximises their pay-off from the best-case scenario. Such a strategy is known as *maximax*.

Changing behaviour patterns over time. Behaviour may also change over time as firms learn about the consequences of their actions and the competitive environment changes. For example, firms may compete hard for a time (in price or non-price terms) and then realise that it is making them all worse off. Firms may then start to collude and jointly raise prices and reduce advertising. Later, after a period of tacit collusion, competition may break out again. This may be sparked off by the entry of a new firm, by the development of a new product design, by a change in market demand, or simply by one or more firms no longer being able to resist the temptation to 'cheat'. In short, the behaviour of particular oligopolists may change quite radically over time as they find out new information.

The objectives of firms. Finally, we have been assuming that firms behave selfishly – that they make decisions with the sole purpose of maximising profits. In reality, people's actions are likely to be influenced by their moral values. Businesspeople may be unwilling to behave ruthlessly or dishonestly, or to undertake profitable activities that they regard as unfair. In Chapter 9, we examine some of the consequences of pursuing goals other than ruthless profit maximisation.

Given the lack of perfect information, uncertainty about the rationality of rivals and varying objectives of firms, simple game theory cannot predict with any accuracy what price, output and level of advertising firms will choose in the real world.

Definitions

Credible threat (or promise) One that is believable to rivals because it is in the threatener's interests to carry it out.

Maximin The strategy of choosing the policy whose worst possible outcome is the least bad. Maximin is usually a low-risk strategy.

Maximax The strategy of choosing the policy that has the best possible outcome. Maximax is usually a high-risk strategy.

Section summary

1. Game theory is a way of modelling behaviour in strategic situations where the outcome for an individual or firm depends on the choices made by others. Thus game theory examines various strategies that firms can adopt when the outcome of each is not certain.

2. One of the simplest types of 'game' is a simultaneous single-move or single-period game. They are often presented in normal form: i.e. as a pay-off matrix. Some simultaneous single-move games have predictable outcomes, no matter what assumptions each firm makes about its rivals' behaviour. Such games are known as dominant-strategy games. Many other simultaneous games are more complicated and either one or both firms do not have a dominant strategy. The Nash equilibrium is a useful way to predict the most likely outcome in any of these games.

3. If a simultaneous game is repeated, the equilibrium can change. The final result depends on a number of factors such as whether the end date of the game is known.

4. In sequential-move games play passes from one 'player' to the other sequentially. Firms will respond not only to what firms do, but what they say they will do. To this end, a firm's threats or promises must be credible if they are to influence rivals' decisions.

5. A firm may gain a strategic advantage over its rivals by being the first one to take action (e.g. to launch a new product). The second mover may gain an advantage if it can commit in advance to behave in a certain manner. A decision tree can be constructed to show the possible sequence of moves in a multiple-move game.

8.4 PRICE DISCRIMINATION

Up to now we have assumed that firms sell each unit of output for the same price. This is known as *uniform pricing*. However, if a firm is able to charge *more* than one price, it might be able to increase profits. It could do this if it can charge a higher price to those customers who are willing to pay more and a lower price to those consumers who would only buy it at a lower price. A strategy of charging more than one price is known as *price discrimination*. However, care needs to be taken when explaining the precise meaning of this concept, as vague definitions can sometimes lead to it being incorrectly applied.

If the costs to the firm of supplying different customers does not vary then price discrimination is defined as the practice of selling the same or similar products to different customers for different prices. If the costs of supplying different customers *does* vary then the definition is slightly more complicated. It is defined as the practice of selling the same or similar product at different prices and the difference in price cannot be fully accounted for by any difference in the cost of supply.

 If customers were all charged the same price for a product could this ever be classed as an example of price discrimination? Explain your answer.

Economists traditionally distinguish between three different types of price discrimination.

First-degree price discrimination is where the seller of the product charges each consumer the maximum price he or she is prepared to pay for each unit. It is sometimes called 'perfect price discrimination' or 'personalised pricing'.

Definitions

Price discrimination Where a firm sells the same product at different prices.

First-degree price discrimination Where the seller of the product charges each consumer the maximum price they are prepared to pay for each unit.

Second-degree price discrimination Where a firm offers consumers a range of different pricing options for the same or similar product. Consumers are then free to choose whichever option they wish, but the price is often dependent on some factor such as the quantity purchased.

In reality, first-degree price discrimination is more of a theoretical benchmark than a viable business strategy because it is very unlikely that sellers could obtain reliable information on the maximum amount people are willing to pay. However, there may be some real-world cases where sellers can implement a person-specific pricing strategy that approaches one of first-degree price discrimination. For example, stallholders in a street market and second-hand car dealers will attempt to do this when haggling with their customers.

Second-degree price discrimination is where a firm offers consumers a range of different pricing options for the same or similar product. Consumers are then free to choose whichever option they wish but the lower prices are conditional on factors such as:

■ The quantity of the product purchased. In order to obtain the good at a lower price the customer has to purchase a certain quantity of the good or service.

■ The use of coupons/vouchers. To be eligible to purchase the product for a lower price customers have to produce a voucher or coupon that they have collected: e.g. from a flyer inside a local newspaper or from the Internet.

■ When the product is purchased. For example, some goods are priced at a higher level when they are first released onto the market. Rail fares are higher at peak times than at off-peak times.

■ The version of the product purchased. Firms can produce different versions of the same core product that have different levels of actual or perceived quality: e.g. value ranges of own-label products sold in supermarkets. This is called 'versioning'. Once example of versioning is the 'damaged goods strategy' where firms create a lower quality version of its good by deliberately damaging the product. It does this by removing some features or reducing its performance characteristics. Note that versioning is not *pure* price discrimination because the product is slightly different.

Third-degree price discrimination is where a firm divides consumers into different groups based on some characteristic that is (a) relatively easy to observe; (b) informative about consumers' willingness to pay; (c) legal; and (d) acceptable to the consumer. The firm then charges a different price to consumers in different groups, but the same

Table 8.3	Examples of third-degree price discrimination
Characteristic	**Example**
Age	16–25 or senior rail card; half-price children's tickets in the cinema.
Gender	'Ladies' night' in a bar or club where men pay the full price for drinks while women can get the same drinks at a discounted price.
Nationality	In several countries, foreign visitors are charged higher entrance fees than locals to various tourist sites.
Location	Pharmaceutical companies often charge different prices for the same medicine/drug in different countries. Consumers in the USA are often charged more than those from other countries.
Occupation	Apple, Microsoft and Orange™ provide price discounts to employees of educational institutions.
Business or individual	Publishers of academic journals charge much lower subscription rates to individuals than university libraries.
Past buying behaviour	Firms often charge new customers a lower price than existing customers for the same product or service as an 'introductory offer'.

price to all consumers in the same group. Some examples include charging different prices based on age, occupation, geographical location and past buying behaviour. See Table 8.3 for some specific examples.

Conditions necessary for price discrimination to operate

As we shall see, a firm will be able to increase its profits if it can engage in price discrimination. But under what

Definition

Third-degree price discrimination Where a firm divides consumers into different groups based on some characteristic that is relatively easy to observe and informative about how much consumers are willing to pay. The firm then charges a different price to consumers in different groups, but the same price to all the consumers within a group.

BOX 8.6 **WHAT'S THE TRAIN FARE TO LONDON?** *CASE STUDIES AND APPLICATIONS*

Price discrimination on the trains

Ask the question 'What's the fare to London?' at ticket enquiries, and you may receive any of the following replies:

■ Do you want 1st or standard class?
■ Do you want single or return?
■ How old are you?
■ Do you have a railcard (Family & Friends, 16–25, Disabled Person, Senior, Two Together)?
■ Will you be travelling on a weekday?
■ Will you be travelling out before 9:30am?
■ Will you be leaving London between 4pm and 6:30pm?
■ Are you able to book your ticket in advance?
■ Do you need to be flexible about the time and date of your journeys, or are you willing to pre-commit to a specific train?

1. *Look at each of the above questions. In each case, decide whether price discrimination is being practised. If it is, is it sensible for train operators to practise it? How are the train operators able to identify travellers with different price elasticities of demand?*
2. *Are these various forms of price discrimination in the traveller's interest?*

You can check out the range of ticket types and prices by going to the National Rail website at www.nationalrail.co.uk and selecting a journey.

| BOX 8.7 | PEAK-LOAD PRICING | EXPLORING ECONOMICS |

Charging more when it costs more to produce

A common form of price discrimination is **peak-load pricing**. This is where people are charged more at times of peak demand and less at off-peak times. Take the case of a holiday. If you look through the brochures or online, you will see that high-season prices are often considerably higher than low-season prices. Similarly, call charges for telephones are often much higher during weekdays than in the evenings and at weekends. Other examples of peak-load (or 'peak-period') pricing are rail and airfares, prices in cinemas and restaurants (higher in the evenings) and charges made by health and sports clubs (higher at weekends and in the evenings).

The reason for the higher prices charged at peak times has partly to do with elasticity of demand. Demand is less elastic at peak times. For example, many commuters have little option but to pay higher rail fares at peak times. This is genuine price discrimination.

But often the higher charges also have to do with higher marginal costs incurred at peak times and, as such, are not true price discrimination. With various fixed factors (such as plant and equipment), marginal costs are likely to rise as output expands to meet higher demand. This could be due to diminishing returns to the variable factors; or it could be due to having to use additional equipment with higher operating costs.

Take the case of electricity. At off-peak times, the power stations with the lowest operating costs will be used. These are normally the wind, nuclear and coal-fired stations. At periods of peak demand, however, stations with higher operating costs, such as oil-fired and gas-fired stations, will have to be brought online. (Both oil- and gas-fired stations are relatively cheap to build, but have higher running costs, largely because of the more expensive fuel.) As a result, the marginal cost of generating electricity is higher at peak times than at off-peak times.

But what are the profit-maximising peak and off-peak prices? These are illustrated in the diagram, which shows units per hour (e.g. of electricity). There are two demand (AR) curves – peak and off-peak – and their corresponding marginal revenue (MR) curves. Profit is maximised in either period at the output where $MR = MC$ (points a and b respectively). In the peak period, this will be at the higher price P_{peak}. There are two reasons why the price is higher. First, demand is less elastic. This is demonstrated by the fact that price is a higher percentage above MR in the peak period than in the off-peak period. Second, marginal cost is higher in the peak period.

1. How likely is it that domestic customers will be able to switch consumption of electricity to off-peak periods? How likely is it that businesses will be able to do so?
2. If, over time, consumers are encouraged to switch their consumption to off-peak periods, what will happen to peak and off-peak prices?
3. To what extent is peak-load pricing in the interests of consumers?
4. Is total consumption likely to be higher or lower with a system of peak and off-peak prices as opposed to a uniform price at all times?

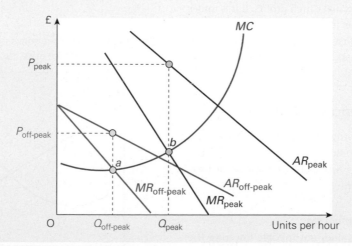

Definition

Peak-load pricing Price discrimination (second or third degree) where a higher price is charged in peak periods and a lower price in off-peak periods.

circumstances will it be able to charge discriminatory prices? There are three conditions that must be met:

■ The firm must be able to set its price. Thus price discrimination will be impossible under perfect competition, where firms are price takers. In other words, firms practising price discrimination must have some market power.

- The markets must be separable. Consumers in the low-priced market must not be able to resell the product in the high-priced market. For example, children must not be able to resell a half-priced child's cinema ticket for use by an adult.
- Demand elasticity must differ in each market. The firm will charge the higher price in the market where demand is less elastic, and thus less sensitive to a price rise.

Advantages to the firm

Price discrimination allows the firm to earn a higher revenue from any given level of sales. Let us examine the case of third-degree price discrimination.

Figure 8.12 represents a firm's demand curve. If it is to sell 200 units without price discrimination, it must charge a price of P_1. The total revenue it earns is shown by the green area. If, however, it can practise third-degree price discrimination by selling 150 of those 200 units at the higher price of P_2, it will gain the pink area in addition to the green area in Figure 8.12.

Explain why, if the firm can practise first-degree price discrimination by selling every unit at the maximum price each consumer is prepared to pay, its revenue from selling 200 units will be the green area plus the pink area in Figure 8.13.

Another advantage to the firm of price discrimination is that it may be able to use it to drive competitors out of business. If a firm has a monopoly in one market (e.g. the home market), it may be able to charge a high price due to relatively inelastic demand, and thus make high profits. If it is under oligopoly in another market (e.g. the export market), it may use the high profits in the first market to subsidise a very low price in the oligopolistic market, thus forcing its competitors out of business.

Profit-maximising prices and output

Assuming that the firm wishes to maximise profits, what discriminatory prices should it charge and how much should it produce? Let us first consider the case of first-degree price discrimination.

First-degree price discrimination

Since an increase in sales does not involve lowering the price for any unit save the *extra* one sold, the extra revenue gained from the last unit (MR) will be its price. Thus profit is maximised at Q_1 in Figure 8.14, where $MC = MR$ ($= P$ of the *last* unit).

Third-degree price discrimination

Assume that a firm sells a given product (such as window cleaning services) and can split its customers into two groups, based on location, where people in market H have a

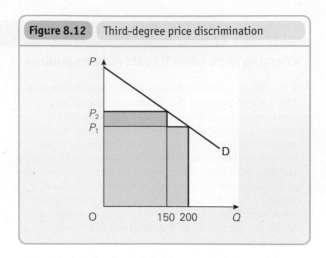

Figure 8.12 Third-degree price discrimination

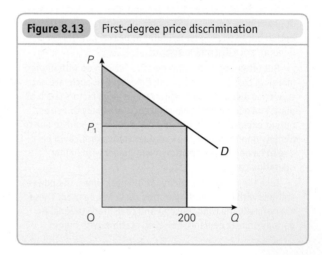

Figure 8.13 First-degree price discrimination

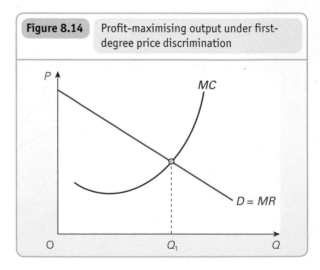

Figure 8.14 Profit-maximising output under first-degree price discrimination

higher average income than people in market L. This is illustrated in Figure 8.15.

It is highly probable that most consumers with the higher incomes would be willing to pay more for the product than those on low incomes. Panel (a) in Figure 8.15 illustrates the demand curve for the firm's product in the high-income

Figure 8.15 Profit-maximising output under third-degree price discrimination

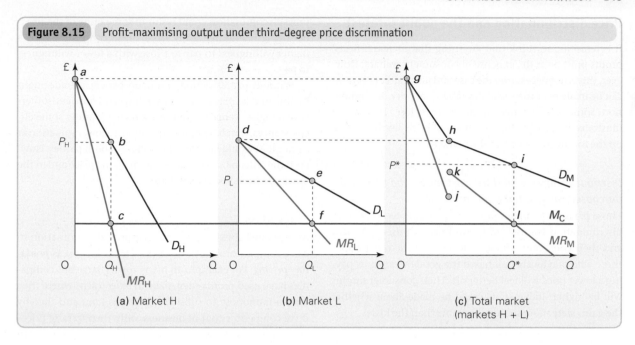

(a) Market H

(b) Market L

(c) Total market
(markets H + L)

market, market H, while panel (b) illustrates the demand curve for those in the low-income market, market L.

Equilibrium for a single-price firm. If the firm were unable to split its customers into these two groups, then a market demand curve could be derived. This is illustrated in panel (c) and is obtained by horizontally aggregating the demand curves in panel (a) and (b). The market demand curve between points g and h is the same as the demand curve in market H between points a and b. This is because no consumer in market L is willing to pay a price above d. As the price falls below d, consumers in both market H and market L are willing to buy the good, so horizontal aggregation of both demand curves must take place from this point onwards. This creates a kink in the market demand curve at point h. This kink also creates a discontinuity in the MR curve between points j and k. To simplify the explanation it is also assumed that the firm's marginal cost is constant and it has no fixed costs. Thus $AC = MC$.

To understand how a firm would behave if it could only set one price for all of its customers we need to focus on the market demand curve in panel (c). If it was a profit-maximising firm then it would produce where the market MR (i.e. MR_M) = MC. This occurs at point l in panel (c) of Figure 8.15. It would therefore produce an output of Q^* and sell all of this output at the same price of P^*.

Equilibrium under third-degree price discrimination. What happens if the firm could now charge a different price to the customers in market H from those in market L? At the single price of P^* the price elasticity of demand in market H is lower than it is in market L. (Note that demand is nevertheless elastic in both markets at this price as MR is positive). Therefore the firm could increase its profits by charging a price above P^* in market H and below P^* in market L. Once again this can be illustrated in Figure 8.15.

In market H the profit-maximising firm should produce where $MR_H = MC$. Therefore it should sell an output of Q_H for a price of P_H.

In market L the profit-maximising firm should produce where $MR_L = MC$ at point f. Therefore it should sell an output of Q_L for a price of P_L.

Note that P_L is below P^*, while P_H is above P^*. Also, because the demand curves are linear, the total output sold is the same under third-degree price discrimination as it is under uniform pricing: i.e. $Q^* = Q_H + Q_L$. We will see later in the chapter that this is a key point when considering whether or not price discrimination is in the public interest.

 How easy do you think it would for a firm to split customers into different groups based on their incomes?

*LOOKING AT THE MATHS

We can use calculus to work out the profit-maximising prices and outputs in each of the two markets *H* and *L* in Figure 8.15. If we know the demand functions in each of the two markets, *H* and *L*, we can derive the total revenue functions in each market (TR_H and TR_L) and hence in the two markets together ($TR = TR_H + TR_L$). Total profit is given by

$$T\Pi = TR_H + TR_L - TC$$

To find the maximum-profit output in each market, we (partially) differentiate the total profit equation with respect to output in each of *H* and *L* and set each equal to zero and solve for Q_H and Q_L (see pages A:9–13 for how calculus is used to find a maximum value). We can then substitute these values of Q_H and Q_L in the respective demand functions to work out P_H and P_L.

Maths Case 8.3 on the student website shows how this is done by using a worked example.

Price discrimination and the public interest

It is tempting to think that anything that increases firms' profits must be at the expense of consumers' welfare. However, this is not necessarily the case and no clear-cut decision can be made over the social desirability of price discrimination. Some people benefit from it; others lose. This can be illustrated by considering the effects of price discrimination on the following aspects of the market.

Distribution effects on those customers who previously purchased the good at a uniform price

Those paying the higher price will probably feel that price discrimination is unfair to them. Price has risen for them and their consumer surplus is lower. On the other hand, those who previously purchased the good but are now paying a lower price will feel better off. Their consumer surplus will be higher. Judgements could be made about whether the gains were more socially desirable than the losses.

The impact of any extra sales

In Figure 8.15, the quantity of sales under price discrimination remained the same as under uniform pricing. However, in some circumstances the quantity of sales may increase. There may be some consumers, such as pensioners, who previously could not afford to buy the good when the firm used uniform pricing. The lower price, made possible by price discrimination, now enables them to purchase the good. These extra sales will have a positive impact on the welfare of society. They will increase both consumer surplus and profit.

Misallocation effects

Price discrimination may cause a negative allocation effect. Under uniform pricing the product is allocated through the price mechanism to those consumers who value it the most, given their incomes. The implementation of third-degree price discrimination could result in some units of the product being reallocated away from those consumers with a higher willingness to pay to those with a lower willingness to pay.

Without any restrictions, mutually beneficial trade might be able to take place between the buyers. Those consumers with a higher valuation of the good could, under some circumstances, purchase it from those with a lower valuation at a price that would improve the welfare of both parties. However, the seller blocks this resale from taking place and in the process reduces society's welfare.

Competition

As explained above, a firm may use price discrimination to drive competitors out of business. This is known as **predatory pricing**. For example, in many towns, large bus companies have used profits they make in *other* towns where they have a monopoly to subsidise their bus fares and thereby drive competitors out of business, only then to raise prices above those that the competitors had been charging. On the other hand, a firm might use the profits from its high-priced market to break into another market and withstand a possible price war. Competition is thereby increased.

Profits

Price discrimination raises a firm's profits. This could be seen as an undesirable redistribution of income in society, especially if the average price of the product is raised. On the other hand, the higher profits may be reinvested and lead to innovation or lower costs in the future.

> **Definition**
>
> **Predatory pricing** Where a firm sets its prices below average cost in order to drive competitors out of business.

| BOX 8.8 | JUST THE TICKET? | CASE STUDIES AND APPLICATIONS |

Price discrimination in the cinema

One of the commonest forms of price discrimination is where children are charged a lower price than adults, whether on public transport or for public entertainment. Take the case of cinema tickets. In most cinemas, children pay less than adults during the day. In the evening, however, many cinemas charge both adults and children the same price.

But why do cinemas charge children less during the day? After all, the child is seeing the same film as the adult and occupying a whole seat. In other words, there is no difference in the 'product' that they are 'consuming'. And why are children charged the higher price in the evenings, given that the seat and the film are the same as during the day?

The answer has to do with revenue maximisation and the price elasticity of demand. Once a cinema has decided to show a film, the marginal costs of an additional customer are zero. There are no additional staffing, film-hire, electricity or other costs. With marginal costs equal to zero, profits will be maximised where marginal revenue is also equal to zero: in other words, where total revenue is maximised.

Take the case of a cinema with 500 seats. This is illustrated in the diagrams, which show the demand and marginal revenue curves for both adults and children. It is assumed that the elasticity of demand for children's tickets is greater than that for adults' tickets. Diagram (a) shows demand during the late afternoon (i.e. after school). Here the demand by children is relatively high compared with adults, but the overall demand is low. Diagram (b) shows demand during the evening. Here there is a higher overall level of demand, especially by adults, many of whom work during the day.

For the afternoon screening (diagram (a)), revenue is maximised from children by charging them a price of £8.00,

(b) *Number of tickets (evening and total)*

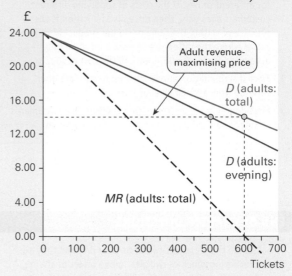

i.e. at the point on the demand curve where $MR = 0$. At this price, 200 child tickets will be sold.

Assuming that the same adult price is charged in both the afternoon and the evening, we need to look at the *total* demand for full-priced tickets (i.e. for both afternoon and evening screenings) in order to ascertain the revenue-maximising price. This will be a price of £14.00, where total adult $MR = 0$ (see diagram (b)). This will lead to 100 adult tickets being sold in the afternoon and 500 in the evening.

But why are reduced-price tickets not available for children in the evening? In diagram (b), the sale of low-priced tickets for children would lead to demand exceeding the 500-seat capacity of the cinema. Each time an adult was turned away because the seat had already been sold to a child, the cinema would lose.

(a) *Number of tickets (afternoon)*

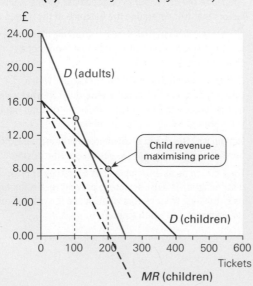

1. Which type of price discrimination is the cinema pursuing: first, second or third degree? Could it pursue either of the other two types?
2. If all cinema seats could be sold to adults in the evenings at the end of the week, but only a few on Mondays and Tuesdays, what price discrimination policy would you recommend to the cinema in order for it to maximise its weekly revenue?
3. Would the cinema make more profit if it could charge adults a different price in the afternoon and the evenings?
4. Would you advise that the cinema extend its practice of price discrimination to include other groups? If so, which groups should be targeted?
5. Are there any other advantages, beyond the additional revenues generated, to having more people in the cinema? Are there any disadvantages?

Section summary

1. If the costs to the firm of supplying different customers do not vary, then price discrimination is the practice of selling the same or similar products to different customers for different prices. If the costs of supplying different customers *does* vary, then price discrimination is the practice of selling the same or similar product at different prices where the difference in price cannot be fully accounted for by the difference in the cost of supply.

2. Price discrimination allows the firm to earn a higher revenue from a given level of sales.

3. First-degree price discrimination is where the consumer is charged the maximum he or she is prepared to pay.

Second-degree price discrimination is where the consumer is offered a range of different prices for the same or similar product. They are free to choose whichever option they wish but the lower prices are conditional on some features of the purchase. Third-degree price discrimination is where consumers are divided into groups and the groups with the lower price elasticity of demand are charged the higher prices.

4. Whether price discrimination is in the consumer's interest or not is uncertain. Some individuals will gain and some will lose

END OF CHAPTER QUESTIONS

1. Assume there are just two firms (X and Y) and they are considering which of two alternative prices to charge. The decisions are made simultaneously: i.e. without either firm knowing the choice of its rival. This various profits are illustrated in the following pay-off matrix.

Table 8.4	Profits for firms X and Y at different prices

		X's price	
		£25	£19
Y's price	£20	**A** £6m, £6m	**B** £2m, £5m
	£15	**C** £4m, £3m	**D** £4m, £4m

(a) What is firm Y's best response to each of the different prices firm X could charge? Does firm Y have a dominant strategy?

(b) What is firm X's best response to each of the different prices firm Y could charge? Does firm X have a dominant strategy?

(c) What is/are the Nash equilibrium/equilibria? What is the most likely outcome of this game? Explain your answer.

2. Assume that a monopolistically competitive industry is in long-run equilibrium. On a diagram like Figure 8.1(b), show the effect of a fall in demand on a firm's price and profit in (a) the short run and (b) the long run.

3. In what ways is a monopolistically competitive firm likely to be less efficient than one under perfect competition?

4. Are there any shops in your area that stay open later than others? If so, does this affect the prices they charge? Why do you think this is?

5. Give three examples of oligopolistic industries. In what ways do the firms in each of these industries compete? Why do they choose to compete in the way that they do?

6. Why, under oligopoly, might a particular industry be collusive at one time and yet highly price competitive at another?

7. What is meant by the prisoners' dilemma game when applied to the behaviour of oligopolists? Discuss some factors that will determine the outcome of the game?

8. What three characteristics must a strategic move have if it is to be successful in altering the behaviour of a competitor later in the game?

9. Give two examples of price discrimination. Which category of price discrimination are they? In what ways do the consumers gain or lose? What information would you need to be certain in your answer?

10. Explain why the rise in e-commerce might increase the number of firms engaging in person-specific pricing.

11. For a firm to be able to implement a strategy of price discrimination it must be able to prevent resale amongst its customers. What factors would make it more difficult for a consumer to resell a good?

Online resources

Additional case studies on the student website

8.1 **Edward Chamberlin and Joan Robinson.** A portrait of the two economists who developed the model of monopolistic competition.

8.2 **The motor vehicle repair and servicing industry.** A case study of monopolistic competition.

8.3 **The corner shop and the hypermarket.** A case study in non-price competition: how the corner shop can survive competition from the big supermarkets.

8.4 **Curry wars.** Monopolistic competition in the take-away food market.

8.5 **Bakeries: oligopoly or monopolistic competition.** A case study on the bread industry, showing that small-scale local bakeries can exist alongside giant national bakeries.

8.6 **Is beer becoming more concentrated.** A study of oligopoly in the brewing industry. There have been mergers between large brewers, but a rise in small breweries.

8.7 **'Rip-off Britain'.** This examines the evidence for oligopolistic collusion in the car, supermarket and banking industries.

8.8 **Fair wars in the skies?** The effect of the entry of low-cost airlines on air fares.

8.9 **A product's life cycle.** How market conditions vary at different stages in a product's life.

8.10 **Advertising and the public interest.** Does the consumer benefit from advertising?

Maths Case 8.1 Calculating the profit-maximising price of a price leader. Using equations for demand, revenue and cost curves.

Maths Case 8.2 Deriving the Cournot equilibrium. An algebraic example.

Maths Case 8.3 Calculating the profit-maximising prices under third-degree price discrimination. Using calculus to find the profit-maximising output and price in each market and to compare the profit with and without price discrimination.

Websites relevant to Chapters 7 and 8

Numbers and sections refer to websites listed in the Web Appendix and hotlinked from this book's website at **www.pearsoned. co.uk/sloman.**

- For news articles relevant to this and the previous chapter, see the *Economics News* section on the student website.
- For general news on companies and markets, see websites in section A, and particularly A2, 3, 4, 5, 8, 9, 18, 21, 23, 24, 25, 26, 35, 36. See also A38, 39, 42, 43 and 44 for links to newspapers worldwide; and A40 and 41 for links to economics news articles from newspapers worldwide.
- For sites that look at competition and market power, see sites E4, 10, 15, 16, 19, 20, 22; G7, 8. See also links in I7, 11 and 14.
- For information on OPEC (Box 8.3), see site H6.
- For sites with resources on game theory, see C23; I11; D4; C20.
- For a site that contains a number of open-access computer-based games on oligopoly and game theory that can be played between students, see sites D13–19.
- For models and simulations on pricing and price discrimination use the search feature in site D3.

9 Chapter

The Behaviour of Firms

The traditional theories of the firm that we have been looking at in the previous three chapters assume that firms aim to maximise profits. Although this is an accurate assumption for many firms, for many it is not.

Some firms would *like* to maximise profits, but have insufficient information to enable them to do so. Others do not even want to maximise profits, if that means sacrificing some other aim, such as rapid growth or increased market share.

In this chapter, we focus on the behaviour of decision makers in firms. We look at various aims they might pursue as an alternative to maximum profits: aims such as maximum sales revenue or maximum growth. We also examine the implications of pursuing alternative aims for the profitability of the firm and for the prices paid by the consumer.

Many firms, especially larger ones, are complex organisations, with different individuals and departments pursuing their own agenda. What happens when these various goals come into conflict? How does conflict get resolved? What are the implications for consumers and other 'stakeholders'? We examine these issues in section 9.5.

Finally, we ask how prices are determined in practice. If firms do not use marginal revenue and marginal cost concepts in setting their prices, or if they are not aiming to achieve maximum profits, how do they choose the price to charge? As we shall see, firms often base their prices on average cost.

9.1 PROBLEMS WITH TRADITIONAL THEORY

The traditional profit-maximising theories of the firm have been criticised for being unrealistic. The criticisms are mainly of two sorts: (a) that firms wish to maximise profits but for some reason are unable to do so; or (b) that firms have aims other than profit maximisation. Let us examine each in turn.

Difficulties in maximising profit

One criticism of traditional theory is that firms do not use *MR* and *MC* concepts. This may well be true, but firms could still arrive at maximum profit by trial and error adjustments of price, or by finding the output where *TR* and *TC* are furthest apart. Provided they end up maximising profits, they will be equating *MC* and *MR*, even if they did not adopt that as a strategy. In this case, traditional models will still be useful in predicting price and output.

Lack of information

The main difficulty in trying to maximise profits is a *lack of information*.

Firms may well use accountants' cost concepts not based on opportunity cost. If it were thereby impossible to measure true profit, a firm would not be able to maximise profit except by chance.

> *What cost concepts are there other than those based on opportunity cost? Would the use of these concepts be likely to lead to an output greater or less than the profit-maximising one?*

More importantly, firms are unlikely to know even approximately their demand curves and hence their *MR* curves. Even though they will know how much they are selling, this only gives them one point on their demand curve and no point at all on their *MR* curve. In order to make an informed guess of marginal revenue, they would need an idea of how responsive demand will be to a change in price.

But how are they to estimate this price elasticity? Market research may help. But this may be unreliable.

The biggest problem in estimating the firm's demand curve is in estimating the actions and reactions of *other* firms and their effects. Even under collusion there will still be a

considerable uncertainty.

As we saw in Chapter 8, game theory may help a firm decide its price and output strategy. But for this to be accurate, it requires that a firm knows the consequences for its profits of each of the possible reactions of its rivals. In reality, no firm will have this information, because it will not know

for sure how consumers will respond to each of its rivals' alternative strategies.

Time period

Finally, there is the problem of deciding the time period over which the firm should be seeking to maximise profits. Firms operate in a changing environment. Demand curves shift; supply curves shift. Some of these shifts occur as a result of factors outside the firm's control, such as changes in competitors' prices and products. Some, however, change as a direct result of a firm's policies, such as an advertising campaign or the installation of new equipment. The firm is not, therefore, faced with static cost and revenue curves from which it can read off its profit-maximising price and output. Instead it is faced with a changing and unpredictable set of curves. If it chooses a price and output that maximises profits this year, it may be entirely the wrong decision months, or even weeks, later.

Take a simple example. The firm may be considering whether to invest in new equipment. If it does, its costs will rise in the short run and thus short-run profits will fall. On the other hand, if the quality of the product thereby increases, demand is likely to increase over the longer run. Also, variable costs will decrease if the new equipment is more efficient. In other words, long-run profit is likely to increase, but probably by an uncertain amount.

Given these problems in trying to work out complex strategies to maximise profits, managers may fall back on simple rules of thumb or mental shortcuts for pricing and output decisions (see page 225).

Alternative aims

An even more fundamental attack on traditional theory is that firms do not even *aim* to maximise profits (even if they could).

The traditional theory of the firm assumes that it is the *owners* of the firm who make price and output decisions. It is reasonable to assume that owners *will* want to maximise profits. The question is, however, whether the owners do in fact make the decisions.

In *public limited companies* the shareholders are the owners. Presumably they will want the firm to maximise profits so as to increase their dividends and the value of their shares. Shareholders elect directors. Directors in turn employ professional managers who are often given considerable discretion in making decisions. There is therefore a *separation between the ownership and control* of a firm. (See Case Study 9.1 on the student website for an examination of the legal structure of firms.)

So what are the objectives of managers? Will *they* want to maximise profits, or will they have some other aim?

We can assume that they want to *maximise their own utility*. They may, for example, pursue higher salaries, greater power or a more prestigious company car. Different managers in the same firm may well pursue different aims. These aims may conflict with profit maximisation.

Definition

Public limited company A company owned by its shareholders. Shareholders' liability is limited to the value of their shares. Shares may be bought and sold publicly – on the stock market.

BOX 9.1   WHAT DO YOU MAXIMISE?

Managers are only human too

You are a student studying economics. So what do you maximise?

Do you attempt to maximise the examination marks you will get? If so, you will probably have to spend most of each week studying. Obviously you will have to have breaks for food and sleep, and you will need some recreation, but you will need to spend most of your time studying.

What is more likely is that you will, in some rather vaguely defined way, try to maximise your happiness. Getting good marks in your exams is just one element contributing to this aim, and you will have to weigh it against the opportunity cost of studying – namely, time not spent out with friends, playing sport, working for money, etc.

To argue that managers seek to maximise profits to the exclusion of everything else is rather like arguing that you seek to maximise your exam marks. Managers' happiness (or utility) will depend on many factors, including their salaries, the pleasantness of their job, their power and the friendship of their colleagues.

Achieving profits may be an important aim (after all, it does contribute to a manager's utility), but the effort required to make additional profits will involve an opportunity cost to the manager – having, say, to work longer hours or firing a close colleague.

1. *When are increased profits in the manager's personal interest?*
2. *Does the way you allocate your time between study and leisure vary at different times of the year? If so, why?*

Managers will still have to ensure that *sufficient* profits are made to keep shareholders happy, but that may be very different from *maximising* profits.

Alternative theories of the firm to those of profit maximisation, therefore, tend to assume that large firms are *profit satisficers*. That is, managers strive hard for a minimum target level of profit, but are less interested in profits above this level.

Such theories fall into two categories: first, those theories that assume that firms attempt to maximise some other aim, provided that sufficient profits are achieved (these are examined in section 9.3); and second, those theories that assume that firms pursue a number of potentially conflicting aims, of which sufficient profit is merely one (these are examined in section 9.5).

KEY IDEA 24

The nature of institutions and organisations is likely to influence behaviour. There are various forces influencing people's decisions in complex organisations. Assumptions that an organisation will follow one simple objective (e.g. short-run profit maximisation) are thus too simplistic in many cases.

Make a list of six possible aims that a manager of a high street department store might have. Identify some conflicts that might arise between these aims.

Definitions

Profit satisficing Where decision makers in a firm aim for a target level of profit rather than the absolute maximum level.

Section summary

1. There are two major types of criticism of the traditional profit-maximising theory: (a) firms may not have the information to maximise profits; (b) they may not even want to maximise profits.

2. Lack of information on demand and costs and on the actions and reactions of rivals, and a lack of use of opportunity cost concepts, may mean that firms adopt simple 'rules of thumb' for pricing.

3. In large companies, there is likely to be a separation between ownership and control. The shareholders (the owners) may want maximum profits, but it is the managers who make the decisions, and managers are likely to aim to maximise their own utility rather than that of the shareholders. This leads to profit 'satisficing'.

9.2   BEHAVIOURAL ECONOMICS OF THE FIRM

Is firm behaviour consistent with the rational choice model?

Section 5.2 in Chapter 5 introduced behavioural economics, the field of study that integrates some simple insights from psychology into standard economic theory. We saw how ideas such as heuristics, loss aversion, present bias and reciprocity can sometimes predict human behaviour more effectively than the traditional approach.

The focus in Chapter 5 was on consumer behaviour. In this chapter, we consider how behavioural economics can be applied to the theory of the firm. For example, in what ways might managerial decision making deviate from that predicted by rationality? How might a firm's actions be affected by managers who have a strong preference for fairness?

Some potential heuristics

Firms operate in complex environments, dealing with imperfect information and uncertainty about both the present and the future. Trying to work out and implement a profit-maximising strategy in these situations is a cognitively demanding task that places great strain on a manager's computational capacity. Rather like consumers, managers may respond by using heuristics (rules of thumb/mental shortcuts) to simplify things. Some heuristics might include the following:

Copying the strategy of the most profitable businesses in the market. This is only possible if a firm can observe the actions and profits made by its rivals. If some firms follow a strategy of imitation in an oligopolistic market, it might lead to more intense competition, with lower prices and higher output. Some research has also found that firms which simply imitate do at least as well as those that successfully calculate their own profit-maximising strategy.

Focusing on relative rather than absolute profits. It is easier to see if a firm is making more profit than its competitors than if it is making the maximum profit possible. Therefore managers may judge their success by comparing their firm's performance with that of their rivals. There may also be financial incentives to behave in this way as bonuses are often based on relative, as opposed to absolute, profits.

This type of behaviour may lead to firms implementing strategies that reduce their own profits (e.g. an aggressive price war) if it reduces the profits of their rivals by a greater amount. Section 9.5 discusses how having multiple goals may also lead to managers focusing on their relative performance.

Making a satisfactory/target level of profit. Instead of constantly looking for new opportunities to maximise profits in a dynamic market, managers may instead only change a firm's strategy when its profits fall below some target level.

The most influential early exponents of this approach were Richard Cyert and James March[1] (see section 9.5 for more detail). Their research made use of case studies of four multinational firms. They used the observations obtained to develop models of the firm, where decisions resulted from a sequence of behaviours. Their work highlighted the limitations of the neoclassical assumption of profit maximisation and proved to be highly influential in two ways. First it led to the study of behaviour, both of firms and the individual decision makers with them. Second, the research methods used have been adopted by experimentalists, not only in economics, but across the social sciences.

 Which is easier – for managers to make decisions that maximise profits or for consumers to make decisions that maximise their utility? Discuss some of the arguments in favour of each case.

Managerial preferences for fairness

As we saw in Chapter 8, the behaviour of a firm in an oligopoly depends on how it thinks its rivals will react to its actions. In collusive oligopoly firms agree to limit competition in order to maximise joint profits. Game theory allows us to examine these strategic decisions in more depth. A consistent assumption is that firms are attempting to maximise profits and believe that their rivals will always behave in a rational and selfish manner (i.e. try to maximise their own profits). But is this always a reasonable assumption?

Rather than being rational profit maximisers, some managers may have a strong preference for fairness. In particular, they may care about the equitable distribution of profits between firms in their industry. If a profit-maximising firm takes actions that enable it to obtain a larger share of the profits, firms with managers who have a strong preference for fairness might be willing to take costly actions to punish them. By costly, we mean actions that reduce the firm's own profits as well as those of its rivals. Many research experiments have found evidence of people being willing to reduce their own earnings to punish other 'players' for what they consider to be unfair behaviour.

Preferences for fairness may increase the chances of collusive oligopoly by reducing the likelihood of cheating. Take the following example. Imagine an industry that is dominated by two large firms (firm A and firm B). These two firms make a collusive agreement to charge prices above the competitive level for an indefinite period of time. If they both stick to the deal they split the higher level of industry profits between them. We explained in Chapter 8 how the chances of both firms sticking to the deal depends on a number of factors, including the expected size of any punishment for cheating. What impact do fairness preferences have on the size of expected punishment?

Assume the sole objective of the managers at firm A is to maximise profits, while those at firm B have a strong preference for fairness. If they both stick to the terms of the collusive agreement, the managers at firm B will think the outcome is fair.

If firm A knows that firm B has this strong preference for fairness this will have an impact on its expected costs of cheating. It knows that firm B will be willing to take further actions that reduce its own profits as long as it reduces the profits of firm A by a greater amount. This helps to equalise the profits between the two businesses, something firm B values, even though they both end up with lower profits. If firm A anticipates this more aggressive response from the fairness-minded firm B, this will deter it from cheating in the first place. What about firm B? If firm A sticks to the agreement, firm B will not cheat because it believes the outcome to be fair.

1 Richard Cyert and James March, *A Behavioural Theory of the Firm* (Blackwell, 1963).

BOX 9.2 HOW FIRMS INCREASE PROFITS BY UNDERSTANDING 'IRRATIONAL' CONSUMERS

In section 5.2 we looked at behavioural economics as applied to consumer behaviour. We examined some of the reasons why people might not always act in the way that traditional economics predicts. This suggests that there may be an opportunity for business to increase profits by taking this 'irrationality' into account.

The role of 'special offers'

We all love a bargain and firms know this. If you walk around any supermarket, or look at online shopping sites, you will notice how many special deals are offered to entice us. 'Sale price'; 'Reduced'; '15% off'; 'Free delivery'; 'Everything must go'.

One thing that these all have in common is that they are only available for a limited time. Behavioural economists suggest that the combination of a special offer and a looming deadline pushes us into a state of excitement. We buy in a frenzy and fail to compute whether the benefits are worth the cost. In particular, there is evidence that we spend money on items that we would not have bought at the same price if there wasn't a special offer involved. We see the original price as a signal of quality and the reduced price as an unmissable opportunity.

The cost of inaction

Have you ever joined a gym? Every January thousands of people do, when they make new year's resolutions to get fit and lose weight. By March most of them have stopped going. A report published in January 2011 suggested that Britons are wasting millions of pounds each year on unused memberships.[1] We could argue that this is a result of poor information (we underestimate the effort required and overestimate the pleasure involved) or of uncertainty (we can't anticipate how we will feel about visiting the gym later in the year). However, neither of these factors explains why we fail to cancel unused gym memberships once the contract allows us to do so.

The answer lies in our tendency to inertia and procrastination; we intend to cancel the membership and the associated direct debit, yet we fail to do so. This inertia is demonstrated in a number of other markets – households have a legal right to switch energy suppliers, yet the majority fail to do so unless they are targeted by salespeople. Many people take out savings accounts which offer high interest

rates for a limited period – but then forget, or can't be bothered, to switch to other accounts at the end of the introductory period. As with the failure to cancel gym membership, the intention may be there, but our inertia leads to failure to maximise our utility.

Alternative contracts

If firms make profits from our inertia, they may also vary contracts to respond to our own understanding of our failure to behave rationally. There is an argument that suggests that at least some consumers will recognise the irrational behaviour that is costing them money. Does this mean that fitness clubs face losing members and lower profits? Not necessarily; some companies seek to appeal to the 'informed consumer' and to extend their customer base by offering rolling contracts, and by offering a 'no-frills' experience.

In 2010, two Harvard graduates set up a business, Gym-Pact, which bought group gym memberships from a number of existing gyms. Gym-Pact then sold on these memberships; but rather than a regular deal, they offered 'motivational' contracts to individuals, who pay more if they miss their regular workouts. The pair came up with this idea after studying behavioural economics as part of their degree; they learnt that people react more strongly to immediate certainties than to future possibilities.

This business model turned out to be short-lived. However, the founders did not give up on the principle. By 2014, Gym-Pact had become Pact, a business that brings together members who commit to working out, to logging their food intake and to eating vegetables. Those who succeed are rewarded with small cash sums, of up to £5 per day. Those who fail are charged for their lack of willpower. Pact makes money as the intermediary.

1. *Insurance companies are keen to offer their customers ongoing renewal, where the annual premium is automatically charged to a credit card. Explain the advantages to the company? Are there benefits to the customers in this arrangement?*
2. *UK consumer protection laws require that goods offered at 'sale prices' have previously been offered at the higher price for at least 28 days. Why is this in the customer's interest?*
3. *Think of two or three things that you intend to do when you 'get around to it'? Are there any business opportunities that might arise from this type of procrastination?*

1 'Britons spend £37 m a year on wasted gym memberships and slimming classes', *Daily Mail,* 13 May 2017.

In reality, the outcome of these examples of strategic interdependence will depend on a number of factors, including (a) the knowledge each firm has about the preferences of its rivals and (b) the strength of its own fairness preferences compared with its desire to make profits.

Some potential biases

Economists have long identified over-optimism as a trait seen in many people. Adam Smith commented that 'the

chance of gain is by every man, more or less over-valued, and the chance of loss is by most men under-valued'.[2] A number of factors may make over-optimism even greater among managers than the population as a whole.

2 See: Adam Smith, *An Inquiry into the Nature and Causes of the Wealth of Nations,* book 1, chapter 10, para. 29.

Why might it present problems for a firm if managers are over-confident? Can you think of any reason why CEOs might be more inclined to optimism than the population average?

There is also survey evidence that managers include sunk costs as well as avoidable costs, when making pricing decisions.[3] This can lead to different prices from those set by a profit-maximising firm (we examine cost-based pricing in section 9.6).

 Why may managers choose to set prices that cover all costs, including sunk costs?

Can firms make use of behavioural economics?

Firms might be able to make use of behavioural economics if they are rational but their customers use heuristics or make systematic mistakes. Indeed, there is evidence that firms have been making use of some of its principles for many years. For example, they develop marketing strategies that do not concentrate solely on price, but are tailored to consumers' (sometimes irrational) preferences. Examples include offering 'buy one, get one free' and loyalty points. In Box 9.2 we look at some examples of how businesses can bring the lessons of behavioural economics into their pricing and marketing.

Of course there are other aspects to running a business than understanding consumer behaviour. Since, for most firms labour is a major input, it will be important to account for the motivation of employees – to ensure that they work hard and that their actions are aligned with the interests of the firm. Mechanisms of reward (and possibly punishment) may be most effective if the behaviour of workers and their preference for fairness is fully understood. This is considered in more detail in Chapter 10.

 Are there other points in the supply chain/production process where firms could make use of a better understanding of behavioural economics?

Section summary

1. Behavioural economics is relevant for understanding why and how the aims and strategies of firms deviate from traditional profit maximisation. This deviation is in part explained by managers using various mental shortcuts or heuristics to simplify complex decisions made in conditions of uncertainty. Some examples include imitation and focusing on performance.

2. Since firms are managed by individuals, who are motivated by a number of possible factors such as fairness, we should not be surprised if companies do not always appear to adopt 'selfish' strategies. The strength and awareness of any preferences for fairness will help to determine the equilibrium outcome in the market.

3. Firms can make use of the principles identified in behavioural economics to increase profits. Opportunities may arise in the relationship with consumers, particularly when looking at marketing and pricing. There may also be examples where greater understanding of behaviour can be used to inform contracts with employees, or with suppliers.

4. Levels of optimism and attitudes to risk will vary among owners and managers. If a firm is unwilling to make bold decisions it may increase its chances of survival, but will pay for this with lower profits. Over-cautious strategies may also leave a firm vulnerable, if its competitors are able to gain market share by being bold.

9.3 ALTERNATIVE MAXIMISING THEORIES

Long-run profit maximisation

The traditional theory of the firm is based on the assumption of *short-run* profit maximisation. Many actions of firms may be seen to conflict with this aim and yet could be consistent with the aim of **long-run profit maximisation**. For example, policies to increase the size of the firm or the firm's share of the market may involve heavy advertising or low prices to the detriment of short-run profits. But if this results in a larger market share, the resulting economic power may enable the firm to make larger profits in the long run.

At first sight, a theory of long-run profit maximisation would seem to be a realistic alternative to the traditional short-run profit-maximisation theory. In practice, however, the theory is not a very useful predictor of firms' behaviour and is very difficult to test.

A claim by managers that they were attempting to maximise long-run profits could be an excuse for virtually any policy. When challenged as to why the firms had, say,

---

Definition

Long-run profit maximisation An alternative theory which assumes that managers aim to shift cost and revenue curves so as to maximise profits over some longer time period.

---

[3] See for example: Steve Buchheit and Nick Feltovich, 'Experimental evidence of a sunk-cost paradox: a study of pricing behavior in Bertrand–Edgeworth duopoly', *University of Aberdeen Discussion Paper, 2008-4* (April 2008).

BOX 9.3   WHEN IS A THEORY NOT A THEORY?

Have you heard the joke about the man sitting in a railway carriage who was throwing pieces of paper out of the window? A fellow traveller was curious and asked him why he kept doing this.

'It keeps the elephants down', was the reply.
'But', said the other man, 'there are no elephants around here.'
'I know', said the first man. 'Effective, isn't it?'

Let's reformulate this joke.

Once upon a time there was this boss of a company who kept doing strange things. First he would spend a massive amount of money on advertising, and then stop. Then he would pay a huge wage increase 'to keep his workforce

happy'. Then he would close the factory for two months to give everyone a break. Then he would move the business, lock, stock and barrel, to a new location.

One day he was talking to an accountant friend, who asked, 'Why do you keep doing these strange things?'

'I have to do them to make the business profitable', was the reply.
'But your business is profitable', said the accountant.
'I know. It just goes to show how effective my policies are.'

1. *Why might it be difficult to refute a theory of long-run profit maximisation?*
2. *If a theory cannot in principle be refuted, is it a useful theory?*

---

undertaken expensive research or high-cost investment, or had engaged in a damaging price war, the managers could reply 'Ah, yes, but in the long run it will pay off.' This is very difficult for shareholders to refute (until it is too late!).

Even if long-run profit maximisation *is* the prime aim, the means of achieving it are extremely complex. The firm will need a plan of action for prices, output, investment, etc., stretching from now into the future. But today's pricing and marketing decisions affect tomorrow's demand. Therefore, future demand curves cannot be taken as given. Today's investment decisions will affect tomorrow's costs. Therefore, future cost curves cannot be taken as given either. These shifts in demand and cost curves will be very difficult to estimate with any precision. Quite apart from this, the actions of competitors, suppliers, unions, the future state of the economy, and so on are difficult to predict. Thus the picture of firms making precise calculations of long-run profit-maximising prices and outputs is an unrealistic one.

It may be useful, however, simply to observe that firms, when making current price, output and investment decisions, try to judge the approximate effect on new entrants, consumer demand, future costs, etc., and try to avoid decisions that would appear to conflict with long-run profits. Often this will simply involve avoiding making decisions (e.g. cutting price) that may stimulate an unfavourable result from rivals (e.g. rivals cutting their price).

Managerial utility maximisation

One of the most influential of the alternative theories of the firm has been that developed by O. E. Williamson[4] in the 1960s. Williamson argued that, provided satisfactory levels of profit are achieved, managers often have the discretion to

choose what policies to pursue. In other words, they are free to pursue their *own* interests. And what are the managers' interests? To maximise their own utility, argued Williamson.

Williamson identified a number of factors that affect a manager's utility. The four main ones were salary, job security, dominance (including status, power and prestige) and professional excellence.

Of these only salary is *directly* measurable. The rest have to be measured indirectly. One way of doing this is to examine managers' expenditure on various items, and in particular on *staff*, on *perks* (such as a company car) and on *discretionary investment*. The greater is the level of expenditure by managers on these items, the greater is likely to be their status, power, prestige, professional excellence and job security, and hence utility.

Having identified the factors that influence a manager's utility, Williamson developed several models in which managers seek to maximise their utility. He used these to predict managerial behaviour under various conditions and argued that they performed better than traditional profit-maximising theory.

One important conclusion was that average costs are likely to be higher when managers have the discretion to pursue their own utility. For example, perks and unnecessarily high staffing levels add to costs. On the other hand, the resulting 'slack' allows managers to rein in these costs in times of low demand (see page 269). This enables them to maintain their profit levels. To support these claims he conducted a number of case studies. These did indeed show that staff and perks were cut during recessions and expanded during booms, and that new managers were frequency able to cut staff without influencing the productivity of firms.

Sales revenue maximisation (short-run)

Perhaps the most famous of all alternative theories of the firm is that developed by William Baumol in the late 1950s.

---

4 O. E. Williamson, *The Economics of Discretionary Behaviour* (Prentice Hall, 1964), p. 3.

TC 9
p129

This is the theory of *sales revenue maximisation*. Unlike the theories of long-run profit maximisation and managerial utility maximisation, it is easy to identify the price and output that meet this aim – at least in the short run.

So why would managers want to maximise their firm's sales revenue? The answer is that the success of managers, and in particular sales managers, may be judged according to the level of the firm's sales. Sales figures are an obvious barometer of the firm's health. Managers' salaries, power and prestige may depend directly on sales revenue. The firm's sales representatives may be paid commission on their sales. Thus sales revenue maximisation may be a more dominant aim in the firm than profit maximisation, particularly if it has a dominant sales department.

Sales revenue will be maximised at the top of the TR curve at output Q_1 in Figure 9.1. Profits, by contrast, would be maximised at Q_2. Thus, for given total revenue and total cost curves, sales revenue maximisation will tend to lead to a higher output and a lower price than profit maximisation.

> **?** Draw a diagram with MC and MR curves. Mark the output (a) at which profits are maximised; (b) at which sales revenue is maximised.

The firm will still have to make sufficient profits, however, to keep the shareholders happy. Thus firms can be seen to be operating with a profit constraint. They are *profit satisficers*.

The effect of this profit constraint is illustrated in Figure 9.2. The diagram shows a total profit ($T\Pi$) curve. (This is found by simply taking the difference between TR and TC at each output.) Assume that the minimum acceptable profit is Π (whatever the output). Any output greater than Q_3 will give a profit less than Π. Thus the sales revenue maximiser that is also a profit satisficer will produce Q_3, not Q_1. Note, however, that this output is still greater than the profit-maximising output Q_2.

Figure 9.2 Sales revenue maximising with a profit constraint

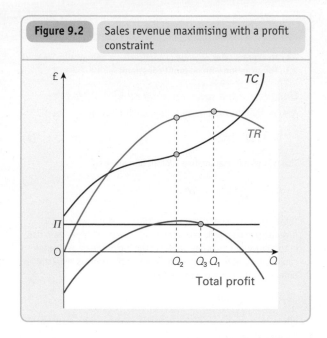

If the firm could maximise sales revenue and still make more than the minimum acceptable profit, it would probably spend this surplus profit on advertising to increase revenue further. This would have the effect of shifting upwards the TR curve and also the TC curve (since advertising costs money).

Sales revenue maximisation will tend to involve more advertising than profit maximisation. The profit-maximising firm will advertise up to the point where the marginal revenue of advertising equals the marginal cost of advertising (assuming diminishing returns to advertising). The firm aiming to maximise sales revenue will go beyond this, since further advertising, although costing more than it earns the firm, will still add to total revenue. The firm will continue advertising until surplus profits above the minimum have been used up.

> **?** Since advertising increases a firm's costs, will prices necessarily be lower with sales revenue maximisation than with profit maximisation?

Growth maximisation

Rather than aiming to maximise *short-run* revenue, managers may take a longer-term perspective and aim for *growth maximisation* in the size of the firm. They may directly gain

Figure 9.1 Sales-revenue-maximising output

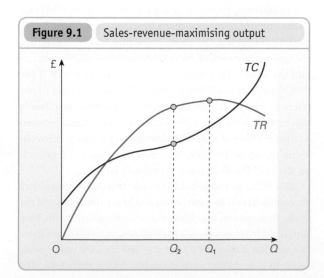

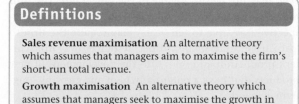

Definitions

Sales revenue maximisation An alternative theory which assumes that managers aim to maximise the firm's short-run total revenue.

Growth maximisation An alternative theory which assumes that managers seek to maximise the growth in sales revenue (or the capital value of the firm) over time.

*LOOKING AT THE MATHS

We can express sales revenue maximisation algebraically. We start with the situation with no profit constraint.

Unconstrained sales revenue maximisation

Assume that the total revenue function is given by

$$TR = bQ - cQ^2 \qquad (1)$$

This will give a straight-line *MR* function given by

$$MR = \frac{dTR}{dQ} = b - 2cQ$$

Total revenue is maximised where $MR = 0$, since, when total revenue is maximised, any increase in output will give a zero rise in total revenue. In other words, at the top of the total revenue curve in Figures 9.1 and 9.2, the slope of the curve is zero (the tangent to the curve is horizontal). Thus:

$$MR = b - 2cQ = 0$$

i.e.

$$2cQ = b$$

i.e.

$$Q = \frac{b}{2c} \qquad (2)$$

Thus, if the total revenue function were

$$TR = 120 - 3Q^2$$

then, from equation (2), total revenue would be maximised at an output (*Q*), where

$$Q = \frac{b}{2c} = \frac{120}{2 \times 3} = 20$$

Constrained sales revenue maximisation

If there is a profit constraint, we can write the objective function as Max *TR*, subject to $(TR - TC) \geq T\Pi^*$ where $T\Pi^*$ is the minimum profit that must be achieved. Assume that the *TR* and *TC* functions are given by

$$TR = bQ - cQ^2$$

and

$$TC = a + dQ - eQ^2 + gQ^3$$

Note that these two equations match the shapes of the *TR* and *TC* curves in Figures 9.1 and 9.2. The constraint can now be written:

$$TR - TC = -a + (b - d)Q + (e - c)Q^2 - gQ^3 \geq T\Pi^*$$

We can use this to solve for *Q*. An example of this is given in Maths Case 9.1 on the student website.

---

utility from being part of a rapidly growing 'dynamic' organisation; promotion prospects are greater in an expanding organisation since new posts tend to be created; larger firms may pay higher salaries; managers may obtain greater power in a larger firm.

Growth is probably best measured in terms of a growth in sales revenue, since sales revenue (or 'turnover') is the simplest way of measuring the size of a business. An alternative would be to measure the capital value of a firm, but this will depend on the ups and downs of the stock market and is thus a rather unreliable method.

If a firm is to maximise growth, it needs to be clear about the time period over which it is setting itself this objective. For example, maximum growth over the next two or three years might be obtained by running factories to absolute maximum capacity, cramming in as many machines and workers as possible, and backing this up with massive advertising campaigns and price cuts. Such policies, however, may not be sustainable in the longer run. The firm may simply not be able to finance them. A longer-term perspective (say, five to ten years) may require the firm to 'pace' itself, and perhaps to direct resources away from current production and sales into the development of new products that have a potentially high and growing long-term demand.

Growth may be achieved either by internal expansion or by merger.

Growth by internal expansion

Internal growth requires an increase in sales, which requires an increase in the firm's productive capacity. In order to increase its *sales,* the firm is likely to engage in extensive product promotion and to try to launch new products. In order to increase *productive capacity,* the firm will require new investment. Both product promotion and investment will require finance.

In the short run, the firm can finance growth by borrowing, by retaining profits or by a new issue of shares. What limits the amount of finance that a firm can acquire, and hence the rate at which it can grow? If the firm *borrows* too much, the interest payments it incurs will make it difficult to maintain the level of dividends to shareholders. Similarly, if the firm *retains* too much *profit,* there will be less available to pay out in dividends. If it attempts to raise capital by a *new issue of shares,* the distributed profits will have to be divided between a larger number of shares. Whichever way it finances investment, therefore, the more it invests, the more the dividends on shares in the short run will probably fall.

This could lead shareholders to sell their shares, unless they are confident that *long-run* profits and hence dividends will rise again, thus causing the share price to remain high in the long run. If shareholders do sell their shares, this will cause share prices to fall. If they fall too far, the firm runs the risk of being taken over and of certain managers losing their jobs. The

TC 1
p11

takeover constraint therefore requires that the growth-maximising firm distribute sufficient profits to avoid being taken over.

In the long run, a rapidly growing firm may find its profits increasing, especially if it can achieve economies of scale and a bigger share of the market. These profits can then be used to finance further growth.

Growth through vertical integration

If market conditions make growth through increased sales difficult, then a firm may choose to grow through vertical integration. This has a number of advantages.

Economies of scale. These can occur by the business performing complementary stages of production within a single business unit. The classic example of this is the steel manufacturer combining the furnacing and milling stages of production, saving the costs that would have been required to reheat the iron had such operations been undertaken by independent businesses. Clearly, for most firms, the performing of more than one stage on a single site is likely to reduce transport costs, as semi-finished products no longer have to be moved from one plant to another.

Reduced uncertainty. A business that is not vertically integrated may find itself subject to various uncertainties in the marketplace. Examples include uncertainty over future price movements, over supply reliability or over access to markets.

Barriers to entry. Vertical integration may give the firm greater power in the market by enabling it to erect entry barriers to potential competitors. For example, a firm that undertakes backward vertical integration and acquires a key input resource may effectively close the market to potential new entrants, either by simply refusing to supply a competitor, or by charging a very high price for the input, such that new firms face an absolute cost disadvantage.

 See if you can identify two companies that are vertically integrated and what advantages they gain from such integration.

The major problem with vertical integration is that it may reduce the firm's ability to respond to changing market demands. A business that integrates may find itself tied to its own supply source. If, by contrast, it were free to choose between suppliers, inputs might be obtained at a lower price than the firm could achieve by supplying itself.

Many firms are finding that it is better *not* to be vertically integrated but to focus on their core business and to outsource their supplies, their marketing and many other functions. That way they put alternative suppliers and distributors in competition with each other.

Growth through diversification

An alternative internal growth strategy to vertical integration is that of diversification. A good example of a highly diversified company is Virgin. Its interests include planes, trains, finance, music, mobile phones, holidays, hotels, wine, cinemas, broadband, health care, publishing, balloon flights and even space travel.

If the current market is saturated or in decline, diversification might be the only avenue open to the business if it wishes to maintain a high growth performance. In other words, it is not only the level of profits that may be limited in the current market, but also the growth of sales.

Diversification also has the advantage of spreading risks. If a business produces a single product in a single market, it is vulnerable to changes in that market's conditions. If a farmer produces nothing but potatoes and the potato harvest fails, the farmer is ruined. If, however, the farmer produces a whole range of vegetables, or even diversifies into livestock, then they are less subject to the forces of nature and the unpredictability of the market.

Growth by merger

A merger may be the result of the mutual agreement of two firms to come together. Alternatively, one firm may put in a takeover bid for another. This involves the first firm offering to buy the shares of the second for cash, to swap them for shares in the acquiring company, or to issue fixed-interest securities (debentures). The shareholders of the second firm then vote on whether to accept the offer. (Technically this is an 'acquisition' or 'takeover' rather than a merger, but the term 'merger' is generally used to include both mutual agreements and acquisitions.)

There are three types of merger:

- A *horizontal merger* is where firms in the same industry and at the same stage of production merge. For example, in October 2016 AB-InBev (the biggest brewing business in the world) announced that it had completed its £79 billion takeover of SABMiller (the second biggest brewing in the world). This merger is discussed in more detail in Box 14.3 (page 431).
- A *vertical merger* is where firms in the same industry but at different stages in the production of a good merge: e.g. during 2015 and 2016, Ikea purchased a number of forests in Romania to gain greater control over the supply of wood it uses to produces furniture.

KI 24
p252

Definitions

Takeover constraint The effect that the fear of being taken over has on a firm's willingness to undertake projects that reduce distributed profits.

Horizontal merger Where two firms in the same industry at the same stage in the production process merge.

Vertical merger Where two firms in the same industry at different stages in the production process merge.

■ A *conglomerate merger* is where firms in different industries merge: e.g. Google has acquired approximately 200 firms across a range of different sectors including robotics, video broadcasting, education and smoke alarms. In April 2015, it purchased Thrive Audio, a business that makes headphones for 3D sound.

Motives for merger

But why do firms want to take over others? Economists have identified a number of possible motives.

Merger for growth. Mergers provide a much quicker means to growth than does internal expansion. Not only does the firm acquire new capacity, it also acquires additional consumer demand. There is a danger for growth-maximising firms, however, from being taken over themselves. If they are growing rapidly and yet have a relatively low profit and a low stock market value, they will be attractive to predators.

Merger for economies of scale. Once the merger has taken place, the constituent parts can be reorganised through a process of 'rationalisation'. The result can be a reduction in costs. For example, only one head office will now be needed. Reduced costs are a way of increasing profits and thereby increasing the rate of growth. In fact, the evidence suggests that most mergers result in few if any cost savings: either potential economies of scale are not exploited due to a lack of rationalisation, or diseconomies result from the disruptions of reorganisation. New managers installed by the parent company are often seen as unsympathetic, and morale may go down.

Merger for monopoly power. Here the motive is to reduce competition and thereby gain greater market power and larger profits. With less competition, the firm will face a less elastic demand and will be able to charge a higher percentage above marginal cost. This obviously fits well with the traditional theory of the firm.

 Which of the three types of merger (horizontal, vertical and conglomerate) are most likely to lead to (a) reductions in average costs; (b) increased market power?

Merger for increased market valuation. A merger can benefit shareholders of *both* firms by leading to a potential increase in the stock market valuation of the merged firm. If both sets of shareholders believe that they will make a capital gain, then they are more likely to give the go-ahead to the merger.

In practice, however, there is little evidence to suggest that mergers lead to a capital gain. In the early stages of a merger boom, as in 2005–6, when some good deals may be had, the share price of acquiring firms may rise. But as the merger boom develops, more marginal firms are acquired. Take the merger boom of the late 1990s. In some 80 per cent of cases, there was a significant fall in the share value of the acquiring firm.

Merger to reduce uncertainty. There are two major sources of uncertainty for firms. The first is the behaviour of rivals.

Mergers, by reducing the number of rivals, can correspondingly reduce uncertainty. At the same time they can reduce the costs of competition (e.g. by reducing advertising). The second source of uncertainty is the economic environment. In a period of rapid change, such as often accompanies a boom, firms may seek to protect themselves by merging with others.

Merger due to opportunity. Sometimes mergers occur simply as a consequence of opportunities that suddenly and unexpectedly arise. Such mergers are largely unplanned and thus virtually impossible to predict. Dynamic business organisations are constantly on the lookout for such opportunities.

Other motives. Other motives for mergers include:

■ Getting bigger so as to make the firm less likely to be taken over itself.
■ Merging with another firm to prevent it being taken over by an unwanted predator (the 'White Knight' strategy).
■ Asset stripping. This is where a firm buys another and then breaks it up, selling off the profitable bits and probably closing down the remainder.
■ Empire building. This is where owners or managers like the power or prestige of owning or controlling several (preferably well-known) companies.
■ Broadening the geographical base of the company by merging with a firm in a different part of the country or the world.
■ Reducing levels of taxation. It has been argued that a number of takeovers in the pharmaceutical industry have been motivated by the desire to reduce the company's tax bill. For example, the American pharmaceutical company Pfizer made a $100 billion bid to purchase the UK business, AstraZeneca, in April 2014. The plan was to merge the two companies into a holding company with its tax domicile in the UK and thus being liable to UK corporation tax of 20 per cent (or even 10 per cent on profits from patented inventions – the Patent Box scheme) rather than US corporation tax of nearly 40 per cent. Even allowing for various foreign incomes and tax exemptions, Pfizer was still paying around 27.5 per cent in tax in 2013 and thus the merger would allow it to make considerable tax savings. The bid, however, ultimately failed.

These theories, alongside the general area of mergers and acquisitions, are the subject of ongoing research, but most are in need of greater empirical investigation and support.

 1. Which of the above theories overlap and in what way?
2. Why do you think it is difficult to find adequate empirical support for any of them?

Definitions

Conglomerate merger Where two firms in different industries merge.

Mergers and the relationship between growth and profit
In order for a firm to be successful in a takeover bid, it must be sufficiently profitable to finance the takeover. Thus the faster it tries to grow and the more takeovers it attempts, the higher must be its profitability.

In addition to being an obvious means to the growth of the firm, mergers may be a means of increasing profits, since mergers can lead to both lower average costs through economies of scale and higher average revenue through increased market power over prices. These profits in turn may be seen as a means of financing further growth.

It can therefore be seen that, whichever way it is financed, growth is closely linked to profits. High profits can help a firm grow. Rapid growth can lead to a rapid growth in profits.

These are not inevitable links, however. For example, long-run profits may not increase if a firm invests in risky projects or projects with a low rate of return. Expansion alone is no guarantee of profits. Also, high profits will not necessarily lead to growth if a large proportion is distributed to shareholders and only a small proportion is reinvested. High profits may help growth, but they do not guarantee it.

Growth through strategic alliances

One means of achieving growth is through the formation of *strategic alliances* with other firms. They are a means whereby business operations can be expanded relatively quickly and at relatively low cost, and are a common way in which firms can deepen their involvement in global markets.

There are many types of strategic alliance between businesses, covering a wide range of alternative collaborative arrangements.

Joint ventures. A *joint venture* is where two or more firms decide to create, and jointly own, a new independent organisation. Hulu, the television on demand and streaming business, is a joint venture between Disney, 21st Century Fox, NBCUniversal and Time Warner.

Consortia. In recent years, many consortia have been created. Camelot, the company that runs the UK National Lottery, and Trans Manche Link, the company that built the Channel Tunnel, are two examples. A *consortium* is usually created for very specific projects, such as major civil engineering work. As such they have a focused objective, and once the project is completed, the consortium is usually dissolved.

Franchising. A less formal strategic alliance is where a business agrees to *franchise* its operations to third parties. McDonald's, Costa and Coca-Cola are good examples of businesses that use a franchise network. In such a relationship, the franchisee is responsible for manufacturing and/or selling, and the franchiser retains responsibility for branding and marketing.

Subcontracting. Like franchising, *subcontracting* is a less formal source of strategic alliance, where companies maintain their independence. When a business subcontracts, it employs an independent business to manufacture or supply some service rather than conduct the activity itself. Car manufacturers are major subcontractors. Given the multitude and complexity of components that are required to manufacture a car, the use of subcontractors to supply specialist items, such as brakes and lights, seems a logical way to organise the business.

Networks. **Networks** are less formal than any of the above alliances. A network is where two or more businesses work collaboratively but without any formal relationship binding one to the other. Such a form of collaboration is highly prevalent in Japan. Rather than a formal contract regulating the behaviour of the partners to the agreement, their relationship is based upon an understanding of trust and loyalty.

Why form strategic alliances?
As a business expands, possibly internationally, it may well be advantageous to join with an existing player in the market. Such a business would have local knowledge and an established network of suppliers and distributors.

In addition, strategic alliances allow firms to share risk. The Channel Tunnel and the consortium of firms that built it is one such example. The construction of the Channel Tunnel was a massive undertaking and far too risky for any single firm to embark upon. With the creation of a consortium, risk was spread and the various consortium members were able to specialise in their areas of expertise.

Projects that might have prohibitively high start-up costs, or running costs, may become feasible if firms co-operate and pool their capital. In addition, an alliance of firms, with their combined assets and credibility, may find it easier to generate finance, whether from investors in the stock market or from the banking sector.

Definitions

Strategic alliance Where two firms work together, formally or informally, to achieve a mutually desirable goal.

Joint venture Where two or more firms set up and jointly own a new independent firm.

Consortium Where two or more firms work together on a specific project and create a separate company to run the project.

Franchise A formal agreement whereby a company uses another company to produce or sell some or all of its product.

Subcontracting Where a firm employs another firm to produce part of its output or some of its input(s).

Network An informal arrangement between businesses to work together towards some common goal.

| BOX 9.4 | MERGER ACTIVITY |

A worldwide perspective

What have been the trends, patterns and driving factors in mergers and acquisitions[1] (M&As) around the world over the past 25 years? An overview is given is given in chart (a).

The 1990s

The early 1990s saw relatively low M&A activity as the world was in recession, but as world economic growth picked up, so worldwide M&A activity increased. Economic growth was particularly rapid in the USA, which became a major target for many acquisitions.

There was also an acceleration in the process of 'globalisation'. With the dismantling of trade barriers around the world and increasing financial deregulation, international competition increased. Companies felt the need to become bigger in order to compete more effectively.

In Europe, M&A activity was boosted by the development of the Single Market, which came into being in January 1993. Companies took advantage of the abolition of trade barriers in the EU, which made it easier for them to operate on an EU-wide basis. As 1999 approached, and with it the arrival of the euro, so European merger activity reached fever pitch, stimulated also by the strong economic growth experienced throughout the EU.

By the 2000s, the number of annual worldwide M&As was three times the level in 1990. Very large deals included a €29.4 billion marriage of pharmaceutical companies Zeneca of the UK and Astra of Sweden in 1998, a €205 billion takeover of telecoms giant Mannesmann of Germany by Vodafone of the UK in 1999 and a €50.8 billion takeover of Orange™ of the UK by France Telecom in 2000.

Other sectors in which merger activity was rife included financial services and the privatised utilities sector. In the UK, in particular, most of the privatised water and electricity companies were acquired, with buyers attracted by the sector's monopoly profits. French and US buyers were prominent.

The 2000s

The number of cross-border deals peaked at 10 517 in 2000 and had a combined total value of over $960 billion. However, a worldwide economic slowdown after 2000 led to a fall in both the number and value of mergers throughout most of the world. The value of cross-border M&As in 2003 was $165 billion – a fall of 83 per cent from the peak of three years earlier. Activity began to increase again after 2003 as economic growth in the world economy began to accelerate. Two major target regions were (a) the 10 countries that joined the EU in 2004 plus Russia and (b) Asian countries, especially India and China.

In 2007, the number of cross-border mergers reached a new peak of 12 044 with a combined market value of over $1000 billion. However, the Great Recession of 2008–9 led to both the number and value of cross-border deals falling dramatically. Recession is a difficult time for deal making and the number of withdrawn mergers – that is, where two firms agree in principle to merge but later pull out of the deal – increased. As diagram (a) shows, the value of cross-border M&As in 2009 was $288 billion – a fall of 72 per cent from the record high in 2007.

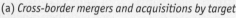

(a) *Cross-border mergers and acquisitions by target*

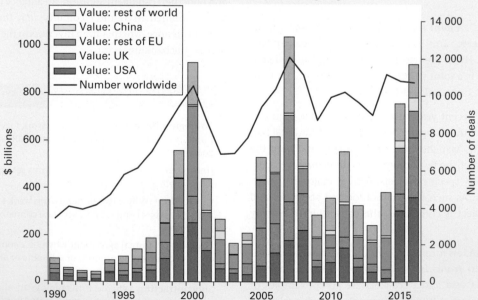

Note: The data cover only those deals that involve an acquisition of an equity of more than 10%.
Source: 'Cross Border Mergers & Acquisitions', *World Investment Report Annex Tables* (UNCTAD, June 2017), Tables 9 and 11.

The 2010s

With the faltering recovery of 2010 there was a small increase in global M&As. However, the eurozone crisis and fears about the state of the public finances in the USA had a negative impact on the number of deals in 2012 and 2013.

Economic growth and growing business confidence saw M&A activity grow quickly again in 2015. The combined market value of deals was over $700 billion – the highest value since the financial crisis, with nine deals of over $50 billion. The ability of firms to borrow money cheaply because of historically low interest rates, slow rates of internal growth and large cash reserves were seen as important drivers behind this increase. The USA, with its accelerating rate of economic growth, was a very popular target country.

Given the uncertainty generated by the Brexit vote in the UK and the election of President Trump in the USA, many observers were surprised to see continued strong growth in M&A activity in 2016.

The worldwide pattern of cross-border M&A activity has also changed between the mid-1990s and the post-financial crisis period of 2010–15, although 2015 proved to be different from the rest of the post-crisis period. Diagram (b) illustrates three trends.

- First, North America saw a fall in its global share of cross-border M&As from 24.6 per cent in the mid-1990s to 20.1 per cent between 2010 and 2015; and its share measured by value fell from 32.2 per cent to 30.4 per cent. However, its share by value in 2015 was unusually high at 43 per cent compared with an average of 19.7 per cent over the previous five years.
- Second, Asian countries (excluding Japan) saw a dramatic increase in their share of the number of cross-border M&As from 7.7 per cent in the mid-1990s to 16 per cent for the period 2010–15. Their share of the value increased from 5.2 per cent to 12 per cent. Two nations in the region, China and India, have been particularly attractive because their economies have grown rapidly; they have low costs, cheap skilled labour and low tax rates. However M&A investment in both countries fell significantly in 2015. In the case of China, it fell from $54.9 billion in 2014 to $9.66 billion in 2015.
- Third, EU countries saw a reduction in their share of cross-border M&As from 49.4 per cent to 39.8 per cent and a fall in their share of the value from 42.1 per cent to 37.7 per cent.

Different types and consequences of M&A activity

When viewed in terms of long-run trends, cross-border M&As have become more common as globalisation has gathered pace. In the mid-1990s they accounted for about 16 per cent of all deals, whereas now they account for over 40 per cent.

Although the number of cross-border deals in the UK in 2016 was less than domestic deals, the *value* of cross-border deals was far higher than domestic ones. The Office for National Statistics reported that the value of M&As, where a foreign company purchased a UK company, was £187.4 billion[2] – the highest figure since records began in 1969.

Cross-border M&As can be an effective strategy for firms that want to gain large-scale entry into an overseas market. One motivating factor for AB-InBev's takeover of SABMiller is to gain access to the fast-growing beer market in Africa. However, these types of takeover can raise concerns about national sovereignty: i.e. the extent to which governments have control over their industrial base when foreign firms own businesses in the domestic economy. For example, following concerns expressed by the South African government, AB-InBev made a

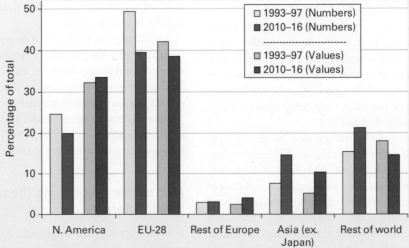

(b) *Cross-border mergers and acquisitions by target region (% of total number and value)*

Source: 'Cross Border Mergers & Acquisitions', *World Investment Report Annex Tables* (UNCTAD, June 2017), Tables 9 and 11.

commitment to maintain permanent employment in that country at the same level for at least five years.

Horizontal cross-border mergers

These are the most common type of merger. A horizontal merger or acquisition of a domestic firm by an overseas firm may not alter the number of firms competing in the sector if the foreign firm merely replaces an existing firm. Its presence may generate greater competition and innovation in the industry if the new owners bring with them fresh ideas.

If the foreign firm is already present in the domestic economy and it then takes over a rival, the number of firms in the industry is reduced. This could lead to less competition and higher prices. Alternatively, the newly merged firm may benefit from lower costs that it can pass on to its customers in the form of lower prices.

Vertical cross-border mergers

Vertical and conglomerate cross-border M&As are less common than their horizontal counterparts, but also come with potential costs as well as benefits. For example, a backward vertical M&A can help a firm compete globally by reducing its supply costs, but it can impose harsh terms on suppliers in the domestic economy where it operates in order to achieve this. Forward vertical M&A into the retail sector can help a foreign firm secure a domestic market and offer customers a better service. However, they may now move away from supplying rival retailers on comparable terms so that customer choice is reduced.

Conglomerate cross-border mergers

There was a wave of these mergers in the 1960s as firms tried to diversify, but they are now far less popular. The tendency instead has been for many companies to try to become more focused, by selling off parts of the business that are not seen as 'core activities'. For example, in October 2012, the conglomerate Kraft Foods split its business into a global snacks business, named Mondelez International, and a food business, named Kraft Foods Group. In 2015, Kraft Foods Group merged with Heinz to become Kraft Heinz.

There is no doubt that many M&As have been good for society and are a sign of a healthy capital market. However, evidence has found that approximately two-thirds of deals fail to achieve the anticipated gains.

1. Are the motives for merger likely to be different in a recession from those in a period of rapid economic growth? What would you predict about the pattern of mergers over the next few years, given the current state of the economy?
2. Use newspaper and other resources to identify the anticipated benefits (extra revenue and lower costs) of a recent cross-border merger. Do you think they are realistic?

1 By 'acquisitions' we mean takeovers or the acquiring of at least 5 per cent of a company's shares.
2 'Mergers and acquisitions involving UK companies: Oct to Dec 2016', *Statistical Bulletin* (ONS).

The past 30 years have seen a flourishing of strategic alliances. They have become a key growth strategy for business both domestically and internationally. They are seen as a way of expanding business operations quickly without the difficulties associated with the more aggressive approach of acquisition or the more lengthy process of merger.

Growth through going global

In many respects, a firm's global strategy is simply an extension of its strategy within its own domestic market. However, opening up to global markets can provide an obvious means for a business to expand its markets and spread its risks. It is also a means of reducing costs, whether through economies of scale or from accessing cheap sources of supply or low-wage production facilities.

A firm's global growth strategy may involve simply exporting or opening up factories abroad, or it may involve merging with businesses abroad or forming strategic alliances. As barriers to trade and to the international flow of capital have reduced, so more and more businesses have sought to become multinational. The result is that the global business environment has tended to become more and more competitive.

Equilibrium for a growth-maximising firm

What will a growth-maximising firm's price and output be? Unfortunately there is no simple formula for predicting this.

In the short run, the firm may choose the profit-maximising price and output – so as to provide the greatest funds for investment. On the other hand, it may be prepared to sacrifice some short-term profits in order to mount an advertising campaign. It all depends on the strategy it considers most suitable to achieve growth.

In the long run, prediction is more difficult still. The policies that a firm adopts will depend crucially on the assessments of market opportunities made by managers. But this involves judgement, not fine calculation. Different managers will judge a situation differently

TC 9 p129

One prediction can be made: growth-maximising firms are likely to diversify into different products, especially as they approach the limits to expansion in existing markets.

Alternative maximising theories and the public interest

It is difficult to draw firm conclusions about the public interest.

 TC 3 p26

In the case of sales revenue maximisation, a higher output will be produced than under profit maximisation, but the consumers will not necessarily benefit from lower prices, since more will be spent on advertising – costs that will be reflected in a higher price.

In the case of growth and long-run profit maximisation, there are many possible policies that a firm could pursue. To the extent that a concern for the long run encourages firms to look to improved products, new products and new techniques, the consumer may benefit from such a concern. To the extent, however, that growth encourages a greater level of industrial concentration through merger, the consumer may lose from the resulting greater level of monopoly power.

As with the traditional theory of the firm, the degree of competition a firm faces is a crucial factor in determining just how responsive it will be to the wishes of the consumer.

How will competition between growth-maximising firms benefit the consumer?

Section summary

1. Rather than seeking to maximise short-run profits, a firm may take a longer-term perspective. It is very difficult, however, to predict the behaviour of a long-run profit-maximising firm, since (a) different managers are likely to make different judgements about how to achieve maximum profits and (b) demand and cost curves may shift unpredictably both in response to the firm's own policies and as a result of external factors.

2. Managers may seek to maximise their own utility, which, in turn, will depend on factors such as salary, job security and power within the organisation. However, given that managerial utility depends on a range of variables, it is difficult to use the theory to make general predictions of firms' behaviour.

3. Managers may gain utility from maximising sales revenue. They will, however, still have to ensure that a satisfactory level of profit is achieved. The output of a firm which seeks to maximise sales revenue will be higher than that for a profit-maximising firm. Its level of advertising will also tend to be higher. Whether price will be higher or lower depends on the relative effects on demand and cost of the additional advertising.

4. Many managers aim for maximum growth of their organisation, believing that this will help their salaries, power, prestige, etc.

5. Growth may be by internal expansion. This can be financed by ploughing back profits, by share issue, or by borrowing. Whichever method a firm uses, it will require sufficient profits to avoid becoming vulnerable to a takeover.

6. Vertical integration can reduce a firm's costs through various economies of scale. It can also help to reduce uncertainty, as the vertically integrated business could secure supply routes and/or retail outlets.

7. Growth may be by merger. Mergers can be horizontal, vertical or conglomerate. Merger activity tends to occur in waves. Various motives have been suggested for mergers, including growth, economies of scale, market power, increased share values, reduction in uncertainty, and simply taking advantage of opportunities as they occur.

8. One means of achieving growth is through the formation of strategic alliances with other firms. They have the advantage of allowing easier access to new markets, risk sharing and capital pooling. Many firms' growth strategy includes expansion abroad.

9. As with long-run profit-maximising theories, it is difficult to predict the price and output strategies of a growth-maximising firm. Much depends on the judgements of particular managers about growth opportunities.

10. Alternative aims will benefit the consumer to the extent that they encourage firms to develop new products and to find more efficient methods of production. They may be against the consumer's interest to the extent that they lead firms to engage in extensive advertising or to merge with a resulting increased concentration of market power.

9.4 ASYMMETRIC INFORMATION AND THE PRINCIPAL–AGENT PROBLEM

Principals and agents

A useful way to think about alternative maximisation theories is as examples of the *principal–agent problem.* Let us examine this problem.

One of the features of a complex modern economy is that people (principals) have to employ others (agents) to carry out their wishes. If you want to sell a house, it is more convenient to go to an estate agent than to do it yourself.

These agents have specialist knowledge and can save you, the principal, a great deal of time and effort. It is an example of the benefits of the specialisation and division of labour.

It is the same with firms. They employ people with specialist knowledge and skills to carry out specific tasks. Companies frequently employ consultants to give them advice, or engage the services of specialist firms such as an advertising agency. Even employees of a company can be seen as 'agents' of their employer. In the case of workers, they can be seen as the agents of management. Junior managers are the agents of senior management. Senior managers are the agents of the directors, who are themselves agents of the shareholders. Thus in large firms there is often a complex chain of principal–agent relationships.

Asymmetric information

But these relationships have an inherent danger for the principal: there is *asymmetric information* between the two sides.

The agent knows more about the situation than the principal – of course, this is part of the reason why the principal employs the agent in the first place. The danger is that the agent may well not act in the principal's best interests, and may be able to get away with it because of the principal's imperfect knowledge. The estate agent may try to convince the vendor that it is necessary to accept a lower price, while the real reason is to save the agent time, effort and expense.

In firms, too, agents may not act in the best interests of their principals. For example, workers may be able to get away with not working very hard, preferring instead an easy

Definitions

Asymmetric information Where one party in an economic relationship (e.g. an agent) has more information than another (e.g. the principal).

BOX 9.5   THE US SUB-PRIME HOUSING CRISIS

Obvious in hindsight

The causes of the financial crisis of 2007–8, and of the subsequent global recession, are numerous and complex. However, there was one factor which made a major contribution to the collapse of confidence in the banking sector – the increased rate of mortgage defaults in the US housing market.

Background to the crisis

Up to 2006, the USA had experienced over a decade of sharply increasing house prices alongside growth in the number of homeowners, attracted by the promise of high returns. Over this period the US financial system was awash with funds flowing in from growing economies in Asia, and interest rates were low. The result was an easing of credit conditions and a sharp increase in the availability of mortgages. Home ownership was approaching 70 per cent, a historic high and an increase of around 7 per cent on the previous decade. Many of these new buyers were on low incomes, or had poor credit ratings – collectively they are known as *sub-prime borrowers*.

In 2006, the housing market in the USA peaked and values started to fall. This had an immediate effect on consumer confidence and demand for owner-occupied housing fell sharply, leading to a collapse in house prices. The 'house price bubble' had burst.

As the world moved into a recession, many borrowers found it hard to maintain their mortgage payments, particularly those on low incomes who had borrowed large amounts. The resulting high level of defaults and foreclosures (or repossessions) had an immediate and serious impact on the value of financial institutions across the world.

Sub-prime borrowers

Why was the sub-prime market so vulnerable to falling house prices? The answer lies in both the amount of lending that took place and the type of mortgages that were taken out by these borrowers. The role of mortgage-brokers, who acted as agents, also proved to be crucial.

Borrowers with low incomes were mostly sold adjustable-rate mortgages, which left them vulnerable to future interest rate rises. In addition, they were encouraged to accept deals with fixed lower payments in the first few years and higher rates after that, regardless of interest rate adjustments. The result was that they would often see mortgage payments double, or even treble, after a couple of years. For most this would present a major problem, since their wages were unlikely to have risen that fast.

However, the brokers had a solution; over the period of increasing house prices sub-prime borrowers were easily able to refinance their housing loans when the time came for higher payments. This ensured that the sub-prime borrowers could retain their properties while the brokers generated further transaction fees. But once prices started to fall, this option disappeared and so the numbers defaulting on their mortgages increased sharply.

Securitisation of sub-prime debt

Since the mid-1990s, many financial institutions have chosen not to hold mortgages through to the end of their term, retaining the associated risk. Instead, they have sold them on to other investors in the form of mortgage-backed securities (MBSs). This practice increased the incentives for banks to offer mortgages to sub-prime borrowers, since now they did not have to bear the full risk of default throughout a 20- or 25-year term.

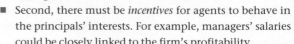

life. Similarly, given the divorce between the ownership and control of a company, managers (agents) may pursue goals different from those of shareholders (principals). Thus *X inefficiency* is likely to occur (see Box 7.5).

So asymmetric information creates a problem for principals – known as the ***principal–agent problem***:

> **KEY IDEA 25**
>
> ***The principal–agent problem.*** Where people (principals), as a result of a lack of knowledge, cannot ensure that their best interests are served by their agents. Agents may take advantage of this situation to the disadvantage of the principals.

So how can principals tackle the problem? There are two elements in the solution:

- The principals must have some way of *monitoring* the performance of their agents. For example, a company might employ efficiency experts to examine the operation of its management.

- Second, there must be *incentives* for agents to behave in the principals' interests. For example, managers' salaries could be closely linked to the firm's profitability.

Alternative theories of the firm therefore place considerable emphasis on incentive mechanisms in explaining the behaviour of managers and the resulting performance of their companies.

In a competitive market, managers' and shareholders' interests are more likely to coincide. Managers have to ensure

Definitions

Principal–agent problem Where people (principals), as a result of lack of knowledge, cannot ensure that their best interests are served by their agents.

The rate of securitisation increased sharply between 1997 and 2007, with 75 per cent of sub-prime mortgages being sold on to third parties by 2006. It played a pivotal role in the financial crisis (see pages 558–66). Once the US housing market collapsed, the effect was felt not only by American mortgage lenders, but also by financial institutions and investors across the world, all of whom had bought mortgage-backed securities or similar financial instruments.

The role of asymmetric information

One question of interest is what light can behavioural economics and the role of asymmetric information shed on the sub-prime market and the broader financial crisis. There is little doubt that throughout the market, economic principals (and agents for that matter) were not in possession of complete information and thus were unable to make rational decisions in the way that traditional theory would predict.

The opportunity for asymmetric information arose, in part, because mortgage brokers, acted as agents for the principals. Since they were paid by transaction fees, their incentive was to complete as many mortgages as possible, regardless of the possibility of future default; this is an example of *moral hazard* (see page 135).

In particular:

- Sub-prime borrowers were permitted to self-certify their incomes; this provided them with a mechanism to conceal full information about their earnings/debts. Why would they do this? They may have suffered from present bias and other types of bounded rationality associated with making probabilistic judgements.

- There is evidence that many borrowers were not given full, or clear, information about the escalating payments that they would face under their repayment plans. As a result they could not anticipate the problems they would face after two or three years.

- The commissions received by brokers were not transparent; thus borrowers could not readily identify the motives that lay behind being sold products that would require refinancing after some years.

- The financial institutions that bought mortgage-backed securities relied on credit ratings agencies to verify the risks involved. These agencies consistently rated the instruments as lower risk than they turned out to be. It is a matter of debate as to whether this was done deliberately, or as a consequence of over-reliance on risk-reducing practices. No matter, the result was that high-risk, sub-prime mortgages ended up in the portfolios of investors who would not have bought them if they had had full information.

1. *Why was the market for sub-prime mortgages sustainable from 1996 to 2005? Explain how this changed in 2006.*
2. *The credit ratings agencies were paid by the companies that had been heavily involved in the market for sub-prime mortgages. Explain why this presents a moral hazard.*
3. *Financial regulation has endowed the judgements of the three credit ratings agencies with legal backing and has protected them from competition. Explain why this presented a problem in the process of securitisation.*
4. *If you were set the task of preventing similar sub-prime issues in the future, what regulations would you put in place?*

that the company remains efficient or it may not survive the competition and they might lose their jobs. In monopolies and oligopolies, however, where supernormal profits can often be relatively easily earned, the interests of shareholders and managers are likely to diverge. Here it will be in shareholders' interests to institute incentive mechanisms that ensure that their agents, the managers, are motivated to strive for profitability.

The adverse impact of asymmetric information

If effective monitoring and incentive systems cannot be found, then asymmetric information might prevent firms from achieving the most efficient outcomes. Consider the example of a small business seeking finance for investment purposes. Banks and financial institutions are unlikely to have full access to information about the business or the individuals who own it. Since investment opportunities often also involve some uncertainty about

the future, the likely outcome is a lower level of lending than is desirable.

 Explain why the existence of asymmetric information may be damaging for both parties in an economic exchange, not only for the one who has incomplete information.

Firms also face asymmetric information about the quality of supplies and the ability of customers to pay; the latter may be a particular issue for transactions that take place between firms and where credit is extended. If firms recognise these issues when writing contracts, they may be able to address the problem and achieve better outcomes. But often the problem only becomes apparent when it is too late.

On occasion the impact of asymmetric information can be so serious that the consequences are devastating, not only for the individual market, but also for the wider economy. One example of this is examined in Box 9.5.

Section summary

1. The problem of managers not pursuing the same goals as the owners is an example of the *principal–agent problem*. Agents (in this case, the managers) may not always carry out the wishes of their principals (in this case, the owners).

2. Possible solutions for owners are to (a) monitor the performance of managers, and (b) create incentives for managers to behave in the owners' interests. If they are ineffective then asymmetric information may prevent firms from achieving their most efficient outcomes.

9.5   MULTIPLE AIMS

Satisfying and the setting of targets

Large firms are often complex institutions with many departments (sales, production, design, purchasing, personnel, finance, etc.). Each department is likely to have its own specific set of aims and objectives, which may come into conflict with those of other departments. These aims in turn will be constrained by the interests of shareholders, workers, customers and creditors (collectively known as *stakeholders*), who will need to be kept sufficiently happy.

In many firms, targets are set for production, sales, profit, stockholding, etc. If, in practice, target levels are not achieved, a 'search' procedure will be started to find out what went wrong and how to rectify it. If the problem cannot be rectified, managers will probably adjust the target downwards. If, on the other hand, targets are easily achieved, managers may adjust them upwards. Thus the targets to which

managers aspire depend to a large extent on the success in achieving *previous* targets. Targets are also influenced by expectations of demand and costs, by the achievements of competitors and by expectations of competitors' future behaviour. For example, if it is expected that the economy is likely to move into recession, sales and profit targets may be adjusted downwards.

Definitions

Stakeholders (in a company) People who are affected by a company's activities and/or performance (customers, employees, owners, creditors, people living in the neighbourhood, etc.). They may or may not be in a position to take decisions, or influence decision taking, in the firm.

BOX 9.6 | **STAKEHOLDER POWER?**

Who governs the firm?

The concept of the 'stakeholder economy' became fashionable in the late 1990s. Rather than the economy being governed by big business, and rather than businesses being governed in the interests of shareholders (many of whom are big institutions, such as insurance companies and pension funds), the economy should serve the interests of everyone. But what does this mean for the governance of firms?

The stakeholders of a firm include customers, employees (from senior managers to the lowest-paid workers), shareholders, suppliers, lenders and the local and national communities.

The supporters of a stakeholding economy argue that *all* these interest groups ought to have a say in the decisions of the firm. Trade unions or workers' councils ought to be included in decisions affecting the workforce, or indeed all company decisions. They could be represented on decision-making bodies and perhaps have seats on the board of directors. Alternatively, the workforce might be given the power to elect managers.

Banks or other institutions lending to firms ought to be included in investment decisions. In Germany, where banks finance a large proportion of investment, banks are represented on the boards of most large companies.

Local communities ought to have a say in any projects (such as new buildings or the discharge of effluent) that affect the local environment. Customers ought to have more say in the quality of products being produced: for example, by being given legal protection against the production of shoddy or unsafe goods.

Where interest groups cannot be directly represented in decision making, companies ought to be regulated by the government in order to protect the interests of the various groups. For example, if farmers and other suppliers to supermarkets are paid very low prices, then the purchasing behaviour of the supermarkets could be regulated by some government agency.

But is this vision of a stakeholder economy likely to become reality? Trends in the international economy suggest that the opposite might be occurring. The growth of multinational corporations, with their ability to move finance and production to wherever it is most profitable, has weakened the power of employees, local interest groups and even national governments.

Employees in one part of the multinational may have little in the way of common interests with employees in another. In fact, they may vie with each other: for example, over which plant should be expanded or closed down. With new 'flexible labour markets', firms are making more use of casual, part-time, temporary or agency workers. These employees are generally 'outsiders' to decision making within the firm (see Box 10.8).

Also, the widespread introduction of share incentive schemes for managers has increasingly made profits their driving goal. Finally, the policies of opening up markets and deregulation – policies that have been adopted by many governments round the world in recent years – have again weakened the power of many stakeholders.

Nevertheless, many firms in recent years have put greater emphasis on 'corporate social responsibility' (CSR), seeing it as important to have an ethical dimension to their business practices. Whether this is a genuine commitment to the interests of society, or simply an attempt to win a larger market by gaining a good public image, clearly varies from firm to firm. CSR and business ethics are explored in Case Study 9.4 on the student website.

 Are customers' interests best served by profit-maximising firms, answerable primarily to shareholders, or by firms where various stakeholder groups are represented in decision taking?

If targets conflict, the conflict could be settled by a bargaining process between managers. In this case, the outcome of the bargaining will depend on the power and ability of the individual managers concerned and the governance structure in which they operate. Thus a similar set of conflicting targets may be resolved differently in different firms.

Organisational slack

Since changing targets often involves search procedures and bargaining processes and is therefore time-consuming, and since many managers prefer to avoid conflict, targets tend to be changed fairly infrequently. Business conditions, however, often change rapidly. To avoid the need to change

targets, therefore, managers will tend to be fairly conservative in their aspirations. This leads to the phenomenon known as *organisational slack* – a term coined by Cyert and March (see above page 253)

When the firm does better than expected, it will allow slack to develop. This slack can then be taken up if the firm does worse than expected. For example, if the firm

---

Definitions

Organisational slack Where managers allow spare capacity to exist, thereby enabling them to respond more easily to changed circumstances.

produces more than it planned, it will build stocks of finished goods and draw on them if subsequently production falls. It would not, in the meantime, increase its sales target or reduce its production target. If it did, and production then fell below target, the production department might not be able to supply the sales department with its full requirement.

Thus keeping targets fairly low and allowing slack to develop allows all targets to be met with minimum conflict.

Organisational slack, however, adds to a firm's costs. If firms are operating in a competitive environment, they may be forced to cut slack in order to survive. In the 1970s, many Japanese firms succeeded in cutting slack by using *just-in-time* methods of production. These involve keeping stocks to a minimum and ensuring that inputs are delivered as required. Clearly, this requires that production is tightly controlled and that suppliers are reliable. Many firms today have successfully cut their warehouse costs by using such methods. These methods are examined in Box 10.8.

Multiple goals: predictions of behaviour

Conservatism

Some firms may be wary of change, seeing it as risky. They may prefer to stick with current practices. This could apply to pricing policies, marketing techniques, product design and range, internal organisation of the firm, etc. This is simple heuristics: if it works, stick with it.

If something does not work, managers will probably change it, but again they may be cautious: perhaps imitating successful competitors.

This safe, satisficing approach makes prediction of any given firm's behaviour relatively straightforward. You simply examine its past behaviour. Making generalisations about all such cautious firms, however, is more difficult. Different firms will have established different rules of behaviour depending on their experiences of their own particular market.

Comparison with other firms

Managers may judge their success by comparing their firm's performance with that of rivals. For example, growing market share may be seen as a more important indicator of 'success' than simple growth in sales. Similarly, they may compare their profits, their product design, their technology or their industrial relations with those of rivals. To many managers it is *relative* performance that matters, rather than absolute performance.

What predictions can be made if this is how managers behave? The answer is that it depends on the nature of competition in the industry. The more profitable, innovative and efficient are the competitors, the more profitable, innovative and efficient will managers try to make their particular firm.

The further ahead of their rivals that firms try to stay, the more likely it is that there will be a 'snowballing' effect, with each firm trying to outdo the other.

 Will this type of behaviour tend to lead to profit maximisation?

Satisficing and the public interest

Firms with multiple goals will be satisficers. The greater the number of goals of the different managers, the greater is the chance of conflict, and the more likely it is that organisational slack will develop. Satisficing firms are therefore likely to be less responsive to changes in consumer demand and changes in costs than profit-maximising firms. They may thus be less efficient.

On the other hand, such firms may be less eager to exploit their economic power by charging high prices, or to use aggressive advertising, or to pay low wages.

The extent to which satisficing firms do act in the public interest will, as in the case of other types of firm, depend to a large extent on the amount and type of competition they face, and their attitudes towards this competition. Firms that compare their performance with that of their rivals are more likely to be responsive to consumer wishes than firms that prefer to stick to well-established practices. On the other hand, they may be more concerned to 'manipulate' consumer tastes than the more traditional firm.

 Are satisficing firms more likely to suffer from X inefficiency (see Box 7.5) than firms which seek to maximise profit or sales revenue?

Definitions

Just-in-time methods Where a firm purchases supplies and produces both components and finished products as they are required. This minimises stockholding and its associated costs. It does, however, put pressure on the supply chain and increases the probability that on occasion firms may not be able to meet demand – for example in times of bad weather.

9.6 PRICING IN PRACTICE

What is the typical procedure by which firms set prices? Do they construct marginal cost and marginal revenue curves (or equations) and find the output where they are equal? Do they then use an average revenue curve (or equation) to work out the price at that output?

As we saw in section 9.1, firms often do not have the information to do so, even if they wanted to. In practice, firms look for rules of pricing that are relatively simple to apply.

Cost-based pricing

One approach is *average cost* or *mark-up pricing*. Here producers work out the price by simply adding a certain percentage (mark-up) for profit on top of average costs (average fixed costs plus average variable costs). It is a very straightforward heuristic.

$$P = AFC + AVC + \text{profit mark-up}$$

Choosing the mark-up

The level of profit mark-up on top of average cost will depend on the firm's aims: whether it is aiming for high or even maximum profits, or merely a target based on previous profit. It will also depend on the likely actions of rivals and their responses to changes in this firm's price and how these responses will affect demand.

If a firm could estimate its demand curve, it could then set its output and profit mark-up at levels that will avoid a shortage or surplus. Thus in Figure 9.3 it could choose a lower

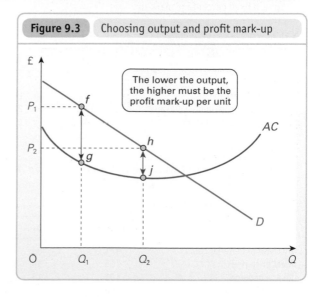

Figure 9.3 Choosing output and profit mark-up

The lower the output, the higher must be the profit mark-up per unit

output (Q_1) with a higher mark-up (fg) or a higher output (Q_2) with a lower mark-up (hj), depending on its aims. If the firm could not estimate its demand curve, it could adjust its mark-up and output over time by a process of trial and error, according to its success in meeting profit and sales aims.

Definitions

Average cost or mark-up pricing Where firms set the price by adding a profit mark-up to average cost.

BOX 9.7   HOW DO COMPANIES SET PRICES?

In 1996, the Bank of England published a survey of price-setting behaviour in 654 UK companies.[1] Among other things, the survey sought to establish what factors influenced companies' pricing decisions. The results are shown in table (a).

Companies were asked to rank alternative methods of pricing of their main product . . . The most popular response was that prices were set with respect to market conditions. The top preference[2] for almost 40 per cent of respondents was that prices were set at the highest level that the market could bear. An additional 25 per cent of respondents stated that they set prices in relation to their competitors – this was the second choice most popular among companies . . .

The survey also confirmed the importance of company-specific factors. The first preference of about 20 per cent of respondents was that price was made up of a direct cost per unit plus a variable percentage mark-up . . . A further 17 per cent of companies, particularly retailing companies, stated that they priced on the basis of costs plus a fixed percentage mark-up.

Cost plus mark-ups tended to be more important for small companies . . . which cannot afford expensive market research.

The survey also sought to establish those factors which could cause prices to change – either up or down (see table (b)).

The Bank survey asked companies to rank those factors most likely to push prices up or down. It found that there were substantial differences between the factors that influenced price increases and those that influenced price decreases. First, many more companies said that cost rises were likely to push prices up than said that cost reductions were likely to push prices down. Second, a rise in demand seemed less likely to lead to a price increase than a fall in demand was to lead to a price cut . . .

The importance of strategic interaction with competitors suggests that when contemplating a price cut, companies need to consider the chance of sparking off a price war . . . The finding that companies were much more likely to match rival price falls than they are to follow rival price rises appears to support the importance of strategic behaviour.

(a) *How are prices determined?*

	1st	%	2nd	%	3rd	%
Market level	257	39	140	21	78	12
Competitors' prices	161	25	229	35	100	15
Direct cost plus variable mark-up	131	20	115	18	88	14
Direct cost plus fixed mark-up	108	17	49	8	42	6
Set by customer	33	5	52	8	47	7
Regulatory agency	11	2	3	1	5	1

Source: S. Hall, M. Walsh and T. Yates, 'How do UK companies set prices?', *Bank of England Quarterly Bulletin,* May 1996, Table D, p. 188.

(b) *Factors leading to a rise or fall in price*

Rise	Number[a]	%	Fall	Number[a]	%
Increase in material costs	421	64	Decrease in material costs	186	28
Rival price rise	105	16	Rival price fall	235	36
Rise in demand	101	15	Fall in demand	146	22
Prices never rise	26	4	Prices never fall	75	12
Increase in interest rates	18	3	Decrease in interest rates	8	1
Higher market share	14	2	Lower market share	69	11
Fall in productivity	5	1	Rise in productivity	22	3

[a]Numbers citing a scenario as most important.
Note: Top preferences only.
Source: S. Hall, M. Walsh and T. Yates, 'How do UK companies set prices?', *Bank of England Quarterly Bulletin,* May 1996, Table D, p. 188.

More recent surveys

Europe-wide survey.   A European study of 2006 reported similar results to the 1996 UK survey. This European study brought together surveys conducted by nine Eurosystem national central banks on the price-setting behaviour of over 11 000 European firms.[3]

The research found that price-setting behaviour is consistent across Europe, with mark-up pricing the dominant strategy in the eurozone and price discrimination widely practised. The asymmetries noted above with respect to price increases and decreases were also seen.

Further Bank of England survey.   In 2008, the Bank of England conducted another survey of price-setting behaviour. This time 693 firms responded, with a spread across industry consistent with shares in UK GDP. The findings broadly supported those of the 1996 survey.

KI 24
p252

KI 23
p222

(c) *Most important factors leading to a rise or fall in price*

Price rise	Rank	Price reduction	Rank
Increase in cost of labour	1	Actual decline in demand	1
Increase in the prices of fuel, raw materials or other inputs	2	Actual price reduction by domestic competitor(s)	2
Actual rise in demand	3	Expected decline in demand	3
Increasing costs arising out of regulation	4	Significant reduction in market share	4
Actual price increase by domestic competitor(s)	5	Expected price reduction by domestic competitor(s)	5
Expected rise in demand	6	Decrease in the prices of fuel, raw materials or other inputs	6
Increase in financing costs	7	Decrease in cost of labour	7
Expected price increase by one or more of your domestic rivals	8	Decrease in costs arising out of regulation	8

Source: Jennifer Greenslade and Miles Parker, 'Price-setting behaviour in the United Kingdom', *Bank of England Quarterly Bulletin*, 2008 Q4.

[The survey revealed that] different factors influenced price rises and price falls. Higher costs – in particular, labour costs and raw materials – were the most important driver behind price rises, whereas lower demand and competitors' prices were the main factor resulting in price falls.[4]

Companies were asked to rank the importance of 11 factors in determining both price rises and price reductions. Table (c) shows the eight most important 6 in determining price changes (based on share of companies responding 'important' or 'very important').

Unlike the 1996 survey, companies were asked about *expected* changes in key variables, including demand, costs and rivals' prices. These were important determinants for many companies.

The survey confirmed that a majority of firms use mark-up pricing, with 58 per cent describing it as 'very important'. More than half of these firms *adjust* their mark-up according to market conditions. Competitors' prices and market demand are the two most important factors leading to a fall in price. The increase in the cost of labour and prices of fuel and raw materials are the two most important factors leading to a price rise.

Price flexibility

Evidence from the USA[5] and the eurozone study suggests that the frequency and magnitude of price changes varies enormously from product to product.

Generally speaking, the greater the share of raw materials in a product, the more often its price moves: petrol prices change, on average, in five months out of six in both America and Europe; the prices of fresh food are altered far more frequently than those of processed food. The prices of services are stickier than those of goods. This may be because services tend to be more labour-intensive than goods, and because wages are stickier (downwards, anyway) than other prices.[6]

For most products, prices change relatively infrequently in Europe, with retail prices changing on average just over once per year. In the USA, sales are much more common, especially with clothes, furniture and processed food. The prices of

services also change more frequently in the USA. In Europe services are more regulated and wages (a large proportion of the cost of most services) are less flexible.

How often individual prices move is an important question. Shifts in prices are like the traffic lights of an economy, signalling to people to buy more of this and less of that, to spend or to save, or to find new jobs. If the lights change readily, resources can be redirected smoothly; if they get stuck, so does the economy. In particular, if neither prices nor wages fall easily, the cost in output and jobs of reducing inflation can be high. Sticky prices also mean that an inflationary shock – an increase in oil prices, say – can take a long time to work its way through the system.[7]

As far as the magnitude of price changes is concerned, in both the USA and Europe, price changes are typically much bigger than the rate of inflation. In Europe, average price increases are 8 per cent and average price reductions 10 per cent.

1. Which of the following is more likely to be consistent with the aim of maximising profits: pricing on the basis of (a) cost per unit plus a variable percentage mark-up; (b) cost per unit plus a fixed percentage mark-up?
2. Explain the differences between the importance attached to the different factors leading to price increases and those leading to price reductions.
3. Why do you think percentage price changes are bigger than the rate of inflation?

1 Simon Hall, Mark Walsh and Tony Yates, 'How do UK companies set prices?', *Bank of England Quarterly Bulletin*, May 1996.
2 Companies were able to show more than one response as their top preference. This means the total percentage of companies expressing first preferences for all of the explanations of price determination exceeds 100 per cent.
3 Silvia Fabiani et al., 'What firms' surveys tell us about price-setting behavior in the euro area', *International Journal of Central Banking*, September 2006.
4 Jennifer Greenslade and Miles Parker, 'New insights into price-setting behaviour in the United Kingdom', *Bank of England Working Paper No. 395* (Bank of England, July 2010).
5 Emi Nakamura and Jón Steinsson, 'Five facts about prices: a re-evaluation of menu cost models', Harvard University, May 2007.
7 Ibid.

The equilibrium price and output

Is it possible to identify an equilibrium price and output for the firm that sets its prices by adding a mark-up to average cost? To answer this we can identify a supply curve for the firm.

If a firm is aiming for a particular profit *per unit* of output and does not adjust this target, the firm's supply curve is derived by adding the mark-up to the *AC* curve. This is shown by curve S_1 in Figure 9.4. If, however, a firm is aiming for a particular level of *total* profit, and does not adjust this target, its supply curve will be like curve S_2. The greater the output, the less the profit per unit needs to be (and hence the less the mark-up) to give a particular level of total profit.

In either case, price and quantity can be derived from the intersection of demand and supply. Price and output will change if the demand or cost (and hence supply) curve shifts.

The main problem here is in predicting the demand curve, since it depends not only on consumer tastes but on the prices and behaviour of competitors. In practice, firms will usually base their assumptions about future sales on current figures, add a certain percentage to allow for growth in demand and then finally adjust this up or down if they decide to change the mark-up.

Variations in the mark-up

In most firms, the mark-up is not rigid. In expanding markets, or markets where firms have monopoly/oligopoly power, the size of the mark-up is likely to be greater. In contracting markets, or under conditions of rising costs and constant demand, a firm may well be forced to accept lower profits and thus reduce the mark-up.

Multi-product firms often have different mark-ups for their different products depending on their various market conditions. Such firms will often distribute their overhead costs unequally between their products. The potentially most profitable products, often those with the least elastic demands, will probably be required to make the greatest contribution to overheads.

The firm is likely to take account of the actions and possible reactions of its competitors. It may well be unwilling to change prices when costs or demand change, for fear of the reactions of competitors (see the discussion of kinked demand curve theory on pages 231–2). If prices are kept constant but costs change, either due to a movement along the *AC* curve in response to a change in demand, or due to a shift in the *AC* curve, the firm must necessarily change the size of the mark-up.

All this suggests that, whereas the mark-up may well be based on a target profit, firms are often prepared to change their target and hence their mark-up, according to market conditions.

1. *If the firm adjusts the size of its mark-up according to changes in demand and the actions of competitors, could its actions approximate to setting price and output where MC = MR?*
2. *Some firms set their prices by adding a mark-up to average variable cost (the mark-up would be larger to include an element to cover fixed cost). Why might this make pricing easier for the firm? (See Box 6.7.)*

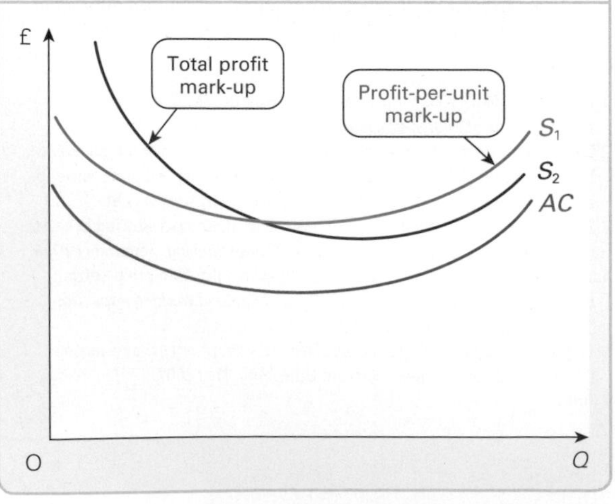

*LOOKING AT THE MATHS

Using a mark-up approach to find the profit-maximising price

Could the firm use a mark-up approach to set the *profit-maximising* price? It could, provided it bases its mark-up on marginal cost (*MC*), rather than average cost, and provided it knows the price elasticity of demand ($P\epsilon_D$) for its product. The rule is:

$$P = \frac{MC}{1 + (1/P\epsilon_D)}$$

This is simply the formula for the profit-maximising price that we derived in section 7.3 (see page 205), except that we have used *MC* rather than *MR* (where profits are maximised, *MC* = *MR*). Proof of this formula is given in Maths Case 7.2 on the student website.

Thus if *MC* = £10 and $P\epsilon_D = -5$, the firm should charge a price of

$$\frac{£10}{1 + (1/-5)} = \frac{£10}{1 - 1/5} = \frac{£10}{0.8} = £12.50$$

The weakness of this pricing rule is that it applies only at the profit-maximising output. If the firm is currently a long way from that output, *MC* and $P\epsilon_D$ may diverge considerably from the values that the firm should use in its calculation. If, however, the firm is producing relatively near to its profit-maximising output, the rule can give a price that is a close approximation to the profit-maximising price.

Figure 9.4   A firm's supply curve based on average cost

£

Total profit mark-up

Profit-per-unit mark-up

S_1

S_2

AC

O   Q

Section summary

1. Many firms set prices by adding a profit mark-up to average cost. This cost-plus pricing is most likely when firms are profit satisficers or when they do not have the information to find the price that will equate marginal cost and marginal revenue.

2. The mark-up could be based on achieving a target level of either *total* profit or profit per unit. In either case, a supply curve can be derived by adding the corresponding mark-up to the average cost curve.

3. For firms keen to increase profit, the size of the mark-up can be varied as market conditions permit the target profit to be increased.

END OF CHAPTER QUESTIONS

1. Assume that a firm faces a downward-sloping demand curve. Draw a diagram showing the firm's *AR, MR, AC* and *MC* curves. (Draw them in such a way that the firm can make supernormal profits.) Mark the following on the diagram:

   (a) The firm's profit-maximising output and price.

   (b) Its sales-revenue-maximising output and price.

   (c) Its sales-maximising output and price (subject to earning at least normal profit).

   Could the answer to (a) and (b) ever be the same?

   Could the answer to (b) and (c) ever be the same?

2. Would it be possible for firms to calculate their maximum-profit output if they did not use marginal cost and marginal revenue concepts?

3. What is meant by the principal–agent problem? Give two examples of this problem that you have come across in your own experience.

4. 'A firm will always prefer to make more profit rather than less.' Do you agree with this statement? Is it compatible with alternatives to the profit-maximising theory of the firm?

5. A firm under monopoly or oligopoly that aims to maximise sales revenue will tend to produce more than a firm that aims to maximise profits. Does this conclusion also apply under (a) perfect competition and (b) monopolistic competition, given that there is freedom of entry?

6. What are the potential costs and benefits of mergers to (a) shareholders; (b) managers; (c) customers?

7. Why is it difficult to test the assumption that firms seek to maximise *long-run* profits?

8. Do behavioural theories of the firm allow us to make any predictions about firms' prices and output?

9. Are 'special offers' likely to benefit consumers?

Online resources

Additional case studies on the student website

9.1. The legal structure of firms. A study of the different types of legal identity that a firm can take – from the sole proprietor to the partnership to the limited company.

9.2. Inside the firm. An examination of alternative organisation structures of firms.

9.3. The Body Shop. A case study of 'alternative business values'.

9.4. Corporate social responsibility. An examination of social responsibility as a goal of firms and its effect on business performance.

9.5. The global information economy and strategic alliances. The way forward for companies such as America Online?

9.6. Downsizing and business organisation. The case of IBM.

9.7. Vouchers and discounts. This case examines the rise of Groupon and looks at its business practices.

9.8. J. K. Galbraith. A portrait of this pioneer of alternative theories of the firm and critic of traditional neoclassical analysis and free-market capitalism.

Maths Case 9.1 Sales revenue maximising with a profit constraint. Part 1: Using simple algebra to find the sales-revenue-maximising output.

Maths Case 9.2 Sales revenue maximising with a profit constraint. Part 2: Using the Lagrangian approach.

Websites relevant to this chapter

Numbers and sections refer to websites listed in the Web Appendix and hotlinked from this book's website at **www.pearsoned.co.uk/sloman**.

- For news articles relevant to this chapter, see the *Economics News* section on the student website.
- For general news relevant to alternative strategies, see websites in section A, and particularly A2, 3, 8, 21, 23, 25, 26, 35, 36. See also A38, 39, 42, 43 and 44 for links to newspapers worldwide, and A40 and 41 for links to economics news articles on particular search topics from newspapers worldwide.
- For student resources relevant to this chapter, see sites C1–7, 9, 10, 14, 19.
- For information on mergers, see sites B3, 43; E4, 10, 18, 20; G1 and 8.
- For data on small and medium-sized enterprises, see the database in B3 or E10.
- For information on pricing, see site E10 and the sites of the regulators of the privatised industries: E15, 16, 19, 22.
- For sites with games and experiments examining the behaviour of firms see D13, 14, 16–20.

The Theory of Distribution of Income

Why do film stars, footballers and investment bankers earn such large incomes? Why, on the other hand, do cleaners, hospital porters and workers in clothing factories earn very low incomes? These are the types of question that the theory of distribution seeks to answer. It attempts to explain why some people are rich and others poor.

The explanation for differences in wages lies in the working of labour markets. In sections 10.1 and 10.2, we will consider how labour markets operate. In particular, we will focus on the determination of wage rates in different types of market: ones where employers are wage takers, ones where they can choose the wage rate, and ones where wage rates are determined by a process of collective bargaining. In the final two sections, we turn to capital and land and ask what determines the rewards that their owners receive.

This chapter examines the theory of income distribution by showing how the rewards to factors of production (labour, capital and land) depend on market conditions. Chapter 11, on the other hand, looks at income distribution in practice. It looks at inequality and poverty and at government policies to tackle the problem.

10.1 WAGE DETERMINATION UNDER PERFECT COMPETITION

Perfect labour markets

When looking at the market for labour, it is useful to distinguish between perfect and imperfect markets. Although in practice few labour markets are totally perfect, many are at least approximately so.

The assumptions of perfect labour markets are similar to those of perfect goods markets. The main one is that everyone is a *wage taker*. In other words, neither employers nor employees have any economic power to affect wage rates. This situation is not uncommon. Small employers are likely to have to pay the 'going wage rate' to their employees, especially when the employee is of a clearly defined type, such as an electrician, a bar worker, a data analyst or a porter. As far as employees are concerned, being a wage taker means competing with other identical (or very similar) workers. It also means not being a member of a union and therefore not being able to use collective bargaining to push up the wage rate.

The other assumptions of a perfect labour market are as follows:

Freedom of entry. There are no restrictions on the movement of labour. Workers are free to move to different jobs or to areas of the country where wages are higher. There are no barriers erected by, say, unions, professional associations or the government. Of course, it takes time for workers to change jobs and maybe to retrain. This assumption therefore applies only in the long run.

Perfect knowledge. Workers are fully aware of what jobs are available at what wages and with what conditions of

Definition

Wage taker An employer or employee who has no power to influence the market wage rate.

employment. Likewise, employers know what labour is available and how productive that labour is.

Homogeneous labour. It is usually assumed that, in perfect markets, workers of a given category are identical in terms of productivity. For example, it would be assumed that all bricklayers are equally skilled and motivated.

 Which of the above assumptions do you think would be correct in each of the following cases?
(a) Supermarket checkout operators.
(b) Agricultural workers.
(c) Crane operators.
(d) Economics teachers.
(e) Call-centre workers.
(f) Professional footballers.
(g) Bar workers.

Wage rates and employment under perfect competition are determined by the interaction of the market demand and supply of labour. This is illustrated in Figure 10.1(a).

Generally, it would be expected that the supply and demand curves slope the same way as in goods markets. The higher the wage paid for a certain type of job, the more workers will want to do that job and, generally, the more hours each will be willing to work. This gives an upward-sloping supply curve of labour. On the other hand, the higher the wage that employers have to pay, the less labour they will employ. They may produce less, or they may substitute other factors of production, like machinery, for labour. Thus the demand curve for labour slopes downwards.

Figure 10.1(b) shows how an individual employer has to accept this wage. The supply of labour to that employer is infinitely elastic. In other words, at the market wage W_m, there is no limit to the number of workers available to that employer (but no workers at all will be available below it: they will all be working elsewhere). At the market wage W_m, the employer will employ Q_1 hours of labour.

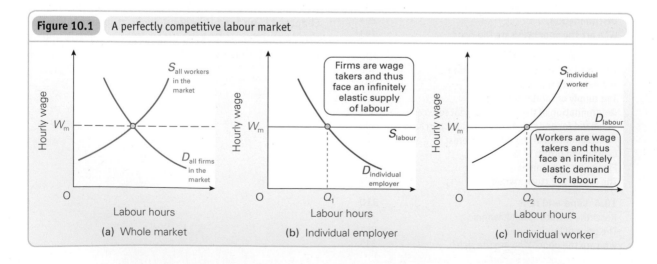

| Figure 10.1 | A perfectly competitive labour market |

(a) Whole market   (b) Individual employer   (c) Individual worker

BOX 10.1 **LABOUR AS A FACTOR OF PRODUCTION** EXPLORING ECONOMICS

Is this any way to treat a worker?

The theory that wages depend on demand and supply is often referred to as the 'neoclassical' theory of wages. Treated as pure theory, it is value free and does not involve moral judgements. It does not say, for example, whether the resulting distribution of income is fair or just.

In practice, however, the neoclassical theory is often used in such a way as to imply moral judgements. It is a theory that tends to be associated with the political right and centre: those who are generally in favour of markets and the capitalist system. Many on the political left are critical of its implied morality. They make the following points:

- By treating labour as a 'factor of production', it demeans labour. Labour is not the same as a piece of land or a machine.
- It legitimises the capitalist system, where some people own land and capital while others have only their own labour. It implies that people have a right to income from their property even if that property is unequally distributed among the population.
- It implies that labour has no rights to the goods that it produces. These goods are entirely the property of the employer, even though it is the workers who made them.

Karl Marx (1818–83) was highly critical of these values and the way that the capitalist system led to extremes of wealth and poverty. He argued that labour was the only true source of value. After all, it is labour that makes machines, labour that works the land, labour that mines coal and other natural resources. Property, he argued, is therefore a form of theft. When capitalists extract profits from their enterprises, he continued, they are stealing part of the value produced by labour.

Neoclassical economists defend their position against the Marxist 'labour theory of value' by arguing the following:

- They are merely describing the world. If people want to draw pro-capitalist conclusions from their theory, then that is up to them.
- If the labour theory of value is used in any practical way to evaluate costs and output, it will lead to a misallocation of resources. Labour is not the only scarce resource. Land, for example, is also scarce and needs to be included in calculations of costs, otherwise it will be used wastefully.

 Assume that it is agreed by everyone that it is morally wrong to treat labour as a mere 'factor of production', with no rights over the goods produced. Does this make the neoclassical theory wrong?

Figure 10.1(c) shows how an individual worker also has to accept this wage. In this case it is the demand curve for that worker that is infinitely elastic. In other words, there is as much work as the worker chooses to do at this wage, but none at all above it.

We now turn to look at the supply and demand for labour in more detail.

The supply of labour

We can look at the supply of labour at three levels: the supply of hours by an individual worker, the supply of workers to an individual employer, and the total market supply of a given category of labour. Let us examine each in turn.

The supply of hours by an individual worker

Work involves two major costs (or 'disutilities') to the worker:

- When people work they sacrifice leisure.
- The work itself may be unpleasant or tedious.

Each extra hour worked will involve additional disutility. This **marginal disutility of work** (*MDU*) will tend to *increase* as people work more hours. There are two reasons for this. First, the less leisure they have left, the greater is the disutility they experience in sacrificing a further hour of leisure. Second, any unpleasantness they experience in

doing the job tends to increase due to boredom, tiredness, or frustration.

 Re-word the explanation of marginal disutility of work in terms of the marginal utility of leisure.

This increasing marginal disutility (see Figure 10.2(a)) will tend to give an upward-sloping supply curve of hours by an individual worker (see Figure 10.2(b)). The reason is that, in order to persuade people to work more hours, a higher hourly wage must be paid to compensate for the higher marginal disutility incurred. This helps to explain why overtime rates are higher than standard rates.

Under certain circumstances, however, the supply of hours curve might bend backwards (see Figure 10.3). The reason is that when wage rates go up, two opposing forces operate on the individual's labour supply.

On one hand, with higher wage rates people tend to work more hours, since time taken in leisure now involves a greater sacrifice of income and hence consumption. They

Definition

Marginal disutility of work The extra sacrifice/ hardship to a worker of working an extra unit of time in any given time period (e.g. an extra hour per day).

Figure 10.2 | Marginal disutility of work and an individual's supply of labour

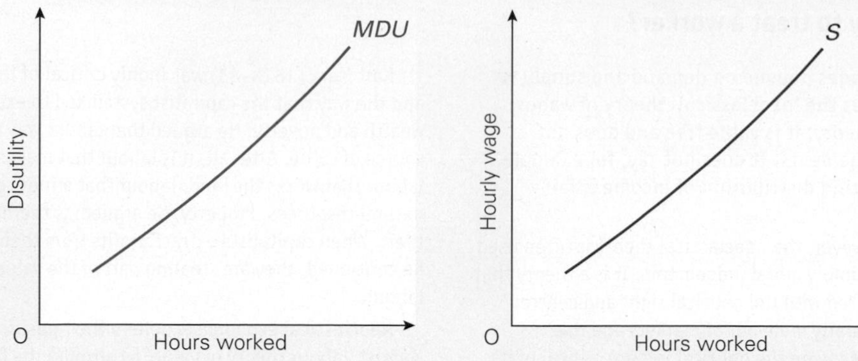

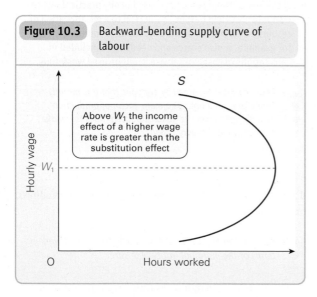

(a) The marginal disutility of hours worked

(b) The supply of hours worked

Figure 10.3 | Backward-bending supply curve of labour

> Above W_1 the income effect of a higher wage rate is greater than the substitution effect

thus substitute income (i.e. work) for leisure. This is called the **substitution effect** of the increase in wage rates.

On the other hand, people may feel that with higher wage rates they can afford to work less and have more leisure. This is called the **income effect**. It reflects the fact that leisure is a *normal good,* one which is consumed in greater quantities as incomes rise.

With two effects working in opposite directions, the relative size of the effects determines the slope of the individual's supply curve. At lower wage rates, it is generally assumed that the substitution effect outweighs the income effect. A rise in the wage rate acts as an incentive and encourages a person to

work more hours. At higher wage rates, however, the income effect might outweigh the substitution effect. As wages rise, people may feel they can afford to give up some consumption in exchange for more leisure time.

If the wage rate becomes high enough for the income effect to outweigh the substitution effect, the supply curve will begin to slope backwards. This occurs above a wage rate of W_1 in Figure 10.3.

These considerations are particularly important for a government when thinking about policies on income tax. Conservative governments have often argued that cuts in income taxes are the equivalent of giving people a pay rise, and that they provide an incentive for people to work harder. This analysis is only correct, however, if the substitution effect dominates. If the income effect dominates, people will work *less* after the tax cut. These questions are examined in Chapter 11.

The supply of labour to an individual employer

Under perfect competition, the supply of labour to a particular firm will be perfectly elastic, as in Figure 10.1(b). The firm is a 'wage taker' and thus has no power to influence wages. Take the case of a small firm that wishes to employ a temporary receptionist via an agency. It has to pay the 'going rate', and presumably will be able to employ as many receptionists as it likes (within reason) at that wage rate.

The market supply of a given type of labour

This will typically be upward sloping, as in Figure 10.1(a). The higher the wage rate offered in a particular type of job, the more people will want to do that job.

Definitions

Substitution effect of a rise in wage rates Workers will tend to substitute income for leisure as leisure now has a higher opportunity cost. This effect leads to *more* hours being worked as wage rates rise.

Income effect of a rise in wage rates Workers get a higher income for a given number of hours worked and may thus feel they need to work *fewer* hours as wage rates rise.

KI 7
p36

*BOX 10.2 USING INDIFFERENCE CURVE ANALYSIS TO DERIVE THE INDIVIDUAL'S SUPPLY CURVE OF LABOUR

EXPLORING ECONOMICS

TC 1
p11

Indifference curve analysis (see section 4.3) can be used to derive the individual's supply curve of labour. The analysis can show why the supply curve may be backward bending.

Assume that an individual can choose the number of hours to work and has 12 hours a day to divide between work and leisure (the remaining 12 being for sleep, shopping, travelling, etc.). In the diagram, with an hourly wage rate of £10, budget line B_1 shows all the possible combinations of daily income and leisure hours. For example, at point x the individual has an income of £80 by working eight hours and having four hours of leisure.

At an hourly wage of £20, the budget line becomes B_2, and at an hourly wage of £25 it becomes B_3.

The choice of hours worked at different wage rates

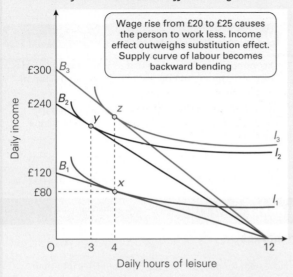

Wage rise from £20 to £25 causes the person to work less. Income effect outweighs substitution effect. Supply curve of labour becomes backward bending

The diagram also shows three indifference curves. Each indifference curve shows all those combinations of income and leisure that give the individual a particular level of utility. The curves are bowed in towards the origin, showing that increasingly higher incomes are necessary to compensate for each hour of leisure sacrificed. Curve I_3 shows a higher level of utility than I_2, and I_2 a higher level than I_1.

At a wage rate of £10 per hour, the individual can move along budget line B_1. Point x shows the highest level of utility that can be achieved. The individual thus supplies eight hours of labour (and has four hours of leisure).

At the higher wage rate of £20 per hour, the individual is now on budget line B_2 and maximises utility at point y by working nine hours. Thus the higher wage has encouraged the individual to work one more hour. So far, then, the individual's supply curve would be upward sloping: a higher wage rate leads to more labour hours supplied.

At the still higher wage rate of £25 per hour, the individual is on budget line B_3, and now maximises utility at point z. But this means that only eight hours are now worked. The supply curve has begun to bend backwards. In other words, the individual is now in a position to be able to afford to take more time off in leisure. The income effect has begun to offset the substitution effect.

KI 7
p36

1. Using the analysis developed in Chapter 4, try to show the size of the income and substitution effects when moving from point x to point y and from point y to point z.
2. Illustrate on an indifference diagram the effect on the hours a person works of (a) a cut in the rate of income tax; (b) the introduction of a weekly tax credit, worth £30 to all adults irrespective of income.

The *position* of the market supply curve of labour depends on the number of people willing and able to do the job at each given wage rate. This depends on three things:

- The number of qualified people. Of course, if the job is unskilled then a large number of people will be 'qualified'.
- The non-wage benefits or costs of the job, such as the pleasantness of the working environment, job satisfaction or dissatisfaction, status, the degree of job security, pensions and other fringe benefits.
- TC 1
p11 The wages and non-wage benefits in alternative jobs.

A change in the wage rate will cause a movement along the supply curve. A change in any of these other three determinants will shift the whole curve.

 Which way will the supply curve shift if the wage rates in alternative jobs rise?

The elasticity of the market supply of labour

How responsive will the supply of labour be to a change in the wage rate? If the market wage rate goes up, will a lot more labour become available or only a little? We looked at elasticity of demand and supply in Chapter 3; a similar analysis is used for the labour market. Thus the responsiveness (elasticity) depends on (a) the difficulties and costs of changing jobs and (b) the time period under consideration.

TC 6
p68

Another way of looking at the elasticity of supply of labour is in terms of the ***mobility of labour***: the willingness and ability of labour to move to another job, whether in a

Definition

Mobility of labour The willingness and ability of labour to move to another job.

different location (geographical mobility) or in a different industry (occupational mobility). The mobility of labour (and hence the elasticity of supply of labour) will be higher when there are alternative jobs in the same location, when alternative jobs require similar skills, and when people have good information about these jobs. It is also much higher in the long run, when people have the time to move or to acquire new skills and when the education system has time to adapt to the changing demands of industry.

1. *Assume that there is a growing demand for computer programmers. As a result more people train to become programmers. Does this represent a rightward shift in the supply curve of programmers, or merely the supply curve becoming more elastic in the long run, or both? Explain.*
2. *Which is likely to be more elastic, the supply of coal miners or the supply of shop assistants? Explain.*

If the demand for a particular category of worker increases, the wage rate will rise. The more inelastic the supply of labour, the higher the rise will be. Workers already employed in that industry will get the benefit of that rise, even though they are doing the same job as before. They are now earning a premium above the wage that was necessary to attract them into the industry in the first place. This premium is called *economic rent*. Case Study 10.1 on the student website explores this concept and its relationship with the elasticity of supply of labour.

The demand for labour: the marginal productivity theory

In the traditional 'neoclassical' theory of the firm, which we examined in Chapters 8 and 9, it is assumed that firms aim to maximise profits. The same assumption is made in the neoclassical theory of labour demand. This theory is generally known as *marginal productivity theory*.

The profit-maximising approach
How many workers will a profit-maximising firm want to employ? The firm will answer this question by weighing up the costs of employing extra labour against the benefits. It will use exactly the same principles as in deciding how much output to produce.

Definition

Economic rent The excess that a factor of production is paid over the amount necessary to keep it in its current employment.

Marginal productivity theory The theory that the demand for a factor depends on its marginal revenue product.

BOX 10.3 IMMIGRATION AND THE UK LABOUR MARKET

Free movement of people and the single European market

On 23 June 2016, a majority of those who voted in the UK referendum on membership of the European Union (EU) voted 'leave'. Many commentators argue that a major reason for the result was the desire of many people to see an end to the free movement of people to the UK from the EU.

The free movement of people is one of the four key principles that underpins the EU's single market (the others being free movement of goods, services and capital). The full implications of this rule for patterns of migration became clear when the so-called EU8 countries (Czech Republic, Estonia, Hungary, Latvia, Poland, Slovakia and Slovenia) joined the EU in 2004.

When new countries gain EU membership, existing countries are usually given the option of introducing transitional arrangements. This typically involves the placing of restrictions on the free movement of citizens from new member states for a period of up to seven years. Most existing members of the EU decided to use this option following the accession of the EU8 countries. Without controls, they feared that their labour markets would become overwhelmed by a large inflow of new economic migrants.

The UK, along with Sweden and Ireland, chose a different course of action. They decided against any transitional arrangements and allowed immediate free movement for people from the EU8 countries into their labour markets.

The impact of this decision on the volume of immigration was quite dramatic. The number of EU8 nationals living in the UK increased from 125 000 in 2004 to over a million in 2012. Immigration from the EU as a proportion of total immigration into the UK increased from around 10 per cent in 1990 to 44 per cent in 2016.

Given this larger-than-expected immigration from 2004, the UK government decided to introduce transitional arrangements for the full seven-year period after Bulgaria and Romania joined the EU in 2007. Citizens from these countries had to apply to the Home Office to obtain authorisation to take a job. Restrictions were lifted when the seven-year period came to an end in 2014.

Impact of EU immigration on the UK economy

What impact has this big increase in immigration had on the labour market in the UK and the economy more generally? The predictions of economic theory are inconclusive. At the microeconomic level, we would expect an increase both in labour supply and in the elasticity of supply. This could result in lower rates of wages and employment for the UK-born labour force.

In the goods market, the firm will maximise profits where the marginal cost of an extra unit of *goods* produced equals the marginal revenue from selling it: $MC = MR$.

In the labour market, the firm will maximise profits where the marginal cost of employing an extra *worker* equals the marginal revenue that the worker's output earns for the firm: MC of labour $= MR$ of labour. The reasoning is simple. If an extra worker adds more to a firm's revenue than to its costs, the firm's profits will increase. It will be worth employing that worker. But as more workers are employed, diminishing returns to labour will set in (see page 151). Each extra worker will produce less than the previous one, and thus bring in less revenue for the firm. Eventually, the marginal revenue from extra workers will fall to the level of their marginal cost. At that point, the firm will stop employing extra workers. There are no additional profits to be gained from employing further workers. Profits are at a maximum.

KI 19
p151

Measuring the marginal cost and revenue of labour

Marginal cost of labour (MC_L). This is the extra cost of employing one more worker. Under perfect competition, the firm is too small to affect the market wage. It faces a horizontal supply curve (see Figure 10.1(b) on page 278). Thus the additional cost of employing one more person will simply be the wage: $MC_L = W$.

Marginal revenue of labour (MRP_L). The marginal revenue that the firm gains from employing one more worker is called the **marginal revenue product** of labour. The MRP_L is found by multiplying two elements – the *marginal physical product* of labour (MPP_L) and the marginal revenue gained by selling one more unit of output (MR):

$$MRP_L = MPP_L \times MR$$

The MPP_L is the extra output produced by the last worker. Thus if the last worker produces 100 tonnes of output per week (MPP_L), and if the firm earns an extra £4 for each additional tonne sold (MR), then the worker's MRP is £400. This extra worker is adding £400 to the firm's revenue.

The profit-maximising level of employment for a firm

The MPP curve was illustrated in Figure 6.3 (see page 159). As more workers are employed, there will come a point when diminishing returns set in (point b). The MPP_L curve thus

CASE STUDIES AND APPLICATIONS

Immigrants also buy goods and services, so at a macroeconomic level we would expect a general increase in demand. This would have a positive impact on the demand for labour.

In order to see which effect is stronger, a number of studies have analysed UK labour market data.

In March 2014, a government report[1] was published which synthesised the research up until this point. It concluded that there was little evidence of long-term damage to British workers' prospects, with the labour market adjusting in both booms and times of recession, albeit more slowly in the latter.

In 2016, a study by the Centre for Economic Performance[2] found that UK-born workers in those parts of the country that had the highest levels of EU immigration did not experience bigger falls in wages and employment than the rest of the country. It also found that EU immigration had little impact on the pay and jobs of low-skilled workers.

What is more, according to a University College London study,[3] between 2000 and 2012, EU immigrants made a substantial net contribution to UK finances, paying considerably more in taxes than claiming in benefits.

Immigration has remained a controversial issue. Commonly held views of its impact on the labour market often seem at odds with the available evidence. Opposition to high levels of immigration has also been driven by a number of non-economic reasons.

At the time of writing, the exact nature of the controls that will be imposed on immigrants from the EU is uncertain. For example, will the government impose a work permit system similar to the one that already applies to non-EU immigrants? Will the rules be stricter or more lenient?

If new controls significantly reduce immigration, it will be interesting to see the impact it has on the UK economy. No doubt economists will be analysing the data.

Draw a diagram illustrating the UK's decision to open up labour markets to workers from the Accession countries. Show the situation both before and after. Consider both the position and slope of the labour supply curve and the impact on the number employed and on wages. Would you expect there to be any movement in the demand for labour?

1 *Impacts of Migration on UK Native Employment* (Home Office and Department for Business, Innovation and Skills, March 2014).

2 Jonathan Wadsworth, Swati Dhingra, Gianmarco Ottaviano and John Van Reenen, *Brexit and the Impact of Immigration on the UK* (Centre for Economic Performance, May 2016).

3 Christian Dustmann and Tommaso Frattini, *The Fiscal Effects of Immigration to the UK* (Centre for Research and Analysis of Migration, University College London, November 2013).

Figure 10.4   The profit-maximising level of employment

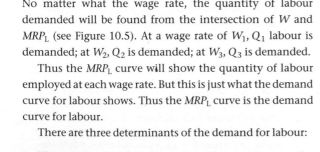

slopes down after this point. The MRP_L curve will be a similar shape to the MPP_L curve, since it is merely being multiplied by a constant figure, MR. (Under perfect competition MR equals P and does not vary with output.) The MRP_L curve is illustrated in Figure 10.4, along with the MC_L 'curve'.

 Why is the MC_L curve horizontal?

Profits will be maximised at an employment level of Q_e, where MC_L (i.e. W) $= MRP_L$. Why? At levels of employment below Q_e, MRP_L exceeds MC_L. The firm will increase profits by employing more labour. At levels of employment above Q_e, MC_L exceeds MRP_L. In this case, the firm will increase profits by reducing employment.

TC 8
p109

Derivation of the firm's demand curve for labour

No matter what the wage rate, the quantity of labour demanded will be found from the intersection of W and MRP_L (see Figure 10.5). At a wage rate of W_1, Q_1 labour is demanded; at W_2, Q_2 is demanded; at W_3, Q_3 is demanded.

Thus the MRP_L curve will show the quantity of labour employed at each wage rate. But this is just what the demand curve for labour shows. Thus the MRP_L curve is the demand curve for labour.

There are three determinants of the demand for labour:

- The wage rate. This determines the position *on* the demand curve, i.e. the quantity demanded.
- The productivity of labour (MPP_L). This determines the position *of* the demand curve.
- The demand for the good being produced. The higher the demand for the good, the higher its price, and hence the higher will be the MR, and the MRP_L. This too determines the position of the demand curve. It shows how the demand for labour (and other factors) is a

*LOOKING AT THE MATHS

The marginal product of labour can be expressed using calculus. It is the rate of increase in output of good X with respect to changes in the quantity of labour:

$$MPP_L = \frac{\partial X}{\partial L}$$

The marginal revenue product of labour is thus given by

$$MRP_L = MR\frac{\partial X}{\partial L}$$

Profits are maximised at the level of employment (L) where $W = MRP_L$: i.e. where

$$W = MR\frac{\partial X}{\partial L} \tag{1}$$

We can easily move from this to the level of profit-maximising *output* of good X (where $MC = MR$). Rearranging equation (1), we get

$$\frac{W}{\partial X/\partial L} = MR \tag{2}$$

But, assuming that labour is the only variable factor, the marginal cost (of output) is the extra cost of employing labour (the only extra cost) *per unit of output*. In other words:

$$MC = \frac{W}{\partial X/\partial L} \tag{3}$$

i.e.

$$MC = MR$$

Thus, not surprisingly, the profit-maximising employment of labour (where $W = MRP_L$) will yield the profit-maximising output (where $MC = MR$).

Figure 10.5   Deriving the firm's demand curve for labour

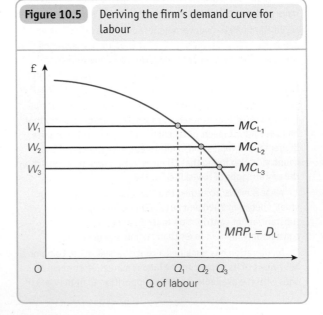

derived demand: i.e. one derived from the demand for the good. For example, the higher the demand for houses, and hence the higher their price, the higher will be the demand for bricklayers.

A change in the wage rate is represented by a movement *along* the demand curve for labour. A change in the productivity of labour or the demand for the good *shifts* the curve.

Derivation of the industry demand curve for labour
This is not simply the sum of the demand curves of the individual firms. The firm's demand curve is based on a constant P and MR, no matter how many workers the firm employs (this is one of the assumptions of perfect competition). In Figure 10.6, when the wage rate falls from W_1 to W_2 the firm will employ more labour by moving from *a* to *b* along its demand curve MRP_1.

The trouble with this analysis is that when the wage rate falls, it will affect *all* employers. They will all want to employ more labour. But when they do, the total industry output will increase, and hence P (and MR) will be pushed down. This will shift the firm's MRP curve to the left and lead to a lower level of employment at point *c*. Therefore, when we allow for the effect of lower wages on the market price of the good, the firm's demand curve for labour will be the *green* line passing through points *a* and *c*.

Thus the *industry* demand curve for labour is the (horizontal) sum of the *green* lines for each firm, and is therefore less elastic than the firm's MRP curve.

 What will determine the elasticity of this curve?

The elasticity of demand for labour
KI 9 p66 The elasticity of demand for labour (with respect to changes in the wage rate) will be greater:

- The greater the price elasticity of demand for the good. A fall in W leads to higher employment and more output. This will drive P down. If the market demand for the good is elastic, this fall in P will lead to a lot more being sold and hence to a lot more people being employed.
- The easier it is to substitute labour for other factors and vice versa. If labour can be readily substituted for other **KI 7 p36** factors, then a reduction in W will lead to a large increase in labour used to replace these other factors.
- The greater the elasticity of supply of complementary factors. If the wage rate falls, a lot more labour will be demanded if plenty of complementary factors can be obtained at little increase in their price.

Definition

Derived demand Demand for a factor of production that depends on the demand for the good that uses it.

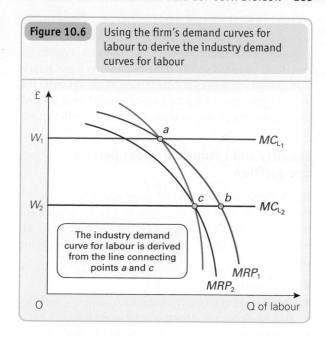

Figure 10.6 Using the firm's demand curves for labour to derive the industry demand curves for labour

- The greater the elasticity of supply of substitute factors. If the wage rate falls and more labour is used, less substitute factors will be demanded and their price will fall. If their supply is elastic, a lot less will be supplied and therefore a lot more labour will be used instead.
- The greater the wage cost as a proportion of total costs. If wages are a large proportion of total costs and the wage rate falls, total costs will fall significantly; therefore production will increase significantly, and so too will the demand for labour.
- The longer the time period. Given sufficient time, firms can respond to a fall in wage rates by reorganising their production processes to make use of the now relatively cheap labour.

 For each of the following jobs, check through the above list of determinants (excluding the last), and try to decide whether demand would be relatively elastic or inelastic: firefighters; telesales operators; app developers; bus drivers; accountants; farm workers; car workers.

Wages and profits under perfect competition

The wage rate (W) is determined by the interaction of demand and supply in the labour market. It will be equal to the value of the output that the last person produces (MRP_L).

Profits to the individual firm arise from the fact that the MRP_L curve slopes downwards (diminishing returns). Thus the last worker adds less to the revenue of firms than was added previously by workers already employed.

If *all* workers in the firm receive a wage equal to the MRP of the *last* worker, everyone but the last worker will receive a wage less than their MRP. This excess of MRP_L over W of previous workers provides a surplus to the firm over its wages bill (see Figure 10.7). Part of this will be required for paying non-wage costs; part will be profits for the firm.

Perfect competition between firms ensures that profits are kept down to *normal* profits. If the surplus over wages is such that *supernormal* profits are made, new firms will enter the industry. The price of the good (and hence MRP_L) will fall, and the wage rate will be bid up, until only normal profits remain.

Equality and inequality under perfect competition

The mythical world of perfect wage equality

Under certain very strict assumptions, a perfectly competitive market will lead to perfect equality of wage rates. All workers will earn exactly the same. These strict assumptions are as follows:

- All workers have identical abilities.
- There is perfect mobility of labour.
- All jobs are equally attractive to all workers.
- All workers and employers have perfect knowledge.
- Wages are determined entirely by demand and supply.

Given these assumptions, if consumer demand rose in any industry, the demand for labour would rise. As a result, wage rates would begin to rise. Immediately workers would flood into this industry, attracted by the higher wages. Very quickly, then, wage rates would be competed back down to the level in the rest of the economy. Likewise if wage rates began to fall in any industry, workers would leave, thereby eliminating any labour surplus and preventing the fall in wage rates.

Under these conditions, therefore, not only would the labour supply curve to a *firm* be infinitely elastic, but so too would the labour supply curve to each *industry* at the universal wage rate.

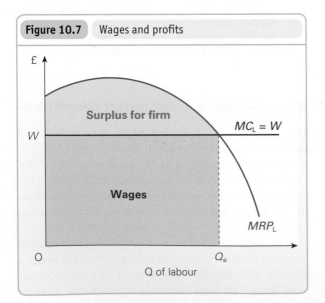

Of course, in the real world these conditions do not hold and we do not see perfectly competitive labour markets.

Huge inequalities of wages exist. But even if markets *were* perfect, inequality would be expected to persist.

Causes of inequality under perfect competition

In the short run, inequality will exist under perfect competition because it takes time for changes in demand and supply conditions to bring new long-run equilibria. Thus expanding industries will tend to pay higher wage rates than contracting industries.

But even after enough time has elapsed for all adjustments to be made to changes in demand and supply, long-run wage differentials will still exist for the following reasons:

- Workers do not have identical abilities.
- Workers are not perfectly mobile, even in the long run. People have different preferences about where they want to live and the jobs they like to do. They may not have access to training or may be unable to afford to retrain. Workers may not have the innate talent to do particular jobs, even if they did retrain.
- Jobs differ enormously in terms of the skills they require and in terms of their pleasantness or unpleasantness.

What is more, since demand and supply conditions are constantly changing, long-run general equilibrium throughout the economy will never be reached.

Who are the poor? Who are the rich?

The lowest paid will be those whose labour is in low demand or high supply. Low demand will be due to low demand for the good or low labour productivity. High supply will be due to low mobility out of industries in decline or to a surplus of people with the same skills or qualifications. Thus, for example, workers who possess few skills, are working in contracting industries, do not want to move from the area and will not or cannot retrain will be low paid.

The highly paid will be those whose labour is in high demand or low supply. Thus workers who possess skills or talents that are in short supply, especially if those skills take a long time for others to acquire, and those who are working in expanding industries, will tend to earn high wages.

Although the movement of labour from low-paid to high-paid jobs will tend to reduce wage differentials, considerable inequality will persist even under perfect competition. It is, therefore, not possible to eliminate poverty and inequality by 'freeing up' markets and encouraging workers to 'stand on their own feet' or 'get on their bikes'.

Furthermore, in the real world there exist many market imperfections, which tend to make inequality greater. These imperfections are examined in the next section.

Finally, income inequality under capitalism will also arise from the unequal distribution of the ownership of land and capital. Even under perfect competition, considerable inequality will therefore exist if wealth is concentrated in the hands of the few.

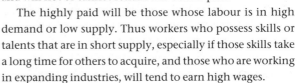

Figure 10.7 Wages and profits

Section summary

1. Wages in a perfect market are determined by supply and demand.

2. The supply curve of hours by an individual worker reflects the increasing marginal disutility of work. Its shape depends on the relative sizes of the substitution and income effects of a wage change. The substitution effect is positive: higher wages encourage people to work more by substituting wages for leisure. The income effect, however, is negative: higher wages make people feel that they can afford to enjoy more leisure. If the income effect is bigger than the substitution effect, the supply curve for labour hours will bend backwards.

3. The supply of labour to a particular employer under perfect competition is infinitely elastic.

4. The market supply is typically upward sloping. Its elasticity depends on labour mobility.

5. The demand for labour depends on a worker's marginal revenue product. This is the extra revenue that a firm will gain from the output of an extra worker. The profit-maximising firm will continue taking on extra workers until MRP_L is equal to MC_L ($= W$ under perfect competition).

6. The elasticity of demand for labour depends on the elasticity of demand for the good being produced, the ease of substituting labour for other factors and vice versa, the elasticity of supply of substitute and complementary factors, wages as a proportion of total costs, and the time period involved.

7. Although market forces will tend to lead to the elimination of differentials as workers move from low-paid to high-paid jobs, nevertheless inequality can persist even under perfect competition. People have different abilities and skills; people are not perfectly mobile; and jobs differ in their labour requirements.

8. Inequality is also caused by market imperfections and by unequal ownership of land and capital.

10.2 WAGE DETERMINATION IN IMPERFECT MARKETS

In the real world, firms and/or workers are likely to have the power to influence wage rates: they are not wage takers. This is one of the major types of labour market imperfection.

TC 3
p26

When a firm is the only employer of a certain type of labour, this situation is called a **monopsony**. A monopsony may arise in a market for particular types of labour; Royal Mail is a monopsony employer of postal workers. Alternatively, and more commonly, it may arise in a local market. Thus a factory may be the only employer of certain types of labour in that district. When there are just a few employers, this is called **oligopsony**. Oligopsony is much more common than monopsony, just as in goods markets oligopoly is much more common than monopoly.

In monopsonistic or oligopsonistic labour markets the employers have market power. Workers too may have market power as members of unions. When a single union bargains on behalf of a certain type of labour, it is acting as a monopolist. When there is more than one union, they are oligopolists.

When a monopsonist employer faces a monopolist union, the situation is called **bilateral monopoly**.

Definitions

Monopsony A market with a single buyer or employer.

Oligopsony A market with just a few buyers or employers.

Bilateral monopoly Where a monopsony buyer faces a monopoly seller.

Firms with market power in employing labour (monopsony, etc.)

Monopsonists (and oligopsonists too) are 'wage setters', not 'wage takers'. A large employer in a small town, for example, may have considerable power to resist wage increases or even to force wage rates down. The National Health Service has considerable power in setting wages for health workers in the UK.

KI 22
p190

Such firms face an upward-sloping supply curve of labour. This is illustrated in Figure 10.8. If the firm wants to take on more labour, it will have to pay a higher wage rate

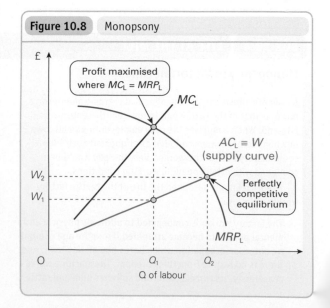

Figure 10.8 Monopsony

to attract workers away from other industries. But conversely, when employing less labour it will be able to pay a lower wage rate.

The supply curve shows the wage rate that must be paid to attract a given quantity of labour. The wage it pays is the *average cost* to the firm of employing labour (AC_L). The supply curve is also therefore the AC_L curve.

The *marginal cost* of employing one more worker (MC_L) will be above the wage (AC_L). The reason is that the wage rate has to be raised to attract extra workers. The MC_L will thus be the new higher wage paid to the new employee *plus* the small rise in the total wages bill for existing employees: after all, they will have to be paid the higher wage too.

The profit-maximising employment of labour would be at Q_1, where $MC_L = MRP_L$. The wage paid would thus be W_1.

If this had been a perfectly competitive labour market, equilibrium employment would have been at the higher level Q_2, with the wage rate at the higher level W_2, where $W = MRP_L$. The monopsonist is therefore forcing the wage rate down by restricting the number of workers employed.

1. *The following table shows data for a monopsonist employer. Fill in the missing figures. How many workers should the firm employ if it wishes to maximise profits?*

Number of workers	Wage rate (£)	Total cost of labour (£)	Marginal cost of labour (£)	Marginal revenue product (£)
1	100	100		
			110	230
2	105	210		
			120	240
3	110	330		
			...	240
4	115	...		
			...	230
5	120	...		
			...	210
6	125	...		
			...	190
7	130	...		
			...	170
8	135	...		
			...	150
9	140	...		

2. *Will a monopsony typically also be a monopoly? Give examples of monopsonists that are not monopolists, and monopolists that are not monopsonists.*

Labour with market power (union monopoly or oligopoly)

The extent to which unions will succeed in pushing up wage rates depends on their power and willingness to take action. It also depends on the power of firms to resist and on their ability to pay higher wages. In particular, the scope for unions to gain a better deal for their members depends on the sort of market in which the employers are producing.

If the employers are producing under perfect or monopolistic competition, wage rates will only rise at the expense of employment. Firms are earning only normal profit. Thus if unions force up wage rates, the marginal firms will make losses and eventually leave the industry. Fewer workers will be employed. The fall in output will lead to higher prices. This will enable the remaining firms to pay a higher wage rate.

Figure 10.9 illustrates these effects. If unions succeed in raising the wage from W_1 to W_2, employment will fall from Q_1 to Q_2. There will be a surplus of people ($Q_3 - Q_2$) wishing to work in this industry for whom no jobs are available.

The union faces a second effect. Not only will jobs be lost as a result of the higher wage rate, but there is also a danger that those who are unemployed as a result might undercut the union wage.

In a competitive goods market, wage rates can only be increased without a reduction in the level of employment if, as part of the bargain, the productivity of labour is increased. This is called a ***productivity deal***. The *MRP* curve,

Definition

Productivity deal Where a union agrees to changes in working practices that will increase output per worker. This may be in return for a rise in the wage rate.

BOX 10.4 **LIFE AT THE MILL**

Monopsony in Victorian times

A dramatic illustration of the effects of extreme monopsony power is that of the textile mill in nineteenth-century England. When a mill was the only employer in a small town, or when factory owners colluded as oligopsonists, things could be very bad for the worker. Very low pay would be combined with often appalling working conditions.

Friedrich Engels described the life of the textile factory worker as follows:

> The factory worker is condemned to allow his physical and mental powers to become atrophied. From the age of eight he enters an occupation which bores him all day long. And there is no respite from this boredom. The machine works ceaselessly. Its wheels, belts and spindles hum and rattle

ceaselessly in his ears, and if he thinks of taking even a moment's rest, the overlooker is always there to punish him with a fine. It is nothing less than torture of the severest kind to which the workers are subjected by being condemned to a life-sentence in the factory, in the service of a machine which never stops.[1]

1. *Why did competition between employers not force up wages and improve working conditions?*
2. *Were the workers making a 'rational economic decision' when they chose to work in such factories?*

1 F. Engels, *The Condition of the Working Class in England,* translated by W. O. Henderson and W. H. Chaloner (Basil Blackwell, 1971), pp. 199–200.

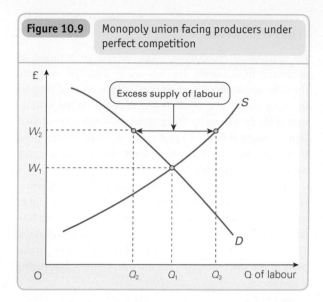

Figure 10.9 Monopoly union facing producers under perfect competition

and hence the demand curve in Figure 10.9, shifts to the right.

 Which of the following unions find themselves in a weak bargaining position for the above reasons?
(a) The shopworkers' union (USDAW).
(b) The tube and train drivers' union (ASLEF).
(c) The farm workers' union (part of Unite).

In a competitive market, then, the union is faced with the choice between wages and jobs. Its actions will thus depend on its objectives.

If it wants to *maximise employment,* it will have to content itself with a wage of W_1 in Figure 10.9, unless productivity deals can be negotiated. At W_1, Q_1 workers will be employed. Above W_1 fewer than Q_1 workers will be *demanded.* Below W_1 fewer than Q_1 workers will be *supplied.*

If the union is more concerned with securing a higher wage rate, it may be prepared to push for a wage rate above W_1 and accept some reduction in employment. This is more likely if the reduction can be achieved through **natural wastage**. This is where people retire, or take voluntary redundancy, or simply leave for another job.

Firms and labour with market power (bilateral monopoly)

It is common to find the strongest unions where there is a monopsonistic labour market. In these circumstances we can think of the union monopoly as a counterweight to the

Definition

Natural wastage Where a firm wishing to reduce its workforce does so by not replacing those who leave or retire.

power of a monopsony employer. What will the wage rate be under these circumstances? What will the level of employment be? Unfortunately, economic theory cannot give a precise answer. There is no 'equilibrium' level as such. Ultimately, the wage rate and the level of employment will depend on the relative bargaining strengths and skills of unions and management.

Strange as it may seem, unions may be in a stronger position to make substantial gains for their members when they are facing a powerful employer. There is often considerable scope for them to increase wage rates *without* this leading to a reduction in employment, or even for them to increase both the wage rate *and* employment. Figure 10.10 shows how this can be so.

Assume first that there is no union. The monopsonist will maximise profits by employing Q_1 workers at a wage rate of W_1. (Q_1 is where $MRP_L = MC_L$.)

What happens when a union is introduced into this situation? Wage rates will now result from negotiation between unions and management. Once a wage rate has been agreed, the employer can no longer drive the wage rate down by employing fewer workers. If it tries to pay less than the agreed wage, it may well be faced by a strike, and thus have a zero supply of labour.

Similarly, if the employer decides to take on *more* workers, it will not have to *increase* the wage rate, as long as the negotiated wage is above the free-market wage: as long as the wage rate is above that given by the supply curve S_1.

The effect of this is to give a new supply curve that is horizontal up to the point where it meets the original supply curve. Assume that the union succeeds in negotiating a wage rate of W_2 in Figure 10.10. The supply curve will be horizontal at this level to the left of point x. To the right of this point it will follow the original supply curve S_1, since to acquire

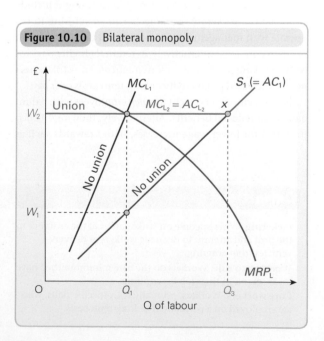

Figure 10.10 Bilateral monopoly

more than Q_3 workers the employer would have to raise the wage rate above W_2.

If the supply curve is horizontal to the left of point x at a level of W_2, so too will be the MC_L curve. The reason is simply that the extra cost to the employer of taking on an extra worker (up to Q_3) is merely the wage rate: no rise has to be given to existing employees. If MC_L is equal to the wage, the profit-maximising level of employment ($MC_L = MRP_L$) will now be where $W = MRP_L$. At a negotiated wage rate of W_2, the firm will therefore choose to employ Q_1 workers.

What this means is that the union can push the wage rate right up from W_1 to W_2 and the firm will still *want* to employ Q_1. In other words, a wage rise can be obtained *without* a reduction in employment.

 If the negotiated wage rate were somewhere between W_1 and W_2, what would happen to employment?

The union could go further still. By threatening industrial action, it may be able to push the wage rate above W_2 and still insist that Q_1 workers are employed (i.e. no redundancies). The firm may be prepared to see profits drop right down to normal level rather than face a strike and risk losses. The absolute upper limit to wages will be that at which the firm is forced to close down.

Collective bargaining

Sometimes when unions and management negotiate, *both* sides can gain from the resulting agreement. For example, the introduction of new technology may allow higher wages, improved working conditions and higher profits. Usually, however, one side's gain is the other's loss. Higher wages mean lower profits.

In collective bargaining, there are various threats or promises that either side can make. Union *threats* might include strike action, **picketing**, **working to rule** or refusing to co-operate with management: for example, in the introduction of new technology. Alternatively, in return for higher wages or better working conditions, unions might *offer* no-strike agreements, increased productivity or long-term deals over pay.

In turn, employers might *threaten* employees with redundancies or reduced benefits. Alternatively, they might *offer*, in return for lower wage increases, better rewards such as productivity bonuses, profit-sharing schemes, more holiday or greater job security.

The outcome of negotiations. The success of a union in achieving its demands depends on its financial strength, the determination of its members and the level of support from the public in general. It also depends on the willingness of the firm to make concessions and on its profitability. Firms earning substantial profits are in a much better position to pay wage increases than firms operating in a highly competitive environment.

The wage settlement may be higher if the union represents only **core workers**. It may be able to secure a higher wage rate at the expense of non-members, who might lose their jobs or be replaced by part-time or temporary workers. The core workers can be seen as **insiders**. Their union(s) can prevent the unemployed – the **outsiders** – from competing wages down.

Industrial action imposes costs on both unions and firms. Union members lose pay. Firms lose revenue. It is usually in both sides' interests, therefore, to settle by negotiation. Nevertheless, to gain the maximum advantage, each side must persuade the other that it will carry out its threats if pushed.

The approach described so far has essentially been one of confrontation. The alternative is for both sides to concentrate on increasing the total net income of the firm by co-operating on ways to increase efficiency or the quality of the product. This approach is more likely when unions and management have built up an atmosphere of trust over time.

 Recall the various strategies that rival oligopolists can adopt. What parallels are there in union and management strategies?

The role of government in collective bargaining

The government can influence the outcome of collective bargaining in a number of ways. One is to try to set an example. It may take a tough line in resisting wage demands by public-sector workers, hoping thereby to persuade employers in the private sector to do likewise.

Additionally, it could set up mechanisms to assist in arbitration or conciliation. For example, in the UK, the Advisory, Conciliation and Arbitration Service (ACAS) is largely funded by the Department of Business, Innovation and Skills (BIS) and conciliates in over 1000 disputes each year.

Definitions

Picketing Where people on strike gather at the entrance to the firm and attempt to dissuade workers or delivery vehicles from entering.

Working to rule Workers do the bare minimum they have to, as set out in their job descriptions.

Core workers Workers, normally with specific skills, who are employed on a permanent or long-term basis.

Insiders Those in employment who can use their privileged position (either as members of unions or because of specific skills) to secure pay rises.

Outsiders Those out of work or employed on a casual, part-time or short-term basis, who have little or no power to influence wages or employment.

Another approach is to use legislation. The government could pass laws that restrict the behaviour of employers or unions; that set a minimum wage rate (see Box 11.2); that prevent discrimination against workers on various grounds. The UK Conservative governments between 1979 and 1997 put considerable emphasis on reducing the power of trade unions and making labour markets more 'flexible'. Several Acts of Parliament were passed. These effectively ended *closed-shop* agreements, made secret ballots mandatory and outlawed political strikes and *secondary action*. It was also made unlawful for employers to deny employment on the grounds that an applicant does not belong to a union, or indeed to penalise them for joining a union.

The effect of these measures was considerably to weaken the power of trade unions in the UK.

The efficiency wage hypothesis

We have seen that a union may be able to force an employer to pay a wage above the market-clearing rate. But it may well be in firms' interests to pay higher wage rates, even in non-unionised sectors.

One explanation for this is the *efficiency wage hypothesis*. This states that the productivity of workers rises as the wage rate rises. As a result, employers may be willing to offer wage rates above the market-clearing level, attempting to balance increased wage costs against gains in productivity. But why might higher wage rates lead to higher productivity? There are three main explanations.

Less 'shirking'

In many jobs it is difficult to monitor the effort individuals put into their work. Workers may thus get away with shirking or careless behaviour. This is an example of the principal–agent problem (see section 9.4 and Box 10.9). The worker, as an agent of the employer (the principal), is not necessarily going to act in the principal's interest.

The business could attempt to reduce shirking by imposing a series of sanctions, the most serious of which would be dismissal. The higher the wage rate, the greater will be the cost to the individual of dismissal, and the less likely it is, therefore, that workers will shirk. The business will benefit not only from the additional output but also from a reduction in the costs of having to monitor workers' performance. As a consequence the *efficiency wage rate* for the business will lie above the market-determined wage rate.

Reduced labour turnover

If workers receive on-the-job training or retraining, then to lose a worker once the training has been completed is a significant cost to the business. Labour turnover, and hence its associated costs, can be reduced by paying a wage above the market-clearing rate. By paying such a wage rate the business is seeking a degree of loyalty from its employees.

Morale

A simple reason for offering wage rates above the market-clearing level is to motivate the workforce – to create the feeling that the firm is a 'good' employer that cares about its employees. As a consequence, workers might be more industrious and more willing to accept the introduction of new technology (with the reorganisation and retraining that it involves).

The paying of efficiency wages above the market-clearing wage will depend upon the type of work involved. Workers who occupy skilled positions, especially where the business has invested time in their training (thus making them costly to replace) are likely to receive efficiency wages considerably above the market wage. By contrast, workers in unskilled positions, where shirking can be easily monitored, where little training takes place and where workers can be easily replaced, are unlikely to command an 'efficiency wage premium'. In such situations, rather than keeping wage rates high, the business will probably try to pay as little as possible.

Other labour market imperfections

The possession of power by unions and/or firms is not the only way in which real-world labour markets diverge from the perfectly competitive model.

- Workers or employers may have imperfect information.
- Wages may respond very slowly to changes in demand and supply, causing disequilibrium in labour markets to persist.
- Firms may not be profit maximisers. Likewise workers may not seek to maximise their 'worker surplus' – the excess of benefits from working (i.e. wages) over the disutility of working (displeasure in doing the job and lost leisure).

Some of the forms and effects of these three imperfections are examined in Case Study 10.3. on the student website.

Definitions

Closed shop Where a firm agrees to employ only union members.

Secondary action Industrial action taken against a company not directly involved in a dispute (e.g. a supplier of raw materials to a firm whose employees are on strike).

Efficiency wage hypothesis The hypothesis that the productivity of workers is affected by the wage rate that they receive.

Efficiency wage rate The profit-maximising wage rate for the firm after taking into account the effects of wage rates on worker motivation, turnover and recruitment.

BOX 10.5 THE RISE AND DECLINE OF THE LABOUR MOVEMENT IN THE UK

Modern trade unionism had its birth with the industrial revolution of the eighteenth and nineteenth centuries. Unions were seen as a means of improving the lot of industrial workers, most of whom suffered low pay and poor working conditions. But, with great hostility from employers, membership grew slowly. By the end of the nineteenth century, only just over 10 per cent of manual workers were in an effective union.

The big change came after the First World War, when returning troops demanded that the sacrifices made should be rewarded. Membership of trade unions increased sharply as workers sought to improve wages and working conditions. By 1920, 45 per cent of the total labour force (8.3 million workers) were in trade unions.

But it was after the Second World War that the trade union movement in the UK really became established as a substantial economic and political force. This can be explained by three crucial trends:

- The growth in the public sector meant that government was itself becoming increasingly responsible for determining wages and conditions of service for many workers.
- In their attempt to control inflation in the 1960s and 1970s, governments sought to impose an 'incomes policy' constraining wage increases. To be successful, this required acceptance by the trade union movement.
- The philosophy of many post-war governments was to govern by consent. Social contracts and discussions between government, employers and unions gave the union movement considerable influence over economic decision making.

Union power grew steadily during the 1950s and 1960s, so much so that attempts were made by successive governments to curb its influence. However, such moves attracted fierce and widespread opposition, and legislation was in many cases abandoned. The trade union movement had become very powerful by the late 1970s with over 13 million members. The number of working days lost because of labour disputes peaked at 29 974 in 1979.

The election of the Conservative government in 1979 ushered in a new wave of trade union reform, eroding and removing many rights and privileges acquired by unions over the years.

Trade union membership stood at just below 6.5 million in 2015, around half of that seen in the late 1970s. This can be explained by a number of factors: the shift to a service-based economy; continued privatisation and the introduction of private-sector management practices, such as local pay bargaining; and contracted-out services in many of the remaining parts of the public sector. More women working and more part-time and casual work, with many people having no guaranteed hours (so-called 'zero-hour contracts'), are also contributory factors, as are the attitudes of many firms to union recognition. In many cases an aggressive management style and a highly competitive environment have made it virtually impossible for unions to gain bargaining rights in the private sector.

Union membership remains high in parts of the public sector, such as education where over 50 per cent of employees were union members in 2015. But even in these areas there is little doubt that their power has declined.

In the light of these changes, many unions have adopted a 'new realism', accepting single-union agreements and supporting flexible working practices and individualised pay packets based on performance (see Box 10.8).

However, not all the unions have lost their power. The British Medical Association is an example of a union

BOX 10.6 HOW USEFUL IS MARGINAL PRODUCTIVITY THEORY?

Reality or the fantasy world of economists?

The marginal productivity theory of income distribution has come in for a lot of criticism. Is this justified?

To start with, marginal productivity theory has been criticised for assuming perfect competition. It doesn't! Rather, it merely states that to maximise profits an employer will employ workers up to the point where the worker's marginal cost equals the extra revenue added by that worker: $MC_L = MRP_L$. This applies equally under perfect competition, monopsony and oligopsony.

What it does say is that, if there is perfect competition, then the worker's wage will equal MRP_L. It certainly does not say that $W = MRP_L$ in other market structures.

A second criticism is that employers do not behave in this 'marginal way', weighing up each additional worker's costs and revenues for the firm. There are three possible reasons for this.

Ignorance of the theory of profit maximisation. The employer may use some rule of thumb, but nevertheless is attempting to maximise profits.

This is a criticism of the theory only if the theory is supposed to describe how employers actually behave. It does not. It merely states that, if firms are attempting to maximise profits, they will in fact be equating MC_L and MRP_L, whether they realise it or not!

A worker's marginal productivity cannot be calculated. When workers are part of a team, it is not usually possible to separate out the contribution to output of each individual. What is the marginal productivity of a cleaner, a porter or even a member of a production line? Similarly, it may not be possible to separate the contribution of workers from that of their tools. A lathe operator is useless without a lathe, as is a lathe without a lathe operator.

This is a more fundamental criticism. Nevertheless it is possible to amend the theory to take this into account. First, an employer can look at the composition of the team, or the partnership of worker and tools, and decide whether any

(although it doesn't choose to use that title) which has protected the pay and power of doctors against a very large employer. For example, it organised and co-ordinated the junior doctor strikes in 2016 in the long-running dispute with the government over contracts.

The RMT Union, which represents workers on London Underground, has been very successful in protecting its members' jobs and securing pay rises. Working closely with two other unions, ASLEF and TSSA, it has achieved above-inflation pay deals, improved working conditions and shorter hours for tube staff. ASLEF and the RMT have also been involved in the

long-running dispute with Southern (Govia Thameslink Railway Ltd) over who was responsible for closing train doors. Critics point out that this has been at the expense of inconvenience to other workers, with regular strikes taking place. However, others would cite it as an example of the benefits of a strong union, protecting its members from monopsony power.

 What factors, other than the ones identified above, could account for the decline in union membership in recent years?

Trade union membership in Great Britain as a percentage of employees

Source: Based on *Trade Union Statistics 2016*, Table 1.2b (BIS and ONS).

reorganisations or alternative production methods will increase the firm's profitability (i.e. increase revenue more than costs). Second, the employer can decide whether to expand or contract the overall size of the team, or the number of workers plus machines. Here the whole team or the worker plus machine is the 'factor of production' whose marginal productivity must be weighed against its costs.

Firms are not always profit maximisers.   This is a criticism only if the theory states that firms are. As long as the theory is merely used to describe what would happen if firms maximised profits, there is no problem.

This criticism, then, is really one of how the theory is used. And even if it is used to predict what will actually happen in the real world, it is still relatively accurate in the large number of cases where firms' behaviour diverges only slightly from profit maximising. It is clearly wrong in other cases.

Moral issues.   A final criticism is the moral one. If economists focus their attention exclusively on how to maximise profits, it might be concluded that they are putting their seal of approval on this sort of behaviour. Of course, economists will respond by saying that they are doing no such thing: they are confining themselves to positive economics. Nevertheless, the criticism has some force. What an economist chooses to study is in part a normative decision.

 Do any of the following contradict marginal productivity theory: (a) wage scales related to length of service (incremental scales); (b) nationally negotiated wage rates; (c) discrimination; (d) firms taking the lead from other firms in determining this year's pay increase?

BOX 10.7 THE PERSISTENT GENDER PAY GAP?

(a) *Average hourly pay, excluding overtime, for full-time UK employees, aged 18 and over, 1970–2016 (£ per hour)*

	1970	1974	1978	1982	1986	1990	1994	1998	2002	2004	2008	2012	2016
Men	0.67	1.05	2.00	3.55	4.82	6.89	8.65	10.65	12.92	13.73	15.53	16.52	17.38
Women	0.42	0.71	1.48	2.62	3.58	5.28	6.88	8.39	10.32	11.21	12.92	14.07	14.96
Women's pay as a % of men's	63.1	67.4	73.9	73.9	74.3	76.6	79.5	78.8	79.9	81.6	83.2	85.2	86.1

Source: Table 1.6a: Annual Survey of Hours and Earnings (National Statistics, 2016).

(b) *Average hourly pay, excluding overtime, for selected occupations, full-time UK employees on adult rates, 2016 (£ per hour)*

Occupation	Men	Women	Women's pay as a % of men's
Bar staff	7.52	7.55	100.4
Social workers	17.81	17.62	98.9
Nurses	17.29	17.01	98.4
Call centre workers	9.45	9.20	97.4
Chefs	9.44	9.12	96.6
Hairdressers, barbers	8.15	7.83	96.1
Police officers (sergeant and below)	18.76	17.97	95.8
Solicitors	26.73	25.53	95.5
Secondary school teachers	23.45	22.04	94.0
Sales and retail assistants	9.58	8.78	91.6
Laboratory technicians	12.57	10.78	85.8
Librarians	16.82	14.16	84.2
Human resource managers/directors	31.08	25.20	81.1
Medical practitioners	36.41	29.02	79.7
Assemblers and routine operatives	12.36	9.55	77.3
Economists and statisticians	32.78	22.31	68.1
Chief executives and senior officials	58.04	39.34	67.8
All occupations	17.38	14.96	86.1
Average *gross weekly* pay (incl. overtime)	691.10	562.10	81.3
Average weekly paid hours (incl. overtime)	40.2	37.6	
Average weekly overtime	1.4	0.5	

Source: Table 14.6a: *Annual Survey of Hours and Earnings* (National Statistics, 2016).

The data in the tables above clearly indicate that there is a gender pay gap – women earn less than men for the same category of work. How much less depends on how earnings are measured. Based on earnings per hour for full-time employees, women on average earned just under 14 per cent less than men in 2016. This wage gap has narrowed gradually over the years, falling from 37 per cent in 1970 to its current levels (see table (a) above). Based on earnings per hour for part-time employees, women on average earned just under 16 per cent less than men in 2016.

A similar picture can be seen throughout the EU.[1] In 2015, women's average hourly pay was 83.7 per cent of men's for the economy as a whole. The gender pay gap varies from one country to another. In Italy and Luxembourg it was only 5.5 per cent, whereas in Estonia it was 26.9 per cent. For full-time workers it varied from −0.4 per cent in Italy to 20.1 per cent in Latvia.

It is important not to confuse the gender pay gap with unequal pay. Unequal pay refers to situations where men and women receive different rates of pay even though they are doing exactly the same job. This is illegal under the 2010 Equality Act. It probably still exists in some workplaces but it is very difficult to tell how significant it is in the economy as a whole.

Unequal pay provides one possible explanation for the gender pay gap but there are also a number of other reasons. For example, the existence of occupational segregation will be a contributing factor. Women are far more likely to be employed in poorly paid occupations. However, there must be other explanations as quite substantial pay gaps persist within particular occupations – see table (b).

1. *If we were to look at weekly rather than hourly pay and included the effects of overtime, what do you think would happen to the pay differentials in table (a)?*
2. *In table (b), which of the occupations have a largely female workforce?*

Discrimination

Discrimination can be another major factor in determining wages. It can take many forms: it can be by race, gender, sexual orientation, age, class, religion, etc.; it can occur in many different aspects of society. This section is concerned with *economic discrimination*, where workers of identical ability receive different pay for doing the same job, or are given different chances of employment or promotion.

So why has the pay gap persisted? There are a number of possible reasons:

- The marginal productivity of labour in typically female occupations may be lower than in typically male occupations. This may in part be due to simple questions of physical strength. Very often, however, it is due to the fact that women tend to work in more labour-intensive occupations. If there is less capital equipment per female worker than there is per male worker, then it would be expected that the marginal product of a woman would be less than that of a man. Evidence from the EU as a whole suggests that occupational segregation is a significant factor in explaining pay differences.

- Many women take career breaks to have children. For this reason, employers are sometimes more willing to invest money in training men (thereby increasing their marginal productivity) and more willing to promote men. A study by the Institute for Fiscal Studies (IFS)[2] estimated that for every year a woman takes away from work her earnings fall by 2 per cent below those who remain in work.

- Women tend to be less geographically mobile. If social norms are such that the man's job is seen as somehow more 'important' than the woman's, then a couple will often move for the man to get promotion. The woman, however, will have to settle for whatever job she can get in the same locality as her partner.

- A smaller proportion of women workers are members of unions than men. Even when they are members of unions, these are often in jobs where unions are weak (e.g. clothing industry workers and shop assistants).

- Part-time workers (mainly women) have less bargaining power, less influence and less chance of obtaining promotion. The IFS study found that when women switch from full-time to part-time work their hourly wage does not fall immediately. However, over time their growth in earnings falls behind those of people working full-time.

- Custom and practice. Many jobs done wholly or mainly by women continue to be low-paid, irrespective of productivity.

Why has the gender pay gap narrowed in the past 20 years? The IFS research suggests that the main reason is the increasing proportion of women who are now educated to 'A' level and degree standard. However, the same study also found that the gender wage gap for the highly educated has not really changed over the same period. The difference in pay between male and female graduates is approximately the same is it was in the late 1990s.

One reason for this is the possibility that in many jobs women are discriminated against when it comes to promotion, especially to senior positions. This is sometimes referred to as *people*

appointing in their own image: i.e. men favouring male applicants.

The government established the Davies review in 2010[3] to examine the under-representation of women on the boards of FTSE 100 and 350 companies. In 2011, only 12.5 per cent of FTSE 100 board members were female. The first Davies report recommended a number of initiatives for businesses to improve this situation and set a target of 25 per cent by 2015. This figure was met (26.1 per cent in 2015) and Lord Davies set a new target of 33 per cent by 2020.

The government has also introduced a number of other initiatives to try to close the gender pay gap including:

- Shared parental leave. This was introduced in April 2015 and enables parents to share up to 50 weeks of leave, of which 37 is paid. At present, the take-up of the scheme has been low – approximately 5 per cent.

- Requirement on larger firms to publish pay data. Companies employing more than 250 people will have to publish information about their employee pay as it was on 5 April 2017. The information must include the mean gender gap for basic pay as well as bonuses. It also has to include the proportion of men and women in each quarter of the pay structure. Firms have until April 2018 to produce the data or they will be contacted by the Equalities and Human Rights Commission.

- Women in Finance Charter. This is a pledge for greater balance in the financial services. In March 2017, HM Treasury announced that 122 firms had signed the Women in Finance Charter.

It will be interesting to see what impact these policies have on the gender pay gap in the future.

3. *If employers were forced to give genuinely equal pay for equal work, how would this affect the employment of women and men? What would determine the magnitude of these effects?*
4. *How could family policy ensure that parents are able to work, while reducing pay differentials?*
5. *What measures could a government introduce to increase the number of women getting higher-paid jobs?*

1 *Gender Pay Gap Statistics* (Eurostat, March 2017).
2 *The Gender Wage Gap* (Institute for Fiscal Studies, August 2016).
3 *Improving the Gender Balance on British Boards, Davies Review Five Year Summary* (October 2015).

Take the case of racial discrimination by employers. Figure 10.11 illustrates the wages and employment of black and white workers by a firm with monopsony power which practises racial discrimination against black workers. Let us assume that there is no difference in the productivity of black and white workers. Let us also assume for simplicity that there is an equal number of black workers and white workers available at any given wage rate. Finally, let us assume that there are no laws to prevent the firm discriminating in terms of either wages or employment.

BOX 10.8 FLEXIBLE LABOUR MARKETS AND THE FLEXIBLE FIRM

New work practices for old?

The past 35 years have seen sweeping changes in the ways that firms organise their workforces. Global recessions combined with rapid changes in technology led many firms to question the wisdom of appointing workers on a permanent basis to specific jobs. Instead, they want the flexibility to respond to changing situations. If demand falls, they want to be able to reduce labour without facing large redundancy costs. If demand rises, they want rapid access to additional labour. If technology changes they want to have the flexibility to move workers around, or to take on new workers in some areas and lose workers in others.

What many firms seek, therefore, is flexibility in employing and allocating labour. What countries are experiencing is an increasingly flexible labour market, as workers and employment agencies respond to the new 'flexible firm'.

There are three main types of flexibility in the use of labour:

- *Functional flexibility*. This is where an employer is able to transfer labour between different tasks within the production process. It contrasts with traditional forms of organisation where people were employed to do a specific job, and then stuck to it. A functionally flexible labour force will tend to be multi-skilled and relatively highly trained.
- *Numerical flexibility*. This is where the firm is able to adjust the size and composition of its workforce according to changing market conditions. To achieve this, the firm is likely to employ a proportion of its labour on a part-time or casual basis, or even subcontract specialist requirements. An increasingly common practice is for workers to be on 'zero-hour contracts', where the employee has no guaranteed hours at all and where actual hours may vary on a weekly basis.
- *Financial flexibility*. This is where the firm has flexibility in its wage costs. In large part it is a result of functional and numerical flexibility. Financial flexibility can be achieved by rewarding individual effort and productivity rather than paying a given rate for a particular job. Such rates of pay are increasingly negotiated at the local level rather than being nationally set. The result is not only a

widening of pay differentials between skilled and unskilled workers, but also growing differentials in pay between workers within the same industry but in different parts of the country.

The diagram shows how these three forms of flexibility are reflected in the organisation of a *flexible firm*, an organisation quite different from that of the traditional firm. The most significant difference is that the labour force is segmented. The core group, drawn from the *primary labour market*, will be composed of functionally flexible workers, who are generally on secure full-time permanent contracts. Such workers will be relatively well paid and receive wages reflecting their scarce skills.

The periphery, drawn from the *secondary labour market*, is more fragmented than the core, and can be subdivided into a first and a second peripheral group. The first peripheral group is composed of workers with a lower level of skill than

The flexible firm

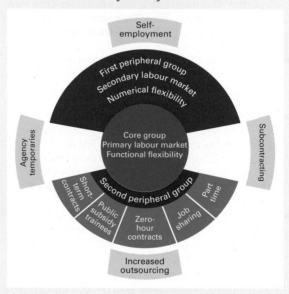

Definitions

Functional flexibility Where employers can switch workers from job to job as requirements change.

Numerical flexibility Where employers can change the size of their workforce as their labour requirements change.

Financial flexibility Where employers can vary their wage costs by changing the composition of their workforce or the terms on which workers are employed.

Flexible firm A firm that has the flexibility to respond to changing market conditions by changing the composition of its workforce.

Primary labour market The market for permanent full-time core workers.

Secondary labour market The market for peripheral workers, usually employed on a temporary or part-time basis, or a less secure 'permanent' basis.

those in the core, skills that tend to be general rather than firm-specific. Thus workers in this group can be drawn from the external labour market, often through agencies. Such workers may be employed on full-time contracts, but they will generally face less secure employment than those workers in the core.

The business gains a greater level of numerical flexibility by drawing labour from the second peripheral group. Here workers are employed on a variety of short-term, part-time contracts, often again through agencies. Some of these workers may be working from home, or online from another country, such as India, where wage rates are much lower. Workers in this group have little job security.

As well as supplementing labour in the first peripheral group, the second periphery can also provide high-level specialist skills. In this instance the business can subcontract or hire self-employed labour, minimising its commitment to such workers. The business thereby gains both functional and numerical flexibility simultaneously.

The Japanese model

The application of new flexible working patterns is becoming more prevalent in businesses in the UK and elsewhere in Europe and North America. In Japan, flexibility has been part of the business way of life for many years and was crucial in shaping the country's economic success in the 1970s and 1980s. In fact, we now talk of a Japanese model of business organisation, which many of its competitors seek to emulate.

The model is based around four principles:

- *Total quality management (TQM).* This involves all employees working towards continuously improving all aspects of quality, both of the finished product and of methods of production.
- *Elimination of waste.* According to the 'just-in-time' (JIT) principle, businesses should take delivery of just sufficient quantities of raw materials and parts, at the right time and place. Stocks are kept to a minimum and hence the whole system of production runs with little, if any, slack. For example, supermarkets today have much smaller storerooms relative to the total shopping area than they did in the past, and take more frequent deliveries.

- *A belief in the superiority of team work.* Collective effort is a vital element in Japanese working practices. Team work is seen not only to enhance individual performance, but also to involve the individual in the running of the business and thus to create a sense of commitment.
- *Functional and numerical flexibility.* Both are seen as vital components in maintaining high levels of productivity.

The principles of this model are now widely accepted as being important in creating and maintaining a competitive business in a competitive marketplace.

Recent UK experience

Within the EU, prior to the recession of 2008–9, the UK was one of the most successful countries in cutting unemployment and creating jobs. Much of this has been attributed to increased labour market flexibility.

One of the puzzles of the downturn that took place from 2008 is how 'little' unemployment occurred in the UK. Of course, if you were one of the 1.6 million people unemployed in 2017, then the use of this term may stick in your throat. However, it remains a fact that, relative to output, fewer people were out of work than economic models predicted. One argument is that this happened because of the flexibility of reducing hours per worker or pay per hour rather than laying workers off. As a result, other EU member states, such as Italy and Germany, have sought to emulate many of the measures the UK has adopted.

1. *Is a flexible firm more likely or less likely to employ workers up to the point where their $MRP = MC_L$?*
2. *Would you expect the advent of flexible firms to alter the gender balance of employment and unemployment?*
3. *If a firm is trying to achieve flexibility in its use of labour, do you think this would be harder or easier in a period of recession? Explain why.*
4. *Assume workers in a firm are allowed to choose between a 20 per cent reduction in pay or 20 per cent of the workforce being laid off. What factors would influence the workers' choice?*

Figure 10.11(a) shows the *MC* and *MRP* curves for black workers. If there were no discrimination, employment of black workers would be at Q_{B_1}, where $MRP_B = MC_B$. The wage rate paid to black workers would be W_{B_1}.

Definition

Economic discrimination Where workers of identical *ability* are paid different wages or are otherwise discriminated against because of race, age, sex, etc.

Figure 10.11(b) shows the position for white workers. Again, if there were no discrimination, Q_{W_1} white workers would be employed at a wage of W_{W_1}: the same wage as that of black workers. (Note that in each case the *MRP* curve is drawn on the assumption that the number of workers employed from the other ethnic group is constant.)

If the firm now discriminates against black workers, it will employ workers along a lower curve, $MRP_B - x$ (where x can be seen as the discriminatory factor). Employment of black workers will thus be at the lower level of Q_{B_2} and the wage they receive will be at the lower level of W_{B_2}.

BOX 10.9 **BEHAVIOUR AT WORK**

EXPLORING
ECONOMICS

What motivates employees?

Much of the work of behavioural economists concentrates on the rationality assumption used in theories of consumer behaviour. Do these models accurately predict consumer behaviour? Do consumers sometimes behave in a manner which is systematically at odds with the rationality assumption: i.e. by including sunk costs and getting excited by special offers? These are all interesting questions. Yet most of us spend as much as 25 per cent of our lives as workers and so our behaviour in the labour market also merits attention.

Dan Ariely, Professor of Psychology and Behavioural Economics at Duke University, is one of the best-known researchers on the subject. In his second book, *The Upside of Irrationality*,[1] he looks at our behaviour at work and identifies a number of areas where some experimental findings appear to contradict the predictions of economic theory.

We care about what we produce

One area that Ariely looked at was how we feel both about what we produce, and about what happens to it. Economic theory suggests workers will be motivated by the rewards they receive for their work and the associated costs. It doesn't ascribe emotions to the outcome of our labour.

Ariely set up an experiment where participants built Lego models; they were paid for each model – at a diminishing rate – and could choose how many to build. There were two sets of participants. Each knew that the models would eventually be disassembled, but for the first set this happened out of their sight after they had finished building. The second set saw the models broken up in front of them, almost immediately.

How did the 'workers' react to these different circumstances? Those who saw their models remain in a valuable state built an average of more than ten models each, and 68 per cent of them continued to produce when the price of their labour fell below a dollar. In contrast, those whose models were destroyed in front of them built an average of just over seven models and only 20 per cent were prepared to work for less than a dollar per model. Ariely concludes from this and other experiments that we are more productive when our labour has meaning; when the outputs are valued.

Bonuses and incentives

There has been a great deal of discussion about bankers' bonuses in the past few years; hardly surprising given the number of banks that taxpayers around the world have bailed out. The response from financial institutions has been predictable: if they are to retain their best staff and get them to perform in the best possible way, they have to offer large bonuses.

It may be true that bonuses are an important part of recruitment and retention, but is it true that they increase productivity? Ariely and his colleagues tested this in a series of experiments, offering participants a variety of bonuses to reward achievement in a series of tasks. By doing this in India, where average incomes are very low, they were able to offer bonuses ranging from a day's wage through to the equivalent of five months' earnings.

Their findings were striking; those offered low and medium bonuses performed at about the same level, with a 'very good' performance on the tasks set around 30 per cent of the time. What about those who stood to gain more? Surely very large bonuses would concentrate the mind (and body, for some of the tasks were physical) and induce better performance? Well large bonuses certainly did have a noticeable effect and the results were striking. Those who could get up to five months' pay achieved a 'very good' performance less than 10 per cent of the time!

What happened? It seems that very large bonuses can lead to considerably worse performance. The pressure and the fear of not achieving the bonus combine to give a level of stress that diminishes performance, rather than enhances it.

Dan Ariely's experiment suggests that large bonuses are counter-productive. But do bonuses work at all? A research project led by Roland Fryer at Harvard University suggests not. In a study of a pay-for-performance programme in more than 200 schools in New York City, he looked at the impact of providing incentives to teachers. He found that offering bonuses to staff did not increase student achievement; furthermore there was no impact on teacher absences or on staff retention. So, in the real world, as in the laboratory, it seems that incentivising staff may not be a simple matter of offering cash, despite what the banks claim.

Lessons for employers

Academics believe that studying behaviour is inherently valuable and, of course, writers like Dan Ariely can also excite the attention and interest of a wider audience. Yet there is also an opportunity for employers to make use of these findings. Staff surveys often highlight concern about quality of outputs, in-house communications and the need to feel part of decision making. If firms are able to gain a better understanding of workers' motivation and to set rewards and incentives that account for this, the outcome may be higher productivity and a happier workforce.

1. *Dan Ariely suggests that bonuses should be based on an average of the previous five years' performance. Explain why this might lead to better performance than a simple annual bonus.*
2. *In Chapter 6, we identified specialisation and division of labour as a source of economies of scale. How might this principle be altered if we care about the finished product of our labour?*

1 Dan Ariely, *The Upside of Irrationality* (Harper Collins 2010).

How will discrimination against black workers affect wages and employment of white workers? Let us consider two cases.

In the first case, assume that the employer practises economic discrimination purely in the negative sense: i.e. it discriminates against black workers but employs white

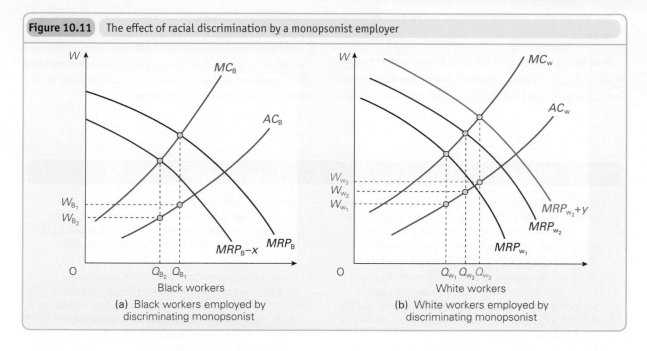

Figure 10.11 The effect of racial discrimination by a monopsonist employer

(a) Black workers employed by discriminating monopsonist

(b) White workers employed by discriminating monopsonist

workers on profit-maximising principles. Thus white workers would be employed up to that point where their MC equals their MRP. But the fact that fewer black workers are now being employed will mean that for any given quantity of white workers there will be fewer workers employed in total, and therefore the MRP of white workers will have increased. In Figure 9.11(b), the white workers' MRP curve has shifted to MRR_{W_2}. This has the effect of raising employment of white workers to Q_{W_2} and the wage rate to W_{W_2}.

Firms may, however, also practise economic discrimination *in favour* of certain groups. Figure 10.11(b) also illustrates this second case, where the employer practises economic discrimination in favour of white workers. Here the firm will employ workers along a higher curve, $MRR_{W_2} + y$, where y is the discriminatory factor. The effect is further to increase the wage rate and level of employment of white workers, to W_{W_3} and Q_{W_3} respectively.

 What effect will the discrimination by the firm have on the wages and employment of black workers in other firms in the area if (a) these other firms discriminate against black workers; (b) they do not discriminate?

If the government now legislates for equal pay for equal work, then employers that discriminate will respond by further cutting back on black workers. The answer to *this* problem would seem to be for the government to pass laws that insist not only that black workers be paid the same as white workers for doing the same job, but also that they be treated equally when applying for jobs.

The type of discrimination considered so far can be seen as 'irrational' if the firm wants to maximise profits. After all, to produce a given amount of output, it would be paying out more in wages to employ white workers than black workers.

In a competitive market environment, such firms may be forced to end discrimination simply to survive the competition from non-discriminating rivals. It, however, the firm has market power, it will probably be making sufficient profits to allow it to continue discriminating. The main pressure to end discrimination is then likely to come from unions, customers, shareholders or race relations organisations.

Other examples of non-economic discrimination stem from unequal educational opportunities. If the educational system discriminates against black children, they are likely to end up with poorer qualifications. They have less *human capital* invested in them. Under these circumstances, employers, preferring to employ the best-qualified applicants, are likely to choose white people. This is particularly so in the more highly paid jobs that require a higher level of educational attainment. Tackling this problem at source means tackling weaknesses early on in the education system and breaking what has come to be known as the cycle of deprivation.

Who are the poor? Who are the rich?

To the list we made at the end of section 10.1 we can now add the following factors that will tend to make people poor:

- Lack of economic power, not belonging to a union or belonging to a union with only weak bargaining power.
- Ignorance of better job opportunities.
- Lack of will or ability to search for a better job.

Definition

Human capital The qualifications, skills and expertise that contribute to a worker's productivity.

- Discrimination against them by employers or fellow workers.

Thus before the advent of the minimum wage many people of Asian origin, especially women, working in the garment industry in back-street 'sweatshops' earned pitifully low wages.

Conversely, belonging to a powerful union, working for a profitable employer which nevertheless is not a ruthless profit maximiser, being aware of new job opportunities and having the 'get up and go' to apply for better jobs, and being white, male and middle-class are all factors that help to contribute to people earning high wages.

Section summary

1. If a firm is a monopsony employer, it will employ workers to the point where $MRP_L = MC_L$. Since the wage is below MC_L, the monopsonist, other things being equal, will employ fewer workers at a lower wage than would be employed in a perfectly competitive labour market.

2. If a union has monopoly power, its power to raise wage rates will be limited if the employer operates under perfect or monopolistic competition in the goods market. A rise in wage rates will force the employer to cut back on employment.

3. In a situation of bilateral monopoly (where a monopoly union faces a monopsony employer), the union may have considerable scope to raise the wage rate above the monopsony level, without the employer wishing to reduce the level of employment. There is no unique equilibrium wage. The wage will depend on the outcome of a process of collective bargaining between union and management.

4. Each side can make various threats or promises. The outcome of the bargaining will depend on the relative power, attitudes and bargaining skills of both sides, the firm's profitability and the information each side has about the other. The outcome also depends on the legal framework within which the negotiations take place.

5. Power is not the only factor that makes actual wage determination different from the perfectly competitive model. Firms and workers may have imperfect knowledge of the labour market; disequilibrium in labour markets may persist; firms may not be profit maximisers (see Case Study 10.3 on the student website).

6. Firms may exercise discrimination (by race, sex, age, etc.) in their employment policy. By discriminating against a particular group, an employer with market power can drive down the wages of the members of that group. Unless firms are forced not to discriminate, equal pay legislation may well lead to a reduction in the employment of members of groups that are discriminated against.

10.3 CAPITAL AND PROFIT

The non-human factors of production

In the final two sections of the chapter, we consider the market for *other* factors of production. These can be divided into two broad groups.

Land. This includes all those productive resources supplied by nature: in other words, not only land itself, but also all natural resources. (We examine land in section 10.4.)

Capital. This includes all manufactured products that are used to produce goods and services. Thus capital includes such diverse items as a blast furnace, a bus, a computer, a factory building and a screwdriver.

The capital goods described above are physical assets and are known as *physical* capital. The word 'capital' is also used to refer to various *paper* assets, such as shares and bonds. These are the means by which firms raise finance to purchase physical capital, and are known as *financial* capital. Being merely paper assets, however, they do not count as factors of production. Nevertheless, financial markets have an important role in determining the level of investment in physical capital, and we shall be examining these markets on pages 307–9.

Factor prices versus the price of factor services

A feature of most non-human factors is that they last a period of time. A machine may last 10 years; an oil well may last 50 years before it is exhausted; farmland will last forever if properly looked after. We must therefore distinguish between the income the owner will get from *selling* the factor and that which the owner will get from *using* it or *hiring* it out.

- The income from selling the factor is the factor's *price*. Thus a machine might sell for £20 000, or a hectare of farming land for £15 000.
- The income gained from using a factor is its *return,* and the income gained from hiring a factor out is its *rental*. This income represents the value or price of the factor's *services*, expressed per period of time. Thus a machine

might earn a firm £1000 per year. A hectare of land might earn a landowner £600 rent per year.

Obviously, the price of a factor will be linked to the value of its services. The price that a hectare of land will fetch if sold will depend on the return or rent that can be earned on that land. If it is highly productive farmland, it will sell for a higher price than a piece of scrubby moorland.

 When we were looking at wage rates, were we talking about the price of labour or the price of labour services? Is this distinction between the price of a factor and the price of factor services a useful one in the case of labour? Was it in Roman times?

The profit-maximising employment of land and capital

 On the demand side, the same rules apply for land and capital as for labour, if a firm wishes to maximise profits. Namely, it should demand factors up to the point where the marginal cost of the factor equals its marginal revenue product: $MC_f = MRP_f$. This same rule applies whether the firm is buying the factor outright, or merely renting it.

Figure 10.12 illustrates the two cases of perfect competition and monopsony. In both cases the *MRP* curve slopes downwards. This is another illustration of the law of diminishing returns, but this time applied to land or capital. For example, if a farmer increases the amount of land farmed while *holding other factors constant,* diminishing returns to land will occur. If the same number of farm workers and the same amount of agricultural machinery and fertilisers are used but on a larger area, then returns per hectare will fall.

In Figure 10.12(a) the firm is a price taker. The factor price is given at P_{f_1}. Profits are maximised at Q_{f_1} where $MRP_f = P_f$ (since $P_f = MC_f$).

In Figure 10.12(b) the firm has monopsony power. The factor price will vary, therefore, with the amount that the firm uses. The firm will again use factors to the point where $MRP_f = MC_f$. In this case, it will mean using Q_{f_2} at a price of P_{f_2}.

What is the difference between buying a factor and renting it? Although the $MRP_f = MC_f$ rule remains the same, there are differences. As far as buying the factors is concerned, the MC_f is the extra outlay for the firm in *purchasing* one more unit of the factor; and the MRP_f is all the revenue produced by that factor over its *whole life* (but measured in terms of what this is worth when purchased: see pages 304–6). In the case of renting, MC_f is the extra outlay for the firm in rent *per period,* while MRP_f is the extra revenue earned from it *per period.*

The demand for capital services

What we are talking about in this section is the hiring of capital equipment for a period of time (as opposed to buying it outright). The analysis is virtually identical to that of the demand for labour. As with labour, we can distinguish between an individual firm's demand and the whole market demand.

Individual firm's demand

Take the case of a small painting and decorating firm thinking of hiring some scaffolding in order to complete a job. It could use ladders, which it already owns, but the job would take longer to complete. If it hires the scaffolding for one day, it can perhaps shorten the job by, say, two or three days. If it hires it for a second day, it can perhaps save another one or two days. Hiring it for additional days may save extra still. But diminishing returns are occurring: the longer the scaffolding is up, the less intensively it will be

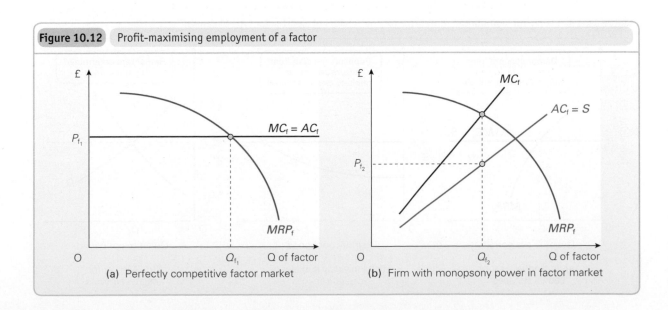

Figure 10.12 Profit-maximising employment of a factor

(a) Perfectly competitive factor market

(b) Firm with monopsony power in factor market

used, and the less additional time it will save. Perhaps for some of the time it will be used when ladders could have been used equally easily.

The time saved allows the firm to take on extra work. Thus each extra day the scaffolding is hired gives the firm extra revenue. This is the scaffolding's marginal revenue product of capital (MRP_K). Diminishing returns mean that it has the normal downward-sloping shape (see Figure 10.12).

Market demand

The market demand for capital services is derived in exactly the same way as the market demand for labour (see Figure 10.6 on page 285). It is the horizontal sum of the MRP_K curves of the individual firms, corrected for the fact that increased use of capital will increase output, drive down the price of the good and hence reduce MRP. This means that the market demand curve for capital is steeper than the horizontal sum of the demand curves (MRP_K) of all the firms in the market.

 Under what circumstances would the market demand for renting a type of capital equipment be (a) elastic; (b) inelastic? (Clue: turn back to page 285 and see what determines the elasticity of demand for labour.)

The supply of capital services

It is necessary to distinguish (a) the supply *to* a single firm, (b) the supply *by* a single firm and (c) the market supply.

Supply to a single firm

This is illustrated in Figure 10.13(a). The small firm renting capital equipment is probably a price taker. If so, it faces a horizontal supply curve at the going rental rate (R_e). If, however, it has monopsony power, it will face an upward-sloping supply curve as in Figure 10.12(b).

Supply by a single firm

This is illustrated in Figure 10.13(b). On the demand side, the firm is likely to be a price taker. It has to accept the going rental rate (R_e) established in the market. If it tries to charge more, then customers are likely to turn to rival suppliers.

But what will the individual supplier's *supply* curve look like? The theory here has a lot in common with perfect competition in the goods market (see pages 193–5): the supply curve is the firm's MC curve, only here the MC is the extra cost of supplying one more unit of capital equipment for rent over a given time period.

The problem with working out the marginal cost of renting out capital equipment is that the equipment probably cost a lot to buy in the first place, but lasts a long time. How then are these large costs to be apportioned to each new rental? The answer is that it depends on the time period under consideration.

The short run. In the short run, the hire company is not buying any new equipment: it is simply hiring out its existing stock of equipment. In the case of the scaffolding hire firm, the marginal costs of doing this will be as follows:

■ Depreciation. Scaffolding has second-hand value. Each time the scaffolding is hired out it deteriorates, and thus its second-hand value falls. This loss in value is called 'depreciation'.

■ Maintenance and handling. Hiring out equipment involves labour time (e.g. in the office) and possibly transport costs; the equipment may need servicing after being hired out.

These marginal costs are likely to rise relatively slowly. For each extra day a piece of equipment is hired out, the company will incur the same or only slightly higher additional costs. This gives a relatively flat supply curve of capital services in Figure 10.13(b) up to the hire company's maximum

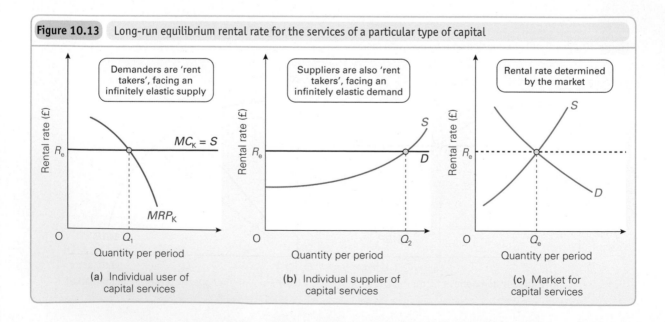

Figure 10.13 Long-run equilibrium rental rate for the services of a particular type of capital

(a) Individual user of capital services

(b) Individual supplier of capital services

(c) Market for capital services

capacity. Once the scaffolding firm is hiring out all its scaffolding, the supply curve becomes vertical.

 Assume now that the firm has monopoly power in hiring out equipment, and thus faces a downward-sloping demand curve. Draw in two such demand curves on a diagram like Figure 10.13(b), one crossing the MC curve in the horizontal section, and one in the vertical section. How much will the firm supply in each case and at what price? (You will need to draw in MR curves too.) Is the MC curve still the supply curve?

The long run. In the long run, the hire company will consider purchasing additional equipment. It can therefore supply as much as it likes in the long run. The supply curve will be relatively elastic, or if it is a price taker itself (i.e. if the scaffolding firm simply buys scaffolding at the market price), the supply curve will be horizontal. This long-run supply curve will be vertically higher than the short-run curve, since the long-run *MC* includes the cost of purchasing each additional piece of equipment.

Maths Case 10.1 on the student website shows how this marginal cost can be calculated.

Market supply

This is illustrated in Figure 10.13(c). The market supply curve of a particular type of capital service is the sum of the quantities supplied by all the individual firms.

In the short run, the market supply will be relatively inelastic, given that it takes time to manufacture new equipment and that stocks of equipment currently held by manufacturers are likely to be relatively small. Also, capital is *heterogeneous*: i.e. one piece of capital equipment is not the same as another. If there is a shortage of scaffolding, you cannot use a cement mixer instead: people would fall off! Finally, hire companies may be unwilling to purchase (expensive) new equipment immediately there is a rise in demand: after all, the upsurge in demand may turn out to be short-lived.

 If supply is totally inelastic, what determines the rental value of capital equipment in the short run?

In the *long run*, the supply curve of capital services will be more elastic because extra capital equipment can be produced. It will not be horizontal, however, but upward sloping. Its elasticity will depend on the elasticity of supply of capital equipment to the hire companies.

Determination of the price of capital services

As Figure 10.13(c) shows, in a perfect market the market rental rate for capital services will be determined by the interaction of market demand and supply. Note that the analysis here parallels that of the determination of the equilibrium wage in a given labour market (see Figure 10.1 on page 278).

 What will happen to the demand for capital services and the equilibrium rental if the price of some other factor, say labour, changes? Assume that wage rates fall. Trace through the effects on a three-section diagram like Figure 10.13. (Clue: a fall in wages will reduce costs and hence the price of the product, so that more will be sold; and it will make labour cheaper relative to capital.)

BOX 10.10 STOCKS AND FLOWS — EXPLORING ECONOMICS

The discussion of the rewards to capital and land leads to a very important distinction: that between stocks and flows.

A stock is a quantity of something held. A landowner may own 200 hectares. A farmer may have a barn with 500 tonnes of grain. You may have £1000 in a savings account. These are all stocks: they are all quantities held at a given point in time.

A flow is an increase or decrease in quantity over a specified period. The landowner may buy another 10 hectares during the year. The farmer may use 10 tonnes of grain from the barn each week as animal feed. You may save £10 per month.

Wages, rent and interest are all rewards to flows. Wages are the amount paid for the services of a person's labour for a week or month. Rent is the amount paid per period of time to use the services of land. Likewise, interest is the reward paid to people per year for the use of their money.

If an asset is sold, its value is the value of the stock. It is a simple payment at a single point in time for the transfer of a whole asset. Thus the price of land and the price of capital are stock concepts.

An important example of stocks and flows arises with capital and investment. If a firm has 100 machines, that is a stock of capital. It may choose to build up its stock by investing. Investment is a flow concept. The firm may choose to invest in 10 new machines each year. This may not add 10 to the stock of machines, however, as some may be wearing out (a negative flow).

KEY IDEA 26 *Stocks and flows.* A stock is a quantity of something at a given point in time. A flow is an increase or decrease in something over a specified period of time. This is an important distinction and a common cause of confusion.

 Which of the following are stocks and which are flows?
(a) Unemployment.
(b) Redundancies.
(c) Profits.
(d) A firm's stock market valuation.
(e) The value of property after a period of inflation.

If there is monopsony power on the part of the users of hired capital, this will have the effect of depressing the rental rate below the MRP_K (see Figure 10.12(b)). If, on the other hand, there is monopoly power on the part of hire companies, the analysis is similar to that of monopoly in the goods market (see Figure 7.8 on page 205). The firm, by reducing the supply of capital for hire, can drive up the rental rate. It will maximise profit where the marginal revenue from hiring out the equipment is equal to the marginal cost of so doing: at a rental rate (price) *above* the marginal cost.

*Demand for and supply of capital for purchase

The alternative to hiring capital is to buy it outright. This section examines the demand and supply of capital for purchase.

The demand for capital: investment

How many computers will an engineering firm want to buy? Should a steelworks install another blast furnace? Should a removal firm buy another furniture lorry? These are all **investment** decisions. Investment involves purchasing of additional capital.

The demand for capital, or 'investment demand', by a profit-maximising firm is based on exactly the same principles as the demand for labour or the demand for capital services. The firm must weigh up the marginal revenue product of that investment (i.e. the money it will earn for the firm) against its marginal cost.

The problem is that capital is durable. It goes on producing goods, and hence yielding revenue for the firm, for a considerable period of time. Calculating these benefits therefore involves taking account of their timing.

There are two ways of approaching the problem: the *present value* approach and the *rate of return* approach. In both cases, the firm is comparing the marginal benefits with the marginal costs of the investment.

Present value approach.   To work out the benefit of an investment (its *MRP*), the firm must estimate all the future earnings it will bring and then convert them to a **present value**. It can then compare this with the cost of the investment. Let us take a simple example.

Assume that a firm is considering buying a machine. It will produce £1000 per year (net of operating costs) for four years and then wear out and sell for £1000 as scrap. What is the

benefit of this machine to the firm? At first sight the answer would seem to be £5000. This, after all, is the total income earned from the machine. Unfortunately, it is not as simple as this. The reason is that money earned in the future is less beneficial to the firm than having the same amount of money today: if the firm has the money today, it can earn interest on it by putting it in the bank or reinvesting it in some other project.

To illustrate this, assume that you have £100 today and can earn 10 per cent interest by putting it in a bank. In one year's time that £100 will have grown to £110, in two years' time to £121, in three years' time to £133.10 and so on. This process is known as *compounding*.

The principle of discounting. People generally prefer to have benefits today rather than in the future. Thus future benefits have to be reduced (discounted) to give them a present value.

It follows that if someone offered to give you £121 in two years' time, that would be no better than giving you £100 today, since, with interest, £100 would grow to £121 in two years. What we say, then, is that, with a 10 per cent interest rate, £121 in two years' time has a *present value* of £100.

The procedure of reducing future value back to a present value is known as *discounting*.

When we do discounting, the rate we use is called the *rate of discount*: in this case, 10 per cent. The formula for discounting is as follows:

$$PV = \sum \frac{R_t}{(1 + r)^t}$$

where PV is the present value, R_t is the revenue from the investment in year t, r is the rate of discount (expressed as a decimal: e.g. 10% = 0.1) and $\sum$ is the sum of each of the years' discounted earnings.

So what is the present value of the investment in the machine that produced £1000 for four years and then is sold as scrap for £1000 at the end of the four years? According to the formula it is:

$$\begin{array}{cccc} \text{Year 1} & \text{Year 2} & \text{Year 3} & \text{Year 4} \\ = \dfrac{£1000}{1.1} + & \dfrac{£1000}{(1.1)^2} + & \dfrac{£1000}{(1.1)^3} + & \dfrac{£2000}{(1.1)^4} \end{array}$$

$= £909 + £829 + £751 + £1366$

$= £3852$

Definitions

Investment The purchase by the firm of equipment or materials that will add to its stock of capital.

Present value approach to appraising investment This involves estimating the value *now* of a flow of future benefits (or costs).

Compounding The process of adding interest each year to an initial capital sum.

Discounting The process of reducing the value of future flows to give them a present valuation.

Rate of discount The rate that is used to reduce future values to present values.

Thus the present value of the investment (i.e. its *MRP*) is £3852, *not* £5000 as it might seem at first sight. In other words, if the firm had £3852 today and deposited it in a bank at a 10 per cent interest rate, the firm would earn exactly the same as it would by investing in the machine.

So is the investment worthwhile? It is now simply a question of comparing the £3852 benefit with the cost of buying the machine. If the machine costs less than £3852, it will be worth buying. If it costs more, the firm would be better off keeping its money in the bank.

The difference between the present value of the benefits (PV_b) of the investment and its cost (C) is known as the ***net present value*** (*NPV*).

$$NPV = PV_b - C$$

If the *NPV* is positive, the investment is worthwhile.

> *What is the present value of a machine that lasts three years, earns £100 in year 1, £200 in year 2 and £200 in year 3, and then has a scrap value of £100? Assume that the rate of discount is 5 per cent. If the machine costs £500, is the investment worthwhile? Would it be worthwhile if the rate of discount were 10 per cent?*

Rate of return approach. The alternative approach when estimating whether an investment is worthwhile is to calculate the investment's *rate of return*. This rate of return is known as the firm's ***marginal efficiency of capital*** (*MEC*) or ***internal rate of return*** (*IRR*).

We use the same formula as for calculating present value:

$$PV = \sum \frac{R_t}{(1 + r)^t}$$

KI 27
p304

and then calculate what value of *r* would make the *PV* equal to the cost of investment: in other words, the rate of discount that would make the investment just break even. Say this worked out at 20 per cent. What we would be saying is that the investment would just cover its costs if the current rate of interest (rate of discount) were 20 per cent. In other words, this investment is equivalent to receiving 20 per cent interest: it has a 20 per cent rate of return (*MEC*).

Details of how to calculate the internal rate of return, along with a worked example, are given in Maths Case 10.2 on the student website.

So should the investment go ahead? Yes, if the actual rate of interest (*i*) is less than 20 per cent. The firm is better off

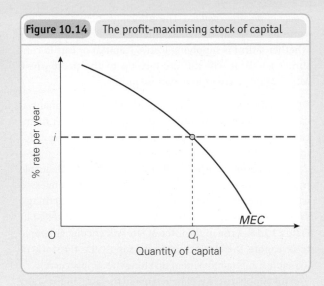

Figure 10.14   The profit-maximising stock of capital

investing its money in this project than keeping it in the bank: i.e. if *MEC* > *i* the investment should proceed.

This is just one more application of the general rule that if $MRP_f > MC_f$ then more of the factor should be used: only in this case, *MRP* is expressed as a rate of return (*MEC*), and *MC* is expressed as a rate of interest (*i*).

TC 8
p109

The profit-maximising position is illustrated in Figure 10.14. As the firm invests more, and thus builds up its stock of capital, so *MEC* will fall due to diminishing returns. As long as *MEC* is greater than *i*, the firm should invest more. It should stop when the stock of capital has reached Q_1. Thereafter it should cut investment to a level just sufficient to replace worn-out machines, and thus keep the capital stock at Q_1.

KI 19
p151

The risks of investment. One of the problems with investment is that the future is uncertain. The return on an investment will depend on the value of the goods it produces, which will depend on the goods market. But future markets depend on consumer tastes, the actions of rivals and the whole state of the economy, none of which can be known with certainty. Investment is thus risky.

Risk may also be incurred in terms of the output from an investment. Take the case of prospecting for oil. An oil company may have a major strike, but it may simply drill dry well after dry well. If it does get a major strike, and hence earn a large return on its investment, these profits will not be competed away by competitors prospecting in other fields, because they too still run the risk of drilling dry holes.

KI 11
p76

How is this risk accounted for when calculating the benefits of an investment? The answer is to use a higher rate of discount. The higher the risk, the bigger the risk premium that must be added to the rate.

The supply of capital

It is necessary to distinguish the supply of *physical* capital from the supply of *finance* to be used by firms for the purchase of capital.

Definitions

Net present value of an investment The discounted benefits of an investment minus the cost of the investment.

Marginal efficiency of capital or **internal rate of return** The rate of return of an investment: the discount rate that makes the net present value of an investment equal to zero.

Supply of physical capital. The principles here are just the same as those in the goods market. It does not matter whether a firm is supplying lorries (capital) or cars (a consumer good): it will still produce up to the point where $MC = MR$ if it wishes to maximise profits.

Supply of finance. An economy will have a stock of financial capital (or 'loanable funds') held in banks and other financial institutions. These funds can be borrowed by firms for investment in new physical capital.

KI 26
p303

When people save, this will build up the stock of loanable funds. This flow of saving represents the resources released when people refrain from consumption. Among other things, saving depends on the rate of interest. This is illustrated in Figure 10.15. A rise in the interest rate will encourage people to save more, thereby increasing the supply (i.e. the stock) of loanable funds (a movement up along the supply curve).

This supply curve will be relatively inelastic in the short run, since the flow of saving over a short time period (say, a month) will have only a relatively small effect on the total stock of funds. Over a year, however, the effect would be 12 times bigger. The longer the time period, therefore, the more elastic the supply curve.

Saving also depends on the level of people's incomes, their expectations of future price changes, and their willingness to sacrifice present consumption in order to be able to have more in the future. A change in any of these other determinants will shift the supply curve.

*Determination of the rate of interest

The rate of interest is determined by the interaction of supply and demand in the market for loanable funds. This is illustrated in Figure 10.15. As we have seen, supply represents accumulated savings.

The demand curve includes the demand by households for credit and the demand by firms for funds to finance their investment. The curve slopes downwards for two reasons.

First, households will borrow more at lower rates of interest. It effectively makes goods cheaper for them to buy. Second, it reflects the falling rate of return on investment as investment increases. This is simply due to diminishing returns to investment. As rates of interest fall, it will become profitable for firms to invest in projects that have a lower rate of return: the quantity of loanable funds demanded thus rises.

Equilibrium will be achieved where demand equals supply at an interest rate of i_e and a quantity of loanable funds $£_e$.

How will this market adjust to a change in demand or supply? Assume that there is a rise in demand for capital equipment, due, say, to an improvement in technology that increases the productivity of capital. There is thus an increase in demand for loanable funds. The demand curve shifts to the right in Figure 10.15. The equilibrium rate of interest will rise and this will encourage more savings. The end result is that more money will be spent on capital equipment.

Capital and profit

What does the analysis so far tell us about the amount of profit that firms will earn? After all, profit is the reward that the owners of firms get from owning and using capital.

Remember from Chapter 7 the distinction between normal and supernormal profit. In a perfectly competitive world, all supernormal profits will be competed away in the long run.

Another way of putting this is that a perfectly competitive firm in the long run will earn only a *normal rate of return* on capital. This means that the return on capital (after taking risk into account) will be the same as if the owners of capital had simply deposited their money in a bank instead. If a firm's capital yields a higher rate of return than this normal level (i.e. supernormal returns), other firms will be attracted to invest in similar capital. The resulting increased level of capital will increase the supply of goods. This, in turn, will lower the price of the goods and hence lower the rate of return on capital until it has fallen back to the normal level.

 Can a perfectly competitive firm earn a supernormal rate of return on capital if it continuously innovates?

If, however, capital owners have monopoly/oligopoly power and can thus restrict the entry of new firms or the copying of innovations – for example, by having a patent on a particular process – they can continue to get a supernormal return on their capital.

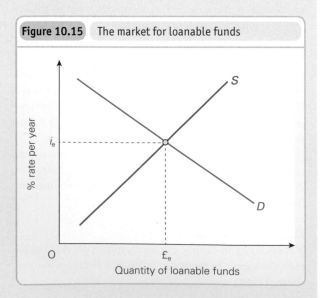

Figure 10.15   The market for loanable funds

Definition

Normal rate of return The rate of return (after taking risks into account) that could be earned elsewhere.

Financing investment

Sources of business finance

A firm can finance capital investment in one of three major ways:

- Internal funds (i.e. retained profits).
- Borrowing from the banking sector.
- Issuing new shares (equities) or debentures (fixed-interest loan stock).

The largest source of finance for investment in the UK is firms' own internal funds (i.e. ploughed-back profits). Given, however, that business profitability depends in large part on the general state of the economy, internal funds as a source of business finance are likely to vary considerably across the business cycle. When profits are squeezed in a recession, this source of investment will decline.

Other sources of finance, which include borrowing and the issue of shares and debentures, are known as 'external funds'. These are then categorised as short-term, medium-term or long-term sources of finance.

Short-term finance.   This is usually in the form of a short-term bank loan or overdraft facility, and is used by business as a form of working capital to aid it in its day-to-day business operations.

Medium-term finance.   This again is provided largely by banks, usually in the form of a loan with set repayment targets. It is common for such loans to be made at a fixed rate of interest, with repayments being designed to fit in with the business's expected cash flow. Bank lending has been the most volatile source of business finance, and has been particularly sensitive to the state of the economy. While part of the reason is the lower demand for loans during a recession, part of the reason is the caution of banks in granting loans if prospects for the economy are poor. In 2008, there was a reduction in the willingness of banks to grant loans to businesses following the credit crunch. This is examined in more detail in sections 18.2 and 22.2.

Long-term finance.   Long-term finance, especially in the UK, tends to be acquired through the stock market. It will usually be in the form of **shares** (or **equities**). This is where members of the public or institutions (such as pension funds) buy a part-ownership in the company and, as a result, receive dividends on those shares. The dividends depend on the amount of profit the company makes and distributes to shareholders. The proportion of business financing from this source clearly depends on the state of the stock market.

In the late 1990s, with a buoyant stock market, the proportion of funds obtained through share issue increased. Then with a decline in stock market prices from 2000 to 2003, this proportion fell. In 2008, there were very substantial falls in the values of shares, further reducing the ability of firms to raise finance. The recovery in share prices seen in 2013 gave rise to hope that firms would be able to fund the investment needed to increase growth back to pre-recession levels.

Alternatively, firms can issue **debentures** (or **company bonds**). These securities are fixed-interest loans to firms. Debenture holders have a prior claim on company shares. Their interest must be paid in full before shareholders can receive any dividends.

Despite the traditional reliance on the stock market for external long-term sources of finance, there has been a growing involvement of banks in recent years. Prior to the credit crunch in 2008, banks had become more willing to provide finance for business start-ups and for diversification. This has been less apparent since and there is a concern that banks are inherently cautious. This risk aversion results in a problem of 'short-termism', with bankers often demanding a quick return on their money or charging high interest rates, and being less concerned to finance long-term investment.

Comparison of the UK with other European countries.   In other European countries, notably Germany and France, the attitude towards business funding is quite different from that in the UK. In these countries banks provide a significant amount of long-term, fixed-rate finance. This provides a much more stable source of finance and creates an environment where banks are much more committed to the long-run health of companies.

The role of the stock market

The London Stock Exchange operates as both a primary and secondary market in capital.

*As a **primary market.***   The primary market is where public limited companies (see Case Study 9.1 on the student website) can raise finance by issuing new shares (equities) or fixed interest securities, whether to new shareholders or to existing ones. To raise finance on the Stock Exchange a business must be 'listed'. The Listing Agreement involves directors agreeing to abide by a strict set of rules governing behaviour and levels of reporting to shareholders. Companies must have at least three years' trading experience and

---

Definitions
Shares (equities) A part-ownership of a company. Companies' distributed profits are paid to shareholders in the form of dividends according to the number of shares held.
Debentures (company bonds) Fixed-interest loans to firms. These assets can be traded on the stock market and their market price is determined by demand and supply.
Primary market in capital Where shares are sold by the issuer of the shares (i.e. the firm) and where, therefore, finance is channelled directly from the purchasers (i.e. the shareholders) to the firm.

make at least 25 per cent of their shares available to the public. In March 2017, there were 937 UK and 271 international companies on the Official List.

As well as those on the Official List, there are approximately 1000 companies on what is known as the Alternative Investment Market (AIM). Companies listed here tend to be young but with growth potential, and do not have to meet the strict criteria or pay such high costs as companies on the Official List.

In 2016, nearly £16 billion's worth of new equity capital was raised through 427 main market issues and £266 billion's worth of fixed interest securities through 1672 main market issues. In addition, £4.8 billion's worth of capital was raised on the AIM.

As a secondary market. The Stock Exchange enables investors to sell *existing* shares and debentures to one another. In March 2017, on an average day £5.5 billion's worth of trading in equities and other securities took place.

The advantages and disadvantages of using the stock market to raise capital

As a market for raising capital, the stock market has a number of advantages:

- It brings together those that wish to invest and companies that seek investment, and does so in a relatively low-cost way. It thus represents a way that savings can be mobilised to generate output.
- Firms that are listed on the Stock Exchange are subject to strict regulations. This is likely to stimulate investor confidence, making it easier for business to raise finance.
- The process of merger and acquisition is facilitated by having a share system, which in turn increases competition for corporate control (see pages 210–11).

The main weaknesses of the stock market for raising capital are:

- The cost to a business of getting listed can be immense, not only in a financial sense, but also in being open to public scrutiny. Directors' and senior managers' decisions will often be driven by how the market is likely to react, rather than by what they perceive to be in the business's best interests. They always have to think about the reactions of those large shareholders in the City that control a large proportion of their shares.

- In the UK, it is often claimed that the market suffers from *short-termism*. Investors on the Stock Exchange are mainly concerned with a company's short-term performance and its share value. In responding to this, the business might neglect its long-term performance and potential.

Is the stock market efficient?

One of the arguments made in favour of the stock market is that it acts as an arena within which share values can be accurately or efficiently priced. If new information comes onto the market concerning a business and its performance, this will be quickly and rationally transferred into the business's share value. This is known as the *efficient market hypothesis*. For example, if an investment analyst found that, in terms of its actual and expected dividends, a particular share was underpriced and thus represented a 'bargain', the analyst would advise investors to buy. As people then bought the shares, their price would rise, pushing their value up to their full worth. So by attempting to gain from inefficiently priced securities, investors will encourage the market to become more efficient.

How efficient, then, is the stock market in pricing securities? Is information rationally and quickly conveyed into the share's price? Or are investors able to prosper from the stock market's inefficiencies?

We can identify three levels of efficiency.

The weak form of efficiency. Share prices often move in cycles that do not reflect the underlying performance of the firm. If information is imperfect, those with a better understanding of such cycles gain from buying shares at the trough and selling them at the peak of the cycles. They are taking advantage of the market's inefficiency.

Increasing numbers of investment analysts are using technical models to track share cycles. As they do so and knowledge becomes more perfect, so the market will become more efficient and the cycles will tend to disappear. But why?

As more people buy a company's shares as the price falls towards its trough, extra demand will prevent the price falling so far. Similarly, as people sell as the price rises towards its peak, so this extra supply will prevent the price rising so far. This is an example of stabilising speculation (see pages 71–2). As more and more people react in this way, so the cycle all but disappears. When this happens, *weak efficiency* has been achieved.

Definitions

Secondary market in capital Where shareholders sell shares to others. This is thus a market in 'second-hand' shares.

Short-termism Where firms and investors take decisions based on the likely short-term performance of a company, rather than on its long-term prospects. Firms may thus sacrifice long-term profits and growth for the sake of a quick return.

Efficient (capital) market hypothesis The hypothesis that new information about a company's current or future performance will be quickly and accurately reflected in its share price.

Weak efficiency (of share markets) Where share dealing prevents cyclical movements in shares.

The semi-strong form of efficiency. **Semi-strong efficiency** is when share prices adjust fully to publicly available information. In practice, not all investors will interpret such information correctly: their knowledge is imperfect. But increasingly more advice is available to shareholders (through stockbrokers, newspapers, online commentators, published accounts, etc.), and more shares are purchased by professional fund managers. The result is that the interpretation of public information becomes more perfect and the market becomes more efficient in the semi-strong sense.

If the market were efficient in the semi-strong sense, then no gain could be made from studying a company's performance and prospects, as this information would *already* be included in the current share price. In selecting shares, you would do just as well by pinning the financial pages of a newspaper on the wall, throwing darts at them, and buying the shares the darts hit!

The strong form of efficiency. If the stock market showed the **strong form of efficiency**, then share prices would fully reflect *all* available information – whether public or not. For this to be so, all 'inside' information would have to be reflected in the share price the moment the information became available.

If the market is *not* efficient at this level, then people who have access to privileged information will be able to make large returns from their investments by acting on such information. For example, directors of a company would know if the company was soon to announce better-than-expected profits. In the meantime, they could gain by buying shares in the company, knowing that the share price would rise when the information about the profits became public. Gains made from such 'insider dealing' are illegal. However, proving whether individuals are engaging in it is very difficult. By the time of its replacement by the Financial Conduct Authority in April 2013, the Financial Services Authority had secured just 23 convictions for insider dealing, prompting criticism that it was toothless.

Given the penalties for insider dealing and the amount of private information that firms possess, it is unlikely that all such information will be reflected in share prices. Thus the strong form of stock market efficiency is unlikely to hold.

 Would the stock market be more efficient if insider dealing were made legal?

If stock markets were fully efficient, the expected returns from every share would be the same. The return is referred to as the **yield**: this is measured as the dividends paid on the share as a percentage of the share's market price. For example, if you hold shares whose market price is £1 per share and you receive an annual dividend of 3p per share, then the yield on the shares is 3 per cent. But why should the expected returns on shares be the same? If any share was expected to yield a higher-than-average return, people would buy it; its price would rise and its yield would correspondingly fall.

It would only be unanticipated information, therefore, that would cause share prices to deviate from that which reflected expected average yields. Such information must, by its nature, be random, and as such would cause share prices to deviate randomly from their expected price, or follow what we call a **random walk**. Evidence suggests that share prices do tend to follow random patterns.

Challenging the efficient market hypothesis

The efficient markets hypothesis has been challenged by critics who laid the blame for the financial crisis in 2007–8 on unfounded belief in rational markets. They argued that regulators failed to understand the role that exuberance plays in financial markets. If investors are 'caught up' in the belief that share prices (or property values) will continue to increase in value, regardless of underlying information, then the result will be a bubble – a situation where assets are traded above their fundamental value.

According to behavioural economists, bubbles can be explained by a number of psychological factors. Among these are paying too little attention to the past, over-confidence, over-optimism and herding. In short, people pay too much for assets because they remember recent returns more than historical averages, because they take more notice of economic good news than bad and because everyone else is doing it. Asset bubbles are vulnerable to breaking on the basis of changes in beliefs, as we saw in the collapse of the US housing market from 2006 and the subsequent stock market crash.

What does this imply for policy makers? The argument might be made that an asset bubble is simply a magnification of any market, with both losers and winners; this does not suggest a need for intervention. However, this ignores the macroeconomic consequences of the bubble, consequences which were clearly seen from 2007 on. Behaviourists therefore believe that effective financial regulation must take account of irrationality.

Definitions

Semi-strong efficiency (of share markets) Where share prices adjust quickly, fully and accurately to publicly available information.

Strong efficiency (of share markets) Where share prices adjust quickly, fully and accurately to all available information, both public and that only available to insiders.

Yield on a share The dividend received per share expressed as a percentage of the current market price of the share.

Random walk Where fluctuations in the value of a share away from its 'correct' value are random, i.e. have no systematic pattern. When charted over time, these share price movements would appear like a 'random walk': like the path of someone staggering along drunk!

Section summary

1. It is necessary to distinguish between buying the services of land (by renting) or capital (by hiring) and buying them outright.

2. The profit-maximising employment of land and capital services will be where the factor's *MRP* is equal to its price (under perfect competition) or its *MC* (where firms have monopsony power).

3. The demand for capital services will be equal to MRP_K. Due to diminishing returns, this will decline as more capital is used.

4. The supply of capital services to a firm will be horizontal or upward sloping depending on whether the firm is perfectly competitive or has monopsony power. The supply of capital services by a firm in the short run is likely to be relatively elastic up to its maximum use, and then totally inelastic. In the long run, the supplying firm can purchase additional capital equipment for hiring out. The long-run supply curve will therefore be very elastic, but at a higher rental rate than in the short run, given that the cost of purchasing the equipment must be taken into account in the rental rate.

5. The market supply of capital services is likely to be highly inelastic in the short run, given that capital equipment tends to have very specific uses and cannot normally be transferred from one use to another. In the long run, it will be more elastic.

6. The price of capital services is determined by the interaction of demand and supply.

7. The demand for capital for purchase will depend on the return it earns for the firm. To calculate this return, all future earnings from the investment have to be reduced to a present value by discounting at a market rate of interest (discount). If the present value exceeds the cost of the investment, the investment is worthwhile. Alternatively, a rate of return from the investment can be calculated and then this can be compared with the return that the firm could have earned by investing elsewhere.

8. The supply of finance for investment depends on the supply of loanable funds, which in turn depends on the rate of interest, on the general level of thriftiness and on expectations about future price levels and incomes.

9. The rate of interest will be determined by the demand and supply of loanable funds. When deciding whether to make an investment, a firm will use this rate for discounting purposes. If, however, an investment involves risks, the firm will require a higher rate of return on the investment than current market interest rates.

10. Business finance can come from internal sources (ploughed-back profits) or from external ones. External sources of finance include borrowing and the issue of shares.

11. The stock market operates as both a primary and a secondary market in capital. As a primary market it channels finance to companies as people purchase new shares and debentures. It is also a market for existing shares and debentures.

12. The stock market helps to stimulate growth and investment by bringing together companies and people who want to invest in them. By regulating firms and by keeping transaction costs of investment low, it helps to ensure that investment is efficient.

13. The stock market does impose costs on firms, however. It is expensive for firms to be listed and the public exposure may make them too keen to 'please' the market. It can also foster short-termism.

14. The stock market is relatively efficient. It achieves weak efficiency by reducing cyclical movements in share prices. It achieves semi-strong efficiency by allowing share prices to respond quickly and fully to publicly available information. Whether it achieves strong efficiency by adjusting quickly and fully to all information (both public or insider), however, is more doubtful.

10.4 LAND AND RENT

Rent: the reward to landowners

We turn now to land. The income it earns for landowners is the *rent* charged to the users of the land. This rent, like the rewards to other factors, is determined by demand and supply.

What makes land different from other factors of production is that it has an inelastic supply. In one sense, this is obvious. The total supply of land in any area is fixed.

In another sense, supply is not *totally* inelastic. Land can be improved. It can be cleared, levelled, drained, fertilised, etc. Thus the supply of a certain type of land can be increased by expending human effort on improving it. The question is whether *land* has thereby increased, or whether the

improvements constitute *capital* invested in land, and if so whether the higher rents that such land can earn really amount to a return on the capital invested in it.

To keep the analysis simple, let us assume that land *is* fixed. Let us take the case of an area of 10 000 hectares surrounding the village of Oakleigh. This is shown as a vertical supply 'curve' in Figure 10.16. The demand curve for that land will be like the demand curve for other factors of production. It is the *MRP* curve and slopes down due to diminishing returns from land. The equilibrium rent is r_e, where demand and supply intersect.

Notice that the level of this rent depends entirely on *demand*. If a new housing development takes place in Oakleigh, due perhaps to a growth in employment in a nearby

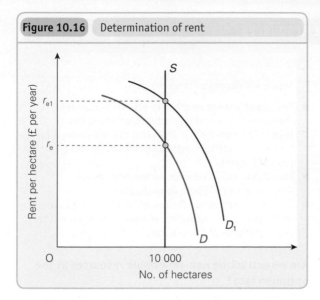

Figure 10.16 Determination of rent

1. We defined the factor of production 'land' to include raw materials. Does the analysis of rent that we have just been looking at apply to raw materials?
2. The supply of land in a particular area may be totally inelastic, but the supply of land in that area for a specific purpose (e.g. growing wheat) will be upward sloping: the higher the price of wheat and thus the higher the rent that wheat producers are prepared to pay, the more will be made available for wheat production. What will determine the elasticity of supply of land for any particular purpose?

The price of land

Not all land is rented: much of it is bought and sold outright. Its price will depend on what the purchaser is prepared to pay, and this will depend on the land's rental value.

Let us say that a piece of land can earn £1000 per year. What would a person be prepared to pay for it? There is a simple formula for working this out:

$$P = \frac{R}{i} \tag{1}$$

where P is the price of the land, R is the rent per year and i is the market rate of interest.

Let us assume that the market rate of interest is 10 per cent (i.e. 0.1). Then according to the formula, a purchaser would be prepared to pay

$$\frac{£1000}{0.1} = £10\,000$$

Why should this be so? If a person deposits £10 000 in the bank, with an interest rate of 10 per cent this will earn that person £1000 per year. Assuming our piece of land is guaranteed to earn a rent of £1000 per year, then provided it costs less than £10 000 to buy, it is a better investment than putting money in the bank. The competition between people to buy this land will drive its price up until it reaches £10 000.

This is just another example of equilibrium being where marginal cost equals marginal benefit. This can be demonstrated by rearranging equation (1) to give

$$Pi = R$$

Remember that the equilibrium price of the land (P) is £10 000 and that the rate of interest (i) is 0.1. If you borrow the £10 000 to buy the land, it will cost you £1000 per year in interest payments (i.e. Pi). This is your annual marginal cost. The annual marginal benefit will be the rent (R) you will earn from the land.

1. What price would the same piece of land sell for if it still earned £1000 rent per year, but if the rate of interest were now (a) 5 per cent; (b) 20 per cent?
2. What does this tell us about the relationship between the price of an asset (like land) and the rate of interest?

town, the demand curve will shift to D_1 and the equilibrium rent will rise to r_{e1}. But the supply of land remains fixed at 10 000 hectares. Landowners will earn more rent, but they themselves have done nothing: the higher rent is a pure windfall gain.

So why are rents in the centre of London many times higher per hectare than they are in the north of Scotland? The answer is that demand is very much higher in London.

Demand for land depends on its marginal revenue product. Thus it is differences in the *MRP* of land that explain the differences in rent from one area to another. There are two reasons for differences in *MRP*. Remember that *MRP* = *MPP* (marginal physical product of the factor) × *MR* (marginal revenue of the good produced by that factor).

Differences in MPP. Land differs in productivity. Fertile land will produce a higher output than deserts or moorland. Similarly, land near centres of population will be of much more use to industry than land in the middle of nowhere.

What other factors will determine the MPP of land for industry?

Differences in MR. The higher the demand for a particular good, the higher its price and marginal revenue, and hence the higher the demand and rent for the land on which that good is produced. Thus if the demand for housing rises relative to the demand for food, the rent on land suitable for house building will rise relative to the rent on agricultural land.

To summarise: rents will be high on land that is physically productive (high *MPP*) and produces goods in high demand (high *MR*).

BOX 10.11   THE ECONOMICS OF NON-RENEWABLE RESOURCES

What happens as stocks diminish?

As world population rises, so the demands on resources continue to grow. Some of these resources are renewable. Water resources are replenished by rain. The soil, if properly managed, can continue to grow crops. Felled forests can be replanted. Of course, if we use these resources more rapidly than they are replenished, stocks will run down. We are all aware of the problems of seas that are overfished, or rainforests that are cleared, or reservoirs that are inadequate to meet our growing demand for water.

But whereas these resources can be replenished, others cannot. These are known as non-renewable resources. What determines the price of such resources and their rate of depletion? Will we eventually run out of resources such as oil, coal, gas and various minerals? To answer these questions, we need to distinguish between the available stock of such resources, and their use (a flow). The greater their use, the faster the stocks run down.

**KI 26
p303**

Price increases over time

As stocks run down, so the price of the resources will tend to increase. Thus we can all expect to pay more for fossil fuels as remaining reserves are depleted. Owners of the reserves (e.g. mine owners and owners of oil wells) will thus find the value of their assets increasing. But how quickly will prices rise? In a perfect market, they will rise at the market rate of return on other assets (of equivalent risk). This is known as the Hotelling rule, named after Harold Hotelling who developed the argument in the early 1930s.

To understand why this is so, consider what would happen if the price of oil rose more slowly than the rate of return on other assets. People who owned oil wells would find that the value of their oil reserves was increasing less rapidly than the value of other assets. They might as well sell more oil now and invest the money in other assets, thereby getting a higher return. The extra oil coming to the market would depress the current oil price, but also reduce reserves, thereby creating a bigger shortage for the future and hence a higher future price. This would cause oil prices to rise more quickly over time (from the new lower base). Once the rate of price increase has risen to equal the rate of return on other assets, equilibrium has occurred. There will no longer be an incentive for the oil to be extracted faster.

The current price

But what determines the current price level (as opposed to its rate of increase)? This will be determined by supply and demand for the extracted resource (its flow).

In the case of a resource used by households, demand will depend on consumer tastes, the price of other goods, income, etc. Thus the greater the desire for using private cars, the greater the demand for petrol. In the case of minerals used by firms, demand will depend on the marginal revenue product of the resources. In either case, a rise in demand will cause a rise in the resource's price.

Supply will depend on three things:

- The rate of interest on other assets. As we have seen, the higher the rate of interest, the faster will the resource be extracted, in order that the mine owners (or well owners) can reinvest their profits at these higher rates of interest.
- The stock of known reserves. As new reserves are discovered, this will push down the price.
- The costs of extraction. The lower the costs, the greater will be the amount extracted, and hence the lower will be the market price of the resource.

Are we extracting non-renewable resources at the optimum rate?

If there are limited reserves of fossil fuels and other minerals, are we in danger that they will soon run out? Should we be more concerned with conservation?

In fact, the market provides an incentive to conserve such resources. As reserves run down, so the price of non-renewable resources will rise. This will create an incentive to discover alternatives. For example, as fossil fuels become more expensive, so renewable sources of energy, such as solar power, wind power and wave power, will become more economical. There will also be a greater incentive to discover new techniques of power generation and to conserve energy.

**TC 5
p50**

Markets, however, are imperfect. As we shall see in Chapter 12, when we consume natural resources, we do not take into account the full costs. For example, the burning of fossil fuels creates harmful environmental effects in the form of acid rain and the greenhouse effect, but these 'external' costs are not included in the price we pay.

**TC 3
p26**

Then there is the question of the distribution of income between present and future generations. If non-renewable resources are going to be expensive in the future, should we not be conserving these resources today in order to help our descendants? The problem is that consumers may well act totally selfishly, saying, 'Why should we conserve resources? By the time they run out, we will be dead.' We almost certainly do care about the welfare of our children and grandchildren, but what about our great-great-grandchildren, whom we will never meet?

**KI 4
p14**

1. *Will the market provide incentives for firms to research into energy-conserving techniques, if energy prices at present are not high enough to make the use of such techniques profitable?*
2. *How will the existence of monopoly power in the supply of resources influence their rate of depletion?*
3. *If the current generation wants to consume all non-renewable resources, is there any market solution to prevent this happening? (We will return to this in Chapter 13.)*

Who are the poor? Who are the rich?

We have been building up an answer to these questions as this chapter has progressed. The final part of the answer concerns the ownership of land and capital. Many people own no land or capital at all. These people will therefore earn no profit, rent or interest.

For those who are fortunate enough to own productive assets, their income from them will depend on (a) the quantity they own and (b) their rental value.

The quantity of assets owned

This will depend on the following:

- Inheritance. Some people have rich parents who leave them substantial amounts of land and capital.
- Past income and savings. If people have high incomes and save a large proportion of them, this helps them to build up a stock of assets.
- Skill in investment (entrepreneurial skill). The more skilful people are in investing and in organising production, the more rapidly will their stock of assets grow.
- Luck. When people open up a business, there are usually substantial risks. The business might flourish or fail.

The rental value

This is the income earned per unit of land and capital. It will depend on the following:

- The level of demand for the factor. This depends on the factor's *MRP*, which in turn depends on its physical productivity (*MPP*) and the demand for the good it produces and hence the good's *MR*.
- The elasticity of demand for the good. The greater the monopoly power that capital owners have in the goods market, the less elastic will be the demand for the product and the greater will be the supernormal returns they can earn on their capital.
- The elasticity of supply of the factor. The less elastic its supply, the more factor owners can gain from a high demand. The high demand will simply push up the level of economic rent that the factor will earn.

- The total factor supply by other factor owners. The further to the left the total factor supply curve, the higher the level of economic rent that each unit of the factor can earn for any given level of demand.

Thus if you are lucky enough to have rich parents who leave you a lot of money when you are relatively young; if you are a skilful investor and save and reinvest a large proportion of your earnings; if you own assets that few other people own, and which produce goods in high demand: then you may end up very rich.

If you have no assets, you will have no property income at all. If at the same time you are on a low wage or are unemployed, then you may be very poor indeed.

Section summary

1. Rent on land, like the price of other factor services, is determined by the interaction of demand and supply. Its supply is totally inelastic (or nearly so). Its demand curve is downward sloping and will equal the *MRP* of land.

2. The price of land depends on its potential rental value (its marginal benefit) and the repayment costs of borrowing

to pay for the land (its marginal cost). Equilibrium is where the two are equal.

3. People's income depends not only on their wages but on whether they own any land or capital, and, if they do, the rental value of these assets. This is the final element in determining the distribution of income in the economy.

END OF CHAPTER QUESTIONS

1. The wage rate that a firm has to pay and the output it can produce vary with the number of workers as follows (all figures are hourly):

Number of workers	1	2	3	4	5	6	7	8
Wage rate (AC_L) (£)	3	4	5	6	7	8	9	10
Total output (TPP_L)	10	22	32	40	46	50	52	52

Assume that output sells at £2 per unit.

   (a) Copy the table and add additional rows for TC_L, MC_L, TRP_L and MRP_L. Put the figures for MC_L and MRP_L in the spaces between the columns.

   (b) How many workers will the firm employ in order to maximise profits?

   (c) What will be its hourly wage bill at this level of employment?

   (d) How much hourly revenue will it earn at this level of employment?

   (e) Assuming that the firm faces other (fixed) costs of £30 per hour, how much hourly profit will it make?

   (f) Assume that the workers now formed a union and that the firm agreed to pay the negotiated wage rate to all employees. What is the maximum to which the hourly wage rate could rise without causing the firm to try to reduce employment below the level of (b) above? (See Figure 10.10.)

   (g) What would be the firm's hourly profit now?

2. If a firm faces a shortage of workers with very specific skills, it may decide to undertake the necessary training

▶

itself. If, on the other hand, it faces a shortage of unskilled workers, it may well offer a small wage increase in order to obtain the extra labour. In the first case, it is responding to an increase in demand for labour by attempting to shift the supply curve. In the second case, it is merely allowing a movement along the supply curve. Use a demand and supply diagram to illustrate each case. Given that elasticity of supply is different in each case, do you think that these are the best policies for the firm to follow? What would happen to wages and economic rent if it used the second policy in the first case?

3. Why do the world's top footballers earn millions of pounds per year, while the top lacrosse players are paid less than the equivalent of £30 000?

4. For what reasons is the median hourly wage rate of women some 16 per cent lower than that of men in the UK, and the average gross weekly pay, including overtime, more than 21 per cent less?

5. Given the analysis of bilateral monopoly, if the passing of minimum wage legislation forces employers to pay higher wage rates to low-paid employees, will this necessarily cause a reduction in employment?

6. Using a diagram like Figure 10.13, demonstrate what will happen under perfect competition when there is an increase in the productivity of a particular type of capital. Consider the effects on the demand, price (rental rate) and quantity supplied of the services of this type of capital.

7. What factors could cause a rise in the market rate of interest?

8. How is the market price of land related to its productivity?

9. In recent years there have been a number of changes in planning laws to make it easier for commercial properties to be converted to housing. What would be the impact on property values?

Online resources

Additional case studies on the student website

10.1 **Economic rent and transfer earnings.** This examines a way of classifying the earnings of a factor of production and shows how these earnings depend on the elasticity of supply of the factor.

10.2 **Telecommuters.** This case study looks at the rise of telecommuting, whereby people are able to work from home utilising modern technology.

10.3 **Other labour market imperfections.** This looks at the three imperfections identified on page 291: namely, imperfect information, persistent disequilibria in labour markets and non-maximising behaviour by firms or workers.

10.4 **Profit sharing.** An examination of the case for and against profit sharing as a means of rewarding workers.

10.5 **Holidays: good for workers; bad for employers?** An examination of holiday entitlements in the USA and Europe and their effects on workers and business.

Maths Case 10.1 Calculating the long-run cost of supplying additional equipment for rent. A worked example.

Maths Case 10.2 Calculating the internal rate of return. A worked example.

Websites relevant to this chapter

See sites listed at the end of Chapter 11 on page 346.

Microeconomic Policy

We now turn to the application of microeconomics and its role in government policy. In Part C we looked at *how* market economies function at a micro level. In Part D we examine the various policies that can be adopted to deal with shortcomings of the market system.

There are various questions that governments will ask. How much monopoly power is too much? How equal do we want the distribution of income to be? How can we make markets more efficient? How can we protect the environment and prevent the depletion of resources? How can we prevent climate change?

In Chapter 11 we look at policies that address the distribution of income. In Chapter 12 we examine the issue of market failure and consider the potential for government intervention. Finally, in Chapters 13 and 14 we turn to government policies with respect to the environment and business.

11

Inequality, Poverty and Policies to Redistribute Income

In Chapter 10 we saw that there are considerable differences in wage rates, and that these depend on market conditions. Similarly, we saw that differences in rewards to owners of capital and land also depend on their respective markets.

But differences in factor rewards are only part of the explanation of inequality. In this chapter, we open out the analysis. We take a more general look at why some people are rich while others are poor, and consider the overall degree of inequality in our society: a society that includes the super-rich, with their luxury yachts, and people living in slum conditions, with not enough to feed themselves or their children. We will see how the gap between rich and poor has tended to widen over time.

We will show how inequality can be measured so that we can make comparisons over time and between countries. We will also look at how incomes are distributed between particular groups, whether by occupation, age, sex, household composition or geographical area.

The second part of the chapter considers what can be done to reduce inequality. Is the solution to tax the rich heavily, so that the money can be redistributed to the poor? Or might this discourage people from working so hard? Would it be better, then, to focus on benefits and increase the support for the poor? Or might this discourage people from taking on work for fear of losing their benefits? We look at the attitudes of governments and at some of the debates taking place today over how to reduce inequality without discouraging effort or initiative.

11.1 INEQUALITY AND POVERTY

Inequality is one of the most contentious issues in the world of economics and politics. Some people have incomes far in excess of what they need to enjoy a luxurious lifestyle, while others struggle to purchase even necessities.

The need for some redistribution from rich to poor is broadly accepted across the political spectrum. Thus the government taxes the rich (and those who most would agree are not rich) and transfers some of the proceeds to the poor, either as cash benefits or as benefits in kind. Nevertheless, there is considerable disagreement as to the appropriate *amount* of redistribution.

Whether the current distribution of income is desirable or not is a normative question. Economists therefore should not specify how much the government should redistribute incomes. However, economists do have a role to play in the analysis of inequality and in assessing the impact of policies. They can do the following:

- Identify the extent of inequality and analyse how it has changed over time.
- Explain why a particular level of income distribution occurs and what causes inequality to grow or to lessen.
- Examine the relationship between equality and other economic objectives such as efficiency.
- Identify various government policies to deal with problems of inequality and poverty.
- Examine the effects of these policies, both on inequality itself and on other questions such as efficiency, inflation and unemployment.
- Examine the effect of other policies, such as the reduction of the budget deficit, on inequality and poverty.

Types of inequality

There are a number of different ways of looking at the distribution of income and wealth.

The distribution of income

There are three broad ways of examining the distribution of income. First we can look at how evenly incomes are distributed among the population. This is known as the *size distribution of income*. It can be expressed between *households*, or between *individual earners*, or between *all individuals*. It can be expressed either *before* or *after* the deduction of taxes and the receipt of benefits. For example, we might want to know the proportion of pre-tax national income going to the richest 10 per cent of households.

Then there is distribution between different *factors of production*, known as the *functional distribution of income*. At the *broader* level, we could look at the distribution between the general factor categories: labour, land and capital. At a *narrower* level, we could look at distribution within the factor categories. Why are some jobs well paid while others are

badly paid? Why are rents higher in some areas than in others? We looked at this distribution in Chapter 10.

Finally, there is the question of the *distribution of income by class of recipient*. This can be by *class of person*: women, men, single people, married people, people within a particular age group or ethnic group, and so on. Alternatively, it can be by *geographical area*. Typically, this is expressed in terms of differences in incomes between officially defined regions within a country.

The distribution of wealth

Income is a *flow*. It measures the receipt of money per period of time (e.g. £25 000 per year). Wealth, by contrast, is a stock (see Box 10.10). It measures the value of a person's assets at a particular point in time. The distribution of wealth can be measured as a size distribution (how evenly it is distributed among the population); as a functional distribution (the proportion of wealth held in various forms, such as dwellings, land, company shares, bank deposits, etc.); or according to the holders of wealth, classified by age, sex, geographical area, etc.

Analysis of incomes below a certain level: the analysis of poverty

A major problem here is in defining just what is meant by poverty. The dividing line between who is poor and who is not is necessarily arbitrary. Someone who is classed as poor in the UK may seem rich to an Ethiopian.

The extent and nature of poverty can be analysed in a number of ways:

- The number or proportion of people or households falling into the category.
- The occupational distribution of poverty.
- The geographical distribution of poverty.
- The distribution of poverty according to age, sex, ethnic origin, marital status, educational attainment, etc.

Definitions

Size distribution of income Measurement of the distribution of income according to the levels of income received by individuals (irrespective of source).

Functional distribution of income Measurement of the distribution of income according to the source of income (e.g. from employment, from profit, from rent, etc.).

Distribution of income by class of recipient Measurement of the distribution of income between the classes of person who receive it (e.g. homeowners and non-homeowners or those in the north and those in the south).

It is not possible in this chapter to look at all aspects of inequality in the UK. Nevertheless some of the more important facts are considered, along with questions of their measurement and interpretation.

The size distribution of income in the UK

Figure 11.1 shows the size distribution of income in the UK. It covers income from all sources. In each chart, households are grouped into five equal-sized groups or *quintiles*, from the poorest 20 per cent of households up to the richest 20 per cent. (The general term for division into equal-sized groups is *quantiles*.) The following points can be drawn from these statistics:

- In 2015/16, the richest 20 per cent of households earned just over 48 per cent of national income, and even after the deduction of taxes this was still 40 per cent.
- The poorest 20 per cent, by contrast, earned a mere 4.1 per cent of national income, and even after the receipt of cash benefits this had risen to only 7.8 per cent.

Inequality grew dramatically in the 1980s and did not begin to fall again until 2000, and then only very slightly. Between 1977 and 2015/16 the post-tax-and-benefits share of national income of the bottom 40 per cent of households

fell from 23 per cent to 20.2 per cent, while the share of the top 20 per cent grew from 37 per cent to 40 per cent.

As measured by quintiles or even deciles (10 equal-sized groups), income inequality in the UK has changed relatively little in the past few years. However, those on the very highest incomes – the top 1 per cent and especially the top 0.1 per cent – have seen an enormous growth in their incomes, with the very rich getting a lot richer. Although there was a slight fall in the top income group's share of national income directly following the financial crisis, the gap has widened again since. A similar picture has emerged in many other developed countries.

Effects of taxes and benefits.   As we shall see in section 11.2, by taxing the rich proportionately more than the poor, taxes can be used as a means of reducing inequality. In the UK, however, indirect taxes (e.g. on tobacco and alcohol) are paid proportionately more by the poor and so have the opposite effect. In 2015/16, the lowest-earning quintile of households paid 11 per cent of their gross income (original income plus cash benefits) in direct taxes (e.g. income tax, national insurance) while the highest-earning quintile paid 22.8 per cent.[1] When we look at indirect taxes, however, we see that the poorest quintile paid 29.7 per cent of their gross income in such taxes while the richest quintile paid only 15 per cent. This more than offsets the redistributive effect from direct tax being paid proportionately more by the rich. The top quintile paid approximately 38 per cent of their gross income in tax while the bottom quintile paid approximately 40 per cent.

Redistribution of income in the UK, therefore, is achieved mainly through the benefits system.

1 *The Effects of Taxes and Benefits on Household Income: Financial Year Ending 2015* (National Statistics, May 2016).

Definitions

Quintiles Divisions of the population into five equal-sized groups (an example of a quantile).

Quantiles Divisions of the population into equal-sized groups.

| **Figure 11.1** | Size distribution of UK income by quintile group of households, 2015/16 |

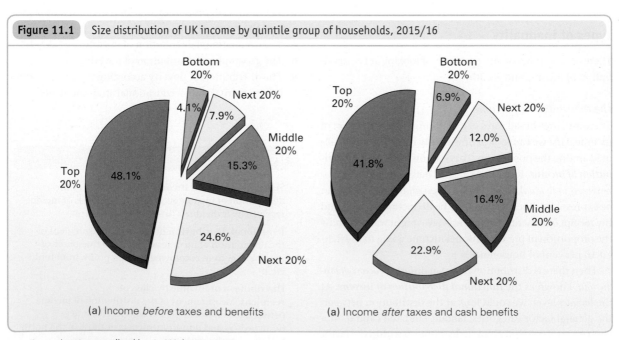

(a) Income *before* taxes and benefits

(a) Income *after* taxes and cash benefits

Note: Figures do not necessarily add up to 100 due to rounding.
Source: Based on data in *Household Disposable Income and Inequality 2015/16,* Table 1 (ONS, January 2017).

Measuring the size distribution of income

Apart from tables and charts, two of the most widely used methods for measuring inequality are the *Lorenz curve* and the *Gini coefficient.*

Lorenz curve

Figure 11.2 shows the **Lorenz curve** for the UK based on pre-tax (but post-benefit) incomes.

The horizontal axis measures percentages of the population from the poorest to the richest. Thus the 40 per cent point represents the poorest 40 per cent of the population. The vertical axis measures the percentage of national income they receive.

The curve starts at the origin: zero people earn zero incomes. If income were distributed totally equally, the Lorenz curve would be a straight 45° line. The 'poorest' 20 per cent of the population would earn 20 per cent of national income; the 'poorest' 60 per cent would earn 60 per cent, and so on. The curve ends up at the top right-hand corner, with 100 per cent of the population earning 100 per cent of national income.

In practice, the Lorenz curve will 'hang below' the 45° line. Point *x,* for example, shows a country where the poorest 50 per cent of households receive only 24 per cent of national income. The further the curve drops below the 45° line, the greater will be the level of inequality.

The Lorenz curve is quite useful for showing the change in income distribution over time. From 1949 to 1979 the curve for the UK moved inwards towards the 45° line, suggesting a lessening of inequality. Then from 1979 to 1990 it moved downwards away from the 45° line, suggesting a deepening of inequality. Since 1990 it has remained approximately the same.

The problem with simply comparing Lorenz curves by eye is that it is imprecise. This problem is overcome by using Gini coefficients.

Gini coefficient

The **Gini coefficient** is a precise way of measuring the position of the Lorenz curve. It is the ratio of the area between the Lorenz curve and the 45° line to the whole area below the 45° line. In Figure 11.2 this is the ratio of the shaded area *A* to the whole area (*A* + *B*), sometimes expressed as a percentage.

If income is equally distributed so that the Lorenz curve follows the 45° line, area *A* disappears and the Gini coefficient is zero. As inequality increases, so does area *A,* and the Gini coefficient rises. In the extreme case of total inequality, where one person earns the whole of national income, area *B* would disappear and the Gini coefficient would be 1. Thus the Gini coefficient will be between 0 and 1. The higher the figure, the greater is the measure of inequality.

In 1979, the *gross income* (original income plus cash benefits) Gini coefficient in the UK was 0.30 (see Figure 11.3). With the growth in inequality during the 1980s, the

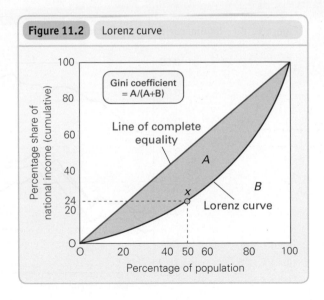

Figure 11.2 Lorenz curve

coefficient steadily increased and stood at 0.39 in 1990. Since then it has remained relatively stable (fluctuating between 0.35 and 0.39). The *post-tax* coefficient (gross income minus both direct and indirect taxes) rose even more dramatically – from 0.29 in 1979 to 0.41 in 1990. It was 0.35 in 2015/16 (see Figure 11.3). In terms of *disposable income* (gross income minus just direct taxes), a similar pattern emerged, but by excluding indirect taxes, which, as we have seen, are paid proportionately more by the poor, the Gini coefficient was lower in all years.

Figure 11.4 shows the Gini coefficients for a selection of countries for the latest year available from 2013 to 2015. These are based on *disposable income*: that is, income after the deduction of taxes and the receipt of cash benefits (transfers). They also include the value of goods produced for own consumption as an element of self-employed income. As you can see, Iceland had the lowest Gini coefficient (0.246) and hence was the most equal. Other Scandinavian countries were also relatively equal. The most unequal country in the sample was South Africa (0.620), followed by China (0.556). The average of the 34 developed countries that form the Organisation for Economic Co-operation and Development (OECD) was 0.333, more equal than both the USA (0.390) and the UK (0.360).

Gini coefficients have the advantage of being relatively simple to understand and use. They provide a clear way of comparing income distribution either in the same country at different times, or between different countries.

Definitions

Lorenz curve A curve showing the proportion of national income earned by any given percentage of the population (measured from the poorest upwards).

Gini coefficient The area between the Lorenz curve and the 45° line divided by the total area under the 45° line.

Figure 11.3   UK Gini coefficients: 1977 to 2015/16

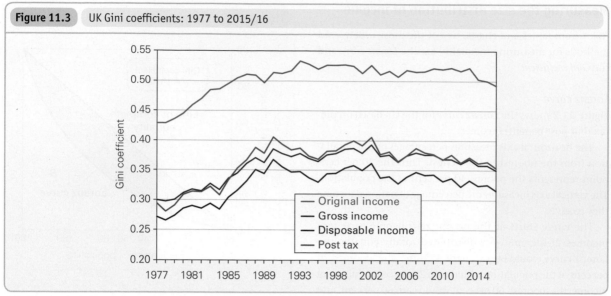

Note: From 1994/5 the figures refer to financial years ending in the year shown.
Source: *Household Disposable Income and Inequality* (ONS, 2017).

Figure 11.4   Gini coefficients for selected countries, based on disposable income: latest year, 2013–15

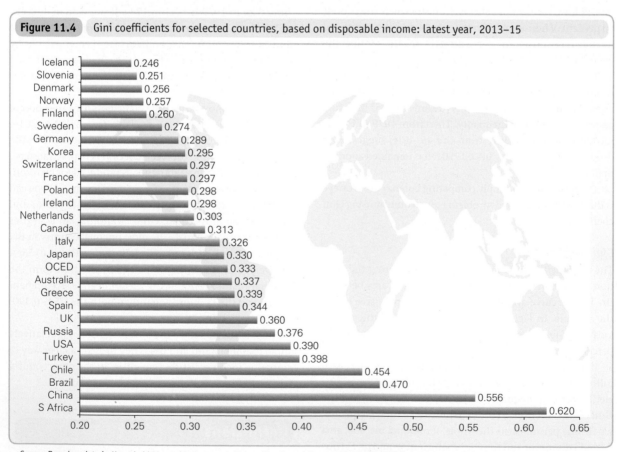

Source: Based on data in *Household Disposable Income and Inequality, financial year ending 2016* (ONS dataset, January 2017)

| **Figure 11.5** | Lorenz curves for two countries with the same Gini coefficients |

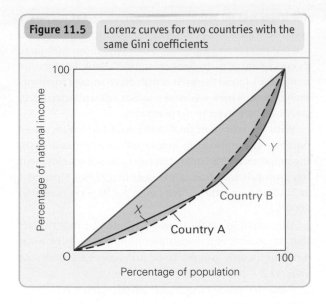

However, they cannot take into account all the features of inequality. Take the case of the two countries illustrated in Figure 11.5. If area *X* is equal to area *Y,* they will have the same Gini coefficient, and yet the pattern of their income distribution is quite different.

Also it is important to note what statistics are used in the calculation. Are they pre-tax or post-tax; do they include benefits; do they include non-monetary incomes (such as food grown for own consumption: a major item in many developing countries); are they based on individuals, households or tax units?

 In which country in Figure 11.5 would you expect to find the highest number of poor people? Describe how income is distributed in the two cases.

Ratios of the shares in national income of two quantile groups

This is a very simple method of measuring income distribution. A ratio quite commonly used is that of the share of national income of the *bottom 40 per cent* of the population to that of the *top 20 per cent.* Thus if the bottom 40 per cent earned 15 per cent of national income and the top 20 per cent earned 50 per cent of national income, the ratio would be 15/50 = 0.3. The lower the ratio, therefore, the greater the inequality. Some figures are shown in Table 11.1.

As can be seen from the table, South Africa is the most unequal country with a ratio of just 0.10 (its Gini coefficient in 2011 was 0.634). Zambia and Brazil also have high levels of inequality. Some of the former communist countries such as Hungary and Romania have greater levels of equality. Generally, advanced countries are more equal than developing countries. Western European countries typically have a ratio of between 0.4 and 0.65. For example, the UK has a figure of 0.49. The USA, however, is less equal, with a ratio of around 0.33.

1. *Why do you think that the ratios for developing countries are lower than those for developed countries?*
2. *Make a list of reasons why the ratios of the bottom 40 per cent to the top 20 per cent may not give an accurate account of relative levels of inequality between countries.*
3. *What would the ratio be if national income were absolutely equally distributed?*

Do earnings statistics give a true representation of inequality?

Although the size distribution of income gives a good first indication of inequality, there are various factors that need to be taken into account when interpreting the statistics.

The first is the diminishing marginal utility of income. If a rich person spends twice as much as a poor person, does that mean that they get twice as much utility? The answer is probably no. The more you earn and spend, the less additional utility you will get for each extra amount spent (see page 131). Part of the reason is that you buy more luxurious versions of products. The argument here is that a car costing £40 000 will not give you four times as much utility as one costing £10 000.

The second factor concerns the interpretation of changes in inequality over time. The past 30 years have seen income increases skewed towards the rich, with the top 10 per cent of income earners getting a lot richer, while the incomes of the poor have risen very little. As we have seen, from 1979 to 2015/16 the Gini coefficient of post-tax income in the UK rose from 0.29 to 0.36.

Although it appears from these figures that inequality has grown rapidly, there may have been factors that mitigate against this. As people earn more, they spend proportionately more on services, such as childcare and personal trainers, and on luxury goods such as designer clothing and fast cars, and proportionately less on items such as basic foodstuffs and clothing. The argument here is that if the prices of these more luxurious goods and services rise faster than

KI 13
p105

| **Table 11.1** | National income share of the poorest 40 per cent of the population as a pro-portion of the share of the richest 20 per cent |

Country	Quantile ratio
South Africa	0.10
Zambia	0.17
Brazil	0.19
USA	0.33
India	0.46
UK	0.49
Hungary	0.55
Romania	0.62

Source: World Development Indicators: Distribution of Income or Consumption, Table 1.3 (The World Bank, various years).

those of more basic goods, the poor will experience a lower inflation rate than the rich. This is what happened over the period 1990–2005, meaning that inequality did not rise as fast as the simple statistics would suggest.

More recently, however, the inflation rate of the poor has overtaken that of the rich. Prices of food and energy have risen faster than those of luxury goods. This would suggest that more recent statistics may have *understated* the growth in inequality.

The third factor that needs to be taken into account when assessing inequality is the distribution of *wealth*. We consider this below (pages 325–6).

The functional distribution of income in the UK

Distribution of income by source

Figure 11.6 shows the sources of household incomes in 1977 and 2015/16. Wages and salaries constitute by far the largest element. However, their share fell from 73 per cent to 63 per cent of national income between 1977 and 2015/16. Conversely, the share coming from total cash benefits and pensions rose from 16 per cent to 25 per cent, reflecting the growing proportion of the population past retirement age, the proportion of the population on low incomes and the stage of the economic cycle.

In contrast to wages and salaries, investment income (dividends, interest and rent) accounts for a relatively small percentage of household income – a mere 3 per cent in 2015/16. Nevertheless, some groups, typically elderly people, rely on savings interest as a key source of income. With policy makers reducing interest rates in 2008 in response to the credit crunch, many of these people suffered falls in their income. Nominal interest rates have remained at historically

low levels and for much of the 2009–17 period they have been below inflation. This has meant that for most savers real interest rates were negative. Conversely, those with large mortgages linked to the Bank of England's Bank Rate ('tracker mortgages'), found themselves with much smaller payments each month. There was thus a major redistributive effect away from net savers to net borrowers.

With the growth of small businesses and the increased numbers of people being 'employed' on a freelance basis, the proportion of incomes coming from self-employment has grown. It rose from 7 per cent in 1977 to 8 per cent in 2015, although this is lower than the 10 per cent seen in 2000/1.

The overall shares illustrated in Figure 11.6 hide the fact that the sources of income differ quite markedly between different income groups. These differences are shown in Table 11.2.

Column (1) shows that higher-income groups get a larger proportion of their income from wages and salaries than do lower-income groups. This can be largely explained by examining column (5). As would be expected, the poor tend to get a larger proportion of their incomes in cash benefits from the government than do people further up the income scale.

One feature to note is that the proportion of income coming from profits, rent and interest (column (3)) varies little between the income groups. In fact only for those people in the top 1 or 2 per cent is it significantly higher. The conclusion from this, plus the fact that investment incomes account for only 3 per cent of household incomes in total, is that incomes from capital and land are of only relatively minor significance in explaining income inequality.

The major cause of differences in incomes between individuals in employment is the differences in wages and salaries between different occupations.

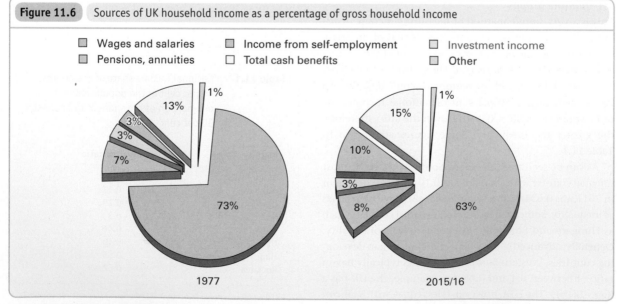

| Figure 11.6 | Sources of UK household income as a percentage of gross household income |

Source: Based on data in *Income and Source of Income for all UK Households*, Table 18 (National Statistics, 2017).

| Table 11.2 | Sources of UK household income as a percentage of total gross household income by quintile groups: 2015/16 |

Gross household weekly incomes (quintiles)	Wages and salaries (1)	Income from self-employment (2)	Income from investments (3)	Pensions and annuities (4)	Total cash benefits (5)	Other (6)	Total (7)
Lowest 20%	30	8	2	7	52	1	100
Next 20%	41	5	1	10	41	2	100
Middle 20%	60	7	1	10	20	2	100
Next 20%	69	7	2	11	10	1	100
Highest 20%	72	10	4	9	3	2	100
All households	63	8	3	10	15	1	100

Source: *Household Disposable Income and Inequality,* Table 2 (National Statistics, 2017).

Distribution of wages and salaries by occupation

Differences in full-time wages and salaries are illustrated in Figure 11.7. This shows the average gross weekly pay of full-time adult workers in selected occupations in 2016. As you can see, there are considerable differences in pay between different occupations. The causes of differences in wage rates from one occupation to another were examined in Chapter 10.

 If fringe benefits (such as long holidays, company cars and health insurance) were included, do you think the level of inequality would increase or decrease? Explain why.

Since the late 1970s, wage differentials have widened. Part of the explanation lies in a shift in the demand for labour. Many firms have adopted new techniques which require a more highly educated workforce. Wage rates in some of these skilled occupations have increased substantially.

At the same time, there has been a decline in the number of unskilled jobs in industry and, along with it, a decline in the power of unions to represent such people. Where low-skilled jobs remain, there will be pressure on employers to reduce wage costs if they are competing with companies based in developing countries, where wage rates are much lower.

| Figure 11.7 | Average gross weekly earnings (excluding overtime) of UK full-time adult employees (£): 2016 |

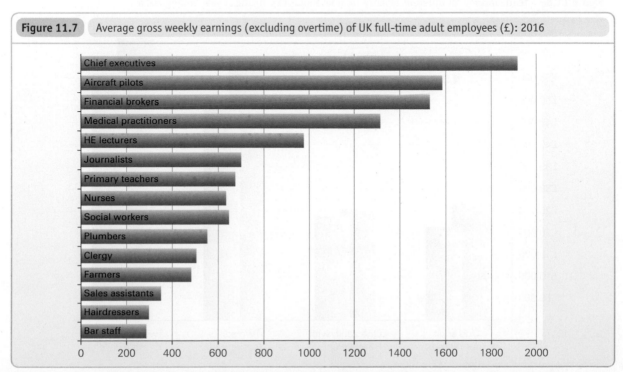

Source: Based on data in of the *Annual Survey of Hours and Earnings,* Table 14.2a (National Statistics, 2016).

As prospects for unskilled people decline in industry, so people with few qualifications increasingly compete for low-paid, service-sector jobs (e.g. in supermarkets and fast-food outlets). The growth in people seeking part-time work has also kept wage rates down in this sector.

Other determinants of income inequality

Differences in household composition

Other things being equal, the more dependants there are in a household, the lower the income will be *per member* of that household. Figure 11.8 gives an extreme example of this. It shows the average household income in the UK in 2015/16 of four different categories of household.

Households containing one adult with children had slightly less gross income than households with only one adult. This means that they had a very much lower income *per member* of the household. This, however, was offset somewhat by the tax and benefits system, with the households with one adult and children having slightly more disposable income than households with just one adult. Disposable income *per member* of the household, however, was still considerably less.

There is a twin problem for many large households. Not only may there be relatively more children and elderly dependants, but also the total household income will be reduced if one of the adults stays at home to look after the family or works only part-time.

Differences by gender

Box 10.7 on pages 294–5 looked at some of the aspects of income inequality between the sexes. In 2016, the average gross weekly pay for full-time female employees was £562.10. For male employees it was £697.1. There are three important factors to note:

- Women are paid less than men in the same occupations. You will see this if you compare some of the occupations in Table (b) in Box 10.7.
- Women tend to be employed in lower-paid occupations than men.
- Women do less overtime than men (on average, 0.5 hours per week, compared with 1.5 for men).

 List the reasons for each of the three factors above. (Re-read section 10.2 and Box 10.7 if you need help.)

Differences in the geographical distribution of income

Figure 11.9 shows the gross yearly household incomes in different regions of the UK in 2014/15. Differences in incomes between the regions reflect regional differences in industrial structure, unemployment and the cost of living. As can be seen from the figure, average incomes are significantly lower in the North- East than in the South East of England and in London.

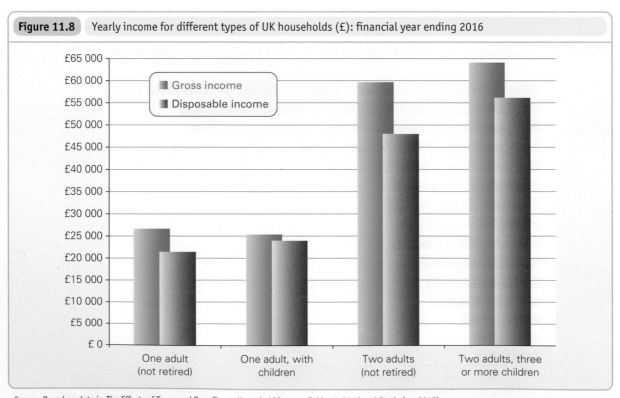

| **Figure 11.8** | Yearly income for different types of UK households (£): financial year ending 2016 |

Source: Based on data in *The Effects of Taxes and Benefits on Household Income,* Table 27 (National Statistics, 2017)

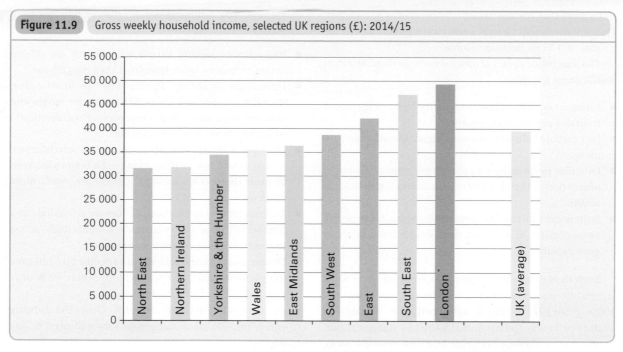

Figure 11.9 Gross weekly household income, selected UK regions (£): 2014/15

Source: Based on data in *The Effects of Taxes and Benefits on Household Income*, Table 28 (ONS, 2016).

On a more local level, there are considerable differences in incomes between affluent areas and deprived areas. It is at this level that some of the most extreme examples of inequality can be observed, with 'leafy' affluent suburbs only a mile or two away from run-down estates. Regional inequality and local inequality are explored in Case Study 23.14 on the student website.

The distribution of wealth

Wealth is difficult to measure. Being a *stock* of assets (such as a house, land, furniture, personal possessions and investments), it has an easily measurable value only when it is sold. What is more, individuals are not required to keep any record of their assets. Only when people die and their assets are assessed for inheritance tax does a record become available. Official statistics are thus based on HMRC data of the assets of those who have died that year. These statistics are suspect for two reasons. First, the people who have died are unlikely to be a representative sample of the population. Second, many items are excluded, such as household and personal items, and items passed automatically to the surviving partner.

Figure 11.10 shows the composition of UK marketable wealth. Residential property is the largest component of wealth (51.7 per cent), followed by bank deposits and cash (15.7 per cent).

Inequality of wealth is far greater than inequality of income. The wealthiest 20 per cent of the adult population owned 64 per cent of aggregate total wealth in 2012–14 – 117

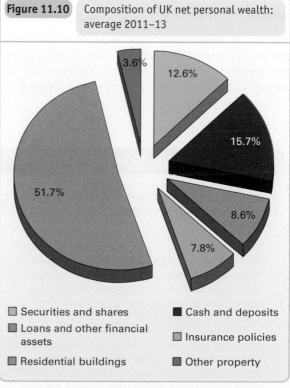

Figure 11.10 Composition of UK net personal wealth: average 2011–13

☐ Securities and shares ◼ Cash and deposits
☐ Loans and other financial assets ☐ Insurance policies
◼ Residential buildings ◼ Other property

Source: Based on of *UK Personal Wealth Statistics*, Table 13.1 (HMRC, September 2016).

KI 26
p303

times more than the least wealthy 20 per cent of households. The Gini coefficient for total wealth was 0.63 compared with a figure of 0.36 for post-tax income.

The four major causes of inequality in the distribution of wealth are as follows:

- Inheritance. This allows inequality to be perpetuated from one generation to another.
- Income inequality. People with higher incomes can save more.
- Different propensities to save. People who save a larger proportion of their income will build up a bigger stock of wealth.
- Entrepreneurial and investment talent/luck. Some people are successful in investing their wealth and making it grow rapidly.

Even though wealth is highly concentrated, there was a significant reduction in inequality of wealth up to the early 1990s. From 1971 to 1991 the Gini coefficient of wealth fell a full 16 percentage points from 0.80 to 0.64. A major reason for this was the increased taxation of inherited wealth. Since 1991, however, this reduction in inequality has been reversed somewhat. This can be explained by lower levels of inheritance tax and substantial rises in property prices and share values.

Causes of inequality

We turn now to identify the major causes of inequality. The problem has many dimensions and there are many factors that determine the pattern and depth of inequality. It is thus wrong to try to look for a single cause, or even the major one. The following are possible determinants of inequality:

- Inequality of wealth. People with wealth are able to obtain an income other than from their own labour.
- Differences in ability. People differ in intelligence, strength, etc. Some of these differences are innate and some are acquired through the process of 'socialisation' – education, home environment, etc.
- Differences in attitude. Some people are adventurous, willing to take risks, willing to move for better jobs, keen to push themselves forward. Others are much more cautious.
- Differences in qualifications. These are reflections of a number of things: ability, attitudes towards study, access to good education, income of parents, etc.
- Differences in hours worked. Some people do a full-time job plus overtime, or a second job; others work only part-time.
- Differences in job utility/disutility. Other things being equal, unpleasant or dangerous jobs will need to pay higher wages.
- Differences in power. Monopoly power in the supply of factors or goods, and monopsony power in the demand for factors, is unequally distributed in the economy.

- Differences in the demand for goods. Factors employed in expanding industries will tend to have a higher marginal revenue product because their output has a higher market value.
- Differences in household composition. The greater the number of dependants relative to income earners, the poorer the average household member will be (other things being equal).

Consider from the following passage whether it is reasonable or even possible to compare poverty today with poverty in the 1800s.

> Every great city has one or more slums, where the working class is crowded together. True, poverty often dwells in hidden alleys close to the palaces of the rich; but, in general, a separate territory has been assigned to it, where, removed from the sight of the happier classes, it may struggle along as it can.
>
> The houses are occupied from cellar to garret, filthy within and without, and their appearance is such that no human being could possibly wish to live in them . . . the filth and tottering ruin surpass all description. Scarcely a whole window-pane can be found, the walls are crumbling, doorposts and window-frames loose and broken, doors of old boards nailed together, or altogether wanting in this thieves' quarter, where no doors are needed, there being nothing to steal. Heaps of garbage

and ashes lie in all directions, and the foul liquids emptied before the doors gather in stinking pools. Here live the poorest of the poor, the worst-paid workers with thieves and the victims of prostitution indiscriminately huddled together . . . and those who have not yet sunk in the whirlpool of moral ruin which surrounds them, sinking daily deeper, losing daily more and more of their power to resist the demoralising influence of want, filth, and evil surroundings.[1]

1. *If we were to measure poverty today and in the nineteenth century in absolute terms, in which would there be the greater number of poor?*
2. *If we measure poverty in relative terms, must a society inevitably have a problem of poverty, however rich it is?*

1 F. Engels, *The Condition of the Working Class in England* (Progress Publishers, 1973), pp. 166–7.

- Discrimination by race, sex, age, social background, etc.
- Degree of government support. The greater the support for the poor, the less will be the level of inequality in the economy.
- Unemployment. When unemployment levels are high, this is one of the major causes of poverty.

 Which of the above causes are reflected in differences in the marginal revenue product of factors?

Government attitudes towards inequality

Attitudes of the right.   The political right sees inequality as having an important economic function. Factor price differences are an essential part of a dynamic market economy. They are the price signals that encourage resources to move to sectors of the economy where demand is growing, and away from sectors where demand is declining. If the government interferes with this process by taxing high incomes and subsidising low incomes, working people will not have the same incentive to gain better qualifications, to seek promotion, to do overtime, or to move for better jobs. Similarly, owners of capital will not have the same incentive to invest.

If inequality is to be reduced, claims the political right, it is better done by encouraging greater factor mobility. If factor supply curves are more elastic (greater mobility), then any shifts in demand will cause smaller changes in factor prices and thus less inequality. But how is greater mobility to be encouraged? The answer, they say, is to create a culture of self-help: where people are not too reliant on state support; where they will look for higher incomes of their own

volition. At the same time, they argue that the monopoly power of unions to interfere in labour markets should be curtailed. The net effect of these policies, they claim, would be to create a more competitive labour market which would help to reduce inequality as well as promoting economic growth and efficiency.

State support, say those on the right, should be confined to the relief of 'genuine' poverty. Benefits should be simply a minimum safety net for those who cannot work (e.g. the sick or disabled), or on a temporary basis for those who, through no fault of their own, have lost their jobs. Even at this basic level, however, the right argues that state support can discourage people from making more effort.

Attitudes of the centre and left.   Although many in the political centre and on the left accept that there is a trade-off between equality and efficiency, they tend to see it as a far less serious problem. They claim that questions of efficiency and growth are best dealt with by encouraging investment. They argue that this can be achieved by creating an environment of industrial democracy where workers participate in investment decisions. This common purpose is in turn best achieved in a more equal and less individualistically competitive society. The left also sees a major role for government in providing support for investment: for example, through government-sponsored research, by investment grants or by encouraging firms to get together and plan a co-ordinated strategy.

These policies to achieve growth and efficiency, claims the left, will leave the government freer to pursue a much more active policy on redistribution.

Section summary

1. Inequality can be examined by looking at the size distribution of income, the functional distribution of income, the distribution of income by recipient, the distribution of wealth, or the extent and nature of poverty.

2. An analysis of the size distribution of income in the UK shows that inequality has grown over the past 30 to 40 years.

3. The size distribution of income can be illustrated by means of a Lorenz curve. The greater the inequality, the more bowed the curve will be towards the bottom right-hand corner.

4. Size distribution can also be measured by a Gini coefficient. This will give a figure between 0 (total equality) and 1 (total inequality). Income distribution can also be measured as the ratio of the share of national income of a given lower income quantile to that of a higher income quantile.

5. Wages and salaries constitute by far the largest source of income, and thus inequality can be explained mainly in

terms of differences in wages and salaries. Nevertheless, state benefits are an important moderating influence on inequality and constitute the largest source of income for the poorest 20 per cent of households. Investment earnings are only a minor determinant of income except for the richest 1 or 2 per cent.

6. Other determinants of income inequality include differences in household composition, gender and where people live.

7. The distribution of wealth is less equal than the distribution of income.

8. Attitudes towards government redistribution of income vary among political parties. The political right stresses the danger that redistributive policies may destroy incentives. The best approach to inequality, according to the right, is to 'free up' markets so as to encourage greater mobility. The left, by contrast, sees fewer dangers in reducing incentives and stresses the moral and social importance of redistribution from rich to poor.

BOX 11.2 MINIMUM WAGE LEGISLATION

A way of helping the poor?

The Labour government introduced a statutory UK minimum wage in April 1999. The rate was set at £3.60 per hour for those aged 22 and over, and £3.00 for those between 18 and 21. In 2004, an additional rate was introduced for 16 and 17 year-olds and in 2010 for apprentices aged 16–18 and those aged 19 in the first year of their apprenticeship. In 2015, George Osbourne announced that a new statutory 'national living wage' would be introduced in April 2016. This is effectively a new higher minimum wage for those workers aged 25 and above.

The rates are increased every year and were set at the following levels for 2017/18.

- 25 and over   £7.50
- 21 to 24   £7.05
- 18 to 20   £5.60
- Under 18   £4.05
- Apprentice   £3.50

As of January 2017, 22 of out the 28 EU member countries had a national minimum wage. The rates vary among the member states from €2.19 in Latvia to €11.53 in Luxembourg. Once adjustments have been made to take account of the different price levels, the ratio between the highest and lowest rates falls from 8.5:1 to 3.3:1. The UK has the seventh highest figure.

The call for a minimum wage in the UK grew during the 1990s as the number of low-paid workers increased. There were many people working as cleaners, security guards and shop assistants who were receiving very low rates of pay, sometimes less than £2 per hour. Several factors explain the growth in the size of the low-pay sector.

Lower demand for unskilled labour. Increased unemployment since the early 1980s had shifted the balance of power from workers to employers. Employers were able to force many wage rates downwards, especially those of unskilled workers.

Growth in part-time employment. Changes in the structure of the UK economy, particularly the growth in the service sector and the growing proportion of women seeking work, had led to an increase in part-time employment and zero hours contracts, with many part-time workers not receiving the same rights and hourly pay as their full-time equivalents until 2000.

Changes in labour laws. The abolition of 'wages councils' in 1993, which had set legally enforceable minimum hourly rates in various low-paid industries, and the introduction of various new laws to reduce the power of labour (see page 290) had left low-paid workers with little protection.

Assessing the arguments

The principal argument against imposing a national minimum wage concerns its impact on employment. If you raise wage rates above the equilibrium level, there will be surplus labour: i.e. unemployment (see Figure 10.9 on page 289). However, the impact of a national minimum wage on employment is not so simple.

In the case of a firm operating in competitive labour and goods markets, the demand for low-skilled workers is relatively wage sensitive. Any rise in wage rates, and hence prices, by this firm alone would lead to a large fall in sales and hence in employment. But given that all firms face the minimum wage, individual employers are more able to pass on higher wages in higher prices, knowing that their competitors are doing the same.

When employers have a degree of monopsony power, however, it is not even certain that they would want to reduce

---

The marginal rate of income tax is the rate that people pay on additional income. In most countries, the marginal rate increases in bands as people earn more. In many countries, there is a main marginal rate of tax that most people pay. This is known as the standard or **basic rate of tax**.

The *average* rate is a person's total income tax as a fraction of total income. This will always be less than the marginal rate, since part of a person's income will be tax-free; and for higher tax rate payers, part will be taxed at lower rates.

Definition

Basic rate of tax The main marginal rate of tax, applying to most people's incomes.

Individuals' social security contributions. In the UK these are known as national insurance contributions (NICs). These are like income taxes in that they are generally charged as a percentage of a person's income, the marginal rate varying with income. Unlike other taxes, which are paid into a common fund to finance government expenditure, they are used to finance *specific* expenditure: namely, pensions and social security. Although they do not officially count as 'taxes', to all intents and purposes they are so.

Table 11.3 and Figure 11.11 show the marginal and average rates of income tax and social security contributions in England, Wales and Northern Ireland in 2017/18. Notice that above £100 000, the personal allowance is reduced by £1 for each £2 earned. This is equivalent to an extra 20 per cent for the next £23 000 (i.e. £11500 × 2).

employment. Remember what we argued in Figure 10.10 (on page 289) when we were examining the effects of unions driving up wages. The argument is the same with a minimum wage. The minimum wage can be as high as W_2 and the firm will still want to employ as many workers as at W_1. The point is that the firm can no longer drive down the wage rate by employing fewer workers, so the incentive to cut its workforce has been removed.

In the long run, the effect on unemployment will depend on the extent to which the higher wages are compensated by higher labour productivity.

Evidence from the USA and other countries suggested that modest increases in the minimum wage had a neutral effect upon employment. Similarly in the UK, there is little evidence to suggest that from 1999 employers responded by employing fewer workers. In fact, until 2008, unemployment rates fell every year, due to the buoyant economy and increasing labour market flexibility (see Box 10.8).

Whether there would continue to be little effect if the minimum wage were to rise substantially is another matter. The question for policy makers, then, seems to be how high the minimum wage can be set before unemployment begins to rise.

Impact of the minimum wage in the UK

The Low Pay Commission estimated that 2.3 million people (8.5 per cent of workers) would be on one of the minimum wage rates from April 2017. This figure was below 500 000 in 2001. If the increases in the NLW are introduced as planned, then by 2020 3.3 million workers will be covered. Evidence suggests that that there is also a *ripple effect* on workers earning just above the minimum wage rates. The growth in pay in 2015/16 for those in the bottom quarter of the pay distribution (i.e. earning up to £9 per hour) was greater than the average.

There has been criticism of the UK government for 'hijacking' the term 'National Living Wage'. The term 'living wage' has been used for several years by the Living Wage Foundation. It is independently calculated each year by the Resolution Foundation 'based on what employees and their families need to live'. In 2017, it was £9.75 in London and £8.45 in other parts of the UK for all workers over 18.

One concern for economists, when assessing the national minimum wage, is that living costs, and particularly housing costs, vary substantially across the economy. For example, 22 per cent of workers in the local authority of West Somerset are covered by the latest rates, whereas the figure for Westminster is just 3 per cent. There have been suggestions that *local* minimum wages rates should be set to ensure both a fairer and a more efficient allocation of resources.

Of course, a weakness of using a minimum wage as a means of relieving poverty is that it only affects the employed; yet one of the main causes of poverty is unemployment. This, in part, explains the focus on getting adults into work as the major plank of poverty relief policy in the UK. It is apparent that a minimum wage rate cannot be the sole answer to poverty and must be considered in conjunction with benefits.

1. *If an increase in wage rates for low-paid workers leads to their being more motivated, how would this affect the marginal revenue product and the demand for such workers? What implications does your answer have for the effect on employment in such cases? (See page 291 on the efficiency wage hypothesis.)*
2. *If a rise in the minimum wage encourages employers to substitute machines for workers, will this necessarily lead to higher long-term unemployment in (a) that industry and (b) the economy in general?*

Table 11.3	UK[1] marginal income tax and national insurance rates: 2017/18

Income per annum (£)	Marginal income tax rate (%)	Marginal NIC rate (%)	Marginal income tax plus NIC rate (%)
0–8164	0	0	0
8165–11 500	0	12	12
11 501–45 000	20	12	32
45 001–100 000	40	2	42
100 001–123 000	40 + 20	2	62
123 001–150 000	40	2	42
Above 150 000	45	2	47

1 The structure is very similar in Scotland but the Scottish Government used its devolved powers to leave the income threshold at which people pay 40 per cent income tax at £43 000 in 2017/18.

Employers' social security contributions. Employers also have to pay social security contributions on behalf of their employees. These are paid per employee. In some countries, small firms pay reduced rates.

Tax on corporate income. In the UK this is known as corporation tax. It is a tax on the profits of limited companies. In most countries, there are lower rates for small companies. Profits can usually be offset against capital expenditure and interest payments when working out the tax liability. This effectively means that profits that are reinvested are not taxed.

Tax on capital gains. This is a tax payable when a person sells assets, such as property or shares. It is payable on the gain in value of these assets since a set date in the past, or since they were purchased if this was after the set date.

Figure 11.11 UK[2] marginal and average rates of income tax plus national insurance contributions, 2017/18

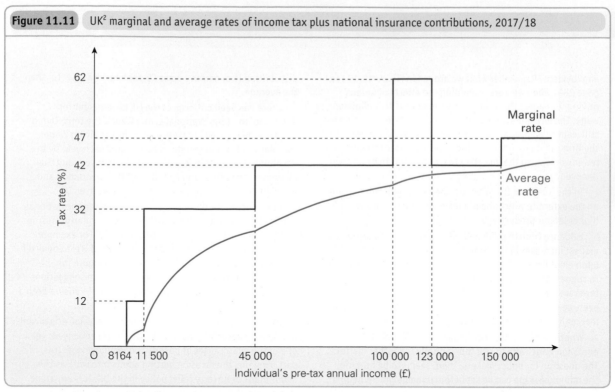

2 The threshold at which people pay 40 per cent income tax in Scotland is £43 000 in 2017/18

Taxes on wealth. These are taxes on assets held or acquired by individuals. One form of wealth tax in most countries is that on inherited assets or assets transferred before a person's death. Another is taxes based on the value of a person's property. This is a particularly common form of local taxation (the others being local income tax, local business tax and local sales tax).

Poll taxes. These are fixed-sum charges per head of the population, irrespective of the person's income. Very few countries use such taxes as they are regarded as unfair. A poll tax (or 'community charge') was introduced in Scotland in 1989 and in England and Wales in 1990 as the new form of local tax, replacing the property tax called 'rates', which was based on property values. But it was massively unpopular with the electorate, leading to demonstrations and riots, and was replaced by 'council tax' (again based on property values) in 1993.

Indirect taxes

There are three main types of indirect tax, all of which are taxes on *expenditure.*

General expenditure taxes. An example of this is **value added tax (VAT)**. This is the main indirect tax throughout the EU. VAT is paid on the value that firms add to goods and services at each stage of their production and distribution. For example, if a firm purchases supplies costing £10 000 and

with them produces goods that it sells for £15 000 (before VAT), it is liable to pay VAT on the £15 000 minus £10 000: in other words, on the £5000 value it has added. Suppliers must provide invoices to show that the VAT has already been paid on all the inputs.

The example in Table 11.4 can be used to show how the tax eventually gets passed on to the consumer. For simplicity's sake, assume that the rate of VAT is 20 per cent and that each firm uses only one supplier.

The value added at each stage plus VAT adds up to the total amount paid by the consumer: £48 000 in this case. The total VAT paid, therefore, amounts to a tax on the consumer. In the example, the £8000 VAT is 20 per cent of the (pre-tax) consumer price of £40 000.

The rates of VAT in the various EU countries are considered in Box 24.10. Each country has a standard rate and up to two lower rates for basic goods and services. Standard rates vary between 15 and 27 per cent, but are typically between 20 and 25 per cent.

Definition

Value added tax (VAT) A tax on goods and services, charged at each stage of production as a percentage of the value added at that stage.

Table 11.4 Calculating VAT: an example where the rate of VAT is 20%

	Value added (1)	VAT (2)	Value added plus VAT (3)	Price sold to next stage (4)
Firm A sells raw materials to firm B for £12 000	£10 000	£2000	£12 000	£12 000
Firm B processes them and sells them to a manufacturer, firm C, for £21 600	£8 000	£1600	£9 600	£21 600
Firm C sells the manufactured goods to a wholesaler, firm D, for £30 000	£7 000	£1400	£8 400	£30 000
Firm D sells them to a retailer, firm E, for £36 000	£5 000	£1000	£6 000	£36 000
Firm E sells them to consumers for £48 000	£10 000	£2000	£12 000	£48 000
	£40 000 +	**£8000** =	**£48 000**	

Many other countries levy general expenditure taxes at a *single* stage (either wholesale or retail). These taxes are called *purchase taxes* and will normally be a percentage of the price of the good at that stage.

Excise duties. These are taxes on particular goods and services: for example, petrol and diesel, alcoholic drinks, tobacco products and gambling. They are a single-stage tax levied on the manufacturer. For example, duty on beer in the UK depends on its alcoholic strength measured as alcohol by volume (ABV). If the ABV of the beer is between 2.8 per cent and 7.5 per cent then the rate of duty in 2017/18 is 19.08 pence per litre for each 1 per cent of ABV. This means that the duty paid on a 5 per cent ABV pint of beer would be 54p. Duty is paid in addition to VAT.

VAT is an ***ad valorem tax***. This means that the tax is levied at a *percentage* of the value of the good. The higher the value of the good, the higher the tax paid. Excise duties, by contrast, are a ***specific tax***. This means that they are levied at a *fixed amount,* irrespective of the value of the good. Thus the duty on a litre of unleaded petrol is the same for a cut-price filling station as for a full-price one.

Customs duties. Economists normally refer to these as ***tariffs***. They are duties on goods imported from outside the country.

 To what extent do (a) income tax, (b) VAT and (c) a poll tax meet the various requirements for a good tax system on pages 328–9 above? (Some of the answers to this question are given below.)

Details of tax rates in the UK are given in Case Study 11.3 on the student website. This case study also examines how progressive or regressive the various types of tax are.

The balance of taxation

Table 11.5 shows the balance of the different types of tax in selected countries. Some striking differences can be seen between the countries. In France, income and capital gains

---

Definition

Ad valorem tax A tax on a good levied as a percentage of its value. It can be a single-stage tax or a multi-stage tax (as with VAT).

Specific tax A tax on a good levied at a fixed amount per unit of the good, irrespective of the price of that unit.

Tariff A tax on imported goods.

Table 11.5 Balance of taxation in selected countries (2015)

Types of tax as percentage of GDP	France	Germany	Japan	Sweden	UK	USA
Personal income tax and capital gains tax	8.6	9.9	6.1	12.5	9.1	10.7
Social security: employee and self-employed contributions	5.6	7.4	6.9[1]	2.7	2.5	3.2
Social security: employer contributions	11.3	6.6	5.8[1]	7.0	3.5	3.1
Corporate taxes	2.1	1.7	4.3	3.0	2.5	2.2
Payroll taxes	1.6	0.0	0.0	4.6	0.0	0.0
Taxes on property and wealth	4.1	1.1	2.6	1.1	4.1	2.7
Taxes on goods and services	11.1	10.1	6.8	12.3	10.7	4.4
Other taxes	1.1	0.1	0.0	0.1	0.1	0.1
Total taxes	45.5	36.9	32.0[1]	43.3	32.5	26.4

1 2014.
Source: Extracted from Revenue statistics tables in *StatExtracts* (OECD).

taxes account for only 18.9 per cent of tax revenue, whereas in the USA they account for 40.5 per cent. In the UK, social security contributions (national insurance) are a lower percentage of total taxes than in other countries, whereas taxes on property (mainly the council tax) are a higher percentage of total taxes.

There is also a big difference between countries in the proportion of taxes paid by companies and that paid by individuals. Corporate taxes, payroll taxes and employer social security contributions account for 33.0 per cent of taxes and 15.0 per cent of GDP[3] in France. In the USA they account for only 20.1 per cent of taxes and just 5.3 per cent of GDP.

In terms of total taxes, again there are large differences between countries. In France 45.5 per cent of GDP is paid in tax whereas in the USA the figure is only 26.4 per cent.

Taxes as a means of redistributing income

If taxes are to be used as a means of achieving greater equality, the rich must be taxed proportionately more than the poor. The degree of redistribution will depend on the degree of 'progressiveness' of the tax. In this context, taxes may be classified as follows:

- **Progressive tax**. As people's income (Y) rises, the percentage of their income paid in the tax (T) rises. In other words, the *average* rate of tax (T/Y) rises.
- **Regressive tax**. As people's income rises, the percentage of their income paid in the tax falls: T/Y falls.
- **Proportional tax**. As people's income rises, the percentage of their income paid in the tax stays the same: T/Y is constant.

In other words, progressiveness is defined in terms of what happens to the average rate of tax as incomes rise. (Note that it is not defined in terms of the *marginal* rate of tax.)

1. *If a person earning £10 000 per year pays £1000 in a given tax and a person earning £20 000 per year pays £1600, is the tax progressive or regressive?*
2. *A proportional tax will leave the distribution of income unaffected. Why should this be so, given that a rich person will pay a larger absolute amount than a poor person?*

An extreme form of regressive tax is a lump-sum tax (e.g. a poll tax). This is levied at a fixed *amount* (not rate) irrespective of income.

Figure 11.12 illustrates these different categories of tax. Diagram (a) shows the total amount of tax that a person pays. With a progressive tax, the curve gets progressively steeper, showing that the average rate of tax (T/Y) rises. The marginal rate of tax ($\Delta T/\Delta Y$) is given by the slope. Thus between points x and y the marginal tax rate is 40 per cent.

Diagram (b) shows the average rates. With a proportional tax, a person pays the same amount of tax on each pound earned. With a progressive tax, a larger proportion is paid by a rich person than by a poor person, and vice versa with a regressive tax.

The more steeply upward sloping the average tax curve, the more progressive is the tax, and the more equal will be the post-tax incomes of the population.

> ## Definition
>
> **Progressive tax** A tax whose average rate with respect to income rises as income rises.
>
> **Regressive tax** A tax whose average rate with respect to income falls as income rises.
>
> **Proportional tax** A tax whose average rate with respect to income stays the same as income rises.

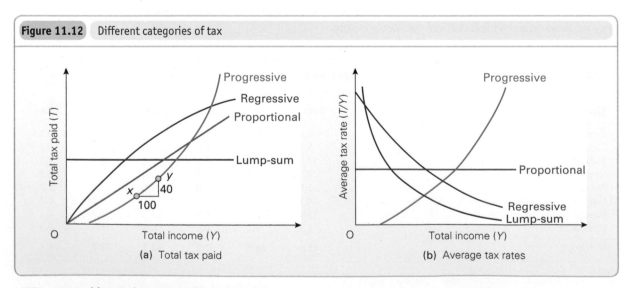

Figure 11.12 Different categories of tax

(a) Total tax paid

(b) Average tax rates

3 GDP is a measure of the nation's income: we will be examining how it is measured in the appendix to Chapter 15.

Problems with using taxes to redistribute incomes

How successfully can taxes redistribute income, and at what economic cost?

Problems in achieving redistribution

How to help the very poor. Taxation takes away income. It can thus reduce the incomes of the rich. But no taxes, however progressive, can *increase* the incomes of the poor. This will require subsidies (i.e. benefits).

But what about tax cuts? Can bigger tax cuts not be given to the poor? This is possible only if the poor are already paying taxes in the first place. Take the two cases of income tax and taxes on goods and services.

■ *Income tax.* If the government cuts income tax, then anyone currently paying it will benefit. A cut in tax *rates* will give proportionately more to the rich, since they have a larger proportion of taxable income relative to total income. An increase in personal *allowances,* on the other hand, will give the same *absolute* amounts to everyone above the new tax threshold. This will therefore represent a smaller proportionate gain to the rich. In either case, however, there will be no gain at all to those people below the tax threshold. They paid no income tax in the first place and gain nothing at all from income tax cuts.

KI 9
p66

■ *Taxes on goods and services.* Since these taxes are generally regressive, any cut in their rate will benefit the poor proportionately more than the rich. A more dramatic effect would be obtained by cutting the rate most on those goods consumed relatively more by the poor.

The government may not wish to cut the overall level of taxation, given its expenditure commitments. In this case, it can switch the burden from regressive to progressive taxes, if it wishes to benefit the very poor.

Tax evasion and tax avoidance. The higher the rates of tax, the more likely are people to try to escape paying some of their taxes.

TC 5
p81

People who are subject to higher rates of income tax will be more tempted not to declare all their income. This tax *evasion* will be much easier for people not paying all their taxes through a pay-as-you-earn (PAYE) scheme. This will include the self-employed and people doing casual work on top of their normal job ('moonlighting'). Furthermore, richer people can often reduce their tax liability – engage in *tax avoidance* – by a careful use of various legal devices such as trusts and tax loopholes such as being allowed to offset 'business expenses' against income.

Part of the government's justification for abolishing income tax rates above 40 per cent in 1988 was that many people escaped paying these higher taxes. Nevertheless, in 2009 the Labour Chancellor, Alistair Darling, announced that a new top rate of 50 per cent would be introduced in 2010/11. He forecast that this would bring an extra £3 billion

per year in tax revenues. However, in 2011, the Office for Budget Responsibility suggested that the overall increases were likely to be much lower than this and HMRC figures suggested that £100 million a year would be lost in avoidance.

In 2013, the Coalition reduced the top rate to 45 per cent. It is difficult, if not impossible, to calculate the exact effect of these marginal changes.

Why may a steeply progressive income tax which is designed to achieve greater vertical equity lead to a reduction in horizontal equity?

Undesired incidence of tax. High rates of income tax on high wage earners may simply encourage employers to pay them higher wages. At the other end of the scale, tax cuts for low-paid workers may simply allow employers to cut wages. In other words, part of the incidence of income taxes will be borne by the employer and only part by the employee. Thus attempting to make taxes more 'progressive' will fail if employers simply adjust wages to compensate.

The incidence of income tax is determined by the elasticity of supply and demand for labour. In Figure 11.13, the initial supply and demand curves for labour (before the imposition of the tax) intersect at point (1), giving Q_1 labour employed at a wage of W_1. Now an income tax is imposed. This shifts the labour supply curve vertically upwards by the amount of the tax, giving the new labour supply curve, $S + \text{tax}$. The new equilibrium is reached at point (2) with Q_2 labour employed at a (gross) wage of W_2.

KI 9
p66

The incidence of the tax is as follows:

■ The total tax revenue for the government is shown by the total shaded area.
■ Workers' take-home pay is cut from W_1 to $W_2 - \text{tax}$. Their share of the tax is thus area A.
■ Employers have to pay workers a rise of $W_2 - W_1$. They pay area B.

If the supply curve of labour of well-paid workers is relatively elastic, as shown in Figure 11.13, there will only be a

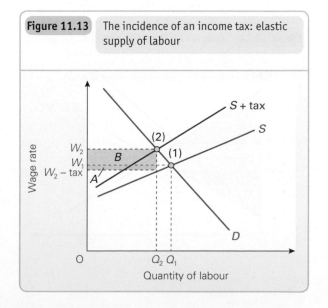

Figure 11.13 The incidence of an income tax: elastic supply of labour

relatively slight fall in take-home pay (the workers' share of the tax is relatively small). The tax will, therefore, have only a relatively slight redistributive effect away from this group of workers.

1. Do poor people gain more from a cut in income tax with an elastic or an inelastic supply of labour? Is the supply of unskilled workers likely to be elastic or inelastic?
2. Draw two diagrams like Figure 11.13, one with a steep demand curve and one with a shallow demand curve. How does the elasticity of demand affect the incidence of the income tax?

Of course, income taxes are not imposed on workers in one industry alone. People therefore cannot move to another industry to avoid paying taxes. This fact will cause a relatively inelastic supply response to any rise in income tax, since the only alternative to paying the income tax is to work less. The less elastic this response, the more will the burden of the tax fall on the taxpayer and the more effectively can income taxes be used to redistribute incomes.

The economic costs of redistribution

If redistribution is to be achieved through *indirect* taxes, this can lead to market distortions.

Take first the case of an indirect tax applied to one good only. Assume for simplicity that there is universal perfect competition. Raising the price of this good relative to other goods will introduce a market distortion. Consumption will shift away from this good towards other goods that people preferred less at the original prices. What is more, the loss to consumers and producers (other things being equal) will be greater than the gain to the community from the tax revenue. This is illustrated in Figure 11.14.

With no tax, price will be at P_1 and output at Q_1, where demand equals supply. By imposing a tax on the good, the supply curve shifts upwards to S + tax. Price rises to P_2 and output falls to Q_2. Producers are left with $P_2 -$ tax. What are the various losses and gains?

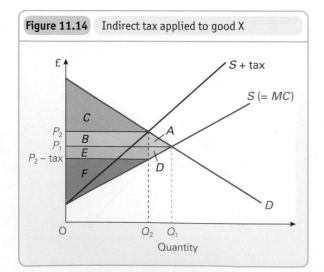

Figure 11.14   Indirect tax applied to good X

Consumers, by having to pay a higher price, lose consumer surplus (see section 4.1). Originally their consumer surplus was areas $A + B + C$. With the price now at P_2, the consumer surplus falls to area C alone. The loss to consumers is areas $A + B$.

Producers, by receiving a lower price after tax and selling fewer units, lose profits. In the simple case where there are no fixed costs of production, total profits are simply the sum of all the marginal profits ($P (= MR) - MC$) on each of the units sold. Thus before the tax is imposed, firms receive total profits of areas $D + E + F$. After the tax is imposed, they receive a profit of area F alone. The loss in profits to producers is therefore areas $D + E$.

The total loss to consumers and producers is areas $A + B + D + E$. The gain to the government in tax revenue is areas $B + E$: the tax rate times the number of units sold (Q_2). There is thus a net loss to the community of areas $A + D$. This is known as the *deadweight loss of the tax*.

However, if the money raised from the tax is redistributed to the poor, their gain in welfare is likely to exceed the loss in welfare from the higher tax. The reason is that a pound sacrificed by the average consumer is probably of less value to them than a pound gained by a poor person.

What is more, if the tax is applied at a uniform rate to *all* goods, there is no distortion resulting from reallocation between goods. This is one of the major justifications for having a single rate of VAT.

Of course, in the real world, markets are highly imperfect and there is no reason why taxes will necessarily make these imperfections worse. In fact, it might be desirable on efficiency grounds to tax certain goods and services, such as cigarettes, alcohol, petrol and gambling, at higher rates than other goods and services. We will examine these arguments in the next chapter.

Although there are costs of redistribution, there are also benefits extending beyond those to whom income is redistributed. If redistribution to the poor reduces crime, vandalism and urban squalor, then it is not just the poor who gain: it is everyone, both financially in terms of reduced policing and social work costs, and more generally in terms of living in a happier and less divided society.

Taxation and incentives

Another possible economic cost of high tax rates is that they may act as a disincentive to work, thereby reducing national output and consumption. This whole question of incentives is highly charged politically. According to the political

Definition

Deadweight loss of an indirect tax The net loss of consumer plus producer surplus (after adding in the tax revenue) from the imposition of an indirect tax.

right, there is a trade-off between output and equity. High and progressive income taxes can lead to a more equal distribution of income, but a smaller national output. Alternatively, if taxes are cut there will be a bigger national output, but less equally divided. If many on the left are correct, however, we can have both a more equal society *and* a bigger national output: there is no trade-off.

The key to analysing these arguments is to distinguish between the *income effect* and the *substitution effect* of a tax rise. Raising taxes does two things:

- It reduces incomes. People may therefore work *more* in an attempt to maintain their consumption of goods and services. This is the **income effect**.
- It reduces the opportunity cost of leisure. An extra hour taken in leisure now involves a smaller sacrifice in consumption, since each hour less worked involves less sacrifice in after-tax income. Thus people may substitute leisure for consumption, and work *less*. This is the **substitution effect**.

The relative size of the income and substitution effects is likely to differ for different types of people and different types of tax change.

Different types of people

The *income* effect is likely to dominate for people with long-term commitments: for example, those with families, or those with mortgages and other debts. They may feel forced to work *more* to maintain their disposable income. Clearly for such people, higher taxes are *not* a disincentive to work. The income effect is also likely to be relatively large for people on higher incomes, for whom an increase in tax rates represents a substantial cut in income.

The *substitution* effect is likely to dominate for those with few commitments: those whose families have left home, the single and second income earners in families where that second income is not relied on for 'essential' consumption. A rise in tax rates for these people is likely to encourage them to work less.

> ### Definitions
>
> **Income effect of a tax rise** Tax increases reduce people's incomes and thus encourage people to work more.
>
> **Substitution effect of a tax rise** Tax increases reduce the opportunity cost of leisure and thus encourage people to work less.

BOX 11.3 THE LAFFER CURVE

EXPLORING ECONOMICS

Having your cake and eating it

Professor Art Laffer was one of President Reagan's advisers during his first administration (1981–4). He was a strong advocate of income tax cuts, arguing that substantial increases in output would result.

He went further than this. He argued that tax cuts would actually increase the amount of tax revenue that the government earned.

If tax cuts cause income to rise (due to incentives) proportionately more than the tax rate has fallen, then tax revenues will increase. These effects are illustrated by the now famous 'Laffer' curve.

If the average tax rate were zero, no revenue would be raised. As the tax rate is raised above zero, tax revenues will increase. The curve will be upward sloping. Eventually, however, the curve will peak (at tax rate t_1). Thereafter tax rates become so high that the resulting fall in output more than offsets the rise in tax rate. When the tax rate reaches 100 per cent, the revenue will once more fall to zero, since no one will bother to work.

The curve may not be symmetrical. It may peak at a 40 per cent, 50 per cent, 60 per cent or even 90 per cent rate. Nevertheless, Laffer and others on the political right argued that tax rates were above t_1. In fact, most evidence suggests that tax rates in most countries were well below t_1 in the 1980s and certainly are now, given the cuts in

income tax rates that have been made around the world over the past 20 years.

1. *What is the elasticity of supply of output with respect to changes in tax rates at a tax rate of t_1? What is it below t_1? What is it above t_1?*
2. *If the substitution effect of a tax cut outweighs the income effect, does this necessarily mean that the economy is to the right of point t_1?*

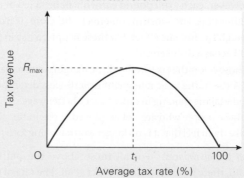

Total tax revenue

Although high income earners may work more when there is a tax *rise,* they may still be discouraged by a steeply progressive tax *structure.* If they have to pay very high marginal rates of tax, it may simply not be worth their while seeking promotion or working harder (see Boxes 11.3 and 11.4).

> 1. *Who is likely to work harder as a result of a cut in income tax rates, a rich person or a poor person? Why? Would your answer be different if personal allowances were zero?*
> 2. *How will tax cuts affect the willingness of women to return to employment after having brought up a family?*

Different types of tax change

A government may wish to raise income taxes in order to redistribute incomes through higher benefits. There are three main ways it can do so: raising the higher rates of tax; raising the basic rate; and reducing tax allowances.

Raising the higher rates of tax. This may seem the most effective way of redistributing incomes: after all, it is only the rich who will suffer. There are, however, serious problems:

- The income effect will be relatively small, since it is only that part of incomes subject to the higher rates that will be affected. The substitution effect, however, could be relatively high. Rich people are likely to put a higher premium on leisure, and may well feel that it is not worth working so hard if a larger proportion of any increase in income is taken in taxes.

- It may discourage risk-taking by businesspeople.
- The rich may be more mobile internationally, so there may be a 'brain drain'. This criticism was made by the then Mayor of London, Boris Johnson, when discussing the effect of a 50 per cent tax rate on the financial sector.

Raising the basic rate of tax. As we have seen, the income effect is likely to be relatively large for those with higher incomes, especially if they have substantial commitments like a large mortgage. For such people, a rise in tax rates is likely to act as an incentive.

For those just above the tax threshold, there will be very little extra to pay on *existing* income, since most of it is tax-free. However, each *extra* pound earned will be taxed at the new higher rate. The substitution effect, therefore, is likely to outweigh the income effect. For these people, a rise in tax rates will act as a disincentive.

For those below the tax threshold, the marginal rate remains at zero. A rise in the basic rate might nevertheless deter them from undertaking training in order to get a better wage.

For those people who are not employed, a rise in tax rates may make them feel that it is no longer worth looking for a job.

Reducing tax allowances. For all those above the old tax threshold, there is no *substitution* effect at all. The rate of tax has not changed. However, there is an *income* effect. The effect is like a lump-sum tax. Everyone's take-home pay is cut by a fixed sum, and people will need to work harder to

make up some of the shortfall. This type of tax change, however, is highly regressive. If everyone pays the same *amount* of extra tax, this represents a bigger percentage for poorer people than richer people. In other words, there may be no negative incentive effects, but it is not suitable as part of a policy to redistribute incomes more equally!

The conclusion from the theoretical arguments is that tax changes will have very different effects depending on (a) whom they affect and (b) the nature of the change.

> 1. *A key policy of the UK Coalition government, achieved in April 2014, was to raise the personal income tax allowance to £10 000. This was accompanied by the gradual removal of the same allowance from those earning over £100 000 (see Table 11.3 on page 331). Evaluate these policies.*
> 2. *What would the effects be of cuts in (i) the basic rate of tax (ii) the top rate of tax?*
> 3. *What tax changes (whether up or down) will have a positive incentive effect and also redistribute incomes more equally?*

One final point should be stressed. For many people, there is no choice in the amount they work. The job they do dictates the number of hours worked, irrespective of changes in taxation.

Evidence

All the available evidence suggests that the effects of tax changes on output are relatively small. Labour supply curves seem highly inelastic to tax changes.

Benefits

Benefits can be either cash benefits or benefits in kind.

Cash benefits

Means-tested benefits. **Means-tested benefits** are available only to those whose income (and savings in some instances) fall below a certain level. To obtain such benefits, therefore, people must apply for them and declare their personal circumstances to the authorities. Examples include housing benefit and income support, the safety net that exists for all in the UK.

The benefits could be given as grants or merely as loans. They could be provided as general income support or for the meeting of specific needs, such as rents, fuel bills and household items.

Universal benefits. **Universal benefits** are those that everyone is entitled to, irrespective of their income, if they fall

---

Definitions

Means-tested benefits Benefits whose amount depends on the recipient's income or assets.

Universal benefits Benefits paid to everyone in a certain category irrespective of their income or assets.

An application of indifference curve analysis[1]

Will tax cuts provide an incentive for people to work more? This question can be analysed using indifference curves (see section 4.3). The analysis is similar to that developed in Box 10.2. It is assumed that individuals can choose how many hours a day to work.

The position with no income tax

Diagram (a) shows the situation without income tax.

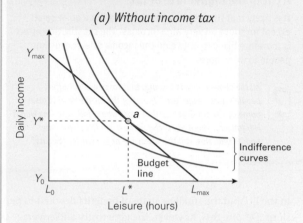

(a) Without income tax

The budget line shows the various combinations of leisure and income open to an individual at a given wage rate.

Why is the budget line straight? What would it look like if overtime were paid at higher rates per hour?

The indifference curves show all the combinations of income and leisure that give the person equal satisfaction. The optimum combination of income and leisure is at Y^* and L^* where the individual is on the highest possible indifference curve: point a.

The position with income tax

Now let us introduce a system of income taxes. This is illustrated in diagram (b).

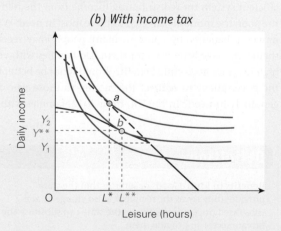

(b) With income tax

Assume that the tax has the following features:

- Up to an income of Y_1 no tax is paid: Y_1 is the individual's personal allowance.
- From Y_1 to Y_2 the basic rate of tax is paid. The budget line is flatter, since less extra income is earned for each extra hour of leisure sacrificed.
- Above Y_2 the higher rate of tax is paid. The budget line becomes flatter still.

The individual illustrated in the diagram will now choose to earn a take-home pay of Y^{**} and have L^{**} hours of leisure: point b. Note that this is more leisure than in the no-tax situation (point a). In this diagram, then, the tax has acted as a disincentive. The substitution effect has outweighed the income effect.

Redraw diagram (b), but in such a way that the income effect outweighs the substitution effect.

A cut in the basic tax rate

We can now analyse the effects of tax cuts. A cut in the basic rate is shown in diagram (c).

The tax cut makes the budget line steeper above point q (the tax threshold).

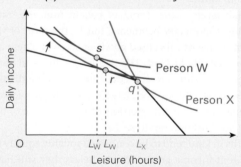

(c) Cut in the basic rate of tax

For people on the tax threshold – like person X – the cut in the basic rate makes no difference. Person X was originally taking L_x hours of leisure (point q) and will continue to do so.

For people above the tax threshold – like person W – the tax cut will enable them to move to a higher indifference curve. Person W will move from point r to point s. The way this diagram is drawn, point s is to the left of point r. This means that person W will work more: the substitution effect is greater than the income effect.

Try drawing two or three diagrams like diagram (c), with the tangency point at different points along the budget line to the left of q. You will find that the further to the left you move, the less likely is the substitution effect to outweigh the income effect: i.e. the more likely are people to work less when given a tax cut.

1 This box is based on D. Ulph, 'Tax cuts: will they work?', *Economic Review*, March 1987.

A rise in the tax threshold

Diagram (d) shows a rise in personal allowances while the tax rates stay the same.

(d) Increase in the tax threshold

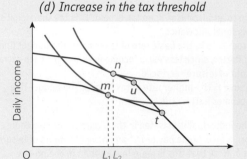

The point at which people start paying taxes rises from point *t* to point *u*. The slope of the budget line remains the same, however, since the tax rates have not changed.

For people paying taxes, the increase in allowances represents a lump-sum increase in income: there will thus be an income effect. But since tax rates have not changed, there is no substitution effect. People therefore work less. The person in the diagram moves from point *m* to point *n*, taking L_2 rather than L_1 hours in leisure.

 Will people actually on the old tax threshold (i.e. those whose indifference curve/budget line tangency point is at t) work more or less? Try drawing it.

A cut in the higher rate of tax

It is likely that the income effect of this will be quite small except for those on very high incomes. The substitution effect is therefore likely to outweigh the income effect, causing people to work more.

 All the above analysis assumes that taxes will not affect people's gross wage rates. If part of the incidence of taxes is borne by the employer, so that gross wages fall, after-tax wages will fall less. There will therefore be a smaller shift in the budget line. How will this affect the argument for tax cuts?

---

into a certain category or fulfil certain conditions (these conditions might include a contributions record). Examples include state pensions, and certain unemployment, sickness and invalidity benefits.

Benefits in kind

Individuals receive other forms of benefit from the state, not as direct monetary payments, but in the form of the provision of free or subsidised goods or services. These are known as **benefits in kind**. The two largest items in most countries are health care and education. They are distributed very unevenly, however, largely due to the age factor. Old people use a large proportion of health services, but virtually no education services.

Benefits in kind tend to be consumed roughly equally by the different income groups. Nevertheless they still have some equalising effect, since they represent a much larger proportion of poor people's income than rich people's. They still have a far smaller redistributive effect, however, than cash benefits.

Figure 11.15 shows the expenditure on social protection benefits in selected European countries. These include unemployment, sickness, invalidity, maternity, family, survivors' and housing benefits and state pensions. They are mainly cash benefits, but do include some benefits in kind. They exclude health and education.

As you can see, the benefits vary significantly from one country to another. Part of the reason for this is that countries differ in their rates of unemployment and in the age structure of their population. Thus Ireland has a very low percentage of people over 65, compared with other countries

in the EU and the smallest share of benefits devoted to pensions. Despite this, however, the generosity and coverage of benefits varies considerably from country to country, reflecting, in part, the level of income per head.

Also, you will see from chart (b) that benefits were generally greater in 2013 than in 1990. This is a largely a reflection of the higher rates of unemployment in 2013, and hence more people in receipt of unemployment benefits.

The system of benefits in the UK and their redistributive effects are examined in Case Study 11.5 on the student website.

Benefits and the redistribution of income

It might seem that means-tested benefits are a much more efficient system for redistributing income from the rich to the poor: the money is directed to those most in need. With universal benefits, by contrast, many people may receive them who have little need for them. Do families with very high incomes need child benefit? Would it not be better for the government to redirect the money to those who are genuinely in need? In the UK, from 2012, families with at

---

Definition

Benefits in kind Goods or services that the state provides directly to the recipient at no charge or at a subsidised price. Alternatively, the state can subsidise the private sector to provide them.

Figure 11.15   Social protection benefits in various European countries

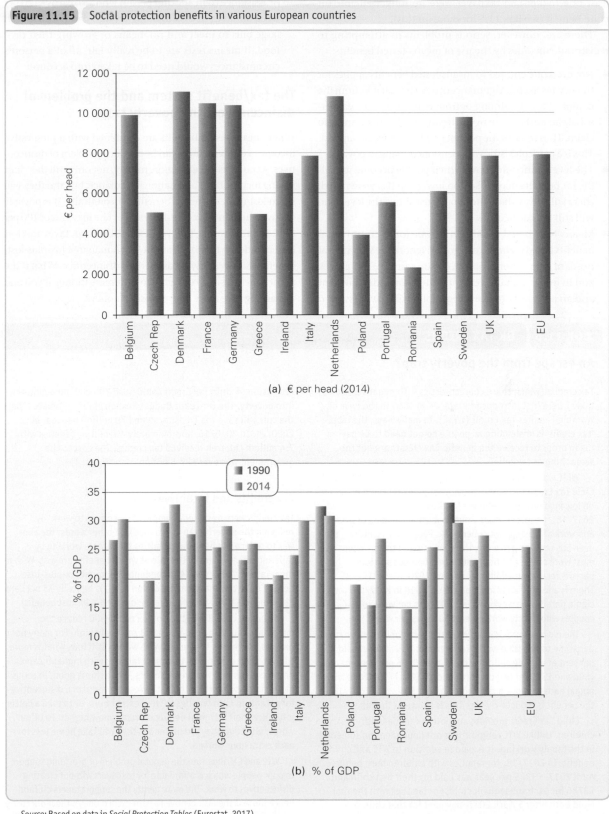

(a) € per head (2014)

(b) % of GDP

Source: Based on data in *Social Protection Tables* (Eurostat, 2017).

KI 3
p13

least one higher-rate taxpayer were no longer eligible for child benefit (see Box 11.5 for more on this).

There are, however, serious problems in attempting to redistribute incomes by the use of means-tested benefits:

- Not everyone entitled to means-tested benefits applies for them, whether from ignorance of what is available, from the complexities of claiming or from reluctance to reveal personal circumstances or from a feeling that it is demeaning to claim. Thus some of the poorest families receive no support. This is a particular issue with pensioners living in poverty.

- The level of income above which people become ineligible for benefits may be set too low. Even if it were raised, there will always be some people just above the level who will still find difficulties.

- Means tests based purely on *income* (or even universal benefits based on broad categories) ignore the very special needs of many poor people. A person earning £120 a week and living in a small, well-appointed flat with a low rent and an allotment to grow vegetables will have less need

of assistance than another person who also earns £120 per week but lives in a cold, draughty and damp house with large bills to meet and no means of growing their own food. If means tests are to be really fair, *all* of a person's circumstances would need to be taken into account.

The tax/benefit system and the problem of disincentives: the poverty trap

When means-tested benefits are combined with a progressive income tax system, there can be a serious problem of disincentives. As poor people earn more money, not only will they start paying income taxes and national insurance, but also they will begin losing means-tested benefits. Theoretically, it is possible to have a marginal tax-plus-lost-benefit rate in excess of 100 per cent. In other words, for every extra £1 earned, taxes and lost benefits add up to more than £1. High marginal tax-plus-lost-benefit rates obviously act as a serious disincentive. What is the point of getting a job or trying to earn more money if you end up earning little more or even losing money?

BOX 11.5   **UK TAX CREDITS**

An escape from the poverty trap?

Tax credits (which share characteristics with negative income taxes) were first introduced in the UK in 1999 in the form of Working Families Tax Credit (WFTC). In many ways, the label 'tax credit' is misleading as people do not need to be paying tax in order to receive the benefit. Tax credits are not the same thing as tax relief.

WFTC was replaced in 2003 by Working Tax Credit (WTC) and Child Tax Credit (CTC). WTC provides support for working people on low incomes. To be eligible for the basic amount (£1960 in 2017/18), people without children must be aged 25 or over and work at least 30 hours per week. People with children, the over-50s returning to work, the over-60s and the disabled must work at least 16 hours per week. Couples and lone parents receive an additional amount (£2010 in 2017/18). There is a further additional payment (£810 in 2017/18) for a single parent who works at least 30 hours per week, or for couples who jointly work at least 30 hours per week.

The payment provides an incentive for people to move from part-time to full-time work. Recipients of WTC also get paid 70 per cent of eligible childcare costs up to £175 per week for one child and £300 for two or more children (2017/18). For each pound earned above a threshold amount (£6420 in 2017/18), the benefit is reduced by 41p. This is known as the taper.

Child Tax Credit provides support to families with children. Unlike WTC, eligibility is not dependent on someone in the family working. It is paid in addition to WTC and child benefit. In 2017/18, for families with children born before 6 April 2017, £3325 per year was paid for their first child and £2780 for each subsequent child. For families with the first child born after 5 April 2017, payment for that child was reduced to £2780. For families with the third or subsequent child born after 5 April 2017, there was no WTC paid at all for these children. Such families thus received a maximum of £5560 no matter how many children they have.

In 2014/15, 872 000 families with more than two children claimed tax credits. Some campaign groups argued that the

restriction of Child Tax Credit could push 200 000 more children into poverty. The Office for Budget Responsibility estimates that the cuts will save the Treasury some £70 million per year by 2020/21. In 2015/16, approximately 4.4 million families with 7.4 million children received tax credits. The cost to the government was over £27.5 billion.

Tax credits and incentives

Tax credits were designed to improve incentives to work, by reducing the poverty trap (see above). In other words, the aim was to reduce the financial penalties for parents working by tapering off more slowly the rate at which benefits are lost. With a taper rate of 41 per cent, the combined marginal tax-plus-lost-benefit rate (the 'marginal deduction rate') is typically 73 per cent (20% income tax + 12% national insurance + 41% lost benefit)

Although the introduction of tax credits did reduce the marginal deduction rate, it remains relatively high. For many poor parents, therefore, the incentive to work is still low. What is more, a lower taper rate means that *more* families with higher incomes become eligible to receive payments. While this is good, in terms of providing support for them, the result is more of a disincentive for parents in such families to work extra hours, or to take a better job, since their marginal deduction rate is now higher. In other words, although they are better off, they will take home less for each extra hour worked.

WTC and CTC illustrate the general problem of providing support to poor people which is affordable for taxpayers without creating disincentives to work. The more gently the support tapers off (and hence the less the disincentive to earn extra money), the more costly it is to finance, and hence higher tax rates are needed elsewhere. The problems with using negative income taxes are explored in Case Study 11.6 on the student website.

A major criticism of tax credits lies in the complexity of the system. This has two consequences: first, it is estimated that of the 7 million households eligible for the benefits, over 2 million

This situation is known as the **poverty trap**. People are trapped on low incomes with no realistic means of bettering their position.

The problem of the poverty trap could be overcome by switching to a system of universal benefits unrelated to income. For example, *everyone* could receive a flat payment from the state fixed at a sufficiently high level to cover their basic needs. There would still be *some* disincentive, but this would be confined to an income effect: people would not have the same need to work if the state provided a basic income. But there would no longer be the disincentive to work caused by a resulting *loss* of benefits (a substitution effect). In addition, a system of universal benefits is relatively cheap to administer, avoiding the need for costly means-testing.

The big drawback with universal benefits, however, is their cost. If they were given to everyone and were large enough to help the poor, their cost would be enormous. Thus, although the benefits themselves would not create much disincentive effect, the necessary taxation to fund them probably would.

There is no ideal solution to this conundrum. On the one hand, the more narrowly benefits are targeted on the poor, the greater is the problem of the poverty trap. On the other hand, the more widely they are spread, the greater is the cost of providing any given level of support to individuals. One compromise proposal is that of a **negative income tax**. This is examined in Case Study 11.6 on the student website. Box 11.5 examines the use of tax credits – which have similarities with a negative income tax – in the UK.

> ## Definitions
>
> **Poverty trap** Where poor people are discouraged from working or getting a better job because any extra income they earn will be largely or entirely taken away in taxes and lost benefits.
>
> **Negative income tax** A combined system of tax and benefits. As people earn more, they gradually lose their benefits until beyond a certain level they begin paying taxes.

CASE STUDIES AND APPLICATIONS

fail to claim them; second, the system is administratively costly and prone to errors.

A universal approach

In 2011, Iain Duncan Smith, the then Secretary of State for Work and Pensions, announced plans to make fundamental reforms to the benefit system by introducing a new Universal Credit (UC).

His intention was to 'simplify the system to make work pay and combat worklessness and poverty'.[1] The new credit was described as an integrated working-age credit providing a basic allowance with additional elements for children, disability, housing and caring. It differs from the system that it is gradually replacing, in that it supports people both in and out of work, replacing Working Tax Credit, Child Tax Credit, Housing Benefit, Income Support, income-based Jobseeker's Allowance and income-related Employment and Support Allowance. (Note that although it is called Universal Credit, it is not a universal benefit and is means-tested.)

The design of UC is intended to address concerns raised about tax credits by:

- Introducing smoother taper rates and so lessening the impact of the poverty trap.
- Removing the distortions that over-reward individuals working a certain number of hours, notably 16 or 30 hours with Working Tax Credits.
- Bringing together in-work and out-of-work benefits, and reducing the risks and transactions costs for those moving into work.
- Reducing administrative costs, with benefits being overseen by a single body, the Department for Work and Pensions.

Although UC originally offered higher levels of support, cuts announced in the July 2015 budget make the payments far less generous. The government is also applying stronger levels of conditionality on claimants.

Unfortunately, achieving simplicity in a benefit system has proved more complex than Iain Duncan Smith had anticipated. There have been numerous setbacks in the implementation of the new system, which has been dogged by design errors, problems with IT systems and cost over-runs. It is gradually being introduced into different areas of the country and by December 2016, 430 000 people were receiving UC. When the scheme finally becomes fully operational, this number will increase to approximately 7 million. In July 2016, the government announced that, due to further delays, the scheme would not be fully implemented until 2022 – five years later than originally planned.

A number of people receiving UC have suffered considerable hardship. Claimants have to wait six weeks for their first payment and some families have found it difficult to cope with this delay. According to evidence presented to the Work and Pensions Select Committee, 920 out of 1058 housing association tenants in Halton Merseyside who had been moved onto UC had rent arrears averaging £600.

1. *Economists sometimes refer to an 'unemployment trap'. People are discouraged from taking work in the first place. Explain how such a 'trap' arises. Will the Universal Credit create an unemployment trap? What are the best ways of eliminating, or at least reducing, the unemployment trap?*
2. *Universal Credit involves a single monthly payment direct to the claimant's bank account. This replaces fortnightly payments, some in the form of cashable cheques, and rent payments direct to landlords. What additional support do you anticipate claimants would need?*

1 *White Paper Universal Credit: Welfare that Works*, www.gov.uk/government/publications/universal-credit-welfare-that-works

Conclusions

Redistribution is not costless. Whether it takes place through taxes or benefits or both, it can pose a problem of disincentives. The size of the disincentive problem varies from one tax to another and from one benefit to another, and in some cases there may even be an incentive effect: for example, when the income effect of a tax outweighs the substitution effect. It is therefore important to estimate the particular effects of each type of proposal not only on income distribution itself, but also on economic efficiency.

Ultimately, the questions of how much income should be redistributed, and whether the costs are worth bearing,

are normative questions, and ones that an economist cannot answer. They are moral and political questions. Unfortunately there is no mechanism for measuring the 'utility' gained by the poor and lost by the rich so that any net gain from redistribution can be weighed up against lost output. For example, the benefit that a person receives from a cooker or an electric fire cannot be measured in 'utils' or any other 'psychic unit'. What people are prepared to pay for the items is no guide either, since a poor person obviously cannot afford to pay nearly as much as a rich person, and yet will probably get the same if not more personal benefit from them.

Section summary

1. Government intervention in the economy through taxation and government expenditure has a number of purposes including redistribution, the correction of market distortions and macroeconomic stabilisation.

2. There are various requirements of a good tax system, including horizontal and vertical equity; payment according to the amount of benefit received; being cheap to collect, difficult to evade, non-distortionary and convenient to the taxpayer and the government; and having the minimum disincentive effects.

3. Taxes can be divided into those paid directly to the authorities (direct taxes: e.g. income tax) and those paid via a middle person (indirect taxes: e.g. VAT).

4. Taxes can be categorised as progressive, regressive or proportional. Progressive taxes have the effect of reducing inequality. The more steeply progressive they are, the bigger is the reduction in inequality.

5. There are various limitations to using taxes to redistribute incomes. First, they cannot on their own increase the incomes of the poor. (Cutting taxes, however, can help the poor if the cuts are carefully targeted.) Second, high taxes on the rich may encourage evasion or avoidance. Third, higher income taxes on the rich will probably lead to their employers paying higher (gross) wages.

6. Using indirect taxes to redistribute incomes involves costs of resource reallocation.

7. Raising taxes has two effects on the amount that people wish to work. On the one hand, people will be encouraged

to work more in order to maintain their incomes. This is the income effect. On the other hand, they will be encouraged to substitute leisure for income (i.e. to work less), since an hour's leisure now costs less in forgone income. This is the substitution effect. The relative size of the income and substitution effects will depend on the nature of the tax change. The substitution effect of a tax rise is more likely to outweigh the income effect for those with few commitments, for people just above the tax threshold and in cases where the highest rates of tax are increased.

8. Benefits can be cash benefits or benefits in kind. Means-tested cash benefits include support for poor families and for low-paid people. Universal benefits include state pensions and child benefit. Benefits in kind include health care, education and free school meals.

9. Means-tested benefits can be specifically targeted to those in need and are thus more 'cost effective'. However, there can be serious problems with such benefits, including limited take-up, some relatively needy people falling just outside the qualifying limit, and inadequate account being taken of all relevant circumstances affecting a person's needs.

10. The poverty trap occurs when the combination of increased taxes and reduced benefits removes the incentive for poor people to earn more. The more steeply progressive this combined system is at low incomes, the bigger is the disincentive effect.

BOX 11.6   **WHAT THE FUTURE HOLDS**

Approaches to pensioner poverty in the UK

While much of the focus since 1997 has been on child poverty, politicians have also been concerned about the plight of pensioners. After all, unlike children, they have the vote. And with an ageing population, the numbers of pensioners are increasing.

For most of the first decade of this century, the analysis was relatively simple: many pensioners are poor and pensioner poverty needs to be addressed. Pensioner incomes had fallen relative to those of the working population, as pensions were up-rated in line with prices rather than wages. Increasing life expectancy and changing labour markets combined to leave nearly three million pensioners living in poverty by 1998.

Policy responses included more generous means-tested benefits and the introduction of a number of universal benefits for pensioners, such as free bus travel and winter fuel allowances. The result was that by 2009 the number of pensioners living in poverty had fallen by one-third to around two million.

Intergenerational equity

More recently, the focus has moved to looking at the question of equity between different generations. With many reliant on incomes from savings and personal pensions, older people have suffered from low or even negative real interest rates since 2008. Younger people with mortgages and other debts, by contrast, have benefited from these low real interest rates. Then there is the question of the fruits of economic growth. Should only companies and wage earners benefit from economic growth, or should the retired benefit too?

Many people, however, are concerned that pensioners as a group are getting more than their fair share of national income. They argue that it is those under 30 who are worst off. Those born between the 1940s and mid-1960s have benefited from a range of financial and social factors, including free higher education and generous final salary pension schemes. Many have built up substantial wealth in the form of housing equity, buying initially when prices were very low. This will enable them to have a comfortable retirement.

The situation is very different for the young, who face higher education fees of up to £9250 per annum, high house prices so they remain unaffordable for many, final salary pension schemes closed and retirement ages likely to increase beyond 70. What is more, they face higher taxes to pay for past spending, for the costs of the bank bailouts in 2008 and for the effects of climate change.

UK government policy

One of the most important elements of recent government policy has been the so-called 'triple lock'. Introduced in 2012, this guarantees that the annual increase in the state pension is by whichever one of the following is greatest – the increase in average earnings, the increases in the consumer price index, or 2.5 per cent. Research by the Institute for Fiscal Studies[1] indicated that between 2010 and 2016 the state pension increased by 22.2 per cent. During the same period, average earnings increased by 7.6 per cent and prices increased by 12.3 per cent. The current government is committed to the policy until 2020, although a number of people have argued that its cost is unsustainable. The Government's Actuary Department estimates that the triple lock increases the cost of the state pension by approximately £6 billion per year.

Rather than focusing on just those who are already pensioners, the government has also introduced policies to encourage those of working age to save more for their future retirement. In particular, the government has introduced an auto-enrolment programme. This aims to make sure that people have a retirement savings policy to top up their state pension. Every employer with at least one employee now has to enrol them automatically into a low-cost workplace pension scheme if they meet certain requirements – they must be over the age of 22 and earn at least £10 000 per year. The minimum contribution rate into the pension scheme is 2 per cent with at least 1 per cent paid by the employer. This increases to 5 per cent in April 2018 with a minimum of 2 per cent paid by the employer. The government has also introduced greater flexibility into how people can use their pension savings as they approach retirement.

Despite these measures, the amounts being saved by many people are still well below the levels required to provide a decent retirement income.

1. *Why has the government legislated for the new national pension scheme to involve auto-enrolment? (Hint, think back to section 5.2 page 144)*
2. *The last two governments have used universal benefits, such as winter fuel allowances and free bus travel, as part of their approach to eliminating pensioner poverty. What are the advantages (and disadvantages) of this approach?*
3. *If you could find out, with some associated probability, when you might die, would you choose to find out? How might the answer affect the way you live today?*

1 *Would You Rather? Further Increases in the State Pension Age v Abandoning the Triple Lock* (IFS, February 2017).

END OF CHAPTER QUESTIONS

1. Using the data shown on the pie charts in Figure 11.1, construct two Lorenz curves (on the same diagram), corresponding to the before- and after-tax income figures. Interpret and comment on the diagram you have drawn.

2. Can taxes be used to relieve poverty?

3. In what ways might the views of different politicians on what constitutes a 'good' tax system conflict?

4. Distinguish between proportional, progressive and regressive taxation. Could a progressive tax have a constant marginal rate?

5. Consider the cases for and against a poll tax.

6. Under what circumstances would a rise in income tax act as (a) a disincentive and (b) an incentive to effort?

7. What is meant by the poverty trap? What design of benefit system would offer the best solution to the problem of the poverty trap?

8. How would you go about deciding whether person A or person B gets more personal benefit from each of the following: (a) an electric fire; (b) a clothing allowance of £x; (c) free higher education; (d) child benefit? Do your answers help you in deciding how best to allocate benefits?

9. Just under two million pensioners were identified as living in poverty in the UK in 2016. In the same year it was estimated that the total property wealth of pensioner households had grown to a record high of £1.031 trillion. What does this imply about inequality and poverty?

Online resources

Additional case studies on the student website

11.1 How can we define poverty? This examines different definitions of poverty and, in particular, distinguishes between absolute and relative measures of poverty.

11.2 Adam Smith's maxims of taxation. This looks at the principles of a good tax system as identified by Adam Smith.

11.3 Taxation in the UK. This case study looks at the various types of tax in the UK. It gives the current tax rates and considers how progressive the system is.

11.4 The poll tax. This case charts the introduction of the infamous poll tax (or 'community charge') in the UK and its subsequent demise.

11.5 The system of benefits in the UK. A description of the various benefits used in the UK and their redistributive effects.

11.6 Negative income tax and redistribution. How effectively can a negative income tax redistribute income without causing adverse incentive effects?

11.7 The squeezed middle. What have been the effects on people on 'middle incomes' of attempts by successive governments to support poor families?

11.8 Increased life expectancy. This examines the likely future impact on individuals and economies of people living longer.

Websites relevant to Chapters 10 and 11

Numbers and section refer to websites listed in the Web Appendix and hotlinked from this book's website at **www.pearsoned.co.uk/sloman**.

■ For news articles relevant to this and the previous chapter, see the *Economics News* section on the student website.

■ For general news on labour markets, see websites in section A, and particularly A1, 2, 4, 5 and 7. See also 40 and 41 for links to economics news articles from newspapers worldwide.

■ For data on labour markets, see links in B1, especially to the National Statistics site. Also see B18, B19 and H3. For international data on labour markets, see the ILO datasets in the ESDS International site (B35) (you will need to log in, available free to all students in UK higher education).

■ For information on international labour standards and employment right, see site H3.

■ Site I11 contains links to *Human Resources* and *Employment* in the *Business* section.

■ Links to the TUC and Confederation of British Industry sites can be found at E32 and 33.

■ For information on poverty and the redistribution of income, see B18; E9, 13, 30, 31, 36; G5, 13; H3.

■ For student resources relevant to these two chapters, see sites C1–7, 9, 10, 19, 28.

■ For simulations and for information and various articles on the labour market see site D3.

12

Markets, Efficiency and the Public Interest

In Chapter 11 we examined the problem of inequality. In this chapter we turn to examine another major area of concern. This is the question of the efficiency (or inefficiency) of markets in allocating resources.

First we show how a perfect market economy could under certain conditions lead to 'social efficiency'. In section 12.2 we examine the real world and show how real-world markets fail to meet social goals. These failures provide the major arguments in favour of government intervention in a market economy. We then turn to discuss the alternative ways in which a government can intervene to correct these various market failings.

If the government is to replace the market and provide goods and services directly, it will need some way of establishing their costs and benefits. Section 12.4 looks at 'cost–benefit analysis'. This is a means of establishing the desirability of a public project such as a new motorway or a new hospital. Finally, in section 12.5, we look at the case for restricting government intervention. We examine the advantages of real-world markets and the drawbacks of government intervention.

12.1 EFFICIENCY UNDER PERFECT COMPETITION

Perfect competition has been used by many economists and policy makers as an ideal against which to compare the benefits and shortcomings of real-world markets.

As was shown in Chapter 7, perfect competition has various advantages for society. Under perfect competition, firms' supernormal profits are competed away in the long run by the entry of new competitors. As a result, firms are forced to produce at the bottom of their average cost curves. What is more, the fear of being driven out of business by the entry of new firms forces existing firms to try to find lower-cost methods of production, thus shifting their *AC* curves downwards.

 Perhaps the most wide-reaching claim for perfect competition is that under certain conditions it will lead to a *socially efficient* use of a nation's resources.

Social efficiency: 'Pareto optimality'

If it were possible to make changes in the economy – changes in the combination of goods produced or consumed, or changes in the combination of inputs used – and if these changes benefited some people without anyone else being made worse off, economists would describe this as an *improvement in social efficiency*, or a **Pareto improvement**, after Vilfredo Pareto, the Italian social scientist (see Case Study 12.1 on the student website).

> ? *Do you agree that, if some people gain and if no one loses, then this constitutes an 'improvement' in the well-being of society? Does it depend who gains? Would it be possible to improve the well-being of society without a Pareto improvement?*

When all Pareto improvements have been made – in other words, when any additional changes in the economy would benefit some people only by making others worse off – the economy is said to be *socially efficient*, or Pareto optimal. What we shall show is that under certain conditions a perfect market will lead to **Pareto optimality**.

But a word of caution. Just because social efficiency is achieved in a particular market environment, it does not necessarily make that environment *ideal*. It may be a *necessary* condition for an ideal allocation of resources that all Pareto improvements are made. It is not *sufficient,* however. If, for example, the government redistributed income from the rich to the poor, there would be no Pareto improvement, since the rich would lose. Thus both an equal and a highly unequal distribution of income could be Pareto optimal, and yet it could be argued that a more equal distribution is socially more desirable. For the moment, however, we will ignore questions of fairness and just focus on social efficiency.

So why may a perfect market lead to social efficiency? The following sections explain.

The simple analysis of social efficiency: marginal benefit and marginal cost

Remember how we defined 'rational' choices. A rational person will choose to do an activity if the gain from so doing exceeds any sacrifice involved. In other words, whether as a producer, a consumer or a worker, a person will gain by expanding any activity whose marginal benefit (*MB*) exceeds its marginal cost (*MC*) and by contracting any activity whose marginal cost exceeds its marginal benefit. Remember that when economists use the term 'cost', they are referring to 'opportunity cost': in other words, the *sacrifice* of alternatives. Thus when we say that the marginal benefit of an activity is greater than its marginal cost, we mean that the additional benefit gained exceeds any sacrifice in terms of alternatives forgone.

Thus the economist's rule for **rational economic behaviour** is that a person should expand or contract the level of any activity until its marginal benefit is equal to its marginal cost. At that point, the person will be acting efficiently in his or her own private interest. Only when *MB = MC* can no further gain be made. This is known as a situation of **private efficiency**.

By analogy, *social* efficiency will be achieved where, for any activity, the marginal benefit to *society* (*MSB*) is equal to the marginal (opportunity) cost to *society* (*MSC*).

$$MSB = MSC$$

> **KEY IDEA 28**
>
> **Allocative efficiency (simple formulation)** in any activity is achieved where marginal benefit equals marginal cost. Private efficiency is achieved where marginal private benefit equals marginal private cost (*MB = MC*). Social efficiency is achieved where marginal social benefit equals marginal social cost (*MSB = MSC*).

Definitions

Pareto improvement Where changes in production or consumption can make at least one person better off without making anyone worse off.

Social efficiency A situation of Pareto optimality.

Pareto optimality Where all possible Pareto improvements have been made: where, therefore, it is impossible to make anyone better off without making someone else worse off.

Rational economic behaviour Doing more of those activities whose marginal benefit exceeds their marginal cost and doing less of those activities whose marginal cost exceeds their marginal benefit.

Private efficiency Where a person's marginal benefit from a given activity equals the marginal cost.

But why is social efficiency (i.e. Pareto optimality) achieved at this point? If *MSB* were greater than *MSC*, there would be a Pareto improvement if there were an increase in the activity. For example, if the benefits to consumers from additional production of a good exceed the cost to producers, the consumers could fully meet the cost of production in the price they pay, and so no producer loses, and yet there would still be a net gain to consumers. Thus society has gained. Likewise if *MSC* were greater than *MSB*, society would gain from a decrease in production.

Economists argue that under certain circumstances the achievement of *private* efficiency will result in *social* efficiency also. Two major conditions have to be fulfilled, however:

■ There must be *perfect competition* throughout the economy. This is examined in the following sections.

■ There must be *no externalities*. Externalities are additional costs or benefits of production or consumption experienced by people other than the producers and consumers directly involved in the transaction. They are sometimes referred to as spillover or third-party costs or benefits. Pollution is an example. It is a cost that society experiences from production, but it is not a cost that the individual producer has to pay. In the *absence* of externalities, the only costs or benefits to society are the ones that the individual producer or consumer experiences: i.e. marginal social benefit (*MSB*) is the same as marginal private benefit (*MB*), and marginal social cost (*MSC*) is the same as marginal private cost (*MC*).

To understand just how social efficiency is achieved, we must look at how people maximise their interests through the market.

Achieving social efficiency through the market

Consumption: MU = P

The marginal benefit to a consumer from the consumption of any good is its marginal utility. The marginal cost is the price the consumer has to pay.

As demonstrated in section 4.1, the 'rational' consumer will maximise consumer surplus where $MU = P$: in other words, where the marginal benefit from consumption is equal to the marginal cost of consumption. Do you remember the case of Tanya and her purchases of petrol? (See page 108.) She goes on making additional journeys and hence buying extra petrol as long as she feels that the journeys are worth the money she has to spend: in other words, as long as the marginal benefit she gets from buying extra petrol (its marginal utility to her) exceeds its marginal cost (its price). She will stop buying extra petrol when its marginal utility has fallen (the law of diminishing marginal utility) to equal its price. At that point, her consumer surplus is maximised: she has an 'efficient' level of consumption.

Assume that the price of a good falls. How will an 'efficient' level of consumption be restored?

Figure 12.1 Maximum total surplus under perfect competition

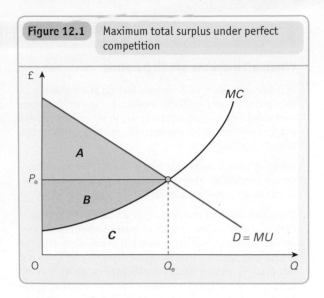

As we have seen, an individual's consumer surplus is maximised at the output where $MU = P$. With all consumers doing this, and all facing the same market price, their collective consumer surplus will be maximised. This is illustrated in Figure 12.1. Consumers' total utility is given by the area under the demand (*MU*) curve (areas $A + B + C$). Consumers' total expenditure is $P \times Q$ (areas $B + C$). Consumer surplus is the difference between total utility and total expenditure: in other words, the area between the price and the demand curve (area A).

Production: P = MC

The marginal benefit to a producer from the production of any good is its marginal revenue (which under perfect competition will be the same as the price of the good). As demonstrated in section 6.6, the 'rational' firm will maximise its profit where its marginal revenue (i.e. the price under conditions of perfect competition) is equal to its marginal cost of production. This is the same thing as saying that it will produce where the marginal benefit from production is equal to the marginal cost from production.

Profit is the excess of total revenue over total costs. A related concept is that of **total producer surplus** (TPS). This is the excess of total revenue over total *variable* costs: $TPS = TR - TVC$. In other words, total producer surplus is total profit plus fixed costs: $TPS = T\Pi + TFC$. But since there are no marginal fixed costs (by definition), both producer surplus and profit will be maximised at the same output.

Definitions

Externalities Costs or benefits of production or consumption experienced by people *other* than the producers and consumers directly involved in the transaction. They are sometimes referred to as 'spillover' or 'third-party' costs or benefits.

Total producer surplus Total revenue minus total variable costs ($TR - TVC$): in other words, total profit plus total fixed costs ($T\Pi + TFC$).

When all markets are in balance

In previous chapters we have been looking at individual markets: goods markets and factor markets. But any change in one market is likely to have repercussions in other markets. And changes in these other markets will probably affect other markets, and so on.

The point about a market economy is that it is like an interconnected web. Understanding these connections helps us understand the concept of an 'economy'.

If we started with an economy where all markets were in equilibrium, we would have a state of **general equilibrium**. Then let's assume that a change occurs in just one market – say a rise in oil prices resulting from increased demand from China and other rapidly growing newly industrialised countries. This will have knock-on effects throughout the economy. Costs, and hence prices, will rise in oil-consuming industries. Consumption will fall for the products of these industries and rise for substitute products which do not use oil, or use less of it. Some motorists will be encouraged to use public transport or cycle. This could have knock-on effects on the demand for houses, with people choosing to live nearer to their work. This could then have effects on the various parts of the construction industry. You can work out some of these effects for yourself.

You will quickly see that a single change in one industry can set off a chain reaction throughout the economy. If there is just the one initial change, things will settle to a new general equilibrium where all markets are back in balance with demand equal to supply. In practice, of course, economic 'shocks' are occurring all the time and thus the economy is in a constant state of flux with no stable general equilibrium.

The concept of general equilibrium is a *threshold concept* because it gives us an insight into how market forces apply to a *whole* economy, and not just to its individual parts. It is about seeing how the whole jigsaw fits together and how changes ripple throughout the economy.

Many other subjects use the concept of general equilibrium. Take meteorology. We could study a single weather system, such as a low pressure area or a cold front. But, to make sense of the development and movement of such systems, we need to see them as part of a bigger picture: as part of the whole world's weather system, which at any time is moving towards a general equilibrium in response to various changes.

For instance, in the short term, we can see how weather systems respond to the changing seasons: for example, how pressure systems move northwards in the northern hemisphere summer. In the longer term, we could model how world weather systems will respond to climate change. Will the resulting general equilibrium be one where sea levels rise; where the Gulf Stream is turned off, with much of north-western Europe becoming colder; where the deserts of north Africa spread to southern Europe; and so on?

But in economics, understanding general equilibrium is not just about understanding and predicting the output of the various industries that make up the economy. It can help us make value judgements and formulate policy. As we shall see in Threshold Concept 11 (see page 353), under certain conditions, general equilibrium can be seen as *socially efficient*. These conditions are (a) perfect competition and (b) an absence of externalities.

If social efficiency is seen as desirable, then one policy implication might be to try to make markets as perfect as possible and to 'internalise' externalities. In this chapter we examine whether such policies should be adopted and, if so, what form should they take?

1. *If general equilibrium is achieved when all markets have responded to a change and its knock-on effects, and if such changes are constantly occurring, will general equilibrium actually be achieved? Does your answer have any implications for policy?*
2. *If social efficiency is seen as desirable (a normative issue), should policy always be geared to achieving this?*

Total producer surplus for all firms in the market is shown in Figure 12.1. Total revenue (i.e. total expenditure) is $P \times Q$ (areas $B + C$). Total variable cost is the area under the MC curve (area C): i.e. it is the sum of all the marginal costs of each unit produced. Producer surplus is thus the area between the price and the MC curve (area B).

Private efficiency in the market: MU = MC

KI 28 p348

TC 2 p26

In Figure 12.1, both consumer surplus and producer surplus are maximised at output Q_e. This is the equilibrium output under perfect competition. Thus, under perfect competition, the market will ensure that **total surplus** (areas $A + B$), sometimes called **total private surplus**, is maximised. At this output, $MU = P = MC$.

At any output other than Q_e total surplus will be less. If output were below Q_e, then MU would be above MC: total surplus would be increased by producing more. If output

were above Q_e, then MU would be below MC: total surplus would be increased by producing less.

Social efficiency in the market: MSB = MSC

Provided the two conditions of (a) perfect competition and (b) the absence of externalities are fulfilled, Pareto optimality (i.e. social efficiency) will be achieved. Let us take each condition in turn.

KI 28 p348

Definition

General equilibrium Where all the millions of markets throughout the economy are in a simultaneous state of equilibrium.

Total (private) surplus Total consumer surplus $(TU - TE)$ plus total producer surplus $(TR - TVC)$.

Perfect competition. Perfect competition will ensure that private efficiency is achieved:

$$MU = MC \text{ (for all producers and all consumers)}$$

No externalities. In the absence of externalities, $MSB = MU$ (i.e. the benefits of consumption within society are confined to the direct consumers) and $MSC = MC$ (i.e. the costs of production to society are simply the costs paid by the producers). Thus

$$MSB = MU = P = MC = MSC$$

i.e.

$$MSB = MSC$$

With no externalities, the total surplus shown in Figure 12.1 will represent **total social surplus**.

Inefficiency would arise if (a) competition were not perfect and so marginal revenue were *not* equal to price and as a result marginal cost were not equal to price; or (b) there were externalities and hence either marginal social benefit were different from marginal utility (i.e. marginal *private* benefit) or marginal social cost were different from marginal (private) cost. We examine such 'market failures' in section 12.2.

1. *If monopoly power existed in an industry, would production be above or below the socially efficient level (assuming no externalities)? Which would be greater, MSB or P?*

2. *Assuming perfect competition and no externalities, social efficiency will also be achieved in factor markets. Demonstrate that this will be where*

$$MSB_f = MRP_f = P_f = MDU_f = MSC_f$$

   (where MRP is the marginal revenue product of a factor, MDU is the marginal disutility of supplying it, and f is any factor – see section 10.1).

3. *Why will marginal social benefit not equal marginal social costs in the labour market if there exists (a) union monopoly power and/or (b) firms with monopsony power?*

Interdependence, efficiency and the 'invisible hand': the simple analysis of general equilibrium

If there is perfect competition and an absence of externalities throughout the economy, then the whole economy,

Definition

Total social surplus Total benefits to society from consuming a good minus total costs to society from producing it. In the absence of externalities, total social surplus is the same as total (private) surplus.

when in equilibrium, will be socially efficient. A state of general Pareto optimality will exist.

No economy, however, is static. Conditions of demand and supply are constantly changing. Tastes change, technology changes and so on. Thus old patterns of consumption and production will cease to be Pareto optimal. Nevertheless, provided there is perfect competition and no externalities, forces will come into play to restore Pareto optimality.

In this perfect market economy, Pareto optimality is restored not by government action, but rather by the individual actions of producers, consumers and factor owners all seeking their own self-interest. It is as if an 'invisible hand' were working to guide the economy towards social efficiency (see Box 1.5).

The economic system will respond to any change in demand or supply by a whole series of subsequent changes in various interdependent markets. Social efficiency will thereby be restored. The whole process can be illustrated with a diagram showing the circular flow of income (see Figure 12.2).

Assume, for example, that tastes change such that the marginal utility of a particular good rises. This is illustrated on the right-hand side of the diagram by a shift in the MU curve (i.e. the demand curve) from MU_1 to MU_2 (i.e. D_1 to D_2). This will lead to the following sequence of events, which you can follow round the diagram in an anti-clockwise direction.

Consumer demand

The rise in marginal utility (i.e. the rise in marginal social benefit of the good, MSB_g) leads to increased consumption. The resulting shortage will drive up the market price.

Producer supply

The rise in the market price will mean that price is now above the marginal (social) cost of production. It will thus be profitable for firms to increase their production. This in turn will lead to an increase in marginal cost (a movement up along the marginal cost curve) due to diminishing returns. There is a movement up along the supply curve from point *a*. Price will continue to rise until equilibrium is reached at P_2Q_2 (point *b*), where $MSB_{g_2} = MSC_g$.

Factor demand

The rise in the price of the good will lead to an increase in the marginal revenue product of factors that are employed in producing the good. The reason for this is that the marginal *revenue* product of a factor is its marginal *physical* product multiplied by the *price* of the good (see section 10.1). The marginal physical product is unchanged, but since the price of the good has now gone up, the output of factors will be worth correspondingly more. The following takes just one factor (*f*) as an example.

Figure 12.2 The interdependence of goods and factor markets

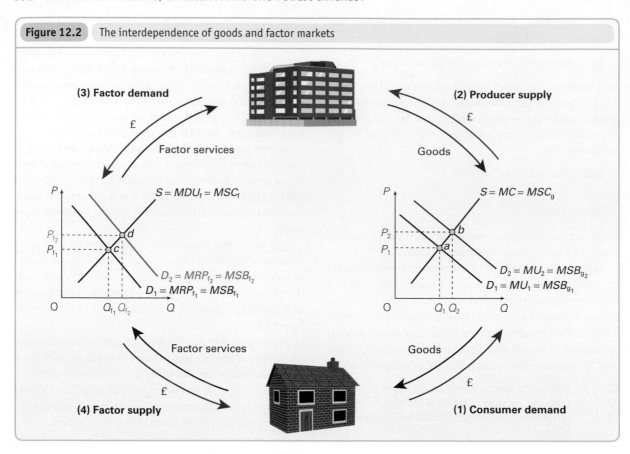

A rise in the value of the factor's output (due to the higher price of the good) will make its marginal revenue product higher than its marginal cost to the firm. This will increase the demand for the factor. Factor demand shifts to $D_2 (= MRP_{f_2} = MSB_{f_2})$. This in turn will drive up the price of the factor.

Factor supply

The rise in the price of the factor will raise the marginal benefit of supplying it (and hence the marginal social benefit). This will mean that the marginal benefit now exceeds the marginal cost (the marginal disutility, MDU_f) of supplying the factor. There is thus a movement up along the factor supply curve from point c as more units of the factor are supplied. The price of the factor will continue to rise until equilibrium is reached at $P_{f_2}Q_{f_2}$ (point d), where $MSB_{f_2} = MSC_f$.

The process of adjustment does not end here. If supernormal profits are made, new firms will enter. Similarly, if factor rewards are supernormal, new factors will be attracted from other industries. This in turn will affect prices and hence quantities in *other* industries in both goods and factor markets.

In other words, a single change in tastes will create a ripple effect throughout the economy, through a whole series of interdependent markets. Eventually, long-run equilibrium will be restored with $MSB = MSC$ in all markets. The economy has returned to a position of Pareto optimality. And all this has taken place with no government intervention. It is the 'invisible hand' of the market that has achieved this state of social efficiency.

These arguments form a central part of the neoclassical case for laissez-faire: the philosophy of non-intervention by the government. Under ideal conditions, it is argued, the free pursuit of individual self-interest will lead to the social good. Since intervention is always associated with costs, the neoclassical case says that the optimal approach is to allow this move to the social good to take place, unimpeded.

1. Trace through the effects in both factor and goods markets of the following: (a) an increase in the productivity of a particular type of labour; (b) an increase in the supply of a particular factor.
2. Show in each case how social efficiency will initially be destroyed and then how market adjustments will restore social efficiency.

The following pages examine social efficiency in more detail. You may omit these and skip straight to section 12.2 (page 356) if you want to.

THRESHOLD CONCEPT 11   ALLOCATIVE EFFICIENCY: PRIVATE AND SOCIAL   THINKING LIKE AN ECONOMIST

Economics is concerned with the allocation of scarce resources. Whenever choices are made, whether by consumers, firms, the government or any other agency, a choice is being made about the allocation of resources.

When you buy a T-shirt costing £10, you are choosing to allocate £10 of your money to the purchase – £10 that could have been spent on something else. But have you allocated your money in the best way?

Similarly, when a firm chooses to produce one product rather than another, or to use technique A rather than some alternative technique, it is choosing to allocate its resources in particular ways. But are these the best ways?

The question is whether the resources have been allocated *efficiently*. We define an efficient allocation of resources as one which brings the maximum benefit for that level of costs. In other words, no gain would be made by reallocating resources in some alternative way. Thus your decision to spend £10 on a T-shirt is an efficient allocation of your resources, if it brings you more benefit (i.e. utility) for the £10 than could any other purchase. The firm's decision to use technique A is an efficient one if it leads to a higher rate of profit: if the marginal benefit (i.e. marginal revenue) relative to the marginal cost is greater than for any other technique.

What we are talking about here is 'allocative efficiency'. It is a *threshold concept* because to understand it is to understand how to make the most of scarce resources: and scarcity is the core problem of economics for all of us. It is obvious that poor people on very limited incomes will want to spend their money as efficiently as possible. But even exceedingly rich people, who can buy anything they want, are still likely to have limited time or opportunities.

Allocative efficiency is a threshold concept for another reason. We need to see how it relates to *social* objectives. If people all individually achieve their own *private efficiency*, does this mean that society will have an efficient allocation of resources? The answer is no. The reason is that our decisions often have consequences for *other* people: our actions have external costs and/or benefits. These externalities mean that private efficiency and *social efficiency* diverge. We need to understand how and why, and how social efficiency can be achieved.

Then there is the question of equity. Just because everyone is allocating their resources in the best possible way for them, and even if there were no externalities, it does not follow that the allocation of resources is *fair*. However efficiently rich people spend their money, most people would still argue that it is socially desirable to redistribute part of rich people's income to the poor through the tax and benefit system.

KI 4
p14

1. *Why might consumers not always make efficient consumption decisions?*
2. *Explain the meaning of social efficiency using the concept of Pareto improvements.*

---

*The intermediate analysis of social efficiency: marginal benefit and marginal cost ratios

In practice, consumers do not consider just one good in isolation. They make choices between goods. Likewise, firms make choices as to which goods to produce and which factors to employ. A more satisfactory analysis of social efficiency, therefore, considers the choices that firms and households make.

Whether as a producer, consumer or worker, a person will gain by expanding activity X relative to activity Y if

$$\frac{MB_X}{MB_Y} > \frac{MC_X}{MC_Y}$$

The reason is straightforward. Activity X is giving a greater benefit relative to its cost than is activity Y. Only when

$$\frac{MB_X}{MB_Y} = \frac{MC_X}{MC_Y}$$

can no further gain be made by switching from the one activity to the other. At this point, people will be acting efficiently in their own private interest.

By analogy, social efficiency is achieved where the social marginal benefit ratio of two goods is equal to the social marginal cost ratio.

 Social efficiency (equi-marginal formulation) is achieved where the marginal social benefit ratios are equal to the marginal social cost ratios for any two alternatives. In the case of two alternatives X and Y, this will be where

$$\frac{MSB_X}{MSB_Y} = \frac{MSC_X}{MSC_Y}$$

KEY IDEA 29

As with the simple analysis of social efficiency, it can be shown that, provided there is perfect competition and no externalities, the achievement of private efficiency will result in social efficiency also. This will be demonstrated in the following sections.

*Efficiency in the goods market (intermediate analysis)

Private efficiency under perfect competition

Consumption.   The optimum combination of two goods X and Y consumed for any consumer is where

$$\frac{MU_X}{MU_Y} \text{ (i.e. } MRS) = \frac{P_X}{P_Y}$$

KI 14
p111

The *marginal rate of substitution in consumption (MRS)* (see page 115) is the amount of good Y that a consumer would be willing to sacrifice for an increase in consumption of good X (i.e. $\Delta Y/\Delta X$). $MRS = MU_X/MU_Y$ since, if X gave twice the marginal utility of Y, the consumer would be prepared to give up two of Y to obtain one of X (i.e. $MRS = 2/1$).

If MU_X/MU_Y were greater than P_X/P_Y, how would consumers behave? What would bring consumption back to equilibrium where $MU_X/MU_Y = P_X/P_Y$?

Production. The optimum combination of two goods X and Y produced for any producer is where

$$\frac{MC_X}{MC_Y} \text{ (i.e. } MRT) = \frac{P_X}{P_Y}$$

The *marginal rate of transformation in production (MRT)* is the amount of good Y that the producer will have to give up producing for an increase in production of good X (i.e. $\Delta Y/\Delta X$) if total costs of production are to remain unchanged. $MRT = MC_X/MC_Y$ since, if the marginal cost of good X were twice that of Y, the firm's costs would remain constant if it gave up producing two of Y in order to produce an extra X (i.e. $MRT = 2/1$).

If MC_X/MC_Y were greater than P_X/P_Y, how would firms behave? What would bring production back into equilibrium where $MC_X/MC_Y = P_X/P_Y$?

Social efficiency under perfect competition

In each of the following three cases, it will be assumed that there are no externalities.

Social efficiency between consumers. If MU_X/MU_Y for person a is greater than MU_X/MU_Y for person b, *both* people would gain if person a gave person b some of good Y in exchange for some of good X. There would be a Pareto improvement. The Pareto optimal distribution of consumption will therefore be where

$$\frac{MU_X}{MU_Y} \text{ person a} = \frac{MU_X}{MU_Y} \text{ person b} = \frac{MU_X}{MU_Y} \text{ person c} \cdots$$

i.e. *MRS* is the same for all consumers.

But this will be achieved *automatically* under perfect competition, since each consumer will consume that combination of goods where $MU_X/MU_Y = P_X/P_Y$ and all consumers face the *same* (market) prices and hence the *same* P_X/P_Y.

Social efficiency between producers. If MC_X/MC_Y for producer g is greater than MC_X/MC_Y for producer h, then if producer g produced relatively more Y and producer h produced relatively more X, the same output could be produced at a lower total cost (i.e. with less resources). There would be a Pareto improvement. The Pareto optimal distribution of production between firms is therefore where

$$\frac{MC_X}{MC_Y} \text{ producer g} = \frac{MC_X}{MC_Y} \text{ producer h} = \frac{MC_X}{MC_Y} \text{ producer i} \cdots$$

i.e. *MRT* is the same for all producers.

This too will be achieved *automatically* under perfect competition, since each producer will maximise profits where $MC_X/MC_Y = P_X/P_Y$ and all producers face the *same* (market) prices and hence the *same* P_X/P_Y.

Social efficiency in exchange. If MU_X/MU_Y (i.e. *MRS*) for all consumers is greater than MC_X/MC_Y (i.e. *MRT*) for all producers, then there would be a Pareto improvement if resources were reallocated to produce relatively more X and less Y.

Assume the *MRS* (i.e. $\Delta Y/\Delta X$) = 3/1 and the *MRT* (i.e. $\Delta Y/\Delta X$) = 2/1. Consumers will be prepared to give up three units of Y to obtain one unit of X, and yet producers only have to sacrifice producing two units of Y to produce one unit of X. Thus consumers can pay producers in full for extra units of X they produce and there will still be a net gain to consumers. There has been a Pareto improvement.

The Pareto optimal allocation of resources is where

Social MRS (SMRS) = *Social MRT (SMRT)*

Assuming no externalities, this will be achieved automatically under perfect competition, since (a) with no externalities, social and private marginal rates of substitution will be the same, and similarly social and private marginal rates of transformation will be the same, and (b) P_X/P_Y is the same for all producers and consumers. In other words:

$$SMRS = MRS_{\text{all consumers}} = \frac{MU_X}{MU_Y} \text{ all consumers} = \frac{P_X}{P_Y}$$

and

$$SMRT = MRT_{\text{all producers}} = \frac{MC_X}{MC_Y} \text{ all producers} = \frac{P_X}{P_Y}$$

i.e.

SMRS = *SMRT*

Thus the pursuit of private gain, it is argued, has led to the achieving of social efficiency. This is an important conclusion. It is clearly very attractive to people (and to many politicians) to think that, simply by looking after their own interests, social efficiency will thereby be achieved!

This is illustrated graphically in Figure 12.3. A production possibility curve (the red line) shows the various combinations of two goods X and Y that can be produced (see pages 14–17). Its slope is given by $\Delta Y/\Delta X$ and shows how much Y must be given up to produce 1 more of X. Its slope, therefore, is the marginal rate of transformation (*MRT*).

Social indifference curves can be drawn showing the various combinations of X and Y that give particular levels of satisfaction to consumers as a whole. Their slope is given by $\Delta Y/\Delta X$ and shows how much Y consumers are prepared to give up to obtain one more unit of X. Their slope, therefore, is the marginal rate of substitution in consumption (*MRS*).

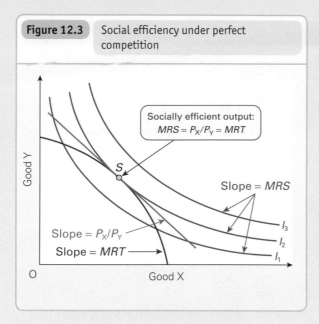

Figure 12.3 Social efficiency under perfect competition

Socially efficient output:
$MRS = P_X/P_Y = MRT$

Good Y

S

Slope = MRS

I_3
I_2
I_1

Slope = P_X/P_Y
Slope = MRT

O   Good X

The Pareto optimal combination of goods is at point S, where the production possibility curve is tangential to the highest possible indifference curve. At any other point on the production possibility curve, a lower level of consumer satisfaction is achieved. The slope of the tangent at S is equal to both MRT and MRS, and hence also to P_X/P_Y.

If production were at a point on the production possibility curve below point S, describe the process whereby market forces would return the economy to point S.

*Efficiency in the factor market (intermediate analysis)

A similar analysis can be applied to factor markets, showing that perfect competition and the absence of externalities will lead to efficiency in the use of factors between firms. Assume that there are two factors: labour (L) and capital (K).

If MPP_L/MPP_K for firm g is greater than MPP_L/MPP_K for firm h, then if firm g were to use relatively more labour and firm h relatively more capital, more could be produced for the same total input. There would be a Pareto improvement.

The Pareto optimum distribution of factors between firms will therefore be where

$$\frac{MPP_L}{MPP_K}_{\text{firm g}} = \frac{MPP_L}{MPP_K}_{\text{firm h}} = \frac{MPP_L}{MPP_K}_{\text{firm i}} \cdots$$

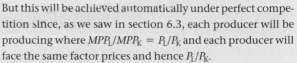

But this will be achieved automatically under perfect competition since, as we saw in section 6.3, each producer will be producing where $MPP_L/MPP_K = P_L/P_K$ and each producer will face the same factor prices and hence P_L/P_K.

Provided there are no externalities, the marginal private benefit of labour to a firm (MPP_L) will equal the marginal social benefit of labour (MSB_L). The same applies to capital. Thus $MPP_L/MPP_K = MSB_L/MSB_K = P_L/P_K$. Similarly on the cost side, if there are no externalities, then $MC_L/MC_K = MSC_L/MSC_K = P_L/P_K$. Therefore:

$$\frac{MSB_L}{MSB_K} = \frac{MSC_L}{MSC_K}$$

*The intermediate analysis of general equilibrium

General equilibrium is where equilibrium exists in all markets. Under perfect competition and in the absence of externalities, general equilibrium will give Pareto optimality.

If any change in the conditions of demand or supply occurs, this disequilibrium will automatically create a whole series of interdependent reactions in various markets.

Assume, for example, that tastes change such that MU_X rises and MU_Y falls. This will lead to the following sequence of events in the goods market.

MU_X/MU_Y will now be greater than P_X/P_Y. Thus consumers buy more X relative to Y. This causes MU_X/MU_Y to fall (due to diminishing marginal utility) and P_X/P_Y to rise (due to a relative shortage of X and a surplus of Y), helping to restore equilibrium where $MU_X/MU_Y = P_X/P_Y$. The rise in P_X/P_Y causes P_X/P_Y to be greater than MC_X/MC_Y. Thus firms produce more X relative to Y. This causes MC_X/MC_Y to rise (due to diminishing returns), helping to restore equilibrium where $P_X/P_Y = MC_X/MC_Y$. This process of price and quantity adjustment thus continues until once more

$$\frac{MU_X}{MU_Y} = \frac{P_X}{P_Y} = \frac{MC_X}{MC_Y}$$

Similar adjustments will take place in the factor market. The price of those factors used in producing good X will be bid up and those used in producing Y will be bid down. This will encourage factors to move from industry Y and into industry X. The whole process of adjustment continues until equilibrium and Pareto optimality are restored in all goods and factor markets.

Section summary

1. Social efficiency (Pareto optimality) will be achieved when it is not possible to make anyone better off without making someone else worse off. This will be achieved if people behave 'rationally' under perfect competition providing there are no externalities.

2. Rational behaviour involves doing more of any activity whose marginal benefit (MB) exceeds its marginal cost (MC) and less of any activity whose marginal cost exceeds its marginal benefit. The optimum level of consumption or production for the individual consumer or firm will be where $MB = MC$. This is called a situation of 'private efficiency'.

3. In a perfectly competitive goods market, the consumer will achieve private efficiency where $MU = P$, and the producer where $P = MC$. Thus $MU = MC$. In the absence of externalities, private benefits and costs will equal social benefits and costs. Thus $MU = MSB$ and $MC = MSC$. Thus $MSB = MSC$: a situation of social efficiency (Pareto optimality).

4. Given perfect competition and an absence of externalities, if the equality of marginal benefit and marginal cost is destroyed in any market (by shifts in demand or supply), price adjustments will take place until general equilibrium is restored where $MSB = MSC$ in all markets: a situation of general Pareto optimality.

*5. The rational producer or consumer will choose the combination of any two pairs of goods where their marginal benefit ratio is equal to their marginal cost ratio. Consumers will achieve private efficiency where

$$\frac{MU_X}{MU_Y} \text{ (i.e. } MRS\text{)} = \frac{P_X}{P_Y}$$

Producers will achieve private efficiency where

$$\frac{P_X}{P_Y} = \frac{MC_X}{MC_Y} \text{ (i.e. } MRT\text{)}$$

Thus:

$$\frac{MU_X}{MU_Y} = \frac{MC_X}{MC_Y}$$

In the absence of externalities, this will give a situation of social efficiency where

$$\frac{MSB_X}{MSB_Y} = \frac{MSC_X}{MSC_Y}$$

*6. Similarly, in factor markets, social efficiency will be achieved if there is perfect competition and an absence of externalities. This will be where the MSB ratio for any two factors is equal to their MSC ratio.

*7. Again assuming perfect competition and an absence of externalities, general equilibrium will be achieved where there is a socially efficient level of production, consumption and exchange in all markets: where the MSB ratio for any pair of goods or factors is equal to the MSC ratio.

12.2 THE CASE FOR GOVERNMENT INTERVENTION

The discussion above considered what happens 'under ideal conditions', but in the real world, markets fail to achieve social efficiency. Part of the problem is the existence of externalities, part is a lack of perfect competition. Even if those were not considerations, we are also faced with markets that may take a long time to adjust to any disequilibrium given short-run immobility of factors. What is more, social efficiency (i.e. Pareto optimality) is not the only economic goal of society. Markets may also fail to the extent that they fail to achieve other objectives such as greater equality and faster growth. In this section we explore the various categories of market failure.

> **KEY IDEA 30**
>
> *Markets generally fail to achieve social efficiency.* There are various types of market failure. Market failures provide one of the major justifications for government intervention in the economy.

Externalities

The market will not lead to social efficiency if the actions of producers or consumers affect people other than themselves: in other words, when there are *externalities* (side effects).

> **KEY IDEA 31**
>
> *Externalities are spillover costs or benefits.* Where these exist, even an otherwise perfect market will fail to achieve social efficiency.

Whenever other people are affected beneficially, there are said to be **external benefits**. Whenever other people are affected adversely, there are said to be **external costs**.

Thus the full cost to society (the **social cost**) of the production of any good is the private cost faced by firms plus any externalities of production. Likewise the full benefit to society (the **social benefit**) from the consumption of any

Definitions

External benefits Benefits from production (or consumption) experienced by people *other* than the producer (or consumer) directly involved in the transaction.

External costs Costs of production (or consumption) borne by people *other* than the producer (or consumer) directly involved in the transaction.

Social cost Private cost plus externalities in production.

Social benefit Private benefit plus externalities in consumption.

Figure 12.4 Negative externality in production

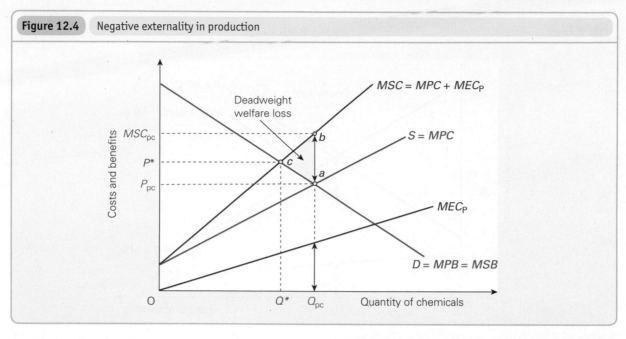

good is the private benefit enjoyed by consumers plus any externalities of consumption.

In the following section we will consider four different types of externality. (In each case, we will assume that the market is in other respects perfect.)

External costs of production (MSC > MPC) with no external cost/benefits of consumption

When a chemical firm dumps waste in a river or pollutes the air, the community bears additional costs to those borne by the firm. There are marginal external costs MEC_P of chemical production. This is illustrated in Figure 12.4. In this example we assume that the external costs begin with the first unit of production and increase at a constant rate.

The marginal *social* cost (*MSC*) of chemical production equals the marginal private costs (*MPC*) plus the MEC_P. This means that the *MSC* curve is above the *MPC* curve. The vertical distance between them is equal to the MEC_P. It is also assumed that there are no externalities in consumption, which means that the marginal social benefit (*MSB*) curve is the same as the marginal private benefit (*MPB*) curve.

Competitive market forces, with producers and consumers responding only to private costs and benefits, will result in a market equilibrium at point *a* in Figure 12.4: i.e. where demand equals supply. The market equilibrium price is P_{pc} while the market equilibrium quantity is Q_{pc}.

At P_{pc}, *MPB* is equal to *MSB*. The market price reflects both the private and social benefits from the last unit consumed. However, the presence of external costs in production means that *MSC* > *MPC*.

The **socially optimal output** would be Q^*, where $P = MSB = MSC$. This is illustrated at point *c* and clearly shows how external costs of production in a perfectly competitive market result in overproduction: i.e. $Q_{pc} > Q^*$. From society's point of view too much waste is being dumped in rivers.

At the market equilibrium (Q_{pc}) there is a **deadweight welfare loss** when compared with the socially optimal output (Q^*). In this context, deadweight welfare loss represents the excess of social costs over social benefits at all outputs above Q^*. At Q_{pc}, this is given by the shaded area, *abc*. Put another way, moving from Q_{pc} to Q^* would represent a *gain* in *social surplus* of the area *abc*.

One of the reasons why external costs cause problems in a free-market economy is because no one has legal ownership of factors such as the air or rivers., Therefore, nobody has the ability either to prevent or to charge for their use as a dumping ground for waste. Such a 'market' is *missing*. Control must, therefore, be left to the government, local authorities or regulators.

Other examples of external costs of production include extensive farming that destroys hedgerows and wildlife, and global warming caused by CO_2 emissions from power stations, industry and transport.

External benefits of production (MSC < MPC) with no external costs /benefits of consumption

If companies in the forestry industry plant new woodlands, there is a benefit not only to the companies themselves, but also to the world through a reduction of CO_2 in the atmosphere (forests are a carbon sink). In this case there are marginal external benefits of production (MEB_P). These are

Definitions

Socially optimal output The output where $MSC = MSB$: the output where total social surplus is maximised.

Deadweight welfare loss from externalities The loss of social surplus at the competitive market equilibrium compared with the social optimum where $MSC = MSB$.

Social surplus Total social benefits minus total social costs.

Figure 12.5   Positive externality in production

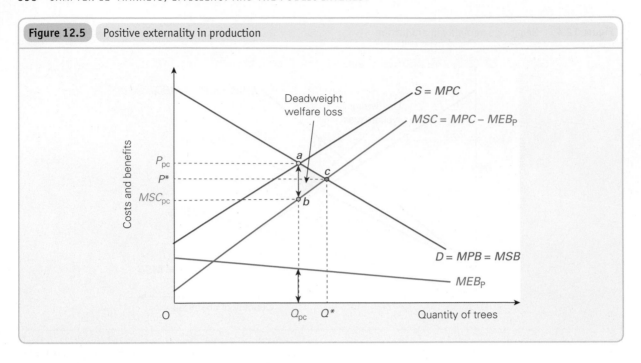

shown in Figure 12.5. We assumed that they begin with the first tree planted but that the marginal benefit declines with each additional tree. In other words, the MEB_P is a downward sloping line.

 Why are marginal external benefits typically likely to decline as output increases? Why in some cases might marginal external benefits be constant at all levels of output or even increase as more is produced?

Given these positive externalities, the marginal *social* cost (MSC) of providing timber is less than the marginal private cost: $MSC = MPC - MEB_P$. This means that the MSC curve is *below* the MPC curve. The vertical distance between the curves is equal to the MEB_P. Once again it is assumed that there are no externalities in consumption so that $MSB = MPB$.

Competitive market forces will result in an equilibrium output of Q_{pc} where market demand ($=MPB$) equals market supply ($=MPC$) (point *a*). The socially efficient level of output, however, is Q^*: i.e. where $MSB = MSC$ (point *c*). The external benefits of production thus result in a level of output *below* the socially efficient level. From society's point of view not enough trees are being planted. The deadweight welfare caused by this underproduction is illustrated by the area *abc*. Output is not being produced between Q_{pc} and Q^* even though $MSB > MSC$.

Another example of external benefits in production is that of research and development. An interesting recent example has been the development of touchscreen technology for tablets and mobile phones. If other firms have access to the results of the research, then clearly the benefits extend beyond the firm which finances it. Since the firm only receives the private benefits, it may conduct a less than optimal amount of research. In turn, this may reduce the pace of innovation and so negatively affect economic growth over the longer term.

External costs of consumption (MSB < MPB) with no external costs/benefits of production (MSC = MPC)

Drinking alcohol can sometimes lead to marginal external costs of consumption. For example, there are the extra nightly policing costs to deal with the increased chance of social disorder. Public health costs may also be greater as a direct consequence of peoples' drinking behaviour: e.g. through an increase in hospitalisations. It may also lead to a number of alcohol-related road accidents. These marginal external costs of consumption (MEC_c) result in the marginal social benefit of alcohol consumption being lower than the marginal private benefit: i.e. $MSB = MPB - MEC_c$.

This is illustrated in Figure 12.6 where the MSB curve is below the MPB curve. In this example, it is assumed that there are no externalities in production so that $MSC = MPC$.

Competitive market forces will result in an equilibrium output of Q_{pc} (point *a*), whereas the socially efficient level of output is Q^*: i.e. where $MSB = MSC$ (point *c*). The external costs of consumption result in a level of output *above* the socially efficient level: i.e. $Q_{pc} > Q^*$. From society's point of view too much alcohol is being produced and consumed. The deadweight welfare caused by this overconsumption is illustrated by the area *abc*.

Other possible examples of negative externalities of consumption include taking a journey by car, noisy music in public places, litter, using a mobile phone while driving and the smoke from cigarettes (passive smoking).

Figure 12.6 Negative externality in consumption

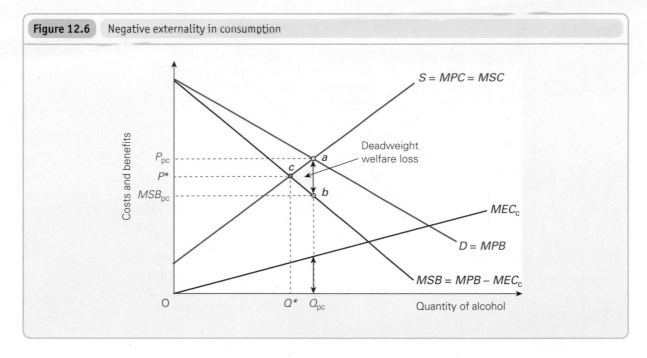

External benefits of consumption (MSB > MPB) with no external costs/benefits of production (MSC = MPC)

How do people travel to a city centre to go shopping on a Saturday? How do they travel to a football match? If they use the train then other people benefit, as there is less congestion and exhaust fumes and fewer accidents on the roads. These marginal external benefits of consumption (MEB_C) result in the marginal social benefit of rail travel being *greater* than the marginal private benefit (i.e. $MSB = MPB + MEB_C$).

This is illustrated in Figure 12.7 where the *MSB* curve is above the *MPB* curve. The vertical distance between the curves is equal to the MEB_C. Once again it is assumed that there are no externalities in production so that $MSC = MPC$.

External benefits of consumption result in a level of output below the socially efficient level: i.e. $Q_{pc} < Q^*$. From society's point of view not enough journeys are being made on the train. The deadweight welfare loss caused by this underconsumption is illustrated by the area *abc*.

Other examples of external benefits of consumption include the beneficial effects for other people from someone using a deodorant, parents getting their children vaccinated, and people planting flowers in their front garden.

To summarise: whenever there are external benefits, there will be too little produced or consumed. Whenever there are external costs, there will be too much produced or consumed. The market will not equate *MSB* and *MSC*.

The above arguments have been developed in the context of perfect competition with prices determined by demand and supply. Externalities can also occur in all other types of market.

1. Give other examples of each of the four types of externality.
2. Redraw Figure 12.4, only this time assume there is only one producer that is a monopoly. How does the existence of market power affect the relationship between the private and social optimum positions?
3. Redraw Figure 12.4, only this time assume that at low levels of production the good generates no external costs. Only once a certain output is reached (Q*) does the production of additional units generate rising marginal external costs.

Public goods

There is a category of goods where the positive externalities are so great that the free market, whether perfect or imperfect, may not produce at all. They are called **public goods**. In order to understand exactly what a public good is it is important to discuss two of its key characteristics – **non-rivalry** and **non-excludability**. Before looking specifically at public goods, let us explore the concepts of rivalry and excludability in more detail.

Definitions

Public good A good or service that has the features of non-rivalry and non-excludability and as a result would not be provided by the free market.

Non-rivalry Where the consumption of a good or service by one person will not prevent others from enjoying it.

Non-excludability Where it is not possible to provide a good or service to one person without it thereby being available free for others to enjoy.

Figure 12.7   Positive externality in consumption

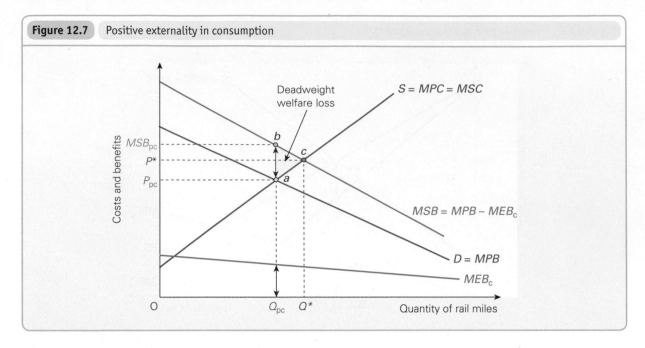

The degree of rivalry

Rivalry occurs when one person's consumption of a good reduces the amount of it that is available for other consumers. Goods can vary in their degree of rivalry.

Perfectly rivalrous goods. At one extreme are goods that are *perfectly* rivalrous. A good has this characteristic if, as one or more people increase their consumption of the product, it prevents all other or 'rival' consumers from enjoying it. This is typical with non-durable goods such as food, alcohol and fuel. For example, imagine that you have purchased a bar of chocolate for your own consumption. Each chunk of the chocolate bar that you eat means that there is less available for other or 'rival' consumers to enjoy. They cannot eat the same piece that you have eaten! The good gets 'used up' when it is consumed.

Many durable goods such as mobile phones also have the property of being rivalrous. For example, if you use your mobile phone it usually prevents other people from using it. Although the mobile phone does not get 'used up', only one person can usually consume the benefits it provides at a time: e.g. sending a text or calling someone.

Perfectly non-rivalrous goods. At the other extreme are goods that have the property of being perfectly non-rivalrous. A good has this characteristic if as one or more people increase their consumption of the product it has no impact on the ability of other, or 'rival', consumers to enjoy the good. For example, imagine that you turn on either your television or tablet to watch a live football match or an episode of your favourite TV programme. Your decision to watch the programme has no impact on the ability of other people to enjoy watching the same programme on a

different device. The television set may be rivalrous but the broadcast is not.

Goods with a degree of rivalry and non-rivalry. In reality, many goods and services will be neither perfectly rival nor non-rival. For example, it may be possible for more than one person to enjoy watching a video clip on a mobile phone. However, a 'crowding effect' will soon occur. As additional people try watching the video it will prevent others from seeing it on the same phone.

There are a number of goods and services that may have the characteristic of being relatively non-rival with low numbers of consumers, before becoming more rivalrous at high levels of consumption. For example, some goods cover a comparatively small geographic area. Here overcrowding, and hence rivalry, will become an issue with relatively few consumers. Viewing a carnival procession, for example, may be non-rivalrous with just a few observers, but quickly any location along the route will become crowded and a good view becomes rivalrous. Another example is enjoying open spaces sitting on a beach: space becomes more rivalrous as the beach fills up with people. In other cases, such as access to the Internet, rivalry might only set in beyond very high levels of usage, when global demand is exceptionally high.

Rather than trying to categorise many goods as either rivalrous or non-rivalrous it makes more sense to think of them as having different *degrees* of rivalry. They could be placed on a scale of rivalry as illustrated along the horizontal axis in Figure 12.8.

 How rivalrous in consumption are each of the following: (a) a can of drink; (b) public transport; (c) a radio broadcast; (d) the sight of flowers in a public park?

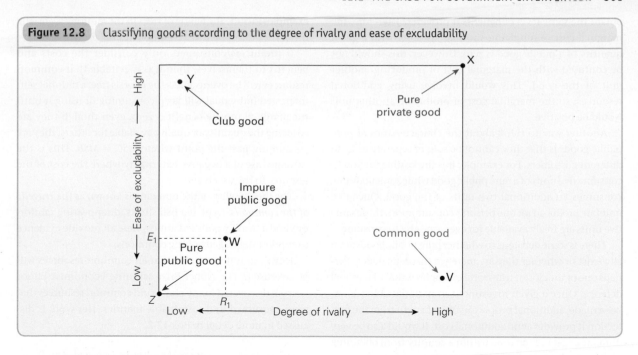

Figure 12.8 Classifying goods according to the degree of rivalry and ease of excludability

The ease of excludability

Excludability occurs when the supplier of a good can restrict who consumes it. This is the case for goods sold in the market. Suppliers allow only those consumers who are prepared to pay for the good to have it. Just as with rivalry, goods vary in their ease of excludability

Easily excludable goods. At one extreme, some goods have the property of being very easily excludable. In this case a relatively low-cost and effective system can be implemented which guarantees that only those people who have paid for the good are able to enjoy the benefits it provides. The system must also prevent anyone who does not pay from obtaining any of the benefits that consuming the good provides. For example, although television broadcasts have a high degree of non-rivalry, a relatively straightforward and reasonably effective system of encryption could be implemented to exclude non-payers from watching the programmes. If this were not possible then pay television channels and pay-per-view broadcasting could not exist. YouTube has also introduced a number of subscription channels.

Advances in technology may also change the ease of excludability for any given good or service over time.

Perfectly non-excludable goods. At the other extreme there may be some goods for which excludability is impossible: i.e. they have the property of being non-excludable. A good has this characteristic if it is too costly or simply not feasible to implement a system that would effectively prevent those people who have not paid from enjoying the benefits it provides.

In some circumstances it may be theoretically possible to exclude non-payers, but in reality the transaction costs involved are too great. For example, it may be very difficult to prevent anyone from fishing in the open ocean or enjoying the benefits of walking in a country park.

Once again, many goods will be neither perfectly excludable nor non-excludable. In these cases it makes more sense to think about the differing levels of ease with which non-payers can be excluded from consuming the good. This is also illustrated in Figure 12.8, this time up the vertical axis.

Pure private goods

Good X in Figure 12.8 is a pure private good. It is very easy to exclude any non-payers from the consuming the product, which is perfectly rivalrous. A pure private good is one where the benefits can be enjoyed only by the consumer who owns (or rents) it.

In reality, many goods will be close to point X and have significant degrees of rivalry and ease of excludability. Products that fall into this category can normally be provided by the market mechanism.

Pure public goods

Good Z in Figure 12.8, by contrast, has the characteristics of being perfectly non-rival and completely non-excludable. This is a known as a ***pure public good***. Once a given quantity of a pure public good is produced, everyone can

Definition

Pure public good A good or service that has the characteristics of being perfectly non-rival and completely non-excludable and, as a result, would not be provided by the free market.

obtain the same level of benefits it provides. Therefore, the marginal cost of supplying another customer with a given quantity of a public good is zero. However, this should not be confused with the marginal cost of producing another unit of the good. This would involve using additional resources; so the marginal cost of producing another unit would be positive.

Another way to think about the characteristics of pure public goods is that they cannot be sold in separate units to different customers. For example, it is impossible for you to consume five units of a pure public good while somebody else consumes an additional two units of the good. Once five units are produced for one person's consumption, those same five units are freely available for everyone else to consume.

There is some debate as to whether pure public goods actually exist or whether they are merely a theoretical idea. Perhaps one of the closest real-world examples is that of national defence. Once a given investment in national defence has been made, additional people can often benefit from the protection it provides at no additional cost. It would also be very difficult to exclude anyone within a country from obtaining the benefits from the increase in security.

To what extent is national defence a pure public good? Can it ever be rivalrous or excludable in consumption.

Impure pure goods

Good W in Figure 12.8 is an example of an **impure public good**. It has a low level of rivalry, without being perfectly rivalrous, and it is difficult, but not impossible, to exclude non-payers. In reality, many public goods will fall into this category, with some being more impure than others. We will see later that as the degree of rivalry and ease of excludability fall it becomes increasingly difficult for the good to be provided by the market mechanism.

Club goods. Good Y has a low degree of rivalry but exclusion is relatively easy. This is called a **club good**. Wireless Internet connection on a train or in a café are examples of a club good if a password is required; other examples include subscription TV services, such as Netflix or Amazon Prime.

Common good or resource. Good V has a high degree of rivalry but the exclusion of non-payers is very difficult. This is called a **common good or resource**. The high degree of rivalry means that the quantity or quality of the common resource available to one person is negatively affected by the number of other people who consume or make use of the same resource. Because it is difficult to exclude non-payers, a common resource is also potentially available to everyone, free of charge.

Fishing in the open ocean is an example. In the absence of intervention, fishing boats can catch as many fish as is possible. There is no 'owner' of either the fish or the sea to stop them. As one fishing boat catches more fish, it means there is less available for other fishing boats: fish are *rivalrous*. Other

examples include the felling of trees in the rainforests and the use of the atmosphere as a common 'dump' for emissions.

If producers/consumers only consider the costs and benefits to themselves, then it is inevitable that common resources will be overused. As the good is free, a rational self-interested individual will keep consuming or using it until the marginal private benefit is zero, even though they are reducing the quantity or quality available for others; they are consuming past the point where $MSC = MSB$. This is the extreme case of a negative externality where the cost of the resource to the user is zero.

The inevitability of the outcome is known as the **tragedy of the commons**. Depleted fish stocks, disappearing rainforests and a heavily polluted atmosphere all provide evidence to support the tragedy of the commons.

However, is it inevitable that all common resources will be overused? The Nobel Prize winning economist Elinor Ostrom discovered many real-world common resources that were consumed in a sustainable manner. Her work is discussed in more detail in Box 12.2.

1. *To what extent can the following be regarded as common resources? (a) Rainforests; (b) children's playgrounds in public parks; (c) silence in a library; (d) the Internet.*
2. *Where would you place each of the following in Figure 12.8: (a) an inner city road at 3:00am; (b) an inner city road at 8:00am; (c) a toll motorway at 3:00am; (d) a toll motorway at 8:00am?*

The efficient level of output for a pure public good

The socially efficient level of output is the quantity at which the marginal social benefit is equal to the marginal social cost. In a competitive market without externalities the marginal social benefit curve is the same as the market demand curve.

The market demand curve for a private good illustrates the sum of all the quantities demanded by all consumers at each possible price. Different consumers will each want to purchase varying amounts at each price. These different individual demands at each price are simply added together in order to derive the market demand curve for a private good. This is known as horizontal aggregation or summation of individual demand curves.

Definitions

Impure public good A good that is partially non-rivalrous and non-excludable.

Club good A good which has a low degree of rivalry but is easily excludable.

Common good or resource A good or resource that has a high degree of rivalry but the exclusion of non-payers is difficult

Tragedy of the commons When resources are commonly available at no charge, people are likely to overexploit them.

The market demand curve for a pure public good cannot be derived in the same way, because consumers are unable to purchase and consume different quantities of the good. Once a given amount of a pure public good is produced for one customer, every other customer can consume that same amount at no additional cost.

Therefore, instead of thinking about how much people are willing to buy at each different price, we have to work out how much people are willing to pay *in total* for each possible level of output. In other words, we have to add together the maximum amount each consumer is willing to pay for each possible level of output. This is illustrated in Figure 12.9.

To keep the example simple it is assumed that there are just two consumers of the public good – Dean and Jon. In most real-world examples there would be many more. The maximum amount Dean would be willing to pay to consume the 10th unit of the good is illustrated at point *a* on his demand curve (D_D) and is £30. The maximum amount Jon would be willing to pay for the 10th unit of the good is illustrated at point *b* on his demand curve (D_J) and is £50.

Therefore, if we simply add these willingness-to-pay figures together we obtain the marginal benefit to society from producing the tenth unit of the public good. This is illustrated at point *c* and is £80. This provides us with one point on the marginal social benefit curve. If we continue this exercise for each different level of output, the marginal social benefit (MSB) can be derived as illustrated in Figure 12.9. The curve has been derived in this example by vertically aggregating Dean's and Jon's individual demand curves: $MSB = D_D + D_J$.

Producing a public good would normally have the same characteristics as producing a private good. Costs would vary with output in a very similar manner. Therefore the marginal cost (MC) for the market as a whole would be derived in the same way as it would be for a private good: i.e. by adding together the quantities that each firm would want to supply at each price – the horizontal summation of all the individual firms' marginal cost curves. Hence it is drawn as an upward-sloping line.

Assuming there are no externalities in production, the private marginal cost curve is the same as the social marginal cost curve ($MC = MSC$). The socially efficient quantity can be found where $MSC = MSB$, which is at point *f* at an output level of 16.

Provision of pure public goods and the free-rider problem

Assume a private firm produced 16 units of the good and charged Jon a price of £20 per unit (point *e*) and Dean £12 per unit (point *d*). These prices would equal their maximum willingness to pay for 16 units. If Jon acts in a perfectly rational and selfish manner we can predict that he will not pay for the good. Why? Because once the 16 units are produced he can consume them whether he has paid for them or not. He can act as a *free-rider* by enjoying the benefits of a good which have been paid for by Dean.

Unfortunately for Jon, if Dean thinks the same way, then he will not pay for the good either. If neither of them pays for the good then the firm will not generate any revenue and

KEY IDEA 32

The free-rider problem. People are often unwilling to pay for things if they can make use of things other people have bought. This problem can lead to people not purchasing things that would be to the benefit of them and other members of society to have.

Definition

Free-rider problem When it is not possible to exclude other people from consuming a good that someone has bought.

Figure 12.9 The efficient output of a pure public good

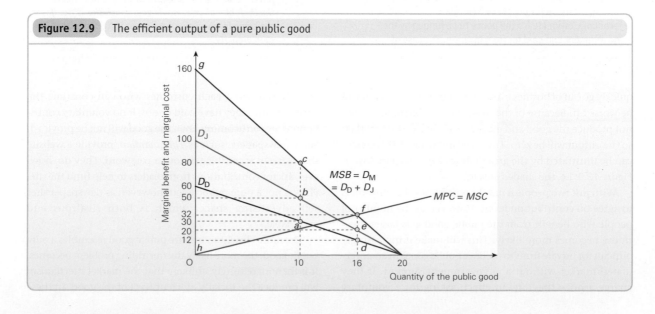

BOX 12.1 THE POLICE AS A PUBLIC SERVICE

Could some aspects of policing be provided privately?

A good example of a good or service that has public-good properties is policing. Take the case of police officers on the beat. They are providing a general service to the community by deterring and detecting crime.

The cost to individuals of privately employing their own police officers would be considerable. For most people this cost would far outweigh the benefits. However, the impact of having police officers on the beat would benefit many individuals in a community.

Voluntary contributions from local residents for local policing

Perhaps local residents could all privately contribute a relatively small amount towards the costs of employing the police officers and collectively enjoy the benefits.

This idea might seem rather strange, but this is exactly what the residents of Frinton-on-Sea in Essex have done. Following cuts in police services, 400 of the 4000 residents have been making a voluntary contribution of £2 per week to fund a private security firm, AGS, to patrol the streets from 7:00pm to 7:00am. The money was collected door to door following a leaflet campaign. The security staff who patrol the streets have exactly the same powers as any other private citizen.

Why is it unlikely that everyone would contribute? Employing security staff to deter crime in a whole town has public-good properties. If one member of the community benefits from the lower chance of a crime being committed, it does not prevent other members of the community from enjoying the same benefits. The deterrence effect is not 'used up' in consumption and so has a very low degree of rivalry.

It would also be very difficult to prevent someone in the local community from benefiting, even if they had not paid towards the costs of the scheme. In the Frinton-on-Sea example, the owner of AGS has stated that 'we don't avoid the streets where people are not paying'.

Because it is difficult to exclude non-payers and there is a strong incentive for people to free-ride, this provides an economic rationale for the police to be funded by the government and paid for from taxation. The case of

Frinton-on-Sea is very unusual and it will be interesting to see if enough people continue to make the voluntary contributions in order for the business to remain viable.

KI 32
p363

Policing where there is no free-rider problem

But do all aspects of policing have a free-rider problem? The answer is no. When there is a *specific* task of guarding specific property, policing could be provided by the market. This is in fact done by security firms. Security guards are employed by banks, shops, etc., to prevent theft or criminal damage to their property. In these cases, the private benefits are perceived to exceed the private costs.

Should such security services be provided privately or are they better provided by the police? Since the *private* benefits in such cases are large, there is a strong argument for charging the recipient. But why should the service be provided by private security firms? Could the police not charge firms for specific guard duties? The problem here is that, if private security firms were not allowed to operate, the police would have a monopoly and could charge very high prices unless the prices were regulated by the government. Also, the quality of the service might be poorer than that provided by private security companies which were competing against each other for business.

On the other hand, the police are likely to bring greater expertise to the job. There are also economies of scale to be gained: for example, the police may have knowledge of criminal activities in other parts of the area which may pose a threat to the particular property in question. Finally, there is the problem that private security guards may not show the same level of courtesy as the police in dealing with the public (or criminals for that matter).

1. *The police charge football clubs for policing inside football grounds, but make no charge for policing outside the ground. Explain this approach.*
2. *Could other aspects of policing make use of market forces? Examine the case for charging to investigate the theft of a bicycle. Would your conclusion differ if the crime involved an attack on an individual rather than property?*

---

quickly go out of business. As a result, both Dean and Jon will be worse off. Because of the free-riding problem, firms cannot produce the good and make a profit in a private market; so the output will be zero. The social inefficiency this creates can be illustrated by the area of deadweight welfare loss in Figure 12.9: i.e. the shaded area *fgh*.

With just two people it may be possible for the consumers to agree on contribution levels. However, as the number of people who benefit from the public good gets larger, free-riding becomes more likely. This will make it increasingly difficult for private firms to produce public goods in an unregulated market without any government support. If they charge a price they are, in effect, asking for a voluntary

contribution from each customer who can consume the good, whether they have paid or not. If no voluntary contributions are forthcoming, then the good will not be provided. Some newspapers, such as *The Guardian,* provide a website that is freely accessible without a password. They do, however, ask for contributions from readers to help fund the site. (This is not a pure public good, however, as newspaper sites sell advertising space, which is both rivalrous and excludable.)

The more closely an impure public good resembles a pure public good, the more likely the free-riding problem becomes. It is then increasingly unlikely that the market mechanism will produce the socially efficient level of the good. In these

| BOX 12.2 | A COMMONS SOLUTION | EXPLORING ECONOMICS |

Making the best use of common resources

To avoid the tragedy of the commons, one solution is to change the status of such resources. There are two obvious ways of doing this.

The first is for the government or an intergovernmental agency either to take over the resources or to regulate their use. Thus a national or local government could pass laws preventing people from tipping waste onto common land or into rivers. Alternatively, groups of governments could act collectively to regulate activities. An example here is the EU's common fisheries policy or international agreements to ban whaling.

The second is to privatise such resources. Common land could be sold or given to private landowners. Such land would then have the property of excludability. This solution clearly raises questions of fairness. How should the land be divided up? If it is sold, how should the previous users of the resource be compensated – if at all? In the 'enclosure movement' in Britain in the eighteenth and nineteenth centuries, common lands were often acquired by wealthy aristocracy and hedges put around them. Poor peasants, who had previously used the land, either had to rent it from the landlords or left the land and were forced to take low-paid work in the cities.

But is there any way for resources to stay as common resources without them being overexploited? After all, economic theory would seem to suggest that the overexploitation of such resources is inevitable: that common ownership will end in tragedy.

Social attitudes towards common resources

In practice, many common resources are used sustainably without government regulation.

When economists began to look at how systems of commonly managed resources actually worked, they found to their surprise that they often worked quite well. Swiss Alpine pastures; Japanese forests; irrigation systems in Spain and the Philippines. All these were examples of commons that lasted for decades. Some irrigation networks held in common were more efficiently run than the public and private systems that worked alongside them. Though there were failures, too, it seemed as if good management could stave off the tragedy.[1]

The crucial factor here is whether a sense of individual responsibility can be fostered and whether mechanisms can be found for the users to act collectively to manage the resources – a form of quasi-government. Also, there has to be some agreement about what is a fair use of such resources and, in many cases, rules will have to be developed.

In *Governing the Commons,* which was published in 1990, Elinor Ostrom of Indiana University described the rules needed to keep a commons going. She showed that there are almost always elaborate conventions over who can use

resources and when. What you take out of a commons has to be proportional to what you put in. Usage has to be compatible with the commons' underlying health (i.e., you cannot just keep grazing your animals regardless). Everyone has to have some say in the rules. And people usually pay more attention to monitoring abuses and to conflict resolution than to sanctions and punishment.[2]

Sometimes the rules of behaviour can be deeply embedded in culture. Thus indigenous peoples operating on marginal lands, such as the Aborigines in Australia or the San in the Kalahari, have a culture that respects common resources and puts sustainability at the heart of its philosophy.

Land is fundamental to the wellbeing of Aboriginal people. The land is not just soil or rocks or minerals, but a whole environment that sustains and is sustained by people and culture. For Indigenous Australians, the land is the core of all spirituality and this relationship and the spirit of 'country' is central to the issues that are important to Indigenous people today.[3]

But if rules are not embedded in culture, how can they be made to stick? One way is through the development of pressure groups, such as Friends of the Earth or local community action groups.

Mrs Ostrom suggests the so-called 'miracle of the Rhine' – the clean-up of Europe's busiest waterway – should be seen as an example of successful commons management because it was not until local pressure groups, city and regional governments and non-governmental organisations got involved that polluters were willing to recognise the costs they were imposing on others, and cut emissions. An intergovernmental body (the International Commission for the Protection of the Rhine) did not have the same effect.[4]

The importance of Elinor Ostrom's work was recognised when she was awarded the Nobel Prize in Economic Sciences in 2009.

1. *Is there any way in which people's behaviour towards the global commons can be changed so as to reduce the problem of climate change?*
2. *List some factors which would make successful management of common resources achievable. You might want to think about the number of people, the stability of the population and the role of traditions. What others can you identify?*

1 'Commons sense', *The Economist,* 31 July 2008.
2 Ibid.
3 Australian Indigenous cultural heritage, www.australia.gov.au/about-australia/australian-story/austn-indigenous-cultural-heritage
4 'Commons sense', *The Economist,* 31 July 2008.

circumstances the good may have to be provided by the government or by the government subsidising private firms.

Note that not all goods and services produced by the public sector come into the category of public goods and services. Thus education and health are publicly provided, but they *can* be, and indeed are, privately provided as well.

> 1. *Give some other examples of public goods. Does the provider of these goods (the government or local authority) charge for their use? If so, is the method of charging based on the amount of the good that people use? Is it a good method of charging? Could you suggest a better method?*
> 2. *Name some goods or services provided by the government or local authorities that are not public goods.*
> 3. *Are there ways in which we could overcome the free-rider problem? Start by thinking about the provision of a public good amongst a group of friends or neighbours.*

Market power

Lack of Pareto optimality

KI 22 p190

Whenever markets are imperfect, whether as pure monopoly or monopsony or as some form of imperfect competition, the market will fail to equate *MSB* and *MSC*. Pareto optimality will not be achieved.

This is illustrated in Figure 12.10, which shows revenue and cost curves for a monopolist. It assumes no externalities. The socially efficient (Pareto optimal) output is Q_2, where $MSB = MSC$. The monopolist, however, produces the lower output Q_1, where $MR = MC$.

> *Referring back to Figure 10.8 on page 287, and assuming that the MRP_L curve represents the marginal social benefit from the employment of a factor, and that the price of the factor represents its marginal social cost (i.e. assuming no externalities), show that a monopsony will employ less than the Pareto optimal amount of factors.*

Deadweight loss under monopoly

Once again the welfare loss can be illustrated by using the concepts of *consumer* and *producer surplus*. The two concepts are illustrated in Figure 12.11, which is similar to Figure 12.10. The diagram shows an industry that is initially under perfect competition and then becomes a monopoly (but faces the same revenue and cost curves).

Under *perfect competition* the industry will produce an output of Q_{pc} at a price of P_{pc}, where $MC (= S) = P (= AR)$: i.e. at point *a*. Consumer surplus is shown by areas 1 + 2 + 3, and producer surplus by areas 4 + 5. Total surplus (i.e. consumer plus producer surplus) is maximised at this output (see Figure 12.1 on page 349).

What happens when the industry is under *monopoly*? The firm will produce where $MC = MR$, at an output of Q_m and a price of P_m (at point *b* on the demand curve). Total revenue is $P_m \times Q_m$ (areas 2 + 4 + 6). Total cost is the area under the MC curve (area 6). Thus the producer surplus is areas 2 + 4. This is clearly a *larger* surplus than under perfect competition

(since area 2 is larger than area 5). The consumer surplus, however, will fall dramatically. With consumption at Q_m, total utility is given by areas 1 + 2 + 4 + 6, whereas consumer expenditure is given by areas 2 + 4 + 6. Consumer surplus, then, is simply area 1. (Note that area 2 has been transformed from consumer surplus to producer surplus.)

Total surplus under monopoly is therefore areas 1 + 2 + 4: a smaller surplus than under perfect competition. 'Monopolisation' of the industry has resulted in a loss of total surplus of areas 3 + 5. The producers' gain has been more than offset by the consumers' loss. This loss of surplus is known as the *deadweight welfare loss of monopoly*.

KI 30 p356

Definition

Deadweight welfare loss of monopoly The loss of consumer plus producer surplus in monopoly or other imperfect markets (when compared with perfect competition).

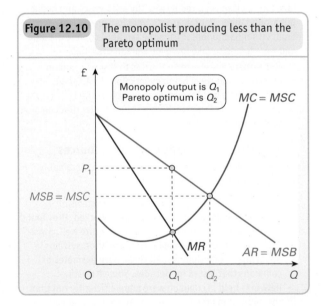

Figure 12.10 The monopolist producing less than the Pareto optimum

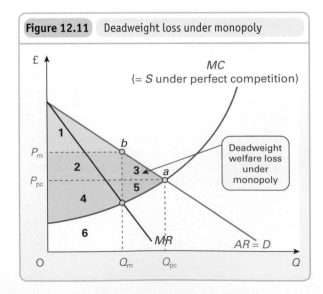

Figure 12.11 Deadweight loss under monopoly

*LOOKING AT THE MATHS

Total consumer surplus (*TCS*) equals total utility minus total expenditure (i.e. total revenue). Total producer surplus (*TPS*) equals total revenue minus total variable cost. Thus total surplus (*TS*) is given by:

$$TS = TCS + TPS = (TU - TR) + (TR - TVC) = TU - TVC$$

Assuming that the demand curve traces out the marginal utility curve (see pages 109–10), this allows us to derive the total utility function. To do this, you would need to use the technique of integration. Assuming that the total utility function is

$$TU = bQ - cQ^2$$

and that the total variable cost function is

$$TVC = jQ - kQ^2 + lQ^3$$

this will give a total surplus function of

$$TS = (bQ - cQ^2) - (jQ - kQ^2 + lQ^3) \tag{1}$$

To find the level of deadweight welfare loss, we would then subtract total surplus under perfect competition from that under monopoly. To do this, we would solve equation (1) first for Q_{pc} and then for Q_m and then subtract the second from the first. A worked example of this is given in Maths Case 12.1 on the student website.

Conclusions

The firm with market power uses fewer factors and produces less output than the Pareto optimum. It also causes deadweight welfare loss. To the extent, however, that the firm seeks aims *other* than profit maximisation and thus may produce more than the profit-maximising output, so these criticisms must be relaxed.

As was shown in Chapter 7, there are possible social *advantages* from powerful firms: advantages such as economies of scale and more research and development. These advantages may outweigh the lack of Pareto optimality. It can be argued that an ideal situation would be where firms are large enough to gain economies of scale and yet are somehow persuaded or compelled to produce where $P = MC$ (assuming no externalities).

With oligopoly and monopolistic competition, further wastes may occur because of possibly substantial resources involved in non-price competition. Advertising is the major example. It is difficult to predict just how much oligopolists will diverge from the Pareto optimum, since their pricing and output depends on their interpretation of the activities of their rivals.

 Why will Pareto optimality not be achieved in markets where there are substantial economies of scale in production?

Other market failures

Imperfect information

Perfect competition assumes that consumers, firms and factor suppliers have perfect knowledge of costs and benefits. In the real world, there is often a great deal of ignorance and uncertainty. Thus people are unable to equate marginal benefit with marginal cost.

KI 15
p129

Consumers purchase many goods infrequently. Cars, washing machines and other consumer durables fall into this category, as do houses. Consumers may not be aware of the quality of such goods until they have purchased them, by which time it is too late. Advertising may contribute to people's ignorance by misleading them as to the benefits of a good.

Firms are often ignorant of market opportunities, prices, costs, the productivity of factors (especially white-collar workers), the activity of rivals, etc.

Many economic decisions are based on expected future conditions. Since the future can never be known for certain, many decisions may turn out to be wrong.

TC 9
p129

In some cases, it may be possible to obtain the information through the market. There may be an agency that will sell you the information or a newspaper or magazine that contains the information. In this case, you will have to decide whether the cost to you of buying the information is worth the benefit it will provide you. A problem here is that you may not have sufficient information to judge how reliable the information is that you are buying!

 1. *Assume that you wanted the following information. In which cases might you (i) buy perfect information, (ii) buy imperfect information, (iii) be able to obtain information without paying for it, (iv) not be able to obtain information?*
   (a) Which washing machine is the most reliable?
   (b) Which of two vacant jobs is more satisfying?
   (c) Which builder will repair my roof most cheaply?
   (d) Which builder is the best value for money?
   (e) How big a mortgage would it be wise for me to take out?
   (f) Should I take a degree or get a full-time job?
   (g) What brand of washing powder washes whiter?
   (h) Will a house need any work done on it over the next few years?
2. *Make a list of pieces of information that a firm might want to know, and consider whether it could buy the information and how reliable that information might be.*
3. *What has been the impact of the Internet on the provision of information?*

Asymmetric information. One form of imperfect information occurs when different sides in an economic relationship have different amounts of information. This, as we saw on page 266, is known as 'asymmetric information' and is at the heart of the principal–agent problem.

KI 25
p267

Take the case of a firm (the principal) using the services of a bank (the agent) to finance its investments. The bank is likely to have a much better knowledge of its range of products and of the current state of financial markets and may mis-sell products to the firm in order to earn a larger profit for the bank. For example, it could provide loans at fixed rates of interest, knowing that rates were likely to fall. The firm would end up being locked into paying a higher rate of interest than if it had taken out a variable rate loan and the bank would consequently make more profit. This practice came to light in 2012, with banks accused of mis-selling such products to some 28 000 small and medium-sized enterprises (SMEs).

Immobility of factors and time lags in response

Even under conditions of perfect competition, factors may be very slow to respond to changes in demand or supply. Labour, for example, may be highly immobile both occupationally and geographically. This can lead to large price changes and hence to large supernormal profits and high wages for those in the sectors of rising demand or falling costs. The long run may be a very long time coming!

> **KEY IDEA 33**
>
> **The problem of time lags.** Many economic actions can take a long time to take effect. This can cause problems of instability and an inability of the economy to achieve social efficiency.

In the meantime, there will be further changes in the conditions of demand and supply. Thus the economy is in a constant state of disequilibrium and the long run never comes. As firms and consumers respond to market signals and move towards equilibrium, so the equilibrium position moves and the social optimum is never achieved.

Whenever monopoly/monopsony power exists, the problem is made worse if firms or unions put up barriers to the entry of new firms or factors of production.

Protecting people's interests

Dependants.   People do not always make their own economic decisions. They are often dependent on decisions made by others. Parents make decisions on behalf of their children; partners on each other's behalf; younger adults on behalf of old people; managers on behalf of shareholders; etc. This, again, is an example of the principal–agent issue.

KI 25
p267

A free market will respond to these decisions, however good or bad they may be, and whether or not they are in the interests of the dependant. Thus the government may feel it necessary to protect dependants.

Give examples of how the government intervenes to protect the interests of dependants from bad economic decisions taken on their behalf.

Poor economic decision making by individuals on their own behalf.   The government may feel that people need protecting from poor economic decisions that they make on their *own* behalf. As we discussed in Chapter 5, this may be a particular problem when the benefits from consuming a good are immediate while the cost happens at some point in the future. People may place too much weight on the immediate benefits and too little weight on the long-run costs of their decisions. Products where this might be an issue include tobacco, alcohol and fast/unhealthy food.

On the other hand, the government may feel that people consume too little of things that are good for them: things such as education, preventative health care and sports facilities. Such goods are known as ***merit goods***. The government could either provide them free or subsidise their production; it could also make their consumption compulsory (e.g. as with fluoride added to water in many areas).

How do merit goods differ from public goods?

Other objectives

As we saw in Chapter 11, one of the major criticisms of the free market is the problem of *inequality*. The Pareto criterion gives no guidance, however, as to the most desirable distribution of income. A redistribution of income will benefit some and make others worse off. Thus Pareto optimality can be achieved for *any* distribution of income. Pareto optimality merely represents the efficient allocation of resources for any *given* distribution of income.

KI 4
p14

In addition to social efficiency and greater equality, we can identify other social goals: goals such as moral behaviour (however defined), enlightenment, social consciousness, co-operation, the development of culture, fulfilment, freedom from exploitation, and freedom to own, purchase and inherit property. The unfettered free market may not be very successful in achieving social efficiency. It may be even less successful in achieving many other social goals.

Finally, the free market is unlikely to achieve simultaneously the *macroeconomic objectives* of rapid economic growth, full employment, stable prices and a balance of international payments. These problems, and methods of government intervention that may be used to deal with them, are examined in later chapters.

Conclusions

It is not the role of economists to make judgements as to the relative importance of social goals. Economics can only consider the means to achieving stated goals. First, therefore,

> **Definition**
>
> **Merit goods** Goods that the government feels people will underconsume and which therefore ought to be subsidised or provided free.

the goals have to be clearly stated by the policy makers. Second, they have to be quantifiable so that the effectiveness of different policies can be compared. Certain goals, such as growth in national income, changes in the distribution of income and greater efficiency, are relatively easy to quantify. Others, such as enlightenment, are virtually impossible to quantify. For this reason, economics tends to concentrate on the means to achieving a relatively narrow range of goals. The danger is that, by concentrating on a limited number of goals, economists may well influence policy makers into doing the same, and thus into neglecting other social goals.

KI 6
p29

Different objectives are likely to conflict. For example, economic growth may conflict with greater equality. In the case of such 'trade-offs', all the economist can do is to demonstrate the effects of a given policy, and leave the policy makers to decide whether the benefits in terms of one goal outweigh the costs in terms of another goal.

TC 1
p11

 How do the economic policies of the major political parties differ? How far can an economist go in assessing these policies?

Section summary

1. Real-world markets will fail to achieve Pareto optimality. What is more, there are objectives other than social efficiency, and real-world markets may fail to achieve these too.

2. Externalities are costs and benefits of consumption experienced by people other than those directly involved in the transaction. Whenever there are external costs, the market will (other things being equal) lead to a level of production and consumption *above* the socially efficient level. Whenever there are external benefits, the market will (other things being equal) lead to a level of production and consumption *below* the socially efficient level.

3. Public goods have the characteristics of being non-rival and non-excludable. Once a given quantity of a pure public good is produced, everyone can obtain the same level of benefit it provides. They will tend to be underprovided by the market. Without government intervention it would not be possible to prevent people having a 'free ride' and thereby escaping any contributions to their cost of production.

4. Common resources are likely to be overused – a problem known as the 'tragedy of the commons'. This is because people are unlikely to take into account the effect of their use of such resources on other people.

5. Monopoly power will (other things being equal) lead to a level of output below the socially efficient level. It will

lead to a deadweight welfare loss: a loss of consumer plus producer surplus.

6. Imperfect information may prevent people from consuming or producing at the levels they would otherwise choose. There may be an asymmetry of information between buyers and sellers, which can result in a principal–agent problem. Information, however, may sometimes be provided (at a price) by the market.

7. Markets may respond sluggishly to changes in demand and supply. The time lags in adjustment can lead to a permanent state of disequilibrium and to problems of instability.

8. In a free market there may be inadequate provision for dependants and an inadequate output of merit goods; there are likely to be macroeconomic problems and problems of inequality and poverty; finally, there may be a whole series of social, moral, attitudinal and aesthetic problems arising from a market system.

9. These being normative questions, the economist cannot make ultimate pronouncements on the rights and wrongs of the market. The economist can, however, point out the consequences of the market and of various government policies, and also the trade-offs that exist between different objectives.

12.3 FORMS OF GOVERNMENT INTERVENTION

Faced with all the problems of the free market, what is a government to do?

There are several policy instruments that a government can use. At one extreme, it can totally replace the market by providing goods and services itself. At the other extreme, it can merely seek to persuade producers, consumers or workers to act differently. Between the two extremes, the government has a number of instruments that it can use to change the way markets operate. These include taxes, subsidies, laws and regulatory bodies.

Before looking at different forms of government intervention and their relative merits, it is first necessary to look at a general problem concerned with all forms of intervention. This is known as the ***problem of the second best***.

Definition

Problem of the second best The difficulty of working out the best way of correcting a specific market distortion if distortions in other parts of the market continue to exist.

BOX 12.3　SHOULD HEALTH-CARE PROVISION BE LEFT TO THE MARKET?

A case of multiple market failures

TC 3
p26

In the UK, the National Health Service provides free hospital treatment, a free general practitioner service, and free prescriptions for certain categories of people. Their marginal cost to the patient is thus zero. Of course, these services use resources and they thus have to be paid for out of taxes.

But why are these services not sold directly to the patient, thereby saving the taxpayer money? There are, in fact, a number of reasons why the market would fail to provide the optimum amount of health care.

The issue of equity

KI 4
p14

This is a problem connected with the distribution of income. Because income is unequally distributed, some people will be able to afford better treatment than others, and the poorest people may not be able to afford treatment at all. On grounds of equity, therefore, it is argued that health care should be provided free – at least for those on low incomes.

The concept of equity that is usually applied to health care is that individuals should be able to access treatment according to their medical need rather than according to their ability to pay.

　1.　Does this argument also apply to food and housing?

Difficulty of predicting future medical needs

If you were suddenly taken ill and required a major operation, it could be very expensive if you had to pay. On the other hand, you may go through life requiring very little if any medical treatment. In other words, there is great uncertainty about your future medical needs. As a result it would be very difficult to plan your finances and budget for possible future medical expenses if you had to pay for treatment.

Medical insurance could provide a solution to this problem if the probability of requiring different treatments (a) can be

estimated and (b) is independent across different individuals. There would also have to be no serious problems of adverse selection or moral hazard. Even if an effective market for medical insurance could be established there would still remain a problem of equity. Would the chronically sick or very old be able to obtain cover and, if so, would they be able to afford the premiums? This issue of 'gaps' in an insurance-based system means that some form of intervention on grounds of equity may be needed, even if most provision is private.

KI 16
p135

KI 17
p135

　2.　Give some examples of adverse selection and moral hazard that might occur with medical insurance (see section 5.1, pages 133–6).

Externalities

Health care generates a number of benefits *external* to the patient. If you are cured of an infectious disease, for example, it is not just you who benefits but also others, since you will not infect them. In addition, if you have a job you will be able to get back to work, thus reducing the disruption there. These external benefits of health care could be quite large.

KI 31
p356

If sick people have to pay the cost of their treatment, they may decide not to be treated – especially if they are poor. They will consider the costs and benefits they might experience, but will probably not take into account the effect that their illness has on other people. The market, by equating *private* benefits and costs, would produce too little health care.

Information problems and patient ignorance

Markets only function well to allocate resources efficiently if the consumer has the knowledge to make informed decisions. For many products we purchase, there is reasonably good information and so we can judge which products/services we will like the most.

In an ideal free market, where there are no market failures of any sort (the 'first-best' world), there would be no need for government intervention at all. If in this world there did then arise just one failure, in theory its correction would be simple. Say a monopoly arose, or some externality (e.g. pollution) was produced by a particular firm, with the result that the marginal social cost was no longer equal to the marginal social benefit. In theory, the government should simply intervene to restore production to the point where $MSC = MSB$. This is known as the **first-best solution**.

Of course, the real world is not like this. It is full of imperfections. What this means is that, if one imperfection is 'corrected' (i.e. by making $MSB = MSC$), it might aggravate problems elsewhere. For example, if a local authority introduces residents-only parking in an inner city area to prevent

commuters parking there, they may simply park just outside the area, thus imposing additional costs on people living there.

Give some examples of how correcting problems in one part of the economy will create problems elsewhere.

Definition

First-best solution　The solution of correcting a specific market distortion by ensuring that the whole economy operates under conditions of social efficiency (Pareto optimality).

In the case of health care the situation is different. Much of the information is complex and a patient might require specialist knowledge to understand it. The one-off nature of many treatments also means that patients are unable to learn from repeat purchases.

In some circumstances the demand for health care might be urgent. In these cases people do not have the time to shop around and may be unable to make rational decisions because of heightened emotional distress. For these reasons a patient has to rely on the professional advice of others. They have to

enter an agency relationship with a doctor or health-care provider.

For example, if you have a pain in your chest, it may be simple muscular strain, or it may be a symptom of heart disease. You rely on the doctor (the *supplier* of the treatment) to give you the information: to diagnose your condition. The key issue is whether the incentives of the doctor and the patient are aligned.

If health care was provided through the market, unscrupulous doctors might advise more expensive treatment than is necessary; they might even have an agreement with certain drugs companies that they will try to persuade you to buy an expensive branded product rather than an identical cheaper version. This problem will also exist in an insurance-based system, where the doctor may be even more inclined to oversupply if the patient has sufficient cover.

If people had to pay, those suffering from the early stages of a serious disease might not consult their doctor until the symptoms become very acute, by which time it might be too late to treat the disease, or very expensive to do so. With a health service that is free at the point of use, however, a person is more likely to receive an earlier diagnosis of serious conditions.

Oligopoly

If doctors and hospitals operated in the free market as profit maximisers, it is unlikely that competition would drive down their prices. Instead they might collude to fix standard prices for treatment, so as to protect their incomes. Even if doctors did compete openly, it is unlikely that consumers would have enough information to enable them to 'shop around' for the best value.

We have to be careful: to argue that the market system will fail to provide an optimal allocation of health-care resources does not in itself prove that *free provision* will result in optimal provision. For example, with no charge for GP appointments it is likely that some patients will consult their doctors over trivial complaints. The result will be consumption beyond the socially efficient point.

In the USA there is much more reliance on *private medical insurance*. Alternatively, the government may simply *subsidise* health care, so as to make it cheaper rather than free. This is the case with prescriptions and dental treatment in the UK, where many people only have to pay part of the cost of treatment. Also, the government can *regulate* the behaviour of the providers of health care, to prevent exploitation of the patient. Thus only people with certain qualifications are allowed to operate as doctors, nurses, pharmacists, etc.

3. *If health care is provided free at the point of consumption, the demand is likely to be high. How is this high demand likely to be dealt with? Is this a good way of dealing with the issue?*

4. *Go through each of the market failings identified in this box. In each case, consider what alternative policies are open to a government to tackle them. What are the advantages and disadvantages of these alternatives?*

5. *Does the provision of free health care mean that it needs to be publicly produced? What would be the advantages, and disadvantages, of private provision?*

As the first-best solution of a perfectly efficient, distortion-free world is obviously not possible, the **second-best solution** needs to be adopted. Essentially this involves seeking the best compromises. This means attempting to minimise the *overall* distortionary effects of the policy measure. Some second-best *rules* can be applied in certain cases.

Definition

Second-best solution The solution to a specific market distortion that recognises distortions elsewhere and seeks to minimise the overall distortionary effects to the economy of tackling this specific distortion.

We will examine these in the following sections as we look at specific policy measures.

Taxes and subsidies

A policy instrument particularly favoured by many economists is that of taxes and subsidies. They can be used for two main microeconomic purposes: (a) to promote greater social efficiency by altering the composition of production and consumption: and (b) to redistribute incomes. We examined their use for the second purpose in Chapter 11. Here we examine their use to achieve greater social efficiency.

When there are imperfections in the market (such as externalities or monopoly power), Pareto optimality will not be achieved. Taxes and subsidies can be used to correct these imperfections. Essentially the approach is to tax those goods or activities where the market produces too much, and subsidise those where the market produces too little.

Taxes and subsidies to correct externalities

The first-best solution. The *first-best solution* when there is only one market imperfection is simple: the government should impose a tax equal to the marginal external cost (or grant a subsidy equal to the marginal external benefit). This is known as a *Pigouvian tax* (or *Pigouvian subsidy*).

Previously, we examined the impact of external costs of pollution created by the chemical industry as a whole. We will now focus on one firm in that industry, which otherwise is perfectly competitive. Assume that this particular chemical company emits smoke from a chimney and thus pollutes the atmosphere. This creates external costs for the people who breathe in the smoke. The marginal social cost of producing the chemicals thus exceeds the marginal private cost to the firm: $MSC > MPC$. This is illustrated in Figure 12.12.

In this example, it is assumed the external pollution cost begins with the first unit of production but remains constant. Hence the MEC_P is drawn as a horizontal line. The vertical distance between the MPC and MSC curves is equal to the MEC_P. The firm produces Q_1 where $P = MPC$ (its

profit-maximising output), but in doing so takes no account of the external pollution costs it imposes on society.

If the government now imposes a tax on production equal to the marginal pollution cost, it will effectively 'internalise' the externality. The firm will have to pay an amount equal to the external cost it creates. It will therefore now maximise profits at Q_2, which is the socially optimal output where $MSB = MSC$.

By analogy, if a firm produced an external benefit, then in the first-best world it ought to be given a subsidy equal to that marginal external benefit.

Note that a tax or subsidy ought to be directed as closely as possible to the source of the externality. For example, if a firm trains labour, and that creates a benefit to society, then ideally it ought to be given a subsidy for each person trained, rather than a general output subsidy. After all, an output subsidy not only encourages the firm to train more people (the desired effect), but also encourages it to use more capital and raw materials (an undesired side effect). This is a general maxim of welfare economics: *a distortion should be corrected at source if side-effect problems are to be avoided.*

Second-best tax and subsidy policies. In reality, the government must tackle imperfections in a world that has many other imperfections. Figure 12.13 shows a firm that both produces an external cost ($MSC > MPC$) and *also* has monopoly power. It will maximise profits at Q_1 where $MPC = MR$ (point *x*).

The socially efficient level of output in this case is Q_2, where MSB equals MSC. Note that in this case, the welfare loss from a monopoly is actually less than if the market were perfectly competitive: i.e. the extent of overproduction is lower. The perfectly competitive equilibrium would be at point *c*, with price P_{pc} and output Q_{pc}.

KI 31
p356

KI 30
p356

KI 28
p348

> ## Definition
>
> **Pigouvian tax (or subsidy)** A tax (or subsidy) designed to 'internalise' an externality. The marginal rate of a Pigouvian tax (or subsidy) should be equal to the marginal external cost (or benefit).

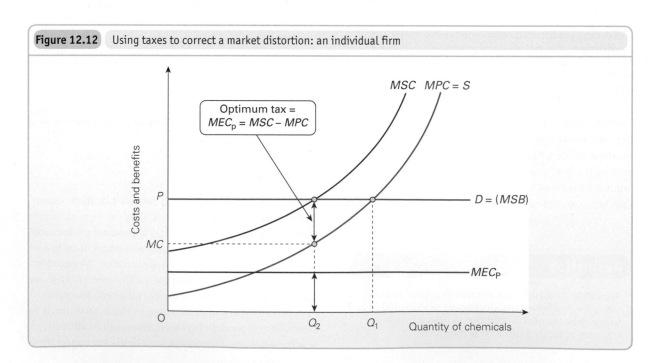

Figure 12.12 Using taxes to correct a market distortion: an individual firm

| BOX 12.4 | DEADWEIGHT LOSS FROM TAXES ON GOODS AND SERVICES | EXPLORING ECONOMICS |

The excess burden of taxes

Taxation can be used to correct market failures, but taxes can have adverse effects themselves. One such effect is the deadweight loss that results when taxes are imposed on goods and services (see page 336).

The diagram shows the demand and supply of a particular good. Equilibrium is initially at a price of P_1 and a level of sales of Q_1 (i.e. where $D = S$). Now an excise tax is imposed on the good. The supply curve shifts upwards by the amount of the tax, to S + tax. Equilibrium price rises to P_2 and equilibrium quantity falls to Q_2. Producers receive an after-tax price of P_2 − tax.

Consumer surplus falls from areas $1 + 2 + 3$, to area 1 (the green area). Producer surplus falls from areas $4 + 5 + 6$ to area 6 (the blue area). Does this mean, therefore, that total surplus falls by areas $2 + 3 + 4 + 5$? The answer is no, because there is a gain to the government from the tax revenue (and hence a gain to the population from the resulting government expenditure). The revenue from the tax is known as the **government surplus**. It is given by areas $2 + 4$ (the pink area).

But even after including government surplus, there is still a fall in total surplus of areas $3 + 5$. This is the deadweight loss of the tax. It is sometimes known as the **excess burden**.

Does this loss of total surplus from taxation imply that taxes on goods are always a 'bad thing'? The answer is no. This conclusion would follow only in a 'first-best' world where there were no market failures: where competition was perfect, where there were no externalities and where income distribution was optimum. In such a world, the loss of surplus from imposing a tax on a good would represent a reduction in welfare.

In the real world of imperfect markets and inequality, taxes can do more good than harm. As we have shown in this section, they can help to correct for externalities; and as we showed in the previous chapter, they can be used as a means of redistributing incomes. Nevertheless, the excess burden of taxes is something that ideally ought to be considered when weighing up the desirability of imposing taxes on goods and services, or of increasing their rate.

1. *How far can an economist contribute to this normative debate over the desirability of an excise tax?*
2. *What is the excess burden of a lump-sum tax? (For a clue, see Figure 12.14.)*

Deadweight loss from an indirect tax

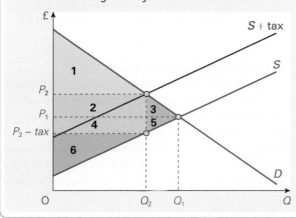

Definitions

Government surplus (from a tax on a good) The total tax revenue earned by the government from sales of a good.

Excess burden (of a tax on a good) The amount by which the loss in consumer plus producer surplus exceeds the government surplus.

To provide an incentive for the monopolist to produce Q_2, a tax of $a − b$ must be imposed (since at point a, $MR = MPC$ + tax). This tax is *less* than the full amount of the externality because of the monopoly power. Were the monopolist to be charged a tax *equal* to the externality (so that its MPC + tax curve was equal to the MSC curve), it would maximise profits at point y, at a price of P_3 and an output of Q_3. This would not be socially efficient, since MSB would now be *above MSC*.

Taxes to correct for monopoly

So far we have considered the use of taxes to correct for externalities. Taxes can also be used to regulate the behaviour of monopolies and oligopolies.

If the government wishes to tackle the problem of excessive monopoly profits, it can impose a *lump-sum* tax on the

monopolist. An example of such a tax was the 'windfall tax', imposed by the UK government in 1997. This was on the profits of various privatised utilities. In 2005, another tax was imposed on the 'excess' profits of oil companies operating in the North Sea. There were also numerous calls in 2008 to impose a windfall tax on energy companies, but this was never implemented. The use of a lump-sum tax is illustrated in Figure 12.14.

Being of a fixed amount, a lump-sum tax is a fixed cost to the firm. It does not affect the firm's marginal cost. It shifts the AC curve upwards.

Profits continue to be maximised where $MC = MR$, at an output of Q_1 and a price of P_1. But profits are reduced from areas $1 + 2$ to area 1 alone. Area 2 now represents the amount of tax paid to the government. If the lump-sum tax were large enough to make the AC + lump-sum tax curve

Figure 12.13   Using taxes to correct for externalities: firms with monopoly power

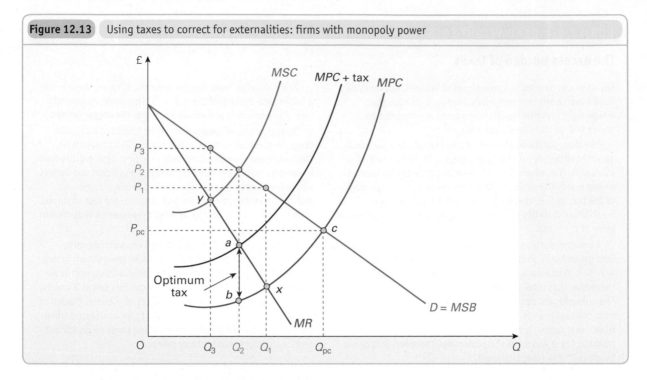

Figure 12.14   Using a lump-sum tax to reduce monopoly profits

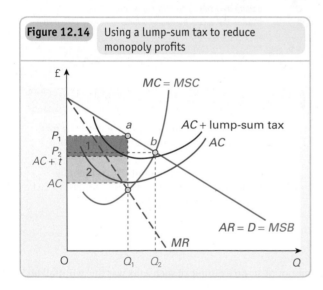

 What could we say about the necessary subsidy if the MR curve crossed the horizontal axis to the left of point b?

Advantages of taxes and subsidies

Many economists favour the tax/subsidy solution to market imperfections (especially the problem of externalities) because it still allows the market to operate. It forces firms to take on board the full social costs and benefits of their actions; as we have seen, this is often described as *internalising the externality*. Furthermore, once the policy is in place, taxes and subsidies can be adjusted according to the magnitude of the problem.

Moreover, if firms are taxed for polluting, they are encouraged to find cleaner ways of producing. The tax acts as an incentive over the longer run to reduce pollution. Likewise, by subsidising *good* practices, firms are given the incentive to adopt more good practices.

The most suitable situation for imposing a pollution tax is when there is a clearly measurable emission, like a particular chemical waste. The government can then impose a tax per litre or per tonne of that waste.

Disadvantages of taxes and subsidies

Infeasibility of using different tax and subsidy rates.   Each firm produces different levels and types of externality and operates under different degrees of imperfect competition. It would be administratively very difficult and expensive to charge every offending firm its own particular tax rate (or grant every relevant firm its own particular rate of subsidy). Even in the case of pollution where it is possible to measure

cross the demand curve at point *a*, *all* the supernormal profits would be taken as tax.

If the government also wants to increase the monopolist's output to the socially efficient level of Q_2, and wants it to charge a price of P_2, it could do this with a careful combination of a per-unit subsidy (which will shift both the *AC* and the *MC* curves downwards) and a lump-sum tax. The required level of subsidy will be that which shifts the *MC* curve downwards to the point where it intersects *MR* at output Q_2. Then a lump-sum tax would be imposed that would be big enough to shift the *AC* curve back up again so that it crosses the demand curve at point *b*.

a firm's emissions, there would still have to be a different tax rate for each pollutant and even for each environment, depending on its ability to absorb the pollutant.

Lack of knowledge. Even if a government did decide to charge a tax equal to each offending firm's marginal external costs, it would still have the problem of measuring those costs and apportioning blame. The damage to lakes and forests from acid rain has been a major concern since the beginning of the 1980s. But just how serious is that damage? What is its current monetary cost? How long lasting is the damage? Just what and who are to blame? These questions cannot be answered precisely. It is thus impossible to fix the 'correct' pollution tax on, say, a particular coal-fired power station.

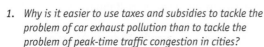

1. *Why is it easier to use taxes and subsidies to tackle the problem of car exhaust pollution than to tackle the problem of peak-time traffic congestion in cities?*
2. *CFCs in fridges were known to cause environmental damage and their use has been banned in most countries. Why has this approach been adopted rather than the tax solution?*

Changes in property rights

One cause of market failure is the limited nature of property rights. If someone dumps a load of rubble in your garden, you can insist that it is removed. If, however, someone dumps a load of rubble in their *own* garden, which is next door to yours, what can you do? You can still see it from your window. It is still an eyesore. But you have no property rights over the next-door garden.

Property rights define who owns property, to what uses it can be put, the rights other people have over it and how it may be transferred. By *extending* these rights, individuals may be able to prevent other people from imposing costs on them or charge them for doing so.

The socially efficient level of charge would be one that was equal to the marginal external cost (and would have the same effect as the government charging a tax on the firm of that amount: see Figure 12.12). The ***Coase theorem***[1] states that when there are well-defined property rights and there are no bargaining or negotiation costs, then the socially efficient charge *will* be levied. But why?

> ### Definition
>
> **Coase theorem** When there are well-defined property rights and zero bargaining costs, then negotiations between the party creating the externality and the party affected by the externality can bring about the socially efficient market quantity.

Let us take the case of river pollution by a chemical works that imposes a cost on people fishing in the river. If property rights to the river were now given to the fishing community, they could impose a charge on the chemical works per unit of output. If they charged *less* than the marginal external cost, they would suffer more from the last unit (in terms of lost fish) than they were being compensated. If they charged *more,* and thereby caused the firm to cut back its output below the socially efficient level, they would be sacrificing receiving charges that would be greater than the marginal suffering. It will be in the sufferers' best interests, therefore, to charge an amount *equal* to the marginal externality.

Alternatively, the property rights to the river could be awarded to the chemical works. In this situation the fishing community could offer payments to the firm on condition that it did not pollute the river.

One interesting result is that the efficient solution to the problem caused by the externality does not depend on which party is assigned the property rights: i.e. the fishing community or the chemical works. All that matters is that the property rights are fully assigned to either one or the other and that there are no bargaining costs.

If the sufferers had no property rights, show how it would still be in their interests to 'bribe' the firm to produce the socially efficient level of output.

In most instances, however, this type of solution is totally impractical. It is impractical when *many* people are *slightly* inconvenienced, especially if there are many culprits imposing the costs. For example, if I were disturbed by noisy lorries passing by my house, it would not be practical to negotiate with every haulage company involved. What if I wanted to ban the lorries from the street but my next-door neighbour wanted to charge them 10p per journey? Who gets their way?

The extension of private property rights becomes more practical where the parties involved are few in number, are easily identifiable and where the costs are clearly defined. Thus a noise abatement Act could be passed which allowed me to prevent my neighbours from playing noisy radios, having noisy parties or otherwise disturbing the peace in my home. The onus would be on me to report them. Or I could agree not to report them if they paid me adequate compensation.

But even in cases where only a few people are involved, there may still be the problem of litigation. I may have to incur the time and expense of taking people to court. Justice may not be free, and thus there may be concerns about equity. The rich can afford 'better' justice. They can employ top lawyers. Even if I have a right to sue a large company for dumping toxic waste near me, I may not have the legal muscle to win.

Finally, there is the broader question of equity. Although the socially efficient outcome does not depend on who has the property rights, the equity of the outcome will. Extending the rights of property owners may favour the rich, who tend to have more property, at the expense of the poor. Ramblers may get great pleasure from strolling across a great country estate, along public rights of way. If the owner's property rights were now extended to exclude the ramblers, would this be a social gain?

Of course, equity considerations can also be dealt with by altering property rights, but in a different way. *Public* property, like parks, open spaces, libraries and historic buildings, could be extended. Also, the property of the rich could be redistributed to the poor. Here it is less a question of the rights that ownership confers, and more a question of altering the ownership itself.

1. To what extent could property rights (either public or private) be successfully extended and invoked to curb the problem of industrial pollution (a) of the atmosphere; (b) of rivers; (c) by the dumping of toxic waste; (d) by the erection of ugly buildings; (e) by the creation of high levels of noise?

2. What protection do private property rights in the real world give to sufferers of noise (a) from neighbours; (b) from traffic; (c) from mobile phones on public transport?

Laws prohibiting or regulating undesirable structures or behaviour

Laws are frequently used to correct market imperfections. This section examines three of the most common cases.

Laws prohibiting or regulating behaviour that imposes external costs

Laws can be applied both to individuals and to firms. In the case of individuals, it is illegal to drive when drunk. Drunk driving imposes costs on others in the form of accidents and death. Other examples include the banning of (a) smoking in public places (b) using mobile phones while driving.

In the case of firms, various polluting activities could be banned or restricted; safety standards could be imposed in the place of work; building houses or factories could be prohibited in green-belt areas.

In the case of common resources, restrictions could be placed on their use. For example, in the case of fishing grounds, governments could limit the size of fleets, impose quotas on catches or specify the types of net to be used. In extreme cases, they could ban fishing altogether for a period of time to allow fish stocks to recover. In order to be able to enforce restrictions, many governments have extended their 'territorial waters' to 200 miles from their coast.

Advantages of legal restrictions

- They are simple and clear to understand and are often relatively easy to administer. Inspectors or the police can conduct spot checks to see that the law is being obeyed.
- When the danger is very great, it might be much safer to ban various practices altogether rather than to rely on

taxes or on individuals attempting to assert their property rights through the civil courts.

- When a decision needs to be taken quickly, it might be possible to invoke emergency action. For example, in a city it would be simpler to ban or restrict the use of private cars during a chemical smog emergency than to tax their use (see Case Study 13.5 on the student website).

Disadvantages of legal restrictions. The main problem is that legal restrictions tend to be a rather blunt weapon. If, for example, a firm were required to reduce the effluent of a toxic chemical to 20 tonnes per week, it would have no incentive to reduce it further. With a tax on the effluent, however, the more the firm reduced the effluent, the less tax it would pay. Thus with a system of taxes there is a *continuing* incentive to cut pollution.

Laws to prevent or regulate monopolies and oligopolies

Governments often introduce laws that prohibit various types of collusive activities, the misuse of market power by a dominant firm and mergers or takeovers that would result in a substantial lessening of competition. These will be examined in detail in Chapter 14.

How suitable are legal restrictions in the following cases? (a) Ensuring adequate vehicle safety; (b) reducing traffic congestion; (c) preventing the abuse of monopoly power; (d) ensuring that mergers are in the public interest; (e) ensuring that firms charge a price equal to marginal cost.

Laws to prevent firms from exploiting people's ignorance

Given that consumers have imperfect information, consumer protection laws can make it illegal for firms to sell shoddy or dangerous goods, or to make false or misleading claims about their products.

The problem is that the firms most likely to exploit the consumer are often the ones that are most elusive when it comes to prosecuting them.

Regulatory bodies

A more subtle approach than banning or restricting various activities involves the use of regulatory bodies.

Having identified possible cases where action might be required (e.g. potential cases of pollution or the abuse of monopoly power), the regulatory body would probably conduct an investigation and then prepare a report containing its findings and recommendations. It might also have the power to enforce its decisions, or this might be up to some higher authority.

An example of such a body is the UK's Competition and Markets Authority, the work of which is examined in section 14.1. Other examples are the bodies set up to regulate the privatised utilities: e.g. Ofwat (the Office of Water Services). These are examined in section 14.2.

The advantage of this approach is that a case by-case method can be used and, as a result, the most appropriate solution adopted. However, investigations may be expensive and time-consuming, only a few cases may be examined and offending firms may make various promises of good behaviour which, if not followed up by the regulatory body, may not in fact be carried out.

 What other forms of intervention are likely to be necessary to back up the work of regulatory bodies?

Price controls

Price controls could be used to prevent a monopoly or oligopoly from charging excessive prices. Currently, sections of various privatised industries, such as water and rail industries, are restricted in their ability to raise their prices (see section 14.2).

Price controls could also be used with the objective of redistributing incomes. Prices could be fixed either above or below equilibrium. Thus (high) minimum farm prices can be used to protect the incomes of farmers, and minimum wage legislation can help those on low incomes. On the consumption side, (low) maximum rents might be put in place with the intention of helping those on low incomes afford housing, and price ceilings on food or other essentials during a war or other emergency can ensure everyone can afford such items. However, as was argued in section 3.1, the problem with price controls is that they cause shortages (in the case of low prices) or surpluses (high prices).

Provision of information

When imperfect information is a reason for market failure, the direct provision of information by the government or one of its agencies may help to correct that failure. An example is the information on jobs provided by job centres to those looking for work. This will speed up the 'matching process' between the unemployed and employers. It helps the labour market to work better and increases the elasticity of supply of labour.

Another example is the provision of consumer information – for example, on the effects of smoking, or of the benefits of eating vegetables. Another is the provision of government statistics on prices, costs, employment, sales trends, etc. This enables firms to plan with greater certainty.

In what way is the provision of information a public good? Do all the examples above come into the category of public goods? Give some other examples of information that is a public good. (Clue: refer back to the characteristics of public goods in section 12.2 and do not confuse a public good with something merely provided by the government which could also be provided by the private sector.)

The direct provision of goods and services

In the case of public goods and services, such as streets, pavements, seaside illumination and national defence, the market may completely fail to provide the socially efficient amount because of free-riding. Government may have to finance the optimal provision of the public good by requiring compulsory payments from members of society. One way of obtaining the compulsory payments is through the central/local tax system.

Before collecting the money the government needs to try to work out the socially efficient amount of the public good to finance. How could the real-world equivalent of point *f* in Figure 12.9 be identified in practice? The solution is to identify all the costs and benefits to society and to weight them appropriately. This is where cost–benefit analysis comes in – the subject of section 12.4.

Once the compulsory payments have been collected, the central government, local government or some other government agency could then manage the production of the goods or services directly. Alternatively, they could pay private firms to do so.

The government could also provide goods and services directly which are *not* public goods. Examples include health and education. There are four reasons why such things are provided free or well below cost.

Social justice. Society may feel that these things should not be provided according to ability to pay. Rather, as *merit goods,* they should be provided according to need.

Large positive externalities. People other than the consumer may benefit substantially. If a person decides to get treatment for an infectious disease, other people benefit by not being infected. A free health service thus helps to combat the spread of disease.

Dependants. If education were not free, and if the quality of education depended on the amount spent, and if parents could choose how much or how little to buy, then the quality of children's education would depend not just on their parents' income, but also on how much they cared. A government may choose to provide such things free in order to protect children from 'bad' or 'foolish' parents. A similar argument is used for providing free prescriptions and dental treatment for all children.

Imperfect information. Consumers may not realise how much they will benefit. If they had to pay, they might choose (unwisely) to go without. Providing health care free may persuade people to consult their doctors before a complaint becomes serious.

Public ownership

This is different from direct provision, in that the goods and services produced by publicly owned (nationalised) industries are sold in the market. The costs and benefits of public ownership are examined in detail in section 14.2.

Section summary

1. If there were a distortion in just one part of the economy, the 'first-best' solution would be possible. This would be to correct that one distortion. In the real world, where there are many distortions, the first-best solution will not be possible. The second-best solution will be to seek the best compromise that minimises the *relative* distortions between the industry in question and other parts of the economy.

2. Taxes and subsidies are one means of correcting market distortions. In the first-best world, externalities can be corrected by imposing tax rates equal to the size of marginal external costs, and granting rates of subsidy equal to marginal external benefits. In the second-best world, taxes and subsidies can be used to correct externalities that create *relative* distortions between this industry and others, or externalities that exist along with other distortions within this industry.

3. Taxes and subsidies can also be used to affect monopoly price, output and profit. Subsidies can be used to persuade a monopolist to increase output to the competitive level. Lump-sum taxes can be used to reduce monopoly profits without affecting price or output.

4. Taxes and subsidies have the advantages of 'internalising' externalities and of providing incentives to reduce external costs. On the other hand, they may be impractical to use when different rates are required for each case, or when it is impossible to know the full effects of the activities that the taxes or subsidies are being used to correct.

5. An extension of property rights may allow individuals to prevent others from imposing costs on them. This is not practical, however, when many people are affected to a small degree, or where several people are affected but differ in their attitudes towards what they want doing about the 'problem'.

6. Laws can be used to tackle various market failures. Legal controls are often simpler and easier to operate than taxes, and are safer when the danger is potentially great. However, they tend to be rather a blunt weapon.

7. Regulatory bodies can be set up to monitor and control activities that are against the public interest (e.g. anti-competitive behaviour of oligopolists).

8. The government may provide information in cases where the private sector fails to provide an adequate level. It may also provide goods and services directly. These could be either public goods or other goods where the government feels that provision by the market is inadequate.

---

*12.4 COST–BENEFIT ANALYSIS

Cost–benefit analysis (CBA) is a technique used to help governments decide whether to go ahead with various projects such as a new motorway, a bypass, an underground line, a hospital, a health-care programme, a dam, and so on. The analysis seeks to establish whether the benefits to society from the project outweigh the costs, in which case the project should go ahead; or whether the costs outweigh the benefits, in which case it should not.

CBAs are usually commissioned either by a government department or by a local authority. Unlike the techniques of project evaluation used by private firms, which take into account only *private monetary* costs and benefits, CBA takes into account *externalities* and private *non-monetary* costs and benefits as well. Thus a cost–benefit study of a proposed new road might attempt to assess the external costs of noise to local residents and destruction of wildlife as well as the direct costs and benefits to motorists.

The procedure

The procedure at first sight seems fairly straightforward.

- All costs and benefits are identified. These include all private monetary and non-monetary costs and benefits and all externalities.

- A monetary value is assigned to each cost and benefit. This is essential if costs and benefits are to be added up: a common unit of measurement must be used. As might be expected, assigning monetary values to externalities like noise, pollution and the quality of life is fraught with difficulties and may involve subjective decisions.

- Account is taken of the likelihood of a cost or benefit occurring. The simplest way of doing this is to multiply the monetary value of a cost or benefit by the probability of its occurrence. This is called the *expected value*. So if there were a 60 per cent chance of a cost of £100 occurring, it would be valued at £60.

- Account is taken of the timing of the costs and benefits. Thus £100 of benefits received today would be regarded as more desirable than having to wait, say, 10 years to

Definitions

Cost–benefit analysis The identification, measurement and weighing up of the costs and benefits of a project in order to decide whether or not it should go ahead.

Expected value The value of a possible outcome multiplied by the probability of its occurrence.

receive the £100. Likewise it is a greater sacrifice to pay £100 today than to have to pay it within 10 years. Thus future costs and benefits must be reduced in value to take this into account. Discounting techniques (similar to those we examined in section 10.3: see pages 304–6) are used for this purpose.

- Some account may also be taken of the distribution of the costs and benefits. Is it considered fair that, although some people will gain from the project, others will lose? Will the losers be compensated in any way?

- A recommendation is then made by weighing up the costs and benefits. In the simplest terms, if the benefits exceed the costs, it will be recommended that the project goes ahead.

Each of these stages involves a number of difficulties. These are examined in the following sections.

Identifying the costs and benefits

Identifying costs and benefits is relatively easy, although there are some problems in predicting what types of external effect are likely to occur.

Costs

Direct (private) monetary costs. These include all the construction costs and the operating and maintenance costs.

External costs. These fall into two categories:

- *Monetary costs,* such as the loss of profits to competitors. Thus in the case of a CBA of a tunnel under a river, external monetary costs would include the loss of profits to ferry operators.

- *Non-monetary costs,* such as pollution, spoiling the landscape, noise and various other forms of inconvenience to local residents. In some projects, such as a tunnel, these costs will be confined largely to the construction phase. With other projects, however, such as a new airport, there may be considerable externalities resulting from its operation (e.g. noise). These non-monetary externalities are usually the most difficult costs to identify.

Benefits

Direct (private) monetary benefits. These are also easy to identify. They consist of the revenues received from the users of the project. The direct monetary benefits of a toll bridge, for example, are the tolls paid.

Private non-monetary benefits. These are the benefits to consumers over and above what they actually pay: in other words, the consumer surplus. For example, if a bridge had a toll of £1.50, and yet a person was prepared to pay £3 if necessary to avoid the long trip round the estuary, then the person's consumer surplus is £1.50. Total consumer surplus is thus the area between the demand curve (which shows

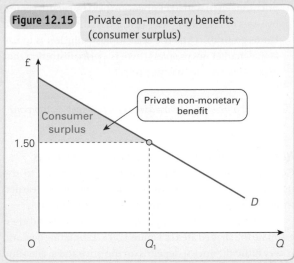

Figure 12.15 Private non-monetary benefits (consumer surplus)

what people are willing to pay) and the price charged. This is illustrated in Figure 12.15.

External benefits. These are the benefits to the non-users of the project. For example, the Victoria Underground line CBA identified external benefits to road users in central London. The roads would become less congested as people used the new Underground line. Usually these benefits are non-monetary benefits, but sometimes they may result in direct financial gain (e.g. higher profits to companies from reduced transport costs on less crowded roads).

Measuring the costs and benefits

Identifying costs and benefits may be relatively easy: measuring them is another matter. Difficulties in measurement depend on the type of cost and benefit. There are four types.

Direct private monetary costs and benefits

These would seem to be the simplest to measure. Normally the simple financial costs and revenues are used. In the case of a new Underground line, for example, such costs would include excavation, construction and capital costs (such as new rolling stock) and the operating costs (such as labour, electricity and maintenance). Revenues would be the fares paid by travellers. There are two problems, nevertheless:

- What *will* these financial costs and revenues be? It is all very well using current prices, but prices rise over time, and at different and unpredictable rates. Also, it is difficult to forecast demand and hence revenues. There is thus a large element of *uncertainty.*

- The prices will often be distorted by the existence of monopoly power. Should this be taken into account? In an otherwise perfect world (the first-best situation), the answer would be yes. But in the real world, where price distortions exist throughout the economy, actual prices should normally be used. In the case of a proposed Underground line, for example, it makes sense to use market prices, given that market prices are paid by car drivers and by users of taxis and buses (the alternatives to using the Underground). Thus the second-best solution is to use actual market prices *unless* there is a price distortion that applies *only* to the specific project.

 What price should be used when there is such a distortion?

Non-monetary private benefits: consumer surplus

Consumer surplus is a private benefit – it accrues to the users of the project – but is not part of the money earned from the project. There are two ways of estimating it.

The first way is to estimate the demand curve and then estimate the shaded area in Figure 12.15. Estimating demand is very difficult, since it depends on the price and availability of substitutes. The demand for the Channel Tunnel depends on the price, frequency and convenience of ferry crossings. It also depends on the overall level of activity in the economy and perhaps the world generally. Thus estimates of air traffic (essential information when deciding whether to build a new airport) have often been proved wrong as the world economy has grown more rapidly or less rapidly than previously forecast.

Another problem is that the consumer surplus gained from the project (e.g. the Channel Tunnel) may replace some of the albeit smaller consumer surplus from a competing service (e.g. cross-Channel ferries). In this case, the non-monetary private benefit is merely the *additional* consumer surplus of those who switch, but still the *full* consumer surplus of those who would not otherwise have crossed the Channel. This makes calculation less straightforward.

An alternative approach is to focus on specific non-monetary benefits to consumers. This approach is more useful when the service is to be provided free and thus no estimate of a demand curve can be made. Assume that a new motorway saves 20 000 hours of travelling time per week. (This, of course, will first have to be estimated, and again a prediction will have to be made of the number of people using the motorway.) How is this 20 000 hours to be evaluated? In the case of businesspeople and lorry drivers, the average hourly wage rate will be used to estimate the value of each labour hour saved. In the case of leisure time, there is less agreement on how to value an hour saved. Usually it is simply assumed to be some fraction of the average hourly wage. This method is somewhat arbitrary, however, and a better approach, though probably impractical, would be to attempt to measure how the travellers themselves evaluate their time.

Another way of measuring time saved would be to see how much money people would be prepared to spend to save travelling time. For example, how much extra would people be prepared to pay for a taxi that saved, say, 10 minutes over the bus journey? This method, however, has to take account of the fact that taxis may be more desirable for other reasons too, such as comfort.

 How would you attempt to value time that you yourself save (a) getting to work; (b) going on holiday; (c) going out in the evening?

Monetary externalities

These would normally be counted at face value. Thus the external monetary costs of a new Underground line would include the loss of profits to taxi and bus companies. The external monetary benefits of a new motorway would include the profits to be made by the owners of the motorway service stations.

Non-monetary externalities

These are likely to be the hardest to measure. The general principle employed is to try to find out how much people would be prepared to pay to obtain the benefits or avoid the costs, if they were able to do so. There are two approaches here.

Ask people (questionnaires). Take the case of noise from an airport or motorway. People could be asked how much they would need to be compensated. There are two problems with this:

- *Ignorance.* People will not know just how much they will suffer *until* the airport or motorway is built.
- *Dishonesty.* People will tend to exaggerate the compensation they would need. After all, if compensation is actually going to be paid, people will want to get as much as possible. But even if it is not, the more people exaggerate the costs to themselves, the more likely it is that they can get the project stopped.

These problems can be lessened if people are questioned who have already experienced a similar project elsewhere. They have less to gain from being dishonest.

Make inferences from people's behaviour. Take the case of noise again. In similar projects elsewhere, how have people actually reacted? How much have they spent on double glazing or other noise insulation? How much financial loss have they been prepared to suffer to move somewhere quieter? What needs to be measured, however, is not just the financial cost, but also the loss of consumer surplus. The Roskill Commission in 1968 examined the siting of a third London airport. It attempted to evaluate noise costs, and looked at the difference in value of house prices round Gatwick compared with elsewhere. A problem with this approach is in finding cases elsewhere that are directly comparable. Were the four potential sites for the third London airport directly comparable with Gatwick?

Another example of externalities would be a reduction in accidents from a safer road. How is this to be measured? Obviously there are the monetary benefits from reduced medical expenditures. But how would you value a life saved? This question is examined in Box 12.5.

*BOX 12.5   WHAT PRICE A HUMAN LIFE?

A difficult question for cost–benefit analysis

TC 1
p11

Many projects involve saving lives, whether they be new hospitals or new transport systems. This is obviously a major benefit, but how is a life to be evaluated?

Some people argue: 'You can't put a price on a human life: life is priceless.' But just what are they saying here? Are they saying that life has an *infinite* value? If so, this project must be carried out *whatever* the costs, and even if other benefits from it were zero! Clearly, when evaluating lives saved from the project, a value less than infinity must be given.

Other people might argue that human life cannot be treated like other costs and benefits and put into mathematical calculations. But what are these people saying? That the question of lives saved should be excluded from the cost–benefit study? If so, the implication is that life has a *zero* value! Again this is clearly not the case.

So if a value somewhere between zero and infinity should be used, what should it be?

Some economists have suggested that a life be valued in terms of a person's future earning potential. But this implies that the only value of a person is as a factor of production. Would the life of a disabled person, for example, who is unable to work and draws state benefit, be given a *negative* value? Again this is clearly not the solution. It would also value the life of a banker considerably higher than that of most other workers; an approach that would be hard to justify politically!

Can any inferences be drawn from people's behaviour?

How much are people prepared to spend on safety: on making their car roadworthy, on buying crash helmets, etc.? This approach too has serious drawbacks. People are wishful thinkers. They obviously do not want to be killed, but simply believe that accidents happen to other people, not to them.

Then again, there are the problems of estimating the effects on other people: on family and friends. Can the amount that people are willing to spend on life insurance be a guide here? Again, people are optimists and in any case may be cash-constrained. Also, it is not the family and friends who buy the insurance; it is the victim, who may not take the effect on others fully into account.

The Department for Transport[1] puts a value of £1 873 498 on a life saved from a road safety project (in 2015 prices). This is based partly on the (discounted) average value of individuals' lost output for the rest of their lives (£620 466), partly on emergency services and hospital costs (£23 548), partly on the costs of insurance and damage to property (£11 561) and partly on the human cost based on people's willingness to pay (if they had to) for the enjoyment of life over and above the consumption of goods and services plus costs to family and friends (£1 217 923). The US Department of Transportation, by contrast, uses the much higher average valuation of $9.4 million (in 2015 prices).

1. Can you think of any other ways of getting a more 'rational' evaluation of human life? Would the person's age make any difference?
2. If you had to decide whether more money from a hospital's budget were to be spent on hip replacements (which do not save lives, but do dramatically improve the quality of the patient's life), or on heart transplants (which do save lives, but are expensive), how would you set about making a rational decision?
3. If different values are used in different countries, does this have implications for policy makers? Does your answer change if different departments within a government use varying valuations?

1 *Reported Road Casualties Great Britain, Annual Report: 2015,* Table RAS60003 (Department of Transport, 2016).

How would you evaluate (a) the external effects of building a reservoir in an area of outstanding natural beauty; (b) the external effects of acid rain pollution from a power station?

Risk and uncertainty

KI 11
p76

Taking account of *risk* is relatively straightforward. The value of a cost or benefit is simply multiplied by the probability of its occurrence.

The problem is that *risk* is less frequent than *uncertainty*. As was explained in section 4.3, in the case of uncertainty all that is known is that an outcome *might* occur. The likelihood of its occurring, however, is uncertain.

How then can uncertainty be taken into account? The best approach is to use **sensitivity analysis**. Let us consider two cases.

Individual uncertain outcomes

A range of possible values can be given to an uncertain item in the CBA: for example, damage from pollution. Table 12.1 illustrates two possible cases.

The lowest estimate for pollution damage is £10 million; the highest is £50 million. In case A, given a very high margin of benefits over *other* costs, the project's desirability is *not* sensitive to different values for pollution damage. Even with the highest value (£50 million), the project still yields a net benefit.

Definition

Sensitivity analysis Where a range of possible values of uncertain costs and benefits are given to see whether the project's desirability is sensitive to these different values.

BOX 12.6 **HS2: IS IT REALLY WORTH IT?**

The case for (and against) High Speed Rail in the UK

In January 2009, the Department for Transport published a report[1] into various options for a new high speed rail network in the UK. It concluded that an initial route between London and the West Midlands would be the best way forward. The then Labour government acted swiftly. It set up a company, High Speed Two Limited (HS2 Ltd), tasked with further investigating the proposals and providing advice on factors such as connectivity with the existing network and further extensions of the line to cities in the north of England and in Scotland.

In 2011, the first section of the route was confirmed as running from London Euston to Birmingham Curzon Street. After three years of parliamentary scrutiny, legislation was finally passed in February 2017 which meant work on construction of the line could finally begin. A completion date for phase 1 was set for December 2026.

HS2 Ltd has also made an economic case for the 'V'-shaped second phase of the project. The two routes will take services from Birmingham Curzon Street to Manchester Piccadilly and to Leeds. The finalised route from Birmingham to Manchester was announced in November 2016, while Birmingham to Leeds remains under discussion.

HS2 Ltd also examined the possibility of further extending the service to Scotland. In May 2015, it announced that there was 'no business case' for this extension.

The rationale for HS2

HS2 Ltd published a detailed analysis of the potential benefits of this infrastructure project in February 2011. The report focused on both phases of the project and stated that:

> The economic appraisal of a transport scheme seeks to cover the full economic costs and full economic benefits of a scheme and to quantify these in monetary terms. . . . we look at some of the wider economic impacts on the UK economy, using Department for Transport guidance to quantify and value these impacts. The appraisal of quantified benefits provides a numerical result, a 'benefit–cost ratio' or BCR. This ratio represents the level of benefit per pound (£) spent by Government (e.g. if a scheme generates £2 of benefit for every £1 spent this is presented as a BCR of 2.0).[2]

The report identified the following as the most important benefits of the scheme:

- Reduced journey times.
- Additional capacity resulting in reduced crowding and waiting times.
- Improved connectivity that would help to rebalance the economy: i.e. the greatest benefits would be for the regions outside of London.
- Environmental benefits from people substituting road and air travel for HS2.
- Improving links with key international gateways.

There was considerable public debate about the estimated costs and benefits published in the initial report. Following criticism of the estimates, HS2 Ltd extended and updated its initial analysis and a new set of estimated costs and benefits were published in October 2013.[3] The net benefits were slightly lower than in the 2011 report – mainly due to a £10bn rise in the projected costs of the scheme. The main findings are summarised in the table.

Quantified benefits and costs (£ billions) of the Y network (2011 PV/prices) and the resulting benefit–cost ratio (BCR)

(1) Transport user benefits	Business £40.5bn
	Other £19.3bn
(2) Other quantifiable benefits (excl. carbon)	£0.8bn
(3) Loss to government of indirect taxes	−£2.9 bn
(4) Net transport benefits = (1) + (2) + (3)	**£57.7bn**
(5) Wider economic impacts (WEIs)	£13.3bn
(6) Net benefits including WEIs (4) + (5)	**£71.0bn**
(7) Capital costs	£40.5bn
(8) Operating costs	£22.1bn
(9) Total costs = (7) + (8)	**£62.6bn**
(10) Revenues	£31.1bn
(11) Net costs to government = (9) − (10)	**£31.5bn**
(12) BCR without WEIs (ratio) = (4)/(11)	**1.8**
(13) BCR with WEIs (ratio) = (6)/(11)	**2.3**

Source: *Economic Case for HS2*, Table 15 (Department for Transport, October 2013).

The estimated values of the two largest benefits of the project help to illustrate the complexity of the economic assessment, and the sensitivity of results to any assumptions used in the analysis.

HS2 Ltd estimated that reductions in crowding would generate just over £7.5bn of benefits – 11 per cent of the total net benefits of the full network. The key assumption here is that the capacity of the rail network is beginning to reach its limit and the growth in the demand for rail travel will continue at a similar rate in the future. For example, the number of passenger journeys and total distance travelled by rail doubled between 1993/94 and 2013/14.

To estimate demand, the report uses the elasticity of rail demand to changes in GDP. This requires forecasting GDP over very long periods of time, which involves high levels uncertainty.

To deal with this uncertainty, a demand cap is used in the analysis. This is a rather arbitrary assumption that growth in demand for rail travel will cease at some predetermined point in the future. The benefits in the table above are estimated by introducing a demand cap in 2036. This assumes that there is no growth in the demand for rail travel for 57 years: i.e. from 2036 to 2093. If the cap is introduced at a later point the estimated benefits increase significantly. For example, if it is introduced in 2049 the BCR increases from 2.3 to 4.5.

Will the demand for rail travel increase in the future if the economy continues to grow? One factor that might influence this relationship is technological developments. In particular, improvements in Internet availability/speed and broadband width might lead to more people working from home and thus reducing the demand for travel at any given level of GDP. The effect could also be in the opposite direction, with more people travelling by train if they are able to make productive use of the travel time. Thus the impact of technology is very uncertain.

The benefits of time saved

The most significant projected advantage of HS2 is the value of the time saved by business, commuter and leisure travellers. For example, the following reductions in travel time have been forecast:

- Birmingham to London: 1hr 21mins to 49mins.
- Birmingham to Leeds: 2hrs to 57mins.
- Manchester to London: 2hr 8mins to 1hr 8mins.

HS2 Ltd estimated that the total time saved was worth £37bn or 44 per cent of the total benefits of the project. How did HS2 Ltd calculate this figure?

It tried to find out how much people are willing to pay for shorter journey times. The values of non-work travel time were estimated by using the results from surveys of motorists carried out in 1994. In these surveys people were asked to choose between journey options (i.e. different prices and times) for a hypothetical trip. From the responses, a value of £6.04 was placed on each hour for a leisure traveller.

No surveys such as these have been carried out with business travellers; so the value of their time was estimated using a cost-savings approach. This assumes that any travel time saved can be put to productive use in the workplace. The value of this work was estimated by using the gross wage of workers who use the train for business purposes. Taking this approach, a figure of £31.96 was estimated for each hour of time saved per person.

There is considerable uncertainty and debate about the use of each of these figures. For example, the survey used to value non-work time is very dated. It is also very difficult to adjust the figures to account for business travellers being able to use some of their travel time productively: i.e. checking/responding to emails, writing reports and doing other work. The HS2 Ltd results assume that people cannot use *any* of their time on a train productively. If further research finds that travellers do use a large proportion of their time productively, then the benefits of HS2 will be considerably lower than have been estimated.

Overall, the report found that the HS2 scheme would produce economic benefits of £71.6bn. Comparing this with estimated net costs (after revenues) of £31.5bn, the result would be a BCR of 2.3 – enough to recommend that the scheme go ahead. It should be noted, however, that this *excludes* environmental impacts, which were assessed for Phase 1 in a separate report[4].

Opposition to HS2

HS2 has been subject to a great deal of opposition, particularly from those directly affected by the proposed route. Two major groups, *Stop HS2* and *HS2 Action Alliance,* have been established to campaign against the building of infrastructure. Eighteen local authorities have also create a group called *51m* which is also opposed to the project.

Both the Institute of Economic Affairs[5] and Adam Smith Institute[6] have published reports that question the reliability of the estimated project costs. Given the expensive tunnelling and technically complex work in urban areas both reports argued that the final costs could be in excess of £80bn. The forecasts have already increased from £33bn to £50bn.

A major study by the House of Lords Economic Affairs Committee published in March 2015[7] also argued that the government had not made a convincing case for continuing with the project. In particular, the report questioned the assumption that the rail network had a capacity issue. The authors argued that rail usage data indicated that there was no existing overcrowding problem on long-distance trains and there was unlikely to be one in the near future.

It also questioned the premise that the greatest benefits would go to the regions outside of London because evidence from other countries suggests that firms in London may actually benefit the most. For example, shorter travel times mean that their employees can live further away and benefit from lower house prices. In order to boost the economies in the north of England, the report argues that investment should be focused on improving regional transport link between cities other than London.

Despite the criticisms, the government has remained committed to the general approach. Chris Grayling, the Transport Secretary, stated in February 2017 that:

> HS2 will be the world's most advanced passenger railway and the backbone of our rail network. Royal Assent is a major step towards significantly increasing capacity on our congested railways for both passengers and freight; improving connections between the biggest cities and regions; generating jobs, skills and economic growth and helping build an economy that works for all.[8]

With time-frames that stretch over decades, it will be a long wait until we find out whose views were correct: those thinking the scheme will prove to be a driver for economic growth, or those who are convinced it will be an expensive white elephant.

(continued)

HS2: IS IT REALLY WORTH IT? (continued)

1. Why is this type of cost–benefit analysis so complex?
2. 'The "losers" will be compensated, so there is no reason for them to protest.' Assess this statement with reference to HS2.
3. Explain why companies in London might benefit as much from HS2 as those in Manchester.

1 *Britain's Transport Infrastructure – High Speed Two* (Department for Transport, January 2009).
2 *Economic Case for HS2 – the Y Network and London–West Midlands* (Department for Transport, February 2011).
3 *Economic Case for HS2* (Department of Transport, October 2013).
4 *Review of HS2 London to West Midlands Appraisal of Sustainability* (Department for Transport, January 2012).
5 *HS2 Decision is Economically Unjustifiable* (IEA, October 2016).
6 *Network Fail: Getting UK Rail Back on Track* (Adam Smith Institute, September 2016).
7 *The Economics of High Speed 2* (House of Lords, March 2015).
8 *Full Speed Ahead as HS2 gets Royal Assent* (gov. uk, 25 February 2017).

	Total costs other than pollution (£m)	Total pollution cost (£m)	Total benefits (£m)	Net benefits (total benefits – total costs) (£m)
	100	10	200	90
Case A	100	20	200	80
	100	50	200	50
	140	10	160	10
Case B	140	20	160	0
	140	50	160	−30

Table 12.1 Effect of different estimates of the costs of production on the viability of a project

- Subtract the costs from the benefits for each year, to give a net benefit for each year.
- Discount each year's net benefit to give it a present value.
- Add up all of these present values. This gives a *net present value (NPV)*.
- If the *NPV* is greater than zero, the benefits exceed the costs: the project is worthwhile.

Maths Case 12.2 on the student website gives a worked example.

Choosing the discount rate

Apart from the problems of measuring the costs and benefits, there is the problem of choosing the rate of interest/discount.

If it were a private-sector project, the firm would probably choose the market rate of interest as its rate of discount. This is the rate that it would have to pay to borrow money to finance the project.

In the case of CBA, however, it is argued that the government ought to use a *social rate of discount*. This rate should reflect society's preference for present benefits over future benefits. But just what is this rate? If a high rate is chosen, then future net benefits will be discounted more, and projects with a long life will appear less attractive than projects yielding a quick return. Since the government has a responsibility to future generations and not just to the present one, it is argued that a relatively low discount rate should be chosen.

In case B, however, the project's desirability *is* sensitive to pollution damage. If the damage exceeds £20 million, the project becomes undesirable. In this case, the government will have to decide whether it is prepared to take the gamble.

A number of uncertain outcomes

When there are several uncertain outcomes the typical approach is to do three cost–benefit calculations: the most optimistic (where all the best possible outcomes are estimated), the most pessimistic (where all the worst possible outcomes are estimated) and the most likely (where all the middle-of-the-range outcomes are estimated). This approach can give a good guide to just how 'borderline' the project is.

Discounting future costs and benefits

KI 27 p304

As we saw in section 10.3, discounting is a procedure for giving a present value to costs and benefits that will not occur until some time in the future.

Discounting in CBA

The procedure is as follows:

- Work out the costs and benefits for each year of the life of the project.

Imagine that a specific public project yields a return of 13 per cent (after taking into account all social costs and benefits), whereas a 15 per cent private return could typically be earned by projects in the private sector. How would you justify diverting resources from the private sector to this project?

Definition

Social rate of discount A rate of discount that reflects society's preferences for present benefits over future ones.

Inevitably, the choice of discount rate is arbitrary. As a result, the analysis will normally be conducted using two or three alternative discount rates to see whether the outcome is sensitive to the choice of discount rate. If it is, then again the project will be seen as borderline.

CBA and the distribution of costs and benefits

Virtually all projects involve gainers and losers. For example, the majority may gain from the construction of a new motorway, but not those whose homes lie alongside it. So how is the distribution of costs and benefits to be taken into account?

The strict Pareto criterion

According to the strict Pareto criterion, a project is unequivocally desirable only if there are some gains and *no one* is made worse off. But are there likely to be any projects that fulfil this criterion? If there are always losers then let us think about a situation where the losers are compensated. Thus we can now state that a project would be accepted only if the gainers *fully* compensated the losers, with the gainers still being better off after doing so.

In practice, this never happens. Often compensation is simply not paid. Even when it is, the recipients rarely feel as well off as before, and there will still be many who do not get compensation. Also, the compensation is usually paid not by the project users, but by the general taxpayer (who will thus be *worse* off).

The Hicks–Kaldor criterion

To get round this problem, J. R. Hicks and N. Kaldor suggested an alternative criterion. This states that a project is desirable if it leads to a *potential* Pareto improvement: in other words, if the gainers could *in principle* fully compensate the losers and still have a net gain, even though in practice they do not pay any compensation at all.

This criterion is what lies behind conventional CBA. If the benefits of a project are greater than the costs, then in principle the losers could be fully compensated with some net benefits left over.

But what is the justification for using this test? The losers, after all, will still lose. Its advocates argue that questions of *efficiency* should be kept separate from questions of *equity*. Projects, they argue, should be judged on efficiency grounds. They are efficient if their benefits exceed their costs. Questions of fairness in distribution, on the other hand, should be dealt with through the general system of taxation and welfare.

This is a 'useful' argument because it lets the proponents of the project off the hook. Nevertheless, the problem still remains that some people will lose. People do not like living near a new motorway, airport or power station. These people cannot expect to receive special welfare benefits from general taxation.

Thus other economists have argued that more specific account should be taken of distributional effects when *measuring* costs and benefits.

Taking specific account of distributional consequences

One way this could be done would be to give a higher weighting to the costs of individual, as opposed to corporate, losers. The justification is simple. The pain for one person of losing £10 000 is greater than the collective pain of 10 000 people losing just £1 each. Just how much higher this weighting should be, however, is a matter of judgement, not of precise calculation.

Another way distribution can be taken into account is to give a higher weighting to the costs incurred by poor people than to those incurred by rich people. For example, assume that a new airport is built. As a result, house prices nearby fall by 10 per cent. A rich person's house price falls from £2 000 000 to £1 800 000 – a loss of £200 000. A poor person's house price falls from £200 000 to £180 000 – a loss of £20 000. Is the loss to the rich person eight times as painful as that to the poor person? Probably not. It is argued, therefore, that the poorer people are, the higher the weighting that should be given to each £1 lost. Just what this weighting should be, however, is controversial.

Section summary

1. Cost–benefit analysis (CBA) can help a government decide whether or not to go ahead with a particular public project, or which of alternative projects to choose. CBA involves a number of stages.

2. All costs and benefits must be identified. These include the direct costs of constructing and operating the project, the direct monetary benefits to the operators and the consumer surplus of the users. They also include external costs and benefits to non-users.

3. Direct monetary costs and benefits are relatively easy to measure. Nevertheless there is still uncertainty about their *future* values. Also, there is a problem if prices are distorted.

4. Non-monetary private benefit (consumer surplus) is difficult to estimate because of the difficulty of estimating the shape and position of the demand curve. The alternative approach is to focus on specific non-monetary benefits, such as journey time saved, and then to evaluate how much people would be prepared to pay for them if they could.

5. Monetary externalities would normally be counted at face value. Non-monetary externalities are much more difficult to estimate. The approach is to try to estimate the value that consumers would put on them in a market environment. Questionnaire techniques could be used, or inferences could be drawn from people's actual behaviour elsewhere.

6. Figures would then have to be adjusted for risk and uncertainty.

7. Discounting techniques would then have to be used to reduce future benefits and costs to a present value.

8. The study may also take distributional questions into account. The Hicks–Kaldor criterion suggests a compensation test for deciding whether a project is desirable. But given that in practice full compensation would be unlikely, the distributional questions may need to be taken into account more specifically.

9. Having adjusted the costs and benefits for risk and uncertainty, timing and distributional effects, a recommendation to go ahead with the project will probably be given if its net present value (NPV) is positive: in other words, if the discounted social benefits exceed the discounted social costs.

12.5 GOVERNMENT FAILURE AND THE CASE FOR THE MARKET

Government intervention in the market can itself lead to problems. The case for non-intervention (laissez-faire) or very limited intervention is not that the market is the *perfect* means of achieving given social goals, but rather that the problems created by intervention are greater than the problems overcome by that intervention.

TC 7
p81

Drawbacks of government intervention

Shortages and surpluses. If the government intervenes by fixing prices at levels other than the equilibrium, this will create either shortages or surpluses (see section 3.1).

If the price is fixed *below* the equilibrium, there will be a shortage. For example, if the rent of social housing is fixed below the equilibrium in order to provide affordable housing for low-income households, demand will exceed supply. In the case of such shortages the government will have to adopt a system of waiting lists, or rationing, or giving certain people preferential treatment. Alternatively it will have to allow allocation to be on a first-come, first-served basis or allow queues to develop. Underground markets are also likely to develop (see page 82 and Case Study 3.2 on the book's website).

If the price is fixed *above* the equilibrium price, there will be a surplus. Such surpluses are wasteful, and high prices may protect inefficient producers. (The problem of food surpluses in the EU was examined in section 3.4.)

 What are the possible arguments in favour of fixing prices (a) below and (b) above the equilibrium? Are there any means of achieving the same social goals without fixing prices?

Poor information. The government may not know the full costs and benefits of its policies. It may genuinely wish to pursue the interests of consumers or any other group, and yet may be unaware of people's wishes or misinterpret their behaviour.

KI 15
p129

Bureaucracy and inefficiency. Government intervention involves administrative costs. The more wide-reaching and detailed the intervention, the greater the number of people and material resources that will be involved. These resources may be used wastefully and the effect on welfare may not be an improvement on the free-market situation. Think back to the problem of scarcity we discussed in Chapter 1; if we 'use up' resources on managing intervention, we need to be sure that the outcome is markedly better than without intervention.

Lack of market incentives. If government intervention removes market forces or reduces their effect (by the use of subsidies, welfare provisions, minimum wages, etc.), it may remove certain useful incentives. Subsidies may allow inefficient firms to survive. Welfare payments may discourage people from working. The market may be imperfect, but it does tend to encourage efficiency by allowing the efficient to receive greater rewards.

Shifts in government policy. Industrial performance may suffer if government intervention changes too frequently. It makes it difficult for firms to plan if they cannot predict tax rates, subsidies, wage controls, etc. Shifts in policy are also likely to involve costs for both business and public-sector providers. This may result in wasted resources.

Lack of freedom for the individual. Government intervention may involve a loss of freedom for individuals to make economic choices. The argument is not just that the pursuit of individual gain is seen to lead to the social good, but that it is desirable in itself that individuals should be as free as possible to pursue their own interests with the minimum of government interference, and with that minimum being largely confined to the maintenance of laws consistent with the protection of life, liberty and property.

 Go through the above arguments and give a reply to the criticisms made of government intervention.

Advantages of the free market

Although markets in the real world are not perfect, even imperfect markets can be argued to have positive advantages over government provision or even government regulation.

Automatic adjustments. Government intervention requires administration. A free-market economy, on the other hand, leads to the automatic, albeit imperfect, adjustment to demand and supply changes.

Even under oligopoly, it is claimed, the competition between firms will be enough to encourage firms to produce goods that are desirable to consumers and at not excessively high prices, and will encourage more efficient production methods. Cases of pure monopoly with total barriers to entry are extremely rare.

Dynamic advantages of the free market. The chances of making high monopoly/oligopoly profits will encourage capitalists to invest in new products and new techniques. Prices may be high initially, but new firms will sooner or later break into the market and competition will ensue. If the government tries to correct the misallocation of resources under monopoly/oligopoly, either by regulating monopoly power or by nationalisation, any resulting benefits could be outweighed by a loss in innovation and growth. This is one of the major arguments put forward by the neo-Austrian libertarian school – a school that passionately advocates the free market (see Box 12.7).

 Are there any features of free-market capitalism that would discourage innovation?

A high degree of competition even under monopoly/oligopoly. Even though an industry at first sight may seem to be highly monopolistic, competitive forces may still work for the following reasons.

- A fear that excessively high profits might encourage firms to attempt to break into the industry (assuming that the market is contestable).
- Competition from closely related industries (e.g. coach services for rail services, or electricity for gas).
- The threat of foreign competition. Additional competition was one of the main purposes behind the Single European Act which led to the abolition of trade barriers within the EU in 1993 (see section 25.4).
- Countervailing powers. Large, powerful producers often sell to large, powerful buyers. For example, the power of detergent manufacturers to drive up the price of washing powder is countered by the power of supermarket chains to drive down the price at which they purchase it. Thus power is to some extent neutralised.
- The competition for corporate control (see pages 210–11).

Should there be more or less intervention in the market?

No firm conclusions can be drawn in the debate between those who favour more and those who favour less government intervention, for the following reasons:

- The debate involves normative issues that cannot be settled by economic analysis. For example, it could be argued that freedom to set up in business and freedom from government regulation are desirable *for their own sake*. As a fundamental ethical point of view, this can be disputed, but not disproved.
- In principle, the issue of whether a government ought to intervene in any situation could be settled by weighing up the costs and benefits of that intervention. Such costs and benefits, however, even if they could be identified, are extremely difficult, if not impossible, to measure, especially when the costs are borne by different people from those who receive the benefits and when externalities are involved.
- Often the effect of more or less intervention simply cannot be predicted: there are too many uncertainties.

Nevertheless, economists can make a considerable contribution to analysing problems of the market and the effects of government intervention. Chapters 13 and 14 illustrate this by examining specific problem areas.

BOX 12.7 MISES, HAYEK AND THE MONT PELERIN SOCIETY

The birth of post-war libertarianism

After the Second World War, governments in the Western world were anxious to avoid a return to the high levels of unemployment and poverty experienced in the 1930s. The free market was seen to have failed. Governments, it was therefore argued, should take on the responsibility for correcting or counteracting these failings. This would involve various measures such as planning, nationalisation, the restriction of monopoly power, controls on prices, the macroeconomic management of the economy and the provision of a welfare state.

But this new spirit of intervention deeply troubled a group of economists and other social scientists who saw it leading to an erosion of freedom. In 1947, this group met in a hotel in the Swiss Alps. There they formed the Mont Pelerin Society: a society pledged to warn against the dangers of socialism and to advocate the freedom for individuals to make their own economic choices.

Two of the most influential figures in the society were the Austrians Ludwig von Mises (1881–1973) and Friedrich von Hayek (1899–1992). They were the intellectual descendants of the nineteenth-century 'Austrian school'. Carl Menger, the originator of the school, had (along with Jevons and Walras (see Box 4.2)) emphasised the importance of individuals' marginal utility as the basis of demand. The Austrian school of economists was famous for its stress on individual choice as the basis for rational economic calculation and also for its advocacy of the free market.

Mises and Hayek (the 'neo-Austrians' as they became known) provided both a critique of socialism and an advocacy of the free market. There were two main strands to their arguments.

The impossibility of rational calculation under socialism

In his famous book *Socialism* (1922), Mises argued that centrally planned socialism was logically incapable of achieving a rational allocation of resources. Given that scarcity is the fundamental economic problem, all societies, whether capitalist or socialist, will have to make choices. But rational choices must involve weighing up the costs and benefits of alternatives. Mises argued that this cannot be done in a centrally planned economy. The reason is that costs and benefits can be measured only in terms of money prices, prices which reflect demand and supply. But such prices can be established only in a market economy.

In a centrally planned economy, prices will be set by the state and no state will have sufficient information on demand and supply to set rational prices. Prices under centrally planned socialism will thus inevitably be arbitrary. Also, with no market for land or capital these factors may not be given a price at all. The use of land and capital, therefore, may be highly wasteful.

Many democratic socialists criticised Mises' arguments that rational prices *logically* cannot be established under socialism. In a centrally planned economy, the state can in theory, if it chooses, set prices so as to balance supply and demand. It can, if it chooses, set an interest rate for capital and a rent for land, even if capital and land are owned by the state. And certainly in a mixed-market socialist economy, prices will merely reflect the forces of demand and supply that have been modified by the state in accordance with its various social goals.

Hayek modified Mises' arguments somewhat. He conceded that some imperfect form of pricing system could be established under socialism, even under centrally planned socialism. Hayek's point was that such a system would inevitably be inferior to capitalism. The problem was one of imperfect information under socialism.

Calculation of costs and benefits requires knowledge. But that knowledge is dispersed amongst the millions of consumers and producers throughout the economy. Each consumer possesses unique information about his or her own tastes; each manager or worker possesses unique information

Section summary

1. Government intervention in the market may lead to shortages or surpluses; it may be based on poor information; it may be costly in terms of administration; it may stifle incentives; it may be disruptive if government policies change too frequently; it may remove certain liberties.

2. By contrast, a free market leads to automatic adjustments to changes in economic conditions; the prospect of monopoly/oligopoly profits may stimulate risk taking and hence research and development and innovation; there may still be a high degree of actual or potential competition under monopoly and oligopoly.

3. It is impossible to draw firm conclusions about the 'optimum' level of government intervention. This is partly due to the normative nature of the question, partly due to the difficulties of measuring costs and benefits of intervention/non-intervention, and partly due to the difficulties of predicting the effects of government policies, especially over the longer term.

about his or her own job. No government could hope to have this knowledge. Planning will inevitably, therefore, be based on highly imperfect information.

The market, by contrast, is a way of co-ordinating this dispersed information: it co-ordinates all the individual decisions of suppliers and demanders, decisions based on individuals' own information. And it does it all without the need for an army of bureaucrats.

> The economic problem of society is thus not merely a problem of how to allocate 'given' resources – if 'given' is taken to mean given to a single mind which deliberately solves the problem set by these 'data'. It is rather a problem of how to secure the best use of resources known to any of the members of society, for ends whose relative importance only these individuals know. Or, to put it briefly, it is a problem of the utilization of knowledge not given to anyone in its totality.[1]

Lack of dynamic incentives under socialism

A planned socialist economy will, according to Mises and Hayek, lack the incentives for people to take risks. Even a 'market socialist' society, where prices are set so as to equate demand and supply, will still lack the crucial motivating force of the possibility of large personal economic gains. Under capitalism, by contrast, a firm that becomes more efficient or launches a new or improved product can gain huge profits. The prospect of such profits is a powerful motivator.

> Without the striving of entrepreneurs (including the shareholders) for profit, of the landlords for rent, of the capitalists for interest and the labourers for wages, the successful functioning of the whole mechanism is not to be thought of. It is only the prospect of profit which directs production into those channels in which the demands of the consumer are best satisfied at least cost. If the prospect of profit disappears the mechanism of the market loses its mainspring, for it is only this prospect

which sets it in motion and maintains it in operation. The market is thus the focal point of the capitalist order of society; it is the essence of capitalism. Only under capitalism, therefore, is it possible; it cannot be 'artificially' imitated under socialism.[2]

In addition to these economic criticisms of socialism, Mises and Hayek saw government intervention as leading down the road towards totalitarianism. The more governments intervened to correct the 'failings' of the market, the more this tended to erode people's liberties. But the more people saw the government intervening to help one group of people, the more help they would demand from the government for themselves. Thus inexorably the role of the state would grow and grow, and with it the size of the state bureaucracy.

In the early years after the war, the Mont Pelerin Society had little influence on government policy. Government intervention and the welfare state were politically popular.

In the late 1970s, however, the society, along with other similar libertarian groups, gained increasing influence as a new breed of politicians emerged who were wedded to the free market and were looking for an intellectual backing for their beliefs.

Libertarian thinkers such as Hayek and Milton Friedman (see Case Study 16.2 on the student website) had a profound effect on many right-wing politicians, and considerably influenced the economic programmes of the Thatcher, Reagan and both Bush (Snr and Jnr) administrations.

 Do the arguments of Mises and Hayek necessarily infer that a free market is the most desirable alternative to centrally planned socialism?

1 F. von Hayek, 'The use of knowledge in society', *American Economic Review* (September 1945), p. 519.
2 L. von Mises, *Socialism: An Economic and Sociological Analysis* (Jonathan Cape, 1936), p. 138.

END OF CHAPTER QUESTIONS

1. Assume that a firm discharges waste into a river. As a result, the marginal social costs *(MSC)* are greater than the firm's marginal private costs *(MPC)*. The following table shows how *MPC, MSC, AR* and *MR* vary with output.

Output	1	2	3	4	5	6	7	8
MPC (£)	23	21	23	25	27	30	35	42
MSC (£)	35	34	38	42	46	52	60	72
TR (£)	60	102	138	168	195	219	238	252
AR (£)	60	51	46	42	39	36.5	34	31.5
MR (£)	60	42	36	30	27	24	19	14

   (a) How much will the firm produce if it seeks to maximise profits?

   (b) What is the socially efficient level of output (assuming no externalities on the demand side)?

   (c) How much is the marginal external cost at this level of output?

   (d) What size tax would be necessary for the firm to reduce its output to the socially efficient level?

   (e) Why is the tax less than the marginal externality?

   (f) Why might it be equitable to impose a lump-sum tax on this firm?

   (g) Why will a lump-sum tax not affect the firm's output (assuming that in the long run the firm can still make at least normal profit)?

2. Why might it be argued that a redistribution of consumption, while not involving a Pareto improvement, could still be desirable?

3. Assume that a country had no state education at all. For what reasons might the private education system not provide the optimal allocation of resources to and within education?

4. Why might it be better to ban certain activities that cause environmental damage rather than to tax them?

5. Distinguish between publicly provided goods, public goods and merit goods.

6. Consider the advantages and disadvantages of extending property rights so that everyone would have the right to prevent people imposing any costs on them whatsoever (or charging them to do so).

7. The food industry provides a great deal of information about its products. Why, despite this, does the government run various campaigns about healthy eating?

8. Should all investment be subject to a social cost–benefit appraisal?

9. Make out a case for (a) increasing and (b) decreasing the role of the government in the allocation of resources.

Online resources

Additional case studies on the student website

12.1 Vilfredo Pareto (1843–1923). A profile of a key figure in the development of welfare economics.

12.2 Can the market provide adequate protection for the environment? This explains why markets generally fail to take into account environmental externalities.

12.3 Catastrophic risk. This examines how a cost–benefit study could put a monetary value on a remote chance of a catastrophe happening (such as an explosion at a nuclear power station).

12.4 Evaluating the cost of aircraft noise. This case study looks at the method used by the Roskill Commission, which in the 1960s investigated the siting of a third major London airport.

12.5 CBA of the Glasgow canal project. A cost–benefit study carried out in the late 1980s on the restoration of the Glasgow canal system.

12.6 Meeting the Kyoto Protocol. This examines the options open to the EU in meeting the targets set under international climate change agreements. It illustrates the use of cost–benefit analysis.

12.7 Public choice theory. This examines how economists have attempted to extend their analysis of markets to the field of political decision making.

Maths Case 12.1 Calculating deadweight welfare loss. A worked example.

Maths Case 12.2 Calculating net present value. The use of discounting techniques in CBA.

Websites relevant to this chapter

See sites listed at the end of Chapter 14 on page 441.

Environmental Policy

Just how far should things be left to the market in practice? Just how much should a government intervene? These are clearly normative questions, and the answers to them may depend on a person's politics. Politicians on the right tend to favour a lesser degree of intervention while those on the left generally prefer more intervention.

In the final two chapters of Part D we examine some topics that illustrate well the possible strengths and weaknesses of both the market and government intervention. In Chapter 13 we look closely at the environment, an area where the existence of externalities results in substantial market failure. We start by considering the broader environmental issues and then turn to alternative policies for dealing with pollution and urban traffic congestion.

As we shall see, the economist's approach is to focus on both the costs and the benefits of various policies and how these costs and benefits can be weighed up. Scientists are the ones who need to assess whether global warming is a real phenomenon and to determine the physical consequences of our actions, such as the degree of warming that might result from a particular level of CO_2 emissions. But it is economists who must assess the implications for various policies to deal with the problems.

13.1 ECONOMICS OF THE ENVIRONMENT

Scarcely a day goes by without some environmental issue featuring in the news: another warning about global warming, a company fined for illegally dumping waste, a drought or flood blamed on pollution, poor air quality in our major cities. Attempts by policy makers to improve the environment also cause controversy and hit the headlines: for example, the impact of government climate change policies on the size of customers' energy bills.

Nearly everyone would like a cleaner, more attractive environment but there are deep disagreements about how much people should pay for it. Environmental improvement normally comes at a cost: whether in cleaning up waste or pollution, or in terms of the higher price we might need to pay for 'green' products, such as organic foods, low-emission cars and electricity from renewable sources.

Economists are concerned with choices, and rational choices involve weighing up costs and benefits. Increasingly, people are recognising that such costs and benefits ought to include the effects on the environment: the effects on the planet we share with each other and with future generations.

The environmental problem

Why is the environment used in such a suboptimal way? Why are policies that try to address these environmental issues always so controversial? To answer these questions we have to understand the nature of the economic relationship between humans and the natural world.

We all benefit from the environment in three ways:

- as an amenity to be enjoyed;
- as a source of primary products (food, raw materials and other resources);
- as a place where we can dump waste.

The relationship between these uses and the rest of the economy are illustrated in Figure 13.1. Unfortunately, having more of one of these benefits usually means having less of another.

The use of the environment as a productive resource reduces its amenity value. Intensive agriculture, with hedges and woods removed, spoils the beauty of the countryside and can lead to a decline in animal and plant species. Mines and quarries are ugly. Commercial forestry is often at the expense of traditional broad-leaved forests.

Similarly, the use of the environment as a dump for waste reduces its amenity value. The environment becomes dirtier and uglier. The burning of fossil fuels dumps CO_2 into the atmosphere and contributes towards global warming.

 Using examples, discuss the conflicts between using the environment as a productive resource and as a dump?

These conflicts have always existed, but are they getting worse? Let us examine the arguments.

Figure 13.1   The economy and the environment

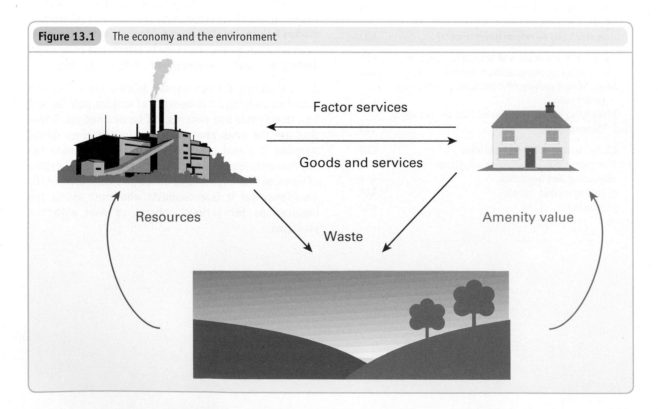

Population pressures and limited resources

As we saw in Box 6.1, as more people crowd on to the fixed supply of world land, so diminishing returns to labour will occur. If food output per head is to remain constant, let alone increase, land must be made to yield more and more. One answer has been to use increasing amounts of fertiliser and pesticides. Likewise, if the increasing world population is to have higher levels of material consumption, this will generate increased demands for natural resources, many of which are non-renewable and generate pollution. With the rapid growth of countries such as China and India, the pressures on the environment are already growing sharply.

The environment is able to absorb most types of waste up to certain levels of emission. Beyond such levels, however, environmental damage is likely to accelerate. Other things being equal, as population and waste grow, so environmental degradation is likely to grow at a faster rate.

Cause for optimism?

Despite population pressures, there are various factors that are helping to reduce environmental degradation.

Technological developments. Many newer industrial processes are cleaner and make a more efficient use of resources, leading to less waste and a slowdown in the rate of extraction of various minerals and fossil fuels. For example, the amount of CO_2 emitted per $ of GDP has fallen from 0.475kg in 1990 to 0.354kg in 2013 (at 2011 prices). What is more, the production of less waste, or the recycling of waste, is often in the commercial interests of firms: it allows them to cut costs. In 2013, the Department of Energy and Climate Change estimated that large firms in the UK could contribute £1.9 billion in net social benefits if they spent money on energy saving investments. Much of this would be in the form of lower costs for the firms themselves. Firms thus have an incentive both to use such technology and also to research into cleaner and more resource-efficient techniques.

Increased price of non-renewable resources. As we saw in Box 10.11 (see page 312), as resources become scarcer, so their prices rise. This encourages people to use less of them, either by using more efficient technology or by switching to renewable alternatives as they become available.

Public opinion. As knowledge about environmental damage has grown, so too has pressure from public opinion to do something about it. Many firms see the opportunity to gain commercially from having a 'green image' and to publicise their positive attitude towards corporate social responsibility. In addition, governments see electoral advantage in policies to create a cleaner, greener environment.

Despite these developments, however, many aspects of environmental degradation continue to worsen.

Global emissions have continued to increase. For example, CO_2 tonnes per capita have risen from 4.059 in 2002 to 4.996 in 2014. A UN Environment Report[1] published in November 2016 concluded that by 2030 emissions would be 12 to 14 gigatonnes above the levels required to limit the growth in global warming to 2°C.

An OECD report[2] published in 2012 identified and classified environmental issues according to a traffic-light system as serious (red light), moderate (amber light) or satisfactory (green light). The following four challenges were identified as most urgent (and badged as red light); climate change, biodiversity, water and the health impacts of pollution.

An optimum use of the environment

If the current levels of pollution and environmental degradation are too high, then can we identify an optimum use of the environment? To do this, we have to go back to first principles of efficiency and also look at our attitudes towards *sustainability*.

Different approaches to sustainability

We can identify four different approaches to the environment and sustainability.

The free-market approach. At the one extreme, we could regard the world as there purely for ourselves: a resource that belongs to individual property owners to do with as they choose, or a 'common asset', such as the air and seas, for individuals to use for their own benefit. In this view of the world, we are entitled simply to weigh up the marginal costs and benefits to ourselves of any activity. Sustainability is achieved in this free-market world only to the extent that resource prices rise as they become scarce and to the extent that environmentally friendly technologies are in firms' (or consumers') private interests.

The social efficiency approach. A somewhat less extreme version of this view is one that takes the social costs and benefits of using the environment into account: i.e. the costs and benefits not only to the direct producer or consumer, but to people in general. Here we would apply the standard rules for social efficiency: use resources to provide goods/services until the marginal social benefit equals the marginal social cost Even though this approach does take into account environmental externalities (such as pollution), it is only to the extent that they adversely affect *human beings*.

Within this general approach, however, more explicit account can be taken of sustainability, by including the

---

1 *The Emissions Gap Report, 2016* (UN Environment, November 2016).
2 *OECD Environmental Outlook to 2050* (OECD, March 2012).

BOX 13.1   A STERN WARNING

Economists can offer solutions, but they can't solve the problem

The analysis of global warming is not just for climate scientists. Economists have a major part to play in examining its causes and consequences and the possible solutions. And these solutions are likely to have a major impact on business.

Perhaps the most influential study of climate change in recent times was the Stern Review of 2006. This was an independent review lead by Sir Nicholas Stern, the then head of the Government Economic Service and former chief economist of the World Bank. Here was an economist using the methods of economics to analyse perhaps the most serious problem facing the world.

Climate change presents a unique challenge for economics: it is the greatest and widest-ranging market failure ever seen. The economic analysis must therefore be global, deal with long time horizons, have the economics of risk and uncertainty at centre stage, and examine the possibility of major, non-marginal change.[1]

Dealing with long time horizons presents some interesting problems. The benefits to society from acting on climate change today will occur in the future. The problem is that the cost of these policies will be felt today: e.g. higher prices and less consumption.

In order to carry out an assessment of environmental policies, therefore, the future social benefits need to be *discounted* (see pages 304–6 and 384–5) so that they can be compared with the current social costs. But what social discount rate should be chosen? This is a major issue as the results obtained from any economic assessment that involve costs and benefits over such a long period of time are very sensitive to the discount rate used. Stern used a relatively low social discount rate, which meant that the future benefits and costs were more highly valued. Some economists criticised the report, claiming that a much higher discount rate should have been chosen.

First the bad news . . .

According to the Stern Report, if no action were taken, global temperatures would rise by some 2–3°C within the next 50 years. As a result the world economy would shrink by an average of up to 20 per cent. The economies of the countries most seriously affected by floods, drought and crop failure could shrink by considerably more. Rising sea levels could displace some 200 million people; droughts could create tens or even hundreds of millions of 'climate refugees'.

. . . Then the good

However, Stern concluded that these consequences could be averted – and at relatively low cost – if action were taken early enough. According to the report, a sacrifice of just 1 per cent of global GDP (global income) could be enough to stabilise greenhouse gases to a sustainable level. To achieve this, action would need to be taken to cut emissions from their various sources (see the chart). This would involve a mixture of four things:

- Reducing consumer demand for emissions-intensive goods and services.
- Increased efficiency, which can save both money and emissions.
- Action on non-energy emissions, such as avoiding deforestation.
- Switching to lower-carbon technologies for power, heat and transport.

As one might expect from a report produced by an economist, the policy proposals focused on altering incentives. This could involve taxing polluting activities; subsidising green alternatives, including the development of green technology;

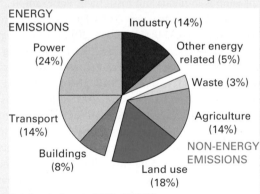

Greenhouse gas emissions in 2000, by source

Total emissions in 2000: 42 GtCO₂e.

Energy emissions are mostly CO_2 (some non-CO_2 in industry and other energy related).

Non-energy emissions are CO_2 (land use) and non-CO_2 (agriculture and waste).

Source: *Stern Review on the Economics of Climate Change*, Office of Climate Change (OCC) (Stern Review, 2006), Executive Summary, Figure 1 based on data drawn from World Resources Institute Climate Analysis Indicators Tool (CAIT) on-line database version 3.0.

---

costs of our use of the environment today to *future* generations. For example, we could take into account the effects of climate change not just on ourselves, but on our children and their descendants. Depending on people's views on 'intergenerational' equity, a higher or lower weighting could be given to future (as opposed to present) costs and benefits (see page 384 on the choice of a social discount rate).

The conservationist approach.   Many environmentalists argue that our responsibilities should not be limited to each other, or even to future generations, but should include the environment for its own sake. Such a view would involve downplaying the relative importance of material consumption and economic growth, and putting greater emphasis on the maintenance of ecosystems. Growth in consumption would be ethically acceptable only if it led to no (or only very minor)

KI 27
p304

establishing a price for carbon through trading carbon (see section on tradable permits on pages 401–403 below) and regulating its production; and encouraging behavioural change through education, better labelling of products and encouraging public debate.

Heeding the warnings?

So just over 10 years after the Stern Report, how much progress has been made? We have already seen on page 393 that the OECD is very concerned about the environmental impact on growth and is pressing for a global response. So are national governments therefore acting with urgency?

In 2014, the Intergovernmental Panel on Climate Change (IPCC) issued its *Fifth Assessment Report (AR5)*[2] – the first one had been published in 1990. This major document consists of three working group reports and an overarching synthesis. The first working group looked at the physical science. The second considered impacts, adaptation and vulnerability, while the third focused on mitigation of climate change. Economists contributed substantially to both the second and third groups.

The report on impact[3] confirmed that the effects of climate change are already occurring on all continents and across the oceans. It concluded that the world is ill-prepared for the risks that climate change brings.

As with Stern, it stated that there are currently opportunities to respond to such risks, though this will be difficult to manage with high levels of warming.

The report details the impacts of climate change to date, the future risks from a changing climate, and the opportunities for effective action to reduce risks. It identifies vulnerable people, industries and ecosystems around the world. It finds that risk from a changing climate comes from vulnerability (lack of preparedness) and exposure (people or assets in harm's way) overlapping with hazards (triggering climate events or trends). Each of these three components can be a target for smart actions to decrease risk.

Adaptation to reduce the risks from a changing climate is now starting to occur, but with a stronger focus on reacting to past events than on preparing for a changing future. According to Chris Field, the Co-Chair of Working Group II:

> Climate-change adaptation is not an exotic agenda that has never been tried. Governments, firms, and communities around the world are building experience

with adaptation. This experience forms a starting point for bolder, more ambitious adaptations that will be important, as climate and society continue to change.[4]

Less than a month after this report, the working group on mitigation published its own findings.[5] It summarised the diverse options open to policy makers and reaffirmed the conclusion that the worst effects of climate can be prevented, if action is taken.

Part of the Mitigation report takes the form of a summary for policy makers. It acknowledges that substantial reductions in emissions will require major changes in investment patterns. The report finds that some progress in policy development has been achieved, particularly at a national level. These policies are often at sectoral level and involve the regulatory, financial and information measures that economists have recommended for some time.

There is, however, a substantial time lag between the implementation of policies and the impact on the environment. AR5 found that since 2008 emission growth has not yet deviated from the previous trend. Of course, a major characteristic of climate change is that it is not restricted by national boundaries. This highlights the potential for international co-operation and we look at this further in Box 13.4 on page 406.

The IPPC is currently working on its sixth Assessment Report, which will be published in 2022.

1. *Would it be in the interests of a business to reduce its carbon emissions if this involved it in increased costs?*
2. *How is the concept of 'opportunity cost' relevant in analysing the impact of business decisions on the environment?*
3. *The Stern Report was produced in 2006. Why has progress to date been slow? Does this reflect a lack of political will or scepticism about the extent of climate change?*

1 *Stern Review on the Economics of Climate Change, Executive Summary* (HM Treasury, 2006).
2 *The Fifth Assessment Report (AR5)* (IPCC, 2014).
3 *Climate Change 2014: Impacts, Adaptation, and Vulnerability, from Working Group II of the IPCC* (IPCC, 2014).
4 'IPCC Report: "severe and pervasive" impacts of climate change will be felt everywhere', *UN and Climate Change* (UN, 31 March 2014).
5 *Climate Change 2014: Mitigation from Climate Change, from Working Group III of the IPCC* (IPCC, 2014).

environmental degradation. Maintenance of the environment is thus seen as an ethical *constraint* on human activity.

The Gaia approach. The strongest approach to sustainability involves a fundamentally different ethical standpoint. Here the Earth itself, and its various natural species of animals and plants, have moral rights. According to this *Gaia philosophy*, people are seen as mere custodians of the

Definition

Gaia philosophy The respect for the rights of the environment to remain unharmed by human activity. Humans should live in harmony with the planet and other species. We have a duty to be stewards of the natural environment, so that it can continue to be a self-maintaining and self-regulating system.

planet: the planet does not belong to them, any more than a dog belongs to the fleas on its back! This view of the environment is similar to that held by some indigenous peoples living in marginal areas, such as the Aborigines in Australia and the San (Bushmen) of the Kalahari, and to various other 'hunter-gatherer' peoples in developing countries. Their ethic is that the land they leave their descendants should be as good as, if not better than, the land they inherited from their ancestors. Conservation is a 'prime directive'. This approach to the environment has been dubbed the 'deep green' approach.

Making optimum decisions concerning the environment

Choice between these four approaches is essentially normative, and therefore we cannot as economists stand in judgement between them.

Nevertheless, economists can help in identifying optimum decisions *within* a given set of values. Most environmental economists adopt an approach that is consistent with the social efficiency view, which can be easily modified to fit the conservationist view. The main area for disagreement is over the *value* to be placed on specific environmental costs and benefits.

Let us take the case of the production of a good by a firm in a perfectly competitive market that yields benefits to consumers, but which involves pollution to the environment. What is the optimum level of output of the good? The choices are illustrated in Figure 13.2.

The line $MEC_{pollution}$ shows the external costs of pollution from each additional unit of the good produced by the firm. This diagram is very similar to Figure 12.12 on page 372. However, we now assume that up to Q_1 there are no external costs: the environment can cope with the waste generated. We also assume that the curve gets steeper as output increases because the environment is increasingly unable to cope with

the waste. The marginal external costs of pollution therefore accelerate.

A profit-maximising firm will produce Q_4 units of output, with external pollution costs of C_4. The *socially* efficient level of output (where $MSB = MSC$), however, is Q_3, with the lower external costs of pollution, C (We are assuming that there are no other externalities.) Identifying this socially efficient level of output is not easy in practice, since it requires us to *measure* pollution costs, and that is fraught with problems. These problems were considered in section 12.4.

A more conservationist approach could be to set a maximum pollution cost of, say, C_2. This would reduce the optimum output to Q_2. A Gaian approach would be to restrict output to Q_1 in order to prevent any pollution. Of course, as we move towards 'greener' approaches, so it becomes more important to look for less polluting methods for producing this good (causing the $MEC_{pollution}$ curve to shift downwards), and for alternative goods that involve less pollution (thus reducing the need to consume this good).

Market failures

What is clear from all the attitudes towards sustainability, other than the free-market one, is that the market system will fail to provide adequate protection for the environment. In fact, the market fails for various reasons.

Externalities. We saw above (Figure 13.2) how pollution could be classified as a 'negative externality' of production or consumption. In the case of production, there are marginal external costs (*MEC*), which means that the marginal social costs (*MSC*) are greater than the marginal private costs (*MC*) to the polluter. The failure of the market system to equate *MSC* and marginal social benefit (*MSB*) is due to either consumers or firms lacking the appropriate property rights.

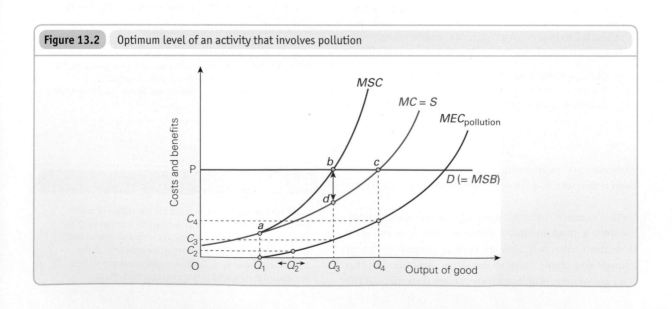

Figure 13.2   Optimum level of an activity that involves pollution

The environment as a common resource. The air, the seas and many other parts of the environment are not privately owned. It is argued that they are a global 'commons'. As such it is extremely difficult to exclude non-payers from consuming the benefits they provide. Because of this property of 'non-excludability', the environment can often be consumed at a zero price. If the price of any good or service to the user is zero, there is no incentive to economise on its use.

Many parts of the environment, however, are *scarce*: there is *rivalry* in their use. As people increase their use of the environment, it may prevent other or rival consumers from enjoying it. This could lead to the *tragedy of the commons* (see page 362).

Ignorance. There have been many cases of people causing environmental damage without realising it, especially when the effects build up over a long time. Take the case of aerosols. It was not until the 1980s that scientists connected their use to ozone depletion. Even when the problems are known to scientists, consumers may not appreciate the full environmental costs of their actions. So even if people would like to be more 'environmentally friendly' in their activities, they might not have the knowledge to be so.

Intergenerational problems. The environmentally harmful effects of many activities are long term, whereas the benefits are immediate. Thus consumers and firms are frequently prepared to continue with various practices and leave future generations to worry about their environmental consequences. The problem, then, is a reflection of the importance that people attach to the present relative to the future.

Look through the categories of possible market failings in section 12.2. Are there any others, in addition to the four we have just identified, that will result in a socially inefficient use of the environment?

Section summary

1. The environment benefits humans in three ways: as an amenity, as a source of primary products and as a dump for waste.

2. Given the increasing population pressures and the demands for economic growth, the pressures on the environment are likely to grow. These pressures can be lessened, however, with the use of cleaner technology, a more efficient use of natural resources and 'greener' behaviour of consumers, firms and governments.

3. The concept of an 'optimum' use of the environment depends on people's attitudes towards sustainability. These attitudes vary from regarding the environment simply as a resource for human use at the one extreme to seeing the environment as having moral rights at the other.

4. Under the social efficiency approach to sustainability, the optimum output of a good is where the marginal external environmental cost is equal to the marginal net benefit to users (assuming no other externalities).

5. The market fails to achieve a socially efficient use of the environment because large parts of the environment are a common resource, because production or consumption often generates environmental externalities, because of ignorance of the environmental effects of our actions, and because of a lack of concern for future generations.

13.2 POLICIES TO TACKLE POLLUTION AND ITS EFFECTS

Environmental policy can take many forms. However, it is useful to put the different types of policy into three broad categories: (a) those that attempt to work through the market by changing property rights or by changing market signals (e.g. through the use of charges, taxes or subsidies); (b) those that involve the use of laws, regulations and controls (e.g. legal limits on the volume of sulphur dioxide emissions); (c) those that attempt to combine the approaches (e.g. 'cap and trade'). The following sections will examine each of these three categories in more detail.

Market-based policies

The policies that a government adopts to reduce pollution will depend on its attitudes towards sustainability: on how 'green' it is.

If governments adopt a social efficiency approach to sustainability, environmental problems are seen to be the result of prices not reflecting marginal social costs and benefits. In this section, we look at ways in which markets can be adjusted so that they do achieve social efficiency.

Extending private property rights

If those suffering from pollution, or causing it, are granted property rights, then charges can be introduced for the right to pollute. According to the Coase theorem (see page 375), this would result in the socially efficient level of output being achieved.

We can use Figure 13.2 to illustrate the Coase theorem. If output is initially less than Q_3, the marginal profit to the polluter will exceed the external costs the pollution imposes on the sufferers. In this case, if the sufferers impose a charge on the polluter that is greater than the sufferers' marginal pollution cost but less than the polluter's marginal profit, both sides will benefit from more of the good being produced. Such a situation can continue up to Q_3. Beyond Q_3, the marginal pollution cost exceeds the marginal profit. There is no charge that would compensate for the victim's suffering and leave enough over for the polluter to make a profit. Equilibrium output is therefore at Q_3, the socially efficient output.

Similarly, if the polluting *firm* is given the right to pollute, victims could offer a payment to persuade it not to pollute. The victims would be prepared to pay only up to the cost to them of the pollution. The firm would cut back production only provided the payment was at least as great as the loss in profit. This would be the case at levels of output above Q_3. Once output falls below Q_3, the maximum payment that the victim would be prepared to pay would be less than the minimum that the firm would be prepared to accept. Again, equilibrium would be at Q_3.

Extending private property rights in this way is normally impractical whenever there are many polluters and many victims. But the principle of the victims paying polluters to reduce pollution is sometimes followed by governments. Thus, one element of the 2015 Paris Agreement on tackling climate change is for the developed countries to provide £66 billion of financial assistance to the developing countries to help them reduce greenhouse gas emissions (see Box 13.3 for more details).

In addition, there are sometimes direct environmental gains to be made from extending private property rights to individuals. In many developing countries, tenant farmers or squatters in urban slums have no incentive to invest in the land where they work or live. Give such people secure property rights, however, and they are more likely to take care of the property. For example, farmers are much more likely to plant trees if they know they have the right to the wood or fruit several years later.

Introducing charges for use of the environment

We previously discussed how the environment can be thought of as a common or natural resource where the user pays no price. For example, the emissions created by a coal burning power station can be spewed into the atmosphere at no cost to the firm even though it imposes costs on society. A firm could also use resources from the environment in its production process at a zero price. For example, it could extract water, cut down trees for timber or extract minerals out of the ground (assuming it owned or rented the land). With a zero price these resources will tend to be depleted at rate that is not optimal for society: i.e. too quickly.

To overcome these problems the government could introduce **environmental charges** for use of resources that would otherwise be free to the user. Thus *emissions charges* could be levied on firms discharging waste. Another example is the use of *user charges* to households for rubbish collection. If a social efficiency approach to sustainability is taken, the optimum level of environmental use would be where the

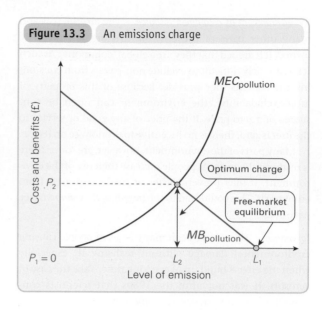

Figure 13.3 An emissions charge

marginal social benefits and costs of that use were equal. This is illustrated in Figure 13.3, which shows the emission of toxic waste into a river by a chemical plant.

It is assumed that all the benefits from emitting the waste into the river accrue to the firm (i.e. there are no external benefits). Marginal private and marginal social benefits are thus the same ($MB = MSB$). The curve slopes downwards because, with a downward-sloping demand for the good, higher output results in lower marginal benefit, and so too will the waste associated with it.

But what about the marginal costs? Without charges, the marginal private cost of using the river for emitting the waste is zero. The pollution of the river, however, imposes an external cost on those using it for fishing or water supply. The marginal external cost rises as the river becomes less and less able to cope with increased levels of emission. As there is no private cost, the marginal social cost is the same as the marginal external cost.

Without a charge, the firm will emit L_1, since this is where its private marginal cost ($= 0$) equals its private marginal benefit. The socially efficient level of emission is L_2 and the socially efficient level of emission charge, therefore, is P_2.

If these charges are to achieve a reduction in pollution, they must be a charge *per unit* of emissions or resource use (as in Figure 13.3). *Fixed total* charges, by contrast, such as water rates or council tax, will *not* encourage households to cut back on water use or reduce domestic refuse, since this will not save them any money: such charges have a *marginal*

Definitions

Environmental charges Charges for using natural resources (e.g. water or national parks), or for using the environment as a dump for waste (e.g. factory emissions or sewage).

rate of zero. If the firm in Figure 13.3 were charged a fixed total pollution fee, it would still choose to emit L_1 waste.

Environmental ('green') taxes and subsidies

Rather than charging for environmental use, a tax could be imposed on the output (or consumption) of a *good,* wherever external environmental costs are generated. Such taxes are known as **green taxes**. In this case, the good already has a market price but this price is below the marginal cost to society: the tax has the effect of increasing the price, thus pushing it closer to the *MSC*.

To achieve a socially efficient output, the rate of tax should be equal to the marginal external cost (i.e. distance $b-d$ in Figure 13.2 on page 396) and so make the price equal to *MSC*. As such, it should fully internalise the costs of the externality.

An alternative is to subsidise activities that reduce pollution (such as the installation of loft insulation). Here the rate of subsidy should be equal to the marginal external benefit.

Although green taxes and subsidies are theoretically a means of achieving social efficiency, they do have serious limitations (see Box 13.2).

Draw a diagram like Figure 13.2, only this time assume that the activity has the effect of reducing pollution, with the result that there are marginal external benefits. Identify the socially optimal level of the activity. What would be the level of subsidy required to achieve this level of activity?

Non-market-based policies

Command-and-control systems (laws and regulations)

One way of tackling pollution has been to set maximum permitted levels of emission or resource use, or minimum acceptable levels of environmental quality, and then to fine firms contravening these limits. Measures of this type are known as **command-and-control (CAC) systems**. Clearly, there have to be inspectors to monitor the amount of pollution, and the fines have to be large enough to deter firms from exceeding the limit.

Virtually all countries have environmental regulations of one sort or another. For example, the EU has over 230 items of legislation covering areas such as air and water pollution, noise, the marketing and use of dangerous chemicals, waste management, the environmental impacts of new projects (such as power stations, roads and quarries), recycling, depletion of the ozone layer and global warming.

Typically, there are three approaches to devising CAC systems.[3]

- **Technology-based standards**. The focus could be on the amount of pollution generated, irrespective of its environmental impact. As technology for reducing pollutants improves, so tougher standards could be imposed, based on the 'best available technology' (as long as the cost were not excessive). For example, the European Union

introduced a directive in 1992, called Euro 1, which set permitted levels of harmful emissions from new petrol and diesel cars in the European Economic Area for the following – Nitrogen Oxide (NOx), Carbon Monoxide (CO), Hydrocarbons (HC) and Particulate Matter (PM). In September 2015, the sixth version of the directive, Euro 6, came into effect. For new diesel cars, it imposed the following restrictions – CO: 0.5g/km; NOx: 0.08g/km; PM: 0.005g/km. Companies, such as Volkswagen, breaking these rules led to the so-called *dieselgate scandal*.

- **Ambient-based standards**. Here the focus is on the environmental impact. For example, standards could be set for air or water purity. Depending on the location and the number of polluters in that area, a given standard would be achieved with different levels of discharge. If the object is a cleaner environment, this approach is more efficient than technology-based standards.

- **Social-impact standards**. Here the focus is on the effect on people. Thus tougher standards would be imposed in densely populated areas. Whether this approach is more efficient than that of ambient-based standards depends on the approach to sustainability. If the objective is to achieve social efficiency, human-impact standards are preferable. If the objective is to protect the environment for its own sake (a deeper green approach), ambient standards would be preferable.

Assessing CAC systems. Given the uncertainty over the environmental impacts of pollutants, especially over the longer term, it is often better to play safe and set tough emissions or ambient standards. These could always be relaxed at a later stage if the effects turn out not to be so damaging, but it might be too late to reverse damage if the effects turn out

---

Definitions

Green tax A tax on output designed to charge for the adverse effects of production on the environment. The socially efficient level of a green tax is equal to the marginal environmental cost of production.

Command-and-control (CAC) systems The use of laws or regulations backed up by inspections and penalties (such as fines) for non-compliance.

Technology-based standards Pollution control that requires firms' emissions to reflect the levels that could be achieved from using the best available pollution control technology.

Ambient-based standards Pollution control that requires firms to meet minimum standards for the environment (e.g. air or water quality).

Social-impact standards Pollution control that focuses on the effects on people (e.g. on health or happiness).

---

3 See R. K. Turner, D. Pearce and I. Bateman, *Environmental Economics* (Harvester Wheatsheaf, 1994), p. 198.

| BOX 13.2 | GREEN TAXES |

Are they the perfect answer to the problem of pollution?

Countries are increasingly making use of 'green' taxes to discourage pollution. The Office for National Statistics estimated that environmental taxes raised £45.974 billion of revenue for the UK government in 2015 (7.4 per cent of total taxes and national insurance) and that households paid an average of £761 in green taxes in 2013. The table shows some of the more important environmental taxes that have been used in the UK. Taxes on hydrocarbon oils (i.e. duty on petrol and diesel) are by far the most significant and account for nearly 60 per cent of total revenue from all environmental taxes.

Environmental tax revenue in the UK as a percentage of GDP has remained broadly stable over the past 20 years at between 2 to 3 per cent. The chart shows how the UK compares with other countries.

As can be seen, they are higher than average in Scandinavian countries, reflecting the strength of their environmental concerns. They are lowest in the USA.

There are various problems, however, with using taxes to tackle pollution.

Identifying the socially efficient tax rate. It will be difficult to identify the $MEC_{pollution}$ curve for each firm (see Figure 13.2), given that each one is likely to produce different amounts of pollutants for any given level of output. Even if two firms produce identical amounts of pollutants, the environmental damage might be quite different, because the ability of the environment to cope with it will differ between the two locations. Also, the human impact will vary. We can

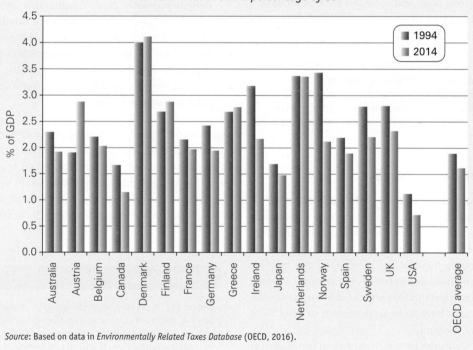

Green tax revenues as a percentage of GDP

Source: Based on data in *Environmentally Related Taxes Database* (OECD, 2016).

to be more serious. Taxes may be a more sophisticated means of reaching a socially efficient output, but CAC methods are usually more straightforward to devise, easier to understand by firms and easier to implement.

Voluntary agreements

Rather than imposing laws and regulations, the government can seek to enter into voluntary agreements (VAs) with firms for them to cut pollution. For example, the UK government operates a system of climate change agreements (CCAs). These are voluntary agreements by firms to

reduce energy use and carbon dioxide (CO_2) emissions in return for a reduction in the Climate Change Levy (a tax on fuel bills).

VAs may involve a formal contract, and hence be legally binding, or they may be looser commitments by firms. VAs will be helped if (a) companies believe that this will improve their image with customers and hence improve sales; (b) there is an underlying threat by the government of introducing laws and regulations should voluntary agreements fail; (c) there are financial incentives (as with CCAs).

Environmental taxes and charges in the UK

Tax	Revenue £ millions (2015)
Tax on hydrocarbon oils (i.e. petrol and diesel)	27 415
Climate Change Levy	1 743
Renewables Obligations (energy)	3 691
Emissions Trading Scheme	552
CRC Energy Efficiency Scheme	535
Air Passenger Duty	3 119
Rail franchise premia	1 546
Vehicle Excise Duty	
Households	4 787
Businesses	1 112
Landfill Tax	1 083
Aggregates Levy	354
Other	37
Total	**45 974**

Source: *Environmental Taxes,* Table 1 (ONS, 5 July 2016).

add to these issues the fact that harmful effects are likely to build up over time, and predicting this is fraught with difficulty.

Problems of demand inelasticity   The less elastic the demand for the product, the less effective will a tax be in cutting production and hence in cutting pollution. Thus taxes on petrol (where we know demand is inelastic) would have to be very high to make significant reductions in the exhaust gases that contribute towards global warming and acid rain.

Problems with international trade   If a country imposes pollution taxes on its industries, its products will become less competitive in world trade. To compensate for this, it may be necessary to give the industries tax rebates for exports. Also, taxes would have to be imposed on imports of competitors'

products from countries where there is no equivalent green tax.

Effects on employment   Reduced output in the industries affected by green taxes will lead to a reduction in employment. If, however, the effect was to encourage investment in new cleaner technology, employment might not fall. Furthermore, employment opportunities could be generated elsewhere, if the extra revenues from the green taxes were spent on alternative products (e.g. buses and trains rather than cars).

Redistributive effects   Many green taxes are regressive. The poor spend a higher proportion of their income on domestic fuel than the rich. A 'carbon tax' on such fuel therefore has the effect of redistributing incomes away from the poor. The poor also spend a larger proportion of their income on food than the rich do. Taxes on agriculture, designed to reduce the intensive use of fertilisers and pesticides, also tend to hit the poor proportionately more than the rich.

Not all green taxes, however, are regressive. The rich spend a higher proportion of their income on motoring than the poor (see Figure 13.4 on page 409). Thus petrol and other motoring taxes could have a progressive effect.

Despite these problems, such taxes can still move output closer to the socially efficient level. What is more, they do have the major advantage of providing a continuing incentive to firms to find cleaner methods of production and thereby save more on their tax bills.

1. *Is it a good idea to use the revenues from green taxes to subsidise green alternatives (e.g. using petrol taxes for subsidising rail transport)? Consider the implications for wider tax policy in your answer.*
2. *If a green tax is highly regressive, does this mean that a government concerned with inequality should avoid implementing it? Consider the long-term impact of climate change on welfare, in your answer.*

Firms often prefer VAs to regulations, because they can negotiate such agreements to suit their own particular circumstances and build them into their planning. The result is that the firms may be able to meet environmental objectives at lower cost. This clearly helps their competitive position.

Education

People's attitudes are very important in determining the environmental consequences of their actions. Fortunately for the environment, people are not always out simply to

maximise their own narrow self-interest. They are sometimes willing to pay higher prices for 'green products' and keen to recycle products wherever possible. There is evidence that peoples' attitudes have changed markedly over the past few decades. Partly this is due to education and better environmental information.

Tradable permits

A policy measure that has grown in popularity in recent years is that of *tradable permits*, also known as a 'cap-and-trade' system. This is a combination of command-and-control and market-based systems.

Capping pollution

Initially, some criteria have to be set in order to determine which factories, power plants and installations will be covered by the scheme. Policy makers then have to set a limit or 'cap' on the total volume of pollution these organisations will be collectively allowed to produce before any financial penalties are incurred.

Once an aggregate cap has been set, pollution permits, known as allowances, are either issued or sold to the firms. Each allowance held by a firm gives it the right to produce a given volume of pollution. The total volume of all the allowances should be equal to the size of the aggregate cap set by the authorities. The quantity of allowances awarded in subsequent years to each firm is then reduced by a certain percentage – the cap is tightened – to give firms an incentive to invest in more environmentally friendly technology.

The number of permits allocated to an individual plant, factory or installation at the beginning of the scheme are often based on its current level of pollution. This approach is known as **grandfathering**. A major criticism of this method is that it seems unfair on those firms that have already invested in cleaner technology. Why should they be required to make the same reductions in the future as firms currently using older polluting technology? An increasing number of allowances are now auctioned – see Box 13.4.

All firms covered by the scheme must monitor and report the levels of pollution from their production. At the end of the year they must then submit enough allowances to the authorities to match the level of pollution they have caused. Each allowance can only be used once. If a firm fails to submit enough allowances then it is subject to heavy fines.

The EU ETS scheme. The biggest cap-and-trade system in the world is the European Union's Emissions Trading Scheme (EU ETS) – for more details see Box 13.4. It covers energy-intensive installations in four broad sectors that have emissions above certain threshold levels. The four sectors are energy (electricity, oil, coal), ferrous metals (iron, steel), minerals (cement, glass, ceramics) and wood pulp

(paper and card). The EU set a total cap on the aggregate CO_2 emissions produced by organisations in these sectors of 2 039 152 882 tonnes for 2013. The cap has been set to decline by 1.74 per cent each year to 2020, so the figure for 2017 was 1 889 411 334 tonnes.

Trading under a cap-and-trade system

The 'trade' part of the scheme refers to the ability of firms to buy and sell allowances in a secondary market once they have been allocated by the authorities. However, in what circumstances would a firm wish either to buy or to sell an allowance?

Take the example of an organisation that estimates it will not have enough permits at the end of the year to match its forecast level of pollution. If it cannot reduce its pollution, say by installing new equipment, or if it is too costly to do so, then it can purchase extra permits.

In order to buy permits (allowances) in the secondary market there must be other firms that have excess permits and hence are willing to sell. These may be firms which have recently made large investments in a more energy-efficient production process.

The price that firms pay to buy, or receive from selling, the allowances in the secondary market will depend on the levels of demand and supply. These will be heavily influenced by the initial number of permits allocated by the authorities, the state of the economy and developments in technology.

The principle of tradable permits can be used as the basis of international agreements on pollution reduction – see Box 13.3 for more details.

Assessing the system of tradable permits

It is argued that one major advantage of the cap-and-trade system over most command-and-control methods is that it can reduce pollution at a much lower cost to society. This can be illustrated by using the following simple example.

TC 2
p26

Assume there are just two firms that each own one plant that pollutes the environment. Firm A and B's production processes currently result in 2000 tonnes of CO_2 being emitted into the atmosphere each year – 1000 tonnes by each firm. Decreasing emissions of CO_2 would cost firm A £100 per tonne, whereas it would cost firm B £200 per tonne.

Assume that the government wishes to reduce emissions from 2000 to 1600 tonnes. It could do this by setting an emissions cap on both firms of 800 tonnes of CO_2. Each would be given permits for that amount. Without the possibility of trading the permits, firm A would have to spend £20 000 to comply with the cap (200 tonnes × £100), while firm B would have to spend £40 000 (200 tonnes × £200). Thus the cost to society of reducing total emissions from 2000 to 1600 tonnes is £60 000.

With trading, however, the cost can be reduced below £60 000. If the two firms traded permits at a price somewhere between £100 and £200 per tonne, say £150, both could gain. Firm A would have an incentive to reduce its emissions

Definitions

Tradable permits Firms are issued or sold permits by the authorities that give them the right to produce a given level of pollution. Firms that do not have sufficient permits to match their pollution levels can purchase additional permits to cover the difference, while those that reduce their pollution levels can sell any surplus permits for a profit.

Grandfathering Where the number of emission permits allocated to a firm is based on its current levels of emission (e.g. permitted levels for all firms could be 80 per cent of their current levels).

to 600 tonnes, costing £40 000 (400 × £100). It could then sell the unused permits (200 tonnes) to firm B for £30 000 (200 × £150), which could then maintain emissions at 1000 tonnes. The net cost to firm A is now only £10 000 (£40 000 − £30 000), rather than the £20 000 from reducing its production to 800 without trade. The cost to Firm B is £30 000, rather than the £40 000 from reducing its production to 800.

Society will have achieved the same total reduction in pollution (i.e. from 2000 tonnes to 1600 tonnes) but at a much lower cost: i.e. £40 000 instead of £60 000. The smaller increase in costs means that price increases in the sector for consumers will be lower than they would otherwise have been.

One potential drawback of using tradable permits is that it could result in pollution being concentrated in certain geographic areas. Some other problems are discussed Box 13.3.

Comparison with CAC systems. In theory, the same outcome could be obtained in a CAC system if the policy makers knew the compliance costs of the different firms. In this case, an emission standard of 600 tonnes could be placed on firm A and a 1000 tonnes on firm B. However, this would require the authorities collecting enormous amounts of detailed information on plant-specific costs in order to calculate the appropriate emissions standard for each business. The cap-and-trade system allows policy makers to achieve the same outcome without the need to collect such large amounts of detailed information.

Comparison with green taxes/charges. An interesting comparison can also be made between tradable permits and green taxes or charges. With the cap-and-trade scheme, the authorities determine the quantity of pollution, while the market determines the price. With a green tax, the authorities determine the price of pollution, while the market determines the quantity. In certain circumstances, green taxes and tradable permits will produce the same outcome.

 What determines the size of the administrative costs of a system of tradable permits? For what reasons might green taxes be cheaper to administer than a system of tradable permits?

How much can we rely on governments?

If governments are to be relied upon to set the optimum green taxes or regulations, several conditions must be met.

First, they must have the will to protect the environment. But governments are accountable to their electorates and must often appease various pressure groups, such as representatives of big business. In the USA, for example, there has been great resistance to cuts in greenhouse gases from the automobile, power and various other industries, many of which have powerful representation in Congress. So there must be the political will in a country if significant environmental improvements are to be made. One of the problems

here is that many of the environmental effects of our actions today will be on future generations; but governments are elected by today's generation, and today's generation may not be prepared to make the necessary sacrifices. This brings us back to the importance of education.

Second, it must be possible to identify just what the optimum is. This requires a clear set of objectives concerning sustainability and any conflicts between human and ecological objectives. It also requires a knowledge of just what are the environmental effects of various activities, such as the emission of CO_2 into the atmosphere, and that is something on which scientists disagree.

Finally, there is the problem that many environmental issues are global and not just local or national. Many require concerted action by governments around the world. The history of international agreements on environmental issues, however, is one plagued with difficulties between countries, which seem more concerned with their own national interests. To understand the difficulties of reaching international agreements, we can draw on game theory (see section 8.3).

Game theory and international agreements

Assume that the world would benefit from a reduction in greenhouse gases and that these benefits would exceed the costs of having to cut back on activities (such as motoring or the generation of electricity) that release such gases into the atmosphere. What would be in the interests of an *individual* country, such as the USA? Its optimum solution would be for *other* countries to cut their emissions, while maintaining its own levels. This approach would yield most of the benefits to the USA and none of the costs. However, when *all* countries refuse to cut emissions, no one gains! This is an example of the *prisoners' dilemma* (see Box 8.5, page 237), and is illustrated in Table 13.1.

Table 13.1	Outcomes for countries from strategies of pollution reduction

		Other countries' strategy		
		All cut pollution	Some cut pollution	None cut pollution
USA's strategy	Cut pollution	A Moderate net gain for all	B Small loss for USA; gain for countries not cutting pollution	C Large loss for USA; slight gain for other countries
	Don't cut pollution	D High gain for USA; small gain for other countries	E Fairly high gain for USA; loss for other countries	F No gain for any country

BOX 13.3 INTERNATIONAL CO-ORDINATION ON CLIMATE CHANGE

From the Kyoto Protocol to the Paris Agreement

In 1992, governments from around the world met at Rio de Janeiro and established the United Nations Framework Convention on Climate Change (UNFCC). The aim of the UNFCC is to limit the concentration of greenhouses gas in the atmosphere to avoid climate change. Representatives from the countries involved in the UNFCC have met annually since 2005. These meetings are known as 'Conferences of the Parties of UNFCC' or more simply 'COP'.

The third meeting, COP3, took place in Kyoto in Japan in 1997, where a draft accord was agreed to reduce greenhouse gas emissions by 5.2 per cent (based on 1990 levels) by the year 2012.

To become a legally binding treaty, the Kyoto Protocol had to be signed and ratified by nations accounting for at least 55 per cent of greenhouse gas emissions. In March 2001, the US government announced that it would not ratify the accord so the 55 per cent target was not met until the Russian parliament voted to sign the agreement in October 2004.

The treaty finally came into force on 16 February 2005 and was ratified by 192 parties in total. Of these, 39 Annex 1 countries (those that are developed or 'in transition') agreed to specific emissions reductions. For example, the UK had a 12.5 per cent reduction target for 2012.

Market-based systems

Although not originally envisaged in this way, the agreement turned climate change into a market, where the right to pollute can be bought and sold through a system of emissions credits. These credits can be earned by reducing emission levels below those agreed or by creating conditions that help to minimise the impact of greenhouse gases on global warming: for example, by planting forests (which absorb carbon).

Within the Kyoto Protocol there are three distinct market-based mechanisms:

- Emissions trading;
- Joint implementation (JI);
- Clean Development Mechanism (CDM).

Emissions trading. The countries that ratified the Kyoto Protocol are allowed to trade amongst themselves rights to emit six greenhouse gases. If a country reduces emissions below its agreed limit, it can sell the additional reduction as a credit. If a country is finding it difficult to cut emissions, it can buy these credits within a type of marketplace. (Box 13.4 explains how CO_2 emissions trading began within the EU in January 2005.)

Joint implementation. Under Article 6 of the protocol, an industrialised country can earn credits by investing in projects that reduce emissions in other industrialised countries (primarily former Soviet countries). These credits, in this case called 'emission reduction units' (ERUs), then reduce the country's own requirement to cut emissions.

Clean Development Mechanism. This is similar to the joint implementation process above, but involves a country or company from the industrialised world earning credits, in this case called 'certified emissions reductions' (CERs), by investing in emissions reduction schemes in *developing* countries. For example, a typical CDM or JI project might involve installing solar panels, planting forests, or investing in a factory producing energy-efficient light bulbs.

Assessing the Kyoto Protocol

The Kyoto Protocol was criticised on a number of grounds. For example:

- Many commentators argued that the 5.2 per cent target was too low. The Intergovernmental Panel on Climate Change estimated that a 60 to 80 per cent cut in greenhouse gas emissions from 1990 levels is required to avert serious climate disruption.
- Some of the reduction in emissions that did take place would have happened anyway. For example, Russia had CO_2 emissions considerably below its 1990 level and so had a large number of emission credits for sale. However, this was not the result of Russian environmental policy, but rather the consequence of the collapse of much of Russian industry in the early 1990s and the replacing of dirty inefficient factories with more profitable cleaner ones.
- Only a relatively small number of developed countries agreed to set emission targets at a national level. Developing countries such as China, India, Brazil and Mexico were under no obligation to reduce emissions, although they did have to monitor and report the levels. Rapid economic growth in these countries over the past 20 years means that they are responsible for an increasing

---

Assume that there is an international agreement (as at the Kyoto summit in December 1997) to cut emissions. If all countries stick to the agreement, the outcome is cell A: a moderate gain to all. What should Congress do? Whatever other countries do (all stick to the agreement, some stick to it, none stick to it), it will be in the USA's interests *not* to stick to it: this is the dominant strategy. Cell D is preferable to Cell A; E is preferable to B; F is preferable to C. But when *all* countries reason like this, the world ends up in Cell F, with no cut in pollution. Cell F is worse for all countries than Cell A.

Only if countries believe that the other countries will (a) ratify the agreement and (b) stick to it once it is ratified will the agreement be likely to succeed. This requires trust on all sides as well as the ability to monitor the outcomes.

share of global emissions. It is estimated that China and India alone are now responsible for a third of global carbon discharges.

■ The USA government, under the George W. Bush presidency, significantly weakened the effectiveness of the treaty by opting out of the protocol. It introduced its own Clear Skies and Global Climate Change Initiatives in February 2002. This provided tax incentives to encourage renewable energy schemes and fuel efficiency schemes, but businesses were not obliged to meet any CO_2 targets.

From Kyoto to Paris

In December 2007, COP13 took place in Bali. As the provisions of the Kyoto agreement ended in 2012, delegates agreed on a new roadmap to make much deeper cuts in emissions. It was hoped that a final accord would be reached in December 2009 at COP15 in Copenhagen. After a fortnight of wrangling between leaders, however, all that resulted was a non-binding 'accord'. This merely recognised the need for keeping global temperature rises to a maximum of 2°C without any specific commitments to achieving that goal.

In December 2010, a modest agreement was accomplished, following a two-week summit held in Cancún in Mexico (COP16). This included the establishment of a 'Green Climate Fund' by rich nations to help poor countries finance climate change investments.

In 2011, Canada became the first country to announce its withdrawal from the Kyoto Accord. It argued that Kyoto was not effective as neither China nor the USA were part of the Accord and several countries outside the EU were falling well short of their Kyoto targets. Japan and Russia announced that they would not adopt any further Kyoto targets in the post-2012 period.

An extension to the Kyoto Protocol to run from 2012 to 2020 was agreed in Doha, Qatar in December 2012 (COP18); only 37 parties (predominately European countries and Australia) had binding targets.

In December 2015, COP21 took place in Paris. After two weeks of intense haggling, the Paris Climate Accord was agreed. This was the first new global climate deal in 18 years.

All parties agreed to the following:

■ All countries need to take action to reduce emissions so that global temperatures rise by less than 2°C above their pre-industrial levels. Further efforts should be made to limit this increase to 1.5°C.

■ A recognition that the pledges made by all countries before the conference would only limit the increase in global temperatures to 2.7°C in the best-case scenario.

■ Actions need to be taken so that at some point between 2050 and 2100 global emissions are equal to the amount that can be absorbed by natural sinks (i.e. trees, soil, etc.) and carbon-capturing technology.

■ By 2020, £66 billion should be raised by richer developed countries to assist poorer developing countries with the cost of switching to renewable energy.

None of these objectives are legally binding. They are aspirational goals rather than commitments. However, unlike the Kyoto Protocol, all the signatories, rather than just the richer nations, have made one important legal obligation.

Each country is now committed to produce and submit a climate change plan for public scrutiny every five years. Common standards of reporting are being introduced so it becomes much easier for the world to scrutinise the actions of each individual country. In particular, it will become far easier to observe (a) how much pollution a country produces; (b) what policies it is using or plans to introduce to reduce its emissions; (c) how well these policies are working.

On 5 October 2016 the threshold for the implementation of the agreement was reached as 55 parties responsible for 55 per cent of total global greenhouse emissions had ratified the treaty. The agreement officially came into force on 4 November 2016. But Donald Trump announced in early 2017 that the USA was pulling out of the agreement. However, he later indicated that he might possibly reverse the decision.

During the past 25 years of intergovernmental climate change conferences, global emissions have continued to rise. It will be interesting to see if the avoidance of 'global shame' proves to be a more effective incentive than any financial penalties.

 Explain who are likely to be the 'winners' and 'losers' as a result of talks on carbon dioxide emissions. Use the concepts of game theory to illustrate your argument.

The other major problem area concerns equity. Most countries will feel that they are being asked to do too much and that others are being asked to do too little. Developed countries will want to adopt a grandfathering approach. The starting point with this approach would be current levels of pollution. Every country would then be required to make the same percentage cut. Developing countries, on the other hand, will want the bulk of the cuts, if not all of them, to be made by the developed countries. After all, the rich countries produce much higher levels of pollutants per capita than do the poor countries, and curbing growth in developing countries would have a far more serious impact on levels of absolute poverty.

 How does an international negotiation 'game' differ from the prisoners' dilemma game?

BOX 13.4   TRADING OUR WAY OUT OF CLIMATE CHANGE

The EU carbon trading system

The EU introduced a carbon Emissions Trading Scheme (EU ETS) in January 2005 as its principal policy to meet environmental targets set by the international treaty, the Kyoto Protocol (which entered into force in February 2005) (see Box 13.3). Article 17 of this treaty supported the use of emissions trading and a similar scheme in the USA had already reduced emissions of both sulphur dioxide and nitrous oxide. The EU ETS created a market in carbon permits or allowances. Its ultimate objective is to give companies greater financial incentives to reduce their emissions of CO_2.

Phases I and II

The first phase of the scheme ran from January 2005 until December 2007. Around 12 000 industrial plants across 27 countries were allocated approximately 2.2 billion CO_2 permits, called Emission Unit Allowances (EUAs). Each EUA issued to a firm gives it the right to emit one tonne of carbon dioxide into the atmosphere. The factories covered by the scheme were collectively responsible for around 40 per cent of the EU's CO_2 emissions each year.

Companies that do not have enough EUAs to match their annual emissions can purchase additional EUAs to cover the difference, while those that reduce their emissions are able to sell any surplus EUAs for a profit. Companies are able to trade directly with each other or via brokers operating throughout Europe.

At the end of December 2007 all existing allowances became invalid and the second Trading Period began, to last until the end of 2012. Although this was run under the same general principles as Trading Period 1, it also allowed companies to use 'Joint Implementation' and 'Clean Development Mechanism' credits earned under the Kyoto Protocol's project-based mechanisms (see Box 13.3). In other words, companies could offset emissions in the EU against emission reductions they achieve in countries outside the EU.

Phase III

Phase III of the EU ETS came into operation on 1 January 2013. It built on the experience gained from operating Phases I and II of the system and included two significant changes.

Move to an EU-wide cap.   The cap on total emissions in both Phases I and II of the system were set in a decentralised manner. Each member state had to develop a National Allocation Plan (NAP). The NAP set out the total cap on emissions for that country, the total quantity of EUAs that

would be issued and how they would be assigned to each industrial plant or factory. Each NAP had to be approved by the European Commission before it could be implemented. The numerous NAPs have been replaced in Phase III of the EU ETS by a single EU-wide cap on the volume of emissions and on the total number of EUAs to be issued. The size of this EU-wide cap is to be reduced by 1.74 per cent per year so that permitted emissions in 2020 are 21 per cent lower than 2005.

Move to auctioning permits.   In Phase I and II of the EU ETS the majority of EUAs were freely allocated to the plants and factories covered by the scheme. The grandfathering method (see page 402) was used to determine the number of EUAs each factory would receive: i.e. it was based on their current emissions. The European Commission allowed member states to auction up to a maximum of 5 per cent of the EUAs in Phase 1 and 10 per cent in Phase II. However, this option was seldom chosen.

In Phase III a big increase is planned in the proportion of EUAs that are auctioned. Since 2013 most of the firms in the power sector have already had to purchase all of their allowances by auction. The average in other sectors is planned to increase from 20 per cent in 2013 to 70 per cent by 2020. Only firms in manufacturing and the power industry in certain member states will continue to be allocated the majority of their allowances at no charge.

It has also been recommended by the EU that half of the revenue generated from the auctions should be used to fund measures to reduce greenhouse gas emissions.

In December 2009, the EU also agreed to a '20-20-20' package to tackle climate change. This would involve cutting greenhouse gases by 20 per cent by 2020 compared with 1990 levels, raising the use of renewable energy sources to 20 per cent of total energy usage and cutting energy consumption by 20 per cent.

Much of the emissions reductions would be achieved by tighter caps under the ETS, with binding national targets for non-ETS sectors, such as agriculture, transport, buildings and services. However, over half of the reductions could be achieved by international carbon trading, where permits could be bought from abroad: e.g. under the Clean Development Mechanism.

Assessing the ETS

The introduction of the world's largest market-based policy to address climate change was welcomed by many economists and policy makers. However, others have raised concerns about both the operation of the scheme and its likely impact on overall emissions.

The size of the cap. What matters crucially for the impact of the scheme is the total number of permits issued by the authorities: i.e. the size of the overall cap. If the supply of the permits is high in the secondary market then the price will be relatively low and firms will lack the necessary incentives to invest in new energy-efficient technology.

Some people have argued that the number of EUAs issued in the past has been far too generous. One reason for this may have been the decentralised manner in which the EUAs were allocated through the NAPs. This gave some countries a strong incentive to game the system by setting an aggregate cap in its NAP that was greater than the volume of emissions actually being produced. By doing this, costs could be kept down for firms operating in that country, which would help to maintain its national economic competitiveness.

Another reason why the number of EUAs may have been too great is because of successful lobbying of governments by firms. In particular, they may have exaggerated claims about the potential negative impact of issuing fewer EUAs on their costs and future competitiveness.

This over-allocation of EUAs clearly seems to have been a problem in Phase I of the scheme. Emission levels across the EU actually rose by 1.9 per cent while the price of EUAs fell from a peak of €30 to just €0.02.

The scrutiny of NAPs by the EU became more rigorous in Phase II of the scheme and the cap on emissions was tightened by 7 per cent. However, there were still big variations between countries, and it appears that the Commission still had limited capacity to check the accuracy of each NAP. Phase III of the system seems to have addressed some of these issues with the removal of the NAPs and the introduction of a single EU-wide cap.

Move from free allocation of permits to auctions. Another major issue with Phases I and II of the scheme was that the majority of EUAs were freely allocated to plants and factories. It was argued by many policy makers that this was important because firms needed time to adjust gradually to a system where they would have to start paying for the pollution they generated. Some people were particularly concerned that selling the permits for a positive price would have large

adverse effects on some firms' costs. This might make it increasingly difficult for them to compete with companies outside the EU. However, after the system was introduced, there were accusations that firms in the power sector had simply used the free allocation of permits to make 'windfall profits'.

The increasing use of auctioning in Phase III of the scheme has been adopted to address this issue. It is also assumed that, after eight years of experience with permits, firms will be better able to adapt to having to buy EUAs.

Transport emissions

From 2012, the EU ETS scheme was also extended to aircraft emissions. Originally the scheme was supposed to cover emissions from all flights either arriving or departing from airports in the EU. Following a huge outcry from the aviation industry, the scheme was temporarily amended so that it would only include flights whose arrival and departure were both at EU airports. This was known as 'Stop the Clock' and an initial cap was set at 86 million tonnes of CO_2.

Plans to bring shipping emissions within the scheme have been delayed. Shipping is a large and growing source of emissions. As a first step towards cutting these, the European Commission has proposed that owners of large ships using EU ports should report their verified emissions from 2018.

Similarly, road transport, responsible for around 20 per cent of all emissions, remains outside the scheme.

Overall, it is still difficult to assess the impact of the EU ETS, even though it has been in operation for over 12 years. Disaggregating the effect of emission allowances from the effects of other economic factors and policy changes is enormously complicated.

The excess supply of allowances remains an issue. The EU has tried to address this problem by introducing *backloading*. This involves withholding allowances from the auction process – 400 million in 2014, 300 million in 2015 and 200 million in 2016. Managing any future supply–demand imbalances will continue to be a major priority for EU policy makers.

 Consider a situation where all firms are of identical size and each is allocated credits that allows it to produce 10 per cent less than its current emissions. How would this compare with a situation where permits are allocated to 90 per cent of firms only? Consider both efficiency and equity in your answer.

Section summary

1. One approach to protecting the environment is to use the market. This can be done by extending private property rights. In many cases, however, this approach is impractical. Another approach is to impose charges for using the environment or taxes per unit of output. The problem with these methods is in identifying the appropriate charges or tax rates, since these will vary according to the environmental impact.

2. Another approach is to use command-and-control systems, such as making certain practices illegal or putting limits on discharges. This is a less sophisticated alternative to taxes or charges, but it is safer when the environmental costs of certain actions are unknown. Other alternatives to market-based approaches include voluntary agreements and education.

3. Tradable permits are a mix of command-and-control and market-based systems. Firms are given permits to emit a certain level of pollution and then these can be traded.

   A firm that can relatively cheaply reduce its pollution below its permitted level can sell this credit to another firm that finds it more costly to do so. The system is an efficient and administratively cheap way of limiting pollution to a designated level. It can, however, lead to pollution being concentrated in certain areas and can reduce the pressure on firms to find cleaner methods of production.

4. Although governments can make a major contribution to reducing pollution, government action is unlikely to lead to the perfect outcome (however defined). Governments may be more concerned with short-run political considerations and will not have perfect information. What is more, given that many environmental effects spill over national borders, governments may 'play games' internationally to try to reduce the costs to their country of any international action to protect the environment.

13.3 THE ECONOMICS OF TRAFFIC CONGESTION

Traffic congestion is a problem faced by many countries, especially in large cities and at certain peak times. This problem has grown at an alarming rate as people have become increasingly reliant on their cars. Vehicles stuck in traffic jams impose huge costs on countries.

It is not only the motorist that suffers. Congested streets make life less pleasant for the pedestrian, and increased traffic leads to increased accidents and significant problems of pollution.

Between 1960 and 2015 road traffic in Great Britain rose by 338 per cent, whereas the length of public roads rose by only 26 per cent (albeit some roads were widened). Most passenger and freight transport travels by road. In 2015, 89 per cent of passenger kilometres (see Table 13.2) and 76 per cent of freight tonnage kilometres in Great Britain were by

road, whereas rail accounted for just under 10 per cent of passenger traffic and 9 per cent of freight tonnage. The total percentage of passenger kilometres by road peaked at 94 per cent in the mid-1990s before falling to its current figure.

Average weekly household expenditure on transport in the financial year 2015/16 was £72.70, equating to 14 per cent of total expenditure. The vast majority of this was on motoring costs, with only £4.10 and £1.30 spent per week on train and bus/coach travel respectively.

Should the government do anything about the problem? Is traffic congestion a price worth paying for the benefits we gain from using cars? Are there things that can be done to ease the problem without generally inconveniencing the traveller?

Table 13.2	Passenger transport in Great Britain: percentage of passenger kilometres					
Year	Cars, vans and taxis	Motor cycles	Buses and coaches	Bicycles	Rail	Air (UK)
1952	26.6	3.2	42.2	10.5	17.4	0.1
1962	56.5	3.3	24.5	3.1	13.2	0.4
1972	75.9	0.9	13.9	0.9	7.9	0.5
1982	80.5	2.0	9.5	1.3	6.1	0.6
1992	86.0	0.7	6.3	0.7	5.6	0.7
2002	85.5	0.7	6.0	0.6	6.2	1.1
2015	82.9	0.6	5.0	0.7	9.8	1.1

Source: Based on data from Table TSGB0101, *Transport Statistics of Great Britain database 2016* (Department for Transport, January 2017).

We will look later in this section at various schemes and at their relative costs and benefits. But first it is necessary to examine the existing system of allocating road space to see the extent to which it meets or fails to meet society's transport objectives.

The existing system of allocating road space

The allocation of road space depends on both demand and supply. Demand is by individuals who base their decisions on largely private considerations. Supply, by contrast, is usually by central government or local authorities. Let us examine each in turn.

Demand for road space (by car users)

The demand for road space can be seen largely as a *derived* demand. What people want is not the car journey for its own sake, but to get to their destination. The greater the benefit they gain at their destination, the greater the benefit they gain from using their car to get there.

The demand for road space, like the demand for other goods and services, has a number of determinants. If congestion is to be reduced, it is important to know how responsive demand is to a change in any of these: it is important to consider the various elasticities of demand.

Price.   This is the *marginal cost* to the motorist of a journey. It includes petrol, oil, maintenance, depreciation and any toll charges.

 Are there any costs associated with motoring that would not be included as marginal costs? Explain why.

The price elasticity of demand for motoring tends to be relatively low. There can be a substantial rise in the price of petrol, for example, and there will be only a modest fall in traffic.

Estimates of the short-run price elasticity of demand for road fuel in industrialised countries typically range from -0.1 to -0.5. Long-run elasticities are somewhat higher, but are still generally inelastic.[4]

The low price elasticity of demand suggests that schemes to tackle traffic congestion that merely involve raising the costs of motoring will have only limited success.

In addition to monetary costs, there are also the time costs of travel. The opportunity cost of sitting in your car is the next best alternative activity you could have been pursuing – relaxing, working, sleeping or whatever. Congestion, by increasing the duration of the journey, increases the opportunity cost.

Income.   As incomes rise, car ownership and usage increase substantially. Demand for road space is elastic with respect to income.

Figure 13.4 shows motoring costs as a percentage of UK household expenditure by quintile groups of household income. The higher the household income, the higher the percentage of income spent on motoring. Indeed, the richest quintile's expenditure on motoring is double that of the poorest as a percentage of household expenditure. Clearly, the income elasticity of demand is significantly greater than 1.

This is also reflected in international statistics of car ownership. Figure 13.5 shows the growth of car ownership between 1980 and 2014 in selected European countries. As national incomes have risen, so has the proportion of car

4 See: *Road Traffic Demand Elasticities* (Department for Transport, 2015).

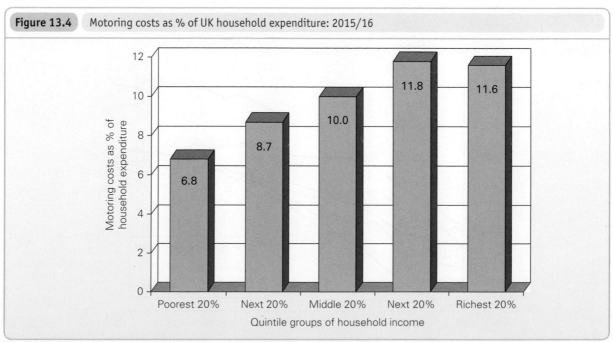

Figure 13.4   Motoring costs as % of UK household expenditure: 2015/16

Source: Based on data in Table 3.2 in *Family Spending Reference Tables, 2016* (National Statistics, February 2017).

ownership. People see car transport as a 'luxury good' compared with alternatives such as public transport, walking or cycling. Also, the growth of suburbs has meant that many people travel longer distances to work.

The implication of this is that, if countries continue to experience economic growth, car ownership and usage are likely to increase substantially: a conclusion in line with most forecasts.

Price of substitutes. If bus and train fares came down, people might switch from travelling by car. The cross-price elasticity, however, is likely to be relatively low, given that most people regard these alternatives as a poor substitute for travelling in their own car. Cars are seen as more comfortable and convenient.

The 'price' of substitutes also includes the time taken to travel by these alternatives. The quicker a train journey is compared with a car journey, the lower will be its time cost to the traveller and thus the more people will switch from car to rail.

Price of complements. Demand for road space will depend on the price of cars. The higher the price of cars, the fewer people will own cars and thus the fewer cars there will be on the road.

 Is the cross-price elasticity of demand for road space with respect to the price of cars likely to be high or low?

Demand will also depend on the price of complementary services, such as parking. A rise in car parking charges will reduce the demand for car journeys. But here again the cross elasticity is likely to be relatively low. In most cases, the motorist will either pay the higher charge or park elsewhere, such as in side streets.

 Go through each of the determinants we have identified so far and show how the respective elasticity of demand makes the problem of traffic congestion difficult to tackle.

Tastes/utility. Another factor explaining the preference of many people for travelling by car is the pleasure they gain from it compared with alternative modes of transport. Car ownership is regarded by many people as highly desirable, and once accustomed to travelling in their own car most people are highly reluctant to give it up.

One important feature of the demand for road space is that it fluctuates. There will be periods of peak demand, such as during the rush hour or at holiday weekends. At such times, roads can get totally jammed. At other times, however, the same roads may be virtually empty.

Supply of road space

The supply of road space can be examined in two contexts: the short run and the long run.

The short run. In the short run, as we have seen, the supply of road space is constant. When there is no congestion, supply is more than enough to satisfy demand. There is spare road capacity. At times of congestion, there is pressure on this fixed supply. Maximum supply for any given road is reached at the point where there is the maximum flow of vehicles per minute along the road.

The long run. In the long run, the authorities can build new roads or improve existing ones. This will require an assessment of the costs and benefits of such schemes.

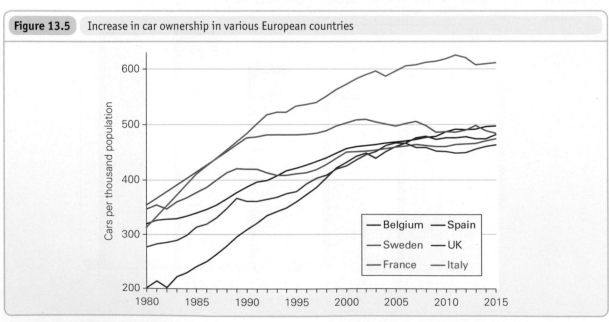

Figure 13.5 Increase in car ownership in various European countries

Source: Based on data in *Eurostat* (tsdpc340).

Identifying a socially efficient level of road usage (short run)

The existing system of *government* provision of roads and *private* ownership of cars is unlikely to lead to an optimum allocation of road space. So how do we set about identifying just what the social optimum is?

In the short run, the supply of road space is fixed. The question of the short-run optimum allocation of road space, therefore, is one of the optimum *usage* of existing road space. It is a question of *consumption* rather than supply. For this reason we must focus on the road user, rather than on road provision.

A socially efficient level of consumption occurs where the marginal social benefit of consumption equals its marginal social cost ($MSB = MSC$). So what are the marginal social benefits and costs of using a car?

Marginal social benefit of road usage

Marginal social benefit equals marginal private benefit plus externalities. Marginal private benefit is the direct benefit to the car user and is reflected in the demand for car journeys, the determinants of which we examined above. External benefits are few. The one major exception occurs when drivers give lifts to other people.

Marginal social cost of road usage

Marginal social cost equals marginal private cost plus externalities. Marginal private costs to the motorist include the costs of petrol, wear and tear, tolls, etc. They also include the time costs of travel. There may also be substantial external costs. These include the following.

Congestion costs: time.   When a person uses a car on a congested road, it will add to the congestion. This will therefore slow down the traffic even more and increase the journey time of other car users.

This is illustrated in Table 13.3 (which uses imaginary figures).

Column (1) shows the number of cars travelling along a given road per minute. Column (2) shows the time taken for each car and thus can be seen as the marginal time cost to a motorist of making this journey. It is thus the *private* marginal time cost. With up to three cars per minute there is no congestion and therefore the traffic flows freely, each car taking 5 minutes to complete the journey. As traffic increases beyond this, however, the road becomes progressively more congested, and thus journey times increase. It is not just the additional cars that are forced to travel more slowly, but *all* the cars on the road. The extra cars thus impose a congestion cost on existing users of the road. By the time seven cars per minute are entering the road, journey time has increased to 16 minutes.

Column (3) shows the sum of the journey times of all the motorists on the road. For example, with six cars on the road, each taking 11 minutes, total journey time for all six is 66 minutes. Column (4) shows the increase in total journey time as one more car enters the road. Thus when the seventh car enters the road, total journey time increases from 66 to 112 minutes: an increase of 46 minutes. This is the additional cost to *all* road users: in other words, the marginal *social* cost. But of these 46 minutes, 16 are the private marginal costs incurred by the extra motorist. Only the remaining 30 minutes are *external* costs imposed on other road users. These external costs are shown in column (5).

 Complete Table 13.3 up to 9 cars per minute, assuming that the journey time increases to 24 minutes for the eighth car and 35 minutes for the ninth car.

Time costs can be converted into money costs if we know the value of people's time. If time were valued at 10p per minute, the congestion costs (external costs) imposed by the seventh car would be £3 (i.e. 30 minutes × 10p per minute). Case Study 13.4 on the student website examines the method used in the UK for estimating the value of time (in the context of evaluating new road schemes).

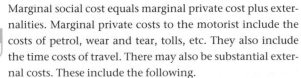

Table 13.3   Time taken to travel between two points along a given road

Traffic density (cars entering road per minute)	Journey time per car (marginal private time cost: in minutes)	Total journey time for all cars (total time cost: in minutes)	Extra total journey time as traffic increases by one more car (marginal social time cost: in minutes)	Additional time cost imposed on other road users by one more car (marginal external time cost: in minutes)
(1)	(2)	(3) = (1) × (2)	(4) = Δ(3)	(5) = (4) − (2)
1	5	5	5	0
2	5	10	5	0
3	5	15	5	0
4	6	24	9	3
5	8	40	16	8
6	11	66	26	15
7	16	112	46	30

Congestion costs: monetary. Congestion increases fuel consumption, and the stopping and starting increases the costs of wear and tear. When a motorist adds to congestion, therefore, there will be additional monetary costs imposed on other motorists. A table similar to Table 13.3 could be drawn to illustrate this.

Environmental costs. When motorists use a road, they reduce the quality of the environment for others. Cars emit fumes and create noise. This is bad enough for pedestrians and other car users, but can be particularly distressing for people living along the road. Driving can cause accidents, a problem that increases as drivers become more impatient as a result of delays. Also, as we saw in section 13.1, exhaust gases contribute to global warming and acid rain.

The socially efficient level of road usage

The point where the marginal social benefit of car use is equal to the marginal social cost can be illustrated on a diagram. In Figure 13.6, costs and benefits are shown on the vertical axis and are measured in money terms. Thus any non-monetary costs or benefits (such as time costs) must be given a monetary value. The horizontal axis measures road usage in terms of cars per minute passing a specified point on the road.

For simplicity it is assumed that there are no external benefits from car use and that therefore marginal private and marginal social benefits are the same. The *MSB* curve is shown as downward sloping. The reason for this is that different road users put a different value on this particular journey. If the marginal (private) cost of making the journey were high, only those for whom the journey had a high marginal benefit would travel along the road. If the marginal cost of making the journey fell, more people would make the journey: people choosing to make the journey at the point at which the marginal cost of using their car had fallen to the level of their marginal benefit. Thus the greater the number of cars in any given time period, the lower the marginal benefit.

The marginal (private) cost curve (*MC*) is likely to be constant up to the level of traffic flow at which congestion begins to occur. This is shown as point *a* in Figure 13.6. Beyond this point, marginal cost is likely to rise as time costs increase and as fuel consumption rises.

The marginal *social* cost curve (*MSC*) is drawn above the marginal private cost curve. The vertical difference between the two represents the external costs. Up to point *b*, external costs are simply the environmental costs. Beyond point *b*, there are also external congestion costs, since additional road users slow down the journey of *other* road users. These external costs get progressively greater as the volume of traffic increases (as column (5) of Table 13.3 illustrated).

The actual level of traffic flow will be at Q_1, where marginal private costs and benefits are equal (point *e*). The socially efficient level of traffic flow, however, will be at the lower level of Q_2, where marginal social costs and benefits are equal (point *d*). In other words, the existing system of allocating road space is likely to lead to an excessive level of road usage.

Identifying a socially optimum level of road space (long run)

In the long run, the supply of road space is not fixed. The authorities must therefore assess what new road schemes (if any) to adopt. This will involve the use of some form of *cost–benefit analysis* (see section 12.4).

The socially efficient level of construction will be where the marginal social benefit from construction is equal to the marginal social cost. This means that schemes should be adopted as long as their marginal social benefit exceeds their marginal social cost.

But how are these costs and benefits assessed in practice? Case Study 13.4 on the student website examines the procedure used in the UK.

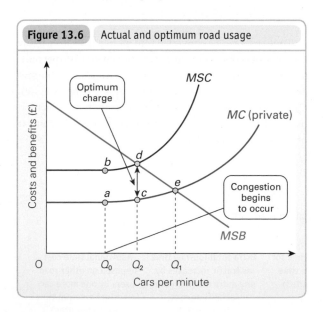

Figure 13.6 Actual and optimum road usage

Section summary

1. Increased car ownership and car usage have led to a growing problem of traffic congestion.

2. The allocation of road space depends on demand and supply. Demand depends on the price to motorists of using their cars, incomes, the cost of alternative means of transport, the price of cars and complementary services (such as parking), and the comfort and convenience of car transport. The price and cross-price elasticities of demand for car usage tend to be low: many people are unwilling to switch to alternative modes of transport. The income elasticity, on the other hand, is high. The demand for cars and car usage grows rapidly as incomes grow.

3. The short-run supply of road space is fixed. The long-run supply depends on government road construction programmes.

4. The existing system of government provision of roads and private ownership of cars is unlikely to lead to the optimum allocation of road space.

5. In the short run, with road space fixed, allocation depends on the private decisions of motorists. The problem is that motorists create two types of external cost: pollution costs and congestion costs. Thus $MSC > MC$. Because of these externalities, the actual use of road space (where $MB = MC$) is likely to be greater than the optimum (where $MSB = MSC$).

6. In the long run, the socially efficient amount of road space will be where $LRMSB = LRMSC$. New road schemes should be adopted as long as their $LRMSB > LRMSC$. Governments must therefore conduct some form of cost–benefit analysis in order to estimate these costs and benefits.

13.4 URBAN TRANSPORT POLICIES

We now turn to look at different solutions to traffic congestion. These can be grouped into three broad types: direct provision, regulation and legislation, and changing market signals.

Direct provision (supply-side solutions)

The road solution

One obvious solution to traffic congestion is to build more roads. There are, however, serious problems with this approach.

The objective of equity. The first problem concerns *equity*. After all, social efficiency is not the only possible economic objective. For example, when an urban motorway is built, those living beside it will suffer from noise and fumes. Motorway users gain, but the local residents lose. The question is whether this is fair.

The more the government tries to appeal to the car user by building more and better roads, the fewer will be the people who use public transport, and thus the more will public transport decline. Those without cars lose, and these tend to be from the most vulnerable groups – poor, elderly and disabled people, and children.

Building more roads may lead to a *potential* Pareto improvement: in other words, if the gainers had fully to compensate the losers (e.g. through taxes or tolls), they would still have a net gain. The problem is that such compensation is rarely if ever paid. There is thus no actual Pareto improvement.

Congestion may not be solved. Increasing the amount of road space may encourage more people to use cars.

A good example is the London orbital motorway, the M25. In planning the motorway, not only did the government underestimate the general rate of traffic growth, but it also underestimated the direct effect it would have in encouraging people to use the motorway rather than using some alternative route, or some alternative means of transport, or even not making the journey at all. It also underestimated the effect it would have in encouraging people to live further from their place of work and to commute along the motorway. The result is that there is now serious congestion on the motorway and many sections have been widened from the original dual three-lane model to dual four, five and, in some parts, six lanes.

Thus new roads may simply generate extra traffic, with little overall effect on congestion in the long term.

The environmental impact of new roads. New roads lead to the loss of agricultural land, the destruction of many natural habitats, noise, the splitting of communities and disruption to local residents. To the extent that they encourage a growth in traffic, they add to atmospheric pollution and a depletion of oil reserves. It is thus important to take account of these costs when assessing new road schemes. The problem, however, is that these environmental costs are frequently ignored, or only considered as an afterthought and not taken seriously. Part of the problem is that they are difficult to assess, and part is that there is often a strong road lobby which persuades politicians to ignore or play down environmental considerations.

Government or local authority provision of public transport

An alternative supply-side solution is to increase the provision of public transport. If, for example, a local authority ran a local bus service and decided to invest in additional buses, open up new routes and operate a low-fare policy, these services might encourage people to switch from using their cars.

To be effective, this would have to be an attractive alternative. Many people would switch only if the buses were frequent, cheap, comfortable and reliable, and if there were enough routes to take people close to where they wanted to go.

 What other types of transport could be directly provided by the government or a local authority?

A policy that has proved popular with many local authorities is to adopt park-and-ride schemes. Here the authority provides free or cheap out-of-town parking and cheap bus services from the car park to the town centre. These schemes are likely to be most effective when used in combination with charges for private cars entering the inner city.

Regulation and legislation

An alternative strategy is to restrict car use by various forms of regulation and legislation.

Restricting car access

One approach involves reducing car access to areas that are subject to high levels of congestion. The following measures are widely used: bus and cycle lanes, 'high occupancy vehicle lanes' (confined to cars with two or more occupants), pedestrian-only areas and no entry to side streets from main roads.

There is a serious problem, with these measures, however. They tend not to solve the problem of congestion, but merely to divert it. Bus lanes tend to make the car lanes more congested; no entry to side streets tends to make the main roads more congested; and pedestrian-only areas often make the roads round these areas more congested, with drivers adopting side streets as 'rat-runs'.

Parking restrictions

An alternative to restricting road access is to restrict parking. If cars are not allowed to park along congested streets, this will improve the traffic flow. Also, if parking is difficult, this will discourage people from using their cars to come into city centres.

Apart from being unpopular with people who want to park, there are some serious drawbacks with parking restrictions:

- People may well 'park in orbit', driving round and round looking for a parking space, and in the meantime adding to congestion.

- People may park illegally. This may add to rather than reduce congestion, and may create a safety hazard.
- People may feel forced to park down side streets in residential areas, thereby causing a nuisance for residents.

Changing market signals

The solution favoured by many economists is to use the price mechanism. As we have seen, one of the causes of traffic congestion is that road users do not pay the full marginal social costs of using the roads. If they could be forced to do so, a social optimum usage of road space could be achieved.

In Figure 13.6 (page 412) this would involve imposing a charge on motorists of $d-c$. By 'internalising' the congestion and environmental externalities in this way, traffic flow will be reduced to the social optimum of Q_2.

So how can these external costs be charged to the motorist? There are several possible ways.

Extending existing taxes

Three major types of tax are levied on the motorist: fuel tax (duty per litre plus VAT), taxes on new cars and car licences. Could increasing these taxes lead to the optimum level of road use being achieved?

Increasing the rates of new car tax and car licences may have *some* effect on reducing the total level of car ownership, but will probably have little effect on car use. The problem is that these taxes do not increase the *marginal* cost of car use and so do not discourage you from using your car.

Unlike the other two, fuel taxes are a marginal cost of car use. The more you use your car, the more fuel you use and the more fuel tax you pay. They are also mildly related to the level of congestion, since fuel consumption tends to increase as congestion increases. Nevertheless, they are not ideal. The problem is that *all* motorists would pay an increase in fuel tax, even those travelling on uncongested roads. To have a significant effect on congestion, there would have to be a very large increase in fuel taxes and this would be very unfair on those who are not causing congestion, especially those who have to travel long distances. Also, as the fuel protests in recent years have shown, increasing fuel taxes could make the government very unpopular.

 Would a tax on car tyres be a good way of restricting car usage?

Introducing new taxes

An alternative to extending existing taxes is to introduce new ones. One that has received much attention in recent times has been the taxing of car parking spaces, particularly those provided by businesses for their employees. The problem with taxing car parking, however, is similar to that of restricting car parking places: people may simply try to park on neighbouring streets (a negative externality imposed on residents), and may spend longer driving around trying to find a space (thereby adding to congestion in the process).

Road pricing

Taxes are inevitably an indirect means of tackling congestion. Charging people for using roads, on the other hand, where the size of the charge reflects the marginal social cost,

is a direct means of achieving an efficient use of road space. The higher the congestion, the higher should be the charge. This would encourage people not only to look for alternative means of transport, but also to travel, wherever possible, at off-peak times.

Variable tolls. Tolls are used in many countries, and could be adapted to reflect marginal social costs.

One obvious problem, however, is that, even with automatic tolls, there can be considerable tailbacks at peak times. Another problem is that they may simply encourage people to use minor roads into cities, thereby causing congestion on these roads. Cities have networks of streets and thus in most cases it is not difficult to avoid the tolls. Finally, if the tolls are charged to people *entering* the city, they will not affect *local* commuters. But it is these short-distance commuters *within* the city who are most likely to be able to find some alternative means of transport and who thus could make a substantial contribution to reducing congestion.

Area charges. One simple and practical means of charging people to use congested streets is the area charge. People would have to pay (normally by the day) for using their car in a city centre. Earlier versions of this scheme involved people having to purchase and display a ticket on their car, rather like a 'pay-and-display' parking system.

More recently, electronic versions have been developed. The introduction of the London Congestion Charge in February 2003 is an example. Car drivers must pay a standard charge of £11.50 per day to enter the inner London area (or 'congestion zone') any time between 7:00 and 18:00, Monday to Friday. Payment can be made by various means, including post, Internet, telephone, text message and at various shops and petrol stations. Drivers can obtain a £1 discount per day if they use an auto payment system, and are charged £14 if they pay before midnight the following day.

Cars entering the congestion zone have their number plate recorded by camera and a computer check then leads to a penalty charge of £130 being sent to those who have not paid.

A report by Transport for London estimated that traffic levels had fallen by 10 per cent in the first 10 years of the London Congestion Charge, although average traffic speeds have also fallen. One unanticipated benefit of the scheme is that it appears to have reduced the number of traffic accidents by 40 per cent.

The charge is not a marginal one in the sense that it does not vary with the degree of congestion or the amount of time spent or distance travelled by a motorist within the zone. This is an intrinsic problem of area charges. Nevertheless,

their simplicity makes the system easy to understand and relatively cheap to operate.

The London system does not address pollution directly. However, under the 'greener vehicle discount', cars that emitted 100g/km of CO_2 or less were exempt from the charge. This led to a big increase in low-emission diesel cars in London as they qualified for the discount. This prompted Transport for London to replace the 'greener vehicle discount' in April 2013 with the 'Ultra Low Emission Discount'. Vehicles will now have to either be purely electric or emit 75g/km of CO_2 or less to qualify.

The London Mayor, Sadiq Khan, announced that from October 2017 a new additional £10 emissions surcharge will be payable for older vehicles to enter the London Congestion Charge Zone. This *T-Charge* will be applied to cars and vans that do not meet Euro 4 standards.

There does appear to be a growing commitment to combine both congestion and emission external costs within the charge.

Variable electronic road pricing. The scheme most favoured by many economists and traffic planners is that of variable electronic road pricing. It is the approach that can most directly relate the price that the motorist is charged to the specific level of marginal social cost. The greater the congestion, the greater the charge imposed on the motorist. Ideally, the charge would be equal to the marginal congestion cost plus any marginal environmental costs additional to those created on non-charged roads.

Various systems have been adopted in various parts of the world, or are under consideration. One involves devices in the road which record the number plates of cars as they pass. Alternatively, cars may be required to be fitted with sensors. Charges are registered to cars on a central computer and owners are billed. Several cities around the world, including Barcelona, Dallas, Orlando, Lisbon, Oklahoma City and Oslo, are already operating such schemes.

Another system involves having a device installed in the car into which a 'smart card' is inserted. Beacons or overhead gantries automatically charge the cards at times of congestion. Such a system was introduced in 1997 on Stockholm's ring road, and in 1998 in Singapore (see Box 13.5).

With both these systems, the rate can easily be varied electronically according to the level of congestion (and pollution). The rates could be in bands and the current bands displayed by the roadside and/or broadcast on local radio so that motorists knew what they were being charged.

The most sophisticated scheme would involve equipping all vehicles with a receiver. Their position is located by satellites, which then send this information to a dashboard unit, which deducts charges according to location, distance travelled, time of day and type of vehicle. The charges can operate through either smart cards or central computerised billing. It is likely that such schemes would initially be confined to lorries.

BOX 13.5   ROAD PRICING IN SINGAPORE

Part of an integrated transport policy

Singapore has some 280 vehicles per kilometre of road (this compares with 271 in Hong Kong, 222 in Japan, 77 in the UK, 75 in Germany and 37 in the USA). The average car in Singapore is driven some 17 500 kilometres per year, but with low car ownership (see below), this translates into a relatively low figure for kilometres travelled by car per person. Part of the reason is that Singapore has an integrated transport policy. This includes the following:

- A 171-kilometre-long mass rail transit (MRT) system with five main lines, 102 stations and subsidised fares. Trains are comfortable, clean and frequent. Stations are air-conditioned.
- A programme of building new estates near MRT stations.
- Cheap, frequent buses, serving all parts of the island.
- A modest expansion of expressways.

But it is in respect to road usage that the Singaporean authorities have been most innovative.

Area licences

The first innovation came in 1975 when the Area Licensing Scheme (ALS) was introduced. The city centre was made a restricted zone. Motorists who wished to enter this zone had to buy a ticket (an 'area licence') at any one of 33 entry points. Police were stationed at these entry points to check that cars had paid and displayed. This scheme was extended to the major expressways in 1995 with the introduction of the Road Pricing Scheme (RPS).

The Vehicle Quota System

In 1990, the government also introduced restrictions on the number of new cars, known as the Vehicle Quota System. In order to register and drive a new vehicle in Singapore, the owner has to purchase a Certificate of Entitlement (COE) which is valid for 10 years. The quantity of COEs issued by the government is limited and the number available each year is announced in April. The COEs are then sold to the public via monthly auctions which are operated in a similar manner to those on the eBay system. Buyers specify a maximum price and bids are automatically revised upwards until that maximum price is reached. The price of COEs increases until the quantity demanded is just equal to the number of certificates on offer.

Partly as a result of the quota system, there are only 114 private cars per 1000 population. As you can see from Figure 13.5 on page 410, this is only a fraction of the figure for European countries.

A problem with the licences is that they are a once-and-for-all payment, which does not vary with the amount people use their car. In other words, their marginal cost (for additional miles driven) is zero. Many people feel that, having paid such a high price for their licence, they ought to use their car as much as possible in order to get value for money!

Electronic road pricing

With traffic congestion steadily worsening, it was recognised that something more had to be done. In 1998, a new Electronic Road Pricing Scheme (ERP) replaced the Area Licensing Scheme for restricted areas and the Road Pricing Scheme for expressways. This alternative not only saves on police labour costs, but enables charge rates to be varied according to levels of congestion, times of the day and locality. How does it work?

All vehicles in Singapore are fitted with an in-vehicle unit (IU). Every journey made requires the driver to insert a smart card into the IU. On specified roads, overhead gantries read the IU and deduct the appropriate charge from the card. If a car does not have sufficient funds on its smart card, the car's details are relayed to a control centre and a fine is imposed. The system has the benefit of operating on three-lane highways and does not require traffic to slow down.

The ERP system operates on roads subject to congestion and charges can vary every 5, 20 or 30 minutes according to predicted traffic flows. Rates are published in advance for a three-month period: e.g. from 20 February until 30 April 2017. A review of traffic conditions takes place every quarter and the results can lead to rates being adjusted in future periods. The system is thus very flexible to allow traffic to be kept at the desired level.

One potential problem with charging different rates at different times is that some drivers may substantially speed up or slow down as they approach the gantries to avoid paying higher ERP charges. To try to overcome this problem the ERP rates are adjusted gradually for the first five minutes of a time slot with either new higher or lower charges.

The authorities in Singapore are now testing the use of a Global Navigation Satellite System. This would remove the need for the overhead gantries. It would also make it possible to alter the size of the charge with the length of the congested road the driver has travelled along. There are plans for this system to become operational in 2020.

The ERP system was expensive to set up, however. Cheaper schemes have been adopted elsewhere, such as Norway and parts of the USA. These operate by funnelling traffic into a single lane in order to register the car, but they have the disadvantage of slowing the traffic down.

One message is clear from the Singapore solution. Road pricing alone is not enough. Unless there are fast, comfortable and affordable public transport alternatives, the demand for cars will be highly price inelastic. People have to get to work!

 Explain how, by varying the charge debited from the smart card according to the time of day or level of congestion, a socially optimal level of road use can be achieved.

Despite the enthusiasm for such schemes amongst economists, there are nevertheless various problems associated with them:

■ Estimates of the level of external costs are difficult to make.

■ Motorists have to be informed in advance what the charges will be, so that they can plan the timing of their journeys.

■ There may be political resistance. Politicians may therefore be reluctant to introduce road pricing for fear of losing popular support.

■ If demand is relatively inelastic, the charges might have to be very high to have a significant effect on congestion.

■ The costs of installing road-pricing equipment could be very high.

■ If road pricing were introduced only in certain areas, shoppers and businesses would tend to move to areas without the charge.

■ A new industry in electronic evasion may spring up!

Subsidising alternative means of transport

An alternative to charging for the use of cars is to subsidise the price of alternatives, such as buses and trains. But cheaper fares alone may not be enough. The government may also have to invest directly in or subsidise an *improved* public transport service: more frequent services, more routes, more comfortable buses and trains.

Subsidising public transport need not be seen as an alternative to road pricing: it can be seen as complementary. If road pricing is to persuade people not to travel by car, the alternatives must be attractive. Unless public transport is seen by the traveller as a close substitute for cars, the elasticity of demand for car use is likely to remain low. This problem is recognised by the UK government, which encourages local authorities to use various forms of road pricing and charges on businesses for employee car parking spaces on condition that the revenues generated are ploughed back into improved public transport. All local authorities have to produce five-year Local Transport Plans covering all forms of transport. These include targets for traffic reduction and increases in the use of public transport.

Subsidising public transport can also be justified on grounds of equity, since it is used most by low-income groups.

 Which is preferable: general subsidies for public transport, or cheap fare policies for specific groups (such as children, students and pensioners)?

Conclusions

It is unlikely that any one policy can provide the complete solution. Certain policies or mixes of policies are better suited to some situations than others. It is important for governments to learn from experiences both within their own country and in others, in order to find the optimum solution to each specific problem.

Section summary

1. There are various types of solution to traffic congestion. These include direct provision by the government or local authorities (of additional road space or better public transport); regulation and legislation (such as restricting car access – by the use of bus and cycle lanes, or pedestrian-only areas – and various forms of parking restrictions); changing market signals (by the use of taxes, by road pricing, and by subsidising alternative means of transport).

2. Problems associated with building additional roads include the decline of public transport, attracting additional traffic onto the roads, and environmental costs.

3. The main problem with restricting car access is that it tends merely to divert congestion elsewhere. The main problem with parking restrictions is that they may actually increase congestion.

4. Increasing taxes is effective in reducing congestion only if it increases the marginal cost of motoring. Even when it does, as in the case of additional fuel tax, the additional cost is only indirectly related to congestion costs, since it applies to all motorists and not just those causing congestion.

5. Road pricing is the preferred solution of many economists. By the use of electronic devices, motorists can be charged whenever they add to congestion. This should encourage less essential road users to travel at off-peak times or to use alternative modes of transport, while those who gain a high utility from car transport can still use their cars, but at a price. Variable tolls and area charges are alternative forms of congestion pricing, but are generally less effective than the use of variable electronic road pricing.

6. If road pricing is to be effective, there must be attractive substitutes available. A comprehensive policy, therefore, should include subsidising efficient public transport. The revenues required for this could be obtained from road pricing.

BOX 13.6   THE ECONOMY AND THE ENVIRONMENT

Green growth: a way forward

Recessions are generally bad news: output and jobs are lost, and both consumers and businesses face uncertainty. Yet in the short run, a slump may have positive environmental effects. Between 2007 and 2008 road traffic fell by 0.8 per cent, with further falls of 0.9 and 1.6 per cent in 2009 and 2010 respectively.[1] Probable causes were lower incomes, less freight being transported and fewer people driving to work. Non-renewable resources are depleted more slowly in a downturn, as households reduce consumption, increase recycling and reuse items that they might have discarded in a boom.

In other ways, however, a recession may lead to faster environmental degradation. Businesses are less likely to invest in clean technologies; consumers may put off replacing vehicles with more energy-efficient models; governments may choose to divert resources from environmental initiatives to job creation schemes.

Economic growth and the green agenda

Think back to the first chapter of this book, where we identified the fundamental economic problem of scarcity. We demonstrated how economic growth can provide a solution; allowing us to produce more and so satisfy more of our wants and needs. (We consider economic growth in more detail in Chapters 15 and 23).

In general, economists and politicians have presented economic growth as a 'good thing', resulting in higher levels of welfare and giving society the opportunity to redistribute further to reduce poverty. However, there has been less wholehearted support from the green lobby. Economic growth has been portrayed as fundamentally harmful with a widespread acceptance of the principle that there is a trade-off between growth and degradation of the environment.

The idea that growth may not be beneficial is not a new one. In 1848, John Stuart Mill wrote, 'Towards what ultimate point is society tending by its industrial progress? When the progress ceases, in what condition are we to expect that it will leave mankind?' In 1973, an influential collection of essays by E. F. Schumacher called *Small is Beautiful* was published (see Case Study 1.1 on the student website). This work led the debate on growth and its impact on well-being – a debate that continues today.

If you spend your time thinking that the most important objective of public policy is to get growth up from 1.9 per cent to 2 per cent and even better 2.1 per cent we're pursuing a sort of false god there. We're pursuing it first of all because, if we accept that, we will do things to the climate that will be harmful, but also because all the evidence shows that beyond the sort of standard of living which Britain has now achieved, extra growth does not

END OF CHAPTER QUESTIONS

1. Assume that as traffic density increases along a given stretch of road, there comes a point when traffic begins to slow down. The following table gives the times taken for a car to travel the stretch of road (in minutes) according to the number of cars entering the road per minute.

Cars entering the road	5	6	7	8	9	10	11
Journey time		10	10	11	13	16	22	30

(a) Copy out the table and add the following rows: (i) total journey time for all cars; (ii) extra journey time as traffic increases by one more car (marginal social time cost); (iii) additional time cost imposed on other road users for each additional car entering the road (marginal external time cost). (See Table 13.3.)

(b) Assume that time is valued at 10p per minute. On a graph, plot the marginal private time cost (journey time) and the marginal social time cost.

(c) Assume that electronic road pricing is introduced. What charge should be levied when traffic density reaches (i) 6 cars per minute; (ii) 8 cars per minute; (iii) 11 cars per minute?

(d) What additional information would you need in order to work out the socially efficient traffic density on this particular stretch of road?

2. Assume that there are several chemical firms in an industry, each one producing different levels of an effluent, whose damage to the environment depends on the location of the firm. Compare the relative merits of using green taxes, tradable permits and controls as means of achieving the socially optimum levels of effluent from these firms.

automatically translate into human welfare and happiness.[2] (*Lord Turner, Previously Chair of the UK Financial Services Authority*)

In 2010, the New Economics Foundation published a report, titled 'Growth isn't possible. Why we need a new economic direction'. In this they argued that economic growth is constrained by the finite capacity of the earth's resources.[3]

However, given the levels of poverty seen across the world, a reduced commitment to growth must imply continuing inequality or an acceptance that industrialised countries will experience lower standards of living. This is unthinkable to many, who instead focus on achieving growth in a sustainable manner: one that allows for increased welfare while ensuring the long-term health of the planet. Much of the OECD's work in the environmental arena concentrates on this aspect – hardly surprising, given its remit to support global development. In 2012, it highlighted three issues which governments should consider in formulating growth policies:

■ Putting a price on carbon emissions and other pollution.
■ Supporting green innovation and ensuring that this spreads across national borders.
■ Fostering private investment in capital that will support growth with cleaner technologies.

The OECD acknowledges that various governments across the world are making efforts to promote greener development. The European Union's *Growth Strategy for 2020*, Korea's National Strategy and five-year plan for Green Growth, the green development focus of China's 12th five-year Plan and South Africa's *New Growth Path* and *Green Economy Accord* are just a few examples.

1. *The UK government introduced a 'scrappage scheme' in 2009 to run for one year. Under this, motorists were given a £2000 grant towards the cost of a new car. To qualify they had to trade in a car that was more than 10 years old, which would then be scrapped. Explain how this scheme might be justified in the middle of a recession. Should there have been any restrictions on the new cars eligible for the grant?*
2. *Growth is largely seen as being associated with economic efficiency. Explain how it may also be an important issue when considering equity.*
3. *Under what circumstances will private investment be attracted to 'green' projects? Is there a role for government here?*

1 Transport Statistics Great Britain 2013, Department of Transport.
2 Quoted in *Growth Isn't Possible. Why We Need a New Economic Direction* (New Economics Foundation, 25 January 2010).
3 Ibid.

3. Make out a case from a deep green perspective for rejecting the 'social efficiency' approach to the environment.
4. Why might efforts to address the issue of global warming be hampered by a lack of understanding of probability amongst the general public?
5. In 2007, China overtook the USA as the world's largest emitter of CO_2. Yet USA per capita emissions are three times those of China. What issues arise from this in the formulation of a global policy to reduce CO_2 emissions?
6. Make out a case for adopting a policy of individual tradable carbon permits, allocated to all citizens within a country. Could such a policy be extended globally?
7. Compare the relative merits of increased road fuel taxes, electronic road pricing and tolls as means of reducing urban traffic congestion.
8. Why is the price inelasticity of demand for private car transport a problem when formulating a policy for the reduction of traffic congestion? What could be done to

change the price elasticity of demand in a desirable direction?
9. How would you set about measuring the external costs of road transport?
10. Many London councils now have residents' street parking permits, with charges that vary according to the carbon emissions of the registered vehicle. Explain the thinking behind this policy.
11. Since 2008, the UK government has provided free off-peak bus travel for the over-60s in England and Wales. What do you think the impact of this policy has been on car usage? Is there a case for extending the policy to (a) bus travel for pensioners at all times of the day, as is the case in Scotland; (b) bus travel for all?
12. In 2010, the number of air passengers using UK airports fell by 3.4 per cent compared with 2009. In 2015, passengers were 5.5 per cent up compared with 2014. Can we deduce anything about people's attitude to the environment and their behaviour from these data?

Online resources

Additional case studies on the student website

13.1 Perverse subsidies. An examination of the use of subsidies around the world that are harmful to the environment.

13.2 Selling the environment. This looks at the proposals made at international climate conferences to use market-based solutions to global warming.

13.3 Environmental auditing. Are businesses becoming greener? A growing number of firms are subjecting themselves to an 'environmental audit' to judge just how 'green' they are.

13.4 Evaluating new road schemes. The system used in the UK of assessing the costs and benefits of proposed new roads.

Websites relevant to this chapter

See sites listed at the end of Chapter 14 on page 441.

Government Policy towards Business

In this chapter we continue our examination of government policy to tackle market imperfections. The focus here is on the problem of market power. We examine various policies the government or its agencies can use to prevent firms abusing a monopolistic or oligopolistic position.

In section 14.1 we examine 'competition policy'. We will see that the targets of such policy include the abuse of monopoly power, the problem of oligopolistic collusion, and mergers that will result in the firm having a dominant position in the market.

Then in section 14.2, we look at privatisation and the extent to which privatised industries should be regulated to prevent them abusing their market power. We also consider whether it is possible to introduce enough competition into these industries to make regulation unnecessary.

The relationship between government and business is always likely to be complex. Governments face the twin pressures of having to ensure consumer protection while needing a dynamic and profitable business environment that will ensure high levels of employment, output and growth. In this chapter we see the conflicts that can arise as a consequence.

14.1   COMPETITION POLICY

Competition, monopoly and the public interest

Most markets in the real world are imperfect, with firms having varying degrees of market power. But will this power be against the public interest? This question has been addressed by successive governments in framing legislation to deal with monopolies and oligopolies.

It might be thought that market power is always 'a bad thing', certainly as far as the consumer is concerned. After all, it enables firms to make supernormal profit, which implies they may be 'exploiting' the consumer. The greater the firm's power, the higher will prices be relative to the costs of production. Also, a lack of competition removes the incentive to become more efficient.

But market power is not necessarily a bad thing. Firms may choose not to fully exploit their position of power – perhaps thinking that very high profits would encourage other firms to overcome entry barriers, or perhaps because they are not aggressive profit maximisers. Even if they do make large supernormal profits, they may still charge a lower price than more competitive sectors of the industry because of their economies of scale. Finally, they may use profits for research and development and for capital investment. The consumer might then benefit from new or improved products at lower prices.

Competition policy could ban various structures. For example, there could be restrictions on mergers leading to market share of more than a certain amount. Most countries, however, focus on whether the practices of particular monopolists or oligopolists are anti-competitive. Some practices may be made illegal, such as price fixing by oligopolists; others may be assessed on a case-by-case basis. Such an approach does not presume that the existence of power is against the public interest, but rather that certain uses of that power may be.

 Try to formulate a definition of 'the public interest'.

The targets of competition policy

There are three possible targets of competition policy.

Abuse of the existing power of monopolies and oligopolies: monopoly policy

Monopoly policy seeks to prevent firms from abusing a dominant market position: i.e. misusing their economic power. Although it is referred to as 'monopoly' policy, it also applies to large oligopolists facing very limited competition. For example, most competition agencies consider a market share greater than 50 per cent as strong evidence that a firm has a dominant position. Once a position of dominance has been identified, the competition agencies usually weigh up the gains and losses to the public of the firm's behaviour.

As we saw in Figure 7.8 (on page 205), faced with the same cost curves as an industry under perfect competition, a monopoly will charge a higher price, produce a lower output and make a larger profit. This is called an *exploitative abuse* – a business practice that directly harms the customer. Other examples include reductions in product quality, limited product ranges and poor levels of customer service. However, a monopolist may achieve substantial economies of scale, with lower costs and a price below the competitive price (see Figure 7.11 on page 207). It may also retain profits for investment and research and development (R&D). This may result in better products and/or lower prices.

Thus the government (or regulatory authority, if separate from the government) has to work out whether a reduction in price would lower R&D and other investment, and whether the consumer would gain in the long run.

Competition authorities have tended to avoid investigating allegations of exploitative abuses because of the challenges involved with correctly identifying and correcting for this type of behaviour. For example, measuring differences between price and costs is very difficult in reality and requires the processing of large amounts of complex information supplied by the firm involved. Regulating prices is also a complicated process. For these reasons, competition agencies have spent most of their time investigating allegations of *exclusionary abuses*.

Exclusionary abuses. These are business practices that limit or prevent effective competition from either actual or potential rivals, for example by creating strategic barriers to entry. Exclusionary abuses may be a necessary condition before firms can implement the more direct exploitative abuses. If a business successfully limits or prevents competition today it may enable the firm to exploit consumers by charging higher prices in the future.

Some of the more frequently cited examples of exclusionary abuses in competition cases include:

- *Predatory pricing.* Prices are set by a dominant firm below its average variable costs with the sole intent of driving its competitor(s) out of business.

Definitions

Exploitative abuse A business practice that directly harms the customer. Examples include high prices and poor quality.

Exclusionary abuses Business practices that limit or prevent effective competition from either actual or potential rivals.

- *Exclusivity rebates/discounts.* Customers are offered special deals if they agree to make 'all or most' of their purchases of the product from the dominant firm. See Box 14.2 for an interesting real-world example.
- *Tying.* This is where a firm controlling the supply of a first product (the tying product), insists that its customers buy a second product (the tied product) from it rather from its rivals.
- *Refusal to supply and margin squeeze.* This occurs where a vertically integrated firm has a dominant position in an upstream market (e.g. components) but faces competition in later stages of the production process (e.g. assembly). If competitors in the downstream market are completely reliant on the supply of some input from the dominant firm in the upstream market, then the dominant firm could *refuse to supply* them. Its aim would be to drive them out of business, thereby giving it a dominant position in the downstream market too. Rather than blatantly refusing to supply its downstream competitors, a more subtle approach for the dominant firm would be to charge high prices for the input so that its rivals are unable to cover their costs and therefore go out of business. This is called **margin squeeze**.
- *Price discrimination.* This would be an abuse if the lower prices are used to drive competitors out of business.
- *Vertical restraints.* This is where a supplying firm imposes conditions on a purchasing firm (or vice versa). For example, a manufacturer may impose rules on retailers about displaying the product or the provision of after-sales service, or it may refuse to supply certain outlets (e.g. perfume manufacturers refusing to supply discount chemist shops).

The growth of power through mergers and acquisitions: merger policy

The aim of merger policy is to have oversight of prospective mergers. The authorities will weigh up gains and losses to the public and the impact on the broader economy, and prevent or modify those that are considered to be against the public interest.

On the plus side, the merged firms may be able to rationalise and reduce costs. Horizontal mergers in particular may allow economies of scale to be gained, with production on fewer sites and more intensive utilisation of capital and labour. Also, a more efficient use may be made of warehousing and transport fleets, with distribution in greater bulk.

There may also be potential benefits with vertical mergers. It may be possible to concentrate various stages in the production process on one site, with consequent savings in transport and handling costs.

There are also cost savings that apply to all types of merger: horizontal, vertical and conglomerate. Central services such as finance and human resources (HR) can be merged and rationalised. Greater financial strength may allow the merged firm to drive down the prices charged by

its suppliers and the combined profits may allow larger-scale investment and R&D.

However, mergers inevitably lead to a greater concentration of economic power, which could be used against the consumer's interests. This is particularly true of horizontal mergers, which will result in fewer firms and reduced consumer choice. But even conglomerate mergers can lead to anti-competitive activities. A conglomerate can use profits gained in one market where it already has monopoly power to *cross-subsidise* prices in a competitive market, thereby driving out competitors.

 What are the possible disadvantages of vertical mergers?

In deciding how tough to be with mergers, the government must consider how this will affect firms' behaviour. If the government adopts a liberal policy, this may actually encourage firms to be more efficient. If the managers of a firm are aware that it could be taken over, there is a greater incentive to ensure that the firm is strong and that it is perceived by shareholders to be more profitable than it would be under alternative ownership. This competition for corporate control (see pages 210–11) may lower costs and benefit the consumer. It may, however, make firms keener to exploit any monopoly power, enabling the takeover of other firms, or persuading shareholders not to vote for being taken over.

Government policy towards corporate control will need to ensure that potential mergers encourage competition rather than reduce it.

Oligopolistic collusion: restrictive practice policy

In most countries, the approach towards oligopolistic collusion, known as **restrictive practices**, tends to be more prohibitive than for mergers and monopoly power. This is because there is a much smaller chance that agreements to restrict, limit or prevent competition will ever be in the interests of society. The most likely outcome is higher joint profits for the firms and higher prices for the customer.

Definitions

Tying Where a firm is only prepared to sell a first product (the tying good) on the condition that its consumers buy a second product from it (the tied good).

Margin squeeze Where a vertically integrated firm with a dominant position in an upstream market deliberately charges high prices for an input required by firms in a downstream market to drive them out of business.

Vertical restraints Conditions imposed by one firm on another which is either its supplier or its customer.

Cross-subsidise To use profits in one market to subsidise prices in another.

Restrictive practices Where two or more firms agree to adopt common practices to restrict competition.

Examples of restrictive practices that are commonly cited in competition cases include

- *Horizontal price fixing.* These are direct or indirect agreements between rival firms to fix prices above competitive levels. There are a number of different ways that firms can make price agreements:
  - Set a minimum level below which prices will not be reduced.
  - Adhere to a published price list.
  - Increase prices by a fixed absolute or percentage amount.
  - Charge customers the same amount for delivery.
  - Pass on all additional costs in higher prices.
- *Market sharing.* These are agreements on how to distribute markets or customers between the firms. This could be done by geographical area, type of product or type of customer. For example, two or more supermarket chains could agree to open only one supermarket in each district.
- *Limit production.* Firms agree quotas on how much each should produce.
- *Bid rigging.* In response to a call for tenders, firms agree to discuss bids with one another rather than submitting them independently. They could agree on high-priced bids, with one of the firms (agreed in turn, possibly) submitting a slightly lower price. Or one or more of them may agree not to submit a bid, withdraw a bid, or submit a bid at an artificially high price.
- *Information sharing.* Firms share sensitive information with one another, such as future plans on pricing, product design and output.

 Are all such agreements necessarily against the interests of consumers?

Banning formal cartels is relatively easy. Preventing tacit collusion is another matter. It may be very difficult to prove that firms are making informal agreements behind closed doors.

Competition policy in the European Union

Relevant EU legislation is contained in Articles 101 and 102 of the 2009 Treaty of the Functioning of the European Union (TFEU). Additional regulations covering mergers came into force in 1990 and were amended in 2004. Further minor amendments have since been introduced, and many of these focus on specific market regulation.

TC 7
p81

Definition

Bid rigging Where two or more firms secretly agree on the prices they will tender for a contract. These prices will be above those that would have been submitted under a genuinely competitive tendering process.

Article 101 is concerned with restrictive practices and Article 102 with the abuse of market power. The Articles focus on firms trading between EU members and do not cover monopolies or oligopolies operating solely within a member country. They are implemented by the European Commission (EC), which monitors compliance, investigates behaviour and imposes fines where unlawful conduct is identified.

Firms can appeal against EC judgments to the *General Court* – formerly known as the *Court of First Instance*. The General Court has the power to overturn decisions made by the EC and is able to amend the size of any fines. The EC and/or the firms involved in the case can appeal against decisions made by the *General Court* to the *European Court of Justice*. However, appeals to the *European Court of Justice* can only be made on points of law.

EU restrictive practices policy

Article 101 covers agreements between firms, joint decisions and concerted practices that prevent, restrict or distort competition. In other words, it covers all types of oligopolistic collusion that are against the interests of consumers.

The legislation is designed to prevent collusive *behaviour* not oligopolistic *structures* (i.e. the simple existence of co-operation between firms). For example, agreements between oligopolists are exempt from Article 101 if they meet all of the following conditions: (a) they directly enhance the quality of the good/service for the customer; (b) they are the only way to do so; (c) they do not eliminate competition; (d) consumers receive a fair share of the resulting benefits.

If companies are found guilty of undertaking any anti-competitive practices that are in contravention of Article 101 such as those discussed above, they are ordered to cease the activity with immediate effect and are subject to financial penalties.

Fines. Table 14.1 illustrates the largest fines imposed by the EC on individual companies involved in cartel activity.

Four of the largest seven fines relate to just one case. The EC ruled in July 2016 that the truck producers MAN, Volvo/Renault, Daimler, Iveco and DAF were guilty of operating a cartel.[1] In particular, they colluded over the factory price of

Table 14.1	Highest EC cartel fines per firm		
Year	**Firm**	**Case**	**Amount in €**
2016	Daimler	Trucks	1 008 766 000
2016	DAF	Trucks	752 679 000
2008	Saint-Gobain	Car glass	715 000 000
2012	Philips	TV/computer monitor tubes	705 296 000
2012	LG Electronics	TV/computer monitor tubes	687 537 000
2016	Volvo/Renault	Trucks	670 448 000
2016	Iveco	Trucks	494 606 000

1 'Commission fines truck producers €2.93 billion for participating in a cartel', Press release (European Commission, 19 July 2016).

trucks for 14 years and agreed to pass on the compliance costs of stricter EU emissions rules to their customers.

The size of any fine imposed on an organisation depends on a number of factors. Initially, the authorities calculate the annual revenue generated by the firms from the sales of the products directly influenced by the activities that restricted competition. These are referred to as the 'relevant sales'. For example, in the paper envelope case referred to in Box 14.1, the Commission estimated that the company 'Bong' had made sales worth €140 million from the cartel activities it had undertaken with four other companies.

The initial size of the basic fine is then calculated by taking a percentage of the value of these annual relevant sales, up to a maximum of 30 per cent, but typically between 15 and 20 per cent. The percentage chosen is based on the severity of the abuse, which depends on factors such as the market shares of the companies involved and the size of the geographical area affected by the practices.

Once this initial figure has been calculated it is then multiplied by the number of years the firms have been in contravention of Article 101. In the case of the truck manufacturers, this 'duration multiplier' was 14.

An additional amount is then added to the size of the fine and is known as an 'entry fee'. This is once again calculated as a percentage of the value of the firm's relevant sales. However, this figure is not adjusted by a duration multiplier.

The figure is then adjusted for either aggravating or mitigating factors. For example, the fine on a company could be increased if it was a repeat offender or seen as the 'ringleader', or reduced if it was judged to have been far less actively involved in the cartel's activities.

The final size of the basic fine imposed on a firm is capped and cannot be greater than 10 per cent of that firm's annual total revenue. This is only likely to affect fines where the cartel activities form a large part of the firm's business (as was the case in the paper envelope investigation discussed in Box 14.1).

Reducing fines through co-operation with the Commission. The size of this basic fine can be reduced if members of a cartel provide information that helps the Commission with its investigations. Such firms would be granted a 'Leniency Notice'. To qualify for this they would have to provide detailed information about cartel meetings and exactly how the anti-competitive practices operated. The first company to supply this type of information can be granted full immunity and not have to pay anything (Type 1A leniency) if this is a new case the company is bringing to the Commission's notice. If it is already being investigated by the Commission, the first company to provide detailed information would *possibly* receive full immunity at the discretion of the Commission (Type 1B leniency). In the truck manufacturing case, MAN was awarded full immunity under Type 1A leniency as it had revealed the existence of the cartel to the Commission in the first place. It, therefore, did not have to pay a fine.

Other companies supplying information can be given reduced fines (Type 2 leniency). The second company to come forward with this type of information can receive a reduction of up to 50 per cent, the third of up to 30 per cent and any firm after this of up to 20 per cent.

Firms can receive a further 10 per cent reduction if they accept the Commission's decision and the size of any financial penalties imposed on them. This is referred to as a Settlement. By speeding up the final decision process it can reduce the administrative costs to the parties involved and avoid the legal costs of any possible appeals.

The aim of all these reductions is to encourage firms to co-operate with the authorities. They further increase the incentive for each firm to cheat on the other members of the cartel to avoid any financial penalties.

EU monopoly policy

Article 102 relates to the abuse of a dominant market position and has also been extended to cover mergers. The implementation of the policy follows a two-stage process.

First, the EC has to define the relevant market: i.e. identify which products and suppliers are close substitutes for one another. Then it has to decide if the firm has a dominant position in this market. To do so it will look at factors such as market shares, the position of competitors, the bargaining strength of customers, measures of profitability and the existence of any significant barriers to entry – see the case in Box 14.2 for an example.

Second, if the evidence confirms that the firm does have a dominant position, the EC will then assess whether the firm is using its market power to restrict competition. As previously discussed, the focus tends to be on exclusionary as opposed to exploitative abuses of power.

If a business is found guilty of engaging in exclusionary abuses that contravene Article 102, such as those discussed on page 422, they are ordered to cease the activities with immediate effect and are subject to financial penalties.

The fines for any infringements of Article 102 are calculated in a very similar manner to those for infringements of Article 101: a percentage is taken of the annual revenue generated from the sale of the products affected by the illegal conduct. This figure is then multiplied by a duration multiplier but, unlike the cartel fine, no entry fee is charged.

Article 102 also contains some guidance on how a dominant firm can defend its behaviour on efficiency grounds. The business has to prove each of the following:

■ Any efficiencies are the direct result of the exclusionary conduct.
■ The same efficiencies could not be achieved by the firm engaging in different behaviour that is less anti-competitive.
■ The efficiencies produced by the exclusionary conduct outweigh any of its negative effects.
■ The conduct does not result in the removal of all or most of the competition in the market.

BOX 14.1 FIXING PRICES AT MINI-GOLF MEETINGS?

The EU approach to cartels

In September 2010, the European Commission began an investigation into the market for both standardised and customised paper envelopes in the EU. In December 2014, the Commission found Bong (of Sweden), GPV and Hamelin (of France), Mayer-Kuvert (of Germany) and Tompla (of Spain) guilty of participating in activities that restricted competition in this market. The meetings at which the details of the cartel arrangements were discussed were referred to by the participating firms as 'golf' or 'mini-golf' meetings!

The cartel arrangements directly affected the market for envelopes in Denmark, France, Germany, Norway, Sweden and the UK. The firms were judged to have been involved in the following restrictive practices that were in violation of Article 101:

- allocating customers amongst members of the cartel: i.e. agreeing not to target customers that 'belonged' to other firms;
- agreeing on price increases;
- co-ordinating responses to tenders initiated by major European customers;
- exchanging commercially sensitive information on customers and sales volumes.

Details of the sales of the companies and the fines imposed are given in the table.

The proportion of the value of sales used to calculate the size of the fine was set at 15 per cent in this case (see row 2 of the table). Four out of the five firms began taking part in the

		Bong	GPV group	Hamelin	Meyer-Kuvert	Tompla
1.	Value of relevant sales (€)	140 000 000	125 086 629	185 521 000	70 023 181	143 316 000
2.	Percentage (15%) of the value of relevant sales (€)	21 000 000	18 762 994	27 828 15	10 503 477	21 497 00
3.	Duration multiplier	4.5	4.5	4.416	4.5	4.5
4.	Duration multiplier × 15% of sales (€)	94 500 000	84 433 475	122 889 110	47 265 646	96 738 300
5.	Plus the entry fee (€) (= row 2)	21 000 000	18 762 994	27 828 150	10 503 477	21 497 400
6	Basic fine (€) (= rows 4 + 5)	115 500 000	103 196 000	150 717 260	57 769 000	118 235 000
7	Final fine	3 118 000	1 651 000	4 996 000	4 991 000	4 729 000

EU merger policy

Under current regulations (2004), mergers and acquisitions (M&As) are prohibited which would significantly reduce competition in the EU.[2] For example, a merger could be blocked if there were concerns that the newly created firm would have significant market power and lead to higher prices for consumers.

Therefore, the EU investigates 'large' M&As that have an 'EU dimension'. A merger or acquisition is judged as having an 'EU dimension' when no more than two-thirds of each firm's EU-wide business is conducted in a single member state. If a firm does conduct more than two-thirds of its business in one country, then investigation of the merger would be the responsibility of that member state's competition authority.

Thresholds. M&As are deemed 'large' if they exceed one or other of two turnover thresholds.

The first threshold is exceeded if (a) the firms involved have combined worldwide sales greater than €5 billion and (b) at least two of the firms individually have sales of more than €250 million within the EU.

The second threshold is exceeded if (a) the firms involved have combined worldwide sales of more than €2.5 billion; (b) in each of at least three member states, combined sales of all firms involved are greater than €100 million; (c) in each of the three member states, at least two of the firms each have domestic sales greater than €25 million; and (d) EU-wide sales of each of at least two firms is greater than €100 million.

If either of these thresholds is exceeded and the intended merger or acquisition is judged to have an EU dimension, then formal notification of the intention has to be made by the firms to the European Commission. There were 362 notifications in 2016 and the figure has been around 300 per year since 1998.

Investigations. Once a notification is made, the Commission must carry out a preliminary investigation (Phase 1), which is normally completed within 25 days working days. At the end of Phase 1 the majority of cases (over 90 per cent) are usually settled and the merger is either allowed to proceed unconditionally or subject to certain conditions being met. These conditions usually relate to the sale of some of the assets of the newly formed business. See Box 14.3 for an interesting example.

2 See http://ec.europa.eu/competition/mergers/overview_en.html

cartel on 8 October 2003 and their involvement in anti-competitive activities lasted until 22 April 2008. Therefore, for these firms the duration multiplier (row 3) was set at 4.5. Hamelin was judged to have entered the cartel a month later than the other participants so the multiplier in its case was set at 4.416. A percentage rate of 15 per cent was also used to calculate the entry fee (row 5). The final figures for the basic amounts of the fine are illustrated in row 7 of the table, which the Commission rounded down to the nearest €1000.

It was considered to be an exceptional case as the sales of envelopes affected by the cartel activities made up a large fraction of each firm's total turnover. Therefore, the unadjusted basic fines would exceed the 10 per cent cap on turnover set by the authorities. The fines were reduced in a way that took account of (a) the value of affected sales for each firm as a proportion of their turnover and (b) the level of involvement in the restrictive practices. Unfortunately, the size of each firm's basic fine, after these adjustments, are not published in the non-confidential report.

Under the Commission's 2006 Leniency Notice we do know that Tompla received a 50 per cent reduction in the size of its adjusted basic fine, Hamelin received a reduction of 25 per cent and Mayer-Kuvert received a reduction of 10 per cent. All five firms obtained an additional 10 per cent reduction for agreeing to the Settlements and not taking their cases to court. Two firms also claimed that they were unable to pay the fine without getting into serious final difficulties and were granted a further reduction.

The final sizes of the fines paid by the companies are illustrated in the final row of the table.

Commissioner Margrethe Vestager in charge of competition policy said:

> Everybody uses envelopes. When cartelists raise the prices of everyday household objects they do so at the expense of millions of Europeans. The Commission's fight against cartels penalises such behaviour and also acts as a deterrent, protecting consumers from harm. On this case we have closed the envelope, sealed it and returned it to the sender with a clear message: don't cheat your customers, don't cartelise.[1]

 Why might global cartels be harder to identify and eradicate than cartels solely located within the domestic economy? What problems does this raise for competition policy?

1 'Antitrust: Commission on fines five envelope producers over 19.4 million in cartel settlement'. Press release (European Commission, 11 December 2014).

In a small number of cases competition concerns are raised at the end of Phase 1 and a decision is made to refer the proposed merger to a formal, in-depth investigation (Phase 2). In 2016, eight of the 362 notifications made to the EC proceeded to Phase 2. Theses investigations must normally be completed within 90 working days or 110 in complex cases.

At the end of Phase 2 there are three possibilities: (a) the merger is allowed to proceed with no conditions attached; (b) the merger is allowed to proceed subject to certain conditions being met; (c) the merger is prohibited.

Assessment of the process. The process of EU merger control is thus very rapid and administratively inexpensive. The regulations are also potentially quite tough. M&As are prohibited if they *significantly impede effective competition* (the 'SIEC' test), either by creating or strengthening a dominant firm or by making collusion with other firms, formal or tacit, more likely. But as well as being quite tough, the regulations are also flexible, since they recognise that M&As *may* be in the interests of consumers if they result in cost reductions. In such cases they are permitted.

This flexibility has led to criticism that the Commission has been too easily persuaded by firms, allowing mergers to go ahead with few, if any restrictions. Indeed, since the current M&A control measures were put in place in 1990 over 6500 M&As have been notified, but only around 250 have been referred to Phase 2 of the process and, of these, only 25 have been prohibited (as of February 2017).

The only M&A prohibited in 2016 related to competition between mobile network operators in the UK. The Commission blocked the acquisition of *O2* by Hutchinson (owner of *Three*) because it believed it would significantly reduce competition: i.e. it would reduce the number of mobile phone operators from four to three and result in customers paying higher prices.

The small number of prohibited mergers highlights a problem for EU policy makers: there is a trade-off between encouraging competition within the EU and supporting European companies to become world leaders. The ability to compete in *world* markets normally requires that companies are large, which may well lead to them having monopoly power within the EU.

 To what extent is Article 102 consistent with both these points of view?

BOX 14.2   EXPENSIVE CHIPS?

The biggest fine in EU monopoly policy history

In May 2004, the European Commission (EC) launched a formal investigation into the business conduct of Intel following complaints submitted by Advanced Micro Devices (AMD) in October 2000 and November 2003. These complaints focused on the behaviour of Intel in the market for microprocessors. These computer chips, also known as Central Processing Units (CPUs), are the most important hardware component in the manufacture of computers. AMD argued that Intel was using its dominance in this market to act in ways that contravened Article 102 of the Treaty on the Functioning of the European Union (TFEU).

EU monopoly policy follows a two-stage process and is similar to the approach adopted by most national competition agencies such as the Competition and Markets Authority in the UK.

Stage 1

The first element in stage 1 of the policy is the identification of the relevant market. This involves survey work to establish which products and suppliers are regarded as close substitutes for one another by the majority of customers.

After carrying out this analysis in the Intel case, the EC concluded that the relevant product market was x86 CPUs. Intel tried, but failed, to convince the authorities that CPUs with a non-x86 architecture should also be included in the definition of the market. All parties did agree that the market for x86 CPUs was global, as computer manufacturers competed on a worldwide basis, CPUs were the same in all regions of the world and the cost of shipping CPUs was small compared to the cost of manufacture.

Having identified the relevant market, the next phase of stage 1 is to assess whether the firm has a dominant position. This involves looking at a number of factors such as market shares, the position of competitors, barriers to entry/expansion and measures of profitability.

Data indicated that Intel's share of the x86 CPU market was approximately 80 per cent over the whole six-year period investigated. The EC typically treats market shares of over 50 per cent as one important indicator of market power. The competition authorities also found evidence of substantial barriers to entry. In particular, the production of CPUs requires considerable sunk investments in R&D, manufacturing facilities and branding. They noted that no new businesses had entered the market in the previous 10 years, while a number had exited, including Rise™ Technology, SGS-Thomson, IBM and Texas Instruments. This left Intel with only one significant rival – AMD. All of this evidence led the EC to conclude that Intel did have a dominant position in the market for x86 CPUs.

Having a dominant position is not in itself unlawful under Article 102. However, the legislation does state that firms in a dominant position have a special responsibility not to abuse their market power by restricting competition either in the market in which they are dominant or in adjacent markets.

Stage 2

In stage 2 of the investigation, the authorities focus on the behaviour of the firm. Final judgements are made about business practices that are potential examples of market abuse. Intel was found guilty of engaging in the following two activities that were seen as examples of exclusionary abuses.

- Discounts were given to four major computer manufacturers (Dell, Lenovo™, HP and NEC) and to the retailer Media-Saturn on the condition that these businesses purchased all or most of their x86 CPUs from Intel.
- Direct payments were made to HP, Acer® and Lenovo on the condition that they postponed or cancelled the launch of products containing x86 CPUs manufactured by AMD.

The fine

The EC imposed a record fine on Intel and ordered the firm to cease the two practices immediately. The size of the fine in monopoly cases is calculated by the EC in the following way.

A proportion of the annual revenue generated by the dominant firm from the sale of the products affected by its illegal conduct is adjusted by a 'duration multiplier' which depends on how many years the abuse lasted.

Typically, it is the annual revenue figure from the final year of the unlawful behaviour that is used in the calculation. For Intel® this was the value of its x86 CPU sales in the whole European Economic Area (EEA) for the business year ending December 2007. Given its confidential nature, this figure was not published in the final report. The proportion of annual revenue was set at 5 per cent. It can be up to a maximum of 30 per cent depending on the seriousness of the infringement. The EC judged that the duration of the exclusionary abuses was from October 2002 to December 2007 – a period of five years and three months. The duration multiplier, however, was set at 5.5 rather than 5.25.

The fine can be reduced if the firm co-operates with the Commission by more than the minimum that is legally required and also terminates the abusive conduct as soon as the Commission intervenes. Neither of these factors applied in the Intel case, so no reductions to the fine were applied.

The final fine was set at €1.06bn.[1] This was the highest financial sanction ever imposed by the EC for abuse of a dominant market position. Intel's annual turnover for the business year ending December 2008 was €25.555bn so the fine was less than 10 per cent of its global turnover – within the limits set by the EC.

Intel challenged the decision by appealing to the General Court. In 2014 (10 years after the investigation began), the General Court announced that it was upholding the EC's decision and Intel was forced to pay the €1.06bn fine.[2] At the time of writing Qualcom®, a manufacturer of chipsets for smartphones and tablets, is being investigated by the EC in a very similar case.[3]

1. *What methods are commonly used by competition authorities to define the relevant market?*
2. *Why might a firm involved in a monopoly case, such as Intel, try to convince the competition authorities to define the relevant market as broadly as possible?*
3. *Using some examples, explain the difference between exploitative and exclusionary abuse.*

1 'Commission imposes fine of €1.06 bn on Intel', Press release (European Commission, 13 May 2009).
2 'Commission welcomes General Court judgment upholding its decision', Press release (European Commission, 12 June 2014).
3 'Commission sends two Statements of Objections to Qualcomm', Press release (European Commission, 8 December 2015).

UK competition policy

There have been substantial changes to UK competition policy since the first legislation was introduced in 1948. The current approach is based on the 1998 Competition Act and the 2002 Enterprise Act, together with Part 3 of the 2013 Enterprise and Regulatory Reform Act.

The Competition Act brought UK policy in line with EU policy, detailed above. The Act has two key sets (or 'chapters') of prohibitions. Chapter I prohibits various restrictive practices, and mirrors EU Article 101. Chapter II prohibits various abuses of monopoly power, and mirrors Article 102. The Enterprise Act strengthened the Competition Act and introduced new measures for the control of mergers.

The 2013 Enterprise and Regulatory Reform Act set up of a new body, the Competition and Markets Authority (CMA), to carry out investigations into particular markets suspected of not working in the best interests of consumers and being in breach of one or more of the Acts. It could make rulings, as we shall see below. Firms affected by a CMA ruling have the right of appeal to the independent Competition Appeal Tribunal (CAT), which can uphold or quash the ruling.

UK restrictive practices policy

The 1998 Competition Act brought UK restrictive practices policy into line with EU policy. In particular, the calculation of fines for anti-competitive behaviour, such as the examples discussed on pages 424–5, was made comparable to the approach used by the European Commission. For example, the size of the available financial penalties was increased so it could be up to 10 per cent of the firm's annual turnover. Also a leniency programme was developed with Type A and B immunity corresponding to EC Type 1A and 1B immunity (see pages 424–5) and Type C immunity corresponding to EC Type 2 immunity.

In December 2016, the CMA ruled that five modelling agencies were guilty of regularly exchanging information and fixing minimum prices for modelling fees.[3] Fines totalling £1.5 million were imposed on the businesses involved. The companies launched an appeal so will not qualify for settlement reductions.

In January 2017, two companies involved in the supply of furniture products, Thomas Armstrong (Timber) Ltd and Hoffman Thornwood Ltd, admitted their involvement in market sharing, price fixing and bid-rigging activities.[4] They were fined a total of £2.8 million. This figure included a 20 per cent reduction as part of the new settlement procedure. A third business involved in the cartel, BHK Ltd, was not fined as it received Type A immunity under the CMA's leniency programme.

The biggest difference between UK and EU policy was created with the passing of the 2002 Enterprise Act. This made it a *criminal* offence for individuals to implement arrangements that enabled price fixing, market sharing, restrictions in production and bid-rigging irrespective of whether there are appreciable effects on competition. Convicted offenders can receive a prison sentence of up to five years and/or an unlimited fine. Prosecutions can be brought by the Serious Fraud Office or the CMA.

Assessing the policy. When the 2002 Act was introduced it was anticipated that it would result in 6–10 prosecutions per year. In reality, the authorities found the policy more difficult to implement and only three cases were prosecuted between 2002 and 2015, and only one of them successfully: in 2008, three UK executives were jailed for their part in organising a cartel in the marine hose industry.[5] A case against four BA executives accused of fixing the prices of transatlantic flights collapsed in 2010, while in 2015 the bosses of two companies, Galglass and Kondea, were cleared of fixing the prices of liquid storage tanks.[6] The boss of the third business involved in the alleged cartel pleaded guilty and received a sentence of six months in prison!

In order to address some of the issues involved with implementing the policy, the 2013 Act included a number of legal amendments to try to make it easier for the CMA to bring successful prosecutions against executives involved in cartel behaviour.

UK monopoly policy

The Chapter II prohibition of the 1998 Competition Act closely mirrors Article 102 of the TFEU. Investigations by the CMA follow the same two-stage process to establish whether the firm (a) has a dominant position and, if so, (b) is using its dominant position to carry out either exploitative or exclusionary abuses. Fines are calculated in a very similar manner to the EC and can be up to 10 per cent of worldwide turnover. One difference between UK and EC policy is that the CMA has the power to ban senior managers from serving as a director of a UK company for up to 15 years.

A recent example of an exploitative abuse case occurred in the pharmaceutical sector. In December 2016, the CMA judged that the pharmaceutical manufacturer Pfizer and distributor Flyn Pharma were guilty of charging excessive and unfair prices for the anti-epilepsy drug Phenytoin Sodium. In September 2012, the price of a 100mg packet of these tablets was increased from £2.83 to £67.50! The CMA imposed a record-high fine on Pfizer of £84.2 million.

In common with other competition authorities, UK agencies have tended to focus on behaviour that is alleged to have excluded competitors from the market. For example, in February 2016 GlaxoSmithKline, the manufacturer of the anti-depressant drug Paroxetine, was fined over £37 million by the CMA for making payments to suppliers of non-branded

---

3 www.gov.uk/government/news/model-agencies-fined-15-million-for-price-collusion

4 www.gov.uk/government/news/28-million-fine-for-furniture-parts-cartel

5 www.gov.uk/cma-cases/marine-hose-criminal-cartel-investigation

6 www.gov.uk/cma-cases/criminal-investigation-into-the-supply-of-galvanised-steel-tanks-for-water-storage

versions of this same drug in return for these businesses delaying their entry into the market.

UK merger policy

The framework for merger and acquisition (M&A) policy is set out in the 2002 Enterprise Act. A merger or acquisition can be investigated by the CMA if the resulting company meets one of two conditions: (a) it has a UK turnover that exceeds £70 million or (b) it has a market share of 25 per cent or above. The CMA's assessment is made solely on competition issues. More specifically, M&As can be prevented if they are likely to result in a substantial lessening of competition (SLC).

The final judgement is left to the CMA, apart from in a few exceptional circumstances when a minister can intervene – where the proposed merger or acquisition would have an impact on national security, media plurality or the stability of the financial system. For example, the government intervened in 2008 and allowed the proposed merger between Lloyds TSB and the troubled bank HBOS to go ahead, overruling any objections raised by the competition authorities.

One unusual aspect of UK policy is that there are no obligations on the participating firms to pre-notify the authorities about a merger that meets either of the two conditions. A voluntary notice can be made or the CMA can initiate an investigation following information received from third parties. Around 30 to 40 per cent of merger investigations are typically instigated by the CMA as no notification had been made by the firms involved.

A merger can also be completed before it has been officially cleared by the CMA. If the CMA then decides to prevent it, the firms face the costs of having to split the business back into two separate entities. The 2013 Act increased the CMA's power to force companies to reverse integration activities undertaken prior to an investigation.

The investigation. In other respects UK policy is similar to EU policy. The CMA conducts a preliminary or Phase 1 investigation to see whether competition is likely to be threatened. The 2013 Act introduced a statutory deadline of 40 working days to complete Phase 1 of the process.

At the end of this period the CMA has to decide whether there is a significant chance that the merger would result in a substantial lessening of competition. Sometimes the firms involved will offer to take certain actions to help address any competition concerns. These are known as Undertakings in Lieu (UILs) and usually involve commitments to sell some of the assets of the newly formed business.

If the CMA concludes that there might still be a SLC, it begins Phase 2 of the process, which is a much more in-depth assessment. At the end of this process if no SLC issues are raised, or if they are addressed by any UILs, the merger is allowed to go ahead.

In 2016/17, only five out of the 57 Phase 1 cases were referred for a Phase 2 investigation; 39 cases were cleared unconditionally; nine were cleared after UILs were accepted while one case was judged not to qualify. For example, the CMA cleared the takeover of the private health-care business, Priory Group, by Acadia Healthcare in November 2016 following a Phase 1 investigation. Acadia had made a UIL to sell 21 hospitals if the merger was cleared.

There is a 24-week statutory time limit for Phase 2 decisions to be made. This can be extended in special circumstances by up to eight weeks. The membership of the team that carries out Phase 2 of the process differs from that which carried out Phase 1 of the investigation. The reasoning behind this is that it is thought to be useful to get a 'fresh pair of eyes' to look at a case. Some M&As are abandoned during the Phase 2 investigations. If the investigations get to the end of Phase 2 the CMA makes one of the following decisions:

- *Unconditional clearance of the merger.* In 2016/17, this happened in 1 out of the 8 cases. For example, in December 2016 the acquisition of LeapFrog by VTech was cleared after a Phase 2 investigation. These two businesses are leading suppliers of toys for learning including tablets for children.

- *Conditional clearance subject to the firms taking certain actions that are legally binding.* These are referred to as 'remedies' and typically involve commitments to sell certain parts of the newly merged business. In 2016/17 this happened in 5 out of the 8 cases. For example, in September 2016 the merger between Ladbrokes and Coral (the second and third largest retail bookmakers in the UK) was given Phase 2 clearance by the CMA with remedies. The newly merged firm had to accept an obligation to sell around 350 to 400 betting shops to a suitable purchaser or purchasers to maintain acceptable levels of competition in some local areas.

- *Prohibition of the merger.* In the 13 years between 2004/5 and 2016/17 only 10 mergers were prohibited out of the 134 Phase 2 investigations that took place. In October 2016, the takeover of Trayport, a company that produces software for utilities trading, by Intercontinental Exchange was prohibited by the CMA.

 If anti-monopoly legislation is effective enough, is there ever any need to prevent mergers from going ahead?

Assessment of competition policy

Most commentators agree that it is correct for monopoly policy in both the EU and UK to concentrate on anti-competitive practices and their effects rather than simply on the existence of market dominance. After all, economic power is a problem only when it is abused. When, by contrast, it enables firms to achieve economies of scale, or more finance for investment, the result can be of benefit to consumers. In other words, the assumption that structure determines conduct and performance (see page 190) is not necessarily true, and certainly it is not necessarily true that market power is always bad and competitive industries are always good.

Secondly, most commentators favour the stricter and more prohibitive approach taken towards restrictive practices. The policing and penalties for infringements of Article 101 and Chapter I have become more severe in recent years. For example, the fines imposed by the EC for the period 1990–94 totalled just under €350m. For the period 2010–14 the figure was over €7.5bn.

A problem with any policy to deal with collusion is the difficulty in rooting it out. When firms do all their deals 'behind closed doors' and are careful not to keep records or give clues, then collusion can be very hard to spot. The Leniency Notice was introduced to address this issue.

Merger policy remains the most controversial area of competition policy, with criticisms that far too many are allowed to go ahead. Specific areas of contention with UK policy are whether: (a) firms should be forced to notify the authorities of proposed mergers and be prevented from undertaking any integration activities until the merger is cleared; (b) there

---

BOX 14.3   MEGABREW

The merger between the two biggest breweries in the world

On 13 October 2015, the management team of SABMiller (the second largest brewing business in the world) agreed in principle to a $108 billion takeover offer from AB-InBev (the largest brewing business in the world). Given the size and global nature of these two businesses it soon became obvious that the deal would need to be cleared by numerous competition authorities before it could be completed. This included those of the European Union.

The relevant legislation in Europe that addresses Mergers and Acquisitions (M&As) is the Merger Regulation that came into force on 1 May 2004. Businesses involved in a merger or acquisition that have an 'EU dimension' are obliged to pre-notify the European Commission (EC) and obtain clearance before going ahead with the deal. AB-InBev formally notified the European Authorities of its intention to acquire SABMiller on 30 March 2016.

Once official notification has been received, the EC launches a Phase 1 investigation that usually has to be completed in 25 working days. The investigation focuses on whether the M&A would 'significantly impede effective competition, in the internal market or in a substantial part of it, in particular as a result of the creation or strengthening of a dominant market position' (Article 2(2) and (3)).[1]

Although AB-InBev and SABMiller were the biggest two brewers in the world, Heineken® and Carlsberg are the largest in the EU. However, the EC was still concerned that the acquisition of SABMiller by AB-InBev might significantly impede effective competition in member states as it would result in the amalgamation of the third and fourth largest brewers by volume. Unconditional clearance of the deal would have resulted in the same business owning many of the best-selling premium lager brands in Europe including Stella Artois, Beck's, Budweiser, Corona, Peroni, Miller, Pilsner Urquell and Grolsh®.

The investigation

As part of any Phase 1 investigation, the management of the businesses involved can have 'State of Play meetings' with officials from the EC. At these meetings, EC staff can raise any competition concerns they have with the deal and the businesses can respond by offering to take specific actions that they hope will address any issues. The most common action is a commitment to sell off some of the assets of the newly merged business.

Any commitments must be made no later than 20 days following the formal notification of the merger. If a commitment is made it results in the time-frame for the Phase 1 investigation being extended from 25 to 35 working days.

From the beginning of the 'State of Play' meetings, AB-Inbev's management team recognised the competition issues of the takeover deal for markets in western Europe. On 8 April 2016, they made a commitment to sell all of SABMiller's businesses in France, Italy, the Netherlands and the UK as a potential remedy for the competition concerns. A price of €2.55 billion for the sale of the assets was agreed with Asahi (the largest Japanese brewery). It included the Peroni, Grolsch and Meantime brands. Following this commitment, the EC extended the deadline for the Phase 1 investigation to 24 May.

At subsequent 'State of Play meetings', EC officials expressed the view that this commitment was not enough to address all their concerns. In particular, they were worried about the impact of the deal on competition in eastern European markets. On 27 April (just inside the 20-working-day deadline) AB-InBev responded by announcing a commitment to sell off all of SABMiller's businesses in the Czech Republic, Hungary, Poland, Romania and Slovakia. This included the following brands: Pilsner Urquell (the best-selling beer in the Czech Republic); Kozel and Tyskie (popular beers in Poland) and Dreher (a best-selling beer in Hungary).

On 24 May the European Commission announced that it would clear the takeover subject to all of the commitments being completed.[2] In order to get the deal approved by the end of Phase 1 of the investigation, AB-Inbev had to agree to sell virtually all of SABMiller's European businesses. In December 2016, it announced the sale of the eastern European businesses to Asahi for a price of €7.3bn.

1. *What threshold criteria need be met before a merger is classed as having a European dimension?*
2. *Discuss the different types of decision made by the European Commission at the end of Phase 1 investigations.*
3. *Compare and contrast the merger notification systems used in the European Union and the UK.*

1 'Competition policy', *Fact Sheets on the European Union* (European Parliament).
2 'Commission approves AB InBev's acquisition of SABMiller, subject to conditions', Press release (European Commission, 24 May 2016).

should be a return to a broad public interest test rather than judging mergers purely by their impact on competition.

A review of the whole UK competition regime published by the National Audit Office in February 2016 was critical of the relatively few number of cases investigated. Between 2012 and 2014 the UK authorities issued enforcement fines of £65 million (in 2015 prices). Over the same period the German competition authorities issued fines of £1.4 billion. One explanation for this smaller number of cases may be fear of failure by the CMA. Many firms believe that they have a far greater chance of getting infringement decisions overturned in the UK than in other countries. This fear of successful appeals may deter the CMA from beginning the cases in the first place.

At the time of writing, there is some uncertainty about the impact of the UK's exit from the European Union on competition policy. The current system is referred to as a 'One Stop Shop'. Cases are investigated by either the CMA or the EC but not by both of them. If the UK leaves the Single Market, then both the CMA and EC may have to investigate the same cases. This could result in a big increase in the workload of the CMA. Firms may also face a situation where two different agencies producing contradictory conclusions: i.e. one prohibits while the other clears the same merger.

 If two or more firms were charging similar prices, what types of evidence would you look for to prove that this was collusion rather than coincidence?

Section summary

1. Competition policy in most countries recognises that monopolies, mergers and restrictive practices can bring both costs and benefits to the consumer. Generally, though, restrictive practices tend to be more damaging to consumers' interests than simple monopoly power or mergers.

2. European Union legislation applies to firms trading between EU countries. Article 101 applies to restrictive practices. Article 102 applies to dominant firms. There are also separate merger control provisions.

3. UK legislation is covered largely by the 1998 Competition Act, the 2002 Enterprise Act and the 2013 Enterprise and Regulatory Reform Act. The Chapter I prohibition of the 1998 Act applies to restrictive practices and is similar to EU Article 101. The Chapter II prohibition applies to dominant firms and is similar to Article 102. Under the 2002 Act, certain cartel agreements became a criminal offence, and mergers over a certain size must be investigated by the Competition and Markets Authority (CMA).

4. The focus of both EU and UK legislation is on anti-competitive practices rather than on the simple existence of agreements between firms or market dominance. Practices that are found, after investigation, to be detrimental to competition are prohibited and heavy fines can be imposed, even for a first offence.

14.2 PRIVATISATION AND REGULATION

Nationalisation and privatisation

One solution to market failure, advocated by some on the political left, is nationalisation. If industries are not being run in the public interest by the private sector, then bring them into public ownership. This way, so the argument goes, the market failures can be corrected. Problems of monopoly power, externalities, inequality, etc. can be dealt with directly if these industries are run with the public interest, rather than private gain, at heart.

Most nationalisation in the UK took place under the Labour government of 1945–51, when coal, railways, gas and steel were nationalised. The Labour Party at the time saw nationalisation not just as a means of correcting market failures, but as something that was morally desirable. It was seen to be much fairer and less divisive to have a society based on common ownership of the means of production than one where people were divided into separate classes: workers and capitalists.

By the mid-1970s, however, it became increasingly clear that the nationalised industries were inefficient and also a source of much industrial unrest. A change of policy was introduced from the early 1980s, when successive Conservative governments engaged in an extensive programme of 'privatisation', returning virtually all of the *nationalised industries* to the private sector. These, included telecommunications, gas, water, steel, electricity and the railways.

By 1997, the year the Conservatives left office, with the exception of the rail industry in Northern Ireland and the water industry in Northern Ireland and Scotland, the only nationalised industry remaining in the UK was the Post Office (including post offices and mail). The Post Office and

Definition

Nationalised industries State-owned industries that produce goods or services that are sold in the market.

Royal Mail were split in 2012 and Royal Mail was privatised in October 2013. Post Office Ltd remains state owned but, under the 2011 Postal Services Act, there is the option for it to become a mutual organisation in the future.

Other countries have followed similar programmes of privatisation in what has become a worldwide phenomenon. Privatisation has been seen by many governments as a means of revitalising inefficient industries and as a golden opportunity to raise revenues to ease budgetary problems.

In 2008, however, many governments returned to using nationalisation – this time to 'rescue' banks which were at risk of going bankrupt. This was facilitated by the EU giving permission for member states to support financial institutions, subject to conditions under EU state aid rules. The use of nationalisation in this *macro*economic context of national or international economic crises is examined in section 24.4.

How desirable is privatisation?

Arguments for privatisation

Market forces. The first argument is that privatisation will expose these industries to market forces, from which will flow the benefits of greater efficiency, faster growth and greater responsiveness to the wishes of the consumer. There are three parts to this argument.

■ Greater competition in the market. If privatisation involves splitting an industry into competing parts (for example, separate power stations competing to sell electricity to different electricity distribution companies), the resulting competition may drive costs and prices down.
■ Greater competition for finance. After privatisation a company has to finance investment through the market: it must issue shares or borrow from financial institutions. In doing so, it will be competing for funds with other companies, and thus must be seen as capable of using these funds profitably.
■ Accountability to shareholders. Shareholders want a good return on their shares and will thus put pressure on the privatised company to perform well. If the company does not make sufficient profits, shareholders will sell their shares. The share price will fall and the company will be in danger of being taken over. The market for corporate control (see pages 210–11) thus provides incentives for private firms to be efficient. There has been considerable takeover activity in the water and electricity industries, with most of the regional electricity companies and several of the water companies being taken over, often by non-UK companies.

Reduced government interference. In nationalised industries, managers may frequently be required to adjust their targets for political reasons. At one time they may have to keep prices low as part of a government drive against inflation. At another they may have to increase their prices substantially in order to raise extra revenue for the government and help finance tax cuts. At another they may find their investment programmes cut as part of a government economy drive.

Privatisation frees the company from these constraints and allows it to make more rational economic decisions and plan future investments with greater certainty.

Financing tax cuts. The privatisation issue of shares earns money directly for the government and thus reduces the amount it needs to borrow. Effectively, then, the government can use the proceeds of privatisation to finance tax cuts.

There is a danger here, however, that in order to raise the maximum revenue the government will want to make the industries as potentially profitable as possible. This may involve selling them as monopolies. But this, of course, would probably be against the interests of the consumer.

Potential problems with privatisation

The markets in which privatised industries operate are unlikely to be perfect. What is more, the process of privatisation itself can create problems.

Natural monopolies. The market forces argument for privatisation largely breaks down if a public monopoly is simply replaced by a private monopoly, as in the case of the water companies. Critics of privatisation argue that at least a public-sector monopoly is not out to maximise profits and thereby exploit the consumer.

Some industries have such great economies of scale that there is only room for one firm in the industry. They are natural monopolies. The best examples of natural monopolies are the various grids that exist in the privatised utilities: the national electricity grid, the national gas pipe network, the network of railway lines. These grids account for a relatively high proportion of the total costs of these industries.

In Figure 14.1, assume that the total industry output is Q_1. With just one company in the industry, long-run average cost is therefore $LRAC_1$. Now assume that the industry is split into two equal-sized companies, each with its own grid. If total output remains at Q_1, the two firms will produce Q_2 each at the higher long-run average cost of $LRAC_2$.

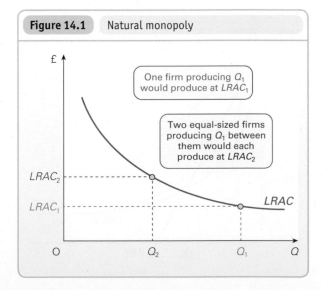

Figure 14.1 Natural monopoly

One firm producing Q_1 would produce at $LRAC_1$

Two equal-sized firms producing Q_1 between them would each produce at $LRAC_2$

It is potentially more efficient, therefore, to have a single monopoly supplier whenever there is a natural monopoly. It avoids wasteful duplication.

The problem is that the monopoly producer in a free market could use its power to drive up prices. The long-run profit-maximising position is illustrated in Figure 14.2. The monopolist produces Q_m at a price P_m and at a cost of $LRAC_m$.

If, however, the industry remained nationalised, or if it was privatised but regulated, it could be run as a monopoly and thus achieve the full economies of scale. And yet it could be directed to set a price that just covered costs (including normal profits), and thus make no more profit than a highly competitive industry. In Figure 14.2, it would produce Q_n at a price of P_n. We examine regulation later in this section.

KI 31
p356 *Planning and the co-ordination of industry.* Road use and road construction affect the demand for railways and vice versa. Decisions in the coal, electricity, gas and oil industries (and to a large extent in the steel industry) all affect each other. If these industries were nationalised, it should make their decisions easier to co-ordinate in the public interest and could help the sensible planning of the nation's infrastructure. If these industries were under private enterprise, however, either there would be little co-ordination, or alternatively co-ordination might degenerate into oligopolistic collusion, with the consumer losing out. In the extreme case, the same company may have a monopoly in more than one industry. For example, in some regions of the UK, one company runs both buses and trains.

Problems of externalities and inequality. Various industries may create substantial external benefits and yet may be privately unprofitable. A railway or an underground line, for example, may considerably ease congestion on the roads, thus benefiting road as well as rail users. Other industries may cause substantial external costs. Nuclear power stations may produce nuclear waste that is costly to dispose of safely, and/or provides hazards for future generations. Coal-fired power stations emit CO_2 and cause acid rain.

For reasons of equity, it can be argued that various transport services should be subsidised in order to keep them going and/or to keep their prices down. For instance, it can be argued that rural bus services should be kept operating at KI 4
p14 subsidised prices and that certain people (e.g. pensioners) should be charged lower prices.

Will such externalities and issues of equity be ignored under privatisation? The advocates of privatisation argue that externalities can be dealt with by appropriate taxes, subsidies and regulations even if the industry is privatised. Likewise, questions of fairness and social justice can be dealt with by subsidies or regulations. A loss-making bus service can be subsidised so that it can be run profitably by a private bus company.

Critics argue that externalities are widespread and need to be taken into account by the industry itself and not just by an occasionally intervening government.

In assessing these arguments, a lot depends on the effectiveness of government legislation and regulation.

To what extent can the problems with privatisation be seen as arguments in favour of nationalisation?

Regulation: identifying the optimum price and output

Privatised industries, if left free to operate in the market, will have monopoly power; they will create externalities; and they will be unlikely to take into account questions of fairness. An answer to these problems is for the government or some independent agency to regulate their behaviour so that they produce at the socially optimum price and output.

Exactly what this optimum is depends on what problems need to be taken into account. Take three cases. In the first, the privatised industry is a monopoly (perhaps it is a natural monopoly), but there are no other problems. In the second case, there are also externalities to be considered, and in the third, questions of fairness too.

The privatised industry is a monopoly

The 'first-best' situation: $P = MC$. Assume that all other firms in the economy are operating under perfect competition, and thus producing where $P = MC$. This is the imaginary 'first-best' situation. If this were so, the privatised company should be required to follow the same pricing rule: $P = MC$. As we saw in section 12.1, this will give the Pareto optimal KI 28
p348 output, where total consumer plus producer surplus is maximised (see pages 348–51).

The theory of the 'second best': $P = MC + Z$. Now let us drop the assumption that the rest of the economy operates under perfect competition. If other industries on average are charging a price, say, 10 per cent above MC, then the theory of the second best suggests that the privatised company

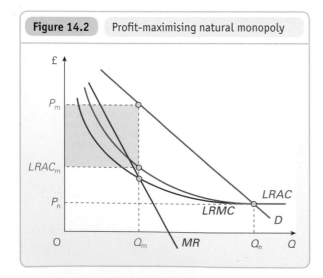

Figure 14.2 Profit-maximising natural monopoly

should also charge a price 10 per cent above *MC*. At least that way it will not cause a diversion of consumption away from relatively low-cost industries (at the margin) to a relatively high-cost one. The second-best rule is therefore to set $P = MC + Z$, where Z in this case is 10 per cent.

The privatised industry produces externalities

In the first-best situation the privatised industry should produce where price equals marginal social (not private) cost: $P = MSC$. The second-best solution is to produce where $P = MSC + Z$ (where Z is the average of other industries' price above their *MSC*).

The difficulty for the regulator in applying these rules in practice is to identify and measure the externalities: not an easy task! (See section 12.4.)

The behaviour of the privatised industry involves questions of fairness

If the government wishes the regulator to insist on a price below *MC* because it wishes to help certain groups (e.g. pensioners, children, rural dwellers, those below certain incomes), what should this price be?

In practice, one of two simple rules could be followed. Either the industry could be required to charge uniform prices, despite higher costs for supplying certain categories of people (this could apply, for example, to rural customers of a privatised postal service); or a simple formula could be used (e.g. half price for pensioners and children). These are often the only practical solutions given the impossibility of identifying the specific needs of individual consumers.

Two further questions arise:

- Should the lower price be subsidised by central or local government, or by the privatised company and hence by other users of the service (i.e. by them paying higher prices)? Justice would suggest that support should come from the community as a whole – the taxpayer – and not just from other users of the service.

- If people require help, should they not be given general tax relief or benefits, rather than specifically subsidised services? For example, should pensioners not be paid better pensions, rather than be charged reduced fares on buses?

1. In the case of buses, subsidies are often paid by local authorities to support various loss-making routes. Is this the best way of supporting these services?
2. In the case of postal services, profitable parts of the service cross-subsidise the unprofitable parts. Should this continue if the industry is privatised?

The long run

In the short run, certain factors of production are fixed in supply. For example, electricity output can be increased by using existing power stations more fully, but the number of power stations is fixed. There will thus be a limit to the

amount of electricity that can be generated in the short run. As that limit is approached, the marginal cost of electricity is likely to rise rapidly. For example, oil-fired power stations, which are more costly to operate, will have to be brought on line.

In the long run, all factors are variable. New power stations can be built. The long-run marginal costs therefore will probably not rise as more is produced. In fact, they may even fall due to economies of scale.

Long-run marginal costs, however, unlike short-run marginal costs, will include the extra capital costs of increasing output. The long-run marginal cost of electricity will thus be all the extra costs of producing one more unit: namely, the extra operating costs (fuel, labour, etc.) plus the extra capital costs (power stations, pylons, etc.).

The rule for the optimum long-run price and output is simple. The regulator should require the industry to produce where price equals long-run marginal social cost (*LRMSC*). This is illustrated in Figure 14.3.

In the short run, optimum price and output are P_S and Q_S where $P = $ (short-run) *MSC*. This might mean that production is at quite a high cost: existing capital equipment is being stretched and diminishing returns have become serious.

In the long run, then, it will be desirable to increase capacity if $LRMSC < MSC$. Optimum long-run price and output are thus at P_L and Q_L where $P = LRMSC$.

This is the rule for the first-best situation. In the second-best situation, the industry should produce where $P = LRMSC + Z$ (where Z is the average of other industries' price above their *LRMSC*).

If the regulator imposed such rules, would they cause the firm to make a loss if it faced a downward-sloping LRMSC curve? (Clues: Where would the LRAC curve be relative to the LRMC curve? What would be the effect of externalities and the addition of the Z factor on the price?)

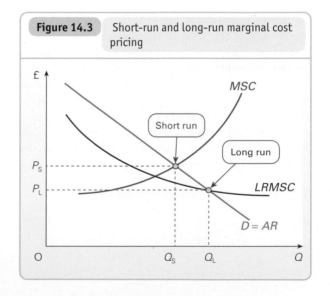

Figure 14.3 Short-run and long-run marginal cost pricing

Regulation in the UK

To some extent the behaviour of privatised industries may be governed by general monopoly and restrictive practice legislation. For example, in the UK privatised firms can be investigated by the Competition and Markets Authority (CMA). In addition to this there may be separate regulatory offices to oversee the structure and behaviour of each of the privatised utilities. In the UK these regulators are as follows: the Office for Gas and Electricity Markets (Ofgem), the Office of Communications (Ofcom) (for telecommunications and broadcasting), the Office of Rail and Road (ORR) and the Office of Water Services (Ofwat).

The regulators set terms under which the industries have to operate. For example, the ORR sets the terms under which rail companies have access to the track and stations. The terms set by the regulator can be reviewed by negotiation between the regulator and the industry. If agreement cannot be reached, the CMA acts as an appeal court and its decision is binding.

The regulator for each industry also sets limits to the prices that certain parts of the industry can charge (see Case Study 14.6 on the student website). These parts are those where there is little or no competition: for example, the charges made to electricity and gas retailers by National Grid, the owner of the electricity grid and major gas pipelines.

Price-setting formulae were largely of the 'RPI minus X' variety (although other factors, including competition and excessive profits, are also taken into account). What the RPI minus X formula means is that the industries can raise their prices by the rate of increase in the retail price index (RPI) (i.e. by the rate of inflation) *minus* a certain percentage (X) to take account of expected increases in efficiency. Thus if the rate of inflation were 3 per cent, and if the regulator considered that the industry (or firm) could be expected to reduce its costs by 2 per cent (X = 2%), then price rises would be capped at 1 per cent. The RPI − X system is thus an example of *price-cap regulation*. The idea of this system of regulation is that it will force the industry to pass cost savings on to the consumer. In 2013, Ofgem replaced RPI − X with RIIO (Revenue = Incentives + Innovation + Outputs). The aim of these price controls is to encourage more innovation.

Whether these price controls will result in marginal cost pricing depends on what the price was in the first place. If the price was equal to marginal cost, and if the X factor is the amount by which the regulator expects the *MC* curve to shift downwards (after taking inflation into account), then the formula could result in marginal cost pricing.

Why might it equally result in average cost pricing?

Assessing the system of regulation in the UK

The system that has evolved in the UK has various advantages over that employed in the USA and elsewhere, where regulation often focuses on the level of profits (see Case Study 14.6 on the student website).

■ It is a discretionary system, with the regulator able to judge individual examples of the behaviour of the industry on their own merits. The regulator has a detailed knowledge of the industry which would not be available to government ministers or other bodies such as the CMA. The regulator could thus be argued to be the best body to decide on whether the industry is acting in the public interest.

■ The system is flexible, since it allows for the licence and price formulae to be changed as circumstances change.

■ The 'RPI minus X' formula provides an incentive for the privatised firms to be as efficient as possible. If they can lower their costs by more than X, they will, in theory, be able to make larger profits and keep them. There is thus a continuing pressure on them to cut costs. (In countries where profits rather than prices are regulated, there is little incentive to increase efficiency, since any cost reductions must be passed on to the consumer in lower prices, and do not, therefore, result in higher profits.)

There are, however, some inherent problems with the regulation as it has been operated in the UK:

■ The 'RPI minus X' formula was designed to provide an incentive for firms to cut costs. But if regulators underestimated the scope for cost reductions resulting from new technology and reorganisation, and set X too low, firms could make excessive profits. Where this has happened, regulators have changed the value of X after only one or two years. Alternatively, one-off price cuts have been ordered, as happened when the water companies were required by Ofwat to cut prices by an average of 10 per cent in 2000. In either case, this then removes the incentive for the industry to cut costs. What is the point of being more efficient if the regulator is merely going to take away the extra profits?

■ With RPI minus X reducing firms' profits, the outcome may be reduced investment and innovation. Given the need for greater investment in power generation, in 2013 Ofgem introduced a new system for controlling prices in the distribution part of the energy sector. This is called RIIO (Revenue = Incentives + Innovation + Outputs).

Definition

Price-cap regulation Where the regulator puts a ceiling on the amount by which a firm can raise its price.

This is a new performance-based model which aims to incentivise innovation and a reduction of future costs. It also allows the climate change agenda to be addressed as part of the price control process.

- Regulation has become increasingly complex. This makes it difficult for the industries to plan and may lead to a growth of 'short-termism' as firms are subjected to short-term changes in regulation or government intervention. It is likely to result in resources being wasted as the industry spends time and energy trying to outwit the regulator.

- Alternatively, there is the danger of *regulatory capture*. As regulators become more and more involved in their industry and get to know the senior managers at a personal level, so they are increasingly likely to see the managers' point of view and will thus become less tough.

- The regulators could, instead, be 'captured' by the government. Rather than being totally independent, there to serve the interests of the consumer, they might bend to pressures from the government to do things that might help the government win the next election.

One way in which the dangers of ineffective or over-intrusive regulation can be avoided is to replace regulation with competition wherever this is possible. Indeed, one of the major concerns of the regulators has been to do just this. (See Box 14.4 for ways in which competition has been increased in the electricity industry.)

Increasing competition in the privatised industries

Where natural monopoly exists, competition is impossible in a free market. Of course, the industry could be broken up by the government, with firms prohibited from owning more than a certain percentage of the industry. But this would lead to higher costs of production. Firms would be

operating further back up a downward-sloping long-run average cost curve.

But many parts of the privatised industries are not natural monopolies. Generally, it is only the grid that is a natural monopoly. In the case of gas and water, it is the pipelines. It would be wasteful to duplicate these. In the case of electricity, it is the power lines: the national grid and the local power lines. In the case of the railways, it is the track.

Other parts of these industries, however, have generally been opened up to competition (with the exception of water). Thus there are now many producers and sellers of electricity and gas. This is possible because they are given access, by law, to the national and local electricity grids and gas pipelines.

To help the opening up of competition, regulators have sometimes restricted the behaviour of the established firms (like BT or British Gas), to prevent them using their dominance in the market as a barrier to entry of new firms.

As competition has been introduced into these industries, so price-cap regulation has been progressively abandoned. The intention is ultimately to confine price regulation to the operation of the grids: the parts that are natural monopolies.

Even for the parts where there is a natural monopoly, they could be made contestable monopolies. One way of doing this is by granting operators a licence for a specific period of time. This is known as *franchising*. This has been the approach used for the railways (see Case Study 14.8 on the student website). Once a company has been granted a franchise, it has the monopoly of passenger rail services over specific routes. But the awarding of the franchise can be highly competitive, with rival companies putting in competitive bids, in terms of both price (or, in the case of many of the train operating companies, the level of government subsidy required) and the quality of service.

Another approach is to give all companies equal access to the relevant grid. For example, regional electricity companies have to charge the same price for using their local power lines to both rival companies and themselves.

But despite attempts to introduce competition into the privatised industries, they are still dominated by giant companies, which retain considerable market power. This is a long way from perfect competition and there is scope for price leadership or other forms of oligopolistic collusion. Although regulation through the price formula has been progressively abandoned as elements of competition have been introduced, the regulators have retained an important role in preventing collusion and the abuse of monopoly power.

Definitions

Regulatory capture Where the regulator is persuaded to operate in the industry's interests rather than those of the consumer.

Franchising Where a firm is granted the licence to operate a given part of an industry for a specified length of time.

BOX 14.4   SELLING POWER TO THE PEOPLE

The impact of privatisation and competition in the electricity industry

Competition is generally seen as better than regulation as a means of protecting consumers' interests, but there is evidence that this requires a strong regulatory framework to be retained. The electricity industry provides a good case study on the impact of the introduction of competition into a privatised industry.

The industry before privatisation

Under nationalisation, the industry in England and Wales was organised as a monopoly with the Central Electricity Generating Board (CEGB) supplying 99 per cent of all electricity. It operated the power stations and transmitted the electricity round the country via the national grid. However, the CEGB did not sell electricity directly to the consumer; rather it sold it to 12 regional boards, which in turn supplied it to the consumer.

Privatisation of the industry

Non-nuclear generation in England and Wales was privatised in 1990 as two companies: National Power (with just over 50 per cent of capacity) and PowerGen (with nearly 30 per cent). Nuclear power stations were privatised in 1996.

The 12 regional boards were privatised in 1991 as separate regional electricity companies (RECs), which were responsible for local distribution and supply to consumers. They were also permitted to build their own power stations if they chose. The RECs jointly owned the national grid, but it was run independently. It was eventually sold as a separate company in 1996. The national grid is now managed and operated by National Grid Electricity Transmission plc, a subsidiary of the multinational business National Grid.

The diagram shows the structure of the industry. Electricity is produced by the *generators* (the power stations).

The electricity is *transmitted* along the power lines of the national grid to different parts of the country. It is then transmitted locally by the *distributors*. There are currently 14 licensed distribution network operators (DNOs) in Britain which are responsible for the distribution of electricity from the high voltage transmission grid to businesses and households.

At the time of privatisation an Office of Electricity Regulation (OFFER) was set up to control prices in parts of the industry where there was no competition. OFFER was later merged with the gas regulator to become the Office of Gas and Electricity Markets (Ofgem). Where prices have been controlled, this has been of the $RPI - X$ variety (see page 436). For example, the charges paid by the generators and the suppliers to the National Grid Electricity Transmission company are regulated in this way, as this part of the business is considered to be a natural monopoly. The same is true for the DNOs, as each has a natural monopoly in the region for which it is responsible. In 2013 Ofgem replaced the $RPI - X$ price controls with Revenue = Incentives + Innovation + Outputs (RIIO). As the name suggests, these set targets to encourage innovation.

The rationale behind introducing the new structure was to increase competition, thereby making regulation increasingly unnecessary. But given the natural monopoly market structure in both transmission and distribution, where was the competition supposed to come from?

It was hoped that competition would be possible at two levels: at the *wholesale* level, with generators competing with each other to sell to suppliers; and at the *retail* level, with suppliers competing to sell to customers. Let us examine each of these markets in turn.

The electricity industry in England and Wales

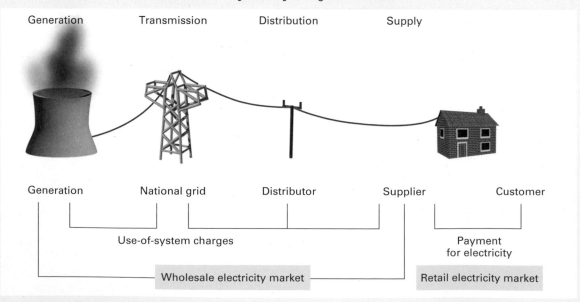

Competition in the wholesale market for electricity: NETA and BETTA

From 2001 in England and Wales electricity was traded in the wholesale market under the New Electricity Trading Arrangements (NETA). In April 2005, this system was extended to Scotland and renamed the British Electricity Trading and Transmission Arrangements (BETTA). Participants in the market include generators, suppliers, large commercial consumers of electricity and traders (i.e. dealers).

In this market, bulk electricity is traded 'forward' in bilateral contracts between individual buyers and sellers. A forward contract means that a price is agreed today for an amount of electricity to be traded over a particular period in the future, which could be as soon as the next day or could be three or more years hence. The long forward contracts are to allow generators to plan to build extra capacity.

Of course, the future price will be based on anticipated demand, and demand in practice may turn out quite differently. To allow for this, BETTA operates a 'central balancing mechanism'. This is a system of buying and selling additional electricity where necessary to ensure that demand actually balances supply second by second. In practice, only about 2 per cent of electricity has to be traded under the balancing mechanisms; the remainder is traded in the forward contracts.

Concerns were expressed that, with the market dominated by the 'Big Six' major producers, 'liquidity'[1] had declined since 2001 and was low compared to that of many other countries and other commodity markets. A low level of liquidity makes it difficult for firms to enter the market and operate as a non-vertically integrated market participant.

Competition in the retail market for electricity

Since 1999 all customers, whether domestic or business, have been able to choose their supplier. Over that period there have been several new entrants into the supplier market, including various gas companies diversifying into electricity supply.

By 2001, 38 per cent of customers had switched suppliers at least once and the former regional monopoly suppliers' market share had fallen to 70 per cent. In the light of this Ofgem announced that competition was sufficiently developed to allow all regulation of the retail market to be removed by April 2002.

However, the rise of the Big Six, which resulted from mergers and takeovers in the industry, meant that by 2004 they had a 99 per cent share of the retail market. With the rise of smaller independent retailers, this had fallen to 85 per cent by 2016 – still a substantial share.

The CMA inquiry

In 2014, the CMA launched the most comprehensive and wide-ranging review of the energy market since privatisation. This followed a number of investigations carried out by the sector regulator, Ofgem, in response to concerns about the functioning of the energy market. For example, between 2004 and 2014 average domestic electricity prices increased by 75 per cent in real terms. One important issue is whether this was the result of market power or simply reflected rising costs in the sector.

Earlier Ofgem investigations

Ofgem published the results from its first investigation into the market in 2009. The Energy Supply Probe concluded that there was no evidence of collusion in the retail market but proposed a number of remedies to help the market work more effectively. This included improvements in the way information on bills was presented to customers.

In late 2010 Ofgem launched its Retail Market Review (RMR).[3] This report recognised that some improvements had been made but that energy bills were still too complex, making it difficult for consumers to find the best deals. For example, there were over 300 different tariffs available to domestic users! The review recommended that tariffs should be calculated on simple per-unit pricing and energy suppliers limited to offering only four different deals – 'the four-tariff rule'.

After carrying out these reviews, Ofgem concluded that its powers as a market regulator were insufficient to determine whether barriers were blocking effective competition. In June 2014, it referred the energy market to the CMA for a full investigation.

The CMA inquiry

The inquiry took two years to complete and the final report was published in June 2016.[4] Some of its key findings were:

- The wholesale market for electricity was working effectively with no evidence of firms exploiting any market power.
- Vertical integration between the suppliers and generators was not having any negative impact on consumers. Independent electricity generators were able to compete effectively with those that were vertically integrated with the energy suppliers.
- A number of new firms had successfully entered the retail market and had increased their market shares.
- A significant number of customers did not actively engage in the market by shopping around for the best deals. For example, in a survey of 7000 domestic customers carried out as part of the inquiry, 34 per cent of respondents stated that they had never considered switching energy supplier.
- Approximately 70 per cent of the customers of the Big Six were on a standard variable tariff (SVT). Customers are placed on these default pricing schemes if they fail to shop around and actively choose a deal.
- The tariffs available to those people who did shop around closely followed changes in industry costs. However, the gap between SVT and industry costs had increased significantly in recent years.
- The majority of customers using prepayment meters were on SVTs because of low levels of competition. This was partly due to the limitations of non-smart meters.
- The restriction on the number of tariffs imposed by Ofgem following its 2010 review had had a negative impact on competition. It forced some firms to withdraw pricing schemes that had previously benefited many customers.
- A large number of small businesses (those employing fewer than 10 people) were on expensive default schemes. The tariffs available to these businesses were not published by the energy suppliers but were instead the outcome of individual-level negotiation.

In response to these findings, the CMA made the following recommendations:

- The creation of a database that includes the details of customers who have been on the SVT for three years or more. Energy suppliers would have access to this database to offer better deals for these customers. The aim of this reform was to reduce switching costs.
- The 'four-tariff' rule on energy suppliers should be scrapped.
- Energy companies supplying businesses employing fewer than 10 people should publish the different available tariffs to increase transparency and make it easier for these small businesses to choose the best deal.
- A temporary price cap (2017–20) should be introduced for those customers using prepayment meters.

The most controversial aspect of the report was a disagreement amongst its panel members over the policy option of imposing a price cap on SVTs for all customers. Four of the five panel members concluded that it would undermine competition, while the other panel member, Martin Cave, believed that a price cap was required in the short term to address the lack of competitive pressure on SVTs.

The outcome

Ofgem agreed to implement the CMA's recommendations. In February 2017, it announced that a temporary price cap for customers using prepayment meters would come into effect in April 2017. The level of the cap would vary by meter type and region. It would also be reviewed every six months and remain in place until 2020. It also announced that the database would be available in 2018.

Controversy continues about the possibility of introducing a price cap for all customers on SVTs. In March 2017, there was continued speculation that the government might impose price controls and Conservative MP John Penrose called for a 'relative price cap' to be introduced. This would force energy suppliers to price their most expensive tariffs such as the SVT at no more than 6 per cent above their cheapest deal.

In October 2017 the Government published draft legislation for the introduction of a price cap on the most expensive SVTs. It will be interesting to see how competition and regulation in the electricity industry continues to evolve over the next few years.

1. *Wholesale and retail energy markets are expected to deliver on a number of targets including competitive pricing, environmental objectives and equity. Explain why this may present problems.*
2. *Why do you think switching rates have been so low in the retail energy market?*
3. *Assess some of the arguments for and against the use of price caps for all customers on SVTs.*

1 Ofgem defines liquidity as the ability to quickly buy or sell a desired commodity or financial instrument without causing a significant change in its price and without incurring significant transaction costs. An important feature of a liquid market, it says, is that it has a large number of buyers and sellers willing to transact at all times. A high level of liquidity is seen as being good because it enables new players to enter the market and reduces the ability of incumbents to manipulate it (*Utility Week*, 3 September 2009).
2 'Energy supply probe', *Market Review and Reform* (Ofgem).
3 'Retail market review', *Market Review and Reform* (Ofgem).
4 'Energy Market Investigation: Overview' (Competition and Market Authority, 24 June 2016).

Section summary

1. From around 1983 the Conservative government in the UK embarked on a large programme of privatisation. Many other countries have followed suit.

2. The economic arguments for privatisation include: greater competition, not only in the goods market but in the market for finance and for corporate control; reduced government interference; and raising revenue to finance tax cuts.

3. The economic arguments against privatisation of utilities include the following: the firms are likely to have monopoly power because their grids are natural monopolies; it makes overall planning and co-ordination of the transport and power sectors more difficult; and the industries produce substantial externalities and raise questions of fairness in distribution.

4. Regulators could require firms to charge the socially efficient price. In the first-best world, this will be where price equals marginal social cost. In the real world, this is not the case given that prices elsewhere are not equal to marginal social costs. Ideally, prices should still *reflect* marginal social costs, but there are difficulties in identifying and measuring social costs.

5. In the long run, the optimum price and output will be where price equals long-run marginal social cost. If $LRMSC < MSC$, it will be desirable to invest in additional capacity.

6. Regulation in the UK has involved setting up regulatory offices for the major privatised utilities. These use negotiation and bargaining to persuade the industries to behave in the public interest and set the terms under which firms can operate (e.g. access rights to the respective grid).

7. As far as prices are concerned, the industries have generally been required to abide by an '*RPI* minus *X*' formula, or some variant of it, in all sectors where there is a lack of competition. This means that potential cost reductions are passed on to the consumer while allowing them to retain any additional profits gained from cost reductions greater than *X*. This has provided them with an incentive to achieve even greater increases in efficiency, but may not have incentivised innovation.

8. Many parts of the privatised industries are not natural monopolies. In these parts, competition has been seen as a more effective means of pursuing the public interest. Various attempts have been made to make the privatised industries more competitive, often at the instigation of the regulator. Nevertheless, considerable market power remains in the hands of many privatised firms, and thus regulators need to be able to retain the ability to prevent the abuse of monopoly power.

END OF CHAPTER QUESTIONS

1. Should governments or regulators always attempt to eliminate the supernormal profits of monopolists/oligopolists?

2. Compare the relative merits of banning certain types of market *structure* with banning certain types of market *behaviour*.

3. Consider the argument that whether an industry is in the public sector or private sector has far less bearing on its performance than the degree of competition it faces.

4. If two or more firms are charging similar prices, does this imply that collusion is taking place? What evidence would you need to determine the existence of collusion?

5. There exists a view that the UK is too small an economy to benefit from competition in many industries, with firms failing to reach minimum efficient scale. What does this imply for competition policy?

6. Should regulators of utilities that have been privatised into several separate companies allow (a) horizontal mergers (within the industry); (b) vertical mergers; (c) mergers with firms in other industries?

7. Summarise the relative benefits to consumers of (a) privatising a nationalised industry, (b) keeping it in the public sector but introducing competition.

8. If an industry regulator adopts an $RPI - X$ formula for price regulation, is it desirable that the value of X should be adjusted as soon as cost conditions change?

9. Examine the case for public ownership of an industry where a natural monopoly exists.

10. If price regulation results in lower profits, will this always imply lower investment? How might a government incentivise innovation in a regulated industry?

11. Price-cap regulation was abandoned in the gas and electricity industries because the regulator (Ofgem) felt that there was sufficient competition. Consider whether this was a wise decision.

Online resources

Additional case studies on the student website

14.1 **Cartels set in concrete, steel and cardboard.** This examines some of the best-known Europe-wide cartels of recent years.
14.2 **Taking your vitamins – at a price.** An examination of a global vitamins cartel and the action taken against it by the EU.
14.3 **A lift to profits?** The EC imposes a record fine on four companies operating a lift and escalator cartel.
14.4 **Misleading advertising.** Do firms intentionally mislead consumers and, if so, what can government do?
14.5 **Payday loans.** This case examines the rise of payday loans and looks at attempts to control their harsh terms and sky-high interest rates in order to protect the poor and vulnerable.
14.6 **Price-cap regulation in the UK.** How $RPI - X$ regulation has been applied to the various privatised industries.
14.7 **Regulation US-style.** This examines rate-of-return regulation: an alternative to price-cap regulation.
14.8 **The right track to reform?** How successful has rail privatisation been in the UK?
14.9 **Privatisation in transition economies.** This extended case study examines state ownership under former communist countries of the USSR and how the transition of these countries to market economies involved a process of privatisation.
14.10 **Forms of privatisation in transition countries.** This focuses on how different types of privatisation are likely to affect the way industries are run.

Websites relevant to Chapters 12–14

Numbers and sections refer to websites listed in the Web Appendix and hotlinked from this book's website at **www.pearsoned.co.uk/sloman**.

- For news articles relevant to this and the previous chapter, see the *Economics News* section on the student website.
- For general news on market failures and government intervention, see websites in section A, and particularly A1–5, 9, 18, 19, 21, 24, 31, 35. See also links to newspapers worldwide in A38, 39, 43 and 44; and see A40 and 41 for links to economics news articles from newspapers worldwide.
- UK and EU departments relevant to competition policy can be found at sites E4 and 10; G7, 8.
- UK regulatory bodies can be found at sites E4, 11, 15, 16, 18, 19, 22, 29.
- For information on taxes and subsidies, see E25, 30, 36; G13. For use of green taxes (Box 13.2), see H5; G11; E2, 14, 30.

- For information on health and the economics of health care (Box 12.3), see E8; H8. See also links in I8 and 11.
- For sites favouring the free market, see C17; E34. See also C18 for the development of ideas on the market and government intervention.
- For policy on the environment and transport, see E2, 7,11, 14, 21, 29; G10, 11. See also H11.
- For student resources relevant to these three chapters, see sites C1–7, 9, 10, 19.

Foundations of Macroeconomics

Why do economies sometimes grow rapidly, while at other times they suffer from recession? Why, if people want to work, do they sometimes find themselves unemployed? Why do economies experience inflation (rising prices), and does it matter if they do? Why do exchange rates change and what will be the impact of such changes on imports and exports? Why do individuals, firms and governments borrow and what are the implications of borrowing and debt for the economic health of countries? These macroeconomic issues affect all countries, and economists are called on to try to find explanations and solutions.

In the next two chapters we will be looking at these issues and giving you a preliminary insight into the causes of these problems and what governments can do to tackle them. In the second of these chapters (Chapter 16) we shall see how macroeconomics has developed over the years as economists have sought to explain the macroeconomic problems of the time – right up to the financial crisis and recession of recent years.

An Introduction to Macroeconomic Issues and Ideas

We turn now to macroeconomics. This will be the subject of the second half of this book. As we have already seen, microeconomics focuses on individual markets. It studies the demand for and supply of, for example, oranges, music downloads, petrol and haircuts; bricklayers, doctors, office accommodation and computers. It examines the choices people make between goods, and what determines their relative prices and the relative quantities produced.

In macroeconomics we take a much broader view. We examine the economy as a whole. We still examine demand and supply, but now it is the total level of spending in the economy and the total level of production. In other words, we examine aggregate demand and aggregate supply.

We still examine output, employment and prices, but now it is national output and its rate of growth, national employment and unemployment, and the general level of prices and their rate of increase (i.e. the rate of inflation).

In this chapter, we identify the major macroeconomic issues facing society. Among these is the volatility of the economy. This volatility is perhaps most evident in the fluctuations we see in the economy's output, but we observe it too in other macroeconomic variables, such as unemployment and inflation.

By providing an overview of macroeconomics, this chapter provides the platform necessary to analyse in subsequent chapters some of the key debates of our time.

15.1 AN OVERVIEW OF KEY MACROECONOMIC ISSUES

Macroeconomics examines various issues affecting whole economies. Many of these are the big issues on which elections are won or lost.

Is the economy growing and, if so, how rapidly? How can we avoid, or get out of, recessions? What causes unemployment and how can the rate be got down? Why is inflation sometimes a problem and what can be done to keep rates of inflation at modest levels? Conversely, why do prices sometimes fall, and does this itself create a problem? What will happen to interest rates? How big a problem is government debt? Are financial institutions lending too much or too little? What affects a country's balance of trade in goods and services? How attractive is the country as a destination for investment by foreign businesses?

Major macroeconomic issues

The questions we have just identified give you a flavour of the macroeconomic issues that we will be studying in the following chapters. For simplicity, we will group them under the following headings: economic growth, unemployment, inflation, economic relationships with the rest of the world, the financial well-being of individuals, businesses and government and the relationship between the financial system and the economy. While we will be studying other issues too, such as consumer behaviour and taxation, these still link to these major macroeconomic issues and, more generally, to how economies function.

The purpose of this section is to provide you with some background on these key issues and to look at some key macroeconomic data. This allows us to put these issues into context before later considering them in more depth.

Economic growth and the business cycle

One of the most basic concerns for macroeconomists is understanding what affects the level of an economy's output and, in turn, what causes it to rise or fall. *Economic growth* is the term economists use to describe the change in the level of an economy's output from period to period. The rate of economic growth measures the percentage change in output. This is usually measured over short periods, such as 12 or 3 months. If we measure the *rate of growth* over a 12-month period we are measuring the economy's annual rate of growth, while if we measure it over a 3-month period we are measuring the quarterly rate of growth.

One of the most important observations to make about economic growth is its *volatility*. This is evident from Figure 15.1, which plots the annual rates of growth of a selection of economies.

KI 34
p445

KEY
IDEA
34

Economies suffer from inherent instability. As a result, economic growth and other macroeconomic indicators tend to fluctuate.

Definitions

Rate of economic growth The percentage increase in national output, normally expressed over a 12-month or 3-month period.

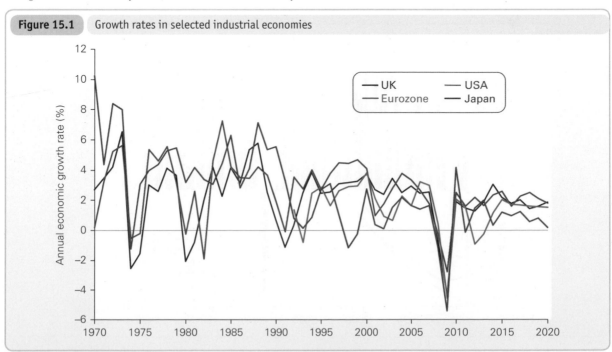

| **Figure 15.1** | Growth rates in selected industrial economies |

Notes: 2017 to 2020 based on forecasts; eurozone figures are the weighted average of the countries using the euro in any given year; the euro was introduced in 1999; the eurozone figures before 1999 are the weighted average of the original members.
Source: Based on data in *AMECO Database*, European Commission, DGECFIN.

Countries rarely experience stable economic growth; instead, growth rates tend to fluctuate. Understanding the volatility of economic growth and its effects is the focus of much analysis by macroeconomists. After all, fluctuating activity levels are likely to affect the behaviour and well-being of many of us. In 2009, for example, the UK economy shrank by 4.5 per cent, unemployment levels rose from 1.6 million during 2007 to 2.7 million by 2011 and the government experienced a 4.5 per cent fall in its receipts between tax years 2007/8 and 2009/10.

The significance of the volatility of short-term economic growth makes it our next threshold concept. It is the volatility of growth that gives rise to the well-known phenomenon of the **business cycle**. The business cycle refers to the fluctuations we observe in the path traced out from period to period in an economy's output level. Because rates of economic growth affect an economy's output path, the more growth rates vary the more marked are the fluctuations in this path.

TC 12
p447

To illustrate the effect of fluctuating growth rates on an economy's output path consider Figure 15.2. This shows the volume of output and the annual rate of economic growth in three advanced economies, France, the UK and the USA, since 1990.

The fluctuating nature of economic growth is most starkly illustrated in the late 2000s. In 2009 the volume of output shrunk by around 3 per cent in France and the USA compared with the year before and by 4.5 per cent in the UK. Compare this, for example, with growth rates in the period 1998–2000, when output rose by over 3 per cent per year in all three countries.

The key point here is that if the rate of growth from year to year were constant, then the bars would be the same height and the output level lines would be smoothly upward sloping.[1] Clearly, this is not the case and it is the fluctuations in short-term growth rates, including periods when economic growth is very weak or even negative, that gives rise to the business cycle. In other words, economies experience neither constant growth nor continued expansion.

We will refer frequently to the volatility of economies in the second half of the book. But, given its central importance to much of the subsequent analysis we will provide an overview of economists' thinking on this important issue in section 15.3.

Definitions

Business cycle or trade cycle The periodic fluctuations of national output. Periods of rapid growth are followed by periods of low growth or even decline in national output.

---

[1] With the index plotted on the vertical axis, a constant growth rate would be shown by a line whose slope gradually increased, as a constant percentage increase would give a steeper line, the higher the index. For example, a 5 per cent annual growth rate from an index of 100 in year 1, would give an index of 105 in year 2, whereas a 5 per cent annual growth rate from an index of 200 in, say, year 10 would give an index of 210 in year 11. Thus the slope between years 10 to 11 would be twice that between years 1 and 2 and yet the growth rate would be identical. If the vertical axis were measured in a *log scale*, then a constant growth rate would be shown as a straight line.

Figure 15.2   Output paths and growth rates of France, UK and USA

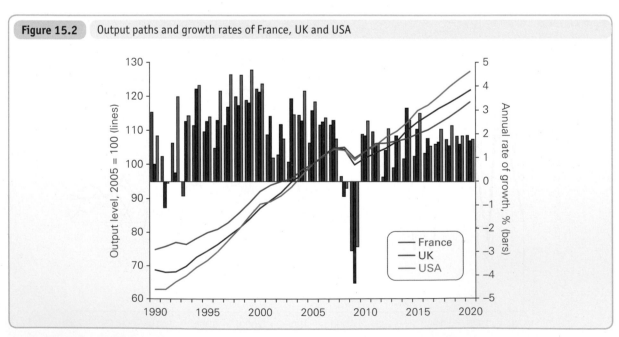

Notes: Data for 2017 onwards are based on forecasts.
Source: Based on data in *World Economic Outlook Database* (IMF, October 2017).

| THRESHOLD CONCEPT 12 | SHORT-TERM GROWTH IN A COUNTRY'S OUTPUT TENDS TO FLUCTUATE | THINKING LIKE AN ECONOMIST |

Countries rarely experience stable economic growth. Instead they experience *business cycles*. Periods of rapid economic growth can be followed by periods of low growth or even negative growth (falling output).

Explaining volatility

Sometimes rising or falling output can be explained by the deliberate actions of governments or central banks (such as the Bank of England). For example, a rise in government spending, a reduction in taxes or a reduction in interest rates may stimulate the economy and raise the rate of economic growth.

But fluctuations in economic growth can often be explained by the working of the market system.

Some economists see the problem as rooted in fluctuations in *aggregate demand*: in other words, in the total demand for the economy's goods and services, whether by individuals or firms (see page 459). What is more, changes in the demands of individuals and firms may interact with each other, affecting the character of the business cycle. For example, a rise in consumer expenditure could stimulate firms to invest in order to build up capacity to meet the extra demand. This, in turn, generates more employment, additional national income and

so more consumption. A similar effect could occur if banks felt able to lend more in response to the growing economy, which would further stimulate the economy as these funds are spent.

Other economists see the problem as rooted in fluctuations in *aggregate supply*: in other words, in the total amount of goods and services firms plan to supply at a given level of prices (see page 462). These 'real-business-cycle' economists argue that changes in aggregate supply occur if the price, availability or effectiveness of the inputs in firms' production processes are in some way affected. One example could be technological changes that boost output and employment. Often such changes come in waves, which would contribute to the observed volatility of output.

But whatever the cause, it is vital to recognise the fundamental instability of market economies. This is what makes the volatility in short-term growth rates a threshold concept.

1. *If people believe that the economy's output level is about to fall, how may their actions aggravate the problem?*
2. *Why will some people suffer more than others from a downturn in economic activity?*

Longer-term economic growth

Although growth rates fluctuate, most economies experience positive growth over the longer term. In other words, most economies have output paths that trend upwards over time. We can see this in Figure 15.2, for example. Therefore, we need to distinguish between short-run and long-run economic growth.

While an analysis of short-run growth involves understanding the determinants of the business cycle, analysing long-run economic growth involves understanding what affects a country's capacity to produce. This is because, for growth to be sustained over the longer term, the economy's capacity must increase.

Table 15.1 shows the average annual growth in output by decade since the 1960s for selected countries. As you can see, the differences between countries are quite marked. There are also big differences between the growth rates of individual countries in different periods. Look, for example, at the figures for Japan. From being an 'economic miracle' in the 1960s, by the 1990s Japan had become a laggard, with growth rates well below the OECD average.

The final column of the table takes an even longer-term perspective by focusing on the average annual rate of economic growth from 1960 to 2019. We still observe differences in growth rates, even when averaged over many years.

Table 15.1	Economic growth rates (average % per annum)						
	1960s	1970s	1980s	1990s	2000s	2010s	1960–2019
Australia	4.9	3.4	3.4	3.2	3.2	2.7	3.5
Canada	5.3	4.1	2.9	2.4	2.1	2.1	3.2
France	5.6	3.7	2.4	2.0	1.4	1.3	2.7
Germany	4.4	3.3	2.0	2.2	0.8	1.8	2.4
Ireland	4.4	4.7	3.1	7.0	3.8	5.1	4.7
Italy	5.8	4.0	2.6	1.5	0.5	0.2	2.4
Japan	10.1	5.2	4.4	1.5	0.6	1.3	3.9
Spain	7.8	3.9	2.7	2.7	2.8	0.9	3.5
UK	3.4	2.6	2.7	2.1	1.8	1.9	2.4
USA	4.5	3.2	3.1	3.2	1.8	2.2	3.0
OECD[a]	5.3	3.7	2.9	2.6	1.8	2.0	3.1

[a]The Organisation for Economic Co-operation and Development (OECD) is an organisation of 35 major industrialised countries.
Note: Figures for 2017–19 are forecasts.
Source: OECD.

While some of the differences may not appear particularly large, it is important to bear in mind is that even small differences in the figures have potentially significant implications for economic development and the well-being of nations when you consider that these differences are being compounded year after year.

 Compare economic growth rates in the early 2010s with those in other periods. What explanations can you offer for the differences?

Unemployment

The inherent instability of economies has implications for the number of people in work and so for the number unable to find work. After all, higher levels of economic activity will tend to decrease unemployment numbers, while reduced economic activity will tend to increase them.

In addition, many countries have seen significant effects on the labour market of rapid industrial change, technological advance and globalisation. Hence, labour markets need to be able to adapt to the dynamic environment in which they operate, not only for the sake of those who are made unemployed, but also because it represents a waste of human resources and because unemployment benefits are a drain on government revenues.

Unemployment can be expressed either as a number (e.g. 1.5 million) or as a percentage (e.g. 5 per cent). The most usual definition that economists use for the **number unemployed** is: *those of working age who are without work, but who are available for work at current wage rates*. If the figure is to be expressed as a percentage, then it is a percentage of the total **labour force**. The labour force is defined as *those in employment plus those unemployed*. Thus if 30 million people were employed and 1.5 million people were unemployed, the **unemployment rate** would be:

$$\frac{1.5}{30 + 1.5} \times 100 = 4.76\%$$

When comparing unemployment across countries it is sensible to compare *rates* of unemployment. Table 15.2 shows average unemployment rates across a sample of

countries since the 1960s. It shows how in the 1980s and early 1990s unemployment rates were significantly higher than in the 1960s and 1970s. Then, in the late 1990s and early 2000s, it fell in some countries, such as the UK and USA. In others, such as Germany and France, it remained stubbornly high. However, the global financial crisis and subsequent economic slowdown meant that unemployment rates were to rise generally in the late 2000s and into the early 2010s.

We take a preliminary look at the nature and causes of unemployment in section 15.5.

 Have unemployment rates generally risen or fallen over the decades or is there no discernible pattern? Does the answer vary by country?

Inflation

By inflation we mean a general rise in prices throughout the economy. Government policy here is to keep inflation both low and stable. One of the most important reasons for this is that it will aid the process of economic decision making. For example, businesses will be able to set prices and wage rates, and make investment decisions with far more confidence.

The **rate of inflation** measures the annual percentage increase in prices. Typically, when we hear about inflation it is in relation to *consumer* prices. The UK government publishes

Definitions

Number unemployed (economist's definition) Those of working age who are without work, but who are available for work at current wage rates.

Labour force The number employed plus the number unemployed

Unemployment rate The number unemployed expressed as a percentage of the labour force.

Rate of inflation The percentage increase in prices over a 12-month period.

Table 15.2	Average unemployment rates (%)						
	1960s	1970s	1980s	1990s	2000s	2010s	1960–2019
Australia	1.7	3.8	7.6	8.8	5.5	5.4	5.5
Canada	5.0	6.7	9.4	9.5	7.0	7.1	7.5
France	1.7	3.1	7.6	9.7	8.4	9.7	6.7
Germany	0.7	2.0	5.8	7.8	8.9	5.0	5.0
Ireland	5.3	7.5	14.2	12.1	5.4	10.4	9.2
Italy	4.8	5.9	8.4	10.2	7.9	10.9	8.0
Japan	1.3	1.7	2.5	3.1	4.7	3.7	2.8
Spain	2.4	4.5	16.3	18.0	11.2	20.8	12.2
UK	1.6	3.5	9.5	8.0	5.4	6.3	5.7
USA	4.8	6.2	7.3	5.8	5.5	6.4	6.0

Note: Figures for 2017–19 are forecasts.

Source: *AMECO* (European Commission, Economic and Financial Affairs).

a consumer prices index (CPI) each month, and the rate of inflation is the percentage increase in that index over the previous 12 months. This index is used throughout the EU, where it generally goes under its full title of the harmonised index of consumer prices (HICP). The HICP covers virtually 100 per cent of consumer spending (including cross-border spending) and uses sophisticated weights for each item (see Appendix 1, page A:7 for an analysis of weighting in indices).

In most developed countries, governments now have a target for the rate of consumer price inflation. This is frequently around 2 per cent, as is the case in the UK, USA and eurozone. Central banks, such as the Bank of England, the US Federal Reserve Bank (the Fed) and the European Central Bank, then adjust interest rates to try to keep inflation on target (we see how this works in Chapter 22). The advent of inflation-rate targeting has tended to narrow differences in inflation rates between countries, as have the increasing economic ties between countries.

Table 15.3 helps to show how, in recent years, people in many developed economies have become accustomed to inflation rates of around 2 or 3 per cent. Yet it was many years ago that inflation in most developed countries was in double figures. Many countries saw relatively high rates of inflation during the 1970s, with the inflation rate in the UK, for example, reaching 24 per cent in 1975.

Today inflation rates are significantly lower and some countries have experienced periods of negative inflation rates or what is sometimes called 'deflation'.

We will take a preliminary look at the factors affecting rates of inflation in section 15.6.

Would it matter if all prices rose by 20 per cent, but everyone's income also rose by 20 per cent? (We consider this issue in section 15.6.)

Foreign trade and global economic relationships

A county's macroeconomic environment is shaped not only by domestic conditions but also by its economic relationships with other countries. These relationships evolve as the global economy develops and the world order changes. Take, for example, the rapid economic growth observed over the past couple of decades or more in economies like China and India, just to name a couple.

International economic relationships also evolve as countries or groups of countries come together to shape their economic relationships with other economies. Following the UK referendum on EU membership in 2016, the decision to leave meant that, over time, a new set of economic relationships between the UK and its foreign partners would emerge.

One way of viewing the economic relationship between a country and other economies is through its **balance of payments account**. This records all transactions between the residents of that country and the rest of the world. These transactions enter as either debit items or credit items. The debit items include all payments *to* other countries: these include the country's purchases of imports, the investments it makes abroad and the interest and dividends paid to people abroad who have invested in the country. The credit items include all receipts *from* other countries: these include the sales of exports, inflows of investment into the country and earnings of interest and dividends from abroad.

The sale of exports and any other receipts earn foreign currency. The purchase of imports or any other payments abroad requires foreign currency. If a country starts to spend more foreign currency than it earns, then its balance of payments will go into deficit. If the government does nothing to correct the

Definitions

Balance of payments account A record of the country's transactions with the rest of the world. It shows the country's payments to or deposits in other countries (debits) and its receipts or deposits from other countries (credits). It also shows the balance between these debits and credits under various headings

	1960s	1970s	1980s	1990s	2000s	2010s	1960–2019
Table 15.3 Average consumer price inflation rates (%)							
Australia	2.5	9.8	8.4	2.5	3.2	2.3	4.8
Canada	2.5	7.4	6.5	2.2	2.1	1.8	3.8
France	3.9	8.8	7.4	1.9	1.7	1.2	4.2
Germany	2.4	4.9	2.9	2.6	1.6	1.4	2.6
Ireland	4.0	12.7	9.3	2.3	3.2	0.6	5.4
Italy	3.7	12.3	11.2	4.2	2.3	1.3	5.8
Japan	5.3	9.0	2.5	1.2	−0.3	0.5	3.7
Spain	5.6	14.4	10.2	4.2	3.0	1.3	6.5
UK	3.5	12.6	7.1	3.3	1.9	2.3	5.1
USA	2.3	7.1	5.6	3.0	2.6	1.9	3.8

Notes: Figures for 2017–19 are forecasts; Ireland 1960–1975, Central Statistics Office.
Source: OECD.

balance of payments deficit, the *exchange rate* of the country's currency must fall. The exchange rate is the rate at which one currency exchanges for another. For example, the exchange rate of the pound into the dollar might be £1 = $1.40.

A falling exchange rate (e.g. from $1.40 to $1.20) is a problem because it pushes up the price of imports and so reduces people's purchasing power and can fuel inflation. This was the situation facing the UK in the aftermath of the vote to leave the European Union, when the pound fell sharply. Exchange-rate fluctuations can also be problematic because they can cause great uncertainty for traders and can damage international trade and economic growth.

What are the underlying causes of balance of payments problems? How do the balance of payments and the exchange rate relate to the other macroeconomic issues? What are the best policies for governments to adopt? We take an initial look at these questions in section 15.7 and then examine them in more detail in Chapters 25 and 26.

Financial well-being

The financial system is an integral part of most economies. Financial markets, financial institutions and *financial instruments* have become increasingly important in determining the financial well-being of nations, organisations, government and people. The increasing importance of the financial system to economies is known as *financialisation*.

The most immediate evidence of financialisation is the extent to which many of us interact with financial institutions and our use of financial instruments. Financialisation is most frequently associated with the level of indebtedness of *economic agents*, such as households and firms, to banks. In the UK, for example, by the end of 2016 households had debt outstanding borrowed from banks and building societies to the value of £1.3 trillion.

The importance of financial stability and the problem of financial distress. It is important for policy makers to ensure the stability of the financial system and the general financial well-being of economic agents. This importance was most starkly demonstrated by the events surrounding the financial crisis of 2007–9, when many banks looked as if they might become bankrupt. The crisis showed starkly how the financial distress of banks and other financial institutions can lead to global economic turmoil. Because of the global interconnectedness of financial institutions and markets, problems can spread globally like a contagion.

And it was not just financial institutions that were distressed in the late 2000s; we also witnessed financially distressed households and businesses, many of which were burdened by unsustainable levels of debt.

Subsequently, the financial distress was to affect government too, especially in advanced economies. Governments were burdened by growing levels of debt as they spent more to offset rapidly weakening private-sector spending. At the same time, tax revenues fell because of weakening economic growth. The consequence has been a prolonged period during which many governments have felt it necessary to tighten their budgets. And this constraint on government spending has been a brake on economic growth.

Financial accounts. In thinking about financial well-being or distress, three key accounts can be considered. These are compiled for the main sectors of the economy: the household, corporate and government sectors, and the whole economy.

First, there is the *income account* which records the various *flows* of income (a credit) alongside the amounts either spent or saved (debits). Economic growth refers to the annual real growth in a country's income flows (i.e. after taking inflation into account).

Next, there is the *financial account*. There are two elements here. First, we can record financial *flows,* which determine the net acquisition of financial wealth by each sector. These comprise new saving, borrowing or repayments. Reductions in the flows of borrowing, in countries like the UK and USA, were very important in explaining the credit crunch and subsequent deep recession of the late 2000s/early 2010s.

The other element of the financial account is its **balance sheet**. A balance sheet is a record of *stocks* of **assets** and **liabilities** of individuals or institutions. An asset is something owned by or owed to you. A liability is a debt: i.e. something you owe to someone else. In the case of the financial account, we have a complete record of the stocks of financial assets (arising from saving) and financial liabilities (arising from borrowing) of a sector, and include things such as currency, bank deposits, loans, bonds and shares. The flows of borrowing during the 2000s meant that many individual and organisations experienced a significant increase in stocks of financial liabilities.

Definitions

Exchange rate The rate at which one national currency exchanges for another. The rate is expressed as the amount of one currency that is necessary to purchase *one unit* of another currency (e.g. £1.20 = £1).

Financial instruments Tradable financial assets, such as shares ('equities'), bonds, foreign currency and bank account deposits.

Financialisation A term used to describe the process by which financial markets, institutions and instruments becoming increasingly significant in economies.

Economic agents People or institutions making economic decisions. These could be individuals as consumers, workers, borrowers or savers, or firms, governments or other public institutions.

Balance sheet A record of the stock of assets and liabilities of an individual or institution.

Asset Possessions of an individual or institution, or claims held on others.

Liability Claims by others on an individual or institution; debts of that individual or institution.

Finally, there is the *capital account,* which looks at flows and stocks of *physical* assets and liabilities. Again, there are two elements. The first records the capital *flows* of the various sectors, which occur when acquiring or disposing of physical assets, such as property and machinery. The second records the *stock* of physical wealth held by the various sectors.

The national balance sheet.   This is a measure of the wealth of a country (i.e. the nation's financial and physical stock of net assets). It shows the *composition* of a country's wealth and the contribution of each of the main *sectors* of the economy.

The balance of a sector's or country's stock of financial and non-financial assets over its financial liabilities is referred to as its **net worth**. An *increase* in the net worth of the sectors or the whole country implies greater financial well-being. However, during the 2000s many sectors experienced increases in net worth as asset values rose, despite the rising stock of financial liabilities. Subsequently, the increase in the stock of liabilities was not financially sustainable and asset prices were to fall.

These various accounts are part of an interconnected story detailing the financial well-being of a country's households, companies and government. To illustrate how, consider what would happen if, over a period of time, you were to spend more than the income you receive. This would result in your income account deteriorating. To finance your excess spending you could perhaps draw on any financial wealth that you have accumulated through saving. Alternatively, you might fund some of your spending through a loan from a financial institution, such as a bank. Either way, your financial balance sheet will deteriorate. Or you may dispose of some physical assets, such as property. However your excess spending is financed, your capital balance will deteriorate: your net worth declines.

The importance of balance-sheet effects in influencing behaviour and, hence, economic activity has been increasingly recognised by both economists and policy makers, especially since the financial crisis of 2007–9. Understanding these effects and their consequences is crucial in devising the most appropriate policies.

 Balance sheets affect people's behaviour. The size and structure of governments', institutions' and individuals' liabilities (and assets too) affect economic well-being and can have significant effects on behaviour and economic activity.

Government macroeconomic policy

From the above issues we can identify a series of macroeconomic policy objectives that governments might typically pursue:

- High and stable economic growth.
- Low unemployment.
- Low inflation.
- The avoidance of balance of payments deficits and excessive exchange rate fluctuations.
- A stable financial system and the avoidance of excessively financially distressed sectors of the economy, including government itself.

Unfortunately, these policy objectives may conflict. For example, a policy designed to accelerate the rate of economic growth may result in a higher rate of inflation, a balance of payments deficit and excessive lending. Governments are thus often faced with awkward policy choices.

 Societies face trade-offs between economic objectives. For example, the goal of faster growth may conflict with that of greater equality; the goal of lower unemployment may conflict with that of lower inflation (at least in the short run). This is an example of opportunity cost: the cost of achieving one objective may be achieving less of another. The existence of trade-offs means that policy makers must make choices.

Definitions

Net worth The market value of a sector's stock of financial and non-financial wealth.

Section summary

1. Macroeconomics, like microeconomics, looks at issues such as output, employment and prices; but it looks at them in the context of the whole economy.

2. Economies are inherently volatile, as evidenced by fluctuations in short-term economic growth rates. These fluctuations cause an economy's output path to fluctuate, generating what economists call the business cycle.

3. Among the macroeconomic goals that are generally of most concern to governments are: economic growth, reducing unemployment, reducing inflation, avoiding balance of payments and exchange rate problems, a stable financial system and the avoidance of excessively financially distressed economic agents.

4. Unfortunately, these goals are likely to conflict. Governments may thus be faced with difficult policy choices.

15.2 MEASURING NATIONAL INCOME AND OUTPUT

A consistent theme of section 15.1 was the inherent volatility of economies. One of the principal ways in which we observe this is through the volatility of national income or output. But just how do we measure national income or output? The measure we use is called *gross domestic product (GDP)*.

This section focuses on how GDP is calculated. It also looks at difficulties in interpreting GDP statistics. Can the figures be meaningfully used to compare one country's standard of living with another? The appendix to this chapter goes into more detail on the precise way in which the statistics for GDP are derived.

The three ways of measuring GDP

GDP can be calculated in three different ways, which should all result in the same figure. These three methods can be understood in the context of the *circular flow of income model,* which we introduced in Chapter 1 (see page 17). This model allows us to trace the resources and, as its name suggests, the income flows that pass between the major groups in the economy.

A simplified version of the model is shown in Figure 15.3. In the diagram, the economy is divided into two major groups: *firms* and *households.* Each group has two roles. Firms are producers of goods and services; they are also the employers of labour and other factors of production. Households (which include all individuals) are the consumers of goods and services; they are also the suppliers of labour and various other factors of production.

The first method of measuring GDP is to add up the value of all the goods and services produced in the country, industry by industry. In other words, we focus on firms and add up all their production. This first method is known as the *product method.*

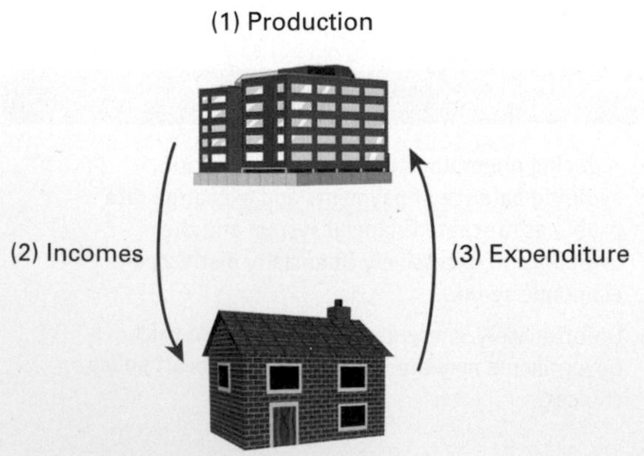

The production of goods and services generates incomes for households in the form of wages and salaries, profits, rent and interest. The second method of measuring GDP, therefore, is to add up all these incomes. This is known as the *income method.*

The third method focuses on the expenditures necessary to purchase the nation's production. In this simple model of the circular flow of income, whatever is produced is sold. The value of what is sold must therefore be the value of what is produced. The *expenditure method* measures this sales value.

Because of the way the calculations are made, the three methods of calculating GDP *must* yield the same result. In other words,

$$\text{national product} = \text{national income}$$
$$= \text{national expenditure}$$

In the appendix to this chapter, we look at each of the three methods in turn, and examine the various factors that have to be taken into account to ensure that the figures are accurate.

Taking account of inflation

If we are to make a sensible comparison of one year's national income with another, we must take inflation into account. For example, if this year national income is 10 per cent higher than last year, but at the same time prices are also 10 per cent higher, then the average person will be no better off at all. There has been no *real* increase in income (see discussion in Appendix 1 at the end of the book on page A:6).

KI 40 pA:6

An important distinction here is between *nominal GDP* and *real GDP. Nominal* GDP, sometimes called 'money GDP', measures GDP in the prices ruling at the time and thus takes no account of inflation. *Real* GDP, sometimes called 'GDP at constant prices', measures GDP in the prices that ruled in some particular year – the *base year.* Thus we could measure each year's GDP in, say, 2015 prices. This would enable us to see how much *real* GDP had changed from one year to another. In other words, it would eliminate increases in money GDP that were merely due to an increase in prices.

TC 13 p453

The official statistics give both nominal and real figures. (Case Study 15.1 on the student website shows in more detail how real GDP figures are calculated.) Figure 15.4 shows nominal GDP and GDP at constant 2015 prices since 1955 in the

Figure 15.3 The circular flow of income

(1) Production

(2) Incomes

(3) Expenditure

Definitions

Gross domestic product (GDP) The value of output produced within the country over a 12-month period.

Nominal GDP GDP measured at current prices.

Real GDP GDP after allowing for inflation: i.e. GDP measured in *constant* prices, in other words in terms of the prices ruling in some base year.

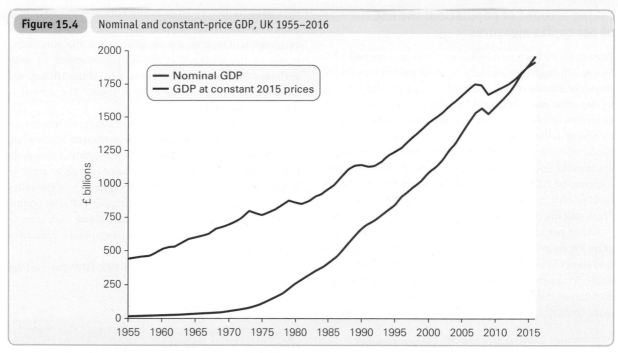

| Figure 15.4 | Nominal and constant-price GDP, UK 1955–2016 |

Source: Based on *Time Series Data,* series YBHA and ABMI (Office for National Statistics).

UK. If we had mistakenly used the nominal GDP figures to compare the size of output between these two dates we would have thought that the economy was over 100 times larger. In fact, the real figures show the UK economy was actually only 4.3 times larger in 2016 than in 1955.

As well as revealing the extent of long-term economic growth, the real figures also show the *variability* of economic growth from year to year. We can see falls in output in the mid-1970s, early 1980s and early 1990s that are not directly observable from nominal GDP. Instead, nominal GDP continued to increase because of rising price levels. However, in 2009 output fell by over 4.2 per cent, which meant that even nominal GDP fell. In other words, price rises were not enough to offset a substantial decline in the volume of output.

THRESHOLD CONCEPT 13 **THE DISTINCTION BETWEEN REAL AND NOMINAL VALUES**   THINKING LIKE AN ECONOMIST

Which would you rather have: (a) a pay rise of 5 per cent when inflation is 2 per cent, or (b) a pay rise of 10 per cent when inflation is 9 per cent? Which debt would you rather have: (a) one where the interest rate is 10 per cent and inflation is 8 per cent, or (b) one where the interest rate is 5 per cent and the inflation rate is 1 per cent?

To answer these questions, you need to distinguish between real and nominal values. *Nominal values* are measured in current prices and take no account of inflation. Thus in the questions above, the nominal pay rises are (a) 5 per cent and (b) 10 per cent; the nominal interest rates are (a) 10 per cent and (b) 5 per cent. In each case it might seem that you are better off with alternative (b).

But if you opted for answers (b), you would be wrong. Once you take inflation into account, you would be better off in each case with alternative (a). What we need to do is to use real values. Real values take account of inflation. Thus in the first question, although the nominal pay rise in alternative (a) is 5 per cent, the real pay rise is only 3 per cent, since 2 of the 5 per cent is absorbed by higher prices. You are only 3 per cent better off in terms of what you can buy. In alternative (b) the real pay rise is

only 1 per cent, since 9 of the 10 per cent is absorbed by higher prices. Thus in real terms, alternative (a) is better.

In the second question, although in alternative (a) you are paying 10 per cent in nominal terms, your debt is being reduced in real terms by 8 per cent and thus you are paying a real rate of interest of only 2 per cent. In alternative (b), although the nominal rate of interest is only 5 per cent, your debt is being eroded by inflation by only 1 per cent. The real rate of interest is thus 4 per cent. Again, in real terms, you are better off with alternative (a).

The distinction between real and nominal values is a threshold concept, as understanding the distinction is fundamental to assessing statistics about the economy.

It's easy to make the mistake of using nominal figures when we should really be using real ones. This is known as 'money illusion': the belief that a rise in money terms represents a real rise.

 When comparing two countries' GDP growth rates, does it matter if we use nominal figures, provided we use them for both countries?

Taking account of population: the use of per capita measures

The figures we have been looking at up to now are *total* GDP figures. Although they are useful for showing how big the total output or income of one country is compared with another, we are often more interested in output or income *per head*. Luxembourg obviously has a much lower total national income than the UK, but it has a higher GDP per head. In 2009 China overtook Japan to become the second largest economy in the world, and some estimate that it will become the biggest economy by 2025. But these are total figures. Despite China's rapid growth, it is estimated that by 2020 GDP per capita in China will still be only around 20 per cent of that of the USA.

Other per capita measures are sometimes useful. For example, measuring GDP per head of the *employed* population allows us to compare how much the average worker produces. A country may have a relatively high GDP per head of population, but also have a large proportion of people at work. Its output per worker will therefore not be so high.

 By what would we need to divide GDP in order to get a measure of labour productivity per hour?

Taking account of exchange rates: the use of PPP measures

There is a big problem with comparing GDP figures of different countries. They are measured in the local currency and thus have to be converted into a common currency (e.g. dollars or euros) at the current exchange rate. But the exchange rate may be a poor indicator of the purchasing power of the currency at home. For example, £1 may exchange for, say, 150 yen. But will £1 in the UK buy the same amount of goods as ¥150 in Japan? The answer is almost certainly no.

To compensate for this, GDP can be converted into a common currency at a ***purchasing-power parity rate***. This is a rate of exchange that would allow a given amount of money in one country to buy the same amount of goods in another country after exchanging it into the currency of the other country. For example, the OECD publishes PPP rates against the US dollar for all OECD currencies. Using such rates to measure GDP gives the ***purchasing-power standard (PPS) GDP***.

Box 15.1 compares GDP with PPS GDP for various countries.

> ## Definitions
>
> **Purchasing-power parity (PPP) exchange rate** An exchange rate corrected to take into account the purchasing power of a currency. $1 would buy the same in each country after conversion into its currency at the PPP rate.
>
> **Purchasing-power standard (PPS) GDP** GDP measured at a country's PPP exchange rate.

BOX 15.1 WHICH COUNTRY IS BETTER OFF?

CASE STUDIES AND APPLICATIONS

Comparing national income statistics

Using PPS GDP figures can give a quite different picture of the relative incomes in different countries than using simple GDP figures. The table shows the GDP per head and PPS GDP per head in various countries. The figures are expressed as a percentage of the average of the EU-15 countries (i.e. those that were members prior to the entry of 10 new members in May 2004).

Thus in 2017, GDP per head in Denmark was estimated to be 45 per cent higher than the EU-15 average. But, because of higher Danish prices, the average person in Denmark could buy only 15 per cent more goods and services. By contrast, GDP per head in the Czech Republic was only 51 per cent of the EU-15 average but, because of lower prices in the Czech Republic, the average person there could buy 82 per cent as much as the average citizen of the EU-15 countries.

 Referring to the figures in the table, which countries' actual exchange rates would seem to understate the purchasing power of their currency?

GDP per head as a percentage of the EU-15 average, 2017

	GDP per head	GDP (PPS) per head
Poland	34.8	65.6
Greece	49.4	62.7
Czech Republic	50.8	82.1
Portugal	54.3	71.6
Spain	73.0	85.5
Italy	82.3	88.4
France	99.6	97.0
UK	104.7	99.1
Japan	107.0	96.9
Germany	113.8	113.4
Canada	120.6	105.4
Netherlands	122.9	118.8
Sweden	139.9	114.7
Denmark	145.4	115.4
Australia	152.9	113.3
USA	163.4	133.5
Ireland	172.0	169.5
Luxembourg	284.6	251.3

Notes: Figures based on forecasts; EU-15 = the 15 members of the EU prior to the accession of additional countries in May 2004.
Source: *AMECO database*, Table 6.2 (European Commission, DGECFIN).

Do GDP statistics give a good indication of a country's standard of living?

If we take into account both inflation and the size of the population, and use figures for *real* per capita PPS GDP, will this give us a good indication of a country's standard of living? The figures *do* give quite a good indication of the level of production of goods and the incomes generated from it, provided we are clear about the distinctions between the different measures.

But when we come to ask the more general question of whether the figures give a good indication of the welfare or happiness of the country's citizens, then there are serious problems in relying exclusively on GDP statistics.

Problems of measuring national output

The main problem here is that the output of some goods and services goes unrecorded and thus the GDP figures will understate the nation's output. There are two reasons why items are not recorded.

Non-marketed items. If you employ a decorator to paint your living room, this will be recorded in the GDP statistics. If, however, you paint the room yourself, it will not. Similarly, if a nanny is employed by parents to look after their children, this childcare will form part of GDP. If, however, a parent stays at home to look after the children, it will not. The exclusion of these 'do-it-yourself' and other home-based activities means that the GDP statistics understate the true level of production in the economy.

If over time there is an *increase* in the amount of do-it-yourself activities that people perform, the figures will also understate the *rate of growth* of national output. On the other hand, if in more and more families both partners go out to work and employ people to look after their children, this will overstate the rate of growth in output. The childcare that was previously unrecorded now enters into the GDP statistics.

 If we were trying to get a 'true' measure of national production, which of the following activities would you include: (a) washing-up; (b) planting flowers in the garden; (c) playing an educational game with children in the family; (d) playing any game with children in the family; (e) cooking your own supper; (f) cooking supper for the whole family; (g) reading a novel for pleasure; (h) reading a textbook as part of studying; (i) studying holiday brochures? Is there a measurement problem if you get pleasure from the do-it-yourself activity itself as well as from its outcome?

The 'underground' or 'shadow' economy. The underground economy consists of illegal and hence undeclared transactions. These could be transactions where the goods or services are themselves illegal, as with drugs, guns and prostitution. Alternatively, they could be transactions that are illegal only in that they are not declared for tax purposes. For example, to avoid paying VAT, a garage may be prepared to repair your car slightly more cheaply if you pay cash. Another example is that of 'moonlighting', where people do extra work outside their normal job and do not declare the income for tax purposes. For example, an electrician employed by a building contractor during the day may rewire people's houses in the evenings, again for cash. Unemployed people may do casual jobs that they do not declare, to avoid losing benefits.

Problems of using GDP statistics to measure welfare

GDP is essentially an indicator of a nation's *production*. But production may be a poor indicator of society's well-being for the following reasons.

Production does not equal consumption. Production is desirable only to the extent that it enables us to *consume* more. If GDP rises as a result of a rise in *investment,* this will not lead to an increase in *current* living standards. It will, of course, help to raise *future* consumption.

The same applies if GDP rises as a result of an increase in exports. Unless there is a resulting increase in imports, it will be consumers abroad that benefit, not domestic consumers.

Production has human costs. If production increases, this may be due to technological advance. If, however, it increases as a result of people having to work harder or longer hours, its net benefit will be less. Leisure is a desirable good, and so too are pleasant working conditions, but these items are not included in the GDP figures.

GDP ignores externalities. The rapid growth in industrial society is recorded in GDP statistics. What the statistics do not record are the environmental side effects: the polluted air and rivers, the ozone depletion, the problem of global warming. If these external costs were taken into account, the *net* benefits of industrial production might be much less.

 Name some external benefits that are not included in GDP statistics.

The production of certain 'bads' leads to an increase in GDP. Some of the undesirable effects of growth may in fact *increase* GDP! Take the examples of crime, stress-related illness and environmental damage. Faster growth may lead to more of all three. But increased crime leads to more expenditure on security; increased stress leads to more expenditure on health care; and increased environmental damage leads to more expenditure on environmental clean-up. These expenditures *add* to GDP. Thus, rather than reducing GDP, crime, stress and environmental damage actually increase it.

Total GDP figures ignore the distribution of income. If some people gain and others lose, we cannot say that there has been an unambiguous increase in welfare. A typical feature of many rapidly growing countries is that some people grow very rich while others are left behind. The result is a growing inequality. If this is seen as undesirable, then clearly total GDP statistics are an inadequate measure of welfare.

Conclusions

If a country's citizens put a high priority on a clean environment, a relaxed way of life, greater self-sufficiency, a less materialistic outlook, more giving rather than selling, and greater equality, then such a country will probably have a lower GDP than a similarly endowed country where the pursuit of wealth is given high priority. Clearly, we cannot conclude that the first country will have a lower level of well-being.

However, this does not mean that we should reject GDP statistics as a means of judging economic performance. While GDP statistics are not a good measure of economic welfare, they are an effective measure of *output* or *income*, and should be seen in that context.

BOX 15.2	CAN GDP MEASURE NATIONAL HAPPINESS?	EXPLORING ECONOMICS

An alternative perspective on well-being

The domains of national well-being

GDP is not a complete measure of economic welfare; nor is it meant to be. Consequently, there is considerable interest in alternative methods of establishing the level of human well-being and happiness.

In 2010 the UK's Office for National Statistics launched its *Measuring National Well-being (MNW) programme.*[1] The principal aim was to develop a set of national statistics which would both help people to gain a better understanding of well-being and allow well-being to be monitored. The data, for instance, would enable policy makers to make more informed policy decisions by better understanding the impact of their choices across society.

The MNW programme has identified a series of 'domains' with associated measures. There are 10 domains: personal well-being, our relationships, health, what we do, education and skills, where we live, personal finance, the economy, governance and the natural environment. These 10 domains produce a series of indicators – 43 as of 2016.

In the three-year period to September 2016 the ONS reported that of the 35 measures where data allowed for comparison, 22 measures had improved, 5 showed no overall change and 8 deteriorated.

Domains such as 'personal finance' and 'where we live' included several indicators showing improvement. For example, real median disposable income rose, the number of people reporting financial hardship fell and the number accessing the natural environment weekly rose.

Meanwhile the number of crimes against the person (per thousand of the population) had risen and the numbers reporting satisfaction with their job and with the amount of leisure time fell.

Personal well-being and social capital

Since 2011, adults in the UK over 16 have been asked the following four questions in an attempt to monitor individual well-being:

- Overall, how satisfied are you with your life nowadays?
- Overall, to what extent do you feel the things you do in your life are worthwhile?
- Overall, how happy did you feel yesterday?
- Overall, how anxious did you feel yesterday?

Respondents give their answers using a scale of 0 to 10 where 0 is 'not at all' and 10 is 'completely'.

Since 2013 the ONS has published regional indicators of personal well-being. In its review of personal well-being in financial year 2015/16,[2] the ONS reports that the average level of personal well-being was highest in Northern Ireland. One possible explanation, it argues, might be higher levels of feelings of belonging to a neighbourhood and a sense that people are prepared to help others. These are elements of what is known as ***social capital***. Social capital captures social connections and networks which affect the cohesiveness of societies. Our social connections, whether through relationships with family and friends, local communities or wider society, help to bind societies together.

As well as affecting personal well-being, social capital is important for national well-being and has economic significance. Examples of the impact of social capital include the economic value of the informal care of the sick and vulnerable, the provision of local amenities through volunteers or social enterprise, the economic benefits from membership of clubs, societies and other organisations, including the social bonds that are created.

Our understanding of both national and individual well-being continues to evolve. However, it is, of course, debatable how close any measures of well-being can come to measuring such a thing. Further, how should the results of such investigations help governments devise policy? Will governments be any closer to measuring the costs and benefits of any policy decisions?

1. *Is well-being the same as happiness or utility?*
2. *For what reasons might a person have a high income but a poor level of well-being?*

1 *Measuring National Well-being in the UK, Domains and Measures: September 2016* (Office for National Statistics, September 2016).
2 *Personal Well-being across the UK, 2015/16* (Office for National Statistics, July 2016).

Definitions

Social capital (OECD definition) Networks, together with shared norms, values and understandings, that facilitate co-operation within or among groups.

Section summary

1. National income is usually expressed in terms of gross domestic product. This is simply the value of domestic production over the course of the year. It can be measured by the product, expenditure or income methods.

2. Real national income takes account of inflation by being expressed in the prices of some base year.

3. In order to compare living standards of different countries, national income has to be expressed per capita and at purchasing-power parity exchange rates.

4. Even if it is, there are still problems in using national income statistics for comparative purposes. Certain items will not be included: items such as non-marketed products, services in the family and activities in the underground economy. Moreover, the statistics include certain 'bads' and ignore externalities, and they also ignore questions of the distribution of income.

15.3 THE BUSINESS CYCLE

The distinction between actual and potential growth

Economies are volatile as evidenced by the volatility of growth. They experience not only periods of expansion but also periods when growth is negative – when output levels contract. For many, the defining feature of the business cycle is the very absence of growth in times of recession.

The published statistics on growth show **actual growth**: the percentage change in national output over a period of time. As we saw in section 15.1, this is commonly measured over a year (12 months) or a quarter (3 months).

We should be careful to distinguish between actual growth and potential growth. **Potential growth** is the speed at which the economy *could* grow. It is the percentage annual increase in the economy's *capacity* to produce: the rate of growth in *potential output*.

Potential output (i.e. potential GDP) is the level of output when the economy is operating at 'normal capacity utilisation'. This allows for firms having a planned degree of spare capacity to meet unexpected demand or for hold-ups in supply. It also allows for some unemployment as people move from job to job. Because potential output is normal-capacity output, it is somewhat below full-capacity output, which is the absolute maximum that could be produced with firms working flat out.

The output gap. The difference between actual and potential output is known as the **output gap**. Thus if actual output exceeds potential output, the output gap is positive: the economy is operating above normal capacity utilisation. If actual output is below potential output, the output gap is negative: the economy is operating below normal capacity utilisation. Box 15.3 looks at the output gap since 1970 for five major industrial economies.

Assume that the actual growth rate is less than the potential growth rate. This will lead to an increase in spare capacity and probably an increase in unemployment. In turn, the output gap will become less positive or perhaps more negative, depending on the economy's starting point.

In contrast, if the actual growth rate were to exceed the potential growth rate, there would be a reduction in spare capacity and the output gap would become less negative or more positive. However, periods when actual growth exceeds potential growth can only be temporary. In the long run, the actual growth rate will be limited to the potential growth rate.

Factors affecting potential output and potential growth

Although our focus in section 15.3 is on short-term volatility and hence on actual growth, it is worth briefly considering the principal factors that contribute to potential economic growth. We look at this in much more depth in Chapter 23.

Explanations tend to focus on the role of the economy's resources. This is the 14th of our threshold concepts, which states that long-term growth in a country's output depends on a growth in the quantity and/or productivity of its resources.

First, there is the issue of quantity. An increase in resources, whether they are natural resources, labour or capital, enables the economy's potential output to increase.

Definitions

Actual growth The percentage increase in national output actually produced.

Potential growth The percentage increase in the capacity of the economy to produce.

Potential output. The sustainable level of output that could be produced in the economy: i.e. one that involves a 'normal' level of capacity utilisation and does not result in rising inflation.

Output gap The difference between actual and potential output. When actual output exceeds potential output, the gap is positive. When actual output is less than potential output, the gap is negative.

Second, there is the issue of the effectiveness or productivity of resources. An increase in the effectiveness of the resources used, perhaps through advances in technology, improved labour skills or improved organisation, also enables growth in potential output.

Although the growth in potential output varies to some extent over the years – depending on the rate of advance of technology, the level of investment and the discovery of new raw materials – it nevertheless tends to be much steadier than the growth in actual output.

 How might the volatility of an economy affect the growth of potential output?

The hypothetical business cycle

Actual growth tends to fluctuate. In some years, countries will experience high rates of economic growth: the country experiences a boom. In other years, economic growth is low or even negative: the country experiences a slowdown or recession.[2] This cycle of expansion and slowdown causes fluctuations in the path of output.

Figure 15.5 illustrates a hypothetical business cycle. While it is a stylised representation of the business cycle, it is useful for illustrating four identifiable 'phases' of the cycle.

2 In official statistics, a recession is defined as when an economy experiences falling real GDP (negative growth) for two or more successive quarters.

1. *The upturn.* In this phase, a contracting or stagnant economy begins to recover, and growth in actual output resumes, or begins to accelerate.
2. *The expansion.* During this phase, there is rapid economic growth: the economy is booming. A fuller use is made of resources, and the gap between actual and potential output narrows.
3. *The peaking out.* During this phase, growth slows down or even ceases.
4. *The slowdown, recession or slump.* During this phase, there is little or no growth or even a decline in output. Increasing slack develops in the economy. The economy is operating with a negative output gap.

A word of caution: do not confuse a high *level* of output with a high rate of *growth* in output. The level of output is highest in phase 3. The rate of growth in output is highest in phase 2 (i.e. where the curve is steepest).

 Figure 15.5 shows a decline in actual output in recession. Redraw the diagram, only this time show a mere slowing down of growth in phase 4.

Long-term output trend

A line can be drawn showing the trend of national output over time (i.e. ignoring the cyclical fluctuations around the trend). This is shown as the dashed line in Figure 15.5. If, over time, firms on average operate with a 'normal' degree of capacity utilisation (a zero output gap), the trend output

---

| THRESHOLD CONCEPT 14 | LONG-TERM GROWTH IN A COUNTRY'S OUTPUT DEPENDS ON A GROWTH IN THE QUANTITY AND/OR PRODUCTIVITY OF ITS RESOURCES | THINKING LIKE AN ECONOMIST |

In the short term, economic growth is likely to be influenced by changes in aggregate demand. If the economy is in recession, an expansion in aggregate demand will help to bring the economy out of recession and move it closer to full employment.

Actual output, however, cannot continue growing faster than potential output over the longer term. Firms will start reaching capacity and actual growth will then have to slow. The rate of potential growth thus places a limit to the rate of actual growth over the longer term.

What then determines the rate of growth in potential output? The answer lies on the supply side. It depends on the rate of growth of factors of production. There are two key elements here. The first is growth in the *quantity* of factors: growth in the size of the workforce, of the available land and raw materials, and of the stock of capital. The second is productivity growth. This involves elements such as growth in the educational attainments and skills of the workforce, growth in technology, and growth in the efficiency with which resources are used.

To recognise the importance of resources and their productivity in determining long-term growth is a threshold concept. It helps in understanding the importance of designing appropriate supply-side policies: policies that focus on increasing aggregate supply rather than managing aggregate demand. It is easy to worry too much about the short term.

This is not to say that the short term should be neglected. The famous economist John Maynard Keynes argued that it was fundamentally important to focus on aggregate demand and the short term to avoid severe economic fluctuations, with the twin problems of high unemployment in recessions and high inflation in periods of unsustainably high growth. He used the famous phrase, 'In the long term we're all dead.'

But although we all have to die sometime, we may have many years left to reap the benefits of appropriate supply-side policy. And even if we don't, our children will.

1. *Give some examples of supply-side policy (see Chapter 23 for some ideas if you are stuck).*
2. *If there is an increase in aggregate supply, will this result in an increase in potential growth?*

line will be the same as the potential output line. Also, if the average level of capacity that is unutilised stays constant from one cycle to another, the trend line will have the same slope as the full-capacity output line. In other words, the trend (or potential) rate of growth will be the same as the rate of growth of capacity.

If, however, the level of unutilised capacity changes from one cycle to another, then the trend line will have a different slope from the full-capacity output line. For example, if unemployment and unused industrial capacity *rise* from one peak to another, or from one trough to another, the trend line will move further away from the full-capacity output line (i.e. it will be less steep).

 If the average percentage (as opposed to the average level) of capacity that was unutilised remained constant, would the trend line have the same slope as the potential output line?

The business cycle in practice

The hypothetical business cycle illustrated in Figure 15.5 is nice and smooth and regular. Drawing it this way allows us to make a clear distinction between each of the four phases. In practice, however, business cycles are highly irregular. They are irregular in two important ways:

- *The length of the phases.* Some booms are short-lived, lasting only a few months or so. Others are much longer, lasting perhaps several years. Likewise some recessions are short while others are long.
- *The magnitude of the phases.* Sometimes in phase 2 there is a very high rate of economic growth, perhaps 4 per cent per annum or more. On other occasions in phase 2 growth is much gentler. Sometimes in phase 4 there is a recession, with an actual decline in output, as occurred in 2008–9. On other occasions, phase 4 is merely a 'pause', with growth simply being low.

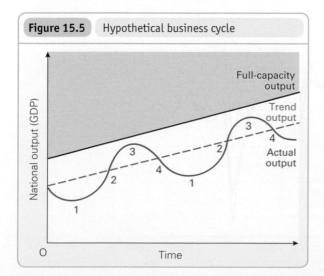

Figure 15.5   Hypothetical business cycle

An international business cycle

All countries tend to experience business cycles. Typically the timing is similar from one country to another. In other words, there is an international business cycle. Figure 15.6 shows the annual rate of growth in real GDP in the global economy alongside that in the UK and USA. Global growth rates varied from 5.6 per cent in 2007 to just below zero in 2009.

Figure 15.6 illustrates how global economic volatility is mirrored, at least in part, by the economic volatility in the UK and USA. More generally, this suggests that countries' business cycles have both a national and a global component. With increased global economic ties, many countries have seen the global component increase in its relative importance.

Aggregate demand and the business cycle

The focus of much of the analysis of business cycles is on fluctuations in *aggregate demand* (*AD*). This is the total spending on goods and services made within the country ('domestically produced goods and services'). It consists of spending by four groups of people: consumers on goods and services (*C*), firms on investment (*I*), the government on goods, services and investment (such as education, health and new roads) (*G*) and people abroad on this country's exports (*X*). From these four we have to subtract any imports (*M*) since aggregate demand refers only to spending on *domestic* firms. Thus

$$AD = C + I + G + X - M$$

Periods of rapid growth are associated with periods of rapid expansion of aggregate demand. Periods of recession are associated with a decline in aggregate demand.

Fluctuations in private-sector expenditure

When analysing the role played by the private sector as a source of economic volatility, it makes sense to begin by looking at consumer spending. This is because, by value, it is the largest expenditure component of aggregate demand. In the UK, for example, it frequently accounts for over 60 per cent of national income. This means that even small fluctuations in consumer expenditure can be significant for aggregate demand. As Figure 15.7 shows, annual rates of economic growth mirror fairly closely those in real household consumption.

Definitions

Aggregate demand   Total spending on goods and services produced in the economy. It consists of four elements, consumer expenditure (*C*), investment (*I*), government expenditure (*G*) and the expenditure on exports (*X*), less any expenditure on foreign goods and services (*M*). Thus $AD = C + I + G + X - M$.

BOX 15.3   OUTPUT GAPS

A measure of excess or deficient demand

If the economy grows, how fast and for how long can it grow before it runs into inflationary problems? On the other hand, what minimum rate must be achieved to avoid rising unemployment?

To answer these questions, economists have developed the concept of 'output gaps'.[1] The output gap is the difference between actual output and potential output, i.e. normal-capacity output.

If actual output is below potential output (the gap is negative), there will be a higher than normal level of unemployment as firms are operating below their normal level of capacity utilisation. There will, however, be a downward pressure on inflation, resulting from a lower than normal level of demand for labour and other resources.

If actual output is above potential output (the gap is positive), there will be excess demand and a rise in inflation.

Generally, the gap will be negative in a recession and positive in a boom. In other words, output gaps follow the course of the business cycle.

Measuring the output gap

But how do we measure the output gap? There are two principal statistical techniques.

De-trending techniques.   This approach is a purely mechanical exercise which involves smoothing the actual GDP figures. In doing this, it attempts to fit a trend growth path. This is illustrated by the dashed line in Figure 15.5. The main disadvantage of this approach is that it is not grounded in economic theory and therefore does not account for those factors likely to determine normal-capacity output.

Production function approach.   Many institutions, such as the European Union, use an approach which borrows ideas from economic theory. Specifically, this uses the idea of a production function which relates output to a set of inputs. Estimates of potential output are generated by using statistics on the size of a country's capital stock (see Box 23.1), the potential available labour input and, finally, the productivity or effectiveness of these inputs in producing output.

In addition to these statistical approaches, use could be made of *business surveys*. In other words, we ask businesses directly about normal capacity working and current levels of output. However, survey-based evidence can provide only a broad guide to rates of capacity utilisation and whether there is deficient or excess demand.

International evidence

The chart shows output gaps for five countries from 1970 estimated using a production function approach. What is apparent from the chart is that all the countries have experienced significant output gaps, both positive and negative. This is consistent with a core theme of this chapter and one to which we will return repeatedly throughout the second half of the book: economies are inherently volatile. In other words, countries experience business cycles.

The chart shows that the characteristics of countries' business cycles can differ, particularly in terms of depth and duration. But we also see evidence of an international business cycle (see page 459), which results from national cycles appearing to share characteristics. This global component of countries' business cycles is clearly evident in the late 2000s and into the 2010s. Increasing global interconnectedness from financial and trading links meant that the financial crisis of the late 2000s spread like a contagion.

While output gaps vary from year to year, over the longer term the average output gap tends towards zero. As we can see from the table, this means that for our selection of countries from 1970 the actual rate of economic growth is approximately the same as the potential rate.

Figure 15.6   UK and global economic growth

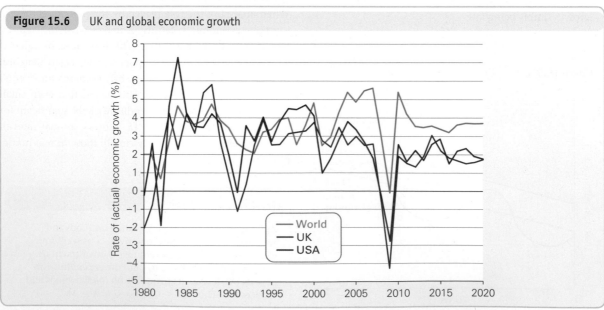

Note: Figures from 2017 are forecasts
Source: World Economic Outlook Database (IMF, October 2017)

Average annual growth in actual and potential output, %
(1970–2018)

	Average annual growth rates (%)	
	Actual output (real GDP)	**Potential output**
Germany	2.04	2.05
Ireland	4.79	4.77
France	2.24	2.24
UK	2.21	2.20
USA	2.71	2.75

Source: *AMECO database* (European Commission, DGECFIN).

Under what circumstances would potential output (i.e. a zero output gap) move further away from the full-capacity output ceiling shown in Figure 15.5?

1 See C. Giorno et al., 'Potential output, output gaps and structural budget balances', *OECD Economic Studies*, no. 24 (1995), p. 1.

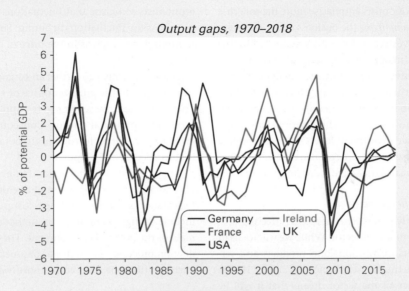

Output gaps, 1970–2018

Note: Figures for Germany based on West Germany prior to 1992; figures from 2017 based on forecasts.
Source: Based on data from *AMECO database* (European Commission, DGECFIN).

Figure 15.7	Annual growth of UK consumption, investment and output

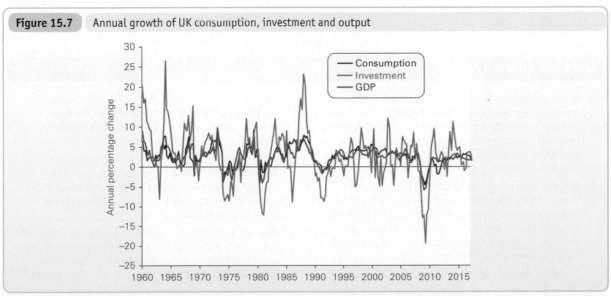

Note: Annual growth rates are calculated using constant-price data.
Source: Based on data in *Quarterly National Accounts*, series KGZ7, KG7T and IHYR (National Statistics).

Yet this still leaves many important questions to be addressed. What factors affect consumption? Which are most important? How do changes in consumption then affect the macroeconomic environment? Are the effects always the same? These are questions we will examine in section 17.1.

Another component of aggregate demand is investment. If we look again at Figure 15.7, we can see that fluctuations in the annual rate of growth of real investment spending (also known as gross capital formation) are considerably greater than those in output (real GDP).

It appears then that the volatility of investment is one of the factors contributing to the ups and downs of the business cycle. However, this does not mean that the fluctuations in investment are the primary cause of the economy's short-term volatility. They can be, but, as we will discuss in Chapter 17, some economists emphasise more the role that investment plays in *amplifying* the business cycle. The argument here is that investment decisions are affected by the growth in national income. Rising national income may encourage firms to invest to meet increasing demand. But this also has the effect of increasing aggregate demand, which further boosts national income. In contrast, an economy experiencing weak growth, or one where national income is contracting, might see investment levels fall, perhaps very sharply. This, of course, weakens aggregate demand, further amplifying already weak or negative economic growth.

The role of the financial sector

One sector that clearly plays a crucial role in affecting economic activity is the financial sector. While we will focus in detail on the markets, institutions and products and services which comprise the financial sector in Chapter 18, the economic significance of the sector means that it will be referred to frequently in subsequent chapters.

Given the financial crisis of the late 2000s, the interest in the role that the financial sector might play in affecting the business cycle is unsurprising. Some economists argue that the financial sector is a major *source* of economic volatility.

Some go as far as to say that the behaviour of financial institutions through their lending and investments generates unsustainable economic growth which inevitably ends with an economic downturn.

Other economists argue that the financial sector *amplifies* economic shocks. The argument here is not that financial institutions are the source of fluctuations in economic growth but rather that they magnify the shocks that affect the economy. They can do this by boosting lending when growth is strong or reducing lending when growth is weak.

Aggregate supply and the business cycle

While much of the economic analysis of business cycles stresses the importance of fluctuations in aggregate demand, economists recognise that fluctuations in *aggregate supply* can also cause fluctuations in output. Sudden sharp changes to input prices, such as in the price of oil, can be one such cause.

Some economists go further and argue that shifts in aggregate supply are the *primary* source of economic volatility. They argue that these aggregate supply shocks affect the economy's potential output. Consequently, the business cycle is the result of fluctuations in potential output, which in turn affect actual output.

They argue that economies are frequently affected by supply shocks, many of which might be described as 'technological shocks'. As well as changes to input prices, these could include changes to production methods, the regulatory climate or the political environment. These shocks affect production processes and levels of productivity. Some of these changes affect potential output positively, some negatively.

Definitions

Aggregate supply The total amount that firms plan to supply at any given level of prices.

Section summary

1. Actual growth must be distinguished from potential growth. The actual growth rate is the percentage annual increase in the output that is actually produced, whereas potential growth is the percentage annual increase in the capacity of the economy to produce (whether or not this capacity is utilised).

2. Actual growth will fluctuate with the course of the business cycle. The hypothetical business cycle can be broken down into four phases: the upturn, the expansion, the peaking out, and the slowdown or recession. In practice, the length and magnitude of these phases will vary: the cycle is thus irregular.

3. Countries' business cycles may have both national and international components. The international component has tended to increase over time as countries have become increasingly interconnected, for example through trade and growing financial ties.

4. Explanations of the business cycle tend to focus on fluctuations originating in aggregate demand. This requires a deeper understanding of the behaviour of the components of aggregate demand, including that of private-sector behaviour.

5. However, fluctuations in aggregate supply can also result in economic instability. Some economists go further and argue that business cycles can result from fluctuations in potential output caused by frequent technology shocks.

15.4 THE CIRCULAR FLOW OF INCOME

As we have seen, the economic choices of people, businesses and organisations can have profound effects for the macroeconomy. One model which allows us to develop an understanding of the impact of these choices for economic growth and which does so by focusing on aggregate demand is the *circular flow of income model*.

We encountered the circular flow model in section 15.2 when looking at how we measure GDP. Consider Figure 15.8. As before, the economy is divided into two major groups: *firms* and *households*. Each group has two roles. Firms are producers of goods and services; they are also the employers of labour and other factors of production. Households (which include all individuals) are the consumers of goods and services; they are also the suppliers of labour and various other factors of production. In the diagram there is an inner flow and various outer flows of incomes between these two groups.

Before we look at the various parts of the diagram, a word of warning. Do not confuse *money* and *income*. Money is a *stock* concept. At any given time, there is a certain quantity of money in the economy (e.g. £1 trillion). But that does not tell us the level of national *income*. Income is a *flow* concept (as is expenditure). It is measured as so much *per period of time*. The relationship between money and income depends on how rapidly the money *circulates*: its 'velocity of circulation'. (We will examine this concept in detail later on: see pages 495 and 588.) If there is £1 trillion of money in the economy and each £1 on average is paid out as income twice per year, then annual national income will be £2 trillion.

The inner flow, withdrawals and injections

The inner flow

Firms pay money to households in the form of wages and salaries, dividends on shares, interest and rent. These payments are in return for the services of the factors of production – labour, capital and land – that are supplied by households. Thus on the left-hand side of the diagram, money flows directly from firms to households as 'factor payments'.

Households, in turn, pay money to domestic firms when they consume domestically produced goods and services (C_d). This is shown on the right-hand side of the inner flow. There is thus a circular flow of payments from firms to households to firms and so on.

If households spend *all* their incomes on buying domestic goods and services, and if firms pay out *all* this income they receive as factor payments to domestic households, and if the velocity of circulation does not change, the flow will continue at the same level indefinitely. The money just goes round and round at the same speed and incomes remain unchanged.

 Would this argument still hold if prices rose?

In the real world, of course, it is not as simple as this. Not all income gets passed on round the inner flow; some is *withdrawn*. At the same time, incomes are injected into the flow from outside. Let us examine these withdrawals and injections.

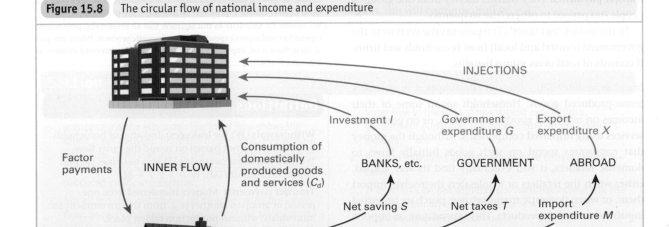

Figure 15.8 The circular flow of national income and expenditure

INJECTIONS

Investment *I*   Government expenditure *G*   Export expenditure *X*

BANKS, etc.   GOVERNMENT   ABROAD

Net saving *S*   Net taxes *T*   Import expenditure *M*

Factor payments   INNER FLOW   Consumption of domestically produced goods and services (C_d)

WITHDRAWALS

15.5 UNEMPLOYMENT

Understandably one of the most emotive of all macroeconomic issues is that of unemployment, not least because of the very personal costs to those affected by unemployment. Box 15.4 considers in more detail these and the broader costs to the economy of unemployment.

In this section, we look briefly at the potential causes of unemployment. What does the volatility of economies mean for unemployment? Is unemployment merely the result of the business cycle? If not, what other factors might be important? Before addressing these questions we do two things. First, we look at how we measure unemployment. Second, we look at evidence on the composition of unemployment and the duration that people are unemployed.

Claimant unemployment and standardised unemployment

Two common measures of unemployment are used in official statistics. The first is *claimant unemployment*. This is simply a measure of all those in receipt of unemployment-related benefits. Claimant statistics have the advantage of being very easy to collect. However, they exclude all those of working age who are available for work at current wage rates, but who are *not* eligible for benefits. The net effect is that the claimant statistics tend to understate the true level of unemployment. They are also sensitive to government changes in the eligibility conditions for unemployment-related benefits.

Because of the weaknesses of claimant statistics many governments use the *standardised unemployment rate* as the main measure of unemployment. In this measure, the unemployed are defined as people of working age who are without work, available to start work within two weeks and *actively seeking employment* or waiting to take up an appointment.

This is the measure used by the International Labour Organization (ILO) and the Organisation for Economic Co-operation and Development (OECD), two international organisations that publish unemployment statistics for many countries. The figures are compiled from the results of national labour force *surveys*. A representative cross-section of the population is asked whether they are employed, unemployed (using the above definition) or economically inactive. From their replies, national rates of unemployment can be extrapolated. In the UK, the Labour Force Survey is conducted quarterly.

As we have seen, the standardised rate is likely to be higher than the claimant rate to the extent that it includes people seeking work who are nevertheless not entitled to claim benefits. However, it will be lower to the extent that it excludes those who are claiming benefits and yet who are not actively seeking work.

Generally, the standardised rate is significantly higher than the claimant rate. Over the five-year period from 2012 to 2016, for example, the average claimant count rate in the UK was 3.7 per cent while the average standardised unemployment rate (for all aged 16 and over) was 6.8 per cent.

 How does the ILO/OECD definition differ from the economist's definition? What is the significance of the phrase 'available for work at current wage rates' in the economist's definition?

The composition of unemployment

Unemployment rates can vary enormously between countries and between different groups within countries. In part, this is likely to reflect structural factors. Countries and regions within countries can, for example, have very different labour markets. Countries often have very different policies on unemployment, training schemes, redundancy, etc., and demonstrate very different attitudes of firms towards their workers.

Table 15.4 highlights differences between countries, age groups and men and women for the period from 2009 to 2016.

In many countries, female unemployment has traditionally been higher than male unemployment. Causes have included differences in education and training, discrimination by employers, more casual or seasonally related employment among women and other social factors. In many countries, as highlighted by Table 15.4, the position has changed in recent years. One important reason has the decline in many of the older industries, such as coal and steel, which employed mainly men.

Table 15.4 does, however, show some stark differences in unemployment rates across different age groups. Rates in the under-25 age group are higher than the average, and substantially so in many countries. Higher youth unemployment rates can be explained by the suitability (or unsuitability) of the qualifications of school leavers, the attitudes of employers to young people, and the greater willingness of young people to spend time unemployed looking for a better job or

Definitions

Claimant unemployment Those in receipt of unemployment-related benefits.

Standardised unemployment rate The measure of the unemployment rate used by the ILO and the OECD. The unemployed are defined as persons of working age who are without work, are available to start work within two weeks and either have actively looked for work in the last four weeks or are waiting to take up an appointment.

Table 15.4   Standardised unemployment rates by age and gender, average 2009–2016

	All ages			Less than 25 years			25 to 74 years		
	Total	Male	Female	Total	Male	Female	Total	Male	Female
Eurozone (19 countries)	10.7	10.6	10.9	22.3	22.8	21.7	9.6	9.3	9.8
Belgium	8.0	8.2	7.8	21.5	22.2	20.7	6.8	6.9	6.7
France	9.8	9.9	9.8	24.1	24.4	23.6	8.3	8.2	8.4
Germany	5.6	5.9	5.3	8.4	14.0	7.6	5.3	5.5	5.0
Greece	20.9	18.0	24.8	45.8	40.5	52.0	19.2	16.5	22.7
Ireland	12.1	14.4	9.3	25.0	29.4	20.2	10.6	12.8	7.9
Italy	10.5	9.6	11.6	34.8	33.3	37.0	8.7	8.0	9.9
Netherlands	6.0	5.6	6.4	11.4	11.8	11.0	5.0	4.6	5.4
Norway	3.7	4.0	3.3	9.2	10.5	7.9	2.8	3.0	2.5
Poland	8.8	8.4	9.3	23.3	22.1	25.0	7.4	7.0	7.9
Portugal	13.2	13.1	13.3	31.8	30.7	33.1	11.6	11.6	11.7
Spain	22.0	21.4	22.8	47.5	48.3	46.4	19.9	19.2	20.8
Sweden	7.9	8.1	7.7	22.8	23.9	21.5	5.7	5.8	5.6
UK	6.9	7.4	6.4	18.4	20.6	15.9	5.0	5.3	4.7
USA	7.5	7.8	7.0	15.1	16.6	13.4	6.2	6.5	6.0

Source: Based on data from *Statistics Database* (Eurostat, European Commission).

BOX 15.4   **THE COSTS OF UNEMPLOYMENT**   EXPLORING ECONOMICS

Who loses and by how much?

The most obvious cost of unemployment is to the unemployed themselves. There is the direct financial cost of the loss in their earnings. Then there are the personal costs of being unemployed. The longer people are unemployed, the more dispirited they may become. Their self-esteem is likely to fall, and they are more likely to succumb to stress-related illness.

Beyond the unemployed themselves, there are the costs to their family and friends. Personal relations can become strained, and there may be an increase in domestic violence and the number of families splitting up.

Then there are the broader costs to the economy. Unemployment represents a loss of output. In other words, actual output is below potential output. Apart from the loss of disposable income to the unemployed themselves, this underutilisation of resources leads to lower incomes for other people too:

- The government loses tax revenues, since the unemployed pay no income tax and national insurance and, given that the unemployed spend less, they pay less VAT and excise duties. The government also incurs administrative costs associated with the running of benefit offices. It may also have to spend extra on health care, the social services and the police.
- Firms lose the profits that could have been made if there had been full employment.
- Other workers lose any additional wages they could have earned from higher national output.

What is more, the longer people remain unemployed, the more deskilled they tend to become. This scarring effect reduces potential as well as actual income.

 Why have the costs to the government of unemployment benefits not been included as a cost to the economy?

Finally, there is some evidence that higher unemployment leads to increased crime and vandalism. This obviously imposes a cost on the sufferers.

The costs of unemployment are to some extent offset by benefits. If workers voluntarily quit their jobs to look for better ones, then they must reckon that the benefits of a better job more than compensate for their temporary loss of income. From the nation's point of view, a workforce that is prepared to quit jobs and spend a short time unemployed will be a more adaptable, more mobile workforce – one that is responsive to changing economic circumstances. Such a workforce will lead to greater allocative efficiency in the short run and more rapid economic growth over the longer run.

Long-term involuntary unemployment is quite another matter. The costs clearly outweigh any benefits, both for the individuals involved and for the economy as a whole. A demotivated, deskilled pool of long-term unemployed is a serious economic and social problem.

 Which of the above costs would be recorded as a reduction in GDP?

waiting to start a further or higher education course. The difference in rates is less in Germany, which has a well-established apprenticeship system.

The duration of unemployment

A few of the unemployed may never have had a job and maybe never will. For most, however, unemployment lasts only a certain period. For some it may be just a few days while they are between jobs. For others it may be a few months. For others – the long-term unemployed – it could be several years. Figure 15.9 shows the composition of standardised unemployment in the UK for all aged 16 and over by duration.

What determines the average duration of unemployment? There are three important factors here.

The number unemployed (the size of the stock of unemployment). Unemployment is a 'stock' concept (see Box 10.10). It measures a *quantity* (i.e. the number unemployed) at a particular *point in time*. The higher the stock of unemployment, the longer will tend to be the duration of unemployment. There will be more people competing for vacant jobs.

The rate of inflow and outflow from the stock of unemployment. The people making up the unemployment total are constantly changing. Each week some people are made redundant or quit their jobs. They represent an inflow to the stock of unemployment. Other people find jobs and thus represent an outflow from the stock of unemployment. The various inflows and outflows are shown in Figure 15.10.

Unemployment is often referred to as 'the pool of unemployment'. This is quite a good analogy. If the water flowing into a pool exceeds the water flowing out, the level of water in the pool will rise. Similarly, if the inflow of people into unemployment exceeds the outflow, the level of unemployment will rise.

The duration of unemployment will depend on the *rate* of inflow and outflow. The rate is expressed as the number of people per period of time. The bigger the flows are relative to the total number unemployed, the less will be the average duration of unemployment. This is because people move into and out of the pool more quickly, and hence their average stay will be shorter.

1. *If the number unemployed exceeded the total annual outflow, what could we conclude about the average duration of unemployment?*

2. *Make a list of the various inflows to and outflows from employment from and to (a) unemployment; (b) outside the workforce.*

The phase of the business cycle. The duration of unemployment also depends on the phase of the business cycle. At the onset of a recession, unemployment will rise, but as yet the average length of unemployment is likely to have been relatively short. Once a recession has lasted for a period of time, however, people will on average have been out of work longer, and this long-term unemployment is likely to persist even when the economy is pulling out of recession.

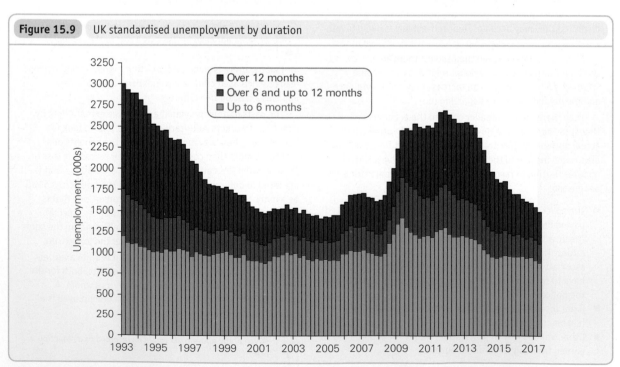

Figure 15.9 UK standardised unemployment by duration

Source: Based on data from dataset *UNEM01 SA: Unemployment by age and duration (seasonally adjusted)* (ONS).

Figure 15.10 Flows into and out of unemployment

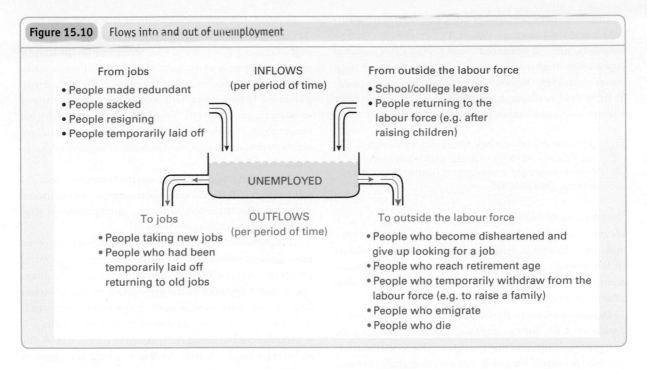

The average duration of unemployment (D_U) will equal the stock of unemployment (U) as a proportion of the outflow (F) from unemployment.

$$D_U = \frac{U}{F}$$

Thus the bigger the stock of unemployment relative to the outflow from it, the longer will unemployment last. Taking the UK figures for 2015, where the number unemployed (U) was 1.78 million and the total outflow from unemployment (F) was 3.44 million:

$$D_U = \frac{1.781}{3.344} = 0.533$$

Thus the average duration of unemployment was 0.533 years or 195 days. By contrast, in 2012, the average duration was $2.572/3.945 = 0.652$ years or 239 days.

Causes of unemployment

There are various possible causes of unemployment. It is important when thinking about policies to tackle unemployment to understand its determinants. The following are among those most commonly identified by economists.

Real wage rates

Nominal wage rates are the actual value of wage rates paid to workers. The real wage rate is the wage rate expressed in terms of its purchasing power to workers and the purchasing cost to employers. In other words, the real wage is the nominal wage corrected for inflation.

$$W_r = \frac{W_n}{P}$$

where W_r is the real wage rate; W_n is the nominal wage rate; and P is the price index (e.g. the CPI).

Real-wage unemployment occurs when trade unions use their monopoly power to drive wages *above* the market-clearing level. It could also be caused by the government setting the national minimum wage too high.

A rise in real wage rates increases the effective cost to firms of employing workers. This is because the wage rates paid by firms have increased *relative* to the prices of their goods and services. Excessive real wage rates were blamed by the Conservative governments under Thatcher and Major for the high unemployment of the 1980s and 1990s. The possibility of higher real-wage unemployment was also one of the reasons for their rejection of a national minimum wage.

Definition

Real-wage unemployment Disequilibrium unemployment caused by real wages being driven up above the market-clearing level.

One effect of high real wage rates, however, may help to reduce real-wage unemployment. The extra wages paid to those who are still employed could lead to extra *consumer* expenditure. Higher real wage rates increase the purchasing power of workers. This addition to aggregate demand could, in turn, lead to firms demanding more labour, as they attempt to increase output to meet the extra demand.

 If the higher consumer expenditure and higher wages subsequently led to higher prices, what would happen to (a) real wages; (b) unemployment (assuming no further response from unions)?

The phase of the business cycle

We have seen throughout this chapter how volatile economies are. Changes in output associated with the business cycle will result in changes in employment and unemployment. In a recession, unemployment is likely to rise, whereas in a boom, it is likely to fall.

Demand-deficient is the name we give to unemployment associated with falling aggregate demand. As aggregate demand falls, firms find that they are unable to sell their current level of output. For a time they may be prepared to build up stocks of unsold goods, but sooner or later they will start to cut back on production and cut back on the amount of labour they employ.

TC 12
p447

As aggregate demand begins to grow again and firms increase output, so demand-deficient unemployment will start to fall again. Because demand-deficient unemployment fluctuates with the business cycle, it is sometimes referred to as *cyclical unemployment*. Figure 15.11 shows the fluctuations in unemployment in industrialised economies. If you compare this figure with Figure 15.1 on page 445, you can see how unemployment tends to rise in recessions and fall in booms.

Demand-deficient unemployment is also referred to as 'Keynesian unemployment', after John Maynard Keynes (see pages 492 and 498 below and Case Study 16.6 on the student website for a profile of the great economist), who saw a deficiency of aggregate demand as the cause of the high unemployment between the two world wars. Today, many economists are known as 'Keynesian'. Although there are many strands of Keynesian thinking, these economists all see aggregate demand as important in determining a nation's output and employment.

The more that aggregate demand fluctuates, the more significant the cyclical component of unemployment becomes. But what affects the amount that unemployment rises following a fall in aggregate demand?

One consideration is the magnitude and persistence of the fall in aggregate demand. This will affect the aggregate demand for labour. A large or enduring downturn could result in a large rise in unemployment as the aggregate demand for labour falls. On the other hand, a small or transitory downturn is more likely to have a smaller impact on unemployment.

Another consideration is the extent to which, if at all, the *real* average wage rate falls. A fall in real wage rates reduces the effective cost to firms of employing workers and thus helps to offset some of the fall in employment that arises from the general reduction in firms' demand for labour. The UK has a relatively 'flexible' labour market with many

Definition

Demand-deficient or cyclical unemployment
Disequilibrium unemployment caused by a fall in aggregate demand with no corresponding fall in the real wage rate.

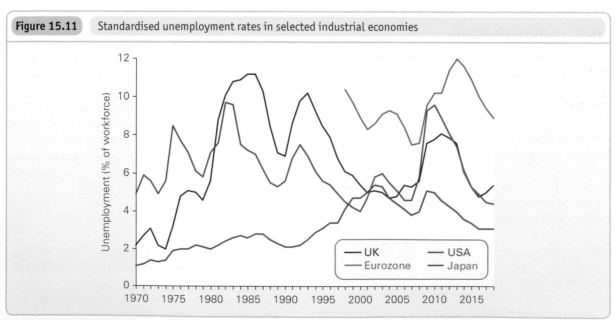

Figure 15.11   Standardised unemployment rates in selected industrial economies

Notes: 2017 to 2018 based on forecasts; eurozone figures are the weighted average of the countries using the euro in any given year.
Source: Based on data in *AMECO Database* (European Commission, DGECFIN).

people on zero-hour, part-time or 'self-employed' contracts and having no union representation. In the recession that followed the financial crisis in the late 2000s, many workers faced cuts in real wages, but unemployment rose less than in some other countries with less flexible labour markets.

 Is it only in the interest of workers to resist falls in real wage rates?

For some Keynesian economists, however, the problem is much more fundamental than a downward stickiness in real wages. For them the problem is that the low level of aggregate demand causes an *equilibrium* in the *goods* market at an output that is too low to generate full employment. Firms' supply is low (below the full-employment level of supply) because aggregate demand is low.

This low-level equilibrium in the goods market, and the corresponding disequilibrium in the labour market, may *persist*. This is the result of a lack of confidence on the part of firms. After all, why should firms produce more and take on more workers if they believe that the recession will persist and that they will therefore not sell any more? The economy remains trapped in a low-output equilibrium. In such cases, a fall in real wages would not cure the unemployment. In fact, it might even make the problem worse.

 If this analysis is correct, namely that a reduction in wages will reduce the aggregate demand for goods, what assumption must we make about the relative proportions of wages and profits that are spent (given that a reduction in real wage rates will lead to a corresponding increase in rates of profit)?

Information

Frictional (search) unemployment occurs when people leave their jobs, either voluntarily or because they are sacked or made redundant, and are unemployed for a period of time while they are looking for a new job. They may not get the first job they apply for, despite a vacancy existing and despite their being suitably qualified.

The problem is that information is imperfect. Employers are not fully informed about what labour is available; workers are not fully informed about what jobs are available and what they entail. Both employers and workers, therefore, have to search: employers searching for the right labour and workers searching for the right jobs.

One obvious remedy for frictional unemployment is to provide better job information through government job centres, private employment agencies or the media. Another much more controversial remedy is for the government to reduce the level of unemployment benefit. This will make the unemployed more desperate to get a job and thus prepared to accept a lower wage.

Structural change

Structural unemployment occurs where the structure of the economy changes. Many countries have witnessed rapid structural change over recent years. This has seen employment in some industries expand while in others it has contracted. There are two main reasons for this.

A change in the pattern of demand. Some industries experience declining demand. This may be due to a change in consumer tastes as certain goods go out of fashion; or it may be due to competition from other industries or from competition overseas. For example, consumer demand may shift away from coal and to other fuels. This will lead to structural unemployment in mining areas.

A change in the methods of production (technological unemployment). New techniques of production often allow the same level of output to be produced with fewer workers (see Case Study 15.11 on the student website). This is known as 'labour-saving technical progress'. Unless output expands sufficiently to absorb the surplus labour, people will be made redundant. This creates **technological unemployment**. An example is the loss of jobs in the banking industry caused by the increase in the number of cash machines and by the development of telephone and Internet banking.

Structural unemployment often occurs in particular regions of the country when industries located in those regions decline or introduce labour-saving technology. When it does, it is referred to as **regional unemployment**.

The level of structural unemployment depends on three factors:

- The degree of *regional concentration* of industry. The more that industries are concentrated in particular regions, the greater will be the level of structural unemployment if particular industries decline. For example, the collapse in the South Wales coal-mining industry led to high unemployment in the Welsh valleys.
- The *speed of change* of demand and supply in the economy. The more rapid the rate of technological change or the shift in consumer tastes, the more rapid will be the rate of redundancies.

Definitions

Frictional (search) unemployment Equilibrium unemployment that occurs as a result of imperfect information in the labour market. It often takes time for workers to find jobs (even though there are vacancies) and in the meantime they are unemployed.

Structural unemployment Equilibrium unemployment that arises from changes in the pattern of demand or supply in the economy. People made redundant in one part of the economy cannot immediately take up jobs in other parts (even though there are vacancies).

Technological unemployment Structural unemployment that occurs as a result of the introduction of labour-saving technology.

Regional unemployment Structural unemployment occurring in specific regions of the country.

Figure 15.13   Selection of annual UK inflation rates

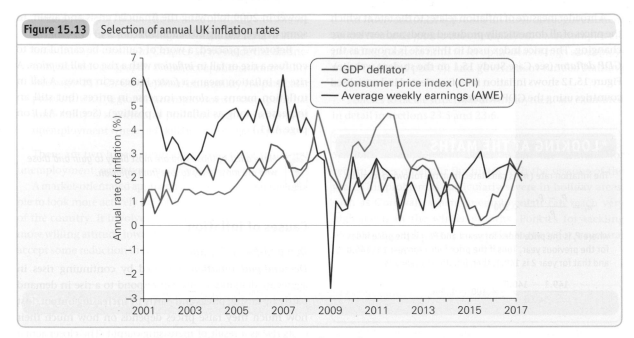

Notes: AWE is the average regular weekly pay (including bonuses) over the latest three months.
Source: Based on *Time Series Data,* series IHYU, D7G7 and KAC3 (ONS).

demand by raising their prices. On the other hand, the greater the spare capacity, the more will firms respond by raising output and the less by raising prices.

Sometimes there may be a *single* increase in demand (or a 'demand shock'). This could be due, for example, to an increased level of government expenditure. The effect is to give a *single* rise in the price level. Although this causes inflation in the short run, once the effect has taken place, inflation will fall back to zero. For inflation to persist, there must be *continuing* increases in aggregate demand and thus continuing rises in the price level. If inflation is to rise, the rate of increase in aggregate demand must also rise.

Demand-pull inflation is typically associated with a booming economy. Many economists therefore argue that it is the counterpart of demand-deficient unemployment. When the economy is in recession, demand-deficient unemployment is high, but demand-pull inflation is low. When, on the other hand, the economy is near the peak of the business cycle, demand-pull inflation is high, but demand-deficient unemployment is low.

Cost-push inflation

Cost-push inflation is associated with continuing rises in costs which occur *independently* of aggregate demand.

If firms face a rise in costs, they will respond partly by raising prices and passing the costs on to the consumer, and partly by cutting back on production. Just how much firms raise prices and cut back on production depends on the impact of price changes on aggregate demand. The less responsive is aggregate demand to price changes, the less will sales fall as a result of any price rise. This allows firms to pass on more of the rise in their costs to consumers as higher prices. On the other hand, the more sensitive aggregate

demand is to price changes, the less able are firms to pass on their higher costs to consumers: hence prices rise by less.

Note that the effect on output and employment is the opposite of demand-pull inflation. With demand-pull inflation, output and hence employment tends to rise. With cost-push inflation, however, output and employment tends to fall.

As with demand-pull inflation, we must distinguish between *one-off* increases in cost (a 'supply shock') from *continuing* increases. If there is a one-off increase in costs, there will be a one-off rise in the price level. For example, if the government raises the excise duty on petrol and diesel, there will be a single rise in fuel prices and hence in firms' fuel costs. This will cause *temporary* inflation while the price rise is passed on through the economy. Once this has occurred, prices will stabilise at the new level and the rate of inflation will fall back to zero again. If cost-push inflation is to continue over a number of years, therefore, then costs must *continually* increase. If cost-push inflation is to *rise,* the rate of increase in costs must also rise.

Sources of cost-push inflation.   Rises in costs may originate from a number of different sources, such as trade unions pushing up wages, firms with monopoly power raising prices in order to increase their profits, or increases in international commodity prices. With the process of globalisation and

BOX 15.5   THE COSTS OF INFLATION

Who loses and by how much?

A lack of growth is obviously a problem if people want higher living standards. Unemployment is obviously a problem, both for the unemployed themselves and also for society, which suffers a loss in output and has to support the unemployed. But why is inflation a problem? If prices go up by 10 per cent, does it really matter? Provided your wages kept up with prices, you would have no cut in your living standards.

If people could correctly anticipate the rate of inflation and fully adjust prices and incomes to take account of it, then the costs of inflation would indeed be relatively small. For us as consumers, they would simply be the relatively minor inconvenience of having to adjust our notions of what a 'fair' price is for each item when we go shopping. For firms, they would again be the relatively minor costs of having to change price labels, or prices in catalogues or on menus, or adjust slot machines. These are known as **menu costs**.

In reality, people frequently make mistakes when predicting the rate of inflation and are not able to adapt fully to it. This leads to the following problems, which are likely to be more serious the higher the rate of inflation becomes and the more the rate fluctuates.

Redistribution.   Inflation redistributes income away from those on fixed incomes and those in a weak bargaining position, to those who can use their economic power to gain large pay, rent or profit increases. It redistributes wealth to those with assets (e.g. property) that rise in value particularly rapidly during periods of inflation, and away from those with types of savings that pay rates of interest below the rate of inflation and hence whose value is eroded by inflation. Elderly people who rely on the interest from their savings may be particularly badly hit by rapid inflation.

Uncertainty and lack of investment.   Inflation tends to cause uncertainty among the business community, especially when the rate of inflation fluctuates. (Generally, the higher the rate of inflation, the more it fluctuates.) If it is difficult for firms to predict their costs and revenues, they may be discouraged from investing. This will reduce the rate of economic growth. On the other hand, as will be explained below, policies to reduce the rate of inflation may themselves reduce the rate of economic growth, especially in the short run. This may then provide the government with a policy dilemma.

Balance of payments.   Inflation is likely to worsen the balance of trade. If a country suffers from relatively high inflation, its exports will become less competitive in world markets. At the same time, imports will become relatively cheaper than home-produced goods. Thus exports will fall and imports will rise. This is known an international substitution effect. As a result, the balance of trade will deteriorate and/or the exchange rate will fall. Both of these effects can cause problems.

Resources.   Extra resources are likely to be used to cope with the effects of inflation. Accountants and other financial experts may have to be employed by companies to help them cope with the uncertainties caused by inflation.

The costs of inflation may be relatively mild if inflation is kept to single figures. They can be very serious, however, if inflation gets out of hand. If inflation develops into 'hyperinflation', with prices rising perhaps by several hundred per cent or even thousands per cent per year, the whole basis of the market economy will be undermined. Firms constantly raise prices in an attempt to cover their soaring costs. Workers demand huge pay increases in an attempt to stay ahead of the rocketing cost of living. Thus prices and wages chase each other in an ever-rising inflationary spiral. People will no longer want to save money. Instead they will spend it as quickly as possible before its value falls any further. People may even resort to barter in an attempt to avoid using money altogether. (Case Study 15.14 on the student website looks at historical cases of hyperinflation in Germany in the 1920s, Serbia in the 1990s and Zimbabwe in the 2000s.)

1. *Do you personally gain or lose from inflation? Why?*
2. *Make a list of those who are most likely to gain and those who are most likely to lose from inflation.*

---

increased international competition, cost-push pressures have tended to decrease in recent years. One major exception has been the oil shocks that have occurred from time to time. For example, the near tripling of oil prices from $51 per barrel in January 2007 to $147 per barrel in July 2008, and again from $41 a barrel in January 2009 to $126 a barrel in April 2011, put upward pressure on costs and prices around the world.

Temporary supply shocks can come from bad harvests. Longer-term supply-side problems can come from the depletion of natural resources, such as the gradual running down of North Sea oil, pollution of the seas and hence a decline in incomes for nations with large fishing industries, and, perhaps the most devastating of all, the problem of 'desertification' in sub-Saharan Africa.

Definition

Menu costs of inflation The costs associated with having to adjust price lists or labels.

BOX 15.6   THE PHILLIPS CURVE

Is higher inflation the price for lower unemployment?

If inflation tends to be higher when the economy is booming and if unemployment tends to be higher in recessions, does this mean that there is a 'trade-off' between inflation and unemployment: that lower unemployment tends to be associated with higher inflation, and lower inflation with higher unemployment? Such a trade-off was observed by the New Zealand economist Bill Phillips (see Case Study 15.15 on the student website), and was illustrated by the famous **Phillips curve**.

The original Phillips curve

In 1958, Phillips showed the statistical relationship between wage inflation and unemployment in the UK from 1861 to 1957. With wage inflation (ω) on the vertical axis and the unemployment rate (U) on the horizontal axis, a scatter of points was obtained. Each point represented the observation for a particular year. The curve that best fitted the scatter has become known as the 'Phillips curve'. It is illustrated in Figure (a) and shows an inverse relationship between inflation and unemployment.[1]

Given that wage increases over the period were approximately 2 per cent above price increases (made possible because of increases in labour productivity), a similar-shaped, but lower curve could be plotted showing the relationship between *price* inflation and unemployment.

The curve has often been used to illustrate the effects of changes in aggregate demand. When aggregate demand rose (relative to potential output), inflation rose and

unemployment fell: there was an upward movement along the curve. When aggregate demand fell, there was a downward movement along the curve.

There was also a second reason given for the inverse relationship. If wages rose, the unemployed might have believed that the higher wages they were offered represented a *real* wage increase. That is, they might not have realised that the higher wages would be 'eaten up' by price increases: they might have suffered from **money illusion**. They would thus have accepted jobs more readily. The average duration of unemployment therefore fell. This is a reduction in *frictional* unemployment.

The Phillips curve was bowed in to the origin. The usual explanation for this is that, as aggregate demand expanded, at first there would be plenty of surplus labour, which could meet the extra demand without the need to raise wages very much. But as labour became increasingly scarce, firms would find they had to offer increasingly higher wages to obtain the labour they required, and the position of trade unions would be increasingly strengthened.

The *position* of the Phillips curve depended on *non*-demand factors causing inflation and unemployment: frictional and structural unemployment; and cost-push, structural and expectations-generated inflation. If any of these non-demand factors changed so as to raise inflation or unemployment, the curve would shift outwards to the right. The relative stability of the curve over the hundred years or so observed by Phillips suggested that these non-demand factors had changed little.

The Phillips curve seemed to present governments with a simple policy choice. They could trade off inflation against unemployment. Lower unemployment could be bought at the cost of higher inflation, and vice versa. Unfortunately, the experience since the late 1960s has suggested that no such simple relationship exists beyond the short run.

The breakdown of the Phillips curve

From about 1967 the Phillips curve relationship seemed to break down. The UK, and many other countries in the Western world too, began to experience growing unemployment *and* higher rates of inflation.

Figure (b) shows price inflation (π) and (standardised) unemployment in the UK from 1960. From 1960 to 1967 a curve similar to the Phillips curve can be fitted through the data (the red line). From 1968 to the early 1990s, however, no simple picture emerges. Certainly the original Phillips

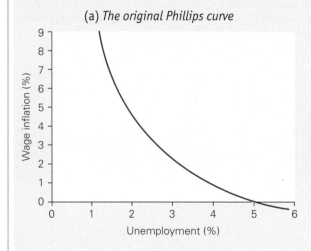

(a) *The original Phillips curve*

The interaction of demand-pull and cost-push inflation
Demand-pull and cost-push inflation can occur together, since wage and price rises can be caused both by increases in aggregate demand and by independent causes pushing up costs. Even when an inflationary process *starts* as either demand-pull or cost-push, it is often difficult to separate the two. An initial cost-push inflation may encourage the government to expand aggregate demand to offset rises in unemployment. Alternatively, an initial demand-pull

Definitions

Phillips curve A curve showing the relationship between (price) inflation and unemployment. The original Phillips curve plotted wage inflation against unemployment for the years 1861–1957

Money illusion When people believe that a money wage or price increase represents a real increase: in other words, they ignore or underestimate inflation.

EXPLORING
ECONOMICS

(b) *Breakdown of the Phillips curve*

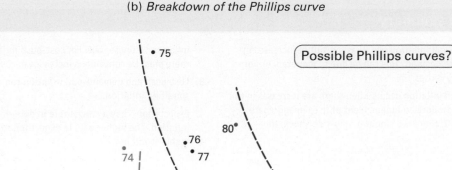

Possible Phillips curves?

Source: Based on data from the Office for National Statistics; forecasts based on data from *World Economic Outlook Database* (IMF).

curve could no longer fit the data; but whether the curve shifted to the right and then back again somewhat (the broken lines), or whether the relationship broke down completely, or whether there was some quite different relationship between inflation and unemployment, is not clear by simply looking at the data.

Since 1997, the Bank of England has been targeting inflation (see section 22.3). For much of this period the 'curve' would seem to have become a virtually horizontal straight line. However, from the late 2000s, against a backdrop of significant economic volatility and uncertainty, the range of inflation rates increased despite inflation rate targeting. A contributory factor to this was the volatility experienced in commodity prices. In the middle of the 2010s, for example, inflation fell

below the target as commodity prices fell reflecting sluggish demand in the eurozone and elsewhere.

Over the years, there has been much debate among economists about the relationship between inflation and unemployment. The controversy will be examined in later chapters and particularly in Chapter 21. One thing does seem clear, however: the relationship is different in the short run and the long run.

 Assume that there is a trade-off between unemployment and inflation, traced out by a 'Phillips curve'. What could cause a leftward shift in this curve?

1 Phillips' estimated equation was $\omega = -0.9 + 9.638U^{-1.394}$.

inflation may strengthen the power of certain groups, which then use this power to drive up costs.

Expectations and inflation

 Workers and firms take account of the *expected* rate of inflation when making decisions.

Imagine that a union and an employer are negotiating a wage increase. Let us assume that both sides expect a rate of

inflation of 5 per cent. The union will be happy to receive a wage rise somewhat above 5 per cent. That way the members would be getting a *real* rise in incomes. The employers will be happy to pay a wage rise somewhat below 5 per cent. After all, they can put their price up by 5 per cent, knowing that their rivals will do approximately the same. The actual wage rise that the two sides agree on will thus be somewhere around 5 per cent.

Now let us assume that the expected rate of inflation is 10 per cent. Both sides will now negotiate around this benchmark, with the outcome being somewhere round about 10 per cent. Thus the higher the expected rate of inflation, the higher will be the level of pay settlements and price rises, and hence the higher will be the resulting *actual* rate of inflation.

Just how expectations impact on inflation depends on how they are formed. We examine this in Chapter 21.

Section summary

1. Demand-pull inflation occurs as a result of increases in aggregate demand. This can be due to monetary or non-monetary causes.

2. Cost-push inflation occurs when there are increases in the costs of production independent of rises in aggregate demand. If there is a single supply-side shock, the inflation will peter out. For cost-push inflation to persist, there must be continuous increases in costs.

3. Cost-push and demand-pull inflation can interact to form spiralling inflation.

4. Expectations play a crucial role in determining the rate of inflation. The higher people expect inflation to be, the higher it will be.

15.7 THE OPEN ECONOMY

All countries trade with and have financial dealings with the rest of the world. In other words, all countries are **open economies**. Indeed, over time the economies of nations have become ever more intimately linked. Key drivers of this global interconnectedness of economies are globalisation, financialisation and improved communications.

Global interconnectedness means economic events in one part of the world, such as changes in interest rates or a downturn in economic growth, can have myriad knock-on effects for the international community at large – from the international investor, to the foreign exchange dealer, to the domestic policy maker, to the business which exports or imports, or which has subsidiaries abroad. Consequently, the international component of countries' business cycles has tended to become ever more important.

The balance of payments account

The flows of money between residents of a country and the rest of the world are recorded in the country's **balance of payments account**.

Receipts of money from abroad are regarded as *credits* and are entered in the accounts with a positive sign. *Outflows* of money from the country are regarded as *debits* and are entered with a negative sign.

There are three main parts of the balance of payments account: the *current account,* the *capital account* and the *financial account*. Each part is then subdivided. We shall look at each part in turn, and take the UK as an example. Table 15.5 gives a summary of the UK balance of payments for 2016, while also providing an historical perspective.

The current account
The **current account** records payments for imports and exports of goods and services, plus incomes flowing into and out of the country, plus net transfers of money into and out of the country. It is normally split into four subdivisions.

The trade in goods account. This records imports and exports of physical goods (previously known as 'visibles'). Exports result in an inflow of money and are therefore a credit item. Imports result in an outflow of money and are therefore a debit item. The balance of these is called the **balance on trade in goods** or **balance of visible trade** or **merchandise balance**. A *surplus* is when exports exceed imports. A *deficit* is when imports exceed exports.

The trade in services account. This records imports and exports of services (such as transport, tourism and insurance). Thus the purchase of a foreign holiday would be a debit, since it represents an outflow of money, whereas the purchase by an overseas resident of a UK insurance policy would be a credit to the UK services account. The balance of these is called the *services balance*.

Definitions

Open economy One that trades with and has financial dealings with other countries.

Balance of payments account The record of all the economic transactions between the residents of a specific country with the rest of the world for a specific time period, typically a year or a quarter. It records all the inflows and outflows of money under various headings. Inflows are recorded as credits; outflows are recorded as debits.

Current account of the balance of payments The record of a country's imports and exports of goods and services, plus incomes and transfers of money to and from abroad.

Balance on trade in goods or balance of visible trade or merchandise balance Exports of goods minus imports of goods.

Table 15.5 UK balance of payments

	2016		Average 1987–2016 as % of GDP
	£m	% of GDP	
CURRENT ACCOUNT			
Balance on trade in goods	−135 391	−6.9	−4.1
Balance on trade in services	92 378	4.7	2.4
Balance of trade	**−43 013**	**−2.2**	**−1.7**
Income balance	−50 417	−2.6	−0.3
Net current transfers	−22 025	−1.1	−0.8
Current account balance	**−115 455**	**−5.9**	**−2.7**
CAPITAL ACCOUNT			
Capital account balance	**−1 344**	**−0.1**	**0.0**
FINANCIAL ACCOUNT			
Net direct investment	184 345	9.4	−0.6
Portfolio investment balance	139 194	7.1	2.8
Other investment balance	−175 851	−9.0	0.5
Balance of financial derivatives	−21 615	−1.1	0.0
Reserve assets	−6 511	−0.3	−0.2
Financial account balance	**119 562**	**6.1**	**2.6**
Net errors and omissions	**−2 763**	**−0.1**	**0.2**
Balance	**0**	**0.0**	**0.0**

Source: *Balance of Payments* (ONS).

The balance of both the goods and services accounts together is known as the **balance on trade in goods and services** or simply the **balance of trade**.

Income flows. These consist of wages, interest and profits flowing into and out of the country. For example, dividends earned by a foreign resident from shares in a UK company would be an outflow of money (a debit item).

Current transfers of money. These include government contributions to and receipts from the EU and international organisations, and international transfers of money by private individuals and firms for the purpose of *consumption.* Transfers out of the country are debits. Transfers into the country (e.g. money sent from Greece to a Greek student studying in the UK) would be a credit item.

The **current account balance** is the overall balance of all the above four subdivisions. A *current account surplus* is where credits exceed debits. A *current account deficit* is where debits exceed credits. Figure 15.14 shows the current account balances of a selection of countries as a proportion of their GDP since 1960. The chart shows how global imbalances on the current account have tended to increase over time, particularly since the 1980s. In conjunction with Table 15.5 we can also see that the UK has consistently run a current account deficit over the past three decades or so. This has been driven by a large trade deficit in goods.

? Why are the US and UK current balances approximately a 'mirror image' of the Japanese and German current balances?

The capital account

The **capital account** records the flows of funds, into the country (credits) and out of the country (debits), associated with the acquisition or disposal of fixed assets (e.g. land or intangibles, such as patents and trademarks), the transfer of funds by migrants, the payment of grants by the government for overseas projects, debt forgiveness by the government and the receipt of money for capital projects (e.g. from the EU's Agricultural Guidance Fund).

As Table 15.5 shows, the balance on the capital account is small in comparison to that on the current and financial accounts.

The financial account [1]

The **financial account** of the balance of payments records cross-border changes in the holding of shares, property, bank deposits and loans, government securities, etc. In

---

Definitions

Balance on trade in goods and services or **balance of trade** Exports of goods and services minus imports of goods and services.

Balance of payments on current account The balance on trade in goods and services plus net investment incomes and current transfers.

Capital account of the balance of payments The record of the transfers of capital to and from abroad.

Financial account of the balance of payments The record of the flows of money into and out of the country for the purposes of investment or as deposits in banks and other financial institutions.

| Figure 15.14 | Current account balance as percentage of GDP in selected countries |

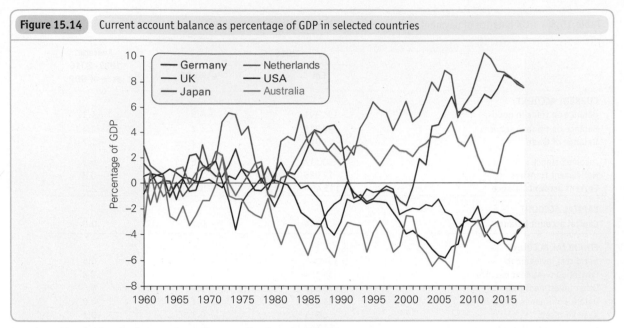

Note: Figures from 2017 based on forecasts; German figures are West Germany up to 1991.
Source: Based on data in *AMECO Database* (European Commission, DGECFIN).

other words, unlike the current account, which is concerned with money *incomes,* the financial account is concerned with the purchase and sale of *assets*. Case Study 15.16 on the student website considers some of the statistics behind the UK's financial account.

Investment (direct and portfolio).   This account covers primarily long-term investment.

■ *Direct investment.* This involves a significant and lasting interest in a business in another country. If a foreign company invests money from abroad in one of its branches or associated companies in the UK, this represents an inflow of money when the investment is made and is thus a credit item. (Any subsequent profit from this investment that flows abroad will be recorded as an *investment income outflow* on the current account.) Investment abroad by UK companies represents an outflow of money when the investment is made. It is thus a debit item.

Note that what we are talking about here is the acquisition or sale of assets: e.g. a factory or farm, or the takeover of a whole firm, not the imports or exports of equipment.

■ *Portfolio investment.* This relates to transactions in debt and equity securities which do not result in the investor having any significant influence on the operations of a particular business. If a UK resident buys shares (equity securities) in an overseas company, this is an outflow of funds and is hence a debit item.

Other financial flows.   These consist primarily of various types of short-term monetary movement between the UK and the rest of the world. Deposits by overseas residents in banks in the UK and loans to the UK from abroad are credit items, since they represent an inflow of money. Deposits by UK residents in overseas banks and loans by UK banks to

overseas residents are debit items. They represent an outflow of money.

Short-term monetary flows are common between international financial centres to take advantage of differences in countries' interest rates and changes in exchange rates.

1. *Why may inflows of short-term deposits create a problem?*
2. *Where would interest payments on short-term foreign deposits in UK banks be entered on the balance of payments account?*

Note that in the financial account, credits and debits are recorded *net*. For example, UK investment abroad consists of the net acquisition of assets abroad (i.e. the purchase *less* the sale of assets abroad). Similarly, foreign investment in the UK consists of the purchase *less* the sale of UK assets by foreign residents. Note that in either case the flow could be in the opposite direction. For example, if UK residents purchased fewer assets abroad than they sold, this item would be a net credit, not a debit (there would be a net return of money to the UK).

By recording financial account items net, the flows seem misleadingly modest. For example, if UK residents deposited an extra £100bn in banks abroad but drew out £99bn, this would be recorded as a mere £1bn net outflow on the other financial flows account. In fact, *total* financial account flows vastly exceed current plus capital account flows.

Flows to and from the reserves.   The UK, like all other countries, holds reserves of gold and foreign currencies. From time to time the Bank of England (acting as the government's agent) will sell some of these reserves to purchase sterling on the foreign exchange market. It does this normally as a means of supporting the rate of exchange (see below). Drawing on reserves represents a *credit* item in the balance of payments accounts: money drawn from the reserves represents an *inflow* to the balance of payments (albeit an outflow from the reserves account). The reserves can thus be used to support a deficit elsewhere in the balance of payments.

Conversely, if there is a surplus elsewhere in the balance of payments, the Bank of England can use it to build up the reserves. Building up the reserves counts as a debit item in the balance of payments, since it represents an outflow from it (to the reserves).

When all the components of the balance of payments account are taken together, the balance of payments should exactly balance: credits should equal debits. As we shall see below, if they were not equal, the rate of exchange would have to adjust until they were, or the government would have to intervene to make them equal.

When the statistics are compiled, however, a number of errors are likely to occur. As a result, there will not be a balance. To 'correct' for this, a *net errors and omissions* item is included in the accounts. This ensures that there will be an exact balance. The main reason for the errors is that the statistics are obtained from a number of sources, and there are often delays before items are recorded and sometimes omissions too.

 With reference to the above, provide an assessment of the UK balance of payments in each of the years illustrated in Table 15.5.

Figure 15.15 graphically summarises the main accounts of the UK's balance payments: current, capital and financial accounts. It presents each as a percentage of national income (see also right-hand column of Table 15.5). In conjunction with the net errors and omissions item, which averages close to zero over the long run, we can see how the accounts

combine to give a zero overall balance. For much of the period since the late 1980s, current account deficits have been offset by surpluses on the financial account.

What causes deficits to occur on the various parts of the balance of payments? The answer has to do with the demand for and supply of sterling on the foreign exchange market. Thus before we can answer the question, we must examine this market and in particular the role of the rate of exchange.

Exchange rates

An exchange rate is the rate at which one currency trades for another on the foreign exchange market.

If you live in the UK and go abroad, you will need to exchange your pounds into euros, dollars, Swiss francs or whatever. You will get the money at the exchange rate in operation at the time you draw it from a cash machine abroad or from a bank: for example, €1.15 to the pound, or $1.25 to the pound.

It is similar for firms. If an importer wants to buy, say, some machinery from Japan, it will require yen to pay the Japanese supplier. It will thus ask the foreign exchange section of a bank to quote it a rate of exchange of the pound into yen. Similarly, if you want to buy some foreign stocks and shares, or if companies based in the UK want to invest abroad, sterling will have to be exchanged into the appropriate foreign currency.

Likewise, if Americans want to come on holiday to the UK or to buy UK assets, or US firms want to import UK goods or to invest in the UK, they will require sterling. They will get it at an exchange rate such as £1 = $1.25. This means that they will have to pay $1.25 to obtain £1 worth of UK goods or assets.

Exchange rates are quoted between each of the major currencies of the world. These exchange rates are constantly

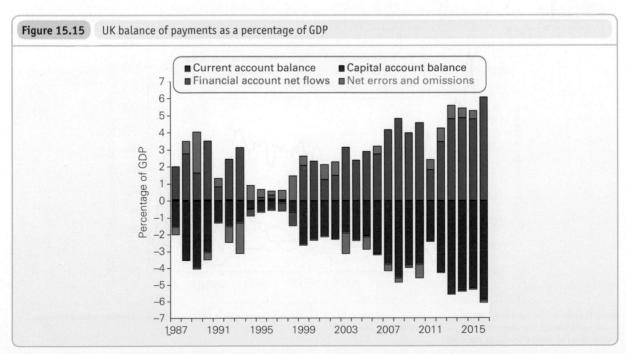

Figure 15.15 UK balance of payments as a percentage of GDP

Source: Based on *Time Series Data* (ONS).

changing. Minute by minute, dealers in the foreign exchange dealing rooms of the banks are adjusting the rates of exchange. They charge commission when they exchange currencies. It is important for them, therefore, to ensure that they are not left with a large amount of any currency unsold. What they need to do is to balance the supply and demand of each currency: to balance the amount they purchase to the amount they sell. To do this, they will need to adjust the price of each currency, namely the exchange rate, in line with changes in supply and demand.

Not only are there day-to-day fluctuations in exchange rates, but also there are long-term changes in them. Figure 15.16 shows the average quarterly exchange rates between the pound and various currencies since 1980.

One of the problems in assessing what is happening to a particular currency is that its rate of exchange may rise against some currencies (weak currencies) and fall against others (strong currencies). In order to gain an overall picture of its fluctuations, therefore, it is best to look at a weighted average exchange rate against all other currencies. This is known as the *exchange rate index*. The weight given to each currency in the index depends on the percentage of UK trade in goods and services done with countries using that currency. The weights are revised annually. Figure 15.16 also shows the sterling exchange rate index based on 2005 = 100.

 From looking at Figure 15.16, how has the pound 'fared' compared with the US dollar and the yen from 1980? What conclusions can be drawn about the relative movements between these currencies?

Note that all the exchange rates must be consistent with each other. For example, if £1 exchanged for $1.50 or 150 yen, then $1.50 would have to exchange for 150 yen directly (i.e. $1 = 100 yen), otherwise people could make money by moving around in a circle between the three currencies in a process known as *arbitrage*.

The determination of the rate of exchange in a free market

In a free foreign exchange market, the rate of exchange is determined by demand and supply. This is known as a *floating exchange rate*, and is illustrated in Figure 15.17.

For simplicity, assume that there are just two countries: the UK and the USA. When UK importers wish to buy goods from the USA, or when UK residents wish to invest in the USA, they will *supply* pounds on the foreign exchange market in order to obtain dollars. The higher the exchange rate, the more dollars they will obtain for their pounds. This will effectively make US goods cheaper to buy, and investment more profitable. Thus the *higher* the exchange rate, the *more*

Definitions

Exchange rate index A weighted average exchange rate expressed as an index, where the value of the index is 100 in a given base year. The weights of the different currencies in the index add up to 1

Arbitrage Buying an asset in a market where it has a lower price and selling it again in another market where it has a higher price and thereby making a profit.

Floating exchange rate When the government does not intervene in the foreign exchange markets, but simply allows the exchange rate to be freely determined by demand and supply.

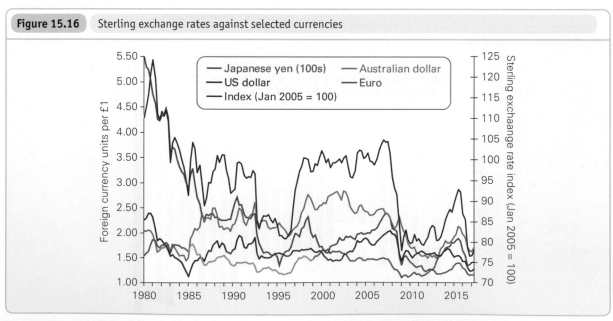

Figure 15.16 Sterling exchange rates against selected currencies

Notes: The euro was introduced in 1999, with notes and coins circulating from 2001. The euro figures prior to 1999 (in grey) are projections backwards in time based on the average exchange rates of the currencies that made up the euro.
Source: Based on data in *Time Series Data* (ONS).

Figure 15.17   Determination of the rate of exchange

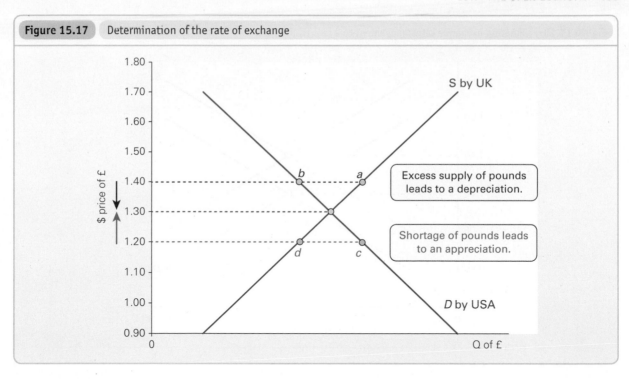

pounds will be supplied. The supply curve of pounds, therefore, typically slopes upwards.

When US residents wish to purchase UK goods or to invest in the UK, they will require pounds. They *demand* pounds by selling dollars on the foreign exchange market. The lower the dollar price of the pound (the exchange rate), the cheaper it will be for them to obtain UK goods and assets, and hence the more pounds they are likely to demand. The demand curve for pounds, therefore, typically slopes downwards.

The equilibrium exchange rate is where the demand for pounds equals the supply. In Figure 15.17 this is at an exchange rate of £1 = $1.30. But what is the mechanism that equates demand and supply?

If the current exchange rate were above the equilibrium, the supply of pounds being offered to the banks would exceed the demand. For example, in Figure 15.17, if the exchange rate were $1.40, there would be an excess supply of pounds of *a* − *b*. The banks, wishing to make money by *exchanging* currency, would have to lower the exchange rate in order to encourage a greater demand for pounds and reduce the excessive supply. They would continue lowering the rate until demand equalled supply.

Similarly, if the rate were below the equilibrium, say at $1.20, there would be a shortage of pounds of *c* − *d*. The banks would find themselves with too few pounds to meet all the demand. At the same time, they would have an excess supply of dollars. The banks would thus raise the exchange rate until demand equalled supply.

In practice, the process of reaching equilibrium is extremely rapid. The foreign exchange dealers in the banks are continually adjusting the rate as new customers make new demands for currencies. What is more, the banks have to watch each other closely since they are constantly in competition with each other and thus have to keep their rates in line. The dealers receive minute-by-minute updates on their computer screens of the rates being offered around the world.

Shifts in the currency demand and supply curves

Any shift in the demand or supply curves will cause the exchange rate to change. This is illustrated in Figure 15.18, which shows the euro/sterling exchange rate. If the demand and supply curves shift from D_1 and S_1 to D_2 and S_2 respectively, the exchange rate will fall from €1.40 to €1.20. A fall in the exchange rate is called a *depreciation.* A rise in the exchange rate is called an *appreciation*.

But why should the demand and supply curves shift? The following are the major possible causes of a depreciation:

- *A fall in domestic interest rates.* UK rates would now be less competitive for savers and other depositors. More UK residents would be likely to deposit their money abroad (the supply of sterling would rise), and fewer people abroad would deposit their money in the UK (the demand for sterling would fall).

KI 8
p46

KI 5
p22

Definitions

Depreciation A fall in the free-market exchange rate of the domestic currency with foreign currencies.

Appreciation A rise in the free-market exchange rate of the domestic currency with foreign currencies.

Figure 15.18 Floating exchange rates: movement to a new equilibrium

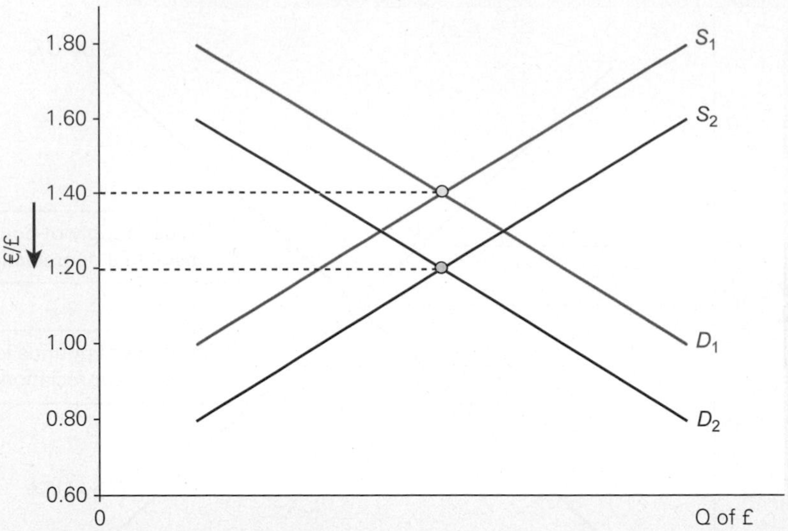

- *Higher inflation in the domestic economy than abroad.* UK exports will become less competitive. The demand for sterling will fall. At the same time, imports will become relatively cheaper for UK consumers. The supply of sterling will rise.
- *A rise in domestic incomes relative to incomes abroad.* If UK incomes rise, the demand for imports, and hence the supply of sterling, will rise. If incomes in other countries fall, the demand for UK exports, and hence the demand for sterling, will fall.
- *Relative investment prospects improving abroad.* If investment prospects become brighter abroad than in the UK, perhaps because of better incentives abroad, or because of worries about an impending recession in the UK, again the demand for sterling will fall and the supply of sterling will rise.

BOX 15.7 DEALING IN FOREIGN EXCHANGE

CASE STUDIES AND APPLICATIONS

A daily juggling act

Imagine that a large car importer in the UK wants to import 5000 cars from Japan costing ¥15 billion. What does it do?

It will probably contact a number of banks' foreign exchange dealing rooms in London and ask them for exchange rate quotes. It thus puts all the banks in competition with each other. Each bank will want to get the business and thereby obtain the commission on the deal. To do this it must offer a higher rate than the other banks, since the higher the ¥/£ exchange rate, the more yen the firm will get for its money. (For an importer a rate of, say, ¥160 to £1 is better than a rate of, say, ¥140.)

Now it is highly unlikely that any of the banks will have a spare ¥15 billion. But a bank cannot say to the importer, 'Sorry, you will have to wait before we can agree to sell them to you.' Instead the bank will offer a deal and then, if the firm agrees, the bank will have to set about obtaining the ¥15 billion. To do this, it must offer to obtain pounds for Japanese who are *supplying* yen at a sufficiently *low* ¥/£ exchange rate.

(The lower the ¥/£ exchange rate, the fewer yen the Japanese will have to pay to obtain pounds.)

The banks' dealers thus find themselves in the delicate position of wanting to offer a *high* enough exchange rate to the car importer in order to gain its business, but a *low* enough exchange rate in order to obtain the required amount of yen. The dealers are thus constantly having to adjust the rates of exchange in order to balance the demand and supply of each currency.

In general, the more of any foreign currency that dealers are asked to supply (by being offered sterling), the lower will be the exchange rate they will offer. In other words, a higher supply of sterling pushes down the foreign currency price of sterling (see Figure 15.18).

> *Assume that a firm based in the USA wants to import Scotch whisky from the UK. Describe how foreign exchange dealers will respond.*

KI 8
p46

- *Speculation that the exchange rate will fall.* If businesses involved in importing and exporting, and also banks and other foreign exchange dealers, think that the exchange rate is about to fall, they will sell pounds *now* before the rate does fall. The supply of sterling will thus rise. People thinking of buying pounds will wait until the rate does fall and hence, in the meantime, the demand for sterling will fall. Speculation thus helps to bring about the very effect people had anticipated (see pages 70–73).

- *Longer-term changes in international trading patterns.* Over time the pattern of imports and exports is likely to change as (a) consumer tastes change, (b) the nature and quality of goods change and (c) the costs of production change. If, as a result, UK goods become less competitive than, say, German or Japanese goods, the demand for sterling will fall and the supply will rise. These shifts, of course, are gradual, taking place over many years.

> ? Go through each of the above reasons for shifts in the demand for and supply of sterling and consider what would cause an appreciation of the pound.

Exchange rates and the balance of payments

In a free foreign exchange market, the balance of payments will *automatically* balance. But why?

The credit side of the balance of payments constitutes the demand for sterling. For example, when people abroad buy UK exports or assets, they will demand sterling in order to pay for them. The debit side constitutes the supply of sterling. For example, when UK residents buy foreign goods or assets, the importers of them will require foreign currency to pay for them. They will thus supply pounds. A floating exchange rate ensures that the demand for pounds always equals the supply. It thus also ensures that the credits on the balance of payments are equal to the debits: that the balance of payments balances.

This does not mean that each part of the balance of payments account will separately balance, but simply that any current account deficit must be matched by a capital plus financial account surplus and vice versa.

For example, suppose initially that each part of the balance of payments *did* separately balance. Then let us assume that interest rates rise. This will encourage larger short-term financial inflows as people abroad are attracted to deposit money in the UK: the demand for sterling would shift to the right (e.g. from D_2 to D_1 in Figure 15.18). It will also cause smaller short-term financial outflows as UK residents keep more of their money in the country: the supply of sterling shifts to the left (e.g. from S_2 to S_1 in Figure 15.18). The financial account will go into surplus. The exchange rate will appreciate.

As the exchange rate rises, this will cause imports to be cheaper and exports to be more expensive. The current account will move into deficit. There is a movement up along the new demand and supply curves until a new equilibrium is reached. At this point, any financial account surplus is matched by an equal current (plus capital) account deficit.

Section summary

1. The balance of payments account records all payments to and receipts from foreign countries. The current account records payments for imports and exports, plus incomes and transfers of money to and from abroad. The capital account records all transfers of capital to and from abroad. The financial account records inflows and outflows of money for investment and as deposits in banks and other financial institutions; it also includes dealings in the country's foreign exchange reserves.

2. The whole account must balance, but surpluses or deficits can be recorded on any specific part of the account.

3. The rate of exchange is the rate at which one currency exchanges for another. Rates of exchange are determined by demand and supply in the foreign exchange market. Demand for the domestic currency consists of all the credit items in the balance of payments account. Supply consists of all the debit items.

4. The exchange rate will depreciate (fall) if the demand for the domestic currency falls and/or the supply increases. These shifts can be caused by increases in domestic prices or incomes relative to foreign ones, reductions in domestic interest rates relative to foreign ones, worsening investment prospects at home compared with abroad, or the belief by speculators that the exchange rate will fall. The opposite in each case would cause an appreciation (rise).

APPENDIX: CALCULATING GDP

As explained in section 15.2, there are three ways of estimating GDP. In this appendix, we discuss each method in more detail. We also look at some alternative measures of national income.

The product method of measuring GDP

This approach simply involves adding up the value of everything produced in the country during the year: the output of cars, timber, lollipops, shirts, etc.; and all the myriad of services, such as football matches, haircuts, bus rides and insurance services. In the national accounts these figures are grouped together into broad categories such as manufacturing, construction and distribution. The figures for the UK economy for 2015 are shown in Figure 15.19.

When we add up the output of various firms, we must be careful to avoid *double counting*. For example, if a manufacturer sells a television to a retailer for £600 and the retailer sells it to the consumer for £800, how much has this television contributed to GDP? The answer is *not* £1400. We do not add the £600 received by the manufacturer to the £800 received by the retailer: that would be double counting. Instead we either just count the final value (£800) or the *value added* at each stage (£600 by the manufacturer + £200 by the retailer).

The sum of all the values added at each of the stages of production by all the various industries in the economy is known as *gross value added at basic prices (GVA)*.

Some qualifications

Stocks (or inventories). We must be careful only to include the values added in the *particular year in question*. A problem here is that some goods start being produced *before* the year begins. Thus when we come to work out GDP, we must ignore the values that had previously been added to stocks of raw materials and goods. Similarly, other goods are only sold to the consumer *after* the end of the year. Nevertheless we must still count the values that have been added during *this* year to these stocks of partially finished goods.

A final problem concerned with stocks is that they may increase in value simply due to increased prices. This is known as **stock (or inventory) appreciation**. Since there has been no real increase in output, stock appreciation must be deducted from value added.

Government services. The output of private industry is sold on the market and can thus be easily valued. This is not the case with most of the services provided by the government. Such services (e.g. health and education) should be valued in terms of what they cost to provide.

Ownership of dwellings. When a landlord rents out a flat, this service is valued as the rent that the tenant pays. But owner-occupiers living in their own property do not pay rent and yet they are 'consuming' a similar 'service'. Here a rental value for owner-occupation is 'imputed'. In other words, a figure corresponding to a rent is included in the GDP statistics under the heading 'letting of property' in the real estate activities category.

Taxes and subsidies on products. Taxes paid on goods and services (such as VAT) and any subsidies on products are *excluded* from gross value added (GVA), since they are not part of the value added in production. Nevertheless the way GDP is measured throughout the EU and most other countries of the world is at *market prices*: i.e. at the prices actually paid at each stage of production. Thus **GDP at market prices** (sometimes referred to simply as GDP) is GVA *plus* taxes on products *minus* subsidies on products.

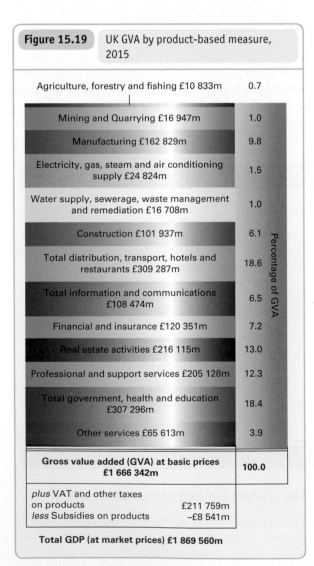

Figure 15.19	UK GVA by product-based measure, 2015	
Agriculture, forestry and fishing £10 833m		0.7
Mining and Quarrying £16 947m		1.0
Manufacturing £162 829m		9.8
Electricity, gas, steam and air conditioning supply £24 824m		1.5
Water supply, sewerage, waste management and remediation £16 708m		1.0
Construction £101 937m		6.1
Total distribution, transport, hotels and restaurants £309 287m		18.6
Total information and communications £108 474m		6.5
Financial and insurance £120 351m		7.2
Real estate activities £216 115m		13.0
Professional and support services £205 128m		12.3
Total government, health and education £307 296m		18.4
Other services £65 613m		3.9
Gross value added (GVA) at basic prices £1 666 342m		**100.0**
plus VAT and other taxes on products	£211 759m	
less Subsidies on products	−£8 541m	
Total GDP (at market prices) £1 869 560m		

Percentage of GVA

Definitions

Gross value added at basic prices (GVA) The sum of all the values added by all industries in the economy over a year. The figures exclude taxes on products (such as VAT) and include subsidies on products

Stock (or inventory) appreciation The increase in monetary value of stocks due to increased prices. Since this does not represent increased output, it is not included in GDP

GDP (at market prices) The value of output (or income or expenditure) in terms of the prices actually paid. GDP = GVA + taxes on products − subsidies on products.

The income method of measuring GDP

The second approach focuses on the incomes generated from the production of goods and services. This must be the same as the sum of all values added, since value added is simply the difference between a firm's revenue from sales and the costs of its purchases from other firms. This difference is made up of wages and salaries, rent, interest and profit: the incomes earned by those involved in the production process.

Since GDP is the sum of all values added, it must also be the sum of all incomes generated: the sum of wages and salaries, rent, interest and profit.

> *If a retailer buys a product from a wholesaler for £80 and sells it to a consumer for £100, then the £20 of value that has been added will go partly in wages, partly in rent and partly in profits. Thus £20 of income has been generated at the retail stage. But the good actually contributes a total of £100 to GDP. Where, then, is the remaining £80 worth of income recorded?*

Figure 15.20 shows how these incomes are grouped together in the official statistics. By far the largest category is 'compensation of employees': in other words, wages and salaries. As you can see, the total in Figure 15.20 is the same as in Figure 15.19, although the components are quite different. In other words, GDP is the same whether calculated by the product or the income method.

Some qualifications

Stock (inventory) appreciation. As in the case of the product approach, any gain in profits from inventory appreciation must be deducted, since they do not arise from a real increase in output.

Transfer payments. GDP includes only those incomes that arise from the production of goods and services. We do not, therefore, include *transfer payments* such as social security benefits, pensions and gifts.

Direct taxes. We count people's income *before* the payment of income and corporation taxes, since it is this *gross* (pre-tax) income that arises from the production of goods and services.

Taxes and subsidies on products. As with the product approach, if we are working out GVA, we measure incomes before the payment of taxes on products or the receipt of subsidies on products, since it is these pre-tax-and-subsidy incomes that arise from the value added by production. When working out GDP, however, we add in these taxes and subtract these subsidies to arrive at a *market price* valuation.

The expenditure method of measuring GDP

The final approach to calculating GDP is to add up all expenditure on final output (which will be at market prices). This will include the following:

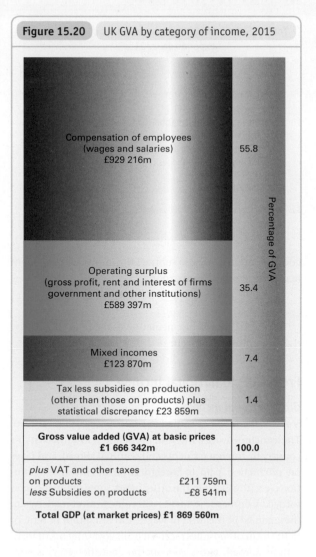

Figure 15.20   UK GVA by category of income, 2015

- *Consumer expenditure (C).* This includes all expenditure on goods and services by households and by non-profit institutions serving households (NPISH) (e.g. clubs and societies).

- *Government expenditure (G).* This includes central and local government expenditure on final goods and services. Note that it includes non-marketed services (such as health and education), but excludes transfer payments, such as pensions and social security payments.

- *Investment expenditure (I).* This includes investment in capital, such as buildings and machinery. It also includes the value of any increase (+) or decrease (−) in inventories, whether of raw materials, semi-finished goods or finished goods.

- *Exports of goods and services (X).*

We then have to *subtract* imports of goods and services (M) from the total in order to leave just the expenditure on *domestic* product. In other words, we subtract the part of consumer expenditure, government expenditure and investment that

Table 15.6	UK GDP at market prices by category of expenditure, 2015	
	£ million	% of GDP
Consumption expenditure of households and NPISH (C)	1 216 113	65.0
Government final consumption (G)	360 828	19.3
Gross capital formation (I)	327 855	17.5
Exports of goods and services (X)	510 340	27.3
Imports of goods and services (M)	−548 908	−29.4
Statistical discrepancy	3 332	0.2
GDP at market prices	**1 869 560**	**100.0**

Source: UK National Accounts, The Blue Book: 2016 (ONS).

Table 15.7	UK GDP, GNY and NNY at market prices, 2015
	£ million
Gross domestic product (GDP)	**1 869 560**
Plus net income from abroad	−37 016
Gross national income (GNY)	**1 832 544**
Less capital consumption (depreciation)	245 144
Net national income (NNY)	**1 587 400**

Source: UK National Accounts, The Blue Book: 2016 Tables (ONS).

goes on imports. We also subtract the imported component (e.g. raw materials) from exports.

$$\text{GDP (at market prices)} = C + I + G + X - M$$

Table 15.6 shows the calculation of the 2015 UK GDP by the expenditure approach.

From GDP to national income

Gross national income

Some of the incomes earned in this country will go abroad. These include wages, interest, profit and rent earned in this country by foreign residents and remitted abroad, and taxes on production paid to foreign governments and institutions (e.g. the EU). On the other hand, some of the incomes earned by domestic residents will come from abroad. Again, these can be in the form of wages, interest, profit or rent, or in the form of subsidies received from governments or institutions abroad. Gross *domestic* product, however, is concerned only with incomes generated *within* the country, irrespective of ownership. If, then, we are to take 'net income from abroad' into account (i.e. these inflows minus outflows), we need a new measure. This is *gross national income (GNY)*.[6] It is defined as follows:

GNY at market prices = GDP at market prices
+ Net income from abroad

Thus GDP focuses on the value of domestic production, whereas GNY focuses on the value of incomes earned by domestic residents.

Net national income

The measures we have used so far ignore the fact that each year some of the country's capital equipment wears out or becomes obsolete: in other words, they ignore capital depreciation. If we subtract from gross national income an allowance for *depreciation* (or 'capital consumption' as it is called in the official statistics), we get *net national income (NNY)*.

NNY at market prices = GNY at market prices
− Depreciation

Table 15.7 shows the 2015 GDP, GNY and NNY figures for the UK.

Although NNY gives a truer picture of a nation's income than GNY, economists tend to use the gross figures because depreciation is hard to estimate accurately.

Households' disposable income

Finally, we come to a measure that is useful for analysing consumer behaviour. This is called *households' disposable income*. It measures the income that people have available for spending (or saving): i.e. after any deductions for income tax, national insurance, etc. have been made. It is the best measure to use if we want to see how changes in household income affect consumption.

How do we get from GNY at market prices to households' disposable income? As GNY measures the incomes that firms receive from production[7] (plus net income from abroad), we must deduct that part of their income that is *not* distributed to households. This means that we must deduct taxes that firms pay – taxes on goods and services (such as VAT), taxes on profits (such as corporation tax) and any other taxes – and add in any subsidies they receive. We must then subtract

Definitions

Gross national income (GNY) GDP plus net income from abroad.

Depreciation The decline in value of capital equipment due to age, or wear and tear.

Net national income (NNY) GNY minus depreciation.

Households' disposable income The income available for households to spend: i.e. personal incomes after deducting taxes on incomes and adding benefits.

6 In the official statistics, this is referred to as GNI. We use Y to stand for income, however, to avoid confusion with investment.

7 We also include income from any public-sector production of goods or services (e.g. health and education) and production by non-profit institutions serving households.

allowances for depreciation and any undistributed profits. This gives us the gross income that households receive from firms in the form of wages, salaries, rent, interest and distributed profits.

To get from this to what is available for households to spend, we must subtract the money that households pay in income taxes and national insurance contributions, but add all benefits to households, such as pensions and child benefit: in other words, we must *include* transfer payments.

Households' disposable income = GNY at market prices
− Taxes paid by firms + Subsidiesreceived by firms
− Depreciation − Undistributed profits − Personal taxes
+ Benefits

Section summary

1. The product method measures the values added in all parts of the economy. Care must be taken in the evaluation of stocks, government services and the ownership of dwellings.

2. The income method measures all the incomes generated from domestic production: wages and salaries, rent, interest and profit. Transfer payments are not included, nor is stock appreciation.

3. The expenditure method adds up all the categories of expenditure: consumer expenditure, government expenditure, investment and exports. We then have to deduct the element of each that goes on imports in order to arrive at expenditure on domestic products. Thus $GDP = C + G + I + X - M$.

4. GDP at market prices measures what consumers pay for output (including taxes and subsidies on what they buy). Gross value added (GVA) measures what factors of production actually receive. GVA, therefore, is GDP at market prices minus taxes on products plus subsidies on products.

5. Gross national income (GNY) takes account of incomes earned from abroad (+) and incomes earned by people abroad from this country (−). Thus GNY = GDP plus net income from abroad.

6. Net national income (NNY) takes account of depreciation of capital. Thus NNY = GNY − depreciation.

7. Personal disposable income is a measure of household income after the deduction of income taxes and the addition of benefits.

END OF CHAPTER QUESTIONS

1. In 1974, the UK economy shrank by 2.5 per cent before shrinking by a further 1.5 per cent in 1975. However, actual GDP rose by 13 per cent in 1974 and by 24 per cent in 1975. What explains these apparently contradictory results?

2. Economists sometimes refer to the 'twin characteristics of economic growth'. What are these characteristics?

3. (i) What do you understand by the term financialisation? (ii) How might we assess the financial well-being of households?

4. Explain how equilibrium would be restored in the circular flow of income if there were a fall in investment.

5. Explain the circumstances under which an increase in pensions and child benefit would (a) increase national income; (b) leave national income unaffected; (c) decrease national income.

6. For what reasons might GDP be a poor indicator of (i) the level of development of a country; (ii) its rate of economic development?

7. (i) Will the rate of actual growth have any effect on the rate of potential growth? (ii) For what possible reasons may one country experience a persistently faster rate of economic growth than another?

8. Why will investment affect both actual (short-term) growth and the long-term growth in potential output? What will be the implications if these two effects differ in magnitude?

9. At what phase of the business cycle is the average duration of unemployment likely to be the highest? Explain.

10. Consider the most appropriate policy for tackling each of the different types of unemployment.

11. Do any groups of people gain from inflation?

12. If everyone's incomes rose in line with inflation, would it matter if inflation were 100 per cent or even 1000 per cent per annum?

13. Imagine that you had to determine whether a particular period of inflation was demand-pull, or cost-push, or a combination of the two. What information would you require in order to conduct your analysis?

14. Explain how the current account of the balance of payments is likely to vary with the course of the business cycle.

15. The overall balance of payments must always balance. If this is the case, why might a deficit on one part of the balance of payments be seen as a problem?

16. List some factors that could cause an increase in the credit items of the balance of payments and a decrease in the debit items. What would be the effect on the exchange rate (assuming that it is freely floating)? What effect would these exchange rate movements have on the balance of payments?

17. Explain how you would derive a figure for households' disposable income if you were starting from a figure for GDP.

Online resources

Additional case studies on the student website

15.1 **The GDP deflator.** An examination of how GDP figures are corrected to take inflation into account.

15.2 **Taking into account the redistributive effects of growth.** This case study shows how figures for economic growth can be adjusted to allow for the fact that poor people's income growth would otherwise count for far less than rich people's.

15.3 **Simon Kuznets and the system of national income accounting.** This looks at the work of Simon Kuznets, who devised the system of national income accounting that is used around the world. It describes some of the patterns of economic growth that he identified.

15.4 **Is stability always desirable?** Should firms sometimes be a given short, sharp shock?

15.5 **Theories of growth.** From dismal economics to the economics of optimism.

15.6 **The costs of economics growth.** Is more necessarily better?

15.7 **How big is the underground economy?** This case study looks at the factors that determine the size of the underground economy.

15.8 **The use of ISEW.** This looks at an alternative measure of economic well-being popular among environment groups: the Index of Sustainable Economic Welfare.

15.9 **Technology and employment.** Does technological progress create or destroy jobs?

15.10 **Cost-push illusion.** When rising costs are not a case of cost-push inflation.

15.11 **Disinflation.** The experience of Europe and Japan.

15.12 **Hyperinflation.** This looks at the extraordinarily high rates of inflation experienced in Germany in the early 1920s, Serbia and Montenegro in the 1990s and more recently in Zimbabwe.

15.13 **A. W. Phillips (1914–75).** A portrait of the discoverer of the Phillips curve, the New Zealand Economist, Bill Phillips.

15.14 **Making sense of the financial balances on the balance of payments.** An examination of the three main components of the financial account.

Websites relevant to this chapter

Numbers and sections refer to websites listed in the Web Appendix and hotlinked from this book's website at **www.pearsoned.co.uk/sloman.**

■ For news articles relevant to this chapter, see the *Economics News Articles* link from the book's website.

■ For general news on macroeconomic issues, both national and international, see websites in section A, and particularly A1–5, 7–9, 20–25, 31. See also links to newspapers worldwide in A38, 39, 42, 43 and 44, and the news search feature in Google at A41.

■ For macroeconomic data, see links in B1; also see B4 and 12. For UK data, see B2, 3 and 34. For EU data, see B38 and 47. For US data, see B15, 17 and 25. For international data, see B15, 21, 24, 31, and 35. For links to datasets, see I7, 18 and 23.

■ For UK data on specific topics, such as unemployment or GDP, search site B3.

■ For international data on balance of payments and exchange rates, see *World Economic Outlook* in H4 and *OECD Economic Outlook* in B21 (also in section B of B1).

■ For UK data on balance of payments, search 'Pink Book' on site B3.

■ For exchange rates, see A1, 3; B34; F2.

16 Chapter

The Development of Macroeconomic Thinking: a Historical Perspective

In this second and final chapter of Part E we provide an overview of how macroeconomics has developed over the past 100 years or so. In reading this chapter you will see how macroeconomic debates and theories have been shaped by real-world events, such as the Great Depression of the 1930s, the rapid inflation of the 1970s or the global economic and financial crisis of the late 2000s. You will also see how the development of economic ideas has affected actual policy, such as the granting of independence to central banks and the pursuit of inflation targets.

The unfolding of the 'macroeconomic story' allows us to see how different theories and approaches have developed. It also helps us to understand where there is greatest agreement among economists and where controversies remain. Although we urge you to read this chapter as it really helps put macroeconomics into historical context, it is not essential and you can, if your lecturer recommends it, move directly to Chapter 17.

had predicted that there would be virtually full employment. Any unemployment would simply be the frictional and structural unemployment of people being 'between jobs'.

Part of the cause of the Depression was the decision in 1925 by Winston Churchill, the Chancellor of the Exchequer, to return to the gold standard following the UK's withdrawal from it in 1914 at the outbreak of the First World War. The decision was made to return at the pre-war rate of £1 = $4.86. But with many export markets lost in the war and a rapid rise in imports for rebuilding the economy, the balance of payments was in severe deficit. The UK's trade deficit had risen to 5 per cent by 1925.

To correct the UK's trade position required severely deflationary policies. The aim was to drive wage rates down, reduce costs and restore the competitiveness of exports. The result, however, was a severe recession: the UK economy contracted by an estimated 3.1 per cent in 1926.

But while in Britain output slumped and unemployment soared, most of the rest of the industrialised world initially experienced a boom. But in 1929, after a decade of rapid growth and a huge rise in share values, Wall Street crashed. This sent the US economy plunging into deep recession, with the rest of the world following suit. As the world economy slumped, so did international trade. With a collapse of its exports, Britain dived even deeper into depression. 1931 saw the UK economy contract by 4.6 per cent.

Eventually, in 1932, Britain was forced to leave the gold standard and allow the pound to depreciate. (Case Study 16.4 on the student website looks at the bitter experience of the return to the gold standard in 1925 and its aftermath.)

The deflationary policies of the 1920s seemed to be directly responsible for increasing unemployment. Many critics argued that the government ought deliberately to *expand* aggregate demand. However, the Treasury and other classical economists rejected the analysis that unemployment was caused by a lack of demand; they also rejected policies of reflation (e.g. increased government expenditure).

The classical Treasury view on unemployment

Would deflation of demand not lead to unemployment? According to the Treasury view, unemployment would occur only if labour markets *failed to clear*: if real wage costs did not fall sufficiently.

The Treasury concluded that people should be encouraged to take wage cuts. This would also help to reduce prices and restore export demand, thus correcting the balance of payments. People should also be encouraged to save. This would, via flexible interest rates, lead to more investment and hence a growth in output and demand for labour.

The classical Treasury view on public works

In the 1920s and 1930s, some politicians and economists argued that unemployment could be reduced if the government pursued a programme of public works: building roads, hospitals, houses, etc. The Treasury view was that this would not work and could have costly side effects.

A programme of public works could be funded in three ways: from extra taxation, from extra government borrowing or by printing extra money. *None* of these three ways would, according to the classical Treasury view, solve the unemployment problem.

- *Extra taxation* would merely have the effect of reducing the money that consumers would spend on private industry. Extra public-sector demand would thus be offset by a fall in private-sector demand.
- If the government *borrowed more,* it would have to offer higher interest rates in order to persuade people to buy the additional government securities. The private sector would

---

Definition

Crowding out Where increased public expenditure diverts money or resources away from the private sector.

BOX 16.1 · BALANCE THE BUDGET AT ALL COSTS

Fiscal policy in the early 1930s

The budget must be balanced. All government expenditure should be financed from taxation. This was orthodox opinion in the 1920s.

But as unemployment increased during the Great Depression (see Figure 16.1), spending on unemployment benefits (the most rapidly growing item of government expenditure) threatened the balanced budget principle. Other spending had to be cut to restore balance. The result was more unemployment, and hence the payment of more unemployment benefits.

Treasury officials and classical economists called for cuts in unemployment benefits. The May Committee, set up to

investigate the budgetary problem, recommended a 20 per cent reduction. Even the Labour government, elected on a mandate to tackle the unemployment problem, proposed a 10 per cent reduction in 1931. This contributed to its subsequent collapse.

Philip Snowden, Labour's Chancellor of the Exchequer, remarked in 1931 how pensioners had returned their pension books and children sent in their savings to help the nation balance its budget. And yet, as Keynes argued, it was not saving that was necessary to cure the unemployment, but spending. Government deficits were *desirable*. Attempts to balance the budget merely deflated the economy further and deepened the problem of unemployment.

| BOX 16.2 | THE CROWDING-OUT EFFECT | EXPLORING ECONOMICS |

When public expenditure replaces private

Critics of the use of government expenditure to stimulate output and employment often refer to the problem of *crowding out*. In its starkest form, the argument goes like this.

There is no point in the government embarking on a programme of public works to bring the economy out of recession. If it attempts to spend more, it can do so only by reducing private expenditure. The effect on total spending will be zero. This crowding out can take two main forms.

Resource crowding out

This is when the government uses resources such as labour and raw materials that would otherwise be used by the private sector. If the economy is operating near full capacity, then if resources are used by the government, they cannot at the same time be used by private companies.

The argument is far less convincing, however, if there is slack in the economy. If the government merely mobilises otherwise *idle* resources, there need be no reduction in private-sector output. In fact, if private-sector firms have spare capacity, they will respond to the higher demand by producing more themselves: aggregate demand will stimulate extra production.

Financial crowding out

This occurs when extra government spending diverts *funds* from private-sector firms and thus deprives them of the finance necessary for investment.

If the government spends more (without raising taxes or printing more money), it will have to borrow more and will therefore have to offer higher rates of interest. Private companies will then have to offer higher rates of interest themselves in order to attract funds. Alternatively, if they borrow from banks, and banks have less funds, the banks will charge them higher interest rates. Higher interest rates will discourage firms from borrowing and hence discourage investment.

The weakness with this argument is that it assumes that the supply of money is fixed. If the government spends more but *increases* the amount of money in the economy, it need not deprive the private sector of finance. Interest rates will not be bid up.

But would that not be inflationary? Not if there are idle resources and hence the extra money can be spent on extra output. Only if *resource* crowding out takes place would it be inflationary.

 Could resource crowding out take place at less than full employment?

then have to offer higher interest rates, to compete for funds. As interest rates went up, private borrowing would go down. Thus public investment would *crowd out* private investment (see Box 16.2). This debate was to be revisited many years later when, following the financial crisis and subsequent economic downturn of the late 2000s, government borrowing rose sharply (see Figure 16.1).

■ According to the quantity theory of money, printing extra money would simply lead to inflation. The argument here is that a rise in aggregate demand would simply lead to a rise in the price level with no increase in national output and, hence, employment. A re-emergence of inflation, which had been eliminated in the early 1920s, would further erode the competitiveness of British goods,

jeopardising the return to the gold standard at the pre-war exchange rate.

Treasury orthodoxy insisted, therefore, that government should attempt to balance its budget, even if this meant cutting welfare benefits to the rising numbers of unemployed (see Box 16.1). The governments of the 1920s and early 1930s followed these classical recommendations. They attempted to balance their budgets and rejected policies of reflation. Yet mass unemployment persisted.

It is interesting to note that the policy of reducing deficits through cuts in government expenditure, even at a time of recession, was a central part of the UK Coalition government's policy in the early 2010s.

Section summary

1. The classical analysis of output and employment is based on the assumption that markets clear. More specifically, it assumes that there are flexible wages, flexible prices and flexible rates of interest. The result will be that demand and supply are equated in the labour market, in the goods market and in the market for loanable funds.

2. Given that markets will clear, Say's law will operate. This law states that supply creates its own demand. In other words, the production of goods and services will generate incomes for households, which in turn will generate consumption expenditure, ensuring that the goods are sold. If any incomes are not directly spent on domestic goods, flexible prices will help to ensure that any money withdrawn is reinjected. Flexible interest rates will ensure that investment equals saving, and flexible prices and wages will ensure that exports equal imports. Provided the government balances its budget, withdrawals will equal injections and Say's law will hold.

3. The classical economists based their analysis of prices on the quantity theory of money. This states that the level of prices is directly related to the quantity of money (M) in the economy. Their position can be demonstrated using the equation of exchange:

$$MV = PY$$

where V is the velocity of circulation, P is the price index and Y is real national income expressed in the prices of the base year. The classical economists assumed that V and Y were not affected by changes in the money supply and could thus be regarded as 'constants'. From this it follows that

$$P = f(M)$$

Increases in the money supply simply lead to inflation.

4. In 1925, Britain returned to the gold standard system of fixed exchange rates at the pre-war rate. But given the massive balance of payments deficit at this rate, it had to pursue tough deflationary policies. The result was mass unemployment.

5. The classical economists saw the remedy to the problem as lying in reductions in wages and prices. According to the classical theory, this would allow Say's law to operate and full employment to be restored. They rejected public works as the solution, arguing that it would lead to crowding out if financed by borrowing, and to inflation if financed by printing money.

16.3 THE KEYNESIAN REVOLUTION

Keynes' rejection of classical macroeconomics

The main critic of classical macroeconomics was John Maynard Keynes. In his major work, *The General Theory of Employment, Interest and Money* (1936), he rejected the classical assumption that markets would clear. Disequilibrium could persist and mass unemployment could continue. There are two crucial markets in which disequilibrium could persist.

The labour market

Workers would resist wage cuts. Wages were thus 'sticky' downwards. In a recession, when the demand for labour is low, wages might not fall far or fast enough to clear the labour market. Consequently, there would exist demand-deficient unemployment (see section 15.5).

But even if wage cuts could be introduced, as advocated by classical economists, Keynes rejected that as the solution to demand deficiency. Workers are also consumers. A cut in workers' wages would mean less consumer spending. Firms would respond to this by further reducing their demand for labour, which would more than offset the reduction in wages. Wage rates would not fall fast enough to clear the market. Disequilibrium would worsen. The recession would deepen.

Employers might well find that labour was cheaper to employ, but if demand for their product were falling, they would hardly be likely to take on more labour.

The market for loanable funds

Keynes also rejected the classical solution of increased saving as a means of stimulating investment and growth. Again the problem was one of market disequilibrium.

An increase in saving will cause a disequilibrium in the market for loanable funds. An increase in the supply of loanable funds will lead to the real rate of interest for loanable funds falling. But an increase in saving also means a fall in consumption. Consequently, firms will sell less and will thus be discouraged from investing. This results in a fall in the demand for loanable funds. The rate of interest would have to fall further to clear the market, perhaps considerably so.

The demand for investment, according to Keynes, depends very much on business confidence in the future. A slide into recession could shatter such confidence. The resulting fall in investment would deepen the recession.

The problem of disequilibrium in the market for loanable funds is made worse, according to Keynes, because neither saving nor investment is very responsive to changes in interest rates, and thus very large changes in interest rates would be necessary if equilibrium were ever to be restored after any

| BOX 16.3 | WILL WAGE CUTS CURE UNEMPLOYMENT? | EXPLORING ECONOMICS |

Keynes' dismissal of the classical remedy

In *The General Theory of Employment, Interest and Money*, Keynes rejects the classical argument that unemployment is due to excessive wages. In Chapter 2 he argues:

> [T]he contention that the unemployment which characterises a depression is due to a refusal by labour to accept a reduction of money wages is not clearly supported by the facts. It is not very plausible to assert that unemployment in the United States in 1932 was due either to labour obstinately refusing to accept a reduction of money wages or to its obstinately demanding a real wage beyond what the productivity of the economic

machine was capable of furnishing. Wide variations are experienced in the volume of employment without any apparent change either in the minimum real demands of labour or in its productivity. Labour is not more truculent in the depression than in the boom – far from it. Nor is its physical productivity less. These facts from experience are a *prima facie* ground for questioning the classical analysis.[1]

1 J. M. Keynes, *The General Theory of Employment, Interest and Money* (Macmillan, 1967), p. 9.

---

change in the supply of loanable funds (saving) or demand for loanable funds (investment).

Keynes also rejected the simple quantity theory of money. Increases in money supply will not necessarily lead merely to rises in prices. If there is a lot of slack in the economy, with high unemployment, idle machines and idle resources, an increased spending of money may lead to substantial increases in real income (Y) and leave prices (P) little affected.

If the government were to cut money supply in an attempt to reduce prices, the major effect might be to reduce output and employment instead. In terms of the quantity equation, a reduction in M may lead to a reduction in output and hence real income Y rather than a reduction in P.

All these arguments meant a rejection of Say's law. Far from supply creating demand and thus ensuring full employment, Keynes argued that it was *demand that created supply*. If aggregate demand rose, firms would respond to the extra demand by producing more and employing more people. But a fall in demand would lead to less output and rising unemployment.

Keynes' central point was that an unregulated market economy *could not ensure sufficient demand*. Governments should therefore abandon laissez-faire, and should intervene to *control* aggregate demand.

Keynes' analysis of employment and inflation

Keynes' analysis of unemployment can be explained most simply in terms of the circular flow of income (see Figure 16.2). Keynes himself did not use this exact model, but it clearly explains the essence of his argument.

If injections (J) do not equal withdrawals (W), a state of disequilibrium exists. What will bring them back into equilibrium, however, is not a change in prices (of labour or of loanable funds), but rather a change in *national income* and *employment*.

Start with a state of equilibrium, where injections equal withdrawals, but with substantial unemployed resources (as was the case in the Great Depression). If there is now a

rise in injections – for example, a rise in government expenditure – aggregate demand ($C_d + J$) will be higher. Firms will respond to this increased demand by using more labour and other resources and thus paying out more incomes (Y) to households. Household consumption will rise and so firms will sell more.

Firms will respond by producing more, and thus using more labour and other resources. Household incomes will rise again. Consumption and hence production will rise again, and so on. There will thus be a multiplied rise in incomes and employment. This is known as the ***multiplier effect*** and is an example of the 'principle of cumulative causation'. Cumulative causation refers to where an initial event can cause an ultimate effect that is much larger. It is our final threshold concept and we examine it in detail in Chapter 17 (see page 535).

TC 15 p535

Definition

Multiplier effect An initial increase in aggregate demand of £xm leads to an eventual rise in national income that is greater than £xm.

Figure 16.2   The circular flow of income

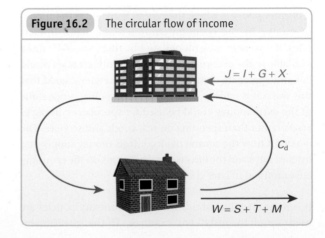

$$J = I + G + X$$

$$C_d$$

$$W = S + T + M$$

The process, however, does not go on for ever. Each time household incomes rise, households save more, pay more taxes and buy more imports. In other words, withdrawals rise. When withdrawals have risen to match the increased injections, equilibrium will be restored and national income and employment will stop rising. The process can be summarised as follows:

$$J > W \rightarrow Y\uparrow \rightarrow W\uparrow \text{ until } J = W$$

Similarly, an initial fall in injections (or rise in withdrawals) will lead to a multiplied fall in national income and employment:

$$J < W \rightarrow Y\downarrow \rightarrow W\downarrow \text{ until } J = W$$

Thus equilibrium in the circular flow of income can be at *any* level of output and employment.

If aggregate demand is too low, there will be a recession and high unemployment. The equilibrium output level would be considerably below that consistent with the full employment of the economy's resources. In this case, argued Keynes, governments should intervene to boost aggregate demand. There are two policy instruments that they can use.

Fiscal policy

Fiscal policy is where the government alters the balance between government expenditure (*G*) and taxation (*T*). By engaging in fiscal policy, government can alter the balance between injections and withdrawals. In this way, it controls aggregate demand. Faced with a recession, it should raise *G* and/or lower *T*. In other words, the government should run a budget deficit rather than a balanced budget. There will then be a multiplier effect:

$$G\uparrow \text{ or } T\downarrow \rightarrow J > W \rightarrow Y\uparrow \rightarrow W\uparrow \text{ until } J = W$$

The larger the multiplier effect the larger the eventual increase in output following the initial increase in aggregate demand.

Monetary policy

Monetary policy is where the central bank alters the supply of money in the economy and/or manipulates interest rates. If it were to raise money supply, there would be more available in the economy for spending, interest rates would fall and aggregate demand would rise. Keynes argued that this was a less reliable policy than fiscal policy, since some of the extra money could be used for speculating in paper assets rather than spending on real goods and services. The details of how the central bank controls money supply and interest rates and the effects of such actions on the economy are examined in later chapters.

It is most effective if both fiscal and monetary policies are used simultaneously. For example, if the government undertook a programme of public works (fiscal policy) and financed it through increases in money supply (monetary policy), there would be no crowding out. There would be a significant rise in output and employment.

 What would be the classical economists' criticisms of this argument?

If aggregate demand rises too much, however, inflation becomes a problem. (This was the case during the Second World War, with the high expenditure on the war effort.) As the economy's full-capacity output is approached, with more and more firms reaching their full capacity and with fewer and fewer idle resources, so additional increases in aggregate demand lead more and more to higher prices rather than higher output. The aggregate level of employment therefore becomes unresponsive to an increase in the effective demand for output. Thus, the level of output when this situation arises is sometimes referred as to the 'full-employment output level'.

 If a rise in aggregate demand were to encourage firms to invest more, how would this influence the size of the rise in real GDP?

Governments faced with the resulting demand-pull inflation should, according to Keynes, use *contractionary* fiscal and monetary policies to reduce demand. Contractionary fiscal policy would involve reducing government expenditure and/or raising taxes. Contractionary monetary policy would involve reducing the rate of growth of money supply and/or raising interest rates. Keynes argued that here too fiscal policy was the more reliable, but again that the best solution was to combine both policies.

The Keynesian policies of the 1950s and 1960s

By the end of the Second World War, the economic consensus had changed and this was to have a direct impact on economic policy making in many countries. The dominance of classical economics was to be replaced by Keynesian ideas. From 1945 up to the mid-1970s, many governments around the world, including Conservative and Labour governments in the UK, pursued Keynesian **demand-management policies** in an attempt to stabilise the economy and avoid excess or deficient demand.

> ## Definitions
>
> **Monetary policy** Where the central bank alters the supply of money in the economy and/or manipulates interest rates.
>
> **Demand-management policies** Demand-side policies (fiscal and/or monetary) designed to smooth out the fluctuations in the business cycle.

When the economy began to grow too fast, with rising inflation and balance of trade deficits, the government adopted *deflationary* (contractionary) fiscal and monetary policies. When inflation and the balance of payments were sufficiently improved, but probably with recession looming, threatening rising unemployment and little or no growth, governments adopted *reflationary* (expansionary) fiscal and monetary policies. This succession of deflationary and reflationary policies to counteract the effect of the business cycle became known as **stop–go policies** (see Case Study 16.7 on the student website for an account of 'fine-tuning' in the UK).

As Figure 16.1 shows (see page 492), during the 1950s and 1960s, inflation in the UK averaged 4 per cent and unemployment a mere 1.7 per cent (see also Case Study 16.8 on the student website). Low rates of inflation and unemployment were experienced in other industrialised countries too.

Nevertheless, from the mid-1960s onwards there was increasing criticism of short-term demand-management policies. Criticisms included the following:

■ *Economic fluctuations still existed.* The policies had mixed success in stabilising economies. The business cycle remained. Some economists even claimed that demand-management policies made fluctuations worse. The main reason given was the time it took for policies to be adopted and to work. If time lags are long enough, a deflationary policy may begin to work only when the economy has already turned down into recession. Likewise, a reflationary policy may begin to work only when the economy is already booming, thus further fuelling inflation.

■ *Neglect of structural problems.* Some economists argued that an over-concentration on short-term policies of

stabilisation meant that underlying structural problems in economies were neglected. This was particularly significant in the UK since its post-war growth rate of around 2¾ per cent per annum was appreciably lower than that of other industrialised countries.

■ *Balance of payments problems.* Countries like the UK and the USA had persistent balance of trade deficits. At the time, with virtually fixed rates of exchange (something we shall examine in Chapter 25), a *depreciation* of the exchange rate was not an option for correcting balance of payments deficits. This meant that Keynesian reflationary policies were not always possible in recessions. The reason was that *deflationary* policies had to be pursued instead to bring prices down to boost exports and dampen demand to reduce imports.

■ *Breakdown of the simple Phillips curve.* The simple Phillips curve relationship between inflation and unemployment was breaking down (see Box 15.6). If reflationary policies were the cure for unemployment and deflationary policies were the cure for inflation, what policies should be pursued when both inflation *and* unemployment were rising?

■ *Focus on aggregate demand.* Perhaps the most fundamental criticism of all came from a group of economists called 'monetarists'. They rejected Keynesianism as a whole, with its concentration on demand. They returned to the earlier classical analysis, with its concentration on supply, and extended it to take account of the increasingly important role of *price expectations* in explaining 'stagflation' – the problem of slow growth and rising unemployment (i.e. stagnation) combined with rising inflation (see the next section).

From the mid-1970s onwards, the Keynesian/monetarist split between economists was often reflected in countries' political systems. For example, in the UK the Conservative leadership embraced monetarism, whereas the other political parties continued to embrace variants of Keynesianism.

Definition

Stop–go policies Alternate deflationary and reflationary policies to tackle the currently most pressing of the four problems that fluctuate with the business cycle.

Section summary

1. Keynes rejected the classical assumption that all markets would clear. Disequilibrium could persist in the labour market. A fall in aggregate demand would not simply lead to a fall in wages and prices and a restoration of the full-employment equilibrium. Instead there would be demand-deficient unemployment: as demand fell, there would be less demand for labour.

2. Disequilibrium could also persist in the market for loanable funds. As aggregate demand fell, and with it business confidence, so the demand for loanable funds for investment would shrink. Reductions in interest rates would be insufficient to clear the market for loanable funds.

3. Keynes also rejected the simple quantity theory. If there is slack in the economy, an expansion of the money supply can lead to an increase in *output* rather than an increase in prices.

4. Keynes argued that there would be a multiplier effect from changes in injections or withdrawals. A rise in investment,

for example, would cause a multiplied rise in national income, as additional expenditures flowed round and round the circular flow, stimulating more and more production and thus generating more and more real income.

5. If the economy is operating below full employment, the government can use fiscal and/or monetary policies to boost aggregate demand and thereby take up the slack in the economy. Excessive aggregate demand, however, causes inflation. Deflationary fiscal and monetary policies can be used to remove this excess demand.

6. Keynesianism became the orthodoxy of the 1950s and 1960s. Governments used fiscal (and to a lesser extent monetary) policies to manage the level of aggregate demand.

7. After the mid-1960s, however, there was growing criticism of Keynesian demand management. Economies still fluctuated and the various macroeconomic problems seemed to be getting worse.

16.4 THE RISE OF THE MONETARIST AND NEW CLASSICAL SCHOOLS

Sowing the seeds of a new orthodoxy

As we saw in section 16.3, the Keynesian orthodoxy began to break down during the 1960s. This breakdown can be seen in the context of a more volatile macroeconomic environment (see Figure 16.3). The high inflation and low growth of the 1970s stimulated macroeconomic debates. As we shall see, some of the resulting developments were to

have a significant impact on macroeconomics, helping to shape a new orthodoxy.

In charting the path to a new orthodoxy, we begin by considering the rise of the monetarist and new classical schools. A feature that distinguished both schools from the Keynesian orthodoxy was the belief that the market economy can deliver macroeconomic stability. Government

---

Figure 16.3 UK macroeconomic indicators, 1950–2018

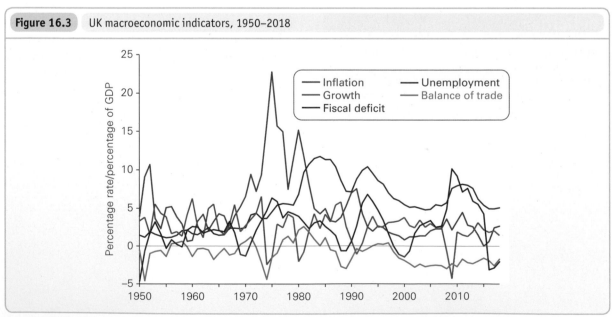

Notes: (i) Inflation is the annual rate of consumer price inflation; (ii) Unemployment rate is the standardised unemployment rate as % of UK workforce; (iii) Growth is the annual growth in constant-price GDP; (iv) Balance of trade is the balance on goods and services as % of GDP; and (v) Fiscal deficit is public sector net borrowing as a % of GDP; (v) Figures from 2016 are forecasts.
Source: Based on data from *Three Centuries of Data* (Bank of England), June 2016 and various forecasts.

intervention, they argued, can be a contributory factor to macroeconomic *instability*.

The monetarist counter-revolution

The chief advocate of monetarism was Milton Friedman, Professor of Economics at Chicago University and recipient of the Nobel Memorial Prize in Economics in 1976 (see Case Study 16.9 on the student website). Monetarists returned to the old classical theory as the basis for their analysis, and extended it to take account of the growing problem of *stagflation* – low growth accompanied by high inflation.

At the heart of monetarism is the *quantity theory of money*, which, as we saw earlier, was central to the classical analysis of inflation (see section 16.2). Friedman examined the historical relationship between money supply and prices, and concluded that inflation was 'always and everywhere a monetary phenomenon'. If money supply over the long run rises faster than the potential output of the economy, inflation will be the inevitable result.

Monetarists argued that over the long run, in the equation $MV = PY$, both V and Y are independently determined and are not, therefore, affected by changes in M. Any change in money supply (M), therefore, will only affect prices (P). In other words, the *neutrality of money* (see section 16.2) holds in the long run.

Monetarists drew two important conclusions from their analysis.

- The rising inflation from the mid 1960s onwards was entirely due to the growth in money supply increasingly outstripping the growth in output. If money supply rises, they argued, then the resulting rise in aggregate demand will lead to higher output and employment only in the short run. But soon people's expectations will adjust. Workers and firms come to expect higher wages and prices. Their actions then ensure that wages and prices *are* higher. Thus after a short period, perhaps one or two years, the extra demand is fully taken up in inflation, and so output and employment fall back again. Then governments are tempted to raise money supply and aggregate demand again in a further attempt to get unemployment down. The effect of this over several years is for the inflation rate to get higher and higher.

- Reducing the rate of growth of money supply will reduce inflation without leading to long-run increases in unemployment. It *will* lead to temporary increases in unemployment, they argued, as the demand for goods and labour fall. But as price and wage inflation adjust down to this new level of demand, unemployment will fall. This process will be hindered and high unemployment is likely to persist if workers continue demanding excessive wage increases, or if firms and workers continue to expect high inflation rates.

Monetarists argued that inflation is damaging to the economy. Inflation creates uncertainty for businesspeople and so reduces investment while also reducing a country's competitiveness in international trade. They saw it as essential, therefore, for governments to keep a tight control over money supply and advocated the setting of money supply *targets*. Modest and well-publicised targets should help to reduce the *expected* rate of inflation. Targets for the growth of the money supply were central to the 'medium-term financial strategy' from the late 1970s to the mid-1980s of the UK governments of Margaret Thatcher.

TC 9 p129

A vertical long-run Phillips curve

Monetarist analysis implied that the long-run Phillips curve is vertical at the equilibrium rate of unemployment. The equilibrium rate is frequently referred to as the **natural rate of unemployment** by monetarists. This is illustrated in Figure 16.4. It is the rate consistent with the economy being at its potential or 'long-run' level. It is therefore argued to be determined principally by structural factors. Though not directly measurable, it can be thought of as capturing structural and frictional unemployment (see section 15.5).

In the *short run,* higher aggregate demand will reduce the unemployment rate below the natural rate. This is because there is a *real* increase in aggregate demand. But in the long run an increase in aggregate demand is fully absorbed by higher inflation. Therefore, a monetary expansion will

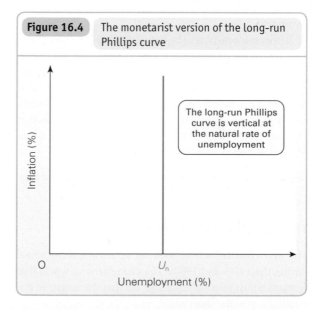

Figure 16.4 The monetarist version of the long-run Phillips curve

The long-run Phillips curve is vertical at the natural rate of unemployment

Inflation (%)

O

U_n

Unemployment (%)

Definitions

Stagflation A term used to refer to the combination of stagnation (low growth and high unemployment) and high inflation.

Natural rate of unemployment The rate of unemployment consistent with market clearing in the labour market. It is the rate of unemployment at which the vertical long-run Phillips curve cuts the horizontal axis.

increase output and employment in the short run, but not so in the long run, when money neutrality holds. The key to understanding why is the role of expectations.

Friedman argued that, in forming expectations of inflation, people learn from experience. If, for example, in the previous period, they under-predicted the rate of inflation, then this period they will adapt: they will revise their expectations of inflation upwards. This type of behaviour is thus known as **adaptive expectations**.

Assume that the economy is in equilibrium with unemployment at its natural rate (U_n) and that the authorities engage in a monetary expansion. This increases aggregate demand, resulting in an excess demand for goods and labour. The effect of this is to cause prices and nominal wages to rise. Even though *real* wages have not risen, workers could be 'fooled' into supplying more labour, believing that the rise in nominal wages represented a real rise. In fact, prices typically rise more quickly than nominal wages, resulting in a *fall* in real wages. Consequently, firms increase their demand for labour; output expands and the unemployment rate falls below its natural rate.

Gradually workers recognise that their real wages have fallen following the monetary expansion. This puts further upward pressure on money wages. In the long run, as expectations of inflation converge on actual inflation, all the extra demand is absorbed in higher inflation. Output falls to its potential level and unemployment rises back to the natural rate.

If unemployment is to be reduced in the long run, therefore, this vertical Phillips curve must be shifted to the left. This will be achieved by a reduction in the natural (equilibrium) rate of unemployment (U_n), *not* by an increase in demand. To reduce the natural rate, argued the monetarists, **supply-side policies** would be needed. These are policies that focus on increasing *potential* output by increasing the quantity and/or productivity of factors of production.

 Give some examples of supply-side policies that would help to reduce the natural rate of unemployment.

The new classical school

The **new classical school** took on increasing significance during the 1970s and 1980s. The monetarist view was that markets adjust relatively quickly, but that there may be disequilibrium in the short run.

 In contrast, new classical economists believed that markets clear continuously. The implication of **continuous market clearing** for the labour market is that there is no demand-deficient unemployment: wage flexibility equates the demand and supply of labour. The only unemployment is 'voluntary' unemployment, where unemployed people choose not to take jobs on offer, preferring, perhaps, to spend time looking for better-paid employment. The assumption of continuous market clearing has another important implication: the distinction between the short run and long run breaks down.

 Is voluntary unemployment the same as frictional unemployment?

Another key assumption of the new classical school is **rational expectations**. This means that economic agents use all available information and predict inflation, or any other macroeconomic variable, as well as they can. The important point here is that, unlike with adaptive expectations, economic agents avoid making the same error repeatedly. Therefore, errors are random. This means that, on average, economic agents' expectations of inflation are correct.

The implication of continuous market clearing combined with rational expectations is that a change in aggregate demand will simply cause a change in prices, not a change in output and employment, even in the short run. This applies equally to both a rise and a fall in aggregate demand.

But, with continuous market clearing and rational expectations, how did new classical models explain the fluctuations in output and unemployment associated with the business cycle?

Monetary surprises

The first strand of new classical models focused on how imperfect information could generate unexpected inflation. The work was led by Professor Robert Lucas, who, like Friedman, spent much of his career at the University of Chicago. Lucas was a recipient of the Nobel Memorial Prize in Economics in 1995 (see Box 21.3).

Monetary surprise models show how *unexpected* changes in monetary policy can result in both firms and workers changing their supply decisions such that the economy temporarily deviates from equilibrium. Consider an unexpected monetary expansion that causes aggregate demand to grow more than expected and, in turn, results in the inflation rate

Definitions

Adaptive expectations hypothesis The theory that people base their expectations of inflation on past inflation rates.

Supply-side policies Policies to increase *potential* output. Such policies focus on increasing the quantity and/or productivity of resources.

New classical school A body of economists who believe that markets are highly competitive and clear very rapidly; any expansion of demand will feed through virtually instantaneously into higher prices, giving a vertical short-run as well as a vertical long-run Phillips curve.

Continuous market clearing The assumption that all markets in the economy continuously clear so that the economy is permanently in equilibrium.

Rational expectations Expectations based on the *current* situation. These expectations are based on the information people have to hand. While this information may be imperfect and therefore people will make errors, these errors will be random.

being higher than expected. If, as wages and prices rise, workers and firms wrongly believe that the *real* price of their labour and output has increased, they will supply more.

Conversely, an unexpected monetary contraction would see labour supply and output fall. This time, workers and firms wrongly believe that a fall in wages and prices represents a real fall in the price of labour and output.

 Why are monetary surprises less likely with independent central banks pursuing an inflation target? Would monetary surprises still be possible in such circumstances?

 The key to economic fluctuations in monetary surprise models is the errors in expected inflation that arise from imperfect information. Once economic agents recognise these errors, output and employment return to their equilibrium levels. In the presence of continuous market clearing and rational expectations, *anticipated* changes in economic policy have no effect on output and employment, which remain at their equilibrium levels. This prediction is known as the *policy ineffectiveness proposition*.

The monetary surprise models and the policy ineffectiveness proposition are highly contentious. Two principal objections have been raised.

The first objection is the assumption of *continuous market clearing.* As we shall see in the next section, a key Keynesian response has been to explore why instead prices might adjust only *slowly* in clearing product and labour markets. If prices do adjust slowly then economic policy can have real effects on output and employment, even in the presence of rational expectations.

The second objection is the conclusion of *money neutrality,* whereby expected changes in monetary policy do not affect output. Could the business cycle be explained only by monetary *surprises*? It was this second concern that some new classical economists attempted to address with the development of real business cycle models.

Real business cycles

 Like the monetary surprise models, **real business cycle** *theories* also assume continuous market clearing and rational expectations. However, real business cycle theories challenge the traditional understanding of the business cycle as

fluctuations in real GDP around potential (natural) output (see section 15.3). Instead, it is argued, the business cycle is created by movements in potential output itself: in other words, shifts in aggregate supply, not aggregate demand. These movements come from frequent 'shocks' that hit the economy which permanently affect the path of the economy's output over time.

Real business cycle (RBC) theories typically focus on supply-side shocks. These shocks are also known as 'impulses' and frequently take the form of technology shocks. Technology shocks can, in theory, refer to anything that affects production processes and levels of productivity. For example, a technological breakthrough in telecommunications could positively affect potential output while a decline in energy sources could negatively affect potential output.

 Would an intensification of government regulation constitute a positive or negative economic shock in RBC models?

Real business cycle theory challenges the traditional view that technology is important largely when explaining the *long-term* rate of economic growth and development. Instead, frequent technology shocks are also seen as an important explanation of business cycles. Therefore, real business cycle theories dispense with the distinction between the business cycle and long-term economic growth; supply-side shocks are important both in the short run and in the long run.

The economic effects of shocks to the economy, such as those from technological change, are assumed to reflect the optimal decisions of economic agents (firms, households, government, etc.). In making consumption and production choices, economic agents take into account the impact of their choices not only in the current period, but in all future periods too.

This means that an expansion in the economy's output (e.g. from a technological breakthrough) reflects purposeful decisions by firms to increase output and workers to increase their labour supply. On the other hand, declining output (e.g. from a less business-friendly regulatory climate) reflects decisions by firms to reduce output and workers to reduce labour supply.

The role of representative agents.   Real business cycle models use representative agents (i.e. a typical person or firm) to analyse and illustrate the impact of economic shocks. They are assumed to allocate their time between work and leisure so as to maximise their lifetime satisfaction.

Consider the effect of a positive technology shock. Again, this could be a technological breakthrough. This enables the representative agent to produce and earn more now. If they believe that the benefits of this positive shock will be relatively short-lived, the incentive to work and earn more now is especially strong. Therefore, following positive economic shocks economic agents actively choose to work more. In doing so, output rises. Some of the increased income from

---

Definitions

Policy ineffectiveness proposition The conclusion drawn from new classical models that when economic agents anticipate changes in economic policy, output and employment remain at their equilibrium (or natural) levels

Real business cycle theories The new classical theory which explains fluctuations in real GDP in terms of economic shocks, especially technology shocks, and which have persistent effects on potential output.

the additional production is invested, increasing levels of investment. This further increases the economy's potential output, so raising possible future output levels.

When economic shocks are negative, such as from a decline in energy sources, economic agents choose to work less. Such shocks reduce current output levels and reduce levels of investment. The effect is to reduce possible future output levels.

 Assume that there is a positive economic shock and the economy expands. Why may it continue to expand for some time? Why may the expansion eventually cease and be followed by a recession?

Government policies

Governments up to the late 1970s responded to rising unemployment by boosting aggregate demand (the balance of payments permitting). This, however, as monetarists and new classical economists predicted, led only to more inflation, fuelled by rising expectations of inflation (see Figure 16.3 on page 502). When governments eventually did curb the growth in aggregate demand, it took time for expectations to adjust downwards.

As we saw earlier, to help bring inflationary expectations down, the UK government from the late 1970s to the mid-1980s set targets for the growth of money supply. This was largely consistent with monetarist principles. In the short term, however, the effect was a rise in unemployment. As can be seen in Figure 16.3, the standardised UK unemployment rate rose to as high as 12 per cent by 1984.

Nevertheless, the pursuit of these policies did, according to monetarists, lead to a dramatic fall in the rate of inflation. Inflationary expectations fell and wage rises moderated. In 1980, the inflation rate was 15 per cent; by 1986, it had fallen to 3 per cent. Eventually the rise in unemployment was to be reversed too.

The rise of monetarist and new classical macroeconomics was to be reflected in economic policy during the 1980s in many countries, though particularly so in the USA and the UK. The result was that governments were again to place a greater reliance on the market. The UK saw policies of privatisation and deregulation pursued; union power curbed; and tax rates cut. Controls over the financial system were reduced, with banks given much more freedom to expand their activities (we examine this in Chapter 18). This 'supply-side' revolution was designed to increase incentives to work, to invest and to innovate. We explore these market-orientated supply-side policies in section 23.5.

Section summary

1. Monetarists argued that there is a close correlation between the rate of growth of the money supply and the rate of inflation. Increases in money supply cause increases in aggregate demand, which in turn cause inflation. Along with the classical economists, they argued that output and employment are determined independently of money supply (at least in the long run). This means that a deflationary policy to cure inflation will *not* in the long run cause a fall in output or a rise in unemployment.

2. Monetarists thus argued that the long-run Phillips curve is vertical. Its position along the horizontal axis will depend on the level of equilibrium or 'natural' unemployment.

3. Building on monetarist ideas, early new classical macroeconomic models focused on how monetary surprises induce short-term deviations in unemployment from its natural rate. However, under the assumptions of continuous market clearing and rational expectations, unemployment does not deviate from its natural rate if monetary policy is anticipated.

4. Real business cycle theorists argue that the business cycle is the result of frequent economic shocks, such as technology shocks, which affect the path of potential output. Economic outcomes, including the path of real GDP, are the result of optimal choices made by rational economic agents under continuous market clearing.

16.5 THE KEYNESIAN RESPONSE

Market imperfections

Monetarist and new classical ideas reshaped macroeconomics radically during the 1970s and 1980s. These ideas affected policy making with increasing emphasis placed on the supply side of the economy. Governments began to place less emphasis on using its discretion over monetary and fiscal policy to fine-tune the economy.

Many Keynesians could agree with monetarists and new classical economists on one point. If demand is expanded too fast and for too long, inflation will result and there will be a certain amount of unemployment of labour (and other resources too) that cannot be eliminated simply by expanding aggregate demand. However, they rejected the notion that the policy ineffectiveness proposition always holds. Because of the behaviour of markets, they argued, governments could intervene through policies designed to affect aggregate demand and make a positive difference.

A large number of academic Keynesians began a research agenda focused on gaining a better understanding of *aggregate supply*. The motivation was to develop stronger theoretical explanations of why markets may be slow to adjust. Consequently, a large amount of work was undertaken into market imperfections and the frictions which cause prices to be 'sticky'. Much of the focus was to establish stronger *microeconomic* foundations. The group of Keynesians who have taken this approach have been subsequently labelled **new Keynesians**.

Menu costs and nominal price rigidity

The assumption of continuous market clearing is seen by many Keynesian as the most controversial of the new classical assumptions. New Keynesians have focused on the *frictions* that may cause prices to adjust only slowly following economic shocks, especially to aggregate demand.

New Keynesians argue that firms are often operating in imperfectly competitive markets (see Chapter 8). Therefore, firms are price-makers rather than price-takers as portrayed in the perfectly competitive model (see Chapter 7). In other words, firms set not just quantity but also price.

However, a firm's product price may exhibit *stickiness* in the presence of demand shocks because of the *menu costs* of price changes (see Box 15.5, page 475). Menu costs include both the physical costs to firms in updating price lists and the costs incurred in determining and negotiating prices with customers and suppliers.

If the menu costs to an individual firm are larger than the profit lost from not adjusting prices, then the rational firm will not change its prices. When price rigidity is commonplace throughout the economy, any change in aggregate demand can have a significant effect on national *output*.

Consider a decrease in demand for a representative profit-maximising firm with power to affect both price and output. Intuitively, we would expect the firm to reduce both output and prices. The extent of both would be ordinarily determined by the rule for the profit-maximising level of output: marginal revenue (*MR*) equals marginal cost (*MC*) (see Chapter 6). However, if frictions, such as those arising from menu costs, result in price stickiness, then output will fall further. The stickiness in prices causes the quantity demanded to fall more than it otherwise would do following the initial decline in demand. Box 16.4 analyses menu costs more formally.

 Illustrate the effect of a fall in demand for an imperfectly competitive firm (a) in the presence of menu costs and (b) in the absence of menu costs.

The significance of price rigidities is that changes in aggregate demand can have significant effects on an economy's actual output. Therefore, in the presence of such frictions to market adjustment, governments may need to intervene to affect the level of aggregate demand.

Such frictions are also important because they mean that changes in the money supply can affect the economy's output. In other words, money ceases to be neutral as predicted by real business cycle theory: it can have real effects on the economy.

 What technological developments are likely to have reduced menu costs in recent years?

Sources of other frictions and imperfections

The extensive new Keynesian literature that has developed since the 1980s has identified a series of other market imperfections. These imperfections can help to reinforce the nominal rigidity in product prices arising from menu costs and so increase fluctuations in real GDP. Imperfections include the following:

- *Price inelasticity of demand.* Where competition is limited, demand will be less elastic. Under such circumstances a firm will be under less pressure to reduce prices if demand falls. In an economic downturn, therefore, firms may prefer to reduce output than cut prices.
- *Anticipating other firms' pricing strategy.* If firms' products are close substitutes for one another, they are likely to be very wary of cutting prices for fear of retaliation from their rivals. They may prefer to reduce output during a downturn rather than risk a price war.
- *Sticky nominal wages.* Wage rates are largely determined through negotiation between workers and employers. The presence of contracts allows both sides to avoid the costs incurred in frequent wage negotiations and provide both with a degree of certainty. Even in the absence of contracts, workers are likely to be resistant to cuts in their money wages. They may prefer a reduction in hours, or the non-replacement of workers who leave, rather than take a cut in wages. Indeed, the flexibility of hours, often with 'zero hours contracts', where workers have no

---

Definitions

New Keynesians Economists who seek to explain how market imperfections and frictions can result in fluctuations in real GDP and the persistence of unemployment.

guaranteed hours, but simply are allocated hours on a weekly or monthly basis, means that employers are more likely to adjust hours than wage rates.

- *Real wage rigidity.* New Keynesians argue that equilibrium real wage rates may be above market clearing levels. The result can be involuntary unemployment. As we saw in section 10.2 (page 291), the *efficiency wage hypothesis* maintains that firms may pay wage rates *above* market levels in order to provide an incentive for workers. The implication that new Keynesians draw is that, in a downturn, a firm may be reluctant to cut real wages for fear of lowering morale and thereby reducing productivity.

  Insider–outsider theories emphasise the power of employees in resisting real wage cuts. Those currently employed (the *insiders*, see page 290) may, through their unions or close relationships with their employers, or because of the possession of specific skills, be able to prevent the unemployed (the *outsiders*) from competing wages down.

TC 5
p50

Definitions

Efficiency wage hypothesis The hypothesis that the productivity of workers is affected by the wage rate that they receive.

Insiders Those in employment who can use their privileged position (either as members of unions or because of specific skills) to secure pay rises, or resist wage cuts, despite an excess supply of labour (unemployment).

Outsiders Those out of work or employed on a casual, part-time or short-term basis, who have little or no power to influence wages or employment.

- *Sources of finance.* During a downturn, both internal and external sources of finance for investment may diminish. The decline in demand will reduce profit and hence internal sources. What is more, banks may be less willing to lend, seeing risks rising in a downturn. The result is a decline in investment. During a boom, by contrast, sources

KI 11
p76

| BOX 16.4 | MENU COSTS | EXPLORING ECONOMICS |

How sticky prices amplify fluctuations in output

Menu costs are any costs incurred by firms when changing prices. These include not only costs to firms of updating price lists, such as the costs of printing new menus in restaurants from which the name of the concept is derived, but also costs in developing new price strategies, in negotiating new contracts and in the very processing of the information around the new price structure that customers will need to undertake.

Menu costs, it is argued, may create a stickiness or rigidity in firms' prices because they are reluctant to change prices even when faced with a change in demand. In other words, menu costs create a friction to the adjustment of nominal (actual) product prices to economic shocks. The more widespread is such price rigidity the more significant can be the effect of a change in aggregate demand on national output.

To illustrate the effect of price rigidity on output, consider the diagram of a monopolistically competitive firm. The firm's demand curve (D_1) is downward sloping, the elasticity depending on how close its competitors' products are as substitutes to its own. The marginal revenue (MR_1) curve lies below the demand curve (average revenue curve) because, in reducing price to sell more units, all units attract the lower price (see Chapter 7 pages 218–20). For simplicity, we assume that marginal cost (MC) is constant across all output levels.

The firm experiences a decrease in demand for its product because of a decrease in aggregate demand in the economy. Before the decrease in aggregate demand, the firm is producing at output level Q_1, where marginal cost (MC) equals marginal revenue (MR_1), and selling its output at price P_1. Its profit is represented by the area CP_1DE.

The decrease in demand results in a leftward movement in both the demand curve (D_1 to D_2) and the marginal revenue

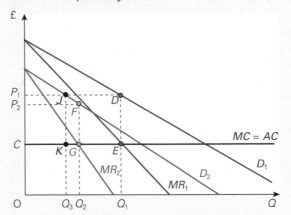

Price frictions and the monopolistically competitive firm

curve (MR_1 to MR_2). In the absence of frictions, our price-setting firm will reduce price from P_1 to P_2 and output from Q_1 to Q_2. Profit falls to CP_2FG.

However, if frictions, such as those arising from menu costs, result in price stickiness, then output will fall further. If price remains at P_1 then output falls to Q_3. Hence, output has fallen by the additional amount equivalent to $Q_2 - Q_3$. Profits fall to CP_1JK. But, the key point is that firms will be willing to incur this forsaken profit, $CP_2FG - CP_1JK$, if the menu costs incurred in reducing prices are greater.

Illustrate the effect of nominal price rigidities on output if the firm's demand increases because of a rise in aggregate demand.

of funds for investment are likely to increase. These 'pro-cyclical' changes in the availability of finance are thus likely to exacerbate existing fluctuations in real GDP.

- *Attitudes towards debt.* In a boom, consumer and business confidence is likely to encourage borrowing. Debts are likely to rise. In a recession, however, with people more anxious about the future, consumers and firms may seek to reduce their debts by curbing spending. These effects could be reinforced by risk-averse financial institutions which reduce lending, seeing it as riskier when firms are more likely to go out of business or individuals more likely to lose their jobs. Again, this means that bank lending tends to be pro-cyclical and exacerbates existing fluctuations in real GDP.

KI 11
p76

Hysteresis

In the early 1980s there was a recession, or slowdown, throughout the industrialised world. Unemployment rose to unprecedented levels. But as the world began to recover, unemployment remained stubbornly high. This focused minds on the extent to which current rates of unemployment affect the future path of unemployment. Could there be a persistence or inertia in unemployment rates? And, if so why?

Keynesians argued that the rise in unemployment, though largely caused by a lack of demand, could not simply be reversed by a *rise* in demand. The recession had itself *caused* higher rates of unemployment to become embedded in the economy. The reason is that during a recession, many people become deskilled and/or demoralised and firms become more cautious about taking on workers, preferring to manage with a smaller, more efficient workforce. What is more, as we saw above, people who remain employed (the *insiders*) are often able to secure wage increases for themselves, and prevent the unemployed (the *outsiders*) from competing wages down. Many of the unemployed thus remain unemployed.

This persistence of high unemployment that characterised many developed economies through the 1980s and into the 1990s and once more in the late 2000s and into the 2010s is known as *hysteresis*. This term, used in physics, refers to the lagging or persistence of an effect, even when the initial cause has been removed. In our context, it refers to the persistence of unemployment even when the initial demand deficiency no longer exists.

Past rates of aggregate demand and unemployment were thus affecting the *natural rate of unemployment,* or what some

Keynesians refer to as the ***non-accelerating-inflation rate of unemployment (NAIRU)***.

Strictly speaking, the natural rate and the NAIRU are theoretically different, though the concepts are often used interchangeably. The natural rate of unemployment is the unemployment rate consistent with market clearing in the labour market. It depends on structural factors affecting labour demand and supply. On the other hand, the NAIRU is the rate of unemployment in a world characterised by market imperfections and frictions at which the inflation rate is steady in the short term, say the next 12 months or so.

Why has UK unemployment been less persistent following the recession of 2008–10 than following that in the early 1980s? In other words, why has hysteresis been less of a problem in the UK in recent times?

Government intervention

Targeted government intervention may be needed to help smooth the path of aggregate demand. A substantial increase in demand may be necessary if the economy is in danger of falling into deep recession, as was the case in 2008–9. The debate then concerns the form that this intervention should take.

TC 7
p81

One approach is for the government to increase its expenditure on public works such as roads, school building and housing. The advantages of such infrastructural projects is that they can directly impact on the economy's potential output and, because they have a relatively low import content, increased expenditure on such projects does not lead to balance of payments problems.

Thereafter, the government should maintain a high and stable demand by appropriate demand-management policies. This should keep unemployment down and set the environment for long-term investment and growth.

Definitions

Hysteresis The persistence of an effect even when the initial cause has ceased to operate. In economics, it refers to the persistence of unemployment even when the demand deficiency that caused it no longer exists.

Non-accelerating-inflation rate of unemployment (NAIRU) The rate of unemployment consistent with steady inflation in the near term, say, over the next 12 months.

Section summary

1. A group of Keynesian economists sometimes referred to as 'new Keynesians' responded to the monetarist/new classical challenge by building models highlighting market imperfections, including frictions that affect the adjustment of markets to shocks. These imperfections were argued to provide a rationale for government intervention.

2. Keynesians argued that unemployment caused initially by a recession (a deficiency of demand) may persist even when the economy is recovering. This 'hysteresis' may be due to the deskilling of labour, a decline in firms'

capacity, insiders preventing outsiders from bidding down the wage rate, or firms being cautious about taking on extra labour when the recovery does come.

3. Whereas monetarist and new classical macroeconomists generally favoured policies of freeing up markets, Keynesians generally favoured a rather more interventionist approach by the government. Through appropriately targeted fiscal measures, governments can help to smooth the business cycle and limit the adverse effects on the economy's future potential output.

16.6 AN EMERGING CONSENSUS UP TO THE CRISIS OF 2008

The Great Moderation and a new mainstream consensus

The period from the early 1990s up to the financial crisis of the late 2000s was to be known as the 'Great Moderation'. The period was characterised in many developed countries by low and stable inflation and continuous economic growth. As Figure 16.3 shows (see page 502), the UK was no exception. From 1994 to 2007 annual UK growth averaged 2.9 per cent while the annual rate of consumer price inflation averaged 1.75 per cent.

The period of the Great Moderation also saw the emergence of a new mainstream macroeconomic consensus. The new consensus built on elements from the new classical and new Keynesian schools of thought. In particular, it combined the idea from real business cycle theory of the economy being hit by frequent random shocks, particularly supply shocks, with the new Keynesian idea of market imperfections that then affect the adjustment process of the economy to the shocks.

The new consensus macroeconomics argued that there is no long-run trade-off between inflation and unemployment, with the natural rate of unemployment and the economy's potential output being determined by supply-side or structural factors. The new Keynesian market imperfections, therefore, explain the deviations of output from its potential or long-run level.

DSGE models – the new consensus macro model

The new consensus has been identified with the development of elaborately technical models of the economy. One particularly well-known group of models are known as *dynamic stochastic general equilibrium models* or *DSGE models* for short.

The dynamic nature of DSGE models. DSGE models of the economy are a fusion of new Keynesian and new classical ideas. In these models, forward-looking rational economic agents (individuals and firms) make choices to maximise their welfare. They attempt to achieve the best outcome outcomes in any given set of circumstances. These choices are affected by future uncertain outcomes and so evolve as events unfold and changes occur in agents' rational expectations. Hence, the models are *dynamic*.

The stochastic element in DSGE models. The economy is hit by frequent random (stochastic) 'shocks'. These **stochastic shocks** generate uncertainty for economic agents. Crucially, it is these shocks and hence the uncertainty that they generate that result in the economy's output deviating from what would otherwise be a predictable growth path. These deviations or disturbances also affect the economy's future growth path. In other words, the effects persist. This means that new consensus models combine an analysis of both short-term and long-term economic growth.

 Give some examples of stochastic shocks.

Definitions

Dynamic stochastic general equilibrium (DSGE) models) Models that seek to explain macroeconomic phenomena by examining the microeconomic behaviour of rational forward-looking individual economic agents acting in a variety of market conditions. The microeconomic equilibria are subject to random shocks, such as technological change, political events or changes in the supply of natural resources.

Stochastic shocks Shocks that are random and hence unpredictable, or predicable only as occurring within a range of values.

The types of shock considered by new consensus economists are quite broad. On the supply side, shocks included, for instance, changes in the price mark-up (over marginal cost) of imperfectly competitive firms, changes in the cost to firms of external finance relative to internal finance, or productivity shocks. On the demand side, shocks include changes to the 'impatience' of economic agents and therefore their preference for spending now relative to the future, and changes in expected future consumption, in government spending or in interest rates.

General equilibrium.   DSGE models seek to understand macroeconomic aggregates, such as real GDP, by analysing the interaction of economic agents in markets. They take a 'bottom-up approach' by analysing the macroeconomy through the interaction of representative agents in different markets which all tend to equilibrium. This explains why DSGE models are *general equilibrium* models.

Market imperfections and frictions.   DSGE models typically assume monopolistically competitive firms and monopolistically competitive labour markets. Furthermore, they incorporate a number of frictions to price adjustment drawn from new Keynesian developments (see page 510). The exact nature of competition in product and labour markets and the frictions applied in the models can vary. This allows economists and policy makers to analyse how these imperfections affect the way in which economic shocks impact on the economy.

Constrained policy discretion

In the UK, as in many other industrialised countries, the Great Moderation was a period when policy makers frequently spoke about the importance of policies that help to foster a stable economic environment and that are conducive to long-term economic growth and prosperity. This led to the birth of what economists call **constrained discretion**: a set of rules or principles providing a framework for economic policy.

Constrained discretion typically involves the use of targets, such as an inflation target or a public-sector deficit or debt ceiling. The key is to affect the *expectations* of the public, for example in relation to inflation.

?   *Does the use of public-sector deficit targets rule out the use of fiscal policy to reduce economic fluctuations associated with the business cycle?*

In many countries, governments handed over the operation of monetary policy to central banks. In the UK, in 1997 the Bank of England was granted independence to determine interest rates to meet an inflation rate target.

The new classical models of the late 1970s and early 1980s played an important role in developing the theoretical foundations for central bank independence. If a short-term trade-off between inflation and unemployment only arises because of *unanticipated* changes in monetary policy then, new classical economists argued, it makes sense to remove the temptation for governments to use expansionary monetary policy unexpectedly.

In the longer term, in the absence of central bank independence or transparent inflation rate targeting, the result is likely to be higher inflationary expectations and higher actual inflation. Output and unemployment will be at their natural levels. This is because the general public is only too aware of governments' incentive to want to induce faster growth by loosening monetary policy and creating 'surprise' inflation. Economic agents therefore push up the inflation rate by revising their inflationary expectation upwards, so choking off any increase in output and employment. This excessive inflation is known as **inflation bias**.

The elimination of inflation bias is commonly identified as a key economic benefit of central bank independence. By sticking to an inflation target, a central bank can create the stable environment necessary for the market to flourish: expectations will adjust to the target rate of inflation (assuming central banks are successful in achieving the target) and firms will be able to plan with more confidence. Investment is thereby encouraged and this, in turn, encourages a growth in potential output. In other words, sticking to the targets creates the best environment for the expansion of aggregate *supply*.

From the mid-1990s to 2007/8, these policies seemed to be successful. But then things went horribly wrong!

> ### Definitions
>
> **Constrained discretion** A set of principles or rules within which economic policy operates. These can be informal or enshrined in law.
>
> **Inflation bias** Excessive inflation that results from people raising their expectations of the inflation rate following expansionary demand management policy, encouraging government to loosen policy even further.

Section summary

1. During the 1990s a new mainstream consensus began to develop. It drew ideas principally from the new classical and new Keynesian schools. Central to most new consensus models are representative forward-looking economic agents who form rational expectations.

2. Dynamic Stochastic General Equilibrium (DSGE) models became the standard model of the economy. These allowed economists to model the impact of frequent economic shocks under certain assumptions about competition in product and labour markets and the speed with which these markets adjust to equilibrium.

3. Government policy moved to one of constrained discretion, with fiscal and monetary targets. This, it was argued, would provide the stable environment for the mixed market system to flourish and for firms and consumers to take a longer-term perspective.

16.7 THE FINANCIAL CRISIS AND THE SEARCH FOR A NEW CONSENSUS

The financial crisis and its aftermath

Throughout the late 1990s/early 2000s, many banks had massively increased their lending. Also many mortgages were granted, especially in the USA, to people unlikely to be able to repay them, especially if house prices stopped rising. This 'sub-prime debt' made banks very vulnerable to an economic downturn or to worries by depositors about banks' viability.

In 2007, several smaller banks were in difficulties and some had to be bailed out. Then, in 2008, Lehman Brothers in the USA collapsed and was liquidated. With many of the world's major banks being seen as having too little capital, there was a real danger that many more would collapse. Lending between banks dried up and several banks had to be bailed out by their governments. There was a sharp reduction in banks' lending to customers.

The financial crisis led to a deep recession in many developed countries. In the USA, for example, the economy shrank by 2.8 per cent in 2009, while in the UK it shrank by 4.3 per cent (see Figure 16.3 on page 502).

The impact of the banking crisis on the economy was on such a scale that important debates followed. These debates challenged the new macroeconomic consensus; after all, why had so few economists predicted the global financial crisis? Indeed, Queen Elizabeth II, on a visit to the London School of Economics in November 2008, asked why economists had got it so wrong. But economists were not slow in providing explanations.

Economists' explanations. Economists on the right tended to argue that the banking crisis was the result of too much government intervention. Such intervention, it was argued, had distorted incentives such that banks believed that they would not be allowed to fail (a moral hazard: see page 135). Consequently, financial institutions took excessive risks, expanding their balance sheets aggressively with too little loss-absorbing capital.

Economists on the left tended to argue that the banking crisis was the result of too *little* intervention. Financial institutions had been too lightly regulated and it was this that had resulted in excessive risk-taking. Some on the left argue that the banking sector is prone to excessive lending during times of prosperity, which ultimately lays the seeds for financial crises (see Box 9.4 on page 262). Therefore, the financial system is an important contributory factor to the business cycle (see section 15.3). Banks should be required to build their capital base in times of rapid growth so that they have sufficient reserves in times of recession.

There are some who argue that tighter regulation should not simply involve increasing the loss-absorbing capital that banks are required hold, which has been the mainstream response since the crisis. Rather, they would advocate a return to controls on the flows of credit, a policy which many countries began abandoning from the late 1970s.

Fiscal expansion to fiscal austerity

Despite disagreement about the causes of the financial crisis, the immediate priorities of policy makers were to ensure the stability of the financial system and to mitigate the effects on aggregate demand of the limited levels of credit now available for households and firms. There was initially a general consensus on the medicine to be applied.

The initial expansionary policies. First, vast amounts of liquidity were supplied to the banking sector. Second, fiscal stimulus packages were used to boost aggregate demand. In other words, the consensus was that central banks and governments needed to act.

This was not a time for passive economic policy. Rules and frameworks were loosened or applied more flexibly and in some cases even abandoned completely. We discuss this in more detail in Chapter 22.

Followed by austerity policies. This consensus was to be relatively short-lived, however, as many countries saw a marked deterioration in the state of their public finances. Governments began running relatively large fiscal deficits which needed financing. These deficits were worsened by governments having to bail out banks and by the recession which saw tax revenues fall and the number claiming benefits rising.

Cutting the deficit became the new priority of many governments, including the UK's Coalition government formed in 2010. In the UK, as illustrated in Figure 16.3 on page 502, the government's deficit had now reached in excess of 10 per cent of GDP. Consequently, in a short space of time the UK witnessed a fiscal policy yo-yo with fiscal austerity (spending cuts and tax rises) replacing fiscal loosening.

This was not confined to the UK. In the eurozone the *sovereign debt crisis* became so serious that Greece, Portugal, Ireland and later Cyprus had to receive bailouts from European funds and the IMF. In return they were obliged to agree to severe fiscal austerity measures.

Debates over policy. In the light of this turmoil, debates re-emerged amongst academics and policy makers over the economic costs of fiscal deficits and of public expenditure crowding out private expenditure. In effect, we were witnessing a re-run of some the debates of the 1920s and 1930s between classical and Keynesian economists (see pages 496–7).

Those on the political left took a more Keynesian line, believing that cutting the deficit too quickly would endanger the economic recovery, with private-sector demand unable to offset the cuts to public expenditure.

Those on the political right argued in favour of rapid deficit reduction. Without this, they claimed, there would be upward pressure on interest rates as the confidence in the government's finances was undermined and as the public sector competed with the private sector for scarce resources. This was the line taken in the UK by the Coalition government.

Debates about the state of macroeconomics

While the financial crisis raised debates amongst academics and policy makers about its causes and its remedies, it also fuelled a debate about the state of macroeconomics. The new mainstream consensus came under scrutiny. We have seen how this consensus brought together ideas from different schools of thought and, in particular, from new classical and new Keynesian economists.

However, it is important to recognise that the views of macroeconomists in relation to key issues, particularly the flexibility of prices, the role of expectations, the impact of changes in aggregate demand on economic activity and the role of government policy (see section 16.2), tend to fall along a spectrum, rather than being in some very specific camp.

At one end of the *spectrum of views* are those who see the free market as working well and who generally blame macroeconomic problems on excessive government intervention. At the other are those who see the free market as fundamentally flawed.

Then there are economists who were never party to the consensus. In particular, objections were raised by a group of Keynesians who have become known as *post-Keynesians*. They highlight some of the key features of Keynes' *General Theory* to explain why economies are not self-correcting. In particular, they stress the importance of what Keynes called 'animal spirits', or what is today known as sentiment or confidence. Changes in confidence can have fundamental effects on the behaviour of economic agents. For instance, the mood of the country's business community can be crucial in determining firms' investment and output decisions. Without appropriate demand-management policy, this mood can remain depressed into the long term.

Post-Keynesians and other *heterodox economists* also challenge most of the microeconomic assumptions on which other more 'mainstream' macroeconomic theories are based. Firms, for example, are not cold, rational profit maximisers, making calm calculations based on marginal analysis. Instead, firms make output decisions largely in response to anticipated demand, again based on their *confidence* in their market. The result is that anticipated demand changes are likely to lead to *output* and *employment* changes, not price changes.

Post-Keynesians tend to focus on a country's *institutions* and *culture* to explain how firms and consumers respond to economic stimuli. In other words, they try to base their explanations and policies on real-world institutional and behavioural information rather than on abstract models.

TC 9
p129

KI 24
p252

Definitions

Sovereign debt crisis The financial and economic problems caused by excessive public-sector debt and by the fear that governments will be unable to raise sufficient finance to repay maturing debt.

Post-Keynesians Economists who stress the importance of institutional and behavioural factors, and the role of confidence in explaining the state of the economy. They argue that firms are more likely to respond to changes in demand by changing output rather than prices.

Heterodox economists Economists who reject the assumptions of neoclassical economics, in particular the assumptions of rational optimising behaviour. They highlight the importance of institutional behaviour and factors influencing human behaviour.

Two economists disagree over what would have been the best way of tackling the problem of unemployment arising from the credit crunch and recession. For what reasons might they disagree? Are these reasons positive or normative?

Emergence of a new consensus?

While some groups, including post-Keynesians, have consistently voiced their concerns about the new consensus, a more broad-based debate began to develop in the aftermath of the financial crisis. The debate extended to the macroeconomics curriculum being taught in universities. Conferences and working parties have considered both what should be taught and how it should be taught.

Problems with relying on micro foundations

One concern is the extent to which the new consensus had focused too heavily on developing microeconomic foundations and thereby applying a 'bottom-up' approach to analysing macroeconomic aggregates. In the process, often very technical and mathematical models emerged. These were based on the assumption that people typically behave rationally – known as representative agents with rational expectations. Some economists note that the acronym spelt out by 'representative agents with rational expectations' is RARE! This is a reminder of the importance of the behavioural assumptions we attach to economic agents in our economic models.

KI 12
p97

Another issue with a purely 'bottom-up' approach to macroeconomic analysis is the fallacy of composition. We first came across this in Chapter 3 (see page 97) in the context of poor harvests. When one farmer alone has a poor harvest their own revenue falls, but if all farmers have poor harvests total revenue may well rise. More generally, what applies in one case does not necessarily apply when repeated in all cases. This is important in macroeconomics because we are analysing aggregates. For this reason the fallacy of composition is also known as the *paradox of aggregates.*

The paradox of thrift. The most commonly cited paradox of aggregates is the paradox of thrift (see Box 16.5). If just a few individuals increase their propensity to save, their saving increases and they can consume more in the future. However, if this is repeated across all individuals, it can lead to a fall in aggregate saving because the fall in consumption causes firms to produce less, which reduces national income.

The example of the paradox of thrift illustrates the importance, when building macroeconomic models, of taking into account not only how individuals behave but how they *interact*. Consequently, it also illustrates how aggregate or group behaviour impacts on individual behaviour and well-being.

A contemporary example of the paradox of thrift is the attempt by economic agents to improve their financial well-being following the financial crisis. To reduce their debts many people cut back on their spending. The general effect

of this was a decline in sales, output and jobs. Additionally, people sought to sell assets, such as property and shares. However, because large numbers of people looked to do likewise, the value of property, shares and other assets fell. Therefore, rather than individuals seeing their net worth increase as they sold assets, group behaviour resulted in the aggregate net worth of economic agents actually falling. For this reason it is known as the *paradox of debt*.

The paradox of thrift and the paradox of debt are illustrations of what, in this context, is known as *downward causation*: group behaviour affects individual behaviour and well-being.

The importance of the financial sector

Unsurprisingly, given the financial crisis, there has been a keen debate around the assumptions made about the financial system in economic models. Financial frictions and imperfections had been incorporated in new consensus models, albeit to varying degrees. However, the financial crisis illustrates the importance of the *behavioural assumptions* we make about financial institutions and the way in which we model their *interaction* with other economic agents. Financial institutions need to be both fully and appropriately incorporated in macroeconomic models. As the financial crisis showed, the behaviour of financial institutions can be acutely destabilising.

Areas of general agreement?

As we have seen, the financial crisis and its aftermath have re-energised long-standing macroeconomic debates, while also fuelling important debates about the state of macroeconomics in the 2010s. Nonetheless, we can attempt to identify some general points of agreement that have emerged in recent years, at least among the majority of economists.

■ In the short run, changes in aggregate demand can have a significant effect on output and employment. If there is a collapse in demand, as in 2008, governments and/or central banks should intervene through expansionary fiscal and/or monetary policies. Only a few extreme new classical economists would disagree with this proposition.

BOX 16.5 | **THE PARADOX OF THRIFT**

When prudence is folly

The classical economists argued that saving was a national virtue. More saving would lead via lower interest rates to more investment and faster growth. Keynes was at pains to show the opposite. Saving, far from being a national virtue, could be a national vice.

Remember the fallacy of composition (see Box 3.5 on page 97). Just because something is good for an individual, it does not follow that it is good for society as a whole. This fallacy applies to saving. If individuals save more, they will increase their consumption possibilities in the future. If society saves more, however, this may *reduce* its future income and consumption. As people save more, they will spend less. Firms will thus produce less. There will thus be a multiplied *fall* in income. The phenomenon of higher saving leading to *lower* national income is known as 'the paradox of thrift'.

But this is not all. Far from the extra saving encouraging more investment, the lower consumption will *discourage* firms from investing. There will then be a further multiplied fall in national income.

The paradox of thrift had in fact been recognised before Keynes, and Keynes himself referred to various complaints about 'underconsumption' that had been made back in the sixteenth and seventeenth centuries:

> In 1598 Laffemas . . . denounced the objectors to the use of French silks on the grounds that all purchasers of French luxury goods created a livelihood for the poor, whereas the miser caused them to die in distress. In 1662 Petty justified 'entertainments, magnificent shews, triumphal arches, etc.', on the ground that their costs flowed back into the pockets of brewers, bakers, tailors, shoemakers and so forth . . . In 1695 Cary argued that if everybody spent more, all would obtain larger incomes 'and might then live more plentifully'.[1]

But despite these early recognitions of the danger of underconsumption, the belief that saving would increase the prosperity of the nation was central to classical economic thought.

 When is an increase in saving desirable?

1 J. M. Keynes, *The General Theory of Employment, Interest and Money* (Macmillan, 1967), pp. 358–9.

- In the long run, changes in aggregate demand will have much less effect on output and employment and much more effect on prices. In fact, many economists say that there will be no effect at all on output and employment, and that the whole effect will be on prices. There is still a substantial body of Keynesians, however, especially post-Keynesians, who argue that changes in aggregate demand will have substantial effects on long-term output and employment via changes in investment and hence in potential output.

- There is no simple long-run trade-off between inflation and unemployment. There is still disagreement, however, as to whether there is no relationship between them at all (i.e. the long-run Phillips curve is vertical), or whether they are connected indirectly via the long-term effects of changes in aggregate demand, for example, on investment or the overall skillset of a country's workforce.

- Expectations have an important effect on the economy. There is still disagreement, however, as to whether it is people's expectations of price changes or of output changes that are more important. Also, it is difficult to model people's expectations when these can so easily be affected by random shocks; and where optimism can sometimes build in a burst of 'irrational exuberance' or pessimism descend in a cloud of despondency, while at other times optimism or pessimism can quickly fade.

- Excessive growth in the money supply will lead to inflation. Some economists argue that the quantity theory of money holds in the long run (i.e. that inflation is entirely due to increases in the money supply). Others argue that the relationship is more general. Nevertheless, the consensus is that governments should avoid allowing the money supply to grow too rapidly.

- Controlling inflation through control of the money supply, however, is difficult, since money supply itself is not easy to control. Even if it were possible to control money supply accurately, there is a time lag between changes in money supply and the resulting changes in inflation. This makes a precise control of inflation by this means very difficult. Most economists, therefore, argue that it is easier to control inflation by controlling interest rates, since this directly affects aggregate demand. Most central banks around the world today therefore use interest rate changes to achieve a target rate of inflation.

- If the economy is in deep recession, most economists agree that it may be necessary to expand the money supply, rather than relying on cuts in interest rates. However, monetary expansion (known as 'quantitative easing') does not directly affect spending. Banks have to be willing to lend the extra money and individuals and firms have to be willing to borrow and spend it.

- Macroeconomic policy should not focus exclusively on the demand side. Long-term growth depends primarily on changes in supply (i.e. in potential output). It is important, therefore, for governments to develop an effective supply-side policy if they want to achieve faster economic growth. There is still disagreement, however, over the forms that supply-side policy should take: should it focus on freeing up the market, or should it focus on various forms of government intervention to compensate for market deficiencies?

■ Governments' ability to control their country's macroeconomic destiny is being increasingly eroded by the process of globalisation. As countries become more and more interdependent, and as capital moves more and more freely around the globe, so there is a growing need for co-ordinated policies between governments to tackle problems of global recessions or excessive exchange rate fluctuations. This lesson was brought home in 2008, when it became obvious that most countries were experiencing a collapse in aggregate demand following the banking crisis and the credit crunch. Leaders discussed common policy approaches at several international summits, including both bank rescue packages and expansionary fiscal and monetary policies.

It is perhaps too soon to say, particularly in the aftermath of the economic and financial crisis of 2007–9 and in the more recent rise in populism and the questioning of 'establishment' ideas, what the future holds for the mainstream macroeconomic consensus. Nevertheless, economists are actively debating developments in the subject and what should be in the university macroeconomic curriculum.

As the book progresses, we will be looking at the various areas of agreement and disagreement in more detail. One thing is certain: these are incredibly fascinating times to be studying macroeconomics.

Section summary

1. During the 1990s a new mainstream consensus began to develop. It drew ideas principally from the new classical and new Keynesian schools. Central to most new consensus models are representative forward-looking economic agents who form rational expectations.

2. Dynamic stochastic general equilibrium (DSGE) models became the standard models of the economy. These allowed economists to examine the impact of frequent economic shocks under certain assumptions about competition in product and labour markets and the speed with which these markets adjust to equilibrium.

3. There are many shades of opinion among economists, from extreme new classical economists who advocate almost complete laissez-faire to post-Keynesian and heterodox economists who focus much more on individual and institutional behaviour and who see markets as having many failings. In between comes a whole spectrum of opinions and theories about the relative effectiveness of markets and the government in achieving the various macroeconomic goals.

4. The financial crisis and its aftermath reignited long-standing debates about policy, while also fuelling debates about the state of macroeconomics. Key concerns included the importance that had been placed on developing models with microeconomic foundations, the appropriateness of the behavioural assumptions of economic agents and assumptions made around the role of the financial system.

5. Despite these disagreements, most economists would agree on the following points: changes in aggregate demand have a direct effect on output and employment in the short run, but either no effect or a far less certain effect in the long run; there is no simple long-run trade-off between inflation and unemployment; expectations have an important effect on the economy, but can be affected in ways that are not easy to predict; excessive growth in the money supply causes inflation; it is easier to achieve inflation targets by controlling interest rates than by controlling money supply; monetary expansion is an important policy tool in tackling recession; changes on the supply side of the economy are the major determinant of long-term growth; globalisation reduces individual countries' ability to control their economies.

END OF CHAPTER QUESTIONS

1. In a given economy, the supply of money is £10 billion; the velocity of circulation of money (spent on final goods and services) is 3; and the price index is 2.00.
   (a) What is the level of real national income?
   (b) How much have prices risen (in percentage terms) since the base year?
   (c) Assume that money supply increases by 10 per cent and that the velocity of circulation remains constant. By what percentage will prices rise if
      (i) there is no increase in real national income;
      (ii) real national income increases by 10 per cent;
      (iii) real national income increases by 5 per cent?

2. In what way will the nature of aggregate supply influence the effect of a change in aggregate demand on prices and real national income?

3. Criticise the classical theory that higher government spending will necessarily crowd out private spending.

4. Criticise the use of increasing government expenditure as a means of reducing unemployment.

5. In what way may short-term demand-management policies help to stabilise the economy? What problems occur in the use of such policies?

6. What explanations can you give for the increase in *both* unemployment and inflation in the 1970s?

7. What do you understand by the policy ineffectiveness proposition? On what assumptions is the proposition based?

8. Identify a series of possible frictions which could affect the speed with which markets adjust or which affect the nature of market equilibria.

9. What is meant by *hysteresis* when applied to unemployment? How do you account for this phenomenon in the 1980s?

10. What will cause people to expect higher rates of inflation? How will expectations of inflation affect the actual rate of inflation?

11. Explain how pro-cyclical lending criteria applied by financial institutions could amplify fluctuations in real GDP.

12. What is meant by the paradox of aggregates? Of what importance might they be for how we analyse macroeconomic problems?

Online resources

Additional case studies on the student website

16.1 The equation of exchange. This examines two more versions that are commonly used: the Fisher version and the Cambridge version.

16.2 Money and inflation in ancient Rome. A very early case study of the quantity theory of money: how the minting of extra coins by the Romans caused prices to rise.

16.3 Thomas Malthus, David Ricardo and Jean-Baptiste Say. A look at the work of three of the most famous classical economists and their degree of optimism or pessimism about the working of the free market.

16.4 The Great Depression and the return to the gold standard. A time of great hardship and sacrifice.

16.5 Classical 'remedies' for unemployment. How the policies advocated by the classical economists to cure unemployment would, according to Keynes, make the problem worse.

16.6 John Maynard Keynes (1883–1946). A profile of the great economist.

16.7 A little bit less of this and a little bit more of that. Fine-tuning in 1959 and 1960.

16.8 Milton Friedman (1912–2006). A profile of the most influential of the monetarist economists.

16.9 Spectrum of views. An overview of the different schools of macroeconomic thought.

Websites relevant to this chapter

See sites listed at the end of Chapter 17 on page 540.

Macroeconomic Models, Theories and Policy

We now build on the foundations of Part E. We will see why economies grow over the longer term but fluctuate in the short term and what governments can do to prevent these fluctuations.

In the following three chapters, we look at what determines the level of national income and the role that money plays in the process. Then, in Chapters 20 and 21 we look at the relationship between inflation and unemployment. In Chapter 22, we look at government policy to stabilise the economy. Finally, in Chapter 23, we turn to the long run and ask how economies can sustain faster growth.

2000   2005   2010   2015

Short-run Macroeconomic Equilibrium

In this chapter we look at the determination of national income, employment and inflation in the short run: i.e. over a period of up to around two years. The analysis is based on the model developed by Keynesians. Although many economists argue that this is not appropriate for analysing the performance of the macroeconomy over the longer term, most agree that the analysis is essentially true over the short term.

The model assumes that aggregate demand determines the level of economic activity in the economy. In other words, the nation's production and employment depend on the amount of spending. Too little spending will lead to unemployment. More spending will stimulate firms to produce more and employ more people. Too much spending, however, will cause inflation. This chapter examines this relationship between aggregate demand and national income (GDP), employment and inflation.

One important simplifying assumption is made: the rate of interest is fixed. This allows us for the time being to ignore what is happening to the amount of money in the economy. A fixed interest rate effectively means that the supply of money will passively rise or fall as aggregate demand rises or falls. In other words, if spending rises and hence the demand for money from the banking system also rises, there will be a corresponding increase in the amount of money made available and hence no need for interest rates to rise. In subsequent chapters, we will drop this assumption and take specific account of the role of money in the economy.

17.1 BACKGROUND TO THE THEORY

The relationship between aggregate demand and national income

This chapter explains what determines the level of national income (GDP) in the short run. It is based on the model developed by John Maynard Keynes, back in the 1930s (see Case Study 16.6 on the student website).

The basic explanation is quite simple: the level of production in the economy depends on the level of aggregate demand. If people buy more, firms will produce more in response to this, providing they have spare capacity. If people buy less, firms will cut down their production and lay off workers. But just *how much* will national income rise or fall as aggregate demand changes? We will answer this as the chapter progresses.

First, let us return to the circular flow of income that we looked at in Chapter 15. This is illustrated in Figure 17.1. Looking at the bottom of the diagram, the consumption of domestically produced goods (C_d) and the three withdrawals (W) – net saving (S), net taxes (T) and spending on imports (M) – all depend on the level of national income (Y). In fact, in the model, national income must always equal consumption of domestic goods plus withdrawals: there is nothing else people can do with their incomes!

$$Y \equiv C_d + W$$

Moving now to the top part of Figure 17.1, total spending in the economy on the goods and services of domestic firms is what we have already defined as aggregate demand (AD). In the Keynesian model that we are examining in this chapter, it is normally referred to as *aggregate expenditure (E)*. Aggregate expenditure consists of C_d plus the three injections (J): investment in the domestic economy (I), government purchases in the domestic economy (G) and expenditure from abroad on the country's exports (X).

$$AD \equiv E \equiv C_d + J$$

In equilibrium, withdrawals equal injections. (We demonstrated this in Chapter 15.) Since national income (Y) is simply withdrawals plus C_d, and aggregate expenditure (E) is simply injections plus C_d, it follows that in equilibrium national income must equal aggregate expenditure. To summarise:

$$W = J$$
$$\therefore C_d + W = C_d + J$$
$$\therefore Y = E \, (= AD)$$

Whenever aggregate expenditure ($C_d + J$) exceeds national income ($C_d + W$), injections will exceed withdrawals. Firms will respond to the extra demand by producing more and hence employing more factors of production. National income will thus rise. But as national income rises, so too will saving, imports and the amount paid in taxes: in other words, withdrawals will rise. Withdrawals will go on rising until they equal injections: until a new equilibrium has been reached. To summarise:

$$J > W \rightarrow Y \uparrow \rightarrow W \uparrow \text{ until } W = J$$

But *how much* will national income rise when aggregate demand (expenditure) rises? What will the new equilibrium level of national income be? To answer this question we must examine the relationship between national income and the component parts of the circular flow of income: consumption, withdrawals and injections. This relationship is shown in the Keynesian '45° line diagram'.

Introducing the Keynesian 45° line diagram

In this model, it is assumed that the levels of consumption and withdrawals are determined by the level of national income. Since national income is part of the model, we say that consumption and withdrawals are *endogenous*. This means that they vary with one of the other components of the model (i.e. income). Injections, however, are assumed to be *exogenous*: they are determined independently of what is going on in the model; they do *not* depend on the level of national income.

We will justify these assumptions later. First we must look at how the diagram is constructed, and at the

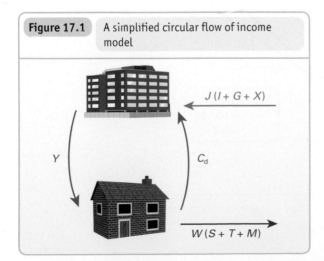

Figure 17.1 A simplified circular flow of income model

$J (I + G + X)$

Y

C_d

$W (S + T + M)$

Definitions

Aggregate expenditure (E) Aggregate demand in the Keynesian model: i.e. $C_d + J$.

Endogenous variable A variable whose value is determined by the model of which it is part.

Exogenous variable A variable whose value is determined independently of the model of which it is part.

significance of the 45° line, which is shown in Figure 17.2. We plot real national income (i.e. national income matched by output) on the horizontal axis, and the various component parts of the circular flow (C_d, W and J) on the vertical axis. If the two axes are plotted to the same scale, then at every point on the 45° line the items on each axis are equal.

But what items on the vertical axis will always equal national income (Y), which is plotted on the horizontal axis? The answer is $C_d + W$, since, by definition, $Y = C_d + W$. For example, if Y were £100 billion, then $C_d + W$ must also be £100 billion (see Figure 17.2).

We turn now to look at each of the components of the circular flow and see how they fit into the 45° line diagram.

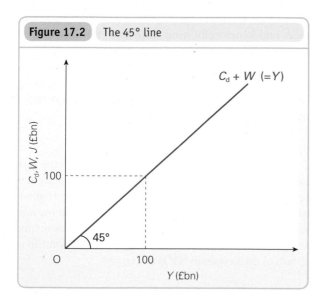

Figure 17.2   The 45° line

Consumption

We will need to distinguish total consumption (C) from that part of consumption that goes purely on the output of domestically produced goods (C_d). C_d excludes expenditure taxes (e.g. VAT) and expenditure on imports.

We start by looking at *total* consumption.

The consumption function

As national income increases, so does consumption. The reason is simple: if people earn more, they can afford to spend more. The relationship between consumption and income is expressed by the **consumption function**:

$$C = f(Y)$$

It can be shown graphically on the 45° line diagram (see Figure 17.3 which is based on Table 17.1). The consumption function slopes upwards. This illustrates that, as national income rises, so does consumption. To keep the analysis simple, the consumption function is drawn as a straight line.

At very low levels of income, the consumption function will lie above the 45° line. When a nation is very poor, most people may be forced to spend more than they earn merely to survive. They usually do this by borrowing or drawing on savings. Above a certain level of income, however (£500 billion in Figure 17.3), the consumption function will lie

Definition

Consumption function The relationship between consumption and national income. It can be expressed algebraically or graphically.

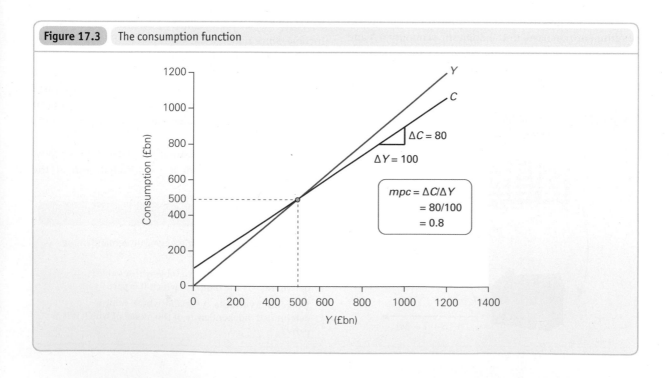

Figure 17.3   The consumption function

Table 17.1	$C = f(Y)$

National income (£bn)	Consumption (£bn)
0	100
100	180
200	260
300	340
400	420
500	500
600	580
700	660
800	740
900	820
1000	900
1100	980

below the 45° line. People will spend less than they earn. The remainder will go on saving and taxes.

The higher the level of national income, the smaller the proportion that will be consumed: people can afford to save proportionately more, and will have to pay proportionately more in taxes. It follows that the slope of the consumption function is less than that of the 45° line.

The marginal propensity to consume.   The slope of the consumption function is given by the **marginal propensity to consume**. This is the proportion of any increase in national income that goes on consumption.[1] In Table 17.1, for each £100 billion rise in national income there is an £80 billion rise in consumption. Thus the marginal propensity to consume is £80 billion/£100 billion = 80/100 or 4/5 or 0.8. The formula is

$$mpc = \Delta C / \Delta Y$$

In Figure 17.3, the consumption function is a straight line: it has a *constant* slope, and hence the *mpc* is also constant.

It is possible that as people get richer they will spend a smaller and smaller fraction of each rise in income (and save a larger fraction). Why might this be so? What effect will it have on the shape of the consumption function?

The other determinants of consumption

Of course, people's incomes are not the only determinants of the amount they consume. There are several other determinants.

Taxation.   The higher the level of income taxes, the less will people have left to spend out of their gross income: consumption depends on **disposable income**.

---

1 The *mpc* is normally defined as the proportion of a rise in *disposable* national income that goes on consumption, where disposable income is income *after taxes*. By defining it the way we have done (i.e. as the proportion of *gross* income that goes in consumption), the analysis is simpler. The conclusions remain the same.

Expected future incomes.   Many people take into account both current and expected future incomes when planning their current and future consumption. You might have a relatively low income when you graduate, but can expect (you hope!) to earn much more in the future.

You are thus willing to take on more debts now in order to support your consumption, not only as a student but shortly afterwards as well, anticipating that you will be able to pay back these loans later. It is similar with people taking out a mortgage to buy a house. They might struggle to pay the interest at first, but hope that this will become easier over time.

KI 10 p70

In fact, the financial system (such as banks and building societies) plays an important part in facilitating this *smoothing of consumption* by households. You can look to borrow or draw on accumulated savings from the past when your current income is low. The hope is that you can then pay back the loans or replenish your savings later on when your income is higher. Therefore, the financial system can provide households with greater flexibility over when to spend their expected future incomes.

The financial system and attitudes of lenders.   The financial sector provides households not only with longer-term loans but also short-term credit. This short-term credit enables transactions to take place by bridging short-term gaps between income and expenditure. This helps to explain why short-term rates of change in household spending, say from one quarter of the year to the next, are often less variable than those in disposable income.

But financial institutions can affect the growth in consumption if their ability and willingness to provide credit changes. The global financial crises of the second half of the 2000s saw credit criteria tighten dramatically. A tightening of credit practices, such as reducing overdraft facilities or reducing income multiples (the size of loans made available relative to household incomes), tends to weaken consumption growth. This is because the growth of consumption becomes more dependent on the growth of current incomes. Consequently, there is a growth in the number of *credit-constrained households*.

Definitions

Marginal propensity to consume The proportion of a rise in national income that goes on consumption: $mpc = \Delta C / \Delta Y$.

Disposable income Household income after the deduction of taxes and the addition of benefits.

Consumption smoothing The act by households of smoothing their levels of consumption over time despite facing volatile incomes.

Credit-constrained households Households which are limited in their ability to borrow against expected future incomes.

In contrast, a relaxation of lending practices, as seen in many countries during the 1980s, can strengthen consumption growth. This allows households more readily to borrow against future incomes: there are fewer credit-constrained households.

Changes in interest rates can affect household spending by affecting how expensive loans are to 'service'. **Debt-servicing costs** are the costs incurred in repaying the loans and the interest payments on the loan. Where the rate of interest on debt is variable, any changes in interest rates affect the cost of servicing the debt. This can be especially important for mortgages. In the UK, where a large proportion of mortgage-payers are on a variable mortgage rate, changes in mortgage rates can have a sizeable impact on their debt-servicing costs. This then has significant implications for the proportion of income that a household needs to set aside to pay the mortgage.

Wealth and household sector balance sheets. By borrowing and saving, households accumulate financial liabilities (debts), financial assets (savings) and physical assets (mainly property). The household sector's *financial* balance sheet details the sector's holding of financial assets and liabilities, while its *capital* balance sheet details its physical assets. Its balance of financial assets over liabilities is the household sector's net *financial wealth.* The household sector's *net worth,* as recorded in the capital balance sheet, is the sum of its net financial wealth and its physical wealth.

Changes on the household sector's balance sheets affect the sector's financial health – sometimes referred to as its level of *financial distress.* Such changes can significantly affect short-term prospects for household spending. For instance, a declining net worth to income ratio is an indicator of greater financial distress. This could be induced by falling house prices or falling share prices. In response to this, we might see the sector engage in *precautionary* or *buffer-stock* saving. Such saving is a means by which households build up a buffer stock of wealth which acts as a form of insurance or protection. Alternatively, households may look to repay some of their outstanding debt.

Therefore, the impact of worsening household balance sheets may be to weaken spending, while improvements on the balance sheets may strengthen the growth of consumption. Household balance sheets are discussed in Box 17.2.

Consumer sentiment. If people are uncertain about their future income prospects, or fear unemployment, they are likely to be cautious in their spending. Surveys of consumer confidence are closely followed by policy makers (see Box 17.3) as an indicator of the level of future spending.

Expectations of future prices. If people expect prices to rise, they tend to buy durable goods such as furniture and cars before this happens.

The distribution of income. The poor have a higher *mpc* than the rich, with very little left over to save. A redistribution of national income from the poor to the rich will therefore tend to reduce the total level of consumption in the economy.

Tastes and attitudes. If people have a 'buy now, pay later' mentality, or a craving for consumer goods, they are likely to have a higher level of consumption than if their tastes are more frugal. The more 'consumerist' and materialistic a nation becomes, facilitated by the financial system, the higher will its consumption be for any given level of income.

The age of durables. If people's cars, carpets, clothes, etc., are getting old, they will tend to have a high level of 'replacement' consumption, particularly after a recession when they had cut back on their consumption of durables. Conversely, as the economy reaches the peak of the boom, people are likely to spend less on durables as they have probably already bought the items they want.

Movements along and shifts in the consumption function

The effect on consumption of a change in national income is shown by a movement *along* the consumption function. A change in any of the other determinants is shown by a *shift* in the consumption function.

 What effect will the following have on the mpc: (a) the rate of income tax rises; (b) the economy begins to recover from recession; (c) people anticipate that the rate of inflation is about to rise; (d) the government redistributes income from the rich to the poor? In each case sketch what would happen to the consumption function.

Long-run and short-run consumption functions

The long-run consumption function is likely to be steeper than the short-run one (see Figure 17.4).

In the short run, people may be slow to respond to a rise in income. Perhaps they are cautious about whether their higher income will last, or are slow to change their consumption habits. In the short run, then, people may have a relatively low *mpc.* In the long run, however, people have time to adjust their consumption patterns.

Assuming that national income rises over time, the long-run consumption function will be intersected by a series of short-run ones. Each year's short-run function will be above the previous year's.

 Which is likely to show the greater variation from one person to another at any given level of income: the short-run mpc or the long-run mpc?

Definition

Debt-servicing costs The costs incurred when repaying debt, including debt interest payments.

Figure 17.4 Long-run and short-run consumption functions

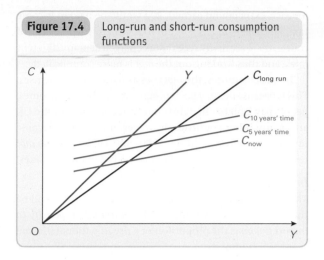

Figure 17.5 The consumption of domestic product

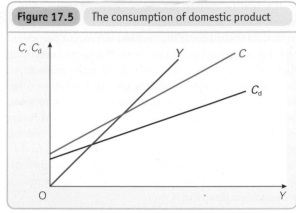

Consumption of domestically produced goods (C_d)

The parts of consumption that go on imports and indirect taxes constitute withdrawals from the circular flow of income and thus do not contribute to aggregate demand. We shall concentrate on the part of consumption that *does*: namely, the consumption of domestic product (C_d). The C_d function lies below the C function, as in Figure 17.5. The gap between them constitutes imports of consumer goods and indirect taxes.

Withdrawals

All three withdrawals – net saving, net taxes and import expenditure – depend on the level of national income. They are thus all *endogenously* determined within the model.

Net saving

As with consumption, the major determinant of net saving (i.e. saving minus consumer borrowing and drawing on past savings) is income. As income increases, and a decreasing fraction of it goes on consumption, so an increasing fraction of it will be saved. The rich can afford to save a larger proportion of their income than the poor.

The proportion of an increase in national income that is saved is given by the **marginal propensity to save** (*mps*).

$$mps = \Delta S / \Delta Y$$

Other determinants of saving. To a large extent these are the same as the other determinants of consumption, since most things that encourage people to spend more will thereby encourage them to save less.

> **KI 26**
> **p303**

Definition

Marginal propensity to save The proportion of an increase in national income saved: $= \Delta S / \Delta Y$.

---

*LOOKING AT THE MATHS

Let us examine the relationship between C and C_d a bit more closely. When people make consumption decisions, this is largely based on their *disposable* income (Y_{dis}), where disposable income is income after the payment of income taxes and the receipt of benefits. We use the term 'net income taxes (T_Y)' to refer to income taxes minus benefits. Thus

$$Y_{dis} = Y - T_Y$$

Also, people tend not to distinguish between domestic goods and imports when they make consumption decisions. Let us then focus on total consumption (C), not just the consumption of domestic products (C_d).

To get a better understanding of people's consumption behaviour, we could express the marginal propensity to consume *all products* (domestic and imported) relative to *disposable* income. Let us call this term *mpc'* (rather than *mpc* or *mpc$_d$*) where

$$mpc' = \frac{\Delta C}{\Delta Y_{dis}} = \frac{\Delta C}{\Delta Y - \Delta T_Y} \tag{1}$$

To get from C to C_d, we would have to subtract the amount spent on imports (M) and the part of consumer expenditure paid in indirect taxes, such as VAT and excise duties, (T_E). Thus

$$C_d = C - M - T_E \text{ or } C = C_d + M + T_E$$

Thus

$$\Delta C = \Delta C_d + \Delta M + \Delta T_E \tag{2}$$

Substituting equation (2) in equation (1) gives

$$mpc' = \frac{\Delta C_d + \Delta T_E + \Delta M}{\Delta Y - \Delta T_Y} \tag{3}$$

Contrast this with the *mpc$_d$*, where

$$mpc_d = \frac{\Delta C_d}{\Delta Y} \tag{4}$$

It might be easy to get the impression that saving is merely what is left over after consumption has taken place. In fact, for many people the decision to save is a purposeful one. For example, they might be saving up for something they are eager to buy but cannot afford at the moment, or they may be saving for retirement. Or, as we saw above (page 524), they may undertake precautionary or buffer stock saving to insure themselves against the possibility of future income loss, such as from unemployment or theft. Indeed, people may be encouraged to save *more* by various factors, such as changes in pension provisions, new government-sponsored saving schemes or uncertainty about the macroeconomic environment.

 Go through each of the determinants of consumption that were listed in the previous section and consider how they will affect saving. Are there any determinants of consumption that will not cause saving to rise if consumption is caused to fall?

Net taxes

As national income increases, so the amount paid in tax will also increase. The **marginal tax propensity** (*mpt*) is the proportion of an increase in national income paid in taxes:[2]

$$mpt = \Delta T / \Delta Y$$

The *mpt* depends on tax rates. In a simple world where there was only one type of tax, which was charged at a constant rate – for example, an income tax of 20 per cent – the *mpt* would be given directly by the tax rate. In this example,

for each extra pound earned, 20p would be paid in income tax. The $mpt = \Delta T / \Delta Y = 20/100 = 0.20$. In practice, of course, there are many types of tax charged at many different rates, and thus working out the *mpt* is more complicated.

In most countries, the *mpt* rises as national income rises. This is because income tax is progressive. At higher incomes, people pay a higher marginal rate of income tax. In the UK and many other countries, however, income tax became much less progressive in the 1980s and 1990s, but the *mpt* remained roughly the same because of rises in indirect taxes.

Imports

The higher the level of national income, the higher will be the amount spent on imports. The **marginal propensity to import** (*mpm*) is the proportion of a rise in national income that goes on imports:

$$mpm = \Delta M / \Delta Y$$

2 We have defined net taxes as taxes minus benefits (i.e. the net flow from the household sector to the government). For our purposes, then, the *mpt* is the proportion of any rise in income going in taxes and reduced benefits.

Definitions

Marginal tax propensity The proportion of an increase in national income paid in tax: $= \Delta T / \Delta Y$.

Marginal propensity to import The proportion of an increase in national income that is spent on imports: $mpm = \Delta M / \Delta Y$.

---

*BOX 17.1 USING CALCULUS TO DERIVE THE *MPC*

 EXPLORING ECONOMICS

The consumption function can be expressed as an equation. For example, the consumption function of Table 17.1 and Figure 17.3 is given by the equation:

$$C = 100 + 0.8Y \tag{1}$$

 Try using this equation to derive the figures in Table 17.1.

From this equation we can derive an equation for *mpc*. It is found by differentiating the consumption function. Remember from previous calculus boxes what it is we are doing when we differentiate an equation. We are finding its rate of change. Thus by differentiating the consumption function, we are finding the rate of change of consumption with respect to income. But this is what we mean by the *mpc*.

The difference between using differentiation and the formula $\Delta C / \Delta Y$ is that with the former we are looking at the *mpc* at a single point on the consumption function. With the $\Delta C / \Delta Y$ formula we were looking at the *mpc* between two points.

Differentiating equation (1) gives

$$mpc = dC/dY = 0.8 \tag{2}$$

Note that, since the consumption function is a straight line in this case, the *mpc* (which measures the slope of the consumption function) is constant.

What would we do to find the *mpc* of a non-linear (curved) consumption function? The procedure is the same.

Assume that the consumption function is given by the following equation:

$$C = 250 + 0.9Y - 0.0001Y^2 \tag{3}$$

The *mpc* is given by *dC / dY:*

$$mpc = 0.9 - 0.0002Y$$

1. First of all, try constructing a table like Table 17.1 and then graph the consumption function that it gives. What is it about equation (3) that gives the graph its particular shape?
2. What are the values of mpc at incomes of (a) 200; (b) 1000?
3. What happens to the value of mpc as national income increases? Is this what you would expect by examining the shape of the consumption function?

Note that we only count that part of the expenditure on imports that actually goes abroad. Amounts retained by the retailer, the wholesaler and the importer, and amounts paid in indirect taxes, are excluded.

Whether the *mpm* rises or falls as national income rises depends on the nature of a country's imports. If a country imports predominantly basic goods, which have a relatively low income elasticity of demand, the rate of increase in their consumption would tail off rapidly as incomes increase. The *mpm* for such a country would thus also rapidly decrease.

If, however, a country's imports were mainly of luxury goods, they would account for an increasing proportion of any rise in national income: the *mpm* would rise.

 If a country imports a whole range of goods whose average income elasticity of demand is the same as for home-produced goods, will the mpm rise or fall as national income rises?

The determinants of the level of imports. Apart from national income, there are a number of other determinants of the level of imports:

- *Relative prices.* If the prices of home-produced goods go up relative to the prices of imports, the level of imports will rise. The rate of exchange is a major influence here. The higher the rate of exchange, the cheaper will imports be and hence the more will be spent on them.
- *Tastes.* If consumer tastes shift towards foreign goods and services, imports will rise. For example, it might become more popular to go abroad for your holidays.
- *Relative quality.* If the quality of foreign goods and services increases relative to that of domestic goods and services, imports will rise.
- *The determinants of consumption.* Since imports of goods and services are part of *total* consumption (as opposed to C_d), the various determinants of consumption that we looked at on pages 522–4 will also be determinants of imports.

The total withdrawals function

Remember that withdrawals consist of the three elements: net saving, net taxes and imports, all of which rise as national income rises. A withdrawals function along with the corresponding consumption of domestic goods function is shown in Figure 17.6.

Note the relationship between the C_d and W curves. The steeper the slope of the one, the flatter the slope of the other. The reason for this is that C_d and W add up to total national income (Y):

$$Y = C_d + W$$

Since the 45° line measures $C_d + W$, the distance between the C_d function and the 45° line must equal withdrawals. Thus at point *x*, where national income is £100 billion and

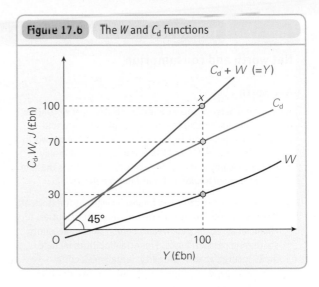

Figure 17.6 The *W* and C_d functions

C_d is £70 billion, W must be £30 billion – the gap between C_d and the 45° line.

The marginal propensity to withdraw

The formula for the **marginal propensity to withdraw** (*mpw*) is as we would expect:

$$mpw = \Delta W / \Delta Y$$

The *mpw* is the slope of the withdrawals function. Note that, since $W = S + T + M$, *mpw* must equal *mps* + *mpt* + *mpm*. For example, if for any rise in national income, 1/10 were saved, 2/10 paid in net taxes, and 2/10 spent on imports, then 5/10 must be withdrawn.

Note also that, since $C_d + W = Y$, $mpc_d + mpw$ must add up to 1. For example, if the country spends, say, 3/5 of any rise in income on domestically produced goods, the remaining 2/5 must go on withdrawals.

 If the slope of the C_d function is 3/4, what is the slope of the W function?

Injections

In simple Keynesian theory, injections are assumed not to depend on the level of national income: they are *exogenously* determined. This means that the injections function is drawn as a horizontal straight line. Injections will be at a given level irrespective of the level of national income.

Definition

Marginal propensity to withdraw The proportion of an increase in national income that is withdrawn from the circular flow: $mpw = \Delta W / \Delta Y$, where $mpw = mps + mpt + mpm$.

BOX 17.2 | THE HOUSEHOLD SECTOR BALANCE SHEETS

Net worth and consumption

Net worth

The national balance sheet details a country's net worth (i.e. wealth). This aggregates the net worth of the household, corporate and public sectors. We consider here the net worth of the household sector and the extent to which this may influence consumption (*C*).[1] The sector's net worth is the sum of its *net financial wealth* and *non-financial assets*.

- The household sector's net financial wealth is the stock of financial assets minus the stock of financial liabilities. Financial assets include wealth held in savings accounts, shares and pension funds. Financial liabilities include debts secured against property, largely residential mortgages, and unsecured debts, such as overdrafts and unpaid balances on credit cards.
- The stock of non-financial assets largely comprises the sector's residential housing wealth. Therefore, this is affected by changes in house prices.

The table summarises the net worth of the UK household sector. By the end of 2015 the sector had a stock of net worth estimated at £10.20 trillion compared with £2.84 trillion at

the end of 1995 – an increase of 258 per cent. This, of course, is a nominal increase, not a real increase, as part of it merely reflects the rise in asset prices.

To put the size of net worth and its components into context, we can express them relative to annual disposable income or GDP. This shows that the household sector's net worth in 2015 was equivalent to 8.2 times the flow of household disposable income in that year, or 5.4 times GDP. In 1995 it was 5.0 times and 3.4 times respectively.

The ratio of the sector's net worth to disposable income has typically increased year on year. An important factor behind this long-term rise has been the rise of non-financial assets (mainly housing). This increased from £1.26 trillion (219 per cent of disposable income) in 1995 to £4.38 trillion (446 per cent of disposable income) in 2007. It then fell in 2008, the year of the financial crisis, but then rose again each year up to 2015, reaching £5.64 trillion (452 per cent of disposable income).

In contrast, net financial wealth to disposable income has been more volatile, without the marked upward trend seen in non-financial assets. The ratio of net financial wealth to

Summary of household-sector balance sheets, 31 December 1995 and 2015

	1995			2015		
	£ billions	% of disposable income	% of GDP	£ billions	% of disposable income	% of GDP
Financial assets	2 143.8	373.1	256.2	6 310.9	506.2	337.0
Financial liabilities	556.4	96.8	66.5	1 750.9	143.4	93.5
Net financial wealth	**1 587.4**	**276.3**	**189.7**	**4 560.0**	**365.8**	**243.5**
Non-financial assets	1 257.6	218.9	150.3	5 636.7	452.2	301.0
Net worth	**2 844.9**	**495.2**	**340.0**	**10 196.7**	**817.9**	**544.5**

Source: Based on data from *National Balance Sheet* and *Quarterly National Accounts* (National Statistics).

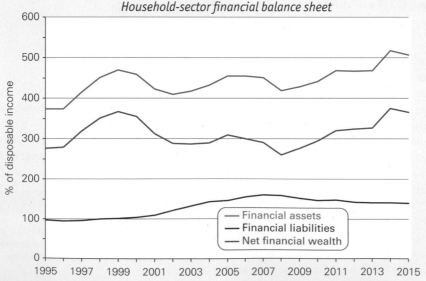

Source: Based on data from *National Balance Sheet* and *Quarterly National Accounts* (National Statistics).

disposable income in 2015, for example, was almost the same as that in 1999. However, this does not mean that the absolute value of financial wealth of the household sector has not risen. In fact, it increased by 188 per cent from 1995 to 2015, though considerably less than the 348 per cent by which net non-financial assets rose. Net worth rose by 258 per cent.

Financial balance sheet

The household sector has experienced significant growth in the size of its financial balance sheet. This is captured by the chart, which shows the components of net financial wealth: financial assets and liabilities.

The ratio of financial liabilities to disposable income rose from 97 per cent in 1995 to 160 per cent in 2007; people were taking on more and more debt relative to their incomes, fuelled by the ease of accessing credit – both consumer credit (loans and credit card debt) and mortgages. Then, in the aftermath of the credit crunch, the ratio began to fall. By 2015 the ratio had fallen to 140 per cent.

The longer-term increase in the sector's debt-to-income ratio up to 2007 meant that interest payments involved increasingly significant demands on household budgets and hence on the discretionary income households had for spending. This is likely to have made the sector's spending more sensitive to changes in interest rates. For example, increases in interest rates can place a substantially larger burden on households, adversely affecting aggregate demand as households curb their expenditures.

Higher debt-to-income levels can also fuel people's concerns about the potential risks arising from debt. If the prospects for income growth are revised down or become more uncertain, people may decide to cut their spending in order to pay off some of their debts.

Non-financial assets

In absolute terms, the financial liabilities of the household sector more than tripled between 1995 and 2015 (see the table). But the long-term accumulation of household debt needs to be seen in the context of the growth in the value of non-financial assets, particularly property. However, while UK house price values have risen by around 10 per cent per annum over the past 50 years, they are very volatile in the short term.

House price volatility is important because it makes the net worth of the household sector volatile too. Furthermore, the impact of house price volatility on net worth has grown. This is because high long-term average rates of growth in house prices have meant that a larger proportion of household sector net worth is now held in property. In 1995, 38 per cent of the household sector's net worth came from the value of dwellings; by 2015 it had risen to 51 per cent.

Volatility in house prices may have the following effects on the spending and saving choices of households:

A precautionary effect. The volatility in net worth from volatile house prices (and potentially the prices of other assets, such as shares) can induce volatility in consumption. If asset prices are falling, households may respond by cutting their spending and increasing saving. This, as we saw on page 524, is a *precautionary or buffer-stock effect.* Conversely, higher asset prices enable households to reduce saving and spend more.

A collateral effect. As house prices rise households' *housing equity* rises, while falling house prices reduce housing equity. Housing equity is the difference between the value of a property and the value of any outstanding loan secured against it. House price movements affect the collateral that households have to secure *additional* lending. They affect the extent to which households are credit constrained.

When house prices are rising it may enable households to borrow resources which can then be used to fund consumption, to purchase other assets (e.g. shares) or to repay other debts. On the other hand, when house prices fall households have less collateral to secure additional resources. They become more credit constrained.

Case Study 17.5 on the student website details the patterns in housing equity withdrawal and consumer spending in the UK.

 Draw up a list of the various factors that could affect the household sector's net worth and then consider how these could impact on consumer spending.

1 The household sector in the official statistics also includes 'non-profit institutions serving households (NPISH)' such as charities, clubs and societies, trade unions, political parties and universities.

| BOX 17.3 | SENTIMENT AND SPENDING |

Does sentiment help forecast spending?

Keynesian economists have frequently pointed to the importance of confidence or sentiment in influencing expenditure decisions. Each month, consumers and firms across the European Union are asked a series of questions, the answers to which are used to compile indicators of consumer and business confidence. For instance, consumers are asked about how they expect both their own financial position and the general economic situation to change over the coming 12 months. For each question, they are offered various options, such as 'get a lot better, 'get a lot worse', and balances are then calculated based on the number of positive and negative replies.[1]

Chart (a) plots economic sentiment in the EU across industry as a whole, consumers and the construction industry since 1990. The chart shows the volatility of economic sentiment. This volatility is more marked amongst businesses than consumers and, in particular, in the construction sector.

Now compare the volatility of economic sentiment in Chart (a) with the annual rates of growth in household consumption and gross capital formation (investment), shown in Chart (b). Capital spending in the EU is significantly more volatile than household spending. Therefore, the extent of the volatility in economic sentiment is reflected in patterns of expenditure.

What is less clear is the extent to which changes in sentiment *lead* to changes in spending. In fact, a likely scenario is that spending and sentiment interact. High rates of spending growth may result in high confidence through

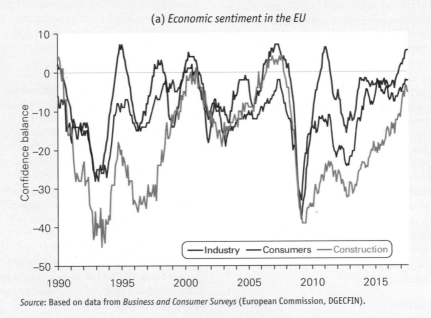

(a) *Economic sentiment in the EU*

Source: Based on data from *Business and Consumer Surveys* (European Commission, DGECFIN).

The injections function is the vertical addition of the investment, government expenditure and export functions, each of which is a horizontal straight line.

The assumption that injections are independent of national income makes the theory simpler. (It is possible to drop this assumption, however, without destroying the theory.) But is the assumption sufficiently realistic? Let us examine each of the injections in turn.

Investment

There are five major determinants of investment.

Increased consumer demand. Investment is to provide extra capacity. This will only be necessary, therefore, if consumer demand increases. The bigger the increase in consumer demand, the more investment will be needed.

You might think that, since consumer demand depends on the level of national income, investment must too, and

that therefore our assumption that investment is independent of national income is wrong. But we are not saying that investment depends on the *level* of consumer demand; rather it depends on *how much it has risen*. If income and consumer demand are high but *constant,* there will be no point in firms expanding their capacity: no point in investing.

The relationship between investment and *increased* consumer demand is examined by the 'accelerator theory'. We will look at this theory in section 17.4.

Expectations. Since investment is made in order to produce output for the future, investment must depend on firms' expectations about future market conditions.

The cost and efficiency of capital equipment. If the cost of capital equipment goes down or machines become more efficient, the return on investment will increase. Firms will invest more. Technological progress is an important determinant here.

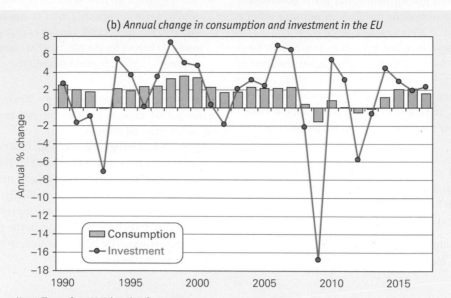

(b) *Annual change in consumption and investment in the EU*

Notes: Figures from 2017 based on forecasts.
Source: Based on data in *AMECO Database* (European Commission, DGECFIN).

TC 9
p129

economic growth, which in turn leads to more spending. The reverse is the case when economic growth is subdued: low spending growth leads to a lack of confidence, which results in low spending growth and so low rates of economic growth.

What makes measures of confidence particularly useful is that they are published monthly. By contrast, measures of GDP and spending are published annually or quarterly and with a considerable time delay. Therefore, measures of confidence are extremely timely for policy makers and provide them with very useful information about the likely path of spending and output growth.

What factors are likely to influence the economic sentiment of (i) consumers; and (ii) businesses? Could the trends in the economic sentiment indicators for consumers and businesses diverge?

1 More information on the EU programme of business and consumer surveys can be found at http://ec.europa.eu/economy_finance/db_indicators/surveys/index_en.htm

The rate of interest. The higher the rate of interest, the more expensive it will be for firms to finance investment, and hence the less profitable will the investment be. Just how responsive total investment in the economy is to changes in interest rates is a highly controversial issue and we will return to it later.

Availability of finance. Investment requires financing. Retained earnings provide one possible source. Alternatively, they could seek finance from banks, or perhaps issue debt instruments, such as bonds, or issue new shares. Therefore, difficulties in raising finance, such as seen in the late 2000s and early 2010s, can limit investment.

So if these are the main determinants of investment, does it mean that investment is totally independent of the level of national income? Not quite. Replacement of worn-out or outdated equipment *will* depend on the level of national income. The higher the current level of national income, the greater will be the stock of capital and therefore the more will need replacing each year. It is also possible that, if the level of national income is high and firms' profits are high, they will be able to *afford* more investment. However, it is not a gross distortion of reality to assume that investment and the level of national income are independent, at least in the short run.

Government purchases

Government spending on goods and services in any year is independent of the level of national income. In the months preceding the Budget each year, spending departments make submissions about their needs in the coming year. These are discussed with the Treasury and a sum is allocated to each department. That then (excepting any unforeseen events) fixes government expenditure on goods and services for the following financial year.

Thus, again, for our purposes we can take government purchases as independent of national income in the short term. Even if tax revenues turn out to be more or less than expected, this will not influence that year's government spending. The government can end up running either a budget surplus ($T = G$) or a budget deficit ($G = T$).

Over the longer term, however, government purchases *will* depend on national income. The higher the level of national income, the higher is the amount of tax revenue that the government receives, and hence the more it can afford to spend. The governments of richer nations clearly spend much more than those of developing countries.

Exports

Exports are sold to people abroad, and thus depend largely on *their* incomes, not on incomes at home. Nevertheless, there are two indirect links between a country's national income and its exports:

- Via other countries' circular flows of income. If domestic incomes rise, more will be spent on imports. But this will cause a rise in other countries' incomes and lead them to buy more imports, part of which will be this country's exports.

- Via the exchange rate. A rise in domestic incomes will lead to a rise in imports. Other things being equal, this will lead to a depreciation in the exchange rate. This will make it cheaper for people in other countries to buy this country's exports. Export sales will rise.

However, it is useful in simple Keynesian models to assume that exports are determined independently of domestic national income.

Note that, although the injections function is assumed to be constant with respect to income and is drawn as a horizontal straight line, this does not mean that it will be constant *over time*. Investment can suddenly rise or virtually collapse as the confidence of businesspeople changes. Exports can change too with shifts in the exchange rate or with speculation. The injections line, then, is constantly shifting up and down.

Section summary

1. In the simple Keynesian model, equilibrium national income is where withdrawals equal injections, and where national income equals the total expenditure on domestic products: where $W = J$ and where $Y = E$.

2. The relationships between national income and the various components of the circular flow of income can be shown on a 45° line diagram. In such a diagram, C, C_d and W are endogenous variables. Each one rises as income rises. The relationships can also be expressed in terms of marginal propensities. The marginal propensity is given by $\Delta V/\Delta Y$ (where V is the variable in question).

3. Apart from being determined by national income, consumption is determined by wealth, taxation, the availability and cost of credit, expectations about future prices and incomes, the distribution of income, tastes and attitudes, and the average age of durables. Consumption of domestic product (C_d) is total consumption minus imports of goods and services and minus indirect taxes and plus subsidies on goods and services.

4. Like consumption, withdrawals (S, T and M) vary with national income. Net saving is also determined by the various factors that determine consumption: if these factors cause consumption to rise, then, except in the case of a cut in income taxes, they will cause saving to fall and vice versa. Net tax revenues, apart from being dependent on incomes, depend on the rates of tax and benefits that the government sets and how progressive or regressive they are. Imports depend on the relative prices and quality of domestic and foreign goods, total consumption and tastes.

5. In the simple Keynesian model, injections are assumed to be exogenous variables. They are therefore drawn as a horizontal straight line in the 45° line diagram. In practice, there will be *some* relationship between injections and national income. Replacement investment depends to some extent on the level of output; government purchases depend to some extent on the level of tax revenues; and exports depend on exchange rates and foreign incomes, both of which will depend on the level of imports. Nevertheless, in the short run it is reasonable to assume that injections are independent of national income.

6. The determinants of investment include the rate of interest, the size of increases in consumer demand, the cost and efficiency of capital equipment, and expectations about prices, consumer demand, interest rates and other costs.

17.2 THE DETERMINATION OF NATIONAL INCOME

Equilibrium national income

We can now put the various functions together on one diagram. This is done in Figure 17.7. Note that there is a new line on the diagram that we have not looked at so far. This is the aggregate expenditure (i.e. the aggregate demand) function. We defined aggregate expenditure as $C_d + J$. Graphically, then, the E function is simply the C_d function shifted upwards by the amount of J.

Equilibrium national income can be found in either of two ways.

$W = J$

Withdrawals equal injections at point x in Figure 17.7. Equilibrium national income is thus Y_e. If national income were below this level, say at Y_1, injections would exceed withdrawals (by an amount $a - b$). This additional net expenditure injected into the economy would encourage firms to produce more and hence cause national income to rise. But as people's incomes rose, so they would save more, pay more taxes and buy more imports. In other words, withdrawals would rise. There would be a movement up along the W function. This process would continue until $W = J$ at point x.

If, on the other hand, national income were at Y_2, withdrawals would exceed injections (by an amount $c - d$). This deficiency of demand would cause production and hence national income to fall. As it did so, there would be a movement down along the W function until again point x was reached.

$Y = E$

If $W = J$, then $C_d + W = C_d + J$. In other words, another way of describing equilibrium is where national income ($Y \equiv C_d + W$) equals aggregate expenditure ($E \equiv C_d + J$).

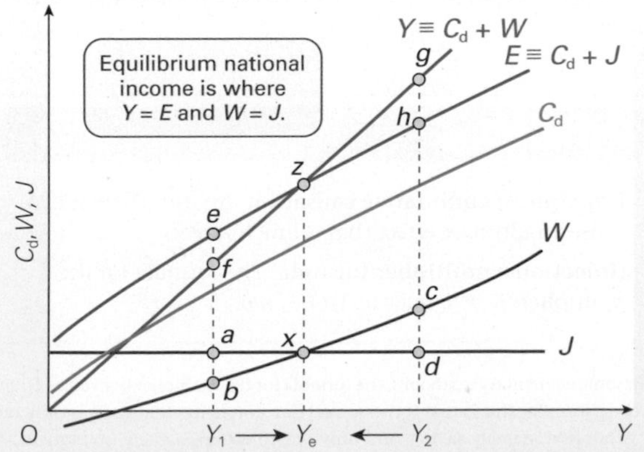

This is shown at point z in Figure 17.7. This is where the expenditure function ($C_d + J$) crosses the 45° line ($C_d + W$).

If aggregate expenditure exceeded national income, say at Y_1, there would be excess demand in the economy (of $e - f$). In other words, people would be buying more than was currently being produced. Firms would find their stocks dwindling and would therefore increase their level of production. In doing so, they would employ more factors of production. National income would thus rise. As it did so, consumption and hence aggregate expenditure would rise. There would be a movement up along the expenditure function. But because not all the extra income would be consumed (i.e. some would be withdrawn), expenditure would rise less quickly than income (the E line is flatter than the Y line). As income rises towards Y_e, the gap between Y and E gets smaller. Once point z is reached, $Y = E$. There is then no further tendency for income to rise.

If national income exceeded national expenditure, at say Y_2, there would be insufficient demand for the goods and services currently being produced. Firms would find their stocks of unsold goods building up. They would thus respond by producing less and employing fewer factors of production. National income would thus fall and go on falling until Y_e was reached.

 Why is it the case that $a - b = e - f$, and $c - d = g - h$?

The multiplier: the withdrawals and injections approach

When injections rise (and continue at the higher level), this will cause national income to rise. But by how much?

In fact, national income will rise by *more* than injections: Y rises by a *multiple* of the rise in J.

$$\Delta Y > \Delta J$$

The number of times that the increase in income (ΔY) is greater than the increase in injections (ΔJ) is known as the *multiplier* (k).

$$k = \Delta Y / \Delta J$$

Thus if a £10 billion rise in injections caused a £30 billion rise in national income, the multiplier would be 3.

What causes the multiplier effect? The answer is that, when extra spending is injected into the economy, it will

---

Figure 17.7 Equilibrium national income

Equilibrium national income is where $Y = E$ and $W = J$.

$Y \equiv C_d + W$
$E \equiv C_d + J$

Definition

(Injections) multiplier The number of times by which a rise in income exceeds the rise in injections that caused it: $K = \Delta Y / \Delta J$.

then stimulate further spending, which in turn will stimulate yet more spending and so on. For example, if firms decide to invest more, this will lead to more people being employed and hence more incomes being paid to households. Households will then spend part of this increased income on domestically produced goods (the remainder will be withdrawn). This increased consumption will encourage firms to produce more goods to meet the demand. Firms will thus employ more people and other factors of production. This leads to even more incomes being paid out to households. Consumption will thus increase yet again. And so the process continues.

The multiplier is an example of an important principle in economics: that of *cumulative causation*. This is the last of our 15 threshold concepts.

Note that in this simple Keynesian theory we are assuming that prices are constant (i.e. that there is no inflation) and hence that any increase in income is a *real* increase in income matched by extra production. So when we talk about extra injections into the economy causing extra spending, it is the extra *output* that this spending generates that we are concerned with. If the multiplier were 3, for example, this would mean that an injection of £1 of expenditure into the economy would lead to an increase in *output* of £3.

But even if there were limitless resources, an increase in injections would not cause national income to go on rising for ever: the multiplier is not infinite. Each time people receive extra income, they will save some of it, pay some of it in taxes and spend some of it on imports: in other words, withdrawals will rise. Eventually, as income goes on rising, all the extra injections will have leaked away into the three withdrawals. At that point, the multiplier process will have ceased; a new equilibrium will have been reached.

What determines the size of the multiplier? This can be shown graphically using either withdrawals and injections or income and expenditure. The income/expenditure approach will be examined shortly. For now we will use the withdrawals/injections approach. This is illustrated in Figure 17.8.

Assume that injections rise from J_1 to J_2. Equilibrium will move from point *a* to point *b*. Income will thus rise from Y_{e_1} to Y_{e_2}. The multiplier is therefore

$$\frac{Y_{e_2} - Y_{e_1}}{J_2 - J_1} \left(\text{i.e.} \frac{\Delta Y}{\Delta J} \right)$$

It can be seen that the size of the multiplier depends on the slope of the W function. Remember that the slope of the W function is given by the marginal propensity to withdraw ($\Delta W/\Delta Y$). The less steep the line (and hence the lower the *mpw*), the bigger will be the rise in national income: the bigger will be the multiplier.

 Try this simple test of the above argument. Draw a series of W lines of different slopes, all crossing the J line at the same point. Now draw a second J line above the first. Mark the original equilibrium and all the new ones corresponding

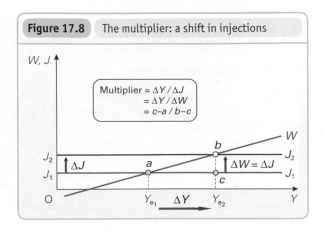

Figure 17.8 The multiplier: a shift in injections

Multiplier = $\Delta Y / \Delta J$
= $\Delta Y / \Delta W$
= $c-a / b-c$

to each of the W lines. It should be quite obvious that the flatter the W line is, the more Y will have increased.

The point here is that the less is withdrawn each time extra income is generated, the more will be recirculated and hence the bigger will be the rise in national income. The size of the multiplier thus varies inversely with the size of the *mpw*. The bigger the *mpw*, the smaller the multiplier; the smaller the *mpw*, the bigger the multiplier. In fact, the **multiplier formula** simply gives the multiplier as the inverse of the *mpw*:

$$k = 1/mpw$$

or alternatively, since $mpw + mpc_d = 1$ and thus $mpw = 1 - mpc_d$,

$$k = 1/(1 - mpc_d)$$

Thus if the *mpw* were $^1/_4$ (and hence the mpc_d were $^3/_4$), the multiplier would be 4. So if *J* increased by £10 billion, *Y* would increase by £40 billion.

But why is the multiplier given by the formula $1/mpw$? This can be illustrated by referring to Figure 17.8. The *mpw* is the slope of the *W* line. In the diagram, this is given by the amount $(b - c)/(c - a)$. The multiplier is defined as $\Delta Y/\Delta J$. In the diagram, this is the amount $(c - a)/(b - c)$. But this is merely the inverse of the *mpw*. Thus the multiplier equals $1/mpw$.[3]

Definitions

Principle of cumulative causation An initial event can cause an ultimate effect that is much larger.

(Injections) multiplier formula The formula for the multiplier: $K = 1/mpw$ or $1/(1 - mpc_d)$.

[3] In some elementary textbooks, the formula for the multiplier is given as $1/mps$. The reason for this is that it is assumed (for simplicity) that there is only one withdrawal, namely saving, and only one injection, namely investment. As soon as this assumption is dropped, $1/mps$ becomes the wrong formula.

THRESHOLD CONCEPT 15   CUMULATIVE CAUSATION

Economic effects can snowball

Once an economy starts to expand, growth is likely to gather pace. Once it starts slowing down, this can gather pace too and end up in a recession. There are many other examples in economics of things getting 'onto a roll'. A rising stock market is likely to breed confidence in investors and encourage them to buy. This 'destabilising speculation' (see pages 72–3) will then lead to further rises in share prices. A fall in stock market prices can lead to panic selling of shares. The booming stock market of the late 1990s and 2003–8, and the falls in the early 2000s and 2008–9 are good examples of this (see chart in Box 2.3 on page 54).

This phenomenon of things building on themselves is known as 'cumulative causation' and occurs throughout market economies. It is a *threshold concept* because it helps us to understand the built-in instability in many parts of the economy and in many economic situations.

Central to explaining cumulative causation is people's psychology. Good news creates confidence and this optimism causes people to behave in ways that build on the good news. Bad news creates pessimism and this leads to people behaving cautiously, which tends to reinforce the bad news.

Take two regions of an economy: an expanding region and a declining region. The expansion of the first region encourages workers to move there in search of jobs. The optimism in the

area causes long-term investment as firms have confidence in an expanding market. This encourages house building and other forms of investment in infrastructure and services. And so the region thrives. Meanwhile, the declining region suffers from deprivation as unemployment rises. This encourages people to move away and businesses to close. There is a further decline in jobs and further migration from the region.

Cumulative causation does not just occur at a macro level. If a company is successful, it is likely to find raising extra finance easier; it may be able to use its power more effectively to outcompete rivals. Giant companies, such as Microsoft, can gain all sorts of economies of scale, including network economies (see Case Study 7.4 on the student website), all of which help the process of building their power base. Success breeds success.

1. *How might cumulative causation work at the level of an individual firm that is losing market share?*
2. *Are there any market forces that work against cumulative causation? For instance, how might markets help to arrest the decline of a depressed region of the economy and slow down the expansion of a booming region?*

*LOOKING AT THE MATHS

The multiplier can be expressed as the first derivative of national income with respect to injections.

$$k = \frac{dY}{dJ}$$

Since in equilibrium $J = W$, it is also the first derivative of income with respect to withdrawals. Thus

$$k = \frac{dY}{dW}$$

The marginal propensity to withdraw (i.e. the slope of the withdrawals curve) is found by differentiating the withdrawals function:

$$mpw = \frac{dW}{dY} = \frac{1}{k}$$

Thus

$$k = \frac{1}{mpw}$$

The algebra of the multiplier is explored in Maths Case 17.1 on the student website, which does not use calculus, and Maths Case 17.2, which does.

A shift in withdrawals

A multiplied rise in income can also be caused by a fall in withdrawals. This is illustrated in Figure 17.9.

The withdrawals function shifts from W_1 to W_2. This means that, at the old equilibrium of Y_{e_1}, injections now exceed withdrawals by an amount $a - b$. This will cause national income to rise until a new equilibrium is reached at Y_{e_2} where $J = W_2$. Thus a downward shift of the withdrawals function of $a - b(\Delta W)$ causes a rise in national income of $c - a(\Delta Y)$. The multiplier in this case is given by $\Delta Y/\Delta W$: in

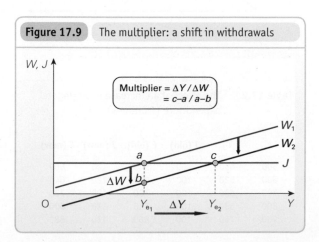

Figure 17.9   The multiplier: a shift in withdrawals

other words, $(c - a)/(a - b)$. Note that the multiplier is based on the *initial* fall in withdrawals. Once the multiplier effect has worked through, withdrawals will have risen back to equal injections at point c.

Why is the 'withdrawals multiplier' strictly speaking a negative figure?

The multiplier: the income and expenditure approach

The multiplier can also be demonstrated using the income/expenditure approach. Assume in Figure 17.10 that the aggregate expenditure function shifts to E_2. This could be due either to a rise in one or more of the three injections, or to a rise in the consumption of domestically produced goods (and hence a fall in withdrawals). Equilibrium national income will rise from Y_{e_1} to Y_{e_2}.

What is the size of the multiplier? The initial rise in expenditure was $b - a$. The resulting rise in income is $c - a$. The multiplier is thus $(c - a)/(b - a)$.

The effect is illustrated in Table 17.2. Consumption of domestic product (C_d) is shown in column 2 for various levels of national income (Y). For every £100 billion rise in Y, C_d

rises by £80 billion. Thus the $mpc_d = 0.8$. Assume initially that injections equal £100 billion at all levels of national income. Aggregate expenditure (column 4) equals $C_d + J$. Equilibrium national income is £700 billion. This is where $Y = E$.

Now assume that injections rise by £20 billion to £120 billion. Aggregate expenditure is now shown in the final column and is £20 billion higher than before at each level of national income (Y). At the original equilibrium national income (£700 billion), aggregate expenditure is now £720 billion. This excess of E over Y of £20 billion will generate extra incomes and continue doing so as long as E remains above Y. Equilibrium is reached at £800 billion, where once more $Y = E$. The initial rise in aggregate expenditure of £20 billion (from £700bn to £720bn) has led to an eventual rise in both national income and aggregate expenditure of £100 billion. The multiplier is thus 5 (i.e. £100bn/£20bn). But this is equal to $1/(1 - 0.8)$ or $1/(1 - mpc_d)$.

1. *What determines the slope of the E function?*
2. *How does the slope of the E function affect the size of the multiplier? (Try drawing diagrams with E functions of different slopes and see what happens when they shift.)*

The multiplier: a numerical illustration

The multiplier effect does not work instantaneously. When there is an increase in injections, whether investment, government expenditure or exports, it takes time before this brings about the full multiplied rise in national income.

Consider the following example. Let us assume for simplicity that the *mpw* is $1/2$. This will give an mpc_d of $1/2$ also. Let us also assume that investment (an injection) rises by £160 million and stays at the new higher level. Table 17.3 shows what will happen.

As firms purchase more machines and construct more factories, the incomes of those who produce machines and those who work in the construction industry will increase by £160 million. When this extra income is received by households, whether as wages or profits, half will be withdrawn ($mpw = 1/2$) and half will be spent on the goods and services of domestic firms. This increase in consumption thus generates additional incomes for firms of £80 million over and above the initial £160 million (which is still being generated

TC 15
p535

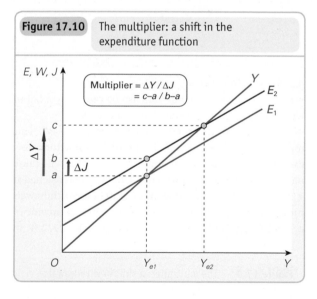

Figure 17.10 The multiplier: a shift in the expenditure function

Multiplier = $\Delta Y / \Delta J$
= $c - a / b - a$

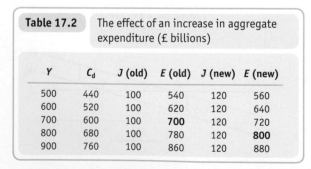

Table 17.2 The effect of an increase in aggregate expenditure (£ billions)

Y	C_d	J (old)	E (old)	J (new)	E (new)
500	440	100	540	120	560
600	520	100	620	120	640
700	600	100	**700**	120	720
800	680	100	780	120	**800**
900	760	100	860	120	880

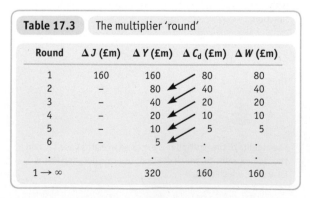

Table 17.3 The multiplier 'round'

Round	ΔJ (£m)	ΔY (£m)	ΔC_d (£m)	ΔW (£m)
1	160	160	80	80
2	–	80	40	40
3	–	40	20	20
4	–	20	10	10
5	–	10	5	5
6	–	5	.	.
.		.	.	.
$1 \to \infty$		320	160	160

BOX 17.4 | DERIVING THE MULTIPLIER FORMULA

An algebraic proof

The formula for the multiplier can be derived using simple algebra. First of all, remember how we defined the multiplier:

$$k \equiv \Delta Y/\Delta J \qquad (1)$$

and the marginal propensity to withdraw:

$$mpw \equiv \Delta W/\Delta Y \qquad (2)$$

If we now take the inverse of equation (2), we get

$$1/mpw \equiv \Delta Y/\Delta W \qquad (3)$$

But in equilibrium we know that $W = J$. Hence any change in injections must be matched by a change in withdrawals and vice versa, to ensure that withdrawals and injections remain equal. Thus

$$\Delta W = \Delta J \qquad (4)$$

Substituting equation (4) in equation (3) gives

$$1/mpw = \Delta Y/\Delta J \, (= k)$$

i.e. the multiplier equals $1/mpw$.

---

in each time period). When this additional £80 million of incomes is received by households (round 2), again half will be withdrawn and half will go on consumption of domestic product. This increases national income by a further £40 million (round 3). And so each time we go around the circular flow of income, national income increases, but by only half as much as the previous time ($mpc_d = {}^1/_2$).

If we add up the additional income generated in each round (assuming the process goes on indefinitely), the total will be £320 million: twice the rise in injections. The multiplier is 2.

The bigger the mpc_d (and hence the smaller the mpw), the more will expenditure rise each time national income rises, and hence the bigger will be the multiplier.

*The multiplier: some qualifications

(This section examines the multiplier formula in more detail. You may omit it without affecting the flow of the argument.)

Some possible errors can easily be made in calculating the value of the multiplier. These often arise from a confusion over the meaning of terms.

The marginal propensity to consume domestic product
Remember the formula for the multiplier:

$$k = 1/(1 - mpc_d)$$

It is important to realise just what is meant by the mpc_d. It is the proportion of a rise in households' gross (i.e. pre-tax-and-benefit) income that actually accrues to domestic firms. It thus excludes that part of consumption that is spent on imports and that part which is paid to the government in VAT and other indirect taxes.

Up to now we have also been basing the mpc on gross income. As Case Study 17.2 on the student website shows, however, the mpc is often based on *disposable* (i.e. post-tax-and-benefit) income. After all, when consumers decide how much to spend, it is their disposable income rather than their gross income that they will consider. So how do we derive

the mpc_d (based on gross income) from the mpc based on disposable income (mpc')? To do this, we must use the following formula:

$$mpc_d = mpc'(1 - t_E)(1 - t_Y) - mpm$$

where t_Y is the marginal rate of income tax, and t_E is the marginal rate of expenditure tax.

To illustrate this formula consider the following effects of an increase in national income of £100 million. It is assumed that $t_Y = 20$ per cent, $t_E = 10$ per cent and $mpc = 7/8$. It is also assumed that the mps (from gross income) $= 1/10$ and the mpm (from gross income) $= 13/100$. Table 17.4 sets out the figures.

Gross income rises by £100 million. Of this, £20 million is taken in income tax ($t_Y = 20$ per cent). This leaves a rise in disposable income of £80 million. Of this, £10 million is saved ($mps = 1/10$) and £70 million is spent. Of this, £7 million goes in expenditure taxes ($t_E = 10$ per cent) and £13 million leaks abroad ($mpm = 13/100$). This leaves £50 million that goes on the consumption of domestic product ($mpc_d = 50/100 = {}^1/_2$). Substituting these figures in the above formula gives:

$$
\begin{aligned}
mpc_d &= mpc(1 - t_E)(1 - t_Y) - mpm \\
&= \frac{7}{8}\left(1 - \frac{1}{10}\right)\left(1 - \frac{2}{10}\right) - \frac{13}{100} \\
&= \left(\frac{7}{8} \times \frac{9}{10} \times \frac{8}{10}\right) - \frac{13}{100} \\
&= \frac{63}{100} - \frac{13}{100} = \frac{50}{100} = \frac{1}{2}
\end{aligned}
$$

Table 17.4 Calculating the mpc_d

	ΔY	$-$	ΔT_Y	$=$	ΔY_{dis}		
(£m)	100		20		80		
	ΔY_{dis}	$-$	ΔS	$=$	ΔC		
£m)	80		10		70		
	ΔC	$-$	ΔT_E	$-$	ΔM	$=$	ΔC_d
(£m)	70		7		13		50

TC 15
p535

Note that the mpc_d, mps, mpm and mpt are all based on the rise in *gross* income, not disposable income. They are 50/100, 10/100, 13/100 and 27/100 respectively.

Maths Case 17.3 on the student website derives the multiplier formula when the propensities to consume, save and import are all based on *disposable* as opposed to gross income.

Assume that the rate of income tax is 15 per cent, the rate of expenditure tax is 12.5 per cent, the mps is $^1/_{20}$, the mpm is $^1/_8$ and the mpc (from disposable income) is $^{16}/_{17}$. What is the mpc_d? Construct a table like Table 17.4, assuming again that national income rises by £100 million.

The effects of changes in injections and withdrawals on other injections and withdrawals

In order to work out the size of a multiplied rise or fall in income, it is necessary to know first the size of the initial *total* change in injections and/or withdrawals. The trouble is that a change in one injection or withdrawal can affect others. For example, a rise in income taxes will reduce not only consumption, but also saving, imports and the revenue from indirect taxes. Thus the total rise in withdrawals will be *less* than the rise in income taxes.

Give some other examples of changes in one injection or withdrawal that can affect others.

Section summary

1. Equilibrium national income can be shown on the 45° line diagram at the point where $W = J$ and $Y = E$.

2. If there is an increase in injections (or a reduction in withdrawals), there will be a multiplied rise in national income. The multiplier is defined as $\Delta Y/\Delta J$.

3. The size of the multiplier depends on the marginal propensity to withdraw (mpw). The smaller the mpw, the less will be withdrawn each time incomes are generated round the circular flow, and thus the more will go round again as *additional* demand for domestic product. The multiplier formula is $k = 1/mpw$ or $1/(1 - mpc_d)$.

*4. When working out the size of the multiplier, you must be careful to identify clearly the mpc_d (which is based on *gross* income and only includes expenditure that actually accrues to domestic firms) and not to confuse it with the mpc based on *disposable* income (which includes consumption of imports and the payment of indirect taxes). It is also necessary to identify the *full* changes in injections and withdrawals on which any multiplier effect is based.

17.3 THE SIMPLE KEYNESIAN ANALYSIS OF UNEMPLOYMENT AND INFLATION

'Full-employment' national income

The simple Keynesian theory assumes that there is a maximum level of national output, and hence real income, which can be obtained at any one time. If the equilibrium level of income is at this level, there will be no deficiency of aggregate demand. This level of income is referred to as the *full-employment level of national income*. In practice, there would still be some unemployment at this level because of structural, frictional and seasonal unemployment (see section 15.5).

Governments of the 1950s, 1960s and early 1970s aimed to achieve this full-employment income (Y_F), if inflation and the balance of payments permitted. To do this, they attempted to manipulate the level of aggregate demand.

Many countries around the world in the late 2000s used fiscal and monetary policies to stimulate aggregate demand in an attempt to combat a deepening recession (see Chapter 16 page 512).

The deflationary gap

If the equilibrium level of national income (Y_e) is *below* the full-employment level (Y_F), there will be excess capacity in the economy and hence demand-deficient unemployment.

There will be what is known as a ***deflationary*** or ***recessionary gap***. This is illustrated in Figure 17.11.

Definitions

Full-employment level of national income The level of national income at which there is no deficiency of demand.

Deflationary or recessionary gap The shortfall of national expenditure below national income (and injections).

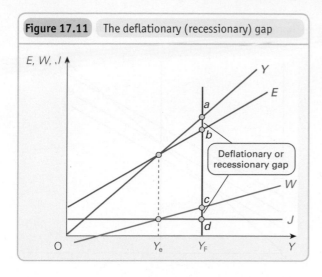

Figure 17.11 The deflationary (recessionary) gap

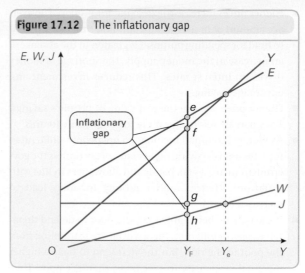

Figure 17.12 The inflationary gap

The full-employment level of national income (Y_F) is represented by the vertical line. The equilibrium level of national income is Y_e, where $W = J$ and $Y = E$. The deflationary gap is $a - b$: namely, the amount that the E line is below the 45° line at the full-employment level of income (Y_F). It is also $c - d$: the amount that injections fall short of withdrawals at the full-employment level of income.

Note that the size of the deflationary gap is *less* than the amount by which Y_e falls short of Y_F. This provides another illustration of the multiplier. If injections were raised by $c - d$, income would rise by $Y_F - Y_e$. The multiplier is thus given by

$$\frac{Y_F - Y_e}{c - d}$$

In this simple Keynesian model, then, the cure for demand-deficient unemployment is to close the deflationary gap. An increase in aggregate expenditure is needed. This could be achieved by an expansionary *fiscal* policy of increasing government expenditure and/or lowering taxes, or by an expansionary *monetary* policy of reducing interest rates and increasing the amount of money in the economy, thereby encouraging extra consumption and investment. Either way, if the deflationary gap is successfully closed, there will be a multiplied rise in income of $Y_F - Y_e$. Equilibrium national income will be restored to the full-employment level.

The inflationary gap

If, at the full-employment level of (real) income, aggregate expenditure exceeds national income, there will be a problem of *excess* demand. Y_e will be above Y_F. The problem is that Y_F represents a real ceiling to output. In the short run, real national income *cannot* expand beyond this point.[4] Y_e

cannot be reached. The result will therefore be demand-pull inflation.[5]

This situation involves an ***inflationary gap***. This is the amount by which aggregate expenditure exceeds national income or injections exceed withdrawals at the full-employment level of national income. This is illustrated by the gaps $e - f$ and $g - h$ in Figure 17.12.

To eliminate this inflation, the inflationary gap must be closed by either raising withdrawals or lowering injections, or some combination of the two, until Y_e equals Y_F. A reduction in aggregate expenditure could be achieved through a deliberate government policy of deflation. This could be either a contractionary *fiscal* policy of lowering government expenditure and/or raising taxes, or a contractionary *monetary* policy of raising interest rates and reducing the amount of money in the economy.

Even if the government does not actively pursue a deflationary policy, the inflationary gap may still close *automatically*, though this may take some time. The mechanisms by which this could occur would move the E line down and the J line up and/or the W line up. These include the following:

- Higher domestic prices will lead to fewer exports being sold and more imports being bought in preference to the now dearer home-produced goods. The precise effect will depend on what happens to exchange rates – a subject we explore in Chapter 26.

Definition

Inflationary gap The excess of national expenditure over income (and injections over withdrawals) at the full-employment level of national income.

---

4 Note that the horizontal axis in the 45° line diagram represents *real* national income. If incomes were to rise by, say, 10 per cent but prices also rose by 10 per cent, real income would not have risen at all. People could not buy any more than before. In such a case, there will have been no rightward movement along the horizontal axis.

5 Except with increased overtime working. In this simple model, we assume that this is not possible.

- Higher prices increase the demand for money. The average amount of money that people and firms would need to hold for spending purposes is greater. In the absence of an increase in the money supply, the shortage of money drives up interest rates. This reduces investment and encourages saving.
- Higher prices reduce the real value of people's savings. They may therefore save more to compensate for this.
- As money (nominal) incomes go up, people will tend to find themselves paying higher rates of tax (unless the government increases tax bands and allowances in line with inflation). Hence, higher money incomes lead to increased taxes.
- If the rich are better able than the poor to defend themselves against inflation, there will be a redistribution from the poor to the rich. But the rich tend to have a higher marginal propensity to save (*mps*) than the poor. Thus saving will rise and consumption will fall.

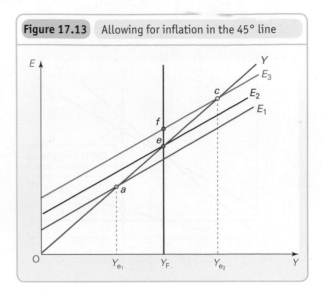

Figure 17.13 Allowing for inflation in the 45° line

 The present level of a country's exports is £12 billion; investment is £2 billion; government expenditure is £4 billion; total consumer spending (not C_d) is £36 billion; imports are £12 billion; and expenditure taxes are £2 billion. The economy is currently in equilibrium. It is estimated that an income of £50 billion is necessary to generate full employment. The mps is 0.1, the mpt is 0.05 and the mpm is 0.1.

(a) Is there an inflationary or deflationary gap in this situation?

(b) What is the size of the gap? (Don't confuse this with the difference between Ye and Y_F.)

(c) What would be the appropriate government policies to close this gap?

The multiplier and the full-employment level of national income

The simple analysis of the preceding pages implies that up to the full-employment level of national income (Y_F), output and employment can increase with no rise in prices at all. There is no inflation because the economy's deflationary gap is being closed. Hence, increases in aggregate expenditure set in motion the multiplier process resulting in a multiplied increase in real national income.

At Y_F no further rises in output are possible. Any further rise in aggregate demand is entirely reflected in higher prices. An inflationary gap opens. Hence, the additional demand no longer generates an increase in output. There is no increase in real national income because the real value of expenditure has not increased. Additional sums of spending on domestically produced goods and service are purely *nominal* reflecting only higher prices. The volume of purchases and, hence, the level of output is unchanged.

In this simple model, therefore, resource constraints become effective at the full-employment national income

level. Up to this point, additional demand generates increases in output without inflation. At the full-employment national income level any further increases in aggregate demand generate only inflation. The multiplier process ceases to operate. We can use the 45° line diagram to illustrate these ideas as shown in Figure 17.13.

Assume that the economy is initially at Y_{e_1} where E_1 crosses the 45° line. Now let us assume that there is a rise in aggregate demand. The E line shifts to E_2 resulting in a full multiplied rise in real income. Therefore, equilibrium national income rises to Y_F.

Consider now a further rise in aggregate demand which causes the E line to shift to E_3. An inflationary gap opens up, illustrated by the gap $e - f$. This time the increase in demand will be reflected only in higher prices with no increase in output. Equilibrium real income will be unchanged. If there is no compensating increase in money supply, the E line will fall back to E_2. The means by which this happens are those we identified above as the automatic mechanisms that tend to close an inflationary gap.

Unemployment and inflation at the same time

Our simple model implies that either inflation *or* unemployment can occur, but not both simultaneously. Two important qualifications need to be made to this analysis to explain the occurrence of both unemployment *and* inflation at the same time.

First, there are *other* types of inflation and unemployment not caused by an excess or deficiency of aggregate demand: for example, cost-push and expectations-generated inflation; frictional and structural unemployment.

Thus, even if a government could manipulate national income so that the equilibrium income level, Y_e, and full-employment income level, Y_F, coincided, this would not eliminate all inflation and unemployment – only demand-pull inflation and demand-deficient unemployment. Keynesians argue, therefore, that governments should use a whole package of policies, each tailored to the specific type of problem. But certainly one of the most important of these policies will be the management of aggregate demand.

Second, not all firms operate with the same degree of slack. Thus a rise in aggregate demand can lead to *both* a reduction in unemployment *and* a rise in prices: some firms responding to the rise in demand by taking up slack and hence increasing output; other firms, having little or no slack, responding by raising prices; others doing both. Similarly, labour markets have different degrees of slack and therefore the rise in demand will lead to various mixes of higher wages and lower unemployment.

 How does the above argument about firms' responses to a rise in demand relate to the shape of their marginal cost curves?

These types of argument were used to justify a belief in a downward-sloping Phillips curve (see Box 15.6) by the majority of economists and politicians in the 1960s and into the 1970s. A modified version of these arguments is still used today by Keynesian economists. This is examined in more detail in Chapter 21.

The problem is that if there is a trade-off between unemployment and inflation, demand management policies used to make one of the objectives better will succeed only in making the other one worse. It then becomes a matter of political judgement which of the objectives is the right one to direct demand management policies towards. Is *inflation* public enemy number one, or is it *unemployment*?

KI 36
p451

The multiplier and inflation

We saw earlier how the multiplier process is affected by the constraint posed by the full-employment national income level. We have now introduced the argument that inflation can begin to occur *before* the full-employment level of income is reached. This means that increases in aggregate demand no longer increase real national income by the full extent of the multiplier even before the full-employment output level is reached.

We might expect inflationary pressures to become more significant, and the size of the multiplier to become smaller, the closer the economy is to the full-employment national income level. This is because an increasingly large part of the increase in demand is being reflected in higher prices and a smaller part in higher output.

Section summary

1. If equilibrium national income (Y_e) is below the full-employment level of national income (Y_F), there will be a deflationary (recessionary) gap. This gap is equal to $Y - E$ or $W - J$ at Y_F. This gap can be closed by expansionary fiscal or monetary policy, which will then cause a multiplied rise in national income (up to a level of Y_F) and will eliminate demand-deficient unemployment.

2. If equilibrium national income exceeds the full-employment level of income, the inability of output to expand to meet this excess demand will lead to demand-pull inflation. This excess demand gives an inflationary gap, which is equal to $E - Y$ or $J - W$ at Y_F. This gap can be closed by deflationary policies.

3. This simple analysis tends to imply that aggregate demand can expand up to Y_F without generating inflation. In practice, inflationary pressures are likely to emerge at lower levels of national income, but become more significant as national income approaches its full-employment level. As it does so, resource constraints and bottlenecks are increasingly likely to occur.

4. An initial rise in aggregate demand (and an upward shift in the E curve) will be eroded to the extent that inflation reduces the real value of this demand: the E curve will shift back downwards again somewhat, unless there is a further boost to demand.

17.4 THE KEYNESIAN ANALYSIS OF THE BUSINESS CYCLE

Volatility of aggregate demand

In the previous sections of the chapter we developed the simple Keynesian model. The model shows how fluctuations in aggregate demand can have multiplied effects on output and employment. This is an important insight because we know that economies are inherently volatile. Therefore, Keynesian analysis of the business cycle focuses on fluctuations in aggregate demand.

The instability of aggregate demand, Keynesians argue, is central to explaining the business cycle. In the upturn (phase 1), aggregate demand starts to rise. It rises rapidly in the expansionary phase (phase 2). It then slows down and may start to fall in the peaking-out phase (phase 3). It then falls or remains relatively stagnant in the recession (phase 4) (see Figure 15.5 on page 460).

Keynesians also argue that market imperfections or frictions can magnify the impact of the instability on aggregate

BOX 17.5   ALLOWING FOR INFLATION IN THE 45° LINE DIAGRAM

The relationship between the AD/AS framework and the Keynesian cross

In this box we consider more formally how we can extend the simple Keynesian model to *allow* for inflation. In other words, the price level is no longer assumed to be constant. Here we introduce a new model: the aggregate demand (*AD*) and aggregate supply (*AS*) model. This is a model we develop later (in Chapter 20) and just the bare bones of the model are considered here.

The *AD/AS* framework enables us to incorporate prices within the context of aggregate demand and aggregate supply. In this box we show the relationship between this framework and the 45° line diagram, known as the 'Keynesian Cross'.

The *AD/AS* model

Consider the top half of the diagram, part (a). AD_1 and AS are representative aggregate demand and aggregate supply curves. They show how aggregate demand and supply vary with the overall level of prices in the economy (*P*). The *AD* curve is downward sloping while the *AS* curve is upward sloping. But what is the economics behind these curves?

The aggregate demand curve (AD).   The downward-sloping *AD* curve captures the idea that economic agents will demand fewer domestically produced goods and services as the economy's general price level rises (a movement upwards along the curve). Reasons for this include:

- people switching from domestic products to now relatively cheaper imported products;
- an increase in the demand for money (to pay the higher prices), which pushes up interest rates and reduces spending;

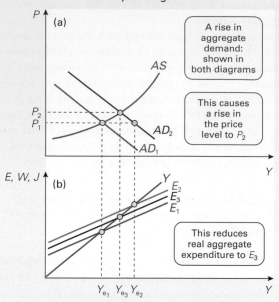

Allowing for inflation in the 45° line and AD/AS diagrams

> A rise in aggregate demand: shown in both diagrams

> This causes a rise in the price level to P_2

> This reduces real aggregate expenditure to E_3

- a decrease in the real value of people's savings, which increases the incentive to save;
- people perhaps finding that they are paying a larger proportion of their incomes in taxes as money incomes rise.

A *shift* in the AD curve will occur if, for any given price level, there is a change in any of the components of aggregate

---

demand. For instance, the reluctance of firms to change prices because of menu costs (the costs incurred in adjusting prices) could see them change output levels substantially in response to fluctuations in demand (see section 16.5). When there are frictions to prices adjusting then changes in aggregate demand will tend to have larger effects on output and employment levels: the multiplier effect is larger.

The volatility of aggregate demand must reflect the volatility of the expenditure components: *C, I, G, X* and *M*. However, Keynesians argue that central to the volatility of aggregate demand is the volatility of private-sector spending. Hence, this volatility will often require the authorities to devise appropriate stabilisation policies to iron out the fluctuations in economic activity that result. A more stable economy, they argue, provides a better climate for investment. With more investment, *potential* output grows more rapidly. This, given appropriate demand management policy, then allows a faster growth in actual output to be maintained. We examine demand management policies (fiscal and monetary) in Chapter 22.

Instability of investment: the accelerator

Of the expenditure components that comprise aggregate demand the most volatile is investment (*I*). To illustrate this volatility consider Figure 17.14, which shows the annual rate of growth in investment for a sample of industrialised countries.

When an economy begins to recover from a recession, investment can rise very rapidly. When the growth of the economy slows down, however, investment can fall dramatically, and during a recession it can all but disappear. Since investment is an injection into the circular flow of income, these changes in investment will cause multiplied changes in income and thus heighten a boom or deepen a recession.

The theory that relates investment to *changes* in national income is called the **accelerator theory**. The term 'accelerator' is used because a relatively modest rise in national income can cause a much larger percentage rise in investment.

When there is no change in income and hence no change in consumption, the only investment needed is a relatively

demand. For an example, an increase in consumer confidence may encourage increased consumer spending (C) and so the AD curve shifts to the right.

The aggregate supply curve (AS).   The upward-sloping AS curve shows firms supplying more as the economy's general price level rises. The curve is drawn on the assumption that various things remain constant. These include wage rates and other input prices, technology and the total supply of factors of production. Because we are holding wages and other input prices constant, as the prices of firms' products rise it becomes profitable for them to expand their output.

The aggregate supply curve will shift if any of the variables that are held constant when we draw the curve now change. For example, a rise in wage rates throughout the economy reduces the amount that firms wish to produce at any level of prices. The AS curve shifts to the left.

The Keynesian cross model

The bottom half of the diagram, part (b), is the 45° line diagram – the Keynesian cross model. Alongside the 45° line ($Y = C_d + W$) are three aggregate expenditure lines (E_1, E_2 and E_3), which show aggregate demand (E) dependent on the level of national income.

Combining AD/AS and the 45° line models

We are now in a position to combine our two models. Assume initially that the economy is in equilibrium at national income level Y_{e_1}, where aggregate demand (AD_1) equals aggregate supply (AS) and where the aggregate expenditure line (E_1) crosses the 45° line.

Now assume that there is a rise in aggregate demand caused, say, by an increase in consumer confidence that results in a rise in consumption. In part (a) of the diagram the AD curve sifts rightwards from AD_1 to AD_2. Meanwhile in part (b), the E line shifts to E_2.

If this rise in demand were to lead to a full multiplied rise in real income, equilibrium income would rise to Y_{e_2}. For this to happen we would require the AS curve in part (a) to be a flat horizontal line, with no general price rises resulting from the increase in the aggregate demand. If, as is more likely, prices do rise, giving an upward-sloping AS curve, the increase in aggregate demand from AD_1 to AD_2 results in the price level rising to P_2.

Hence, part of the increase in demand is reflected in higher prices and only *part* is reflected in higher output. Equilibrium real income therefore rises only to Y_{e_3} and not Y_{e_2}. In other words, it does not rise by the full extent of the multiplier.

In part (b) of the diagram, the effect of the higher prices is to reduce the real value of expenditure (E). In other words, a given amount of money buys fewer goods. If there is no compensating increase in money supply (which would shift the AD curve further to the right in diagram (a)), the E line must fall to the point where it intersects the 45° line at a real income of Y_{e_3}; the E line must fall to E_3.

TC 13
p453

 Assume that the AS curve is flat up to the full-employment national income level, Y_F, after which it becomes vertical. Combining the AD/AS and 45° line models, illustrate the effect on the multiplier of an increase in AD at output levels below Y_F and at Y_F.

Figure 17.14   Annual growth in investment

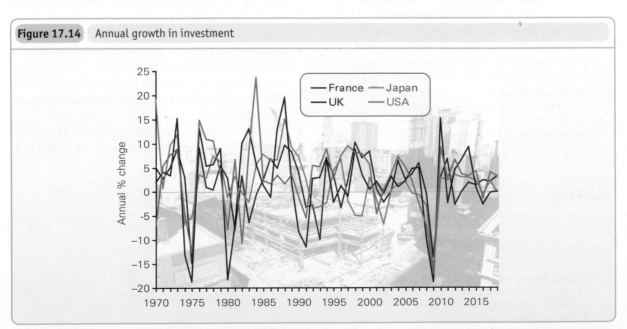

Notes: Investment growth is the growth in gross capital formation (gross fixed capital formation plus net change in inventories plus net acquisitions less disposal of valuables).
Source: Based on data in *AMECO Database, European Commission, DGECFIN.*

small amount of replacement investment for machines that are wearing out or have become obsolete. When income and consumption increase, however, there will have to be *new* investment in order to increase production capacity. This is called *induced investment* (I_i). Once this has taken place, investment will fall back to mere replacement investment (I_r) unless there is a further rise in income and consumption.

Thus induced investment depends on *changes* in national income (ΔY):

$$I_i = \alpha \, \Delta Y$$

where α is the amount by which induced investment depends on changes in national income, and is known as the **accelerator coefficient**. Thus if a £1 million *rise* in national income caused the *level* of induced investment to be £2 million, the accelerator coefficient would be 2.

The size of α depends on the economy's **marginal capital/output ratio** ($\Delta K/\Delta Y$). If an increase in the country's capital stock of £2 million (i.e. an investment of £2 million) is required to produce £1 million extra national output, the marginal capital/output ratio would be 2. Other things being equal, the accelerator coefficient and the marginal capital/output ratio will therefore be the same.

How is it that the cost of an investment to a firm will exceed the value of the output that the investment will yield? Surely that would make the investment unprofitable? (Clue: the increase in output refers to output over a specific time period, usually a year.)

Definitions

Accelerator theory The level of investment depends on the rate of change of national income, and as a result tends to be subject to substantial fluctuations.

Induced investment Investment that firms make to enable them to meet extra consumer demand.

Accelerator coefficient The level of induced investment as a proportion of a rise in national income: $\alpha = I_i/\Delta Y$.

Marginal capital/output ratio The amount of extra capital (in money terms) required to produce a £1 increase in national output. Since $I_i = \Delta K$, the marginal capital/output ratio $\Delta K/\Delta Y$ equals the accelerator coefficient (α).

The following example (see Table 17.5) illustrates some important features of the accelerator. It looks at the investment decisions made by a firm in response to changes in the demand for its product. The firm is taken as representative of firms throughout the economy. The example is based on various assumptions:

- The firm's machines last exactly 10 years and then need replacing.
- At the start of the example, the firm has ten machines in place, one 10 years old, one 9 years old, one 8 years old, one 7, one 6 and so on. Thus one machine needs replacing each year.
- Machines produce exactly 100 units of output per year. This figure cannot be varied.
- The firm always adjusts its output and its stock of machinery to match consumer demand.

The example shows what happens to the firm's investment over a six-year period when there is first a substantial rise in consumer demand, then a levelling off and then a slight fall. It illustrates the following features of the accelerator.

- *Investment will rise when the growth of national income (and hence consumer demand) is rising ($\Delta Y_{t+1} > \Delta Y_t$).* Years 1 to 2 illustrate this (see Table 17.5). The rise in consumer demand is zero in year 1 and 1000 units in year 2. Investment rises from 1 to 11 machines. The growth in investment may be considerably greater than the growth in consumer demand, giving a large accelerator effect. Between years 1 and 2, consumer demand doubles but investment goes up by a massive *11* times!
- *Investment will be constant even when national income is growing, if the increase in income this year is the same as last year ($\Delta Y_{t+1} = \Delta Y_t$).* In years 2 to 3, consumer demand continues to rise by 1000 units, but investment is constant at 11 machines.
- *Investment will fall even if national income is still growing, if the rate of growth is slowing down ($\Delta Y_{t+1} < \Delta Y_t$).* In years 3 to 4, consumer demand rises by 500 units (rather than 1000 units as in the previous year). Investment falls from 11 to 6 machines.
- If national income is constant, investment will be confined to replacement investment only. In years 4 to 5,

Table 17.5   The accelerator effect

				Year			
	0	1	2	3	4	5	6
Quantity demanded by consumers (sales)	1000	1000	2000	3000	3500	3500	3400
Number of machines required	10	10	20	30	35	35	34
Induced investment (I_i) (extra machines)		0	10	10	5	0	0
Replacement investment (I_r)		1	1	1	1	1	0
Total investment ($I_i + I_r$)		1	11	11	6	1	0

investment falls to the one machine requiring replacement.

- *If national income falls, even if only slightly, investment can be wiped out altogether.* In years 5 to 6, even though demand has fallen by only 1/35, investment will fall to zero. Not even the machine that is wearing out will be replaced.

In practice, the accelerator will not be as dramatic and clear-cut as this. The effect will be extremely difficult to predict for the following reasons:

- Many firms may have spare capacity and/or carry stocks. This will enable them to meet extra demand without having to invest.
- The willingness of firms to invest will depend on their confidence in *future* demand (see Box 17.3). Firms are not going to rush out and spend large amounts of money on machines that will last many years if it is quite likely that demand will fall back again the following year.

- Firms may make their investment plans a long time in advance and may be unable to change them quickly.
- Even if firms do decide to invest more, the producer goods industries may not have the capacity to meet a sudden surge in demand for machines.
- Machines do not as a rule suddenly wear out. A firm could thus delay replacing machines and keep the old ones for a bit longer if it was uncertain about its future level of demand.

All these points tend to reduce the magnitude of the accelerator and make it very difficult to predict. Nevertheless, the effect still exists. Firms still take note of changes in consumer demand when deciding how much to invest.

Box 17.6 looks at how fluctuations in investment in the UK specifically have typically been far more severe than fluctuations in national income. However, similar findings can be observed in many countries (see also Figure (b) in Box 17.3 on page 531). This tends to support the idea that significant accelerator effects contribute towards the instability of economies.

The multiplier/accelerator interaction

If there is an initial change in injections or withdrawals, then theoretically this will set off a chain reaction between the multiplier and the accelerator. For example, if there is a rise in government expenditure, this will lead to a multiplied rise in national income. But this *rise* in national income will set off an accelerator effect: firms will respond to the rise in income and the resulting rise in consumer demand by investing more. But this rise in investment constitutes a further rise in injections and thus will lead to a second multiplied rise in income. If this rise in income is larger than the first, there will then be a second rise in investment (the accelerator), which in turn will cause a third rise in income (the multiplier). And so the process continues indefinitely.

But does this lead to an exploding rise in national income? Will a single rise in injections cause national income to go on rising for ever? The answer is no, for two reasons. The first is that national income, in real terms, cannot go on rising faster than the growth in potential output. It will bump up against the ceiling of full employment, whether of labour or of other resources.

A second reason is that, if investment is to go on rising, it is not enough that national income should merely go on *rising*: instead, national income must *rise faster and faster*. Once the growth in national income slows down, investment will begin to fall, and then the whole process will be reversed. A fall in investment will lead to a fall in national income, which will lead to a massive fall in investment. The multiplier/accelerator interaction is shown more formally in Table 17.6. A numerical example is given in Case Study 17.8 on the student website.

Fluctuations in stocks

Firms hold stocks (inventories) of finished goods. These stocks tend to fluctuate with the course of the business cycle, and these fluctuations in stocks themselves contribute to fluctuations in output.

Imagine an economy that is recovering from a recession. At first, firms may be cautious about increasing production.

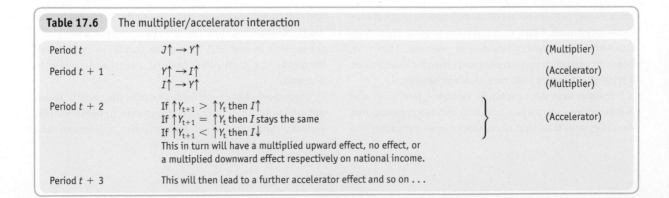

Table 17.6	The multiplier/accelerator interaction	
Period t	$J\uparrow \rightarrow Y\uparrow$	(Multiplier)
Period $t + 1$	$Y\uparrow \rightarrow I\uparrow$	(Accelerator)
	$I\uparrow \rightarrow Y\uparrow$	(Multiplier)
Period $t + 2$	If $\uparrow Y_{t+1} > \uparrow Y_t$ then $I\uparrow$	
	If $\uparrow Y_{t+1} = \uparrow Y_t$ then I stays the same	(Accelerator)
	If $\uparrow Y_{t+1} < \uparrow Y_t$ then $I\downarrow$	
	This in turn will have a multiplied upward effect, no effect, or a multiplied downward effect respectively on national income.	
Period $t + 3$	This will then lead to a further accelerator effect and so on . . .	

BOX 17.6   HAS THERE BEEN AN ACCELERATOR EFFECT IN THE UK?

The volatility of investment

If we look at the period from 1960 to 2016, the average annual rate of increase in GDP was 2.5 per cent while that for investment was only slightly higher at 2.8 per cent. But the key point is that investment is highly volatile. Economic growth has fluctuated with the business cycle; but investment has been subject to far more violent swings.

If we look at the chart we can see that the fastest annual rate of increase in GDP was 9.8 per cent (Q1 1973), while the sharpest rate of decline was 6.1 per cent (Q1 2009). By contrast, the fastest annual rate of increase in investment was 26.4 per cent (Q1 1964), while the sharpest rate of decline was 20.7 per cent (Q2 2009).

These figures are consistent with the accelerator theory, which argues that the *level* of investment depends on the *rate*

of change of national income. A relatively small percentage change in national income can give a much bigger percentage change in investment.

The ups and downs in GDP and investment do not completely match because there are additional factors that determine investment other than simply changes in national income. These factors include interest rates, the availability of finance, exchange rates and businesses' expectations of future demand.

1. Can you identify any time lags in the graph? Why might there be time lags?
2. Why does investment in the construction and producer goods industries tend to fluctuate more than investment in retailing and the service industries?

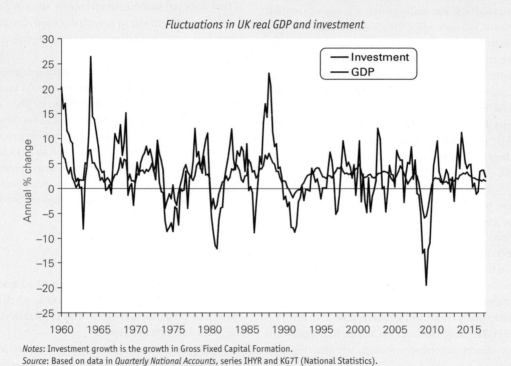

Fluctuations in UK real GDP and investment

Notes: Investment growth is the growth in Gross Fixed Capital Formation.
Source: Based on data in *Quarterly National Accounts*, series IHYR and KG7T (National Statistics).

Doing so may involve taking on more labour or making additional investment. Firms may not want to make these commitments if the recovery could soon peter out. They may, therefore, run down their stocks rather than increase output. Initially the recovery from recession will be slow.

If the recovery does continue, however, firms will start to gain more confidence and will increase production. Also, they will find that their stocks have got rather low

and will need building up. This gives a further boost to production, and for a time the growth in output will exceed the growth in demand. This extra growth in output will then, via the multiplier, lead to a further increase in demand.

Once stocks have been built up again, the growth in output will slow down to match the growth in demand. This slowing down in output will, via the accelerator and multiplier, contribute to the ending of the expansionary phase of the business cycle.

As the economy slows down, firms will find their stocks building up. Unless they cut back on production immediately, this increase in stocks cushions the effect of falling demand on output and employment.

If the recession continues, however, firms will be unwilling to go on building up stocks. But as firms attempt to reduce their stocks back to the desired level, production will fall *below* the level of sales, despite the fact that sales themselves are lower. This could lead to a dramatic fall in output and, via the multiplier, to an even bigger fall in sales.

Eventually, once stocks have been run down to the minimum, production will have to rise again to match the level of sales. This will contribute to a recovery and the whole cycle will start again.

Fluctuations in borrowing and debt

During an upswing, when confidence is high, businesses will be more willing to borrow to invest and consumers will be more willing to borrow to spend. At the same time, banks will be more willing to lend, being confident in people's ability to repay. The extra borrowing and lending fuel the expansion. Private debt as a percentage of GDP thus tends to rise.

During a recession, banks are less willing to lend and both firms and consumers are less willing to borrow, fearing their ability to repay. Indeed, many people will seek to reduce their debts by increasing repayments. The reduction in borrowing and debt will push the economy deeper into recession.

We explored these balance sheet effects in Box 17.2 (page 528).

Determinants of the course of the business cycle

We are now in a position to paint a more complete Keynesian picture of the business cycle. We need to answer two key questions: (a) why do booms and recessions last for several months or even years, and (b) why do they eventually come  to an end – what determines their turning points? Let us examine each in turn.

Why do booms and recessions persist?

Time lags.   It takes time for changes in injections and withdrawals to be fully reflected in changes in national income, output and employment. The multiplier process takes time.

Moreover, consumers, firms and government may not all respond immediately to new situations.

'Bandwagon' effects.   Once the economy starts expanding, expectations become buoyant. People think ahead and adjust their expenditure behaviour: they consume and invest more now. Likewise in a recession, a mood of pessimism may set in. The effect is cumulative. The multiplier and accelerator interact: they feed on each other.

Group behaviour.   Individual consumers and businesses may take their lead from others and so mimic their behaviour. This helps to reinforce bandwagon effects.

For example, during the 2000s many financial institutions loosened their lending criteria. This helped to fuel unsustainable property booms in several countries, including the UK, Ireland and the USA. They engaged in a competitive race, offering ever more favourable terms for borrowers. Often the borrowers could only repay if their assets (e.g. property) appreciated in value, as they tend to do in a boom – but not in a recession.

This rush to lend meant that many banks over-extended themselves and operated with too little capital. This made them much more vulnerable to financial crises and much more likely to cut back lending dramatically in a downturn – as indeed they did from 2008.

Group behaviour can therefore help to amplify economic upturns and downturns. By modelling representative agents with rational expectations, it is argued, we may we fail to understand how the interaction between economic agents can affect macroeconomic aggregates (see Chapter 16 page 514).

Why do booms and recessions come to an end?

Ceilings and floors.   Actual output can go on growing more rapidly than potential output only as long as there is slack in the economy. As full employment is approached and as more and more firms reach full capacity, so a ceiling to output will be reached.

At the other extreme, there is a basic minimum level of consumption that people tend to maintain. During a recession, people may not buy many luxury and durable goods, but they will continue to buy food and other basic goods. There is thus a floor to consumption.

The industries supplying these basic goods will need to maintain their level of replacement investment. Also, there will always be some minimum investment demand as firms feel the need to install the latest equipment. There is thus a floor to investment too.

Echo effects.   Durable consumer goods and capital equipment may last several years, but eventually they will need replacing. The replacement of goods and capital purchased in a previous boom may help to bring a recession to an end.

The accelerator. For investment to continue rising, consumer demand must rise at a faster and faster rate. If this does not happen, investment will fall back and the boom will break.

TC 9
p129

Sentiment and expectations. A change of sentiment and a sense that current rates of growth will not be sustained can lead people to adjust their spending behaviour, so contributing to the very slowdown that was expected. The impact of this will be amplified by bandwagon effects and group behaviour.

Random shocks. National or international political, social, institutional or natural events can affect the mood and attitudes of firms, governments and consumers, or the conditions under which they operate, and thus affect aggregate demand. Changes in world oil prices, a war, an election or a banking crisis are all examples.

Changes in government policy. In a boom, a government may become most worried by inflation, balance of payments deficits and rising levels of private debt, and thus pursue contractionary policies. In a recession, it may become most worried by unemployment and lack of growth and thus pursue expansionary policies. These government policies, if successful, will bring about a turning point in the cycle.

Keynesians argue that governments should attempt to reduce cyclical fluctuations by using active stabilisation policies. A more stable economy will encourage investment and allow a faster growth in output to be maintained. The policy traditionally favoured by Keynesians is *fiscal policy*. This is the subject of Chapter 22.

An analysis of the factors contributing to each of the four phases of the business cycle is given in Case Study 17.10 on the student website.

Section summary

1. Keynesians explain cyclical fluctuations in the economy by examining the causes of fluctuations in the level of aggregate demand.

2. A major part of the Keynesian explanation of the business cycle is the instability of private-sector expenditure. Investment is the most volatile component of aggregate demand. The accelerator theory explains this volatility. It relates the level of investment to changes in national income and consumer demand. An initial increase in consumer demand can result in a very large percentage increase in investment; but as soon as the rise in consumer demand begins to level off, investment will fall; and even a slight fall in consumer demand can reduce investment to virtually zero.

3. The accelerator effect will be dampened by the carrying of stocks, the cautiousness of firms, forward planning by firms and the inability of producer goods industries to supply the capital equipment.

4. The interaction of the multiplier and accelerator will cause cycles.

5. Fluctuations in stocks and in levels of borrowing and debt are also major contributors to the business cycle.

6. Keynesians identify other causes of cyclical fluctuations, such as time lags, 'bandwagon' effects, ceilings and floors to output, echo effects, swings in government policy and random shocks.

END OF CHAPTER QUESTIONS

1. An economy is currently in equilibrium. The following figures refer to elements in its national income accounts.

	£ billions
Consumption (total)	60
Investment	5
Government expenditure	8
Imports	10
Exports	7

(a) What is the current equilibrium level of national income?

(b) What is the level of injections?

(c) What is the level of withdrawals?

(d) Assuming that tax revenues are £7 billion, how much is the level of saving?

(e) If national income now rose to £80 billion and, as a result, the consumption of domestically produced goods rose to £58 billion, what is the *mpcd*?

(f) What is the value of the multiplier?

  (g) Given an initial level of national income of £80 billion, now assume that spending on exports rises by £4 billion, spending on investment rises by £1 billion, whilst government expenditure falls by £2 billion. By how much will national income change?

  (h) Given this new level of national income, assume that full employment is achieved at a national income of £100 billion. Is there an inflationary or a deflationary gap?

  (i) What is the size of this gap?

2. What is the relationship between the *mpc,* the *mpcd* and the *mpw*?

3. Why will the short-run consumption function be different from the long-run consumption function?

4. Construct a table similar to Table 17.3 (on page 536), only this time assume that the *mpcd* is ¾. Show that national income will increase by £640 million.

5. Assume that the multiplier has a value of 3. Now assume that the government decides to increase aggregate demand in an attempt to reduce unemployment. It raises government expenditure by £100 million with no increase in taxes. Firms, anticipating a rise in their sales, increase investment by £200 million, of which £50 million consists of purchases of foreign machinery. How much will national income rise? (Assume *ceteris paribus.*)

6. What factors could explain why some countries have a higher multiplier than others?

7. How can the interaction of the multiplier and the accelerator explain cyclical fluctuations in national income?

8. Why is it difficult to predict the size of the accelerator?

Online resources

Additional case studies on the student website

17.1 How does consumption behave? The case looks at evidence on the relationship between consumption and disposable income from the 1950s to the current day.

17.2 Keynes' views on the consumption function. An analysis of how the assumptions made by Keynes affect the shape of the consumption function.

17.3 Consumption and saving in practice. An international comparison of consumption and saving rates over time.

17.4 The relationship between income and consumption. This examines three different theories of the consumption function – the absolute income hypothesis, the relative income hypothesis and the permanent income hypothesis. Each one is based on different assumptions about consumer behaviour.

17.5 Trends in housing equity withdrawal (HEW). An analysis of the patterns in HEW and consumer spending.

17.6 An international comparison of household wealth and indebtedness. An examination of households' financial assets and liabilities relative to disposable income in seven developed countries (the G7).

17.7 Business expectations and their effects on investment. An examination of business surveys in Europe and the effects of business sentiment on investment.

17.8 The multiplier/accelerator interaction. A numerical example showing how the interaction of the multiplier and accelerator can cause cycles in economic activity.

17.9 Heavenly cycles. An examination of the claim by Jevons in the late nineteenth century that the business cycle depends on the sunspot cycle!

17.10 The phases of the business cycle. A demand-side analysis of the factors contributing to each of the four phases.

Maths Case 17.1 Calculating the value of the multiplier. Examining the algebra.

Maths Case 17.2 Calculating the value of the multiplier. Using calculus.

Maths Case 17.3 Calculating the value of the multiplier with marginal propensities based on disposable income. Examining the algebra.

Websites relevant to this Chapters 16 and 17

Numbers and sections refer to websites listed in the Web Appendix and hotlinked from this book's website at **www.pearsoned.co.uk/sloman**.

- For news articles relevant to this and the previous chapter, see the *Economics News* section on the student website.

- For general news on national economies and the international economy, see websites in section A, and particularly A1–5, 7–9, 13, 20–26, 31, 33, 35, 36. See also links to newspapers worldwide in A38, 39, 42, 43 and 44, and the news search feature in Google at A41.

- For information on the development of ideas, see C12, 18.

- For data on economic growth, employment and the business cycle, see links in B1; also see B4 and 12. For UK data, see B3, 5 and 34. For EU data, see B38 and 47. For US data, see B15 and the *Data* section of B17. For international data, see B15, 21, 24, 31, 33, 35, 37, 40, 43 and 46.

- For a model of the economy (based on the Treasury model), see *The Virtual Chancellor* (site D1). The model allows you to devise your own Budget.

- For student resources relevant to this chapter, see sites C1–7, 9, 10, 19, 28.

18 Chapter

Banking, Money and Interest Rates

In this chapter and the next, we are going to look at the role that money and financial institutions play in an economy. The financial crisis that developed during the late 2000s demonstrated vividly the significance of the financial system to modern-day economies. It is generally recognised that changes in the amount of money can have a powerful effect on all the major macroeconomic indicators, such as inflation, unemployment, economic growth, interest rates, exchange rates and the balance of payments. But the financial crisis did more than this: it demonstrated the systemic importance of financial institutions.

There continues to be a vibrant debate about how, if at all, we can avoid a repeat of the recent financial crisis. Governments and regulators worldwide are grappling with many very important questions. For instance, are some financial institutions simply *too big to fail*? How can we ensure that banks operate with adequate loss-absorbing capacity? Can we prevent financial institutions from contributing to excessive cycles in the credit extended to households and firms? Can we better align the incentives of banks with those of the wider community? These and other questions about financial institutions are considered here.

The chapter begins by defining what is meant by money and examining its functions. Then in sections 18.2 and 18.3 we look at the operation of the financial sector of the economy and its role in determining the supply of money. It is here where we consider the possible causes of the financial crisis, its impact on financial institutions themselves and some of the responses by central banks to the problems faced by financial institutions and, as a result, the economy.

In section 18.4 we turn to look at the demand for money. What we are asking is: how much of people's assets do they want to hold in the form of money? Finally, in section 18.5 we put supply and demand together to see how free-market interest rates – which have a crucial impact on aggregate demand – are determined.

18.1 THE MEANING AND FUNCTIONS OF MONEY

Before going any further we must define precisely what we mean by 'money' – not as easy a task as it sounds. Money is more than just notes and coin. In fact the main component of a country's money supply is not cash, but deposits in banks and other financial institutions. Only a very small proportion of these deposits is kept by the banks in their safes or tills in the form of cash. The bulk of the deposits appear merely as bookkeeping entries in the banks' accounts.

This may sound very worrying. Will a bank have enough cash to meet its customers' demands? The answer in the vast majority of cases is yes. Only a small fraction of a bank's total deposits will be withdrawn at any one time, and banks always seek to ensure that they have the ability to meet their customers' demands. The chances of banks running out of cash are very low indeed. The only circumstance where this could become possible is if people lost confidence in a bank and started to withdraw money in what is known as a 'run on the bank'. This happened with the Northern Rock bank in 2008. But in these circumstances the central bank or government would intervene to protect people's deposits by making more cash available to the bank or, in the last resort, by nationalising the bank (as happened with Northern Rock).

What is more, the bulk of all but very small transactions are not conducted in cash at all. By the use of cheques, credit cards and debit cards, most money is simply transferred from the purchaser's to the seller's bank account without the need for first withdrawing it in cash.

What items should be included in the definition of money? To answer this we need to identify the functions of money.

The functions of money

The main purpose of money is for buying and selling goods, services and assets: i.e. as a 'medium of exchange'. It also has three other important functions. Let us examine each in turn.

A medium of exchange

In a subsistence economy, where individuals make their own clothes, grow their own food, provide their own entertainments, etc., people do not need money. If people want to exchange any goods, they will do so by barter. In other words, they will do swaps with other people.

The complexities of a modern developed economy, however, make barter totally impractical for most purposes (see Case Study 18.1 on the student website). What is necessary is a **medium of exchange** that is generally acceptable as a means of payment for goods and services and as a means of payment for labour and other factor services. 'Money' is any such medium.

To be a suitable physical means of exchange, money must be light enough to carry around, must come in a number of denominations, large and small, and must not be easy to forge (the attributes of money are explored in Case Study 18.2 on the student website). Alternatively, money must be in a form that enables it to be transferred indirectly through some acceptable mechanism. For example, money in the form of bookkeeping entries in bank accounts can be transferred from one account to another by the use of such mechanisms as debit cards and direct debits.

A means of storing wealth

People need a means whereby the fruits of today's labour can be used to purchase goods and services in the future. People need to be able to store their wealth: they want a

Definition

Medium of exchange Something that is acceptable in exchange for goods and service.

BOX 18.1 MONEY SUPPLY, NATIONAL INCOME AND NATIONAL WEALTH

EXPLORING ECONOMICS

Don't confuse the supply of money with the money value of national income. National income is a *flow* concept. It measures the value of the nation's output per year. Money supply, by contrast, is a *stock* concept. At any one point in time, there is a given amount of money in the economy.

But what if the money supply increases? Will the national income increase by that amount? No, because the extra money will usually be spent more than once per year on final goods and services. The rise in national income would thus be greater than the rise in money supply. On the other hand, some of the extra spending may simply result in higher prices. *Real* national income will rise by less than national income measured at current prices.

So if money supply is not the same as national *income,* is it the same as national *wealth?* After all, wealth is a stock concept. Again the answer is no. The nation's wealth consists of its *real* assets: land, buildings, capital equipment, works of art, etc. People may well hold part of their wealth in the form of money, it is true, but this is not wealth as far as the nation is concerned: if it were, the government could make us all wealthier by simply printing more money! Money represents wealth to the individual only to the extent that it represents a claim on *real* goods and services. It has nothing to do with national wealth.

means of saving. Money is one such medium in which to hold wealth. It can be saved.

A means of evaluation

Money allows the value of goods, services or assets to be compared. The value of goods is expressed in terms of prices, and prices are expressed in money terms. Money also allows dissimilar things, such as a person's wealth or a company's assets, to be added up. Similarly, a country's GDP is expressed in money terms. Money thus serves as a 'unit of account'.

 Why may money prices give a poor indication of the value of goods and services?

A means of establishing the value of future claims and payments

People often want to agree today the price of some future payment. For example, workers and managers will want to agree the wage rate for the coming year. Firms will want to sign contracts with their suppliers specifying the price of raw materials and other supplies. Money prices are the most convenient means of measuring future claims.

What should count as money?

What items, then, should be included in the definition of money? Unfortunately, there is no sharp borderline between money and non-money.

Cash (notes and coin) obviously counts as money. It readily meets all the functions of money. Goods (fridges, cars and cabbages) do not count as money. But what about various financial assets, such as bank accounts, building society accounts and stocks and shares? Do they count as money? The answer is: it depends on how narrowly money is defined. The narrowest definition of money includes just cash (i.e. notes and coins). Broader definitions include various types of bank account, and broader definitions still include various financial assets as well. We examine the different definitions in the UK and the eurozone in Box 18.4.

 In terms of the broad definition of money, would a deposit account passbook count as money?

In order to understand the significance of different measures of the money supply and the ways in which money supply can be controlled, it is first necessary to look at the various types of account in which money can be held and at the various financial institutions involved.

Section summary

1. Money's main function is as a medium of exchange. In addition, it is a means of storing wealth, a means of evaluation and a means of establishing the value of future claims and payments.

2. What counts as money depends on how narrowly it is defined. All definitions include cash, but they vary according to what other financial assets are included.

18.2 THE FINANCIAL SYSTEM

The role of the financial sector

Banks and other financial institutions are known as **financial intermediaries**. They provide a link between those who wish to lend and those who wish to borrow. In other words, they act as the mechanism whereby the supply of funds is matched to the demand for funds. In this process, they provide five important services.

Expert advice

Financial intermediaries can advise their customers on financial matters: on the best way of investing their funds and on alternative ways of obtaining finance. This should help to encourage the flow of savings and the efficient use of them.

Expertise in channelling funds

Financial intermediaries have the specialist knowledge to be able to channel funds to those areas that yield the highest return. They also have the expertise to assess risks and to refuse loans for projects considered too risky or to charge a risk premium to others. This all encourages the flow of saving as it gives savers the confidence that their savings will earn a good rate of interest. Financial intermediaries also help to ensure that projects that are potentially profitable will be able to obtain finance. They help to increase allocative efficiency.

Definition

Financial intermediaries The general name for financial institutions (banks, building societies, etc.) which act as a means of channelling funds from depositors to borrowers.

Maturity transformation

Many people and firms want to borrow money for long periods of time, and yet many depositors want to be able to withdraw their deposits on demand or at short notice. If people had to rely on borrowing directly from other people, there would be a problem here: the lenders would not be prepared to lend for a long enough period. If you had £100 000 of savings, would you be prepared to lend it to a friend to buy a house if the friend was going to take 25 years to pay it back? Even if there was no risk whatsoever of your friend defaulting, most people would be totally unwilling to tie up their savings for so long.

This is where a bank or building society comes in. It borrows money from a vast number of small savers, who are able to withdraw their money on demand or at short notice. It then lends the money to house purchasers for a long period of time by granting mortgages, which are typically paid back over 20 to 30 years. This process whereby financial intermediaries lend for longer periods of time than they borrow is known as *maturity transformation*. They are able to do this because with a large number of depositors it is highly unlikely that they would all want to withdraw their deposits at the same time. On any one day, although some people will be withdrawing money, others will be making new deposits.

This does not mean that maturity transformation is without risks for financial institutions. Maturity transformation implies a maturity mismatch between the liabilities and assets on institutions' balance sheets. This needs managing. Box 18.2 considers the potential risks of maturity transformation for financial institutions and the wider economy.

 What dangers are there in maturity transformation for (a) financial institutions; (b) society generally?

Risk transformation

KI 11
p76
You may be unwilling to lend money directly to another person in case they do not pay up. You are unwilling to take the risk. Financial intermediaries, however, by lending to large numbers of people, are willing to risk the odd case of default. They can absorb the loss because of the interest they earn on all the other loans. This spreading of risks is known as *risk transformation*. What is more, financial intermediaries may have the expertise to be able to assess just how risky a loan is.

 Which of the above are examples of economies of scale?

Transmission of funds

In addition to channelling funds from depositors to borrowers, certain financial institutions have another important function. This is to provide a means of transmitting payments. Thus by the use of debit cards, credit cards, the Internet and telephone banking, cheques, direct debits, etc., money can be transferred from one person or institution to another without having to rely on cash.

The banking system

Types of bank

By far the largest element of money supply is bank deposits. It is not surprising, then, that banks play an absolutely crucial role in the monetary system. Banking can be divided into two main types: retail banking and wholesale banking. Most banks today conduct both types of business and are thus known as 'universal banks'.

Retail banking. **Retail banking** is the business conducted by the familiar high street banks, such as Barclays, Lloyds, HSBC, Royal Bank of Scotland, NatWest (part of the RBS group) and Santander. They operate bank accounts for individuals and businesses, attracting deposits and granting loans at published rates of interest.

Wholesale banking. The other major type of banking is **wholesale banking**. This involves receiving large deposits from and making large loans to companies or other banks and financial institutions; these are known as **wholesale deposits and loans**.

As far as companies are concerned, these may be for short periods of time to account for the non-matching of a firm's payments and receipts from its business, or they may be for longer periods of time, for various investment purposes. As these wholesale deposits and loans are very large sums of money, banks compete against each other for them and negotiate individual terms with the firm to suit the firm's particular requirements.

In the past, there were many independent wholesale banks, known as *investment banks*. These included famous names such as Morgan Stanley, Rothschild, S G Hambros and Goldman Sachs. With the worldwide financial crisis of the

---

Definitions

Maturity transformation The transformation of deposits into loans of a longer maturity.

Risk transformation The process whereby banks can spread the risks of lending by having a large number of borrowers.

Retail banking Branch, telephone, postal and Internet banking for individuals and businesses at published rates of interest and charges. Retail banking involves the operation of extensive branch networks.

Wholesale banking Where banks deal in large-scale deposits and loans, mainly with companies and other banks and financial institutions. Interest rates and charges may be negotiable.

Wholesale deposits and loans Large-scale deposits and loans made by and to firms at negotiated interest rates.

late 2000s, however, most of the independent investment banks merged with universal banks which conduct both retail and wholesale activities.

The rise of large universal banks has caused concern, however. In the UK in 2010, the Coalition government set up the Independent Commission on Banking (ICB). It was charged with investigating the structure of the banking system. It proposed *functional separation*: the ring-fencing of retail and wholesale banking. It argued that the core activities of retail banks needed isolating from the potential contagion from risky wholesale banking activities.

The principal recommendations of the ICB were accepted and the Financial Services (Banking Reform) Act became law in December 2013. The Act defines *core activities* as facilities for accepting deposits, facilities for withdrawing money or making payments from deposit accounts and the provision of overdraft facilities. It gives regulators the power to exercise ring-fencing rules to ensure the effective provision of core activities. These include restricting the power of a ring-fenced body to enter into contracts and payments with other members of the banking group. The Act also gives the regulator powers to restructure or split banks up to safeguard their future.

It was agreed that the ring-fencing of UK banking groups would become effective from the start of January 2019. The UK government decided that banks with more than £25 billion of core retail deposits would be ring-fenced. Banks which were to be functionally separated from the rest of their groups were to be known as ring-fenced banks or RFBs.

Building societies

These UK institutions specialise in granting loans (mortgages) for house purchase. They compete for the savings of the general public through a network of high street branches. Unlike banks, they are not public limited companies, their 'shares' being the deposits made by their investors. In recent years, many of the building societies have converted to banks (including all the really large building societies except the Nationwide).

In the past, there was a clear distinction between banks and building societies. Today, however, they have become much more similar, with building societies now offering current account facilities and cash machines, and retail banks granting mortgages. As with the merging of retail and wholesale banks, this is all part of a trend away from the narrow specialisation of the past and towards the offering of a wider and wider range of services. This was helped by a process of *financial deregulation*.

In fact, banks and building societies are both examples of what are called *monetary financial institutions (MFIs)*. This term is used to describe all deposit-taking institutions, including central banks (e.g. the Bank of England).

MFIs also lend and borrow wholesale funds to and from each other, and deposit with and borrow from the central bank. Up to the financial crisis of 2008/9, there had been a marked growth in wholesale funding. In many countries, including the UK, this contributed to the growth in the size of banks' balance sheets. Wholesale funds can be distributed amongst banks by means of a series of financial instruments. These instruments are typically short term and acquired in markets known as *money markets*.

During the financial crisis many forms of inter-bank lending virtually dried up in many countries. MFIs became increasingly fearful of other MFIs defaulting on loans. In response to the crisis, the Bank of England and other central banks, such as the Federal Reserve Bank in the USA, supplied extra money to MFIs to ensure the security of these institutions and the stability of the financial system. It did this by purchasing various assets from them with money it had, in effect, created (see Box 18.4).

Deposit taking and lending

Balance sheets

Banks and building societies provide a range of *financial instruments*. These are financial claims, either by customers on the bank (e.g. deposits) or by the bank on its customers (e.g. loans). They are best understood by analysing the balance sheets of financial institutions, which itemise their liabilities and assets. A financial institution's liabilities are those financial instruments involving a financial claim on the financial institution itself. As we shall see, these are largely *deposits* by customers, such as current and savings accounts. Its assets are financial instruments involving a financial claim on a third party: these are *loans,* such as personal and business loans and mortgages.

The total liabilities and assets for UK MFIs are set out in a balance sheet in Table 18.1. The aggregate size of the balance sheet in 2017 was equivalent to almost four times the UK's annual GDP. This is perhaps the simplest indicator of the significance of banks in modern economies, like the UK.

Both the *size* and *composition* of banks' balance sheets have become the focus of the international community's effort to ensure the stability of countries' financial systems. The growth of the aggregate balance sheet in the UK is considered in Box 18.2. But, it is to the composition of the balance sheet that we now turn. To do this, we focus on banks' liabilities and assets.

KI 11 p76

KI 26 p303

Definitions

Financial deregulation The removal of or reduction in legal rules and regulations governing the activities of financial institutions.

Monetary financial institutions (MFIs) Deposit-taking institutions including banks, building societies and the Bank of England.

Money market The market for short-term debt instruments, such as government bills (Treasury bills), in which financial institutions are active participants.

Financial instruments Financial products resulting in a financial claim by one party over another.

Table 18.1 Balance sheet of UK banks and building societies: August 2017

Sterling liabilities	£bn	%	Sterling assets	£bn	%
Sight deposits		45.2	Notes and coin	10.9	0.3
UK banks, etc.	160.9		Balances with Bank of England		10.9
UK public sector	19.1		Reserve balances	417.6	
UK private sector	1376.0		Cash ratio deposits	4.6	
Non-residents	181.2		Market loans		13.3
Time deposits		29.5	UK banks, etc.	379.2	
UK banks, etc.	305.6		UK banks' CDs, etc.	3.0	
UK public sector	16.1		Non-residents	134.0	
UK private sector	639.4		Bills of exchange	4.1	0.1
Non-residents	173.8		Reverse repos	299.3	7.7
Certificates of deposit (CDs)	185.9	4.8	Investments	485.1	12.5
Repos	273.8	7.1	Advances	2047.9	52.8
Sterling capital & other funds	451.5	11.7	Other assets	90.5	2.3
Other liabilities	59.8	1.6			
Total sterling liabilities	3842.8	100.0	**Total sterling assets**	3876.2	100.0
Liabilities in other currencies	4250.6		Assets in other currencies	4217.2	
Total liabilities	**8093.5**		**Total assets**	**8093.5**	

Source: Based on data in *Bankstats* (Bank of England), Table B1.4. Data published September 2017.

Liabilities

Customers' deposits in banks (and other deposit-taking institutions such as building societies) are **liabilities** to these institutions. This means simply that the customers have the claim on these deposits and thus the institutions are liable to meet the claims.

There are five major types of liability: sight deposits, time deposits, certificates of deposit (CDs), 'repos' and capital.

Sight deposits. **Sight deposits** are any deposits that can be withdrawn on demand by the depositor without penalty. In the past, sight accounts did not pay interest. Today, however, there are many sight accounts that do. In fact, there is quite aggressive competition nowadays between banks to offer apparently very attractive interest rates on such accounts, although these are often on balances up to a relatively small amount.

The most familiar form of sight deposits are current accounts at banks. Depositors are issued with chequebooks and/or debit cards (e.g. Visa debit or MasterCard's Maestro) that enable them to spend the money directly without first having to go to the bank and draw the money out in cash. In the case of debit cards, the person's account is electronically debited when the purchase is made. This process is known as EFTPOS (electronic funds transfer at point of sale). Money can also be transferred between individuals and businesses through direct debits, standing orders and Internet banking transfers.

An important feature of current accounts is that banks often allow customers to be overdrawn. That is, they can draw on their account and make payments to other people in excess of the amount of money they have deposited.

Time deposits. **Time deposits** require notice of withdrawal. However, they normally pay a higher rate of interest than

sight accounts. With some types of account, a depositor can withdraw a certain amount of money on demand, but there will be a penalty of so many days' lost interest. They are not chequebook or debit-card accounts, although some allow customers to use cash cards. The most familiar form of time deposits are the deposit and savings accounts in banks and the various savings accounts in building societies. No overdraft facilities exist with time deposits.

A substantial proportion of time deposits are from the banking sector. Inter-bank lending grew over the years as money markets were deregulated and as deposits were moved from one currency to another to take advantage of different rates of interest between different countries. A large proportion of overseas deposits are from foreign banks.

Certificates of deposit. **Certificates of deposit** are certificates issued by banks to customers (usually firms) for large deposits of a fixed term (e.g. £100 000 for 18 months). They can be sold by one customer to another, and thus provide a

Definitions

Liabilities All legal claims for payment that outsiders have on an institution.

Sight deposits Deposits that can be withdrawn on demand without penalty.

Time deposits Deposits that require notice of withdrawal or where a penalty is charged for withdrawals on demand.

Certificates of deposit (CDs) Certificates issued by banks for fixed-term interest-bearing deposits. They can be resold by the owner to another party.

means whereby the holders can get money quickly if they need it without the banks that have issued the CDs having to supply the money. (This makes them relatively 'liquid' to the depositor but 'illiquid' to the bank: we examine this below.) The use of CDs has grown rapidly over the past two decades. Their use by firms has meant that, at a wholesale level, sight accounts have become less popular.

Sale and repurchase agreements (repos).   If banks have a temporary shortage of funds, they can sell some of their financial assets to other banks or to the central bank – the Bank of England in the UK and the European Central Bank in the eurozone (see below) – and later repurchase them on some agreed date, typically a fortnight later. These **sale and repurchase agreements (repos)** are in effect a form of loan – the bank borrowing for a period of time using some of its financial assets as the security for the loan. One of the major assets to use in this way are government bonds (issued when the government borrows), normally called 'gilt-edged securities' or simply 'gilts' (see below). Sale and repurchase agreements involving gilts are known as gilt repos. Gilt repos play a vital role in the operation of monetary policy (see section 22.3).

Capital and other funds.   This consists largely of the share capital in banks. Since shareholders cannot take their money out of banks (although they can sell them to other investors on the stock market), share capital provides a source of funding to meet sudden increases in withdrawals from depositors and to cover bad debts.

It is vital that banks have sufficient capital. As we shall see, an important part of the response to the financial crisis has been to require banks to hold relatively larger amounts of capital. At the beginning of 2017, the aggregate amount of sterling capital held by banks based in the UK was equivalent to 12 per cent of their sterling liabilities.

Assets

A bank's financial *assets* are its claims on others. There are three main categories of assets.

Cash and reserve balances in the central bank (Bank of England in the UK, ECB in the eurozone). Banks need to hold a certain amount of their assets as cash. This is largely used to meet the day-to-day demands of customers. They also keep 'reserve balances' in the central bank. In the UK these earn interest at the Bank of England's repo rate (or 'Bank Rate' as it is called), These are like the banks' own current accounts and are used for clearing purposes (i.e. for settling the day-to-day payments between banks). They can be withdrawn in cash on demand. With inter-bank lending being seen as too risky during the crisis of the late 2000s, many banks resorted to depositing surplus cash in the Bank of England, even though Bank Rate was lower than the inter-bank lending rate or LIBOR ('London inter-bank offered rate') (see Box 18.3).

In the UK, banks and building societies are also required to deposit a small fraction of their assets as 'cash ratio deposits' with the Bank of England. These cannot be drawn on demand and earn no interest.

As you can see from Table 18.1, cash and balances in the Bank of England account for a very small proportion of banks' assets. The vast majority of banks' assets are in the form of various types of loan – to individuals and firms, to other financial institutions and to the government. These are 'assets' because they represent claims that the banks have on other people. Loans can be grouped into two types: short and long term.

Short-term loans.   These are in the form of market loans, bills of exchange or reverse repos. The market for these various types of loan is known as the money market.

- **Market loans** are made primarily to other financial institutions. This inter-bank lending consists of (a) money lent 'at call' (i.e. reclaimable on demand or at 24 hours' notice); (b) money lent for periods up to one year, but typically a few weeks; (c) CDs (i.e. certificates of deposits made in other banks or building societies).
- **Bills of exchange** are loans either to companies (**commercial bills**) or to the government (**Treasury bills**). These are, in effect, an IOU, with the company issuing them (in the case of commercial bills), or the government (in the case of Treasury bills), promising to pay the holder a specified sum on a particular date (the 'maturity date'), typically three months later. Since bills do not pay interest, they are sold below their face value, i.e. at a 'discount', but redeemed on maturity at face value. This enables the purchaser, in this case the bank, to earn a return. The market for new or existing bills is therefore known as the **discount market**.

Definitions

Sale and repurchase agreements (repos) An agreement between two financial institutions whereby one in effect borrows from another by selling its assets, agreeing to buy them back (repurchase them) at a fixed price and on a fixed date.

Assets Possessions or claims on others.

Market loans Short-term loans (e.g. money at call and short notice).

Bills of exchange Certificates promising to repay a stated amount on a certain date, typically three months from the issue of the bill. Bills pay no interest as such, but are sold at a discount and redeemed at face value, thereby earning a rate of discount for the purchaser.

Commercial bills Bills of exchange issued by firms.

Treasury bills Bills of exchange issued by the Bank of England on behalf of the government. They are a means whereby the government raises short-term finance.

Discount market An example of a money market in which new or existing bills, such as Treasury bills or Commercial bills, are bought and sold at a discount below their face value: i.e. the value at which they will be redeemed on maturity.

BOX 18.2 THE GROWTH OF BANKS' BALANCE SHEETS

The rise of wholesale funding

Banks' traditional funding model relied heavily on deposits as the source of funds for loans. However, new ways for financial institutions to access funds to generate new loans evolved. These reflected the deregulation of financial markets and the rapid pace of financial innovation.

Seeds of the crisis

Increasingly, financial institutions made greater use of *wholesale funds*. These are funds from other financial institutions. This coincided with the growth in a process known as securitisation. This involves the conversion of non-marketable banks' assets, such as residential mortgages, which have regular income streams (e.g. from payments of interest and capital) into securities, which can be bought and sold on financial markets. These provide lenders who originate the loans with a source of funds for further loans. The growth of securitisation is discussed in more detail in Box 18.3.

With an increasing use of money markets by financial institutions, vast sums of funds became available for lending. One consequence of this, as illustrated in the chart, was an expansion of the aggregate balance sheet of banks. The balance sheet grew from £2.6 trillion (2¾ times GDP) at the start of 1998 to £8.5 trillion (5½ times GDP) at the start of 2010.

The growth in banks' balance sheets was accompanied by a change in their composition. First, the profile of banks' assets became less liquid as they extended more long-term credit to households and firms. Assets generally became more risky too, as banks increasingly granted mortgages of 100 per cent or more of the value of houses – a problem for banks if house prices fell and they were forced to repossess.

Second, there was a general increase in the use of fixed-interest bonds as opposed to ordinary shares (equities) for raising capital. The ratio of bonds to shares is known as the *gearing* (or *leverage*) ratio. The increase in leverage meant

that, prior to the financial crisis, banks were operating with lower and lower levels of loss-absorbing capital, such as ordinary shares. If banks run at a loss, dividends on shares can be suspended; payments to bond holders cannot. This meant that as the crisis unfolded, policy makers were facing a liquidity problem, not among one or two financial institutions, but across the financial system generally.

The market failure we are describing is a form of *co-ordination failure* and is an example of the *fallacy of composition*. When one bank pursues increased earnings by borrowing from and lending to other financial institutions, this is not necessarily a problem. But, if many institutions expand their balance sheets by borrowing from and lending to *each other,* then it becomes a problem for the whole financial system. The apparent increase in liquidity for individual banks, on which they base credit, is not an overall increase in liquidity for the financial system as a whole. The effect is to create a credit bubble.

The dangers of the bubble for the financial system and beyond were magnified by the increasingly tangled web of interdependencies between financial institutions, both nationally and globally. There was a danger that this complexity was masking fundamental weaknesses of many financial institutions and too little overall liquidity.

Financial crisis

Things came to a head in 2007 and 2008. Once one or two financial institutions failed, such as Northern Rock in the UK in August 2007 and Lehman Brothers in the USA in September 2008, the worry was that failures would spread like a contagion. Banks could no longer rely on each other as their main source of liquidity.

The problems arising from the balance sheet expansion, increased leverage and a heightened level of maturity

---

The price paid for bills will depend on demand and supply. For example, the more Treasury bills that are offered for sale (i.e. the higher the supply), the lower will be their equilibrium price, and hence the higher will be their rate of return (i.e. their rate of interest, or 'rate of discount').

Normally, a bank will buy commercial bills only if they have been first 'accepted' by another financial institution (typically an investment bank). This means that the investment bank will redeem the bill (i.e. pay up) on

the maturity date, if the firm issuing the bill defaults on payment. Of course the investment bank charges for this insurance (or 'underwriting'). Bills that have been accepted in this way are known as **bank bills**.

■ *Reverse repos*. When a sale and repurchase agreement is made, the financial institution purchasing the assets (e.g. gilts) is, in effect, giving a short-term loan. The other party agrees to buy back the assets (i.e. pay back the loan) on a set date. The assets temporarily held by the bank making the loan are known as 'reverse repos'. Reverse

---

Definitions

Gearing or leverage (US term) The ratio of debt capital to equity capital: in other words, the ratio of borrowed capital (e.g. bonds) to shares.

Co-ordination failure When a group of firms (e.g. banks) acting independently could have achieved a more desirable outcome if they had co-ordinated their decision making.

Bank bills Bills that have been accepted by another financial institution and hence insured against default.

Reverse repos Gilts or other assets that are purchased under a sale and repurchase agreement. They become an asset to the purchaser.

KI 26
p303

KI 35
p451

KI 12
p97

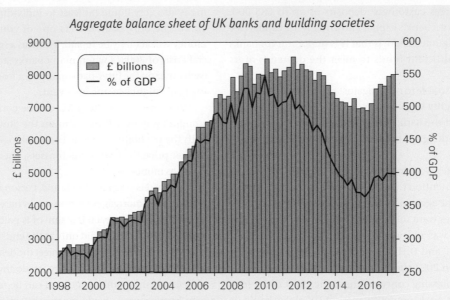

Aggregate balance sheet of UK banks and building societies

Legend: £ billions, % of GDP

Note: Since 2010 all loans securitised by MFIs are recorded on MFI balance sheets.

Sources: (i) Data showing liabilities of banks and building societies based on series LPMALOA and RPMTBJF (up to the end of 2009) and RPMB3UQ (from 2010) from *Statistical Interactive Database*, Bank of England (data published 29 September 2017, not seasonally adjusted). (ii) GDP data from *Quarterly National Accounts* series YBHA, Office for National Statistics (GDP figures are the sum of the latest four quarters).

mismatch meant that central banks around the world, including the Bank of England, were faced with addressing a liquidity problem of huge proportions. They had to step in to supply central bank money to prevent a collapse of the banking system.

Subsequently, the Basel Committee on Banking Supervision (see pages 564–5) agreed a set of measures, to be applied globally, designed to ensure the greater financial resilience of banks and banking systems. It is notable from the chart how from the early 2010s there was a reduction of the aggregate balance sheet of banks resident in the UK. By the middle of 2017 the aggregate balance sheet was close to £8 trillion, the equivalent to four times GDP: this compares with a figure of nearly £8.5 trillion in early 2010 – over 550 per cent of GDP.

What are the potential costs and benefits for financial institutions, lenders and borrowers and for the wider economy arising from maturity transformation? Are these dangers an inherent and unavoidable consequence of maturity transformation?

repos are typically for one week, but can be for as little as overnight or as long as one year.

Longer-term loans. These consist primarily of loans to customers, both personal customers and businesses. These loans, also known as advances, are of four main types: fixed-term (repayable in instalments over a set number of years – typically, six months to five years), overdrafts (often for an unspecified term), outstanding balances on credit card accounts, and mortgages (typically for 25 years).

Banks also make investments. These are partly in government bonds (gilts), which are effectively loans to the government. The government sells bonds, which then pay a fixed sum each year as interest. Once issued, they can then be bought and sold on the stock exchange. Banks are normally only prepared to buy bonds that have less than five years to maturity (the date when the government redeems the bonds). Banks also invest in various subsidiary financial institutions and in building societies.

Taxing the banks

Bank levy. In January 2011, the UK introduced the bank levy: a tax on the *liabilities* of banks and building societies operating in the UK. For banking groups with their headquarters in the UK the levy applies to their global balance sheet; for subsidiaries of non-UK banks it applies just to their UK activities. The tax is founded on two key principles. First, the revenues raised should be able to meet the full fiscal costs of any future support for financial institutions. Second, it should provide banks with incentives to reduce risk-taking behaviour and so reduce the likelihood of future financial crises.

The UK bank levy has two rates: a full rate on taxable liabilities with a maturity of less than one year and a half rate on taxable liabilities with a maturity of more than one year. This differential is intended to discourage excessive short-term borrowing by the banks in their use of wholesale funding.

Not all liabilities are subject to the levy. First, it is not imposed on the first £20 billion of liabilities. This is to encourage small banks (note that the largest UK banks, such as HSBC, Barclays and RBS, each have liabilities of over £2 trillion). Second, various liabilities are excluded. These are: (a) gilt repos; (b) retail deposits insured by public schemes such as the UK's Financial Services Compensation Scheme, which guarantees customers' deposits of up to £85 000; (c) a large part of a bank's capital known as Tier 1 capital (see below) – the argument here is that it is important for banks to maintain sufficient funds to meet the demands of its depositors.

Banks are also able to offset against their taxable liabilities holdings of highly liquid assets, such as Treasury bills and cash reserves at the Bank of England. These exclusions and deductions are designed to encourage banks to engage in less risky lending.

The levy rates were initially set at 0.075 and 0.0375 per cent with the intention that the levy raise at least £2.5 billion each year. As the aggregate balance sheets of banks began to shrink, the rates were increased several times. Then in the 2015 Budget it was announced that the levy rates, which at time were 0.21 and 0.105 per cent, were to be gradually reduced until in 2021 they would be 0.1 and 0.05 per cent. With some expressing concerns about the effect of the levy on the international competitiveness of UK global banks, it was also announced that from 2021 the levy would apply only to UK balance sheets.

Bank corporation tax surcharge. The 2015 Budget also saw the announcement of a new 8 per cent corporation tax surcharge on banks. This marked a shift in the tax base from banks' balance sheets to their profits. The 8 per cent surcharge was introduced in January 2016 for all banks with annual profits over £25 million. With the main corporation tax rate at 18 per cent when introduced, the surcharge on banks meant that their effective corporation tax rate was 26 per cent. The Office for Budget Responsibility estimated at the time of the announcement that the surcharge would raise £6.5 billion between 2016/17 and 2020/21. It also forecast that revenues from the bank levy would fall from £3.1 billion to £2.2 billion.

Liquidity, profitability and capital adequacy

As we have seen, banks keep a range of liabilities and assets. The balance of items in this range is influenced by three important considerations: profitability, liquidity and capital adequacy.

Profitability

Profits are made by lending money out at a higher rate of interest than that paid to depositors. The average interest rate received by banks on their assets is greater than that paid by them on their liabilities.

Liquidity

The *liquidity* of an asset is the ease with which it can be converted into cash without loss. Cash itself, by definition, is perfectly liquid.

Some assets, such as money lent at call to other financial institutions, are highly liquid. Although not actually cash, these assets can be converted into cash virtually on demand with no financial penalty. Other short-term inter-bank lending is also very liquid (at least to individual banks: see Box 18.2). The only issue here is one of confidence that the money will actually be repaid. This was a worry in the financial crisis of 2008/9 when many banks stopped lending to each other on the inter-bank market for fear that the borrowing bank might become insolvent.

Other assets, such as gilts, can be converted into cash straight away by selling them on the Stock Exchange, but with the possibility of some financial loss, given that their market price fluctuates. Such assets, therefore, are not as liquid as money at call.

Other assets are much less liquid. Personal loans to the general public or mortgages for house purchase can be redeemed by the bank only as each instalment is paid. Other advances for fixed periods are repaid only at the end of that period.

Banks must always be able to meet the demands of their customers for withdrawals of money. To do this, they must hold sufficient cash or other assets that can be readily turned into cash. In other words, banks must maintain sufficient liquidity.

1. *If a bank buys a £500 000 Treasury bill at the start of its 91-day life for £480 000, at roughly what price could it sell it to another financial institution after 45 days? Why is it not possible to predict the precise price when the bill is first purchased?*
2. *Suppose there were a sudden surge in demand for cash from the general public. Would the existence of inter-bank market loans help to meet the demand in any way?*

The balance between profitability and liquidity

Profitability is the major aim of banks and most other financial institutions. However, the aims of profitability and liquidity tend to conflict. In general, the more liquid an asset, the less profitable it is, and vice versa. Personal and business loans to customers are profitable to banks, but highly illiquid. Cash is totally liquid, but earns no profit. Thus financial institutions like to hold a range of assets with varying degrees of liquidity and profitability.

For reasons of profitability, the banks will want to 'borrow short' (at low rates of interest, as are generally paid on current accounts) and 'lend long' (at higher rates of interest, as are normal on personal loans). The difference in the average maturity of loans and deposits is known as the **maturity gap**. In general terms, the larger the maturity gap between loans

---

Definitions

Liquidity The ease with which an asset can be converted into cash without loss.

Maturity gap The difference in the average maturity of loans and deposits.

and deposits, the greater the profitability. For reasons of liquidity, however, banks will want a relatively small gap: if there is a sudden withdrawal of deposits, banks will need to be able to call in enough loans.

The ratio of an institution's liquid assets to total assets is known as its *liquidity ratio*. For example, if a bank had £100 million of assets, of which £10 million were liquid and £90 million were illiquid, the bank would have a 10 per cent liquidity ratio. If a financial institution's liquidity ratio is too high, it will make too little profit. If the ratio is too low, there will be the risk that customers' demands may not be able to be met: this would cause a crisis of confidence and possible closure. Institutions thus have to make a judgement as to what liquidity ratio is best – one that is neither too high nor too low.

Balances in the central bank, short-term loans (i.e. those listed above) and government bonds with less than 12 months to maturity would normally be regarded as liquid assets.

 Why are government bonds that still have 11 months to run regarded as liquid, whereas overdrafts granted for a few weeks are not?

As Box 18.2 explains, over the years, banks had reduced their liquidity ratios (i.e. the ratio of liquid assets to total assets). This was not a problem as long as banks could always finance lending to customers by borrowing on the inter-bank market. In the late 2000s, however, banks became increasingly worried about bad debt. They thus felt the need to increase their liquidity ratios and hence cut back on lending and chose to keep a higher proportion of deposits in liquid form. In the UK, for example, banks substantially increased their reserve accounts at the Bank of England.

Secondary marketing and securitisation

As we have seen, one way of reconciling the two conflicting aims of liquidity and profitability is for financial institutions to hold a mixture of liquid and illiquid assets. Another way is through the *secondary marketing* of assets. This is where holders of assets sell them to someone else before the maturity date. This allows banks to close the maturity gap for liquidity purposes, but maintain the gap for profitability purposes.

Certificates of deposit (CDs) are a good example of secondary marketing. CDs are issued for fixed-period deposits in a bank (e.g. one year) at an agreed interest rate. The bank does not have to repay the deposit until the year is up. CDs are thus illiquid liabilities for the bank, and they allow it to increase the proportion of illiquid assets without having a dangerously high maturity gap. But the holder of the CD in the meantime can sell it to someone else (through a broker). It is thus liquid to the holder. Because CDs are liquid to the holder, they can be issued at a relatively low rate of interest and thus allow the bank to increase its profitability.

Another example of secondary marketing is when a financial institution sells some of its assets to another financial institution. The advantage to the first institution is that it gains liquidity. The advantage to the second one is that it gains profitable assets. The most common method for the sale of assets has been through a process known as *securitisation*.

Securitisation occurs when a financial institution pools some of its assets, such as residential mortgages, and sells them to an intermediary known as a *special purpose vehicle (SPV)*. SPVs are legal entities created by the financial institution. In turn, the SPV funds its purchase of the assets by issuing bonds to investors (noteholders). These bonds are known as *collateralised debt obligations* (CDOs). The sellers (e.g. banks) get cash now rather than having to wait and can use it to fund loans to customers. The buyers make a profit if the income yielded by the CDOs are as expected. Such bonds can be very risky, however, as the future cash flows may be *less* than anticipated.

The securitisation chain is illustrated in Figure 18.1. The financial institution looking to sell its assets is referred to as the 'originator' or the 'originator-lender'. Working from left to right, we see that the originator-lender sells its assets to another financial institution, the SPV, which then bundles assets together into CDOs and sells them to investors (e.g. banks or pension funds) as bonds. Now working from right to left, we see that by purchasing the bonds issued by the SPV, the investors provide the funds for the SPV's purchase

Definitions

Liquidity ratio The proportion of a bank's total assets held in liquid form.

Secondary marketing Where assets are sold before maturity to another institution or individual. The possibility of secondary marketing encourages people or institutions to buy assets/grant loans in the primary market, knowing that they can sell them if necessary in the secondary market. The sale of existing shares and bonds on the stock market is an example of secondary marketing.

Securitisation Where future cash flows (e.g. from interest rate or mortgage payments) are turned into marketable securities, such as bonds. The sellers (e.g. banks) get cash immediately rather than having to wait and can use it to fund loans to customers. The buyers make a profit by buying below the discounted value of the future income. Such bonds can be very risky, however, as the future cash flows may be less than anticipated.

Special purpose vehicle (SPV) Legal entity created by financial institutions for conducting specific financial functions, such as bundling assets together into fixed-interest bonds and selling them.

Collateralised debt obligations (CDOs) These are a type of security consisting of a bundle of fixed-income assets, such as corporate bonds, mortgage debt and credit card debt.

BOX 18.3 THE RISE OF SECURITISATION

Spreading the risk or securing a crisis?

The conflict between profitability and liquidity may have sown the seeds for the credit crunch that affected economies across the globe in the second half of the 2000s.

To understand this, consider the size of the 'advances' item in the banking sector's balance sheet – nearly 53 per cent of the value of sterling assets (see Table 18.1). The vast majority of these are to households. Advances secured against property have, in recent times, accounted for around 80 per cent by value of all household advances. Residential mortgages involve institutions lending long.

Securitisation of debt

One way in which individual institutions can achieve the necessary liquidity to expand the size of their mortgage lending (illiquid assets) is through *securitisation*. Securitisation grew especially rapidly in the UK and USA. In the UK this was particularly true amongst banks; building societies have historically made greater use of retail deposits to fund advances.

Securitisation is a form of financial engineering. It provides banks (originator-lenders) with liquidity and enables them to engage in further lending opportunities. It provides the special purpose vehicles with the opportunity to issue profitable securities.

In the period up to 2010 most securitisations in the UK saw the original loans moving off the balance sheet of MFIs and onto the balance sheet of the special purpose vehicle (SPV) issuing the collateralised debt obligations (CDOs). From 2010, however, all securitisations are detailed on the balance sheets of MFIs, including previous securitisations which, as a result, have been brought back on to the balance sheets of MFIs.

The chart shows the rapid growth in the flows of securitised secured loans from an estimated £8 billion in 2000 to over £100 billion by 2008. This increase in securitisation reflects the strong demand amongst investors for CDOs. The attraction of these fixed-income products for the noteholders was the potential for higher returns than on (what were) similarly rated products. However, investors have no recourse should people with mortgages fall into arrears or, worse still, default on their mortgages.

Risk and the sub-prime market

The securitisation of assets is not without risks for all those in the securitisation chain and consequently for the financial system as a whole.

The pooling of advances in itself *reduces* the cash-flow risk facing investors. However, there is a **moral hazard** problem here (see page 135). The pooling of the risks may encourage originator-lenders to lower their credit criteria by offering higher income multiples (advances relative to annual household incomes) or higher loan-to-value ratios (advances relative to the price of housing).

Towards the end of 2006, the USA witnessed an increase in the number of defaults by households on residential mortgages. This was a particular problem in the sub-prime market – higher-risk households with poor credit ratings. Similarly, the number falling behind with their payments rose. This was on the back of rising interest rates.

These problems in the US sub-prime market were the catalyst for the liquidity problem that beset financial systems in 2007 and 2008. Where these assets were securitised, investors, largely other financial institutions, suffered from the contagion arising from arrears and defaults.

KI 17
p135

---

of the lender's assets. The SPV is then able to use the proceeds from the bond sales (CDO proceeds) to provide the originator-lender with liquidity.

The effect of secondary marketing is to reduce the liquidity ratio that banks feel they need to keep. It has the effect of increasing their maturity gap.

Dangers of secondary marketing. There are dangers to the banking system, however, from secondary marketing. To the extent that banks individually feel that they can operate with a lower liquidity ratio, so this will lead to a lower national liquidity ratio. This may lead to an excessive expansion of credit (illiquid assets) in times of economic boom.

Definitions

Moral hazard The temptation to take more risks when you know that someone else will cover the risks if you get into difficulties. In the case of banks taking risks, the 'someone else' may be another bank, the central bank or the government.

| Figure 18.1 | Securitisation chain |

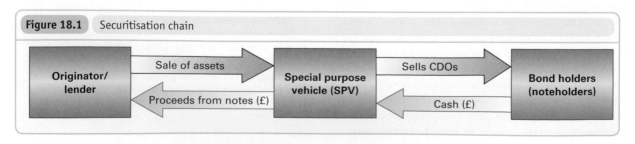

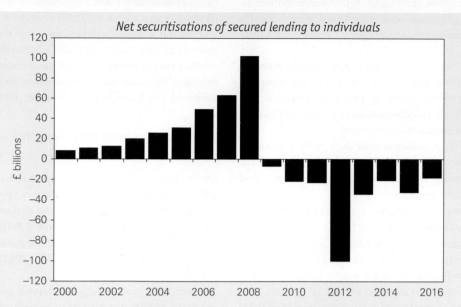

Net securitisations of secured lending to individuals

Note: Data up to 2010 relate to changes in other specialist lenders' sterling net securitisations of secured lending to individuals and housing associations. From 2010 data relate to changes in resident MFI sterling securitised loans secured on dwellings to individuals.

Sources: Based on data from *Statistical Interactive Database*, Bank of England, series LPMVUJD (up to 2010) and LPMB8GO (data published 29 March 2017).

Securitisation also spread the contagion across the world. Investors are global, so that advances, such as an American family's residential mortgage, supporting CDOs are effectively travelling across national borders. This resulted in institutions having to write off debts, a deterioration of their balance sheets, the collapse in the demand for securitised assets and the drying up of liquidity.

The chart shows the collapse of the market for securitised secured lending after the financial crisis. Indeed, the 2010s were to be characterised by banks *buying back* CDOs from SPVs, including unsold ones. A similar pattern was observed in many countries. This process was accelerated by central banks, which began to accept securitised assets in exchange for liquidity, either as part of programmes of quantitative easing (see Box 22.10) or other liquidity insurance mechanisms (see pages 568–9 for a discussion of liquidity insurance in the UK).

 Does securitisation necessarily involve a moral hazard problem?

Also, there is an increased danger of banking collapse. If one bank fails, this will have a knock-on effect on those banks which have purchased its assets. In the specific case of securitisation, the strength of the chain is potentially weakened if individual financial institutions move into riskier market segments, such as **sub-prime** residential mortgage markets. Should the income streams of the originator's assets dry up – for instance, if individuals default on their loans – then the impact is felt by the whole of the chain. In other words, institutions and investors are exposed to the risks of the originator's lending strategy.

The issue of securitisation and its impact on the liquidity of the financial system during the 2000s is considered in Box 18.3.

KI 11
p76

Capital adequacy

In addition to sufficient liquidity, banks must have sufficient capital (i.e. funds) to allow them to meet all demands from depositors and to cover losses if borrowers default on payment. Capital adequacy is a measure of a bank's capital relative to its assets, where the assets are weighted according to the degree of risk. The more risky the assets, the greater the amount of capital that will be required.

A measure of capital adequacy is given by the **capital adequacy ratio (CAR)**. This is given by the following formula:

$$CAR = \frac{\text{Common Equity Tier 1 capital} + \text{Additional Tier 1 capital} + \text{Tier 2 capital}}{\text{Risk-weighted assets}}$$

Definitions

Sub-prime debt Debt where there is a high risk of default by the borrower (e.g. mortgage holders who are on low incomes facing higher interest rates and falling house prices).

Capital adequacy ratio (CAR) The ratio of a bank's capital (reserves and shares) to its risk-weighted assets.

Common equity Tier 1 capital includes bank reserves (from retained profits) and ordinary share capital (equities), where dividends to shareholders vary with the amount of profit the bank makes. Such capital thus places no burden on banks in times of losses as no dividend need be paid. What is more, unlike depositors, shareholders cannot ask for their money back.

Additional Tier 1 (AT1) capital consists largely of preference shares. These pay a fixed dividend (like company bonds). But although preference shareholders have a prior claim over ordinary shareholders on company profits, dividends need not be paid in times of loss.

Tier 2 capital is 'subordinated debt' with a maturity greater than five years. Subordinated debt holders only have a claim on a failing company after the claims of all other bondholders have been met.

Risk-weighted assets are the value of assets, where each type of asset is multiplied by a risk factor. Under the internationally agreed Basel II accord, cash and government bonds have a risk factor of zero and are thus not included. Inter-bank lending between the major banks has a risk factor of 0.2 and is thus included at only 20 per cent of its value; residential mortgages have a risk factor of 0.35; personal loans, credit card debt and overdrafts have a risk factor of 1; loans to companies carry a risk factor of 0.2, 0.5, 1 or 1.5, depending on the credit rating of the company. Thus the greater the average risk factor of a bank's assets, the greater will be the value of its risk-weighted assets, and the lower will be its CAR.

The greater the CAR, the greater the capital adequacy of a bank. Under Basel II, banks were required to have a CAR of at least 8 per cent (i.e. 0.08). They were also required to meet two supplementary CARs. First, banks needed to hold a ratio of Tier 1 capital to risk-weighted assets of at least 4 per cent and, second, a ratio of ordinary share capital to risk-weighted assets of at least 2 per cent. It was felt that these three ratios would provide banks with sufficient capital to meet the demands from depositors and to cover losses if borrowers defaulted. The financial crisis, however, meant a rethink.

Strengthening international regulation of capital adequacy and liquidity

Capital adequacy. In the light of the financial crisis of 2008/9, international capital adequacy requirements were strengthened by the *Basel Committee on Banking Supervision*, with a first draft in 2010/11 and a final agreement in December 2017. The new 'Basel III' capital requirements, as they are called, will be phased in by 2022. They are summarised in Figure 18.2.

From 2013, banks continued to need a CAR of at least 8 per cent (i.e. 0.08). But, by 2015 were required to operate with a ratio of CET1 to risk-weighted assets of at least 4.5 per cent. From 2016 began a phased introduction of a *capital conservation buffer* raising the CET1 ratio to no less than 7 per cent by 2022. This increases the overall CAR to at least 10.5 per cent.

On top of this, national regulators are required to assess the financial resilience across all financial institutions under

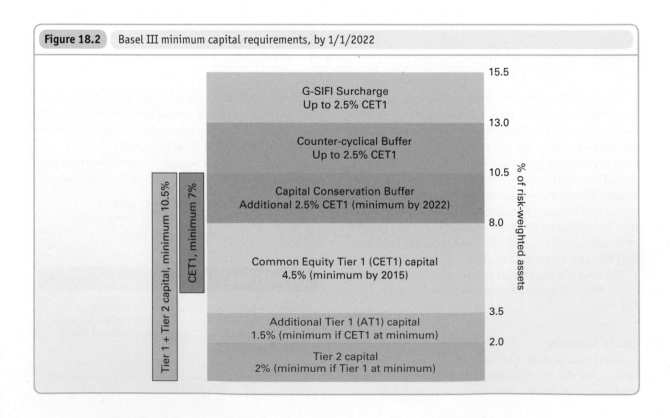

Figure 18.2 Basel III minimum capital requirements, by 1/1/2022

its jurisdiction, particularly in light of economic conditions. This is *macro-prudential regulation*. If necessary, regulators will then apply a *counter-cyclical buffer* to all banks so increasing the CET1 ratio by up to a further 2.5 per cent. This will allow financial institutions to build up a capital buffer in boom times to allow it to be drawn on in times of recession or financial difficulty. It should also help to reduce the likelihood of financial institutions destabilising the economy by amplifying the business cycle.

Large global banks, known as *global systemically important banks* (G-SIBs), will be required to operate with a CET1 ratio of up to 3.5 per cent higher than other banks. The global and systemic importance of these institutions is scored against a series of indicators which determine the magnitude of their additional capital requirements. These indicators include their size and the extent of cross-border activity. The reason for this extra capital requirement – or a *G-SIB systemic buffer* – is that the failure of such an institution could trigger a global financial crisis. This means that the overall CAR for very large financial institutions from 2022 can be as high as 15.5 per cent (see Figure 18.2).

> **?** What are the economic arguments for larger 'systemically important banks' (SIBs) having an additional capital requirement?

In the UK it was decided that individual ring-fenced banks (RFBs), as well as large building societies which hold more than £25 billion in deposits, would be required to hold an additional capital buffer in excess of the Basel III requirements. These financial institutions have been identified as domestic systemically important banks (D-SIBs). Hence, this buffer is also referred as the *D-SIB systemic buffer*. UK bank groups identified as G-SIBs containing a ring-fenced bank are subject to two systemic buffers: the G-SIB systemic buffer at the group level and the D-SIB buffer at the level of the ring-fenced bank.

The UK's domestic systemic buffer depends on the size of risk-weighted assets, with the initial plan for additional capital requirement of up to 3 per cent of these assets. However, depending on the judgement of the Financial Policy Committee, whose job is to ensure the financial resilience of the UK financial sector, the asset bands and the systemic buffer rates applied can be reviewed and adjusted if necessary.

To supplement the risk-based capital requirements, the Basel III framework introduced a *non-risk-based leverage ratio*. Described by regulators as a complementary to the risk-based framework, this requires financial institutions to operate with a Tier 1 capital-to-asset ratio of 3 per cent. In contrast to the risk-based ratios, the assets in the denominator in this ratio are *not* weighted by risk factors.

The impact of the Basel III's capital adequacy requirements was to increase the capital cushions of many banks significantly. Indeed, many exceeded the Basel III requirements, even those for 2022.

Nonetheless, discussions were to continue around the calculation of risk-weighted assets. Because of the complexity of banks' asset structures, which tend to vary significantly from country to country, it is difficult to ensure that banks are meeting the Basel III requirements. Under proposed amendments, banks would have to compare their own calculations with a 'standardised' model. Their own calculations of risk-based assets would then not be allowed to be lower than 60–90 per cent (known as 'the output floor') of the standardised approach.

There were some concerns raised by some European banks which claimed that this would penalise them, as some of their assets are less risky than the equivalent assets in other countries. For example, Germany argued that mortgage defaults have been rare and thus German mortgage debt should be given a lower weighting than US mortgage debt, where defaults have been more common. If all assets were assessed according to the output floor, several banks, especially in Europe, would be judged to be undercapitalised.

In December 2017 the Basel Committee finally agreed to adopt a revised standardised approach to assessing credit risk. First, financial institutions would not be required to adopt such a 'mechanistic' approach to assessing asset risk. Second, the output floor for the risk weighting of assets was set at 72.5 per cent, meaning that the risk of an asset, such as a mortgage, could not be set at less than 72.5 per cent of the level used by regulators in their standardised models.

Liquidity. The financial crisis highlighted the need for banks not only to hold adequate levels of capital but also to manage their liquidity better. The Basel III framework includes a *liquidity coverage ratio* (LCR). This requires that financial institutions have high quality liquid assets (HQLAs) to cover the expected net cash flow over the next 30 days. From its implementation in 2015, the minimum LCR ratio (HQLAs relative to the expected 30-day net cash flow) will rise from 60 per cent to 100 per cent by 2022.

Net stable funding ratio (NSFR). As part of the Basel III reforms, a *net stable funding ratio* (NSFR) was to become a regulatory standard from 2018. This takes a longer-term view of the funding profile of banks by focusing on the reliability of liabilities as a source of funds, particularly in circumstances of extreme stress. The NSFR is the ratio of stable liabilities to assets likely to require funding (i.e. assets where there is a likelihood of default).

On the liabilities side, these will be weighted by their expected reliability– in other words, by the stability of these

---

Definitions

Macro-prudential regulation Regulation which focuses not on a single financial institution but on the financial system as a whole and which monitors its impact on the wider economy.

Global systemically important banks (SIBs) Bank identified by a series of indicators as being significant players in the global financial system.

funds. This weighting will reflect the maturity of the liabilities and the propensity of lenders to withdraw their funds. For example, Tier 1 and 2 capital will have a weighting of 100 per cent; term deposits with less than one year to maturity will have a weighting of 50 per cent; and unsecured wholesale funding will have a weighting of 0 per cent. The result of these weightings is a measure of *stable funding*.

On the assets side, these will be weighted by the likelihood that they will have to be funded over the course of one year. This means that they will be weighted by their liquidity, with more liquid assets requiring less funding. Thus cash will have a zero weighting, while more risky assets will have weightings up to 100 per cent. The result is a measure of *required funding*.

Banks will need to hold a stable-liabilities-to-required-funding ratio (NSFR) of at least 100 per cent.

The central bank

The Bank of England is the UK's **central bank**. The European Central Bank (ECB) is the central bank for the countries using the euro. The Federal Reserve Bank of America (the Fed) is the USA's central bank. All countries with their own currency have a central bank. They fulfil two vital roles in the economy.

The first is to oversee the whole monetary system and ensure that banks and other financial institutions operate as stably and as efficiently as possible.

The second is to act as the government's agent, both as its banker and in carrying out monetary policy.

The Bank of England traditionally worked in very close liaison with the Treasury, and there used to be regular meetings between the Governor of the Bank of England and the Chancellor of the Exchequer. Although the Bank may have disagreed with Treasury policy, it always carried it out. In 1997, however, the Bank of England was given independence to decide the course of monetary policy. In particular, this meant that the Bank of England and not the government would now decide interest rates.

Another example of an independent central bank is the European Central Bank (ECB), which operates the monetary policy for the eurozone countries. Similarly, the Fed is independent of both the President and Congress, and its chair is generally regarded as having great power in determining the country's economic policy. Although the degree of independence of central banks from government varies considerably around the world, there has been a general move in recent years to make central banks more independent.

Within their two broad roles, central banks typically have a number of different functions. Although we will consider the case of the Bank of England, the same principles apply to other central banks, such as the ECB and the Fed.

It issues notes

The Bank of England is the sole issuer of banknotes in England and Wales. (In Scotland and Northern Ireland, retail banks issue notes.) The issue of notes is done through the Issue Department, which organises their printing. This is one of two departments of the Bank of England. The other is the Banking Department, through which it deals with banks.

Table 18.2 shows the consolidated balance sheet across the two departments of the Bank of England for the end of March 2016. As we shall discuss shortly, the balance sheet of the Bank of England was to expand markedly following the financial crisis. This was the case for many central banks across the world.

On the balance sheet we see the outstanding value of the banknote issue (notes in circulation). The amount of

---

Definitions

Central bank Banker to the banks and the government. It oversees the banking system, implements monetary policy and issues currency.

Table 18.2   Consolidated balance sheet of the Bank of England: 31 March 2016

Liabilities	£bn	%	Assets	£bn	%
Notes in circulation	69.8	16.5	Ways and means advance to National Loans Fund	0.4	0.1
Reserve balances	312.2	73.8	Short-term open market operations	0.0	0.0
Short-term open market operations	0.0	0.0	Long-term open market operations	18.7	4.4
Cash ratio deposits	4.1	1.0	Sterling denominated bond holdings	10.0	2.4
Other sterling liabilities	20.6	4.9	Loans to Asset Purchase Facility	375.0	88.6
Capital and reserves (equity)	4.5	1.1	Other sterling assets	0.8	0.2
Foreign currency public securities issued	4.2	1.0	Foreign currency reserve assets	4.2	1.0
Other foreign currency liabilities	7.8	1.8	Other foreign currency assets	14.2	3.4
Total	**423.2**	**100.0**	**Total**	**423.2**	**100.0**

Source: Bank of England Consolidated Balance Sheet 31 March 2016 (Bank of England, published 4 July 2017).

banknotes issued by the Bank of England depends largely on the demand for notes from the general public. If people draw more cash from their bank accounts, the banks will have to draw more cash from their balances in the Bank of England. These balances are held in the Banking Department. The Banking Department will thus have to acquire more notes from the Issue Department, which will simply print more in exchange for extra government or other securities supplied by the Banking Department.

It acts as a bank

To the government. It keeps the two major government accounts: the 'Exchequer' and the 'National Loans Fund'. Taxation and government spending pass through the Exchequer. Government borrowing and lending pass through the National Loans Fund. The government tends to keep its deposits in the Bank of England (the public deposits item in the balance sheet) to a minimum. If the deposits begin to build up (from taxation), the government will probably spend them on paying back government debt. If, on the other hand, it runs short of money, it will simply borrow more.

To banks. Banks' deposits in the Bank of England consist of reserve balances and cash ratio deposits (see Table 18.2). The reserve balances are used for clearing purposes between the banks but are also a means by which banks can manage their liquidity risk. Therefore, the reserve balances provide banks with an important buffer stock of liquid assets.

To overseas central banks. These are deposits of sterling (or euros in the case of the ECB) made by overseas authorities as part of their official reserves and/or for purposes of intervening in the foreign exchange market in order to influence the exchange rate of their currency.

It operates the government's monetary policy

The Bank of England's Monetary Policy Committee (MPC) sets Bank Rate at its regular meetings. This nine-member committee consists of four experts appointed by the Chancellor of the Exchequer and four senior members of the Bank of England, plus the Governor in the chair.

By careful management of the liquidity of the financial system the Bank of England aims to keep interest rates in line with the level decided by the MPC. It is able to do this through operations in the money markets. These are known as **open-market operations (OMOs)**. If shortages of liquidity are driving up short-term interest rates above the desired level, the Bank of England purchases securities (gilts and/or Treasury bills) on the open market: e.g. through reverse repos (a repo to the banks). This releases liquidity into the financial system and puts downward pressure on interest rates. Conversely, if excess liquidity is driving down interest rates, the Bank of England will sell more securities. When these are purchased, this will reduce banks' reserves and thereby put upward pressure on interest rates.

In normal times the Bank of England manages the aggregate amount of reserves through weekly auctions of 1-week repos. It also agrees with commercial banks an *average* amount of overnight reserve balances they would hold over the period between MPC meetings. Individual banks are then able to deposit or borrow reserves using the Bank of England's **operational standing facilities.** Banks deposit reserves at the deposit facility rate if they have an excess of reserves or borrow reserves from the Bank of England if they are short of reserves through overnight repo operations priced at the lending facility rate. The deposit rate is set below the Bank Rate, while the borrowing rate is set above the Bank Rate. This process is known as **reserve averaging**.

The operational standing facilities are designed to provide banks with excess or surplus reserves an incentive to trade them with other banks. Banks would prefer to borrow reserves at a lower interest rate or deposit reserves at a higher interest rate than they can through the operational standing facilities. By managing the aggregate amount of reserves, agreeing an average overnight holding of reserves and providing operational standing facilities, the Bank of England aims to establish a 'corridor' for inter-bank rates between its lending and deposit rates.

From its inception in March 2006 up until the middle of 2007 the corridor system kept short-term money market rates close to Bank Rate. But then, with growing concerns about the solvency of banks, the inter-bank market ceased to operate effectively and banks were forced to make greater use of the more costly operational standing facilities and draw reserves from the Bank. In other words, banks could no longer trade reserves with each other (in order to meet their average reserve target) at a lower cost than by using the Bank's standing facilities.

As the financial crisis unfolded it became increasingly difficult for the Bank to meet its monetary policy objectives while maintaining financial stability. New policies were thus adopted. October 2008 also saw the Bank of England stop short-term open-market operations. The key priority was now ensuring sufficient liquidity and so the focus switched to longer-term OMOs.

Definitions

Open-market operations (OMOs) The sale (or purchase) by the authorities of government securities in the open market in order to reduce (or increase) money supply and thereby affect interest rates.

Operational standing facilities Central bank facilities by which individual banks can deposit reserves or borrow reserves.

Reserve averaging The process whereby individual banks manage their average level of overnight reserves between MPC meetings using the Bank of England's operational standing facilities and/or the inter-bank market.

The advent of quantitative easing. March 2009 saw the Bank begin its programme of **quantitative easing (QE)** (see Box 22.10). The aim was to increase the amount of money in the financial system and thereby stimulate bank lending and hence aggregate demand. QE involved the Bank creating electronic money and using it to purchase assets, mainly government bonds, predominantly from non-deposit-taking financial institutions, such as unit trusts, insurance companies and pension funds. These institutions would then deposit the money in banks, which could lend it to businesses and consumers for purposes of spending.

Given this large quantity of 'new money' being supplied to the banking system it was decided to end the practice of banks voluntarily setting their own reserve targets between meetings of the MPC. Instead, all reserves were now to be remunerated at the official Bank Rate. The effect of remunerating all reserves was to replace the 'corridor system' with a 'floor system' since no commercial bank would be willing to lend surplus reserves at any rate lower than the Bank Rate. Therefore, the inter-bank rate would not fall below the Bank Rate.

The Bank of England's programme of asset purchases were conducted by a subsidiary of the Bank of England, known as the Asset Purchase Facility (APF). We can see the effect of these asset purchases in the Bank of England's balance sheet in Table 18.2: by far the largest item on the assets side is 'Loans to Asset Purchase Facility'. Another way of seeing their effect is through the increase in the Bank of England's sterling reserve liabilities (see Figure 18.3). These are the monies held by commercial banks in their accounts with the central bank, either for purposes of settling accounts with other commercial banks or for managing their liquidity.

Although the financial crisis saw changes to the Bank's monetary framework, the Bank argued that, in normal times, the reserves averaging framework remained an effective framework for implementing monetary policy. The case for resuming the framework was thus to be kept under review.

It provides liquidity, as necessary, to banks

Financial institutions engage in maturity transformation. While most customer deposits can be withdrawn instantly, financial institutions will have a variety of lending commitments, some of which span many years. Hence, the Bank of England acts as a 'liquidity backstop' for the banking system. It attempts to ensure that there is always an adequate supply of liquidity to meet the legitimate demands of depositors in banks.

Banks' reserve balances provide them with some liquidity insurance. However, the Bank of England needs other means by which to provide both individual banks and the banking system with sufficient liquidity. The financial crisis, for instance, saw incredible pressure on the aggregate liquidity of financial system. The result is that the UK has three principal insurance facilities:

Definitions

Quantitative easing (QE) A deliberate attempt by the central bank to increase the money supply by buying large quantities of securities through open-market operations. These securities could be securitised mortgage and other private-sector debt or government bonds.

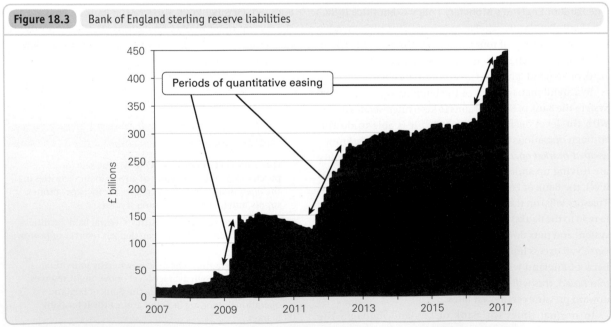

Figure 18.3   Bank of England sterling reserve liabilities

Source: Based on data from *Statistical Interactive Database*, series LPMBL22 (Bank of England) (data published 29/9/17).

Index long-term repos (ILTRS). Each month the Bank of England provides MFIs with reserves for a six-month period secured against collateral and indexed against the Bank Rate. Financial institutions can borrow reserves against different levels of collateral. These levels reflect the quality and liquidity of the collateral. The reserves are distributed through an auction where financial institutions indicate, for their particular level of collateral, the number of basis points over the Bank Rate (the 'spread') they are prepared to pay. Successful bidders pay a uniform price: this is the clearing price at which the Bank of England's preparedness to lend reserves has been met. The Bank of England will provide a greater quantity of reserves if, from the bids, it observes a greater demand for it to provide liquidity insurance.

Discount window facility (DWF). This on-demand facility allows financial institutions to borrow government bonds (gilts) for 30 days against different classes of collateral. They pay a fee to do so. The size of the fee is determined by both the level of collateral and the size of the collateral being traded. Gilts are long-term government debt instruments used by government as a means of financing its borrowing. Gilts can be used in repo operations as a means of securing liquidity. In this way, financial institutions are performing a liquidity upgrade of their collateral. However, the Bank may agree to lend cash rather than gilts if gilt repo markets cease to provide the necessary amount of liquidity, perhaps because the cost of doing so becomes prohibitively high. Financial institutions can look to roll over the funds obtained from the DWF beyond the normal 30 days.

Contingent term repo facility (CTRP). This is a facility which the Bank of England can activate in exceptional circumstances. As with the ILTRS, financial institutions can obtain liquidity secured against different levels of collateral through an auction. However, the terms, including the maturity of the funds, are intended to be more flexible.

It oversees the activities of banks and other financial institutions

The Bank of England requires all recognised banks to maintain adequate liquidity: this is called **prudential control**.

In May 1997, the Bank of England ceased to be responsible for the detailed supervision of banks' activities. This responsibility passed to the Financial Services Authority (FSA). But the financial crisis of the late 2000s raised concerns about whether the FSA, the Bank of England and HM Treasury where sufficiently watchful of banks' liquidity and the risks of liquidity shortage. Some commentators argued that a much tighter form of prudential control needed to be imposed.

In 2013, a new regulatory framework came into force, with an enhanced role for the Bank of England.

First, the Bank's *Financial Policy Committee* became responsible for **macro-prudential regulation**. This type of regulation takes a broader view of the financial system. It considers, for instance, its health or resilience to possible shocks and its propensity to create macroeconomic instability through credit creation.

Second, the prudential regulation of individual firms was transferred from the FSA to the *Prudential Regulation Authority,* a subsidiary of the Bank of England.

Third, the *Financial Conduct Authority (FCA)* took responsibility for consumer protection and the regulation of markets for financial services. The FCA is an independent body accountable to HM Treasury. The FSA was wound up.

1. *Would it be possible for an economy to function without a central bank?*
2. *What effect would a substantial increase in the sale of government bonds and Treasury bills have on interest rates?*

It operates the government's exchange rate policy

The Bank of England manages the country's gold and foreign currency reserves on behalf of the Treasury. This is done through the **exchange equalisation account**. The Treasury sets the Bank an annual remit for the management of the account (for example, setting a limit on changes in the level of reserves).

By buying and selling foreign currencies on the foreign exchange market, the Bank of England can affect the exchange rate. For example, if there were a sudden selling of sterling (due, say, to bad trade figures and a resulting fear that the pound would depreciate), the Bank of England could help to prevent the pound from falling by using reserves to buy up pounds on the foreign exchange market. Intervention in the foreign exchange market is examined in detail in Chapter 25.

The money markets

We now turn to the money markets where participants, including financial institutions, are able to lend and borrow to and from each other. In these markets debts typically have maturities of less than one year.

It has been traditional to distinguish money markets from another set of financial markets known as **capital markets**. In capital markets borrowing typically takes place over a longer

---

Definitions

Prudential control The insistence by the Bank of England that recognised banks maintain adequate liquidity.

Macro-prudential regulation Regulation that focuses on the overall stability of the financial system and its resilience to shocks.

Exchange equalisation account The gold and foreign exchange reserves account in the Bank of England.

Capital market A financial market where longer-term debt instruments, like government bonds (gilts), can be bought and sold.

duration. Capital markets include the market for ordinary shares and longer-term government debt instruments, known in the UK as gilts, which pay periodic fixed payments (known as 'coupons'). However, as we shall see, the boundaries in practice between these markets are rather difficult to pinpoint.

Central banks are also important participants in money markets. It is through the money markets that a central bank exercises control over interest rates. As we have seen throughout this chapter, the financial system has evolved rapidly and the money markets are no exception. This has widened the lending and borrowing opportunities for financial institutions.

We take the case of the London money market, which is normally divided into the 'discount' and 'repo' markets and the 'parallel' or 'complementary' markets.

 What how might the development of new financial instruments affect a central bank's conduct of monetary policy?

The discount and repo markets

The discount market. The discount market is the market for commercial or government bills. In the UK, government bills are known as Treasury bills and operations are conducted by the Debt Management Office, usually on a weekly basis. Treasury Bills involve short-term lending, say for one or three months, which, in conjunction with their low default risk, make them highly liquid assets. These markets are examples of **discount markets** because the instruments being traded are issued at a discount. In other words, the redemption price of the bills is greater than the issue price. The redemption price is fixed, but the issue price depends on demand and supply in the discount market. The rate of discount on bills can be calculated by the size of the discount relative to the redemption value and is usually expressed as an annual rate.

The discount market is also known as the 'traditional market' because it was the market in which many central banks traditionally used to supply central bank money to financial institutions. For instance, if the Bank of England wanted to increase liquidity in the banking system it could purchase from the banks Treasury bills which had yet to reach maturity. This process is known as **rediscounting**. The Bank of England would pay a price below the face value, thus effectively charging interest to the banks. The price could be set so that the 'rediscount rate' reflected the Bank Rate.

The repo market The emergence of the repo market is a more recent development dating back in the UK to the 1990s. As we saw earlier, repos have become an important source of wholesale funding for financial institutions. But they have also become an important means by which central banks can affect the liquidity of the financial system both to implement monetary policy and to ensure financial stability.

By entering into a repo agreement the Bank of England can buy securities, such as gilts, from the banks (thereby supplying them with money) on the condition that the banks buy them back at a fixed price and on a fixed date. The repurchase price will be above the sale price. The difference is the equivalent of the interest that the banks are being charged for having what amounts to a loan from the Bank of England. The repurchase price (and hence the 'repo rate') is set by the Bank of England to reflect the Bank Rate chosen by the MPC.

The Bank of England first began using repo operations to manage the liquidity of the financial system in 1997 when it undertook daily operations, with the repurchases of securities usually occurring two weeks after the initial sale. This system was refined so that in 2006 operations became weekly and the repurchase period typically shortened to one week.

However, the financial crisis caused the Bank to modify its repo operations to manage liquidity for both purposes of monetary policy, but increasingly to ensure financial stability. These changes included a widening of the securities eligible as collateral for loans, a move to longer-term repo operations and a suspension of short-term repo operations.

So central banks, like the Bank of England, are prepared to provide central bank money through the creation of bank reserves. Central banks are thus the ultimate guarantor of sufficient liquidity in the monetary system and, for this reason, are known as the **lender of last resort**.

The parallel money markets

Like repo markets, complementary or parallel money markets have grown rapidly in recent years. In part, this reflects the opening up of markets to international dealing, the deregulation of banking and money market dealing and the desire of banks to keep funds in a form that can be readily switched from one form of deposit to another, or from one currency to another.

Examples of parallel markets include the markets for *certificates of deposit* (CDs), *foreign currencies markets* (dealings in foreign currencies deposited short term in the country) and *the inter-bank market*. We focus here on the important inter-bank market (details on other parallel markets can be found in Case Study 18.11 on the student website).

The inter-bank market. The inter-bank market involves wholesale loans from one bank to another over periods from one day to up to several months. Banks with surplus liquidity lend to other banks, which then use this as the basis for loans to individuals and companies.

Definitions

Discount market The market for corporate bills and Treasury bills whose initial price is below the redemption value.

Rediscounting bills of exchange Buying bills before they reach maturity.

Lender of last resort The role of the Bank of England as the guarantor of sufficient liquidity in the monetary system.

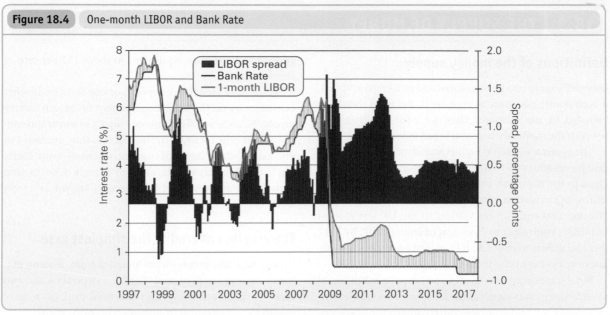

Figure 18.4 One-month LIBOR and Bank Rate

Source: Based on data from *Statistical Interactive Database*, series IUMABEDR and IUMAVYRA (Bank of England) (data published 1/11/17).

The rate at which banks lend to each other is known as the IBOR (inter-bank offered rate). The IBOR has a major influence on the other rates that banks charge. In the euro-zone, the IBOR is known as Euribor. In the UK, it is known as the LIBOR (where 'L' stands for 'London'). As inter-bank loans can be anything from overnight to 12 months, the IBOR will vary from one length of loan to another.

Inter-bank interest rates tend to be higher than those in the discount and repo markets and sensitive to the aggregate level of liquidity in the financial system. As Figure 18.4 shows, during the financial crisis of 2008 inter-bank lending rates rose significantly above the Bank Rate. At the same time lending virtually ceased as banks became worried that the bank they were lending to might default.

 Why should Bank of England determination of the rate of interest in the discount and repo markets also influence rates of interest in the parallel markets?

Section summary

1. Central to the financial system are the retail and wholesale arms of banks. Between them they provide the following important functions: giving expert advice, channelling capital to areas of highest return, maturity transformation, risk transformation and the transmission of payments. During the financial crisis the systemic importance of some of these banks meant they had to be rescued by governments. They were seen as too important or too big to fail (TBF).

2. Banks' liabilities include both sight and time deposits. They also include certificates of deposit and repos. Their assets include: notes and coin, balances with the Bank of England, market loans, bills of exchange (Treasury bills and commercial bills), reverse repos, advances to customers (the biggest item – including overdrafts, personal loans, credit card debt and mortgages) and investments (government bonds and inter-bank investments). In the years up to 2008 they had increasingly included securitised assets.

3. Banks aim to make profits, but they must also have a sufficient capital base and maintain sufficient liquidity. Liquid assets, however, tend to be relatively unprofitable and profitable assets tend to be relatively illiquid. Banks therefore need to keep a balance of profitability and liquidity in their range of assets.

4. The Bank of England is the UK's central bank. It issues notes; it acts as banker to the government, to banks and to various overseas central banks; it ensures sufficient liquidity for the financial sector; it operates the country's monetary and exchange rate policy.

5. The money market is the market in short-term deposits and loans. It consists of the discount and repo markets and the parallel money markets.

6. Through repos the Bank of England can provide liquidity to the banks at the rate of interest chosen by the Monetary Policy Committee (Bank Rate). It is always prepared to lend in this way in order to ensure adequate liquidity in the economy. The financial crisis saw the Bank adapt its operations in the money market and introduce new mechanisms for providing liquidity insurance, including the Discount Window Facility and longer-term repos.

7. The parallel money markets consist of various markets in short-term finance between various financial institutions.

18.3 THE SUPPLY OF MONEY

Definitions of the money supply

If money supply is to be monitored and possibly controlled, it is obviously necessary to measure it. But what should be included in the measure? Here we need to distinguish between the monetary base and broad money.

The *monetary base* (or 'high-powered money') consists of cash (notes and coin) in circulation outside the central bank. Thus, in the eurozone, the monetary base is given by cash (euros) in circulation outside the ECB.[1] In 1970, the stock of notes and coins in circulation in the UK was around £4 billion, equivalent to 7 per cent of annual GDP. By 2017 this had grown to over £80 billion, but equivalent to only just over 4 per cent of annual GDP.

But the monetary base gives us a very poor indication of the effective money supply, since it excludes the most important source of liquidity for spending: namely, bank deposits. The problem is which deposits to include. We need to answer three questions:

- Should we include just sight deposits, or time deposits as well?
- Should we include just retail deposits, or wholesale deposits as well?
- Should we include just bank deposits, or building society (savings institution) deposits as well?

In the past there has been a whole range of measures, each including different combinations of these accounts. However, financial deregulation, the abolition of foreign exchange controls and the development of computer technology have led to huge changes in the financial sector throughout the world. This has led to a blurring of the distinctions between different types of account. It has also made it very easy to switch deposits from one type of account to another. For these reasons, the most usual measure that countries use for money supply is *broad money*, which in most cases includes both time and sight deposits, retail and wholesale deposits, and bank and building society (savings institution) deposits.

In the UK, this measure of broad money is known as M4. In most other European countries and the USA it is known as M3. There are, however, minor differences between countries in what is included. (Official UK and eurozone measures of money supply are given in Box 18.4.)

In 1970, the stock of M4 in the UK was around £25 billion, equivalent to 48 per cent of annual GDP. By 2017 this had grown to £2.3 trillion, equivalent to about 115 per cent of annual GDP.

As we have seen, bank deposits of one form or another constitute by far the largest component of (broad) money supply. To understand how money supply expands and contracts, and how it can be controlled, it is thus necessary to understand what determines the size of bank deposits. Banks can themselves expand the amount of bank deposits, and hence the money supply, by a process known as 'credit creation'.

The creation of credit: the simplest case

To illustrate this process in its simplest form, assume that banks have just one type of liability – deposits – and two types of asset – balances with the central bank (to achieve liquidity) and advances to customers (to earn profit).

Banks want to achieve profitability while maintaining sufficient liquidity. Assume that they believe that sufficient liquidity will be achieved if 10 per cent of their assets are held as balances with the central bank. The remaining 90 per cent will then be in advances to customers. In other words, the banks operate a 10 per cent liquidity ratio.

Assume initially that the combined balance sheet of the banks is as shown in Table 18.3. Total deposits are £100 billion, of which £10 billion (10 per cent) are kept in balances with the central bank. The remaining £90 billion (90 per cent) are lent to customers.

Now assume that the government spends more money – £10 billion, say, on roads or hospitals. It pays for this with cheques drawn on its account with the central bank. The people receiving the cheques deposit them in their banks. Banks return these cheques to the central bank and their balances correspondingly increase by £10 billion. The combined banks' balance sheet now is shown in Table 18.4.

But this is not the end of the story. Banks now have surplus liquidity. With their balances in the central bank having

Table 18.3		Banks' original balance sheet	
Liabilities	**£bn**	**Assets**	**£bn**
Deposits	100	Balances with the central bank	10
		Advances	90
Total	100	Total	100

Definitions

Monetary base Notes and coin outside the central bank.

Broad money Cash in circulation plus retail and wholesale bank and building society deposits.

---

1 Before 2006, there used to be a measure of narrow money called 'M0' in the UK. This included cash in circulation outside the Bank of England and banks' non-interest-bearing 'operational balances' in the Bank of England, with these balances accounting for a tiny proportion of the whole. Since 2006, the Bank of England has allowed banks to hold interest-bearing reserve accounts, which are much larger than the former operational balances. The Bank of England thus decided to discontinue M0 as a measure and focus on cash in circulation as its measure of the monetary base.

BOX 18.4 | **UK AND EUROZONE MONETARY AGGREGATES**

How long is a piece of string?

UK measures

There are two main measures of the money supply in the UK: cash in circulation (i.e. outside the Bank of England) and M4. Cash in circulation is referred to as the 'monetary base' or 'narrow money' and M4 is referred to as 'broad money' or simply as 'the money supply'. In addition, there is a measure called 'Retail deposits and cash in M4' (previously known as M2). This measure excludes wholesale deposits.

The definitions are as follows:

Cash in circulation. This is all cash held outside the Bank of England: in other words by individuals, firms, banks and the public sector.

Retail deposits and cash in M4. Cash in circulation with the public (but not cash in banks and building societies) + private-sector *retail* sterling deposits in banks and building societies.

M4. Retail deposits and cash in M4 + private-sector wholesale sterling deposits (including repos) in banks and building societies + private-sector holdings of sterling certificates of deposit, commercial paper and other short-term paper issued by MFIs.

Table (a) gives the figures for these aggregates for the end of August 2017.

(a) *UK monetary aggregates, end August 2017 (not seasonally adjusted)*

	£ billion
Cash in circulation (i.e. outside the Bank of England)[a]	82.46
− Cash in banks and cash held outside the UK[a,b]	−8.10
+ Private-sector retail bank and building society deposits	1 586.07
= **Retail deposits and cash in M4**	**1 660.44**
+ Private-sector wholesale bank and building society deposits + CDs	667.83
= **M4**	**2 328.26**

a Cash in circulation is calculated mid-month and thus the figure slightly understates the end-month value.
b Row 4 minus rows 3 and 1.
Source: Based on data in *Bankstats* (Bank of England), Tables A1.1.1 and A2.2.1. Data published September 2017.

 Why is cash in banks and building societies not included in M4?

Eurozone measures

Although the ECB uses three measures of the money supply, they are different from those used by the Bank of England. The narrowest definition (M1) includes overnight deposits (i.e. call money) as well as cash, and is thus much broader than the UK's narrow money measure. The broadest eurozone measure (M3) is again broader than the UK's broadest measure (M4), since the eurozone measure includes various other moderately liquid assets. The definitions of the three eurozone aggregates are:

M1. Cash in circulation with the public + overnight deposits.

M2. M1 + deposits with agreed maturity up to two years + deposits redeemable up to three months' notice.

M3. M2 + repos + money-market funds and paper + debt securities with residual maturity up to two years.

Table (b) gives the figures for UK money supply for each of these three ECB measures – again, for the end of August 2017.

(b) *UK money supply using ECB measures: end August 2017 (not seasonally adjusted)*

		£ billion
	Currency in circulation	75.09
+	Overnight deposits	1 610.09
=	**M1**	**1 685.49**
+	Deposits with agreed maturity up to 2 years	168.93
+	Deposits redeemable up to 3 months' notice	485.45
=	**M2**	**2 339.87**
+	Repos	327.65
+	Money market funds and paper	114.47
=	**M3**	**2 781.99**

Note: M1, M2 and M3 estimates relate to non-MFI residents, excluding central government and contain deposits in all currencies.
Source: Based on data in *Bankstats* (Bank of England), Table A2.2.1. Data published September 2017.

 What are the benefits of including these additional items in the broad measure of money supply?

---

increased to £20 billion, they now have a liquidity ratio of 20/110, or 18.2 per cent. If they are to return to a 10 per cent liquidity ratio, they need only retain £11 billion as balances at the central bank (£11 billion/£110 billion = 10 per cent). The remaining £9 billion they can lend to customers.

Assume now that customers spend this £9 billion in shops and the shopkeepers deposit the cheques in their bank accounts. When the cheques are cleared, the balances in the central bank of the *customers'* banks will duly be debited by £9 billion, but the balances in the central bank of the shop-keepers' banks will be credited by £9 billion, leaving overall balances in the central bank unaltered. There is still a surplus of £9 billion over what is required to maintain the 10 per cent liquidity ratio. The new deposits of £9 billion in the

Table 18.4 The initial effect of an additional deposit of £10 billion

Liabilities	£bn	Assets	£bn
Deposits (old)	100	Balances with the central bank (old)	10
Deposits (new)	10	Balances with the central bank (new)	10
		Advances	90
Total	110	Total	110

shopkeepers' banks, backed by balances in the central bank, can thus be used as the basis for further loans. Ten per cent (i.e. £0.9 billion) must be kept back in the central bank, but the remaining 90 per cent (i.e. £8.1 billion) can be lent out again.

When the money is spent and the cheques are cleared, this £8.1 billion will still remain as surplus balances in the central bank and can therefore be used as the basis for yet more loans. Again, 10 per cent must be retained and the remaining 90 per cent can be lent out. This process goes on and on until eventually the position is as shown in Table 18.5.

The initial increase in balances with the central bank of £10 billion has allowed banks to create new advances (and hence deposits) of £90 billion, making a total increase in money supply of £100 billion.

This effect is known as the **bank deposits multiplier**. In this simple example with a liquidity ratio of 1/10 (i.e. 10 per cent), the bank deposits multiplier is 10. An initial increase in deposits of £10 billion allowed total deposits to rise by £100 billion. In this simple world, therefore, the bank deposits multiplier is the inverse of the liquidity ratio (l).

Bank deposits multiplier $= 1/l$

> **?** If banks choose to operate a 20 per cent liquidity ratio and receive extra cash deposits of £10 million,
> (a) How much credit will ultimately be created?
> (b) By how much will total deposits have expanded?
> (c) What is the size of the bank deposits multiplier?

Table 18.5 The full effect of an additional deposit of £10 billion

Liabilities	£bn	Assets	£bn
Deposits (old)	100	Balances with the central bank (old)	10
Deposits (new: initial)	10	Balances with the central bank (new)	10
(new: subsequent)	90	Advances (old)	90
		Advances (new)	90
Total	200	Total	200

*LOOKING AT THE MATHS

The process of credit creation can be expressed mathematically as the sum of an infinite series. If a is the proportion of any deposit that is lent by banks, where $a = 1 - l$, then total deposits will expand by

$$D_r = D_0(1 + a + a^2 + a^3 + \dots)$$
$$= D_0(1/1 - a)$$
$$= D_0(1/l) \tag{1}$$

Thus if there were an initial additional deposit (D_0) of £100 and if $a = 0.8$, giving a liquidity ratio (l) of 0.2, total deposits would expand by £100 × 1/0.2 = £500. The bank deposits multiplier is 5.

Proof of equation (1) is given in Maths Case 18.1 on the student website.

Note that the maths of the bank deposits multiplier is very similar to that of the Keynesian expenditure multiplier of section 17.2 (see Maths Case 17.1 on the student website). The economics, however, is quite different. The Keynesian multiplier is concerned with the effects of increased demand on real national output. The bank deposits multiplier is simply concerned with money creation.

The creation of credit: the real world

In practice, the creation of credit is not as simple as this. There are three major complications.

Banks' liquidity ratio may vary

Banks may choose a different liquidity ratio. At certain times, banks may decide that it is prudent to hold a bigger proportion of liquid assets. For example, if banks are worried about increased risks of default on loans, they may choose to hold a higher liquidity ratio to ensure that they have enough to meet customers' needs. This was the case in the late 2000s when many banks became less willing to lend to other banks for fear of the other banks' assets containing subprime debt. Banks, as a result, hoarded cash and became more cautious about granting loans.

On the other hand, there may be an upsurge in consumer demand for credit. Banks may be very keen to grant additional loans and thus make more profits, even though they have acquired no additional assets. They may simply go ahead and expand credit, and accept a lower liquidity ratio.

Customers may not want to take up the credit on offer. Banks may wish to make additional loans, but customers may not want to borrow. There may be insufficient demand. But will

> **Definition**
>
> **Bank deposits multiplier** The number of times greater the expansion of bank deposits is than the additional liquidity in banks that causes it: $1/l$ (the inverse of the liquidity ratio).

the banks not then lower their interest rates, thus encouraging people to borrow? Possibly; but if they lower the rate they charge to borrowers, they must also lower the rate they pay to depositors. But then depositors may switch to other institutions such as building societies.

 How will an increased mobility of savings and other capital between institutions affect this argument?

Banks may not operate a simple liquidity ratio

The fact that banks hold a number of fairly liquid assets, such as short-term loans to other banks on the inter-bank market, bills of exchange and certificates of deposit, makes it difficult to identify a simple liquidity ratio. For example, if banks use £1 million in cash to purchase £1 million of bills, can we assume that the liquidity ratio has remained exactly the same? In other words, can we assume that **near money** assets, such as bills, are just as liquid as cash? If we assume that they are not, then has the liquidity ratio fallen? If so, by how much?

Banks do not see a clear-cut dividing line between liquid and non-liquid assets. They try to maintain a rough balance across the liquidity range, but the precise composition of assets will vary as interest rates on the various assets vary, and as the demands for liquidity vary.

In practice, therefore, the size of the bank deposits multiplier will vary and is thus difficult to predict in advance.

 Is the following statement true: 'The greater the number of types of asset that are counted as being liquid, the smaller will be the bank deposits multiplier'?

Some of the extra cash may be withdrawn by the public

If extra cash comes into the banking system, and as a result extra deposits are created, part of them may be held by households and non-bank firms (known in this context as the **non-bank private sector**) as cash outside the banks. In other words, some of the extra cash leaks out of the banking system. This will result in an overall multiplier effect that is smaller than the full bank deposits multiplier. This overall multiplier is known as the **money multiplier**. It is defined as the rise in total money supply expressed as a proportion of the rise in the monetary base that caused it: $\Delta M_s / \Delta M_b$ (where M_s is total broad money supply and M_b is the monetary base). Box 18.5 shows how the money multiplier is calculated.

The broad money multiplier in the UK

In the UK, the principal money multiplier measure is the broad money multiplier. This is given by $\Delta M4 / \Delta M_b$, where M_b in this case is defined as cash in circulation with the public plus banks' interest-bearing deposits (reserve accounts) at the Bank of England.

Another indicator of the broad money multiplier is simply the ratio of the *level* of (as opposed to the change in) M4 relative to the *level* of cash in circulation with the public and banks' reserve accounts at the central bank. This 'levels'

relationship is shown in Figure 18.5 and helps us to analyse the longer-term relationship between the stocks of broad money and the monetary base.

From Figure 18.5 we can see how broad money grew rapidly relative to the monetary base during the late 1980s and into the early 1990s. From the early 1990s to the mid-2000s, the level of M4 relative to the monetary base fluctuated in a narrow range.

From May 2006 the Bank of England began remunerating banks' reserve accounts at the official Bank Rate. This encouraged banks to increase their reserve accounts at the Bank of England and led to a sharp fall in the broad money multiplier. It then decreased further during 2009. The significant decline in the ratio of broad to narrow money in 2009, in 2011/12 and again in 2016/17 coincided with the Bank of England's programme of asset purchases (quantitative easing) which led to a large increase in banks' reserves. The point is that the increase in the monetary base did not lead to the same percentage increase in broad money, as banks were more cautious about lending and chose to keep higher reserves. The policy of quantitative easing is discussed more in Chapter 22.

In the next section we focus on those factors which help to explain movements in the money multiplier and changes in the money supply.

 Which would you expect to fluctuate more, the money multiplier ($\Delta M4 / \Delta cash$), or the simple ratio, M4/cash, illustrated in Figure 18.4?

What causes money supply to rise?

Money supply can change for a number of reasons. We consider five sets of circumstances which can cause the money supply to *rise*.

Central bank action

The central bank may decide that the stock of money is too low and that this is keeping up interest rates and restraining spending in the economy. In such circumstances, it may choose to create additional money.

As we saw above, this was the case following the financial crisis of 2007/8 when the Bank of England and the US Federal Reserve Bank embarked on programmes of quantitative easing. QE involves the central bank creating electronic (narrow) money which is used to purchase assets, mainly government bonds. When the recipients of this money

---

Definitions

Near money Highly liquid assets (other than cash).

Non-bank private sector Households and non-bank firms. In other words, everyone in the country other than banks and the government (central and local).

Money multiplier The number of times greater the expansion of money supply is than the expansion of the monetary base that caused it: $\Delta M_s / \Delta M_b$.

Figure 18.5	UK money multiplier

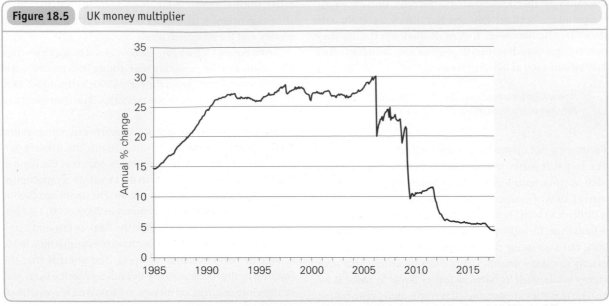

Source: Based on series LPMBL22 (reserves), LPMAVAB (notes and coin) and LPMAUYN (M4) from Statistical Interactive Database, Bank of England (data published 29 September 2017, seasonally adjusted except for reserves)

(mainly non-bank financial institutions) deposit it in banks, the banks can then lend it to businesses and consumers for spending and, through the bank deposits multiplier, broad money would increase.

As we can see from Figure 18.6, however, this was not enough to prevent UK broad money supply falling for much of the first half of the 2010s.

Banks choose to hold a lower liquidity ratio

If banks collectively choose to hold a lower liquidity ratio, they will have surplus liquidity. The banks have tended to choose a lower liquidity ratio over time because of the increasing use of direct debits and debit card and credit card transactions.

Surplus liquidity can be used to expand advances, which will lead to a multiplied rise in broad money supply (e.g. M4).

---

*BOX 18.5 | **CALCULATING THE MONEY MULTIPLIER** | EXPLORING ECONOMICS

The money multiplier (m) is the rise in total money supply (ΔM_s) divided by the rise in the monetary base (ΔM_b):

$$m = \Delta M_s / \Delta M_b \qquad (1)$$

The total money supply (M_s) consists of deposits in banks and building societies (D) plus cash held by the public (C). Thus a rise in money supply would be given by

$$\Delta M_s = \Delta D + \Delta C \qquad (2)$$

The monetary base (M_b) consists of bank and building society reserves (R) plus cash held by the public (C). Thus a rise in the monetary base would be given by

$$\Delta M_b = \Delta R + \Delta C \qquad (3)$$

Thus, by substituting equations (2) and (3) into equation (1), the money multiplier is given by

$$m = \frac{\Delta D + \Delta C}{\Delta R + \Delta C} \qquad (4)$$

Assume now that banks wish to hold a given fraction (r) of any rise in deposits in the form of reserves, i.e.

$$r = \Delta R / \Delta D \qquad (5)$$

and that the public wishes to hold a given fraction (c) of any rise in its deposits as cash, i.e.

$$c = \Delta C / \Delta D \qquad (6)$$

If we now divide the top and bottom of equation (4) by ΔD, we get

$$m = \frac{\Delta D/\Delta D + \Delta C/\Delta D}{\Delta R/\Delta D + \Delta C/\Delta D} = \frac{1 + c}{r + c} \qquad (7)$$

Thus if c were 0.2 and r were 0.1, the money multiplier would be

$$(1 + 0.2)/(0.1 + 0.2) = 1.2/0.3 = 4$$

i.e.

$$\Delta M_s = 4 \times \Delta M_b$$

1. *If c were 0.1 and r were 0.01, by how much would money supply expand if the monetary base rose by £1 million?*
2. *Money supply (M4) includes wholesale as well as retail deposits. Given that firms will wish to keep only a very small fraction of a rise in wholesale deposits in cash (if any at all), how will a change in the balance of wholesale and retail deposits affect the value of c and hence of the money multiplier?*

| Figure 18.6 | Annual rate of growth of M4 |

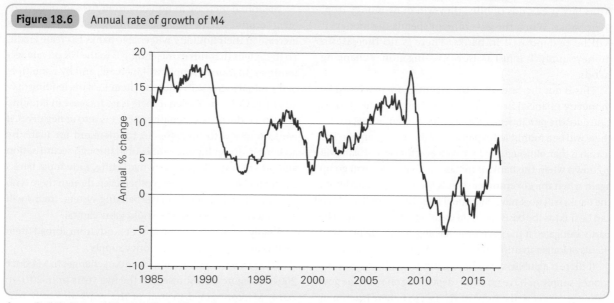

Source: *Statistical Interactive Database* (Bank of England), series LPMVQJW (data published 29/9/17, seasonally adjusted).

An important trend up to the late 2000s was the growth of the use of wholesale funds by financial institutions. Table 18.1 showed that short-term loans to other banks (including overseas banks) are now the largest element in banks' liquid assets. These assets may be used by a bank as the basis for expanding loans and thereby starting a chain of credit creation.

But although these assets are liquid to an individual bank, they do not add to the liquidity of the banking system as a whole. By using them for credit creation, the banking system is operating with a lower *overall* liquidity ratio.

This was a major element in the banking crisis of 2008. By operating with a collectively low liquidity ratio, banks were vulnerable to people defaulting on debt, such as mortgages. The problem was compounded by the holding of sub-prime debt in the form of securitised assets. Realising the vulnerability of other banks, banks became increasingly unwilling to lend to each other. The resulting decline in inter-bank lending reduced the amount of credit created, thereby depressing the money supply (see Figure 18.6).

 What effects do debit cards and cash machines (ATMs) have on (a) banks' prudent liquidity ratios; (b) the size of the bank deposits multiplier?

The non-bank private sector chooses to hold less cash

Households and firms may choose to hold less cash. Again, the reason may be a greater use of cards, direct debits, etc. This means that a greater proportion of the cash base will be held as deposits in banks rather than in people's wallets, purses or safes outside banks. The extra cash deposits allow banks to create more credit.

The previous two reasons for an expansion of broad money supply (M4) are because more credit is being created for a given monetary base. As Figure 18.5 showed, the money multiplier rose substantially in the late 1980s and early 1990s and then gradually up to 2006.

The next two reasons for an expansion of money supply are reasons why the monetary base itself might expand.

An inflow of funds from abroad

When sterling is used to pay for UK exports and is deposited in UK banks by the exporters, credit can be created on the basis of it. This leads to a multiplied increase in the domestic money supply.

The money supply will also expand if depositors of sterling in banks overseas then switch these deposits to banks in the UK. This is a direct increase in the money supply. In an open economy like the UK, movements of sterling and other currencies into and out of the country can be very large, leading to large fluctuations in the money supply.

A public-sector deficit

A public-sector deficit is the difference between public-sector expenditure and public-sector receipts. To finance a public-sector deficit, the government has to borrow money by selling interest-bearing securities (Treasury bills and gilts). The precise amount of money the public sector requires to borrow in any one year is known in the UK as the **public-sector net cash requirement (PSNCR)**. In general, the bigger the deficit, the greater will be the growth in the money supply. Just how the money supply will be affected, however, depends on who buys the securities.

Consider first the case where government securities are purchased by the non-bank private sector. When people or

---

Definitions

Public-sector net cash requirement (PSNCR) The (annual) deficit of the public sector, and thus the amount that the public sector must borrow.

firms buy the bonds or bills, they will draw money from their banks. When the government spends the money, it will be re-deposited in banks. There is no increase in money supply. It is just a case of existing money changing hands.

This is not the case when the securities are purchased by monetary financial institutions, including the central bank. Consider the purchase of Treasury bills by commercial banks: there will be a multiplied expansion of the money supply. The reason is that, although banks' balances at the central bank will go down when the banks purchase the bills, they will go up again when the government spends the money. In addition, the banks will now have additional liquid assets (bills), which can be used as the basis for credit creation. This effect could be partly mitigated if the government is able to issue debt instruments of longer maturity (gilts) since these are less liquid.

If there is a public-sector *surplus* this will either reduce the money supply or have no effect, depending on what the government does with the surplus. The fact that there is a surplus means that the public sector is spending less than it receives in taxes, etc. The initial effect, therefore, is to reduce the money in the economy: it is being 'retired' in the central bank.

If, however, the government then uses this money to buy back securities from the non-bank private sector, the money will merely return to the economy, and there will be no net effect on money supply.

 If the government borrows but does not spend the proceeds, what effect will this have on the money supply if it borrows from:
(a) the banking sector;
(b) the non-bank private sector?

The flow-of-funds equation

All these effects on money supply can be summarised using a *flow-of-funds equation*. This shows the components of a change in money supply (ΔM_s). The following flow-of-funds equation is the one most commonly used in the UK, that for M4. It consists of four items (or 'counterparts' as they are known):

ΔM4	*equals*	PSNCR	(Item 1)
	minus	Sales of public-sector debt to (or plus purchases of public-sector debt from) the non-bank private sector	(Item 2)
	plus	Banks' and building societies' sterling net lending to the UK private sector	(Item 3)
	plus	External effect	(Item 4)

Public-sector borrowing (item 1) will lead to a direct increase in the money supply, but not if it is funded by selling bonds and bills to the non-bank private sector. Such sales (item 2) have therefore to be subtracted from the public-sector net cash requirement (PSNCR). But conversely, if the government buys back old bonds from the non-bank private sector, this will further increase the money supply.

The initial increase in liquidity from the sale of government securities to the banking sector is given by item 1. This increase in their liquidity will enable banks to create credit. To the extent that this extra lending is to the UK private sector (item 3), money supply will increase, and by a multiple of the initial increase in liquidity (item 1). Bank lending may also increase (item 3) even if there is no increase in liquidity or even a reduction in liquidity (item 1 is zero or negative), if banks respond to increases in the demand for loans by accepting a lower liquidity ratio, or if, through securitisation and other forms of secondary marketing, individual banks gain extra liquidity from each other, even though there is no total increase in liquidity in the banking system. Item 3 will be reduced if banks choose to hold more capital.

Finally, if there is a net inflow of funds from abroad (item 4), this too will increase the money supply.

Table 18.6 shows the components of changes in M4 since 2004. As Figure 18.6 showed, in the five years from 2010 to 2014, M4 contracted in four of the years and only rose slightly in the other one (2013). The period was also characterised by large public-sector deficits. Consider 2011, when the public-sector net cash requirement (item 1) was close to £120 billion. Deficits tend to increase the money supply. However, this effect was counteracted by sales of government debt to the non-bank private sector (item 2), by an outflow of funds abroad (item 4), but, more especially, by a very large decrease in the flow of bank lending (item 3). Indeed, the negative figure for net lending indicates that the private non-bank sector was repaying existing debts more than it was acquiring new debt. This phenomenon was observed frequently throughout the early 2010s. It is an example of a balance-sheet effect (see pages 450–51) which helped to reduce the growth of the money supply.

The relationship between money supply and the rate of interest

Simple monetary theory often assumes that the supply of money is totally independent of interest rates. This is illustrated in Figure 18.7. The money supply is *exogenous*. It is assumed to be determined by the government or central bank ('the authorities'): what the authorities choose it to be, or what they allow it to be by their choice of the level and method of financing the public-sector deficit.

In practice, however, even if narrow money were to be tightly controlled by the central bank (which it is not), it

---

> **Definitions**
>
> **Flow-of-funds equation** The various items making up an increase (or decrease) in money supply.
>
> **Exogenous money supply** Money supply that does not depend on the demand for money but is set by the authorities.

Table 18.6 Counterparts to changes in M4 (£m)

	PSCNR (+) (Public sector Net Cash Requirement) (1)	Sales (−)/ Purchases (+) to/ from non-bank private sector (2)	Banks' and building societies net lending to UK private sector (less increase in bank's capital) (3)	External effect: inflows (+)/ outflows (−) (4)	Total change in M4
2004	40 066	−32 477	116 390	1 846	98 233
2005	40 452	−11 037	152 816	2 829	150 409
2006	35 643	−22 916	238 694	−34 269	166 593
2007	35 044	−3 846	296 104	−77 272	191 138
2008	102 821	−52 230	199 272	108 494	259 666
2009	192 586	31 845	80 417	−183 161	135 092
2010	153 055	−33 941	−128 603	−28 662	−34 617
2011	118 660	−16 027	−122 386	−33 703	−52 810
2012	100 083	24 566	−16 971	−127 466	−19 819
2013	73 370	−2 251	−26 060	−36 358	3 504
2014	98 476	−94 045	−174 056	146 112	−23 338
2015	83 486	−28 721	46 430	−88 233	5 801
2016	83 676	389	96 557	−53 230	132 999

Note: White shaded rows are years in which the stock of M4 contracted.
Source: Based on data in *Bankstats* (Bank of England), Table A3.2. Data published September 2017.

Figure 18.7 The supply of money curve: exogenous money supply

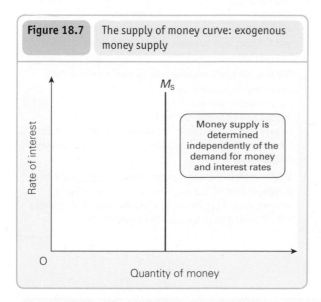

Money supply is determined independently of the demand for money and interest rates

Figure 18.8 The supply of money curve: endogenous money supply

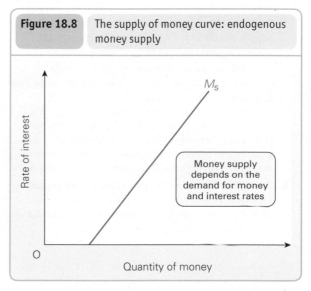

Money supply depends on the demand for money and interest rates

would be very hard to have a precise control of broad money. More complex models, therefore, and especially Keynesian models, assume that money supply is *endogenous*: that it depends on the demand for money. The argument is that higher money demand will result in higher interest rates and in higher levels of money supplied. The result is an upward-sloping money supply curve, as in Figure 18.8. The reasons for this are as follows:

■ Increases in money supply may occur as a result of banks expanding credit in response to the demand for credit. This assumes that banks have surplus liquidity in the first place, or are happy to operate with lower liquidity, or can increase liquidity through secondary marketing of otherwise illiquid assets, or can obtain liquidity from the central bank through repos. Higher demand for credit will drive up interest rates, making it more profitable for banks to supply more credit.

■ Higher interest rates may encourage depositors to switch their deposits from sight accounts (earning little or no interest) to time accounts. Since money is less likely to

Definition

Endogenous money supply Money supply that is determined (at least in part) by the demand for money.

be withdrawn quickly from time accounts, banks may feel the need to hold less liquidity, and therefore may decide to increase credit, thus expanding the money supply.

- Higher interest rates attract deposits from overseas. This increases the money supply to the extent that the Bank of England does not allow the exchange rate to appreciate in response.

To summarise: an increase in demand for money raises interest rates, which in turn increases the quantity of money supplied (see sections 18.4 and 18.5): a movement along an upward-sloping money supply curve.

Some economists go further still. They argue that not only is money supply endogenous, but the 'curve' is effectively horizontal; money supply expands passively to match the demand for money. In practice, the shape varies with the confidence of MFIs. In periods of optimism, banks may be willing to expand credit to meet the demand from customers. In periods of pessimism, such as that following the financial crisis, banks may be very unwilling to grant credit when customers seek it.

Section summary

1. Money supply can be defined in a number of different ways, depending on what items are included. A useful distinction is between narrow money and broad money. Narrow money includes just cash, and possibly banks' balances at the central bank. Broad money also includes deposits in banks and possibly various other short-term deposits in the money market. In the UK, M4 is the preferred measure of broad money. In the eurozone it is M3.

2. Bank deposits are a major proportion of broad money supply. The expansion of bank deposits is the major element in the expansion of the money supply.

3. Bank deposits expand through a process of credit creation. If banks' liquid assets increase, they can be used as a base for increasing loans. When the loans are redeposited in banks, they form the base for yet more loans, and thus a process of multiple credit expansion takes place. The ratio of the increase of deposits to an expansion of banks' liquidity base is called the 'bank deposits multiplier'. It is the inverse of the liquidity ratio.

4. In practice, it is difficult to predict the precise amount by which money supply will expand if there is an increase in cash. The reasons are that banks may choose to hold a different liquidity ratio; customers may not take up all the credit on offer; there may be no simple liquidity ratio given the range of near money assets; and some of the extra cash may leak away into extra cash holdings by the public.

5. Money supply will rise if (a) banks choose to hold a lower liquidity ratio and thus create more credit for an existing amount of liquidity; (b) people choose to hold less cash outside the banks; (c) there is a net inflow of funds from abroad; (d) the government runs a public-sector deficit and finances it by borrowing from the banking sector or from abroad.

6. The flow-of-funds equation shows the components of any change in money supply. A rise in money supply equals the public-sector net cash requirement (PSNCR) *minus* sales of public-sector debt to the non-bank private sector, *plus* banks' lending to the private sector (less increases in banks' capital), *plus* inflows of money from abroad.

7. Simple monetary theory assumes that the supply of money is independent of interest rates. In practice, a rise in interest rates (in response to a higher demand for money) will often lead to an increase in money supply.

18.4 THE DEMAND FOR MONEY

The motives for holding money

The demand for money refers to the desire to hold money: to keep your wealth in the form of money, rather than spending it on goods and services or using it to purchase financial assets such as bonds or shares. It is usual to distinguish three reasons why people want to hold their assets in the form of money. Note that we are talking here about broad money: M4 in the UK.

The transactions motive

Since money is a medium of exchange, it is required for conducting transactions. But since people receive money only at intervals (e.g. weekly or monthly) and not continuously, they require to hold balances of money in cash or in current accounts.

The precautionary motive

Unforeseen circumstances can arise, such as a car breakdown. Thus individuals often hold some additional money as a precaution. Firms too keep precautionary balances because of uncertainties about the timing of their receipts and payments. If a large customer is late in making payment, a firm may be unable to pay its suppliers unless it has spare liquidity.

TC 9
p129

The speculative or assets motive

Certain firms and individuals who wish to purchase financial assets, such as bonds, shares or other securities, may prefer to wait if they feel that their price is likely to fall. In the meantime, they will hold money balances instead. This speculative demand can be quite high when the price of securities is considered certain to fall. Money when used for this purpose is a means of temporarily storing wealth.

Similarly, people who will require foreign currency at some time in the future (people such as importers, holidaymakers, or those thinking of investing abroad or in foreign securities) may prefer to wait before exchanging pounds into the relevant foreign currencies if they believe that the sterling price of these currencies is likely to fall (the pound is likely to appreciate).

The transactions plus precautionary demand for money: L_1

The transactions plus precautionary demand for money is termed L_1. 'L' stands for *liquidity preference*: that is, the desire to hold assets in liquid form. Money balances held for these two purposes are called *active balances*: money to be used as a medium of exchange. What determines the size of L_1?

The major determinant of L_1 is nominal national income (i.e. national income at current prices). The higher people's money income, the greater their (nominal) expenditure and the bigger their demand for active balances. The frequency with which people are paid also affects L_1. The less frequently they are paid, the greater the level of money balances they will require to tide them over until the next payment.

 Will students in receipt of a loan, grant or an allowance who receive the money once per term have a high or a low transactions demand for money relative to their income?

The rate of interest has some effect on L_1, albeit rather small (see Figure 18.9). At high rates of interest, people may choose to spend less and save more of their income, e.g. by buying shares. The effect is likely to be bigger on the precautionary demand: a higher interest rate may encourage people to risk tying up their money. Firms' active balances are more likely to be sensitive to changes in r than those of individuals.

KI 9
p66

Other determinants of L_1 include the season of the year: people require more money balances at Christmas, for example. Also, any other factors that affect consumption will affect L_1.

The increased use of credit cards in recent years has reduced both the transactions and precautionary demands. Paying once a month for goods requires less money on average than paying separately for each item purchased. Moreover, the possession of a credit card reduces or even eliminates the need to hold precautionary balances for many people. On the other hand, the increased availability of cash machines, the convenience of debit cards and the ability to earn interest on current accounts have all encouraged people to hold more money in bank accounts. The net effect has been an increase in the demand for (broad) money.

The speculative (or assets) demand for money: L_2

The speculative demand for money balances is termed L_2. Money balances held for this purpose are called *idle balances*.

People who possess wealth, whether they are wealthy or simply small savers, have to decide the best form in which to hold that wealth. Do they keep it in cash in a piggy bank, or in a current account in a real bank; or do they put it in some interest-bearing time account; or do they buy stocks and shares or government bonds; or do they buy some physical asset such as a car or property?

In making these decisions, people will have to weigh up the relative advantages and disadvantages of the various alternative assets. Assets can be compared according to two criteria: liquidity and the possibility of earning income.

TC 1
p11

Just as we saw in the case of a bank's assets, these two criteria tend to conflict. The more liquid an asset is, the lower is likely to be the income earned from holding it. Thus cash is totally liquid to the holder: it can be used to buy other assets (or spent on goods) instantly, but it earns no interest. Shares, on the other hand, are not very liquid since they cannot be

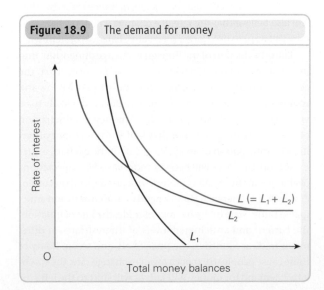

Figure 18.9 The demand for money

Rate of interest (vertical axis)

Total money balances (horizontal axis)

$L (= L_1 + L_2)$

L_2

L_1

O

Definitions

Liquidity preference The demand for holding assets in the form of money.

Active balances Money held for transactions and precautionary purposes.

Idle balances Money held for speculative purposes: money held in anticipation of a fall in asset prices.

sold instantly at a guaranteed price. (They can be sold pretty well instantly, but if share prices are depressed, a considerable loss may be incurred in so doing. In other words, they are a risky means of holding wealth.) But shares have the potential of earning quite a high income for the holder, not only in terms of the dividends paid out of the firms' profits, but also in terms of the capital gain from any increase in the shares' prices.

> *Buying something like a car is at the other end of the spectrum from holding cash. A car is highly illiquid, but yields a high return to the owner. In what form is this 'return'?*

There are three major determinants of the speculative demand for money. Let us examine each in turn.

The rate of interest (or rate of return) on assets

In terms of the operation of money markets, this is the most important determinant. The higher the rate of return on assets, such as shares and bonds, the greater the opportunity cost of holding money and therefore the lower the speculative demand for money.

The rate of return on assets varies inversely with their price. Take the case of a government bond (which pays a fixed sum of money throughout its life). Assume that the government issued a £100 bond at a time when interest rates were 10 per cent. Thus the bond must pay £10 per year. Although the government will not redeem bonds until their maturity date, which could well be 20 years from when they were issued, holders can sell bonds at any time on the stock market. Their market price will reflect (nominal) market rates of interest. Assume, for example, that interest rates fall to 5 per cent. What will happen to the market price of the bond paying £10 per year? It will be driven up to £200. At that price, the £10 per year is worth the current market rate of 5 per cent. Thus the market price of bonds varies inversely with the rate of interest.

Expectations of changes in the prices of securities and other assets

If people believe that share prices are about to rise rapidly on the stock market, they will buy shares and hold smaller speculative balances of money. If they think that share prices will fall, they will sell them and hold money instead. Some clever (or lucky) individuals anticipated the 2007–8 stock market decline (see figure in Box 2.3 on page 54). They sold shares and 'went liquid'.

If the market price of securities is high, the rate of interest (i.e. the rate of return) on these securities will be low. Potential purchasers of these securities will probably wait until their prices fall and the rate of interest rises. Similarly, existing holders of securities will probably sell them while the price is high, hoping to buy them back again when the price falls, thus making a capital gain. In the meantime, therefore, large speculative balances of money will be held. L_2 is high.

If, on the other hand, the rate of interest is high, then L_2 is likely to be low. To take advantage of the high rate of return on securities, people buy them now instead of holding on to their money.

> *Would the demand for securities be low if their price was high, but was expected to go on rising?*

The relationship between L_2 and the rate of interest is again shown in Figure 18.9. The inverse relationship between the rate of interest and L_2 gives a downward-sloping curve.

Speculative demand and the exchange rate

In an open economy like the UK where large-scale movements of currencies across the foreign exchanges take place, expectations about changes in the exchange rate are a major determinant of the speculative demand for money.

If people believe that the pound is likely to appreciate, they will want to hold sterling until it does appreciate. For example, if the current exchange rate is £1 = $1.25 and speculators believe that it will shortly rise to £1 = $1.50, then if they are correct they will make a 25¢ per £1 profit by holding sterling. The more quickly is the exchange rate expected to rise, the more will people want to hold sterling (as money). If, however, people believe that it will be a slow rise over time, they will want to buy sterling assets (such as UK government bonds) rather than money, since such assets will also earn the holder a rate of interest.

Conversely, if people believe that the exchange rate is likely to fall in the near future, they will economise on their holdings of sterling, preferring to hold their liquid assets in some other currency – the one most likely to appreciate against other currencies.

Graphically, changes in expectations about the exchange rate will have the effect of shifting the L_2 curve in Figure 18.9.

There is a further complication here. Expectations about changes in the exchange rate will themselves be influenced by the interest rate (relative to overseas interest rates). If the UK rate of interest goes up, people will want to deposit their money in the UK. This will increase the demand for sterling on the foreign exchange market: there will be a short-term financial inflow into the UK (the financial account of the balance of payments will go into surplus). The effect will be to drive up the exchange rate. Thus if people believe that the UK rate of interest will rise, they will also believe that the rate of exchange will appreciate, and they will want to hold larger speculative balances of sterling.

The introduction of the 'foreign exchange dimension' into our analysis will have two effects on the L_2 curve. First, the curve will become more *elastic*. If the rate of interest is low and is thought likely to rise, the speculative demand is likely to be very high. Not only will people hold money in anticipation of a fall in security prices, but they will also hold money (sterling) in anticipation of an appreciation of the exchange rate.

Second, the curve will become more *unstable*. Expectations of changes in the exchange rate do not just depend on current domestic interest rates. They depend on the current and anticipated future state of the balance of trade, the rate of inflation, the current and anticipated levels of interest rates in other major trading countries, the price of oil, and so on. If any of these cause people to expect a lower exchange rate, the speculative demand for money will fall: L_2 will shift to the left.

Which way is the L2 curve likely to shift in the following cases?
(a) The balance of trade moves into deficit.
(b) People anticipate that foreign interest rates are likely to rise substantially relative to domestic ones.
(c) The domestic rate of inflation falls below that of other major trading countries.
(d) People believe that the pound is about to depreciate.

The total demand for money: $L_1 + L_2$

Figure 18.9 also shows the total demand for money balances (L). This is found by the horizontal addition of curves L_1 and L_2. This curve is known as the 'liquidity preference curve' or simply the demand for money curve.

Any factor, other than a change in interest rates, that causes the demand for money to rise will shift the L curve to the right. For example, a rise in national income will cause L_1 to increase, and thus L will shift to the right.

Additional effects of expectations

 We have talked about expectations and their importance in determining the speculative demand for money. In particular, we have looked at (a) the effect of interest rates on people's anticipations of future security prices and (b) the effect of expectations about exchange rate movements. There are two other ways in which expectations can influence the demand for money, and make it more unstable.

Expectations about prices. If people expect prices to rise, they may reduce their money balances and purchase goods and assets now, before prices do rise. This will tend to shift L to the left. (Note, though, that once prices have risen, people will need more money to conduct the same amount of transactions.)

Expectations of interest rate levels over the longer term. If people come to expect that interest rates will normally be higher than they used to be, then any given interest rate will seem lower relative to the 'normal' rate than it used to be. People will be more inclined to hold speculative balances of money in anticipation of a rise in interest rates. This will tend to shift L upwards.

In an era of uncertainty about inflation, interest rates and exchange rates, people's expectations will be hard to predict. They will be volatile and susceptible to rumours and political events. In such circumstances, the L curve itself will be hard to predict and will be subject to considerable shifts. Generally, it is likely that the greater the uncertainty, the greater will be the preference for liquidity, and the greater the risk of tying wealth up in illiquid assets.

*LOOKING AT THE MATHS

The demand for money (L) can be expressed by the following function:

$$L = L_1 + L_2$$
$$= l_1(PY, f, i) + l_2(i, er^e)$$
$$= l_1(PY, f, (r + \pi^e)) + l_2((r + \pi^e), er^e) \quad (1)$$

This states that L_1 is a function l_1 of nominal national income (i.e. real national income (Y) multiplied by the price index (P)), the frequency with which people are paid (f) and the nominal rate of interest (i), which equals the real rate of interest (r) on alternative assets to money plus the expected rate of inflation (π^e). L_2 is a function of the nominal rate of interest (i) and the expected value of the exchange rate er^e.

The advantage of specifying a relationship in this way is that it gives a simple way of representing a situation where something depends on a number of determinants. It is a convenient shorthand. Indeed, a more complex function could easily be specified where the demand for money depends on a longer list of variables. The one above, however, identifies the main determinants. By putting plus and minus signs under each of the terms, we could also identify whether the relationship with each of the determinants is a positive or negative one (i.e. whether the respective partial derivative is positive or negative). Equation (1) could thus be written

$$L = l_1(PY, f, i) + l_2(i, er^e) \quad (2)$$
$$\quad + \; - \; - \qquad - \; +$$

This merely states that the demand for money will rise as PY and er^e rise and f and i fall.

Section summary

1. The three motives for holding money are the transactions, precautionary and speculative (or assets) motives.
2. The transactions-plus-precautionary demand for money (L_1) depends primarily on the level of nominal national income, the frequency with which people are paid and institutional arrangements (such as the use of credit or debit cards). It also depends to some degree on the rate of interest.
3. The speculative demand for money (L_2) depends on the rate of return on assets and on anticipations about future movements in security prices (and hence their rate of return) and future movements in exchange rates. If security prices are anticipated to fall or the exchange rate to rise, people will hold more money balances.
4. The demand for money is also influenced by expectations of price changes and the levels of interest rates over the longer term.

18.5 EQUILIBRIUM

Equilibrium in the money market

Equilibrium in the money market is where the demand for money (L) is equal to the supply of money (M_s). This equilibrium is achieved through changes in the *nominal* rate of interest (i). To make the analysis more straightforward, we assume there is no inflation (π). Hence, the nominal rate of interest (i) is the same as the real rate of interest (r) (we drop this assumption in later chapters).

In Figure 18.10, equilibrium is achieved with a nominal rate of interest i_e and a quantity of money M_e. If the rate of interest were above i_e, people would have money balances surplus to their needs. They would use these to buy shares, bonds and other assets. This would drive up the price of these assets and drive down the rate of interest.

As the rate of interest fell, so there would be a contraction of the money supply (a movement down along the M_s curve) and an increase in the demand for money balances, especially speculative balances (a movement down along the liquidity preference curve). The interest rate would go on falling until it reached i_e. Equilibrium would then be achieved.

Similarly, if the rate of interest were below i_e, people would have insufficient money balances. They would sell securities, thus lowering their prices and raising the rate of interest until it reached r_e.

A shift in either the M_s or the L curve will lead to a new equilibrium quantity of money and rate of interest at the new intersection of the curves. For example, a rise in the supply of money will cause the rate of interest to fall.

In practice, there is no one single rate of interest. Equilibrium in the money markets, therefore, will be where demand and supply of each type of financial asset separately balance.

If, for example, there were excess demand for short-term loans (such as one-month inter-bank lending) and excess supply of money to invest in long-term assets (such as bonds), short-term rates of interest would rise relative to long-term rates. Generally, however, different interest rates tend to move roughly together as the overall demand for money and other liquid assets (or their supply) changes. Thus interest rates may generally rise or generally fall.

Table 18.7 gives some examples of the rates of interest on various financial instruments in the UK. It shows how the various rates of interest move together. As we saw in section 18.2, the Bank of England conducts open-market operations to affect the general structure of the economy's interest rates and, in turn, the inflation rate. We can see how significant reductions to the policy rate (Bank Rate) were mirrored by falls in other interest rates.

What patterns in interest rates emerged between 2008 and 2017?

Equilibrium in the foreign exchange market

Changes in the money supply also affect the foreign exchange market. In a free foreign exchange market, equilibrium will be achieved by changes in the exchange rate. Assume that the money supply increases. This has three direct effects:

■ Part of the excess money balances will be used to purchase foreign assets. This will therefore lead to an increase in the supply of domestic currency coming on to the foreign exchange markets.
■ The excess supply of money in the domestic money market will push down interest rates. This will reduce the return on

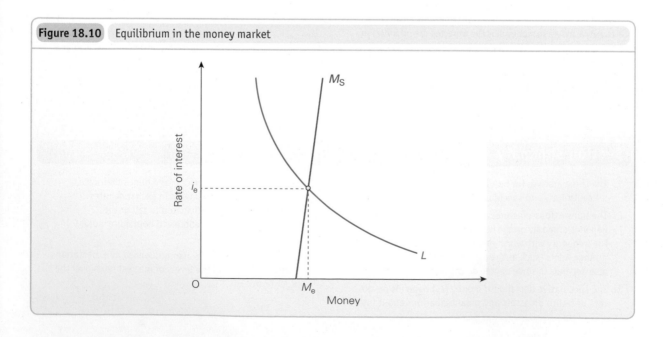

Figure 18.10 Equilibrium in the money market

Table 18.7 Selected rates of interest: January 1997 to September 2017 (monthly averages)

Financial instrument	Period of loan	Rate of interest, per cent per annum					
		Average Jan 1997– Sept 2008	Average Oct 2008– Sept 2017	Jan 1997	Sept 2008	Jan 2009	Sept 2017
Call money	Overnight	4.89	0.51	5.90	4.89	1.33	0.21
Gilt repos	1 week	5.09	0.54	5.91	4.92	1.43	0.21
Inter-bank loans	1 month	5.25	0.64	6.14	5.57	1.71	0.29
Treasury bills	3 months	5.05	0.44	6.07	4.95	1.29	0.08
British government securities[1]	20 years	4.81	3.32	7.74	4.64	4.48	1.91
Bank and building society mortgages[2]	Variable (25 years typical)	6.87	4.32	7.18	6.95	4.73	4.32
Credit card	–	17.58	17.26	22.14	16.12	16.09	17.96
Official Bank Rate (policy rate)	–	5.18	0.56	5.94	5.00	1.60	0.25

1 Zero coupon, nominal yields (series IUMALNZC).
2 Standard variable rate for UK MFIs (series IUMTLMV).
Source: Statistical Interactive Database (Bank of England). Data published October 2017.

domestic assets below that on foreign assets. This, like the first effect, will lead to an increased demand for foreign assets and thus an increased supply of the domestic currency on the foreign exchange market. It will also reduce the demand for domestic assets by those outside the country, and thus reduce the demand for the domestic currency.

■ Speculators will anticipate that the higher supply of the domestic currency will cause the exchange rate to depreciate. They will therefore sell domestic currency and buy foreign currencies before the expected depreciation takes place.

The effect of all three is to cause the exchange rate to depreciate.

 Trace through the effects on the foreign exchange market of a fall in the money supply.

*LOOKING AT THE MATHS

Equilibrium in the money market is where demand and supply of money are equal. From Box 18.5, the money supply (M_s) equals the monetary base (M_b) multiplied by the money multiplier:

$$M_s = M_b\left(\frac{1 + c}{rs + c}\right)$$

Note that this is the more complex version of the money multiplier that we examined in Box 18.5, not the simple bank deposits multiplier developed in the text.

From the 'Looking at the maths' panel on page 583, the demand for money (L) is given by

$$L = l_1(PY, f, (r + \pi^e) + l_2((r + \pi^e), er^e)$$

Thus, in equilibrium,

$$M_s = L$$

that is

$$M_b\left(\frac{1 + c}{rs + c}\right) = l_1(PY, f, (r + \pi^e) + l_2((r + \pi^e), er^e) \quad \textbf{(1)}$$

At first sight, this equation looks quite daunting, but what we have done is to bring together money supply and demand, each of which has been separately derived in a set of simple stages. In one single equation (equation (1)) we have completed a jigsaw made up of several simple parts.

Section summary

1. Equilibrium in the money market is where the supply of money is equal to the demand. Equilibrium will be achieved through changes in the nominal rate of interest.

2. A rise in money supply causes money supply to exceed money demand. This causes interest rates to fall and a movement down along both the supply of money curve and the demand for money curve until money supply is equal to money demand.

3. Equilibrium in the foreign exchange market is where the demand and supply of a currency are equal. A rise in money supply causes interest rates to fall. The rise in money supply plus the fall in interest rates causes an increased supply of domestic currency to come on to the foreign exchange market and a reduced demand for the domestic currency. This causes the exchange rate to depreciate.

END OF CHAPTER QUESTIONS

1. Imagine that the banking system receives additional deposits of £100 million and that all the individual banks wish to retain their current liquidity ratio of 20 per cent.
   (a) How much will banks choose to lend out initially?
   (b) What will happen to banks' liabilities when the money that is lent out is spent and the recipients of it deposit it in their bank accounts?
   (c) How much of these latest deposits will be lent out by the banks?
   (d) By how much will *total* deposits (liabilities) eventually have risen, assuming that none of the additional liquidity is held outside the banking sector?
   (e) How much of these are matched by (i) liquid assets; (ii) illiquid assets?
   (f) What is the size of the bank deposits multiplier?
   (g) If one-half of any additional liquidity is held *outside* the banking sector, by how much less will deposits have risen compared with (d) above?

2. What is meant by the terms *narrow money* and *broad money*? Does broad money fulfil all the functions of money?

3. How does money aid the specialisation and division of labour?

4. What enables banks safely to engage in both maturity transformation and risk transformation?

5. Why do banks hold a range of assets of varying degrees of liquidity and profitability?

6. What is meant by the securitisation of assets? How might this be (a) beneficial and (b) harmful to banks and the economy?

7. What were the causes of the credit crunch and the banking crisis of the late 2000s?

8. If the government reduces the size of its public-sector net cash requirement, why might the money supply nevertheless increase more rapidly?

9. Why might the relationship between the demand for money and the rate of interest be an unstable one?

10. What effects will the following have on the equilibrium rate of interest? (You should consider which way the demand and/or supply curves of money shift.)
    (a) Banks find that they have a higher liquidity ratio than they need.
    (b) A rise in incomes.
    (c) A growing belief that interest rates will rise from their current level.

Online resources

Additional case studies on the student website

18.1 **Barter: its use in Russia in the 1990s.** When barter was used as an alternative to money.

18.2 **The attributes of money.** What distinguishes it from other assets?

18.3 **From coins to bank deposit money.** This case traces the evolution of modern money.

18.4 **Gresham's law.** This examines the famous law that 'bad money drives good money out of circulation'.

18.5 **German banking.** This case compares the tradition of German banks with that of UK retail banks. Although the banks have become more similar in recent years, German banks have a much closer relationship with industry.

18.6 **Residential mortgages and securitisation.** Was the bundling of residential mortgage debt into securitised assets the cause of the 2008 credit crunch?

18.7 **Bailing out the banks.** An overview of the concerted efforts made to rescue the banking system in the crisis of 2007–9.

18.8 **The Bank of England's response to the financial crisis.** Focusing on the Bank of England, this case shows the timeline of the responses between 2007 and 2012.

18.9 **Making money grow.** A light-hearted illustration of the process of credit creation.

18.10 **Consolidated MFI balance sheet** A look at the *consolidated* balance sheet of UK monetary and financial institutions, including the Bank of England

18.11 **Parallel money markets.** A description of the variety of short-term financial instruments available in the parallel money markets.

18.12 **Are the days of cash numbered?** Are credit and debit cards and direct money transfers replacing cash transactions?

Maths Case 18.1 Calculating the value of the bank multiplier. Looking at the algebra.

Websites relevant to this chapter

See sites listed at the end of Chapter 19 on page 621.

The Relationship between the Money and Goods Markets

In Chapter 17 we saw how equilibrium national output was determined. In other words, we looked at macro-economic equilibrium in goods markets. In Chapter 18 we saw how equilibrium was determined in the money market. In this chapter we combine the analysis of the two chapters.

In section 19.1 we examine how changes in money supply affect real national income. In other words, we see how changes in money markets are transmitted through to goods markets: how monetary changes affect real output. Then, in section 19.2, we look at things the other way round. We examine the effects on money markets and interest rates of changes in the goods market. For example, if aggregate demand increases and firms start to produce extra goods, to what extent will money markets act as a constraint on this process?

In the remaining sections we look at the interplay of goods and money markets. In doing so, we introduce models which allow us to study how these markets interact. In section 19.3 the interaction is analysed in the contemporary context of central banks setting interest rates to target the rate of inflation. In doing so, we introduce a relatively new model: the *IS/MP* model. In the Appendix to the chapter we introduce the more traditional model: the *IS/LM* model. This helps us to see how the two markets interact when interest rates adjust to bring about equilibrium in the money market.

19.1 THE EFFECTS OF MONETARY CHANGES ON NATIONAL INCOME

In this section we examine the impact on the economy of changes in money supply and interest rates: how they affect aggregate demand and how this, in turn, affects national income and prices. A simple way of understanding the issues is in terms of the *quantity theory of money*.

The quantity theory of money

In section 16.2 (page 495), we looked at the following version of the quantity equation:

$$MV = PY$$

In case you did not study Chapter 16, let us state the theory again. First a definition of the terms: M is the supply of money; V is the income velocity of circulation (the number of times money is spent per year on national output (GDP)); P is the price index (where the index $= 1$ in the base year); and Y is the real value of national income ($=$ national output) for the year in question (i.e. GDP measured in base-year prices).

MV is the total spending on national output. For example, if total money supply (M) was £1 trillion and each pound was spent on average twice per year (V) on national output, then total spending on national output (MV) would equal £2 trillion for that year. MV is thus simply (nominal) aggregate demand, since total spending on national output consists of the four elements of aggregate demand: consumer spending (C), investment expenditure (I), government purchases (G), and expenditure on exports less expenditure on imports ($X - M$), all measured in current prices.

PY is the money value of national output: in other words, GDP measured at *current* prices. For example, if real national income (Y) (i.e. in base-year prices) were £1 trillion, and the price index (P) were 2 (in other words, prices were twice as high as in the base year), then the value of national output in current prices would be £2 trillion.

TC 13
p453

Because of the way we have defined the terms, MV must equal PY. A simple way of looking at this is that MV and PY are both ways of measuring GDP. MV measures it in terms of national *expenditure*. PY measures it in terms of the value of what is *produced*.

The effect of a change in money supply

If money supply (M) changes, how will it affect the other three elements of the quantity equation? Will a rise in money supply simply lead to a rise in prices (P), or will there be a rise in real national income (Y): i.e. a rise in real GDP? What will happen to the velocity of circulation (V)? Can we assume that it will remain constant, or will it change?

Clearly the relationship between money supply and prices depends on what happens to V and Y. What happens to them has been the subject of considerable debate between economists over the years. Keynesians have generally had different views from monetarists and new classical economists.

Essentially there are two issues. In this chapter we look at the first one: the variability of V. If V is constant, a change in money supply (M) will directly affect nominal aggregate demand (MV) and hence nominal national income (PY). If, however, V varies, a change in M may have a much less predictable effect on PY.

The second issue is examined in Chapter 20. This concerns the variability of Y. Will a rise in aggregate demand lead to increased employment and output (Y), or will it simply lead to higher prices (P), or some combination of the two?

TC 12
p447

1. If V is constant, will (a) a £10 million rise in M give a £10 million rise in MV; (b) a 10 per cent rise in M give a 10 per cent rise in MV?
2. If both V and Y are constant, will (a) a £10 million rise in M lead to a £10 million rise in P; (b) a 10 per cent rise in M lead to a 10 per cent rise in P?

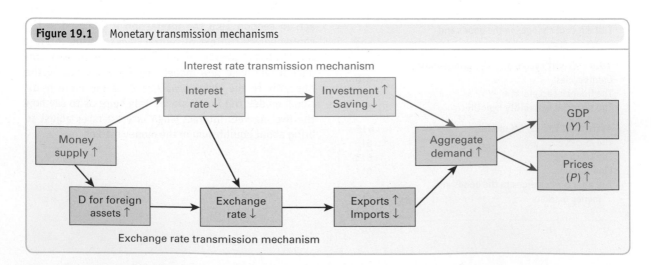

Figure 19.1 Monetary transmission mechanisms

Two principal means by which a rise in money supply can cause a rise in aggregate demand are the *interest rate transmission mechanism* and the *exchange rate transmission mechanism*. These are illustrated in Figure 19.1. We start with the interest rate transmission mechanism.

The interest rate transmission mechanism

The interest rate transmission mechanism is summarised in the top part of Figure 19.1. It shows the process by which changes in interest rates, following a change in the money supply, can affect aggregate demand.

When analysing expenditure decisions, it is typically *real* interest rates that are important. Consumers and producers are interested in the additional future volumes of consumption and production respectively that their investment, borrowing or saving today will enable them to enjoy.

The *realised* ('*ex post*') real rate of interest (r) received on savings or paid on borrowing is the nominal (actual) interest rate (i) *less* the rate of inflation (π). However, for savers and borrowers it is the future rate of inflation that is relevant in their decision making. Of course, future inflation rates cannot be known with certainty and, instead, people must form *expectations* of inflation. Hence, the perceived real interest rate when the decision is made ('*ex ante*') is the nominal interest rate (i) *less* the *expected* rate of inflation (π^e).

We assume in the following analysis of the short term that prices are constant and that the expected rate of

> **TC 13**
> **p453**

Definitions

Interest rate transmission mechanism How a change in money supply affects aggregate demand via a change in interest rates.

Exchange rate transmission mechanism How a change in money supply affects aggregate demand via a change in exchange rates.

inflation is zero. Therefore, a change in real interest rates is equivalent to that in nominal interest rates.

Figure 19.2 allows us to analyse the interest rate transmission mechanism in more detail. It is a three-stage process.

> **KI 5**
> **p22**

Money market and interest rates (stage 1). Figure 19.2(a) shows the money market. The horizontal axis shows real money balances (the real purchasing power of money); the vertical axis shows the real interest rate (r). With the economy's price level held constant, an increase in nominal money supply increases the supply of real balances (M): e.g. from M to M'. This, in turn, leads to a surplus of real money balances at the initial equilibrium real interest rate r_1, and hence a fall in the real rate of interest from r_1 to r_2.

> **?** *What is the opportunity cost of holding money? Is it the real or the nominal rate of interest? Explain.*

Interest rates and investment (stage 2). Figure 19.2(b) shows the relationship between real investment levels (I) and the real rate of interest. A fall in the real rate of interest from r_1 to r_2 leads to a rise in investment (and any other interest-sensitive expenditures) from I_1 to I_2. Note that it also encourages consumers to spend, since borrowing through credit cards and personal loans is now cheaper. At the same time, it discourages saving.

Investment and national income (stage 3). Figure 19.2(c) is the Keynesian withdrawals and injections diagram we discussed in Chapter 17. With no change in the economy's price level, a rise in investment leads to a full multiplied rise in real national income from Y_1 to Y_2. If saving fell, there would also be a downward shift in the W line, which would further amplify the effects on real national income and national output from the fall in the real rate of interest.

However, the increase in real income to Y_2 shown in Figure 19.2(c) does not take into account the likelihood that any rise in real income will lead to a rise in the demand for real balances from the rise in the transactions demand

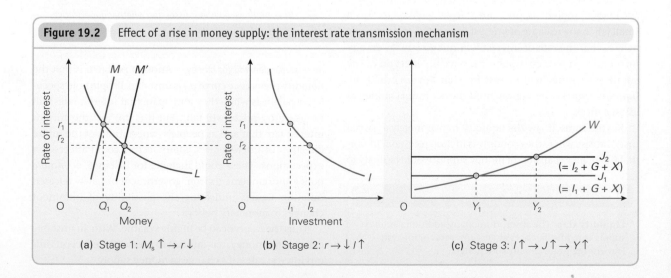

Figure 19.2 Effect of a rise in money supply: the interest rate transmission mechanism

(a) Stage 1: $M_s \uparrow \rightarrow r \downarrow$

(b) Stage 2: $r \rightarrow \downarrow I \uparrow$

(c) Stage 3: $I \uparrow \rightarrow J \uparrow \rightarrow Y \uparrow$

for money, L_1. In other words, L will shift to the right in Figure 19.2(a), and thus r will not fall as much as illustrated. Thus investment (Figure 19.2(b)) and real national income (Figure 19.2(c)) will not rise as much as illustrated either.

The overall effect of a change in money supply on national income will depend on the size of the effect in each of the three stages. This will depend on the shapes of the curves in each of the three diagrams and whether they are likely to shift. The effect will be bigger:

- the less elastic the liquidity preference curve (L): this will cause a bigger change in the rate of interest;
- the more interest-elastic the investment curve (I): this will cause a bigger change in investment;
- the lower the marginal propensity to withdraw (mpw), and hence the flatter the withdrawals function: this will cause a bigger multiplied change in national income and aggregate demand.

The problem is that stages 1 and 2 may be both weak and unreliable, especially in the short run. This problem is stressed by Keynesians.

Problems with stage 1: the money–interest link

An interest-elastic demand for money. According to Keynesians, the speculative demand for money is highly responsive to changes in interest rates. If people believe that the rate of interest will rise, and thus the price of bonds and other securities will fall, few people will want to buy them now. Instead there will be a very high demand for money and near money as people prefer to hold their assets in liquid form. The demand for money will therefore be very elastic in response to changes in interest rates.

If demand for money is interest elastic, the demand-for-money curve (the liquidity preference curve, L) will be relatively flat and may even be infinitely elastic at some minimum interest rate. This is the point where everyone believes interest rates cannot go any lower and sooner or later will rise, and therefore no one wants to buy bonds.

With a very gently sloping L curve (as in Figure 19.3), a rise in (real) money supply from M to M' will lead to only a small fall in the real rate of interest from r_1 to r_2. Once people believe that the rate of interest will not go any lower, any further rise in money supply will have no effect on r. The additional money will be lost in what Keynes called the **liquidity trap**. People simply hold the additional money as idle balances.

Keynes himself saw the liquidity trap as merely a special case: the case where the economy is in deep recession. In normal times, an expansion of money supply would be likely to

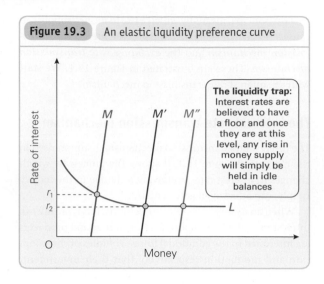

Figure 19.3 An elastic liquidity preference curve

> **The liquidity trap:** Interest rates are believed to have a floor and once they are at this level, any rise in money supply will simply be held in idle balances

have *some* effect on interest rates. But in a deep recession an expansion of money supply may have no effect on the economy.

The possibility that additional real money balances might simply find themselves lost in a liquidity trap, with individuals and firms unwilling to spend it, was of concern to policy makers who responded to the financial crisis of the late 2000s by increasing the money supply.

In the UK, with the Bank of England's base rate at 0.5 per cent, the money supply was increased by the Bank purchasing gilts in exchange for central bank money (see Box 22.10 on quantitative easing). The hope was that this would increase bond prices as well as other asset prices, so reducing interest rates even further throughout the economy and hence further reducing the cost of borrowing. In turn, it was hoped that this would generate higher rates of spending growth than would otherwise have been the case.

In practice, the effectiveness of such policies is constrained by a liquidity trap. Extra real money balances may be held as additional liquidity rather than boosting spending.

 How might we go about assessing whether quantitative easing actually worked?

An unstable demand for money. Another problem is that the liquidity preference curve (L) is unstable. People hold speculative balances when they anticipate that interest rates will rise (security prices will fall). But it is not just the current interest rate that affects people's expectations of the future direction of interest rates. Many factors could affect such expectations. These could include, for instance, economic policy announcements from government or newly released inflation figures indicating the possibility of imminent changes to monetary policy.

Thus the L curve can be highly volatile. With an unstable demand for money, it is difficult to predict the effect on various interest rates of a change in money supply.

Definition

Liquidity trap The absorption of any additional money supply into idle balances at very low rates of interest, leaving aggregate demand unchanged.

A policy of *targeting* money supply (whether nominal or real) can be criticised for similar reasons. A volatile demand for money can cause severe fluctuations in interest rates if the supply of money is kept constant (see Figure 19.4). These fluctuations will cause further uncertainty and further shifts in the speculative demand for money. Targeting the money supply can therefore add to the volatility of the velocity of circulation (V).

Problems with stage 2: the interest rate–investment link

An interest-inelastic investment demand. In the 1950s and 1960s, many Keynesians argued that investment was unresponsive to interest rate changes: that the I curve in Figure 19.2(b) was steep (as in Figure 19.5). In these circumstances, a very large change in real interest rates would be necessary to have any significant effect on investment and aggregate demand.

KI 9
p66

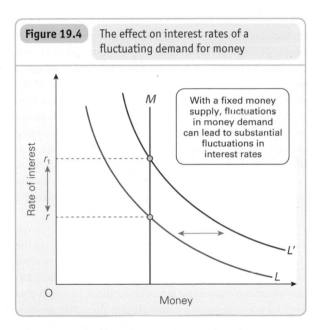

Figure 19.4   The effect on interest rates of a fluctuating demand for money

With a fixed money supply, fluctuations in money demand can lead to substantial fluctuations in interest rates

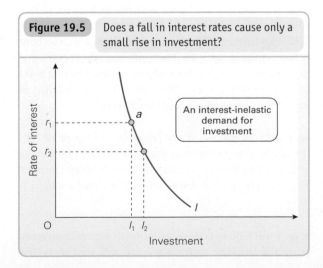

Figure 19.5   Does a fall in interest rates cause only a small rise in investment?

An interest-inelastic demand for investment

Investment, it was argued, depends on confidence in future markets. If confidence is high, firms will continue to invest even if interest rates are high. They can always pass the higher costs on to the consumer. If confidence is low, firms will not invest even if interest rates are low and borrowing is cheap. Evidence seemed to confirm the interest inelasticity of investment demand.

TC 9
p129

Few Keynesians hold this extreme position today. The evidence for an inelastic investment demand has been challenged. Just because investment was not significantly higher on occasions when interest rates were low, it does not follow that investment is unresponsive to interest rate changes. There may have been changes in *other* factors that helped to *curb* investment: in other words, the I curve shifted to the left. For example, a fall in consumer demand would both cause the low interest rate *and* discourage investment.

> **?** *Figure 19.5 shows a steep investment demand curve. If the real rate of interest falls from r_1 to r_2, there is only a small rise in investment from I_1 to I_2. Now draw a much more elastic I curve passing through point a. Assume that this is the true I curve. Show how the rate of interest could still fall to r_2 and investment still only rise to I_2 if this curve were to shift.*

Even if fixed investment in plant and machinery is not very interest sensitive, other components of aggregate demand may well be: for example, investment in stocks, consumer demand financed through credit cards, bank loans or hire purchase, and the demand for houses financed through mortgages.

The process of financialisation (see section 15.1), some economists argue, may have made aggregate demand more interest-rate sensitive. Increased levels of indebtedness to financial institutions, for example, means that the real expenditure of people and firms is potentially more sensitive to interest rate changes than in the past. This is because debt-servicing costs have a more significant effect on the income they have to spend.

Interest rate changes can generate sizeable *cash flow effects* for highly indebted people and firms. For example, when interest rates fall, the interest payments on those debts subject to variable interest rates fall too, giving people/firms more money to spend. However, it does reduce the interest receipts on savings. The net effect on aggregate demand will depend on which of these two counteracting effects is stronger. Evidence tends to suggest that it is debtors who have the higher marginal propensity to consume. Therefore, the overall effect of a fall in interest rates would be to generate a positive cash flow. This helps to boost aggregate expenditure and so reinforce the interest rate mechanism.

An unstable investment demand. Investment is notoriously volatile (see section 17.5). It is sensitive to a multitude of factors other than the rate of interest, which means that the investment curve in Figure 19.5 can shift erratically. These factors include, for example, business optimism, credit conditions and the availability of finance.

KI 34
p445

To analyse the effect of interest rate changes given an unstable investment curve consider Figure 19.6. Assume that the initial investment demand curve is given by I_1. Now assume that the central bank reduces interest rates from r_0 to r_1. Other things being equal, the level of investment will rise from Q_0 to Q_1. However, the fall in real interest rates might be accompanied by other changes that affect investment too. For example, if firms believe that the economy will now pull out of recession, their confidence will increase. Firms may also believe that this growth will help to improve their balance sheets and hence their financial well-being, while financial institutions might be more confident to provide finance. The investment curve will shift to I_2 and investment will increase quite markedly to Q_2.

If, on the other hand, firms become more pessimistic about the business environment in which they operate, their confidence may well decrease. Again, this could affect credit conditions, with financial institutions now less confident to provide finance. The investment curve will shift to I_3 and the level of investment will actually fall to Q_3.

What we have seen here is that the effectiveness of monetary (and fiscal policy) is dependent on how people respond. Its effectiveness is therefore dependent on a range of factors, many of which are peculiar to that moment in time. Nonetheless, monetary policy is likely to be more effective if people have confidence in its effectiveness. This *psychological* effect can be quite powerful. This helps to explain the co-ordinated responses of central bankers to the financial crisis of 2007–9 and the concerted attempts to inject extra liquidity into the banking system. By doing so they were trying to reassure individuals and firms that the measures would work. Further expansions of liquidity by central banks during the 2010s were again, in part, an attempt to reassure investors, despite the tightening of fiscal policy as governments grappled with mounting public-sector debt.

The exchange rate transmission mechanism

A second transmission mechanism is the *exchange rate transmission mechanism*. This is illustrated in the bottom half of Figure 19.1 on page 588 and graphed in Figure 19.7. This mechanism backs up the interest rate mechanism. It includes the exchange rate as an intermediate variable between changes in the money supply and changes in aggregate demand.

Figure 19.7 shows that there are four stages in this exchange rate transmission mechanism. We continue to assume that the economy's price level is constant in the short term and that the expected rate of inflation is 'anchored' at zero.

Money market and interest rates (stage 1).   In Figure 19.7(a), a rise in money supply causes a fall in domestic interest rates from r_1 to r_2.

Interest rates and foreign exchange market (stage 2).   In Figure 19.7(b), the fall in domestic interest rates leads to an increased outflow of short-term finance from the country as people demand more foreign assets instead. There will also be a reduced inflow, as depositors seek to take advantage of relatively higher interest rates abroad. The supply of the domestic currency on the foreign exchange market rises from S_1 to S_2 and the demand falls from D_1 to D_2. This causes a depreciation of the exchange rate from er_1 to er_2 (assuming the authorities allow it). In addition, part of the increased money supply will be used to buy foreign assets directly, further contributing to the rightward shift in the supply curve. What is more, the depreciation in the exchange rate may be speeded up or amplified by speculation.

Exchange rates and net exports (stage 3).   In Figure 19.7(c), the depreciation of the exchange rate causes a rise in demand for exports (X), since they are now cheaper for people abroad to buy (there is a movement down along the X curve). It also causes a fall in demand for imports (M), since they are now more expensive (there is a movement up along the M curve). Note that the rise in exports and fall in imports gives a current account balance of payments surplus (assuming a previous balance). This is matched by the financial account deficit resulting from the lower interest rate encouraging people to buy foreign assets and people abroad buying fewer of this country's assets. We examine these balance of payments effects in more detail in Chapter 25.

Net exports and national income (stage 4).   In Figure 19.7(d), the rise in exports (an injection) and a fall in imports (a withdrawal) will cause a multiplied rise in national income. The equilibrium level of real national income rises from Y_1 to Y_2.

Stage 1 will tend to be more powerful in a more open economy. The liquidity preference curve will tend to be less

KI 10
p70

KI 35
p451

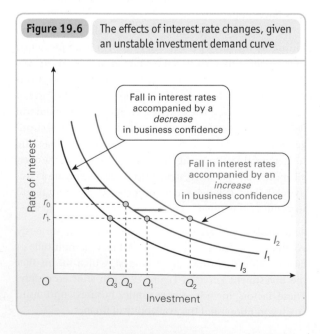

Figure 19.6   The effects of interest rate changes, given an unstable investment demand curve

Fall in interest rates accompanied by a *decrease* in business confidence

Fall in interest rates accompanied by an *increase* in business confidence

Rate of interest

r_0
r_1

I_2
I_1
I_3

O Q_3 Q_0 Q_1 Q_2

Investment

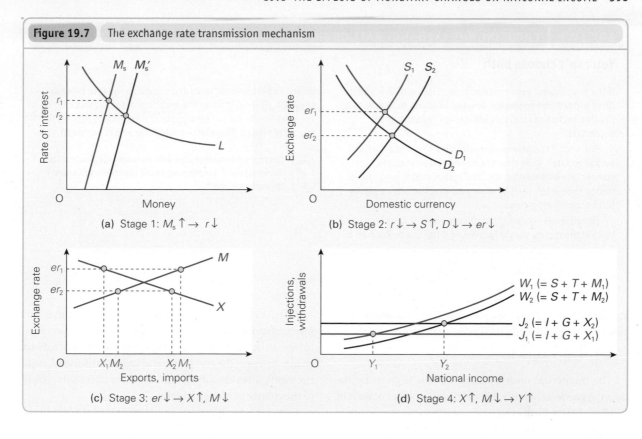

Figure 19.7   The exchange rate transmission mechanism

(a) Stage 1: $M_s \uparrow \rightarrow r \downarrow$

(b) Stage 2: $r \downarrow \rightarrow S \uparrow, D \downarrow \rightarrow er \downarrow$

(c) Stage 3: $er \downarrow \rightarrow X \uparrow, M \downarrow$

(d) Stage 4: $X \uparrow, M \downarrow \rightarrow Y \uparrow$

elastic because, as interest rates fall, people may fear a depreciation of the domestic currency and switch to holding other currencies. Just how strong stage 1 will be depends on *how much* people think the exchange rate will depreciate.

Stage 2 is likely to be very strong indeed. Given the openness of international financial markets, international financial flows can be enormous in response to interest rate changes. Only a relatively small change in interest rates is necessary to cause a relatively large financial flow. Monetarists and new classical economists stress the importance of this effect. Any fall in interest rates, they argue, will have such a strong effect on international financial flows and the exchange rate that the rise in money supply will be relatively quickly and fully transmitted through to aggregate demand.

Stage 3 may be rather limited in the short run as the demand and supply of both imports and exports may be relatively inelastic in the short run. Given time, however, consumers and firms may be more responsive and the effects on imports and exports correspondingly larger. However, the size of the effect depends on people's expectations of exchange rate movements. If people think that the exchange rate will fall further, importers will buy *now* before the rate does fall. Exporters, on the other hand, will hold back as long as possible before shipping their exports. These actions will tend to push the exchange rate down. But such speculation is very difficult to predict as it depends on often highly volatile expectations.

 If importers and exporters believe that the exchange rate has 'bottomed out', what will they do?

Stage 4 is the familiar multiplier, only this time triggered by a change in imports and exports.

Again, as with the interest rate transmission mechanism, the full effect is unlikely as to be as large as that illustrated. This is because the increased real national income (Y) will cause an increased *transactions* demand for money. This will shift the L curve to the right in Figure 19.7(a), and thus lead to a smaller fall in the rate of interest than that illustrated.

The overall effect via the exchange rate transmission mechanism can still be quite strong, but the precise magnitude is usually highly unpredictable.

The effects of changes in money supply will also depend on just how free the exchange rate is. If the government intervenes to 'peg' (i.e. fix) the exchange rate or to prevent excessive fluctuations, the transmission mechanism will not work in the way described. Alternative exchange rate systems (or 'regimes', as they are called) are examined in Chapter 25.

The portfolio balance effect

Money can also impact on the economy through a process of 'portfolio adjustment': a mechanism that was stressed by monetarists. If money supply increases, people will have more money than they need to hold. They will spend this

---

BOX 19.1 **CHOOSING THE EXCHANGE RATE OR THE MONEY SUPPLY**   *EXPLORING ECONOMICS*

You can't choose both

If the government expands the money supply, then interest rates will fall and aggregate demand will tend to rise. With a floating exchange rate, this will cause the currency to depreciate.

But what if the government attempts to maintain a fixed exchange rate? To do this it must keep interest rates comparable with world rates. This means that it is no longer free to choose the level of money supply. The money supply has become endogenous.

The government can't have it both ways. It can choose the level of the money supply (providing it has the techniques to

do so) and let interest rates and the exchange rate be what they will. Or it can choose the exchange rate, but this will then determine the necessary rate of interest and hence the supply of money. These issues are explored in Chapter 25.

 Can the government choose both the exchange rate and the money supply if it is prepared to use the reserves to support the exchange rate?

---

surplus. Much of this spending will go on goods and services, thereby directly increasing aggregate demand:

$$M_s\uparrow \rightarrow M_s > M_d \rightarrow AD\uparrow$$

The theoretical underpinning for this is given by the *theory of* **portfolio balance**. People have a number of ways of holding their wealth: as money, or as financial assets such as bills, bonds and shares, or as physical assets such as houses, cars and televisions. In other words, people hold a whole portfolio of assets of varying degrees of liquidity – from cash to property.

If money supply expands, people may find themselves holding more money than they require: their portfolios are unnecessarily liquid. Some of this money will be used to purchase financial assets, and some to purchase *goods and services.* As more assets are purchased, this will drive up their price. This will effectively reduce their 'yield'. For bonds and other financial assets, this means a reduction in their rate of interest. For goods and services, this means a reduction in their marginal utility/price ratio: a higher level of consumption will reduce their marginal utility and drive up their price. The process will stop when a balance has been restored in people's portfolios. In the meantime, there will have been extra consumption and hence a rise in aggregate demand.

 Do you think that this is an accurate description of how people behave when they acquire extra money?

Definition

Portfolio balance The balance of assets, according to their liquidity, that people choose to hold in their portfolios.

Many Keynesian economists, however, argue that this mechanism may be weak and unreliable. What is more, a rise in money supply may itself come about as a result of a direct change in one of the components of aggregate demand, making it difficult to identify how much of any effect is due solely to the change in money supply.

Consider an increase in government expenditure financed by purchases of Treasury bills by the banking system. Will any impact on output and prices come primarily from the extra liquidity in the balance sheets of households and firms, or will it come directly from the higher government expenditure?

Even if there is a direct increase in liquidity (e.g. through quantitative easing) without any accompanying change in government expenditure or taxation, the effect of this additional liquidity will depend on the extent to which banks use it to extend new credit. This, in turn, will depend on the *demand* for credit, which in a recession may fall as people try to rein in their spending.

The question then is the extent to which any extra money will be passed on around the economy. Box 19.2 looks at this process.

Portfolio balance and the interest rate mechanism

The holding of a range of assets in people's portfolios can strengthen the interest rate transmission mechanism by making the liquidity preference curve less elastic (curve *L* in Figure 19.2(a) on page 589 is relatively steep). The reason is that speculative balances of money may now have a much smaller role. But why?

A reduction in the rate of interest (*r*) following an increase in the money supply may well make bond holding less attractive, but this does not mean that the extra money will be mainly held in idle balances. Again, it can be used to

TC 6 p68

purchase other assets such as property. Idle balances may expand only slightly.

 Redraw the three diagrams of Figure 19.2 with a steeper L curve. Show how an increase in money supply will have a larger effect on national income.

How stable is the velocity of circulation?

Short-run variability of V

Most economists agree that there is some variability of the velocity of circulation (*V*) in the short run if the money supply is changed. To the extent that interest rates and yields do fall with an expansion of the money supply, people may well hold somewhat larger money balances: after all, the interest sacrificed by not holding bonds, etc., has been reduced. If people hold relatively more money, the velocity of circulation is thereby reduced, thus reducing the effect on aggregate demand. Furthermore, the direct mechanism (i.e. the portfolio balance mechanism) may take time to operate. In the meantime, *V* will fall.

Also, the demand for money can shift unpredictably in the short run with changing expectations of prices, interest rates and exchange rates. Thus *V* is unpredictable in the short run, and so is the effect of monetary policy on aggregate demand. For these reasons, changing the money supply may not be an effective means of short-run demand management.

Long-run stability of V

The main claim of monetarists is that the velocity of circulation (*V*) is relatively stable over the longer run, and any changes that do occur are the predictable outcome of institutional changes, such as the increased use of credit cards (see Box 19.3).

One explanation of why *V* remains relatively stable in the long run, despite an increase in money supply, is that sufficient time has elapsed for the direct mechanism to have worked fully through.

Another explanation is the effect on inflation and consequently on interest rates. This works as follows.

Assume an initial increase in money supply. Interest rates fall. *V* falls. But if money supply goes on rising and hence expenditure goes on rising, inflation will rise. This will drive up *nominal* interest rates (even though *real* interest rates will stay low). But in choosing whether to hold money or to buy assets, it is the nominal rate of interest that people look at, since that is the opportunity cost of holding money. Thus people economise on money balances and *V* rises back again.

In extreme cases, *V* will even rise to levels higher than before. This is likely if people start speculating that prices will rise further. People will rush to buy goods and assets before their prices rise further. This action will help to push the prices up even more. This form of destabilising speculation took place in the hyperinflation of Germany in the 1920s and in Zimbabwe in the years up to 2008, as people spent their money as quickly as possible (see Case Study 15.12 on the student website).

With a predictable *V* in the longer run, monetarists have claimed that monetary policy is the essential means of controlling long-term aggregate demand. For this reason, they have favoured a longer-term approach to monetary policy, including targets for the growth of the money supply (see page 503).

In the 1990s and 2000s, most governments adopted a policy of setting a target for the rate of inflation. This involves the central bank controlling aggregate demand by choosing an appropriate rate of interest. In these circumstances, the money supply must be *passively* adjusted to ensure that the chosen rate of interest is the equilibrium rate. This means expanding the money supply in line with the increase in real national income (*Y*) and the targeted increase in the price level (*P*). These rules were somewhat relaxed, however, following the recession of 2008/9 and subsequent rises in inflation. Preventing a double-dip recession became more important than strictly adhering to a (short-run) inflation target.

We explore inflation targeting and its effects in section 19.4. We explore the operation of monetary policy in section 22.3.

BOX 19.2   PARTY GAMES AND THE VELOCITY OF MONEY

Are you ready for a game of pass-the-parcel?

What will be the effect of an increase in money supply on spending, output and prices? To address this we need to understand how money supply interacts with money demand. This requires an analysis of the velocity of circulation of money (V).

An interesting way of thinking about V and what it might mean for the economy is to consider changes in money in the context of a game of pass-the-parcel! Assume there has been an increase in money supply and that this causes individuals and firms to have *excess* money balances. In response, they can look to pass the excess on to somebody else and, of course, if that individual or firm also has excess money balances they too will look to pass it on. The consequence is a game of pass-the-parcel, where the parcel is money and the passing occurs through spending. The quicker the 'parcel' is passed, the higher will V be. If the extra spending is not matched by extra output (Y), then we would expect prices (P) to rise too.

But what if the increase in money occurred at a time when people are looking to increase their money holdings? This time there will be little impact on spending (and, in turn, output and prices) as people hold on tightly to the parcel and refuse to play the game. In this case the velocity of circulation would fall.

The growth in money and spending

One way of assessing the extent to which the non-bank private sector might be holding excess money balances is to compare the annual growth in broad money with the annual growth in nominal spending (nominal GDP). Chart (a) is an indicator of the *excess nominal money balances* of the UK's non-bank private sector.

Positive values show excess money holdings: the velocity of circulation has slowed. This was the situation through the second half of the 1980s and much of the 2000s. To restore the balance of their portfolios, individuals and firms would be expected to pass the parcel more quickly, so causing the velocity of circulation to increase again. In turn, this increased spending would be expected to result in increasing economic activity, but perhaps in inflationary pressures too.

On the other hand, negative values indicate a deficit of liquid funds: the velocity of circulation has increased. This was the situation during the first half of the 2010s. To restore balance in this case, individuals and firms would be expected to increase money balances and so pass the parcel more slowly. The reduction in spending would act to constrain economic activity and limit any potential inflationary pressures.

Money balances in different sectors

Our excess money balance indicator is an imperfect indicator of short-term activity and potential price movements, however, not least because the non-bank private sector comprises three groups: households, non-financial corporations (firms) and other financial corporations (e.g. insurance companies, pension funds and unit trusts). The key

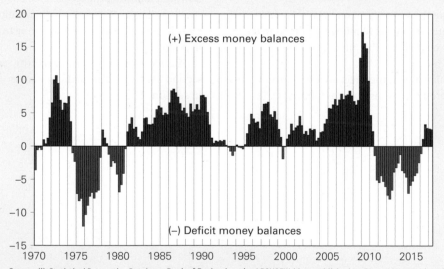

(a) *Annual money growth minus annual spending growth*

Source: (i) *Statistical Interactive Database*, Bank of England, series LPQVQJW (data published 29 September 2017) and (ii) *Quarterly National Accounts*, Office for National Statistics, series YBHA.

point is that the implications for spending, economic activity and prices may depend on which of these three groups is experiencing excess or deficit money balances. Moreover, the ways in which these groups adjust their portfolios can have quite different economic effects.

Chart (b) shows, alongside the annual rate of growth of M4, the growth in the stock of M4 held by each of the groups comprising the non-bank private sector since 2000. From the second half of the 2000s we observe markedly contrasting rates of growth in their money holdings. The particular concern of the Bank of England was the dramatic slowdown from 2008 in the growth of broad money holdings of households and firms (non-financial corporations). This was not entirely surprising given the substantial retrenchment of lending and so of credit creation by financial institutions.

As if the negative impact of this on spending growth was not enough, households and firms were also looking to rebuild their balance sheets and reduce their debt exposure. An important element of this was their increased demand for money balances. In what were incredibly uncertain times, and with the markets for shares and housing depressed, households and firms looked to increase the liquidity of their portfolios. It was almost as if the music for our game of

pass-the-parcel had stopped. Inevitably, the growth in nominal spending fell sharply, economic activity floundered and the economy entered into recession.

By contrast, broad money holdings of other financial corporations (OFCs) grew rapidly in the late 2000s before declining in the early 2010s.

Some of the initial rise in money holdings by OFCs related to unsold liquid securities issued by Special Purpose Vehicles (SPVs) to fund the purchase of securitised assets, such as residential mortgages, from banks (see section 18.2). However, some of the increased money holdings were the result of quantitative easing, with OFCs exchanging gilts for money from the Bank of England. This increased the liquidity of OFCs' balance sheets. If money holdings are excessive, they can be passed on by purchasing other assets. In doing so, asset prices tend to rise and their yields fall. Therefore, it was hoped that amongst the positive effects of passing-the-parcel would be lower borrowing costs, a boost to the wealth of asset holders and increased economic activity.

 What can we infer from charts (a) and (b) about the stability of the velocity of circulation in the short run? What can we learn from chart (b) about the association between the growth of money holdings and that in nominal GDP?

(b) *Annual growth rates of broad money and nominal GDP*

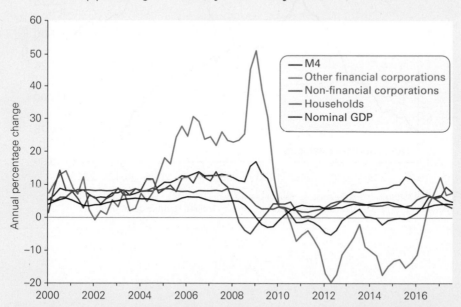

Sources: (i) *Statistical Interactive Database*, Bank of England, series LPQVVHK, LPQVVHQ, LPQVVHW and LPQVQJW (data published 30 October 2017) and (ii) *Quarterly National Accounts*, Office for National Statistics, series YBHA.

BOX 19.3 **THE STABILITY OF THE VELOCITY OF CIRCULATION**

What is the evidence?

How stable is the velocity of circulation (*V*) in practice? Does the evidence support the monetarist case that it is relatively stable or the Keynesian case that it fluctuates unpredictably, at least in the short run? Unfortunately, the facts do not unequivocally support either side.

The evidence

How has *V* behaved over time? To answer this we need to measure *V*. A simple way of doing this is to use the formula $V = PY/M$ (rearranging the terms in the quantity equation $MV = PY$). Thus we need to measure *PY* and *M*. *PY* is simply the money value of national output: in other words, GDP at current prices. The value of *M* (and hence *V*) will depend on which measure of the money supply we use.

The diagram shows how the velocities of circulation in the UK of both broad money (M4) and narrow money (notes and coin) have changed over the years.

The long run

Broad money. Long-term increases in the velocity of broad money from 1973 to 1979 are explained by the increase in money substitutes and credit cards, and thus smaller holdings of money balances.

The decrease after 1980 reflects falling inflation and nominal interest rates, with people being increasingly prepared to hold money in sight accounts; the growth in wholesale deposits (which earn interest); and people putting a larger proportion of their savings into bank and building society accounts, attracted by higher real interest rates and new types of high-interest instant-access accounts. As the pace of these changes slowed, so the fall in velocity became gentler after 1990.

However, in the second half of the 2000s the velocity of broad money once again fell sharply. The financial and

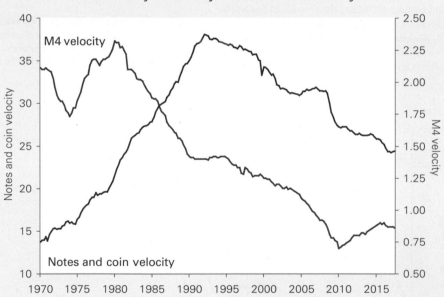

Velocities of circulation for narrow and broad money

Sources: (i) *Statistical Interactive Database*, Bank of England, series LPMAVAB and LPQAUYN (data published 1 November 2017) and (ii) *Quarterly National Accounts*, Office for National Statistics, series YBHA.

economic upheaval of this period is likely to have increased the demand for liquid assets.

Then, after the effects of the financial crisis waned and spending began to grow again, so the velocity of circulation increased. The size of people's desired money balances gradually decreased as confidence slowly grew.

Narrow money.   The velocity of narrow money more than doubled between 1974 and 1993. One reason for this was the increased use of credit and debit cards, which reduced the amount of cash people needed to hold. The growth of cash machines also reduced the need to hold so much cash, given that many people could easily obtain more at any time. The relatively smaller amount of cash thus circulated faster. But, as with broad money, these changes in the velocity of narrow money ceased in the early 1990s.

During the 2000s, the velocity of narrow money actually fell back to levels seen in the late 1980s. Low inflation rates, by reducing the opportunity cost of holding cash, contributed to the fall during the first half of 2000s. As with broad money, the impact of the economic and financial crisis contributed to a further fall in the velocity of narrow money during the second half of the 2000s.

But, unlike broad money velocity, narrow money velocity has continued to fall. Part of the reason has to do with the continuing rapid growth of purchases with cards. This has been fuelled by the growth in online sales and by the use of contactless card payments. At the same time, with continuing record low interest rates, the opportunity cost of holding narrow money has been very low.

The point made by monetarists is that these changes are predictable and gradual and do not, therefore, undermine the close relationship between *M* and *PY*.

The short run

Evidence shows periods when the velocity of circulation has been relatively stable in the short run, especially during the 1990s. However, this is largely because changes in money supply were not used to manipulate aggregate demand and hence national income. However, in response to the financial crisis of the late 2000s, the Bank of England embarked on a policy known as quantitative easing to increase the money supply. As we discussed in Box 19.2 the success of this was to depend on the responses of individuals and firms and so the extent to which *V* would fluctuate.

The direction of causality

Monetary and real changes often work together – especially in the long run. An expansionary fiscal policy over a number of years will increase public-sector borrowing, which, in turn, will lead to an increase in money supply (*M*). If the fiscal policy increases nominal national income (*PY*), *V* may well as a result remain constant. But it does not follow from this that it was the growth in *M* that *caused* the growth in *PY*. On the few occasions when fiscal and monetary policy work in opposite directions, the evidence is unclear as to which has the bigger effect – especially as the time period is rarely long enough for the full effects to be identified.

What we are concerned about here is the direction of causality. Changes in aggregate demand may go together with changes in money supply. But is it higher money supply causing higher aggregate demand, or the other way round, or the two simply occurring simultaneously?

Monetarists argue that increases in money supply cause (nominal) aggregate demand to expand (with a lag of perhaps a few months). For them money supply is exogenous: determined independently by the central bank. Keynesians, by contrast, argue that higher aggregate demand causes an increased demand for bank loans, and banks are only too happy to create the necessary credit, thus expanding the money supply. For them, money supply is endogenous.

 Why might it be difficult to establish the direction of causality from the evidence?

Section summary

1. The quantity equation $MV = PY$ can be used to analyse the possible relationship between money and prices. Whether and how much increases in money supply (M) affect the price level (P) depends on whether the velocity of circulation (V) and the level of real national income (Y) are independent of money supply (M).

2. The interest rate transmission mechanism works as follows: (a) a rise in money supply causes money supply to exceed money demand; assuming that expected inflation is fixed, real interest rates fall; (b) this causes investment to rise; (c) this causes a multiplied rise in national income; but (d) as national income rises, so the transactions demand for money rises, thus preventing quite such a large fall in interest rates.

3. The effect will be weak if the demand-for-money curve (L) is elastic and the investment demand curve is inelastic. The effects may also be unreliable because of an unstable and possibly inelastic investment demand.

4. The exchange rate transmission mechanism works as follows: (a) a rise in money supply causes interest rates to fall; (b) the rise in money supply plus the fall in interest rates causes an increased supply of domestic currency to come on to the foreign exchange market; this causes the exchange rate to fall; (c) this causes increased exports and reduced imports, and hence a multiplied rise in national income.

5. According to the theory of portfolio balance, if people have an increase in money in their portfolios, they will attempt to restore portfolio balance by purchasing assets, including goods. Thus an increase in money supply is transmitted directly into an increase in aggregate demand.

6. The demand for money is more stable in the long run than in the short run. This leads to a greater long-run stability in V (unless it changes as a result of other factors, such as institutional arrangements for the handling of money).

19.2 THE MONETARY EFFECTS OF CHANGES IN THE GOODS MARKET

If there is an expansion in one of the components of aggregate demand (C, I, G or $X - M$), what will be the monetary effects? Will the current level of money supply act as a constraint on the growth in national income? In other words, will an expansion of one component of aggregate demand, such as government expenditure, be at the expense of another component, such as investment?

The monetary effects of an increase in injections

Let us assume that business confidence grows and that, as a result, the level of investment increases. Let us also assume that there is a given quantity of real money balances in the economy and, further, that prices are constant in the short term. Will the rise in investment lead to a full multiplier effect on national income?

The effect of the rise in investment is illustrated in Figure 19.8. In Figure 19.8(a), the rise in investment leads to a rise in injections to J_2. Other things being equal, the real level of national income would rise to Y_2. But this increase in real national income also leads to a rise in the transactions demand for money. The rise in demand for real money balances leads to the demand-for-money curve in Figure 19.8(b) shifting from L to L'.

If the central bank does not wish to allow the real value of the economy's money supply to rise, the higher demand for money will force it to raise interest rates to r_2. The effect of higher real interest rates is to reduce the level of investment. The overall rise in injections will be smaller than the rise from J_1 to J_2. Also net saving (i.e. saving minus borrowing) will rise as the higher real interest rate acts as both an incentive for

households to save and a disincentive for them to borrow. This causes an upward shift in the W curve. The result is that the real level of national income will not rise as far as Y_2. In the extreme case, there would be no rise in real national income at all.

If, however, the central bank responds to the increase in investment by expanding the real money supply to $M_s{}'$, there will be no change in the real rate of interest and hence no dampening effect on either the volume of investment or consumption.

 Assume that the government cuts its expenditure and thereby runs a public-sector surplus.
(a) What will this do initially to equilibrium national income?
(b) What will it do to the demand for money and initially to interest rates?
(c) Under what circumstances will it lead to
  (i) a decrease in money supply;
  (ii) no change in money supply?
(d) What effect will (i) and (ii) have on the rate of interest compared with its original level?

Crowding out

Another example of the monetary constraints on expansion in the goods market is the phenomenon known as *financial crowding out*. This is where an increase in public-sector spending reduces private-sector spending (see Box 16.2 on page 497).

Definition

Financial crowding out Where an increase in government borrowing diverts money away from the private sector.

To illustrate the effects, assume that previously the government has had a balanced budget, but that now it chooses to expand the level of government expenditure without raising additional taxes. As a result, it runs a budget deficit ($G > T$). But this deficit will have to be financed by borrowing. This increased borrowing will lead to an increase in the money supply if it is financed by sales of government debt to financial institutions, especially debt with shorter maturity. Alternatively, if it is financed by selling bills or bonds outside the banking sector, there will be no increase in the money supply.

The effect can once more be shown in Figure 19.8. A rise in government spending on goods and services will cause injections to rise to J_2 and, other things being equal, real national income will rise to Y_2. But, as with the case of increased investment, this increase in real national income will lead to a rise in the demand for real money balances. In Figure 19.8(b), the demand-for-money curve shifts from L to L'.

If public-sector borrowing is financed in such a way as to allow the real money supply to expand to M_s', there will be no change in the real interest rate and no crowding-out effect. If, however, the real money supply is not allowed to expand, interest rates will rise to r_2. This in turn will reduce investment: crowding out will occur. Injections will fall back again below J_2. In the extreme case, injections could even fall back to J_1 and thus real national income return to Y_1. Here crowding out is total.

The extent of crowding out

Just how much crowding out will occur when there is an expansionary fiscal policy, but when the supply of real money balances is *not* allowed to expand, depends on two things.

The responsiveness (elasticity) of the demand for money to a change in interest rates. If the demand is relatively elastic (as in Figure 19.9(a)), the increase in demand, represented by a horizontal shift in the liquidity preference curve from L to L', will lead to only a small rise in real interest rates. If, however, the demand is relatively inelastic (as in Figure 19.9(b)), the same horizontal shift will lead to a bigger rise in real interest rates.

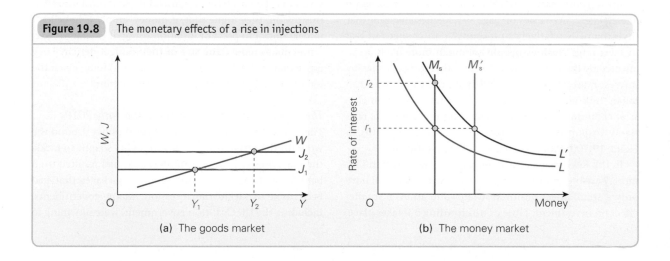

Figure 19.8   The monetary effects of a rise in injections

(a) The goods market

(b) The money market

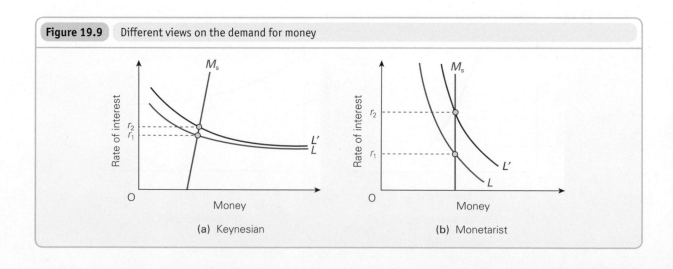

Figure 19.9   Different views on the demand for money

(a) Keynesian

(b) Monetarist

Taking exchange rate effects into account

Will fiscal policy be crowded out in an open economy with floating exchange rates? Assume that the government increases its expenditure but does not allow the money supply to expand: a case of pure fiscal policy. What will happen?

- The increased government expenditure will increase the demand for money (see Figure 19.8(b)).
- This will drive up interest rates – the amount depending on the elasticity of the liquidity preference curve.
- This will lead to an inflow of finance from abroad, which in turn will lead to an appreciation of the exchange rate.
- The higher exchange rate will reduce the level of exports

(an injection) and increase the level of imports (a withdrawal). This will add to the degree of crowding out.

Thus in an open economy with floating exchange rates, an expansionary fiscal policy will be crowded out not only by higher interest rates, but also by a higher exchange rate.

We have argued that the short-term inflow of finance following a rise in the rate of interest will drive up the exchange rate. Are there any effects of expansionary fiscal policy on the demand for imports (and hence on the current account) that will go some way to offsetting this?

As we saw in section 19.1, Keynesians generally see the liquidity preference curve as being more elastic than do monetarists and new classical economists. They therefore argue that a rise in money demand normally leads to only a relatively modest rise in interest rates.

The responsiveness (elasticity) of investment to a change in interest rates.   As we saw on page 591, Keynesians argue that investment is relatively unresponsive to changes in real interest rates. Businesspeople are much more likely to be affected by the state of the market for their product than by interest rates. Thus in Figure 19.10(a), there is only a small fall in the volume of investment. Monetarists and new classical economists, however, argue that investment is relatively responsive to changes in interest rates. Thus in Figure 19.10(b), there is a bigger fall in investment.

In the Keynesian case, therefore, the rise in demand for money arising from an expansionary fiscal policy will have only a small effect on interest rates and an even smaller effect on investment. Little or no crowding out takes place.

In fact, the expansion of demand might cause an increase in investment through the accelerator effect (see pages 542–5).

Monetarists and new classical economists argue that interest rates will rise significantly and that there will be a severe effect on investment. Crowding out is substantial. For this reason, they argue that, if money supply is to be kept under control to prevent inflation rising, it is vital for governments to reduce the size of their budget deficit. They argue that, in the long run, crowding out is total, given the long-run stability of the velocity of circulation.

The debate about crowding out in the early 2010s

There was a general tightening of fiscal policy around the world in the early 2010s, as governments sought to tackle the huge rises in public-sector debt that had resulted from bank bailouts and the fiscal stimulus packages that had been used to tackle the recession. Many governments, including the UK Coalition government, were unwilling to

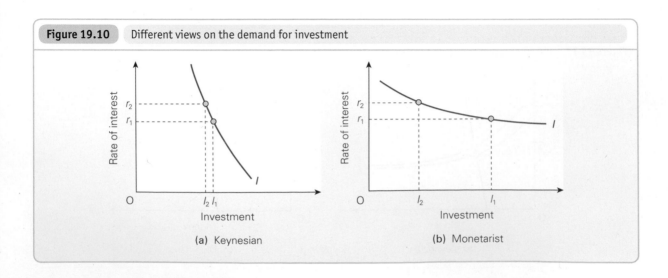

Figure 19.10   Different views on the demand for investment

(a) Keynesian

(b) Monetarist

adopt a more expansionary fiscal policy for fear of crowding out private-sector investment and 'spooking' the markets that they were not serious about deficit reductions.

However, bankers and many economists were urging a relaxing of fiscal restraint. For example, a report by economists at Bank of America/Merrill Lynch stated that:

> while fiscal austerity could help the long-run outlook, near-term fiscal consolidation threatens the recovery in developed economies. . . . Interest rates are already quite low, signalling limited market pressure to reduce deficits. As a result, near-term fiscal austerity would do little to lower rates. Moreover, companies are flush with cash. Investment is low because of a lack of confidence in the recovery – not because government borrowing is crowding them out.[1]

Is money supply exogenous or endogenous?

Money supply is *exogenous* (independently determined) if it can be fixed by the authorities and if it does not vary with aggregate demand and interest rates. The money supply 'curve' would be vertical, as in Figure 19.9(b). It would shift only if the government or central bank *chose* to alter the money supply.

Money supply is *endogenous* (determined within the model) if it is determined by aggregate demand and hence the demand for money: banks expanding or contracting credit in response to customer demand. In such a case, the money supply curve would be upward sloping or even horizontal. The more that money supply expands in response to an increase in aggregate demand, the more gently upward sloping the money supply curve would be.

The more elastic the money supply curve, the less will money act as a constraint on expansion in the goods market, and the less will a rise in government expenditure crowd out private expenditure. In other words, the less will real interest rates rise in response to a rise in the demand for real money balances.

The extreme monetarist position is that money supply is wholly exogenous. The extreme Keynesian position is that money supply is wholly endogenous: money simply passively expands to meet the demand for money.

In reality, money supply is partly exogenous and partly endogenous. The authorities are able to influence money supply, but banks and other financial institutions have considerable scope for creating credit in response to rises in demand. If control of the money supply is adopted as the basis for policy, the authorities must reduce the endogenous element to a minimum.

The authorities in many countries recognise the difficulties in controlling the money supply directly. They therefore influence the supply of money indirectly by controlling interest rates and hence the demand for money.

Sometimes, however, in extreme circumstances, the authorities may attempt to control money supply directly. As we saw in Chapter 18, central banks in several countries, including the USA, the UK, Japan and eventually the eurozone, injected large amounts of liquidity into their financial systems in response to the financial crisis. The aim was to stabilise their economies and to stimulate bank lending. This use of 'quantitative easing' is examined in section 22.2 (Boxes 22.5 and 22.10).

Section summary

1. Changes in injections or withdrawals will have monetary implications. If there is a rise in investment with no change in the supply of real money balances, the increased demand for money will drive up real interest rates and reduce both investment and consumption. The resulting rise in real income will be smaller.

2. Similarly, if there is a fiscal expansion and *no* change in the money supply, the increased demand for money will again drive up the real interest rate. This will to some extent crowd out private expenditure and thus reduce the effectiveness of the fiscal policy.

3. The extent of crowding out will depend on the shape of the liquidity preference curve and the investment demand curve. The less elastic the demand for money, and the more elastic the investment demand, the more crowding out will take place, and the less effective will fiscal policy be.

4. If there is a rise in aggregate demand, money supply may rise in response to this. The more elastic the supply of money curve, the less crowding out will take place.

5. Money supply is not totally exogenous. This makes it hard for the authorities to control it precisely. Generally, therefore, central banks try to control *interest rates* and attempt to alter liquidity to back this up. Sometimes, however, they may take more deliberate steps to inject extra liquidity into the financial system.

1 Quoted in Stephanie Flanders, 'Restraint or stimulus? Markets and governments swap role', *BBC News*, 7 September 2011.

19.3 MODELLING THE INTERACTION OF MONETARY POLICY AND THE GOODS MARKET

The goods and money markets

In this chapter, we have shown that there are two key markets in the economy at macroeconomic level, and that these two markets interact. The first is the goods market; the second is the money market. Each of these two markets has been analysed by using a model.

In the case of the goods market, the model is the Keynesian injections/withdrawals model. Any change in injections or withdrawals will cause national income to change. For example, a rise in government expenditure shifts the *J* line upwards and causes a rise in equilibrium real national income. In other words, an increase in the demand for goods and services causes a (multiplied) rise in the output of goods and services (assuming that there are sufficient idle resources).

In the case of the money market, the model is the one showing the real demand for money (*L*) and the real supply of money (*M*) and their effect on the rate of interest. A change in the supply or demand for money will cause the equilibrium rate of interest to change. Monetary policy operates directly in this market, either by affecting the supply of money or by operating on interest rates.

What we have shown in this chapter is that the two markets *interact*: that changes in one market cause changes in the other. Therefore, we need a model which allows us to *combine* the goods and money markets. The traditional approach has been through a model known as the *IS/LM* model. The *IS* curve is based on equilibrium in the goods market; the *LM* curve is based on equilibrium in the money market. By examining the interaction of both markets we can see the implication for interest rates *and* output.

In many countries, including the UK, interest rates have become the key tool of monetary policy, with money supply controlled directly only in extreme circumstances. A (nominal) interest rate is announced by the central bank and then it supplies a given level of reserves to banks (central bank money), taking into account the real demand for money, so that the announced interest rate is the equilibrium one. Central banks do this principally to affect aggregate demand so as to meet an inflation rate target (normally set by the government). In both the UK and the eurozone, the target inflation rate is 2 per cent.

Under inflation targeting the authorities use monetary policy to affect equilibrium in the goods market. Therefore, the modern approach to modelling the interaction between the goods and money markets retains the *IS* curve as the *IS* curve relates to equilibrium in the goods market. However, the *LM* curve is replaced with a 'monetary policy curve' – the *MP* curve. The *MP* curve captures the interest rate choices of central bank.

The traditional *IS/LM* model can be found in the Appendix to this chapter. We now develop the *IS/MP* model.

The *IS* curve

Deriving the IS curve

To explain how the *IS* curve is derived, let us examine Figure 19.11, which as you can see is in two parts. The top part shows the familiar Keynesian injections and withdrawals diagram, only in this case, for simplicity, we are assuming that saving is the only withdrawal from the circular flow of income, and investment the only injection. The levels of saving (*S*) and investment (*I*) are *real* levels and in equilibrium $I = S$ (i.e. $J = W$). The bottom part of Figure 19.11 shows the *IS* curve. This shows all the various combinations of real interest rates (*r*) and real national income (*Y*) at which $I = S$.

Assume initially that the real interest rate is r_1. Both investment and saving are affected by the level of real interest rates, and thus, other things being equal, an interest rate of r_1 will give particular investment and saving schedules. Let us say that, in the top part of Figure 19.11, these are shown by the curves I_1 and S_1. The equilibrium level of real national income will be where $I = S$, i.e. at Y_1. Thus in the lower part of Figure 19.11, an interest rate of r_1 will give a level of output Y_1. Thus point *a* is one point on the *IS* curve. At an interest rate of r_1 the goods market will be in equilibrium at output Y_1.

Now what will happen if the real rate of interest changes? Let us assume that it falls to r_2. This will cause a rise in investment and a fall in saving. A rise in investment is shown in the top part of Figure 19.11 by a shift in the investment line to I_2. Likewise a fall in saving is shown by a shift in the saving curve to S_2. This will lead to a multiplied rise in income to Y_2 (where $I_2 = S_2$). This corresponds to point *b* in the lower diagram, which therefore gives a second point on the *IS* curve.

Thus *lower* real interest rates are associated with *higher* real national income, if equilibrium is to be maintained in the goods market ($I = S$).

The elasticity of the IS curve

The elasticity of the *IS* curve (i.e. the responsiveness of real national income to changes in real interest rates) depends on two factors.[2]

The responsiveness of investment and saving to interest rate changes. The more investment and saving respond to a

---

2 Note that, as with demand and supply curves, the elasticity of the *IS* curve will vary along its length. Therefore we should really talk about the elasticity at a particular point on the curve, or between two points.

change in the real rate of interest, the bigger will be the vertical shift in the I and S curves in the top part of Figure 19.11, and thus the bigger will be the effect on national income. The bigger the effect on national income, the more elastic will be the IS curve.

The size of the multiplier. This is given by 1/*mps* (i.e. 1/*mpw* in the full model). The *mps* is given by the slope of the S curve. The flatter the curve, the bigger the multiplier. The larger the value of the multiplier, the bigger will be the effect on real national income of any rise in investment and fall in saving, and the more elastic therefore will be the IS curve. Thus the flatter the S curve in the top part of Figure 19.11, the flatter the IS curve in the bottom part.

> ? *In a complete model where there were three injections (I, G and X) and three withdrawals (S, T and M), what else would determine the shape of the 'JW' curve?*

Keynesians argue that the IS curve is likely to be fairly inelastic. The reason they give is that investment is not very responsive to changes in real interest rates: the demand-for-investment curve in Figure 19.2(b) on page 589 is relatively inelastic. Saving also, claim Keynesians, is unresponsive to real interest rate changes. The effect of this is that there will only be a relatively small shift in the I and S curves in response to a change in interest rates, and thus only a relatively small change in national income.

Monetarists, by contrast, argue that investment and saving are relatively responsive to changes in real interest rates and that therefore the IS curve is relatively elastic.

Shifts in the IS curve

A change in real interest rates will cause a *movement along* the IS curve. As we saw in Figure 19.11, a reduction in interest rates from r_1 to r_2 causes a movement *along* the IS curve from point *a* to point *b*. Hence as real interest rates fall, real aggregate demand increases.

A change in any *other* determinant of investment or saving, however, will *shift* the whole curve. The reason is that it will change the equilibrium level of real national income at any given real rate of interest.

An increase in investment, other than as a result of a fall in real interest rates, will shift the IS curve to the *right*. This could happen, for example, if there were an increase in business confidence. A rise in business confidence *at the current real interest rate* will cause an upward shift of the I curve in the top part of Figure 19.11, which will cause a multiplied rise in real income. Thus in the lower part of Figure 19.11 a higher equilibrium real income is now associated with each level of the real interest rate: the IS curve has shifted to the right. Likewise, for any given real interest rate, a fall in saving, and hence a rise in consumption, would also shift the IS curve to the right.

In a complete model (with three injections and three withdrawals), where the IS curve was a '$J = W$' curve rather than a simple '$I = S$' curve, similar shifts would result from changes in other injections or withdrawals. Thus an expansionary fiscal policy that increased government expenditure on goods and services (G) or cut taxes (T) would shift the 'IS' curve (i.e. the JW curve) to the right.

> ? *In a complete JW model, what else would cause the JW curve (a) to shift to the right; (b) to shift to the left?*

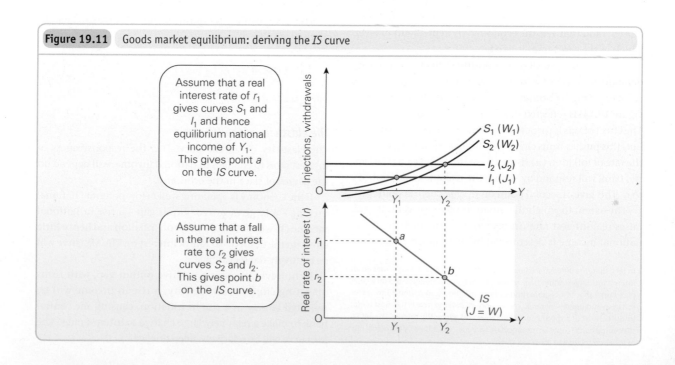

Figure 19.11   Goods market equilibrium: deriving the *IS* curve

Assume that a real interest rate of r_1 gives curves S_1 and I_1 and hence equilibrium national income of Y_1. This gives point *a* on the *IS* curve.

Assume that a fall in the real interest rate to r_2 gives curves S_2 and I_2. This gives point *b* on the *IS* curve.

The *MP* curve

Deriving the MP curve

To help analyse the monetary policy (*MP*) curve consider Figure 19.12. Unlike the *IS* curve, which was developed as part of the *IS/LM* model (see Appendix to this chapter) in the 1930s, the *MP* curve is a relatively new model, developed in the context of inflation targeting by central banks.[3]

In controlling inflation, the central bank adjusts the nominal policy rate. In simple terms, this is the rate of interest at which it is prepared to supply liquidity to financial institutions. Hence, this rate then affects other interest rates in the economy. For ease of exposition we begin our analysis by assuming a single representative interest rate. As we saw earlier (see page 589), it is the *real* rate of interest that is key in affecting aggregate demand.

Since, the *ex ante* real interest rate is the nominal interest rate (i) *less* the expected rate of inflation (π^e), the central bank needs to account for inflation rate expectations when deciding on the nominal interest rate. In the short term we assume an *inertia* in the adjustment of expectations. This means that the expected rate of inflation is constant or 'anchored' at any moment in time. Any adjustment to inflationary expectations in response to changes in actual inflation occurs with a lag.

The central bank is assumed to raise *real* interest rates when inflation rises above the target (π^*) and to lower them when inflation falls below the target. To raise the real rate of interest (r) the nominal rate of interest (i) must rise relative to the expected rate of inflation (π^e). Similarly, for the real rate of interest to fall the nominal interest rate must fall relative to the expected rate of inflation.

The *MP* curve is drawn as upward sloping. To understand why, assume that the economy represented in Figure 19.12 is at point *a* with real national income Y_1 and real interest rates r_1. Assume too that inflation is currently at the target rate (π^*) and that Y_1 is the economy's potential output level, which in the short term is fixed.

Now assume that there is a positive 'shock' to aggregate demand because of a rise in consumer confidence that reduces saving by households. This (as we shall see later in Figure 19.14) is reflected in a rightward shift of the *IS* curve. The effect of this is to increase real national income, say to Y_2. But, this pushes firms closer to full capacity and so results in the rate of inflation (π) rising above the target (π^*). The central bank will respond by raising the real rate of interest, say to r_2. This gives a second point on the *MP* curve at point *b*.

The extent to which the inflation-targeting central bank raises real interest rates in response to the increase in real national income is determined by its forecasts of how the

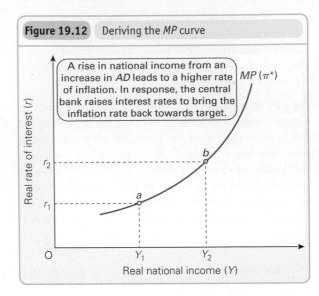

Figure 19.12 Deriving the *MP* curve

> A rise in national income from an increase in *AD* leads to a higher rate of inflation. In response, the central bank raises interest rates to bring the inflation rate back towards target.

transmission mechanisms of monetary policy identified in section 19.1 will affect inflation. Therefore, the *MP* curve represents the *short-term* response of the central bank. The adjustment process of the economy to economic shocks will determine subsequent monetary policy changes. We will consider these issues further in Chapters 20 and 21 when looking at the interaction between aggregate demand and supply both in the short and long run.

The short-term response of the central bank to a positive demand-side shock is to raise real interest rates: a move up the *MP* curve. But what if the economy had experienced a negative shock to aggregate demand? Because the fall in real national income causes the rate of inflation to fall below the target rate, the central bank responds by lowering the real rate of interest.

The relationship underpinning the *MP* curve can be summarised as follows:

$$Y\uparrow \rightarrow \pi > \pi^* \rightarrow r\uparrow$$

$$Y\downarrow \rightarrow \pi < \pi^* \rightarrow r\downarrow$$

The elasticity of the MP curve

The elasticity of the *MP* curve, i.e. the responsiveness of interest rates to changes in national income, will depend on the degree of slack in the economy.

If the economy is operating well below potential national income – a large negative output gap – a rise in national income (Y) will have little effect on inflation and hence little effect on the desired real rate of interest (r). The *MP* curve will be relatively flat (elastic).

If, however, there is a positive output gap, with firms operating close to full capacity, a rise in income will be reflected largely in a rise in inflation, causing the central bank to make a relatively large change to interest rates. The *MP* curve will be relatively steep (inelastic).

---

3 In fact, there are different versions of the *MP* curve. One version focuses on an interest rate target, rather than an inflation target. Another focuses on a complex target that is a combination of both inflation and national income or inflation and unemployment. The version we develop here is the most useful in the context of a specific inflation target and where the interest rate set by the central bank is only an intermediate variable determined by the actual rate of inflation relative to the target rate.

This means that the curve is likely to get steeper as national income rises, as in Figure 19.12. The closer the economy gets to full employment – i.e. the smaller the negative output gap or the bigger the positive output gap – the less slack there is in the economy. The less the slack, the more firms are likely to respond to a rise in demand by raising real prices (i.e. raising their prices above the rate of inflation) and the greater the resulting rise in inflation and the rise in central bank interest rates.

Shifts in the MP curve

A particular *MP* curve assumes a particular central bank target, a given expected rate of inflation and a particular level of potential income. If any one of these changes, a new *MP* curve will have to be drawn.

Change in the target rate of inflation. If the central bank chooses to raise the target rate of inflation, the *MP* curve will shift downwards. Any given level of national income and hence inflation will result in a lower central bank interest rate.

An inflationary shock. If there is a cost-push inflationary shock, such as a rise in inflationary expectations, an oil price increase or a substantial rise in the minimum wage, the *MP* curve will shift upwards. For any given level of national income (Y), there will be a higher rate of inflation and thus the central bank will choose a higher real rate of interest.

KI 10
p70

Change in central bank policy. If, instead of targeting just inflation, the central bank chooses to target national income or a combination of inflation and national income (known as a Taylor rule: we examine Taylor rules in section 22.4 on pages 705–706), then the *MP* curve will change shape. For example, putting a greater emphasis on targeting

a particular level of national income will make the *MP* curve steeper, as changes in national income will cause the central bank to make larger changes in interest rates than it would have done if it targeted inflation alone. In the extreme case of targeting just national income and not inflation at all, the curve would be vertical at the targeted level of national income.

Alternatively, the central bank may target unemployment alongside inflation. Again this will tend to make the curve steeper the more closely unemployment is aligned to national income. For example, the Fed in the USA has a dual mandate: it is required to target not only inflation but also increasing employment.

Change in potential national income. Potential national income is likely to rise over time. This rise in aggregate supply is the result of increased investment, new technology, greater labour efficiency, etc. A rise in potential national income will shift the *MP* curve to the right, as a given rate of inflation will be associated with a higher level of national income.

 If the central bank targets real national income rather than inflation, what will be the shape of the MP curve?

Equilibrium

Equilibrium national income and the rate of interest are given by the intersection of the *IS* and *MP* curves. This is shown as point *a* in Figure 19.13, giving equilibrium national income of Y_e and an interest rate of r_e.

To demonstrate why this is an equilibrium, consider what would happen if national income were not at Y_e but at Y_1. According to the *MP* curve (point *b*), the higher inflation associated with this higher level of national income would

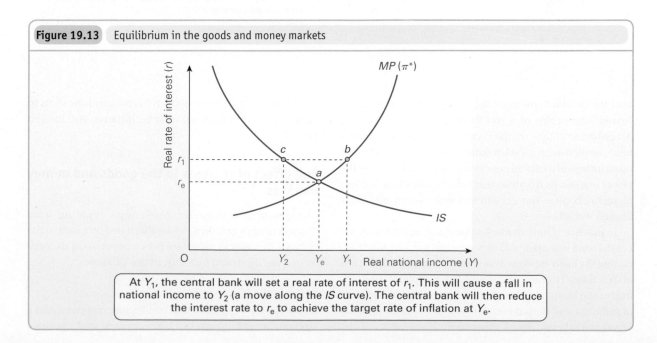

Figure 19.13 Equilibrium in the goods and money markets

At Y_1, the central bank will set a real rate of interest of r_1. This will cause a fall in national income to Y_2 (a move along the *IS* curve). The central bank will then reduce the interest rate to r_e to achieve the target rate of inflation at Y_e.

*LOOKING AT THE MATHS

Equilibrium in the *IS/MP* model is where the two functions, *IS* and *MP*, are equal. The simplest mathematical representation of this is where both *IS* and *MP* are simple linear (i.e. straight-line) functions. The *IS* function could be expressed as

$$r = a - bY \qquad (1)$$

In other words, the higher the real rate of interest (r), the lower will be the level of aggregate demand and hence real national income (Y).[1] This is consistent with a downward-sloping *IS* curve.

The *MP* function can be written as

$$r = c + dY \qquad (2)$$

In other words, the higher the level of real national income (and hence the higher the rate of inflation), the higher will be the real rate of interest set by the central bank. This is consistent with an upward-sloping *MP* curve.

Equation (2) can be derived from the relationships between inflation (π) and national income and between inflation and the rate of interest. The relationship between inflation and national income is given by

$$\pi = e + f(Y - Y_p) \qquad (3)$$

where Y_p is potential national income. The greater the excess of actual (short-run) income over potential income (i.e. the bigger the positive output gap), the higher will be the rate of inflation.

The relationship between inflation and the rate of interest is given by the central bank response function, which, in its simplest form, is given by

$$r = g + h(\pi - \pi^*) \qquad (4)$$

where π^* is the target rate of inflation. The higher the actual inflation rate is relative to the target rate, the higher will be the rate of interest set by the central bank. Substituting equation (4) in equation (3) gives

$$r = g + h(e + f(Y - Y_p) - \pi^*) \qquad (5)$$

Assuming that Y_p and π^* are constant, equation (5) can be simplified as equation (2):

$$r = c + dY \qquad (2)$$

We can then solve for *Y* from equations (1) and (2) by setting the two equations equal. Thus

$$a - bY = c + dY$$

that is

$$bY + dY = a - c$$

giving

$$Y = \frac{a - c}{b + d}$$

Note that a change in any of the factors affecting *Y*, other than *r*, will shift the *IS* curve. Such factors include taxes, government expenditure, the exchange rate, expectations about income and prices, and so on.

Similarly, a change in any of the factors affecting *r*, other than *Y*, will shift the *MP* curve. Such factors include potential national income (Y_p), cost pressures, inflationary expectations and the inflation target (π^*).

The IS function can be written as

$$Y = IS(r, G, t, X, M, er, Y^e \ldots)$$

where G is government expenditure, t is the tax rate, X and M are the levels of exports and imports, er is the exchange rate, Y^e is the expected level of real national income and '. . .' represents other unspecified determinants.

Write an MP function in the form r = MP($-----$) identifying each of the determinants.

1 Note that although equation (1) shows *r* as a function of *Y*, the model in fact has *Y* as the dependent variable. In other words, *r* determines *Y*. We express equation (1) this way to make it consistent with equation (2), where *r* is the dependent variable.

KI 8
p46

lead the central bank to set an interest rate of r_1. But this higher interest rate of r_1 will dampen aggregate demand. According to point *c* on the *IS* curve, the goods market will be in equilibrium at a level of national income of Y_2. This will cause inflation to fall and hence the central bank to lower the rate of interest. As it does so, there will be a movement down along the *IS* curve and a rise in national income until equilibrium is reached at Y_e.

In practice, if the two markets are not in equilibrium, the central bank will attempt to move straight to r_e and Y_e by forecasting the likely movements in the economy and the results of its actions. The Bank of England, for example, at the meetings of the Monetary Policy Committee, examines forecasts of inflation and output contained in its quarterly *Inflation Report* and other models of the economy.

The next step in the analysis is to consider how shifts in either curve affect national income, inflation and interest rates.

Full effect of changes in the goods and money markets

Changes in goods market equilibrium resulting from changes to aggregate demand are illustrated by a shift in the *IS* curve. Changes to monetary policy or potential national income are illustrated by a shift in the *MP* curve.

Shifts in the IS curve

Assume in Figure 19.14(a) that equilibrium is at point *a*, at a level of national income of Y_1. Now assume that a positive demand shock occurs resulting in a rightward shift in the *IS* curve from IS_1 to IS_2. This could arise, for example, because confidence rises and economic agents decide to increase spending or because of a loosening of fiscal policy (e.g. an increase in government purchases). This causes national income and inflation to rise. The central bank responds to the higher inflation by raising the rate of interest. There is a movement up along the *MP* curve. Equilibrium is reached at point *b* at a level of national income of Y_2 and a rate of interest of r_2.

Shifts in the MP curve

As we noted earlier, many countries have adopted some form of inflation targeting. However, inflation targeting can take many different forms and the policy rule can be changed or adapted. For example, the Federal Reserve from 2008 and the Bank of England from 2013 supplemented their existing policy frameworks with forward guidance: statements about the likely path of future interest rates. The intention was to signal that interest rates were likely to remain low for some time given the fragile economic conditions following the financial crisis. The hope was that this would give economic agents confidence to bring forward spending.

To illustrate a change to the monetary policy rule using the *IS/MP* framework, consider the case where the central bank now sets a lower interest rate for any given level of output and rate of inflation. The effect of this looser monetary policy rule is to move the *MP* curve vertically downwards. This is illustrated by a move from MP_1 to MP_2 in Figure 19.14(b). The central bank reduces the nominal rate of interest so as to give a real rate of interest of r_3. As a result there is a movement along the *IS* curve to point *c* and national income rises to Y_3.

A positive supply-side shock would have a similar effect. An example is a rise in potential income. This again can be illustrated by a shift in the *MP* curve from MP_1 to MP_2 in Figure 19.14(b). With a rise in potential income, a higher level of actual income is now associated with any given rate of inflation and hence central bank interest rate.

 What other examples of supply-side shocks would cause the MP curve to move vertically downwards?

Shifts in the both curves

If potential national income increases and also aggregate demand, actual income can rise without imposing extra inflationary pressures. This is illustrated in Figure 19.14(c). National income rises to Y_3. The central bank does not need to raise interest rates as there is no upward movement in inflation.

Size of the effect on national income of shifts in either or both curves

The magnitude of a change in income resulting from a shift in one or both curves depends not only on the size of the shift, but in the shape of the curves.

- The effect of a shift in the *IS* curve will be bigger, the flatter is the *MP* curve and the steeper the *IS* curve. When *MP* is relatively flat (e.g. when there is plenty of slack in the economy), a rightward shift in *IS* will lead to only a small rise in the real rate of interest (*r*) by the central bank. If *IS* is steep (i.e. aggregate demand being relatively unresponsive to changes in interest rates), this rise in *r* will lead to only a small curtailing of investment. In these two circumstances, the dampening effect on investment and consumption is limited. There will be a large increase in national income (*Y*).
- The effect of a shift in the *MP* curve will be bigger when the *MP* curve is steep (e.g. when the economy is near full employment) and the *IS* curve is relatively flat. When the *MP* curve is steep, there will be a relatively large downward shift in the *MP* curve for any fall in the inflation target and hence a relatively large fall in *r*. When *IS* is relatively flat, this fall in *r* will lead to a relatively large increase in investment and hence *Y*.
- The effect of a shift in either curve will be bigger if matched by a similar shift in the other curve.

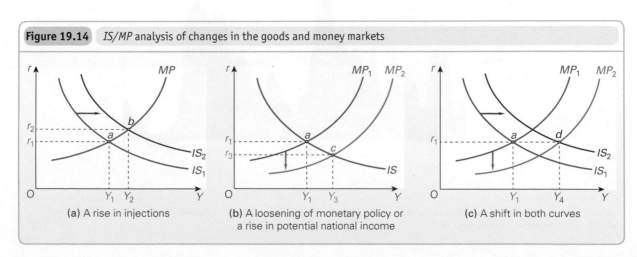

Figure 19.14 *IS/MP* analysis of changes in the goods and money markets

(a) A rise in injections

(b) A loosening of monetary policy or a rise in potential national income

(c) A shift in both curves

Section summary

1. The *IS/MP* model allows us to model the interaction between the goods and the money market. The model shows the relationship between national income and interest rates where central bankers set interest rates.

2. Equilibrium in the goods market is shown by the *IS* curve. This shows all the combinations of the real rate of interest and national income where investment (*I*) equals saving (*S*) (or, in a complete Keynesian model, where injections equal withdrawals). As the rate of interest rises, so investment will fall and saving will rise: therefore equilibrium national income will fall. The *IS* curve is thus downward sloping.

3. The *MP* curve shows the real rate of interest that the central bank would choose at any particular level of national income. We assume that the rate of inflation rises with the level of national income. The central bank

will thus raise the real rate of interest (i.e. the nominal rate plus the rate of inflation) as national income rises. This gives an upward sloping *MP* curve. A higher potential national income, by putting downward pressure on inflation at any given level of actual national income, will shift the *MP* curve to the right. A lower inflation target will shift the curve downward.

4. Equilibrium occurs where *IS* = *MP*. At this point the goods market is in equilibrium at the real interest rate chosen by the central bank.

5. A shift in either curve will lead to a new equilibrium. The resulting size of the change in real national income and real interest rates will depend on the size of the shift and the shape of the other curve.

19.4 CREDIT CYCLES AND THE GOODS MARKET

Credit cycles

The flows of credit extended by financial institutions can vary considerably from period to period. This is shown in Figure 19.15, which plots annual flows of credit from monetary financial institutions (MFIs) to households and private non-financial corporations in the UK from 1965. The flows are measured relative to GDP, allowing us to make better comparisons of the magnitude of credit flows over time.

As you can see, there were heightened flows of credit in the late 1980s and the early-to-mid 2000s. In each case, this

was then followed by a period of significantly weaker credit growth and, for non-financial corporations, even net repayments of outstanding lending.

In analysing the interaction between the goods and money markets it is therefore important to understand how these cycles arise and what impact they have on aggregate demand and national output. We look at two theories of the instability of credit and the effect on the economy: the *financial accelerator* and the *financial instability hypothesis*.

Figure 19.15 Annual flows of credit from MFIs

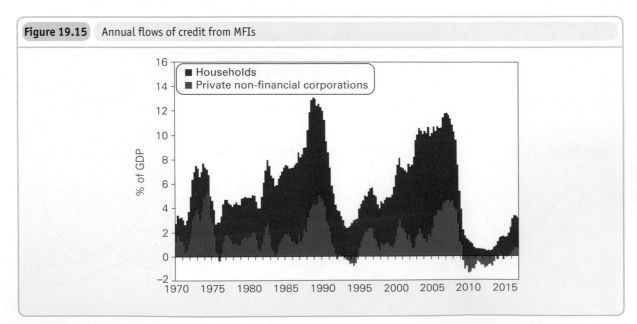

Source: (i) *Statistical Interactive Database*, Bank of England, series LPQVWNV and LPQVWNQ (data published 29 September 2017) and (ii) *Quarterly National Accounts*, Office for National Statistics, series YBHA.

The financial accelerator

The *financial accelerator* explains how financial institutions can amplify the business cycle. They tend to lend more when macroeconomic conditions are improving or already strong, but less when they deteriorate.

The reason for this behaviour is that financial institutions use the macroeconomic environment as a basis for assessing the riskiness of their lending and the probability of default. A booming economy encourages banks to lend more; a recession makes them much more cautious.

This behaviour amplifies the effects of economic shocks. Positive economic shocks are magnified by increasing credit flows, while negative economic shocks are magnified by a weakening of credit flows.

Interest rate differentials

One way in which credit conditions can vary with macroeconomic conditions is through their impact on interest rate differentials. The financial system is characterised by a range of interest rates rather than a single interest rate. To simplify, we can assume that there is a representative real borrowing rate (r_b) and a representative real interest rate on savings (r_s). The differential between the two rates ($r_b - r_s$) reflects the risks attached to lending to economic agents and the costs incurred by financial institutions in screening clients and then in arranging and managing loans. The bigger the risk, the bigger the differential.

The interest rate differential can amplify economic fluctuations because the interest rate differential frequently varies across the course of business cycle. The differential tends to fall in a boom and rise in a slowdown or recession.

But why does the differential fall in a boom? As far as lending is concerned, banks and other financial institutions may see rising output levels as a signal that lending is becoming less risky. After all, the financial well-being of economic agents typically improves as national income rises. Consequently, banks tend to reduce the differential of borrowing rates over saving rates in periods of rapid economic growth. This is an example of the use of *heuristics* (see section 5.2, page 138) – banks using the macroeconomic situation to develop simple decision-making rules.

At the same time, with economic agents gaining more confidence, they may decide to spend more and reduce their level of savings. Banks may thus offer higher interest rates on savings, further reducing the differential between borrowing and saving rates.

Definition

Financial accelerator The amplification of effects on the macroeconomy from economic shocks because of changes in the pricing and supply of credit by financial institutions.

Availability of credit

A second way in which lending behaviour may vary across the business cycle is through changes in the volume of credit made available by financial institutions. Credit criteria are relaxed in a boom, as banks see rising output and incomes as a signal that lending is less risky. In a slowdown or recession, by contrast, lending is seen as more risky and hence credit criteria are tightened.

Taken together, varying interest rate differentials and varying credit constraints could therefore result in credit flows being strongly pro-cyclical.

The interaction between the multiplier and the financial accelerator

The effect of the financial accelerator is to *increase* the marginal propensity to consume domestically produced goods. To understand why, recall that the mpc_d is the proportion of the rise in output which is spent on domestic goods and services. As output rises, credit constraints weaken and the borrowing rate of interest (r_b) falls for a given saving interest rate (r_s). This means that investment (I) and consumption (C) rise as output rises. Hence, we have an *additional* channel by which increases in real national income cause aggregate expenditures to rise.

The financial accelerator has the effect of making the marginal propensity to consume domestically produced goods (mpc_d) bigger. Consequently, the measurable multiplier effect from increases in aggregate demand is bigger too. This is because the normal multiplier effects, whereby rising incomes increase spending, are supplemented by additional credit flows which facilitate further additional spending.

The financial accelerator and the IS/MP framework

Because the financial accelerator makes the overall multiplier bigger, the *IS* curve is more *elastic*. This is illustrated in Figure 19.16. When applying the *IS/MP* framework in the presence of interest rate differentials we need to identify

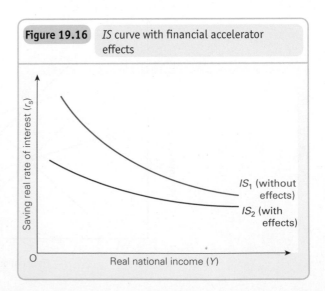

Figure 19.16   *IS* curve with financial accelerator effects

which interest rate is on the vertical axis. Since rates on saving typically track the central bank rate most closely, we now label the vertical axis the real interest rate on saving (r_s).

IS_1 shows the IS curve in the absence of financial accelerator effects, while IS_2 incorporates financial accelerator effects. This curve is flatter, as a given fall in saving rates will produce a bigger rise in national income as borrowing rates will have fallen more as the interest rate differential narrows and credit becomes more readily available.

The flatter curve, IS_2, is shown as converging on IS_1 as output rises. This is because the interest rate differential declines and credit constraints weaken. Conversely, at lower levels of output credit constraints become tighter and the borrowing rate becomes relatively higher, so causing aggregate expenditure to be increasingly lower than it otherwise would be. In other words, we can think of financial market imperfections increasing as output falls (for a given level of potential output).

At each point on the IS curve the goods market is in equilibrium. As we illustrated in Figure 19.11 this means that injections (J) equal withdrawals (W). With the incorporation of an interest rate differential, we can think of our IS curve as showing the combination of the real interest rate on saving (r_s) and real national income (Y) that ensures that $J = W$.

The effects of consumer confidence. Consider now the effect of an increase in consumer confidence. In the presence of financial accelerator effects there is a larger rightward movement of the IS curve than would otherwise be the case. This is because as output rises (as the IS curves shifts rightwards) the financial market imperfections lessen. At each real interest rate on saving (r_s) there is a lower interest rate differential than before along with reduced credit constraints.

These additional effects further increase spending and, hence, output.

Another way of analysing the effect on output of an increase in consumer confidence is to consider upward shifts of the IS curve. The magnitude of the financial market imperfections grow smaller as the level of output rises. But, at any particular level of output, at any moment in time, they are fixed. Hence, these imperfections have no effect on the extent to which the IS curve moves upwards when consumer confidence rises. This is useful because we can now show more clearly how financial accelerator effects magnify the impact of demand shocks on output. We do this in Figure 19.17.

Assume the economy is at point a with the real interest on saving (and the real central bank policy rate) at r_1 and real national income at Y_1. Curve IS_1 represents the economy in the presence of financial accelerator effects . It is flatter than IS'_1, which illustrates the position with no financial accelerator effects.

The rise in consumer confidence causes an equivalent upward movement of both IS curves. This is represented by the vertical distance $b−a$ at the initial level of output, Y_1. In the presence of financial accelerator effects the IS curve moves to IS_2 while in the absence of financial accelerator effects the IS curve moves to IS'_2.

The new short-run equilibrium in the absence of the financial accelerator is at point c. From this we can see that output has increased from Y_1 to Y_2. However, with financial accelerator effects the new equilibrium is at point d and this represents an increase in output from Y_1 to Y_3. Therefore, the financial accelerator leads to an additional increase in output equivalent to $Y_3 − Y_2$. This captures the additional effects on aggregate demand as the interest rate differential falls and banks relax their lending criteria.

Figure 19.17 Financial accelerator: positive demand-side shock

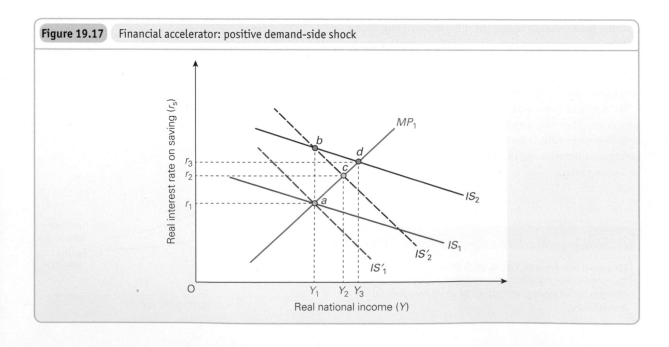

The interest rate on saving increases by more following the rise in consumer confidence in the presence of the financial accelerator. Since the real interest rate on saving tracks the real policy rate, this reflects the larger increase in the real interest rate by the central bank. The financial accelerator causes a larger rise in output, which leads to a larger rise in the rate of inflation.

The increase in the saving (and central bank) interest rate is captured by the move up and along the MP curve. This will put upward pressure on the interest rate on borrowing (r_b). However, the fall in the interest rate differential ($r_b - r_s$) that occurs as output increases tends to decrease the interest rate on borrowing. We would tend to expect the borrowing rate to rise following the rise in confidence. But if it does rise, it will rise by less than otherwise in the presence of financial accelerator effects.

The financial instability hypothesis

The second theory of credit cycles is the ***financial instability hypothesis (FIH)***. This theory argues that the volume of credit flows goes through stages which are ultimately destabilising for the economy. As flows of credit increase unsustainably as, it is argued, they inevitably do, they cause the health of the balance sheets of people and businesses to deteriorate. This then results in a period of consolidation during which spending growth is subdued.

The hypothesis argues that the financial system generates unsustainable growth in the goods market. Our appetite for goods and services is fed by increasing flows of credit which increasingly place greater strain on people's ability to meet their debt obligations. Eventually, the financial distress is too great and the growth in aggregate demand ends, perhaps very abruptly, as people take steps to improve their financial well-being.

The financial instability hypothesis is associated with American economist Hyman Minsky (1919–96). He argued that financial cycles are an inherent part of the economic cycle and are the primary source of fluctuations in real GDP. He argued that the accumulation of debt by people and businesses is not only pro-cyclical, but destabilising. While Minsky himself focused on the accumulation of debt by businesses, the role of the mortgage market in generating unsustainable stocks of household debt during the 2000s (see Box 18.2) has meant that his ideas are now frequently applied across the whole of the private sector.

The extension of credit by financial institutions can be seen to go through three different stages: financial tranquillity, financial fragility and financial bust. During each of these stages both the credit criteria of banks and the ability of borrowers to afford their debts vary.

Minsky argued that credit flows will tend to increase after a period of sustained growth. This causes banks and investors to develop a heightened euphoria and confidence in the economy and in the returns of assets. Economists refer to this as ***irrational exuberance***, which results in people and businesses taking on bigger debts to acquire assets. These debts increasingly stretch their financial well-being. A point is reached, perhaps triggered by an economic shock or a tightening of economic policy, when the euphoria stops and confidence is replaced with pessimism. This moment is now commonly referred to as a ***Minsky moment***.

The result of a Minsky moment is that lenders reduce their lending, and economic agents look to increase their net worth (i.e. reduce debts or increase savings) to ensure their financial well-being. However, the result of these individual actions causes a decline in spending and in national income. The collapse in aggregate demand from financial distress therefore leads to a ***balance-sheet recession*** or economic downturn. Furthermore, by selling assets to improve financial well-being, the value of assets falls. This paradoxical reduction of net worth is known as the paradox of debt (see Chapter 16, page 514).

Minsky believed that credit cycles are inevitable in a free-market economy. Hence, the authorities will need to take action to moderate credit cycles. The significance given to macro-prudential regulation by policy makers (see section 18.3) in the response to the financial crisis is recognition of the dangers posed to the economy by credit cycles.

Definitions

Financial instability hypothesis The theory that the economy goes through stages of credit accumulation which initially fuel aggregate demand but because of increasing financial distress eventually see a collapse in aggregate demand.

Irrational exuberance Where banks and other economic agents are over-confident about the economy and/or financial markets and expect economic growth to remain stronger and/or asset prices to rise further than warranted by evidence. The term is associated with the economist Robert Shiller and his book *Irrational Exuberance* (2000) and with the former US Federal Reserve Chairman, Alan Greenspan.

Minsky moment A turning point in a credit cycle where a period of easy credit and rising debt is replaced by one of tight credit and debt consolidation.

Balance-sheet recession A recession or economic slowdown caused by a collapse in aggregate demand arising from the actions of financially distressed people and businesses.

BOX 19.5 THE FINANCIAL ACCELERATOR AND FLUCTUATIONS IN AGGREGATE DEMAND

Illustrating financial accelerator effects using the Keynesian cross

Financial market imperfections

New Keynesians emphasise how market imperfections contribute to economic volatility (see pages 506–507). The financial accelerator shows how imperfections in the financial system can amplify the ups and downs associated with the business cycle.

TC 15 p535

According to the financial accelerator, the state of the economy affects the lending behaviour of financial institutions, which, in turn, affects aggregate demand and the real economy. Because of this feedback to the economy itself the business cycle is amplified. If we assume that financial institutions take rising levels of real GDP as a signal that lending is less risky and falling levels that it is more risky, then credit flows may become acutely pro-cyclical.

The financial accelerator and the 45° line diagram (Keynesian cross)

As national income rises, the financial accelerator effects are *additional* to the normal multiplier (and accelerator) effects which act to increase expenditures. The impact of the financial accelerator is to make the aggregate expenditure line in the Keynesian cross diagram *steeper*. This is illustrated in Figure (a). It shows a particular economy's aggregate expenditure. In the absence of financial accelerator effects the aggregate expenditure line is E_1, while in the presence of financial accelerator effects it is E_2. This reflects the idea that with financial accelerator effects the economy would have a bigger marginal propensity to consume domestically produced goods (mpc_d). The two lines grow closer as real

national income rises because credit constraints lessen and the interest rate differential narrows (see page 611).

We can use the Keynesian cross diagram to illustrate the amplification of fluctuations in output arising from fluctuations in aggregate demand. We do this in Figure (b). For ease of illustration we assume that, with or without financial accelerator effects, the economy is initially at income level Y_1.

Consider now the effect of a given increase in autonomous expenditures: i.e. expenditures unrelated to real national income, such as investment (I) or government purchases (G). This results in both of the E lines moving vertically upwards by the same distance.

From the diagram we can see that, in the absence of the financial accelerator, output rises from Y_1 to Y_2. However, in the presence of the financial accelerator, output rises from Y_1 to Y_3. The financial accelerator effects lead to an additional increase in output equivalent to $Y_3 - Y_2$. This captures how the additional credit flows, which arise as the economy expands, generate additional expenditure.

The more significant the financial accelerator effects, the steeper is the E line and the more output fluctuates in response to shocks to aggregate demand.

1. Is it possible for the aggregate expenditure line to be steeper than the 45° line in the presence of financial accelerator effects?
2. What has happened to the interest rate on borrowing (r_b) and the interest rate on saving (r_s) in the two scenarios shown in Figure (b)?

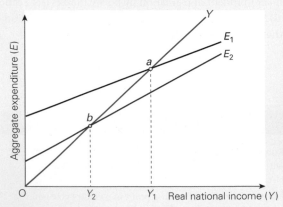

(a) *Financial accelerator and aggregate expenditure line*

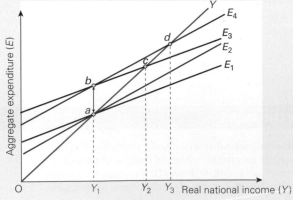

(b) *Financial accelerator and output fluctuations*

Section summary

1. The financial accelerator amplifies the impact on the economy of economic shocks. The lending behaviour of financial institutions is argued to be dependent on the state of the economy. Increasing output levels may weaken credit constraints and reduce the differential between interest rates on borrowing and on saving. Conversely, falling output levels increase credit constraints and the differential between interest rates on borrowing and saving.

2. The financial accelerator increases the size of the multiplier. The impact on real national income of demand-side shocks is amplified by changes in the pricing and supply of credit by financial institutions.

3. The financial instability hypothesis (FIH) characterises economies as progressing through stages. In the first stage people and businesses accumulate more debt. The accumulation of debt is driven by an over-confidence and euphoria and, hence, by an irrational exuberance.

4. The FIH predicts that debt accumulation will initially boost aggregate demand. However, as debt-servicing obligations progressively increase, the growth in aggregate demand will begin to weaken. A Minsky moment is reached when financial distress causes a collapse in aggregate demand. The result is a balance-sheet recession or slowdown.

APPENDIX: THE *IS/LM* MODEL

In Section 19.3 we applied a framework known as the *IS/MP* model to analyse the interaction between monetary policy and the goods market. This framework recognises that many central bankers today attempt to achieve a target rate of inflation. They do this by seeking to influence the structure of interest rates in the economy and thereby to affect aggregate demand. We look at central bank objectives and their evolution in greater detail in Chapter 22.

The predecessor to the *IS/MP* model was the *IS/LM model*. As with the *IS/MP* model, *IS/LM* model allows us to examine the effects of changes originating in the money or goods markets on *both* national income *and* interest rates: it shows what the equilibrium will be in both the goods and the money markets simultaneously. The difference with the *IS/MP* model is that there is no inflation target. Instead, interest rates are purely market determined. The central bank is assumed to conduct monetary policy through changes in money supply.

As we saw earlier, the *IS* curve is based on equilibrium in the goods market. The *LM* curve is concerned with equilibrium in the money market. It shows all the various combinations of interest rates and national income at which the demand for money (L) equals the supply (M). The *LM* curve is different from the *MP* curve in that it analyses how the interest rate adjusts to help bring money demand into equilibrium with money supply. In other words, the interest rate equilibrates the money market at any given level of national income.

In constructing the *IS/LM* model we assume, for simplicity, that prices are constant, i.e. there is an absence of inflation. Therefore, there is no difference between the nominal interest rate (i) and real interest rate (r).

The *IS* curve

We analysed the *IS* curve in depth in section 19.3, so only a brief overview is provided here. The curve shows combinations of national income and interest rates at which planned expenditure equals national income. This occurs when the flow of injections (J) is matched by the flow of withdrawals (W). Hence, when we consider all injections (I, G and X) and withdrawals (S, T and M), rather than just investment and saving, we may think of the curve as a *JW* curve.

When the real rate of interest (r) rises, there is a fall in investment and a fall in saving. This will lead to a multiplied fall in income. Thus *higher* interest rates are associated with *lower* national income, if equilibrium is to be maintained in the goods market ($J = W$). The *IS* curve is therefore drawn as downward sloping, as illustrated in Figure 19.11 on page 605.

A change in *interest rates* causes movements *along* the *IS* curve. Changes in any *other* determinant of injections and withdrawals *shift* the whole curve. The reason is that it will change the equilibrium level of national income at any given rate of interest. For example, if, in response to a decline in their net worth, firms reduce their investment at *the current interest rate* (resulting in a downward shift of the *I* curve in the top part of Figure 19.11), there is a multiplied fall in national income. Thus a lower equilibrium income is now associated with each level of the interest rate. The *IS* curve has shifted to the left.

The *LM* curve

Deriving the LM *curve*

To explain how the *LM* curve is derived consider Figure 19.18. The left-hand part of the diagram is the

Definition

IS/LM **model** A model showing simultaneous equilibrium in the goods market ($I = S$) and the money market ($L = M$).

Figure 19.18   Money market equilibrium: deriving the *LM* curve

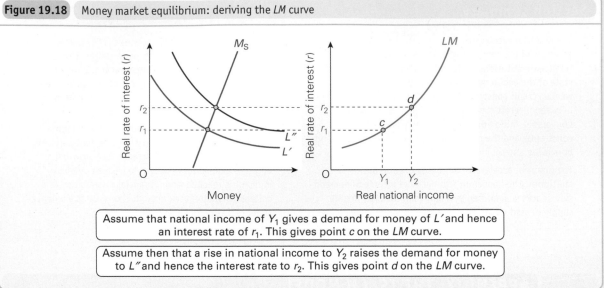

Assume that national income of Y_1 gives a demand for money of L' and hence an interest rate of r_1. This gives point *c* on the *LM* curve.

Assume then that a rise in national income to Y_2 raises the demand for money to L'' and hence the interest rate to r_2. This gives point *d* on the *LM* curve.

familiar money market diagram, showing a liquidity preference (demand for money) curve (*L*) and a supply of money curve (*M*).

At any given level of national income, there will be a particular level of transactions-plus-precautionary demand for money, and hence a given overall demand-for-money curve (*L*). Let us assume that, when national income is at a level of Y_1 in the right-hand part of Figure 19.18, the demand-for-money curve is L'. With the given money supply curve M_s, the equilibrium rate of interest will be r_1. Thus point *c* is one point on the *LM* curve. At a level of national income Y_1, the money market will be in equilibrium at a rate of interest of r_1. (Note that we are assuming that the money supply curve is not totally exogenous; in other words, the curve is upward sloping. In simple *IS/LM* models, the money supply curve is (unrealistically) assumed to be vertical.)

Now what will happen if the level of national income changes? Let us assume that national income rises to Y_2. The effect is to increase the transactions-plus-precautionary demand for money. The *L* curve shifts to the right: to, say, L''. This will cause the rate of interest to rise to the new equilibrium level of r_2. This therefore gives us a second point on the *LM* curve (point *d*).

Thus *higher* national income leads to a greater demand for money and hence *higher* interest rates if equilibrium is to be maintained in the money market. The *LM* curve is therefore upward sloping.

The elasticity of the LM curve

The elasticity of the *LM* curve (i.e. the responsiveness of interest rate changes to a change in national income) depends on two factors.[4]

4 Note that the rate of interest is the dependent variable and the level of national income is the independent variable. Thus the more elastic is the *LM* curve (i.e. the more responsive interest rates are to changes in national income), the *steeper* it will be.

The responsiveness of the demand for money to changes in national income. The greater the marginal propensity to consume, the more will the transactions demand for money rise as national income rises, and thus the more the *L* curve will shift to the right. Hence the more the equilibrium interest rate will rise, and the steeper will be the *LM* curve.

The endogeneity of money will lessen this effect. In the case of an upward-sloping money supply curve (as in Figure 19.18), the less steep it is, the more will money supply expand in response to a rise in the demand for money and the less will interest rates rise. Hence the flatter will be the *LM* curve. Where money supply simply expands passively to meet any rise in demand, the *LM* curve will be horizontal.

The responsiveness of the demand for money to changes in interest rates. The more the demand for money responds to a change in interest rates, the flatter will be the liquidity preference curve in the left-hand part of Figure 19.18. The flatter the *L* curve, the less will the equilibrium interest rate change for any given horizontal shift in the *L* curve (arising from a change in *Y*). The less the equilibrium interest rate changes, the flatter will be the *LM* curve.

The Keynesian and monetarist views on the shape of the *LM* curve reflect their respective views on the elasticity of the *L* curve. Keynesians argue that the *L* curve is likely to be relatively flat given the responsiveness of the speculative demand for money to changes in interest rates and the endogeneity of money. They thus argue that the *LM* curve is correspondingly relatively flat (depending, of course, on the scales of the axes). Monetarists, on the other hand, argue that the *LM* curve is relatively steep. This is because they see the demand for money as insensitive to changes in interest rates and the supply of money as being exogenous.

Shifts in the LM curve

A change in *national income* will cause a movement *along* the *LM* curve to a new equilibrating interest rate. Thus in Figure 19.18 a rise in national income from Y_1 to Y_2 leads to a movement along the *L* curve from point *c* to point *d* and hence a rise in the rate of interest from r_1 to r_2.

A change in any *other* determinant of the demand and supply of money will *shift* the whole curve. The reason is that it will change the equilibrium level of interest associated with any given level of national income.

An increase in the demand for money, other than as a result of a rise in income, will shift the *L* curve to the *right*. This could be due to people being paid less frequently, or a greater use of cash, or increased speculation that the price of securities will fall. This increased demand for money will raise the equilibrium rate of interest at the current level of national income. The *LM* curve will shift upwards.

An increased supply of money by the authorities will shift the M_s curve to the right. This will lower the rate of interest (in the left-hand part of Figure 19.18). This will shift the *LM* curve downwards: a lower rate of interest will be associated with any given level of national income.

Draw a diagram like Figure 19.18, only with just one L curve. Assume that the current level of national income is Y_1. Now assume that the supply of money decreases. Show the effect on
(a) the rate of interest;
(b) the position of the LM curve.

Equilibrium

The *IS* curve shows all the combinations of the rate of interest (*r*) and national income (*Y*) at which the *goods* market is

in equilibrium. The *LM* curve shows all the combinations of *r* and *Y* at which the *money* market is in equilibrium. *Both* markets will be in equilibrium where the curves intersect. This is at r_e and Y_e in Figure 19.19.

But what would happen if both markets were not simultaneously in equilibrium? How would equilibrium be achieved?

Let us suppose that the current level of real national income is Y_1. This will create a demand for money that will lead to an equilibrium real interest rate of r_1 (point *a* on the *LM* curve). But at this low interest rate, the desired level of investment and saving would generate an income of Y_2 (point *b* on the *IS* curve). Thus national income will rise. But as national income rises, there will be a movement up along the *LM* curve from point *a*, since the higher income will generate a higher demand for money and hence push up interest rates. And as interest rates rise, so the desired level of investment will fall and the desired level of saving will rise so as to reduce the equilibrium level of national income below Y_2. There will be a movement back up along the *IS* curve from point *b*. Once the interest rate has risen to r_e, the actual level of income will be at the equilibrium level (i.e. *on* the *IS* curve). Both markets will now be in equilibrium.

Assume that national income is initially at Y_2 in Figure 19.19. Describe the process whereby equilibrium in both markets will be achieved.

Full effects of changes in the goods and money markets

IS/LM analysis can be used to examine the full effects of changes in the goods market. Such changes are illustrated

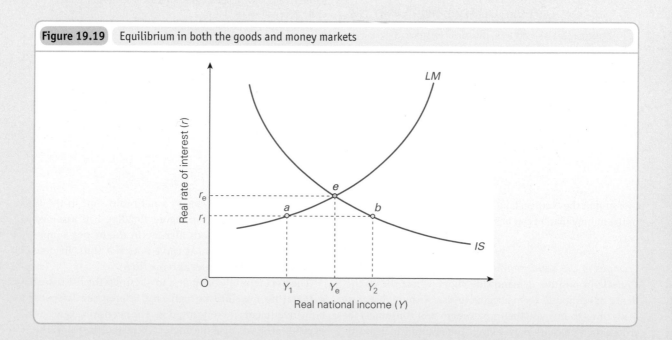

Figure 19.19 Equilibrium in both the goods and money markets

*LOOKING AT THE MATHS

Equilibrium in the *IS/LM* model is where the two functions, *IS* and *LM*, are equal. The simplest mathematical representation of this is where both *IS* and *LM* are simple linear (i.e. straight-line) functions. The *IS* function could be expressed as

$$r = a - bY \qquad (1)$$

In other words, the higher the rate of interest (*r*), the lower will be the level of aggregate demand and hence national income (*Y*).[1] This is consistent with a downward-sloping *IS* curve.

The *LM* function can be written as

$$r = g + hY \qquad (2)$$

In other words, the higher the level of real national income (and hence the higher the demand for money), the higher will be the real rate of interest. This is consistent with an upward-sloping *LM* curve.

We can then solve for *Y* by setting the two equations equal. Thus

$$a - bY = g + hY$$

that is

$$bY + hY = a - g$$

giving

$$Y = \frac{a - g}{h + b}$$

More complex IS and LM functions

In practice, neither function is likely to be linear. Both *IS* and *LM* are likely to be curves rather than straight lines. To understand why, we need to look at the other determinants of *Y* in the case of the *IS* curve and of *r* in the case of the *LM* curve. Let us first examine the *IS* function.

Real national income consists of five elements:

$$Y = C + I + G + X - M \qquad (3)$$

or

$$Y = C(Y,T,r,\pi^e) + I(r,\pi^e,\Delta Y) + G + X(er) - M(Y,T,r,\pi^e,er) \qquad (3a)$$

Equation (3a) is simply an expansion of equation (3) listing the key determinants of each of the variables in equation (3), where *T* is taxes, π^e is expected inflation and *er* is the exchange rate. Investment being a function of changes in national income (ΔY) is the accelerator effect. Thus an *IS* function could be expressed as

$$Y = IS(r, T, \pi^e, \Delta Y, G, er) \qquad (4)$$
$$\quad\;\; - - + \;\; + \;\; + -$$

All the variables in this function are contained in equation (3a). It is highly likely that the relationship between *Y* and most, if not all, these variables is non-linear (i.e. contains squared or higher power terms).

The sign under each of the variables indicates the direction in which *Y* changes when the variable changes. For example, the negative sign under the *T* term means that a rise in taxes would lead to a *fall* in *Y*. Put another way, the sign indicates the sign of the partial derivative of *Y* with respect to each variable. For example, the positive sign under the expected inflation term (π^e) means that when you differentiate *Y* with respect to π^e, you end up with a positive number. This simply means that a rise in π^e leads to a *rise* in *Y*.

Note that a change in *r* would lead to a movement along the *IS* curve. A change in any of the other determinants in equation (4) would shift the curve. A rise in any of the determinants with a positive sign would result in a rightward shift in the curve; a rise in any of the determinants with a negative sign would result in a leftward shift.

Turning to the *LM* function, this can be expressed as

$$r = LM\left(Y, \frac{M_s}{P}, \pi^e, er^e, f\right)$$
$$\quad\;\; + \; - \; + \; + \; - \qquad (5)$$

where M_s / P is the real money supply, π^e is the expected rate of inflation, er^e is the expected exchange rate and *f* is the frequency with which people are paid. The *LM* curve assumes equilibrium in the money market. It therefore represents all the combinations of *r* and *Y* where the real demand for money is equal to the real supply. The real supply of money is given by the term M_s / P and the real demand for money depends on the other terms in equation (5) (see page 583).

A rise in *Y* would cause a movement up along the *LM* curve. A rise in any of the other determinants would shift the curve: upwards in the case of the determinants with a positive sign; downwards in the case of those with a negative sign.

As with the *IS* function, it is highly likely that the relationship between *r* and most, if not all, the variables in the *LM* function is likely to be non-linear.

Maths Case 19.1 on the student website shows how equilibrium in the *ISLM* model can be derived from specific *IS* and *LM* functions.

1 Note that although equation (1) shows *r* as a function of *Y*, the model in fact has *Y* as the dependent variable. In other words, *r* determines *Y*. We express equation (1) this way to make it consistent with equation (2), where *r* is the dependent variable.

TC 13
p453

---

by a shift in the *IS* curve. Likewise, the full effects of changes in the money market can be illustrated by a shift in the *LM* curve.

Changes in the goods market

Consider a positive demand-side shock where the confidence of economic agents begins to rise. Assume that this leads firms to increase their investment and consumers to reduce their precautionary saving. The resulting increase in

aggregate expenditure leads to a rightward shift in the *IS* curve. This is illustrated in Figure 19.20(a). It is assumed that there is no exogenous increase in the money supply and that, therefore, the *LM* curve does not shift. Income rises to Y_2, but interest rates also rise (to r_2).

The rise in the rate of interest to r_2 restricts the rise in real national income, since the higher real interest rate dampens both investment and consumption. The net rise in aggregate expenditure is less than the original increase. The steeper the

LM curve, the less national income rises. The equilibrating effect of interest rates in the money market therefore 'chokes off' some of the increase in national income originating from the positive demand-side shock.

The *IS/LM* framework allows us to see how monetary policy could accommodate the positive demand-side shock. If money supply is expanded to meet the extra demand for money, then interest rates will not have to rise. This is illustrated in Figure 19.20(c). The rightward shift in the *IS* curve is matched by a downward shift in the *LM* curve. The rate of interest remains at r_1 and there is a full multiplied rise in national income to Y_4.

In the context of the early 2010s, central banks like the Federal Reserve and the Bank of England were keen that monetary policy should stimulate economic recovery. While remaining watchful of inflation, monetary policy was predominantly geared to supporting the still fragile economic recovery. This saw the authorities boost the money supply through asset purchases (see Box 22.10). One effect of this was to put downward pressure on the general structure of interest rates. As we saw in section 18.5, there is not a single interest rate. Rather, there is a myriad of interest rates on a range of financial instruments.

The *IS/LM* framework demonstrates nicely the policy dilemma that faced the authorities in the early 2010s as aggregate demand recovered: how quickly to put the brakes on quantitative easing. To do so too quickly ran the risk of stalling the recovery as general interest rates rose, even if the authorities maintained a low policy rate. As our analysis in section 19.4 showed, interest rate differentials tend to be greatest when output levels are relatively low. The authorities therefore looked to apply the monetary policy handbrake gently.

Changes in the money market

Now consider an increase in money supply. The *LM* curve shifts downwards. This is illustrated in Figure 19.20(b). Interest rates fall and this encourages an increase in borrowing and hence an increase in investment and consumption. This is shown by a movement down along the *IS* curve. National income rises. Equilibrium is reached at a rate of interest of r_3 and a national income of Y_3.

The fall in the rate of interest means that some of the extra money is absorbed in idle balances and is not all used to finance additional expenditure and this reduces the resulting increased national income. The effect on national income also depends on the elasticity of the *IS* curve. The steeper the *IS* curve, the less will national income rise. This will be the case when investment is relatively insensitive to cuts in interest rates.

If, however, the rise in money supply is accompanied by an autonomous rise in injections (for example, a rise in government expenditure), then the effect can be much bigger. If the downward shift in the *LM* curve is matched by a rightward shift in the *IS* curve, then the effect is once more illustrated in Figure 19.20(c).

To summarise: the effect on national income of a change in either market depends on the slope of the *IS* and *LM* curves.

■ The flatter the *LM* curve and the steeper the *IS* curve, the bigger will be the effect of a shift in the *IS* curve. When *LM* is relatively flat, a rightward shift in *IS* will lead to only a small rise in the rate of interest (r). If *IS* is steep, this rise in r will lead to only a small curtailing of investment. In these two circumstances, the dampening effect on investment and consumption is limited. There will be a large increase in real national income (Y).

■ The effect of a shift in the *LM* curve will be bigger when the liquidity preference curve (L) (e.g. in Figure 19.18(a)) is steep and the *IS* curve is relatively flat. When *L* is steep, there will be a relatively large downward shift in the *LM* curve for any given increase in the money supply and hence a relatively large fall in r. When *IS* is relatively flat, this fall in r will lead to a relatively large increase in investment and hence Y.

■ The effect of a shift in either curve will be bigger if matched by a similar shift in the other curve.

 On a diagram similar to Figure 19.19, trace through the effects of (a) a fall in investment and (b) a fall in the money supply. On what does the size of the fall in national income depend?

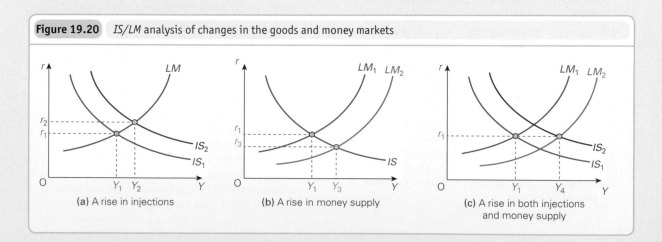

Figure 19.20   *IS/LM* analysis of changes in the goods and money markets

(a) A rise in injections

(b) A rise in money supply

(c) A rise in both injections and money supply

Appendix summary

1. The *IS/LM* model allows equilibrium to be shown in both goods and money markets simultaneously. The model shows the relationship between national income and interest rates.

2. Equilibrium in the goods market is shown by the *IS* curve. As the rate of interest rises, so investment will fall and saving will rise: thus equilibrium national income will fall. The *IS* curve is thus downward sloping.

3. A change in interest rates will cause a movement along the *IS* curve. A change in anything else that affects national income causes a shift in the *IS* curve.

4. Equilibrium in the money market is shown by the *LM* curve. This shows all the combinations of national income and the rate of interest where the demand for money (*L*) equals the supply (*M*). As national income rises, so the demand for money will rise: thus the equilibrium rate of interest in the money market will rise. The *LM* curve is therefore upward sloping.

5. A change in national income will cause a movement along the *LM* curve. A change in anything else that affects interest rates (i.e. a change in the demand or supply of money other than as a result of a change in national income) will shift the *LM* curve.

6. Simultaneous equilibrium in both goods and money markets (i.e. the equilibrium national income *and* the equilibrium rate of interest) is where *IS* = *LM*.

7. A change in injections or withdrawals will shift the *IS* curve. A rise in injections will shift it to the right. This will cause a rise in both national income and the rate of interest. The steeper the *IS* curve and the flatter the *LM* curve, the bigger will be the rise in income and the smaller the rise in the rate of interest.

8. A rise in money supply will shift the *LM* curve downwards. This will cause a fall in interest rates and a rise in national income. The rise in national income will be larger, the flatter is the the *IS* curve and the steeper the liquidity preference curve (*L*) and hence the bigger the downward shift in the *LM* curve for any given increase in the money supply.

END OF CHAPTER QUESTIONS

1. Using one or more diagrams like Figures 19.2, 19.7, 19.8, 19.9 and 19.10, illustrate the following:

   (a) The effect of a contraction in the money supply on national income. Refer to both the interest rate and exchange rate transmission mechanisms and show how the shapes of the curves affect the outcome.

   (b) The effect of a fall in investment on national income. Again show how the shapes of the curves affect the outcome. Specify your assumptions about the effects on the supply of money.

2. Controlling the money supply is sometimes advocated as an appropriate policy for controlling inflation. What implications do different assumptions about the relationships between *M* and *V,* and *M* and *Y,* in the equation *MV* = *PY* have for the effectiveness of this policy?

3. Why may an expansion of the money supply have a relatively small effect on national income? Why may any effect be hard to predict?

4. What impact might the balance sheets of economic agents have on the influence of interest rates in affecting aggregate expenditure?

5. Why does the exchange rate transmission mechanism strengthen the interest rate transmission mechanism?

6. Explain how the holding of a range of assets in people's portfolios may help to create a more direct link between changes in money supply and changes in aggregate demand.

7. Explain how financial crowding out can reduce the effectiveness of fiscal policy. What determines the magnitude of crowding out?

8. What determines the shape and position of the *IS* curve?

9. What determines the shape and position of the *MP* curve?

10. Using the *IS/MP* model analyse the possible effect of an increase in aggregate expenditure on output, the real interest rate and inflation.

11. Using the *IS/MP* model analyse how a lower bound on real interest rates might cause the economy to enter a deflationary spiral following a significant decrease in aggregate expenditure.

12. What impact does the financial accelerator have on the marginal propensity to consume domestically produced goods *(mpc_d)*? How does this affect the *IS* curve?

13. Illustrate the impact on the *IS* curve of a general increase in interest rate differentials following a credit market disruption like that experienced during the financial crisis of the late 2000s.

14. Using the *IS/MP* framework illustrate how the financial accelerator affects the extent of the fall in output following a negative demand-side shock.

15. What implication does the financial instability hypothesis have for the balance sheets of different sectors of the economy?

*16. Using the *IS/LM* model analyse under what circumstances will (a) a rise in investment and (b) a rise in money supply cause a large rise in national income?

Online resources

Additional case studies on the student website

19.1 Crowding out. This case looks at a different version of crowding out from that analysed in section 19.2.

19.2 Sir John Hicks. A profile of the developer of *IS/LM* analysis.

Maths Case 19.1 Using *IS* and *LM* equations to find the equilibrium national income and interest rate. Using the algebra in a worked example.

Websites relevant to Chapters 18 and 19

Numbers and sections refer to websites listed in the Web Appendix and hotlinked from this book's website at **www.pearsoned.co.uk/sloman.**

- For news articles relevant to this and the previous chapter, see the *Economics News* section on the student website.

- For general news on money and banking, see websites in section A, and particularly A1–5, 7–9, 20–22, 25, 26, 31, 36.

- For monetary and financial data (including data for money supply and interest rates), see section F and particularly F2. Note that you can link to central banks worldwide from site F17. See also the links in B1.

- For monetary targeting in the UK, see F1 and E30. For monetary targeting in the eurozone, see F6 and 5.

- For links to sites on money and monetary policy, see the *Financial Economics* sections in I7, 11, 17.

- For student resources relevant to Chapters 18 and 19, see sites C1–7, 9, 10, 12, 19.

Aggregate Supply, Inflation and Unemployment

The focus so far of Part F has been to develop a better understanding of aggregate demand. We have looked at a variety of influences on aggregate demand and its components, including the effects of financial institutions and money markets. Now we consider in more detail the interaction of aggregate demand and aggregate supply. We will see that the effects of changes in aggregate demand on output, employment and prices depend crucially on the responsiveness of aggregate supply.

We begin this chapter by constructing the aggregate demand and supply (*AD/AS*) model. We then apply the model to analyse demand-pull and cost-push inflation, including the subsequent effects on prices and output that can result from these sources of inflation. In the next section (section 20.3) we extend this model to the modern context of inflation targeting by central banks. The model highlights the dynamic nature of economies and, hence, the importance of considering the subsequent effects that can arise from economic shocks.

The adjustment of economies to shocks is a theme we pursue further in the final two sections of the chapter. First, we focus on the role the labour market plays in determining the interaction between aggregate demand and supply. In doing so, we distinguish between classical and Keynesian perspectives on the labour market. Finally, we take a broader look at debates around output determination. We analyse the contrasting the views of different macroeconomic schools on the behaviour of markets, the flexibility of aggregate supply and the role of expectations.

20.1 THE *AD/AS* MODEL

Our focus to this point as been on developing an understanding of aggregate demand. This is a sensible starting point since fluctuations in aggregate demand are generally argued to be the primary source of fluctuations in the economy's output path. However, to understand economic fluctuations more fully we need to analyse the interaction between aggregate demand and aggregate supply.

The problem with the circular flow model and the Keynesian multiplier model is that they take no account of just how firms make supply decisions: they assume that firms simply respond to demand. But supply decisions, as well as being influenced by current levels of demand, are also influenced by prices and costs. To be able to analyse the impact of changes in aggregate demand on national income *and* prices we make use of the aggregate demand–aggregate supply (*AD/AS*) model. This is illustrated in Figure 20.1. Note that the aggregate supply curve we shall be examining is the short-run curve (*SRAS*), as explained below.

As with demand and supply curves for individual goods, we plot quantity on the horizontal axis, except that now it is the *total quantity of national output,* (real) GDP; and we plot price on the vertical axis, except that now it is the *general* price level. Because the general price level relates to the prices of all domestically produced goods and services it is also known as the *GDP deflator*.

We now examine each curve in turn.

The aggregate demand curve

In Chapter 15 we saw how aggregate demand consists of four elements: consumer spending (*C*), private investment (*I*), government expenditure on goods and services (*G*) and expenditure on exports (*X*) less expenditure on imports (*M*). Thus:

$$AD = C + I + G + X - M$$

The aggregate demand curve shows how much national output (GDP) will be demanded at each level of prices. But why does the *AD* curve slope downwards? Why will people demand less as prices rise? There are two effects that can cause this: income effects and substitution effects.

Income effects

For many people, when prices rise, their wages will not rise in line, at least not in the short run. There will therefore tend to be a redistribution of income away from wage earners (and hence consumers) to those charging the higher prices – namely, firms. Thus for consumers there has been an *income effect* of the higher prices. The rise in prices leads to a cut in real incomes and therefore people will spend less. Aggregate demand will fall. The *AD* curve will be downward sloping, as in Figure 20.1.

To some extent this will be offset by a rise in profits, but it is unlikely that much of the additional profits will be spent by firms on investment, especially if they see consumer expenditure falling; and any increase in dividends to

Definition

GDP deflator The price index of all final domestically produced goods and services: i.e. all those items that contribute towards GDP.

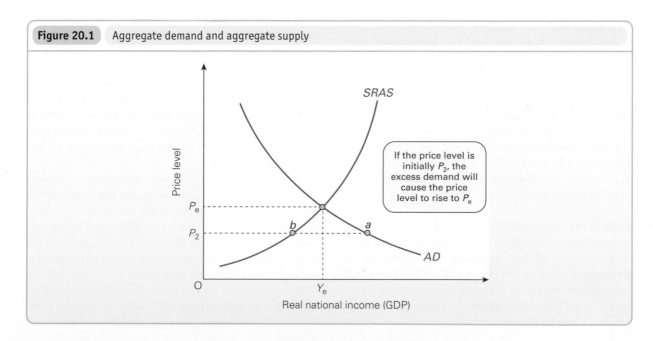

Figure 20.1 Aggregate demand and aggregate supply

shareholders will take a time before it is paid, and then may simply be saved rather than spent. To summarise: if prices rise more than wages, the redistribution from wages to profits is likely to lead to a fall in aggregate demand.

Clearly, this income effect will not operate if wages rise in line with prices. Real incomes of wage earners will be unaffected. In practice, as we shall see at several places in this book, in the short run wages do lag behind prices.

An income effect is also likely to occur as a result of progressive taxes. As prices and incomes rise, so people will find that they are paying a larger proportion of their incomes in taxes. As a result, they cannot afford to buy so much.

Substitution effects

In the *micro*economic situation, if the price of one good rises, people will switch to alternative goods. This is the substitution effect of that price rise and helps to explain why the demand curve for a particular good will be downward sloping. At a *macro*economic level we can identify three main reasons why people will demand fewer products as prices.

- An **international substitution effect**. If prices rise, people will be encouraged to buy fewer of the country's products and more imports instead (which are now relatively cheaper); the country will also sell fewer exports (which are now less competitive). Thus imports (a withdrawal) will rise and exports (an injection) will fall. Aggregate demand, therefore, will be lower.

- An **inter-temporal substitution effect**. As prices rise, people will need more money to pay for their purchases. With a given supply of money in the economy, this will have the effect of driving up interest rates (see section 19.1). The effect of higher interest rates will be to discourage borrowing and encourage saving, with individuals postponing current consumption in favour of future consumption. The effect will be a reduction in spending and hence in aggregate demand.

- **Real balance effect.** If prices rise, the value of people's savings will be eroded. They may thus save more (and spend less) to compensate.

The shape of the aggregate demand curve

We have seen that both the income and substitution effects of a rise in the general price level will cause the aggregate demand for goods and services to fall. Thus the *AD* curve is downward sloping. The bigger the income and substitution effects, the more elastic will the curve be.

Shifts in the aggregate demand curve

The aggregate demand curve can shift inwards (to the right) or outwards (to the left), in exactly the same way as the demand curve for an individual good. A rightward shift represents an increase in aggregate demand, whatever the price level; a leftward shift represents a decrease in aggregate demand, whatever the price level.

> ### Definitions
>
> **International substitution effect** As prices rise, people at home and abroad buy less of this country's products and more of products from abroad.
>
> **Inter-temporal substitution effect** Higher prices may lead to higher interest rates and thus less borrowing and more saving. Current consumption falls; future consumption (from the higher savings) rises.
>
> **Real balance effect** As the price level rises, so the value of people's money balances will fall. They will therefore spend less in order to increase their money balances and go some way to protecting their real value.

A shift in the aggregate demand curve will occur if, for any given price level, there is a change in any of its components – consumption, investment, government expenditure or exports minus imports. Thus if the government decides to spend more, or if consumers spend more as a result of lower taxes, or if business confidence increases so that firms decide to invest more, the *AD* curve will shift to the right.

The aggregate supply curve

The aggregate supply (*AS*) curve shows the amount of goods and services that firms are willing to supply at each level of prices. We focus here on the *short-run AS* curve (*SRAS* curve). When constructing this curve, we assume that various other things remain constant. These include wage rates and other input prices, technology and the total supply of factors of production (labour, land and capital).

Why do we assume that wage rates and other input prices are constant? Wage rates are frequently determined by a process of collective bargaining and, once agreed, will typically be set for a whole year, if not two. Even if they are not determined by collective bargaining, wage rates often change relatively infrequently. So too with the price of other inputs: except in perfect, or near perfect markets (such as the market for various raw materials), firms supplying capital equipment and other inputs tend to change their prices relatively infrequently. They do not immediately raise them when there is an increase in demand or lower them when demand falls. Thus there is a 'stickiness' in both wage rates and the price of many inputs.

The short-run aggregate supply curve slopes upwards, as shown in Figure 20.1. In other words, the higher the level of prices, the more will be produced. The reason is simple. Because we are holding wages and other input prices constant, then as the prices of their products rise, firms' profitability at each level of output will be higher than before. This will encourage them to produce more.

But what *limits* the increase in aggregate supply in response to an increase in prices? In other words, why is the *SRAS* curve not horizontal? There are two main reasons:

■ *Diminishing returns.* With some factors of production fixed in supply, notably capital equipment, firms experience a diminishing marginal physical product from their other factors, and hence have an upward-sloping marginal cost curve. In microeconomic analysis the upward-sloping cost curves of firms explain why the supply curves of individual goods and services slope upwards. Here in macroeconomics we are adding (horizontally) the supply curves of all goods and services and thus the aggregate supply curve also slopes upwards.

■ *Growing shortages of certain variable factors.* As firms collectively produce more, even inputs that can be varied

may increasingly become in short supply. Skilled labour may be harder to find, and certain raw materials may be harder to obtain.

Thus rising costs explain the upward-sloping short-run aggregate supply curve. The more steeply costs rise as production increases, the less elastic will the aggregate supply curve be. It is likely that, as the level of national output (i.e. national income) increases and firms reach full-capacity working, so marginal costs will rise faster. The *SRAS* curve will thus tend to get steeper (as shown in Figure 20.1).

Box 20.1 considers further the microeconomic foundations of the *SRAS* curve.

BOX 20.1   SHORT-RUN AGGREGATE SUPPLY

The importance of microeconomic foundations

To understand the shape of the short-run *AS* curve, it is necessary to look at its microeconomic foundations. How will *individual* firms and industries respond to a rise in demand? What shape will their individual supply curves be?

In the short run, we assume that firms respond to the rise in demand for their product *without* considering the effects of a general rise in demand on their suppliers or on the economy as a whole. We also assume that the prices of inputs, including wage rates, are constant.

In the case of a profit-maximising firm under monopoly or monopolistic competition, there will be a rise in price and a rise in output. In diagram (a), profit-maximising output rises from where $MC = MR_1$ to where $MC = MR_2$. Just how much price changes compared with output depends on the slope of the marginal cost (*MC*) curve.

(a) *Short-run response of a profit-maximising firm to a rise in demand*

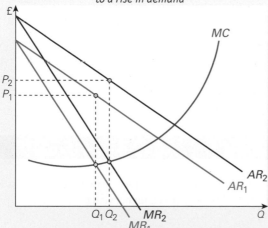

The nearer the firm is to full capacity, the steeper the *MC* curve is likely to be. Here the firm is likely to find diminishing returns setting in rapidly, and it is also likely to have to use more overtime with correspondingly higher unit labour costs. If, however, the firm is operating well below capacity, it can

probably supply more with little or no increase in price. Its *MC* curve may thus be horizontal at lower levels of output.

Under oligopoly, where there is a tendency for prices to be more stable, firms may respond to an increase in demand without raising prices, even if their costs rise somewhat.

When there is a general rise in demand in the economy, the *aggregate* supply response in the short run can be seen as simply the sum of the responses of all the individual firms. The short-run *AS* curve will look something like that in diagram (b).

(b) *The SRAS curve and the effect of an increase in AD*

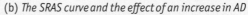
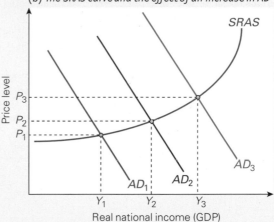

If there is generally plenty of spare capacity, a rise in aggregate demand (e.g. from AD_1 to AD_2) will have a big effect on output and only a small effect on prices. However, as more and more firms find their costs rising as they get nearer to full capacity, so the *AS* curve becomes steeper. Further increases in aggregate demand (e.g. from AD_2 to AD_3) will have bigger effects on prices and smaller effects on output (GDP).

A general rise in prices, of course, means that individual firms were mistaken in assuming that a rise in price from P_1 to P_2 in diagram (b) was a *real* price rise (i.e. relative to prices elsewhere).

 What is happening to real wage rates as we move up the SRAS curve?

Shifts in the short-run aggregate supply curve

The *SRAS* curve will shift if there is a change in any of the variables that are held constant when we plot the curve. Several of these variables, notably technology, the labour force and the stock of capital, change only slowly – normally shifting the curve gradually to the right. This represents an increase in potential output.

By contrast, wage rates and other input prices can change significantly in the short run, and are thus the major causes of shifts in the short-run supply curve. For example, a general rise in wage rates throughout the economy reduces the amount that firms wish to produce at any level of prices. The aggregate supply curve shifts to the left. A similar effect will occur if other costs, such as oil prices or indirect taxes, increase.

Equilibrium

Equilibrium in the macroeconomy occurs when aggregate demand and aggregate supply are equal. In Figure 20.1, this is at the price level P_e and national income (GDP) of Y_e. To

demonstrate this, consider what would happen if aggregate demand exceeded aggregate supply: for example, at P_2 in Figure 20.1. The resulting shortages throughout the economy would drive up prices. This would encourage firms to produce more: there would be a movement up *along* the *AS* curve. At the same time, the increase in prices would reduce the level of aggregate demand: that is, there would also be a movement back up *along* the *AD* curve. The shortage would be eliminated when price had risen to P_e.

TC 4
p47

Shifts in the AD or SRAS curves

If the *AD* or *SRAS* curve shifts, there will be a movement along the other curve to the new point of equilibrium. For example, if there is a cut in income taxes and a corresponding increase in consumer demand, the *AD* curve will shift to the right. This will result in a movement up along the *SRAS* curve to the new equilibrium point: in other words, to a new higher level of national income and a higher price level. The more elastic the *SRAS* curve, the more will output rise relative to prices.

Section summary

1. An aggregate demand curve shows the relationship between aggregate demand ($C + I + G + X - M$) and the price level. The curve is downward sloping because of income and substitution effects.

2. If a rise in the price level causes wage rises to lag behind or causes a rise in the proportion of income paid in income tax, then consumers will respond to the resulting fall in their real incomes by cutting consumption. This is the income effect.

3. If a rise in the price level causes (a) imports to rise and exports to fall, (b) people to spend less and save more because of a rise in interest rates and possibly (c) people to spend less in order to maintain the value of their bank balances, these effects too will result in a fall in the level of aggregate demand. These are all substitution effects.

4. If the determinant of any component of aggregate demand (other than the price level) changes, the aggregate demand will shift.

5. The short-run aggregate supply (*SRAS*) curve is upward sloping. This reflects the fact that at higher prices, firms will find it profitable to supply more. The curve will be more elastic, the less rapidly diminishing returns set in and the more elastic the supply of variable factors.

6. The *SRAS* curve will shift to the left (upwards) if wage rates or other costs rise independently of a rise in aggregate demand.

7. Equilibrium in the economy occurs when aggregate demand equals aggregate supply. A rise in the price level will occur if there is a rightward shift in the aggregate demand curve or a leftward shift in the short-run aggregate supply curve.

20.2 *AD/AS* AND INFLATION

We first analysed inflation in section 15.6. There we identified two principal types of inflation: demand-pull and cost-push inflation. Demand-pull inflation is caused by continuing rises in aggregate demand while cost-push inflation is caused by continuing rises in costs, which occur *independently* of aggregate demand.

We can use our aggregate demand and supply framework to further our understanding of demand-pull and cost-push inflation. In particular, we can think about the possible subsequent effects on output and prices that might arise from these types of inflation. This illustrates the dynamic nature

of economies: macroeconomic fluctuations or shocks frequently set in motion a chain of events.

TC 15
p535

Demand-pull inflation

Demand-pull inflation can be represented by *continuous* shifts of the *AD* curve to the right. In Figure 20.2, the *AD* curve shifts to the right and continues doing so. A single increase in *AD* caused by a *positive* demand shock only causes inflation in short run. Once the price level has settled at its new higher level, the inflation rate falls back to zero.

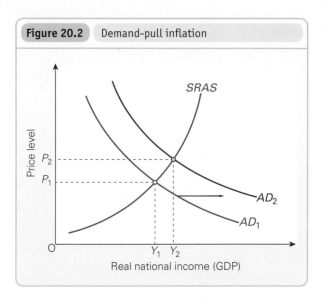

Figure 20.2 Demand-pull inflation

AD curve goes on shifting to the right, the price level will go on rising and there will be demand-pull inflation. There will be a movement from point *a* to *b* to *c* in Figure 20.3(b).

An important part of the subsequent adjustment process comes from the *interdependence of firms*. Rising aggregate demand will lead firms throughout the economy to raise their prices (in accordance with the short-run *AS* curve). But as raw material and intermediate good producers raise their prices, this will raise the costs of production further up the line. A rise in the price of steel will raise the costs of producing cars and washing machines. At the same time, workers, experiencing a rise in demand for labour, and seeing the prices of goods rising, will demand higher wages. Firms will be relatively willing to grant these wage demands, since they are experiencing buoyant demand.

The effect of all this is to raise firms' costs, and hence their prices. As prices rise for any given level of output, the short-run *AS* curve shifts upwards.

All other things being equal, this will lead to a falling back of output but a further rise in prices as the economy moves to point *d*.

If there was to be a further rise in demand, we might perhaps observe a further outward movement of the *AD* curve, say to point *e*, but a further rise in prices. Then the *SRAS* curve will probably continue shifting upwards and the economy will move to point *f*.

If the source of the increase in demand was to cease or government now makes the control of inflation its main policy objective, then this may stop further increases in aggregate demand. Aggregate supply may continue shifting upwards for a while as cost increases and expectations feed through. The economy moves to point *g*. In the extreme case, point *g* may be vertically above point *a*. The only effect of the shift in *AD* to AD_3 has been inflation.

For demand-pull inflation to continue, the rightward shifts of the *AD* curve must also continue; for demand-pull inflation to rise, the rightward shifts must get faster.

Subsequent effects

In illustrating demand-pull inflation in Figure 20.2, we have analysed the short-term effects on output and the price level. Crucially, we have assumed that the factors taken as given in constructing the short-run aggregate *supply* curve remain constant. But eventually the *SRAS* curve will start shifting. In Figure 20.3 we analyse how this might happen and what this could mean subsequently for the economy's price level and output.

As before, assume that aggregate demand rises. In Figure 20.3(a), there is some increase in output, and the price level rises from P_0 to P_1. If demand goes on rising, so that the

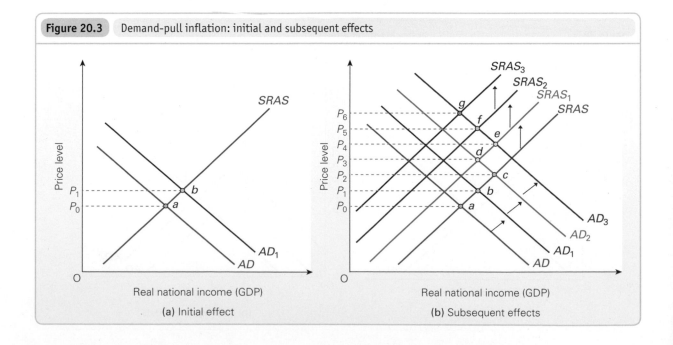

Figure 20.3 Demand-pull inflation: initial and subsequent effects

(a) Initial effect

(b) Subsequent effects

Note that, although costs in Figure 20.3(b) have increased and hence the *AS* curves have shifted upwards, this is not *cost-push* inflation because the rise in costs is the result of the rise in *demand*.

Whatever the output and price paths that result from rising (or falling) demand, the analysis illustrates the dynamic nature of economies. The responses of economic agents, the interdependencies that exist between them and the workings of markets are important in determining the adjustment processes that take place following economic shocks. This is crucial too when thinking about cumulative causation: i.e. the ideas that economic effects can snowball. Multiple changes can result from an initial economic shock or set of events. In section 20.4 we focus on the role of the labour market in determining adjustment processes.

How would the shifts in the SRAS curve be affected if, in response to rising output levels, firms increased their investment expenditures?

Cost-push inflation

Cost-push inflation can be represented by *continuous* shifts of the *SRAS* curve upwards to the left. This is illustrated in Figure 20.4. As with our analysis of demand-pull inflation, we need to distinguish between single shifts and continuous shifts of the *SRAS* curve when looking at cost-push inflation. A single *negative* supply shock will cause only temporary inflation. If cost-push inflation is to continue, the *SRAS* curve must keep shifting upwards to the left. Similarly, for the rate of cost-push inflation to rise, these shifts of the *SRAS* curve must get faster.

If we compare Figures 20.2 and 20.4, we can see that demand-pull and cost-push inflation have the opposite effect on output. This is because it is *positive* demand shocks

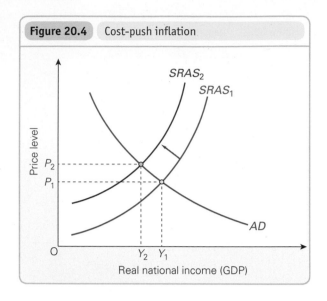

Figure 20.4   Cost-push inflation

but *negative* supply shocks that cause price levels to rise. Therefore, with demand-pull inflation output and hence employment tend to rise. On the other hand, with cost-push inflation output and employment tend to fall.

Subsequent effects

In illustrating cost-push inflation to this point, the aggregate demand curve has been unaffected by the shifts in the *SRAS* curve. After a time, this is unlikely to remain the case. We use Figure 20.5 to consider how the *AD* curve might be affected subsequently.

Assume that there is some exogenous increase in costs: a sharp increase in world oil prices, or an increase in wages due to increased trade union activity, or firms raising prices to cover the costs of a rise in interest rates. In Figure 20.5(a), the *SRAS* curve shifts to $SRAS_1$. Prices rise to P_1 and there is a fall in national output.

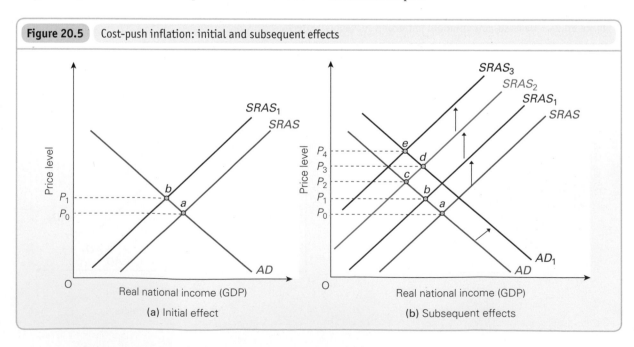

Figure 20.5   Cost-push inflation: initial and subsequent effects

(a) Initial effect

(b) Subsequent effects

If these increases in costs continue for some time, the *SRAS* curve will go on shifting upwards. Price rises will continue and there is cost-push inflation. The economy will move from point *a* to *b* to *c* in Figure 20.5(b). Continuous upward shifts in the *SRAS* curve are particularly likely if there is a continuing struggle between different groups (e.g. unions and employers' organisations) for a larger share of national income.

After a time, aggregate demand is likely to rise. This may be due to the government using expansionary fiscal and monetary policies to halt the falling output and employment. Or it may be due to money supply expanding endogenously as workers and firms need larger money balances to allow for increasingly costly transactions. Aggregate demand shifts to AD_1 and there is a movement to point *d*.

There may be a further increase in costs and a movement to point *e*, and then a further increase in aggregate demand and so on. Again, the dynamics of the adjustment process following the initial effect in Figure 20.5(a) will shape the actual path that prices and national output take in Figure 20.5(b).

Note this time that, although demand has increased, this is not *demand-pull* inflation because the rise in demand is the result of the upward pressure on *costs*.

BOX 20.2 COST-PUSH INFLATION AND SUPPLY SHOCKS   EXPLORING ECONOMICS

It is important to distinguish a *single* supply shock, such as a rise in oil prices or an increase in VAT or excise duties, from a continuing upward pressure on costs, such as workers continually demanding increases in real wages above the level of labour productivity, or firms continually using their monopoly power to increase the real value of profits.

A single supply shock will give a *single* upward movement in the *SRAS* curve. Prices will move to a new higher equilibrium. An example occurred in the UK in January 2011, with the rise in VAT from 17.5 to 20 per cent. Cost-push inflation in this case is a *temporary* phenomenon. Once the new higher price level has been reached, the cost-push inflation disappears.

Sometimes these supply-side shocks can themselves be the result – at least partially – of an increase in demand elsewhere in the world. An example of this occurred during 2008 when the prices of materials and fuels used by industry began rising sharply, partly in response to the rapid growth in developing countries, such as China and India. As we can see from the chart, this caused the rate of input price inflation amongst manufacturers to rise to 35 per cent. This spike in

prices was temporary, however, as the global downturn acted to depress the demand for inputs and led to a fall in their prices – at least for a while.

But what if there is continuous upward pressure on costs? In this case, cost-push inflation is likely to continue, resulting in repeated shifts of the *SRAS* curve. During 2010, as the global economy began to recover, the prices of materials and fuels began to rise sharply once again. This raised concerns that the global slowdown had only acted as a temporary brake on rising input prices.

This created a dilemma for central banks, like the Bank of England, which are charged with meeting inflation rate targets. Should they raise interest rates to slow the growth in aggregate demand, even if much of the cause of consumer price inflation was emanating from the supply side?

 Give some examples of single shocks and continuing changes on the demand side. Does the existence of multiplier and accelerator effects make the distinction between single shocks and continuing effects more difficult to make on the demand side than on the supply side?

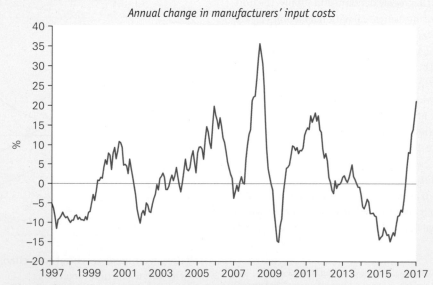

Annual change in manufacturers' input costs

Note: Manufacturers' inputs costs include materials, fuels and climate levy.
Source: Based on data from *Producer Price Index - Statistical bulletin time series dataset*, series K646 (National Statistics).

Section summary

1. Demand-pull inflation occurs where there are continuous rightward shifts in the *AD* curve. Subsequently we would expect the *SRAS* curve to start shifting. This might occur as rising costs are passed from firm to firm, which then acts to shift the *SRAS* curve upwards.

2. Cost-push inflation occurs where there are continuous upward shifts in the *AS* curve. Subsequently we may expect to see *AD* start shifting rightwards. This might occur if the supply of money increases to meet the demand for more liquidity as transactions become increasingly costly.

20.3 AGGREGATE DEMAND AND SUPPLY WITH INFLATION TARGETING: THE *DAD/DAS* MODEL

A more modern version of the aggregate demand and supply model plots aggregate demand and supply, not against the level of prices, but against the rate of inflation. This model has become known as the *DAD/DAS* model, where *DAD* stands for 'dynamic aggregate demand' and *DAS* stands for 'dynamic aggregate supply'.[1]

As with the *IS/MP* model, which we looked at in section 19.3, the *DAD/DAS* model has been developed to incorporate an important feature of contemporary monetary policy: central banks setting interest rates to meet an inflation target (or a more complex target). We will explore in more detail developments in monetary policy and the objectives of central bankers in Chapter 22.

Together, we can use both models to analyse the interaction of the goods and money markets for national income, real interest rates and inflation.

Aggregate demand and supply plotted against inflation

The *DAD/DAS* model is illustrated in Figures 20.6 and 20.7.

In this version of aggregate demand and supply, the horizontal axis, as before, measures real national income (Y). The vertical axis, however, measures the *rate of inflation*, not the *level* of prices. The aggregate demand and supply curves are labelled *DAD* and *DAS* to distinguish them from the curves in the normal aggregate demand and supply diagram. We also add a line showing the target rate of inflation (π_{target}).

Before we look at the properties of the model, let us examine each of the three lines in turn. The first two are illustrated in Figure 20.6.

The inflation target line

This is simply a horizontal line at the target rate of inflation (π_{target}). If inflation is above target, real interest rates will be raised by the central bank. If it is below target, real interest rates will be cut.[2]

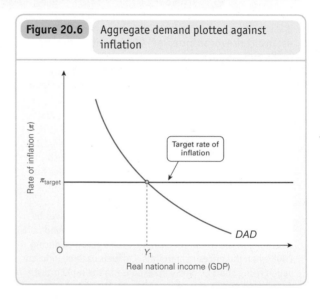

Figure 20.6 Aggregate demand plotted against inflation

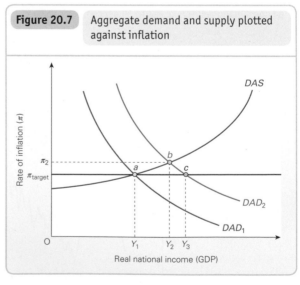

Figure 20.7 Aggregate demand and supply plotted against inflation

If the government or central bank changes the target, the line will shift to the new target rate.

---

[1] As the model has developed over recent years, different names have been given to the two curves. In earlier editions of this book, we used the terms *ADI* and *ASI*, meaning aggregate demand and aggregate supply plotted against inflation. We have switched to *DAD* and *DAS* for this edition as this has now become the more common terminology. The model, however, is exactly the same as in previous editions.

[2] Note that, in practice, although it is the nominal rate of interest (i) that the central bank changes, the objective is to affect the real rate of interest (r) in order to meet the inflation target.

The dynamic aggregate demand curve

As with the normal *AD* curve, the *DAD* curve is downward sloping. In other words, a higher rate of inflation leads to a lower level of (real) aggregate demand. But why?

The reason is simple. It consists of a two-stage process.

1. If the rate of inflation (π) goes above the target level, the central bank will raise the *real* rate of interest (r). In other words it will raise the nominal rate *more* than the rise in the inflation rate. Thus if the rate of inflation goes up from a targeted 2 per cent to 3 per cent, the nominal interest rate (i) must rise by more than 1 percentage point in order to achieve a rise in the real interest rate.

2. The higher real rate of interest will then reduce (real) aggregate demand (*AD*), through both the interest rate and exchange rate mechanisms (see pages 589–93). In terms of the *IS/MP* framework, there is a movement leftward along the *IS* curve.

To summarise:

$$\pi\uparrow \rightarrow r\uparrow \rightarrow AD\downarrow$$

Similarly, a fall in the rate of inflation will cause the central bank to lower the real rate of interest. This will then lead to an increase in aggregate demand.

The slope of the DAD curve. The slope of the *DAD* curve depends on the strength of the two stages. The curve will be flatter:

■ the more the central bank adjusts real interest rates in response to a change in inflation. The faster the central bank wants to get inflation back to its target level and the less concerned it is about cutting back on aggregate demand and hence output and employment, the larger will interest rate changes be;

■ the more responsive investment, consumption and exports (i.e. the components of aggregate demand) are to a change in interest rates.

A movement along the DAD curve. This will be caused by a change in the rate of inflation. If inflation rises, there will be a movement up the curve as the central bank raises the real rate of interest and this causes real income to fall. When *inflation* begins to fall in response to the higher rate of interest, there will be a movement back down the curve again.

The position of the DAD curve. A given *DAD* curve represents a given monetary policy (the vertical position of the *MP* curve for a given inflation target). The particular *DAD* curve in Figure 20.6 intersects with the inflation target line at a real income of Y_1. This means that if inflation is on target, real national income will be Y_1. The central bank will need to consider whether this is consistent with long-term equilibrium in the economy: in other words, whether Y_1 is the *potential* level of national output: i.e. the level of real national income with a zero output gap (see Box 15.3 on page 460). If it is, then the monetary policy it has chosen is appropriate.

A shift in the DAD curve. Any factor that causes aggregate demand to change, other than the central bank responding to inflation being off-target, will cause the *DAD* curve to shift. A rightward shift represents an increase in aggregate demand. A leftward shift represents a decrease.

Examples of a rightward shift include cuts in tax rates, an increase in government expenditure and a rise in consumer or business confidence. These also cause the *IS* curve to shift rightwards in the *IS/MP* model (see page 605).

The *DAD* curve will also shift to the right if the government or central bank sets a higher target rate of inflation. The reason is that this will lead to lower interest rates at every level of inflation. This causes the *MP* curve to move vertically downwards.

The curve will also shift if the central bank *changes* its monetary policy, such that it no longer wants Y_1 to be the equilibrium level of national income. For example, if Y_1 in Figure 20.6 were below the potential level, and there was therefore demand-deficient unemployment, the central bank would want to reduce real interest rates in order to achieve a higher level of aggregate demand at the target rate of inflation. This will shift the *DAD* curve to the right. In other words, each rate of inflation along this new *DAD* curve would correspond to a lower real rate of interest (r) and hence a higher level of aggregate demand.

But what determines the level of Y? This is determined by the interaction of aggregate demand and aggregate supply. To show this we introduce a third line: the *DAS* curve.

The dynamic aggregate supply curve

The *DAS* curve, like the normal *AS* curve, is upward sloping. In the short run it will be relatively flat. In the long run it will be relatively steep, if not vertical at the potential level of national income. The curve illustrated in Figure 20.7 is the short-run *DAS* curve. But why is it shaped this way? Why will a higher rate of inflation lead to higher real national income?

Assume that the economy is currently generating a real national income of Y_1 and that inflation is on target (π_{target}). Equilibrium is at point *a*. Assume also that Y_1 represents the long-run potential level of output.

Now assume that consumer confidence rises, and that, as a result, the *DAD* curve shifts to DAD_2. Firms will respond to the higher aggregate demand partly by raising prices more than the current (i.e. target) rate of inflation and partly by increasing output: there is a movement along the *DAS* curve. Equilibrium moves to point *b*, where $DAD = DAS$.

But why will firms raise output as well as prices? The reason is that wage rises lag behind price rises. This is because of the time it takes to negotiate new wage rates and the fact that people were probably anticipating that inflation would stay at its target level. The higher prices now charged by firms will generate bigger profit margins for them, and thus they will be willing to supply more.

Over time, however, if the higher demand persists, wage rises would get higher. This would be the result of firms trying to obtain more labour to meet the higher demand and of unions seeking wage increases to compensate for the higher rate of inflation. Thus, assuming no increase in productivity, the DAS curve would shift upwards and continue doing so until real national income returned to the potential level Y_1. The long-run DAS curve would be vertical through point a.

Response to changes in aggregate demand and supply

A rise in aggregate demand

Assume, in Figure 20.7, that there has been a rise in real aggregate demand and that the DAD curve has shifted to DAD_2. Assume also that Y_1 is the potential level of national output. If inflation remained at its target level, the economy would move to point c, with national income increasing to Y_3. But as firms respond partly by increasing prices more rapidly, equilibrium is reached at point b. In other words, there has been a movement up along the (short-run) DAS curve from point a to point b and back up along the new DAD curve from point c to point b. This movement along curve DAD_2 is the result of the higher interest rates imposed by the central bank in response to inflation rising to π_2.

But equilibrium at point b is above the target rate. This is unsustainable, even in the short run. One of two things must happen. The first option is for the central bank (or government) to accept a higher target rate of inflation: i.e. π_2. But if it does this, real income can only remain above its potential level in the short run. Soon, higher prices will feed through into higher wages and back into higher prices, and so on. The DAS curve will shift upwards.

The second option – the only effective option in the long run – is for the central bank to reduce aggregate demand back to DAD_1. This will mean changing monetary policy, such that a higher real rate of interest is chosen for each rate of inflation. This tighter monetary policy shifts the DAD curve to the left.

In other words, if the central bank is adhering strictly to an inflation target, any rise in real aggregate demand can have only a temporary effect, since the higher inflation that results will force the central bank to bring aggregate demand back down again.

The one exception to this would be if the higher aggregate demand encouraged firms to invest more. When the effects of this on aggregate supply began to be felt in terms of higher output, the short-term DAS curve itself would shift to the right, leading to a new equilibrium to the right of point a. In such a case, there would have been a long-term increase in output, even though the central bank was sticking to an inflation target.

 Using a graph similar to Figure 20.7, trace through the effect of a reduction in aggregate demand.

A rise in aggregate supply

Assume now that aggregate supply rises. This could be a temporary 'supply shock', such as a cut in oil prices or a good harvest, or it could be a permanent increase caused, say, by technical progress. Let us take each in turn.

A temporary supply shock. In Figure 20.8, initial equilibrium is at point a, with curves DAD_1 and DAS_1 intersecting at point a, at the target rate of inflation. The rise in aggregate supply causes the DAS curve temporarily to shift from DAS_1 to DAS_2. Inflation thus falls below the target rate. As a result, the central bank reduces the real rate of interest (r). The effect is to increase aggregate demand. This is shown by a movement *along* curve DAD_1 from point a to point d. Inflation falls to π_3 and real national income rises to Y_4. Since this is only a temporary increase in aggregate supply, the central bank will not change its monetary policy. The DAD curve, therefore, will not shift.

As the supply shock subsides, aggregate supply will fall again. The DAS curve will shift back from DAS_2 to DAS_1, causing inflation to rise again. The result is a move back up the DAD_1 curve from point d to point a.

1. Trace through the effect of an adverse supply shock, such as a rise in oil prices.
2. What determines the amount that national income fluctuates when there is a temporary shift in the DAS curve?

A permanent increase in aggregate supply. Now assume that DAS_2 represents a permanent shift. As before, the reduction in inflation causes the central bank to reduce interest rates. If there is no change in monetary policy, there would be simply be, once more, a movement from point a to point d with inflation now at π_3.

Once the central bank realises that the rise in aggregate supply is permanent, it will want to move to equilibrium at point e. To do this it will have to *change* its monetary policy and adopt a lower real interest rate at each rate of inflation (a shift downwards of the MP curve, as in Figure 19.14(b) on page 609)). This will shift the DAD curve to DAD_2. If it does this, equilibrium will be restored at the target rate of inflation. Y_5 will be the new sustainable level of real national income.

In other words, the central bank, by maintaining an inflation target, will allow aggregate demand to expand sufficiently to accommodate the full rise in aggregate supply.

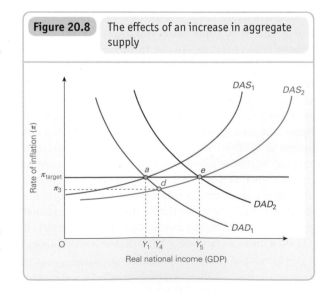

Figure 20.8   The effects of an increase in aggregate supply

In Chapter 22 we explore policies to control aggregate demand. In section 22.4, we look at whether it is best for a central bank to target inflation or whether it should adopt an alternative target. We also look at the more general issue of whether governments ought to set targets and stick to them, or whether they should allow themselves more discretion in managing the economy.

In the next chapter we expand our analysis of aggregate demand and supply to take account of unemployment and also the role of expectations. We look at how the various schools of thought model the macroeconomy in this more complete framework.

BOX 20.3   ANALYSING DEMAND-PULL AND COST-PUSH INFLATION USING THE *DAD/DAS* MODEL

EXPLORING ECONOMICS

Types of inflation under a policy of inflation targeting

We can use the *DAD/DAS* model to analyse the implications of demand-pull and cost-push pressures under a policy of inflation targeting.

The diagram below is similar to Figure 20.8. Assume that the central bank operates with an inflation target of π_{target} and that the economy is currently in equilibrium at point *a* with dynamic aggregate demand and supply given by DAD_1 and DAS_1 respectively. Real national income is at the potential (or 'natural') level of Y_1.

Demand-pull inflation

If there is a rise in aggregate demand to DAD_2, this will result in demand-pull pressures on inflation. The government or central bank could respond in either of two ways.

■ Fiscal or monetary policy could be tightened to shift the *DAD* curve back to DAD_1, thereby maintaining inflation at the target level.
■ A new higher inflation target could be adopted (e.g. π_2), allowing an equilibrium at point *b*. Note, however, that if the potential level of income remains at Y_1, Y_2 will not be sustainable. In the long run, the *DAS* curve will drift upwards, pushing inflation above the new higher target level. A tighter monetary policy (DAD_3) would then be needed to bring national income back down to the potential level, Y_1.

Cost-push inflation

If costs now rise faster than the rate of inflation (a *real* rise in costs), the *DAS* line will shift upwards (e.g. to DAS_2). Again, the government or central bank could respond in either of two ways.

■ The central bank could stick to its target and adopt a tighter monetary policy. In this case the *DAD* curve will shift to the left to give an equilibrium at point *c* at the target rate of inflation. The potential level of output is now at the lower level of Y_3.
■ The central bank could be given a higher target rate of inflation (π_2) to prevent real income falling. It will thus expand aggregate demand and the *DAD* line will shift to DAD_3. Equilibrium would now be at point *d*. The problem with this second approach is that if there has been a long-term reduction in potential output to Y_3 (as opposed to a one-off supply-side shock that is later reversed), there will be further upward pressure on inflation: the *DAS* curve will continue shifting upwards as long as real national income remains above Y_3. It will only be possible to keep to the target rate of inflation, at any level, if *DAD* is allowed to fall so that it intersects with *DAS* at Y_3.

 If cost-push pressures reduce the potential level of real national income (e.g. from Y_1 to Y_3 in the diagram), why do demand-pull pressures not increase the potential level of real national income (e.g. from Y_1 to Y_2 in the diagram)?

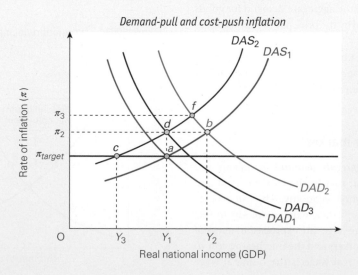

Demand-pull and cost-push inflation

Section summary

1. The effects of adhering to an inflation target can be illustrated in a modified version of the aggregate demand and supply diagram. Inflation, rather than the price level, is plotted on the vertical axis. The aggregate demand curve in this diagram (labelled *DAD*) is downward sloping. This is because higher inflation encourages the central bank to raise interest rates and this leads to a fall in real national income.

2. The aggregate supply (*DAS*) curve in the short run is upward sloping. This is because wage rises lag behind price rises and thus firms are encouraged to supply more in response to a rise in demand knowing that their profits will increase.

3. If aggregate demand rises, the *DAD* curve will shift to the right. The rate of inflation will rise above its target level. This is shown by a movement up the *DAS* curve and back up the new *DAD* curve to the new intersection point (as in Figure 20.7). The movement up the new *DAD* curve is in response to the higher interest rate now set by the central bank as it attempts to bring inflation back down to its target level.

4. Since the new equilibrium is above the target rate of inflation, the central bank must change to a tighter monetary policy and raise the real rate of interest. This shifts the *DAD* curve back to the left, and equilibrium is restored back at its original level. The rise in aggregate demand (unless accompanied by a rightward shift in aggregate supply) has had only a temporary effect on real national income.

5. A rise in aggregate supply (unless merely a temporary supply shock) will have a permanent effect on real national income. A rightward shift in aggregate supply will lead to an initial equilibrium at a rate of inflation below target and some rise in real national income as the rate of interest is reduced (as in Figure 20.8). The equilibrium is now below the target rate of inflation. The central bank must therefore change to a looser monetary policy and reduce the real rate of interest. This will shift the *DAD* curve to the right, causing a further rise in real national income that now fully reflects the rise in aggregate supply.

20.4   THE LABOUR MARKET AND AGGREGATE SUPPLY

Labour is a vital factor of production and so an important element of the aggregate supply relation we have considered in the previous sections of this chapter. The wage rate, quantity and quality of labour all, in one way or another, affect aggregate supply.

But the demand for labour is a derived demand: firms demand labour because of the goods and services it helps to produce. The level of aggregate demand for goods and services (*AD*) therefore affects the aggregate demand for labour in the economy (*AD*$_L$). Yet the aggregate demand for goods and services is itself affected by the price paid by firms for the labour it employs.

All of this illustrates the importance of the labour market to the behaviour of the economy. Therefore, we now take a closer look at how the labour market works.

Modelling the labour market

Figure 20.9 shows the **aggregate demand** for labour and **aggregate supply** of labour: that is, the total demand and supply of labour in the whole economy. The *real* average wage rate is plotted on the vertical axis. As we saw in section 15.5, this is the average wage rate expressed in terms of its purchasing power to workers and the purchasing cost to employers. Therefore, the real wage is the nominal wage corrected for inflation.

Definitions

Aggregate demand for labour curve A curve showing the total demand for labour in the economy at different average real wage rates.

Aggregate supply of labour curve A curve showing the total number of people willing and able to work at different average real wage rates.

Figure 20.9   Disequilibrium unemployment

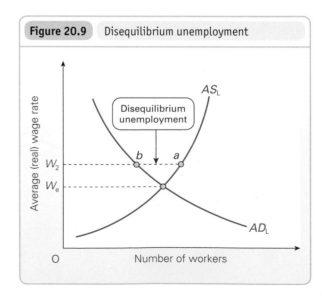

The aggregate supply of labour curve (AS_L) shows the number of workers *willing to accept jobs* at each real wage rate. This curve is relatively inelastic, since the size of the labour force at any one time cannot change significantly. Nevertheless it is not totally inelastic because (a) a higher wage rate will encourage some people to enter the labour market (e.g. parents raising children), and (b) the unemployed will be more willing to accept job offers rather than continuing to search for a better-paid job.

The aggregate demand for labour curve (AD_L) slopes downwards. This is an extension of the microeconomic demand for labour curve (see section 10.1) and is based on the assumption of diminishing returns to labour. For a given capital stock, the more people are employed, the lower their marginal productivity. Thus firms take on more labour only if there is a fall in the real wage rate to compensate them for the lower output produced by the additional workers. On the other hand, the higher the real wage rate, the more will firms attempt to economise on labour and to substitute other factors of production for labour.

The labour market is in equilibrium at a real wage of W_e – where the demand for labour equals the supply.

If the wage rate were above W_e, the labour market would be in a state of disequilibrium. At a wage rate of W_1, there is an excess supply of labour of $a - b$. This is called ***disequilibrium unemployment***.

For disequilibrium unemployment to occur, two conditions must hold:

- The aggregate supply of labour must exceed the aggregate demand for labour.
- There must be a 'stickiness' in wages. In other words, the wage rate must not immediately fall to W_e, the market-clearing wage.

Even when the labour market *is* in equilibrium, however, not everyone looking for work will be employed. Some people will hold out, hoping to find a better job. This is illustrated in Figure 20.10.

Figure 20.11 Disequilibrium and disequilibrium unemployment

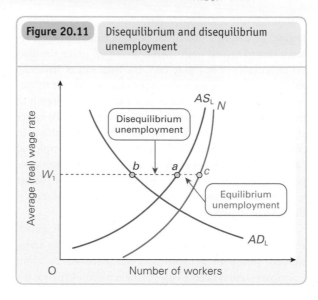

The curve N shows the total number in the labour force. The horizontal difference between it and the aggregate supply of labour curve (AS_L) represents the excess of people looking for work over those actually willing to accept jobs. Q_e represents the equilibrium level of employment and the distance $d - e$ represents the ***equilibrium level of unemployment***. This is sometimes known as the ***natural level of unemployment***.

Note that the AS_L curve gets closer to the N curve at higher wages. The reason for this is that the higher the wages that are offered to the unemployed, the more willing they will be to accept jobs.

Figure 20.11 shows both equilibrium *and* disequilibrium unemployment. At a wage of W_1, disequilibrium unemployment is $a - b$; equilibrium unemployment is $c - a$; thus total unemployment is $c - b$.

We are now able to relate the concepts of equilibrium and disequilibrium unemployment to our discussion of the causes of unemployment in Chapter 15 (see pages 469–72). Real wage unemployment and demand-deficient unemployment are types of disequilibrium unemployment while structural, frictional and seasonal unemployment are types of equilibrium unemployment.

Figure 20.10 Equilibrium unemployment

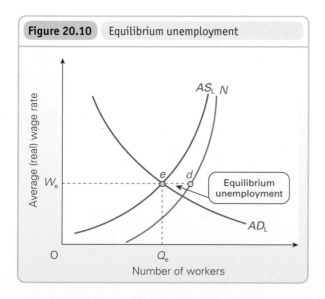

Definitions

Disequilibrium unemployment Unemployment resulting from real wage rates in the economy being above the equilibrium level.

Equilibrium ('natural') unemployment The difference between those who would like employment at the current wage rate and those willing and able to take a job.

Disequilibrium unemployment

Real-wage unemployment is disequilibrium unemployment caused by real wages being driven up above the market-clearing level. In Figure 20.9, the wage rate is driven up *above* W_e. There are a variety of possible reasons for this, as we saw in section 15.5. Some argue that it is the result of trade unions using their monopoly power to drive wages above the market-clearing or, more generally, those in employment ('*insiders*') preventing the unemployed ('*outsiders*') from competing wages down. An alternative perspective is that firms may pay wage rates *above* market levels in order to provide an incentive for workers. This is the basis of the *efficiency wage hypothesis.*

Demand-deficient or cyclical unemployment is associated with fluctuations in aggregate demand. In the recessionary phase of a business cycle demand-deficient unemployment is likely to rise; as the economy expands it is likely to fall.

Demand-deficient unemployment is illustrated in Figure 20.12. Assume initially that the economy is at the peak of the business cycle. The aggregate demand for and supply of labour are equal at the current wage rate of W_1. There is no disequilibrium unemployment. Now assume that the economy moves into recession. Consumer demand falls and as a result firms demand less labour. The demand for labour shifts to AD_{L_2}. If there is a resistance to wage cuts, such that the real wage rate remains fixed at W_1, there will now be disequilibrium unemployment of $Q_1 - Q_2$.

Some Keynesians focus on the reluctance of real wage rates to fall from W_1 to W_2. Others, as we saw in Chapter 15, argue that the focus should be on the low level of aggregate demand. This, they argue, causes an equilibrium in the goods market at an output level that is too low to generate full employment. The disequilibrium in the labour market is the result of the low equilibrium output level in the goods market.

Equilibrium (or natural) unemployment

Although there may be overall *macro*economic equilibrium, with the *aggregate* demand for labour equal to the *aggregate* supply, and thus no disequilibrium unemployment, at a *micro*economic level supply and demand may not match. There may be excess demand for labour (vacancies) in some markets and excess supply (unemployment) in others.

Two commonly identified sources for these mismatches are skills and geography. There may be vacancies for computer technicians and unemployment in the steel industry, but unemployed steel workers cannot immediately become computer technicians. Even if the working population were relatively adaptable and therefore mobile between different sectors of the economy, there is still the potential problem that those unemployed may be in different geographical locations from where vacancies are located.

Then there is the problem of *imperfect information*. There is considerable turnover or churn in the labour market, with some individuals being made redundant or quitting their jobs while others are finding work. But employers are not fully informed about the labour available, while workers are not fully informed about what jobs are available and what they entail. The result is a process of search which sees employers searching for the right labour and workers for the right jobs.

The longer people search for a job, the better the wage offers they are likely to be made. This is illustrated in Figure 20.13 by the curve W_o. It shows the highest wage offer that the typical worker will have received since being unemployed.

When they first start looking for a job, people may have high expectations of getting a good wage. The longer they are unemployed, however, the more anxious they are likely to be to get a job, and therefore the lower will be the wage they are prepared to accept. The curve W_a shows the wage that is acceptable to the typical worker.

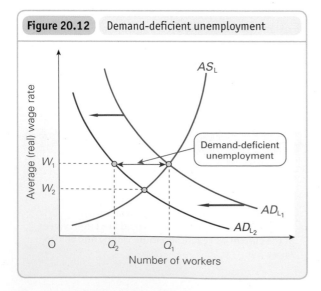

Figure 20.12 Demand-deficient unemployment

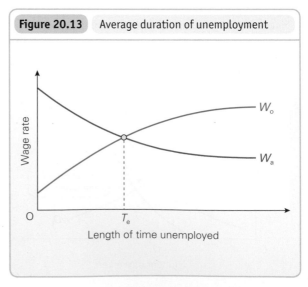

Figure 20.13 Average duration of unemployment

Why are W_o and W_a drawn as curves rather than straight lines?

The average duration of unemployment will be T_e. That is, workers will remain unemployed until they find a job at an acceptable wage.

By improving the flow of job information, for example through government spending on job centres, the intention is to make the curve W_o reach its peak earlier. This has the effect of shifting the intersection of W_o and W_a to the left.

Other economists advocate reducing levels of unemployment benefit. The argument here is that this incentivises the unemployed to take work by making them more prepared to accept a lower wage. It will therefore have the effect of shifting the W_a curve downwards and again of shifting the intersection of W_o and W_a to the left.

The classical model of labour markets and aggregate supply

The classical model is based on the 'classical' assumptions that real wage rates are flexible in the long run and that people are fully aware of price and wage changes, and hence do not believe that a given percentage pay increase will make them better off when prices are rising by the same percentage. In other words, people do not suffer from *money illusion*.

Figure 20.14(a) shows again our aggregate demand and supply of labour diagram. The equilibrium real wage is W_e, where $AD_L = AS_L$, with Q_e workers employed. There is no disequilibrium unemployment at this real wage rate, but there is some equilibrium or natural unemployment. As we saw above, this is largely made up of frictional and structural unemployment. It is represented by the distance $(b - a)$.

With flexible prices and wage rates in the long run, *real wage rates* will also be flexible in the long run. This ensures that long-run employment is kept at Q_e.

The equilibrium in the labour market is matched by a corresponding equilibrium in the goods market, which is shown in Figure 20.14(b). The level of real national income corresponding to the natural level of employment is known as the *natural level of income (or output)*. This is just another name for the *potential level of output* (Y_p): i.e. where there is a zero output gap (see Box 15.3, on page 460). The natural level of income is shown in the diagram as Y_p.

Now assume that aggregate demand for goods rises. This is shown by a rightward move of the aggregate demand curve from AD_1 to AD_2. It causes a movement up the short-run aggregate supply curve, $SRAS_1$, from point e to point f. The price level rises from P_1 to P_2. This causes the real wage to fall below W_e, say to W_1 in Figure 20.14(a). But at this real wage rate there is an excess demand for labour of $d - c$. This drives up the money (nominal) wage rate until the *real* wage rate has returned to W_e. Thus equilibrium employment is at Q_e and output is at its natural level irrespective of changes in aggregate demand.

Q_e would change only if there were some *exogenous* shift in the AD_L or AS_L curve (e.g. a growth in the working population would cause N and AS_L to shift to the right; a growth in labour productivity would cause AD_L to shift to the right). In turn, this would affect the economy's natural level of output.

 Assume that there is a fall in aggregate demand (for goods). Trace through the short-run and long-run effect on employment.

The time taken for national output and employment to return to their natural levels will depend on the speed with

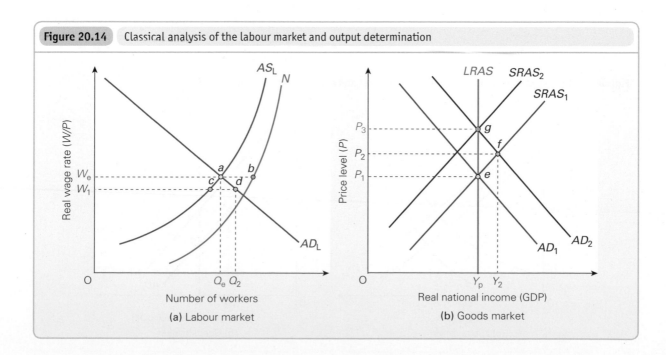

Figure 20.14 Classical analysis of the labour market and output determination

(a) Labour market

(b) Goods market

which money wages adjust. However, any disequilibrium experienced in the labour market will be temporary. Indeed, a group of economists known as new classical economists (see section 16.4) argue that wage and price flexibility is very great, especially with increased numbers of part-time and short-term jobs. This flexibility is so great that both goods and labour markets clear virtually instantaneously. This is the assumption of *continuous market clearing* (see page 504).

Consequently, the speed of adjustment in the labour market to changes in aggregate demand means that there will be very little in the way of fluctuations in employment and output around their natural levels. Only if the change in aggregate demand was *unexpected* might there be any more significant effect on output and employment (see section 16.4, pages 504–505). For this reason some economists refer to the short-run aggregate supply curve as the 'surprise aggregate supply curve'.

It is argued that once people recognise the impact that demand shocks have had on the prices of goods and services and, in turn, on their real wages, the labour market will readily adjust to equilibrium. As it does, the short-run (or surprise) aggregate supply curve moves readily to intersect the aggregate demand curve at the natural level of output.

> ## Definitions
>
> **Money illusion** The belief that a *money* change in wages or prices represents a *real* change.
>
> **Natural level of real income (or output)** The level of output consistent with the equilibrium or 'natural' level of employment.

Keynesian models of labour markets and aggregate supply

Keynesians take a very different view of labour markets, arguing that they are characterised by imperfections and frictions. In particular, they point to labour markets exhibiting considerable wage inflexibility. Employers bargain with unions and usually set wage rates for a whole year. Even in non-unionised firms, wage rates are still often set for a year.

A negative output gap. The inflexibility of wages and of prices in goods markets is a concern when an economy experiences a fall in aggregate demand. This is because it can lead to significant falls in the *quantities* of output and employment. Compare this with the classical model, where the adjustment occurs through *prices*. In the classical model a fall in aggregate demand for goods (a leftward shift of the *AD* curve) causes prices in the goods market to fall. This eliminates the excess supply of goods in the goods market. Meanwhile, in the labour market money wages fall. This is driven by an excess supply of labour from real wages being higher because of lower goods prices. The proportionate fall in money wages matches the fall in goods prices so that the real wage rate is restored at its equilibrium level.

Keynesians argue that if there is a fall in consumer demand, firms usually respond *not* by cutting wages. Instead they lay off workers, cut hours, institute early retirement or do not replace workers when they leave. In the short run, therefore, wages in many sectors of the economy are insensitive to a fall in demand.

Consider an economy characterised by equilibrium in the labour and goods market. In Figure 20.15(a), employment is Q_e and the only unemployment is equilibrium unemployment of $b - a$. Meanwhile, real national income (output) is the natural level Y_1 and the economy's price level is P_1.

Assume now the case of a fall in aggregate demand, represented by a leftward shift of the aggregate demand curve

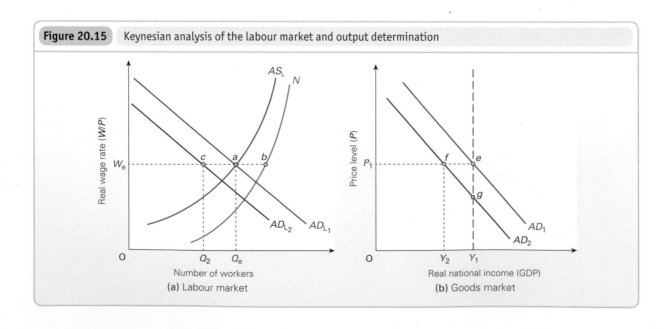

Figure 20.15 Keynesian analysis of the labour market and output determination

(a) Labour market

(b) Goods market

from AD_1 to AD_2 in Figure 20.15(b). However, the aggregate price level does not adjust following the fall in aggregate demand. Firms find that they cannot sell all the goods they previously did. Hence, the adjustment to the fall in aggregate demand occurs solely through a fall in the quantity of output. The *SRAS* curve becomes a horizontal line at price level P_1 in Figure 20.15(b) and output falls from Y_1 to Y_2.

In the labour market, the stickiness of nominal wages means that, with nominal wages and prices not affected by the fall in demand, real wages are unaffected too. Hence, with a lower aggregate demand for goods but real wages still at their full-employment real wage rate, firms reduce their *effective* demand for labour. This is represented in Figure 20.15(a) by a fall in the aggregate demand for labour from AD_{L_1} to AD_{L_2}. Firms thus reduce employment from Q_e to Q_2. There is now demand-deficient unemployment of $a - c$. *Total* unemployment is $b - c$.

But what about the *long* run? Clearly it depends on how long the long run is. Many Keynesians argue that prices and especially wages exhibit a degree of inflexibility over quite a

long period of time, and over this period of time, therefore, the aggregate supply curve would not be vertical. In other words, it could take some considerable time for the economy to move from point f in Figure 12.15(b) to point g. The result could be an economy stuck at an output level below its potential. In such a scenario, Keynesians argue, governments can play a important role by helping to stimulate aggregate demand.

The possibility of a low-output equilibrium is a significant insight. But, can the current analysis explain positive output gaps: i.e. output levels above potential output?

A positive output gap. Again, assume that the economy is characterised by equilibrium in both the goods and labour market. In the presence of sticky prices in the goods market the increase in aggregate demand (a rightward shift of the *AD* curve) is reflected in full by an increase in output. There is no effect on the real wage. Hence, in the labour market, firms' effective demand for labour rises (a rightward shift of the AD_L curve). If we assume that workers choose to supply this additional demand, despite being off their AS_L curve, then employment rises to produce the additional goods.

Section summary

1. The goods and labour markets are interdependent. A rise in aggregate demand in the goods market will lead to a rise in the aggregate demand for labour.

2. Equilibrium in the labour market is where the aggregate demand and supply of labour are equal. However, even in equilibrium, there is likely to be some unemployment. This 'equilibrium unemployment' occurs when there are people unable or unwilling to fill job vacancies. This could be frictional or structural unemployment.

3. Disequilibrium unemployment occurs when real wage rates are above the level that will equate the aggregate demand and supply of labour. In the case of demand-deficient unemployment, the disequilibrium in the labour market may correspond to a low-output equilibrium in the

goods market. A fall in real wage rates may be insufficient to remove the deficiency of demand in the labour market.

4. Classical economists argue that prices and wages respond quickly to changes in aggregate demand and supply. A fall in aggregate demand will quickly result in a fall in prices, with equilibrium remaining at the natural level of output. Likewise, nominal wages will quickly fall and there will be no disequilibrium unemployment.

5. Keynesian economists argue that, because of sticky prices and wages, a fall in demand in the goods market will lead to a fall in output and a fall in employment; disequilibrium unemployment will occur. The slower prices and wages are to adjust, the longer it is likely to persist.

20.5   *AD/AS* AND MACROECONOMIC CONTROVERSIES

In this chapter we have introduced the *AD/AS, DAD/DAS* and AD_L/AS_L models. These models allow us to analyse the interaction of aggregate demand and aggregate supply in determining the economy's output, price and employment levels. The nature of this interaction and, in particular, the way in which the economy adjusts to economic shocks highlights important differences between economists. In this final section of the chapter we discuss some of these differences and the implications they have for policy.

Most of the debate in macroeconomics has centred on the working of the market mechanism: just how well or how badly it achieves various macroeconomic objectives. We

focus here on three major areas of disagreement: (a) how flexible are wages and prices, (b) how flexible is aggregate supply; (c) what is the role of expectations? We examine each in turn.

Controversy 1: the flexibility of prices and wages

Generally, the political right has tended to ally with those economists who argue that prices and wages are relatively flexible. Markets tend to clear, they say, and clear fairly quickly.

Disequilibrium unemployment is likely to be fairly small, according to their view, and normally only a temporary, short-run phenomenon. Any long-term unemployment, therefore, will be equilibrium (or 'natural') unemployment. To cure this, they argue, encouragement must be given to the free play of market forces: to a rapid response of both firms and labour to changes in market demand and supply, to a more rapid dissemination of information on job vacancies, and generally to greater labour mobility, both geographical and occupational.

There are some on the political right, however, who argue that in the short run wages may not be perfectly flexible. This occurs when unions attempt to keep wages above the equilibrium. In this case, disequilibrium unemployment may continue for a while. The solution here, they argue, is to curb the power of unions so that wage flexibility can be restored and disequilibrium unemployment cured.

The political centre and left have tended to ally with economists who reject the assumption of highly flexible wages and prices. There exists, they argue, frictions and market imperfections. If there is a deficiency of demand for labour in the economy, for example during a recession, there will be a resistance from unions to cuts in real wages and certainly to cuts in money wages. Any cuts that do occur will be insufficient to eliminate the disequilibrium, and will anyway serve only to reduce aggregate demand further, so that workers have less money to spend. The aggregate demand for labour curve in Figure 20.15 (see page 638) would shift further to the left.

The prices of goods may also be inflexible in response to changes in demand. As industry became more concentrated and more monopolistic over the years, firms, it is argued, became less likely to respond to a general fall in demand by cutting prices. Instead, they were likely to build up stocks if they thought the recession was temporary, or cut production and hence employment if they thought the recession would persist. It is also argued that many firms use cost-plus methods of pricing. If wages are inflexible downwards, and if they form a major element of costs, prices will also be inflexible downwards.

Thus, according to those who criticise the right, markets cannot be relied upon automatically to correct disequilibria and hence cure disequilibrium unemployment.

 Why are real wages likely to be more flexible downwards than money wages?

The process of globalisation has helped to offset the growth in market power in many industries in recent years. Competition from China and India, for example, has made prices in many markets more flexible. In other markets, however, particularly in the service sector, international competition is less relevant and in others, global giants, such as Apple, Monsanto, Boeing and GlaxoSmithKline, have considerable price-setting power.

Controversy 2: the flexibility of aggregate supply

The question here is, how responsive is national output (i.e. aggregate supply), and hence also employment, to a change in aggregate demand?

The arguments centre on the nature of the aggregate supply curve (*AS*). Three different *AS* curves are shown in Figure 20.16. In each of the three cases, it is assumed that the government raises aggregate demand through the use of fiscal and/or monetary policy. Aggregate demand shifts from AD_1 to AD_2. The effect on prices and output will depend on the shape of the *AS* curve.

Some economists, generally supported by the political right, argue that output is not determined by aggregate demand, except perhaps in the very short run. Instead, the rise in aggregate demand will simply lead to a rise in prices. They therefore envisage an *AS* curve like that in Figure 20.16(a).

If the government wants to expand aggregate supply and get more rapid economic growth, it is no good, they argue, concentrating on demand. Instead, governments should concentrate directly on supply by encouraging enterprise and competition, and generally by encouraging markets to operate more freely. For this reason, this approach is often labelled ***supply-side economics***.

Their critics, however, argue that a rise in aggregate demand will lead to a rise in output. In the extreme case where actual output is well below potential output, prices will not rise at all. In this case, the *AS* curve is like that in Figure 20.16(b). Output will rise to Y_2 with the price level remaining at P.

Others argue that both prices and output will rise. In this case, the short-term curve will be like that in Figure 20.16(c). If there is plenty of slack in the economy – idle machines, unemployed labour, etc. – output will rise a lot and prices only a little. But as slack is taken up, the *AS* curve becomes steeper. Firms, finding it increasingly difficult to raise output in the short run, simply respond to a rise in demand by raising prices.

As we discussed in Chapter 16, a new macroeconomic consensus has emerged in recent times. It is generally agreed that the short-run *AS* curve is similar to that in Figure 20.16(c), but that in the long run, given time for prices and wages to adjust, the curve is much steeper, if not vertical. Any increase in aggregate demand will simply result in higher prices.

Definition

Supply-side economics An approach which focuses directly on aggregate supply and how to shift the aggregate supply curve outwards.

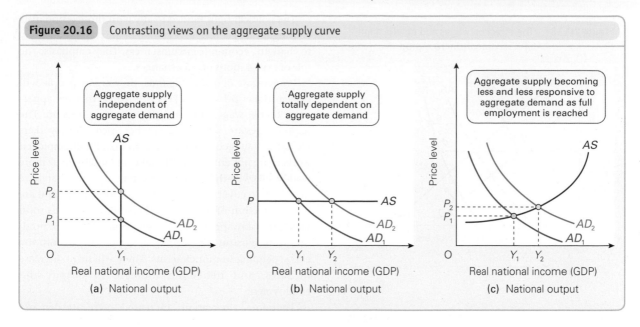

Figure 20.16   Contrasting views on the aggregate supply curve

(a) National output

(b) National output

(c) National output

Aggregate demand and investment

There is not total agreement, however, that changes in aggregate demand have no long-term effect on output. One way in which changes in aggregate demand can have a lasting impact on output is if these affect firms' investment plans.

Assume there is a rise in aggregate demand. As a result, firms may be encouraged to invest in new plant and machinery (the accelerator effect). In so doing, they may well be able to increase output significantly in the long run with little or no increase in their prices. This would make their long-run *MC* curves much flatter than their short-run *MC* curves.

In Figure 20.17, the short-run *AS* curve (*SRAS*) shifts to the right. Equilibrium moves from point *a* to *b* to *d*. In this case, the long-run *AS* curve (*LRAS*) joining points *a* and *d* becomes more elastic. There is a relatively large increase in output and a relatively small increase in price.

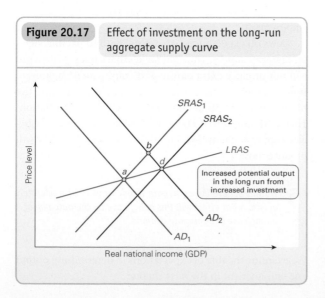

Figure 20.17   Effect of investment on the long-run aggregate supply curve

The *LRAS* curve will be flatter and possibly even downward sloping if the investment involves the introduction of new cost-reducing technology, or if firms generally experience economies of scale. It will be steeper if the extra investment causes significant shortages of materials, machinery or labour. This is more likely when the economy is already operating near its full-capacity output.

1. *Will the shape of the LRAS curve here depend on just how the 'long' run is defined?*
2. *If a shift in the aggregate demand curve from AD to AD₁ in Figure 20.17 causes a movement from point a to point d in the long run, would a shift in aggregate demand from AD₁ to AD cause a movement from point d back to point a in the long run?*

The possibility that increases in aggregate demand can stimulate higher levels of investment, and so bring about higher capacity and a higher aggregate supply, has clear policy implications. For example, Keynesian economists argued for a package of measures to expand aggregate demand following the banking crisis of 2008. An expansion in aggregate demand, through fiscal and monetary policies, would, they argue, result in higher investment and hence an increase in capacity of the economy, which would allow economic recovery to be sustained.

Hysteresis

The possibility of economic *hysteresis* provides another means by which fluctuations in aggregate demand may generate long-term real effects on the economy. As you may have seen in section 16.5, page 509, hysteresis refers to the lagging or persistence of an effect, even when the initial cause has been removed. In other words, an equilibrium position depends on the path taken to arrive there. In this context, hysteresis would be where long-run aggregate

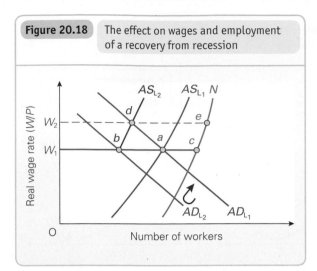

Figure 20.18 The effect on wages and employment of a recovery from recession

KI 33
p368

supply depends on what has been happening to aggregate demand and supply in the short run.

To illustrate this, we apply a Keynesian view of goods and labour markets, assuming that both prices and wages are sticky. Now assume that the economy goes into recession, with a corresponding rise in demand-deficient unemployment and a fall in output. In Figure 20.18, the effective aggregate demand for labour curve has fallen from AD_{L_1} to AD_{L_2}. Demand-deficient unemployment is $a - b$ (the short-run effect).

As the recession persists, those previously laid off may not be readily re-employable, especially if they have been out of work for some time and have become deskilled and demoralised. The aggregate supply of labour curve shifts to the left, perhaps as far as AS_{L_2}. In such a case, there would now no longer be an excess supply of labour that firms regard as 'employable' ($AD_{L_2} = AS_{L_2}$). There is no downward pressure on real wages: a long-run equilibrium has been reached. The implication of this is that the long-run aggregate supply (of goods) curve is *not* vertical. A leftward shift in aggregate demand has led to a long-run fall in output.

Assume now that the government pursues a reflationary policy, and that the aggregate demand for labour shifts back to AD_{L_1}. There will be a move up along AS_{L_2} to point d. Unemployment is now $e - d$, higher than the original level of $c - a$.

Controversy 3: the role of expectations in the working of the market

How quickly and how fully will individuals and firms anticipate changes in prices and changes in output? How are their expectations formed, and how accurate are they? What effect do these expectations have? This has been the third major controversial topic.

TC 9
p129

The political right tended to ally with those economists who argue that people's expectations adjust rapidly and fully to changing economic circumstances. They emphasise the role of expectations of *price* changes.

If aggregate demand expands, they argue, people will expect higher prices. Workers will realise that the apparently higher wages they are offered are an illusion. The higher wages are 'eaten up' by higher prices. Thus workers are not encouraged to work longer hours, and unemployed workers are not encouraged to take on employment more readily. Likewise the higher prices that firms can charge are necessary to cover higher wages and other costs, and are not a reflection of higher real demand. Firms thus soon realise that any apparent increased demand for their products is an illusion. Their price rises will fully absorb the extra spending in money terms. There will be no increase in sales, and hence no increase in output and employment.

Therefore, they argue, increased aggregate demand merely fuels inflation and can do no more than give a very temporary boost to output and employment. If anything, the higher inflation could damage business confidence and thus worsen long-term output and employment growth by discouraging investment.

Those who criticise this view argue that the formation of expectations is more complex than this. Whether people expect an increase in demand to be fully matched by inflation depends on the current state of the economy and how any increase in demand is introduced.

If there is a lot of slack in the economy (if unemployment is very high and there are many idle resources) and if an increase in demand is in the form, say, of direct government spending on production (on roads, hospitals, sewers and other infrastructure) then output and employment may quickly rise. Here the effect of expectations may be beneficial. Rather than expecting inflation from the increased demand, firms may expect faster growth and an expansion of markets. As a result, they may choose to invest, and this in turn will produce further growth in output and employment.

Views on expectations, therefore, tend to parallel views on aggregate supply. The right argues that a boost to demand will not produce extra output and employment: aggregate supply is inelastic (as in Figure 20.16(a)) and therefore the higher demand will merely fuel expectations of inflation. Their critics argue that a boost to demand can increase aggregate supply and employment. If firms expect this, they will produce more.

 If firms believe the aggregate supply curve to be moderately elastic, what effect will this belief have on the outcome of an increase in aggregate demand?

We examine the role of expectations in determining output and employment in the next chapter.

BOX 20.4	COMMON GROUND BETWEEN ECONOMISTS?	EXPLORING ECONOMICS

Identifying areas of agreement

The financial crisis of the late 2000s helped to reignite long-standing debates amongst macroeconomists. Up to that point a new macroeconomic consensus was developing. This brought under one large tent a group of macroeconomists modelling the interaction of representative forward-looking economic agents in markets characterised by varying degrees of imperfections where shocks regularly hit economies.

The models were a fusion of new Keynesian and new classical ideas (see Chapter 16 for more on 'macroeconomic schools of thought'). The models were argued to provide insights into how economies adjust to new equilibria in the face of economic shocks. The focus would be on the paths taken by key macroeconomic variables such as output, employment and inflation.

The financial crisis raised several concerns about the new mainstream macroeconomic approach. Had the approach to modelling become too mathematical? Did it, therefore, not sufficiently account for the effects, for instance, of human behaviour and the way in which humans interact? Had it placed too much faith in the ability of markets to deliver socially desirable outcomes? Had it taken too little account of the financial system and the financial well-being of economic agents?

These and many other questions continue to be debated. Nonetheless, we can still identify areas of common ground between many economists over many issues. Hence, some degree of macroeconomic consensus may be argued to have survived the financial crisis. We summarise here three general areas of agreement first introduced in section 16.6 (see pages 514–16).

1. Fluctuations in aggregate demand can have significant effects on output and employment in the short term

With the exception of extreme new classical economists, most economists would accept that the short-run aggregate supply (*SRAS*) curve is *upward sloping,* albeit getting steeper as potential output is approached. There are two major implications of this analysis.

- Reductions in aggregate demand can cause reductions in output and increases in unemployment. In other words, too little spending will cause a recession.
- An expansion of aggregate demand by the government (whether achieved by fiscal or monetary policy, or both) will help to pull an economy out of a recession. There may be considerable time lags, however, before the economy fully responds to such expansionary policies.

2. Changes in aggregate demand will have much less effect on output and employment and much more effect on prices in the longer term

As we have seen, new classical economists and others argue that the long-run aggregate supply (*LRAS*) curve is vertical.

Some Keynesian economists agree, but argue that the long run might be quite a long time. Others, while arguing that the *LRAS* curve is not vertical, would still see it as less elastic than the short-run aggregate supply curve. Nevertheless, some Keynesians argue that changes in aggregate demand *will* have substantial effects on long-term output and employment via changes in investment and hence in potential ('full-employment') output.

3. Expectations have important effects on the economy

Virtually all economists argue that expectations are crucial in determining the success of government policy on unemployment and inflation. Whatever people expect to happen, their actions will tend to make it happen.

If people believe that an expansion of money supply will merely lead to inflation (the monetarist and new classical position), then it will. Firms and workers will adjust their prices and wage rates upwards. Firms will make no plans to expand output and will not take on any more labour. If, however, people believe that an expansion of demand will lead to higher output and employment (the Keynesian position), then, via the accelerator mechanism, it will.

Similarly, just how successful a deflationary policy is in curing inflation depends in large measure on people's expectations. If people believe that a deflationary policy will cause a recession, then firms will stop investing and will cut their workforce. If they believe that it will cure inflation and restore firms' competitiveness abroad, firms may increase investment.

To manage the economy successfully, therefore, the government must convince people that its policies will work. This is as much a job of public relations as of pulling the right economic levers. It is one of the reasons for making central banks independent. If people believe that the central bank will not be swayed from its task of keeping inflation on target, either by public opinion or by political pressure, then people will come to expect low inflation.

In Chapter 21 we will look further at the importance of expectations, particularly inflationary expectations. We will also consider the process by which people's expectations are formed.

1. *If constant criticism of governments in the media makes people highly cynical about any government's ability to manage the economy, what effect will this have on the performance of the economy?*
2. *Suppose that, as part of the national curriculum, everyone in the country had to study economics up to the age of 16. Suppose also that the reporting of economic events by the media became more thorough (and interesting!). What effects would these developments have on the government's ability to manage the economy? How would your answer differ if you were a Keynesian from if you were a new classicist?*

Section summary

1. Over the years there has been considerable debate among economists and politicians about how the market mechanism works at a macroeconomic level.

2. The right has tended to argue (a) that prices and wages are relatively flexible, (b) that aggregate supply is determined independently of aggregate demand and (c) that people's price and wage expectations adjust rapidly to shifts in aggregate demand so as to wipe out any output effect.

3. The centre and left to varying degrees have argued (a) that prices and wages are inflexible downwards, (b) that aggregate supply is relatively elastic when there is slack in the economy and (c) aggregate supply can be responsive to changes in aggregate demand in the longer term because of, for example, economic hysteresis or positive expectations of output and employment.

END OF CHAPTER QUESTIONS

1. For what reasons might the long-run aggregate supply curve be (a) vertical; (b) upward sloping; (c) downward sloping?

2. How would you attempt to assess whether a particular period of inflation was the result of cost-push or demand-pull pressures?

3. Repeat the analysis undertaken in Figure 20.5 to consider the possible subsequent effects following a period of demand-pull deflation.

4. What implications would a vertical short-run aggregate supply curve have for the effects of demand management policy?

5. What would cause (a) a steep *DAD* curve; (b) a gently sloping *DAD* curve? Compare the short-run and long-run effects of (i) a temporary adverse supply shock and (ii) a permanent supply reduction under each of (a) and (b).

6. Under what circumstances would a rightward shift in the *DAD* curve lead to a *permanent* increase in real national income?

7. For what reasons may the natural level of unemployment increase?

8. Assume that there is a positive technological shock. How would this impact on the equilibrium level of employment and the economy's potential output? Illustrate using diagrams of both the labour and goods markets.

9. How might fluctuations in aggregate demand lead to changes in output even under the assumption of continuous market clearing?

10. Given the Keynesian explanation for the persistence of high levels of unemployment after the recessions of the early 1980s and early 1990s, what policies would you advocate to reduce unemployment in the years following a recession?

Online resources

Additional case studies on the student website

20.1 The factors shaping the *LRAS*. This case looks at three important factors shaping the *AS* curve in the long run.

20.2 Do people volunteer to be unemployed? Is it useful to make the distinction, often made, between voluntary and involuntary unemployment?

20.3 Getting predictitons wrong. How incorrect predictions can lead to a rise or fall in output in the new classical model.

Websites relevant to this chapter

See sites listed at the end of Chapter 22 on page 712.

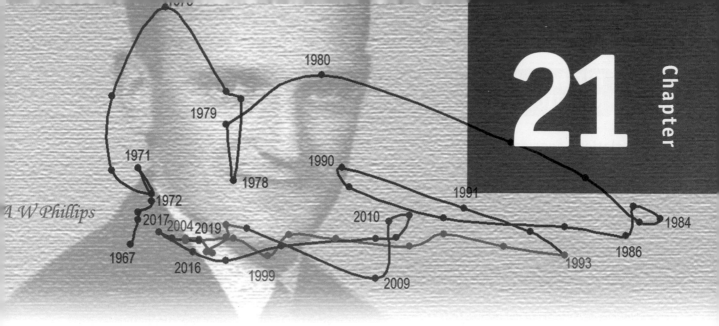

A W Phillips

The Relationship between Inflation, Unemployment and Output

In this chapter we turn to the relationship between inflation and unemployment. We examine a range of alternative perspectives. Once more we shall see that a crucial element here is the response of aggregate supply to a change in aggregate demand, in this case reflected in the shape of the Phillips curve. If aggregate supply responds to changes in aggregate demand, then a rise in aggregate demand should lead to a fall in unemployment, but will probably lead to a rise in inflation.

We shall see that the behaviour of markets and the formation of expectations are especially important in affecting the unemployment/inflation relationship, both in the short run and in the long run.

Around the world many central banks target inflation, often supplemented by other macroeconomic objectives. We look at how the analysis of the inflation/unemployment relationship has led many government to delegate monetary policy to their central banks. Finally, by integrating the Phillips curve framework with the *DAD/DAS* framework introduced in Chapter 20, we begin to consider how central banks can affect the adjustment paths of economies that face frequent economic shocks.

The expectations-augmented Phillips curve (*EAPC*)

In Chapter 20 we discussed the interaction of aggregate demand and supply and the impact on output and prices from the frequent shocks that affect the economy. We saw how the adjustment process is affected, among other things, by the behaviour of product and labour markets and by expectations. In this section we look at the importance of inflationary expectations in affecting macroeconomic outcomes. To do so, we introduce an alternative way of looking at the macroeconomy: the *expectations-augmented Phillips curve (EAPC)*.

The *EAPC* was a major contribution to our understanding of the relationship between unemployment and inflation made by Milton Friedman (see Case Study 16.8 on the student website) and others in the late 1960s. They incorporated people's expectations about the future level of prices into the Phillips curve.

The original Phillips curve stems from the inverse relationship identified by Bill Phillips between wage inflation and unemployment for the UK from 1861 to 1957 (see Box 15.6). It appeared to offer a trade-off between inflation against unemployment. Lower unemployment could be bought at the cost of higher inflation, and vice versa, through changes in aggregate demand (relative to potential output).

Friedman argued that the theoretical trade-off implied by the simple Phillips curve relationship relied on permanent changes in the *real* wage. For the rate of unemployment to remain below its natural rate, i.e. the equilibrium rate, workers would need to supply labour at below the equilibrium real wage rate (e.g. W_e in Figure 20.10 on page 635). Friedman argued that this was implausible other than in the short term and that wage inflation would surely catch up with consumer price inflation to restore the real wage equilibrium.

Hence, Friedman believed that the theory underpinning the original Phillips curve relationship had failed to incorporate people's expectations of inflation.

In its simplest form, this expectations-augmented Phillips curve may be expressed as

$$\pi = f(1/U) + \pi^e + k \qquad (1)$$

This states that the rate of price inflation (π) depends on three things.

- First, it is a function (f) of the inverse of unemployment ($1/U$). This is simply the original Phillips curve relationship. A rise in aggregate demand will lead to a fall in unemployment (a rise in $1/U$) and a rise in inflation: e.g. a movement from point a to point b in Figure 21.1.
- Second, the expected rate of inflation π^e must be added to the inflation that would result simply from the level of excess demand represented by $(1/U)$.

- Third, if there are any exogenous cost pressures on inflation (k) (such as increases in international commodity prices), this must be added too.

Thus if people expected a 3 per cent inflation rate ($\pi^e = 3\%$) and if excess demand were causing demand-pull inflation of 2 per cent ($f(1/U) = 2\%$) and exogenous increases in costs were adding another 1 per cent to inflation ($k = 1\%$), actual inflation would be $3 + 2 + 1 = 6$ per cent.

By augmenting the Phillips curve with expectations, we move from a single curve to a family of Phillips curves. The vertical position of each curve is determined by inflationary expectations (π^e) and any exogenous costs pressures (k). If we assume that on average $k = 0$, then we can simplify the *EAPC* framework so that each expectations-augmented Phillips curve is associated with a particular rate of inflationary expectations.

In Figure 21.1, points a and c both represent a hypothetical economy with unemployment at its natural rate, U_n. However, in the case of point a it is assumed that people's inflationary expectations are π_1, while at point c they are π_2. If we start at point a and aggregate demand expands so that, in the short run, inflation rises and unemployment falls but expected inflation stays at π_1, there will be a movement up along curve $EAPC_1$ to, say, point b. But this is not the end of the story; inflationary expectations will adjust. Once they do, the *EAPC* will shift upwards to $EAPC_2$. Unless there is a further rise in aggregate demand, the original rise in aggregate demand will simply

> ### Definition
>
> **Expectations-augmented Phillips curve** A (short-run) Phillips curve whose position depends on the expected rate of inflation.

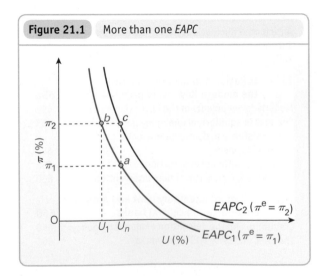

Figure 21.1 More than one *EAPC*

KI 36 p451

result in higher inflation and the economy moves to point c, with unemployment rising back to the natural rate, U_n.

But by what process do people form their inflationary expectations? We can identify two principal forms of expectations: adaptive and rational expectations. We examine each in turn. We will see that the response of inflation and unemployment to a rise in aggregate demand differs according to how expectations are formed.

 Assume the economy is represented by EAPC₁ in Figure 21.1. Illustrate the effects of positive and negative inflation shocks on the curve.

Adaptive expectations

If we assume that people base their expectations of inflation on past inflation rates, then they form what are called **adaptive expectations**. If, for example, last year people underpredicted the rate of inflation, then this year they will adapt by revising their expectations of inflation upwards.

The simplest form of adaptive expectations is to assume that people use last year's actual inflation rate (π_{t-1}) as their prediction for the expected rate of inflation this year (π_t^e):

$$\pi_t^e = \pi_{t-1}$$

Box 21.1 considers more sophisticated versions of adaptive expectations.

Rational expectations

The adaptive expectations hypothesis, it is argued, suffers from a serious flaw: it assumes that people base their expectations on the past. So if inflation is on an upward trend, the future of inflation will always be underestimated. Similarly, inflation will always be overestimated if it is on a downward trend. Thus people will normally be wrong.

But people will soon realise that it is not rational to base their expectations blindly on the past. They will look at the *current* situation and what is likely to affect inflation. Thus, it is argued, adaptive expectations cannot be a rational basis of behaviour.

Rational expectations are not based on past rates of inflation. Instead they are based on the current state of the economy and the current policies being pursued by the government. Workers and firms look at the information available to them – at the various forecasts that are published, at various economic indicators and the assessments of them by various commentators, at government pronouncements, and so on. From this information they predict the rate of inflation as well as they can. It is in this sense that the expectations are 'rational': people use their reason to assess the future on the basis of current information.

But forecasters frequently get it wrong, and so do economic commentators! And the government does not always do what it says it will. Thus workers and firms base their expectations on *imperfect information*. Other versions assume that they may make very poor use of information. But either way, people frequently forecast incorrectly. The crucial point about the rational expectations theory, however, is that these errors in prediction are *random*. People's predictions of inflation are just as likely to be too high as too low.[1]

 TC 9 p129

Definition

Adaptive expectations Where people adjust their expectations of inflation in the light of what has happened to inflation in the past.

---

*BOX 21.1 | **BASING EXPECTATIONS ON THE PAST** | EXPLORING ECONOMICS

More sophisticated adaptive expectations models

More complex adaptive expectations models assume that π^e is a weighted average of past rates of inflation:

$$\pi_t^e = a\pi_{t-1} + b\pi_{t-2} + c\pi_{t-3}\dots + m\pi_{t-n} \qquad (1)$$

where $a + b + c\dots + m = 1$, and where $a > b > c$, etc.

In other words, people will base their expectations of inflation on the actual inflation rates over the last few time periods (e.g. months, quarters or years), but with the last

period's inflation having a bigger influence on people's expectations than the previous period's and so on.

In times of rapidly *accelerating* inflation, people may adjust their expectations of inflation upward by the amount that inflation *rose* last period ($\Delta\pi_{t-1}$). This gives:

$$\Delta\pi_t^e = \Delta\pi_{t-1} \qquad (2)$$

 Under what circumstances will term a in equation (1) be large relative to terms b, c etc.?

---

1 The rational expectations hypothesis can be stated as:

$$\pi_t = \pi_{t-1} + \left(\sum_{t=1}^{t=\infty}\varepsilon_t\right)(\varepsilon = 0)$$

In other words, the rate of inflation for any time period (π_t) will be the rate that people expected in that time period (π_t^e) plus an error term (e_t). This error term may be quite large but is equally likely to be positive or negative. Thus when you sum ($\sum$) the error terms over the years (strictly speaking, to infinity), the positive and negative values will cancel each other out and the sum will therefore be zero.

Short-run and long-run perspectives

As we saw in Chapter 16, Friedman and other monetarists argued that there exists a long-run Phillips curve (*LRPC*) which is vertical at the natural (equilibrium) rate of unemployment. Only in the *short run* would higher aggregate demand reduce the unemployment rate below the natural rate (and raise output above its potential level). In the long run there would be no *real* increase in aggregate demand.

The idea that unemployment will return to its natural rate (and output to its potential level) following fluctuations in aggregate demand is commonly referred to as the ***natural rate hypothesis***. Although initially associated with monetarists, the hypothesis has become more widely incorporated into macroeconomic models.

However, not all economists accept that the natural rate of unemployment is unaffected by fluctuations in aggregate demand. As discussed in section 20.5, Keynesian economists, for example, have developed theories exploring how changes in aggregate demand can have effects on physical and human capital. These effects, they argue, can result in a non-vertical *LRPC* (and *LRAS* curve).

In understanding the long-run relationship between inflation and unemployment, it is important to analyse the adjustment of economies to economic shocks. Short-run adjustments to fluctuations in aggregate demand involve movements along expectation-augmented Phillips curves. Hence, the *EAPC* provides us with a framework to analyse the implications for inflation and the labour market from the frequent fluctuations in aggregate demand.

The way in which people form expectations is an important factor in determining how economies adjust to shocks. We have already seen that people may form adaptive or rational expectations. This is the case for their expectations of inflation and also other macroeconomic variables, such as output.

Another important factor affecting the adjustment processes of economies is the speed with which markets clear through the adjustment of prices to equate demand and supply.

Market clearing

In models which assume market clearing, prices are deemed to be flexible and so adjust to bring about equilibrium between demand and supply. In the labour market, for example, wages are not sticky downwards, at least not in the long run. There can be no long-run disequilibrium unemployment: no long-run deficiency of demand.

However, within the modern fusion of macroeconomic ideas (see section 16.6 and Box 20.4) models vary according to the speed with which markets are assumed to adjust. The more rapid is the process of market clearing the more quickly unemployment will, other things being equal, adjust to its natural rate.

The assumption made by new classical economists (see section 16.4) is that of *continuous* market clearing. This means that markets experience a very rapid adjustment of prices resulting in them clearing continuously. On the other hand, New Keynesian economists (see section 16.5) argue that there are frictions which impede and slow the adjustment of markets to economic shocks.

We now consider the effect of a range of views about both expectations and the degree of market clearing on the inflation/unemployment trade-off. We begin in section 21.2 with original monetarist thinking which combines adaptive expectations of inflation with the assumption that markets are relatively flexible.

Definition

Natural rate hypothesis The theory that, following fluctuations in aggregate demand, unemployment will return to a natural rate. This rate is determined by supply-side factors, such as labour mobility.

Section summary

1. A refinement of the simple Phillips curve involves the incorporation of people's expectations about the rate of inflation. This gives an expectations-augmented Phillips curve.

2. One explanation of how people form these expectations is given by the adaptive expectations hypothesis. In its simplest form, the hypothesis states that the expected rate of inflation this year is what it actually was last year: $\pi_t^e = \pi_{t-1}$.

3. An alternative process by which expectations are formed is known as rational expectations. This assumes that people base their expectations of inflation on a rational assessment of the current situation. People may predict wrongly, but they are equally likely to underpredict or to overpredict. On average, over the years, it is assumed that they will predict correctly.

4. Those who support the natural rate hypothesis argue that fluctuations in aggregate demand have no long-term effect on unemployment, which will adjust to its natural rate. Hence, the economy is characterised by an *LRPC* which is vertical at the natural rate of unemployment. The natural rate is determined by supply-side factors.

5. Though the natural rate hypothesis has become increasingly accepted by economists other than just monetarists, it is not universally accepted. The *EAPC* provides a framework to study the adjustment of economies to shocks and their longer-term impact on the inflation–unemployment relationship.

6. The formation of expectations and the flexibility of markets are two important factors in determining the long-term inflation–unemployment relationship.

The short-run trade-off

As we have seen in the previous section, monetarists argued that the natural rate of unemployment is determined independently of aggregate demand. Consequently, the long-run Phillips curve is vertical. In the long run it is supply-side policies that affect levels of structural and frictional unemployment. However, in the short run unemployment may deviate from its natural rate. To understand why, we develop a simple model of the economy.

The model is based on two key assumptions. First, prices adjust relatively quickly to ensure equilibrium between demand and supply in goods and labour markets Second, people form adaptive expectations of inflation.

To make the analysis more straightforward, we assume that they use last year's actual inflation rate year (π_{t-1}) as their prediction for the expected rate of inflation this year (π_t^e):

$$\pi_t^e = \pi_{t-1} \tag{2}$$

Also we assume that the economy's inflation rate last year was zero, no inflation is expected and there are no exogenous cost pressures on inflation ($k = 0$ in equation (1) on page 646).

In Figure 21.2 the economy is initially at point a with both actual and expected inflation of zero. The goods and labour markets are in equilibrium: $AD = AS$ and unemployment is at its natural rate, U_n.

Increase in aggregate demand. Assume that there is an increase in real aggregate demand. The economy moves to, say, point b along the expectations-augmented Phillips curve, *EAPC*$_0$. The rate of inflation rises from zero to π_1.

But, with people still expecting zero inflation, the labour market sees a fall in the average real wage rate, leading to a rise in the demand for labour. Assuming that workers are fooled into supplying the additional labour despite the fall in real wages, unemployment falls below its natural rate to U_1.

If we now move ahead a year, people will have revised their expectations of inflation upwards to π_1. The result is that the Phillips curve has shifted up vertically by π_1 to *EAPC*$_1$. If *nominal* aggregate demand (i.e. demand purely in monetary terms, irrespective of the level of prices) continues to rise at the same rate, the whole of the increase will now be absorbed in higher prices. *Real* aggregate demand will fall back to its previous level and the economy will move to point c on the long-run Phillips curve. Unemployment will return to its natural rate, U_n, consistent with the natural rate hypothesis. There is no *demand-pull* inflation now ($f(1/U) = 0$), but inflation is π_1 per cent due to inflationary expectations.

Decrease in aggregate demand. Assume that the economy is at point c in Figure 21.2. It now experiences a decrease in the growth of nominal demand. Real aggregate demand falls. Let us assume that there is downward pressure on inflation such that the inflation rate falls to zero. The economy moves down *EAPC*$_1$ to point d. In the labour market the expected average real wage rate increases because the expected inflation rate is π_1. The demand for labour falls and unemployment rises above its natural rate, U_n to U_2.

The following year the expected rate of inflation will fall to zero. The *EAPC* moves vertically down to *EAPC*$_0$. If the growth in nominal aggregate demand remains at its new lower rate, with inflation now at zero, the economy will again be at point a on the long-run Phillips curve. Unemployment is again at its natural rate.

The accelerationist hypothesis

The preceding analysis helps to show that when people form adaptive expectations of inflation, unemployment can deviate from its natural rate following changes in aggregate demand even if markets clear fairly quickly. This raises the theoretical possibility that governments could keep unemployment below the natural rate. But this would come at a cost, since to do so it must raise nominal aggregate demand at ever-increasing rates.

Each time government is able to raise the nominal growth in aggregate demand there is a transitory period when real aggregate demand rises too. But inflationary expectations then rise to reflect higher inflation rates. This is mirrored in the labour market by real wages being driven

---

Figure 21.2 *EAPC* and the natural rate hypothesis

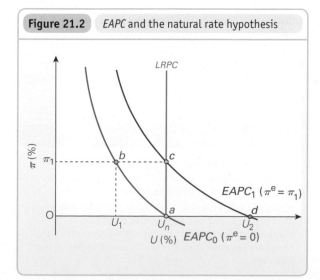

back up to their equilibrium level. Hence, for the government to keep unemployment below its natural rate it needs to keep raising the growth in nominal aggregate demand – in other words, it must increase nominal aggregate demand faster and faster. This, of course, means that nominal aggregate demand needs to grow at more than the rate of inflation. However, the rate of inflation is itself getting progressively higher as people are continually raising their inflationary expectations.

The theory that unemployment can be reduced below the natural rate only at the cost of accelerating inflation is known as the *accelerationist hypothesis*. Box 21.2 considers a numerical example of the hypothesis.

Stagflation and Phillips loops

In the 1970s, many countries experienced 'stagflation' – a simultaneous rise in unemployment and inflation. Monetarists used the adaptive expectations model to explain why this occurred. The explanation involved clockwise Phillips loops and rightward shifts in the long-run Phillips curve.

Clockwise Phillips loops

Consider a 10-year cycle. This is illustrated in Figure 21.3. The economy starts at position *a* in year 0. There is no inflation and the economy is at the natural rate of unemployment. The government pursues an expansionary policy over the next three years in order to reduce unemployment. The economy moves up through points *b, c* and *d*.

The government then starts worrying about inflation. It allows unemployment to rise somewhat, but as it is still below U_n there is still demand-pull inflation. The economy moves to point *e*. The government now allows unemployment to rise to U_n, but the Phillips curve still shifts up as expectations catch up with last year's inflation. The economy moves from point *e* to point *f*.

Thereafter the government allows unemployment to rise further, and the economy eventually returns to point *a,* via points *g, h, i* and *j*. The economy has thus moved through a clockwise loop.

Stagflation is easy to see. From points *d* to *f*, both unemployment *and* inflation are rising. What is more, several points are to the 'north-east' of other earlier points. For example, point *g* is north-east of point *c*. In other words, inflation *and* unemployment in year 6 (point *g*) are higher than in year 2 (point *c*).

 Under what circumstances would a Phillips loop be (a) tall and thin; (b) short and wide?

Rightward shifts in the long-run Phillips curve

If frictional or structural unemployment rises (due, say, to increased unemployment benefits), U_n will increase. The long-run Phillips curve will shift to the right.

Assume that the economy was initially on the long-run Phillips curve with $U_n = 8$ per cent and a stable inflation rate of 5 per cent. U_n now rises to 12 per cent. The government uses demand-management policy to keep the rise in unemployment to only 10 per cent. But this is now *below* U_n and thus inflation will increase. Thus both inflation *and* unemployment have risen.

Phillips loops and the political business cycle

The monetarist adaptive expectations model can also be applied to illustrate how the path of unemployment and inflation can follow a cycle mirroring the election cycle. In other words, policy makers may attempt to engineer a path for the macroeconomy that increases its probability of election. This path is known as the *political business cycle*.

The theory suggests that the discretionary policy choices of government can purposefully destabilise the economy. Therefore, it is argued, governments should be made to adopt policy rules.

Imagine that a politically naïve government has been fulfilling election promises to reduce unemployment, cut taxes and increase welfare spending. In Figure 21.3 this is shown by a move from points *a* to *b* to *c*. However, by the time the next election comes, inflation is accelerating and unemployment is rising again. The economy is moving from point *d* to *e* to *f*. This is unlikely to be a successful strategy for a vote-maximising government.

What the political business cycle model suggests is that at the start of their electoral terms, governments will engineer a recession and begin to squeeze down inflationary expectations. Assuming the economy is already at point *f* as a result of previous political business cycles, it will look to move the economy from point *f* to *g* to *h*.

But people are assumed to have short memories. Therefore, the government looks to engineer a pre-election boom and be rewarded for its economic management over the latter part of the election period. Unemployment falls, but inflation continues falling because of expectations adjusting downwards. The economy moves from point *h* to *i* to *j* to *a*.

 How would the political business cycle be affected if governments were able to choose when to hold elections?

Definitions

Accelerationist hypothesis The theory that unemployment can be reduced below the natural rate only at the cost of accelerating inflation.

Political business cycle The theory that governments, after being elected, will engineer an economic contraction, designed to squeeze out inflation. They will then later engineer a pre-election boom to appeal to the electorate.

BOX 21.2 THE ACCELERATIONIST HYPOTHESIS

The race to outpace inflationary expectations

Let us trace the course of inflation and expectations over a number of years in an imaginary economy. To keep the analysis simple, assume there is no growth in the economy and no exogenous cost pressures on inflation ($k = 0$ in equation (1) on page 646).

Year 1. Assume that at the outset, in year 1, there is no inflation of any sort; that none is expected; that $AD = AS$; and that equilibrium unemployment is 8 per cent. The economy is at point a in the diagram.

Year 2. Now assume that the government expands aggregate demand in order to reduce unemployment. Unemployment falls to 6 per cent. The economy moves to point b along $EAPC_1$. Inflation has risen to 4 per cent, but people, basing their expectations of inflation on year 1, still expect zero inflation. There is therefore no shift as yet in the Phillips curve. $EAPC_1$ corresponds to an expected rate of inflation of zero. (See Case Study 21.1 on the student website for an explanation of why the short-run Phillips curve slopes downwards.)

Year 3. People now revise their expectations of inflation to the level of year 2. The Phillips curve shifts up by 4 percentage points to $EAPC_2$. If *nominal* aggregate demand (i.e. demand purely in monetary terms, irrespective of the level of prices) continues to rise at the same rate, the whole of the increase will now be absorbed in higher prices. *Real* aggregate demand will fall back to its previous level and the economy will move to point c. Unemployment will return to 8 per cent. There is no *demand-pull* inflation now ($f(1/U) = 0$), but inflation is still 4 per cent due to expectations ($\pi^e = 4$ per cent).

Year 4. Assume now that the government expands real aggregate demand again so as to reduce unemployment once more to 6 per cent. This time it must expand nominal aggregate demand by more than it did in year 2, because this time, as well as reducing unemployment, it also has to validate the 4 per cent expected inflation. The economy moves to point d along $EAPC_2$. Inflation is now 8 per cent.

Year 5. Expected inflation is now 8 per cent (the level of actual inflation in year 4). The Phillips curve shifts up to $EAPC_3$. If at the same time the government tries to keep unemployment at 6 per cent, it must expand nominal aggregate demand 4 per cent faster in order to validate the 8 per cent expected inflation. The economy moves to point e along $EAPC_3$. Inflation is now 12 per cent.

Year 6 onwards. To keep unemployment at 6 per cent, the government must continue to increase nominal aggregate demand by 4 per cent more than the previous year. As the expected inflation rate goes on rising, the Phillips curve will go on shifting up each year.

Construct a table like the one in the diagram, only this time assume that the government wishes to reduce unemployment to 5 per cent. Assume that every year from year 1 onwards the government is prepared to expand aggregate demand by whatever it takes to do this. If this expansion of demand gives $f(1/U) = 7$ per cent, fill in the table for the first six years. Do you think that after a couple of years people might begin to base their expectations differently?

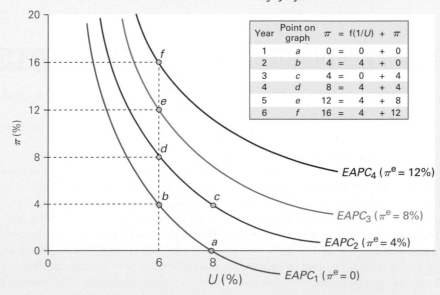

The accelerationist theory of inflation

Year	Point on graph	π	=	f(1/U)	+	π
1	a	0	=	0	+	0
2	b	4	=	4	+	0
3	c	4	=	0	+	4
4	d	8	=	4	+	4
5	e	12	=	4	+	8
6	f	16	=	4	+	12

$EAPC_4$ ($\pi^e = 12\%$)

$EAPC_3$ ($\pi^e = 8\%$)

$EAPC_2$ ($\pi^e = 4\%$)

$EAPC_1$ ($\pi^e = 0$)

Figure 21.3   Clockwise Phillips loops

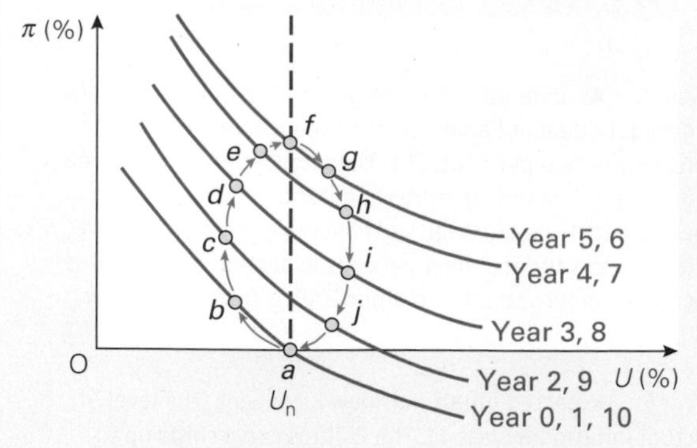

or fiscal policy can have no *long-run* effect on unemployment. They can only be used to influence the inflation rate.

Ultimately, monetary and fiscal policies merely move the economy up or down the vertical long-run Phillips curve. An expansionary policy, for example, could only ever bring a *temporary* reduction in unemployment below U_n. Moreover, demand-side policy can be destabilising, especially if used by governments to court electoral popularity.

To reduce unemployment permanently, *supply-side* policies should be used. These could either be market-orientated policies of removing impediments to the working of the market (see section 23.5) or interventionist policies, such as improving education and training or the country's transport and communications infrastructure (see section 23.6). By reducing frictional and/or structural unemployment, such policies will shift the long-run Phillips curve back to the left.

Policy implications

The implications of the monetarist application of the expectations-augmented Phillips curve are that monetary

Section summary

1. The monetarist model assumes that markets are relatively flexible. But the assumption of adaptive expectations allows unemployment to deviate from the natural rate in the short term. People can be fooled, allowing unemployment and output to fluctuate.

2. If there is excess demand in the economy, producing upward pressure on wages and prices, initially unemployment will fall. The reason is that workers and firms will believe that wage and price increases represent *real* wage and price increases respectively. Thus workers are prepared to take jobs more readily and firms choose to produce more. But as people's expectations adapt upwards to these higher wages and prices, so

ever-increasing rises in nominal aggregate demand will be necessary to maintain unemployment below the natural rate. Price and wage rises will accelerate: i.e. inflation will rise.

3. The long-run Phillips curve, according to this analysis, is thus vertical at the natural rate of unemployment.

4. Stagflation can be explained in this model either by a movement from 9 o'clock to 12 o'clock round a clockwise Phillips loop, or by a rightward shift in the vertical Phillips curve combined with a mild expansionary policy.

5. The model also illustrates how governments can benefit electorally by generating a political business cycle.

21.3 INFLATION AND UNEMPLOYMENT: THE NEW CLASSICAL POSITION

New classical assumptions

Economists of the *new classical school* (see section 16.4) go further than the traditional monetarist theory described above. They argue that unless there are unexpected or 'surprise' events, there is no short-run trade-off between inflation and unemployment. The *EAPC* therefore represents a short-run trade-off between inflation and unemployment only in the presence of surprise events. It mirrors the *SRAS* curve which, as we saw in section 20.4, some refer to as the 'surprise aggregate supply curve'.

The argument that there is normally *no* trade-off between unemployment and inflation, even in the short run, is based on two key assumptions:

- Prices and wages are flexible so that markets clear continuously.
- Expectations are 'rational', but are based on imperfect information.

Continuous market clearing.   The new classical position is that markets clearly continuously. This is likely, they argue, in modern economies with flexible labour markets (see Box 10.8 on pages 296–7) and facing global competition. There is thus no disequilibrium unemployment, even in the short run. All unemployment, therefore, is *equilibrium* unemployment, or 'voluntary unemployment' as new classical economists tend to call it. Increases in unemployment are therefore due to an increase in the natural level of unemployment, as people choose not to take jobs because of a lack of incentives to do so.

Rational expectations. The monetarist analysis of the previous section was based on *adaptive* expectations. New classical analysis, by contrast, is based on *rational* expectations. As we saw above, these are assumed to diverge only randomly from the actual rate of inflation. On average they are assumed to be correct.

Anticipated fluctuations in aggregate demand

If markets continuously clear and if people are correct in their expectations, then fluctuations in aggregate demand will have no impact on unemployment either in the short run or long run. The only effect is on the rate of inflation.

In the new classical (rational expectations) model, unlike the adaptive expectations model, there is *no* lag in expectations. If their information is correct, people will rationally predict that output and employment will stay at the natural level. They predict that any change in *nominal* aggregate demand will be reflected purely in terms of changes in prices,

and that real aggregate demand will remain the same. If real aggregate demand remains the same, so will the demand for and supply of labour and the demand for and supply of goods. Thus, even in the *short* run, output and employment will stay at the natural level.

Is the assumption of rational expectations on its own sufficient for anticipated demand shocks to have no impact on economic activity even in the short run?

We can use Figure 21.4 to illustrate the adjustment of the economy under continuous market clearing, rational expectations and anticipated demand shocks. Assume that the economy is at point *a* with unemployment at its natural rate, U_n, and an actual and expected inflation rate of zero. Now assume that government increases aggregate demand. With rational expectations and no surprises, people fully anticipate that the inflation rate will rise to π_1. $EAPC_0$, which is based on expectations of zero inflation, cannot be moved along. The moment that aggregate demand rises people correctly anticipate an inflation rate of π_1. Thus the whole *EAPC* moves vertically upwards to $EAPC_1$. As a result, the economy moves *directly* from point *a* to point *c*.

BOX 21.3 | **THE RATIONAL EXPECTATIONS REVOLUTION** | EXPLORING ECONOMICS

Trying to 'unfool' the economics profession

The rational expectations revolution swept through the economics profession in the 1970s in a way that no other set of ideas had done since Keynes. Although largely associated with the free-market, non-interventionist wing of economics, the rational expectations revolution has been far more wide-reaching. Even economists implacably opposed to the free market nevertheless incorporated rational expectations into their models. Hence, rational expectations became part of the mainstream consensus that emerged up to the financial crisis of the late 2000s (see section 16.6).

The rational expectations revolution is founded on a very simple idea. People base their expectations of the future on the information they have available. They don't just look at the past, they also look at current information, including what the government is saying and doing and what various commentators have to say.

The new classical economists use rational expectations in the following context. If the *long-run* Phillips curve is vertical, so that an expansionary policy will in the end merely lead to inflation, it will be difficult for the government to fool people that this will not happen. If employers, unions, city financiers, economic advisers, journalists, etc., all expect this to happen, then it will: and it will happen in the *short run*. Why should firms produce more in response to a rise in demand if their costs are going to rise by just as much? Why should higher wages attract workers to move jobs, if wages everywhere are going up? Why should firms and unions not seek price and wage rises fully in line with the expected inflation?

But can the government not surprise people? The point here is that 'surprising' people really only means 'fooling' them – making them believe that an expansionary policy really *will* reduce unemployment. But why should the public be fooled? Why should people believe smooth-talking government ministers rather than the whole host of critics of the government, from the opposition, to economic commentators, to the next-door neighbour?

The rational expectations school revised the old saying 'You can't fool all the people all the time' to 'You can hardly fool the people at all'. And if that is so, argue the new classical economists, unemployment can only momentarily be brought below its natural level.

Two of the most famous rational expectations economists are Robert Lucas and Thomas Sargent. Robert Lucas, like Milton Friedman and many other famous conservative economists, has his academic base in the University of Chicago, where he has been a professor since 1974. In 1995, like Milton Friedman in 1976, Lucas was awarded the Nobel prize in economics. Tom Sargent is Professor of Economics at New York University and senior fellow at the Hoover Institution of Stanford University. He was Professor of Economics at Chicago in the 1990s.

In recent years, rational expectations have been incorporated into models characterised by market imperfections and frictions, such as those developed by new Keynesians (see section 16.5). In this context, government policy *can* be effective. For example, supply-side policies can be directed to removing market distortions.

Figure 21.4 Anticipated and unanticipated changes in *aggregate demand*

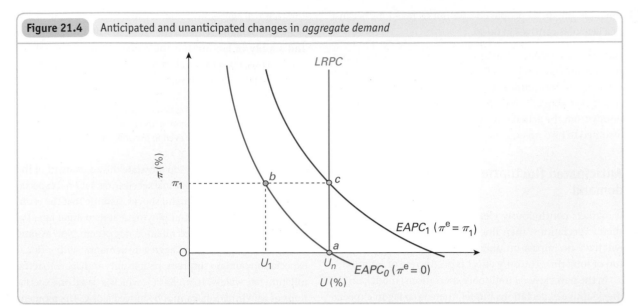

Surprise fluctuations in aggregate demand

Although over time people's expectations are assumed to be correct on average, it is more than likely that in any one period they will be wrong. Economic shocks, which for instance lead to unexpected changes in aggregate demand, mean that households and businesses are subject to 'surprises' (see section 16.5).

To illustrate the economic effects of unexpected fluctuations in aggregate demand, assume again that the economy is point *a* in Figure 21.4 above. The government now increases aggregate demand, but the size of the increase is unexpected. Prices and wages thus also rise more than people expect.

Consider first the potential impact in the labour market. If workers believe that they are getting a higher *real* wage

---

BOX 21.4   FORECASTING THE WEATHER

CASE STUDIES AND APPLICATIONS

An example of rational expectations

'What's the weather going to be like tomorrow?' If you are thinking of having a picnic, you will want to know the answer before deciding.

So what do you do? You could base your assessment on past information. Yesterday was fine; so was the previous day. Today is glorious. So, you think to yourself, it's a good bet that tomorrow will be fine too. If, on the other hand, the weather has been very changeable recently, you may feel that it's wiser not to take the risk. These 'forecasts' are examples of *adaptive* expectations: your forecasts are based on the actual weather over the past few days.

But would you really base such a crucial decision as to whether or not to have a picnic on something so unreliable? Wouldn't you rather take on board more information to help you make up your mind?

The first thing that might come to mind is the old saying that a British summer is three fine days and a thunderstorm. We've just had the three fine days, you think to yourself, so perhaps we'd better stay at home tomorrow.

Or, being a bit more scientific about it, you look at the weather forecast. Seeing loads of sunshine symbols all over the map, you decide to take a chance.

Basing your expectations in this way on current information (including even seeing whether there is a red sky that night) is an example of *rational* expectations.

So you go on your picnic and, guess what, it rains! 'I bet if we had decided to stay at home, it would have been fine', you grumble, as you eat your soggy sandwiches.

What you are acknowledging is that your decision was made on *imperfect* information. But the decision was still rational. It was still the best decision you could have made on the information available to you.

Weather forecasters make mistakes. But they are probably just as likely to get it wrong in predicting a sunny day as in predicting a wet day. It is still rational to base your decisions on their forecasts provided they are reasonably accurate.

 Under what circumstances might weather forecasters have a tendency to err on the side of pessimism or optimism? If you knew this tendency, how would this affect your decisions about picnics, hanging out the washing or watering the garden?

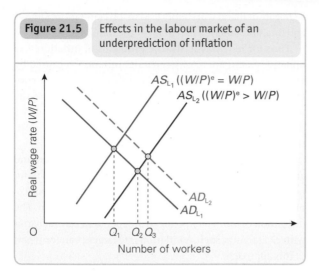

Figure 21.5 Effects in the labour market of an underprediction of inflation

But with firms underpredicting the rate of inflation too, the effect on employment is more complicated. On the one hand, with a rise in prices firms will want to produce more; their demand for labour will, therefore, tend to increase. For example, it might shift to AD_{L_2} in Figure 21.5, and thus employment would rise to Q_3. On the other hand, given that they are underpredicting the rate of inflation, they will believe that any given level of money wages (W) represents a higher level of *real* wages $(W/P)^e$ than it really does (W/P). They will tend, therefore, to employ *fewer* people at each wage rate, and the demand-for-labour curve will shift to the left. Thus, depending on which way the AD_L curve shifts, firms could employ more or less labour than Q_2.

The result of the surprise increase in aggregate demand is that workers or firms or both experience money illusion. This increases the employment of labour and output of goods. If we return to Figure 21.4, the surprise causes a move along an *EAPC*. If for simplicity we assume that the surprise occurred with people's expectations of inflation remaining at zero then the increase in demand would cause unemployment to fall below the natural rate, say to U_1. Once the surprise becomes apparent then the *EAPC* shifts upwards, eventually reaching $EAPC_2$. If the growth of demand then remains at the same rate, long-run equilibrium is represented by point *c*.

(W/P) than they really are, such that $(W/P)^e > W/P$, they will supply more labour. In Figure 21.5, the labour supply curve shifts from AS_{L_1} to AS_{L_2}. Employment rises above the natural level Q_1 (where expectations are correct), to Q_2. If only labour (and not firms) had underpredicted the rate of inflation, this rise in employment to Q_2 would the only short-run effect.

THE BOY WHO CRIED 'WOLF'

A government had better mean what it says

Do you remember the parable of the boy who cried 'Wolf!'?

There was once this little village on the edge of the forest. The villagers used to keep chickens, but when no one was around wolves would come out of the forest and carry off the chickens. So one of the boys in the village was given the job of keeping a lookout for wolves.

One day for a joke the boy called out 'Wolf, wolf! I see a wolf!' even though there was none. All the villagers came rushing out of their houses or back from the fields to catch the wolf. As you might expect, they were very angry to find that it was a false alarm.

The next day, thinking that this was great fun, the boy played the same trick again. Everyone came rushing out, and they were even more angry to find that they had been fooled again. But the boy just grinned.

The next day, when everyone was away in the fields, a wolf stalked into the village. The boy, spotting the animal, cried out 'Wolf, wolf! I see a wolf!' But the people in the fields said to each other 'We're not going to be fooled this time. We've had enough of his practical jokes.' And so they carried on working. Meanwhile, back in the village, the wolf was killing all the chickens.

You can probably guess what the villagers said when they returned in the evening to find just a large pile of feathers.

A government says 'We will take tough action to bring the rate of inflation down to 2 per cent.' Now of course this might be a 'joke' in the sense that the government doesn't really expect to succeed or even seriously to try, but is merely attempting to persuade unions to curb their wage demands. But if unions *believe* in both the government's intentions and its ability to succeed, the 'joke' may pay off. Some unions may well moderate their pay demands.

But some may not. What is more, the government may decide to give tax cuts to boost its popularity and stimulate growth, knowing that union pay demands are generally quite moderate. As a result, inflation soars.

But can the government get away with it a second or third time? It's like the boy who cried 'Wolf!' After a time, people will simply not believe the government. If they see the government boosting aggregate demand, they will say to themselves, 'Here comes inflation. We'd better demand higher wages to compensate.'

  Does this parable support the adaptive or the rational expectations hypothesis?

What would the process of adjustment to the unanticipated size of the increase in aggregate demand look like if people had adjusted their inflationary expectation upwards from zero but to a rate less than π_1?

Policy implications

If the new classical 'surprise model' is correct, anticipated changes in aggregate demand will have no effect on output and employment. *Unanticipated* changes in aggregate demand will have some effect, but only for as long as it takes people to realise their mistake and for their wages and prices to be corrected. Given rational expectations, people can be fooled in this way only by luck. There is no way that a government can *systematically* use demand management policy to keep output and employment above the natural level.

The new classical economists therefore totally reject Keynesian demand management policy, even in the short run. Monetary policy should be used to control inflation, but neither fiscal nor monetary policy can be used systematically to increase output and employment. Similarly, there is no fear of a deflationary monetary policy reducing output and employment and leading to a recession. The reduction in aggregate demand will simply lead to lower inflation. Output and unemployment will remain at the natural level.

Thus for new classicists, the problems of inflation and unemployment are totally separate. Inflation is caused by excessive growth in the money supply and should be controlled by monetary policy. Unemployment will be at the natural rate and should be reduced by supply-side policies designed to increase the incentives to work. In this respect, their views echo monetarist sentiments too.

To prevent unanticipated changes in aggregate demand and thus to prevent unemployment deviating from its natural level, new classical economists advocate the announcement of clear monetary rules and then sticking to them. The delegation of monetary policy to independent central banks with clear remits, such as inflation rate targets, can form part of this approach.

1. *If the government announced that it would, come what may, reduce the growth of money supply to zero next year, what (according to new classical economists) would happen? How might their answer be criticised?*
2. *For what reasons would a new classical economist support the policy of the Bank of England publishing its inflation forecasts and the minutes of the deliberations of the Monetary Policy Committee?*

Section summary

1. New classical theories assume continuous market clearing with flexible prices and wages in the short run as well as in the long run. It also assumes that people base their expectations of inflation on a rational assessment of the *current* situation.

2. People may predict wrongly, but they are equally likely to underpredict or to overpredict. On average, over the years, they will predict correctly.

3. The assumptions of continuous market clearing and rational expectations imply that only unexpected fluctuations in aggregate demand will cause unemployment to deviate from its natural rate. There can be no short-run trade-off between inflation and unemployment when changes in aggregate demand are anticipated.

4. If people correctly predict the rate of inflation, they will correctly predict that any increase in nominal aggregate demand will simply be reflected in higher prices. Total output and employment will remain the same: at the natural level.

5. If people underpredict the rate of inflation, they will believe that there has been a *real* increase in aggregate demand, and thus output and employment will increase. But they are just as likely to overpredict the rate of inflation, in which case they will believe that real aggregate demand has fallen. The result is that output and employment will fall.

6. When the government adopts fiscal and monetary policies, people will rationally predict their effects. Given that people's predictions are equally likely to err on either side, fiscal and monetary policies are useless as means of controlling output and employment.

21.4   INFLATION AND UNEMPLOYMENT: THE MODERN KEYNESIAN POSITION

Keynesians in the 1950s and early 1960s looked to aggregate demand to explain inflation and unemployment. Their approach was typically that of the inflationary/deflationary gap model (see pages 538–9). Although they recognised the existence of some cost-push inflation and some equilibrium unemployment, these factors were seen as relatively constant. As a result, there was thought to be a relatively stable inverse relationship between inflation and unemployment, as depicted by the Phillips curve. Governments could trade off inflation against unemployment by manipulating aggregate demand.

Modern developments of the Keynesian model

Keynesians still see aggregate demand as playing the crucial role in determining the rate of inflation and the levels of output and employment. They still argue that the free market works inefficiently: it frequently fails to clear; price signals are distorted by economic power; most wages and many prices are 'sticky'; and, most important, the free market is unlikely to settle at full employment.

They still argue, therefore, that it is vital for governments to intervene actively to prevent either a slump in demand or an overexpansion of demand.

Nevertheless, the Keynesian position has undergone some major modifications in recent years (see section 16.5). This has been in response to apparent shifts in the Phillips curve and the inability of the traditional Keynesian model to explain it.

The breakdown of the Phillips curve in the 1970s and the growing problem of 'stagflation' (see page 680) led many Keynesians to focus on cost-push causes of inflation. These causes included increased power and militancy of trade unions, a growing concentration of monopoly power in industry, and rising oil and other commodity prices. The effect was to push the short-run Phillips curve outwards.

Later, with a decline in industrial unrest in the 1990s and a growth of international competition keeping prices down, the Phillips curve apparently shifted inwards again. Keynesians attributed this partly to a *decline* in cost-push inflation. (These cost-push explanations are examined in Case Study 21.3 on the student website.)

More recently, Keynesian analysis has incorporated three major modifications:

- An increased importance attached to equilibrium unemployment.
- A rationale for the persistence of demand-deficient unemployment.
- The incorporation of the theory of expectations: either adaptive or rational.

Changes in equilibrium unemployment

Changes in structural unemployment

Most Keynesians include growth in equilibrium unemployment as part of the explanation of the apparent rightward shift in the Phillips curve in the 1970s and 1980s. As we noted in Chapter 16, rather than the natural rate, some Keynesians prefer to speak of the *non-accelerating-inflation rate of unemployment,* which is known more simply as the NAIRU. This acknowledges that there exist market imperfections. The NAIRU can be thought of as the rate of

unemployment that is consistent with steady inflation in the near term.

Keynesians highlight the considerable structural rigidities that existed in the economy in a period of rapid industrial change. The changes include the following:

- Dramatic changes in technology. The microchip revolution, for example, made many traditional jobs obsolete.
- Competition from abroad. The introduction of new products from abroad, often of superior quality to domestic goods, or produced at lower costs, had led to the decline of many older industries: e.g. the textile industry.
- Shifts in demand away from the products of older labour-intensive industries to new 'high-tech' capital-intensive products.

Keynesians argue that the free market simply could not cope with these changes without a large rise in structural/technological unemployment. Labour was not sufficiently mobile – either geographically or occupationally – to move to areas where there were labour shortages or into jobs where there were skill shortages. A particular problem here was the lack of investment in education and training, with the result that the labour force was not sufficiently flexible to respond to changes in demand for labour.

1. *What effect did these developments have on (a) the Phillips curve; (b) the aggregate supply curve?*
2. *What policy implications follow from these arguments?*

From the mid-1980s up to the financial crisis of the late 2000s, structural unemployment was thought to have fallen as labour markets become more flexible and as various government supply-side policies took effect (see Chapter 24).

Hysteresis

If a recession causes a rise in unemployment which is not then fully reversed when the economy recovers, there is a problem of hysteresis (see page 509). Recessions can lead to a growing number of people becoming both deskilled and demotivated. What is more, many firms, in an attempt to cut costs, cut down on training programmes. In these circumstances, a rise in aggregate demand would not simply enable the long-term unemployed to be employed again. The effect is a rightward shift in the Phillips curve: a rise in the NAIRU. To reverse this, argue Keynesians, the government should embark on a radical programme of retraining.

Recessions also cause a lack of investment. The reduction in their capital stock means that many firms cannot respond to a recovery in demand by making significant increases in output and taking on many more workers. Instead they are more likely to raise prices. Unemployment may thus fall only modestly and yet inflation may rise substantially. The NAIRU increases: the Phillips curve shifts to the right.

These arguments hold in reverse. A period of sustained growth can reduce the NAIRU: the Phillips curve shifts to the left.

Are hysteresis effects likely to be asymmetrical (i.e. of different magnitude) following an economic boom rather than an economic slowdown?

The persistence of demand-deficient unemployment

Monetarists and new classical economists argue that markets, including the labour market, clear quickly, if not continuously. Keynesians point to frictions in the labour market which may prevent real wages from falling and helping to eliminate demand-deficient unemployment. Two major explanations for the persistence of real wage rates above equilibrium are efficiency wages and insider power. While we first came across these in Chapter 16 (see pages 506–509), we revisit them here in the context of the inflation–unemployment relationship.

■ *Efficiency wages.* Wage rates work not only to balance the demand and supply of labour but also to motivate workers. If real wage rates are reduced when there is a surplus of labour (demand-deficient unemployment), then those workers already in employment may become dispirited and work less hard. If, on the other hand, firms keep wage rates up, then by maintaining a well-motivated workforce, by cutting down on labour turnover and by finding it easier to attract well-qualified labour, firms may find that their costs are reduced: a higher real wage rate is thus more profitable for them. The maximum-profit real wage rate (the *efficiency wage rate*: see pages 291) is likely to be above the market-clearing real wage rate. Demand-deficient unemployment is likely to persist.
■ *Insider power.* If those still in employment (the insiders) are members of unions while those out of work (the outsiders) are not, or if the insiders have special skills or knowledge that give them bargaining power with employers while the outsiders have no influence, then there is no mechanism whereby the surplus labour – the outsiders – can drive down the real wage rate and eliminate the demand-deficient unemployment.

These two features help to explain why real wage rates did not fall during the recessions of the early 1980s and early 1990s. With the more flexible labour markets of more recent years, however, real wages did fall consistently in the period following the financial crisis (see Figure 15.13 on page 474). Over the period 2009–13, the annual rate of consumer price inflation typically exceeded annual earnings growth by 1.6 percentage points.

 How might the possibility of labour shirking affect the real wage firms are willing to pay?

The incorporation of expectations

Some Keynesians incorporate adaptive expectations into their models. Others incorporate rational expectations.

Either way, their models differ from monetarist and new classical models in two important respects:

■ Prices and wages are not perfectly flexible. Markets are characterised by various frictions and imperfections.
■ Expectations influence *output* and *employment* decisions, not just pricing decisions.

Price and wage rigidities are likely to be greater *downwards* than upwards. It is thus necessary to separate the analysis of a decrease in aggregate demand from that of an increase.

Expansion of aggregate demand

Unless the economy is at full employment or very close to it, Keynesians argue that an expansion of demand *will* lead to an increase in output and employment, even in the long run after expectations have fully adjusted.

In Figure 21.6, assume that the economy has a fairly high level of unemployment (U_1) but at the same time some cost inflation. Inflation is constant at π_1, with expectations of inflation at π_1 also. The economy is at point *a*.

Now assume that the economy begins to recover. Aggregate demand rises. As there is plenty of slack in the economy, output can rise and unemployment fall. The economy moves to point *b* on short-run Phillips curve I. The rise in inflation will feed through into expectations. The short-run Phillips curve will shift upwards. With adaptive expectations, it will initially shift up, say, to curve II.

But will the short-run Phillips curve not go on shifting upwards as long as there is any upward pressure on inflation? Keynesians reject this argument for two reasons:

■ If there is a gradual but sustained expansion of aggregate demand, firms, seeing the economy expanding and seeing their orders growing, will start to invest more and make longer-term plans for expanding their labour force. People will generally *expect* a higher level of output, and this optimism will cause that higher level of output to be produced. In other words, expectations will affect output

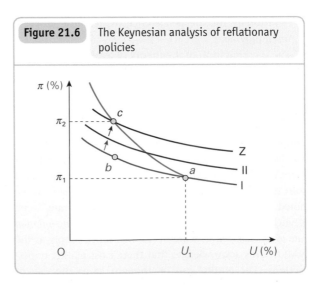

Figure 21.6 The Keynesian analysis of reflationary policies

and employment as well as prices. The Phillips curve will shift downwards to the left, offsetting (partially, wholly or more than wholly) the upward shift from higher inflationary expectations. The NAIRU has fallen.

■ If U_1 includes a considerable number of long-term unemployed, then the expansion of demand may be *initially* inflationary, since many of the newly employed will require some retraining (a costly exercise). But as these newly employed workers become more productive, their lower labour costs may offset any further upward pressure on wages from the expansion of demand. At the same time, the higher investment may embody new, more productive, techniques that will also help to prevent further acceleration in costs. These factors occurred in the 1990s as the economy recovered from recession.

It is quite likely that these effects can prevent any further rises in inflation. Inflation can become stable at, say, π_2, with the economy operating at point *c*. The short-run Phillips curve settles at position *Z*. There is thus a long-run downward-sloping Phillips curve passing through points *a* and *c*. What this analysis is assuming is that, in the medium to long run, the NAIRU itself is responsive to changes in real aggregate demand.

 Would it in theory be possible for this long-run Phillips curve to be horizontal or even upward sloping over part of its length?

If expectations are formed rationally rather than adaptively, there will merely be a quicker movement to this long-run equilibrium. If people rationally predict that the effect of government policy will be to move the economy to point *c*, then their predictions will bring this about. All rational expectations do is to bring the long run about much sooner! The theory of rational expectations on its own does not provide support specifically for either the new classical or the Keynesian position.

The lesson here for governments, however expectations are formed, is that a sustained, but moderate, increase in aggregate demand can lead to a sustained growth in aggregate supply. What should be avoided is an excessive and unsustainable expansion of aggregate demand, as occurred in the late 1980s in the UK and in the late 1990s in the USA. This will lead to a boom, only to be followed by a 'bust' and a consequent recession.

Contraction of aggregate demand

Many Keynesians argue that the short-run Phillips curve is kinked at the current level of real aggregate demand. A reduction in real aggregate demand will have only a slight effect on inflation, since real wages are sticky downwards. Unions may well prefer to negotiate a reduction in employment levels, preferably by natural wastage (i.e. not replacing people when they leave), rather than accept a reduction in real wages. Thus in Figure 21.7, to the right of point *a*, the short-run Phillips curve is very shallow.

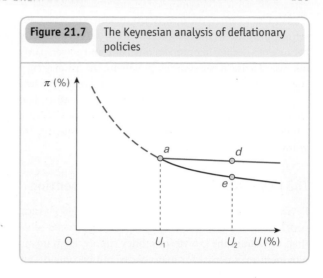

Figure 21.7 The Keynesian analysis of deflationary policies

As long as this curve is not totally horizontal to the right of *a*, the introduction of expectations into the analysis will cause the short-run curve to shift downwards over time (if unemployment is kept above U_1) as people come to expect a lower rate of inflation.

With *adaptive* expectations, however, the curve could shift downwards very slowly indeed. If a movement from point *a* to point *d* represents only a 1 per cent reduction in inflation, and if it takes, say, two years for this to be fully reflected in expectations, then if unemployment is kept at U_2, inflation will reduce (i.e. the curve shift downwards) by only 0.5 per cent a year. This may be totally unacceptable politically if inflation is already at very high levels, and if U_2 is also very high.

Even with *rational* expectations the response may be too slow. If there is a resistance from unions to receiving increases in wages below the current rate of inflation, or if they are attempting to 'catch up' with other workers, then even if they rationally predict the correct amount by which inflation will fall, inflation will fall only slowly. People will rationally predict the *resistance* to wage restraint, and sure enough, therefore, inflation will fall only slowly.

The worst scenario is when the government, in its attempt to eliminate inflation, keeps unemployment high for a number of years. As the core of long-term unemployed workers grows, an increasing number of workers become deskilled and therefore effectively unemployable. The effective labour supply is reduced, and firms find there is no longer a surplus of employable labour *despite* high unemployment. The NAIRU increases. A long-term equilibrium is reached at, say, point *e* with still substantial inflation. The *long*-run Phillips curve too may thus be relatively shallow to the right of point *a*.

 Some economists argue that recessions generate unemployment 'scarring' (i.e. various negative outcomes for the people unemployed and possibly broader society too). What might these scarring effects be and what is likely to be their longer-term impact?

As we saw earlier, the downward stickiness of wages was significantly less in the recession of 2008/9. This was partly because of a decline in union membership and power, partly because of a rise in part-time employment, the use of agency staff and the use of zero-hour contracts, and partly because of a willingness of people to accept lower wages rather than face the possibility of redundancy. This greater flexibility of labour markets gave a steeper Phillips curve to the right of point *a* than in previous recessions.

The Keynesian criticism of non-intervention

Keynesians are therefore highly critical of the new classical conclusion that governments should not intervene other than to restrain the growth of money supply. High unemployment may persist for many years and become deeply entrenched in the economy if there is no deliberate government policy of creating a steady expansion of demand.

Countries in the eurozone, such as Greece, Portugal and Spain, which have had to seek bailouts because of their high levels of debt have found themselves in this position. A condition of being granted bailouts has been to reduce public-sector debt. This has ruled out Keynesian expansionary fiscal policy. The very high levels of unemployment in these countries, especially amongst the young (rates of over 50 per cent in Greece and Spain in the 15–24 age group), has resulted in a problem of entrenchment and hysteresis that will make reductions in unemployment slow and difficult to achieve.

 Why is it important in the Keynesian analysis for there to be a steady expansion of demand?

Section summary

1. Modern Keynesians incorporate expectations into their analysis of inflation and unemployment. They also see an important role for cost-push factors and changes in equilibrium unemployment in explaining the position of the Phillips curve.

2. A growth in equilibrium unemployment in the 1970s and 1980s was caused by rapid changes in technology, greater competition from abroad and more rapid changes in demand patterns. It was also due to the persistence of unemployment beyond the recessions of the early 1980s and early 1990s and, to a lesser extent, the early 2010s, because of a deskilling of labour during the recessions (an example of hysteresis). The effect of increased equilibrium unemployment was to shift the Phillips curve to the right.

3. Demand-deficient unemployment may persist because real wage rates may be sticky downwards, even into the longer term. This stickiness may be the result of efficiency real wage rates being above market-clearing real wage rates and/or outsiders not being able to influence wage bargains struck between employers and insiders.

4. If expectations are incorporated into Keynesian analysis, the Phillips curve will become steeper in the long run (and steeper in the short run too in the case of rational expectations). It will not become vertical, however, since people will expect changes in aggregate demand to affect output and employment as well as prices.

5. If people expect a more rapid rise in aggregate demand to be sustained, firms will invest more, thereby reducing unemployment in the long run and not just increasing the rate of inflation. The NAIRU will fall. The long-run Phillips curve will be downward sloping.

6. The short- and long-run Phillips curves may be kinked. Reductions in real aggregate demand may have only a slight effect on inflation if real wage rates are sticky downwards.

21.5 INFLATION, UNEMPLOYMENT AND OUTPUT: CREDIBILITY AND CENTRAL BANKS

This chapter has examined alternative views on the relationships between unemployment and inflation. To do so we have used a Phillips curve framework. In this final section we examine these relationships in the modern context of central banks operating within targets.

We first look at why many governments have delegated the operation of monetary policy to central banks: i.e. giving them independence in setting interest rates and/or determining the money supply. Then we see how the Phillips curve and *DAD/DAS* frameworks can be used to analyse the determination of inflation, unemployment and output in the context of central banks operating with an inflation target.

Credibility and the delegation of monetary policy

If the natural rate hypothesis holds then policy makers cannot use demand management policy to affect real GDP (output) or the rate of unemployment, except, perhaps, in the short run. Output must adjust to its potential level, and unemployment to its natural rate. Depending on the process by which people form their inflationary expectations and the speed by which markets adjust to shocks, the movement of the goods and labour markets to equilibrium could be very rapid.

The increased interest among economists since the 1960s in the natural rate hypothesis has been one of the key reasons for governments delegating monetary policy to central banks, sometimes through legal statute. In the UK, for example, the Bank of England was given operational independence over monetary policy in 1997.

This delegation is usually for the making of policy decisions, such as setting interest rates or whether to engage in quantitative easing. Normally, governments still decide what the policy objective(s) of the central bank should be – whether it is to achieve a target rate of inflation set by the government, or to do this while being mindful of other objectives, such as economic growth and lower unemployment.

The case for delegating monetary policy was briefly presented in Chapter 16 (see page 511). As we saw there, the principal argument is that delegation will remove the inflation bias that can result from political interference in monetary policy. It is tempting for governments to boost aggregate demand and to try to reduce unemployment below the natural rate by the time of the next election. When governments behave in this way, it is likely to result in higher inflation – an **inflation bias**. We look at a model of inflation bias in Box 21.6.

The *EAPC* and *DAD/DAS* frameworks

EAPC *and* DAS *curves*

To understand the relationship between inflation and unemployment, it is therefore important to do so within the context of delegated monetary policy. To do this, we combine the dynamic aggregate demand and supply (*DAD/DAS*) analysis, which we looked at in section 20.3, with the expectations-augmented Phillips curve (*EAPC*) analysis of this chapter. Figure 21.8 illustrates the two models.

Figure 21.8(b) shows *DAD* and *DAS* curves. The *DAD* curve explicitly incorporates an inflation target pursued by a delegated central bank (see page 631). As we shall see, the *DAS* curve turns out to be closely related to the *EAPC*.

Figure 21.8(a) shows the expectations-augmented Phillips curve. The downward-sloping short-run *EAPC* illustrates the short-run trade-off between unemployment and inflation. A rise in aggregate demand (e.g. from point *a* to point *b*) will result in a movement up along the curve: there will be lower unemployment but at the cost of higher inflation. Meanwhile, the dynamic short-run aggregate supply (*DAS*) curve, (see page 631), shows a *positive* relationship between output and inflation: a rise in aggregate demand will result in a movement up along the curve (e.g. from point *a'* to point *b'*). Thus the *DAS* curve is essentially an alternative representation of the *EAPC*. However, rather than the rate of unemployment, we plot real national income (*Y*) on the horizontal axis.

The slopes of both the *DAS* curve and the *EAPC* therefore capture the potential short-run trade-off between inflation

---

> **Definition**
>
> **Inflation bias** The tendency of governments to pursue excessively expansionary monetary policies for political reasons, resulting in higher inflation than if the central bank was charged with targeting inflation.

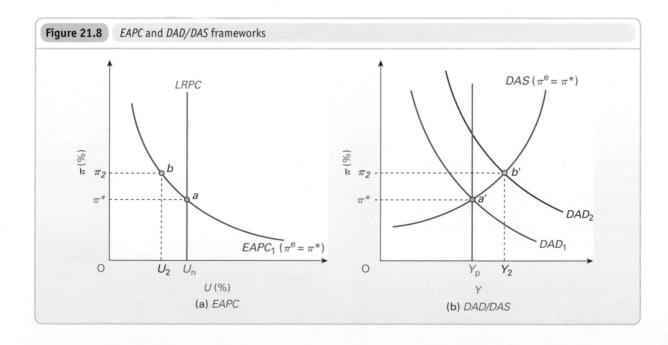

Figure 21.8 *EAPC* and *DAD/DAS* frameworks

(a) *EAPC*

(b) *DAD/DAS*

*BOX 21.6 | INFLATION BIAS

A new classical 'surprise' model

We can use the expectations-augmented Phillips curve (*EAPC*) framework and a new classical 'surprise' model to examine how excessive inflation arises. People are assumed to form rational expectations and markets clear rapidly.

The diagram shows various expectations-augmented Phillips curves (*EAPC*). We assume an absence of exogenous inflation shocks ($k = 0$) so that each *EAPC* reflects only differences in the expected inflation rate (π^e): the higher the expected rate, the vertically higher the *EAPC*.

The diagram also includes a series of government indifference curves. Each one depicts a particular level of satisfaction (or happiness) of the government. In this model, the government, not the central bank, has control of monetary policy. At any point along a particular indifference curve the government derives a given level of satisfaction from the various combinations of unemployment and inflation shown.

Note that, because higher rates of unemployment and inflation *reduce* satisfaction, the government's satisfaction is higher on those indifference curves that are closer to the origin. For example, satisfaction is higher on I_1 than it is on I_2, and so on. Note also that because we are measuring *undesirable* things on each axis, the curves slope differently from the traditional indifference curves which we examined in section 4.3: the ones here are bowed out, rather than bowed in.

 How would the policy maker's indifference curves be affected by the extent of their aversion to inflation?

The incentive for the government to stimulate the economy

Assume that the economy is currently at point *a* with both the goods and labour markets in equilibrium. People's expectations of inflation are zero. Given this, the government's optimal inflation–unemployment choice is at point *b*, with lower unemployment of U_1 but inflation of π_1. This is the highest level of government satisfaction that can be achieved along curve $EAPC_1$. The government's satisfaction is likely to be mirrored by the wider public it serves. Indeed, if

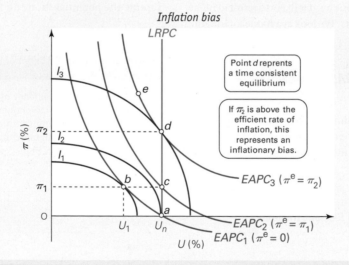

Inflation bias

> Point *d* reprents a time consistent equilibrium

> If π_2 is above the efficient rate of inflation, this represents an inflationary bias.

$EAPC_3$ ($\pi^e = \pi_2$)

$EAPC_2$ ($\pi^e = \pi_1$)

$EAPC_1$ ($\pi^e = 0$)

and economic activity. The latter is captured by unemployment in the case of the *EAPC* curve but by output (real national income) in the case of the *DAS* curve. Meanwhile, the vertical position of both curves is determined by inflationary expectations (π^e) and exogenous inflationary shocks (k). Higher inflationary expectations or negative inflationary shocks result in both curves moving vertically upwards. We shall return to Figure 21.8 below.

Okun's law

There exists a well-known relationship that captures the cyclical relationship between unemployment and output, known as **Okun's law**. The law is named after Arthur Okun

who in a 1962 paper investigated the relationship between unemployment and output in the USA. His work suggested that for every 1 percentage point that US unemployment was above its natural rate, US output would be 3 per cent below its potential output.

Definition

Okun's law The name given to the negative statistical relationship between the unemployment rate and deviations of output from potential output.

an election was to be held around this time its chances of electoral success are increased – people preferring lower unemployment (and higher output) and being prepared to put up with slightly higher inflation

To get to point *b*, the government needs to surprise the public by relaxing monetary policy, for example by providing greater liquidity to the financial system and so putting downward pressure on real interest rates (see section 19.1). The loosening of monetary policy then raises aggregate demand.

However, point *b* is not sustainable. People will revise their inflationary expectations upwards. Consequently, real aggregate demand will fall back to the economy's potential output level and unemployment will rise again to its natural rate. If nominal aggregate demand was to continue to grow at the new rate, the economy would settle at point *c*, with higher inflation (π_1) than before.

While the government can only temporarily increase its satisfaction by generating surprise inflation, it may, nonetheless, feel that this is worth doing, especially if it helps it to win an election.

The response of the public: the issue of the government's credibility

But of course the public knows that any gain is likely to be temporary. Workers, for instance, know that any temporary increase in economic activity would be followed a period where their real wages fall. Therefore, one possibility is that people keep their inflationary expectations sufficiently high that the government no longer benefits from generating further inflation and creating a surprise economic boom.

Consider point *d* in the diagram. Again, the economy is in equilibrium with unemployment at its natural rate. But, unlike the situation when the economy was at point *a*, the government no longer benefits from a surprise loosening of monetary policy. In simple terms, the now much higher inflation rate acts as a disincentive to government to generate surprise inflation. People would react badly to even higher inflation. The additional satisfaction to the

government, therefore, from moving to say point *e* and reducing unemployment is outweighed by the dissatisfaction generated by the higher inflation.

Point *d* is described as a 'consistent equilibrium'. The reason is that if the government says that it wants to target an inflation rate of π_2, this will be a ***time-consistent policy announcement***. This means that there is no incentive, once people have set their inflationary expectations, for the government to generate surprise inflation and conduct monetary policy inconsistent with validating this high inflation rate. An inflation announcement of π_2 is therefore *credible*. People believe that the government will stick to it.

By contrast, the government stating that it wants to target point *a*, with zero inflation, is a ***time-inconsistent policy announcement***. Once people have set their inflationary expectations at zero, the government then has an incentive to generate surprise inflation. In other words, it conducts monetary policy which generates a positive inflation rate. A zero inflation rate announcement by the government thus lacks ***credibility***: government has an incentive to renege on it. Credible policies, on the other hand, are ones that, once that they have been announced by policy makers, people believe will be carried through.

In the diagram, the credible inflation rate is π_2. At any point on the *LRPC* with an inflation rate below π_2 (i.e. below point *d*) there is an incentive for government to create surprise inflation.

If π_2 is above the rate that could be seen as desirable for the efficient functioning of the economy (generally thought by central banks to be around 2 per cent: see table in Box 21.7), then the government could be said to exhibit *inflationary bias*. If, for example, π_2 were 5 per cent and the efficient rate of inflation were 2 per cent, the government would be exhibiting an inflationary bias of 3 per cent (i.e. 5% − 2%).

 How would inflation bias be affected if the government placed considerable importance on its future reputation for controlling inflation?

Since Okun's law shows a close relationship between unemployment and output, movements along either *EAPCs* or *DAS* curves capture cyclical volatility: a boom would be represented by a movement up both curves (e.g. from *a* to *b* in Figure 21.8(a) and from *a'* to *b'* in Figure 21.8(b); a recession would be represented by a movement down both curves. Both curves can be used to analyse the business cycle and to debate the extent to which fluctuations in aggregate demand have enduring effects on economic activity.

 Why might changes in the unemployment rate not match one-for-one changes in the output gap?

Definitions

Time-consistent policy announcement A policy announcement where there is an incentive for the policy maker to stick to it over time.

Time-inconsistent policy announcement A policy announcement where there is an incentive for the policy maker to renege on it at a future date.

Credibility (of policies) Policies that people believe the government will carry out once they have been announced.

BOX 21.7   INFLATION TARGETING

The fashion of the age

Many countries have turned to inflation targeting as their main macroeconomic policy. The table gives the targets for a selection of countries (as of 2017).

Part of the reason is the apparent failure of discretionary macroeconomic policies. Discretionary fiscal and monetary policies suffer from time lags, from being used for short-term political purposes and from failing to straighten out the business cycle. But if discretionary policies have seemed not to work, why choose an inflation target rather than a target for the money supply or the exchange rate?

Money supply targets were adopted by many countries in the 1980s, including the UK, and this policy too was largely a failure. Money supply targets proved very difficult to achieve. As we have seen, money supply depends on the amount of credit banks create, and this is not easy for the authorities to control. Then, even if money supply is controlled, this does not necessarily mean that aggregate demand will be controlled: the velocity of circulation may change. Nevertheless, many countries do still target the money supply, although in most cases it is not the main target.

Exchange rate targets, as we shall see in Chapter 25, may have serious disadvantages if the equilibrium exchange rate is not the one that is being targeted. The main instrument for keeping the exchange rate on target is the rate of interest. But, as we shall see in Box 22.9 (on page 701), if the rate of interest is being used to achieve an exchange rate target, it cannot be used for other purposes, such as controlling aggregate demand or inflation. Raising interest rates to achieve an exchange rate target may lead to a recession.

Inflation targets have proved relatively easy to achieve. There may be problems at first, if the actual rate of inflation is way above the target level. The high rates of interest necessary to bring inflation down may cause a recession. But once inflation has been brought down and the objective is then simply to maintain it at the target level, most countries have been relatively successful. And the more successful they are, the more people will expect this success to be

maintained, which in turn will help to ensure this success.

So, have there been any problems with inflation targeting? Ironically, one of the main problems lay in its success. With worldwide inflation having fallen, and with global trade and competition helping to keep prices down, there was now less of a link between inflation and the business cycle. Booms no longer seemed to generate the inflation they once did. Gearing interest rate policy to maintaining low inflation could still see economies experiencing unsustainable booms, followed by recessions. Inflation may be controlled, but the business cycle may not be.

Some argue that the low interest rates seen in many countries during the first half of the 2000s helped to fuel unsustainable flows of lending. These boosted asset prices, including housing, which generated even higher levels of confidence among borrowers and lenders alike. However, by encouraging further investments that increasingly stretched the financial well-being of economic agents, the point was reached when a significant retrenchment by banks, business and people became inevitable.

Then there is the periodic problem of rising world inflation resulting from rapidly developing economies, such as China, India and Brazil. The resulting rise in food and commodity prices pushes up inflation rates around the world. Too strict an adherence to an inflation target could see higher interest rates and slow economic growth. This was a problem in many countries just after the financial crisis in 2010–12. Several countries, including the UK, had only just emerged from recession and their governments were embarking on a significant fiscal consolidation. Central banks faced a policy conundrum with the macroeconomic environment characterised on the one hand by increasing inflationary pressures but on the other by often sizeable negative output gaps. In fact, most central banks were to keep interest rates at historic lows.

 Why may there be problems in targeting (a) both inflation and money supply; (b) both inflation and the exchange rate?

Country	Inflation target (%)	Details
Australia	2–3	Average over the medium term
Brazil	4.5	Tolerance band of ±1.5 percentage points
Canada	2	Tolerance band of ±1 percentage points
Chile	3	Tolerance band of ±1 percentage point
Czech Republic	2	Tolerance band of ±1 percentage point
Eurozone	<2 but close to it	Average for eurozone as a whole; over medium term
Hungary	3	Tolerance band of ±1 percentage point
Iceland	2.5	
Israel	1–3	
Japan	2	
Mexico	3	Tolerance band of ±1 percentage point
New Zealand	2	Tolerance band of ±1 percentage point
Norway	2.5	
Peru	2	Tolerance band of ±1 percentage point
Poland	2.5	Tolerance band of ±1 percentage point
South Africa	3–6	
South Korea	2	Target for 2016–18
Sweden	2	
Switzerland	<2	
Thailand	2.5	Tolerance band of ±1.5 percentage points
UK	2	Forward-looking inflation target; tolerance band of ±1 percentage point

Source: Various central bank websites (see BIS central bank hub; see also *Central Bank News*).

KI 34
p445

KI 35
p451

KI 36
p451

Central banks and the DAD curve

The *DAD* curve allows us to analyse the economy in the modern context of central banks whose macroeconomic objectives include targeting inflation. Box 21.7 provides an indication of the number of central banks targeting, to one degree or another, the rate of inflation.

The *DAD* curve shows a *negative* relationship between output and the rate of inflation. As we saw in section 20.2, this is explained by central banks responding to higher inflation by raising nominal and real interest rates. The extent to which they do raise interest rates will reflect their policy remits and, hence, their aversion to inflation. The impact of higher interest rates on aggregate demand will then depend on the transmission mechanisms through which changes in real interest rates operate (see section 19.1).

The *slope* of the *DAD* curve is flatter the more inflation averse the central bank and the more interest-rate elastic is aggregate demand (see page 631). Meanwhile, *shifts* in the *DAD* curve will be caused by exogenous shocks to aggregate demand – in other words, changes to aggregate demand brought about by factors other than the rate of inflation causing the central bank to adjust interest rates.

How would financial accelerator effects (see section 19.4) affect the DAD curve?

Combining the EAPC and DAD/DAS frameworks

Because of the close relationship between changes in unemployment and output, much of the earlier analysis in this chapter using the *EAPC* framework could readily have been undertaken through the lens of the *DAS* curve alongside the *DAD* (dynamic aggregate demand) curve. To illustrate this, let us return to Figure 21.8.

Assume that the economy is in equilibrium with inflation at the target rate π^*, unemployment at its natural rate U_n and output at its potential level Y_p. This is represented by point a in the *EAPC* framework, and by point a' in the *DAD/DAS* framework. Now assume that there is an unexpected increase in aggregate demand. The increase in aggregate demand causes the *DAD* curve to move rightwards from DAD_1 to DAD_2 in Figure 21.8(b).

The economy expands in the short run. In the *DAD/DAS* framework we move along the *DAS* curve to point b' and output expands to Y_2. This is mirrored in the *EAPC* framework by a movement along $EAPC_1$ from a to b. We can also see from both diagrams that the short-run boost in economic activity (fall in the unemployment rate and rise in output) is accompanied by a rise in the rate of inflation from π^* to π_2.

The role of the central bank. Our interest throughout this chapter has been on how the economy adjusts to shocks, such as an increase in aggregate demand. Hence, we have been concerned about the role that markets and expectations play in that adjustment. The incorporation of the *DAD*

curve allows us to take this one step further and consider the effect of central banks in this adjustment. Hence, how would central banks with inflation rate targets affect the relationship between inflation and unemployment or output?

For simplicity, assume that an inflation-targeting central bank responds to the rise in aggregate demand by tightening its monetary stance. Assume also that it does this under the belief that the increase in aggregate demand will persist for some time and that the increase will not affect the economy's *potential* output.

By tightening monetary policy, and hence shifting the *DAD* curve leftwards from DAD_2 to DAD_1, the central bank can also help to keep inflationary expectations anchored at π^*. (If inflationary expectations were to adjust upwards this would lead to a vertical upward movement of both the *EAPC* and the *DAS* curve. This would generate a different adjustment path.)

Of course, the analysis here is based on a series of assumptions. Throughout the chapter we have seen that economists hold different views about the ways in which economies behave in the face of frequent economic shocks. The point here is that the central banks are an important factor in shaping this behaviour.

Indeed, if people believe that central banks will be successful in keeping inflation roughly at the target rate, this is likely to affect the shape of the *EAPC* and make it much flatter. We can see from the chart in Box 15.6 (see page 476) that variations in UK inflation in recent years have been relatively small, while variations in unemployment have been quite considerable. Some of the changes in unemployment have been due to changes in labour markets, and especially a greater labour market flexibility causing a movement left in the natural rate of unemployment (or NAIRU). But some have been due to fluctuations in real aggregate demand. For example, there was a large rise in unemployment in 2008 and 2009, following the financial crisis.

The central bank's remit. The more assiduous the central bank is perceived to be in keeping to the inflation target, the flatter the *EAPC* and *DAS* curve will be. People's expectations will be anchored at the target rate. If, however, the central bank's remit was also to be mindful of output and employment and, as a result, it was prepared to accept some fluctuations in inflation, the *EAPC* and *DAS* curve will be steeper.

Box 21.8 looks at how the *EAPC* and *DAD/DAS* frameworks can be combined to help analyse how economies might adjust in the face of supply side shocks.

The divergent views of different economists – from the market flexibility assumption of the new classicists to the market imperfections assumption of modern Keynesians – have different implications for macroeconomic policy.

The next chapter looks at demand-side policy – both fiscal and monetary. It also looks at whether the approach to them should be one based on rules (such as a target for

BOX 21.8	INFLATION SHOCKS AND CENTRAL BANKS	EXPLORING ECONOMICS

Combining the *EPAC* and *DAD/DAS* frameworks

As we saw in section 21.1, the vertical position of the expectations-augmented Phillips curve (*EAPC*) is determined by the expected rate of inflation (π^e) and by exogenous cost pressures on inflation (k). Since the dynamic aggregate supply (*DAS*) curve is an alternative representation of the *EAPC*, these factors also affect the vertical position of the *DAS*. We combine both frameworks here to analyse an adverse supply-side shock ($k > 0$). We assume that this takes the form of a temporary period of higher commodity price inflation.

Assume that the economy is in equilibrium with no output gap ($Y = Y_p$), unemployment at its natural rate U_n and inflation at its target rate π^*. This is represented by point *a* in the *EAPC* framework (Figure (a)), and by point *a'* in the *DAD/DAS* framework (Figure (b)). There then occurs an increase in commodity price inflation which causes a rise in the rate at which firms' real non-labour costs increase.

The *EAPC* and *DAS* curve move vertically upwards because the rate of inflation is now higher at any level of economic activity (unemployment or output). The *EAPC* moves from $EAPC_1$ to $EPAC_2$ and the *DAS* curve from DAS_1 to DAS_2. The equivalent vertical differences *ac* and *a'c'* reflect the exogenous cost factor k.

The rate of inflation π rises above its target rate π^*. The response of the central bank is to raise the real rate of interest to dampen inflation. Even though the shock may be thought to be temporary, the central bank is likely to see the

raising of interest rates as necessary to keep inflationary expectations anchored at the target inflation rate. More generally, the extent to which rates rise will be determined by the remit of the central bank. This is reflected in the slope of *DAD* curve with a more inflation-averse central bank having a flatter *DAD* curve.

As real interest rates rise and real aggregate demand falls, there is a movement along the *DAD* curve from *a'* to *b'*. This is reflected in the *EAPC* framework by a move from *a* to *b*. The economy experiences both a negative output gap and higher inflation. Therefore, the economy incurs a period of *stagflation*. The more inflation-averse is the central bank, the larger will be the fall in output but the smaller the rise in inflation.

However, as the negative supply shock subsides the *DAS* curve and *EAPC* move back vertically downwards. As they do, real interest rates fall. Eventually the economy will have adjusted to its original equilibrium.

1. *If the supply-side shock persists, explain how the economy will move to points c and c'.*
2. *Draw five separate graphs, known as impulse response functions, to plot the path of the unemployment rate, inflation, output, nominal interest rates and real interest rates (y-axis) against time (x-axis) to reflect the analysis in this box.*

KI 36
p451

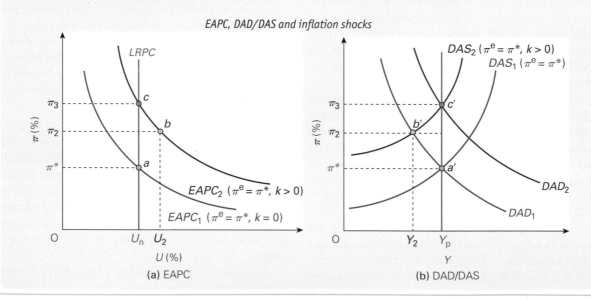

EAPC, DAD/DAS and inflation shocks

(a) EAPC

(b) DAD/DAS

public-sector borrowing or a target for inflation) or one based on discretion, where policies are varied according to circumstances.

The chapter then concludes by developing an integrated model of the economy bringing together the *IS/MP, DAD/*

DAS and *EAPC* frameworks and relates them to macroeconomic policy.

Then in Chapter 23 we look at the supply side of the economy: at the causes of growth in potential output and supply-side policy.

Section summary

1. Many governments around the world have delegated monetary policy to their central banks. Consequently, many central banks are charged with targeting inflation, though their remits are often supplemented by other macroeconomic objectives.

2. New classical and monetarist ideas have helped provide the theoretical justifications for central bank independence. Delegating monetary policy, it is argued, can eliminate the inflation bias that would otherwise arise from monetary policies lacking credibility.

3. Policy announcements lack credibility and are time inconsistent when there is an incentive for policy makers to renege on them. By depoliticising monetary policy, it is argued that low inflation target announcements become more credible. This allows people to reduce their inflationary expectations thereby reducing actual inflation.

4. The dynamic aggregate supply curve is an alternative representation of the expectations-augmented Phillips curve, but with real national income rather than unemployment on the horizontal axis. We can view the behaviour of the economy and the relationship between inflation and economic activity through either the *EAPC* or the *DAD/DAS* frameworks.

5. The incorporation of the dynamic aggregate demand curve allows us to consider more formally the role of inflation-targeting central banks in affecting the behaviour of economies that are frequently hit by economic shocks, such as fluctuations in aggregate demand.

END OF CHAPTER QUESTIONS

1. Assume that inflation depends on two things: the level of aggregate demand, indicated by the inverse of unemployment $(1/U)$, and the expected rate of inflation $(\pi^e{}_t)$. Assume that the rate of inflation (π_t) is given by the equation

$$\pi_t = (48/U - 6) + \pi^e{}_t$$

Assume initially (year 0) that the actual and expected rate of inflation is zero.

   (a) What is the current (natural) rate of unemployment?

   (b) Now assume in year 1 that the government wishes to reduce unemployment to 4 per cent and continues to expand aggregate demand by as much as is necessary to achieve this. Fill in the rows for years 0 to 4 in the following table. It is assumed for simplicity that the expected rate of inflation in a given year $(\pi^e{}_t)$ is equal to the actual rate of inflation in the previous year (π_{t-1}).

Year	U	$48/U-6$	+	π^e	=	π
0	...	...	+	...	=	...
1	...	...	+	...	=	...
2	...	...	+	...	=	...
3	...	...	+	...	=	...
4	...	...	+	...	=	...
5	...	...	+	...	=	...
6	...	...	+	...	=	...
7	...	...	+	...	=	...

   (c) Now assume in year 5 that the government, worried about rising inflation, reduces aggregate demand sufficiently to reduce inflation by 3 per cent in that year. What must the rate of unemployment be raised to in that year?

   (d) Assuming that unemployment stays at this high level, continue the table for years 5 to 7.

2. In the accelerationist model, if the government tries to maintain unemployment below the natural rate, what will determine the speed at which inflation accelerates?

3. What is the difference between adaptive expectations and rational expectations?

4. How can adaptive expectations of inflation result in clockwise Phillips loops? Why would these loops not be completely regular?

5. For what reasons may the NAIRU increase?

6. What is meant by inflation bias? What factors affect the potential magnitude of inflation bias?

7. Using the integrated *DAD/DAS* and *EAPC* framework, analyse the effect of an unexpected increase in aggregate demand assuming that markets adjust relatively rapidly. Compare the adjustment path of the economy when inflationary expectations remain anchored with that when expectations are based on actual inflation in the previous period.

8. In what sense is it true to say that the Phillips curve is horizontal today?

Online resources

Additional case studies on the student website

21.1 **Explaining the shape of the short-run Phillips curve.** This shows how money illusion on the part of workers can explain why the Phillips curve is downward sloping.

21.2 **The quantity theory of money restated.** An examination of how the vertical long-run *AS* curve in the adaptive expectations model can be used to justify the quantity theory of money.

21.3 **Cost-push factors in Keynesian analysis.** How Keynesians incorporated cost-push inflation into their analysis of shifts in the Phillips curve.

Websites relevant to this chapter

See sites listed at the end of Chapter 22 on page 712.

Fiscal and Monetary Policy

Both fiscal and monetary policy can be used to control aggregate demand. Excessive growth in aggregate demand can cause unsustainable short-term growth and higher rates of inflation. Too little aggregate demand can result in a recession, with negative growth and rising unemployment.

Fiscal policy seeks to control aggregate demand by altering the balance between government expenditures and taxation. Monetary policy seeks to control aggregate demand by directly controlling money supply or by altering the rate of interest and then backing this up by any necessary changes in money supply.

In the first three sections of this chapter we examine fiscal and monetary work; how effective they are likely to be in controlling aggregate demand; and what are the potential pitfalls in their use.

We then turn to consider the arguments as to how much discretion or control policy makers should have over fiscal and monetary policy. Should governments adopt fixed targets for policy (e.g. inflation targets) or should they adjust policies according to circumstances? This is a debate reinvigorated by the global financial and economic crisis of the late 2000s and the sluggish growth of many economies since.

Finally, we integrate the *EAPC, IS/MP* and *DAD/DAS* models from earlier chapters. This allows us to analyse simultaneously the relationships between unemployment, output, inflation and interest rates in the context of central banks with specific macroeconomic objectives, such as an inflation rate target. We then apply the framework to focus on the possible adjustment paths of economies hit by shocks and what this means for the paths of key macroeconomic variables.

22.1 FISCAL POLICY AND THE PUBLIC FINANCES

Fiscal policy involves the government manipulating the level of government expenditure and/or rates of tax. An *expansionary* fiscal policy will involve raising government expenditure (an injection into the circular flow of income) or reducing taxes (a withdrawal from the circular flow). A *deflationary* (i.e. a contractionary) fiscal policy will involve cutting government expenditure and/or raising taxes.

But why might government wish to change its fiscal position? In other words, what are the roles for fiscal policy?

Roles for fiscal policy

Aggregate demand

Fiscal policy may be used to affect aggregate demand. There are two principal reasons for this.

Prevent the occurrence of fundamental disequilibrium in the economy. The government may wish to remove any severe deflationary or inflationary gaps. Hence, expansionary fiscal policy could be used to prevent an economy experiencing a severe or prolonged recession, such as that experienced in the Great Depression of the 1930s or in 2008/9 when substantial tax cuts and increased government expenditure were used by many countries, including the UK and the USA, to combat the onset of recession. Likewise, deflationary fiscal policy could be used to prevent rampant inflation, such as that experienced in the 1970s.

Stabilisation policies. The government may wish to smooth out the fluctuations in the economy associated with the business cycle. This involves reducing government expenditure or raising taxes when the economy begins to boom. This will dampen down the expansion and prevent 'overheating' of the economy, with its attendant problems of rising inflation and a deteriorating current account balance of payments. Conversely if a recession looms, the government should cut taxes or raise government expenditure in order to boost the economy.

If these stabilisation policies are successful, they will amount merely to 'fine-tuning'. Problems of excess or deficient demand will never be allowed to get severe. Any movement of aggregate demand away from a steady growth path would be quickly 'nipped in the bud'.

Aggregate supply

Fiscal policy can also be used to influence aggregate supply. For example, government can increase its expenditure on education, training and infrastructure, or give tax incentives for investment and research and development. Such initiatives would be intended to increase the rate of growth of the economy's potential output and reduce the natural rate of unemployment. Supply-side policies are considered in more detail in Chapter 23.

In section 22.2 we look at how fiscal policy can be used. But, first it is important to understand some of the terminology of government spending and taxation and some of the key fiscal indicators.

Government finances: some terminology

Government

When analysing government finances the term 'government' is often used interchangeably with that of 'general government'. It is important to note that general government includes both *central* and *local* government. Separate balance sheets can be presented for each. An analysis of both may be particularly important in countries where local government has considerable autonomy from central government, such as varying tax rates or raising money by issuing debt instruments.

The terms **budget deficit** and **budget surplus** are frequently used in the context of government, and especially central government. In fact, these terms can be applied to any organisation to assess its financial well-being by comparing expenditure with revenues.

If general government's expenditure (including benefits) exceeds its revenue from taxation it would be running a budget deficit, sometimes known simply at the **general government deficit**. Conversely, when general government's revenues exceed its expenditure there is a **general government surplus**.

For most of the past 50 years, governments around the world have run budget deficits. In the late 1990s and early 2000s, however, many countries, the UK included, made substantial efforts to reduce the size of general government deficits, and some achieved budget surpluses for periods of time. The position changed dramatically in 2008/9, however, as governments around the world increased their expenditure and cut taxes in an attempt to stave off recession. Government deficits in many countries soared.

Definitions

Fiscal policy Policy to affect aggregate demand by altering the balance between government expenditure and taxation.

Budget deficit The excess of an organisation's spending over its revenues. When applied to government it is the excess of its spending over its tax receipts.

Budget surplus The excess of an organisation's revenues over its expenditures. When applied to government it is the excess of its tax receipts over its spending.

General government deficit (or surplus) The combined deficit (or surplus) of central and local government.

Table 22.1   General government deficits/surpluses and debt as a percentage of GDP

	General government deficits (−) or surpluses (+)		General government debt	
	Average 1997–2007	Average 2008–18	Average 1997–2007	Average 2008–18
Belgium	−0.7	−3.2	104.3	103.2
France	−2.6	−4.4	62.3	88.9
Germany	−2.4	−0.6	61.6	72.4
Greece	−6.3	−7.4	102.8	161.5
Ireland	+1.6	−7.9	35.6	85.8
Italy	−2.9	−3.1	104.6	123.9
Japan	−5.9	−6.2	152.4	228.6
Netherlands	−0.6	−2.2	51.7	61.8
Portugal	−4.2	−5.5	58.5	114.9
Spain	−0.5	−6.7	51.0	82.0
Sweden	+0.9	−0.2	52.3	39.7
UK	−1.6	−5.9	38.9	80.3
USA	−2.7	−7.4	60.5	99.5
Eurozone	−2.1	−3.1	68.6	87.3

Note: Data for 2017–18 are forecasts.

Source: Based on data from *AMECO database*, Tables 16.3 and 18.1 (European Commission, DG ECFIN).

Deficits, debt and borrowing. To finance their deficits, governments will have to borrow (e.g. through the issue of bonds (gilts) or Treasury bills). As we saw in section 18.3, this will lead to an increase in the money supply to the extent that the borrowing is from the banking sector. The purchase of bonds or Treasury bills by the (non-bank) private sector, however, will not lead to an increase in the money supply.

Deficits represent *annual* borrowing: a flow concept. The accumulated deficits over the years (minus any surpluses) gives total *debt*: a stock concept. It is the total amount owed by the government. Central and general government debt are known as **national debt** and **general government debt** respectively.

Note that the national debt is not the same thing as the country's overseas debt. In the case of the UK, only around 27 per cent of national debt is owed overseas. The remainder is owed to UK residents. In other words, the government finances its budget deficits largely by borrowing at home and not from abroad.

Table 22.1 shows general government deficits/surpluses and debt for selected countries. They are expressed as a proportion of GDP.

Why are historical and international comparisons of deficit and debt measures best presented as proportions of GDP?

As you can see, in the period from 1997 to 2007, all the countries, with the exception of Ireland and Sweden, ran an average deficit. In the period from 2008 to 2018 the average deficits increased for most countries. And the bigger the deficit, the faster debt increased.

Public sector

To get a more complete view of public finances, we would need to look at the entire public sector: namely, central government, local government and public corporations.

There is one important caveat to this: we have to be aware that corporations can transfer between the public and private sectors (a result of privatisation or nationalisation). Consequently, public finance statistics can be distorted by such movements. As we shall see in Chapter 24, in recent times many countries have privatised major industries, such as transport, energy and telecommunications.

The financial crisis of the late 2000s saw various banking corporations transferred wholly or partly to the public sector (nationalisation) in order to ensure their survival and the stability of the financial system. In the UK, this included banking groups such as Lloyds, Northern Rock and the Royal Bank of Scotland. The hope was to return these institutions to the private sector in due course. Case 22.1 on the student website discusses the UK government's financial interventions during the financial crisis and their cost to the public purse.

Definitions

National debt The accumulated deficits of central government. It is the total amount owed by central government, both domestically and internationally.

General government debt The accumulated deficits of central plus local government. It is the total amount owed by general government, both domestically and internationally.

Current and capital expenditures. In presenting the public finances, it has become the custom to distinguish between **current** and **capital expenditures**. Current expenditures involve the operational expenditures of the public sector, including the wages and salaries of public-sector staff, and the payments of welfare benefits. Capital expenditures are public-sector investment. Examples include expenditure on roads, hospitals and schools. Like all types of investment, they give rise to a stream of benefits over time.

So why might we wish to distinguish between current and capital expenditures? One reason for the distinction is that capital expenditures generate long-term economic benefits which can be enjoyed into the future. In other words, by benefiting more than just the current generation, capital expenditure may help to promote intergenerational fairness.

Another reason is that capital expenditures can increase potential output and thereby positively affect future growth rates. This, in turn, could increase future tax revenues and help to provide more sustainable foundations for the public finances over the longer term.

However, the distinction between current and capital expenditures and the associated reasons for it is not without issues. Teachers and doctors, for instance, whose wages form part of public-sector current expenditure, would reasonably argue that their work generates benefits for future generations.

Figure 22.1 shows the scale and composition of public-sector expenditures in the UK since the 1960s. The figures are presented as shares of GDP. Over the period, total spending has averaged 40 per cent of GDP, current spending 34 per cent of GDP and capital spending just 6 per cent of GDP. However, a closer inspection of the chart shows that capital spending by the UK government decreased consistently as a proportion of GDP from the late 1960s through to 2000. It then rose during the 2000s but has since declined again (but not as fast as current expenditure).

 What could have driven the changes in the composition of UK public expenditure? Do such changes matter?

Final expenditure and transfers. We can also distinguish between *final expenditure* on goods and services, and *transfers*. This distinction recognises that the public sector directly adds to the economy's aggregate demand through its spending on goods and services, including the wages of public-sector workers, but also that it redistributes incomes between individuals and firms. Transfers include subsidies and benefit payments, such as payments to the unemployed.

Public-sector borrowing and debt. If the public sector spends more than it earns, it will have to finance the deficit

---

Definitions

Current expenditure Recurrent spending on goods and factor payments.

Capital expenditure Investment expenditure; expenditure on assets.

Final expenditure Expenditure on goods and services. This is included in GDP and is part of aggregate demand.

Transfers Transfers of money from taxpayers to recipients of benefits and subsidies. They are not an injection into the circular flow but are the equivalent of a negative tax (i.e. a negative withdrawal).

Figure 22.1 UK Public-sector current and capital expenditures

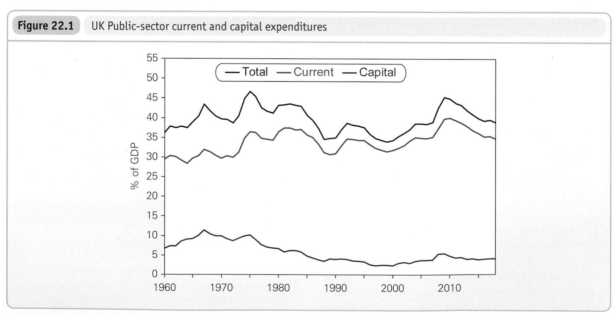

Note: Data based on financial years; forecasts from 2017/18.
Sources: Public Finances Databank, Office for Budget Responsibility.

through borrowing, known as *public-sector net borrowing (PSNB)*. The principal form of borrowing is through the sale of gilts (bonds). The precise amount of money the public sector needs to borrow in any one year is known as the *public-sector net cash requirement (PSNCR)*. It differs slightly from the PSNB because of time lags in the flows of public-sector incomes and expenditure.

As with central and general government debt, *public-sector debt* is the current stock of the accumulated deficits over the years. In assessing the sustainability of this stock of debt – a theme we return to shortly – it is usual to focus on *public-sector net debt*. This is the sector's gross debt less its liquid assets, which comprise official reserves and deposits held with financial institutions.

Key fiscal indicators

Sustainability of the public finances

We can use a range of fiscal indicators to assess the financial position of government and the whole public sector. The most commonly used indicators are those that convey information about the prudence or sustainability of the public sector's finances.

We can identify four measures which, in one way or another, allow us to say something about prudence or sustainability. First is *public-sector net borrowing* (or its close counterpart in the public-sector net cash requirement); second is *public-sector net debt*. As we have seen, the first captures the relative flow of the public sector's receipts in comparison to its total expenditure, while the second measures the accumulated debt stock that has arisen from the sector's deficits.

A third indicator of sustainability is the *public-sector current budget deficit*. If public-sector revenues are less than the sum of its *current* expenditures, then the public sector runs a deficit on the current budget. This means that the public sector, by not even meeting the full cost of its current expenditures out of its receipts, is also unable to meet any of the cost of its capital expenditures. As well as implications for the immediate sustainability of public finances, the constraints that a current budget deficit can place on capital expenditures could, as we discussed above, have implications for future economic growth and for the well-being of future generations.

TC 14
p458

The fourth indicator of sustainability is the *primary surplus (or deficit)*. This occurs when public-sector receipts are greater (or less) than public-sector expenditures *excluding* interest payments. The primary surplus is important for analysing the path of the *public-sector debt-to-GDP ratio*. For this ratio to fall requires that the public sector operates a given primary surplus-to-GDP ratio.

KI 26
p303

To see this a little more readily we can use a rule of thumb that connects the primary surplus-to-GDP (S_p/Y_n) ratio and the public-sector debt-to-GDP (D/Y_n) ratio. Each ratio is

calculated using nominal values, so Y_n, for example, is nominal GDP. Then, to calculate the required primary surplus-to-GDP ratio to maintain the current value of the public-sector debt-to-GDP ratio, we multiply the current debt-to-GDP ratio (D/Y_n) by the sum of the *real* rate of interest (r) minus the *real* economic growth rate ($\Delta Y_r/Y_r$). This gives us what is referred to as the 'debt sustainability rule':

$$\frac{S_p}{Y_n} = \frac{D}{Y_n} \times \left(r - \frac{\Delta Y_r}{Y_r} \right) \qquad (1)$$

To illustrate the sustainability arithmetic, consider a country where the public-sector net debt-to-GDP ratio (D/Y_n) is currently 0.5 (i.e. 50 per cent). Assume that the real interest rate on borrowing (r) is 3 per cent and the annual real rate of economic growth ($\Delta Y_r/Y_r$) is 1 per cent. For the debt-to-GDP ratio to remain at its current level, the country will need to run a primary surplus equivalent to 1 per cent of GDP ($0.5 \times (3 - 1)$). If, however, the current debt-to-GDP ratio were currently 1 (i.e. 100 per cent), then it would need to run a primary surplus-to GDP ratio of 2 per cent ($1 \times (3 - 1)$).

Thus a country where the average real interest rate on public debt instruments (r) is greater than the real economic growth rate ($\Delta Y_r/Y_r$) will have to run primary surpluses for its debt-to-GDP ratio to fall. Furthermore, the required primary surplus-to-GDP ratio will be higher if the country has an already high debt-to-GDP ratio. In other words, the sustainability arithmetic tends to get more difficult for governments to comply with, the higher their existing debt-to-GDP ratio.

 What primary balance-to-GDP ratio would a country need to run to sustain a debt-to-GDP ratio of 60 per cent if the real interest rate is 2 per cent and economic growth is 4 per cent?

Definitions

Public-sector net borrowing (PSNB) The difference between the expenditures of the public sector and its receipts from taxation and the revenues from public corporations.

Public-sector net cash requirement (PSNCR) The (annual) deficit of the public sector, and thus the amount that the public sector must borrow. In the UK the principal measure, which takes into account financial transactions by the public sector, is known as the public-sector net cash requirement.

Public-sector net debt Gross public-sector debt minus liquid financial assets.

Public-sector current budget deficit The amount by which public-sector expenditures classified as current expenditures exceed public-sector receipts.

Primary surplus (or deficit) The situation when the sum of public-sector expenditures excluding interest payments on public-sector debt is less than (greater than) public-sector receipts.

Figure 22.2   UK public-sector deficit balances and debt stock

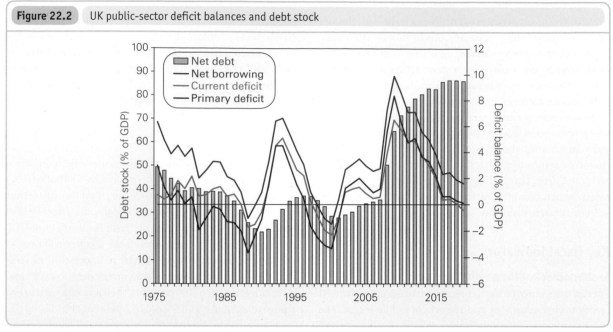

Note: Data based on financial years; forecasts from 2017/18.
Sources: Public Finances Databank, Office for Budget Responsibility.

Figure 22.2 shows the four key fiscal indicators for the UK since 1975. During this time, net borrowing has averaged 3.4 per cent, the current deficit 1.4 per cent and the primary deficit 1.0 per cent of GDP. We can also see how the deterioration in the deficit balances and the interventions to help shore up the financial system in the late 2000s led to a marked increase in the public-sector net debt-to-GDP ratio.

The business cycle and the public finances

When analysing the fiscal indicators, it is important to recognise that their values are affected by the state of the economy. In other words, there is both a structural and a cyclical component determining the path of our fiscal measures.

If the economy is booming, with people earning high incomes, the amount paid in taxes will be high. In a booming economy the level of unemployment will be low. Thus the amount paid out in unemployment benefits will also be low. The combined effect of increased tax revenues and reduced benefits is to improve public-sector balances, such as public-sector net borrowing. Indeed, rather than a reduced deficit there could be public-sector surplus. By contrast, if the economy were depressed, tax revenues would be low and the amount paid in benefits would be high. The public-sector deficit would thus be high.

 How is the public-sector debt-to-GDP ratio likely to be affected by the state of the economy?

Definition

Structural deficit (or surplus) The public-sector deficit (or surplus) that would occur if the economy were operating at the potential level of national income: i.e. one where there is a zero output gap.

Since, therefore, the values of fiscal indicators are not entirely due to deliberate government policy, they may not give a very good guide to government intentions or to the longer-term financial well-being of government. By cyclically-adjusting measures of public-sector deficits or surpluses we remove their cyclical component. The deficit or surplus that would arise if the economy were producing at the potential level of national income is termed the ***structural deficit or surplus***. Remember that the potential level of national income is where there is no excess or deficiency of aggregate demand: where the output gap is zero (see page 457 and Box 15.3).

This relationship between the public-sector deficit or surplus and the state of the economy is illustrated in Figure 22.3. The tax revenue function is upward sloping. Its slope depends on tax rates. The government expenditure function (which in this diagram includes transfer payments, such as unemployment benefits) is drawn as downward sloping, showing that at higher levels of income and employment

Figure 22.3   National income and the size of the public-sector deficit or surplus

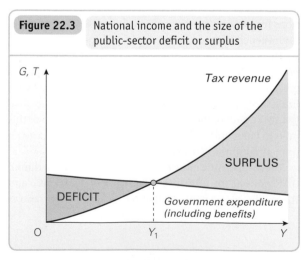

BOX 22.1 **PRIMARY SURPLUSES AND SUSTAINABLE DEBT**

The fiscal arithmetic of government debt

One way of thinking about the sustainability of the public finances is the conditions needed for the public sector's debt-to-GDP ratio to cease rising. It turns out that given an existing debt-to-GDP ratio (D/Y_n), an expected annual real rate of interest on public-sector debt (r) and an expected annual rate of real economic growth ($\Delta Y_r/Y_r$) the public sector needs to run a particular primary surplus-to-GDP ratio (S_p/Y_n). As explained in the text, this sustainability condition can be written as:

$$\frac{S_p}{Y_n} = \frac{D}{Y_n} \times \left(r - \frac{\Delta Y_r}{Y_r} \right)$$

A primary surplus occurs when the public sector's revenues are greater than its expenditures when excluding its interest payments on its debts. Only in the case where the economic growth rate is greater than the real interest rate can the public sector run a primary deficit without its debt-to-GDP ratio rising.

General government and the financial crisis

Concerns about the sustainability of public-sector finances were put into sharp focus following the financial crisis of 2007–8. Governments in many countries made interventions to shore up their financial systems and to support aggregate demand as private-sector expenditures fell sharply.

The following table helps us to understand the evolution of the finances of general government in a sample of advanced economies following the financial crisis. The table shows the debt-to-GDP ratio in each country in 2008 and 2016. It also shows the average primary surplus-to-GDP ratio and economic growth rate over the period from 2009 to 2016

as well as the average real short-term interest rate for each economy. The latter should be treated as indicative of the average interest rate facing government on its debt. The actual interest costs could be somewhat different, not least because of the turbulence in government debt markets during this period and because, more generally, governments issue a range of debt instruments with different terms to maturity.

The final column of the table shows an estimate for each country of their required primary surplus-to-GDP ratio to maintain the initial debt-to-GDP ratio in 2008 based on the average real interest rate and growth rate that they subsequently experienced from 2009 to 2016. In most cases countries would have been able to run primary deficits, as indicated by the negative values. Despite this, if we compare the required primary balance values with the actual values we can see that only Germany ran a primary balance which exceeded that needed to stabilise the debt-to-GDP ratio.

Hence, other than in Germany, the countries in our sample experienced primary balances that fell short of the values needed to stabilise the debt-to-GDP ratio. Furthermore, in many cases the debt-to-GDP ratio rose very sharply indeed. This is important because it needs even healthier primary balances in the future for countries to maintain the now higher debt-to-GDP ratio. Consequently, the sustainability constraints become ever more binding on the fiscal choices of governments. This reduces their ability to use fiscal policy to cushion economies against adverse economic shocks.

 Some argue that the sustainability arithmetic is even more significant for countries in the eurozone. What might be the explanation for this argument?

General government fiscal indicators

| | General government gross debt-to-GDP, % | | 2009–16 averages | | | |
| | | | Primary surplus-to-GDP) (%) | Real short-term interest rates (%) | Economic growth (% p.a.) | Required primary surplus-to-GDP (%) |
	2008	2016				
France	68.0	96.0	−2.6	0.1	0.6	−0.4
Germany	65.1	68.3	1.2	−0.5	1.0	−1.0
Greece	109.4	179.0	−3.7	0.4	1.0	−0.6
Ireland	42.4	75.4	−6.6	0.8	4.7	−1.7
Portugal	71.7	130.4	−2.3	−0.3	−0.5	0.2
Spain	39.5	99.4	−5.2	−0.3	−0.2	−0.1
UK	50.2	89.3	−4.1	−1.0	1.2	−1.1
USA	72.8	107.4	−4.3	−0.8	1.5	−1.7
Japan	184.6	238.6	−5.1	0.6	0.6	0.0

Source: Based on data in *AMECO database* (European Commission, DGECFIN).

KI 26
p303

less is paid out in benefits. As can be clearly seen, there is only one level of income (Y_1) where there is a public-sector financial balance. Below this level of income there will be a public-sector deficit. Above this level there will be a surplus. The further income is from Y_1, the bigger will be the deficit or surplus.

The fiscal stance

The government's *fiscal stance* refers to whether it is pursuing an expansionary or contractionary fiscal policy. Does the fact that countries such as the UK, which in most years run public-sector deficits, mean that their government's fiscal stance is mainly expansionary? Would the mere existence of a surplus mean that the stance was contractionary? The answer is no. Whether the economy expands or contracts depends on the balance of *total* injections and *total* withdrawals.

What we need to focus on is *changes* in the size of the deficit or surplus. If the deficit this year is lower than last year, then (*ceteris paribus*) aggregate demand will be lower this year than last. The reason is that either government expenditure (an injection) must have fallen, or tax revenues (a withdrawal) must have increased, or a combination of the two.

To conclude, the size of the deficit or surplus is a poor guide to the stance of fiscal policy. A large deficit *may* be due to a deliberate policy of increasing aggregate demand, but it may be due simply to the fact that the economy is depressed.

Section summary

1. The public sector comprises general government and public corporations. There exist a range of fiscal indicators that allow us to analyse the fiscal position and well-being of the public sector or its component sectors.

2. Key fiscal indicators include those that assess the sustainability of the public sector's finances. We can estimate a required primary surplus-to-GDP ratio needed to prevent the ratio of public-sector debt to GDP from rising. Countries with higher existing debt-to-GDP ratios, higher real interest costs and lower real rates of economic growth will need to operate larger primary surpluses (or smaller deficits) to prevent the ratio from rising further.

3. The government's fiscal policy influences the size of its budget deficit or surplus. Its size alone, however, is a poor guide to the government's fiscal stance. A large deficit, for example, may simply be due to the fact that the economy is in recession and therefore tax receipts are low. A better guide is whether the change in the deficit or surplus will be expansionary or contractionary.

22.2 THE USE OF FISCAL POLICY

The fiscal choices of government relate to decisions about public expenditures and taxation. These choices can shape future government receipts or expenditures. For example, the design of a country's income tax or benefits system evolves over time. As governments make policy changes they shape the tax and benefit systems, including their relationship with macroeconomic variables such as national income or unemployment.

More generally, today's choices by government can commit future governments to certain expenditure and taxation flows. Indeed, some expenditure and taxation receipts *automatically* change as the macroeconomic environment changes. For example, income tax receipts automatically increase as nominal national income increases. The design of the income tax system and the rates and bands determine just how much receipts will change as nominal national income changes.

However, governments also make *discretionary* choices which deliberately manipulate taxes or levels of spending to affect current levels of aggregate demand, regardless of the automatic effects that occur across the business cycle. These decisions may then be reversed as economic conditions change. For example, Box 22.2 (and Case Study 22.1 on the student website) discusses the fiscal measures taken by the UK government following the financial crisis. These measures initially focused on stimulating aggregate demand. Then, as the policy focus shifted to reducing the burgeoning public-sector deficit, fiscal policy was tightened.

In this section we begin by considering how expenditure and taxation flows automatically change across the business cycle and, in so doing, help to stabilise the economy. We then move on to discuss why governments might make deliberate changes to taxation and government expenditures and how effective they may be in managing the economy.

Automatic fiscal stabilisers

We saw from Figure 22.3 that the size of the public-sector surplus or deficit will automatically vary according to the level of national income. The effect of this will be to reduce

---

Definition

Fiscal stance How expansionary or contractionary the Budget is.

the level of fluctuations in national income without the government having to take any deliberate action.

Taxes whose revenues rise as national income rises and benefits that fall as national income rises are called **automatic stabilisers**. They have the effect of reducing the size of the multiplier, reducing both upward and downward movements of national income. Thus, in theory, the business cycle should be dampened by such built-in stabilisers. The more taxes rise or benefits fall, the bigger will be the *mpt* (the net marginal tax propensity). Remember that we defined this as the proportion of any rise in income going in taxes and reduced benefits. The bigger the *mpt,* the smaller will be the multiplier and the greater will be the stabilising effect.

 Draw an injections and withdrawals diagram, with a fairly flat W curve. Mark the equilibrium level of national income. Now draw a second steeper W curve passing through the same point. This second W curve would correspond to the case where tax rates were higher. Assuming now that there has been an increase in injections, draw a second J line above the first. Mark the new equilibrium level of national income with each of the two W curves. You can see that national income rises less with the steeper W curve. The higher tax rates are having a dampening effect on the multiplier.

The effectiveness of automatic stabilisers

Automatic stabilisers have the obvious advantage that they act instantly as soon as aggregate demand fluctuates. By contrast, it may take some time before the government can institute discretionary changes in taxes or government expenditure, especially if forecasting is unreliable.

Nevertheless, automatic stabilisers can never be the complete answer to the problem of fluctuations. Their effect is merely to reduce the multiplier – to reduce the severity of fluctuations, not to eliminate them altogether.

In addition, they tend to suffer two specific drawbacks: adverse effects on aggregate supply and the problem of 'fiscal drag'. Let us examine each in turn.

Adverse supply-side effects

High tax rates may discourage effort and initiative. The higher the marginal tax rate (*mpt*), the greater the stability provided by the tax system. But the higher tax rates are, the more likely they are to create a disincentive to work and to invest. For example, steeply progressive income taxes may discourage workers from doing overtime or seeking promotion. A higher marginal rate of income tax is equivalent to a higher marginal cost of working. People may prefer to work less and substitute leisure for income. The substitution effect of more progressive taxes may thus outweigh the income effect. These issues were examined in detail in section 11.2 (see pages 336–8).

High unemployment benefits may increase equilibrium unemployment. High unemployment benefits, by reducing the hardship of being unemployed, may encourage people to spend longer looking for the 'right' job rather than taking the first job offered. This has the effect of increasing unemployment and thus of shifting the Phillips curve to the right. This is because a longer average period of job search represents a higher level of friction in the economy and thus a higher natural (or equilibrium) level of unemployment.

High income-related benefits may create a poverty trap. The higher the level of income-related benefits and the more steeply they taper off, the greater will be the problem of the 'poverty trap'. What is the point in unemployed people seeking jobs, or people in very low-paid jobs seeking better ones, if as a result they lose their benefits and end up being little or no better off than before? The more that people are discouraged in this way, the lower will be the level of aggregate supply. (The question of the poverty trap was also examined in Chapter 11 (see pages 342–3).)

The problem of fiscal drag

Automatic stabilisers help to reduce upward and downward movements in national income. This is fine if the current level of income is the *desirable* level. But suppose that there is currently a deep recession in the economy, with mass unemployment. Who would want to stabilise the economy at this level?

In these circumstances, if the economy began to recover, the automatic stabilisers would act as a drag on the expansion. This is known as **fiscal drag**. By reducing the size of the multiplier, the automatic stabilisers reduce the magnitude of the recovery. Similarly, they act as a drag on discretionary policy: the more powerful the automatic stabilisers are, the bigger the change in *G* or *T* that would be necessary to achieve a given change in national income.

Discretionary fiscal policy

Automatic stabilisers cannot prevent fluctuations. They merely reduce their magnitude. If there is a fundamental disequilibrium in the economy or substantial fluctuations in other injections and withdrawals, the government may choose to *alter* the level of government expenditure or the rates of taxation. This is known as **discretionary fiscal policy**. It involves *shifting* the *J* and *W* lines.

Definitions

Automatic fiscal stabilisers Tax revenues that rise and government expenditure that falls as national income rises. The more they change with income, the bigger the stabilising effect on national income.

Fiscal drag The tendency of automatic fiscal stabilisers to reduce the recovery of an economy from recession.

Discretionary fiscal policy Deliberate changes in tax rates or the level of government expenditure in order to influence the level of aggregate demand.

In the UK, changes in taxation and some changes in government expenditure are announced by the Chancellor of the Exchequer in the Budget (now held in the autumn). Some of these changes apply to the coming financial year; some apply to the next financial year or even the one after that.

Since Budgets are normally held only once per year, 'fine-tuning' aggregate demand on a week-by-week or month-by-month basis is left to monetary policy – to changes in interest rates (see section 22.3). Very occasionally, however, changes are made between Budgets. Thus in September 2008 the government raised the threshold above which stamp duty must be paid on house purchase in an attempt to help first-time buyers. Then, in the Pre-Budget Report of November 2008, as recession deepened, VAT was cut and planned public-sector projects were brought forward (see Box 22.2).

Note that discretionary changes in taxation or government expenditure, as well as being used to alter the level of aggregate demand (fiscal policy), are also used for other purposes, including the following:

- *Altering aggregate supply*. Examples include tax incentives to encourage people to work more, or increased government expenditure on training or on transport infrastructure (e.g. roads and railways). We look at such 'supply-side policies' in Chapter 23.
- *Altering the distribution of income*. As Chapter 11 explained, taxation and benefits are the government's major means of redistributing incomes from the rich to the poor.

Let us now compare the relative effects of changing government expenditure and changing taxes. Will a £100 million increase in government expenditure have the same effect as a £100 million cut in taxes? Will the multiplier be the same in each case?

Discretionary fiscal policy: changing G

If government expenditure on goods and services (roads, health care, education, etc.) is raised, this will create a full multiplied rise in national income. The reason is that all the money gets spent and thus all of it goes to boosting aggregate demand.

Show the effect of an increase in government expenditure by using (a) the injections and withdrawals diagram; (b) the income/expenditure diagram (see Figures 17.8 and 17.10 on pages 534 and 536).

Discretionary fiscal policy: changing T

Cutting taxes by £1 million will have a smaller effect on national income than raising government expenditure on goods and services by £1 million. The reason is that cutting taxes increases people's *disposable* incomes, of which only *part* will be spent. Part will be withdrawn into extra savings, imports and other taxes. In other words, not all the tax cuts will be passed on round the circular flow of income as extra expenditure.

The proportion of the cut in taxes that will be withdrawn is given by the *mpw,* and the proportion that will circulate round the flow is given by the mpc_d. Thus if the mpc_d were 4/5, the tax multiplier would only be 4/5 of the normal multiplier.[1] If the mpc_d were 2/3, the tax multiplier would only be 2/3 of the normal multiplier, and so on. The formula for the tax multiplier (k_t) becomes

$$k_t = mpc_d \times k$$

Thus if the normal multiplier were 5 (given an mpc_d of 4/5), the tax multiplier would be $4/5 \times 5 = 4$. If the normal multiplier were 4 (given an mpc_d of 3/4), the tax multiplier would be $3/4 \times 4 = 3$, and so on. It should be obvious from this that the tax multiplier is always 1 less than the normal multiplier:

$$k_t = k - 1$$

Since the tax multiplier is smaller than the government expenditure multiplier, to achieve a given rise in income through tax cuts would therefore require a bigger budget deficit than if it were achieved through increased government expenditure. In other words, the required tax cut would be bigger than the required government expenditure increase.

Why will the multiplier effect of government transfer payments such as child benefit, pensions and social security be less than the full multiplier effect given by government expenditure on goods and services? Will this 'transfer payments multiplier' be the same as the tax multiplier? (Clue: will the recipients of such benefits have the same mpc_d as the average person?)

The effectiveness of discretionary fiscal policy

How successful will discretionary fiscal policy be? Can it 'fine-tune' demand? Can it achieve the level of national income that the government would like it to achieve?

There are two main problem areas with discretionary fiscal policy. The first concerns the *magnitude* of the effects. If G or T is changed, how much will *total* injections and withdrawals change? What will be the size of the multiplier? How much will a change in aggregate demand affect output and employment, and how much will it affect prices?

The second concerns the *timing* of the effects. How quickly can policy be changed and how quickly will the changes affect the economy?

Problems of magnitude

Before changing government expenditure or taxation, the government will need to calculate the effect of any such change on national income, employment and inflation. Predicting these effects, however, is often very unreliable for a number of reasons.

---

1 Strictly speaking, the tax multiplier is negative, since a *rise* in taxes causes a *fall* in national income.

Predicting the effect of changes in government expenditure

A rise in government expenditure of £x may lead to a rise in total injections (relative to withdrawals) that is smaller than £x. This will occur if the rise in government expenditure *replaces* a certain amount of private expenditure. For example, a rise in expenditure on state education may dissuade some parents from sending their children to private schools. Similarly, an improvement in the National Health Service may lead to fewer people paying for private treatment.

Crowding out. If the government relies on **pure fiscal policy** – that is, if it does not finance an increase in the budget deficit by increasing the money supply – it will have to borrow the money from the non-bank private sector. It will thus be competing with the private sector for finance and will have to offer higher interest rates. This will force the private sector also to offer higher interest rates, which may discourage firms from investing and individuals from buying on credit. Thus government borrowing *crowds out* private borrowing. In the extreme case, the fall in consumption and investment may completely offset the rise in government expenditure, with the result that aggregate demand does not rise at all.

Figure 22.4 illustrates the extent of crowding out. (It is the same as Figure 19.8 on page 601.) The rise in government expenditure shifts the injections line from J_1 to J_2 in Figure 22.4(a). The full multiplier effect of this would be a rise in national income to Y_2. However, the increased government expenditure leads to an increased demand for money. In Figure 22.4(b), the liquidity preference curve shifts to L'. This raises the real interest rate to r_2. Note that we are assuming that the money supply is purely *exogenous* – i.e. does not vary with the demand for money – and that, therefore, the money supply 'curve' is a vertical straight line (M_s).

The higher real rate of interest reduces investment. The injections line falls below J_2, and, as a result, national income does not rise as far as Y_2. The amount by which actual income falls short of Y_2 measures the extent of crowding out.

The amount of crowding out from pure fiscal policy depends on three things:

- The shape of the L curve. The flatter the curve, the less will interest rates rise. A greater amount of liquidity will be released from idle balances and there will be a bigger increase in the velocity of circulation.
- Whether money supply is exogenous. If the extra demand for money leads to banks creating extra credit, the money supply curve will be upward sloping, not vertical. The more money is created, the flatter will be the M_s curve, the less interest rates will rise and the less will be the crowding out.
- The responsiveness of investment (and consumption) to a change in real interest rates. The more responsive investment is to a rise in real interest rates, the more will the J curve shift downwards and the bigger will be the crowding-out effect.

If the fiscal policy is not *pure* fiscal policy, if the extra government borrowing is financed by borrowing from the banking sector, then the supply of money curve will shift to the right. If it were to shift as far as M'_s, the real rate of interest would remain at r_1 and there would be no crowding out.

 How do people's expectations influence the extent of crowding out?

Predicting the effect of changes in taxes

A cut in taxes, by raising people's real disposable income, increases not only the amount they spend but also the amount they save. The problem is that it is not easy to predict the relative size of these two increases. In part it depends on whether people feel that the cut in tax is only temporary, in which case they may simply save the extra disposable income, or permanent, in which case they may adjust their consumption upwards.

Definition

Pure fiscal policy Fiscal policy that does not involve any change in money supply.

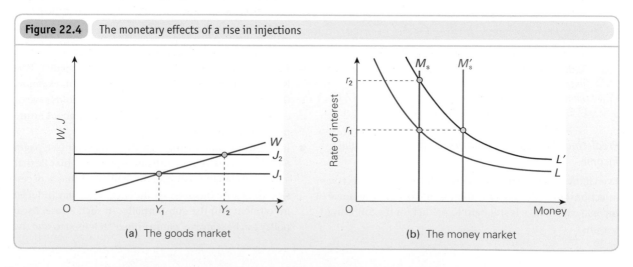

Figure 22.4 The monetary effects of a rise in injections

(a) The goods market

(b) The money market

BOX 22.2 THE FINANCIAL CRISIS AND THE UK FISCAL POLICY YO-YO

Trying to find the balance between rules and discretion

Fiscal rules prior to the financial crisis

On being elected in 1997, the UK's Labour government introduced two fiscal rules.

The golden rule. First, under its 'golden rule', it pledged over the cycle to achieve a *current budget balance,* where total receipts equal total current expenditures (i.e. excluding capital expenditures). This rule was designed not to unduly inhibit the automatic stabilisers from working and recognised both the current and future economic benefits of investment spending.

Sustainable investment rule. Second, under its 'sustainable investment rule', the government set itself the target of maintaining public-sector net debt at no more than 40 per cent of GDP, again averaged over the economic cycle. This rule, in conjunction with the golden rule, was designed to signal to the public the government's commitment to sustainable public finances.

The rules provided a framework within which discretionary policy choices would be made. They inevitably placed some constraints on these choices but the economic benefits were thought to be worthwhile – until the financial crisis began to unfold.

What followed was an initial expansionary policy as attempts were made to mitigate the worst of the economic slowdown. But then, with a new government in place and with a burgeoning budget deficit, the UK turned rapidly to a policy of fiscal consolidation. Within a short space of time the stance of fiscal policy changed markedly: a fiscal policy yo-yo.

Expansionary discretion

The impact of the financial crisis on economic growth in the UK was stark. The UK economy entered recession in the second quarter of 2008. After having expanded by an average of 2.8 per cent per year in the five-year period ending in 2007, the UK economy contracted in 2008 by 0.6 per cent and then by 4.3 per cent in 2009.

The severity of the economic downturn, the government argued, required more discretion than its fiscal policies allowed it. Consequently, its fiscal rules were lifted. The hope was that they could be reinstated in due course.

In the Pre-Budget Report of November 2008, amongst other measures, the Labour government introduced a 13-month cut in VAT from 17.5 per cent to 15 per cent. It also brought forward from 2010/11 £3 billion of capital spending on projects such as motorways, new social housing, schools and energy efficiency.

The effect of the capital spending projects was to increase public-sector gross investment to 5.3 per cent and 5.5 per cent of GDP in 2008/9 and 2009/10 respectively (see Figure 22.1 on page 672). In the previous 10 years the typical amount of public-sector gross investment spending had been just 3.1 per cent of GDP.

Meanwhile, as the chart shows, total government spending (excluding financial interventions) began to rise rapidly, fuelled by rising transfer payments on the back of the faltering economy, peaking at just over 45 per cent in 2009/10.

The UK came out of recession in the second quarter of 2009 after five consecutive quarters of declining output which saw the economy shrink by 6.3 per cent. Meanwhile, the rate of unemployment, which had stood at 5.2 per cent at the start of 2008, peaked at 8 per cent in early 2010 and stood at 7.8 per cent in May when 13 years of Labour government came to an end. Not only did this mark a change of government as a Conservative–Liberal Democrat coalition took charge, but it also a marked a change in the direction of fiscal policy.

Consolidation and the fiscal mandate

In 2009/10, public-sector net borrowing hit 9.9 per cent of GDP, up from 2.6 per cent in 2007/8 (see the chart). Consequently, public-sector net debt grew rapidly (see Figure 22.2 on page 674). From £557 billion (35.5 per cent of GDP) in 2007/8 it rose to £1.0 trillion (64.8 per cent of GDP) by 2009/10.

The response of the new government was to begin a policy of consolidation. The framework for this was to be known as the *fiscal mandate*. The initial mandate was for a balanced current budget (after adjusting for the position in the economic cycle) five years ahead. Therefore, at the end of a rolling five-year forecast period public-sector receipts should

 Do theories of the long-run and short-run consumption function help us to understand consumer reactions to a change in taxes? (See section 17.1 and Case Studies 17.1, 17.2, 17.3 and 17.4 on the student website.)

Predicting the resulting multiplied effect on national income

Even if the government *could* predict the net initial effect on injections and withdrawals, the extent to which national income will change is still hard to predict for the following reasons:

■ The size of the *multiplier* may be difficult to predict. This is because the mpc_d and mpw may fluctuate. For example, the amount of a rise in income that households save or consume will depend on their expectations about future price and income changes.

■ Induced investment through the *accelerator* (see pages 542–5) is also extremely difficult to predict. It may be that a relatively small fiscal stimulus will be all that is necessary to restore business confidence, and that induced investment will rise substantially. In such a case, fiscal policy can be seen as a 'pump primer'. It is used to *start* the

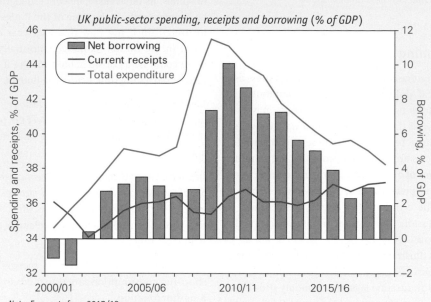

UK public-sector spending, receipts and borrowing (% of GDP)

Note: Forecasts from 2017/18.
Source: *Public Finances Databank*, Office for Budget Responsibility.

at least equal public-sector current expenditures, after adjusting for the economy's output gap. This mandate was supplemented by a target for public-sector net debt as a percentage of GDP to be falling by 2015/16.

To achieve this, the government embarked on a series of spending cuts and tax rises. This started with a 'discretionary consolidation' of £8.9 billion in 2010/11 comprising spending cuts of £5.3 billion and tax increases worth £3.6 billion. It was announced that the consolidation would continue up to 2015/16. By the end of 2015/16 the government planned to have delivered a discretionary consolidation of £122 billion, with £99 billion coming from discretionary reductions in spending and £23 billion from tax increases. As it turned out, however, in real terms total public-sector spending fell by just 1.5 per cent between 2010/11 and 2014/15.

The principal fiscal objectives were thus not met during the 2010–15 parliamentary period, although the government claimed that 'significant progress' had been made on its fiscal consolidation.

During the 2015–20 Parliament, the fiscal mandate was to be amended. This ultimately resulted in a looser set of rules, with targets (a) to reduce cyclically adjusted public-sector net borrowing to below 2 per cent of GDP by 2020/21 and (b) for public-sector net debt as a percentage of GDP be falling in 2020/21. The government believed that these rules struck a balance between ensuring the long-term sustainability of the public finances and providing government with sufficient discretion to provide further support for the economy, particularly with the uncertainty arising from of the UK's move to leave the European Union.

 Is it possible to design a fiscal framework that is sufficiently flexible to deal with all the shocks and events that economies face?

process of recovery, and then the *continuation* of the recovery is left to the market. But for pump priming to work, businesspeople must *believe* that it will work. Business confidence can change very rapidly and in ways that could not have been foreseen a few months earlier.

- The behaviour of commercial banks may also be hard to predict. Credit conditions may be pro-cyclical, perhaps significantly so, resulting in a financial accelerator (see pages 611–13). In the presence of financial accelerator effects small changes in fiscal policy can have amplified effects on national income.

- Multiplier/accelerator interactions. If the initial multiplier and accelerator effects are difficult to estimate, their interaction will be virtually impossible to estimate. Small divergences in investment from what was initially predicted will become magnified as time progresses.

Random shocks

Forecasts cannot take into account the unpredictable, such as the attack on the World Trade Center in New York in September 2001. Even events that, with hindsight, should have been predicted, such as the banking crisis of 2007–9, often are not. Unfortunately, unpredictable or unpredicted events do occur and may seriously undermine the government's fiscal policy.

 Give some examples of these random shocks.

Problems of timing

Fiscal policy can involve considerable time lags. If these are long enough, fiscal policy could even be *de*stabilising. Expansionary policies taken to cure a recession may not come into effect until the economy has *already* recovered and is experiencing a boom. Under these circumstances, expansionary policies are quite inappropriate: they simply worsen the problems of overheating. Similarly, contractionary policies taken to prevent excessive expansion may not take effect until the economy has already peaked and is plunging into recession. The contractionary policies only deepen the recession.

This problem is illustrated in Figure 22.5. Path (a) shows the course of the business cycle without government intervention. Ideally, with no time lags, the economy should be dampened in stage 2 and stimulated in stage 4. This would make the resulting course of the business cycle more like path (b), or even, if the policy were perfectly stabilising, a straight line.

With time lags, however, contractionary policies taken in stage 2 may not come into effect until stage 4, and expansionary policies taken in stage 4 may not come into effect until stage 2. In this case, the resulting course of the business cycle will be more like path (c). Quite obviously, in these circumstances 'stabilising' fiscal policy actually makes the economy less stable.

There are five possible lags associated with fiscal policy.

Time lag to recognition. Since the business cycle can be irregular and forecasting unreliable, governments may be unwilling to take action until they are convinced that the problem is serious.

Time lag between recognition and action. Most significant changes in government expenditure have to be planned well in advance. The government cannot increase spending on motorways overnight or suddenly start building new hospitals. As far as taxes are concerned, these can normally be changed only at the time of the Budget, and will not be instituted until the new financial year or at some other point in the future. As Budgets normally occur annually, there could be a considerable time lag if the problems are recognised a long time before the Budget.

Time lag between action and changes taking effect. A change in tax rates may not immediately affect tax payments, as some taxes are paid in arrears and new rates may take a time to apply.

Time lag between changes in government expenditure and taxation and the resulting change in national income, prices and employment. The multiplier round takes time. Accelerator effects take time. The multiplier and accelerator go on interacting. It all takes time.

Consumption may respond slowly to changes in taxation. The short-run consumption function tends to be flatter than the long-run function.

If the fluctuations in aggregate demand can be forecast, and if the lengths of the time lags are known, then all is not lost. At least the fiscal measures can be taken early and their delayed effects can be taken into account.

Fiscal rules

Given the problems of pursuing active fiscal policy, many governments in recent years took a much more passive approach. Instead of the policy being changed as the economy changes, countries applied a set of fiscal rules. These rules typically relate to measures of government deficits and to the stock of accumulated debt. Taxes and government expenditure can then be planned to meet these rules.

However, designing rules for fiscal policy can be problematic. Economies are regularly hit by shocks. Some shocks may

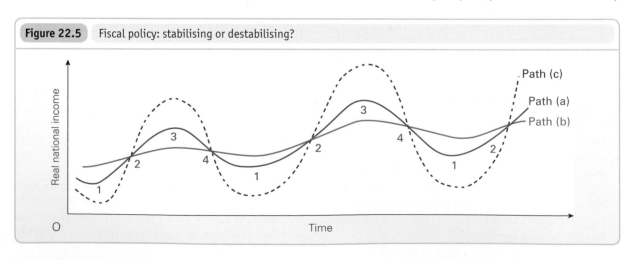

Figure 22.5 Fiscal policy: stabilising or destabilising?

BOX 22.3   RIDING A SWITCHBACK

A parable for Chancellors

Imagine that you are driving a car along a straight but undulating road. These undulations are not regular: some of the hills are steep, some are gentle; some are long, some are short.

You are given the instruction that you must keep the car going at a constant speed. To do this, you will need to accelerate going up the hills and brake going down them.

There is a serious problem, however. The car is no ordinary car. It has the following distinctly unusual features:

■ The front windscreen and side windows are blacked out, so you cannot see where you are going! All you can see is where you have been by looking in your rear-view mirror.
■ The brake and accelerator pedals both work with a considerable and unpredictable delay.
■ The car's suspension is so good that you cannot feel whether you are going up or downhill. You can only judge this by looking in your mirror.
■ Finally (you are relieved to know), the car has a special sensor and automatic steering that keep it in the correct lane.

As you are going along, you see that the road behind you is higher, and you realise that you are going downhill. The car gets faster and faster. You brake – but nothing happens. In your zeal to slow the car down, you put your foot down on the brake as hard as you can.

When the brake eventually does come on, it comes on very strongly. By this time, the car has already reached the bottom of the hill. As yet, however, you do not realise this and are still braking. But now the car is going up the next hill with the brakes still on. Looking in your mirror, you eventually realise this. You take your foot off the brake and start accelerating. But the pedals do not respond. The car is still slowing down rapidly, and you only just manage to reach the top of the hill.

Then, as you start going down the other side, the brakes eventually come off and the accelerator comes on . . .

This famous parable – first told by Frank Paish, Professor of Economics at the LSE, some 40 years ago – demonstrates how 'stabilising' activity can in fact be destabilising. When applied to fiscal policy, long and uncertain time lags can mean that the government can end up stimulating the economy in a boom and contracting it in a slump.

So what should be done? One alternative, of course, would be to try to reduce the time lags and to improve forecasting. But failing this, the best policy may be to do nothing: to take

a 'steady as you go' or 'fixed throttle' approach to running the economy. Going back to the car analogy, a fixed throttle will not prevent the car from going faster downhill and slower uphill, but at least it will not make the speed even more irregular.

A recent version of the parable

In an article in the *New Statesman* on what Keynes' response would have been to the recovery and getting the public-sector deficit down, Vince Cable, the then UK Business Secretary, wrote:

> As in many economic policy disputes, much of the ideological rhetoric conceals different forecasting assumptions – in respect of the cyclical, as opposed to structural, deficit; the influence of asset prices on consumer behaviour; the impact of the unorthodox monetary policy of quantitative easing (QE) and its interaction with the velocity of circulation of money; and the weight to be attached to business confidence and sentiment in financial markets. Amid such uncertainty, economic policymaking is like driving a car with an opaque windscreen, a large rear-view mirror and poor brakes.[1]

So what are the policy implications of this uncertainty and the time lags in response to government policy initiatives? The Coalition government saw the answer in a fiscal rule of getting the deficit down and thereby restoring long-term confidence in financial markets and encouraging private investment.

Critics of the government argued that policy needed to be flexible and responsive to current circumstances. Even with the time lags associated with fiscal policy, it was probably better to ease back on cutting the deficit so quickly if demand appeared to falter rather than just sticking with the planned government expenditure cuts.

But at least there were the automatic fiscal stabilisers – the car's accelerator would automatically come on and the brake would be eased if the economy slowed down.

  What would a fixed throttle approach to fiscal policy involve?

1 Vince Cable, 'Keynes would be on our side', *New Statesman*, 12 January 2011.

---

require more discretion than the current rules allow for. Hence, how flexible should any rules be?

Following the severe disruption to the global economy that occurred with the credit crunch of 2008, countries around the world resorted to discretionary fiscal policy to boost aggregate demand. Many abandoned fiscal rules – at least temporarily. However, rules were generally reinstated

around the world as the global economy pulled out of recession. In Boxes 22.2 and 22.4 we detail how the fiscal rules in the UK and the eurozone, respectively, evolved following the events of the late 2000s.

In section 22.4 we review the debate concerning constraints on a government's discretion – over both its fiscal and its monetary policies.

BOX 22.4   THE EVOLVING FISCAL FRAMEWORK IN THE EUROPEAN UNION

Constraining government discretion over fiscal policy

Preparing for the euro

In signing the Maastricht Treaty in 1992, the EU countries agreed that to be eligible to join the single currency (i.e. the euro), they should have sustainable deficits and debts. This was interpreted as follows: the general government deficit should be no more than 3 per cent of GDP and general government debt should be no more than 60 per cent of GDP, or should at least be falling towards that level at a satisfactory pace.

But in the mid-1990s, several of the countries that were subsequently to join the euro had deficits and debts substantially above these levels (see chart). Getting them down proved a painful business. Government expenditure had to be cut and taxes increased. These fiscal measures, unfortunately, proved to be powerful! Unemployment rose and growth remained low.

The EU Stability and Growth Pact (SGP)

In June 1997, at the European Council meeting in Amsterdam, the EU countries agreed a Stability and Growth Pact (SGP). Under the SGP, governments adopting the euro should seek to balance their budgets (or even aim for a surplus) averaged over the course of the business cycle, and deficits should not exceed 3 per cent of GDP in any one year. A country's deficit was permitted to exceed 3 per cent only if its GDP declined by at least 2 per cent (or 0.75 per cent with special permission from the Council of Ministers). Otherwise, countries with deficits exceeding 3 per cent were required to make deposits of money with the European Central Bank. These would then become fines if the excessive budget deficit were not eliminated within two years.

There were two main aims of targeting a zero budget deficit over the business cycle. The first was to allow automatic stabilisers to work without 'bumping into' the 3 per cent deficit ceiling in years when economies were slowing. The second was to allow a reduction in government debts as a proportion of GDP (assuming that GDP grows on average at around 2–3 per cent per year).

From 2002, with slowing growth, Germany, France and Italy breached the 3 per cent ceiling (see chart)). By 2007,

however, after two years of relatively strong growth, deficits had been reduced well below the ceiling.

But then the credit crunch hit. As the EU economies slowed, so deficits rose. To combat the recession, in November 2008 the European Commission announced a €200 billion fiscal stimulus plan, mainly in the form of increased public expenditure; €170 billion of the money would come from member governments and €30 billion from the EU, amounting to a total of 1.2 per cent of EU GDP. The money would be for a range of projects, such as job training, help to small businesses, developing green energy technologies and energy efficiency. Most member governments quickly followed in announcing how their specific plans would accord with the overall plan.

The combination of the recession and the fiscal measures pushed most eurozone countries' budget deficits well above the 3 per cent ceiling, as the chart shows. The recession in EU countries deepened markedly in 2009, with GDP declining by 4.5 per cent in the eurozone as a whole, and by 5.6 per cent in Germany, 5.5 per cent in Italy, 3.6 per cent in Spain and 2.9 per cent in France. Consequently, the deficits were not seen to breach SGP rules.

In some cases, countries' public finances deteriorated unsustainably. Following high-profile rescue packages to Greece, Ireland and Portugal involving the International Monetary Fund and EU, the EU established a funding mechanism for eurozone countries in financial difficulties, known as the European Stability Mechanism. This became operational in October 2012. As well as taking on the management of existing rescue packages, financial assistance was granted subsequently to Spain and Cyprus.

The Fiscal Compact

With many countries experiencing burgeoning deficits and some countries requiring financial assistance, the SGP was no longer seen as a credible vehicle for constraining deficits: it needed reform. The result was an intense period of negotiation that culminated in early 2012 with a new intergovernmental treaty on limiting spending and borrowing. The treaty, known as the Fiscal Compact, requires

Section summary

1. Automatic fiscal stabilisers are tax revenues that rise, and benefits that fall, as national income rises. They have the effect of reducing the size of the multiplier and thus reducing cyclical upswings and downswings.

2. Automatic stabilisers take effect as soon as aggregate demand fluctuates, but they can never remove fluctuations completely. They also create disincentives and act as a drag on recovery from recession.

3. Discretionary fiscal policy is where the government deliberately changes taxes or government expenditure in

order to alter the level of aggregate demand. Changes in government expenditure on goods and services have a full multiplier effect. Changes in taxes and benefits, however, have a smaller multiplier effect. The tax multiplier has a value 1 less than the full multiplier.

4. There are problems in predicting the magnitude of the effects of discretionary fiscal policy. Expansionary fiscal policy can act as a pump primer and stimulate increased private expenditure, or it can crowd out private expenditure. The extent to which it acts as a pump primer

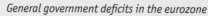

General government deficits in the eurozone

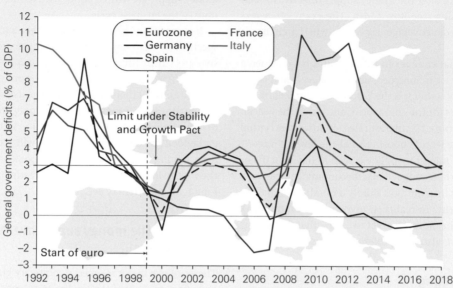

Note: Data from 2017 based on forecasts.
Source: Based on data in *Statistical Annex to the European Economy* (European Commission).

that from January 2013 national governments not only abide by the excessive deficit procedure of the SGP but also keep structural deficits no higher than 0.5 per cent of GDP.

Structural deficits are that part of a deficit not directly related to the economic cycle and so would exist even if the economy were operating at its potential output. In the cases of countries with a debt-to-GDP ratio significantly below 60 per cent, the structural deficit is permitted to reach 1 per cent of GDP. Finally, where the debt-to-GDP ratio exceeds 60 per cent, countries should, on average, reduce it by one-twentieth per year.

The average structural deficit across the eurozone fell from 4.3 per cent of GDP in 2010 to 1.1 per cent in 2016. This improvement was mirrored in most individual eurozone countries, with particularly large improvements in Greece (−10 to +3.7 per cent) and Ireland (−9.9 to −1.9 per cent),

which had received financial assistance but with conditions attached that they cut spending and raise taxes. Nonetheless, most countries still had structural deficits in excess of the target levels of the Fiscal Compact.

Where a national government is found by the European Court of Justice not to comply with the Fiscal Compact, it has the power to fine that country up to 0.1 per cent of GDP payable to the European Stability Mechanism (ESM). The ESM is a fund from which loans are provided to support a eurozone government in severe financial difficulty; alternatively it can be used to purchase that country's bonds in the primary market.

 If there is a danger of recession, should governments loosen the straitjacket of fiscal policy targets?

depends crucially on business confidence – something that is very difficult to predict beyond a few weeks or months. The extent of crowding out depends on monetary conditions and the government's monetary policy.

5. There are five possible time lags involved with fiscal policy: the time lag before the problem is diagnosed, the lag between diagnosis and new measures being announced, the lag between announcement and implementation, the lag while the multiplier and accelerator work themselves out, and the lag before

consumption fully responds to new economic circumstances.

6. In recent years, many governments preferred a more passive approach towards fiscal policy. Targets were set for one or more measures of the public-sector finances, and then taxes and government expenditure were adjusted so as to keep to the target.

7. Nevertheless, in extreme circumstances, as occurred in 2008/9, governments were prepared to abandon rules and give a fiscal stimulus to their economies.

22.3 MONETARY POLICY

The Bank of England's Monetary Policy Committee (MPC) regularly meets to set the Bank Rate and possibly consider whether or not to alter the money supply directly through quantitative easing (see Box 22.10). The event often gets considerable media coverage, especially when a change is expected.

The fact is that changes in interest rates have gained a central significance in macroeconomic policy. And it is not just in the UK. Whether it is the European Central Bank setting interest rates for the eurozone countries, or the Federal Reserve Bank setting US interest rates, or any other central bank around the world choosing what the level of interest rates should be, monetary policy is seen as having a major influence on a whole range of macroeconomic indicators.

But is setting interest rates simply a question of making an announcement? In reality, it involves the central bank intervening in the money market to ensure that the interest rate announced is also the *equilibrium* interest rate.

The policy setting

In framing its monetary policy, the government must decide on what the goals of the policy are. Is the aim simply to control inflation, or does the government wish also to affect output and employment, or does it want to control the exchange rate?

The government also has to decide the role of the central bank in carrying out monetary policy. There are three possible approaches.

In the first, the government both sets the policy and decides the measures necessary to achieve it. Here the government would set the interest rate, with the central bank simply influencing money markets to achieve this rate. This first approach was used in the UK before 1997.

The second approach is for the government to set the policy *targets,* but for the central bank to be given independence in deciding interest rates. This is the approach adopted in the UK today. The government has set a target rate of CPI inflation of 2 per cent, but then the MPC is free to choose the rate of interest.

The third approach is for the central bank to be given independence not only in carrying out policy, but in setting the policy target itself. The ECB, within the statutory objective of maintaining price stability over the medium term, has decided on the target of keeping inflation below, but close to, 2 per cent over the medium term.

Finally, there is the question of whether the government or central bank should take a long-term or short-term perspective. Should it adopt a target for inflation or money supply growth and stick to it come what may? Or should it adjust its policy as circumstances change and attempt to 'fine-tune' the economy?

We will be looking primarily at *short-term* monetary policy: that is, policy used to keep to a set target for inflation or money supply growth, or policy used to smooth out fluctuations in the business cycle.

It is important first, however, to take a longer-term perspective. Governments generally want to prevent an excessive growth in the money supply over the longer term. Likewise they want to ensure that money supply grows enough and that there is not a shortage of credit, such as that during the credit crunch. If money supply grows too rapidly over the longer term, then high inflation is likely to become embedded in the economy, which will feed inflationary expectations; if money supply grows too slowly, or even falls, then recession is likely to result, investment may fall and long-term growth may be subdued.

Control of the money supply over the medium and long term

There are two major sources of monetary growth: (a) banks choosing to hold a lower liquidity ratio (probably in response to an increase in the demand for loans); (b) public-sector borrowing financed by borrowing from the banking sector. If the government wishes to restrict monetary growth over the longer term, it could attempt to control either or both of these.

Banks' liquidity ratio

The central bank could impose a statutory **minimum reserve ratio** on the banks, *above* the level that banks would otherwise choose to hold. Such ratios come in various forms. The simplest is where the banks are required to hold a given minimum percentage of deposits in the form of cash or deposits with the central bank. Other versions are where they are required to hold a given minimum percentage of certain specified types of deposit in the form of various liquid assets. This was the system used in the UK up to 1981. Various types of liquid asset had to add up to at least 12.5 per cent of certain 'eligible liabilities'.

The effect of a minimum reserve ratio is to prevent banks choosing to reduce their cash or liquidity ratio and creating more credit. This was a popular approach of governments in many countries in the past. Some countries imposed very high ratios indeed in their attempt to slow down the growth in the money supply.

Definition

Minimum reserve ratio A minimum ratio of cash (or other specified liquid assets) to deposits (either total or selected) that the central bank requires banks to hold.

Minimum reserve ratios also have the effect of reducing the bank deposits multiplier, since, for any expansion of the monetary base, *less* credit can be created. For example, if banks would otherwise choose a 10 per cent cash ratio, and if the central bank imposes a 20 per cent cash ratio, the bank deposits multiplier is reduced from 10 (= $1/^1/_{10}$) to 5 (= $1/^1/_5$).

A major problem with imposing restrictions of this kind is that banks may find ways of getting round them. After all, normally banks would like to lend and customers would like to borrow. It is very difficult to regulate and police every single part of countries' complex financial systems.

Nevertheless, attitudes changed substantially after the excessive lending of the mid-2000s. The expansion of credit had been based on 'liquidity' achieved through secondary marketing between financial institutions and the growth of securitised assets containing sub-prime debt (see pages 558–63 and Box 18.3). After the credit crunch and the need for central banks or governments to rescue ailing banks, such as Northern Rock and later the Royal Bank of Scotland in the UK and many other banks around the world, there were calls for greater regulation of banks to ensure that they had sufficient capital and operated with sufficient liquidity and that they were not exposed to excessive risk of default. As we saw in section 18.2, a number of measures were taken.

Public-sector deficits

In section 18.3, we showed how government borrowing tends to lead to an increase in money supply. To prevent this, deficits must be financed by selling *bonds* (as opposed to bills, which could well be taken up by the banking sector, thereby increasing money supply). However, to sell extra bonds the government will have to offer higher interest rates. This will have a knock-on effect on private-sector interest rates. The government borrowing will thus crowd out private-sector borrowing and investment.

If governments wish to reduce monetary growth and yet avoid financial crowding out, they must therefore reduce deficits. It is partly for this reason that many governments have constrained fiscal policy choices by applying fiscal rules or agreements, such as the 'fiscal mandate' in the UK or the Fiscal Compact in the eurozone (see Boxes 22.2 and 22.4).

How could long-term monetary growth come about if the government persistently ran a public-sector surplus?

Long-term monetary control and inflation

Although there are issues with achieving long-term control of the money supply, there is widespread agreement that it is important to do so. The argument is that *increasing* the money supply cannot increase output in the long run; all that will happen is an increase in prices.

2 See European Central Bank, www.ecb.int/mopo/intro/role/html/index. en.html

It is argued that in the long run – after all adjustments in the economy have worked through – a change in the quantity of money in the economy will be reflected in a change in the general level of prices. But it will not induce permanent changes in real variables such as real output or unemployment.

This general principle, referred to as the **long-run neutrality of money**, underlies much macroeconomic thinking. Real income or the level of employment are, in the long term, essentially determined by real factors, such as technology, population growth or the preferences of economic agents.[2]

If inflation is to be kept under control, therefore, it is important to control the supply of money. And if long-term control is to be achieved, it is also important not to allow excessive expansion (or contraction) of the money supply in the short term too. But what instruments does a central bank have at its disposal? We examine these next.

The operation of monetary policy in the short term

Assume that inflation is above its target rate and that the central bank wishes to operate a tighter monetary policy in order to reduce aggregate demand and so the rate of inflation. What can it do?

Aggregate demand is dependent on real interest rates (r). Assuming that in the short term the central bank is able to take the expected rate of inflation (π^e) as given, any change in the nominal rate of interest (i) will be matched by an equivalent change in the real rate of interest (r).

For any given supply of money (M_s) there will be a particular equilibrium real rate of interest at any one time: where the supply of money (M_s) equals the demand for money (L). This is shown as r_1 in Figure 22.6.

Thus to operate a tighter monetary policy, the authorities can do one of the following:

- Reduce money supply and accept whatever equilibrium interest rate results. Thus if money supply is reduced to Q_2 in Figure 22.6, a new higher rate of interest, r_2, will result.
- First raise interest rates to r_2 and then manipulate the money supply to reduce it to Q_2. The more endogenous the money supply is, the more this will occur automatically through banks adjusting credit to match the lower demand at the higher rate of interest and the less the central bank will have to take deliberate action to reduce liquidity.

Definition

Long-run neutrality of money Changes in money supply over the long run will only affect prices and not real output or employment.

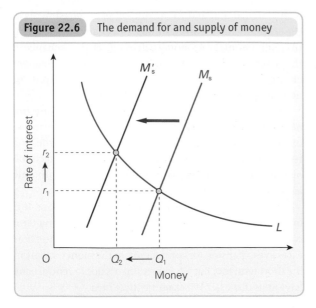

Figure 22.6   The demand for and supply of money

We thus focus on the two major approaches to monetary policy: (a) controlling the money supply and (b) controlling interest rates.

Techniques to control the money supply

There are two broad approaches to controlling the money supply.

The first is alter the level of liquidity in the banking system, on which credit is created. Suppose, for example, that banks operate a rigid 10 per cent cash ratio and have just two types of asset: cash and advances. Suppose also that the authorities are able to reduce cash in banks by £1 million. With a bank multiplier of 10 (= 1/cash ratio), advances must be reduced by £9 million, and hence (broad) money supply by £10 million (see Table 22.2).

 If banks operated a rigid 5 per cent cash ratio and the government reduced cash in banks by £1 million, how much must credit contract? What is the bank deposits multiplier?

The second approach is to alter the size of the bank deposits multiplier, by altering the ratio of reserves to deposits. Thus if the bank deposits multiplier can be reduced, credit will have to be reduced for any given reserve base.

Before they can apply techniques of monetary control, the authorities must make two preliminary decisions:

- Should a statutory minimum reserve or a minimum liquidity ratio be imposed on the banks, or should the banks be allowed to choose whatever ratios they consider to be prudent?
- Should the authorities attempt to control a range of liquid assets, or should they focus on controlling just the monetary base?

There are four techniques that a central bank could use to control the money supply. Assume in each case that the central bank wishes to *reduce* money supply.

Open-market operations

Open-market operations (OMOs) are the most widely used of the four techniques around the world. They alter the monetary base (cash in circulation outside the central

There is another possibility. This is to keep interest rates low (at r_1), but also reduce money supply to a level of Q_2. The trouble here is that the authorities cannot both control the money supply *and* keep interest rates down without running into the problem of disequilibrium. Since the demand for money now exceeds the supply by $Q_1 - Q_2$, some form of credit rationing would have to be applied.

Credit rationing was widely used in the past, especially during the 1960s. The aim was to keep interest rates low, so as not to discourage investment, but to restrict credit to more risky business customers and/or to consumers. In the UK the Bank of England could order banks to abide by such a policy, although in practice it always relied on persuasion. The government also, from time to time, imposed restrictions on hire-purchase credit, by specifying minimum deposits or maximum repayment periods.

Such policies were progressively abandoned around the world from the early 1980s. They were seen to stifle competition and prevent efficient banks from expanding. Hire-purchase controls could badly hit certain industries (e.g. cars and other consumer durables), whose products are bought largely on hire-purchase credit. What is more, with the deregulation and globalisation of financial markets up to 2007, it had become very difficult to ration credit. If one financial institution was controlled, borrowers could simply go elsewhere.

With the excessive lending in sub-prime markets that had triggered the credit crunch of 2007–9, however, there were calls around the world for tighter controls over bank lending. But this was different from credit rationing as we have defined it. In other words, tighter controls, such as applying counter-cyclical buffers of capital to all banks (see pages 564–5), would be used to prevent reckless behaviour by banks, rather than to achieve a particular level of money at a lower rate of interest.

Table 22.2	Reducing the money supply		
Change in liabilities		**Change in assets**	
Deposits	£10m ↓	Cash	£1m ↓
		Advances	£9m ↓

Definition

Open-market operations The sale (or purchase) by the authorities of government securities in the open market in order to reduce (or increase) money supply.

bank). This then affects the amount of credit that banks can create and hence the level of broad money (M4 in the UK; M3 in the eurozone).

Open-market operations involve the sale or purchase by the central bank of government securities (bonds or bills) in the open market. These sales or purchases are *not* in response to changes in the level of government deficits/surpluses. Rather, they are being conducted to implement monetary policy. Hence, they are best understood in the context of an unchanged deficit.

Assume that the central bank wishes to *reduce* the money supply. It will conduct OMOs so as to reduce financial institutions' reserves. It can do this by borrowing from financial institutions against government securities. To do so, it will use reverse repos on banks' balance sheets: i.e. temporarily selling government securities, with an agreement to buy them back later. These securities include government bonds or short-term Treasury or central bank bills. Alternatively the central bank can sell securities outright.

The borrowing against securities or the direct sale of securities reduces the reserve balances of financial institutions at the central bank. If the reduction in banks' balances brings bank reserves below their prudent ratio (or statutory ratio, if one is in force), banks will reduce advances. There will be a multiple contraction of credit and hence of (broad) money supply. (Details of how open-market operations work in the UK are given in Box 22.5.)

The effect will be limited if the extra securities are bills (as opposed to bonds) and if some are purchased by banks. The reduction in one liquid asset (balances with the central bank) will be offset to some extent by an increase in another liquid asset (bills). Open-market operations are more likely to be effective in reducing the money supply, therefore, when conducted in the bond market.

1. *Explain how open-market operations could be used to increase the money supply.*
2. *Why would it be difficult for a central bank to predict the precise effect on money supply of open-market operations?*

Adjusting central bank lending to the banks

In most countries, the central bank is prepared to provide extra money to banks (through rediscounting bills, gilt repos or straight loans). If banks obtain less money in this way, they will have to cut back on lending. Less credit will be created and broad money supply will thereby be reduced.

Whether or not banks *choose* to obtain extra money from the central bank depends on (a) the rate of interest charged by the central bank (i.e. its discount rate, repo rate or lending rate); and (b) its willingness to lend (or repurchase securities).

In some countries, it is the policy of the central bank to keep its interest rate to banks *below* market rates, thereby encouraging banks to borrow (or sell back securities) whenever such facilities are available. By controlling the amount

of money it is willing to provide at these low rates, the central bank can control the monetary base and hence the amount of credit that banks can create.

In other countries, such as the UK and the eurozone countries, it is not so much the amount of money made available that is controlled, but rather the rate of interest (or discount). The higher this rate is relative to other market rates, the less willing will banks be to borrow and, hence, the lower will be the monetary base. Raising the central bank's interest rate, therefore, has the effect of reducing the money supply.

In some countries, central banks operate two rates: a main repo rate (or 'refinancing rate') on a set amount of money that the central bank wants to be made available, and a higher rate (a penal rate) used for 'last-resort' lending to banks short of liquidity. The European Central Bank operates such a system (see Box 22.7). Its higher rate is known as the 'marginal lending facility rate'.

Some central banks, including the ECB, have a third, lower rate. This is the rate they are willing to pay banks for short-term deposits of surplus money in the central bank. In some countries this rate became negative (a charge on banks) in the mid-2010s to encourage banks to lend money rather than merely keeping it on deposit at the central bank.

In response to the credit crunch of the late 2000s, central banks in several countries extended their willingness to lend to banks. The pressure on central banks to act as the 'liquidity backstop' grew as the inter-bank market ceased to function effectively in distributing reserves and, hence, liquidity between financial institutions. As a result, inter-bank rates rose sharply relative to the central bank's main rate. Increasingly, the focus of central banks was on providing the necessary liquidity to ensure the stability of the financial system. Yet, at the same time, by providing more liquidity, central banks were ensuring that monetary policy was not being compromised. The additional liquidity was needed to alleviate the upward pressure on market interest rates.

Changing the method of funding the national debt

Rather than focusing on controlling the monetary base (as in the case of the above two techniques), an alternative is for the authorities to attempt to alter the overall liquidity position of the banks. An example of this approach is a change by the authorities (the Debt Management Office in the UK) in the balance of **funding** the national debt. To reduce money supply the authorities issue more bonds and fewer bills. Banks' balances with the central bank will be little affected, but to the extent that banks hold fewer bills,

> ### Definition
>
> **Funding (in monetary policy)** Where the authorities alter the balance of bills and bonds for any given level of government borrowing.

BOX 22.5 THE OPERATION OF MONETARY POLICY IN THE UK

What goes on at Threadneedle Street?

The Bank of England (the 'Bank') does not normally attempt to control money supply directly. Instead it seeks to control interest rates. There are two principal elements to the framework in which it conducts monetary policy. First, it conducts *open-market operations* (OMOs) to adjust the aggregate amount of banks' reserves. Second, *standing facilities* allow individual banks to borrow reserves overnight directly from the Bank or to deposit reserves overnight at the Bank.

The framework is designed to determine short-term interest rates, which then have a knock-on effect on longer-term rates, as returns on different forms of assets must remain competitive with each other.

Normal operation of the monetary framework

The Monetary Policy Committee (MPC) of the Bank of England meets several times per year to decide on Bank Rate. Changes in the Bank Rate are intended to affect the whole structure of interest rates in the economy, from inter-bank rates to bank deposit rates and rates on mortgages and business loans. The monetary framework works to affect the general structure of interest rates, principally by affecting short-term *inter-bank rates*.

Central to the process are the reserve accounts of financial institutions at the Bank of England (see section 18.2, page 566). From the inception of the current system in May 2006, commercial banks have agreed with the Bank of England the average amount of reserve balances they would hold between MPC meetings. So long as the average over the month is within a small range, the reserves are remunerated at Bank Rate.

In order for individual banks to meet their reserve targets, the Bank of England needs to provide sufficient reserves. To do so, it uses OMOs. In normal circumstances, the Bank of England conducts short-term OMOs every week (on a Thursday) at Bank Rate. The size of the weekly OMO is adjusted to help banks maintain reserves at the target level and to reflect variations in the amount of cash withdrawn or deposited in banks.

To supply reserves the Bank of England will either enter into short-term repo operations, lending against collateral ('high-quality' government securities), or buy securities outright. Although there is usually a shortage of liquidity in the banking system, in some weeks there may be a surplus. This would ordinarily drive market interest rates down. Depending on the Bank Rate, the Bank may look to reduce banks' reserves. To do this it can sell government securities on a repo basis, invite bids for Bank of England one-week sterling bills or sell outright some of its portfolio of securities.

At the end of the period between MPC interest rate decisions, the Bank of England conducts a 'fine-tuning' OMO. This is conducted on a Wednesday – the day before the MPC decision on interest rates. The idea is to ensure that banks meet their reserve targets as closely as possible. This OMO could expand or contract liquidity as appropriate.

Longer-term finance is available through longer-term open market operations. Prior to the financial crisis of the late 2000s, longer-term OMOs would normally be conducted once per month. As well as the outright purchase of gilts, the Bank would conduct repo lending with 3-, 6-, 9- or 12-month maturities.

---

there will be a reduction in their liquidity and hence a reduction in the amount of credit created. Funding is thus the conversion of one type of government debt (liquid) into another (illiquid).

One problem with this approach is that bonds are likely to command a higher interest rate than bills. By switching from bills to bonds, the government will be committing itself to these interest rates for the life of the bond.

 If the Bank of England issues £1 million of extra bonds and buys back £1 million of Treasury bills, will there automatically be a reduction in credit by a set multiple of £1 million?

Variable minimum reserve ratios

If banks are required to maintain a statutory minimum reserve ratio and if the central bank is free to alter this ratio, it can use it as a means of controlling the money supply. It does this by affecting not the monetary base, but the size of the bank multiplier.

Assume that there are just two types of asset: cash and advances, and that banks are required to maintain a

minimum 10 per cent cash ratio (a ratio above that which the banks would have chosen for reasons of prudence). The bank multiplier is thus 10 ($= 1/^1/_{10}$). Assume that banks' total assets are £100 billion, of which £10 billion are cash reserves and £90 billion are advances. This is illustrated in the first part of Table 22.3.

Now assume that the central bank raises the minimum reserve ratio to 20 per cent. Banks still have £10 billion cash reserves, and so they have to reduce their advances to £40 billion (giving total assets of £50 billion, of which the £10 million cash is the required 20 per cent). This is shown in the second part of Table 22.3. The bank multiplier has been reduced to 5 ($= 1/^1/_5$).

In the past, central banks that imposed minimum reserve ratios on the banks tended to vary them in this way as a means of altering the money supply for any given monetary base. For example, several of the EU countries used this technique before joining the euro. Increasingly, countries that still have minimum reserve ratios are relying on open-market operations or direct lending to banks, rather than on varying the ratio. This is the case with the ECB, which has a fixed

The rate of interest on the repos is market determined. Banks bid for the money and the funds are offered to the successful bidders. The bigger the demand for these funds by banks and the lower the supply by the Bank of England, the higher will be the interest rate that banks must pay. By adjusting the supply, therefore, the Bank of England can look to influence longer-term interest rates too.

With the aggregate amount of banks' reserves determined by the Bank of England's OMOs, the task now is for individual banks to meet their agreed reserve targets. This requires that they manage their balance sheets and, in particular, their level of liquidity. In doing so, commercial banks can make use of either the *inter-bank* market or the 'standing facilities' at the Bank of England. These standing facilities allow individual banks to borrow overnight (secured against high-quality collateral) at a rate *above* Bank Rate or to deposit reserves with the Bank at a rate *below* Bank Rate. Consequently, banks will trade reserves with each other if inter-bank rates fall within the corridor created by the interest rates of the standing facilities.

The financial crisis and the monetary framework

The financial crisis meant that normal OMOs were no longer sufficient to maintain liquidity for purposes of monetary policy. There was a severe liquidity crisis – one which posed grave risks for financial stability.

In response, from January 2009 the Bank of England deliberately injected narrow money in a process known as 'quantitative easing' (see Box 22.10). This involved the Bank of England purchasing assets, largely gilts, from financial institutions. The Bank argued that its asset purchase programme was an important monetary policy tool in meeting its inflation rate target.

Between January 2009 and July 2012 the Bank of England injected £375 billion through the purchase of gilts. In August 2016, following the UK's vote to leave the European Union and concerns about deteriorating prospects for growth, the Bank of England decided to increase its gilt purchases by a further £60 billion and in addition to purchase up to £10 billion of UK corporate bonds.

As a result of this significant increase in aggregate reserves, banks were no longer required to set reserve targets. The supply of reserves was now being determined by MPC policy decisions. All reserves were to be remunerated at the Bank Rate.

Furthermore, short-term OMOs were temporarily suspended. Long-term repo operations continued but these were modified to allow financial institutions to sell a wider range of securities. It also adapted its means of providing liquidity insurance (see section 18.2, pages 566–9). This includes the introduction of the Discount Window Facility (DWF), which enables banks to borrow government bonds (gilts) against a wide range of collateral which can then be used in repo operations to secure liquidity.

 Assume that the Bank of England wants to raise interest rates. Trace through the process by which it achieves this.

Table 22.3	Effect of raising the minimum reserve ratio from 10% to 20%						
Initial position: 10% reserve ratio				**New position: 20% reserve ratio**			
Liabilities		**Assets**		**Liabilities**		**Assets**	
Deposits	£100bn	Reserve assets	£10bn	Deposits	£50bn	Reserve assets	£10bn
		Advances, etc.	£90bn			Advances, etc.	£40bn
Total	£100bn	Total	£100bn	Total	£50bn	Total	£50bn

reserve ratio.[3] Nevertheless, in January 2012 it was lowered from 2 per cent to 1 per cent in a 'one-off' effort to increase lending. It remains at 1 per cent. The USA, however, still uses variable minimum reserve ratios as a monetary policy tool, although increasingly less so (see Box 22.6).[4]

3 It was lowered from 2 per cent to 1 per cent in January 2012.
4 In one sense, it could be argued that the imposition of a minimum reserve ratio is a *form* of credit rationing. It restricts the ability of banks to expand credit as much as they would like for the amount of reserves they hold. In Figure 22.6, however, higher minimum reserves would still shift the *supply* curve, given that this curve measures broad money and not the monetary base. It is for this reason that we considered minimum reserve ratios under the heading of 'techniques to control the money supply'.

Difficulties in controlling money supply

The authorities may experience considerable difficulties in controlling broad money supply. Difficulties occur whether they focus on doing this via control of narrow money – the 'monetary base' – or whether they attempt to control a wider range of liquid assets.

Problems with monetary base control
Assume that the authorities seek to control narrow money: i.e. notes and coin. This could be done by imposing a statutory cash ratio on banks. Assume that a statutory ratio of 10

BOX 22.6 CENTRAL BANKING AND MONETARY POLICY IN THE USA

How the 'Fed' works

The central bank in the USA is called the Federal Reserve System (or 'Fed'). It was set up in 1913 and consists of 12 regional Federal Reserve Banks, each of which is responsible for distributing currency and regulating banks in its region. But despite its apparent regional nature, it is still a national system. The Federal Reserve Board, based in Washington, decides on monetary policy and then the Federal Open Market Committee (FOMC) decides how to carry it out. The FOMC meets eight times a year. The Fed is independent of both the President and the Congress, and its chairman is generally regarded as having great power in determining the country's economic policy.

Its macroeconomic objectives include low inflation, sustainable economic growth, low unemployment and moderate long-term interest rates. Of course, these objectives may well conflict from time to time. In such a case, an assessment has to be made of which is the most pressing problem.

When there is no threat of rising inflation, the Fed may use monetary policy aggressively to pursue these other goals. Thus, from January to December 2001, with the US economy moving into recession, the FOMC cut interest rates 10 times. In January the rate was 6 per cent; by December it was down to 1.75 per cent.

Even when inflation is rising, the Fed may still cut interest rates if the economy is slowing. With the onset of the credit crunch of 2007/8, the Fed cut rates several times. In August 2007, the rate was 5.25 per cent. By August 2008 it had been cut to 2 per cent, even though inflation was rising. Then as inflation fell and recession deepened, rates were cut again to stand at between 0 and 0.25 per cent by December 2008.

The Fed's policy instruments

To carry out its objectives, the FOMC has traditionally had three policy instruments.

Open-market operations. The most important one is *open-market operations*. These are conducted through the Federal Reserve Bank of New York, which buys and sells Treasury bills and government bonds. For example, if the FOMC wishes to increase money supply, the New York Fed will buy more of these securities. The purchasers, whether they be banks,

corporations or individuals, will have their bank accounts duly credited. In other words, the Fed credits the accounts of sellers with a deposit and this enables a multiple increase in credit.

The discount rate. The second policy instrument is the *discount rate.* Known as the 'federal funds rate', this is the rate of interest at which the Fed is willing to lend to banks, thereby providing them with liquidity on which they can create credit. This is known as 'lending through the discount window'. If this rate is raised, banks are discouraged from borrowing, and credit is thereby squeezed. Since 1995, the FOMC has published its target federal funds rate. Sometimes this rate merely mirrors other market rates and is not, therefore, an active instrument of policy. On other occasions, however, the Fed changes it ahead of other market rates in order to signal its intentions to tighten (or loosen) monetary policy.[1]

Variable minimum reserve requirements. Banks are legally required to hold a certain minimum percentage of eligible deposit liabilities as reserves. Interest is paid on these reserves. The reserve requirement is dependent on the size of a bank's eligible deposit liabilities. Banks with an amount of liabilities falling within an adjustable exemption range have no reserve requirement. Above this is the 'low-reserve tranche' range. As of January 2017, banks with eligible deposit liabilities within this range must hold 3 per cent of deposits in reserves. Banks with an eligible deposit total in excess of this must hold 10 per cent in reserves.

Currently the only deposit accounts subject to reserve requirements are transaction accounts, which include sight accounts ('checking accounts') and time deposits. The Fed can vary the types of deposits subject to the reserve requirement as well as the size and number of bands and the reserve ratios. Given that any change in the reserve ratio causes a multiplied effect on advances, changes are made only occasionally and by a small amount.

Response to the credit crunch

With the credit crunch of 2007/8 and the difficulties of banks in obtaining finance from the inter-bank market, the Fed extended its activities. It made considerable liquidity

---

per cent is imposed. Then provided the authorities control the supply of cash by, say, open-market operations, it would seem that they can thereby control the creation of credit and hence deposits. There would be a bank multiplier of 10. For every £1 million decrease in cash held by the banks, money supply would fall by £10 million. There are serious problems, however, with this form of **monetary base control**:

■ Banks could hold cash in excess of the statutory minimum. For a time, therefore, they could respond to any

restriction of cash by the authorities by simply reducing their cash ratio towards the minimum, rather than having to reduce credit.

Definition

Monetary base control Monetary policy that focuses on controlling the monetary base (as opposed to broad liquidity).

available to banks by swapping Treasury bills for hard-to-trade securities, such as mortgage-backed bonds and other securitised assets, including those backed by student loans. It also extended the period of its short-term loans through the discount window and was now willing to lend not only to retail banks but to investment banks and mortgage lenders too.

Then in October 2008, the US government adopted a $700 billion rescue package for the ailing US financial system. This was known as the Troubled Asset Relief Program (TARP). The plan was to purchase 'distressed assets' including collateralised debt obligations (see section 18.2). The purchases were designed to provide liquidity for the holders of these CDOs, to stabilise the financial system and, in turn, encourage bank lending. In return for participating in TARP, financial institutions effectively gave the US Treasury part-ownership. Revisions to the TARP programme saw the first $250 billion allocated for the programme used to purchase preference shares from nine of the largest US banks. Subsequently, purchases of toxic assets took place, including mortgage-backed securities.

The US government's measures were backed up the Fed, which embarked on an aggressive policy of increasing the money supply through the purchase of long-term securities. The first round of quantitative easing (QE1) was announced in November 2008 with the intention to purchase $100 billion of corporate debt issued by government-sponsored financial enterprises and $500 billion of mortgage-backed securities (MBSs), including MBSs guaranteed by the two main mortgage lenders Fannie Mae and Freddie Mac, which had recently been nationalised to save them from collapse.

In March 2009, the Fed announced that it would increase its purchases of debt issued by government-sponsored financial enterprises by a further $100 billion and its purchases of MBSs by a further $750 billion. The hope was to stimulate bank lending and revive the collapsed housing market. It also announced that it would purchase $300 billion of longer-term Treasury securities

Despite these measures the economy remained fragile. In November 2010 a second round of quantitative easing (QE2) was announced. Between November 2010 and June 2011 it expanded its holding of longer-term Treasury securities by $600 billion. The aim was 'to promote a stronger pace of economic recovery'.

In September 2011, the Fed announced that in the period up to June 2012 it would buy up to $400 billion of long-term government bonds in the market and sell an equal amount of shorter-dated ones (of less than three years). The plan became known as 'Operation Twist'. It is a way of altering the *funding* of national debt, rather than directly altering the monetary base. The idea was to drive up the price of long-term bonds and hence drive down their yield and thereby drive down long-term interest rates. The hope was to stimulate investment and longer-term borrowing. The plan was expanded in June 2012 with the sale of a further $267 billion in Treasury securities by the end of the year.

In September 2012, the US Federal Reserve bank launched a third round of quantitative easing (QE3). The Fed would buy mortgage-backed securities of $40 billion per month, extended to $85 billion per month in December 2012. And this would go on for as long as it took for the employment market to show significant improvement. It was this open-ended commitment which made QE3 different from QE1 and QE2. Under QE1 and QE2, the Fed purchased $2.3 trillion of assets.

In December 2013, the Federal Reserve announced the start of a tapering of its quantitative easing programme. In other words, monthly purchases of MBSs and longer-term Treasury securities were reduced. The conclusion of QE3 was formally announced in October 2014 after accumulating assets of $2.5 trillion.

As the rate of US economic growth increased to over 2 per cent by 2014 and as unemployment fell, so it was expected that interest rates would eventually begin to rise and that more 'normal' times would return. In December 2015, the Fed raised the federal funds rate by 0.25 percentage points (the first increase since June 2006) and by another 0.25 percentage points in December 2016 and in March and June 2017 (see Figure 22.8 on page 695).

1. In what ways is the Fed's operation of monetary policy (a) similar to and (b) different from the Bank of England's?
2. Could there be a potential moral hazard problem arising out of the actions taken by the Fed and the US government in response to the financial crisis?

1 For details of the Fed's interest rate policy, see www.federalreserve.gov/fomc/fundsrate.htm

- Unless cash ratios were imposed on every single financial institution, the control of certain institutions' lending would merely shift business to other uncontrolled institutions, including overseas ones. Banks operate in a global market. Thus UK banks can do business with UK borrowers using money markets abroad, thereby diverting potentially profitable business away from London. This is an example of Goodhart's law (see Box 22.8 on page 700).
- Alternatively, if those banks subject to statutory cash requirements were short of cash, they could attract cash away from the uncontrolled institutions.

The switching of business away from controlled banks is known as *disintermediation*. To avoid this problem and to allow the greatest freedom of competition between financial institutions, the alternative is to use monetary base control with no *statutory* cash ratio.

Definition

Disintermediation The diversion of business away from financial institutions that are subject to controls.

But two major problems with monetary base control, with or without a statutory cash ratio, are the most serious of all. The first is that central banks *are always prepared to increase the monetary base, through repos or rediscounting, if it is demanded.* This makes it virtually impossible to have a precise control of the monetary base.

The second is the size and variability of the money multiplier. As we saw in section 18.3 (pages 575–6), the money multiplier is the number of times greater the rise in (broad) money supply is than the rise in the monetary base. As Figure 18.5 (see page 576) demonstrates, the broad money multiplier can be highly variable. In other words, controlling the monetary base would have a highly unpredictable effect on the money supply.

For these reasons, the support for monetary base control has waned in recent years.

1. *Trace through the effects of a squeeze on the monetary base from an initial reduction in cash to banks' liquidity being restored through gilt repos. Will this restoration of liquidity by the central bank totally nullify the initial effect of reducing the supply of cash? (Clue: what is likely to happen to the rate of interest?)*
2. *Given the difficulties of monetary base control, would you expect cash in circulation and broader measures of the money supply, such as M4, to rise and fall by the same percentage as each other?*

Problems with controlling broad money supply

One solution to the problems of monetary base control would be for the authorities to attempt to control broader money supply directly. In the UK, targets for the growth in broad money were an important part of monetary policy from 1976 to 1985. The UK has not targeted money supply growth since the 1980s, however. The European Central Bank has a 'reference value' of 4.5 per cent for M3 growth of the euro (see Box 18.4 on page 573 for a definition of M3). This, however, is only a guideline and not a strict target.

How would such a policy work? Assume that the authorities want to operate a tight monetary policy. They sell bonds on the open market. Banks, now short of cash, obtain money from the central bank through rediscounting bills or through repos. Thus although the central bank has been obliged to restore the amount of cash it had withdrawn from the system, there has been a decrease in bills and short-term bonds held by the banks. Banks' *overall* liquidity has thus been reduced. Such measures could be backed up by changing the funding methods.

But as with monetary base control, there are problems with attempting to control broad money supply. Banks may be prepared to reduce their liquidity ratio. This is likely if they already have surplus liquidity, or if their customers are prepared to switch from sight to time accounts (for which banks require fewer cash reserves). This will involve offering higher interest rates on time accounts, and hence charging higher interest rates on bank loans. But if the demand for

loans is relatively insensitive to interest rate changes, this will have little effect on credit or on overall deposits.

The use of open-market operations or funding to reduce money supply involves selling more bonds. But if potential purchasers believe interest rates will rise in the future (highly likely when the government is attempting to operate a tighter monetary policy), they will hold off buying bonds now and may even attempt to sell bonds before bond prices fall. Thus the authorities may be forced into a large immediate increase in bond interest rates.

In circumstances where the central bank wants to *increase* broad money, the problem can be even more serious. Purchasing bonds may increase liquidity in the banking sector, but (a) people may not want to borrow if the economy is going into recession and people are trying to cut back on spending; (b) banks may be reluctant to lend, preferring to keep the extra liquidity in reserve as a precaution against people defaulting on debts. These were the problems facing various central banks around the world which were to engage in quantitative easing (see Box 22.10) following the financial crisis of the late 2000s and the subsequent economic slowdown.

Perhaps the biggest problem is the effect on interest rates.

The effect on interest rates

A policy of controlling money supply can lead to severe fluctuations in real interest rates. This can cause great uncertainty for business and can be very damaging to long-term investment and growth.

The problem is more acute if the overall demand for money is inelastic and is subject to fluctuations. In Figure 22.7, with money supply controlled at M_s, even a fairly moderate increase in demand from L to L' leads to a large rise in real interest rates from r to r_1.

And yet, if the authorities are committed to controlling money supply, they will have to accept that equilibrium interest rates may well fluctuate in this way.

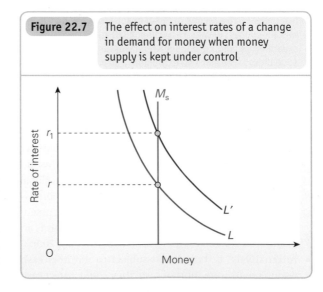

Figure 22.7 The effect on interest rates of a change in demand for money when money supply is kept under control

Because of the above difficulties in controlling the money supply directly, countries have become increasingly reliant on controlling interest rates (backed up, normally, by open-market operations).

Techniques to control interest rates

The approach to monetary control today in many countries is to focus directly on interest rates. Normally an interest rate change will be announced, and then open-market operations will be conducted by the central bank to ensure that the money supply is adjusted so as to make the announced interest rate the *equilibrium* one. Figure 22.8 shows central bank (nominal) interest rates in the UK, USA and the eurozone since 2005.

Central banks look to affect *real* interest rates through their monetary operations that affect nominal interest rates. Assuming inflationary expectations are constant in the short term, then, by announcing a particular change in nominal rates, this results in an equivalent change in real interest rates. Thus, in Figure 22.6 (on page 688), the central bank announces a rise in nominal interest rates which corresponds to an equivalent rise in real interest rates from r_1 to r_2 and then conducts open-market operations to ensure that the money supply is reduced from Q_1 to Q_2.

In the UK, since the Bank of England was made independent in 1997, interest rate changes have been made by the Bank's Monetary Policy Committee (MPC) at its meetings, which take place eight times per year. These are then backed up through the Bank's operations in the gilt repo and discount markets (see Box 22.5). Similarly, in the eurozone, the ECB's Governing Council decides on interest rates every six weeks (see Box 22.7).

Let us assume that the central bank decides to raise interest rates. What does it do? In general, it will seek to keep banks short of liquidity. This will happen automatically on any day when tax payments by banks' customers exceed the money they receive from government expenditure. This excess is effectively withdrawn from banks and ends up in the government's account at the central bank. Even when this does not occur, issues of government debt will effectively keep the banking system short of liquidity.

This 'shortage' can then be used as a way of forcing through interest rate changes. Banks will obtain the necessary liquidity from the central bank through gilt repos or by selling it back (rediscounting) bills. The central bank can *choose the rate of interest to charge* (i.e. the gilt repo rate or the bill rediscount rate). This will then have a knock-on effect on other interest rates throughout the banking system.

The effects can be illustrated in Figure 22.9, both parts of which assume that the central bank wishes to raise the real interest rate (the real repo or discount rate) from r_1 to r_2.

In Figure 22.9(a), it is assumed that banks are short of liquidity and are seeking to sell gilts to the central bank on a repo basis. It is assumed that the central bank will supply as much cash (i.e. demand as many gilts through repos) as banks choose, but only at the central bank's chosen repo rate. The demand for gilts is thus perfectly elastic at the central bank's repo rate. The supply curve of gilts by the banks represents their demand for cash from the central bank, and hence is *downward* sloping: the lower the real repo rate, the cheaper it is for the banks to obtain cash. If the central bank raises the real repo rate to r_2 (via a rise in the nominal rate), banks will supply fewer gilts (i.e. demand less cash from the central bank). If there is less liquidity in the banking system, the money supply will fall.

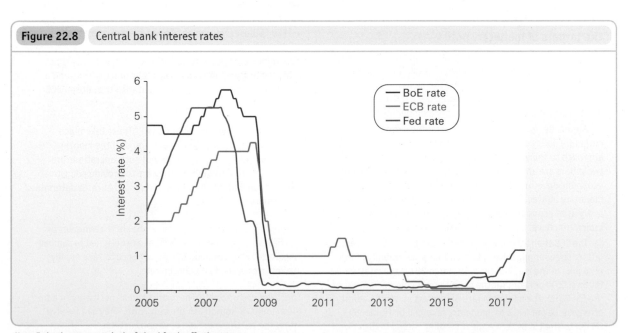

Figure 22.8 Central bank interest rates

Note: Federal reserve rate is the federal funds *effective* rate.
Source: Federal Reserve Bank, European Central Bank and Bank of England.

BOX 22.7   MONETARY POLICY IN THE EUROZONE

The role of the ECB

The European Central Bank (ECB) is based in Frankfurt and is charged with operating the monetary policy of those EU countries that have adopted the euro. Although the ECB has the overall responsibility for the eurozone's monetary policy, the central banks of the individual countries, such as the Bank of France and Germany's Bundesbank, were not abolished. They are responsible for distributing euros and for carrying out the ECB's policy with respect to institutions in their own countries. The whole system of the ECB and the national central banks is known as the European System of Central Banks (ESCB).

In operating the monetary policy of a 'euro economy' roughly the size of the USA, and in being independent from national governments, the ECB's power is enormous and is equivalent to that of the Fed (see Box 22.6). So what is the structure of this giant on the European stage, and how does it operate?

The structure of the ECB

The ECB has two major decision-making bodies: the Governing Council and the Executive Board.[1]

The Governing Council consists of the members of the Executive Board and the governors of the central banks of each of the eurozone countries. The Council's role is to set the main targets of monetary policy and to oversee the success (or otherwise) of that policy. It also sets interest rates at six-weekly meetings. Decisions are by simple majority. In the event of a tie, the president has the casting vote.

The Executive Board consists of a president, a vice-president and four other members. Each serves for an eight-year, non-renewable term. The Executive Board is responsible for implementing the decisions of the Governing Council and for preparing policies for the Council's consideration. Each member of the Executive Board has a responsibility for some particular aspect of monetary policy.

The targets of monetary policy

The overall responsibility of the ECB is to achieve price stability in the eurozone. The target is a rate of inflation below, but close to, 2 per cent over the medium term. It is a weighted average rate for all the members of the eurozone, not a rate that has to be met by every member individually.

Alongside its definition of price stability, the ECB's monetary policy strategy comprises what it calls 'a two-pillar approach to the analysis of the risks to price stability'. These two pillars are any analysis of monetary developments and of economic developments. The former includes an analysis of monetary aggregates, including M3. The latter includes an analysis of economic activity, the labour market, cost indicators, fiscal policy and the balance of payments.

The ECB then attempts to 'steer' short-term interest rates to influence economic activity to maintain price stability in the euro area in the medium term. In March 2017, the rates were as follows: 0.00 per cent for the main 'refinancing operations' of the ESCB (i.e. the minimum rate of interest at which liquidity is offered once per week to 'monetary financial institutions' (MFIs) by the ESCB); a 'marginal lending' rate of 0.25 per cent

(for providing overnight support to the MFIs); and a 'deposit rate' of −0.40 per cent (the rate paid to MFIs for depositing overnight surplus liquidity with the ESCB). The negative deposit rate meant that banks were being charged for 'parking' money with the ECB rather than lending it. The hope was that this would encourage banks to lend to each other or to households and businesses and, consequently, stimulate the economy.

The operation of monetary policy

The ECB sets a minimum reserve ratio. The ratio is designed primarily to prevent excessive lending and hence the need for excessive borrowing from the central bank or from other financial institutions. This, in turn, should help to reduce the volatility in interest rates.

The minimum reserve ratio was not designed, however, to be used to make changes in monetary policy. In other words, it was not used as a variable minimum reserves ratio, and for this reason it was set at a low level. From 1 January 1999 to 17 January 2012 the ratio (also known as the reserve coefficient) was 2 per cent of key liquid and relatively liquid liabilities. However, as of 18 January 2012 the ratio was reduced to 1 per cent in an attempt to help stimulate bank lending. In other words, it was now being used for the first time as part of an active monetary policy. However, it has not been used for this purpose since.

The main instrument for keeping the ECB's desired interest rate as the equilibrium rate is open-market operations in government bonds and other recognised assets, mainly in the form of repos. These repo operations are conducted by the national central banks, which must ensure that the repo rate does not rise above the marginal overnight lending rate or below the deposit rate.

The ECB uses four types of open-market operations:

Main refinancing operations.   These are short-term repos with a maturity of one week. They take place weekly and are used to maintain liquidity consistent with the chosen ECB interest rate.

Longer-term refinancing operations.   These take place monthly and typically have a maturity of three months. Longer maturities are available, but such operations are conducted more irregularly. They are to provide additional longer-term liquidity to banks as required at rates determined by the market, not the ECB.

Fine-tuning operations.   These can be short-term sales or purchases of short-term assets. They are designed to combat unexpected changes in liquidity and hence to keep money market rates at the ECB's chosen rate.

Structural operations.   These are used as necessary to adjust the amount of liquidity in the eurozone. They can involve either the purchase or sale of various assets.

ECB independence

The ECB is one of the most independent central banks in the world. It has very little formal accountability to elected politicians. Although its president can be called before the European Parliament, the Parliament has virtually no powers to influence the ECB's actions. Until its January 2015 meeting, its deliberations were secret and no minutes of Council meetings were published. Subsequently, an account of meetings is published (usually with a lag of around two weeks) with an explanation of the policy stance. However, the minutes do not include details of how Council members voted or of future policy intentions, unlike the minutes published by the Bank of England which, from 2015, are available at the time of the policy announcement.

There is one area, however, where the ECB's power is limited by politicians and this concerns the exchange rate of the euro. Under the Maastricht Treaty, EU finance ministers have the responsibility for deciding on exchange rate policy (even though the ECB is charged with carrying it out). If the finance ministers want to stop the exchange rate of the euro rising, in order to prevent putting EU exporters at a competitive disadvantage, this will put pressure on the ECB to lower interest rates, which might run directly counter to its desire to meet its inflation and money supply targets. This is an example of the principle of 'targets and instruments'. If you have only one instrument (the rate of interest), it cannot be used to achieve two targets (the exchange rate and inflation) if these two targets are in conflict (see Box 22.9).

Financial crisis

The financial crisis put incredible strains on commercial banks in the eurozone and, hence, on the ECB's monetary framework. Consequently, monetary operations were gradually modified.

A Securities Market Programme (SMP) began in May 2010 designed to supply liquidity to the ailing banking system. It allowed for ECB purchases of central government debt in the secondary market (i.e. not directly from governments) as well as purchases both in primary and secondary markets of private-sector debt instruments. By June 2012, €214 bn of purchases had been made, largely of government bonds issued by countries experiencing financing difficulties, including Portugal, Ireland, Greece and Spain.

The SMP was supplemented in December 2011 by the introduction of three-year refinancing operations (LTROs) worth €529.5 billion and involving some 800 banks. These were cheap loans (repos) to the banks by the ECB. These were followed in January by a fall in the minimum reserve ratio to 1 per cent (as we saw above).

By the end of February 2012, a further €489.2 billion of three-year loans to 523 banks took place, taking the total to over €1 trillion. The hope was that the funds would help financially distressed banks pay off maturing debt and again increase their lending.

Then in September 2012 with worries about the continuing difficulties of some eurozone countries, such as Greece, Spain

and Italy, to borrow at affordable rates and possibly, as a result, their being driven from the euro, the ECB announced a replacement for the SMP programme. This would involve a more extensive programme of purchasing existing government bonds with up to three years of maturity in the secondary market. The aim would be to drive down these countries' interest rates and thereby make it cheaper to issue new bonds when old ones matured. These Outright Monetary Transactions (OMTs) were in principle unlimited, with the ECB president, Mario Draghi, saying that the ECB would do 'whatever it takes' to hold the single currency together.

Critics argued that this was still not enough to stimulate the eurozone economy and help to bring countries out of recession. The principal problem, it was argued, was that OMTs would differ from the quantitative easing programmes used in the UK and the USA. ECB purchases of these bonds would not increase the eurozone money supply as the ECB would sell off other assets to compensate. This process is known as *sterilisation*.

Despite the eurozone economy contracting by 0.6 per cent in 2012 and by a further 0.4 per cent in 2013, OMTs had still not been used. Nonetheless, the ECB argued that the announcement that it was prepared to intervene had acted to prevent 'self-reinforcing fears' in sovereign bond markets.

Subsequent measures were to follow. In June 2014, the ECB announced that it was adopting a negative deposit rate (see above), that it was embarking on a further series of targeted long-term refinancing operations so as to provide long-term loans to commercial banks at cheap rates until September 2018, and that it would stop sterilising its SMP programme.

Quantitative easing. Finally, in September 2014, it announced that it would be commencing quantitative easing by purchasing marketable debt instruments, including public-sector bonds and asset-backed private-sector securities, such as securitised mortgages and commercial loans (see section 18.2). From March 2015 until March 2016 the average monthly purchase was €60 billion, which was increased to €80 billion from April 2016 before being reduced back to €60 billion from April 2017. Purchases were intended to be carried out until the end of 2017, dependent on economic conditions in the eurozone.

 What are the arguments for and against publishing the minutes of the meetings of the ECB's Governing Council and Executive Board?

1 See www.ecb.int/ecb/orga/decisions/govc/html/index.en.html
2 'The use of a minimum reserve system by the European System of Central Banks in Stage Three', www.ecb.europa.eu/press/pr/date/1998/html/pr981013_3.en.html

Definition

Sterilisation Actions taken by a central bank to offset the effects of foreign exchange flows or its own bond transactions so as to leave money supply unchanged.

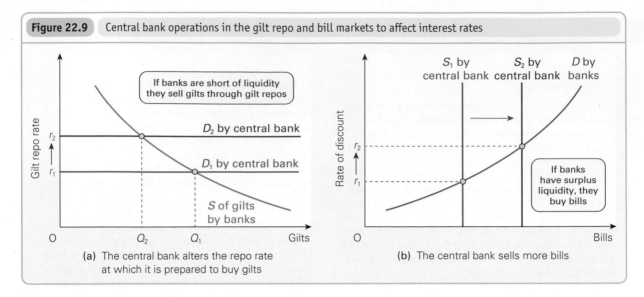

Figure 22.9 Central bank operations in the gilt repo and bill markets to affect interest rates

(a) The central bank alters the repo rate at which it is prepared to buy gilts

(b) The central bank sells more bills

In the event of banks having a surplus of liquidity, Figure 22.9(b) applies. Here banks are seeking to use their surplus liquidity to *buy* bills from the central bank. Their demand curve is *upward* sloping: the higher the rate of discount (i.e. the lower the price that banks have to pay for bills), the more the banks will demand. In this case, the central bank can raise the rate of discount by offering more bills for sale. By increasing the supply of bills from S_1 to S_2, it can increase the equilibrium real rate from r_1 to r_2.

In both cases, the central bank will first decide on the repo rate (or discount rate) and then adjust the supply or demand of gilts or bills to ensure that the chosen rate is the equilibrium rate (see Boxes 22.5, 22.6 and 22.7 for details of how the Bank of England, the Fed and the ECB do this in practice).

A change in the repo rate will then have a knock-on effect on other interest rates. For example, in the UK, banks normally automatically adjust their base rates (to which they gear their other rates) when the Bank of England announces a change in the Bank Rate (i.e. the nominal repo rate). Thus a 0.25 percentage point rise in Bank Rate will normally mean a 0.25 percentage point rise in banks' deposit rates, overdraft rates, etc.

Changes in Bank Rate, however, will not necessarily have an *identical* effect on other interest rates. In section 19.4 we saw how some economists argue that interest rate differentials, such as those between saving and borrowing products, can be dependent on the macroeconomic environment. Economic growth may help to reduce the cost of borrowing relative to the return on saving, which further fuels spending and aggregate demand.

While interest rate differentials may vary across the business cycle, they can also be affected by disruptions in the functioning of financial markets. The financial crisis of the late 2000s can be seen in this light, with interest rate differentials between borrowing and saving or deposit rates rising sharply. This is illustrated in Figure 22.10, which shows the UK's Bank Rate alongside the average mortgage rate and one-month LIBOR (*inter-bank* lending rate).

Because of the financial crisis, inter-bank rates did not follow Bank Rate changes precisely. The chart illustrates how during the height of the credit crunch in 2008, the LIBOR diverged considerably from Bank Rate as banks became reluctant to lend to each other for fear that banks would default on their loans. From 2011, however, the inter-bank rate converged once more with Bank Rate.

Similarly, the average mortgage rate did not fall nearly as much as Bank Rate in 2008/9. But, unlike the inter-bank rate, the higher spread between Bank Rate and mortgage rate persisted through the 2010s.

 How could we model a credit market disruption and its impact on interest rate differentials using the Keynesian cross (Keynesian 45° line) diagram?

Problems with controlling interest rates

Even though central bank adjustment of the repo rate is the current preferred method of monetary control in most countries, it is not without its difficulties. The problems centre on the nature of the demand for loans. If this demand is (a) unresponsive to interest rate changes or (b) unstable because it can be significantly affected by other determinants (e.g. anticipated income or foreign interest rates), it will be very difficult to control by controlling the rate of interest.

Problem of an inelastic demand for loans

If the demand for loans is inelastic, as in Figure 22.11, any attempt to reduce demand (e.g. from Q_1 to Q_2) will involve large rises in real interest rates (r_1 to r_2). The problem will be compounded if the demand curve shifts to the right, due, say, to a consumer spending boom. High interest rates lead to the following problems:

- They may discourage long-term investment (as opposed to current consumption) and hence long-term growth.
- They add to the costs of production, to the costs of house purchase and generally to the cost of living. They are thus cost inflationary.
- They are politically unpopular, since the general public do not like paying higher interest rates on overdrafts, credit cards and mortgages.

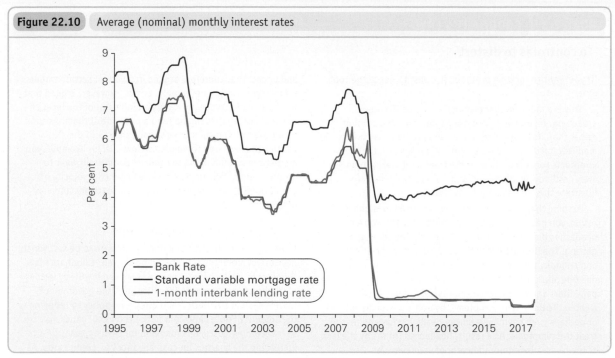

Figure 22.10 Average (nominal) monthly interest rates

Source: Based on series IUMABEDR (Bank Rate), IUMTLMV (mortgage rate) and IUMAVNEA (inter-bank rate) from *Statistical Interactive Database* (Bank of England) (data published 7 December 2017).

- The authorities may need to ensure a sufficient supply of longer-term securities so that liquidity can be constrained. This could commit the government to paying high rates on these bonds for some time.
- High interest rates encourage inflows of money from abroad. This makes it even more difficult to restrain bank lending. This drives up the exchange rate. A higher exchange rate makes domestic goods expensive relative to goods made abroad. This can be very damaging for export industries and industries competing with imports. Many firms in the UK suffered badly between 1997 and 2007 from a high exchange rate, caused partly by higher interest rates in the UK than in the eurozone and the USA.

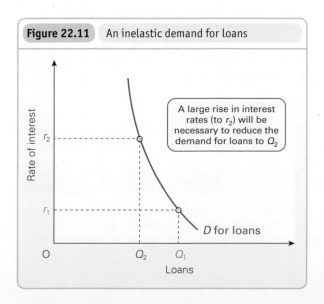

Figure 22.11 An inelastic demand for loans

A large rise in interest rates (to r_2) will be necessary to reduce the demand for loans to Q_2

Evidence suggests that the demand for loans may indeed be quite inelastic, especially in the short run. Although investment plans may be curtailed by high interest rates, borrowing to finance current expenditure by many firms cannot easily be curtailed. Similarly, while householders may be discouraged from taking on new mortgages, they may find it difficult to reduce current expenditure as a means of reducing their credit card debt. What is more, although high interest rates may discourage many firms from taking out long-term fixed-interest loans, some firms may merely switch to shorter-term variable-interest loans.

Problem of an unstable demand

Accurate monetary control requires the authorities to be able to predict the demand curve for money. Only then can they set the appropriate level of interest rates. Unfortunately, the demand curve may shift unpredictably, making control very difficult. The major reason is *speculation*:

- If people think interest rates will rise and bond prices fall, in the meantime they will want to hold their assets in liquid form. The demand for money will rise.
- If people think exchange rates will rise, they will demand sterling while it is still relatively cheap. The demand for money will rise.
- If people think inflation will rise, the transactions demand for money may rise. People spend now while prices are still relatively low.
- If people think the economy is going to grow faster, the demand for loans will increase as firms seek to increase their investment.

BOX 22.8   GOODHART'S LAW

'To control is to distort'

'If you want to tackle a problem, it's best to get to the root of it.'

This is a message that economists are constantly preaching. If you merely treat the symptoms of a problem rather than its underlying causes, the problem may simply manifest itself in some other form. What is more, the symptoms (or lack of them, if the treatment makes them go away) will now be a poor indicator of the problem. Let's illustrate this with a medical example.

Assume that you suffer from deteriorating eyesight. As a result, you get increasingly bad headaches. The worse the headaches become, the worse it suggests your eyesight is getting. The headaches are thus a symptom of the problem and an indicator of the problem's magnitude. So what do you do? One approach is to treat the symptoms. You regularly take painkillers and the headaches go away. But you haven't treated the underlying problem – by getting stronger glasses, or perhaps even having eye surgery – all you have done is to treat the symptoms. As a result, headaches (or rather the lack of them) are now a poor indicator of your eyesight.

If you control the indicator rather than the underlying problem, the indicator ceases to be a good indicator. 'To control [the indicator] is to distort [its use as an indicator].' This is *Goodhart's law* and it has many applications in economics, especially when targets are set by the government. Let us take the example of a money supply target.

KEY IDEA 37

Goodhart's law: Controlling a symptom (i.e. an indicator) of a problem will not cure the problem. Instead, the indicator will merely cease to be a good indicator of the problem.

Money as an indicator of aggregate demand

Monetarists from the 1960s argued that the level of money supply determines the level of nominal aggregate demand and prices. They therefore argued in favour of setting targets for the growth of money supply. Critics, however, argued that the level of money supply is only an indicator of the level of nominal aggregate demand (and a poor one at that). As soon as you start to control money supply, they said, the relationship between them breaks down. If, for example, you restrict the amount of money and yet people still want to borrow, money will simply circulate faster (the velocity of circulation (*V*) will rise), and hence aggregate demand may not decline.

The choice of money supply target

If targets for the growth of money supply are to be set, which measure of money supply should be chosen? Goodhart's law suggests that whichever measure is chosen it will, by virtue of its choice, become a poor indicator. If the government targets cash in circulation and directs its policy to reducing the amount of notes and coin in the economy, banks may try to reduce their customers' demand for cash by, say, increasing the charges for cash advances on credit cards. As a result, cash may well be constrained, but M4 may well go on rising.

The choice of institutions

If bank advances are a good indicator of aggregate demand, the government may choose to control bank lending. But as soon as it does so, bank lending will become a poor indicator. If people's demand for loans is still high and bank loans are becoming difficult to obtain, people will simply go elsewhere to borrow money. If you regulate part of the financial system, you are likely to end up merely diverting business to other parts which are unregulated.

1. *Give some everyday examples of Goodhart's law.*
2. *How may the use of targets in the health service (such as getting waiting lists down) provide an example of Goodhart's Law?*

TC 9 p129

It is very difficult for the authorities to predict what people's expectations, and hence speculation, will be. Speculation depends largely on world political events, rumour and 'random shocks'.

If the demand curve shifts very much, and if it is inelastic, monetary control will be very difficult. Furthermore, the central bank will have to make frequent and sizeable adjustments to interest rates. These fluctuations can be very damaging to business confidence and may discourage long-term investment.

Why does an unstable demand for money make it difficult to control the supply of money?

The net result of an inelastic and unstable demand for money is that substantial interest rate changes may be necessary to bring about the required change in aggregate demand. For example, central banks had to cut interest rates to virtually zero in their attempt to tackle the global recession of the late 2000s. Indeed, as we see in Box 22.9, central banks took to other methods as the room for interest rate cuts simply disappeared.

Using monetary policy

It is impossible to use monetary policy as a precise means of controlling aggregate demand. It is especially weak when it

Definition

Goodhart's law Controlling a symptom of a problem or only one part of the problem will not cure the problem: it will simply mean that the part that is being controlled now becomes a poor indicator of the problem.

| BOX 22.9 | USING INTEREST RATES TO CONTROL *BOTH* AGGREGATE DEMAND *AND* THE EXCHANGE RATE | EXPLORING ECONOMICS |

A problem of one instrument and two targets

Assume that the central bank is worried about excessive growth in the money supply and rising inflation. It thus decides to raise interest rates. One effect of these higher interest rates is to attract deposits into the country (causing a financial account surplus) and thus drive up the exchange rate. This makes imports cheaper and exports less competitive. This will result in a current account deficit, which will match the financial (plus capital) account surplus.

Now let us assume that the central bank becomes worried about the damaging effect on exports and wants to reduce the exchange rate. If it uses interest rates as the means of achieving this, it will have to lower them: lower interest rates will cause deposits to flow out of the country, and this will cause the rate of exchange to depreciate.

But there is a dilemma here. The central bank wants high interest rates to contain inflation, but low interest rates to help exporters. If interest rates are the only policy instrument, one objective will have to be sacrificed for the other.

Another example, but this time the reverse case, was when the UK voted to leave the EU in June 2016. Worried about the possible dampening effect on investment and economic

growth from worries about trade relationships, the Bank of England *lowered* Bank Rate from 0.5 to 0.25 per cent and backed this up with another round of quantitative easing. However, the worries about UK trade also drove down the exchange rate, which increased the price of imports and increased inflation – at least temporarily. If the Bank of England had wanted to dampen this inflation, it would have to have *raised* Bank Rate. Clearly, it could not both lower and raise Bank Rate at the same time.

These examples illustrate a rule in economic policy: you must have at least as many instruments as targets. If you have two targets (e.g. low inflation and a low exchange rate), you must have at least two policy instruments (e.g. interest rates and one other).

1. *Give some other examples of the impossibility of using one policy instrument to achieve two policy objectives simultaneously.*
2. *If the central bank wanted to achieve a lower rate of inflation and also a higher exchange rate, could it under these circumstances rely simply on the one policy instrument of interest rates?*

is pulling against the expectations of firms and consumers, and when it is implemented too late. However, if the authorities operate a tight monetary policy firmly enough and long enough, they should eventually be able to reduce lending and aggregate demand. But there will inevitably be time lags and imprecision in the process.

An expansionary monetary policy is even less reliable. If the economy is in recession, no matter how low interest rates are driven, people cannot be forced to borrow if they do not wish to. Firms will not borrow to invest if they predict a continuing recession.

A particular difficulty in using interest rate reductions to expand the economy arises if the repo rate is nearly zero but this is still not enough to stimulate the economy. The problem is that (nominal) market interest rates cannot be negative (except in the case for overnight deposits by banks in the central bank), for clearly nobody would be willing to lend in these circumstances. The UK and many eurozone countries were in this position in the early 2010s. They found themselves caught in the 'liquidity trap' (see pages 590). Despite record low interest rates and high levels of liquidity, borrowing and lending remained low given worries about fiscal austerity and its dampening effects on economic growth.

One way in which central banks, like the Federal Reserve, the Bank of England and the ECB, attempted to encourage

spending following the financial crisis of the late 2000s was by publicly indicating the expected path of future interest rates. By stating that interest rates were likely to remain low for some time, central banks hoped that *forward guidance* would give economic agents confidence to bring forward their spending.

Despite these problems, changing interest rates can be quite effective in the medium term. After all, they can be changed very rapidly. There are not the time lags of implementation that there are with various forms of fiscal policy. Indeed, since the early 1990s, most governments or central banks have used interest rate changes as the major means of keeping inflation and/or aggregate demand under control.

In the UK, the eurozone and many other countries, the government or central bank sets a target for the rate of inflation for the medium term. In the UK, the target is 2 per cent CPI inflation in two years' time plus or minus 1 per cent. In the eurozone, the target is a rate of CPI inflation[5] below, but close to, 2 per cent over the medium term (where the precise period is unspecified). If forecasts suggest that inflation is going to be off-target, interest rate changes are announced, and then appropriate open-market operations are conducted to support the new interest rate. The use of such targets is examined in section 22.4.

One important effect of changing interest rates in this very public way is that it sends a clear message to people that inflation *will* be kept under control. People will therefore be more likely to adjust their expectations accordingly and keep their borrowing in check.

5 In the eurozone the CPI is known as the 'harmonised index of consumer prices (HICP)'.

BOX 22.10 **QUANTITATIVE EASING**

Rethinking monetary policy in hard times

As the economies of the world slid into recession in 2008, central banks became more and more worried that the traditional instrument of monetary policy – controlling interest rates – was insufficient to ward off a slump in demand.

Running out of options?

Interest rates had been cut at an unprecedented rate. Central banks were reaching the end of the road for interest rate cuts. The Fed was the first to be in this position. It had made several cuts in the target federal funds rate – the overnight rate at which the Fed lends to banks. By December 2008 it had been cut to a range between 0 and 0.25 per cent. Meanwhile in the UK, Bank Rate had fallen to 0.5 per cent by March 2009. But you cannot, in most cases, cut nominal rates below zero – otherwise you would be paying people to borrow money, which would be like giving people free money!

The problem was that there was an acute lack of willingness of banks to lend and firms and consumers to borrow as people saw the oncoming recession. So the cuts in interest rates were not having enough effect on aggregate demand.

Increasing the money supply

So what were central banks to do? The answer was to increase money supply directly, in a process known as *quantitative easing*. This involves an aggressive version of open-market operations, where the central bank buys up a range of assets, such as securitised mortgage debt and long-term government bonds. The effect is to pump large amounts of additional cash into the economy in the hope of stimulating demand and, through the process of credit creation, to boost broad money too.

In the USA, in December 2008, at the same time as the federal funds rate was cut to a range of 0 to 0.25 per cent, the Fed was already embarking on large-scale quantitative easing. As we saw in Box 22.6, the Fed began buying hundreds of billions of dollars worth of mortgage-backed securities on the open market and planned also to buy large quantities of long-term government debt.

The Federal Open Market Committee (the interest rate setting body in the USA) said that, 'The focus of the committee's policy going forward will be to support the functioning of financial markets and stimulate the economy through open-market operations and other measures that sustain the size of the Federal Reserve's balance sheet at a high level.' The result was that considerable quantities of new money were injected into the system. At the conclusion of three rounds of QE in October 2014 it had purchased assets of $2.5 trillion.

A similar approach was adopted in the UK. In January 2009, the Bank of England was given powers by the Treasury to buy on the open market up to £50 billion of existing government bonds (gilts) and high-quality private-sector assets, such as corporate bonds and commercial paper. The purchases from non-bank financial institutions were with newly created electronic money. But this was only the start.

In March 2009, as the recession deepened, the Chancellor agreed to increase the scale of purchases, so beginning the second and substantive phase of quantitative easing. These purchases, mainly government bonds (gilts) resulted in a substantial increase in banks' reserves at the Bank of England and hence in the Bank's balance sheet (see Table 18.2 on page 566). By July 2012, asset purchases had been made totalling £375 billion. In August 2016, with concerns about the prospects for the UK economy following the vote to leave the European Union, the Bank of England increased its gilt purchases by a further £60 billion to £435 billion.

Section summary

1. Control of the growth in the money supply over the longer term will normally involve governments attempting to restrict the size of their deficits. Whilst this is relatively easy once inflation has been brought under control, it can lead to serious problems if inflation is initially high. Increases in taxes and cuts in government expenditure are not only politically unpopular, but could also result in a recession.

2. In the short term, the authorities can use monetary policy to restrict the growth in aggregate demand in one of two major ways: (a) reducing money supply directly; (b) reducing the demand for money by raising interest rates.

3. The money supply can be reduced directly by using open-market operations. This involves the central bank selling more government securities and thereby reducing banks' reserves when their customers pay for them from their bank accounts. Alternatively, the central bank can reduce the amount of lending or rediscounting it is prepared to do (other than as a last-resort measure). Rather than

Definition

Quantitative easing A deliberate attempt by the central bank to increase the money supply by buying large quantities of securities through open-market operations. These securities could be securitised mortgage and other private-sector debt or government bonds.

Additionally, it agreed to purchase up to £10 billion of UK corporate bonds.

The ECB was more reticent about adopting quantitative easing. But with growth in the eurozone averaging only 0.4 per annum from 2011 to 2014 and deflation emerging towards the end of 2014, a programme of quantitative easing began in March 2015 at a rate of €60 billion per month. Initially, the scheme was to run to September 2016 with total purchases of up to €1.08 trillion. However, with the inflation rate averaging zero per cent in early 2016, the scheme was extended into 2017, with monthly purchases rising in March 2016 to €80 billion (and including corporate bonds for the first time). However, with eurozone growth beginning to increase, monthly purchases fell back to €60 billion per month from April 2017, but the scheme was extended to the end of 2017. Total asset purchases were expected to be around €2.3 trillion.

The transmission mechanism of asset purchases

By financing asset purchases through the creation of central bank reserves, quantitative easing involves increasing the amount of narrow money. It can also, indirectly, increase broad money. There are two principal ways in which this can happen.

The first is through the effects on asset prices and yields. When non-bank financial intermediaries, including insurance companies and pension funds, sell assets to the central bank they can use the money to purchase other assets. In doing so, this will drive up their prices. This, in turn, reduces the yields on these assets (at a higher price there is less dividend or interest per pound spent on them), which should help to reduce interest rates and make the cost of borrowing cheaper for households and firms, so boosting aggregate demand.

Also, for those holding these now more expensive assets there is a positive wealth effect. For instance, households with longer-term saving plans involving securities will now have greater financial wealth. Again, this will boost spending.

The second mechanism is through bank lending. Banks will find their reserve balances increase as those selling assets deposit the proceeds in their bank accounts. This will increase the liquidity ratio of banks, which could encourage them to grant more credit.

However, it is all very well increasing the monetary base, but a central bank cannot force banks to lend or people to borrow. That requires confidence. We observed in Box 18.6 the continued weakness of bank lending to the non-bank private sector through the late 2000s and into the early 2010s.

This is not to say that quantitative easing failed in the UK and elsewhere: growth in credit and broad money could have been weaker still. However, it does illustrate the potential danger of this approach if, in the short run, little credit creation takes place. In the equation $MV = PY$, the rise in (narrow) money supply (M) may be largely offset by a fall in the velocity of circulation (V) (see pages 591–9).

On the other hand, there is also the danger that if this policy is conducted for too long, the growth in money supply could prove to be excessive, resulting in inflation rising above the target level. It is therefore important for central banks to foresee this and turn the monetary 'tap' off in time. This would involve 'quantitative tightening' – selling assets that the central bank had purchased, thereby driving down asset prices and driving up interest rates.

 Would it be appropriate to define the policy of quantitative easing as 'monetarist'?

---

controlling the monetary base in either of these two ways, the central bank could adjust its funding of the national debt. This would involve increasing the sale of bonds relative to bills, thereby reducing banks' liquid assets. Finally, it could operate a system of variable minimum reserve ratios. Increasing these would force banks to cut back the amount of credit they create.

4. Controlling either the monetary base or broad liquidity in the short term, however, is difficult given that central banks are always prepared to provide liquidity to the banks on demand. Even if the authorities are successful in controlling the money supply, there then arises the problem of severe fluctuations in interest rates if the demand for money fluctuates and is relatively inelastic.

5. The current method of control in the UK and many other countries involves the central bank influencing interest rates by its operations in the gilt repo and discount markets. The central bank keeps banks short of liquidity and then supplies them with liquidity, largely through gilt repos, at its chosen interest rate (gilt repo rate). This

then has a knock-on effect on interest rates throughout the economy.

6. With an interest-inelastic demand for loans, however, changes in interest rates may have to be very large to bring the required changes in monetary growth. High interest rates are politically unpopular and discriminate against those with high borrowing commitments. They also drive up the exchange rate, which can damage exports. Controlling aggregate demand through interest rates is made even more difficult by fluctuations in the demand for money. These fluctuations are made more severe by speculation against changes in interest rates, exchange rates, the rate of inflation, etc.

7. It is impossible to use monetary policy as a precise means of controlling aggregate demand in the short term. Nevertheless, controlling interest rates is a rapid way of responding to changing forecasts, and can be an important signal to markets that inflation will be kept under control, especially when, as in the UK and the eurozone, there is a firm target for the rate of inflation.

22.4 THE POLICY-MAKING ENVIRONMENT

Debates over the control of demand have shifted ground somewhat in recent years. There is now less debate over the relative effectiveness of fiscal and monetary policy in influencing aggregate demand. There is general agreement that a *combination* of fiscal and monetary policies will have a more powerful effect on demand than either used separately.

Economists have become increasingly interested in the environment within which policy is made. In this section we analyse debates around the extent to which governments ought to pursue active demand management policies or adhere to a set of policy rules.

Those in the Keynesian tradition prefer discretionary policy – changing policy as circumstances change. Those in the monetarist and new classical tradition prefer to set firm rules (e.g. targets for inflation, public deficits or growth in the money supply) and then stick to them.

KI 34 p445

The case for rules

There are two important arguments against discretionary policy and for rules: the political incentives of governments and time lags.

Political behaviour

Politicians may attempt to manipulate the economy for their own political purposes – such as the desire to be re-elected. As we saw in section 21.2 when discussing the *political business cycle* (see page 650), the government, if not constrained by rules, may overstimulate the economy some time before an election so that growth is strong at election time. After the election, the government strongly dampens the economy to deal with the higher inflation which is now beginning to accelerate, and to create enough slack for another boost in time for the next election.

A less extreme version is where governments from time to time use monetary and fiscal policy to try to boost their popularity. The manipulation of policy instruments is not necessarily systematic or regular in the way that the political business cycle model implies. Nonetheless, the manipulation is intended to court short-term favour with the public and may store up problems for the economy and, in the case of fiscal policy, for the public finances.

It is argued that when politicians behave in this way, fiscal policy may exhibit a **deficit bias**. Because governments are more willing to use their discretion to loosen fiscal policy than they are to tighten fiscal policy, persistent deficits and a rising debt-to-GDP ratio can result. Table 22.1 (on page 671) provides some support for this. Therefore, fiscal rules may be needed to ensure the long-term sustainability of public finances.

It is also argued that politically motivated policy makers can lose *credibility* concerning sound economic management. This can lead to higher inflationary expectations, uncertainty and lower long-term investment. Trade unions are likely to bargain for increases in wages that protect their purchasing power should government loosen its policy

stance to try and boost its popularity. The result could be an *inflation bias*, with inflation typically higher than it would otherwise be, but with unemployment no lower.

As we saw in section 21.5 (and Box 21.6), the possibility of inflation bias (see pages 660–63) is one of the principal arguments behind the move in many countries for the delegation of monetary policy to central banks.

Time lags with discretionary policy

Both fiscal and monetary policies can involve long and variable time lags. These can make policy at best ineffective and at worst destabilising (see Figure 22.5 on page 682). Taking the measures *before* the problem arises, and thus lessening the problem of lags, is usually not an option since forecasting tends to be unreliable.

KI 33 p368

In contrast, by setting and sticking to rules, and then not interfering further, the government can provide a sound fiscal and monetary framework in which there is maximum freedom for individual initiative and enterprise, and in which firms are not cushioned from market forces and are therefore encouraged to be efficient. By the government setting a target for a steady reduction in the growth of money supply, or a target for the rate of inflation, and then resolutely sticking to it, people's expectations of inflation will be reduced, thereby making the target easier to achieve.

This sound and stable monetary environment, with no likelihood of sudden contractionary or expansionary fiscal or monetary policy, will encourage firms to take a longer-term perspective and to plan ahead. This could then lead to increased capital investment and long-term growth.

KI 15 p129

The optimum situation is for all the major countries to adhere to mutually consistent rules, so that their economies do not get out of line. This will create more stable exchange rates and provide the climate for world growth (we explore this issue in section 26.1).

Advocates of this point of view in the 1970s and 1980s were monetarists and new classical macroeconomists, but support for the setting of targets was to become widespread. As we have seen, in both the UK and the eurozone countries, targets are set for both inflation and public-sector deficits.

 Would it be desirable for all countries to stick to the same targets?

The case for discretion

Keynesians typically reject the argument that rules provide the environment for high and stable growth. Demand, argue Keynesians, is subject to many and sometimes violent

> ### Definitions
>
> **Deficit bias** The tendency for frequent fiscal deficits and rising debt-to-GDP ratios because of the reluctance of policy makers to tighten fiscal policy.

exogenous shocks: e.g. changes in expectations, domestic political events (such as an impending election), financial market effects (such as the credit crunch), world economic factors (such as the global economic recession of 2008–9) or world political events (such as a war). The resulting shifts in injections or withdrawals cause the economy to deviate from a stable full-employment growth path.

Any change in injections or withdrawals will lead to a cumulative effect on national income via the multiplier and accelerator and via changing expectations. These endogenous effects take time and interact with each other, and so a process of expansion or contraction can last many months before a turning point is eventually reached.

Since the exogenous changes in demand occur at irregular intervals and are of different magnitudes, the economy is likely to experience cycles of irregular duration and of varying intensity.

Given that the economy is inherently unstable and is buffeted around by various exogenous shocks, Keynesians argue that the government needs actively to intervene to stabilise the economy. Otherwise, the uncertainty caused by unpredictable fluctuations will be very damaging to investment and hence to long-term growth in potential output (quite apart from the short-term effects of recessions on actual output and employment).

If demand fluctuates in the way Keynesians claim, and if the policy of having a money supply or inflation rule is adhered to, interest rates must fluctuate. But excessive fluctuations in interest rates will discourage long-term business planning and investment. What is more, the government may find it difficult to keep to its targets. This too may cause uncertainty and instability.

Problems with targets

Assume that the government or central bank decides to set policy rules. Should they stick to these rules, come what may? What degree of flexibility should be designed into any rules? Should policy makers at least have the discretion to *change* the rules, even if only occasionally?

For example, when a target has been in force for some time, it may cease to be the appropriate one. Economic circumstances might change. For example, a faster growth in productivity or a large increase in oil revenues may increase potential growth and thus warrant a faster growth in money supply. Or an extended period of relatively low inflation may warrant a lower inflation target.

If an inflation target is chosen, then again the problem of Goodhart's Law is likely to apply. If people believe that their central bank will be successful in achieving its inflation target, then those expectations will feed into their inflationary expectations, and not surprisingly the target will be met.

The problem with inflation targets therefore is that they can become consistent with both a buoyant and a depressed economy. In other words, the Phillips curve may become *horizontal*. Consequently, as we explained in section 21.5, the *DAS* curve too becomes horizontal (at least up to near full capacity in the economy). Shifts in the *DAD* curve will

simply lead to changes in real national income. Thus achieving an inflation target may not tackle the much more serious problem of creating stable economic growth and an environment which will encourage long-term investment.

In extreme cases, as occurred in 2008, the economy may slow down rapidly and yet cost-push factors may cause inflation to rise. Strictly adhering to an inflation rate target in these circumstances would demand *higher* interest rates, which could further restrict growth. A similar argument applied to the UK after the Brexit vote. The fall in the pound threatened to push up inflation and yet the Bank of England decided to cut Bank Rate. The aim was to ward off a downswing in the economy.

But if rules should not be stuck to religiously, does this mean that the policy makers can engage in fine-tuning? Keynesians today recognise that fine-tuning may not be possible; nevertheless, significant and persistent excess or deficient demand *can* be corrected by demand management policy. For example, the actions taken in the late 2000s following the financial crisis by several central banks to cut interest rates substantially, and by governments to increase expenditures and to cut taxes, helped to stave off even deeper recessions.

Improvements in forecasting, a willingness of governments to act quickly and the use of quick-acting policies can all help to increase the effectiveness of discretionary demand management.

 Under what circumstances would adherence to money supply targets lead to (a) more stable interest rates and (b) less stable interest rates than pursuing discretionary demand management policy?

Central banks and a Taylor rule

Given the potential problems in adhering to simple inflation rate targets, many economists have advocated the use of a *Taylor rule*.[6] A Taylor rule takes two objectives into account – (1) inflation and (2) either real national income or unemployment – and seeks to get the optimum degree of stability of the two. The degree of importance attached to each of the two objectives can be decided by the government or central bank. The central bank adjusts interest rates when either the rate of inflation diverges from its target or the level of real national income (or unemployment) diverges from its potential (or natural) level.

Definitions

Taylor rule A rule adopted by a central bank for setting the rate of interest. It will raise the interest rate if (a) inflation is above target or (b) real national income is above the potential level (or unemployment is below the natural rate). The rule states how much interest rates will be changed in each case.

---

6 Named after John Taylor, from Stanford University, who in a 1993 paper, 'Discretion versus policy rules in practice' (*Carnegie-Rochester Conference Series on Public Policy 39* (North-Holland, 1993)), proposed a representative monetary policy rule based on the rate of inflation over the past four quarters and the percentage deviation of real GDP from a target.

KI 34
p445

TC 15
p535

KI 34
p445

A general form of the Taylor rule can be written as follows:

$$r = r^* + b(\pi - \pi^*) + c(Y - Y_p) \tag{2}$$

where r is the real rate of interest set by the central bank; r^* is the real rate of interest consistent with long-run equilibrium in the economy, also known as 'the natural real interest rate'; π is the current rate of inflation; π^* is the target rate of inflation, Y is the current level of real national income and Y_p the potential level of real national income.

What this equation says is that if inflation goes above its target, or if real national income rises above its potential level, the central bank will raise the real rate of interest, the amount depending on the values of b and c respectively. John Taylor proposed that for every 1 per cent that inflation rises above its target level, real interest rates should be raised by 0.5 percentage points (i.e. nominal rates should be raised by 1.5 percentage points), and that for every 1 per cent that real national income rises above its potential level, real interest rates should be raised by 0.5 percentage points (i.e. nominal rates should be raised by 0.5 percentage points).

 The terms 'doves' and 'hawks' are frequently used to describe central banks. How do these terms relate to the Taylor rule?

Taylor rules and the DAD/DAS framework

We can illustrate the economic significance of the relative weights in the Taylor rule given by the central bank to inflation (b) and real national income (c) using the *DAD/DAS* framework introduced in section 20.2. Consider Figure 22.12. It shows two alternative *DAD* (dynamic aggregate demand) curves. Assume that the economy is currently at point a, with inflation on target and real national income at Y_p, which happens to be the potential level. Now assume that inflation rises to π_1. As this is above the target level, the central bank raises the rate of interest. This causes real national income to fall and is represented by a movement up along the *DAD* curve.

If the central bank puts a high weight on controlling inflation rather than on stabilising real national income around its potential level, the curve will be relatively flat, like DAD_1 in Figure 22.12. The bank will be prepared to raise interest rates a lot and, as a result, see real national income fall a lot in the short term.

If, however, it puts a relatively high weight on stabilising real national income around its potential level, the curve will be relatively steep, like DAD_2. The bank will not be prepared to see real national income fall very much and will thus only raise interest rates modestly.

Thus the central bank has to trade off inflation stability against real income stability. Its Taylor rule shows its optimum trade-off and is illustrated by the slope of the *DAD* curve.

Conclusions

The following factors provide us with a framework to help analyse the relative merits of rules or discretion.

- The confidence of people in the effectiveness of either discretionary policies or rules: the greater the confidence, the more successful is either policy likely to be.
- The degree of self-stabilisation of the economy (in the case of rules), or conversely the degree of inherent instability of the economy (in the case of discretion).
- The size and frequency of exogenous shocks to demand: the greater they are, the greater the case for discretionary policy.
- In the case of rules, the ability and determination of governments to stick to the rules and the belief by the public that they will be effective.
- In the case of discretionary policy, the ability of governments to adopt and execute policies of the correct magnitude, the speed with which such policies can be effected and the accuracy of forecasting.

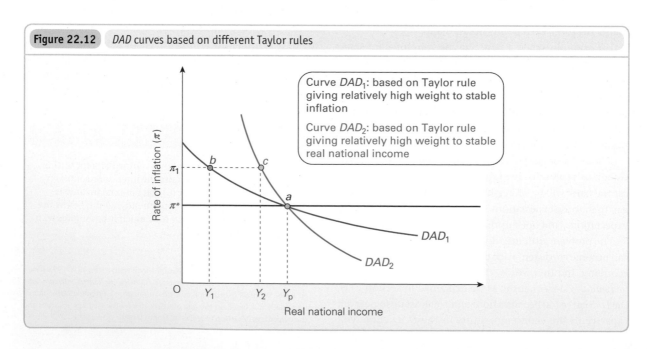

Figure 22.12 *DAD* curves based on different Taylor rules

Curve DAD_1: based on Taylor rule giving relatively high weight to stable inflation

Curve DAD_2: based on Taylor rule giving relatively high weight to stable real national income

22.5 CENTRAL BANKS, ECONOMIC SHOCKS AND THE MACROECONOMY: AN INTEGRATED MODEL

Developing an integrated macroeconomic model

Shocks regularly hit economies. The adjustment of economies is affected, in part, by the way in which people and the markets in which they interact subsequently behave.

But then there is the behaviour of policy makers too. In recent decades there has been a general shift to place some constraints on the discretion of policy makers. This is particularly so in the case of monetary policy, with many countries having delegated monetary policy to central banks. The result is that many central banks now have macroeconomic remits which include targeting inflation. This objective is often supplemented with a requirement that the central bank be mindful of the implications of its monetary policy for other macroeconomic variables, such as growth or employment.

The purpose of this section is to develop an integrated model of an economy bringing together the *IS/MP, DAD/DAS* and *EAPC* frameworks. It is developed in the modern context of central banks with monetary policy rules, which include the targeting of inflation. Specifically, we model the possible response of a series of endogenous macroeconomic variables – output, unemployment inflation and interest rates – to exogenous economic shocks. These responses characterise the dynamics of economies. We consider first a demand shock and then a supply shock.

Assumptions and simulations

In developing our integrated model we necessarily make certain assumptions. Yet these assumptions affect the adjustment paths of our key variables to the shocks. Consequently, it is important to think about the sensitivity of our results to any changes in our assumptions. It is for this reason that forecasters will run simulations and then compare the response of the economy to shocks under different assumptions. These assumptions include, for example, the monetary policy rule, the speed at which prices in goods and labour markets adjust and the formation of expectations.

We will assume that the central bank behaves according a Taylor rule and adjusts real interest rates in response to deviations in the rate of inflation from its target ($\pi - \pi^*$) and real national income from its potential level ($Y - Y_p$). We assume too that input prices exhibit a degree of stickiness in the short run which enables a short-run trade between inflation and economic activity. We will show that this is reinforced when past inflation rates determine expectations of inflation.

Demand-side shocks

Constant inflationary expectations

Figure 22.13 combines the three principal models that we have used to analyse the macroeconomy. Diagrams (a) and (b) combine the expectations-augmented Phillips curve (*EAPC*) and *DAD/DAS* models, as shown previously in section 21.5. The economy is assumed to be in long-run equilibrium. From these two models, we can see that unemployment is at the natural rate (U_n) (point a'), real national income at potential level (Y_p) (point a), the rate of inflation is at the target rate (π^*) and the expected rate of inflation is equal to the target rate ($\pi^e = \pi^*$).

From the *IS/MP* model in diagram (c), we can see that the central bank is setting a real rate of interest r^* (point a''). With the economy in long-run equilibrium at Y_p this interest rate is referred to as the economy's equilibrium or 'natural' real interest.

Short-run adjustment to a rise in aggregate demand. Now assume that there is a rise in aggregate demand from, say, a rise in consumer confidence. The *DAD* and *IS* curves shift to the right, to DAD_2 and IS_2 respectively. The rise in aggregate demand causes a rise in real national income, but also a rise in inflation. This is shown by a movement upwards along the short-run *DAS* curve to point b in diagram (b), which corresponds to movement upwards along the expectations-augmented Phillips curve to point b' in diagram (a).

In response to the higher rate of inflation of π_1, the central bank raises the nominal rate of interest (i) more than the rise in inflation (π), thereby raising the *real* rate of interest (r). The extent to which the real interest rate rises depends on how strictly the central bank targets inflation stabilisation.

Figure 22.13   Increase in real aggregate demand with anchored inflationary expectations

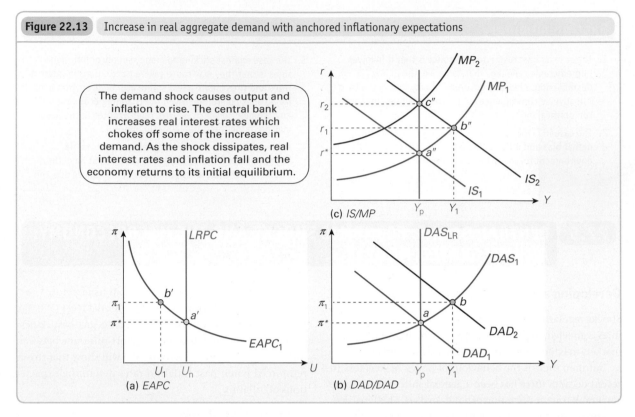

The demand shock causes output and inflation to rise. The central bank increases real interest rates which chokes off some of the increase in demand. As the shock dissipates, real interest rates and inflation fall and the economy returns to its initial equilibrium.

(c) *IS/MP*

(a) *EAPC*

(b) *DAD/DAD*

Consequently, there is a movement upwards along a short-run *MP* curve in diagram (c). A new short-run equilibrium is reached at point b'', with a real interest rate of r_1.

With the economy's real national income above its potential level and the unemployment rate below its natural rate, inflation rises to π_1 – above the target rate (π^*).

Long-term adjustment.   The analysis now turns to the longer-term adjustment path of the economy (assuming inflationary expectations remained anchored).

A likely scenario, given the volatility of economies, is that the positive demand-side shock will gradually subside. If so, the *DAD* will move leftwards in diagram (b). As aggregate demand falls we slide back down the short-run *DAS* curve and the rate of inflation falls. This movement is mirrored by a corresponding movement down the *EAPC* in diagram (a). As the inflation rate falls the central bank reduces real interest rates. The nominal interest rate falls by more than the fall in the rate of inflation. Eventually, the economy returns to the original long-run equilibrium.

Another possibility is that the positive demand-shock may persist for some time – or that the central bank may forecast that it will. In this case, if the central bank is to return the economy to point *a* in diagram (b) with inflation on target and real national income at the potential level, it must shift the *DAD* curve back again. It does this by adopting a tighter monetary policy (i.e. a higher real interest rate for each rate of inflation). It thus raises the real interest rate above r_1, initially to r_2, as shown in diagram (c). In other words, the *MP* curve will shift upwards to MP_2.

The effect of the tighter monetary policy will be to shift the DAD_2 curve back towards DAD_1 and equilibrium will be

restored at point *a*. This is matched in diagram (a) by a move from b' to a'. In diagram (c), the tighter monetary policy is represented by a movement up *along* curve IS_2 to point c''.

 How will the composition of aggregate demand at points c'' and a'' in Figure 22.13(c) differ?

Adaptive inflationary expectations

Up to this point we have assumed that inflationary expectations are 'anchored'. We now consider how the economy's adjustment to a demand shock is affected if people's inflationary expectations *adjust* during this process. We assume that there is a lag in the adjustment of inflationary expectations with people using past inflation rates as a predictor of current inflation rates.

Each *EAPC,* short-run *DAS* curve and short-run *MP* curve is based on a given expected rate of inflation, which will directly impact on the actual rate of inflation. But what happens in the next time period when expectations adjust? The answer is that each short-run curve shifts upwards *if the* expected rate of inflation rises, and shifts downwards *if* it falls. This is illustrated in Figure 22.14.

Again we assume that at the initial equilibrium real national income is at its potential level (Y_p), unemployment is at the natural rate (U_n) and that expected inflation is the actual (targeted) inflation ($\pi^e = \pi^*$).). Finally, the natural real rate of interest is r^*.

An initial positive demand shock.   Now, as before, assume there is a positive demand shock with a rise in consumer confidence. To make the analysis more straightforward we will assume that the shock lasts two periods, at which point

Figure 22.14 | Increase in real aggregate demand with adaptive inflationary expectations

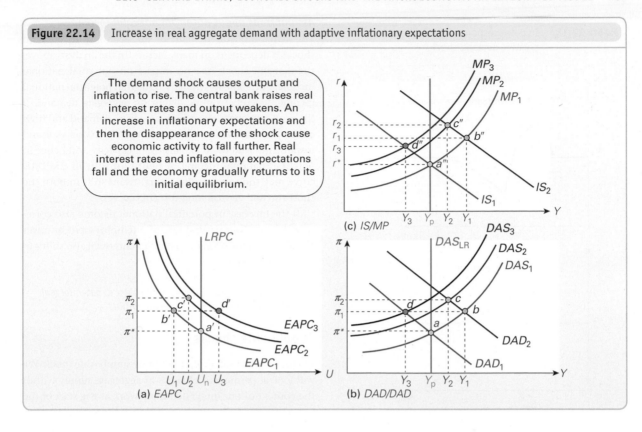

The demand shock causes output and inflation to rise. The central bank raises real interest rates and output weakens. An increase in inflationary expectations and then the disappearance of the shock cause economic activity to fall further. Real interest rates and inflationary expectations fall and the economy gradually returns to its initial equilibrium.

(c) IS/MP

(a) EAPC

(b) DAD/DAD

demand conditions return to their previous state. This rise in aggregate demand shifts the *DAD* curve to DAD_2 and the *IS* curve to IS_2. In the short run there is a movement along the DAS_1 and MP_1 curves to point b and b'' respectively.

The rise in real aggregate demand and in economic activity is mirrored by the move along $EAPC_1$ from point a' to b'. In the process, the rate of inflation rises from π^* to π_1. The central bank raises nominal and real interest rates, which chokes off some of the increase in aggregate demand. The extent to which it raises rates again depends on the monetary policy rule (and hence the shape of the *MP* and *DAD* curves).

Adjustment of inflationary expectations. We now assume that in the second period people raise their inflationary expectations to the now higher rate of inflation π_1, which, in turn, drives up the actual rate of inflation. This causes an upward shift in the *EAPC* and the *DAS* and *MP* curves, say to $EAPC_2$, DAS_2 and MP_2.

The central bank responds to the further rise in the rate of inflation by increasing real interest rates, which rise to r_2. The new short-run equilibrium in the second period sees the inflation rate at π_2, real national income fall from Y_1 to Y_2 and unemployment rise from U_1 to U_2. Thus, while the inflation rate is higher, economic activity falls back following its initial increase.

We now move into the third period. Inflationary expectations rise further to π_2. This is in response to the higher inflation rate experienced in the second period. Consequently, the *EAPC* and the *DAS* and *MP* curves shift upwards again, say to $EAPC_3$, DAS_3 and MP_3 respectively. But the aggregate demand shock is assumed now to disappear so that the *DAD* curve shifts leftwards back to its original position DAD_1. Therefore,

the economy moves from point c to d in the *DAD/DAS* model and point c' to d' in the *EAPC* model. As it does, output falls below its potential level and unemployment rises above its natural rate. The central bank now reduces real interest rates in response, but because inflation is still above its target rate, the real interest rate r_3 is still above its natural level r^*.

Over the following periods, economic activity recovers as inflation and expected inflation fall. As it does so, the *EAPC* and the *DAS* and *MP* curves shift downwards. The economy therefore returns to its initial long-run equilibrium. The quicker expectations adjust, the sooner the economy will return to its long-run equilibrium.

 If expectations were formed rationally with no time lags, what would be the implications for short-run DAS curves and for the response to a rise in aggregate demand?

Impulse response functions. The adjustment path of key macroeconomic variables to economic shocks can be represented in diagrams known as ***impulse response functions***. In Figure 22.15 we show the impulse response functions for output (real national income) and real interest rates consistent with the analysis in Figure 22.14. These time paths illustrate how both output and real interest rates adjust following the shock in period 1. For example, we can see clearly how output falls below its potential level during

> ### Definition
>
> **Impulse response functions** The time paths of key macroeconomic variables following economic shocks.

KI 34 p445

TC 9 p129

KI 34 p445

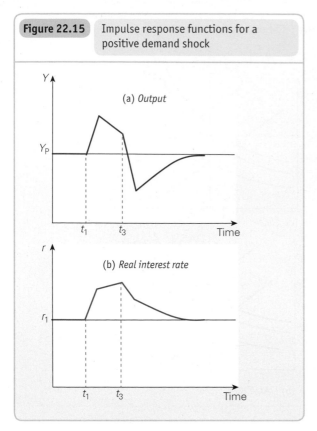

Figure 22.15 Impulse response functions for a positive demand shock

(a) *Output*

(b) *Real interest rate*

period 3. Both variables are assumed to gradually return to their original equilibrium levels

Based on the analysis in Figure 22.14, what would an impulse response function look like for the rate of inflation?

Assumptions about potential national income

The actual adjustment path of the economy to demand shocks is dependent on many factors. In the analysis above, the demand shock had no impact on potential national income. But, some Keynesians argue that potential national income depends to some extent on aggregate demand. If the economy experiences high aggregate demand and high output, this may encourage investment, both domestic and inward, and lead to an expansion of capacity and hence in potential national income. A rightward shift in the *DAD* curve may thus also result in a rightward shift in both the short-run and vertical long-run *DAS* curves.

If the increase in potential national income also corresponds to a lower natural rate of unemployment or lower NAIRU, the vertical long-run Phillips curve will also shift – in this case to the left.

 Under what circumstances would a rise in potential real income not result in a fall in the NAIRU?

Supply-side shocks

We finish by considering a temporary supply-side shock. We will look at permanent changes in aggregate supply within the context of our integrated framework at the start of the next chapter, which focuses on long-term economic growth.

We assume that there is a one-period negative economic shock, say caused by higher commodity price inflation. We also assume that people form their inflationary expectations adaptively based on the previous period's inflation rate.

In Figure 22.16 the economy is at its long-run equilibrium when the inflationary shock occurs. There is now a higher

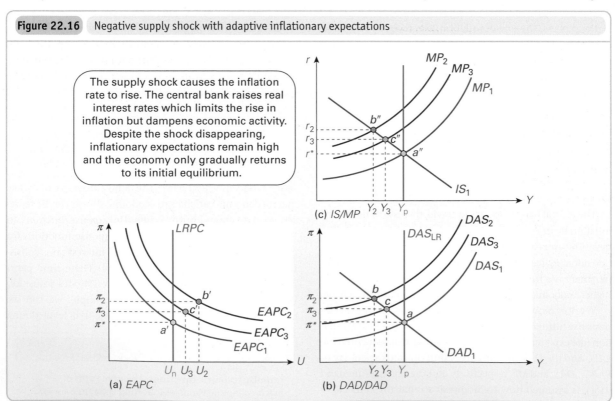

Figure 22.16 Negative supply shock with adaptive inflationary expectations

The supply shock causes the inflation rate to rise. The central bank raises real interest rates which limits the rise in inflation but dampens economic activity. Despite the shock disappearing, inflationary expectations remain high and the economy only gradually returns to its initial equilibrium.

(c) *IS/MP*

(a) *EAPC*

(b) *DAD/DAD*

Inflation rate at any of level of economic output or unemployment because of the exogenous cost pressures. This has the effect of causing the *EAPC* and the *DAS* and *MP* curves to shift vertically upwards to $EAPC_2$, DAS_2 and MP_2 respectively. We can see from diagram (b) that we therefore move upwards along the *DAD* curve from point *a* to point *b*. The central bank raises real interest rates in response to the higher rate of inflation. In diagram (c) real interest rates rise from r^* to r_2. The extent of the rise again depends on the monetary policy rule. The more the central bank targets inflation stabilisation the more that the economy contracts.

Despite the dampening effect on inflation from the fall in output, in the following period inflationary expectations rise. Hence, although the initial inflationary shock has now disappeared, the *EAPC* and the *DAS* and *MP* curves remain above their initial position. Thereafter, they gradually shift downwards as inflationary expectations fall, for example to $EAPC_3$, DAS_3 and MP_3. As they do, real interest rates fall and economic activity increases: real national income increases and the rate of unemployment falls. Eventually, the economy returns to its initial long-run equilibrium.

Based on the analysis in Figure 22.16 what would the impulse response functions look like for output, unemployment, inflation and real and nominal interest rates?

Section summary

1. Many central banks nowadays are tasked with using monetary policy to help deliver pre-defined macroeconomic objectives. This frequently involves targeting inflation.

2. By combining the *EAPC, DAD/DAS* and *IS/MP* models it is possible to analyse the relationships between output, unemployment, inflation and interest rates in a contemporary policy-making context.

3. The combined frameworks can be used to analyse the effects of demand and supply shocks. Different adjustment paths for the economy result from different assumptions about the workings of the economy.

4. We can plot the adjustment paths for key macroeconomic variables following demand or supply shocks. The time plots are known as impulse response functions.

END OF CHAPTER QUESTIONS

1. What are the problems of relying on automatic fiscal stabilisers to ensure a stable economy at full employment?

2. Does it matter if a country has a large national debt as a proportion of its national income?

3. If the government is running a budget deficit, does this mean that national income will increase?

4. Of what significance are primary deficits or surpluses for the dynamics of a government's debt-to-GDP ratio?

5. What factors determine the effectiveness of discretionary fiscal policy?

6. Why is it difficult to use fiscal policy to 'fine-tune' the economy?

7. Assume that a bank has the following simplified balance sheet, and is operating at its desired liquidity ratio:

Liabilities	(£m)	Assets	(£m)
Deposits	100	Balances with central bank	10
		Advances	90
	100		100

Now assume that the central bank repurchases £5 million of government bonds on the open market. Assume that the people who sell the bonds all have their accounts with this bank and keep a constant amount of cash outside the bank.

(a) Draw up the new balance sheet directly after the purchase of the bonds.

(b) Now draw up the eventual balance sheet after all credit creation has taken place.

(c) Would there be a similar effect if the central bank rediscounted £5 billion of Treasury bills?

(d) How would such open-market operations affect the rate of interest?

8. Is it possible for the government to target the money supply over the longer term without targeting the level of public-sector net borrowing?

9. What are the mechanics whereby the central bank raises the rate of interest?

10. What is Goodhart's law? How is it relevant to (a) monetary policy; (b) using assignment grades to assess a student's ability; (c) paying workers according to the amount of output they produce; (d) awarding local authority contracts to cleaning or refuse disposal companies on the basis of tendered prices?

11. 'It is easier to control the monetary base than broader money, but it is less relevant to do so.' Do you agree with this statement?

12. Compare the relative merits of targeting (a) the money supply; (b) the exchange rate; (c) the rate of inflation.

13. Is there a compromise between purely discretionary policy and adhering to strict targets?

14. Assume that the economy is at potential output and the natural rate of unemployment and that inflation is at

KI 36
p451

the target rate set for the central bank by the government. In each of the following scenarios apply the integrated *EAPC, DAD/DAS* and *IS/MP* framework to analyse the economy's adjustment path.

(a) A temporary fall in aggregate demand under the assumption that inflationary expectations remain anchored.

(b) A temporary fall in aggregate demand where inflationary expectations are based on the rate of inflation in the previous period.

(c) A temporary positive supply shock where inflationary expectations are based on the rate of inflation in the previous period.

Online resources

Additional case studies on the student website

22.1 Banks, taxes and the fiscal costs of the financial crisis. A discussion of the government's financial interventions during the financial crisis and their impact on the public finances.

22.2 The national debt. This explores the question of whether it matters if a country has a high national debt.

22.3 Trends in public expenditure. This case examines attempts to control public expenditure in the UK and relates them to the crowding-out debate.

22.4 Injections against the contagion. The use of discretionary fiscal policy in the late 1990s.

22.5 Any more G and T? Does the Code for Fiscal Stability mean that the UK government balances its books? An examination of the evidence.

22.6 Discretionary fiscal policy in Japan. Attempts by successive Japanese governments since 1992 to bring the economy out of recession though expansionary fiscal policy.

22.7 Credit and the business cycle. This case traces cycles in the growth of credit and relates them to the business cycle. It also looks at some of the implications of the growth in credit.

22.8 Effective monetary policy versus banking efficiency and stability. This case examines potential conflicts between banking stability, efficiency and the effective operation of monetary policy.

22.9 Should central banks be independent of government? An examination of the arguments for and against independent central banks.

22.10 The Bank of England and Taylor rules. A comparison of the Bank of England's monetary policy rule with a simple Taylor rule.

22.11 *IS/MP*, policy and the aftermath of the banking crisis. Using the *IS/MP* framework we analyse the banking crisis and the subsequent recession and slow recovery.

22.12 Fiscal and monetary policy in the UK. An historical overview of UK fiscal and monetary policy.

22.13 *IS/LM* analysis of fiscal and monetary policy. An illustration of how we can use the *IS/LM* framework to examine the effects of fiscal and monetary policy taking into account both the goods and money markets.

Websites relevant to this chapter and Chapters 20 and 21

Numbers and sections refer to websites listed in the Web Appendix and hotlinked from this book's website at **www.pearsoned.co.uk/sloman.**

- For news articles relevant to this chapter, see the *Economics News Articles* link from the book's website.

- For general news on fiscal and monetary policies, see websites in section A, and particularly A1–5. See also links to newspapers worldwide in A38, 39, 42, 43 and 44, and the news search feature in Google at A41. See also links to economics news in A42.

- For information on UK fiscal policy and government borrowing, see sites E30, 36; F2. See also sites A1–8 at Budget time.

- For a model of the economy (based on the Treasury model), see *The Virtual Chancellor* (site D1). In the model you can devise your own Budget.

- For monetary policy in the UK, see F1, C21 and E30. For monetary policy in the eurozone, see F6 and 5. For monetary policy in the USA, see F8. For monetary policy in other countries, see the respective central bank site in section F or in site F17.

- For demand-side policy in the UK, see the latest Budget Report (e.g. section on maintaining macroeconomic stability) at site E30.

- For inflation targeting in the UK and eurozone, see sites F1 and 6.

- For student resources relevant to this chapter, see sites C1–7, 9, 10, 12, 19, 21. Also see site D10 (*The Virtual Chancellor*).

Long-term Economic Growth and Supply-side Policies

In this chapter we turn our attention to the determinants of long-run economic growth. All developed countries have experienced economic growth over the past 60 years, but rates have differed significantly from one country to another. We look at some of these differences in section 23.1.

If an economy is to achieve sustained economic growth over the longer term, there must be a sustained increase in potential output. An important ingredient for long-term economic growth is the growth in labour productivity. This, in turn, depends on two major factors: a growth in the amount of capital that workers use, and technological progress. We can see these two elements if we look around us. Take a modern car factory, with its high-tech robot-driven equipment: it is no surprise that workers' productivity is much higher than it was, say, 30 years ago. Take a modern office, with powerful computers: again it is no surprise that today's office staff are much more productive than their counterparts of past years.

In section 23.2 we look at the effects of an increase in the rate of capital investment when there is no change in technology. As we shall see, the effect will simply be growth to a new higher level of national income, not a permanently higher rate of economic growth. If economic growth is to be higher over the long term, therefore, there must be an increase in the rate of technological progress. We look at how this affects economic growth in section 23.3.

In the final three sections we look at various policy options to increase aggregate supply. Supply-side policies can be put into two broad categories: market orientated and interventionist. Market-orientated policies focus on 'freeing up' markets and improving market incentives. They involve policies such as tax cuts, privatisation and deregulation. Interventionist policies, by contrast, focus on ways of countering the inadequacies of markets through direct government provision of transport infrastructure, training or R&D, or financial support for private provision.

23.1 INTRODUCTION TO LONG-TERM ECONOMIC GROWTH

Twin characteristics of growth

Our focus so far in Part F has been on economic volatility. This is not surprising given that economies are inherently volatile and often experience significant fluctuations in economic activity. Yet when we step back and look at the longer span of history, these short-term fluctuations take on less significance. What we see is that economies tend to experience long-term economic growth.

These twin characteristics of growth are nicely captured in Figure 23.1, which plots for the UK both the *level* of real GDP and annual percentage *changes* in real GDP. It shows that while the rate of economic growth is volatile, the volume of output grows over time.

The rate of long-term economic growth in developed nations, such as the UK, has meant that average living standards have improved markedly. When measured in terms of real GDP per head, all developed nations are considerably richer today than they were, say, 50 or 60 years ago.

The picture, however, is not one of universal improvement. People are not necessarily happier; there are many stresses in modern living; the environment is in many respects more polluted; inequality has increased in most countries, especially over the past 20 years; for many people work is more demanding and the working day is longer than in the past; there is more crime and more insecurity. Hence, 'more' is not always 'better'.

Nevertheless, most people *want* more consumer goods; they want higher incomes. In this chapter, we examine what causes long-term economic growth, and how it can be increased. We leave you to judge whether a materially richer society is a better society.

Long-run growth and the *DAD/DAS* and *IS/MP* models

Sustained economic growth over the longer term requires a sustained increase in *potential output*. This means that there has to be a continuous rightward shift in aggregate supply. When viewed through the *DAD/DAS* model, long-run growth therefore means a continuous rightward shift of the

KI 2
p10

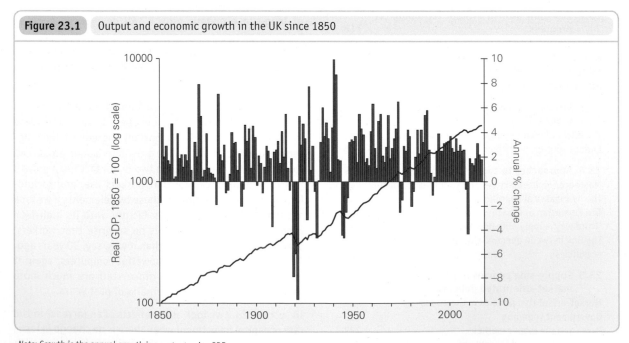

Figure 23.1 Output and economic growth in the UK since 1850

Note: Growth is the annual growth in constant-price GDP.
Sources: 1850–1948 based on data from Bank of England available at http://www.bankofengland.co.uk/publications/quarterlybulletin/threecenturiesofdata.xls; from 1949 based on data from *Quarterly National Accounts* series ABMI and IHYP (National Statistics).

Figure 23.2   Long-term growth in integrated *DAD/DAS* and *IS/MP* framework

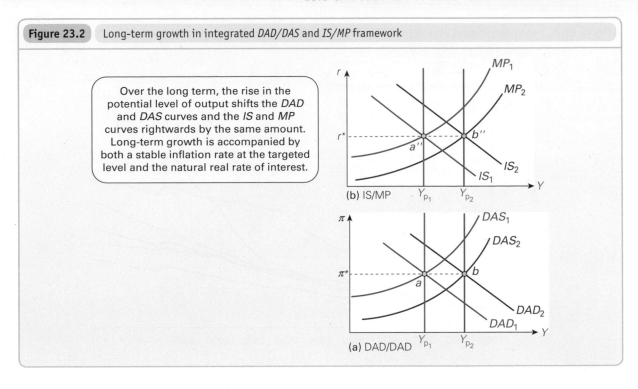

Over the long term, the rise in the potential level of output shifts the *DAD* and *DAS* curves and the *IS* and *MP* curves rightwards by the same amount. Long-term growth is accompanied by both a stable inflation rate at the targeted level and the natural real rate of interest.

DAS curve. The rate of growth in potential output is then the rate at which the curve shifts rightwards.

We can use Figure 23.2 to illustrate the process of long-run growth through a simplified version of our integrated macroeconomic framework introduced in the previous chapter. It combines the *DAD/DAS* and *IS/MP* models. The relationship between the labour market and long-term growth is discussed as we go through the chapter.

 Does a rise in potential real income result in a fall in the natural rate of unemployment?

Assume initially that the economy is at equilibrium characterised by output (real national income) at the potential level (Y_{P_1}), inflation at the target rate (π^*) and the interest rate at the natural rate (r^*). Now assume that potential output rises from Y_{P_1} to Y_{P_2}. We will look at how this might happen later in the chapter.

The DAD/DAS model (Figure 23.2(a))

The *DAS* curve moves rightwards – say to DAS_2. The size of the shift reflects the increase in the economy's productive capabilities. If the extra capacity is used, this also has the effect of increasing the real national income of the country; people are now able to make more purchases. There is also likely to be a rightward shift in the *DAD* curve. If the extra real income generated by the increase in potential output generates an equivalent amount of additional real spending, the *DAD* curve will shift to DAD_2. (This would be when Say's law is operative: see page 494.) In such a case, actual output would increase by the same amount as potential output: i.e. $Y_{P_2} - Y_{P_1}$.

If, however, the rise in potential output did not translate into sufficient extra spending, the *DAD* curve would not shift sufficiently to the right to give a new equilibrium at Y_{P_2} – a negative output gap would emerge. In such a case, discretionary fiscal and/or monetary policy may be required to shift the *DAD* curve to DAD_2.

Generally, however, over a time span of several years, periods of deficient demand are likely to be matched by periods of excess demand. In the long run, therefore, rightward shifts in the *DAS* curve would be matched by equivalent rightward shifts in the *DAD* curve. In other words, in the long run, economies tend towards equilibrium at the potential level of national income as markets and expectations adjust.

The IS/MP model (Figure 23.2(b))

In this model, the *MP* curve also shifts rightwards by the increase in potential output (i.e. from MP_1 to MP_2). This occurs because, with more productive capacity, the rate of inflation is now lower at any level of output. Hence, the central bank can now set a lower real rate of interest at any particular level of output than previously.

Meanwhile, if the extra capacity generates extra demand, the *IS* curve will shift to the right too. In periods of negative or positive output gaps, however, the shift in the *IS* curve is likely to fall short of or exceed the rightward shift in the *MP* curve. Over time, however, the rightward shift in the *IS* curve is likely to match the rightward shift in the *MP* curve as markets clear and expectations adjust.

 Explain the mechanisms whereby the DAD and IS curves will shift by the same amount as the DAS and MP curves in the long run.

| Figure 23.3 | Long-term output growth (real GDP, 1960 = 100) |

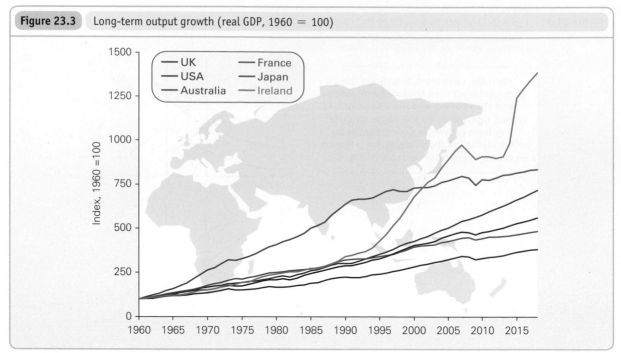

Note: Data from 2017 based on forecasts.
Source: Based on data in *AMECO* Database (European Commission, DGECFIN).

Growth over the decades

Despite economic volatility, most countries have experienced long-term economic growth. Figure 23.3 shows the path of real GDP (output) in six developed economies, including the UK, from 1960. As you can see, the fluctuations in output appear relatively minor compared with the long-term growth in output.

Such growth cannot be explained by a closing of the gap between actual and potential output: by an expansion of aggregate demand leading to a fuller use of resources. Instead, the explanation lies on the supply side. Countries' economic *capacity* has increased.

Comparing the growth performance of different countries

An increase in economic capacity is reflected in a growth in the average output per head of the population (per capita). Table 23.1 shows the average *annual* rate of growth in output per capita and output per employed person for several *developed* countries since the 1960s, alongside that for output (real GDP). The effect of even very small differences can have a significant effect when looked at over many years.

As you can see from Table 23.1, there has been a considerable difference in the rates of growth experienced by the different countries. Such differences have implications for the longer-term living standards of countries' populations. However, if economic growth is to give an indication of an increase in living standards, it has to be measured per head of the population.

| Table 23.1 | Average annual percentage growth rates, 1961–2018 |

	Real GDP	Real GDP per capita	Real GDP per worker
Australia	3.5	1.9	1.6
Canada	3.1	1.9	1.2
France	2.8	2.1	2.3
Germany	2.4	2.1	1.9
Ireland	4.7	3.8	3.5
Italy	2.4	2.1	2.2
Japan	3.8	3.2	3.2
Netherlands	2.7	2.0	1.9
New Zealand	2.7	1.5	1.1
Norway	3.1	2.4	2.0
Spain	3.4	2.6	2.7
UK	2.4	1.9	1.8
USA	3.0	2.0	1.6

Notes: (i) Figures from 2017 based on forecasts; (ii) German figures based on West Germany only up to 1991.
Source: Based on data from *AMECO database* (European Commission, DGECFIN).

Table 23.2 considers the average annual growth rates from 1993 to 2018, both overall and per capita, for a wider range of countries than we have so far considered. Canada and America had faster absolute growth rates than the UK, but after taking into account their more rapid increase in populations, they experienced a slightly lower per capita growth rate. Russia and South Korea, with a decline in their populations, experienced higher growth per capita than absolute growth.

Table 23.2	Average annual growth rates 1993–2018 at constant prices: total and per capita	
	Real GDP	**Real GDP per capita**
Australia	3.3	1.8
Brazil	2.5	1.3
Canada	2.5	1.4
China	9.4	8.7
Ethiopia	8.1	5.5
France	1.5	1.0
Germany	1.3	1.2
India	7.0	5.3
Ireland	5.5	4.3
Italy	0.6	0.3
Jamaica	0.8	0.1
Japan	0.8	0.7
Malaysia	5.4	3.2
Netherlands	1.9	1.5
New Zealand	3.1	1.9
Nigeria	5.1	2.3
Norway	2.2	1.3
Russia	1.5	1.7
Singapore	5.5	3.3
South Korea	3.7	4.1
Spain	2.1	1.4
The Gambia	3.3	0.2
UK	2.1	1.6
USA	2.5	1.5

Note: Figures from 2016 based on forecasts.
Source: Authors' calculations based on data from *World Economic Outlook Database*, October 2016 (International Monetary Fund).

In general, GDP per capita in the richer developed countries have grown at a slower rate than the less rich ones. The result has been a narrowing of the gap. For example, in 1950 GDP per head in the USA (in purchasing-power standard terms) was 2.5 times that in West Germany and 20 times that in Japan. By 2018, GDP per head in the USA was estimated to be only 19 per cent higher than that in Germany and 49 per cent higher than that in Japan.

This *convergence in GDP per head*, however, has not been universal across the world. Although countries like Brazil, China, India and many other Asian countries have grown very rapidly, and in recent years some of the poorer African countries too, there remain others, often blighted by war or corruption or rapid population growth rates, where real GDP per capita has grown at pitifully slow rates, and in some cases has even declined. We examine the causes of low growth in developing countries in sections 26.3 to 26.5.

Although recent generations have come to expect economic growth, it is a relatively new phenomenon. For most of the last 2000 years, countries have experienced virtually static output per head over the long term. Economic growth has become significant only once countries have undergone an industrial revolution, and it is only with the technological advances of the twentieth and now the twenty-first centuries that long-term growth rates of 2 per cent or more have been achieved.

The causes of economic growth

The sources of economic growth can be grouped into two broad categories:

- An increase in the *quantity* of factors. Here we would include an increase in the workforce or the average number of hours that people work, an increase in raw materials (e.g. discoveries of oil) and an increase in capital. Of these,

Definition

Convergence in GDP per head The tendency for less rich developed countries to catch up with richer ones. Convergence does not apply to many of the poorer developing countries, however; the gap between them and richer countries has tended to widen.

TC 14
p458

*LOOKING AT THE MATHS

Since 1961, the UK economy has grown on average by 2.4 per cent per annum. This means that it has doubled in size roughly every 29 years. Over the same period, the Australian economy has grown by an average of 3.5 per cent per annum. As a result, its economy has doubled in size roughly every 20 years.

But how do we work out these numbers of years? To do this we use logarithms. To find the number of years, n, that it takes an economy to grow by a factor x (e.g. 2 in the case of a doubling), we divide the log of x by the log of the factor by which the economy is growing each year, g (so $g = 1.024$ for 2.4% and $g = 1.035$ for 3.5%):

$$n = \frac{\log x}{\log g}$$

We can use our calculators to find the logs. Thus, in the case of the UK:

$$n = \frac{\log x}{\log g} = \frac{\log 2}{\log 1.024} = 29.2$$

and in the case of Australia:

$$n = \frac{\log x}{\log g} = \frac{\log 2}{\log 1.035} = 20.1$$

In practice, these figures are only approximate as the two countries' growth rates varied from year to year.

 How long would it take an economy, like China, growing at an annual rate of close to 10 per cent to (a) double in size; (b) triple in size?

for most countries, it is an increase in the capital stock, brought about by investment, that is the most important source of growth. The amount of capital per worker – the capital/labour ratio (K/L) – has increased over time and has resulted in a greater output per worker (Y/L).

■ An increase in the *productivity* of factors. Here we would include an increase in the skills of workers, a more efficient organisation of inputs by management and more productive capital equipment. Most significant here is technological progress. Developments of computer technology, of new techniques in engineering, of lighter,

stronger and cheaper materials, of digital technology in communications and of more efficient motors have all contributed to a massive increase in the productivity of capital. Machines today can produce much more output than machines in the past and cost the same to manufacture.

In the next two sections, we will examine these two sources of growth and focus first on capital accumulation (an increase in the *quantity* of capital) and then on technological progress (an increase in the *productivity* of factors).

Section summary

1. Economies are inherently volatile in the short run. But most countries experience growth over the long term. The determinants of long-term economic growth lie primarily on the supply side. Long-term growth is therefore consistent with continuous rightwards shifts of the *AS* or *DAS* curves.

2. Most developed countries have experienced average annual rates of economic growth of 2 per cent or more over the last 50 years, but there have been considerable differences between countries.

3. The income gap between developed countries has tended to narrow as the less rich ones have grown faster than the richer ones. Some of the poorest countries of the world, however, have experienced very low rates of growth, with the result that the gap between them and richer countries has widened.

4. The determinants of economic growth can be put into two broad categories: an increase in the quantity of factors and an increase in the productivity of factors.

23.2 ECONOMIC GROWTH WITHOUT TECHNOLOGICAL PROGRESS

Capital accumulation

An increase in capital per worker will generally increase output. In other words, the more equipment that is used by people at work, the more they are likely to produce. But to increase capital requires investment, and that investment requires resources – resources that could have been used for producing consumer goods. Thus more investment means diverting resources away from producing finished goods into producing machines, buildings and other capital equipment. This is the opportunity cost of investment.

If we take a simple circular flow of income model, with saving as the only withdrawal and investment as the only injection, then saving will be equal to investment ($S = I$). An increase in saving, therefore, will enable more investment and more output for the future. Thus sacrifices today, in terms of more saving and less consumption, will mean more output and hence possibly more consumption for the future.

A model of economic growth

A country's percentage rate of economic growth (g) depends crucially on two factors:

■ The amount of extra capital that is required to produce an extra unit of output per year: i.e. the marginal capital/

output ratio (k). The greater the marginal capital/output ratio, the lower will be the output per year that results from a given amount of investment.

■ The percentage of national income that a country saves (s). The higher this percentage, the greater the amount of investment that can be financed.

There is a simple formula that relates the rate of economic growth to these two factors. It is known as the *Harrod–Domar model* (after the two economists, Sir Roy Harrod and Evsey Domar, who independently developed the model). The formula is:

$$g = s/k$$

Thus if a country saved 10 per cent of its national income ($s = 10\%$), and if £4 of additional capital were required to produce £1 of extra output per annum ($k = 4$), then the rate of economic growth would be 10%/4 = 2.5 per cent.

Definition

Harrod–Domar model A model that relates a country's rate of economic growth to the proportion of national income saved and the ratio of capital to output.

? *What would be the rate of economic growth if 20 per cent of national income were saved and invested and the marginal capital/output ratio was $\frac{5}{2}$?*

However, we need to make two qualifications to this simple model.

Declining marginal efficiency of capital. The first relates to the marginal capital/output ratio (k). Since the ratio measures how much additional capital is needed to produce one more unit of output it reflects the effectiveness of additional capital. In fact, the ratio is the inverse of the *marginal efficiency of capital* (see page 305).

We can define the nation's marginal efficiency of capital (MEC) as the annual extra output (ΔY) yielded by an increase in the capital stock, relative to the cost of that extra capital (ΔK).

$$MEC = \frac{\Delta Y}{\Delta K} = \frac{\Delta Y}{I}$$

Thus if £4 of extra capital yielded an additional annual income of £1, the marginal efficiency of capital would be $^1/_4$. Since the marginal capital/output ratio (k) is $1/MEC$, then k must equal 4.

KI 19
p151

The marginal efficiency of capital is likely to decline (and the marginal capital/output ratio to increase) as the amount of capital per worker increases. This is because of diminishing returns to capital.

Increasing replacement investment. The second qualification is that a proportion of investment has to be used for replacing worn-out or obsolete equipment. The problem here is that the larger the capital stock, the greater the proportion of investment that will be needed for replacement purposes, and the smaller the proportion that can be used for increasing the size of the capital stock.

Growth to a long-run equilibrium level of national income

KI 8
p46

Let us now incorporate these two qualifications into a model of growth. This is known as the neoclassical or 'Solow' growth model, after the MIT economics professor and Nobel Prize winner, Robert Solow. In this model, we are assuming for simplicity that the size of the workforce is constant. Any increase in the capital stock, therefore, means an increase in the average amount of capital per worker.

The model is illustrated in Figure 23.4. The size of the capital stock (K) is measured on the horizontal axis; the level of national output (Y) is measured on the vertical axis.

KI 19
p151

We start by looking at the effects of a growth in the capital stock on national output (i.e. on real national income (Y)). This is shown by the green output curve. As the capital stock increases, so output increases, but at a diminishing rate (the curve gets less and less steep). The reason for this is the law of diminishing returns: in this case, diminishing returns to capital. For example, if, in an office, you start equipping workers with computers, at first output will increase very rapidly. But as more and more workers have their own

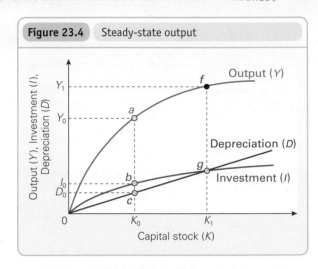

Figure 23.4 Steady-state output

computer rather than having to share, so the rate of increase in output slows down. When everyone has their own, output is likely to be at a maximum. Any additional computers (of the same specification) will remain unused.

Increased output will mean increased saving and hence increased investment (the amount depending on the level of i). This is shown by the blue investment (I) curve. In this simple model, the vertical distance between the Y and I curves represents consumption ($C = Y - I$).

KI 26
p303

The magenta (D) line shows the amount of depreciation of capital that takes place, and hence the amount of replacement investment required. The bigger the capital stock, the larger the amount of replacement investment required.

Assume initially that the size of the capital stock is K_0. This will generate an output of Y_0 (point a). This output, in turn, will generate saving and investment of I_0, but of this, D_0 will have to be used for replacement purposes. The difference ($b - c$) will be available to increase the size of the capital stock. The capital stock will thus increase up to K_1 (point g). At this point, all investment will be required for replacement purposes. Output will therefore cease growing. Y_1 represents the **steady-state level of national income**.

Effect of an increase in the saving rate

In the simple model, $g = s/k$ (or $g = s \times MEC$), an increase in the saving rate (s) will increase the growth rate (g). When we take into account diminishing returns to capital and depreciation, however, an increase in the saving rate will lead to only a temporary increase in output, and to no long-term *growth* at all!

Definition

Steady-state level of national income The long-run equilibrium level of national income. The level at which all investment is used to maintain the existing capital stock at its current level.

*LOOKING AT THE MATHS

Steady-state equilibrium in the Solow growth model is achieved where investment (I) equals depreciation (D).

Investment is assumed to be a given fraction (s) of the level of national income Y, where national income is a function of the total capital stock (K): $Y = f(K)$. Thus

$$I = sY$$
$$= s \times f(K) \qquad (1)$$

Depreciation in the model is assumed to be a fixed proportion (d) of the capital stock (K). Thus

$$D = dK \qquad (2)$$

In steady-state equilibrium, given that $I = D$, from equations (1) and (2) we can write

$$s \times f(K) = dK$$

Thus

$$K = \frac{s \times f(K)}{d}$$

Thus if we know the production function ($Y = f(K)$), the saving rate (s) and the depreciation rate (d), we can solve for the steady-state equilibrium value of K and hence also for Y. Maths Case 23.1 on the student website gives a worked example of this.

| BOX 23.1 | GETTING INTENSIVE WITH CAPITAL |

How quickly does it grow?

In this box we take a look at two issues relating to capital. First, we consider what counts as capital in a country's national accounts. Second, we compare the growth of the capital stock in a sample of developed economies and then see how this compares with their rates of economic growth.

What is capital?

In a country's national accounts, capital consists of non-financial *fixed assets*. It does not include goods and services transformed or used up in the course of production; these are known as *intermediate goods and services*. Furthermore, it does not relate directly to the stock of human capital: the skills and attributes embodied in individuals that affect production (see Box 23.3).

A country's stock of fixed assets can be valued at its replacement cost, regardless of its age: this is its gross value. It can also be valued at its written-down value known as its net value. The net value takes into account the *consumption of capital* which occurs through wear and tear (depreciation) or when capital becomes naturally obsolescent.

The table shows that the estimated net capital stock of the UK in 2015 was £4.35 trillion. This is considerably less than the estimate of human capital of £19.9 trillion (see Box 23.3). To put this into context, this is 2.3 times the value of (annual) GDP.

The table shows that there are five broad categories of fixed assets. The largest of these by value is *dwellings,* which includes houses, bungalows and flats. Residential housing yields rental incomes for landlords and, more generally, provides all of us with important consumption services, most notably shelter.

The second largest component by value is *other buildings and structures*. This includes buildings, other than residential dwellings, and most civil engineering and construction work. It includes structures such as factories, schools and hospitals and the country's railway track.

The third largest component is *ICT and other machinery equipment*. It includes telecommunications equipment, computer hardware, office machinery and hardware as well as weapon systems equipment.

KI 26
p303

UK net capital stock

Type	2015			average real annual change, %	
	£ billions	% of fixed assets	% of GDP	1996–2015	2009–2015
Dwellings (excluding land)	1 785.0	41.0	95.3	1.3	0.4
Other buildings and structures	1 592.6	36.6	85.0	2.1	1.6
ICT, other machinery and equipment	672.4	15.4	35.9	2.9	1.1
Intellectual property products	197.5	4.5	10.5	−2.0	−2.0
Transport equipment	99.8	2.3	5.3	1.8	3.0
Cultivated biological resources	6.6	0.2	0.4	0.7	4.4
All fixed assets	4 353.9	100.0	232.5	1.9	1.0

Source: Based on data from *Capital Stocks, Consumption of Fixed Capital, 2016* and *Quarterly National Accounts* (series YBHA) (National Statistics).

The fourth largest is *intellectual property products*. These include intangible fixed assets such as R&D, mineral exploration, software and databases, and original literary and artistic works.

Next by value is *transport equipment*. This includes equipment for moving people and objects such as lorries for haulage, buses, railway rolling stock and civil aircraft.

The smallest component is *cultivated biological resources*. This includes livestock for breeding, vineyards, orchards and forests.

The final two columns of the table look at the annual growth in the stock of capital. The first of these shows that, on average, from 1996 to 2015 the volume of the UK capital stock increased by 1.9 per cent per year. This was largely driven by growth in 'ICT, other machinery and equipment' and in 'other buildings and

This is illustrated in Figure 23.5. If the saving rate increases, the investment curve will shift upwards. This is shown by a shift from I_1 to I_2. Investment is now above that which is necessary to maintain the capital stock at K_1. The capital stock will grow, therefore, and so will national income. But this growth is only temporary. Once the capital stock has risen to K_2, all the new higher level of investment will be absorbed in replacing capital ($I = D$ at point n). National income stops rising. Y_2 represents the new steady-state national income.

Does this mean, therefore, that there is no long-term gain from an increase in the saving rate? There *is* a gain, to the extent that income per worker is now higher (remember that we are assuming a constant labour force), and this higher income will be received not just once, but every year from now on as long as the saving rate remains at the new higher level. There is no increase in the long-term *growth rate*, however. To achieve that, we would have to look to the other determinants of growth.

Human capital and education

The analysis of Figures 23.4 and 23.5 need not be confined to the stock of *physical* capital: machines, buildings, tools, etc. It can also apply to *human capital*. Human capital, as we saw in Chapter 10, refers to the skills and expertise of workers that have been acquired through education and

EXPLORING ECONOMICS

structures'. Since 2009, the annual growth rate has fallen to just 1 per cent per year.

How quickly does capital grow? An international comparison

In models of economic growth an important measure of how much capital is being used is the amount of capital per person employed (per worker). This is also known as *capital intensity*. In the chart we plot the ratio of capital per worker in 2018 to that in 1960 (x-axis) against the ratio of output (real GDP) per worker in 2015 to that in 1960 (y-axis) in a selection of developed countries.

For each country we observe an increase in capital intensity, although the rates of capital accumulation differ quite significantly. The data show that the UK ranks relatively low in terms of capital accumulation. In the UK the capital stock per worker is 2.3 times higher in 2018 than in 1960. This compares with, for example, Japan, where it is 5.6 times higher, or France, where it is 3.7 times higher.

We would expect that the higher the level of capital per worker, the greater will be the level of output per worker. This is largely borne out in the chart. However, while there is a strong statistical association between capital accumulation and economic growth, there are other factors that impact on long-term growth. Three of these are technological progress, *human capital* and the efficiency with which capital is deployed. We examine these later in this chapter.

1. *How does human capital (the skills and expertise of the workforce) fit into a national account's definition of capital?*
2. *Does the composition of a country's capital affect its long-run economic growth?*

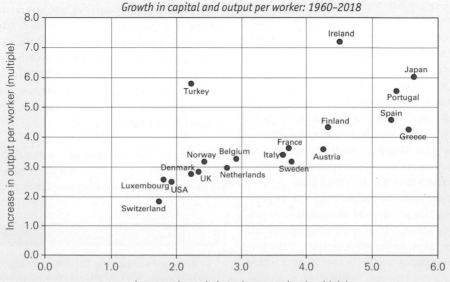

Growth in capital and output per worker: 1960–2018

Note: Figures from 2017 are forecasts.

Source: Based on data from AMECO database (European Commission).

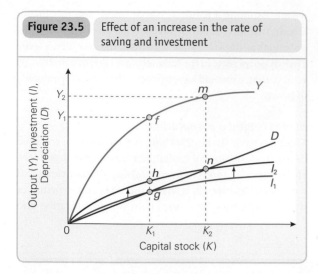

Figure 23.5 Effect of an increase in the rate of saving and investment

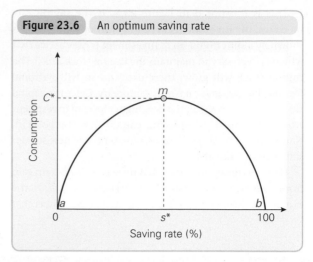

Figure 23.6 An optimum saving rate

training. If part of saving is used for investment in education and training, then the productivity of workers will rise, and so will output.

In Figures 23.4 and 23.5, therefore, the horizontal axis measures both physical and human capital. An increase in either has the effect of increasing the steady-state level of national income. In Boxes 23.1 and 23.3 we consider both how physical and human capital respectively are treated in countries' national accounts and at their rates of accumulation.

 If there were a gradual increase in the saving rate over time, would this lead to sustained economic growth?

An optimum rate of saving?

KI 6
p29 If an increase in the saving rate does at least lead to a higher level of output, is there an *optimum* level of saving? Clearly we would need to define 'optimum'. One definition would be where *consumption* per head is maximised.

Assuming a fixed population and a fixed workforce, higher saving will do two things. First, it will directly decrease consumption, since what is saved is not directly spent. Second, as we have seen, it will lead to higher output and hence higher income. So, with a higher saving rate, consumption will be a smaller proportion, but of a higher income. This implies that there will be some optimum saving rate at which consumption is maximised. This is illustrated in Figure 23.6.

If the saving rate is zero, the capital stock will be zero. Output and consumption will thus be zero (point *a*). As saving rises above zero, so the capital stock will grow, as will output and consumption. At the other extreme, if the saving rate were 100 per cent, although the capital stock would be high, all of the nation's income would go on maintaining that capital stock: there would be no consumption (point *b*). A saving rate somewhere between 0 and 100 per cent, therefore, will give the maximum consumption. In

Figure 23.6, this is a rate of s^*, giving a level of consumption of C^* (point *m*). This is sometimes known as the **golden-rule saving rate**.

Evidence suggests that all countries have saving rates below the golden-rule level. Thus increases in saving rates would result in increases in consumption.

 If this is true, why do people not increase their rate of saving?

An increase in the workforce

An increase in the workforce, or in the number of hours worked by the existing workforce, will have the effect of shifting both the Y and I lines upwards in Figures 23.4 and 23.5. In other words, if a given amount of capital is used by more workers or for longer periods, output and hence saving and investment will increase. As more labour hours are used with any given amount of capital, diminishing returns to labour will set in. Output will grow, but at a diminishing rate. The marginal and average product of labour will fall (see Figure 6.1 on page 152). Thus although national output has risen (the new steady-state income is higher), the output per labour hour is less.

The effect on GDP per head of the population

If the rise in total hours worked is the result of an increased **participation rate** (i.e. a greater proportion of the population

---

Definition

Golden-rule saving rate The rate of saving that maximises the level of long-run consumption.

Participation rate The percentage of the working-age population that is part of the workforce.

wishing to work) or of people working longer hours, then GDP per capita will be higher, even though output per hour worked will be lower. If, however, the increased hours worked are the result of an increased *population,* with no increase in the participation rate or number of hours worked per worker, then, because of diminishing returns to labour, output per head of the population will have gone down: GDP per capita will be lower.

KI 19
p151

?
1. *If there were a higher participation rate and GDP per capita rose, would output per worker also have risen?*
2. *If people worked longer hours and, as a result, GDP per capita rose, how would you assess whether the country was 'better off'?*

If, however, there is an increase in both labour *and* capital, GDP per capita need not fall, even with the same number of hours worked per head. There are likely to be constant returns to scale. For example, if country A has double the population and double the capital stock of country B, its GDP is likely to be approximately double, and its GDP per head approximately the same.

What should be clear from the above analysis is that, without technological progress or some other means of increasing output from a given quantity of inputs, long-term growth cannot be sustained.

Section summary

1. An increased saving rate will lead to higher investment and hence to an increase in the capital stock. This, in turn, will lead to a higher level of national income.

2. A larger capital stock, however, will require a higher level of replacement investment. Once this has risen to absorb all the extra investment, national income will stop rising: growth will cease. A steady-state level of national income has been achieved. An increased saving rate will therefore lead only to a rise in output, not to a long-term rise in the rate of growth.

3. An optimum rate of saving could be defined as one where consumption per head is maximised. This is sometimes known as the 'golden-rule saving rate'.

4. An increase in the workforce will lead to higher total output, but unless accompanied by an increase in the capital stock, it will generally lead to a reduction in output per worker.

23.3   ECONOMIC GROWTH WITH TECHNOLOGICAL PROGRESS

The effect of technological progress on output

Technological progress has the effect of increasing the output from a given amount of investment. This is shown in Figure 23.7. Initial investment and income curves are I_1 and Y_1; steady-state income is at a level of Y_1 (point f). A technological advance has the effect of shifting the Y line upwards, say to Y_2. The higher income curve leads to a higher investment curve (for a given *rate* of saving). This is shown by curve I_2. The new long-term equilibrium capital stock is thus K_2, and the new steady-state level of income is Y_2 (point p).

If there is a 'one-off' technological advance, the effect is the one we have just illustrated. Income rises to a higher level, but does not go on rising once the new steady-state level has been reached. But technological progress marches on over time. New inventions are made; new processes are discovered; old ones are improved. In terms of Figure 23.7, the Y curve *goes on* shifting upwards over time.

The faster the rate of technological progress, the faster will the Y curve shift upwards and the higher will be the rate of economic growth. This is illustrated in Figure 23.8, which shows the increase in output over time. The faster the rate of technological progress, the higher the rate of growth of output.

Maths Case 23.2 on the student website explores the algebra of technological progress.

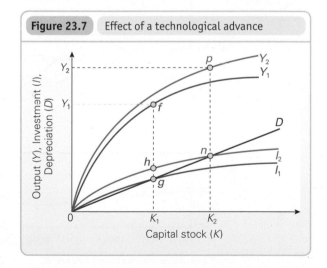

Figure 23.7   Effect of a technological advance

The effect of an increase in the saving rate with a given rate of technological progress

Figure 23.9 shows the combined effects of an increased saving rate and continuing technological progress. The rate of technological progress gives the slope of the

BOX 23.2   LABOUR PRODUCTIVITY

How effective is UK labour?

A country's potential output depends on the productivity of its factors of production. There are two common ways of measuring labour productivity. The first is *output per worker*. This is the most straightforward measure to calculate. All that is required is a measure of total output and employment.

A second measure is *output per hour worked*. This has the advantage that it is not influenced by the *number* of hours worked. So for an economy like the UK, with a very high percentage of part-time workers on the one hand, and long average hours worked by full-time employees on the other, such a measure would be more accurate in gauging worker efficiency.

Both measures focus solely on the productivity of labour. In order to account directly for the productivity of capital we need to consider the growth in *total* factor productivity (*TFP*). This measure analyses output relative to the amount of factors used. Changes in total factor productivity over time provide a good indicator of technical progress.

International comparisons of labour productivity

Charts (a) and (b) show comparative productivity levels of various countries and the G7 using GDP per hour worked. Chart (a) shows countries' productivity relative to the UK. As you can see, GDP per hour worked is lower in the UK than the other countries with the exception of Japan. For example, in 2016, compared with the UK, output per hour was 34.5 per cent higher in Germany, 29 per cent higher in France and 28 per cent higher in the USA.

Compared with the rest of the G7 countries, UK output per worker was 18 per cent lower, which means that the productivity gap remains at an historic high. A major explanation of lower productivity in the UK is the fact that for decades it has invested a smaller proportion of its national income than most other industrialised nations. Nevertheless, until 2006 the gap had been narrowing with the rest of the G7. This was because UK productivity, although lower than in many other countries, was growing faster. This can be seen chart (b). Part of the reason for this was the inflow of investment from abroad.

Chart (c) compares labour productivity across both measures. Workers in the USA and the UK work longer hours than those in France and Germany. Thus whereas output *per hour worked* in the USA is on par with that in France and Germany, output *per person employed* in the USA is about 23 per cent higher than in France and 27 per cent higher than in Germany.

The evidence points to UK labour productivity being *lower* than that in the USA, France and Germany on both measures but higher than that in Japan.

In understanding the growth in labour productivity it is generally agreed that we need to focus on three issues: physical capital (see Box 23.1), human capital (see Box 23.3) and innovation and technological progress. The significance of these for the UK productivity gap is considered further in Case Study 23.2 on the student website.

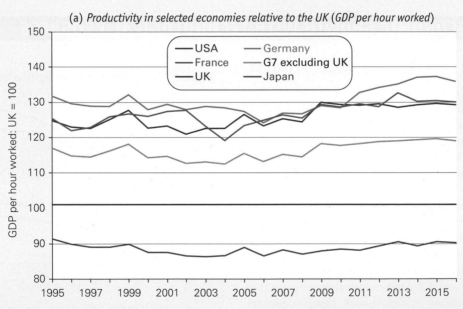

(a) *Productivity in selected economies relative to the UK (GDP per hour worked)*

Note: Figures are current-price GDP per hour worked.
Source: Based on data in *International Comparisons of Productivity* (National Statistics, 2017).

---

steady-state growth path. This is the growth path for any given saving rate. The saving rate determines the *position* (as opposed to slope) of the curve. Assume that the economy is on steady-state growth path 1. Then, at time t_1, there is an increase in the saving rate. This has the effect of increasing output and the economy will move towards

Definition

Steady-state growth path The growth path for a given saving rate (where growth results from technological progress).

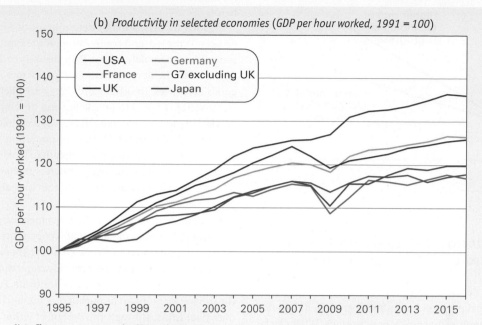

(b) *Productivity in selected economies (GDP per hour worked, 1991 = 100)*

Note: Figures are constant-price GDP per hour worked.
Source: Based on data in *International Comparisons of Productivity* (National Statistics, 2017).

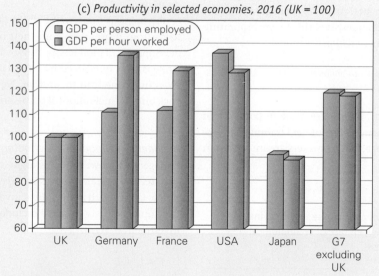

(c) *Productivity in selected economies, 2016 (UK = 100)*

Note: Figures are current-price GDP per hour worked/person employed.
Source: Based on data in *International Comparisons of Productivity* (National Statistics, 2017).

*What could explain the differences in productivity between
the five countries in chart (c), and why do the differences vary
according to which of the two measures is used?*

steady-state growth path 2. But the full effect does not take place immediately, since new capital equipment takes time to plan and install and then to generate additional income, part of which will be used for more investment. Thus the actual growth path will follow the green line, gradually converging on steady-state growth path 2.

Endogenous growth theory

It should be clear from what we have argued that an increase in technological progress is essential if a country wants to achieve faster rates of growth in the long term. But is this purely in the lap of the scientists and engineers? In the Solow growth model that we have been considering up

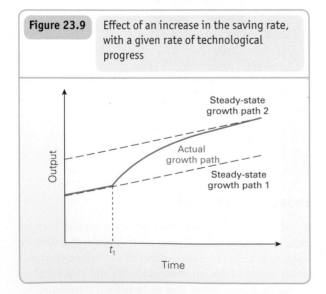

Figure 23.8 Effect of technological progress on growth rates

appropriate policies that might, for example, make their country a world leader in innovation and technological advancement, especially if this helps to sustain higher long-run rates of economic growth, and so higher standards of living.

In such models, a major determinant of technological progress is the size and composition of the capital stock. As economies accumulate capital, they are likely to devote more resources to the development and maintenance of capital goods industries. In other words, they are likely to have a larger sector devoted to producing and developing capital goods. This, in turn, can raise the rate of technological progress and enable further capital accumulation. A virtuous circle is created. Consequently, rather than looking at capital accumulation and technological progress as separate sources of long-term economic growth, the two are arguably interdependent.

Investment in research and development can be encouraged through the use of patents and copyrights. These provide some protection to firms, enabling them to capture more of the benefits from their own ideas and thus providing them with an incentive to create and innovate. Furthermore, the striving for profit or the pursuit of competitive advantage over rival firms, through the design of either innovative products and services or the most cost-efficient production processes, are incentives that can drive this innovation and creativity.

But there are limits to the ability of firms to exclude other firms from prospering from their own ideas, such as the development of products, processes and people. The virtuous circle is thus reinforced by externalities: the spill-over of ideas from one firm to another. New ideas cannot be put back into the metaphorical bottle once its lid is off.

to now, this is the type of assumption made. In other words, technological progress is simply a 'given': it is exogenously determined.

Whilst the neoclassical model identifies the importance of technological progress for enduring growth, it does not offer governments actual policy prescriptions. What can be done to speed up the rate of innovation? Can governments adopt policies that encourage scientific breakthroughs and technological developments? An *endogenous growth model* attempts to answer such questions this by incorporating technological advancement *within* the model.

 What is endogenous about endogenous growth theory?

Endogenous growth models stress the importance of research and development, education and training and fostering innovation. Hence, policy makers are interested in

A model of endogenous technological progress

Endogenous growth models argue two things. The first is that technological progress is *dependent* on various economic factors such as the rate of investment in research and development. This could be included as an element in the investment (*I*) term, i.e.

$$I = I_n + I_c$$

where I_n is investment in research and development of new technology (it could also include investment in training) and

Figure 23.9 Effect of an increase in the saving rate, with a given rate of technological progress

> ### Definition
>
> **Endogenous growth models** Models where the rate of growth depends on the rate of technological progress and diffusion, both of which depend on institutions, incentives and the role of government.

I_c is investment in capital that uses current technology. The greater the value of I_n/I_c, the faster will the Y curve shift upwards in Figure 23.4 (see page 719) and the steeper will be the steady-state growth path in Figure 23.9. Any policy, then, that increases the proportion of national income being devoted to R&D and training will increase the long-run rate of economic growth.

The second factor is the responsiveness of national income to new technologies ($\Delta Y/I_n$). This will depend in part on the extent to which innovations spill over to other firms, which duplicate or adapt them, thereby adding to the increase in national income (ΔY). The greater the value of Δ/I_n, the greater will be the rate of economic growth: the steeper will be the steady-state growth path.

The values of I_n and $\Delta Y/I_n$ are thought to depend on structural and institutional factors within the economy and on the role of government. These include:

- attitudes of business, such as their inclination to take risk;
- willingness of financial institutions to lend support to investment opportunities;
- tax incentives and government grants, for instance support for R&D;
- a research infrastructure (e.g. laboratories and the number and skills of researchers);
- the degree of competition to develop new products and processes and/or to reduce costs;
- the magnitude of external spillovers from the generation of new products, processes and techniques;
- the stock of human capital.

As we have seen, endogenous growth models try to explain how the economy's production function shifts upwards over time. In some cases the production function may also become steeper. In other words, a given rise in the capital stock will cause a larger rise in national income. The reason is that the benefits of the output from investment are not confined just to the firms doing the investing. Rather, some benefits spill over to other firms. For example, firms may be able to duplicate or develop other firms' ideas. Consequently, these spillovers may positively impact on the overall marginal product of capital.

---

*LOOKING AT THE MATHS

The above endogenous growth model can be expressed algebraically as follows:

$$\Delta Y/Y = v(I_n/Y)$$

This states that the rate of economic growth ($\Delta Y/Y$) depends on the proportion of national income devoted to R&D and training (I_n/Y) by an amount v.

The higher the value of I_n/Y and the higher the value of v, the steeper will be the steady-state growth path.

 Do all investment projects generate significant spillovers?

Policy implications

If there is a virtuous circle arising from firms investing and innovating, how can governments encourage this? Many economists argue that this requires supply-side policies. Examples include policies to influence research and development, education and training, industrial organisation and work practices – in other words, policies to affect aggregate supply directly.

There is less agreement, however, as to whether these policies should focus on delivering market solutions or involve greater state intervention. We look at this debate in the final sections of this chapter.

But encouraging investment does not just depend on effective supply-side policies. It also depends on the stability of the macroeconomic environment. It is not easy to plan ahead in times of great economic uncertainty. In the years following the financial crisis of 2007–8, uncertainty led to lower levels of investment and innovation in many countries. In the UK, for example, investment in the period 1997 to 2006 averaged 18.2 per cent of GDP; in the period 2009 to 2016, it averaged 16.3 per cent. The result was that productivity and potential income grew at a slower rate. In the decade following the financial crisis, annual productivity growth in advanced economies dropped to 0.3 per cent – down from around 1 per cent in the years before the crisis. If productivity growth had continued at 1 per cent, overall GDP in advanced economies would be some 5 per cent higher than it is today.[1]

By contrast, the less the volatility in output (real GDP), the greater will be the confidence of business to innovate and invest and the higher will be the growth in potential income.

The idea that economic shocks can have persistent or enduring effects on the path of potential output has become a feature of many macroeconomic models (see section 16.6). These shocks can originate from both the demand and supply sides. Either way, we need to understand the mechanisms by which such shocks are propagated and their significance for longer-term growth.

Some economists, however, argue that, given the inherent volatility of economies, governments *should* be more proactive. For example, imperfections in the financial system which result in credit cycles can have marked effects on flows of investment, including spending on research and development. They argue that governments have a role to play in helping to stabilise aggregate demand so as to support and encourage firms to invest and increase potential output.

1 See Christine Lagarde (Managing Director, International Monetary Fund), 'Reinvigorating productivity growth', *IMF Speeches*, 3 April 2017.

BOX 23.3 UK HUMAN CAPITAL

Estimating the capabilities of the labour force

The OECD (2001) defines human capital as the 'knowledge, skills, competencies and attributes embodied in individuals that facilitate the creation of personal, social and economic well-being'.[1] Hence, trends in human capital have implications for a range of economic-related issues, including economic growth, unemployment, life satisfaction, the inequality of income, wealth and opportunity and also for social cohesiveness. But how we do we go about measuring human capital?

Measuring human capital

In estimating an individual's human capital, a common approach is to estimate the present value of an individual's *remaining lifetime labour income*. This can be done for representative individuals in categories defined by gender, age and educational attainment. An assumption is then made about the working life of individuals. In compiling the UK estimates it is assumed that the remaining lifetime labour income of individuals aged 65 and over is zero. Then an approach known as backwards recursion is applied.

Backwards recursion involves first estimating the remaining lifetime labour income of someone aged 64 with a particular gender, age and educational level. The remaining lifetime income in this case is simply their current labour income. For someone aged 63 it is their current labour income plus the present value of the remaining lifetime income of someone aged 64 with the same gender, age and educational level. This continues back to someone aged 16. In calculating the remaining lifetime labour income of representative individuals account is also taken of the probability that their level of educational attainment may rise and with it their expected future earnings.

Further working assumptions are necessary to complete the calculations. Two of the most important are: the rate of

labour productivity growth is 2 per cent per annum and the discount rate is 3.5 per cent per annum, as recommended by HM Treasury's *Green Book* (2003) when undertaking appraisal and evaluation studies in central government.

Two measures of the stock of human capital are estimated. The first is for *employed human capital*. It is based on estimating the lifetime labour income of those in employment. The second is *full human capital*. It includes the human capital of the unemployed. This assumes that the human capital of those currently unemployed should be valued at the remaining lifetime labour income of employed individuals with the same characteristics (gender, age and educational attainment). It ignores any so-called scarring effects from being unemployed, such as the depreciation of job-specific or transferable skills. Such effects are likely to increase with the duration of unemployment.

Estimates of human capital

The chart shows estimates of employed and full human capital in the UK since 2004. Both follow broadly similar patterns. Between 2004 and 2007, prior to the financial crisis, the stock of human capital increased by an average of 2.7 per cent per annum. Employed and full human capital fell in each year from 2009 to 2013. The fall in full human capital was, however, a little less pronounced because of the impact of rising unemployment on the employed human capital estimates.

On the back of a resumption of real wage growth and a rise in employment, the value of the stock of human capital, particularly employed human capital, began growing from 2014. In 2015 human capital values grew by over 4 per cent, with full human capital stock reaching £19.9 trillion (10.6 times GDP) and employed human capital £19.2 trillion (10.3 times GDP).

Section summary

1. A higher long-term rate of growth will normally require a faster rate of technological progress.

2. The rate of technological progress determines the slope of the steady-state growth path (i.e. the rate of steady-state growth). If there is a rise in the saving rate, this will shift the steady-state growth path upwards (parallel) and the

   actual growth path will gradually move from the lower to the higher path.

3. Endogenous growth theory argues that the rate of technological progress and its rate of diffusion depend on economic institutions and incentives. Supply-side policy could be used to alter these.

In Box 23.1 we saw that the net value of the UK's physical capital was £4.35 trillion (2.3 times GDP). Therefore, in 2015, the value of the stock of human capital was estimated to be around 4.6 times higher than the stock of physical capital.

We can also analyse the *distribution* of human capital by a particular characteristic, such as educational attainment. In 2015, it is estimated that 37.3 per cent of UK employed human capital was embodied in the 28.0 per cent of the population who have a degree (or equivalent). In contrast, only 5.1 per cent of employed human capital was embodied in

the 8.8 per cent of the working-age population with no formal qualifications.

1. *Are human capital and physical capital substitutes or complements?*
2. *What characteristics might policy makers choose to focus on when analysing the distribution of human capital?*

1 *The Well-Being of Nations: The Role of Human and Social Capital* (Centre for Educational Research and Innovation, OECD, 2001).

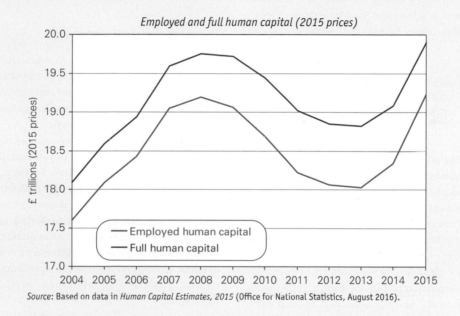

Employed and full human capital (2015 prices)

Source: Based on data in *Human Capital Estimates, 2015* (Office for National Statistics, August 2016).

23.4 APPROACHES TO SUPPLY-SIDE POLICY

Macroeconomic objectives and supply-side policies

Long-term growth

Supply-side policies are policies designed to increase the quantity and/or productivity of the inputs used in production. If effective, such policies will increase potential output

Definition

Supply-side policies Government policies that attempt to influence aggregate supply directly, rather than through aggregate demand.

and thus, as we saw in section 23.1, shift the *AS* or *DAS* curves to the right. The more effective these policies are, the faster will potential output grow over time and the faster will the *AS* and *DAS* curves shift rightwards.

As we saw earlier in the chapter, an important influence on the pace of long-term growth is technological progress. Supply-side policies may therefore be directed at encouraging research and development. Specific measures might include increasing incentives for firms to take advantage of new ideas and innovations by investing in new capital, new production processes and perhaps organisational structures. But they will also need workers and managers with the tools, skills and flexibility to take full advantage of these innovations.

Thus supply-side policies to encourage economic growth are likely to focus not just on research and development, but also on education and training, infrastructure, industrial organisation, work practices and the whole range of incentives that may be necessary to make the best use of new ideas and techniques.

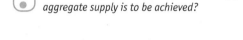

Why do Keynesians argue that, even in the long run, demand-side policies will still be required if faster growth in aggregate supply is to be achieved?

Employment and unemployment

The cure for demand-deficient unemployment may lie on the demand side, but other types of unemployment require supply-side solutions.

Equilibrium unemployment – frictional, structural, etc. – is caused by rigidities or imperfections in the market. There is a mismatching of aggregate supply and demand, and vacancies are not filled despite the existence of unemployment. The problem is that labour is not sufficiently mobile, either occupationally or geographically, to respond to changes in the job market. Labour supply for particular jobs is too inelastic.

Supply-side policies aim to influence labour supply by helping workers to be more responsive to changes in job opportunities. They may also aim to make employers more adaptable and willing to operate within existing labour constraints. Alternatively, they may seek to reduce the monopoly power of unions to drive real wages above the equilibrium.

Successful supply-side policies that reduce equilibrium unemployment and increase employment and human capital also increase potential output. A rising stock of employed human capital (see Box 23.3) can contribute to the development of new products, processes and techniques and hence to the development of higher-quality capital. As we saw in the analysis of endogenous growth theories, there is also the potential that knowledge spillovers hasten progress. These spillovers are a form of externality with some of the benefits captured or consumed by others. In other words, these new ideas can then be developed by others.

Inflation

If inflation is caused by cost-push pressures, supply-side policy can help to reduce it in three ways:

- By reducing the power of unions and/or firms (for example, by the use of anti-monopoly legislation) and thereby encouraging more competition in the supply of labour and/or goods.

- By preventing people from exercising that power by some form of prices and incomes policy. (Such policies were used in the 1970s: see Case Study 23.7 on the student website.)

- By encouraging increases in productivity through retraining, or by investment grants to firms, or by tax incentives, etc.

The new classical approach

New classical economists argue that demand-side policy (by which they mean monetary policy) can only control inflation; it cannot affect growth and employment. Supply-side policy is the appropriate policy to increase output and reduce the level of unemployment.

New classical economists advocate policies to 'free up' the market: policies that encourage private enterprise, or provide incentives and reward initiative. Section 23.5 examines these *market-orientated supply-side policies*.

This part of the new classical agenda has much in common with the *neo-Austrian/libertarian school* (see Box 12.7). The argument here is that a free market, with the absolute minimum of government interference, will provide the dynamic environment where entrepreneurs will be willing to take risks and develop new products and new techniques.

The neo-Austrians go further. They also argue that the prospect of monopoly profits is often what provides a major motivation for firms to take risks. The search to achieve market advantages through new products and new techniques is just as important a part of competition, they argue, as competition in the market for existing goods. Thus private property rights are a key element in neo-Austrian thought: the right to keep the fruits of innovation and investment, with minimum taxation.

Definition

Market-orientated supply-side policies Policies to increase aggregate supply by freeing up the market.

Neo-Austrian/libertarian school A school of thought that advocates maximum liberty for economic agents to pursue their own interests and to own property.

The Keynesian approach

Modern Keynesians do not just advocate the management of demand. They also advocate supply-side policies, but generally of a more *interventionist* nature (e.g. training schemes, or policies to encourage firms to set up in areas of high unemployment).

The appropriate balance between demand- and supply-side policies depends on the degree of slack in the economy. In a recession, the immediate policy requirement is to increase aggregate *demand* rather than aggregate supply. Over the long term, however, supply-side policies will be needed to increase potential output and to reduce equilibrium (structural and frictional) unemployment.

 Does this mean that Keynesians would advocate using supply-side policies only at times of full employment?

'Third Way' supply-side policies

During the early years of the Labour government in the UK from 1997 under Tony Blair, there was much discussion of a 'Third Way' between the unfettered market system advocated by many of those on the right and the interventionist approach advocated by those on the left. The Third Way borrows from the right in advocating incentives, low taxes and free movements of capital. It also borrows from the left in advocating means whereby governments can provide support for individuals in need while improving economic performance by investing in the country's infrastructure, such as its transport and telecommunication systems, and in its social capital, such as schools, libraries and hospitals.

Its main thrust is the concept of helping people to help themselves. Thus unemployment policies should be focused on helping the unemployed become employable, with unemployment benefits linked to the obligation actively to look for work. Growth policies should be a mixture of strengthening market incentives and keeping taxes low, regulation to encourage more competition and prevent monopoly abuse, and providing improved infrastructure and improved education and training.

To some extent, this approach has been continued by subsequent UK governments through the 2010s, albeit with somewhat more emphasis on freeing up the market.

The link between demand-side and supply-side policies

Policies can have both demand-side and supply-side effects. For example, many supply-side policies involve increased government expenditure, whether on retraining schemes, on research and development projects, or on industrial relocation. They will therefore cause a rise in aggregate demand (unless accompanied by a rise in taxes). Similarly, supply-side policies of tax cuts designed to increase incentives will increase aggregate demand (unless accompanied by a cut in government expenditure). It is thus important to consider the consequences for demand when planning various supply-side policies.

Likewise, demand management policies often have supply-side effects. If a cut in interest rates boosts investment, there will be a multiplied rise in national income: a demand-side effect. But that rise in investment will also create increased productive capacity: a supply-side effect.

Definition

Interventionist supply-side policies Policies to increase aggregate supply by government intervention to counteract the deficiencies of the market.

Section summary

1. Supply-side policies, if successful, will shift the *AS* and *DAS* curves to the right, and possibly shift the Phillips curve downwards/to the left.

2. An important role for supply-side policies is to help increase productivity and, in particular, promote more rapid technological progress and its adoption by business. By doing so, this can raise the long-term rate of economic growth.

3. Demand-side policies (fiscal and monetary) may be suitable for controlling demand-pull inflation or demand-deficient unemployment, but supply-side policies will be needed to control the other types of inflation and unemployment.

4. New classical and neo-Austrian economists favour market-orientated supply-side policies. Keynesians tend to favour interventionist supply-side policies. The Third Way advocates carefully targeted government intervention, regulation, welfare and education programmes to encourage people better to help themselves and markets to work more effectively.

5. Supply-side policies often have demand-side effects, and demand-side policies often have supply-side effects. It is important for governments to take these secondary effects into account when working out their economic strategy.

23.5 SUPPLY-SIDE POLICIES IN PRACTICE: MARKET-ORIENTATED POLICIES

Market-orientated policies in the 1980s

Radical market-orientated supply-side policies were first adopted in the early 1980s by the Thatcher government in the UK and the Reagan administration in the USA. The essence of these policies was to encourage and reward individual enterprise and initiative, and to reduce the role of government; to put more reliance on market forces and competition, and less on government intervention and regulation. The policies were thus associated with the following:

- Reducing government expenditure so as to release more resources for the private sector.
- Reducing taxes so as to increase incentives.
- Reducing the monopoly power of trade unions so as to encourage greater flexibility in both wages and working practices and to allow labour markets to clear.

- Reducing the automatic entitlement to certain welfare benefits so as to encourage greater self-reliance.
- Reducing red tape and other impediments to investment and risk-taking.
- Encouraging competition through policies of deregulation and privatisation.
- Abolishing exchange controls and other impediments to the free movement of capital.

Such policies were increasingly copied by other governments around the world. Today most countries have adopted some or all of the above measures.

Government spending

The desire by many governments to cut government expenditure is not just to reduce the size of deficits and hence

---

BOX 23.4 THE SUPPLY-SIDE REVOLUTION IN THE USA

CASE STUDIES AND APPLICATIONS

'Reaganomics' and beyond

In both the UK and the USA, the 1980s proved to be years of radical political and economic change. Traditional economic and political practices were replaced by new and often controversial policies, although in theory many of the ideas advocated were based on old principles of laissez-faire capitalism.

In the USA, the era of 'Reaganomics' began in January 1981 when Ronald Reagan became President. With this new administration came a radical shift in policy aimed at directly tackling the supply side of the economy. This policy strategy involved four key strands:

- A reduction in the growth of Federal (central government) spending.
- A reduction in individual and corporate tax rates.
- A reduction in Federal regulations over private enterprise.
- A reduction in inflation through tight monetary policy.

On all four points, President Reagan was to achieve a degree of success. Federal spending growth was reduced even though military spending rocketed. Tax rates fell dramatically. Deregulation was speeded up. Inflation at first was stabilised and then fell sharply.

These supply-side measures were hailed as a great success by Republicans, and followers in both the UK and the USA were quick to advocate an even bigger reduction in the government's role.

Critics remained sceptical and pointed to the costs of Reaganomics. Huge budget deficits plagued the Reagan administration and the Bush Snr, Clinton and Bush Jnr

administrations that followed. The massive tax cuts were not matched by an equivalent cut in public expenditure; nor did they produce a sufficiently high rate of economic growth, through which additional tax revenues were to balance the budget. In the 1980s, 'civilian' or welfare spending was cut repeatedly in preference to the huge military budget. This led to increasing social hardship.

And such hardship still existed under George W. Bush. Indeed, with the onset of the credit crunch, things were to get worse as many poor people lost their houses. The emphasis had remained on cutting welfare and tightening requirements to receive state assistance. Critics claim that, even though the numbers on welfare might have fallen over the years, individuals and families remained in poverty, being forced to work for poverty wages as welfare support dwindled. The revolution was far from complete and its benefits to all social groups have been far from even.

The financial crisis of the late 2000s and the subsequent need for fiscal consolidation led to much debate, not only in the USA, about the form the fiscal consolidation should take and, more generally, about the role the state should play in modern economies. Whether, in such circumstances, current or future administrations will succeed in providing greater support for the poor without jeopardising the 'supply-side revolution' remains to be seen.

 Are market-orientated supply-side policies incompatible with policies to redistribute national income more equally?

reduce the growth of money supply; it is also an essential ingredient of their supply-side strategy.

The public sector is portrayed as more bureaucratic and less efficient than the private sector. What is more, it is claimed that a growing proportion of public money has been spent on administration and other 'non-productive' activities, rather than on the direct provision of goods and services.

Two things are needed, it is argued: (a) a more efficient use of resources within the public sector and (b) a reduction in the size of the public sector. This would allow private investment to increase with no overall rise in aggregate demand. Thus the supply-side benefits of higher investment could be achieved without the demand-side costs of higher inflation.

In practice governments have found it very difficult to cut their share of expenditure in GDP. However, many countries were faced with trying to do this after the financial crisis and global economic slowdown of the late 2000s (see Figure 23.10). Governments found that this means making difficult choices, particularly concerning the level of services and the provision of infrastructure.

 Why might a recovering economy (and hence a fall in government expenditure on social security benefits) make the government feel even more concerned to make discretionary cuts in government expenditure?

Taxes and the labour market

Over time, governments in many countries have cut the marginal rate of income tax. Here we consider the case of the UK.

In 1979, the standard marginal rate of income tax was 33 per cent, with higher rates rising to 83 per cent. By 2008 the standard rate was 20 per cent and the higher rate was 40 per cent. From 2010, an additional 50 per cent tax rate was implemented for incomes in excess of £150 000, largely as a means of plugging the deficit in the public finances. This was subsequently reduced to 45 per cent from 2013.

Cuts in the marginal rate of income tax are claimed to have five beneficial effects: people work longer hours; more people wish to work; people work more enthusiastically; employment rises; unemployment falls. These are big claims. Are they true?

People work longer hours

A cut in the marginal rate of income tax has a *substitution effect* inducing people to work more and also an *income effect* causing people to work less. (At this point, you should review the arguments about the incentive effects of tax cuts: see pages 336–40.) Evidence suggests that the two effects will roughly cancel each other out. Anyway, for many people there is no such choice in the short run. There is no chance of doing overtime or working a shorter week. In the long run, there may be some flexibility in that people can change jobs.

More people wish to work

This applies largely to second income earners in a family, mainly women. A rise in after-tax wages may encourage more women to look for jobs. It may now be worth the cost in terms of transport, childcare, family disruption, etc. The effects of a 1 or 2 per cent cut in income tax rates, however, are likely to be negligible. A more significant effect may be

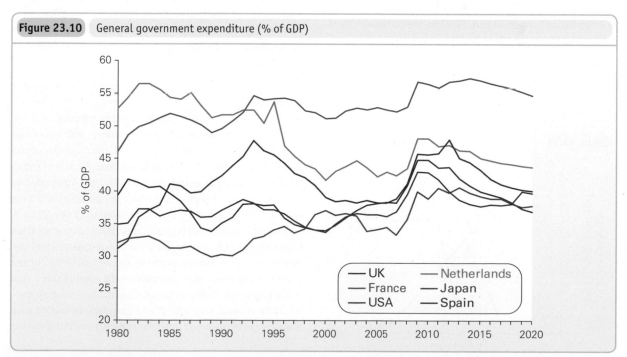

Figure 23.10   General government expenditure (% of GDP)

Notes: Data from 2017 based on forecasts.
Source: Based on data from *World Economic Outlook Database* (IMF) and *AMECO* database (European Commission).

achieved by raising tax allowances. Part-time workers, especially, could end up paying no taxes. Of course, if unemployment is already high, the government will not want to increase the labour force.

People work more enthusiastically

There is little evidence to test this claim. The argument, however, is that people will be more conscientious and will work harder if they can keep more of their pay.

Employment rises

If wages are flexible, total employment will rise. This is illustrated in Figure 23.11. The N curve shows the total labour force. The AS_L curve shows the number of people who are actually qualified and willing to do the specific jobs they are offered at each (after-tax) wage rate. Equilibrium is where the aggregate demand for labour (AD_L) is equal to the labour cost to the employer (i.e. the pre-tax wage rate). Assume an initial income tax per worker of $a - b$. The equilibrium employment will be Q_1. Workers receive an after-tax wage W_1 and thus supply Q_1 labour. Employers' labour cost is the pre-tax wage lc_1. At this wage, they demand Q_1 labour.

If the income tax per worker now falls to $c - d$, equilibrium employment will rise to Q_2. Firms will employ more workers because their labour costs have fallen to lc_2. More workers will take up jobs because their after-tax wages have risen to W_2.

Unemployment falls

One of the causes of natural (equilibrium) unemployment highlighted by new classical economists is the cushioning provided by unemployment benefit. If income tax rates are cut, there will be a bigger difference between after-tax wage rates and unemployment benefit. More people will be motivated to 'get on their bikes' and look for work.

In Figure 23.11, the horizontal gap between N and AS_L represents equilibrium unemployment. With a cut in

income tax per worker from $a - b$ to $c - d$, equilibrium unemployment will fall from $e - b$ to $f - d$.

What would happen to the AS_L curve and the level of unemployment if unemployment benefits were increased?

Despite the cuts in marginal rates of income tax in many countries, it has been commonplace for these to be offset by significant increases in other taxes. For example, in the UK, VAT was raised from 8 to 15 per cent per cent in 1979, to 17.5 per cent in 1992 and to 20 per cent in 2011.[2] The marginal rate of national insurance contributions for employees was 6.5 per cent in 1979; by 2011 it had risen to 12 per cent. The net effect was that government's receipts as a proportion of GDP were largely unchanged at just under 40 per cent.

Does this mean that there were no positive incentive effects from the 1979–97 Conservative government's tax measures?

To the extent that tax cuts do succeed in increasing take-home pay, there is a danger of 'sucking in' imports. In the UK, there is a high income elasticity of demand for imports. Extra consumer incomes may be spent on foreign-made electronic goods, foreign cars, holidays abroad and so on. Tax cuts can therefore have a serious effect on the current account of the balance of payments.

Taxes, business and investment

A number of financial incentives can be given to encourage investment. Selective intervention in the form of grants for specific industries or firms is best classified as an interventionist policy and will be examined in section 23.6. Market-orientated policies seek to reduce the general level of taxation on profits, or to give greater tax relief to investment.

TC 5
p50

A cut in taxes on business profits.   A cut in corporation tax (the tax on business profits) will increase after-tax profits. This will leave more funds for ploughing back into investment. Also, the higher after-tax return on investment will encourage more investment to take place. In 1983, the main rate of corporation tax in the UK stood at 52 per cent. A series of reductions have taken place since then. By 2011 the main rate had been halved to 26 per cent; by 2017 it had fallen to 19 per cent; by 2020 the rate is due to have fallen to 17 per cent.

The UK government hopes that such low corporation tax rates will make the country an attractive destination for business investment. However, the danger of countries cutting taxes to make them more internationally competitive is that it is a prisoners' dilemma game. Countries cannot all have lower taxes than each other! You may simply end up with global taxes being lower and governments receiving less tax

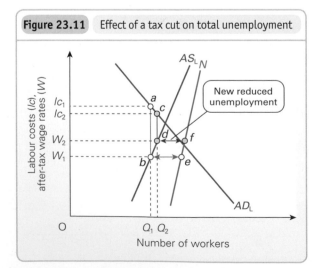

Figure 23.11 Effect of a tax cut on total unemployment

---

2 The rate was cut to 15 per cent in December 2008 for 13 months as part of the government's fiscal stimulus package.

revenue. Governments thus have to make a judgement as to whether or not cutting taxes will stimulate other countries to do the same.

Tax relief or other incentives for investment. Another approach to increase investment is through the use of allowances or R&D expenditure credits. Investment allowances enable firms to offset the cost of investment against their pre-tax profit, thereby reducing their tax liability. R&D expenditure credits operate by providing firms with cash payments for a proportion of their R&D expenditure which, although subject to tax, nonetheless increase their net profit.

Successive governments have applied such R&D incentives. For example, in the UK small and medium-sized enterprises (SMEs) can offset multiple research and development costs against corporation tax. Since April 2015, the rate of relief for small and medium-sized enterprises was 230 per cent: taxable profits are reduced by £230 for every £100 of R&D expenditure. Meanwhile, from April 2016 larger companies can claim a taxable credit worth 11 per cent of R&D expenditures.

Since April 2013, firms have been subject to a lower rate of corporation tax on profits earned from their patented inventions and certain other innovations. The idea is that firms will be provided with financial support to innovate where this results in their acquiring patents. Patents provide protection for intellectual property rights. Firms are liable to corporation tax on the profits attributable to qualifying patents at a reduced rate of 10 per cent.

Reducing the power of labour

In Figure 23.12, if the power of unions to push wage rates up to W_1 were removed, then (assuming no change in the demand curve for labour) wage rates would fall to W_e. Disequilibrium unemployment ($Q_2 - Q_1$) would disappear. Employment would rise from Q_1 to Q_e.

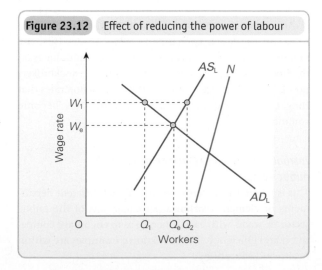

Figure 23.12   Effect of reducing the power of labour

Equilibrium unemployment, however, will rise somewhat as the gap between gross and effective labour supply widens. With the reduction in wage rates, some people may now prefer to remain on unemployment benefits.

If labour costs to employers are reduced, their profits will probably rise. This could encourage and enable more investment and hence economic growth. If the monopoly power of labour is reduced, then cost-push inflation will also be reduced.

The Thatcher government took a number of measures to weaken the power of labour. These included restrictions on union closed shops, restrictions on secondary picketing, financial assistance for union ballots, and enforced secret ballots on strike proposals (see Chapter 10). It also set a lead in resisting strikes in the public sector.

As labour markets have become more flexible, with increased part-time working and short-term and zero-hour contracts, and as the process of globalisation has exposed more companies to international competition, so this has further eroded the power of labour in many sectors of the economy.

 Is the number of working days lost through disputes a good indication of (a) union power; (b) union militancy?

A danger in driving down wages through increased competition in the labour market is that it reduces the incentive for firms to increase labour productivity. One cause of the UK's significantly lower output per hour than its major competitors (see chart (c) in Box 23.2) is that hourly wages are lower in many industries.

Reducing welfare

New classical economists claim that a major cause of unemployment is the small difference between the welfare benefits of the unemployed and the take-home pay of the employed. This causes voluntary unemployment (i.e. frictional unemployment). People are caught in a 'poverty trap': if they take a job, they lose their benefits (see pages 342–3).

A dramatic solution to this problem would be to cut unemployment benefits. Unlike policies to encourage investment, this supply-side policy would have a very rapid effect. It would shift the effective labour supply curve to the right. In Figure 23.13, equilibrium unemployment would fall from $a - b$ to $c - d$ if real wage rates were flexible downwards; or from $a - b$ to $a - e$ if they were not flexible. In the case of non-flexible real wage rates, the reduction in equilibrium unemployment would be offset by a rise in disequilibrium unemployment ($e - b$).

Because workers would now be prepared to accept a lower wage, the average length of job search by the unemployed would be reduced. In Figure 23.14, the average duration of unemployment would fall from T_1 to T_2.

 Would a cut in benefits affect the W_o curve? If so, with what effect?

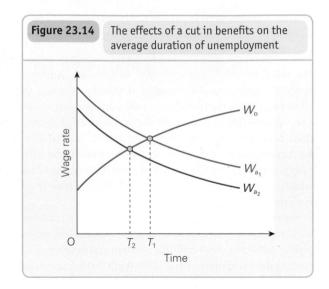

Figure 23.13 The effects of a cut in benefits on the number unemployed

Figure 23.14 The effects of a cut in benefits on the average duration of unemployment

A major problem is that with changing requirements for labour skills, many of the redundant workers from the older industries are simply not qualified for new jobs that are created. What is more, the longer people are unemployed, the more demoralised they become. Employers would probably be prepared to pay only very low wage rates to such workers. To persuade these unemployed people to take these low-paid jobs, the welfare benefits would have to be slashed. A 'market' solution to the problem, therefore, may be a very cruel solution. A fairer solution would be an interventionist policy: a policy of retraining labour.

Another alternative is to make the payment of unemployment benefits conditional on the recipient making a concerted effort to find a job. In the jobseeker's allowance scheme introduced in the UK in 1996, claimants must be available for, and actively seeking, work and must sign a 'Claimant Commitment', which sets out the types of work the person is willing to do, and their plan to find work. Payment can be refused if the claimant refuses to accept the offer of a job.

Policies to encourage competition

If the government can encourage more competition, this should have the effect of increasing national output and reducing inflation. Five major types of policy have been pursued under this heading.

Privatisation

If privatisation simply involves the transfer of a natural monopoly to private hands (as with the water companies), the scope for increased competition is limited. However, where there is genuine scope for competition (e.g. in the supply of gas and electricity), privatisation can lead to increased efficiency, more consumer choice and lower prices (but see Box 14.4 on page 438).

Alternatively, privatisation can involve the introduction of private services into the public sector (e.g. private contractors providing cleaning services in hospitals, or refuse collection for local authorities). Private contractors may compete against each other for the franchise. This may well lower the cost of provision of these services, but the quality of provision may also suffer unless closely monitored. The effects on unemployment are uncertain. Private contractors may offer lower wages and thus may use more labour. But if they are trying to supply the service at minimum cost, they may employ less labour.

Deregulation

This involves the removal of monopoly rights. In 1979, the UK's National Bus Corporation lost its monopoly of long-distance coach haulage. Private operators were now allowed to compete. This substantially reduced coach fares on a number of routes. In 1986, competition was allowed in providing local bus services (see Case Study 23.5 on the student website).

An example in the private sector was the so-called 'Big Bang' on the Stock Exchange in 1986. Under this, the monopoly power of 'jobbers' to deal in stocks and shares on the Stock Exchange was abolished. In addition, stockbrokers now compete with each other in the commission rates that they charge, and online share dealing has become commonplace.

Introducing market relationships into the public sector

This is where the government tries to get different departments or elements within a particular part of the public sector to 'trade' with each other, so as to encourage competition and efficiency. The best-known examples are within health and education.

KI 24
p252

One example is the UK's National Health Service. In 2003, the government introduced a system of 'foundation trusts'. Hospitals can apply for foundation trust status. If successful, they are given much greater financial autonomy in terms of purchasing, employment and investment decisions. Applications are judged by Monitor, the independent health regulator. By April 2017, there were 155 NHS foundation trusts. Critics argue that funds have been diverted to foundation hospitals away from the less well-performing hospitals where greater funding could help that performance. In the 2012 Health and Social Care Act the government proposed that in due course all NHS hospitals become foundation trusts.

As far as general practice is concerned, groups of GP practices are formed into Clinical Commissioning Groups (CCGs). These are responsible for arranging most of the NHS services within their boundaries. A key principle of the system is to give GPs a choice of 'providers' with the hope of reducing costs and driving up standards.

Public–private partnerships

Public–private partnerships (PPS) are a way of funding public expenditure with private capital. In the UK the *Private Finance Initiative* (PFI), as it was known, began in 1992. The PFI meant that a private company, after a competitive tender, would be contracted by a government department or local authority to finance and build a project, such as a new road or a prison. The government then pays the company to maintain and/or run it, or simply rents the assets from the company. The public sector thus becomes a purchaser of services rather than a direct provider itself.

Critics claim that PFI projects have resulted in low quality of provision and that cost control has often been poor, resulting in a higher burden for the taxpayer in the long term. What is more, many of the projects have turned out to be highly profitable, suggesting that the terms of the original contracts were too lax.

In 2012, the UK government published reforms to the PFI process following concerns about the quality of provision and the costs being incurred. The public sector now takes stakes of up to 49 per cent in new private finance projects (PF2 projects). PF2 projects no longer include 'soft services', such as cleaning and catering. The benefits and costs of PFI and PF2 are explored in Case 23.4 on the student website.

Free trade and free capital movements

The opening up of international trade and investment is central to a market-orientated supply-side policy. One of the first measures of the Thatcher government (in October 1979) was to remove all exchange controls, thereby permitting the free inflow and outflow of capital, both long term and short term. Most other industrialised countries also removed or relaxed exchange controls during the 1980s and early 1990s.

The Single European Act of 1987, which came into force in 1993, was another example of international liberalisation. As we shall see in section 24.4, it created a 'single market' in the EU: a market without barriers to the movement of goods, services, capital and labour.

Critics have claimed that in the short term industries may be forced to close by the competition from cheaper imported products, which can have a major impact on employment in the areas affected. A major election promise of the Trump campaign was that 'putting America first' would involve a move away from free trade and giving specific protection to US industries, such as vehicles and steel. We examine the arguments for and against protection in section 24.2.

Section summary

1. Market-orientated supply-side policies aim to increase the rate of growth of aggregate supply by encouraging private enterprise and the freer play of market forces.

2. Reducing government expenditure as a proportion of GDP is a major element of such policies.

3. Tax cuts can be used to encourage more people to take up jobs, and to encourage people to work longer hours and more enthusiastically. They can be used to reduce equilibrium unemployment and encourage employers to take on more workers. Likewise, tax cuts for businesses or increased investment allowances may encourage higher investment. The effects of tax cuts depend on how people respond to incentives. For example, people will work longer hours only if the substitution effect outweighs the income effect.

4. Reducing the power of trade unions by legislation could reduce disequilibrium unemployment and cost-push inflation. It could also lead to a redistribution of income to profits, which could increase investment and growth (but possibly lead to greater inequality).

5. A reduction in welfare benefits, especially those related to unemployment, will encourage workers to accept jobs at lower wages and thus decrease equilibrium unemployment.

6. Various policies can be introduced to increase competition. These include privatisation, deregulation, introducing market relationships into the public sector, public–private partnerships and freer international trade and capital movements.

23.6 SUPPLY-SIDE POLICIES IN PRACTICE: INTERVENTIONIST POLICIES

The case for intervention

Many interventionist policies come under the general heading of **industrial policy**: the government taking an active role to support investment in industry and to halt the decline of the manufacturing sector (see Box 23.3). The basis of the case for government intervention is that the free market is likely to provide too little research and development, training and investment.

As we saw in section 23.3, there are potentially large external benefits from research and development. Hence, the social rate of return on investment may be much higher than the private rate of return. Investment that is privately unprofitable for a firm may therefore still be economically desirable for the nation.

Similarly, investment in training may continue yielding benefits to society that are lost to the firms providing the training when the workers leave.

Investment often involves risks. Firms may be unwilling to take those risks, since the costs of possible failure may be too high. When looked at nationally, however, the benefits of investment might well have substantially outweighed the costs, and thus it would have been socially desirable for firms to have taken the risk. Successes would have outweighed failures.

For decades, the UK has had a lower level of investment relative to GDP than other industrialised countries. This is illustrated in Table 23.3. It could be argued, therefore, that there is a particularly strong case in the UK for government intervention to encourage investment.

Imperfections in the capital market

Imperfections in the capital market may result in investment not being financed, even though it is privately profitable. Banks in the UK, unlike banks in France, Germany and Japan, have not traditionally been a source of finance for long-term investment by firms.

Similarly, if firms rely on raising finance by the issue of new shares, this makes them very dependent on the stock market performance of their shares, which depends on current profitability and expected profitability in the near future, not on long-term profitability. Shareholders, who are mainly financial institutions, tend to demand too high a dividend rate from the companies in which they invest. This, in part, is due to competition between financial institutions to attract savers to buy their savings packages. The result is that there is less profit left over for ploughing back into investment. The fear of takeovers (the competition for corporate control) again makes managers overconcerned to keep shareholders happy. Finally, floating successful companies on the Stock Exchange provides a large windfall gain to the original owners. This encourages entrepreneurs to *set up* companies, but discourages them from making *long-term* commitments to them. This has all led to the UK disease of 'short-termism': the obsession with short-term profits and the neglect of investment that yields profits only after a number of years.

Finally, in the case of ailing firms, if the government does not help finance a rescue investment programme, there may be substantial social costs from job losses. The avoidance of these social costs may make the investment socially, if not privately, profitable.

 How would the radical right reply to these arguments?

Examples of interventionist supply-side policy

Nationalisation

This is the most extreme form of intervention, and one that most countries have in the past rejected, given the world-wide trend of privatisation. Nevertheless, many countries have stopped short of privatising certain key transport and power industries, such as the railways and electricity

Table 23.3	Gross capital formation (investment), % of GDP				
	1980s	**1990s**	**2000s**	**2010s**	**1980–2019**
Australia	27.0	24.9	26.8	26.1	26.2
Belgium	22.0	22.9	23.0	23.3	22.8
Canada	22.2	19.9	21.9	23.9	22.0
Denmark	20.5	20.2	22.3	19.9	20.7
France	22.8	21.0	22.4	22.8	22.2
Germany	26.2	24.1	20.3	19.6	22.6
Ireland	22.5	20.3	26.2	25.2	23.5
Italy	23.3	20.2	21.1	17.9	20.6
Japan	31.1	30.7	24.7	23.1	27.4
Netherlands	22.7	23.2	21.7	20.0	21.9
Norway	28.8	23.7	22.9	27.8	25.8
Spain	22.3	23.2	28.3	20.6	23.6
UK	20.5	19.5	17.7	16.7	18.6
USA	23.3	21.4	21.9	19.6	21.6

Note: Data from 2017 based on forecasts.
Source: Based on data from *World Economic Outlook* database (IMF, October 2017).

Definition

Industrial policies Policies to encourage industrial investment and greater industrial efficiency.

BOX 23.5   A NEW APPROACH TO INDUSTRIAL POLICY   EXPLORING ECONOMICS

Industrial policy attempts to increase investment and halt or slow the shrinking of the industrial sector. As with many other areas of economic policy, industrial policy throughout most of the world has undergone a radical reorientation in recent years. The government's role has shifted from one of direct intervention in the form of subsidies and protecting industry from competition, to one of focusing upon the external business environment and the conditions that influence its competitiveness.

The reasons for such a change are both philosophical and structural:

- The rise of the political right in the 1980s led to a shift away from interventionist and towards market-based supply-side policy.
- Growing government debt, and a desire to curb public expenditure, acted as a key incentive to reduce the state's role in industrial affairs. This was argued to be one of the driving forces behind the European privatisation process since the 1980s.
- Industry, during the 1980s, became progressively more global in its outlook. As such, its investment decisions were increasingly being determined by external environmental factors, especially the technology, productivity and labour costs of its international competitors.

The new approach to industrial policy, being widely adopted by many advanced countries, is to focus on improving those factors that shape a nation's competitiveness. This involves shifting away from particular sectors to targeting what are referred to as 'framework conditions for industry'.

Policies include the following:

- The promotion of investment in physical and human capital. Human capital in particular, and the existence of a sound skills base, are seen as crucial for attracting global business and ensuring long-run economic growth.
- A reduction in non-wage employment costs, such as employers' social security and pension contributions. Many governments see these costs as too high and as a severe limitation on competitiveness and employment creation.
- The promotion of innovation and the encouragement of greater levels of R&D.
- Support for small and medium-sized enterprises. SMEs have received particular attention due to their crucial role in enhancing innovation, creating employment and contributing to skills development, especially in high-tech areas.
- The improvement of infrastructure. This includes both physical transport, such as roads and railways, and information highways.
- The protection of intellectual property by more effective use of patents and copyright. By reinforcing the law in these areas it is hoped to encourage firms to develop new products and commit themselves to research.

These policies, if they are to be truly effective, are likely to require co-ordination and integration, since they represent a radical departure from traditional industrial policy.

1. *In what senses could these new policies be described as (a) non-interventionist; (b) interventionist?*
2. *Does globalisation, and in particular the global perspective of multinational corporations, make industrial policy in the form of selective subsidies and tax relief more or less likely?*

KI 24
p252

---

generation. Having these industries under public ownership may result in higher investment than if they were under private ownership. Thus French governments have invested heavily in the state-owned railway system. This has resulted in fast, efficient rail services, with obvious benefits to rail users and the economy generally.

Nationalisation may also be a suitable solution for rescuing vital industries suffering extreme market turbulence. This was the case in 2008 with many banks. With the credit crunch, overexposure to risky investments in securitised subprime debt, inadequate levels of capital, declining confidence and plummeting share prices, many banks were taken into full or partial public ownership. In the UK, Northern Rock and Bradford & Bingley were fully nationalised, while the government took a temporary majority shareholding in the Royal Bank of Scotland and Lloyds Banking Group.

Direct provision

Improvements in infrastructure – such as a better motorway system – can be of direct benefit to industry. Alternatively, the government could provide factories or equipment to specific firms. Following the financial crisis and the economic volatility that followed, the IMF, OECD and other international organisations began calling for greater international expenditure on infrastructure as a way of increasing not only potential output but also aggregate demand.

Funding research and development (R&D)

To increase a country's research and development, the government could fund universities or other research institutes through various grants, perhaps allocated by research councils. Alternatively, it could provide grants or tax relief to private firms to carry out R&D.

As we saw in section 23.5, the UK uses the tax system to encourage research and development (R&D). Despite this, UK gross expenditure on R&D as a percentage of GDP has been significantly lower than that of its main economic rivals (see Figure 23.15). This has contributed to a productivity gap between the UK and other G7 countries (see Box 23.2).

The UK's poor R&D record has occurred even though a sizeable number of UK-based companies are among the world's largest R&D spending companies, albeit within a

TC 5
p50

Figure 23.15 Gross expenditure on R&D (% of GDP)

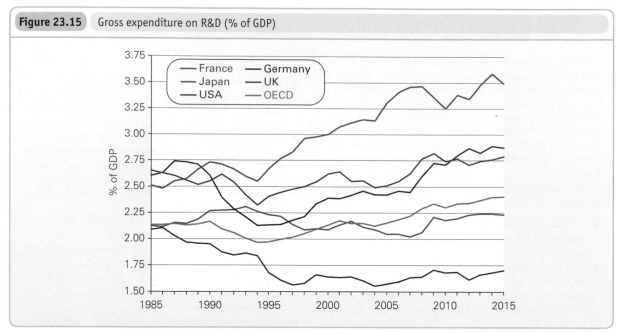

Note: OECD = 35 members (as of April 2017) of the Organisation for Economic Co-operation and Development.
Source: *Gross Domestic Spending on R&D* (OECD, 2017).

narrow range of industries, such as pharmaceuticals, finance and aerospace. In part, this reflects the limited R&D expenditure by government. But, it also reflects the low R&D intensity across the private sector. In other words, total R&D expenditure by British firms has often been low *relative* to the income generated by sales.

Training and education

It is generally recognised by economists and politicians alike that improvements in training and education can yield significant supply-side gains. Indeed, the UK's failure to invest as much in training as many of its major competitors is seen as a key explanation for the persistent productivity gap with many other advanced countries.

The government may set up training schemes, or encourage educational institutions to make their courses more vocationally relevant, or introduce new vocational qualifications. Alternatively, the government can provide grants or tax relief to firms which themselves provide training schemes.

Education and training in the UK. From April 2017 in England, the Education and Skills Funding Agency (ESFA) took over responsibility for funding education and training for children, young people and adults. Hence, as well as the funding of education for pupils aged 5 to 16 it has responsibility for overseeing education and training for those aged 16 to 19 and apprenticeships and adult education.

As part of the government's strategy to support apprenticeships, the Apprenticeship Levy was introduced from April 2017. This saw employers with an annual wage bill of £3 million or more having to pay a levy of 0.5 per cent towards the funding of apprenticeships. Employers in England can then use funds in their apprenticeship accounts to pay for apprenticeship training and assessment with the payment dependent, in part, on the level of the apprenticeship: i.e. the equivalent educational level. For smaller employers the government will pay up to 90 per cent of their training and assessment costs, although in the case of companies with fewer than 50 employees 100 per cent of these costs are paid for if the apprentices are aged between 16 and 18.

Figure 23.16 shows the steady expansion in the number of starts on government-funded apprenticeships in England between 2006/7 and 2009/10, followed by a more significant expansion in the early 2010s before then levelling off at around 500 000 per annum. While each age group has seen an increase in the number of apprenticeships, the growth in the number of learners aged 25 and over starting apprenticeships has been particularly rapid.

Nonetheless, the recent growth in apprenticeships has to be seen in the context of the relatively low starting point compared with other countries. The National Audit Office in 2012 identified that only 5 per cent of employers in England (2010) were offering apprenticeships compared with 24 per cent in Germany (2008) and 30 per cent in Australia (2009).

Alternative approaches to training in the UK, Germany, France and the USA are examined in Case 23.10 on the student website.

Advice, information and collaboration

The government may engage in discussions with private firms in order to find ways to improve efficiency and innovation. It may bring firms together to exchange information and create a climate of greater certainty or it may bring

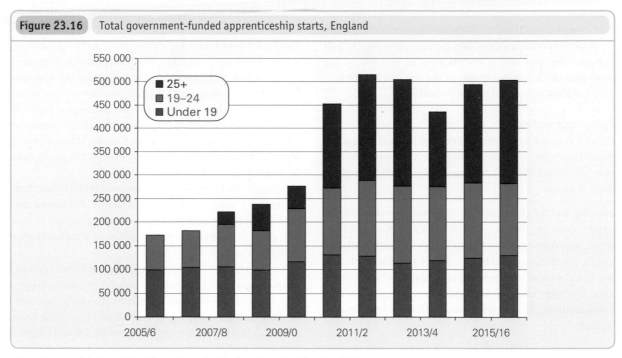

Figure 23.16 Total government-funded apprenticeship starts, England

Source: Based on data from *FE Data Library: Apprenticeships* (Department for Education, 2017).

firms and unions together to try to create greater industrial harmony. It can provide various information services to firms: technical assistance, the results of public research, information on markets, etc.

Local Enterprise Partnerships (LEPs) are an example of partnerships created between local government and businesses in England. LEPs began in 2011 and their aim is to promote local economic development. As well as facilitating the flow of information between public and private organisations, LEPs agree on local strategic economic objectives. They can seek funds from central government through 'Local Growth Deals' or co-ordinate the establishment of enterprise zones (see below) to meet these objectives.

> *What are the advantages and disadvantages of local collaborations, such as LEPs, as compared to geographically larger collaboration?*

Regional and urban policy

Causes of regional imbalance

In addition to adopting supply-side measures that focus on the economy as a whole, governments may decide to target specific regions of the economy. Certain parts of the country suffer from lower economic growth and higher unemployment than others. These can be broad regions, such as the North East of England or Calabria in southern Italy, or much smaller areas, such as parts of inner cities. These regional and urban problems normally result from structural problems – the main one being the decline of certain industries, such as mining or heavy manufacturing

industry, which had previously been concentrated in those areas.

When an area declines, there will be a downward *regional multiplier effect*. The decline in demand and loss of jobs lead to less money being spent in the local community; transport and other service industries lose custom. The whole region becomes more depressed.

In addition, labour may be geographically immobile. The regional pattern of industrial location may change more rapidly than the labour market can adjust to it. Thus jobs may be lost in the depressed areas more rapidly than people can migrate from them. Unemployment rises. Even when people do leave the area, this can compound the downward multiplier effect as spending further declines.

If the capital market functioned well, this could help to arrest the decline. If wages were lower and land were cheaper in the depressed areas, capital would be attracted there. In practice, capital, like labour, is often relatively immobile. *Existing* capital stock is highly immobile. Buildings and most

> **Definition**
>
> **Regional multiplier effects** When a change in injections into or withdrawals from a particular region causes a multiplied change in income in that region. The regional multiplier (k_r) is given by $1/mpw_r$, where the import component of mpw_r consists of imports into that region either from abroad or from other regions of the economy.

machinery cannot be moved to where the unemployed are! *New* capital is much more mobile. But there may be insufficient new investment, especially during a recession, to halt regional decline, and investors may be put off by the depressed and run-down nature of the area, the lack of suitably qualified labour and lack of infrastructure.

Policy approaches

Policies targeted at specific regions (or sectors) tend to be more interventionist in nature. Interventionist policies involve encouraging firms to move. Such policies include the following.

Subsidies and tax concessions in the depressed regions. Businesses could be given general subsidies, such as grants to move, or reduced rates of corporation tax. Alternatively, grants or subsidies could be specifically targeted at increasing employment (e.g. reduced employers' national insurance contributions) or at encouraging investment (e.g. investment grants or other measures to reduce the costs of capital).

The provision of facilities in depressed regions. The government or local authorities could provide facilities, such as land and buildings at concessionary, or even zero, rents to incoming firms; or spend money on improving the infrastructure of the area (roads and communications, technical colleges, etc.).

The siting of government offices in the depressed regions. The government could move some of its own departments out of the capital and locate them in areas of high unemployment. The siting of the vehicle licensing centre in Swansea is an example.

Recent regional policy for England draws heavily on the first two of these. As we saw earlier, Local Enterprise Partnership (LEPs) have been a key mechanism used by the government in bringing together local authorities, firms and organisations. Subsequently, LEPs have been used to drive forward the development of Enterprise Zones. First established in 2012, these zones are specific geographic locations where firms can benefit from reduced planning restrictions, tax breaks and improved infrastructure, including access to superfast broadband. The number of zones has grown from 24 in 2012 to 48 in April 2017.

Many of the Enterprise Zones encourage clustering: businesses in the same sector grouping together. The hope is that they can mutually benefit from external economies of scale (see page 187) such as co-operation and technological developments.

To benefit from clustering effects, the zones typically focus on specific sectors, such as automotive and transport (e.g. the MIRA technology park near Hinckley, Leicestershire), renewable energy (e.g. the Humber Enterprise Zone) or science and innovation (e.g. Loughborough and Leicester Enterprise Zone).

The danger of such an approach, particularly given the relatively small geographic areas of many LEPs and Enterprise Zones, is that they may merely divert investment away from other areas rather than resulting in *additional* investment.

Case Study 23.14 on the student website is an extended case study of regional and urban policy in both the UK and the EU.

 How might clustering effects be incorporated into endogenous growth theories?

Section summary

1. Those in favour of interventionist industrial policy point to failings of the market, such as the externalities involved in investment and training, the imperfections in the capital market and the short-term perspective of decision makers.

2. Interventionist supply-side policy can take the form of grants for investment and research and development, advice and persuasion, the direct provision of infrastructure and the provision, funding or encouragement of various training schemes.

3. Regional and local disparities arise from a changing pattern of industrial production. With many of the older

industries concentrated in certain parts of the country and especially in the inner cities, and with an acceleration in the rate of industrial change, so the gap between rich and poor areas has widened.

4. Regional disparities may persist because of capital and labour immobility and regional multiplier effects.

5. Policies targeted at specific regions or sectors tend to be interventionist in their approach. These include subsidies, tax concessions and the provision of facilities in depressed regions.

BOX 23.6   UNEMPLOYMENT AND SUPPLY-SIDE POLICIES

Two approaches

Countries have had varying degrees of success in reducing unemployment through appropriate supply-side policies.

In 2006, the OECD put countries into four groups according to their policies towards labour markets. The first two groups have been successful in cutting unemployment. The other two have not.

The first group, labelled 'mainly English-speaking' by the OECD (Japan, South Korea and Switzerland are honorary Anglophones), tends to have weaker job protection, less generous unemployment benefits and thinner tax wedges than the average. Its employment rate is comfortably higher than the OECD average; its jobless rate [5.3 per cent] is comfortably lower [than the OECD average of 7.5 per cent]. In the second, 'northern European' group (Scandinavia, the Netherlands, Austria and Ireland), taxes and unemployment benefits are high and workers hard to fire. Yet the average employment rate is a little higher than the first group's and the unemployment rate a little lower [4.8 per cent].

There are two reasons why the second group can match the first. Their product markets are, like those of the first group, fairly loosely regulated, making the whole economy more dynamic. And they spend much more on schemes intended to ensure that the unemployed try hard to find work: in return for high benefits, they must accept that their search for a job will be closely watched and that some work-seeking programmes may be compulsory. That high unemployment benefits are a disincentive to seek work is not in doubt; but it seems that a sufficiently diligent and well-funded employment service can offset their effects. . . .

Countries in the third group – mainly southern European ones, plus France and Germany – tend to pay high benefits too. But they have not offset these with labour-market programmes on the scale of the second group, and their product markets are more protected. [Unemployment in this group averages 9.0 per cent.]

In the last group, which includes the Czech Republic, Poland and Slovakia, benefits are low. But workers are not especially easy to fire; little is spent on pushing the jobless into work; and product markets are more regulated than in any other group. [Unemployment in this group averages 15.1 per cent.][1]

1. How would you classify the approaches of the first two groups in terms of whether they are 'market-orientated' or 'interventionist'?
2. Is there an even more effective approach to reducing unemployment that uses elements of each?

1 'Intricate workings', *The Economist,* 17 June 2006.

END OF CHAPTER QUESTIONS

1. For what reasons do countries experience very different long-run rates of economic growth from each other?

2. Why do developed countries experience a degree of convergence over time? Would you expect there to be total convergence of GDP per head?

3. If increased investment (using current technology) does not lead to increased long-run economic growth, does it bring any benefits?

4. What determines the rate of depreciation of capital? What would happen if the rate of depreciation fell?

5. What is meant by the 'steady-state economic growth path'? What determines its slope?

6. What is the significance of the term 'endogenous' in endogenous growth theory? What, according to this theory, determines the long-run rate of economic growth?

7. Under what circumstances would a higher rate of investment lead to a higher rate of economic growth?

8. What determines the rate of growth in total factor productivity?

9. What policy prescriptions do the neoclassical and endogenous growth theories offer policy makers who are looking to raise their country's long-run growth rate?

10. For what possible reasons may a country experience a persistently faster rate of economic growth than another?

11. What is the relationship between 'successful' supply-side policies and unemployment in (i) the short run and (ii) the long run, according to (a) Keynesian and (b) monetarist assumptions?

12. Why might market-orientated supply-side policies have undesirable side effects on aggregate demand?

13. What type of tax cuts are likely to create the greatest (a) incentives, (b) disincentives to effort?

14. Is deindustrialisation necessarily undesirable?

15. In what ways can interventionist industrial policy work *with* the market, rather than against it? What are the arguments for and against such policy?

16. What are the arguments for and against relying entirely on *discretionary* regional and urban policy?

17. Select a European country other than the UK and compare its regional and urban policy with that of the UK.

Online resources

Additional case studies on the student website

23.1 Growth accounting. This case study identifies various factors that contribute to economic growth and shows how their contribution can be measured.

23.2 Productivity performance and the UK economy. A detailed examination of how the UK's productivity compares with that in other countries.

23.3 The USA: is it a 'new economy'? An examination of whether US productivity increases are likely to be sustained.

23.4 Assessing PFI. An analysis of this 'third way' approach to funding public sector projects.

23.5 Deregulating the UK bus industry. Has this led to greater competition and improved services?

23.6 The R&D Scoreboard. An international comparison of spending by companies on R&D.

23.7 Controlling inflation in the past. This case study looks at the history of prices and incomes policies in the UK.

23.8 UK industrial performance. This examines why the UK has had a poorer investment record than many other industrial countries and why it has suffered a process of 'deindustrialisation'.

23.9 Technology and economic change. How to get the benefits from technological advance.

23.10 Alternative approaches to training and education. This compares approaches to training and education in the UK with those in other countries.

23.11 Assistance to small firms in the UK. An examination of current government measures to assist small firms.

23.12 Small-firm policy in the EU. This looks at the range of support available to small and medium-sized firms in the EU.

23.13 Welfare to work. An examination of the UK Labour government's policy of providing support to people looking for work.

23.14 Regional and urban policy. This case looks at the causes of regional imbalance and urban decay and at the approaches to regional and urban policy in the UK and EU.

Maths Case 23.1 Finding the steady-state equilibrium in the Solow model. Using the algebra in worked example.

Maths Case 23.2 The effect of technological progress in the Solow model. Using the algebra in a worked example.

Websites relevant to this chapter

Numbers and sections refer to websites listed in the Web Appendix and hotlinked from this book's website at **www.pearsoned.co.uk/sloman**.

- For news articles relevant to this chapter, see the *Economics News* section on the student website.
- For general news on unemployment, inflation, economic growth and supply-side policy, see websites in section A, and particularly A1–13, 18, 19, 21, 35, 37. See also links to newspapers worldwide in A38, 39, 42, 43 and 44, and the news search feature in Google at A41.
- For data on unemployment, inflation and growth, see links in B1; also see B4 and 12. For UK data, see B3 and 34. For EU data, see B38 and 47. For US data, see the data section of B17. For international data, see B15, 21, 24, 31, 33, 43 and 46. For links to datasets, see B28; I23.
- For specific data on UK unemployment, search site B3. For international data on unemployment, see G1; H3 and 5.
- For information on the development of ideas, including information on classical, Keynesian, monetarist, new classical and new Keynesian thought, see C18.
- For the current approach to UK supply-side policy, see the latest Budget Report (e.g. sections on productivity and training) at site E30. See also sites E5, 9, 10, 18, 36 and 40.
- For support for a market-orientated approach to supply-side policy, see C17 and E34.
- For information on training in the UK and Europe, see sites E5; G5, 14.
- For information on the support for small business in the UK, see site E38.
- For information on regional policy in the UK, see site E2; and in the EU, see site G12.
- For student resources relevant to these three chapters, see sites C1–7, 9, 10, 19.

The World Economy

'Globalisation' is a word frequently used nowadays. It captures one of the key features of economics today: that it is global in nature. International trade and international financial flows have often grown at exceedingly rapid rates in recent decades. The result is that economies around the globe are highly interconnected so that what happens in one country can have profound effects on others.

In Chapter 24 we focus on international trade, looking at the benefits it brings, but also at the costs that can be incurred. This is important when analysing the calls, by some, for greater protectionism. Are people right to fear international competition? The chapter concludes by reflecting on the potential longer-term implications for the UK from the vote in 2016 to leave the European Union.

With the growth in international trade and financial flows Chapter 25 focuses on the potential for countries to be more vulnerable to balance of payments problems and exchange rate fluctuations. It analyses the relationships between a country's balance of payments and its exchange rate.

Chapter 26 looks at particular aspects of global and regional interdependence. In this context, it analyses the euro and how economic and monetary union (EMU) operates, whether the adoption of the euro by 19 EU countries has been of benefit to them and reflects on the future of the euro. Chapter 26 concludes by looking at the poorest countries of the world, whose development depends so much on the economic policies of the rich.

24 Chapter

International Trade

Without international trade we would all be much poorer. There would be some items like pineapples, coffee, cotton clothes, foreign holidays and uranium that we would simply have to go without. Then there would be other items like wine and spacecraft that we could produce only very inefficiently. International trade has the potential to benefit all participating countries. This chapter explains why.

Totally free trade, however, may bring problems to countries or to groups of people within those countries. Many people argue strongly for restrictions on trade. Textile workers see their jobs threatened by cheap imported cloth. Car manufacturers worry about falling sales as customers switch to Japanese or other East Asian models. But are people justified in fearing international competition, or are they merely trying to protect some vested interest at the expense of everyone else? Section 24.2 examines these arguments and also looks at world attitudes towards trade restrictions.

A step on the road to freer trade is for countries to enter free trade agreements with just a limited number of other countries. Examples include the EU and more recently the North American Free Trade Association (NAFTA – the USA, Canada and Mexico). We consider such 'preferential trading systems' in section 24.3. Then, in section 24.4, we look in more detail at the EU and the development of the 'single European market'. We finish by considering some of the possible economic implications for the UK from the vote in 2016 to leave the European Union. The focus here is on the supply-side effects of the UK's new trading relationship with the EU and the rest of the world.

This chapter may be studied after Chapter 12 or Chapter 14 if you prefer.

24.1   THE ADVANTAGES OF TRADE

The growth of world trade

Trade values

In 1960 the (nominal) value of world merchandise exports (i.e. the exports of goods) was estimated at $130 billion. By 2016 this had grown to over $16 trillion. Figure 24.1 helps to put this into perspective by showing both the value of world merchandise exports and their value as a percentage of GDP. From just under 10 per cent in 1960, by 2008 they had grown to 25.5 per cent of GDP. Indeed, from 1960 to 2008 the value of world trade had typically grown at more than twice the rate of the value of world output. However, since the financial crisis of 2007–8, this trend has been reversed. By 2016, world merchandise exports had fallen to 21 per cent of world GDP.

Another way of looking at world trade is through the sum of both exports *and* imports. This is commonly used to capture the openness of economies. Table 24.1 shows total merchandise trade as a percentage of GDP for various countries. As you can see, in all cases the proportion was higher in the 2010s than in 1960s, and in some cases considerably higher.

Which countries' merchandise trade had fallen as a percentage of GDP between the 2000s and the period from 2010 to 2015? Explain why.

So far our focus has been on the trade of goods. But countries trade services too. Commercial services include manufacturing services on physical inputs (e.g. oil refining,

assembly of electronics and packing), maintenance and repair, transport, construction, insurance and financial services, telecommunications and private health and education services. In 2016 the global value of exports of commercial services was $4.9 trillion, the equivalent of 6.5 per cent of GDP. This was an increase from just $191 billion or 3 per cent of GDP in 1976.

Table 24.1	Merchandise trade, percentage of GDP					
	1960s	1970s	1980s	1990s	2000s	2010–15
Australia	25.0	24.6	27.0	29.3	34.3	33.5
Canada	32.1	39.9	45.0	55.0	59.0	51.7
China	6.8	9.1	24.5	36.2	51.6	43.7
France	20.5	30.0	35.6	37.1	44.4	44.8
Germany	n.a.	33.6	42.7	41.0	60.0	70.5
Ireland	57.2	75.0	89.7	104.0	92.7	76.2
India	8.6	8.9	11.1	16.2	27.2	38.6
Italy	22.1	32.0	34.6	33.1	41.5	46.7
Japan	18.1	20.1	20.5	15.4	22.6	28.4
Netherlands	78.1	80.7	83.0	86.3	111.3	142.2
New Zealand	32.2	40.2	43.7	43.3	44.6	42.3
UK	31.0	38.7	39.3	37.1	37.0	42.2
USA	6.9	11.7	14.4	16.8	19.7	22.9
World	**17.7**	**26.5**	**30.9**	**32.9**	**43.5**	**48.4**

Note: Merchandise trade as a share of GDP is the sum of merchandise exports and imports divided by the value of GDP, all in current US dollars.
Source: World Bank (series TG.VAL.TOTL.GD.ZS).

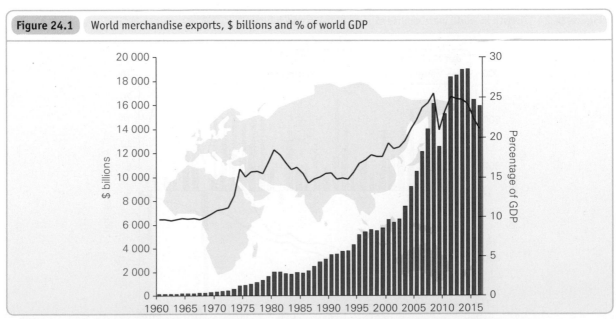

Figure 24.1   World merchandise exports, $ billions and % of world GDP

Sources: Merchandise exports data, *WTO Merchandise Trade Values Annual Dataset*, (WTO); World GDP data, series NY.GDP.MKTP.CD (World Bank).

Table 24.2	Trade in commercial services, percentage of GDP			
	1980s	**1990s**	**2000s**	**2010–15**
USA	3.5	4.7	5.3	6.8
UK	10.7	11.2	16.2	19.3
China	2.2	5.9	7.7	5.9
Germany	8.7	8.6	12.7	15.5
France	10.8	11.2	13.4	16.9
Netherlands	19.3	21.6	27.2	34.3
World	**7.3**	**8.4**	**10.7**	**12.3**

Note: Trade in commercial services as a share of GDP is the sum of exports and imports in commercial services divided by the value of GDP, all in current US dollars.
Source: World Bank (series BG.GSR.NFSV.GD.ZS).

Table 24.2 shows the sum of exports and imports in commercial services as a percentage of GDP in various countries since the 1980s – these countries were the largest exporters by value of commercial service in 2015. Though the flows are much smaller than those of merchandise goods, we still observe a significant increase in international flows of commercial services over the whole period and, with the exception of China, the percentages were higher in the period 2010 to 2015 than in the 2000s.

Trade volumes

The dollar value of recorded global trade is affected by changes in prices and exchange rates as well as the volumes traded. Therefore, by adjusting the dollar value of trade flows for changes in export and import prices we are able to estimate the change in the *volumes* of goods being traded.

Figure 24.2 shows the growth in the value and volume of world merchandise exports from 1980. Over the period as a whole the value of merchandise exports grew at annual rate of 4.6 per cent. After accounting for changes in the prices of countries' exports, the volume of exports is estimated to have grown by 1.7 per cent per year.

The chart also shows the actual year-to-year changes in the values and volumes of merchandise exports. There are some significant differences between the change in values and volumes. Take, for example, 2015 when the value of merchandise exports fell by around 13.5 per cent. In contrast, the volume of exports rose by 2.5 per cent. The difference is largely attributable to the large fall in commodity prices in 2015 with, for example, global energy prices falling by as much as 45 per cent.

From Figure 24.2 we can see the significant negative impact of the global financial crisis at the end of the 2000s on the volume of merchandise exports. In 2009, the volume of worldwide merchandise exports fell by approximately 12 per cent (while their value declined by 23 per cent). This was the biggest contraction in global trade since the Second World War. Despite the initial rebound in 2010 the average rate of growth in the volume of exports from 2011 to 2016 was only 2.8 per cent compared to the 5.3 per cent average experienced from 1981 to 2007. This was partly attributable to weaker global economic growth: the world economy grew by 2.5 per cent per annum from 2011 to 2016 compared with 3.1 per cent from 1981 to 2007. Notably, larger developing economies, such as China, saw their growth weaken and in some cases, such as Brazil, economies went into recession.

 If the volume of merchandise exports falls by less than their value what can be infer about what has happened to the prices of merchandise exports'?

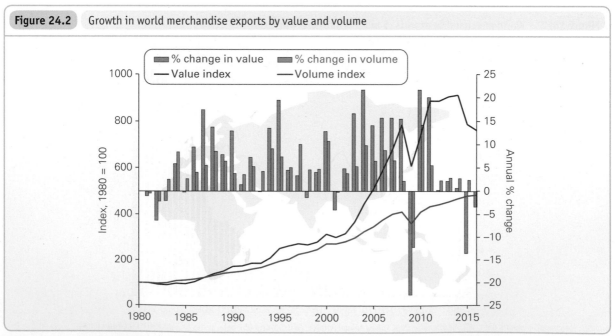

Figure 24.2   Growth in world merchandise exports by value and volume

Sources: Based on data from *Time Series on International Trade*, statistics database (SDB), (WTO).

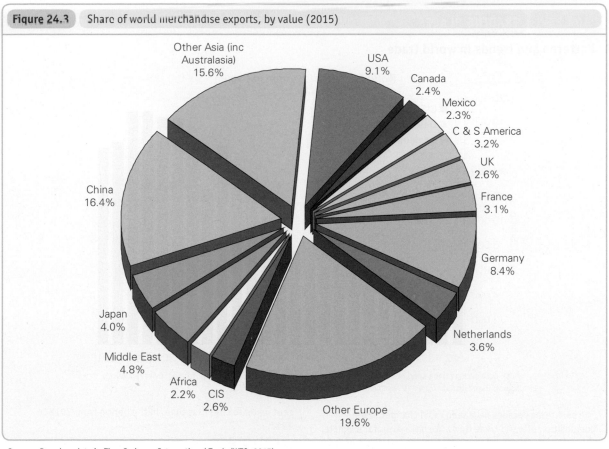

Figure 24.3 Share of world merchandise exports, by value (2015)

Other Asia (inc Australasia) 15.6%
USA 9.1%
Canada 2.4%
Mexico 2.3%
C & S America 3.2%
UK 2.6%
France 3.1%
Germany 8.4%
Netherlands 3.6%
Other Europe 19.6%
CIS 2.6%
Africa 2.2%
Middle East 4.8%
Japan 4.0%
China 16.4%

Sources: Based on data in *Time Series on International Trade* (WTO, 2017).

Trading nations

Developed economies have until recently dominated world trade. In 2016, they accounted (by value) for 54 per cent of world merchandise exports and 57 per cent of world merchandise imports (see Figure 24.3). Their share of world trade, however, has tended to decline over time. Thirty years earlier, they accounted for nearly 80 per cent of merchandise exports and imports (see Box 24.1). The reason for this changing global pattern in trade is that many of the countries with the most rapid *growth* in exports can now be found in the developing world.

The growth in merchandise exports from the group of developing nations collectively known as the BRICS[1] (Brazil, Russia, India, China and South Africa) has been especially rapid. Between them they accounted for just 5.4 per cent of the value of world exports in 1994. In 2016

they accounted for 18.2 per cent of world exports (see Figure 24.4). More recently, other countries, such as Mexico, Turkey, Cambodia and Vietnam, have joined the ranks of rapidly growing 'newly industrialised' developing countries.

Box 24.1 looks in more detail at the leading trading nations and at the countries with which they trade.

1 Sometimes the term is used to refer just to the first four countries. When South Africa is excluded, the term is written BRICs rather than BRICS.

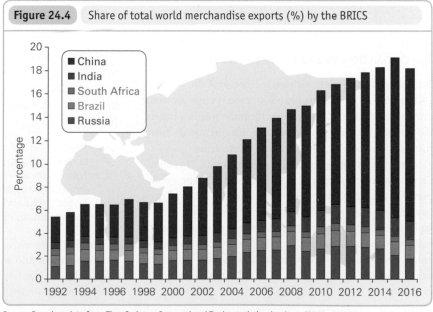

Figure 24.4 Share of total world merchandise exports (%) by the BRICS

Legend: China, India, South Africa, Brazil, Russia

Source: Based on data from *Time Series on International Trade*, statistics database (SDB), (WTO).

BOX 24.1 **TRADING PLACES**

Patterns and trends in world trade

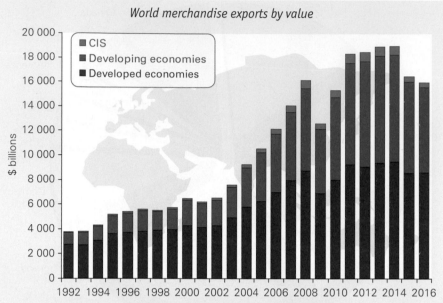

World merchandise exports by value

Note: data exclude Hong Kong re-exports; CIS = Commonwealth of Independent States (former Soviet republics).
Source: Based on data from *WTO Merchandise Trade Values Annual Dataset*, (WTO).

The past three decades have seen rapid changes in the composition of world trade flows. We have seen, for example, the rising importance of the BRICS and, in particular, of China (see Figure 24.4). More generally, the dominance of world trade by the developed nations has weakened. The chart shows the value of world exports since 1992 originating from developed countries, developing countries and the Commonwealth of Independent States (former Soviet republics).

In 1992, the percentage of world merchandise exports originating from developed countries was 73 per cent. In 2016, the percentage had fallen to 54 per cent, though this reflected a rebound after the ratio fell just below the 50 per cent mark, for the first time, in the period from 2012 to 2014.

Table (a) shows the world's top five merchandise exporters and importers by value for 2015. It also shows trade figures for the UK. The four largest exporting nations are also the four largest importers of goods and services.

Trade partners

But who do countries trade with? Table (b) looks at the trading partners of the world's leading trading countries. The table shows that trading blocs (see section 24.3) and geography matter. For instance, in the case of Germany over one-half of its trade is with other EU countries. Similarly,

---

Specialisation as the basis for trade

TC 1
p11

Why do countries trade with each other, and what do they gain from it? The reasons for international trade are really only an extension of the reasons for trade *within* a nation. Rather than people trying to be self-sufficient and do everything for themselves, it makes sense to specialise.

Firms specialise in producing certain goods. This allows them to gain economies of scale and to exploit their entrepreneurial and management skills and the skills of their labour force. It also allows them to benefit from their particular location and from the ownership of any particular capital equipment or other assets they might possess. With the revenues firms earn, they buy in the inputs they need from other firms and the labour they require. Firms thus trade with each other.

Countries also specialise. They produce more than they need of certain goods. What is not consumed domestically is exported. The revenues earned from the exports are used to import goods that are not produced in sufficient amounts at home.

Why does the USA not specialise as much as General Motors or Texaco? Why does the UK not specialise as much as Tesco? Is the answer to these questions similar to the answer to the questions 'Why does the USA not specialise as much as Luxembourg?' and 'Why does Tesco or Unilever not specialise as much as the local butcher?'?

But which goods should a country specialise in? What should it export and what should it import? The answer is that it should specialise in those goods in which it has a *comparative advantage*. Let us examine what this means.

(a) *Top trading countries by value and world share, 2015*

Rank	Exporters	$ billion	Share		Rank	Importers	$ billion	Share
1	China	2275	13.8		1	USA	2306	13.8
2	USA	1505	9.1		2	China	1682	10.1
3	Germany	1329	8.1		3	Germany	1050	6.3
4	Japan	625	3.8		4	Japan	648	3.9
5	Netherlands	567	3.4		5	UK	626	3.7
9	UK	460	2.8		8	Netherlands	506	3.0

Source: *World Trade Statistical Review 2016*, Table A6 (WTO, 2016).

(b) *Merchandise trade by destination and origin (2015)*

(i) *Exports*

China		USA		Germany		Japan		UK	
Destinations	**%**	**Destinations**	**%**	**Destinations**	**%**	**Destinations**	**%**	**Destinations**	**%**
1 USA	18.0	Canada	18.6	EU 27	57.8	USA	20.2	EU 27	43.8
2 EU 28	15.6	EU 28	18.2	USA	9.5	China	17.5	USA	14.9
3 Hong Kong	14.6	Mexico	15.7	China	6.0	EU 28	10.6	Switzerland	7.3
4 Japan	6.0	China	7.7	Switzerland	4.2	S Korea	7.0	China	5.9
Other	45.8	Other	39.7	Other	22.5	Other	44.7	Other	28.1

(ii) *Imports*

Origins	%	Origins	%	Origins	%	Origins	%	Origins	%
1 EU 28	12.4	China	21.8	EU 27	57.1	China	25.7	EU 27	55.1
2 S Korea	10.4	EU 28	18.9	China	9.7	EU 28	11.4	China	10.0
3 USA	9.0	Canada	13.0	USA	6.4	USA	10.9	USA	9.2
4 Taiwan	8.6	Mexico	12.9	Switzerland	4.6	Australia	5.6	Norway	3.2
Other	59.6	Other	33.4	Other	22.2	Other	46.5	Other	22.7

Source: Trade profiles, Statistics database (WTO).

one-third of the value of the USA's exports and one-quarter of its imports can be attributed to Canada and Mexico, members of the North American Free Trade Association (NAFTA) (see page 774).

 Does the fact that world trade has increased at a much faster rate than world GDP (at least up until the financial crisis) highlight the limitations of trade as a driver of economic growth?

The law of comparative advantage

Countries have different endowments of factors of production. They differ in population density, labour skills, climate, raw materials, capital equipment, etc. These differences tend to persist because factors are relatively immobile between countries. Obviously land and climate are totally immobile, but even with labour and capital there are more restrictions on their international movement than on their movement within countries. Thus the ability to supply goods differs between countries.

What this means is that the relative cost of producing goods varies from country to country. For example, one country may be able to produce one fridge for the same cost as 6 tonnes of wheat or 3 MP4 players, whereas another country may be able to produce one fridge for the same cost

as only 3 tonnes of wheat but 4 MP4 players. It is these differences in relative costs that form the basis of trade.

At this stage, we need to distinguish between *absolute advantage* and *comparative advantage*.

Absolute advantage

When one country can produce a good with less resources than another country, it is said to have an **absolute advantage** in that good. If France can produce grapes with less resources than the UK, and the UK can produce barley

KI 2
p10

> **Definition**
>
> **Absolute advantage** A country has an absolute advantage over another in the production of a good if it can produce it with less resources than the other country.

with less resources than France, then France has an absolute advantage in grapes and the UK an absolute advantage in barley. Production of both grapes and barley will be maximised by each country specialising and then trading with the other country. Both will gain.

Comparative advantage

The above seems obvious, but trade between two countries can still be beneficial even if one country could produce *all* goods with less resources than the other, providing the *relative* efficiency with which goods can be produced differs between the two countries.

Take the case of a developed country that is absolutely more efficient than a less developed country at producing both wheat and cloth. Assume that with a given amount of resources (labour, land and capital) the alternatives shown in Table 24.3 can be produced in each country.

Despite the developed country having an absolute advantage in both wheat and cloth, the less developed country (LDC) has a *comparative advantage* in wheat, and the developed country has a comparative advantage in cloth.

This is because wheat is relatively cheaper in the LDC: only 1 square metre of cloth has to be sacrificed to produce 2 kilos of wheat, whereas 8 square metres of cloth would have to be sacrificed in the developed country to produce 4 kilos of wheat (i.e. 2 square metres of cloth for every 1 kilo of wheat). In other words, the opportunity cost of wheat is four times higher in the developed country (8/4 compared with 1/2).

 KI 2 p10

On the other hand, cloth is relatively cheaper in the developed country. Here the opportunity cost of producing 8 square metres of cloth is only 4 kilos of wheat, whereas in the LDC 1 square metre of cloth costs 2 kilos of wheat. Thus the opportunity cost of cloth is four times higher in the LDC (2/1 compared with 4/8).

 Draw up a similar table to Table 24.3, only this time assume that the figures are: LDC 6 wheat or 2 cloth; DC 8 wheat or 20 cloth. What are the opportunity cost ratios now?

To summarise: countries have a comparative advantage in those goods that can be produced at a lower opportunity cost than in other countries.

If countries are to gain from trade, they should export those goods in which they have a comparative advantage and import those goods in which they have a comparative disadvantage. From this we can state a *law of comparative advantage*.

> **KEY IDEA 38**
> *The law of comparative advantage.* Provided opportunity costs of various goods differ in two countries, both of them can gain from mutual trade if they specialise in producing (and exporting) those goods that have relatively low opportunity costs compared with the other country.

Table 24.3	Production possibilities for two countries			
			Kilos of wheat	Square metres of cloth
Less developed country	Either	2	or	1
Developed country	Either	4	or	8

See Case Study 24.1 on the student website for Ricardo's original statement of the law in 1817.

But why do they gain if they specialise according to this law? And just what will that gain be? We will consider these questions next. TC 1 p11

The gains from trade based on comparative advantage

Before trade, unless markets are very imperfect, the prices of the two goods are likely to reflect their opportunity costs. For example, in Table 24.3, since the less developed country can produce 2 kilos of wheat for 1 square metre of cloth, the *price* of 2 kilos of wheat will roughly equal the price of 1 square metre of cloth.

Assume, then, that the pre-trade exchange ratios of wheat for cloth are as follows:

LDC : 2 wheat for 1 cloth
Developed country : 1 wheat for 2 cloth (i.e. 4 for 8)

Both countries will now gain from trade, provided the exchange ratio is somewhere between 2:1 and 1:2. Assume, for the sake of argument, that it is 1:1, that 1 wheat trades internationally for 1 cloth. How will each country gain? TC 2 p26

The LDC gains by exporting wheat and importing cloth. At an exchange ratio of 1:1, it now only has to give up 1 kilo of wheat to obtain a square metre of cloth, whereas before trade it had to give up 2 kilos of wheat.

The developed country gains by exporting cloth and importing wheat. Again at an exchange ratio of 1:1, it now has to give up only 1 square metre of cloth to obtain 1 kilo of wheat, whereas before it had to give up 2 square metres of cloth.

Thus both countries have gained from trade.

> **Definitions**
>
> **Comparative advantage** A country has a comparative advantage over another in the production of a good if it can produce it at a lower opportunity cost: i.e. if it has to forgo less of other goods in order to produce it.
>
> **Law of comparative advantage** Trade can benefit all countries if they specialise in the goods in which they have a comparative advantage.

The actual exchange ratios will depend on the relative prices of wheat and cloth after trade takes place. These prices will depend on total demand for and supply of the two goods. It may be that the trade exchange ratio is nearer to the pre-trade exchange ratio of one country than the other. Thus the gains to the two countries need not be equal. (We will examine these issues below.)

1. Show how each country could gain from trade if the LDC could produce (before trade) 3 wheat for 1 cloth and the developed country could produce (before trade) 2 wheat for 5 cloth, and if the exchange ratio (with trade) was 1 wheat for 2 cloth. Would they both still gain if the exchange ratio was (a) 1 wheat for 1 cloth; (b) 1 wheat for 3 cloth?
2. In question 1, which country gained the most from a trade exchange ratio of 1 wheat for 2 cloth?

Simple graphical analysis of comparative advantage and the gains from trade: constant opportunity cost

The gains from trade can be shown graphically using production possibility curves. Let us continue with the example of the developed and less developed countries that we looked at in Table 24.3, where both countries produce just two goods: wheat and cloth.

Table 24.4	Pre-trade production possibilities				
	Less developed country			Developed country	
	Wheat (million kg)	Cloth (million m²)		Wheat (million kg)	Cloth (million m²)
A	1000	0	g	500	0
B	800	100	h	400	200
C	600	200	i	300	400
D	400	300	j	200	600
E	200	400	k	100	800
F	0	500	l	0	1000

For simplicity, assume that the pre-trade opportunity costs of cloth in terms of wheat in the two countries do not vary with output: i.e. there are *constant opportunity costs* of cloth in terms of wheat of 2/1 in the LDC and 1/2 in the developed country. Let us assume that the pre-trade production possibilities are as shown in Table 24.4.[2]

2 Note that, for simplicity, it is assumed that the size of the two economies is similar. The LDC can still have an *absolute* disadvantage in both goods, however, because it may take many more resources to produce these goods. For example, it may have a very much larger population than the developed country and hence a very much lower output per person.

A parable of comparative advantage

Imagine that you and a group of friends are fed up with the rat race and decide to set up a self-sufficient community. So you club together and use all your savings to buy an old run-down farmhouse with 30 acres of land and a few farm animals.

You decide to produce all your own food, make your own clothes, renovate the farmhouse, make all the furniture, provide all your own entertainment and set up a little shop to sell the things you make. This should bring in enough income to buy the few items you cannot make yourselves.

The day comes to move in, and that evening everyone gathers to decide how all the jobs are going to be allocated. You quickly decide that it would be foolish for all of you to try to do all the jobs. Obviously it will be more efficient to specialise. This does not necessarily mean that everyone is confined to doing only one job, but it does mean that each of you can concentrate on just a few tasks.

But who is to do which job? The answer would seem to be obvious: you pick the best person for the job. So you go down the list of tasks. Who is to take charge of the renovations? Pat has already renovated a cottage, and is brilliant at bricklaying, plastering, wiring and plumbing. So Pat would seem to be the ideal person. Who is to do the cooking? Everyone agrees on this. Pat makes the best cakes, the best quiches and the best Irish stew. So Pat is everyone's choice

for cook. And what about milking the sheep? 'Pat used to keep sheep', says Tarquin, 'and made wonderful feta cheese.' 'Good old Pat!' exclaims everyone.

It doesn't take long before it becomes obvious that 'clever-clogs' Pat is simply brilliant at everything, from planting winter wheat, to unblocking drains, to doing the accounts, to tie-dyeing. But it is soon realised that, if Pat has to do everything, nothing will get done. Even Chris, who has never done anything except market research, would be better employed milking the sheep than doing nothing at all.

So what's the best way of allocating the jobs so that the work gets done in the most efficient way? Sharon comes up with the solution. 'Everyone should make a list of all the jobs they could possibly do, and then put them in order from the one they are best at to the one they are worst at.'

So this is what everyone does. And then people are allocated the jobs they are *relatively* best at doing. Chris escapes milking the sheep and keeps the accounts instead. And Pat escapes with an eight-hour day!

If Pat took two minutes to milk the sheep and Tarquin took six, how could it ever be more efficient for Tarquin to do it?

Figure 24.5   Effect of trade on consumption possibilities

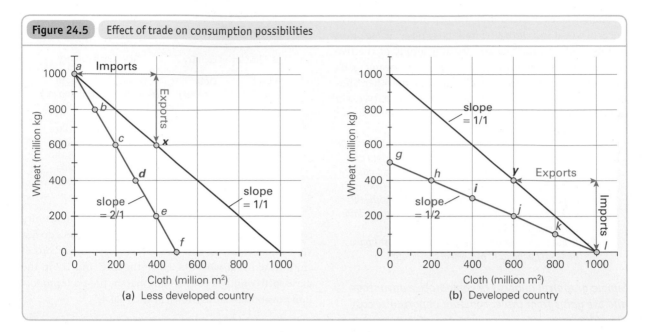

(a) Less developed country

(b) Developed country

For each 100 extra square metres of cloth that the LDC produces, it has to sacrifice 200 kilos of wheat. For each extra 100 kilos of wheat that the developed country produces, it has to sacrifice 200 square metres of cloth. Straight-line pre-trade production possibility 'curves' can thus be drawn for the two countries with slopes of (minus) 2/1 and (minus) 1/2 respectively. These lines illustrate the various total combinations of the two goods that can be produced and hence consumed. They are shown as the blue lines in Figure 24.5.

Assume that before trade the LDC produces (and consumes) at point *d*: namely, 400 million kilos of wheat and 300 million square metres of cloth; and that the developed country produces at point *i*: namely, 300 million kilos of wheat and 400 million square metres of cloth.

If they now trade, the LDC, having a comparative advantage in wheat, will specialise in it and produce at point *a*. It will produce 1000 million kilos of wheat and no cloth. The developed country will specialise in cloth and produce at point *l*. It will produce 1000 million square metres of cloth and no wheat.

For simplicity, let us assume that trade between the two countries takes place at an exchange ratio of 1:1 (i.e. 1 kilo of wheat for 1 square metre of cloth). This means that the two countries can now *consume* along the red lines in Figure 24.5: at, say, points *x* and *y* respectively. At point *x* the LDC consumes 600 million kilos of wheat (a gain of 200 million kilos over the pre-trade position) and 400 million square metres of cloth (a gain of 100 million square metres over the pre-trade position). At point *y* the developed country consumes 400 million kilos of wheat (a gain of 100 million kilos over the pre-trade position) and 600 million square metres of cloth (a gain of 200 million square metres over the pre-trade position). Thus trade has allowed both countries to increase their consumption of both goods.

TC 2 p26

To summarise: before trade, the countries could only consume along their production possibility curves (the blue lines); after trade, they can consume along the higher red lines.

KI 39 p760

Note that in this simple two-country model total production and consumption of the two countries for each of the two goods must be the same, since one country's exports are the other's imports. Thus if the LDC produces at point *a* and consumes at point *x*, the developed country, producing at point *l*, must consume at point *y*. The effects on trade of the two countries consuming at points *x* and *y* are shown in Table 24.5.

As complete specialisation has taken place in our example, the LDC now has to import all its cloth and the developed country has to import all its wheat. Thus, given the exchange ratio of 1:1, the LDC exports 400 million kilos of wheat in exchange for imports of 400 million square metres of cloth. (These imports and exports are also shown in Figure 24.5.)

The final two columns of Table 24.5 show that trade has increased the total production and consumption of the two countries.

1. *Draw a diagram with the same two countries and with the same production possibilities and exchange ratio as in Figure 24.5. But this time show how much would be imported and exported for each country if, after trade, the LDC consumes 500 million kilos of wheat. Fill the figures in on a table like Table 24.5.*

2. *If the opportunity cost ratio of wheat for cloth is 1/2 in the LDC, why is the slope of the production possibility curve 2/1? Is the slope of the production possibility curve always the reciprocal of the opportunity cost ratio?*

3. *Show (graphically) that, if the (pre-trade) opportunity cost ratios of the two countries were the same, there would be no gain from trade – assuming that the production possibility curves were straight lines and did not shift as a result of trade.*

Table 24.5 The production and consumption gains from trade

	Less developed country			Developed country			Total	
	Production	Consumption	Imports (−)/ Exports (+)	Production	Consumption	Imports (−)/ Exports (+)	Production	Consumption
No trade								
Wheat (million kg)	400	400	0	300	300	0	700	700
Cloth (million m²)	300	300	0	400	400	0	700	700
With trade								
Wheat (million kg)	1000	600	+400	0	400	−400	1000	1000
Cloth (million m²)	0	400	−400	1000	600	+400	1000	1000

International trade and its effect on factor prices

Countries tend to have a comparative advantage in goods that are *intensive in their abundant factor.* Canada has abundant land and hence it is cheap. Therefore Canada specialises in grain production since grains are land-intensive. South Asian countries have abundant supplies of labour with low wage rates, and hence specialise in clothing and other labour-intensive goods. Europe, Japan and the USA have relatively abundant and cheap capital, and hence specialise in capital-intensive manufactured goods.

Trade between such countries will tend to lead to greater equality in factor prices. For example, the demand for labour will rise in labour-abundant countries like India if they specialise in labour-intensive goods. This will push up wage rates in these low-wage countries, thereby helping to close the gap between their wage rates and those of the developed world. Without trade, wage rates would tend to be even lower.

Increasing opportunity costs and the limits to specialisation and trade

In practice, countries are likely to experience increasing opportunity costs (and hence have bowed-out production possibility curves). The reason for this is that, as a country increasingly specialises in one good, it has to use resources that are less and less suited to its production and which were more suited to other goods. Thus ever-increasing amounts of the other goods have to be sacrificed. For example, as a country specialises more and more in grain production, it has to use land that is less and less suited to growing grain.

These increasing costs as a country becomes more and more specialised lead to the disappearance of its comparative cost advantage. When this happens, there will be no point in further specialisation. Thus whereas a country like Germany has a comparative advantage in capital-intensive manufactures, it does not produce only manufactures. It would make no sense not to use its fertile lands to produce food or its forests to produce timber. The opportunity costs of diverting all agricultural labour to industry would be very high.

Thus increasing opportunity costs limit the amount of a country's specialisation and hence the amount of its trade. There are also other limits to trade:

- Transport costs may outweigh any comparative advantage. A country may be able to produce bricks more cheaply than other countries, but their weight may make them too expensive to export.

KI 2
p10

BOX 24.3 **TRADE AS EXPLOITATION?**

EXPLORING ECONOMICS

Does free trade exploit cheap labour abroad?

People sometimes question the morality of buying imports from countries where workers are paid 'pittance' wages. 'Is it right', they ask, 'for us to support a system where workers are so exploited?' As is often the case with emotive issues, there is some truth and some misunderstanding in a point of view like this.

First the truth. If a country like the UK trades with a regime that denies human rights, and treats its workers very badly, we may thereby be helping to sustain a corrupt system. We might also be seen to be lending it moral support. In this sense, therefore, trade may not help the cause of the workers in these countries. It is arguments like these that were used to support the imposition of trade sanctions against South Africa in the days of apartheid.

Now the misunderstanding. If we buy goods from countries that pay low wages, we are *not* as a result contributing to their low-wage problem. Quite the reverse. If countries like India export textiles to the West, this will help to *increase* the wages of Indian workers. If India has a comparative advantage in labour-intensive goods, these goods will earn a better price by being exported than by being sold entirely in the domestic Indian market. Provided *some* of the extra revenues go to the workers, they will gain from trade.

 Under what circumstances would a gain in revenues by exporting firms not lead to an increase in wage rates?

KI 4
p14

- It may be the factors of production, rather than the goods, that move from country to country. Thus developed countries, rather than exporting finished goods to LDCs, may invest capital in LDCs to enable manufactures to be produced there. Also, labour may migrate from low-wage to high-wage countries.
- Governments may restrict trade (see section 24.2).

The terms of trade

What price will our exports fetch abroad? What will we have to pay for imports? The answer to these questions is given by the *terms of trade*.

To simplify matters, suppose there is only one exported good and only one imported good. In this case, the terms of trade are defined as P_x/P_m, where P_x is the price of the exported good and P_m is the price of the imported good. This is the reciprocal of the exchange ratio: for example, if 2x exchange for 1m (an exchange ratio of 2/1), the price of x will be half the price of m. The terms of trade will be 1/2.

1. If 4x exchange for 3m, what are the terms of trade?
2. If the terms of trade are 3, how many units of the imported good could I buy for the money earned by the sale of 1 unit of the exported good? What is the exchange ratio?

In the real world where countries have *many* exports and imports, the **terms of trade** are given by

Average price of exports
—————————————————
Average price of imports

expressed as an index, where price changes are measured against a base year in which the terms of trade are assumed to be 100. Thus if the average price of exports relative to the average price of imports has risen by 20 per cent since the base year, the terms of trade will now be 120. The terms of

trade for selected countries are shown in Figure 24.6 (with 2010 as the base year).

If the terms of trade rise (export prices rising relative to import prices), they are said to have 'improved', since fewer exports now have to be sold to purchase any given quantity of imports. Changes in the terms of trade are caused by changes in the demand for and supply of imports and exports, and by changes in the exchange rate.

 In Figure 24.6, which countries' terms of trade improved in the 2000s?

The terms of trade and comparative advantage

Assuming there are two goods, x and m, trade can be advantageous to a country as long as the terms of trade P_x/P_m are different from the opportunity cost ratios of the two goods, given by MC_x/MC_m. For example, if the terms of trade were greater than the opportunity cost ratio $(P_x/P_m > MC_x/MC_m)$, it would benefit the country to produce more x for export in return for imports of m, since the relative value of producing x (P_x/P_m) is greater than the relative cost (MC_x/MC_m).

With increasing opportunity costs, however, increasing specialisation in x will lead to MC_x rising (and MC_m falling), until $P_x/P_m = MC_x/MC_m$. At this point, there can be no more gain from further specialisation and trade: the maximum gain has been achieved and comparative cost advantages have been exhausted.

Definition

Terms of trade The price index of exports divided by the price index of imports and then expressed as a percentage. This means that the terms of trade will be 100 in the base year.

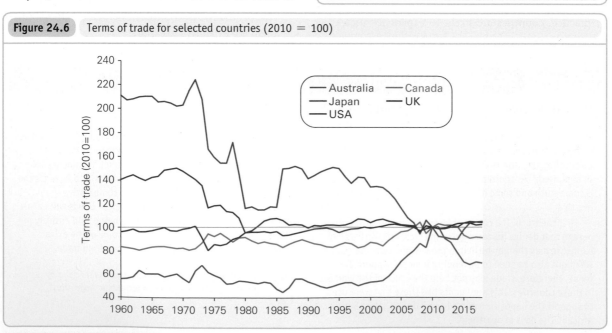

Figure 24.6 Terms of trade for selected countries (2010 = 100)

Note: Data from 2017 are based on forecasts.
Source: Based on data in *AMECO Database* (European Commission, DGECFIN).

Figure 24.7 Determination of the price of an individual traded good

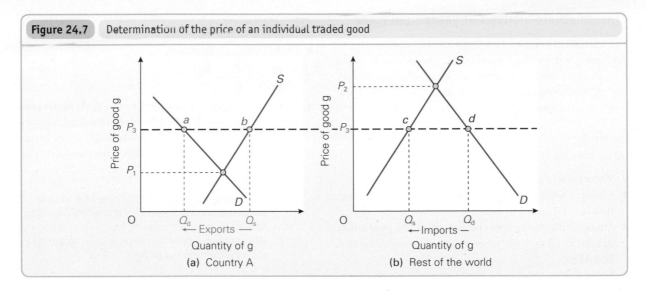

(a) Country A

(b) Rest of the world

The determination of the terms of trade

When countries import and export many goods, the terms of trade will depend on the prices of all the various exports and imports. These prices will depend on the demand and supply of each traded good and their elasticities in the respective countries. Take the case of good g in which country A has a comparative advantage with respect to the rest of the world. This is illustrated in Figure 24.7.

Demand and supply curves of good g can be drawn for both country A and the rest of the world. (The upward-sloping supply curves imply increasing opportunity costs of production.) Before trade, country A has a low equilibrium price of P_1 and the rest of the world a high equilibrium price of P_2. After trade, price will settle at P_3 in both countries (assuming no transport costs), where total demand by both country A and the rest of the world together equals total supply, and thus where the imports of g into the rest of the world ($d - c$) equal the exports from country A ($b - a$). The position of P_3 relative to P_1 and P_2 will depend on the elasticities of demand and supply.

A similar analysis can be conducted for all the other traded goods – both exports and imports of country A. The resulting prices will allow country A's terms of trade to be calculated.

Draw a similar diagram to Figure 24.7 showing how the price of an individual good imported into country A is determined.

The analysis is complicated somewhat if different national currencies are involved, since the prices in each country will be expressed in its own currency. Thus to convert one country's prices to another currency will require knowledge of the rate of exchange: e.g. for the USA and the UK it might be \$1.50 = £1. But under a floating exchange rate system, the rate of exchange will depend in part on the demand for and supply of imports and exports. If the rate of exchange depreciates – say, from \$1.50 = £1 to \$1.25 = £1 – the UK's terms of trade will worsen. Exports will earn less foreign currency per pound: e.g. £1 worth of exports will now be worth only \$1.25 rather than \$1.50. Imports, on the other hand, will be more expensive: e.g. \$6 worth of imports previously cost £4; they now cost £4.80.

Why will exporters probably welcome a 'deterioration' in the terms of trade?

In a world of many countries and many goods, an individual country's imports and exports may have little effect on world prices. In the extreme case, the country may face prices totally dictated by the external world demand and supply. The country in this case is similar to an individual firm under perfect competition. The country is too small to influence world prices, and thus faces a horizontal demand curve for its exports and a horizontal supply curve for its imports. In foreign currency terms, therefore, the terms of trade are outside its control. Nevertheless, these terms of trade will probably be to its benefit, in the sense that the gains from trade will be virtually entirely received by this small country rather than the rest of the world. It is too small for its trade to depress the world price of its exports or drive up the price of its imports.

In general, a country's gains from trade will be greater the less elastic its own domestic demand and supply of tradable goods are, and the more elastic the demand and supply of other countries. You can see this by examining Figure 24.7. The less elastic the domestic demand and supply, the bigger will be the effect of trade on prices faced by that country. The more the trade price differs from the pre-trade price, the bigger the gain.

KI 8
p46

TC 6
p68

*Intermediate analysis of gains from trade

The analysis of section 12.1 (pages 353–5) can be used to demonstrate the welfare gains from trade and the limits to specialisation under conditions of increasing opportunity cost. A simple two-good model is used, and the pre-trade position is compared with the position with trade.

Pre-trade

Let us make the following simplifying assumptions:

- There are two goods, x and m.
- Country A has a comparative advantage in the production of good x.
- There are increasing opportunity costs in the production of both x and m. Thus the production possibility curve is bowed out.
- Social indifference curves can be drawn, each one showing the various combinations of x and m that give society in country A a particular level of utility.

Figure 24.8 shows the pre-trade position in country A. Production and consumption at P_1C_1 will give the highest possible utility. (All other points on the production possibility curve intersect with lower indifference curves.)

If there is perfect competition, production will indeed be at P_1C_1. There are four steps in establishing this:

- The slope of the production possibility curve $(-\Delta m/\Delta x)$ is the marginal rate of transformation (MRT), and equals MC_x/MC_m (see pages 354–5). For example, if the opportunity cost of producing 1 extra unit of x (Δx) was a sacrifice of 2 units of m $(-\Delta m)$, then an extra unit of x would cost twice as much as an extra unit of m: i.e. $MC_x/MC_m = 2/1$, which is the slope of the production possibility curve, $-\Delta m/\Delta x$.
- The slope of each indifference curve $(-\Delta m/\Delta x)$ is the marginal rate of substitution in consumption (MRS), and equals MU_x/MU_m. For example, if x had three times the

marginal utility of m $(MU_x/MU_m = 3)$, consumers would be willing to give up 3m for 1x $(-\Delta m/\Delta x = 3)$.

- Under perfect competition,

$$\frac{MC_x}{MC_m} = \frac{P_x}{P_m} = \frac{MU_x}{MU_m}$$

- Thus the domestic pre-trade price ratio P_x/P_m under perfect competition must equal the slope of the production possibility curve (MC_x/MC_m) and the slope of the social indifference curve (MU_x/MU_m). This is the case at P_1C_1 in Figure 24.8.

> 1. If production were at point a in Figure 24.8, describe the process whereby equilibrium at point P_1C_1 would be restored under perfect competition.
> 2. Why would production be unlikely to take place at P_1C_1 if competition were not perfect?

With trade

If country A has a comparative advantage in good x, the price of x relative to m is likely to be higher in the rest of the world than in country A: i.e. world P_x/P_m > pre-trade domestic P_x/P_m. This is shown in Figure 24.9. The world price ratio is given by the slope of the line WW. With this new steeper world price ratio, the optimum production point will be P_2 where MRT (the slope of the production possibility curve) = world P_x/P_m (the slope of WW).

With production at P_2, the country can by trading consume *anywhere* along this line WW. The optimum consumption point will be C_2 where MRS (the slope of the indifference curve) = world P_x/P_m (the slope of WW). Thus trade has allowed consumption to move from point C_1 on the lower indifference curve I_1 to point C_2 on the higher indifference curve I_2. There has thus been a gain from trade. Perfect competition will ensure that this gain is realised, since production at P_2 and consumption at C_2 meet the equilibrium condition that

$$\frac{MC_x}{MC_m} = \frac{P_x}{P_m} = \frac{MU_x}{MU_m}$$

How much will be imported and how much will be exported? With production at P_2 and consumption at C_2, country A will import $C_2 - D$ of good m in exchange for exports of $P_2 - D$ of good x.

Similar diagrams to Figure 24.9 can be drawn for other countries. Since they show equilibrium for both imports and exports on the *one* diagram, economists refer to them as **general equilibrium diagrams** (see page 355 for another example).

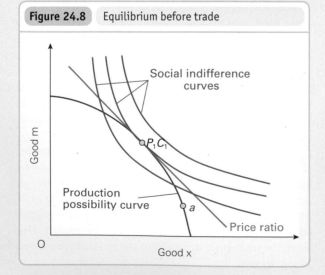

Figure 24.8 Equilibrium before trade

Good m

Social indifference curves

P_1C_1

Production possibility curve

a

Price ratio

O

Good x

Definition

General equilibrium diagrams (in trade theory)
Indifference curve/production possibility curve diagrams that show a country's production and consumption of both imports and exports.

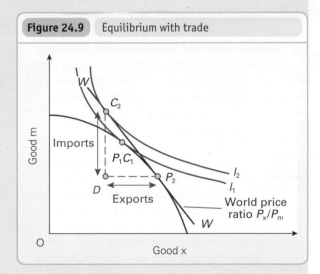

Figure 24.9 Equilibrium with trade

1. *Draw a similar diagram to Figure 24.9, only this time assume that the two goods are good a measured on the vertical axis and good b measured on the horizontal axis. Assume that the country has a comparative advantage in good a. (Note that the world price ratio this time will be shallower than the domestic pre-trade price ratio.) Mark the level of exports of a and imports of b.*
2. *Is it possible to gain from trade if competition is not perfect?*

Other reasons for gains from trade

Decreasing costs

Even if there are no initial comparative cost differences between two countries, it will still benefit both to specialise in industries where economies of scale (either internal or external) can be gained, and then to trade. Once the economies of scale begin to appear, comparative cost differences TC 2
p26 will also appear, and thus the countries will have gained a comparative advantage in these industries.

A similar argument applies to different models of the same product (e.g. different models of cars or electrical goods). Several countries, by specialising in just one or two models each, can gain the full economies of scale and hence a comparative advantage in their particular model(s). Then, through trade, consumers can gain from having a wider KI 38
p752 range from which to choose. Much of the specialisation that international trade permits is of this nature.

The decreasing cost reason for trade is particularly relevant for small countries where the domestic market is not large enough to support large-scale industries. Thus exports form a much higher percentage of GDP in small countries such as Singapore than in large countries such as the USA.

Would it be possible for a country with a comparative disadvantage in a given product at pre-trade levels of output to obtain a comparative advantage in it by specialising in its production and exporting it?

Differences in demand

Even with no comparative cost differences and no potential economies of scale, trade can benefit both countries if demand conditions differ.

If people in country A like beef more than lamb, and people in country B like lamb more than beef, then rather than A using resources better suited for lamb to produce beef and B using resources better suited for producing beef to produce lamb, it will benefit both to produce beef *and* lamb and to export the one they like less in return for the one they like more.

Increased competition

If a country trades, the competition from imports may stimulate greater efficiency at home. This extra competition may prevent domestic monopolies/oligopolies from charging high prices. It may stimulate greater research and development and the more rapid adoption of new technology, thereby increasing the economy's longer-term growth rate. It may lead to a greater variety of products being made available to consumers.

Trade as an 'engine of growth'

In a growing world economy, the demand for a country's exports is likely to grow, especially when these exports have a high income elasticity of demand. This provides a stimulus to growth in the exporting country.

Non-economic advantages

There may be political, social and cultural advantages to be gained by fostering trading links between countries.

The competitive advantage of nations

The theory of comparative advantage shows how countries can gain from trade, but why do countries have a comparative advantage in some goods rather than others?

One explanation is that it depends on the resources that countries have. If a country has plenty of land, then it makes sense to specialise in products that make use of this abundant resource. Thus Canada produces and exports wheat. If a country has a highly skilled workforce and an established research base, then it makes sense to specialise in high-tech products and export these. Thus Germany exports many highly sophisticated manufactured products. By contrast, many developing countries with plentiful but relatively low-skilled workers specialise in primary products or simple manufactured products.

In other words, countries should specialise in goods which make intensive use of their abundant resources. But this still does not give enough detail as to why countries specialise in the precise range of products that they do. Also, why do countries both export and import the *same* products? Why do many countries produce and export cars, but also import many cars?

According to Porter,[3] there are four key determinants of why nations are highly competitive in certain products but less so in others.

Available resources.   These include 'given' resources, such as raw materials, population and climate, but also specialised resources that have been developed by humans, such as the skills of the labour force, the amount and type of capital, the transport and communications infrastructure, and the science and technology base. These specialised resources vary in detail from one country to another and give them a competitive advantage in very specific products. Once an industry has started to develop, this may attract further research and development, capital investment and training, all of which are very specific to that industry. This then further builds the country's competitive advantage in that industry. Thus the highly developed engineering skills and equipment in Germany give it a competitive advantage in producing well-engineered cars.

Demand conditions in the home market.   The more discerning customers are within the country, the more this will drive the development of each firm's products and the more competitive the firm will then become in international markets. The demand for IT solutions within the USA drove the development of the software industry and gave companies such as Microsoft, Intel and Google an international advantage.

Strategy, structure and rivalry of firms.   Competition between firms is not just in terms of price. Competitive rivalry extends to all aspects of business strategy, from product design, to marketing, to internal organisation, to production efficiency, to logistics. The very particular competitive conditions within each industry can have a profound effect on the development of firms within that industry and determine whether or not they gain an international competitive advantage. Strategic investments and rivalry gave Japanese electronic companies an international competitive advantage.

Related and supporting industries.   Firms are more likely to be successful internationally if there are well-developed supporting industries within the home economy. These may be industries providing specialist equipment or specialist consultancy, or they may simply be other parts of the main value chain, from suppliers of inputs to distributors of the firms' output. The more efficient this value chain, the greater the competitive advantage of firms within the industry.

KEY IDEA 39

The competitive advantage of nations is the ability of countries to compete in the market for exports and with potential importers to their country. The competitiveness of any one industry depends on the availability and quality of resources, demand conditions at home in that industry, the strategies and rivalry of firms within the industry and the quality of supporting industries and infrastructure. It also depends on government policies, and there is also an element of chance.

The above four determinants of competitive advantage are interlinked and influence each other. For example, the nature of related and supporting industries can influence a firm's strategic decision about whether to embark on a process of vertical integration or de-integration. Similarly, the nature of related and supporting industries depends on demand conditions in these industries and the availability of resources.

With each of the four determinants, competitive advantage can be stimulated by appropriate government supply-side policies, such as a supportive tax regime, investment in transport and communications infrastructure, investment in education and training, competition policy and sound macroeconomic management of the economy. Also, chance often has a large part to play. For example, any pharmaceutical company which discovers a cure for AIDS or for various types of cancer will give a significant competitive advantage to the country in which it is based.

3 Michael E. Porter, *The Competitive Advantage of Nations* (The Free Press, 1998).

Section summary

1. Countries can gain from trade if they specialise in producing those goods in which they have a comparative advantage: i.e. those goods that can be produced at relatively low opportunity costs. This is merely an extension of the argument that gains can be made from the specialisation and division of labour.

2. If two countries trade, then, provided that the trade price ratio of exports and imports is between the pre-trade price ratios of these goods in the two countries, both countries can gain. They can both consume *beyond* their production possibility curves.

3. With increasing opportunity costs there will be a limit to specialisation and trade. As a country increasingly

specialises, its (marginal) comparative advantage will eventually disappear. Trade can also be limited by transport costs, factor movements and government intervention.

4. The terms of trade give the price of exports relative to the price of imports. Additional trade can be beneficial if the terms of trade (P_x/P_m) are greater than the relative marginal costs of exports and imports (MC_x/MC_m).

5. A country's terms of trade are determined by the demand and supply of imports and exports and their respective elasticities. This will determine the prices at which goods are traded and affect the rate of exchange. A country's gains from trade will be greater the less elastic its own

domestic demand and supply of tradable goods, and the more elastic the demand and supply of other countries.

*6. Trade allows countries to achieve a higher level of utility by consuming on a higher social indifference curve. The maximum gain from trade is achieved by consuming at the point where the world price ratio is tangential to both the production possibility curve and a social indifference curve. This would be achieved under perfect competition.

7. Gains from trade also arise from decreasing costs (economies of scale), differences in demand between

countries, increased competition from trade and the transmission of growth from one country to another. There may also be non-economic advantages from trade.

8. Comparative advantage is related to competitive advantage. Countries tend to have a competitive advantage in those industries where specialist resources have been developed, where products have been developed in response to changing consumer demands, where business strategy is conducive and where there is a network of supporting industries and infrastructure.

24.2 ARGUMENTS FOR RESTRICTING TRADE

Most countries have not pursued a policy of totally free trade. Their politicians know that trade involves costs as well as benefits. In this section, we will attempt to identify what these costs are, and whether they are genuine reasons for restricting trade.

Although countries may sometimes contemplate having completely free trade, they usually limit their trade. However, they certainly do not ban it altogether. The sorts of questions that governments pose are (a) should they have freer or more restricted trade and (b) in which sectors should restrictions be tightened or relaxed? Ideally, countries should weigh up the marginal benefits against the marginal costs of altering restrictions, although just *what* benefits and costs should be taken into account, and what weighting should be attached to them, may be highly contentious. For example, should external costs and benefits be considered and should these include *global* externalities?

Methods of restricting trade

Tariffs (customs duties). These are taxes on imports and are usually **ad valorem tariffs**: i.e. a percentage of the price of the import. Tariffs that are used to restrict imports are most effective if demand is elastic (e.g. when there are close domestically produced substitutes). Tariffs can also be used as a means of raising revenue, but in this case they are more effective if demand is inelastic. They can in addition be used to raise the price of imported goods to prevent 'unfair' competition for domestic producers.

Quotas. These are limits imposed on the quantity of a good that can be imported. Quotas can be imposed by the government, or negotiated with other countries which agree 'voluntarily' to restrict the amount of exports to the first country.

Exchange controls. These include limits on how much foreign exchange can be made available to importers (financial quotas), or to citizens travelling abroad, or for investment. Alternatively, they may take the form of charges for the purchase of foreign currencies.

Import licensing. The imposition of exchange controls or quotas often involves requiring importers to obtain licences. This makes it easier for the government to enforce its restrictions.

Embargoes. These are total government bans on certain imports (e.g. drugs) or exports to certain countries (e.g. to enemies during war).

Administrative barriers. Regulations may be designed to exclude imports: examples include customs delays and excessive paperwork.

Procurement policies. This is where governments favour domestic producers when purchasing equipment (e.g. defence equipment).

Dumping. Alternatively, governments may favour domestic producers by subsidising their exports in a process known as **dumping**. The goods are 'dumped' at artificially low prices in the foreign market.

Arguments in favour of restricting trade

Economic arguments having some general validity

The infant industry argument. Some industries in a country may be in their infancy, but have a potential comparative advantage. This is particularly likely in developing countries. Such industries are too small yet to have gained economies of scale; their workers are inexperienced; they lack back-up facilities, such as communications networks and specialist suppliers. They may have only limited access to

TC 7 p81

Definitions

Ad valorem tariffs Tariffs levied as a percentage of the price of the import.

Dumping Where exports are sold at prices below marginal cost – often as a result of government subsidy.

BOX 24.4   FREE TRADE AND THE ENVIRONMENT

Do whales, rainforests and the atmosphere gain from free trade?

International trade provides an outlet for hardwood from the rainforests, for tiger parts for medicines, for chemicals and other industrial products produced with little regard for safety or environmental standards, and for products produced using electricity generated from low-cost, high-sulphur, highly polluting coal.

The problem is that countries are likely to export goods that they can produce at a relatively low opportunity cost. But these opportunity costs are *private* costs. They do not take into account externalities. This is a powerful argument against free trade based on free-market prices.

Surely, though, the developed countries use taxes, legislation and other means to prevent the abuse of the environment? They may do, but this does not stop them importing products from countries that do not.

In reply, the advocates of free trade argue that it is up to each country to decide its own environmental standards. If a poor country produces a product in a cheap polluting way, the gains from exporting it may more than offset the environmental damage done.

There is some strength in this argument provided (a) the government of that country has done a proper study of the costs and benefits involved, including the external costs; and (b) the externalities are confined to within the country's borders. Unfortunately, in many cases neither of these conditions holds. Much of the pollution generated from industrial production has global effects (e.g. global warming).

As countries such as China and India take an increasingly large share of world exports of industrial products (see Figure 24.4), so these problems are likely to grow. Both countries have much lower environmental protection standards than those in Europe and North America.

 Should the world community welcome the use of tariffs and other forms of protection by the rich countries against imports of goods from developing countries that have little regard for the environment?

 KI 31 p356

---

finance for expansion. Without protection, these **infant industries** will not survive competition from abroad.

Protection from foreign competition, however, will allow them to expand and become more efficient. Once they have achieved a comparative advantage, the protection can then be removed to enable them to compete internationally.

Similar to the infant industry argument is the *senile industry argument*. This is where industries with a potential comparative advantage have been allowed to run down and can no longer compete effectively. They may have considerable potential, but be simply unable to make enough profit to afford the necessary investment without some temporary protection. This is one of the most powerful arguments used to justify the use of special protection for the automobile and steel industries in the USA.

KI 3 p13

 How would you set about judging whether an industry had a genuine case for infant/senile industry protection?

To reduce reliance on goods with little dynamic potential.   Many developing countries have traditionally exported primaries: foodstuffs and raw materials. The world demand for these, however, is fairly income inelastic, and thus grows relatively slowly. In such cases, free trade is not an engine of growth. Instead, if it encourages countries' economies to become locked into a pattern of primary production, it may prevent them from expanding in sectors like manufacturing that have a higher income elasticity of demand. Since 2000, for example, the value of exports of manufactures has typically been in excess of 70 per cent of the value of all merchandise exports. There may thus be a valid argument for protecting or promoting manufacturing industry. (We explore these arguments in section 26.4.)

To prevent dumping and other unfair trade practices.   A country may engage in dumping by subsidising its exports. The result is that prices may no longer reflect comparative costs. Thus the world would benefit from tariffs being imposed to counteract such practices.

 Does the consumer in the importing country gain or lose from dumping?

It can also be argued that there is a case for retaliating against countries that impose restrictions on your exports. In the *short* run, both countries are likely to be made worse off by a contraction in trade. But if the retaliation persuades the other country to remove its restrictions, it may have a longer-term benefit. In some cases, the mere threat of retaliation may be enough to get another country to remove its protection.

 TC 5 p50

To prevent the establishment of a foreign-based monopoly.   Competition from abroad, especially when it involves dumping or predatory pricing (see pages 246 and 761), could drive domestic producers out of business. The foreign company, now having a monopoly of the market, could charge high prices with a resulting misallocation of resources.

 KI 22 p190

All of the above arguments suggest that governments should adopt a 'strategic' approach to trade. ***Strategic trade theory*** (see Box 24.5) argues that protecting certain industries allows a net gain *in the long run* from increased competition in the market. This argument has been used to justify the huge financial support given to the aircraft manufacturer Airbus, a consortium based in four European countries. The subsidies have allowed it to compete with Boeing, which would otherwise have a monopoly in many types of passenger aircraft. Airlines and their passengers worldwide, it is argued, have benefited from the increased competition.

To spread the risks of fluctuating markets. A highly specialised economy – Zambia with copper, Cuba with sugar – is highly susceptible to world market fluctuations. Greater diversity and greater self-sufficiency can reduce these risks.

To reduce the influence of trade on consumer tastes. It is a mistake to assume that fixed consumer tastes dictate the pattern of production through trade. Multinational companies through their advertising and other forms of sales promotion may influence consumer tastes. Thus some restriction on trade may be justified in order to reduce this 'producer sovereignty'.

In what ways may free trade have harmful cultural effects on developing countries?

Definitions

Infant industry An industry that has a potential comparative advantage, but which is as yet too underdeveloped to be able to realise this potential.

Strategic trade theory The theory that protecting/supporting certain industries can enable them to compete more effectively with large monopolistic rivals abroad. The effect of the protection is to increase long-run competition and may enable the protected firms to exploit a comparative advantage that they could not have done otherwise.

BOX 24.5 STRATEGIC TRADE THEORY

An argument for protection?

Lester Thurow is professor of management and economics and former dean in the Sloan School of Management at the Massachusetts Institute of Technology (MIT), and an economics journalist and editor. He is also one of the USA's best-known and most articulate advocates of 'managed trade'.

Thurow (and others) have been worried by the growing penetration of US markets by imports from Japan and Europe and also from China and many other developing countries. Their response is to call for a carefully worked-out strategy of protection for US industries.

The *strategic trade theory* that they support argues that the real world is complex. It is wrong, they claim, to rely on free trade and existing comparative advantage. Particular industries will require particular policies of protection or promotion tailored to their particular needs:

- Some industries will require protection against unfair competition from abroad – not just to protect the industries themselves, but also to protect the consumer from the oligopolistic power that the foreign companies will gain if they succeed in driving the domestic producers out of business.
- Other industries will need special support in the form of subsidies to enable them to modernise and compete effectively with imports.
- New industries may require protection to enable them to get established – to achieve economies of scale and build a comparative advantage.
- If a particular foreign country protects or promotes its *own* industries, it may be desirable to retaliate in order to persuade the country to change its mind.

The arguments of strategic trade theorists are criticised by economic liberals. If the USA is protected from cheap imports from Asia, they claim, all that will be achieved is a huge increase in consumer prices. The car, steel, telecommunications and electrical goods industries might

find their profits bolstered, but this is hardly likely to encourage them to be more efficient.

Another criticism of managed trade is the difficulty of identifying just which industries need protection, and how much and for how long. Governments do not have perfect knowledge. What is more, the political lobbyists from various interested groups are likely to use all sorts of tactics – legal or illegal – to persuade the government to look favourably on them. In the face of such pressure, will the government remain 'objective'? No, say the liberals.

So how do the strategic trade theorists reply? If it works for China and Japan, they say, it can work for the USA. What is needed is a change in attitudes. Rather than industry looking on the government as either an enemy to be outwitted or a potential benefactor to be wooed, and government looking on industry as a source of votes or tax revenues, both sides should try to develop a partnership – a partnership from which the whole country can gain.

But whether sensible, constructive managed trade is possible given the political context in which decisions would need to be made is a highly debatable point. 'Sensible' managed trade, say the liberals, is just pie in the sky. However, with the election of Donald Trump, who has vowed to 'put America first', calls for specific protection of certain industries in the USA may receive a more sympathetic hearing than from previous administrations. But whether increased protection will help to increase efficiency and regain comparative advantage remains to be seen.

Airbus, a consortium based in four European countries, has received massive support from the four governments, in order to enable it to compete with Boeing, which until the rise of Airbus had dominated the world market for aircraft. To what extent are (a) air travellers; (b) citizens of the four countries likely to have gained or lost from this protection? (See Case Study 24.8 on the student website.)

To prevent the importation of harmful goods. A country may want to ban or severely curtail the importation of things such as drugs, pornographic literature and live animals.

To take account of externalities. Free trade will tend to reflect private costs. Both imports and exports, however, can involve externalities. The mining of many minerals for export may damage the health of miners; the production of chemicals for export may involve pollution; the importation of juggernaut lorries may lead to structural damage to houses; shipping involves large amounts of CO_2 emissions (some 3 to 5 per cent of total world emissions) (see Box 24.4).

In recent years some politicians and green groups have called for the imposition of 'carbon tariffs'. The rate of tariff would reflect the amount of carbon emitted in the production of the good being imported. Such tariffs would be hard to implement, however. Assessing and valuing the carbon emitted would be very difficult and could lead to arbitrary tariff rates. Also, domestic goods would have to be subject to similar taxes.

Economic arguments having some validity for specific groups or countries

The arguments considered so far are of general validity: restricting trade for such reasons could be of net benefit to the world. There are other arguments, however, that are used by individual governments for restricting trade, where their country will gain, but at the *expense* of other countries, such that there will be a net loss to the world. Such arguments include the following.

The exploitation of market power. If a country, or a group of countries, has market power in the supply of exports (e.g. South Africa with diamonds, OPEC with oil) or market power in the demand for imports (e.g. the USA or other large, wealthy countries), it can exploit this power by intervening in trade.

Let us first take the case of a country, or a group of countries acting as a cartel, which has monopoly power in the sale of a particular export: for example, West African countries in the sale of cocoa. But let us assume that there are many individual producers that are therefore price takers and are thus not in a position to exploit the country's overall market power. In Figure 24.10, these price-taking firms will collectively produce at point *a* where $P = MC$. Market equilibrium is at a trade price of P_1 and an output of Q_1.

The country's profit, however, would be maximised at point *b* where $MC = MR$, with output at the lower level of Q_2. By imposing an export tax of $P_2 - P_3$, therefore, the country can maximise its gain from this export. Producers will receive P_3 and will therefore supply Q_2. Market price will be P_2.

? 1. How much would be the total tax revenue for the government?
2. Will the individual producers gain from the export tax?

Now let us take the case of a country that has *monopsony* power in the demand for an import. This is illustrated in

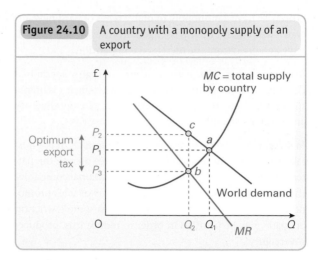

Figure 24.10 A country with a monopoly supply of an export

Figure 24.11. Without intervention, equilibrium will be at point *d* where demand equals supply. Q_1 would be purchased at a price of P_1.

But the marginal cost of imports curve will be *above* the supply curve because, given the country's size, the purchase of additional imports would drive up their price. This means that the cost of additional imports would be the new higher price (given by the supply curve) *plus* the rise in expenditure on the imports that would previously have been purchased at a lower price. The country will maximise its gain from trade at point *f* by importing Q_2, where demand equals marginal cost. Consumption can be reduced to Q_2 if the government imposes a tariff of $P_3 - P_2$. This is known as the **optimum tariff**. The country now only pays P_2 to importers. Consumers have to pay P_3 (i.e. P_2 plus the tariff).

Definition

Optimum tariff A tariff that reduces the level of imports to the point where marginal social cost equals marginal social benefit.

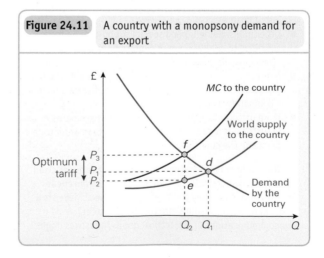

Figure 24.11 A country with a monopsony demand for an export

The country gains from such intervention, but only at the expense of the other countries with which it trades.

To protect declining industries.   The human costs of sudden industrial closures can be very high. In areas heavily reliant on a declining industry, such as coal mining areas, or 'rust belt' towns in the USA or cities like Detroit, there can be huge costs to the individuals losing their jobs. Their lack of transferable skills may make them occupationally highly immobile. What is more, regional multiplier effects can compound the direct loss of income and consumption. In such circumstances, temporary protection may be warranted to allow industries that have lost comparative advantage to decline more slowly, or even to encourage inward investment in new more efficient technology (making senile industries new 'infants'). Such policies will be at the expense of the consumer, who will be denied access to cheaper foreign imports. Nevertheless, such arguments have gained huge support from populist movements in the USA and elsewhere and protection for such industries form part of President Trump's 'America first' policies.

To improve the balance of payments.   Under certain special circumstances, when other methods of balance of payments correction are unsuitable, there may be a case for resorting to tariffs (see Chapter 25).

'Non-economic' arguments

A country may be prepared to forgo the direct economic advantages of free trade – consumption at a lower opportunity cost – in order to achieve objectives that are often described as 'non-economic':

- It may wish to maintain a degree of self-sufficiency in case trade is cut off in times of war. This may apply particularly to the production of food and armaments.
- It may decide not to trade with certain countries with which it disagrees politically.
- It may wish to preserve traditional ways of life. Rural communities or communities based on old traditional industries may be destroyed by foreign competition.
- It may prefer to retain as diverse a society as possible, rather than one too narrowly based on certain industries.

Pursuing such objectives, however, involves costs. Preserving a traditional way of life, for example, may mean that consumers are denied access to cheaper goods from abroad. Society must therefore weigh up the benefits against the costs of such policies.

---

*BOX 24.6   THE OPTIMUM TARIFF OR EXPORT TAX

EXPLORING ECONOMICS

Using calculus

The size of the optimum export tax depends on the price elasticity of demand ($P\epsilon_d$). You can see this if you imagine rotating the demand and *MR* curves in Figure 24.10. The less elastic the demand curve, the bigger will be the optimum export tax. The formula for the optimum export tax rate is

$$t = 1/P\epsilon_d$$

The proof of this is as follows.

In Figure 24.10, the optimum tax rate is

$$(P_2 - P_3) \div P_2 \tag{1}$$

From the point of view of the country (as opposed to individual producers) this is simply

$$(P - MR) \div P \tag{2}$$

Remember from Box 2.6 (on page 64) that price elasticity of demand is given by

$$P\epsilon_d = \frac{-dQ}{dP} \times \frac{P}{Q} \tag{3}$$

Remember also, from Box 6.10 (on page 183), that

$$MR = \frac{dTR}{dQ} = \frac{d(P \cdot Q)}{dQ} \tag{4}$$

From the rules of calculus:

$$\frac{d(P \cdot Q)}{dQ} = \frac{dP \cdot Q + dQ \cdot P}{dQ} \tag{5}$$

$$\therefore P - MR = P - \frac{dP \cdot Q + dQ \cdot P}{dQ} \tag{6}$$

$$\frac{P}{P - MR} = \frac{P}{P - \dfrac{dP \cdot Q + dQ \cdot P}{dQ}} \tag{7}$$

$$= 1 - \frac{P}{P - \dfrac{dP \cdot Q + dQ \cdot P}{dQ}} \tag{8}$$

Again from the rules of calculus:

$$= 1 - \left(\frac{dQ \cdot P}{dP \cdot Q} + \frac{dQ \cdot P}{dQ \cdot P} \right) \tag{9}$$

$$= 1 - \frac{dQ \cdot P}{dP \cdot Q} - 1 \tag{10}$$

$$= \frac{-dQ \cdot P}{dP \cdot Q} = P\epsilon_d \tag{11}$$

$\therefore$ from equations (2) and (11):

$$\frac{P - MR}{P} = \text{optimum tax rate} = \frac{1}{P\epsilon_d}$$

See if you can devise a similar proof to show that the optimal import tariff, where a country has monopsony power, is $1/P\epsilon_s$ (where $P\epsilon_s$ is the price elasticity of supply of the import).

If economics is the study of choices of how to use scarce resources, can these other objectives be legitimately described as 'non-economic'?

Problems with protection

TC 1
p11
Tariffs and other forms of protection impose a cost on society. This is illustrated in Figure 24.12. It illustrates the case of a good that is partly home produced and partly imported. Domestic demand and supply are given by D_{dom} and S_{dom}. It is assumed that firms in the country produce under perfect competition and that therefore the supply curve is the sum of the firms' marginal cost curves.

Let us assume that the country is too small to affect world prices: it is a price taker. The world price is given, at P_w, and world supply to the country (S_{world}) is perfectly elastic. At P_w, Q_2 is demanded, Q_1 is supplied by domestic suppliers and hence $Q_2 - Q_1$ is imported.

Now a tariff is imposed. This shifts up the world supply curve to the country by the amount of the tariff. Price rises to $P_w + t$. Domestic production increases to Q_3, consumption falls to Q_4, and hence imports fall to $Q_4 - Q_3$.

What are the costs of this tariff to the country? Consumers are having to pay a higher price, and hence consumer surplus falls from ABC to ADE. The cost to consumers in lost

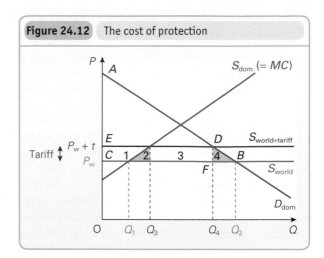

Figure 24.12   The cost of protection

consumer surplus is thus $EDBC$ (i.e. areas $1 + 2 + 3 + 4$). *Part* of this cost, however, is redistributed as a *benefit* to other sections in society. *Firms* face a higher price, and thus gain extra profits (area 1): where profit is given by the area between the price and the MC curve. The *government* receives extra revenue from the tariff payments (area 3): i.e. $Q_4 - Q_3 \times$ tariff. These revenues can be used, for example, to reduce taxes.

BOX 24.7   GIVING TRADE A BAD NAME

Arguments that don't add up

'Why buy goods from abroad and deny jobs to workers in this country?'

This is typical of the concerns that many people have about an open trade policy. However, these concerns are often based on arguments that do not stand up to close inspection. Here are four of them.

'Imports should be reduced since they lower the standard of living.

The money goes abroad rather than into the domestic economy.' Imports are consumed and thus add directly to consumer welfare. Also, provided they are matched by exports, there is no net outflow of money. Trade, because of the law of comparative advantage, allows countries to increase their standard of living: to consume beyond their production possibility curve (see Figures 24.5 and 24.9).

'Protection is needed from cheap foreign labour.'

Importing cheap goods from, say, Indonesia, allows more goods to be consumed. The UK uses less resources by buying these goods through the production and sale of exports than by producing them at home. However, there will be a cost to certain UK workers whose jobs are lost through foreign competition.

'Protection reduces unemployment.'

At a microeconomic level, protecting industries from foreign competition may allow workers in those industries to retain their jobs. But if foreigners sell fewer goods to the UK, they will not be able to buy so many UK exports. Thus unemployment will rise in UK export industries. Overall unemployment, therefore, is little affected, and in the meantime the benefits from trade to consumers are reduced. Temporary protection given to declining industries, however, may help to reduce structural unemployment.

'Dumping is always a bad thing, and thus a country should restrict subsidised imports.'

Dumping may well reduce world economic welfare: it goes against the law of comparative advantage. The importing country, however, may well gain from dumping. Provided the dumping is not used to drive domestic producers out of business and establish a foreign monopoly, the consumer gains from lower prices. The losers are the taxpayers in the foreign country and the workers in competing industries in the home country.

Go through each of these five arguments and provide a reply to the criticisms of them.

But *part* of this cost is not recouped elsewhere. It is a net cost to society (areas 2 and 4).

Area 2 represents the extra costs of producing $Q_3 - Q_1$ at home, rather than importing it. If $Q_3 - Q_1$ were still imported, the country would only be paying S_{world}. By producing it at home, however, the costs are given by the domestic supply curve ($=MC$). The difference between MC and S_{world} (area 2) is thus the efficiency loss on the production side.

Area 4 represents the loss of consumer surplus by the reduction in consumption from Q_2 to Q_4. Consumers have saved area FBQ_2Q_4 of expenditure, but have sacrificed area DBQ_2Q_4 of utility in so doing – a net loss of area 4.

The government should ideally weigh up such costs against any benefits that are gained from protection.

 In this model, where the country is a price taker and faces a horizontal supply curve (the small country assumption), is any of the cost of the tariff borne by the overseas suppliers?

Apart from these direct costs to the consumer, there are several other problems with protection. Some are direct effects of the protection; others follow from the reactions of other nations.

Protection as 'second best'.   Many of the arguments for protection amount merely to arguments for some type of government intervention in the economy. Protection, however, may not be the best way of dealing with the problem, since protection may have undesirable side effects. There may be a more direct form of intervention that has no side effects. In such a case, protection will be no more than a second-best solution.

For example, using tariffs to protect old, inefficient industries from foreign competition may help prevent unemployment in those parts of the economy, but the consumer will suffer from higher prices. A better solution would be to subsidise retraining and investment in those areas of the country in *new, efficient* industries – industries with a comparative advantage. In this way, unemployment is avoided, but the consumer does not suffer.

Even if the *existing* industries were to be supported, it would still be better to do this by paying them subsidies than by putting tariffs on imports. This argument can be expressed in terms of Figure 24.12. As we have seen, a tariff imposes costs on the consumer of areas $1 + 2 + 3 + 4$. In the current example, area 2 may be a cost worth paying in order to increase domestic output to Q_3, (and hence reduce unemployment). Areas 1 and 3, as argued above, are merely *redistributed* elsewhere (to firms and the government respectively). But this still leaves area 4. This is a side-effect cost not recouped elsewhere.

A *subsidy,* on the other hand, would not have involved this side-effect cost. In order to raise output to Q_3, a rate of subsidy the same as the tariff rate would have to be given to producers. This would raise the amount they receive per unit

to $P_w + t$. They would choose to supply Q_3. The price to the consumer, however, would *remain at the world price P_w*. There would thus be no cost to the consumer. The cost of the subsidy to the taxpayer would be areas $1 + 2$. Area 1 would be redistributed to firms as extra profit. Area 2, as argued above, may be worth paying to achieve the desirable output and employment consequences.

If the aim is to increase output, a *production* subsidy is the best policy. If the aim is to increase employment, an *employment* subsidy is the best policy. In either case, to use *protection* instead would be no more than second best, since it would involve side effects.

To conclude: the best policy is to tackle the problem directly. Unless the aim is specifically to reduce imports (rather than help domestic industry), protection is an indirect policy, and hence never more than second best.

 1. What would be the 'first-best' solution to the problem of an infant industry not being able to compete with imports?
2. Protection to allow the exploitation of monopoly/ monopsony power can be seen as a 'first-best' policy for the country concerned. Similarly, the use of tariffs to counteract externalities directly involved in the trade process (e.g. the environmental costs of an oil tanker disaster) could be seen to be a first-best policy. Explain why.

World multiplier effects.   If the UK imposes tariffs or other restrictions, imports will be reduced. But these imports are other countries' exports. A reduction in their exports will reduce the level of injections into the 'rest-of-the-world' economy, and thus lead to a multiplied fall in rest-of-the-world income. Which in turn will lead to a reduction in demand for UK exports. This, therefore, tends to undo the benefits of the tariffs.

 What determines the size of this world multiplier effect?

Retaliation.   If the USA imposes restrictions on, say, imports from the EU, then the EU may impose restrictions on imports from the USA. Any gain to US firms competing with EU imports is offset by a loss to US exporters. What is more, US consumers suffer, since the benefits from comparative advantage have been lost.

The increased use of tariffs and other restrictions can lead to a trade war: each country cutting back on imports from other countries. In the end, everyone loses.

Protection may allow firms to remain inefficient.   By removing or reducing foreign competition, protection may reduce firms' incentive to reduce costs. Thus if protection is being given to an infant industry, the government must ensure that the lack of competition does not prevent it 'growing up'. Protection should not be excessive and should be removed as soon as possible.

Bureaucracy. If a government is to avoid giving excessive protection to firms, it should examine each case carefully. This can lead to large administrative costs.

Corruption. Some countries that have an extensive programme of protection suffer from corruption. Home producers want as much protection as possible. Importers want as much freedom as possible. It is very tempting for both groups to bribe officials to give them favourable treatment.

The World Trade Organization

After the Wall Street crash of 1929 (when prices on the US stock exchange plummeted), the world plunged into the Great Depression (see pages 495–9). Countries found their exports falling dramatically, and many suffered severe balance of payments difficulties. The response of many countries was to restrict imports by the use of tariffs and quotas.

Of course, this reduced other countries' exports, which encouraged them to resort to even greater protectionism. The net effect of the Depression and the rise in protectionism was a dramatic fall in world trade. The volume of world trade in manufactures fell by more than a third in the three years following the Wall Street crash. Clearly there was a net economic loss to the world from this decline in trade.

After the Second World War there was a general desire to reduce trade restrictions, so that all countries could gain the maximum benefits from trade. There was no desire to return to the beggar-my-neighbour policies of the 1930s.

In 1947, 23 countries got together and signed the General Agreement on Tariffs and Trade (GATT). By 2017, there were 164 members of its successor organisation, the World Trade Organization (WTO), which was formed in 1995. Between them, the members of the WTO account for around 98 per

---

| BOX 24.8 | THE DOHA DEVELOPMENT AGENDA |

A new direction for the WTO?

Globalisation, based on the free play of comparative advantage, economies of scale and innovation, has produced a genuinely radical force, in the true sense of the word. It essentially amplifies and reinforces the strengths, but also the weaknesses, of market capitalism: its efficiency, its instability, and its inequality. If we want globalisation not only to be efficiency-boosting but also fair, we need more international rules and stronger multilateral institutions.[1]

In November 1999, the members of the World Trade Organization met in Seattle in the USA. What ensued became known as the 'Battle of Seattle' (see Case Study 24.3 on the student website). Anti-globalisation protesters fought with police; the world's developing economies fell out with the world's developed economies; and the very future of the WTO was called into question. The WTO was accused of being a free trader's charter, in which the objective of free trade was allowed to ride roughshod over anything that might stand in its way. Whatever the issue – the environment, the plight of developing countries, the dominance of trade by multinationals – free trade was king.

At Seattle, both the protesters and developing countries argued that things had gone far enough. The WTO must redefine its role, they argued, to respect *all* stakeholders. More radical voices called for the organisation to be scrapped. As Pascal Lamy, the EU Trade Commissioner, made clear in the speech quoted above, rules had to be strengthened, and the WTO had to ensure that the gains from trade were fairer and more sustainable.

The rebuilding process of the WTO began in Doha, Qatar, in 2001. The meeting between the then 142 members of the WTO concluded with the decision to launch a new round of WTO trade talks, to be called the Doha Development Agenda (DDA). As with previous trade rounds, the talks were designed to increase the liberalisation of trade. However, this time such a goal was to be tempered by a policy of strengthening assistance to developing economies.

At Doha it was agreed that the new trade talks would address questions such as:

- *Sustainable development and the environment.* In the past, international trade agreements always seemed to take precedence over international environmental agreements, even though they are legally equivalent. The hope this time was to achieve greater coherence between various areas of international policy making.

- *Trade and development.* The Doha round would attempt to address a number of issues of concern to developing countries as they become more integrated into the world's trading system. These included improving access to markets in developed countries and strengthening the special treatment that developing countries received, such as the ability to maintain higher rates of tariff protection.

Other areas identified for discussion include: greater liberalisation of agriculture; rules to govern foreign direct investment; the co-ordination of countries' competition policies; the use and abuse of patents on medicines; and the needs of developing countries.

The talks were originally scheduled for completion by January 2005, but this deadline was extended several times as new talks were arranged and failed to reach agreement. A particular sticking point was the unwillingness of rich countries, and the USA and the EU in particular, to make sufficient reductions in agricultural protection, given the pressure from their domestic farmers. The USA was unwilling to make substantial cuts in agricultural subsidies and the EU in agricultural tariffs.

cent of world trade. The aims of GATT, and now the WTO, have been to liberalise trade.

WTO rules

The WTO requires its members to operate according to various rules. These include the following:

- *Non-discrimination.* Under the 'most favoured nations clause', any trade concession that a country makes to one member must be granted to *all* signatories. The only exception is with free trade areas and customs unions (such as the EU). Here countries are permitted to abolish tariffs between themselves while still maintaining them with the rest of the world.
- *Reciprocity.* Any nation benefiting from a tariff reduction made by another country must reciprocate by making similar tariff reductions itself.
- *The general prohibition of quotas.*

- *Fair competition.* If unfair barriers are erected against a particular country, the WTO can sanction retaliatory action by that country. The country is not allowed, however, to take such action without permission.
- *Binding tariffs.* Countries cannot raise existing tariffs without negotiating with their trading partners.

Unlike the GATT, the WTO has the power to impose sanctions on countries breaking trade agreements. If there are disputes between member nations, these will be settled by the WTO, and if an offending country continues to impose trade restrictions, permission will be granted for other countries to retaliate.

For example, in March 2002, the Bush administration imposed tariffs on steel imports into the USA in order to protect the ailing US steel industry (see Case Study 24.6 on the student website). The EU and other countries referred the case to the WTO, which in December 2003 ruled that they

There was also unwillingness on the part of large developing countries, such as India and Brazil, to reduce protection to their industrial and service sectors. What is more, there were large divergences in opinion between developing countries on how much they should reduce their own agricultural protection.

Breakdown of the talks

The talks seemed finally to have broken down at a meeting in Geneva in July 2008. Despite the willingness of developing countries to reduce industrial tariffs by more than 50 per cent, and that of the USA and the EU to make deep cuts in agricultural subsidies and tariffs, the talks foundered over the question of agricultural protection for developing countries. This was item 18 on a 'to-do' list of 20 items; items 1 to 17 had already been agreed. China and India wanted to protect poor farmers by retaining the ability to impose temporary tariffs on food imports in the event of a drop in food prices or a surge in imports. The USA objected. When neither side would budge, the talks collapsed.

Many commentators, however, argued that failure was no catastrophe. The gain from total liberalisation of trade would have boosted developing countries' GDP by no more than 1 per cent. And anyway, tariffs were already at an all-time low, demonstrating the extent to which progress had already been made. But with the global economic downturn of 2008–9, there were worries that protectionism would begin to rise again. This was a classic prisoners' dilemma (see pages 235–7 and 403–5). Policies that seemed to be in the interests of countries separately would be to the overall determinant of the world. The Nash equilibrium of such a 'game', therefore, is one where countries are generally worse off. As it turned out, the worries were largely unfounded – at least in the short term.

The Bali Package and the push to agreement

In December 2013, agreement was reached on a range of issues at the WTO's Bali Ministerial Conference and these were adopted in November 2014 by the General Council. The agreement means a streamlining of trade to make it 'easier, faster and cheaper', with particular focus on the promotion of development, boosting the trade of the least developed countries and allowing developing countries more options for providing food security, as long as this does not distort international trade.

This was the first significant agreement of the round and goes some way to achieving around 25 per cent of the goals set for the Doha round.

Then in December 2015, at the Ministerial Conference in Nairobi, another historic agreement was made on various trade initiatives that should provide particular benefits to the WTO's poorest members. This 'Nairobi Package' contains six Ministerial Decisions on agriculture, cotton and issues related to least developed countries, including a commitment to abolish export subsidies for farm exports.

While many issues remain outstanding, some progress has been made. However, many governments, including the USA, have indicated that this could well be the end of the road for the Doha round. Indeed, the Trump presidency may usher in a new wave of protectionism around the world, with populist movements blaming free trade for the decline of many traditional sectors, with a loss of jobs and increased social deprivation.

 Does the process of globalisation mean that the role of the WTO is becoming less and less important?

1 'Global policy without democracy' (speech by Pascal Lamy, EU Trade Commissioner, given in 2001).

were illegal. This ruling made it legitimate for the EU and other countries to impose retaliatory tariffs on US products. President Bush consequently announced that the steel tariffs would be abolished.

 Could US action to protect its steel industry from foreign competition be justified in terms of the interests of the USA as a whole (as opposed to the steel industry in particular)?

The greater power of the WTO has persuaded many countries to bring their disputes to it. From January 1995 to April 2017 the WTO had considered, or was considering, 524 disputes (compared with 300 by GATT over the whole of its 48 years).

Trade rounds

Periodically, member countries have met to negotiate reductions in tariffs and other trade restrictions. There have been eight 'rounds' of such negotiations since the signing of GATT in 1947. The last major round to be completed was the Uruguay round, which began in Uruguay in 1986, continued at meetings around the world and culminated in a deal being signed in April 1994. By that time, the average tariff on manufactured products was 4 per cent and falling. In 1947 the figure was nearly 40 per cent. The Uruguay round agreement also involved a programme of phasing in substantial reductions in tariffs and other restrictions up to the year 2002 (see Case Study 24.2 on the student website).

Despite the reduction in tariffs, many countries have still tried to restrict trade by various other means, such as quotas and administrative barriers. Also, barriers have been particularly high on certain non-manufactures. Agricultural protection in particular has come in for sustained criticism by developing countries. High fixed prices and subsidies given

to farmers in the EU, the USA and other advanced countries mean that the industrialised world continues to export food to many developing countries that have a comparative advantage in food production! Farmers in developing countries often find it impossible to compete with subsidised food imports from the rich countries.

The most recent round of trade negotiations began in Doha, Qatar, in 2001 (see Box 24.8). The negotiations have focused on both trade liberalisation and measures to encourage development of poorer countries. In particular, the Doha Development Agenda, as it is called, is concerned with measures to make trade fairer so that its benefits are spread more evenly around the world. This would involve improved access for developing countries to markets in the rich world. The Agenda is also concerned with the environmental impacts of trade and development.

The negotiations were originally due to be completed in 2005, but, as Box 24.8 explains, deadlines continued to be missed. However, some progress was made at Ministerial Conference in 2013 and 2015. The Bali Package agreed in 2013 made commitments to streamline trade, boost trade among least developed countries and provide 'food security' for developing countries. The deal was proclaimed as the first substantial agreement since the WTO was formed in 1995. This was followed in 2015 by the 'Nairobi Package' which built on the Bali package by agreeing on actions in the areas of agriculture, cotton with particular relevance to the least developed countries. This included a commitment to begin to abolish export subsidies for farm exports. Nonetheless, considerable work remained in meeting the goals set in Doha. And with the rise in populist anti-globalisation movements and with the election of Donald Trump, it looks as if the Nairobi Package may be the high point of freer trade for some time to come.

Section summary

1. Countries use various methods to restrict trade, including tariffs, quotas, exchange controls, import licensing, export taxes, and legal and administrative barriers. Countries may also promote their own industries by subsidies.

2. Reasons for restricting trade that have some validity in a world context include the infant industry argument; the inflexibility of markets in responding to changing comparative advantage, dumping and other unfair trade practices; the danger of the establishment of a foreign-based monopoly; the problems of relying on exporting goods whose market is growing slowly or even declining; the need to spread the risks of fluctuating export prices; and the problems that free trade may adversely affect consumer tastes, may allow the importation of harmful goods and may not take account of externalities.

3. Often, however, the arguments for restricting trade are in the context of one country benefiting even though other

countries may lose more. Countries may intervene in trade in order to exploit their monopoly/monopsony power. In the case of imports, the optimum tariff would be that which would reduce consumption to the level where price was equal to the country's marginal cost. In the case of exports, the optimum export tax would be that which reduced production to the level where the country's marginal revenue was equal to marginal cost. Other 'beggar-my-neighbour' arguments include the protection of declining industries and improving the balance of payments.

4. Finally, a country may have other objectives in restricting trade, such as remaining self-sufficient in certain strategic products, not trading with certain countries of which it disapproves, protecting traditional ways of life or simply retaining a non-specialised economy.

5. In general, trade brings benefits to countries, and protection to achieve one objective may be at a very high

opportunity cost. Other things being equal, there will be a net loss in welfare from restricting trade, with any gain in government revenue or profits to firms being outweighed by a loss in consumer surplus. Even if government intervention to protect certain parts of the economy is desirable, restricting trade is unlikely to be a first-best solution to the problem, since it involves side-effect costs. What is more, restricting trade may have adverse world multiplier effects; it may encourage retaliation; it may allow inefficient firms to remain inefficient; it may involve considerable bureaucracy and possibly even corruption.

6. Most countries of the world are members of the WTO and in theory are in favour of moves towards freer trade. The Uruguay round brought significant reductions in trade restrictions, both tariff and non-tariff.

7. The latest, the Doha round, focuses on trade liberalisation and aims to spread the benefits of trade across developing countries. It has yet to be concluded, but progress has been made since 2013. There is some doubt, however, as to whether any further progress will be made and whether the round, therefore, is effectively over.

24.3   PREFERENTIAL TRADING

The world economy has, over time, seen the formation of a series of trade blocs. These have often been based upon regional groupings of countries, such as the European Union (EU) or the North American Free Trade Agreement (NAFTA). Such trade blocs are examples of *preferential trading arrangements*. These arrangements involve trade restrictions with the rest of the world, and lower or zero restrictions between the members.

Although trade blocs clearly encourage trade between their members, many countries outside the blocs complain that they benefit the members at the expense of the rest of the world. For many developing economies, in need of access to the most prosperous nations in the world, this represents a significant check on their ability to grow and develop.

Types of preferential trading arrangement

There are three possible forms of such trading arrangements.

Free trade areas

A *free trade area* is where member countries remove tariffs and quotas between themselves, but retain whatever restrictions *each member chooses* with non-member countries. Some provision will have to be made to prevent imports from outside coming into the area via the country with the lowest external tariff.

Customs unions

A *customs union* is like a free trade area, but in addition members must adopt *common* external tariffs and quotas with non-member countries.

Common markets

A *common market* is where member countries operate as a *single* market. As with a customs union, there are no tariffs and quotas between member countries and there are

common external tariffs and quotas. But a common market goes further than this. A full common market includes the following features:

- *A common system of taxation.* In the case of a *perfect* common market, this will involve identical rates of tax in all member countries.

- *A common system of laws and regulations governing production, employment and trade.* For example, in a perfect common market, there would be a *single* set of laws governing issues such as product specification (e.g. permissible artificial additives to foods, or levels of exhaust emissions from cars), the employment and dismissal of labour, mergers and takeovers, and monopolies and restrictive practices.

- *Free movement of labour, capital and materials, and of goods and services.* In a perfect common market, this will involve a total absence of border controls between member states, the freedom of workers to work in any member country and the freedom of firms to expand into any member state.

- *The absence of special treatment by member governments of their own domestic industries.* Governments are large

Definitions

Preferential trading arrangements A trade agreement whereby trade between the signatories is freer than trade with the rest of the world.

Free trade area A group of countries with no trade barriers between themselves.

Customs union A free trade area with common external tariffs and quotas.

Common market A customs union where the member countries act as a single market with free movement of labour and capital, common taxes and common trade laws.

purchasers of goods and services. In a perfect common market, they should buy from whichever companies within the market offer the most competitive deal and not show favouritism towards domestic suppliers: they should operate a *common procurement policy*.

The definition of a common market is sometimes extended to include the following two features of *economic and monetary union*:

■ *A fixed exchange rate between the member countries' currencies*. In the extreme case, this would involve a single currency for the whole market.

■ *Common macroeconomic policies*. To some extent, this must follow from a fixed exchange rate, but in the extreme case it will involve a single macroeconomic management of the whole market, and hence the abolition of separate fiscal or monetary intervention by individual member states.

We will examine European economic and monetary union in section 26.2.

The direct effects of a customs union: trade creation and trade diversion

By joining a customs union (or free trade area), a country will find that its trade patterns change. Two such changes can be distinguished: trade creation and trade diversion.

Trade creation

Trade creation is where consumption shifts from a high-cost producer to a low-cost producer. The removal of trade barriers allows greater specialisation according to comparative advantage. Instead of consumers having to pay high prices for domestically produced goods in which the country has a comparative disadvantage, the goods can now be obtained more cheaply from other members of the customs union. In return, the country can export to them goods in which it has a comparative advantage.

For example, suppose that the most efficient producer in the world of good x is France. Assume that, before it joined the EU in 2004, Poland had to pay tariffs on good x from France. After joining the EU, however, it was then able to import good x from France without paying tariffs. There was a gain to Polish consumers. This gain is illustrated in Figure 24.13. Curves S_{Pol} and D_{Pol} show the domestic supply and demand curves in Poland. The diagram assumes for simplicity that Poland is a price taker as an importer of good x from France: the EU price is given.

The diagram shows that, before joining the EU, Poland had to pay the EU price *plus* the tariff (i.e. P_1). At P_1 Poland produced Q_2, consumed Q_1 and thus imported $Q_1 - Q_2$. With the removal of tariffs, the price fell to P_2. Consumption increased to Q_3 and production fell to Q_4. Imports thus increased to $Q_3 - Q_4$. Trade had been created.

The gain in welfare from the removal of the tariff is also illustrated in Figure 24.13. A reduction in price from P_1 to P_2

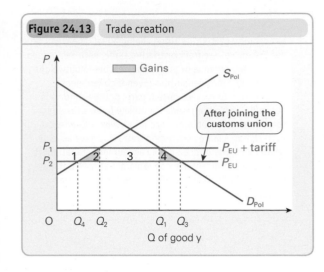

Figure 24.13 Trade creation

leads to an increase in Polish consumer surplus of areas 1 + 2 + 3 + 4. On the other hand, there is a loss in profits to domestic producers of good x of area 1 and a loss in tariff revenue to the government of area 3. There is still a net gain, however, of areas 2 + 4.

The increased consumption of wine in the UK after joining the EU may be seen as trade creation.

Trade diversion

Trade diversion is where consumption shifts from a lower-cost producer outside the customs union to a higher-cost producer within the union.

Assume that the most efficient producer of good y in the world was Russia – outside the EU. Assume that, before membership, Poland paid a similar tariff on good y from any country, and thus imported the product from Russia rather than the EU.

After joining the EU, however, the removal of the tariff made the EU product cheaper, since the tariff remained on the Russian product. Consumption thus switched to a higher-cost producer. There was thus a net loss in world efficiency. As far as Poland was concerned, consumers still gained, since they were paying a lower price than before, but this time the loss in profits to Polish producers plus the loss

---

Definition

Trade creation Where a customs union leads to greater specialisation according to comparative advantage and thus a shift in production from higher-cost to lower-cost sources.

Trade diversion Where a customs union diverts consumption from goods produced at a lower cost outside the union to goods produced at a higher cost (but tariff-free) within the union.

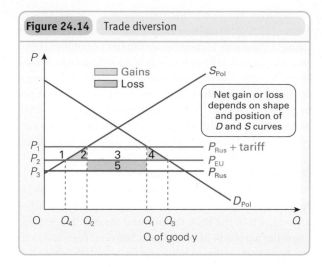

Figure 24.14 Trade diversion

in tariff revenue to the Polish government might have out-weighed these gains, giving a net loss.

These benefits and costs are shown in Figure 24.14. For simplicity it assumes a constant Russian and EU price (i.e. that their supply curves to Poland are infinitely elastic). The domestic supply curve (S_{Pol}) is upward sloping, and is assumed to be equal to marginal cost.

Before joining the EU, Poland was importing good y from Russia at a price P_1 (i.e. the Russian price plus the tariff). Poland thus consumed Q_1, produced Q_2 domestically and imported the remainder, $Q_1 - Q_2$. On joining the EU, it was now able to consume at the EU (tariff-free) price of P_2. (Note that this is above the tariff-free Russian price, P_3.) What are the gains and losses to Poland?

- Consumers' gain: Polish consumer surplus rises by areas 1 + 2 + 3 + 4.
- Producers' loss: Polish producer surplus (profit) falls by area 1.
- Government's loss: previously tariffs of areas 3 + 5 were paid. Now no tariffs are paid. The Polish government thus loses this revenue.

There is thus a net gain of areas 1 + 2 + 3 + 4 minus areas 1 + 3 + 5, i.e. areas 2 + 4 minus area 5. If, however, area 5 is bigger than area 2 + 4, there is a net loss.

When trade *diversion* takes place, therefore, there may still be a net gain, but there may be a net loss. It depends on circumstances.

TC 1
p11

TC 1 p11

? *Under which of the following circumstances is there likely to be a net gain from trade diversion? (Refer to Figure 24.14.)*
(a) A small difference between the EU price and the Russian pre-tariff price, and a large difference between the EU price and the Russian price with the tariff, or vice versa.
(b) Elastic or inelastic Polish demand and supply curves.
(c) The Polish demand and supply curves close together or far apart.

A customs union is more likely to lead to trade diversion rather than trade creation:

- When the union's external tariff is very high. Under these circumstances, the abolition of the tariff within the union is likely to lead to a large reduction in the price of goods imported from other members of the union.
- When there is a relatively small cost difference between goods produced within and outside the union. Here the abolition of even relatively low tariffs within the union will lead to internally produced goods becoming cheaper than externally produced goods.

Longer-term effects of a customs union

The problem with the above analysis is that it assumes *static* demand and supply curves: in other words, supply and demand curves that are unaffected by changes in trading patterns. In reality, if a country joins a customs union, the curves are likely to shift. Membership itself affects demand and supply – perhaps beneficially, perhaps adversely.

Longer-term advantages (economic) include the following:

- Increased market size may allow a country's firms to exploit (*internal*) *economies of scale*. This argument is more important for small countries, which have therefore more to gain from an enlargement of their markets.
- *External economies of scale.* Increased trade may lead to improvements in the infrastructure of the members of the customs union (better roads, railways, financial services, etc.). This in turn could bring bigger long-term benefits from trade between members, and from external trade too, by making the transport and handling of imports and exports cheaper.
- The bargaining power of the whole customs union with the rest of the world may allow member countries to gain *better terms of trade*. This, of course, will necessarily involve a degree of political co-operation between the members.
- *Increased competition* between member countries may stimulate efficiency, encourage investment and reduce monopoly power. Of course, a similar advantage could be gained by the simple removal of tariffs with any competing country.
- Integration may encourage a more rapid spread of technology.

Longer-term disadvantages (economic) include the following:

- *Resources may flow from a country* to more efficient members of the customs union, or to the geographical centre of the union (so as to minimise transport costs). This can be a major problem for a *common market* (where there is free movement of labour and capital). The country could become a depressed 'region' of the community, with adverse regional multiplier effects.

- If integration encourages greater co-operation between firms in member countries, it may also encourage *greater oligopolistic collusion,* thus keeping prices to the consumer higher. It may also encourage mergers and takeovers which would increase monopoly power.
- *Diseconomies of scale.* If the union leads to the development of very large companies, they may become bureaucratic and inefficient.
- The *costs of administering* the customs union may be high. This problem is likely to be worse, the greater the intervention in the affairs of individual members.

It is extremely difficult to assess these arguments. To decide whether membership has been beneficial to a country requires a prediction of what things would have been like if it had not joined. No *accurate* predictions of this sort can be made, and they can never be tested. Also, many of the advantages and disadvantages are very long term, and depend on future attitudes, institutions, policies and world events, which again cannot be predicted.

In addition, some of the advantages and disadvantages are distinctly political, such as 'greater political power' or 'loss of sovereignty'.

 How would you set about assessing whether or not a country had made a net long-term gain by joining a customs union? What sort of evidence would you look for?

Preferential trading in practice

Preferential trading has the greatest potential to benefit countries whose domestic market is too small, taken on its own, to enable them to benefit from economies of scale, and where they face substantial barriers to their exports. Most developing countries fall into this category, and as a result many have attempted to form preferential trading arrangements.

Examples in Latin America and the Caribbean are the Latin American Integration Association (LAIA), the Andean Community, the Central American Integration System (SICA) and the Caribbean Community (CARICOM). In 1991, a Southern Common Market (MerCoSur) was formed, consisting of Argentina, Brazil, Paraguay and Uruguay. Venezuela joined in 2012. It has a common external tariff and most of its internal trade is free of tariffs.

The Association of South-East Asian Nations (ASEAN) was formed in 1967 when six nations (Brunei, Indonesia, Malaysia, the Philippines, Singapore and Thailand) agreed to work towards an ASEAN Free Trade Area (AFTA). ASEAN now has 10 members (the new countries being Vietnam, Laos, Myanmar and Cambodia) with a population of over 620 million people and is dedicated to increased economic co-operation within the region.

By 2010, virtually all tariffs between the six original members had been eliminated and both tariff and non-tariff barriers are falling quickly for both original and new members. The ASEAN Economic Community (AEC) was established in 2015, ahead of schedule.

In Africa, the Economic Community of West African States (ECOWAS) has been attempting to create a common market between its 15 members which has a combined population of around 350 million. The West African franc is used in eight of the countries and another six plan to introduce a common currency, the eco. However, the launch of this has been delayed several times and it is now not expected until at least 2020. The ultimate goal is to combine the two currency areas and adopt a single currency for all member states.

North American Free Trade Agreement (NAFTA)

Along with the EU, NAFTA is one of the two most powerful trading blocs in the world. It came into force in 1994 and consists of the USA, Canada and Mexico. These three countries agreed to abolish tariffs between themselves in the hope that increased trade and co-operation would follow. Tariffs between the USA and Canada were phased out by 1999, and tariffs between all three countries were eliminated as of 1 January 2008. Many non-tariff restrictions remain, although new ones are not permitted. However, the Trump administration has threatened to break this rule with the erection of new barriers against Mexican imports.

NAFTA members hope that, with a market similar in size to the EU, they will be able to rival the EU's economic power in world trade. NAFTA is, however, at most only a free trade area and not a common market. Unlike the EU, it does not seek to harmonise laws and regulations, except in very specific areas such as environmental management and labour standards. Member countries are permitted total legal independence, subject to the one proviso that they must treat firms of other member countries equally with their own firms – the principle of 'fair competition'. Nevertheless, NAFTA has encouraged a growth in trade between its members, most of which is trade creation rather than trade diversion.

Case Study 24.7 on the student website looks at the costs and benefits of NAFTA membership to the three countries involved.

Asia-Pacific Economic Co-operation forum (APEC)

The most significant move towards establishing a more widespread regional economic organisation in East Asia appeared with the creation of the Asia-Pacific Economic Co-operation (APEC) in 1989. APEC links 21 economies of the Pacific rim, including Asian, Australasian and North and South American countries (19 countries, plus Hong Kong and Taiwan). These countries account for over half of global GDP and almost half of the world's trade. At the 1994 meeting of APEC leaders, it resolved to create a free trade area across the Pacific by 2010 for the developed industrial countries, and by 2020 for the rest.

This preferential trading area is by no means as advanced as NAFTA and is unlikely to move beyond a free trade area. Within the region there exists a wide disparity across a range of economic and social indicators. Such disparities create a wide range of national interests and goals. Countries are unlikely to share common economic problems or concerns. In addition, political differences and conflicts within the region are widespread, reducing the likelihood that any organisational agreement beyond a simple economic one would succeed. Nevertheless, freer trade has brought economic benefits to the countries involved.

The longest established and most comprehensive of preferential trading arrangements is the European Union. The next section is devoted to examining its evolution from a rather imperfect customs union to a common market (though still not perfect).

The Trans-Pacific Partnership

The Trans-Pacific Trade Partnership (TPP) is an agreement between 12 Pacific-rim countries – Australia, Brunei, Canada, Chile, Japan, Malaysia, Mexico, New Zealand, Peru, Singapore, the USA and Vietnam, but not China. It was signed by the 12 countries in February 2016, but has yet to be ratified by the countries' governments. On coming into office in January 2017, Donald Trump withdrew the USA from the agreement, making ratification of the agreement by the remaining countries difficult.

The agreement is more than a simple free trade agreement. In terms of trade it involves the removal of many non-tariff barriers as well as most tariff barriers. It also has elements of a single market. For example, it contains many robust and enforceable environmental protection, human rights and labour standards measures. It also allows for the free transfer of capital by investors in most circumstances.

However, it also established an 'investor–state dispute settlement' (ISDS) mechanism. This allows companies from any of the now 11 countries to sue governments of any other countries in the agreement for treaty violations, such as giving favourable treatment to domestic companies, the seizing of companies' assets or controls over the movement of capital. Critics of ISDS claim that it gives too much power to companies and may prevent governments from protecting their national environment or domestic workers and companies.

China, South Korea, Indonesia, the Philippines, Thailand and Colombia have expressed an interest in joining and it may be that these and the 11 members will find a way of progressing with the agreement without the USA. A key question is whether a growing international antipathy to trade deals will extend beyond the USA to current and prospective members.

Section summary

1. Countries may make a partial movement towards free trade by the adoption of a preferential trading system. This involves free trade between the members, but restrictions on trade with the rest of the world. Such a system can be either a simple free trade area, or a customs union (where there are common restrictions with the rest of the world), or a common market (where in addition there is free movement of capital and labour, and common taxes and trade laws).

2. A preferential trading area can lead to trade creation where production shifts to low-cost producers within the area, or to trade diversion where trade shifts away from lower-cost producers outside the area to higher-cost producers within the area.

3. There is a net welfare gain from trade creation: the gain in consumer surplus outweighs the loss of tariff revenue and the loss of profit to domestic producers. With trade diversion, however, these two losses may outweigh the gains to consumers: whether they do depends on the size of the tariffs and on the demand for and supply of the traded goods.

4. Preferential trading may bring dynamic advantages of increased external economies of scale, improved terms of trade from increased bargaining power with the rest of the world, increased efficiency from greater competition between member countries, and a more rapid spread of technology. On the other hand, it can lead to increased regional problems for members, greater oligopolistic collusion and various diseconomies of scale. There may also be large costs of administering the system.

5. There have been several attempts around the world to form preferential trading systems. The two most powerful are the European Union and the North American Free Trade Association (NAFTA).

24.4 THE EUROPEAN UNION

Historical background

The European Economic Community was formed by the signing of the Treaty of Rome in 1957 and came into operation on 1 January 1958.

The original six member countries of the EEC (Belgium, France, Italy, Luxembourg, the Netherlands and West Germany) had already made a move towards integration with the formation of the European Coal and Steel Community in 1952. This had removed all restrictions on trade in coal, steel and iron ore between the six countries. The aim had been to gain economies of scale and allow more effective competition with the USA and other foreign producers.

The EEC extended this principle and aimed eventually to be a full common market with completely free trade between members in all products, and with completely free movement of labour, enterprise and capital.

All internal tariffs between the six members had been abolished and common external tariffs established by 1968. But this still only made the EEC a *customs union,* since a number of restrictions on internal trade remained (legal, administrative, fiscal, etc.). Nevertheless the aim was eventually to create a full common market.

In 1973 the UK, Denmark and Ireland became members. Greece joined in 1981, Spain and Portugal in 1986, and Sweden, Austria and Finland in 1995. In May 2004, a further 10 countries joined: Cyprus, the Czech Republic, Estonia, Hungary, Latvia, Lithuania, Malta, Poland, Slovakia and Slovenia. Bulgaria and Romania joined in 2007. The last new member is Croatia, which joined in 2013. With the UK scheduled to leave the EU in 2019, there will then be 27 members.

Montenegro, Serbia and Turkey ('accession countries') are in negotiations to join and Albania and the former Yugoslav Republic of Macedonia have applied to join ('candidate countries'). However, with concerns throughout the EU with immigration, cultural assimilation and financial costs, it is doubtful that any of these countries will succeed in joining.

From customs union to common market

The EU is clearly a customs union. It has common external tariffs and no internal tariffs. But is it also a common market? For many years, there have been *certain* common economic policies.

Common Agricultural Policy (CAP).   The Union has traditionally set common high prices for farm products. This has involved charging variable import duties to bring foreign food imports up to EU prices and intervention to buy up surpluses of food produced within the EU at these above-equilibrium prices (see section 3.4). Although the main method of support has shifted to providing subsidies (or 'income support') unrelated to current output, this still represents a *common* economic policy.

Regional policy.   EU regional policy provides grants to firms and local authorities in relatively deprived regions of the Union (see Case Study 23.14 on the student website).

Competition policy.   EU policy here has applied primarily to companies operating in more than one member state (see section 14.1). For example, Article 101 of the Treaty of Lisbon prohibits agreements between firms operating in more than one EU country (e.g. over pricing or sharing out markets) which adversely affect competition in trade between member states (see page 424–5).

Harmonisation of taxation.   VAT is the standard form of indirect tax throughout the EU. However, there are substantial differences in VAT rates between member states, as there are with other tax rates.

 What would be the economic effects of (a) different rates of VAT, (b) different rates of personal income tax and (c) different rates of company taxation between member states if there were no other barriers to trade or factor movements?

Social policy.   In 1989 the European Commission presented a *social charter* to the heads of state. This spelt out a series of worker and social rights that should apply in all member states (see Case Study 24.9 on the student website). These rights were grouped under 12 headings covering areas such as the guarantee of decent levels of income for both the employed and the non-employed, freedom of movement of labour between member countries, freedom to belong to a trade union and equal treatment of men and women in the labour market. However, the charter was only a recommendation and each element had to be approved separately by the European Council of Ministers.

The social chapter of the Maastricht Treaty (1991) attempted to move the Community forward in implementing the details of the social charter in areas such as maximum hours, minimum working conditions, health and safety protection, information and consultation of workers, and equal opportunities.

 Would the adoption of improved working conditions necessarily lead to higher labour costs per unit of output?

Despite these various common policies, in other respects the Community of the 1970s and 1980s was far from a true common market: there were all sorts of non-tariff barriers such as high taxes on wine by non-wine-producing countries, special regulations designed to favour domestic producers, governments giving contracts to domestic producers (e.g. for defence equipment), and so on.

The category often cited by businesses as being the most important single barrier was that of regulations and norms. In some cases, the regulations merely added to the costs of imports. But in the cases of many mechanical engineering and telecommunications products, technical and health and safety regulations sometimes ruled out foreign imports altogether.

Moves towards a single market

The Single European Act of 1986, which came into force in July 1987, sought to remove these barriers and to form a genuine common market by the end of 1992 (see Box 24.10).

One of the most crucial aspects of the Act was its acceptance of the principle of **mutual recognition**. This is the

---

Definition

Mutual recognition The EU principle that one country's rules and regulations must apply throughout the EU. If they conflict with those of another country, individuals and firms should be able to choose which to obey.

principle whereby if a firm or individual is permitted to do something under the rules and regulations of *one* EU country, it must also be permitted to do it in all other EU countries. This means that firms and individuals can choose the country's rules that are least constraining.

Mutual recognition also means that individual governments can no longer devise special rules and regulations that keep out competitors from other EU countries (see Box 24.9). Here was the answer to the dilemma of how to get all EU countries to agree to common sets of rules and regulations. All that was required was that they recognised the rules and regulations applying in each other's countries. However, there was a danger that governments would end up competing against each other to provide the lightest set of regulations in order to attract firms to invest in their country. This could be to the detriment of consumers and workers.

Thus *some* common sets of rules and regulations were still required. One other feature of the Single European Act helped here. This was the institution of *majority* voting in questions of harmonisation of rules and regulations. Previously, unanimous approval had been necessary. This had meant that an individual country could veto the dismantling of barriers. This new system of majority voting, however, does not currently apply to the harmonisation of taxes, although the European Commission continues to propose that majority voting be extended to taxation while recognising that 'there is no need for across the board harmonisation' of taxes.

The benefits and costs of the single market

It is difficult to quantify the benefits and costs of the single market, given that many occur over a long period, and it is hard to know to what extent the changes that are taking place are the direct result of the single market.

One study conducted in 1998 did, nevertheless, estimate the benefits in terms of increased consumption (see Table 24.6). This found that the benefits to the smaller, lower-income countries, such as Portugal and Greece, were the greatest. Such estimates, however, do depend crucially on the assumptions made and are thus open to substantial error.

Then in 2012, the European Commission published *20 Years of the European Single Market*. This stated that, 'The GDP of the EU27 was 2.13% – or €233 billion – higher in 2008 than it would have been without the Single Market. This can be equated to around €500 extra in income per EU citizen. Between 1992 and 2008, the Single Market helped to create 2.77 million new jobs.'

Even though the precise magnitude of the benefits is difficult to estimate, it is possible to identify the *types* of benefit that have resulted, many of which have been substantial.

Trade creation. The expansion of trade within the EU has reduced both prices and costs, as countries have been able to exploit their comparative advantage. Member countries have specialised further in those goods and services that they can produce at a comparatively low opportunity cost.

KI 39
p760

Or when is a liqueur not a liqueur?

Crème de Cassis is an alcoholic blackcurrant drink made by the French firm Cassis de Dijon. Added to white wine, it makes the drink kir. It is not just the French who like drinking kir; it is also, among others, the Germans. In this seemingly innocent fact lay the seeds for the dismantling of some of the most serious trade barriers in Europe!

The story starts back in 1978. The West German company Rewe Zentral AG wanted to import Cassis, but found that under West German law it could not. The problem was that Cassis does not contain enough alcohol to be classed as a liqueur, and it also fell outside any other category of alcoholic drink that was permitted by West German law.

But Rewe was not to be put off. It started legal proceedings in Europe to challenge the German law. The basis of Rewe's case was that this law discriminated against non-German companies. After much legal wrangling, the European Court of Justice in Luxembourg ruled that Germany had no right to prevent the importation of a product that was legitimately on sale in another member country (i.e. France). The only exceptions to this ruling would be if the product was barred for reasons of consumer protection, health or fair trade. None of these applied to Cassis, so the Germans can

now drink kir to their hearts' content without having to become smugglers.

But what of the implications of the case? These are enormous and were spelt out in the Single European Act: 'the Council may decide that provisions in force in a member state must be recognised as being equivalent to those applied by another'. In other words, individuals and firms can choose which country's sets of regulations suit them the best and then insist that they be applied in *all* member states.

'Mutual recognition' of each other's laws tends to lead to deregulation, as people choose those countries' laws that give them the greatest freedom. This appeals to economic and political liberals. Equally, it worries those who argue that regulations and laws on industrial standards have been instituted for a purpose, and should not be undone just because some other member country has not been wise enough to institute them itself.

 How has the Cassis de Dijon ruling affected the balance of power in the EU between (a) individual states and the EU as a whole; (b) governments and the courts?

BOX 24.10 FEATURES OF THE SINGLE MARKET

Since 1 January 1993 trade within the EU has operated very much like trade within a country. In theory, it should be no more difficult for a firm in Marseilles to sell its goods in Berlin than in Paris. At the same time, the single market allows free movement of labour and involves the use of common technical standards.

The features of the single market are summed up in two European Commission publications.[1] They are:

- Elimination of border controls on goods within the EU: no more long waits.
- Free movement of people across borders.
- Common security arrangements.
- No import taxes on goods bought in other member states for personal use.
- The right for everyone to live in another member state.
- Recognition of vocational qualifications in other member states: engineers, accountants, medical practitioners, teachers and other professionals able to practise throughout Europe.
- Technical standards brought into line, and product tests and certification agreed across the whole EU.
- Common commercial laws – making it attractive to form Europe-wide companies and to start joint ventures.
- Public contracts to supply equipment and services to state organisations now open to tenders across the EU.

So what does the single market mean for individuals and for businesses?

Individuals

Before 1993, if you were travelling in Europe you had a 'duty-free allowance'. This meant that you could only take goods up to the value of €600 across borders within the EU without having to pay VAT in the country into which you were importing them. Now you can take as many goods as you like from one EU country to another, provided they are for your own consumption. But to prevent fraud, member states may ask for evidence that the goods have been purchased for the traveller's own consumption if they exceed specified amounts.

Individuals have the right to live and work in any other member state. Qualifications obtained in one member state must be recognised by other member states.

Firms

Before 1993 all goods traded in the EU were subject to VAT at every internal border. This involved some 60 million customs clearance documents at a cost of some €70 per consignment.[2]

This has all now disappeared. Goods can cross from one member state to another without any border controls: in fact, the concepts of 'importing' and 'exporting' within the EU no longer officially exist. All goods sent from one EU country to another will be charged VAT only in the country of destination. They are exempt from VAT in the country where they are produced.

One of the important requirements for fair competition in the single market is the convergence of tax rates. Although income tax rates, corporate tax rates and excise duties still differ between member states, there has been some narrowing in the range of VAT rates. Higher rates of VAT on luxury goods were abolished and countries are allowed to have no more than two lower rates of at least 5 per cent on 'socially necessary' goods, such as food and water supply.

There is now a lower limit of 15 per cent on the standard rate of VAT. Actual rates in January 2017 nonetheless varied from 17 per cent in Luxembourg to 27 per cent in Hungary. However, during the early 2010s several countries, including the UK, Ireland, Greece and Portugal increased their standard rate of VAT as a means of reducing their budget deficits (see sections 22.2 and 22.4). One effect of this is that the vast majority of EU countries now have a standard rate of VAT between 20 and 25 per cent.

 In what ways would competition be 'unfair' if VAT rates differed widely between member states?

1 *A Single Market for Goods* (Commission of the European Communities, 1993); *10 Key Points about the Single European Market* (Commission of the European Communities, 1992).
2 *A Single Market for Goods* (Commission of the European Communities, 1993).

Table 24.6	Gains from the single market

Countries	Extra consumption as % of GDP
France, Germany, UK, Italy	2–3
Denmark	2–5
Netherlands, Spain	3–4
Belgium, Luxembourg	4–5
Ireland	4–10
Greece	5–16
Portugal	19–20

Source: C. Allen, M. Gasiorek and A. Smith, 'The competition effects of the single market in Europe', *Economic Policy* (1998).

Reduction in the direct costs of barriers. This category includes administrative costs, border delays and technical regulations. Their abolition or harmonisation has led to substantial cost savings, shorter delivery times and a larger choice of suppliers.

Economies of scale. With industries based on a Europe-wide scale, many firms can now be large enough, and their plants large enough, to gain the full potential economies of scale (see Box 6.9 on pages 174–5). Yet the whole European market is large enough for there still to be adequate competition. Such gains have varied from industry to industry depending on the minimum efficient scale of a plant or firm. Economies of scale have also been gained from mergers and other forms of industrial restructuring.

Greater competition. Increased competition between firms has led to lower costs, lower prices and a wider range of products available to consumers. This has been particularly so in newly liberalised service sectors such as transport, financial services, telecommunications and broadcasting. In the long run, greater competition can stimulate greater innovation, a greater flow of technical information and the reorganisation ('rationalisation') of production to increase efficiency.

Despite these gains, the single market has not received universal welcome within the EU. Its critics argue that, in a Europe of oligopolies, unequal ownership of resources, rapidly changing technologies and industrial practices, and factor immobility, the removal of internal barriers to trade has merely exaggerated the problems of inequality and economic power. More specifically, the following criticisms are made.

Radical economic change is costly. Substantial economic change is necessary to achieve the full economies of scale and efficiency gains from a single European market. These changes necessarily involve redundancies – from bankruptcies, takeovers, rationalisation and the introduction of new technology. The severity of this structural and technological unemployment depends on (a) the pace of economic change and (b) the mobility of labour – both occupational and geographical. Clearly, the more integrated markets become across the EU, the less the costs of *future* change.

Adverse regional multiplier effects. Firms are likely to locate as near as possible to the 'centre of gravity' of their markets and sources of supply. The geographical expansion of firms' markets to potentially encompass the whole of the EU can tend to attract capital and jobs away from the edges of the Union to its geographical centre.

In an ideal market situation, areas like the south of Italy or Portugal, should attract resources from other parts of the Union. Since they are relatively depressed areas, wage rates and land prices are lower. The resulting lower industrial costs should encourage firms to move into the areas. In practice, regional multiplier effects may worsen the problem (see page 741). As capital and labour (and especially young and skilled workers) leave the extremities of the Union, so these regions are likely to become more depressed. If, as a result, their infrastructure is neglected, they then become even less attractive to new investment.

 Has the problem of adverse regional multiplier effects been made better or worse by the adoption of a single European currency? (This issue is explored in section 26.3.) (Clue: without a single currency, how would the devaluation of the drachma (the former Greek currency) have affected a depressed Greek economy?)

The development of monopoly/oligopoly power. The free movement of capital can encourage the development of giant 'Euro-firms' with substantial economic power. Indeed, recent years have seen some very large European mergers (see Box 9.4 on pages 262–3). This can lead to higher, not lower, prices and less choice for the consumer. It all depends on just how effective competition is, and how effective EU competition policy is in preventing monopolistic and collusive practices.

Trade diversion. Just as increased trade creation has been a potential advantage from completing the internal market, so trade diversion has been a possibility too. This is more likely if *external* barriers remain high (or are even increased) and internal barriers are *completely* abolished.

 Is trade diversion more likely or less likely in the following cases? (a) European producers gain monopoly power in world trade. (b) Modern developments in technology and communications reduce the differences in production costs associated with different locations. (c) The development of the internal market produces substantial economies of scale in many industries.

Perhaps the biggest objection raised against the single European market is a political one: the loss of national sovereignty. Governments find it much more difficult to intervene at a microeconomic level in their own economies. This was one of the key arguments in the debate over the Britain's future within Europe in the run-up to the EU referendum in 2016 (see section 24.5).

Why may the newer members of the Union have the most to gain from the single market, but also the most to lose?

Completing the internal market

Despite the reduction in barriers, the internal market is still not 'complete'. In other words, various barriers to trade between member states still remain. Thus, in June 1997, an Action Plan was adopted by the European Council. Its aim was to ensure that all barriers were dismantled by the launch of the euro in January 1999.

In 1997, what is now known as Single Market Scoreboard was established to monitor the progress in dismantling trade barriers. This is now published annually and shows progress towards the total abandonment of any forms of internal trade restrictions (see Case Study 24.11 on the student website). It shows the percentage of EU Single Market Directives still to be transposed into national law. To counteract new barriers, the EU periodically issues new Directives. If this process is more rapid than that of the transposition of existing Directives into national law, the transposition deficit increases.

In addition to giving each country's 'transposition deficit', the Scoreboard identifies the number of infringements of the internal market that have taken place. The hope is that the 'naming and shaming' of countries will encourage them to make more rapid progress towards totally free trade within the EU.

In 1997, the average transposition deficit of member countries was 6.3 per cent. By 1999, this had fallen to 3.5 per cent and by 2016 to 0.7 per cent. However, by the beginning of 2017 it had risen 1.5 per cent. But this was largely due to an exceptional number of new directives waiting to be transposed and the deficit was expected to return to between 0.5 and 0.7 per cent. Despite this success, national governments have continued to introduce *new* technical standards, several of which have had the effect of erecting new barriers to trade. Also, infringements of single market rules by governments have not always been dealt with. The net result is that, although trade is much freer today than in the early 1990s, especially given the transparency of pricing with the euro, there still do exist various barriers, especially to the free movement of goods.

 If there have been clear benefits from the single market programme, why do individual member governments still try to erect barriers, such as new technical standards?

The effect of the new member states

Given the very different nature of the economies of many of the new entrants to the EU, and their lower levels of GDP per head, their potential gain from membership has been substantial. The gains come through trade creation, increased competition, technological transfer and inward investment, both from other EU countries and from outside the EU.

A study in 2004 concluded that Poland's GDP would rise by 3.4 per cent and Hungary's by almost 7 per cent.[4] Real wages would rise, with those of unskilled workers rising faster than those of skilled workers, in accordance with these countries' comparative advantage. There would also be benefits for the existing 15 EU countries from increased trade and investment, as well as cheaper inputs, but these would be relatively minor in comparison to the gains to the new members.

A European Commission Report produced in April 2009, five years after the enlargement,[5] found that the expansion had been a win–win situation for both old and new members. There had been significant improvements in the standard of living in new member states and they had benefited from modernisation of their economies and more stabilised institutions and laws. In addition, enterprises in old member states had enjoyed opportunities for new investment and exports, and there had been an overall increase in trade and competition between the member states.

When Lithuania adopted the euro in 2015 the number of countries using the euro had reached 19. Hence, in future years trade within the EU is likely to continue to grow as a proportion of GDP. We examine the benefits and costs of the single currency and the whole process of economic and monetary union in the EU in section 26.2.

4 M. Maliszewska, 'Benefits of the single market expansion for current and new member states', *Studia i Analizy* (Centrum Analiz Spoleczno – Ekonomicznych, 2004).
5 'Five years of an enlarged EU – economic achievements and challenges', *European Economy 1 2009* (Commission of the European Communities).

Section summary

1. The European Union is a customs union in that it has common external tariffs and no internal ones. But virtually from the outset it has also had elements of a common market, particularly in the areas of agricultural policy, regional policy, monopoly and restrictive practice policy, and to some extent in the areas of tax harmonisation and social policy.

2. Nevertheless, there have been substantial non-tariff barriers to trade within the EU, such as different tax rates, various regulations over product quality, licensing, state procurement policies, educational qualification requirements, financial barriers, various regulations and norms, and subsidies or tax relief to domestic producers.

3. The Single European Act of 1987 sought to sweep away these restrictions and to establish a genuine free market within the EU: to establish a full common market. Benefits from completing the internal market have included trade creation, cost savings from no longer having to administer barriers, economies of scale for firms now able to operate on a Europe-wide scale, and greater competition leading to reduced costs and prices, greater flows of technical information and more innovation.

4. Critics of the single market point to various changes in industrial structure that have resulted, bringing problems of redundancies and closures. They also point to adverse regional multiplier effects as resources are attracted to the geographical centre of the EU, to possible problems of market power with the development of giant 'Euro-firms', and to the possibilities of trade diversion.

5. The actual costs and benefits of EU membership to the various countries vary with their particular economic circumstances – for example, the extent to which they gain from trade creation, or lose from adverse regional multiplier effects – and with their contributions to and receipts from the EU budget.

6. These cost and benefits in the future will depend on just how completely the barriers to trade are removed, on the extent of monetary union and on any further enlargements to the Union.

24.5 THE UK AND BREXIT

On 23 June 2016, the UK held a referendum on whether to remain a member of the EU. By a majority of 51.9 per cent to 48.1 per cent of the 72.1 per cent of the electorate who voted, Britain voted to leave the EU.

In the run-up to the vote there was heated debate on the merits and costs of membership and of leaving ('Brexit'). Although many of the arguments were concerned with sovereignty, security and other political factors, many of the arguments centred on whether there would be a net *economic* gain from either remaining or leaving.

However, as we have previously discussed, assessing the benefits of membership of customs unions and, in this case, of the EU is fraught with difficulties. Hence, forecasting the economic impact of the decision is difficult. The effects of either remaining or leaving were likely to be very different in the long run from the short run and, of course, long-run forecasts are highly unreliable as the economy is likely to be affected by so many unpredictable events.

Nonetheless, the tools of economics provide a framework in which we can discuss the *potential* economic benefits and costs of the UK's membership of the European Union as compared with the alternatives outside the EU.

Alternative trading arrangements

An analysis of the longer-term economic effects of the UK leaving the European Union depend on the nature of its future trading relationship with the EU. Three main possibilities were suggested.

The first was 'the Norwegian model', where Britain leaves the EU, but joins the European Economic Area (EEA), giving access to the single market, but removing regulation in some key areas, such as fisheries and home affairs.

The second possibility is the negotiation of bilateral agreements. These fall under three types:

- 'The Swiss model' where the UK negotiates a series of bilateral agreements with the EU, including selective or general access to the single market.
- 'The Canadian model' where the UK forms a comprehensive trade agreement with the EU to lower customs tariffs and other barriers to trade.
- 'The Turkish model' where the UK forms a customs union with the EU. In Turkey's case the agreement relates principally to manufactured goods.

At the extreme, the UK could make a complete break from the EU and simply use its membership of the WTO to make trade agreements. Table 24.7 summarises the possible alternative trading relationships between the UK and the EU.

Of these alternatives, the most likely seems a 'hard Brexit', which means leaving both the single market and the customs union. Indeed, in a speech in January 2017, the Prime Minister, Theresa May, stated that the UK 'cannot possibly' remain in the single market, as that would mean 'not leaving the EU at all. So we do not seek membership of the Single market. Instead, we seek the greatest possible access to it through a new, comprehensive, bold and ambitious 'Free Trade Agreement'.[6]

After the triggering of Article 50 in March 2017 (which begins formal Brexit talks), the EU negotiators also made clear that leaving the EU means sacrificing the right of access to the single market and customs union. What is more, any trade deals between the UK and the EU could only be considered once the terms of the 'divorce' settlement had been finalised.

Long-term growth, trade and Brexit

The effects of the decision to leave the EU will take many years to become clear. Many of these effects will depend on the impact that the decision has for the UK's long-term rate of growth. In Chapter 23 we saw that long-term growth requires continuous increases in potential output. Hence, a longer-term analysis of the vote to leave can be expected to focus on its impact on the economy's productive potential.

The important point here is that for most countries it is important to consider their long-term growth and well-being within the context of a global economy with markedly greater levels of openness and trade flows than in the past.

TC 14 p458

Since the UK joined the EU in 1973 the openness of the UK economy has increased rapidly. Figure 24.15 shows the ratio of the total flow of imports and exports of goods and services to GDP since the 1970s. Over this period the ratio has doubled from 30 per cent to 60 per cent.

Adverse effects of Brexit

In its 2016 analysis of the possible long-term implications of Brexit, the UK Treasury argued that the country's openness to trade and investment had been a key factor behind the growth in the economy's potential output.[7] Hence, maintaining this openness, it argued, would be important for long-term growth and so for raising living standards. Positive supply-side effects from openness might include:

KI 39 p760

- Increasing *market opportunities* which enable firms to exploit internal economies of scale (see pages 162–4 and 759).
- Increasing *competition* encourages firms to improve their productivity to maintain their market share and so encourages the adoption of new technologies and processes.
- *Technology transfer.* Technological know-how can be passed between firms in international supply chains,

6 Speech given by Theresa May at Lancaster House, 17 January 2017.

7 *EU Referendum: HM Treasury analysis key facts* (HM Treasury, 18 April 2016), www.gov.uk/government/news/eu-referendum-treasury-analysis-key-facts

Table 24.7 Alternative trading relationships with the EU

		Tariffs	Customs union and external trade	Non-tariff barriers/other policy and regulatory issues
EU membership		Full tariff-free trade	Common external tariffs No customs costs Access to EU Free Trade Agreements (FTAs)	Alignment of regulations, standards and specifications Non-discriminatory access for markets for services
EEA (Norway)		Some tariffs on agriculture and fisheries	Custom costs apply No access to EU Free Trade Agreements (FTAs)	Limited coverage of agricultural and fisheries Compliance with most EU rules and standards, including free movement of people and social policy
Bilateral agreements	Switzerland	Some tariffs on agriculture	Custom costs apply No access to EU Free Trade Agreements (FTAs)	Minimises non-tariff barriers in areas covered by agreements Limited coverage of services No financial services passport Complies with EU rules in sector covered by agreements, including free movement of people and social policy
	Canada	Some tariffs on agriculture Tariffs for transitional period on manufactured goods	Custom costs apply No access to EU Free Trade Agreements (FTAs)	No financial services passport Compliance with EU standards for firms importing into EU
	Turkey	Tariff exemptions apply only to manufactured goods and processed agricultural goods	No custom costs for manufactured goods Align external trade policy with EU	No financial services passport No special access for services Adopts EU product standards Compliance with environmental standards linked to goods and to rules on competition and state aid
WTO membership		EU external tariffs apply	Custom costs apply No access to EU Free Trade Agreements (FTAs)	No financial services passport Compliance with EU standards for firms importing into EU

Source: Adapted from *EU Referendum: HM Treasury analysis key facts*, HM Treasury, 18 April 2016, www.gov.uk/government/news/eu-referendum-treasury-analysis-key-facts

Figure 24.15 UK trade in goods and services as a percentage of GDP

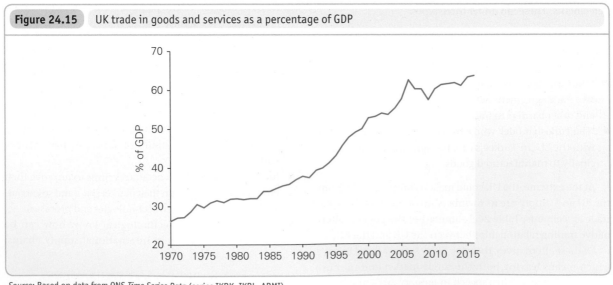

Source: Based on data from ONS *Time Series Data* (series IKBK, IKBL, ABMI).

through internationally mobile workers or new international entrants.

The Treasury's analysis attempted to estimate the average impact on households of the UK leaving the EU by modelling the adverse impacts on the supply-side of the economy from lower levels of openness. To do so it considered three new relationships with the EU (see Table 24.7) and annual losses 15 years after leaving. With a Norwegian-type deal, households would be £2600 worse off each year; a Swiss deal would lead to a £4300 annual loss of GDP per household and a complete exit would create a household loss per annum of £5200. It found that tax receipts would be lower and that the overall benefit to the UK of being in the EU, relative to another arrangement, would be between 3.4 per cent and 9.5 per cent of GDP, depending on the exact 'new deal'.

The OECD suggested that Brexit would be like a tax, pushing up the costs and weakening the economy. Its analysis indicated that by 2020, GDP would be at least 3 per cent lower than it otherwise would have been, making households £2200 worse off. By 2030, these figures would be 5 per cent and £3200. It continues that:

> In the longer term, structural impacts would take hold through the channels of capital, immigration and lower technical progress. In particular, labour productivity would be held back by a drop in foreign direct investment and a smaller pool of skills. The extent of forgone GDP would increase over time . . . The effects would be even larger in a more pessimistic scenario and remain negative even in the optimistic scenario.[8]

The OECD analysis points to the *structural change* the UK economy will experience. The growth in openness experienced by the UK economy has occurred within the context of EU membership. Membership has influenced the patterns of trade and investment. It has provided the framework in which businesses have operated – for example, the development of supply chains across EU member countries. Structural changes accompanying Brexit, the OECD argued, would have negative supply-side effects.

 Can we incorporate trade effects into endogenous growth models?

Opportunities from Brexit

Despite the pessimistic forecasts from the vast majority of economists about a British exit, there was a group of eight economists in favour of Brexit.[9] They claimed that leaving the EU would lead to a stronger economy, with higher GDP, a faster growth in real wages, lower unemployment and a smaller gap between imports and exports. The main argument to support the claims was that the UK would be more able to pursue trade creation freed from various EU rules and regulations. In other words, there would be positive supply-side effects.

While disagreement about the impact on the UK's exit from the EU was to be expected, there was agreement that these effects would work primarily through their impact on the supply-side.

However, perhaps less clear was the likely *distributional* effects of the UK's exit. While openness and its associated movements in people, goods, services and capital impact on an economy's productive capabilities, there can be significant distributional effects too. Trade can impact on different sectors differently. Consequently, a more complete analysis of Brexit or of trading relationships more generally needs to take account of the possible distributional effects.

 What particular sectors might a distributional analysis of the impact of trade consider?

---

8 *The Economic Consequences of Brexit: A taxing decision* (OECD, 25 April 2016), www.oecd.org/economy/the-economic-consequences-of-brexit-a-taxing-decision.htm

9 www.economistsforbrexit.co.uk (now Economists for Free Trade: www.economistsforfreetrade.com/)

Section summary

1. Following a referendum in June 2016 the UK voted to leave the European Union. The longer-term economic effects for the UK were expected to depend crucially on the nature of its future trading relationship with the EU.

2. Much of the economic analysis of Brexit has focused on the long-term implications for growth and living standards. Economic theory gives us a framework through which we can analyse the possible supply-side effects of Brexit.

3. Economists have largely argued that the decision to leave would result in negative supply-side effects. Brexit, they argue, would impede cross-border trade with its EU's partners and so reduce the UK's openness to trade and investment. This then adversely affects productivity growth and so living standards.

4. Some economists, however, have argued that outside of the EU the UK would be free of EU rules and regulations and would be able to create trade. The supply-side benefits would help to raise long-term growth and living standards.

5. Trade and the openness of economies has distributional effects. A more complete economic assessment of Brexit therefore requires that we take into account such effects.

END OF CHAPTER QUESTIONS

1. Imagine that two countries, Richland and Poorland, can produce just two goods, computers and coal. Assume that for a given amount of land and capital, the output of these two products requires the following constant amounts of labour:

	Richland	Poorland
1 computer	2	4
100 tonnes of coal	4	5

Assume that each country has 20 million workers.

(a) Draw the production possibility curves for the two countries (on two separate diagrams).

(b) If there is no trade, and in each country 12 million workers produce computers and 8 million workers produce coal, how many computers and tonnes of coal will each country produce? What will be the total production of each product?

(c) What is the opportunity cost of a computer in (i) Richland; (ii) Poorland?

(d) What is the opportunity cost of 100 tonnes of coal in (i) Richland; (ii) Poorland?

(e) Which country has a comparative advantage in which product?

(f) Assuming that price equals marginal cost, which of the following would represent possible exchange ratios?
   (i)   1 computer for 40 tonnes of coal;
   (ii) 2 computers for 140 tonnes of coal;
   (iii) 1 computer for 100 tonnes of coal;
   (iv) 1 computer for 60 tonnes of coal;
   (v)   4 computers for 360 tonnes of coal.

(g) Assume that trade now takes place and that a computer exchanges for 65 tonnes of coal. Both countries specialise completely in the product in which they have a comparative advantage. How much does each country produce of its respective product?

(h) The country producing computers sells 6 million domestically. How many does it export to the other country?

(i) How much coal does the other country consume?

(j) Construct a table like Table 24.4 to show the no-trade and with-trade positions of each country.

2. If capital moves from developed to less developed countries, and labour moves from less developed to developed countries, what effects will these factor movements have on wage rates and the return on capital in the two types of country?

3. What factors determine a country's terms of trade?

4. Go through each of the arguments for restricting trade (both those of general validity and those having some validity for specific countries) and provide a counter-argument for not restricting trade.

5. If countries are so keen to reduce the barriers to trade, why do many countries frequently attempt to erect barriers?

6. What factors will determine whether a country's joining a customs union will lead to trade creation or trade diversion?

7. Why is it difficult to estimate the magnitude of the benefits of completing the internal market of the EU?

8. Look through the costs and benefits that we identified from the completion of the internal market. Do the same costs and benefits arise from the enlarged EU of 27 members?

9. Consider the process of Brexit negotiations since the triggering of Article 50 (to leave the EU) at the end of March 2017. What model of trade relations with the EU27 is likely to be the end result of the negotiations?

10. Is a 'hard Brexit' (reverting to WTO rules and negotiating bilateral trade deals) necessarily an inferior alternative for the UK to remaining in the European single market or, at least, in the customs union?

Online resources

Additional case studies on the student website

24.1 David Ricardo and the law of comparative advantage. The original statement of the law of comparative advantage by David Ricardo back in 1817.

24.2 The Uruguay round. An examination of the negotiations that led to substantial cuts in trade barriers.

24.3 The World Trade Organization. This looks at the various opportunities and threats posed by this major international organisation.

24.4 The Battle of Seattle. This looks at the protests against the WTO at Seattle in November 1999 and considers the arguments for and against the free trade policies of the WTO.

24.5 Banana, banana. The dispute between the USA and the EU over banana imports.

24.6 Steel barriers. This examines the use of tariffs by the George W. Bush administration in 2002 to protect the ailing US steel industry.

24.7 Assessing NAFTA. Who are the winners and losers from NAFTA?

24.8 Strategic trade theory. The case of Airbus.

24.9 The social dimension of the EU. The principles of the social charter.

24.10 **The benefits of the single market.** Evidence of achievements and the Single Market Action Plan of 1997.

24.11 **The internal market scoreboard.** Keeping a tally on progress to a true single market.

Websites relevant to this chapter

Numbers and sections refer to websites listed in the Web Appendix and hotlinked from this book's website at **www.pearsoned.co.uk/sloman.**

- For news articles relevant to this chapter, see the *Economics News* section on the student website.
- For general news on international trade, see websites in section A, and particularly A1–5, 7–9, 21, 23, 24, 25, 31. See also links to newspapers worldwide in A38, 39, 42, 43 and 44, and the news search feature in Google at A41.
- For international data on imports and exports, see site H16 > *Documents, data and resources* > *Statistics*. See also *World Economic Outlook* in H4. The ESDS International site (B35) has links to World Bank, IMF, OECD, UN and Eurostat datasets (but you will need to register, which is free to all UK higher education students).
- For UK data, see site B1 (site 1). See also B34. For EU data, see B38 > *Foreign trade and current balance*; see also B47 (Ameco online) sections 10 and 11.
- For discussion papers on trade, see H4 and 7.
- For trade disputes, see H16.
- For various pressure groups critical of the effects of free trade and globalisation, see H13, 14.
- For information on various preferential trading arrangements, see H20–23.
- For EU sites relating to trade, see G7, 8, 13, 20, 21, 22.
- For student resources relevant to this chapter, see sites C1–7, 9, 10, 19.

Australia	Dollar	1.4036	1.746...
China	Yuan	9.214	12.09...
East Carib.	Dollar	3.7042	5.151...
Hungary	Forint	272.78	360.8...
Japan	Yen	116.40	144.6...
Maldives	Rufiyaa	23.148	29.10...

25 Chapter

The Balance of Payments and Exchange Rates

We live in a world in which events in one country or group of countries can have profound effects on other countries. Look at what happened in 2007/8. Excessive sub-prime mortgage lending in the USA led to huge losses for many financial institutions. With such debt securitised into bonds held by financial institutions across the world, the credit crunch rapidly became global.

As globalisation has increased, with trade and international financial movements having grown much more rapidly than countries' GDP, and, in general, having become much freer, so countries' vulnerability to balance of payments problems and exchange rate fluctuations has increased.

This chapter explores the relationships between a country's balance of payments and its exchange rate. In particular, we ask whether a country should allow its exchange rate to be determined entirely by market forces, with the possible instability that this brings, or whether it should attempt to fix its exchange rate to another currency (such as the US dollar), or at the very least attempt to reduce exchange rate fluctuations through central bank intervention in the foreign exchange market. We also look at the experience of countries in operating different types of exchange rate system.

25.1 ALTERNATIVE EXCHANGE RATE REGIMES

Policy objectives: internal and external

A country is likely to have various **internal** and **external** **policy objectives**. *Internal* objectives include such things as economic growth, low unemployment and low inflation. *External* objectives include such things as avoiding current account balance of payments deficits, encouraging international trade and preventing excessive exchange rate fluctuations. Internal and external objectives may come into conflict, however.

A simple illustration of potential conflict is with the objectives of *internal balance* and *external balance*.

Internal balance. This is where the economy is at the potential level of national income: i.e. where the output gap is zero (see Box 15.3 on page 460). This can be expressed in various ways, depending on the model of the economy and the policy objectives being pursued.

Thus, in the simple Keynesian model, internal balance is where the economy is at the *full-employment* level of national income: i.e. where Y_e (equilibrium national income) = Y_f (full-employment national income) (see Chapter 17). In the monetarist and new classical models, it would be where the economy is on the vertical Phillips curve with stable inflation. In the context of inflation targeting, it would be where meeting the inflation target is consistent with achieving potential national income: i.e. where the *DAD* crosses the *DAS* curve at the targeted inflation rate (see Figure 20.7 on page 630).

If there is initially internal balance and then aggregate demand falls, in the short run output will fall below the potential level and disequilibrium unemployment will occur. Internal balance will be destroyed. The stickier wages and prices are, the longer it will take for internal balance to be restored.

External balance. This is the term for a *balance of payments* equilibrium. In the context of floating exchange rates, it is normally used in the narrow sense of a current account balance, and therefore also a capital plus financial account balance.

In the context of a fixed exchange rate, or an exchange rate target, it is often used more loosely to refer merely to a *total currency flow balance*. This is where the total demand and supply of the currency are equal at the targeted exchange rate with *no need for intervention from the reserves*: in other words, where any current account deficit is matched by a surplus on the other two accounts, and vice versa.

Conflicts between internal and external balance

It may, however, be difficult to achieve internal and external balance simultaneously. This is illustrated in Figure 25.1. Assume in Figure 25.1(b) that the exchange rate is er_1. Currency demand and supply curves are given by D and S_1 and

there is no central bank intervention. Thus er_1 is the *equilibrium* exchange rate and there is external balance in the loose sense. Assume also that there is external balance in the narrow sense: i.e. a current account balance.

Let us also assume, however, that there is a recession. This is illustrated in Figure 25.1(a). Equilibrium national income is Y_{e_1}, where W_1 equals J_1. There is a deflationary gap: Y_{e_1} is below the full-employment level, Y_F. There is no *internal* balance.

Now assume that the government expands aggregate demand through fiscal policy in order to close the deflationary gap and restore internal balance. It raises injections to J_2 and reduces withdrawals to W_2. National income rises to Y_{e_2}. But this higher national income leads to an increased demand for imports. The supply of sterling will shift to S_2 in Figure 25.1(b). There is now a current account deficit, which destroys external balance in the narrow sense. If the government maintains the exchange rate at er_1 (by buying sterling from the reserves), external balance will be destroyed in the loose sense too.

External balance in the loose sense could be restored by allowing the exchange rate to depreciate to er_2, so that the demand and supply of sterling are equated at the new lower exchange rate.

But will this also correct the current account deficit and restore external balance in the narrow sense? It will go *some* way to correcting the deficit, as the lower exchange rate will make imports relatively more expensive and exports relatively cheaper. The amount that imports fall and exports rise will depend on their price elasticity of demand.

But there may also be an effect on the financial account. The higher aggregate demand will lead to a higher demand for money. This will drive up interest rates unless money supply is allowed to expand to offset the higher demand for money. If interest rates rise, this will lead to an inflow of finance (a financial account surplus). In Figure 25.1(b), the supply curve of sterling would shift to the left and the demand curve to the right. The exchange rate would not

---

Definitions

Internal policy objectives Objectives relating solely to the domestic economy.

External policy objectives Objectives relating to the economy's international economic relationships.

Internal balance Where the equilibrium level of national income is at the desired level.

External balance Narrow definition: where the current account of the balance of payments is in balance (and thus also the capital plus financial accounts). Loose definition: where there is a total currency flow balance at a given exchange rate.

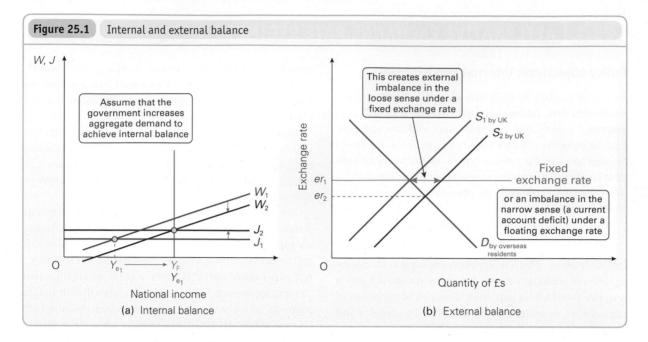

Figure 25.1 Internal and external balance

(a) Internal balance

(b) External balance

therefore fall as far as er_2. If the positive effect of higher interest rates on the financial account was bigger than the negative effect of higher imports on the current account, the exchange rate would actually *appreciate*.

Either way, there will be a current account deficit and an equal and opposite financial plus capital account surplus. Narrow external balance has not been restored in the short term. (We explore the long-term current account balance under floating exchange rates in section 25.3.)

Figure 25.2 shows the effect of various 'shocks' that can affect both internal and narrow external balance.

1. *Assume that there is both internal and narrow external balance. Now assume that as a result of inflation being below target, the central bank cuts interest rates. Into which of the four quadrants in Figure 25.2 will the economy move?*

2. *Imagine that there is an inflationary gap, but a current account equilibrium. Describe what will happen if the government raises interest rates in order to close the inflationary gap. Assume first that there is a fixed exchange rate; then assume that there is a floating exchange rate.*

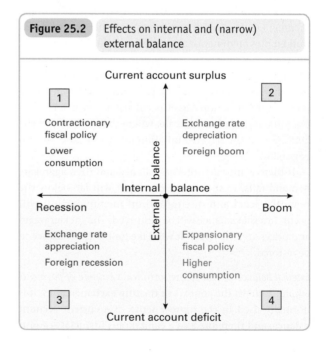

Figure 25.2 Effects on internal and (narrow) external balance

The ability of the economy to correct these imbalances depends on the *exchange rate regime*. We examine alternative exchange rate regimes in the final part of this section, but first we must distinguish between nominal and real exchange rates.

Nominal and real exchange rates

A nominal exchange rate is simply the rate at which one currency exchanges for another. All exchange rates that you see quoted in the newspapers, on television or the Internet, or at travel agents, banks or airports, are nominal rates. Up to this point we have solely considered nominal rates.

The *real exchange rate* is the exchange rate index adjusted for changes in the prices of imports (measured in foreign currencies) and exports (measured in domestic prices): in other words, adjusted for the terms of trade. Thus if a country has a higher rate of inflation for its exports than the weighted average inflation of the imports it buys from other countries, its real exchange rate index (RERI) will rise relative to its nominal exchange rate index (NERI).

TC 13
p453

BOX 25.1	THE BALANCE OF TRADE AND THE PUBLIC-SECTOR BUDGET BALANCE	EXPLORING ECONOMICS

A case of twin deficits?

We have seen that the external situation can affect the ability of an economy to achieve internal balance (where actual income is at the potential level). But it also impacts on the *composition* of aggregate demand. This is most readily demonstrated by observing the relationship between the *public sector's budget balance* and *the balance of trade*.

Consider the circular flow of income model that we introduced in Chapter 15. There we saw that actual (as opposed to planned) withdrawals from the circular flow (net saving (S) plus net taxes (T) plus imports (M)) must equal injections (investment (I) plus government expenditure (G) plus exports (X)):

$$S + T + M = I + G + X \qquad (1)$$

The public sector's budget balance is simply the difference between its receipts (taxation and operating receipts, net of transfer expenditures) and its spending on goods and services, or $T - G$. The balance of trade is the difference between expenditure on exports and imports, or $X - M$. If we rearrange equation (1) slightly we find:

$$(T - G) = (X - M) + (I - S) \qquad (2)$$

This tells us that if the public sector runs a budget surplus ($T - G$ is positive), there is a likelihood that the trade balance will be in surplus too. We can see from equation (2) that this will depend on the extent to which investment (I) and saving (S) differ from each other. In the case where investment and saving are equal, then a budget surplus would be exactly matched by a trade surplus, or a budget deficit by an identical trade deficit. The latter gives rise to the term 'the *twin deficits*'.

The chart plots the UK's public-sector budget balance as measured by public-sector net borrowing (see section 22.1) and its balance of trade. Each is presented as a percentage of GDP.

First, we see that from 1955 to 2016 the public sector typically ran a deficit with public-sector net borrowing averaging 2.8 per cent of GDP. Consequently, the public sector has been acting as a net injector of income. Second, we see that the balance of trade has more often than not been negative, with an average deficit of 0.9 per cent of GDP.

The size of the net withdrawal from the trade deficit does not quite match the net injection from the public sector. This means that private-sector investment expenditure has been *less* than private saving ($I < S$). It also reinforces the arguments that we examined in Chapters 16 and 22 that public-sector deficits can reduce private investment. This is known as *crowding out*. In the UK, public-sector borrowing has been financed partly through foreign borrowing from running a trade deficit and partly from the private saving that is not used for private investment.

 If the exchange rate depreciated, how would this affect the trade and budget balances?

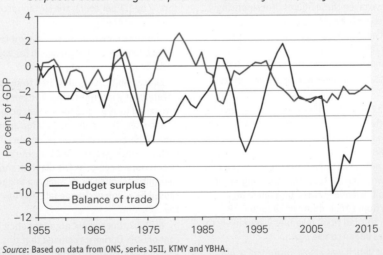

UK public-sector budget surplus and balance of trade, % of GDP

Source: Based on data from ONS, series J5II, KTMY and YBHA.

Definitions

Exchange rate regime The system under which the government allows the exchange rate to be determined.

Real exchange rate A country's exchange rate adjusted for changes in the domestic currency prices of its exports relative to the foreign currency prices of its imports. If a country's prices rise (fall) relative to those of its trading partners, its real exchange rate will rise (fall) relative to the nominal exchange rate.

The real exchange rate index can be defined as:

$$\text{RERI} = \text{NERI} \times P_X/P_M$$

where P_X is the domestic currency price index of exports and P_M is the foreign currencies weighted price index of imports. Thus if (a) a country's inflation is 5 per cent higher than the trade-weighted average of its trading partners (P_X/P_M rises by 5 per cent per year) and (b) its nominal exchange rate depreciates by 5 per cent per year (NERI falls by 5 per cent per year), its real exchange rate index will stay the same.

Take another example: if a country's export prices rise faster than the foreign currency prices of its imports (P_X/P_M rises), its real exchange rate will appreciate relative to its nominal exchange rate.

The real exchange rate thus gives us a better idea of the *quantity* of imports a country can obtain from selling a given quantity of exports. If the real exchange rate rises, the country can get more imports for a given volume of exports.

Figure 25.3 shows the nominal and real exchange rate indices of sterling. As you can see, the real exchange rate has tended to rise over time *relative* to the nominal exchange rate. This is because the UK has often experienced higher rates of inflation than the weighted average of its trading partners.

Table 25.1 shows that the size of the UK's *inflation rate differential* with the eurozone since the 1970s. During this period the UK rate of inflation has typically been 1 percentage point higher than the weighted average of the eurozone economies.

Table 25.1 also shows the average percentage change in the nominal and real sterling exchange rate indices since the 1970s. Over this period the nominal sterling exchange rate index has on average fallen by 1.3 per cent per year. However, after adjusting for the domestic price of exports and the foreign currency price of imports, the real sterling exchange rate index has fallen by 0.4 per cent per year. Hence, since 1970 the UK has experienced a small *real* depreciation of sterling.

 By looking at the nominal and real exchange rate changes in Table 25.1 can we identify periods during which the UK's terms of trade rose?

BOX 25.2 **THE UK'S BALANCE OF PAYMENTS DEFICIT**

A cyclical problem or a long-term trend?

In the late 1980s, the UK current account balance of payments moved sharply into deficit, as the chart shows. In 1989, the current account deficit was 4.1 per cent of GDP – then a historic high. Opinions differed dramatically, however, as to how seriously we should have taken these figures. Not surprisingly, the government claimed that the problem was merely temporary and was not something to cause serious concern. The opposition parties (also not surprisingly) saw the figures as disastrous and a sign that the economy was badly off-course.

So who was correct? In fact there was an element of truth in both these claims.

The government was correct to the extent that the severity of the deficit partly reflected the unprecedented boom of the late 1980s. An average growth rate of real GDP of 4.2 per cent between 1984 and 1988 had led to a huge increase in imports. Since the boom could not be sustained, the growth in imports was bound to slow down. Another factor contributing to the deficit was the fall in oil revenues caused by a fall in oil prices. Oil exports fell from £16.1 billion in 1985 to £5.9 billion in 1989. Again, this fall in oil revenues was unlikely to continue once oil prices began to rise again.

The current account deficit was also a mirror image of the financial account surplus. This had been caused by a rise in interest rates, used to slow the economy down. As short-term finance flowed into the country to take advantage of the higher interest rate, so this drove the exchange rate up: the real exchange rate index rose by 4.25 per cent in 1988 (see Figure 25.3). The higher exchange rate contributed to the fall in exports and the rise in imports.

But the opposition parties were also correct. The severity of the deficit reflected an underlying weakness of the UK's trading position. If the deficit had been merely a cyclical

problem associated with the boom phase of the business cycle, the current account should have gone into *surplus* in the early 1990s as the economy moved into recession. But even in the depths of the recession in 1991 (the economy shrank by 1.1 per cent), the current account deficit was still 1.3 per cent of GDP.

The government, however, sought to place a large portion of the blame on a falling demand for exports as the rest of the world began to move into recession.

Subsequent events appeared to support the Conservative government's interpretation. The world economy was recovering in 1994 and the current account deficit virtually disappeared. But then, with a large appreciation of sterling from 1996, and an even larger appreciation of the real exchange rate (see Figure 25.3), the current account started to deteriorate again, as the diagram shows. Optimists claimed that this was, once more, simply a temporary situation, caused by a high exchange rate and low growth in demand in the eurozone.

By 2007, the current account deficit had reached 3.5 per cent of GDP. Optimists claimed that this was, once more, simply a temporary situation, caused by a high exchange rate and a relatively slower rate of growth in demand in the eurozone. Pessimists once more pointed to underlying supply-side weaknesses, with a deterioration in exports of goods not being matched by a rise in services exports.

With the financial crisis of 2007/8 and the subsequent recession hitting the UK economy particularly badly, the fall in confidence led to a depreciation in the exchange rate. Between October 2007 and October 2013 the sterling effective exchange rate fell in nominal terms by 20 per cent and in real terms by 13.5 per cent.

Table 25.1	Inflation rate differential and annual rate of change in sterling exchange rate indices		
	Inflation rate differential	Nominal exchange rate index	Real exchange rate index
1970–74	0.8	–3.2	–1.6
1975–79	5.8	–4.0	0.3
1980–84	0.1	–0.8	–0.8
1985–89	1.8	–1.3	–0.8
1990–94	0.8	–2.5	–1.5
1995–99	0.5	3.2	3.5
2000–04	–1.1	0.1	–0.6
2005–09	0.2	–4.5	–4.0
2010–14	0.4	1.5	2.7
2015–16	0.3	–2.3	–2.2
1970–2016	1.0	–1.3	–0.4

Note: Inflation rate differential is the difference between the annual % change in GDP deflator in the UK and the weighted average across the Eurozone.
Source: Based on data from *Effective Exchange Rate Indices* (Bank for International Settlements) and series NY.GDP.DEFL.KD.ZG (World Bank).

The real exchange rate also gives a better idea than the nominal exchange rate of how competitive a country is. The lower the real exchange rate, the more competitive will be the country's exports be. For example, Figure 25.3 shows that the UK became less competitive between 1996 and 2001, and remained at similarly uncompetitive levels until 2008, thanks not only to a rise in the nominal exchange rate index, but also to higher inflation than its trading partners.

Alternative exchange rate regimes

There are a number of possible exchange rate regimes. They all lie somewhere between two extremes. These two extreme regimes are a *totally fixed rate* and a *freely floating rate*.

In the case of a *fixed rate*, the government or central bank will almost certainly have to intervene in the foreign exchange market in order to maintain that rate, and will probably have to take internal policy measures too.

In the case of a *freely floating rate*, there is no government intervention in the foreign exchange market. Exchange rates fluctuate according to market forces – according to changes

KI 15 p129

CASE STUDIES AND APPLICATIONS

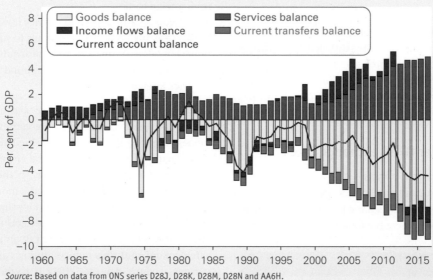

UK balance of payments as a % of GDP, 1960–2016

Legend: Goods balance, Services balance, Income flows balance, Current transfers balance, Current account balance

Source: Based on data from ONS series D28J, D28K, D28M, D28N and AA6H.

But this was not enough to prevent a further deterioration in the current account from 2011. By 2014, the current account deficit had risen to a new historic high: 4.7 per cent of GDP in 2014. By this point the deficit on the balance of trade in *goods* had risen to close to 7 per cent of GDP.

Pessimists again pointed to a much deeper malaise in the UK exporting sector and claimed that successive supply-side reforms had made too little difference. Indeed, recent governments have stressed the need for a 'rebalancing' of the economy towards greater exports and investment.

With the Brexit vote of 2016, the issue gained greater urgency as the government sought to secure trade deals to compensate for a lack of automatic access to the EU single market. With the fall in sterling since the vote, it was hoped that this would, at least, give exporters a price advantage.

So should we worry about balance of payments deficits? What effect do they have on exchange rates, inflation, growth, unemployment, etc.? What should the government do? These are questions we shall look at in this chapter.

| Figure 25.3 | Sterling nominal and real exchange rate indices (Jan 1970 = 100) |

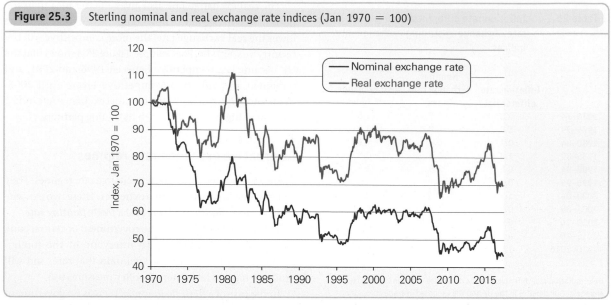

Note: Exchange rate indices are BIS narrow indices comprising 27 countries, re-based by the authors, Jan 1970 = 100.

Source: Based on data from *effective exchange rate indices* (Bank for International Settlements).

in the demand for and supply of currencies on the foreign exchange market. Changes in the exchange rate may well affect internal policy objectives, however, and thus cause the government to take various internal policy measures.

> *What adverse internal effects may follow from (a) a depreciation of the exchange rate; (b) an appreciation of the exchange rate?*

Between these extremes there are a number of **intermediate regimes**, where exchange rates are partly left to the market, but where the government intervenes to influence the rate. These intermediate regimes differ according to how much the government intervenes, and thus according to how much flexibility of the exchange rate it is prepared to allow.

Correction under fixed exchange rates

Foreign exchange intervention

Unless the demand for and supply of the domestic currency on the foreign exchange markets are equal at the fixed rate – unless, in other words, there is a total currency flow balance

---

Definitions

Totally fixed exchange rate Where the government takes whatever measures are necessary to maintain the exchange rate at some stated level.

Freely floating exchange rate Where the exchange rate is determined entirely by the forces of demand and supply in the foreign exchange market with no government intervention whatsoever.

Intermediate exchange rate regimes Where the government intervenes to influence movements in the exchange rate.

– the central bank will have to intervene in the market and buy or sell the domestic currency to make up the difference. This is illustrated in Figure 25.4, which looks at the case of the UK.

Figure 25.4(a) shows the case of a currency flow deficit (an excess of pounds) of an amount $a - b$. The Bank of England thus has to purchase these excess pounds by drawing on its foreign exchange reserves, or by borrowing foreign currency from foreign banks.

In Figure 25.4(b), there is a currency flow surplus of $c - d$. In this case, the Bank of England has to supply $c - d$ additional pounds to the market, and will acquire foreign currencies in exchange. It can use these to build up reserves or to pay back foreign loans.

Foreign exchange market intervention and the money supply. Maintaining a fixed exchange rate causes changes in the money supply. If the rate is maintained above the equilibrium (Figure 25.4(a)), there is a total currency flow deficit. The Bank of England buys pounds. It thereby withdraws them from circulation and reduces the money supply.

The effect of this reduction in money supply is to raise the equilibrium rate of interest. This attracts financial inflows and improves the financial account. It also dampens aggregate demand, and thus reduces imports and improves the current account. The net effect is to reduce the overall currency flow deficit and thus reduce the gap $a - b$ in Figure 25.4(a). The problem here, of course, is that the lower aggregate demand may well result in a recession.

If the rate is maintained *below* equilibrium (Figure 25.4(b)), there is a total currency flow surplus. The Bank of England supplies additional pounds (which are spent by people abroad on UK exports, etc., and are thus injected into the UK economy). It thereby increases the money supply.

The effect of the increased money supply is to reduce interest rates. This worsens the financial account and, by

Figure 25.4 Central bank intervention to maintain a fixed exchange rate

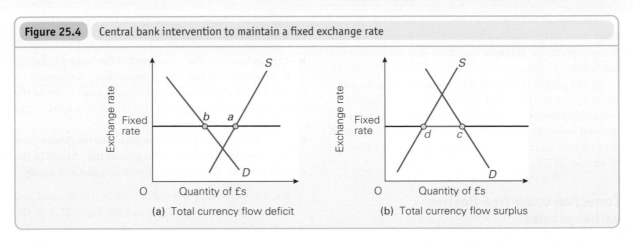

(a) Total currency flow deficit

(b) Total currency flow surplus

boosting aggregate demand, increases imports. The currency flow surplus is reduced. The gap $d - c$ narrows.

Sterilisation. If the Bank of England did not want the money supply to alter, it would have to counter these effects with other monetary measures: e.g. open-market operations. Thus when there is a deficit and money supply falls, the Bank of England could buy back government bonds from the general public, thereby restoring the money supply to its previous level. This will prevent the economy moving into recession.

This process of countering the effects on money supply of a balance of payments deficit or surplus is known as *sterilisation*.

 Describe the open-market operations necessary to sterilise the monetary effects of a balance of payments surplus. Would this in turn have any effect on the current or financial accounts of the balance of payments?

There is a problem with sterilisation, however. If the money supply is not allowed to change, the currency flow deficit or surplus will persist. In the case of a deficit, a recession may be avoided, but the central bank will have to continue using reserves to support the exchange rate. But reserves are not infinite. Sooner or later they will run out! A recession may be inevitable.

Correcting the disequilibrium

If a balance of payments deficit persists, and reserves continue to dwindle or foreign debts mount, the government will have to tackle the underlying disequilibrium. If the exchange rate is to remain fixed, it must shift the demand and supply curves so that they intersect at the fixed exchange rate.

It can use contractionary fiscal and monetary policies for this purpose. Such policies have two main effects on the current account: an income effect (*expenditure reducing*) and a substitution effect between home and foreign goods (*expenditure switching*).

KI 7
p36

Expenditure reducing. Contractionary policy reduces national income. This in turn reduces expenditure, including expenditure on imports, shifting the supply of sterling

curve to the left in Figure 25.4(a). The bigger the marginal propensity to import, the larger the shift.

There is a possible conflict here, however, between external and internal objectives. The balance of payments may improve, but unemployment is likely to rise and the rate of growth to fall.

KI 36
p451

 Under what circumstances would (a) contractionary and (b) expansionary policies cause no conflict between internal and external objectives?

Expenditure switching. If contractionary policies reduce the rate of inflation below that of foreign competitors, exports will become relatively cheaper compared with foreign competing goods and imports will become relatively more expensive compared with home-produced alternatives. Some foreign consumers will switch to UK exports. The more elastic the demand, the bigger the switch. Some UK consumers will switch from imports to home-produced goods. Again, the more elastic the demand, the bigger the switch. Demand in both cases will be more elastic the closer UK goods are as substitutes for foreign goods.

TC 6
p68

To the extent that contractionary policies result in expenditure switching rather than expenditure reducing, so this reduces the conflict between balance of payments and employment objectives.

Definitions

Sterilisation Where the government uses open-market operations or other monetary measures to neutralise the effects of balance of payments deficits or surpluses on the money supply.

Expenditure changing (reducing) from a contraction: the income effect Where contractionary policies lead to a reduction in national income and hence a reduction in the demand for imports.

Expenditure switching from a contraction: the substitution effect Where contractionary policies lead to a reduction in inflation and thus cause a switch in expenditure away from imports and towards exports.

Expenditure switching can also be achieved by placing restrictions on imports (tariffs and/or quotas) or the subsidising of exports. But this would conflict with the objective of free trade.

To the extent that fiscal and monetary policies affect interest rates, so this will affect the financial account of the balance of payments. Higher interest rates will increase the demand for sterling and will thus lead to an improvement on the financial account. (The implications of this are explored in section 25.2.)

Correction under free-floating exchange rates

Freely floating exchange rates should automatically and immediately correct any balance of payments deficit or surplus: by depreciation and appreciation respectively. Foreign exchange dealers simply adjust the exchange rate so as to balance their books – in line with demand and supply.

As with fixed rates, an income effect and a substitution effect of the correction process can be distinguished. But the nature of the income and substitution effects of depreciation/appreciation is quite different from that of deflation. It is only the substitution effect that corrects the disequilibrium. The income effect makes the problem *worse*! First the substitution effect: ***expenditure switching***.

Expenditure switching (the substitution effect)

The process of adjustment. Assume a higher rate of inflation in the UK than abroad. As domestic prices rise relative to the price of imports, more imports will be purchased. The supply of pounds curve will shift to the right (to S_2 in Figure 25.5). UK exports will now be relatively more expensive for foreigners. Less will be sold. The demand for pounds curve will shift to the left (to D_2).

Foreign exchange dealers will now find themselves with a glut of unsold pounds. They will therefore lower the exchange rate (to er_2 in Figure 25.5). The amount that the exchange rate has to change depends on:

- The amount that the curves shift. Thus large differences in international inflation rates or large differences in international interest rates will cause large shifts in the demand for and supply of currencies, and hence large movements in exchange rates.
- The elasticity of the curves. The less elastic the demand and supply curves of sterling, the greater the change in the exchange rate for any given shift in demand and supply.

But what determines the elasticity of the demand and supply curves? This is examined in Case Study 25.1 on the student website.

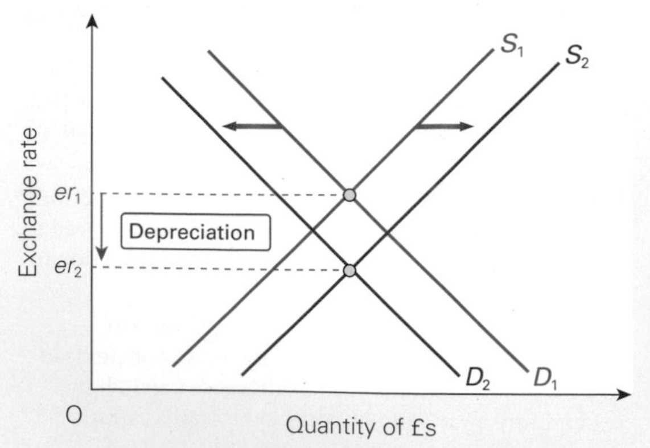

Expenditure changing (the income effect)

Depreciation, as well as affecting relative prices, will affect national income. This will cause ***expenditure changing***.

We have already established that, as the exchange rate falls, so more exports will be sold and less imports purchased: this was the substitution effect. But this is only an initial effect.

Exports are an injection into, and imports a withdrawal from, the circular flow of income. There will thus be a multiplied rise in national income. This income effect (expenditure *increasing*) reduces the effectiveness of the depreciation. Two situations can be examined.

A rise in national income and employment, but no change in prices. Assume that there are substantial unemployed resources, so that an increase in aggregate demand will raise output and employment but not prices. As national income rises, so imports rise (thereby tending to offset the initial fall), but exports are unaffected.

This is illustrated by the line $(X - M)_1$ in Figure 25.6. At low levels of national income, spending on imports is low; thus exports (X) exceed imports (M). $X - M$ is positive. As national income and hence imports rise, $X - M$ falls, and after a point becomes negative. Thus the $X - M$ line is downward sloping.

Figure 25.5 Adjustment of the exchange rate to a shift in demand and supply

Definitions

Expenditure switching from depreciation: the substitution effect Where a lower exchange rate reduces the price of exports and increases the price of imports. This will increase the sale of exports and reduce the sale of imports.

Expenditure changing (increasing) from depreciation: the income effect Where depreciation, via the substitution effect, will alter the demand for imports and exports, and this, via the multiplier, will affect the level of national income and hence the demand for imports.

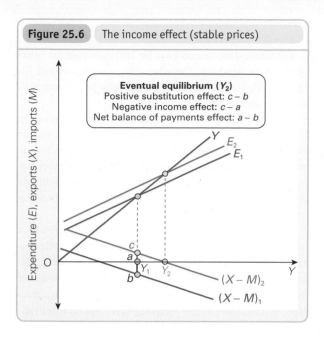

Figure 25.6   The income effect (stable prices)

Eventual equilibrium (Y_2)
Positive substitution effect: $c - b$
Negative income effect: $c - a$
Net balance of payments effect: $a - b$

Assume an initial equilibrium national income at Y_1, where national income (Y) equals national expenditure (E_1), but with imports exceeding exports by an amount $a - b$. The exchange rate thus depreciates.

This will cause a substitution effect: exports rise and imports fall. The $X - M$ line therefore shifts upwards. But this in turn causes an income effect. Aggregate demand rises, and the E line shifts upwards.

An eventual internal and external equilibrium is reached at Y_2, where $Y = E_2$ and $(X - M)_2 = 0$.

The positive substitution effect of this depreciation is $c - b$. The negative income effect is $c - a$. The net effect is thus only $a - b$, which is the size of the initial deficit. Had it not been for this negative income effect, a smaller depreciation would have been needed.

At least in this case, the income effect is having a desirable *internal* consequence: reducing unemployment.

A rise in prices.   If the economy is near full employment, the rise in aggregate demand from depreciation will make that depreciation even less effective. Not only will the higher demand lead directly to more imports, it will also lead to higher inflation. There will thus be an adverse substitution effect too. This will partially offset the beneficial substitution effect of the depreciation. The higher inflation will have the effect of shifting the $X-M$ line back down again somewhat.

In the extreme case, where money supply expands to accommodate the rise in aggregate demand, $X-M$ may simply return to its original position. The depreciation will fail to correct the balance of payments disequilibrium. In Figure 25.5, the fall in the exchange rate to er_2 will simply lead to a further rightward shift in supply and a leftward shift in demand, until the gap between them is the same as it was at er_1.

To offset the income effect, a government may feel it necessary to back up a currency depreciation with deflationary demand management policies.

Intermediate exchange rate regimes

There are a number of possible intermediate systems between the two extremes of totally fixed and completely free-floating exchange rates.

Adjustable peg.   The **adjustable peg** system is towards the fixed end of the spectrum. Exchange rates are fixed (or 'pegged') for a period of time – perhaps several years.

In the short and medium term, therefore, correction is the same as with a totally fixed system. Central banks have to intervene in the foreign exchange market to maintain the rate. If a deficit persists, then deflationary or other policies must be adopted to *shift* the currency demand and supply curves. This will be a problem, however, if there already exist substantial unemployed resources.

In the long term, if a fundamental disequilibrium occurs, the currency can be repegged at a lower or higher rate. Adjusting the peg downwards is known as **devaluation**. Adjusting it upwards is known as **revaluation**.

Alternatively, more frequent smaller adjustments could be made, thus moving the system away from the fixed end of the spectrum.

Managed floating.   The **managed floating** system is towards the free-floating end of the spectrum. Exchange rates are not pegged: they are allowed to float. But the central bank intervenes from time to time to prevent excessive exchange rate fluctuations. It is thus a form of 'managed flexibility'.

Under such a system, the central bank does not seek to maintain a long-term or even medium-term disequilibrium rate. Rather it tries to allow an 'orderly' exchange rate adjustment to major changes in demand and supply, while preventing the violent short-term swings that can occur with a totally free float (swings arising from currency speculation).

To back up the central bank's use of reserves, it may also alter interest rates to prevent exchange rate fluctuations. If,

Definitions

Adjustable peg A system whereby exchange rates are fixed for a period of time, but may be devalued (or revalued) if a deficit (or surplus) becomes substantial.

Devaluation Where the government repegs the exchange rate at a lower level.

Revaluation Where the government repegs the exchange rate at a higher level.

Managed floating A system of flexible exchange rates, but where the government intervenes to prevent excessive fluctuations or even to achieve an unofficial target exchange rate.

for example, there were a large-scale selling of the domestic currency, the central bank could raise interest rates to counter this effect and prevent the exchange rate from falling.

 How would raising interest rates in this way affect the balance between the current and financial accounts of the balance of payments?

The degree of currency stability sought, and hence the degree of intervention required, will vary from country to country and from government to government. At one extreme, the government may intervene only if exchange rate fluctuations become very severe; at the other extreme, the government may try to maintain the exchange rate at some unofficial target level.

Crawling peg. The **crawling peg** system is midway between managed floating and the adjustable peg system. Instead of making large and infrequent devaluations (or revaluations), the government adjusts the peg by small amounts, but frequently – say, once a month, as the equilibrium exchange rate changes.

Joint float. Under a **joint float** a group of countries have a fixed or adjustable peg system between their own currencies, but jointly float against all other currencies.

Exchange rate band. With an **exchange rate band** the government sets a lower and an upper limit to the exchange rate: say, £ = $1.60 and £1 = $1.80. It then allows the exchange rate to fluctuate freely within these limits. It will intervene, however, if the rate hits the floor or the ceiling.

Exchange rate bands could be narrow (say ±1 per cent) or wide (say ±15 per cent).

Exchange rate bands can be incorporated in other systems – the band could be adjustable, crawling or fixed. For example, Figure 25.7 illustrates a crawling peg system with an exchange rate band.

The exchange rate mechanism (ERM) of the European Monetary System (EMS), which pre-dated the euro, was an example of a joint float against non-member currencies and an adjustably pegged exchange rate band with member currencies (see section 26.2). The ERM2 system for Denmark (and potentially for other members of the EU in preparation to join the euro) is similar.

All these intermediate systems are attempts to achieve as many as possible of the advantages of both fixed and flexible exchange rates, with as few as possible of the attendant disadvantages. To assess any of these compromise systems, therefore, we must examine the advantages and disadvantages of fixed and flexible exchange rates. We do this in the next two sections.

Definitions

Crawling peg A system whereby the government allows a gradual adjustment of the exchange rate.

Joint float Where a group of currencies pegged to each other jointly float against other currencies.

Exchange rate band Where a currency is allowed to float between an upper and lower exchange rate, but is not allowed to move outside this band.

Figure 25.7 The crawling peg within exchange rate bands

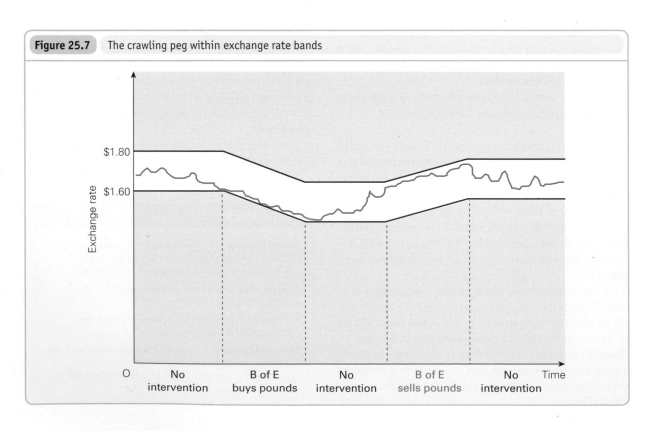

Section summary

1. There may be a conflict in achieving both internal and external balance simultaneously. The nature of the conflict depends on the exchange rate regime that the country adopts.

2. Nominal exchange rates are simply the rates at which one currency exchanges for another. Real exchange rates take account of differences in inflation rates between import and export prices and are a measure of the competitiveness of a country's exports.

3. Under a fixed exchange rate system, the government will have to intervene whenever the equilibrium exchange rate ceases to coincide with the fixed rate. If the equilibrium rate falls below the fixed rate, the government will have to buy in the domestic currency on the foreign exchange market. This will have the effect of reducing the money supply. Likewise, selling the domestic currency in order to prevent an appreciation will increase money supply. The government can prevent these changes in money supply by the use of appropriate open-market operations or other monetary measures. This is known as 'sterilisation'. Sterilisation, however, means that the disequilibrium is likely to go uncorrected.

4. If a deficit (or surplus) persists under a fixed rate, the government can attempt to shift the currency demand and supply curves. To cure a deficit, it can use contractionary fiscal or monetary policies. These have two effects. Deflation leads to a fall in national income (the income effect) and hence a fall in the demand for imports. It also leads to a fall in inflation and hence a switch in demand from foreign goods to home-produced goods (the substitution effect).

5. Correction under free-floating exchange rates also involves an income and a substitution effect. If there is a deficit, the exchange rate will depreciate. This will make imports more expensive and exports cheaper, and hence there will be a substitution effect as imports fall and exports rise.

6. The income effect of a depreciation, however, reduces its effectiveness. The rise in exports and fall in imports (i.e. the substitution effect of a depreciation) will lead to a multiplied rise in national income, which will cause imports to rise back again somewhat. The bigger this income effect, the bigger will be the depreciation necessary to achieve equilibrium in the foreign exchange market. Correction is made more difficult if any depreciation leads to increases in domestic prices and hence to a second substitution effect – only this time an adverse one.

7. There are intermediate exchange rate regimes between the extremes of fixed rates and free-floating rates. The exchange rate may be fixed for a period of time (the adjustable peg); or it may be allowed to change gradually (the crawling peg); or the government may merely intervene to dampen exchange rate fluctuations (managed floating); or the exchange rate may be allowed to fluctuate within a band, where the band in turn may be fixed, adjustable or crawling.

25.2 FIXED EXCHANGE RATES

In this section we examine the causes of balance of payments problems under fixed nominal exchange rates, in both the short run and the long run. First, in an optional section, we look at short-run causes and whether balance will be restored. We then look at longer-run, more fundamental causes of balance of payments problems. Finally, we assess the desirability of fixed exchange rates.

*Effects of shocks under fixed exchange rates

Under fixed exchange rates, it is unlikely that internal and external balance can persist for long without government intervention. Various macroeconomic 'shocks', such as changes in injections or withdrawals, or changes in international interest rates, are constantly occurring. These are likely to destroy either internal or external balance or both. Even with government intervention, it may still be very difficult, if not impossible, to restore both balances. Correction of balance of payments disequilibria will come into conflict with the other macroeconomic goals of growth, full employment and stable prices.

How the economy responds to shocks under fixed exchange rates, and which policy measures are most effective in dealing with the resultant disequilibria, depend on two things: (a) whether the shocks are internal or external; (b) the flexibility of wages and prices, which, in turn, depends on the time period under consideration.

Response to an internal shock

Let us assume that there is a fall in aggregate demand, caused by a fall in consumer demand or investment, or by a rise in saving.

Short-run effect. In the short run, prices and especially wages tend to be relatively inflexible (this is a central assumption of Keynesian analysis). The fall in aggregate demand will lead to a recession. Internal balance will be destroyed. In a closed economy, the central bank would probably reduce interest rates to boost the economy, either to tackle the recession directly or because forecast inflation had fallen below its target level.

In an open economy under fixed exchange rates, however, this is not possible. But why?

The lower aggregate demand will lead to a fall in imports, resulting in a *current account* surplus. There is an opposite effect on the *financial account,* however. The reduced aggregate demand will lead to a fall in the demand for money and hence downward pressure on interest rates. If interest rates were allowed to fall, there would be a resulting financial outflow and hence a financial account deficit.

But which would be the larger effect: the current account surplus or the financial account deficit? This depends on the marginal propensity to import (*mpm*) and the mobility of international finance. The higher the *mpm,* the bigger the current account surplus. The higher the international mobility of finance, the bigger the financial outflow and hence the bigger the financial account deficit. In today's world of massive financial flows across the foreign exchanges, international finance is highly, if not perfectly, mobile. If the central bank allows interest rates to fall, the financial account deficit will therefore exceed the current account surplus.

To prevent this happening, interest rates must not be allowed to fall or, at least, must fall only very slightly – just enough for the resulting financial account deficit to match the current account surplus. With hardly any fall in interest rates, money supply must thus be allowed to contract to match the fall in the demand for money.

Thus to maintain the fixed exchange rate (without massively draining reserves) interest rates will be determined by the balance of payments. They cannot be used for domestic purposes, such as targeting inflation, targeting real national income or some combination (e.g. a Taylor rule: see pages 705–6). Internal imbalance will persist in the short run.

Long-run effect.   In the long run, there will be much greater, if not perfect, price and wage flexibility. Under new classical assumptions, such flexibility will exist in the short run too. This flexibility will ensure that internal balance is restored. The Phillips curve is vertical at the natural rate of unemployment.

But, with a fixed exchange rate, will it also ensure external balance? Again, let us assume that people decide to spend less and save more. As in the short run, this will lead to a *current account* surplus. This time, however, the effect is much bigger. In the short run, there was little or no price effect (i.e. no substitution effect) since there was little change in inflation. There was only an income effect from reduced imports caused by the recession. In the long run, however, the lower real aggregate demand reduces inflation. Assuming that inflation falls below that of trading partners, the *real* exchange rate falls. This makes exports relatively cheaper and imports relatively more expensive. This causes exports to rise and imports to fall.

The resulting rise in aggregate demand not only helps to eliminate the recession, but also helps to reduce the current account surplus.

Thus, despite a fixed *nominal* exchange rate, wage and price flexibility cause the *real* exchange rate to be flexible. This helps restore overall external balance. Nevertheless, a current account surplus may persist. Indeed, as the surplus is used to buy foreign assets, so, over time, these will yield an income, further crediting the current account.

But what is clear is that, although interest rates are determined by the need to maintain a fixed nominal exchange rate, wage and price flexibility in the long run will eventually restore internal balance. The question is, how long will the long run be? How long will the recession persist? If it is too long, and if interest rates cannot be cut, then can expansionary fiscal policy be used? We examine this in Box 25.3.

Response to an external shock

Assume now that there is a fall in demand for exports.

Short-run effect.   The fall in exports causes the current account to go into deficit. It also reduces aggregate demand, causing a multiplied fall in national income. This reduces the demand for imports: the larger the *mpm,* the bigger the reduction in imports. Aggregate demand will go on falling until the lower injections are matched by lower withdrawals. But the current account deficit will not be eliminated, since the fall in withdrawals to match the fall in exports consists only partly of lower imports; part will consist of lower saving and lower tax receipts.

The reduction in aggregate demand reduces the transactions demand for money, putting downward pressure on interest rates. This would result in a financial outflow and hence a *financial account* deficit, making the overall currency flow deficit worse. To prevent this happening, the central bank must prevent interest rates from falling by reducing the money supply (through open-market operations). Indeed, given the current account deficit, interest rates may have to be slightly higher than they were originally in order to create a financial account surplus sufficient to offset the current account deficit. This will make the recession worse.

Long-run effect.   The reduction in aggregate demand will put downward pressure on domestic inflation. This will help to reduce the real exchange rate and hence correct the current account deficit. It will also restore internal balance. Again, however, without fiscal policy, the long run may be some time in coming. The recession may persist.

> *Trace through the short-run and long-run internal and external effects (under a fixed exchange rate) of (a) a fall in domestic saving; (b) a rise in the demand for exports.*

Causes of longer-term balance of payments problems under fixed exchange rates

With moderately flexible prices, current account balance may eventually be restored after 'one-off' shocks. However, long-term continuing shifts in the demand and supply of imports and exports can make balance of payments problems persist. We will examine four causes of these long-term shifts.

BOX 25.3   THE EFFECTIVENESS OF FISCAL AND MONETARY POLICIES UNDER FIXED EXCHANGE RATES

Monetary policy

Monetary policy is not very effective under fixed exchange rates.

Assume that the central bank, worried by rising inflation, wishes to reduce the growth in nominal aggregate demand. It thus reduces the rate of growth in money supply. This drives up interest rates and causes a fall in real national income.

What effect will this have on the balance of payments? The lower national income reduces expenditure on imports and hence leads to a surplus on the current account. Also, the higher interest rates encourage an inflow of finance and hence a surplus on the financial account too. This balance of payments surplus will *increase* money supply again and reduce interest rates back towards the original level. Aggregate demand will rise back towards its original level. Monetary policy has been ineffective.

But rather than changing the *supply* of money, can the government not directly alter interest rates? The problem here is that, in order to maintain the rate of exchange at the fixed level, the government's room for manoeuvre is very limited. For example, if it raises interest rates, the resulting inflow of finance will cause a balance of payments surplus. The government could, for a period of time, simply build up reserves, but it may not want to do this indefinitely.

The problem is more serious if the economy is in recession and the central bank wants to increase aggregate demand by *reducing* interest rates. The financial outflow will force the central bank to buy in the domestic currency by using its reserves. But it can do this for only so long. Eventually, it will be forced to raise interest rates again in order to stem the drain on the reserves. In today's world, with little in the way of exchange controls and with massive amounts of short-term international liquidity, such flows can be enormous. This gives the central bank virtually no discretion over changing interest rates. Interest rates will have to be kept at a level so as to maintain the exchange rate. In the case of *perfect* mobility of international finance, interest rates must be kept at world rates. Monetary policy will be totally ineffective.

Fiscal policy

Fiscal policy is much more effective.

Assume that there is a recession and the government wishes to increase aggregate demand. It thus cuts taxes and/or raises government expenditure. This raises national income and increases expenditure on imports. Also, higher inflation raises the real exchange rate. This makes exports less competitive and imports relatively cheaper. The current account moves into deficit.

The increase in aggregate demand will raise the demand for money and hence put upward pressure on interest rates. This will lead to an inflow of finance and a financial account surplus. To prevent this swamping the current account deficit, the central bank must prevent interest rates from rising very much. In the case of an infinitely elastic supply of finance, interest rates must not be allowed to rise at all.

Thus money supply must be allowed to expand to keep interest rates down. This expansion of the money supply thus reinforces the expansionary fiscal policy and prevents crowding out.

Thus a high level of international financial mobility enhances the effectiveness of fiscal policy.

 Suppose that under a managed floating system the central bank is worried about high inflation and wants to keep the exchange rate up in order to prevent import prices rising. To tackle the problem of inflation, it raises interest rates. What will happen to the current and financial accounts of the balance of payments?

Different rates of inflation between countries. If a country has persistently higher rates of inflation than the countries with which it trades, it will have a growing current account deficit. Exports and import substitutes will become less and less competitive as its real exchange rate appreciates.

Different rates of growth between countries. If a country grows faster than the countries with which it trades, its imports will tend to grow faster than its exports.

Income elasticity of demand for imports higher than for exports. If the income elasticity of demand for imports is relatively high, and the income elasticity of demand for exports is relatively low, then as world incomes grow, the country's imports will grow faster than its exports. This has been a particular problem for many developing countries: they import manufactured goods and capital equipment, whose demand grows rapidly, and export primary products – food and raw materials – whose demand, until recent years, has grown relatively slowly (see section 26.4).

Long-term structural changes

- Trading blocs may emerge, putting up tariff barriers to other countries. Australian and New Zealand exports were adversely affected when the UK joined the EEC.
- Countries may exercise monopoly power to a greater extent than previously. The OPEC oil price increases of 1973/4 and 1978/9 are examples.
- Countries may develop import substitutes. Thus plastics and other synthetics have in many cases substituted for rubber and metals, worsening the balance of payments of traditional primary exporters.

■ The nature and quality of a country's products may change. Thus Japan has shifted from producing low-quality simple manufactured goods in the 1950s to producing high-quality sophisticated manufactured goods today. This helped increase its exports.

To maintain a fixed exchange rate under such circumstances, governments have to take measures to correct the disequilibria. They can use demand-side policies (fiscal and monetary: see Box 25.3), supply-side policies or protectionist policies.

Advantages of fixed exchange rates

Many economists are opposed to fixed exchange rates, for reasons to be examined shortly. Nevertheless, many businesspeople are in favour of relatively rigid exchange rates. The following arguments are used.

Certainty. With fixed exchange rates, international trade and investment become much less risky, since profits are not affected by movements in the exchange rate.

Little or no speculation. Provided the rate is absolutely fixed – and people believe that it will remain so – there is no point in speculating. For example, between 1999 and 2001, when the old currencies of the eurozone countries were still used, but were totally fixed to the euro, there was no speculation that the German mark, say, would change in value against the French franc or the Dutch guilder.

> ? When the UK joined the ERM in 1990, it was hoped that this would make speculation pointless. As it turned out, speculation forced the UK to leave the ERM in 1992. Can you reconcile this with the argument that fixed rates discourage speculation?

Automatic correction of monetary errors. If the central bank allows the money supply to expand too fast, the resulting extra demand and lower interest rates will lead to a balance of payments deficit. This will force the central bank to intervene to support the exchange rate. Either it must buy the domestic currency on the foreign exchange market, thereby causing money supply to fall again (unless it sterilises the effect), or it must raise interest rates. Either way this will have the effect of correcting the error.

Preventing governments pursuing 'irresponsible' macroeconomic policies. If a government deliberately and excessively expands aggregate demand – perhaps in an attempt to gain short-term popularity with the electorate – the resulting balance of payments deficit will force it to constrain demand again (unless it resorts to import controls).

Disadvantages of fixed exchange rates

The new classical view

New classicists make two crucial criticisms of fixed rates.

Fixed exchange rates make monetary policy ineffective. Interest rates must be used to ensure that the overall balance of

payments balances. As a result, money supply must be allowed to vary with the demand for money in order to keep interest rates at the necessary level. Thus monetary policy cannot be used for domestic purposes (see Box 25.3). Inflation depends on world rates, which may be high and domestically unacceptable. If the central bank tries to reduce inflation by attempting to reduce money supply and raise interest rates, the current and financial accounts will go into surplus. Money supply will thus increase until domestic inflation rises back to world levels.

Fixed rates contradict the objective of having free markets. Why fix the exchange rate, when a simple depreciation or appreciation can correct a disequilibrium? In the new classical world where markets clear, and supply and demand are relatively elastic, why not treat the foreign exchange market like any other, and simply leave it to supply and demand?

The Keynesian view

In the Keynesian world, wages and prices are relatively 'sticky', and demand-deficient unemployment and cost-push inflation may persist. As such, there is no guarantee of achieving both internal and external balance simultaneously when exchange rates are fixed. This leads to the following problems.

Balance of payments deficits can lead to a recession. A balance of payments deficit can occur even if there is no excess demand. As we saw above, this could be caused by different rates of growth or different rates of inflation from trading partners, a higher income elasticity of demand for imports than for exports, and so on. If protectionism is to be avoided, and if supply-side policies work only over the long run, the government will be forced to reduce the rate of growth of aggregate demand. This will lead to higher unemployment and possibly a recession.

If wages and prices are sticky downwards, the contraction may have to be severe if a significant improvement in the *current* account is to be made. Here, reliance would have to be placed largely on lower *incomes* reducing the demand for imports. If the deflation is achieved through higher interest rates, however, an improvement on the *financial* account may remove the need for a severe deflation, especially given the high degree of financial mobility that exists nowadays. Nevertheless, the rate of interest may still be higher than that desired for purely internal purposes.

If a country has a *persistent* current account deficit, it may need to have persistently higher interest rates than its competitors and suffer persistently lower growth rates as a result. It will also tend to build up short-term debts, as money is put on deposit in the country to take advantage of the higher interest rates. This can make the problem of speculation much more acute if people come to believe that the fixed rate cannot be maintained (see below).

Competitive deflations leading to world depression. If deficit countries deflated, but surplus countries reflated, there would be no overall world deflation or reflation. Countries may be quite happy, however, to run a balance of payments surplus and build up reserves. Countries may thus competitively deflate – all trying to achieve a balance of payments surplus. But this is beggar-my-neighbour policy. Not all countries can have a surplus! Overall, the world must be in balance. Such policies lead to general world deflation and a restriction in growth.

Problems of international liquidity. If trade is to expand, there must be an expansion in the supply of currencies acceptable for world trade (dollars, euros, gold, etc.): there must be adequate **international liquidity**. Countries' reserves of these currencies must grow if they are to be sufficient to maintain a fixed rate at times of balance of payments disequilibrium. Conversely, there must not be excessive international liquidity. Otherwise the extra demand that would result would lead to world inflation. It is important under fixed exchange rates, therefore, to avoid too much or too little international liquidity. The problem is how to maintain adequate control of international liquidity. The supply of dollars, for example, depends largely on US policy, which may be dominated by the US internal economic situation rather than by any concern for the well-being of the international community. Similarly, the supply of euros depends on the policy of the European Central Bank, which is governed by the internal situation in the eurozone countries.

 Why will excessive international liquidity lead to international inflation?

Speculation. If speculators believe that a fixed rate simply cannot be maintained, speculation is likely to be massive.

If there is a huge deficit, there is no chance whatsoever of a revaluation. Either the rate will be devalued or it will remain the same. Speculators will thus sell the domestic currency. After all, it is a pretty good gamble: heads they win (devaluation); tails they don't lose (no devaluation). This speculative selling will worsen the deficit, and may itself force the devaluation. Speculation of this sort had disastrous effects on some South East Asian currencies in 1997 (see Case Study 25.3 on the student website) and on the Argentinean peso in 2002 (see Case Study 26.10).

 To what extent do Keynesians and new classicists agree about the role of fixed exchange rates?

Postscript

An argument used in favour of fixed rates is that they prevent governments from pursuing inflationary policies. But if getting inflation down is desirable, why do governments not pursue an anti-inflationary policy directly? Today, many governments make inflation targeting the goal of monetary policy and many do so by delegating monetary policy to the central bank to enhance the credibility of inflation targeting. Most, however, have floating exchange rates.

Definition

International liquidity The supply of currencies in the world acceptable for financing international trade and investment.

Section summary

*1. Macroeconomic shocks are constantly occurring. Whether internal and external balance will be restored under a fixed exchange rate, following a shock, depends on price and wage flexibility and on the time period.

*2. In the short run there is a degree of wage and price inflexibility. If there is a fall in aggregate demand, the resulting fall in national income will reduce the demand for imports. This will cause a current account surplus. The fall in aggregate demand will also reduce the demand for money and put downward pressure on interest rates. This will cause a financial account deficit. This effect can be large, given the high mobility of international finance. Interest rates are thus constrained by the need for the financial account to balance the current account.

*3. In the long run, with wage and price flexibility, the real exchange rate can change. This will help to restore both internal and external balance.

4. Over the longer term, balance of payments disequilibria under fixed exchange rates can arise from different rates of inflation and growth between countries, different

income elasticities of demand for imports and exports, and long-term structural changes.

5. Under fixed exchange rates, monetary policy will not be very effective, but fiscal policy will be much more effective.

6. Fixed exchange rates bring the advantage of certainty for the business community, which encourages trade and foreign investment. They also help to prevent governments from pursuing irresponsible macroeconomic policies.

7. Both new classical and Keynesian economists, however, see important disadvantages in fixed exchange rates. New classical economists argue that they make monetary policy totally ineffective, and that they run counter to the efficiency objective of having free markets. Keynesians argue that fixed rates can lead to serious internal imbalance with perhaps a persistent recession; that with competitive deflations a recession can be worldwide; that there may be problems of excessive or insufficient international liquidity; and that speculation could be very severe if people came to believe that a fixed rate was about to break down.

25.3 FREE-FLOATING EXCHANGE RATES

Floating exchange rates and the freeing of domestic policy

With a freely floating exchange rate there can be no overall balance of payments disequilibrium. Foreign exchange dealers will constantly adjust the exchange rate to balance their books, so that the demand for and supply of any currency are equal.

This, therefore, removes the balance of payments constraint on domestic policy that exists under a fixed exchange rate. No reserves are required, since there is no central bank intervention to support the exchange rate. The government would seem free to pursue whatever domestic policy it likes. Any resulting effects on the balance of payments are simply and automatically corrected by a depreciation or appreciation of the exchange rate.

In reality, however, things are not quite so simple. Even under a totally free-floating exchange rate, some constraints on domestic policy may be imposed by the effects of these exchange rate movements. For example, a depreciation of the exchange rate increases the price of imports. If the demand for imports is relatively inelastic, this may lead to a higher rate of inflation.

Response to shocks under a floating exchange rate

Internal shocks

Let us assume that there is a rise in aggregate demand that causes inflation. For the moment, however, let us also assume that monetary policy maintains real interest rates at international levels. For simplicity, let us assume that there is no inflation abroad. How will a floating exchange rate system cope with this internal shock of a rise in aggregate demand? The exchange rate will simply depreciate to maintain the competitiveness of exports and import substitutes.

For example, assume an initial exchange rate of £1 = $2. A UK product costing $2 in the USA will earn £1 for the UK exporter. If UK inflation now causes prices to double, the exchange rate will roughly halve. If it falls to £1 = $1, then the same product costing $2 in the USA will now earn £2 for the UK exporter, which in *real* terms is the same amount as before. This is the ***purchasing-power parity theory***. This states

that domestic price changes will be offset by (nominal) exchange rate changes, thereby maintaining the same relative prices between countries as before.

If this is the case, need firms worry about losing competitiveness in world markets if domestic inflation is higher than world inflation?

If we now drop the assumption that real interest rates are maintained at the same level as abroad, the purchasing-power parity theory will break down. Let us assume that the rise in aggregate demand causes a rise in UK real interest rates. This could be either the effect of the higher demand for money pushing up interest rates, or a deliberate act of the central bank to bring the inflation rate back down to the target level.

There are now two effects on the exchange rate. The higher aggregate demand and higher inflation rate will cause the current account to move into deficit, thereby putting downward pressure on the exchange rate. The higher real interest rates, however, will cause the financial account to move into surplus as depositors choose to hold their money in pounds. This will put upward pressure on the exchange rate. Whether the exchange rate actually falls or rises depends on which of the two effects is the bigger. In today's world of huge international financial flows, the effect on the financial account is likely to be the larger one: the exchange rate will thus *appreciate*. The greater the interest elasticity of supply of such flows, the greater the appreciation.

But either way, because of the financial account effect, the new equilibrium exchange rate will be above the purchasing-power parity rate. This will adversely affect export industries, since the exchange rate has not fallen sufficiently (if at all) to compensate for their higher sterling price. It will also adversely affect domestic industries that compete with imports, since again the exchange rate has not fallen sufficiently to retain their competitiveness with imports. The current account thus remains in deficit, matched by an equal and opposite financial plus capital account surplus.

This is a position that has characterised the UK for several years. As we saw in Table 25.1, the rate of inflation has frequently been above that of major trading partners, while the current account has been persistently in deficit (see Box 25.2) and the capital plus financial account persistently in surplus (see Figure 15.15 on page 481).

The positive inflation rate differential between the UK and its major trading partners (see Table 25.1) has often meant higher UK interest rates. This was the case following the delegation of monetary policy to the Bank of England in 1997 with its remit to meet an inflation rate target. The resulting interest rate differential contributed to an appreciating real exchange rate in the late 1990s, which remained persistently high up to the onset of the financial crisis (see Figure 25.3).

Definition

Purchasing-power parity theory The theory that the exchange rate will adjust so as to offset differences in countries' inflation rates, with the result that the same quantity of internationally traded goods can be bought at home as abroad with a given amount of the domestic currency.

The carry trade. The problem for current account deficit countries has often been made worse by the **carry trade**, especially in the period running up to the financial crisis. This involves international investors taking advantage of nominal interest rate differences between countries.

Prior to the financial crisis of 2008, current account deficit countries, such as the UK, Australia and New Zealand, typically had relatively high interest rates, while current account surplus countries such as Japan and Switzerland had relatively low ones. It was thus profitable to borrow, say, yen at the low interest rate that obtains in Japan, exchange it into sterling and deposit the money at the higher interest rate available in the UK. If there was no change in the exchange rate between the pound and the yen, the investor made a profit equal to the difference in the interest rates.

If, however, the higher interest rates in the UK and other deficit countries were simply to compensate investors for the risk of currency depreciation, then there would be no excessive inflow of finance. The benefit of the higher interest rate would be offset by a depreciating currency. But the carry trade had the effect of making deficit currencies *appreciate*, thereby further boosting the carry trade by speculation of further exchange rate rises.

Thus the currencies of deficit countries appreciated, making their goods less competitive and worsening their current account deficit. Between 1996 and 2006, the average current account deficits as a percentage of GDP for Australia, the USA and the UK were 4.3, 3.8 and 1.5 respectively. Between January 1996 and December 2006, the broad-based *real* exchange rate index of the Australian dollar appreciated by 17.1 per cent, of the US dollar by 3.8 per cent and of sterling by some 23.5 per cent.

Currencies of surplus countries depreciated, making their goods more competitive and further boosting their current account surpluses. For example, between 2004 and 2006 the average current account surpluses as a percentage of GDP for Japan and Switzerland were 3.7 and 14.2 respectively. Their short-term interest rates averaged a mere 0.1 and 1.0 per cent respectively (compared with 3.4, 4.7 and 5.7 per cent for the USA, the UK and Australia). Yet between January 2004 and December 2006, the *real* exchange rate index of the yen depreciated by 20.6 per cent while that of the Swiss franc depreciated by 6.0 per cent.

With the credit crunch of 2007/8, however, short-term flows of finance declined significantly. This had the effect of reducing the carry trade and its effect on exchange rates.

Hence, the current account became relatively more significant in determining exchange rates. The currencies of deficit countries, such as the UK and USA, began to depreciate and those of surplus countries, such as Japan and Switzerland, began to appreciate. Between September 2007 and September 2008, the *real* exchange rate indices of the US dollar and sterling depreciated by 2.3 and 13.3 per cent respectively; the yen and the Swiss franc appreciated by 2.6 and 2.7 per cent.

External shocks

Now let us assume that the rest of the world goes into recession (but with no change in international interest rates). The demand for UK exports will fall. This will lead to a depreciation of the exchange rate. This in turn will boost the demand for UK exports and domestic substitutes for imports. This boost to demand again will help to offset the dampening effect of the world recession.

Floating exchange rates thus help to insulate the domestic economy from world economic fluctuations.

 Will there be any cost to the UK economy from a decline in the demand for exports resulting from a world recession?

The path to long-run equilibrium

If there is a single shock, and if there is initially both internal balance and also external balance in the narrow sense (i.e. a current account balance), eventually both internal balance and current account balance will be restored. Current account balance will be restored by a change in the exchange rate that restores purchasing-power parity. This is illustrated in Figure 25.8.

Assume that the country experiences the same long-term rate of inflation as its trading partners and that, therefore, the nominal exchange rate follows the same path as the real exchange rate. Assume also that there are no *long-term* changes to cause an appreciation or depreciation and that, therefore, the long-term equilibrium exchange rate is constant over time. This is shown by the horizontal line at er_L.

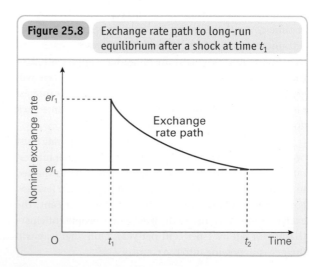

Figure 25.8 Exchange rate path to long-run equilibrium after a shock at time t_1

BOX 25.4   THE PRICE OF A BIG MAC

The Economist's guide to purchasing-power parity rates

At least once a year *The Economist* publishes its 'Big Mac index'. It is a light-hearted attempt to see if currencies are exchanging at their purchasing-power parity rates. The test is the price at which a 'Big Mac' McDonald's hamburger sells in different countries! According to this simplified version of the purchasing-power parity theory, exchange rates should adjust so that a Big Mac costs the same in dollars everywhere.

If a Big Mac is taken as representative of all goods and services, then in January 2017, with a Big Mac selling for $5.06 in the USA, but only the equivalent of $2.83 in China, this implies that the Chinese yuan was undervalued by 44 per cent.

As we can see from the table, it was not the only Asian currency to be undervalued in Big Mac PPP terms. The Malaysian ringgit and the Thai baht, for instance, were also substantially undervalued. In Malaysia a Big Mac cost 8.00 ringgits, while in Thailand it cost 119 bahts. With, at the time, exchange rates of 4.47 ringgits and 35.57 bahts to the dollar, this meant that in Malaysia a Big Mac cost $1.79, while in Thailand it cost $3.35. This implied that the Malaysian ringgit was undervalued in Big Mac PPP terms by 65 per cent while the Thai baht was undervalued by 34 per cent.

In India, the nearest product is a 'Maharajah Mac', which uses chicken rather than beef. Given that the meat accounts for less than 10 per cent of a burger's cost, it is a fair approximation to use this rather than a Big Mac. In January 2017, with a price of $2.49 at the dollar–rupee exchange rate, this implied that the rupee was undervalued by 51 per cent.

While Asia was often found to be the cheapest place to eat a burger, Europe tended to be more expensive. For instance, the Swiss franc was estimated to be 25 per cent overvalued. At the prevailing exchange rate of 1.02 francs to the dollar, a Big Mac in Switzerland cost the equivalent of $6.35. For a Big Mac to cost the same in Switzerland as in America, the exchange rate would have had to be 1.28 francs to the dollar.

The hamburger standard

Country	Big Mac price in dollars at current exchange rate	Under (−) or over (+) valuation against the dollar (%)
Egypt	1.46	−71
Malaysia	1.79	−65
South Africa	1.89	−63
Russia	2.15	−57
Mexico	2.23	−56
Poland	2.30	−55
Indonesia	2.33	−54
Hong Kong	2.48	−51
India	2.49	−51
Turkey	2.75	−46
China	2.83	−44
Peru	3.24	−36
Japan	3.26	−36
Thailand	3.35	−34
Argentina	3.47	−31
Chile	3.64	−28
South Korea	3.68	−27
UK	3.73	−26
Singapore	3.89	−23
Eurozone[a]	4.06	−20
New Zealand	4.19	−17
Denmark	4.22	−17
Uruguay	4.35	−14
Canada	4.51	−11
USA[b]	5.06	0
Brazil	5.12	1
Venezuela	5.25	4
Sweden	5.26	4
Norway	5.67	12
Switzerland	6.35	25

a Weighted average of member countries.
b Average of New York, Chicago, San Francisco and Atlanta.

Now assume, as before, that there is a rise in aggregate demand and a resulting rise in interest rates. This occurs at time t_1. As the demand for imports rises, the current account goes into deficit. Higher interest rates, however, lead to a financial inflow and an immediate appreciation of the exchange rate to er_1. But then the exchange rate will gradually fall back to its long-run rate as the higher interest rates curb demand and interest rates can thus come back down.

What determines the level of er_1? This exchange rate must be high enough to balance the gain from the higher interest rate against the fact that the exchange rate will be expected to depreciate again back to its long-run equilibrium level er_L. For example, if the interest rate rises by 1 per cent, the exchange rate must rise to the level where people anticipate that it will fall by 1 per cent per year. Only that way will finance stop flowing into the country.

 Describe the exchange rate path if there were a single shock that caused interest rates to fall. What determines the magnitude and speed of changes in the exchange rate in such a scenario?

Speculation

In the real world, shocks are occurring all the time. Also, there is considerable uncertainty over the future course of the exchange rate path. What is more, things are made more complicated by the activities of speculators. As soon as any exchange rate change is anticipated, speculators will buy or sell the currency.

Assume, for example, that there is a rise in UK inflation above international rates, but no change in interest rates. This causes a fall in the demand for exports and hence a fall in the demand for sterling (assuming a price elasticity of

Across the eurozone a Big Mac in January 2017 cost on average €3.88. With an exchange rate of €1 = $1.05, the eurozone Big Mac cost $4.06, implying an undervaluation of the euro of 20 per cent.

So what of the UK? A Big Mac in January 2017 cost an average of £3.09. At the exchange rate at the time of £1 = $1.21, this meant a Big Mac cost $4.63 in the UK. This implies an *undervaluation* of 26 per cent. Yet as recently as July 2014 the Big Mac index was indicating an overvaluation of sterling, albeit a small overvaluation of 3 per cent. The significant change reflects a Brexit effect. In particular, the uncertainty generated, the short-term relaxation of the Bank of England's monetary stance (see Box 22.10) and the expectation that long-term growth would be adversely affected.

International patterns

Generally, richer, developed countries' currencies seem to be overvalued and poorer ones' undervalued (exceptions in the table being Brazil and Venezuela). The explanation lies in differences in local costs, such as rents and wages. These are higher in rich countries. According to David Parsley, of Vanderbilt University, and Shang-Jin Wei, of the International Monetary Fund, non-traded inputs, such as labour, rent and electricity, account for between 55 and 64 per cent of the price of a Big Mac.[1]

With lower rents and wages,

you would expect average prices to be cheaper in poor countries than in rich ones because labour costs are lower. This is the basis of the so-called 'Balassa-Samuelson effect'. Rich countries have much higher productivity and hence higher wages in the traded-goods sector than poor countries do. Because firms compete for workers, this also pushes up wages in non-tradable goods and services, where rich countries' productivity advantage is smaller.[2]

A Big Mac index is now produced adjusting for GDP per capita. In January 2017, it still suggested that the Indian rupee and Chinese yuan were undervalued, but now by only 10 and 6 per cent respectively. On the other hand, the Thai baht was now overvalued by as much as 14 per cent. While this adjustment may capture some of the differences between countries, such as in labour costs, it cannot capture differences attributable to transportation costs, or to consumer tastes which affect the amount consumers are willing to pay.

Also, exchange rates can diverge from their PPP values because of factors influencing the *financial account* of the balance of payments: factors such as actual and expected interest rate differentials, investment prospects and speculation about exchange rate movements.

Nevertheless, despite the limitation of the original Big Mac index, it does give some indication of whether a currency is above or below its long-term equilibrium rate.

1. *If the Chinese yuan is undervalued by 44 per cent in PPP terms against the US dollar and the Swiss franc overvalued by 25 per cent, what implications does this have for the interpretation of Chinese, Swiss and US GDP statistics?*
2. *Why do developing countries' currencies tend to be undervalued relative to those of developed countries (see table)?*
3. *At the time the table was compiled, the Big Mac PPP rate for the Norwegian krone was $1 = kr9.68. What was the market exchange rate?*

1 David C. Parsley and Shang-Jin Wei, 'A prism into the PPP puzzles: the microfoundations of Big Mac real exchange rates', *NBER Working Paper No. 10074* (National Bureau of Economic Research, November 2003), www.nber.org/papers/w10074
2 *The Economist*, 30 July 2011.

---

demand greater than 1), and a rise in imports and hence a rise in the supply of sterling. This is illustrated in Figures 25.9 and 25.10. The exchange rate depreciates from er_1 to er_2. Speculators seeing the exchange rate falling can react in one of two ways. The first is called *stabilising speculation*; the second is called *destabilising speculation* (see section 3.2).

Stabilising speculation

KI 10 p70

This occurs when speculators believe that any exchange rate change will soon be reversed.

In our example, speculators may anticipate that the central bank will raise interest rates or take some other measure to reduce inflation. They thus believe that the exchange rate will appreciate again. As a result, they buy more pounds and sell fewer. But this very act of speculation causes the appreciation they had anticipated.

This is illustrated in Figure 25.9. Inflation has caused the demand for and supply of pounds to shift from D_1 and S_1 to

Figure 25.9   Stabilising speculation

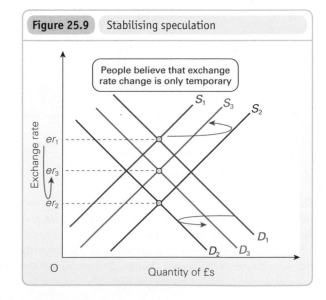

People believe that exchange rate change is only temporary

BOX 25.5 THE EURO/DOLLAR SEESAW

Ups and downs in the currency market

For periods of time, world currency markets can be quite peaceful, with only modest changes in exchange rates. But with the ability to move vast sums of money very rapidly from one part of the world to another and from one currency to another, speculators can suddenly turn this relatively peaceful world into one of extreme turmoil – a turmoil that can be very damaging for business.

In this box we examine the huge swings of the euro against the dollar since the euro's launch in 1999.

First the down . . .

On 1 January 1999, the euro was launched and exchanged for $1.16. By October 2000 the euro had fallen to $0.85. The main cause of this 27 per cent depreciation was the growing fear that inflationary pressures were increasing in the USA and that, therefore, the Federal Reserve Bank would have to raise interest rates. At the same time, the eurozone economy was growing only slowly and inflation was well below the 2 per cent ceiling set by the ECB. There was thus pressure on the ECB to cut interest rates.

The speculators were not wrong. As the diagram shows, US interest rates rose, and ECB interest rates initially fell, and when eventually they did rise (in October 1999), the gap between US and ECB interest rates soon widened again.

In addition to the differences in interest rates, a lack of confidence in the recovery of the eurozone economy and a continuing confidence in the US economy encouraged investment to flow to the USA. This inflow of finance (and lack of inflow to the eurozone) further pushed up the dollar relative to the euro.

The low value of the euro meant a high value of the pound and other currencies relative to the euro. This made it very difficult for companies outside of the eurozone to export to eurozone countries and also for those competing with imports from the eurozone (which had been made cheaper by the fall in the euro).

In October 2000, with the euro trading at around 85¢, the ECB plus the US Federal Reserve Bank (America's central bank), the Bank of England and the Japanese central bank all intervened on the foreign exchange market to buy euros. This arrested the fall, and helped to restore confidence in the euro.

. . . Then the up

The position completely changed in 2001. With the US economy slowing rapidly and fears of an impending recession, the Federal Reserve Bank reduced interest rates 11 times during the year: from 6.5 per cent at the beginning of the year to 1.75 per cent at the end (see the chart). Although the ECB also cut interest rates, the cuts were relatively modest: from 4.75 at the beginning of the year to 3.25 at the end. With eurozone interest rates now considerably above US rates, the euro began to rise.

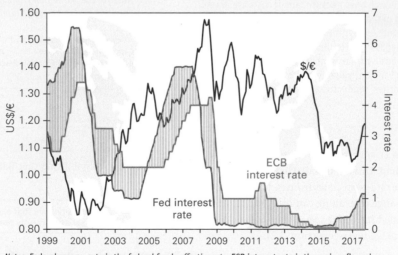

Fluctuations between the euro and the dollar

Notes: Federal reserve rate is the federal funds *effective rate*; ECB interest rate is the main refinancing operations rate.

Sources: $/€ based on data from ONS, series THAP and AUSS; interest rate data from *Federal Reserve Bank and European Central Bank*.

D_2 and S_2, and the exchange rate to fall from er_1 to er_2. Stabilising speculation then shifts the curves back again, to D_3 and S_3, and the exchange rate rises again to er_3.

The action of speculators in this case, therefore, prevents excessively large exchange rate changes. In general, stabilising speculation occurs whenever speculators believe that the exchange rate has 'overreacted' to the current economic situation.

Draw a similar diagram to Figure 25.9, showing how an initial appreciation of the exchange rate would similarly be reduced by stabilising speculation.

In addition, a massive deficit on the US balance of payments current account, and a budget deficit nearing 4 per cent of GDP, made foreign investors reluctant to invest in the American economy. In fact, investors were pulling out of the USA. One estimate suggests that European investors alone sold $70 billion of US assets during 2002. The result of all this was a massive depreciation of the dollar and appreciation of the euro, so that by December 2004 the exchange rate had risen to $1.36: a 60 per cent appreciation since June 2001!

In 2004–5, with the US economy growing strongly again, the Fed raised interest rates several times, from 1 per cent in early 2004 to 5.25 by June 2006. The ECB kept interest rates constant at 2 per cent until early 2006. The result was that the euro depreciated against the dollar in 2005. But then the rise of the euro began again as the US growth slowed and eurozone growth rose and people anticipated a narrowing of the gap between US and eurozone interest rates.

In 2007 and 2008, worries about the credit crunch in the USA led the Fed to cut interest rates to stave off recession. In August 2007, the US federal funds rate was 5.25 per cent. It was then reduced on several occasions to stand at between 0 and 0.25 per cent by December 2008. The ECB, in contrast, kept the eurozone rate at 4 per cent for the first part of this period and even raised it to 4.25 per cent temporarily in the face of rapidly rising commodity prices. As a result, short-term finance flooded into the eurozone and the euro appreciated again, from $1.37 in mid-2007 to $1.58 in mid-2008.

... Then the steps down

Eventually, in September 2008, with the eurozone on the edge of recession and predictions that the ECB would cut interest rates, the euro at last began to fall. It continued to do so as the ECB cut rates. However, with monetary policy in the eurozone remaining tighter than in the USA, the euro began to rise again, only falling once more at the end of 2009 and into 2010 as US growth accelerated and speculators anticipated a tightening of US monetary policy.

Growing worries in 2010 about the level of government deficits and debt in various eurozone countries, such as Greece, Portugal, Spain, Italy and Ireland, contributed to speculation and thus growing volatility of the euro. Throughout the first part of 2010 investors became increasingly reluctant to hold the euro, as fears of debt default mounted. As such, the euro fell substantially from

$1.44 in January 2010 to $1.19 in June – a 17 per cent depreciation.

Then, as support was promised by the ECB and IMF to Greece in return for deficit reduction policies, and similar support could be made available to other eurozone countries with severe deficits, fears subsided and the euro rose again. By the end of October 2010, the euro was trading at $1.39. In April 2011, the euro increased to a high of $1.44.

Then began a dramatic fall in the euro as concerns grew over the eurozone's sluggish recovery and continuing high debt levels. Speculators thus believed that eurozone interest rates would have to continue falling. The ECB cut the main interest rate from 1.5 per cent in October 2011 in a series of steps to 0.05 per cent by September 2014.

With the ECB reducing interest rates and people increasingly predicting the introduction of quantitative easing (QE), the euro depreciated during 2014. Between March and December 2014 it depreciated by 11 per cent against the dollar, while the euro exchange rate index depreciated by 4 per cent. With the announced programme of QE being somewhat larger than markets expected, in the week following the announcement in January 2015, the euro fell a further 2.3 per cent against the dollar, and the euro exchange rate index also fell by 2.3 per cent. The result was that the euro was trading at its lowest level against the US dollar since April 2003.

With the long-awaited rise in US interest rates starting in December 2015, a fall in the main EU rate to 0 per cent in March 2016 and the announcement that the ECB's quantitative easing programme would continue to at least the end of 2017, the euro remained weak against the dollar.

The path of the euro shows that interest rate volatility and divergence in interest rates between the USA and the eurozone have been a major factor in the exchange rate volatility between the euro and the dollar – itself a cause of uncertainty in international trade and finance. However, more recently concerns over the fiscal health of national eurozone governments have played a particularly important role in explaining fluctuations in the euro.

 Find out what has happened to the euro/dollar exchange rate over the past 12 months. (You can find the data from the Bank of England's Statistical Interactive Database at www.bankofengland.co.uk/boeapps/iadb/newintermed.asp.) Explain why the exchange rate has moved the way it has.

Destabilising speculation

 This occurs when speculators believe that exchange rate movements will continue in the same direction.

In our example, speculators may believe that inflation will not be brought under control. They anticipate a continuing fall in the exchange rate and thus sell *now* before the

exchange rate falls any further. In Figure 25.10, this speculation causes the demand and supply curves to shift further, to D_3 and S_3, and causes the exchange rate to fall further, to er_3.

Eventually, however, this destabilising speculation could cause **overshooting**, with the exchange rate falling well below the purchasing-power parity rate. At this point speculators,

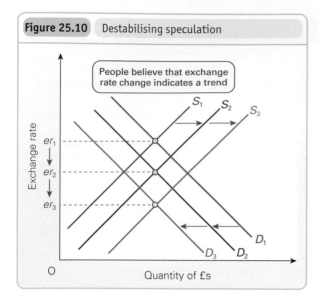

Figure 25.10 Destabilising speculation

believing that the rate will rise again, will start buying pounds again. This causes the exchange rate to rise.

Obviously, governments prefer stabilising to destabilising speculation. Destabilising speculation can cause severe exchange rate fluctuations. The resulting uncertainty is very damaging to trade. It is very important, therefore, that governments create a climate of confidence. People must believe that the government can prevent economic crises from occurring.

Conclusion

Whatever speculators anticipate will happen to the exchange rate, their actions will help to bring it about. If they think the sterling exchange rate will fall, they will sell pounds, hence causing it to fall. Thus speculators as a whole will gain. This applies to both stabilising and destabilising speculation.

 If speculators on average gain from their speculation, who loses?

Advantages of a free-floating exchange rate

The advantages and disadvantages of free-floating rates are to a large extent the opposite of those of fixed rates.

Automatic correction. The government simply lets the exchange rate move freely to the equilibrium. In this way,

Definition

Exchange rate overshooting Where a fall (or rise) in the long-run equilibrium exchange rate causes the actual exchange rate to fall (or rise) by a greater amount before eventually moving back to the new long-run equilibrium level.

balance of payments disequilibria are automatically and instantaneously corrected without the need for specific government policies – policies that under other systems can be mishandled.

No problem of international liquidity and reserves. Since there is no central bank intervention in the foreign exchange market, there is no need to hold reserves. A currency is automatically convertible at the current market exchange rate. International trade is thereby financed.

Insulation from external economic events. A country is not tied to a possibly unacceptably high world inflation rate, as it is under a fixed exchange rate. It can choose its own inflation target. It is also to some extent protected against world economic fluctuations and shocks (see pages 802–4).

Governments are free to choose their domestic policy. Under a fixed rate, a government may have to deflate the economy even when there is high unemployment. Under a floating rate, the government can choose whatever level of domestic demand it considers appropriate, and simply leave exchange rate movements to take care of any balance of payments effect. This is a major advantage, especially when the effectiveness of deflation is reduced by downward wage and price rigidity, and when competitive deflation between countries may end up causing a world recession.

Disadvantages of a free-floating exchange rate

Despite these advantages, there are still some serious problems with free-floating exchange rates.

Speculation. Short-run instability can be lessened by stabilising speculation, thus making speculation advantageous. If, due to short-run inelasticity of demand, a deficit causes a very large depreciation, speculators will buy pounds, knowing that in the long run the exchange rate will appreciate again. Their action therefore helps to lessen the short-run fall in the exchange rate.

Nevertheless, in an uncertain world where there are few restrictions on currency speculation, where the fortunes and policies of governments can change rapidly, and where large amounts of short-term deposits are internationally 'footloose', speculation can be highly destabilising in the short run. Considerable exchange rate overshooting can occur.

An example of such overshooting occurred between June 2008 and March 2009 when the pound depreciated 14 per cent against the euro, 28 per cent against the US dollar and 34 per cent against the yen (see Figure 15.16 on page 482). The nominal sterling exchange rate index fell 16 per cent and the real index by 15 per cent. Speculators were predicting that interest rates in the UK would fall further than in other countries and stay lower for longer. This was because the recessionary implications of a highly financialised economy such as the UK following the financial crisis were expected to be deeper. Consequently, inflation was expected to undershoot the Bank of England's 2 per cent target and perhaps even become negative. But the fall in the exchange rate represented considerable overshooting and both the nominal and real exchange rate indices rose by 9 per cent between March and June 2009.

This is just one example of the violent swings in exchange rates that have occurred in recent years. They even occur under managed floating exchange rate systems where governments have attempted to dampen such fluctuations!

The continuance of exchange rate fluctuations over a number of years is likely to encourage the growth of speculative holdings of currency. This can then cause even larger and more rapid swings in exchange rates.

KI 11 p76 *Uncertainty for traders and investors.* The uncertainty caused by currency fluctuations can discourage international trade and investment. To some extent, the problem can be overcome by using the *forward exchange market*. Here traders agree with a bank today the rate of exchange for some point in the future (say, in six months' time). This allows traders

to plan future purchases of imports or sales of exports at a known rate of exchange. Of course, banks charge for this service, since they are taking upon themselves the risks of adverse exchange rate fluctuations.

This will not help long-term investment, however, where decisions are made based on anticipated costs and revenue flows for many years to come. The possibility of exchange rate appreciation may well discourage firms from investing abroad.

 Why would banks not be prepared to offer a forward exchange rate to a firm for, say, five years from now?

Definition

Forward exchange market Where contracts are made today for the price at which a currency will be exchanged at some specified future date.

BOX 25.6 | **THE EFFECTIVENESS OF MONETARY AND FISCAL POLICIES UNDER FLOATING EXCHANGE RATES** | *EXPLORING ECONOMICS*

With a floating exchange rate, monetary policy is strong and fiscal policy is weak (the reverse of the case with fixed exchange rates).

Monetary policy

Assume that the economy is in recession and the central bank wishes to increase aggregate demand. It thus reduces interest rates. Three effects follow, each contributing to the effectiveness of the monetary policy.

1. *The expansionary monetary policy directly increases aggregate demand.* The size of the effect here depends on the amount that interest rates change and the elasticity of aggregate demand in response to the changes in interest rates.
2. *The exchange rate depreciates.* Higher aggregate demand increases imports and (via higher prices) reduces exports. This and the lower interest rates reduce the demand for and increase the supply of domestic currency on the foreign exchange market. The exchange rate thus depreciates.

    This reinforces the increase in domestic demand. A lower exchange rate makes exports less expensive again and therefore increases their demand (an injection). Imports become more expensive again and therefore their demand falls (a withdrawal). There is thus a *further* multiplied rise in income.
3. *Speculation may cause initial exchange rate overshooting.* Lower interest rates cause speculative financial outflows in anticipation of the depreciation. This causes the exchange rate to fall below its eventual rate – to overshoot, thus causing a further rise in aggregate demand.

This is only a short-term effect, however, since speculators will stop selling the domestic currency when the rate has gone so low that they feel it must rise again (back towards the purchasing-power parity level) sufficiently fast to offset the lower interest rates they are now getting. The greater the mobility of international finance and the better the information of the speculators, the shorter will the short run be.

Fiscal policy

Fiscal policy is relatively weak under a floating rate. Again, let us assume that the objective is to raise aggregate demand to combat a recession. The government thus reduces taxes and/or increases its expenditure. The rise in aggregate demand raises imports and (via higher prices) reduces exports. This effect on the current account of the balance of payments puts downward pressure on the exchange rate.

The higher aggregate demand, however, increases the transactions demand for money and hence *raises* interest rates. These higher interest rates will lead to financial inflows. This will put upward pressure on the exchange rate, which is likely to swamp the downward pressure from the current account deficit. There will therefore be an *appreciation* of the exchange rate. This will increase imports and reduce exports, thus reducing aggregate demand again, and reducing the effectiveness of the fiscal expansion.

 Compare the relative effectiveness of fiscal and monetary policies as means of reducing aggregate demand under a system of floating exchange rates.

Lack of discipline on the domestic economy. Governments may pursue irresponsibly inflationary policies. Also, unions and firms may well drive up wages and prices, without the same fear of losing overseas markets or of the government imposing deflationary policies. The depreciation resulting from this inflation will itself fuel the inflation by raising the price of imports.

Conclusion

Neither fixed nor free-floating exchange rates are free from problems. For this reason, governments have sought a compromise between the two, the hope being that some intermediate system will gain the benefits of both, while avoiding most of their disadvantages.

One compromise was tried after the Second World War. This was the *adjustable peg*. Another is the system that replaced the adjustable peg in the early 1970s and continues for much of the world today. This is the system of *managed floating*. We examine these systems in the next section.

Section summary

1. Under a free-floating exchange rate, the balance of payments will automatically be kept in balance by movements in the exchange rate. This removes the *balance of payments* constraint on domestic policy. It does not, however, remove external constraints entirely.

2. According to the purchasing-power parity theory, any changes in domestic prices will simply lead to equivalent changes in the exchange rate, leaving the international competitiveness of home-produced goods unaffected. If, however, internal shocks cause changes in interest rates, there will be a change in the *financial* account balance. This will influence exchange rates and destroy the purchasing-power parity theory. The current account will go out of balance (in an equal and opposite way to the financial account).

3. This problem is made more acute by the carry trade, whereby people borrow money in low interest rate (current account surplus) countries and deposit them in high interest rate (current account deficit) countries. This causes deficit countries' exchange rates to appreciate, thereby worsening their current account deficit.

4. External shocks will be reflected in changes in exchange rates and will help to insulate the domestic economy from international economic fluctuations.

5. Exchange rate movements are highly influenced by speculation. If speculators believe that an appreciation or depreciation is merely temporary, their activities will help to stabilise the exchange rate. If, however, they believe that an exchange rate movement in either direction will continue, their activities will be destabilising and cause a bigger movement in the exchange rate.

6. The advantages of free-floating exchange rates are that they automatically correct balance of payments disequilibria; they eliminate the need for reserves; and they give governments a greater independence to pursue their chosen domestic policy.

7. On the other hand, a completely free exchange rate can be highly unstable, made worse by destabilising speculation. This may discourage firms from trading and investing abroad. What is more, a flexible exchange rate, by removing the balance of payments constraint on domestic policy, may encourage governments to pursue irresponsible domestic policies for short-term political gain.

25.4 EXCHANGE RATE SYSTEMS IN PRACTICE

The adjustable peg system: 1945–73

After the collapse in 1931 of the fixed exchange rate system of the gold standard (see section 16.2), the huge scale of the initial disequilibria caused wild swings in exchange rates. Many countries resorted to protectionism, given the great uncertainties associated with free trade under fluctuating exchange rates.

The Bretton Woods system

In 1944, the allied countries met at Bretton Woods in the USA to hammer out a new exchange rate system: one that would avoid the chaos of the 1930s and encourage free trade, but that would avoid the rigidity of the gold standard. The compromise they worked out was an adjustable peg system that lasted until 1971.

Under the **Bretton Woods system** there was a totally fixed dollar/gold exchange rate ($35 per ounce of gold). The USA guaranteed that it would freely convert dollars into gold. It was hoped that this would encourage countries to hold dollars as their major reserve currency. After all, if dollars were freely convertible into gold, they were as good as gold. All other countries pegged their exchange rate to the dollar.

To prevent temporary, short-term fluctuations in the exchange rate, central banks *intervened* on the foreign exchange markets using their foreign reserves. This enabled them to maintain the pegged rate within a 1 per cent band.

If the disequilibrium became more serious, governments were supposed to pursue policies of *deflation* or *reflation*. In the meantime, in the case of a deficit, the central bank might have insufficient reserves to maintain the exchange rate. The International Monetary Fund was set up to provide such liquidity. All countries were required to deposit a quota of funds with the IMF, depending on the size of their trade. The IMF would then lend to countries in balance of payments deficit to enable them to maintain their exchange rate. The more a country had to borrow from the IMF, the more the IMF would insist that it pursued appropriate deflationary policies to correct the disequilibrium.

If the deficit became severe, countries could *devalue*: the pegged rate could be adjusted (in consultation with the IMF).

 Under this system, how would you expect countries to respond to a balance of payments surplus? Would a revaluation benefit such countries?

Advocates of an adjustable peg system argue that the Bretton Woods arrangement made a significant contribution to the long boom of the 1950s and 1960s.

■ Since rates were fixed for a long period of time – perhaps many years – uncertainty was reduced and trade was encouraged.

■ Pegged rates, plus the overseeing role of the IMF, prevented governments from pursuing irresponsible policies, and helped to bring about an international harmonisation of policies. They kept world inflation in check.

■ If a deficit became severe, countries could devalue. This prevented them being forced into a depression or into adopting protectionist policies. The IMF ensured an orderly process of devaluation.

However, there were two serious weaknesses with the system. These became more and more apparent during the 1960s, and eventually led to the system's downfall.

Problems of adjustment to balance of payments disequilibria

To avoid internal policy being governed by the balance of payments, and to avoid being forced into a depression, countries with a fundamental deficit were supposed to devalue. There were several difficulties here, however.

■ Identifying whether a deficit was fundamental. Governments were frequently overoptimistic about the future balance of payments position.

■ If devaluation did take place, it could be very disruptive to firms. A devaluation suddenly alters the costs and revenues of importers and exporters by a substantial amount.

If a devaluation is felt to be imminent, it can cause great uncertainty and may make them reluctant to take on new trade commitments.

 Would this uncertainty have a similar or a different effect on exporting companies and companies using imported inputs?

■ At first a devaluation might make a current account deficit *worse*: the *J-curve effect*. The price elasticities of demand for imports and exports may be low in the short run (see Case Study 25.1 on the student website). Directly after devaluation, few extra exports may be sold, and more will have to be paid for imports that do not have immediate substitutes. There is thus an initial deterioration in the balance of trade before it eventually improves. In Figure 25.11, devaluation takes place at time t_1. As you can see, the diagram has a J shape.

For these reasons, countries in deficit tended to put off devaluing until they were forced to by a crisis. The reluctance of countries to devalue caused other problems.

Stop-go policies. Countries had to rely much more on deflation as a means of curing deficits. The UK in particular found that, whenever the economy started to grow, the balance of payments went into deficit. This forced the government to curb demand again through fiscal and/or monetary policies.

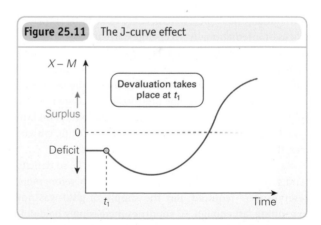

Figure 25.11 The J-curve effect

Devaluation takes place at t_1

Definition

Bretton Woods system An adjustable peg system whereby currencies were pegged to the US dollar. The USA maintained convertibility of the dollar into gold at the rate of $35 to an ounce.

J-curve effect Where a devaluation causes the balance of payments first to deteriorate and then to improve. The graph of the balance of payments over time thus looks like a letter J.

Speculation. If countries delayed devaluing until a deficit became really severe, an eventual large devaluation became inevitable. This provided a field day for speculators: they could not lose, and there was a high probability of a substantial gain.

Large-scale disruption. The delay in devaluing plus the build-up of speculative pressure could cause the devaluation to be very large when it eventually came. This could be highly disruptive.

Countries' balance of payments deficits could be reduced and adjustment made easier if surplus countries were willing to revalue. There was a reluctance to do this, however, by countries such as Japan. Revaluation was strongly opposed by exporters (and producers of import substitutes), who would find it suddenly more difficult to compete. What is more, there were not the same pressures for surplus countries to revalue as there were for deficit countries to devalue. A lack of reserves can force deficit countries to devalue. Surplus countries, however, may be quite happy to carry on building up reserves.

The USA was not allowed to devalue when in deficit. The onus was on other countries to revalue, which they were reluctant to do. Hence large US deficits persisted. The problem of these deficits was linked to the second major problem area: that of international liquidity.

Problems of international liquidity and the collapse of the system

With an adjustable peg system, there have to be sufficient stocks of internationally acceptable currencies or other liquid assets. This 'international liquidity' is necessary both to finance trade and to provide enough reserves for central banks to support their currencies whenever there is a currency flow deficit. Under the Bretton Woods system, there were three main sources of liquidity: gold, dollars and IMF quotas. But since IMF quotas were only in existing currencies, they were not a source of *additional* liquidity.

As world trade expanded (see section 24.1), so deficits (and surpluses) were likely to be larger, and therefore more reserves were required. But the supply of gold was not expanding fast enough, so countries increasingly held dollars. After all, dollars earned interest. The willingness to hold dollars enabled the USA to run large balance of payments deficits. All the USA needed to do to pay for the deficits was to 'print' more dollars, which other countries were prepared to accept as reserves.

US balance of payments deficits in the 1960s got steadily worse. The financing of the Vietnam War, in particular, deepened the deficit. Dollars flooded out of the USA. World liquidity thus expanded rapidly, fuelling world inflation. Furthermore, the rapid growth in overseas dollar holdings meant that US gold reserves were increasingly inadequate to guarantee convertibility. Some countries, fearful that the USA might eventually be forced to suspend convertibility,

chose to exchange dollars for gold. US gold reserves fell, creating a further imbalance and a deepening of the crises.

Despite various attempts to rescue the system, with its overreliance on the dollar, it eventually collapsed. The dollar was devalued against gold by 8 per cent in December 1971. In June 1972 the pound was floated. Over the following year, other countries followed suit, and despite a further dollar devaluation the system was finally abandoned in 1973. By mid-1973 gold was trading at $120 per ounce.

 Why would the adjustable peg system have been less suitable in the world of the mid-1970s than it was back in the 1950s?

Managed floating

The world has been on a floating exchange rate system since the breakdown of the Bretton Woods system in the early 1970s. This allows adjustment to be made to the inevitable shifts in demand and supply, shifts that got more extreme in the early 1970s with a quadrupling of oil prices in 1973–4 and rapid changes in world trading patterns. Domestic policy has been largely freed from balance of payments constraints. At the same time, *managed* floating was claimed to allow adjustment to be more gentle, ideally avoiding wild swings in the exchange rate aggravated by speculation.

Some minor currencies remain pegged (but adjustable) to a major currency such as the dollar, but float along with it against other currencies. Other currencies are pegged to each other, but jointly float against the rest of the world. The most notable examples of this have been the currencies of the exchange rate mechanism (ERM) of the European Monetary System (see section 26.2) and now the members of ERM2 (see page 796).

Some countries allow their currencies to float freely. Most countries, however, from time to time have attempted to stabilise their exchange rate, and have thus been operating a system of 'managed flexibility'.

If the country decides to adopt a managed floating system, how could the central bank prevent the exchange rate from falling? There are two main methods:

- Using reserves or foreign loans to purchase domestic currency on the foreign exchange market.
- Raising interest rates to attract short-term financial inflows.

Problems with managed floating since 1972

Managing the exchange rate involved problems, however. Governments needed to know when to intervene, what exchange rate level they should aim to maintain, and how persistently they should try to maintain that rate in the face of speculative pressure.

Predicting the long-term equilibrium exchange rate

Differing inflation rates between countries will require exchange rate adjustments to maintain purchasing-power parity. It is not correct, however, for governments to assume that this will be the *only* cause of shifts in the long-term equilibrium exchange rate. For example, the 1973–4 and 1979–80 oil crises caused fundamental and unpredictable changes in currency demand and supply. So too did other factors, such as the dismantling of trade barriers within the EU, protectionist measures adopted in different parts of the world, changes in technology and changes in tastes.

It is therefore very difficult for the government to predict what the long-term equilibrium will be, and what proportion of any exchange rate movement is therefore due to *long-term* and what proportion merely to *short-term* phenomena.

The growth in speculative financial flows

The OPEC oil price increase in 1973–4 caused huge balance of payments deficits for oil importers. The OPEC countries could not spend all of these surpluses on additional imports since (a) they did not have the capacity to consume such a huge increase in imports and (b) the oil-importing countries did not have the capacity to supply such a huge increase in exports. The surpluses were thus largely invested in short-term dollar (and, to a lesser extent, other major currency) assets. This created a large capacity for short-term loans by Western banks. These moneys could be rapidly shifted from one world financial centre to another, depending on which country had the most favourable interest rates and exchange rates. This created a massive capacity for speculation, and thus made it difficult for countries to control exchange rates by currency sales alone.

KI 10
p70

Over the years, the scale of speculative flows has continued to increase. Foreign exchange market data from the Bank for International Settlements show that in 2016 some $5 trillion was passing across the international exchanges every day. Reserves and access to foreign loans are simply inadequate to prevent concerted speculative selling.

To manage the exchange rate, therefore, central banks would have to rely much more on using interest rates.

Conflicts with internal policy

Using interest rates to support the exchange rate has become more and more unpopular as countries have preferred to use interest rates to keep inflation at or below a target level.

KI 36
p451

As a result of these problems, countries have increasingly opted for a system of freely floating exchange rates. The UK experience is considered in Box 25.7.

 Would any of these problems be lessened by the world returning to an adjustable peg system? If so, what sort of adjustable peg system would you recommend?

The volatility of exchange rates

KI 34
p445

Exchange rates have become extremely volatile. We continue to observe this volatility when we adjust for changes in the prices of exports (measured in domestic prices) relative to the prices of imports (measured in foreign currencies). In other words, the *real* exchange rate is volatile too (see Figure 25.12). This means that nominal exchange rates have typically moved more than the relative prices of exported and imported goods and services.

As a result of exchange rate volatility, currencies can gain or lose several percentage points in the space of a few days. These changes can then make all the difference between profit and loss for trading companies. There are a number of reasons for this volatility:

- Inflation or money supply targets. Central banks may have to make considerable changes to interest rates in order to keep to their targets. These in turn cause exchange rate fluctuations.

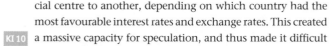

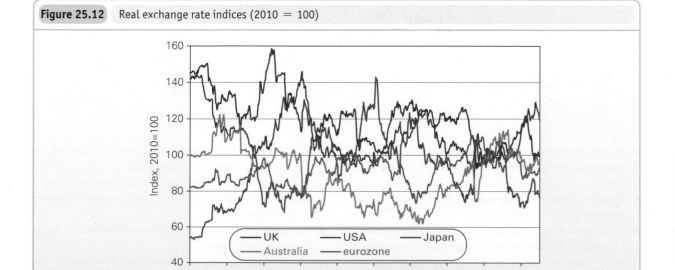

Note: Exchange rate indices are BIS narrow indices comprising 27 countries; prior to the introduction of the euro in 1999, eurozone figures are weighted average exchange rates of currencies that made up to the euro.
Source: Based on data from *Effective Exchange Rate Indices* (Bank for International Settlements).

BOX 25.7   STERLING SINCE THE 1990S

The sterling seesaw

Between October 1990 and September 1992, sterling was in the ERM, at a central rate of £1 = 2.95 German marks, with permitted fluctuations of ±6 per cent against any other ERM currency. However, this exchange rate proved unsustainably high and the UK was forced out of the ERM by a massive wave of speculation. Within two months of this, sterling had depreciated by some 15 per cent.

Since 1992, the UK has adopted a virtually free-floating exchange rate. Between 1992 and 1996, fluctuations in the exchange rate were relatively minor. The government was now targeting inflation, and with inflation coming down, it was at first able to reduce interest rates. But this mirrored reductions in inflation and interest rates in other countries, and thus there was little need for exchange rate changes.

A rise in sterling

By the beginning of 1996, however, speculators began buying pounds, believing that the exchange rate would appreciate.

They saw that the economy was now beginning to grow quite rapidly, and was likely to continue doing so, given that an election was coming up. Inflation was thus likely to rise and this would force the government to raise interest rates. Indeed, by mid-1996 interest rates bottomed out *and began to rise*.

When the new Labour government was elected in 1997, the Bank of England was made independent. Over the following months, the Bank raised interest rates several times in order to bring the inflation down to the target level. The effect was to further fuel a large-scale appreciation of sterling. Between January 1996 and April 1998, the *real* exchange rate index rose by 28 per cent (see chart). This made it *more* difficult for UK exporters and industries competing with imports.

From 1998 to 2007 the pound was well above its purchasing-power parity rate. This was largely the result of UK interest rates being higher than eurozone and Japanese rates, and frequently above US rates too.

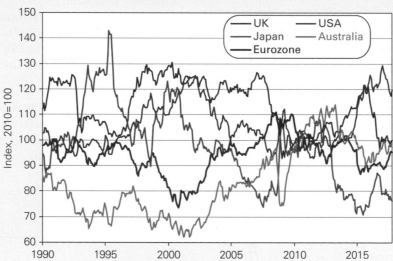

Real exchange rate indices (2010 = 100)

Note: Exchange rate indices are BIS narrow indices comprising 27 countries.
Source: Based on data from *Effective Exchange Rate Indices* (Bank for International Settlements).

- A huge growth in international financial markets. This has encouraged the international transfer of money and capital.
- The abolition of exchange controls in most industrialised countries.
- The growth in information technology. The simple use of a computer can transfer capital and finance internationally in a matter of seconds.
- The preference for liquidity. With the danger of currency fluctuations, companies prefer to keep their financial capital as liquid as possible. They do not want to be locked into assets denominated in a declining currency.

- The growing speculative activities of trading companies. Many large companies have a team of dealers to help manage their liquid assets: to switch them from currency to currency in order to take advantage of market movements.
- The growing speculative activities of banks and other financial institutions.
- The growing belief that rumour and 'jumping on the bandwagon' are more important determinants of currency buying or selling than cool long-term appraisal. If people *believe* that speculation is likely to be destabilising, their actions will ensure that it is. Many companies

With the growth of the carry trade (see page 803), this had helped keep the exchange rate above the PPP rate. The overvaluation of the pound continued to put both the export and import competing sectors in the UK under great competitive pressure. The current account remained in deficit and in most years deteriorated (see the chart in Box 25.2 on page 790).

A fall in sterling

In late 2007, at last the pound began depreciating. With the effects of speculation, this became rapid. Worries about recession suggested that the Bank of England would reduce interest rates – as indeed it did: Bank Rate fell from 5 per cent in October 2008 to 0.5 per cent in March 2009.

But other central banks were reducing their rates too, so why did the pound depreciate while other currencies, including the Japanese yen and Australian dollar, appreciated. There were various reasons for this:

- The cut in the Bank Rate was greater than in the eurozone.
- There were worries that the recession would be deeper and more prolonged in the UK than elsewhere and that low interest rates would therefore persist for longer than in other countries.
- Investment in the UK was seen as more risky than in other countries, given the importance of the financial services sector in the UK (a sector badly hit by the credit crunch) and the more rapid rise in government borrowing than in many other countries.
- Commodity prices were rising, which pushed up the exchange rates for commodity exporting countries, such as Australia.

Significantly, the carry trade began to unwind. With the onset of recession, the UK's high current account deficit was no longer seen as a reason to expect relatively high interest rates. Many who had borrowed in yen or other low interest rate currencies to purchase sterling, now began selling sterling and returning to the original currencies, causing such currencies to appreciate substantially.

Between September 2008 and September 2010 the real sterling exchange rate depreciated by 8 per cent while the real exchange rate of the Japanese yen appreciated by 20 per cent. This appreciation of the yen prompted the Japanese central bank in September 2010 to begin intervening in the foreign exchange markets by selling yen and buying dollars.

Rising again

Eventually, in mid-2013, sterling began to rise. With recovery gaining momentum more rapidly in the UK than in the eurozone, speculators were predicting that the Bank of England would raise rates before the ECB and that this would cause the pound to appreciate. The actions of speculators ensured that this occurred.

The Brexit fall

On 23 June 2016, the UK held a referendum on whether to remain a member of the EU. As soon as it became clear that the UK had voted to leave the EU the pound began to fall sharply. Investor concern about the UK's future trading relationships and its likely negative impact on long-term growth, coupled with the Bank of England's reduction in Bank Rate from 0.5 to 0.25 per cent, a further round of quantitative easing (see Box 22.10) and the potential for further monetary loosening helped to fuel a marked fall in sterling.

Six weeks after the vote, sterling had depreciated by 10.8 per cent against the dollar and 9.3 per cent against the euro compared with directly before the referendum. By the end of 2016, the real sterling exchange rate index was some 15 per cent lower than at the end of 2015, while the euro index was up by 1 per cent and the US dollar up by 5 per cent.

1. *Identify two factors in the UK economy which help to explain the appreciation of the real exchange rate after 1996.*
2. *What longer-term determinants are there of the sterling exchange rate index?*

---

involved in international trade and finance have developed a 'speculative mentality'.
- The growing belief that governments are powerless to prevent currency movements. As short-term capital (or 'hot money') grows relative to official reserves, it is increasingly difficult for central banks to stabilise currencies through exchange market intervention.

Although most governments and firms dislike highly volatile exchange rates, few today advocate a return to fixed exchange rates, or a system like the Bretton Woods one. In fact, apart from the Gulf states, very few countries still peg their currencies to the dollar. Even China, which from 1997 to 2005 was pegged to the dollar at $1 = 8.27$ yuan, has moved to a managed float based round the weighted average of a basket of currencies. In May 2017, the yuan was trading at 6.90 to the dollar – an appreciation of 20 per cent since 2005.

Despite the preference of most countries for floating exchange rates, suggestions have been made for reducing volatility. We examine some of these in Chapter 26.

BOX 25.8   **DO INFLATION RATES EXPLAIN LONGER-TERM EXCHANGE RATE MOVEMENTS?**

Does PPP hold in the long run?

As we have seen in section 25.4, exchange rates have become extremely volatile. We can see from Figure 25.1 (page 788) that the trade-weighted *real* exchange rate of sterling exhibits considerable volatility. The real exchange rate adjusts for the terms of trade. The significance of movements in the real exchange rate is that it demonstrates that purchasing-power parity (PPP) fails to hold in the short run.

But does PPP hold in the long run? If so, differences in countries' inflation rates need to be reflected in changes in exchange rates. In this box, we consider whether long-term inflation rate differentials between the UK and nine other countries have been reflected in long-term movements in the foreign currency price of sterling, i.e. in the number of foreign currency units per £.

Consider the chart. On the horizontal axis is plotted the average annual percentage change in the number of foreign currency units per £1 from 1976 to 2016. Positive values indicate that sterling appreciated against that currency; negative values that it depreciated. For instance, sterling appreciated by 0.95 per cent per annum against the Swedish krona, but depreciated by 2.56 per cent per annum against the Japanese yen.

On the vertical axis is plotted the inflation differential; this measures the difference between the average annual rate of inflation in the UK and that in each of the other nine countries. For instance, the average annual British inflation rate was 3.96 percentage points higher than in Japan, but 0.79 percentage points lower than in New Zealand.

If inflation differentials are to be reflected in exchange rate changes we would expect to see the observations for the nine countries lying along the downward-sloping blue line. This links positive values of the inflation differential with the equivalent percentage depreciation; this would be consistent with PPP holding in the long run.

Eight of our nine observations lie to various degrees *above* the blue line. This tells us that that for the inflation rate differential with each country, sterling has appreciated more or depreciated less than might be expected. This means that the *real* exchange rate of sterling has *appreciated* against each country's currency over the period of analysis.

Take Japan as an example. As we noted above, the inflation rate differential with the UK is 3.96 percentage points per annum. The higher rate of inflation in the UK means that the exchange rate would need to depreciate by 3.96 per cent per annum to compensate. Although sterling has indeed depreciated against the yen, it has done so by only 2.56 per cent per annum.

New Zealand is slightly *below* the blue line, consistent with sterling having appreciated less or depreciated more than we would have expected (a depreciation of the real sterling exchange rate). In fact, the real depreciation of sterling against the New Zealand dollar is relatively small. While the average UK annual rate of inflation was 0.79 percentage points lower, the nominal appreciation of sterling was 0.65 percentage points.

From observing the data, it would appear that long-term inflation differentials do affect movements in bilateral exchange rates. However, it also appears that we need to take into account more than just inflation differentials in understanding exchange rate movements. Other causes of exchange rate movements include changes in relative interest rates, various international shocks, longer-term shifts in demand and supply for imports and exports, and speculation.

 Identify two factors in the UK economy which help to explain the appreciation of the real exchange rate.

Inflation differentials and appreciation of sterling, 1976–2016

Source: Exchange rate calculations based on bilateral sterling exchange rates from *ONS*; Inflation rate calculations based on GDP deflator data from *AMECO*.

Section summary

1. Under the Bretton Woods system (1945–71), currencies were pegged to the US dollar. The rate was supported from countries' reserves and if necessary with loans from the IMF. If there was a moderate disequilibrium, countries were supposed to use deflationary/reflationary policies. If the disequilibrium became severe, they were supposed to devalue/revalue.

2. The system was claimed to bring certainty for business and a constraint on governments pursuing irresponsible fiscal and monetary policies, while avoiding the problem of a recession if a balance of payments deficit became severe.

3. However, it was sometimes difficult to identify whether a deficit was severe enough to warrant a devaluation; a devaluation itself could be very disruptive for firms; and devaluation at first could make the deficit worse (the J-curve effect). If a country was reluctant to devalue, it would have to rely on deflation and a possible recession to tackle a balance of payments deficit.

4. Problems for deficit countries were made worse by an unwillingness of surplus countries to revalue or reflate.

5. Dollars were the main source of international liquidity under the Bretton Woods system. The USA, by creating dollars to pay for balance of payments deficits, caused excessive liquidity. This caused worldwide inflation, a lack of confidence in the USA and an eventual collapse of the system.

6. Since the early 1970s the world has largely been on a managed floating exchange rate system. The degree of intervention varies from country to country and from time to time.

7. In theory, managed floating can give the necessary degree of exchange rate flexibility in a world where shifts in currency demand and supply have become much larger. It can also release domestic policy from being dominated by balance of payments considerations. At the same time, the intervention could (in theory) prevent violent exchange rate fluctuations and allow a more orderly adjustment to new equilibrium exchange rates.

8. Nevertheless, there are problems under managed floating of predicting long-term equilibrium exchange rates. What is more, with the massive growth in 'hot money' since the early 1970s, it has become increasingly difficult for countries on their own to counteract speculation. The main instrument of intervention has become the rate of interest. There may be a conflict, however, in using interest rates both to control exchange rates *and* to control the domestic economy.

9. Sterling exchange rates have shown considerable volatility over the years, with large divergences from the purchasing-power parity rate. For example, the rise in UK interest rates in 1997–8 caused a large appreciation of sterling, much to the consternation of exporters. The cut in interest rates in 2008 was accompanied by an equally large depreciation.

10. The volatility of exchange rates around the world has grown. Reasons include: a growth in international financial markets and a liberalisation of international financial movements combined with easier computer transfer of funds, a growth in speculative activities and a growing belief in the impotence of governments acting on their own to stabilise rates.

*APPENDIX: THE OPEN ECONOMY AND *ISLM* ANALYSIS

In this appendix, we show how the *ISLM* analysis that we examined in the appendix to Chapter 19 can be extended to incorporate the open economy. We will first assume a fixed rate of exchange and then later a free-floating rate.

Analysis under a fixed exchange rate

The BP *curve*

We start by introducing a third curve, the *BP* (balance of payments) curve. This curve, like the *IS* and *LM* curves, plots a relationship between the rate of interest (*r*) and the level of national income (*Y*). All points along the *BP* curve represent a position of *balance of payments equilibrium.*

We assume that prices are fixed in the short run; hence a change in the real interest rate (*r*) corresponds to an equivalent change in the nominal rate of interest (*i*). The *BP* curve slopes upwards from left to right (see Figure 25.13). Increases

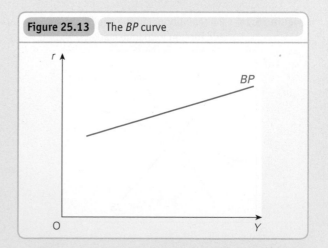

Figure 25.13   The *BP* curve

in the rate of interest (*r*) will cause the financial account to move into surplus as finance is attracted into the country. Increases in real national income (*Y*), in contrast, will cause the current account to move into deficit as more imports are purchased. If the overall balance of payments is to stay in equilibrium, current account deficits must be matched by financial (plus capital) account surpluses and vice versa. Thus a rise in *Y* must be accompanied by a rise in *r*, and reductions in *Y* must be accompanied by reductions in *r*. The *BP* curve therefore slopes upwards. Any point below the *BP* line represents a position of overall deficit; any point above the line, a position of surplus.

The slope of the *BP* curve depends on two factors.

The marginal propensity to import (mpm = $\Delta M/\Delta Y$). The higher the *mpm,* the steeper will be the *BP* curve. The reason is that with a high *mpm* there will be a correspondingly large rise in imports for any given rise in national income. This will cause a large current account deficit. To maintain an overall balance of payments equilibrium, this will require a correspondingly large financial account surplus. This in turn will require a large rise in interest rates. Thus the bigger the *mpm,* the larger the rise in interest rates that will be necessary to restore balance of payments equilibrium, and hence the steeper will be the BP curve.

The elasticity of supply of international finance. The greater the elasticity of supply of international finance, the less will be the rise in interest rates necessary to attract an inflow of finance and thereby restore balance of payments equilibrium after a rise in national income, and hence the flatter will be the *BP* curve. In the case of a perfectly elastic supply of international finance, the BP curve will be horizontal at the world rate of interest.

Equilibrium in the model

If we now put the *BP* curve on an *ISLM* diagram, we have the position shown in Figure 25.14. Point *a* represents full equilibrium. At r_1 and Y_1, investment equals saving (point *a* is on the *IS* curve), the demand for money equals the supply

(point *a* is also on the *LM* curve), and finally the balance of payments is in balance (point *a* is also on the *BP* curve).

But what is the mechanism that ensures that all three curves intersect at the same point? To answer this question, let us assume that the three curves just happen to intersect at the same point, and then let us examine the effects of changes in fiscal and monetary policies, which shift the *IS* and *LM* curves respectively. Will equilibrium be restored? The answer is yes, via a change in the money supply. Let us examine fiscal and monetary policy changes in turn.

Fiscal policy under fixed exchange rates

An expansionary fiscal policy, i.e. a rise in government spending and/or a reduction in tax, will have the effect of shifting the *IS* curve to the right (e.g. to IS_2 in Figure 25.15). The reason is that for any given rate of interest there will be a higher equilibrium level of national income than before.

This will increase national income, but the extra demand for money that results will drive up interest rates. In a *closed* economy, equilibrium would now be at point *b* (r_2, Y_2), where $IS_2 = LM_1$. But in our open economy model, this equilibrium is *above the BP curve*. There is a balance of payments surplus. The reason for this is that the higher interest rates have caused a financial account surplus that is bigger than the current account deficit that results from the higher national income.

Such a surplus will cause the money supply to rise as funds flow into the country. This will in turn cause the *LM* curve to shift to the right. Equilibrium will finally be achieved at point *c* (r_3, Y_3), where $IS_2 = LM_2 = BP$. Thus under these conditions, the monetary effect of the change in the balance of payments will *reinforce* the fiscal policy and lead to a bigger rise in national income.

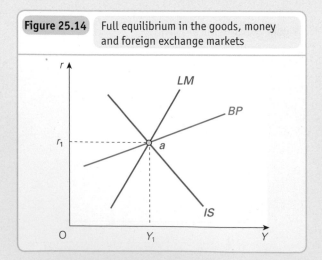

Figure 25.14 Full equilibrium in the goods, money and foreign exchange markets

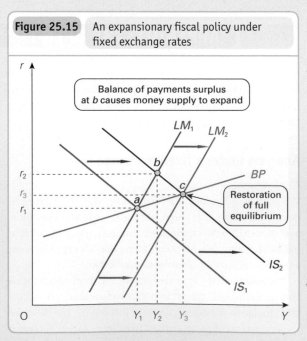

Figure 25.15 An expansionary fiscal policy under fixed exchange rates

What will be the effect of an expansionary fiscal policy on interest rates and national income if there is a perfectly elastic supply of international finance?

If the *BP* curve were steeper than the *LM* curve, the effect would be somewhat different. (Remember the *BP* curve will be steep if there is a high *mpm* and an inelastic supply of international finance.) This is illustrated in Figure 25.16.

Under these circumstances, an initial rise in national income to Y_2 (where $IS_2 = LM_1$) will cause a balance of payments *deficit* (point *b* is *below the BP curve*). The reason is that this time the current account deficit is bigger than the financial account surplus (due to a large *mpm* and a small inflow of finance). This will reduce the money supply and cause the *LM* curve to shift to the left. Equilibrium will be achieved at point *c*, where $LM_2 = IS_2 = BP$.

When the *BP* curve is steeper than the *LM* curve, therefore, the monetary effect of the change in the balance of payments will *dampen* the effect of the fiscal policy and lead to a smaller rise in national income.

Monetary policy under fixed exchange rates

An expansionary monetary policy will cause the *LM* curve to shift to the right (e.g. to LM_2 in Figure 25.17). The increased supply of money will drive down the rate of interest and increase national income. In a closed economy, equilibrium would now be at point *b* (r_2, Y_2), where $LM_2 = IS$. But in an open economy, this extra demand will have sucked in extra imports, and the lower interest rate will have led to net financial outflows. There will be a balance of payments deficit: point *b* is below the *BP* curve.

The balance of payments deficit will cause the money stock to fall as money flows abroad. This will cause the *LM*

curve to shift back again to its original position. The economy will return to its initial equilibrium at point *a*.

Thus under a fixed exchange rate regime, monetary policy alone will have *no long-term effect* on national income and employment. Only when accompanied by an expansion in aggregate demand (either through fiscal policy or through an autonomous rise in investment or a fall in savings) will an expansion of money supply lead to higher national income.

1. *Why does this conclusion remain the same if the BP curve is steeper than the LM curve?*
2. *Trace through the effects of a fall in exports (thereby shifting the BP curve).*
3. *Show what will happen if there is (a) a rise in business confidence and a resulting increase in investment; (b) a rise in the demand for money balance (say, for precautionary purposes).*

Analysis under free-floating exchange rates

As the exchange rate changes, the *BP* curve will shift (see Figure 25.18). If the *IS* and *LM* curves intersect *above* the *BP* curve, there will be a balance of payments surplus. This will cause the exchange rate to appreciate. The appreciation will cause the surplus to disappear. This in turn will cause the *BP* curve to shift upwards.

Similarly, if the *IS* and *LM* curves intersect *below* the *BP* curve, the resulting balance of payments deficit will cause a depreciation and a downward shift of the *BP* curve. Thus the *BP* curve will always shift so that it intersects where the *IS* and *LM* curves intersect.

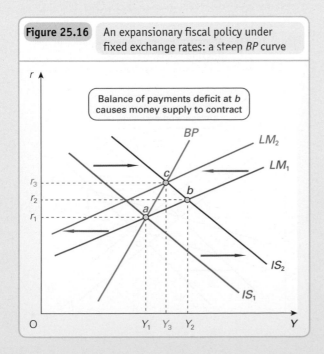

Figure 25.16 An expansionary fiscal policy under fixed exchange rates: a steep *BP* curve

Balance of payments deficit at *b* causes money supply to contract

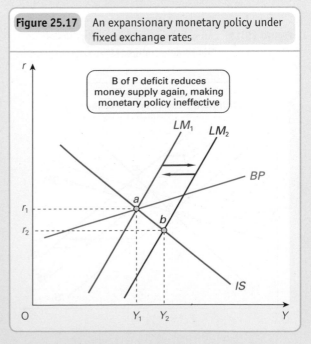

Figure 25.17 An expansionary monetary policy under fixed exchange rates

B of P deficit reduces money supply again, making monetary policy ineffective

Fiscal policy under floating exchange rates

Assume that the government pursues a reflationary fiscal policy. The *IS* curve shifts to *IS*₂ in Figure 25.19.

At point *b*, where the *LM* curve and the new *IS* curve intersect, there is a balance of payments surplus (due to higher financial inflows attracted by the higher rate of interest). This causes the exchange rate to appreciate and the *BP* curve to shift upwards.

But the higher exchange rate will cause a fall in exports and a rise in imports. This fall in aggregate demand will cause the *IS* curve to shift back towards the left. The new equilibrium will be at a point such as *c*. This represents only a modest change from point *a*. Thus under a floating exchange rate the effects of fiscal policy may be rather limited.

The effect will be stronger, however, the steeper the *BP* curve. In Figure 25.20, the *BP* curve is steeper than the *LM*

curve. This time a rise in the *IS* curve from *IS*₁ to *IS*₂ will lead to a balance of payments *deficit* and hence a *depreciation* of the exchange rate. The *BP* curve will shift *downwards*. The depreciation will cause a rise in exports and a fall in imports. This *rise* in aggregate demand will cause the *IS* curve to shift to the *right*. The new equilibrium will be at point *c*, which is at a higher level of national income, *Y*₃. Under these circumstances, the balance of payments effect makes fiscal policy stronger.

Under what circumstances would an expansionary fiscal policy have no effect at all on national income?

Figure 25.20 An expansionary fiscal policy under floating exchange rates: steep *BP* curve

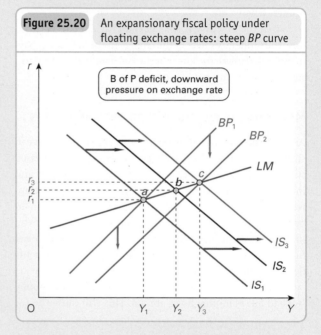

Figure 25.18 Movements of the *BP* curve under floating exchange rates

---

Figure 25.19 An expansionary fiscal policy under floating exchange rates

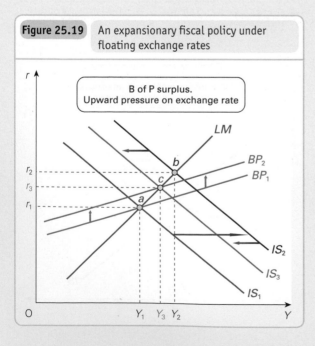

Figure 25.21 An expansionary monetary policy under floating exchange rates

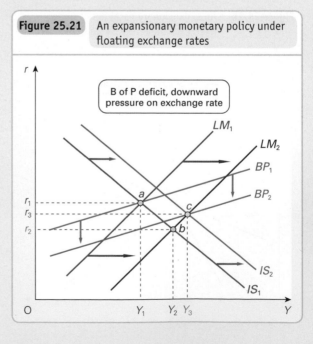

Monetary policy under floating exchange rates

An expansionary monetary policy will shift the *LM* curve to the right, to LM_2 in Figure 25.21. In a closed economy, equilibrium would now be at point *b*.

In an open economy under a floating exchange rate, the fall in the rate of interest will cause the exchange rate to depreciate and the *BP* curve to shift downwards. The depreciation will cause exports to rise and imports to fall. This increase in aggregate demand will shift the *IS* curve to the right. The new equilibrium will thus be at point *c*, where $LM_2 = IS_2 = BP_2$. This represents a large change from the initial point *a*.

Thus monetary policy can have a substantial effect on the level of national income under a system of floating exchange rates.

 What will determine the size of the shift in the BP curve in each case?

Appendix summary

1. A *BP* curve can be added to an *ISLM* diagram. It shows all the combinations of national income and interest rates at which the balance of payments is in equilibrium. The curve is upward sloping, showing that a rise in national income (causing a current account deficit) will require a rise in interest rates to give a counterbalancing financial account surplus.

2. The lower the *mpm* and the more elastic the supply of international finance, the flatter will be the *BP* curve.

3. Under a fixed exchange rate, the flatter the *BP* curve, the larger will be the effect on national income of an expansionary fiscal policy. Provided the *BP* curve is flatter than the *LM* curve, an expansionary fiscal policy will cause a balance of payments surplus (via its effect of increasing interest rates). The resulting increase in money supply will strengthen the initial effect of the fiscal policy.

4. Monetary policy under fixed exchange rates will have no effect on national income. Any expansion of money supply will, by depressing interest rates, simply lead to a balance of payments deficit and thus a reduction in the money supply again.

5. Under a floating exchange rate an appreciation will shift the *BP* curve upwards and a depreciation will shift it downwards.

6. If the *BP* curve is flatter than the *LM* curve, fiscal policy under a floating exchange rate will be dampened by the resulting changes in the exchange rate. An expansionary fiscal policy will lead to an appreciation (due to the effects of higher interest rates), which in turn will dampen the rise in aggregate demand.

7. Monetary policy will have a relatively large effect on aggregate demand under floating rates. A rise in money supply will reduce interest rates and raise aggregate demand. This will cause a balance of payments deficit and thus a depreciation. This in turn will lead to a further expansion of aggregate demand.

END OF CHAPTER QUESTIONS

1. Assume a free-floating exchange rate. Draw a diagram like Figure 25.6 (on page 759), only this time show an initial equilibrium national income with a balance of payments surplus.
    (a) Mark the size of the surplus.
    (b) Show the resulting shifts in the $(X-M)$ and the *E* curves.
    (c) Mark the eventual equilibrium.
    (d) Show the size of the income and substitution effects (of the change in the exchange rate).
    (e) Under what circumstances will the income effect be (i) 'desirable'; (ii) 'undesirable'?
    (f) Could the income effect of the change in the exchange rate ever be larger than the substitution effect?

2. Compare the relative effectiveness of fiscal and monetary policy under (a) fixed; (b) free-floating exchange rates. How is the effectiveness influenced by the elasticity of supply of international finance?

3. What will be the effects on the domestic economy under free-floating exchange rates if there is a rapid expansion in world economic activity? What will determine the size of these effects?

4. The following table shows a selection of nominal exchange rate indices (effective exchange rates) for the years 2010 to 2016, based on 2010 = 100.
    (a) Explain what is meant by an exchange rate index/ an effective exchange rate.
    (b) Calculate the annual rate of appreciation or depreciation for each currency for each year from 2010.

(continued)

	2010	2011	2012	2013	2014	2015	2016
Australian $	100.0	107.10	109.32	103.23	97.87	88.75	89.35
US $	100.0	95.48	98.24	99.36	102.33	115.24	120.33
Japanese yen	100.0	105.72	107.21	87.09	81.50	76.57	88.30
Sterling	100.0	99.37	103.17	101.06	108.09	114.10	102.73
Euro	100.0	100.49	95.83	100.10	102.47	95.10	98.48
Chinese yuan	100.0	100.19	105.92	111.87	114.71	125.65	119.91

Source: Based on data from Bank for International Settlements.

(c) Calculate the percentage appreciation or depreciation of each currency when comparing 2016 with 2010.

5. For what reasons might the exchange rate diverge from the purchasing-power parity rate over the longer term?

6. Why does exchange rate overshooting occur? What determines its magnitude?

7. Consider the argument that in the modern world of large-scale, short-term international capital movements, the ability of individual countries to affect their exchange rate is very limited.

8. If speculators had better information about future exchange rates, would their actions be more or less stabilising than at present?

*9. Using *ISLMBP* analysis, trace through the effect of (a) a deflationary fiscal policy and (b) a deflationary monetary policy under (i) a fixed exchange rate; (ii) a free-floating exchange rate.

Online resources

Additional case studies on the student website

25.1 The Marshall–Lerner condition. An analysis of the determinants of the elasticities of demand and supply of a currency.

25.2 The gold standard. A historical example of fixed exchange rates.

25.3 Currency turmoil in the 1990s. Two examples of speculative attacks on currencies: first on the Mexican peso in 1995; then on the Thai baht in 1997.

25.4 The euro, the US dollar and world currency markets. An analysis of the relationship between the euro and the dollar.

Websites relevant to this chapter

See sites listed at the end of Chapter 26 on page 861.

26 Chapter

Economies in an Interdependent World

With the growth in globalisation, countries have become increasingly dependent on each other. In the first section, we explore the nature of the interdependence of economies and why countries are so vulnerable to international fluctuations. We then look at what can be done to create a greater co-ordination of international economic policies and consider the role of the G7 and G20 countries in this process.

The extreme solution to currency instability is for countries to adopt a common currency. In section 26.2, we look at the euro and how economic and monetary union (EMU) operates. Has the adoption of a single currency by 19 EU countries been of benefit to them? How have the members sought to tackle the problems of some of the member states?

Then we turn to the economic problems of the poorer countries of the world. These include all the countries of Africa and Latin America and most of the countries of Asia. More than three-quarters of the world's population lives in these countries. As Theodore Schultz said when accepting the Nobel Prize in Economics in 1979:

> Most of the people of the world are poor, so if we knew the economics of being poor we would know much of the economics that really matters.

In section 26.3 we look at the nature and extent of their poverty and the means by which it can be measured. Then, in section 26.4, we look at the trade relations between the poorer countries and the advanced industrialised world. As we shall see, most developing countries are highly dependent for their development, or lack of it, on their relationships with the rich world.

The final section looks at one of the most serious problems facing poorer countries: the problem of huge international debts. We look at various measures to reschedule debts so as to reduce repayments. We also look at various moves to cancel some of the debts, especially of the poorest countries.

26.1   GLOBALISATION AND THE PROBLEM OF INSTABILITY

We live in an interdependent world. Countries are affected by the economic health of other countries and by their governments' policies. Problems in one part of the world can spread like a contagion to other parts, with perhaps no country immune.

There are two major ways in which this process of 'globalisation' affects individual economies. The first is through trade. The second is through financial markets.

Interdependence through trade

So long as nations trade with one another, the domestic economic actions of one nation will have implications for those which trade with it. For example, if the US administration feels that the US economy is growing too fast, it might adopt various contractionary fiscal and monetary measures, such as higher tax rates or interest rates. US consumers will not only consume fewer domestically produced goods, but also reduce their consumption of imported products. But US imports are other countries' exports. A fall in these other countries' exports will lead to a multiplier effect in these countries. Output and employment will fall.

Changes in aggregate demand in one country thus send ripples throughout the global economy. The process whereby changes in imports into (or exports from) one country affect national income in other countries is known as the *international trade multiplier*.

 Assume that the US economy expands. What will determine the size of the multiplier effect on other countries?

The more open an economy, the more vulnerable it will be to changes in the level of economic activity in the rest of the world. This problem will be particularly acute if a nation is heavily dependent on trade with one other nation (e.g. Canada on the USA) or one other region (e.g. Switzerland on the EU).

Until very recently, international trade had been growing as a proportion of countries' national income for many years. This is illustrated in Figure 26.1, which shows the ratio of the sum of global exports and imports of goods and services to global GDP since 1960. This is the measure of openness we introduced in Chapter 24 (see page 747). Over the period, the ratio has risen from 24 per cent to around 60 per cent.

With most nations still committed to freer trade, and with the WTO overseeing the dismantling of trade barriers, so international trade may continue growing as a proportion of world GDP. This will increase countries' interdependence and their vulnerability to world trade fluctuations, such as the global recession of the late 2000s. World output fell by 2.1 per cent in 2009 (at market exchange rates), while the volume of goods and services (imports and exports) fell by 10.5 per cent. This was the biggest contraction in global trade since the Second World War.

> ### Definition
>
> **International trade multiplier** The effect on national income in country B of a change in exports (or imports) of country A.

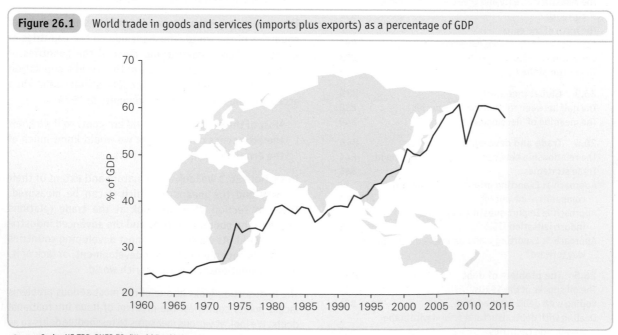

| Figure 26.1 | World trade in goods and services (imports plus exports) as a percentage of GDP |

Source: Series NE.TRD.GNFS.ZS (World Bank).

There is some doubt, however, over world attitudes towards free trade. With the growth in protectionist rhetoric under the Trump administration and in other countries, it is possible that world trade may have peaked as a proportion of GDP – at least for the time being.

 Are exports likely to continue growing faster than GDP indefinitely? What will determine the outcome?

Financial interdependence

International trade has grown rapidly over the past 30 years, but international financial flows have grown much more rapidly. Trillions of dollars are traded across the foreign exchanges each day. Many of the transactions are short-term financial flows, moving to where interest rates are most favourable or to currencies where the exchange rate is likely to appreciate. This has meant that non-deposit financial institutions like pension funds, insurance companies and investment trusts have become important players on foreign exchange markets.

In Chapter 18 we identified a variety of financial instruments. The global nature of financial systems means that these financial instruments readily cross national borders. It also means that financial institutions operating in one country will have liabilities to foreign residents (individuals and institutions).

Figure 26.2 shows the growth in the claims of foreign residents on banks operating in the UK which take the form of sterling-denominated sight deposits, time deposits and repos. Holdings by foreign residents of these three financial instruments rose from £135 billion at the beginning of 1998 (11 per cent of sterling liabilities) to nearly £630 billion in April 2008

(21 per cent of sterling liabilities). By March 2017, following the global banking crisis and subsequent consolidation by banks of their balance sheets, the value of these liabilities was £446 billion (12 per cent of sterling liabilities), but this was still well above the 1998 values, even after taking inflation into account.

Another demonstration of global financial interdependence is the foreign holdings of government securities. Figure 26.3 shows the importance of foreign demand for British gilts, i.e. for long-term British government securities. At the start of 1987, about £15 billion worth of gilts were held overseas, the equivalent to 11 per cent of holdings of gilts. By 2008, the total had risen to £191 billion or 36 per cent of all holdings. Then, with government borrowing rising rapidly in the aftermath of the financial crisis, foreign holdings rose rapidly, but not as rapidly as domestic holdings, so that by the start of 2017, although foreign holding had risen to close to £525 billion, the percentage had fallen to 28 per cent of holdings.[1] In Box 26.1 we consider the significance of foreign purchases of American government debt.

A stark example of global financial interdependence was the collapse of the sub-prime credit markets in the USA in the late 2000s, which spread like a contagion to cause a global recession. Household debt in many advanced economies, including the UK and USA, had grown markedly as a proportion of household disposable income. Between 1995 and 2007, the stock of debt held by UK households increased from around 100 per cent to 175 per cent of annual disposable income (see Box 17.2). In the USA over the same period, the stock of household debt increased from 95 to 145 per cent of annual disposable income.

1 Note that this still means that the bulk of national debt is held by residents in the UK. In other words, most of what the government owes is in the form of the savings by UK individuals and companies.

Figure 26.2 Selected sterling liabilities of UK banks to non-domestic residents

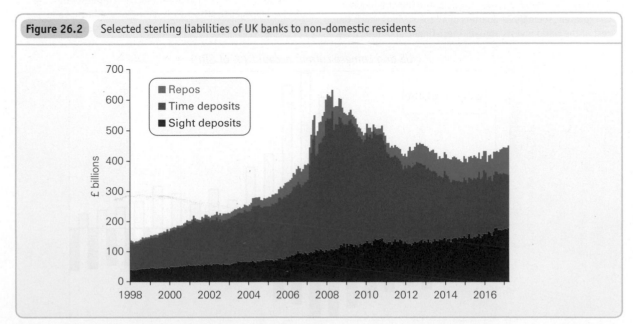

Note: Data include building societies from 2010; data are not seasonally adjusted.
Source: Based on series RPMTBFF, RPMTBFM, RPMTBFT (up to end of 2009) and RPMB3OM, RPMB3TM and RPMB3WM (from 2010) from *Statistical Interactive Database*, Bank of England (data published 30 August 2017).

| Figure 26.3 | Overseas holdings of British government gilts |

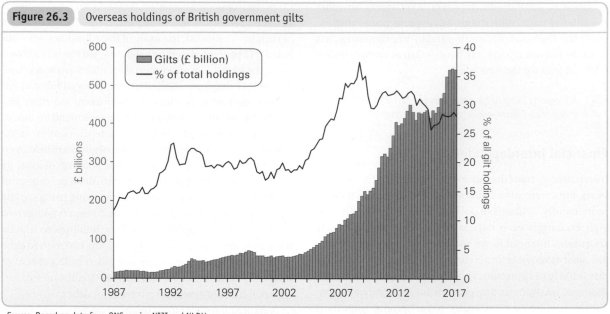

Source: Based on data from ONS, series NIJI and NLDU.

BOX 26.1   ECONOMIC AND FINANCIAL INTERDEPENDENCIES: TRADE IMBALANCE IN THE US AND CHINA

Is the world paying for excessive American expenditure?

America's current account deficit

In 2016, the USA had a current account deficit of $481 billion – the equivalent of 2.6 per cent of GDP (see chart). American current account deficits are not new. Over the 20-year period up to 2016, the US current account deficit has averaged 3.6 per cent of GDP, reaching as high as 5.9 per cent in 2006.

The current account deficit is offset by an equal and opposite capital-plus-financial account surplus, much of which consists of the purchase of US government bonds and Treasury bills. These massive inflows to the USA are thought to represent some three-quarters of all the savings which the rest of the world invests abroad. These financial inflows have permitted the persistence of sizeable US current account deficits.

To attract such large inflows, it might be expected that US interest rates would have to be high. Yet for much of the 2000s they were at historically low levels. Nominal interest rates from mid-2003 to mid-2004 were a mere 1 per cent (see chart in Box 25.5 on pages 806–7) and real rates were close to minus 1.5 per cent. Similarly, since the financial crisis of the late 2000s, interest rates have been very low by comparison with other countries. How is it, then, that with such low interest rates, the USA has managed to attract such vast inflows of finance and thereby maintain such a large financial account surplus?

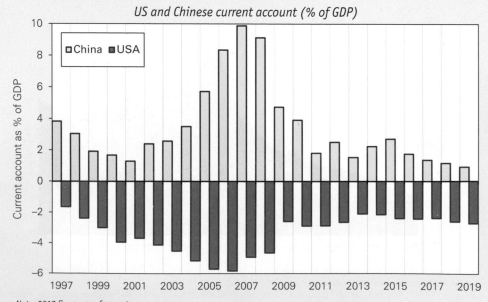

US and Chinese current account (% of GDP)

Note: 2017 figures are forecasts.
Source: Based on data from *World Economic Outlook Database* (IMF).

As we discussed in section 18.2, the growth of domestic credit has been facilitated both by financial deregulation, including the removal of capital controls, and the greater use by financial institutions of wholesale funding. The process of securitisation (see page 561–3), for instance, enabled financial institutions to raise capital from financial investors across the globe in order to provide domestic households with both mortgages and short-term credit. In other words, the aggressive expansion of domestic banks' balance sheets was funded by international financial flows.

KI 35 p451

Financial deregulation and innovation has therefore created a complex chain of interdependencies between financial institutions, financial systems and economies. But this chain is only as strong as its weakest link. In the financial crisis of the late 2000s overly aggressive lending practices by banks in one part of the world impacted on financial investors worldwide. As US interest rates rose from 2004 to 2007 (see figure in Box 25.5), the income flows from American households to banks began to dry up; US households began to fall in arrears and, worse still, default on their loans. But these income flows were the source of the return for global financial investors who had purchased collateralised debt obligations (see page 561). Hence, the new financial order meant the contagion went international.

KI 35 p451

Global financial interdependence also means that changes in interest rates in one country can affect the economies of other countries. Assume that the Federal Reserve Bank in the USA, worried about rising inflation, decides to raise interest rates. What will be the effect on business in America's trading partners? There are three major effects.

- If aggregate demand in America falls, so will its expenditure on imports from firms abroad, thus directly affecting businesses exporting to the USA. With a decline in their exports, aggregate demand in these other countries falls.
- The higher interest rate in the USA will tend to drive up interest rates in other countries. This will depress investment. Again, aggregate demand will tend to fall in these countries.

CASE STUDIES AND APPLICATIONS

China's appetite for dollars

Several Asian currencies, including the Chinese yuan (or 'renminbi'), were pegged to the dollar and had been running large current account surpluses. For instance, the Chinese current account surplus was running as high as 8 to 9 per cent of GDP during the 2000s (see chart). Instead of letting the yuan appreciate against the dollar, the Chinese central bank used the surpluses to buy dollars.

There were three perceived advantages in doing this. First, it allowed China to *build up reserves* and thereby bolster its ability to resist any future speculative attacks on its currency. Chinese foreign exchange reserves rose from around $170 billion in 2000 to $4 trillion in 2014 – a staggering 24-fold increase. The effect was a huge increase in global liquidity and hence money supply.

Second, and more important, it *kept their exchange rates low* and thereby helped to keep their exports competitive. This helped to sustain their rapid rates of economic growth. Third, it helped to *keep US interest rates down* and therefore boost US spending on Asian exports.

In 2005, the Chinese, after much international pressure, agreed to revalue the yuan and would then peg it against a basket of currencies with subsequent further revaluations. Between July 2005 and July 2008 the yuan was allowed to appreciate by around 18 per cent against the US dollar while the exchange rate index rose by 7 per cent (the exchange rate index of the US dollar fell by 15 per cent).

But, with the global economic downturn biting in 2008 and concerns about slowing Chinese export growth, the Chinese authorities effectively fixed the yuan once again.

This remained the case until June 2010 when again the yuan was revalued. Between June 2010 and January 2014 the yuan appreciated a further 12 per cent against the US dollar. Therefore, over the period from July 2005 to January 2014 the yuan had appreciated by around 33 per cent against the US dollar.

China's economic slowdown

The managed appreciation of the yuan, coupled with the slowdown of the global economy, saw China's current account surplus begin to wane, falling from 9 per cent of GDP in 2008 to $1\frac{1}{2}$ per cent by 2013. Meanwhile, though still sizeable, the USA's current account deficit had shrunk. By 2013 the deficit had fallen to 2.2 per cent of GDP – less than half the level of the mid-2000s.

China's economic growth rate, which had been as high as 14 per cent in 2007, had fallen back to around 8 per cent in 2012 and 2013 and to around 7 per cent in 2014 to 2016 (see figure in Box 1.4 on page 22). This weakening of growth reflected a sharp decline in the growth of China's exports of goods and services. While export volumes grew by 24 per cent per annum from 2002 to 2007, from 2012 to 2016 export growth was just 4 per cent per annum and the indication pointed to the slowdown gathering pace (the IMF has forecast an annual export growth of under 3 per cent from 2017 to 2022).

In late 2014, China's central bank began cutting interest rates in response to weaker growth. Then, in August 2015, it took the step to devalue the yuan by 2 per cent against the US dollar. However, this raised concerns of further devaluations and loosening of monetary policy. Hence, the yuan began falling more sharply.

KI 10 p70

The central bank responded by *selling* dollars to curb the depreciation. Despite this, the yuan depreciated by over 6 per cent against the now rising dollar in 2016 on the back of rising US interest rates (see Box 25.5). Hence, private capital was now being attracted to the USA, while China was experiencing 'capital flight'. In its efforts to support the yuan, China's stock of foreign exchange reserves are estimated to have fallen by $830 billion during 2015 and 2016 to a little over $3 trillion (a fall of nearly 22 per cent).

Examine the merits for the Chinese of (a) floating the yuan freely; (b) pegging it to a trade-weighted basket of currencies.

■ The higher interest rate will attract an inflow of funds to the USA from other countries. This will cause the dollar to appreciate relative to other currencies, which will make these other countries' exports to the USA more competitive and imports from the USA relatively more expensive. This will result in an improvement in the current account of the USA's trading partners: their exports rise and imports fall. This represents a *rise* in aggregate demand in these countries – the opposite from the first two effects.

 What will be the effect on the UK economy if the European Central Bank cuts interest rates?

International business cycles

There is an old saying: 'If America sneezes, the rest of the world catches a cold.' Viruses of a similar nature regularly infect the world economy. The credit crunch of 2007/8 resulting from defaults on US sub-prime debt was a dramatic example of this. As a consequence of both trade and financial interdependence, the world economy, like the economy of any individual country, tends to experience periodic fluctuations in economic activity – an *international* business cycle. The implication of this is that countries will tend to share common problems and concerns at the same time. At one time, the most pressing problem may be world inflationary pressures; at another time, it may be a world recession.

In order to avoid 'beggar-my-neighbour' policies, it is better to seek *common* solutions to these common problems: i.e. solutions that are international in scope and design rather than narrowly based on national self-interest. For example, during a world recession, countries are likely to suffer from rising unemployment. Policies that lead to a depreciation of the exchange rate (such as cutting interest rates) will help to stimulate demand by making exports cheaper and imports more expensive. But this will then only worsen the trade balance of other countries, whose aggregate demand will thus fall. The first country is thus tackling its own unemployment at the expense of rising unemployment in other countries.

However, if other nations (which will also be experiencing higher unemployment) can be convinced to co-ordinate their policy actions, an expansionary *international* economic policy will benefit all. In addition to the resulting rise in their imports, all nations will also experience rising export sales.

Even if national policies are not in the strictest sense co-ordinated, discussions between nations regarding the nature and magnitude of the problems they face may help to improve the policy-making process.

 Give some examples of beggar-my-neighbour policies.

The need for international policy co-ordination

Global economic interdependence and an international business cycle can aid the process of international co-operation between countries. For instance, in response to the financial crisis of the late 2000s world leaders were seriously worried that the whole world would plunge into recession. What was needed was a co-ordinated policy response from governments and central banks. This came in October 2008 when governments in Britain, Europe, North America and other parts of the world injected some $2 trillion of extra capital into banks.

Countries frequently meet in various groupings – from the narrow group of the world's seven richest countries (the G7) to broader groups such as the G20, which, in addition to the G7 and other rich countries, also includes larger developing countries, such as China, India, Brazil and Indonesia.

Today the G20 is considered to be the principal economic forum for discussing global economic and other concerns and for considering policy responses. In effect, the emergence of the G20 as the premier global forum recognises two important developments:

■ First, there has been a remarkable growth seen in emerging economies such as India and China (see sections 24.1 and 26.4).

■ Second, the increasing scale of interdependency through trade and finance typically requires a co-ordinated response from a larger representation of the international community.

Global interdependence also raises questions about the role that international organisations like the World Trade Organization (WTO) and the International Monetary Fund (IMF) should play. The WTO's role is to encourage freer trade. We considered its role in section 24.2. The IMF's remit is to promote global growth and stability, to help countries through economic difficulty and to help developing economies achieve macroeconomic stability and reduce poverty. In response to the global economic and financial crisis of the late 2000s, the IMF's budget was substantially increased and it became more actively involved with what were previously defined as 'strong performing economies'.

International harmonisation of economic policies

The five main underlying causes of exchange rate movements are divergences in *interest rates, growth rates, inflation rates, current account balance of payments* and *government deficits*. Table 26.1 shows the variation in the levels of these indicators across a sample of nine countries. These divergences still remain considerable.

An important issue for G8 and G20 meetings is how to generate world economic growth without major currency fluctuations. To achieve this it is important that there is a

Table 26.1   International macroeconomic indicators

		Australia	Canada	China	France	Ireland	Germany	Japan	UK	USA
Nominal exchange rate index (annual % change)	1997–2001	−3.4	−1.6	2.7	−2.3	−1.2	−2.8	0.3	3.5	4.2
	2002–2006	5.7	5.3	−2.5	1.3	4.0	0.9	−4.2	−0.4	−2.6
	2007–2011	4.9	1.6	3.8	−0.8	−0.4	−1.0	2.8	−4.0	−2.7
	2012–2016	−3.1	−4.2	4.1	−1.1	−2.0	−0.8	−4.0	0.8	3.9
Short–term (3-month) nominal interest rates (%)	1997–2001	5.2	4.6	5.1	3.7	4.6	3.7	0.4	6.1	5.3
	2002–2006	5.7	3.0	3.0	2.6	2.6	2.6	0.3	4.3	2.6
	2007–2011	4.7	2.1	3.2	2.5	2.5	2.5	0.4	2.8	1.9
	2012–2016	2.4	1.0	3.2	0.1	0.1	0.1	0.1	0.6	0.3
Economic growth (% change in real GDP)	1997–2001	3.8	4.1	8.3	3.0	9.2	2.1	0.6	3.2	3.7
	2002–2006	3.1	6.7	6.2	1.3	3.5	3.2	2.1	2.8	2.9
	2007–2011	2.8	1.3	10.6	0.7	−0.7	1.3	−0.2	0.2	0.6
	2012–2016	2.7	1.8	7.3	0.8	8.0	1.2	1.2	2.1	2.1
Consumer price inflation (% change in CPI)	1997–2001	2.3	1.9	0.3	1.2	3.0	1.2	0.1	1.4	2.5
	2002–2006	2.5	1.9	1.8	1.8	1.5	2.4	0.7	2.1	4.1
	2007–2011	2.9	1.9	3.7	1.8	0.8	1.8	4.5	3.2	2.2
	2012–2016	1.9	1.4	2.1	0.8	0.5	1.0	0.7	1.5	1.3
Current account balance (% of GDP)	1997–2001	−3.8	0.4	2.4	3.4	0.8	−0.9	2.4	−1.4	−3.0
	2002–2006	−1.9	3.1	2.8	2.4	0.9	1.0	0.8	−3.4	−5.1
	2007–2011	−4.5	−1.7	5.9	−0.7	−4.1	6.0	−4.1	−2.7	−3.6
	2012–2016	−3.5	−3.2	2.2	−0.9	3.2	7.6	1.9	−4.3	−2.5
Unemployment rate (% of labour force)	1997–2001	7.2	7.8	3.2	9.9	6.3	8.7	4.4	5.9	4.5
	2002–2006	6.3	5.6	6.4	9.3	4.6	7.2	4.9	5.2	3.3
	2007–2011	4.9	7.2	4.1	8.6	10.4	7.3	4.5	6.9	7.6
	2012–2016	5.7	7.1	4.1	10.2	11.3	4.9	3.7	6.4	6.3
General government surplus (% of GDP)	1997–2001	0.2	1.0	−1.9	−2.1	2.3	−1.9	−6.9	0.1	−0.6
	2002–2006	1.0	−0.5	−2.5	−3.3	−2.2	−1.1	−4.1	−3.2	−2.6
	2007–2011	−2.7	−2.0	−0.4	−5.0	−13.1	−1.7	−7.0	−7.0	−8.6
	2012–2016	−2.9	−1.4	−1.7	−3.9	−4.0	0.3	−5.8	−5.3	−4.8

Sources: *Stat Extracts* (OECD); *World Economic Outlook database* (IMF); *AMECO database* (European Commission) and *Federal Reserve Economic Data*.

harmonisation of economic policies between nations. In other words, it is important that all the major countries are pursuing consistent policies aiming at common international goals.

But how can policy harmonisation be achieved? As long as there are significant domestic differences between the major economies, there is likely to be conflict, not harmony. For example, if one country, say the USA, is worried about the size of its budget deficit, it may be unwilling to respond to world demands for a stimulus to aggregate demand to pull the world economy out of recession. What is more, speculators, seeing differences between countries, are likely to exaggerate them by their actions, causing large changes in exchange rates. The G8 countries have therefore sought to achieve greater *convergence* of their economies. But whilst convergence may be a goal of policy, in practice it has proved more elusive.

Referring to Table 26.1, in what respects was there greater convergence between these countries in the period 2012–16 than in the period 2002–6?

Because of a lack of convergence, there are serious difficulties in achieving international policy harmonisation:

- Countries' budget deficits and national debt may differ substantially as a proportion of their national income. This puts very different pressures on the interest rates necessary to service these debts. In 2016, the UK had a general government gross debt to GDP ratio of 89 per cent. This compared with 41 per cent for Australia,

Definition

International harmonisation of economic policies Where countries attempt to co-ordinate their macroeconomic policies so as to achieve common goals.

Convergence of economies When countries achieve similar levels of growth, inflation, budget deficits as a percentage of GDP, balance of payments, etc.

68 per cent for Germany, 92 per cent for Canada, 97 per cent for France and 239 per cent for Japan.

- Harmonising rates of monetary growth or inflation targets would involve letting interest rates fluctuate with the demand for money. Without convergence in the demand for money, interest rate fluctuations could be severe.
- Harmonising interest rates would involve abandoning monetary, inflation and exchange rate targets (unless interest rate 'harmonisation' meant adjusting interest rates so as to maintain monetary or inflation targets or a fixed exchange rate).
- Countries have different internal structural relationships. A lack of convergence here means that countries with higher endemic *cost* inflation would require higher interest rates and higher unemployment if international inflation rates were to be harmonised, or higher inflation if interest rates were to be harmonised.
- Countries have different rates of productivity increase, product development, investment and market penetration. A lack of convergence here means that the growth in exports (relative to imports) will differ for any given level of inflation or growth.

- Countries may be very unwilling to change their domestic policies to fall in line with other countries. They may prefer the other countries to fall in line with them!

If any one of the five – interest rates, growth rates, inflation rates, current account balance of payments or government deficits – could be harmonised across countries, it is likely that the other four would then not be harmonised.

Total convergence and thus total harmonisation may not be possible. Nevertheless, most governments favour some movement in that direction: some is better than none. To achieve this, co-operation is necessary.

Although co-operation is the ideal, in practice discord often tends to dominate international economic relations. The reason is that governments are normally concerned with the economic interests of other countries only if they coincide with those of their own country. This, however, can create a prisoners' dilemma problem (see pages 235–7 and 403–5). With each country looking solely after its own interests, the world economy suffers and everyone is worse off.

 If total convergence were achieved, would harmonisation of policies follow automatically?

Section summary

1. Changes in aggregate demand in one country will affect the amount of imports purchased and thus the amount of exports sold by other countries and hence their national income. There is thus an international trade multiplier effect.

2. Changes in interest rates in one country will affect financial flows to and from other countries, and hence their exchange rates, interest rates and national income.

3. To prevent problems in one country spilling over to other countries and to stabilise the international business cycle will require co-ordinated policies between nations.

4. Currency fluctuations can be lessened if countries harmonise their economic policies. Ideally this will involve achieving compatible growth rates, inflation rates, balance of payments and government deficits (as percentages of GDP) and interest rates. The attempt to harmonise one of these goals, however, may bring conflicts with one of the other goals.

5. Leaders of the G8 and G20 countries meet at least annually to discuss ways of harmonising their policies. Usually, however, domestic issues are more important to the leaders than international ones, and frequently they pursue policies that are not in the interests of the other countries.

26.2 EUROPEAN ECONOMIC AND MONETARY UNION (EMU)

The ultimate way for a group of countries to achieve greater currency stability between themselves is to adopt a single currency and, therefore, to have a common central bank and a common monetary policy – to form an *economic and monetary union (EMU)*. This is what has happened in the EU, with countries coming together to adopt a single currency – the euro. The euro began in 1999, with notes and coins circulating from 2002. Initially 11 countries joined; by 2015 there were 19 members.

Definition

Economic and monetary union (EMU) The adoption by a group of countries of a single currency with a single central bank and a single monetary policy. In the EU the term applies to the countries that have adopted the euro.

The ERM (exchange rate mechanism)

The forerunner to EMU was the *exchange rate mechanism (ERM)*. This was an adjustable peg system, where members pegged their exchange rates to each other while floating against the rest of the world. This encouraged trade between the members and enabled the combined reserves of all member countries to prevent excessive fluctuations of their currencies with the rest of the world.

Under the system, each currency was given a central exchange rate with each of the other ERM currencies in a grid. However, fluctuations were allowed from the central rate within specified bands, typically of up to 0.25 per cent. The central rates were adjusted from time to time by agreement. All the currencies floated jointly with currencies outside the ERM.

If a currency approached the upper or lower limit against *any* other ERM currency, intervention would take place to maintain the currencies within the band. This would take the form of central banks in the ERM selling the strong currency and buying the weak one. It could also involve the weak currency countries raising interest rates and the strong currency countries lowering them.

The ERM in practice

The ERM came into existence in March 1979 and the majority of the EU countries were members. The UK, however, initially chose not to join. Spain joined in 1989, the UK in 1990 and Portugal in April 1992.

Sterling entered the ERM at a central rate of £1 = 2.95 German marks with permitted fluctuations of ±6 per cent against any other ERM currency. This rate proved unsustainable. German interest rates were rising to dampen inflationary pressures partly fuelled by substantial public expenditures following the reunification of Germany. US interest rates by contrast were falling to help stimulate economic growth in the face of recession. The result was a large outflow of capital from the USA, much of it going to Germany. The effect was to push up the value of the German mark. Consequently, currencies like sterling and the Italian lira were repeatedly at the bottom of their permitted exchange rate band with the mark. This was despite high and rising interest rates and, in the case of the UK, despite the economy sliding rapidly into recession.

In September 1992, things reached a crisis point. On 16 September – known thereafter as 'Black Wednesday' – the UK and Italy were forced to suspend their membership of the ERM. Both currencies were floated and depreciated substantially.

Turmoil returned in the summer of 1993, with pressure this time on the French franc. In response, EU finance ministers agreed to adopt very wide ±15 per cent bands, though with bands this wide it hardly seemed like a 'pegged' system at all. Within months, however, the crisis passed and exchange rate fluctuations began to fall within a very narrow range and for most of the time within ±2.25 per cent.

Italy rejoined the ERM in November 1996 as part of its bid to join the single European currency. Austria joined in 1995, Finland in 1996 and Greece in 1998. By the time the ERM was replaced by the single currency in 1999, only Sweden and the UK were outside the ERM.

The Maastricht Treaty and the road to the single currency

The ERM was conceived as a stage on the road to complete economic and monetary union (EMU) of member states. Details of the path towards EMU were finalised in the Maastricht Treaty, which was signed in February 1992. The timetable for EMU involved the adoption of a single currency by 1999 at the latest.

Before they could join the single currency, member states were obliged to achieve convergence of their economies. Each country had to meet five convergence criteria:

- Inflation: should be no more than 1.5 per cent above the average inflation rate of the three countries in the EU with the lowest inflation.
- Interest rates: the rate on long-term government bonds should be no more than 2 per cent above the average of the three countries with the lowest inflation rates.
- Budget deficit: should be no more than 3 per cent of GDP at market prices.
- National debt: should be no more than 60 per cent of GDP at market prices.
- Exchange rates: the currency should have been within the normal ERM bands for at least two years with no realignments or excessive intervention.

Before the launch of the single currency, the Council of Ministers had to decide which countries had met the convergence criteria and would thus be eligible to form a *currency union* by fixing their currencies permanently to the euro. Their national currencies would effectively disappear.

At the same time, a European System of Central Banks (ESCB) would be created, consisting of a European Central Bank (ECB) and the central banks of the member states. The ECB would be independent, both from governments and from EU political institutions. It would operate the monetary policy on behalf of the countries that had adopted the single currency.

Definitions

Exchange rate mechanism A semi-fixed system whereby participating EU countries allow fluctuations against each other's currencies only within agreed bands. Collectively they float freely against all other currencies.

Currency union A group of countries (or regions) using a common currency.

The birth of the euro

In March 1998, the European Commission ruled that 11 of the 15 member states were eligible to proceed to EMU in January 1999. The UK and Denmark were to exercise their opt-out, and Sweden and Greece failed to meet one or more of the convergence criteria. (Greece joined the euro in 2001.)

All 11 countries unambiguously met the interest rate and inflation criteria, but doubts were expressed by many 'Eurosceptics' as to whether they all genuinely met the other three criteria.

- *Exchange rates.* Neither Finland nor Italy had been in the ERM for two years and the Irish punt was revalued by 3 per cent on 16 March 1998. However, the Commission regarded these three countries as being sufficiently close to the reference value.
- *Government deficits.* All 11 countries met this criterion, but some countries only managed to achieve a deficit of 3 per cent or below by taking one-off measures, such as a special tax in Italy and counting privatisation receipts in Germany. Yet, under the Stability and Growth Pact, eurozone countries would be required to keep their deficits within the 3 per cent limit (see Box 22.4). The concern was that countries that only just met this criterion at time of entry would find it difficult to keep within the limit in times of recession or slow growth. This proved to be the case with France and Germany from 2002 to 2005.
- *Government debt.* Only four countries had debts that did not exceed 60 per cent (France, Finland, Luxembourg and the UK). However, the Maastricht Treaty allowed countries to exceed this value as long as the debt was 'sufficiently diminishing and approaching the reference value at a satisfactory pace'. Critics argued that this phrase was interpreted too loosely.

The euro came into being on 1 January 1999, but euro banknotes and coins were not introduced until 1 January 2002. In the meantime, national currencies continued to exist alongside the euro, but at irrevocably fixed rates. The old notes and coins were withdrawn a few weeks after the introduction of euro notes and coins.

Ten new members joined the EU in May 2004, and another two in January 2007. Under the Maastricht Treaty, they were all required to make preparations for joining the euro by meeting the convergence criteria and being in a new version of the exchange rate mechanism with a wide exchange rate band. Under ERM II, euro candidate countries must keep their exchange rates within ± 15 per cent of a central rate against the euro. Estonia, Lithuania and Slovenia were the first to join ERM II in June 2004 with Latvia, Cyprus, Malta and Slovakia following in 2005. Slovenia adopted the euro in 2007, Malta and Cyprus in 2008, Slovakia in 2009, Estonia in 2011, Latvia in 2014 and Lithuania in 2015, making a total of 19 countries using the euro.

Advantages of the single currency

EMU has several major advantages for its members.

Elimination of the costs of converting currencies. With separate currencies in each of the EU countries, costs were incurred each time one currency was exchanged into another. The elimination of these costs, however, was probably the least important benefit from the single currency. The European Commission estimated that the effect was to increase the GDP of the countries concerned by an average of only 0.4 per cent and perhaps less so for those countries with well-developed financial markets.

Increased competition and efficiency. Not only does the single currency eliminate the need to convert one currency into another (a barrier to competition), but it has brought more transparency in pricing, and has put greater downward pressure on prices in high-cost firms and countries. This, of course, does not necessarily favour business, which might find its profits squeezed, but it generally benefits consumers. Although there has been some price convergence across the eurozone, it has not been as extensive as many thought it would be.

Elimination of exchange rate uncertainty (between the members). Removal of exchange rate uncertainty has helped to encourage trade between the eurozone countries. Perhaps more importantly, it has encouraged investment by firms that trade between these countries, given the greater certainty in calculating costs and revenues from such trade.

In times of economic uncertainty, such as the credit crunch of 2008, exchange rate volatility between countries can be high, as we saw with the experience of sterling. However, if the UK had adopted the euro, the uncertainty created by this volatility for the UK in its trade with the eurozone countries would have been eliminated.

Increased inward investment. Investment from the rest of the world is attracted to a eurozone of some 340 million inhabitants, where there is no fear of internal currency movements. As well as potentially increasing its global share of FDI, by removing the uncertainty arising from possible exchange rate volatility between its 19 members, the eurozone countries may experience less volatility in FDI flows than would otherwise be the case.

Lower inflation and interest rates. A single monetary policy forces convergence in inflation rates (just as inflation rates are very similar between the different regions within a country). With the ECB being independent from short-term political manipulation, this has resulted in a low average inflation rate in the eurozone countries. This, in turn, has helped to convince markets that the euro will be strong relative to other currencies. The result is lower long-term rates of interest. This, in turn, further encourages investment in the eurozone countries, both by member states and by the rest of the world.

KI 11
p76

Opposition to EMU

European monetary union has, however, attracted considerable criticism. Many 'Eurosceptics' see within it a surrender of national political and economic sovereignty. Their arguments are essentially ones of principle.

Others, including those more sympathetic to monetary union in principle, raise concerns about the design of the monetary and fiscal systems within which monetary union operates – a design that, in principle, can be amended (see Boxes 22.4 and 22.7).

Arguments against EMU in principle

The lack of national currencies.   This is a serious problem if an economy is at all out of harmony with the rest of the Union. For example, if countries such as Greece and Spain have higher rates of inflation (due, say, to greater cost-push pressures), then how are they to make their goods competitive with the rest of the Union? With separate currencies these countries could allow their currencies to depreciate. With a single currency, however, they could become depressed 'regions' of Europe, with rising unemployment and all the other problems of depressed regions within a country. This might then require significant regional policies – policies that might not be in place or, if they were, would be seen as too interventionist by the political right.

How might multiplier effects (the principle of cumulative causation) lead to prosperous regions becoming more prosperous and less prosperous regions falling even further behind?

Proponents of EMU argue that it is better to tackle the problem of high inflation in such countries by the disciplines of competition from other EU countries, than merely to feed that inflation by keeping separate currencies and allowing repeated depreciation, with all the uncertainty that they bring.

What is more, the high-inflation countries tend to be the poorer ones with lower wage levels (albeit faster wage *increases*). With the increased mobility of labour and capital as the single market deepens, resources are likely to be attracted to such countries. This could help to narrow the gap between the richer and poorer member states.

The critics of EMU counter this by arguing that labour is relatively immobile, given cultural and language barriers. Thus an unemployed worker in Dublin could not easily move to a job in Turin or Helsinki. What the critics are arguing here is that the EU is not an *optimal currency area* (see Box 26.2).

Loss of separate monetary policies.   Perhaps the most serious criticism is that the same rate of interest must apply to all eurozone countries: the 'one-size-fits-all' problem. The trouble is that while one country might require a lower rate of interest in order to ward off recession (such as Portugal, Ireland and Greece in 2010–11), others might require a higher one to prevent inflation. Furthermore, some countries may be more sensitive to interest changes than others, hence the optimal change in interest rates for one country may represent too much or too little of a change in another.

The greater the convergence between economies within the eurozone, the less serious this problem is. Consequently, it was hoped that, with common fiscal rules and free trade, these divergences would diminish over time. Eurosceptics, however, argue that there has been increasing divergence between members especially in terms of the size of government deficits and debt and the confidence of the financial markets in countries' ability to tackle these deficits.

Asymmetric shocks.   A third and related problem for members of a single currency occurs in adjusting to a shock when that shock affects members to different degrees. Such occurrences are known as **asymmetric shocks**. For example, the banking crisis affected the UK more severely than other countries, given that London is a global financial centre. This problem is more serious, the less the factor mobility between member countries and the less the price flexibility within member countries.

This problem, however, should not be overstated. Divergences between economies are often the result of a lack of harmony between countries in their demand-management policies. This is impossible in the eurozone in the case of monetary policy, and more difficult in the case of fiscal policy, due in part, to the constraints of the Growth and Stability Pact and Fiscal Compact (see Box 22.4). Also, many of the shocks that face economies today are global and have similar (albeit not identical) effects on all countries. Adjustment to such shocks would often be better with a single co-ordinated policy, something that is much easier with a single currency and a single central bank.

Even when shocks are uniformly felt in the member states, however, there is still the problem that policies adopted centrally will have different effects on each country. This is because the transmission mechanisms of economic policy (i.e. the way in which policy changes impact on economic variables like growth and inflation) vary across countries.

Criticisms of the current design of EMU

Others, who are currently critical of the design of EMU, argue that with appropriate changes, the problems could be significantly reduced.

> ## Definitions
>
> **Optimal currency area** The optimal size of a currency area is the one that maximises the benefits from having a single currency relative to the costs. If the area were increased or decreased in size, the costs would rise relative to the benefits.
>
> **Asymmetric shocks** Shocks (such as an oil price increase or a recession in another part of the world) that have different-sized effects on different industries, regions or countries.

TC 15
p535

BOX 26.2   OPTIMAL CURRENCY AREAS

When it pays to pay in the same currency

Imagine that each town and village used a different currency. Think how inconvenient it would be having to keep exchanging one currency into another, and how difficult it would be working out the relative value of items in different parts of the country.

Clearly, there are benefits to using a common currency, not only within a country but across different countries. The benefits include greater transparency in pricing, more open competition, greater certainty for investors and the avoidance of having to pay commission when you change one currency into another. There are also the benefits from having a single monetary policy if that is delivered in a more consistent and effective way than by individual countries.

So why not have a single currency for the whole world? The problem is that the bigger a single currency area gets, the more likely the conditions are to diverge in the different parts of the area. Some parts may have high unemployment and require expansionary policies. Others may have low unemployment and suffer from inflationary pressures. They may require *contractionary* policies.

What is more, different members of the currency area may experience quite different shocks to their economies, whether from outside the union (e.g. a fall in the price of one of their major exports) or from inside (e.g. a prolonged strike). These 'asymmetric shocks' would imply that different parts of the currency area should adopt different policies. But with a common monetary policy and hence common interest rates, and with no possibility of devaluation/revaluation of the currency of individual members, the scope for separate economic policies is reduced.

The costs of asymmetric shocks (and hence the costs of a single currency area) will be greater, the less the mobility of labour and capital, the less the flexibility of prices and wage rates, and the fewer the alternative policies there are that can be turned to (such as fiscal and regional policies).

So is the eurozone an optimal currency area? Certainly strong doubts have been raised by many economists.

- Labour is relatively immobile.
- There are structural differences between the member states.
- The transmission effects of interest rate changes are different between the member countries, given that countries have different proportions of borrowing at variable interest rates and different proportions of consumer debt to GDP.
- Exports to countries outside the eurozone account for different proportions of the members' GDP, and thus their economies are affected differently by a change in the rate of exchange of the euro against other currencies.
- Wage rates are relatively inflexible.
- Under the Stability and Growth Pact and the Fiscal Compact (see Box 22.4), the scope for using discretionary fiscal policy is curtailed except in times of severe economic difficulty (as in 2009).

This does not necessarily mean, however, that the costs of having a single European currency outweigh the benefits. Also, the problems outlined above should decline over time as the single market develops. Finally, the problem of asymmetric shocks can be exaggerated. European economies are highly diversified; there are often more differences *within* economies than between them. Thus shocks are more likely to affect different industries or localities, rather than whole countries. Changing the exchange rate, if that were still possible, would hardly be an appropriate policy in these circumstances.

 Why is a single currency area likely to move towards becoming an optimal currency area over time?

Monetary policy.   In the case of monetary policy, it is argued that the ECB's remit makes it especially inflation-averse. Hence, it will tend to be more 'hawkish' and less proactive in response to economic downturns in the eurozone, particularly if the downturn is accompanied by a persistence in inflation or by rising rates of inflation.

Some argue that the hawkishness of the ECB is most clearly seen when comparing its monetary stance with other central banks in the aftermath of the financial crisis (see Box 22.7). Concerned by the above-target consumer price inflation rates that had resulted from the rising rates of global commodity inflation before the financial crisis, the ECB was cautious in relaxing monetary policy. In comparison, central banks such as the US Federal Reserve, the Bank of England and the Bank of Japan were more 'dovish' and aggressively relaxed monetary policy (see Boxes 22.5 and 22.6). Indeed, it was not until late in 2014 that the ECB announced that it would be starting a programme of

quantitative easing, around the very time that the Federal Reserve's programme was winding down.

Critics also point to the underlying weakness of a single currency operating alongside separate *national* government debt issues. The greater the divergence of the eurozone countries, in terms of growth, inflation, deficits, debt and the proportions of debt securities maturing in the short term, the greater this problem becomes.

Fiscal policy.   Under the Stability and Growth Pact (SGP), countries were supposed to keep public-sector deficits below 3 per cent of GDP and their stocks of debt below 60 per cent of GDP (see Box 22.4 on page 684). However, the Pact was not rigidly enforced. Furthermore, because the rules allowed for discretion in times of recession, deficits and debt rose sharply in the late 2000s (see Table 22.1 on page 671).

Subsequently, efforts have been made to change the framework within which national governments make their fiscal choices. The result is the Fiscal Compact, signed in March 2012 (see Box 22.4). This reaffirmed the Stability and Growth Pact rules, but added other requirements. For example, eurozone countries would now be required to keep *structural deficits* at or below 0.5 per cent of GDP and tougher penalties would be imposed on countries breaking the rules.

There are those who argue that, for eurozone members to benefit fully from monetary union, tighter fiscal rules alone are insufficient. Instead, they advocate greater fiscal harmonisation. In other words, the problem, they say, is one of incomplete integration.

 By what means would a depressed country in an economic union with a single currency be able to recover? Would the market provide a satisfactory solution to its problems or would (union) government intervention be necessary, and if so, what form could that intervention take?

Future of the euro

When Lithuania adopted the euro on 1 January 2015 it became the nineteenth country to do so. Yet debates around the advantages and disadvantages of EMU intensified as the ongoing Greek debt crisis raised the prospect of Greece's exit from the euro (Grexit).

The Greek crisis

The perilous state of Greece's public finances had already seen two international bailouts agreed. These involved the IMF, the European Commission and the ECB – the so-called 'Troika' – and were worth €240 billion. However, these loans were contingent on the Greek government undertaking a series of economic measures, including significant fiscal tightening. However, the fiscal austerity measures contributed to a deterioration of the macroeconomic environment.

Matters came to a head at the end of 2014 when the final tranches of the Greek bailout programme were suspended by the Troika. This followed the formation in December 2014 of a Syriza-led Greek government which had fought the election on an anti-austerity platform.

What followed was a drawn-out set of negotiations between Greece and its international creditors. With no agreement on further aid to Greece yet reached, Greece was unable to meet a €1.55 billion repayment to the IMF on 30 June 2015. This made Greece the first developed country to have defaulted on a loan from the IMF. Meanwhile, conditions for Greek citizens continued to deteriorate. In July the ECB announced that it would maintain its emergency liquidity assurance for the Greek financial system at levels agreed at the end of June. Without further credit for an already financially distressed banking system, capital controls were imposed with strict limits on withdrawals from bank accounts.

In August 2015, the Greek government and its international creditors reached an agreement on the terms of a third bailout worth €85 billion over three years. Further austerity measures continued. These were required in order for the periodic release of funds, but they were to place further strains on an already weak economy.

Concerns continued to grow, however, that the fiscal arithmetic (see section 22.1) to sustain Greece's current public sector debt-to-GDP ratio simply did not add up. Larger and larger primary surpluses were needed merely to sustain the current national debt, thereby requiring further fiscal austerity and structural reform. Some, including the IMF, were arguing that only debt relief would ensure the long-term sustainability of Greece's public finances.

For the time being at least, Grexit had been avoided. Yet the Greek debt crisis brought to the fore fundamental questions about the future of the euro and the conditions under which it would be beneficial for other EU member states to join or for existing members to exit.

The single currency and gains from trade

The benefits from a country being a member of a single currency are greater the more it leads to trade with other members of the single currency. Table 26.2 shows for a sample of member states of the European Union (including the UK), the proportion of their exports and imports to and from other member states. From the table we can see that about two-thirds of trade in the EU is between member states. However, there are considerable differences in the importance of intra-EU trade for member states.

On the basis of intra-industry trade, it might be argued that countries like Greece and Malta (and the UK, had it chosen to join when a member of the EU) have least to gain from being part of a single currency with other EU nations. But we need to consider other factors too. The theory of optimal currency areas (see Box 26.2) suggests, for example, that the degree of convergence between economies and the flexibility

Table 26.2	Intra-European Union exports and imports, % of total exports or imports			
	Exports		**Imports**	
	2002–8	**2009–16**	**2002–8**	**2009–16**
EU-28	68.4	64.0	64.9	62.4
UK	58.9	48.6	55.3	50.6
Slovakia	87.4	84.8	75.4	75.2
Netherlands	79.6	76.2	51.2	46.3
Portugal	79.0	72.6	77.5	74.7
Belgium	76.6	72.0	71.9	66.4
Spain	72.7	65.9	65.0	58.6
Eurozone (19 countries)	68.8	64.1	65.3	62.5
France	65.3	60.0	69.0	68.1
Greece	64.9	51.4	59.8	50.9
Lithuania	64.9	60.2	60.7	61.3
Germany	64.4	58.7	64.9	64.5
Ireland	63.6	58.5	67.3	65.5
Italy	61.8	55.8	60.1	56.5
Malta	47.8	43.0	72.4	69.8

Source: Based on data from *AMECO database* (European Commission, DGECFIN).

of labour markets are important considerations for countries considering the costs of relinquishing their national currency.

The more similar economies are, the more likely it is that they will face similar or symmetric shocks which can be accommodated by a common monetary policy. Furthermore, greater wage flexibility and mobility of labour provide mechanisms for countries within a single currency to remain internationally competitive.

Table 26.3 shows a series of macroeconomic indicators for a sample of countries within the eurozone. From it we can see that there remain considerable differences in the macroeconomic performance of these countries, reflecting continuing differences in the structures of their economies. These differences were exacerbated by the financial crisis of the late 2000s and the subsequent deterioration of the macroeconomic environment.

Among the differences captured by Table 26.3 is the contrasting trade positions of eurozone economies. In the period 2002–8 Greece and Spain ran large current account deficits, averaging 12 and 7 per cent of GDP respectively. By contrast, Germany ran a current account surplus of around 4.5 per cent of its GDP.

In the absence of nominal exchange rate adjustments, countries like Greece and Spain, looking to a fall in the *real* exchange rate to boost competitiveness, need to have relatively lower rates of price inflation (see pages 788–91 and Box 25.8 on page 816 on nominal and real exchange rates). Therefore, in a single currency productivity growth and wage inflation take on even greater importance in determining a country's competitiveness.

In Table 26.3, labour productivity is captured by the growth in output per hour worked. Again significant variations exist. Where labour productivity growth is lower, it needs lower nominal wage growth to help prevent countries losing their competitiveness. Even in countries where labour productivity is higher, as is often observed in countries with lower levels of income, their competitive position will deteriorate if wage growth exceeds productivity growth. In this scenario unit labour costs (labour costs per unit of output) will increase. In the period from 2002 to 2008, Table 26.3 shows unit labour costs increasing at between 3 and 4 per cent per annum in Greece, Spain and Italy compared with close to zero in Germany. This, other things being equal, puts these countries at a competitive disadvantage.

The euro and the fiscal framework

The discussion so far highlights the importance of economic convergence in affecting the benefits and costs of being a member of the euro. Fiscal policy can provide some buffer against asymmetric shocks by enabling transfers of income to those areas experiencing lower rates of economic

---

Table 26.3 Macroeconomic indicators for eurozone, 2002–16

	2002–8							2009–16						
	UK	Eurozone	France	Germany	Greece	Italy	Spain	UK	Eurozone	France	Germany	Greece	Italy	Spain
Economic growth (% p.a.)	4.3	1.8	1.6	1.3	3.4	0.8	3.1	1.2	0.4	0.6	1.0	−3.6	−0.8	−0.2
Output gap (% of potential output)	1.1	1.0	1.7	−0.3	3.5	1.1	2.5	−2.1	−2.1	−1.4	−0.8	−9.3	−2.8	−5.3
Growth in potential output (% p.a.)	2.3	1.8	1.7	1.3	2.9	0.9	3.5	1.1	0.7	1.0	1.2	−1.8	−0.4	0.2
Unemployment rate (%)	5.1	8.5	8.3	9.4	9.4	7.5	10.2	6.9	10.7	9.8	5.6	20.9	10.5	22.0
Current account (% of GDP)	−2.1	0.5	−0.1	4.4	−11.7	−1.2	−7.0	−2.1	1.9	−2.4	7.1	−5.5	−0.2	−0.8
Growth in output per hour worked (% p.a.)	1.7	0.9	1.2	1.2	1.7	−0.1	0.5	0.1	0.9	0.8	0.7	−1.1	0.0	1.4
Growth in unit labour costs (% p.a.)	2.6	2.0	2.0	0.1	4.3	3.1	3.8	1.4	1.2	1.3	2.0	−0.6	1.2	−0.5
Economy-wide inflation rate (%)	−0.8	2.1	2.1	1.0	3.3	2.5	3.6	1.4	1.0	0.8	1.5	−0.2	1.1	0.2

Notes: (i) Unit labour costs are the ratio of compensation per employee to real GDP per person employed; (ii) the economy-wide inflation rate is the annual rate of change of the GDP deflator.
Source: Based on data from *AMECO database* (European Commission, DGECFIN) and OECD.stat (OECD).

growth. Therefore, the fiscal framework within which the euro operates is important when considering the future of the euro.

To date, the eurozone has resisted a centralisation of national budgets. In a more centralised (or federal) system we would see automatic income transfers between different regions and countries. A country, say Greece, affected by a negative economic shock would pay less tax revenues and receive more expenditures from a central eurozone budget, while in a country, say Germany, experiencing a positive shock the opposite would be the case.

Since national budgets in the eurozone remain largely decentralised, fiscal transfers are principally determined by national fiscal frameworks. But the ability of these to offset the effects of negative economic shocks is constrained by the sustainability of national budgets. This is important because it places limits on the ability of national governments to use fiscal policy to offset the effects of negative economic shocks.

When analysing the sustainability of national budgets, economists look at the balance needed between spending and revenues to prevent the ratio of the stock of public-sector debt to annual GDP from rising. The key here is the flow of receipts compared to those expenditures other than the interest payments on servicing the existing public-sector debt. If receipts are greater than expenditures excluding interest payments then a *primary surplus* occurs (see page 673). A primary surplus is needed to maintain the debt-to-GDP ratio if the effective real rate of interest payable on public-sector debt is greater than the economy's economic growth rate. Furthermore, the required size of the primary

surplus-to-GDP ratio rises the lower is the rate of economic growth relative to the real interest rate and the larger is the existing debt-to-GDP ratio.

Table 26.4 shows the public-sector debt-to-GDP ratios in a sample of eurozone economies in 2008 and 2016 alongside the factors that affect the path of the ratio. In other words, the table provides important insights into the sustainability of levels of public-sector debt of eurozone economies (see Box 22.1 for an analysis of the 'fiscal arithmetic' of countries outside of the eurozone).

The final column of the table provides a rule-of-thumb estimate of the average primary surplus-to-GDP ratio needed to maintain the 2008 debt stock-to-GDP ratio. It can then be compared with the average primary surplus-to-GDP ratio the countries ran from 2009 to 2016. Belgium, Germany, Italy and Malta ran primary balances close to or in excess of that needed to maintain existing debt-to-GDP levels. Other countries, including Greece, Spain and Ireland, ran primary balances that fell short of that needed to prevent the debt-to-GDP ratio from rising.

The table also illustrates considerable differences between countries in the state of their public finances. Therefore, in a decentralised fiscal environment countries with an already high debt-to-GDP ratio, such as Greece, Italy and Portugal, will find it considerably more difficult to mitigate through fiscal policy the impact of future adverse economic shocks. Consequently, the sustainability of the current decentralised approach to fiscal policy in the eurozone is likely to be crucial in determining the future for the euro and those countries using the euro.

Table 26.4	Debt sustainability in the eurozone				

	General government gross debt-to-GDP, %		2009–16 averages			
	2008	**2016**	**Primary surplus-to-GDP, %**	**Real short-term interest rates, %**	**Economic growth, % p.a.**	**Required primary surplus-to-GDP, %**
Eurozone	68.6	91.3	−1.0	−0.4	0.4	−0.5
Belgium	92.5	105.9	−0.2	−0.7	0.8	−1.4
France	68.0	96.0	−2.6	0.1	0.6	−0.4
Germany	65.1	68.3	1.2	−0.5	1.0	−1.0
Greece	109.4	179.0	−3.7	0.4	−3.7	4.5
Ireland	42.4	75.4	−6.6	0.8	4.7	−1.7
Italy	102.4	132.6	1.1	−0.5	−0.7	0.3
Lithuania	14.6	40.2	−2.3	−0.2	1.0	−0.2
Malta	62.7	58.3	0.7	−0.9	3.8	−3.0
Netherlands	54.8	62.3	−1.6	−0.4	0.5	−0.5
Portugal	71.7	130.4	−2.3	−0.3	−0.5	0.2
Slovakia	28.5	51.9	−2.6	−0.6	1.9	−0.7
Spain	39.5	99.4	−5.2	−0.3	−0.2	−0.1

Note: A negative primary surplus ratio indicates a country running a primary deficit.

Source: AMECO database (European Commission, DGECFIN).

Section summary

1. One means of achieving greater currency stability is for a group of countries to peg their exchange rates with each other and yet float jointly with the rest of the world. The exchange rate mechanism of the EU (ERM) was an example. Members' currencies were allowed to fluctuate against other member currencies within a band. The band was ±2.25 per cent for the majority of the ERM countries until 1993.

2. The need for realignments seemed to have diminished in the late 1980s as greater convergence was achieved between the members' economies. Growing strains in the system, however, in the early 1990s led to a crisis in September 1992. The UK and Italy left the ERM. The bands were widened in 1993 to ±15 per cent, although in practice fluctuations were kept within ±2.25 per cent for most of the time from 1993 to the start of the euro in 1999.

3. The ERM was seen as an important first stage on the road to complete economic and monetary union.

4. The euro was born on 1 January 1999. Twelve countries adopted it, having at least nominally met the Maastricht convergence criteria. Euro notes and coins were introduced on 1 January 2002, with the notes and coins of the old currencies withdrawn a few weeks later.

5. The advantages claimed for EMU are that it eliminates the costs of converting currencies and the uncertainties associated with possible changes in inter-EU exchange rates. This encourages more investment, both inward and by domestic firms. What is more, a common central bank, independent from domestic governments, provides the stable monetary environment necessary for a convergence of the EU economies and the encouragement of investment and inter-Union trade.

6. Critics claim, however, that it makes adjustment to domestic economic problems more difficult. The loss of independence in policy making is seen by such people to be a major issue, not only because of the loss of political sovereignty, but also because domestic economic concerns may be at variance with those of the Union as a whole. A single monetary policy is claimed to be inappropriate for dealing with asymmetric shocks. What is more, countries and regions at the periphery of the Union may become depressed unless there is an effective regional policy.

7. The Greek sovereign debt crisis raised concerns about the future of the euro. Considerable differences remain in key macroeconomic indicators. This includes differences in the growth of labour productivity and unit labour costs, which are especially significant in the absence of nominal exchange rate adjustments.

8. There are also considerable differences in the financial health of the public finances of eurozone governments. This is significant because it affects the ability of national governments to use fiscal policy to absorb the adverse economic effects of negative shocks.

26.3 GLOBAL INEQUALITY

The gulf between rich and poor countries

KI 4
p14

The typical family in North America, western Europe, Japan and Australasia has many material comforts: plentiful food to eat; a house or apartment with electricity and running hot and cold water; an inside toilet connected to an underground sewerage system; access to free or affordable health care and education; numerous consumer durables; holidays away from home; visits to the cinema, concerts, sports events, etc. There are some people, it is true, who are very poor and, indeed, the problem of poverty in many developed countries has worsened in recent years. But it is only a small minority that cannot afford the basics of life, such as adequate food, shelter and clothing.

KI 1
p7

In most of Africa and large parts of Asia and Latin America, the picture is quite different. The majority of people live in poverty. For them life is a daily struggle for survival. Affluence does exist in these countries, but here it is the fortunate few who can afford good food, good housing and the various luxury items that typify life in the industrialised world.

A large proportion of the inhabitants live in the countryside. For many, this means living in a family with many children and working on a small amount of land with too little income to buy adequate agricultural machinery, fertilisers or pesticides. With a rapid growth in population there is less and less land to go round. As land is passed on from generation to generation, it is divided up between the offspring into smaller and smaller plots. Many who cannot make ends meet are forced to sell their land to the local landlords. Then as landless labourers they have to accept very low-paid jobs on the large farms or plantations. Others try to survive by borrowing, hoping to be able to pay off their debts with future crop sales. But often the only source of finance is again the local landlord who charges exorbitant rates of interest. As a result, they end up in a state of 'debt bondage' where they can never pay off their debts, but year in year out have to give part of their crops to the landlord as interest.

KI 19
p151

Others come to the rapidly growing cities. In the cities, at least there are some jobs. But typically more people migrate to the cities than there are jobs available. Thus the number of unemployed in the cities has grown inexorably. People are forced to do anything to earn a living: selling wares on street corners, or working as casual labourers, domestic servants or shoe shiners; some resort to prostitution and crime, others merely beg.

All round the outskirts of cities throughout the developing world, shanty towns mushroom as the poor flock in from the countryside. Families crowd into one- or two-roomed shacks, often with no electricity, no water and no sanitation. There are schools in these towns, but often parents cannot afford to allow their children to attend. Instead they have to send them out to work to supplement the family's meagre income. In some emerging countries, programmes to provide work and education in the shanty towns have helped reduce the problem somewhat; in other countries, the problem continues to worsen.

Statistics cannot give the complete picture, but they can give us some indication of the gulf between rich and poor countries. Table 26.5 gives some details.

In 2015, some 84 per cent of the world's population lives in developing countries (low- and middle-income countries), but these people earn only 54 per cent of global GNY[2] (in purchasing-power parity terms). In fact, as Figure 26.4 shows, this share has been rising over time. In 1990, developing countries' share of GNY was only 44 per cent. Despite this overall increase across developing countries, the poorest economies have experienced relatively little change in their share of global income.

In high-income countries, the average GNY per head in 2015 was just over $41 900. In low-income countries it was a mere $619. Even in purchasing-power parity terms, the figures were $46 100 and $1600 respectively. The gulf between rich and poor countries can also be seen in other basic indicators, including health, life expectancy and literacy. This is illustrated in Table 26.5, which shows a series of indicators under one of four categories: size of the economy, poverty and quality of life, promoting sustainability and gender development.

2 GNY (gross national income): see appendix to Chapter 15.

Table 26.5   Selected development indicators

		Low-income economies	Lower-middle-income economies	Upper-middle-income economies	High-income economies	World
Economy	Population (2015, billions)	638.3	2927.5	2593.9	1187.1	7346.7
	Population growth (p.a., 2011–15)	2.8	1.5	0.8	0.6	1.2
	GNY (2015, PPP, $ trillions)	1.0	18.8	40.6	54.8	115.0
	GNY per capita (2015, PPP, $)	1602	6409	15 670	46 135	15 659
	Growth in real GNY per capita (%. 2011–15)	2.0	3.9	n.a.	1.1	0.9
Poverty and quality of life	Under-5 mortality rate (per 1000 births, 2011–15)	82.5	56.7	10.1	5.8	45.8
	Primary school completion rate (number in last grade as % of those of entrance age, 2014)	65.9	91.0	110.4	98.2	90.1
	Growth in output per person employed (%, 2012–16)	2.2	3.1	3.3	0.8	1.8
Promoting sustainability	Population in 2015 with access to improved sanitation services (%)	28.3	52.0	80.0	99.4	67.5
	Population in 2014 with access to electricity (%)	28.3	79.8	98.7	100.0	85.3
	Population using the internet (%, 2011–15)	6.3	20.8	45.3	76.9	37.7
Gender development	Male life expectancy (years, 2015)	60.2	65.8	72.5	78.2	69.6
	Female life expectancy (years, 2015)	63.4	69.4	77.0	83.5	73.8
	Firms with female top manager (% of firms)	14.0	19.2	19.7	19.2	18.6
	Women in parliament (% of parliamentarians, 2016)	23.9	17.7	24.1	26.5	23.0

Notes: (i) Low-income economies are those with GNY per capita of $1025 or less in 2015; lower-middle income, $1026 – $4035; upper-middle income, $4036–$12 475; and high income, $12 476 or more; (ii) n.a. = not available.
Source: Based on data from Databank (World Bank).

Figure 26.4 World GNY in PPP terms (2011 prices)

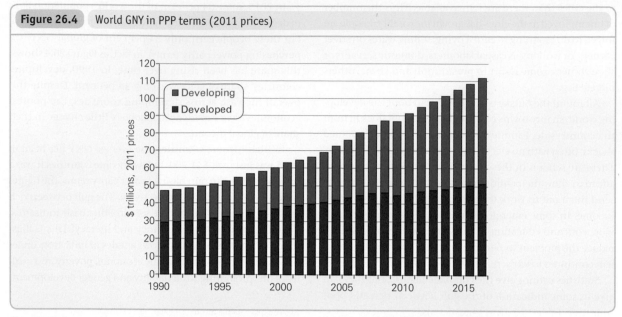

Note: Developing countries are classified as low, lower-middle and upper-middle-income economies; developed economies are high-income economies.
Source: Based on data from *Databank* (World Bank), series NY.GNP.MKTP.PP.KD.

Nevertheless, as the table shows, growth in GNY per capita over recent years has been faster in developing countries than in rich countries. The income gap between the developed and developing world has been narrowing.

The meaning of 'development'

Countries want to develop. But just what do we mean by 'development'? Clearly it is a normative concept. Its definition will depend on the goals that the economist assumes societies want to achieve. So how do economists define and measure development?

The basic needs approach

A starting point is to identify the basic needs that people have if they are to be able to realise their potential as human beings. Different economists have identified various lists of requirements, including the following items:

- Adequate food, shelter, warmth and clothing.
- Universal access to education.
- Availability of adequate health care.
- Availability of non-demeaning jobs.
- Sufficient free time to be able to enjoy social interaction.
- Freedom to make one's own economic decisions.
- Freedom to participate in the decisions of government and other bodies that affect one's life.

What other items might be included as basic needs?

There are four major problems with defining development in terms of a basic list of requirements.

The first is in deciding *what to include.* Any definition of *economic* development would clearly include people's *material* standard of living. But should development include social and political factors such as 'self-esteem', freedom from servitude and freedom of religion?

The second problem is in *measuring each of the items.* It is possible to measure such things as income per head, literacy rates and mortality rates. It is much more difficult, however, to measure the achievement of social and political objectives such as self-esteem.

The third problem is in arriving at a *single measure* of the level of development. You cannot add the average calorific intake to the number of doctors and nurses to the percentage of homes having various basic amenities such as running water. You can meaningfully add things up only if they are expressed in the same units, or if appropriate *weights* are attached to each of the items. Clearly, the assigning of any such weights would be highly controversial.

The fourth problem is in deciding the importance of the *distribution* of the various items. If, say, the average calorific intake increases, but the poorest sections of the population have less to eat, has the country really experienced an increase in the level of development?

However, many economists argue that the basic needs approach does provide a useful 'checklist' to see whether a country's development is broadly based or confined to just one or two indicators.

Would it be possible with this basic needs approach to say
(a) that one country was more developed than another;
(b) that one country was developing faster than another?

Using GNY to measure development

The desire to have a single measure for development and thus to be able to make simple comparisons between countries has led to the universal use of real gross national income (GNY) per capita as the main indicator. It has some major advantages:

- It takes into account virtually all the goods and services produced in a country, and converts them into a single measure by the use of market prices.
- Although markets are by no means perfect, they do reflect the strength of demand and the opportunity costs of supply.
- The rules for the measurement of GNY are universally agreed.
- Virtually all countries compile GNY statistics.
- Although not every item that affects human welfare is included in GNY, a sustained rise in GNY is generally agreed to be a *necessary* condition for a sustained rise in welfare.
- There is a fairly close correlation between the level of per capita GNY and other indicators such as mortality rates, literacy rates, and calorific and protein intake.

However, there are four fundamental criticisms of relying on simple GNY per capita as an indicator of development.

Many items are excluded. Much of production that does not get bought and sold will escape being recorded. This is a particular problem with rural societies that are largely sub-sistence-based. People grow their own food, build their own houses, make their own clothes and provide their own entertainment. GNY statistics are therefore likely to *under-state* the level of production in these societies.

On the other hand, as these societies 'develop', the size of the market sector is likely to grow. A larger proportion of people's consumption will be of items they have purchased and which therefore do enter into GNY statistics. Thus GNY figures will *overstate* the rate of growth of production and consumption.

As an economy becomes more urbanised, there is likely to be a growth in *external* costs of production and consumption, such as pollution and crime. Traditional ways of life will be destroyed; people may find themselves increasingly in a competitive, uncaring environment. Again the growth in GNY is likely to *overstate* the growth in human welfare.

Market prices may be highly distorted. GNY is based on market prices, but these prices may be distorted. Markets are often highly fragmented, and there is little competition to ensure that prices reflect undistorted marginal costs. Companies often have considerable monopoly power to push up prices of man-ufactured goods; landlords often have power to push up rents; governments may impose price controls on food; employers with monopsony power may be able to pay very low wages.

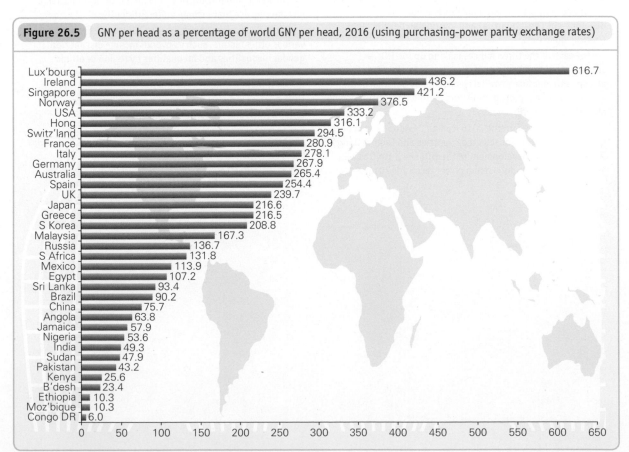

Figure 26.5 GNY per head as a percentage of world GNY per head, 2016 (using purchasing-power parity exchange rates)

Lux'bourg	616.7
Ireland	436.2
Singapore	421.2
Norway	376.5
USA	333.2
Hong	316.1
Switz'land	294.5
France	280.9
Italy	278.1
Germany	267.9
Australia	265.4
Spain	254.4
UK	239.7
Japan	216.6
Greece	216.5
S Korea	208.8
Malaysia	167.3
Russia	136.7
S Africa	131.8
Mexico	113.9
Egypt	107.2
Sri Lanka	93.4
Brazil	90.2
China	75.7
Angola	63.8
Jamaica	57.9
Nigeria	53.6
India	49.3
Sudan	47.9
Pakistan	43.2
Kenya	25.6
B'desh	23.4
Ethiopia	10.3
Moz'bique	10.3
Congo DR	6.0

Source: Based on data from *Databank* (World Bank), series NY.GNP.PCAP.PP.CD.

How would a redistribution of income to the powerful be likely to affect GNY?

Exchange rates may not reflect local purchasing power. GNY statistics are initially compiled in terms of the domestic currency. For purposes of international comparison they then have to be converted into a common currency – usually the US dollar – at the current exchange rate. But exchange rates reflect demand and supply of *traded* goods; they do not reflect the prices of *non-traded* goods. Generally, the price of non-traded goods and services in developing countries will be lower than the price of similar goods and services in advanced countries. The *level* of GNY is therefore likely to *understate* the level of production in poor countries. If, on the other hand, the proportion of traded goods increases over time, the *growth* of GNY will again *overstate* the growth in production.

It is much better, therefore, to estimate GNY using purchasing-power parity (PPP) exchange rates. Even if this is

---

BOX 26.3   THE HUMAN DEVELOPMENT INDEX (HDI)

A measure of human welfare?

Since 1990, the United Nations Development Programme (UNDP) has published an annual Human Development Index (HDI). This is an attempt to provide a more broadly based measure of development than GDP or GNY. HDI is the average of three indices based on three sets of variables: (i) life expectancy at birth, (ii) education (a weighted average of (a) the mean years that a 25-year-old person or older has spent in school and (b) the number of years of schooling that a 5-year-old child is expected to have over their lifetime) and (iii) real GNY per capita, measured in US dollars at purchasing-power parity exchange rates. The 188 countries are then placed in one of four equal-sized groups according to their HDI: very high human development (top quartile), high human development (next quartile), medium human development (next quartile) and low human development (bottom quartile).

For each of the three indices making up the HDI, a sophisticated formula is used. Thus the index for GNY attempts to measure material well-being by building in the assumption of a rapidly diminishing marginal utility of income above average world levels.

The table, based on the 2016 Human Development Report, gives the 2015 HDIs for selected countries and their rankings. It also shows the development of the HDI since 1990 as well as GNY per capita in purchasing power terms for 2015.

The final column of the table shows the divergence between the HDI and GNY per capita rankings in 2015. A positive number shows that a country has a higher ranking for HDI than GNY per capita. As can be seen, the rankings differ substantially in some cases between the two measures. For some countries, such as Australia, Ireland and Cuba, GNY *understates* their relative level of human development, whereas for others, such as the United Arab Emirate, Kuwait and Nigeria, GNY per capita *overstates* their relative level of human development. Thus South Africa (PPP) GNY per capita is 62 per cent higher than that of Cuba and yet its HDI is lower.

The point is that countries with similar levels of national income may use that income quite differently.

Recently, work has been done to adjust HDI figures for various other factors, such as overall income distribution, gender inequalities and inequalities by region or ethnic group. Thus the overall HDI can be adjusted downwards to reflect greater degrees of inequality. Alternatively, separate HDIs can be produced for separate regions or ethnic groups, or for women and men within a country.

1. *For what reasons are HDI and per capita GDP rankings likely to diverge?*
2. *Why do Kuwait and South Africa have such a large negative figure in the final column of the table?*

done, however, massive differences remain in GNY per head between rich and poor countries. This is illustrated in Figure 26.5, which shows GNY per head at PPP exchange rates as a percentage of the estimated world GNY per head.

Simple GNY per head ignores the distribution of income.   Since the early 1980s, many developing countries have achieved relatively rapid growth in per capita GNY as they have sought overseas investment, privatised their industries and cut the levels of public provision. But with a deepening of poverty, a growing inequality in the distribution of income and an increase in unemployment, few would argue that this constitutes genuine 'development'.

Many who have advocated the concentration on GNY and its rate of growth have argued that, while the rich may be the first to benefit from prosperity, gradually the benefits will 'trickle down' to the poor. In practice, the wealth has failed to trickle down in many countries. The rich have got richer while the poor have got poorer.

EXPLORING ECONOMICS

Human Development Index for selected countries (2015)

		Human Development Index (HDI)				GNY per head in 2015 (PPP $, 2011 prices)		GNY (PPP$) rank minus HDI rank
		2015	2010	2000	1990	Ranking	$	
	Very high human development							
1	Norway	0.949	0.939	0.917	0.849	6	67 614	5
2	Australia	0.939	0.927	0.899	0.866	9	56 364	7
2	Switzerland	0.939	0.932	0.888	0.831	20	42 822	18
4	Germany	0.926	0.912	0.860	0.801	16	45 000	12
5	Singapore	0.925	0.911	0.820	0.718	2	78 162	−3
7	Netherlands	0.924	0.911	0.878	0.830	14	46 326	7
8	Ireland	0.923	0.909	0.857	0.762	18	43 798	10
10	Canada	0.920	0.903	0.867	0.849	11	53 245	1
10	United States	0.920	0.910	0.884	0.860	21	42 582	11
16	United Kingdom	0.909	0.902	0.866	0.775	25	37 931	9
17	Japan	0.903	0.884	0.856	0.814	26	37 268	9
21	France	0.897	0.882	0.849	0.779	24	38 085	3
38	Saudi Arabia	0.847	0.803	0.742	0.698	53	21 665	15
42	United Arab Emirates	0.840	0.824	0.798	0.726	7	66 203	−35
51	Kuwait	0.800	0.792	0.786	0.713	3	76 075	−48
	High human development							
54	Uruguay	0.795	0.780	0.742	0.692	73	14 952	19
59	Malaysia	0.789	0.774	0.725	0.643	45	24 620	−14
60	Palau	0.788	0.770	0.741	..	59	19 470	−1
68	Cuba	0.775	0.780	0.686	0.676	114	7 455	46
79	Brazil	0.754	0.724	0.685	0.611	77	14 145	−2
87	Thailand	0.740	0.720	0.649	0.574	91	11 295	4
90	China	0.738	0.700	0.592	0.499	82	13 345	−8
101	Tonga	0.721	0.712	0.674	0.648	131	5 284	30
	Medium human development							
119	South Africa	0.666	0.638	0.629	0.621	88	12 087	−31
131	India	0.624	0.580	0.494	0.428	125	5 663	−6
139	Bangladesh	0.579	0.545	0.468	0.386	140	3 839	1
139	Ghana	0.579	0.554	0.485	0.455	142	3 464	3
146	Kenya	0.555	0.530	0.447	0.473	152	2 881	6
147	Pakistan	0.550	0.525	0.450	0.404	134	5 031	−13
	Low human development							
152	Nigeria	0.527	0.500	..	..	127	5443	−25
154	Zimbabwe	0.516	0.452	0.427	0.499	170	1588	16
165	Sudan	0.490	0.463	0.399	0.331	139	3846	−26
170	Malawi	0.476	0.444	0.387	0.325	182	1073	12
174	Ethiopia	0.448	0.411	0.283	..	175	1523	1
187	Niger	0.353	0.323	0.255	0.212	184	889	−3
188	Central African Republic	0.352	0.361	0.314	0.320	188	587	0

Source: Based on data from *2016 Human Development Report* (United Nations Development Programme, 2016).

Given the weaknesses of GNY, but given the desirability of having a single measure of development, various composite indicators have been constructed. The most widely used is the *Human Development Index (HDI)*, which is a combined measure of life expectancy, education and GDP per head at PPP exchange rates. This index is examined in Box 26.3.

Section summary

1. There are a number of ways of categorising countries according to their level of development.

2. The level of development of a country can be defined in terms of the extent to which it meets basic needs for human life. There is no universal agreement, however, about which items should be measured or about how to measure and weight them. Nevertheless, the approach provides a useful indicator of whether development is broadly based and how rapidly the most serious problems of poverty are being tackled.

3. The most widely used measure of development is GNY per head at PPP exchange rates. However, there are serious problems with using GNY: many items may be excluded, especially for a more subsistence-based society; prices may be highly distorted; and the statistics ignore the question of the distribution of income. Another widely used measure is the Human Development Index.

26.4 TRADE AND DEVELOPING COUNTRIES

The role of international trade is one of the most contentious issues in development economics. Should countries adopt an open trading policy with few if any barriers to imports? Should governments actively promote trade by subsidising their export sector? Or should they restrict trade and pursue a policy of greater self-sufficiency? These are issues that we will be looking at in this section.

Whether it is desirable that developing countries should adopt policies of more trade or less, trade is still vital. Certain raw materials, capital equipment and intermediate products that are necessary for development can be obtained only from abroad. Others *could* be produced domestically, but only at much higher cost.

The relationship between trade and development

What makes the issue of trade so contentious is the absence of a simple relationship between trade and development. Instead the relationship is complex and determined by a series of interactions between variables affecting both trade and development. Furthermore, while some countries have managed to use trade as an engine for economic growth and wider human development, others, despite trade liberalisation, have seen relatively little improvement in either their export performance or in human development.

In constructing a trade and development index, the UN[3] identified three broad groups of influences or dimensions which interact and affect a country's trade and development performance. Within these broad groups are various indicators which themselves interact. We consider briefly these three dimensions and some of the indicators within each dimension.

Structural and institutional dimension

Human capital. This relates to the skills and expertise of the workforce which affect a country's performance and its productivity. Education and health are key influences here. As well as affecting the economic growth of a country, higher educational attainment and better health conditions positively impact on social and human development.

Physical infrastructure. Infrastructure affects a country's productive capacity and so its potential output. Poor transport infrastructure, for example, is thought to be a major impediment to a country's export performance.

Financial environment. Credit is important to producers and consumers alike in helping to finance both short-term and longer-term commitments. For instance, it enables firms to finance day-to-day operational purchases but also longer-term investments in fixed assets such as buildings and machinery.

Institutional quality. This relates to issues of governance not just of firms themselves, but also to institutions, largely governmental.

3 Developing Countries in International Trade 2005: Trade and Development Index (United Nations, 2005).

Environment sustainability. The argument here is that excessive activity, particularly at the early stages of development, can result in environmental degradation. This can adversely affect human development and, in turn, economic development.

Trade policies and process dimension

Openness to trade. In the absence of market failures and externalities, trade liberalisation is argued to be a driver of development. However, there can be significant human costs in the transition process.

Effective access to foreign markets. The success of a country's export performance is crucially dependent on its effective access to markets. Barriers to access include tariffs and non-tariff barriers, such as regulatory standards in the markets of recipient countries. A wider definition of 'effective' access recognises other factors too. These might include the size of foreign markets, transport links, the characteristics of the goods being exported – for example how differentiated they are – as well as the cost of the exported goods.

Levels of development dimension

The third series of factors affecting both trade and human development relate to existing levels of development. In section 26.3 we discussed some of the issues in defining and measuring development. But, in general terms, we can think of the relevant development issues here as encompassing three components: economic development, social development and gender development.

Trade strategies

Despite the complexity of the relationship between trade and development, countries' policies towards trade typically go through various stages as they develop.

Primary outward-looking stage. Traditionally, developing countries have exported primaries – minerals such as copper, cash crops such as coffee and non-foodstuffs such as cotton – in exchange for manufactured consumer goods. Having little in the way of an industrial base, if they want to consume manufactured goods, they have to import them.

Secondary inward-looking stage. In seeking rapid economic development, most developing countries drew lessons from the experience of the advanced countries. The main conclusion was that industrialisation was the key to economic success.

But industrialisation required foreign exchange to purchase capital equipment. This led to a policy of *import-substituting industrialisation*, which involved cutting back on non-essential imports and thereby releasing foreign exchange. Tariffs and other restrictions were imposed on those imports for which a domestic substitute existed or which were regarded as unimportant.

Secondary outward-looking stage. Once an industry had satisfied domestic demand, it had to seek markets abroad if expansion was to continue. What is more, as we shall see, import substitution brought a number of serious problems for developing countries. The answer seemed to be to look outward again, this time to the export of manufactured goods. Many of the most economically successful developing countries (especially Hong Kong, Singapore, South Korea, Taiwan and, more recently, China, India and Indonesia) have owed their high growth rates to a rapid expansion of manufactured exports.

We will now examine the three stages in more detail.

Approach 1: Exporting primaries – exploiting comparative advantage

The justification for exporting primaries

Despite moves towards import substitution and secondary export promotion, many developing countries still rely heavily on primary exports. Three major arguments have traditionally been used for pursuing a policy of exporting primaries. In each case the arguments have also been used to justify a policy of free or virtually free trade.

Exporting primaries exploits comparative advantage. Traditional trade theory implies that countries should specialise in producing those items in which they have a comparative advantage: i.e. those goods that can be produced at relatively low opportunity costs. For most developing countries, this means that a large proportion of their exports should be primaries.

The reasons for differences in comparative costs were examined by two Swedish economists, Eli Heckscher and Bertil Ohlin. They believed that comparative cost differences arise from differences in factor endowments. The **Heckscher–Ohlin theory** states that *a country should specialise in those goods that are intensive in the country's abundant factor.* The more abundant a factor, the relatively cheaper it is likely to be, and thus the lower will be the opportunity cost of producing goods that are intensive in its use. Thus labour-abundant developing countries should specialise in labour-intensive products. By exporting these products, which will typically be primaries, they can earn the foreign exchange to import goods that use large amounts of capital and other resources that are in short supply.

> ### Definitions
>
> **Import-substituting industrialisation** A strategy of restricting imports of manufactured goods and using the foreign exchange saved to build up domestic substitute industries.
>
> **Heckscher–Ohlin version of comparative advantage** A country has a comparative advantage in those goods that are intensive in the country's relatively abundant factor.

According to this theory, international trade would lead not only to higher consumption, but also to *factor price equalisation*: i.e. the erosion of income inequalities between trading nations. For example, if wage rates are low in developing countries, trade will increase the demand for their labour-intensive products and thereby push up wage rates. International trade will also erode income differentials *within* countries. The demand for exports will increase the demand for the relatively cheap factors, and imports will reduce the demand for the relatively expensive ones. Thus the cheap factors will go up in price and the expensive ones will come down.

1. *What effect will trade have on the price of capital in developing and developed countries?*
2. *It is sometimes claimed that trade with developing countries is unjust because it leads to the importation of goods produced at pitifully low wages. How can the Heckscher-Ohlin theory be used to refute this claim? Is there any validity in the claim? (See Box 24.3.)*

Exporting primaries provides a 'vent for surplus'. Trade offers a **vent for surplus**: i.e. a means of putting to use resources that would otherwise not be used. These surpluses occur where the domestic market is simply not big enough to consume all the available output of a particular good. There is far too little demand within Zambia to consume its potential output of copper. The same applies to Namibian uranium and Peruvian tin.

Exporting primaries provides an 'engine for economic growth'. According to this argument, developing countries benefit from the growth of the economies of the developed world. As industrial expansion takes place in the rich North, this creates additional demand for primaries from the poor South. In more recent years, the rapid growth in China, India and other industrialising developing countries saw a rapid growth in demand for commodities, many produced in the least developed countries. This drove up commodity prices in the first decade of the 2000s and benefited primary exporters (see Figure 26.6 on page 847). However, as we shall see, commodity prices can be very volatile; indeed, they fell in the first part of the 2010s.

Traditional trade theory in the context of development

There are several reasons for questioning whether the above arguments justify a policy of relying on primary exports as the means to development.

Comparative costs change over time. Over time, with the acquisition of new skills and an increase in the capital stock, a developing country that once had a comparative advantage in primaries may find that it now has a comparative advantage in certain *manufactured* products, especially those that are more labour-intensive and use raw materials of which the country has a plentiful supply. The market, however, cannot necessarily be relied upon to bring about a smooth transition to producing such products.

Concentrating on primary production may hinder growth. The theory of comparative advantage shows how trade allows a country to consume beyond its production possibility curve (see pages 753–4). As its economy grows, however, this production possibility curve will *shift outwards*. By concentrating on primaries, the curve may shift outwards more slowly than if the country had pursued a policy of industrialisation. In other words, economic growth may be slower from a policy of exporting primaries than from a policy of industrialisation.

The benefits from trade may not accrue to the nationals of the country. If a mine or plantation is owned by a foreign company, it will be the foreign shareholders who get the profits from the sale of exports. In addition, these companies may bring in their own capital and skilled labour from abroad. The benefits gained by the local people will probably be confined to the additional wages they earn. With these companies being in a position of monopsony power, the wages are often very low.

In recent years the Fair Trade movement has focused attention on the low incomes received by many primary producers and their lack of market power. Only a tiny fraction of the price you pay for coffee, tea or bananas goes to local growers.

Why does this argument make GNY a better indicator of development than GDP? (See the appendix to Chapter 15.)

Trade may lead to less equality. Trade shifts income distribution in favour of those factors of production employed intensively in the export sector. If exports are labour intensive, greater equality will tend to result. But if they are land or raw material intensive, trade will redistribute income in favour of large landowners or mine owners.

Exporting primary exports may involve external costs. Mining can lead to huge external costs, such as the despoiling of the countryside and damage to the health of miners. Mines and plantations can lead to the destruction of traditional communities and their values.

These arguments cast doubt on whether a policy of relying on free trade in primary exports is the best way of achieving economic development. Various trends in the international economy have also worked against primary exporters, causing them serious balance of payments problems.

Balance of payments problems: long term

Long-term trends in international trade have caused problems for primary exporting countries in various ways.

Low income elasticity of demand for primary products.   As world incomes grow, so a smaller proportion of these incomes is spent on primaries. Since food is a necessity, consumers, especially in rich countries, already consume virtually all they require. A rise in incomes, therefore, tends to be spent more on luxury goods and services, and only slightly more on basic foodstuffs. The exceptions are certain 'luxury' imported foodstuffs such as exotic fruits. In the case of raw materials, as people's incomes grow, they tend to buy more and more expensive products. The extra value of these products, however, arises not from the extra raw materials they might contain, but from their greater sophistication.

This argument, however, has not always applied in recent years. The rapid growth of countries such as China and India, where people spend a relatively large proportion of any increase in their income on food, has led to periods of rapidly rising world food prices (see Figure 26.6). This has been aggravated by poor harvests in many parts of the world and by switching land to growing crops for biofuels instead of food. This has raised concerns among developing countries about 'food security' and hence the ability of people to afford foodstuffs. There has also been a rapid growth in demand by such countries for raw materials as inputs into the construction industry and the expanding industrial sector.

Agricultural protection in advanced countries.   Faced with the problem of a slowly growing demand for food produced by their own farmers, advanced countries increasingly imposed restrictions on imported food. Reducing these restrictions has been one of the main aims of the Doha Development Agenda (the latest round of WTO trade negotiations: see Box 24.8 on pages 768–9).

Technological developments.   Synthetic substitutes have in many cases replaced primaries in the making of consumer durables, industrial equipment and clothing. Also, the process of miniaturisation, as microchips have replaced machines, has meant that less and less raw materials have been required to produce any given amount of output.

Rapid growth in imports.   There tends to be a high income elasticity of demand for imported manufactures. This is the result partly of better-off people in developing countries being able to afford luxury goods, and partly of the development of new tastes as people are exposed to the products of the developed world – products such as Coca-Cola®, Levi® jeans, mobile phones and iPods®. In fact, the whole process has been dubbed 'Coca-Colanisation'. Because of a lack of domestic substitutes, the price elasticity of demand for manufactured imports is low. This gives market power to the overseas suppliers of these imports, which tends to raise their price relative to exports.

The terms of trade.   Between 1980 and 2000, the prices of many primary products declined. For instance, the nominal price index in 2000 for beverages (coffee and tea) was only one-third of its level in the late 1970s – and even less than that in real terms. This reflected the slow growth in demand for primaries and led to a *decline* in the terms of trade for primary exporters. This is because they were having to export more and more in order to buy any given quantity of imports, such as manufactured goods.

As Figure 26.6 shows, a quite different picture emerged in the 2000s. As the demand for food and raw materials grew rapidly, reflecting the rapid growth of China and various

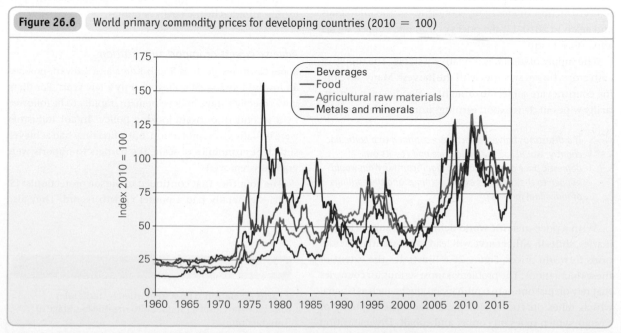

Figure 26.6   World primary commodity prices for developing countries (2010 = 100)

Source: Based on data from *World Bank Commodity Price Data (The Pink Sheet)*, (Commodity Markets, World Bank).

other emerging economies, so primary commodity prices rose sharply.

This was to come to an abrupt halt with the world recession of 2008–9, when primary product prices fell sharply. But, the resumption of global growth saw primary commodity prices climb once more and in many cases to levels considerably higher than before the world recession. But then, with a slowing in global growth, commodity prices fell, so that by January 2016 the aggregate commodity price index had returned to the level of 2006 – before the financial crisis. Nevertheless, this was still some 80 per cent higher than in January 2000 (in nominal terms). It then drifted up slowly over the coming months.

Balance of payments problems: short term

There are also problems for primary exporting countries in the *short term*.

As we have just seen, the prices of primary products can be subject to large fluctuations. This causes great uncertainty for primary exporters. The current account of the balance of payments fluctuates wildly, which tends to cause large swings in exchange rates or requires massive government intervention to stabilise them.

Price fluctuations are caused partly by the low price elasticity of demand and supply of primaries, but also by substantial *shifts* in their demand and supply.

The demand for *food* tends to be relatively stable, but that for minerals varies with the business cycle and tends to vary more than the demand for consumer goods. The reason is the *accelerator principle* (see section 17.4). Since the *level* of investment demand depends on the size of *changes* in consumer demand, investment will fluctuate much more than consumer demand. But since many minerals are inputs into *capital* equipment, their demand is also likely to fluctuate more than consumer demand. For example, with the boom in construction in emerging economies in the mid-2000s and again in 2010–11, the prices of iron ore, copper, nickel and lead shot up.

The supply of minerals is relatively stable. The supply of cash crops, however, varies with the harvest. Many developing countries are subject to drought or flood, which can virtually wipe out their export earnings from the relevant crop.

 If a disastrous harvest of rice were confined to a particular country, would (a) the world price and (b) its own domestic price of rice fluctuate significantly? What would happen to the country's export earnings and the earnings of individual farmers?

With a price-inelastic world demand and supply for primaries, shifts in either curve will lead to substantial fluctuations in world prices. Figure 26.6 illustrates the extent of these fluctuations. The problem is most serious for countries that rely on just one or two primary products, such as Ghana, which relies on cocoa, and the Democratic Republic of Congo, which relies on copper and cobalt. Diversification into other primaries would help to reduce their exposure.

Approach 2: Import-substituting industrialisation (ISI)

 TC 7 p81

Dissatisfaction with relying on primary exporting has led most countries to embark on a process of *industrialisation*. The newly industrialised countries (NICs), such as China, Malaysia, Brazil and India, are already well advanced along the industrialisation road. Other developing countries have not yet progressed very far, especially the poorest African countries.

The most obvious way for countries to industrialise was to cut back on the imports of manufactures and substitute them with home-produced manufactures. This could not be done overnight: it had to be done in stages, beginning with assembly, then making some of the components, and finally making all, or nearly all, of the inputs into production. Most developing countries have at least started on the first stage. Several of the more advanced developing countries have component-manufacturing industries. Only a few of the larger NICs, such as China, India, Brazil and South Korea, have built extensive capital goods industries.

The method most favoured by policy makers was **tariff escalation**. Here tariff rates (or other restrictions) increased as one moved from the raw materials to the intermediate product to the finished product stage. Thus finished goods had higher tariffs than intermediate products. This encouraged assembly plants, which were protected by high tariffs from imported finished products, and were able to obtain components at a lower tariff rate.

One of the problems with ISI was that countries were desperately short of resources to invest in industry. As a result, a policy of ISI usually involved encouraging investment by multinational companies. But even without specific 'perks' (e.g. tax concessions, cheap sites, the cutting of red tape), multinationals would still probably be attracted by the protection afforded by the tariffs or quotas.

Adverse effects of import substitution

Some countries, such as South Korea and Taiwan, pursued an inward-looking ISI policy for only a few years. For them it was merely a stage in development, rapidly to be followed by a secondary outward-looking policy. Infant industries were initially given protection, but when they had achieved sufficient economies of scale, the barriers to imports were gradually removed.

The countries that continued to pursue protectionist ISI policies generally had a poorer growth record. They also

---

Definition

Tariff escalation The system whereby tariff rates increase the closer a product is to the finished stage of production.

BOX 26.4 WHEN DRIVING AND ALCOHOL DO MIX

A case of import substitution in Brazil

Two major changes in world trade hit Brazil in the 1970s. The first was the fourfold increase in world oil prices. Brazil has very little oil of its own. The second was the slump in the world sugar cane market as a result of northern countries' protection of their sugar beet industries. Brazil was a major cane sugar exporter.

Faced with a resulting large increase in its import bill and a slump in its sugar exports, the Brazilian government came up with an ingenious solution. It could use surplus sugar cane to make alcohol, which could then be used instead of petrol for cars. Farmers were given subsidies to grown sugar cane.

Large distilleries were set up to convert the sugar cane into alcohol. At the same time, cars were produced (e.g. VW Beetles) that could run on alcohol (ethanol) rather than petrol.

Thus by one measure two problems were alleviated. By 1985, more than 90 per cent of cars produced in Brazil were designed to burn alcohol.

Then, with the decline in oil prices from the mid-1980s, the relative cost efficiency of alcohol-powered cars declined: at times it was cheaper to import oil than to produce alcohol. The government cut subsidies and by 1997 less than 1 per cent of cars produced in Brazil were alcohol-powered.

The dual-fuel solution

A more flexible solution was found in 2003 with the introduction of dual-fuel cars that could run on either alcohol or petrol or a mixture of the two. This gave consumers the chance of using whichever fuel was the cheapest at the time. The popularity of these 'flexi-fuel' cars gave a welcome boost to the sugar cane and ethanol industries.

However, despite the number of dual-fuel cars and vans in Brazil reaching over 80 per cent of the total in the early 2010s, the industry began to experience difficulties. The deteriorating macroeconomic climate depressed car usage and the purchase of new cars. Furthermore, in looking to control inflation the government was subsidising petrol prices and, with the price of oil falling from 2014, the effect was to make the use of ethanol less competitive compared with petrol. Again, the effect was to dampen the demand for ethanol.

The government subsequently took steps to revive the biofuel sector. It terminated its subsidies of petrol and also increased the proportion of ethanol in petrol from 25 per cent to 27.5 per cent.

The story illustrates the danger of basing major schemes on terms of trade existing at a particular time. If these terms of trade subsequently change, the schemes could prove to be uneconomical.

A new era for the biofuels industry

Brazil also increased its support for another import-substituting drive: to displace diesel fuel with fuel produced from soybeans. To do this, parliament approved measures to increase the percentage of biodiesel required in diesel fuel by 1 per cent a year, from 7 per cent in 2016 to 10 per cent in 2019.

Perhaps this support for biodiesel will help to revive the vehicle industry in Brazil. But soya-based biodiesel can have very damaging effects on the environment. It is far less energy-efficient than sugar cane as a source of fuel and it absorbs less carbon per hectare as it grows. In fact, given that rainforest is being cleared to grow soya, the net effect is to reduce carbon capture substantially.

 Could a case be made out for a flexible tax on oil imports to ensure that it was always profitable to produce alcohol?

---

tended to suffer from other problems, such as a deepening of inequality. The development of the modern industrial sector was often to the detriment of the traditional sectors and also to the export sector.

The criticisms of ISI are numerous, and include the following.

It ran directly counter to the principle of comparative advantage. Rather than confining ISI to genuine infant industries and then gradually removing the protection, ISI was applied indiscriminately to a whole range of industries. Countries ended up producing goods in which they had a comparative *disadvantage*.

 If a country specialises in a good in which it has a comparative disadvantage, where will it be consuming with respect to its production possibility curve?

KI 38
p752

It cushioned inefficient practices and encouraged the establishment of monopolies. Without competition from imports, many of the industries were highly inefficient and wasteful of resources. What is more, in all but the largest or most developed of the developing countries the domestic market for many manufactures is small. If a newly established industry is to be large enough to gain the full potential economies of scale, it must be large relative to the market. This means that it will have considerable monopoly power.

 KI 22 p190

It involved artificially low real interest rates. To encourage capital investment in the import-substituting industries, governments often intervened to keep interest rates low. This encouraged the use of capital-intensive technology with a consequent lack of jobs. It also starved other sectors (such as agriculture) of much-needed finance, and it discouraged saving.

It led to urban wages above the market-clearing level. Wage rates in the industrial sector, although still low compared with advanced countries, are often considerably higher than in the traditional sectors.

- They are pushed up by firms seeking to retain labour in which they have invested training.
- Governments, seeking to appease the politically powerful urban industrial working class, have often passed minimum wage laws.
- Trade unions, although less widespread in developing than in advanced countries, are mainly confined to the new industries.

Higher industrial wages again encourage firms to use capital-intensive techniques.

It involved overvalued exchange rates. Restricting imports tends to lead to an appreciation of the exchange rate. This makes non-restricted imports cheaper. This then discourages the production of domestic goods, such as food and component parts, which compete with those imports. Also, a higher exchange rate discourages exports. Exports tend to be priced in dollars. If the exchange rate appreciates, domestic currency will buy more dollars; or put another way, a dollar will exchange for less domestic currency. Thus exporters will earn less domestic currency as the exchange rate appreciates.

Why is an overvalued exchange rate likely to encourage the use of capital-intensive technology?

It did not necessarily save on foreign exchange. Many of the new industries were highly dependent on the importation of raw materials, capital equipment and component parts. These imported inputs, unlike imports of finished goods, were often supplied by a single firm, which could thus charge monopoly prices. What is more, a large proportion of the extra incomes generated by these industries tended to be spent on imports by the new urban elites.

Protection was not applied evenly. Many different tariff rates were used in one country: in fact, a policy of tariff escalation demands this. In addition, governments often used a whole range of other protectionist instruments, such as the licensing of importers, physical and value quotas, and foreign exchange rationing. These were often applied in a haphazard way. The result was that protection was highly uneven.

Income distribution was made less equal. Additional incomes generated by the modern sector tended to be spent on modern-sector goods and imported goods. Thus there was a multiplier effect *within* the modern sector, but virtually none between the sectors. Also, as we saw above, an overvalued exchange rate leads to a bias against agriculture, and thus further deepens the divide between rich and poor. Finally, the relatively high wages of the modern sector encourage workers to migrate to the towns, where many, failing to get a job, live in dire poverty.

Social, cultural and environmental costs. A policy of ISI often involved imposing an alien set of values. Urban life can be harsh, competitive and materialistic. Moreover, a drive for industrialisation may involve major costs to the environment, as a result of waste products from new industries and a lack of sewage systems in poor areas.

Finally, import substitution is necessarily limited by the size of the domestic market. Once that is saturated, ISI can come to an abrupt halt. At that stage, further expansion can come only from exporting; but if these industries have been over-protected, they will be unable to compete in world markets.

This has been a long list of problems and different economists put different emphases on them. Neoclassical economists stress the problems of market distortions, arguing that ISI leads to great inefficiency. Neo-Marxist economists, on the other hand, stress the problems of *dependency*. Many of the new industries will be owned by multinational companies, which import unsuitable technologies. The countries will then become dependent on imported inputs and foreign sources of capital. (See Case Study 26.6 on the student website.)

Approach 3: Exporting manufactures – a possible way forward?

The countries with the highest rates of economic growth are those that have successfully made the transition to being exporters of manufactures. Table 26.6 gives some examples.

The transition from inward-looking to outward-looking industrialisation

How is a country to move from import substituting to being outward-looking? One approach is to take it industry by industry. When an industry has saturated the home market and there is no further scope for import substitution, it should then be encouraged to seek markets overseas. The trouble with this approach is that, if the country is still protecting other industries, there will probably still be an overvalued exchange rate. Thus specific subsidies, tax concessions or other 'perks' would have to be given to this industry to enable it to compete. The country would still be highly interventionist, with all the distortions and misallocation of resources that this tends to bring.

The alternative is to wean the whole economy off protection. Three major things will need doing:

- A devaluation of the currency in order to restore the potential profitability of the export sector.

Definition

Dependency Where the development of a developing country is hampered by its relationships with the industrialised world.

- A dismantling of the various protective measures that had biased production towards the home market.
- A removal or relaxing of price controls.

But these are things that cannot be done 'at a stroke'. Firms may have to be introduced gradually to the greater forces of competition that an outward-looking trade policy brings. Otherwise there may be massive bankruptcies and a corresponding massive rise in unemployment.

The benefits from a secondary outward-looking policy
The advocates of outward-looking industrialisation make a number of points in its favour.

It conforms more closely to comparative advantage. Countries pursuing an open trade regime will be able to export only goods in which they have a comparative advantage. The resources used in earning a unit of foreign exchange from exports will be less than those used in saving a unit of foreign exchange by replacing imports with home-produced goods. In other words, resources will be used more efficiently.

Economies of scale. If the home market is too small to allow a firm to gain all the potential economies of scale, these can be gained by expanding into the export market.

Increased competition. By having to compete with foreign companies, exporters will be under a greater competitive pressure than industries shielded behind protective barriers. This will encourage (a) resource saving in the short run, both through their better *allocation* and through reductions in X inefficiency (see Box 7.5), and (b) innovation and investment, as firms attempt to adopt the latest technology, often obtained from developed countries.

Increased investment. To the extent that outward-looking policies lead to a greater potential for economic growth, they may attract more foreign capital. To the extent that they lead to increased incomes, additional saving will be generated, especially given that the *marginal* propensity to save may be quite high. The extra savings can be used to finance extra investment.

It can lead to more employment and a more equal distribution of income. According to the Heckscher–Ohlin theory, the manufactured goods in which a country will have a comparative advantage are those produced by labour-intensive techniques. Export expansion will thus increase the demand for labour relative to capital, and create more employment. The increased demand for labour will tend to lead to a rise in wages relative to profits.

 Will the adoption of labour-intensive techniques necessarily lead to a more equal distribution of income?

It removes many of the costs associated with ISI. Under a policy of ISI, managers may spend a lot of their time lobbying politicians and officials, seeking licences (and sometimes paying bribes to obtain them), adhering to norms and regulations or trying to find ways around them. If an outward-looking policy involves removing all this, managers can turn their attention to producing goods more efficiently.

Drawbacks of an export-orientated industrialisation strategy
The export of manufactures is seen by many developed countries as very threatening to their own industries. Their response has often been to erect trade barriers. These barriers have tended to be highest in the very industries (such as textiles, footwear and processed food) where developing countries have the greatest comparative advantage. Even if the barriers are *currently* low, developing countries may feel that it is too risky to expand their exports of these products for fear of a future rise in barriers. Recognising this problem, the World Trade Organization is very keen to ensure fair access for developing countries to the markets of the rich world. This has been a core focus of the Doha Round of trade negotiations (see Box 24.8 on pages 768–9).

Consider the arguments from the perspective of an advanced country for and against protecting its industries from imports of manufactures from developing countries.

The successes of developing countries such as China, Malaysia and South Korea in exporting manufactures (see Table 26.6) do not imply that other developing countries will have similar success. As additional developing countries attempt to export their manufactures, they will be facing more and more competition from each other.

Another problem is that, if a more open trade policy involves removing or reducing exchange and capital controls, the country may become more vulnerable to speculative attack. This was one of the major contributing factors to the East Asian crisis of the late 1990s (see Case Study 26.2 on the student website). Gripped by currency and stock market speculation, and by banking and company insolvency, many countries of the region found that economic growth had turned into a major recession. The 'miracle' seemed to be over. Nevertheless, the countries with the fewest distortions fared the best during the crisis. Thus Singapore and Taiwan, which are open and relatively flexible, experienced only a slowdown, rather than a recession.

Exporting manufactures may thus be a very risky strategy for the least developed countries, such as many in Africa. Perhaps the best hope for the future may be for a growth in manufacturing trade *between* such developing countries. That way they can gain the benefits of specialisation and economies of scale that trade brings, while at the same time producing for a growing market. The feasibility of this approach depends on whether developing countries can agree to free trade areas or even customs unions between themselves (see section 24.3).

There does, however, seem to be a strong movement in this direction. The share of trade between developing countries (so-called South–South trade) in total world exports has doubled over the past 20 years, to over 25 per cent. Manufactured goods now account for nearly 60 per cent of South–South trade, respectively.

| BOX 26.5 | THE EVOLVING COMPARATIVE ADVANTAGE OF CHINA |

Riding the dragon

Comparative advantage enables specialisation and trade and this can be one of the key factors that helps a country to grow and develop. During the 1990s and 2000s, China experienced an average rate of growth of just over 10 per cent per year. Its emergence as an economic power is due to many things, but its ability to exploit its *comparative advantage* is certainly one such factor.

A country's comparative advantage often derives from its abundant resources and China used its abundance of cheap labour. With labour costs estimated to be between 60 and 90 per cent lower than in the USA, it was this that attracted many manufacturing companies to China, making a range of products using moderately and low-skilled jobs.

According to the 2016 World Investment Report, China (excluding Hong Kong) was the world's third largest *recipient* of foreign direct investment (FDI) with investment of $136 billion (6.3 per cent of the country's gross fixed capital formation). This meant China was the recipient of around 8 per cent of global FDI.

Lu Zheng, the Director of the Institute of Industrial Economics under the Chinese Academy of Social Sciences, said that 'it [China's comparative advantage] will last at least two decades and play an important role in promoting China's economic growth'.

However, it is not just the quantity of labour that explained China's dominance in manufacturing. While many of its workers are low-skilled, many are educated. Furthermore, Paul Krugman notes another key factor:

China's dominant role in the export of many labor-intensive manufactured goods surely reflects its

combination of relatively abundant labor and relatively high manufacturing competence.[1]

It is unsurprising that companies would take advantage of lower costs of production and locate factories in China. But while China has benefited from this, many developed nations have seen a decline in their manufactured exports. Countries like the UK and USA gradually adjusted and moved to exploit their comparative advantage in the services sector. They saw a comparative disadvantage emerge in manufactured items. This changing comparative advantage as a country develops is well-documented and could it be that China will soon begin to see its own comparative advantage change?

Rising labour costs

China's low labour costs are crucial, but these have been rising, as workers demand higher wages, shorter hours and greater benefits. Data suggest that labour costs have been growing at some 20 per cent per year.

The first effect of this has been for some labour-intensive businesses to migrate towards inland China, where labour costs are lower.

However, in other cases the move has been more significant. With a comparative advantage in low-cost labour disappearing, some labour-intensive businesses have left China, moving to other nations which can boast cheap labour, such as Bangladesh, Cambodia, Indonesia and Vietnam. This is especially the case for companies specialising in the production of clothes and shoes.

But the story will not stop there. These industries require labour and as long as this remains the case, when a country

| Table 26.6 | Growth rates and export performance of selected secondary outward-looking countries |

	Average 1985–2015			2015		
	Annual growth in real GDP	Annual growth in real GDP per capita	Annual growth rate of exports	GDP per capita	Exports	Share of manufactures in merchandise exports (%)
	(%)	(%)	(%)	(PPP, $)	(% of GDP)	
Brazil	2.8	1.4	5.8	15 474	12.9	38.1
China	9.8	8.8	6.7	14 451	22.0	94.3
Hong Kong	4.4	3.4	8.5	56 923	201.6	65.7
India	6.4	4.6	11.0	6 105	20.0	70.6
Malaysia	5.8	3.5	7.9	26 950	29.2	66.9
Singapore	6.2	3.9	9.4	85 382	176.5	77.0
South Korea	6.0	5.2	11.2	34 647	45.9	89.6
Low-income economies	3.5	0.8	5.8	1 636	20.6	n.a.
Middle-income economies	4.4	2.9	5.1	10 891	25.1	66.2
Low and middle-income economies	4.4	2.8	5.3	9 931	25.1	65.9
High-income economies	2.4	1.7	5.4	45 648	31.3	65.7
World	3.0	1.5	5.2	15 691	29.5	68.8

Source: Based on data from *Databank* (World Bank).

begins to grow this will lead to higher wage demands, which in turn will raise costs. Production will shift once more.

Moving up the value chain

So, what does this mean for China? When the USA and Europe lost their comparative advantage in the production of manufactured products, they had to look elsewhere. They developed a comparative advantage in the production of products requiring highly skilled labour and increasingly specialised in the services sector. However, with rising costs in emerging economies, more manufacturing, especially of high-value products, is being returned to these developed nations.

Research from 2013 considers the iPhone and electronics manufacturing in terms of comparative advantage and the value chain. Whilst the data on gross trade statistics confirm the decline of US competitiveness in this industry, the 'value-added trade statistics reveal the rising robustness of the United States' comparative advantage in electronics'. The suggestion is that, while China dominates in the sale of many finished exports, the simple sales data actually overstate China's productive capacity. Developed countries, such as the USA, the UK and Japan, often contribute to the value of the final products in terms of intellectual capital, design and technology.[2]

China will need to follow the pattern of the Western economies; its companies and workers will need to move up the value chain to find products that they can specialise in, which are not easily transferable to lower-wage countries.[3] This is no easy task, as moving up the value chain will involve entering into direct competition with countries that have had time to develop their comparative advantage.

China's reliance on cheap labor has powered the country's economy to unprecedented heights. But China's manufacturing sector is running into problems these days: squeezed from one end by places with even lower labor costs, such as Laos and Vietnam, and yet struggling to move to higher ground making more advanced products because of competition from developed nations such as Germany and the United States.[4]

Despite the rising costs of production in China, it does have other factors that will ensure continued investment and production. In particular, the expansion of industrial clusters, such as Shenzhen, may help China to maintain its competitive advantage for many years.[5]

The changing nature of comparative advantage can cause problems for workers, businesses and countries, but benefits also emerge through greater competition, choice and innovation. The next few decades are likely to see some significant changes in the structure of industry in all countries.

 Why are countries likely to see their comparative advantage change as they develop?

1 Paul Krugman, 'Increasing returns in a comparative advantage world', in Robert M. Stern, *Comparative Advantage, Growth, and the Gains from Trade and Globalization* (World Scientific, 2011), Chapter 7, p. 45.
2 Lauren Dai, 'The comparative advantage of nations: How global supply chains change our understanding of comparative advantage', *M-RCBG Associate Working Paper Series, no. 15* (May 2013).
3 Mohan Kompella, 'China, comparative advantage and moving up the value chain', *The Story of Business* blog, 25 November 2012.
4 Jia Lynn Yang, 'China's manufacturing sector must reinvent itself, if it's to survive', *The Washington Post*, 23 November 2012.
5 'The Boomerang effect', *The Economist*, 21 April 2012.

Section summary

1. Trade is of vital importance for the vast majority of developing countries, and yet most developing countries suffer from chronic balance of trade deficits.

2. Developing countries have traditionally been primary exporters. This has allowed them to exploit their comparative advantage in labour-intensive goods and has provided a market for certain goods that would otherwise have no market at home.

3. There are reasons for questioning the wisdom of relying on traditional primary exports, however. With a low world income elasticity of demand for many primary products, with the development of synthetic substitutes for minerals and with the protection of agriculture in developed countries, the demand for primary exports from the developing world has grown only slowly. At the same time, the demand for manufactured imports into developing countries has grown rapidly. Until recently, the result was a decline in the terms of trade. The rapid growth in demand for primary products from China and India has, to some extent, reversed this trend and the terms of trade have improved for many primary exporters.

4. Import-substituting industrialisation (ISI) was seen to be the answer to the problems of primary exporting. ISI was normally achieved in stages, beginning with the finished goods stage and then working back towards the capital goods stage. ISI, it was hoped, would allow countries to benefit from the various long-term advantages associated with manufacturing.

5. For many countries, however, ISI brought as many problems, if not more, than it solved. It often led to the establishment of inefficient industries, protected from foreign competition and facing little or no competition at home either. It led to considerable market distortions, with tariffs and other forms of protection haphazardly applied; to overvalued exchange rates, with a resulting bias against exports and the agricultural sector generally; to a deepening of inequalities and to large-scale social problems as the cities expanded, as poverty and unemployment grew and as traditional values were undermined; to increased dependency on imported inputs; and to growing environmental problems.

6. The most rapidly growing of the developing countries are those that have pursued a policy of export-orientated industrialisation. This has allowed them to achieve the benefits of economies of scale and foreign competition, and to specialise in goods in which they have a comparative advantage (i.e. labour-intensive goods) and yet which have a relatively high income elasticity of demand. Whether countries that have pursued ISI can successfully turn to an open, export-orientated approach will depend to a large extent on the degree of competition they face not only from advanced countries but also from other developing countries.

26.5 THE PROBLEM OF DEBT

Perhaps the most serious of all balance of payments problems in the world today is that faced by some of the poorest developing countries. Many of them experience massive financial outflows year after year as a result of having to 'service' debt (i.e. pay interest and make the necessary repayments). Much of this debt has been incurred in their attempts to finance development. Figure 26.7 shows the growth of external debt (as a proportion of national income) that began in the early 1970s.

The oil shocks of the 1970s

In 1973–4, oil prices quadrupled and the world went into recession. Oil imports cost much more and export demand was sluggish. The current account deficit of oil-importing developing countries rose from 1.1 per cent of GNY in 1973 to 4.3 per cent in 1975.

It was not difficult to finance these deficits, however. The oil surpluses deposited in commercial banks in the industrialised world provided an important additional source of finance. The banks, flush with money and faced with slack demand in the industrialised world, were very willing to lend. Bank loans to developing countries rose from $3 billion in 1970 to $12 billion in 1975. These flows enabled developing countries to continue with policies of growth.

The world recession was short-lived, and with a recovery in the demand for their exports and with their debts being eroded by high world inflation, developing countries found it relatively easy to service these increased debts (i.e. pay interest and make the necessary capital repayments).

In 1979–80 world oil prices rose again (from $15 to $38 per barrel). This second oil shock, like the first one, caused a large increase in the import bills of developing countries. But the full effects on their economies this time were very much worse (see Figure 26.7), given the debts that had been accumulated in the 1970s and given the policies adopted by the industrialised world after 1979.

But why were things so much worse this time?

- The world recession was deeper and lasted longer (1980–83), and when recovery came, it came very slowly. Developing countries' current account balance of payments deteriorated sharply. This was due both to a marked slowing down in the growth of their exports and to a fall in their export prices.
- The tight monetary policies pursued by the industrialised countries led to a sharp increase in interest rates, and the resulting fall in inflation meant, therefore, that there was a very sharp increase in real interest rates. This greatly increased developing countries' costs of servicing their debts as can be seen in Figure 26.8.
- The problem was made worse by the growing proportion of debt that was at variable interest rates. This was largely due to the increasing proportion of debt that was in the form of loans from commercial banks.

Figure 26.8 shows how after 1979 debt servicing costs as a proportion of national income rose across developing countries, making it increasingly difficult for them to service their debts. Then in 1982 Mexico, followed by several other countries such as Brazil, Bolivia, Zaire and Sudan, declared that it would have to suspend payments. There was now a debt crisis, which threatened not only the debtor countries, but also the world banking system.

Coping with debt: rescheduling

There have been two dimensions to tackling the debt problems of developing countries. The first is to cope with difficulties in servicing their debt. This usually involves some form of rescheduling of the repayments. The second

Figure 26.7 External debt as a percentage of gross national income (GNY)

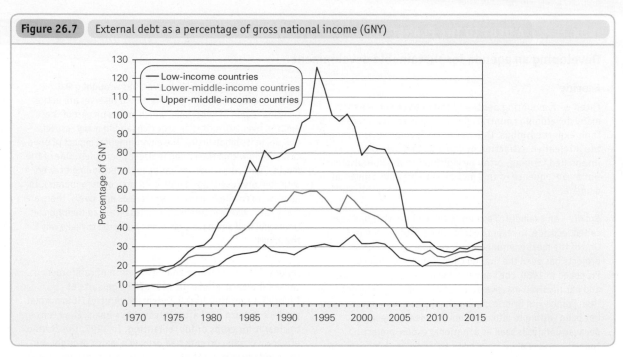

Source: Based on data from *Databank* (World Bank), series DT.DOD.DECT.GN.ZS.

dimension is to deal with the causes of the problem. Here we will focus on rescheduling.

Rescheduling official loans

Official loans are renegotiated through the Paris Club. Industrialised countries are members of the club, which arranges terms for the rescheduling of their loans to developing countries. Agreements normally involve delaying the date for repayment of loans currently maturing, or spreading the repayments over a longer period of time. Paris Club agreements are often made in consultation with the IMF, which works out a programme with the debtor country for tackling its underlying economic problems.

Several attempts have been made since the mid-1980s to make rescheduling terms more generous, with longer periods before repayments start, longer to repay when they do start, and lower interest rates. In return, the developing countries have had to undertake various 'structural adjustment programmes' supervised by the IMF (see below).

But despite the apparent advances made by the Paris Club in making its terms more generous, the majority of low-income countries failed to meet the required IMF conditions, and thus failed to have their debts reduced. What is more, individual Paris Club members were often reluctant to reduce debts unless they were first convinced that other members were 'paying their share'. Nevertheless, some creditor countries unilaterally introduced more generous terms and even cancelled some debts.

The net effect of rescheduling, but only very modest debt forgiveness, can be seen in Figures 26.7 and 26.8. By the mid-1990s average debt service ratios had fallen from the levels of

the mid-1980s and yet the ratio of total debt to GNY was higher. There were thus growing calls for the cancellation of debts (see below).

Rescheduling commercial bank loans

After the declarations by Mexico and other countries of their inability to service their debts, there was fear of an imminent collapse of the world banking system. Banks realised that disaster could be averted only by collective action of the banks to reschedule debts. Banks were prepared to reschedule some of the debts and to provide some additional loans in return for debtor countries undertaking structural adjustment (as described below). Additional loans, however, fell well short of the amount that was needed. Nevertheless, banks were increasingly setting aside funds to cover bad debt, and thus the crisis for the banks began to recede.

As banks felt less exposed to default, so they became less worried about it and less concerned to negotiate deals with debtor countries. Many of the more severely indebted countries, however, found their position still deteriorating rapidly. What is more, many of them were finding that the IMF adjustment programmes were too painful (often involving deep cuts in government expenditure) and were therefore abandoning them. Thus, in 1989, US Treasury Secretary Nicholas Brady proposed measures to *reduce* debt.

The *Brady Plan* involved the IMF and the World Bank lending funds to debtor countries to enable them to repay debts to banks. In return for this instant source of liquidity, the banks would have to be prepared to accept repayment of less than the full sum (i.e. they would sell the debt back to the country at a discount). To benefit from such deals, the debtor

BOX 26.6 | A DEBT TO THE PLANET

Developing an agenda for sustainable development

Ecocide

Faced with mounting debts and the need to service them, many developing countries have attempted to increase their export earnings. One way of achieving this is through the intensified extraction of minerals and ores or intensified farming, often by multinational corporations. But a consequence of this may be massive environmental damage.

Brazil. An example of a country forced into what has been called 'ecocide' in response to its huge debt burden is Brazil. One of the most environmentally damaging of all Brazilian projects has been the Grande Carajas iron ore project. Proposed in 1980, the Carajas scheme cost some $62 billion and has involved massive deforestation of an area larger than France and Britain combined. The Brazilian government has been willing to allow this environmental damage because Carajas is seen as a 'national export project'. Indeed, various plans have been approved for further mining activity in the area. In July 2013, for example, the Carajas Serra Sul S11D Iron Project, the largest iron ore mine project in the world, was approved and production began in December 2016, with supply expected to reach 90 million metric tonnes by 2018.

Venezuela. Another example of ecocide has occurred in Venezuela. The country has huge gold reserves – some 12 per cent of the world total. With the fall in oil prices in the 1990s, and hence a fall in revenues for Venezuela, one of the world's leading oil exporters, the Venezuelan authorities sought to exploit the country's gold reserves more aggressively. By 1994, the state had contracted out some 436 sites, covering 12 839 km². By 2000, this had risen to 30 000 km² (an area the size of Belgium), earning revenue of some $250 million per year.

The extraction of gold, however, has wrought great environmental damage. The richest gold reserves are in the Guayana region of Venezuela, which makes up part of the Amazon river basin. It is an area rich, and in many respects unique, in its biodiversity. The environmental impact of open-cast mining within the region is already being felt. One of the most serious consequences has been the poisoning of rivers with mercury (used to separate gold from other minerals). In addition to the destruction of the forests and rivers, there are many cases where indigenous peoples have had their human rights violated and have even been murdered to make way for the mines.

Indonesia. The misuse and destruction of rainforests caused dramatic effects in 1997. In large parts of Indonesia (another highly indebted country), it is normal practice to burn land after forests have been felled, either to clear it for crops or for replanting. In 1997, the El Niño effect on ocean currents had caused a major drought and the forest fires got out of hand. As a result, air pollution on a massive scale affected many countries in South East Asia. Most of Indonesia, Malaysia and Singapore became covered with a haze of dense smoke. The international air pollutant index has a scale on which readings above 500 are considered extremely hazardous. In parts of Malaysia readings of 1200 were recorded – equivalent to smoking a couple of packs of cigarettes a day. Schools and airports were closed, and income from tourism was lost throughout the region.

Biodiesel. A recent case of ecocide is the production of palm oil as a biofuel. The environmental justification was that the carbon dioxide given off by burning the fuel is offset by the carbon absorbed by growing the oil palm trees. But this has turned out to be only part of the story. The production of the

---

countries would have to agree to structural adjustment programmes. Several such agreements were negotiated; much of the debt reduction has involved debt swaps of one sort or another (see Case Study 26.16 on the student website).

 What are the relative advantages and disadvantages to a developing country of rescheduling its debts compared with simply defaulting on them (either temporarily or permanently)?

Dealing with debt: structural reform within the developing countries

The IMF has typically demanded that debtor countries pursue severe structural adjustment programmes before it has been prepared to sanction the rescheduling of debts. Such programmes have included:

- Tight fiscal and monetary policies to reduce government deficits, reduce interest rates and reduce inflation.

- Supply-side reforms to encourage greater use of the market mechanism and greater incentives for investment.
- A more open trade policy and devaluation of the currency in order to encourage more exports and more competition.

These policies, however, often brought extreme hardship as countries were forced to deflate. Unemployment and poverty increased and growth slowed down or became negative. Even though in the long run some developing countries emerged as more efficient and better able to compete in international trade, in the short run the suffering for many was too great to bear. Popular unrest and resentment against the IMF and the country's government led to riots in many countries and a breakdown of law and order.

A more 'complete' structural adjustment would extend beyond simple market liberalisation and tough monetary policies to much more open access to the markets of the rich countries (the subject of much of the Doha Round

additional palm oil has involved either cutting down rainforest, which, apart from being a much more efficient carbon absorber than oil palm trees, is habitat for many endangered species, or the draining and burning of peat lands, which sends huge amounts of carbon dioxide into the atmosphere.

The Rio Declaration

In recent years, there has been growing international awareness of the scale of the environmental destruction that is taking place. In particular, the rich countries have begun to realise that they too might suffer from this destruction, with its consequences for global warming and the loss of many unique species of plants and animals. Increasingly, international agencies such as the IMF and the World Bank are taking ecological issues into account when considering appropriate development and adjustment programmes.

Many in the developed world now realise that development must be sustainable. It is no good trying to secure 'development' for the current generation if, in the process, the environment is damaged and future generations suffer. This is a message that has been well understood by indigenous peoples for countless generations, especially those living on marginal lands: from the Aborigines of the Australian outback to the tribes of the African bush. It is seen as a moral imperative that the land bequeathed by one's ancestors should be passed on in just as good a state to one's descendants (see pages 395–6).

In 1992 in Rio de Janeiro, the United Nations Conference on Environment and Development (UNCED) put forward a programme for environmentally responsible development. In Agenda 21 it set out various policies that could be carried out by the international community. The policies, which were approved by 178 countries, included: targeting aid to projects that helped improve the

environment (such as providing clean water); research into environmentally friendly farming methods; and programmes that help reduce population growth (such as family planning and education).

The test of such sentiments, however, is action. To monitor this, a Commission on Sustainable Development (CSD) was established in December 1992. In 2003, it set out a programme until 2015. Every two years from 2004 there was a particular focus for action, including themes around water, sanitation, sustainable development, climate change, forestry and biodiversity.

2030 Agenda for Sustainable Development

In September 2015, the UN adopted the 2030 Agenda for Sustainable Development. This saw a commitment to 17 Sustainable Development Goals and 169 targets, building on the Millennium Development Goals. The aim, the UN argued, is to end poverty, protect the planet and ensure prosperity for all.

The overseer of the progress in meeting the goals and targets of the sustainable development agenda was to be a body known as the High Level Political Forum (HLPF). As with the CSD, the HLPF was to meet periodically, again with meetings arranged around particular themes. For instance, the theme of its 2017 meeting was eradicating poverty and promoting prosperity in a changing world.

1. *If reductions in developing countries' debt are in the environmental interests of the whole world, then why have developed countries not gone much further in reducing or cancelling the debts owed to them?*
2. *Would it be possible to devise a scheme of debt repayments that would both be acceptable to debtor and creditor countries and not damage the environment?*

negotiations: see Box 24.8), to more aid and debt relief being channelled into health and education, and to greater research and development in areas that will benefit poor people (e.g. into efficient labour-intensive technology and into new strains of crops that are suitable for countries' specific climate and soil conditions, and which do not require large amounts of chemicals).

Dealing with debt: debt forgiveness

By the end of the 1990s, the debt burden of many of the poorest countries had become intolerable. Despite portions of their debt being written off under Paris Club terms, the debts of many countries were still rising. Between 1980 and 2000, the debt of sub-Saharan Africa had increased some $3\frac{1}{2}$ times, from $61 billion to $212 billion. Some countries, such as Ethiopia and Mozambique, were spending nearly half their export earnings on merely servicing their debt.

Even with substantial debt rescheduling and some debt cancellation, highly indebted countries were being forced to make savage cuts in government expenditure, much of it on health, education and transport. The consequence was a growth in poverty, hunger, disease and illiteracy. African countries on average were paying four times more to rich countries in debt servicing than they were spending on health and education: it was like a patient giving a blood transfusion to a doctor! The majority of these countries had no chance of 'growing their way out of debt'. The only solution for them was for a more substantial proportion of their debt to be written off.

The heavily indebted poor countries (HIPC) initiative

In 1996, the World Bank and the IMF launched the HIPC initiative. A total of 42 countries, mainly in Africa, were identified as being in need of substantial debt relief. This number was subsequently reduced to 39, of which 33 are in

Figure 26.8 Debt servicing costs as a percentage of gross national income (GNY)

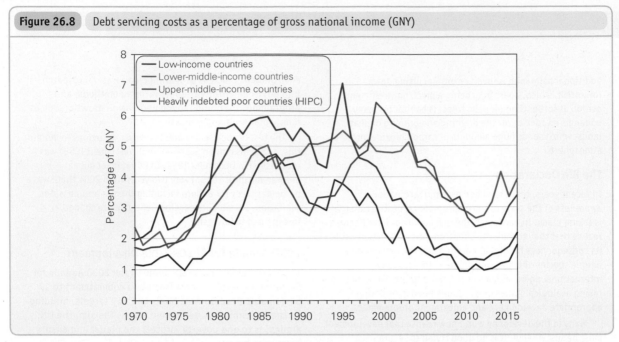

Source: Based on data from *Databank* (World Bank), series DT.TDS.DECT.GN.ZS.

Africa. The object of the initiative has been to reduce the debts of such countries to 'sustainable' levels by cancelling debts above 200–250 per cent of GDP (this was reduced to 150 per cent in 1999 and to a lower level still for five countries).

The HIPC process involved countries passing through two stages. In the first stage, eligible countries had to demonstrate a track record of 'good performance'. This means that they had to satisfy the IMF, the World Bank and the Paris Club that they were undertaking adjustment measures, such as cutting government expenditure and liberalising their markets. It also involved the countries preparing a Poverty Reduction Strategy Paper (PRSP) to show how they would use debt relief to tackle poverty, and especially how they would improve health and education. Once the IMF and the World Bank were satisfied that the country was making sufficient progress, the 'decision point' was reached and the level of debt relief would be determined. The country would then enter the second stage. All 39 countries have now reached this stage.

During this second stage, some interim debt relief is provided. Meanwhile the country must establish a 'sound track record' by implementing policies established at the decision point and based on the PRSP. The length of this stage depends on how long it takes the country to implement the policies. At the end of the second stage, the country reaches the 'completion point' and debts are cancelled (as agreed at the decision point) by the various creditors, on a pro rata basis, to bring the debt to the sustainable threshold.

In 2006, debt relief for the HIPCs that reached the completion point was extended under the Multilateral Debt Relief Initiative (MDRI). This involves cancelling multilateral debt incurred before 2004.

By 2017, 36 of the HICPs had reached the completion point and were receiving MRDI relief, and three were at the pre-decision point. It is estimated that by the end of 2015 $76 billion had been cancelled under the HIPC programme and a further $50 billion under MDRI. The debt stocks of the 36 post-decision-point HIPCs had been reduced by over 97 per cent, while poverty-reducing expenditure as a share of government revenue had increased from 42 per cent in 1999 to 45 per cent in 2015. The effect on various debt indicators is shown in Table 26.7. As you can see, the improvement has been dramatic.

Despite this substantial relief, the programme has been heavily criticised for taking too long and imposing excessively harsh conditions on the HIPC countries. The required reductions in government expenditure have led to deep cuts in basic health and education, and deflationary policies have led to reductions in investment.

Then there are the non-HIPCs. Many of these countries are also suffering debts which divert a large percentage of their income from poverty relief. Just because non-HIPCs can manage to service their debts, it does not make it desirable that they should be forced to do so.

Table 26.7 Debt indicators of 36 post-decision-point HIPCs

	1999 (%)	2015 (%)
Present value of debt-to-exports	457	87
Present value of debt-to-GDP	114	22
Debt service-to-exports	18	6
Present value of debt-to-revenue	552	126
Debt service-to-revenue	22	9

Source: Debt Relief Facts, April 2017 (The World Bank).

According to many charities, such as Oxfam, a much better approach would be to target debt relief directly at poverty reduction, with the resources released being used for investment in fields such as health, education, rural development and basic infrastructure. The focus, they argue, should be on what countries can afford to pay *after* essential spending on poverty relief and human development.

 Imagine that you are an ambassador of a developing country at an international conference. What would you try to persuade the rich countries to do in order to help you and other poor countries overcome the debt problem? How would you set about persuading them that it was in their own interests to help you?

Should all debt be cancelled and aid increased?

In recent years there have been growing calls for the cancellation of debts and a significant increase in aid, especially for the poorest developing countries, many ravaged by war, drought or AIDS. The United Nations has for many years called on wealthy countries to give 0.7 per cent of their GDP in aid.

In 2016 the net flow of aid, i.e. official development assistance (ODA), from the 29 donor countries plus European Union institutions which comprise the OECD's Development Assistance Committee (DAC) amounted to $143 billion, a mere 0.3 per cent of gross national income (GNY). As

Figure 26.9 shows, many countries fail to meet the UN target. The UK has met the target since 2013. In 2015 the UK parliament passed legislation requiring government to meet the 0.7 per cent foreign aid target.

As we have seen, the HIPC and MDRI relief has reduced such countries' debt dramatically. However, as of 2015 low-income countries' external debt still amounted to close to $110 billion and developing countries as a whole owed some $6.7 trillion. Then there is the plight of many non-HIPC countries, such as Kenya, which could be argued to be in greater need of debt relief than some HIPC countries.

The argument against debt cancellation and a substantial increase in aid is that this could represent a 'moral hazard' (see page 135). Once the burden of debt had been lifted and aid had been increased, countries might be tempted to squander the money. It might also encourage them to seek further loans, which might again be squandered.

For this reason, much of the disbursement of funds by donor countries, the IMF and other agencies has been conditional on countries pursuing policies of fiscal restraint and supply-side reform. But also, in recent years, conditionality has required recipient countries to pursue key poverty-reducing projects, such as health, education, clean water and other basic infrastructure projects. (Case Study 26.15 on the student website examines some of the issues surrounding aid.)

Figure 26.9 Official Development Assistance by DAC countries, per cent of GNY, 2016

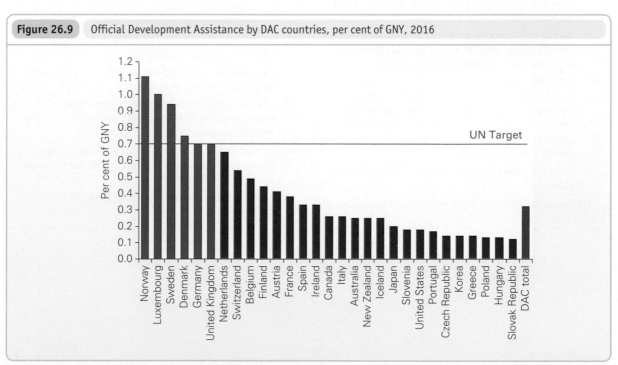

Source: Based on data from *International Development Statistics* online databases (OECD).

Section summary

1. After the 1973 oil crisis, many developing countries borrowed heavily in order to finance their balance of trade deficits and to maintain a programme of investment. After the 1979 oil price rises the debt problem became much more serious. There was a world recession and real interest rates were much higher. Debt increased dramatically, and much of it at variable interest rates.

2. Rescheduling can help developing countries to cope with increased debt in the short run and various schemes have been adopted by creditor countries and the banks.

3. If the problem is to be tackled, however, then either debts have to be written off – something that banks have been increasingly forced to do – or the developing countries themselves must take harsh corrective measures. The IMF has traditionally favoured 'structural adjustment' policies of deflation and market-orientated supply-side policies. An alternative is to use debt relief and aid to invest in health, education, roads and other infrastructure.

4. In 1996, the World Bank and the IMF launched the HIPC initiative to help reduce the debts of heavily indebted poor countries to sustainable levels. HIPC relief has been criticised, however, for being made conditional on the debtor countries pursuing excessively tough IMF adjustment programmes, for having an excessively long qualifying period and debt sustainability thresholds that are too high, and for delays in its implementation. A better approach might be to target debt relief directly at programmes to help the poor.

END OF CHAPTER QUESTIONS

1. Under what circumstances does a growth in financial flows make exchange rates less stable?

2. Assume that countries in the eurozone decide to pursue a deflationary fiscal policy. What effect is this likely to have on the UK economy?

3. It is often argued that international convergence of economic indicators is a desirable objective. Does this mean that countries should all seek to achieve the same rate of economic growth, monetary growth, interest rates and budget deficits as a percentage of their GDP, etc.?

4. Did the exchange rate difficulties experienced by countries under the ERM strengthen or weaken the arguments for progressing to a single European currency?

5. Assume that just some of the members of a common market like the EU adopt full economic and monetary union, including a common currency. What are the advantages and disadvantages to those members joining the full EMU and to those not?

6. Is the eurozone an optimal currency area? Explain your answer.

7. How are asymmetric shocks dealt with within a country? To what extent can this process be mirrored within the eurozone?

8. Would the world benefit from the general imposition of controls on the movement of international finance?

9. Compare the relative merits of using GNY statistics with those of various basic needs indicators when assessing both the level and the rate of a country's economic development.

10. If a developing country has a comparative advantage in primary products, should the government allow market forces to dictate the pattern of trade?

11. What are the advantages and disadvantages for a developing country of pursuing a policy of ISI?

12. Should all developing countries aim over the long term to become *exporters* of manufactured products?

13. How would you attempt to assess whether the technology used by an industry in a developing country was 'inappropriate'?

14. To what extent was the debt crisis of the early 1980s caused by inappropriate policies that had been pursued by the debtor countries?

15. Assess the operation and success of the HIPC programme.

Online resources

Additional case studies on the student website

26.1 **High oil prices.** What is their effect on the world economy?

26.2 **Crisis in South East Asia.** Causes of the severe recession in many South East Asian countries in 1997/8.

26.3 **The 1997/8 crisis in Asia: the role played by the IMF.**

26.4 **The Tobin tax.** An examination of the proposed tax, named after the economist James Tobin, imposed at a very small rate (of 0.05 to 0.5 per cent) on all foreign exchange transactions, or on just capital and financial account transactions.

26.5 **Converging on the euro.** Did the 11 countries that adopted the euro in 1999 genuinely meet the convergence criteria?

26.6 **Theories of development.** This looks at different approaches to the analysis of poverty and development.

26.7 **Multinational corporations and developing countries.** This examines whether multinational investment is a net benefit to developing countries.

26.8 **A miracle gone wrong.** Lessons from East Asia.

26.9 **Ethical business.** An examination of the likelihood of success of companies which trade fairly with developing countries.

26.10 **Argentina in crisis.** An examination of the collapse of the Argentinean economy in 2001/2, the default on its debts and the subsequent recovery.

26.11 **Structural problems within developing countries.** An analysis of problems around the neglect of agriculture, inappropriate technology and unemployment in developing countries.

26.12 **Unemployment in developing countries.** This looks at three models that have been developed to explain Third World unemployment.

26.13 **The Building BRICS of development.** A look at the importance of development for emerging economies.

26.14 **The great escape.** This case examines the problem of capital flight from developing countries to rich countries.

26.15 **Economic aid.** Does aid provide a solution to the debt problem?

26.16 **Swapping debt.** Schemes to convert a developing country's debt into other forms, such as shares in its industries

Websites relevant to Chapters 25 and 26

Numbers and sections refer to websites listed in the web appendix and hotlinked from this book's website at **www.pearsoned.co.uk/sloman.**

■ For news articles relevant to this and the previous chapter, see the *Economics News* section on the student website.

■ For general news on countries' balance of payments and exchange rates, see websites in section A, and particularly A1–5, 7–9, 20–25, 31, 35, 36. For articles on various aspects of economic development, see A27, 28; I9. See also links to newspapers worldwide in A38, 39, 42, 43 and 44, and the news search feature in Google at A41.

■ For international data on balance of payments and exchange rates, see *World Economic Outlook* in H4 and *OECD Economic Outlook* in B21 (also in sections 10 and 8 of B1). See also the trade topic in I14. The International macrodata section of the UK Data Service site (B35) has links to World Bank, IMF, OECD, UN and Eurostat datasets (but you will need to register first, a service free to all UK higher education students).

■ For UK data on balance of payments, search site B3 for 'balance of Payments' or the 'Pink Book'. See also B34. For EU data, see B38 > *Economic Forecasts* (click on latest year), tables 36–44; see also B47 (Ameco online) sections 10 and 11.

■ For exchange rates, see A1, 3; B5, 34; F2, 6, 8. For real and nominal exchange rate indices, see B45.

■ For discussion papers on balance of payments and exchange rates, see H4 and 7.

■ For various pressure groups critical of the effects of free trade and globalisation, see H13 and 14.

■ For information on EMU, see sites G1, 2, 3 and 6; F3–6 and 9.

■ For the United Nations Development Programme and also its Human Development Reports, see site H17.

■ For data on debt, search for 'International debt statistics' in DataBank on site B24.

■ For student resources relevant to these two chapters, see sites C1–7, 9, 10, 19.

Postscript: *The Castaways or Vote for Caliban*

The Pacific Ocean –
A blue demi-globe.
Islands like punctuation marks.

A cruising airliner,
Passengers unwrapping pats of butter.
A hurricane arises,
Tosses the plane into the sea.

Five of them flung onto an island beach,
Survived.

Tom the reporter.
Susan the botanist.
Jim the high-jump champion.
Bill the carpenter.
Mary the eccentric widow.

Tom the reporter sniffed out a stream of drinkable water.
Susan the botanist identified a banana tree.
Jim the high-jump champion jumped up and down and gave them each a bunch.
Bill the carpenter knocked up a table for their banana supper.
Mary the eccentric widow buried the banana skins,
But only after they had asked her twice.

They all gathered sticks and lit a fire.
There was an incredible sunset.

Next morning they held a committee meeting.
Tom, Susan, Jim and Bill
Voted to make the best of things.
Mary, the eccentric widow, abstained.

Tom the reporter killed several dozen wild pigs.
He tanned their skins into parchment
And printed the *Island News* with the ink of squids.

Susan the botanist developed new strains of banana
Which tasted of chocolate, beefsteak, peanut butter,
Chicken and bootpolish.

Jim the high-jump champion organised organised games
Which he always won easily.
Bill the carpenter constructed a wooden water wheel
And converted the water's energy into electricity.
Using iron ore from the hills, he constructed lampposts.

They all worried about Mary, the eccentric widow,
Her lack of confidence and her –
But there wasn't time to coddle her.

The volcano erupted, but they dug a trench
And diverted the lava into the sea
Where it formed a spectacular pier.
They were attacked by pirates but defeated them
With bamboo bazookas firing
Sea-urchins packed with home-made nitro-glycerine.
They gave the cannibals a dose of their own medicine
And survived an earthquake thanks to their skill in jumping.

Tom had been a court reporter
So he became a magistrate and solved disputes.
Susan the botanist established
A university which also served as a museum.
Jim the high-jump champion
Was put in charge of law enforcement –
Jumped on them when they were bad.
Bill the carpenter built himself a church,
Preached there every Sunday.

But Mary the eccentric widow . . .
Each evening she wandered down the island's main street,
Past the Stock Exchange, the Houses of Parliament,
The prison and the arsenal.
Past the Prospero Souvenir Shop,
Past the Robert Louis Stevenson Movie Studios,
Past the Daniel Defoe Motel
She nervously wandered and sat on the end of the pier of lava.

Breathing heavily,
As if at a loss,
As if at a lover,
She opened her eyes wide
To the usual incredible sunset.

Adrian Mitchell

1. *Had the castaways reduced their problem of scarcity by the end of the poem?*
2. *Could the 'usual incredible sunset' be described as an economic good?*

© Adrian Mitchell. Available in *Adrian Mitchell's Greatest Hits*, 1991.
  Reprinted by permission of PFD on behalf of Adrian Mitchell.

Educational Health Warning! Adrian Mitchell asks that none of his poems be used in connection with any examination whatsoever.

Appendix 1: Some Techniques of Economic Analysis

As you will see if you flick back through the pages, there are many diagrams and tables and several equations. But this does not mean that there are many mathematical techniques that you will have to master in order to study this book. In fact there are relatively few techniques, but they are ones which we use many times in many different contexts. You will find that if you are new to the subject, you will very quickly become familiar with these techniques. If you are not new to the subject, perhaps you could reassure your colleagues who are!

On some university courses, however, you will take mathematics to a higher level. To meet your needs there are a number of optional 'Looking at the Maths' sections scattered throughout the book. These use maths to express arguments that have just been covered in words or diagrams. Most of these 'Looking at the Maths' sections also refer to 'Maths Cases' on the student website. These cases consist of worked examples and also have one or more questions at the end for you to test your understanding of the relevant technique. The answers to these questions are also given on the student website.

But please note that the 'Looking at the Maths' sections are purely optional and will not be suitable for many courses. In such cases you can simply ignore them.

Diagrams as pictures

On many occasions, we use diagrams simply to provide a picture of a relationship. Just as a photograph in a newspaper can often depict an event much more vividly than any verbal account, so too a diagram in economics can often picture a relationship with a vividness and clarity that could never be achieved by words alone.

For example, we may observe that as people's incomes rise, they spend a lot more on entertainment and only a little more on food. We can picture this relationship very nicely by the use of a simple graph.

In Figure A1.1, an individual's income is measured along the horizontal axis and expenditure on food and entertainment is measured up the vertical axis. There are just two lines on this diagram: one showing how the expenditure on entertainment rises as income rises, the other how the expenditure on food rises as income rises. Now we could use a diagram like this to plot actual data. But we may simply be using it as a sketch – as a picture. In this case we do not necessarily need to put figures on the two axes. We are simply showing the relative *shapes* of the two curves. These shapes tell us that the person's expenditure on entertainment rises more quickly than that on food, and that above a certain level of income the expenditure on entertainment becomes greater than that on food.

 What else is the diagram telling us?

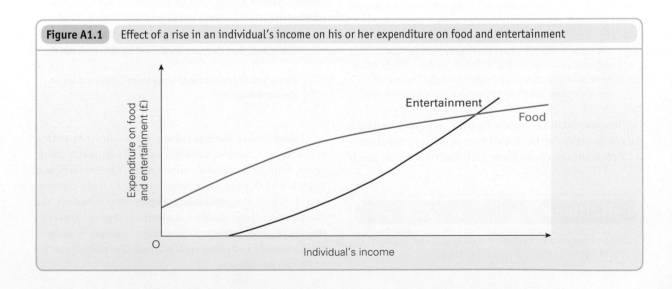

Figure A1.1 Effect of a rise in an individual's income on his or her expenditure on food and entertainment

Table A1.1   UK unemployment, 2010 Q1–2017 Q2

	2010				2011				2012				2013			
	Q1	Q2	Q3	Q4	Q1	Q2	Q3	Q4	Q1	Q2	Q3	Q4	Q1	Q2	Q3	Q4
Unemployment (millions)	2.53	2.49	2.47	2.50	2.48	2.54	2.66	2.68	2.63	2.58	2.54	2.54	2.54	2.52	2.48	2.36

	2014				2015				2016				2017	
	Q1	Q2	Q3	Q4	Q1	Q2	Q3	Q4	Q1	Q2	Q3	Q4	Q1	Q2
Unemployment (millions)	2.21	2.06	1.96	1.87	1.83	1.85	1.75	1.69	1.69	1.64	1.61	1.59	1.54	0.00

Source: Based on *Time Series Data,* series MGSC (ONS, 2017).

Representing real-life statistics

In many cases, we will want to depict real-world data. We may want to show, for example, how unemployment has changed over the years in a particular country, or how income is distributed between different groups in the population. In the first we will need to look at *time-series* data. In the second we will look at *cross-section* data.

Time-series data

Table A1.1 shows the level of UK unemployment between the first quarter of 2010 and the second quarter of 2017. A table like this is a common way of representing **time-series data**. It has the advantage of giving the precise figures, and is thus a useful reference if we want to test any theory and see if it predicts accurately.

Notice that in this particular table the figures are given quarterly. Depending on the period of time over which we want to see the movement of a variable, it may be more appropriate to use a different interval of time. For example, if we wanted to see how unemployment had changed over the past 50 years, we might use annual figures or even average figures for longer periods of time. If, however, we wanted to see how unemployment had changed over the course of a year, we would probably use monthly or even weekly figures.

 The table in Box 1.1 shows time-series data for four different variables for four different countries. Would there have been any advantage in giving the figures for each separate year? Would there have been any disadvantage?

Time-series data can also be shown graphically. In fact the data from a table can be plotted directly on to a graph. Figure A1.2 plots the data from Table A1.1. Each dot on the graph

corresponds to one figure from the table. The dots are then joined up to form a single line. Thus if you wanted to find the level of unemployment at any time between 2010 Q1 and 2017 Q2, you would simply find the appropriate date on the horizontal axis, read vertically upward to the line you have drawn, then read across to find the level of unemployment.

Although a graph like this cannot give you quite such an accurate measurement of each point as a table does, it gives a much more obvious picture of how the figures have moved over time and whether the changes are getting bigger (the curve getting steeper) or smaller (the curve getting shallower). We can also read off what the likely figure would be for some point *between* two observations.

 What was the level of unemployment midway between quarter 1 and quarter 2 of 2014?

It is also possible to combine *two* sets of time-series data on one graph to show their relative movements over time. Table A1.2 shows the figures for UK economic growth for the same time period. Figure A1.3 plots these data along with those from Table A1.1. This enables us to get a clear picture of how unemployment and the rate of economic growth moved in relation to each other over the period in question. Note that we use a different vertical scale for the two variables. This is inevitable given that they are measured in different units.

 How would it be possible to show three different lines on the same diagram?

All developed countries publish time-series data for the major macroeconomic variables such as national income, prices, employment and unemployment, interest rates, and imports and exports. Microeconomic data on the distribution of income, the performance of particular industries, the distribution of household expenditure, and so on, appear in the official government statistics. Firms, consumers' associations, charities and other organisations also publish microeconomic statistics.

Definitions

Time-series data Information depicting how a variable (e.g. the price of eggs) changes over time.

Figure A1.2 UK unemployment, 2010 Q1–2017 Q2

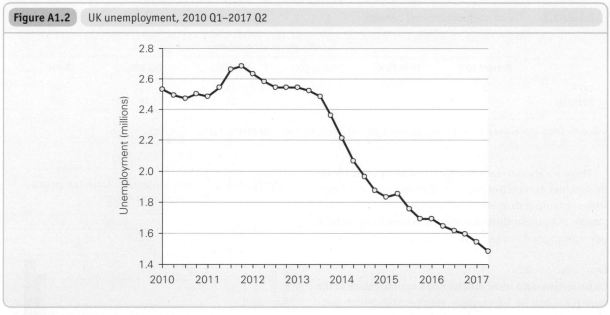

Source: Based on *Times Series Data*, series MGSC (ONS).

Table A1.2 UK economic growth, 2010 Q1–2017 Q2 (% increase over equivalent quarter in previous year)

	2010				2011				2012				2013			
	Q1	Q2	Q3	Q4	Q1	Q2	Q3	Q4	Q1	Q2	Q3	Q4	Q1	Q2	Q3	Q4
Economic growth (%)	0.8	2.1	2.6	2.3	2.3	1.3	1.2	1.3	1.2	1.0	1.8	1.3	1.5	2.1	1.7	2.4

	2014				2015				2016				2017			
	Q1	Q2	Q3	Q4	Q1	Q2	Q3	Q4	Q1	Q2	Q3	Q4	Q1	Q2		
Economic growth (%)	2.6	3.1	3.1	3.5	2.8	2.4	1.8	1.7	1.6	1.7	2.0	1.9	2.1	0.0		

Source: Based on *Time Series Data,* series IHYR (ONS, 2017).

Figure A1.3 UK unemployment and annual economic growth, 2010 Q1–2017 Q2

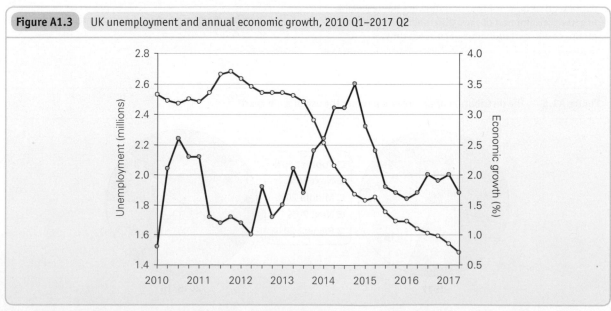

Source: Based on *Times Series Data*, series MGSC and IHYR (ONS).

Table A1.3	Income before taxes and benefits					
	Quintile groups of households					
	Bottom 20%	Next 20%	Middle 20%	Next 20%	Top 20%	Total
1977	3	10	18	26	42	100
2015/16	4	8	15	25	48	100

Source: *The Effects of Taxes and Benefits on Household Income, financial year ending 2016,* Table 29 (ONS, 2017).

There are also several sources of data freely available on the Internet. Section B of Appendix 2 gives a number of websites containing datasets. These websites can be accessed directly from the hotlinks section of this book's own website (www.pearsoned.co.uk/sloman).

Cross-section data

Cross-section data show different observations made at the same point in time. For example, they could show the quantities of food and clothing purchased at various levels of household income, or the costs to a firm or industry of producing various quantities of a product.

Table A1.3 gives an example of cross-section data. It shows the distribution of household income in the UK before the deduction of taxes and the addition of benefits. It puts households into five equal-sized groups (or 'quintiles') according to their income. Thus the poorest 20 per cent of households are in one group, the next poorest 20 per cent are in the next and so on. Looking just at the 2015/16 figures, they show that the poorest 20 per cent earned just 4 per cent of total household incomes, whereas the richest 20 per cent earned 48 per cent.

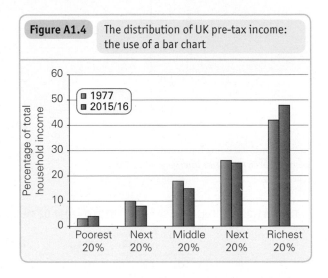

Figure A1.4	The distribution of UK pre-tax income: the use of a bar chart

Cross-section data like these are often represented in the form of a chart. Figure A1.4 shows the data as a *bar chart,* and Figure A1.5 as two *pie charts.*

It is possible to represent cross-section data at two or more different points in time, thereby presenting the figures as a time series. In Table A1.3, figures are given for just two time periods. With a more complete time series we could graph the movement of the shares of each of the five groups over time.

 Could bar charts or pie charts be used for representing time-series data?

Definition

Cross-section data Information showing how a variable (e.g. the consumption of eggs) differs between different groups or different individuals at a given time.

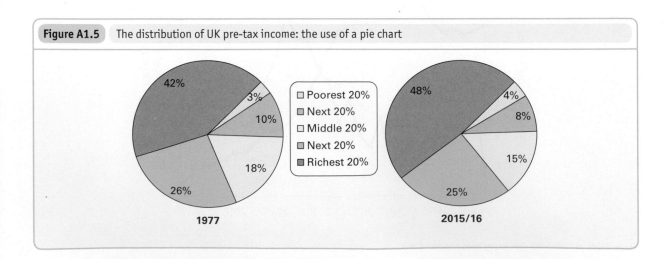

Figure A1.5	The distribution of UK pre-tax income: the use of a pie chart

Legend:
- □ Poorest 20%
- ▣ Next 20%
- □ Middle 20%
- ▣ Next 20%
- ▣ Richest 20%

1977: 42%, 3%, 10%, 18%, 26%

2015/16: 48%, 4%, 8%, 15%, 25%

Getting a true picture from the statistics

'There are lies, damned lies and statistics.' This well-known saying highlights the abuse of statistics – abuse, unfortunately, that is commonplace. Have you noticed how politicians always seem to be able to produce statistics to 'prove' that they are right and that their opponents are wrong? And it's not just politicians. Newspapers frequently present statistics in the most 'newsworthy' way; companies try to show their performance in the most flattering way; pressure groups fighting for a cause (such as the protection of the environment) again present statistics in the way that best supports their case.

It is not difficult to present data in such a way as to give a grossly distorted picture of a situation. Let us have a look at some of the most common examples.

Selective use of data

This is where people select only those statistics that support their case and ignore those that do not. For example, assume that unemployment has risen but inflation has fallen. The government highlights the inflation statistics to show how successful its policies have been. The opposition parties do the opposite: they concentrate on the unemployment statistics to demonstrate the failure of government policy.

Graphical presentation of data

Two graphs may present exactly the same data and yet convey a quite different impression about them. Figure A1.6 shows how the amount that people buy of a particular foodstuff varies with their income. It is based on the information in Table A1.4.

Diagram (a) shows *exactly the same* information as diagram (b), and yet at a glance it would seem from diagram (a) that people buy a lot more as their incomes rise, whereas from diagram (b) it would seem that people only buy a little more.

Clearly the choice of *scales* for the two axes will determine the shape of the graph.

1. If the vertical scale for Figure A1.2 ran from 0 to 5 million, how would this alter your impression of the degree to which unemployment had changed?
2. What are the advantages and disadvantages of presenting data graphically with the axes starting from zero?

Use of absolute or proportionate values

'People are paying more taxes now than they did when the government came to office', claims the opposition.

'Since coming into office we have cut taxes substantially', claims the government.

So who is right? Do we pay more or less tax? Quite possibly they are both right. If incomes have risen, we probably do pay more tax in total. After all, the more we earn, the greater the sum of money we will be paying in income tax; and the more we spend, the more we will be paying out in VAT. Thus in *absolute* terms we probably are paying more in taxes.

On the other hand, if the government has cut the rates of tax, we may be paying a smaller *proportion* of our income. In other words, a smaller proportion of a larger total can still represent an absolute increase.

Ignoring questions of distribution

'The average person has become better off under this government', claims a minister.

'Poverty has increased steeply under this government', claims the opposition. 'More than half the population are worse off now than when the government came to office.'

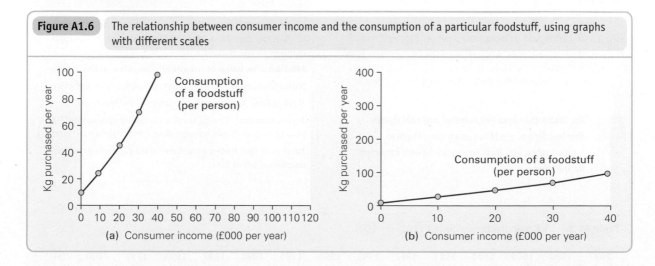

Figure A1.6 The relationship between consumer income and the consumption of a particular foodstuff, using graphs with different scales

(a) Consumer income (£000 per year)

(b) Consumer income (£000 per year)

Table A1.4 Annual purchases per person of a particular foodstuff

Consumer income (£ per year)	0	10 000	20 000	30 000	40 000
Foodstuff purchased per person (kg per year)	10	25	45	70	100

Surely, this time one of the claims must be wrong? But again, both could be right. The term 'average' normally refers to the **mean**. The mean income is simply the total national income divided by the number in the population: i.e. income *per head*. If this is what is meant by the average, then the government may well be correct. Income per head may have risen.

If, however, a small number of people have got a lot richer and the rest have got a little poorer, the **median** income will have fallen. The median income is the income of the *middle* person. For example, if the population were 50 million, the median income would be the income of the 25 millionth richest person. This person's income may have fallen.

Real or nominal values

'Incomes have risen by 2 per cent this last year', claims the government.

'The standard of living has fallen', claims the opposition.

One of the most common abuses of statistics is deliberately switching between real and nominal figures, depending on what message you want to give your audience. **Nominal** figures are the simple monetary values at the prices ruling at the time. For example, if you earned a wage of £500 per week last year and are earning £510 per week this year, then in nominal terms your wage has risen by 2 per cent.

But what if prices have risen by 3 per cent? Your 2 per cent increase in wages will in fact buy you 1 per cent *less*. Your **real** wages have gone down by 1 per cent. In other words, to show how much better or worse off a person or nation is, the nominal figure must be corrected for inflation.

Thus:

Real growth = Nominal growth − Inflation

1. *If a bank paid its depositors 3 per cent interest and inflation was 5 per cent, what would be the real rate of interest?*
2. *Has your real income gone up or down this last year?*

KEY IDEA 40

The distinction between nominal and real figures
Nominal figures are those using current prices, interest rates, etc. Real figures are figures corrected for inflation.

The time chosen for comparison

'Between 1982 and 1990, Britain's real growth rate averaged 3.5 per cent per year', boasted the Conservative government of the time.

'Between 1979 and 1993, Britain could only manage a real growth rate of 1.6 per cent per year', chided the opposition.

Again, both were correct, but they had chosen either to include or to ignore the periods from 1979 to 1982 and from 1990 to 1993 when the real growth rate was negative.

Index numbers

Time-series data are often expressed in terms of **index numbers**. Consider the data in Table A1.5. It shows index numbers of manufacturing output in the UK from 1985 to 2013.

One year is selected as the **base year** and this is given the value of 100. In our example this is 2013. The output for other years is then shown by their percentage variation from 100. For 1987 the index number is 90.0. This means that manufacturing output was 10.0 per cent lower in 1987 than in 2013. The index number for 2007 is 108.9. This means that manufacturing output was 8.9 per cent higher in 2007 than in 2013.

 Does this mean that the value of manufacturing output in 2007 was 8.9 per cent higher than 2013 in money terms?

The use of index numbers allows us to see clearly any upward and downward movements and to make an easy comparison of one year with another. For example, Table A1.5 shows quite clearly that manufacturing output fell from

Definitions

Mean (or arithmetic mean) The sum of the values of each of the members of the sample divided by the total number in the sample.

Median The value of the middle member of the sample.

Nominal values Money values measured at *current* prices.

Real values Money values corrected for inflation.

Index number The value of a variable expressed as 100 plus or minus its percentage deviation from a base year.

Base year (for index numbers) The year whose index number is set at 100.

Table A1.5 UK manufacturing output (2013 = 100)

1987	1988	1989	1990	1991	1992	1993	1994	1995	1996	1997	1998	1999	2000	2001
90.0	96.6	100.4	100.3	95.2	95.2	96.6	101.1	102.6	103.4	105.2	105.6	106.2	108.5	106.9

2002	2003	2004	2005	2006	2007	2008	2009	2010	2011	2012	2013	2014	2015	2016
104.6	104.0	105.9	105.9	108.2	108.9	105.8	95.9	100.3	102.5	101.0	100.0	102.9	102.7	103.5

Source: Time Series Data, series K22A (ONS, 2017).

1990 to 1991 and did not surpass its 1989 level until 1994. It fell again from 2007 to 2009 and from 2011 to 2013.

Using index numbers to measure percentage changes

To find the annual percentage growth rate in any one year we simply look at the percentage change in the index from the previous year. To work this out we use the following formula:

$$\left(\frac{I_t - I_{t-1}}{I_{t-1}}\right) \times 100$$

where I_t is the index in the year in question and I_{t-1} is the index in the previous year.

Thus to find the growth rate in manufacturing output from 1987 to 1988 we first see how much the index has risen $(I_t - I_{t-1})$. The answer is $96.6 - 90.0 = 6.6$. But this does *not* mean that the growth rate is 6.6 per cent. According to our formula, the growth rate is equal to

$$\frac{96.6 - 90.0}{90.0} \times 100$$
$$= 6.6/90.0 \times 100$$
$$= 7.3$$

 What was the growth rate in manufacturing output from (a) 2005 to 2006; (b) 2008 to 2009?

The price index

Perhaps the best known of all price indices is the **consumer prices index (CPI)**. It is an index of the prices of goods and services purchased by the average household. Movements in this index, therefore, show how the cost of living has changed. Annual percentage increases in the CPI are the commonest definition of the rate of inflation. Thus if the CPI went up from 100 to 110 over a 12 month period, we would say that the rate of inflation was 10 per cent.

 If the CPI went up from 150 to 162 over 12 months, what would be the rate of inflation?

The use of weighted averages

The CPI is a **weighted average** of the prices of many items. The index of manufacturing output that we looked at previously was also a weighted average, an average of the output of many individual products.

To illustrate how a weighted average works, consider the case of a weighted average of the output of just three industries, A, B and C. Let us assume that in the base year (year 1) the output of A was £7 million, of B £2 million and of C £1 million, giving a total output of the three industries of £10 million. We now attach weights to the output of each industry to reflect its proportion of total output. Industry A is given a weight of 0.7 because it produces seven-tenths of total output. Industry B is given a weight of 0.2 and industry C a weight of 0.1. We then simply multiply each industry's index by its weight and add up all these figures to give the overall industry index.

The index for each industry in year 1 (the base year) is 100. This means that the weighted average index is also 100. Table A1.6 shows what happens to output in year 2. Industry A's output falls by 10 per cent, giving it an index of 90 in year 2. Industry B's output rises by 10 per cent and industry C's output rises by 30 per cent, giving indices of 110 and 130, respectively. But as you can see from the table, despite the fact that two of the three industries have had a rise in output, the total industry index has *fallen* from 100 to 98. The reason is that industry A is so much larger than the other two that its decline in output outweighs their increase.

The consumer prices index is a little more complicated. This is because it is calculated in two stages. First, products are grouped into categories such as food, clothing and services. A weighted average index is worked out for each group. Thus the index for food would be the weighted average of the indices for bread, potatoes, cooking oil, etc. Second, a weight is attached to each of the groups in order to work out an overall index.

Functional relationships

Throughout economics we examine how one economic variable affects another: how the purchases of cars are affected

Definitions

Consumer prices index (CPI) An index of the prices of goods bought by a typical household.

Weighted average The average of several items where each item is ascribed a weight according to its importance. The weights must add up to 1.

Table A1.6   Constructing a weighted average index

| Industry | Weight | Year 1 | | Year 2 | |
		Index	Index times weight	Index	Index times weight
A	0.7	100	70	90	63
B	0.2	100	20	110	22
C	0.1	100	10	130	13
Total	1.0		100		98

by their price; how consumer expenditure is affected by taxes, or by incomes; how the cost of producing washing machines is affected by the price of steel; how the rate of unemployment is affected by the level of government expenditure. These relationships are called **functional relationships**. We will need to express these relationships in a precise way, preferably in the form of a table or a graph or an equation.

Simple linear functions

These are relationships which produce a straight line when plotted on a graph. Let us take an imaginary example of the relationship between total value added tax receipts in an economy (V) and the level of consumer expenditure (C). This functional relationship can be written as:

$$V = f(C)$$

This is simply shorthand for saying that VAT receipts are a function of (i.e. depend on) the level of consumer expenditure.

If we want to know just *how much* VAT revenue will be at any given level of consumer expenditure, we will need to spell out this functional relationship. Let us do this in each of the three ways.

As a table. Table A1.7 gives a selection of values of C and the corresponding level of V. It is easy to read off from the table the level of VAT receipts at one of the levels of consumer expenditure listed. It is clearly more difficult to work out the level of VAT receipts if consumer expenditure is £23.4 billion or £47.6 billion.

As a graph. Figure A1.7 plots the data from Table A1.7. Each of the dots corresponds to one of the points in the table. By joining the dots up into a single line we can easily read off the value for VAT receipts at some level of consumption other than those listed in the table. A graph also

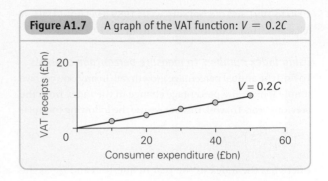

Figure A1.7   A graph of the VAT function: $V = 0.2C$

has the advantage of allowing us to see the relationship at a glance.

It is usual to plot the *independent variable* (i.e. the one that does not depend on the other) on the horizontal or x-axis, and the *dependent variable* on the vertical or y-axis. In our example, VAT receipts *depend* on consumer expenditure. Thus VAT receipts are the dependent variable and consumer expenditure is the independent variable.

As an equation. The data in the table can be expressed in the equation

$$V = 0.2C$$

This would be the equation if the VAT rate were 20 per cent on all goods and services.

An equation has the major advantage of being precise. We could work out *exactly* how much would be paid in VAT at any given level of consumption.

This particular function starts at the origin of the graph (i.e. the bottom left-hand corner). This means that when the value of the independent variable is zero, so too is the value of the dependent variable.

When a graph does not pass through the origin its equation will have the form

$$y = a + bx$$

where y stands for the dependent variable and x for the independent variable, and a and b will have numbers assigned in an actual equation. For example, the equation might be

$$y = 4 + 2x$$

This would give Table A1.8 and Figure A1.8.

Definition

Functional relationships The mathematical relationships showing how one variable is affected by one or more others.

Table A1.7   A VAT function

Consumer expenditure (£bn per year)	VAT receipts (£bn per year)
0	0
10	2
20	4
30	6
40	8
50	10

Table A1.8 $y = 4 + 2x$

x	y
0	4
1	6
2	8
3	10
4	12
5	14

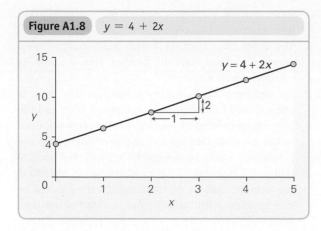

Figure A1.8 $y = 4 + 2x$

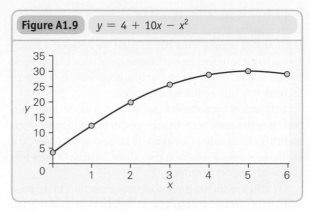

Figure A1.9 $y = 4 + 10x - x^2$

Notice two things about the relationship between the equation and the graph:

- The point where the line crosses the vertical axis (at a value of 4) is given by the constant (a) term. If the a term is negative, the line will cross the vertical axis *below* the horizontal axis.
- The slope of the line is given by the b term. The slope is 2/1: for every 1 unit increase in x there is a 2 unit increase in y.

 On a diagram like Figure A1.8 draw the graphs for the following equations: $y = -3 + 4x; y = 15 - 3x.$

Note that in the second equation of the question, the x term is negative. This means that y and x are *inversely related*. As x increases, y decreases.

Non-linear functions

With these functions the equation involves a squared term (or other power terms). Such functions will give a curved line when plotted on a graph. As an example, consider the following equation:

$$y = 4 + 10x - x^2$$

Table A1.9 and Figure A1.9 are based on it.

As you can see, y rises at a decelerating rate and eventually begins to fall. This is because the negative x^2 term is becoming more and more influential as x rises and eventually begins to outweigh the $10x$ term.

 What shaped graph would you get from the equations $y = -6 + 3x + 2x^2$ *and* $y = 10 - 4x + x^2$?

(If you cannot work out the answer, construct a table like Table A1.9 and then plot the figures on a graph.)

*Elementary differentiation

In several starred boxes and *Looking at the Maths* sections we use some elementary calculus. The part of calculus we use is called **differentiation**. This is a technique to enable us to calculate the rate of change of a variable. The purpose of this section is not to explain why differentiation involves the procedures it does, but simply to state the rules that are necessary for our purposes. You will need to consult a maths book if you want to know how these rules are derived.

First, let us see when we would be interested in looking at the rate of change of a variable. Take the case of a firm thinking of expanding. It will want to know how much its costs will increase as its output increases. It will want to know the rate of change of costs with respect to changes in output.

Let us assume that it faces a cost function of the form

$$C = 20 + 5Q + Q^2 \qquad (1)$$

where C is the total cost of production and Q is the quantity produced. Table A1.10 and Figure A1.10 are derived from this equation.

The rate of increase in its costs with respect to increases in output is given by the *slope* of the cost curve in Figure A1.10. The steeper the slope, the more rapidly costs increase. At

Table A1.9 $y = 4 + 10x - x^2$

x	y
0	4
1	13
2	20
3	25
4	28
5	29
6	28
7	25

Definition

Differentiation A mathematical technique to find the rate of change of one variable with respect to another.

point *a* the slope of the curve is 11. This is found by drawing the tangent to the curve and measuring the slope of the tangent. At this point on the curve, what we are saying is that for each one unit increase in output there is an £11 increase in costs. (Obviously as the graph is curved, this rate of increase will vary at different outputs.)

This rate of increase in costs is known as the **marginal cost**. It is the same with other variables that increase with quantity: their rate of increase is known as *marginal*. For example, *marginal revenue* is the rate of increase of sales revenue with respect to output.

We can use the technique of differentiation to derive a marginal from a total equation: in other words, to derive the slope of the total curve. Let us assume that we have an equation:

$$y = 10 + 6x - 4x^2 + 2x^3 \tag{2}$$

When we differentiate it, we call the new equation dy/dx: this stands for the rate of increase in y (dy) with respect to the increase in x (dx).

The rules for differentiating a simple equation like equation (2) are very straightforward.

1. You delete the constant term (10). The reason for this is that, being constant, by definition it will not cause an increase in y as x increases, and it is the *increase* in y that we are trying to discover.

2. You delete the x from the x term which has no power attached, and just leave the number. Thus the term $6x$ becomes simply 6.

3. For any term with a power in it (a square, a cube, etc.), its value should be *multiplied* by the power term and the power term reduced by one. Thus in the term $4x^2$, the 4 would be multiplied by 2 (the power term), and the power term would be reduced from 2 to 1 (but x to the power of 1 is simply x). After differentiation, therefore, the term becomes $8x$. In the term $2x^3$, the 2 would be multiplied by 3 (the power term), and the power term would be reduced from 3 to 2. After differentiation, therefore, the term becomes $6x^2$.

Applying these three rules to the equation

$$y = 10 + 6x - 4x^2 + 2x^3 \tag{2}$$

gives

$$dy/dx = 6 - 8x + 6x^2 \tag{3}$$

To find the rate of change of y with respect to x at any given value of x, therefore, you simply substitute that value of x into equation (3).

Thus when $x = 4, dy/dx = 6 - (8 \times 4) + (6 \times 16) = 70$. In other words, when $x = 4$, for every 1 unit increase in x, y will increase by 70.

Returning to our cost function in equation (1), what is the marginal cost equation? Applying the three rules to the equation

$$C = 20 + 5Q + Q^2 \tag{1}$$

gives

$$dC/dQ = 5 + 2Q \tag{4}$$

Thus at an output of 3, the marginal cost (dC/dQ) is $5 + (2 \times 3) = 11$, which is the slope of the tangent to point *a*.

Table A1.10	$C = 20 + 5Q + Q^2$

x	y
0	20
1	26
2	34
3	44
4	56
5	70
6	86
7	104
8	124

What would be the marginal cost equation if the total cost equation were

$$C = 15 + 20Q - 5Q^2 + Q^3?$$

What would be the marginal cost at an output of 8?

Finding the maximum or minimum point of a curve

The other important use we can make of calculus is to find the maximum or minimum point of a curve. This has a number of important applications. For example, a firm may want to know the minimum point on its average cost curve (a curve which

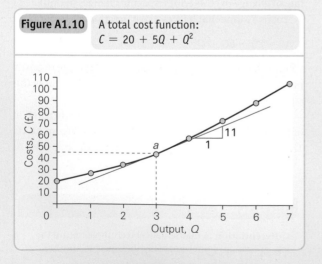

Figure A1.10 A total cost function:
$C = 20 + 5Q + Q^2$

Definition

Marginal cost The rate of increase in costs with respect to output.

*BOX A1.1   WHEN IS GOOD NEWS REALLY GOOD?

Are things getting better or merely getting worse more slowly?

From the second quarter of 2008 unemployment rose continuously for several months. By the third quarter of 2009 unemployment had increased by some 0.75 million. What good news could the government possibly draw from this?

Governments, always in search of any glimmer of good economic news, proclaimed that unemployment was rising more slowly (in other words, that the rate of increase in unemployment was *falling*). This was perfectly correct.

To show this, let us assume that N is the number of people out of work. The rate of change of unemployment is therefore given by dN/dt (where t is time). A positive figure for dN/dt represents a rise in unemployment, a negative figure a fall. Its value is given by the slope of the green line in the diagram. From the second quarter of 2008 this figure was positive. Bad news!

But the government sought a rosier interpretation. By using a second-order derivative, d^2N/dt^2, it could show that the rate of increase in unemployment from early 2009 had been falling. The value of this is given by the *slope* of the red line in the diagram and by the level of the green line. The government proclaimed that this was evidence that the economy was beginning to recover. Good news!

The use of calculus in this manner is a two-edged sword and such statistical sophistry is open to the political opposition, who could at a later date, if they so wished, claim that a fall in unemployment was bad economic news. Dare they?

 If the opposition were indeed to claim that a fall in unemployment was bad news, what would have to be the value of d^2N/dt^2: positive or negative?

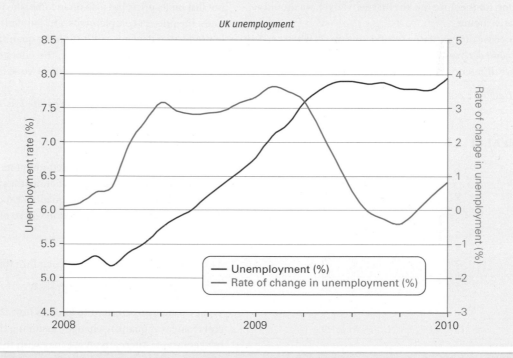

UK unemployment

shows how costs per unit of output vary as output increases). Also it is likely to want to know the output at which it will earn maximum profit. Let us examine this particular case.

Assume that the equation for total profit (Π) is:

$$\Pi = -20 + 12Q - Q^2 \qquad (5)$$

This gives profit at various outputs as shown in Table A1.11. The corresponding graph is plotted in Figure A1.11.

 What is the meaning of a negative profit?

It can be seen at a glance that profits are maximised at an output of 6 units. But we could have worked this out directly

from the profit equation without having to draw up a table or graph. How is this done?

Remember that when we differentiate a curve, the equation we get (known as 'the first derivative') gives us the slope of the curve. You can see that at the point of maximum profit (the top of the curve) its slope is zero: the tangent is horizontal. So all we have to do to find the top of the curve is to differentiate its equation and set it equal to zero.

Given that

$$\Pi = -20 + 12Q - Q^2 \qquad (5)$$

then:

$$d\Pi/dQ = 12 - 2Q \qquad (6)$$

Setting this equal to zero gives:

$$12 - 2Q = 0$$
$$\therefore \quad 2Q = 12$$
$$\therefore \quad Q = 6$$

Thus profits are maximised at an output of 6 units: the result we obtained from the table and graph.

The second derivative test

There is a problem with this technique, however. How can we tell from equation (6) that we have found the *maximum* rather than the *minimum?* The problem is that *both* the maximum *and* the minimum points of a curve have a zero slope.

The answer is to conduct a **second derivative test**. This involves differentiating the equation a second time. This gives the rate of change of the *slope* of the original curve. If you look at Figure A1.11, as output increases, the tangent moves from being upward sloping, to horizontal, to downward sloping. In other words, the slope is getting less and less. Its rate of change is *negative*. Thus if we differentiate the equation for the slope (i.e. the first derivative), we should get a negative figure.

When we differentiate a second time we get what is called the **second derivative**. It is written d^2y/dx^2.

If we differentiate equation (6):

$$d\Pi/dQ = 12 - 2Q \tag{6}$$

Table A1.11	$\Pi = -20 + 12Q - Q^2$

Q	Π
0	−20
1	−9
2	0
3	7
4	12
5	15
6	16
7	15
8	12
9	7
10	0

Figure A1.11 A total profit function:
$\Pi = -20 + 12Q - Q^2$

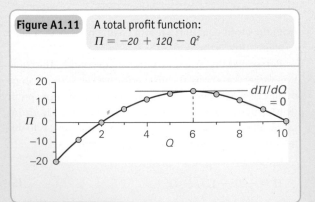

we get:

$$d^2\Pi/dQ^2 = -2 \tag{7}$$

(Note that the rules for differentiating a second time are the same as for the first time.) Given that the second derivative in this case is negative, we have demonstrated that we have indeed found the maximum profit point (at $Q = 6$), and not the minimum.

Given the following equation for a firm's average cost (AC), i.e. the cost per unit of output (Q):

$$AC = 60 - 16Q + 2Q^2$$

(a) At what output is AC at a minimum?
(b) Use the second derivative test to prove that this is a minimum and not a maximum.

Partial differentiation

Many relationships in economics involve more than two variables. For example, the demand for a product depends not just on its price, but also on income, the price of substitutes, the price of complements, etc. Similarly, a firm's cost of production depends not just on the quantity of output it produces, but also on wage rates, the prices of the various materials it uses, the productivity of its workers and machinery, and so on.

Such relationships can be expressed as a function as follows:

$$y = f(x_1, x_2, x_3, \ldots x_n)$$

where x_1, x_2, etc. are the various determinants of y.

Let us take a simple example where a firm's total cost (TC) depends on just two things: the quantity produced (Q) and the wage rate (W). The cost function will be of the form

$$TC = f(Q,W)$$

Assume that in the case of a particular firm the function is

$$TC = 20 + 10Q - 4Q^2 + 2Q^3 + 6W \tag{8}$$

What we are likely to want to know is how this firm's total cost changes as quantity changes, assuming the wage rate is held constant. Alternatively we may wish to know how its total cost changes as the wage rate changes, assuming that output is held constant. To do this we use the technique of

Definitions

Second derivative test If on differentiating an equation a second time the answer is negative (positive), the point is a maximum (minimum).

Second derivative The rate of change of the first derivative, found by differentiating the first derivative.

partial differentiation. This involves the same technique as simple differentiation but applied to just the one variable that is not held constant.

Thus to find the rate of change of costs with respect to quantity in equation (8), we differentiate the equation with respect to Q and ignore the W term. We ignore it as it is held constant and is thus treated like the constant (20) term in the equation. Using the rules of differentiation, the *partial derivative* is thus

$$\frac{\partial TC}{\partial Q} = 10 - 8Q + 6Q^2 \qquad (9)$$

Note that instead of using the symbol 'd' that we used in simple differentiation, we now use the symbol '∂'. Apart from that, the rules for partial differentiation are exactly the same as with simple differentiation.

If we now wanted to see how this firm's costs vary with the wage rate for any given output, then we would partially differentiate equation (8) with respect to W, giving

$$\frac{\partial TC}{\partial W} = 6$$

In other words, for each £1 rise in the wage rate, total cost would rise by £6.

Assume that the demand for a product is given by the following function:

$$Q_D = 1000 - 50P + 2P^2 + 10Ps + Ps^2$$

where Q_D is the quantity demanded, P is the price of the good and P_S is the price of a substitute good. What is the partial derivative of this demand function with respect to (a) the price of the good; (b) the price of the substitute good? Interpret the meaning of each partial derivative.

Definitions

Partial differentiation A mathematical technique used with functions containing two or more independent variables. The technique is used to find the rate of change of the dependent variable with respect to a single independent variable assuming that the other independent variables are held constant.

Partial derivative The partial derivative of a function of two or more independent variables is the derivative with respect to just one of those variables, while holding the others constant.

Appendix summary

1. Diagrams in economics can be used as pictures: to sketch a relationship so that its essentials can be perceived at a glance.

2. Tables, graphs and charts are also used to portray real-life data. These can be time-series data or cross-section data or both.

3. In order to get a true picture from economic data it is important to be aware of various ways that statistics can be abused: these include a selective use of data, a choice of axes on a graph to make trends seem more or less exaggerated or to make a curve more or less steep, confusing absolute and relative values, ignoring questions of distribution, confusing nominal and real values, and selecting the time period to make the statistics look the most favourable or unfavourable.

4. Presenting time-series data as index numbers gives a clear impression of trends and is a good way of comparing how two or more series (perhaps originally measured in different units) have changed over the same time period. A base year is chosen and the index for that year is set at 100. The percentage change in the value of a variable is given by the percentage change in the index (I). The formula is

$$\left(\frac{I_t - I_{t-1}}{I_{t-1}}\right) \times 100$$

Several items can be included in one index by using a weighted value for each of the items. The weights must add up to 1, and each weight will reflect the relative importance of that particular item in the index.

5. Functional relationships can be expressed as an equation, a table or a graph. In the linear (straight-line) equation $y = a + bx$, the a term gives the vertical intercept (the point where the graph crosses the vertical axis) and the b term gives the slope. When there is a power term (e.g. $y = a + bx + cx^2$), the graph will be a curve.

*6. Differentiation can be used to obtain the rate of change of one variable with respect to another. The rules of differentiation require that in an equation of the form

$$y = a + bx + cx^2 + dx^3$$

the a term disappears, the bx term simply becomes b, the cx^2 term becomes $2cx$, the dx^3 becomes $3dx^2$ and so on, with each extra term being multiplied by its power term and its power term being reduced by 1.

*7. To find the value of the x term at which the y term is at a maximum or minimum, the equation should be differentiated and set equal to zero. To check which it is – maximum or minimum – the second derivative should be calculated. If it is negative, then setting the first derivative equal to zero has yielded a maximum. If the second derivative is positive, then setting the first derivative to zero has yielded a minimum value.

Appendix 2: Websites

All the following websites can be accessed from this book's own website (http://www.pearsoned.co.uk/sloman). When you enter the site, click on **Hot Links.** You will find all the following sites listed. Click on the one you want and the 'hot link' will take you straight to it.

The sections and numbers below refer to the ones used in the websites listed at the end of each chapter. Thus if the list contained the number A21, this would refer to the *Conversation* site.

(A) General news sources

As the title of this section implies, the websites here can be used for finding material on current news issues or tapping into news archives. Most archives are offered free of charge. However, some do require you to register. As well as key UK and American news sources, you will also notice some slightly different places from where you can get your news, such as *The Moscow Times* and *The Japan TImes*. Check out site numbers 38. *Refdesk,* 43. *Guardian World News Guide* and 44. *Online newspapers* for links to newspapers across the world. Try searching for an article on a particular topic by using site number 41. *Google News Search.*

1. BBC news
2. The Economist
3. The Financial Times
4. The Guardian
5. The Independent
6. ITN
7. The Observer
8. The Telegraph
9. Aljazeera
10. The New York Times
11. Fortune
12. Time Magazine
13. The Washington Post
14. The Moscow Times (English)
15. Pravda (English)
16. Straits Times (Singapore)
17. New Straits Times (Malaysia)
18. The Scotsman
19. The Herald
20. Euromoney
21. The Conversation
22. Market News International
23. Bloomberg Businessweek
24. International Business Times
25. CNN Money
26. Vox (economic analysis and commentary)
27. Asia News Network
28. allAfrica.com
29. Greek News Sources (English)
30. France 24 (English)
31. Euronews
32. Australian Financial Review
33. Sydney Morning Herald
34. The Japan Times
35. Reuters
36. Bloomberg
37. David Smith's EconomicsUK.com
38. Refdesk (links to a whole range of news sources)
39. Newspapers and Magazines on World Wide Web
40. Yahoo News Search
41. Google News Search
42. ABYZ news links
43. Guardian World News Guide
44. Online newspapers

(B) Sources of economic and business data

Using websites to find up-to-date data is of immense value to the economist. The data sources below offer you a range of specialist and non-specialist data information. Universities have free access to the *UK Data Service* site (site 35 in this set), which is a huge database of statistics. Site 34, the *Treasury Pocket Databank,* is a very useful source of key UK and world statistics, and is updated monthly; it can be saved as an Excel file. The Economics Network's *Economic data freely available online* (site 1) gives links to various sections in over 40 UK and international sites.

1. Economics Network gateway to economic data
2. Office for Budget Responsibility
3. Office for National Statistics
4. Data Archive (Essex)
5. Bank of England Statistical Interactive Database
6. UK Official Statistics (GOV.UK)
7. Nationwide House Prices Site
8. House Web (data on housing market)
9. Economist global house price data
10. Halifax House Price Index
11. House prices indices from ONS)

12. Penn World Table
13. Economist economic and financial indicators
14. FT market data
15. Economagic
16. Groningen Growth and Development Centre
17. AEAweb: Resources for economists on the Internet (RFE): data
18. Joseph Rowntree Foundation
19. OECD iLibrary statistics
20. Energy Information Administration
21. OECDStat
22. CIA world statistics site (World Factbook)
23. Millennium Development Goal Indicators Database
24. World Bank Data
25. Federal Reserve Bank of St Louis, US Economic Datasets (FRED)
26. Ministry of Economy, Trade and Industry (Japan)
27. Financial data from Yahoo
28. DataMarket
29. Index Mundi
30. Knoema: Economics
31. World Economic Outlook Database (IMF)
32. Telegraph shares and markets
33. Key Indicators (KI) for Asia and the Pacific Series (Asia Development Bank)
34. Treasury Pocket Databank (source of UK and world economic data)
35. UK Data Service (incorporating ESDS)
36. BBC News, market data
37. NationMaster
38. Statistical Annex of the European Economy
39. Business and Consumer Surveys (all EU countries)
40. Gapminder
41. EcEdWeb data
42. WTO International Trade Statistics database
43. UNCTAD trade, investment and development statistics (UNCTADstat)
44. London Metal Exchange
45. Bank for International Settlements, global nominal and real effective exchange rate indices
46. Vizala (international data)
47. AMECO database
48. The Conference Board data
49. Institute for Fiscal Studies: tools and resources
50. European Central Bank (ECB): statistics

(C) Sites for students and teachers of economics

The following websites offer useful ideas and resources to those who are studying or teaching economics. It is worth browsing through some just to see what is on offer. Try out the first four sites, for starters. The *Internet for Economics* (site 8) is a very helpful tutorial for economics students on using the Internet.

1. The Economics Network
2. Teaching Resources for Undergraduate Economics (TRUE)
3. Ecedweb
4. Studying Economics
5. Economics and Business Education Association
6. Tutor2U
7. Council for Economic Education
8. Internet for Economics (tutorial on using the Web)
9. Econoclass: Resources for economics teachers
10. Teaching resources for economists (RFE)
11. METAL – Mathematics for Economics: enhancing Teaching And Learning
12. Federal Reserve Bank of San Francisco: Economics Education
13. Excel in Economics Teaching (from the Economics Network)
14. EcEdWeb resources
15. Dr. T's EconLinks: Teaching Resources
16. Online Opinion (Economics)
17. Free to Choose TV from the Idea Channel
18. History of Economic Thought
19. Resources For Economists on the Internet (RFE)
20. Games Economists Play (non-computerised classroom games)
21. Bank of England education resources
22. Why Study Economics?
23. Economic Classroom Experiments
24. Veconlab: Charles Holt's classroom experiments
25. Embedding Threshold Concepts
26. MIT Open Courseware in Economics
27. EconPort
28. ThoughtCo. – Economics

(D) Economic models, simulations and classroom experiments

Economic modelling is an important aspect of economic analysis. There are several sites that offer access to a model or simulation for you to use, e.g. *Virtual Chancellor* (where you can play being Chancellor of the Exchequer). Using such models can be a useful way of finding out how economic theory works within a specific environment. Other sites link to games and experiments, where you can play a particular role, perhaps competing with other students.

1. Virtual Chancellor
2. Virtual Factory
3. Interactive simulation models (Economics Web Institute)
4. Classroom Experiments in Economics (Pedagogy in Action)
5. MobLab
6. Economics Network Handbook, Chapter on Simulations, Games and Role-play
7. Experimental Economics Class Material (David J Cooper)

8. Simulations
9. Experimental economics: Wikipedia
10. Software available on the Economics Network site
11. RFE Software
12. Virtual Worlds
13. Veconlab: Charles Holt's classroom experiments
14. EconPort Experiments
15. Denise Hazlett's Classroom Experiments in Macroeconomics
16. Games Economists Play
17. Finance and Economics Experimental Laboratory at Exeter (FEELE)
18. Classroom Expernomics
19. The Economics Network's Guide to Classroom Experiments and Games
20. Economic Classroom Experiments (Wikiversity)

(E) UK government and UK organisations' sites

If you want to see what a government department is up to, then look no further than the list below. Government departments' websites are an excellent source of information and data. They are particularly good at offering information on current legislation and policy initiatives.

1. Gateway site (GOV.UK)
2. Department for Communities and Local Government
3. Prime Minister's Office
4. Competition & Markets Authority
5. Department for Education
6. Department for International Development
7. Department for Transport
8. Department of Health
9. Department for Work and Pensions
10. Department for Business, Energy & Industrial Strategy
11. Environment Agency
12. Department of Energy and Climate Change
13. Low Pay Commission
14. Department for Environment, Food & Rural Affairs (Defra)
15. Office of Communications (Ofcom)
16. Office of Gas and Electricity Markets (Ofgem)
17. Official Documents OnLine
18. Office for Budget Responsibility
19. Office of Rail and Road (ORR)
20. The Takeover Panel
21. Sustainable Development Commission
22. Ofwat
23. National Statistics (ONS)
24. List of ONS releases from UK Data Explorer
25. HM Revenue & Customs
26. UK Intellectual Property Office
27. Parliament website
28. Scottish Government
29. Scottish Environment Protection Agency
30. HM Treasury
31. Equality and Human Rights Commission
32. Trades Union Congress (TUC)
33. Confederation of British Industry (CBI)
34. Adam Smith Institute
35. Chatham House
36. Institute for Fiscal Studies
37. Advertising Standards Authority
38. Businesses and Self-employed
39. Campaign for Better Transport
40. New Economics Foundation
41. Financial Conduct Authority
42. Prudential Regulation Authority

(F) Sources of monetary and financial data

As the title suggests, here are listed useful websites for finding information on financial matters. You will see that the list comprises mainly central banks, both within Europe and further afield. The links will take you to English language versions of non-English speaking countries' sites.

1. Bank of England
2. Bank of England Monetary and Financial Statistics
3. Banque de France (in English)
4. Bundesbank (German central bank)
5. Central Bank of Ireland
6. European Central Bank
7. Eurostat
8. US Federal Reserve Bank
9. Netherlands Central Bank (in English)
10. Bank of Japan (in English)
11. Reserve Bank of Australia
12. Bank Negara Malaysia (in English)
13. Monetary Authority of Singapore
14. Bank of Canada
15. National Bank of Denmark (in English)
16. Reserve Bank of India
17. Links to central bank websites from the Bank for International Settlements
18. The London Stock Exchange

(G) European Union and related sources

For information on European issues, the following is a wide range of useful sites. The sites maintained by the European Union are an excellent source of information.

1. Business, Economy, Euro (EC DG)
2. European Central Bank
3. EU official website
4. Eurostat
5. Employment, Social Affairs and Inclusion (EC DG)
6. Reports, Studies and Booklets on the EU

7. Internal Market, Industry, Entrepreneurship and SMEs (EC DG)
8. Competition (EC DG)
9. Agriculture and Rural Development (EC DG)
10. Energy (EC DG)
11. Environment (EC DG)
12. Regional Policy (EC DG)
13. Taxation and Customs Union (EC DG)
14. Education, Youth, Sport and Culture (EC DG)
15. European Patent Office
16. European Commission
17. European Parliament
18. European Council
19. Mobility and Transport (EC DG)
20. Trade (EC DG)
21. Maritime Affairs and Fisheries (EC DG)
22. International Cooperation and Development (EC DG)
23. Financial Stability, Financial Services and Capital Markets Union (EC DG)

(H) International organisations

This section casts its net beyond Europe and lists the Web addresses of the main international organisations in the global economy. You will notice that some sites are run by charities, such as Oxfam, while others represent organisations set up to manage international affairs, such as the International Monetary Fund and the United Nations.

1. UN Food and Agriculture Organization (FAO)
2. United Nations Conference on Trade and Development (UNCTAD)
3. International Labour Organization (ILO)
4. International Monetary Fund (IMF)
5. Organisation for Economic Co-operation and Development (OECD)
6. OPEC
7. World Bank
8. World Health Organization (WHO)
9. United Nations (UN)
10. United Nations Industrial Development Organization (UNIDO)
11. Friends of the Earth
12. Institute of International Finance
13. Oxfam
14. Christian Aid (reports on development issues)
15. European Bank for Reconstruction and Development (EBRD)
16. World Trade Organization (WTO)
17. United Nations Development Programme
18. UNICEF
19. EURODAD – European Network on Debt and Development
20. NAFTA
21. South American Free Trade Areas

22. ASEAN
23. APEC

(I) Economics search and link sites

If you are having difficulty finding what you want from the list of sites above, the following sites offer links to other sites and are a very useful resource when you are looking for something a little bit more specialist. Once again, it is worth having a look at what these sites have to offer in order to judge their usefulness.

1. Gateway for UK official sites
2. Alta Plana
3. Data Archive Search
4. Inomics (information on economics courses and jobs)
5. Ideas: RePEc bibliographic database
6. Wikidata
7. Portal site with links to other sites (Economics Network)
8. EcEdWeb
9. Global goals 2030 (link to economic development resources)
10. Development Data Hub
11. DMOZ Open Directory: Economics (legacy site)
12. Web links for economists from the Economics Network
13. EconData.Net
14. Yale university: 75 Sources of Economic Data, Statistics, Reports, and Commentary
15. Excite Economics Links
16. Internet Resources for Economists
17. Trade Map (trade statistics)
18. Resources for Economists on the Internet
19. UK University Economics Departments
20. Economics education links
21. Development Gateway
22. Find the Data
23. Data on the Net
24. National Bureau of Economic Research links to data sources

(J) Internet search engines

The following search engines have been found to be useful.

1. Google
2. Bing
3. Whoosh UK
4. Excite
5. Zanran (search engine for data and statistics)
6. Search.com
7. MSN
8. Economics search engine (from RFE)
9. Yahoo
10. Ask
11. Lycos
12. Webcrawler
13. Metacrawler: searches several search engines

Threshold Concepts and Key Ideas

THRESHOLD CONCEPTS

KEY IDEAS

Glossary

Abduction   Using pieces of evidence to develop a plausible explanation. This can then be tested by gathering more evidence.

Absolute advantage   A country has an absolute advantage over another in the production of a good if it can produce it with less resources than the other country can.

Accelerationist hypothesis/theory   The theory that unemployment can only be reduced below the natural rate at the cost of accelerating inflation.

Accelerator coefficient   The level of induced investment as a proportion of a rise in national income: $\alpha = I_i/\Delta Y$.

Accelerator theory   The *level* of investment depends on the *rate of change* of national income, and as result tends to be subject to substantial fluctuations.

Active balances   Money held for transactions and precautionary purposes.

Actual growth   The percentage increase in national output actually produced.

Ad valorem tariffs   Tariffs levied as a percentage of the price of the import.

Ad valorem tax   A tax on a good levied as a percentage of its value. It can be a single-stage tax or a multi-stage tax (such as VAT).

Adaptive expectations hypothesis   The theory that people base their expectations of inflation on past inflation rates.

Adjustable peg   A system whereby exchange rates are fixed for a period of time, but may be devalued (or revalued) if a deficit (or surplus) becomes substantial.

Adverse selection (in general)   A market process whereby either buyers, sellers or products with certain unobservable characteristics (e.g. high risk or low quality) are more likely to enter the market at the current market price. This process can have a negative impact on economic efficiency and cause some potentially profitable markets to collapse.

Adverse selection in the insurance market   Where customers with the least desirable characteristics from the sellers' point of view are more likely to purchase an insurance policy at a price based on the average risk of all the potential customers.

Aggregate demand   Total spending on goods and services made in the economy. It consists of four elements, consumer spending (*C*), investment (*I*), government spending (*G*) and the expenditure on exports (*X*), less any expenditure on imports of goods and services (*M*): $AD = C + I + G + X - M$.

Aggregate demand for labour curve   A curve showing the total demand for labour in the economy at different levels of real wage rates.

Aggregate expenditure (*E*)   Aggregate demand in the Keynesian model: i.e. $C_d + J$.

Aggregate supply of labour curve   A curve showing the total number of people willing and able to work at different average real wage rates.

Aggregate supply   The total amount of output in the economy.

Allocative efficiency   A situation where the current combination of goods produced and sold gives the maximum satisfaction for each consumer at their current levels of income. Note that a redistribution of income would lead to a different combination of goods that was allocatively efficient.

Alternative theories of the firm   Theories of the firm based on the assumption that firms have aims other than profit maximisation.

Ambient-based standards   Pollution control that requires firms to meet minimum standards for the environment (e.g. air or water quality).

Appreciation (of a currency)   A rise in the free-market exchange rate of the domestic currency with foreign currencies.

Arbitrage   The practice of taking advantage of price differentials in markets by buying in the low-priced markets and selling in the high-priced ones. The practice of buying and selling will tend to eliminate the price differentials. Interest rate arbitrage involves borrowing at low interest rates and lending at high rates. This will tend to eliminate the interest rate differentials.

Arc elasticity   The measurement of elasticity between two points on a curve.

Assets   Possessions of an individual or institution, or claims held on others.

Asymmetric information   Where one party in an economic relationship (e.g. an agent) has more information than another (e.g. the principal).

Asymmetric shocks   Shocks (such as an oil price increase or a recession in another part of the world) that have different-sized effects on different industries, regions or countries.

Automatic fiscal stabilisers   Tax revenues that rise and government expenditure that falls as national income rises. The more they change with income, the bigger the stabilising effect on national income.

Average (total) cost   Total cost (fixed plus variable) per unit of output: $AC = TC/Q = AFC + AVC$.

Average cost pricing or **mark-up pricing**   Where firms set the price by adding a profit mark-up to average cost.

Average fixed cost   Total fixed cost per unit of output: $AFC = TFC/Q$.

Average physical product   Total output (TPP) per unit of the variable factor in question: $APP = TPP/Q_v$.

Average rate of income tax   Income taxes as a proportion of a person's total (gross) income: T/Y.

Average revenue   Total revenue per unit of output. When all output is sold at the same price average revenue will be the same as price: $AR = TR/Q = P$.

Average variable cost   Total variable cost per unit of output: $AVC = TVC/Q$.

Backwards induction   A process by which firms think through the most likely outcome in the last period of competition and then work backwards step by step, thinking through the most likely outcomes in earlier periods of competition.

Balance of payments account   The record of all the economic transactions between the residents of a specific country with the rest of the world for a specific time period, typically a year or a quarter. It records all the inflows and outflows of money under various headings. Inflows are recorded as credits; outflows are recorded as debits.

Balance of payments on current account   The balance on trade in goods and services plus net investment income and current transfers.

Balance on trade in goods or **balance of visible trade** or **merchandise balance**   Exports of goods minus imports of goods.

Balance on trade in goods and services (or balance of trade)   Exports of goods and services minus imports of goods and services.

Balance on trade in services   Exports of services minus imports of services.

Balance sheet   A record of the stock of assets and liabilities of an individual or institution.

Balance-sheet recession   A recession or economic slowdown caused by a collapse in aggregate demand arising from the actions of financially distressed people and businesses.

Bank bills   Bills that have been accepted by another institution and hence insured against default.

Bank (or deposits) multiplier   The number of times greater the expansion of bank deposits is than the additional liquidity in banks that causes it: $1/L$ (the inverse of the liquidity ratio).

Barometric firm price leadership   Where the price leader is the one whose prices are believed to reflect market conditions in the most satisfactory way.

Barriers to entry   Anything that prevents or impedes the entry of firms into an industry and thereby limits the amount of competition faced by existing firms.

Barter economy   An economy where people exchange goods and services directly with one another without any payment of money. Workers would be paid with bundles of goods.

Base year (for index numbers)   The year whose index number is set at 100.

Basic needs approach   The attempt to measure development in terms of a country's ability to meet the basic requirements for life.

Basic rate of tax   The main marginal rate of tax, applying to most people's incomes.

Behavioural theories of the firm   Theories that attempt to predict the actions of firms by studying the behaviour of various groups of people within the firm and their interactions under conditions of potentially conflicting interests.

Benefit principle of taxation   The principle that people ought to pay taxes in proportion to the amount they use government services.

Benefits in kind   Goods or services which the state provides directly to the recipient at no charge or at a subsidised price. Alternatively, the state can subsidise the private sector to provide them.

Bid rigging   Where two or more firms secretly agree on the prices they will tender for a contract. These prices will be above those that would have been submitted under a genuinely competitive tendering process.

Bilateral monopoly   Where a monopsony buyer faces a monopoly seller.

Bill of exchange   A certificate promising to repay a stated amount on a certain date, typically three months from the issue of the bill. Bills pay no interest as such, but are sold at a discount and redeemed at face value, thereby earning a rate of discount for the purchaser.

Bounded rationality   When the ability to make rational decisions is limited by lack of information or the time necessary to obtain such information or by a lack of understanding of complex situations.

Bretton Woods system   An adjustable peg system whereby currencies were pegged to the US dollar. The USA maintained convertibility of the dollar into gold at the rate of $35 to an ounce.

Broad money in UK (M4)   Cash in circulation plus retail and wholesale bank and building society deposits.

Budget deficit   The excess of central government's spending over its tax receipts.

Budget line   A graph showing all the possible combinations of two goods that can be purchased at given prices and for a given budget.

Budget surplus   The excess of central government's tax receipts over its spending.

Buffer stocks   Stocks of a product used to stabilise its price. In years of abundance, the stocks are built up. In years of low supply, stocks are released on to the market.

Business cycle or **trade cycle**   The periodic fluctuations of national output round its long-term trend.

Capital   All inputs into production that have themselves been produced: e.g. factories, machines and tools.

Capital account of the balance of payments   The record of the transfers of capital to and from abroad.

Capital adequacy ratio (CAR)   The ratio of a bank's capital (reserves and shares) to its risk-weighted assets.

Capital expenditure   Investment expenditure; expenditure on assets.

Capital market   A financial market where longer-term debt instruments, like government bonds (gilts), can be bought and sold.

Carry trade   Borrowing at low interest rates and then using it to buy assets that earn higher rates. In foreign exchange markets, the carry trade involves borrowing money in a currency of a country where interest rates are low and exchanging it for another currency where the country pays higher interest rates.

Cartel   A formal collusive agreement.

Central bank   Banker to the banks and the government. It oversees the banking system, implements monetary policy and issues currency.

Centrally planned or command economy   An economy where all economic decisions are taken by the central authorities.

Certainty equivalent   The guaranteed amount of money that an individual would view as equally desirable as the expected value of a gamble. Where a person is risk averse, the certainty equivalent is less than the expected value.

Certificates of deposit (CDs)   Certificates issued by banks for fixed-term interest-bearing deposits. They can be resold by the owner to another party.

Ceteris paribus   Latin for 'other things being equal'. This assumption has to be made when making deductions from theories.

Change in demand   This is the term used for a shift in the demand curve. It occurs when a determinant of demand *other* than price changes.

Change in supply   The term used for a shift in the supply curve. It occurs when a determinant *other* than price changes.

Change in the quantity demanded   The term used for a movement along the demand curve to a new point. It occurs when there is a change in price.

Change in the quantity supplied   The term used for a movement along the supply curve to a new point. It occurs when there is a change in price.

Claimant unemployment   Those in receipt of unemployment-related benefits.

Classical model   A macroeconomic model that assumes prices and wages are fully flexible.

Clearing system   A system whereby inter-bank debts are settled.

Closed shop   Where a firm agrees to employ only union members.

Club good   A good which has a low degree of rivalry but is easily excludable.

Coase theorem   When there are well-defined property rights and zero bargaining costs, then negotiations between the party creating the externality and the party affected by the externality can bring about the socially efficient market quantity.

Cobb–Douglas production function   Like other production functions, this shows how output (*TPP*) varies with inputs of various factors (F_1, F_2, F_3, etc.). In the simple two-factor case it takes the following form:

$$TPP + f(F_1, F_2) + aF_1^{\alpha}F_2^{\beta}$$

If $\alpha + \beta = 1$, there are constant returns to scale; if $\alpha + \beta > 1$, there are increasing returns to scale; if $\alpha + \beta < 1$, there are decreasing returns to scale.

Collateralised debt obligations (CDOs)   These are a type of security consisting of a bundle of fixed-income assets, such as corporate bonds, mortgage debt and credit card debt.

Collusive oligopoly   Where oligopolists agree (formally or informally) to limit competition between themselves. They may set output quotas, fix prices, limit product promotion or development, or agree not to 'poach' each other's markets.

Collusive tendering   Where two or more firms secretly agree on the prices they will tender for a contract. These prices will be above those which would be put in under a genuinely competitive tendering process.

Command-and-control (CAC) systems   The use of laws or regulations backed up by inspections and penalties (such as fines) for non-compliance.

Command economy   An economy where all economic decisions are made by a central planning process.

Commercial bills   Bills of exchange issued by firms.

Common good or resource   A good or resource that has a high degree of rivalry but the exclusion of non-payers is difficult.

Common market   A customs union where the member countries act as a single market with free movement of labour and capital, common taxes and common trade laws.

Comparative advantage   A country has a comparative advantage over another in the production of a good if it can produce it at a lower opportunity cost: i.e. if it has to forgo less of other goods in order to produce it.

Competition for corporate control   The competition for the control of companies through takeovers.

Complementary goods   A pair of goods consumed together. As the price of one goes up, the demand for both goods will fall.

Compounding   The process of adding interest each year to an initial capital sum.

Compromise strategy   A strategy whose worst outcome is better than under a high-risk strategy and whose best outcome is better than under a low-risk strategy.

Conglomerate merger   When two firms in different industries merge.

Consortium Where two or more firms work together on a specific project and create a separate company to run the project.

Constant-cost industry An industry where average costs stay constant as the size of the industry expands.

Constrained discretion A set of principles or rules within which economic policy operates. These can be informal or enshrined in law.

Consumer durable A consumer good that lasts a period of time, during which the consumer can continue gaining utility from it.

Consumer prices index (CPI) An index of the weighted average of the prices of goods and services bought by a typical household. Its annual rate of change gives CPI inflation and is the measure used by most countries, including the UK, for their inflation target.

Consumer sovereignty A situation where firms respond to changes in consumer demand without being in a position in the long run to charge a price above average cost.

Consumer surplus The excess of what a person would have been prepared to pay for a good (i.e. the utility) over what that person actually pays.

Consumers' share of a tax on a good The proportion of the revenue from a tax on a good that arises from an increase in the price of the good.

Consumption The act of using goods and services to satisfy wants. This will normally involve purchasing the goods and services.

Consumption function The relationship between consumption and national income. It can be expressed algebraically or graphically.

Consumption of domestically produced goods and services (C_d) The direct flow of money payments from households to firms.

Consumption smoothing The act by households of smoothing their levels of consumption over time despite facing volatile incomes.

Contingent convertible debt instruments (Co-Cos) Debt instruments, like corporate bonds, which may be converted into equity capital when a trigger point, such as the level of financial distress of a corporation, is reached.

Continuous market clearing The new classical assumption that all markets in the economy continuously clear so that the economy is permanently in equilibrium.

Convergence in GDP per head The tendency for less rich developed countries to catch up the richer ones. Convergence does not apply to many of the poorer developing countries, however, where the gap between them and richer countries has tended to widen.

Convergence of economies When countries achieve similar levels of growth, inflation, budget deficits as a percentage of GDP, balance of payments, etc.

Co-ordination failure When a group of firms (e.g. banks) acting independently could have achieved a more desirable outcome if they had co-ordinated their decision making.

Core workers Workers, normally with specific skills, who are employed on a permanent or long-term basis.

Cost–benefit analysis The identification, measurement and weighing up of the costs and benefits of a project in order to decide whether or not it should go ahead.

Cost-plus pricing (full-cost pricing) (another name for mark-up pricing) When firms price their product by adding a certain profit 'mark-up' to average cost.

Cost-push inflation Inflation caused by persistent rises in costs of production (independently of demand).

Countervailing power When the power of a monopolistic/oligopolistic seller is offset by powerful buyers who can prevent the price from being pushed up.

Cournot equilibrium Where each of two firm's actual output is the same as what the other firm predicted it would produce: where the two firms' reaction curves cross.

Cournot model of duopoly A model where each firm makes its price and output decisions on the assumption that its rival will produce a particular quantity.

Crawling peg A system whereby the government allows a gradual adjustment of the exchange rate.

Credibility (of policies) Policies that people believe the government will carry out once they have been announced.

Credible threat (or promise) One that is believable to rivals because it is in the threatener's interests to carry it out.

Credit-constrained households Households which are limited in their ability to borrow against expected future incomes.

Credit crunch A sudden reduction in the availability of loans or credit from banks and other financial institutions.

Cross-price elasticity of demand The percentage (or proportionate) change in quantity demanded of one good divided by the percentage (or proportionate) change in the price of another.

Cross-price elasticity of demand (arc formula) $\Delta Q_{DA}/\text{average } Q_{DA} + \Delta P_B/\text{average } P_B$.

Cross-section data Information showing how a variable (e.g. the consumption of eggs) differs between different groups or different individuals at a given time.

Cross-subsidise To use profits in one market to subsidise prices in another.

Crowding out Where increased public expenditure diverts money or resources away from the private sector.

Cumulative causation (principle of) When an initial change causes an eventual change that is larger.

Currency union A group of countries (or regions) using a common currency.

Current account balance of payments Exports of goods and services minus imports of goods and services plus net incomes and current transfers from abroad. If inflows of money (from the sale of exports, etc.) exceed outflows of money (from the purchase of imports, etc.) there is a 'current account surplus' (a positive figure). If outflows exceed inflows there is a 'current account deficit' (a negative figure).

Current expenditure (by the government) Recurrent spending on goods and factor payments.

Customs union A free trade area with common external tariffs and quotas.

Deadweight loss of an indirect tax The loss of consumers' plus producers' surplus from the imposition of an indirect tax.

Deadweight welfare loss of monopoly The loss of consumers' plus producers' surplus in monopoly or other imperfect markets (when compared with perfect competition).

Deadweight welfare loss from externalities The loss of social surplus at the competitive market equilibrium compared with the social optimum where $MSC = MSB$.

Debentures (company bonds) Fixed-interest loans to firms. These assets can be traded on the stock market and their market price is determined by demand and supply.

Debt servicing Paying the interest and capital repayments on debt.

Debt-servicing costs The costs incurred when repaying debt, including debt interest payments.

Deciles Divisions of the population into ten equal-sized groups (an example of a quantile).

Decision tree (or game tree) A diagram showing the sequence of possible decisions by competitor firms and the outcome of each combination of decisions.

Decreasing-cost industry An industry where average costs decrease as the size of the industry expands.

Deduction Using a theory to draw conclusions about specific circumstances.

Deficit bias The tendency for frequent fiscal deficits and rising debt-to-GDP ratios because of the reluctance of policy makers to tighten fiscal policy.

Deflationary (or recessionary) gap The shortfall of national expenditure below national income (and injections below withdrawals) at the full-employment level of national income.

Deflationary policy Fiscal or monetary policy designed to reduce the rate of growth of aggregate demand.

Demand curve A graph showing the relationship between the price of a good and the quantity of the good demanded over a given time period. Price is measured on the vertical axis; quantity demanded is measured on the horizontal axis. A demand curve can be for an individual consumer or group of consumers, or more usually for the whole market.

Demand function An equation which shows the mathematical relationship between the quantity demanded of a good and the values of the various determinants of demand.

Demand-management policies Demand-side policies (fiscal and/or monetary) designed to smooth out the fluctuations in the business cycle.

Demand schedule (market) A table showing the different total quantities of a good that consumers are willing and able to buy at various prices over a given period of time.

Demand schedule for an individual A table showing the different quantities of a good that a person is willing and able to buy at various prices over a given period of time.

Demand-deficient or **cyclical unemployment** Disequilibrium unemployment caused by a fall in aggregate demand with no corresponding fall in the real wage rate.

Demand-pull inflation Inflation caused by persistent rises in aggregate demand.

Demand-side policies Policies designed to affect aggregate demand: fiscal policy and monetary policy.

Demand-side policy Government policy designed to alter the level of aggregate demand, and thereby the level of output, employment and prices.

Dependency Where the development of a developing country is hampered by its relationships with the industrialised world.

Depreciation (of a currency) A fall in the free-market exchange rate of the domestic currency with foreign currencies.

Depreciation (of capital) The decline in value of capital equipment due to age, or wear and tear.

Deregulation Where the government removes official barriers to competition (e.g. licences and minimum quality standards).

Derived demand The demand for a factor of production depends on the demand for the good which uses it.

Destabilising speculation Where the actions of speculators tend to make price movements larger.

Devaluation Where the government re-pegs the exchange rate at a lower level.

Differentiation A mathematical technique to find the rate of change of one variable with respect to another.

Diminishing marginal rate of substitution The more a person consumes of good X and the less of good Y, the less additional Y will that person be prepared to give up in order to obtain an extra unit of X: i.e. $\Delta Y/\Delta X$ diminishes.

Diminishing marginal returns When one or more factors are held fixed, there will come a point beyond which the extra output from additional units of the variable factor will diminish.

Diminishing marginal utility As more units of a good are consumed, additional units will provide less additional satisfaction than previous units.

Diminishing marginal utility of income Where each additional pound earned yields less additional utility than the previous pound.

Direct income support or direct aid A fixed grant to farmers that does not vary with current output. It may be based on acreage, number of livestock or past output.

Direct monetary transmission mechanism A change in money supply having a direct effect on aggregate demand.

Direct taxes Taxes on income and wealth. Paid directly to the tax authorities on that income or wealth.

Dirty floating (managed flexibility)   A system of flexible exchange rates but where the government intervenes to prevent excessive fluctuations or even to achieve an unofficial target exchange rate.

Discount factor   The value today of deciding to consume a good one period in the future as a proportion of the value when it is actually consumed.

Discount market   An example of a money market in which new or existing bills, such as Treasury bills or commercial bills, are bought and sold at a discount below their face value: i.e. the value at which they will be redeemed on maturity.

Discounting   The process of reducing the value of future flows to give them a present valuation.

Discounting: exponential   A method of reducing future benefits and costs to a present value. The discount rate depends on just how much less, from the consumer's perspective, *future* utility and costs (from a decision made today) are than gaining the utility/incurring the costs *today*.

Discretionary fiscal policy   Deliberate changes in tax rates or the level of government expenditure in order to influence the level of aggregate demand.

Diseconomies of scale   Where costs per unit of output increase as the scale of production increases.

Disequilibrium unemployment   Unemployment resulting from real wage rates in the economy being above the equilibrium level.

Disguised unemployment   Where the same work could be done by fewer people.

Disintermediation   The diversion of business away from financial institutions which are subject to controls.

Disposable income   Household income after the deduction of taxes and the addition of benefits.

Distribution of income by class of recipient   Measurement of the distribution of income between the classes of person who receive it (e.g. homeowners and non-homeowners or those in the North and those in the South).

Diversification   This is where a firm expands into new types of business.

Dominant firm price leadership   When firms (the followers) choose the same price as that set by a dominant firm in the industry (the leader).

Dominant strategy game   Where the firm's optimal strategy remains the same irrespective of what it assumes its rivals are going to do.

Downward causation   The name given to the impact on individual behaviour or well-being of aggregate or group effects. This is an example of cumulative causation (Threshold Concept 15).

Dumping   When exports are sold at prices below marginal cost – often as a result of government subsidy.

Duopoly   An oligopoly where there are just two firms in the market.

Dynamic stochastic general equilibrium (DSGE models)   Models that seek to explain macroeconomic phenomena by examining the microeconomic behaviour of rational forward-looking individual economic agents acting in a variety of market conditions. The microeconomic equilibria are subject to random shocks, such as technological change, political events or changes in the supply of natural resources.

Econometrics   The science of applying statistical techniques to economic data in order to identify and test economic relationships.

Economic agents   People or institutions making economic decisions. These could be individuals as consumers, workers, borrowers or savers, or firms, governments or other public institutions.

Economic and monetary union (EMU)   The adoption by a group of countries of a single currency with a single central bank and a single monetary policy. In the EU the term applies to the countries that have adopted the euro.

Economic discrimination   When workers of identical *ability* are paid different wages or are otherwise discriminated against because of race, age, sex, etc.

Economic efficiency   A situation where each good is produced at the minimum cost and where individual people and firms get the maximum benefit from their resources.

Economic model   A formal presentation of an economic theory.

Economic rent   The excess that a factor is paid over the amount necessary to keep it in its current employment.

Economies of scale   When increasing the scale of production leads to a lower long-run cost per unit of output.

Economies of scope   When increasing the range of products produced by a firm reduces the cost of producing each one.

ECU (European Currency Unit)   The predecessor to the euro: a weighted average of EU currencies. It was used as a reserve currency and for the operation of the exchange rate mechanism (ERM).

Effective rate of protection   The percentage increase in an industry's domestic value added resulting from protection given to that industry.

Efficient (capital) market hypothesis   The hypothesis that new information about a company's current or future performance will be quickly and accurately reflected in its share price.

Efficiency (technical)   The firm is producing as much output as is technologically possible given the quantity of factor inputs it is using.

Efficiency wage hypothesis   The hypothesis that the productivity of workers is affected by the wage rate that they receive.

Efficiency wage rate   The profit-maximising wage rate for the firm after taking into account the effects of wage rates on worker motivation, turnover and recruitment.

Elastic demand (with respect to price)   Where quantity demanded changes by a larger percentage than price. Ignoring the negative sign, it will have a value greater than 1.

Elasticity   A measure of the responsiveness of a variable (e.g. quantity demanded or quantity supplied) to a change in one of its determinants (e.g. price or income).

EMS (The European Monetary System, mark 1)   A system, prior to the euro, whereby EU countries co-operated to achieve greater exchange rate stability. It involved use of the exchange rate mechanism (the ERM).

Endogenous growth models   Models which demonstrate that the rate of economic growth depends on the rate of technological progress and diffusion, both of which depend on institutions, incentives and the role of government.

Endogenous money supply   Money supply that is determined (at least in part) by the demand for money.

Endogenous variable   A variable whose value is determined by the model of which it is part.

Endowment effect (or **divestiture aversion**)   The hypothesis that people ascribe more value to things when they own them than when they are merely considering purchasing or acquiring them – in other words, when the reference point is one of ownership rather than non-ownership.

Engel curve   A line derived from indifference analysis showing how much of a good people will demand at different levels of income.

Entrepreneurship   The initiating and organising of the production of new goods, or the introduction of new techniques, and the risk taking associated with it.

Envelope curve   A long-run average cost curve drawn as the tangency points of a series of short-run average cost curves.

Environmental charges   Charges for using natural resources (e.g. water or national parks), or for using the environment as a dump for waste (e.g. factory emissions or sewage).

Equation of exchange $MV = PY$. The total level of spending on GDP (MV) equals the total value of goods and services produced (PY) that go to make up GDP.

Equilibrium   A position of balance. A position from which there is no inherent tendency to move away.

Equilibrium price   The price where the quantity demanded equals the quantity supplied: the price where there is no shortage or surplus.

Equilibrium ('natural') unemployment   The difference between those who would like employment at the current wage rate and those willing and able to take a job.

Equi-marginal principle   Consumers will maximise total utility from their incomes by consuming that combination of goods where $MU_a/P_a = MU_b/P_b = MU_c/P_c \ldots = MU_n/P_n$.

Equities   Company shares. Holders of equities are owners of the company and share in its profits by receiving dividends.

Equity   A distribution of income that is considered to be fair or just. Note that an equitable distribution is not the same as an equal distribution and that different people have different views on what is equitable.

ERM (the exchange rate mechanism)   A system of semi-fixed exchange rates used by most of the EU countries prior to adoption of the euro. Members' currencies were allowed to fluctuate against each other only within agreed bands. Collectively they floated against all other currencies.

Excess burden (of a tax on a good)   The amount by which the loss in consumer plus producer surplus exceeds the government surplus.

Excess capacity (under monopolistic competition)   In the long run, firms under monopolistic competition will produce at an output below their minimum-cost point.

Exchange equalisation account   The gold and foreign exchange reserves account in the Bank of England.

Exchange rate   The rate at which one national currency exchanges for another. The rate is expressed as the amount of one currency that is necessary to purchase *one unit* of another currency (e.g. €1.20 = £1).

Exchange rate band   Where a currency is allowed to float between an upper and lower exchange rate, but is not allowed to move outside this band.

Exchange rate index   A weighted average exchange rate expressed as an index where the value of the index is 100 in a given base year. The weights of the different currencies in the index add up to 1.

Exchange rate mechanism   See *ERM*.

Exchange rate overshooting   Where a fall (or rise) in the long-run equilibrium exchange rate causes the actual exchange rate to fall (or rise) by a greater amount before eventually moving back to the new long-run equilibrium level.

Exchange rate: real   A country's exchange rate adjusted for changes in the domestic currency prices of its exports relative to the foreign currency prices of its imports. If a country's prices rise (fall) relative to those of its trading partners, its real exchange rate will rise (fall) relative to the nominal exchange rate.

Exchange rate regime   The system under which the government allows the exchange rate to be determined.

Exchange rate transmission mechanism   How a change in money supply affects aggregate demand via a change in exchange rates.

Exclusionary abuses (in business)   Business practices that limit or prevent effective competition from either actual or potential rivals.

Exogenous money supply   Money supply that does not depend on the demand for money but is set by the authorities.

Exogenous variable   A variable whose value is determined independently of the model of which it is part.

Expansion path   The line on an isoquant map that traces the minimum-cost combinations of two factors as output increases. It is drawn on the assumption that both factors can be varied. It is thus a long-run path.

Expected value   The average value of an outcome of an activity when the same activity takes place many times.

Expectations-augmented Phillips curve A (short-run) Phillips curve whose position depends on the expected rate of inflation.

Expenditure changing (increasing) from depreciation: the income effect Where depreciation, via the substitution effect, will alter the demand for imports and exports, and this will, via the multiplier, affect the level of national income and hence the demand for imports.

Expenditure changing (reducing) from deflation: the income effect Where deflationary policies lead to a reduction in national income and hence a reduction in the demand for imports.

Expenditure switching from deflation: the substitution effect Where deflationary policies lead to a reduction in inflation and thus cause a switch in expenditure away from imports and also towards exports.

Expenditure switching from depreciation: the substitution effect Where a lower exchange rate reduces the price of exports and increases the price of imports. This will increase the sale of exports and reduce the sale of imports.

Exploitative abuse (in business) A business practice that directly harms the customer. Examples include high prices and poor quality.

Exponential discounting A method of reducing future benefits and costs to a present value. The discount rate depends on just how much less, from the consumer's perspective, *future* utility and costs (from a decision made today) are than gaining the utility/incurring the costs *today*.

Explicit costs The payments to outside suppliers of inputs.

External balance (in the economy) Narrow definition: where the current account of the balance of payments is in balance (and thus also the capital plus financial accounts). Loose definition: where there is a total currency flow balance at a given exchange rate.

External benefits Benefits from production (or consumption) experienced by people *other* than the producer (or consumer) directly involved in the transaction.

External costs Costs of production (or consumption) borne by people *other* than the producer (or consumer) directly involved in the transaction.

External diseconomies of scale Where a firm's costs per unit of output increase as the size of the whole *industry* increases.

External economies of scale Where a firm's costs per unit of output decrease as the size of the whole *industry* grows.

External policy objectives Objectives relating to the economy's international economic relationships.

Externalities Costs or benefits of production or consumption experienced by people *other* than the producers and consumers directly involved in the transaction. They are sometimes referred to as 'spillover' or 'third-party' costs or benefits.

Factor price equalisation The tendency for international trade to reduce factor price inequalities both between and within countries.

Factors of production (or resources) The inputs into the production of goods and services: labour, land and raw materials, and capital.

Fallacy of composition What applies to the individual does not necessarily apply to the whole.

Final expenditure Expenditure on goods and services. This is included in GDP and is part of aggregate demand.

Financial accelerator The amplification of effects on the macroeconomy from economic shocks because of changes in the pricing and supply of credit by financial institutions.

Financial account of the balance of payments The record of the flows of money into and out of the country for the purposes of investment or as deposits in banks and other financial institutions.

Financial crowding out When an increase in government borrowing diverts money away from the private sector.

Financial deregulation The removal of or reduction in legal rules and regulations governing the activities of financial institutions.

Financial flexibility Where employers can vary their wage costs by changing the composition of their workforce or the terms on which workers are employed.

Financial instability hypothesis During periods of economic growth, economic agents (firms and individuals) tend to borrow more and MFIs are more willing to lend. This fuels the boom. In a period of recession, economic agents tend to cut spending in order to reduce debts and MFIs are less willing to lend. This deepens the recession. Behaviour in financial markets thus tends to amplify the business cycle.

Financial instruments Financial products resulting in a financial claim by one party over another.

Financial intermediaries The general name for financial institutions (banks, building societies, etc.) which act as a means of channelling funds from depositors to borrowers.

Financialisation A term used to describe the process by which financial markets, institutions and instruments becoming increasing significant in economies.

Fine-tuning The use of demand management policy (fiscal or monetary) to smooth out cyclical fluctuations in the economy.

First-best solution The solution of correcting a specific market distortion by ensuring that the whole economy operates under conditions of social efficiency (Pareto optimality).

First-degree price discrimination Where the seller of the product charges each consumer the maximum price he or she is prepared to pay for each unit.

First-mover advantage When a firm gains from being the first one to take action.

Fiscal drag The tendency of automatic fiscal stabilisers to reduce the recovery of an economy from recession.

Fiscal policy Policy to affect aggregate demand by altering the balance between government expenditure and taxation.

Fiscal stance How deflationary or reflationary the Budget is.

Fixed costs Total costs that do not vary with the amount of output produced.

Fixed exchange rate (totally) Where the government takes whatever measures are necessary to maintain the exchange rate at some stated level.

Fixed factor An input that cannot be increased in supply within a given time period.

Flat organisation Where the senior management communicate directly with those lower in the organisational structure, bypassing middle management.

Flexible firm A firm that has the flexibility to respond to changing market conditions by changing the composition of its workforce.

Floating exchange rate When the government does not intervene in the foreign exchange markets, but simply allows the exchange rate to be freely determined by demand and supply.

Flow An amount of something occurring over a *period of time*: e.g. production per week, income per year, demand per week. (Contrasts with *stock*.)

Flow-of-funds equation The various items making up an increase (or decrease) in money supply.

Forward exchange market Where contracts are made today for the price at which currency will be exchanged at some specified future date.

Framing The way in which a choice is presented or understood. A person may make different decisions depending on whether a choice is presented optimistically or pessimistically.

Franchising Where a firm is given the licence to operate a given part of an industry for a specified length of time.

Free trade area A group of countries with no trade barriers between themselves.

Freely floating exchange rate Where the exchange rate is determined entirely by the forces of demand and supply in the foreign exchange market with no government intervention whatsoever.

Free-market economy An economy where all economic decisions are taken by individual households and firms and with no government intervention.

Free-rider problem When it is not possible to exclude other people from consuming a good that someone has bought.

Frictional (search) unemployment Equilibrium unemployment which occurs as a result of imperfect information in the labour market. It often takes time for workers to find jobs (even though there are vacancies) and in the meantime they are unemployed.

Full-employment level of national income The level of national income at which there is no deficiency of demand.

Functional distribution of income Measurement of the distribution of income according to the source of income (e.g. from employment, from profit, from rent, etc.).

Functional flexibility Where employers can switch workers from job to job as requirements change.

Functional relationships The mathematical relationship showing how one variable is affected by one or more others.

Funding (in monetary policy) Where the authorities alter the balance of bills and bonds for any given level of government borrowing.

Future price A price agreed today at which an item (e.g. commodities) will be exchanged at some set date in the future.

Futures or forward market A market in which contracts are made to buy or sell at some future date at a price agreed today.

Gaia philosophy The respect for the rights of the environment to remain unharmed by human activity. Humans should live in harmony with the planet and other species. We have a duty to be stewards of the natural environment, so that it can continue to be a self-maintaining and self-regulating system.

Game theory (or the theory of games) A mathematical method of decision making in which alternative strategies are analysed to determine the optimal course of action for the interested party, depending on assumptions about rivals' behaviour. Widely used in economics, game theory is also used as a tool in biology, psychology and politics.

GDP (gross domestic product at market prices) The value of output (or income or expenditure) in terms of the prices actually paid. GDP = GVA + taxes on products − subsidies on products.

GDP deflator The price index of all final domestically produced goods and services: i.e. all those items that contribute towards GDP.

Gearing or **leverage** (US term) The ratio of debt capital to equity capital: in other words, the ratio of borrowed capital (e.g. bonds) to shares.

General equilibrium A situation where all the millions of markets throughout the economy are in a simultaneous state of equilibrium.

General equilibrium diagrams (in trade theory) Indifference curve/production possibility curve diagrams that show a country's production and consumption of both imports and exports.

General government debt The accumulated deficits of central plus local government. It is the total amount owed by general government, both domestically and internationally.

General government deficit (or surplus) The combined deficit (or surplus) of central and local government.

Geographical immobility The lack of ability or willingness of people to move to jobs in other parts of the country.

Giffen good An inferior good whose demand increases as its price increases as a result of a positive income effect larger than the normal negative substitution effect.

Gini coefficient The area between the Lorenz curve and the 45° line divided by the total area under the 45° line.

Global systemically important banks (SIBs) Banks identified by a series of indicators as being significant players in the global financial system.

GNY (gross national income) GDP plus net income from abroad.

Gold standard The system whereby countries' exchange rates were fixed in terms of a certain amount of gold and whereby balance of payments deficits were paid in gold.

Golden-rule saving rate The rate of saving that maximises the level of long-run consumption.

Goodhart's law Controlling a symptom of a problem or only one part of the problem will not *cure* the problem: it will simply mean that the part that is being controlled now becomes a poor indicator of the problem.

Government bonds or **'gilt-edged securities'** A government security paying a fixed sum of money each year. It is redeemed by the government on its maturity date at its face value.

Government surplus (from a tax on a good) The total tax revenue earned by the government from sales of a good.

Grandfathering Where the number of emission permits allocated to a firm is based on its *current* levels of emission (e.g. permitted levels for all firms could be 80 per cent of their current levels).

Green tax A tax on output designed to charge for the adverse effects of production on the environment. The socially efficient level of a green tax is equal to the marginal environmental cost of production.

Gross domestic product (GDP) The value of output produced within the country over a 12-month period.

Gross national income (GNY) GDP plus net income from abroad.

Gross value added at basic prices (GVA) The sum of all the values added by all industries in the economy over a year. The figures exclude taxes on products (such as VAT) and include subsidies on products.

Growth maximisation An alternative theory that assumes that managers seek to maximise the growth in sales revenue (or the capital value of the firm) over time.

Harrod–Domar model A model that relates a country's rate of economic growth to the proportion of national income saved and the ratio of capital to output.

Heckscher–Ohlin version of comparative advantage A country has a comparative advantage in those goods that are intensive in the country's relatively abundant factor.

Heterodox economists Economists who reject the assumptions of neoclassical economics, in particular the assumptions of rational optimising behaviour. They highlight the importance of institutional behaviour and factors influencing human behaviour.

Heuristics A mental short-cut or rule of thumb that people use when trying to solve complex problems. Heuristics reduce the computational effort required but sometimes lead to systematic errors.

H-form organisation (holding company) Where the parent company holds interests in a number of subsidiary companies.

Historic costs The original amount the firm paid for factors it now owns.

Hit-and-run competition A strategy whereby a firm is willing to enter a market and make short-run profits and then leave again when the existing firm(s) cut prices. Costless exit makes hit-and-run behaviour more likely.

Horizontal equity The equal treatment of people in the same situation.

Horizontal merger When two firms in the same industry at the same stage in the production process merge.

Households' disposable income The income available for households to spend: i.e. personal incomes after deducting taxes on incomes and adding benefits.

Human capital The qualifications, skills and expertise that contribute to a worker's productivity.

Human Development Index (HDI) A composite index made up of three elements: an index for life expectancy, an index for school enrolment and adult literacy, and an index for GDP per capita (in PPP$).

Hysteresis The persistence of an effect even when the initial cause has ceased to operate. In economics, it refers to the persistence of unemployment even when the demand deficiency that caused it no longer exists.

Identification problem The problem of identifying the relationship between two variables (e.g. price and quantity demanded) from the evidence when it is not known whether or how the variables have been affected by *other* determinants. For example, it is difficult to identify the shape of a demand curve simply by observing price and quantity when it is not known whether changes in other determinants have *shifted* the demand curve.

Idle balances Money held for speculative purposes: money held in anticipation of a fall in asset prices.

Illegal (or **shadow** or **underground**) **markets** Where people ignore the government's price and/or quantity controls and sell illegally at whatever price equates illegal demand and supply.

Imperfect competition The collective name for monopolistic competition and oligopoly.

Implicit costs Costs which do not involve a direct payment of money to a third party, but which nevertheless involve a sacrifice of some alternative.

Import-substituting industrialisation (ISI) A strategy of restricting imports of manufactured goods and using the foreign exchange saved to build up domestic substitute industries.

Impulse response functions The time paths of key macroeconomic variables following economic shocks.

Impure public good A good that is partially non-rivalrous and non-excludable.

Incidence of tax The distribution of the burden of tax between sellers and buyers.

Income and expenditure account or **profit and loss account** A record of the flows of incomes, expenditure and saving of an individual or institution.

Income effect (of a price change) The effect of a change in price on quantity demanded arising from the consumer becoming better or worse off as a result of the price change.

Income effect of a rise in wage rates Workers get a higher income for a given number of hours worked and may thus feel they need to work *fewer* hours as wage rates rise.

Income effect of a tax rise Tax increases reduce people's incomes and thus encourage people to work more.

Income elasticity of demand The percentage (or proportionate) change in quantity demanded divided by the percentage (or proportionate) change in income.

Income elasticity of demand (arc formula) ΔQ_D/average $Q_D \Delta Y$/average Y.

Income–consumption curve A line showing how a person's optimum level of consumption of two goods changes as income changes (assuming the price of the goods remains constant).

Increasing-cost industry An industry where average costs increase as the size of the industry expands.

Increasing opportunity costs of production When additional production of one good involves ever increasing sacrifices of another.

Independence (of firms in a market) Where the decisions of one firm in a market will not have any significant effect on the demand curves of its rivals.

Independent risks Where two risky events are unconnected. The occurrence of one will not affect the likelihood of the occurrence of the other.

Index number The value of a variable expressed as 100 plus or minus its percentage deviation from a base year.

Indifference curve A line showing all those combinations of two goods between which a consumer is indifferent: i.e. those combinations that give the same level of utility.

Indifference map A graph showing a whole set of indifference curves. The further away a particular curve is from the origin, the higher the level of satisfaction it represents.

Indifference set A table showing the same information as an indifference curve.

Indirect monetary transmission mechanism A change in money supply affecting aggregate demand indirectly via some other variable.

Indirect taxes Taxes on expenditure (e.g. VAT). They are paid to the tax authorities, not by the consumer, but indirectly by the suppliers of the goods or services.

Indivisibilities The impossibility of dividing a factor into smaller units.

Induced investment Investment that firms make to enable them to meet extra consumer demand.

Induction Constructing general theories on the basis of specific observations.

Industrial policies Policies to encourage industrial investment and greater industrial efficiency.

Industry's infrastructure The network of supply agents, communications, skills, training facilities, distribution channels, specialised financial services, etc., that supports a particular industry.

Inelastic demand (with respect to price) Where quantity demanded changes by a smaller percentage than price. Ignoring the negative sign, it will have a value less than 1.

Infant industry An industry that has a potential comparative advantage, but which is as yet too underdeveloped to be able to realise this potential.

Inferior goods Goods whose demand *decreases* as consumer incomes increase. Such goods have a negative income elasticity of demand.

Inflation A general rise in the level of prices throughout the economy.

Inflation bias Excessive inflation that results from people raising their expectations of the inflation rate following expansionary demand management policy, encouraging government to loosen policy even further.

Inflation rate (annual) The percentage increase in prices over a 12-month period.

Inflationary gap The excess of national expenditure over income (and injections over withdrawals) at the full-employment level of national income.

Informal sector The parts of the economy that involve production and/or exchange, but where there are no money payments.

Infrastructure (industry's) The network of supply agents, communications, skills, training facilities, distribution channels, specialised financial services, etc. that supports a particular industry.

Injections (J) Expenditure on the production of domestic firms coming from outside the inner flow of the circular flow of income. Injections equal investment (I) plus government expenditure (G) plus expenditure on exports (X).

(Injections) multiplier The number of times by which a rise in income exceeds the rise in injections that caused it: $k = \Delta Y/\Delta J$.

(Injections) multiplier formula The formula for the multiplier: $k = 1/mpw$ or $1/(1-mpc_d)$.

Input–output analysis This involves dividing the economy into sectors where each sector is a user of inputs from and a supplier of outputs to other sectors. The technique examines how these inputs and outputs can be matched to the total resources available in the economy.

Insiders Those in employment who can use their privileged position (either as members of unions or because of specific skills) to secure pay rises despite an excess supply of labour (unemployment).

Interdependence (under oligopoly) One of the two key features of oligopoly. Each firm will be affected by its rivals' decisions. Likewise its decisions will affect its rivals. Firms recognise this interdependence. This recognition will affect their decisions.

Interest rate transmission mechanism How a change in money supply affects aggregate demand via a change in interest rates.

Intermediate exchange rate regimes Where the government intervenes to influence movements in the exchange rate.

Internal balance (of an economy) Where the equilibrium level of national income is at the desired level.

Internal policy objectives (national) Objectives relating solely to the domestic economy.

Internal rate of return The rate of return of an investment: the discount rate that makes the net present value of an investment equal to zero.

International harmonisation of economic policies Where countries attempt to co-ordinate their macroeconomic policies so as to achieve common goals.

International liquidity The supply of currencies in the world acceptable for financing international trade and investment.

International substitution effect As prices rise, people at home and abroad buy less of this country's products and more of products from abroad.

International trade multiplier The effect on national income in Country B of a change in exports (or imports) of Country A.

Inter-temporal substitution effect Higher prices may lead to higher interest rates and thus less borrowing and more saving. Current consumption falls; future consumption (from the higher savings) rises.

Intervention price (in the CAP) The price at which the EU is prepared to buy a foodstuff if the market price were to be below it.

Interventionist supply-side policies Policies to increase aggregate supply by government intervention to counteract the deficiencies of the market.

Investment The production of items that are not for immediate consumption. This can include investment in plant and equipment; such investment builds the stock of firms' capital and yields a flow of future output. Investment also includes adding to stocks of goods or resources which are not sold or used in the current period, but will be in the future.

Irrational exuberance Where banks and other economic agents are over confident about the economy and/or financial markets and expect economic growth to remain stronger and/or asset prices to rise further than warranted by evidence.

IS/LM model A model showing simultaneous equilibrium in the goods market ($I = S$) and the money market ($L = M$).

Isocost A line showing all the combinations of two factors that cost the same to employ.

Isoquant A line showing all the alternative combinations of two factors that can produce a given level of output.

J-curve effect Where a devaluation causes the balance of trade first to deteriorate and then to improve. The graph of the balance of trade over time thus looks like a letter J.

Joint float Where a group of currencies pegged to each other jointly float against other currencies.

Joint supply Where the production of more of one good leads to the production of more of another.

Joint venture Where two or more firms set up and jointly own a new independent firm.

Just-in-time methods Where a firm purchases supplies and produces both components and finished products as they are required. This minimises stock holding and its associated costs. It does, however, put pressure on the supply chain and increases the probability that on occasion firms may not be able to meet demand – for example in times of bad weather.

Kinked demand theory The theory that oligopolists face a demand curve that is kinked at the current price, demand being significantly more elastic above the current price than below. The effect of this is to create a situation of price stability.

Labour All forms of human input, both physical and mental, into current production.

Labour force The number employed plus the number unemployed.

Land (and raw materials) Inputs into production that are provided by nature: e.g. unimproved land and mineral deposits in the ground.

Law of comparative advantage Trade can benefit all countries if they specialise in the goods in which they have a comparative advantage.

Law of demand The quantity of a good demanded per period of time will fall as price rises and will rise as price falls, other things being equal (*ceteris paribus*).

Law of diminishing (marginal) returns When one or more factors are held fixed, there will come a point beyond which the extra output from additional units of the variable factor will diminish.

Law of large numbers The larger the number of events of a particular type, the more predictable will be their average outcome.

Lender of last resort The role of the Bank of England as the guarantor of sufficient liquidity in the monetary system.

Leverage (US term) or **gearing** The ratio of debt capital to equity capital: in other words, the ratio of borrowed capital (e.g. bonds) to shares.

Liability Claim by others on an individual or institution; debt of that individual or institution.

Liabilities All legal claims for payment that outsiders have on an institution.

Libertarian school A school of thought that advocates maximum liberty for economic agents to pursue their own interests and to own property.

Limit pricing Where a monopolist (or oligopolist) charges a price below the short-run profit-maximising level in order to deter new entrants.

Liquidity The ease with which an asset can be converted into cash without loss.

Liquidity preference   The demand for holding assets in the form of money.

Liquidity ratio   The proportion of a bank's total assets held in liquid form.

Liquidity trap   The absorption of any additional money supply into idle balances at very low rates of interest, leaving aggregate demand unchanged.

Lock-outs   Union members are temporarily laid off until they are prepared to agree to the firm's conditions.

Long run   The period of time long enough for *all* factors to be varied.

Long run under perfect competition   The period of time that is long enough for new firms to enter the industry.

Long-run average cost curve   A curve that shows how average cost varies with output on the assumption that *all* factors are variable. (It is assumed that the least-cost method of production will be chosen for each output.)

Long-run marginal cost   The extra cost of producing one more unit of output assuming that all factors are variable. (It is assumed that the least-cost method of production will be chosen for this extra output.)

Long-run neutrality of money   Changes in money supply over the long run will only affect prices and not real output or employment

Long-run profit maximisation   An alternative theory of the firm which assumes that managers aim to *shift* cost and revenue curves so as to maximise profits over some longer time period.

Long-run shut-down point   This is where the *AR* curve is tangential to the *LRAC* curve. The firm can just make normal profits. Any fall in revenue below this level will cause a profit-maximising firm to shut down once all costs have become variable.

Lorenz curve   A curve showing the proportion of national income earned by any given percentage of the population (measured from the poorest upwards).

Macro-prudential regulation   Regulation which focuses not on a single financial institution but on the financial system as a whole and which monitors its overall stability, its resilience to shocks and its impact on the wider economy.

Macroeconomics   The branch of economics that studies economic aggregates (grand totals): e.g. the overall level of prices, output and employment in the economy.

Managed flexibility (dirty floating)   A system of flexible exchange rates but where the government intervenes to prevent excessive fluctuations or even to achieve an unofficial target exchange rate.

Margin squeeze   Where a vertically integrated firm with a dominant position in an upstream market deliberately charges high prices for an input required by firms in a downstream market to drive them out of business.

Marginal benefit   The additional benefit of doing a little bit more (or 1 unit more if a unit can be measured) of an activity.

Marginal capital/output ratio   The amount of extra capital (in money terms) required to produce a £1 increase in national output. Since $I_i = \Delta K$, the marginal capital/output ratio $\Delta K/\Delta Y$ equals the accelerator coefficient α.

Marginal consumer surplus   The excess of utility from the consumption of one more unit of a good (MU) over the price paid: $MCS = MU - P$.

Marginal cost (of an activity)   The additional cost of doing a little bit more (or 1 unit more if a unit can be measured) of an activity.

Marginal cost (of production)   The cost of producing one more unit of output: $MC = \Delta TC/\Delta Q$.

Marginal disutility of work   The extra sacrifice/hardship to a worker of working an extra unit of time in any given time period (e.g. an extra hour per day).

Marginal efficiency of capital or **internal rate of return**   The rate of return of an investment: the discount rate that makes the net present value of an investment equal to zero.

Marginal physical product   The extra output gained by the employment of one more unit of the variable factor: $MPP = \Delta TPP/\Delta Q_v$.

Marginal productivity theory   The theory that the demand for a factor depends on its marginal revenue product.

Marginal propensity to consume   The proportion of a rise in national income that goes on consumption: $mpc = \Delta C/\Delta Y$.

Marginal propensity to import   The proportion of an increase in national income that is spent on imports: $mpm = \Delta M/\Delta Y$.

Marginal propensity to save   The proportion of an increase in national income saved: $mps = \Delta S/\Delta Y$.

Marginal propensity to withdraw   The proportion of an increase in national income that is withdrawn from the circular flow: $mpw = \Delta W/\Delta Y$, where $mpw = mps + mpt + mpm$.

Marginal rate of factor substitution   The rate at which one factor can be substituted by another while holding the level of output constant: $MRS = \Delta F_1/\Delta F_2 = MPP_{F2}/MPP_{F1}$.

Marginal rate of income tax   The income tax rate. The rate paid on each *additional* pound earned: $\Delta T/\Delta Y$.

Marginal rate of substitution (between two goods in consumption)   The amount of one good (Y) that a consumer is prepared to give up in order to obtain one extra unit of another good (X): i.e. $\Delta Y/\Delta X$.

Marginal revenue   The extra revenue gained by selling one more unit per time period: $MR = \Delta TR/\Delta Q$.

Marginal revenue product (of a factor)   The extra revenue a firm earns from employing one more unit of a variable factor: $MRP_{factor} = MPP_{factor} MR_{good}$.

Marginal tax propensity   The proportion of an increase in national income paid in tax: $mpt = \Delta T/\Delta Y$.

Marginal utility   The extra satisfaction gained from consuming one extra unit of a good within a given time period.

Market   The interaction between buyers and sellers.

Market clearing   A market clears when supply matches demand, leaving no shortage or surplus.

Market demand schedule   A table showing the different total quantities of a good that consumers are willing and able to buy at various prices over a given period of time.

Market for loanable funds   The market for loans from and deposits into the banking system.

Market loans   Short-term loans (e.g. money at call and short notice).

Market-orientated supply-side policies   Policies to increase aggregate supply by freeing up the market.

Mark-up   A profit margin added to average cost to arrive at price.

Marshall–Lerner condition   Depreciation will improve the balance of payments only if the sum of the price elasticities of demand for imports and exports is greater than 1.

Maturity gap   The difference in the average maturity of loans and deposits.

Maturity transformation   The transformation of deposits into loans of a longer maturity.

Maximax   The strategy of choosing the policy that has the best possible outcome. Maximax is usually a high-risk strategy.

Maximin   The strategy of choosing the policy whose worst possible outcome is the least bad. Maximin is usually a low-risk strategy.

Maximum price   A price ceiling set by the government or some other agency. The price is not allowed to rise above this level (although it is allowed to fall below it).

Mean (or arithmetic mean)   The sum of the values of each of the members of the sample divided by the total number in the sample.

Means-tested benefits   Benefits whose amount depends on the recipient's income or assets.

Median   The value of the middle member of the sample.

Medium of exchange   Something that is acceptable in exchange for goods and services.

Menu costs of inflation   The costs associated with having to adjust price lists or labels.

Merchandise balance   See *Balance of trade in goods*.

Merit goods   Goods which the government feels that people will underconsume and which therefore ought to be subsidised or provided free.

M-form (multi-divisional form) of corporate organisation   Where the firm is split into a number of separate divisions (e.g. different products or countries), with each division then split into a number of departments.

Microeconomics   The branch of economics that studies individual units: e.g. households, firms and industries. It studies the interrelationships between these units in determining the pattern of production and distribution of goods and services.

Minimum price   A price floor set by the government or some other agency. The price is not allowed to fall below this level (although it is allowed to rise above it).

Minimum reserve ratio   A minimum ratio of cash (or other specified liquid assets) to deposits (either total or selected) that the central bank requires banks to hold.

Minsky moment   A turning point in a credit cycle where a period of easy credit and rising debt is replaced by one of tight credit and debt consolidation.

Mixed command economy   A planned economy that nevertheless makes some use of markets.

Mixed economy   An economy where economic decisions are made partly by the government and partly through the market. In practice all economies are mixed.

Mixed market economy   A market economy where there is some government intervention.

Mobility of labour   The willingness and ability of labour to move to another job.

Monetarists   Those who attribute inflation solely to rises in money supply.

Monetary base   Notes and coin outside the central bank.

Monetary base control   Monetary policy that focuses on controlling the monetary base (as opposed to broad liquidity).

Monetary financial institutions (MFIs)   Deposit-taking institutions including banks, building societies and the Bank of England.

Monetary policy   Where the central bank alters the supply of money in the economy and/or manipulates interest rates.

Money illusion   When people believe that a *money* change in wages or prices represents a *real* change: in other words, they ignore or underestimate inflation.

Money market   The market for short-term debt instruments, such as government bills (Treasury bills), in which financial institutions are active participants.

Money multiplier   The number of times greater the expansion of money supply is than the expansion of the monetary base that caused it: $\Delta Ms/\Delta Mb$.

Monopolistic competition   A market structure where, like perfect competition, there are many firms and freedom of entry into the industry, but where each firm produces a differentiated product and thus has some control over its price.

Monopoly   A market structure where there is only one firm in the industry.

Monopsony   A market with a single buyer or employer.

Moral hazard   Where one party to a transaction has an incentive to behave in a way which reduces the pay-off to the other party: for example, the temptation to take more risks when you know that someone else will cover the risks if you get into difficulties. In the case of banks taking risks, the 'someone else' may be another bank, the central bank or the government.

Moral hazard (in insurance)   Customers taking more risks when they have insurance than when they don't have insurance.

Multiplier (injections multiplier)   The number of times a rise in income exceeds the rise in injections that caused it. $k = \Delta Y/\Delta J$.

Multiplier effect   An initial increase in aggregate demand of £x million leads to an eventual rise in national income that is greater than £x million.

Multiplier formula (injections multiplier)   The formula for the multiplier is $k = 1/mpw$ or $1/(1-mpc_d)$.

Mutual recognition   The EU principle that one country's rules and regulations must apply throughout the EU. If they conflict with those of another country, individuals and firms should be able to choose which to obey.

Nash equilibrium   The position resulting from everyone making their optimal decision based on their assumptions about their rivals' decisions. Without collusion, there is no incentive for any firm to move from this position.

National debt   The accumulated deficits of central government. It is the total amount owed by central government, both domestically and internationally.

National expenditure on domestic product (E)   Aggregate demand in the Keynesian model: i.e. $C_d + J$.

Nationalised industries   State-owned industries that produce goods or services that are sold in the market.

Natural level of real income or output   The level of output in monetarist analysis where the vertical long-run aggregate supply curve cuts the horizontal axis.

Natural level of unemployment   The level of equilibrium unemployment in monetarist and new classical analysis measured as the difference between the (vertical) long-run gross labour supply curve (N) and the (vertical) long-run effective labour supply curve (AS_L).

Natural monopoly   A situation where long-run average costs would be lower if an industry were under monopoly than if it were shared between two or more competitors.

Natural rate hypothesis   The theory that, following fluctuations in aggregate demand, unemployment will return to a natural rate. This rate is determined by supply-side factors, such as labour mobility.

Natural rate of unemployment   The rate of unemployment at which there is no excess or deficiency of demand for labour. The rate of unemployment consistent, therefore, with a constant rate of inflation: the rate of unemployment at which the vertical long-run Phillips curve cuts the horizontal axis.

Natural wastage   When a firm wishing to reduce its workforce does so by not replacing those who leave or retire.

Near money   Highly liquid assets (other than cash).

Negative income tax   A combined system of tax and benefits. As people earn more they gradually lose their benefits until beyond a certain level they begin paying taxes.

Neo-Austrian/libertarian school   A school of thought that advocates maximum liberty for economic agents to pursue their own interests and to own property.

Net investment   Total investment minus depreciation.

Net national income (NNY)   GNY minus depreciation.

Net present value of an investment   The discounted benefits of an investment minus the cost of the investment.

Net worth   The market value of a sector's stock of financial and non-financial wealth.

Network (business)   An informal arrangement between businesses to work together towards some common goal.

Network economies (or network externalities)   The benefits a consumer obtains from consuming a good or service increase with the number of other people who use the same good or service.

Neutrality of money (long run)   Changes in money supply over the long run will only affect prices and not real output or employment.

New classical school   The school of economists which believes that markets clear virtually instantaneously and that expectations are formed 'rationally'. Any expansion of demand will feed through virtually instantaneously into higher prices, giving a vertical short-run as well as a vertical long-run Phillips curve.

New Keynesians   Economists who seek to explain how market imperfections and frictions can result in fluctuations in real GDP and the persistence of unemployment. They argue that governments may have to expand aggregate demand when demand-deficient unemployment is persistent.

Nominal GDP   GDP measured at current prices.

Nominal national income   National income measured at current prices.

Nominal values   Money values measured at *current* prices.

Non-accelerating-inflation rate of unemployment (NAIRU)   The rate of unemployment consistent with steady inflation in the near term, say, over the next 12 months.

Non-bank private sector   Households and non-bank firms: in other words, everyone in the country other than banks and the government (central and local).

Non-collusive oligopoly   Where oligopolists have no agreement between themselves either formal, informal or tacit.

Non-excludability   Where it is not possible to provide a good or service to one person without it thereby being available free for others to enjoy.

Non-price competition   Competition in terms of product promotion (advertising, packaging, etc.) or product development.

Non-rivalry   Where the consumption of a good or service by one person will not prevent others from enjoying it.

Normal-form game   Where the possible pay-offs from different strategies or decisions are presented as a matrix.

Normal goods   Goods whose demand increases as consumer incomes increase. They have a positive income elasticity of demand. Luxury goods will have a higher income elasticity of demand than more basic goods.

Normal profit   The opportunity cost of being in business: the profit that could have been earned in the next best alternative business. It is counted as a cost of production.

Normal rate of return   The rate of return (after taking risks into account) that could be earned elsewhere.

Normative statement   A value judgement.

Nudge theory   The theory that positive reinforcement or making the decision easy can persuade people to make a particular choice. They are 'nudged' into so doing.

Numerical flexibility   Where employers can change the size of their workforce as their labour requirements change.

Occupational immobility   The lack of ability or willingness of people to move to other jobs irrespective of location.

Okun's law   The name given to the negative statistical relationship between the unemployment rate and deviations of output from potential output.

Oligopoly   An market structure where there are few enough firms to enable barriers to be erected against the entry of new firms.

Oligopsony   A market with just a few buyers or employers.

Open economy   One that trades with and has financial dealings with other countries.

Open-market operations   The sale (or purchase) by the authorities of government securities in the open market in order to reduce (or increase) money supply or influence interest rates.

Operational standing facilities   Central bank facilities by which individual banks can deposit reserves or borrow reserves.

Opportunity cost   Cost measured in terms of the value of the best alternative forgone.

Optimal currency area   The optimal size of a currency area is the one that maximises the benefits from having a single currency relative to the costs. If the area were increased or decreased in size, the costs would rise relative to the benefits.

Optimum tariff   A tariff that reduces the level of imports to the point where the country's marginal social cost equals marginal social benefit.

Organisational slack   Where managers allow spare capacity to exist, thereby enabling them to respond more easily to changed circumstances.

Output gap   The difference between actual and potential output. When actual output exceeds potential output, the gap is positive. When actual output is less than potential output, the gap is negative.

Outsiders   Those out of work or employed on a casual, part-time or short-term basis, who have little or no power to influence wages or employment.

Overheads   Costs arising from the general running of an organisation, and only indirectly related to the level of output.

Paradox of debt (or paradox of deleveraging)   The paradox that one individual can increase his or her net worth by selling assets, but if this is undertaken by a large number of people aggregate net worth declines because asset prices fall.

Paradox of thrift   If society saves more, this may *reduce* its future income and consumption. The reason is that as people save more, they will spend less. Firms will thus produce less. There will thus be a multiplied *fall* in income.

Pareto improvement   Where changes in production or consumption can make at least one person better off without making anyone worse off.

Pareto optimality   Where all possible Pareto improvements have been made: where, therefore, it is impossible to make anyone better off without making someone else worse off.

Partial derivative   The partial derivative of a function of two or more independent variables is the derivative with respect to just one of those variables, while holding the others constant.

Partial differentiation   A mathematical technique used with functions containing two or more independent variables. The technique is used to find the rate of change of the dependent variable with respect to a single independent variable assuming that the other independent variables are held constant.

Participation rate   The percentage of the working-age population that is part of the workforce.

Partnership   A firm owned by two or more people. They each have unlimited liability for the firm's debts.

Peak-load pricing   Price discrimination (second or third degree) where a higher price is charged in peak periods and a lower price in off-peak periods.

Perfect competition   A market structure where there are many firms, none of which is large; where there is freedom of entry into the industry; where all firms produce an identical product; and where all firms are price takers.

Perfectly contestable market   A market where there is free and costless entry and exit and the monopolist cannot immediately respond to entry.

Phillips curve   A curve showing the relationship between (price) inflation and unemployment. The original Phillips curve plotted *wage* inflation against unemployment for the years 1861–1957.

Picketing   When people on strike gather at the entrance to the firm and attempt to persuade workers or delivery vehicles from entering.

Pigouvian tax (or subsidy)   A tax (or subsidy) designed to 'internalise' an externality. The marginal rate of a Pigouvian tax (or subsidy) should be equal to the marginal external cost (or benefit).

Plant economies of scale   Economies of scale that arise because of the large size of the factory.

Point elasticity   The measurement of elasticity at a point on a curve. The formula for price elasticity of demand using the point elasticity method is: $dQ/dP \times P/Q$, where dQ/dP is the inverse of the slope of the tangent to the demand curve at the point in question.

Policy ineffectiveness proposition   The conclusion drawn from new classical models that when economic agents anticipate changes in economic policy, output and employment remain at their equilibrium (or natural) levels.

Political business cycle   The theory that governments, after being elected, will engineer an economic contraction, designed to squeeze out inflation. They will then later engineer a pre-election boom to appeal to the electorate.

Poll tax A lump-sum tax per head of the population. Since it is a fixed *amount*, it has a marginal rate of zero with respect to both income and wealth.

Polluter pays principle The principle that polluters ought to be charged (e.g. through green taxes) for the external environmental costs that they generate.

Pooling risks (for an insurance company) The more policies and insurance company issues and the more independent the risks of claims from these policies are, the more predictable will be the number of claims.

Portfolio balance The balance of assets, according to their liquidity, that people choose to hold in their portfolios.

Positive statement A value-free statement which can be tested by an appeal to the facts.

Post-Keynesians Economists who stress the importance of institutional and behavioural factors, and the role of business confidence in explaining the state of the economy. They argue that firms are more likely to respond to changes in demand by changing output rather than prices.

Potential growth The percentage increase in the capacity of the economy to produce.

Potential output The sustainable level output that could be produced in the economy: i.e. one that involves a 'normal' level of capacity utilisation and does not result in rising inflation.

Poverty trap (for developing countries) When countries are too poor to save and invest enough to achieve real per capita growth.

Poverty trap (for individuals) Where poor people are discouraged from working or getting a better job because any extra income they earn will be largely taken away in taxes and lost benefits.

Predatory pricing Where a firm sets its prices below average cost in order to drive competitors out of business.

Preferential trading arrangements A trade agreement whereby trade between the signatories is freer than trade with the rest of the world.

Present bias Time-inconsistent behaviour whereby people give greater weight to present pay-offs relative to future ones than would be predicted by standard discounting techniques.

Present value approach to appraising investment This involves estimating the value *now* of a flow of future benefits (or costs).

Present value (in consumption) The value a person places today on a good that will not be consumed until some point in the future.

Price benchmark A price which is typically used. Firms, when raising prices will usually raise it from one benchmark to another.

Price discrimination Where a firm sells the same product at different prices.

Price elasticity of demand (arc formula) ΔQ/average $Q \div \Delta P$/average P. The average in each case is the average between the two points being measured.

Price elasticity of demand ($P\epsilon_D$) The percentage (or proportionate) change in quantity demanded divided by the percentage (or proportionate) change in price: $\%\Delta Q_D \div \%\Delta P$.

Price elasticity of supply ($P\epsilon_S$) The percentage (or proportionate) change in quantity supplied divided by the percentage (or proportionate) change in price: $\%\Delta Q_S \div \%\Delta P$.

Price elasticity of supply (arc formula) ΔQ_S/average $Q_S \div \Delta P$/average P.

Price mechanism The system in a market economy whereby changes in price in response to changes in demand and supply have the effect of making demand equal to supply.

Price taker A person or firm with no power to be able to influence the market price.

Price-cap regulation Where the regulator puts a ceiling on the amount by which a firm can raise its price.

Price–consumption curve A line showing how a person's optimum level of consumption of two goods changes as the price of one of the two goods changes (assuming that income and the price of the other good remain constant).

Prices and incomes policy When the government seeks to restrain price and wage increases. This may be in the form of a voluntary agreement with firms and/or unions, or there may be statutory limits imposed.

Primary labour market The market for permanent full-time core workers.

Primary market in capital Where shares are sold by the issuer of the shares (i.e. the firm) and where, therefore, finance is channelled directly from the purchasers (i.e. the shareholders) to the firm.

Primary surplus (or deficit) The situation when the sum of public-sector expenditures excluding interest payments on public-sector debt is less than (greater than) public-sector receipts.

Principal–agent problem Where people (principals), as a result of lack of knowledge, cannot ensure that their best interests are served by their agents.

Principle of cumulative causation An initial event can cause an ultimate effect that is much larger.

Prisoners' dilemma Where two or more firms (or people), by attempting independently to choose the best strategy for whatever the other(s) are likely to do, end up in a worse position than if they had co-operated in the first place.

Private efficiency Where a person's marginal benefit from a given activity equals the marginal cost.

Private limited company A company owned by its shareholders. Shareholders' liability is limited to the value of their shares. Shares can only be bought and sold privately.

Producers' share of a tax on a good The proportion of the revenue from a tax on a good that arises from a reduction in the price to the producer (after the payment of the tax).

Product differentiation   When one firm's product is sufficiently different from its rivals' to allow it to raise the price of the product without customers all switching to the rivals' products. A situation where a firm faces a downward-sloping demand curve.

Production   The transformation of inputs into outputs by firms in order to earn profit (or meet some other objective).

Production function   The mathematical relationship between the output of a good and the inputs used to produce it. It shows how output will be affected by changes in the quantity of one or more of the inputs used in production, holding the level of technology constant.

Production possibility curve   A curve showing all the possible combinations of two goods that a country can produce within a specified time period with all its resources fully and efficiently employed.

Productive efficiency   A situation where firms are producing the maximum output for a given amount of inputs, or producing a given output at the least cost. The least-cost combination of factors for a given output.

Productivity deal   When, in return for a wage increase, a union agrees to changes in working practices that will increase output per worker.

Profit (rate of)   Total profit (T) as a proportion of the total capital employed (K): $r = T/K$.

Profit and loss account or **income and expenditure account**   A record of the flows of incomes, expenditure and saving of an individual or institution.

Profit satisficing   Where decision makers in a firm aim for a target level of profit rather than the absolute maximum level.

Profit-maximising rule   Profit is maximised where marginal revenue equals marginal cost.

Progressive tax   A tax whose average rate with respect to income rises as income rises.

Proportional tax   A tax whose average rate with respect to income stays the same as income rises.

Prudential control   The insistence by the Bank of England that recognised banks maintain adequate liquidity.

Public good   A good or service that has the features of non-rivalry and non-excludability and as a result would not be provided by the free market.

Public limited company   A company owned by its shareholders. Shareholders' liability is limited to the value of their shares. Shares may be bought and sold publicly – on the Stock Exchange.

Public-sector current budget deficit   The amount by which public-sector expenditures classified as current expenditures exceed public-sector receipts

Public-sector net borrowing (PSNB)   The difference between the expenditures of the public sector and its receipts from taxation and the revenues from public corporations.

Public-sector net cash requirement (PSNCR)   The (annual) deficit of the public sector, and thus the amount that the public sector must borrow. This can differ from the PSNB because of the timing of receipts and expenditures. The term is only used in the UK.

Public-sector net debt   Gross public-sector debt minus liquid financial assets.

Public-sector surplus or **public-sector debt repayment (PSDR)**   The (annual) surplus of the public sector, and thus the amount of debt that can be repaid when public-sector income exceeds public-sector expenditures.

Purchasing-power parity (PPP) exchange rate   An exchange rate corrected to take into account the purchasing power of a currency. $1 would buy the same in each country after conversion into its currency at the PPP rate.

Purchasing-power parity theory   The theory that the exchange rate will adjust so as to offset differences in countries' inflation rates, with the result that the same quantity of internationally traded goods can be bought at home as abroad with a given amount of the domestic currency.

Purchasing-power standard (PPS) GDP   GDP measured as a country's PPP exchange rate.

Pure fiscal policy   Fiscal policy which does not involve any change in money supply.

Pure public good   A good or service that has the characteristics of being perfectly non-rivalrous and completely non-excludable and as a result, would not be provided by the free market.

Quantiles   Divisions of the population into equal-sized groups.

Quantitative easing (QE)   A deliberate attempt by the central bank to increase the money supply by buying large quantities of securities through open-market operations. These securities could be securitised mortgage and other private sector debt or government bonds. When banks and other financial institutions lend the money, broad money expands by a multiple of this through the process of credit creation.

Quantity demanded   The amount of a good a consumer is willing and able to buy at a given price over a given period of time.

Quantity theory of money   The price level (P) is directly related to the quantity of money in the economy (M).

Quasi-rent   Temporary economic rent arising from short-run supply inelasticity.

Quintiles   Divisions of the population into five equal-sized groups (an example of a quantile).

Quota (set by a cartel)   The output that a given member of a cartel is allowed to produce (production quota) or sell (sales quota).

Random walk   Where fluctuations in the value of a share away from its 'correct' value are random: i.e. have no systematic pattern. When charted over time, these share price movements would appear like a 'random walk': like the path of someone staggering along drunk!

Rate of discount   The rate that is used to reduce future values to present values.

Rate of economic growth   The percentage increase in output, normally expressed over a 12-month or 3-month period.

Rate of inflation (annual) The percentage increase in the level of prices over a 12-month period.

Rate of profit Total profit (T) as a proportion of the capital employed (K): $r = T/K$.

Rational choices Choices that involve weighing up the benefit of any activity against its opportunity cost so that the decision maker successfully maximises his or her objective: e.g. happiness or profits.

Rational consumer A person who weighs up the costs and benefits to themselves of each additional unit of a good purchased.

Rational consumer behaviour The attempt to maximise total consumer surplus.

Rational economic behaviour Doing more of activities whose marginal benefit exceeds their marginal cost and doing less of those activities whose marginal cost exceeds their marginal benefit.

Rational expectations Expectations based on the *current* situation. These expectations are based on the information people have to hand. Whilst this information may be imperfect and therefore people will make errors, these errors will be random.

Rational producer behaviour When a firm weighs up the costs and benefits of alternative courses of action and then seeks to maximise its net benefit.

Rationalisation The reorganising of production (often after a merger) so as to cut out waste and duplication and generally to reduce costs.

Rationing Where the government restricts the amount of a good that people are allowed to buy.

Reaction function (or curve) This shows how a firm's optimal output varies according to the output chosen by its rival (or rivals).

Real balance effect As the price level rises, so the value of people's money balances will fall. They will therefore *spend* less in order to increase their money balances and go some way to protecting their real value.

Real business cycle theory The new classical theory which explains cyclical fluctuations in terms of shifts in aggregate supply, rather than aggregate demand.

Real exchange rate A country's exchange rate adjusted for changes in the domestic currency prices of its exports relative to the foreign currency prices of its imports. If a country's prices rise (fall) relative to those of its trading partners, its real exchange rate will rise (fall) relative to the nominal exchange rate.

Real GDP GDP after allowing for inflation: i.e. GDP measured in *constant* prices, in other words in terms of the prices ruling in some base year.

Real income Income measured in terms of how much it can buy. If your *money* income rises by 10 per cent, but prices rise by 8 per cent, you can only buy 2 per cent more goods than before. Your *real* income has risen by 2 per cent.

Real national income National income after allowing for inflation: i.e. national income measured in constant prices: i.e. in terms of the prices ruling in some base year.

Real values Money values corrected for inflation.

Real-wage unemployment Disequilibrium unemployment caused by real wages being driven up above the market-clearing level.

Recession A period where national output falls for two successive quarters or more.

Recessionary (or deflationary) gap The shortfall of national expenditure below national income (and injections below withdrawals) at the full-employment level of national income.

Reciprocity (in economics) Where people's behaviour is influenced by the effects it will have on others.

Recognised banks Banks licensed by the Bank of England. All financial institutions using the word 'bank' in their title have to be recognised by the Bank of England. This requires them to have paid-up capital of at least £5 million and to meet other requirements about their asset structure and range of services.

Rediscounting bills of exchange Buying bills before they reach maturity.

Reference dependent loss aversion Where people value (or 'code') outcomes as either losses or gains in relation to a reference point. This can mean that losses are disliked more than would be predicted by standard diminishing marginal utility.

Reflationary policy Fiscal or monetary policy designed to increase the rate of growth of aggregate demand.

Regional Development Agencies (RDAs) Nine agencies, based in English regions, which initiate and administer regional policy within their area.

Regional multiplier effects When a change in injections into or withdrawals from a particular region causes a multiplied change in income in that region. The regional multiplier (k_r) is given by $1/mpw_r$, where the import component of mpw_r consists of imports into that region either from abroad or from other regions of the economy.

Regional unemployment Structural unemployment occurring in specific regions of the country.

Regression analysis A statistical technique which allows a functional relationship between two or more variables to be estimated.

Regressive tax A tax whose average rate with respect to income falls as income rises.

Regulatory capture Where the regulator is persuaded to operate in the industry's interests rather than those of the consumer.

Relative price The price of one good compared with another (e.g. good X is twice the price of good Y).

Replacement costs What the firm would have to pay to replace factors it currently owns.

Resale (or retail) price maintenance Where the manufacturer of a product (legally) insists that the product should be sold at a specified retail price.

Reserve averaging The process whereby individual banks manage their average level of overnight reserves between MPC meetings using the Bank of England's operational standing facilities and/or the inter-bank market.

Residual demand curve A firm's residual demand curve illustrates the relationship between the output it produces and the market price for the product, holding constant the output produced by other firms.

Restrictive practice Where two or more firms agree to adopt common practices to restrict competition.

Retail banks 'High street banks'. Banks operating extensive branch networks and dealing directly with the general public, with published interest rates and charges.

Retail deposits and loans Deposits and loans made through bank/building society branches at published interest rates.

Retail price index (RPI) An index of the prices of goods bought by a typical household.

Revaluation Where the government re-pegs the exchange rate at a higher level.

Reverse repos When gilts or other assets are *purchased* under a sale and repurchase agreement. They become an asset to the purchaser.

Risk When a (desirable) outcome of an action may or may not occur, but the probability of its occurring is known. The lower the probability, the greater the risk involved in taking the action.

Risk averse Where a person is not prepared to take a gamble even if the odds of gaining are favourable.

Risk loving Where a person is willing to take a gamble even if the odds of gaining are unfavourable.

Risk neutral Where a person is willing to take a gamble if the odds are favourable and is unwilling if the odds are unfavourable.

Risk premium The expected value of a gamble minus a person's certainty equivalent.

Risk transformation The process whereby banks can spread the risks of lending by having a large number of borrowers.

Sale and repurchase agreement (repos) An agreement between two financial institutions whereby one in effect borrows from another by selling it assets, agreeing to buy them back (repurchase them) at a fixed price and on a fixed date.

Sales revenue maximisation An alternative theory of the firm based on the assumption that managers aim to maximise the firm's short-run total revenue.

Say's law Supply creates its own demand. In other words, the production of goods will generate sufficient demand to ensure that they are sold.

Scarcity The excess of human wants over what can actually be produced to fulfil these wants.

Search theory This examines people's behaviour under conditions of ignorance where it takes time to search for information.

Seasonal unemployment Unemployment associated with industries or regions where the demand for labour is lower at certain times of the year.

Second best (problem of) The difficulty of working out the best way of correcting a specific market distortion if distortions in other parts of the market continue to exist.

Second derivative The rate of change of the first derivative: found by differentiating the first derivative.

Second derivative test If on differentiating an equation a second time the answer is negative (positive), the point is a maximum (minimum).

Secondary action Industrial action taken against a company not directly involved in a dispute (e.g. a supplier of raw materials to a firm whose employees are on strike).

Secondary labour market The market for peripheral workers, usually employed on a temporary or part-time basis, or a less secure 'permanent' basis.

Secondary market in capital Where shareholders sell shares to others. This is thus a market in 'second-hand' shares.

Secondary marketing Where assets are sold before maturity to another institution or individual. The possibility of secondary marketing encourages people or institutions to buy assets/grant loans in the primary market, knowing that they can sell them if necessary in the secondary market. The sale of existing shares and bonds on the stock market is an example of secondary marketing.

Second-best solution The solution to a specific market distortion that recognises distortions elsewhere and seeks to minimise the overall distortionary effects to the economy of tackling this specific distortion.

Second-degree price discrimination Where a firm offers consumers a range of different pricing options for the same or similar product. Consumers are then free to choose whichever option they wish but the price is often dependent on some factor such as the quantity purchased.

Securitisation Where future cash flows (e.g. from interest rate or mortgage payments) are turned into marketable securities, such as bonds. The sellers (e.g. banks) get cash now rather than having to wait and can use it to fund loans to customers. The buyers make a profit by buying below the discounted value of the future income. Such bonds can be very risky, however, as the future cash flows may be less than anticipated.

Self-fulfilling speculation The actions of speculators tend to cause the very effect that they had anticipated.

Semi-strong efficiency (of share markets) Where share prices adjust quickly, fully and accurately to publicly available information.

Sensitivity analysis Where a range of possible values of uncertain costs and benefits are given to see whether the project's desirability is sensitive to these different values.

Sequential move game One firm (the first mover) makes and implements a decision. Rival firms (second movers) can observe the actions taken by the first mover before making their own decisions.

Set-aside   A system in the EU of paying farmers not to use a certain proportion of their land.

Shadow (or **illegal** or **underground**) **markets**   Where people ignore the government's price and/or quantity controls and sell illegally at whatever price equates illegal demand and supply.

Shares (equities)   A part ownership of a company. Companies' distributed profits are paid to shareholders in the form of dividends according to the number of shares held.

Short run (in production)   The period of time over which at least one factor is fixed.

Short run under perfect competition   The period during which there is insufficient time for new firms to enter the industry.

Short-run shut-down point   This is where the AR curve is tangential to the AVC curve. The firm can only just cover its variable costs. Any fall in revenue below this level will cause a profit-maximising firm to shut down immediately.

Short selling   The practice of borrowing an asset (for a fee) and selling it, hoping that the price will fall so that it can then be purchased and returned to the lender. The difference between the sale and purchase price (minus the fee) is thus profit to the short seller.

Short-termism   Where firms and investors take decisions based on the likely short-term performance of a company, rather than on its long-term prospects. Firms may thus sacrifice long-term profits and growth for the sake of a quick return.

Sight deposits   Deposits that can be withdrawn on demand without penalty.

Simultaneous single-move game   A game where each player has just one move, where each player plays at the same time and acts without knowledge of the actions chosen by other players.

Size distribution of income   Measurement of the distribution of income according to the levels of income received by individuals (irrespective of source).

Social benefit   Private benefit plus externalities in consumption.

Social capital (OECD definition)   Networks, together with shared norms, values and understandings, that facilitate co-operation within or among groups.

Social cost   Private cost plus externalities in production.

Social efficiency   A situation of Pareto optimality: where all possible Pareto improvements have been made: where, therefore, it is impossible to make anyone better off without making someone else worse off.

Social efficiency (improvement in)   A Pareto improvement: where changes in production or consumption can make at least one person better off without making anyone worse off.

Social rate of discount   A rate of discount that reflects *society's* preferences for present benefits over future ones.

Social surplus   Total social benefits minus total social costs.

Social-impact standards   Pollution control that focuses on the effects on people (e.g. on health or happiness).

Socially optimal output   The output where $MSC = MSB$: the output where total social surplus is maximised.

Sole proprietorship   A firm owned by one person. That person has unlimited liability.

Sovereign debt crisis   The financial and economic problems caused by excessive public-sector debt and by the fear that governments will be unable to raise sufficient finance to repay maturing debt.

Special drawing rights (SDRs)   Additional liquidity created by the IMF. SDRs give countries the right to borrow a certain amount of additional funds from the IMF, with no requirement for extra deposits (quotas).

Special purpose vehicle (SPV)   Legal entities created by financial institutions for conducting specific financial functions, such as bundling assets together into fixed interest bonds and selling them.

Specialisation and division of labour   Where production is broken down into a number of simpler, more specialised tasks, thus allowing workers to acquire a high degree of efficiency.

Specific tax   A tax on a good levied at a fixed amount per unit of the good, irrespective of the price of that unit.

Speculation   Where people make buying or selling decisions based on their anticipations of future prices.

Speculators   People who buy (or sell) commodities or financial assets with the intention of profiting by selling them (or buying them back) at a later date at a higher (lower) price.

Spot price   The current market price.

Spreading risks (for an insurance company)   The more policies an insurance company issues and the more independent the risks of claims from these policies are, the more predictable will be the number of claims.

Stabilising speculation   Where the actions of speculators tend to reduce the magnitude of price fluctuations.

Stagflation   A term used to refer to the combination of stagnation (low growth and high unemployment) and high inflation.

Stakeholders (in a company)   People who are affected by a company's activities and/or performance (customers, employees, owners, creditors, people living in the neighbourhood, etc.). They may or may not be in a position to take decisions, or influence decision taking, in the firm.

Standardised unemployment rate   The measure of the unemployment rate used by the ILO and OECD. The unemployed are defined as persons of working age who are without work, available to start work within two weeks and either have actively looked for work in the last four weeks or are waiting to take up an appointment.

Steady-state growth path   The growth path for a given saving rate (where growth results from technological progress).

Steady-state level of national income   The long-run equilibrium level of national income. The level at which all investment is used to maintain the existing capital stock at its current level.

Sterilisation Actions (e.g. open-market operations) taken by a central bank to offset the effects of foreign exchange flows or its own bond transactions so as to leave money supply unchanged.

Stochastic shocks Shocks that are random and hence unpredictable, or predicable only as occurring within a range of values.

Stock An amount of something (inputs, goods, money, etc.) existing at a point of time. (Contrasts with *flow*.)

Stock (or inventory) appreciation The increase in monetary value of stocks due to increased prices. Since this does not represent increased output, it is not included in GDP.

Stop–go policies Alternate deflationary and reflationary policies to tackle the currently most pressing of the four problems which fluctuate with the business cycle.

Strategic alliance Where two firms work together, formally or informally, to achieve a mutually desirable goal.

Strategic trade theory The theory that protecting/supporting certain industries can enable them to compete more effectively with large monopolistic rivals abroad. The effect of the protection is to increase long-run competition and may enable the protected firms to exploit a comparative advantage that they could not have done otherwise.

Strong efficiency (of share markets) Where share prices adjust quickly, fully and accurately to all available information, both public and that only available to insiders.

Structural public-sector deficit (or surplus) The public-sector deficit (or surplus) that would occur if the economy were operating at the potential level of national income: i.e. one where there is a zero output gap.

Structural unemployment Equilibrium unemployment that arises from changes in the pattern of demand or supply in the economy. People made redundant in one part of the economy cannot immediately take up jobs in other parts (even though there are vacancies).

Structuralists Economists who focus on specific barriers to development and how to overcome them.

Subcontracting Where a firm employs another firm to produce part of its output or some of its input(s).

Sub-prime debt Debt where there is a high risk of default by the borrower (e.g. mortgage holders who are on low incomes facing higher interest rates and falling house prices).

Subsistence production Where people produce things for their own consumption.

Substitute goods A pair of goods which are considered by consumers to be alternatives to each other. As the price of one goes up, the demand for the other rises.

Substitutes in supply These are two goods where an increased production of one means diverting resources away from producing the other.

Substitution effect of a price change The effect of a change in price on quantity demanded arising from the consumer switching to or from alternative (substitute) products.

Substitution effect of a rise in wage rates Workers will tend to substitute income for leisure as leisure now has a higher opportunity cost. This effect leads to *more* hours being worked as wage rates rise.

Substitution effect of a tax rise Tax increases reduce the opportunity cost of leisure and thus encourage people to work less.

Substitution effect – international As prices rise, people at home and abroad buy less of this country's products and more of products from abroad.

Sunk costs Costs that cannot be recouped (e.g. by transferring assets to other uses). Examples include specialised machinery or the costs of an advertising campaign.

Supernormal profit also known as **pure profit, economic profit, abnormal profit,** or simply **profit**) The excess of total profit above normal profit.

Supply curve A graph showing the relationship between the price of a good and the quantity of the good supplied over a given period of time.

Supply schedule A table showing the different quantities of a good that producers are willing and able to supply at various prices over a given time period. A supply schedule can be for an individual producer or group of producers, or for all producers (the market supply schedule).

Supply-side economics An approach which focuses directly on aggregate supply and how to shift the aggregate supply curve outwards.

Supply-side policies Government policies that attempt to alter the level of aggregate supply directly (rather than through changes in aggregate demand). Such policies aim to increase *potential* output. They focus on increasing the quantity and/or productivity of resources.

Surplus on the current budget The amount by which public-sector receipts exceed those expenditures classified as current expenditures.

Sustainability (environmental) The ability of the environment to survive its use for economic activity.

Sustainable output The level of national output corresponding to no excess or deficiency of aggregate demand.

Switching costs The costs to a consumer of switching to an alternative supplier.

Systemically important banks (SIBs) Banks identified by a series of indicators as being significant players in the global financial system.

Tacit collusion Where oligopolists take care not to engage in price cutting, excessive advertising or other forms of competition. There may be unwritten 'rules' of collusive behaviour such as price leadership.

Takeover bid Where one firm attempts to purchase another by offering to buy the shares of that company from its shareholders.

Takeover constraint The effect that the fear of being taken over has on a firm's willingness to undertake projects that reduce distributed profits.

Target real wage theory The theory that unions bargain for target real wage increases each year irrespective of the level of real growth in the economy.

Tariff escalation The system whereby tariff rates increase the closer a product is to the finished stage of production.

Tariffs (or import levies) Taxes on imported products: i.e. customs duties.

Tax allowance An amount of income that can be earned tax-free. Tax allowances vary according to a person's circumstances.

Tax avoidance The rearrangement of one's affairs so as to reduce one's tax liability.

Tax evasion The illegal non-payment of taxes (e.g. by not declaring income earned).

Taylor rule A rule adopted by a central bank for setting the rate of interest. It will raise the interest rate if (a) inflation is above target or (b) real national income is above the sustainable level (or unemployment is below the natural rate). The rule states how much interest rates will be changed in each case.

Technical efficiency The firm is producing as much output as is technologically possible given the quantity of factor inputs it is using.

Technological unemployment Structural unemployment that occurs as a result of the introduction of labour-saving technology.

Technology-based standards Pollution control that requires firms' emissions to reflect the levels that could be achieved from using the best available pollution control technology.

Terms of trade The price index of exports divided by the price index of imports and then expressed as a percentage. This means that the terms of trade will be 100 in the base year.

Theory of the firm (traditional) The analysis of pricing and output decisions of the firm under various market conditions, assuming that the firm wishes to maximise profit.

Third-degree price discrimination Where a firm divides consumers into different groups based on some characteristic that is relatively easy to observe and informative about how much consumers are willing to pay. The firm then charges a different price to consumers in different groups, but the same price to all the consumers within a group.

Tie-in sales Where a firm is only prepared to sell a first product on the condition that its customers by a second product from it.

Time consistency Where a person's preferences remain the same over time. For example, it is time consistent if you plan to buy a book when your student loan arrives and then actually do so when it does.

Time-consistent policy announcement A policy announcement where there is an incentive for the policy maker to stick to it over time.

Time deposits Deposits that require notice of withdrawal or where a penalty is charged for withdrawals on demand.

Time-inconsistent policy announcement A policy announcement where there is an incentive for the policy maker to renege on it at a future date.

Time-series data Information depicting how a variable (e.g. the price of eggs) changes over time.

Total consumer expenditure on a product (TE) (per period of time) The price of the product multiplied by the quantity purchased: $TE = PQ$.

Total consumer surplus The excess of a person's total utility from the consumption of a good (TU) over the amount that person spends on it (TE): $TCS = TU - TE$.

Total cost The sum of total fixed costs and total variable costs: $TC = TFC + TVC$.

Total currency flow on the balance of payments The current plus capital plus financial account balance but excluding the reserves.

Total physical product The total output of a product per period of time that is obtained from a given amount of inputs.

Total (private) surplus Total consumer surplus ($TU - TE$) plus total producer surplus ($TR - TVC$).

Total producer surplus (TPS) Total revenue minus total variable cost ($TR - TVC$): in other words, total profit plus total fixed cost ($T + TFC$).

Total revenue A firm's total earnings from a specified level of sales within a specified period: $TR = P \times Q$.

Total revenue (TR) (per period of time) The total amount received by firms from the sale of a product, before the deduction of taxes or any other costs. The price multiplied by the quantity sold. $TR = P \times Q$.

Total social surplus Total benefits to society from consuming a good minus total costs to society from producing it. In the absence of externalities, total social surplus is the same as total (private) surplus.

Total utility The total satisfaction a consumer gets from the consumption of all the units of a good consumed within a given time period.

Tradable permits Firms are issued or sold permits by the authorities that give them the right to produce a given level of pollution. Firms that do not have sufficient permits to match their pollution levels can purchase additional permits to cover the difference, while those that reduce their pollution levels can sell any surplus permits for a profit.

Trade creation Where a customs union leads to greater specialisation according to comparative advantage and thus a shift in production from higher-cost to lower-cost sources.

Trade cycle or **business cycle** The periodic fluctuations of national output round its long-term trend.

Trade diversion Where a customs union diverts consumption from goods produced at a lower cost outside the union to goods produced at a higher cost (but tariff free) within the union.

Traditional theory of the firm The analysis of pricing and output decisions of the firm under various market conditions, assuming that the firm wishes to maximise profit.

Tragedy of the commons When resources are commonly available at no charge people are likely to overexploit them.

Transfer payments Moneys transferred from one person or group to another (e.g. from the government to individuals) without production taking place.

Transfers (by the government) Transfers of money from taxpayers to recipients of benefits and subsidies. They are not an injection into the circular flow but are the equivalent of a negative tax (i.e. a negative withdrawal).

Treasury bills Bills of exchange issued by the Bank of England on behalf of the government. They are a means whereby the government raises short-term finance.

Trigger strategy Once a firm observes that its rival has broken some agreed behaviour it never co-operates with them ever again.

Tying Where a firm is only prepared to sell a first product (the tying good) on the condition that its consumers buy a second product from it (the tied good).

U-form (unitary form) of corporate organisation Where the managers of the various departments of a firm are directly responsible to head office, normally to a chief executive.

Uncertainty When an outcome may or may not occur and its probability of occurring is not known.

Underemployment Where people who want full-time work are only able to find part-time work.

Underground (or **illegal** or **shadow**) **markets** Where people ignore the government's price and/or quantity controls and sell illegally at whatever price equates illegal demand and supply.

Unemployment The number of people of working age who are actively looking for work but are currently without a job. (Note that there is much debate as to who should officially be counted as unemployed.)

Unemployment rate The number unemployed expressed as a percentage of the labour force.

Unit elastic demand Where quantity demanded changes by the same percentage as price. Ignoring the negative sign, it will have a value equal to 1.

Universal benefits Benefits paid to everyone in a certain category irrespective of their income or assets.

Util An imaginary unit of satisfaction from the consumption of a good.

Value added tax (VAT) A tax on goods and services, charged at each stage of production as a percentage of the value added at that stage.

Variable costs Total costs that vary with the amount of output produced.

Variable factor An input that can be increased in supply within a given time period.

Velocity of circulation The number of times annually that money on average is spent on goods and services that make up GDP.

Vent for surplus When international trade enables a country to exploit resources that would otherwise be unused.

Vertical equity The redistribution from the better off to the worse off. In the case of taxes, this means the rich paying proportionately more taxes than the poor.

Vertical merger When two firms in the same industry at different stages in the production process merge.

Vertical restraints Conditions imposed by one firm on another which is either its supplier or its customer.

Wage–price spiral Wages and prices chasing each other as the aggregate demand curve continually shifts to the right and the aggregate supply curve continually shifts upwards.

Wage taker An employer or employee who has no power to influence the market wage rate.

Weak efficiency (of share markets) Where share dealing prevents cyclical movements in shares.

Weighted average The average of several items where each item is ascribed a weight according to its importance. The weights must add up to 1.

Wholesale banks Banks specialising in large-scale deposits and loans and dealing mainly with companies.

Wholesale deposits and loans Large-scale deposits and loans made by and to firms at negotiated interest rates.

Withdrawals (W) (or leakages) Incomes of households or firms that are not passed on round the inner flow. Withdrawals equal net saving (S) plus net taxes (T) plus expenditure on imports (M): $W = S + T + M$.

Working to rule Workers do the bare minimum they have to, as set out in their job descriptions.

Yield on a share The dividend received per share expressed as a percentage of the current market price of the share.

Index